Oxford Dictionary of National Biography

Volume 6

Oxford Dictionary of National Biography

IN ASSOCIATION WITH

The British Academy

From the earliest times to the year 2000

Edited by

H. C. G. Matthew

and

Brian Harrison

Volume 6

Blackmore–Bowyer

OXFORD
UNIVERSITY PRESS

Great Clarendon Street, Oxford OX2 6DP

Oxford University Press is a department of the University of Oxford.
It furthers the University's objective of excellence in research, scholarship,
and education by publishing worldwide in

Oxford New York

Auckland Bangkok Buenos Aires Cape Town
Chennai Dar es Salaam Delhi Hong Kong Istanbul Karachi
Kolkata Kuala Lumpur Madrid Melbourne Mexico City Mumbai Nairobi
São Paulo Shanghai Taipei Tokyo Toronto

Oxford is a registered trade mark of Oxford University Press
in the UK and in certain other countries

Published in the United States
by Oxford University Press Inc., New York

First published 2004

British Library Cataloguing in Publication Data
Data available

Library of Congress Cataloging in Publication Data
Data available: for details see volume 1, p. iv

ISBN 0-19-861356-3 (this volume)
ISBN 0-19-861411-X (set of sixty volumes)

Text captured by Alliance Phototypesetters, Pondicherry
Illustrations reproduced and archived by
Alliance Graphics Ltd, UK
Typeset in OUP Swift by Interactive Sciences Limited, Gloucester
Printed in Great Britain on acid-free paper by
Butler and Tanner Ltd,
Frome, Somerset

LIST OF ABBREVIATIONS

1 *General abbreviations*

AB	bachelor of arts
ABC	Australian Broadcasting Corporation
ABC TV	ABC Television
act.	active
A$	Australian dollar
AD	*anno domini*
AFC	Air Force Cross
AIDS	acquired immune deficiency syndrome
AK	Alaska
AL	Alabama
A level	advanced level [examination]
ALS	associate of the Linnean Society
AM	master of arts
AMICE	associate member of the Institution of Civil Engineers
ANZAC	Australian and New Zealand Army Corps
appx *pl.* appxs	appendix(es)
AR	Arkansas
ARA	associate of the Royal Academy
ARCA	associate of the Royal College of Art
ARCM	associate of the Royal College of Music
ARCO	associate of the Royal College of Organists
ARIBA	associate of the Royal Institute of British Architects
ARP	air-raid precautions
ARRC	associate of the Royal Red Cross
ARSA	associate of the Royal Scottish Academy
art.	article / item
ASC	Army Service Corps
Asch	Austrian Schilling
ASDIC	Antisubmarine Detection Investigation Committee
ATS	Auxiliary Territorial Service
ATV	Associated Television
Aug	August
AZ	Arizona
b.	born
BA	bachelor of arts
BA (Admin.)	bachelor of arts (administration)
BAFTA	British Academy of Film and Television Arts
BAO	bachelor of arts in obstetrics
bap.	baptized
BBC	British Broadcasting Corporation / Company
BC	before Christ
BCE	before the common (*or* Christian) era
BCE	bachelor of civil engineering
BCG	bacillus of Calmette and Guérin [inoculation against tuberculosis]
BCh	bachelor of surgery
BChir	bachelor of surgery
BCL	bachelor of civil law
BCnL	bachelor of canon law
BCom	bachelor of commerce
BD	bachelor of divinity
BEd	bachelor of education
BEng	bachelor of engineering
bk *pl.* bks	book(s)
BL	bachelor of law / letters / literature
BLitt	bachelor of letters
BM	bachelor of medicine
BMus	bachelor of music
BP	before present
BP	British Petroleum
Bros.	Brothers
BS	(1) bachelor of science; (2) bachelor of surgery; (3) British standard
BSc	bachelor of science
BSc (Econ.)	bachelor of science (economics)
BSc (Eng.)	bachelor of science (engineering)
bt	baronet
BTh	bachelor of theology
bur.	buried
C.	command [identifier for published parliamentary papers]
c.	*circa*
c.	*capitulum pl. capitula*: chapter(s)
CA	California
Cantab.	Cantabrigiensis
cap.	*capitulum pl. capitula*: chapter(s)
CB	companion of the Bath
CBE	commander of the Order of the British Empire
CBS	Columbia Broadcasting System
cc	cubic centimetres
C$	Canadian dollar
CD	compact disc
Cd	command [identifier for published parliamentary papers]
CE	Common (*or* Christian) Era
cent.	century
cf.	compare
CH	Companion of Honour
chap.	chapter
ChB	bachelor of surgery
CI	Imperial Order of the Crown of India
CIA	Central Intelligence Agency
CID	Criminal Investigation Department
CIE	companion of the Order of the Indian Empire
Cie	Compagnie
CLit	companion of literature
CM	master of surgery
cm	centimetre(s)

Cmd	command [identifier for published parliamentary papers]
CMG	companion of the Order of St Michael and St George
Cmnd	command [identifier for published parliamentary papers]
CO	Colorado
Co.	company
co.	county
col. *pl.* cols.	column(s)
Corp.	corporation
CSE	certificate of secondary education
CSI	companion of the Order of the Star of India
CT	Connecticut
CVO	commander of the Royal Victorian Order
cwt	hundredweight
$	(American) dollar
d.	(1) penny (pence); (2) died
DBE	dame commander of the Order of the British Empire
DCH	diploma in child health
DCh	doctor of surgery
DCL	doctor of civil law
DCnL	doctor of canon law
DCVO	dame commander of the Royal Victorian Order
DD	doctor of divinity
DE	Delaware
Dec	December
dem.	demolished
DEng	doctor of engineering
des.	destroyed
DFC	Distinguished Flying Cross
DipEd	diploma in education
DipPsych	diploma in psychiatry
diss.	dissertation
DL	deputy lieutenant
DLitt	doctor of letters
DLittCelt	doctor of Celtic letters
DM	(1) Deutschmark; (2) doctor of medicine; (3) doctor of musical arts
DMus	doctor of music
DNA	dioxyribonucleic acid
doc.	document
DOL	doctor of oriental learning
DPH	diploma in public health
DPhil	doctor of philosophy
DPM	diploma in psychological medicine
DSC	Distinguished Service Cross
DSc	doctor of science
DSc (Econ.)	doctor of science (economics)
DSc (Eng.)	doctor of science (engineering)
DSM	Distinguished Service Medal
DSO	companion of the Distinguished Service Order
DSocSc	doctor of social science
DTech	doctor of technology
DTh	doctor of theology
DTM	diploma in tropical medicine
DTMH	diploma in tropical medicine and hygiene
DU	doctor of the university
DUniv	doctor of the university
dwt	pennyweight
EC	European Community
ed. *pl.* eds.	edited / edited by / editor(s)
Edin.	Edinburgh
edn	edition
EEC	European Economic Community
EFTA	European Free Trade Association
EICS	East India Company Service
EMI	Electrical and Musical Industries (Ltd)
Eng.	English
enl.	enlarged
ENSA	Entertainments National Service Association
ep. *pl.* epp.	*epistola(e)*
ESP	extra-sensory perception
esp.	especially
esq.	esquire
est.	estimate / estimated
EU	European Union
ex	sold by (*lit.* out of)
excl.	excludes / excluding
exh.	exhibited
exh. cat.	exhibition catalogue
f. *pl.* ff.	following [pages]
FA	Football Association
FACP	fellow of the American College of Physicians
facs.	facsimile
FANY	First Aid Nursing Yeomanry
FBA	fellow of the British Academy
FBI	Federation of British Industries
FCS	fellow of the Chemical Society
Feb	February
FEng	fellow of the Fellowship of Engineering
FFCM	fellow of the Faculty of Community Medicine
FGS	fellow of the Geological Society
fig.	figure
FIMechE	fellow of the Institution of Mechanical Engineers
FL	Florida
fl.	*floruit*
FLS	fellow of the Linnean Society
FM	frequency modulation
fol. *pl.* fols.	folio(s)
Fr	French francs
Fr.	French
FRAeS	fellow of the Royal Aeronautical Society
FRAI	fellow of the Royal Anthropological Institute
FRAM	fellow of the Royal Academy of Music
FRAS	(1) fellow of the Royal Asiatic Society; (2) fellow of the Royal Astronomical Society
FRCM	fellow of the Royal College of Music
FRCO	fellow of the Royal College of Organists
FRCOG	fellow of the Royal College of Obstetricians and Gynaecologists
FRCP(C)	fellow of the Royal College of Physicians of Canada
FRCP (Edin.)	fellow of the Royal College of Physicians of Edinburgh
FRCP (Lond.)	fellow of the Royal College of Physicians of London
FRCPath	fellow of the Royal College of Pathologists
FRCPsych	fellow of the Royal College of Psychiatrists
FRCS	fellow of the Royal College of Surgeons
FRGS	fellow of the Royal Geographical Society
FRIBA	fellow of the Royal Institute of British Architects
FRICS	fellow of the Royal Institute of Chartered Surveyors
FRS	fellow of the Royal Society
FRSA	fellow of the Royal Society of Arts

FRSCM	fellow of the Royal School of Church Music
FRSE	fellow of the Royal Society of Edinburgh
FRSL	fellow of the Royal Society of Literature
FSA	fellow of the Society of Antiquaries
ft	foot *pl.* feet
FTCL	fellow of Trinity College of Music, London
ft-lb per min.	foot-pounds per minute [unit of horsepower]
FZS	fellow of the Zoological Society
GA	Georgia
GBE	knight or dame grand cross of the Order of the British Empire
GCB	knight grand cross of the Order of the Bath
GCE	general certificate of education
GCH	knight grand cross of the Royal Guelphic Order
GCHQ	government communications headquarters
GCIE	knight grand commander of the Order of the Indian Empire
GCMG	knight or dame grand cross of the Order of St Michael and St George
GCSE	general certificate of secondary education
GCSI	knight grand commander of the Order of the Star of India
GCStJ	bailiff or dame grand cross of the order of St John of Jerusalem
GCVO	knight or dame grand cross of the Royal Victorian Order
GEC	General Electric Company
Ger.	German
GI	government (*or* general) issue
GMT	Greenwich mean time
GP	general practitioner
GPU	[Soviet special police unit]
GSO	general staff officer
Heb.	Hebrew
HEICS	Honourable East India Company Service
HI	Hawaii
HIV	human immunodeficiency virus
HK$	Hong Kong dollar
HM	his / her majesty('s)
HMAS	his / her majesty's Australian ship
HMNZS	his / her majesty's New Zealand ship
HMS	his / her majesty's ship
HMSO	His / Her Majesty's Stationery Office
HMV	His Master's Voice
Hon.	Honourable
hp	horsepower
hr	hour(s)
HRH	his / her royal highness
HTV	Harlech Television
IA	Iowa
ibid.	*ibidem*: in the same place
ICI	Imperial Chemical Industries (Ltd)
ID	Idaho
IL	Illinois
illus.	illustration
illustr.	illustrated
IN	Indiana
in.	inch(es)
Inc.	Incorporated
incl.	includes / including
IOU	I owe you
IQ	intelligence quotient
Ir£	Irish pound
IRA	Irish Republican Army
ISO	companion of the Imperial Service Order
It.	Italian
ITA	Independent Television Authority
ITV	Independent Television
Jan	January
JP	justice of the peace
jun.	junior
KB	knight of the Order of the Bath
KBE	knight commander of the Order of the British Empire
KC	king's counsel
kcal	kilocalorie
KCB	knight commander of the Order of the Bath
KCH	knight commander of the Royal Guelphic Order
KCIE	knight commander of the Order of the Indian Empire
KCMG	knight commander of the Order of St Michael and St George
KCSI	knight commander of the Order of the Star of India
KCVO	knight commander of the Royal Victorian Order
keV	kilo-electron-volt
KG	knight of the Order of the Garter
KGB	[Soviet committee of state security]
KH	knight of the Royal Guelphic Order
KLM	Koninklijke Luchtvaart Maatschappij (Royal Dutch Air Lines)
km	kilometre(s)
KP	knight of the Order of St Patrick
KS	Kansas
KT	knight of the Order of the Thistle
kt	knight
KY	Kentucky
£	pound(s) sterling
£E	Egyptian pound
L	lira *pl.* lire
l. *pl.* ll.	line(s)
LA	Lousiana
LAA	light anti-aircraft
LAH	licentiate of the Apothecaries' Hall, Dublin
Lat.	Latin
lb	pound(s), unit of weight
LDS	licence in dental surgery
lit.	literally
LittB	bachelor of letters
LittD	doctor of letters
LKQCPI	licentiate of the King and Queen's College of Physicians, Ireland
LLA	lady literate in arts
LLB	bachelor of laws
LLD	doctor of laws
LLM	master of laws
LM	licentiate in midwifery
LP	long-playing record
LRAM	licentiate of the Royal Academy of Music
LRCP	licentiate of the Royal College of Physicians
LRCPS (Glasgow)	licentiate of the Royal College of Physicians and Surgeons of Glasgow
LRCS	licentiate of the Royal College of Surgeons
LSA	licentiate of the Society of Apothecaries
LSD	lysergic acid diethylamide
LVO	lieutenant of the Royal Victorian Order
M. *pl.* MM.	Monsieur *pl.* Messieurs
m	metre(s)

m. *pl.* mm.	membrane(s)
MA	(1) Massachusetts; (2) master of arts
MAI	master of engineering
MB	bachelor of medicine
MBA	master of business administration
MBE	member of the Order of the British Empire
MC	Military Cross
MCC	Marylebone Cricket Club
MCh	master of surgery
MChir	master of surgery
MCom	master of commerce
MD	(1) doctor of medicine; (2) Maryland
MDMA	methylenedioxymethamphetamine
ME	Maine
MEd	master of education
MEng	master of engineering
MEP	member of the European parliament
MG	Morris Garages
MGM	Metro-Goldwyn-Mayer
Mgr	Monsignor
MI	(1) Michigan; (2) military intelligence
MI1c	[secret intelligence department]
MI5	[military intelligence department]
MI6	[secret intelligence department]
MI9	[secret escape service]
MICE	member of the Institution of Civil Engineers
MIEE	member of the Institution of Electrical Engineers
min.	minute(s)
Mk	mark
ML	(1) licentiate of medicine; (2) master of laws
MLitt	master of letters
Mlle	Mademoiselle
mm	millimetre(s)
Mme	Madame
MN	Minnesota
MO	Missouri
MOH	medical officer of health
MP	member of parliament
m.p.h.	miles per hour
MPhil	master of philosophy
MRCP	member of the Royal College of Physicians
MRCS	member of the Royal College of Surgeons
MRCVS	member of the Royal College of Veterinary Surgeons
MRIA	member of the Royal Irish Academy
MS	(1) master of science; (2) Mississippi
MS *pl.* MSS	manuscript(s)
MSc	master of science
MSc (Econ.)	master of science (economics)
MT	Montana
MusB	bachelor of music
MusBac	bachelor of music
MusD	doctor of music
MV	motor vessel
MVO	member of the Royal Victorian Order
n. *pl.* nn.	note(s)
NAAFI	Navy, Army, and Air Force Institutes
NASA	National Aeronautics and Space Administration
NATO	North Atlantic Treaty Organization
NBC	National Broadcasting Corporation
NC	North Carolina
NCO	non-commissioned officer

ND	North Dakota
n.d.	no date
NE	Nebraska
nem. con.	*nemine contradicente*: unanimously
new ser.	new series
NH	New Hampshire
NHS	National Health Service
NJ	New Jersey
NKVD	[Soviet people's commissariat for internal affairs]
NM	New Mexico
nm	nanometre(s)
no. *pl.* nos.	number(s)
Nov	November
n.p.	no place [of publication]
NS	new style
NV	Nevada
NY	New York
NZBS	New Zealand Broadcasting Service
OBE	officer of the Order of the British Empire
obit.	obituary
Oct	October
OCTU	officer cadets training unit
OECD	Organization for Economic Co-operation and Development
OEEC	Organization for European Economic Co-operation
OFM	order of Friars Minor [Franciscans]
OFMCap	Ordine Frati Minori Cappucini: member of the Capuchin order
OH	Ohio
OK	Oklahoma
O level	ordinary level [examination]
OM	Order of Merit
OP	order of Preachers [Dominicans]
op. *pl.* opp.	opus *pl.* opera
OPEC	Organization of Petroleum Exporting Countries
OR	Oregon
orig.	original
OS	old style
OSB	Order of St Benedict
OTC	Officers' Training Corps
OWS	Old Watercolour Society
Oxon.	Oxoniensis
p. *pl.* pp.	page(s)
PA	Pennsylvania
p.a.	per annum
para.	paragraph
PAYE	pay as you earn
pbk *pl.* pbks	paperback(s)
per.	[during the] period
PhD	doctor of philosophy
pl.	(1) plate(s); (2) plural
priv. coll.	private collection
pt *pl.* pts	part(s)
pubd	published
PVC	polyvinyl chloride
q. *pl.* qq.	(1) question(s); (2) quire(s)
QC	queen's counsel
R	rand
R.	Rex / Regina
r	recto
r.	reigned / ruled
RA	Royal Academy / Royal Academician

RAC	Royal Automobile Club
RAF	Royal Air Force
RAFVR	Royal Air Force Volunteer Reserve
RAM	[member of the] Royal Academy of Music
RAMC	Royal Army Medical Corps
RCA	Royal College of Art
RCNC	Royal Corps of Naval Constructors
RCOG	Royal College of Obstetricians and Gynaecologists
RDI	royal designer for industry
RE	Royal Engineers
repr. *pl.* reprs.	reprint(s) / reprinted
repro.	reproduced
rev.	revised / revised by / reviser / revision
Revd	Reverend
RHA	Royal Hibernian Academy
RI	(1) Rhode Island; (2) Royal Institute of Painters in Water-Colours
RIBA	Royal Institute of British Architects
RIN	Royal Indian Navy
RM	Reichsmark
RMS	Royal Mail steamer
RN	Royal Navy
RNA	ribonucleic acid
RNAS	Royal Naval Air Service
RNR	Royal Naval Reserve
RNVR	Royal Naval Volunteer Reserve
RO	Record Office
r.p.m.	revolutions per minute
RRS	royal research ship
Rs	rupees
RSA	(1) Royal Scottish Academician; (2) Royal Society of Arts
RSPCA	Royal Society for the Prevention of Cruelty to Animals
Rt Hon.	Right Honourable
Rt Revd	Right Reverend
RUC	Royal Ulster Constabulary
Russ.	Russian
RWS	Royal Watercolour Society
S4C	Sianel Pedwar Cymru
s.	shilling(s)
s.a.	*sub anno*: under the year
SABC	South African Broadcasting Corporation
SAS	Special Air Service
SC	South Carolina
ScD	doctor of science
S$	Singapore dollar
SD	South Dakota
sec.	second(s)
sel.	selected
sen.	senior
Sept	September
ser.	series
SHAPE	supreme headquarters allied powers, Europe
SIDRO	Société Internationale d'Énergie Hydro-Électrique
sig. *pl.* sigs.	signature(s)
sing.	singular
SIS	Secret Intelligence Service
SJ	Society of Jesus
Skr	Swedish krona
Span.	Spanish
SPCK	Society for Promoting Christian Knowledge
SS	(1) Santissimi; (2) Schutzstaffel; (3) steam ship
STB	bachelor of theology
STD	doctor of theology
STM	master of theology
STP	doctor of theology
supp.	supposedly
suppl. *pl.* suppls.	supplement(s)
s.v.	*sub verbo* / *sub voce*: under the word / heading
SY	steam yacht
TA	Territorial Army
TASS	[Soviet news agency]
TB	tuberculosis (*lit.* tubercle bacillus)
TD	(1) *teachtaí dála* (member of the Dáil); (2) territorial decoration
TN	Tennessee
TNT	trinitrotoluene
trans.	translated / translated by / translation / translator
TT	tourist trophy
TUC	Trades Union Congress
TX	Texas
U-boat	*Unterseeboot*: submarine
Ufa	Universum-Film AG
UMIST	University of Manchester Institute of Science and Technology
UN	United Nations
UNESCO	United Nations Educational, Scientific, and Cultural Organization
UNICEF	United Nations International Children's Emergency Fund
unpubd	unpublished
USS	United States ship
UT	Utah
v	verso
v.	versus
VA	Virginia
VAD	Voluntary Aid Detachment
VC	Victoria Cross
VE-day	victory in Europe day
Ven.	Venerable
VJ-day	victory over Japan day
vol. *pl.* vols.	volume(s)
VT	Vermont
WA	Washington [state]
WAAC	Women's Auxiliary Army Corps
WAAF	Women's Auxiliary Air Force
WEA	Workers' Educational Association
WHO	World Health Organization
WI	Wisconsin
WRAF	Women's Royal Air Force
WRNS	Women's Royal Naval Service
WV	West Virginia
WVS	Women's Voluntary Service
WY	Wyoming
¥	yen
YMCA	Young Men's Christian Association
YWCA	Young Women's Christian Association

2 *Institution abbreviations*

All Souls Oxf.	All Souls College, Oxford
AM Oxf.	Ashmolean Museum, Oxford
Balliol Oxf.	Balliol College, Oxford
BBC WAC	BBC Written Archives Centre, Reading
Beds. & Luton ARS	Bedfordshire and Luton Archives and Record Service, Bedford
Berks. RO	Berkshire Record Office, Reading
BFI	British Film Institute, London
BFI NFTVA	British Film Institute, London, National Film and Television Archive
BGS	British Geological Survey, Keyworth, Nottingham
Birm. CA	Birmingham Central Library, Birmingham City Archives
Birm. CL	Birmingham Central Library
BL	British Library, London
BL NSA	British Library, London, National Sound Archive
BL OIOC	British Library, London, Oriental and India Office Collections
BLPES	London School of Economics and Political Science, British Library of Political and Economic Science
BM	British Museum, London
Bodl. Oxf.	Bodleian Library, Oxford
Bodl. RH	Bodleian Library of Commonwealth and African Studies at Rhodes House, Oxford
Borth. Inst.	Borthwick Institute of Historical Research, University of York
Boston PL	Boston Public Library, Massachusetts
Bristol RO	Bristol Record Office
Bucks. RLSS	Buckinghamshire Records and Local Studies Service, Aylesbury
CAC Cam.	Churchill College, Cambridge, Churchill Archives Centre
Cambs. AS	Cambridgeshire Archive Service
CCC Cam.	Corpus Christi College, Cambridge
CCC Oxf.	Corpus Christi College, Oxford
Ches. & Chester ALSS	Cheshire and Chester Archives and Local Studies Service
Christ Church Oxf.	Christ Church, Oxford
Christies	Christies, London
City Westm. AC	City of Westminster Archives Centre, London
CKS	Centre for Kentish Studies, Maidstone
CLRO	Corporation of London Records Office
Coll. Arms	College of Arms, London
Col. U.	Columbia University, New York
Cornwall RO	Cornwall Record Office, Truro
Courtauld Inst.	Courtauld Institute of Art, London
CUL	Cambridge University Library
Cumbria AS	Cumbria Archive Service
Derbys. RO	Derbyshire Record Office, Matlock
Devon RO	Devon Record Office, Exeter
Dorset RO	Dorset Record Office, Dorchester
Duke U.	Duke University, Durham, North Carolina
Duke U., Perkins L.	Duke University, Durham, North Carolina, William R. Perkins Library
Durham Cath. CL	Durham Cathedral, chapter library
Durham RO	Durham Record Office
DWL	Dr Williams's Library, London
Essex RO	Essex Record Office
E. Sussex RO	East Sussex Record Office, Lewes
Eton	Eton College, Berkshire
FM Cam.	Fitzwilliam Museum, Cambridge
Folger	Folger Shakespeare Library, Washington, DC
Garr. Club	Garrick Club, London
Girton Cam.	Girton College, Cambridge
GL	Guildhall Library, London
Glos. RO	Gloucestershire Record Office, Gloucester
Gon. & Caius Cam.	Gonville and Caius College, Cambridge
Gov. Art Coll.	Government Art Collection
GS Lond.	Geological Society of London
Hants. RO	Hampshire Record Office, Winchester
Harris Man. Oxf.	Harris Manchester College, Oxford
Harvard TC	Harvard Theatre Collection, Harvard University, Cambridge, Massachusetts, Nathan Marsh Pusey Library
Harvard U.	Harvard University, Cambridge, Massachusetts
Harvard U., Houghton L.	Harvard University, Cambridge, Massachusetts, Houghton Library
Herefs. RO	Herefordshire Record Office, Hereford
Herts. ALS	Hertfordshire Archives and Local Studies, Hertford
Hist. Soc. Penn.	Historical Society of Pennsylvania, Philadelphia
HLRO	House of Lords Record Office, London
Hult. Arch.	Hulton Archive, London and New York
Hunt. L.	Huntington Library, San Marino, California
ICL	Imperial College, London
Inst. CE	Institution of Civil Engineers, London
Inst. EE	Institution of Electrical Engineers, London
IWM	Imperial War Museum, London
IWM FVA	Imperial War Museum, London, Film and Video Archive
IWM SA	Imperial War Museum, London, Sound Archive
JRL	John Rylands University Library of Manchester
King's AC Cam.	King's College Archives Centre, Cambridge
King's Cam.	King's College, Cambridge
King's Lond.	King's College, London
King's Lond., Liddell Hart C.	King's College, London, Liddell Hart Centre for Military Archives
Lancs. RO	Lancashire Record Office, Preston
L. Cong.	Library of Congress, Washington, DC
Leics. RO	Leicestershire, Leicester, and Rutland Record Office, Leicester
Lincs. Arch.	Lincolnshire Archives, Lincoln
Linn. Soc.	Linnean Society of London
LMA	London Metropolitan Archives
LPL	Lambeth Palace, London
Lpool RO	Liverpool Record Office and Local Studies Service
LUL	London University Library
Magd. Cam.	Magdalene College, Cambridge
Magd. Oxf.	Magdalen College, Oxford
Man. City Gall.	Manchester City Galleries
Man. CL	Manchester Central Library
Mass. Hist. Soc.	Massachusetts Historical Society, Boston
Merton Oxf.	Merton College, Oxford
MHS Oxf.	Museum of the History of Science, Oxford
Mitchell L., Glas.	Mitchell Library, Glasgow
Mitchell L., NSW	State Library of New South Wales, Sydney, Mitchell Library
Morgan L.	Pierpont Morgan Library, New York
NA Canada	National Archives of Canada, Ottawa
NA Ire.	National Archives of Ireland, Dublin
NAM	National Army Museum, London
NA Scot.	National Archives of Scotland, Edinburgh
News Int. RO	News International Record Office, London
NG Ire.	National Gallery of Ireland, Dublin

NG Scot.	National Gallery of Scotland, Edinburgh
NHM	Natural History Museum, London
NL Aus.	National Library of Australia, Canberra
NL Ire.	National Library of Ireland, Dublin
NL NZ	National Library of New Zealand, Wellington
NL NZ, Turnbull L.	National Library of New Zealand, Wellington, Alexander Turnbull Library
NL Scot.	National Library of Scotland, Edinburgh
NL Wales	National Library of Wales, Aberystwyth
NMG Wales	National Museum and Gallery of Wales, Cardiff
NMM	National Maritime Museum, London
Norfolk RO	Norfolk Record Office, Norwich
Northants. RO	Northamptonshire Record Office, Northampton
Northumbd RO	Northumberland Record Office
Notts. Arch.	Nottinghamshire Archives, Nottingham
NPG	National Portrait Gallery, London
NRA	National Archives, London, Historical Manuscripts Commission, National Register of Archives
Nuffield Oxf.	Nuffield College, Oxford
N. Yorks. CRO	North Yorkshire County Record Office, Northallerton
NYPL	New York Public Library
Oxf. UA	Oxford University Archives
Oxf. U. Mus. NH	Oxford University Museum of Natural History
Oxon. RO	Oxfordshire Record Office, Oxford
Pembroke Cam.	Pembroke College, Cambridge
PRO	National Archives, London, Public Record Office
PRO NIre.	Public Record Office for Northern Ireland, Belfast
Pusey Oxf.	Pusey House, Oxford
RA	Royal Academy of Arts, London
Ransom HRC	Harry Ransom Humanities Research Center, University of Texas, Austin
RAS	Royal Astronomical Society, London
RBG Kew	Royal Botanic Gardens, Kew, London
RCP Lond.	Royal College of Physicians of London
RCS Eng.	Royal College of Surgeons of England, London
RGS	Royal Geographical Society, London
RIBA	Royal Institute of British Architects, London
RIBA BAL	Royal Institute of British Architects, London, British Architectural Library
Royal Arch.	Royal Archives, Windsor Castle, Berkshire [by gracious permission of her majesty the queen]
Royal Irish Acad.	Royal Irish Academy, Dublin
Royal Scot. Acad.	Royal Scottish Academy, Edinburgh
RS	Royal Society, London
RSA	Royal Society of Arts, London
RS Friends, Lond.	Religious Society of Friends, London
St Ant. Oxf.	St Antony's College, Oxford
St John Cam.	St John's College, Cambridge
S. Antiquaries, Lond.	Society of Antiquaries of London
Sci. Mus.	Science Museum, London
Scot. NPG	Scottish National Portrait Gallery, Edinburgh
Scott Polar RI	University of Cambridge, Scott Polar Research Institute
Sheff. Arch.	Sheffield Archives
Shrops. RRC	Shropshire Records and Research Centre, Shrewsbury
SOAS	School of Oriental and African Studies, London
Som. ARS	Somerset Archive and Record Service, Taunton
Staffs. RO	Staffordshire Record Office, Stafford
Suffolk RO	Suffolk Record Office
Surrey HC	Surrey History Centre, Woking
TCD	Trinity College, Dublin
Trinity Cam.	Trinity College, Cambridge
U. Aberdeen	University of Aberdeen
U. Birm.	University of Birmingham
U. Birm. L.	University of Birmingham Library
U. Cal.	University of California
U. Cam.	University of Cambridge
UCL	University College, London
U. Durham	University of Durham
U. Durham L.	University of Durham Library
U. Edin.	University of Edinburgh
U. Edin., New Coll.	University of Edinburgh, New College
U. Edin., New Coll. L.	University of Edinburgh, New College Library
U. Edin. L.	University of Edinburgh Library
U. Glas.	University of Glasgow
U. Glas. L.	University of Glasgow Library
U. Hull	University of Hull
U. Hull, Brynmor Jones L.	University of Hull, Brynmor Jones Library
U. Leeds	University of Leeds
U. Leeds, Brotherton L.	University of Leeds, Brotherton Library
U. Lond.	University of London
U. Lpool	University of Liverpool
U. Lpool L.	University of Liverpool Library
U. Mich.	University of Michigan, Ann Arbor
U. Mich., Clements L.	University of Michigan, Ann Arbor, William L. Clements Library
U. Newcastle	University of Newcastle upon Tyne
U. Newcastle, Robinson L.	University of Newcastle upon Tyne, Robinson Library
U. Nott.	University of Nottingham
U. Nott. L.	University of Nottingham Library
U. Oxf.	University of Oxford
U. Reading	University of Reading
U. Reading L.	University of Reading Library
U. St Andr.	University of St Andrews
U. St Andr. L.	University of St Andrews Library
U. Southampton	University of Southampton
U. Southampton L.	University of Southampton Library
U. Sussex	University of Sussex, Brighton
U. Texas	University of Texas, Austin
U. Wales	University of Wales
U. Warwick Mod. RC	University of Warwick, Coventry, Modern Records Centre
V&A	Victoria and Albert Museum, London
V&A NAL	Victoria and Albert Museum, London, National Art Library
Warks. CRO	Warwickshire County Record Office, Warwick
Wellcome L.	Wellcome Library for the History and Understanding of Medicine, London
Westm. DA	Westminster Diocesan Archives, London
Wilts. & Swindon RO	Wiltshire and Swindon Record Office, Trowbridge
Worcs. RO	Worcestershire Record Office, Worcester
W. Sussex RO	West Sussex Record Office, Chichester
W. Yorks. AS	West Yorkshire Archive Service
Yale U.	Yale University, New Haven, Connecticut
Yale U., Beinecke L.	Yale University, New Haven, Connecticut, Beinecke Rare Book and Manuscript Library
Yale U. CBA	Yale University, New Haven, Connecticut, Yale Center for British Art

3 *Bibliographic abbreviations*

Adams, *Drama*	W. D. Adams, *A dictionary of the drama*, 1: *A–G* (1904); 2: *H–Z* (1956) [vol. 2 microfilm only]
AFM	J O'Donovan, ed. and trans., *Annala rioghachta Eireann / Annals of the kingdom of Ireland by the four masters*, 7 vols. (1848–51); 2nd edn (1856); 3rd edn (1990)
Allibone, *Dict.*	S. A. Allibone, *A critical dictionary of English literature and British and American authors*, 3 vols. (1859–71); suppl. by J. F. Kirk, 2 vols. (1891)
ANB	J. A. Garraty and M. C. Carnes, eds., *American national biography*, 24 vols. (1999)
Anderson, *Scot. nat.*	W. Anderson, *The Scottish nation, or, The surnames, families, literature, honours, and biographical history of the people of Scotland*, 3 vols. (1859–63)
Ann. mon.	H. R. Luard, ed., *Annales monastici*, 5 vols., Rolls Series, 36 (1864–9)
Ann. Ulster	S. Mac Airt and G. Mac Niocaill, eds., *Annals of Ulster (to* AD *1131)* (1983)
APC	*Acts of the privy council of England*, new ser., 46 vols. (1890–1964)
APS	*The acts of the parliaments of Scotland*, 12 vols. in 13 (1814–75)
Arber, *Regs. Stationers*	F. Arber, ed., *A transcript of the registers of the Company of Stationers of London, 1554–1640* AD, 5 vols. (1875–94)
ArchR	*Architectural Review*
ASC	D. Whitelock, D. C. Douglas, and S. I. Tucker, ed. and trans., *The Anglo-Saxon Chronicle: a revised translation* (1961)
AS chart.	P. H. Sawyer, *Anglo-Saxon charters: an annotated list and bibliography*, Royal Historical Society Guides and Handbooks (1968)
AusDB	D. Pike and others, eds., *Australian dictionary of biography*, 16 vols. (1966–2002)
Baker, *Serjeants*	J. H. Baker, *The order of serjeants at law*, SeldS, suppl. ser., 5 (1984)
Bale, *Cat.*	J. Bale, *Scriptorum illustrium Maioris Brytannie, quam nunc Angliam et Scotiam vocant: catalogus*, 2 vols. in 1 (Basel, 1557–9); facs. edn (1971)
Bale, *Index*	J. Bale, *Index Britanniae scriptorum*, ed. R. L. Poole and M. Bateson (1902); facs. edn (1990)
BBCS	*Bulletin of the Board of Celtic Studies*
BDMBR	J. O. Baylen and N. J. Gossman, eds., *Biographical dictionary of modern British radicals*, 3 vols. in 4 (1979–88)
Bede, *Hist. eccl.*	*Bede's Ecclesiastical history of the English people*, ed. and trans. B. Colgrave and R. A. B. Mynors, OMT (1969); repr. (1991)
Bénézit, *Dict.*	E. Bénézit, *Dictionnaire critique et documentaire des peintres, sculpteurs, dessinateurs et graveurs*, 3 vols. (Paris, 1911–23); new edn, 8 vols. (1948–66), repr. (1966); 3rd edn, rev. and enl., 10 vols. (1976); 4th edn, 14 vols. (1999)
BIHR	*Bulletin of the Institute of Historical Research*
Birch, *Seals*	W. de Birch, *Catalogue of seals in the department of manuscripts in the British Museum*, 6 vols. (1887–1900)
Bishop Burnet's History	*Bishop Burnet's History of his own time*, ed. M. J. Routh, 2nd edn, 6 vols. (1833)
Blackwood	*Blackwood's [Edinburgh] Magazine*, 328 vols. (1817–1980)
Blain, Clements & Grundy, *Feminist comp.*	V. Blain, P. Clements, and I. Grundy, eds., *The feminist companion to literature in English* (1990)
BL cat.	*The British Library general catalogue of printed books* [in 360 vols. with suppls., also CD-ROM and online]
BMJ	*British Medical Journal*
Boase & Courtney, *Bibl. Corn.*	G. C. Boase and W. P. Courtney, *Bibliotheca Cornubiensis: a catalogue of the writings … of Cornishmen*, 3 vols. (1874–82)
Boase, *Mod. Eng. biog.*	F. Boase, *Modern English biography: containing many thousand concise memoirs of persons who have died since the year 1850*, 6 vols. (privately printed, Truro, 1892–1921); repr. (1965)
Boswell, *Life*	*Boswell's Life of Johnson: together with Journal of a tour to the Hebrides and Johnson's Diary of a journey into north Wales*, ed. G. B. Hill, enl. edn, rev. L. F. Powell, 6 vols. (1934–50); 2nd edn (1964); repr. (1971)
Brown & Stratton, *Brit. mus.*	J. D. Brown and S. S. Stratton, *British musical biography* (1897)
Bryan, *Painters*	M. Bryan, *A biographical and critical dictionary of painters and engravers*, 2 vols. (1816); new edn, ed. G. Stanley (1849); new edn, ed. R. E. Graves and W. Armstrong, 2 vols. (1886–9); [4th edn], ed. G. C. Williamson, 5 vols. (1903–5) [various reprs.]
Burke, *Gen. GB*	J. Burke, *A genealogical and heraldic history of the commoners of Great Britain and Ireland*, 4 vols. (1833–8); new edn as *A genealogical and heraldic dictionary of the landed gentry of Great Britain and Ireland*, 3 vols. [1843–9] [many later edns]
Burke, *Gen. Ire.*	J. B. Burke, *A genealogical and heraldic history of the landed gentry of Ireland* (1899); 2nd edn (1904); 3rd edn (1912); 4th edn (1958); 5th edn as *Burke's Irish family records* (1976)
Burke, *Peerage*	J. Burke, *A general* [later edns *A genealogical*] *and heraldic dictionary of the peerage and baronetage of the United Kingdom* [later edns *the British empire*] (1829–)
Burney, *Hist. mus.*	C. Burney, *A general history of music, from the earliest ages to the present period*, 4 vols. (1776–89)
Burtchaell & Sadleir, *Alum. Dubl.*	G. D. Burtchaell and T. U. Sadleir, *Alumni Dublinenses: a register of the students, graduates, and provosts of Trinity College* (1924); [2nd edn], with suppl., in 2 pts (1935)
Calamy rev.	A. G. Matthews, *Calamy revised* (1934); repr. (1988)
CCI	*Calendar of confirmations and inventories granted and given up in the several commissariots of Scotland* (1876–)
CClR	*Calendar of the close rolls preserved in the Public Record Office*, 47 vols. (1892–1963)
CDS	J. Bain, ed., *Calendar of documents relating to Scotland*, 4 vols., PRO (1881–8); suppl. vol. 5, ed. G. G. Simpson and J. D. Galbraith [1986]
CEPR letters	W. H. Bliss, C. Johnson, and J. Twemlow, eds., *Calendar of entries in the papal registers relating to Great Britain and Ireland: papal letters* (1893–)
CGPLA	*Calendars of the grants of probate and letters of administration* [in 4 ser.: England & Wales, Northern Ireland, Ireland, and Éire]
Chambers, *Scots.*	R. Chambers, ed., *A biographical dictionary of eminent Scotsmen*, 4 vols. (1832–5)
Chancery records	chancery records pubd by the PRO
Chancery records (RC)	chancery records pubd by the Record Commissions

CIPM	*Calendar of inquisitions post mortem*, [20 vols.], PRO (1904–); also *Henry VII*, 3 vols. (1898–1955)
Clarendon, *Hist. rebellion*	E. Hyde, earl of Clarendon, *The history of the rebellion and civil wars in England*, 6 vols. (1888); repr. (1958) and (1992)
Cobbett, *Parl. hist.*	W. Cobbett and J. Wright, eds., *Cobbett's Parliamentary history of England*, 36 vols. (1806–1820)
Colvin, *Archs.*	H. Colvin, *A biographical dictionary of British architects, 1600–1840*, 3rd edn (1995)
Cooper, *Ath. Cantab.*	C. H. Cooper and T. Cooper, *Athenae Cantabrigienses*, 3 vols. (1858–1913); repr. (1967)
CPR	*Calendar of the patent rolls preserved in the Public Record Office* (1891–)
Crockford	*Crockford's Clerical Directory*
CS	Camden Society
CSP	*Calendar of state papers* [in 11 ser.: *domestic*, *Scotland*, *Scottish series*, *Ireland*, *colonial*, *Commonwealth*, *foreign*, *Spain* [at Simancas], *Rome*, *Milan*, and *Venice*]
CYS	Canterbury and York Society
DAB	*Dictionary of American biography*, 21 vols. (1928–36), repr. in 11 vols. (1964); 10 suppls. (1944–96)
DBB	D. J. Jeremy, ed., *Dictionary of business biography*, 5 vols. (1984–6)
DCB	G. W. Brown and others, *Dictionary of Canadian biography*, [14 vols.] (1966–)
Debrett's Peerage	*Debrett's Peerage* (1803–) [sometimes *Debrett's Illustrated peerage*]
Desmond, *Botanists*	R. Desmond, *Dictionary of British and Irish botanists and horticulturists* (1977); rev. edn (1994)
Dir. Brit. archs.	A. Felstead, J. Franklin, and L. Pinfield, eds., *Directory of British architects, 1834–1900* (1993); 2nd edn, ed. A. Brodie and others, 2 vols. (2001)
DLB	J. M. Bellamy and J. Saville, eds., *Dictionary of labour biography*, [10 vols.] (1972–)
DLitB	Dictionary of Literary Biography
DNB	*Dictionary of national biography*, 63 vols. (1885–1900), suppl., 3 vols. (1901); repr. in 22 vols. (1908–9); 10 further suppls. (1912–96); *Missing persons* (1993)
DNZB	W. H. Oliver and C. Orange, eds., *The dictionary of New Zealand biography*, 5 vols. (1990–2000)
DSAB	W. J. de Kock and others, eds., *Dictionary of South African biography*, 5 vols. (1968–87)
DSB	C. C. Gillispie and F. L. Holmes, eds., *Dictionary of scientific biography*, 16 vols. (1970–80); repr. in 8 vols. (1981); 2 vol. suppl. (1990)
DSBB	A. Slaven and S. Checkland, eds., *Dictionary of Scottish business biography, 1860–1960*, 2 vols. (1986–90)
DSCHT	N. M. de S. Cameron and others, eds., *Dictionary of Scottish church history and theology* (1993)
Dugdale, *Monasticon*	W. Dugdale, *Monasticon Anglicanum*, 3 vols. (1655–72); 2nd edn, 3 vols. (1661–82); new edn, ed. J. Caley, J. Ellis, and B. Bandinel, 6 vols. in 8 pts (1817–30); repr. (1846) and (1970)
DWB	J. E. Lloyd and others, eds., *Dictionary of Welsh biography down to 1940* (1959) [Eng. trans. of *Y bywgraffiadur Cymreig hyd 1940*, 2nd edn (1954)]
EdinR	*Edinburgh Review, or, Critical Journal*
EETS	Early English Text Society
Emden, *Cam.*	A. B. Emden, *A biographical register of the University of Cambridge to 1500* (1963)
Emden, *Oxf.*	A. B. Emden, *A biographical register of the University of Oxford to AD 1500*, 3 vols. (1957–9); also *A biographical register of the University of Oxford, AD 1501 to 1540* (1974)
EngHR	*English Historical Review*
Engraved Brit. ports.	F. M. O'Donoghue and H. M. Hake, *Catalogue of engraved British portraits preserved in the department of prints and drawings in the British Museum*, 6 vols. (1908–25)
ER	The English Reports, 178 vols. (1900–32)
ESTC	*English short title catalogue, 1475–1800* [CD-ROM and online]
Evelyn, *Diary*	*The diary of John Evelyn*, ed. E. S. De Beer, 6 vols. (1955); repr. (2000)
Farington, *Diary*	*The diary of Joseph Farington*, ed. K. Garlick and others, 17 vols. (1978–98)
Fasti Angl. (Hardy)	J. Le Neve, *Fasti ecclesiae Anglicanae*, ed. T. D. Hardy, 3 vols. (1854)
Fasti Angl., 1066–1300	[J. Le Neve], *Fasti ecclesiae Anglicanae, 1066–1300*, ed. D. E. Greenway and J. S. Barrow, [8 vols.] (1968–)
Fasti Angl., 1300–1541	[J. Le Neve], *Fasti ecclesiae Anglicanae, 1300–1541*, 12 vols. (1962–7)
Fasti Angl., 1541–1857	[J. Le Neve], *Fasti ecclesiae Anglicanae, 1541–1857*, ed. J. M. Horn, D. M. Smith, and D. S. Bailey, [9 vols.] (1969–)
Fasti Scot.	H. Scott, *Fasti ecclesiae Scoticanae*, 3 vols. in 6 (1871); new edn, [11 vols.] (1915–)
FO List	*Foreign Office List*
Fortescue, *Brit. army*	J. W. Fortescue, *A history of the British army*, 13 vols. (1899–1930)
Foss, *Judges*	E. Foss, *The judges of England*, 9 vols. (1848–64); repr. (1966)
Foster, *Alum. Oxon.*	J. Foster, ed., *Alumni Oxonienses: the members of the University of Oxford, 1715–1886*, 4 vols. (1887–8); later edn (1891); also *Alumni Oxonienses … 1500–1714*, 4 vols. (1891–2); 8 vol. repr. (1968) and (2000)
Fuller, *Worthies*	T. Fuller, *The history of the worthies of England*, 4 pts (1662); new edn, 2 vols., ed. J. Nichols (1811); new edn, 3 vols., ed. P. A. Nuttall (1840); repr. (1965)
GEC, *Baronetage*	G. E. Cokayne, *Complete baronetage*, 6 vols. (1900–09); repr. (1983) [microprint]
GEC, *Peerage*	G. E. C. [G. E. Cokayne], *The complete peerage of England, Scotland, Ireland, Great Britain, and the United Kingdom*, 8 vols. (1887–98); new edn, ed. V. Gibbs and others, 14 vols. in 15 (1910–98); microprint repr. (1982) and (1987)
Genest, *Eng. stage*	J. Genest, *Some account of the English stage from the Restoration in 1660 to 1830*, 10 vols. (1832); repr. [New York, 1965]
Gillow, *Lit. biog. hist.*	J. Gillow, *A literary and biographical history or bibliographical dictionary of the English Catholics, from the breach with Rome, in 1534, to the present time*, 5 vols. [1885–1902]; repr. (1961); repr. with preface by C. Gillow (1999)
Gir. Camb. opera	*Giraldi Cambrensis opera*, ed. J. S. Brewer, J. F. Dimock, and G. F. Warner, 8 vols., Rolls Series, 21 (1861–91)
GJ	*Geographical Journal*

Gladstone, *Diaries*	*The Gladstone diaries: with cabinet minutes and prime-ministerial correspondence*, ed. M. R. D. Foot and H. C. G. Matthew, 14 vols. (1968–94)
GM	*Gentleman's Magazine*
Graves, *Artists*	A. Graves, ed., *A dictionary of artists who have exhibited works in the principal London exhibitions of oil paintings from 1760 to 1880* (1884); new edn (1895); 3rd edn (1901); facs. edn (1969); repr. [1970], (1973), and (1984)
Graves, *Brit. Inst.*	A. Graves, *The British Institution, 1806–1867: a complete dictionary of contributors and their work from the foundation of the institution* (1875); facs. edn (1908); repr. (1969)
Graves, *RA exhibitors*	A. Graves, *The Royal Academy of Arts: a complete dictionary of contributors and their work from its foundation in 1769 to 1904*, 8 vols. (1905–6); repr. in 4 vols. (1970) and (1972)
Graves, *Soc. Artists*	A. Graves, *The Society of Artists of Great Britain, 1760–1791, the Free Society of Artists, 1761–1783: a complete dictionary* (1907); facs. edn (1969)
Greaves & Zaller, *BDBR*	R. L. Greaves and R. Zaller, eds., *Biographical dictionary of British radicals in the seventeenth century*, 3 vols. (1982–4)
Grove, *Dict. mus.*	G. Grove, ed., *A dictionary of music and musicians*, 5 vols. (1878–90); 2nd edn, ed. J. A. Fuller Maitland (1904–10); 3rd edn, ed. H. C. Colles (1927); 4th edn with suppl. (1940); 5th edn, ed. E. Blom, 9 vols. (1954); suppl. (1961) [see also *New Grove*]
Hall, *Dramatic ports.*	L. A. Hall, *Catalogue of dramatic portraits in the theatre collection of the Harvard College library*, 4 vols. (1930–34)
Hansard	*Hansard's parliamentary debates*, ser. 1–5 (1803–)
Highfill, Burnim & Langhans, *BDA*	P. H. Highfill, K. A. Burnim, and E. A. Langhans, *A biographical dictionary of actors, actresses, musicians, dancers, managers, and other stage personnel in London, 1660–1800*, 16 vols. (1973–93)
Hist. U. Oxf.	T. H. Aston, ed., *The history of the University of Oxford*, 8 vols. (1984–2000) [1: *The early Oxford schools*, ed. J. I. Catto (1984); 2: *Late medieval Oxford*, ed. J. I. Catto and R. Evans (1992); 3: *The collegiate university*, ed. J. McConica (1986); 4: *Seventeenth-century Oxford*, ed. N. Tyacke (1997); 5: *The eighteenth century*, ed. L. S. Sutherland and L. G. Mitchell (1986); 6–7: *Nineteenth-century Oxford*, ed. M. G. Brock and M. C. Curthoys (1997–2000); 8: *The twentieth century*, ed. B. Harrison (2000)]
HJ	*Historical Journal*
HMC	Historical Manuscripts Commission
Holdsworth, *Eng. law*	W. S. Holdsworth, *A history of English law*, ed. A. L. Goodhart and H. L. Hanbury, 17 vols. (1903–72)
HoP, *Commons*	*The history of parliament: the House of Commons* [*1386–1421*, ed. J. S. Roskell, L. Clark, and C. Rawcliffe, 4 vols. (1992); *1509–1558*, ed. S. T. Bindoff, 3 vols. (1982); *1558–1603*, ed. P. W. Hasler, 3 vols. (1981); *1660–1690*, ed. B. D. Henning, 3 vols. (1983); *1690–1715*, ed. D. W. Hayton, E. Cruickshanks, and S. Handley, 5 vols. (2002); *1715–1754*, ed. R. Sedgwick, 2 vols. (1970); *1754–1790*, ed. L. Namier and J. Brooke, 3 vols. (1964), repr. (1985); *1790–1820*, ed. R. G. Thorne, 5 vols. (1986); in draft (used with permission): *1422–1504*, *1604–1629*, *1640–1660*, and *1820–1832*]
IGI	*International Genealogical Index*, Church of Jesus Christ of the Latterday Saints
ILN	*Illustrated London News*
IMC	Irish Manuscripts Commission
Irving, *Scots.*	J. Irving, ed., *The book of Scotsmen eminent for achievements in arms and arts, church and state, law, legislation and literature, commerce, science, travel and philanthropy* (1881)
JCS	*Journal of the Chemical Society*
JHC	*Journals of the House of Commons*
JHL	*Journals of the House of Lords*
John of Worcester, *Chron.*	*The chronicle of John of Worcester*, ed. R. R. Darlington and P. McGurk, trans. J. Bray and P. McGurk, 3 vols., OMT (1995–) [vol. 1 forthcoming]
Keeler, *Long Parliament*	M. F. Keeler, *The Long Parliament, 1640–1641: a biographical study of its members* (1954)
Kelly, *Handbk*	*The upper ten thousand: an alphabetical list of all members of noble families*, 3 vols. (1875–7); continued as *Kelly's handbook of the upper ten thousand for 1878* [1879], 2 vols. (1878–9); continued as *Kelly's handbook to the titled, landed and official classes*, 94 vols. (1880–1973)
LondG	*London Gazette*
LP Henry VIII	J. S. Brewer, J. Gairdner, and R. H. Brodie, eds., *Letters and papers, foreign and domestic, of the reign of Henry VIII*, 23 vols. in 38 (1862–1932); repr. (1965)
Mallalieu, *Watercolour artists*	H. L. Mallalieu, *The dictionary of British watercolour artists up to 1820*, 3 vols. (1976–90); vol. 1, 2nd edn (1986)
Memoirs FRS	*Biographical Memoirs of Fellows of the Royal Society*
MGH	Monumenta Germaniae Historica
MT	*Musical Times*
Munk, *Roll*	W. Munk, *The roll of the Royal College of Physicians of London*, 2 vols. (1861); 2nd edn, 3 vols. (1878)
N&Q	*Notes and Queries*
New Grove	S. Sadie, ed., *The new Grove dictionary of music and musicians*, 20 vols. (1980); 2nd edn, 29 vols. (2001) [also online edn; see also Grove, *Dict. mus.*]
Nichols, *Illustrations*	J. Nichols and J. B. Nichols, *Illustrations of the literary history of the eighteenth century*, 8 vols. (1817–58)
Nichols, *Lit. anecdotes*	J. Nichols, *Literary anecdotes of the eighteenth century*, 9 vols. (1812–16); facs. edn (1966)
Obits. FRS	*Obituary Notices of Fellows of the Royal Society*
O'Byrne, *Naval biog. dict.*	W. R. O'Byrne, *A naval biographical dictionary* (1849); repr. (1990); [2nd edn], 2 vols. (1861)
OHS	Oxford Historical Society
Old Westminsters	*The record of Old Westminsters*, 1–2, ed. G. F. R. Barker and A. H. Stenning (1928); suppl. 1, ed. J. B. Whitmore and G. R. Y. Radcliffe [1938]; 3, ed. J. B. Whitmore, G. R. Y. Radcliffe, and D. C. Simpson (1963); suppl. 2, ed. F. E. Pagan (1978); 4, ed. F. E. Pagan and H. E. Pagan (1992)
OMT	Oxford Medieval Texts
Ordericus Vitalis, *Eccl. hist.*	*The ecclesiastical history of Orderic Vitalis*, ed. and trans. M. Chibnall, 6 vols., OMT (1969–80); repr. (1990)
Paris, *Chron.*	*Matthaei Parisiensis, monachi sancti Albani, chronica majora*, ed. H. R. Luard, Rolls Series, 7 vols. (1872–83)
Parl. papers	*Parliamentary papers* (1801–)
PBA	*Proceedings of the British Academy*

Pepys, *Diary*	*The diary of Samuel Pepys*, ed. R. Latham and W. Matthews, 11 vols. (1970–83); repr. (1995) and (2000)
Pevsner	N. Pevsner and others, Buildings of England series
PICE	*Proceedings of the Institution of Civil Engineers*
Pipe rolls	*The great roll of the pipe for* . . ., PRSoc. (1884–)
PRO	Public Record Office
PRS	*Proceedings of the Royal Society of London*
PRSoc.	Pipe Roll Society
PTRS	*Philosophical Transactions of the Royal Society*
QR	*Quarterly Review*
RC	Record Commissions
Redgrave, *Artists*	S. Redgrave, *A dictionary of artists of the English school* (1874); rev. edn (1878); repr. (1970)
Reg. Oxf.	C. W. Boase and A. Clark, eds., *Register of the University of Oxford*, 5 vols., OHS, 1, 10–12, 14 (1885–9)
Reg. PCS	J. H. Burton and others, eds., *The register of the privy council of Scotland*, 1st ser., 14 vols. (1877–98); 2nd ser., 8 vols. (1899–1908); 3rd ser., [16 vols.] (1908–70)
Reg. RAN	H. W. C. Davis and others, eds., *Regesta regum Anglo-Normannorum, 1066–1154*, 4 vols. (1913–69)
RIBA Journal	*Journal of the Royal Institute of British Architects* [later *RIBA Journal*]
RotP	J. Strachey, ed., *Rotuli parliamentorum ut et petitiones, et placita in parliamento*, 6 vols. (1767–77)
RotS	D. Macpherson, J. Caley, and W. Illingworth, eds., *Rotuli Scotiae in Turri Londinensi et in domo capitulari Westmonasteriensi asservati*, 2 vols., RC, 14 (1814–19)
RS	Record(s) Society
Rymer, *Foedera*	T. Rymer and R. Sanderson, eds., *Foedera, conventiones, literae et cuiuscunque generis acta publica inter reges Angliae et alios quosvis imperatores, reges, pontifices, principes, vel communitates*, 20 vols. (1704–35); 2nd edn, 20 vols. (1726–35); 3rd edn, 10 vols. (1739–45), facs. edn (1967); new edn, ed. A. Clarke, J. Caley, and F. Holbrooke, 4 vols., RC, 50 (1816–30)
Sainty, *Judges*	J. Sainty, ed., *The judges of England, 1272–1990*, SeldS, suppl. ser., 10 (1993)
Sainty, *King's counsel*	J. Sainty, ed., *A list of English law officers and king's counsel*, SeldS, suppl. ser., 7 (1987)
SCH	Studies in Church History
Scots peerage	J. B. Paul, ed. *The Scots peerage, founded on Wood's edition of Sir Robert Douglas's Peerage of Scotland, containing an historical and genealogical account of the nobility of that kingdom*, 9 vols. (1904–14)
SeldS	Selden Society
SHR	*Scottish Historical Review*
State trials	T. B. Howell and T. J. Howell, eds., *Cobbett's Complete collection of state trials*, 34 vols. (1809–28)
STC, 1475–1640	A. W. Pollard, G. R. Redgrave, and others, eds., *A short-title catalogue of* . . . *English books* . . . *1475–1640* (1926); 2nd edn, ed. W. A. Jackson, F. S. Ferguson, and K. F. Pantzer, 3 vols. (1976–91) [see also Wing, *STC*]
STS	Scottish Text Society
SurtS	Surtees Society
Symeon of Durham, *Opera*	*Symeonis monachi opera omnia*, ed. T. Arnold, 2 vols., Rolls Series, 75 (1882–5); repr. (1965)
Tanner, *Bibl. Brit.-Hib.*	T. Tanner, *Bibliotheca Britannico-Hibernica*, ed. D. Wilkins (1748); repr. (1963)
Thieme & Becker, *Allgemeines Lexikon*	U. Thieme, F. Becker, and H. Vollmer, eds., *Allgemeines Lexikon der bildenden Künstler von der Antike bis zur Gegenwart*, 37 vols. (Leipzig, 1907–50); repr. (1961–5), (1983), and (1992)
Thurloe, *State papers*	*A collection of the state papers of John Thurloe*, ed. T. Birch, 7 vols. (1742)
TLS	*Times Literary Supplement*
Tout, *Admin. hist.*	T. F. Tout, *Chapters in the administrative history of mediaeval England: the wardrobe, the chamber, and the small seals*, 6 vols. (1920–33); repr. (1967)
TRHS	*Transactions of the Royal Historical Society*
VCH	H. A. Doubleday and others, eds., *The Victoria history of the counties of England*, [88 vols.] (1900–)
Venn, *Alum. Cant.*	J. Venn and J. A. Venn, *Alumni Cantabrigienses: a biographical list of all known students, graduates, and holders of office at the University of Cambridge, from the earliest times to 1900*, 10 vols. (1922–54); repr. in 2 vols. (1974–8)
Vertue, *Note books*	[G. Vertue], *Note books*, ed. K. Esdaile, earl of Ilchester, and H. M. Hake, 6 vols., Walpole Society, 18, 20, 22, 24, 26, 30 (1930–55)
VF	*Vanity Fair*
Walford, *County families*	E. Walford, *The county families of the United Kingdom, or, Royal manual of the titled and untitled aristocracy of Great Britain and Ireland* (1860)
Walker rev.	A. G. Matthews, *Walker revised: being a revision of John Walker's Sufferings of the clergy during the grand rebellion, 1642–60* (1948); repr. (1988)
Walpole, *Corr.*	*The Yale edition of Horace Walpole's correspondence*, ed. W. S. Lewis, 48 vols. (1937–83)
Ward, *Men of the reign*	T. H. Ward, ed., *Men of the reign: a biographical dictionary of eminent persons of British and colonial birth who have died during the reign of Queen Victoria* (1885); repr. (Graz, 1968)
Waterhouse, *18c painters*	E. Waterhouse, *The dictionary of 18th century painters in oils and crayons* (1981); repr. as *British 18th century painters in oils and crayons* (1991), vol. 2 of *Dictionary of British art*
Watt, *Bibl. Brit.*	R. Watt, *Bibliotheca Britannica, or, A general index to British and foreign literature*, 4 vols. (1824) [many reprs.]
Wellesley index	W. E. Houghton, ed., *The Wellesley index to Victorian periodicals, 1824–1900*, 5 vols. (1966–89); new edn (1999) [CD-ROM]
Wing, *STC*	D. Wing, ed., *Short-title catalogue of* . . . *English books* . . . *1641–1700*, 3 vols. (1945–51); 2nd edn (1972–88); rev. and enl. edn, ed. J. J. Morrison, C. W. Nelson, and M. Seccombe, 4 vols. (1994–8) [see also *STC, 1475–1640*]
Wisden	*John Wisden's Cricketer's Almanack*
Wood, *Ath. Oxon.*	A. Wood, *Athenae Oxonienses* . . . *to which are added the Fasti*, 2 vols. (1691–2); 2nd edn (1721); new edn, 4 vols., ed. P. Bliss (1813–20); repr. (1967) and (1969)
Wood, *Vic. painters*	C. Wood, *Dictionary of Victorian painters* (1971); 2nd edn (1978); 3rd edn as *Victorian painters*, 2 vols. (1995), vol. 4 of *Dictionary of British art*
WW	*Who's who* (1849–)
WWBMP	M. Stenton and S. Lees, eds., *Who's who of British members of parliament*, 4 vols. (1976–81)
WWW	*Who was who* (1929–)

Blackmore, Chewning (1663–1737). *See under* Blackmore, William (1616–1684).

Blackmore, Sir Richard (1654–1729), physician and writer, was born on 22 January 1654 at Corsham, Wiltshire, the third of the four children of Robert Blackmore (*d.* 1681), a wealthy attorney, and Anne Pilsworth, *née* Harris (*fl.* 1633–1676), widow of Edward Pilsworth. According to Giles Jacob, Blackmore was educated at a country school and then at Westminster School for a brief period. On 19 March 1669 he matriculated at St Edmund Hall, Oxford, where he took his BA on 4 April 1674 and MA on 3 June 1676. He continued as tutor at St Edmund Hall and perhaps worked for some time as a schoolmaster.

The year after his father's death Blackmore went to the continent. He first stayed in France, then moved to Geneva, where he composed his first literary work: a Latin epitaph for Thomas Bent, a fellow of Lincoln College, Oxford. From there he went to Italy, where he visited Rome, Venice, and Padua. In Padua he stopped to study medicine at the local university, where he graduated doctor of pure medicine on 24 March 1684. He then returned to England via Germany and Holland, and settled in London to start practice. On 9 February 1685 Blackmore married Mary Adams (*d.* 1728), who was related to an important whig family, the Verneys of Claydon House, Buckinghamshire, who probably helped him in his career. On 12 April 1687, at the *comitia majora extraordinaria*, Blackmore was admitted as a fellow of the Royal College of Physicians. His relationship with the college was turbulent: he was censured for leave-taking without permission and had strong disagreements with the president and the majority of the college, principally over the project to establish a dispensary to provide free drugs for the London poor, something which Blackmore opposed vehemently.

In 1695 Blackmore published *Prince Arthur: an Heroick Poem in Ten Books*, which he stated he had written with the aim of reforming contemporary poetry from the immorality and impiety of the age. The poem, modelled on Virgil's *Aeneid* and based on Geoffrey of Monmouth's *Historia regum Britanniae*, narrates Arthur's defence of the Britons against the usurping Saxons and his final conquest of London. It displays a transparent political allegory, with the pious Arthur representing William III and his ungodly antagonist symbolizing James II. Despite the severe criticism by John Dennis, who in his *Remarks on a Book Entitled Prince Arthur* (1696) reproved Blackmore's 'servile' imitation of Virgil, the tedious digressiveness of the plot, and the inconsequency of its 'fearful' hero, the poem sold well, reaching a third edition.

King William, who had appointed Blackmore as one of his physicians-in-ordinary, was so pleased with the poem as to present him with a medal of gold and then to knight him on 18 March 1697. Blackmore, who always manifested his attachment to the king and the revolution (PRO, C.213/168, chancery: petty bag office, association oath rolls, College of Physicians, London, 1696), was chosen to write the story of Sir George Barclay's plot to murder the king (which was published only in 1723 as *A true and impartial history of the conspiracy against the person and government of King William III, of glorious memory, in the year 1695*). In 1697 a sequel to his first poem appeared, *King Arthur: an Heroic Poem in Twelve Books*, which continued the allegorical treatment of contemporary events with a Virgilian structure and a Miltonic diction; in its preface, however, Blackmore acknowledged the defects of his former epic, rejecting Aristotelian 'rules' for a more sublime style. The poem was greeted with less enthusiasm than *Prince Arthur* and did not go into any further editions.

Sir Richard Blackmore (1654–1729), by R. Williams, pubd *c.*1697 (after John Closterman)

Blackmore was made the object of ridicule and lampoons by the wits he had chastised for their impiety and by the Dispensarians (particularly virulent was Sir Samuel Garth's attack in his *The Dispensary*, 1699), and he decided to retort with the poem *A Satyr against Wit* (1700). The wits, led by Tom Brown, made things worse with the publication of the mocking *Commendatory Verses, on the Author of the Two Arthurs, and the Satyr against Wit* (1700). Blackmore, who in the meantime was engaged in his *Paraphrase on the Book of Job* (1700), a Christian epic with a virtuous and peaceful hero, saw the assault rebutted by his supporters' *Discommendatory Verses, on those which are Truly Commendatory, on the Author of the Two Arthurs, and the Satyr against Wit* (1700). The attacks on Blackmore were further exacerbated when John Dryden accused him of plagiarism of his own project of an Arthurian epic. Dryden described Blackmore (who had offensively portrayed him in *Prince Arthur* and in the *Satyr against Wit*) as a 'Pedant, Canting Preacher, and a Quack' who wrote while travelling from patient to patient, 'to the rumbling of his Coaches Wheels' (J. Dryden, prologue to *The Pilgrim*, 1700, 42, 49). The wits sneered at the 'City Bard' and 'Cheapside Knight', as they labelled Blackmore on account of his residence in Cheapside, both as a poet and a physician who 'killed' his victims with his verses and his pills. This trite stricture aside, Blackmore was considered one of the leaders of the medical profession and his skills were commended by his contemporaries, notably by John Locke. As a physician-in-ordinary to King William (whom he assisted until his death) Blackmore was entitled to a lodging at Hampton Court and to a salary of £100 per half year (PRO, T. 61/16/78). He later held the same post to Queen Anne.

Despite the wits' assault, in 1705 Blackmore published one more epic, *Eliza: an Epic Poem in Ten Books*, a poem on the Spanish (that is, Popish) conspiracies against Elizabeth and protestantism (Anne and the Church of England). Samuel Johnson stated that *Eliza* 'dropped, as it seems, dead-born from the press' (Johnson, *Poets*, 3.81), but the poem did not pass unobserved, for its sardonic portrayal of Roderigo Lopez, the Portuguese physician who made an attempt on Elizabeth's life, was an allegory of John Radcliffe, the eminent physician who was suspected of Jacobite inclinations and had alienated the sympathies of the queen. Blackmore celebrated Queen Anne in her triumphant campaigns in the Seven Years' War, with the long poem *An advice to the poets: a poem occasioned by the wonderful success of her majesty's arms, under the conduct of the duke of Marlborough in Flanders* (1706), and the *Instructions to Vander Bank, a sequel to the Advice to the poets: a poem, occasion'd by the glorious success of her majesty's arms, under the command of the duke of Marlborough, the last year in Flanders* (1709). In 1711 appeared *The Nature of Man*, a physico-theological poem about the effects of climate on man's intellectual faculties, and a tribute to English prosperity and constitutional freedom. It was followed in 1712 by another physico-theological work, *Creation: a Philosophical Poem*, which was highly praised for its lofty, Miltonic style by Dennis, Addison, and, later, by Johnson, who included it in his edition of the English poets. The poem, which was acclaimed as the English *De rerum natura* and went through sixteen editions, becoming the most popular of Blackmore's works, is a confutation of the atomistic theories of Epicurus and his modern followers, and a vindication of the operations of divine providence.

On 13 November 1713 Blackmore and his friend John Hughes started *The Lay-Monk*, published every third week, and which followed the example of *The Spectator* and *The Guardian*. It ceased publication on 15 February 1714, after forty numbers, subsequently collected as *The Lay-Monastery* (1714). With the accession of the Hanoverians, Blackmore was no longer summoned to court as physician-in-ordinary, yet his medical career was still successful: in 1716 the College of Physicians made him censor and, on 22 August 1716, selected him as one of the eight elects, the college's ruling body. Meanwhile he moved residence from Cheapside to Earls Court, Kensington. In 1716 and 1717 Blackmore published two volumes of *Essays upon Several Subjects* (on topics ranging from the immortality of the soul to the origin of civil power). The second volume contained a tirade against Alexander Pope's blasphemous parody of the first psalm of David, which had been surreptitiously printed by the hack publisher Edmund Curll. A feud between Blackmore and Pope started and never really ended, though it remained mostly at a literary level. Blackmore became one of the main butts of Pope and his Scriblerian friends, who ridiculed him as physician in the play *Three Hours after Marriage* (1717), castigated him as poet in *The Dunciad* (1728, 2.247–56), and scoffed at his bombastic verses in the mock treatise *Peri Bathous: of the Art of Sinking in Poetry* (1727). In 1718 *A Collection of Poems on Various Subjects* appeared, containing many of Blackmore's previously published shorter poems and a few new ones.

In 1721 Blackmore published a religious treatise, *Just Prejudices against the Arian Hypothesis*, written 'in the Defence of God's Existence against the Atheist; and in Vindication of the Christian Religion against the Deist; and of the Divinity of Christ against the Arian and Socinian' (p. 11). It was immediately followed by a sequel, *Modern Arians Unmasked* (1721). Blackmore had always been a supporter of the established church: he was a member of the vestry in the parishes of St Vedast, Foster Lane, and St Michael Le Quern, London, where he also served as a verger, and in 1704 was made one of the vice-presidents of the Society for the Propagation of the Gospel in America. In 1721 he published *A New Version of the Psalms of David*, which he strove ineffectually to have adopted in the church. In 1724 the Society for the Propagation of the Gospel undertook to print a selection of Blackmore's psalms, which however never came to press because of the opposition of the bishop of London. Blackmore was not discouraged in his zealous fight for the reformation of the age, and in 1722 sent to the press *Redemption*, a poem on the divinity of Christ, against the Arian hypothesis.

On 22 October 1722, after leaving Kensington to retire to Boxted, Essex, Blackmore resigned his position as an elect of the College of Physicians. In 1723 his last epic poem, *Alfred*, appeared, which he dedicated to Prince Frederick of Hanover with the aim of instilling in him 'just Ideas of political Prudence, and … an honourable Ambition of becoming a publick Blessing' (sig. a2*r*). The poem failed to win him the attention of the court and went unnoticed by the public. Far from the London crowd, in his Boxted retirement, Blackmore dedicated the last years of his life to the writing of various medical treatises, on the plague (1720), the smallpox (1722), consumption, the gout, dropsy (1727), and the spleen. They are imbued with a religious zeal against atheistic and heretic conceptions and earnestly advocate a pragmatic and anti-academic approach to medicine; Blackmore wrote in English instead of Latin to preserve 'the true Dignity and Worth of Physick … as much as can be [from] Philosophical Notions and Scholastick Darkness' (*A Treatise of Consumptions and other Distempers Belonging to the Breast and Lungs*, 1724, xi). Blackmore was a follower of Sir Thomas Sydenham and stressed the importance of experience and observation over pure speculation and erudition, the 'extensive Mechanical Knowledge of Books … that is call'd Misteria Literaria' (*Discourse on the Gout, a Rheumatism, and the King's Evil*, 1726, xxxvii). His strenuous empiricism made him reject the Galenic theory of the four humours, as well as other medical schools based on hypothetical conjecture. He was particularly attracted to the subject of the spleen, to which he had already devoted one of his *Essays on Various Subjects*, and which he investigated in *A Treatise of the Spleen and Vapours* and *A Critical Dissertation upon the Spleen* (both 1725). In 1728 he published one more religious treatise, *Natural Theology, or, Moral Duties Consider'd apart from Positive*.

Blackmore, who in later life suffered from colic, died at Boxted, Essex, on 9 October 1729 and was buried at the parish church there, where a monumental inscription to his memory was erected. His last work, *The Accomplished Preacher*, was posthumously published by his literary executor, the Revd John White of Nayland, Essex, in 1731.

FLAVIO GREGORI

Sources A. Rosenberg, *Sir Richard Blackmore: a poet and physician of the Augustan age* (1953) · E. Hudson Long, 'Notes on Sir Richard Blackmore', *Modern Language Notes*, 58 (1943), 585–9 · Munk, *Roll* · R. C. Boys, *Sir Richard Blackmore and the wits* (1949) · T. F. M. Newton, 'Blackmore's Eliza', *Harvard Studies and Notes in Philology and Literature*, 17 (1935), 113–23 · S. Johnson, *Prefaces, biographical and critical, to the works of the English poets*, 5 (1781) · H. M. Solomon, *Sir Richard Blackmore* (1980) · G. Jacob, *An historical account of the lives and writings of our most considerable English poets* (1720), 9–11 · R. Shiels, *The lives of the poets of Great Britain and Ireland*, ed. T. Cibber, 5 (1753), 177–91 · T. N. Toomey, 'Sir Richard Blackmore, M.D.', *Annals of Medical History*, 4 (1922), 180–88 · M. Kelley, 'Sir Richard Blackmore in the judgment of his fellow writers', *Journal of the History of Medicine and Allied Sciences*, 16 (1961), 186–9 · Foster, *Alum. Oxon.* · D. Boyce, 'The dispensary, Sir Richard Blackmore, and the captain of the wits', *Review of English Studies*, 14 (1938), 453–8 · Wood, *Ath. Oxon.: Fasti* (1815), 379 · G. Clark and A. M. Cooke, *A history of the Royal College of Physicians of London*, 3 vols. (1964–72)

Likenesses R. Williams, mezzotint, pubd *c*.1697 (after J. Closterman?), BM [*see illus.*] · attrib. J. Closterman, oils, RCP Lond. · G. White, mezzotint (after J. Vanderbank), BM, NPG

Wealth at death approx. £3300: will, PRO, PROB 11/633

Blackmore, Richard Doddridge (1825–1900), novelist and fruit farmer, was born on 7 June 1825, at the vicarage, Longworth, Berkshire, the third but second surviving son of the Revd John Blackmore (1794–1858) and his first wife, Anne Basset Knight (1794–1825). Anne was the eldest daughter of the Revd Robert Knight (1764?–1819), vicar of Tewkesbury, Gloucestershire, and of Bayton, Worcestershire, and his second wife, Harriet Mercy Humphreys (1769–1846), after whose maternal grandfather, the nonconformist minister Philip *Doddridge (1702–1751), Richard was named.

Early years and education John Blackmore had been curate-in-charge of Longworth, a few miles south-west of Oxford, since 1820, and supplemented his income by coaching undergraduates. However, before Richard was three months old, typhus struck the village and carried off, among other members of the household, his mother and her twin sister. The baby Richard and his elder brother, Henry (1824–1875), were taken in charge by his mother's

Richard Doddridge Blackmore (1825–1900), by Frederick Jenkins

younger sister Mary Frances Knight (*d.* 1878), whom he described as 'my dearest relative (who was my mother till I got a step one)' (R. Blackmore to Mrs Halliday, 1 July 1875, cited in Dunn, 27). Much of his early childhood was spent with her at the home of his maternal grandmother and uncles at Newton Nottage, Glamorgan, on the north shore of the Bristol Channel. His bereaved father, who had left Longworth after the tragedy, moved back to King's Nympton in his native Devon in 1832. Blackmore also used to visit his paternal grandfather, the Revd John Blackmore (1764–1842), who lived at Combe Martin, in north-west Devon, but held another cure at Oare on the north edge of Exmoor. All these remote and beautiful places were later to feature largely in his fiction, which was haunted by the figure of the homeless orphan baby, and was also coloured by an enthusiasm for antiquarianism and natural history encouraged by his mother's brother the Revd Henry Hey Knight (1795–1857).

In November 1831 Blackmore's father married his second wife, Charlotte Ann Platt; they were to have two daughters and a son. This event, which was followed by Mary Knight's marriage to the Revd Richard Gordon in July 1832, meant that the Blackmore boys again had a permanent home with their father. In 1833 Richard was at Squier's Grammar School, South Molton, Devon, and in 1833–4 at the King's School, Bruton, Somerset. In August 1837 he went to Blundell's School, Tiverton, Devon, where his father had been before him, and where he himself was to send John Ridd, the hero of his most famous novel. His brother did not go with him. Tiverton is some 10 miles east of Culmstock, the village in the Blackdown hills where John Blackmore was curate-in-charge from 1835 to 1841, and Blackmore lived in the town during the week and returned home for Sunday. He lodged with two older boys, Frederick Temple (1821–1902), later archbishop of Canterbury, and his younger brother John, sons of an impoverished widow living at Culmstock; when they left the school in March 1839 Blackmore became a boarder. During his time at Blundell's the day boys, who were educated by the foundation, were subject to appalling persecution by the fee-paying boarders (in 1847 a public scandal led to reform). Blackmore's treatment is sometimes said to have caused his lifelong epilepsy. The main authority for Blackmore's sufferings at Blundell's is F. J. Snell, whose father had been at school with him: he claims that Frederick Temple used to hit him on the head with a hammer, and that Blackmore was given a nickname so vile as to be 'too brutally frank for mature ears' (Snell, 'Richard Doddridge Blackmore', 155). However the picture Blackmore gives of Blundell's in *Lorna Doone* is not a wholly antagonistic one, and his old-fashioned grammar school education laid the foundation for his lifelong devotion to the classics. He became head boy of the school, and gained a school scholarship to Exeter College, Oxford, where he went at the end of 1843 and where he was happy. He graduated with a second-class degree in classics in 1847, and after a short time as a tutor decided to study law; he was called to the bar at the Middle Temple in June 1852, and is said to have practised as a conveyancer for some years.

Marriage and new career On 8 November 1853 at Holy Trinity Church, Gray's Inn Road, London, without the knowledge or approval of his family, Blackmore married Lucy Maguire or McGuire (*c*.1827–1888) of Guernsey, who was a Roman Catholic born in Dublin, and whose father, Edmond Paul Maguire, is unilluminatingly described on the marriage certificate as a government secretary. Her mother was probably named Margaret Lynch. It is said by S. J. Reid that Blackmore had first met her as an undergraduate, while with a college reading party in Jersey which was boarding in her family's house. The marriage proved happy, though childless; Lucy Blackmore became a member of the Church of England, and friendly relations between the couple and the Revd John Blackmore had been established before the latter's death in 1858. Religious and social barriers between lovers were to be a frequent motif in Blackmore's fiction, notably in *Lorna Doone*. The marriage certificate also gives Blackmore's profession as 'writer for the press', which suggests that, like many briefless barristers of the time, he had taken to journalism. It has been said that Blackmore's decision to abandon his career at the bar was connected to his fear of having an epileptic fit in court, rather than a result of any lack of success as a lawyer. Whatever the truth of this, in 1855 he joined the staff of Wellesley House grammar school, Twickenham. Hitherto he and his wife had lived in lodgings in Rochester Square, Camden Town; they now moved to Hampton Wick. In 1857 Henry Hey Knight died and left him enough money to give up teaching, which he is said to have disliked, and buy some land at nearby Teddington, where he built a house, called Gomer House after a favourite dog, planted an orchard, and set up as a market gardener.

Blackmore's fruit farming was his main occupation for the rest of his life, although, perhaps because of his high standards, he lost more money than he made. Even after he had become a successful novelist, he wrote that 'All the time that I can spare from the pen is occupied by the more congenial trowel' (R. Blackmore to Paul H. Hayne, 31 May 1884, cited in Burris, 177). He became an accepted authority on fruit growing, contributing articles on the subject to several reference books, and in September 1894 took part in a fierce controversy in *The Times* on the relative merits of British and Californian fruit. From 1883 until 1892 he served on the fruit and vegetable committee of the Royal Horticultural Society.

The apparently abrupt change of tack from teaching schoolboys Latin and Greek to growing apples and pears should be seen in connection with Blackmore's interest in an ideal of rural life. One of his earlier publications was *The farm and fruit of old: a translation in verse of the first and second georgics of Virgil, by a market gardener* (1862), and his greatest success as a novelist was with an idyll of seventeenth-century Devon, whose hero is also both a classicist and a farmer. Blackmore had always dreamed of 'a house in the country encompassed by a large garden' (*DNB*): in his novels he was again and again to depict a version of the Horatian Happy Man, farming and gardening in obscure domestic bliss in England in the seventeenth, eighteenth, or early nineteenth centuries. He translated Theocritus and Horace as well as Virgil, and allusions to classical literature and mythology pervade his work. It is hard to assess whether the exigencies of farming fruit (which frost or wind may spoil from one day to the next) developed in Blackmore the passionate interest in weather which is so marked a feature of his fiction, or whether his choice of occupation was determined by a pre-existing obsession with the subject.

Blackmore's earliest publications were all verse: two volumes under the pseudonym Melanter ('more black' in Greek), appeared in 1854, and in the following year a patriotic poem on the Crimean War, *The Bugle of the Black Sea: the Fate of Franklin* (1860), was published under his own name. None of them caught the public attention, and even when he did turn to publishing prose fiction, he had no success for some years. *Clara Vaughan* (1864), the story of a girl who grows up hoping to revenge her father's murder, is an autobiographical narrative, partly set in Camden Town, with some effective passages of lush description of nature in north Devon and Corsica, and a complicated plot involving an Italian vendetta. Inspector Cutting is an early literary portrait of a police detective. The book came out in the heyday of the sensation novel, and some reviewers detected the hand of a woman author; Blackmore later defended himself against the charge of having imitated Mary Braddon's *Eleanor's Victory* (3 vols., 1863), another novel about a woman revenging her father's murder. His next novel, *Cradock Nowell: a Tale of the New Forest*, was serialized (1865–6), and, Blackmore wrote, 'spoiled by *Macmillan's Magazine*. I was repeatedly interfered with, and never left to my own course' (R. Blackmore to Nelson Fedden, 17 Feb 1873, cited in Dunn, 116). It appeared in one volume in 1866; a much revised version was published in 1873. Like *Clara Vaughan*, it was set in the present day.

Lorna Doone For his third novel, *Lorna Doone*, begun in February 1865, Blackmore drew on legends and tales circulating in Devon and Somerset associated with the area of north-east Exmoor which he knew from his childhood visits to his Blackmore grandfather, and set his novel in the late seventeenth century, against the background of Monmouth's uprising. John Ridd, a yeoman farmer, recounts the story of his courtship of Lorna, kidnapped as a baby by the outlawed Doones, and brought up in their Exmoor fastness, half-captive, half-queen. The hidden combe becomes a symbolic landscape of initiation and sexual awakening; Lorna is an English Persephone: intermittently visible, shedding her sweetness over the fertile landscape. Her marriage to John symbolizes the appropriation of aristocratic power by the hard-working middle class, while the picture of plenitude and rural festivity at Plovers Barrows offers a fantasy of English communal life in the shadow of war and corrupt government. The first edition of the book did not sell particularly well, but the one-volume cheap edition of 1870 became a best-seller; Blackmore himself believed the story that its sales were boosted by the announcement in October 1870 of the engagement of Princess Louise to the marquess of Lorne (in the novel Lorna is supposed to be descended from the earls of Lorne). Combining romance, adventure, and idyll, *Lorna Doone* has been continuously in print since its publication, though its wide currency among schoolchildren is probably a thing of the past. Like *Robinson Crusoe* and *Gulliver's Travels*, however, it circulated in the twentieth century to a very large extent in abridged and simplified versions (*BL cat.* lists nineteen), not only because of its length and its plentiful digressions, and the fact that the story is filtered through a highly self-conscious and ironic retrospective narrative, but because of the striking difficulty of its language, which abounds in archaic and dialect words and literary and historical allusions. There have been three BBC television versions (in 1963, 1976, and 2000) and seven film versions since 1911, the latest, directed by Andrew Grieve (GB 1990, Working Title), starring Sean Bean as Carver Doone and Billie Whitelaw as Mrs Ridd.

None of Blackmore's other novels ever approached the aesthetic or commercial success of *Lorna Doone*, but his next novel, *The Maid of Sker* (3 vols., 1872), was his own favourite. It is set during the late eighteenth century on both sides of the Bristol Channel, in Newton Nottage and north Devon. Blackmore's intimate knowledge of the localities, his close observation of nature, and his lyrical celebration of weather (a hurricane, a sandstorm), give the story (another lost baby inheritance plot) colour and drama. The narrative is facetiously and bombastically recounted by an untrustworthy Welsh fisherman, Davy Llewelyn. This narrative technique resembles to some extent the subtle use of John Ridd's voice in *Lorna Doone*, without being as successful. Perhaps Blackmore was influenced here by the sentimental comic novels of Edward Bulwer-Lytton, *The Caxtons* (1849) and *My Novel* (1853), of which he wrote 'The Caxton series form to my mind the grandest production of the century' (R. Blackmore to Mrs Halliday, 16 Dec 1876, cited in Dunn, 163). The plot of *The Maid of Sker* is driven by the machinations of the sinister Parson Chowne, one of the worst of Blackmore's many villains, who gets his just deserts by catching hydrophobia and being strangled by a fellow clergyman. The heroine Bardie, a baby found in a boat by Davy, whose baby talk is lovingly recounted, is known to have been based by Blackmore on a niece of his wife's named Eva Pinto Leite (*d.* 1911), who was practically adopted by the childless Blackmores, and kept house for him after Lucy's death.

Private grief and other novels In 1875 Blackmore's brother Henry, a lonely eccentric who, adopting the name of a remote ancestor of the Knights, had changed his name in 1852 to Henry John Turberville, died in a hotel in Yeovil, having made a will leaving his substantial property to the family of the local chemist, to whose daughter he had been engaged. An autopsy revealed the presence of cyanide, and Blackmore made allegations which led to both the chemist's and the doctor's beginning libel proceedings against him. Objections were raised (on grounds of unsound mind and undue influence) by both Blackmore, as next-of-kin and heir-at-law, and the beneficiaries of several earlier wills (who included the atheist and radical Charles Bradlaugh, 1833–1891); after involving Blackmore in a good deal of anxiety the case ended in compromise.

Blackmore's next novel, *Alice Lorraine: a Tale of the South Downs* (3 vols., 1875), an ambitious attempt to depict an early nineteenth-century English Antigone, was so badly reviewed he briefly resolved to abandon novel writing, but a steady stream of novels continued to flow from his pen, and although they never made as much money for him or their publishers as *Lorna Doone* had, he was able to place them as serials and obtain good prices. *Cripps, the Carrier: a Woodland Tale* (3 vols., 1876) is set near Oxford in the winter of 1837–8 and mingles pastoral with satire on the Tractarians. Like many British writers of the time Blackmore resented the piracy of his books in America, but he engaged in cordial correspondence with several of his American fans, and, though he had never visited the United States, or indeed it appears any other foreign country, he made California the setting of *Erema, or, My Father's Sin* (3 vols., 1877), in which, perhaps partly under the influence of his friend the Georgia poet Paul H. Hayne (1830–1886), he gives a sympathetic depiction of the Southern cause. In 1879, shortly after the death of his aunt Mary Gordon, he published anonymously the poem, 'Dominus illuminatio mea', which, placed by Arthur Quiller-Couch at the end of his best-selling *Oxford Book of English Verse, 1250–1900* (1900), achieved fame, although it was not credited to Blackmore for many years. *Mary Anerley: a Yorkshire Tale* (3 vols., 1880), is one of his best novels, again patterned as a search for identity and nourishing communal and domestic life, in this case by the lost baby turned outlaw and smuggler Robin Lyth who loves the heroine, a farmer's daughter. *The Remarkable History of Sir Thomas Upmore* (2 vols., 1884) was an unsuccessful satire, incorporating Blackmore's increasingly choleric views on Gladstonian Liberalism. *Christowell: a Dartmoor Tale* (3 vols., 1882), is one of several novels named after a village and structured as a portrait of a community; its hero has retreated to an inaccessible house and garden to escape a false reputation for cowardice obtained in the Peninsular War. Another is *Springhaven* (3 vols., 1887), admired by many of his fans, a naval tale of the Napoleonic wars, set on the Sussex coast. In some ways an invasion scare story on the model of George Chesney's *The Battle of Dorking* (1871), it has a large cast of characters, mostly residents of the eponymous fishing village, but including both Nelson and Napoleon. In January 1888 Lucy Blackmore died, after many years of chronic invalidism; grief affected all Blackmore's subsequent works, especially *Kit and Kitty: a Story of West Middlesex* (3 vols., 1890), begun in the year of his bereavement, in which he wrote for the first time about his adopted home the Thames valley, setting the novel in the 1850s and 1860s, when he and Lucy were living in Teddington as a young married couple. Kit's wife disappears unaccountably; he is bereft; after an extraordinary series of events she returns and they live happily ever after; the author portrays himself partly as Kit and partly as Uncle Corney, an elderly and grumpy market gardener. Equally elegiac is *Perlycross: a Tale of the Western Hills* (3 vols., 1894) which is, like *Christowell* and *Springhaven*, an anatomy of an entire community. It is set in a village closely modelled on Culmstock, with a hero, a poor widowed curate, modelled on the author's father, in the year 1835, a golden age before the repeal of the corn laws, when 'as yet it was no mockery to cast the fat grain among the clods … Alas, that thy beauty should be of the past, and ground into gritty foreign flour!' (pp. 5–6). The village is struck by a violent storm, and social barriers are overcome for the sake of romance. There are also later works of less importance in prose and verse.

Final years and reputation Blackmore never quite had his due from twentieth-century literary critics, although Max Keith Sutton's 1979 study, written under Northrop Frye's influence, convincingly emphasizes the importance of archetypal patterns to the functioning of his novels. At their best his gift for endowing historical fiction with symbolic resonance, his unsurpassed observation of the natural world, his outstanding power of creating unforgettable visual images (John saving the sheep in *Lorna Doone*, the church struck by lightning in *Christowell*), give his novels qualities which compensate for their lack of organization and their needlessly crabbed language. Blackmore's books do not respond well to fast reading. His superficial nostalgia and conservatism have not recommended him to academic readers and have obscured his deceptively complex narrative techniques and his interest in marshalling a wide variety of mutually contradictory points of view.

Blackmore's own tastes in literature as well as politics were conservative; he was no enthusiast for realism in fiction; nor on the other hand was the late-Victorian flowering of the adventure novel to his taste: he particularly disliked the work of Rider Haggard. But he admired and was on good terms with Hardy, and had a considerable influence on younger regional novelists, such as Hall Caine and Eden Phillpotts. Though there are many witnesses to his charm of manner and generosity, it is hard to avoid the impression that he was sometimes irascible and exacting, especially with his employees. There was a gardener who sabotaged his vines in revenge for being dismissed, and there were housekeeping difficulties (though Blackmore did not take up the offer of help recruiting domestic staff which was made by his lifelong friend Arthur Munby). Throughout his time at Teddington he maintained a running battle with his neighbours the London and South Western Railway Company. After his wife's death he became increasingly infirm and seldom moved far from home. He died at Gomer House, of abdominal cancer, on 20 January 1900 and was buried at Teddington cemetery. There is a memorial in Exeter Cathedral, with a verse inscription by Munby, and a statue of Lorna in Dulverton, while on Exmoor the tourists are still sold postcards of Doone country. CHARLOTTE MITCHELL

Sources M. K. Sutton, *R. D. Blackmore* (1979) · W. H. Dunn, *R. D. Blackmore, the author of Lorna Doone* (1956) · Q. G. Burris, *Richard Doddridge Blackmore* (1930) · *DNB* · F. J. Snell, *Blundell's: a short history of a famous west country school* (1928) · F. J. Snell, *Early associations of Archbishop Temple: a record of Blundell's School and its neighbourhood* (1904) · F. J. Snell, 'Richard Doddridge Blackmore', *Blundell's worthies*, ed. M. L. Banks (1904) · H. H. Knight, 'Account of Newton Nottage, Glamorgan', *Archaeologia Cambrensis*, new ser., 4 (1853), 90–98, 161–80, 229–62 · *IGI* · d. cert. · census returns for Teddington, 1871 · will of John Blackmore (*d.* 1858) · R. Webber and P. A. Ching, *R. D. Blackmore, author and horticulturalist of Teddington*, Borough of Twickenham Local History Society Paper, no. 44 (April 1980) · A. R. B. Thomas, *R. D. Blackmore of Blundell's School* (1984) · E. G. Sandford, ed., *Memoirs of Archbishop Temple, by seven friends*, 2 vols. (1906) · *An inventory of the ancient monuments in Glamorgan*, 4 vols., pt 4: *Domestic architecture from the Reformation to the industrial revolution*; Royal Commission on Ancient and Historical Monuments in Wales and Monmouthshire (1981–) · *DWB* · *Ordnance survey atlas of England and Wales*, Ordnance Survey (1922) · A. D. Fox, ed., *King's School Bruton register enlarged and revised up to May 1911* (1911) · A. Fisher, ed., *The register of Blundell's School* (1904) · private information (2004) [H. Tomlinson, librarian, Priaulx Library, Guernsey; Beatrice Watson, Exebridge]

Archives BL, diary, Add. MS 5771 · Devon RO, school notebooks; papers · Hunt. L., letters and papers · L. Cong., student notes · NL Scot., business corresp. · NL Wales, notebooks · Princeton University, New Jersey, letters and MSS · Richmond Local Studies Library, London, papers · University of Exeter Library, proofs of novels, drafts, and papers · University of Virginia, Charlottesville, corresp., literary MSS, and papers · Westcountry Studies Library, Exeter, autograph novels, etc. | BL, letters to Nelson Fedden, Add. MSS 43688, 44919 · BL, corresp. with Macmillans, Add. MS 54965 · Devon RO, letters to C. J. Down · NL Scot., corresp. with Blackwoods · NL Wales, letters to Johnes family · University of Bristol Library, letters to James Baker

Likenesses photograph, 1882, repro. in Dunn, *R. D. Blackmore* · F. Jenkins, photogravure, NPG [*see illus.*] · relief medallion on memorial tablet, Exeter Cathedral

Wealth at death £16,963 18*s.* 10*d.*: probate, 7 March 1900, *CGPLA Eng. & Wales*

Blackmore, Thomas (*b*. in or before **1740**, *d*. in or after **1780**), engraver, of whose training nothing is known, modelled his style on that of James McArdell, as may be seen in his untitled print of a woman after Frans Hals. He signed twelve mezzotint engravings: James Chaloner Smith noted ten, C. E. Russell mentioned another, and a small mezzotint after van Ostade is known. The earliest of them appear to be a portrait of *Master Bunbury* (the future caricaturist William Henry Bunbury), a private plate after Joshua Reynolds, and four prints published by Ryland and Bryer, probably before 1768; some of these are crude and hard. The portrait of Bunbury may have brought Blackmore to the notice of Reynolds, for five of his prints are after that artist and another is from a painting in his collection. Blackmore's later prints bear dates from 1768 to 1771: one was exhibited at the Society of Artists in 1769 as from 'Mr [Joseph?] Pearson's Duke St York Buildings'. All of his prints, with the exception of his portraits of Bunbury and Samuel Foote and a print after Frans Hals, are uncommon. Nothing else is known of his work, although he may have undertaken two other small unsigned prints, portraits of Lady Coventry and of Miss Lascelles, for Ryland and Bryer, and he could be the Mr Blackmore of 14 Denmark Court, Strand, who exhibited 'An Engraving of a Gentleman', a print which does not appear to have survived, at the Free Society of Artists in 1773. Thomas Dodd confused him with a John Blackmore who made drawings of sculpture in St Albans, Hertfordshire, in 1760; John Blackmore also exhibited three pictures at the Free Society in 1769, giving his address as 'at Mr Wilkes opposite Dorset Street Picadilly'. C. A. LENNOX-BOYD

Sources T. Dodd, 'Memorials of engravers practising in Great Britain, 1550–1800', BL, Add. MS 33394 · Graves, *Soc. Artists* · J. C. Smith, *British mezzotinto portraits*, 1 (1878) · C. E. Russell, *English mezzotint portraits and their states*, 2 vols. (1926) · *DNB*

Blackmore, William (**1616–1684**), clergyman and ejected minister, was born on 24 June 1616, the second son of William Blackmore, a member of London's Fishmongers' Company. He was educated at Merchant Taylors' School in London and matriculated from Lincoln College, Oxford, in 1635; he graduated BA in 1638 and proceeded MA in 1641. Blackmore's first employment in the ministry of the church was in December 1645 at the Essex parish of Pentlow. He owed this position to the parliamentarian committee for plundered ministers, filling the place of the ejected minister Edward Alston.

Blackmore did not remain long at Pentlow and in September 1646 obtained the committee's acceptance of his resignation in order to move to the London parish of St Peter Cornhill. He had been elected by the parishioners of St Peter's in June 1646 to replace Thomas Coleman, the ailing Westminster assembly divine who was the key opponent of the high presbyterianism of men like Blackmore. Unlike the Erastian Coleman, Blackmore believed firmly in the presbyterian system of church government and put into effect the regime of ruling elders at St Peter's. The younger Calamy notes that he was particularly strict in catechizing the young of the parish. Despite his rigid presbyterianism, Blackmore found himself in trouble in April 1647 with the local presbyterian classis. In 1641 he had received deacon's orders from Bishop Prideaux of Worcester, but the fourth London classis demanded that he take full orders before they would permit him to continue to administer the sacrament at St Peter's. In order to test his qualification for the ministry, the fourth classis set Blackmore a telling thesis topic: 'an cui competat ex officio praedicare, competat sacramenta administrare?' ('if a person's office gives him the ability to preach, does it make him competent to administer the sacraments?'). The classis must have known of his competence in this area of theology, for in 1646 London's presbyterian ministers had chosen Blackmore to write the section on ordination by imposition of hands in their treatise on the divine right of presbyterianism, the *Jus divinum regiminis ecclesiastici* (1646).

Blackmore later became a stalwart of the London provincial assembly, the governing synod of London's ramshackle presbyterian system, serving in 1648 as its scribe and later on its ruling grand committee. He was a signatory to the *Testimony to the Truth of Jesus Christ* (1647), a document calling for parliament to be intolerant of religious heterodoxy and fully to support the presbyterian reformation of the church. He was also involved with Sion College, the religious club of civil-war presbyterianism, being elected junior dean in 1658–9 and senior dean in 1660.

As a key London presbyterian Blackmore was involved in the attempts to halt the political crisis of 1648–9. He signed the *Serious and Faithful Representation* (1649) petitioning Lord General Fairfax to put a stop to the king's trial, and later signed the *Vindication of the Ministers of the Gospel* (1649) in defence of that petition. After the execution of Charles I he became involved in the City presbyterian plot to restore Charles II to the throne. He was implicated with Christopher Love, who was later condemned and executed for treason, and was suspended by the Commonwealth regime from his post at St Peter's. Although his freedom was secured by the surety of his elder brother, Sir John Blackmore, later governor of St Helena, the Commonwealth regime replaced Blackmore with Thomas Hodges. However, Blackmore maintained the support of at least seventy of St Peter's vestry, who petitioned the corporation of London on 13 May 1656 for his return to the parish. This caused a division in the parish and a number of parishioners presented a counter-petition in favour of Hodges, complaining of Blackmore's 'dull and heavie ministry'. Blackmore won the dispute and was reinstituted on 17 October 1656. Hodges tried to gain possession of the living again in 1660, but the parliamentary commissioners upheld Blackmore's title as the rector of St Peter's.

Hodges finally won the struggle in 1662 when Blackmore's conscience directed him to join the ranks of the ejected clergy. By the time of the great ejection Blackmore had gathered a respectable estate and used this wealth to retire to the village of Hornchurch in Essex. Here he kept a conventicle in his house and was licensed as a presbyterian during the king's indulgence of 1672. Blackmore married three times: his first wife, Martha, died in 1658; Mary

Chewning, whom he married at St Mary's Islington on 1 May 1660, died in 1678; and his third wife, Sarah Luttrell, survived him and died in March 1694. Blackmore himself died at Hare Street, Essex, in 1684 and on 18 July was buried at Romford in the same county.

Chewning Blackmore (1663–1737), Independent minister, was born on 1 January 1663 and was baptized at St Peter Cornhill on 2 January 1663, the only surviving son of William Blackmore and Mary Chewning. He was educated at John Woodhouse's academy in Sheriffhales in Shropshire because of the ban on nonconformists entering universities, and followed his father into the church. In 1688 he became the assistant to Thomas Badland at the congregational church in Worcester, where he remained for the rest of his life. He married Abigail Higgins in 1694 and together they had two sons: Francis, who was the Presbyterian minister at Evesham (1728–30), Coventry (1730–42), and Worcester (1743–61), and Edward, who became the Presbyterian minister at Stoke, near Malvern. Chewning Blackmore died on 2 August 1737. E. C. VERNON

Sources *The nonconformist's memorial … originally written by … Edmund Calamy*, ed. S. Palmer, 2nd edn, 2 vols. (1777) • *Calamy rev.* • E. C. Vernon, 'The Sion College conclave and London presbyterianism during the English revolution', PhD diss., U. Cam., 1999 • C. E. Surman, ed., *The register-booke of the fourth classis in the province of London, 1646–59*, 2 vols. in 1, Harleian Society, 82–3 (1953) • minutes of provincial assembly, DWL, MS 201.12 • DWL, Blackmore MS • *DNB* • will, PRO, PROB 11/377, fols. 4–5 • *Christian Reformer*, 3rd ser., 7 (1851), 413; 3rd ser., 8 (1852), 1, 218 • *CSP dom.*, 1651, 256, 258 • *Seventh report*, HMC, 6 (1879) • BL, Add. MS 15670, fol. 127
Archives DWL, corresp. and papers
Wealth at death £150 stock in East India Co.; £60 to mortgage of neighbour; three houses, Aldersgate, London, long leasehold: will, PRO, PROB 11/377, fols. 4–5

Blackner, John (1770?–1816), radical and county historian, was born in Ilkeston, Derbyshire. He served an apprenticeship to a stocking maker in his native town, and there married Sarah, *née* Brown, sister of a 'respectable' farmer in Kirk Hallam, Derbyshire, with whom he had four sons and three daughters. Illiterate at the time of his marriage, he taught himself to read and write soon after moving to Nottingham in 1792, where he found profitable work as a lace maker. He was of 'tall and commanding' physique, had natural eloquence, and though mild in private conversation was boisterous, even overbearing, in public. He enjoyed society, and for a time lived a dissipated life of public houses and poaching. He emerged, though, as a leading voice among Nottingham's radical artisan community, publishing political pamphlets, notably *A Few Reflections on the Corn Laws* (1805), and from 1808 contributing regularly to the editorial comment of the *Nottingham Review*, which was unwavering in its opposition to the war with France. In 1810 Blackner was at the centre of a *cause célèbre* when he was sentenced, with three others, to a month's imprisonment for conspiring to resist wage reductions in the lace trade. His close association with the framework-knitters' cause may thereafter have implicated him in Luddism. In July 1812 he was engaged as editor of *The Statesman*, a radical London evening paper, but he soon returned to Nottingham, apparently on account of failing health associated with heavy drinking. The following year he became landlord of a public house, which he renamed the Rancliffe Arms in honour of the town's radical MP Lord Rancliffe, whose candidacy in 1812 Blackner had helped bring about. In 1815 he published his substantial *History of Nottingham*, a valuable reference work and a contemporary record of the political controversies aroused by the French Revolution. Blackner was both a chronicler of and a participant in these disputes, firmly identifying with the 'democrat' party against the 'aristocrat'. For this partisanship his history has been criticized. Blackner was a radical patriot, who advocated the 'rights of man' but defended government by the social élite. A professed deist for much of his life, he turned to Christianity in his declining years, and died in Nottingham on 22 December 1816, survived by his wife. MARK POTTLE

Sources J. C. Warren, 'The life of John Blackner', *Transactions of the Thoroton Society*, 30 (1926), 161–6 • W. H. Wylie, *Old and new Nottingham* (1853), 232–3 • J. Orange, *History and antiquities of Nottingham* (1840), 937–8 • J. Blackner, *The history of Nottingham* (1815) • M. I. Thomis, *Politics and society in Nottingham, 1785–1835* (1969) • *DNB*
Archives Notts. Arch., notebook containing heroic poem, 'The battle of Marengo' | Notts. Arch., biography by J. Crosby
Likenesses mezzotint (after R. Bonington), BM, NPG

Black Ramsay. *See* Ramsay, James (1589?–1638/9).

Blackrie, Alexander (*bap.* 1702, *d.* 1772), surgeon-apothecary, was baptized on 14 June 1702 at the church of St Nicholas, Aberdeen, the seventh of the eleven children of William Blackrie and his wife, Isobel, *née* Fordyce. A merchant's son, he was educated at the grammar school and Marischal College, Aberdeen (1718–22), and went on to be surgeon-general on the Indian establishment. Among his friends was an East India Company director, John Hawkesworth of Bromley, Kent; Blackrie moved to the town in the late 1730s and practised there for the rest of his life. He married about 1740; he and his wife, Ann (*d.* 1749), had a son, William, and a daughter, Elizabeth, who, with a £20,000 dowry, became the first wife of John Scott, the political agent of Warren Hastings.

When in March 1761 Blackrie took Samuel Saunders as his apprentice for seven years with the substantial premium of £84, his practice was described as that of Alexander Blackrie & Co., suggesting an early example of a medical partnership. In October 1763 Blackrie contributed a letter to the *Gentleman's Magazine* criticizing Walter Chittick of Bath (*d.* 1761) for his recently published cure for renal calculi. Blackrie expanded this into *A disquisition on medicines that dissolve the stone. In which Dr. Chittick's secret is considered and discovered* (1766). In 1771 a second part appeared, with a 'considerably improved' version of the first edition. In 1775 the work was translated into French. Initially Blackrie's *Disquisition* attracted only 216 subscribers, but more than 1000 applied for the second edition.

In his will (made on 19 November 1770) Blackrie bequeathed £5 5*s.* to John Hawkesworth and a similar sum to Thomas Wellings, a London druggist. His daughter, the only other beneficiary, inherited his portrait and the copyright of his *Disquisition*. He died in Bromley on 29 May 1772 and was buried on 4 June in the church of St Peter and St Paul, Bromley. JOAN LANE

Sources parish register, St Nicholas, Aberdeen, Aberdeen City RO, 14 June 1702 [baptism] • parish register (burial), St Peter and St Paul, Bromley, Bromley Central Library, 4 June 1772 • parish register (burial), St Peter and St Paul, Bromley, Bromley Central Library [Ann Blackrie], 10 May 1749 • will, PRO, PROB 11/978 • *GM*, 1st ser., 42 (1772), 295 • *Kent: west and the weald*, Pevsner (1976) • *Bromley and District Times* (14 Aug 1931) • *Fasti academiae Mariscallanae Aberdonensis: selections from the records of the Marischal College and University, MDXCIII–MDCCCLX*, 2, ed. P. J. Anderson, New Spalding Club, 18 (1898) • P. J. Wallis and R. V. Wallis, *Eighteenth century medics*, 2nd edn (1988)

Likenesses portrait; formerly in the possession of his daughter

Wealth at death see will, PRO, PROB 11/978

Blackstone, John (1712–1753), apothecary and botanist, was born at Harefield, Middlesex, the eldest of three sons of Edward Blackstone (*d.* 1730), ironmonger and citizen of London, and his wife, Sarah, daughter of Francis Ashby of Brakspeare, Harefield. In 1729 he was apprenticed to Thomas Bearcroft, apothecary in the Strand, Westminster. Following his father's death, his mother took her younger sons to live in Harefield; Blackstone spent his holidays there, became interested in the local flora, and from 1734 began to discover new species.

Blackstone's paternal grandfather, John Blackstone (1650–1712), prominent in the Society of Apothecaries and a benefactor of St Bartholomew's Hospital, had been a friend of Sir Hans Sloane and this probably encouraged the young man to begin corresponding with Sloane, J. J. Dillenius, Isaac Rand, and other eminent botanists. Apart from these letters, he apparently worked alone. Convalescence from an illness during the summer of 1736 kept him at Harefield, enabling further discoveries. Another spell of illness in 1737 forwarded his work, and that year he published his *Fasciculus plantarum circa Harefield sponte nascentium*. It was a small catalogue in alphabetical order, with synonyms taken from other authors, giving the locations, times of flowering, and other details, of 527 local plants, supported by a general description of the soils, aspects, and drainage. It is valuable as the first example of a complete enumeration of a small district, probably 16 to 20 square miles, and as such was much imitated by later collectors.

After completing his apprenticeship Blackstone stayed at Charlbury, Oxfordshire, with his uncle John Blackstone, keeper of Wychwood forest, where he compiled a catalogue of local plants. He then went to Essex, where another uncle owned property; there he extended his interest to mycology as autumn drew on.

Blackstone was made free of the Society of Apothecaries in 1738 and established his own business in Fleet Street, London. On 16 February 1740 he married a widow, Elizabeth Webb, but she died later that year. In October 1742 he married Mary (*d.* 1801), daughter of Richard Abbott, of the Painter–Stainers' Company. Their first daughter (*b.* 1744) died in infancy; a second, Sophia (1748–1827), survived him.

Friendship with the Yorkshireman Ambrose Dawson, physician at St George's Hospital, probably led Blackstone to visit the north of England. Mary Blackstone inherited £500 from her father and this was spent on acquiring property in Harefield. Blackstone gathered his knowledge of 366 rare and local species within England into his *Specimen botanicum quo plantarum plurium rariorum Angliae indigenarum loci naturales illustrantur* (1746), intending to follow this with a second volume. This was the last book published in England on indigenous botany to be based on the classification system of John Ray before that of Linnaeus came into universal favour. Blackstone was beset by failing health and died at Harefield on 11 March 1753. He was buried there, near his parents, on 18 March. Some of his own books were bought by Thomas Birch, secretary of the Royal Society, and later went into the British Library with Birch's bequest. His name was perpetuated in the genus *Blackstonia*. ANITA MCCONNELL

Sources D. H. Kent, 'John Blackstone, apothecary and botanist, 1712–53', *Watsonia*, 1 (1948), 141–8 • H. Trimen and W. T. Thiselton Dyer, *Flora of Middlesex* (1869), 389–91 • 'Some account of John Blackstone, and a notice of "Fasciculus plantarum circa Harefield sponte nascentium" (a catalogue of Harefield plants)', *The Phytologist*, 5 (1861), 145–51 • will, PROB 11/800, sig 71 • GL, Apothecaries' Company apprenticeships, MS 9207

Blackstone, William (*bap.* 1596?, *d.* 1675), settler in America and horticulturist, was born to unknown parents. It has been asserted that he was baptized on 5 March 1595 at Whickham in co. Durham, the son of John Blackstone and his wife, Agnes (*née* Hawley), but there is no entry to this effect in the parish register. A William Blackstone was baptized on 5 March 1596 at Horncastle, Lincolnshire, son of parents of these names. He was admitted a sizar at the puritan-dominated Emmanuel College, Cambridge, on 16 May 1614, and graduated BA early in 1618. Ordained deacon and priest at Peterborough on 23 May 1619, he proceeded MA in 1621.

Soon afterwards dislike of episcopacy, as he later explained, took him to New England. He probably sailed with Robert Gorges in the ship which landed at Wessagusset (later Weymouth) in Massachusetts Bay. The Gorges settlement soon melted away, and Blackstone moved to Shawmut (later Boston), where he had occasional contact with other isolated Englishmen and with Native Americans. For four years from 1630 he co-existed in Boston with the new settlers who arrived with John Winthrop, but his house was on the opposite side of Boston Neck from the main settlement. In 1634 the town of Boston purchased Blackstone's estate, and he moved, probably with servants, to Study Hill, just north of the site where two years later Roger Williams established Providence, and in an area later known as Blackstone River.

For the next forty years Blackstone remained at this spot and had little communion with the outside world, although he occasionally visited Williams, and on 4 July 1659 in Boston he married 34-year-old Sarah (*née* Fisher), widow of John Stevenson, a cobbler who had left her with five children. He officiated at the first recorded prayer book service in Rhode Island, and sometimes preached there. At one point he received an invitation to become minister at York. However, he declined to take up a pastorate. Cotton Mather, who noted that he was 'commonly reckoned' among godly episcopalians, recounted that he was a man 'of a particular humor, and he would never join himself to any of our churches, giving this reason for it: "I came from England, because I did not like the *lord-bishops*; but I can't join you, because I would not be under the *lord-brethren*"' (Mather, 243). Instead he farmed and cultivated roses and apple trees, breeding the first new strain of apples in the colony, yellow sweetings.

Sarah Blackstone died in June 1673 and Blackstone himself on 26 May 1675, aged about eighty. The inventory of his moveable estate totalled £56 3*s*. 6*d*., with an additional three parcels of land not valued, amounting to more than 260 acres. His library of nearly two hundred books, one of the largest in New England at the time, accounted for close to a third of his moveables. A marginal annotation in the inventory states that 'this estate was destroyed and carried away by the Indians': this probably occurred during King Philip's War, which broke out on 20 June that year in Plymouth County, just a few miles away.

Many myths grew up around this man, the so-called 'sage of the wilderness', who deliberately withdrew from society. Tales were told of him travelling round the locality mounted on a white bull, with his nose in a book. Honoured by the protestant episcopal church as a pioneer episcopal clergyman in America and as the first resident of Boston, he features on the Founders' Memorial on Boston Common and at other sites. His pastureland later became North America's first public park.

ROBERT CHARLES ANDERSON

Sources Venn, *Alum. Cant.* • R. C. Anderson, *The great migration begins: immigrants to New England, 1620–1633*, 1 (1995) • C. F. Adams, *Three episodes of Massachusetts history*, 2 vols. (1903) • R. Williams, *The correspondence of Roger Williams*, ed. G. W. LaFantasie, 2 vols. (1988) • C. Mather, *Magnalia Christi Americana*, 2 vols. (1855) • L. Lind, *William Blackstone: sage of the wilderness*, Blackstone Valley Tourism Council [n.d.] • P. F. Eno, 'Blackstone, William', *ANB* • Plymouth colony probate records, 3/1/173–4 • parish register, Whickham, co. Durham [baptism] • parish register, Horncastle, Lincolnshire [baptism]

Wealth at death £56 3*s*. 6*d*.—moveables only: inventory, 28 May 1675, Plymouth colony probate records, 3/1/173–4

Blackstone, Sir William (1723–1780), legal writer and judge, was born on 10 July 1723 in Cheapside, London, the third surviving but posthumous son of Charles Blackstone (*d*. 1723), a citizen silk mercer 'not of great Affluence' (Blackstone, *Reports*, iii), and his wife, Mary, eldest daughter of Lovelace Bigg, a landed gentleman of Chilton Foliat, Wiltshire. In the biographical memoir prefixed to the 1781 edition of Blackstone's *Reports*, compiled by his executor and brother-in-law James Clitherow from 'a short Abstract of every Circumstance of Consequence in his Life written by himself with his accustomed Accuracy' (ibid., ii), Blackstone's paternal grandfather John is described as 'an eminent Apothecary in Newgate Street' (ibid., iii). But it was a medical practitioner from the other side of his family, the London surgeon Thomas Bigg, who gave protection and support to William and his brothers after the loss of their father and subsequent death of their mother during William's childhood. According to Clitherow the 'liberal Educations' which this affectionate uncle provided his three nephews 'supplied the great Loss they had so early sustained, and compensated in a great Degree for their want of more ample Fortunes' (ibid., iv).

Sir William Blackstone (1723–1780), by John Bacon senior, 1784

So William Blackstone followed his two elder brothers into the professions, rather than pursuing his father's trade. But whereas Charles and Henry went from Winchester College to New College, Oxford (where another Bigg uncle was warden), and then into the church, William received a London schooling at the Charterhouse. Enrolled as a fee-paying student in 1730, he became entitled after his mother's death five years later to a free education, provided under the terms of the founder's will for needy, well-recommended boys between the ages of ten and fourteen; Blackstone's nomination came from no less a personage than Sir Robert Walpole, arranged by one of his mother's cousins. While his 'Talents and Industry rendered him the favourite of his Masters', Blackstone's academic performance cannot have disappointed his family and friends (Blackstone, *Reports*, iv). At the age of fifteen he had become head scholar of Charterhouse, 'and although so young, was thought well-qualified to be removed to the University'; he also showed early evidence of literary abilities, not confined to the Latin verse for which in 1737 he won a school prize medal bearing the name and likeness of the poet Milton (ibid.).

Oxford and London, 1738–1753 Blackstone matriculated at Oxford on 1 December 1738, having been admitted to Pembroke College as a commoner the previous day, doubtless in anticipation of his election early next year to one of two Holford exhibitions tenable at Pembroke by scholars from the Charterhouse. Classical studies dominated his first two undergraduate years, and Clitherow relates that he worked 'with unremitting Ardour' towards the BA degree (Blackstone, *Reports*, v). Yet he also continued to find time for literary pursuits, while 'Logic, Mathematicks, and the other Sciences were not neglected'; in particular, he developed what would prove to be a lifelong interest in the theory and practice of architecture (ibid.).

In July 1740 Blackstone was admitted as a candidate for the BCL in the faculty of laws, a course extending over five years after two preliminary years of humane studies, but requiring neither the BA nor MA degree. This shift in direction was seemingly reinforced by his admission to the Middle Temple in November 1741, even if the choice of a legal career was made only reluctantly, and 'with doubtful mind' according to 'The Lawyer's Farewell to his Muse', one of several poems written in his later teens and early twenties ('Select Poems and Translations between the Years 1736 and 1744', cited in the Maggs Bros. catalogue 576 of 1932, 9–10, 73). In view of this ambivalence, it was perhaps fortunate that Blackstone did not yet have to decide whether he would become a civilian, or alternatively a common lawyer.

As membership of the Middle Temple had no residential requirements Blackstone could remain in Oxford, pursue a relatively undemanding course of reading for the BCL (which he received in June 1745), and otherwise follow a wide range of intellectual interests. These are hinted at by the books and manuscripts he ordered up from the stacks of the Bodleian Library, including works of classical letters, theology, church history, and antiquarian studies, as well as legal texts, although the last become more prominent in the 1750s (Bodl. Oxf., MS records e 554–60). One notable product of Blackstone's student days at Oxford was a systematic treatise on architecture, embellished with proficient pen and ink drawings, which exists in preliminary draft as 'An abridgement of architecture', dated July 1743 (Getty Research Institute, special collections, MS 890227). This work, a precursor of Blackstone's later didactic achievements, was completed 'with considerable Additions and Improvements' at All Souls College, where he had been elected to a fellowship in November 1743, after an unsuccessful attempt the previous year (All Souls College, Codrington Library, MS 333, 'Elements of architecture'). Blackstone's first publication was also written at this time, although not printed until 1747, when an anonymous prefatory 'Advertisement' to *The Pantheon: a Vision* explained the author's aim as to 'take a Poetical View of the several Religions that have prevailed in the World', concluding with the Church of England, 'the most pure and Apostolical upon Earth' (G. Bingham, *Dissertations, Essays, and Sermons … to which are Prefixed Memoirs of his Life*, 1804, 1.xxiii–xxv).

Blackstone does not seem to have begun serious study of the common law until January 1746, less than a year before he was called to the bar (on 28 November 1746). In a cheerful letter to Seymour Richmond, a lawyer-uncle on his mother's side, written shortly after reaching 'my new Habitation, (which is at Mr Stoke's a Limner in Arundel-Street)', William depicted his initial encounter with Sir Thomas Littleton's *Tenures* in confident military terms: 'I have stormed one Book of Littleton, & opened my Trenches before the 2d; and I can with Pleasure say I have met with no Difficulty of Consequence' (Warden, 58–61). But whatever intellectual grasp of the common law Blackstone may have acquired, whether before or after call to the bar—and following two years at the Temple he reportedly claimed to have 'made myself pretty well master of it'—he lacked two crucial keys to success: powerful legal or social connections, and the ability to think and argue on his feet. His timing was also bad, because the mid-eighteenth century marked the bottom of a long-term slump in the business of Westminster Hall. Thus he noted in December 1751 that there had been 'not one Determinac'on of any Moment' during the whole of the past Michaelmas term, '& the Courts (except the Chancery) not sitting above an hour in the morning' (Doolittle, 46; *Legal Observer*, 6, 1833, 421). Although the *Reports* published after his death suggest he remained a constant term-time attender at the superior law courts from 1746 until at least 1750, Clitherow states that his subject 'made his Way very slowly, and acquired little Notice and little Practice' (Blackstone, *Reports*, vii). For a man of Blackstone's abilities and ambition, succeeding his uncle in 1749 as recorder of Wallingford, Berkshire—where he later made his family home—can hardly have compensated for lack of success in 'the bustling Practical part' of 'the active Life of Westminster Hall' (Newdigate MSS, CR136/B1488).

All Souls and Oxford University, 1746–1760 At Oxford, by contrast, Blackstone enjoyed congenial friends, a secure collegiate base, and a growing reputation. There was also ample scope to exercise his abundant intellectual energies and emerging administrative skills. At All Souls College, where as early as 1746 he was elected both dean of laws and bursar, almost every aspect of college life benefited from his 'passion for order and efficiency and … immense capacity for hard work' (Sutherland, 'Blackstone and the legal chairs', 230). His architectural interests found practical expression in overseeing the long-delayed completion of the Codrington Library, together with an adjoining building financed, thanks to Blackstone's 'Care and Activity', from the estate of the duke of Wharton (Blackstone, *Reports*, viii). Thereafter he took keen interest in the arranging and cataloguing of the library's books and manuscripts, according to detailed regulations drawn up in his characteristically incisive style (All Souls College, library book, 8 Nov 1751; Craster, 79–82). As bursar he reviewed all leases of college lands, reorganized the college's archives, and even put the capacious new wine cellars under the Codrington Library on a businesslike footing. His financial and legal talents were further deployed in his stewardship of the college's estates from 1749, and given literary form in an expository open letter compiled in 1753 (with subsequent holograph additions) for Benjamin Butler, his friend and successor in office. Another abiding college concern motivated Blackstone's first acknowledged venture into print, the *Essay on Collateral Consanguinity* (1750), in which law, logic, and mathematics were marshalled to defend All Souls's restrictive approach to those seeking privileged access to fellowships on the grounds of their descent from the society's medieval founder.

Far from confining his energies to All Souls, Blackstone emerged as a leading university figure from 1750, when his DCL degree first admitted him to membership of convocation, the major academic forum. His decision in 1753 'no longer to attend the Courts at Westminster' further enhanced his Oxford profile (Newdigate MSS, CR136/B1488). He served for six years from 1753 as assessor, or deputy judge, of the vice-chancellor's court, where he was responsible for various procedural reforms. He had less success in promoting a scheme for the recently completed Radcliffe Camera to become a 'Library of a new Species' by housing manuscripts and drawings from the Bodleian and college collections (I. G. Doolittle, 'William Blackstone and the Radcliffe Camera, 1753', *Bodleian Library Record*, 11, 1982, 47–50). But this failed initiative stands in sharp contrast to the important academic and institutional reforms which Blackstone was primarily responsible for conceiving and implementing during the 1750s.

The first of these involved a direct assault on the oligarchical power of the board of delegates, who were traditionally appointed by successive vice-chancellors to control the university's printing and publishing operations. In 1755 dissatisfaction with the limited output, low profile, and high prices of Oxford's press led to Blackstone's nomination as a delegate, despite vice-chancellorial opposition. He proceeded to conduct a one-man review of the printing house, with particular reference to its cost structure, on which he gathered much detailed information from booksellers and printers in Oxford and London. When his report, *Some Thoughts on the Oxford Press* (1756), was coolly received by his fellow delegates, Blackstone proceeded to publish an open letter, *To the Reverend Dr Randolph, Vice-Chancellor of the University of Oxford* (1757), which comprehensively indicted both the delegates' managerial incompetence and their mode of appointment. Further resistance saw Blackstone threaten to bring the whole matter 'before another less indulgent Tribunal', whereupon the delegates rapidly back-pedalled, adopting virtually all the proposals for remodelling their own role and the operation of the press which Blackstone had helpfully drafted for them (Philip, 45–72, 80).

Blackstone's second major initiative broke a constitutional stranglehold on the university's ability to manage its own affairs which had been imposed by the early seventeenth-century statutes known as the Laudian code. The intention of Archbishop Laud to establish a permanent educational structure for Oxford had succeeded so well that by the mid-eighteenth century the university was widely believed to lack the legal capacity to change its curriculum or internal organization, unless by an unwelcome direct intervention from government. Having confronted this potential obstacle in the course of his campaign to reform the press, Blackstone developed a cogent case against the power of any corporate body to bind its successors, 'who have the same right to *repeal* as the Predecessors had to *enact*' (Sutherland, 'The Laudian Statutes', 199). However, the issue on which the point of principle eventually turned in 1759–60 was a disputed election for the office of chancellor, when questions about the eligibility of candidates and voters led to convocation's enactment of a statute which not only defined its own membership and rights but effectively established the university's legislative independence for the first time since 1636.

The laws of England Blackstone's third significant contribution to his university lay in establishing English law as an academic discipline, initially by presenting a successful course of private lectures, then as the foundation Vinerian professor of common law, and finally with the publication of his acclaimed *Commentaries on the Laws of England* (1765–9). In the summer of 1753, 'finding the Profits of his Profession very inadequate', Blackstone finally resolved to 'retire to his Fellowship and an academical Life', supplemented by whatever he could earn 'as a Provincial Counsel' (Blackstone, *Reports*, x). He simultaneously commissioned a printed prospectus for 'A course of lectures on the laws of England', to be delivered in the hall of All Souls College. Private lecture courses on subjects outside the formal curriculum were no novelty in Hanoverian Oxford. But it seems that Blackstone had originally begun to think about lecturing in anticipation of an impending vacancy in the regius professorship of civil law. Only when it became clear that his candidacy for this chair would be politically unacceptable to the Newcastle–Pelham administration did he turn to a 'Scheme for lectures' on English common law. In so doing he was possibly influenced by private knowledge that the elderly Charles Viner had recently determined to endow a professorship in that subject for a scholar who, like Blackstone, held qualifications in both civil and common law (Newdigate MSS, CR136/B1488).

Blackstone's initial lectures were sufficiently well received to be repeated in 1754, the prospectus for that year representing them as part of a 'Design, for cultivating the Study of the Municipal Law in Oxford' (W. Blackstone, *Proposals for a Course of Lectures*, 1754: Bodl. Oxf., G. A. Oxon. b. 111 (50)). Whatever his shortcomings as an advocate, and despite a manner of delivery which the hostile Jeremy Bentham, who attended his lectures in the early 1760s, later characterized as 'formal, precise, and affected', Blackstone proved highly effective when speaking from a prepared text (G. Jones, introduction, in W. Blackstone, *The Sovereignty of the Law: Selections from Blackstone's 'Commentaries on the Laws of England'*, 1973, xvii). His carefully arranged material was presented in a literate and polished fashion, and not directed exclusively to intending future lawyers, but rather to 'such other Gentlemen of the University, as are desirous to be in some Degree acquainted with the Constitution and legal Polity of their native Country' (Bodl. Oxf., G. A. Oxon. b. 111 (50)). With this general audience firmly in mind Blackstone sought to:

> lay down a general and comprehensive Plan of the Laws of England; to deduce their History and Antiquities; to select and illustrate their Leading Rules, and Fundamental Principles; to explain their Reason and Utility; and to compare them frequently with the Laws of Nature and of other Nations; without dwelling too minutely on the Niceties of Practice, or the more refined Distinctions of particular Cases. (ibid.)

From 1756, the year of Viner's death, successive printed editions of the lecturer's *Analysis of the Laws of England* provided students with 'the Order, and principal Divisions, of his Course' (ibid., viii). Given that neither English university had previously offered any formal instruction in English law, and considering the distinct shortage of accessible introductory texts to that notoriously dry and difficult subject, Blackstone's pioneering exposition was bound to attract attention, both within Oxford and beyond.

Although Blackstone had made himself the obvious—and, as it turned out, sole—candidate for what became the Vinerian chair in English law, establishing Viner's benefaction in a manner acceptable to Blackstone and his supporters was not achieved without considerable wrangling. The eventual comprehensive defeat of various personal and political opponents left a legacy of resentment which outlasted Blackstone's formal election as Vinerian professor in October 1758 and his 'elegant and admired' inaugural lecture, separately published as *A Discourse on the Study of the Law*. But while such animosities may have contributed to his eventual removal from the university, and undoubtedly frustrated his plan to annex a residential foundation of common lawyers to the Vinerian chair, they hardly dented Blackstone's burgeoning reputation outside Oxford. Lord Bute as royal tutor invited Blackstone to present his lectures before the prince of Wales (who received written copies when the lecturer declined to leave his Oxford classes), while the 'high Character of a Professor at Oxford', said to have brought the law's 'Mysterious Business to some System', attracted notice even across the Atlantic (Blackstone, *Reports*, xiii; *Letter Book of John Watts*, ed. D. C. Barck, 1928, 13).

This new-found fame, 'which he justly thought might entitle him to some particular Notice at the Bar', encouraged Blackstone in June 1759 to buy a Middle Temple chamber and resume his London practice, declining an offer of promotion to the now diminished professional dignity of serjeant-at-law in the hope of better things to come (Blackstone, *Reports*, xiii–xiv). But it was not until after his marriage in 1761 and the births of his first children (see below) that a printed version of his lectures appeared. While publication was doubtless always a possibility, the decision to go into print may well have been hastened by threats of a pirate edition from Dublin, as also by concern about the growing circulation of imperfect sets of student notes, recognition that his future did not lie in Oxford, and some sense that his text, sufficiently honed by years of repetition and revision, was unlikely to benefit from further reworking.

The first volume of the *Commentaries on the Laws of England* appeared in 1765, with the remaining three following over the next four years. In some 2000 pages the common law's tortuous complexities were outlined in a manner at once authoritative, clear, elegant, and even engaging. While far from wholly laudatory or uncritical (of procedural complexities or excessively harsh criminal punishments, for example), the *Commentaries* depicted England's constitution and laws as reflecting the natural order of the cosmos, yet also rooted in the nation's distinctive historical development, like 'an old Gothic castle, erected in the days of chivalry, but fitted up for a modern inhabitant' (Blackstone, *Commentaries*, 3.268). Although mounting criticism tempered an initial highly favourable reception, Blackstone's *Commentaries* would become the most celebrated, widely circulated, and influential law book ever published in the English language.

Politics and principles, 1751–1762 Long before making his name as a legal author Blackstone had enjoyed a rather different reputation as the most powerful Oxford academic politician of his day. His leadership from All Souls of a loose-knit tory coalition was indeed responsible for giving that relatively small society unprecedented prominence in university affairs throughout the 1750s. Blackstone's public political career began in 1751, when he took over Sir Roger Newdigate's campaign for one of the university's two parliamentary seats. Although near contemporaries as undergraduates, with a common friend in James Clitherow (whose sister Blackstone married a decade later), Newdigate and Blackstone apparently had not met when the latter wrote from All Souls on 13 January 1751, warning Newdigate that a new candidate threatened to split the vote of those 'Old Interest' dons who had successfully maintained Oxford's intransigence towards successive whig administrations ever since the Hanoverian succession (Newdigate MSS, CR136/B1482–1483, 1485–1486).

Soon after this well-managed by-election launched Newdigate's long career as a university MP, Blackstone's tory sympathies were voiced in the elegiac verses he contributed (albeit under his future brother-in-law's name) to an Oxford anthology mourning the premature death of Prince Frederick (Blackstone, *Reports*, vi–vii). According to his political opponents Blackstone was also responsible for much anonymous journalism in the tory interest during the fiercely fought county election of 1754; he certainly wrote a tract against extending the parliamentary franchise to copyholders, commissioned by candidates in this struggle and published in 1758, together with a pamphlet discrediting revelations of a supposed Jacobite conspiracy in Oxford. His next major political intervention occurred in 1758–9, when he helped the earl of Westmorland become chancellor by arguing that his chief opponent, Lord Litchfield, had rendered himself technically ineligible. The latter's subsequent withdrawal provoked considerable bitterness against Blackstone, even within his own college, which was probably not diminished by the skirmishes preceding modification of the Laudian code in July 1760.

Henceforth Blackstone's growing activities and reputation outside Oxford, coinciding with the tory party's return from the political wilderness at George III's accession, tended to diminish his effectiveness as a university politician. In the fierce chancellorship contest in 1762 he found himself altogether on the wrong side by opposing Litchfield, who was not only ultimately successful but the candidate backed by Bute and Shelburne, those aristocratic patrons who offered Blackstone his best chance of advancement. Despite this embarrassing débâcle, and his eventual departure from Oxford, Blackstone continued to be regarded there as a person of influence, although his last recorded direct intervention in an Oxford political contest, the parliamentary election of 1768, again saw the defeat of his favoured candidate.

Like other aspects of his Oxford career, Blackstone's political activism was doubtless partly motivated by personal ambition. Yet his role in the 1762 chancellorship election hardly suggests a man driven wholly or largely by self-seeking expediency, even if some contemporaries professed difficulty in understanding just what his principles were. During the 1750s Blackstone had been closely identified with Oxford toryism and its oppositionist 'country' values, including hostility to ministerial corruption, and support for greater parliamentary independence through place bills and more frequent elections. Yet he consistently repudiated any 'Tincture of Jacobitism', observing that 'To be subservient to French Views, is no more to be wished by an Englishman, than to German' (Newdigate MSS, CR136/B1492). This tone of sturdy independence was maintained after 1760, even though Blackstone now could and did seek advancement under the crown. As he wrote to Shelburne in October 1762, explaining (but not excusing) his position in the contest for the Oxford chancellorship: 'I think it is essential to the Spirit of Liberty to follow my own Convictions' (Bodl. Oxf., MS Film 2000, MS Shelburne 35, fols. 158–9).

Patronage and parliament, 1758–1770 Of course there was a price to be paid for acting on such assertions. Shelburne, who had attended his lectures as an undergraduate, not only brought Blackstone to Bute's notice, but vigorously promoted his former teacher's career in the opening months of the new reign. While declining nomination as chief justice of Ireland in March 1761, on the stated grounds of 'a provincial Narrowness in my Constitution, that I could rather wish to exert the little Share of Abilities I am Master of … in my own native Country', Blackstone hesitated only momentarily before accepting the offer of a House of Commons seat, for which he had been recommended to Bute by Shelburne as 'a man of business' (Bodl. Oxf., MS Film 1999, MS Shelburne 35, fol. 137). This entry to public life apparently cost Blackstone nothing: indeed he stipulated that it must not 'injure my private Fortune; which is confined within moderate Bounds' (Bodl. Oxf., MS Film 2000, MS Shelburne 35, fol. 139*r–v*). By year's end he was nevertheless pointing out that the preferment he had received to date, which included a patent of precedence at the bar, equivalent to appointment as king's counsel, 'has no Emolument annexed to it' (Bodl. Oxf., MS Film 2000, MS Shelburne 35, fol. 151). When the office of chief justice of Chester went to someone else, he began pressing Shelburne for a seat on the judicial bench proper. However ambitious for a man of Blackstone's relative youth and limited Westminster Hall experience, his failure to achieve this goal until 1770 must in part reflect the withdrawal of Shelburne's support in the aftermath of the 1762 Oxford chancellorship election, as well as Blackstone's somewhat unsatisfactory parliamentary performance (see further below). Contact between the two dropped off markedly from December 1762 onwards; there is no indication that Shelburne helped him to the largely honorific position of solicitor-general to Queen Charlotte which he achieved in 1763, and Blackstone appears to have ceased approaching Shelburne altogether after October 1766, when he vainly sought assistance in recommending his cause to the new lord chancellor (Bodl. Oxf., MS Film 2000, MS Shelburne 35, fols. 153–4, 155–6, 158–9, 162–3, 168–9). While the aristocratic if financially embarrassed Bertie family were important clients, and he was also 'deeply connected' with Lord Suffolk, these ties hardly compensated for the loss of Shelburne's personal connections and influence.

Blackstone needed preferment partly because he had been obliged to abandon his All Souls fellowship on his marriage in May 1761, the same month that he became a bencher of the Middle Temple. Regrettably little is known about his wife, Sarah Clitherow (*d.* 1783), the elder daughter of James Clitherow of Boston House, Brentford, Middlesex, 'with whom he passed near nineteen Years, in the Enjoyment of the purest domestic and conjugal Felicity'—and which (according to her brother) 'he used often to declare, was the happiest part of his Life' (Blackstone, *Reports*, xvi). These sentiments may well have been more than mere conventional rhetoric. Sarah and William had nine children, in whose upbringing and well-being he took a considerable and perhaps somewhat intimidating interest; Henry, his eldest surviving son, later pursued a wholly undistinguished career in Canada, but James, the second-born, eventually followed in his father's footsteps as fellow of All Souls and Vinerian professor. The judge and his wife occasionally travelled together, and having presumably learned to deal with his notoriously short temper, she reportedly objected to 'the Contraction of the Brows, & consequent Sternness of Look' in a contemporary likeness of her husband (Newdigate MSS, CR136/B1500; 'Letters', 16).

Blackstone did not finally quit Oxford until 1766, when he resigned both his chair and the principalship of New Inn Hall, to which he had been appointed by Lord Westmorland, in belated return for his support in the 1758 chancellorship election. Even then he retained some vestigial involvements with both town and gown. As visitor on the Michel foundation of Queen's College (to which he had been formally elected in 1757), he steered the college through the legal and legislative steps required to complete an ambitious building programme and finally secure the benefits of Michel's endowment. As legal adviser to successive earls of Abingdon he sought to improve the value of their entangled family estates as well as to benefit the city and university by promoting a toll bridge over the River Thames at Swinford, and reconstructing the Botley causeway leading west out of Oxford. However, no more is heard of his larger earlier ambition to reform 'Academical Education', by eliminating 'monastic Pedantry' and adapting it 'to Gentlemen of Rank & Fortune' (Bodl. Oxf., MS Film 2000, MS Shelburne 35, fols. 151–2).

Besides growing family responsibilities, the demands of his practice, and scholarly activities associated with the Society of Antiquaries, to which he had been elected following his learned edition of *The Great Charter and Charter of the Forest* (1759) with its substantial 'Introductory discourse', parliamentary business also drew Blackstone away from Oxford. After a first term as member for Hindon (1761–8), Blackstone was returned in 1768 for Westbury, another Wiltshire borough, this time by the influence of his aristocratic client Lord Abingdon. Initially an infrequent and perhaps always 'an indifferent speaker', he followed Bute rather than the Rockingham ministry in opposing repeal of the Stamp Act in 1766 (Namier, 96). While impressed by the substance of his contribution to this debate, one observer thought its manner 'much like that of reading a lecture in College' (P. D. G. Thomas, *British Politics and the Stamp Act Crisis*, 1975, 197). Unsurprisingly Blackstone developed an even greater aversion to parliament 'where' (as he purportedly said) 'amid the Rage of contending Parties, a Man of Moderation must expect to meet with no Quarter from any Side', than he had earlier done to the bar (Blackstone, *Reports*, xx). At the end of a long debate in May 1769 his self-acknowledged 'natural diffidence' left him wordless in the face of George Grenville's claim that his own *Commentaries* confuted his support for John Wilkes's exclusion from parliament (Bodl. Oxf., MS Film 2000, MS Shelburne 35, fol. 153). Subsequent editions were amended to meet this objection, encouraging opposition toasts to 'the *first* edition of Dr Blackstone's Commentaries' (G. Jones, introduction, in W. Blackstone, *The Sovereignty of the Law: Selections from Blackstone's 'Commentaries on the Laws of England'*, 1973, xx). Yet while he had largely endorsed the government stand on Wilkes—despite having voted against general warrants in 1763, and his own claim that he 'could not intirely agree with either the Ministry or the Opposition, in their Conduct with respect to Mr Wilkes'—his parliamentary record overall hardly justifies the charge of unprincipled place-seeking behaviour levelled by Junius in several slashing responses to Blackstone's printed attempts at self-vindication ('A letter to the author of the question stated', in W. Meredith, *Letter to Dr Blackstone*, 1770, 3).

Judge Blackstone's House of Commons career ended formally in February 1770, although his refusal of the office of solicitor-general the month before clearly signalled an intention to retire from public political life. While his initial parliamentary seat was, in his words at the time, 'conferred unsought, & accepted unconditionally', and he had told Shelburne as early as July 1762 that 'my ambition now rises to the Post of an English Judge', the long and bruising controversy over Wilkes must have influenced his acceptance of a puisne justice's place on the court of common pleas, together with a knighthood (Bodl. Oxf., MS Film 2000, MS Shelburne 35, fols. 153–4). In the event Blackstone agreed to respond to Justice Joseph Yates's 'Representation of his infirm State of Health' by replacing him on the busier king's bench, where he sat alongside Lord Mansfield as chief justice (*University of California Chronicle*, 12/4, 1910, 346–7). But he returned to common pleas less than six months later, following Yates's death early in June.

According to Clitherow his subject 'seemed now arrived at the Point he always wished for' (Blackstone, *Reports*, xx). Yet Blackstone's judicial reputation was somewhat mixed. As an assize judge sitting alone he purportedly had more new trials granted on cases decided before him than any of his Westminster colleagues: 'The reason was that, being extremely diffident of his opinion, he never supported it with much warmth or pertinacity in the court above if a new trial was moved for' (Prior, 431–2). Yet on appeals to the full court he often carried his brethren with him, as when in 1772 he delivered the exchequer chamber's opinion which upheld a strict construction of the venerable rule in Shelley's case in the long-running suit of *Perrin* v. *Blake* (A. W. B. Simpson, *Leading Cases in the Common Law*, 1995, chap. 2). Whether with the majority or in dissent, his arguments were always careful and learned. Blackstone's judicial standing might have been enhanced if the case notes published by his executors in somewhat literal-minded accordance with his will had been better prepared for the press, thereby giving less occasion for Mansfield's remark that 'Mr Justice Blackstone's Reports are not very accurate' (J. S. Waterman, 'Mansfield and Blackstone's *Commentaries*', *University of Chicago Law Review*, 1, 1934, 555–7). It is also possible that in reporting his own decisions Blackstone erred on the side of excessive modesty (H. J. Hanbury, 'Blackstone as judge', *American Journal of Legal History*, 3, 1959, 26).

In criminal matters Blackstone displayed characteristic concern 'to keep strictly up to Forms' (Blackstone, *Reports*, xxvii), even when extending 'a Degree of Indulgence' to bail a prisoner from York gaol, deputing a Wallingford attorney to act as deputy clerk of assize for the northern circuit in order to draft the necessary recognizance ('Letters of Sir William Blackstone', 364–5). In 1771 he showed no trace of compassion towards 'a bold artful Man' sentenced to hang for returning from transportation ('I saw nothing in him that made him an Object of Mercy'); but much of his energy and political skills during these years were devoted to the cause of penal reform (BL, Add. MS 61674, fol. 69). As early as April 1770 Blackstone proposed statutory amendments to clarify the law relating to transportation (E. Sussex RO, SAS/RF 18/122–4). Then, in consultation with his former pupil the MP William Eden, he drafted a 'Convict Bill' in 1776, providing for the establishment of 'Penitentiary Houses', or prisons as an alternative to transportation; over the next three years Blackstone 'spared neither Time nor Pains' to further these proposals, and after the Penitentiary Act finally passed in 1779 he continued to work for its implementation. Another successful lobbying campaign, which again relied heavily on Eden and other political contacts, as well as his own 'Industry and Attention' (Blackstone, *Reports*, xxii–xxiii), eventually secured legislation to augment the salaries paid to the puisne judges, and hence their independence from the administration.

Besides additions and corrections to the five successive new editions of the *Commentaries* published between 1770 and 1778, Blackstone also found time for 'Poetical Criticism' (Bodl. Oxf., MS Eng. lett. c.15, fol. 21), some fruits of which were subsequently included in Edward Malone's *Supplement to the Edition of Shakespeare's Plays* (1780) and an 'Investigation of the quarrel between Pope and Addison' published in the second edition of Andrew Kippis's *Biographia Britannica* (1779–93). But his mental energies were outrunning his physical powers. After a partial breakdown in 1758, the last twenty years of Blackstone's life were marked by frequent attacks of gout and vertigo, to which growing corpulence, dislike of physical exercise, and what one contemporary categorized as his 'temperate use' of port all doubtless contributed (Boswell, *Life*, 4.91). In December 1779 'a violent Shortness of Breath' was temporarily relieved by his physicians, but a second attack early next year in London 'baffled all the Art of Medicine', and led to his death, presumably of congestive heart failure, in London on 14 February 1780 at the age of fifty-six (Blackstone, *Reports*, xxiii).

Sir William Blackstone was buried in the family vault he had built in the parish church of St Peter's, Wallingford, the reconstruction of which was yet another project of his final years. His will (PROB 11/1061, fols. 101*v*–105*v*) appointed his 'dear wife' Sarah as executor, alongside her brother James Clitherow. Besides leaving mourning rings to a wide circle of relatives, and his professional library to the first of his sons to take up the law, Blackstone bequeathed a small number of manuscript and early printed law books to All Souls College, together with his collection of the works of William Prynne. Although he was said to have made over £14,000 from his lectures and the *Commentaries*, the full value of his estate is unknown (Prior, 431).

Influence and reputation The influence of Blackstone's *Commentaries* is difficult to exaggerate. Twenty-three successive English and Irish editions had appeared by 1854, together with a plethora of digests and extracts, directed mostly at law students, but also adapted for school use, and the education of young ladies; *The Comic Blackstone* (1844 and later editions) was compiled from instalments first published in *Punch*. There were translations into French, German, Italian, and Russian (vol. 1 only), while Blackstone's *Commentaries* continued to represent England's common law throughout the British imperial diaspora for more than a century after their author's death. The *Commentaries* long dominated legal education in North America, where nearly 100 editions and abridgements had been produced by 1900. Blackstone's other legal, historical, and literary writings received little attention, just as the life of their author has been largely approached via, and overshadowed by, his greatest work.

The immediate fame of both text and author scarcely precluded criticism. By modifying several passages on the civil disabilities of dissenters, Blackstone showed himself anxious to accommodate complaints from their spokesmen Philip Furneaux and Joseph Priestley (K. Haakonssen, ed., *Enlightenment and Religion: Rational Dissent in Eighteenth-Century Britain*, 1996, 191–2). But he left unanswered Jeremy Bentham's *Fragment on Government* (1776), which so effectively portrayed him as a confused and shallow apologist for the status quo that his intellectual and political reputation had barely began to recover before the early twentieth century. However, it is now widely recognized that, in targeting Blackstone's shortcomings as a legal theorist, Bentham deliberately ignored his prime aim and achievement, which was to expound the state of English law in his own day, not to justify it in abstract terms. Re-evaluation of Blackstone's life and work has been hampered by a lack of personal papers, the bulk and diversity of his writings, and his tendency to self-effacement. Recent scholarship has none the less broken much new ground, so there may yet be attained a more balanced and realistic portrait of this ambitious, complex, and multi-talented representative of the English Enlightenment.

WILFRID PREST

Sources W. Blackstone, *Reports of cases determined in the several courts of Westminster-Hall, from 1746 to 1779* (1781) [incl. memoir by J. Clitherow] · *Blackstone and Oxford* (1980) [exhibition catalogue, Bodl. Oxf., 1980] · I. G. Doolittle, *William Blackstone, a biography* (2001) · W. Blackstone, correspondence with R. Newdigate, 1750–79, Warks. CRO, Newdigate papers, CR 136 · W. Blackstone, letters to William Petty, second earl of Shelburne, 1761–6, Bodl. Oxf., Bowood muniments, MS Film 1999–2000, MS Shelburne 35 [most origs. now privately held] · letters from William Blackstone to William Eden, 1778–9, BL, Add. MSS 34415–34416, 46491 · L. S. Sutherland, 'William Blackstone and the legal chairs at Oxford', *Evidence in literary scholarship: essays in memory of James Marshall Osborn* (1979), 229–40 · L. S. Sutherland, 'Political respectability, 1751–1771', *Hist. U. Oxf.* 5: *18th-cent. Oxf.*, 129–61 · L. S. Sutherland, 'The Laudian statutes in the eighteenth century', *Hist. U. Oxf.* 5: *18th-cent. Oxf.*, 191–204 · I. G. Philip, *William Blackstone and the reform of the Oxford University Press in the eighteenth century* (1957) · L. B. Namier, 'Blackstone, William', HoP, *Commons*, *1754–90*, 2.96–7 · 'The letters of Sir William Blackstone in the Hampton L. Carson collection of the Free Library of Philadephia', ed. H. J. Heaney, *American Journal of Legal History*, 1 (1957), 363–78 · M. Lobban, *The common law and English jurisprudence, 1760–1850* (1991) · cellar book, 1750–59, All Souls Oxf., MS D.D. E 331 · All Souls Oxf., MS library book · W. Blackstone, letters to Thomas Walker, 1765–76, Bodl. Oxf., MS D. D. Bertie c. 2/8 · [D. Douglas], *The biographical history of Sir William Blackstone and a catalogue of Sir William Blackstone's works … by a gentleman of Lincoln's Inn* (1782); repr. (New York, 1971) · entry books, 1746–69, Bodl. Oxf., MSS records e. 554–60 · D. A. Lockmiller, *Sir William Blackstone* (1938) · E. Craster, *The history of All Souls College library*, ed. E. F. Jacob (1971) · G. D. Squibb, *Founders' kin: privilege and pedigree* (1972) · P. Langford, 'Tories and Jacobites, 1714–1751', *Hist. U. Oxf.* 5: *18th-cent. Oxf.*, 99–127 · J. L. Barton, 'Legal studies', *Hist. U. Oxf.* 5: *18th-cent. Oxf.*, 593–606 · W. R. Ward, *Georgian Oxford: university politics in the eighteenth century* (1958) · J. Prior, *Life of Edmond Malone, editor of Shakespeare* (1860), 431–2 · L. C. Warden, *The life of Blackstone* (1938) · D. Lieberman, *The province of legislation determined: legal theory in eighteenth-century Britain* (1989) · S. F. C. Milsom,

The nature of Blackstone's achievement (1981) • R. Willman, 'The politics of Blackstone's *Commentaries*: whig or tory?', *Empire and Revolutions: papers presented at the Folger Institute Seminar 'Political thought in the English-speaking Atlantic, 1760–1800'*, ed. G. J. Schochet (1993), 279–308 [directed by J. G. A. Pocock and others] • W. Blackstone, *Commentaries on the laws of England*, 4 vols. (1765–9); facs. edn (1979) [helpful introductions by S. Katz, T. Green, and others, but text does not incorporate Blackstone's editorial corrections] • C. S. Eller, *The William Blackstone collection in the Yale law library: a bibliographical catalogue* (New Haven, 1938) [see no. 56 for Blackstone's editorial corrections to W. Blackstone, *Commentaries*] • R. M. Mersky, 'A bibliography of articles on Blackstone', *American Journal of Legal History*, 3 (1959), 78–87 • *DNB* • will, PRO, PROB 11/1061 fols. 101*v*–105*v* • S. Devereux, 'The making of the Penitentiary Act, 1775–1779', *HJ*, 42 (1999), 405–34 • *IGI* • I. Doolittle, *William Blackstone: a biography* (2001) • Holdsworth, *Eng. law*, 12.702–37

Archives All Souls Oxf., holograph MS of 'Elements of architecture' • All Souls Oxf., law lecture notes • All Souls Oxf., MS cellar book • All Souls Oxf., MS 'dissertation upon the accounts' • All Souls Oxf., MS elements of architecture • All Souls Oxf., MS library book • BL, Add. MSS 34415–46491 • BL, lectures on common law, Add. MSS 36093–36101 • Bodl. Oxf., corresp. relating to Clarendon Press • Bodl. Oxf., MS records e. 554–60 • Law Society, London, lecture notes • LMA, executors' account, MSS ACC 1360/586 • Pembroke College, Oxford, undergraduate exercises, MS 62/1/13 • Warks. CRO, Newdigate MSS, CR 136 | Bodl. Oxf., MS D.D.Bertie c. 2/8 • Bodl. Oxf., MS Film 1999–2000, MS Shelburne 35 • Getty Research Institute, 'An abridgement of architecture', MS 890227 • Glos. RO, corresp. with Granville Sharp, D3549 13/1/825 • Mount Stuart Trust, Isle of Bute, archive, letters to third earl of Bute • NRA, priv. coll., letters to Lord Shelburne • UCL, department of geological sciences, notes by John Wilkinson on his law lectures

Likenesses T. Gainsborough, oils, 1774, NPG, Tate collection • J. Hall, engraving, 1778 (after T. Gainsborough), Middle Temple, London • J. Bacon senior, marble statue, 1784, All Souls Oxf. [*see illus.*] • T. Kettle, oils, 1784, Bodl. Oxf. • P. Bartlett, bronze statue, 1924, Courts of Justice, London • attrib. J. Reynolds, oils, NPG • A. N. Sanders, mezzotint (after T. Gainsborough), BM

Wealth at death substantial; £14,448 1*s*. 7*d*. from sale of self-published *Commentaries*; paid a total of £49 in land tax assessed on properties in and around Wallingford in 1779; mortgages, stock, and other securities, from which Lady Blackstone was to receive an annuity of £280 p.a.: executors' account, LMA, MSS ACC 1360/586/2, 5

Blackton, James Stuart (1875–1941), film pioneer, was born on 5 January 1875 at 121 Broom Spring Lane, Ecclesall Bierlow, Sheffield, the son of Henry Blackton, saw manufacturer, and his wife, Jessie Stuart. The family emigrated in 1885 to America, where after his father's death in 1888 young Jim became its sole supporter as an apprentice carpenter in the Bronx. His artistic ambition first surfaced in an amateur variety act, formed with two other English immigrants, in which he executed rapid sketches and oil paintings. This led to a job with the *New York World*, interviewing and sketching celebrities, then to a commission from Thomas Edison in 1896 to appear as a cartoonist in three short films. Together with one of his stage partners, Albert E. Smith, Blackton acquired an Edison projector which they converted into a camera, and used to produce films from 1897, under the title Vitagraph.

Blackton took the lead in one of their first successes, *The Burglar on the Roof*, shot on an improvised set in downtown New York, and caught the public mood during the war with Spain in a topical allegory, *Tearing Down the Spanish Flag*, using a miniature. In 1903 he supervised the building

James Stuart Blackton (1875–1941), by unknown photographer, 1921 [right, with his colour-camera operator, working on *The Glorious Adventure*]

of America's best-equipped studio, at Flatbush, New Jersey, which enabled the company to make increasingly lavish films and become the leading producer during the nickelodeon boom that started in 1905. He also returned to graphic and trick work with a series of films that laid the foundations for much subsequent animation and special effects, including *Humorous Phases of Funny Faces* and a virtuoso display of single-frame magic in *The Haunted Hotel*.

Showing a remarkable ability to anticipate new trends, Blackton launched a realist drama series, *Scenes of True Life*, in 1908. And as cinema owners sought to attract more sophisticated audiences, he produced one of the first biblical spectacles, *The Life of Moses* (1909), followed by a series of Shakespearian and other classic adaptations. Seeing how different aspects of the business supported each other, Blackton and Smith launched a fan magazine in 1911 and an exclusive Vitagraph cinema on Broadway in 1914, by which time Blackton had become a millionaire, enjoying an affluent Long Island existence, with a succession of yachts and Theodore Roosevelt as his neighbour. Encouraged by Roosevelt, in 1915 he produced a sensational propaganda film, *The Battle-Cry of Peace*, which urged American armament in the face of the war raging in Europe.

As America entered the war, Blackton resigned from Vitagraph and worked briefly for Adolph Zukor's Famous Players, before returning to his native country in 1920 to inject American 'know-how' into the stagnant British post-war cinema. Using the newly developed Prizma colour process, he produced two historical romances, *The Glorious Adventure* (1921) and *The Gypsy Cavalier* (1924): the former starred Lady Diana Manners and was set during the fire of London and the latter featured the French boxing champion Georges Charpentier. When a third period romance, with Lady Diana as *The Virgin Queen*, failed to achieve major success, Blackton returned to Flatbush for the last years of the Vitagraph company. After its sale to Warner Brothers in 1926, he turned to a series of quixotic ventures, including an experimental 3-D film, and in 1930, after losing much of his fortune, an eccentric history of cinema, *The Film Parade*, which he continued to show until his death.

Blackton was married four times. His first marriage, in 1898, was to Isabelle Mabel MacArthur, with whom he had a son and a daughter. The couple divorced in 1906, and in the following year he married an actress in Vitagraph films. This was Paula Hilburn (*d.* 1930), known professionally as Paula Dean, with whom he had two more children. A third marriage, in 1931, was to Helen Stahle, who died at some point in or before 1936. In that year Blackton married another actress, Evangeline Russell (*d.* 1966), who survived him. In his last years, living happily in North Hollywood with his fourth wife, Blackton was supported by the New Deal Works Program Administration and was exploiting a newly invented colour effects process at the time of his death. This was caused by a road accident, in Hollywood, on 13 August 1941. The figure that emerges from his daughter's biography, published in 1985, is a breezy, optimistic, and endlessly inventive, if also gullible, character who embodied much of the brashness and energy of the early years of cinema, as well as the cultural ambition that drove it. IAN CHRISTIE

Sources M. Blackton Trimble, *J. Stuart Blackton: a personal biography by his daughter* (1985) • A. E. Smith and P. A. Koury, *Two reels and a crank* (1952) • D. Gifford, *Who's who of Victorian cinema* (1986) • C. Musser, 'The American Vitagraph, 1897–1901: survival and success in a competitive industry', *Film before Griffith*, ed. J. L. Fell (1983), 22–66 • D. Gomery, 'Blackton, James Stuart', *ANB* • A. Slide, *The big V* (1987) • C. Musser, *The emergence of cinema* (1990) • b. cert.
Archives FILM BFI NFTVA, home footage
Likenesses photograph, 1921, Hult. Arch. [*see illus.*]

Blackwall, Anthony (*bap.* **1672**, *d.* **1730**), classical scholar and schoolmaster, was baptized on 17 July 1672 at Kirk Ireton, Derbyshire, the son of Anthony Blackwall, of Blackwall, a hamlet in that parish. His sister Elizabeth was also baptized there, on 11 May 1674. Having been educated at Derby grammar school he was admitted sizar at Emmanuel College, Cambridge, on 13 September 1690; he graduated BA in 1695 and proceeded MA in 1698. In 1697 he was appointed headmaster of Derby grammar school and lecturer of All Saints', Derby. He was presented to the vicarage of Elvaston, Derbyshire, in 1699, and held it until 1723.

Blackwall was twice married. He and his first wife, whose maiden name was Toplis, had one son, Anthony, who graduated BA from Emmanuel College in 1722. His second wife was the widow of Thomas Cantrell (1649–1698), who was Blackwall's predecessor at Derby School. They had four sons and one daughter: Henry (*d.* 1728), fellow of Emmanuel College; Robert (*b. c.*1704), a dragoon; John (*bap.* 1707, *d.* 1762), attorney at Stoke Golding; William (*b. c.*1708), who died young; and Mary, who married John Pickering on 20 September 1733.

Blackwall established his credentials as a classical scholar in 1706, when he published an edition of the verse of Theognis, with a translation into Latin; it was prefaced by an address in Greek to Joshua Barnes, professor of Greek at Oxford. His next work, *An Introduction to the Classics* (1718), was written for his pupils and proved to have a long shelf-life; it reached a sixth edition in 1746 and was reissued with additions by William Mavor, schoolmaster at Woodstock, as *Blackwall's Introduction to the Classics* in 1809.

In 1722 Blackwall was appointed headmaster of Market Bosworth grammar school, in Leicestershire, and he brought with him his assistant master from Derby, the Revd John Bradbury. He immediately set about expanding the school. A new gable and penthouse was built over the street door in 1723 and the number of pupils rose to an average of seventy. Among his pupils were Richard Dawes, classicist, and Sir Henry Atkins, who presented him to the rectory of Clapham on 12 October 1726. At both Derby and Market Bosworth Blackwall taught from his own Latin grammar, which he was prevailed upon to publish, albeit anonymously, in 1728 as *A new Latin grammar: being a short, clear, and easy introduction of young scholars to the knowledge of the Latin tongue*. His grammar was poorly regarded by Samuel Johnson, who said of him that 'By endeavouring to make the rules of Grammar more simple than was possible, he has only shown that the "easier any subject is in its own nature, the harder it is to make it more easy by explanation"' (Nichols, *Lit. anecdotes*, 1.133).

There was an equally mixed critical reception to Blackwall's final work, *The sacred classics defended and illustrated, or, An essay humbly offered towards proving the purity, propriety, and true eloquence of the writers of the New Testament* (2 pts, 1725). Praised by Philip Doddridge and Thomas Hartwell Horne, its detractors included Edward Bickersteth, William Orme, and Samuel Clarke. John Gilbert Cooper dismissed Blackwall's pretensions to lasting literary merit when he wrote that he was:

> grammatically master of the two dead languages, Greek and Latin, and had *read over* all the ancient authors in both; but, not having by nature of acquisition that happy taste of distinguishing beauties, nor a digestion to assimilate the sense of others into his own understanding, his conceptions were as crude as his address and style were unpleasing. (ibid., 1.131)

Blackwall's second wife had died by 8 June 1728, when he drew up his final will. He was revising the second volume of *The Sacred Classics* until within a few weeks of his death, at the schoolhouse in Market Bosworth on 8 April 1730. JOHN WESTBY-GIBSON, *rev.* S. J. SKEDD

Sources Nichols, *Lit. anecdotes*, 1.130–33; 2.551; 3.332 • B. Tacchella, *The Derby School register, 1570–1901* (1902) • Venn, *Alum.*

Cant. • *IGI* • will, PRO, PROB 11/642, sig. 25 • Allibone, *Dict.* • M. L. Clarke, *Greek studies in England, 1700–1830* (1945)

Likenesses G. Vertue, line engraving, BM, NPG; repro. in A. Blackwall, *The sacred classics defended*, 2nd edn (1727)

Blackwall, John (**1790–1881**), zoologist, was born on 20 January 1790, at 14 St Ann's Square, Manchester, the son of Thomas Blackwall, an Irish linen merchant. He initially worked in partnership with his father, but at the same time developed a keen interest in natural history. In 1821 he joined the Manchester Literary and Philosophical Society, and in the same year published a note on a method of determining the 'mean temperature of the natural day'. He then published a paper in which he developed an argument of John Gough, on the migration of birds. He wrote about fifteen papers on ornithology and a number on a variety of other subjects. In 1827 he was elected fellow of the Linnean Society, in whose *Transactions* he published his first researches on spiders, a subject he was to make his own. In 1834 his papers were collected into one volume and published as *Researches in Zoology* (2nd edn, 1873). He was married and had a son, also called John.

In 1833 Blackwall gave up his business career to dedicate himself entirely to his hobby. He moved to north Wales, and settled at Hendre House, Llanrwst, Denbighshire. With extraordinary dedication and skill, and with the minimum of artificial aids beyond a small lens, he fully described over 300 spiders; 67 of these were new to science. His work was set out in his *History of the Spiders of Great Britain and Ireland* (1861–4), which was beautifully illustrated with plates showing 272 different spiders. The work was delayed for ten years by the illness of the artist, Tiffen West, whom Blackwall curiously does not mention.

Blackwall continued to work until he was eighty-six, when failing eyesight compelled him to stop. He was a recluse who worked alone, unfortunately lacking colleagues in Britain and having little contact with continental scientists. He died at his home at Llanrwst, on 11 May 1881, one of the oldest members of the Linnean Society, of the Manchester 'Lit. and Phil.', and of the British Association. DONALD CARDWELL

Sources *Nature*, 24 (1881), 86–7 • O. Pickard-Cambridge, *The Entomologist*, 14 (1881), 145–50 • C. W. Sutton, *The Entomologist*, 14 (1881), 190 • *Proceedings of the Manchester Literary and Philosophical Society*, 21 (1881–2), 141–2 • *British Birds*, 36 (1933), 301–4 • W. H. Mullens and H. K. Swann, *A bibliography of British ornithology from the earliest times to the end of 1912* (1917), 67–8 • G. H. Locket and A. F. Millidge, *British spiders* (1975), 4–5 • W. S. Bristowe, *The world of spiders* (1958), 15

Archives NHM, report on the structure and uses of the Palpi of the Arancida

Wealth at death £36,492 13*s*. 4*d*.: resworn probate, Dec 1881, *CGPLA Eng. & Wales*

Blackwell, Alexander (*bap.* **1709**, *d.* **1747**), agricultural improver and government agent in Sweden, was baptized in Aberdeen on 10 October 1709. He was the son of Thomas *Blackwell (1660?–1728), professor of theology and principal at Marischal College in Aberdeen, and his wife, Christian (*d.* 1749), daughter of John Johnstoun. His brother, Thomas *Blackwell (1701–1757), was also a professor and principal at Marischal College. Alexander appears to have been the 'black sheep' of his family and little detail is known of his early years, but he is said to have studied at both Aberdeen and Edinburgh universities before moving on to Leiden in the Netherlands. There he apparently studied under Herman Boerhaave in 1725. During his time on the continent he is thought to have travelled to France and Portugal. Although he subsequently became known as a doctor of medicine he does not appear to have sat any exams or obtained an official diploma. By 1730 Blackwell was living in London where he worked as a corrector for the printer Mr Wilkins. During this time he married Elizabeth Blachrie (*bap.* 1707, *d.* 1758) [*see* Blackwell, Elizabeth], the daughter of an Aberdeen merchant, who either wrote or undertook the illustrations for *A Curious Herbal* published in 1737. Blackwell's attempts to establish his own print house resulted in a two-year spell in a debtor's prison when he went bankrupt. Elizabeth allegedly bailed him out of prison by selling illustrations.

Blackwell then turned his attention to agricultural studies and was employed by the duke of Chandos as a superintendent of works at his house, Cannons, at Stanmore, Middlesex. In 1741 Blackwell published *A New Method of Improving Cold, Wet, and Clayey Grounds* on developing soil through its fertilization with lime, or marling, of which there is apparently no surviving copy. This work became known in Sweden, where the botanist Carl von Linne mentioned it. Around this time Blackwell met the Swedish minister in London, K. M. Wasenburg, and made such an impact that he was invited to Sweden. It seems that Blackwell was losing favour with the duke of Chandos and probably welcomed the opportunity to start afresh.

In May 1742 Blackwell arrived in Sweden; after visiting Nicolaus Sahlgren, a director of the Swedish East India Company, in Göteborg he moved on to Jonas Alströmer, a founder of the Academy of Sciences and a major industrialist who had spent seventeen years living and working in London, in Allingsås. Blackwell travelled through south-western Sweden with J. Carlson, Alströmer's brother-in-law, studying local agricultural practices before returning to Allingsås where he conducted his own experiments in both agriculture and animal husbandry.

Blackwell came to the attention of the Swedish king, Frederick I, and submitted a proposal for employment as an agricultural and animal husbandry improver in November and December 1743. His job was largely based on importing sheep from Great Britain. He seems to have found royal favour, for a letter of 28 May 1744 provided a refund for Blackwell's travel expenses and proposed an annual salary of 2000 daler from 1 June. In addition he was given tax exemption, the promise of a 1000 daler annual pension for his wife or children on his death, and was provided with the royal garden of Allestad in 1745 to conduct his studies. Blackwell also published an article in the same year which was sharply criticized by the learned circles who cried plagiarism. Blackwell had similar problems with his reputation as a doctor in Stockholm, as his Swedish peers questioned his lack of medical understanding. Despite this he was apparently appointed royal physician to Frederick I in January 1745, although no proof of this appointment has been found.

Blackwell suddenly became involved in the political intrigues of the Swedish court which divided into two factions of 'hats' and 'caps' following the election of Adolf Frederick as the heir to the throne over the Danish crown prince in 1743. Frederick I's party, the 'caps', looked toward the British court for support, whereas Adolf Frederick's followers tended toward France and Russia. At this point Blackwell appears to have made contact with the British minister in Denmark, Walter Titley, perhaps hoping to enter Danish royal service. He was certainly losing favour in Sweden, and in March 1747 was summoned to the court to provide evidence of his work. At his audience with Frederick I Blackwell suggested instead that Queen Louise of Denmark, who was a British princess, could obtain £100,000 sterling from her father for Sweden's use, so long as Frederick allied himself with the king of Denmark. Frederick sent him to consult other members of his council, and Blackwell allegedly suggested ways of destroying the influence of the 'hats' party. Further details of the plan involved transferring two Swedish regiments, largely consisting of the nobility of the 'hats' party, into British and Danish service to remove them from the court and political influence.

However, Karl Gustav Tessin, councillor, president of both the chancellery and the college of war, and a supporter of the 'hats' faction, became aware of this plan. Blackwell was subsequently arrested on suspicion of attempting to overthrow the king and government of Sweden. At the same time a letter arrived from the Swedish minister in Copenhagen claiming that the Danish king was arming for war. This later was proven false, but caused enough consternation to seal Blackwell's fate. Blackwell was three times subjected to torture in attempts to gain a confession. On 10 June 1747 he was sentenced to death, a sentence confirmed by the state council one month later. Blackwell was executed in Stockholm on 9 August 1747.

A letter, allegedly written by Blackwell and delivered on the day of his death, was published in London claiming that he had worked in Sweden as a doctor and that he was about to die falsely charged with treason. The account of Blackwell's life which accompanies this letter differs significantly from the facts generally accepted, casting doubt on its authenticity. Even a contemporary publication provided little correct information, and the real story of Blackwell remains unclear. Blackwell's trial and all the documents relating to it were kept secret until the mid-nineteenth century. There is, however, no proof to date that Blackwell was engaged in subterfuge with any foreign party, and it is most likely that he was simply used as a scapegoat to bolster Tessin's position at court.

A. N. L. Grosjean

Sources *DNB* • Riksarkivet, Stockholm, biographica microcard 30a Black–Blavier, EO 1251 2/6–3/6 • *A genuine copy of a letter from a merchant in Stockholm, to his correspondent in London. Containing an impartial account of Doctor Alexander Blackwell, his plot, trial, character, and behaviour, both under examination, and at the place of execution. Together with the copy of a paper delivered by Dr. Alexander Blackwell* (1747?) • *Fasti academiae Mariscallanae Aberdonensis: selections from the records of the Marischal College and University, MDXCIII–MDCCCLX*, 2, ed. P. J. Anderson, New Spalding Club, 18 (1898), 29, 51 • *Fasti Scot.*, new edn, 7.358 • *Fasti Scot.*, new edn, 8.711 • E. Naumann, 'Blackwell, Alexander', *Svenskt biografiskt lexicon*, ed. B. Boëthius, 4 (1924), 730–34 • N. Bohman, *Svenska män och kvinnor* (1942), pt 1 • C. G. Malmström, *Sveriges politiska historia* (1897), 3.325–34 • *Chambers's biographical dictionary*, ed. D. Patrick and F. H. Groome (1897) • H. Hofberg, *Svenskt biografiskt handlexicon* (1906), pt 1 • A. Chalmers, ed., *The general biographical dictionary*, new edn, 5 (1812), 358–60
Archives Riksarkivet, Stockholm, biographica microcard collection EO 1251 2/6–3/6
Wealth at death salary of £200 p.a.: Riksarkivet, Stockholm, biographica microcard 30a Black–Blavier, EO 1251 2/6–3/6

Blackwell, Sir Basil Henry (1889–1984), bookseller and publisher, was born on 29 May 1889, at Blackwell's bookshop, 51 Broad Street, Oxford, the only son and younger child of Benjamin Henry Blackwell (1849–1924), bookseller, and his wife, Lydia (Lilla), daughter of John Taylor, a Norfolk farmer. Basil's grandfather, Benjamin Harris Blackwell (1813–1855), had first become a bookseller in Oxford in 1845, but he died prematurely when his elder son, Benjamin Henry, was only six. However, on new year's day 1879 Benjamin Henry opened his shop at Broad Street, and by the time Basil was born the business was well established. The family moved out of the shop to 1 Linton Road, Oxford. Blackwell was educated at a dame-school for boys kept by Wilhelmina and Sarah Mardon and then at Magdalen College School, Oxford. In 1907 he achieved a postmastership at Merton College, Oxford, where he received a third class in classical honour moderations (1909) and a second in *literae humaniores* (1911). Here he met Adrian Mott, who became his publishing partner.

On graduation Blackwell went to work for two years in the London office of Oxford University Press in order to learn about publishing; he was joint editor of a volume of essays for the World's Classics. On new year's day 1913 he joined his father and in September established the publications department separately from the bookshop. In his first year he launched the annual series Oxford Poetry, which included, over thirty years, Robert Graves, W. H. Auden, and Stephen Spender. He also published Edith Sitwell's first three volumes of poetry. His first editorial assistant was the crime writer Dorothy L. Sayers. On 9 September 1914 he married Marion Christine (1888/9–1977), daughter of John Soans, schoolmaster, of Ramsgate. They had two sons and three daughters.

In the next few years (he was rejected for military service because of defective eyesight) Blackwell laid the foundation for the publishing firm of Basil Blackwell and Mott (founded in 1922), which encouraged many young Oxford poets. Blackwell and Adrian Mott were also co-directors of the Shakespeare Head Press, which they saved from bankruptcy, and which allowed them to indulge in fine book production.

However, in 1924 Blackwell's father died and he became chairman of B. H. Blackwell Ltd. This meant that he had to concentrate on the main business of selling new books. This he did reluctantly, as he preferred publishing to bookselling and selling antiquarian books to new books.

Sir Basil Henry Blackwell (1889–1984), by John Ward, 1979

In spite of this, and through the promotion of export in the USA, by 1929 he was one of the most flourishing and influential booksellers in the country. Almost immediately on assuming complete responsibility for the business he successfully opposed a ring of collusive bidders in antiquarian book auctions. In 1925–6 he was elected president of the Antiquarian Booksellers' Association. In 1955, after a further outbreak of collusive bidding, Blackwell had the matter raised vigorously in parliament, and, as a result of the publicity, the Antiquarian Booksellers' Association made a new and even more stringent rule against the practice.

Throughout his life Blackwell served his profession well and exercised considerable influence in the book trade of the United Kingdom. From 1934 to 1936 he was president of the Booksellers' Association. He forged an alliance with Stanley *Unwin (1884–1968), president of the Publishers' Association, on the grounds that booksellers and publishers, so often mutually suspicious, should be brought together in co-operation. At the 1932 Booksellers' Association conference Blackwell, at Unwin's request, had finally succeeded in persuading booksellers to support the book token scheme, which had originally been proposed by a publisher in 1928. In 1934 Blackwell invited Unwin to be joint host to an informal weekend conference of fifty booksellers and publishers in Ripon Hall, Oxford, the beneficial influence of which lasted for many years. At the end of his period of office Blackwell's reputation for approachability, concern for the welfare of the trade, and enthusiasm was such that he was affectionately nicknamed the Gaffer.

By 1938 the bookselling business was flourishing, with expansion into further premises and the establishment of a second publishing business, Blackwell Scientific Publications Ltd. Contrary to the experience of the First World War, and to expectations, the sales of books greatly increased in the Second World War, and in 1945 B. H. Blackwell Ltd and its two associated publishing companies were well set. Blackwell's eldest son, Richard *Blackwell (1918–1980), returned from the war and in the course of the next twenty years gradually assumed responsibility and undertook modernization. Blackwell finally resigned the chairmanship after forty-five years in 1969 to become president, and handed on a business vastly increased, both in reputation and in size, although much of the credit for the post-war expansion overseas belonged to his son, Richard.

For the rest of his life, to within a week of his death, Blackwell continued to attend all board meetings as president, to peruse all accounting statements, and to visit the three main offices. He instinctively supported the attitudes and conventions of a previous age, working long hours in his office and supervising every detail. He believed in paternalism and it was his settled intention that Blackwells should remain independent and controlled only by those members of the family actively concerned with its management. He had the reputation of being one of the best-read people in the country. He wrote no books, but his letters and speeches were entertaining. He contributed the notice of J. G. Wilson to the *Dictionary of National Biography*.

In 1941 Blackwell became a JP for Oxford, and in 1956 he was the first bookseller to be knighted. In 1959 he was elected an honorary fellow of Merton College. He was president of the Classical Association (1964–5), and of the English Association (1969–70). In 1979, on the hundredth anniversary of the founding of B. H. Blackwell Ltd, the University of Oxford made him an honorary DCL. He was also an honorary LLD of Manchester University (1965). But the distinction he cherished most was that of honorary freeman of the city of Oxford, conferred upon him in his eightieth year. Blackwell died of bronchopneumonia at his home, Tubney House, Tubney, near Abingdon, Oxfordshire, on 9 April 1984.

JOHN BROWN, *rev.* CLARE L. TAYLOR

Sources A. L. P. Norrington, *Blackwell's, 1879–1979: the history of a family firm* (1983) · P. J. Anderson and J. Rose, eds., *British literary publishing houses, 1820–1880*, DLitB, 106 (1991) · *WW* · b. cert. · m. cert. · d. cert.

Archives Bodl. Oxf., corresp. with L. G. Curtis; Round Table corresp. · Bodl. Oxf., corresp. with Herbert Davis · U. Glas. L., letters to D. S. MacColl

Likenesses V. Strang, oils, 1969, Blackwell Group Ltd, Oxford · J. Ward, oils, 1979, Blackwell Group Ltd, Oxford [*see illus.*] · photographs, Blackwell Group Ltd, Oxford

Wealth at death £193,289: probate, 27 Sept 1984, *CGPLA Eng. & Wales*

Blackwell, Ebenezer (*d.* 1782), banker, was born in Tewkesbury. In 1731 he joined Martin's Bank, Lombard Street, London, as principal clerk, later becoming a partner and retiring in 1780. In August 1739 George Whitefield entrusted to him the £15 collected for his charity school at Kingswood when he preached on Blackheath, and this brought Blackwell into correspondence with John Wesley. His country home, The Limes, Lewisham, became Wesley's favourite retreat from the pressures of London life. A number of his sermons and other publications were written there and at the end of 1753 he spent five weeks recuperating from a serious illness under the devoted nursing of Blackwell's first wife, Elizabeth (*née* Mowland). On visiting the house in August 1782 with his brother Charles,

Wesley wrote: 'We took one more walk round the garden and meadow, which he took so much pains to improve. Upward of forty years this has been my place of retirement when I could spare two or three days from London' (*Journal of … John Wesley*, 6.363). Elizabeth died on 27 March 1772 and Charles Wesley wrote an elegiac poem commemorating her piety. In the same year Blackwell married Mary Eden, the niece of Robert Lowth, bishop of London. It was at the Blackwells' home that Lowth and Wesley met and exchanged courtesies on 24 November 1777, the day after Wesley preached a sermon for the Humane Society in Lewisham church.

Blackwell's business acumen and experience were always at Wesley's disposal and their correspondence was full of financial as well as spiritual matters. Towards the end of his life he became one of the first trustees of the new City Road Chapel. Over the years he gave generous support to Wesley's charitable activities and Wesley did not hesitate to appeal to him when, for example, the growing number of poor coming to the dispensary at the Foundery Chapel left him desperately short of medicines. Wesley's letter of 4 February 1751 shows how meticulous he was, in his turn, in giving a detailed account of ways in which Blackwell's charitable gifts had been disbursed. At the same time Wesley repeatedly expressed his concern for the spiritual well-being of his Lewisham friend, seeing his 'natural cheerfulness of temper' and fear of being 'singular' as worldly temptations, and expressed the hope that he would be 'not almost only, but altogether a Christian' (16 May 1753, *Letters of … John Wesley*, 3.98–9). He repeatedly warned him of the dangers inherent in being so fully occupied with financial responsibilities: 'Engaging in these temporal affairs is apt to dampen and deaden the soul' (14 May 1747, ibid., 2.97). 'Business itself, when it comes in such a flood upon you, must needs be one of the greatest temptations, since it naturally tends to hinder your waiting upon God … without distraction' (14 Aug 1748, ibid., 2.151). And in asking for Blackwell's help with his wife's financial affairs, Wesley prayed in the same letter that he might

serve with careful Martha's hands
And loving Mary's heart.
(14 May 1751, ibid., 3.67)

Blackwell became Wesley's most trusted confidant, with whom he shared both religious and marital problems. He had known Mrs Vazeille, probably through her first husband, before her marriage to Wesley, and may have been more than a passive observer of the events that led to that less-than-happy union. There was a period at the end of the 1750s when Mrs Wesley came near to effecting an estrangement between them. But the frankness they had nurtured over the years enabled their long association to hold firm. When Blackwell died on 21 April 1782, Charles Wesley wrote verses celebrating his old friend's philanthropy:

Obedient both in word and deed,
By works his genuine faith he showed,
Rejoiced in Jesu's steps to tread
And spent his life in doing good.
(*Journal of … Charles Wesley*, 2.390)

JOHN A. VICKERS

Sources *The journal of the Rev. John Wesley*, ed. N. Curnock and others, 8 vols. (1909–16) · *The letters of the Rev. John Wesley*, ed. J. Telford, 8 vols. (1931) · *The journal of the Rev. Charles Wesley*, ed. T. Jackson, 2 vols. [1849]

Blackwell [*née* Blachrie], **Elizabeth** (*bap.* **1707**, *d.* **1758**), botanical author and artist, was baptized on 22 June 1707 at St Nicholas, Aberdeen, the sixth daughter of a prosperous stocking merchant, William Blachrie (*b. c.*1669) and his wife, Isobel Fordyce. Elizabeth married her second cousin Alexander *Blackwell (*bap.* 1709, *d.* 1747), reportedly eloping to London about 1728. Elizabeth's dowry enabled her husband to establish a printing business at the Atlas, opposite Catherine Street in the Strand, about 1730, but the business foundered and Alexander was incarcerated in the debtors' prison by 1734. Elizabeth decided to extricate her husband from his financial difficulties by applying her artistic talents to drawing and painting lifelike reproductions of medicinal plants. Encouragement came from Sir Hans Sloane, Richard Mead, and apothecary Isaac Rand, director of the botanical garden at Chelsea. Elizabeth took lodgings at 4 Swan Walk in Chelsea, close to the garden where she would find the living models for her botanical drawings. She was assisted in her task by Philip Miller, head of the garden's staff.

Elizabeth Blackwell's *A curious herbal: containing five hundred cuts, of the most useful plants, which are now used in the practice of physick* has been described as 'among the earliest publications on botany by a woman … links an older female tradition of herbal work with an emergent female tradition of botanical illustration' (Shteir, 40). Before her work on the *Curious Herbal* was completed, Elizabeth's son, William, died, and was buried at Chelsea on 3 May 1736. After finishing the drawings Elizabeth engraved them on copper herself, and coloured the 500 prints individually by hand. Alexander assisted with textual translation. Initially published in weekly parts, the first volume, which contained commendations from the Royal College of Physicians, was completed in 1737, the second in 1738 or early 1739. Among those to whom the volumes were dedicated was Elizabeth's uncle by marriage, John Johnstoun, professor of medicine at the University of Glasgow, as well as Richard Mead, Isaac Rand, and other luminaries of the medical profession. The book enjoyed considerable success in the eighteenth century, selling for about £5 for both volumes. A woman of many talents, Elizabeth was personally involved in the accounting and bookkeeping tasks associated with the marketing of her publication, which successfully rescued the family from debt. Although Blackwell's original edition has been seen by some as inferior to the augmented German version published in Nuremburg by J. Trew between 1757 and 1773, it remains aesthetically superior. The text is delicately engraved in her elegant hand (as opposed to the heavy print of the German text) and boasts a more sensible arrangement, with drawings closely integrated with the relevant text. Blackwell's format, as well as the English text, invited lay readership. Elizabeth remained in England when her husband travelled to Sweden in 1742, the year she bore her second son, Alexander, who was baptized at St Paul's, Covent Garden, Westminster, on 7 September 1742. Widowed in 1747 by the execution in Sweden of her husband, after he had become involved in a political intrigue, Elizabeth lived until October 1758. She was buried in the churchyard at Chelsea Old Church.

DOREEN A. EVENDEN

Sources E. Blackwell, *A curious herbal: containing five hundred cuts, of the most useful plants, which are now used in the practice of physick*, 2 vols. (1737–9) · B. Henrey, *British botanical and horticultural literature before 1800*, 2 (1975) · A. B. Shteir, *Cultivating women, cultivating science: Flora's daughters and botany in England, 1760–1860* (1996) · *IGI* · A. Boney, *The lost gardens of Glasgow University* (1988) · J. Dallas, 'Elizabeth Blackwell: a curious herbal containing five hundred cuts of the most useful plants', *Scottish Book Collector*, 5 (1996–7) · T. Faulkner, *An historical and topographical description of Chelsea and its environs*, [new edn], 2 (1829) · J. Bruce, *Lives of eminent men of Aberdeen* (1841) · W. Blunt and S. Raphael, *The illustrated herbal* (1979) · Desmond, *Botanists*, rev. edn · B. Madge, 'Elizabeth Blackwell: the forgotten herbalist?', *Health Information and Libraries Journal*, 18/3 (2001), 144–52

Likenesses Swaine, photomechanical print, Wellcome L.

Blackwell, Elizabeth (1821–1910), physician, was born on 3 February 1821 at Counterslip Street, Bristol, the third daughter and the third of nine children of Samuel Blackwell (*c.*1790–1838), sugar refiner, and his wife, Hannah, daughter of Bristol jewellers (husband and wife) named Lane. Samuel Blackwell, an active Congregationalist and anti-slavery campaigner, was committed to giving his daughters as well as his sons full opportunity to develop their talents and abilities. Following financial problems with his business and the riots in Bristol in 1831, Samuel Blackwell, his children, including the eleven-year-old Elizabeth, and four unmarried sisters emigrated to New York, where he resumed both sugar refining and anti-slavery protest. More business difficulties took the family to Cincinnati in 1838 where Samuel Blackwell died suddenly, leaving his family poorly provided for. Elizabeth and her two elder sisters set up a school to support the family. In 1842 Elizabeth was appointed as head of a girls' school in Kentucky but soon left because of her loathing of slavery. For the next few years she continued to teach, although she disliked it, as the only means of supporting herself while saving for medical training. She had conceived the ambition of entering medicine about 1844, partly because of the suffering of an acquaintance whose modesty had prevented her consulting a male doctor until her uterine cancer was too advanced for any treatment; partly to dissociate the term 'female physician' from abortionists; and, according to her own autobiography, because she did not wish to become dependent on a man through marriage.

Finding a way of realizing this ambition however was not to be easy. Blackwell rejected advice to go to Paris as impractical and to disguise herself as a man as immoral. In 1847, after several years of private study and numerous rejections from medical schools, her application to the small, low-status medical school at Geneva in upstate New York was put to the students by the faculty, confident that a resounding rejection would result. The mischievous students, however, voted unanimously to admit her and then found themselves victims of their own practical joke when, in January 1849, Blackwell graduated MD above all 150 male students, an event that received widespread press coverage across the United States and in Great Britain. Blackwell then returned to Europe for further medical training. In May 1849 she enrolled at La Maternité, the leading school for midwives in Paris, as no Paris hospital would admit her as a doctor. Here Blackwell contracted purulent ophthalmia from a patient which left her blind in one eye and with only partial vision in the other, ending all hope of becoming a surgeon. She visited London where she was admitted as a doctor to all departments of St Bartholomew's Hospital, except that for women, and was much fêted within the social circles associated with the emerging women's movement. In 1850 Blackwell returned to New York and set up in private practice, opening a dispensary for poor women and children in 1853, which later developed into the New York Infirmary for Women, a hospital run by medical women for women. Here she was joined by some of the small but growing number of formally qualified medical women in the United States, including her younger sister Emily. She also lectured extensively on women's health and hygiene. A collection of her lectures was published in 1852 as *The Laws of Life with Special Reference to the Physical Education of Girls*.

In 1858 Blackwell revisited London where, under a clause in the 1858 Medical Act that recognized doctors with foreign degrees practising in Britain before 1858, she was able to have her name entered on the General Medical Council's register (1 January 1859), the only woman so entitled. During this visit, Blackwell gave public lectures, several of which were published, on the value of physiological and medical knowledge to women and on the work of medical women in America. Among those whom she influenced was the young Elizabeth Garrett (1836–1917) who, in 1863, and after her own protracted struggle, was to become the second registered medical woman in Britain. Back in New York in 1859, Blackwell focused her professional activities on developing the infirmary as a hospital providing both services for women patients and sound training for women medical students, although the outbreak of the civil war in 1861 saw her, as a committed emancipationist, active in the attempt to organize women's nursing services for the United States army troops. In 1868 the infirmary's medical school for women was formally opened, with instruction from women as far as was possible without compromising standards, with Elizabeth Blackwell as professor of hygiene and Emily Blackwell as professor of obstetrics and diseases of women. But the relationship between the two sisters became increasingly strained and in 1869 Blackwell decided to return to England where she lived until her death in 1910.

During this last phase of her life, living mainly in London or, from 1879, in Hastings, Blackwell was largely retired from professional medical practice, her income from investments in the United States making earning a living unnecessary. She did hold an appointment as consulting physician at Elizabeth Garrett Anderson's New Hospital for Women in Marylebone, London, and, when the London School of Medicine for Women formally opened in 1875, she was a member of the school's council and a lecturer in midwifery. But it was social reform more generally, particularly in relation to health and hygiene and the role of women in promoting these, that preoccupied her. Among the causes to which Blackwell lent her support, in public and through voluminous private correspondence, were the campaign against the Contagious Diseases Acts in the 1870s and social and sexual purity in the 1880s. She was implacably opposed to animal experimentation and to the adoption of Pasteur's treatment of suspected rabies infections. She was interested in spiritualism and Christo-theosophy. In 1871 she had been among the founders of the National Health Society, which aimed to promote sanitary and hygiene instruction, particularly in schools, under the slogan 'Prevention is better than cure'. She published extensively on these topics, a collection of essays being reprinted in her two volumes of *Essays in Medical Sociology* in 1902, and also on sex education and morality, for example, in *The Human Element in Sex*, first published in 1880. Her autobiography, *Opening the Medical Profession to Women*, was published in 1895. Running through these social reform activities, her writing, and her entire professional career were two more or less constant commitments: her profound opposition to materialist medicine, to what she saw as an amoral scientific approach which explained ill health in terms of chance encounter with germs or physiological malfunctions alone rather than the result of failure to adhere to the essentially moral laws of healthy living; and her elevated views of women's role as guardians of social purity and hence health.

Blackwell propounded a case for women doctors not just on the liberal grounds of equal opportunity for women nor just as a means of ensuring women had access to medical care without compromising their modesty and delicacy. Rather, she argued that women doctors had an invaluable contribution to make to the whole of society through the exercise of their power of 'spiritual maternity' (E. Blackwell, *Erroneous Method in Medical Education*, 1891, 8). For her, a specifically feminine approach could safeguard the links between medicine and morality, emphasizing prevention through hygiene, in line with the sanitarian tradition of public health she adhered to. She fervently beseeched women doctors to reject the materialist tenets of germ theory and the (in her view) excessively interventionist medicine being practised by men. But she did so in the face of mounting evidence in the 1880s and 1890s that women medical students were being socialized into the same values as their male peers, even in the women's medical schools. Privately and, at times, publicly, Blackwell found herself increasingly at odds with the younger women who had followed in her footsteps, the American physician Mary Putnam Jacobi, for example, and, in Britain, Elizabeth Garrett Anderson, neither of whom shared her abhorrence of animal experimentation or major abdominal surgery.

Blackwell's social reform activities brought her a wide range of close associates and friends and she retained close links with her extensive family on both sides of the Atlantic. In 1856 she adopted Kitty Barry, an orphan of Irish origin who was her companion for the rest of her life. In 1907 Blackwell sustained a fall from which she never fully recovered and she died on 31 May 1910 at her home, Rock House, Hastings, shortly after a stroke. She was buried in June in the churchyard at Kilmun on Holy Loch in the west of Scotland, a place where she had loved to spend holidays. M. A. Elston

Sources N. A. Sahli, 'Elizabeth Blackwell, MD (1821–1910): a biography', unpublished PhD diss., University of Pennsylvania, 1974 · E. Blackwell, *Opening the medical profession to women: autobiographical sketches* (1895) · *The Lancet* (11 June 1910), 1657–8 · *BMJ* (18 June 1910), 1523–4 · R. M. Morantz-Sanchez, *Sympathy and science: women physicians in American medicine* (1985) · E. M. Bell, *Storming the citadel: the rise of the woman doctor* (1953) · M. Forster, *Significant sisters: the grassroots of active feminism, 1839–1939* (1984) · R. M. Morantz-Sanchez, 'Feminism, professionalism and germs: the thought of Mary Putnam Jacobi and Elizabeth Blackwell', *American Quarterly*, 34 (1982), 459–78

Archives Col. U., MSS · Harvard U., Radcliffe Institute for Advanced Study, family MSS · L. Cong., family MSS · Medical College of Pennsylvania, Philadelphia · Royal Free Hospital, London, medical school · Women's Library, London | Col. U., Rare Book and Manuscript Library, letters to Barbara Bodichon · NRA, priv. coll., letters to Sir Norman Moore

Likenesses Swaine, photomechanical print, Wellcome L. · drawing (after pencil sketch by Comtesse de Charnacée, 1859), Royal Free Hospital Medical School, London · photograph, Medical College of Pennsylvania, Philadelphia, Archives and Special Collections on Women in Medicine · photographs, L. Cong., Blackwell family MSS

Blackwell, George (1547–1613), archpriest, was born in Middlesex. According to Robert Charnock, his father was 'a pewterer by Newgate in London', perhaps the Thomas Blackwell (*d.* 1553) who was a warden of the Pewter Company in 1547–8. On 27 May 1562 Blackwell was admitted scholar of Trinity College, Oxford, graduating BA in 1563. In 1565 he became probationer and in 1566 perpetual fellow of the college, and in 1567 he was instituted MA. In 1571 six fellows resigned or were ejected from Trinity due to their conservative religious views, among them Blackwell. He moved first to Gloucester Hall, then a refuge for Catholics, and in 1574 to the English College, Douai. It must have been about this time that he met Robert Bellarmine (then professor of theology in Louvain), who in 1607 mentioned having met Blackwell almost forty years before. In 1575 Blackwell was ordained and, on 20 October, graduated bachelor of sacred theology. On 2 November 1576 he left Douai to return to England as a missioner. Two months later it was reported in the English College that his erudition and piety were already having a favourable effect in England, but letters that reached Rheims on 1 December 1578 reported his capture. In 1602 Charnock wrote that 'About twenty years since … you were imprisoned in London; but your brother, being the bishop of London's register, procured your release'. This would have been William Blackwell, perhaps the same who matriculated at Christ Church in 1554–5 and graduated BCL in 1562.

The Council of Trent's condemnation in 1562 of attendance at Church of England services was not published until 1593, and in the meantime a number of Catholic opinions that allowed attendance in order to escape the rigour of the English laws were in circulation. In the winter of 1580–81 Blackwell prepared the notes from which Robert Persons wrote *A Brief Discours Contayning Certayne Reasons why Catholiques Refuse to Goe to Church*, one of the most influential books persuading Catholics to recusancy. For seven or eight years Blackwell lodged in the house of a Mrs Meany in Westminster, in constant fear of capture. On one occasion, when he was concealed in a priest's hole, with guards posted in the house to starve him out, he was rescued by the intervention of the countess of Arundel and Surrey.

After the death of Cardinal Allen (1594) the English mission lacked authoritative leadership, and serious divisions arose between the Jesuits and those secular priests unfavourably disposed towards them. The tensions led to accusations of maladministration of funds against the Jesuit superior Henry Garnet, for whose propriety George Blackwell vouched. To put an end to such dissensions, the disciplinary and financial aspects of the Jesuit and secular missions were divided in 1598. Cardinal Cajetan, protector of the English nation, on 7 March 1598 issued letters appointing George Blackwell archpriest of the secular clergy of England and Scotland. Blackwell's instructions ordered him to work in close consultation with the Jesuit superiors. The English College in Rome was already under Jesuit direction, and in 1598 Thomas Worthington, known to be favourably disposed towards the society, became president of the English College in Douai. The institutions of the English secular clergy were thus controlled by Jesuits or by priests willing to work closely with them, and Blackwell's appointment became the focus of discontent. Feelings of personal slight also played a role: among the seculars there were a number of priests more prominent than him either for their birth or for their erudition, and who had experience in dealing with the questions of conscience arising in the spiritual direction of a substantial household, while Blackwell had long 'had charge onely of a widow gentlewoman' (Law, 1.90–98).

A substantial minority of the secular priests signed a petition which was carried to Rome by William Bishop and Robert Charnock, appealing to the pope to overturn Cardinal Cajetan's arrangements and appoint a bishop. In March 1599 Blackwell suspended three priests for opposing his appointment. On 6 April Clement VIII issued a bull confirming Blackwell's appointment and powers, to which the appellants submitted. Blackwell then insisted that those who had publicly refused to recognize his authority were guilty of schism, and could not carry out their priestly duties until absolved. On 3 May 1600 the faculty of theology of the University of Paris delivered a judgment that the sin of schism had not been committed, but on 29 May Blackwell decreed that this judgment was prejudicial to the dignity of the Holy See and should not be published in England. A second appeal to Rome ensued, drawn up on 17 November. In the winter of 1600–01 Blackwell suspended at least ten priests. On 17 August 1601 the pope issued a breve upholding Blackwell's appointment, criticizing his intransigence, and prohibiting all further controversy on the issue, but it was not promulgated in England until 26 January 1602. In the interval John Mush, Christopher Bagshaw, and Dr Bishop published works attacking Blackwell, and his friends wrote in his defence.

It was probably about this time that Blackwell requested general prayers for his own intention, which was later revealed to be the safe delivery of the Infanta Isabella, then rumoured to be with child. A report to Sir Robert Cecil dated 27 August 1601 gave a description of Blackwell's person and movements as:

> about 50 years of age, his head brownish, his beard more black, cut after the fashion of a spade, of stature indifferent, and somewhat thick, decently attired … Termly he is in London and at this instant as near to Framingham as he well may be (*Salisbury MSS*, 11.363–5)

while in October he was reported as being 'on the Borders'. When in London he lived in the town house of Viscount Montague.

In September 1601 arrangements were made with the privy council that four imprisoned priests should be banished from the realm so that they could go to Rome to pursue the second appeal, the papal rejection of which was not yet known in England. Richard Bancroft was particularly eager for their success, arguing in letters to Cecil that 'all the Catholics almost that are in England' accepted Blackwell's authority, and that 'To be subject to Blackwell is to be subject to Parsons, the vilest traitor that lives, and consequently to the King of Spain' (*Salisbury MSS*, 11.318, 12.204). In response to this 'third' appeal, Clement VIII on 5 October 1602 censured Blackwell's tactlessness and revoked the instruction that he act in consultation with the Jesuit superiors, instead ordering him to communicate no business to members of the society. This completed the institutional separation of the secular and Jesuit missions, and tempers very quickly cooled. In May 1603 Blackwell had a meeting with Mush and Colleton in which a spirit of reconciliation was evident. At James's accession Blackwell wrote a letter to the clergy commanding them 'to labour to give stay and restraint to all bad attempts' against the new government, and in June, through the mediation of John Gage, he revealed the existence of the Bye plot to the authorities. In October he was dangerously ill, and the nuncio in Brussels wrote to the cardinal secretary of state about possible successors, but he soon recovered his health.

Throughout 1604 and 1605 Blackwell exercised his authority unimpeded by disputes. As soon as he became aware, on 7 November 1605, of the Gunpowder Plot he wrote a letter condemning the plot and ordering his priests to instruct all Catholics to behave themselves peaceably in civil matters; on the same day he wrote to Paul V requesting that the pope issue a letter to the same effect, which he did on 28 November. When a new oath of allegiance was formulated as part of the Act for the Better Discovery and Repressing of Popish Recusants (1606), Blackwell wrote and spoke to the clergy in favour of taking it, partly basing himself on the pope's call for civil obedience. He was, however, contradicted by Paul V, who condemned the oath. Bancroft, who drafted the oath with the advice of the former Jesuit Sir Christopher Perkins, had framed it in such words that divisions among Catholics were bound to arise. In particular, the requirement to 'abhor, detest and abjure as impious and heretical' the position that the pope could depose the king and encourage his subjects to murder him, was a rejection of murder to which any Catholic could subscribe, but in phrases which might seem to give the king of England the authority to define heresy, and in such a way as to declare heretics several prominent Catholic theologians who maintained the papal deposing power (without the authority to order murder) as a probable opinion. The archpriest, and a number of other Catholic priests, persisted in defending the licitness of the oath despite the papal condemnation and the contrary opinion of many theologians.

On 24 June 1607 Blackwell, 'comming fromwarde the Charterhouse', where a Mr Leake rented rooms in which some of the archpriest's papers were stored, was apprehended by the pursuivant John Wragg. He was committed first to the Gatehouse in Westminster, then to the Clink in Southwark. Between 25 June and 4 July he was taken to Lambeth Palace seven times to be questioned on his opinion of the oath, and on 4 July he took the oath and wrote a letter to the English clergy exhorting them to do likewise. Cardinal Bellarmine on 18 September wrote a letter to Blackwell deploring his subscription to an oath 'so craftily composed, that no man can detest Treason against the King, and make profession of his Civill subjection, but he must be constrayned perfidiously to denie the Primacie of the Apostolike See' (James I, 39). Blackwell's reply to Bellarmine relied heavily on the distinctions between thesis (a general principle) and hypothesis (a particular application), and between *de fide, formaliter* (a formal issue of doctrine) and *de eo quod est fidei, materialiter* (a material issue arising in connection with doctrine), arguing in particular that the contested passage of the oath was not a rejection of the papal deposing power, but only of certain inferences which might be drawn from it, and of its application to England in current circumstances. He further maintained that he had 'not wavered … in the least point, which certainly and definitely may appertaine to the sublime Majestie, and supreme authoritie of the See Apostolicke … in defence of whose Supremacie in spirituall causes, he is readie to yeeld his life' (*A Large Examination … of M. George Blakwell*, sig. e2v; p. 33).

The position of an Oxford logician was not the clear statement of adherence or rejection that the government and the papacy required. Paul V repeated his condemnation of the oath on 22 September 1607 and, despairing of Blackwell's retraction, on 1 February 1608 deposed him as archpriest and appointed George Birkhead in his stead. The terms in which Blackwell defended the oath appeared to the civil authorities so qualified that he was interrogated on the matter throughout February 1608, and was kept imprisoned until his death in the Clink on 12 January 1613. He maintained to the end that his understanding of the oath of allegiance accorded both with the meaning of the words enacted by parliament and with Catholic doctrine. His conduct towards the appellant clergy and over the oath led the Jesuit historian John Hungerford Pollen to characterize him, perhaps harshly, as 'A man who in easier circumstances might have borne the weight of ecclesiastical dignity creditably, but who was unequal to the strain of those arduous times' (Pollen, 99).

PAUL ARBLASTER

Sources R. Charnock, *An answere to a fraudulent letter of M. George Blackwels, written to Cardinall Caietane, 1596* (1602) · Clement VIII, *Dilecto filio magistro Georgio Blackvello, nostro & sedis apostolicae notario, regni archipresbitero* (1602) · James I, *Triplici nodo, triplex cuneus, or, An apologie for the oath of allegiance* (1607) · *A large examination taken at Lambeth according to his majesties direction, point by point, of M. George Blakwell* (1607/8) · D. A. Bellenger, ed., *English and Welsh priests, 1558–1800* (1984), 40 · Gillow, *Lit. biog. hist.*, 1.224–31 · GL, MS 22179 [communicated by Ian Gadd of the Pewter Society] · H. H. Cotterell, *Old Pewter* (1929), 400 · T. F. Knox and others, eds., *The first and second diaries of the English College, Douay* (1878) · *CSP dom.*, 1595–7; 1603–10, with *addenda*, 1580–1625 · *Calendar of the manuscripts of the most hon. the marquis of Salisbury*, 9–15, HMC, 9 (1902–30) · Boase, *Mod. Eng. biog.*, 1.249–51 · T. McCoog, 'The slightest suspicion of avarice: the finances of the English Jesuit mission', *Recusant History*, 19 (1988–9), 103–23 · J. H. Pollen, *The institution of the Archpriest Blackwell* (1916) · T. G. Law, ed., *The archpriest controversy: documents relating to the dissensions of the Roman Catholic clergy, 1597–1602*, 2 vols., CS, new ser., 56, 58 (1896–8) · J. Bossy, *The English Catholic community, 1570–1850* (1975), chap. 2 · A. O. Meyer, *England and the Catholic church under Queen Elizabeth*, trans. J. R. McKee (1916); repr. with introduction by J. Bossy (1967), 411–50 · P. R. Harris, 'The reports of William Udall, informer, 1605–1612 [pts 1–2]', *Recusant History*, 8 (1965–6), 192–249, 252–84 · T. J. McCann, 'The known style of a dedication is flattery: Anthony Browne, 2nd Viscount Montague of Cowdray, and his Sussex flatterers', *Recusant History*, 19 (1988–9), 396–410 · L. Van Wassenhoven, *Ottavio Mirto Frangipani, nuntius van Vlaanderen, en de Engelsche Katholieken (1598–1606)* (1925) · A. C. Southern, *Elizabethan recusant prose, 1559–1582* (1950), 462 · P. Milward, *Religious controversies of the Elizabethan age* (1977) · J. Bossy, 'Henri IV, the appellants and the Jesuits', *Recusant History*, 8 (1965–6), 80–122

Archives Inner Temple, London, corresp. and papers · LPL, corresp. · Winchester Cathedral

Blackwell, John (1624–1701), government official and colonial governor, was born in St Matthew's parish, London, on 8 March 1624, the eldest son and second of ten children of John Blackwell (1594/5–1658), a puritan-inclined London merchant who at one time supplied the royal household with groceries and who latterly settled in Mortlake in Surrey, and his first wife, Juliana (*d.* 1640). Blackwell was an ensign in the City of London's horse militia as early as 1642 and a cornet in the parliamentary army by 1644; in 1645 he became a captain in Oliver Cromwell's own cavalry regiment, in which he served until June

1648. On 9 June 1647 Blackwell married Elizabeth Smithesby (*d*. 1669), a relative of his father's second wife, Martha Smithesby. They had at least eight children.

From 1645 Blackwell combined his military service with the important post of deputy treasurer-at-wars. As he was a political as well as a religious Independent, his appointment may have been intended to reassure the army, since the war treasurers themselves were London aldermen of Presbyterian persuasion. In 1649 the Rump Parliament rejected a motion to make Blackwell a full treasurer, but in 1652 he became co-treasurer with an obscure backbench MP, and from 1653 with Richard Deane; they were also joint receivers-general of assessments, and thus responsible for the entire system of direct taxation and military expenditure. Blackwell and Deane received a basic salary plus poundage according to the level of military spending. Although Charles Fleetwood, the lord deputy, grumbled about his getting priority for his Irish land claims—Blackwell and his father both having invested in Ireland as adventurers, and part of his own pay arrears being due in this way—two years later John Thurloe, secretary of state, thought his conduct perfectly reasonable. In the 1656–8 parliament, as a member for Surrey Blackwell was active in committees but took little part in the debates.

Although Blackwell might have seemed to be a committed Cromwellian, he like Deane supported the Wallingford House faction, led by Charles Fleetwood and John Lambert, who were responsible for the overthrow of Richard Cromwell as protector and for the return of the Rump in May 1659. If a little less politically active than his colleague Deane, Blackwell too continued to act under the military junta of October–December; and not surprisingly the restored Long Parliament replaced both of them as war treasurers early in 1660. After the Restoration he was one of those perpetually disabled from holding any office. He was able to satisfy royalist investigators that an outpayment which he had made in connection with the king's trial and execution had simply been a routine matter, in no way implicating him in the actual regicide. This was fortunate, since his father had served on the second high court of justice in February–March 1649, which had tried and condemned James Hamilton, first duke of Hamilton, Henry Rich, first earl of Holland, and other royalist leaders in the second civil war of 1648. The elder Blackwell's religious commitment was at least as strong as his son's; he seems to have died in some poverty in early 1658, having previously calculated the debts owing to himself at nearly £36,000.

Blackwell's Irish lands had been confirmed by a special act in the second protectorate parliament of 1656–8. In the autumn of 1659, when he was appointed (very briefly as it turned out) to be a treasury commissioner, he was also elected an alderman of the City of London; early the next year he was excused from this dignity owing to lack of means. At the Restoration his former church and crown lands and those belonging to the Butler (Ormond) family in Ireland were all forfeit, but he managed to retain other Irish interests through the friendship and protection of the first Baron Kingston who, as Sir John King, had been a Cromwellian until 1659. In spite of this Blackwell was threatened with arrest at least once in the 1660s. He seems to have divided his time between Dublin and Chester.

About 1672, having been a widower for some two years, Blackwell married Frances, daughter of the imprisoned republican general, John *Lambert, which hardly argues any diminution in his commitment to the Good Old Cause. They had nine children, one of whom, Lambert Blackwell, became a household official and diplomatic envoy under William III, was knighted, and then made a baronet in 1718: a nice reminder of the continuities between the protectorate and the post-1689 monarchy.

The next phase of Blackwell's career was in the colony of Massachusetts Bay, where he arrived in 1684. In spite of the charter having been called in and the old puritan ruling party apparently crushed, Blackwell rapidly attained considerable influence, as was sourly noted by the ardently imperialistic customs official Edward Randolph. Blackwell produced an ingenious if not wholly convincing scheme for a land bank, to provide credit and to help overcome the colony's chronic shortage of specie. It is not clear whether the plan foundered because of legal or constitutional doubts about the governor's interim council lacking authority to incorporate such a bank, or because of opposition from the mercantile, creditor interest. Blackwell had already been in touch with William Penn when the Quaker proprietor offered him the deputy governorship of the infant colony of Pennsylvania, in a desperate attempt to reassert his authority over the resident Quaker oligarchy based in Philadelphia. Blackwell's effective period as governor lasted only a year, from the end of 1688 to new year 1690, and is generally reckoned a failure. Given the balance of social and political forces and the lack of coercive power, Pennsylvania was in fact ungovernable except by, or with the tacit agreement of, the local élite. The governor expressed his disillusionment in letters to Penn and others: 'the hosts of Musqueetos are worse than armed men: yet the men without Armes worse than they'; he also attacked what he saw as Quaker hypocrisy: 'each praying with his neighbour on First Days, and then preying on him the other six' (*DNB*).

Having declined Penn's offer of a lesser post as receiver-general of all proprietary revenues in the colony, Blackwell returned to Massachusetts in 1690 and then to England in 1693 or 1694. Thereafter he lived in Bethnal Green in east London; he died intestate, and was buried in Kensington on 6 July 1701. The baronetcy bestowed on his son became extinct in 1801. G. E. Aylmer

Sources G. E. Aylmer, *The state's servants: the civil service of the English republic, 1649–1660* (1973) • E. A. R., 'Blackwell, John', HoP, *Commons, 1640–60* [draft] • *The papers of William Penn*, ed. M. M. Dunn, R. S. Dunn, and others, 3 (1986) • GEC, *Peerage* • J. Dorfman, *The economic mind in American civilisation, 1606–1865*, 1 (1947) • D. B. Horn, ed., *British diplomatic representatives, 1689–1789*, CS, 3rd ser., 46 (1932) • J. J. Howard, ed., *Miscellanea Genealogica et Heraldica*, new ser., 1 (1874), 177–8 • Bodl. Oxf., MS Rawl., A. 34, fol. 259

Blackwell, John [*pseud.* Alun] (**1797–1840**), Welsh-language poet and writer, was born at Ponterwyl, Mold,

Flintshire, the son of Peter Blackwell, collier, and his wife, Mary. He received no formal education, and at the age of eleven he was apprenticed as a shoemaker with William Kirkham. From an early age, however, he had shown the greatest avidity for books, and he carried off several prizes offered for poems and essays in the Welsh language, including an award at the eisteddfod at Mold in 1823 for an *awdl* (ode), 'Maes Garmon'. Such activity brought him to the attention of several gentlemen and clergymen, who created a fund for his education. In January 1824 he was sent to Thomas Richards to prepare for university entrance, and in December he entered Jesus College, Oxford; he took the degree of BA in 1828. In the autumn of the latter year, at the royal Denbigh eisteddfod, a prize was awarded him for his beautiful Welsh elegy on the death of Bishop Heber. During his time at Oxford he had read everything that he could find on the history and literature of Wales in the Bodleian and the college library.

In 1829 Blackwell was ordained to the curacy of Holywell, Caernarvonshire. During his residence there he was a principal contributor to the columns of the *Gwyliedydd*, a periodical conducted on the principles of the established church, and in 1832 he won a prize medal at the Beaumaris eisteddfod. In 1833 he was presented by Lord Chancellor Brougham to the living of Maenordeifi in Pembrokeshire. Soon afterwards, at the request of the Society for the Diffusion of Useful Knowledge, he became editor of an illustrated magazine in the Welsh language, entitled *Y Cylchgrawn*, and he conducted it with remarkable ability. On 30 July 1839 he married Matilda, daughter of Jonas Dear, tidewaiter, at Holywell church. Blackwell died on 19 May 1840 at St Mary Street, Cardigan, and was buried at Maenordeifi; a tablet to his memory was placed on the wall of the church there. His poems and essays, with a memoir of his life, were edited by Griffith Edwards of Minera, in a volume entitled *Ceinion Alun* ('The beauties of Alun'; 1851), Alun being Blackwell's bardic name.

THOMPSON COOPER, *rev.* M. CLARE LOUGHLIN-CHOW

Sources G. Edwards, 'Preface', *Ceinion Alun* (1851) • *DWB* • *GM*, 2nd ser., 14 (1840), 100 • R. Williams, *Enwogion Cymru: a biographical dictionary of eminent Welshmen* (1852) • M. Stephens, ed., *The Oxford companion to the literature of Wales* (1986) • m. cert. • d. cert.
Archives NL Wales, letters [copies] | UCL, letters to Society for the Diffusion of Useful Knowledge

Blackwell, (Arthur) John Harvey (1937–1997), publisher, was born on 23 October 1937 at 24 Church Lane, Coventry, the first of three children of Arthur Blackwell (1910–1970), telecommunications planning engineer, and his wife, Alice Lilian Harvey (1906–1993), who prior to marriage was a manager in her family's wholesale warehouse business. John Blackwell (so he was known to family and friends) was baptized into the Roman Catholic church, but did not practise that or any other religion after early childhood. He was educated at King Henry VIII Grammar School, Coventry, from 1946 to 1955, and was awarded an open scholarship at Jesus College, Cambridge, but deferred university entrance to do his national service in the Royal Navy from 1956 to 1958.

The details of Blackwell's military service are clouded in a certain amount of mystery, which he himself encouraged rather than dispelled. It is known that he was trained as a coder, and took a course in Russian at the Joint Services School for Linguists at Crail, Fife. At some point in his naval career he was stationed in Turkey, monitoring Russian radio traffic in the Black Sea region, a clandestine operation from which he had to be hastily airlifted by the American military in circumstances that remain obscure. According to family tradition John did not take his intelligence duties altogether seriously, and claimed to have recorded Russian radio programmes for children at half speed and sent them to the Admiralty for analysis. The story, whether true or not, was certainly in character. He neither sought nor obtained promotion above the rank of leading coder.

At Jesus College, Cambridge, Blackwell read English (1958–61), and met his future wife, Pamela Muriel Jessie Lewis Price (*b.* 1936). They married on 14 July 1966. After graduation John worked in a number of short-term jobs before becoming the editor of the trade journal of the Iron and Steel Institute. From that experience he no doubt acquired some of the detailed knowledge of engineering with which he later impressed several of his authors. At some point in the late 1960s (the exact date is not known) he joined the publishing house of Secker and Warburg, which was then an independent firm headed by Frederick Warburg, shortly to be succeeded by Tom Rosenthal. As the Secker imprint was bought and sold several times in the era of publishing take-overs, and Tom Rosenthal's successors came and went, John Blackwell stayed in post; and the fact that Secker continued to publish a distinguished list of literary fiction in these turbulent times was due in no small measure to the allegiance he inspired in the writers he edited.

Blackwell was a publisher of a kind now virtually obsolete: a senior editor who devoted himself to editing, including the time-consuming business of copy-editing, rather than commissioning. It is not the way to advance up the corporate ladder, but Blackwell was never personally ambitious. He simply cared passionately about publishing good books. He was not a 'creative' editor, though he would comment on work in progress if asked. He preferred to work, by patient questioning and tactful suggestion, on a completed manuscript, tuning and refining it, removing wrinkles and blemishes, and ensuring that nothing in the appearance of the printed page would interfere with the communication of meaning between writer and reader. He was a perfectionist, and, since most novelists wish their work to be as near perfection as possible, his scrupulous editing was highly valued. Among the many writers who benefited from his skills at various times were John Banville, Louis de Bernières, Malcolm Bradbury, Melvyn Bragg, André Brink, J. M. Coetzee, David Lodge, Michael Moorcock, Tim Parks, Tom Sharpe, Angus Wilson, and A. N. Wilson.

In appearance Blackwell was stoop-shouldered, balding, and bespectacled, but he was more athletic than he looked, a habitual cyclist and keen skier. In formal social gatherings he was somewhat shy and reticent, but he was a convivial companion, especially over several glasses of beer or wine, and was regarded with great affection by his colleagues and friends. His working habits were unorthodox and increasingly at odds with the style of modern publishing, especially when Secker and Warburg moved from their cosy quarters in Soho to the open-plan plate-glass offices of the Reed Group's Michelin House in South Kensington. He invariably dressed in jeans and denim jacket, and cycled to work from his home in Clapham, arriving and leaving later than anyone else. The letters he wrote to his authors, and the book reports he circulated to colleagues, composed on an old-fashioned manual typewriter, were legendary for their wit, acuity, and erudition. He excelled as a writer of those short, evocative, and enticing descriptions of books known in the trade as 'blurbs'.

John Blackwell felt increasingly alienated from the ethos of corporate publishing, and when Reed-Elsevier put Secker and Warburg, with several other imprints, up for sale in 1996 he turned freelance and edited a stable of loyal authors from his home in Iveley Road, Clapham. He died there, suddenly and unexpectedly, on 5 November 1997. The cause of death was determined as pulmonary embolism caused by carcinoma of the liver—a condition of which he was unaware. He was cremated at the South London crematorium, Streatham Vale, on 14 November 1997. DAVID LODGE

Sources private information (2004) [Pamela Blackwell, widow; Margaret Ockenden, sister] • D. Lodge, *The Independent* (10 Nov 1997) • D. Franklin, *The Guardian* (14 Nov 1997) • L. de Bernières, *The Guardian* (14 Nov 1997) [postcript] • M. Bradbury, *The Times* (7 Nov 1997)

Blackwell, Richard (1918–1980), bookseller and publisher, was born on 5 January 1918 at 1 Frenchay Road, Oxford, the eldest in the family of two sons and three daughters of Sir Basil Henry *Blackwell (1889–1984), bookseller, and his wife, Marion Christine (1888/9–1977), daughter of John Soans, schoolmaster, of Ramsgate. He was educated at the Dragon School in Oxford. He won a scholarship to Winchester College, and from there a scholarship to New College, Oxford, where he rowed in the first eight; in 1938 he achieved a first class in classical honour moderations. However, the war cut short his academic career, and he did not return later, but was content with a wartime MA (1944). His six and a half years of war service were spent in the Royal Navy, as lieutenant (S), Royal Naval Volunteer Reserve. He saw action and hardship on the Russian convoy route and also in the Mediterranean, where in 1944 he was awarded the DSC. On 23 May 1942 he married Marguerite Brook Holliday (*b*. 1922/3), the daughter of Major Lionel Brook Holliday, industrialist and landowner, of Copgrave Hall, Yorkshire. They had two sons. He was destined for the family firm and in 1946 he joined his father in the bookselling business.

After the war Blackwells enjoyed a high and enviable reputation as one of the best retail booksellers in the English-speaking world, but the actual size of the business in financial terms was modest. It was Richard Blackwell's life work to build a large, complex, and successful international business on this base. He achieved this by foreseeing the spread of English as the main international language, the post-war growth of higher education throughout the world, and the establishment of many new universities and libraries, and thus the opportunities for export. He also promoted specialization in the management of the business.

Richard Blackwell (1918–1980), by unknown photographer

Blackwell travelled widely and took every opportunity for development. He nurtured many small and not so small subsidiary and associated companies in the book trade. The most significant of these was perhaps Blackwell Scientific Publications Ltd. In 1964 he formed, with Oxford University Press as a joint partner, University Bookshops (Oxford) Ltd.. When the Richard Abel library supply business in the United States failed, he developed Blackwell North America Inc. to take over the business. His aim was to develop a worldwide service supplying English periodicals and books to academic and specialist libraries and customers. While Blackwells was always a priority, he also helped to establish the Smaller Business Association (later the Association of Independent Businesses), which upheld the rights of small firms. In 1962 he worked hard for the defence of the net book agreement and played an arduous part in the case itself before the restrictive trade practices court (see R. E. Barker and G. R. Davies, eds., *Books are Different*, 1966). For two years (1966–8) he was president of the Booksellers' Association.

In all business enterprises Blackwell always ensured the ultimate control by the Blackwell family. It was not only a question of seeing his inheritance multiply, it was also his intention that the family business should remain wholly independent and private. During the years of growth Richard Blackwell had been supported by his family, above all his father, his younger brother, Julian, and latterly his two sons, Miles and Nigel, all actively involved in the management of the business. In the early days the guidance of his father was an essential feature in his success, but he steadily took over the main burden of responsibility, becoming managing director in 1966 and chairman in 1969. In 1976 he became chairman of Basil Blackwell Publisher Ltd, the publishing business originally established by his father as Blackwell and Mott. He always down-played his achievement with characteristic modesty and self-effacement.

In 1971 Blackwell was made an honorary DLitt at York University, Ontario, and in 1978 he was elected a fellow of St Cross College, Oxford. He died of cancer at his home, Tubney House, Tubney, near Abingdon, Oxfordshire, on 26 February 1980; his funeral took place on the 29th.

JOHN BROWN, *rev.* CLARE L. TAYLOR

Sources A. L. P. Norrington, *Blackwell's, 1879–1979: the history of a family firm* (1983) • P. J. Anderson and J. Rose, eds., *British literary publishing houses, 1820–1880*, DLitB, 106 (1991) • b. cert. • m. cert. • d. cert.

Likenesses photograph, repro. in Norrington, *Blackwell's* [*see illus.*]

Wealth at death £172,434: probate, 8 May 1980, *CGPLA Eng. & Wales*

Blackwell, Thomas (1660?–1728), Church of Scotland minister and college head, was probably born in Glasgow, the son of a covenanting calenderer, Thomas Blackwell, and his wife, Janet Knox. He was educated at the University of Glasgow, where he apparently earned an MA in 1684. He was licensed to preach on 23 February 1693 and received a call to become a minister from the presbytery of Paisley on 5 April 1693, but his ordination was delayed until 28 August 1694. Blackwell took over the first charge in the Abbey parish, and it would seem that while he was in Paisley he married Christian Johnstoun (*d.* 1749), the daughter of the Glasgow physician John Johnstoun. The couple reputedly had twelve children, of whom four sons and three daughters survived into adulthood, including Thomas *Blackwell the younger (1701–1757), who also distinguished himself as principal of Marischal College and a leading Aberdonian man of letters, and Alexander *Blackwell (*bap.* 1709, *d.* 1747), agricultural improver and government agent in Sweden.

Blackwell transferred to the second charge of St Nicholas Church, Aberdeen, on 9 October 1700, and gradually emerged as a prominent figure in the town. He was made a burgess and in 1716 became patron of Aberdeen's seven incorporated trades. In 1710 he made his mark on the republic of learning with the publication in Edinburgh of two related volumes: *Ratio sacra, or, An appeal unto the rational world, about the reasonableness of revealed religion* (dedicated to the lord provost and town council of Aberdeen) and *Schema sacrum, or, A Sacred Scheme of Natural and Revealed Religion* (dedicated to Sir Hugh Dalrymple, lord president of the court of session). In both works Blackwell sought to demonstrate the congruence of revealed religion with what he considered to be the genuine dictates of reason. Although his sense of the reasonableness of religion was very different from that of the English latitudinarians, he seems to have been receptive to the writings of Edward Stillingfleet, for in his attack on deism he invokes the refutation of Cartesianism and other heterodox philosophical systems added to later editions of Stillingfleet's *Origines sacrae*. Given the deep religious divisions which then existed in Aberdeen and the north-east of Scotland, the *Ratio sacra* was a highly polemical work because Blackwell took aim not only at atheism and irreligion, but also at the Quakers, who were a significant local presence, and at the French mystic Madame Bourignon, whose tenets appealed to many episcopalians in the region.

Because of his staunch defence of presbyterianism Blackwell was appointed professor of divinity at Marischal College, Aberdeen, and preacher at Grey Friars Church on 18 December 1711. Beginning in 1710 he also became increasingly involved in the affairs of the general assembly of the Church of Scotland. In 1711 the moderator of the assembly, William Carstares, chose Blackwell and the Revd Robert Baillie of Inverness to accompany him to London in an attempt to stave off legislation which threatened to destroy presbyterian hegemony in Scotland. But to the delight of Scottish episcopalians, the lobbying of the trio failed to stop the tory ministry from pushing through the Toleration Act and the Act of Patronage in 1712. While in London, Blackwell additionally acted as an agent for the Aberdeen town council, and reported back on matters of political interest. He returned home in June or July 1712 following the publication in London of his tract on pulpit oratory, *Methodus evangelica*, which he had written as a respite from kirk affairs.

In the Jacobite rising which began in September 1715 Blackwell was the only member of the Marischal faculty who remained loyal to George I. He was duly rewarded by the royal commission of visitation appointed in 1717 to purge Marischal of residual Jacobitism; the commissioners retained Blackwell as professor of divinity, and he was confirmed as the new principal by the crown on 30 September 1717. He proved an effective manager of the college, although he provoked the opposition of some of his junior colleagues, and his continuing attacks on episcopalianism prompted a minor pamphlet war in 1722. Blackwell died in Aberdeen in February 1728.

PAUL WOOD

Sources 'Letters from Professor Blackwell, and others, to John Ross of Arnage … MDCCXI–MDCCXVII', *The miscellany of the Spalding Club*, ed. J. Stuart, 1, Spalding Club, 3 (1841), 197–223 • A. M. Munro, 'Epitaphs and inscriptions in St Nicholas Church and churchyard', *Scottish Notes and Queries*, 3 (1889–90), 35–6 • T. Blackwell, *Ratio sacra, or, An appeal unto the rational world, about the reasonableness of revealed religion* (1710) • T. Blackwell, *Schema sacrum, or, A sacred scheme of natural and revealed religion* (1710) • *Fasti Scot.*, new edn • P. J. Anderson and J. F. K. Johnstone, eds., *Fasti academiae Mariscallanae Aberdonensis: selections from the records of the Marischal College and University, MDXCIII–MDCCLX*, 3 vols., New Spalding Club, 4, 18–19 (1889–98) • C. Innes, ed., *Munimenta alme Universitatis Glasguensis / Records of the University of Glasgow from its foundation till 1727*, 1–3, Maitland Club, 72 (1854) • J. Stuart, ed., *Extracts from the* *council register of the burgh of Aberdeen, 1625–1747*, 2 vols., Scottish Burgh RS, 8–9 (1871–2) • R. H. Story, *William Carstares: a character and career of the revolutionary epoch, 1649–1715* (1874)

Likenesses oils, Incorporated Trades of Aberdeen, Aberdeen

Wealth at death approx. £119 10s. 10d.: will, 30 May 1728, NA Scot., CC 1/6/9

Blackwell, Thomas (1701–1757), classical scholar and historian, was born on 4 August 1701 in the city of Aberdeen, second son of Thomas *Blackwell (1660?–1728), one of the ministers of Aberdeen, later professor of divinity, and his wife, Christian Johnstoun (*d.* 1749). His younger brother was Alexander *Blackwell. He was educated at the grammar school of Aberdeen and studied Greek and philosophy at Marischal College, of which his father had become principal in 1717. He graduated AM in 1718 and was presented to the chair of Greek at Marischal in 1723. He went on to teach a number of important figures including a future principal, George Campbell, Alexander Gerard, and James Beattie, and was an important influence on the poet James Macpherson, the compiler of *Ossian*. In October 1748 Blackwell was appointed principal of Marischal College, and introduced a programme of reforms to modernize the curriculum, including a new class taught by himself in ancient history, geography, and chronology. He married Barbara Black (*d.* 1793), daughter of an Aberdeen merchant, probably in 1749; they had no children. In 1752 he took the degree of doctor of laws. As principal, Blackwell was active in promoting the union of Marischal and King's colleges to form a single university in Aberdeen, a project which came to fruition in the fusion of 1860.

Blackwell's main fame is as a writer whose books—*An Enquiry into the Life and Writings of Homer* (1735), *Letters Concerning Mythology* (1748), and *Memoirs of the Court of Augustus* (3 vols., 1753–63)—were pioneering studies in their fields and mark him as a major figure of the Scottish Enlightenment. The *Enquiry* was published anonymously in 1735 and went to five subsequent editions. Blackwell considered why Homer had been the supreme epic poet and concluded that his achievement was explicable almost entirely in terms of natural forces. Homer was the outcome of a specific historical context, social organization, geography, and climate, which combined to shape the culture he represented and which provided an ethos uniquely favourable to epic poetry. The argument was that culture was learned, not inherent; it was the basic means of organizing social institutions and was part of a continually changing process—ideas which were to become the cornerstones of modern cultural anthropology. Blackwell distinguished four periods in Greek history: settlement, growth in civilization, cultural maturity, and decline. A key point of the analysis was the idea of uneven development, an overlap between high civilization in the centres of Greek culture, with a continuation of relative barbarism and its attendant heroic values elsewhere. Advances in civilization brought gains in wealth and sophistication, but also introduced artifice and corruption, a loss of the heroic simplicity and clear moral vision that had distinguished earlier periods. Blackwell declared:

> I am in the case of a noble Historian [Herodotus], who having related the constant Superiority his *Greeks* had over the Inhabitants of the *Assyrian* Vales, concludes 'That it has not been given by the Gods, to one and the same Country, to produce rich Crops and warlike Men:' Neither indeed does it seem to be given to one and the same Kingdom, to be thoroughly civilized, and afford proper Subjects for Poetry … Whoever reflects upon the Rise and Fall of States, will find, that along with their Manners, their *Language* too accompanies them both in their Growth and Decay … It is the *different Periods* or Steps, naturally succeeding in the *Progression of Manners*, that can only account for the Succession of Wit and Literature. (*An Enquiry into the Life and Writings of Homer*, 1735, 26–8, 36, 77)

In the early stages of society language was naturally bold and metaphorical, so that utterance had a rude and energetic quality which it later lost. This was fostered by the clannish nature of early Greek society which limited the growth of centralized power. Blackwell considered the latter inimical to high cultural achievement because of its tendency to foster an artificial 'courtly' style which checked spontaneity and dampened the vigorous localism and particularity characteristic of early poetry at its best, a point he was to develop in his study of Virgil in *Memoirs of the Court of Augustus*. Homer was peculiarly favoured by circumstance, since he had appeared at the beginning of a new cultural phase, but still had personal experience of the old heroic ethos. Although a member of a powerful bardic class, he had been born poor, and could therefore draw upon the rich pool of popular traditions sustained by the common people, which Blackwell regarded as the ultimate source of all literary creativity. Homer had been a strolling bard, a master improviser whose songs had been committed to writing long after his death: the unitary written text being a late development resulting from deliberate editorial intervention in a previously oral process. A set of unique socio-cultural circumstances therefore made Homer's achievement possible, but also unrepeatable.

Letters Concerning Mythology was published, also anonymously, in 1748. The earlier of the nineteen letters came from another hand, but Blackwell completed numbers seven and eight and wrote the remainder of the series. For almost two millennia the mythology of the ancient world had been attacked by Euhemeristic critics who regarded it as a fabulous form of history and saw the gods as deified priests and kings; by Christian apologists to whom the gods were thinly disguised demons; and by modern rationalists who dismissed the whole affair as merely absurd. Blackwell took a different view. He saw mythology as a humane and civilizing influence, arguing that the system possessed enduring significance, and concluding that, interpreted with sympathetic regard to its original allegorical intention, it was a major key to the world-picture of classical antiquity. While 'the old Divinity' had been accepted quite literally by the vulgar, the wise had treated it as a system of abstractions which dealt with reality in symbolic terms, and these Blackwell set himself to unravel. He cast his net wide, discussing not only obviously 'mythical' tales, but also material culture, iconography, ceremonial and ritual, and even proverbial lore, citing an impressive array of learned works in a variety of languages including French, Spanish, Italian, Hebrew, and Arabic. He attempted to distinguish between earlier and later myths by studying their transmission through the various host societies. Once later priestly and literary accretions had been identified and eliminated, the original deeply meaningful mythic stratum and the ancient thought patterns it represented could be recovered. It was important at the same time that mythology be related to the actual practice of ancient religions. The original source of the Orphic mysteries lay in Egypt, and the evidence suggested that the original twelve 'great gods' of ancient Egypt had been mythic creations from the start—great metaphors of the creation and the ordering of the universe. It seemed clear, too, how these abstractions had gradually become objectified as ideas passed from one culture to another. Blackwell was an early proponent of the numen/nomen theory later championed by Max Müller and others, which held that the source of myth lay in a 'disease of language', an intensely figurative habit of expression peculiar to early man which invested everything it touched with metaphoric force resulting in the personification of nature:

> As the early *Egyptian* Rites … were all typical and symbolical, the Type or Symbol came by an easy Transition, not only to signify obscurely, but directly to express the Thing typified … But besides the original Type, any remarkable part of the divine Service, any mystical Mixture as in the Rites of Ceres, any striking posture as in the Feasts of Pan, any uncouth Garb of the Hierophant or Priest, or any uncouth Quality ascribed to the Numen, was enough to fix an Epithet, and that Epithet to wear gradually into a Name. (*Letters Concerning Mythology*, 1748, 189–90)

Blackwell viewed early Jewish beliefs in the context of contemporary Near Eastern cosmographies, subjecting the account of creation in the book of Genesis to comparative analysis with ancient Phoenician texts, and discounting the conventional view of the scriptures as embodying the primal religion of which all the others, with the exception of Christianity, were in varying degrees corruptions. He traced the transformation of Chaldean monotheism into polytheism, as the stars began to be worshipped as lesser deities, demonstrating not only that this had happened, but how it had come about. He was even prepared to explain, if not altogether to defend, priapism and phallic worship. Throughout his wide-ranging and subtle study the basic assumption was that the past was coherent, that its correct interpretation was not only of crucial importance to an enlightened understanding of what it meant to be human, but that, viewed in its own terms, it all made perfect sense.

In *Memoirs of the Court of Augustus* (3 vols., 1753–63), Blackwell disavowed any intention as a mere annalist, presenting himself as a practitioner of intellectual history, what he called 'This difficult Science of Men' (T. Blackwell, *Memoirs of the Court of Augustus*, 1.5). He discussed how people existed in and were defined by society, and went on to explore the forces that had transformed Rome from an obscure Italian hamlet into a great imperial power. The city had been founded in Spartan military virtue and for a long time its government had been popular and democratic, but the constitution was flawed: everything turned upon the quality of the political culture, and if republican virtue waned there was little to prevent an irresistible slide into tyranny. Insufficient separation of powers meant that if the army went bad—and it did—then everything else went with it. The villain of the piece was Julius Caesar who

> dared to point his Sword at his Parent's Throat. He besieged her Towns, trampled upon her Laws, cut off her Consuls, slew her Pretors, pursued her Senators from city to city, and land to land, until he set his unhallowed foot on the Neck of Freedom, and laid Rome's Glory in the Dust. (ibid., 1.192)

A balanced constitution was therefore the indispensable foundation of enduring political success, a lesson underlined by comparative surveys of France, Venice, and the Spanish empire. Blackwell explored how behaviour patterns were moulded by power relations, and in a study of Virgil and Horace demonstrated how the arts were responsive to the political ethos in which they functioned and how they might influence it in turn. This was set within a detailed and racy political history of the later republic and early imperial period from a writer well acquainted with power, and how the greatest of enterprises could be compromised by human weakness, vice, and folly. In Blackwell's urbane and witty pages one might learn how at a meeting of the senate, Cato—to his horror—intercepted a billet-doux to Caesar from his own sister; how the rake Pollio's travelling baggage contained a matching set of nude statues of some half-dozen of the loveliest matrons in Rome, done from the life; how Antony made public love to the actress Cytheris in a golden chariot drawn by lions, an act made doubly offensive to good taste by the fact that she was not even a tragedienne.

Blackwell's contemporary reputation was very considerable, and for nearly half a century he was regarded as the foremost Homeric critic in Europe. But his championship of the Franco-Scots *galant* style, his evident links with a cosmopolitan pan-European intellectual tradition, and his thoroughly Scottish whig politics provoked bitterly hostile criticism from nationalistically minded English commentators like Samuel Johnson. As Scotland lost ground within the union during the nineteenth century, Blackwell was gradually assigned to the legion of the lost whose works it was permissible not to read. There were stirrings of revival during the twentieth century as classical scholars began to re-explore the history of their subject under the influence of the oral-formulaic theories of the American Homeric scholars Milman Parry and Albert Lord whose work he had partly anticipated, but the full range of Blackwell's achievement has yet to be acknowledged. Blackwell died of a consumptive illness in Edinburgh on 6 March 1757. WILLIAM DONALDSON

Sources B. Feldman and R. D. Richardson, 'Thomas Blackwell', *The rise of modern mythology, 1680–1860* (1972), 99–111 ·

W. Donaldson, 'Their songs are of other worlds: Ossian and the Macpherson paradigm', *The highland pipe and Scottish society, 1750–1950* (2000), 5–19 • W. Donaldson, appx, *The highland pipe and Scottish society, 1750–1950* (2000), 448–60 • R. L. Krenis, 'Thomas Blackwell: the literary and historical criticism', *Dissertation Abstracts International*, 35/8 (1975), 5351A–52A • G. Hollingshead, 'Berkeley, Blackwell, and Blackwell's Homer', *Scottish Literary Journal*, 11/1 (1984), 20–35 • *DNB* • H. D. Weinbrot, *Augustus Caesar in 'Augustan' England: the decline of a classical norm* (1978) • F. J. Stafford, *The sublime savage: a study of James Macpherson and the poems of Ossian* (1988) • H. Erskine-Hill, *The Augustan idea in English literature* (1983) • Chambers, *Scots.* (1835) • P. B. Wood, *The Aberdeen Enlightenment: the arts curriculum in the eighteenth century* (1993) • K. Simonsuuri, 'Blackwell and the myth of Orpheus', *Aberdeen and the Enlightenment*, ed. J. J. Carter and J. H. Pittock (1987), 199–206 • F. E. Manuel, *The eighteenth century confronts the gods* (1959)

Archives NA Scot., corresp. with Sir John Clerk • NA Scot., letters to Sir A. Grant • NA Scot., letters to Sir Andrew Mitchell

Likenesses J. Record, etching, pubd 1783 (after J. Richardson, 1735), BM, NPG • J. Richardson, portrait, Morgan L.

Blackwood, Adam (1539–1613), civil lawyer and Roman Catholic polemicist, was born in Dunfermline, Fife, one of at least three children of William Blackwood (*d.* 1547), soldier, and Helen Reid (*d.* 1547/8). His parents died when he was about eight years old, his father in battle at Pinkie, and his mother shortly afterwards. After their deaths he came into the care of his maternal great-uncle, Robert Reid, bishop of Orkney, who *c.*1552 sent him to be educated in Paris. At the university there he was taught by Adrian Turnèbe (Turnebus), a well-known literary figure of the day, and Jean Dorat (Auratus), a poet in Latin and Greek, who inspired Blackwood to follow his example. When his great-uncle died in 1558 after negotiating the marriage between Mary, queen of Scots, and the Dauphin François, Blackwood returned to Scotland. However, the political and religious circumstances proved unwelcoming for a committed Roman Catholic, and he returned quickly to Paris. There, through the support of Mary, he continued his studies, including philosophy. From about 1560 he also spent two years at the University of Toulouse studying civil law, which became the foundation of his later career.

Once his studies were complete Blackwood taught philosophy at Paris, where he was rector in 1567–8. He caught the attention of James Beaton, archbishop of Glasgow and the Scottish ambassador, with his early works, firstly *Caroli IX pompa funebris versiculis expressa per A. B. J. C.* (*juris consultum*), a memorial poem for Charles IX (Paris, 1574), and secondly and more importantly, *De vinculo religionis et imperii libri duo* ('Of the chains of religion and government, in two books'; Paris, 1575). *De vinculo* argued for the legitimacy of state-imposed faith, specifically Roman Catholic, and for state extirpation of heresy. Impressed by Blackwood's arguments, Beaton recommended that Mary appoint him counsellor to the parliament of Poitiers in Poitou, a preferment that she held in her gift as part of her marriage settlement. After Henri III had granted confirmation of his position, Blackwood settled in Poitiers, where *c.*1580 he married Maria Courtinier (*fl.* 1575–1613), the daughter of the king's treasurer there. They had eleven children, four sons and seven daughters.

In Poitiers Blackwood continued his writing career, and remained interested in Scottish affairs. *Adversus Georgii Buchanani dialogum de jure regni apud Scotos pro regibus apologia* ('Apology for kings against George Buchanan's dialogue on the law of government among the Scots'; Poitiers, 1581; Paris, 1588) challenges Buchanan's arguments for the right of subjects to depose unsatisfactory monarchs, on the grounds that a king is set apart once anointed, and can be subject to none but divine judgment. It also repeats a theme of *De vinculo*, connecting heretical belief with political sedition. Blackwood's attack on Buchanan was also rooted in his loyalty to Mary, queen of Scots, whom he is said to have visited in her captivity in England. As well as translating one of her poems into Latin, after her execution he produced *Martyre de la royne d'Écosse*, which described her treatment at the hands of Elizabeth, and included transcriptions of the correspondence, as well as poems attacking Elizabeth at the end of the volume. This was first published in 1587, shortly after the queen's execution; the printer's mark says it was printed by Jean Nafield in Edinburgh, whereas it was in fact printed in Paris, and reprinted in Antwerp in 1588 and 1589. The work, of which there is a nearly contemporary translation into Scots (printed by the Maitland Club in 1834), is evidently partisan, and demonstrates the loyalty Mary aroused in her followers.

After Mary's execution Blackwood did not go to England until 1604, when he visited James VI and I in London. By that point Blackwood's writing was largely confined to religious and poetic material. He wrote a series of spiritual meditations, *Sanctarum precationum proemia* (Poitiers, 1598, 1608), and was the author of a penitential study of the Psalms, *In psalmum Davidis quinquagesimum* (Poitiers, 1608), and a collection of poems, *Varii generis poemata* (Poitiers, 1609), in which appeared his translation of Mary's poem. In 1606 he returned to political writing, when he published his *Inauguratio Jacobi Magnae Britanniae regis*, and in 1612 he added an extra book to *De vinculo* and dedicated it to Henry, prince of Wales.

Blackwood died in 1613, in Poitiers, and was buried in St Porcharius's Church in the town. His contribution to the development of the theory of absolute monarchy can be seen as part of a Scottish Catholic rejection of Buchanan's interpretation of Scottish history, and in his foreshadowing of the 'divine right of kings' an influence on events to come. His contemporary importance in this respect is shown by Gabriel Naudé's publication of his complete works in French and Latin in Paris in 1644, together with a eulogy and an engraving by Picart. NICOLA ROYAN

Sources G. Naudé, 'Eulogy', in *Adami Blackuodæi opera omnia* (Paris, 1644) • D. Irving, *Lives of Scotish writers*, 1 (1839), 161–9 • G. Mackenzie, *The lives and characters of the most eminent writers of the Scots nation*, 3 (1722), 487–513 • J. H. Burns, 'George Buchanan and the anti-monarchomachs', *Scots and Britons: Scottish political thought and the union of 1603*, ed. R. A. Mason (1994), 138–58, esp. 146–52 • J. H. Burns, *The true law of kingship: concepts of monarchy in early modern Scotland* (1996), 209–86 • J. H. Burns, 'Three Scots Catholic critics of George Buchanan', *Innes Review*, 1 (1950), 92–109 • J. Durkan, 'Blackwood, Adam', *DSCHT*

Likenesses monument, c.1613; formerly St Porcharius's Church, Poitiers, 1708 • J. Picart, line engraving, BM, NPG; repro. in A. Blackwood, *Opera omnia*, ed. G. Naudé (1644)

Blackwood, Algernon Henry (1869–1951), writer of supernatural fiction, was born at Wood Lodge, Shooter's Hill, Kent, on 14 March 1869, the second son born to Sir (Stevenson) Arthur *Blackwood (1832–1893), who became permanent secretary to the Post Office, and his wife, Harriet Sydney Montagu (1834–1907), daughter of Conway R. Dobbs, of Castle Dobbs, co. Antrim, Ireland, and widow of George, sixth duke of Manchester. His father, in his youth a man of fashion known as Beauty Blackwood, underwent a conversion while serving in the Crimean War in 1855; he became a leading evangelist, a passion shared by his wife. Algernon, who later described himself as having been a 'dreamy boy', escaped from his repressive upbringing by turning to nature. At Shortlands House near Beckenham, where he lived from the age of eleven, he would climb out of the window at night, launch a boat on the garden pond, and imagine that supernatural beings observed him.

Blackwood's schooling had an unsettling and even traumatic effect on him; he referred to the five schools that he attended as 'my horrible private schools' (Blackwood, *Episodes*, 33). At one of these, in 1881, he was falsely accused by the 'fiendish' evangelical headmaster of stealing a poetry book, an event that 'haunted' him for years. Blackwood looked back 'with disgust at the overstrict, semi-military discipline' (Blackwood, 'Author's note', vi) at the Moravian Brethren school in the German Black Forest, where he spent an 'unhappy' eighteen months from May 1885. Yet the remote setting of this school, 'haunted by elves and dwarfs and peopled by charming legends' (Blackwood, *Episodes*, 25), only increased his worship of nature.

Blackwood's real education did not begin, however, until 1886, when he read Patanjali's *Yoga Aphorisms* and the *Bhagavad Gita* and was converted to Eastern wisdom, to his father's horror. He also 'swallowed whole' the theosophy of Mme Blavatsky, whose claims of an extrasensory spirit realm became a central preoccupation of Blackwood's. He later claimed, 'My fundamental interest, I suppose, is signs and proofs of other powers that lie hidden in us all; the extension, in other words, of human faculty' (Punter, 464).

After father and son visited Canada in 1887, it was decided that Algernon would take up farming. In preparation for this he ostensibly studied agriculture at Edinburgh University during 1888–9, though he became more enthralled by lectures on pathology. For the next nine years he lived a perilous and momentous existence in North America, beginning innocuously enough in Toronto working as an editorial assistant on the *Methodist Magazine* (until the editor discovered his Buddhist inclinations), and then as a dairy farmer and a publican. He succeeded at none of these. Moving to New York in 1892, he floundered again, experimenting with morphine and falling into abject poverty before landing a job as court reporter for the *Evening Sun*. In his vivid autobiography *Episodes before Thirty* (1923), he recalled that reporting for a New York newspaper introduced him to 'vice, crime, horror, terror, and every kind of human degradation' (Blackwood, *Episodes*, 92). About this time he began recounting these 'weird stories', as well as his adventures into the Ontario wilderness, to a fellow Briton, Angus Hamilton. Homesickness drove Blackwood back to England in 1899, where he faced the thrilling prospect of a partnership in the Dried Milk Company. Fortunately for both Blackwood and probably the company, Hamilton reappeared in Blackwood's life and, unbeknown to him, submitted some of his stories to the publisher Eveleigh Nash, who accepted them.

Algernon Henry Blackwood (1869–1951), by Howard Coster, 1929

This first collection, *The Empty House and other Ghost Stories* (1906), as well as the second, *The Listener* (1907), focuses on haunted-house ghost stories. However, the most chillingly evocative and frequently reprinted story in them is an uncanny nature tale, 'The Willows', based on a 2400-mile canoe trip down the Danube that Blackwood made in 1900. With his third volume, *John Silence: Physician Extraordinary* (1908), Blackwood achieved notoriety and success, partly because Nash promoted the book with the largest posters to appear on hoardings and horse-buses that had ever been seen in Britain. More importantly it captivated a society suffering from spiritual malaise in featuring a psychic detective, John Silence (compared with Sherlock Holmes by contemporary reviewers), who treats difficult cases of spiritual affliction.

These early works caused Blackwood to be pigeon-holed

as a ghost-story writer, but he quickly moved on to fanciful novels of psychic adventure. Several of these depict young people possessed of 'old souls' who connect with older male mystical protagonists, notably *Jimbo: a Fantasy* (1909), *The Education of Uncle Paul* (1909), *The Human Chord* (1910), and *A Prisoner in Fairyland* (1913). He dramatized the last-mentioned with Violet Pearn as *The Starlight Express* (1915), for which Sir Edward Elgar composed music. Among Blackwood's more powerful mystical odysseys was *The Centaur* (1911), based on his 1910 voyage to Greece, in which an Irish traveller feels the call of the *Urwelt* and has a vision in the Caucasus of the dawning of the earth. The novel impressed writers as diverse as Rainer Maria Rilke, James Stephens, and Siegfried Sassoon, and was Blackwood's own favourite as well. *The Wave: an Egyptian Aftermath* (1916) is also an exotic psychic adventure, this one involving reincarnation, one of Blackwood's characteristic themes; it sets a precedent in being probably the first novel in English to refer to Freud by name as well as to explore the Oedipus complex in a supernatural context. He continued to produce atmospheric nature tales in *The Lost Valley and other Stories* (1910); *Pan's Garden* (1912); and *Incredible Adventures* (1914). The first includes the often anthologized story 'The Wendigo', dealing with the 'panic of the wilderness' manifested as a great moss-eating beast in the Canadian north.

During the First World War Blackwood experienced some incredible adventures of his own, involving 'code names, invisible ink and hair's breadth escapes' (Ashley, 22) while operating as an undercover agent in Switzerland for British military intelligence. Afterwards Blackwood travelled extensively and associated with the mystics P. D. Ouspensky and Georgi Gurdjieff. He also found time to collaborate on several successful plays, and pen half a dozen more psychical novels, including *The Bright Messenger* (1921), and story collections. Blackwood's friend Wilfred Wilson suggested some of the ideas for one of the latter, *The Wolves of God and other Fey Stories* (1921). Most of the tales deal with the effects of wild animals on man or with animal instincts within man, and several of the best draw on experiences in the Canadian backwoods, including the title story, as well as 'Running Wolf', and 'The Valley of the Beasts'.

In the late 1920s, when the volume of his prose writing was declining, Blackwood achieved high acclaim for his children's story *Dudley and Gilderoy: a Nonsense* (1929). It brings to the fore Blackwood's sense of humour in its description of the London adventures of a renegade parrot and a cat.

In the 1930s and 1940s Blackwood embarked on two new careers, in radio and television; he appeared on Britain's first television show, *Picture Page*, in 1936. By 1947 his regular *Saturday Night Story* spot on television had made him a household name, and in 1949 he was appointed CBE, one of his proudest moments. Late in 1951 his health deteriorated, and on 10 December he died in London of cerebral thrombosis and arteriosclerosis.

One interviewer described Blackwood as being possessed of an 'unusual, singularly fine personality, with its sympathy, sensitiveness, humour, charm, and touches of a most appealing naiveté' (Field, 304). These qualities garnered him a large circle of friends and yet he remained determinedly independent, never marrying. Tall and with striking, rugged features, he relished the open-air life, spending a good deal of his time hiking and skiing in Europe, especially Switzerland.

Altogether Blackwood published over forty books, penning more stories and novels in the realm of the psychological, mystical, and supernatural than any other contemporary. His work is informed by an eclectic framework of ideas, ranging from Eastern mysticism, theosophy, and psychical research to psychoanalysis. Occasionally in his novels Blackwood is too didactic or verbose, but most often he carries the reader along on his flights of poetic fancy. Many of his stories excel at evoking uncanny atmospheres, leading no less an expert than H. P. Lovecraft to refer in 1927 to Blackwood's work as 'some of the finest spectral literature of this or any age'. E. F. Bleiler more recently confirms Blackwood's position as 'the foremost British supernaturalist of the twentieth century'. However, Blackwood's best work defies categorizing by genre; for his powerful and unique exploration of the possibilities of expanded consciousness he deserves wider recognition. GEORGE MALCOLM JOHNSON

Sources M. Ashley, *Starlight man: the extraordinary life of Algernon Blackwood* (2001) • M. Ashley, *Algernon Blackwood: a bio-bibliography* (1987) • A. Blackwood, *Episodes before thirty*, rev edn (1950) • E. F. Bleiler, 'Introduction to the Dover edition', *Best ghost stories of Algernon Blackwood* (1973), v–x • J. R. Colombo, *Blackwood's books* (1981) • A. Blackwood, 'Author's note', *John Silence* (1942), v–vi • L. M. Field, 'What New York did to an English novelist', *Literary Digest International Book Review* (1924), 304–5 [review of Blackwood's *Episodes before thirty*] • D. Hudson, 'A study of Algernon Blackwood', *Essays and Studies by Members of the English Association*, new ser., 14 (1961), 102–14 [repr. as 'Algernon Blackwood', chap. 9 of *Talks with Fuddy and other papers* (1968), 81–91] • S. T. Joshi, 'Algernon Blackwood: the expansion of consciousness', *The weird tale: Arthur Machen, Lord Dunsany, Algernon Blackwood, M. R. James, Ambrose Bierce, H. P. Lovecraft* (1990), 87–132 • H. P. Lovecraft, 'Supernatural horror in literature', *The Recluse*, 1 (1927) [incorporated, after revision, in *The outsider and others* (1939); repr. in *Dagon and other macabre tales* (1965; rev. edn 1986)] • P. Penzoldt, 'Algernon Blackwood', *The supernatural in fiction* (1952), 228–53 • D. Punter, 'Algernon Blackwood', *Supernatural fiction writers: fantasy and horror*, ed. E. F. Bleiler, 1 (1985), 463–70 • D. Scarborough, *The supernatural in modern English fiction* (1917); repr. (1967) • J. Sullivan, 'The visionary ghost story: Algernon Blackwood', *Elegant nightmares: the English ghost story from Le Fanu to Blackwood* (1978), 112–29 • E. Wagenknecht, 'Algernon Blackwood', *Seven masters of supernatural fiction* (1991), 69–94

Archives BBC WAC • Boston College, Massachusetts • Hunt. L. • priv. coll., corresp. • Richmond Local Studies Library, London, corresp. and literary MSS • University of Toronto | BL, corresp. with Macmillans, Add. MS 54972 • BL, letters to Vera Wainwright, Add. MS 54329 • NYPL, Berg collection • State Historical Society of Wisconsin, Madison, August Derleth collection | SOUND BBC WAC

Likenesses W. Tittle, lithograph, 1922, NPG • H. Coster, photographs, 1929, NPG [*see illus.*] • Histed, photograph, repro. in *The Bookman*, 39/2 (Nov 1910) • K. Shackleton, drawing, repro. in 'Algernon Blackwood the mystic', *John O'London's Weekly*, 5/126 (3 Sept 1921) • photographs, Hult. Arch. • photographs, repro. in Blackwood, *Episodes before thirty*

Wealth at death £14,189 1*s*. 4*d*.: probate, 8 Feb 1952, *CGPLA Eng. & Wales*

Blackwood [*née* Lambart], **Lady Alicia** (1818–1913), nurse and philanthropist, was born probably on 29 November 1818 at Eaglehurst, near Ower Green in Hampshire, the daughter of George Frederick Augustus Lambart, Viscount Kilcoursie (1789–1828), and Sarah Coppin (*d.* 1823), the only daughter of J. P. Coppin of Cowley, Oxfordshire. Alicia was baptized in the parish church at Fawley on 13 December 1818. After her eldest brother, Frederick John William, succeeded as eighth earl of Cavan in 1838 Alicia and her brother Oliver George and sisters, Henrietta Augusta and Julia, received a royal patent of precedence giving them the rank of an earl's children.

Alicia Lambart spent her childhood at the Cavan country seats of Eaglehurst in Hampshire and Sharpham Park, near Broomfield in Somerset. Orphaned in 1828, she was probably brought up by relatives and educated at home. On 13 April 1849 she married the Revd James Stevenson Blackwood (*d.* 1882). Blackwood had attended Trinity College, Dublin, where he qualified as a barrister-at-law in 1835. He undertook studies in divinity and was ordained deacon in the Anglican church in 1847; in 1848 he was made a prebendary of Winchester.

The Blackwoods were prominent members of the Evangelical Alliance founded by Edward Bickersteth, a leading evangelical clergyman and Lord Shaftesbury's private counsellor. They took an active part in London's religious and philanthropic life, travelling regularly from Yorkshire to assemble at the alliance headquarters at Exeter Hall, the major public platform for evangelical religious and social campaigns, and the centre of domestic and overseas missionary activities. From 1846 the Evangelical Alliance organized annual meetings for Reformed protestants from England, Ireland, Scotland, the United States, France, Geneva, and Germany. The Blackwoods attended many of these religious meetings, where they made numerous friends, including two young Swedish women, Ebba and Emma Almroth, whom they met at an Evangelical Alliance conference in Lausanne in early 1856.

The war in the Crimea, the fall of Sevastopol, and news of the calamitous situation following the battle of Inkerman 'deeply moved' the Blackwoods and Lady Alicia was spurred into action (Blackwood, 2). She organized a small volunteer party to travel to Scutari and in early November 1854 Lady Alicia, her young Swedish friends, a maidservant, and her husband travelled overland and then by the *La Gange*, a French troopship, arriving at Seraglio Point in mid-December.

From the first days in Scutari, Lady Alicia recorded her experiences in a journal which formed the basis of a wartime memoir, *A narrative of personal experiences and impressions during a residence on the Bosphorus throughout the Crimean War* (1881). In this memoir she related that she presented herself to the authorities as a willing helper, begging to be 'usefully employed' (Blackwood, 49). James Blackwood immediately secured a post as a military chaplain, and when Florence Nightingale was convinced that Lady Alicia was in earnest and willing to work she was asked to take charge of 200 women sheltering in appalling conditions in the foul basements of the great barrack hospital at Scutari. Lady Alicia described the scene as 'a Pandemonium full of cursing and swearing and drunkenness' (Blackwood, 50).

Lady Alicia quickly demonstrated her energy and resourcefulness. Initially she took responsibility for 280 women and infants, many of them the wives, widows, and children of soldiers who had arrived from Varna in wretched condition. While sympathetic to the women's plight, Florence Nightingale regarded them as hindrances to the major task of caring for military casualties. With supplies brought from England, charitable gifts, supplemented with goods bought locally, Lady Alicia set up a women's hospital in a rented house. There, with two 'industrious and respectable' women employed as nurses and laundresses, a resident matron, and Dr Peyton Smith, sent out from Leeds, Lady Alicia began work (Blackwood, 54). Observing the destitute condition of the women, she soon decided to establish a small shop to distribute 'gifts to the women' (ibid., 57) sent from England, and to sell tea, soap, and calico at subsidized prices on two mornings each week. Flannel material and soap were in greatest demand. The women's hospital was supported by private subscriptions. As a result of her appeals in 1855 a charity to aid Lady Alicia's work for soldiers' children was established in England by Lord Kinnaird: the Soldiers' Infant Home was to house 100 children (ibid., 317).

At Scutari, Lady Alicia took charge of a lying-in ward, an invalid hospital, and established a small infants' school with a Sunday school which she supplied with bibles, prayers, and tracts. At the request of Sister Bernadine of the Roman Catholic Sisters of Mercy, Lady Alicia established a small school for the children of German Jewish families who had fled from Kerch by sea. Mainly artisans, the families were destitute and had taken up temporary residence in Pera, inland from Tophana. With assistance from a 'Mr. C—', a German convert employed by the English Society for Promoting Christianity among the Jews, she enrolled fifty-six pupils. By the time peace was proclaimed in Constantinople in March 1856 Lady Alicia recorded that she had 500 women 'more or less' under her charge (Blackwood, 237). Lady Alicia and her chaplain husband worked for fifteen months ministering to the sick and dying. At the end of the war they managed to travel, visiting Balaklava, Inkerman, Chernaya valley, and Cathcart's Hill. They delivered translated bibles and testaments to vanquished Russian soldiers, and travelled to see the khans of Bakhchisaray, the resort of the Karaite Jews in the valley of Jehoshaphat. Lady Alicia recalled that the southern part of the Crimea was reduced to 'one vast cemetery' (Blackwood, 255).

According to Lady Alicia the wartime journal remained untouched until the death in 1880 of Sultan, her favourite horse, acquired in Scutari and transported to England on the Blackwoods' return in July 1856. The horse had remained 'a connecting link between those stirring and deeply interesting times and the present' (Blackwood, 310). Sultan's death prompted Lady Alicia to recount the 'scenes impressed on our memories that can never be effaced and have been since as monitors to check discontent' (Blackwood, 59).

In her *Narrative* Lady Alicia recounted incidents at the women's hospital, conversations with Florence Nightingale and other prominent helpers, and the difficulties in organization. In addition she graphically described the agonies of men dying on the battlefields from wounds and from infectious disease; in freezing winter temperatures frostbite and exposure were constant enemies. Burials, the silent aftermath of battles, rocky cemeteries, and new memorials are poignantly evoked and yet, occasionally offsetting tragedy, Lady Alicia's lively and informative travelogue is reminiscent of Lady Mary Wortley Montague's eighteenth-century Turkish *Letters*. Just as Lady Mary had been, Lady Alicia was an acute observer of Turkish women's manners and customs. In her *Narrative* she conveyed vivid descriptions and opinions on Turkish women's demeanour and dress, and managed to communicate her interest well enough to receive invitations to visit the local women's domestic quarters where she 'fraternised', receiving coffee, a hookah, and sweetmeats (Blackwood, 85–6). She supplied her *Narrative* with illustrations—pencil sketches of Turkish and Crimean scenery. These were also published separately as an album, *Scutari, the Bosphorus, and the Crimea, 24 Sketches* (1857). Her wry humour made light of difficulties, and through her writing Lady Alicia emerges as a venturesome individual with a practical streak, kind, earnest, and deeply religious.

After the Crimean War the Blackwoods returned to the Yorkshire parish of Middleton Tyas, where James Blackwood was appointed vicar. There Lady Alicia applied herself to parish and charitable work, notably for the British and Foreign Bible Society. Correspondence with Florence Nightingale continued sporadically until 1866. On the Revd James Blackwood's retirement in 1874 they moved to Boxmoor House, near Bovingdon in Hertfordshire, where they lived quietly. James Blackwood died in 1882 and Lady Alicia lived on at Boxmoor House continuing her charitable and religious work. She wrote another book, *Six in the Fold, and One: Narratives Drawn from Life*, published by the Religious Tract Society in 1892.

Lady Alicia Blackwood died at Boxmoor House on 30 July 1913 at the age of ninety-four. As the Blackwoods were childless Lady Alicia left the bulk of her estate to her sister-in-law, the Hon. Elizabeth Lambart, and provided legacies to her sister, Lady Julia Bouwens, her nieces and nephews, and close friends. SUZANNE L. G. RICKARD

Sources A. Blackwood, *A narrative of personal experiences and impressions during a residence on the Bosphorus throughout the Crimean War* (1881) · *The Times* (1 Aug 1913) · *Hertfordshire, Hemel Hempstead Gazette and West Herts Advertiser* (2 Aug 1913) · letter, F. Nightingale to Sir H. Verney, 1859?, Wellcome L., MS 8998/14 · m. cert. · d. cert. · census returns, 1881 · *CGPLA Eng. & Wales* (1913) · parish register, Fawley, Hampshire, 13 Dec 1818 [baptism] · C. Woodham-Smith, *Florence Nightingale, 1820–1910* (1950), 180–81, 190, 225 · F. B. Smith, *Florence Nightingale: reputation and power* (1982), 43 · *A calendar of the letters of Florence Nightingale*, ed. S. Goldie (1977) [microfiche] · Allibone, *Dict.* · Burke, *Peerage* (1845) · *Debrett's Peerage* (1995) · Crockford (1865) · Crockford (1882) · L. James, *1854–1856 Crimea: the war with Russia from contemporary photographs* (1981)

Archives BL, Florence Nightingale MSS, Add. MSS 43397, 45796 · Wellcome L., Florence Nightingale MSS

Wealth at death £11,870 9*s*. 4*d*.: probate, 2 Sept 1913, *CGPLA Eng. & Wales*

Blackwood, Sir (Stevenson) Arthur (1832–1893), secretary of the Post Office, was born at Rosslyn Lodge, The Grove, Hampstead, on 22 May 1832, the only son of Arthur Johnstone Blackwood (1808–1874), groom of the privy chamber, and Cecilia Georgiana (*d*. 1881), daughter of the Hon. John Byng, and widow of John Wright of Lenton Hall, Nottinghamshire. Stevenson was the grandson of Vice-Admiral the Hon. Sir Henry *Blackwood and had one sister. The family was of Scottish origin, related to Adam Blackwood, from an Irish branch. Stevenson grew up to be very tall and good-looking, though prone to illness. He became a pupil (1843–4) of the Revd Jeremiah Carver, vicar of Great Sampford, Essex. At Eton College in 1845–8 Blackwood maintained his classics. To learn German he lived at Proseken, Mecklenburg (1848–50). He then matriculated from Trinity College, Cambridge. A keen sportsman, Blackwood possessed 'bright intelligence' (*Record*, 1012), but took no degree, for in 1852 Lord John Russell appointed him to a clerkship at the Treasury. On volunteering in 1854 for the Crimean campaign, Blackwood became deputy assistant commissary-general. He did well, gaining the applause of his men, a Crimean medal with clasps, and a Turkish decoration. His godmother, Charlotte Wright, by sending him a biography of Colonel Holcombe, stimulated a gradual conversion experience. Recalled in December 1855, he was promoted second-class clerk in the Treasury chest division. In 1856 he suffered from a bout of rheumatic fever.

While being encouraged by Catherine Marsh, daughter of Dr William Marsh, to commit himself further to personal faith in Christianity, Blackwood still moved in London society, where he was known as Beauty Blackwood. His conversion was made complete under William Pennefather. He renounced worldly pleasures and began to learn Hebrew. On 16 December 1858, at St George's, Hanover Square, Blackwood married Harriet Sydney Montagu (1834–1907), the daughter of Conway Richard Dobbs of Castle Dobbs, co. Antrim, and the widow of a prominent evangelical peer, George, sixth duke of Manchester. They had three daughters and two sons, of whom the younger, Algernon *Blackwood, became a notable author; his *Episodes before Thirty* (1923) includes reflections on a secluded evangelical upbringing, albeit by loving parents. In successive homes near London, Blackwood held Christian gatherings. At intervals during 1862–92 he published his Bible addresses. Habitually putting his official duties first, he was prone to overworking. In 1870 and 1872 he served on Treasury commissions overseas. In 1873 he succeeded Pennefather as chairman of the annual Mildmay Conference. Although he accepted moderate Holiness teaching, he continued a strong advocate of Reformation principles.

To enable the Treasury to monitor postal affairs, Blackwood was appointed financial secretary of the Post Office in 1874, becoming CB. At St Martin's-le-Grand, the Post

Sir (Stevenson) Arthur Blackwood (1832–1893), by Elliott & Fry, 1890

Office headquarters, he soon came to understand its internal tensions. In April 1880 Blackwood was promoted secretary of the Post Office. His administrative gifts and Christian character—not wholly austere, for he retained through life a boyish quality—made him 'one of the ablest, most successful, and consistent servants of the state' (H. S. Blackwood, 399–400). Scholarly opinion, while perceiving an autocratic tendency, continues to regard him in a favourable light. Under Blackwood postal orders were introduced in 1880, inland parcel post in 1883, and sixpenny telegrams in 1885. At a universal postal congress in Lisbon (1885) Blackwood was prominent: his command of French increased his country's influence, and he received a Portuguese decoration. A new postmaster-general, H. C. Raikes, chose to assert his authority at home, but Blackwood was made KCB in 1887. Thereafter he dropped his first name, becoming known as Sir Arthur Blackwood. In 1890 his decisive action at the beginning of a postal strike prevented disruption from spreading; Raikes approved. In 1891 ill health delayed his departure for a postal congress in Vienna. On arrival, his influence still proved strong. In 1892 influenza left Blackwood considerably weakened. Returning to work in May 1893, he persisted until August with departmental reorganization. Clearly in worse health, he left for better air in the Engadine. Growing weaker, he travelled homewards with difficulty, reaching Harwich almost unconscious. Taken ashore to the Great Eastern Hotel, Parkeston, he died on 2 October from pernicious anaemia. He was buried with his parents in Kensal Green cemetery, London.

J. S. Reynolds

Sources H. S. D. Montagu, Lady Blackwood, ed., *Some records of the life of Stevenson Arthur Blackwood* (1896) • H. F. Buxton, *St Martin's-le-Grand* [Post Office magazine], 4 (1894), 1–16 • [H. S. Montagu], *How he was won for Christ: a record for those who love the memory of Sir S. A. Blackwood* [1893] • *Christian Portrait Gallery* (c.1890), 22–5 • C. Marsh, 'In Memoriam', *Service for the king*, 14 (Nov 1893) • L. E. O'Rorke, *Life and friendships of Catherine Marsh* (1917) • Boase, *Mod. Eng. biog.* • *The Times* (4 Oct 1893), 3 • *The Times* (10 Oct 1893), 6 • *Record* (13 Oct 1893), 1012 • *ILN* (7 Oct 1893), 439, 458 • A. Blackwood, *Episodes before thirty* (1923) • Burke, *Peerage* • M. J. Daunton, *Royal Mail: the Post Office since 1840* (1985) • H. St J. Raikes, *The life and letters of Henry Cecil Raikes* (1898) • F. E. Baines, *Forty years at the Post-Office: a personal narrative*, 1 (1895)

Likenesses wood-engraving, pubd 1875, NPG • Elliott & Fry, photograph, 1890, priv. coll. [*see illus.*] • engraving (after photograph), repro. in *The Christian portrait gallery* (1889), 1.4 • photograph, repro. in Blackwood, *Episodes before thirty*, 32 • photographs (in later life), Post Office Archives, Phoenix Place, London • photographs, NPG • photographs, repro. in Blackwood, *Some records of … S. A. Blackwood*

Wealth at death £14,503 6*s*. 5*d*.: resworn probate, July 1894, *CGPLA Eng. & Wales* (1893)

Blackwood, Beatrice Mary (1889–1975), anthropologist, was born on 3 May 1889 at her parents' home at 3 Marlborough Hill, Marylebone, London, the eldest of the three children of James Blackwood (1822–1911), publisher, and his wife, Mary (1859–1953), a nurse, daughter of John Carter Chamberlayne. She was educated in London at Wycombe House School, and Paddington and Maida Vale high school. In 1908 she won a scholarship to Somerville College, Oxford, where she was awarded a second-class honours degree in English language and literature in 1912.

In 1918 Blackwood took the Oxford diploma in anthropology with distinction and started work as research assistant to Professor Arthur Thomson in the department of human anatomy, then based in the University Museum, Oxford. After two years she was promoted to departmental demonstrator, and then took a BSc degree with a thesis on embryology in 1923. In 1924, as a Laura Spelman Rockefeller scholar, she embarked on a three-year anthropological investigation into the relationship between intelligence and physical type in North America. On her return to Oxford she became university demonstrator in ethnology, a post that was transferred to the Pitt Rivers Museum in 1935, where she remained until retirement.

Blackwood began fieldwork in 1929 in Buka and Bougainville, later part of Papua New Guinea, funded by the American National Research Council. The resulting publication, *Both Sides of Buka Passage* (1935), combined social anthropology, material culture, and technology, reflecting her ability to combine methodological approaches. In 1936, under the aegis of the Pitt Rivers Museum, she worked among the stone tool-using communities in the interior of New Guinea. The hallmark of all Blackwood's fieldwork was her adoption of a cat as companion. In the Upper Watut region, where few locals spoke the lingua franca of pidgin, the cat's antics proved essential in breaking down the barriers of communication between her and the warriors. After nine months her pioneering fieldwork was cut short when the area was declared 'uncontrolled' by the government. Rather than return home she spent the rest of her leave collecting in other, more accessible regions of Papua New Guinea. It is for this fieldwork, published as *The Technology of a Modern Stone Age People in New Guinea* (1950), that she is most fondly remembered as the diminutive woman who braved 'cannibal country' with only a kitten as companion.

After returning to the Pitt Rivers Museum in 1938 Blackwood made a collecting trip to New Mexico, returning early owing to the outbreak of war in 1939. In 1943, as an acknowledgement of her professional achievements as an expert fieldworker, she was awarded the Rivers memorial medal of the Royal Anthropological Institute. During the Second World War the museum closed and Blackwood and the curator, T. K. Penniman, devoted their time to creating a regional and typological card index for all the objects in the Pitt Rivers Museum. After requests from visiting researchers, who realized the value of Blackwood's comprehensive classification system, it was published in 1970 for use in other museums. She was made lecturer in ethnology at Oxford University in 1946. After her retirement in 1959, at the age of seventy, she continued to work at the Pitt Rivers Museum daily and was made an honorary curator in 1965.

Blackwood never married, having reportedly chosen at an early age between marriage and a career. An occasional poet, she wrote humorous verse for family and friends, often making light of arduous conditions in the field. She was made a fellow of the Royal Anthropological Institute in 1921 and a fellow of the Society of Antiquaries in 1943. She died of pneumonia on 29 November 1975 at her home, 11 Wyndham House, Plantation Road, Oxford, within days of her final visit to the museum. She was cremated at Oxford crematorium and her ashes spread in the garden of remembrance there on 4 December.

Chantal Knowles

Sources [H. Bryant], ed., *Somerville College register, 1879–1959* (1961) • *The Times* (2 Dec 1975) • *Oceania*, 46 (1975–6), 234–7 • *American Anthropologist*, 78/2 (June 1976), 321–2 • *Folklore*, 87 (1976), 113–14 • *Oxford Mail* (1 Dec 1975) • private information (2004) • B. Blackwood, curriculum vitae, U. Oxf., Pitt Rivers Museum, manuscript collection • N. Lutkehaus, 'Beatrice Mary Blackwood (1889–1975)', *Woman anthropologists: selected biographies*, ed. U. Gacs, A. Khan, J. McIntyre, and R. Weinberg (1989), 17–22 • b. cert. • d. cert.

Archives U. Oxf., Pitt Rivers Museum, collections • U. Oxf., Pitt Rivers Museum, diaries, field notes, letters, papers | FILM U. Oxf., Pitt Rivers Museum, 2 reels of cine film

Likenesses photograph, 1925, U. Oxf., Pitt Rivers Museum • photograph, 1927, U. Oxf., Pitt Rivers Museum • photograph, 1946, U. Oxf., Pitt Rivers Museum

Blackwood, Lady Caroline Maureen Hamilton-Temple- [*known as* Caroline Blackwood] (**1931–1996**), novelist, was born on 16 July 1931, at 4 Hans Crescent, Knightsbridge, London, the eldest of three children of Basil Sheridan Hamilton-Temple-Blackwood, fourth marquess of Dufferin and Ava (1909–1945), and his wife, Maureen Constance Guinness (1907–1998), socialite and one of the 'fabulous Guinness girls' of the 1920s. Caroline was the great-granddaughter of Edward Cecil *Guinness, first earl of Iveagh (1847–1927), and of Frederick Hamilton-Temple-*Blackwood, first marquess of Dufferin and Ava (1826–1902), governor-general of Canada and viceroy of India. She was scantily educated at Rockport Preparatory School for Boys, Brillantmont School, Lausanne, and Downham School for Girls, Essex, and had an unhappy childhood at the family seat at Clandeboye in Ulster. After a finishing school in Oxford, she came out as a débutante in 1949 at a ball held at Londonderry House. As a teenager she was plump, ungainly, and lacking in confidence; her stockings were always falling down. However, she had huge avid blue eyes and wonderful blonde hair, and after losing weight developed into a captivating beauty and a sensational débutante.

Lady Caroline Maureen Hamilton-Temple-Blackwood (1931–1996), by Lucian Freud, 1954

Blackwood then took a secretarial job with the Hulton Press, and was given small reporting assignments by Claud Cockburn. Ann Fleming introduced Blackwood to the painter Lucian Michael Freud (*b.* 1922), with whom she eloped to Paris in 1952. There she met Picasso, and did not wash for three days after he drew on her hands and fingernails. After their marriage on 9 December 1953 she became a striking figure in London's *haute bohème*: the Gargoyle Club and Colony Room replaced Belgravia drawing-rooms as her haunts. She sat for several of Freud's finest portraits, notably *Girl in Bed*, which testify to her outstanding allure. Cyril Connolly's attentions to Blackwood became so unequivocal that Freud ambushed him in Soho and kicked his shins. She was impressed by the ruthless vision of Freud and of Francis Bacon, and her later fiction was a literary version of their view of humanity.

After her marriage had disintegrated Blackwood moved in 1957 to New York, where she studied acting at the Stella Adler school. She had relationships with the editor of the *London Magazine* Alan Ross (1922–2001) and with the Anglo-American screenwriter Ivan Moffat (1918–2002). She also went to Hollywood, appeared in an Italian film, and had a small part in the television series *Have Gun Will Travel* in the 1950s. Her marriage to Freud was dissolved in Mexico in 1958. Meeting her that year Christopher Isherwood noted, 'Caroline was round eyed as usual, either dumb or scared'. As a dinner guest he thought her 'a frost' (Isherwood, *Diaries*, 1.768, 814). On 15 August 1959, in Yonkers, she married Israel Citkowitz (1909–1974), a composer with a creative block. They had three daughters (although a deathbed admission revealed that Ivan Moffat was the father of Ivana).

In the early 1960s Blackwood began contributing to *Encounter*, the *London Magazine*, and other periodicals on such subjects as beatniks, Ulster sectarianism, women's lib theatre, and New York free schools. Although these articles were elegant, minutely observed, and sometimes wickedly funny, they had, according to Isherwood, a persistent flaw: 'She is only capable of thinking negatively. Confronted by a phenomenon, she asks herself: what is wrong with it?' (Isherwood, *Diaries*, 803). During the mid-1960s she had an affair with Robert Benjamin (Bob) Silvers (*b.* 1929), founder and co-editor of the *New York Review of Books* (1963). Although her marriage to Citkowitz was sundered, he continued to live near her and served as her gentle nanny-duenna until his death.

After returning to London, in April 1970 Blackwood began a relationship with the manic-depressive American poet Robert Traill Spence Lowell (1917–1977), who was then a visiting professor at All Souls College, Oxford. Their son was born on 28 September 1971, and after obtaining divorces from their spouses in Santo Domingo, they married on 21 October 1972 and lived in London, in Milgate, Kent, and later in Castletown, co. Kildare. The sequence of poems in Lowell's *The Dolphin* (1973) provides a disrupted narrative of his involvement with Blackwood and the birth of their son. She was distressed and confused in her reactions to Lowell's manic episodes. She felt useless during his attacks, and afraid of their effects on her children. Her anxieties, alcohol-related illnesses, and late-night tirades exacerbated his condition. The turmoil and tension of their relationship were aggravated by the chaos of their domestic arrangements. During 1976–7 the marriage disintegrated. Lowell died clutching a Freud portrait of Blackwood, in the back seat of a New York taxi, on his way to resume life with his second wife, Elizabeth Hardwick.

Despite their marital anguish, Lowell was crucial to Blackwood's development as a novelist. He encouraged her, as Caroline Blackwood, to assemble her first book, a collection of stories and reportage, with a title from an Ulster protestant marching song, *For All that I Found there* (1973), and a coruscating memoir of her daughter's treatment in a burns unit. Blackwood's first novel, *The Stepdaughter* (1976), is a concise, gripping monologue by a rich, self-pitying woman deserted by her husband in a luxurious New York apartment and tormented by her fat, stodgy stepdaughter. Like much of Blackwood's fictional writing, it has a claustrophobic emotional intensity as it demonstrates how a selfish woman's emotional state distorts her perception and treatment of other people. *The Stepdaughter*, which won the David Higham prize for the best first novel of the year, has Blackwood's hallmark: exactitude, wit, and sensitivity as well as the relentless tone of resentment characteristic of her narratives. Its female fury is chilling.

The tone in much of Blackwood's fiction was that of a prodigious and observant child: knowing, unhappy, and helpless in the power of cruel, devious, or emotionally suffocating adults. This temper was particularly conspicuous in her second novel, *Great Granny Webster* (1977), which was partly based on her own miserable childhood. She depicted an austere and loveless old woman's destructive impact on her daughter and granddaughter. The cumulative effect is of blistering resentment, grief, and despair that nothing can palliate. It impressed Philip Larkin and was also short-listed for the Booker prize.

As a result of the punitive taxation levied by the Callaghan government Blackwood left England in 1977 and took an apartment in the great Georgian house of Castletown in co. Kildare, which was convenient for Guinness family parties. One of her last serious relationships was with the poet and fellow of All Souls College, Oxford, Andrew Harvey (*b.* 1951). The death of her eldest daughter Natalya in 1978 further demoralized her; her love of children had impressed Elizabeth Bishop, but she was sometimes a difficult mother.

In 1980 Blackwood wrote a study of the relations between the duchess of Windsor and her cunning lawyer, Maître Suzanne Blum. This malicious, macabre, zestful, and muddled book proved impossible to publish during Blum's lifetime and was eventually issued as *The Last of the Duchess* (1995). Blackwood's third novel, a misanthropic psychological thriller, *The Fate of Mary Rose* (1981), describes the effect on a Kent village of the rape and murder of a ten-year-old girl, Maureen. Narrated by a selfish historian whose obsessions destroy his domestic life, it is a pitiless investigation of neurosis, cruelty, and panic. *Good Night Sweet Ladies* (1983) is a collection of five short stories. 'Olga' is perhaps the most intensely personal; but Blackwood's depiction of annihilating egotists who are variously bullying, reclusive, vain, or self-deceiving is so implacable and gruesome that the reader can feel as overwhelmed as Lowell did by her late-night tirades. The stories' power and emotional precision are, however, undeniable. Her final novel, *Corrigan* (1984), was least successful. It depicted the effects on a depressed widow of a charming, energetic but sinister cripple who erupts into her life.

Blackwood's later books were based on interviews and vignettes. *On the Perimeter: Caroline Blackwood at Greenham Common* (1984) contained her observations of the peace women's encampment outside an American air base in Berkshire. She also published a personal account of hunting and hunt saboteurs, *In the Pink* (1987). In this reflective yet ghoulish book she deployed her powers at depicting obsessive personalities of both fox-hunters and animal rights activists. Together with Anna Haycraft (Alice

Thomas Ellis) she compiled a cookbook for the expeditious *Darling, you shouldn't have Gone to so much Trouble* (1980). Its recipes by, among others, Tallulah Bankhead, Quentin Crisp, and Roald Dahl, were described by Anita Brookner as '*cuisine grosseur* with a vengeance' (Brookner, 1282).

James Lees-Milne found Blackwood 'a difficult girl' in 1980: 'Chain-smoking, churchyard cough, beautiful blue staring eyes, raddled complexion' (Lees-Milne, 101). She returned to the USA in 1987, settling at Sag Harbor, Long Island. Although her powers were depleted by alcoholism, her occasional writings—such as a vivid memoir of Princess Margaret and Francis Bacon (*New York Review of Books*, 24 Sept 1992)—remained exceptional. She died of cancer on 14 February 1996, at the Mayfair Hotel, Park Avenue and East 65th Street, New York. Her mordant humour was never quelled. On her deathbed Anna Haycraft brought some holy water from Lourdes which was accidentally splashed on her bed-sheets. 'I might have caught my death,' Blackwood muttered (*The Independent*). Before her death she had been working on a novel about a transsexual. RICHARD DAVENPORT-HINES

Sources C. Blackwood, *For all that I found there* (1973) • N. Schoenberger, *Dangerous muse: a life of Caroline Blackwood* (2001) • S. Aronson, 'Sophisticated lady', *Town and Country* (Sept 1993) • *The Independent* (15 Feb 1996) • *The Times* (15 Feb 1996) • *Daily Telegraph* (16 Feb 1996) • C. Isherwood, *Diaries*, ed. K. Bucknell (1996) • I. Hamilton, *Robert Lowell* (1983) • J. Lees-Milne, *Deep romantic chasm*, ed. M. Bloch (2000) • E. Bishop, *One art: selected letters*, ed. R. Giroux (1994) • Sheridan, fifth marquess of Dufferin and Ava, 'Growing up at Clandeboye', *Clandeboye* (1985), 5–9 • H. Moraes, *Henrietta* (1994) • A. Brookner, 'Cuisine menteur', *TLS* (14 Nov 1980) • C. Isherwood, *Lost years*, ed. K. Bucknell (2000) • *New Grove*

Likenesses eight photographs, 1934–53, Hult. Arch. • L. Freud, two oils, 1952, probably priv. coll.; repro. in R. Hughes, ed., *Lucian Freud: paintings* (1987), pl. 13, 14 [exhibition catalogue, Smithsonian Institution, Washington, DC, 15 Sept–29 Nov 1987] • D. Farson, bromide print, *c*.1953, NPG • L. Freud, oils, 1954, Hayward Gallery, London, Arts Council Collection [*see illus.*] • photograph, *c*.1970, repro. in Hamilton, *Robert Lowell*, following p. 402

Wealth at death approx. $3,000,000: Schoenberger, *Dangerous muse*, 295, 306

Blackwood, Christopher (1607/8–1670), Particular Baptist minister, was born in August 1607 or 1608, in Yorkshire, the youngest son of William Blackwood. After matriculating at the age of thirteen from Pembroke College, Cambridge, at Easter 1621, he graduated BA in 1625. He was ordained a priest in the diocese of London on 8 June 1628, at which time he was referred to as having the MA degree. After serving as vicar of Stockbury, Kent, in 1631, he was curate of Rye, Sussex, from 1632 to 1635. On emigrating to New England in 1640, he succeeded John Lathrop as minister at Scituate in Plymouth Colony. After his return to England in 1642, he became rector of Staplehurst, Kent, but resigned after embracing Baptist tenets in 1644. He became convinced that only believer's baptism is valid after hearing the General Baptist Francis Cornwell preach at Cranbrook, Kent, and then studying the matter for a fortnight. The General Baptist messenger (superintendent) William Jeffery baptized him.

Blackwood published his arguments for believer's baptism (including a short catechism on the subject) and against compulsion in matters of conscience in *The Storming of Antichrist, in his Two Last and Strongest Garrisons* (1644), citing the patristics, church councils, protestant reformers, and the puritan Richard Greenham to bolster his case. In this work he attacked a sermon preached by Stephen Marshall in Westminster Abbey as well as Thomas Blake's *The Birth-Priviledge* (1644). To Blake's retort in *Infants Baptisme, Freed from Antichristianisme* (1645), Blackwood responded in *Apostolicall Baptisme* (1645). Thomas Cobbett, minister at Lynn, Massachusetts, criticized the baptismal views of Blackwood, Henry Denne, and others in *A just vindication of the covenant and church estate of children of members as also of their right to baptisme* (1648), and the same year Blackwood published *A Treatise Concerning Deniall of Christ* (1648). From 1646 to 1652 Blackwood resided at Marden, Kent, though in June 1651 he was at Chester with its governor, Colonel Robert Duckenfield.

Following the death of his first wife, Martha, at Marden in 1646, Blackwood married Mary, daughter of Thomas and Mary Hartridge of Pembury, Kent. They had three children: Christopher (*b*. 1650), who was apprenticed to Colonel Richard Lawrence, a prominent Dublin Baptist; Timothy, who became a goldsmith in Dublin; and Phineas, who emigrated to Massachusetts.

Blackwood went to Ireland, settling at Kilkenny by August 1652 through the influence of the governor, Colonel Daniel Axtell; he drew a stipend of £150 p.a. from the civil list in 1653–4. By this time he had embraced the Calvinist principles of the Particular Baptists. Henry Cromwell and several Independent ministers, including Thomas Harrison, unsuccessfully appealed to Blackwood to worship publicly with them, but the terms he offered, including the right openly to condemn any of their views, were unacceptable. By 1 June 1653 he had established a Particular Baptist church at Wexford, and on that day he was a signatory of a letter from Baptists in Ireland to their counterparts in London seeking closer contact and urging that at least two qualified men be sent to exhort the godly in England, Scotland, and Wales. He continued to publish, his next book being *A Soul-Searching Catechism* (2nd edn, 1653), a substantive work of eighty-two pages as well as a brief catechism intended for memorization by servants and children. The former contained a defence of the laying on of hands after baptism. He dedicated *A treatise concerning repentance, wherein also, the doctrine of restitution is handled at large* (1653) to Edmund Ludlow and Miles Corbet, and *Some Pious Treatises* (1654), on such topics as appropriate speech and the resurrection of the body, to Lady Bridget Fleetwood, Oliver Cromwell's daughter. The Independent minister Thomas Harrison described Blackwood as 'the oracle of the anabaptists in Ireland' (Thurloe, 4.90).

By 17 October 1655 Blackwood had gone to Dublin to succeed Thomas Patient as pastor of the Particular Baptist church in Swift's Alley; his successor at Kilkenny was William Wilsby. Shortly thereafter he moved to London, where he became the pastor of a Particular Baptist congregation. The Independent Samuel Winter attacked Blackwood's baptismal doctrine in *The Summe of Diverse Sermons Preached in Dublin* (1656). In December of that year various queries, mostly by Blackwood dealing with compulsion in matters of conscience, were circulated in Limerick, where the Independent Claudius Gilbert refuted them in *The Libertine School'd* (1657). Blackwood signed the address of loyalty from Particular Baptists in Ireland to Oliver Cromwell in 1657. He finally completed his mammoth 900-page *Exposition upon the Ten First Chapters of … Matthew* (1659), which he had begun at Kilkenny and now dedicated to Charles Fleetwood. In it, he modestly wrote, the reader would not find '*the flourishing* garnish *of humane* Eloquence, *nor the glorious* varnish *of* Rhetorical *expressions, but* naked truth' (A3*r*).

During the outbreak of popular hostility against religious radicals at the Restoration, a threat was made against Blackwood's life. He returned to England in 1660, and the following year signed the *Humble Apology* denouncing Thomas Venner's Fifth Monarchist insurrection. In the autumn of 1661 he went to Amsterdam, but he was back in London by October 1662, and shortly thereafter returned to Dublin. Some time before November 1663 the government received a report that his congregation was meeting at Major William Lowe's house in Abbey Green, Dublin, on Sundays and Thursdays. He died, apparently at Dublin, in 1670. His will, dated 27 March 1669 and proved at Dublin on 17 September 1670, bequeathed £280 to his wife, £72 to Phineas, £44 to Timothy, £20 for the printing of his works, and most of his other goods to Christopher.

RICHARD L. GREAVES

Sources B. R. White, ed., *Association records of the Particular Baptists of England, Wales, and Ireland to 1660*, 4 vols. (1971–7), vol. 2, pp. 112–18, 120, 123 · Bodl. Oxf., MS Carte 45, fol. 437*r* · Thurloe, *State papers*, 4.90 · Venn, *Alum. Cant.*, 1/1.162 · St J. D. Seymour, *The puritans in Ireland, 1647–1661* (1912) · T. Grantham, *Christianismus primitivus, or, The ancient Christian religion*, 4 pts in 1 (1678), pt 3, p. 9 · B. R. White, 'Blackwood, Christopher', Greaves & Zaller, *BDBR*, 1.69–70 · R. L. Greaves, *God's other children: protestant nonconformists and the emergence of denominational churches in Ireland* (1997) · A. Laurence, *Parliamentary army chaplains, 1642–1651*, Royal Historical Society Studies in History, 59 (1990) · T. C. Barnard, *Cromwellian Ireland: English government and reform in Ireland, 1649–1660* (1975) · T. W. W. Smart, 'Original letters, hitherto unpublished, of the Rev. Christopher Blackwood, an eminent minister of the seventeenth century', *Baptist Magazine*, 59 (1867), 369–76, 435–40, 519–24, 579–85

Archives Bodl. Oxf., MS Carte 45, fol. 437*r*

Wealth at death over £416

Blackwood, Frederick Temple Hamilton-Temple-, first marquess of Dufferin and Ava (1826–1902), diplomatist, was born on 21 June 1826, in via Maggio, Florence, Italy, the only child of Price Blackwood (1794–1841), formerly captain in the Royal Navy, afterwards fourth Baron Dufferin and Claneboye in the Irish peerage, and his wife, Helen Selina, *née* Sheridan (1807–1867) [*see* Hay, Helen Selina, countess of Gifford]. His mother was aged eighteen when he was born, and their relationship had special tenderness, radiance, and trust: 'You see,' he said, 'my mother and I were young together in the reign of George IV. We shared our youth' (Nicolson, 62). An affectionate and happy child, despite being accidentally blinded in the left eye, he succeeded his father in 1841. He was educated at Mr Walton's school at Hampton, Middlesex, then at Eton College (1839–43) and Christ Church, Oxford (1844–6). He was president of the Oxford Union Society (1847). After a Puseyite phase at Oxford, he retained his faith in the efficacy of prayer. He suffered nervous illnesses during adolescence, and his mother's ambitions for him as a young man caused him anxiety. His guardian, Sir James Graham, was a strong and beneficial influence.

Frederick Temple Hamilton-Temple-Blackwood, first marquess of Dufferin and Ava (1826–1902), by George Frederic Watts, 1881

Irish landowner In 1847 Dufferin visited the famine and typhus districts of co. Kerry and gave a trenchant description of the degradation in his *Narrative of a Journey from Oxford to Skibbereen during the Irish Famine* (1847). Dufferin's position as an Ulster landlord of progressive views was awkward. He thought the Irish were ill-equipped for self-government, but that they might advance under English protection. Ireland's economic problems he regarded as demographic, and therefore soluble by mass emigration. He judged that Irish tenant-rights exploited both landlords and landless peasants. After 1870 he despaired of maintaining proprietary rights in Ireland, and gradually sold his estates in co. Down; he retained only property worth about £8000 a year within a ring fence in the Clandeboye demesne around his house and property at Helen's Bay. He realized £370,000 by land sales in the 1870s. In later life he privately opposed home rule. His family had limited local influence, since the county was dominated by Downshires and Londonderrys. Indeed it was anomalous that while Dufferin's paternal ancestors were tory squires without great incomes, his own manners and sympathies were those of a whig grandee. His pretensions seemed unconvincing to whigs such as Lord Granville, who in 1856 labelled him as 'a poor creature, who does not require any bribe' (Maxwell, 2.134).

Early career Dufferin's early advances were due to Lord John Russell, for whom he always felt grateful devotion. Russell appointed him lord-in-waiting to Queen Victoria in 1849–52 (a post that he resumed under Aberdeen and Palmerston in 1854–8). He was considered almost too handsome by the queen, who later 'thought his Sheridan blood led him to relax social restrictions' (Johnson, 715). On Russell's advice in 1850 he was advanced to a United Kingdom peerage and took his seat in the House of Lords as Baron Clandeboye. His diplomatic career was inaugurated in 1855, when he went as attaché with Russell to the Vienna conference which attempted to settle the Crimean War. Having travelled in the Near East in 1858–9, he was appointed by Russell in July 1860 as British commissioner inquiring into the massacres of Christians in Lebanon. Dufferin conciliated a formidable set of racial, religious, and national antagonisms and secured agreement on the region's future government.

In 1854 Dufferin had sailed his yacht *Foam* to the Baltic, where the Anglo-French fleets were besieging the Russian fort of Bomarsund, and two years later to Iceland, Jan Mayen, and Spitsbergen; his account of this voyage, published as *Letters from High Latitudes*, had a prolonged circulation, and went through many editions; it was admired by both D. H. Lawrence and W. H. Auden. At a ball in 1857 Dufferin was described as 'the crack beau of the room' (Lewin, 2.164). For much of this decade he nursed a chivalrous devotion to Viscountess Jocelyn, whom he 'never ceased to love' (Dufferin to Lady Mount-Temple, 14 Dec 1894, PRO NIre., D 1071 H/03/37). Dufferin married on 23 October 1862 Hariot Georgina Rowan-Hamilton [*see* Blackwood, Hariot Georgina Hamilton-Temple- (1843–1936)]. By royal licence a month earlier he had taken the surname of Hamilton before his patronymic of Blackwood; in 1872 he inserted the further surname of Temple. He and his wife had six sons and three daughters. He proved a wise, proud, and loving father.

Dufferin was appointed lord lieutenant of co. Down in 1864 (he resigned this post with gracious dignity when dying in 1902). He received his first ministerial appointment from Palmerston as under-secretary for India in November 1864. He was transferred to the War Office in a like capacity in 1866. He and his friends hoped for his appointment as viceroy of Ireland in Gladstone's administration of 1868, but it was judged that he lacked 'backbone' (Kimberley, 28), and he was instead made chancellor of the duchy of Lancaster. He regretted his exclusion from the cabinet, but was advanced in the English peerage in November 1871, when he took the titles of Viscount Clandeboye and earl of Dufferin. He was chairman of royal commissions on military education (1868–70) and the design of warships (1871). As the author of *Irish Emigration and the Tenure of Land in Ireland* (1867) and *Mr. Mill's Plan for the Pacification of Ireland Examined* (1868), he was consulted by Gladstone in 1869 about Irish land policy, without satisfaction to either man.

Canada In 1872 Dufferin's friend the duke of Argyll, as secretary of state for India, wished to confer the Indian viceroyalty on him; but he was instead nominated as governor-general of Canada. Dufferin had debts of £299,000 by 1872, of which £135,000 was owed to John Mulholland, afterwards Lord Dunleath, who obtained the Ards estate in settlement. Without his official income, Dufferin would have been obliged to renounce public life, and the proconsular turn to his career saved him from a rupture with Gladstone over Irish policy. British Columbia had lately joined the confederation, and Dufferin was the first governor-general to be installed (25 June 1872) with jurisdiction over the vast territory from the Atlantic to the Pacific. Ably assisted by his wife, he set himself to make the governor-generalship a centre of public interest. He entertained lavishly, travelled incessantly throughout the dominion, and spoke on every possible occasion, encouraging Canadian pride, and promoting Canada overseas. His speeches, then as always, were fluent, elegant, and amusing. Although there was an element of vanity in his techniques which displeased the official classes, he was the most popular of nineteenth-century Canadian governors, and when he visited Washington, DC, Henry Adams reported he 'was a success and developed uncommon social tact' (*Letters of Henry Adams*, 307). The Pacific Railway contract, and his acceptance of the advice of his prime minister, John MacDonald, whom he much admired, on the prorogation of the Canadian parliament (1873) proved the most contentious issues to handle.

Russia and Turkey Having left Canada in October 1878, Dufferin was appointed (to Gladstone's displeasure) by Beaconsfield in February 1879 as British ambassador at St Petersburg. He sought to maintain friendly relations with Russia despite conflicts of interests in Asia and Afghanistan, and resentment at the outcome of the congress of Berlin. He also reported on the nihilist agitations that culminated in the assassination of Alexander II. The Dufferins looked and played their ambassadorial parts to perfection. Dufferin was resplendent but never pompous, and enjoyed games, jokes, and family jollity; St Petersburg, though, was the least congenial of his postings. After the Liberals returned to office, Dufferin was transferred to Constantinople (June 1881). His conduct of this embassy and his shrewdness, lucidity, and confidence in his friends are well attested. His chief diplomatic activity was concerned with the Egyptian crisis, and in November 1882 he went to Egypt as special commissioner. He was entrusted with devising a new constitution for Egypt to remedy the abuses which had provoked the Arabi insurrection. Six months' work resulted in the reforms outlined in the Dufferin report on Egypt, which was published as a state paper in September 1883. Dufferin despised 'the cruelty, imbecility and abuses of Turkish rule', and judged Sultan Abdul Hamid the Terrible had a 'diseased and almost maniacal nature' (dispatch 679, 14 Dec 1883, PRO FO 78/3514).

Viceroy of India In 1884 Dufferin was nominated viceroy of India on the retirement of Lord Ripon. 'Dufferin is popular everywhere, having pleasant manners, ready wit, considerable power as a speaker, and a fair share of Irish "blarney"', Lord Derby noted. 'India is the prize to which he has long looked forward: & apart from ambition, he needs office, having been through much of a fortune not originally large' (Derby diary, 11 Sept 1884, Lpool RO). About this time Dufferin nearly succeeded in selling Clandeboye and the remnant of his estate, but the arrangement failed at a late stage. Dufferin relished the pomp of a viceroy's existence yet disavowed grandiose plans: 'I never had any ambition to distinguish my reign by a sensational policy' (Dufferin to Salisbury, 5 Feb 1888, BL OIOC). As to his personal position, he wrote:

> It is an odd thing to say, but dullness is certainly the characteristic of a viceroy's existence. All the people who surround him are younger than himself; he has no companions or playfellows; even the pretty women who might condescend to cheer him, it is better for him to keep at a distance; and, except occasionally, the business he has to deal with is of a very uninteresting and *terre à terre* description, for, though he would make a great mistake if he drowned himself in too much detail, it is well that he should know everything that goes on. (Dufferin to Sir William Gregory, 1 Jan 1888, India Office, Eur. F 130/29)

The policy of Dufferin's predecessor Lord Ripon, of 'Mid-Lothianizing India' with promises of self-government, had 'divided the country into two camps with Natives and Anglo-Indians yelping at each other from either side of a ditch' (Dufferin to Sir James Stephen, 28 July 1885, CUL). Dufferin enjoined a policy of conciliation and repose; recognizing the growing power of educated Indians, he was sympathetic to the formation of the Indian National Congress (1885–7), although aware of its implications for British hegemony. He promised educated Indians a larger share in provincial administration, but condemned incendiary speechifying. His greatest service was 'the quiet way in which he managed to restore the confidence between the Indian civil service and the Government of India which had been seriously shaken at the end of Ripon's administration', judged Lord Northbrook: 'Dufferin did this without throwing over Ripon' (Northbrook to Curzon, 19 Feb 1902, BL OIOC, Eur. F 111/179). Certainly many officials were devoted to him. 'A slight, spare man, with a strong face and a good figure, and charming in manner, no shyness or awkwardness, a touch of blarney, a quick temper, a slight or more than slight lisp, and a very decided will', wrote Sir Mortimer Durand. 'His speech is slow and rather hesitating, and he writes little, not having been trained to office work, but he is very quick at seizing the points of a subject; a man with more training in dealing with men than in dealing with papers' (Sykes, 152).

Dufferin's experiences in Ireland had given him a practical sympathy with tenants' rights and a distrust of unsound agricultural legislation. This position was reflected in several judicious measures introduced by his administration to protect the Indian peasant from exploitation: the Bengal Tenancy Act (1885), the Oudh Rent Act (1886), and the Punjab Land Tenures Act (1887). Although ethnocentric, he disliked racism. 'We are irritating the natives out here in exactly the same manner as for hundreds of years we have been irritating the Irish', he warned in deprecation of 'that intolerable and vulgar brutality which the strong English race always manifests towards more inferior and sensitive populations' (Dufferin to Sir Harry Verney, 6 Jan 1888, BL OIOC, Eur. F 130/29A).

The Panjdeh incident of March 1885, when Russian forces occupied a district claimed by the Afghans just before a sumptuous visit by the amir of Afghanistan to Rawalpindi, was deftly handled by Dufferin. Hostilities were averted, and after delineation of the Afghan frontier by an Anglo-Russian commission, the Russians ceased their infiltration in central Asia. Dufferin's management of this crisis was enhanced by his knowledge of Russia, gleaned in St Petersburg. The French government, supposing that Anglo-Russian hostilities were inevitable, had meanwhile signed a commercial treaty with upper Burma with the intention of extending their Indo-Chinese protectorate to the Indian frontier. Dufferin's remonstrances to King Thibaw were rejected, and on 20 October war was declared on Burma. Ten thousand troops marched from Rangoon, and after ten days, on 28 November 1885, occupied Mandalay. The Burmese kingdom was annexed on 1 January 1886, although the region was not pacified until after Dufferin's retirement. He was 'perfectly unprejudiced by any Jingo sentimentality' and regarded annexation 'as a great nuisance' bound to entail 'for some time … nothing but trouble and annoyance' (Dufferin to Kimberley, 14 Feb 1886, PRO NIre., D 1071/H/M1/5).

The last months of Dufferin's viceroyalty were disturbed by a press agitation against the Indian army's policy on venereal disease, and particularly by 'English ladies who have constituted themselves the champions of military chastity' (Dufferin to the duchess of Manchester, 6 June 1888, BL OIOC, Eur. F 130/29E). Dufferin retired from India in December 1888. Kipling's poem on this event, 'One Viceroy Resigns', is unfair in its picture of Dufferin drinking until two in the morning; he was notably abstemious, in contrast to many of his ancestors and descendants, who drank heavily. On 17 November 1888 he was advanced in the peerage to become marquess of Dufferin and Ava, and earl of Ava. Kipling wrote of a meeting with him at Naples in 1891:

> unlike the generality of Viceroys, Lord Dufferin *knew*. Of all his revelations and reminiscences, the sentence that stays with me is: 'And so, you know, there can be no room (or was it "allowances"?) for good intentions in one's work'. (Kipling, 94)

Rome and Paris In 1889 Dufferin resumed his diplomatic career as ambassador at Rome. He enjoyed this post, which carried little work but provided the most beautiful embassy in Europe, and enabled him to sail his yawl *The*

Lady Hermione in Mediterranean waters. His most important task was to prevent Italian colonial pretensions in east Africa from causing a serious conflict with Britain. Eventually, in March 1891, a protocol defining British and Italian interests in the region was signed.

Dufferin was appointed British ambassador to France in December 1891 and reached Paris in March 1892. 'No British Ambassador can so perfectly have fulfilled the French ideal of a *grand seigneur*', wrote a guest at the embassy.

> He brought to the discharge of his duties, a tact, charm, knowledge of men and affairs and … a radiant kindliness, that in combination can never have been equalled. Though by no means tall, he was still straight and graceful, and his presence made most men look common. (Armytage, 337–8)

Dufferin was initially vilified by the French press as a proven enemy of France in Syria and Burma, who had been sent to Paris to break the Franco-Russian entente and used secret funds to bribe journalists and statesmen. He was hurt by these criticisms, yet continued to delight his immediate circle. Bertrand Russell, who was an attaché in his Paris embassy, wrote in 1894: 'He is really a delicious man—so perfect and well-rounded. He was very gracious … and … treated me so affectionately' (Russell, 1.105). The most important affair that exercised Dufferin's diplomacy in 1893–6 was 'the scandalous shuffling and the tyrannical injustice of the French' in Siam (Dufferin to Rosebery, 27 July 1893, PRO NIre., D 1071/H/01/1), but he was also concerned with harmonizing Anglo-French colonial rivalries elsewhere. He retired from Paris in October 1896 after surpassing the age limit for an ambassador.

Retirement and death Dufferin received the following appointments and honours: KCB (1861), KP (1863), GCMG (1876), GCB (1883), and GCSI (1884). He was sworn of the privy council in 1868 and of the Irish privy council in 1897. He was elected FRS in 1865, honorary DCL of Oxford University (1879), honorary LLD of Cambridge University (1891), honorary freeman of the City of London (1889) and Edinburgh (1898), lord rector of St Andrews University (1890) and of Edinburgh University (1899), and lord warden of the Cinque Ports (1891). But these honours were tarnished by financial disgrace. He had always been imprudent with money, and had to resign the sinecure office of lord warden in 1895 because he could not afford £700 a year to maintain Walmer Castle. In 1897 he was induced by Whitaker Wright to become chairman of the London and Globe Finance Corporation, which speculated on a reckless scale in mining shares. This company in December 1900 announced its insolvency, and subsequently Wright was proved to be a swindler. Although Dufferin had no complicity in Wright's frauds, he felt implicated in the ruin of investors and himself sustained heavy losses. Also during 1900 his beloved eldest son was killed in the Second South African War and his youngest son was dangerously wounded. He died on 12 February 1902, at Clandeboye, and was buried in the private graveyard there known as the Campo Santo.

Dufferin as patron Dufferin improved his house after coming of age, showed a flair for interior arrangements, and transformed the surrounding fields with an idyllic landscaped park. He built a baronial private entrance at Helen's Bay station with a 2 mile avenue to Clandeboye. In honour of his mother he erected a folly called Helen's Tower, completed in 1862, for which Tennyson at his request wrote a poem. Dufferin once said that, second only to his mother, Sir Walter Scott was the formative influence of his life, and he commissioned several ambitious designs for an enchanted neo-Jacobean castle. With greater funds Dufferin would have proved as important as a private architectural patron as the third marquess of Bute. Instead, he indulged his imaginative gifts as a public patron. He rebuilt Rideau Hall, the Canadian governor-general's residence at Ottawa, and saved the fortifications and citadel at Quebec, which he hoped to transform into an American Carcassonne in the manner of Viollet-le-Duc. At Simla he built a viceregal lodge in the Elizabethan style.

Assessment Dufferin was imaginative, sympathetic, warm-hearted, and gloriously versatile. He pacified Lebanon, won the loyalty of Canadians, settled the principles for the government of Egypt, averted war with Russia, annexed Burma, made a fluent speech in dog-Latin in Iceland, replied in Greek to a Greek address at McGill University, skated Sir Roger de Coverley on a Montreal ice rink, made a lifelong study of Egyptian hieroglyphics, scandalized St Petersburg society by hopping and grunting like a pig while playing Dumb-crambo, startled Paris by bicycling publicly, and conversed in Persian with the shah. He enjoyed discretion, reticence, and good manners. He would never commit himself to an opinion 'until it becomes necessary to arrive at a practical decision' (Dufferin to Sir Mountstuart Grant-Duff, 12 Jan 1896, PRO NIre., D 1071 H/03/54). His charm and gaiety tended to eclipse his more solid virtues; but he was deliberate, tenacious, and unwavering in public policy, and observant and alert in all his dealings. 'I am a great believer in frivolity', he wrote (Dufferin to Lady Agatha Russell, 31 Dec 1887, BL OIOC, Eur. F 130/26E), but this was coupled with a passionate love of justice. 'He had read enormously, and his knowledge of books, pictures, and music was unbounded, while no one was too insignificant … for him to be kind to' (St Helier, 269). He was a man of rare discrimination who wrote elegant verses, sketched attractively, danced with graceful brio, and cultivated many literary friendships. His faults were trivial: he was lazy, vain, and over-sensitive to criticism. The worst charges directed at him—he was called 'the *enfant gâté* ["spoiled child"] of diplomacy' by Lord Rosebery in 1894 (*Private Diaries of … Algernon West*, 146), and 'a delightful literary humbug' by Lord George Hamilton in 1901 (Hamilton to Curzon, 3 Jan 1901, BL OIOC, Eur. C 125/6)—are not so terrible. His life, until the griefs of 1900, was unusually happy; he himself spread an unusual amount of happiness.

RICHARD DAVENPORT-HINES

Sources A. Lyall, *The life of the marquis of Dufferin and Ava*, 2 vols. (1905) • H. G. Nicolson, *Helen's tower* (1937) • C. E. D. Black, *The marquess of Dufferin and Ava* (1903) • A. T. Harrison, *The first marquess of Dufferin and Ava: Whig, Ulster landlord and imperial statesman* (1983) •

G. W. de Kiewit and F. H. Underhill, eds., *Dufferin–Carnarvon correspondence, 1874–78* (1955) • H. E. Maxwell, *Life and letters of George William Frederick, fourth earl of Clarendon*, 2 vols. (1913) • *The diary of Gathorne Hardy, later Lord Cranbrook, 1866–1892: political selections*, ed. N. E. Johnson (1981), 715 • T. H. Lewin, ed., *The Lewin letters … 1756–1884*, 2 vols. (1909), 164 • John, first earl of Kimberley, 'A journal of events during the Gladstone ministry, 1864–74', ed. E. Drus, *Camden miscellany, XXI*, CS, 3rd ser., 90 (1958), 28 • *Letters of Henry Adams, 1858–1891*, ed. W. C. Ford (1930), 307–8 • P. Sykes, *Sir Mortimer Durand* (1926) • R. Kipling, *Something of myself* (1937), 94 • P. Armytage, *By the clock of St James's* (1927), 337–8 • B. Russell, *The autobiography of Bertrand Russell*, 1 (1967), 105 • Lady St Helier [S. M. E. Jeune], *Memories of fifty years* (1909), 269 • *Private diaries of the Rt Hon. Sir Algernon West*, ed. H. G. Hutchinson (1922), 146 • BL OIOC, MS Eur. C 125/6 • Gladstone, *Diaries*

Archives BL OIOC, corresp. relating to India, MS Eur. F 130 • Duke U., Perkins L., corresp. • NA Canada, letters • PRO NIre., corresp. and papers | BL, corresp. with Campbell-Bannerman, Add. MS 41233 • BL, corresp. with Lord Carnarvon, Add. MS 60797 • BL, corresp. with Lord D'Abernon, Add. MSS 48937–48938 • BL, corresp. with Sir Charles Dilke, Add. MS 43883 • BL, corresp. with A. J. Fraser, Add. MSS 44912–44913 • BL, corresp. with W. E. Gladstone, Add. MS 44151 • BL, corresp. with Kingsley, Add. MS 41299 • BL, corresp. with Sir Austen Layard, Add. MSS 39024–39098, *passim* • BL OIOC, corresp. with Sir Henry Durand, MS Eur. D 727 • BL OIOC, corresp. with Sir James Fergusson, MS Eur. E 214 • BL OIOC, letters to Arthur Godley, MS Eur. F 102 • BL OIOC, letters to Sir Mountstuart Grant-Duff, MS Eur. F 234 • BL OIOC, corresp. with Sir Alfred Lyall, MS Eur. F 132 • BL OIOC, corresp. with Lord Northbrook, MS Eur. C 144 • BL OIOC, corresp. with Sir Edward Sladen, MS Eur. E 290 • Bodl. Oxf., corresp. with Benjamin Disraeli • Bodl. Oxf., corresp. with Lord Kimberley • Bodl. Oxf., Monk Bretton MSS • Borth. Inst., letters to Lord Halifax • CAC Cam., corresp. with Lord Randolph Churchill • CKS, letters to Edward Stanhope • CUL, Acton MSS • CUL, corresp. with Lord Hardinge • CUL, Stephen MSS • Devon RO, letters to duke and duchess of Somerset • Glos. RO, letters to Sir Michael Hicks Beach • Hatfield House, Hertfordshire, Salisbury MSS • Hove Central Library, Sussex, letters to Lord Wolseley and Lady Wolseley • Hughenden Manor, Buckinghamshire, Disraeli MSS • King's AC Cam., letters to Le Fanu family • LPL, Benson MSS • LPL, letters to Roundell Palmer • LPL, Tait MSS • LPL, Temple MSS • McMaster University Library, Hamilton, Ontario, corresp. with Sir Charles Crosthwaite • Metropolitan Toronto Reference Library, letters to Lady Dorothy Nevill • NAM, letters to Lord Roberts • NL Ire., letters to G. C. Brodrick • NL Scot., Blackwood MSS • NL Scot., corresp. mainly with Lord Rosebery • NYPL, Berg collection, Gregory MSS • PRO, corresp. with Lord Carnarvon, PRO 30/6 • PRO, corresp. with Lord Cromer, vols. v, vii • PRO, corresp. with Lord Granville, PRO 30/29 • PRO, corresp. with Sir Arthur Nicolson, PRO 30/81 • PRO, corresp. with Lord John Russell, PRO 30/22 • PRO, corresp. with Odo Russell, FO 918 • PRO, letters to Sir William White, FO 364/1–11 • U. Lpool L., Sydney Jones Library, letters to William Rathbone • Yale U., Beinecke L., Locker-Lampson MSS

Likenesses oils, 1831, repro. in Lyall, *Life of the marquess of Dufferin and Ava* • attrib. J. R. Swinton, oils, 1845, presumed Clandeboye, co. Down • A. Scheffer, oils, 1850, repro. in Lyall, *Life of the marquis of Dufferin and Ava*, vol. 1, facing p. 74 • J. R. Swinton, crayon drawing, 1850, repro. in Nicolson, *Helen's tower*, frontispiece • H. T. Wells, portrait, 1873–7, NA Canada; repro. in Kiewit and Underhill, eds., *Dufferin-Carnarvon correspondence*, frontispiece • photographs, *c.*1876, repro. in J. Hall, 'A forest of poles', *The Beaver* [Hudson Bay Company, Winnipeg], 66/3 (June–July 1986), 6, 10 • E. Boehm, statue, 1880–89, Calcutta • Marochetti, bust, 1880–89, probably Clandeboye, co. Down • G. F. Watts, oils, 1881, NPG [*see illus.*] • F. Holl, oils, 1884, probably Clandeboye, co. Down • T. B. Wingman, sketch, 1884, probably Clandeboye, co. Down • E. Norman, oils, *c.*1893, Gov. Art Coll. • B. Constant, oils, 1894, U. Edin.; repro. in Lyall, *Life of the marquis of Dufferin and Ava*, vol. 2, facing p. 240 • Pirou of Paris, photograph, 1896, repro. in D. Dawson, *A soldier diplomat* (1927), facing p. 228 • H. Rae, oils, exh. RA 1901, Clandeboye, co. Down; repro. in Nicholson, *Helen's tower*, facing p. 245 • F. S. Baden-Powell, silhouette, *c.*1902, probably Clandeboye, co. Down • photograph, 1902 (posthumous), PRO NIre., Dufferin and Ava MSS • Ατη [A. Thompson], chromolithograph caricature, NPG; repro. in *VF* (9 April 1870) • H. Furniss, ink sketch, Palace of Westminster, London • C. Holl, stipple (after H. T. Wells; Grillion's Club series), BM, NPG • Klinkicht, wood-engraving (after photograph), BM; repro. in *ILN* (14 Nov 1891) [supplement] • Lock & Whitfield, woodburytype photograph, NPG; repro. in T. Cooper, *Men of mark: a gallery of contemporary portraits* (1876) • Maclure & Macdonald, lithograph, NPG • F. W. Pomeroy, statue, Belfast • C. Silvy, carte-de-visite, V&A • C. W. Walton, lithograph, BM • D. Wehrschmidt, mezzotint and etched remarque (after F. Hall, exh. RA 1885), BM, NG Ire. • oils (as a schoolboy), probably Clandeboye, co. Down • photographs, NPG • silhouette, NPG

Wealth at death £108,548 9*s.* 8*d.*: probate, 17 March 1902, *CGPLA Eng. & Wales*

Blackwood, George Frederick (1838–1880), army officer, was the second son of Major William Blackwood of the Bengal army, and grandson of William *Blackwood, founder of the publishing firm. He was born at Moradabad, Bengal, was educated at the Edinburgh Academy and at Addiscombe College, and was commissioned a second lieutenant in the Bengal artillery on 11 December 1857. He arrived in India during the Indian mutiny, and was at once appointed to command two guns in Colonel Wilkinson's Rohilkhand column. He was promoted first lieutenant on 27 August 1858, and was adjutant first to the Bareilly and Gwalior divisions and then to the 22nd and 19th brigades of Royal Artillery from 1859 to 1864.

Blackwood was promoted captain on 20 February 1867, and in 1872 was appointed to command the artillery attached to General Bourchier's column in the Lushai expedition. He was present at the attacks on Tipai-Mukh, Kungnung, and Taikum. His services were specially mentioned in the general's dispatch of 19 March 1872, and he was promoted brevet major on 11 September. He gave further evidence of his ability as an artillery officer by his able report on the use of guns in such country as that in which he had recently served, with views on the best calibre for mountain guns, which was printed by the Indian government and circulated among its officers. Blackwood was promoted major on 10 February 1875, and after temporarily commanding a battery of Royal Horse Artillery came to England on sick leave. He thus missed the first Afghan campaign of 1878–9, but was in India when, on the news of Cavagnari's death, it was determined to once more occupy both Kabul and Kandahar.

Blackwood was posted to the command of E battery B brigade of Royal Horse Artillery, and ordered to join the force destined for Kandahar. While stationed there the news arrived of the advance of Ayub Khan, and a column was ordered out under the command of Brigadier-General Burrows to assist the wali placed in command by Abdur Rahman Khan and to investigate the strength of the enemy. To that column Blackwood's battery was attached; the column was cut to pieces at the battle of Maiwand on 27 July 1880, where Blackwood was killed and buried in

George Frederick Blackwood (1838–1880), by London Stereoscopic Co.

the field, and two of his guns lost. They were subsequently recovered after Ayub's defeat on 1 September 1880, and were presented to Roberts by the government.

H. M. STEPHENS, *rev.* JAMES LUNT

Sources Lord Roberts [F. S. Roberts], *Forty-one years in India*, 2 (1897) • B. Robson, *The road to Kabul: the Second Afghan War, 1878–1881* (1986) • H. B. Hanna, *The Second Afghan War*, 3 vols. (1899–1910) • L. Maxwell, *My God! Maiwand* (1979) • B. Robson, 'Maiwand, 27th July 1880', *Journal of the Society for Army Historical Research*, 51 (1973) • C. H. T. MacFetridge and J. P. Warren, eds., *Tales of the mountain gunners* (1973) • Boase, *Mod. Eng. biog.*
Archives NL Scot., family corresp. • U. Cam., Centre of South Asian Studies, corresp. and papers
Likenesses London Stereoscopic Co., photograph, repro. in S. H. Shadbolt, *The Afghan campaigns of 1878–1880* (1882) [*see illus.*]
Wealth at death £2641 7*s.* 11*d.*: confirmation, 29 Oct 1880, *CCI*

Blackwood, Hariot Georgina Hamilton-Temple-, marchioness of Dufferin and Ava (1843–1936), vicereine of India, was born on 5 February 1843, the eldest child of four sons and three daughters of Archibald Rowan-Hamilton (1818–1860) of Killyleagh Castle, co. Down, in Ireland, and his wife, Catherine Anne (1820–1919), daughter of the Revd George Caldwell. She married on 23 October 1862, in the drawing-room at Killyleagh Castle, Frederick Hamilton-Blackwood, fifth Baron Dufferin and Claneboye (1826–1902) [*see* Blackwood, Frederick Temple Hamilton-Temple-], who was elevated to the earldom of Dufferin in 1871 and became first marquess of Dufferin and Ava in 1888. They had three daughters and six sons. Theirs was a good-humoured and affectionate marriage. She was a child bride of innocence and beauty who seemed 'delicate but very gentle and pleasing' (*Later Letters of Lady Augusta Stanley*, 91). She matured into a strong, decisive woman with a magnificent presence. 'Of a reserved nature, she gave her love and confidence sparingly but, when she did, the recipient was rich indeed' (Chapman-Huston, 90).

Accompanying her husband to Canada in 1872, Lady Dufferin soon proved to be that rarity, a governor's wife who strengthened her husband's hand. Her popularity was probably unsurpassed among governor-generals' wives in Canada. She was resilient, zestful, attentive, shrewd, and kind, but never blasé or spoilt by her official experiences. Her dignity and devotion to duty were both as natural as they were undeviating. An intrepid traveller in rough or frightening conditions, her endurance and stoicism were formidable. In Canada, as in later postings, it was a distinct advantage that:

> she could spend the night in a rough country sledge, or sleep in her clothes on a truss of hay, and yet appear in the morning as fresh and neat, and spick and span, as though she had had the most elaborate toilet appliances at her disposal. (Hamilton, 122)

She was very unhappy at leaving Canada on 31 August 1878.

In 1879–81 Lady Dufferin was ambassadress at St Petersburg and in 1881–4 at Constantinople. The Dufferins in all their embassies were celebrated for their hospitality and kindness, treating their staff with charming informality; visitors felt as if they were staying in a country-house party. Despite her shyness, she was a consummate actress in amateur theatricals: her lead in Sheridan's *The Critic* at Constantinople in 1881 was a particular success. Notwithstanding her Presbyterian upbringing, she had a great sense of fun and a feeling heart.

The Dufferins arrived in India as viceroy and vicereine in December 1884. Lady Dufferin took lessons in Hindustani and later in photography. An indefatigible organizer, traveller, and hostess, she most memorably used her energies to found the National Association for Supplying Female Medical Aid to the Women of India, often known as the Countess of Dufferin Fund, in 1885. Its purpose was to relieve the suffering by illness and child bearing of Indian women. Her plan was to recruit and train women doctors, nurses, and midwives to provide medical advice and attendance under conditions which respected patients' wishes. With gentle, persistent authority she presided over countless fund-raising meetings; by the time she left India her scheme had been adopted in every province, and there were Countess of Dufferin Fund hospitals and dispensaries for women in all the principal states. This great act of constructive charity was commemorated by Rudyard Kipling in his 'Song of the Women'. She was depressed at leaving India, and the demonstrations of gratitude were unusually numerous and sincere. She was a great benefactor of Indian women, compassionate and uncondescending in her manner, whose initiative introduced Western ideas of hygiene and medicine into many parts of India: her work saved innumerable lives.

Accompanying her husband in his embassies to Italy and France, Lady Dufferin maintained her reputation as the most effective diplomatic wife of her generation. According to George I of Greece, 'there was no lady in Europe who could enter a room like Lady Dufferin' (Nicolson, 145). She retired with her husband to Clandeboye in co. Down in 1896, although for much of her long widowhood she lived in a small house in Tedworth Square, Chelsea. Her sons were always short of money, and she made selfless economies to relieve their burdens.

Hariot Georgina Hamilton-Temple-Blackwood, marchioness of Dufferin and Ava (1843–1936), by Barraud, pubd 1890

Lady Dufferin published her letters to her mother in the form of journals: *Our Viceregal Life in India* (2 vols., 1889), *My Canadian Journal* (1891), and *My Russian and Turkish Journals* (1916). Her books focus on ceremonials, journeys, and festivities rather than high policy, but are vivid, picturesque, and amusing. They establish her near the forefront of nineteenth-century women travel writers. She savoured the ridiculous, but curbed her satiric powers in public. Her unpublished correspondence is often as fluent and elegant as her books. Lady Dufferin received the Crown of India (1884) and the Royal Order of Victoria and Albert (1889), and was created DBE in 1917. The Ottoman sultan and shah of Persia respectively bestowed on her the grand cross of the Chefakat (1883) and the order of the Lion and the Sun (1887).

Lady Dufferin outlived her six sons and her eldest daughter: Archibald, the eldest son, was killed in the Second South African War in 1900; Terence died of pneumonia in 1918; the third son, Sydney, died shortly after birth, on 29 May 1867; the fourth, Ian, died similarly, on 6 August 1868; Basil was killed in action in 1917; and Frederick, the youngest, was lost in an aviation accident in 1930. The eldest daughter, Helen, Viscountess Novar, died in 1930; Lady Dufferin's two younger daughters survived her. The marchioness died of arteriosclerosis and heart failure on 25 October 1936 at her home in 4 Wellesley House, Sloane Square, Chelsea, and was buried on 28 October at Clandeboye. RICHARD DAVENPORT-HINES

Sources PRO NIre., Dufferin and Ava MSS • H. G. Hamilton-Temple-Blackwood [marchioness of Dufferin and Ava], *Our viceregal life in India* (1889) • Marchioness of Dufferin and Ava [H. G. Blackwood], *My Canadian journal* (1891) • H. G. Hamilton-Temple-Blackwood, *My Russian and Turkish journals* (1916) • *The Times* (26 Oct 1936) • H. G. Nicolson, *Helen's tower* (1937) • *Later letters of Lady Augusta Stanley, 1864–1876*, ed. A. V. Baillie and H. Bolitho [1929] • D. Chapman-Huston, *The lamp of memory* (1949) • F. Hamilton, *The vanished pomps of yesterday* (1919) • 'Lady Dufferin's life in India', *The Spectator* (23 Nov 1889), 724–5 • *The Athenaeum* (21 Nov 1891), 678–9 • J. Hall, 'A forest of poles', *The Beaver*, 66 (1986), 4–14 • Lord Dufferin and others, *Clandeboye* (1985) • d. cert. • GEC, *Peerage*

Archives PRO NIre., corresp., journals, and papers | CUL, Templewood MSS

Likenesses Barraud, photograph, pubd 1890, NPG [*see illus.*] • photographs, Mary Evans Picture Library, London • photographs, NA Canada • portraits, Clandeboye, co. Down

Wealth at death £50,996 9*s.* 3*d.*: resworn probate, 5 Jan 1937, *CGPLA Eng. & Wales*

Blackwood, Helen Selina, Lady Dufferin and Claneboye. *See* Hay, Helen Selina, countess of Gifford (1807–1867).

Blackwood, Henry (*d.* 1614), physician, was the son of William Blackwood (*d.* *c.*1547) and Helen Reid (*d.* *c.*1547) and elder brother of the writer Adam *Blackwood, who was also a judge of the parliament of Poitiers. He was born in Dunfermline, and after studying *belles-lettres* and philosophy, was sent by his uncle, Robert Reid, bishop of Orkney, to the University of Paris, where, about 1551, he taught philosophy. After studying medicine he graduated MD, was incorporated a member of the College of Physicians of Paris, and ultimately became dean of the faculty. At one time physician to the duc de Longueville, he was remembered for remaining in Paris to treat patients during an outbreak of plague. Blackwood died in 1614. He edited *In organum Aristotelis commentaria*, *Collatio philosophiae atque medicinae*, and *De claris medicis*, and left in manuscript 'Animadversio in omnes Galeni libros', 'Hippocratis quaedam cum MSS. collata', 'In Alexandrum Trallianum comment.', and 'Locorum quorumdam Plinii explicatio'. *Hippocratis Coi prognosticorum libri tres, cum Latina interpretatione, ad veterum exemplarium fidem emendati et recogniti* (1625) was attributed to him, but was really edited by his son, Henry, professor of medicine and surgery at Paris, who died at Rouen on 17 October 1634. George Blackwood, an uncle, taught philosophy at Paris in 1571, took holy orders, and obtained preferment in France. T. F. HENDERSON, *rev.* RACHEL E. DAVIES

Sources G. Mackenzie, *The lives and characters of the most eminent writers of the Scots nation*, 3 (1722), 479–87 • D. Irving, *Lives of Scotish writers*, 1 (1839), 168–9 • L. Moréri, *Le grand dictionnaire historique*, 18th edn, 8 vols. (1740), vol. 2, p. 489 • Chambers, *Scots.* (1855)

Blackwood, Sir Henry, first baronet (**1770–1832**), naval officer, was born in co. Down, Ireland, on 28 December 1770, the fourth son of Sir John Blackwood, second baronet (*d.* 27 Feb 1799), of Ballyleidy, co. Down, and of his wife, Dorcas, daughter of James Stevenson, who after her husband's death was created a peeress of Ireland, as Baroness Dufferin and Claneboye (*d.* 8 Feb 1807). In April 1781 he entered the navy as a volunteer on the frigate *Artois*,

Sir Henry Blackwood, first baronet (1770–1832), by John Hoppner, 1806

with Captain Macbride, and in her was present at the battle on the Dogger Bank. He afterwards served with captains Montgomery and Whitshed, and for four years in the *Trusty* with Commodore Cosby in the Mediterranean. In 1790 he was signal midshipman on board the *Queen Charlotte* with Lord Howe, by whom he was made lieutenant on 3 November 1790. In 1791 he was in the frigate *Proserpine* with Captain Curzon, and towards the close of that year obtained leave to go to France in order to improve his French. For most of 1792 he was in Paris, and on one occasion was in much danger, having been denounced as a spy, and eventually he had to flee for his life.

Blackwood was almost immediately appointed to the frigate *Active*, from which, a few months later, he was transferred to the *Invincible* at the special request of Captain Pakenham. Of this ship Blackwood was first lieutenant on 1 June 1794, and as such was promoted, along with all the other first lieutenants of the ships of the line, on 6 July. He was immediately appointed to the *Megaera*, and continued in her, attached to the fleet under Lord Howe and afterwards Lord Bridport, until he was promoted captain on 2 June 1795. After a few months in command of the guardship at Hull, Blackwood was appointed to the frigate *Brilliant* (28 guns), which for the next two years was attached to the North Sea Fleet under the command of Admiral Duncan. Early in 1798 the *Brilliant* was sent out to join Admiral Waldegrave on the Newfoundland station; and on 26 July, while standing close in to the Bay of Santa Cruz in quest of a French privateer, she was chased by two large French frigates. By seamanship and courage, Blackwood succeeded in checking the pursuit and in escaping.

Early in 1799 the *Brilliant* returned to England, and Blackwood was appointed to the frigate *Penelope* (36 guns), in which, after a few months of channel service, he was sent to the Mediterranean, and employed during the winter and following spring in the close blockade of Malta. On the night of 30 March 1800 the *Guillaume Tell* (80 guns), taking advantage of a southerly gale and intense darkness, ran out of the harbour. As she passed the *Penelope*, Blackwood immediately pursued. Until dawn, the *Penelope* successfully engaged her with broadsides, inflicting much damage. At five o'clock the *Lion* (64 guns), and some little time afterwards the *Foudroyant* (80 guns), came up, and after a gallant resistance the *Guillaume Tell* surrendered; that she was brought to action at all was due to the *Penelope*. Nelson wrote to Blackwood from Palermo (5 April 1800): 'Your conduct and character on the late glorious occasion stamps your fame beyond the reach of envy. It was like yourself; it was like the Penelope' (*Blackwood*, 7).

On the peace of Amiens in 1802 the *Penelope* was paid off; and in April 1803, when war again broke out, Blackwood was appointed to the *Euryalus* (36 guns). During the next two years he was employed on the coast of Ireland or in the channel, and in July 1805 was sent to watch the movements of the allied fleet under Villeneuve after its defeat by Sir Robert Calder. On his return with the news that Villeneuve had gone to Cadiz, he stopped on his way to London to see Nelson, who went with him to the Admiralty and received his final instructions to resume the command of the fleet without delay. Blackwood, in the *Euryalus*, accompanied him to Cadiz, and was appointed to the command of the inshore squadron, with the duty of keeping the admiral informed of every movement of the enemy. He was offered a line-of-battle ship, but preferred to remain in the *Euryalus*, believing that he would have more opportunity of distinction; for Villeneuve, he was convinced, would not venture out in the presence of Nelson. When he saw the combined fleets outside, Blackwood could not but regret his decision. On the morning of 21 October 1805, in writing to his wife, he added: 'My signal just made on board the Victory—I hope to order me into a vacant line-of-battle ship.' This signal was made at six o'clock, and from that time until after noon, when the shot was already flying thickly over the *Victory*, Blackwood remained on board, receiving the admiral's last instructions, and, together with Captain Hardy, witnessing the codicil to Nelson's will. He was then ordered to return to his ship. 'God bless you, Blackwood,' said Nelson, shaking him by the hand, 'I shall never speak to you again.' As Blackwood himself wrote:

> He not only gave me the command of all the frigates, for the purpose of assisting disabled ships, but he also gave me a latitude seldom or ever given, that of making any use I pleased of his name in ordering any of the sternmost line-of-battle ships to do what struck me as best. (*Nelson Despatches*, 7.226)

Immediately after the battle Lord Collingwood hoisted his flag on board the *Euryalus*, but after ten days removed it to the *Queen*, and the *Euryalus* was sent home with dispatches and with the French admiral. Blackwood was thus in England at the time of Nelson's funeral (8 January 1806), when he acted as train-bearer of the chief mourner, Sir Peter Parker, the aged admiral of the fleet.

After this, Blackwood was appointed to the *Ajax* (80 guns), in which he joined Collingwood off Cadiz on the first anniversary of Trafalgar, and early in the following year was detached with the squadron under Sir John Duckworth in the expedition up the Dardanelles. At the entrance of the straits, on the night of 14 February 1806, the *Ajax* caught fire through the drunken carelessness of the purser's steward, and was totally destroyed, with the loss of nearly half the ship's company. Blackwood himself was picked up hanging on to an oar, almost perished with cold, after nearly an hour in the water. During the subsequent operations in the straits he served as a volunteer on board the flagship, and arrived in England in May.

Blackwood was now offered the situation of pay commissioner at the Navy Board, which he declined, preferring to be appointed to the command of the *Warspite* (74 guns). In this, after some uneventful service in the North Sea, he again went out to the Mediterranean, where the principal duty of the fleet was the very harassing blockade of Toulon. Here, for some time during the summer of 1810, Blackwood commanded the inshore squadron, and on 20 July drove back a sortie made by a much stronger French force. He returned to England at the end of 1812, but remained in command of the *Warspite* for another year. In May 1814, on the occasion of the visit of the allied sovereigns, he was appointed captain of the fleet under the duke of Clarence, a special service which was nominally rewarded by a baronetcy (September 1814). On 4 June 1814 he attained the rank of rear-admiral, and in August 1819 was nominated a KCB, and appointed commander-in-chief in the East Indies, from which station he returned in December 1822. He became vice-admiral in May 1825, and from 1827 to 1830 he was commander-in-chief at the Nore.

Blackwood married three times. On 12 January 1795 he married Jane Mary, *née* Crosbie; she died on 19 January 1798, without surviving children. On 3 June 1799 he married Eliza, daughter of Martin *Waghorn; they had one son (later the second baronet) and she died on 30 October 1802. On 9 May 1803 he married Harriet, *née* Gore; they had several children and she died on 5 May 1851. Two of his sons became captains in the navy.

Still in the full vigour of life, Blackwood died after a short illness, variously stated as typhus or scarlet fever, on 17 December 1832, at Ballyleidy, the seat of his eldest brother, Lord Dufferin and Claneboye. Blackwood was a brilliant officer, possessing all the qualities that were required for sea command. Nelson's opinion, and the authority he deputed at Trafalgar, were the high point of his career. J. K. LAUGHTON, *rev.* ANDREW LAMBERT

Sources G. S. Graham, *Great Britain in the Indian Ocean: a study of maritime enterprise, 1810–1850* (1967) • J. S. Corbett, *The campaign of Trafalgar* (1910) • *Blackwood*, 34 (1833) • J. Marshall, *Royal naval biography*, 1/2 (1823), 642–51 • Burke, *Peerage* • *Letters and despatches of Viscount Nelson*, ed. J. K. Laughton (1886), 7.140, 226

Archives PRO NIre., papers | BL, letters to Lord Nelson, Add. MSS 34915–34931, *passim*

Likenesses J. Hoppner, oils, 1806, NMM [*see illus.*] • C. Turner, mezzotint, pubd 1833 (after J. Hoppner), BM

Blackwood, John (1818–1879), publisher and journal editor, was born on 7 December 1818 at Salisbury Road, Edinburgh, the sixth son of Janet Steuart (1779–1849) and the publisher William *Blackwood (1776–1834). Educated at Edinburgh high school (1826–31), the alma mater of Walter Scott, and at the University of Edinburgh (1831–5), John Blackwood subsequently undertook a three-year tour of continental Europe, accompanied in part by his brothers Robert and Alexander, and chaperoned by his classics tutor, William Hay. On his return in 1838, John Blackwood began an apprenticeship with the London publishers George Whitaker & Co., where he remained until 1840. In December of that year Robert and Alexander, by then heads of the Blackwood firm, decided to open a London office at 22 Pall Mall, and John, now a partner in the firm, was chosen to run it. Over the next five and a half years he established the firm's presence in the capital, making close personal connections with, among others, William Thackeray, Laurence Lockhart, Edward Bulwer-Lytton, and John Delane, later to become editor of *The Times*. Through Delane, with whom he shared lodgings for several years, he was introduced to writers who were later to form a core grouping of *Blackwood's Magazine* contributors, including generals Edward Bruce Hamley and William Hamley, Frederick Hardman (French correspondent of *The Times*), and Laurence Oliphant.

In July 1845, four months after the death of his brother Alexander, John Blackwood returned to Edinburgh to take over as editor of *Blackwood's Edinburgh Magazine*. In 1852, on the death of Robert Blackwood, John assumed control of the firm, working in partnership with his brother Major William Blackwood, who had returned from India in 1848 to manage financial matters. Now financially secure, John Blackwood married Julia Blandford in 1854 and moved into the New Town dwelling of 3 Randolph Crescent. They had a son, John, and a daughter, Mary, who was to write the publishing memoirs of her father in 1898. After Major Blackwood's death from pneumonia in 1861, John reorganized the family business, making his nephew William *Blackwood (1836–1912) a co-partner, and establishing a four-strong editorial team along with William, his London office manager, Joseph Munt Langford, and the Edinburgh office manager, George Simpson. Between them, they strengthened the firm's lists and established its magazine at the forefront of mid-Victorian literary production.

John Blackwood's editorial flair, warmth of character, and friendly openness led to important and lasting literary relationships with leading authors of the mid-nineteenth century. Although conservative and paternalistic in manner, during his thirty-one-year career he was to gain the trust of, and publish, Elizabeth Barrett Browning, Edward Bulwer-Lytton, Charles Lever, Charles Reade, Richard D. Blackmore, Thomas Hardy, Margaret Oliphant, George Henry Lewes, and George Eliot, among others. Anthony Trollope, seeking a place for experimental work, anonymously serialized *Nina Balatka* (1867) and *Linda*

Tressel (1868) in *Blackwood's Magazine*. The experiments were not a success, and it would be another ten years before Trollope's work featured again in the magazine.

Under John Blackwood's guidance, the firm also became involved in publishing travel and exploration works. James Augustus Grant and John Hanning Speke's accounts of searching for the Nile River source in Africa were best-sellers for the firm in 1864 and 1865. Between 1852 and 1879, *Blackwood's Magazine* featured Frederick Hardman on Africa, Richard Burton on India and east Africa, Sir Henry Brackenbury on the Second Anglo-Asante War, Sir Garnet Wolseley on expeditions in Canada and Egypt, and Laurence Oliphant on Japan and the Crimea. But it was undoubtedly John Blackwood's connection with George Eliot, begun in 1857 with the anonymous publication in *Blackwood's Magazine* of *Scenes of Clerical Life*, which was to be one of his greatest contributions to British literary culture; with the exception of *Romola*, John Blackwood was to publish all of her major novels. Although relationships between the author and publisher proved at times fraught and difficult, the result was an unusually strong and personal connection that lasted until Blackwood's death on 29 October 1879 at Strathtyrum, St Andrews, his country home for twenty years. He was buried on 5 November 1879 in the family mausoleum on Calton Hill in Edinburgh. DAVID FINKELSTEIN

Sources F. D. Tredrey, *The house of Blackwood, 1804–1954* (1954) • Mrs G. Porter, *John Blackwood* (1898), vol. 3 of *Annals of a publishing house* (1897–8) • G. S. Haight, *George Eliot: a biography* (1968); repr. (1985) • *A selection from the obituary notices of the late John Blackwood* (privately printed, Edinburgh, 1880) • *Wellesley index*, vol. 1 • *CGPLA Eng. & Wales* (1880)

Archives NL Scot., corresp. • NL Scot., MSS | Bodl. Oxf., letters to Benjamin Disraeli • Herts. ALS, corresp. with Lord Lytton • NL Scot., letters to Lord Brougham

Likenesses J. W. Gordon, oils, exh. RA 1857, Scot. NPG • wood-engraving, pubd 1879 (after photograph by L. Suscipi), NPG; repro. in *ILN* (15 Nov 1879) • oils, Scot. NPG; repro. in Tredrey, *House of Blackwood* • print, NPG • sepia etching, NPG

Wealth at death £51,747 11*s.* 4*d.*: confirmation, 12 Jan 1880, *CCI* • £49,791 10*s.* 8*d.*: corrective value of estate, 18 May 1880, *CCI* • £661 2*s.* 5*d.*: additional estate, eik granted, 30 May 1881, *CCI* • £2152 6*s.* 8*d.*: second eik granted, 24 April 1889, *CCI*

Blackwood, William (1776–1834), publisher and founder of *Blackwood's Edinburgh Magazine*, was born in Edinburgh on 20 November 1776, the second son of Alexander Blackwood (1736–1802), descended from a family of silk mercers, and Janet Drysdale. On finishing his formal education at the age of fourteen, Blackwood entered into a six-year apprenticeship with the Edinburgh booksellers Bell and Bradfute, located in Parliament Square. Through Mrs Bradfute, wife of one of the firm's partners, William Blackwood met his future wife, Janet Steuart (1779–1849). He completed his apprenticeship in 1796, and subsequently undertook further training in other areas of the publishing trade, superintending the Glasgow branch of the Edinburgh publishers Mundell & Co. for a year, serving as a partner with the antiquarian bookseller and auctioneer Robert Ross for another, and working for two years in London in the antiquarian department of the booksellers Cuthill. In 1804 Blackwood opened a shop at

William Blackwood (1776–1834), by Sir William Allan, 1830?

64 South Bridge, Edinburgh, specializing in acquiring and selling rare books. The business was a success, and in October 1805 he married Janet Steuart; in 1806 they moved to Salisbury Road, where their nine children, seven boys and two girls, were born and raised.

By 1810 Blackwood had begun experimenting in publishing, producing historical works and publishing a biography of John Knox. Blackwood's breakthrough occurred in 1811, when he was appointed the Edinburgh agent for the publisher John Murray, becoming an important link in the distribution of the latest works from London. Blackwood consolidated his position in the trade by becoming the agent in March 1813 for James and John Ballantyne, printers of Walter Scott's novels. This arrangement paved the way in 1816 for Blackwood and John Murray to co-publish Walter Scott's *Tales of my Landlord*, comprising the novels *Old Mortality* and *Black Dwarf*. It is said that Scott's response to Blackwood's suggestions for improvements to *Black Dwarf*, made during production and in consultation with William Gifford, editor of Murray's *Quarterly Review*, was an acerbic comment that 'I belong to the Death-Head Hussars who neither give nor receive criticism'. Scott's publishing connection with Blackwood was terminated shortly afterwards.

In 1816 Blackwood moved his firm to the more spacious New Town premises of 17 Princes Street. A second and final move was made to 45 George Street in 1830. By 1817 Blackwood had begun concentrating his business in publishing, and in April of that year he launched the *Edinburgh Monthly Magazine* under the joint editorship of James Cleghorn and Thomas Pringle. Originally envisaged as a 'more nimble, more frequent, more familiar' tory alternative to the whig-orientated quarterly *Edinburgh Review*, the first six issues failed to live up to the publisher's vision. After firing Pringle and Cleghorn, Blackwood took editorial control and relaunched the journal in October 1817 as *Blackwood's Edinburgh Magazine*, with new contributors and editorial input from members of his literary coterie, who included John Gibson Lockhart, John Wilson (Christopher North), and James Hogg. The first issue, which included a new blend of literary and political articles and fiction, anonymous attacks on Leigh Hunt, the 'cockney school' of poetry, and, in the mock biblical 'Chaldee manuscript', a ferociously satirical attack on Edinburgh society, set the tone for future issues. Those who smarted most under the attacks were quick to retaliate, bringing lawsuits and libel actions against the magazine, which Blackwood endured on behalf of his editorial team, some of whom fled Edinburgh for the safety of the Lake District until the furore died down. Frightened by the storm caused by this upstart journal, Baldwin, Cradock & Co. (Blackwood's London agents), and Oliver and Boyd (Blackwood's printers), severed their connections with the firm. Leigh Hunt demanded the identity of 'Z', the anonymous author of the attack on him, and for months pamphlet wars raged between pro- and anti-Blackwood camps. Literary hostilities reached a climax in 1821, when John Gibson Lockhart challenged John Scott, rival editor of the *London Magazine*, to a duel. Lockhart's second, G. H. Christie, faced Scott instead, mortally wounding him with his second shot. Future Blackwoodians were confined by Blackwood to the printed page for their literary quarrels.

Bringing home the first number of his new magazine, Blackwood is said to have presented it to his wife with the words, 'There's ma Maga-zine'. In affectionate parody, the journal became known to future generations of editors, contributors, and readers as 'Maga'. Maga's rising reputation brought competition from London—the *London Magazine*, for example, was begun in 1820 specifically in response to the journal. Blackwood, however, consolidated his initial success by attracting a core of well-placed writers to work for him, including the Irishmen William Maginn and Samuel Ferguson, John Galt, David M. Moir (Delta), and Thomas De Quincey. The magazine also featured occasional reviews by Walter Scott, fiction by Samuel Warren and Susan Ferrier, and work by Samuel Taylor Coleridge. In 1822 the magazine began a regular feature, *Noctes Ambrosianae*, an extremely popular, imaginative series of collaborative, colloquial, and discursive essays combining politics and literary and cultural criticism, written collaboratively by several Blackwood contributors, chief among them being John Wilson, James Hogg, and Robert Sym. After 1825 John Wilson became the main writer of the series, which ran until 1835.

Throughout the 1820s and early 1830s Blackwood turned his firm, William Blackwood & Sons, into the leading Scottish publisher of the period, printing seminal works of fiction, history, and biography. A technique pioneered by Blackwood was the publishing in book form of fiction first serialized in the magazine, predating Charles Dickens's use of such marketing strategies by several years. Works featured in this way included Susan Ferrier's *Marriage* (1818) and *Inheritance* (1824), John Galt's *The Ayrshire Legatees* (1820–21) and *Annals of the Parish* (1821), and David M. Moir's *The Autobiography of Mansie Wauch* (1824–8). Other important Blackwood publications included John Gibson Lockhart's *Peter's Letters to his Kinfolk* (1819) and Thomas Hamilton's *Annals of the Peninsular War* (1829), as well as various learned journals and legal, medical, and theological texts. Blackwood also took on civic responsibilities, becoming a major figure in Edinburgh tory politics as an active member of the Edinburgh town council. He was made a bailie of the city by the council in 1820, and in 1828 was elected commissioner of police, a post he was to discharge with great vigour until shortly before his death at Salisbury Road, Edinburgh, on 16 September 1834. He was buried in the Calton cemetery in Edinburgh. The editorship of the magazine was taken over in 1845 by John *Blackwood, Blackwood's sixth son. The William *Blackwood (1836–1912) who was editor from 1879 was his grandson. DAVID FINKELSTEIN

Sources F. D. Tredrey, *The house of Blackwood, 1804–1954* (1954) · Mrs Oliphant, *William Blackwood and his sons* (1897), vols. 1–2 of *Annals of a publishing house* (1897–8) · I. C. Blackwood, *The early house of Blackwood* (1900) · R. Morrison and C. Baldick, eds., *Tales of terror from Blackwood's Magazine* (1995) · *Wellesley index*, vol. 1

Archives NL Scot., corresp. | BL OIOC, letters to Sir John McNeill, MS Eur. D 1165 · Inst. CE, letters to Thomas Telford · NL Scot., letters to his wife [copies] · NL Scot., letters to J. W. Croker; letters to James Hogg; corresp. with John Lee; letters to William Maginn; letters to James McQueen; corresp. with Sir Walter Scott; letters to John Wilson · U. Edin. L., corresp. with David Laing

Likenesses W. Allan, oils, 1830?, Scot. NPG [*see illus.*] · line engraving (after W. Allan?), Scot. NPG

Blackwood, William (1836–1912), literary editor and publisher, was born on 13 July 1836 at Lucknow, India, eldest son of Major William Blackwood (1810–1861) and Emma Moore. In 1842 he was sent back to the family home in Ainslie Place, Edinburgh, to begin his education at the Edinburgh Academy. After a stint at the University of Edinburgh William completed his education studying at the Sorbonne in Paris (1854–6), and at Heidelberg. In 1857 he entered the family publishing business started by his grandfather William *Blackwood (1776–1834), then co-partnered by his father and his uncle John *Blackwood. His father's death in 1861 led to a reorganization of the company, and in early 1862 William was made a partner in the business, in charge of the London office. As his uncle's right-hand man, William was intimately involved in negotiating with, and publishing, some of the most important writers of the period including George Eliot, Charles Lever, Margaret Oliphant, Anthony Trollope, and A. W. Kinglake.

After John Blackwood's death in 1879 William assumed sole responsibility for the company and its magazine. Blackwood's publishing successes over the next two decades were few but included Anthony Trollope's posthumous *An Autobiography* in 1883. The entrance of David Storr Meldrum as literary adviser in 1894, however, brought a renewed revival to the company's lists and to

William Blackwood (1836–1912), by William Logsdail

the magazine. His literary judgement influenced William Blackwood's decision to publish Stephen Crane, Henry Lawson, Miles Franklin, John Buchan, and Jack London. Perhaps most significant of all were William Blackwood's subsequent literary connections with Joseph Conrad. It was Blackwood who first encouraged and published Conrad, featuring some of his best-known works, such as *Lord Jim* and *Heart of Darkness*, in *Blackwood's Magazine* between 1898 and 1902. Despite later estrangement Conrad always credited Blackwood's 'encouraging and helpful kindness' as having been crucial to his initial development as a writer.

Blackwood, who remained unmarried after an engagement to his second cousin Florence Moore was broken off by her family in 1866, continued to run the company until 1910, when ill health prompted him to hand over much of the daily management to his nephews George and James Blackwood. He died at his home in Gogar Mount, Ratho, just outside Edinburgh, on 10 November 1912, and was buried on 15 November in the city's Dean cemetery.

DAVID FINKELSTEIN

Sources F. D. Tredrey, *The house of Blackwood, 1804–1954* (1954) · Mrs G. Porter, *John Blackwood* (1898), vol. 3 of *Annals of a publishing house* (1897–8) · *Joseph Conrad, letters to William Blackwood and David S. Meldrum*, ed. W. Blackburn (1958) · D. Finkelstein, *An index to Blackwood's Magazine, 1901–1980* (1995) · *The Times* (11 Nov 1912) · *The Scotsman* (16 Nov 1912) · *CCI* (1913)

Archives NL Scot., corresp. · NL Scot., MSS | LUL, senate house corresp. · NL Scot., letters to Lord Brougham · NL Wales, letters to Johnes family

Likenesses photograph, 1890–99, repro. in Blackburn, ed., *Joseph Conrad, letters* (1958) · W. Logsdail, portrait, Messrs. Blackwood & Sons Ltd, Edinburgh [*see illus.*] · oils, repro. in Tredrey, *House of Blackwood* (1954)

Wealth at death £18,840 9*s*. 11*d*.: confirmation, 22 Aug 1913, *CCI*

Blacman [Blakman], **John** (1407/8–1485?), biographer of Henry VI, was born in the diocese of Bath and Wells, and was admitted about 1437 to Merton College, Oxford; he graduated MA, and became a fellow of that college, some two years later. In 1443 he resigned his fellowship, to become a fellow of Henry VI's new foundation of Eton College, where he was precentor from 1444 to 1452. Early in the latter year he was admitted rector of Sapperton, Gloucestershire, while on 3 December 1452 he was appointed warden of King Henry's other foundation, King's Hall at Cambridge. He resigned from Eton in the following year. By this time he had obtained the degree of BTh and qualified as a notary public. On 3 January 1456 he was collated to the deanship of Westbury-on-Trym, Gloucestershire. However, in 1457 or 1458 he resigned from his wardenship and livings, and entered the London Charterhouse.

Blacman commemorated this change in his life by compiling a commonplace book of meditations on death. He describes his state of mind on abandoning the world, associating his anxieties about physical death with the death to all worldly things implicit on entering a Carthusian house, a form of death that he sees as leading to eternal life. About 1465 he moved to Witham Charterhouse in Somerset. His status here, described in 1474 as that of a *clericus reditus* (half monk, half lay brother), gave him the freedom to acquire a large library. In this year he donated to Witham a large collection of Latin books, some copied and annotated by himself, with a note after the sixty-sixth: 'take these, your books, Father, as many as my years' (Bodl. Oxf., MS Laud misc. 154, fols. 1*r*–2*v*). The most comprehensive private collection of devotional texts known from fifteenth-century England, Blacman's library represents a strand in English spirituality dominated by Richard Rolle's emphasis on extremes of physical and emotional excitement. Notably absent are vernacular English works by writers like Nicholas Love and Walter Hilton, representing a more moderate, pastorally orientated form of contemplative instruction geared to the needs and responsibilities of the layman. This imbalance in Blacman's collection is not surprising given his eremitic vocation, but it had wider implications because of his influence on the spirituality of England's most pious and unsuccessful king, Henry VI.

Blacman was brought into close contact with Henry VI when, as precentor at Eton, he was responsible for collective worship at the college and acted as a priest for the king; he celebrated private masses in the king's presence when the king acted as his server. After Henry VI's death in 1471, and probably in 1483 (that is before Richard III moved Henry's body from Chertsey Abbey to Windsor in August 1484), Blacman wrote at Witham his *Collectarium mansuetudinum et bonorum morum regis Henrici VI* ('Compilation of the meekness and good life of Henry VI'). In it he refers to a long series of miracles at the king's tomb at Chertsey, and to others performed during his lifetime. However, this is not a mere work of hagiography, but a unique insight into the private life and limitations of a medieval king, based on the author's personal reminiscences for the period between 1444 and 1461, when Henry lost his throne, and on the eyewitness testimonies of royal associates such as Bishop William Waynflete (*d.* 1486) and the royal chaplain William Kymberley from the period from 1461 to 1471, a period covering the king's wanderings and captivity.

As an Eton fellow, Blacman was in a position to give an accurate account of the unique combination of piety and learning that lay behind Henry's close involvement with his foundation of Eton. He describes how the king met Eton boys at Windsor Castle, and advised them to follow the path of virtue and discouraged them from visiting his corrupting court. Blacman is candid about Henry's political limitations, but this is because he sees them as a sign of the king's religious vocation, his detachment from temporal things. One vivid personal reminiscence describes Blacman and the king engaged in the study of holy books, and the king giving them signs of his most deep devotion. A mighty duke of the realm knocked at the door, and the king said 'They do so interrupt me that by day and night I can hardly snatch a moment to be refreshed' (Blacman, 15–16).

Blacman goes further, and tries to establish that Henry's limitations as king were positive spiritual virtues. He therefore describes the king's insanity in 1453 as the mystical rapture of one 'not conscious of himself or of those about him as if he were in a trance' (Blacman, 16). Henry's neglect of royal display, such as his failure to notice his hat falling off, and his inattention to political realities are celebrated as the sort of indifference to temporal things, 'as if he might gain Christ' (Blacman, 11), that had been espoused by Rolle. Instead Henry is shown to be a visionary, devoted to the cult of the holy cross, and the sufferings of Jesus, and experiencing visions of Christ presiding in human form at the sacrament of the altar.

Blacman's portrait of the king is that of a true follower of Christ, a holy fool who in 1470 forgave the enemies who had wounded him in 1461, and who in 1471 patiently endured mockery, abuse, and violent death; and the compilation explains why this incompetent king remained loved by so many of his people. It also demonstrates the prescience of Walter Hilton's reservations about the social implications of too enthusiastic a following of Rolle's teachings at the expense of fulfilling social responsibilities. Henry VI was decidedly not a successful practitioner of the mixed life, and this seems to have met with Blacman's approval. This was a failing that was to have profound consequences for the peace and stability of fifteenth-century England.

The date of Blacman's death is uncertain but it is thought to have occurred in 1485. His *Compilation* was published in 1510 by Robert Copland, whose text was reprinted by Thomas Hearne in 1732. An English translation by M. R. James appeared in 1919.

JONATHAN HUGHES

Sources Bodl. Oxf., MS Laud misc. 154 · BL, Sloane MS 2515 · R. Lovatt, 'John Blacman: biographer of Henry VI', *The writing of history in the middle ages: essays presented to R. W. Southern*, ed. R. H. L. Davis and J. M. Wallace-Hadrill (1981), 415–44 · R. Lovatt, 'The library of John Blacman and contemporary Carthusian spirituality', *Journal of Ecclesiastical History*, 43 (1992), 195–230 · R. Lovatt, 'A collector of apocryphal anecdotes: John Blacman revisited', *Property and politics: essays in later medieval English history*, ed. T. Pollard (1984), 172–97 · J. Hughes, *Pastors and visionaries: religion and secular life in late medieval Yorkshire* (1988) · J. Blacman, *'Henry the Sixth': a reprint of John Blacman's memoir*, ed. and trans. M. R. James (1919) · *Duo rerum Anglicarum scriptores veteres, Thomas Otterbourne et Joh. Whethamstede*, ed. T. Hearne, 1 (1732) · W. Sterry, *Etoniana*, 56 (1934), 94
Archives BL, Sloane MS 2515 · Bodl. Oxf., MS Laud misc. 154

Bladen, Martin (1680–1746), army officer and politician, was born possibly at Abbey Hatch, Essex, the third son of Nathaniel Bladen (*b.* 1642/3) of Hemsworth, Yorkshire, and his wife, Isabella, the daughter of Sir William *Fairfax of Steeton, Yorkshire. He was thus a relation of Thomas, third Baron Fairfax, the commander-in-chief of the Cromwellian army, and of Thomas, sixth Baron Fairfax, who inherited extensive estates in Virginia and became a great patron of the Washington family. Bladen's sister Elizabeth was to be the mother of Edward *Hawke, first Baron Hawke; Bladen became his guardian and was responsible for his early advancement in the navy.

Bladen was educated at a small private school and then at Westminster School (1695–7); he matriculated at St John's College, Cambridge, in 1697 and in the same year was admitted at the Inner Temple, but did not pursue a career in law. He joined the army, served in the Low Countries and Spain, and became an aide-de-camp to Henri de Massue de Ruvigny, first earl of Galway. In 1709 he was appointed colonel of a regiment of foot raised in Portugal, but he sold the colonelcy in 1710 and retired from the army. As one of Marlborough's colonels he sought to enter politics, but was twice defeated for the seat of Saltash, Cornwall, in 1713 and 1715. Having been appointed to the sinecure of comptroller of the Royal Mint in 1714, he finally won election to parliament at Stockbridge, Hampshire, in 1715. In 1715 he was also elected to the Irish House of Commons, as member for Bandon, a seat he held until 1727. In 1734 he relinquished the representation of Stockbridge and was elected for Maldon, Essex. A political associate of Thomas Pelham-Holles, duke of Newcastle, and Sir Robert Walpole, in 1741 he was rewarded for his services with the safe Admiralty seat of Portsmouth, a constituency he represented until his death, whereupon he was succeeded by his nephew, who was then Sir Edward Hawke.

Bladen's first wife was Mary, the daughter of Colonel Gibbs; with her he had at least two daughters and a son, George Monk Bladen, who seems to have died young. On 3 April 1728 he married Frances (*d.* 1747), the niece and heir of Colonel Joseph Jory and the widow of John Foche, Fouch, or Ffocke, of Aldborough Hatch, Essex. This second marriage brought him great wealth, including vast plantation concerns in the West Indies. He did not, however, make a new will on his second marriage; he named his daughter Isabella and three infant children of 'my very good friend Jane Porter of London Gentlewoman' as his residuary legatees. The only one of the Porter children to survive Bladen was described as 'John Porter otherwise Bladen', suggesting a closer relationship than friendship.

Appointed through Newcastle's influence to the Board of Trade in 1717, Bladen was sent to Paris in 1719 to represent Britain at a conference to determine the boundaries between British and French North America following the peace of Utrecht (1713). In 1732 he again acted as the main British representative at a conference at Antwerp to adjust the tariffs between Britain, the emperor of Germany, and the states general. Something of a literary figure, he published a dull tragi-comedy, *Solon, or, Philosophy No Defence Against Love: with the Masque of Orpheus and Euridice* (1705), and in 1714 an English translation, *Caesar's Commentaries of his Wars in Gaul*, which was dedicated to the duke of Marlborough. Bladen's historical importance, however, is on account of his record twenty-nine years of service at the Board of Trade.

The political importance and influence of the Board of Trade fluctuated in the eighteenth century, but Bladen's attention to business, and hence his grasp of departmental detail and past official precedent, remained constant. In his first three years in office he attended 463 out of the 572 recorded meetings. During the period 1732–42, when the board declined into a refuge for political placemen, Bladen still managed to attend 978 meetings. His application to colonial affairs was widely respected, and a contemporary pun termed him 'Trade' and his less efficient colleagues as merely 'Board'. Bladen became so influential he often controlled the patronage of various colonial offices, especially in North Carolina. He often broke governors of dubious loyalty and ability, and sometimes made governors, although his motives in doing so have been questioned: of the seven governors appointed through his influence, one was his son-in-law, John Tinker, and another, Thomas Bladen of Maryland, was his nephew. His own economic interests in the West Indies may also have been responsible for his hostility towards the New England colonies, especially Massachusetts, which were notorious for their lax attitude towards the laws of trade.

The hand of Bladen is clearly evident throughout the Colonial Office papers covering his tenure. His first important contribution was his role in the 135-page report to the king, on 8 September 1721, on the condition and government of the colonies. The product of fourteen separate meetings of the board, it was a crucial restatement of past British official attitudes which, on account of their importance, came to influence later deliberations of the board regarding official policy. Briefly, the report suggested that British authority and security needed to be strengthened in North America. This could best be achieved, Bladen suggested, by restricting extensive land grants, appointing reliable crown officials, weakening the rising power of the colonial assemblies, raising a revenue by a more efficient collection of royal quitrents, sending regular troops to the colonies, recalling the charters of the proprietary colonies, securing the frontiers by the creation of a coherent system of native alliances to prevent French encroachment, and the creation of a colonial union under the direct supervision of a captain-general sent out from Britain.

Bladen remained a voice for such policies throughout his career. In an attempt to lessen the drift to independence that he perceived to be developing in the New England colonies, especially Massachusetts, and to tie them more closely to the British mercantile system, he undertook in the Commons the defence of the abortive sugar bills of 1731–2, strongly supported the passage of the Hat Act of 1732, and was largely responsible for steering through the house the Molasses Act of 1733. A summary of his colonial policy viewpoints may be found in his personal reports, to Lord Townshend, 'For the settling of Carolina', 1729 (PRO, CO5/4, fols. 159–62); to Newcastle, 'Reasons for the immediate peopling of Nova Scotia', 1735 (*CSP col.*, 41, nos. 592, 454–8); and to Sir Robert Walpole, 'Reasons for appointing a captain-general for the continent of North America', 1739 (Cholmondeley MSS, CUL).

Throughout his career at the board Bladen rarely formulated new policy; his importance lay in keeping alive the older reform policies of the Williamite board. This was crucial in the development of later British colonial policy, and consequently Bladen was possibly the most influential and best-informed official regarding the American colonies between the retirement of William Blathwayt in 1710 and the appointment in 1748 of George, second earl of Halifax, as president of the board. Bladen died on 1 February 1746, and was buried in the chancel of St Dunstan and All Saints, Stepney, Middlesex. Administration of his will was granted to one of his creditors, the Revd John Emmerson. RORY T. CORNISH

Sources J. A. Henretta, *Salutary neglect: colonial administration under the duke of Newcastle* (1972) • T. C. Barrow, *Trade and empire: the British customs service in colonial America, 1660–1775* (1967) • I. K. Steele, *Politics of colonial policy: the board of trade in colonial administration, 1696–1720* (1968) • J. P. Greene, 'Martin Bladen's blueprint for a colonial union', *William and Mary Quarterly*, 17 (1960), 521–30 • A. H. Basye, *The lords commissioners on trade and plantations commonly known as the board of trade, 1748–82* (1925) • P. Haffenden, 'Colonial appointments and patronage under the duke of Newcastle, 1724–1739', *EngHR*, 78 (1963), 417–35 • PRO, PROB 11/754 • *IGI* • Venn, *Alum. Cant.* • Burke, *Gen. GB* (1937) • HoP, *Commons*

Bladen, Thomas (1698–1780), politician and colonial governor, was born in Annapolis, Maryland, the eldest son of William Bladen (1670–1718), placeman and lawyer, and his second wife, Anne, daughter of Garrett and Mary Van Swearingen. Bladen's father, from a prominent Yorkshire family, emigrated to Maryland in 1690; his mother was a native of the colony. Bladen had three younger brothers and two sisters.

Sent by his parents to England for schooling in or before 1712 (possibly at Westminster), Bladen remained in the country until 1742. Little is known of his early career other than his service in parliament, where he was the member for Steyning in Sussex between 1727 and 1734 and for Ashburton, Devon, from 1735 to 1741. On 14 July 1737 Bladen married Barbara, daughter of the financier Sir Theodore *Janssen, first baronet (*c.*1658–1748), and his wife, Williamza Henley (*d.* 1731), daughter of Sir Robert Henley MP.

Bladen's sister-in-law, Mary Janssen, was the wife of Charles Calvert, fifth Baron Baltimore, proprietor of Maryland, and his brother-in-law, William, was the colony's principal secretary from February 1733 until his death about 1741. The Janssen tie was undoubtedly responsible for Bladen's appointment as governor of Calvert's colony. Commissioned in April 1742, Bladen was sworn in six months later. In addition to the governorship he served as surveyor-general of the western shore and as chancellor during the same period. Bladen was undoubtedly in a strong position when he became governor: born in Maryland, he was the brother-in-law of the colony's proprietor; his sister Anne's marriage to Benjamin Tasker linked him to a powerful member of the colony's élite; and he replaced Samuel Ogle, whose relationship with the lower house had deteriorated so badly that Bladen could hardly fail to do better. Nevertheless the impasse between proprietary interests and the anti-proprietary sentiments of the lower house that had made Ogle's tenure so contentious continued unabated under Bladen. He endured these tensions until October 1746 when, on the basis of his 'tactless and quarrelsome' performance in office (Papenfuse and others, 135), he was dismissed.

For the next fifty years Bladen's critics were able to equate his term in office with the partly completed gubernatorial residence—dubbed 'Bladen's folly'—he had been charged to build by Lord Baltimore. By the time that Bladen's ambitious plan exceeded the £4000 assigned by the assembly, and with the second floor and roof still unfinished, the lower house had lost all interest in authorizing the £2000 needed to complete the work. Instead they left the unfinished building as a memorial to the divisions between proprietor and subjects. The lower house might have baulked at spending further funds at any time, but Bladen made his request as he and the delegates differed over the extent to which the house could determine the powers of emissaries to be sent to negotiate with the Iroquois. The residence thus became a pawn in the ongoing struggle that pitted the governor as proprietary representative against delegates defending their own and their constituents' interests against the prerogative.

Dismissed from office, Bladen remained in the colony until the arrival of his successor, the same Samuel Ogle whom he had replaced five years earlier. On 12 May 1747 Bladen and his family returned to London, where they lived, at least initially, in Westminster. Bladen's daughter Harriet (*d.* 1821) married William Anne Capel, fourth earl of Essex (1732–1799), on 3 March 1767, and his daughter Barbara married General Henry St John (1738–1818) on 31 August 1773. Bladen died, probably in London, in 1780. During his lifetime, he had acquired more than 20,000 acres of Maryland land, either by inheritance or patent, but had sold most by the time of his death. The state of Maryland confiscated the remainder in 1782.

Edward C. Papenfuse

Sources E. C. Papenfuse and others, eds., *A biographical dictionary of the Maryland legislature, 1635–1789*, 1 (1979) [pt of the Maryland State Archives biography project] • A. C. Land, *Colonial Maryland—a history* (1981) • R. J. Brugger, *Maryland: a middle temperament* (1988) • J. B. Lawson, 'Bladen, Thomas', HoP, *Commons, 1715–54*

Wealth at death land in two Maryland counties: Papenfuse and others, eds., *Biographical dictionary*, vol. 1, p.136

Blades, James (1901–1999), percussionist and author, was born on 9 September 1901 at 166 Star Road, Peterborough, the eldest among the four sons and one daughter of Thomas Weston Blades (1879–1953), journeyman tailor, and his wife, Catherine Close (*d.* 1921). Jimmy Blades, as he was known, was born into a poor but loving family, which he recalled with great warmth in his first volume of autobiography, *Drum Roll*, published in 1977. Introduced to drumming by an amateur drummer uncle beating with a knife and fork on a dinner plate, he graduated to watching the drummers of the local bands. To help out at home, he took odd jobs; in 1912 he joined the Boy Scouts and at last played a real drum. In July 1915 he left school and joined Brotherhood's engineering firm as an apprentice. Attracted by the many army bands he heard in the war years, he joined up a year later, but his age was soon found out and he was discharged. Although he never completed his apprenticeship as a turner and fitter, his training remained with him all his life, his garages being well-equipped workshops with lathes where he would work on fittings for his instruments and later could adapt instruments with great skill and imagination for handicapped children.

In 1918 Blades visited London and heard the orchestras of the Lyons' Corner House and Alhambra Theatre, which decided for him where his future lay. He bought his first pair of side-drum sticks and began long hours of practice, relegated to the pigsty at the end of the garden at home. He began by helping his uncle and gradually moved to small drumming roles in local amateur groups; eventually he was allowed to take up drumming as a career, obtaining his first professional engagement with Ginnett's Circus at Henley-on-Thames in June 1921. From there he progressed into the silent cinema bands, all the while gradually building up his own collection of percussion instruments. Throughout the 1920s he continued to work in the cinemas, and in the north he also made his first symphonic contacts, as well as marrying Olive Hewitt (1900–1945) in Workington parish church on 29 January 1927. His son Douglas was born on 27 June 1930. He was heard playing in Edinburgh and was invited to London to play at the Crouch End Hippodrome; from there his talents took him to the Holborn Empire, where he eventually played under Roger Quilter and Leslie Woodgate. He became noted for his xylophone and marimba solos, as well as for his natural flair, sober lifestyle, and reliable professionalism. In 1931 he joined the Jerry Hoey band at the Piccadilly Hotel and quickly came to wider public and musical attention, with engagements also for film music and gramophone recordings.

By the end of 1932 Blades was a member of the London Symphony Orchestra; from that time onwards he became a friend and colleague of many famous inter-war solo and orchestral players, and demands for his services increased. After turning down an invitation to settle in

James Blades (1901–1999), by Norman Parkinson, 1953

America, he was invited to play with a number of broadcasting orchestras, including those of Charlie Kunz and Alfredo Campoli. In 1935 he was called upon to provide the sound of the gong used by J. Arthur Rank at the start of every film: he struck the note on a Chinese tam-tam, while Bombardier Billy Wells mimed for the film. With the outbreak of the Second World War he found himself caught up in the orchestral touring of the Entertainments National Service Association at home and in France, an earlier injury precluding subsequent active service. About the same time he was engaged by the London Philharmonic Orchestra and came into contact with Sir Adrian Boult and Sir Malcolm Sargent, the first of many conductors whom he later came to know as friends. Perhaps his most important contribution to the war was his devising and recording of the uncopyable 'V for victory' signal which prefaced every BBC transmission of messages to the resistance groups in occupied Europe.

On 18 April 1945 Blades's wife died, and he entered a period of depression. He concentrated on work and was invited to join in what was for him the first of many performances in the Bartók sonata for two pianos and percussion. He received wonderful support from countless friends in the profession, and was introduced to the oboist Joan Edith Gauntlett Goossens (1919–2000), whom he married in Winchester on 17 June 1948. He enjoyed her love and totally devoted support both on and off the platform to the end, she unselfishly abandoning her own orchestral career to give the attention that his busy life required. Symphonic work increased after the war, and he was in demand at the BBC and with the London Symphony Orchestra. In 1950 he added Stravinsky's *Histoire du soldat* to his repertory of chamber works with important percussion parts, after advising the composer on the layout of the instruments. In 1953 he was in the selected coronation orchestra in Westminster Abbey; he then began a period of long, happy, and productive associations with the English Opera Group, Benjamin Britten, the Aldeburgh Festival, the English Chamber Orchestra, and the Melos Ensemble, which continued to his official retirement from performance in 1971 while still at the height of his powers. As well as creating the percussion instruments for Britten's three church parable operas, he played in the premières of all of Britten's stage operas, coming out of retirement at the composer's request in 1973 to perform in the last opera, *Death in Venice*.

In 1964 James Blades was appointed professor of percussion at the Royal Academy of Music. There he counted Simon Rattle and Evelyn Glennie among his many students; he retired in 1976, although he continued to give masterclasses there until 1 December 1993. His popularity as a lecturer on the instruments of percussion, with his wife, Joan, accompanying him on the piano, had given rise to countless invitations from schools, music societies, festivals, and learned institutions throughout Britain from the mid-1950s onwards. By chance this led him to his first contact with severely handicapped children, with whom he immediately established a rapport. Such was the impact on him that thereafter he and his wife worked for the physically and mentally handicapped, visiting schools and hospitals on their lecture tours without fee. For this work he was appointed OBE in 1971. For his lectures Benjamin Britten wrote his *Timpani Piece for Jimmy* and Malcolm Arnold his *Concert Piece*.

Jimmy Blades was a wonderful communicator and marvellous scholar but wore his scholarship with disarming ease. In 1961 he wrote *Orchestral Percussion Technique* in the Oxford University Press instrumental technique series, and in 1970 he published *Percussion Instruments and their History*, a work astonishing in its comprehensive coverage of world percussion from earliest times to the date of writing. In 1998 he published a second autobiographical volume, *These I have Met* … Jimmy Blades died on 19 May 1999 at his home, 191 Sandy Lane, Cheam, Sutton, survived by his wife. He was cremated on 28 May at the north-east Surrey crematorium, Morden, where his ashes were subsequently scattered. On 14 November 1999 the percussion studio at the Royal Academy of Music was named after him and dedicated to his memory.

Graham Melville-Mason

Sources *The Independent* (24 May 1999) • J. Blades, *Drum roll* (1977) • *The Guardian* (29 May 1999) • J. Blades, *These I have met* … (1998) • *The Times* (25 May 1999) • b. cert. • m. cert. • d. cert. • private information (2004) [Douglas Blades, son]

Archives Royal Academy of Music, London • U. Edin., collection of historical musical instruments | FILM BBC Television Archives | SOUND BBC sound archives

Likenesses N. Parkinson, photograph, 1953, NPG [*see illus.*] • photograph, repro. in *The Independent* • photograph, repro. in *The Guardian* • photograph, repro. in *The Times* • portrait, repro. in

Blades, *Drum Roll*, no. 27, following p. 80 • portrait, repro. in Blades, *These I have met …*

Blades, William (1824–1890), printer and bibliographer, was born on 5 December 1824, in Clapham, Surrey, the third son and the fifth of the nine children of Joseph Blades (*c.*1786–*c.*1860) and his wife, Grace Hainsworth (1792–1863). His parents were both English. His father and uncle were partners with Joseph East in the printing house of East and Blades, later Blades, East, and Blades, of Abchurch Lane. Blades was educated at Stockwell and Clapham grammar schools and bound apprentice to his father's firm on 1 May 1840.

The early 1850s were productive years: Blades was made a partner and in due course succeeded as senior partner in Blades, East, and Blades, which he ran with his younger brother, Rowland. Unusually for a working printer, he early developed an interest in printing history and furthered his education, in the midst of a busy working life, by forming a fine library; it was 'essentially a workshop and his books [were] his tools' (Reed). He began to concentrate on a study of Caxton. Not wanting to take anything on trust, he personally examined—in libraries up and down the country and in the Netherlands, Belgium, and France—more than 450 copies of the products of Caxton's press. His first publication was an introduction to a facsimile of Caxton's *Governayle of Helthe* of 1491 made from Lord Dysart's copy, printed by Blades, East, and Blades, in 'Types expressly cast in pewter' (1858).

The firm specialized in security printing and Blades was able to command the highest standards for the production of all his books and use his contacts with lithographic artists and printers of top calibre, in particular the firm of G. F. Tupper & Sons; the eldest son, George Isaac Frederick Tupper, was an outstandingly skilled lithographic 'writer' who produced a lithographic frontispiece for the *Governayle of Helthe*. This fairly launched Blades on what would, but for business and family commitments, have become his life's work. He infected Tupper with his own enthusiasm and, in the course of tracing individual types and pages from Caxton's works, he made notes on Caxton's types which Blades used in *The Life and Typography of William Caxton* (1861 and 1863). Following Joseph Ames's seminal work in his *Typographical Antiquities* (1749) on dating Caxton's works by their types, Blades classified them systematically in an attempt to assign dates to the undated works. With the help of Tupper, and of Henry Bradshaw at Cambridge, he identified six of the eight Caxton types known today. The biographical volume was based on original documents. Bradshaw was one of the most astute bibliographical minds of all time with as sharp an eye for type variants as Blades who was working with type all the time. Blades had sent Bradshaw a copy of the *Governayle of Helthe*, and in the years leading up to publication of the *Life and Typography* they wrote to each other almost daily on bibliographical subjects. Bradshaw had more leisure to pursue such niceties than Blades, who had to fit his Caxton studies into the interstices of a working printer's life and was soon to be married: 'What with business & evenings lost in visiting future relations', he wrote on the eve of his marriage, '& the feeling that I am not taking pains enough to be correct in my Caxton articles I get quite savage sometimes' (Blades to Bradshaw, 6 Feb 1862). The amount of time he spent on Caxton was beginning to cause family friction and he was forced to press on faster than he wished with publication of volume 2 of his Caxton book: 'for the whole of [the last three months] I have almost entirely neglected my business which has annoyed my uncle & Partner Mr East, and which if continued much longer would lead to disagreeable results' (Blades to Bradshaw, 20 March 1862).

On 29 April 1862 Blades married Eliza Caroline Anne Fletcher (*b. c.*1837). They had seven children. In the succeeding years Blades produced some more facsimile editions and became the acclaimed authority on Caxton, but he published nothing comparable to his *Life and Typography* apart from a slim pamphlet, *How to Tell a Caxton* (1870), which took account for the first time of Jan Veldener, who cut most of Caxton's types. The one-volume octavo revision of his great work, the *Biography and Typography of William Caxton, England's First Printer*, which he published for Caxton's quatercentenary in 1877, has been criticized for failing to include many of Bradshaw's corrections to the earlier work. Professional jealousy may have played some part but the truth is that Blades, as he confessed to Bradshaw, had lost his youthful impetus; 'I am hard at work digesting my quarto volumes into an 8vo … but find it harder to work satisfactorily than I did 14 years ago—neither body nor mind will stand it' (Blades to Bradshaw, 23 Nov 1876).

Blades was also deeply involved in the organization of a Caxton quatercentenary exhibition on the development of printing, a venture conceived as part charitable and part educational; it was intended to raise funds for the Printers' Pension, Almshouse and Orphan Asylum Corporation as well as introducing the working man to fine books on the one hand and showing the latest printing machines and technological developments in printing on the other. Blades threw himself into it heart and soul, procuring for the exhibition some 5000 books, type specimens, letters, and ephemera, loaned by nearly 300 owners and libraries. He wrote 286 letters to owners, helped to put up the display, and wrote one entire section of the massive catalogue.

Later Blades turned to collecting trade tokens in the tradition of coin and medal collecting of earlier centuries—later considered of little academic account. He published several works on printers' tokens, the most important being *Numismata typographica, or, The medallic history of printing, being an account of the medals, jettons, and tokens struck in commemoration of printers and the art of printing* (1883). His most popular work, *The Enemies of Books*, lighthearted in a heavy Victorian way, went into six editions between 1881 and 1886. He continued to take an active interest in bibliography, was a founder of the Library Association in 1877, read papers at several of its annual meetings, and published a series of bibliographical miscellanies (1890). He also helped to found the Bibliographical Society but died before it came into being in 1892.

The world of printing and London civic affairs claimed an increasing part of Blades's time. He was a liveryman of the Scriveners' Company and was involved in the affairs of Candlewick ward, in which his business premises stood. He had progressive views on improving working conditions in the trade and encouraged a strong trade union in his firm. In the early 1880s the works moved to five-storey premises in Appold Street, Finsbury Pavement, London. It was a showplace with the most up-to-date equipment until the whole building was gutted by fire in 1886 and they had to move again, this time to a smaller, four-storey building.

William Blades died on 27 April 1890 at Suffolk House, Clear Road, Sutton, Surrey; his wife survived him. After his death his extensive library formed the foundation collection of the St Bride Printing Library. Two of his sons followed him into the business. Blades's enduring claim to fame rests on his pioneering use of type identification as a method of dating undated early books, a method still used by incunabulists at the beginning of the twenty-first century. ROBIN MYERS

Sources T. B. Reed, 'Memoir of the author, and list of his works', in W. Blades, *The Pentateuch of printing* (1891) • J. Moran, 'William Blades', *The Library*, 5th ser., 16 (1961), 251–66 • V. Harper, 'William Blades (1824–1890): a monograph', diss., Oxford Polytechnic, 1980 • W. Turner Berry, *Catalogue of an exhibition in commemoration of the centenary of William Blades* (1924) [exhibition catalogue, St Bride Foundation Institute, London, 5–11 Dec 1924] • W. Blades, correspondence with H. Bradshaw, 1860–78, CUL, Add. MSS, various series • letters, manuscript notes, and working papers of William Blades, St Bride Institute, London, St Bride Printing Library • G. Bullen, ed., *Caxton celebration, 1877: catalogue of the loan collection of antiquities, curiosities, and appliances connected with the art of printing* (1877) [exhibition catalogue, Western Galleries, South Kensington, London, 1 July – 17 Nov 1877] • William Blades's copy of Bullen, ed., *Caxton celebration, 1877*, interleaved and extra-illustrated, 8 vols., BL, C.61.e.8 • R. Myers, 'William Blades' debt to Henry Bradshaw and G. I. F. Tupper in his Caxton studies: a further look at unpublished documents', *The Library*, 5th ser., 33 (1978), 261–83 • [R. Myers], *Caxtoniana, or, The progress of Caxton studies from the earliest times to 1976* (1976) [exhibition catalogue, St Bride Institute, London, St Bride Printing Library, 20 Sept – 19 Oct 1976] • R. Myers, 'The Caxton celebration of 1877: a landmark in bibliophily', *Bibliophily*, ed. R. Myers and M. Harris (1986), 138–64 • J. Southward, *Catalogue of the William Blades Library* (1899) • *DNB* • *CGPLA Eng. & Wales* (1890)

Archives Norfolk RO, description of Blickling library • St Bride Institute, London, St Bride Printing Library, books, letters, working papers, and notebooks | BL, *Caxton celebration 1877*, catalogue of the exhibition; copy containing letters, prospectuses, minutes, etc. • CUL, corresp. with H. Bradshaw • U. Edin. L., letters to D. Laing

Likenesses bust, St Bride Institute, London, St Bride Printing Library • photograph (in later life), St Bride Institute, London, St Bride Printing Library • wood-engraving (after photograph by Done & Ball), NPG; repro. in *ILN* (10 May 1890)

Wealth at death £19,538 4*s*. 8*d*.: probate, 26 June 1890, *CGPLA Eng. & Wales*

Blagden, Sir Charles (*bap.* **1748**, *d.* **1820**), physician and secretary of the Royal Society, was born at Wotton under Edge in Gloucestershire, where he was baptized on 19 April 1748, a younger son of John Blagden (1715–1750) and Elizabeth Phelps (1716–1784). His family was involved in various ways in the local textile industry. His early education is obscure but he studied medicine at the University of Edinburgh, and graduated MD in 1768.

Blagden was elected a fellow of the Royal Society in 1772, entering a circle of young fellows that included Joseph Banks. In 1776 Blagden was appointed a surgeon in the army and served on the hospital ship HMS *Pigot* in the American War of Independence. Returning to England in 1780, he briefly held an army medical position in Plymouth but longed for the London scientific life. In late 1782 or early 1783 he became an assistant and amanuensis to Henry Cavendish (1731–1810). This association lasted until 1789, coinciding with the most active phase of Blagden's own scientific career. Cavendish provided for Blagden's financial security with an annuity, and a bequest of £15,000 in his will.

On 5 May 1784 Blagden was elected one of the secretaries of the Royal Society amid the dissensions which gripped that institution over the conduct of its autocratic president, Joseph Banks. Blagden was Banks's right-hand man and remained so until he relinquished the secretaryship in 1797. He finally abandoned the pursuit of a medical position in the early 1780s, on assurances that his career would be advanced in other ways. Dissatisfaction with the rate of that advancement created tension with Banks, but it seems to have been dispelled by the knighthood Blagden received in 1792.

Blagden's centrality in the scientific community was ensured by his closeness to Cavendish and to Banks, but also by his day-to-day control of the *Philosophical Transactions* and by his thorough knowledge of the European scientific scene, a knowledge made possible by his command of languages and extensive travel. Blagden visited the continent annually until the outbreak of the French Revolution and travelled in Germany, Italy, Switzerland, and France. He was elected a corresponding member of the Académie des Sciences in 1789 and counted Antoine Lavoisier, P. S. de Laplace, Georges Cuvier, and especially Claude Louis Berthollet among his friends. When travel to the continent was again possible, Blagden spent considerable time in France with the distinguished scientific coterie known as the 'Société d'Arcueil', centred on Berthollet's residence outside Paris.

Most of Blagden's modest scientific output consisted of a dozen contributions to the *Philosophical Transactions* between 1775 and 1813. He also published papers in the *Annales de Chimie*. His first papers for the Royal Society reported experiments, conducted on himself, Banks, and other colleagues, in the tolerance of extreme air temperatures by humans. His most famous work, published in 1788, was his determination that salt lowers the freezing point of water in a simple inverse ratio, subsequently dubbed Blagden's law, even though his finding had been anticipated by Richard Watson in 1771.

Blagden's best known scientific involvement was in the 'water controversy', beginning in 1783, a contest involving the rival claims of Lavoisier, Cavendish, and James Watt to priority in the discovery of the compound nature of water. Ironically this controversy became more heated in the 1830s and 1840s, after the protagonists were dead, than it was at the time. Subsequent interpretations of Blagden's role have shaped his reputation. His involvement in the controversy was manifold: as Cavendish's assistant; as secretary of the Royal Society, with oversight of the publication of some of the papers in question; and as a scientific traveller, who carried news to Lavoisier and his circle in Paris. The most extreme charges suggest that Blagden falsified documents and otherwise tried to ensure his employer Cavendish's priority. These seem unwarranted, though Blagden was cavalier and presumptuous in his behaviour.

Dr Johnson found the gossipy Blagden a 'delightful fellow'. Hannah More regarded him as modest, sensible, and knowing. Benjamin Thompson, Count Rumford, who successfully rivalled Blagden for the hand of the widowed Madame Lavoisier, and whose daughter, Sarah, Blagden once sought in marriage, had less flattering things to say about him. Blagden remained unmarried and childless. He died suddenly of apoplexy on 26 March 1820 at Arcueil, near Paris, the home of his friend Berthollet, and was buried in the cemetery of Père Lachaise in Paris. His will (the estate was less than £50,000) included bequests to his younger brother Richard, a nephew, nieces, and friends. The residuary legatee was his nephew Robert Hale Blagden Hale. DAVID PHILIP MILLER

Sources F. H. Getman, 'Sir Charles Blagden', *Osiris*, 3 (1937), 69–87 • E. L. Scott, 'Blagden, Charles', *DSB* • *DNB* • G. Wilson, *The life of the Honourable Henry Cavendish* (1851) • *Correspondence of the late James Watt on his discovery of the theory of the composition of water*, ed. J. P. Muirhead (1846) • H. B. Carter, *Sir Joseph Banks, 1743–1820* (1988) • catalogue, Glos. RO, Hale family of Alderley MSS, Ref. D1086, v-ix • Charles Blagden to Joseph Banks, 9 Oct 1783, 16 Oct 1783, Dawson Turner copies, Banks correspondence, NHM [vol. 3, 112–15, 127–31] • C. Jungnickel and R. McCormmach, *Cavendish* (1996) • M. Sadoun-Goupil, *Le chimiste Claude-Louis Berthollet, 1748–1822* (1977) • E. Heberden, *William Heberden: physician of the age of reason* (1989) • G. E. Ellis, *Memoir of Sir Benjamin Thompson, Count Rumford* (1871) • G. R. De Beer, 'The diary of Sir Charles Blagden', *Notes and Records of the Royal Society*, 8 (1950–51), 65–89 • parish register (baptisms), Wotton under Edge, 19 April 1748 • *The Banks letters*, ed. W. R. Dawson (1958), 47

Archives Glos. RO, corresp. and family papers • RS, corresp., diary, and papers • Wellcome L., papers • Yale U., Beinecke L., corresp. and papers | FM Cam., S. G. Perceval collection, letters to Sir Joseph Banks • Hunt. L., letters to Elizabeth Montagu • NHM, Banks MSS • RAS, corresp. with Sir William Herschel • RBG Kew, Banks MSS • U. Cam., Sedgwick Museum of Earth Sciences, letters to Edward King

Likenesses T. Phillips, portrait • M. D. Turner, etching (after T. Phillips), BM, NPG • etching (after T. Phillips), repro. in Getman, 'Sir Charles Blagden', 70

Wealth at death under £50,000; bequests of over £9000: will, Glos. RO, D1086/F59

Blagden, Isabella (1816/17–1873), novelist and poet, was born on 30 June 1816 or 1817 in the East Indies. Although the register of the protestant cemetery in Florence gives her father's name as Thomas, and her nationality as Swiss, rumours held that she was the illegitimate daughter of an Englishman and an Indian mother. The uncertainty over the year of her birth arises from different information given on her grave marker and death certificate. In fact, very little is known with any certainty about Isa, as she was commonly known, before her arrival in 1850 in Florence, where she became one of the central figures in the Anglo-Florentine community. She had been educated in England, however, probably at Louisa Agassiz's Ladies School, Regent's Park, where most of the students were children of parents living in India.

By the time Isa Blagden was seventeen she had composed a play that was later privately printed. In 1842 Edward Bulwer Lytton read the work and his positive response encouraged her in literary pursuits; no copy of the play has survived, however. He also inspired her first published work, a poem entitled 'What is Sir Lytton Bulwer's "Zanoni"' (in *The Metropolitan*, July 1842), which was followed by another poem addressed to Lytton and published in the same journal in April 1843. Probably her most interesting poetic effort is 'To George Sand on her Interview with Elizabeth Barrett Browning', inspired by the two writers' meeting in 1852. Encouraged by Elizabeth Barrett Browning, she turned to writing novels: *Agnes Tremorne*, probably the best of her fiction, was published in two volumes in March 1861. Although she had requested it be published under the pseudonym Ivory Beryl, the publisher substituted her real name, and the pseudonym was never used. She later published four other novels including *The Cost of a Secret* (1863) and *The Crown of a Life* (1869). Her fiction has been described as 'quirky and sometimes laboured' (Blain, Clements & Grundy, *Feminist comp.*, 102), and her work is little known in the twenty-first century. In only one instance did she publish verse under her name: 'Voices: Youth, Love and Death' in the *Victoria Regia* (1861) is signed 'Isa Blagden', otherwise her poetry was published under her initials or anonymously.

With comfortable means Isa Blagden resided at Bellosguardo, and is best remembered for her kind and generous nature as a friend and companion to members of the Anglo-Florentine circle, especially the Brownings and the Trollopes. Isa Blagden died in the Villa Castellani, piazza di Bellosguardo, Florence, on 20 January 1873 and was buried on 28 January near her friend Elizabeth Barrett Browning in the protestant cemetery. Linda White Mazini collected some of her verse in *Poems … with a Memoir* (by Alfred Austin) in that same year. SCOTT LEWIS

Sources I. Blagden, *Poems … with a memoir* [by A. Austin] (1873) • R. Browning, *Dearest Isa: Robert Browning's letters to Isabella Blagden*, ed. E. C. McAleer (1951) • W. O. Raymond, '"Our lady of Bellosguardo": a pastel portrait', *University of Toronto Quarterly*, 12 (1943), 499–553 • *The letters of Elizabeth Barrett Browning*, ed. F. G. Kenyon (1897) • T. A. Trollope, *What I remember*, 3 vols. (1887–9) • A. Leighton and M. Reynolds, eds., *Victorian women poets: an anthology* (1995) • Blain, Clements & Grundy, *Feminist comp.* • d. cert.

Archives Baylor University, Waco, Texas, Armstrong Browning Library • Biblioteca Nazionale Centrale, Florence • Boston PL • Eton • FM Cam. • Girton Cam. • Herts. ALS • Hotchkiss Library, Sharon, Connecticut • Hunt. L. • Indiana University, Bloomington • John Murray, London • Kungliga Biblioteket, Stockholm • L. Cong. • Morgan L. • NYPL, Henry W. and Albert A. Berg collection • Princeton University, New Jersey, R. H. Taylor collection •

Smithsonian Institution, Washington, DC, Archives of American Art · Wellesley College, Massachusetts · Yale U.
Likenesses photograph, 1873 (after oil portrait, *c.*1860), Baylor University, Waco, Texas, Armstrong Browning Library

Blagdon, Francis William (*bap.* 1777, *d.* 1819), journalist and author, was baptized on 19 January 1777 at St Paul's, Covent Garden, the son of Thomas and Mary Blagdon. He began his career as a horn-boy employed to sell the *Sun* newspaper whenever it contained any extraordinary news. He then became amanuensis to Dr A. F. M. Willich, a medical writer, who taught him French and German; he also learnt Spanish and Italian, and subsequently described himself as 'professor' of those languages, which probably implies that he endeavoured to earn a living by teaching. At one time he published a *French Interpreter.* In 1802 Blagdon began editing the series Modern Discoveries (1802–3); the first two volumes comprised Vivant Denon's *Travels in Egypt* in the train of Napoleon Bonaparte, the next two included Golberry's *Travels in Africa*, and the remaining four were devoted to Pallas's *Travels in the Southern Provinces of Russia*. The first two works were translated by Blagdon from the French, and the last from the German. His interests ranged from the literary to the historical. In 1803 he commenced publishing with the Revd F. Prevost a literary miscellany entitled *Flowers of Literature*, which continued to appear until 1809, and ran to seven volumes. In 1805 he brought out *A Brief History of Ancient and Modern India*, which was reissued in 1813 as an appendix to Captain Thomas Williamson's *European in India*, and in 1806 he contributed the 'Memoirs' to Orme's *Graphic History of the Life, Exploits, and Death of … Nelson.*

About this time Blagdon became associated with the *Morning Post*, which he helped to edit for some years. The paper was then committed to upholding tory policies and Blagdon's literary activity took a polemical turn; he had already been imprisoned for six months in 1805 for libelling John Jervis, earl of St Vincent, in the matter of his naval administration. The proposal of the whig ministry of 1806 to remove Roman Catholic disabilities induced him to publish an edition of Foxe's book of martyrs, and this appeared as *An universal history of Christian martyrdom … originally composed by John Fox … and now entirely rewritten … by the Rev. J. Milner, M.A.* (1807). The pseudonym 'the Rev. J. Milner' should not have been used, as a well-known Roman Catholic divine, John Milner, was then living.

In 1809 Blagdon came into conflict with political journalist William Cobbett (1762–1835), and in October of that year he launched a Sunday paper, *Blagdon's Weekly Political Register*, in opposition to Cobbett's *Political Register.* Blagdon was ruined by speculation, however, and this paper, as well as the *Phoenix*, another of his ventures, soon came to an end. In 1814 Blagdon published *An historical memento … of the public rejoicings … in celebration of the peace of 1814, and of the centenary of the accession of the house of Brunswick*, and in 1819 a *New Dictionary of Classical Quotations*. Among his other noteworthy compositions were an edition of Dr Johnson's poems, together with his biography, contributed to *The Laurel* in 1808, and a general index compiled for the *British Critic*, volumes 21–43. Blagdon died in obscurity and poverty in June 1819, and a subscription was raised for his destitute widow and children.

A. F. Pollard, *rev.* Nilanjana Banerji

Sources *GM*, 1st ser., 89/2 (1819), 88 · [J. Watkins and F. Shoberl], *A biographical dictionary of the living authors of Great Britain and Ireland* (1816) · Watt, *Bibl. Brit.*, 1.119 · J. D. Reuss, *Alphabetical register of all the authors actually living in Great Britain, Ireland, and in the United Provinces of North-America*, 1 (1804), 109 · E. Smith, *Life of Cobbett* (1878), 2.47–8 · parish register, St Paul's, Covent Garden, City Westm. AC

Blagg, Mary Adela (1858–1944), astronomer, was born on 17 May 1858 at Abbot Hay, Cheadle, Staffordshire, the eldest of the five daughters and four sons of Charles John Blagg, a solicitor of Cheadle, and his wife, Frances Caroline. Other than education at a private boarding-school in London, she lived all her life in Cheadle. Largely self-educated in mathematics, she was attracted to astronomy by attending the university extension lectures of J. A. Hardcastle, who encouraged her to original work in selenography. Hardcastle undertook lunar measuring for his colleague S. A. Saunder (1852–1912), another master at Wellington College, with the support of Professor H. H. Turner, director of the University of Oxford observatory.

In mid-life in 1907 Blagg responded to Turner's appeal for skilled help, and by more than twenty years' indefatigable effort became the longest serving of his sixteen volunteers, helping him advance work of international importance. Blagg sorted out a mass of original variable star observations by Joseph Baxendall, editing the whole by 1918 for discussion by Turner and subsequent publication. This led to eleven joint papers with Turner in *Monthly Notices*. She then used Turner's method of harmonic analysis to make her own analyses and generate light curves for four variables observed by members of the British Astronomical Association, and published six papers of her own.

Blagg achieved repute and made a lasting contribution by her lunar work. In 1900 lunar maps were still based on W. G. Lohrmann's measurements of 1824–36, but only 162 points were known with precision, and nomenclature was confusing. Saunder then applied Turner's method of rectangular co-ordinates developed for the *Astrographic Catalogue*, which made possible the formidable reductions to allow for libration. He determined a large number of secondary control points, gaining an improvement of fifty times in accuracy. In 1905 Saunder proposed an international committee to remedy lunar nomenclature, and the chairman called for an accurate map in mean libration. Untimely deaths brought Mary Blagg to undertake a crucial role in both projects. Dr Julius Franz made fundamental measures of the outer areas, and Saunder of the inner areas; when Franz died, Saunder laid down all the points for the map to be drawn by W. H. Wesley. Through Hardcastle's introduction he had already secured the devoted help of Blagg in compiling a great list of features and their names given by Beer and Madler, Julius Schmidt, Edmund Neison, and W. R. Birt. Saunder's sudden death in 1912 left Turner to publish in 1913 the *Collated List of Lunar*

Formations, which he noted 'is throughout the work of Miss Blagg'.

When the International Astronomical Union (IAU) was formed in 1920, Blagg joined the lunar commission under Turner's presidency. He secured the best photographs from Paris, Mount Wilson, and other observatories. From these, using the positions determined by Franz and Saunder, Blagg had by 1922 drawn the maps for the ten outer portions of the moon, to complete an atlas with the four inner quadrants drawn by Wesley. After 1928 she and Dr K. Muller of Vienna developed a definitive list naming nearly 6000 features, published by the IAU as *Named Lunar Formations* (1935), of which the second volume was the atlas, not surpassed until 1964. The nomenclature remained the basic work, thus meeting Saunder's original aim.

Although of a retiring nature, Blagg did not baulk at criticizing earlier astronomers, and her criticisms were accepted. She undertook masses of tedious work for others, and the originality in her contribution was that she first disentangled the errors of selenographers who had relied on Lohrmann's early measurements and then brought order to the chaos that had accumulated in naming features on the moon. Epitomizing the best amateur tradition, Blagg also published six papers in the *Journal of the British Astronomical Association*. She was one of the first five women to be elected a fellow of the Royal Astronomical Society, in January 1916. Blagg never married. Her name was given to a lunar crater after her death, from long-term heart disease, at her home at High Bank, Cheadle, on 14 April 1944. ROGER HUTCHINS

Sources P. M. Ryves, *Monthly Notices of the Royal Astronomical Society*, 105 (1945), 65–6 · H. H. Turner, 'Introduction', in M. A. Blagg, *Collated list of lunar formations* (1913), v–vi · M. B. Ogilvie, 'Blagg, Mary Adela', in M. B. Ogilvie, *Women in science* (1986), 41 · Annual reports [U. Oxf. observatory] · M. A. Blagg and K. Muller, *Named lunar formations* (1935) · review, *The Observatory*, 58 (1935), 334–5 · b. cert. · d. cert.

Archives MHS Oxf., printed works, C 63–76, D 68–242

Wealth at death £1156 10s. 9d.: probate, 16 May 1944, *CGPLA Eng. & Wales*

Blagge, Robert (*d.* 1522), administrator, was born on an undetermined date, at Northwich, Somerset, the son of Stephen Blagge and his wife, Alice. His early life and career are obscure. He received his training in the law at the Inner Temple, where he was a governor in 1511, and served as clerk to John Fitzherbert, who was king's remembrancer of the exchequer from 1480 to 1502. Following Fitzherbert's death Blagge was, on 16 December 1502, granted for life the office of king's remembrancer; he was admitted on 26 January 1503. The king's remembrancer, invariably a prominent lawyer, supervised a department of the exchequer of audit responsible for auditing royal accounts and collecting crown debts. Blagge became the first remembrancer since 1447 to be raised to the exchequer bench, as third baron, on 27 June 1511. Unlike his predecessors, Blagge was permitted to retain the remembrancer's office, to be exercised by deputy, in a confirmation by letters patent. Subsequently, on 19 November 1515, Blagge secured a new life grant of the remembrancership in reversion for his son Barnabe. However, on Blagge's death in 1522 the office passed to a keeper, John Copewood, and in 1524 the patent of 1515 was declared void on the grounds that Blagge possessed no legal estate in the remembrancership from the date of his elevation to the bench. His successor, Thomas Walsh, surrendered the office upon being appointed fourth baron in 1534.

In 1515 Blagge moved to the centre of royal financial administration with his appointment as surveyor of crown lands alongside Sir Edward Belknap and Bartholomew Westby. He remained active in this office until the year of his death. As a surveyor and a general purveyor of the king's revenue, Blagge proved to be a resourceful and hard-headed administrator. Shortly before his death he was involved in collecting the fines for distraint of knighthood. He also held numerous appointments in local government, being on successive commissions of the peace for Kent and Middlesex, and commissions of sewers for Cambridgeshire, Lincolnshire, Essex, Middlesex, and Hertfordshire.

Blagge acquired a landed estate in Somerset, Wiltshire, Middlesex, and Kent, which was to be divided upon his death between Barnabe, of the Inner Temple, his only living child with his first wife, Katherine, the daughter and heir of Thomas Brown (or Brune) of Kent; and George (1512/13–1551), his only living child from his marriage of 1506 to his second wife, Mary, daughter of John Brooke, seventh Lord Cobham (*d.* 1512), and Margaret, daughter of Edward Neville, Lord Bergavenny. George would receive the larger portion, including estates that came to his father from his second marriage. At the age of twenty-one George was to inherit property in Holloway, Middlesex, and Bristol, and the manors of Severswoke and Grubbswyk, Somerset; at the death of his mother he was to have the manors of Lucton, Barrers, and Broke Montacute, Somerset, and several tenements in Dartford, Kent. George Blagge esquire, of Westminster and Dartford, later became a courtier to Henry VIII and Edward VI, a comptroller of London customs, MP for Bedford and Westminster, and a prominent protestant associate of Sir Thomas Wyatt the elder. He was knighted during the Scottish campaign of 1547. In his will of 8 September 1522 Robert Blagge required that George marry his ward, Mary Coke, if his son consented upon coming of age, but in the event George married Dorothy, daughter of William Badby of Essex; they had three children, including the Elizabethan MP Henry Blagge (*d.* 1596). Barnabe Blagge received a life interest from his father of lands in Dartford, Wilmington, Sutton, and Darenth, Kent, which had in part been his mother's dowry; an inheritance of his father's property in Westminster; and £106 13s. 4d. in money and plate. He died without heirs; the date of his death is not known. An elder son from Robert Blagge's first marriage, Robert, of the Inner Temple, predeceased his father.

Robert Blagge died on 13 September 1522 in London and was buried shortly afterwards in the priory of St Bartholomew beside his first wife. Mary Blagge was executor to his estate; the overseers were his close friends Sir Richard Broke (*d.* 1529), serjeant-at-law, recorder of the city of London, and MP for London, and Nicholas Mynne of London, royal auditor. He left a bequest to his brother-in-law, Thomas Pymme, of Middlesex, foreign apposer of the exchequer (1515–49). His last will and testament revealed a devout character, intent upon deeds of late medieval piety and charity. Blagge was a not untypical lawyer of the opening decades of the sixteenth century who through advantageous marriages and government service rose to a position of influence and socio-economic success.

J. D. Alsop

Sources *LP Henry VIII* • wills, PRO, PROB 11/20, sig. 15; PROB 11/31, sig. 10; PROB 11/33, sig. 1 • J. C. Sainty, ed., *Officers of the exchequer: a list* (1983), 44–5 • *DNB* • HoP, *Commons, 1509–58*, 1.440–42 • *The reports of Sir John Spelman*, ed. J. H. Baker, 1, SeldS, 93 (1977), 150 • *VCH Somerset*, 3.215 • E. Foss, *Biographia juridica: a biographical dictionary of the judges of England … 1066–1870* (1870) • W. C. Richardson, *Tudor chamber administration, 1485–1547* (1952), 256–7, 488 • E. W. Ives, *The common lawyers of pre-Reformation England* (1983), 82, 453 • *The notebook of Sir John Port*, ed. J. H. Baker, SeldS, 102 (1986), xix • F. A. Inderwick and R. A. Roberts, eds., *A calendar of the Inner Temple records*, 1 (1896), xxxix, 11, 23, 30, 32, 68 • will of John Fitzherbert, PRO, PROB 11/13, sig. 18

Wealth at death solvent: will, PRO, PROB 11/20, sig. 15

Blaghd, Earnán de. *See* Blythe, Ernest (1889–1975).

Blagrave, Daniel (*bap.* **1603**, *d.* **1668?**), politician and regicide, was baptized on 20 November 1603 at St Mary's, Reading, the fifth son of Alexander Blagrave (*d.* 1612), a clothier of Southcote Lodge, Berkshire, and his wife, Margaret. A nephew of the mathematician John Blagrave, Daniel entered the Inner Temple in 1637 and was called to the bar in 1648. Before then he emerged as a prominent parliamentarian in Berkshire, as treasurer of the county committee. His greatest influence was in Reading, where he was made an 'assistant' of the corporation (1644), and became 'steward' or recorder (1645). Thereafter he began to make an impression outside the county. He was made an exigenter in the court of common pleas and a master in chancery, and secured election as a recruiter MP for the borough of Reading in June 1648, although only after the resolution of an election dispute. Blagrave was vilified almost immediately in the royalist press, who accused him of securing his seat through bribery, and he would remain a controversial figure for many years. He married, in 1632, Elizabeth (*b.* 1612, *d.* in or after 1672), daughter of Abraham Hull, a London merchant, with whom he had at least two sons.

A friend to the Independents, if not to the army, Blagrave emerged as a prominent MP during the Rump Parliament. He was involved in preparing for the trial of Charles I, during which he was a zealous commissioner who proved willing to sign the death warrant [*see also* Regicides]. He participated in the abolition of the House of Lords, and in introducing the controversial engagement, and secured appointments to many leading committees, not least in relation to the sequestration of delinquents and the sale of confiscated estates and church lands. He became a commissioner for forfeited estates in July 1651. His ambition for preferment and pecuniary office is evident in his frequent letters to Elias Ashmole seeking astrological advice, and his parliamentary activity was closely related to matters wherein he sought promotion. In 1650 the commissioners for compounding expressed fear that his attempt to become steward of forfeited estates in Berkshire conflicted with his positions as an MP and sequestrator, and by the spring of 1653 he faced accusations of having used bribes to secure offices, a practice recommended to him by Ashmole. Such accusations prompted an official investigation which threatened Blagrave's public career in the Commons.

Blagrave survived this investigation, but the absence of parliamentary privilege after the dissolution of the Rump left him open to other prosecutors, notably the corporation of Reading. This dispute, together with growing hostility resulting from his clashes with local presbyterians, probably prevented him from securing a seat in the 1654 parliament. He was also accused of failing to assist in the prosecution of the local astrologer and mystic John Pordage. Blagrave, having examined Pordage, provided written testimony in his defence in 1654, prompting accusations that he, like his wife, was one of Pordage's acolytes. The presbyterians in Reading removed Blagrave from civic office in March 1656, sparking a lengthy battle to reclaim his post, and a bitter factional struggle within the town. Blagrave's party secured his return in another contested parliamentary election in 1656, against the wishes of the ruling élite, and he was returned again in 1659 after another double return, and was restored to his post as recorder.

Active in the restored Rump in 1659, Blagrave favoured civilian rather than military rule but probably withdrew from the Commons upon the readmission of the secluded members in February 1660. He gave way to his son in the Convention Parliament, but was confirmed as the town's recorder until he fled at the Restoration, to avoid prosecution as a regicide. The town promised to hold the post open for him until his return, but Blagrave remained on the continent until his death. He probably died at Aachen in 1668, and was certainly dead by 1672 when Bulstrode Whitelocke received a bequest through Blagrave's widow.

J. T. Peacey

Sources C. G. Durston, 'Berkshire and its county gentry, 1625–1649', PhD diss., U. Reading, 1977 • J. M. Guilding, ed., *Reading records: diary of the corporation*, 4 vols. (1892–6) • Berks. RO, R/AC1/1/5–10 • *JHC*, 3–7 (1642–59) • *CSP dom., 1640–60* • [C. Fowler], *Daemonium meridianum: Satan at noon* (1655) • [C. Fowler], *Daemonium meridianum: Satan at noon. The second part* (1656) • J. Pordage, *Innocencie appearing* (1655) • *Elias Ashmole (1617–1692): his autobiographical and historical notes*, ed. C. H. Josten, 5 vols. (1966 [i.e. 1967]) • D. Underdown, *Pride's Purge: politics in the puritan revolution* (1971) • B. Worden, *The Rump Parliament, 1648–1653* (1974) • M. Noble, *The lives of the regicides* (1798)

Blagrave, John (*b.* before **1560**, *d.* **1611**), mathematician, was the second of four sons of John Blagrave of Bulmershe, near Sonning, Berkshire, and Anne, daughter of Sir Anthony Hungerford of Down Ampney, Gloucestershire. He was born at Reading. The date of his birth is unknown, but he was educated at Reading School and was lent mathematical books by Sir Thomas Parry of Hampstead Marshall, Berkshire, who died in 1560. Blagrave had a house at Swallowfield and lived there and at Southcot Lodge, Reading, let to him by his elder brother, Anthony, on a lease of ninety-six years in 1596.

Blagrave was a practical mathematician. He practised as a land surveyor and was among the first to draw estate maps to scale. He also designed and made instruments, including an astrolabe, which he described in *The Mathematical Jewel* (1585), whose design modified a number of earlier instruments, particularly that of Gemma Frisius. One astrolabe made to Blagrave's design is known to survive. Between 1589 and 1596 he enjoyed the patronage of Sir Francis Knolles, the dedicatee of *Baculum familliare, catholicon sive generale: a booke of the making and use of a staffe, newly invented by the author, called the familiar staffe* (1590), and his family. The 'familiar staffe' is an early example of one of the elaborate universal instruments, whose use was short-lived, designed by contemporary mathematical practitioners. In 1596 Blagrave published *Astrolabium Uranicum generale* and advertised termly visits to London and arrangements to make his instruments available to customers. Blagrave also made sundials and published *The Art of Dyalling* in 1609. He was ranger of the Forest of Dean until 1611. In his will of 1611 Blagrave directed that a stone monument should be erected in St Lawrence's Church, Reading, which would commemorate his skills:

> representing my said mother w[i]th the hungerfordes and our armes by her and my self lyinge vnder her w[i]th this writinge Johannes Blagrauius totus Mathematicus cum matre sepultus restinge my head on a globe and an astrolabe a quadrant rule and compasse lyinge by me.

Blagrave made many bequests to his wife, Dorothy, her daughter, Jane, his relatives, and servants. He also left legacies to enlarge the market-place at Reading and to build a portico to St Lawrence's Church. Among other bequests was the annual sum of 20 nobles to a maidservant of good character who had served one master for five years. To avoid partiality, three servants were to be chosen, one from each of the three parishes of the town and in every fifth year from Southcot, should there be a suitable candidate. Lots were to be cast on Good Friday to select the recipient of the money. Blagrave died on 9 August 1611 and was buried two days later in St Lawrence's Church. An elaborate monument of himself, surrounded by allegorical figures, was erected, which approximated to the directions of his will.

E. M. Thompson, *rev.* Sarah Bendall

Sources will, PRO, PROB 11/118, sig. 74 • F. W. Steer and others, *Dictionary of land surveyors and local map-makers of Great Britain and Ireland, 1530–1850*, ed. P. Eden, 2nd edn, ed. S. Bendall, 2 vols. (1997) • C. Coates, *The history and antiquities of Reading* (1802) • *Biographia Britannica, or, The lives of the most eminent persons who have flourished in Great Britain and Ireland*, 2 (1748), 802–5 • E. G. R. Taylor, *The mathematical practitioners of Tudor and Stuart England* (1954) • Wood, *Ath. Oxon.*, new edn, 2.96–8 • M. Naxton, *Floreat Redingensis: the history of Reading School* (1986) • parish register (baptisms), 11 Aug 1611, St Lawrence's Church, Reading

Archives BL, maps • Bodl. Oxf., maps • Reading Central Library, maps • St John's College, Oxford, maps

Likenesses effigy on monument, 1611, St Lawrence's Church, Reading • D. L., line engraving, repro. in J. Palmer, ed., *The Catholique Planisphaer: which Mr Blagrave calleth the mathematical jewel* (1658) • line print, NPG

Wealth at death annuities initially of £136 8*s*.; single bequests of £504; property in Berkshire, Hampshire, and Wiltshire: will, PRO, PROB 11/118, sig. 74

Blagrave, Joseph (*b.* 1610, *d.* in or before 1682), astrologer, was born in the parish of St Giles, Reading, the youngest of four sons of Alexander Blagrave (*d.* 1639) and his wife, Margaret. He was a nephew of John Blagrave (*d.* 1611), the mathematician, from whom he appears to have inherited a small estate in nearby Swallowfield. What little is known of his personal history is mainly derived from his books. His youth was spent in the study of astronomy and astrology, his later years in philosophy and the practice of physic, on which he wrote:

> Without some knowledge in astronomy one can be no astrologer, and without knowledge in astrology one can be no philosopher, and without knowledge both in astrology and philosophy one can be no good physician, the practice of which must be laid upon the five substantial pillars of time, virtue, number, sympathy, and antipathy. (Blagrave, *Astrological Practice*, preface)

Blagrave's marriage to his wife, Susan, brought him a son, Joseph, in May 1640, but his wife died shortly after the birth, on 2 June.

Blagrave's first appearance as an author was with a series, Ephemerides, with Rules for Husbandry for the years 1658, 1659, 1660, and 1665. No copy of the Ephemeris for 1658 has survived, and the volume for 1660 states that 'it came into but few hands, by reason of the slackness of the printer before it came forth'. Copies for the years 1659 and 1660 are rare. The next work ascribed to Blagrave is *The Epitome of the Art of Husbandry, by J. B., Gent.* (1669). The attribution to Blagrave is likely, since its editor was his nephew, Obadiah Blagrave, a bookseller in St Paul's Churchyard. He published this and all the subsequent works of his uncle, two of which were posthumous. Blagrave's *Astrological Practice of Physick* (1671) certainly appeared in Trinity term for this year, although most copies bear the date 1689, being reprints published in Hilary term 1689/90. His next work was the *Supplement or enlargement to Mr. Nich. Culpepper's English physitian, to which is annexed a new tract for the cure of wounds by gunshot* (1674). The preface to this work is dated 'From my house called Copt Hall, upon the seven bridges in Reading'. Blagrave's last definite, and posthumously published, work is his *Introduction to Astrology*, in three parts (1682). This work contains an engraved portrait of Blagrave at the age of seventy-two and is dedicated to his friend Elias Ashmole the antiquary. Lowndes (W. T. Lowndes, *Bibliographer's Manual*, ed. Bohn, 1, 1864, 214) ascribes to Joseph Blagrave *Planispherium Catholicum*, but this is certainly an error, for the work is a revised version of the *Mathematical Jewel* of John Blagrave, edited by J. Palmer, and published in London in 1658. Another work wrongly ascribed to Blagrave is a manuscript, now lost, 'A remonstrance in favour of antient learning against the proud pretensions of the moderns, more especially in respect to the doctrine of the stars', about 1669 or 1670.

Blagrave's character appears to have been a mixture of earnest piety with a profound belief in the virtues of astrology. One of the cures which he claimed to have effected was that of casting out a dumb devil from a maid at Basingstoke, where, he reported, after he had invoked the name of the Tetragrammaton with that of the blessed Trinity, 'the devil came forth, but invisible, with a great cry and hideous noise, raising a sudden gust of wind, and so vanished' (Blagrave, *Astrological Practice*, 124). The whole story is a curious study in the demonology of the seventeenth century. Blagrave's chief interest lies in his ambiguous status as a leading representative of the long tradition of astrological medicine, at just the time when that tradition was rapidly becoming unacceptable among people of the increasingly powerful 'respectable' sort. In this respect, his complaint in the *Astrological Practice of Physick* speaks for a generation:

> I find that many being unsatisfied concerning the legality of my way of Cure, have refused to come or send unto me for help to cure their infirmities: and many of those who did come, came for the most part privately, fearing either loss of reputation or reproaches from their Neighbours, and other unsatisfied people; and also fearing that what I did, was either Diabolical, or by unlawful means. (ibid., preface)

Blagrave had died before publication of *Introduction to Astrology* in 1682, but the exact date and location of his death are unknown.

C. H. Coote, *rev.* Patrick Curry

Sources J. Blagrave, *Astrological practice of physick* (1671) • *Blagrave's Introduction to astrology*, ed. O. Blagrave (1682) • J. Blagrave, *Blagrave's Supplement or enlargement to Mr. Nich. Culpepper's English physitian* (1674) • P. Curry, *Prophecy and power: astrology in early modern England* (1989), 21, 24, 55, 114 • E. Arber, ed., *The term catalogues, 1668–1709*, 3 vols. (privately printed, London, 1903–6), vol. 1, p. 79; vol. 2, p. 308 • private information (2004) • C. Coates, *The history and antiquities of Reading* (1802), 234 • D. Lysons and S. Lysons, *Magna Britannia: being a concise topographical account of the several counties of Great Britain*, 1 (1806), 545 • J. Granger, *A biographical history of England, from Egbert the Great to the revolution*, 2nd edn, 4 vols. (1775)

Likenesses line engraving (aged seventy-two), BM, NPG; repro. in O. Blagrave, ed., *Blagrave's introduction to astrology*

Blagrave, Thomas (*d.* 1688), musician, was the eldest son of Richard Blagrave (*d.* 1641) and his third wife, Ann (*d.* in or after 1672), who were married at Northwood, Isle of Wight, on 19 February 1622. Richard, of Berkshire ancestry, was a musician at the court of Charles I; Ann was the daughter of a court musician, Thomas Mason, and sister of another, John Mason (whose will mentions members of the Blagrave family, as does that of the musician John Goodwin). Thomas Blagrave deputized for the sackbut player Edward Bassano from December 1637, and in the next year was admitted to the hautboy and sackbut ensemble to assist his father, on whose death in 1641 he inherited a full post. On 14 October 1645 he married Margaret (*d.* 1689), the daughter of Thomas Clarevell (or Clarvox) of Parson's Green, Middlesex, at St Margaret's, Westminster; the marriage was apparently childless.

A signet warrant of July 1681 describes Blagrave as 'a great sufferer for loyalty in the late rebellion', but he

Thomas Blagrave (*d.* **1688**), by unknown artist

nevertheless became one of Cromwell's musicians. At some stage he shared with the older Henry Purcell the bass role of Mustapha in William D'Avenant's *The Siege of Rhodes*, though variant cast lists throw doubt on statements that he participated in the original production of 1656. Pepys became friendly with Blagrave, and on 18 March 1660 recorded giving him a lute 'two years ago' in return for a note for 40*s*. On 21 June 1660 Pepys had a flageolet lesson from Blagrave, and he afterwards mentioned him several times.

Following the Restoration Blagrave was sworn in as a court violinist (18 June 1660), and he thereafter played in the king's band of violins. He was also made a gentleman of the Chapel Royal, of which he was to be chosen clerk of the cheque in 1682. Although he was at Windsor as a wind player on 17 April 1661, it was not until 3 August that year that he regained the place he held before the civil wars.

On 20 April 1662 Pepys visited Blagrave at 'his old house in the Fishyard'; this was in St Margaret's Lane, Westminster, where he lived for the rest of his life (although a poll tax return for 1664 places him on the north side of the Strand). In August 1664 Blagrave became a lay clerk of Westminster Abbey; there in 1666 he succeeded Christopher Gibbons as master of the choristers, a post which he yielded up in 1670 (the accounts assign both events to March, but this may be a book-keeping convenience). Pepys clearly had Blagrave's several posts in mind when, on 20 May 1666, he described him as 'a sober politique man, that gets money and increase of places'.

At Windsor in 1674 Blagrave sang as a countertenor, though at the coronation of James II, in 1685, he sang as a bass. The new reign brought a review of posts, leaving Blagrave with only his place in the chapel. He made his will on 14 May 1686, but lived until 21 November 1688 (he is presumed to have died at Westminster) and was buried in the north cloister of Westminster Abbey three days later; he made small bequests to members of his family, and left a house and land at Teddington, Middlesex, to his wife. She made her will on 5 February 1689, and was buried next to him on 12 October 1689.

Pepys's good opinion of Blagrave was shared by Anthony Wood, who wrote that he was 'a gentile and honest man'. His song 'What conscience say it is in thee' appears in *Select Ayres and Dialogues* (1669); another song, the short but appealing 'What means this strangeness', survives in manuscript. JOHN HARLEY

Sources PRO, lord chamberlain's papers LC3, LC5, LC9; Signet Office docquet book SO3 [calendared in A. Ashbee, *Records of English court music* (1986–96), vols. 1, 2, 3, 5, 8] · Pepys, *Diary* · W. H. Rylands, ed., *The four visitations of Berkshire*, 2 vols., Harleian Society, 56–7 (1907–8) · parish registers, Northwood, Isle of Wight, Isle of Wight RO [marriage: Richard Blagrave and Ann Mason, parents] · A. M. Burke, ed., *Memorials of St Margaret's Church, Westminster* (1914) · overseers' accounts, parish of St Margaret's, 1669–85, City Westm. AC, E182–E300 · muniments, Westminster Abbey Muniment Room, London, WAM 33699, WAM 33703 · archive of Her Majesty's Chapel Royal, St James's Palace, the cheque books [ed. A. Ashbee and J. Harley as *The cheque books of the Chapel Royal* (2000)] · J. L. Chester, ed., *The marriage, baptismal, and burial registers of the collegiate church or abbey of St Peter, Westminster*, Harleian Society, 10 (1876) · will, 14 May 1686, City Westm. AC, dean and chapter, Westminster, original will no. 893 [proved 4 Dec 1688; probate copy: PRO, PROB 11/385, sig. 160] · will, City Westm. AC, dean and chapter, Westminster, original will no. 912 [will of Margaret Blagrave, wife, 5 Feb 1689, proved 17 Oct 1689; probate copy: PRO, PROB 11/396, sig. 133] · will, City Westm. AC, dean and chapter, Westminster, original will no. 1003 [will of John Goodwin, 3 July 1692, proved 20 July 1692; copy at PRO, LC9/259] · PRO, PROB 11/375, q.134; PROB 11/341, q.37 [will of John Hingeston, 12 Dec 1683, proved 16 Feb 1684; will of John Mason, proved 11 March 1673] · A. Wood, Bodl. Oxf., MS Wood D 19 (4) [ed. J. D. Shute in 'Anthony à Wood and his manuscript Wood D 19(4) at the Bodleian Library, Oxford: an annotated transcription', DPhil diss., International Institute for Advanced Studies, Clayton, Missouri, 1979] · F. Sandford, *The history of the coronation of James II and Queen Mary* (1687) · A. Ashbee and D. Lasocki, eds., *A biographical dictionary of English court musicians, 1485–1714*, 2 vols. (1998) · H. W. Shaw, *The succession of organists of the Chapel Royal and the cathedrals of England and Wales from c.1538* (1991) · E. Pine, *The Westminster Abbey singers* (1953)

Likenesses oils, U. Oxf., faculty of music [*see illus.*]

Wealth at death house and land at Teddington, Middlesex; under £100 in other bequests: will, City Westm. AC, original will no. 893, PRO, PROB 11/385, sig. 160; PRO, PROB 11/396, sig. 133 [Margaret Clarevell]

Blagrove, Henry Gamble (1811–1872), violinist, was born at Nottingham on 20 October 1811, the eldest son of the composer and violinist Richard Blagrove, author of *A New and Improved System to the Art of Playing the Violin* (1828), and his wife, Elenor Moss. Taught by his father, he first appeared in public at the age of five, and in 1817 played in London at Drury Lane Theatre in *The Liliputians*, as well as in concerts at the Exhibition Rooms in Spring Gardens. From 1821 he studied with Paolo Spagnoletti, and in 1823 with William Crotch and Franz Cramer as one of the first students of the new Royal Academy of Music. He won the silver medal in 1824, and from 1830 to 1837 was solo violinist in Queen Adelaide's private band. At her wish he went in 1832 to Kassel to study with Spohr, and thereafter played with great success in Vienna and elsewhere.

After returning to England, Blagrove appeared as soloist at the Philharmonic Concerts, served as principal violin at Covent Garden and Drury Lane, performed in Louis Jullien's concerts, and made many other appearances in London and elsewhere; in 1839 he played Spohr's concertante for two violins (op. 48) with the composer at the Norwich festival. On 7 November 1835 he inaugurated the first regular series of chamber concerts in London in the Hanover Square Rooms, and on 17 March 1836 founded the Quartett Concerts there with a quartet whose other members were Henry Gattie, Joseph Dando, and Charles Lucas. These concerts, which established chamber music in Victorian life and lasted until 1859, always included a work by Beethoven but also introduced new music; however, Blagrove left in 1843 to found Blagrove's Quartet Concerts. At Queen Victoria's coronation he led the state band. On 17 August 1841 he married Etheldred, daughter of Henry Combe, with whom he had three children. He returned to Germany in 1858, and later played at the lower Rhine festival in Düsseldorf.

Blagrove's works include some valuable exercises and studies for the violin and a few solos. He was regarded as one of Spohr's best pupils, his tone and technique alike being admirable. Popular with all with whom he came in contact, he was a persevering and successful teacher, notably at the Royal Academy of Music; however, for Walter Macfarren, 'though a talented and estimable individual, his temperament, like his violin playing, was decidedly cold'. After his wife's death, on 8 January 1869, Blagrove's health declined. He was presented with a public testimonial in 1872, but that December had a stroke while playing at a private concert, and he died at his home, 224 Marylebone Road, on the 15th. He was buried at Kensal Green.

His brother **Richard Manning Blagrove** (1827?–1895), viola and concertina player, was born in Nottingham and studied the viola with Henry Hill at the Royal Academy of Music. He was also one of the first to study the concertina seriously. He played a solo at the Hanover Square Rooms on 12 March 1842, and later formed a concertina quartet with Giulio Regondi, George Case, and A. B. Sedgwick; their first concert took place in the Hanover Square Rooms on 12 June 1844. Some concertina works were written for him by Sir George Macfarren. He also appeared as a piano accompanist and a violist, succeeding his old teacher as principal viola in the Philharmonic Concerts and at the Three Choirs festivals until 1894. He taught the viola at the Royal Academy until 1890, then founded a series of concerts at Clapham Hall with his sons Stanley and Arthur and his pianist wife (*née* Freeth). He died at his home, 23 Orlando Road, Clapham, London, on 21 October 1895. JOHN WARRACK

Sources *New Grove* · Brown & Stratton, *Brit. mus.* · *Musical Directory* (1874) · *The Musical Library* [monthly supplement], 3 (1835–6) · W. Macfarren, *Memories: an autobiography* (1905) · *The Times* (21 Sept 1839) · personal knowledge (1885) [*DNB*]

Likenesses wood-engraving, pubd 1872 (after C. V. Bark), NPG; repro. in *ILN* (28 Dec 1872)
Wealth at death under £450: probate, 8 Feb 1873, *CGPLA Eng. & Wales* • £1128 15s. 7d.—Richard Manning Blagrove: probate, 28 Dec 1895, *CGPLA Eng. & Wales*

Blagrove, Richard Manning (1827?–1895). *See under* Blagrove, Henry Gamble (1811–1872).

Blague, Thomas (*c.*1545–1611), dean of Rochester, was a native of Gloucester. He was admitted pensioner at Queens' College, Cambridge, at Easter 1568, seemingly after proceeding BA at Oxford the previous year. While at Queens' he compiled an anthology of classical aphorisms in translation, *A Schoole of Wise Conceytes* (1572). On 18 June 1574 he supplicated at Oxford for the degree of BTh as a bachelor of seven years' standing and proceeded DTh on 2 April 1582. The higher degree was incorporated at Cambridge in 1589.

His successive clerical appointments suggest that Blague was a man not much given to residency. He was instituted rector of Great Braxted, Essex, on 9 September 1570 at the presentation of George Talbot, sixth earl of Shrewsbury, and collated rector of St Vedast, Foster Lane, in the city of London by Archbishop Matthew Parker on 2 September 1571. Appointed one of Parker's household chaplains, he was collated rector of Lambeth by his successor, Edmund Grindal, in 1577, thereafter resigning St Vedast. As chaplain to Grindal he assisted at the consecration of John Aylmer, bishop of London, on 24 March 1577. On 20 July 1580 he was instituted to the rectory of Ewelme, Oxfordshire, on the crown's presentation and (probably in 1582) was appointed a chaplain-in-ordinary to Elizabeth. Presented to the deanery of Rochester by the crown on 14 January 1592, he was installed on 1 February. He resigned Ewelme in 1596 but became rector of Crayford, Kent, in 1599 and in 1604 succeeded Richard Vaughan, newly promoted bishop of London, as rector of Bangor Is-coed, Flintshire.

Blague remained a royal chaplain after the accession of James I, serving a monthly turn in May alongside Anthony Rudd, bishop of St David's, and Henry Hooke, later archdeacon of the West Riding. In this capacity he greeted James I during his progress south to London and preached the Tuesday court sermon in the chapel of the London Charterhouse on 10 May 1603, when the new king, consciously retracing the entry into London of his predecessor in November 1558, stayed there as a guest of Thomas, Lord Howard de Walden, who was to be created earl of Suffolk only weeks later. One of those present—perhaps Henry Hooke or else a member of the Howard family (the epistle dedicatory is signed 'H. H.')—had the sermon (on Psalms 1: 1–2) published, but without submitting the text to Blague himself for correction, 'supposing it to be comfortable a doctrine to others, as he found it delightfull to himselfe' and commending 'the grave and methodicall delivery thereof' (Blague, *Sermon*, epistle dedicatory). The sermon is a felicitous rather than admonitory piece, in which Blague offers advice to his new monarch—the *beatus vir* of the psalm—cautioning him not to take ungodly counsel nor associate with sinners or scorners. Rather he is to delight in and meditate upon the law. Like other royal chaplains that year Blague was at pains to emphasize the new king's obligations as a righteous lawgiver who would exercise justice and mercy.

In 1604—as dean of Rochester, rector of Great Braxted, rector of Lambeth, and rector of Crayford—Blague was blacklisted in a puritan survey of the Essex clergy: he had not come to Great Braxted 'paste once or twice this eighte yeres laste paste'; it was claimed that he derived an annual income of £70 from Great Braxted, £160 from Lambeth, and £120 from Crayford (*A Viewe*, 10). As rector of Lambeth he was responsible for the interment of Archbishop Richard Bancroft in November 1610, and died in possession of all his preferments except St Vedast and Ewelme.

Blague married twice. His first wife, Mary Holborne, whom he married in 1572, died without children, and in 1575 or 1576 he married Alice Brock (*b.* 1560), who, at fifteen, was half her husband's age. The Blagues make frequent appearances in the papers of the doctor and astrologer Simon Forman, whom they consulted many times, in both his capacities. In 1597, for instance, Blague was hoping for the see of Salisbury and asked Forman for a prognostication of his chances of success. His wife, who appears in the astrologer's notebooks as extravagant and promiscuous, wanted advice over her health but more especially about her love affairs, which included a prolonged liaison with Owen Wood, dean of Armagh, as well as a brief involvement with Forman himself. Nevertheless Blague saluted Alice in his will, drawn up on 4 October 1611, a week before he died, for 'her wisdome and fidelitie', and made her his sole executor. Blague died at Lambeth on 11 October 1611 and was buried at the parish church. He was survived by his wife and three sons, John (who became a fellow of Jesus College, Cambridge, and to whom Blague bequeathed his sermon notes 'if he will use them right'), Cornwallis, and Edmund. Their daughter Frances, wife of John Dove, had died in 1604, leaving a daughter whom Blague remembered in his will. About a year after her husband's death Alice married Walter Meysey, keeper of a portion of the Gatehouse prison at Westminster, but they soon separated, largely owing to debts which she brought with her from her first marriage and which she had herself principally incurred. It is not known when she died. NICHOLAS W. S. CRANFIELD

Sources T. Blague, *A sermon preached at the Charterhouse* (1603) • T. Blague, *A schoole of wise conceytes* (1572) • Venn, *Alum. Cant.*, 1.163 • *Fasti Angl., 1541–1857*, [Canterbury] • will, PRO, PROB 11/118, fol. 309 • A. L. Rowse, *Simon Forman: sex and society in Shakespeare's age* (1974) • *A viewe of the state of the clargie within the countie of Essex* [n.d., *c.*1888] • P. E. McCullough, *Sermons at court: politics and religion in Elizabethan and Jacobean preaching* (1998) [incl. CD-ROM] • LPL, Reg. Abbot 1, fol. 389v
Wealth at death died substantially in debt: Rowse, *Simon Forman*, 138–9

Blaikie, Francis (1771–1857), agriculturist and land agent, was born on 24 December 1771 at Holydean in the parish of Bowden, Roxburghshire, the son of Andrew Blaikie, a tenant farmer of Holydean, and his wife, Jane Currie. Francis followed a career in agriculture and moved to England about 1789; he subsequently became agent to the earl of Chesterfield at Bradley in Derbyshire.

In 1810 Blaikie published a pamphlet on the planting and management of forest trees, and in 1814 a further pamphlet followed on the cultivation of Swedish turnips. It was while supervising the earl of Chesterfield's estates that he attracted the notice of Thomas Coke of Holkham (1754–1842), first earl of Leicester, the celebrated pioneer of Norfolk agriculture. On the death of Chesterfield Blaikie became the chief agent of the famous Holkham estate, in 1816.

At Holkham, Blaikie immediately set about reforming the administration, made careful inspections of the farms, and reported on the character and capacity of the individual tenants. Some he found to be old-fashioned in their ideas and too easily satisfied with moderate results, and he offered advice on improvement both directly and by writing further pamphlets on such subjects as the conversion of arable land to pasture and the management of manure (a vital element in improving the light sandy soils of the estate). Subsequently he wrote on hedgerows and hedgerow timber, and on mildew and smut in wheat. Some of his pamphlets reached second and third editions. He also posed technical questions in the *Farmer's Journal* with the object of providing enlightening answers himself.

Very businesslike and insistent on correct office procedures, Blaikie prepared model leases for use on the farms, required the tenants to insure their premises, and advocated the under-drainage of wetlands. He was also an advocate of large farms, believing that the great flocks of sheep needed for manuring the light Norfolk soils could not be maintained on small farms. A large part of the high reputation of the Holkham estate for progressive and successful farming was due not so much to his famous employer but to Blaikie's intelligent and detailed direction, and his agricultural education of the tenants.

> Blaikie was exceedingly expert in the details of agricultural method, a penetrating critic of bad practice, a somewhat solemn figure of efficiency and rectitude, and inexhaustibly devoted to his employer. His was a total identification with the interests of the Coke family, and he saw his role as that of saving his masters from their best instincts. During one financial crisis Blaikie remarked with some feeling that 'Mr Coke's benevolent mind outstrips his resources. It is a virtue in him carried to excess, and for which I see no remedy in this world'. (Richards, 447)

In addition to administering the estate, Blaikie advised on Coke's finances. He was doubtful of the policy of selling distant properties, for example in coalmining areas, in order to buy additional agricultural land in Norfolk; he was also aware that continued income from the family's ownership of the Dungeness lighthouse was uncertain and he believed economies to be necessary. He reduced the large sums spent on elaborate farm buildings, though there was still considerable rebuilding of the farms during his period as agent.

Blaikie himself combined generosity with caution, presenting Coke's daughter Elizabeth with a topaz-and-diamond locket on the occasion of her betrothal while producing at the same time a report on the financial affairs of her prospective husband. With a salary of £550 p.a. (later increased to £650), very respectable remuneration for the period, he managed to make substantial investments in land and turnpikes at Wells, in Norfolk, and when he retired in 1832 he sold the land he had accumulated to Coke for £1200. On his retirement from Holkham Blaikie returned to Scotland and farmed land of his own at St Helens in the parish of Melrose, Roxburghshire, where by 1851 he was employing four labourers and two general servants. He died, unmarried, at St Helens on 17 August 1857 at the age of eighty-six, and was buried at Melrose churchyard. G. E. MINGAY

Sources S. Wade Martins, *A great estate at work: the Holkham estate and its inhabitants in the nineteenth century* (1980) • R. A. C. Parker, *Coke of Norfolk* (1975) • E. Richards, 'The land agent', *The Victorian countryside*, ed. G. E. Mingay, 2 (1981), 439–56 • A. M. W. Stirling, *Coke of Norfolk and his friends*, 2 vols. (1908) • J. Donaldson, *Agricultural biography* (1854) • d. cert.

Likenesses portrait, Holkham, Norfolk; repro. in Martin, *Great estate at work*, 68

Blaikie, Walter Biggar (1847–1928), civil engineer and publisher, was born in Edinburgh on 23 November 1847, the second son of the Revd William Garden *Blaikie (1820–1899), minister at Pilrig, a Disruption father of the Free Church of Scotland, later professor of apologetics and pastoral theology at New College, Edinburgh, and his wife, Margaret Catherine (*d.* 1915), daughter of Walter Biggar, a retired fish merchant resident in Edinburgh. Like his relative Robert Louis Stevenson, with whom he shared a childhood nurse, Blaikie was destined to be a civil engineer. He was educated at Edinburgh Academy and privately in Brussels before attending classes at Edinburgh University and training in the office of B. and E. Blyth, noted railway engineers. He went to India in 1870 to work first for the raja of Kathiawar, and then for the public works department of the government of India, in which he became executive engineer, military works. In 1873 he married Janet Marshall (only daughter of John Macfie of Edinburgh); they had five daughters. The Indian climate suited neither Blaikie's wife nor their first child, so he returned to Scotland on leave and resigned in 1879.

Blaikie was about to emigrate to Australia when he happened to meet, at King's Cross Station, London, Thomas Constable, the queen's printer in Edinburgh, a fellow Edinburgh Academical, and an elder of Pilrig Free Church, who suggested that he try a spell in the printing trade. Six months later he became a partner in T. and A. Constable, Thistle Street, Edinburgh. He settled in Colinton and rose to be company chairman, an authority on the history of Scottish typography, and a printer of fine editions of, among others, the works of R. L. Stevenson.

Passionately interested in non-telescopic astronomy, Blaikie published annually from 1898 until 1920 an elaborate set of star maps designed to help amateurs. His ingenious spherical planisphere calculating device was appreciated by the Greenwich and Edinburgh observatories. He wrote articles for the magazine of the Royal Scottish Geographical Society, of which he was a founder, and for long a member of council. A fellow of the Royal Society of Edinburgh, he was prominent in the Scottish History Society, and a founder and president of the Old Edinburgh Club. He was also a member and office bearer of the Scottish Society of Arts. As generous-hearted as he was brusquely businesslike, he was chairman of the Edinburgh chamber of commerce in 1903–6, and from 1900 to 1920 a manager of the Edinburgh Royal Infirmary.

Blaikie wrote and printed for the Scottish History Society his meticulous *Itinerary of Prince Charles Edward Stuart* (1897) and the substantial volume, *Origins of the Forty-Five* (1916). He put money into the *Scots Observer*, which in 1891 became the London-based *National Observer*. He also helped found the *Celtic Review* and was president of the Royal Celtic Society, 1921–6.

Edinburgh University awarded Blaikie an honorary LLD in 1913. He was a JP and from 1918 a deputy lieutenant of Edinburgh. One daughter married Robert Kilpatrick, managing director of T. and A. Constable. Two others, Alice and Margaret Blaikie, presented his Jacobite pamphlets and manuscripts to the National Library of Scotland as a memorial after his death in an Edinburgh nursing home on 3 May 1928. B. P. LENMAN, *rev.*

Sources *Walter Biggar Blaikie, 1847–1928* (privately printed, Edinburgh, 1929) • *William Garden Blaikie: an autobiography*, ed. N. L. Walker (1901) • Edinburgh Central Public Library, Coll YDA1820B • NL Scot., Blaikie MSS • *CCI* (1928)

Archives NL Scot., collections relating to Jacobites, MSS 278–318, 3128 • NL Scot., letters to Lord Haldane, MSS 6017–6030

Wealth at death £34,442 13*s*. 7*d*.: confirmation, 21 Aug 1928, *CCI*

Blaikie, William Garden (1820–1899), Free Church of Scotland minister and writer, was born in Aberdeen on 5 February 1820, one of ten children and the second son of James Blaikie (1786–1836) of Craigiebuckler and his wife, Jane Garden (*d*. 1857). His father, an advocate, was lord provost of Aberdeen at the time of his death. Educated at Aberdeen grammar school and Marischal College, Aberdeen, Blaikie proceeded to the study of divinity, during which he spent a session (1839–40) at Edinburgh University. Licensed to preach by the presbytery of Aberdeen, he was presented to the parish of Drumblade, Aberdeenshire, by the earl of Kintore, a family friend, and was ordained on 22 September 1842. He adhered to the Free Church at the Disruption the following May and remained in Drumblade until he accepted a call to a new congregation at Pilrig in Edinburgh, to which he was admitted on 1 March 1844.

Social conditions in Pilrig prompted Blaikie to become involved in both the erection of model buildings for rent to workmen, and also in temperance issues. On 20 May 1845 Blaikie married Margaret Catherine Biggar (*d*. 1915) with whom he had fourteen children, though three of them were stillborn, and three more died in infancy. Among those to survive into adulthood was Walter Biggar *Blaikie, civil engineer and publisher. William Blaikie's wife shared in his work and ran a children's home for some twenty years, from which many children emigrated to Canada. Blaikie's *Six Lectures to the Working Classes on the Improvement of their Temporal Condition* (1849), re-issued in 1863 as *Better Days for Working People*, sold 80,000 copies, and brought him to public attention. It prompted a less successful sequel which looked at employers, *Heads and Hands in the World of Labour* (1865). A new church was also built during his ministry.

In 1868 Blaikie was appointed professor of apologetics and pastoral theology at New College, Edinburgh. The presence of another professor and near-namesake in Edinburgh, John Stuart Blackie, proved an embarrassment to Blaikie in that, among other confusions, many of Blackie's eccentricities were attributed to him. This caused him to stress the Garden element of his name thereafter. A student dining-hall was instituted at New College on his initiative, and he promoted the work of the New College settlement. He was honoured with the degree of DD by Edinburgh University in 1864, and that of LLD by Aberdeen University in 1871. From 1874 to 1878 he was convener of the Home Mission committee of the Free Church: during the visit of the American evangelists Moody and Sankey in 1873–4, the Blaikies housed the Moody family, an act typical of a couple who were never too busy to take on another commitment. In 1888 Blaikie was Cunningham lecturer, and in 1892 served as moderator of the Free Church general assembly, the last of the pre-Disruption ministers to do so. He was greatly interested in foreign churches and was one of the founders of the Pan-Presbyterian Alliance, of which he was president from 1888 to 1892, as well as helping to raise money for the Waldenses.

Literary work made constant claims on Blaikie, beginning with the *Free Church Magazine*, which he edited from 1849 to 1853. He also edited the *North British Review* (1860–63), which he gave up on health grounds, though soon after he assisted Thomas Guthrie with the *Sunday Magazine*, briefly assuming sole editorship on Guthrie's death. He edited the *Catholic Presbyterian* (1879–83) and kept up a steady output of books. The most famous of several biographies was *The Personal Life of David Livingstone* (1880), and Blaikie contributed to the early volumes of the *Dictionary of National Biography*.

Increasing deafness led Blaikie to resign his chair in 1897 but he remained active and was only prevented from attendance at the Free Church general assembly by a paralytic seizure from which he died at his home, 2 Tantallon Terrace, North Berwick, on 11 June 1899. Blaikie showed great catholicity of interest while at the same time remaining true to the conservative religious tradition in which he had been raised. Although not a leader of his church in any conventional sense, he was certainly one of its ornaments. LIONEL ALEXANDER RITCHIE

Sources *William Garden Blaikie: an autobiography*, ed. N. L. Walker (1901) • *Fasti Scot.* • *The Scotsman* (12 June 1899) • *ILN* (17 June 1899), 869 • *Free Church of Scotland Monthly* (1 Aug 1899), 184–5 • *WWW*, *1897–1915* • J. Silvester, *Dr W. G. Blaikie, divine and philanthropist*

(1922) • *Walter Biggar Blaikie, 1847–1928* (privately printed, Edinburgh, 1929)
Archives U. Edin., New Coll. L., notes of proceedings of convocation 1842 • U. Edin., New Coll. L., sermon notes | NL Scot., letters to Alexander Campbell Fraser, Dep 208
Likenesses P. Novice, oils, 1853, Scot. NPG • J. Moffat, carte-de-visite, NPG • photograph (in old age), repro. in Walker, ed., *William Garden Blaikie*, facing frontispiece
Wealth at death £3679 16*s*. 9*d*.: confirmation, 8 Sept 1899, *CCI*

Blaímac mac Áeda [Blathmac] (*d.* **665**), joint high-king of Ireland, was one of the numerous sons of *Áed Sláine (*d.* 604), who was the founder of that branch of the Uí Néill which ruled Brega, a district stretching from the River Liffey to the southern part of what is now co. Louth. Síl nÁeda Sláine, 'the seed of Áed Sláine', was the most powerful branch of the southern Uí Néill in the seventh century, during which five of its members were high-kings of Ireland, among them Blaímac. In the regnal lists preserved in twelfth-century manuscripts, and also in the text known as *Baile Chuinn* ('The frenzy of Conn'), probably composed during the reign of *Fínsnechtae Fledach (*d.* 695) late in the seventh century, Blaímac is given as joint king of Tara (high-king of Ireland) with his brother Diarmait. In an account of the battle of Ogoman in 662, however, the Annals of Tigernach and the *Chronicum Scotorum* declare that Blaímac was defeated in that battle by the companions of Diarmait, his brother, and that this was the end of Blaímac's reign and the beginning of Diarmait's. This detail is not found in the annals of Ulster and it may be mistaken. Under 643 the annals of Ulster declare their uncertainty as to who reigned as king of Tara after Domnall mac Áeda (*d.* 642): 'Some historiographers say that four kings, namely Cellach and Conall Cóel and the two sons of Áed Slâne, namely Diarmait and Blathmac [Blaímac], ruled in shared reigns.' Most lists, however, made Blaímac and Diarmait succeed Cellach and Conall Cóel. *Baile Chuinn*'s inclusion of Blaímac and Diarmait among the kings of Tara is probably decisive, since it seems to reflect the particular interests of their nephew Fínsnechtae Fledach and omits Blaímac's two sons, *Cenn Fáelad (*d.* 675) and *Sechnassach (*d.* 671). From the ninth century onwards the joint reign of Blaímac and Diarmait—falling immediately before the great plague of 664–5—was regarded as a golden age and became the focus of many legends.

In 634 Blaímac's brothers, Congal, king of Brega, and Ailill the Harper, were killed by Conall mac Suibni, who had also been the slayer of their father, Áed Sláine. After their death, Diarmait was initially the only surviving brother to be noticed in the annals: he killed Conall mac Suibni to revenge his brothers and his father and he went on to defeat and kill another potential rival, Máel Umai mac Óengusa of another Uí Néill dynasty, Clann Cholmáin Bicc. The surviving sons of Áed Sláine, Blaímac, Diarmait, and Dúnchad, contrived to be on the winning side at the major battle of Mag Roth in 637 as allies of Domnall mac Áeda, whereas their rivals of Mide were allies of the loser, Congal Cáech (*d.* 637). The sons of Áed Sláine thus became the dominant figures among the southern Uí Néill.

The period between 637 and his death, probably of the plague, in 665 seems to have been uneventful for Blaímac. His brother Diarmait continued to take the lead in the military sphere, defeating the kings of Munster and Connacht in 649. The deaths of two of Blaímac's sons in 651 and of another in 660 are not explained in the annals. There may have been difficulties with Diarmait and his sons, but later and uncertain tradition ascribed the deaths of two sons to an exploit by a Leinsterman, Máelodrán. It is unclear where in Brega Blaímac and his sons had their main power: Diarmait's descendants became the kings of southern Brega while those of the elder sons, Congal and Ailill the Harper, ruled northern Brega. Although two of his sons were to be high-kings of Ireland, Blaímac's family thereafter fell into obscurity, suggesting that they may never have established a strong territorial base.

T. M. Charles-Edwards

Sources W. Stokes, ed., 'The annals of Tigernach [8 pts]', *Revue Celtique*, 16 (1895), 374–419; 17 (1896), 6–33, 119–263, 337–420; 18 (1897), 9–59, 150–97, 267–303, 374–91; pubd sep. (1993) • *Ann. Ulster* • G. Murphy, 'On the dates of two sources used in Thurneysen's *Heldensage*: 1. *Baile Chuind* and the date of *Cin Dromma Snechtai*', *Ériu*, 16 (1952), 145–56, esp. 146–9 • W. M. Hennessy, ed. and trans., *Chronicum Scotorum: a chronicle of Irish affairs*, Rolls Series, 46 (1866) • M. A. O'Brien, ed., *Corpus genealogiarum Hiberniae* (Dublin, 1962) • D. Greene, ed., *Fingal Rónáin and other stories* (1955) • F. J. Byrne, *Irish kings and high-kings* (1973)

Blaímac mac Flainn (*d.* **825**). *See under* Iona, abbots of (*act.* 563–927).

Blair, Alexander (**1789–1859**), banker, was born on 18 June 1789, the son of William Blair, a captain in the 13th regiment of foot, and his wife, Margaret Freeland. Nothing seems to be known of his early life, but his commercial education began in a merchant's house in Liverpool. In 1811 he entered the service of the British Linen Bank in Edinburgh. He began as a confidential clerk and, from there, proceeded to the position of assistant secretary. In 1826 he was appointed joint secretary. Two years later the manager and secretary of the bank both resigned, and Blair was appointed joint manager with Thomas Corrie, a director of the bank, who resigned from the board upon his appointment as joint manager. Blair was to be paid £800 plus £100 for a house, while Corrie was paid £1400. On 7 May 1828 Blair married Mary Smith (1800–1872), the daughter of George Smith, a banker. They had one daughter, Mary Elizabeth (1830–1857).

If Blair resented his situation at the British Linen Bank he did not have to endure it for long, for in July 1832 the treasurer of Scotland's oldest bank, the Bank of Scotland, resigned after pressure from his board, and Blair was appointed to the position at a salary of £1200. What the Bank of Scotland needed was a reforming manager who had strong views on financial management and business organization. They found both of these attributes in Blair. He began by reforming the reporting practices in the bank to ensure that he and the board were continuously aware of the position of the bank, and 'he quickly made his mark as an effective banker, at once energetic and disciplined, with an ability for work on accounts, the auditing and control of branches and the huge volume of administrative work required of a Bank Treasurer' (Saville, 301).

This was a difficult time for banks as many new joint-stock banks were being set up, thereby increasing the competitive pressures. The Bank of Scotland's profits continued to be under pressure, and Blair wrote a very incisive treasurer's report for his board. This was a comprehensive review, which considered the bank's internal affairs as well as such topics as joint-stock banking, the role of the Bank of England, and 'the probable intention of the Government upon the subject of the currency' (Checkland, 354). Blair realized that, despite the boom in business, the Bank of Scotland's profits were actually falling. The only real solutions to this problem were a lowering of the deposit rate and the introduction of charges on services (as English banks did), but the Bank of Scotland was unable to act unilaterally. Blair therefore worked for the introduction of a code of conduct for all Scottish banks.

Blair had very sound ideas about how a bank should view its balance sheet, especially its reserve ratios and its dividend policy. It is easy, in reading his letters, to see Blair as the arch conservative banker, and there was much about his demeanour which would confirm this view. But the bank emerged from his period as treasurer as a healthier and larger institution with a reputation for sound judgement and good faith. Under Blair's firm hand a more limited role was allowed to directors and Scottish politicians on the board, and his managerial reforms led to a greater degree of professionalism.

By the later 1840s Blair had become convinced that the Scottish banking system was dangerously weak. His preferred solution was a merger of the three public banks in Edinburgh. Once consolidated, an institution comprising the Bank of Scotland, the Royal Bank of Scotland, and the British Linen Bank would perform in Scotland a role analogous to that of the Bank of England. However, although Blair obtained promises of government support, he was unable to secure approval from his colleagues in the other two banks.

Blair certainly did not believe in untrammelled competition, viewing it as potentially damaging to both the profitability and the stability of the financial system. In the early 1840s he made several efforts to get the Scottish banks to agree to uniform rates of interest for deposits and discounts. However, it usually proved difficult to hold the parties together for very long. Blair conceded that agreements would end when it suited the needs of any individual bank. 'Experience shows', he wrote, 'that the banks have never acted together unless compelled to do so by the state of the money market, and that all proceedings of committees have been disavowed by one or other of the Boards' (Checkland, 391). Nevertheless, the regular meetings which he established between senior bankers became the committee of Scottish bank general managers, the basis for the cartel which operated for more than a century.

Blair skilfully defended Scottish banking principles and methods before a number of parliamentary committees, and he became embroiled in the currency and banking debate. He was a friend of Thomas Tooke, who wrote part of his *History of Prices* (6 vols., 1838–57) in Blair's house at Drylaw. Volume 3 is dedicated to Blair. The passage of the Bank Charter Acts of 1844 and 1845 led to widespread condemnation in Scotland. Blair and other Scottish bankers objected to the degree of banking centralization and control that the acts introduced. Not only did the legislation impose a costly requirement to hold reserve gold, but, by inhibiting the formation of new banks, it supported the cartel over prices operated via the general managers' committee. Although Blair believed that the legislation of 1844 and 1845 was intellectually flawed, he nevertheless conceded that in practice it contained some useful operating principles.

Blair saw himself, or rather his bank, as the policeman of the system, and in the 1830s he led the other public banks in an attempt to discipline what he believed to be the financially irresponsible Western Bank of Scotland. Blair's view of the Western as a potential problem was well founded, for it was the Western's failure in 1857 which did so much damage to the reputation of the Scottish banking system. It was again Blair who led the effort to minimize the damage of the crisis. However, it and the report, and evidence from the select committee on the Bank Acts, 'thoroughly depressed' (Saville, 406) Blair, who was disappointed that the support given by the Bank of Scotland to bolstering the Scottish banking system had not been appreciated. Unfortunately, Blair experienced a personal blow when, in the middle of the crisis, his only child, Mary, died in childbirth. Blair enjoyed indifferent health throughout 1858, and died on 1 February 1859 at his home, Beechwood, Edinburgh, as a result of influenza. He was buried in St John's churchyard, Princes Street, Edinburgh.

Throughout his life Blair took a professional interest in economic debate, but he was also a classical scholar who read the psalms in Hebrew. For recreation he played sacred music on an organ, and otherwise conducted himself in a modest manner. He had a wide circle of correspondents, who included the leading banking theoreticians such as J. R. McCulloch, Lord Overstone, and the MP John Abel Smith.

One of the most highly regarded Scottish bankers of his time, Blair strove to defend the interests of the Bank of Scotland, while also working to transform the nature of the Scottish financial system. Yet while he undoubtedly succeeded in the former role, Blair did not generate enough support for his schemes of bank merger. In the period before the Bank Charter Acts of 1844 and 1845 his arguments did not prove powerful enough to undermine the influence of the Bank of England. 'This failure to maintain the pre-eminence of Scottish banking ideas', Richard Saville has recently concluded, 'rather clouded his judgement in later years and induced a reluctance to take part in national debate, although in purely banking terms he was able to deal with the periodic crises of the banking system' (Saville, 301). CHARLES W. MUNN

Sources C. A. Malcolm, *The Bank of Scotland, 1695–1945* (1945) · A. W. Kerr, *History of banking in Scotland*, 3rd edn (1918) · C. A. Malcolm, *The history of the British Linen Bank* (privately printed, Edinburgh, 1950) · A. Cameron, *Bank of Scotland, 1695–1995: a very singular institution* (1995) · S. G. Checkland, *Scottish banking: a history, 1695–1973* (1975) · R. Saville, *Bank of Scotland: a history, 1695–1995* (1996) · d. cert. · J. F. Mitchell, Some Edinburgh monumental inscriptions, General Register Office for Scotland, Edinburgh
Archives Bank of Scotland, Edinburgh, archives department
Likenesses photograph, Bank of Scotland, Edinburgh, archives department; repro. in Cameron, *Bank of Scotland*

Blair, David [*real name* David Butterfield] (**1932–1976**), ballet dancer, was born David Butterfield on 27 July 1932 at the Royal Halifax Infirmary, Halifax, Yorkshire, the elder child and only son of John Butterfield, moquette weaver, and his wife, Zetté Carolyne Elizabeth Whiteley, both of Halifax, where he received his primary education at Trinity School. As a child he attended local dancing classes and was selected by the Royal Academy of Dancing for extra coaching under its scholarship scheme in the Yorkshire region, which led, when he was fourteen, to the Royal Ballet School, London. Only a year later, in 1947, he joined the Sadler's Wells Theatre Ballet and progressed so quickly that at sixteen he was dancing the exacting *pas de deux* in *Casse noisette* and in 1950 he was made a principal dancer.

From the start Blair's exceptional virtuosity, enhanced by good looks and a most engaging stage presence, endeared him to the public and critics alike in a variety of roles. His first lead in a new choreography came when Michael Somes cast him for his *Summer Interlude*; and a few months later Balanchine chose him for *Trumpet Concerto* at Sadler's Wells Theatre. But it was John Cranko who worked most closely with Blair for several years, developing his talents over a wide range and creating for him, in 1951, the unforgettable Captain Belaye in *Pineapple Poll* to the music of Arthur Sullivan. Blair's portrayal of the dashingly handsome but ludicrously vain captain was a masterpiece of comedy which, combined with his brilliant dancing, helped to establish the ballet as one of the favourite British classics.

In 1953 Blair transferred to the 'parent' company, Sadler's Wells Ballet (later the Royal Ballet) at the Royal Opera House, Covent Garden. The change to a larger company and larger theatre was timely for his artistic development in the classical repertoire, for which his slightly mischievous, boyish charm and exuberance were almost a disadvantage—although of course making him the ideal Franz in *Coppélia*.

Blair soon mastered the noble style and partnered with great distinction all the Royal Ballet ballerinas including Svetlana Beriosova, Violetta Elvin, Annette Page, Rowena Jackson, Anya Linden, Margot Fonteyn, and especially Nadia Nerina, with whom he had an exceptionally successful partnership.

Blair's repertoire with the Royal Ballet included *The Three-Cornered Hat* (1953), *Swan Lake* and *Sleeping Beauty* (1955), *Cinderella* (1956), *Giselle* and *Prince of the Pagodas* (1957), *Petrushka* (1959), and much more. In 1960 Frederick Ashton choreographed one of his greatest works, *La fille mal gardée*, for Nadia Nerina and David Blair, who shared a triumphant success. Blair danced superbly the role of Colas, the country youth, giving him an irresistible air of amiable cheekiness. Another triumph was his Mercutio in Kenneth MacMillan's *Romeo and Juliet*. In 1961, on Michael Somes's retirement, David Blair succeeded him as principal dancer of the Royal Ballet.

Blair had a delightfully fresh enthusiasm for dance even when encountering the ups and downs from which no one is immune—the road is always bumpier at the top than on the way up. But it would be hard to find a man more straightforward, staunch, without malice or guile, warm-hearted, and lovable. He spoke his mind in the forthright manner of a true Yorkshireman and he was also very human—he had a soft shell for criticism.

Blair married in 1957 the ballerina Maryon Lane, who was born Patricia Mills, the daughter of an Irish doctor in Melmouth, Zululand, South Africa. Twin daughters, Diana and Catherine Blair, were born in 1960, and Diana, following her parents' profession, became a member of the Hamburg Ballet.

While still on the top as a dancer, Blair branched out into production with the complete versions of *Swan Lake* (1965) and *Sleeping Beauty* (1966) for the Atlanta Civic Ballet. For American Ballet Theater he produced *Swan Lake* (1967) and *Giselle* (1968). He was also the producer of the Hong Kong Ballet's *Giselle* and a filmed version of *Giselle* starring Carla Fracci and Erik Bruhn (1969).

In the history of British ballet David Blair stands in the forefront of accomplished male dancers. He set a standard of virtuoso dancing in the 1950s that inspired and influenced the following generation. In addition he gave much time and effort, mainly through his involvement with the Royal Academy of Dancing (he was a member of its executive committee from 1971), to the teaching of students and the resettlement of retiring professionals. His was a life devoted to dance and fellow dancers. For services to ballet he was appointed CBE in 1964. In 1973 his farewell to the stage at the Royal Opera House was an overwhelming personal triumph. He was about to take up directorship of the Norwegian Ballet in Oslo when on 1 April 1976 he died suddenly of a heart attack at his home in London, 19 Holland Park Road, Kensington, his wife surviving him.

MARGOT FONTEYN, *rev.*

Sources *The Times* (2 April 1976) · *Dancing Times* (May 1976) · H. Koegler, *The concise Oxford dictionary of ballet* (1977) · personal knowledge (1986) · private information (1986) · J. Kavanagh, *Secret muses: the life of Frederick Ashton* (1996) · *CGPLA Eng. & Wales* (1976) · b. cert.
Likenesses photographs, 1951–65, Hult. Arch.
Wealth at death £80,604: probate, 3 Sept 1976, *CGPLA Eng. & Wales*

Blair, Dame Emily Mathieson (**1890–1963**), nurse and nursing administrator, was born on 12 January 1890 at Boghead, Lenzie, Kirkintilloch, daughter of Hugh Blair, muslin manufacturer, and his wife, Mary Ann, *née* Croll. Blair trained as a nurse at the Western Infirmary, Glasgow, from 1912 to 1916. In July 1916 she was appointed ward sister at the VAD hospital, Higham, where she worked until

February 1917. She was then a sister at the RAF hospital at Halton, near Aylesbury, Buckinghamshire, as a member of Queen Alexandra's Royal Naval Nursing Service (Reserves), and in 1918 she was recommended for a permanent commission with the RAF nursing service, the forerunner of Princess Mary's Royal Air Force Nursing Service (PMRAFNS), formed by royal warrant in 1921. Blair soon showed that her enthusiasm and ability were above average, and that she was tactful in dealing with staff and patients, and in 1923 she was recommended for accelerated promotion.

Blair's first permanent commission was as sister at the Central Hospital, Hampstead, London, and from 1919 to 1922 she was again at the RAF hospital at Halton. Her first tour of duty abroad was to Baghdad Hospital (1922–4). She also worked in Basrah (1926–8), Palestine (1928–30), and Hinaidi, Iraq (1935–7), with intervening spells in Uxbridge, Halton, and Cranwell. After September 1937 she remained in England, working at Halton and Cranwell. She was a senior sister from January 1925, an acting matron from January 1927, and matron from January 1930. On 6 May 1935 she was presented with the king's jubilee medal. In December 1937 she was moved to the Air Ministry, and was appointed as matron-in-chief of the PMRAFNS from January 1938 until her retirement in 1943. On 6 September 1938 she was awarded the Royal Red Cross (first class) by the joint war committee (the wartime union of the British Red Cross Society and the order of St John of Jerusalem). This was given for her exceptional devotion and the competence she had shown while nursing and caring for the sick in RAF hospitals at home and abroad. Blair was mentioned in dispatches on 1 January 1941. She was created a dame of the British empire (military division) on 2 June 1943. She was appointed to the order of St John on 24 February 1944 in the grade of officer sister and given the honorary position of matron-in-chief of the order of St John.

From 1943 to 1947 Blair was matron-in-chief of the joint war committee. When this disbanded she continued as matron-in-chief of the British Red Cross Society from 1947 to 1953. She was awarded the Florence Nightingale medal in 1947 by the international committee of the Red Cross for her great services to nursing. During the war the appointment of all the trained staff in the 250 joint war organizations' hospitals and convalescent homes was her responsibility. She was immensely tactful and able to ensure that in all the hospitals and homes the relationships between the professional nursing staff and the auxiliary nurses from the Red Cross were happy. She also selected many nurses for overseas service. She was on the executive committee of the Red Cross from 1946. When she retired from the British Red Cross Society she was made an honorary life member. A collection was made for her retirement and she was presented with a wireless on 24 November 1953 by Lord Woolton and Lady Limerick, representatives of the British Red Cross Society. She died, unmarried, on 25 December 1963, at 12 Avenue Road, St John's Wood, London, from lung cancer, and her remains were cremated. A memorial service was held on 28 January 1964 at St Clement Danes, London, which was attended by representatives of all the organizations with which she had been associated.

CATHARINE M. C. HAINES

Sources RAF Innsworth, Gloucester, personnel management agency • PRO, AIR 2/93/C 45714; AIR/2/93/CW 1528; C 66031 [air ministry correspondence; establishment of RAF nursing services] • private information (2004) [air historical branch, ministry of defence, Scotland Yard, London; curator of fine art, and the senior keeper, Royal Air Force Museum, Hendon, London; M. Mackie; C. Mulryne, keeper, St John Ambulance collection, Order of St John Museum and Library, Clerkenwell, London; W. J. G. Spencer, PRO] • *WW* (1962) • *WWW, 1961–70* • British Red Cross Society Archives, Grosvenor Square, London • *The Times* (29 Jan 1964) • *Annual Report of the British Red Cross*, 4 (1942–3), 92 • P. G. Cambray and G. G. B. Briggs, eds., *Red Cross & St. John: the official record of the humanitarian services of the war organization of the British Red Cross Society and order of St. John of Jerusalem, 1939–1947* (1949) • b. cert. • d. cert.

Likenesses A. R. Thomson, oils, 1943, RAF Museum, Cosford, Shropshire • photograph, 1943 (with princess royal), repro. in *MTE Journal* (Aug–Sept 1943), 276

Wealth at death £1393: probate, 29 Jan 1964, *CGPLA Eng. & Wales*

Blair, Eric Arthur [*pseud.* George Orwell] (**1903–1950**), political writer and essayist, was born in Motihari, Bengal, India, on 25 June 1903, the only son of Richard Walmesley Blair (1857–1938), a sub-deputy opium agent in the government of Bengal, and his wife, Ida Mabel Limouzin (1875–1943). Richard Blair's great-grandfather Charles Blair (1743–1820), a Scot, had been a rich man, a plantation and slave owner in Jamaica who had married into the English aristocracy; the money had run out by Richard Blair's time, who all his career held poor posts, and was on the move constantly. He married Ida Limouzin, who was eighteen years his junior, late in his career. Her mother was English and her father French; she was born in Penge but had spent most of her life in Moulmein, Burma, where her father was a teak dealer and boat builder. Ida Blair took three-year-old Eric and his older sister, Marjorie, back to England just before the birth of her third and last child, Avril. Eric attended a small Anglican convent school in Henley-on-Thames until he gained a part scholarship to St Cyprian's, a fashionable preparatory school where Cyril Connolly was among his contemporaries. His fees were topped up by his mother's unmarried brother, who like his sister, and totally unlike Richard Blair, seems to have had intellectual interests and ambitions for his nephew.

In *The Road to Wigan Pier* Orwell described his family with sardonic precision as 'lower-upper middle class', that is the 'upper-middle class without money' (*Complete Works*, 5.113–14). Late in his life he wrote a long account of his prep school days, 'Such, such were the joys', that could not be published in his lifetime for fear of libel. Some have taken this to be a literal account of the horrors of an oppressive and socially discriminatory regime, but it is more likely a polemic against private education based on fact and with a reimagined Eric Blair as the observer, hero, or rather anti-hero. However, whether or not he was caned in front of the school for bed-wetting, the school was bad enough.

Eric Arthur Blair [George Orwell] (**1903–1950**), by Felix H. Man, *c.*1947

Education and early life Young Eric crammed for and eventually won a scholarship to Eton College, but once there he rested on his oars, neglecting the set tasks; however, he read widely for himself in the canon of English literature and books by rationalists, freethinkers, and reformers like Samuel Butler, George Bernard Shaw, and H. G. Wells. As a scholarship boy at Eton he was in the College—an intellectual élite thrust into the heart of a social élite. He found a few kindred spirits, including Steven Runciman (later the historian of Byzantium) and his prep school friend Cyril Connolly (the critic and writer). In Connolly's *Enemies of Promise* there are good descriptions of Orwell both at prep school and at Eton. Orwell's contemporaries agree that, without being openly rebellious, he cultivated a mocking, sardonic attitude towards authority. The classical scholar Andrew Gow, who as a young man had taught Orwell, in the mid-1970s remembered him only with irritation and annoyance for having wasted his chance to get to university. It was that kind of attitude that Orwell reacted against.

Following in his father's footsteps, probably more cynically than purposively, Eric was sent to a crammer's to prepare for the Indian Civil Service exams. He scraped just enough marks to be able to join the Burma police in 1921. Burma was then governed as a province of India and did not rate high in the pecking order of 'the Service'. Eric Blair may well have been the only Etonian ever to pass through the police training school at Mandalay to become an assistant superintendent. His fellow recruits were all older than he (though none taller or wearing size eleven boots) and almost all had gone through the First World War. Blair showed a loathing both for the war and for military values, but also some signs of guilt or regret at having missed it. He grew to like the Burmese and to dislike the effect of colonial rule on his fellow British. Like Flory in his first novel, *Burmese Days*, he 'learned to live inwardly, in books and secret thoughts that could not be uttered'. He was not popular in the police and had poor postings: 'In Moulmein in Lower Burma, I was hated by large numbers of people—the only time in my life that I have been important enough for this to happen to me' (*Complete Works*, 10.501). When he wrote about Burma, both in *Burmese Days* and in two of his finest essays, 'Shooting an elephant' and 'A hanging', his contempt for imperial rule and the arrogant pretentiousness of too many of his fellows came bursting out.

Setting out To the dismay of his parents Blair resigned his safe, respectable, and pensionable job while on leave in England from July 1927 and not only resolved to be a writer but took to making journeys among tramps. He lived as a tramp sometimes for a day or two, sometimes for weeks at a time. He said that he wanted to see if the English poor were treated in their own country as the Burmese were treated in theirs. On the whole he thought they were. In spring 1928 he went to Paris to write. As he wrote for an American reference book in 1942, he

> lived for about a year and a half in Paris, writing novels and short stories which no one would publish. After my money came to an end I had several years of fairly severe poverty during which I was, among other things, a dishwasher, a private tutor and a teacher in cheap private schools. (*Complete Works*, 12.147)

But in an introduction to the Ukrainian edition of *Animal Farm* he revealed more:

> I sometimes lived for months on end among the poor and half-criminal elements … who take to the streets, begging and stealing. At that time I associated with them through lack of money, but later their way of life interested me very much for its own sake. (ibid., 19.86–7)

Years later Sir Victor Pritchett described him as a man 'who went native in his own country' (Crick, 276). In this period he called himself 'a Tory anarchist'. At first he did not know what he wanted to write about, and he destroyed two early novels. The poet Ruth Pitter remembers reading early manuscripts: 'How we cruel girls laughed. … He wrote like a cow with a musket' (ibid., 179).

Orwell stuck to it, however, and taught himself to write in his famous plain style. His first book published, *Down and out in Paris and London* (1933), was an account of his tramping days in England, particularly in the hop fields of Kent, and of the poverty he endured while living in Paris trying to write novels. The sales of the book were modest, but it received good notices. He used a pseudonym, George Orwell, partly to avoid embarrassing his parents, partly as a hedge against failure, and partly because he disliked the name Eric, which reminded him of a prig in a Victorian boys' story. His first novel, *Burmese Days*, was published in New York in 1934. Victor Gollancz in London had refused it for fear of libel actions: the novel was obviously written directly from experience. Based partly on teaching in cheap private schools such as The Hawthorns in Hayes where he had a position from 1932 to 1933, and partly on his parents' neighbours in Southwold, he wrote a contrived literary pastiche, *The Clergyman's Daughter* (1935). His schoolteaching had ended when in December 1933 he had a bad attack of pneumonia. In October 1934 he left Southwold and moved to Hampstead, London, where he became a half-time assistant in a secondhand bookshop.

Since 1930 Orwell had been reviewing books and writing sketches and poems for *The Adelphi*, owned and edited by Sir Richard Rees, a disciple of John Middleton Murry. Orwell moved to Hampstead to see more of Rees and also the young writers who called at the *Adelphi* office for a cup of tea, to talk, and to solicit books to review. He became friendly with Jack Common and Rayner Heppenstall, and met Cyril Connolly again after Connolly had reviewed *Burmese Days*. But his world, unlike Connolly's, was not that of fashionable Hampstead drawing-rooms but of Hampstead bohemia: those bitter and often jealous intellectuals, living in bed-sits, making a pint in a pub last a whole evening, fearing rent day, and knowing that the post brought only rejection slips. All this he portrayed in *Keep the Aspidistra Flying* (1936). At this time he himself, like his novel's hero Gordon Comstock, came near to making a cult of failure and to believing that all literary success is 'selling out'.

In January 1936 the left-wing publisher Victor Gollancz, showing great faith in Orwell as a writer, gave him an advance of £500 (then nearly two years' income for Orwell) to write a book about poverty and unemployment. He spent two months in the north of England, living with working people in Wigan, Barnsley, and Sheffield from 31 January to 30 March. On his return he moved to a cheap cottage in Wallington, Hertfordshire. On 9 June, after a short courtship, he married Eileen Maud O'Shaughnessy (1905–1945), who had read English at Oxford, and after running a secretarial agency, was taking a postgraduate diploma in psychology at University College, London. They had met in Hampstead, and hoped to live on his writing, her typing, and running a small village shop.

In Wallington Orwell settled down to write essays including 'Shooting an elephant', sent to John Lehmann for *New Writing*, which established him as minor literary talent. He also wrote *The Road to Wigan Pier* (1937). Gollancz liked the clear and unromantic description of working-class life and coalmining in the first part of the book, but was dismayed by the second part where Orwell announced both his adherence to socialism and his dislike of socialist intellectuals and their admiration for Soviet power. Only with difficulty did Gollancz persuade the selectors of the Left Book Club to publish the book under that banner, and only then with an introduction by himself repudiating his author. 'A writer cannot be a *loyal* member of a political party,' said Orwell (*Complete Works*, 11.167). Yet he was soon to join a political party.

Spain and after When he finished his book in December, Orwell went to Spain to fight for the republic. 'Someone has to kill fascists,' he is alleged to have said. Impatient to be there, he made his own way to Barcelona and joined the POUM militia ('Partido Obrero de Unificación Marxista') on the Aragon front. The POUM was an independent Marxist movement, hated by the Stalinists and in dispute with the Trotskyites. Because he was on a quiet section of the front he tried to transfer to the communist-dominated International Brigades around Madrid, but he became involved in the May troubles in Barcelona. This attempt by the communists to purge the POUM and the Catalan anarchists made him bitterly anti-communist. Upon returning to the front, he was badly wounded in the neck, and was then hunted by the communists while still convalescent. With the help of his wife, Eileen, who had come to Barcelona to work for the Independent Labour Party (ILP), he escaped from Spain at the end of June 1937.

Orwell went back to Wallington and wrote *Homage to Catalonia*, a supreme description of trench life (lice and boredom), but also a trenchant and detailed exposure of how the communists risked the whole republican cause in their lust for power and in their zeal to suppress all other socialists. Gollancz refused to publish it, so Frederick Warburg, who was known as the Trotskyite publisher simply because he took left-wing books that were critical of Stalin, brought out the book in April 1938. Orwell now saw himself as an anti-communist revolutionary socialist; he joined the ILP, and he attended and spoke at their summer schools. *Homage to Catalonia* was much abused and much defended. Its literary merits were hardly noticed, and it sold few copies. Some now think of it as Orwell's finest achievement, and nearly all critics see it as his great stylistic breakthrough: he became the serious writer with the terse, easy, vivid colloquial style.

In March 1938 Orwell had collapsed with a tubercular lesion in one lung and was removed to a sanatorium. Thanks to help from an unknown admirer, the Blairs spent winter 1938–9 in the warmth of Morocco, where he finished *Coming up for Air* (1939), a novel reflecting a foreboding of war and an ironic nostalgia for a lost past. Like all his novels prior to the Second World War, except *A Clergyman's Daughter*, it was not written for the modernist intellectuals: he wanted to reach the audience whom he called the common man, the audience for whom H. G. Wells still wrote and who still read Dickens—those whose only university was the free public library. In fact Orwell's novels did not reach such a wide audience, each selling only between 3000 and 4000 copies.

In his ILP days Orwell claimed that 'the coming war' would be merely a capitalist struggle for the control of colonial markets. As late as July 1939 he wrote 'Not counting Niggers' (a title of savage, Swiftian irony), claiming that British and French leaders did not ask the vast majority of their colonies about whether they wanted to fight. But, when the Second World War broke out, he immediately declared that even Chamberlain's England was preferable to Hitler's Germany. In his essay 'My country, right or left' he stated a left-wing case for patriotism that he developed in *The Lion and the Unicorn*.

In wartime Orwell was rejected for the army several times because of his tuberculosis (a friend said that he tried harder to get into the army than many did to get out), so he moved back to London and joined the part-time Home Guard; for a while he thought that it could become a Catalan-style revolutionary militia. In February 1941 he published *The Lion and the Unicorn*, partly a profound meditation on the English national character and partly a left-wing assertion of patriotism, but also continuing the argument from his Catalan days that the war could be won only if a revolution replaced the old ruling class. But those hopes faded. In August 1941 he became, after a period of painful underemployment, a producer with the Far Eastern section of the BBC, tolerating the job's unaccustomed and uncongenial restraints until November 1943.

In 1939 Orwell had published a volume of essays, *Inside the Whale*. His powers as an essayist were recognized and went from strength to strength. A remarkable series of essays followed when he at last could begin to choose for whom he wrote: notably 'The prevention of literature', 'Politics and the English language', 'Politics versus literature', and 'Writers and Leviathan'. During the war he wrote regularly for Cyril Connolly's *Horizon* and for *Partisan Review* in New York. But some of his best writing came after November 1943, when he was made literary editor of *The Tribune*, a left-wing weekly directed by Aneurin Bevan. His weekly column, 'As I please', ranged through a vast number of topics, some serious and some comic, some political and some literary. He set a model for the lively mixed column soon to be emulated by many other writers not only in Britain. As George Orwell he became a known character, hard-hitting and good-humoured, a quirky socialist but with a love of traditional liberties and pastimes. The private man was, however, very reserved and a compulsive overworker. Both his and Eileen's health became very run down, partly through wartime conditions and partly through physical neglect; yet he persuaded her to adopt a child, Richard.

Brief days of fame Early in 1944 Orwell finished writing *Animal Farm* but at least four leading publishers (Gollancz, T. S. Eliot for Faber, Jonathan Cape, and Collins) turned it down as inopportune while Russia was an ally. It was not published until shortly after the end of the war in Europe. Several critics called it the greatest satire in the English language since Swift's *Gulliver's Travels*, and it brought Orwell instant fame and a huge new and international readership. Harcourt Brace took it after many New York firms had rejected it, and it was a Book of the Month Club selection: it sold 250,000 copies in one year. It was translated into every major language, including some in which it could only be read in smuggled or in samizdat versions. It has survived the late twentieth-century collapse of Soviet power not only because of its plain style—Orwell believed passionately and politically that no meaningful idea was too difficult to be explained in simple terms to ordinary people—but because the satire can touch all power-hungry regimes, left or right, and even some rulers who can be hard to pin down in either category.

Before it appeared Orwell went to France for *The Observer* to report on the liberation, and to Germany to try to witness the opening of the concentration camps, but Eileen died and he came hurrying home. He told people that she died during anaesthetic for a minor operation. In fact she had cancer. She may well not have told him, but it seems somewhat obtuse of him not to have seen that something was badly wrong. Outwardly he bore her death with the stoicism of Orwell, but Eric Blair was deeply hurt and shaken—though by now the public mask had taken over almost entirely. Only a few very old friends called him Eric; new friends, as diverse as Julian Symons, Arthur Koestler, Anthony Powell, and Malcolm Muggeridge, called him George. He stuck to his adopted son, Richard, first on his own, then with the help of a housekeeper. He began writing regularly again for *The Tribune* and *The Observer* and also for the *Manchester Evening News*. He moved to a farmhouse on the northern tip of the remote island of Jura, where, even in Eileen's lifetime, he had resolved to escape, to avoid the distractions of London and to begin work on a new and ambitious book.

Barnhill was indeed remote, 8 miles up a track from the nearest phone, which in turn was 25 miles from a shop in a small village where steamers came twice a week. The journey from London took two days. At first Orwell revelled in the difficulties and seclusion, but soon his younger sister, Avril, followed him, froze out the young housekeeper, and became herself both housekeeper and 'gatekeeper' against unwanted visitors. Brother and sister did not always see eye to eye on who was unwanted or welcome. He worked hard, perhaps too hard, in a small room with a smoky stove, and chain-smoked as usual. In a notebook he wrote that in all his writing life

> there has literally been not one day in which I did not feel that I was idling, that I was behind with the current job, and that my total output was miserably small. Even at the period when I was working ten hours a day on a book, or turning out four or five articles a week, I have never been able to get away from this neurotic feeling, that I was wasting time. (*Complete Works*, 20.204)

Orwell collapsed with tuberculosis with only a first draft of his long-planned new novel finished, which as always 'to me is only ever halfway through'. In a Scottish hospital the new drug streptomycin, obtained from America with the help of David Astor and Aneurin Bevan, was tested on him. Gruesome side-effects resulted, not then controllable, and the treatment was unhappily abandoned. Rested, at least, he returned to Jura, but drove himself hard again and, when his agent and his publisher failed to find a typist who would go to Jura, he sat up in bed and typed the second version of his novel himself. He collapsed again when he had finished.

The resulting novel, *Nineteen Eighty-Four*, published in 1949, immediately elicited diverse interpretations. Critics have seen it as a pessimistic and deterministic prophecy; an allegory on the impossibility of staying human without belief in God; an anti-Catholic diatribe, in which the inquisitor, O'Brien, and the inner party are really the church; a world-hating act of nihilistic misanthropy; a deathbed renunciation of any kind of socialism; or a humanistic and libertarian socialist (almost anarchist) satire against totalitarian tendencies in both his own and other contemporary societies. Isaac Rosenfeld saw it as 'mysticism of cruelty, utter pessimism' (Rosenfeld, 514); and Anthony Burgess as 'a comic novel', or one that 'allows' (Burgess, 20) humour.

Certainly it is the most complex piece of writing Orwell attempted. Jenni Calder in a lecture called it 'a well-crafted novel', perhaps over-crafted; and part of the craft was dramatizing dilemmas and fears of humanity, and not offering easy solutions. But biographically it is clear at least, contrary to much facile opinion, what it is not: it is not a work of unnatural, almost psychotic intensity dashed off by a dying man with a death wish for civilization and regressing to memories of childhood traumas. In fact it was long planned and coolly premeditated, and was neither a conscious nor an unconscious repudiation of Orwell's democratic socialism. Czesaw Miłosz in 1953 reported that in Poland some of his old Communist Party colleagues had read smuggled copies as a manual of power, but that the freer minds had seen it as 'a Swiftian satire': 'The fact that there are writers in the West who understand the functioning of the unusually constructed machine of which they are themselves a part, astounds them and argues against "the stupidity" of the West' (Miłosz, 42). It is arguable whether *Nineteen Eighty-Four* was Orwell's greatest achievement; most critics, and Orwell himself, see *Animal Farm* as his unquestioned literary masterpiece. 'What I have most wanted to do is to make political writing into an art,' he said in his essay of 1946 'Why I write'. He was both a great polemical and a speculative writer: 'Liberty is telling people what they do not want to hear.' He challenges his readers' assumptions in direct terms of homely common sense, forces them to think, but mostly leaves them to reach their own conclusions. He may argue fiercely but never as if authoritatively, which perhaps accounts for his continued popularity.

If seen as Swiftian satire then a lot falls into place: grotesque exaggeration, humour but also deadly seriousness. Orwell raged against the division of the world into spheres of influence by the great powers at the wartime meetings at Yalta and Potsdam; power-hunger and totalitarian impulses wherever they occurred; intellectuals for turning into bureaucrats and betraying the common people; the debasement of language by governments and politicians; the rewriting of history for ideological purposes; James Burnham's thesis in his *Managerial Revolution* that the managers and technocrats are going to take over the world; the existence of a permanent cold war because of the impossibility of a deliberate atomic war; and, not least, the debasement of popular culture by the mass press. He pictured the ministry of truth in *Nineteen Eighty-Four* as producing for the proles not propaganda but 'rubbishy newspapers containing almost nothing but sport, crime and astrology, sensational five-cent novelettes, films oozing with sex, and sentimental songs composed entirely by mechanical means'. Plainly he was getting at the British press of his day. It is doubtful if he had even heard of the Frankfurt school of Marxism which held that social control was maintained in capitalist society by the degradation of literacy rather than by terrorism, but in homely terms Orwell makes the same point.

Last days and afterlife From January to September 1949 Orwell lay in a sanatorium in Gloucestershire. Then he was transferred to University College Hospital in London to be under one of the best chest specialists in England, who had also once treated D. H. Lawrence. The doctors, as was then customary, gave him some hope. In fact they knew that there was none. But he was not told, nor was Sonia Mary *Brownell (1918–1980), a former editorial assistant on Connolly's *Horizon* to whom he had proposed marriage without success in 1945. When he asked her again, she accepted, genuinely hoping to help him and nurse him back to health and, at the worst, perhaps not unwilling to accept the status of widow of an already world-famous author.

Orwell married Brownell on 13 October 1949 and began work on a new novel, as if he thought he would survive; but he also made his will and left precise instructions (fortunately ignored by his widow) about which of his writings to reprint and which to suppress. He read the first reviews of *Nineteen Eighty-Four* and dictated notes for a press release to correct some American reviewers who saw in it an attack on all forms of socialism, not just on all forms of totalitarianism. He reminded them that he was a democratic socialist, that the book was 'a parody', and that he meant only that something like the iron regime could, not would, occur, if we did not all both guard and exercise our liberties. He died on 21 January 1950 of a tubercular haemorrhage and was buried on 26 January at All Saints, Sutton Courtenay. Unexpectedly (for he was an avowed non-believer) he had asked to be buried not cremated, and according to the rites of the Church of England. The language and liturgies of the church were part of the Englishness he felt so deeply.

It is much debated whether Orwell's real genius is as an essayist and descriptive writer rather than as a novelist. In 'Why I write' (1946) he said that

> while my starting point is always a feeling of partisanship, a sense of injustice … [yet] so long as I remain alive and well so I shall continue to feel strongly about prose style, to love the surface of the earth and to take pleasure in solid objects and useless scraps of information.

He said he was not able and did not want 'completely to abandon the world-view that I acquired in childhood'. Above all else, he said, he wanted 'to make political writing into an art' (*Complete Works*, 18.319).

Rarely has a more private and simple man become more famous. Orwell's very name has entered the English language. The word 'Orwellian' conveys the fear of a future for humanity governed by rival totalitarian regimes who rule through suffering, deprivation, deceit, and fear, and who debase language and people equally. But 'Orwell-like' conveys something quite different: a lover of nature, proto-environmentalist, advocate of plain language and plain speaking, humorist, eccentric, polemicist, and someone who could meditate, almost mystically, almost pietistically, on the pleasure and wonder of ordinary things—as in the small, great essay 'Some thoughts on the common toad'.

Even before Orwell's death political battle broke out and has long continued to annex his reputation. Some American editors and writers had genuinely misunderstood *Animal Farm* as a satirical polemic against all forms of socialism, rather than a betrayal of revolutionary egalitarian ideals by Stalin and the Communist Party. By the time of the publication of *Nineteen Eighty-Four* the then powerful *Time* and *Life* magazines chose to ignore the author's standpoint and to present him again as both anti-socialist and anti-communist. If they recognized a distinction in the presence of the post-war Labour government in Britain, they either thought that inevitably it 'would go that way' or that Orwell, had he lived, would have abandoned democratic socialism.

The espousal of Orwell by the American right and free-market liberals made some British socialists immediately brand him as a betrayer of socialism and 'a cold war warrior'. He himself had first coined the phrase 'cold war' in postulating an atomic stalemate. Certainly he was much more alert and aroused than many fellow socialists to the real threat of the communist subversion in western Europe; but he cannot be considered a betrayer of socialism if his reviews and writings are followed right up to the time of his death. Many ex-communists were angry with him for being, as was said, 'prematurely correct' and for giving 'ammunition to the enemy'. One example of such ammunition was that he gave permission without charge for translations of *Animal Farm* into Ukrainian to be made for smuggling into Ukraine by the early Central Intelligence Agency (which helped to fund a cartoon based on the novel released in 1955). He wrote an interesting introduction to explain his own background and his politics. Most of the copies were, by another irony, destroyed by the American military in Austria who were strictly observing the three power agreement. Back then, in the eyes of the left, all Ukrainians were of course fascists, and to complicate matters further some Ukrainians who did get to read his introduction could not (like the editors of *Time*) see any difference between communism and socialism.

The 'old' new left (that is, those who left the Communist Party after Hungary in 1956 but were still Marxists) engaged in a deliberate campaign of both political and literary abuse of Orwell. They still smarted at the impatience he had shown at their earlier illusions and naïvety. To this the 'new' new left of the *New Left Review* (the student generation trying to reform Marxist theory) added two more charges: that he was not a serious theorist and that he was patriotic, comfortable in his Englishness. They seemed with their secular liberationist ideology to be in favour of anybody else's nationalism except their own. Edward Thompson's and Raymond Williams's intense dislike of Orwell was especially curious because all three had a vivid sense of an English radical tradition in perpetual conflict with the conservative account of tradition, the common people versus the establishment.

At least these attacks took Orwell seriously as a 'political writer' which, he said in his essay 'Why I write', had been his main intent since 1936. Many literary figures found it hard to come to terms with his politics and most critical studies in the 1950s and 1960s concentrated on his character and on his books. A Uniform Edition of his books had been published by Secker and Warburg in 1960, but not until 1968 in the four volumes of *The Collected Essays, Journalism and Letters* of 1968, edited by Sonia Orwell (as Sonia Blair, his widow, called herself) and Ian Angus, could the full variety and power of his writing be appreciated. A less Orwellian version of Orwell could then emerge: the Orwell-like speculative, humorous, sardonic, discursive essayist. Even then the last of the four volumes left out several telling political essays and long reviews that Sonia Orwell regarded as 'repetitive' or 'not his best'. These could strengthen the complacent surmise of English writers that he was moving away from political writing back to more conventional novels and *belles lettres*, and the wishful belief of American neo-liberals that he was 'giving all that up', 'that' being democratic socialism. Sonia Blair's friend Mary McCarthy took it for granted that he was moving to the right before his death, as did two major studies of cultural politics in the cold war. But biographical evidence is to the contrary.

The year 1984 saw a carnival of misunderstanding in the media, as if *Nineteen Eighty-Four* had ever been a serious projection or prophecy rather than a Swiftian satire, still less a prediction of a date. But what was remarkable was that by then all Orwell's books and most of his essays had been in print since 1960 and that at conferences large non-academic audiences appeared. Orwell's stature as writer and thinker cannot rival that of George Bernard Shaw or H. G. Wells, but neither of their reputations as popular writers has survived as well, nor have even their major writings remained continuously in print. Perhaps it is this popularity of Orwell in a literal sense that so irritates or embarrasses some critics and writers, either jealous or convinced that he cannot therefore be a serious intellectual writer.

In 1996 a fresh storm broke out when some files in the Public Record Office were routinely opened and *The Guardian* and the *Daily Telegraph* 'revealed' that Orwell had 'spied on' fellow writers for the Foreign Office. (In fact this information had appeared in Bernard Crick's biography of 1980 drawn from Orwell's own papers in University College, London.) Far from spying, he provided a list that he sent to a friend, Celia Kirwan (Arthur Koestler's sister-in-law), who was working in the IRD (information research department), a special unit of the Foreign Office set up by Ernest Bevin. It was a list of writers who, he thought, would be unsuitable for anti-communist propaganda in 1946 when the Soviet Union was subsidizing and infiltrating every kind of cultural conference and event they could. There was a cultural cold war. The *Sunday Telegraph* mocked that an 'icon of the Left has been exposed', and *The Guardian* said that no liberal should ever do such a thing. But Orwell was not a liberal in their sense: his temperament was republican. When the republic was threatened, it had to be defended.

Struggles to appropriate or to denigrate Orwell will continue, as will popular interest in his essays and the documentary books. Four major biographies, with two more appearing in the centenary year 2003, have been produced, and fully reliable texts have been reissued by Secker, in the twenty-volume *Complete Works of George Orwell* (1986–98), and are now followed in the Penguin editions. These are freed from the bowdlerization of publishing in the 1930s, errors, and omissions, thanks to the monumental labours of one of England's leading Shakespearian bibliographers, Peter Davison. After Orwell's death many of the fashionable intellectuals of the time who knew him wrote tributes or assessments as if his character was more noteworthy and important than the quality or content of his writings. But the continued popularity of his writings has settled that argument. His greatest fame and readership have been posthumous.

BERNARD CRICK

Sources B. Crick, *George Orwell: a life*, pbk edn (1982) • P. Stansky and W. Abrahams, eds., *The unknown Orwell* (1972) • P. Stansky and W. Abrahams, eds., *Orwell: the transformation* (1979) • A. Coppard and B. R. Crick, eds., *Orwell remembered* (1994) • M. Shelden, *Orwell: the authorised biography* (1991) • *The complete works of George Orwell*, ed. P. Davison, 20 vols. (1986–98) • G. Woodcock, *The crystal spirit* (1967) • P. Buitenhuis and I. B. Nadel, *George Orwell: a reassessment* (1988) • C. Hitchens, *Orwell's victory* (2002) • C. Miłosz, *The captive mind* (1953) • J. Calder, *Chronicles of conscience: a study of George Orwell and Arthur Koestler* (1968) • A. Burgess, *1985* (1978) • I. Rosenfeld, 'Decency and death', *Partisan Review* (May 1950) • G. Orwell, *Nineteen eighty-four* (1984) [with a critical introduction and annotations by B. Crick]

Archives NRA, corresp. and literary papers • UCL, corresp. and diary • UCL, corresp., literary MSS, and notebooks | UCL, corresp. with Secker and Warburg, publishers

Likenesses photographs, *c*.1945, Hult. Arch. • F. H. Man, photograph, *c*.1947, NPG [*see illus.*] • photographs, UCL, Orwell archive

Wealth at death £9908 14*s*. 11*d*.—in England: probate, 2 Feb 1951, *CGPLA Eng. & Wales*

Blair, Hugh (1718–1800), Church of Scotland minister and university professor, was born in Edinburgh on 7 April 1718, the only child of John Blair, a clerk in the Excise Office, and Martha, daughter of Alexander Ogston, an Edinburgh bookseller, and his wife, Martha, who operated her late husband's bookshop in Parliament Square until 1738. Although his father never attained prominence after losing his inheritance in the unsuccessful Darien scheme, Blair was descended from a prominent Scottish family that included his great-grandfather Robert Blair (1593–1666), a professor at the University of Glasgow and a leading Presbyterian reformer. He was educated at Edinburgh high school and the University of Edinburgh, which he entered in the autumn of 1731 at thirteen. At the university he came under the influence of the professor of logic, John Stevenson, who incorporated the study of English rhetoric and *belles-lettres* into his classes. As he passed through the arts and divinity courses, Blair began to associate with a group of students, mostly a few years younger than himself, who remained his close friends and academic and ecclesiastical colleagues in the moderate party of the Church of Scotland. The roots of Blair's career as an author can be traced to his student days in Edinburgh, when he is supposed to have published *A Poem Sacred to the Memory of the Reverend Mr. James Smith* (1736), no copies of which have survived, and to have co-authored, with his cousin George Bannatine, a poem entitled 'The Resurrection', which circulated in manuscript. In addition his student notes on chronology are believed to have formed the foundation of a volume of *Chronology and History of the World* that first appeared in 1754, under the name of his distant relation in the Church of England, John Blair. In February 1739 Hugh successfully defended his MA thesis, 'De fundamentis et obligatione legis naturae', which argued that benevolence is rooted in natural law. While completing his divinity studies he worked as a tutor, including a stint in the highlands in 1740 as tutor to Simon Fraser, eldest son of Baron Lovat.

Early career in the church On 21 October 1741 Blair was licensed to preach by the presbytery of Edinburgh, and on 23 September 1742 he was ordained as the minister of the little parish of Collessie in Fife, thanks to the patronage of Lord and Lady Leven. Within a few months he was a candidate for the second charge in the Canongate church, then an independent parish, though situated near the heart of Edinburgh. He secured the call to the Canongate after besting a rival, Robert Walker, by a margin of 136 to 82 in a vote among the eligible parishioners, and was translated on 14 July 1743. During his eleven years in the Canongate, Blair steadily developed his reputation as an up-and-coming preacher in the kirk. At the unusually young age of twenty-eight he was elected moderator of the presbytery of Edinburgh, and in that capacity preached a sermon, 'The wrath of man praising God', to open the proceedings on 18 May 1746, one month after the battle of Culloden ended the Jacobite rising led by Charles Edward Stuart. Published in the same year, the sermon was a jeremiad on the 'Forty-Five, interpreted in the style of the Old Testament, as a providential chastising of the British people for their sinful ways—a traditional rhetorical device to which Blair would return in later years. On 1 January 1750 Blair was invited to preach on the occasion of the fiftieth anniversary of the Society in Scotland for the Propagation of Christian Knowledge, and that sermon, 'The importance of religious knowledge to the happiness of mankind', was also published separately. Three years later he edited for the press Frederick Carmichael's posthumous *Sermons on Several Important Subjects*, to which he contributed the preface. Blair has usually been credited with editing another publication of 1753, the Edinburgh edition of Shakespeare's *Works*, but the editor was actually John Reid, the press corrector for the printers, Murray and Cochran.

It was during his Canongate period, on 19 April 1748, that Blair married his first cousin Katherine Bannatine (*d.* 1795), daughter of his uncle James Bannatine, an Edinburgh minister. She was said to be a woman 'of a Masculine Understanding, of a Cheerfull Temper and Amiable

Manners', ideally suited for Blair who, 'Being of an Infantine Disposition, needed a Mate of a Superior and Decisive Mind, on which he could Rely for advice, in all his Doubts and Perplexities, which Occurd almost every Hour' (Carlyle, 'Comparison', 278). In January 1749 the Blairs had a daughter, Katherine, who grew up as an only child after their second child, a son, died in infancy.

On 8 March 1754 Blair was called to Edinburgh proper as the minister of Lady Yester's Church, where he was settled on 11 October. The mid-1750s was a time of intense conflict over the relationship between culture and piety in the Church of Scotland, and Blair was at the centre of the struggle. In 1755–6 he participated in the original *Edinburgh Review*, a short-lived periodical produced by his circle of friends for the purpose of showing off and encouraging Scottish polite learning, in opposition to the straight and narrow Calvinism of the moderates' opponents. Blair is thought to have contributed to the first number the reviews of Francis Hutcheson's *System of Moral Philosophy* and the first two volumes of Bishop Sherlock's *Discourses* (and possibly also Dodsley's *Collection of Poems*), and to the second and last number the reviews of the third volume of Sherlock's *Discourses* and John Jortin's *Six Dissertations upon Different Subjects*. He is also believed to have written about this time two anonymous pamphlets defending his friends David Hume and Henry Home, Lord Kames, against charges of infidelity in the Scottish church courts: *Observations on a pamphlet, entitled an analysis of the moral and religious sentiments contained in the writings of Sopho [Kames], and David Hume, esq.* (1755) and (with three other Edinburgh ministers) *Objections Against the Essays on Morality and Natural Religion Examined* (1756). In December 1756 he took part in a rehearsal of the tragedy *Douglas* by his friend John Home, playing the small part of the maid Anna, but he did not risk the wrath of his fellow churchmen by attending the professional performances of the play that followed.

Blair received an honorary DD degree from the University of St Andrews on 13 June 1757. On 15 June 1758 he took his place as one of the ministers of the High or New Kirk in St Giles's Church, Edinburgh, after a bitter dispute in which the moderates and their political allies in the general assembly managed, by a vote of sixty-four to fifty-four, to overturn a decision by the synod that would have deprived Blair of that prestigious charge. Once settled at St Giles's, Blair cultivated his reputation as a leading figure in the church. He was a member of the church committee that produced a new version of biblical translations and paraphrases (1781) used in worship, and is supposed to have been personally responsible for revising numbers 4, 33, 34, 44, and 45. He was a delegate to the annual general assembly on a number of occasions, but he never participated in its debates and rarely played a leading role in the management of ecclesiastical affairs, at least until after 1780, when the retirement of the moderate leader—his lifelong friend the historian William Robertson—led to Blair's being consulted more often for advice on ecclesiastical matters. He had no enemies in the church and was on excellent terms with Robert Walker, his colleague at St Giles's, a leader of the rival popular party and his former opponent in the election for the Canongate charge, whose life Blair commemorated in a portion of a funeral sermon that was preached on 13 April 1783 and was prefixed to the third volume of Walker's *Sermons on Practical Subjects* in 1784.

Man of letters Meanwhile, Blair was pursuing a second career, as a man of letters and an academic. He was an active participant in the convivial and intellectual club-life that characterized the culture of the Scottish Enlightenment. He was an early member of the Select Society (1754–64) and in 1761 was one of the directors of its offshoot, the Society for Promoting the Reading and Speaking of the English Language. He was a member of the whiggish Revolution Club at Edinburgh, an honorary member of the Belles Lettres Society (elected 8 May 1760), a member of the convivial Oyster Club, and from the early 1760s until the mid-1780s a moderately active member of the *Poker Club, established by his circle of friends to promote the establishment of a Scots militia. He was elected a fellow of the Royal Society of Edinburgh on 17 November 1783, and became one of the four founding presidents of its literary class at their first meeting on the same day.

On 11 December 1759 Blair began delivering public lectures on English language and literature, following the tradition of Adam Smith and Robert Watson, the future historian, who was his relation by marriage. Six months later, on 27 June 1760, the town council of Edinburgh appointed him professor of rhetoric at the University of Edinburgh, with no salary but the right to collect class fees from his students, and on 3 September he was admitted to the university by the senatus academicus. This was the first dedicated chair of English in any university. On 27 April 1762 it was further enhanced by the creation for Blair of the regius chair of rhetoric and *belles-lettres*, with an annual salary of £70 and the continued right to collect class fees. Earlier in 1762 Blair had half-heartedly put himself forward for the vacant principalship of the university, which was given to his friend Robertson, but he seems to have done so merely in order to strengthen his claim for the regius chair, to which he was formally admitted by the senatus academicus on 21 July.

Blair's rise to prominence in the field of rhetoric and *belles-lettres* was closely connected with his leading role in the emergence of the supposedly ancient Celtic bard Ossian during the early 1760s. Learning from friends that a young highlander by the name of James Macpherson possessed samples of ancient Gaelic poetry, Blair arranged for Macpherson's purported translations to appear in a small volume entitled *Fragments of Ancient Poetry, Collected in the Highlands of Scotland*, published in Edinburgh on 14 June 1760, and almost immediately reissued in a second edition which added an additional poem. Blair also wrote the preface to the *Fragments*, which mentioned an 'Epic poem' that might, if recovered, 'serve to throw considerable light upon the Scottish and Irish antiquities' (p. viii). After Macpherson visited the highlands and published in late 1761 the epic poem in question, *Fingal* (1762), Blair expanded a classroom lecture on Ossian into his first major work, *A Critical Dissertation on the Poems of Ossian, the Son of Fingal*. It was published in London in January 1763 in a quarto format, and immediately made his international reputation as a literary critic. That spring Blair visited London, where young James Boswell served as his guide and Samuel Johnson insulted him by doubting in his presence the authenticity of Macpherson's work. Pressed by the growing doubts of Englishmen such as Johnson, along with a few sceptical Scottish friends such as David Hume, Blair produced a second, octavo edition of his *Critical Dissertation* in 1765, which added commentary on Macpherson's second Ossianic epic, *Temora* (1763). It also had an appendix containing testimonial evidence regarding the authenticity of Macpherson's Ossianic poetry, which he hoped would convince even 'that Barbarian Samuel Johnson' (Blair to Hume, 1 July 1765, NL Scot., MS 23153, no. 53). The *Critical Dissertation* (without the appendix) was reissued with very minor changes in 1772, 1784–5, 1790, and 1796, was included in most editions of the poems of Ossian, and was translated into several European languages. But it could not quell the controversy over the extent of Ossian's authenticity, which is still being disputed more than two hundred years later. In the early 1780s Blair was reluctantly drawn into a particularly acrimonious controversy concerning Ossian, generated by charges that in 1765 Thomas Percy had been subjected to a bogus recitation of Ossianic poetry at Blair's Edinburgh house in James's Court.

The house in question was owned by David Hume, who rented it to Blair while the owner was abroad. During the first half of 1769 Blair's little family moved to a 'neat & commodious' house in Argyle Square (James Shaw, 'Nine Months in Scotland, 1795–96', NL Scot., Adv. MS 16.2.15, fol. 53), where Blair was to remain for the rest of his life. On 23 August 1769 the Blairs suffered a severe blow when their beloved daughter Katherine died at the age of twenty. In his grief Blair retired 'for some time from social intercourse and professional labour' (Somerville, 167), and undertook an excursion to the north of England with two clergymen not much older than his daughter, Thomas Somerville and Samuel Charters. Somerville later recollected that Blair remained a good friend for life, and many others found him so as well. He took a particular interest in patronizing younger ministers and writers, such as the African traveller James Bruce, the historian Robert Watson, the miscellaneous writer and clergyman John Logan, and the Scots poet Robert Burns, who called him 'a worthy and most respectable character' in his second commonplace book. But Burns was also aware of Blair's faults as a critic and a man. He spoke with what Burns considered an unpleasant burr, could be vain and prudish, sometimes caring more about propriety than creativity, and all in all seemed to the Ayrshire poet to be 'merely an astonishing proof of what industry and application can do' (Lindsay, 32). However, according to Blair's nephew, James Shaw, 'his vanity … was mixed with so much good nature that it gave offence to no one' (Shaw, 'Nine Months', fol. 13). Blair's contemporary biographer, John Hill, expressed a similar view, and so did his friend Alexander Carlyle, who observed that though 'a vain man' Blair had remarkably little envy or 'malignity', and possessed 'truly a pure mind' (*Autobiography*, 307). In this he was much like his good friend David Hume, with whom he lived in great intimacy, in spite of their differences concerning religion and other matters.

Like most other clergymen affiliated with the moderate party, Blair was staunchly conservative in his political views. Early in the American War of Independence he preached a fast-day sermon against the Americans on 12 December 1776, which so offended James Boswell that it caused him to stop attending Blair's church for a period of time. In opposition to Boswell's claim that in this case 'Resistance is not Rebellion' (Boswell to Blair, 24 Feb 1777, Yale University Library, L59), Blair argued that the Americans were reacting against the fear of oppression rather than against actual oppression, and that therefore 'their resistance is in my view rebellion in its most criminal extent' (*Boswell in Extremes*, 359–60).

Blair's *Sermons* Blair's exchange with Boswell on the American war coincided with his publishing an octavo volume of *Sermons* that evolved into an extraordinarily popular five-volume work. He initially received £100 for the copyright from his friend Alexander Kincaid, bookseller and lord provost of Edinburgh, who was planning to print a small first edition of the work as a favour to the author but died before its appearance. Toward the end of 1776 the London publishers William Strahan and Thomas Cadell purchased shares of the copyright, on the strength of the reputation of the author and a strong recommendation from William Robertson. The book was printed in Edinburgh under the supervision of Kincaid's protégé and successor, William Creech, who sent half a printed sheet containing the book's first sermon to London for Strahan's inspection. Strahan thought little of what he read and on 6 December 1776 sent off an angry letter to Robertson, accusing him of prejudice for having recommended the volume 'so warmly' (NL Scot., MS 3942, fols. 299–300). Samuel Johnson reassured Strahan after reading the first sermon, though Boswell's *Life of Johnson* errs in claiming that Johnson's favourable judgement was instrumental in bringing about the book's publication, which was already assured. The volume was published in Edinburgh on 8 February 1777 and in London on 15 April, and was immediately successful.

Blair produced a second volume in 1780, a third in 1790, and a fourth in 1794, and at the time of his death he was preparing for the press a fifth volume, which appeared posthumously in 1801. In light of the initial response by Strahan, there is considerable irony in the fact that, by the time of his death in 1785, he had printed 33,500 copies of the first two volumes of Blair's *Sermons*, more copies than he printed of any other book. Sales were so strong that the value of the copyright rose to £500 for the second volume and £600 for each of the subsequent volumes, and the publishers periodically gave Blair additional cash gifts that were the functional equivalent of royalties. Thus Blair earned well over £2000 for the four volumes published in his lifetime—a vast sum for any eighteenth-century author, but unheard of for an author of sermons.

The royal family was particularly fond of the work, making it easier for Blair's former student Henry Dundas, the lord advocate of Scotland, to secure for him a pension of £200 per annum, on 25 July 1780. The first volume of the *Sermons* reached a twenty-second edition during Blair's lifetime, and in 1807 the *Critical Review* proclaimed the five-volume collection 'the most popular work in the English language' (vol. 11, 170), excepting *The Spectator*. That popularity seems to have derived from the combination of an elegant prose style, a reassuring philosophy of moral comfort grounded in Christian stoicism, and perceptive psychological insights into human nature.

Final years In 1767 Blair published *Heads of the Lectures on Rhetoric and Belles Lettres, in the University of Edinburgh*, which was reissued in 1771 and 1777. By the early 1780s he was considering publishing the lectures themselves, allegedly because he was worried about the wide circulation of corrupt manuscript copies, but perhaps also because he was then contemplating his retirement from the classroom. *Lectures on Rhetoric and Belles Lettres* appeared in two quarto volumes on 7 June 1783 in London, and on 5 July in Edinburgh. The publishers were once again Strahan, Cadell, and Creech, who paid Blair a handsome fee of £1500. As the author explained to his publishers on 21 June 1783, the work was based 'on plain common sense, so as to be intelligible to all, without any abstruse metaphysics' (NL Scot., MS 3813, fols. 17–18). It also benefited from Blair's comprehensive approach to his subject, which included discussions of the principles of taste and criticism, the rise and development of language, style, and various types of eloquence, both written and oral. Blair's book immediately became the new standard for the study of rhetoric and literary criticism, and was particularly popular and influential in the United States, where the *Sermons* also enjoyed great fame during the first half of the nineteenth century. In July 1784 Blair officially became joint holder of the rhetoric and *belles-lettres* chair with his disciple William Greenfield, who had already begun lecturing and collecting the class fees, while Blair continued to receive the £70 annual salary for life. According to a biographical sketch written just before his death, Blair's pension was raised from £200 to £300 per annum on the occasion of his academic retirement.

On 18 April 1793 Blair preached a patriotic fast-day sermon against the French Revolution and its influence, 'On the love of our country'; it would eventually find its way into the fifth volume of his *Sermons*, consisting mainly of older sermons which he continued to revise for the press throughout the 1790s. He suffered a blow upon the death of his old friend William Robertson in June 1793, another when Robertson's office as principal of the university was not offered to him as an expected courtesy, and still another, far more devastating, when his wife, Katherine, died on 9 February 1795. He lived his last years with his niece and adopted daughter, Elizabeth Hunter, an orphan whom the Blairs had brought into their home shortly after their daughter's death; they passed winters in Argyle Square and summers at a country house called Summerfield, at the seaside in nearby Leith. On 20 May 1796 Blair preached a sermon that was published for the benefit of the Sons of the Clergy under the title *The Compassion and Beneficence of the Deity*. Although pained by gout, he nevertheless remained mentally sharp and active until just before his death, at the age of eighty-two, on 27 December 1800. He was buried in Greyfriars churchyard and left behind a substantial estate, including bonds worth approximately £4000, the Argyle Square house and its furnishings, and a fine library of some 2400 volumes, which were sold at auction in two parts, in April 1801 and April 1816. His personal papers and manuscripts were burned, in accordance with a directive in his will.

RICHARD B. SHER

Sources H. Amory, 'Hugh Blair', *Sale catalogues of libraries of eminent persons*, ed. A. N. L. Munby, 7, ed. H. Amory (1973), 159–64 • *Boswell in extremes, 1776–1778*, ed. C. M. Weis and F. A. Pottle (1970), vol. 10 of *The Yale editions of the private papers of James Boswell*, trade edn (1950–89) • *The autobiography of Dr Alexander Carlyle of Inveresk, 1722–1805*, ed. J. H. Burton (1910) • A. Carlyle, 'A comparison of two eminent characters [Hugh Blair and William Robertson] attempted after the manner of Plutarch', *Anecdotes and characters of the times*, ed. J. Kinsley (1973), 277–82 • 'Dr Hugh Blair', *Public characters of 1800–1801* (1801) • J. Dwyer, *Virtuous discourse: sensibility and community in late eighteenth-century Scotland* (1987) • R. L. Emerson, 'The social composition of Enlightened Edinburgh: the Select Society of Edinburgh, 1754–1764', *Studies on Voltaire and the Eighteenth Century*, 114 (1973), 291–329 • H. F. Harding, introduction, in H. Blair, *Lectures on rhetoric and belles lettres*, 2 vols. (1965), vii–xl • R. D. Harlan, 'William Strahan: eighteenth century London printer and publisher', PhD diss., U. Mich., 1960 • J. Hill, *An account of the life and writings of Hugh Blair* (1807) • W. S. Howell, *Eighteenth-century British logic and rhetoric* (1971) • M. Lindsay, *The Burns encyclopedia*, 3rd edn (1980), 31–3 • W. McDougall, 'Copyright litigation in the court of session, 1738–1749', *Edinburgh Bibliographical Society Transactions*, 5/5 (1971–87), 2–31 • D. D. McElroy, *Scotland's age of improvement: a survey of eighteenth-century literary clubs and societies* (1969) • T. P. Miller, *The formation of college English: rhetoric and belles lettres in the British cultural provinces* (1997) • S. Rizza, 'A bulky and foolish treatise? Hugh Blair's *Critical dissertation* reconsidered', *Ossian revisited*, ed. H. Gaskill (1991), 129–46 • R. M. Schmitz, *Hugh Blair* (1948) • *Fasti Scot.*, new edn, 1.29, 68, 82; 5.134 • R. B. Sher, *Church and university in the Scottish Enlightenment: the moderate literati of Edinburgh* (1985) • R. B. Sher, 'Percy, Shaw, and the Ferguson "cheat": national prejudice in the Ossian wars', *Ossian revisited*, ed. H. Gaskill (1991), 207–45 • T. Somerville, *My own life and times, 1741–1814*, ed. W. Lee (1861) • NL Scot., MS 23153 • NL Scot., Adv. MS 16.2.15 • Yale U., L59

Archives Bodl. Oxf., lecture notes • Morgan L., letters • U. Edin. L., lecture notes | NA Scot., corresp. with Lord Kames • NL Scot., David Hume MSS; Minto papers; Saltoun papers • Yale U., letters to James Boswell

Likenesses D. Martin, oils, *c*.1775, U. Edin. • J. Caldwell, line engraving, 1783 (after D. Martin), BM, NPG; repro. in H. Blair, *Discourse* (1783) • J. Tassie, paste medallion, 1791, Scot. NPG • H. Raeburn, oils, *c*.1795, Canongate Kirk, Edinburgh • J. Kay, line engraving, 1798, BM, NPG • F. Bartolozzi, stipple, pubd 1802 (after H. Raeburn), BM, NPG • H. Raeburn, portrait, repro. in Sher, *Church and university*; priv. coll. • H. Raeburn, portrait, repro. in A. Carlyle, *Anecdotes and characters*, ed. J. Kinsley (1973); priv. coll.

Wealth at death approx. £4000 in bonds; plus Argyle Square house, a fine library, and house in Leith

Blair, James (1655/6–1743), Church of England clergyman and founder of the College of William and Mary, was the son of Peter Blair (*d.* 1673), Church of Scotland minister of

James Blair (1655/6–1743), by Charles Bridges

St Cuthbert's parish, Edinburgh, and his wife, Mary Hamilton (*d.* in or after 1696). He is sometimes described instead as the eldest of four sons and one daughter of Robert Blair, Church of Scotland minister of Alvah, Banffshire, but this is probably an error. Admitted to Marischal College, Aberdeen, in 1668 as a Crombie scholar, aged twelve, Blair the next year matriculated at the University of Edinburgh, and graduated MA on 21 July 1673. He completed his theological studies in 1679, when he was ordained a priest of the Church of Scotland by John Paterson, bishop of Edinburgh. Blair served the parish of Cranston in the presbytery of Dalkeith, 10 miles south-west of Edinburgh, from 11 July 1679 until deprived in 1681.

The privy council of Scotland on 22 December 1681 noted that Blair, like many Scottish episcopalian clergymen, had refused to swear and subscribe to the test oath that acknowledged the Catholic James, duke of York and Albany (later James VII and II), as the head of the Scottish church should James succeed as king of Scotland. Caught in a dilemma, Blair sought the assistance of his former Edinburgh University professor of divinity, Laurence Charteris, who had resigned his academic appointment rather than sign the oath. Charteris wrote to a fellow Scotsman in London, Gilbert Burnet, preacher at the Rolls Chapel, a former professor of divinity at Marischal College, requesting his help on Blair's behalf.

Blair travelled to London where through Burnet's efforts he became an under-clerk (1682–5) of the master of the rolls. Burnet introduced Blair to such prominent church leaders as John Tillotson, later archbishop of Canterbury, and Henry Compton, bishop of London. In 1685 Compton, seeking men to serve the overseas church, appointed Blair to serve Henrico parish in Virginia and four years later appointed him his commissary in the colony. In 1694 Blair became minister of the James City parish, serving until 1710 when he became the parson of Bruton parish in Williamsburg, a post he held until his death.

On 28 April 1687 Blair married Sarah (1670–1713), the seventeen-year-old daughter of the prominent Benjamin Harrison the younger of Wakefield in Surry county, Virginia, a planter and influential member of the colonial council. Blair was linked by marriage to several leading Virginia families. Later his brother Archibald and his nephew John became conspicuous leaders of the house of burgesses and colonial council, establishing for Blair a vital and potent network of political connections. Blair extended his personal fortune and status through his acquisition of land and his financial participation in his brother Archibald Blair's trading store in Williamsburg, and became a prominent defender of the economic and political interests of the provincial gentry.

Doubtless Blair's most significant legacy was the founding and development of the College of William and Mary. The idea for establishing a college in the colony had been current for nearly eighty years. As early as 1619 the Virginia Company of London had moved to grant 10,000 acres to support the founding of the University of Henrico with special attention for an Indian college. At the time English prelates raised £1500 to aid in the project. However, the Good Friday massacre of 1622 at the Henrico settlement had terminated the project. In 1660 the general assembly of the sparsely settled province renewed efforts to found a college with the purpose of providing ministers for the Church of England in Virginia, enabling the education of the colony's young men on religious and classical principles, and propagating Christianity among the native Americans.

Provincial political turmoil and Bacon's rebellion in the 1670s and unsteady constitutional affairs in England during the 1680s suspended plans for a college. Recognizing that from the establishment of the colony in 1607 there had been a chronic shortage of ministers at a convention of the clergy in 1690 Blair proposed the need for establishing a college to educate candidates for the ministry. The parsons in attendance approved of the plan and Blair enlisted the financial support of key provincial leaders, including the governor, Francis Nicholson, and members of the general assembly. Recognizing Blair's influential London contacts the legislature requested that he travel to London to obtain a royal charter and an endowment for the institution. He sailed in 1691 and obtained the support of William III and Mary II for the institution. A royal charter for the College of William and Mary was granted on 8 February 1693, with Henry Compton, bishop of London, designated as chancellor, and Blair as president. He was rewarded with appointment to the colonial council in 1694, a position he held for nearly fifty years.

On Blair's return to Virginia the college, based at Middle Plantation, Virginia, began instruction about 1695 with a handful of students but was exposed to weak financial circumstances and difficulty attracting tutors. In 1699 a joint initiative by Blair and the governor of Virginia, Francis Nicholson, led to Middle Plantation being renamed Williamsburg, replacing Jamestown as Virginia's capital. In 1705 a fire practically reduced the college buildings to ruins and it was not until 1716 that they were rebuilt and classes resumed. Fortunes for the college improved by the late 1720s and Blair spent much of 1726–7 in England raising funds with the assistance of Edmund Gibson, bishop of London. In 1729, nearly three and a half decades after the college opened, Blair entered formally on the duties of his office as president.

During Blair's first three decades in Virginia and as a member of the colonial council he was regularly engaged in controversies with royal governors. Each dispute was shaped by the strong willed temperaments of the combatants, men archly seeking to protect and advance the prerogatives of their offices. Blair's conflicts with the royal officials led to their recall by the Board of Trade. He stridently complained in a 1697 memorial to Bishop Compton, a member of the Board of Trade, that the governor, Sir Edmund Andros, neglected to serve the needs of the church and the college. He argued that twenty-seven of the fifty congregations in the province were without ministers; that parson's salaries were deficient; and that the recently founded college was in need of urgent provincial financial assistance. The commissary also claimed that Andros had withheld granting the use of glebes to several ministers because the vestries had not presented the men to the livings, a situation that led Andros not to intercede and induct the clergymen. A menu of charges suggested that Andros was not fulfilling his royal instruction on ecclesiastical affairs. Both men were summoned by the archbishop of Canterbury, Thomas Tension, to Lambeth Palace in 1697 to discuss the matter. It remains unclear how the objections of both disputants were resolved. None the less Andros resigned his governorship in 1697.

Blair attacked Francis Nicholson, Andros's successor, in 1703, when he complained to Bishop Compton that Nicholson was marked with a personal streak of 'hypocrisy and profaneness'. The controversy between the two men was expanded and included a division of opinion between several members of the colonial council and the rank and file members of the provincial clergy. Joined by five members of the Virginia council Blair presented to Queen Anne in 1703 a memorial disparaging the arbitrariness and maladministration of Nicholson's regime. The governor counter-attacked by summoning the Virginia clergy to a convention at Williamsburg on 25 August 1703 for a discussion of the dispute. After hearing a presentation of the two antagonists, twenty ministers in attendance supported Nicholson's position and noted their satisfaction with his administration. The men concluded that Blair's action had stirred up public contempt for the clergy. They recommended to Bishop Compton that Blair should be required to confine his duties to furthering his ecclesiastical duties with the aid of the colony's well-to-do planters rather than to indulge in such divisive political affairs. Blair's unrelenting criticism forced the Board of Trade to recall Nicholson in 1705.

Blair's political and educational interests overshadowed his career as a deputy of the bishops of London in Williamsburg. Despite his tough-mindedness, persistence, and political acumen, he was not venerated by his fellow clerics, and was warily surveyed by politicians and laymen. In churchmanship he was a latitudinarian, and in 1703 he welcomed the first missionary of the Society for the Propagation of the Gospel to the colonies, the recently converted former Quaker George Keith, to the pulpit of the Jamestown church. Keith was on an assignment to assess the state of the church in the colonies on behalf of the society. Throughout his career Blair had limited contact with the society, as the Church of England was established by statute in Virginia. There was no need for him or the local vestries to rely on the society for a regular supply of ministers to fill vacant pulpits or to pay their salaries. Successive bishops of London aided in the recruitment of clergymen. Blair's view of doctrine was expounded in *Our Saviour's divine sermon on the mount, contained in the fifth, sixth and seventh chapters of St Matthew's gospel, explained, and the practice of it recommended in divers sermons and discourses*, published in four volumes in London in 1722. A second edition appeared in 1732, with a preface by Daniel Waterland.

Blair's third major political opponent was Alexander Spotswood, lieutenant-governor of Virginia from 1710. Their dispute festered for several years and came to a head in 1719 and 1720. Blair outspokenly objected to Spotswood's efforts to impose additional imperial authority over such local institutions as the judiciary, the colonial council, and the right of vestrymen to induct into parishes ministers of their choosing. Following Nicholson's example Spotswood called the clergy to a convention in 1719 with the specific purpose of bluntly challenging Blair's charges. Again the clergy were divided in their support of the commissary and the governor. Yet Spotswood emerged from the controversy a blighted official and in 1722 was recalled by the Board of Trade. The Spotswood dispute was Blair's last feud with a royal governor and for the remainder of his life he called the clergy to convention only once, in 1727. He retained his latitudinarian position to the extent that in December 1739 Blair welcomed George Whitefield to his home and church, when his Anglican counterparts in Philadelphia, New York, and Boston had rejected Whitefield, whose preaching excoriated most of the Church of England clergy. Whitefield preached from the pulpit of Bruton parish church to a congregation that included lieutenant-governor William Gooch and members of the provincial council.

At bottom Blair was a complex personality, at once bold, narrowly tough-minded, self-confident, hot tempered, and politically accomplished. By his offices and longevity Blair was a prominent Virginia public figure. During the absence of the lieutenant-governor, Gooch, from the colony he served for more than a year in the early 1740s as acting governor.

Childless, Blair died in Williamsburg, Virginia, on 1

August 1743, aged eighty-seven, a wealthy man, and was buried at Jamestown church cemetery alongside his wife, who had died on 5 May 1713. His will, dated 5 April 1743, bequeathed to the college his library and £500 for a scholarship for 'breeding a young divine'. The remainder of his £10,000 estate he left to his nephew, John Blair (1687–1771), including 1250 acres of farmland in New Kent and 100 acres of the Richneck Tract; a half interest in the Blair-Prentis store with a value of £6000; as well as unfree servants and other property. He also bequeathed £100 for the education of poor children. JAMES B. BELL

Sources P. Rouse jun., *James Blair of Virginia* (Chapel Hill, NC, 1971) • G. M. Brydon, *Virginia's mother church: and the political conditions under which it grew* (Richmond, Va, 1947), vol. 1 • F. L. Hawks, *Contributions to the ecclesiastical history of the United States of America*, 2 vols. (New York, 1836–9) • *Bishop Burnet's History* • W. B. Sprague, *Annals of the American pulpit, or, Commemorative notices of distinguished American clergymen of various denominations, from the early settlement of the country to the close of the year eighteen hundred and fifty-five*, 9 vols. (New York, 1860–69), vol. 5, pp. 7–9 • J. E. Morpurgo, *Their majesties' Royall Colledge of William and Mary in the seventeenth and eighteenth centuries* (1976) • P. Rouse jun., 'Blair, James', *ANB* • *Fasti Scot.*, new edn, 1.100, 310; 2.126; 8.69, 139 • private information (2004) [J. Rettig]

Archives LPL, letters to bishops of London

Likenesses J. Hargreaves, oils, 1705, College of William and Mary, Williamsburg, Virginia; repro. in Rouse jun., *James Blair*, following p. 146 • C. Bridges, portrait, College of William and Mary, Williamsburg, Virginia, Muscarelle Museum of Art [*see illus.*]

Wealth at death over £10,000: Rouse jun., *James Blair*, 254

Blair, Sir James Hunter, first baronet (1741–1787), banker, was born James Hunter on 26 February 1741 at Ayr, the second of three sons of John Hunter (*d.* *c.*1762), a wealthy merchant and probably banker of Mainholm, later of Brownhill, both in Ayrshire, and Anna, daughter and heir of William Cunningham of Brownhill. He had a younger sister, Elizabeth. Hunter was apprenticed to the Edinburgh banking house of the Coutts brothers in 1756, where he met Sir William Forbes, who became a lifelong friend and colleague. When the Coutts partnership was weakened by the death in 1761 of its principal, John Coutts, Forbes successfully persuaded the family in London to give an interest in the firm to himself and to Hunter, who inherited £5000 from his father's estate in 1762.

The Edinburgh bank traded under the name of John Coutts until 1773, when the name became Sir W. Forbes, J. Hunter & Co., and these two principals conducted the firm in complete harmony until Hunter's death in 1787. Hunter was for some years, but to a lesser extent than Forbes, concerned in the London enterprises of Sir Robert Herries, who had briefly trained with them at the Edinburgh bank.

In December 1770 Hunter married Jane (*d.* 1817), eldest daughter of John Blair of Dunskey House near Portpatrick in Wigtownshire, and they had at least nine children; his wife had six brothers but they all predeceased her, and when Jane inherited her father's estate, in 1777, Hunter assumed the surname of Blair. It was only after this marriage, in the last ten years of his life, that Blair became particularly well known. He had an interest in the development of Portpatrick, the town from which the shortest

Sir James Hunter Blair, first baronet (1741–1787), by John Smart, 1772

crossing to Ireland might be made (to Donaghadee), and he combined this with a concern for urban improvements in Edinburgh. The latter projects were by far the more successful in the long term. Despite his enhancements to the harbour and the provision of better packet-boats, Portpatrick remained little more than a village; it was to be further eclipsed by Stranraer in the steam age.

In 1781 and 1784 Blair represented Edinburgh in parliament. A single speech has been documented, on 4 August 1784, when he argued against the imposition of new duties on linen and cotton and 'proved his extensive knowledge of the trade and manufactures of Scotland. His arguments were pointed and conclusive' (Haden-Guest, 658). A supporter of William Pitt (1759–1806), Blair vacated his seat later in 1784 to make way for Sir Adam Fergusson.

Blair became lord provost of Edinburgh in 1784 and set about schemes to improve the university buildings and, more especially, the accessibility of the city centre from the southern suburbs. His enduring memorial is the south bridge over the Cowgate, which was linked to the earlier north bridge on the opposite side of High Street. The south bridge formed part of a viaduct of twenty-two arches, mostly hidden from view, which carried a new road, flanked by new development, towards Nicolson Street. This major project was bitterly controversial, both because of the levies and tolls proposed for the funding, and because of the longer-term fear that people would migrate to the suburbs to avoid the taxes of the inner city. The Edinburgh historian Hugo Arnot, writing at a time when he believed the scheme had been defeated, denounced it at length as 'iniquitous' and 'absurd' (Arnot, 250); paradoxically his appendix, and the publisher's addendum after Arnot's death in 1786, were almost enthusiastic. The foundation stone of the bridge was laid on 1 August 1785; the structure was completed in the following year, though the new road to the south was not opened for carriages until March 1788. The scheme was a triumph, with building land alongside reputedly fetching £100,000 per acre. Although it is usual also to associate the name of Sir William Forbes with the south bridge venture, Forbes himself wrote of it as being 'the magnificent idea' of his colleague (Forbes, 65).

Blair, who was made a baronet in 1786 as a result of the south bridge construction, did not live to see his ambition fully completed. He had gone to Harrogate in April 1787 for what Forbes called 'a scorbutic complaint' (Forbes, 64), and he died there quite suddenly on 1 July, aged forty-six, 'of a putrid fever' (*GM*, 641). He was widely lamented, as a diligent, cheerful, and gregarious man, shrewd in business and honest in his principles. His caricature by John Kay depicts him as tall and corpulent. Forbes wrote that Blair was 'but little acquainted with books or literature' (Forbes, 65), but that he had won the friendship and respect of Robert Burns, who wrote an elegy on his death. As this poem includes the line 'The drooping arts surround their patron's bier' (Burns, *Poems and Songs*), Forbes's comment might be too severe. Another poem or 'monody' on Blair's death was published in the *Edinburgh Magazine*.

Blair was certainly well acquainted with prominent engineers, including John Smeaton, who worked at Portpatrick, and John Loudon McAdam. He was also interested in agricultural improvements, and raised standards among farmers near his Dunskey estate. He is commemorated by Blair Street and Hunter Square in Edinburgh (appropriately near the south bridge), and probably by Blair Terrace, formerly Blair Street, in Portpatrick. He was buried at Edinburgh, his six sons flanking the coffin on its journey to the Greyfriars churchyard on 11 July 1787. Between his death and his funeral, 'the music bells of Edinburgh' had been silenced (*GM*, 641).

JOHN BOOKER

Sources J. Paterson, *Kay's Edinburgh portraits: a series of anecdotal biographies chiefly of Scotchmen*, ed. J. Maidment, 1 (1885) • W. Forbes, *Memoirs of a banking-house*, ed. [R. Chambers], [2nd edn] (1860) • *GM*, 1st ser., 57 (1787), 641–2 • H. Arnot, *The history of Edinburgh* (1816) • 'Monody on the death of the late Sir J. Hunter Blair', *Edinburgh Magazine, or, Literary Miscellany*, 6 (1787), 43–4 • R. Burns, 'Elegy on the death of Sir James Hunter Blair', *The poems and songs of Robert Burns*, ed. R. Ford (1902) • GEC, *Baronetage* • *Scots Magazine*, 49 (1787), 361–2 • R. R. Cunningham, *Portpatrick through the ages* (1993) • E. Haden-Guest, 'Hunter Blair, James', HoP, *Commons* • A. J. Youngson, *The making of classical Edinburgh, 1750–1840* (1966) • parish register (births and baptisms), Ayr, 26 Feb 1741, 9 March 1741

Archives NRA, priv. coll., papers, incl. political corresp. | NA Scot., letters to Hugh Hamilton of Pinmore • NL Scot., corresp. with Sir William Forbes; papers

Likenesses J. Smart, miniature, 1772, Christies, 12–13 July 1983 [*see illus.*] • J. Kay, caricature etching, 1785, NPG; repro. in Paterson, *Kay's Edinburgh portraits*, vol. 1, p. 1 • J. Kay, group portrait, caricature etching, 1785, BM, NPG • D. Allan, group portrait, oils, priv. coll. • H. Raeburn, portrait (after miniature by J. Smart, 1776), priv. coll. • W. S. Watson, group portrait, oils (*The inauguration of Robert Burns as Poet Laureate of the Lodge Canongate, Kilwinning, 1787*), probably Scot. NPG

Blair, John (*supp. fl. c.*1300), supposed biographer and priest, was the creation of *Hary, the late fifteenth-century author of a life of Sir William Wallace (*d.* 1305). To give authority to his own tendentious and unreliable verse account of his hero's exploits, Hary invented the learned and Paris-trained clerk John Blair, who, having acted as both Wallace's chaplain and his comrade-in-arms, could plausibly be presented as the man who 'first compilid in dyt the Latyne buk Off Wallace lyff' (Hary, 1.89). There is no evidence that such a man as Hary presents in this role ever existed. But it is highly likely that in the shadow cast by the fictional John Blair lies a real-life namesake, the John Blair who became a Glasgow MA in 1461 and was a royal chaplain six years later, when he was paid by James III for translating Sir John Mandeville's *Travels*—a work not without influence on Hary. By 1472 he had become vicar of Maybole in Kyle, Ayrshire, and held that living until at least 1488. This John Blair was surely a friend and adviser of the poet, who paid him the compliment of borrowing his name for the scholarly source required by his epic poem. Among those deceived by Hary's invention was the late sixteenth-century literary historian Thomas Dempster, who attributes to John Blair not only the *Gesta Guliemi Wallas*, but also a treatise entitled *De liberata Tyrannide Scotia*. The works will have had as much objective reality as their author.

HENRY SUMMERSON

Sources *Hary's Wallace*, ed. M. P. McDiarmid, 2 vols., STS, 4th ser., 4–5 (1968–9) • *Thomae Dempsteri Historia ecclesiastica gentis Scotorum, sive, De scriptoribus Scotis*, ed. D. Irving, rev. edn, 1, Bannatyne Club, 21 (1829), 86

Blair, John (*d.* 1782), Church of England clergyman and chronologist, was descended from the Blairs of Balthayock, Perthshire, although precise information about his parents, date of birth, and early years is lacking. He was born and educated in Edinburgh, where he trained for a career in the Church of Scotland along with Hugh Blair, Alexander Carlyle, John Home, William Robertson, and other young men who would become notable for their association with the Scottish Enlightenment. According to Carlyle's memoirs, he obtained his licence to preach in Scotland, but before receiving a Scottish pastoral charge he visited London with a patrimony of several hundred pounds, and ended up taking orders in the Church of England and remaining in London for the rest of his life. His first known position there was as an usher at a school in Hedge Lane.

In the early 1750s Blair issued *Proposals for Printing by Subscription, the General Chronology and History of the World*, a work he is said to have adapted from chronological tables originally devised by his Edinburgh classmate and distant relation, Hugh Blair. *The Chronology and History of the World* was published in London in early summer 1754. The book quickly became the standard work of its kind and was frequently reprinted throughout the eighteenth and nineteenth centuries. To the 1768 edition Blair added a set of fourteen maps and 'A dissertation on the rise and progress of geography', which were also published separately in the same year, and in 1784 an expanded version of his dissertation was published in a smaller duodecimo format. A French translation of *The Chronology and History of the World* appeared in Paris in 1797, and there were several American editions in the 1820s. From 1856 onwards it was known as *Blair's Chronological Tables, Revised and Enlarged*, although the editor of the 1856 London edition, J. Willoughby Rosse, declared in the preface that 'all that remains of *Blair* is the general outline' (xii); a London edition was published with that title as late as 1904.

The success of Blair's book led to the author's election as a fellow of the Royal Society of London in 1755; in the same year he published a paper, 'Agitation of the waters near Reading', in the society's *Transactions*. In 1761 he was elected a fellow of the Society of Antiquaries. In September 1757, through the influence at Leicester House of John Home and Gilbert Elliot, among others, Blair was appointed chaplain to Augusta, princess-dowager of Wales (to whom he later dedicated some editions of his *Chronology and History*), and mathematics tutor to her son Prince Edward, later duke of York, whom he accompanied on a continental tour in 1763–4. He subsequently served as Edward's secretary, and owed to him his appointment as prebendary of Westminster in March 1761, which was later followed by presentation of the dean and chapter of Westminster to the vicarage of Hinckley, to the vicarage of St Bride's, London, in 1771, and to the rectory of St John the Evangelist, Westminster, in 1776. He was also rector of Horton in Buckinghamshire.

Alexander Carlyle called Blair 'a lively agreeable fellow, and one of the most friendly men in the world' (*Autobiography*, ed. Burton, 198), but he also observed that Blair was 'disliked by many people, particularly by [Tobias] Smollett' on account of 'a certain petulant and wrangling humour' and 'his flippancy of speech' (ibid., 353–4). Blair died in Dean's Yard, Westminster, on 24 June 1782. Three years later Thomas Cadell published by subscription a quarto edition of his only religious work, *Lectures on the canon of the scriptures, comprehending a dissertation on the Septuagint version*, which had been delivered in the cathedral church of Westminster. It was dedicated to the king by the author's widow, Anne Persode Blair, who is identified in the anonymous editor's advertisement as the person 'upon whose account the publication was undertaken' (xii). RICHARD B. SHER

Sources *The autobiography of Dr Alexander Carlyle of Inveresk, 1722–1805*, ed. J. H. Burton (1910) • J. Hill, *An account of the life and writings of Hugh Blair* (1807); repr. with introduction by E. V. Macleod (1997) • *Fasti Angl., 1541–1857* • *DNB* • *GM*, 1st ser., 52 (1782), 312

Archives BL, Douglas papers, Egerton MS 2185 • Mount Stuart Trust, Isle of Bute, papers of John Stuart, third earl of Bute • NL Scot., William Robertson papers

Blair, Patrick (*c*.1680–1728), botanist and surgeon, was born at Lethendy, Perthshire, the third son of George Blair (*d*. 1682), a farmer, and his wife, Euphame. Little is known of his early life, and his date of birth is not certain. He was apprenticed to a surgeon-apothecary from the late 1680s, possibly in Coupar Angus, Perthshire, where he was later in practice. Between 1694 and 1697 he was in the Low Countries, mainly Flanders, where he practised surgery and also made botanical observations. His knowledge of continental botanical theories may date from this period. Blair was in Dundee by 1700, and in 1701 advertised a projected anatomical handbook in the *Edinburgh Gazette* (where he is identified as 'surgeon-apothecary of Dundee'). This work was never published, although Blair described it in a letter to James Petiver in 1709.

Blair married Elizabeth or Elspeth Whyte in April 1702. Their son John was baptized in 1703. They had another son, Henry, and two daughters, Elizabeth and Isobell (*d*. 1745).

In April 1706 a female Indian elephant, which had been exhibited around northern Scotland, died near Dundee. Blair was given the opportunity to anatomize it, and with the help of local butchers he skinned the elephant and retrieved the bones, which he mounted for exhibition in Dundee, along with the stuffed skin. He wrote a detailed paper on the elephant's anatomy, which was published in the *Philosophical Transactions* of the Royal Society of London in 1710, and also published as a pamphlet in 1713, under the title of *Osteographia elephantina*. In 1712 Blair was elected a fellow of the Royal Society, and in the same year was granted an MD from King's College, Aberdeen, on the rolls of which he is identified as residing in Coupar Angus. Blair also enrolled an apprentice in Coupar Angus in that year, so presumably he had by then moved there from Dundee. He contributed several more papers to the *Philosophical Transactions*, mainly on botanical subjects. Blair corresponded with Hans Sloane and James Petiver on these topics. He had been introduced to Sloane by Charles Preston in 1705.

In 1713 Blair journeyed to London, staying with Petiver, and visited Jacob Bobart in Oxford on the way back; Bobart, like Blair, upheld Robert Morison's system of classification of plants over that of John Ray. He also travelled to Lichfield to meet Sir John Floyer, with whom he agreed on the value of cold bathing, especially in nervous disorders.

Blair came from a family of Jacobites and was acquainted with the Jacobite physician Archibald Pitcairne, as well as with the earl of Mar. In 1715 Blair joined Lord Nairn's battalion as a surgeon and was taken prisoner at Preston. He was taken to London and imprisoned at Newgate, where he was tried on 31 March 1716, pleaded guilty, and was condemned to death. Sloane and Petiver visited him in prison, and Blair appealed to Sloane and Richard Mead to secure him a pardon. Blair assured Sloane that he had joined the rebel army involuntarily. On the night before his scheduled execution, Blair awaited impatiently the arrival of his expected pardon, which arrived only after midnight.

Blair apparently had some difficulty in re-establishing his practice after his imprisonment. In 1719 he wrote to Sloane asking for a loan to enable him to set up a practice in Newcastle. However, he continued to publish scientific works, including an account of pyloric stenosis in the *Philosophical Transactions* in 1717, probably the earliest account of that condition. He published his *Miscellaneous observations in the practise of physick, anatomy and surgery: with new and curious remarks in botany* in London in 1718.

Blair finally settled about 1720 in Boston, Lincolnshire, where he practised medicine and continued his botanical studies. His *Botanick Essays* appeared in the same year. Blair's interest in botany was both medical and scientific; he was interested in pharmaceutical uses of plants but also investigated their intrinsic properties. In *Botanick*

Essays he discussed the new concept of plant sexuality. However, like many of his British contemporaries, Blair viewed plant reproduction as hermaphroditic, rather than requiring two different sexes. He was an 'ovulist' rather than a 'pollenist', and engaged in controversy over this matter with other botanists, particularly Richard Bradley.

In 1723 Blair published the first volume of his *Pharmaco-botanologia*, an encyclopaedic account of the plants listed in the London pharmacopoeia. The last volume of this work, which took it up to the letter H, appeared in 1728. Blair died at Boston in January 1728.

ANITA GUERRINI

Sources [R. C. Buist], 'The story of a Dundee elephant: Patrick Blair's romantic life', *Dundee Courier and Advertiser* (8 Feb 1928), 11 · P. C. Ritterbush, *Overtures to biology: the speculations of eighteenth-century naturalists* (1964) · A. Stevenson, 'Patrick Blair, surgeon apothecary, Dundee', *Transactions of the Botanical Society* [Edinburgh], 23 (1907), 259–76 · E. Caulfield, 'An early case of pyloric stenosis', *American Journal of Diseases of Children*, 40 (1930), 1069–75 · F. J. Cole, *A history of comparative anatomy* (1944) · *IGI*

Archives NHM, corresp. [copies] · RS, letters and papers | BL, corresp. and papers, Sloane MSS 3321–3222, 3812, 4020, 4025, 4040–4049, 4058, 4065–4066 · Bodl. Oxf., MSS Rawl., Blair papers bound with a copy of Richard Bradley, *Philosophical account of the works of nature* (1721), Western MS 16,068 · University of Dundee, archives, MS 67/1/2, 67/1/11

Blair, Robert (1593–1666), Church of Scotland minister, was the sixth son of John Blair of Windyedge (*d. c.*1598), a merchant in Irvine, Ayrshire, and his wife, Beatrix or Bessie Mure (*d.* 1640s), both of whom traced their descent from landed families. Having 'profited well in my bairnly studies', Blair, between 1611 and 1614, attended the University of Glasgow, where, perceiving himself 'to be inferior to none of my fellow-students', he was smitten by God with a tertian fever for four months 'lest I should be puffed up' (*Life*, 7). Subsequently, when he was studying at night in a haunted room, a spirit fled from him, confirming his faith in God's power. Having graduated MA he spent some time as a schoolmaster before becoming, in 1615, a regent at the university. He was licensed to preach the following year.

Blair opposed the reforms of worship embodied in the five articles of Perth (1618) and the growing power of bishops, and his presbyterianism was strengthened by 'the daft people of Stewarton', as enemies called those involved in the Ayrshire religious revival of 1622, and by visiting ministers confined to Turriff and Inverness for holding views similar to his own. Under increasing pressure to conform he resigned his post in Glasgow University in 1623 and became minister of a congregation in Bangor, co. Down. In the freer atmosphere of Ulster, where any protestant minister was welcome, he was ordained by the bishop of Down even though he had explained his objections to episcopacy. However, Blair was suspended from his ministry in 1631 for having taken part in a great revivalist presbyterian communion at Kirk o' Shotts (Lanarkshire) the previous year. Deposition followed in 1632, and his 27-year-old wife, Beatrix Hamilton, whom he had married on 16 July 1626, was 'perfected' by death in November 1633 (*Life*, 100). Undaunted, he travelled to court in England and persuaded Charles I to order his restoration, but his continued nonconformity led to a second deposition in 1634.

Despairing, Blair and his new wife, Katherine (daughter of Hugh, Lord Montgomery of Airds) embarked for New England in 1636, but when their ship was driven back by storms he concluded that this was a sign that God needed him elsewhere. A favour from God was that his infant son did not die at sea, but on the day they landed in Ireland, having been 'persecuted to the death by the prelates and their followers' (*Life*, 146). Orders were given for Blair's arrest, and he fled to Scotland early in 1637. He lived in Irvine, Ayrshire, and preached in the surrounding area, joining John Livingstone, David Dickson, and other dissident ministers with whom he had worked for many years, in campaigning against the changes in worship embodied in Charles I's new Scottish prayer book. However, Blair despaired of successful resistance to royal policy and decided that it was now God's wish that he should work in France, something he had long contemplated. He accepted an invitation to become preacher to Hepburn's regiment, a Scottish unit in the French service. However, once on board he found the recruits with whom he was to travel 'most profligate, and desperately wicked men' given to 'filthy conversation' (*Life*, 152). On being threatened when he rebuked them, Blair hastily decided that God did not want him to go to France after all, and went ashore.

Following the outbreak of open resistance to the new prayer book in July 1637 and the advent of the national covenant in February 1638 Blair became second minister at Ayr, in July 1638, and sat in the general assembly which abolished episcopacy, but he seems to have been reluctant to become involved in organizing the campaign against royal policies. None the less, the persecution he had endured in Ireland and Scotland had made him a revered figure and the assembly ordered his transfer from Ayr to St Andrews. He 'earnestlie opposed' the move (*Letters and Journals of Robert Baillie*, 1.89), and took up his new post only after the 1639 assembly again ordered him to go. Earlier in 1639 he had acted as chaplain in the Scottish army which had assembled on the borders to oppose the king, and he rejoined the army when it invaded northern England in 1640. Subsequently he went to London as chaplain to the Scots commissioners sent to negotiate a peace settlement. When Charles I visited Scotland in 1641 Blair was chosen to preach before him (8 November), and he preached in Ulster to presbyterians and the Scottish army there for three months in 1642. He was involved with negotiating the solemn league and covenant with England in 1643, and served as a regimental chaplain to a Scottish regiment in England in 1644, being 'an eye and ear witness' to the battle on Marston Moor (*Life*, 172).

In 1645, when a number of royalists were executed in St Andrews in the bitter aftermath of civil war, Blair was present on the scaffold with Sir Robert Spottiswood. Blair's supporters recorded Spottiswood's 'railing discourse' against the covenanters, and asserted that Blair's response was mild: 'It's no wonder to hear the son of a false prophet' (the archbishop of St Andrews) speak so of the faithful and honest servants of Jesus Christ. Spottiswood, says Blair, 'died railing and raging' (*Life*, 180). Royalists, however, spoke of Blair being white with fury and breaking 'out into scurrilous abuse' of Spottiswood, which he bore in 'serene silence' (G. Wishart, *Memoirs of James Marquis of Montrose*, 1893, 171).

Blair was elected moderator of the general assembly of the Church of Scotland on 3 June 1646, and he was one of the ministers subsequently sent to negotiate with Charles I when the king was a prisoner of the Scottish army in England at Newcastle. A few months later Charles agreed to appoint Blair to be his chaplain, regarding him as more acceptable than the other Scottish ministers. Blair accepted the post with reluctance, remaining with the king until, in January 1647, the Scottish army withdrew from England.

Blair opposed the Scottish engagers' attempt to help the king in 1648, and after they were defeated by Cromwell in England he helped persuade the remnants of their army to disband. Sent to England to attend Scottish commissioners there, he sought unsuccessfully to prevent the prosecution and execution of Charles I, and it was rumoured that the king had asked for Blair to accompany him to the scaffold. On his journey home Blair suffered much from gout, and after 'being troubled with the gout, and sometimes more pained with the gravel (his two twins as he used to call them)' (*Life*, 218) he was much less active than in the past, although he was one of the ministers who tried to persuade the marquess of Montrose to repent before his execution in May 1650.

When the Scottish church split into warring factions in 1650 Blair sided with the more moderate resolutioners against the protesters, but he saw the dispute as 'the heart-break of all honest and moderate men' and, being 'displeased with some things on both sides' he worked for reconciliation (*Life*, 301). He was one of those summoned to London in May 1654 by Cromwell to try to resolve the matter, but was unwilling to attend and too ill to do so. He concentrated on his work as parish minister but, worn down by the disputes of hostile factions, in 1660 he unsuccessfully sought permission to move from St Andrews to another parish.

On the restoration of monarchy and episcopacy Blair was removed from the ministry (September 1661) after defiantly preaching in support of presbyterianism. He was at first confined to his room in Edinburgh, but in January 1662 he was ordered instead to confine himself in the parish of Musselburgh. Blair disliked the place and soon obtained permission to move to Kirkcaldy, where he remained for three and a half years. He continued preaching to and worshipping with presbyterian dissidents, but in February 1666, fearing action would be taken against him, he withdrew to Couston, near Aberdour. There his presence still attracted dissidents, but he soon fell ill, 'being worn with old age, but much more with sorrow'. He died on 27 August 1666 and was buried in Aberdour.

As well as his autobiography (which ends in the 1630s) and some Latin verse Blair wrote a preface for James Durham's *The Dying Man's Testimony … a Treatise on Scandal* (1659), and several other works which remained unpublished. Though stubborn in his resistance to episcopacy, Blair seems to have had little taste for controversy or a role in public affairs, and was influential mainly through his preaching, praying, and piety. Robert Baillie, who had been his student, was devoted to him, praising him for 'his great dexteritie; yea greater than any man I know living, to insinuate the fear of God in the hearts of young schollars' (*Letters and Journals of Robert Baillie*, 1.174).

DAVID STEVENSON

Sources *DNB* · *The life of Mr Robert Blair … containing his autobiography*, ed. T. M'Crie, Wodrow Society, 11 (1848) · *The letters and journals of Robert Baillie*, ed. D. Laing, 3 vols. (1841–2) · *Fasti Scot.*, new edn, vol. 5 · J. S. Reid and W. D. Killen, *History of the Presbyterian church in Ireland*, new edn, 3 vols. (1867)
Archives NL Scot., Adv MSS, autobiography

Blair, Robert (1699–1746), poet, was born in Edinburgh, the eldest son of the Revd David Blair (*d.* 1710), minister of the Old Kirk parish in Edinburgh and one of the king's chaplains, and his wife, Euphemia Nisbet, daughter of Alexander Nisbet of Carfin, Lanarkshire. Hugh Blair, who was to become famous as professor of rhetoric and *belles-lettres* at the University of Edinburgh, was his first cousin. Robert was educated at the University of Edinburgh and in the Netherlands, though no specific details of his education remain.

From about 1718 to 1731 Blair resided probably in Edinburgh as an unemployed probationer, finally being licensed to preach by the presbytery of Haddington on 5 August 1729. Prior to his only church living as minister in Haddington presbytery at Athelstaneford, Haddingtonshire, to which he was ordained on 5 January 1731, references to Blair are scant. There is an 'Epistle to Robert Blair' in a miscellany, *Lugubres cantus*, published in Edinburgh in 1719 that provides no biographical detail of its dedicatee. Blair was a member, probably, of the Athenian Society, an Edinburgh literary club whose members included James Thomson, author of *The Seasons*, who may have been Blair's fellow student at Divinity Hall in Edinburgh. In 1720 the Athenians published a volume of verse, the *Edinburgh Miscellany*, that includes the early work of Thomson. Some slight pietistic poems in the book signed by B are usually taken to be by Blair. In 1728 Blair published his *Poem Dedicated to the Memory of … William Law*, 138 lines of elegiac verse in the form of a quarto pamphlet on the professor of moral philosophy at Edinburgh, William Law of Elvingston.

On 11 April 1738 Blair married Isabella (*d.* 1774), the daughter of Professor Law. The couple had five sons, David, William, Francis, Robert *Blair (1741–1811), who was to become Lord Blair of Avontoun, lord president of the Scottish college of justice from 1808, and a man admired by George III, and Archibald; they also had one daughter, Anna. Blair possessed a private fortune and had long relied on this to give him leisure to pursue his two chief interests, English poetry and botany. At Athelstaneford, Blair seems to have continued a rather solitary life of which, Alexander Carlyle, in his *Anecdotes and Characters of the Times*, provides a rather acidic glimpse during 1744,

> I got away time enough next Day to reach Haddington before Dinner; Having past by Athelstaneford where the Minister Mr Robert Blair Author of The Grave, was said to be Dying Slowly; or at any Rate, was so Austere and void of Urbanity, as to make him quite Disagreeable to young People (*Autobiography*, ed. Burton, 49)

At Athelstaneford, Blair worked slowly on *The Grave*, which he had begun while living in Edinburgh. The long genesis of the poem probably resulted from an extreme care not so much born out of perfectionism as out of wariness on the part of Blair, due to a Calvinist cultural climate in Scotland that was only very slowly changing so as to accommodate poetry. The advance of the evangelical revival in Britain in the 1740s licensed the often gloomy, emotional excess that Blair poured into his religious poem and spurred its author to seek publication. In 1742 the poem was finished and Blair sent the manuscript to the great hymnist Dr Isaac Watts, who attempted, unsuccessfully, to interest two London booksellers in publishing it. In 1743 with the help of another English divine, Dr Philip Doddridge, Blair succeeded in having *The Grave* published in quarto and it enjoyed an instantly huge vogue.

The Grave features 767 lines of blank verse and is notable more for its luxuriantly melancholy atmosphere rather than for any profound intellectual ideas. Not entirely even in its quality of writing, the poem does feature passages of exquisite description. Its opening section invokes the grave as 'Eternal King! Whose potent arm sustains / The keys of Hell and Death' (ll. 1–10). In a manner that sets the tone for the rest of the poem, Blair proceeds very morbidly to describe the physical horror of the tomb (ll. 11–27), the eeriness of the churchyard and human loneliness (ll. 28–87), and from there reflects on 'Friendship! mysterious cement of the soul' (ll. 88–110). Returning to contemplation of the grave, the poet considers the foolish vanity of mankind when set against this certainty, producing a fervent *contemptus mundi* (ll. 111–368). The poem next considers the strangeness and imponderability of death and includes some of the piece's finest moments on the fragility of human life and understanding (ll. 369–633). The final 140 lines of the poem bring a far from entirely convincing and rather forced, pietistic meditation on human sin and the resurrection.

As one commentator has noted, '*The Grave* accorded with the Post-Enlightenment vogue of melancholy' (Simpson, 11). Along with Edward Young's *Night Thoughts on Life, Death, and Immortality* (1742–5), Blair's poem initiated a fashion for 'mortuary poems' and Young himself had been inspired to continue in his own, longer project by the success of Blair's work. Blair's poetry is a harbinger of the literary cult of sentiment and paves the way for the melancholy writing of such proto-Romantic writers as Thomas Gray and James Macpherson. The repeated publication of *The Grave* also afforded the opportunity for one of the great Romantic artists, William Blake, to provide illustrations for it in 1808.

In spite of his literary fame, or perhaps because of the awkwardness with which this sat upon a Church of Scotland minister (a number of talented Scottish literary divines found such a co-existence difficult), Blair published nothing else and no literary manuscripts were found posthumously among his effects. Robert Blair died of a fever on 4 February 1746 and was buried in the churchyard at Athelstaneford under a plain stone marked 'R. B.'.

GERARD CARRUTHERS

Sources *Fasti Scot.*, new edn • *The poetical works of Beattie, Blair and Falconer*, ed. G. Gilfilwan (1854) • M. J. Scott, *James Thomson: Anglo-Scot* (1988) • *Autobiography of the Rev. Dr. Alexander Carlyle … containing memorials of the men and events of his time*, ed. J. H. Burton (1860); repr. as *Anecdotes and characters of the times*, ed. J. Kinsley (1973) • K. Simpson, *The Protean Scot* (1988)

Archives JRL, letters to H. Baker

Blair, Robert, Lord Avontoun (**1741–1811**), judge, was born at Athelstaneford, Haddingtonshire, Scotland, the third son of the minister of the parish, the Revd Robert *Blair (1699–1746), author of *The Grave*, and his wife, Isabella (*d.* 1774), eldest daughter of William Law (*d.* 1728) of Elvingston, Haddingtonshire, professor of moral philosophy in the University of Edinburgh.

Blair began his education at the grammar school at Haddington; from there he was sent to the high school at Edinburgh, where he formed a lifelong friendship with Henry Dundas, afterwards Viscount Melville. Thence he was transferred to the university. In 1764 he was admitted a member of the Faculty of Advocates and he soon obtained a considerable practice at the bar, where he and Henry Erskine were often pitted against each other. On 19 May 1786 he married Isabella Cornelia (1766–1857), third and youngest daughter of Colonel Charles Craigie Halkett of Lawhill, Fife. They had a son and three daughters.

In 1789 Blair, having served some years as an advocate-depute and as an assessor for the city of Edinburgh, was appointed solicitor-general for Scotland. About this time he bought a small estate at Avontoun, Linlithgowshire, where he took much pleasure in agricultural pursuits. He continued to occupy his post until the change of ministry that was occasioned by Pitt's death in 1806. During this period he twice refused the offer of a seat on the judicial bench, and in both 1802 and 1805 he declined to accept the office of lord advocate. In 1801 he was elected dean of the Faculty of Advocates. Upon the return of the tory party to power in 1807 he refused the offices of solicitor-general and lord advocate but in the next year, upon the resignation of Sir Ilay Campbell, he accepted the presidency of the college of justice. He had been chosen as a safe pair of hands, his good legal mind more than compensating for a lack of eloquence, at a time of prospective upheaval in the court of session. During his presidency the court was split into two divisions, and rules were introduced to cut down the number of appeals to the House of Lords in an effort to expedite Scottish justice.

Blair died suddenly on 20 May 1811 at his home in George Square, Edinburgh. Melville, who travelled to Edinburgh purposely to attend the funeral, was taken ill and died on the very day that Blair was buried, 28 May. Blair's wife and children survived him, but he left them so badly off that a pension was granted by the crown to his widow and daughters through the instrumentality of Mr Perceval.

G. F. R. BARKER, *rev.* MICHAEL FRY

Sources M. Fry, *The Dundas despotism* (1992) • *Law Review*, 2, 341–52 • J. Kay, *A series of original portraits and caricature etchings … with biographical sketches and illustrative anecdotes*, ed. [H. Paton and others], new edn [3rd edn], 1 (1877), 313–16 • *EdinR*, 59 (1834), 31–2, 281–3 • *Scots Magazine and Edinburgh Literary Miscellany*, 73 (1811), 403–7 • *Fasti Scot.*

Archives NL Scot., opinion books and session papers | NA Scot., corresp. with Lord Melville

Likenesses J. Tassie, paste medallion, 1792, Scot. NPG • J. Kay, caricature etchings, 1793–9, BM, NPG; repro. in Kay, *Original portraits* (1877) • J. Heath, line engraving, pubd 1813 (after H. Raeburn), BM • F. Chantrey, marble statue, Parliament House, Edinburgh, Faculty of Advocates • H. Raeburn, oils, Society of Writers to the Signet, Edinburgh

Blair, Robert (1748–1828), surgeon and maker of optical instruments, was born at Garvald, Haddingtonshire, the son of the minister Archibald Blair and his wife, Janet Barclay. After studying medicine at Edinburgh University he was apprenticed to Francis Balfour, surgeon in the Royal Navy; as a naval surgeon Blair served in the West Indies, during which time he became interested in navigation and its instruments. His proposal for improving the adjustment of Hadley's quadrant for back observations gained him an award of £100 from the commissioners of longitude; his description was published in 1783 as an appendix to the *Nautical Almanac* for 1788 and was also issued separately. Blair returned to Britain in the early 1780s.

In 1785 a regius chair of practical astronomy was established at the University of Edinburgh with the aim of improving navigation and allied arts. Blair was appointed professor, with a yearly salary of £120, and awarded the degree of MD. The following year he was elected to the Royal Society of Edinburgh. As professor, Blair 'enjoyed forty two years of endowed leisure' (Grant, 2.362), for he refused to give lectures on the grounds that he had neither apparatus nor observatory. He declined to attend meetings of the university senate, and indeed was seldom seen, and resided latterly for eight years in London where his son Archibald Blair was an optician.

While at Edinburgh Blair sought to improve the performance of refracting telescopes which relied on achromatic lenses: doublets of flint and crown glass. It was difficult to procure flint glass without defects, and Blair, as others had done before him, hoped to substitute some dense fluid, with a refractive index similar to that of flint glass, which, when in contact with a crown glass lens, would give an image free from colour and distortion. Two patents (1473 of 1785 and 1800 of 1791) were filed in the course of his lengthy experiments; these labours and the successful outcome were reported at two meetings of the Royal Society of Edinburgh in January and April 1791, and published in their transactions in 1794. Blair decided that the most satisfactory form was a triplet, in which a solution of antimony or mercury in hydrochloric acid was sealed in a concavity between two crown glass lenses. For such lenses, he coined the term 'aplanatic', declaring them superior to the common achromatic form, and suitable for telescopes or microscopes. Working with his son, Blair constructed several telescopes equipped with his triplet lenses of apertures between 3 and 4 inches. They were favourably received by astronomers and others; fears that evaporation and loss of transparency would rapidly destroy them were countered by Archibald Blair who in 1827 claimed that lenses made over twenty years previously were still in good condition.

These optical experiments ceased in 1793 when Blair was appointed emeritus first commissioner of the Admiralty's board for the care and custody of prisoners of war, a post which required him to tour naval establishments around Britain. His contribution to sailors' welfare lay in finding a method for preserving lime and lemon juice, and persuading the Admiralty to issue it for long voyages, thus helping to prevent scurvy. Blair later published *Essays on Scientific Subjects* (1818) and *Scientific Aphorisms* (1826), slight works whose contents did not match the promise of their titles. After a long illness he died at Westlock, Berwickshire, on 22 December 1828.

A. M. CLERKE, *rev.* ANITA MCCONNELL

Sources A. Grant, *The story of the University of Edinburgh during its first three hundred years*, 2 vols. (1884) • H. A. Brück, *The story of astronomy in Edinburgh from its beginnings until 1975* (1983) • R. Blair, 'Experiments and observations on the unequal refrangibility of light', *Transactions of the Royal Society of Edinburgh*, 3/2 (1794), 3–76 • A. Blair, 'On the permanency of achromatic telescopes constructed with fluid object glasses', *Edinburgh Journal of Science*, 7 (1827), 336–42 • S. Devlin-Thorp, ed., *One hundred medical and scientific fellows of the Royal Society of Edinburgh, elected from 1783 to 1832* (1981), vol. 1 of *Scotland's cultural heritage* (1981–4)

Archives NMM, Royal Greenwich Observatory • RAS • U. Edin. | NL Scot., Melville MSS, etc.

Likenesses T. Campbell, bust, U. Edin.

Blair, Sir Robert (1859–1935), educational administrator, was born in Wigtown in south-west Scotland on 8 March 1859, the eldest of the ten children of William Blair and his wife, Mary, *née* Hood. His father, a Presbyterian, appears to have had a variety of jobs but was principally a cobbler by trade. Robert attended the Free Kirk school in Wigtown, where he was introduced to classical scholarship and academic rigour. The school catered for children from different social backgrounds, a style of education which he later recalled with approval. He was a pupil teacher at the Garlieston endowed school from 1873 to 1876 before entering Edinburgh University with the help of a bursary from the Edinburgh Galloway Association. The novelist S. R. Crockett was a fellow student and Blair appears as Rob Grier in Crockett's semi-autobiographical *Kit Kennedy* (1899).

After graduating MA in 1880 Blair taught for a short time in Kelso before moving to London in 1881 to take up an appointment at Aske's Hatcham School, New Cross, where he was a master for twelve years. During this period he became increasingly interested in science education, studying part-time for a London University BSc, and eventually taking responsibility for this area of work throughout the school. This experience helped him to secure his next appointment as headmaster of the Cheltenham Science and Technical School. This was followed in 1894 by six years as an inspector with the Scottish education department, after which Blair moved to Ireland, where he became inspector of science and art and subsequently assistant secretary for technical education. He was a member of Alfred Mosely's commission to study American education in 1903.

The period of Blair's greatest influence came with his appointment in June 1904 as the first education officer to the London county council (LCC). Physically impressive (he had 'a magnificent leonine head'), and with a forceful personality, he came to exercise great authority at the LCC. His first task was to effect the fusion of the London school board and the technical education board; his work in this area helped to establish the professional role of the chief officer. He was president of the National Association of Education Officers in 1914 and was knighted in the same year. A strong believer in educating adolescents for employment, he recognized the fundamental importance of technical education. He reorganized technical education in London in 1913, attempting to raise its quality, but his failure to win support from London employers convinced him of the need for compulsory day-continuation schools for all those aged between fourteen and sixteen not in full-time education. As chairman of the Liberal Party's advisory committee on education he was able to exert a significant influence upon H. A. L. Fisher's 1918 Education Act, which gave continuation schools a central role. Compulsory attendance was enforced by the LCC until opposition from employers became overwhelming in the council elections of 1922. In 1924, the year of Blair's retirement, London began the reorganization of elementary schools into junior and senior branches, which he had long advocated.

In 1883 Blair married Ida Kathleen Westrup of Kensington, London, with whom he had four sons and one daughter. He died at his home, 33 Gresham Gardens, Golders Green, Middlesex, on 10 June 1935 and was buried in Hampstead cemetery. DAVID THOMS

Sources *Nature*, 135 (1935), 1065 • R. Blair, 'My schooldays', *Teachers World* (8 June 1927) • D. Thoms, *Policy making in education: Robert Blair and the LCC, 1904–1924* (1980) • *WWW* • b. cert. • *CGPLA Eng. & Wales* (1935)

Archives Heriot-Watt University, Edinburgh, notebooks and papers

Wealth at death £2829 15*s*. 2*d*.: probate, 6 Sept 1935, *CGPLA Eng. & Wales*

Blair, Sonia Mary. *See* Brownell, Sonia Mary (1918–1980).

Blair, William (1741–1782), naval officer, the son of Daniel Blair of Edinburgh, went to sea in merchant ships and, as surgeon's servant, able seaman, and midshipman, in the *Windsor*, *Firebrand*, *Amazon*, *Aleide*, *Hussar*, and *Eolus*, before passing his lieutenant's examination on 30 May 1760. From 9 October 1760 he served as lieutenant in the *Grenado*, *Superb*, *Centurion*, *Salisbury*, and *Grafton*, and then from 6 December 1777 commanded the sloop *Wasp*.

Blair was promoted post captain on 18 April 1778; he was captain of John Byron's flagship, *Princess Royal* (90 guns), at the action off Grenada on 6 July 1779, and was later appointed to the *Nonsuch*. From 2 March 1781 he commanded the *Dolphin* (44 guns). In the hard-fought but indecisive battle of Dogger Bank on 5 August 1781 the *Dolphin*, notwithstanding her small size, took her place in the line of battle. Blair's conduct won for him the approval of the Admiralty and his appointment on 23 August to the *Anson*, a new 64-gun ship, then fitting for service in the West Indies.

In January 1782 Blair sailed in the *Anson* as part of Sir George Rodney's fleet. On 12 April he was killed in action at the battle of the Saintes, the *Anson*, in the leading squadron, having been heavily engaged from the very beginning of the battle.

J. K. LAUGHTON, *rev.* RANDOLPH COCK

Sources commission and warrant books, PRO, ADM 6/19,20,21,22 • lieutenants' passing certificates, PRO, ADM 107/5 f.248 • R. Beatson, *Naval and military memoirs of Great Britain*, 3 vols. (1790) • *GM*, 1st ser., 52 (1782) • W. L. Clowes, *The Royal Navy: a history from the earliest times to the present*, 7 vols. (1897–1903) • *N&Q*, 6th ser., 7 (1883), 122

Archives PRO, ADM 6/19, 20, 21, 22 • PRO, ADM 107/5, fol. 248

Blair, William (1766–1822), surgeon, youngest son of William Blair, surgeon, and Ann Gideon, his wife, was born at Lavenham in Suffolk on 28 January 1766. Educated for the church Blair changed direction to study under John Pearson, surgeon, of Golden Square, London. In 1788 he passed the diploma for membership of the Company of Surgeons, which became the Royal College of Surgeons in 1800; he also took an MA degree at Aberdeen, and at some point married. He was made assistant surgeon to the London Lock Hospital in 1802, and he had appointments to the Finsbury and the Bloomsbury dispensaries in Great Russell Street, the Female Penitentiary in Pentonville, and the New Rupture Society. He was a member of medical societies in London, Paris, Brussels, and Aberdeen. For a time he edited the *London Medical Review and Magazine*. In 1803 he recommenced his series of physiological lectures, illustrated with anatomical preparations, addressed to the nobility and clergy, and to painters, sculptors, and others. He published his syllabus as *Anthropology, or, The natural history of man; with a comparative view of the structure and function of animated beings in general* (1803). The lectures, started 'as occasional amusement to a few friends', had grown imperceptibly 'into the mature state of regular and annual discourses' (Blair, preface).

Blair's other works included: *The Soldier's Friend, or, The Means of Preserving the Health of Military Men* (1798); *Essays on the Venereal Disease and its Concomitant Affections, in Two Parts* (1798–1800); and *The Vaccine Contest respecting Cow-Pox Inoculation … for the Use of Clergymen, Heads of Families, Guardians, etc.* (1806). In this and other publications Blair defended vaccination, mentioning a report of the Royal Jennerian Society and abuse at the London Smallpox Hospital. His *Prostitutes Reclaimed and Penitents Protected, being an Answer to some Objections against the Female Penitentiary* appeared in 1809. This and subsequent publications debated the rehabilitation of prostitutes after care of their venereal infections. Blair's *Correspondence on the Formation, Objects, and Plan of the Roman Catholic Bible Society* (1814) drew him into a controversy with Charles Butler of Lincoln's Inn (*GM*, 1st ser., 84/2, 1814).

Blair also wrote a long and elaborate article entitled 'Cipher', in the eighth volume of Abraham Rees's *Cyclopaedia* (1819); three engraved illustrative plates are inserted under the heading 'Writing by cipher' in the fourth volume of plates (1820). This article was considered the best treatise in the English language on secret writing and the art of deciphering. It included a cipher method invented by Blair, which he declared to be inscrutable; but the key was discovered in 1819 by Michael Gage, who commented that Blair's method was a real improvement on previous ciphers and the first method ever published on a scientific principle. In addition Blair was the author of the article 'Stenography' in Rees's *Cyclopaedia* (vol. 34, 1819, 12), discussing the origins and history of shorthand.

Blair was a very earnest Methodist and worked enthusiastically in the cause of the British and Foreign Bible Society, on whose committee he served and to which he presented his valuable collection of rare editions of the Bible. After his wife's death, on 1 March 1822, he gave up his practice to retire to the country. However, before the preparations for moving to the Colchester area were completed, he died at his residence in Great Russell Street, Bloomsbury, London, on 6 December 1822. He left no children.

THOMPSON COOPER, *rev.* JOHN KIRKUP

Sources *GM*, 1st ser., 92/2 (1822), 646 • examination book, court of examiners, Company of Surgeons, 6 Nov 1788, RCS Eng. • D. I. Williams, *The London Lock, a charitable hospital for venereal disease* (*c.*1996) • private information (2004) • W. Blair, *Anthropology, or, The natural history of man* (1803) • *Some account of the death of William Blair, etc.* (1823) • *Orthodox Journal*, 4 (1816), 139–40

Archives Wellcome L., notes and corresp. relating to inquiry into vaccination

Likenesses G. Cruikshank, etching, 1812 (*An attack on smallpox vaccination and on the Royal College of Physicians' advocation of it*), Wellcome L. • S. Medley, oils (*Founders of the Medical Society of London, 1800*), Lettsom House, London • H. Meyer, oils, St Giles-in-the-Fields, London

Blak, John. *See* Black, John (*d.* 1566).

Blake, Anthony (1707–1787), Roman Catholic archbishop of Armagh, was born in Kilvine, co. Mayo, younger son of Patrick Blake, landowner, of a prominent local family. He was educated locally, in co. Galway, and was probably ordained in Ireland before travelling to St Omer and Louvain for further education. He returned to Ireland in 1731 to take up an appointment in the archdiocese of Tuam, near Galway city. He was elected warden of Galway in 1742, where he presided over a flourishing Catholic community and, in the face of bitter opposition from the town's mayors and from Governor Eyre, built a new church in Middle Street, completed about 1750. In 1756 he was promoted to the bishopric of Ardagh, where he presided over the integration into the diocese of the newly acquired territory of Clonmacnois. He was translated to Armagh in 1758. He may have owed his promotion to his absence from the episcopal meeting in 1757 that was convened to discuss proposals by the government to register Irish priests, a measure frowned upon by Rome. He held a diocesan synod in 1761, which concerned itself with the repression of abuses, especially intemperance, irregularity in the hours and places of worship, and interference of the laity with episcopal rights in collating parishes. Another synod was held in 1764; this concerned itself with financial support for the bishop and the erection of chapels, or mass houses, in the parishes of the diocese. Blake was uncommitted on the regulars' admission controversy in the 1760s, when many bishops argued that Ireland was oversupplied with clergy and that the regulars in particular should be obliged to limit admissions to their houses.

From 1764 onwards Blake's relations with his cathedral chapter deteriorated, owing mainly to his persistent non-residence, his allegedly unfair financial exactions, his failure to perform visitation, and his ill-treatment of clergy, especially with regard to clerical appointments in Dundalk and Drogheda. Blake did live much of the year with his family in co. Galway; he was prompt in his demands for collations and procuration and rather legalistic in his dealings with the clergy, and he fought opposition over several clerical appointments, notably in the parish of Dundalk. Complaints were communicated to *propaganda fide* but Blake defended himself in several long, repetitive letters, one of which reveals that he spent enough time in Armagh to notice the growth of secret agrarian organizations.

After 1772 clerical and lay opposition to Blake grew; John Carpenter, archbishop of Dublin, was deputed by Cardinal Castelli, prefect of *propaganda*, to investigate. Carpenter found in favour of Blake's appointee to Dundalk but laid the blame for the scandal that had been caused on Blake's persistent non-residence. In 1775 *propaganda*, who despaired of Blake's returning permanently to his diocese and who were unconvinced by his argument that his return would expose him to the rigours of penal legislation, suspended Blake and delegated his functions to Bishop Cheevers of Meath. The Munster bishops rallied round Blake, shocked by the effect of clerical opposition on the status of one of their own. As a pledge of his intention to reform Blake returned briefly to his diocese but was back in Galway by 1776. The complaints continued and *propaganda*, disappointed by the performance of Carpenter, Cheevers, and the latter's vicar, Anthony Nowlan, appointed John Troy, bishop of Ossory, to investigate the case. Subject to his acceptance of important conditions, Blake was reinstated. Almost immediately he began preparing for his successor and imposing his restored authority. This brought him into renewed conflict with many of his clergy. *Propaganda* considered imposing Plunkett, the new bishop of Meath, as Blake's coadjutor but Plunkett appears to have refused. Richard O'Reilly, former parish priest of Kilcock, co. Kildare, briefly coadjutor in Kildare, was appointed Blake's coadjutor in 1782.

Blake died in Galway on 29 November 1787 and was buried near the collegiate church of St Nicholas at Browne's Isle. He does not appear to have been widely mourned in Armagh, where his achievements were limited. Well adapted to the low-profile, family-based Catholic church structures of the early to mid-eighteenth century, Blake proved unable or unwilling to adapt to the increasingly high-profile, territorially based organization of the later eighteenth century. In his will he left £27 and some property at Carrowbrowne, co. Galway.

THOMAS O'CONNOR

Sources P. Whelan, 'Anthony Blake, archbishop of Armagh, 1758–1787', *Seanchas Ardmhacha*, 5 (1969–70), 289–323 • C. Carrigan, 'Catholic episcopal wills (1683–1812) (Ulster)', *Archivium Hibernicum*, 1 (1912), 148–200, esp. 157–9, 192 • J. Hagan, ed., 'Miscellanea Vaticano-Hibernica', *Archivium Hibernicum*, 5 (1916), 74–185, esp. 139 • H. Fenning, 'Some problems of the Irish mission, 1733–1774', *Collectanea Hibernica*, 8 (1965), 58–109, esp. 84 • E. Bolster, ed., 'The Moylan correspondence in Bishop's House, Killarney [pt 1]', *Collectanea Hibernica*, 14 (1971), 82–142, esp. 115 • E. MacIysaght, 'Report on documents relating to the wardenship of Galway', *Analecta Hibernica*, 14 (1944), 1–186, esp. 40, 107, 109 • P. E. MacFhinn, 'Scríbhinní ig Cartlainn an Vatican: Tuarascbháil', *Analecta Hibernica*, 16 (1946), 1–280, esp. 87, 201

Archives Sacra Congregazione di Propaganda Fide, Scritt. Rif and Scritt. orig.

Wealth at death over £27; plus landed property: Carrigan, 'Catholic episcopal wills', 157–9

Blake [*née* Boucher]**, Catherine Sophia** (1762–1831), wife and assistant to William Blake, was born in Battersea, Surrey, on 25 April 1762, and baptized there at St Mary's Church on 16 May 1762, the thirteenth child of William Boucher (1714–1794), a market gardener, and his wife, Mary *née* Davis (*d.* 1782). Nothing is known of Catherine's early life until she met William *Blake (1757–1827) in 1781. His proposal having been rejected by another, he turned for solace to Catherine and soon fell in love with the dark-eyed brunette. The couple married on 18 August 1782 in St Mary's, Battersea. They had no children.

Catherine Blake may have been illiterate, or at least limited in penmanship, for she signed the marriage register with an X. Her husband (who called her Kate) taught her to read, write, and assist him in his printmaking activities. She was probably the 'clean hands' person who managed the paper when the couple printed on their engraving press. She took an active role in the production of Blake's illuminated books, beginning in 1788, with both the printing of the plates and their hand colouring. The extent of her contributions as a colourist has never been determined, but she alone bound the volumes in paper wrappers. Catherine also printed intaglio engravings, taking major responsibility for the illustrations in William Hayley's *Life of William Cowper* (1803–4). She drew and painted her own compositions, but only three are extant (Butlin, 1.625–6).

The early years of marriage were not without conflict. After an argument between Catherine and her husband's beloved brother Robert (1762?–1787), William made her apologize humbly. In later years, their bond became very strong; many who knew them considered Catherine the ideal wife and helpmate. She was the most important person in Blake's life, the only one who consistently believed in his visions and genius. Although they were rarely apart, she once remarked, 'I have very little of Mr. Blake's company; he is always in Paradise' (Bentley, *Blake Records*, 221). When the muse was upon him, she sat quietly for hours, late at night, by his side. Catherine was the more practical of the two and managed the family purse. When resources were meagre, she set an empty plate before her husband at mealtime as a reminder of their needs.

The Blakes resided in Felpham, on the Sussex coast, between 1800 and 1803—the only time in their lives they lived outside London and its suburbs. They were at first delighted with their cottage; but by January 1803 both were ill, Catherine suffering from rheumatism (for which she received electrical treatment in 1804) and respiratory complaints. Back in London, the couple was in danger of dire poverty, but found a new patron in the artist John Linnell in 1818.

After Blake's death on 12 August 1827 Catherine lived with Linnell; about six months later she moved to the home of Frederick Tatham, another young artist who had befriended the couple, to serve as housekeeper. She may have completed several of Blake's projects, left unfinished at his death, including his watercolour illustrations to Bunyan's *Pilgrim's Progress*. During her last months Catherine resided at 17 Charlton Street, Fitzroy Square, where she died on 18 October 1831 after suffering from stomach and bowel disorders. Five days later she was buried next to her husband in Bunhill Fields, Finsbury. Extant art works by Catherine Blake are in the collection of the Fitzwilliam Museum, Cambridge (exh. 'William Blake', Tate Britain, 2000).

ROBERT N. ESSICK

Sources G. E. Bentley, *Blake records supplement* (1988) • A. Gilchrist, *Life of William Blake, 'Pictor ignotus'*, 2 vols. (1863) [2nd edn, 2 vols. (1880); ed. R. Todd (1942)] • *The letters of William Blake*, 3rd edn, ed. G. Keynes (1980) • G. E. Bentley, *Stranger from paradise: a biography of William Blake* (2001) • M. Wilson, *Life of William Blake* (1927) • P. Ackroyd, *Blake* (1995) • M. Butlin, *Paintings and drawings of William Blake*, 2 vols. (1981) • G. Keynes, *Complete portraiture of William and Catherine Blake* (1977) • R. Hamlyn and M. Phillips, *William Blake* (2000) [exhibition catalogue, Tate Britain, London, 9 Nov 2000 – 11 Feb 2001, and the Metropolitan Museum of Art, New York, 27 March 2001–24 June 2001]

Likenesses G. Cumberland?, pencil and grey wash, *c.*1785, FM Cam. • W. Blake, pencil drawing, *c.*1803, Tate collection • F. Tatham, pencil drawing, 1828, BM

Blake, Charles (1664–1730), Church of England clergyman and poet, was born on 31 October 1664 at Reading, Berkshire, the son of John Blake, wharfinger, and his wife, Mary, who were later described as 'parents of the highest rank, even for such a town' (Brown and others, 15). He was baptized at St Giles's Church, Reading, on 1 November 1664 and educated at Merchant Taylors' School, London, from 1677/1678 to 1683 and then at St John's College, Oxford, where he 'completely surrendered himself to sound learning' (ibid.): he graduated BA in 1687, and proceeded MA in 1694, BD in 1696, and DD in 1712. He was an accomplished classical linguist and theologian, and acquired 'an outstanding reputation among academics' for his 'intellect and learning' and 'love of piety' (ibid.). He also developed a love of poetry, and composed in 1688 an elegy on the death of Frederick, the great elector, founder of Brandenburg-Prussia and champion of European protestantism, and in 1689 a poem in the style of Virgil's *Eclogues*, 'Hibernia plorans', which empathized with the besieged protestant stronghold of Londonderry. Both poems were published in 1693 in a sixpenny pamphlet, together with Blake's translation from Greek into Latin of the epic poem of Musaeus on Hero and Leander and an extract from Milton's *Paradise Lost*.

Blake became domestic chaplain in 1710 to Sir William Dawes, a high-church tory who achieved episcopal preferment under Queen Anne, and served him while he was bishop of Chester and archbishop of York. Dawes, a younger contemporary of Blake at Merchant Taylors' and St John's College, shared his academic interests and love of poetry and remained a close personal friend until his death in 1724. Blake was appointed successively prebendary of Chester in 1710 and York in 1715, subdean of York in 1716, and archdeacon of York in 1720, and held the benefices of St Sepulchre, London, St Mary the Virgin, Hull, and St Helen, Wheldrake, a substantial living in the gift of the archbishop of York. Unassuming and unambitious, he declined several other preferments and voluntarily resigned others.

Blake appears to have been an efficient ecclesiastical administrator as archdeacon of York and with the archdeacons of the East Riding and Cleveland undertook a major survey of the fabric of the churches in the diocese in 1721–2. However, the foundations, walls, and roofs of the nave and tower of the medieval church at Wheldrake, an open field village in the Vale of York, where he was rector from 1719 until 1730, remained 'in so ruinous a condition' that the congregation later petitioned that they were unable to assemble for 'public worship of Almighty God without manifest danger of their lives' (Brown and others, 6) and the church had to be almost completely rebuilt in 1778. The old timber-framed rectory was also pronounced old-fashioned in 1764 and subsequently extensively altered, but Blake's legacy to the poor of the parish, in the form of bequests amounting to £200, proved more enduring.

The diary of Henry Prescott, deputy registrar of the diocese of Chester, reveals Blake as a devoted scholar, meticulous liturgist, and a genial companion, who occasionally enjoyed a very spruce dinner and more frequently a domestic glass of wine. In the closing years of his life he became 'racked by the pains of gout', until, 'finally overcome', he died, a bachelor, on 22 November 1730 at Wheldrake. He was buried in the churchyard at Wheldrake in the same month and two large marble plaques were placed in the sanctuary of the church recording his own epitaph on his life, together with tributes from his friends, 'since those who were joined to him by nearness of blood had died' (Brown and others, 15).

JOHN A. HARGREAVES

Sources D. R. Brown and others, eds., *Wheldrake: aspects of a Yorkshire village*, Wheldrake Local History Society (1971) • H. B. Wilson, *The history of Merchant-Taylors' School*, 2 vols. (1814) • *Catalogue of chapter records*, York Minster Library, D1/1710–1719 • Foster, *Alum. Oxon.* • *The diary of Henry Prescott, LLB, deputy registrar of Chester diocese*, ed. J. Addy and others, 1, Lancashire and Cheshire RS, 127 (1987) • *The diary of Henry Prescott, LLB, deputy registrar of Chester diocese*, ed. J. Addy and others, 2, Lancashire and Cheshire RS, 132 (1994) • R. V. H. Burke, *Chester Cathedral* (1958) • *VCH Yorkshire East Riding* • last will and testament of Charles Blake, Borth. Inst. • C. J. Robinson, ed., *A register of the scholars admitted into Merchant Taylors' School, from AD 1562 to 1874*, 1 (1882) • Mrs E. P. Hart, ed., *Merchant Taylors' School register, 1561–1934*, 1 (1936) • Reading, St Giles, baptism register, 1664, Berks. RO, D/P 96/1/4

Archives Borth. Inst., York archdeaconry MSS

Wealth at death approx. £1000: will, probate records, Borth. Inst.

Blake, Charles Henry (1794–1872), property speculator, was born in Calcutta, the son of Benjamin Blake, a sea captain who had been plying the route to India since 1775. Soon after 1794 his father left the sea and became an indigo planter in Bengal, and Blake followed his father into this business. In the 1820s he left India for England, but returned to India about 1830. Later he became a rum and sugar manufacturer, an occupation he continued to pursue until he left India for good in 1842 or 1843, the profits from which, no doubt, provided the basis for his speculations in Notting Hill and Notting Dale in North Kensington.

Blake's twenty-year career as an active speculator began in 1850 when he bought 25 acres of undeveloped land on the Ladbroke estate and began to grant building leases. Only two years later, however, he sold this still isolated land (probably at a loss) and bought a smaller but more advantageously situated estate at the top of Lansdowne Hill. Here, in Stanley Crescent, Stanley Gardens, and the north side of Kensington Park Gardens, he built some sixty large, stucco-fronted houses, designed in the Italianate manner by Blake's architect, Thomas Allom, and grouped around the communal gardens which were a distinguishing feature of the layout of the Ladbroke estate. Forty of these houses were built by a direct contract for some £64,000 between Blake and a builder, D. A. Ramsay, and the rest under the usual procedure of building leases granted by Blake.

In 1854, however, the housing boom in North Kensington collapsed, Ramsay was declared bankrupt, and Blake was left with forty unfinished houses on his hands. In 1858 he too was on the verge of insolvency and had to sell his own fine house at 24 Kensington Park Gardens, but he was saved by a revival of the housing market in 1859–60 and soon he was developing other land further north on the west side of Ladbroke Grove.

In the second phase of Blake's career as a building speculator he made full use of the housing boom of the 1860s and of the impending construction of the Hammersmith and City railway line, which traversed Notting Dale to a junction with the Great Western Railway near Paddington, and of which Blake was the principal promoter and a director. In 1862 he had contracted to buy, for about £838 per acre, some 130 acres of the Portobello estate, part of which would be needed for the line; he and the chairman of the railway company (who also had a share in the deal) demanded £10,000 per acre for the ground needed by the railway. Ultimately the price to be paid by the company was settled at £2105 per acre, but both Blake and the chairman resigned as directors, with heavily tarnished reputations. The railway, opened in 1864, proved an instant commercial success and Blake had no difficulty in developing all of the land on either side of Ladbroke Grove between the railway and Kensal Green. In that area he acted as both ground landlord and speculator, granting building leases, making loans to builders, buying and selling improved ground rents, and also selling vacant land, usually at about double the price which he had himself paid. Many of the houses were of the three-storey terraced variety with basements, the plots being usually only 20 feet wide and 60 feet deep. Some of the streets developed by these means achieved nationwide notoriety in the mid-twentieth century as the scene of some of the worst housing conditions in all London.

After 1868 Blake lived in semi-retirement at Bournemouth, where he died at his home, 15 Westover Villas, on 22 March 1872. A monument to him (which no longer exists) was erected in St Peter's Church there. He was survived by his wife, Frances (*d.* 1876), and, subject to her life interest, bequeathed his estate to his two sons and two daughters; the elder son (also named Charles Henry), a barrister, continued to manage the estate for some years. At the time of Blake senior's death his principal property consisted of twenty-four freehold houses on Lansdowne Hill and freehold land and ground rents on the Portobello estate. There were also a number of outstanding mortgages and family charges, and the surplus of assets over liabilities amounted to some £120,000, which yielded a gross income of £3905 per annum. This represented a return of only about 3.25 per cent on the capital invested—not a very high rate for Blake's twenty-two years' assiduous labours, the imminence of ruin in 1859, and a blemished reputation acquired in 1862–4.

F. H. W. SHEPPARD

Sources F. H. W. Sheppard, ed., *Northern Kensington*, Survey of London, 37 (1973), 220–36, 304–12 · d. cert.
Archives LMA
Wealth at death under £35,000: probate, 11 April 1872, *CGPLA Eng. & Wales*

Blake, Cyril McDonald [*called* Midnight Blake] (**1897–1951**), jazz musician, was born on 22 October 1897 in Trinidad, the son of Samuel Blake, cabinet-maker. He served in the merchant navy in the First World War and went to Britain on discharge. In October 1921 he was a member for engagements in Glasgow and Ireland of the Southern Syncopated Orchestra, and he was a survivor of the sinking on 8 October 1921 of the SS *Rowan*, on which the orchestra was travelling to Ireland. This orchestra, which had arrived in Britain in 1919, had originally consisted of African-Americans, but by 1921 many had been replaced by other members of the African diaspora, for whom it served as an initiation into jazz practices. Blake married Olive May Douglas (*b.* 1903/4), a music-hall artiste and daughter of Edward James Douglas, chief ship's steward, in Manchester on 7 November 1923.

By 1926 Blake was performing in clubs in the West End of London. In 1927 or 1928 he moved to Paris. It is believed that he took up the trumpet, which henceforth became his main instrument, only at this time. He was a member of Thompson's Negro Band for the summer season at La Baule, France in 1928, and on an international tour the following winter which took in Hamburg, Amsterdam, Rotterdam, Oslo, Copenhagen, and Madrid. This band had originally been led by the Sierra Leonean trumpeter Egbert E. Thompson, who had died in August 1927. While in Paris Blake also worked with Josephine Baker.

Blake returned to England in March 1933 in the band of the African-American violinist Leon Abbey. For the remainder of the 1930s he worked mainly in London clubs and touring the variety halls in the bands of his elder brother George Lionel Blake (*b.* 1895), a drummer known professionally as Happy Blake, and of Rudolph Dunbar, Leslie Thompson, and others. In 1938 he began an association with the Havana Club, Denman Street, where he was billed as Midnight Blake. The association lasted after he also became band leader at Jig's Club, Wardour Street, in May 1941. His Jig's Club band rapidly established itself as one of the best-regarded jazz groups in wartime London and in December 1941 was the subject of an early experiment in location recording by the Parlophone company. The resulting records captured the band's raw energy, far removed from the polite aspirations of much British jazz of the era.

In the course of the Second World War Blake led bands at other London clubs, including the West One Club in Grafton Street, the Bag O'Nails in Kingly Street, and the Barberina Club in St John's Wood. He was again band leader at the Havana Club from December 1942 until it was closed by the police in April 1943. His bands, which used shifting personnel drawn mainly from among African-Caribbean jazz musicians working in London, made several BBC broadcasts, including a programme devoted to calypsos in June 1942 and one devoted to spirituals in March 1943. In 1944 he led bands at the New Malcolm Club in Commercial Road and at the Chesterfield Officers' Club in Curzon Street. In 1945–7 his bands were resident at the Goose and Gander Club in Baker Street and the Panama Club, South Kensington. However, fashions in jazz were changing, and the small swing groups such as those he led were by then ceasing to be ubiquitous and were attracting a smaller audience.

Like most African-Caribbean musicians involved in jazz in Europe, Blake also had roots in Latin and Caribbean music. As early as 1942 he had been a member of a rumba band led by the Trinidadian pianist Clarry Wears, who had also played in Blake's jazz bands, and Blake appeared with Wears's band in the film *Alibi* (1942). By the late 1940s Blake's own bands were alternating jazz with rumbas and calypsos. With the growing demand for Caribbean music in Britain he formed his Calypso Serenaders in 1949. In 1950 they took part in recording sessions with the Calypsonians Lord Beginner and Lord Kitchener, and in 1951 they toured Germany with Kitchener and others. By this time Blake had fallen ill, and despite surgical intervention he succumbed to cancer at St Pancras Hospital, London, on 3 December 1951. His wife, who reported the death, believed him to be fifty-one, which is just consistent with the age of twenty-two he gave at their marriage in 1923, but the birth date given on his seaman's identity certificate, 22 October 1897, was also on the passport he used to enter Denmark in 1929. A relationship with Florence Eva Dowling early in 1939 led to the birth of a son, Anthony Cyril Dowling, who was acknowledged by his father and was the residual legatee in his will.

HOWARD RYE

Sources J. Cowley, 'Cultural "fusions": aspects of British West Indian music in the USA and Britain, 1918–1951', *Popular Music*, 5 (1985), 81–96 · H. Rye, 'Visiting firemen, 8a: Leon Abbey and his orchestra', *Storyville*, 108 (1983), 207–10 · H. Rye, 'The Southern Syncopated Orchestra', pt 3, *Storyville*, 144 (1990), 227–34 · 'Ginmill on wax: Parlophone's unique recording session at Jig's Club', *Melody Maker* (27 Dec 1941), 5 · 'Cyril Blake's Calypso Serenaders', *Jazz Illustrated*, 1/5 (1950), 6 · J. Cowley, *West Indian gramophone records in Britain, 1927–1950* (1985) · *Melody Maker* (8 Dec 1951), 7 · seaman's identity certificate, PRO, Class BT 350, no. 453028 · m. cert. · d. cert. · b. cert. [Anthony Cyril Dowling, son]

Archives FILM BFI NFTVA | SOUND BL NSA

Likenesses portrait, repro. in *Melody Maker* (27 Dec 1941), 5 · portrait, repro. in *Melody Maker* (7 Feb 1942), 3 · portrait, repro. in *Melody Maker* (14 Nov 1942), 5 · portrait, repro. in *Jazz Illustrated*, 6 · seaman's identity certificate, PRO, class BT 350, no. 453028

Wealth at death £311 9s. 8d.: probate, 18 June 1952, *CGPLA Eng. & Wales*

Blake, (Dominick) Edward (1833–1912), lawyer and politician in Canada, was born on 13 October 1833 at a homestead at Bear River, Adelaide township, Middlesex county, Upper Canada, the elder son of William Hume Blake (1809–1870) and his wife, Catherine (1804/5–1886), the daughter of Joseph Samuel Hume. Both parents were from Galway, Ireland. The Blakes were originally Catholic gentry, but William Hume's branch became protestant. William Hume, a graduate of Trinity College, Dublin, trained for medicine, but abandoned his medical career to emigrate to Upper Canada (later Ontario) in 1832, the year of his marriage to his cousin Catherine. He farmed briefly, during which time Dominick Edward (the first name soon slipped into oblivion) was born, and then in 1833 moved his family to Toronto, where he took up law. He became a prominent lawyer and judge as well as a Reform politician, and attained the positions of solicitor-general and chancellor of Upper Canada.

Edward Blake attended Upper Canada College, Toronto, and then the University of Toronto, where he obtained his BA and the silver medal in classics in 1854. While working for his MA (acquired in 1858), he enrolled as a senior student in law. In 1856 he was called to the bar. He entered into a partnership with Stephen Jarvis, and a year later founded his own law firm, which his brother Samuel Blake joined. He was appointed QC in 1864. In 1858 Blake married a first cousin, Margaret, the second daughter of Revd Benjamin Cronyn, first Anglican bishop of Huron (later London, Ontario). Of their seven children, three sons and one daughter survived.

Blake became the leading Canadian lawyer of his day, arguing many important cases before the judicial committee of the privy council. He consented to be chancellor of the University of Toronto from 1873 to 1900, but refused high judicial offices, including the chancellorship of Ontario, the chief justiceship of the supreme court of

(Dominick) Edward Blake (1833–1912), by Sir Benjamin Stone, 1897

Canada (1875), and membership of the judicial committee of the imperial privy council.

Blake's political career was promising but marked by numerous resignations and positions rejected. In 1867 he was elected as a Liberal to both the newly created federal House of Commons, for the constituency of West Durham, and the Ontario legislature, for South Bruce. He became leader of the opposition for Ontario in 1869, and premier in 1871, but in 1872 resigned when dual representation ended and opted for federal politics.

In Ottawa, Blake helped to expose corruption in John A. Macdonald's Conservative government during the Pacific Scandal, over contracts to build the Canadian Pacific Railway, which led to its resignation in 1873 and defeat in 1874. The Liberals came to power in 1873 under Alexander Mackenzie, although many believed that Blake should have been party leader and prime minister. In 1874 Blake agreed reluctantly to become a minister without portfolio. He resigned from cabinet early the following year, but returned as minister of justice from 1875 to 1877. When he resigned this position he became president of the council, only to resign altogether from the cabinet in 1878, on the eve of the Liberals' defeat at the polls. While minister of justice he was instrumental in curbing imperial judicial powers, including the governor-general's prerogative of pardon, his power to disallow legislation passed by the Canadian parliament, and his right to reserve for the consideration of the British government certain bills enacted by the Canadian parliament.

In 1880 Blake succeeded Mackenzie as leader of the Liberal opposition. Unable to defeat the Conservatives under Macdonald in the elections of 1882 and 1887, he resigned as party leader in the latter year, and was influential in getting Wilfrid Laurier—Canada's first French-speaking party leader and prime minister—chosen as his successor. He retired from Canadian politics in 1892.

During the years of Blake's active involvement in the Liberal Party of Canada the party took on a national perspective, but it remained more a loose coalition of factions than a united party, and needed a strong leader who could instil loyalty. Blake, with his abrasive personality, his cold, rather academic appearance, his cut-and-dried, unemotional, and verbose speeches, and his relentless insistence on principles over people, was not such a leader. As one member commented: 'I looked at his shirt-front and then at his face, and concluded that it didn't matter which I looked at as they were both starched and ironed. He will never be a real leader of men' (Schull, 1975, 216–17).

Always more the intellectual than the politician, Blake helped define the nature of Canadian Liberalism. In an important speech in Aurora, Ontario, in 1874, he appealed for the cultivation of a 'national spirit'—'some common aspiration to be shared' (Underhill, 1957, 11)—as an alternative to what he saw as the crass materialism of the Conservatives' policy of railway building to promote national unity (although Blake's law firm catered to Canada's growing entrepreneurial class, including some of the country's wealthiest railway builders). That national spirit, he argued, could arise from the struggle to obtain greater Canadian autonomy within the British empire, otherwise 'we are four millions of Britons who are not free' (ibid.). He favoured a form of imperial federation in which Canada would cease to be a dependent colony under the British parliament and instead become an equal partner under the British crown. This viewpoint proved unpopular in the Liberal Party, but found favour with the Canadian intellectuals of the Canada First movement, a movement to put Canadian interests first, who looked to Blake—unsuccessfully—to become leader.

Blake consistently opposed the Conservatives' railway-building scheme, especially their desire to construct an expensive transcontinental railway, and the use of taxpayers' money to support the privately owned Canadian Pacific Railway Company. To his dying days he denounced this alliance of government and business, even though it consistently won the Conservative Party votes.

Blake also questioned the Liberal Party's trade policy. He felt that Canada, a country with a small population, needed a high tariff, but one that balanced trade with Britain and the United States, and which, by preventing free trade with the United States, could counteract trends towards political union with America. The issue came to a head in the election of 1891, when protection was advocated by the Conservatives, and unrestricted reciprocity, a form of free trade with the Americans, was favoured by the Liberals. Although Blake opposed his party's position, he kept silent during the election campaign, but the day after the Liberals' defeat he wrote an open letter to his West Durham constituents explaining his objections to unrestricted reciprocity. Ironically, two years later the Liberal Party abandoned its free-trade policy, a shift that helped them come to power in 1896.

By the time of the Liberal victory, Blake had left Canadian politics to join the Irish nationalist party in their struggle for home rule in the British parliament. His deep interest in the Irish question stemmed from his ancestral roots and his belief that resolution of the issue was important both to the empire and to Canada as part of the empire. He believed that home rule in Ireland and other British possessions abroad would strengthen the empire, and hence accorded with his favourable view of imperial federation. Blake was both an Irish nationalist and an imperialist.

From 1892 to 1907 Blake sat in the Commons for South Longford. He became a member of the inner executive of the Irish nationalist group, raised funds for the party, spoke in favour of home rule at public meetings in Britain and North America, and advised fellow MPs. He played some part in the making of the second Home Rule Bill in 1893. But, ironically, he served Canadian Liberalism and Irish nationalism in times when both stagnated.

In 1907 poor health took Blake back to Canada. For the last five years of his life he lived at 449 Jarvis Street in Toronto and made occasional visits to the family cottage on Murray Bay in Quebec. He died at home following a stroke on 1 March 1912. R. Douglas Francis

Sources J. Schull, *Edward Blake*, 2 vols. (1975–6) · M. A. Banks, *Edward Blake, Irish nationalist* (1957) · M. A. Banks, 'The change in liberal party leadership, 1887', *Canadian Historical Review*, 38 (1957), 109–28 · M. A. Banks, 'Edward Blake's relations with Canada during his Irish career, 1892–1907', *Canadian Historical Review*, 35 (1954), 22–42 · F. H. Underhill, 'Edward Blake', *Our living tradition*, ed. C. T. Bissell (1957), 3–28 · F. H. Underhill, 'Edward Blake and Canadian liberal nationalism', *Essays in Canadian history*, ed. R. Flenley (1939), 132–53 · F. H. Underhill, 'Edward Blake, the liberal party and unrestricted reciprocity', *Report of the Canadian Historical Association* (1939), 133–41 · F. H. Underhill, 'Edward Blake, the Supreme Court Act, and the appeal to the privy council, 1875–6', *Canadian Historical Review*, 19 (1938), 292–4 · F. H. Underhill, 'Laurier and Blake, 1882–1891', *Canadian Historical Review*, 20 (1939), 392–408 · F. H. Underhill, 'Laurier and Blake, 1891–1892', *Canadian Historical Review*, 24 (1943), 135–55 · F. H. Underhill, 'Political ideas of the upper Canadian reformers, 1867–1878', *Report of the Canadian Historical Association* (1942), 104–15 · Gladstone, *Diaries* · J. Kendle, *Ireland and the federal solution* (1989)

Archives NA Canada · Public Archives of Ontario, Toronto · University of Toronto | NA Canada, letters to Barry Hayes · NL Ire., letters to J. F. X. O'Brien and John Redmond · TCD, Dillon MSS

Likenesses B. Stone, photograph, 1897, NPG [*see illus.*]

Blake, Elizabeth. *See* Burnet, Elizabeth (1661–1709).

Blake, Sir Ernest Edward (**1845–1920**), civil servant, was born on 1 March 1845 at the new rectory, Bramerton, Norfolk, the sixth child of the eleven children of the Revd Edmund Blake (1812–1883), rector, and his wife, Mary Hobart Sewell (1808–1883), daughter of Joseph Sewell of Norwich. On leaving Norwich grammar school, Blake prepared himself for the civil service first division exams, which he passed second in his year. Appointed assistant junior clerk in the Colonial Office in 1863, his hard work and enthusiasm led him to successive promotions. From 1874 he was private secretary to the secretary of state, the earl of Kimberley. In 1879 he was again promoted, to first class clerk, and became head of the general department of the Colonial Office. He married, on 8 October 1874, Catherine Isabella (*d.* 1902), daughter of Alfred Blyth, a London shipping engineer, with whom he had two sons and one daughter.

Impressed by the energy and skill with which Blake managed the general department, Kimberley, in 1881, appointed him third agent in the office of the crown agents for the colonies, a quasi-government department that acted as the UK commercial and financial agent of the crown colonies and protectorates. His duties involved the organization of the purchase of colonial public goods, worth £500,000 p.a. in 1881 and £1.5 million in 1899, the recruitment of colonial technical officers, and the payment of colonial service pensions and half pay to officers on leave in Britain. On the death of Sir William Sargeaunt, in 1888, and his promotion to second agent, he also became involved in the office's financial activities; under the supervision of the senior agent, Sir Montagu Ommanney, he began to manage colonial UK investments, and eventually took part in the flotation of colonial UK loans.

On the promotion of Ommanney to under-secretary of state at the Colonial Office in 1901 Blake was appointed senior agent and awarded a knighthood. Although he had long sought the post of senior agent it proved to be his downfall. His 1901 reorganization of the office and his autocratic management style so reduced the morale of his staff that, in 1904, they wrote a series of anonymous letters to *The Times* and *Pall Mall Gazette* severally critical of their conditions of work. Similarly, his patronizing and, at times, vindictive treatment of colonial officials and governors led to numerous complaints to the Colonial Office. His reluctance to accept the secretary of state's instructions, which often led to long drawn-out and acrimonious correspondence, created much ill-feeling among Colonial Office officials. The standard of the service provided by the agency also began to decline. The office had started to supply expensive goods that were often subject to long delays, and to construct costly and uneconomic infrastructure projects. Colonial dissatisfaction with the agency was picked up by the press, which, in 1904, revealed that Blake was a director of London Assurance Corporation, the agency's insurance company. Although aware of the relationship, the Colonial Office bowed to pressure and required Blake to resign the directorship. There were also rumours, proved to be correct, that his eldest son, Ernest Stephen Blake, was a director of the agency's shipping agency, that his second son, Edmund Christopher Blake, was employed by the officer's brokers, and that various other relatives were members of crown agent staff. Fearing further criticism the Colonial Office, in 1908, held an inquiry into the agency, which recommended widescale reorganization. Strongly opposed to the findings, Blake demanded that the Colonial Office publish his own views on the inquiry, and, when the request was rejected, resigned in 1909. He died of a heart attack on 30 November 1920 at Woolcombe St Mary's, Uplyme, Devon, where he had recently settled, and was buried at Fetcham in Surrey. DAVID SUNDERLAND

Sources *WWW* • D. Sunderland, 'Agents and principals: the crown agents for the colonies, 1880–1914', DPhil diss., U. Oxf., 1996 • R. F. Shinn, *Arthur Berriedale Keith (1874–1944)* (1990) • *The Times* (8 Dec 1920), 15 • private information (2004)

Archives PRO, CO CAoG

Likenesses cartoon, Archive of the Crown Agents, St Nicholas House, St Nicholas Road, Sutton, Surrey; presented on his retirement • photograph (aged forty?), Archive of the Crown Agents, St Nicholas House, St Nicholas Road, Sutton, Surrey

Wealth at death £23,173 8*s.* 7*d.*: probate, 1 March 1921, *CGPLA Eng. & Wales*

Blake, Sir Francis, first baronet (1707/8–1780), experimental philosopher, was the son of Robert Blake (*d.* 1734), landowner, of Twisell, co. Durham, and his wife, Sarah, daughter of Sir Francis Blake MP (1638–1718), of Ford Castle, Northumberland. His father was of Irish origin and belonged to the Blakes of Menlo Castle, co. Galway, who claimed descent from Richard Caddle, a fourteenth-century sheriff of Connaught. His mother's family, though bearing the same name, was descended from minor Hampshire gentry. His maternal grandfather was a substantial and rising landowner who had made good during the Commonwealth and Restoration, and had given the small estate of Twisell to Robert Blake as a marriage settlement.

Blake was educated at Lincoln College, Oxford, where he matriculated in 1725. On 9 November 1732 he married Isabel (*c.*1710–1741), daughter of Samuel Ayton of West Herrington; they had two sons and two daughters. He inherited the estate of Twisell on his father's death and held on to it, though his title was challenged by descendants of the Selby family who had owned it until the late seventeenth century. When in London, he appears to have resided at Queen Square, Westminster. He rendered active support to the government during the Jacobite rising of 1745, and was created a baronet on 3 May 1774.

In 1741 Blake published *An Explanation of Fluxions, in a Short Essay on the Theory*. He devoted much of his time to mechanics and experimental philosophy, and was elected a fellow of the Royal Society in 1746. He was an active member of the society during the 1750s and 1760s, serving on a committee set up to examine John Canton's experiments on the compressibility of water, and publishing papers in *Philosophical Transactions* on the design of steam engines. He was related to the Delaval family, which included a number of early scientists and industrialists. He died at Tilmouth, Northumberland, on 29 March 1780, and was buried at Houghton-le-Spring, co. Durham. His elder son, Robert, who had been a student at Westminster School, died in 1754 at the age of twenty-one, and was buried in Westminster Abbey, and Blake was succeeded in the baronetcy by his second son, Francis *Blake (1736/7–1818). GORDON GOODWIN, *rev.* JOSEPH GROSS

Sources J. Raine, 'Pedigree of Blake of Twisell Castle', *The history and antiquities of north Durham* (1852), 316 • *A history of Northumberland*, Northumberland County History Committee, 15 vols. (1893–

1940), vol. 11, p. 402 [pedigree of Blake of Ford Castle] · HoP, *Commons* · Burke, *Gen. GB* · RS, MS Ca. 2.47 · election certificate, RS · Foster, *Alum. Oxon.* · W. Betham, *The baronetage of England*, 5 vols. (1801–5)

Blake, Sir Francis, second baronet (1736/7–1818), political writer, was the eldest surviving son of Sir Francis *Blake, first baronet (1707/8–1780), of Twisell Castle, Norham, co. Durham, mathematician, and his wife, Isabel (*c*.1710–1741), second daughter and coheir of Samuel Ayton of West Herrington, co. Durham. He was educated at Westminster School, and possibly at the Middle Temple from June 1755. On 15 January 1756 he was admitted to Trinity Hall, Cambridge, from where he graduated LLB in 1763. He became second baronet on the death of his father on 29 March 1780 and served as high sheriff of Northumberland from 1784 to 1785. In the following years he published his three most significant studies of state finances *The Efficacy of a Sinking Fund of one Million per annum Considered* in 1786, *The Propriety of an Actual Payment of the Public Debt Considered* in 1786, and *The True Policy of Great Britain Considered* in 1787. These, and other pieces, were republished collectively under the title *Political Tracts*, first at Berwick in 1788 and again at London in 1795.

Blake spent some £80,000 on building Fowberry Tower on the banks of the River Till; his project was never completed and the structure was sold to George Colley, an agriculturist, in 1807 for £45,000. Blake married Elizabeth Douglas on 15 April 1772. Their eldest son, also named Francis (1774/5–1860), represented Berwick in parliament between 1826 and 1834 and published severe criticisms on the conduct of the House of Lords in relation to the corn laws. The elder Sir Francis died on 22 May 1818 at Twisell Castle; his son inherited the title and died on 10 September 1860, aged eighty-five.

Gordon Goodwin, *rev.* Philip Carter

Sources *GM*, 3rd ser., 9 (1860), 445–6 · Venn, *Alum. Cant.*
Archives Sheff. Arch., letters to Bacon Frank · U. Durham L., letters to second Earl Grey

Blake, Sir Geoffrey (1882–1968), naval officer, was born on 16 September 1882 at Bramley House, Alverstoke, Hampshire, the son of Thomas Naish Blake (1826–1906), brewer, and his wife, Fanny (1842–1931), daughter of Theophilus Leahy. Educated at Winchester College, he entered the Royal Naval College, Dartmouth, in 1897. In 1903 he was given his first command, torpedo boat 59, and promoted lieutenant. In 1911 he married Jean St John Carr (1888–1963), and they had two daughters. Appointed gunnery officer of *Iron Duke* and promoted commander in 1914, his direction of the ship's gunnery at Jutland resulted in several hits on a German battleship and he was appointed to the DSO. Serving as executive officer on *Queen Elizabeth* (1917–18), he was noted as exceptionally promising for high command. In December 1918 he was promoted captain and in 1919–20 acted as naval attaché in Washington. Blake won further praise as flag captain in *Queen Elizabeth* (1921–3). After the directorship of the Royal Naval Staff College (1926–7), he became chief of staff to the commander-in-chief, Atlantic Fleet (1927–9), and in 1929 was appointed CB and served as first naval member of the New Zealand navy board. Promoted rear-admiral in April 1931, he served as fourth sea lord between 1932 and 1935. Promoted vice-admiral in 1935, he became second in command of the Mediterranean Fleet, earning congratulations for his tactful handling of British interests during the Spanish Civil War, and in May 1937 he was appointed KCB.

Unsparing in his efforts to achieve the highest standards of efficiency, discipline, and seamanship, Blake was highly respected and extremely popular throughout the service. It was confidently expected that ultimately he would become first sea lord. However, in June 1937, while swimming at Malta, he suffered a pulmonary embolism and thrombosis of the leg. He made an excellent recovery but, though the Admiralty was desperate for him to remain in the service, he feared his illness might recur and was anxious about his family's welfare. He retired on 15 January 1938 and took up a post with British Power Boats. Sheafs of letters testified to the navy's anguish at the loss of its most promising vice-admiral.

In 1940 Blake returned as assistant chief of the naval staff (foreign), relieving Admiral Pound, the first sea lord, of some of his burdens. Though Blake was closer to Pound than any other officer (Pound thought he had a greater range of abilities than Andrew Cunningham, whose career profited from Blake's illness), Blake often opposed both Churchill and Pound with vigour. He condemned the assault on the French fleet at Mers al-Kebir in July 1940, defended Vice-Admiral Sir James Somerville when Churchill and Pound, quite unjustifiably, wished to remove him from the command of force H, and described operation Ration, the seizure of French merchantmen, as stupid. He was opposed equally firmly to the dispatch of *Prince of Wales* and *Repulse* to Singapore. When Admiral Harold R. (Betty) Stark went to London in 1942 in command of American naval forces in Europe, Blake was appointed flag officer liaison United States and enjoyed a close relationship with the affable Stark. They oversaw the successful Anglo-American naval co-operation in the battle of the Atlantic and the great combined operations in the Mediterranean and Normandy; for his part, Blake was appointed to the American legion of honour (chief commander). Between 1945 and 1949 he served as gentleman usher of the black rod. He was consulted frequently by post-war first sea lords and died on 18 July 1968 at 42 Burton Court, London.

A charming and good-humoured man of the utmost integrity, he was the Royal Navy's 'lost leader'. Admiral of the Fleet Lord Chatfield intended him to take command of the Home Fleet in September 1940 and become first sea lord in 1943. Had he done so, the Royal Navy would have been directed with acute intelligence, decisiveness, a clear strategic vision, and, probably freedom from major errors.

Michael Simpson

Sources NMM, Blake MSS · *The Times* (24 July 1968) · *The Times* (26 July 1968) · private information (2004) [Mr and Mrs J. Ehrman (family)] · BL, Cunningham MSS · CAC Cam., Somerville MSS ·

Naval Historical Center, Washington, DC, Stark MSS • PRO, Admiralty Records • Admiral of the Fleet Lord Chatfield to Sir Samuel Hoare, 24 May 1937, NMM, Chatfield MSS, CHT 3/1

Archives NMM, corresp. and papers | BL, Cunningham MSS • CAC Cam., corresp. with S. W. Roskill • CAC Cam., Somerville MSS • Naval Historical Center, Washington, DC, Stark MSS

Likenesses photographs (Second World War and early career), NMM

Wealth at death £17,147: probate, 17 Sept 1968, *CGPLA Eng. & Wales*

Blake, George (**1893–1961**), novelist, was born on 28 October 1893 at 60 Forsyth Street, Greenock, Renfrewshire, the fourth child of Matthew Blake, manufacturer of sugar machinery, and his wife, Ursula Scott McCulloch. He was educated at Greenock Academy and studied law at Glasgow University until the outbreak of the First World War. He served in the forces and was wounded at Gallipoli. After the war he entered journalism and wrote for the Glasgow *Evening News*, then edited by the novelist Neil Munro. He married Eliza (Ellie) Malcolm Lawson in 1923, and they had two sons and a daughter.

In 1924 Blake moved to London, where he edited two literary magazines and in 1930 became a director of the publisher Faber and Faber. He was involved in running the Porpoise Press, Edinburgh (which published Neil M. Gunn's *Morning Tide* in 1931) as a subsidiary of Faber. He returned to Scotland in 1932 and lived successively in Helensburgh, Dunbartonshire, Dollar, Clackmannanshire, and Glasgow.

Blake wrote more than twenty novels and many non-fiction works. The autobiographical *Down to the Sea* (1937) demonstrated his lifelong interest in the Clyde and its shipping. His melodramatic first novel, *Mince Collop Close* (1923), preceded more mature work in *Young Malcolm* (1926) and *The Path of Glory* (1929), which drew on his First World War experiences. *The Shipbuilders* (1935), which contrasts the fates of a shipowner and a manual worker during the depression on Clydeside, attracted much attention and was filmed, although some later critics detect a patronizing attitude towards its working-class characters. Blake himself came to believe that he 'had failed with his proletarians … and found his right subject among the *bourgeoisie*' (Blake, 32) when he went on to write a popular series of novels set in Garvel, a fictionalized Greenock. *Late Harvest* (1938) is also set during the depression years, while *The Constant Star* (1945) and *The Westering Sun* (1946) depict the rise and fall of middle-class shipbuilding and shipowning dynasties. The Garvel novels are accurate in historical and social detail, but have not generally been highly regarded as works of literature.

Blake, described as 'a thickset, battering-ram of a man, with a frowning brow and unruly hair' (Reid), was a frequent radio broadcaster and published much literary journalism. He assessed the Scottish kailyard school generously but honestly in *Barrie and the Kailyard School* (1951). His death from a cerebral haemorrhage in the Southern General Hospital, Glasgow, on 29 August 1961 was followed by a private funeral. His wife survived him.

Moira Burgess

Sources *Glasgow Herald* (30 Aug 1961) • A. Reid, 'Ends and means', *Scotland's Magazine*, 55/11 (Nov 1959), 37–8 • G. Blake, *Annals of Scotland, 1895–1955* [1956] • *CCI* (1961)

Archives NL Scot., literary and personal corresp. and papers incl. diary of visit to USA • NL Scot., Greenock letters | BBC WAC, letters • NL Scot., letters to Neil Gunn • NL Scot., letters to Rachel Taylor

Likenesses photograph, 1933, repro. in R. D. Macleod, *Modern Scottish literature* (1933), 24 • photograph, 1959, repro. in Reid, 'Ends and means', 37 • photograph, 1961, repro. in *Glasgow Herald*

Wealth at death £8870 13*s*. 3*d*.: confirmation, 20 Dec 1961, *CCI*

Blake, Henrietta Jex- (**1862–1953**). *See under* Blake, Katharine Jex- (1860–1951).

Blake [*alias* Cross], **James** (**1649–1728**), Jesuit, was born in London. The names of his parents are unknown. In 1669 he went to the English College at Seville in Spain to study for the priesthood and was ordained there in 1673. In 1675 he entered the English province of the Society of Jesus at Watten in the Southern Netherlands. After a year of noviciate and study at Liège he was chosen to escort four students from the English College at St Omer to the English College in Madrid, arriving there in 1677 and remaining until 1683. While in Spain he was named (as James Cross) as one of the Jesuit conspirators in Titus Oates's account of the Popish Plot. From 1685 until 1720 Blake was stationed in London and was briefly a chaplain at the Portuguese embassy chapel; from 1696 to 1701 he was rector of the Jesuit London district and from 1701 to 1704 was the Jesuit provincial superior. His only published works are *Applausus in honorem … Jacobi II* (1685), in which he gave himself the epithet 'Galviensis', suggesting an apparent association with Galway, and *A sermon of the blessed sacrament, preach'd in the chappel of his excellency the Spanish embassador* (1686; reprinted in 1741 in vol. 2 of *A Select Collection of Catholick Sermons*).

At the death of Queen Anne and during the Jacobite rising search was made for Blake. When there was discussion among English Catholics in 1718 about what oath might be taken to George I by those who had previously sworn allegiance to James II, Blake was believed to take a liberal view but denied that he was more liberal than others. Having left London, he was chaplain to Mr Mannocks at Bromley Hall, Colchester, from 1720 and it was probably there that he died between 4 and 13 January 1728, leaving all his effects to Robert Ashmall of Lincoln's Inn.

Geoffrey Holt

Sources H. Foley, ed., *Records of the English province of the Society of Jesus*, 5 (1879), 98, 108, 161, 537; 7 (1882–3), 64, 968 • G. Holt, *The English Jesuits, 1650–1829: a biographical dictionary*, Catholic RS, 70 (1984), 34 • M. Murphy, *St Gregory's College, Seville, 1592–1767*, Catholic RS, 73 (1992), 54 • E. Henson, ed., *The English college at Madrid, 1611–1767*, Catholic RS, 29 (1929), 101, 158, 368 • *The letter book of Lewis Sabran*, ed. G. Holt, Catholic RS, 62 (1971), 119, 304 • catalogues and other records, Archives of the British Province of the Society of Jesus, London • *DNB* • G. Holt, *The English Jesuits in the age of reason* (1993), 54–6 • T. H. Clancy, *English Catholic books, 1641–1700: a bibliography*, rev. edn (1996), 18, nos. 100–01 • Wing, *STC*, B3131–3132 • A. de Backer and others, *Bibliothèque de la Compagnie de Jésus*, new edn, 1, ed. C. Sommervogel (Brussels, 1890), 1532; 8 (Brussels, 1898), 1845 • G. Anstruther, *The seminary priests*, 3 (1976), 18 • J. Warner, letter book, 1678–82, CUL, MS Ll.1.19, fol. 90 • J. O. Payne, ed., *Records of the English Catholics of 1715* (1889), 24–5 • G. Anstruther, 'Abstracts of wills of Essex Catholic interest, V', *Essex Recusant*, 19 (1977), 37–40 • will and probate, PRO, PROB 8/121, fol. 18; PROB 11/619, fol. 2 • T. Oates, *A true narrative of the horrid plot and conspiracy of the popish party* (1679), 10

Wealth at death see will and probate, PRO, PROB 8/121, fol. 18 and PROB 11/619, fol. 2, will; summarized in Payne, *Records of the English Catholics*; Anstruther, 'Abstracts of wills', 38

Blake, John Aloysius (1826–1887), politician, was born at 45 King Street, Waterford, the son of Andrew Blake (*d.* 1829), a Catholic merchant who also held landed property in co. Waterford at Ballinacourty and Kilmeaden, and his wife, Mary (*bap.* 1794, *d.* 1871), daughter of Patrick Gallwey, merchant. All contemporary published sources give the year of his birth as 1826. He was educated at St John's College, Waterford, and at the Government College, Pau, Basses-Pyrénées, France. During his youth there was a rapid growth of political involvement among the Catholic middle class, symbolized by the successful campaigns for Catholic emancipation (1829) and municipal reform (1840). Blake seems to have had a lifelong interest in politics. Elected to Waterford corporation, he was chosen mayor in 1855, and held office for three years running. He was also president of the chamber of commerce in 1858 and 1859.

Blake's mayoralty was marked by two important developments, both initiated by him. The first was the People's Park, formed on waste ground to the east of the city. Begun in 1855, it was formally opened two years later by the lord lieutenant, the seventh earl of Carlisle. Its construction was quite a feat of engineering: marshy land was drained and a new course dug for King John's River. His other initiative was the clearing of slums from the city centre during his third year in office. Barronstrand Street was extended to its present width, and Broad Street created so as to form an open space in the heart of the medieval city.

In 1857 Blake entered parliament as a Liberal, and two years later he and his associates founded the *Citizen* newspaper (later the *Waterford Citizen*) as a mouthpiece for the Liberal interest in the area. He represented Waterford city at Westminster until 1869, when he resigned on being appointed inspector of Irish fisheries. The election of his successor, Ralph Bernal Osborne, occasioned unprecedented mob violence, and Blake's support of Osborne nearly cost him his life—he escaped under an escort of dragoons. In 1880 Blake again stood for election and was returned as home rule MP for co. Waterford. However, disapproving of Parnell's radical style of leadership, he resigned in 1884. In 1886 he became reconciled with Parnell and was returned unopposed in a by-election for co. Carlow.

For many years Blake courted Adelaide Mary Josephine Isabella Power (1834–1911), his junior by several years, the fifth and youngest daughter of Nicholas Mahon Power of Faithlegg. But her father, said to be the richest commoner in Ireland, did not consider Blake a suitable match for his daughter. The couple had to wait until Power died in February 1873, when after a decent interval Adelaide's brother Patrick graciously gave permission for his sister (now aged forty) to marry. This they did on 7 May 1874. The Blakes had no children, but the union was in every other respect a close and happy one.

Blake's unpublished journals show that he was an indefatigable traveller. In addition to visiting much of Europe he also toured Egypt and the Ottoman empire (1878), Algeria (1880), and the Indian subcontinent (1881–2). After resigning his co. Waterford seat in 1884 he was abroad for more than a year, travelling to Japan, China, Australia, New Zealand, and South America; he addressed Irish communities and assessed the potential effects of colonial development on Irish agriculture.

On 22 May 1887 Blake died of a heart attack at Queen Anne's Mansions in London. He was buried in Kensal Green cemetery on 25 May and his widow erected a Celtic cross over his grave. She also had a stained-glass window put up to his memory in Faithlegg church. Her own memorial is the reading-room she built for the residents of Cheekpoint village. She survived her husband for many years, dying on 18 February 1911, aged seventy-six.

The pages of *Hansard* show that Blake was an energetic parliamentarian, addressing the house in support of causes that were not always fashionable or popular. He spoke out on behalf of the temperance movement (a dangerous standpoint for the representative of a city with strong brewing interests) and against the mistreatment of Fenian prisoners. He campaigned for a more humane regime in the country's lunatic asylums, and was ahead of his time in seeking the development of the Irish fishing industry: he was inspector of Irish fisheries, 1869–78, and chairman of the fishery harbours commission (Ireland) from 1883. He published several tracts in support of his favoured causes. As a speaker he was described as 'ready and impressive, of commanding presence, and highly capable of conciliating those who disagreed with him' (Egan, 342). JULIAN C. WALTON

Sources journals of J. A. Blake, 5 vols., priv. coll. [covering most of the period 1862–85] • Burke, *Gen. Ire.* (1976) [Power] • will and associated documents of J. A. Blake, NA Ire. • *Hansard 3* (1857–69); (1880–84); (1886–7) • *Munster Express* (28 May 1887) • *Waterford News* (28 May 1887) • *Waterford Standard* (25 May 1887) • *Dod's Parliamentary Companion* • P. M. Egan, *History, guide and directory of county and city of Waterford* [1895], 177c, 340–42 • wills of subject's parents, and settlement made upon his mother's second marriage, priv. coll. • D. Power, 'A history of the People's Park', *Decies: Journal of the Old Waterford Society*, 52 (1996), 113–44 • K. Kelly, ed., 'Extracts from the census of the city of Waterford, 1821', *Irish Genealogist*, 4/1 (1968), 23

Archives priv. coll., journal [microfilm at Waterford municipal library]

Likenesses N. Blanc fils of Cannes, photograph, priv. coll. • Chancellor of Dublin, photograph, priv. coll. • newspaper sketch, priv. coll., journals of J. A. Blake • photograph, repro. in Egan, *History, guide & directory*, facing p. 24 • photographs, priv. coll., journals of J. A. Blake

Wealth at death £15,667: probate, 8 May 1888, *CGPLA Eng. & Wales* • £3227 5s. 10d.: probate, 28 May 1888, *CGPLA Ire.*

Blake, John Bradby (1745–1773), naturalist, was born on 4 November 1745 in Great Marlborough Street, Westminster, the son of John Blake (*d.* 1790) and his wife, Mary. John Blake was a former East India Company captain and, from the 1760s, the promoter and manager of an extensive organization set up to transport fresh fish overland to a new market in Westminster. Blake sailed to China in 1766 as a supercargo for the East India Company, the practice then being for a supercargo to accompany his ship out and back—a three-year journey. In 1770 the company's directors resolved that in future the supercargoes should reside permanently in Canton (Guangzhou). This allowed Blake to devote his spare time to natural science.

Blake's plan was to obtain seeds of those plants which served the Chinese for food, medicine, manufactures, or other economic uses, and to send back to Europe both seeds and living plants. His hopes that these plants might be propagated in Britain and Ireland, or in the colonies, met with success. Rice from Cochin-China was grown in Jamaica and South Carolina; the tallow-tree (so called from the fatty covering of its seeds) prospered in Jamaica and other parts of North America; and many of the seeds he sent back throve in various botanical gardens near London. Under his direction, a set of drawings of plants was prepared by a Chinese artist, which later found its way into the library of Sir Joseph Banks. Blake also sent back samples of fossils and ores.

In February 1774 Blake was proposed for membership of the Royal Society, but this proposal was withdrawn when it was learned that he had fallen ill and died in Canton on 16 November 1773. He was unmarried, but had amassed sufficient money to leave £1000 to each of his three sisters. ANITA MCCONNELL

Sources BL OIOC, B/82, 144; B/88, 329–31; B/89, 519; B/90, 393 • H. B. Morse, *The chronicles of the East India Company trading to China, 1635–1834*, 1 (1926) • *GM*, 1st ser., 60 (1790), 276 • will of John Blake, PROB 11/1001, sig. 359; PROB 11/1011, sig. 334 • W. M. Stern, 'Fish supplies for London in the 1760s: an experiment in overland transport', *Journal of the Royal Society of Arts*, 118 (1969–70), 360–64, 430–35 • E. Bretschneider, *History of European botanical discoveries in China*, 1 (1898), 52

Likenesses J. Smith, Wedgwood medallion, City Museum and Art Gallery, Stoke

Wealth at death over £3000: will, PRO, PROB 11/1001, sig. 259; 11/1011, sig. 334

Blake, Joseph [*nicknamed* Blueskin] (*c.***1700–1724**), burglar, was born in London to parents 'in tolerable Circumstances' (*Lives of the most Remarkable Criminals*, 1.364). He attended St Giles Cripplegate parish school for about six years, where he was distinguished only by an early 'Inclination to Roguery' (*Select Trials*, 2.160). At about fourteen he was introduced by his school fellow and future companion in crime William Blewitt (hanged for murder in 1726) to the thief-taker Jonathan Wild; contemporary reports state that soon after this fateful meeting Blueskin left school and, spurning all honest employment, 'set up for a Robber' (*Lives of the most Remarkable Criminals*, 1.364). According to one account 'Joe was hardly Fifteen, before he had been in all the Bridewells, and Work-houses about Town' (*Select Trials*, 2.158).

Blake seems to have begun his criminal career in earnest at about seventeen, picking pockets 'in Company with one Edward Pollit' whom he was said to have later impeached in order to save his own life (*History of the Lives*, 72). By 1719 Blueskin—so called presumably because of his dark complexion or facial hair, or as a pun on William Blewitt's surname—had fallen in with the Irish highwayman James Carrick. In 1722 he joined a gang of street robbers led by Robert Wilkinson. At a time when the incidence of violent crime and the 'Insolency' of highwaymen and footpads in and around the metropolis seemed to be reaching epidemic proportions, 'there was scarce a Robbery about the Town … but Bleuskin was concerned in it' (*Lives of the most Remarkable Criminals*, 3.330; *History of the Lives*, preface, unnumbered). In the summer of 1722 several of Blake's associates were apprehended, three of whom were hanged the following September. Blueskin, who it was believed was 'skreen'd … from Justice' by 'his Master', Jonathan Wild, escaped for a time, and when he was arrested in December 1722 was admitted as an evidence against several of his companions, including his old friend William Blewitt (*History of the Lives*, 71). In February 1723 John Levee, Richard Oakey, and Matthew Flood were executed on the basis of Blake's testimony.

After this 'Hanging Work of his Companions' Blake expected both a free pardon and a reward; instead he was committed to the Wood Street compter, where he lay for 'above a Year', subsisting on the charity of his patron Wild (*Select Trials*, 2.160). Blueskin was finally released in the spring of 1724 after 'prevailing with two Gardeners' to stand surety for his good behaviour (ibid., 2.160). According to accounts written after Blake's execution there was scant expectation that such an 'Old Offender' would mend his ways: when one 'Gentleman … then present' wondered aloud 'how long it might be before they saw Blake again at the Old Baily? another answered, about three Sessions'—a response which would prove prophetic (*History of the Lives*, 71; *Select Trials*, 2.160).

Indeed, Blake was no sooner at liberty than he went 'a plundering' with Jack Sheppard: during the summer of 1724 the pair committed several robberies on Hampstead Heath, and on 12 July robbed the house of Sheppard's former master, William Kneebone (*Select Trials*, 2.160). After the burglary Blake and Sheppard approached William Field, a fence who lodged with Blueskin's mother, to dispose of the goods. Field was also a noted evidence known to be in the pay of Jonathan Wild, and whether because Blake's exploits had 'made such a noise about Town, that Jonathan did not think it safe to countenance him any longer', or because Wild objected to Blake's association with Sheppard—who, it was believed, obstinately refused to have any dealings with the 'Thief-Catcher'—it now became clear that the latter was about to cashier his old 'Pensioner' (*Parker's London News*, 7 October 1724; *History of the Lives*, 71; *Narrative of the Robberies*, 16). On 3 October 1724 Blake was apprehended in his St Giles lodgings by Wild and two of his henchmen and was committed to Newgate, charged (along with Sheppard) on Field's evidence with the Kneebone robbery, in which Field professed to have taken part—a claim both Blueskin and Sheppard would vehemently deny at their respective trials.

On 14 October, when Blake was outside the Old Bailey court house waiting to be arraigned, he shared a glass of wine and some 'friendly Discourse' with his old master (*Weekly Journal, or, British Gazetteer*, 17 Oct 1724). When Blueskin asked Wild to put in a word for him, however, the latter blandly informed him that while he would provide him a coffin and 'a good Book or Two', he 'believe[d Blake] must die' (*History of the Remarkable Life*, 195; *Proceedings*, 14–21 Oct 1724). Enraged, Blake whipped a clasp-knife out of his pocket and promptly slit Wild's throat. While the wound did not prove mortal Wild was prevented from testifying at Blake's trial three days later, an otherwise routine affair: after putting up but a feeble defence, aimed primarily at discrediting Field's evidence, Blake was found guilty of burglary and sentenced to death.

Blake's attempt on Wild's life, immortalized in the street ballad *Newgate's Garland*, elevated him to something of the status of a popular hero: 'amongst the Mob' he was viewed as a 'brave Fellow', and by numerous respectable citizens as one of the many unfortunate 'foster children' whom Wild had 'bred … up in the Art of Thieving' only to deliver to the gallows (*Lives of the most Remarkable Criminals*, 1.30; *True and Genuine Account*, 252; *Lives of the most Remarkable Criminals*, 2.47). More cynical contemporaries, while acknowledging that Blake was 'a Dapper, well-set Fellow, of great Strength', dismissed him 'as a mean spirited timorous Wretch', who betrayed most of his associates, and a brute who, upon being locked up after his trial, violently—and in full view of the court—attempted 'Rudeness' with 'a Woman Prisoner' (*Lives of the most Remarkable Criminals*, 1.370–1; *British Journal*, 24 Oct 1724). Sheppard himself was supposed to have characterized the man whom later literature would cast as his staunch sidekick as 'a worthless Companion' and 'a sorry Thief' (*Narrative of the Robberies*, 15).

Blake, while described by the ordinary of Newgate as being serious and even tearful at chapel, showed little remorse for his actions in the days leading up to his execution (except insofar as his attempt on Wild had been unsuccessful)—instead busying himself with various abortive escape attempts (*Select Trials*, 2.160). Even on his way to Tyburn, Blueskin endeavoured (with the tacit consent of spectators) 'to escape out of the Cart', and after this project was prevented stopped at the Griffin tavern in Holborn, 'where he drank and shewed much Insolence and ill Behaviour' (*Evening Post*, 10–12 Nov 1724; *Parker's London News*, 13 Nov 1724). By all accounts, when Blake mounted the scaffold on 11 November 1724 he was so 'disguised in Liquor' as to 'reel and Faulter in his Speech' (*Select Trials*, 2.162).

Andrea McKenzie

Sources *The history of the lives and actions of Jonathan Wild, thief-taker. Joseph Blake alias Bleuskin, foot-pad. And John Sheppard, housebreaker*, 3rd edn (1725) • *The history of the remarkable life of John Sheppard* (1724); repr. in G. H. Maynadier, ed., *The works of Daniel Defoe*, 16 (1903), 167–206 • *The lives of the most remarkable criminals*, 3 vols. (1735) • [D. Defoe], *A narrative of all the robberies, escapes, &c. of John Sheppard … the whole publish'd at the particular request of the prisoner*, 8th edn (1725) [often attributed to D. Defoe] • *Newgate's garland: being a new ballad, shewing how Mr. Jonathan Wild's throat was cut, from ear to ear, with a penknife by Mr. Blake, alias Blueskin, the bold highwayman, as he stood at his trial at the Old-Bailey* (1725) • T. Purney, *The ordinary of Newgate: his account, of the behaviour, confession, and last dying words of the malefactors, that were executed at Tyburn, on Friday the 8th of February, 1722–3* (1723) • *The proceedings on the king's commission of the peace* (1723–4) [Old Bailey sessions papers, 14–21 Oct 1724] • *Select trials at the sessions house in the Old Bailey*, 4 vols. (1742) • *The true and genuine account of the life and actions of the late Jonathan Wild, not made up of fiction and fable, but taken from his own mouth, and collected from papers of his own writing* (1725) [attributed to D. Defoe; repr. in H. Fielding, *Jonathan Wild*, ed. D. Nokes (1982), 223–57] • G. Howson, *Thief-taker general: the rise and fall of Jonathan Wild* (1970)

Blake, Katharine Jex- (1860–1951), classical scholar and college head, was born at Rugby School, Rugby, Warwickshire on 18 November 1860, one of nine daughters and two sons of Thomas William Jex-*Blake (1832–1915), later headmaster of Rugby School and dean of Wells, and his wife, Henrietta Cordery. Katharine's aunt, Sophia Jex-Blake, was a pioneer in the medical education of women; her uncle, John Graham Cordery, was an Indian civil servant and translator of Homer. Henrietta Jex-Blake [*see below*] was her younger sister.

Katharine Jex-Blake, who was, like her sisters, educated at home by masters from Rugby School, went to Girton College, Cambridge, in 1879. With the exception of one year (1884–5) spent as an assistant mistress at Notting Hill high school, she remained in residence at Girton until 1922. In 1882 she became one of the first two Girtonians to gain a first class in part one of the classical tripos, and subsequently became only the second Girtonian to take both parts of this demanding examination. She served as classics lecturer at Girton from 1885 to 1916 and as director of studies in classics from 1902 until 1919. She was appointed vice-mistress in 1903 and mistress in 1916.

Katharine Jex-Blake was first and foremost a scholar, although her greatest contribution to scholarship was as a teacher. Her only published classical work was her translation of Pliny the elder's *Chapters on the History of Art* (1896), in collaboration with her friend Eugenie Sellers (Strong), who wrote the introduction and commentary. Jex-Blake's influence as a teacher, however, extended far beyond Girton. In the early 1920s the classics lecturers at six women's colleges (Girton, Newnham, Bedford, Royal Holloway, Somerville, and Lady Margaret Hall) had been her students. Other prominent pupils were Agnata Ramsay, Katharine McCutcheon, Dorothy Tarrant, Dorothy Brock, Dora Olive Ivens, and Margaret Postgate (later Cole). Her terrifying tutorials, where she exposed the unprepared and exploded the half-baked, became legendary. Most of her students, however, seemed to respect her high standards and appreciated her dry wit and underlying kindness. They also got to know her in more informal settings, through 'Homeric', her weekly readings of Homer with the third-year students, or at meetings of the Classical Club. The college was reportedly delighted when she was elected mistress.

Katharine Jex-Blake proved to be an able administrator in the difficult years of the First World War and its aftermath. She has been described as the 'first truly professional and scholarly modern woman academic and administrator to be mistress of Girton' (Bradbrook, 67). Her contemporaries frequently commented on her clear-

Katharine Jex-Blake (1860–1951), by unknown photographer

eyed, practical approach to problems; her favourite phrase was 'Let us take a concrete case' (*The Times*). During the war she faced a shortage of labour, the rationing of food and fuel, and the fear that students would leave for war work with a resulting loss of tuition fees. In reality only a few students and lecturers left, while the college received three Belgian students without fees and a Serbian at a reduced fee. Always practical, Jex-Blake responded to wartime shortages and inflation by growing vegetables in the garden and keeping pigs on the college grounds.

After the war, when enrolment at Girton increased, Jex-Blake bought a disused army hut and used it for lecture rooms. Under her tenure, student fees, which had been stationary since 1869, were gradually raised to pay for the needed expansion and improvements. In 1919 she presided over the college's jubilee. She also navigated Girton's uneasy relations with Cambridge University. In 1920 a proposal brought before the university senate to give full membership to the members of the women's colleges was rejected amid much acrimony. In 1921 a grace giving women titular degrees was passed (Jex-Blake had taken her own MA from Trinity College, Dublin, several years earlier), and the college began a process of constitutional change in preparation for its royal charter, granted in 1924 under Jex-Blake's successor, her cousin Bertha Phillpotts, later Dame Bertha Newall. There was also pressure from the students at Girton for revision of the college's antiquated social regulations. Katharine Jex-Blake introduced a few modifications, although more changes came with her successors. An old student recalled that she 'bridged the gulf between past and present … by her statesmanship and her clear vision, by her saving sanity, and her sense of humour … [and] by her uncanny knowledge of things she could not possibly know' (Brock, 6).

Upon her retirement from Girton in 1922 Katharine Jex-Blake donated a sum collected in her honour to the college for what became the Jex-Blake fellowship, thus encouraging the advanced study and research that she had had little opportunity to do herself. She remained involved with Girton, serving as a governor and sitting on the council as representative of the old students for ten years. She was made an honorary fellow in 1932. In retirement she served for many years as a member of the council of the Girls' Public Day School Trust, where she continued to use her administrative and practical skills to forward women's education. She died at Nettlesworth, Wickham Hill, Hurstpierpoint, Sussex, on 26 March 1951.

Her sister, **Henrietta Jex-Blake** (1862–1953), college head, was born at Rugby School in June 1862; she did not attend college but instead studied music at the Leipzig Conservatoire, Dresden, and Vienna, becoming an accomplished violinist. From 1899 to 1909 she was headmistress of St Margaret's School, Polmont, in central Scotland, which was founded by her sister's Girton friend Maud Mary Daniel, who wished to replicate the successful girls' school St Leonard's, St Andrews. As headmistress, Henrietta Jex-Blake promoted girls' sports and encouraged many of her pupils to go to university, particularly to Girton.

In 1909 Henrietta Jex-Blake was elected the second principal of Lady Margaret Hall, Oxford. Under her tenure the number of students grew, several large building projects were completed, and the college was incorporated under the Companies Act. She modernized and redecorated the college buildings, often using her own money. A colleague later wrote that 'she held tenaciously to the ideals of her family, believing in the right and duty of women to work in whatever way was most suited to their gifts, irrespective of the mere fact of their sex' (*Brown Book*, 26). She was a strong supporter of women's suffrage and of opening degrees to women. Like her sister she served as principal during the stressful war years and their aftermath. At Oxford, however, women became eligible for degrees in 1920. Henrietta Jex-Blake presented the first candidate for matriculation and was herself awarded an MA by decree. Exhausted by the strains of the war years, looking after her ageing mother, and clashes with the LMH council, who, for example, rejected her proposal of a limited pension plan for tutors and staff, she retired in 1921, a year before her sister.

Henrietta Jex-Blake and her sister travelled frequently together, often spending winters in Italy. In Madrid, they found themselves caught in the chaos of the Spanish Civil War, which they endured with equanimity. Henrietta Jex-Blake served as a governor of the Burlington School and Clapham secondary school, and on the committee for King's College, Campden Hill (later Queen Elizabeth College). In later years, the sisters lived together in Tunbridge

Wells. Henrietta Jex-Blake died at the White House Nursing Home, Gerrards Cross, Buckinghamshire, on 21 May 1953. FERNANDA HELEN PERRONE

Sources *Girton Review*, Easter term (1951) • *The Times* (28 March 1951) • *Daily Telegraph* (28 March 1951) • *Manchester Guardian* (30 March 1951) • M. D. Brock, 'Speech at the farewell roll luncheon to Miss Jex-Blake', *Girton Review*, Easter term (1922) • B. Stephen, *Girton College, 1869–1932* (1933) • M. Bradbrook, *That infidel place* (1969) • K. T. Butler and H. I. McMorran, eds., *Girton College register, 1869–1946* (1948) • *Brown Book* (1953) [Henrietta Jex-Blake] • G. Battiscombe, *Reluctant pioneer: a life of Elizabeth Wordsworth* (1978) • C. Avent and H. Pipe, eds., *Lady Margaret Hall register, 1879–1990* (1990) • *Journal of Education*, 53 (March 1921) • *CGPLA Eng. & Wales* (1953)

Archives Girton Cam. • Lady Margaret Hall, Oxford • Norfolk RO, family papers • Norfolk RO, corresp. and papers [Henrietta Jex-Blake] | Norfolk RO, letters to Henrietta Jex-Blake and Violet Jex-Blake

Likenesses H. von Herkomer, portrait, 1879, Girton Cam. • photograph, 1922, repro. in *Girton Review* • photograph, Girton Cam. [*see illus.*]

Wealth at death £26,521 19*s.* 0*d.*: probate, 11 June 1951, *CGPLA Eng. & Wales* • £17,954 1*s.* 9*d.*—Henrietta Jex-Blake: probate, 11 July 1953, *CGPLA Eng. & Wales*

Blake, Dame Louisa Brandreth Aldrich- (1865–1925), surgeon, was born on 15 August 1865, at the rectory, Chingford, Essex, eldest daughter and second of six children of the Revd Frederick James Aldrich-Blake (formerly Aldrich; 1824–1904), rector of Chingford, and his wife, Louisa Blake Morrison (*d.* 1918). The surname of Blake was assumed by her father on his marriage. Soon after Louisa's birth her father was appointed rector of Welsh Bicknor in Herefordshire. Here she spent her childhood and retained a home throughout her life. She went to school in Great Malvern and Neuchâtel, and then attended Cheltenham Ladies' College. In 1887 she entered the London School of Medicine for Women, graduating MB from London University in 1892 with first-class honours in medicine and obstetrics and BS with first-class honours in 1893. She obtained her MD (London) in 1894 and in 1895 became the first woman to obtain the master of surgery (MS).

Determined on a career in general surgery Miss Aldrich-Blake was appointed, in 1895, as assistant surgeon to the New Hospital for Women (a hospital staffed only by medical women, later renamed the Elizabeth Garrett Anderson Hospital). She subsequently became senior and then consulting surgeon there. Also in 1895 she was the first woman appointed as anaesthetist to the Royal Free Hospital, the teaching hospital for the London School of Medicine for Women. In 1896 she was appointed surgical registrar at the Royal Free, again the first woman to hold the post. In 1919 she was appointed consulting surgeon there, a position she held until her death. She was also consultant to the Canning Town Women's Settlement Hospital in east London from 1897 to 1920. A landowner with private means she never made a large income from her professional practice. Miss Aldrich-Blake published little but was widely respected for her excellent judgement in surgery. She was one of the first surgeons in Britain to undertake Wertheim's operation for carcinoma of the cervix. In 1910 she was elected a fellow of the Royal Society of Medicine.

Dame Louisa Brandreth Aldrich-Blake (1865–1925), by Sir William Orpen, 1921

For most of her professional life Miss Aldrich-Blake was closely associated with the London School of Medicine for Women, being appointed vice-dean in 1906 and dean in 1914. Under her leadership the school almost doubled in size during the First World War, as many young women sought a medical training to make their contribution to the war effort. Miss Aldrich-Blake was herself heavily involved in medical women's war efforts, over and above her roles as medical school dean and consultant surgeon. She helped organize a woman-staffed hospital in Cherbourg in 1914 and worked there in her vacation. In 1915 and 1916 she spent her vacations working at the Anglo-French Red Cross Hospital run by Dr Frances Ivens in Royaumont where she was dubbed 'Madame la Générale' by the patients (Crofton, 58). In 1916 she organized two major initiatives to recruit medical women for war service overseas. She was also visiting surgeon at the Women's Army Auxiliary Corps Hospital in Isleworth during the war years.

Miss Aldrich-Blake was not a campaigning feminist but aimed to establish women's equality with men through professional example, a message she stressed to her students. Miss Aldrich-Blake was noted for her quietness, her readiness to help young women surgeons in their work and as an outstanding administrator and financial planner. She was founding treasurer of the Medical Women's Federation from 1917. After the war ended she was a prime mover in the substantial enlargement of both the Elizabeth Garrett Anderson and the Royal Free hospitals. In 1925, the year of the London School of Medicine's golden jubilee, she was made DBE. Louisa Aldrich-Blake died of cancer on 28 December 1925 at her London home, 17 Nottingham Place, Marylebone, having been engaged in surgery up to the last six weeks of her life. Her funeral was held on 1 January 1926 in St Pancras Church, London, close to the women's medical school and the Elizabeth Garrett Anderson and Royal Free hospitals. Her ashes were taken to her country home in Welsh Bicknor. M. A. ELSTON

Sources Lord Riddell, *Dame Louisa Aldrich-Blake* (1926) • *DNB* • *BMJ* (9 Jan 1926), 69–71 • *The Lancet* (26 Jan 1926) • lecture notes and casebooks, Wellcome L., Medical Women's Federation archives • Royal Free Hospital school of medicine archives, London • E. Crofton, *The women of Royaumont: a Scottish women's hospital on the western front* (1997) • Venn, *Alum. Cant.* [Frederick James Aldrich] • *CGPLA Eng. & Wales* (1926)

Archives Royal Free Hospital, London, school of medicine | Wellcome L., Medical Women's Federation archives, lecture notes and casebooks

Likenesses W. Orpen, oils, 1921, Royal Free Hospital, London, school of medicine [*see illus.*] • H. Salomon, oils, 1926, Wellcome L. • Lafayette Ltd, photograph, Wellcome L. • E. Lutyens, memorial, Tavistock Square, London • oils, Elizabeth Garrett Anderson Hospital, London • photograph, repro. in *The Lancet*, 101 • photographs, Royal Free Hospital, London

Wealth at death £37,829 3*s*. 0*d*.: resworn probate, 26 Feb 1926, *CGPLA Eng. & Wales*

Blake, Malachi (*bap.* **1687**, *d.* **1760**), Presbyterian minister, was born at Blagdon, near Taunton, Somerset, and baptized there on 16 August 1687, the second son of Malachi Blake (1651–1705). He appears to have been educated and trained for the ministry by his father, an itinerant preacher in the south-west of England and afterwards Presbyterian minister at Wellington, Somerset, where he was credited with 'laying the foundation of the dissenting cause' (Murch, 244).

The younger Malachi Blake's first ministerial appointment was at Langport, Somerset, in 1712, and then from 1717 until his death at Bandford Forum, Dorset, where he proved a popular preacher. He was minister there when the town was badly damaged by fire on 4 June 1731. Afterwards he wrote *A Brief Account of the Dreadful Fire at Blandford Forum*, to which he added a sermon and an address to the inhabitants of the town. The work was published for private circulation in 1735. A second edition appeared in the same year and a third in 1736.

In later years Blake suffered increasingly from depression, and he died at Blandford Forum on 15 February 1760, aged seventy-two. His younger brother William (1688–1772), a woolstapler, was father of Malachi (1724–1795), Presbyterian minister of Whitney and Fullwood, and William (1730–1799), Presbyterian minister of Crewkerne.

ALEXANDER GORDON, *rev.* M. J. MERCER

Sources J. Murch, *A history of the Presbyterian and General Baptist churches in the west of England* (1835), 244, 315 • *Protestant Dissenter's Magazine*, 6 (1799), 281 • *Journal of the United Reformed Church Historical Society*, 5 (1994), suppl., 9 • A. Gordon, ed., *Freedom after ejection: a review (1690–1692) of presbyterian and congregational nonconformity in England and Wales* (1917), 217

Archives DWL, letters to P. Doddridge and his wife, New College archives, L1/4/108–10

Blake, Midnight. *See* Blake, Cyril McDonald (1897–1951).

Blake, Nicholas. *See* Lewis, Cecil Day- (1904–1972).

Blake, Robert (*bap.* **1598**, *d.* **1657**), naval and army officer, was baptized on 27 September 1598 at the church of St Mary the Virgin in Bridgwater, Somerset, the eldest of the eight surviving children of Humphrey Blake (*d.* 1625), a merchant of the town, and his wife, Sarah (*d.* 1638), daughter of Humphrey Williams of Plainsfield near Bridgwater. Educated at the free grammar school, Bridgwater, he was admitted to the University of Oxford, studying at St Alban Hall and Wadham College. He graduated on 10 February 1618. Shortly afterwards he stood unsuccessfully for election as a fellow of Merton College.

Early life On the death of his father in 1625 Blake inherited the manor of Crandon-cum-Puriton. He bought a house in Bridgwater and his name appears in the subsidy list for 1628. Some time between 1629 and 1632 he left Bridgwater, and may have become a merchant and travelled on the continent. There is a story that he lived in Schiedam, so he could be the Robert Blake who was admitted to the Company of the Freemen of Dorchester in 1629 and who was trading in masts, deal, and other timber with Schiedam's neighbouring port of Middleburg.

Blake was elected to the Short Parliament in April 1640 as one of the two burgesses for Bridgwater, but failed to keep his seat in elections for the Long Parliament which met in November the same year. He was a strong supporter of the parliament during the first civil war. In March 1643 a plot was formed to admit the royalists to the city of Bristol, which was only thwarted at the last minute. Blake was among those who signed the decree sentencing the plotters to death. When William Waller marched into the west Blake is reputed to have raised a troop of horse and it may well have formed part of the cavalry commanded by Colonel Edward Popham which made a foray against Bridgwater in May. By the time Prince Rupert laid siege to Bristol on 23 July, Blake was the commander of Prior's Hill Fort and repelled all the royalist attempts to storm it. He was still resisting when the parliamentarian governor agreed terms surrendering the city four days later.

Blake next appears at the siege of Lyme Regis in April 1644. He was never the official commander of the garrison but he was, by common consent, the mainspring of the resistance. The royalists outnumbered the defenders by six to one but they failed to make their advantage tell. Lyme was eventually relieved by an army under the earl of Essex. Subsequently Blake was appointed governor of Taunton. After Essex's defeat at Lostwithiel and the indecisive second battle of Newbury, Blake was left isolated and endured three sieges—between October and December 1644, between March and May 1645, and briefly again in June 1645. The successful resistance in the second one in particular made him famous throughout the country and brought him to the attention of the army leaders. In October 1645 Blake and Colonel William Sydenham were sent with 600 men to lay siege to Dunster Castle. Here Blake got a taste of his own medicine. The castle resisted all his attempts to capture it and only surrendered on terms in April 1646 when the royalist cause was lost.

In September 1645 Blake was elected as a 'Recruiter' MP

for Bridgwater. He was also on the Somerset county committee, where his chief concern was the establishment of a presbyterian system of ministers and lay elders within the county. When it finally came into being in March 1648 Blake figured as a lay elder in the Taunton classis. While Blake did not like the Church of England he did not much care for the sects either and suppressed an Independent meeting-house in St Mary Street, Taunton, but by this time he was a republican and opposed to any compromise with the royalists. Taunton was one of the first places to support the vote of no addresses of January 1648, by which the MPs pledged themselves never to negotiate with Charles again. No fighting took place in Somerset during the second civil war but Alexander Popham seems to have been convinced that a rising was imminent. Blake had ceased to be governor of Taunton in September 1647, as part of the programme for the reduction of unnecessary garrisons, but Popham had him reappointed in August 1648. He was back in London in early November but took no part in Pride's Purge or the trial and execution of the king.

The Commonwealth, 1649–1651 In March 1649 the new Commonwealth government appointed three generals-at-sea. Their qualifications for command were to be that they were loyal to the new regime and that they had good military records. Previous naval experience was of small importance as the commander usually consulted his council of officers when he needed navigational advice. The first appointment was that of Richard Deane. He appears to have recommended Blake, who in turn suggested Edward Popham. The first priority, to re-establish order and discipline, which had been badly dented by the mutiny of 1648, was effected smoothly and rapidly. On 21 May the Commonwealth fleet appeared off Kinsale to find a squadron of royalist ships, commanded by Prince Rupert, inside. After drawing lots Popham returned to the Downs. Deane was assigned the task of organizing the transport of Cromwell's army, designed for the reconquest of Ireland, from Milford. Blake was left off Kinsale to watch Rupert.

Cromwell's original intention was to land in Munster but when winds proved consistently contrary the army made for Dublin instead, leaving Blake to a very lonely vigil. All summer Blake kept Rupert penned in the harbour, unable to interfere with the movement of troops from England to Ireland. In September 1649 Cromwell offered Blake the post of major-general of foot in the Irish army but Blake preferred to stay with the fleet. While his political masters were pleased with his performance Blake was not. Just when it looked as if the parliamentarian army would capture the whole royalist fleet, a storm blew Blake off his station and Rupert escaped.

Rupert was no longer a military threat but his attacks on English merchant shipping from his new base in Portugal were costly and embarrassing. In March 1650 Blake was dispatched with a squadron of eleven ships to deal with him. When the king of Portugal refused to expel Rupert, Blake attempted to force his way up the Tagus but he had to retreat, the fire from the forts at the river mouth being far too strong for wooden ships to endure successfully. Faced with the prospect of a long blockade Blake was compelled to change tack. A request was made to King João IV that the English fleet be allowed to water in Oeiras Bay, to which he agreed on condition that no attack was made on Rupert while he was in Portuguese waters. The nearest Spanish port where he could water was Cadiz so, fearing a repeat of the Kinsale escape, Blake reluctantly accepted the limitation.

On 26 May Popham arrived with eight more ships and orders instructing both generals to seize Rupert's ships wherever they might be found, which obliged Blake to abandon his agreement with King João. In reprisal the king arrested the goods and property of the English merchants in Lisbon and expelled Charles Vane, the Commonwealth agent. Rupert's presence was an embarrassment to Portugal, especially as the blockading fleet was now seizing any ships attempting to enter the Tagus, and João tried to push the prince into leaving, but Popham and Blake combined gave the royalists little hope of getting away. Twice João persuaded Rupert to try, each time while part of the parliamentarian fleet was watering at Cadiz. The first attempt was on 22 June but the royalists and their Portuguese and French allies hardly got beyond the Catchops shoals before the powerful Commonwealth ships sent them scuttling back to the Tagus. The second was on 3 September during foggy weather while Popham was away watering, preparatory to returning to England. This time the determination of Blake not to be faced down when his flagship, the *George*, encountered Rupert in the *Constant Reformation*, was enough to persuade the royalists to seek the shelter of Lisbon once more.

The English did not get what they wanted until Popham had left and Blake had given up the close blockade as pointless. Returning from a short cruise in search of French privateers Blake learned that Rupert had left Cadiz. The English pursued his squadron into the Mediterranean, coming up with the royalists just short of Cartagena. One ship was captured and a second forced on shore, the remaining four taking refuge in Cartagena harbour. The Spanish government did not prove as accommodating as that of Portugal. Rather than have their ships and goods seized, the royalists decided to make a run for it on the night of 6–7 November, but they had little knowledge of Cartagena harbour and all four vessels were wrecked. Neither Rupert nor his brother Maurice were present but the destruction of most of their ships had the result of reducing them to naval insignificance.

In spring 1651 Blake was appointed to command a small squadron designed to capture the Isle of Man but before he could sail he was redirected to the Isles of Scilly. The Commonwealth government, fearing a pre-emptive strike by the Dutch, wanted immediate action. Blake's own small force was augmented by the diversion of the squadron under Sir George Ayscue, designed for the recapture of Barbados. Blake quickly grasped that the key to success was the island of Tresco. The first attack was mismanaged by the landing party but a second one was more successful. The island was quickly occupied and two small royalist frigates captured. The surrender of the main island of St Mary's soon followed. The terms were very lenient—there were no reprisals against the islanders and for those royalists who wished for it transport was provided to take them wherever they wanted to go.

By the summer the war with Scotland was reaching crisis point. Cromwell ordered Major-General John Disbrowe into the midlands and Blake came on shore to replace him as the chief officer commanding the west of England, but at the crucial moment news arrived of Popham's death. As Deane was already with the army Blake was the only one of the original three generals-at-sea still active so he was instructed to return to the fleet.

The last action of the year was the reduction of Jersey. This Blake accomplished with his now customary efficiency. He first of all exhausted the defenders by cruising up and down the west coast and round the Corbière Rocks, forcing them to anticipate where he was going to strike by marching parallel to the fleet. Then, night having fallen, an amphibious descent was organized just after high tide when the tired royalists thought that the immediate danger had passed. Once ashore the result was a foregone conclusion.

The First Anglo-Dutch War, 1652–1654 By this time relations with the Dutch had deteriorated so much that war seemed only just over the horizon. The immediate pretext was the English demand that all Dutch ships should strike their flags when in the presence of an English warship and submit to search for contraband of war. In March 1652 the Dutch dispatched a squadron into the channel under Lieutenant-Admiral Tromp to protect incoming Dutch merchant shipping and prevent searches. At first Tromp avoided the small squadrons of Blake and Nehemiah Bourne to prevent arguments about striking the flag but then he received information which led him to believe that the English had stopped and were searching a Dutch merchant fleet off Fairlight. He altered course right into the path of Blake's ships. When Blake fired shots across his bow to try and force him to strike his flag, the Dutchman replied with a broadside and a mêlée ensued which has become known as the skirmish off Dover. Tromp's squadron numbered forty-two. Blake had no more than twelve ships with him and even when Bourne joined in the English were never more than half the Dutch strength. Despite this the English lost no ships; they captured one Dutchman and another was so badly damaged that only the superior Dutch seamanship prevented it from falling into English hands.

The English were eager to force the Dutch to fight pitched battles which they now knew they could win. Blake was dispatched with a fleet of over eighty ships to the Shetland Islands to intercept the Dutch East India fleet, which was reported to be coming home 'north about'. This was a challenge the Dutch could not turn down and Tromp was sent after him, only for both fleets to be caught in a terrible storm on 25–7 July. The English were able to take shelter in Bressay Sound so their fleet, though battered, remained intact. There was no refuge for the Dutch caught off a hostile lee shore. When the weather let up after three days of continuous rain and gale force wind Tromp found that he had only thirty-four ships in company out of a fleet of over 100. Most of the others found some sort of shelter away from the main settlements but six foundered at sea and ten were wrecked. Blake had won a major victory without raising a finger. Ironically seven of the nine East Indiamen successfully rendezvoused with the now much depleted Dutch fleet.

Both fleets returned southwards to find that events in the channel had been much more favourable to the Dutch. A Dutch squadron under Commodore de Ruijter, escorting a merchant convoy, had encountered an English one under Ayscue off Plymouth. The English fought bravely but Ayscue adopted the old charge tactics, which proved inadequate, suggesting that more than superior morale and gunnery were required if complete success were to be achieved over the more experienced and skilful Dutch—a lesson which the winter campaign was to drive home.

By this time Blake was back in the Downs. For the moment the Dutch were impotent. Blake took advantage of the respite to attack a French convoy designed for the relief of Dunkirk in retaliation for the way Mazarin had allowed royalists to sell their prizes in French ports. The result was the surrender of Dunkirk to its Spanish besiegers. Then, mustering all his available force, Blake set off down the channel to try and waylay de Ruijter's returning convoy. He sent on ahead a strong force of the speediest and most weatherly third- and fourth-rate frigates under the command of William Penn, which was to seek out de Ruijter and hold him until Blake could come up with the remainder of the fleet. Penn came in sight of de Ruijter's squadron off Berry Head and went in pursuit but lost it in worsening visibility and approaching darkness. Neither Penn nor Blake saw it again. Sure now that the English were off their own coast, de Ruijter took his fleet over to the French side and got home without trouble. The ease with which Blake had been fooled again suggested that the war might not be as plain sailing as the skirmish off Dover and the Shetland voyage seemed to presage.

As trade was the lifeblood of the Dutch the English stranglehold had to be broken. Tromp was now out of favour and after much dispute a fleet was organized with Cornelis Witte de With, the vice-admiral of Holland, in command, assisted by de Ruijter. As soon as Blake knew the Dutch were at sea his only thought was for a battle. The English ships got under way with all speed and rushed out of the Downs northwards as fast as they could with little regard for order, so much so that Rear-Admiral Bourne's division got left behind. When the English appeared, on 28 September, the Dutch were sailing westward. De With immediately ordered a change of course to SSE with the aim of sailing right past Blake and Penn's squadrons to attack Bourne, who was still trying to get his ships clear of the Downs. The plan was thwarted by an accident. The two leading ships of Penn's squadron, the *Sovereign of the Seas* and the *James*, went aground on a shoal called the Kentish Knock. Neither was seriously damaged but the incident had the effect of halting the English charge and forcing them to turn east straight into the path of the oncoming Dutch. The result was a violent mêlée out of which the English emerged triumphant partly because of their superior firepower and partly because many Dutch captains had no stomach for the fight. The Dutch lost only one ship sunk and one captured but there would have been many more had darkness not fallen before the English could exploit their victory, because the whole fleet had been badly mauled. So much so that all de With's attempts to get the captains to re-engage the next day failed. Even de Ruijter thought such a course would be suicide.

The euphoria induced by the result of Kentish Knock led the Commonwealth to make a serious error. The campaign had been very costly and, believing there would be no further fighting until the spring, a large part of the main fleet was stood down. On the Dutch side Tromp was reinstated because he was the only man who commanded sufficient respect to calm the factious behaviour of the other senior officers. The Dutch had to keep their trade flowing and over 400 merchant ships were awaiting convoy, so Tromp decided on a winter campaign as the only way that they could be got through the channel safely. Blake was in the Downs with forty-two ships but he made no move until Tromp's fleet of eighty-eight men-of-war was approaching the entrance to the channel. A council of war recommended that they sit tight but such was not Blake's way and the English fleet was soon heading south out of the Downs parallel to the Dutch. At first shoals prevented an engagement but once the Varne, the last of these, had been left behind, soon after noon on 30 November, Tromp closed with the English and a violent conflict began between the leading ships of the two fleets. The English, unable to manoeuvre because of the proximity of Dungeness, got much the worst of it. Two English ships, the *Garland* and the *Anthony Bonadventure*, were captured in the fighting and a third, the *Hercules*, was lost when she sailed into the Dutch fleet on her way from Portsmouth to the Downs. The Dutch suffered only one casualty when an accidental spark fired the magazine of Captain Juynbol's ship. The English recoiled on Dover and a major disaster might have occurred if Tromp had followed up his advantage but he regarded escorting the merchant ships to their destinations safely as his main task. When his ships disappeared over the horizon the English heaved a great sigh of relief.

The main reason for the defeat was the failure of the Commonwealth to maintain an adequate fleet. The government was quick to accept its share of responsibility and refused Blake's offer to resign. Yet Blake was not free from blame, rushing into battle with scant regard for the tactical situation, though he himself refused to accept this as the crucial factor. For him the defeat was caused by the failure of a number of his captains to support him properly. His determination to make them do exactly as he wanted, regardless of the cost, runs like a refrain throughout the war. After the skirmish off Dover captains Charles Thorowgood and John Gibbs were dismissed for, allegedly, keeping their ships out of the action. Thorowgood was the senior captain in the fleet. Blake conducted a running battle with another, John Taylor, who had been his flag captain in the Scilly campaign and was now one of those who incurred his wrath after Dungeness, together with four others, among them another distinguished captain, Anthony Young. Most extraordinary of all was his quarrel with his brother Benjamin. As Benjamin was his flag captain at the time his sin must have been to stand up for the others. Many of the ships appear to have been short of ammunition and the captains were angry at the way Blake rode roughshod over the council of war. The government supported Blake, as it had to, issuing a new set of thirty-nine articles of war which made the authority of the commander-in-chief paramount and provided severe punishments for any subordinate who failed to carry out the orders of a superior officer. But all the captains, except one, were later quietly reinstated, though their promotion prospects were irretrievably damaged.

Deane, who had gone on shore to serve in the Scottish campaign, was sent back to sea and Monck was appointed to succeed Popham. Blake welcomed them. While the war had been progressing favourably he was quite happy to command alone but when the prospects darkened he was unwilling to be made the scapegoat. The determination of the government to repair the situation, combined with the influence of Deane, brought more order and method into the conduct of the fleet which was now divided into three squadrons—the red, blue, and white—each with its admiral, vice-admiral, and rear-admiral.

A refurbished fleet of sixty to seventy ships put to sea to prevent Tromp's return. On 18 February 1653 advanced elements of the English fleet spotted the Dutch off Start Point. To begin with the Dutch had a decided advantage. In order to prevent Tromp slipping past, as de Ruijter had done, the English fleet was strung out across the channel. Tromp on the other hand had all his ships well in hand, and the weather gauge. He attacked immediately. The result was that the Blue squadron, commanded by the vice-admiral, William Penn, and leading elements of the Red squadron, among them the *Triumph*, which had Blake and Deane on board, bore the entire brunt of the initial Dutch assault. For over an hour the battle raged south of Portland Bill, over the decks of Penn's squadron and around the little group of ships with the *Triumph*. Blake's flag captain, Andrew Ball, and his secretary were both killed, and Blake himself was seriously wounded in the thigh. The battle began to swing the English way when the rear-admiral, John Lawson, managed to bring the remainder of the Red squadron into the fray. The White squadron, commanded by Monck, had been far away to leeward and took some time to come into play. When it finally did so Tromp was obliged to break off the action for fear that the English frigates would get among his convoy.

For the next two days the English harried the Dutch up the channel until, on the evening of 20 February, they were forced to seek sanctuary under the cliffs of Cap Gris Nez. The English prepared to administer the *coup de grâce* the next morning but when day dawned the Dutch were nowhere to be seen. They had used the shallow draught of their ships to escape over the shoals around the cape. The English claimed that seventeen Dutch men-of-war and forty merchant ships had been either sunk or captured. The Dutch only admitted to twelve but even that showed that the English had achieved a major victory. Yet once again English inexperience had let the Dutch off the hook.

Blake continued to exercise command as a general-at-sea throughout the battle despite his wound, but he seems to have caught a severe cold which turned to a fever and forced him to go on shore. He was ill during March and April and then went to London where he organized a new squadron designed to reinforce the fleet. Meanwhile Deane and Monck had sailed into the North Sea where Tromp once more attempted to contest the English supremacy. The battle of the Gabbard was a stunning victory for the English. The Dutch lost twenty men-of-war and the rest were so badly battered that they were forced to seek the protection of the shoals. The only real casualty on the English side was Richard Deane, killed at the outset of the battle. Blake's squadron did not get to sea early enough to take part but his appearance completed the Dutch rout. The pressures of life at sea brought a recurrence of his illness and he was forced to go on shore once again. During July he was so ill that his life was despaired of. He then made a slow recovery but he missed the final victory at Scheveningen, in which Tromp was killed, and did not return to duty until October.

The crisis of the war had been marked by a prolonged political upheaval. In April 1653 Cromwell had forcibly dissolved what remained of the Long Parliament. After an unsatisfactory experiment with Barebone's Parliament during 1653 Cromwell took power himself in December, as lord protector. He had never liked the war with the United Provinces and the Dutch were unwilling to face another summer campaign, so peace was concluded in spring 1654.

The Mediterranean and the Spanish war, 1654–1657 Blake accepted the new protectorate and was appointed to command a powerful fleet destined for the Mediterranean. The long cruise which ensued had three main phases. The French were planning an attack on Spanish-controlled Naples. A fleet was to sail from Toulon, escorting the troop transports. Blake carried instructions to thwart the intended invasion if he could. When he reached the Strait of Gibraltar he found himself in a dilemma. He received information that the French Brest squadron was intending to sail for the Mediterranean to reinforce the Toulon fleet, picking up four Portuguese warships on the way. He waited a vital three weeks off the strait until he heard that the French had taken refuge in Lisbon and had no intention of stirring so long as he was anywhere around. The result was that when he finally reached Naples on 12 December 1654 he found that the action was all over. The 8000 French, under the duc de Guise, arrived at the beginning of November. After two unsuccessful attempts to storm the city, they retired discomfited on 7 December. Had Blake not delayed in the strait the French expedition would have been destroyed completely.

Another part of Blake's instructions related to the corsairs of Tunis. The English claimed that the Tunisians had broken an agreement of 1646 by seizing a merchant ship called the *Princess*. Blake was to demand the ship's return and compensation for the merchants concerned. In February 1655 Blake sailed to Tunis but the negotiations soon reached an impasse. The dey claimed that the ship had been seized in reprisal for the action of a Captain Mitchell who had sold into slavery a group of Turkish soldiers he was supposed to be transporting to Malta. Blake contemplated offensive action but the harbour of Tunis was too well defended and there was no trade to attack. He inspected the more open roadstead at Porto Farina where the *Princess* and eight frigates lay at anchor. As he was closely watched by the dey's army Blake took no action and the English sailed away to Sicily for supplies. A second round of negotiations in March also proved fruitless because the dey was now confident that there was nothing Blake could do. His belief was reinforced when the English fleet disappeared over the horizon for a second time.

He was soon undeceived. Blake had sounded Porto Farina harbour earlier and he reappeared there suddenly on 2 April. Using the early-morning land breeze the third- and fourth-rate frigates sailed in, covered by the larger ships which bombarded the forts. All nine ships in the roadstead were destroyed and the English ships warped out again without any loss. The successful action made no difference. As Blake well knew the frigates were Turkish ones destined for the attack on Venetian Candia (Crete) and not the property of the dey.

By the time Blake sailed away from Tunis Cromwell had practically finalized the details of an alliance with France and a war with Spain was imminent. An expedition under William Penn had already sailed to attack the Spanish West Indies. Additional orders were sent to Blake to prevent any reinforcements reaching there from Spain so he returned to the Atlantic, posting his fleet off Cadiz. On 16 August 1655 the English fleet came in sight of the Spanish battle fleet. Blake's immediate instinct was to engage but the seas were running high, making it impossible to use the lower tier of guns, so he held away. During the delay he had second thoughts. There had been no declaration of war and he was informed that the Spaniards only intended to escort home the plate fleet. As they were not going to the West Indies he believed that his instructions did not entitle him to begin hostilities and he let them go.

The fleet reached the Downs at the beginning of October 1655, having apparently failed in all its aims. Blake was too late to be of use at Naples. He got no concessions out of the dey and the destruction of the Turkish ships only delayed the capture of Candia (Crete). Cromwell was dismayed by Blake's decision not to attack the Spanish fleet, though he admitted that his instructions were ambiguous. Yet the expedition was seen by everyone as momentous. Blake's presence effectually ruptured French schemes of Mediterranean dominance and forced Mazarin to accept an alliance with England on Cromwell's terms. Tunis may have got away with it but the strength and bellicosity of the English fleet led Algiers to make an agreement and England became a major player in Mediterranean politics. Blake may not have destroyed the Spanish fleet but he effectually prevented any reinforcements reaching the West Indies, saving Penn's mismanaged expedition from total disaster.

Cromwell showed his confidence in Blake by reappointing him to command the new expedition which was to blockade the coast of Spain now that war had been officially declared. He was joined by a new general-at-sea, Edward Mountagu. Mountagu's primary task was to negotiate a treaty with Portugal and Blake may well have been relieved that the political decisions which had plagued his last expedition were now to be transferred to someone else's shoulders. The fleet of thirty-seven powerful ships sailed from the Downs on 17 March 1656. The negotiations proved difficult. Cromwell demanded £50,000 compensation for the damage done by royalist privateers, participation by English merchants in the Brazil trade on favourable terms, freedom of worship for English residents in Portugal, and free access to Portuguese ports for English warships. In return he was prepared to support Portugal in her fight for freedom from Spain which had been going on since 1640. King João wriggled hard and at one point Blake had to convince Mountagu that an attempt by the fleet to force the issue would not work. Blake had learned the lesson of 1650. In the end the Portuguese bowed to necessity. They needed English support badly. The treaty was concluded and the compensation money safely embarked and sent to England.

The English were now faced with the problem of what to do. The greatest prize, the plate fleet, was not expected for some time. Mountagu favoured an expedition to the West Indies but he received no support from the captains who feared the high mortality rate common in the tropics. A close inspection of Cadiz showed that a Porto Farina-style attack would not work. Mountagu had instructions to examine the Rock of Gibraltar to see if it would be suitable as a permanent fleet base. The report was not favourable. A large garrison would be needed and seamen were not suitable material. There was nothing of real importance on offer. Eleven ships were sent home and the rest prepared for a long and wearisome blockade, only varied by respites for victualling and watering at Lisbon and sporadic forays against the more exposed Spanish ports.

On 8 September 1656 the event occurred for which everyone had been waiting. Blake had divided the English fleet into three. Mountagu went with one squadron to negotiate a settlement with the pirates of Salé, in which he was successful, due in no small part to the fear Blake inspired. Blake himself stood off to sea, leaving six of the fittest frigates under Captain Richard Stayner to watch Cadiz. Stayner it was who fell in with the plate fleet as it tried to make a dash for home, believing that the way was clear. Of the eight ships only two escaped. Three were captured, a fourth was sunk, and the other two forced on shore. The English haul was later valued at about £200,000. They were rather disappointed because they thought that it would be much more valuable. In a way they were right. The ships with the most plate on board were the one sunk and one of those forced on shore, but the enduring belief that the war could be paid for with captured Spanish gold and silver was a myth.

Mountagu went home with the proceeds of Stayner's victory, leaving Blake to continue his weary watch off the Spanish coast. The plate fleet Stayner had captured was smaller than usual and information from prisoners indicated that a larger fleet was expected in the new year. When Cromwell heard what Mountagu had to say he had Blake reinforced and the weaker ships replaced so that he could ride the winter out. By this time everyone knew that the English fleet was there and merchant shipping kept away. The only excitement the English had was when a Dutch fleet appeared under de Ruijter. There were rumours that he intended to try and waylay the Portuguese Brazil fleet, which could have been a severe embarrassment. In the end all he did was escort Dutch trade to and from the Mediterranean. The first news of the plate fleet came when an English merchant captain, William Sadlington, reported seeing it on his voyage across the Atlantic. Blake made no move partly because of de Ruijter's presence and partly because he feared that he would miss it en route. Then information reached him that the fleet was at Tenerife and had no intention of moving so long as the English fleet was off the Spanish coast. Still he waited until de Ruijter had gone home and there was no danger to the ships left behind to maintain the blockade. The English sailed for the Canary Islands on 14 April 1657 and sighted Tenerife four days later.

After closely reconnoitring Santa Cruz harbour the English attacked on the morning of 20 April. The larger ships were to use their powerful guns to engage and, if possible, silence the Spanish forts. Twelve third- and fourth-rate frigates under the overall command of Stayner were to use the land breeze to sail into the harbour and get alongside the galleons. Strict instructions were given to sink them and not to try and take prizes. The attack commenced at 8 a.m. As at Porto Farina the English guns proved too strong for the main forts, which were quickly knocked out. The entire foreshore was fortified but the gunners there found that they could not see for smoke and risked hitting their own ships moored in front of them. By 9 a.m. the frigates were moored alongside the Spanish ships. By 11 a.m. all the smaller ships had been struck and many were on fire. The greater galleons were a tougher proposition and the larger ships had to enter the bay in order to complete their destruction, which was not accomplished until about 2 p.m. when the ships of the Spanish admiral and vice-admiral blew up in quick succession.

The most difficult part of the operation now began. The English ships had to warp themselves out of the bay under continuous fire from the forts, where some of the guns had been remounted, and from the foreshore, where, now that their own ships had gone, the gunners could at last see their targets. To make matters worse some of the captains greedily tried to tow their prizes out. Blake had to repeat his orders twice before they consented to fire them and cast off the ropes. It says a good deal for Blake's authority and leadership that they all successfully escaped; Stayner in the *Speaker* was the last to leave, very battered but still afloat.

In one way Blake's victory was a barren one. The Spaniards had had the forethought to transport the plate and bullion into the interior of the island, so the successful outcome of the battle did nothing to swell English coffers. Shortage of money was to force them to scale down their activity within a year. Yet in all other respects what Blake had done was of paramount importance. The victory at Tenerife resounded round Europe and made the English fleet feared far and wide. Santa Cruz harbour was believed to be one of the best defended on the Atlantic coast, a reputation that Nelson was later to find not unjustified. Yet the English fleet had sailed in and sunk all seventeen ships of the plate fleet without losing a single one of its own, an achievement almost unparalleled against land-based guns in naval annals. England may have been embarrassed for money but Blake's fleet had reduced the Spanish to desperate straits. In 1656 all the bullion from the New World had been lost, either to the English or sunk to the bottom of the ocean. The 1657 consignment was safe at Tenerife but the Spanish government could not get at it because of the English blockade. The Spanish armies ground to a halt for lack of money. 1658 was to be a disastrous year which finally forced them to the negotiating table.

The destruction of the plate fleet rendered a large armament off the Spanish coast unnecessary. Leaving a squadron of fourteen ships under Captain John Stokes, Blake sailed for home with the rest. Blake had never really recovered from the wound sustained at Portland. During the Mediterranean cruise of 1654–5 he never set foot on shore, leaving diplomatic contacts to other officers such as Joseph Jordan. Part of the problem was ill health, which got worse in 1656 particularly after Mountagu went home. He was ill and in pain for part of the winter but rallied for the Canary Islands expedition. His state of health was causing concern to the Commonwealth agent Thomas Maynard, who visited him in July 1657. Blake must have known that he had not long to live and he breathed his last on 7 August 1657 as his flagship, the *George*, entered Plymouth Sound.

Blake never married and seems to have been almost totally without interest in women beyond the usual civilities. By his will dated 13 March 1656 he left his manor of Puriton to his brother Humphrey and his house in Bridgwater to his brother Benjamin. Apart from a house in Taunton he had no other property, not even in London, using the apartment at Whitehall to which his official duties entitled him as his residence. He left £3000 in money. After giving £100 each to Bridgwater and Taunton for distribution among the poor, the remainder was divided among his numerous relatives. He was buried in great state in the Henry VII chapel of Westminster Abbey, on 4 September, apparently against his expressed wishes, but at the Restoration his remains were thrown out by the royalists.

Assessment Blake's achievements have led him to be ranked as one of England's three greatest seamen alongside Drake and Nelson, but often for the wrong reasons. In his day naval warfare was in the throes of a revolution but Blake had little part in making it. Regular broadside firing was already standard practice in the parliamentarian fleet and in the East India Company's fleet of defence. Disputes will always rage as to when fighting in a single line ahead became the norm. None of the battles where Blake was in charge show evidence of such tactics, yet this should not detract from his reputation. Neither Drake nor Nelson was a revolutionary and all three stand out for the way they led their fleets and took the tactics of their day to their logical conclusion. Yet, unlike the other two, Blake was not bred to the sea. He was appointed to the command on the strength of his record as a soldier and his loyalty to the Commonwealth, and had to learn the seaman's trade.

To begin with Blake seems to have been ignorant of the power of the guns English ships carried. At the beginning of the Anglo-Dutch War he soundly rated Christopher Myngs for rashness in taking on three Dutch warships single-handed. The skirmish off Dover opened his eyes and at Dungeness he went to the other extreme, rushing into battle with less than half the strength of the Dutch fleet. The critical early stages of Portland saw him treating a sea battle like the siege of Taunton, his ships being tied together so that guns were firing in all directions. Not until the Spanish war did he evolve a system by which he could use them to the greatest effect. The results both the Tunisians and the Spaniards had good cause to rue. How his conception of a battle in the open sea had developed will never be known, because he declined the one chance he had to engage the Spanish battle fleet.

In the same way Blake learned the art of blockade. In 1649 he let Rupert escape from Kinsale. In 1650 he learned first that attempts to force the issue could be counter-productive, then that accepting favours could limit his sphere of action, and finally that the enemy was only likely to emerge if the odds were not too heavily stacked against him. 1656 showed how well he had learned them.

Blake's most enduring contribution was in bringing a disciplined approach to naval warfare. What his captains liked were expeditions in search of plunder and prizes. What they disliked were pitched battles which threatened both life and limb, the irksome discipline which forced to them to spend long months on blockade, and, when they were on detached service, the priority which was given to defending their own merchant shipping over seeking rich pickings by attacking that of the enemy. His experiences before the First Anglo-Dutch War led him to suspect advice given by the traditional council of captains. During the war he was unsparing in his criticism of them. He was undoubtedly behind the new articles of war and supported the hierarchical arrangement of flag officers, introduced after Dungeness, which supplanted the earlier more egalitarian system.

Blake's disciplined approach continued during the Spanish war. He had learned the value of proper scouting and woe betide the frigate captain who abandoned his station to chase potential prizes or who returned before his relief had arrived. Blake was 5 feet 6 inches in height with a squat build and heavy jowled features, the very image of the church militant here on earth, the English 'bear' who struck fear into his subordinates and visiting diplomats alike. So cowed were his captains before Tenerife that when Blake asked for their advice they refused to give it. The battle itself was the culmination of his work when he succeeded in forcing his captains to abandon their prizes in the interests of the operation as a whole.

If that had been all, Blake would not have been able to secure the response he did. In 1648 Lord Saye referred to the seamen with contempt as a group not worth considering in comparison with the soldiers. By 1660 all that had changed, and Blake played a major part in altering perceptions. It is typical of the man that, though most of the £3000 he left were arrears from the civil wars, not claimed until he made his will, he realized that good men would not serve if they were not paid properly. In 1648 Popham had refused the command of a ship probably because becoming a navy captain would have entailed a reduction in his pay. In 1652 senior captains at last reached the pay levels of army colonels, who were their official equals in rank. Blake did not neglect the ordinary seamen either. There had been pay rises in 1642 and 1647 but rates were still poor in comparison with the Dutch and they were raised again. In order to encourage the men the prize regulations were altered so that they were rewarded for ships sunk as well as those captured, in proportion to the number of guns they carried. After Dungeness new regulations covering the sick and wounded were introduced and the interests of the relatives and dependants of captains were safeguarded. The widows and children of senior captains killed in battle were generously compensated. The interregnum governments and the other generals all played their part but only Blake identified himself totally with the interests of the fleet. He had no home life. His captains were his only family; he may have treated them like unruly children but he never asked them to do anything he would not do himself, with the result that they and their crews responded by following him wherever he led. The standards he set were the bench-mark by which later ages were to measure their own performances.

Perhaps Blake's greatest achievement in his own time was to create a unity of purpose when the country was beset by unrest and division. He himself wanted the Church of England to be replaced by a national presbyterian church along the lines laid down by parliament in 1646 and he regarded the sects with distaste. He was a republican. When he became one is not clear but Clarendon may well have been right in thinking that the idea took as early as his university days. While he was far from indifferent to what was happening, he took little active part in politics and, like Sir Henry Vane junior, he may have favoured the forced abdication of the king rather than his execution. He made no difficulty about serving the Commonwealth but he viewed the behaviour of Barebone's Parliament with disfavour, and he accepted the protectorate unenthusiastically as the least damaging alternative. As the earthly Jerusalem he sought became more and more elusive he tried to forget what was happening at home and treated the wars against the Dutch and the Spanish as in the interests of English people everywhere whatever their religious and political opinions. Clarendon again mirrored the extent to which he succeeded. He regarded Blake as an obstacle to a royalist restoration, second only to Cromwell, but he could not disguise his admiration for the 'miraculous' victory at Tenerife which raised the reputation of the English nation throughout Europe to new heights (Clarendon, *Hist. rebellion*, 6.37). MICHAEL BAUMBER

Sources M. L. Baumber, *General-at-sea: Robert Blake and the seventeenth-century revolution in naval warfare* (1989) • J. R. Powell, *Robert Blake: general-at-sea* (1972) • *The letters of Robert Blake*, ed. J. R. Powell, Navy RS, 76 (1937) • Thurloe, *State papers* • *CSP dom.*, 1649–60 • S. R. Gardiner and C. T. Atkinson, eds., *Letters and papers relating to the First Dutch War, 1652–1654*, 6 vols., Navy RS, 13, 17, 30, 37, 41, 66 (1898–1930) • parish register, Bridgwater, 27 Sept 1598 [baptism] • *The visitation of Somersetshire, 1623, with additions from earlier visitations and continuations by R. Mundy*, 1842 [inserted], College of Arms (1838) • Foster, *Alum. Oxon.* • J. Wells, *Wadham College* (1898); facs. edn (1998) • will of Humphrey Blake, 1626, PRO, PROB 11/148, sig. 35 • subsidy list, 1628, PRO, E 174/172/390 • *Report on the manuscripts of F. W. Leyborne-Popham*, HMC, 51 (1899)

Archives Admiral Blake Museum, Bridgwater, letters • Som. ARS, papers and copies of seventeenth-century letters, etc. | East Kent Archives Centre, Dover, corresp. with mayor of Sandwich • Worcester College, Oxford, corresp. mainly with Edward Popham

Likenesses T. Preston, mezzotint, pubd 1740 (after unknown artist), BM, NPG • oils, NMM • oils, Wadham College, Oxford

Wealth at death £3000 plus property

Blake, Sophia Louisa Jex- (1840–1912), physician and campaigner for women's rights, was born on 21 January 1840 at 3 Croft Place, Hastings, Sussex. She was the youngest of the three surviving children of Thomas Jex-Blake (1790–1868), proctor of Doctors' Commons, and his wife, Maria Emily Cubitt (1800/01–1881); the Cubitt family home was at Honing Hall, Norfolk. Sophia's brother Thomas William Jex-*Blake (1832–1915) was headmaster of Rugby School from 1874 to 1887.

Early education and teaching In 1851 the family moved from Hastings to 13 Sussex Square, Brighton. Sophia attended several private boarding-schools in Sussex and London. Although she knew she had no need to earn her living, at seventeen she was planning a career as a schoolteacher. In 1858–9 she studied at Queen's College in Harley Street, London. This school was founded in 1847 with the support of the Governesses' Benevolent Institution; it provided advanced secondary education for women who intended to work as teachers. Jex-Blake's unusual proficiency in mathematics won for her a position as college tutor in this subject while she was still a student, and she retained this post until 1861. For part of this time in London she shared a house in Nottingham Place with Octavia Hill and her family. In 1862 Jex-Blake spent several months in Edinburgh being taught by private tutors. She also helped Elizabeth Garrett to prepare her application to

Sophia Louisa Jex-Blake (1840–1912), by unknown photographer

Edinburgh University for enrolment as a medical student. The two had previously met in London, but during Elizabeth's visit to Edinburgh Jex-Blake learned more about the problems facing women who wished to practise medicine.

The Medical Act of 1858 had established a register that listed the names of Britain's qualified medical practitioners. The recognized qualifications were those awarded by nineteen bodies, including the British universities, the colleges of physicians and surgeons, the Society of Apothecaries of London and the Apothecaries' Hall of Dublin. A foreign qualification was accepted only if it had been obtained before 1858 and the holder was practising in Britain when the act was passed. Elizabeth Blackwell, the USA's first woman doctor, had made a brief working visit to England just in time to meet these requirements. Hers was the only woman's name to appear in the first register, and some observers believed that its inclusion was an error, since the act did not acknowledge the eligibility of women. For this reason Edinburgh University, while not rejecting Elizabeth Garrett's application outright, deferred its decision on the matter indefinitely.

On 21 July 1862 Jex-Blake travelled to Europe. For eight months she filled a temporary vacancy on the teaching staff of the Grand Ducal Institute in Mannheim. Next she planned a visit to the United States of America to observe women's education in that country. She arrived in Boston on 8 June 1865. There she met Dr Lucy Sewall, the resident physician of the New England Hospital for Women and Children. It was to be a lasting friendship. Jex-Blake visited progressive co-educational schools in four states—Massachusetts, Ohio, Michigan, and Missouri. She reported her observations in a book entitled *A Visit to some American Schools and Colleges* which was published in London in 1867.

On her return to Boston Jex-Blake was offered accommodation at the New England Hospital for Women in return for her services as a clerk and nursing assistant. This experience changed the course of her life. She had long been aware that women in her own country, as well as in the United States, often failed to obtain vital medical treatment because they dreaded the insensitive attitudes of many of the male members of the profession; there was undoubtedly an urgent need for women doctors. Furthermore, she now realized that medical practice, rather than teaching, was the occupation best suited to her own ability and interests. Jex-Blake also heard that in September 1865 Elizabeth Garrett had passed the examination conducted by the Society of Apothecaries in London and was now the second woman to have her name on the British register. However, increasing male opposition to the admission of women to the profession caused the society to take steps to prevent this from happening again. In future it would be impossible for a woman to attend some of its lecture courses that were compulsory for examination candidates. Jex-Blake continued to work and study in Boston, but her application to become a student at the Harvard medical school was rejected. In 1868 she moved to New York, where Elizabeth Blackwell was establishing a medical college for women. However, the death of her father in November, shortly after the college opened, compelled Jex-Blake to return home to England.

Attempts to study medicine Jex-Blake's essay 'Medicine as a profession for women' was included in the book *Women's Work and Women's Culture*, edited by Josephine Butler, and was published in 1869. In the same year Jex-Blake applied to enter the medical course at Edinburgh University in the hope that its uncertainty about accepting women students had been resolved. The faculty of medicine accepted her application, but it was overruled by the university court on the grounds that she could not attend the men's classes and it would not be practicable to hold separate classes for just one woman. Jex-Blake soon found four other women, all with excellent academic records, who also wished to study medicine. They were permitted to take the matriculation examination and all passed. On 2 November 1869 they signed the matriculation roll, thereby being recorded as the first women medical students of a British university. The house Jex-Blake rented at 15 Buccleuch Place was close to the university and was the meeting place for the group. As their leader her first task was to arrange their lectures for the first term. The university lecturers, who were paid directly by their students, were not compelled to teach women. Those who agreed to do so charged them very high fees because of the small size of their class; without Jex-Blake's help some of the women could not have met the cost. The women all passed the examinations held at the end of their first term, four of them with distinction, but opposition to their presence increased. At the end of the first year two more women joined the group, which then became known as the '*Edinburgh Seven'.

Edinburgh University's medical students received their clinical training in the wards of the Edinburgh Royal Infirmary, but when the seven applied to attend the infirmary in 1871 a special meeting of the managers was called. Their application was refused for that year. The women's chief opponent was the eminent physician Professor Robert Christison, who believed that the presence of women students would lower the status not only of the university's medical school but of the profession generally. Joseph Lister, the recently appointed professor of surgery, shared this view. Many of the male medical students feared that an influx of women into an already crowded profession would seriously harm their financial prospects; only a few supported the women's cause.

On the afternoon of 18 November 1870 the seven were walking to Surgeons' Hall, Nicholson Street, to take an examination when they encountered a mob of hostile students who shouted abuse and blocked their entry to the hall. They pelted the women with mud and refuse. Then a sympathetic student emerged from the hall; he opened the gate and ushered the women inside. They took their examination and all passed. This incident, known later as 'the riot at Surgeons' Hall', was given wide publicity in the national newspapers and won support for the women's cause. Jex-Blake's addresses to public meetings and her frequent letters to the newspapers helped to maintain this interest. Her book *Medical Women* (1872) outlined women's contribution to medical history. Opponents in the medical profession were also becoming more determined. For two years in succession they excluded women students from the Edinburgh Royal Infirmary. It was not until 1873 that the women students gained limited access to the infirmary wards, but they were then facing another problem.

In January 1872 the university court had decided that degrees could not be granted to women medical students, even if they completed the course and passed all the examinations. Jex-Blake appealed to the Scottish court of session to have the university court's decision overruled. In July the case was heard by the lord ordinary, Lord Gifford. He declared the university court's decision invalid; he said that women were entitled to receive degrees, just as men were. But the university then appealed to a higher court. Early in 1873 a panel of twelve judges found that the university had never been empowered to accept women students, so the women had no legitimate claim to degrees. They were, in effect, expelled. Jex-Blake's group remained in Edinburgh for another year, gaining experience in the wards of the infirmary. Then in March 1874 she began the next phase of her campaign, in London.

The London School of Medicine for Women Jex-Blake's first step was to initiate the founding of the London School of Medicine for Women. With the support of friends she was able to rent suitable premises at 30 Henrietta Street, Brunswick Square. Members of the school's provisional council included Professor Thomas Huxley and Ernest Hart, the editor of the *British Medical Journal*. A number of eminent medical men formed a panel of lecturers. Jex-Blake was the school's secretary, in an unofficial capacity, as she was also one of its students. When the school opened on 12 October 1874 it had fourteen students on its roll, the Edinburgh group having been joined by some newcomers. The future of the school depended on the solution of two problems. First, it had to become affiliated with a major hospital so that its students could receive clinical training. Second, its students required access to examinations that would qualify them for registration by the General Medical Council. A year after the school opened there seemed to be a solution to one of these problems. The Royal College of Surgeons of England offered a licence in midwifery, a qualification that entitled the holder to be registered. Very few men took the examination for the licence, so if women applied they would not seem to be competing with their male colleagues. Jex-Blake and two of her fellow students entered their names as candidates. Senior members of the college could find no legal basis for rejecting their applications. Then, just as the examination was about to be held, the three examiners all resigned and there were no volunteers to replace them. The examination was cancelled for an indefinite period. Two members of parliament, Russell Gurney and James Stansfeld, then gave valuable support to the women's cause. Stansfeld accepted the post of honorary treasurer of the London School of Medicine for Women; he came to know Jex-Blake well. When he and Russell Gurney drafted a private member's bill to enable women to qualify in medicine they relied heavily on information and advice which Jex-Blake gave them.

Russell Gurney's enabling bill was passed by parliament on 11 August 1876. This bill merely stated that all of the nineteen recognized examining bodies were permitted (or enabled) to accept women candidates, but they were not compelled to do so. The supporters of the bill correctly predicted that once the position was clarified some of the examining bodies would admit women. The King and Queen's College of Physicians in Ireland did so a month later. Meanwhile, Jex-Blake, with the support of James Stansfeld, successfully completed negotiations with the London (afterwards the Royal) Free Hospital in Gray's Inn Road. On 15 March 1877 the hospital and the London School of Medicine for Women became affiliated for the teaching of women students. At last British women had access to comprehensive medical training and to registration.

Jex-Blake was not the first woman to take the examination in Dublin. Knowing that if she failed her opponents would be gratified, she decided to test herself by taking an examination in Switzerland. On 10 January 1877 she obtained the MD at Bern. Four months later she passed the examination in Dublin and was duly registered on 14 May. Jex-Blake had expected that she would now be formally appointed honorary secretary of the London School of Medicine for Women, but members of the school council, including James Stansfeld, thought her unsuited to the position. Her forthright, militant approach was no longer appropriate. Now that the two main problems had been solved the school needed the services of a diplomatic secretary to win the goodwill and respect of the medical profession. Another former student was appointed. Feeling severely hurt Jex-Blake decided to return to Edinburgh, where she still had many friends.

Career after qualification There, in June 1878, Jex-Blake opened a medical practice at 4 Manor Place; three months later she established a dispensary (an out-patient clinic) for impoverished women. This was at 73 Grove Street,

Fountainbridge. Both the practice and the dispensary soon became very busy and for three years she carried a heavy work load. Then the death of her mother early in 1881, followed by the death of one of her assistants, made her severely depressed. She closed her practice and left the dispensary in the care of her medical colleagues. For two years she lived the life of a recluse, but by September 1883 she had recovered. She moved to Bruntsfield Lodge, Whitehouse Loan, and reopened her practice. The dispensary was also moved to a larger site, at 6 Grove Street; with the addition of a ward for in-patients it became the Edinburgh Hospital for Women. Jex-Blake also compiled a second edition of *Medical Women*, adding an account of the recent victory; it was published in 1886.

In 1885 the Royal Colleges of Physicians and Surgeons of Edinburgh established a conjoint board to award joint diplomas in medicine and surgery; women candidates would be accepted. When a group of women students appealed to Jex-Blake for help with their training she responded generously. At considerable personal cost she founded the Edinburgh School of Medicine for Women, in Surgeon Square. It opened early in 1887. In its second year the school was disrupted by disputes between Jex-Blake and several of the students who resented her imposition of strict rules of conduct. The rebels succeeded in having another school established—the Medical College for Women, in Chambers Street. Jex-Blake's school eventually closed in 1898.

Over the years Jex-Blake's hospital had continued to grow, as it provided a valuable service to Edinburgh's women. After her retirement in March 1899 the hospital was moved to her former home and was renamed the Bruntsfield Hospital. Jex-Blake spent her retirement in rural Sussex. Her property, Windydene, was a small farm at Mark Cross, some 5 miles south of Tunbridge Wells. Although her heart was failing she enjoyed reading, gardening, and entertaining her many friends, until her death at Windydene on 7 January 1912. She was buried in Rotherfield churchyard, Sussex. One of her close friends, Dr Margaret Todd, later wrote of Sophia Jex-Blake:

> She was impulsive, she made mistakes and would do so to the end of her life: her naturally hasty temper and imperious disposition had been chastened indeed, but the chastening fire had been far too fierce to produce perfection … But there was another side to the picture after all. Many of those who regretted and criticised details were yet forced to bow before the big transparent honesty, the fine unflinching consistency of her life. (Todd)

Shirley Roberts

Sources S. Roberts, *Sophia Jex-Blake: a woman pioneer in nineteenth century medical reform* (1993) • M. Todd, *The life of Sophia Jex-Blake* (1918) • S. Jex-Blake, *Medical women: a thesis and a history*, 2nd edn (1886) • S. Jex-Blake, *A visit to some American schools and colleges* (1867) • I. Thorne, *Sketch of the foundation and development of the London School of Medicine for Women* (1915) • Royal Free Hospital, London, archives of the medical school • J. Stansfeld, 'Medical women', *Nineteenth Century*, 2 (1877), 888–901 • *The life of Sir Robert Christison*, 2 (1886) • *CGPLA Eng. & Wales* (1912) • Burke, *Gen. GB*

Archives Edinburgh Central Reference Library • Francis A. Countway Library of Medicine, Boston • Lothian Health Board Medical Archive Centre • NL Scot. • Royal Free Hospital, London, medical school, letters, application form, and newspaper cuttings • U. Edin., faculty of medicine • Wellcome L. • Women's Library, London | SOUND BBC WAC

Likenesses S. Laurence, portrait, Royal Society of Medicine, 1 Wimpole Street, London • Swaine, photograph, Wellcome L. • photograph, U. Edin. • photograph, State Library of Victoria, Melbourne, Victoria, Australia • photograph, NPG [*see illus.*]

Wealth at death £14,196 3*s*.: probate, 14 Feb 1912, *CGPLA Eng. & Wales*

Blake, Thomas (1596/7–1657), Church of England clergyman and religious controversialist, was born in Staffordshire. He matriculated from Christ Church, Oxford, on 25 October 1616, aged nineteen, graduated BA on 5 May 1620 and proceeded MA on 21 February 1623. By about 1630 he had begun a ministry in Tamworth, on the Staffordshire/Warwickshire border. As he reminded the dedicatees of his first publication, *The Birth Priviledge, or, Covenant-Holinesse of Beleevers* (1644), 'I have served you for Christ a double apprenticeship of yeares almost compleat'. In 1645, following the surrender of Shrewsbury to the parliamentary forces, Blake became vicar of St Alkmund there.

Blake's pamphlet launched him into a sustained controversy over the inclusiveness or exclusiveness of admission to the church's sacraments, conducted with a number of notable protagonists, including eventually his fellow west midlands minister, Richard Baxter of Kidderminster. While he set much store on catechizing the young in order to produce a Christian nation, Blake argued in *The Birth Priviledge* for a latitudinarian largeness: the right to baptism was in his view as wide as the name 'Christian'; visible penitence from the child's parents was sufficient to satisfy the requirements. In *Infants Baptisme, Freed from Antichristianisme* (1645), dedicated to Ruth, Lady Scudamore, he defended the practice against the 'assault' on it, and on his previous work, by the baptist Christopher Blackwood in *The Storming of Antichrist* (1644). Here Blake was ranged with the eminent minister Stephen Marshall, as he was again in *Mr Blakes Answer to Mr Tombes* (1646), a reply to the *Two Treatises* (1645) of another baptist, John Tombes, who had by this time returned to his native west midlands. In 1648 Blake was among the Shropshire ministers who signed the covenant.

In 1650 Blake and a colleague, with their families, left Shrewsbury, probably owing to an outbreak of plague. With Blake suffering from a fever, and subject to suspicion that they might be carrying infection, the party could find only 'mean accommodations' until given hospitality by the Shropshire minister Samuel Hildersham and his wife, Mary. Blake acknowledged their kindness in the dedication to them of his next work, *Vindiciae foederis, or, A Treatise of the Covenant of God Entered with Mankind* (1652): 'for many months we had free and liberal entertainment … in your house I had not only leisure to make a good progresse in this work, but singular accommodation from your accomplisht Library' (sig. A2*v*). He signed the dedication on 4 November 1652 from his study in Tamworth, having in the interim resumed his ministry there and become an assistant to the local committee of triers and ejectors in its work of regulating the clergy of Staffordshire.

Vindiciae foederis resumed the controversy with John

Tombes, but it extended the discussion to consideration of admission to holy communion (on which Blake again advocated inclusiveness), and was also a very oblique attack on Richard Baxter's first work, *Aphorismes of Justification* (1649). Blake respected Baxter, praising him when he could, and only attacked the arguments of *Aphorismes*, not the man. In 1654 three of Baxter's allies, John Humfrey, Henry Bartlett, and Giles Firmin, were urging him to take up the cudgels against Blake, Firmin reporting that 'good men' were being won over to the latter's side (Keeble and Nuttall, 1.150). Baxter duly replied in *Rich. Baxters Apology* (1654) and *Rich. Baxters Confession* (1655). In May or June 1655 Blake wrote in a conciliatory vein to Baxter, thanking him for the gift of the *Apology* and expressing himself 'loath indeed to appear your professed adversary' (ibid., 1.182), but his *The Covenant Sealed* (1655), which included a 'brief answer' to the *Apology*, further antagonized Firmin. On 7 April 1656 Firmin wrote to Baxter that, though he understood that Blake was 'very godly', he dealt 'too slightly in such a solemne ordinance': while he himself did not turn away from the sacrament those whose views on church government differed from his own, he was concerned about the level of ignorance in some of the candidates, which was worthy of 'Heathens' or 'Indians' (ibid., 1.207–8). In reply Baxter pronounced *The Covenant Sealed* 'a Volume of mistakes and passions', but was persuaded 'to handle the Controversie Argumentatively' and to cut out the personal abuse, and advised Firmin to 'keep your eye on the Center, where Mr Blake & you & I are one' (ibid., 1.211–12). This did not prevent Baxter's continuing the exchange in *Certaine Disputations of Right to the Sacraments* (1657).

Blake drew up his will on 11 January 1656, when he was enjoying a 'good measure of health' (PRO, PROB 11/270, sig. 477), but following an illness he died the following year. He was buried in Tamworth church on 11 June 1657. Anthony Burgess, minister of Sutton Coldfield, who delivered at the funeral *Pauls Last Sermon* (1658), remarked on Blake's 'Doctrinall abilities', his wisdom as a spiritual director, his studiousness, and his preaching (pp. 18, 20). In the controversies that had taken place among the godly, to which Burgess had also been a party, he praised Blake for his willingness to vindicate himself publicly and for giving the lie to those who criticized his 'promiscuous admission of all' to the sacraments by his vigilance in catechizing the young. An oration by Samuel Shaw, master at Tamworth school, complemented the picture of a godly pastor. Blake's will was proved by his widow, Jane; as Burgess had noted, he died childless, and his estate was divided between Jane and his brother John, with books and manuscripts left to two clerical nephews, William Blake of Mashfield and Samuel Beresford of Bremingham Alson. WILLIAM LAMONT

Sources Foster, *Alum. Oxon.* • Wood, *Ath. Oxon.*, new edn, 3.431–3 • *Calendar of the correspondence of Richard Baxter*, ed. N. H. Keeble and G. F. Nuttall, 2 vols. (1991) • A. Burgess, *Pauls last sermon* (1658) • W. M. Lamont, *Richard Baxter and the millennium: protestant imperialism and the English revolution* (1979) • H. Boersma, *A hot pepper corn: Richard Baxter's doctrine of justification in its seventeenth-century context of controversy* (Zoetermeer, 1993) • *Walker rev.*, 305 • T. Blake, *Vindiciae foederis* (1653) • will, PRO, PROB 11/270, sig. 477

Archives DWL, corresp.

Wealth at death divided property between wife, brother, and nephew: will, PRO, PROB 11/270, sig. 477

Blake, Thomas William Jex- (1832–1915), headmaster and dean of Wells, was born at 2 Cumberland Terrace, Regent's Park, London, on 26 January 1832, the eldest surviving son of the two sons and four daughters of Thomas Jex-Blake (1790–1868) of Bunwell, Norfolk, and Brighton, proctor of Doctors' Commons, and his second wife, Maria Emily (*d.* 1881), youngest daughter of Thomas Cubitt JP, of Honing Hall, Norfolk. Sophia Louisa Jex-*Blake, the pioneer in the medical education of women, was his youngest sister. He was educated at the Revd Benjamin Guest's Preparatory School at Brighton before being sent to Rugby, where he was a pupil of G. E. L. Cotton. He matriculated as a scholar of University College, Oxford, in 1851, and obtained a first class in classical moderations (1853) and a first class in *literae humaniores* (1855). During his undergraduate days at University College he was greatly influenced by Goldwin Smith. In 1855 Jex-Blake was elected a fellow of Queen's College, after one of the first elections by open competition during the provostship of William Thomson, and in the following year he was ordained. In 1857 he married Henrietta (*d.* 1921), second surviving daughter of John Cordery, an Indian merchant.

Like other able university men obliged to relinquish their fellowships while celibacy restrictions remained in force, Jex-Blake found a vocation as a public-school master. His apprenticeship was served at Marlborough College, where, for one 'half', he was sixth-form master under his former teacher, Cotton, an inspiring head. He then became assistant master (1858–68, taking the 'Twenty') at Rugby under Frederick Temple, his second experience of an inspiring chief. In 1868 he was elected principal of Cheltenham College, a tribute to his reputation, which his services to Cheltenham enhanced. He took the Oxford degrees of BD and DD in 1873.

In February 1874 Jex-Blake was appointed headmaster of Rugby, following the dismissal of Henry Hayman, whose unpopularity with the masters had led to damaging divisions. By tact and wisdom, and with the help of old friends, Jex-Blake restored the school to prosperity, his courteous manners and knowledge of the world being helpful to Rugby in its relations with parents and with the county. He was the first public-school headmaster in England to appreciate the value of art in a liberal education. Owing to his initiative Rugby had an art museum (1879) before any other school in England. His taste for fine pictures owed much to John Ruskin, an influence acknowledged in the introduction to his book *A Long Vacation in Continental Picture Galleries* (1858). At Rugby Jex-Blake built the Temple reading-room and art museum, a new Big School with classrooms under it, completed the new quadrangle, started the modern side, gave a swimming pool in the Close, equipped school workshops under the gymnasium, and enriched the art museum with generous personal gifts.

Jex-Blake's sermons preached at Cheltenham and Rugby (published under the title *Life in Faith*, 1876) illustrate the influence of Arnold, Jowett, and Temple on the school pulpit. He was in the school tradition of broad-churchmanship, which was derived from Thomas Arnold, cooled by the influence of John Stuart Mill and of Oxford liberalism of the 1850s, energized a second time by Frederick Temple, and coloured by the culture of Ruskin. As a headmaster he was mild and benevolent, with a kind manner, which gained him popularity with the boys. He avoided rows with the masters. But some felt he lacked firmness. He was reluctant to resort to expulsion or to enforce rules about superannuation; nor did he use corporal punishment. By 1884 the governing body was concerned that pupil numbers were beginning to fall, and there was talk that the school was becoming slack. In 1887 he resigned from the headship and took up the living of Alvechurch, Worcestershire, to which he was presented by Henry Philpott, bishop of Worcester and chairman of the Rugby governors.

In 1891, on Lord Salisbury's recommendation, Jex-Blake was made dean of Wells, where he remained until 1910. Latterly his political sympathies moved towards Liberal Unionism and tariff reform. Elected FRGS and a member of the Alpine Club, he travelled widely throughout his life, visiting all the European capitals and venturing to north Africa and India. He inherited a family estate of over 300 acres in Norfolk. Jex-Blake died at his London home, 13 Ennismore Gardens, on 2 July 1915. He had two sons and nine daughters, of whom Henrietta Jex-*Blake [*see under* Blake, Katharine Jex-] and Katharine Jex-*Blake became heads of women's colleges at Oxford and Cambridge.

M. E. Sadler, *rev.* M. C. Curthoys

Sources *The Times* (3 July 1915) • private information (1927) • personal knowledge (1927) • Burke, *Gen. GB* • J. Foster, *Oxford men and their colleges* (1893) • *Men and women of the time* (1899) • E. Gaskell, *Norfolk leaders* (1910) • J. B. H. Simpson, *Rugby since Arnold* (1967)
Archives Norfolk RO, corresp. and papers • Rugby School, Warwickshire, album
Likenesses H. G. Herkomer, oils, exh. RA 1891, Rugby School, Warwickshire • J. E. Millais, oils, priv. coll. • R. T. & Co., wood-engraving (after photograph by E. H. Speight), NPG; repro. in *ILN* (28 Feb 1891) • wood-engraving (after photograph by A. G. Tod), NPG; repro. in *ILN* (11 April 1879)
Wealth at death £126,210 14*s.* 6*d.*: resworn probate, 26 July 1915, *CGPLA Eng. & Wales*

Blake, William (1757–1827), engraver, artist, and poet, was born on 28 November 1757 at 28 Broad Street, Soho, London, the third son of James Blake (1723?–1784), a hosier, and his wife, Catherine, *née* Wright (1723–1792), the widow of Thomas Armitage. Blake had four brothers, James (1753–1827), John (*b.* 1755, *d.* before 1760), Robert (1762?–1787), and John (1760–1800?), and one sister, Catherine (1764–1841). Records at St James's, Piccadilly, note the baptism of a Richard Blake in 1762, but this may be an error for Robert. Only James, who continued the family business, and Catherine played roles in Blake's adult life. The younger John was apprenticed to a baker but ran away to 'enlist as a Soldier & died' (Tatham in Bentley, *Records*, 509). William Blake was baptized on 11 December 1757 in St

William Blake (1757–1827), by Thomas Phillips, 1807

James's Church, Piccadilly. Persistent claims that his parents were dissenters are not supported by documentary evidence, but Blake was born into the class of London shopkeepers and artisans known for its hard work in pursuit of financial security and a tendency toward independent opinions in religion and politics.

Childhood, education, and apprenticeship, 1757–1779 Little is known about the outer circumstances of Blake's childhood, but the special character of his inner life made itself apparent at an early age. When walking on Peckham Rye, aged 'eight or ten perhaps', he beheld 'a tree filled with angels' (Gilchrist, 1.7). On another occasion 'his mother beat him for running in & saying that he saw the Prophet Ezekiel under a Tree in the Fields' (Tatham in Bentley, *Records*, 519). At about this same time, Blake showed an interest in the pictorial arts. While still a youth, he began sketching and attending auctions to acquire old and then unfashionable prints after artists such as Raphael, Michelangelo, and Dürer. The intertwining of extrasensory perception and artistic expression continued throughout Blake's life and is integral to his concepts of mind, art, and religion.

Blake's father disapproved of his son's reports about angels in trees, but he was supportive of William's ambitions in the arts, buying for his young connoisseur casts of antique sculpture for copying with pencil or pen. When ten years old Blake began to attend a drawing school directed by Henry Pars—apparently his first contact with formal education. His character and interests indicated that Blake would become an artist; his family's finances would dictate the first step toward such a career.

At the age of fourteen it was time for Blake to begin an apprenticeship. A 'painter of Eminence' (Tatham in Bentley, *Records*, 510)—or, according to Gilchrist, the fashionable engraver William Ryland (1.13)—was first considered as a master, but the fee was too high for the family purse. The Blakes settled instead on James Basire, an old-fashioned line and stipple printmaker who practised the 'mixed method' of preliminary etching followed by engraving. William was apprenticed to Basire on 4 August 1772 for a bond of 50 guineas. Blake probably lived for the traditional period of seven years with his master at 31 Great Queen Street, Lincoln's Inn Fields.

Blake learned from Basire the profession he would practise throughout his life. Gaining the necessary skills involved a good deal of drudgery preparing copperplates and replicating the abstract linear patterns of Basire's graphic technique. Blake mastered his craft quickly—given the 1773 date he later inscribed on 'Joseph of Arimathea among the Rocks of Albion', a plate based on a figure by Michelangelo. The print's competent conventionality gives no hint of Blake's later graphic innovations.

In addition to providing professional instruction, Blake's master introduced him to the intellectual life of London. Basire was engraver to the Royal Society and the Society of Antiquaries, and Blake assisted in the execution of many plates for them. He probably also worked on engravings for Jacob Bryant's *A New System, or, An Analysis of Ancient Mythology* (1774–6), which influenced Blake's later excursions into syncretic myth-making. From these projects, and possibly from authors and publishers who visited Basire's shop, Blake learned about the natural sciences, philology, and archaeology.

Beginning in 1774, Basire sent Blake to Westminster Abbey to make drawings of its medieval monuments and wall paintings for later engraving. This assignment, which probably lasted on and off for three years, may have been prompted by a desire to separate Blake from fellow apprentices and thereby end a quarrel with them (Malkin in Bentley, *Records*, 422). Blake's earliest known drawings record the opening of the coffin of Edward I on 2 May 1774. Later efforts are careful copies of the effigies and tombs of monarchs; many were subsequently engraved in Basire's shop (some probably by Blake) as book illustrations. The sculpture filling the abbey 'appeared as miracles of art, to his Gothicised imagination' (ibid., 423) and shaped Blake's lifelong interest in early British history and medieval art.

A career in the arts, 1779–1787 At the end of his apprenticeship in August 1779, Blake began his career as a journeyman copy engraver. He was hired by the print-publisher Thomas Macklin to execute stipple engravings after Watteau and by several booksellers, including the liberal publisher Joseph Johnson, to engrave illustrations. Many of these were based on designs by Thomas Stothard, a friend of Blake's from at least 1780 and an artist just beginning a career as Britain's most prolific book illustrator. Blake became part of a circle of engravers regularly employed to reproduce Stothard's designs.

Blake's efforts as a commercial engraver in the 1780s are what one would expect for a young man trained in that craft. His ambitions in the arts, however, extended beyond what copy engraving could satisfy—or was expected of engravers. He began training as an original artist by enrolling, probably in July 1779, as a student in the Royal Academy of Arts. After a three-month probation, Blake was granted permission to study works in the academy's collections, featuring casts of classical sculpture, for six years. Among his first compositions was a series of watercolours illustrating the history of England from the legendary arrival of Brutus to the reign of Edward IV. Blake exhibited one design, *The Death of Earl Goodwin*, at the Royal Academy in 1780. Many other drawings based on historical, literary, and biblical subjects followed, with two on the consequences of warfare in the academy's 1784 exhibition and four on the story of Joseph in 1785. These works exhibit the strong outlines and frieze-like arrangement of figures typical of the then dominant neoclassical style, but with an attempt at monumentality influenced by Michelangelo, Raphael, and Blake's contemporary James Barry. Blake was aiming at a career in 'history' painting, then considered the highest genre of pictorial expression.

Blake's circle of friends was growing. In addition to Stothard, Blake became acquainted in the early 1780s with the sculptor John Flaxman, the connoisseur John Hawkins, the artist (and later biographer) John Thomas Smith, and George Cumberland, an amateur artist and collector of early Italian prints. In 1784 Hawkins tried, but failed, to raise funds to send Blake to Italy. Stothard, Flaxman, and Cumberland would play significant roles in Blake's later life. The arts provided a common interest for these young men and prompted activities such as sketching tours. One such, on the River Medway late in the summer of 1780, proved memorable. Stothard, Blake, and another friend strayed too close to the naval base near Upnor Castle and the trio was briefly detained as suspected spies. This may not have been the first time Blake was caught up in political events. A few months earlier, London had been swept by the anti-Catholic Gordon riots. According to Gilchrist (1.35), Blake 'encountered the advancing wave' of the mob and 'was forced … to go along in the very front rank, and witness the storm and burning' of Newgate prison.

Blake's social life in the early 1780s included romantic interests. His first proposal of marriage was rejected. He told his broken-hearted tale to Catherine Sophia Boucher (1762–1831) [*see* Blake, Catherine Sophia], the daughter of a market gardener, and a bond of affection soon developed (Tatham in Bentley, *Records*, 517–18). About a year after first meeting, they were married on 18 August 1782 in the church of St Mary, Battersea. Catherine may have been illiterate, or at least embarrassed by her penmanship, for she signed the register with an X. Blake probably lived in his father's house until his marriage; soon after, the couple took lodgings at 23 Green Street, near Leicester Square. Little is known about Catherine Blake, but she managed the family purse and, in later years, would place an empty plate before her husband at mealtime to remind him of monetary necessities (Gilchrist, 1.313). She was the most important person in Blake's adult life, a constant companion, helpmate, and faithful believer in his genius. The couple had no children.

From the age of twelve Blake had been testing his powers as a poet. Some of these efforts were privately published as *Poetical Sketches* (1783). The collection shows an indebtedness to eighteenth-century verse, but also an uneasiness with its conventions and a desire to reach back to earlier models—Shakespeare, Spenser, and the supposedly ancient works of Ossian—to revivify present sensibilities. The cost of producing the volume was borne by Harriet Mathew, her clergyman husband, and Flaxman, who had introduced Blake into the Mathew home, one 'frequented by most of the literary and talented people of the day' (Smith in Bentley, *Records*, 456). The group included Thomas Taylor 'the Platonist', who apparently instructed Blake in mathematics (Bentley, *Records Supplement*, 94–5). Blake had impressed these worthies by reciting and singing his compositions, but by 1784 he became uncomfortable with their pretentious conversations. His criticism found expression in *An Island in the Moon* (*c.*1784–5), a fragmentary manuscript that playfully satirizes contemporary speculations in the arts and sciences.

It may have been a small inheritance from his father, who died in July 1784, that helped Blake begin a print-publishing partnership with another former Basire apprentice, James Parker. The two families moved to 27 Broad Street, next door to the Blake family home. Blake probably acquired his engraver's rolling press at this time. Only two prints bear the partnership's imprint and the business may have ceased when the Blakes moved to 28 Poland Street, Soho, late in 1785. Blake's first attempt at artistic and financial independence had not prospered.

Graphic inventions, 1787–1789 Blake was exceptionally close to his youngest brother, Robert, who was also set on a career in the arts and was perhaps a lodger with the Blakes. When a quarrel developed between brother and wife, Blake made Catherine apologize humbly to Robert (Gilchrist, 1.58–9). The youth fell ill in the winter of 1786–7 and died in early February. In his exhaustion after the 'last fortnight' of Robert's life, having tended him 'day and night by his bedside', Blake fell into 'an unbroken sleep of three days' and nights' duration' (ibid., 1.59). But his brother's spirit remained alive for Blake and grief turned to inspiration in the following year. 'Robert stood before him in one of his visionary imaginations, and so decidedly directed him' in how to publish his works without 'the expense of letter-press' (Smith in Bentley, *Records*, 460). Whatever its other-worldly origins, Blake's invention of relief etching also developed from his craft as an engraver. His new method was more direct, faster, and required less technical expertise than intaglio printmaking. It permitted Blake the artist to paint his images directly on a copperplate in acid-resistant varnish; Blake the poet could write his words in the same medium. The text must be executed in reverse, so that impressions would print right-way around, but this was only a slight impediment for a trained engraver. After the uncovered areas of the metal were etched away, the images stood in relief and could be inked quickly on, and printed with low pressure from, the surface. The process embodied a unity between conception and execution—a practice that became a principle of Blake's later aesthetic doctrines—rather than the divisions between invention and production embedded in eighteenth-century print technology and its class distinctions among authors and printers, artists and engravers.

Blake's first relief etching, one that includes the related technique of white-line etching, may have been *The Approach of Doom*, a print based on a wash drawing by Robert in his notebook, a treasured memento that Blake used for his own compositions. A combination of words and pictures soon followed: *All Religions are One* and *There is No Natural Religion*, both of 1788, are Blake's first 'Illuminated Books', as he called his new genre in 1793 (Blake, 693). These aphoristic tractates reject rationalist doctrines and welcome the imaginative truths of revealed religions which were, in Blake's view, one with artistic expression.

Blake produced his first illuminated book of poems, *Songs of Innocence*, in 1789. These brief lyrics, their illustrations, and interlinear decorations, reach beyond the genre of children's literature to express Blake's ideal of a unified sensibility incarnate in children, as in Christ. Catherine Blake helped with the presswork and hand colouring of this and other illuminated books and bound the leaves in wrappers. Although he may have exhibited a few of these singular works at Johnson's shop, Blake apparently sold his illuminated books directly to collectors rather than through booksellers. He and his wife thereby had complete control over all stages of production and distribution.

At about the same time that he developed relief etching, Blake was composing a narrative poem, *Tiriel*, his first extensive attempt to create mythic texts by conflating ancient Greek, British, and Hebraic motifs. The format of the *Tiriel* manuscript and its associated wash drawings indicate that it was intended for letterpress publication illustrated with intaglio engravings. In *The Book of Thel* (late 1789), Blake combined for the first time his new mode of illuminated printing with so-called 'prophetic' verse in long lines evocative of allegorical meanings couched in rhetoric alternately gentle and horrific.

Revolution and reaction, 1790–1795 Illuminated printing supplemented, without replacing, Blake's other graphic activities. In 1788 the great print-publishers John and Josiah Boydell hired Blake to execute his largest copy engraving, *Beggar's Opera*, after a painting by William Hogarth. He completed the plate in the summer of 1790 and it may have been the fee (unrecorded, but probably substantial) that permitted the Blakes to move to a fine terrace house at 13 Hercules Buildings, Lambeth. Their relative prosperity in this period is indicated by Tatham's story that Blake's house was robbed of goods valued at £100 (Bentley, *Records*, 522).

London's booksellers continued to use Blake's skills, commissioning him to engrave illustrations for modest volumes of poetry, mathematics, and medicine, and for influential works such as Erasmus Darwin's *The Botanic Garden* (1791) and James Stuart and Nicholas Revett's *The Antiquities of Athens* (vol. 3, 1794). After a brief hiatus in the mid-1780s, perhaps caused by Blake's dilatoriness in completing assignments, Johnson was again his main employer. He appears to have appreciated Blake's abilities as an artist and poet, for he hired him to both design and engrave illustrations for Mary Wollstonecraft's *Original Stories from Real Life* (1791) and agreed to publish Blake's verse narrative, *The French Revolution* (1791), and a small emblem book, *For Children: the Gates of Paradise* (1793). Sales of the latter must have been meagre; the poem never progressed beyond proofs of 'Book the First'. *The French Revolution* set a pattern repeated throughout most of Blake's life: ambitious projects begun with great hopes, only to be cut short by financial or personal failings.

Johnson's commercial importance to Blake's career was matched by his role in introducing Blake to some of England's leading liberal writers and artists, many of whom regularly gathered at the bookseller's. It was probably through Johnson that Blake met and befriended the Swiss-German artist Henry Fuseli, for whose translation of J. C. Lavater's *Aphorisms on Man* (1788) Blake engraved the frontispiece. Other plates based on Fuseli's compositions, similar to Blake's own, followed. Blake may have also met more radical figures in the Johnson coterie, including Joseph Priestley and Thomas Paine. Tatham asserts that Blake warned Paine of imminent arrest, just before he left England in 1792, but the story is questionable (Tatham in Bentley, *Records*, 530; expanded in Gilchrist, 1.95).

Blake and his wife attended an organizational meeting of the New Jerusalem church, which based its doctrines on the writings of Emanuel Swedenborg, on 13 April 1789. Blake was no thoughtless convert; his annotations to two of Swedenborg's works express growing misgivings. These turned to outright rejection in *The Marriage of Heaven and Hell* (1790), Blake's most heterodox illuminated book in both its form, a loose gathering of prose and poetry, and content. Through the 'voice of the Devil' and 'Proverbs of hell' (Blake, 34–5), he parodies Swedenborg, reverses the cosmology of Milton's *Paradise Lost*, pronounces that the sensual is an avenue to the spiritual, and attacks the biblical history and morality constructed by the 'Angels' of the established church. Energy is celebrated as eternal delight, at war with the restraints of reason. The book concludes with 'A Song of Liberty' calling for the revolutionary overthrow of tyrannies religious and secular.

Blake's radical political views continue in *Visions of the Daughters of Albion* (1793). Like *The Book of Thel*, the poem and its designs centre on a female character. Her rape initiates an incantatory protest against exploitation and enslavement influenced by Wollstonecraft and by John Gabriel Stedman, for whose *Narrative* (1796) about a slave revolt in Surinam Blake began engraving illustrations in 1791. *America a Prophecy*, also dated 1793, was the first of Blake's 'Continental Prophecies' that continued through *Europe* (1794) and concluded, somewhat diminished, in *The Song of Los* (1795), divided into sections entitled 'Africa' and 'Asia'. The designs in these books extend beyond direct illustration to establish their own iconographic drama. The texts intermingle figures real (Washington, Franklin) and fictive (Enitharmon, Rintrah), places local (Great George Street) and biblical (Mount Sinai). Blake alludes to contemporary events, but he typically seeks for their ancient origins and millennial conclusions. Three separate engravings of this period, *Albion Rose*, *The Accusers of Theft Adultery Murder*, and *Lucifer and the Pope in Hell*, also herald apocalyptic revolution.

The record of Blake's active engagement with politics is equally complex. Gilchrist claims that Blake was 'a vehement republican' who 'donned the famous symbol of liberty and equality—the *bonnet rouge*—in open day' (1.93–4). But, when Blake learned of 'the Days of Terror' in France in September 1792, he 'assuredly never wore the red cap again' (1.94). His cancellation of three plates in *America*, one containing direct reference to George III, suggests that Blake may have feared prosecution if his views were stated too directly. Perhaps such fears, coupled with a general sense of dread, led Blake to scribble in his notebook, 'I say I shant live five years And if I live one it will be a Wonder June 1793' (Blake, 694).

There is no record of Blake attending political gatherings of any sort; perhaps his anti-deistic convictions separated him from the secular revolutionaries of his day. His singular religious beliefs also seem to have set Blake on a lonely course. There are striking parallels between Blake's poetry and the writings of several radical protestant groups; but, except for the meeting with Swedenborgians in 1789, it may be true that Blake did not 'attend any place of Divine worship' for the last forty years of his life (Smith in Bentley, *Records*, 458).

By October 1793 Blake had built up a stock of illuminated books and other prints sufficient to issue an advertisement 'To the Public'. This handbill includes *Songs of Experience* (1794), the contrary companion to *Songs of Innocence*. Blake first issued *Experience*, etched on the backs of the *Innocence* copperplates, as a separate volume, but soon combined the collections under a general title-page, *Songs of Innocence and of Experience*. Its subtitle, 'Shewing the two contrary states of the human soul', indicates that child and adult are temporal expressions of eternal mental states. Experience enacts a fall into division, but the Bard, 'Who Present, Past, & Future sees' and 'Whose ears have heard, / The Holy Word', can reclaim a unified vision (Blake, 18). Yet these spiritual concerns did not carry Blake away from this world: several poems, including 'The Chimney Sweeper' and 'London', are lyrics of social protest.

Blake's next project in illuminated poetry was potentially enormous—a version of Genesis, perhaps as the first book in the 'Bible of hell' announced in *The Marriage of Heaven and Hell* (Blake, 44). *The First Book of Urizen* (1794) ranges beyond a satanic retelling of the Bible to establish an even more primordial perspective and construct an ur-myth in which material creation—spatial, temporal, and biological—is one with the fall. Urizen and Los, representatives of both cosmic and psychic forces, are the chief actors in the agonistic drama. There is no 'second' book of Urizen; but the brief poems *The Book of Los* and *The Book of*

Ahania, both etched in conventional intaglio in 1795, are fragments of Blake's grand intentions.

Epic ventures, 1795–1800 Blake ceased producing illuminated books in 1795, probably owing to poor sales of all but *Songs of Innocence and of Experience* and the commencement of other, time-consuming projects. In the previous year, Blake had begun to print his relief etchings in dense, glue-based pigments. He used the technique to create a group of twelve large colour prints without accompanying texts in 1795. Most were printed planographically rather than from relief surfaces. They are among his most powerful designs, with subjects ranging from the Bible to Shakespeare and Milton. Word and image were further disengaged when, in 1796, the miniature painter Ozias Humphry commissioned a selection of colour-printed designs without texts from Blake's illuminated books. Blake next separated his colouring medium from printing and began to produce his so-called 'tempera' or 'fresco' paintings on biblical subjects. He exhibited two at the Royal Academy, *The Last Supper* in 1799 and *The Loaves and Fishes* in 1800. The temperas were commissioned by Thomas Butts, a clerk to the commissary general of musters, the government office in charge of military pay. Butts became Blake's major patron for his drawings and paintings, hiring him to execute over eighty watercolours, also illustrating the Bible, between 1800 and 1805. Presumably Butts had financial resources beyond his clerk's salary, but the source of additional funds is not known. Perhaps 'like most government servants of the period, the system of fees and patronage allowed him to acquire a modest fortune' (Ackroyd, 206).

Butts is the source for a famous incident related by Gilchrist. Visiting the Blakes while they lived in Lambeth, Butts found the couple nude in their garden summer house. '"*Come in!*" cried Blake; "*it's only Adam and Eve you know!*" Husband and wife had been reciting passages from *Paradise Lost*, in character' (Gilchrist, 1.115). Although friends who met Blake later in his life and Butts's grandson denied the tale, it does not seem out of character for the man who wrote that 'The nakedness of woman is the work of God' and that 'Art can never exist without Naked Beauty displayed' (Blake, 36, 275). Similarly, Tatham's story (Bentley, *Records*, 521) about how 'Blakes blood boiled' when he saw a boy punished by having his foot tied to a log befits the man who wrote

A Robin Red breast in a Cage
Puts all Heaven in a Rage.
(Blake, 490)

Blake began the largest commercial project of his career in 1795. The publisher Richard Edwards contracted Blake to execute designs for Edward Young's then famous poem, *Night Thoughts*, first published in 1742–6. With his usual attention to what he called 'minute particulars' (Blake, 194), Blake carefully translated Young's words into pictures; but by using his own vocabulary of images, Blake created a visual commentary on the poem. By 1797 Blake had produced 537 large watercolours surrounding the printed text of *Night Thoughts*. The modest fee of £21 was probably based on the expectation of much more to follow for engraving the designs. Forty-three plates grace the 1797 volume, the first of four announced, but Edwards closed his business shortly thereafter and no further instalments appeared. Blake's immense labours had failed to produce profit or fame.

The *Night Thoughts* project inspired two others. Blake's 116 watercolours illustrating the poems of Thomas Gray, which repeat the format of the *Night Thoughts* designs, were commissioned in 1797 by Flaxman as a gift for his wife. Probably in the previous year, Blake began to compose an epic, first titled *Vala* and later changed to *The Four Zoas* as layers of revision accumulated. Like Young's poem, Blake's is divided into 'Nights' and treats some of the same vast subjects—life, death, immortality. Blake wraps these issues in his own mythology centred on the Zoas (Urizen, Los, Luvah, Tharmas) and their female counterparts, or 'emanations'. These beings, their speeches, and contentions, represent phenomena both physical and mental, the two being one in Blake's system. Blake probably worked on the manuscript and its marginal drawings, many sexually explicit, until 1807, but finally abandoned a poem that had spiralled beyond control.

Blake's fortunes waned as the new century approached. In August 1799 he told Cumberland that 'even Johnson & Fuseli have discarded my Graver' (Blake, 704). Lacking these employers, Blake turned increasingly to patrons for his paintings and drawings. Among these were Butts, a good friend by 1799, and Dr John Trusler, who commissioned a watercolour of *Malevolence* and apparently tried to instruct the artist in its composition. Blake could not brook interference with his talents and defended his work in two letters of August 1799, the second implying that Trusler was an 'Idiot' (ibid., 702). Patronage ceased.

Another prospect began more propitiously. Blake had been in contact with the popular writer William Hayley, or at least his son Thomas, a student of Flaxman's, since June 1796. By February 1800 Blake was engraving plates for Hayley's *Essay on Sculpture*. Hayley was dissatisfied with Blake's copy of a portrait of Thomas, but Blake seems not to have reacted as he did with Trusler. The professional relationship became more personal when Thomas died in May and Blake wrote a letter of condolence to Hayley comparing the father's grief to his own when, years earlier, Blake's brother had died at a similarly early age. The growing friendship between the men, each perhaps a replacement for the other's loss, was strengthened by Hayley's tendency to take under his wing talented men who, he believed, needed him to direct their genius. Blake was a good candidate, a man of heightened imagination who also possessed artisanal skills Hayley could use advantageously.

Blake visited Hayley in July 1800 at his home in Felpham on the Sussex coast. There they apparently came to an informal agreement: Blake would take up residence in Felpham—he immediately made arrangements to rent a cottage—and Hayley would engage him on several designing and engraving projects. Blake had confessed to Flaxman, in a letter written just before his trip, that he was emerging 'from a Deep pit of Melancholy' (Blake, 706), a return to optimism stimulated by the developing relationship with Hayley. Letters to friends through the summer evince Blake's overwrought joy as he and his wife prepared to move to their new home. He associated the change in residence, an escape from 'Londons Dungeon dark', with financial and artistic independence, for under Hayley's patronage Blake hoped to be sufficiently compensated, yet able to 'be Poet Painter & Musician as the Inspiration comes' (letter to Cumberland, 1 Sept 1800, in *Blake: an Illustrated Quarterly*, 32, 1998, 4–5). The journey took all day, 18 September. The party included Blake's sister Catherine; the seven chaises of household goods included his rolling press.

Interlude in Felpham, 1800–1803 As his letters indicate, Blake's enthusiasm continued once in Sussex. Hayley received him 'with his usual brotherly affection' and Felpham was certain to prove 'propitious to the Arts' (Blake, 710–11). In a letter to Butts of 2 October 1800 Blake included a poem in couplets testifying to his renewed 'Vision' by the sea (ibid., 713). Hayley provided ample employment: a series of portraits of poets to decorate his library; a broadside etched in relief and white-line of Hayley's poem, 'Little Tom the Sailor'; portrait miniatures; illustrations for a series of ballads authored by Hayley and distributed (with scant success) by his friends; and engravings for Hayley's *Life of William Cowper*. In May 1801 Blake reported to Butts that 'Hayley acts like a Prince' and that Felpham remained 'the sweetest spot on Earth' (ibid., 715).

The first dissonant notes emerged from work associated with the biography of Cowper. Beginning in March 1801, Cowper's cousin Lady Harriet Hesketh criticized Blake's miniature, and later his engraving, based on George Romney's portrait of her beloved relation. More generally, Hayley tried to divert Blake from poetry and history painting and direct him into the practical crafts of copy engraving and miniature portraiture. As Blake later jotted in his notebook:

When H—y finds out what you cannot do
That is the Very thing hell set you to.
(Blake, 506)

Although he assisted Blake in acquiring at least a little Latin, Greek, and Hebrew and thereby elevated the London artisan closer to the society of educated gentlemen, differences in class and taste persisted. Hayley treated Blake as a protégé possessing 'admirable Talents' and 'uncommon powers of mind', but also an 'eccentric Soul' evincing 'Touches of nervous Infirmity' verging on 'Insanity' (Hayley's letters in Bentley, *Records*, 83, 87, 106, 164). The decaying relationship with Hayley was compounded with poor health: Catherine Blake's recurring bouts of rheumatism began in November 1800; husband and wife were both ill in spring 1802 and again in January 1803.

Blake's distresses went beyond professional and medical inconvenience. Growing tensions with his patron created, or at least augmented, profound psychic disturbances; indeed, Hayley's characterizations of Blake's mental states may have been reasonably accurate. Blake initially suffered in silence from Hayley's 'Genteel Ignorance & Polite Disapprobation' (letter to Butts, July 1803, Blake, 730), in part because of pecuniary dependence on Hayley's patronage. Such repression produced anguish and a disruption of those extrasensory perceptions that Blake believed to be one with his imagination. He was increasingly torn between fulfilling commissions from Hayley and from Butts, between his calling as an artist and the advice of his more worldly companions (including Hayley, Flaxman, and possibly Catherine Blake), and between temporal and spiritual responsibilities. This fall into a divided consciousness—a dominant motif in much of Blake's poetry—emerges in his letters from the autumn of 1801 to 1803.

In September 1801 Blake confessed to Butts that his 'Abstract folly hurries' him away from 'Duty & Reality' (Blake, 716). If by 'folly' Blake meant his inner visions, then he had become alienated, however temporarily, from the wellsprings of his art. Unspecified distresses led Blake to write, in November 1802, that he had been 'very unhappy', having 'traveld thro Perils & Darkness', but that he had 'again Emerged into the light of Day' with renewed faith in 'him who is the Express image of God' (ibid., letter to Butts, 720). The restoration was short-lived; for several years, Blake's moods alternated between depression and hope, the former expressed in letters and poems through images of darkness, the latter through images of intense illumination and a turn toward Christ as saviour. By January 1803 Blake hinted that Hayley was the 'source' of his difficulties and stated his determination 'not to remain another winter' in Felpham (ibid., 724–5). This letter to Butts and an equally revelatory one to his brother James record Blake's most intimate observations on his practical circumstances and psychological state. Prompted (or excused) by ill health and the impending end of the lease on his cottage, Blake states his determination to distance himself from Hayley's friendship, now seen as malevolent. But why would Hayley, outwardly so mild, appear to Blake as a sneaking serpent?—Because he was 'jealous' of Blake's talents (ibid., 725). Surprisingly, Blake likens Hayley's motivation to similar feelings on Stothard's part. It is difficult to believe that either the popular author or successful illustrator coveted the abilities of a man they considered an engraver needful of their advice, but Blake became convinced that 'Corporeal Friends are Spiritual Enemies' (ibid., 98). Blake concluded that he could 'alone carry on' his 'visionary studies in London unannoyd' by 'the Doubts of other Mortals' (ibid., letter to Butts, 25 April 1803, 728).

Confrontation and acquittal, 1803–1804 Hayley was aware, by May 1803, of Blake's plans to leave Felpham, but the Blakes were still in their cottage when, on 12 August 1803, a private soldier in the 1st regiment of dragoons, John Scolfield, entered the garden. Not knowing that the man was there on the gardener's invitation, Blake told him to leave. Scolfield refused; heated words were exchanged. Finally Blake, short of stature but not of strength, took Scolfield 'by the Elbows & … pushed him forwards down the road' (letter to Butts, 16 Aug 1803, Blake, 732). The confrontation, witnessed in its final stages by several villagers and Scolfield's fellow soldier John Cock, ended at The Fox inn, a public house where Scolfield may have been drinking. Three days later Scolfield went before the Chichester justice of the peace, John Quantock, and accused Blake of seditious expressions favouring the French and damning the king of England. Blake refuted the charges vigorously but was ordered to appear at the Michaelmas quarter sessions of the court (Bentley, *Records*, 124–8). Blake's bond of £200 was paid by the accused, Hayley, and Joseph Seagrave, a local printer who had worked with both men. At its sessions on 4 October in Petworth, the grand jury returned bills indicting Blake for sedition against king and country and assault against Scolfield. Blake pleaded not guilty, but it would hardly have been inconsistent with Blake's anti-monarchical views, so evident in his work of the 1790s, to have damned the king while struggling with one of his soldiers.

Blake was 'in anguish', as he states among the inscriptions he cut into a glass rummer in August (Bentley, *Records Supplement*, 24). And not without cause, for sedition was a grave charge at a time when England was fearful of Napoleonic invasion on the coastline where Blake resided. The encounter with Scolfield and its legal consequences increased Blake's paranoia and influenced his writings and friendships for years. He was initially grateful to Hayley for his support and regretful of earlier misgivings, even asking Butts to 'burn what I have peevishly written about any friend' (letter, 16 Aug 1803, Blake, 733). Yet gratitude can become a burden and the benefactor insufferable in the mind of the debtor. Such may have led Blake to believe, contrary to all appearances, that Hayley was implicated in a conspiracy against him, and thus to write a few years later in his notebook that Hayley, having failed to

> act upon my wife
> Hired a Villain to bereave my Life.
> (Blake, 506)

The Blakes moved to London in September, staying briefly with James Blake before taking rooms at 17 South Molton Street, Westminster, on the edge of Mayfair. Blake returned to Sussex in October to answer the indictment and again for trial on 11 January 1804 in the Chichester Guildhall. He was represented at trial by Samuel Rose, a London barrister retained and paid by Hayley. Before the duke of Richmond and six other magistrates, Rose opened his defence by acknowledging the seriousness of the charge of sedition, impugning Scolfield's character, and insisting on the defendant's innocence. Rose's speech was cut short by illness, but several witnesses testified on Blake's behalf and he was acquitted of all charges.

Commerce and poetry, 1804 Shortly after his return to London, Blake complained that 'Every Engraver turns away work … Yet no one brings work to me'. He had little taste for the hurly-burly of the commercial arts in 'a City of [character] Assassinations' (letters to Hayley, 7 Oct 1803 and 28 May 1804, Blake, 736, 751). Blake had to rely on friends, principally Fuseli, Flaxman, and Hayley, for engraving commissions. He assisted Hayley in preparation for a biography of Romney and negotiated with the publisher Richard Phillips for an edition of Hayley's ballads with new engravings of Blake's illustrations. Blake invested in the 1805 *Ballads*, but probably lost money. For the Romney biography Blake began to engrave two plates, but only one appeared in the 1809 volume. Commissions for most of the Romney engravings, and for plates in a new edition of the Cowper biography, were given to Caroline Watson, whose softer style Hayley preferred. Blake must have been disappointed, but he told his patron that 'the Idea of Seeing' Watson's *Engraving of Cowper* was 'a pleasing one' (letter, 22 March 1805, Blake, 764). This and other insincerities prompted by financial dependence led Blake to scrawl in his notebook,

> I write the Rascal thanks till he & I
> With Thanks & Compliments are quite drawn dry.

Another couplet addressed 'To H—' summarizes Blake's view of the relationship:

> Thy Friendship oft has made my heart to ake
> Do be my Enemy for Friendships sake.
> (Blake, 506)

In October 1804 Catherine Blake received electrical treatment for her rheumatism that reduced 'the swelling of her legs and knees' (Blake, 756). Blake reported, in this same letter to Hayley, an equally dramatic restoration in his psychic condition. After visiting the Truchsessian Gallery, an exhibition of paintings dubiously attributed to artists such as Michelangelo and Rembrandt, Blake 'was again enlightened with the light' he had enjoyed in his youth. 'I am really drunk with intellectual vision … as I have not been for twenty dark, but very profitable years'. Blake had 'reduced … to his station' the 'Spectrous Fiend'—a personification of those distresses internal and external that had led him astray as an artist, 'incessantly labouring and incessantly spoiling' his work (ibid., 756–7). Blake remained ebullient in early December, telling Hayley that he had 'fought thro a Hell of terrors & horrors … in a Divided Existence now no longer Divided' (ibid., letter, 4 Dec 1804, 758). While it is difficult to discern any significant change in Blake's pictorial art datable to autumn 1804, his improved spirits may have affected his labours as a poet, an activity known to few, and appreciated by none, except for his wife.

When still in Felpham, Blake had begun to compose in his notebook (and probably in separate drafts now lost) a group of short poems integrating his mythic structures and imagery with a more personal, often anguished, voice. A few years later, Blake wrote out in a clear hand ten poems of a similar tenor in what is now known as the Pickering manuscript, including 'The Mental Traveller' and 'Auguries of Innocence'. It may have been about this time that Blake began to rise 'in the middle of the night' and 'write for two hours or more', often with Catherine Blake at his side (Smith in Bentley, *Records*, 475; Gilchrist, 1.316). His renewed poetic instinct culminated in two epics in illuminated printing, *Milton* and *Jerusalem*, dated 1804 on their title-pages. Both evolved out of, and incorporated many passages from, *The Four Zoas* manuscript. As Blake reported to Butts, these interrelated poems were written 'from immediate Dictation ... without Premeditation'. The result was a 'Sublime Allegory' of which Blake was 'the Secretary' for 'Authors ... in Eternity' (letters, 25 April and 6 July 1803, Blake, 729–30). All three poems turn from political revolution and toward mental reconfigurations leading to biblical apocalypse. All three question conventional suppositions about imagination and reality, time and space, self and other, to entertain alternative ways of thinking and being at the core of Blake's visionary literalism.

Milton, not printed until 1810–11, follows the titular hero in a journey of self-discovery and renewal that also reconstructs the bond between Blake and his great predecessor. In the poem's second 'Book', Milton unites with his feminine aspect, Ololon, in progress towards the apocalyptic overcoming of divisions between the sexes, between the living and the dead, and between mind and its projections into the external world. This plot is interwoven with allusions ranging from the Bible to Blake's own life, particularly the difficult relationship with Hayley. The lyric beginning 'And did those feet in ancient time', now well known as the hymn 'Jerusalem', appears in the 'Preface' to *Milton*.

The illuminated book entitled *Jerusalem*, the one hundred plates of which were not completed until 1820, takes for its subject all of history as a record of desire struggling for fulfilment. The cast of characters is vast, with Los (the artist's imagination at work in the material world), Jerusalem and Albion (the female and male portions of divided humanity who must be reunited), the nature goddess Vala, and Jesus playing major roles. The poem is divided into four chapters, each with a preface addressed to a different audience (the Public, the Jews, the Deists, the Christians), and concludes with a vision of consciousness, liberated and empowered, in a post-apocalyptic universe. Blake beautifully hand-coloured one complete copy of *Jerusalem*, but it remained unsold at his death.

Patronage and the arts, 1805–1817 Blake's commercial prospects (and probably his spirits) were again rising when, late in the summer of 1805, he was commissioned by the engraver and would-be publisher Robert H. Cromek to illustrate Robert Blair's poem *The Grave*, first published in 1743. Blake quickly produced about twenty designs for 'the insignificant sum of one guinea each' (Smith in Bentley, *Records*, 464). Fifteen were selected for Blake to engrave, as Cromek announced in a November prospectus. Blake etched one design, *Death's Door*, as an example; Cromek exhibited it, along with the drawings, at his shop. The darkly reticulated white-line etching proved so out of step with contemporary tastes that Cromek soon hired the fashionable engraver Louis Schiavonetti to engrave all twelve designs actually published. Blake's loss of this potentially lucrative commission motivated his detached mood, as 'one who cares little for this World', in his letter of 11 December 1805 to Hayley (Blake, 767). Relations with Cromek may have remained polite until the publisher rejected Blake's dedicatory vignette 'To the Queen' in May 1807. Blake recorded his opinion of Cromek in his notebook:

> Cr— loves artists as he loves his Meat
> He loves the Art but tis the Art to Cheat.
> (ibid., 509)

When *The Grave* finally appeared in 1808, it included a frontispiece based on Thomas Phillips's 1807 portrait of Blake. The painting emphasizes Blake's hypnotic eyes, by all accounts his most prominent feature and even more evident in an anonymous wash drawing (probably a self-portrait) of *c.*1803.

The unhappy results of Blake's dealings with Cromek did not forestall another attempt to reach a wide audience. Blake began preparations in 1806 for a panoramic engraving of Chaucer's Canterbury pilgrims starting on their journey. The project was soon embroiled in controversy. When Blake learned that Stothard was painting a similar scene for Cromek, he believed that the publisher, having first commissioned Blake's design and seen the preliminary drawings, had stolen his idea. Although Stothard was almost certainly innocent of any double-dealing, Blake was furious with his old companion. *Chaucer's Canterbury Pilgrims*, Blake's largest print, found few purchasers when he published it in 1810. The engraving of Stothard's version, published in 1817, was a popular success.

The *Grave* and Canterbury imbroglios, coupled with reactions to his work of the sort represented by Robert Southey's condescending review of the 1805 *Ballads* illustrations, led to Blake's discomfort with commerce in the arts. He felt 'stigmatised as an engraver, who might do tolerably well, if he was not mad' (Malkin in Bentley, *Records*, 424). A few words Blake jotted in his notebook offer an even darker self-description: 'Tuesday Jan[ry]. 20. 1807 between Two & Seven in the Evening—Despair' (Blake, 694).

There are no known commercial engravings from Blake's hand between 1806 and 1813. Sales to Butts of watercolours, paintings, a set of the large colour prints designed in 1795, and several illuminated books became a major source of income. During a five-year period beginning in 1806, Butts paid Blake over £400, including fees for teaching engraving to his son (Bentley, *Records*, 175–6). Among the more important projects were series of watercolours illustrating Milton's major poems. The Revd Joseph Thomas commissioned a group of eight designs for *Comus* in 1801, followed by *Paradise Lost* (1807) and 'On the Morning of Christ's Nativity' (1809). Between 1808 and 1815, Blake produced similar sets for Butts, to which he added twelve illustrations to 'L'allegro' and 'Il penseroso' about 1816–20. Perhaps prompted by the 'Day of Judgment' design he drew for Blair's *Grave*, Blake painted a more elaborate watercolour of that subject for Butts in 1806. A year later, the countess of Egremont commissioned a similar watercolour, for which Blake wrote a detailed description. Patronage supplied what commerce denied.

The 1808 Royal Academy exhibition included two of Blake's watercolours, but a year later he complained that his designs were 'regularly refused' by the academy (Blake, 527). Blake took matters into his own hands and, in May 1809, opened an exhibition of his tempera paintings and watercolours at the family home, 28 Broad Street, now occupied by his brother James. The display may have lasted until June 1810, when Charles and Mary Lamb saw Blake's paintings. Among the sixteen works were 'Apotheoses' ('Prospectus', Blake, 527) of Admiral Nelson, William Pitt, and Napoleon; the tempera of Chaucer's pilgrims; *Satan Calling up his Legions*; and *The Ancient Britons*, Blake's largest painting, commissioned by the Welsh antiquary William Owen Pughe, now lost but reported to have been 10 by 14 feet. A letterpress *Descriptive Catalogue* contains notes on each design, the longest an analysis of Chaucer's characters and the errors in Stothard's portrayal. This catalogue, along with the harshly critical annotations of *c.*1808 to Joshua Reynolds's *Discourses* and the 'Public address' and 'A vision of the last judgment' Blake drafted in his notebook *c.*1810, presents his basic aesthetic concepts: the rejection of classical art in favour of a synthesis of the Hebraic and the Gothic (also boldly stated in the 'Preface' to *Milton* and there intertwined with a rejection of Hayley's tastes), the superiority of line to colour (in part an inheritance from Blake's training as a line engraver), and the unity of conception and execution (in part a reaction against the complaint that Blake could conceive but could not adequately execute his sublime images). As he wrote in the 'Public address', 'Resentment for Personal Injuries' played a role in shaping Blake's views (Blake, 574).

There is no record of sales resulting from the 1809 exhibition. The single review, by Robert Hunt in *The Examiner* on 16 September 1809, mocked the paintings and branded the artist 'an unfortunate lunatic' (Bentley, *Records*, 216). After 1810, even commissions from Butts appear to have slowed as Blake sank deeper into obscurity and into his visions as he laboured on *Jerusalem* and on another painting of the last judgment, measuring 7 feet by 5 and 'containing upwards of one thousand figures' (Smith in Bentley, *Records*, 467), left unsold at Blake's death and now lost. It was during this period that Catherine Blake told the artist Seymour Kirkup, 'I have very little of Mr. Blake's company; he is always in Paradise'. In June 1814, George Cumberland's son found Blake 'still poor still Dirty'—the dirt probably ink from printing copperplates (Bentley, *Records*, 221, 232). After a period of coolness between the two in 1808, Blake was once again on good terms with Flaxman, on whose recommendation Blake received, by September 1814, the commission to engrave Flaxman's thirty-seven outline illustrations to Hesiod. Without this employment, lasting until 1817, and work (also gained with Flaxman's help) engraving illustrations for Rees's *Cyclopaedia* and Wedgwood's catalogue of earthenware, the Blakes might have fallen into dire poverty.

New friends and projects, 1818–1826 The artist John Linnell visited Blake in June 1818 and hired him to etch the preliminary stages of a portrait of James Upton. From this modest beginning developed a relationship that shaped the final nine years of Blake's life. Although Linnell was thirty-five years Blake's junior, they became good friends, attending art exhibitions and the theatre together. After Linnell moved to Hampstead in March 1824, Blake, always a great walker, often made the uphill journey on foot. There he 'sang, in a voice tremulous with age, sometimes old ballads, sometimes his own songs, to [unrecorded] melodies of his own' (Gilchrist, 1.294).

The artist John Varley was among the first in a new circle of friends to which Linnell introduced Blake. During séance-like sessions, beginning in October 1819 and intermittently repeated during the next six years, Blake drew for Varley over one hundred 'Visionary Heads' of persons historical (Edward I, William Wallace) and spiritual (*The Man who Taught Blake Painting in his Dreams*). Varley, prompted by his interests in physiognomy and astrology, apparently believed in the literal presence of these figures. Blake may have taken the conjurations less seriously, yet his belief in the reality of imaginative apperception is consistent with visionary portraiture. Blake developed one of his more bizarre images, *The Ghost of a Flea*, into a tempera painting; Linnell's engravings of the creature's anthropomorphic head were published in Varley's *Treatise on Zodiacal Physiognomy* (1828).

In September 1819 Linnell introduced Blake to his family physician, Robert Thornton, who soon after hired Blake to design illustrations for Ambrose Philips's 'Imitation' of Virgil's first eclogue to appear in the third edition of Thornton's school text of Virgil. Blake first produced a relief etching of four small vignettes. These were rejected, probably for reasons both technical and stylistic. As with the *Grave* project years earlier, Blake had failed to introduce one of his special graphic methods into a commercial publication. He next prepared twenty-one wash drawings—apparently accepted by Thornton and his publishers—and executed seventeen as wood-engravings. These were so ruggedly different from established conventions that they would have been excluded from Thornton's 1821 edition except for praise from several respected artists, including Sir Thomas Lawrence. The images of melancholy and disruption pictured in Blake's only engravings in wood suggest that Virgil's pastoral lament reminded Blake of his own pastoral sojourn in Felpham under Hayley's burdensome patronage.

Blake's financial circumstances had not improved by the early 1820s; indeed, he may have become poorer. In 1821 he sold his collection of old master prints and moved to just two rooms at 3 Fountain Court, Strand. Blake received a charitable grant of £25 from the Royal Academy in June 1822; Thomas Lawrence also assisted with a gift of money. Blake persevered through these trying times, painting in 1821 one of his most mysterious allegorical designs, *The Sea of Time and Space*, illustrating Milton's *Paradise Regained* with twelve watercolours, and in 1822 etching in relief two brief works, *On Homers Poetry* [and] *On Virgil*, a disquisition on the errors of classicism, and *The Ghost of Abel*, a response to Byron's *Cain: a Mystery*. In the latter, Blake emphasizes the need for forgiveness, suggesting that Blake was seeking release from self-defeating anger through the forgiveness of erstwhile enemies.

Linnell's commissions may have been motivated in part by a desire to provide the ageing artist with a regular income. Blake had produced for Butts a series of nineteen watercolour illustrations to the book of Job in 1805–6. Linnell traced these in September 1821; Blake later coloured the tracings and added two more designs. This work provided the basis for the contract, signed by Linnell and Blake on 25 March 1823, to engrave the Job illustrations. The commission provided Blake an income of about £1 a week from 1823 through 1825. The task proved arduous, for Blake engraved the plates without preliminary etching, and the twenty-one designs plus an engraved title-page were not published until March 1825. Blake's graphic retelling of the story begins with Job's blind adherence to the letter of the law; follows Job and his wife through miseries inflicted by Satan, a projection of Job's false vision; and concludes with Job restored to prosperity, the physical sign of his spiritual awakening. Blake's mastery of traditional line engraving in the Job illustrations recalls the Renaissance artists he so much admired, particularly Dürer; but the interplay between darkness and light exhibited throughout the series may have been influenced by Linnell's engraving style. This revival of traditional graphics prompted Blake, probably at some point after 1818, to return to intaglio plates he had executed years earlier, including *Joseph of Arimathea* and the large *Job* and *Ezekiel* separate plates, thoroughly to revise them and add new inscriptions. The emblems *For Children* became *For the Sexes: the Gates of Paradise*.

Through Linnell, a group of young artists met Blake and came to admire him greatly, both for his character and his art. They looked upon him as a seer or Old Testament prophet come to life; in turn, Blake's peace of mind was enhanced by finding a worshipful audience. Samuel Palmer, only nineteen when first recorded in Blake's company in May 1824, would kiss the 'bell-handle' before entering Blake's home, which the group called 'the House of the Interpreter' after a passage in Bunyan's *Pilgrim's Progress* illustrated by one of Blake's white-line etchings (Bentley, *Records*, 292, 295). George Richmond was the most influenced by the figural style of Blake's art. Works by Palmer and Edward Calvert reveal their profound debt to the Virgil wood-engravings, described by Palmer as 'visions of … Paradise; models of the exquisitest pitch of intense poetry' (ibid., 271). This loose brotherhood of Blake followers, one that also included Francis Oliver Finch, Frederick Tatham, and Welby Sherman, called themselves 'The Ancients' and often sought their own intense responses to nature in the environs of Shoreham, Kent, which Blake visited in late summer 1825.

Blake's youthful associations, perhaps rich with memories of the lost bond with his brother Robert, were complemented by gatherings at the home of Linnell's patrons Charles and Elizabeth Aders. There Blake met Henry Crabb Robinson, who had written an article about Blake in 1811 for a German periodical and had discussed Blake's poems with William Wordsworth and Samuel Taylor Coleridge. Late in 1825, Robinson began to record Blake's conversations, including gnomic observations uttered in all honesty, but in such a way as to perplex the audience. Robinson writes in his *Reminiscences* that Blake said:

> the most strange things in the most unemphatic manner, speaking of his *visions* as any man would of the most ordinary occurances. '… I was Socrates'—and then as if he had gone too far in that—'Or a sort of brother—I must have had conversations with him—So I had with Jesus Christ.' … Concerning the imputed Divinity of Jesus Christ He answered—'he is the only God'—but then he added—'and so am I and so are you'. (Robinson in Bentley, *Records*, 538–40)

As in *The Marriage of Heaven and Hell* and the 'Visionary Heads', Blake again intertwined the profound and the playful.

Continued creativity, in spite of declining health, characterizes Blake's final years. He executed a separate etching/engraving of the *Laocoön* *c*.1826, surrounding the famous Hellenistic sculpture with aphorisms on the unity of art and religion and the evils of money and empire. New customers for the *Songs of Innocence and of Experience* led Blake to print and elaborately hand colour five copies in the last three years of his life. In the summer of 1824, long before the Job engravings were completed, Linnell commissioned an even larger project, the illustration of Dante's *Divine Comedy*, which provided Blake an income of about £2 a week. He 'applied himself to learning Italian' (Gilchrist, 1.334) and produced 102 watercolours which, like the seven Dante engravings, remained incomplete at his death. Other endeavours cut short by mortality included twenty-nine watercolour illustrations to Bunyan's *Pilgrim's Progress*, begun in 1824, and an illuminated manuscript of Genesis.

The final months, 1827 Blake began, in the spring of 1825, to have periodic bouts of 'Shivering Fit[s]' and 'Ague'—perhaps a return of the abdominal maladies he had suffered in Felpham (letters to Linnell, Blake, 773–4). Although growing ever weaker in the winter of 1826–7, he carried on heroically with the Dante designs and a small calling card for his old friend Cumberland. In April 1827 Blake told Cumberland that he had been 'near the Gates of Death & have returned very weak & an Old Man feeble & tottering, but not in Spirit & Life not in The Real Man The Imagination which Liveth for Ever' (Blake, 783). A failing liver caused jaundice, but still he laboured on. According to Tatham, in his last few days Blake coloured an impression of the *Ancient of Days* (the frontispiece to *Europe*) and drew Catherine Blake's portrait (Bentley, *Records*, 527–8).

Blake died at 3 Fountain Court on 12 August 1827. Three days later, Richmond informed Palmer that Blake

> died on Sunday Night at 6 Oclock in a most glorious manner. He said He was going to that Country he had all His life wished to see & expressed Himself Happy hoping for Salvation through Jesus Christ—Just before he died His Countenance became fair—His eyes brighten'd and He burst out in Singing of the things he Saw in Heaven. (Bentley, *Records*, 346–47)

The precise cause of Blake's death is not known, but the most detailed analysis of the symptoms suggests biliary cirrhosis, possibly caused by years of inhaling cupreous fumes while etching (Robson and Viscomi). Blake was buried on 17 August at Bunhill Fields, Finsbury, traditionally a cemetery for nonconformists where his parents and other family members were interred. Yet, according to Smith, Blake had requested a funeral service 'of the Church of England' (Bentley, *Records*, 476). Catherine Blake went to live with Linnell, but after about six months she moved to Tatham's home, where she served as housekeeper. In 1829 the earl of Egremont purchased from her Blake's *The Characters in Spenser's Faerie Queene*, a companion to the Canterbury pilgrims painting, for 80 guineas, a sum sufficient to supply her needs for the rest of her life. She died on 18 October 1831, leaving to Tatham the remaining stock of Blake's works, possibly including manuscripts which Tatham destroyed. After reprinting some of Blake's illuminated books, he claimed that most of the copperplates had been stolen (Gilchrist, 1.126); only one small fragment of a relief-etched plate has survived.

Nineteenth-century reputation The mythologizing of Blake's life began with the (embellished?) descriptions of his final days written by friends who considered him a sage. A different characterization emerged in obituaries: Blake was 'one of those ingenious persons … whose eccentricities were still more remarkable than their professional abilities' (*Literary Chronicle*, 1 Sept 1827, in Bentley, *Records*, 351). J. T. Smith's reasonably straightforward memoir of 1828 was followed two years later by Allan Cunningham's more dramatic account of Visionary Blake, a compound of genius and madness. For the next three decades, Blake was remembered primarily as a psychological curiosity, his poetry unknown beyond *Songs of Innocence and of Experience* (first published in letterpress in 1839), his designs little known beyond the illustrations to Blair's *Grave*.

Alexander Gilchrist's *Life of William Blake* (1863) soon belied its subtitle, 'Pictor ignotus', by bringing the man and his work to the attention of a far larger audience than he had previously commanded. Although he rarely indicates his sources, Gilchrist includes information learned from people who had known Blake. Gilchrist died two years before publication; his widow saw the biography through the final stages of its production, assisted by Dante Gabriel Rossetti and his brother William Michael, whose catalogue of Blake's art appeared in the second volume of the work. Arguably the most important book ever published on Blake, Gilchrist's biography sets Blake within his intellectual and social milieu, but presents him as a secular saint—a perspective influenced by Thomas Carlyle's theories of the artist as hero. Growing interest in Blake led to the first exhibition devoted to his art at the Burlington Fine Arts Club (London) in 1876.

Algernon Charles Swinburne, also a Blake enthusiast in the Gilchrist/Rossetti circle, published the first book-length study of Blake's poetry in 1868. A heterodox and revolutionary Blake emerges in Swinburne's critique, one that includes high praise for *The Marriage of Heaven and Hell*. While even Swinburne could do little more with Blake's later poetry than extract brief passages for comment, Edwin John Ellis and William Butler Yeats plunged headlong into the apparent chaos. Unfortunately, their three-volume edition and study of 1893 is marred by poor scholarship, a Procrustean notion of mystic symbolism, and a belief that Blake was Irish.

Twentieth-century reputation John Sampson brought scholarly expertise to the editing of Blake's poetry in 1905, but a full and accurate edition of Blake's writings was still wanting. The challenge was taken up by Geoffrey Keynes, who more than any other individual shaped the public perception of Blake in the twentieth century. In 1921 Keynes published a detailed bibliography of Blake's writings, engraved book illustrations, and texts about him, followed four years later by a complete edition. Keynes continued to produce editions and scholarly essays devoted to Blake until his death in 1982. He was the key figure in founding in 1949 the William Blake Trust, which sponsored publication of facsimiles of the illuminated books (1951–76) and a second series of more affordable reproductions with scholarly introductions (1991–5).

Joseph Wicksteed's commentary on the Job engravings (1910) set a new standard for the study of Blake's pictorial art; S. Foster Damon's *William Blake: his Philosophy and Symbols* (1924) made a similar but more extensive contribution to the study of Blake's ideas and poetry, thereby initiating the critical appreciation of Blake in the United States. His reputation continued to develop in America through the inter-war years, assisted by major collectors (particularly Henry Huntington and Lessing Rosenwald) and a comprehensive exhibition of his works in Philadelphia in 1939; but it was not until 1947, with the publication of Northrop Frye's *Fearful Symmetry*, that Blake's reputation as a poet began an exponential ascent. By setting Blake within a tradition of poetry extending from the Bible to Virgil, Spenser to Milton, Frye's book, more than any other single study, established Blake as a defining presence in the pantheon of English Romantic poetry, the equal of Wordsworth and Coleridge. Seven years later, David Erdman's *Blake: Prophet Against Empire: a Poet's Interpretation of the History of his Own Time*, constructed an alternative foundation for the scholarly understanding of Blake in the second half of the century. Whereas Frye's perspective tended to emphasize a unifying system in Blake's work, nascent at the beginning and fleshed out in the later (and now fully appreciated) epics, Erdman perceived an evolution in response to shifting events in a revolutionary age. Frye's Blake rose above history; Erdman's Blake was fully engaged in time.

By the last two decades of the century, Erdman's view became dominant, as a host of scholars set Blake within various historical and cultural contexts, ranging from printmaking to radical protestant and political groups. Others argued for Blake as a prophet of twentieth-century intellectual fashions, finding him a Marxist, Freudian, or deconstructionist *avant la lettre*. The illuminated books, with their complex interactions between words and pictures, remained at the centre of critical debate, but every document, visual and verbal, received attention. During this same period, all requisite scholarly tools were produced: editions true to Blake's unconventional spelling and punctuation; a concordance to his writings; an exhaustive bibliography; complete catalogues of his paintings, drawings, and prints; several biographies; a journal-of-record devoted to its eponymous hero; and, by the century's final decade, an electronic archive on the internet. 'Blake' signified an academic industry as much as a man.

Blake's influence on the arts and on popular culture forms an important part of his twentieth-century legacy. In 1916 Charles Hubert Parry set to music the 'Jerusalem' lyric from *Milton*; it soon became one of the most sung hymns in the Church of England. The dramatic postures in Blake's Job designs led Keynes to conceive of the ballet *Job*, which débuted in 1931 with music by Ralph Vaughan Williams, stage and costume designs by Gwendolen Raverat, and choreography by Ninette de Valois. Except for his profound effect on Yeats, Blake was not a major influence on twentieth-century British poetry. In America, however, the important poets Theodore Roethke and Allen Ginsberg, and the author and illustrator Maurice Sendak, considered themselves inspired by Blake. His impact on the visual arts was similarly limited, but intensely felt in the 1920s by a group of young printmakers, including Graham Sutherland.

By mid-century Blake had become one of the cultural icons of the English-speaking world. The British Museum, the British Library, and the Tate Gallery housed important collections of his works, as did the National Gallery of Victoria in Melbourne, Australia, and several major institutions in the United States, including the National Gallery of Art, Washington, DC, the Yale University Center for British Art, and the Museum of Fine Arts in Boston. Single drawings and letters fetched at auction more than Blake made in his lifetime; copies of his illuminated books sold for over £1 million. 'The Tyger' from *Songs of Experience* became the most anthologized text in the language, *The Ancient of Days* one of the most widely recognized images. The installation of Jacob Epstein's bust of Blake in Westminster Abbey in 1957 signalled Blake's acceptance by the establishment; in the next decade he became a hero to a youthful counter-culture. 'The road of excess leads to the palace of wisdom' (Blake, 35) and other energetic outbursts in Blake's writings became rallying cries for those advocating political, sensual, and intellectual liberation.

Blake's reputation reached international proportions by the end of the century. Translations of his poetry were complemented by exhibitions of his art in Germany, Italy, Japan, Israel, and Spain. In his homeland, a single sculptural response epitomized Blake's stature. Eduardo Paolozzi's monumental bronze of Isaac Newton, installed in the forecourt of the new British Library in 1995, copies Blake's *Newton* colour print of 1795. Britain entered a new millennium with the image of its greatest scientist, placed at the entry to its greatest repository of knowledge, shaped by the vision of William Blake.

ROBERT N. ESSICK

Sources W. Blake, *Complete poetry and prose*, ed. D. V. Erdman, rev. edn (1982) [source of quotations here] • D. V. Erdman, ed., *A concordance to the writings of William Blake*, 2 vols. (1967) • G. E. Bentley, *Blake records* (1969) [incl. early biographical accounts by B. H. Malkin (1806), J. T. Smith (1828), A. Cunningham (1830), F. Tatham (c.1833), and H. C. Robinson (1852)] • G. E. Bentley, *Blake records supplement* (1988) • A. Gilchrist, *Life of William Blake, 'Pictor ignotus'*, 2 vols. (1863) • A. Gilchrist, *Life of William Blake*, enl. edn, 2 vols. (1880) • A. Gilchrist, *Life of William Blake*, ed. R. Todd, [new edn] (1942) • G. Keynes, *Blake studies: essays on his life and works*, 2nd edn (1971) • G. Keynes, *Complete portraiture of William and Catherine Blake* (1977) • M. Wilson, *Life of William Blake* (1927) • P. Ackroyd, *Blake* (1995) • L. Robson and J. Viscomi, 'Blake's death', *Blake: an Illustrated Quarterly*, 30 (1996), 36–49 • A. Ward, 'William Blake and the hagiographers', *Biography and source studies*, ed. F. R. Karl (1994), 1–24 • G. E. Bentley, Jr., *Blake books: annotated catalogues of William Blake's writings*, rev. edn (1977) • G. E. Bentley, Jr., *Supplement* (1995) [to *Blake books*] • N. Frye, *Fearful symmetry: a study of William Blake* (1947) • D. V. Erdman, *Blake: prophet against empire* (1954) • S. F. Damon, *William Blake: his philosophy and symbols* (1924) • A. C. Swinburne, *William Blake* (1868) • D. Bindman, *Blake as an artist* (1977) • D. V. Erdman, *The illuminated Blake* (1974) • R. N. Essick, *William Blake, printmaker* (Princeton, NJ, 1980) • M. D. Paley, *Energy and the imagination: a study of the development of Blake's thought* (1970) • J. Viscomi, *Blake and the idea of the book* (1993) • M. Eaves, *William Blake's theory of art* (1982) • William Blake archive, www.blakearchive.org

Archives Harvard U., Houghton L., papers • Hunt. L., letters, marginalia, and drawings • L. Cong., papers • Morgan L., MSS • NYPL, Berg Collection, MSS • Princeton University, New Jersey, MSS • Rosenbach Foundation, Philadelphia, MSS • Trinity College, Hartford, Connecticut, papers • Yale U., Beinecke L., MSS | BL, notebook, Add. MS 49460 • BL, corresp. with George Cumberland, Add. MSS 36498, 36501 • City Westm. AC, corresp. with Thomas Butts

Likenesses T. Stothard, group portrait, etching, c.1780–1781, BM • probably by W. Blake, self-portrait, wash drawing, c.1803, priv. coll. • J. Flaxman, pencil, 1804, FM Cam. • J. Flaxman, pencil, c.1804, Yale U. CBA • T. Phillips, oils, 1807, NPG [*see illus.*] • W. Blake, self-portrait, pencil sketch, before 1810, BL, Blake's notebook, p. 67 • J. Linnell, portraits, pencil drawings, 1820–25, FM Cam. • J. Linnell, watercolour on ivory miniature, 1821, FM Cam. • J. S. Deville, plaster cast life mask, 1823, FM Cam., NPG • G. Richmond, drawings, 1825–c.1859, FM Cam. • attrib. C. Blake, pencil, c.1828, FM Cam. • F. Tatham, sepia wash and pencil, c.1830, Yale U. CBA • J. Linnell, watercolour drawing (after his miniature, 1821), NPG • L. Schiavonetti, engraving (after T. Phillips, 1807), repro. in R. Blair, *The grave* (1808)

Blake, William (1773–1821), Presbyterian minister, was born on 29 March 1773 at Crewkerne, Somerset, the second son in the family of five children of William Blake (1730–1799), who was married twice, a former pupil of Philip Doddridge at Northampton and Presbyterian minister at Crewkerne, 1754–98. He came from a long line of Presbyterian ministers in the west of England. The younger Blake was educated at Litton, Dorset, and then at the free school in Crewkerne, before going to the academy at Northampton in 1790, where he studied under John Horsey.

Blake preached for a year at Yeovil in 1793, and was chosen to succeed his father at Crewkerne, where he remained for the rest of his life. A humanitarian in his Christology, he published *Devotional Services for the Public Worship of one True God* (1812) and one of his sermons, *Private Judgement* (1810).

Blake married twice, leaving one son and three daughters. He died on 18 February 1821.

ALEXANDER GORDON, *rev.* ANNE PIMLOTT BAKER

Sources J. Murch, *A history of the Presbyterian and General Baptist churches in the west of England* (1835), 244–8 · S. Smith, *Monthly Repository*, 16 (1821), 262–8
Likenesses M. Haughton, stipple (after F. Webb), NPG

Blakeley, William [*real name* William Stone Baseley] (**1830–1897**), actor, of whose early life nothing is known, played as an amateur at the Gough Street Theatre (later pulled down) and at the Soho Theatre (later named the Royalty). His first professional appearance was at the Theatre Royal, Dublin, with Sir William Don. At the Amphitheatre, Liverpool, he performed as Polonius and in other parts, and he accompanied Edward Sothern on tour, playing Asa Trenchard to his Lord Dundreary in Tom Taylor's *Our American Cousin*. He made his London début on 21 December 1867 at the Prince of Wales's Theatre, Tottenham Street, as Sir Abel Hotspur in Dion Boucicault's *How She Loves Him*, having played the same role at the Prince of Wales's Theatre, Liverpool, in 1863. Among his most notable parts in the next few years were that of the original Bodmin Todder in T. W. Robertson's *Play*, John Chodd senior in a revival of the same author's *Society*, and Mr Tweedie in Yates's *Tame Cats*.

After accompanying Sothern to America in 1880, Blakeley appeared at the Criterion on 23 July 1881 as Jeremiah Deeds in *Flats in Four Stories* (*Les locataires de Monsieur Blondeau*), adapted by G. R. Sims. It was this theatre with which his name was principally associated, and where he played comedy roles in the revivals of F. C. Burnand's *Betsy*, James Albery's *Pink Dominos*, and Taylor's *Still Waters Run Deep*. Some of his most successful original characters at this theatre arose out of his skilful delineation of old men, from Talbot in Gilbert's *Foggerty's Fairy* (1881) to the hen-pecked old General Bletchingley in Burnand's *Headless Man* (1890). At Daly's Theatre in 1895 he appeared as Smoggins in *An Artist's Model* and Duckworth Crabbe in *The Chili Widow*. His last appearance in London was on 17 July 1897 at the Criterion, as Thomas Tyndal in Walter Stokes Craven's *Four Little Girls*.

Besides being what was known as a 'mugger', or maker of comic faces, Blakeley was a genuine comedian, and was particularly successful as Hardcastle in *She Stoops to Conquer*. In showing self-importance, in airs of assumed dignity, and in the revelation of scandalized propriety, he stood alone. Blakeley, who had been married, died at Criterion House, Clovelly Terrace, Walham Green, London, on 8 December 1897, and was buried in Fulham cemetery on 13 December.

Joseph Knight, *rev.* Nilanjana Banerji

Sources *The Era* (11 Dec 1897) · Adams, *Drama* · E. Reid and H. Compton, eds., *The dramatic peerage* [1891] · *The life and reminiscences of E. L. Blanchard, with notes from the diary of Wm. Blanchard*, ed. C. W. Scott and C. Howard, 2 vols. (1891) · personal knowledge (1901) · Boase, *Mod. Eng. biog.* · *ILN* (18 Dec 1897), 877
Likenesses portrait (as Vanderpump), repro. in *ILN*

Blakely, Fletcher (**1783–1862**), non-subscribing Presbyterian minister, was born on 13 May 1783 at Ballyroney, co. Down. He was the youngest son of Joseph Bleakly, a farmer, and was named after the Revd William Fletcher (*d.* 1824), Presbyterian minister of Ballyroney, who gave him his early education; both his parents died when he was very young. In 1799 he entered Glasgow University (at which time he spelled his name Bleakly), and is said to have graduated (*DNB*) though he is not included in the university's roll of alumni. On 19 September 1809 he was ordained by Bangor presbytery as minister of Moneyreagh, co. Down, in succession to Samuel Patton.

In 1810 Blakely married Margaret Lindsay (1783–1825), daughter of David Lindsay of co. Down. They had four children: Jane, who married the Revd William Cochrane; Sarah (1814–1844); David (1816–1854), inspector of Irish national schools; and William Joseph (1818–1842), Unitarian minister at Billingshurst, Sussex.

Although Blakely was raised a Calvinist he gradually turned to Unitarian views. He was the first self-styled 'humanitarian preacher' in Ulster. Under his influence Moneyreagh became so well known for heterodox opinion that it was popularly said of Moneyreagh that it was the place 'where there is one God and no devil'. When, in 1821, the English Unitarians sent John Smethurst (1792–1859) on a mission to Ulster, the Moneyreagh meeting-house was one of the five meeting-houses which were open to him.

In 1829 Blakely led his entire congregation to join the remonstrant secession from the synod of Ulster. He had throughout the previous synodical debates been one of the most powerful associates of Henry Montgomery, the leader of the New Light party, and helped him to form the Remonstrant Synod. On 27 April 1836 a public testimonial bore witness to his 'successful advocacy of the rights of conscience and human freedom'. Locally he also worked hard for popular education, for tenants' rights, and for the promotion of the flax industry. He was a joint editor from 1830 to 1833 of the *Bible Christian*. His early tracts and sermons, published anonymously, include *A Dialogue* (1817), *On the Bible and other Standards of Faith*, which was followed by *The battle of the two dialogues … a conversation between a rev. Covenanter and a rev. Presbyterian on the impropriety of adhering to any standard of faith except the Bible* (1818). In reply to it John Paul, dissenting minister of Carrickfergus (*d.* 1848), published his first work, *Creeds and Confessions Defended* (1819). Blakely's later works were *The Doctrine of the Trinity not Comprised on the Faith* (1846) and *An Explicit Avowal of Truth the Best Mode of Teaching it* (1853). He resigned his charge on 22 September 1857 but continued to preach until his successor, John Jellie, was installed on 27 September 1859. He died on 25 February 1862 at Cradley, Worcestershire, the residence of his son-in-law the Revd William Cochrane. Fletcher Blakely was a prominent Unitarian and a committed advocate of religious and civil liberty. He was buried in the graveyard of Moneyreagh non-subscribing Presbyterian church on 1 March 1862, and a monument was erected there to his memory.

Alexander Gordon, *rev.* David Huddleston

Sources *The Inquirer* (15 March 1862), 211–12 · *Christian Unitarian*, 1 (1862), 123–4 · 'Synodical portraits', *Northern Whig* (24 Sept 1829) · tombstone, Moneyreagh non-subscribing Presbyterian church, Down · W. I. Addison, ed., *The matriculation albums of the University of Glasgow from 1728 to 1858* (1913), 188 · J. McConnell and others, eds.,

Fasti of the Irish Presbyterian church, 1613–1840, rev. S. G. McConnell, 2 vols. in 12 pts (1935–51) · *Christian Unitarian*, 2 (1863), 31, 60–68, 91–101, 140–2, 171 · *Christian Reformer, or, New Evangelical Miscellany*, 8 (1822), 218 · *Christian Reformer, or, Unitarian Magazine and Review*, new ser., 15 (1859), 474 · *Northern Whig* (28 April 1836)

Wealth at death under £100: probate, 24 Sept 1863, *CGPLA Eng. & Wales*

Blakely, Johnston (1781–1814), naval officer in the United States service, was born in Dublin in October 1781. When he was an infant, his parents emigrated to North Carolina. In 1800 he entered the United States Navy and, when the Anglo-American War broke out in 1812, had attained the rank of master commandant. Commanding the *Wasp*, a new, large, heavily armed sloop, he sailed from Portsmouth, New Hampshire, on 1 May 1814. He crossed the Atlantic, and in the channel on 28 June fought and captured the much weaker British brig *Reindeer*, for which congress voted him a gold medal. In September 1814, on another cruise, he captured a merchant vessel and defeated the much weaker British brig *Avon*. When other British warships approached, he ran. The *Wasp* sailed south, captured two or three merchantmen, and was last seen in the Atlantic, west of Portugal, on 9 October; her fate was unknown. For one who fought so few actions and only against decisively weaker opponents, Blakely gained an apparently exaggerated reputation among his compatriots. J. K. LAUGHTON, *rev.* ANDREW LAMBERT

Sources C. McKee, *A gentlemanly and honorable profession: the creation of the U. S. naval officer corps, 1794–1815* (1991) · W. S. Dudley, ed., *The naval war of 1812: a documentary history*, 2 (1992) · A. T. Mahan, *Seapower in its relation to the war of 1812* (1905) · T. Roosevelt, *The naval war of 1812* (1882)

Likenesses I. T. Gimbrede, stipple, NPG; repro. in *Harper's Magazine* (1842), 179

Blakeney, Sir Edward (1778–1868), army officer, born at Newcastle upon Tyne, was the fourth son of Colonel William Blakeney of Newcastle upon Tyne, MP for Athenry in the Irish parliament (1781–3, 1790–1800). He was appointed a cornet in the King's Royal Irish light dragoons on 28 February 1794, lieutenant in an unattached regiment of foot on 24 September 1794, and captain in the 99th foot on 24 December 1794. He accompanied the expedition under Major-General White to the West Indies and was present in British Guiana at the capture of Demerara, Berbice, and Essequibo in 1796; during this service he was taken prisoner by privateers three times. After a short period on half pay he joined the 17th foot as a captain on 8 March 1798, and in 1799 he went with the duke of York's expedition to the Netherlands, taking part in actions on 10 and 19 September and 2 and 6 October. After being promoted major on 17 September 1801, and again going on half pay the following year, he joined the 47th foot on 9 July 1803 and exchanged into the 7th foot on 24 March 1804. In 1807 Blakeney sailed to the Baltic with Lord Cathcart's force, which captured the Danish fleet and secured the surrender of Copenhagen. Appointed brevet lieutenant-colonel on 25 April 1808, he was present with the 1st battalion of the 7th foot at the capture of Martinique in 1809, then led it during the battles of Busaco (27 September 1810) and Albuera (16 May 1811), once the battalion had joined the duke of Wellington in the Peninsula. After recovering from a severe thigh wound suffered at Albuera, on 20 June 1811 as a substantive lieutenant-colonel Blakeney assumed command of both battalions of the 7th, which had been combined after sustaining heavy losses at Albuera. He subsequently commanded the regiment during the action at Aldea de Ponte, the sieges of Ciudad Rodrigo and Badajoz (where he was severely wounded in the arm), and the battles of Vitoria, Pamplona, the Pyrenees, and Nivelle, as well as various minor encounters.

Having been made colonel on 4 June 1814, Blakeney took part in the British expedition to the United States and fought at the battle of New Orleans. Subsequently, he joined the duke of Wellington's allied force in the Netherlands prior to its entry into Paris in 1815, and remained in France with the army of occupation. Appointed KCB on 2 January 1815, he also received the gold cross and one clasp for Martinique, Albuera, Badajoz, Vitoria, and the Pyrenees, and the silver war medal with four clasps for Busaco, Ciudad Rodrigo, Nivelle, and Nive; in 1812 he had been created a knight of the Tower and Sword of Portugal. He married, in 1814, Maria, daughter of Colonel Gardiner of the East India Company's service. She died at Chelsea Hospital, London, on 21 January 1866, aged seventy-six.

Although retaining nominal command of his regiment until 2 June 1825, and being promoted major-general on 27 May 1825, Blakeney commanded the 1st brigade of the army sent to Portugal in 1826. On 20 September 1832 he was appointed colonel of his old regiment, the 7th foot, and he served in Ireland as commander-in-chief from 1836 to 1855. A privy councillor from 7 May 1836 (thereafter appearing in the *Army List* as 'Rt Hon.'), Blakeney was promoted local lieutenant-general on 26 August 1836, substantive lieutenant-general on 28 June 1838, and general on 20 June 1854. He had been appointed GCH in 1836 and GCB on 7 May 1849, before leaving the 7th foot on 21 December 1854 to become colonel of the 1st foot, a post retained until his death. After his return from Ireland he became lieutenant-governor of Chelsea Hospital in London (with a salary of £400 p.a.) on 6 February 1855 and governor (at £500 p.a.) on 25 September 1856. Sir Edward attained the rank of field marshal on 9 November 1862 and was made colonel-in-chief of the rifle brigade on 28 August 1865. He died at Chelsea Hospital on 2 August 1868 and was buried at Twickenham, Middlesex, on 8 August.

G. C. BOASE, *rev.* JOHN SWEETMAN

Sources *Army List* · W. Wheater, ed., *Historical record of the seventh or royal regiment of fusiliers* (1875) · M. Foss, *The royal fusiliers* (1967) · *The royal fusiliers in an outline of military history, 1685–1938*, 3rd edn (1938)

Archives CKS, corresp. | Beds. & Luton ARS, corresp. with Earl de Grey · McGill University, Montreal, McLennan Library, corresp. with duke of Wellington, Lord Fitzroy Somerset, and others, relating to military matters in Ireland

Likenesses R. J. Lane, lithograph, 1840 (after J. Nogues), NPG · G. Sanders, mezzotint (after S. C. Smith), NPG · S. C. Smith, oils; formerly at United Service Club, London

Wealth at death under £45,000: probate, 25 Aug 1868, *CGPLA Eng. & Wales*

Blakeney, Richard Paul (1820–1884), Church of England clergyman, was born in co. Roscommon on 2 June 1820, the son of Richard Blakeney, a Royal Marines officer, and his wife, Susan Maria, elder daughter of John Purdon of Low Park, co. Roscommon. His father's family came originally from Norfolk. He was educated at Mr Sargent's school in Dublin and at Trinity College, Dublin, where he matriculated in 1837, graduated BA in 1842, and took his LLB and LLD in 1852. He was awarded a DD by the University of Edinburgh in 1868.

Blakeney was ordained deacon in 1843 and priest in 1844. His first curacy was at St Paul's, Nottingham, and in 1844 he was appointed perpetual curate of the new district church of Hyson Green, Nottingham. He became involved in local controversies with Roman Catholics, and rapidly acquired a reputation as a protestant polemicist through his involvement in the British Reformation Society. From late 1850 he was employed by John Hope (1807–1893), the barrister and philanthropist, to write tracts for his Edinburgh-based anti-Catholic movement. These works formed the basis of Blakeney's *Manual of the Romish Controversy* (1851) and *Popery in its Social Aspect* (1852).

Blakeney had married first about 1840, but his wife, Anna, was, he subsequently alleged, 'torn from me by the demoniacal machinations of Popery for ten years' (Blakeney to J. Hope, 24 May 1851, NA Scot., Hope MSS). In May 1851 Blakeney's brother carried her off from alleged confinement at Gort in co. Galway and returned her to her husband, who found her to be in a mentally and physically enfeebled state. It would seem that this personal tragedy gave particular intensity to Blakeney's hatred of the Roman Catholic church. Anna Blakeney appears to have died in 1855.

In 1852 Blakeney moved to Birkenhead, as perpetual curate of Christ Church, Claughton. During the subsequent two decades he combined an energetic parochial ministry with national roles as a prominent organizer and writer on behalf of militantly protestant evangelicalism within the Church of England. He was a dominant force in the British Reformation Society, a key opponent of ritualism, and supporter of the Church Association, formed in 1865. His works, which also notably included a *Protestant Catechism* (1854) and *The Book of Common Prayer in its History and Interpretation* (1865), became textbooks for his party. In the meantime he was married a second time in 1856, to Elizabeth Bibby. They had four sons and six daughters, born between 1858 and 1874.

In 1874 Blakeney was appointed vicar of Bridlington, Yorkshire, where he adopted a gentle and effective pastoral style which belied his reputation as a formidable controversialist. He was instrumental in the restoration of Bridlington priory church, and his growing respectability was evidenced by his appointment as a rural dean in 1875 and as a canon of York Minster in 1882. He died at the parsonage in Bridlington on 31 December 1884, after a short illness, and was buried on 6 January 1885 in the shadow of the priory church. At a subsequent memorial meeting the archbishop of York, William Thomson, paid tribute to his unsurpassed learning and unfailing humility of demeanour. Blakeney's brother, John Edward Blakeney (1824–1895), first archdeacon of Sheffield, shared his religious opinions, and won renown as a church builder and ecclesiastical administrator. JOHN WOLFFE

Sources W. Odom, *'A man greatly beloved': memories of life and work of John Edward Blakeney, D.D.* (1895) • *The Record* (2 Jan 1885) • *The Record* (9 Jan 1885) • *The Record* (30 Jan 1885) • NA Scot., Hope MSS, GD253 • J. Wolffe, *The protestant crusade in Great Britain, 1829–1860* (1991) • census returns for Bridlington, Yorkshire, 1881 • *The Times* (2 Jan 1885) • D. M. Lewis, ed., *The Blackwell dictionary of evangelical biography, 1730–1860*, 2 vols. (1995) • Boase, *Mod. Eng. biog.* • *DNB*

Archives NA Scot., corresp. with John Hope, GD 253

Likenesses engraving, 1865, NA Scot., GD253/54/13–14 • O. Ford, medallion on marble memorial tablet, Bridlington Priory Church

Wealth at death £1846 10s.: administration with will, 3 Feb 1885, *CGPLA Eng. & Wales*

Blakeney, William, **Baron Blakeney** (1671/2–1761), army officer, the eldest son in the family of five sons and four daughters of William Blakeney (*d.* 1717/18) and his wife, Elizabeth Bowerman, was born at Mount Blakeney, co. Limerick, Ireland, on 7 September 1671 or 1672. His father was a fairly wealthy country gentleman who represented the borough of Kilmallock in the Irish House of Commons for many years, and he expected his eldest son to lead the same life as himself. During the Rapparee insurrection of 1690 the family retreated to Castle Blakeney, but the young William Blakeney was left to defend the estates with a small military force organized out of his father's tenants—which he did successfully.

Blakeney's early military career is uncertain. He was commissioned as an ensign in 1695 and became a lieutenant on 1 August 1701. His anonymous biographer says he received an ensigncy in Lord Cutt's regiment of foot guards (Coldstream) in 1702 at the siege of Venloo, but there is no evidence of this in the regiment's archives. He continued to serve in Flanders, becoming a lieutenant in the 1st foot guards on 9 March 1708 and lieutenant-colonel in 1712. After the peace of Utrecht came a long period of peace, during which promotion was slow; Blakeney was made lieutenant-colonel of Lord John Kerr's regiment of foot on 3 April 1718, but received no further promotion until 1737.

On 27 January 1737, possibly through the influence of the duke of Richmond, Blakeney became colonel of a regiment of foot on the Irish establishment. In 1739 the regiment was ordered to England in response to the growing crisis with Spain. War was declared on Spain on 19 October, and early in 1740 a large expedition was prepared to attack the Spanish colonies in the West Indies. Blakeney's regiment was selected to go on this service, and Blakeney himself was appointed adjutant-general to the expedition, which was commanded by Charles, Lord Cathcart. Blakeney had gained a solid reputation during the 1730s as a good trainer of officers. A major element of the expeditionary army was to be a regiment of 3000 American levies, raised in the northern colonies, officered partly by local gentry and partly by officers from Britain. In April

Blakeney sailed for New York to assist organizing and disciplining this regiment. In his absence, in August, he was appointed as third brigadier on the expedition.

The Americans began to appear at Jamaica from late September 1740. Blakeney arrived at the end of November, while the main expeditionary army arrived from Britain in late January. Cathcart had died in December 1740, and had been replaced by his second in command, Major-General Thomas Wentworth. Blakeney served throughout the expedition. At Cartagena he registered his objection to the army council of war decision on 8 April 1741 to assault the fort of San Lazar—an attack which ended in disaster. From mid-1741 he acted as Wentworth's second in command. He was present with the army during its occupation of Guantanamo Bay, on the south coast of Cuba, but remained at Kingston during the abortive attack on Porto Bello in March 1742. He returned to England when the expedition was abandoned in the autumn of 1742.

After his return from the West Indies, Blakeney was made lieutenant-governor of Stirling Castle, which was besieged by the Jacobites during the rising of 1745–6. The siege began in early January 1746, and Blakeney vigorously defended the castle, inflicting substantial casualties upon his besiegers, until relieved by the duke of Cumberland's army on 2 February. His good service was not forgotten by George II. Blakeney had been promoted major-general on 20 July 1745. He became lieutenant-general in 1747, and lieutenant-governor of the island of Minorca.

Blakeney went at once to Minorca, and as Lord Tyrawley, the governor, remained in Britain, he was left in chief command for ten years. As Britain and France drifted to war, a French expedition to attack Minorca was dispatched in April 1756 under the duc de Richelieu and Admiral la Galissonnière. They intended to make a rapid attack before reinforcements could reach the garrison. Blakeney had become concerned about the French preparations as early as February but had been unable to achieve much. His only hope was that he could hold out at Fort St Philip, Port Mahon, until reinforcements arrived. Admiral the Hon. John Byng's return to Gibraltar after the inconclusive battle with Galissonnière's fleet on 19 May ended hopes of relief, and Blakeney, after seventy days' defence, surrendered on the honourable terms that his garrison was to be transported to Gibraltar, and not made prisoners of war. Blakeney's gallant defence of Minorca contrasted greatly in the minds of the English people with the apparent failure of Byng to press home his attack. Blakeney gave ambiguous evidence at Byng's trial as to the prospects of resisting the French and reinforcing his garrison. No blame was attached to Blakeney, and he was made a knight of the Bath and Baron Blakeney of Mount Blakeney in the peerage of Ireland. He was MP for Kilmallock from 1725 to 1757. He was a popular figure; a statue of him by Van Most was erected in Dublin, and after his death on 20 September 1761, at the age of eighty-nine, he was buried on 9 October in Westminster Abbey.

Blakeney left no major collection of private papers. His personality and private life are therefore difficult to establish. The anonymous biography written in 1756 presents him as a traditional soldier and gentleman. He was depicted as a soldier of the soldiers, always living among them, enjoying his punch as well as any of them, and beloved by them. In his family relations he was always exemplary; he used to live on his pay, and to allow his brothers to live on his estate of Mount Blakeney. One brother swindled him grossly; but he made no change in his arrangements, and merely transferred his estate to another brother, Robert, who succeeded to the property on Blakeney's death.

H. M. STEPHENS, *rev.* RICHARD HARDING

Sources *Memoirs of the life and actions of General William Blakeney* (1756) • C. Dalton, ed., *English army lists and commission registers, 1661–1714*, 6 vols. (1892–1904) • C. Dalton, *George the First's army, 1714–1727*, 2 vols. (1910–12) • PRO, CO5/41–2 • Royal Arch., Cumberland papers, box 8 • *Army List* (1740) • Burke, *Gen. GB* (1958) • GEC, *Peerage* • R. Harding, *Amphibious warfare in the eighteenth century: the British expedition to the West Indies, 1740–1742*, Royal Historical Society Studies in History, 62 (1991)

Archives PRO, CO5/41–2 • West Highland Museum, Fort William, corresp. relating to the 1745 rebellion | U. Nott. L., corresp. with Henry Pelham

Likenesses J. Faber junior, mezzotint, 1756 (after T. Hudson), BM, NPG • J. Macardell, mezzotint, 1756 (after G. Chalmers), BM, NPG • Van Most, statue, *c.*1757, Dublin • G. Chalmers, oils, Scot. NPG

Blakenham. For this title name *see* Hare, John Hugh, first Viscount Blakenham (1911–1982).

Blakesley, Joseph Williams (1808–1885), dean of Lincoln, was born at 38 Coleman Street, in the city of London, on 6 March 1808, and baptized privately on 22 April. His parents were Jeremiah George and Elizabeth Blaksley, as the name was then spelt. His father, who was a factor, died before his son had reached the age of ten. He entered St Paul's School, London, on 3 October 1819, after which he matriculated with a Stock scholarship and a special exhibition at Corpus Christi College, Cambridge, on 3 November 1827. Among his close friends there were R. Chenevix Trench (subsequently archbishop of Dublin), R. Monckton Milnes (Lord Houghton), Henry Alford, James and Thomas Story Spedding, Alfred Tennyson, and his brothers. His friendships among Trinity men led to his migration from Corpus to Trinity in Lent 1830. As an undergraduate Blakesley was influenced by J. C. Hare and Connop Thirlwall, through their association with the Cambridge Conversazione Society.

Blakesley joined the 'youthful band of friends' forming the celebrated Apostles' club. The club, under the influence of its 'second father', Professor F. D. Maurice, the 'creator not of its form but of its spirit' (*Maurice's Life and Letters*, i. 110), greatly influenced Blakesley. He was the

Clear-headed friend, whose joyful scorn,
Edged with sharp laughter, cuts atwain
The knots that tangle human creeds

to whom Lord Tennyson addressed one of his first published poems.

In 1829 Blakesley was president of the Cambridge Union, and in 1830 was elected to a foundation scholarship. He graduated BA in 1831, MA in 1834, and BD on 5

April 1849. He was a wrangler in the mathematical tripos and was placed third in the classical tripos, where his chief strength lay, subsequently obtaining the senior chancellor's medal. He was elected a fellow of Trinity in 1831, became assistant tutor in 1834, and was tutor from 1839 to 1845. Among his pupils were Lord Lyttelton, Lord Frederick Cavendish, George Denman, A. J. Beresford Hope, and Arthur Cayley.

Blakesley had originally intended to adopt the law as his profession, being admitted at the Inner Temple on 16 April 1831. He had a capacity for expressing opinion and summing up facts, but weak health led him to change his career. He was ordained deacon in 1833 and priest in 1835. In 1834, together with other Trinity liberals, including Sedgwick and Thirlwall, Blakesley announced his opposition to university religious tests. In 1840 he acted as campaign manager to the whig Lord Lyttelton in the election of the university high steward. He twice occupied the university pulpit at Cambridge (1840, 1843); his sermons were published as *Conciones academicae* (1843). In 1850 he was an unsuccessful candidate for the regius chair of divinity.

In 1845 Blakesley left Cambridge to take up the Trinity College living of Ware, Hertfordshire. On 21 August 1845 he married Margaret Wilson Holmes, daughter of Revd Thomas Holmes of Brooke Hall, Norfolk. They had seven sons and four daughters before Margaret Blakesley died in 1880. From 1850 to 1863 he was classical examiner in the University of London. As vicar of Ware he became widely known as the Hertfordshire Incumbent, whose letters in *The Times* newspaper examined social and political subjects of the day. The letters greatly increased his reputation, and in 1863 he received a canonry at Canterbury from Lord Palmerston, with whose political views he fully sympathized. In 1860 Palmerston had offered Blakesley the regius professorship of history at Cambridge in preference to Dr Woodham of Jesus, despite Blakesley's lack of credentials as a modern historian. He became proctor in convocation for his chapter, and was an influential, although very independent, member of the lower house, serving as a regular member of the committee for revision of the translation of the New Testament. Although no scientific theologian, Blakesley took much interest in theological studies, especially in the critical and evidential department. He believed the divine nature of the Bible could not be established by impersonal science but was apprehended by individual conscience. By diminishing rational Christianity as a foundation for belief, he felt he could safely pursue rational biblical criticism. Poor health drove him to Algiers in the winter of 1857–8. On his return he published an account of his sojourn under the title of *Four Months in Algiers, with a Visit to Carthage*.

In 1872 Blakesley succeeded James Jeremie as dean of Lincoln on Gladstone's recommendation. As dean he made Lincoln his home, and devoted himself to the interests of his cathedral and of the city of Lincoln. A practical man, he gave attention to the management of the cathedral, and opposed some of the enthusiastic projects for increasing cathedral activities favoured by his bishop, E. W. Benson. He did not see the cathedral as the mother church of the diocese, but as existing by and for itself. His view of the church was expressed in *Thoughts on the recommendations of the ecclesiastical commission … a letter to W. E. Gladstone* (1873), in which he argued that the church needed variety to retain all channels for talent: the scholar and the antiquary, not just the preacher and bishop.

Blakesley was master of the court of the Mercers' Company in 1864. As one of the governors he took a warm interest in the welfare of St Paul's School. His chief work was an edition of Herodotus for the Bibliotheca Classica. His annotations were chiefly devoted to geographical and historical questions. He contributed articles to the *Quarterly* and *Edinburgh* reviews and other periodicals, and wrote many reviews of books for *The Times* newspaper. He died on 18 April 1885, at the deanery, Lincoln, and was buried on 23 April at St Mary Magdalene, Lincoln.

EDMUND VENABLES, *rev.* ELLIE CLEWLOW

Sources *Saturday Review*, 59 (1885), 533–4 • *The Guardian* (22 April 1885) • private information (1885) • Venn, *Alum. Cant.* • R. Deacon, *The Cambridge Apostles* (1985) • P. Searby, *A history of the University of Cambridge*, 3: *1750–1870*, ed. C. N. L. Brooke and others (1997) • R. Brent, *Liberal Anglican politics: whiggery, religion, and reform, 1830–1841* (1987) • D. A. Winstanley, *Early Victorian Cambridge* (1940) • *Romilly's Cambridge diary, 1842–47: selected passages from the diary of the Rev. Joseph Romilly*, ed. M. E. Bury and J. D. Pickles, Cambridgeshire RS, 10 (1994) • W. W. Rouse Ball and J. A. Venn, eds., *Admissions to Trinity College, Cambridge*, 1 (1916) • A. C. Benson, *The trefoil* (1923) • *Wellesley index* • *GM*, 2nd ser., 24 (1845), 521–2

Archives Herts. ALS, papers mainly relating to the living of Ware • Trinity Cam., scrapbooks of his newspaper articles and book reviews | LPL, letters to A. C. Tait

Likenesses D. Biemann, glass plaque, *c*.1841–1845, V&A

Wealth at death £14,789 6*s*. 10*d*.: will with a codicil, 22 May 1885, *CGPLA Eng. & Wales*

Blakeway, John Brickdale (1765–1826), Church of England clergyman and antiquary, the eldest son of Joshua Blakeway, of Shrewsbury, and Elizabeth, sister of Matthew Brickdale, merchant and MP in several parliaments for the city of Bristol, was born at Shrewsbury on 24 June 1765. He was educated initially in the free school there (1772–5). From 1775 to 1782 he attended Westminster School, from where he went to Oriel College, Oxford, where he graduated BA in 1786 and proceeded MA in 1795. Disappointed in his hopes of election to a fellowship at Oriel, he left the university and entered Lincoln's Inn; he was called to the bar in 1789. He followed the law more for pleasure than as a means of support, and worked on the Oxford circuit, where he was quite successful, despite having a slight speech impediment. The collapse of the family fortunes, however, compelled him to earn his living. The legal profession proved too expensive, and Blakeway resolved to enter the church. He was ordained in 1793.

In 1794 Blakeway was presented by his uncle the Revd Edward Blakeway, then mayor of Shrewsbury, to the ministry of the royal peculiar of St Mary's, Shrewsbury. On his uncle's death in 1795 he became official of the peculiar, and also succeeded to the vicarage of Neen Savage, Shropshire, and the rectory of Felton, Somerset. In October 1797 he married Mary-Elizabeth, youngest daughter of Thomas Wilkieson, a Hamburg and Dutch merchant, formerly of

Blackheath. They were happily married, but had no children. In 1800 he was presented to the vicarage of Kinlet, Shropshire. From 1800 until 1816 he divided his time between Kinlet and Shrewsbury, but, finding it inconvenient to keep up two houses, he gave up Felton and Kinlet in 1816, and subsequently lived only in his native town.

Comfortably settled with his various livings, Blakeway found time to turn to antiquities, which became his favourite pursuit. He was elected fellow of the Society of Antiquaries in 1807. Blakeway's main works are *A History of Shrewsbury* (2 vols., 1825), written in collaboration with Hugh Owen, and *The Sheriffs of Shropshire* (1831).

Although he had suffered from asthma as a child, Blakeway was generally in good health until he began to suffer from a tumour on his hip in around 1823. It was operated on in early 1826, but he died on 10 March 1826 at the Council House, Shrewsbury, which had been his home since 1815. He was buried in St Mary's Church, where a fine Gothic monument, by John Carline, was erected to his memory by his parishioners.

Much of Blakeway's work remained in manuscript. His topographical history of Shropshire was published posthumously by the Shropshire Archaeological Society in 1905–7. His quick mind and good memory, combined with great industry and his legal training, made his work highly respected by contemporaries, although it was increasingly superseded by that of specialist students of the next generation.

THOMPSON COOPER, *rev.* ELIZABETH BAIGENT

Sources *GM*, 1st ser., 96/1 (1826), 277–8, 369–74 • Foster, *Alum. Oxon.* • *Salopian Journal* (15 March 1826) • *Salopian Journal* (22 March 1826) • *Salopian Journal* (29 March 1826) • F. Madan, *A summary catalogue of Western manuscripts in the Bodleian Library at Oxford*, 4 (1897), 636 • memoir, Shropshire Public Library, Walton press cuttings, vol. 7 • C. R. J. Currie and C. P. Lewis, eds., *English county histories: a guide* (1994)

Archives Bodl. Oxf. • Shrops. RRC • Yale U., Beinecke L., Osborn collection

Likenesses C. Hullmandel, lithograph (after P. Corbet), NPG

Blakey, Nicholas (*d.* **1758**), draughtsman and engraver, is principally known for his book illustrations and for several large-scale scenes representing episodes from Britain's early history. He was born in Ireland and by 1747 was studying in Paris. Here, it can be assumed, he developed the late rococo style that can be seen throughout his work but is most notable in his composition of dancing nymphs in a rocaille cartouche. He worked principally for publishers, producing, and sometimes engraving, illustrations to embellish a wide variety of books. Although it is not clear whether he returned from Paris, he regularly collaborated with other noted book illustrators, including L. P. Boitard, Charles Grignion, Simon François Ravenet, and Louis Gérard Scotin, on British publications. This was the team behind the illustrations for Bernard Siegfried Albinus's anatomical publication *Tables of the Skeleton and Muscles of the Human Body* (1749), where Blakey's earliest published designs appear.

Between 1751 and 1753 Blakey worked closely with the painter Francis Hayman, producing frontispieces, very much in Hayman's distinctive style, for *The Works of Alexander Pope* (1751), Jonas Hanway's *An Historical Account of the British Trade over the Caspian Sea* (1753), and J. H. Merchant's *The Revolution in Persia* (1753)—all of which are simply signed 'Blakey del.'. Again produced with Hayman, Blakey's most complex works were designed for a subscription scheme launched by the publishers John and Paul Knapton and Richard Dodsley between 1749 and 1750. Eventually published as part of their *English History Delineated* (1750–52), compositions such as *Alfred in the Isle of Athelney* reveal Blakey's abilities with expression and the human figure, as well as his sensitivity to the contemporary debates surrounding the need for a school of history painting in England. Blakey died in Paris on 20 November 1758, survived by his wife, Elizabeth, who died in 1770.

LUCY PELTZ

Sources B. Allen, *Francis Hayman* (1987) • Anderton catalogues [exhibition catalogues, Society of Artists, BM, print room] • H. Hammelmann, *Book illustrators in eighteenth-century England*, ed. T. S. R. Boase (1975) • Mallalieu, *Watercolour artists* • G. Meissner, ed., *Allgemeines Künstlerlexikon: die bildenden Künstler aller Zeiten und Völker*, [new edn, 34 vols.] (Leipzig and Munich, 1983–) • W. G. Strickland, *A dictionary of Irish artists*, 2 vols. (1913)

Blakey, Robert [*pseud.* Palmer Hackle] (**1795–1878**), radical and historian of philosophy, son of Robert Blakey (*c.*1774–1796), mechanic, and his wife, Elizabeth Laws (*b.* 1773), was born in Manchester Street, Morpeth, Northumberland, on 18 May 1795. His father died when he was nine months old. When he was six, he was taken charge of by his grandmother, also Elizabeth Laws (*c.*1728–1818), a staunch Presbyterian. 'She awakened within me that love of knowledge which has been to me, not only a cold sentiment, but a positive passion from my earliest recollections' (*Memoirs*, 46). From his eighth year he worked almost full time for his uncle, market gardening and making 'corve rods'. In February 1809 he moved to Alnwick, where he became a furrier, learned fishing and shooting, and became a radical in the mould of William Cobbett. His minister, the Revd David Paterson, gave him private tuition which, with his own extensive reading, made him unusually well educated.

In 1815 Blakey returned to Morpeth, selling rabbit fur to hat makers throughout much of England and Scotland. He opened two hat shops and speculated in property. On 11 June 1822 he married Mary Gibb (1791–1858), daughter of Henry and Isabella Gibb of Alnwick. They had six children, of whom four survived—Mary (1823–1895), Isabella Elizabeth (1824–1901), George (1827–1890), and Robert (1828–1855). Blakey 'had at times very indifferent health, and I have known him laid up for months, and never out of doors' (Haslam). He wrote pamphlets and squibs on the Morpeth poor-law fraud (1818–21), contributed to *Cobbett's Register*, the *Black Dwarf*, *Durham Chronicle*, and *Tyne Mercury*, was elected to Morpeth town council in 1835, and became mayor in November 1836. His most important achievements were the founding of the Morpeth Mechanical and Scientific Institution (1825) and the new corporation schools (1837–8), which anticipated by thirty years the Cowper-Temple clause of 1870 on religious teaching in schools. *Cottage Politics* (1837) contains his charges of cruelty against the Morpeth guardians, with their replies. In 1841, in the *Newcastle Journal*, he detailed two appalling cases of their interference in medical treatment, but also admitted making errors in his original accusations.

In 1838 Blakey purchased the *Northern Liberator*, the only Chartist newspaper to attract extensive advertising. He and Thomas Doubleday wrote the leaders, and in 1839 Blakey bought a new press and doubled its size, after which it enjoyed an average circulation of over 2400. His sub-editor, Thomas Devyr, inserted his own 'Address to the middle classes' in the first enlarged issue. The government charged Blakey and his printer, John Bell, with seditious libel. Bell went to prison for six months, but Blakey's case was twice postponed because of illness. His account of what happened is confused, but the case was evidently compromised, and Blakey closed down the *Liberator* in December 1840. The home secretary was privately delighted (Napier, 2.148) and on 25 February 1841 Blakey was merely bound over. The prosecution and closure cost him severe worry and financial loss, made worse by the failure of *The Politician* (June–July 1841).

In philosophical speculation Blakey was an orthodox follower of the intuitive school. His literary career began in 1820 in the *Newcastle Magazine*. He published *An Essay on Moral Good and Evil* in 1831. *History of Moral Science* (2 vols., 1833) established him as a scholarly writer, but after 1834 philosophy gave way for a time to politics and business. In 1840 he moved to London, and in 1841: 'I went to France with my wife and family. Here I resolved to devote all my time and energies to philosophical literature' (*Memoirs*, 115). They moved to Belgium, constantly short of money, but in 1843–4 Blakey made £300 from ghost-writing, and with a friend wrote *Hints on Angling* under the pseudonym Palmer Hackle (1846). He returned to London and brought out his principal work, *History of the Philosophy of Mind* (4 vols., 1848), dedicated to Prince Albert. In 1849 Leopold, king of the Belgians, awarded him a gold medal.

In 1849 Blakey became professor of logic and metaphysics at Queen's College, Belfast. He made a good start, but then missed a whole academic year due to illness, and in October 1851 was dismissed, technically for neglect of duty. During his illness he published *Historical Sketch of Logic* (1851) and, after he recovered, *The Angler's Complete Guide to the Rivers and Lakes of England* (1853), *Rivers and Lochs of Scotland* (1854), and *History of Political Literature* (2 vols., 1855). In 1856 he was elected PhD by the University of Jena.

After 1849 the Blakeys lived in Glasgow, but were at Moffat when Mrs Blakey died in 1858. Blakey returned to London and on 10 December 1859 married Charlotte Esther Aldous, *née* Reynolds (*c.*1799–1878). In 1860 the former Chartist agitator was awarded a pension from the civil list, 'in consideration of his exertions to aid and promote the study of philosophy' (*The Athenaeum*, 11 Aug 1860). He lived for several years at Walford, near Ross-on-Wye, but returned to London in 1873–4. He died on 26 October 1878 at his home, 20 Blomfield Road, Maida Hill, Paddington, and was buried at Kensal Green. Twenty-five of his works appeared between 1831 and 1879. Most can still be read with profit, and his fishing books continue to be of use, if sometimes only as a contrast to modern times—the upper Spey, Blakey notes, is so full of fish that 'one grows absolutely tired of the sport' (Blakey, *Rivers and Lochs of Scotland*, 134). *Hints on Angling* is mentioned in the eighth edition of the *Encyclopaedia Britannica* but, contrary to report, Blakey was not a contributor. His *Angling, or, How to Angle and where to Go* (1854) published at 1*s.* was constantly reprinted and came out in a new edition in 1898, while *History of Political Literature* was republished by Kennicat as recently as 1970. Blakey never finished his memoirs, which must be used with caution, but they mention many contemporaries, from Jack Mitford to Cardinal Newman. Unfortunately his papers and portrait are lost. His daughter Isabella married George Adam Bell of Brooklyn; they had four sons, and their granddaughter Madeline Bell Gilbert had children of her own in New York in 1920. Blakey's last known descendants in Britain were Elizabeth Lewis, *née* Sinclair (*b.* 1897), and Arthur Reginald Sinclair Lewis (*b.* 1918). ROGER HAWKINS

Sources *Memoirs of Dr. Robert Blakey*, ed. H. Miller (1879) · *Men of the time* (1862) · R. Hawkins, *The life of Robert Blakey, 1795–1878* (2003) · R. Blakey, 'The Poor Law Amendment Bill—to Lord Viscount Howick', *Newcastle Journal* (10 April 1841) · C. J. Haslam, *Newcastle Weekly Chronicle* (23 Nov 1878) · T. A. Devyr, *Newcastle Weekly Chronicle* (7 Dec 1878) · T. A. Devyr, *The odd book of the nineteenth century, or, 'Chivalry' in modern days, a personal record of reform—chiefly land reform, for the last fifty years* (privately printed, New York, 1882) · T. W. Moody and J. C. Beckett, *Queen's, Belfast, 1845–1949: the history of a university*, 2 vols. (1959) · W. F. P. Napier, *The life and opinions of General Sir Charles James Napier*, 2 (1857), 148 · *Reports of the presidents of the Queen's colleges* (G. and J. Grierson for HMSO, Dublin, 1851) · *The Athenaeum* (11 Aug 1860), 203 [citation for civil list pension] · Presbyterian baptismal register, Northumbd RO, M1266 · Universitätsarchiv Jena, Bestand M, Nr 451 [MS notes on Blakey's candidature, citation 30 Nov 1856] · *Northern Liberator* (3 Aug 1839); (17 Aug 1839); (29 Feb 1840); (7 March 1840); (14 March 1840); (8 Aug 1840) [contemporary reports of Blakey's prosecution] · *Newcastle Journal* (27 Feb 1841) · *Gateshead Observer* (26 Dec 1840); (27 Feb 1841) [contemporary reports of Blakey's prosecution] · *The Times* (12 Feb 1841) · *Tyne Mercury* (2 March 1841) [contemporary reports of Blakey's prosecution] · Morpeth town council minute book, Northumbd RO, NRO 990/A1 · lease of garden to Blakey's house, Northumbd RO, ZBS 2/60 · census returns for Lambeth, 1841, PRO, HO 107/1056/3, fol. 18 · census return for Moffat, Dumfries, 1851, PRO, ED 5, p. 28, schedule 130 · *CGPLA Eng. & Wales* (1878) · *Littlebury's directory of Herefordshire* (1867) · *Manchester Examiner* (5 April 1872) · W. Senior, notes and memorandum, in R. Blakey, *Angling, or, How to angle and where to go*, rev. W. Senior, new edn (1898) · grave register for All Souls' cemetery, Kensal Green, grave no. 26,406/3/2 [General Cemetery Co. letter] · *The Athenaeum* (2 Nov 1878), 562 · *Newcastle Daily Chronicle* (29 Oct 1878)

Archives King Edward VI High School, Morpeth, King Edward VI Grammar School trustees' minute book and accounts · King Edward VI High School, Morpeth, William Woodman's solicitor's daybook · Newcastle Central Library, anonymous letters to *Tyne Mercury* on electoral corruption of freemen of Morpeth · Newcastle Central Library, tracts, probably by Blakey, in the Morpeth poor law dispute, 1818–21, L942.82 M817M · Northumbd RO, Morpeth, Morpeth Records Centre, assignments of Blakey's leases on 4 May 1840, BMO/D2/51, BMO/D2/52 · Northumbd RO, Morpeth, Morpeth Records Centre, leases of Blakey's hat shop in Bridge Street and of Tenter Close, BMO/D1, 167–8 · Northumbd RO, Morpeth,

Morpeth Records Centre, papers on the Morpeth poor law fraud and dispute, 1818–21, EP28/70/1–14 · Northumbd RO, Morpeth, Morpeth Records Centre, squibs on Morpeth Mechanical and Scientific Institution, ZAN M16/B2, 323 · PRO, assizes papers, ASSI 44–156 part 1 [indictments of Blakey, Bell, Devyr, and others in 1840–41] · PRO, assizes papers, ASSI 41/16 [court minute book for 3 Aug 1840]

Wealth at death under £200: probate, 7 Dec 1878, *CGPLA Eng. & Wales*

Blakhal, Gilbert. *See* Blackhall, Gilbert (*d.* 1671).

Blakiston, Herbert Edward Douglas (1862–1942), college head, was born on 5 September 1862 in the parish of St Mary in the Castle, Hastings, Sussex. He was the eldest of the six children of Douglas Yeoman Blakiston (1832–1914) and Sophia Matilda (1826–1912), daughter of William Dent of Crosby Cote, Yorkshire. Baronets among his ancestors were a source of considerable satisfaction to him. In 1869 his father turned from painting to the church, and in 1871 the family settled at East Grinstead vicarage, Sussex. An atmosphere of impoverished respectability inculcated a frugality and preoccupation with money which he never lost. In later life, his parents leant on him increasingly for moral and financial support.

Blakiston entered Tonbridge School in 1876. He did well, but it was diligence not brilliance that brought him success. In 1881 he won an open scholarship in classics to Trinity College, Oxford. He took a first in *literae humaniores* in 1885, and in 1887 proceeded to holy orders and a fellowship at Trinity.

Trinity was a home so stable, so congenial, that Blakiston never looked beyond its sheltering walls. He was a very shy man, and his few lasting friends were made early in his Oxford career. The early and sudden deaths of his three brothers, followed by those of his two sisters and both parents within four years of each other, left a sad vacuum in his life. He had no close relationships with either sex; he was married to his college. For the whole of his adult life he cared for Trinity College with the same watchful economy and anxious pride he showed for his family's fortunes, and he was soon intimate with every detail of Trinity's history. He was a conscientious tutor and a competent latinist, and his few published articles were carefully written, but his real passion was for the fabric and traditions of his college. His research into the college's administrative archives was painstaking, and he showed equal devotion to the lives of past members. His love was consummated in the publication of a meticulous college history in 1898.

Ever a willing worker, Blakiston held office as senior tutor and junior bursar from 1898 to 1907, when he became assistant, later acting, estates bursar. His was a safe and thrifty pair of hands. In 1907 he was elected president of Trinity, after the fellows' unanimous offer to R. W. Raper had been rejected, and proceeded to the degree of DD. Under his headship Trinity College assumed a character and reputation which were to remain long after his death.

Herbert Edward Douglas Blakiston (1862–1942), by Walter Stoneman, 1933

Many of Blakiston's attitudes hardened during the First World War. Trinity struggled under severe financial constraints. He was tormented by the loss of 155 Trinity men, each known to him personally. Early on he conceived the idea of a new undergraduate library as a prestigious yet practical memorial. He wrote 1500 fund-raising letters, and himself gave over 5 per cent of the building's cost. The design was his own, and he took especial pains over the symbolic ornamentation of the entrance. This Curzonesque attention to detail, combined with characteristic parsimony, did not make Blakiston, or the library, popular with his younger colleagues.

Blakiston can be justly criticized for his snobbishness, his racism, and his anti-feminism. He alone handled applications to the college, and fostered an atmosphere of squirearchical complacency. He fought a grim rearguard action against the admission of Indian students, and strongly opposed women taking Oxford degrees.

Essentially opposed to the centralizing trends of twentieth-century Oxford, Blakiston's involvement with the university was based on the same conservative principles and delight in administrative minutiae as governed his college life. He was proctor in 1899, university auditor from 1903 to 1917, elected to the hebdomadal council in 1915, and vice-chancellor from 1917 to 1920. He came to national prominence in 1899 when he signed a memorial of regret that Cecil Rhodes was to receive the honorary degree of DCL which the university had offered to him seven years earlier. Blakiston's brother John had been killed in the Matabele (Ndebele) uprising of 1896. But public duty outweighed private disapproval, and he never seriously considered exercising his proctorial veto.

From 1922 to 1932 Blakiston was a curator of the university chest, and from 1922 to 1927 he was a delegate of the Clarendon Press. As vice-chancellor his reorganization of the finance board and institution of the reserve fund were deftly efficient. Typically reactionary in his opposition to a university grant from central government, he was dogged in his resistance to perceived interference by the subsequent royal commission appointed in 1919.

Blakiston enjoyed his fleeting appearances in the limelight. But most of his pleasures were solitary: the countryside, antiquarian research, low-church ritual. He relished his contributions to the *Dictionary of National Biography*. Acquaintances described his childlike kindness—and his belittling sarcasm. Favourite undergraduates could not be helped, nor forgiven, enough.

In 1938 Blakiston retired to Boars Hill, Berkshire. He had misread the international situation, and war prevented his anticipated evolution into a college patriarch. Travel was difficult, and Trinity's activities were greatly curtailed. His last years were lonely and frustrated as he witnessed the destruction of the world he had struggled to preserve. Walking near his home on 28 July 1942 Blakiston absent-mindedly stepped in front of a car. He died in the Radcliffe Infirmary, Oxford, on the following day without regaining consciousness, and was cremated at Oxford crematorium on 1 August 1942. He had written his obituary, planned his funeral, and pored over his will. Blakiston's estate was considerable. His main bequests, to Oxford University and to Trinity College, were for the purchase of works of art. He never wanted his own portrait painted, but two, by Allan Gwynne-Jones and Cyril Hinshelwood, were in the possession of Trinity College at the close of the twentieth century.

For much of his life, Blakiston was a recognized Oxford character, even a figure of fun. He was ugly, he wore glasses (the nickname Blinks dated from his adolescence), he was a bad driver, and he made enemies easily. After his death he was quickly reduced to a series of comic anecdotes, redolent of the Victorian common-room tradition he had himself enjoyed. CLARE HOPKINS

Sources H. E. D. Blakiston, 'Memoranda', Trinity College, Oxford, OF 20/G2 • T. F. Higham, *Dr Blakiston recalled: memories of an Oxford 'character' the Rev. Herbert Edward Blakiston, D.D. President of Trinity College, 1907–1938* (1967) • *Manchester Guardian* (31 July 1942) • *The Times* (30 July 1942) • *Oxford Magazine* (5 Nov 1942) • *Trinity College Report* (1941–2) • *Oxford Mail* (6 Aug 1942) • Trinity College admissions register • Trinity College, Oxford, Blakiston MSS

Archives Trinity College, Oxford, corresp. | Trinity College, Oxford, Higham MSS

Likenesses Elliott & Fry, photographs, *c.*1887–*c.*1929, Trinity College, Oxford • Lafayette, photographs, *c.*1899, Trinity College, Oxford • Lafayette, photograph, *c.*1923, Trinity College, Oxford • C. Hinshelwood, oils, *c.*1932, Trinity College, Oxford • W. Stoneman, photograph, 1933, NPG [*see illus.*] • A. Gwynne-Jones, oils, 1943 (after photographs), Trinity College, Oxford • T. F. Higham, cartoon, Trinity College, Oxford

Wealth at death £100,055 19*s.* 3*d.*: resworn probate, 2 Dec 1942, *CGPLA Eng. & Wales*

Blakiston, Hugh Noel (1905–1984), archivist and author, was born on 8 December 1905 at Baumber vicarage, Lincolnshire, the second child of the vicar, the Revd Felix Milburn Blakiston (1874–1941), and his wife, Mary Augusta Fox (1880–1962), who were married on 23 April 1903 at Horncastle parish church. After a highly successful career as king's scholar at Eton College, which included prowess at cricket, membership of the Eton Society, and friendship with, among others, Cyril Connolly, Eric Arthur Blair (George Orwell), and Steven Runciman, Blakiston went up to Magdalene College, Cambridge, where he achieved a first in history. He passed the civil service exam and entered the Public Record Office in 1928. In the search department (the Round Room) his erudition, wit, charm, and radiant good looks at first created a considerable stir, to be replaced later by a climate of scholarly accessibility which endeared him to scores of researchers. In 1938 he shouldered the task of cataloguing the huge corpus of documents and charters in the Eton College Library, for which Eton eventually made him an honorary fellow—the first for over 300 years.

While at the Public Record Office Blakiston found time to advise the Russian Orthodox church in London and the Malaysian government in Kuala Lumpur, and to write the only detective story to be published in the *Burlington Magazine*—an enthralling account of the origins of a Tudor miniature by Nicholas Hilliard. This led to a collection of short stories, mainly about country clergymen, university dons, picnics under the cedar tree, and in the case of one of the most arresting tales, 'Nice Things', the director of the National Gallery. They were published first in the *Cornhill Magazine*, *Harper's Bazaar*, the *New Statesman*, and *World Review*, then in four slim volumes (1951–65), and finally in a collected edition in 1977.

On 10 October 1929 Blakiston married (Rachel) Georgiana Russell (1903–1995), writer, a granddaughter of Lord Arthur Russell, brother of the ninth duke of Bedford. This union, which lasted for fifty-six happy years, produced two daughters (Rachel, a painter and sculptor, and Caroline, an actress). It also led to his passionate interest in Italy and the Risorgimento, and bore fruit in *The Roman Question* (1962), a work of considerable historical research based on the papers of Lord Odo Russell and the labyrinthine tangle of papal affairs between 1858 and 1870. This was followed naturally by a stream of articles, reviews, and lectures, delivered in fluent if idiosyncratic Italian, published as *Inglesi e italiani nel Risorgimento* (1972), and leading to a wide circle of friendships, especially among the Italian *cognoscenti*. He had already made his mark when in 1966 a disastrous flood struck Florence, inundating its treasures. Blakiston took his place on the rescue committee and made sure that 'Archives' featured both in its title and among the recipients of aid. He was elected a fellow of the Società Toscana per la Storia del Risorgimento, and was made a knight of the Italian order of merit; he was also made an OBE for his distinguished career at the Public Record Office, especially for his 'Catalogue of maps', a monument of archival scholarship and a boon to searchers. A more personal tribute appeared on his seventieth birthday—an album handsomely bound by the office binders, full of evocative photographs of his colleagues, and of Noel Blakiston himself, attending a conference in Rome in 1965.

Retirement made little difference to the volume of his activities. In 1975 he published *A Romantic Friendship*, letters from Cyril Connolly which reveal the deep relationship of two young men in 1924–9 and after. The friendship began with Connolly's admiration for the young N's 'dark hair, green eyes, and classic head with the wistfulness of a minor angel in Botticelli' (Connolly, *Enemies of Promise*, chap. 21), and developed into a 'marriage of true minds'. Connolly's last letter (9 February 1963) ends: 'it was so perfect that it could not go forward unless we lived together … and we weren't homosexual' (*Romantic Friendship*, 343). In his preface to the book Blakiston treats the subject with tact and good humour, aptly quoting Dr Johnson to Boswell: 'There are few people whom I take so much to as to you'.

Blakiston continued tirelessly his archival work at Eton, and from 1970 he was chairman of the Chelsea Society, famous for his skill in detecting and thwarting bureaucratic plots to turn his beloved riverside Chelsea into a thoroughfare for continental juggernauts. Retirement also allowed him and Giana more time to entertain their friends. Dinner parties at 6 Markham Square, with its slightly minatory bust of Voltaire in the hall, lasted far into the night, and if, as tended to happen in his later years, memory appeared to fail, such lapses were skilfully diverted with Noel's customary sparkling good nature. His portrait was painted (with Giana) by Anthony Devas in 1940, and by John Ward, for the Society of Dilettanti, in 1976. He died at his home, Parsonage Farm, Bentworth, Hampshire, on 22 December 1984. R. J. B. WALKER

Sources *The Times* (4 Jan 1985) • news sheet, 1985, PRO • personal knowledge (2004) • private information (2004) [Patrick Blakiston, brother; Caroline Blakiston, daughter] • *A romantic friendship: the letters of Cyril Connolly to Noel Blakiston* (1975) • C. Connolly, *Enemies of promise* (1938), 246–77 • J. Lewis, *Cyril Connolly: a life* (1997), 62–8 • b. cert. • m. cert. • d. cert.

Likenesses A. Devas, portrait, priv. coll. • J. Ward, portrait, Brooks's Club, London, Society of Dilettanti

Wealth at death £275,154: probate, 17 May 1985, *CGPLA Eng. & Wales*

Blakiston, John (*bap.* 1603, *d.* 1649), politician and regicide, was baptized on 21 August 1603 at Sedgefield in co. Durham, the third son of Marmaduke Blakiston (1565–1639) and Margaret James (1575–1636). He was apprenticed to Christopher Shafto of Newcastle upon Tyne, probably in 1613, and became a free burgess, as a mercer, in 1627. Later, royalists described him as either a pedlar, butcher, chandler, or shopkeeper, but such disparaging comments cannot detract from the fact that by 1632 he was one of Newcastle's chamberlains. His growing prominence within the town's mercantile community was perhaps assisted by his marriage to Susanna Chamber (*b.* 1607, *d.* in or after 1661), the widow of a local merchant, at All Saints, Newcastle, on 9 November 1626. Blakiston's father was a prebendary of Durham Cathedral and a noted Arminian ally of John Cosin, his son-in-law, who was much criticized by puritan commentators such as Peter Smart. However, Blakiston himself emerged as a puritan during the 1630s. He helped secure a lecturer (William Morton) for Newcastle, and was fined by the high commission in Durham for his attack upon a local minister, Yeldard Alvey.

Blakiston was returned to the Long Parliament for Newcastle in a contested election, being declared eligible to sit on 30 January 1641. He became a zealous reforming member and later parliamentarian, who subscribed £1200 for the Irish Adventure, and whose interests lay in religious reform and local affairs, both because of the royalist threat in the north, and because of the involvement of the Scots in later years. He was styled an 'Annabaptisticall' sectary by royalist commentators (*Mercurius Pragmaticus*, 21–8 Nov 1648, sig. Bbb3*v*), but he seems rather to have been a more moderate puritan whose friends included Independents such as Sidrach Simpson, and presbyterians such as Robert Jenison, and who was prepared to act as a commissioner for scandalous offences and for exclusion from the sacrament in the mid-1640s. Blakiston's deep religious convictions underpinned his attempt to establish a godly ministry in Newcastle, and his attempt to secure a place for Hezekiah Woodward as one of the town's schoolmasters.

During the course of the civil wars Blakiston emerged as an immensely powerful figure among northern parliamentarians, and was made mayor of Newcastle in October 1645. In July 1646 he was named as a commissioner for conserving the peace between England and Scotland. He, along with Sir Arthur Hesilrige, came to dominate political affairs in the region. Once parliamentarian unity disappeared in the mid-1640s Blakiston emerged as a supporter of the Independents, not least in his opposition to the Scots. Denzil Holles called him an 'incendiary' between the two kingdoms, and one of the Independents' 'little Northern Beagles' who were set to work to provoke a confrontation between the covenanters and the New Model Army (Maseres, 1.227, 228). In the north he was aligned with Hesilrige against the interest of Robert Lilburne, causing some acrimony, not least over claims that Blakiston made undue personal gains during the wars and acted to protect local delinquents, including members of his own family. However, the civic leaders in Newcastle defended him against the 'unjust and scandalous reflections' made by Lilburne, and remarked on his 'sincerity' and 'faithfulness', and upon 'how unapt he is to cram himself with the riches of a ruined country' (Bodl. Oxf., MS Tanner 56, fol. 22). At Westminster Blakiston became aligned with the more radical elements in the Commons, and his closest allies were probably Thomas Scot and Sir Henry Vane junior. There is also evidence of a close personal friendship with Philip, Lord Wharton. Blakiston joined those MPs who fled to the safety of the army in the summer of 1647, and was later styled one of the 'Levelling sort', who apparently supported the Levellers' 'large petition' of September 1648 (*Mercurius Pragmaticus*, 22–9 Aug 1648, sig. Cc4). Having indicated his opposition to further negotiations with the king in December 1648, Blakiston was named to the high court of justice for the trial of

Charles I in January 1649, and proved to be one of the most assiduous of the commissioners, attending all but one session in the painted chamber and all four days of the trial, before signing the death warrant [*see also* Regicides]. Although probably a zealous supporter of the constitutional changes of 1649, Blakiston was not named to the council of state, but he was an active member of the Rump Parliament until his death, which occurred some time between 1 June 1649, when he drew up his will, and 6 June, when the Commons awarded £3000 to his widow and children. J. T. PEACEY

Sources R. Howell, 'Newcastle's regicide: the parliamentary career of John Blakiston', *Archaeologia Aeliana*, 4th ser., 42 (1964) · R. Howell, *Newcastle upon Tyne and the puritan revolution: a study of the civil war in north England* (1967) · *JHC*, 2–6 (1640–51) · *CSP dom.*, 1640–49 · D. Underdown, *Pride's Purge: politics in the puritan revolution* (1971) · B. Worden, *The Rump Parliament, 1648–1653* (1974) · will, PRO, PROB 11/215, fol. 342 · C. H. Firth and R. S. Rait, eds., *Acts and ordinances of the interregnum, 1642–1660*, 3 vols. (1911) · W. H. Coates, A. Steele Young, and V. F. Snow, eds., *The private journals of the Long Parliament*, 3 vols. (1982–92) · *The journal of Sir Simonds D'Ewes from the first recess of the Long Parliament to the withdrawal of King Charles from London*, ed. W. H. Coates (1942) · J. R. MacCormack, 'The Irish adventurers and the English civil war', *Irish Historical Studies*, 10 (1956–7), 21–58 · Bodl. Oxf., MS Tanner 56, fol. 22 · F. Maseres, ed., *Select tracts relating to the civil wars in England*, 2 vols. (1815), vol. 1

Wealth at death see will, PRO, PROB 11/215, fol. 342

Blakiston, John (1785–1867). *See under* Blakiston, Thomas Wright (1832–1891).

Blakiston, Thomas Wright (1832–1891), army officer and explorer, was born at Lymington in Hampshire on 27 December 1832, the second of three sons of **John Blakiston** (1785–1867), army officer, and his wife, Jane, daughter of the Revd Thomas Wright of Market Harborough, Leicestershire.

Major John Blakiston was the second son of Sir Matthew Blakiston, second baronet (1761–1806), and his wife, Anne (*d.* 27 November 1862 in her 101st year), daughter of John Rochfort of Clogrenane, co. Carlow, Ireland. He served in the Madras engineers and in the 27th regiment (Enniskillens), participated in the battle of Assaye and the capture of Bourbon, Mauritius, and Java, and fought during the Peninsular War from Vitoria to Toulouse. On 26 September 1814 he married Jane Wright, retiring from active military service around the same time. He published *Twelve Years of Military Adventures* anonymously (1829) and *Twenty Years in Retirement* under his name (1836). He died on 4 June 1867 at Moberley Hall, Cheshire.

His son Thomas was educated at St Paul's Proprietary School at Southsea, and at the Royal Military Academy at Woolwich, from which he obtained a commission in the Royal Artillery on 16 December 1851. He served with his regiment in England, Ireland, and Nova Scotia, and in the Crimea before Sevastopol, where his younger brother Lawrence was killed in the battle of the Redan on 8 September 1855. In 1857 Blakiston was appointed, on the recommendation of Sir Edward Sabine, a member of the scientific expedition for the exploration of British North America between Canada and the Rocky Mountains, under the command of John Palliser. He was principally employed in taking observations on the magnetic conditions and temperature; but in 1858 he crossed the Kutanie and Boundary passes independently, and subsequently published *Report of the Exploration of Two Passes through the Rocky Mountains* (1859).

During the Chinese war of 1859 Blakiston was left in command of a detachment of artillery at Canton (Guangzhou), and there he organized a widely reported exploration of the middle and upper course of the Yangtze (Yangzi), the idea being to ascend the river as far as the Min, and then cross the province of Szechwan (Sichuan), and reach north-western India via Tibet and Lhasa. The party consisted of Blakiston, Lieutenant-Colonel H. A. Sarel, and Dr Alfred Barton, and with the Revd S. Schereschewsky as interpreter, together with four Sikh and three Chinese attendants, it set out from Shanghai on 12 February 1861, convoyed by Vice-Admiral Sir James Hope's squadron, which left the party at Yaan (Ya'an) on 16 March. They reached Pingshan on 25 May, having travelled 1800 miles from Shanghai, 900 miles further than any other Europeans, except the Jesuits in native costume. The country there being subject to considerable insurgency, they were forced to retrace their route on 30 May, reaching Shanghai on 9 July. Blakiston produced a remarkably accurate chart of the river from Hangchow (Hangzhou) to Pingshan, published in 1861, for which he received in 1862 the royal (patron's) medal of the Royal Geographical Society. Blakiston quickly published a substantial account of their journey, *Five Months on the Yang-tsze* (1862), with illustrations by Barton. This remained a standard account for the region for at least the following fifty years.

Towards the end of 1862 Blakiston made a brief visit to Yezo (Hokkaido), the northern island of Japan. Returning to England at the end of the year, he resigned his commission and entered into a business arrangement with a small group of Scottish merchants. Together they registered the West Pacific Company Ltd, on 12 February 1863, to exploit the rich timber resources of the area with the aim of erecting sawmills in Yezo, as well as acting as general shippers between China and Japan. Blakiston, having subscribed nearly half the company's £4400 capital, returned to Japan, via Russia, Siberia, and the Amur River. Settling at the treaty port of Hakodate, then widely regarded as an isolated and storm-battered settlement, he acted as local manager for the company, as well as establishing his own local trading firm, Blakiston, Marr & Co. The West Pacific Company failed to prosper, however. Hostility grew between Blakiston and the Scottish shareholders, local Japanese officials proved increasingly obstructive, and, finally, political turbulence initiated by the Meiji restoration of 1868 badly disrupted trade. With losses of nearly £25,000 the company went into liquidation in July 1869.

Notwithstanding this set-back Blakiston remained in Hakodate, operating as a merchant on his own account. He also designed fortifications for the port, undertook scientific surveys, and soon became the longest established and best-known of the European residents—'le véritable Roi d'Hakodate'—keeping open house for travellers, especially those with scientific interests. In 1872 he contributed to the *Journal of the Royal Geographical Society* a narrative of a journey round Hokkaido, containing information on its topography, climate, forests, fisheries, mines, and population, and first calling attention to the existence of a pre-Ainu race of pit-dwellers.

During Blakiston's residence at Hakodate he cultivated a deep interest in the ornithology of Hokkaido. He made an extensive collection of birds, which was later housed in the University Museum of Natural History at Sapporo, Japan, and in 1878 compiled, with H. Pryer of Yokohama, a pioneering catalogue of the avifauna of Japan (*Ibis*, 4th ser., 2, 1878, 207–50), revised and reprinted in London in 1884. He demonstrated that the birds of Hokkaido belong to the Siberian as distinct from the Manchurian subregion of the Palaearctic region; and the zoo-geographical line of division formed by the Strait of Tsu-garu was termed Blakiston's line in contemporary ornithological literature. In 1883 he read to the Asiatic Society (*Transactions*, 11, 1883) a paper entitled 'Zoological Indications of the Ancient Connexion of the Japan Islands with the Continent'. Seven new species of Japanese birds were named after him. Blakiston also published a book, *Japan in Yezo* (1883), consisting of articles reprinted from the *Japan Gazette* as well as a number of papers in *The Ibis*, *The Chrysanthemum*, the *Transactions of the Asiatic Society of Japan*, and the *Proceedings of the United States National Museum*, on the birds of British North America and Japan. Besides the collection at Sapporo, he gave Japanese birds to the United States National Museum (Smithsonian Institution), and sent living specimens to the gardens of the London Zoological Society.

In 1884, after a visit to Australia, New Zealand, and England, Blakiston retired from his business and left Japan for the United States. He was married relatively late in life, on 16 April 1885, to Anne Mary, daughter of James Dun of Dundaff, London, Ohio. They had a son, Lawrence Wright, and a daughter, Jessie Carmichael. He eventually settled in New Mexico; he died on 15 October 1891 at San Diego, California, and was buried at Columbus, Ohio.

H. E. D. Blakiston, *rev.* Christopher J. Schmitz

Sources *Proceedings* [Royal Geographical Society], new ser., 13 (1891), 728–9 · *The Ibis*, 6th ser., 4 (1892), 190 · *Auk*, 9 (1892), 75–6 · private information (1901, 2004) · Burke, *Peerage* · board minutes, annual returns of capital and shareholders, West Pacific Company, Limited, 1863–72, NA Scot., BT2/129 · T. W. Blakiston, *Japan in Yezo: a series of papers descriptive of journeys undertaken in the island of Yezo, at intervals between 1862 and 1882* (1883)

Archives Hakodate Municipal Library, Japan, letters · University Museum of Natural History, Sapporo, Japan, ornithological collection

Likenesses photograph, repro. in Blakiston, *Japan in Yezo*

Wealth at death under £8000—John Blakiston: probate, 1867, *CGPLA Eng. & Wales*

Blakman, John. *See* Blacman, John (1407/8–1485?).

Blamey, Sir Thomas Albert (1884–1951), army officer, was born at Lake Albert, New South Wales, Australia, on 24 January 1884, seventh of the ten children of Richard Henwood Blamey (*b.* 1846), a small farmer and droving contractor who had migrated from Cornwall, and his wife,

Sir Thomas Albert Blamey (1884–1951), by Ronald K. Monro, 1943

Margaret Louisa Murray (*b.* 1849), who was Australian born. Thomas was educated at Superior Public School, Wagga Wagga, and at Wagga Wagga grammar school; he was a pupil teacher at the New South Wales education department (1899–1903) before moving to Fremantle (Western Australia) as an assistant teacher. He would have become a Methodist minister had he not won a commission in the cadet forces administrative and instructional staff in Melbourne in 1906. On 8 September 1909, aged twenty-five, he married a stockbroker's daughter, thirty-four-year-old Minnie Caroline Millard (1875–1935), in her parents' house in Toorak, Victoria. They had two sons: Charles (*b.* 1910) who joined the Royal Australian Air Force and died in a plane crash in 1932; and Thomas (*b.* 1914) who became a solicitor and served in the Australian Imperial Force (AIF) in the Second World War.

Full of promise and energy, Blamey moved to the Australian military forces as a captain in 1910 and was sent to Staff College at Quetta in India in 1912. There, living initially as a bachelor, he abandoned his straitened Methodism for the more lubricious life of the mess, and wrote his main essay, 'The British empire and the Pacific problem'. The commandant's report noted that Blamey had 'succeeded beyond all expectation' though 'he was not gifted with a large amount of tact' (*AusDB*). When war broke out in 1914, Major Blamey was in London attached to the War Office, but he soon joined the AIF's 1st division headquarters in Egypt as an intelligence officer. He saw some action with the 2nd brigade at the Gallipoli landing on 25 April 1915 and in May was fortunate to survive a fierce shoot-out while on patrol. When the 2nd Australian division was raised Blamey, now temporary lieutenant-colonel, became its assistant adjutant and quartermaster-general.

Blamey moved with the AIF to France, became chief of staff of 1st Australian division, and helped plan its battles on the Somme in 1916 and 1917. From June 1918, as a brigadier, he was chief of staff to Lieutenant-General Sir John Monash's Australian corps. Monash found him 'alert and prehensile' with 'an infinite capacity for taking pains'; while General Sir William Birdwood thought him 'an exceedingly able little man, though by no means a pleasing personality' (*AusDB*). Blamey played a role in planning the battle of Hamel (4 July 1918), the August offensive, and the assault on the Hindenburg line. Though briefly commanding a battalion and a brigade in France, Blamey had not done so in action; his strengths were in staff work rather than on the battlefield itself.

After the war and in his peacetime rank of colonel, Blamey served in various staff posts but became dissatisfied with the army's promotional logjam. In 1925, when 41, he accepted the much more lucrative and prestigious post of chief commissioner of the Victorian police force. While Blamey improved the standards of police organization and education, his approach was autocratic, confrontational and violent, both with the police union and with rioters during the depression. His high living won him little praise from the press, nor did his bungling of an episode when a friend borrowed his police badge and left it in a brothel. Knighted in 1935, Blamey was forced to resign a year later over deceiving the public in a misguided attempt to shield a colleague. Minnie, for years an invalid, had died in 1935, and Blamey at fifty-two found himself alone and unemployed.

For a time Blamey lived on his pension and modest investments, making occasional radio broadcasts on international affairs. Then, in September 1938, as part of its rearmament programme, the Australian government appointed him to organize manpower planning and recruiting. Soon after the declaration of war Blamey, promoted lieutenant-general, was placed in command of the Australian corps in the Middle East. He had married on 5 April 1939 Olga Ora Farnsworth (*b.* 1904), a 35-year-old fashion artist from Melbourne, at St John's Anglican Church, Toorak.

Blamey's battles in the Middle East, were more with the British high command than the enemy. He fought against Generals Wavell and Auchinleck to keep the AIF together and adequately equipped—and usually won; he persuaded General Wilson to move the weight of attack in Syria on to a more advantageous axis; he had the foresight to survey the evacuation beaches in Greece on landing, knowing that with insufficient air cover and armoured support his men would soon be back; and he negotiated the evacuation of the Australians from the Tobruk fortress after they had defied Rommel's forces for over six months. However, his ambiguous conduct towards Australian prime minister R. G. Menzies, while saving Blamey's political skin, helped perpetrate the Greek fiasco in the first place; and his inclusion of his son, an artillery captain, in his staff evacuation plane was an unnecessary indulgence.

Blamey became a full general in September 1941, and, on his return to Australia in early 1942, was appointed commander-in-chief of the Australian military forces, responsible for their rapid expansion to meet the Japanese thrust south. He also became commander of the allied land forces under Douglas MacArthur, the United States general. Either task would have tested most men; Blamey excelled in doing both. His most difficult time came in September–October 1942 when the Japanese were pushing across the Kokoda track and threatening Port Moresby. MacArthur needed a scapegoat and ordered Blamey to New Guinea to assume operational control. Although the turn of the tide of battle was imminent, Blamey sacked two field commanders and accused some of his men of having 'run like rabbits', thereby appeasing MacArthur, saving himself, and making more enemies in the Australian forces.

As American strength built up, Blamey was increasingly sidelined. Still, he was responsible for the high-level planning for the Australians' retaking of Buna and Lae in 1943, and in 1944–5, for the arduous campaigns in the Ramu and Markham valleys, at Wewak, and in the Solomons and Borneo. He mastered the complex logistics of combined arms warfare in the most difficult of terrains, while always carefully monitoring the health of his men. At the war's end, Blamey was one of only a few allied commanders to have survived in post for the duration; he accepted the Japanese regional surrender at Morotai and was a signatory to the final document of surrender at Tokyo Bay.

Blamey's critics, of whom there were many, drew attention to his drinking, gambling, and womanizing, to which John Curtin (Australia's prime minister, 1941–5) replied that he had appointed 'a military leader not a Sunday-School teacher'. They also noticed that he played favourites and his public accounts were sometimes suspect. Still, MacArthur's judgement is fair: he thought Blamey a 'sensual, slothful and doubtful character but a tough commander likely to shine like a power-light in an emergency. The best of the local bunch' (*AusDB*). This whisky-complexioned, pug-faced, rotund little man (he was 5 feet 6 inches tall) was a brilliant staff officer in one world war and a political general of outstanding ability in the next who, for all his faults, successfully fashioned and led Australia's army to victory in the nation's darkest hours.

Losing favour with the Labor leadership after Curtin's death, Blamey was forced to resign in November 1945. He retired to his business affairs, but when the Liberals regained office in 1950 Menzies made him a field marshal—the only Australian to have held that rank. Blamey died of a stroke in the Repatriation General Hospital, Heidelberg, Victoria, on 27 May 1951, and 300,000 attended his state funeral on 30 May. He was cremated at Fawkner crematorium, Melbourne. CARL BRIDGE

Sources D. Horner, *Blamey* (1998) • J. Hetherington, *Blamey*, 1973, Australian War Memorial, Canberra • N. D. Carlyon, *I remember Blamey* (1980) • D. M. Horner, 'Blamey, Sir Thomas Albert', *AusDB*, vol. 13 • P. Dennis and others, *The Oxford companion to Australian military history* (1995) • D. Horner, ed., *The commanders* (1984) • S. F. Rowell, *Full circle* (1974)

Archives Australian War Memorial, Canberra, MSS | Australian War Memorial, Canberra, Carlyon MSS · Australian War Memorial, Canberra, Rowell MSS · National Archives of Australia, Canberra, Shedden MSS · State Library of Victoria, Melbourne, La Trobe Manuscript collection, Olga Blamey TS | FILM Australian War Memorial, Canberra, news footage · BFI NFTVA, documentary footage · BFI NFTVA, news footage · IWM FVA, news footage
Likenesses R. K. Monro, photograph, 1943, Australian War Memorial, Canberra [*see illus.*] · group photograph, 1945, Hult. Arch. · W. Dargie, oils, Naval and Military Club, Melbourne · W. Dargie, oils, Commercial Travellers' Association, Melbourne · R. Ewers, bronze statue, Kings Domain, Melbourne · I. Hele, oils, Australian War Memorial, Canberra
Wealth at death A$27,899: Horner, 'Blamey, Sir Thomas Albert'

Blamire, Susanna (1747–1794), poet, known as the Muse of Cumberland and the Poet of Friendship, was born on 12 January 1747 at Cardew Hall, near Dalston, Cumberland, the youngest of the four children of William Blamire (1703–1758), a yeoman farmer of the Hollin estate (later named The Oaks), and Isabella, *née* Simpson (1709–1753), of the nearby manor of Thackwood Nook, Stockdalewath, whose mother was a Richmond of the neighbouring manor of Highhead Castle. Susanna's parents died when she was a child, and on her father's death she went to live at Thackwood with her widowed aunt, Mary Simpson (1703–1785), a shrewd but unfailingly kind woman. Her brother William, a distinguished naval surgeon, was married to Jane, *née* Christian (1749–1837), sister of John Christian Curwen (1756–1828) MP and agricultural reformer. Susanna's other brother, Richmond, was the London publisher of many of William Gilpin's books on the picturesque.

After briefly attending the dame school at Raughton Head, Susanna is thought to have been taught at home by assistants from the distinguished grammar school at nearby Sebergham, where the poet Josiah Relph had been headmaster. By mid-adolescence she already had a wide and discriminating literary knowledge. She was a tall, sociable, and 'bonny and verra lish young lass' (Blamire, *Poetical Works*, xxiii). Her face was slightly marked by smallpox (which Giacomo Cambruzzi tactfully ignored in his portrait of her of about 1778). Her brother William commented that the most vivacious youths of his day were dull and phlegmatic in comparison with his lively sister. Indeed her passion for dancing was so extreme that if she met travelling musicians on the road she would dismount and dance to a jig or hornpipe.

Blamire often wrote poems beside a stream in her own garden at Thackwood, sometimes playing an air on her guitar or flageolet, and occasionally pinning her verses to oak trees, where they could be read by passers-by. She was able to broaden her horizons, and master the music and phrasing of Scottish song, as a result of her sister Sarah's marriage in 1767 to Colonel Thomas Graeme of Duchray Castle, Stirlingshire, an officer in the Black Watch. She was introduced to a circle at Gartmore House that sympathized with and encouraged her, and she often paid visits to Scotland. She henceforth wrote many songs in the Scots dialect as well as in the Cumbrian. Among the best of the Scots songs are 'What ails this heart o'mine?'; the beautiful, semi-autobiographical 'The Siller Croun'; and 'The Nabob', set to the air 'The Traveller's Return'. The latter is a nostalgic poem with a setting near Duchray Castle that anticipates Robert Burns's 'Auld Lang Syne'. While visiting a relation at Chillingham, in Northumberland, she attracted the attention of Charles Bennet, Lord Ossulston (1743–1822). Maxwell says that Ossulston's father, the third earl of Tankerville, encouraged Susanna to write one of her best sketches of rustic life, a dialogue beginning 'Wey, Ned, man! thou luiks sae down-hearted', a remarkable amalgam of political ferment, involving a political argument that Blamire had overheard between two neighbours on the subject of Thomas Paine's 'Reets o'man' of 1791 (Blamire, *Poetical Works*, xxx). While the earl may indeed have been amused by Susanna's compositions in Cumberland dialect, his death in 1767 makes nonsense of the claim that he requested her to compose 'Wey, Ned, man!'. Blamire and Ossulston had a love affair that was thwarted when in 1767 Ossulston was sent away to prevent marriage. One of the allegories in *Stoklewath*, with its authentic ring of a real lovers' quarrel, points to an angry confrontation some twelve years later between Susanna and Lord Ossulston (now the married fourth earl of Tankerville). This allegory, coupled with the poem 'Hope', a paean to the picturesque, probably set at Painshill Park, suggests that the meeting could have occurred at or near Painshill, only 4 miles distant from the earl's Surrey house at Walton-on-Thames.

While staying in Carlisle, Blamire met William Gilpin's sister, Catherine Gilpin, of Scaleby Castle. They lived together for a while and collaborated on a number of poems including 'The Cumberland Scold'—a 'perfect masterpiece of dramatic dialect poetry' (MacDiarmid). They also jointly composed 'Peer Body', a bawdy version of the traditional song 'Comin' thro' the Rye'. Blamire herself wrote a number of songs in Cumberland dialect about which the Denwoods enthused:

> It is all there in a torrent of rich, lively, homely rhymed sense, hitting off character sketches that are truly delightful, and when we remember that they are the first of their kind in Cumbrian dialect our amazement is not lessened. (Denwood and Denwood, 42)

Blamire detailed her method of composition in 'Epistle to her Friends at Gartmore' (1773), an amusing letter-poem to her Scottish friends Isabella and Elizabeth Graham in which she light-heartedly and cleverly showed the difficulties of writing poetry. This poem was later taken as evidence for Blamire's already being 'a very accomplished poet' who had 'created for this more personal side of her poetry a free-moving, airy, conversational style, such as no one else is using at this period' (Wordsworth, 1).

It is sometimes thought from the concluding verses of 'Wey, Ned, man!' that Blamire was a reactionary, but this is not borne out in her most powerful poem, 'The nun's return to the world, by the decree of the national assembly of France, February 1790', where she expresses unequivocal support for the principles of the French Revolution and a sympathy for the lot of the unenfranchised labourer. Sections of the poem appear to anticipate Byron's 'The Prisoner of Chillon', especially canto 14. The fact that Blamire's nephew William Brown was Annabella Milbanke's tutor makes it possible that Byron could have read a transcript of the poem while at Seaham Manor, immediately following his marriage to Annabella in 1815.

Blamire, who suffered from debilitating recurrent bouts of rheumatic fever, was also an early female practitioner of orthodox medicine, having learned physic from her brother William. In an unpublished Gothic prose allegory she used desert imagery to describe the pain and malaise of a severe attack of her illness and expressed longing for recovery when, significantly, she would again be able to 'dispense blessings to the world as the physician, Counsellor and friend of Mankind' (Susanna Blamire MSS). Her illness was possibly aggravated by her ministrations to the poor; Blamire, as reflected in her poetry, never lost sight of the grim reality that she had seen at first hand when attending the sick in dark, cramped labourers' cottages. Dr William Paley was a friend of the family, and his philosophy of 'moral utilitarianism'—that 'virtue is the doing good to mankind in obedience to the will of God, and for the sake of everlasting happiness' (W. Paley, *Principles of Moral and Political Philosophy*, 2 vols., 1787, 1.41)—would certainly have struck a chord with the warmly altruistic Susanna, and probably influenced her own philosophy.

Susanna Blamire died at 14 Finkle Street, Carlisle, on 5 April 1794, of what is now believed to be rheumatic heart disease. She was buried at Raughton Head church, near Dalston, on 9 April. Many regretted the loss of 'Miss Sukey's' lively and friendly company at 'merry-neets' (late-night social gatherings): 'Weel, weel, t'merrie neets wullent be worth gangin' till at aw, noo that she's gean' (Bullock and Tutor, 21).

Blamire published virtually nothing in her lifetime, and even then anonymously, in magazines and collections such as *Calliope, or, The musical miscelleny* (1788) and Johnson's *Scots Musical Museum* (1790). 'The Chelsea Pensioners' was at first wrongly attributed to Dr James Moor, professor of Greek at the University of Glasgow. Blamire's works were collected for the first time in 1842 by Henry Lonsdale and Patrick Maxwell, who contacted friends and family in search of fragments of her poems, many of which were written on the backs of recipes and letters. Maxwell extolled her as 'unquestionably the best female writer of her age' (Blamire, *Poetical Works*, xxxix). Further unpublished poems were included in Sidney Gilpin's edition of *Songs and Poems by Miss Blamire, together with Songs by her Friend Miss Gilpin* (1866).

Hugh MacDiarmid much regretted Blamire's obscurity and praised her Scottish songs, which in their unsentimental, natural sweetness 'can be set beside the best that have ever been produced by Scotsmen writing in their own tongue' (MacDiarmid). For MacDiarmid, Blamire was a 'sweet Cumbrian singer whose lyric genius bridged the gulf between Scotland and England, and rang its mirthful or sorrowful changes so effectively in the three different linguistic media of Scots, Cumbrian, and English' (ibid.). Blamire has also been credited with anticipating the Romantic view expounded by Coleridge and Wordsworth—that the natural world can be influenced by the power of the mind—as early as 1767:

> Now grief obscures the cheerful sky
> And clouds the sunbeam of her eye
> So does the black descending storm
> The smiling face of heaven deform.
> ('Lament for the Happy Swain')

In her Scots and Cumbrian poems she is understood to have initiated a 'new order, a new magic in freedom of rhythm, in sheer spontaneous lyrical beauty' (Denwood and Denwood, 32).

On 20 March 1994 an inscribed stone in Carlisle Cathedral was dedicated as a bicentennial memorial by Bishop Harland. This coincided with a renewed critical interest in her work. A reprint of her collected poems appeared in 1994. Her biography, *A Passionate Poet: Susanna Blamire, 1747–94* by Christopher Maycock, was published by the Hypatia Trust in 2003.

CHRISTOPHER HUGH MAYCOCK

Sources S. Blamire, *The poetical works, 1842* (1994) [Woodstock facsimile] • *The poetical works of Miss Susanna Blamire*, ed. H. Lonsdale (1842) • 'Jane Blamire's diary, 1763–1830', 2 vols., Wordsworth Trust, Dove Cottage, Grasmere, WLMSA / Blamire, Jane [handwritten transcripts] • C. Maycock, *A passionate poet: Susan Blamire, 1747–94* (2003) • 'The Maycock Blamire manuscripts', Wordsworth Trust, Dove Cottage, Grasmere, WLMSA record nos. 1998.60.1–77 • Susanna Blamire MSS, priv. coll. • H. Lonsdale, *The worthies of Cumberland* (1873) • J. Wordsworth, *Susanna Blamire: poet of friendship, 1747–1794* (1994) • H. MacDiarmid, 'Susanna Blamire (1747–1794)', NL Scot., MS 27069, fols. 40–48 [transcript of transmission, 7 Nov 1947, BBC Scottish Home Service] • BBC Radio Cumbria, 10 Aug 1998, ref. 100898 • private information (2004) [J. J. McGann] • E. R. Denwood and M. Denwood, 'Susanna Blamire, 1747–1794', *Journal of the Lakeland Dialect Society*, 9 (1947) • R. Lonsdale, ed., *Eighteenth-century women poets: an Oxford anthology* (1989) • 'Jane Blamire's diary, 1763–1830', vol. 1, Manx Museum, Douglas, Isle of Man, Manx National Library, accession no. 9381, item 4 [manuscript: shortened, twentieth-century transcript of the nineteenth-century transcript, vol. 1 only] • N. Nicholson, *The Lake District: an anthology* (1988) • B. Willey, *Eighteenth-century background* (1946) • P. J. Bullock and F. E. Tutor, eds., *A history of Dalston parish from early times* (1992–3) • B. Ruddick, 'Susanna Blamire (1747–1794)', 1989, Manchester University, Department of English [typescript appreciation] • Anderson, *Scot. nat.*, vol. 2 • *DNB*

Archives priv. coll. • Wordsworth Trust, Dove Cottage, Grasmere, Maycock Blamire MSS | Manx Museum, Douglas, Isle of Man, Manx National Library, J. Blamire, diary [transcript] • Wordsworth Trust, Dove Cottage, Grasmere, J. Blamire, diary [transcript]

Likenesses G. Cambruzzi, crayon, *c.*1778, repro. in Maycock, *A passionate poet* • portrait, repro. in Maycock, *A passionate poet*

Blamire, William (1790–1862), farmer and politician, was born on 13 April 1790 at The Oaks, near Dalston, Cumberland, the son of William Blamire (1740–1814), yeoman farmer and naval surgeon, and Jane Curwen (1739/40–1837). He came on both sides of his family from long-established Cumberland yeoman farming stock. His mother was the sister of John Christian Curwen, the Cumberland agriculturalist and whig MP, who exerted a major influence on both Blamire's agricultural interests and his political views. Another early influence was William Paley who, as vicar of Dalston, officiated at Blamire's baptism and later gave him informal tuition. In 1799 Blamire became a private pupil of Revd John Fawcett in Carlisle. He was king's scholar at Westminster School, London, from 1805 to 1808 and entered Christ Church, Oxford, with a studentship in 1808 but left the university in 1811 without taking a degree.

Blamire's education had fitted him for a professional career but he preferred practical agricultural experiments, and to these he devoted himself with enthusiasm in the 1810s and 1820s. He attended Curwen's Schoose Farm on his Workington estate, where he learned about animal husbandry, and then travelled extensively in the north-west of England and southern Scotland. At considerable financial cost, since he freely indulged what was in large part a hobby, he became thereby an authority. The contacts he forged with yeoman farmers proved useful to his later political career. To his obituarist in the *Carlisle Journal* he became 'the very idol of the yeomanry; and his name a household word in every hamlet, dale and nook of Cumberland'. His close links with local landed society were decisive in what was a very popular appointment as high sheriff of Cumberland in April 1828 on the death of the incumbent Thomas Parker.

Blamire was a whig and a reformer and worked to secure Curwen's nomination and election as MP for Cumberland in 1818 and 1820. He was one of the largest graziers in the north of England and his political instincts reflected 'country' concerns. He believed in the independence of the landowning classes and—ironically given his career after 1836—was suspicious of central government influence. In 1816, at a public meeting in Cockermouth, he opposed the Liverpool government's attempt to preserve the new income tax in peacetime. Blamire became an MP at the exceptional general election of 1831, which the whigs called after defeats in committee over their parliamentary reform bill. Strongly supported by landowners across the county, he agreed to stand as a reformer alongside Sir James Graham. This involved a challenge, against Graham's advice, to the entrenched political interest of the tory Lowther family and a rare party battle in Cumberland. His success was assured in May when Lowther withdrew from the contest with polls showing that he had less than half the votes cast for Graham and Blamire (453 against 942 and 917 respectively). Blamire's success was part of the pronounced pro-reform swing throughout the country but was widely acclaimed in Cumberland, where large numbers of 40 shilling freeholders had made the frequently difficult journey to the sole polling station in Cockermouth. Blamire celebrated 'the force of public opinion in destroying the magic spell of wealth and unconstitutional influence' (*Carlisle Journal*). He also welcomed support from ordinary clergymen who had forsaken normally tory loyalties, noting tartly: 'You will find no pluralist, no man who holds two livings in the list of Blue [the whig colour in Cumberland] voters' (Lonsdale, 246).

Blamire took his seat on 20 June 1831 and remained an MP until 1836, being returned unopposed for the newly created seat of East Cumberland at the general elections of 1832 and 1835. He spoke rarely and pithily in parliament, and nearly always from the basis of local knowledge. While generally loyal to the whig government on the reform question, he never neglected local concerns. In July 1831 he concurred, against tory objections, that Cockermouth should lose one of its two members since its population was below 4000. He did not neglect to praise his fellow Cumbrians: 'He must … bear witness to the respectability of the constituency … He knew of no place more deserving of two Members, if respectability and independence were to determine the question' (*Hansard* 3, 5, 1831, 488–9). He opposed the government on two other matters. He moved an unsuccessful amendment on 22 June 1831 to have the boundaries of Whitehaven adjusted to remove rural voters from the constituency. In August, in a coded attack on the Lowther interest in west Cumberland, he unsuccessfully opposed the creation of a second county seat, arguing that the 9000 county voters would be freer from electoral influence in one constituency.

Most of Blamire's parliamentary speeches after 1832 concerned property. He opposed the General Registry Bill in January 1832 because of its adverse consequences for copyholders. He stated in July 1833 that new Bank of England charter regulations would damage property owners 'in northern parts of the country … where they had a serious objection to Bank of England paper and preferred country paper, as they had much less difficulty in detecting forgeries' (*Hansard* 3, 18, 1833, 1393–4). On 3 April 1834 he married his cousin, Dorothy, youngest daughter of John Taubman of The Nunnery, Isle of Man, and widow of Colonel Mark Wilkes, the late governor of St Helena. The couple, who had no children, lived in Upper Harley Street, London.

Blamire's most important parliamentary contributions concerned the tithe question and these determined the shape of his future career. His extensive knowledge of Cumberland agriculture convinced him of the damage done to rural society by tithes and of the urgent need for legislation. In 1833 he introduced a bill to suspend the rash of tithe suits under the so-called Tenterden Act of 1832, which had allowed a period of one year during which long-dormant claims could be pressed. His bill, delayed in the Lords, became law in 1834. He made a decisive contribution to the proposals for tithe commutation made by Melbourne's government. His speech to the Commons on 25 March 1836 was made, he said, as 'a practical man' with ample opportunity of observing 'the workings of the tithing system in its various ramifications' (*Hansard* 3, 32, 1836, 607–16). He urged that parties be given time to come to voluntary agreements, since the imposition of compulsory tithe awards would be unnecessarily expensive and might ignore relevant local circumstances. He also stressed the need to safeguard improving landowners from punitively high commutation awards which threatened their investments.

Blamire's speech won warm commendation from both sides of the house. It also led to his being appointed on 22

August 1836 first tithe commissioner under the new Commutation Act. With the two other commissioners, Thomas Wentworth Buller and Richard Jones, he wrestled with the complexities of intricate issues of property right. Blamire was recognized as *primus inter pares* in a job to which he committed enormous time and reserves of energy. He took great care over the appointment as assistant tithe commissioners of practical land agents, since it was their task to negotiate agreements and impose settlements. His determination to let local knowledge and experience carry as much weight as possible within the scope of the act paid rich dividends. The much cheaper voluntary tithe commutation agreements, which his speech of March 1836 had advocated, were effected in almost 58 per cent of all cases. The work of the tithe commission proceeded smoothly. Three-quarters of all tithe awards were completed within the first ten years—a much faster rate of progress than was achieved by the poor-law commissioners—and the tithe commission was able to be wound up on 8 August 1851, virtually laying to rest one of the most contentious areas of property dispute in eighteenth- and early nineteenth-century England.

By this time Blamire's success had brought other administrative duties. On 22 June 1841 he became commissioner for copyholds as well as tithes under new copyhold enfranchisement legislation. The work of the copyhold commission increased substantially when compulsory powers were taken under amending legislation passed in 1852, and it absorbed him until his retirement. Blamire's practical efficiency also impressed Peel, who described him as 'that indefatigable public servant' (Lonsdale, 297). He gave influential evidence (1 July 1844) to the House of Commons select committee on commons' enclosure, in which he estimated that there were 8 million acres of unenclosed waste land in England and Wales, much of which could be brought under cultivation. He was invited on 14 August 1845 to become commissioner in charge of the enclosure of commons and wastes under legislation passed to expedite and reduce the cost of enclosure agreements. Here, again until retirement, he supervised the enclosure of about 350,000 acres of common and waste land. Such was the scale of his work that it has been said that he 'helped to re-make the face of rural England' (Spring, 167).

Blamire was one of a small number of élite administrators who flourished in the new world of government commissions and regulation created in the 1830s and 1840s and who inaugurated a new era of bureaucracy. Long working hours and prolonged absence from rural Cumberland alike took their toll. He endured paralysis of his right arm from 1847, after which he required the assistance of two secretaries to take dictation, and never fully recovered from his wife's death on 20 September 1857. Deteriorating health forced his resignation from all official duties in September 1860, when he received a pension from the lords of the Treasury. His return to Cumberland did not improve his health and he died at his property, Thackwood Nook, 4 miles south-east of Dalston, on the edge of Inglewood Forest, on 12 January 1862. He was buried on 18 January at Raughtonhead churchyard, 1 mile north of his home. ERIC J. EVANS

Sources H. Lonsdale, *The worthies of Cumberland*, 1 (1867) • *DNB* • E. J. Evans, *The contentious tithe* (1976) • E. J. Evans, 'A 19th century tithe dispute and its significance', *Transactions of the Cumberland and Westmorland Antiquarian and Archaeological Society*, new ser., 74 (1974), 159–85 • *Carlisle Journal* (17 Jan 1862) • F. Chance, *Some notable Cumbrians* (1931), 31–9 • J. Wilson, *Dalston parish registers*, 2 (1895) • W. Jackson, 'The Richmonds of Highead', *Transactions of the Cumberland and Westmorland Antiquarian and Archaeological Society*, 2 (1874–5), 108–47 • *Hansard* 3 (1831–6) • R. Kain, *The tithe surveys of England and Wales* (1985) • *Cumberland Pacquet* (April–May 1831) [for election battle in Cumberland] • D. Spring, *The English landed estate in the nineteenth century: its administration* (1963)

Archives Cumbria AS, Carlisle, Lonsdale MSS • UCL, letters to James Brougham

Wealth at death under £4000: administration, 17 Feb 1862, *CGPLA Eng. & Wales*

Blanch, Stuart Yarworth, Baron Blanch (1918–1994), archbishop of York, was born at Viney Hill Farm, Blakeney, Gloucestershire, in the Forest of Dean, on 2 February 1918, by eleven years the youngest of three sons of William Edwin Blanch (1870–1923), farmer, and his wife, Elizabeth, *née* Yarworth (1877–1944). The first five years of his life were remembered by him as a time of idyllic happiness brutally cut short by his father's death in a shooting accident. Subsequently the family moved to London, where he later won a scholarship to Alleyn's School, Dulwich, leaving at the age of eighteen for a post with the Law Fire Insurance Society Ltd in Chancery Lane. After joining the RAF in 1940, his intellectual belief in God was transformed into faith, an experience which came from repeatedly reading the four gospels while on Christmas guard duty at a deserted RAF camp. After some time as a corporal in the RAF police he volunteered for aircrew duties, trained as a navigator, and for eighteen months flew reconnaissance missions over Burma from Calcutta, with the rank of flight lieutenant. During this time he became an Anglican lay reader and applied for ordination. On 10 July 1943 he married Brenda Gertrude (*b.* 1916), daughter of William Arthur Percival Coyte and his wife, Lilian Gertrude, *née* March. Their years of wartime separation were bridged by a remarkable correspondence in which they explored their faith together.

After the war Blanch obtained a place in St Catherine's Society, Oxford, gained a first in theology in 1948, and trained for the ministry at Wycliffe Hall. Ordained in 1949, he served a three-year curacy in the parish of All Saints, Highfield, Oxford. During these Oxford years the first three of the Blanches' five children, Susan, Hilary, and Angela, were born. In November 1952 he became vicar of the Oxfordshire village of Eynsham, where over the next four years a large congregation was built up from a handful of people, and close-knit ecumenical relations were created with the local Roman Catholic, Baptist, and Methodist churches. Here their family was completed with the birth of Timothy in 1953 and Alison in 1955. Returning to Oxford in 1957, Blanch was vice-principal of Wycliffe Hall until appointed in July 1960 as Oriel canon of Rochester Cathedral and first principal of a new theological college

Stuart Yarworth Blanch, Baron Blanch (1918–1994), by Anne-Katrin Purkiss, 1988

established in the old deanery. The college was intended to suit the needs of older men and he developed a syllabus and lifestyle which brilliantly met the need.

In 1966 Blanch became the fifth bishop of Liverpool, coming to a city still scarred by wartime bombing and to a region beset by severe social and economic problems. He effectively oversaw the considerable reorganization of parishes required by massive rehousing programmes, creating the new post of planning officer in the diocese. Universal questions were raised by the preoccupations of the 1960s, while internal church business included urgent matters concerning synodical government, changes in worship, church unity discussions, and the effects of the Second Vatican Council. Blanch matched the moment, relating his Christian faith to a changing world and skilfully managing change in the church. One special skill lay in offering a view of the Bible acceptable to Christians of all persuasions. In cultural and political matters he was persuasive in his view that a serious view of society required a serious view of the Bible, consequently commanding audiences for it outside church circles.

In Liverpool an early and lasting friendship was established with Blanch's ecumenical colleagues the Roman Catholic archbishop, George Andrew Beck, and the Methodist chairman, the Revd Rex Kissack, and they met together with planned regularity. Against a local history of sectarian bitterness the flowering of ecumenical life in Liverpool, known as the 'Mersey miracle', taken forward by their successors, stemmed from this period. It owed much to the ecumenical Call to the North—a process begun in 1969 and culminating at Easter 1973—which arose from a suggestion by Blanch. Having been nurtured by the friendship of Merseyside's church leaders, it found a strong ally in Donald Coggan, then archbishop of York, who in 1969 invited northern church leaders of all traditions to a consultation at Bishopthorpe. This was the first of what became annual overnight gatherings of leaders, later called the Northern Consultation for Mission. With the failure in 1969 of the Anglican–Methodist union scheme, Blanch and Kissack promptly called together a joint Anglican–Methodist synod which met in Liverpool in 1971 and laid foundations for future work. In 1968 Blanch attended the World Council of Churches meeting in Uppsala. He was increasingly in demand as a lecturer, and visited Alabama in 1968 and Bermuda in 1969. The first of his eight books, *The World our Orphanage* (1972), embodied the content of his lectures at a College of Preachers festival in York.

Following Coggan's translation to Canterbury, Blanch was appointed ninety-fourth archbishop of York and enthroned on 25 February 1975. A superb pastor, he presided over a happy diocese and travelled widely in his province. Invitations to lecture multiplied, and in the following eight years he made ten working trips abroad, fulfilling engagements in fifteen countries, including New Zealand, Australia, India, Ceylon, the Gulf states, Israel, America, and Canada, and visiting Northern Ireland and Éire on several occasions. His lecture titles numbered 136 and covered seventy themes. His love of the Old Testament helped forge special links with the Jewish community, particularly in York. At the 1978 Lambeth conference he delivered a series of lectures long remembered by bishops worldwide. A not too frequent but always effective speaker in general synod, his work included membership of its broadcasting commission and chairing its Partners in Mission consultation. No lover of bureaucracy, he was described as the most unecclesiastical of archbishops. In many respects a private man, he had a charismatic gift of friendship and humour, and inspired much affection and faith, his winning personality and delightful voice also making him a popular broadcaster. He wrote six books at York: *For All Mankind* (1976), *The Christian Militant* (1978), *The Burning Bush* (1978), *The Trumpet in the Morning* (1979), *The Ten Commandments* (1981), and *Living by Faith* (1983), the most autobiographical of his writings.

Such work took its toll and early in 1981 Blanch suffered a breakdown. He took only one month off duty, but thereafter he reduced his workload. He resigned in 1983, becoming the first archbishop of York to be made a life peer. He retired to Oxfordshire, living first in Bloxham and then in Shenington, where he took turns in conducting services at his village church. He also undertook four more lecture assignments abroad and wrote two more books, *The Way of Blessedness* (1985) and *Encounters with Jesus* (1988). In retirement his wife, Brenda, herself active in public life in both Liverpool and York, compiled two anthologies, *Learning of God: Readings from Amy Carmichael* (1985), and *Heaven a Dance: an Evelyn Underhill Anthology* (1992). Blanch added forewords and they were a fitting emblem of a splendid marriage. He died of cancer at the Katharine House Hospice, Banbury, Oxfordshire, on 3 June 1994. Retirement years had been saddened by the death of his eldest daughter, Susan, and he was buried alongside her in Shenington churchyard on 9 June. He was survived by his wife, son, and three daughters.

R. H. L. WILLIAMS

Sources R. H. L. Williams, *Stuart Blanch: a life* (2001) · York Minster, Blanch MSS · general synod of the Church of England, *Synod report* · *The Times* (4 June 1994) · *The Independent* (7 June 1994) ·

WWW [forthcoming] · personal knowledge (2004) · private information (2004)
Archives York Minster, literary corresp. and papers | SOUND priv. coll., recorded talks
Likenesses A.-K. Purkiss, photograph, 1988, NPG [*see illus.*] · photograph, repro. in *The Times* · photograph, repro. in *The Independent*

Blanchard, Caroline Cadette. *See* Howard, Caroline Cadette (*b.* 1821, *d.* in or after 1901).

Blanchard, Edward Litt Leman (1820–1889), writer and playwright, was born on 11 December 1820 at 28 Great Queen Street, London, the second son of William *Blanchard (1769–1835), comic actor with the Kembles' Covent Garden company, and his second wife, Sarah Harrold (1784–1875).

After a brief education in Brixton, Surrey, and then Lichfield, Blanchard went with his parents to New York in 1831. Back in London, and forced by his father's death to find employment at an early age, he became sub-editor of Pinnock's *Guide to Knowledge* in 1836. Although he continued to edit periodicals such as *Chambers's London Journal* (1841) and the *New London Magazine* (1845), he also wrote illustrated guidebooks, among them some of Bradshaw's Descriptive Railway Guides. He edited Willoughby's *Shakespeare*, wrote unmemorable novels, and demonstrated his lifelong interest in spiritualism and séances by founding and editing *The Astrologer and Oracle of Destiny* (1845).

Blanchard's most important work, however, was done for the stage, under his own name and the pseudonyms Francesco (or Francisco) Frost and (with T. L. Greenwood) the Brothers Grinn; he wrote innumerable pantomimes, entertainments, farces, and dramas, as well as comic songs such as 'A Norrible Tale' and 'Villikins and his Dinah'. Beginning with a pantomime for amateurs (1839), in which he devised 'trick' staging and played Harlequin, he went on to write annual Christmas pantomimes for the Drury Lane Theatre from 1852 to 1888, as well as for other London and provincial theatres. Sometimes three, even four, of his works were staged concurrently. In these seasonal productions he strove seriously for prettiness and coherence as well as comic effects, and for a moral to adorn the fairy-tales on which many were based. *See Saw Margery Daw, or, Harlequin Holiday and the Island of Ups and Downs* (1856), for example, shows Necessity in her cottage 'with a Prospect of Hard Work in the Distance'. She says:

> those that work are the illustrious,
> And those most noble are the most industrious.

During the last years of his Drury Lane pantomimes he was made increasingly unhappy by interpolated vulgarisms in his text and by the introduction of music-hall performers.

Blanchard also contributed theatrical obituaries, reviews, and articles about the stage to many periodicals, including *Fun*, the *Illustrated Times*, the *Era Almanack and Annual*, *The Observer*, and *The Era*. From 1863 to 1887 he was the drama critic of the *Daily Telegraph*.

Blanchard was one of the kindliest of men and, privately, one of the saddest. In his diary for 11 December 1861 he recorded: 'Have at least the satisfaction of knowing that … I have never injured a living creature' (Scott and Howard, 1.264). His brother William and William's family, however, were a continual and heavy drain on his resources, when his indefatigable work brought him only between £200 and £400 a year; eventually his income rose to £500 but rarely to £600 or £700. His happiness was greatly increased after his marriage to his long-adored Caroline (*b.* 1821, *d.* in or after 1901) [*see* Howard, Caroline Cadette], whom he called Carina, on 11 June 1874. Many years earlier she had married and had gone to New Zealand, and he had lost touch with her, but had never forgotten her. Caroline was a widow by 1874, and this may also have been Blanchard's second marriage. Having begun his career at such an early age, he always seemed much older than he actually was, and his appearance was anything but youthful. His theatrical knowledge was encyclopaedic, and he did not like to admit ignorance of anything being discussed (Watson, 172).

After a long illness Blanchard died at his home, 6 Albert Mansions, 114 Victoria Street, Westminster, on 4 September 1889 of 'general decay', though he was only sixty-eight. He was buried on 10 September in Kensington Hanwell cemetery, Ealing, Middlesex, and left an estate valued at £441. Carina, who had been a tireless worker for the Emigration Society, survived him. She was awarded a civil-list pension of £50 on 24 May 1890.

JANE W. STEDMAN

Sources *The life and reminiscences of E. L. Blanchard, with notes from the diary of Wm. Blanchard*, ed. C. W. Scott and C. Howard, 2 vols. (1891) [incl. poems, correspondence, repr. of articles, and case bk of Blanchard's doctor] · M. R. Booth, preface, to E. L. Blanchard, 'Aladdin, or, Harlequin and the wonderful lamp', *English plays of the nineteenth century*, 5: *Pantomimes, extravaganzas and burlesques* (1976), 337–77 · *The Athenaeum* (7 Sept 1889), 331 · *The Era* (7 Sept 1889), 9 · *Pall Mall Gazette* (5 Sept 1889), 5 · *Pall Mall Gazette* (11 Sept 1889), 5 · *The Times* (6 Sept 1889), 9 · A. Nicholl, *A history of English drama, 1660–1900*, 2nd edn, 4–5 (1955–62), 4.268–9; 5.262–5 · A. E. Wilson, *King Panto: the story of pantomime* (1935), 142–53 · A. E. T. Watson, *A sporting and dramatic career* (1918), 172 · d. cert. · *CGPLA Eng. & Wales* (1889)
Archives BL, letters, as sponsor, to the Royal Literary Fund, loan no. 96
Likenesses Barraud, woodburytype photograph, 1885, NPG; repro. in *The Theatre* (1 Oct 1885) · wood-engraving, 1889, NPG; repro. in *ILN* (14 Sept 1889) · sketch, repro. in J. Hatton, *Reminiscences of J. L. Toole* (1889), vol. 1, p. 137 · woodcut (after photograph by H. Watkins, 1873), NPG; repro. in *Illustrated Review* (13 Feb 1873)
Wealth at death £441 8s. 1d.: probate, 16 Oct 1889, *CGPLA Eng. & Wales*

Blanchard, (Samuel) Laman (1803–1845), author and journalist, was born at Great Yarmouth on 15 May 1803, the only son of Samuel Blanchard and his wife, the widowed Mary Cowell, *née* Laman. There were five other children of the marriage, all of them daughters. In 1804 his father moved to Southwark, establishing himself as a painter and glazier. In 1809 Blanchard entered St Olave's School in Southwark, where he became the chief Latin scholar, but despite the wishes of the master and the school's trustees to send him to a university and maintain him there for two years, his father's strained finances did not allow him to contemplate supporting his son for a third year. On leaving school in 1816 Blanchard became a clerk to Charles Pearson, a proctor in Doctors' Commons, an occupation he found uncongenial. His preference for a literary career was evident in the precocious dramatic sketches ('Flores histrionici') he published in *The Drama* in 1823, sketches marked by the influence of the work of B. W. Procter (Barry Cornwall) and Byron. About 1822 he formed a close and enduring friendship with Douglas Jerrold, and through Jerrold made the acquaintance of the actor John Buckstone. After abandoning a whimsical notion of going with Jerrold to fight with Byron in Greece, Blanchard resolved to dedicate himself to the stage and was briefly engaged by the manager of the Margate Theatre. According to Buckstone, quoted by Bulwer-Lytton, 'a week was sufficient to disgust him with the beggary and drudgery of the country player's life' (Bulwer-Lytton, xii) and he was obliged to return to London penniless and on foot. He subsequently worked as a reader for the printer Bayliss in Fleet Street, the publisher of the *Monthly Magazine*, to which he had already begun to contribute verse and prose.

In 1823 Blanchard married Ann Elizabeth Gates. There were four children of the marriage, three sons and a daughter. Through the influence of his brother-in-law, Nicholas Vigors, he was appointed to an assistant secretaryship at the Zoological Society of London in 1826, holding the post for three years. In this period his literary activity burgeoned, and in 1828 his friend William Harrison Ainsworth published his volume of verse *Lyric Offerings*, a volume dedicated to Charles Lamb. In 1831 he was appointed sub-editor of the *Monthly Magazine*, then under the direction of George Croly, and editor of the *Belle Assemblée*. He contributed verse to both journals. In the following year he also became associated with the Liberal daily the *True Sun*, and when the paper failed in 1836 he assumed the editorship of the short-lived daily *The Constitutional*. From 1836 to 1837 he also directed the *Court Journal* and from 1837 to 1839 the whig evening paper *The Courier*. Following a shift in *The Courier's* ownership and political bias in 1839, a failed attempt was made by, among others, Bulwer-Lytton, to obtain for him either a clerkship or the editorship of the *London Gazette* from the whig government. From 1841 to 1845 he was closely associated with the *Examiner* and for a year from February 1842 he served as sub-editor of *Ainsworth's Magazine*. In 1842 he also directed and contributed to the monthly journal *George Cruikshank's Omnibus*.

In February 1844 Ann Blanchard was struck with what was described at the time as 'paralysis', and after a protracted period of suffering died on 16 December. Distracted by his wife's illness and death, by the pressures of periodical journalism, and by concern for his four children, Blanchard entered an acute depressive state during which symptoms of his wife's paralysis were repeated in him. On 14 February 1845 he committed suicide by cutting his throat with a razor at his home at 11 Union Place, Lambeth Road, London. A coroner's inquest decreed that he was of unsound mind at the time. He was interred the following month at Norwood cemetery.

Blanchard's death occasioned a good deal of supportive activity from his wide circle of literary friends, many of whom raised funds to benefit his orphaned children. Those friends included Douglas Jerrold, Edward Bulwer-Lytton, William Harrison Ainsworth, Thomas Noon Talfourd, Charles Dickens, Leigh Hunt, John Forster, B. W. Procter, Robert Browning, George Cruikshank, W. M. Thackeray, and W. C. Macready. In 1831, at the distraught father's request, Blanchard had arranged the funeral of William Godwin's only son, who had died of cholera in the epidemic of that year. He had also been a steady friend and supporter of Laetitia Landon (L.E.L.) and published a sympathetic appreciation of her career in his *The Life and Literary Remains of L.E.L.* of 1841. He was godfather, and subsequently father-in-law, to Douglas Jerrold's son, William Blanchard, who in 1876 collected his *Poetical Works*. His essay on Harrison Ainsworth, published in *The Mirror* in 1842, was regularly reprinted as a preface to later nineteenth-century editions of Ainsworth's collected works.

Blanchard was described by Bulwer-Lytton as being 'small and slight, though sufficiently well-knit' and his dark features as 'of rather an oriental cast' (Bulwer-Lytton, xxxvi). Ainsworth, referring to the Maclise sketch reproduced in *Sketches from Life*, noted that 'it has his gravest looks, and wants that cordial and bewitching smile which ordinarily lighted up the features' (Ainsworth, 134). Thackeray too remembered 'his keen, kind, beaming Jew face,—a mixture of Mendelsohn and Voltaire' (Thackeray, 347). Defending Blanchard's decision to concentrate on a career in periodical journalism, Thackeray also insisted that 'his education and habits, his quick easy manner, his sparkling hidden fun, constant tenderness, and brilliant good-humour were best employed as they were' (ibid., 346).

Blanchard's prose essays were collected in three volumes by Bulwer-Lytton in 1846 as *Sketches from Life*. In his obituary of Blanchard in *Ainsworth's Magazine* (7 March 1845, 220) Ainsworth remarked that the essays placed Blanchard 'on a level with one whom he admired and knew well—the celebrated Elia'. The first volume contains a substantial memorial essay by Bulwer-Lytton and a lithographic portrait after a drawing by Daniel Maclise. The collected *Poetical Works* of 1876 has on its title page a photographic reproduction of a miniature by Louisa Stuart Costello. Blanchard's *Corporation Characters: Forming a Select Portrait Gathering of Civic Celebrities*, illustrated by Kenny Meadows, appeared posthumously in 1855.

ANDREW SANDERS

Sources E. Bulwer-Lytton, 'Memoir', in S. L. Blanchard, *Sketches from life*, 3 vols. (1846), v–xliv · W. B. Jerrold, 'Memoir', in *The poetical works of Laman Blanchard* (1876), 1–83 · W. M. Thackeray, 'A brother of the press on the history of a literary man', *Fraser's Magazine*, 33 (1846) · d. cert. · d. cert. [Ann E. Blanchard] · W. B. Jerrold, *The life and remains of Douglas Jerrold* (1859) · S. M. Ellis, *William Harrison Ainsworth and his friends* (1911) · W. H. Ainsworth, 'Laman Blanchard and his writings', *New Monthly Magazine*, new ser., 76 (1846), 131–40 · *Wellesley index* · *The letters of Charles Dickens*, ed. M. House,

G. Storey, and others, 1–4 (1965–77) · P. Graham, *West Norwood cemetery: the Dickens connection* (1995) · *The parish of St Mary, Lambeth*, 1 (1951) · *The Times* (17 Feb 1845)

Archives BL, letters to Leigh Hunt, Add. MSS 38109, 38523–38524 · Herts. ALS, letters to Lord Lytton

Likenesses D. Maclise, group portrait, pencil drawing, 1844 (*Charles Dickens reading 'The chimes' to his friends*), V&A · S. Freeman, stipple (after drawing by D. Maclise), repro. in S. L. Blanchard, *Sketches from life*, 2 vols. (1846), frontispiece · D. Maclise, pencil drawing, V&A · photograph (after miniature by L. S. Costello), repro. in L. Blanchard, *Poetical works of Laman Blanchard* (1876), title-page

Blanchard, Thomas (1760–1797), actor and singer, baptized at Bulmer, Yorkshire, on 16 June 1760, was born into a theatrical family. His father, the elder Thomas Blanchard (*fl.* 1760–1787), was a seasoned actor who built a reputation for himself at York and Norwich before joining the Drury Lane company in 1773; his mother, Elizabeth, also enjoyed a theatrical career. The younger Thomas Blanchard was prepared for a life on the stage as a young child, when he was taught to sing and dance. He is thought to have made his theatrical début in Norwich when he was about twelve, and in October 1773 he joined his father at Drury Lane, making his first appearance as Cupid in Whitehead's *A Trip to Scotland*. He took a number of juvenile parts in the 1773–4 season, the most notable being Prince Arthur in Garrick's production of *King John*, and he remained with the Drury Lane company for a further year, singing and playing juvenile roles, before embarking upon a career as an adult actor in the small provincial theatres of Plymouth and Exeter. After two years he was spotted by the managers of the Theatre Royal, Bath, who engaged him for the 1778–9 season. He became popular with the audience there, achieving particular applause as a singer of rustic songs and as a hornpipe dancer.

For the next four years Blanchard toured the west of England with a small troupe of players, though he rejoined the Bath company in 1783. On 19 May 1787 he married Charlotte Wright (*b.* 1761), the daughter of the actor Roger Wright. Miss Wright was already a singer of some repute, having performed at Drury Lane between 1779 and 1783. Following their marriage the Blanchards moved from Bath to London, Thomas having agreed terms with Thomas Harris to join the company at Covent Garden. He made his début there on 3 October 1788, playing the part of Hodge in Bickerstaffe's *Love in a Village*. Blanchard remained at Covent Garden for several seasons, becoming famous for his comic portrayal of simple, rustic characters, notable among them the part of Sim in John O'Keefe's *Wild Oats*. Haslewood records the extent of his popularity at this time, attributing it to the actor's 'unaffected simplicity, and native humour on the Stage, his affability and laudable conduct off it' (Haslewood, 212).

However, despite the warmth of his reception on the London stage, Blanchard was afflicted with chronic stage fright. In an effort to subdue his frequent bouts of anxiety, the actor appears to have turned increasingly to alcohol. He continued to perform at Covent Garden until the end of the 1793–4 season, when he was summarily dismissed from the company on account of his excessive drinking. He then travelled to Scotland, where he accepted an offer from Stephen Kemble to appear at the theatre in Edinburgh. According to the account given in *The Thespian Dictionary*, Kemble was aware of Blanchard's fondness for alcohol and tried his utmost to ensure that his new recruit remained sober. On the afternoon of his Edinburgh début, Kemble invited Blanchard to dinner, thinking it the easiest way to prevent him from becoming drunk. However, while Kemble slept in his armchair, Blanchard helped himself to a bottle of the theatre manager's best brandy. Kemble awoke to discover his star actor insensible, and was obliged to cancel the evening performance. Despite this inauspicious start, Blanchard remained with Kemble's company for two seasons.

In the summer of 1796 Blanchard returned to London. Unable to find work in the theatres, he was obliged to perform at the circus in St George's Fields. At the beginning of the 1797 season he was engaged by the Fishamble Street theatre in Dublin. However, his tenure with that company lasted only a few weeks. He died at his lodgings in Hamilton Row on 30 December 1797, a victim of 'the fatigue he underwent in the late storms' (*GM*, 1st ser., 67, 1797, 1134). He was buried in St Mark's churchyard, Dublin, in January 1798. Charlotte Blanchard continued her stage career after her husband's death, appearing in Dublin and Limerick in 1798. Blanchard's daughters, Elizabeth and Charlotta, also enjoyed brief stage careers. His only son, Thomas John Blanchard (1789–1859), became a pantomime actor. CHARLES BRAYNE

Sources [J. Haslewood], *The secret history of the green rooms: containing authentic and entertaining memoirs of the actors and actresses in the three Theatres Royal*, 2 (1790), 210–15 · *The thespian dictionary, or, Dramatic biography of the present age*, 2nd edn (1805) · *GM*, 1st ser., 67 (1797), 1134 · Highfill, Burnim & Langhans, *BDA* · G. W. Stone, ed., *The London stage, 1660–1800*, pt 4: 1747–1776 (1962) · C. B. Hogan, ed., *The London stage, 1660–1800*, pt 5: 1776–1800 (1968) · W. S. Clark, *The Irish stage in the county towns, 1720–1800* (1965), 351 · *IGI*

Likenesses Thornthwaite, engraving, 1791 (after S. De Wilde), repro. in J. Bell, ed., *Bell's British theatre*, 8 (1797), frontispiece · S. De Wilde, oils (as Ralph in Bickerstaffe's *The maid of the mill*), Garr. Club · S. De Wilde, pencil and watercolour (as Ralph in Bickerstaffe's *The maid of the mill*), Garr. Club

Blanchard, William (1769–1835), actor, was born at Nessgate, York, on 2 January 1769, and for a few years was educated at a private school in that city. Both his father, John Blanchard, a staymaker and hosier, and his mother, Ann Bowzer, or Nancy as she was commonly called, died when he was still a child, and he was left to the care of his uncle, William Blanchard, long well known as the proprietor of the *York Chronicle*. In 1782 he was placed in his uncle's office, but he took such delight in Shakespeare that in 1785 he resolved to become an actor. He joined Welsh's company of travelling comedians at Buxton. His first appearance was as Allan-a-Dale in MacNally's *Robin Hood*. For four years he played under the name of Bentley, but from 1789 he resumed his own name. He took the parts of Achmet, Douglas, and even Romeo. Blanchard next became a manager and opened theatres at Penrith,

Hexham, Barnard Castle, and Bishop Auckland, but he lost a lot of money, and abandoned this occupation to join Brunton's company of players on the Norwich circuit, taking on comic parts.

Blanchard's first appearances in London were at Covent Garden in October 1800, as Bob Acres in Sheridan's *The Rivals* and Crack in Thomas Knight's musical farce *The Turnpike Gate*. He was so successful that he remained at Covent Garden, except for a brief professional visit to America in 1832, continuously for thirty-four years. He was especially noted for playing Shakespeare's Fluellen, Sir Hugh Evans, Menenius, and Polonius. According to Leigh Hunt, his best performance was as the Marquis de Grand-Château in the musical toy show *The Cabinet*. Hunt also praised highly his Russett in Colman's *The Jealous Wife*.

On 15 May 1807 Blanchard's first wife, Susan, an actress, died, leaving behind four children. On 15 October 1808 Blanchard married the Sarah Harrold (1784–1875), a schoolfriend of one of his daughters. They had two sons, William and Edward Litt Laman *Blanchard (1820–1889); the latter later became famous as a writer of pantomimes and Christmas extravaganzas. Blanchard's daughter Elizabeth also took to the stage; she appeared at Covent Garden and the Haymarket and, after marrying Thomas Hamblin about 1824, continued playing under her married name.

In 1831 Blanchard was engaged by Hamblin to appear at the Bowery Theatre, New York, and subsequently performed in Boston and Baltimore. This trip, however, was not very successful, so eventually he returned to England. The last character created by him was that of Counsellor Crowsfoot in Douglas Jerrold's comedy *Nell Gwynne*, produced at Covent Garden in January 1833.

Blanchard's death occurred suddenly. On 6 May 1835 he dined with a friend and left for home at 6 p.m. Some nine hours later he was found in a ditch, having had a fit. Two more attacks followed before he died, on 9 May 1835, at his residence, 1 Camera Square, Chelsea. He was buried in the graveyard of St Luke's Church, Chelsea. Sarah Blanchard survived her husband nearly forty years; she died on 15 February 1875.

Charles Kent, *rev.* Nilanjana Banerji

Sources *The life and reminiscences of E. L. Blanchard, with notes from the diary of Wm. Blanchard*, ed. C. W. Scott and C. Howard, 2 vols. (1891) • *The biography of the British stage, being correct narratives of the lives of all the principal actors and actresses* (1824) • Adams, *Drama* • T. F. D. Croker, *A walk from London to Fulham* (1860) • T. A. Brown, *History of the American stage* (1870) • *Oxberry's Dramatic Biography*, 4/64 (1826) • *The thespian dictionary, or, Dramatic biography of the present age*, 2nd edn (1805) • L. Hunt, *Critical essays on the performers of the London theatres* (1807) • Hall, *Dramatic ports.* • Genest, *Eng. stage*

Likenesses Ridley, engraving, 1805, repro. in *Monthly Mirror*, 19, 217 • G. H. Harlow, group portrait, oils, 1817, Royal Shakespeare Memorial Theatre Museum, Stratford upon Avon • G. Clint, oils, exh. RA 1830, Garr. Club • G. Clint (scene from *The beggar's opera*) • H. Cook, line engraving, BM, NPG; repro. in *European Magazine*, 72 (1817), 3 • S. De Wilde, oils, Garr. Club • portrait, repro. in *Bell's British theatre* (1791) • portrait, repro. in W. Oxberry, *The new English drama* (1823) • portrait, repro. in *Oxberry's Dramatic Biography*, 4/64 • prints, BM, NPG • prints, Harvard TC

Blanchard, William Isaac (*bap.* 1741?, *d.* 1796), stenographer and legal writer, was the grandson of a French refugee and is probably the William Blanchard baptized on 20 December 1741 at St Martin-in-the-Fields, Westminster, London, son of Isaac Blanchard and his wife, Ann Mary Delpeuch. He became a shorthand writer in the Westminster law courts about the year 1767. In 1779, following the court martial of Admiral Augustus Keppel, in which he served as shorthand writer for defence counsel, Blanchard published and sold at his office at 4 Dean Street, Fetter Lane, London, *A Complete System of Short Hand, being an Improvement upon All the Authors whose Systems have yet been made Public*, the first of his two distinct systems of shorthand.

Blanchard recorded, chiefly in London but also elsewhere in the country, numerous proceedings of special commissions, speeches, and trials, such as the speech of Charles James Fox to explain his resignation from the cabinet, 17 July 1782; the trial of William Davies Shipley, dean of St Asaph, for libel, 1784; and the trial of Warren Hastings, 1788–95, which he recorded for defence counsel opposite the government shorthand writer, Joseph Gurney. Presumably Blanchard's reputation as a legal shorthand writer was enhanced by the verbatim publication of his transcribed notes.

In late 1786 or early 1787 Blanchard published his second and more elaborate system, *The Complete Instructor of Short Hand, upon Principles Applicable to the European Languages*. In this work he attacked an unnamed author (Samuel Taylor) whose recently published system, Blanchard claimed, is 'entirely useless for the gentlemen of the law, as it will never suit the language of Westminster-Hall (the only test of a good Short-Hand) neither can it possibly be of the least assistance to students in anatomy' (p. 8). In Blanchard's own system, the writer is 'not reduced to the miserable shift of leaving out a great number of monosyllables [with reference to Taylor's omission of vowels], by doing which it would be impossible to convict a person of perjury upon a trial' (p. 13). Among the subscribers to Taylor's *An Essay Intended to Establish a Standard for an Universal System of Stenography* (1786) was, ironically, Admiral (then Viscount) Keppel, whose defence Blanchard had taken in 1779 and published with Keppel's permission.

While his system never achieved the public acclaim accorded that of Taylor, Blanchard established a reputation as a successful and efficient legal shorthand writer 'of the first note among gentlemen of the law' (*GM*, 1797). His notes recording a speech of an hour and forty minutes by Thomas Erskine required 208 law sheets, which at 72 words per sheet made a total of 14,976 words (*Complete Instructor*, 3), or about 150 words a minute. Present during a famous speech by Richard Brinsley Sheridan at the impeachment trial of Warren Hastings in June 1788, Edward Gibbon recalled:

> As I was waiting in the manager's box, I had the curiosity to inquire of the shorthand writer, how many words a ready and rapid orator might pronounce in an hour? From 7000 to 7500 was his answer. The medium of 7200 will afford 120 words a minute, and two words in each second. But this

computation will only apply to the English language. (Gibbon, 208)

Given Blanchard's references to the suitability of his system for Latin and other languages, it is likely that Gibbon's informant was Blanchard and not a member of the Gurney family.

Blanchard apparently continued as a legal shorthand writer until his death early in 1796, soon after the decease of his wife, who had died, aged fifty-six, in September 1795. PAGE LIFE

Sources *GM*, 1st ser., 65 (1795), 881 [obit. of Blanchard's wife] · *GM*, 1st ser., 67 (1797), 435 [obit. of Peter Blanchard] · A. Kingston, 'Shorthand in literature: 17. Famous eighteenth-century trials and shorthand', *Pitman's Shorthand Weekly*, 36 (1909), 203–4 · J. J. Gold, 'The battle of the shorthand books, 1635–1800', *Publishing History*, 15 (1984), 5–29 · E. Gibbon, *Memoirs of my life and writing*, ed. A. O. J. Cockshut and S. Constantine, bicentenary edn (1994) · J. H. Lewis, *An historical account of the rise and progress of short hand* (privately printed, London, c.1825) · M. Levy, *The history of short-hand writing* (1862) · E. H. Butler, *The story of British shorthand* (1951) · *IGI*

Archives BL, notes, in case of Roos or Ros Barony, Hargrave MS 130, fol. 35 · BL, shorthand reports of trials for treason (Edinburgh) of David Downie and Robert Watt, King's MSS 428–429 [1794] · BL, specimen of miniature writing, Add. MS 4828 · BL, transcriptions of notes of Warren Hastings trial, Add. MSS 1766–1782

Blanche of Lancaster (1346?–1368). *See under* John, duke of Aquitaine and duke of Lancaster, styled king of Castile and León (1340–1399).

Blanche, Ada [*real name* Ada Cecilia Blanche Adams] (**1863–1953**), actress, was born at Musely House, Brixton, London, on 16 July 1863, the daughter of the rising music-hall manager Sam Adams (1837–1893) of the Islington Philharmonic, and his wife, the former Mrs Sarah Ann Bellini (*née* Harris) (1832?–1900), a well-known vocalist and actress, known professionally as Cicely Nott, who had recently played under Chatterton at the Theatre Royal, Drury Lane. Adams, the son of a Ware-based maltster and banker, was professedly descended from Sir Thomas Adams, a seventeenth-century lord mayor of London.

Ada's parents had already separated (after producing five children, all of whom would make a name in the theatre) before the young girl first went on the stage in her early teens. She appeared in Chatterton's children's pantomimes at the Adelphi Theatre, in similar productions at Drury Lane and at the Imperial, and was also seen in juvenile roles in drama, often playing on the same programmes as one or both of her mother and youngest sister 'Little' Addie Blanche. She had her first important adult role at the age of nineteen, when she briefly took over the soprano part of Fiametta, to her mother's Peronella, in Emily Soldene's touring company performance of *Boccaccio*. She left this job to fulfil the kind of substantial pantomime principal boy engagement which would be the backbone of her early career.

In 1883–4 Blanche toured with Lila Clay's all-ladies operetta company, in 1885 with the Holmes Burlesque Company in America, and in 1886 in Britain with her mother and another sister, Edith Blanche, in Dion Boucicault's comedy *Forbidden Fruit*. In 1886 she made her first adult appearance at the mecca of modern burlesque, the Gaiety

Ada Blanche (1863–1953), by unknown photographer

Theatre, cast (alongside Addie) in a small part in the burlesque *Monte Cristo jr.* At the Gaiety she understudied the theatre's top star, Nellie Farren, and when the burlesques were sent on the road, Ada was cast in Farren's parts. In her twenties, she spent most of her time playing burlesque around Britain, but she returned to London to succeed to the title-role in George Edwardes's production of the burlesque *Joan of Arc* and also to play both music-hall engagements and, most particularly—alongside Marie Lloyd, Dan Leno, Little Tich, and other such variety stars—as principal boy in the pantomimes at the Theatre Royal, Drury Lane. She also, apparently, though unbilled, latterly had a hand in the staging of the pantomimes, and Sir Francis Burnand reported that 'as a stage manager for farcical pieces with chorus and dances she ran even "Charley 'Arris" uncommonly hard' (*The Era*, 11 April 1908, 21).

The best theatre part which Ada Blanche found in her middle years was the title-role in *The Telephone Girl*, Burnand's English adaptation of the French vaudeville-operetta *La demoiselle du téléphone*, which she played for several seasons around Britain. However, apart from regular pantomime engagements, London offered her only a brief season in the title-role, Stella de Winton, in *The Royal Star* (1898) and an *in extremis* take-over of Ada Reeve's star role in the unsuccessful *The Medal and the Maid* (1903). She came into her West End own only in her forties when Robert Courtneidge, husband of her actress sister Rosie Nott, became prominent as a producer of musical plays. Courtneidge cast her in older comedy characters in a series of his productions, and she thus created the role of the booming, lost-husband-seeking Mrs Smith alongside the Simplicitas Smith of Dan Rolyat in the long-running *The Arcadians* (1909), the tea-house owner Mitsu, again teamed with Rolyat, in its successor, *The Mousmé* (1911), paired up with Lauri De Frece to supply the chief comedy of *The Pearl Girl* (1913) as the vulgar nouveau-riche Mrs Baxter Brown, and, in more sedate style, the senior Lady Elizabeth Weston in *The Rebel Maid* (1921).

Although Ada Blanche never married, each of her three sisters did. Edith married the producer of *Forbidden Fruit*, John H. Tully, Addie became Mrs William Peacock and the mother of the successful 1910s musical comedy actress Marie Blanche, while Rosie and Courtneidge were the parents of the future comedienne Dame Cicely Courtneidge. Ada spent her retirement years in Yorkshire and west London, and died at St Mary's Guest House, Burlington Lane, Chiswick, on 1 January 1953. She was buried at Nunhead cemetery. KURT GÄNZL

Sources K. Gänzl, *The encyclopedia of the musical theatre*, 2 vols. (1994) · K. Gänzl, *The British musical theatre*, 2 vols. (1986) · *The Era* (1883–1921) · J. Parker, ed., *Who's who in the theatre*, 6th edn (1930) · b. cert.

Likenesses photograph, NPG [*see illus.*]

Wealth at death £4159 10s. 1d.: probate, 17 March 1953, *CGPLA Eng. & Wales*

Blanchflower, Robert Dennis [Danny] **(1926–1993)**, footballer and journalist, was born on 10 February 1926 at 7 Elmdale Street in the Bloomfield district of east Belfast, the eldest child in the family of three sons and two daughters of John Blanchflower, an iron turner in the Belfast shipyards, and his wife, Selina, *née* Ellison. His working-class, Presbyterian family had little interest in sport, though his mother had played football in her youth, for the Roebucks factory team during that brief moment between 1915 and 1923 when women's football threatened to become almost as much an obsession as the male version.

Danny Blanchflower was educated at Ravenscroft public elementary school and did well enough to be awarded a scholarship to Belfast College of Technology. He joined the air training corps there but left early to become an apprentice electrician at the Gallachers' cigarette factory. He also joined the air-raid precautions (ARP) and in 1943 lied about his age in order to join the RAF. As a trainee navigator he was sent on a course to St Andrews University (where he acquired a lifelong love of golf) and in the spring of 1945 was posted to Canada for further training. By April 1946 he was back in Belfast, back at Gallachers, and building a reputation as an outstanding footballer.

Like many working-class boys of his generation, Blanchflower learned to play football at school and on the streets and waste ground of his home town. He was good enough to be chosen for the Belfast Wolf Cub team against their Dublin counterparts in 1937. When the time of year allowed, he could play three times on a Saturday: for the school in the morning, the Boys' Brigade in the afternoon,

Robert Dennis [Danny] **Blanchflower (1926–1993)**, by Mark Gerson, 1962

and a local league team in the evening. During the early part of the war he characteristically formed his own club, Bloomfield United. He was establishing a reputation for himself within the local football subculture and in 1942, shortly before his sixteenth birthday, he was signed as an amateur by the local professional team Glentoran. He returned from military service fitter and stronger and soon won a place in the Glentoran first team, who played in the Irish league. He had thought of returning to St Andrews University, but the offer of a £50 signing-on fee and £3 for playing a game he loved and was good at proved too tempting.

In February 1947 Blanchflower played for the Irish league against the English league. As the opposition included Stanley Matthews, Tommy Lawton, Tom Finney, and Billy Wright and the Irish only lost 4–2 it is hardly surprising that it stimulated his ambition to go east. By now he was playing on the right-hand side of midfield, where his ability to make the telling pass and to see how the game was going far outweighed his shortage of pace. He fell out with Glentoran about money, and in 1948–9 their directors agreed that if an English club wanted him he could have one-third of the transfer fee. Only second-division Barnsley made an offer, because other English clubs thought him neither strong enough nor quick enough to succeed in the faster English game. The fee was £6000, of which Blanchflower collected £700, which did nothing to appease his low opinion of football's ruling élite.

At Barnsley, Blanchflower replaced a local hero, Sidney (Skinner) Normanton, for whom the phrase 'Get stuck in' could have been invented. Blanchflower could tackle too, but his anticipation, interceptions, and perceptive passes soon won over the hard-nosed Oakwell crowd. Certainly the local paper had never seen such a skilful player. As its football correspondent put it, 'the girth of his skill is immense' (Bowler, 53). On 1 October 1949 he won the first of fifty-six caps for Northern Ireland. While playing for Barnsley he lived in Darfield in a bungalow owned by the club and travelled to home matches on public transport with his boots in a brown paper bag. But he wasn't happy.

What disappointed him was the lack of thought, of serious preparation, of any plan or method on the field. He was desperate to practise with the ball but the trainer would not even allow him to return in the afternoon for ball practice because if he did, he said, all the other players would want to do the same. He was impatient for a move to the first division, where more sophisticated attitudes would be found. In March 1951 he was transferred to Aston Villa for £15,000. But he was intensely frustrated to find that things were little different there. The older players did much as they liked and were far from impressed by this incessantly talkative young man who thought he knew much more than they did.

In 1954 Blanchflower seemed on the verge of signing for Arsenal for a then record fee but at the last moment the deal fell through. Instead he went to Tottenham Hotspur for £30,000. It was the best move of his life. Not that it seemed so at first. For one thing Arthur Rowe, who had built the stylish Tottenham team of the early 1950s, had to retire from the manager's job owing to illness. Jimmy Anderson was a much more old-fashioned manager and soon fell out with Blanchflower, from whom he removed the captaincy. A championship team was nevertheless being built up—at least, once Bill Nicholson replaced Anderson as manager in October 1958. It was Nicholson who made the inspired signings of Les Allen, Bill Brown, Dave Mackay, and John White. He disciplined the argumentative Blanchflower by dropping him, but in 1959 reinstated him as captain. Although very different in character, they were both keen on new ways of playing based on what they had seen of the control, passing, movement, and possession of the Brazilians and the Hungarians.

Blanchflower had captained Northern Ireland to the last eight of the world cup in 1958 and in the same year was voted footballer of the year by the football writers. In his early thirties he was at the height of his powers and an intelligent creator of time and space. Tottenham finished third in the first division in 1959–60, having finished eighteenth in 1958–9. On the eve of the 1960–61 season the *Evening Standard*'s Bernard Joy reported a conversation with Blanchflower in which the latter had told him that football was not really about winning, goals, saves, or supporters: 'It's about doing things in style, doing them with a flourish. It's about going out to beat the other lot, not waiting for them to die of boredom. It's about dreaming of the glory of the double' (Bowler, 13). By the end of the season both cup and league had been won (the first time in the twentieth century that any team had won the double), the league with an average of almost three goals a game. But it was the style in which it was done that made Spurs the second-favourite team of most football enthusiasts. An almost certain record of 2½ million people watched their matches. And for Blanchflower it was a personal triumph recognized by a second award as footballer of the year. The FA cup was won again the next year and the European cup winners' cup the year after that, but the glory of 1960–61 could never be recaptured.

Blanchflower was that rare bird, someone who could think and talk about the game as effectively as he played it. He had been writing columns in various papers since his Villa days for the *Birmingham Evening Mail* and then, after his move south, for the *London Evening News*. He had even published in *The Observer* and the *New Statesman*. By the time of retirement in 1964 he had ten years' experience, and he worked for the *Sunday Express* as a columnist from 1964 until 1988.

Like many complicated personalities, Blanchflower had his contradictions. He was a private man, and refused to take part in the television programme *This is your Life* in 1961; but he wanted people to know who he was, and he was the first professional footballer to appear on *Desert Island Discs* (in 1960). He could be charming but also determined to have his own way, opinionated and witty but sometimes intolerant of the views of others. He could be unwilling to change his ideas or compromise. Even in football he was both progressive and romantic: he was a pioneer of more imaginative systems of play, but could be very critical of modern coaches, whom he accused of using tactics to stifle invention. He was articulate but not always easy for young footballers to understand, and this may have partly accounted for his failure to succeed as a manager when he eventually tried, first with Northern Ireland from January 1976 to the summer of 1978, and then when he failed to save Chelsea from relegation in 1978–9. He probably would have liked to manage Tottenham—he had been assistant manager there while still a player—but when Nicholson resigned in 1974 the board shied away from appointing someone so brilliant but unpredictable and outspoken.

Blanchflower was married three times. He and his first wife, Denise (whom he had married in Belfast), divorced in 1953. His second marriage was to Betty Lawson, with whom he had a son and two daughters. That marriage ended in divorce in 1963, the year in which he married Avrille Margaret Dean Hunter. There were two further daughters by this marriage, which ended in divorce in 1976.

Money was a frequent worry for Blanchflower, and he was grateful for a testimonial which brought him £40,000. Towards the end of his life he suffered from Alzheimer's disease and Parkinson's disease. He died at Woodlands Nursing Home, Rookery Road, Staines, Middlesex, on 9 December 1993, of bronchopneumonia after suffering a fall which broke his hip. As his biographer shrewdly noted, he was remembered with more affection than was sometimes bestowed on him in his life. A memorial service was held in St Anne's Cathedral, Belfast, on 14 February 1994.

TONY MASON

Sources D. Bowler, *Danny Blanchflower: a biography of a visionary* (1997) • K. Ferris, *The double: the inside story of Spurs' triumphant 1960–61 season* (1999) • *The Times* (10 Dec 1993) • *The Independent* (10 Dec 1993) • *The Guardian* (16 Oct 2000) • private information (2004) [Gayle Blanchflower] • b. cert. • m. cert. [Avrille Hunter] • d. cert.

Likenesses photographs, *c.*1954–1979, Hult. Arch. • M. Gerson, photograph, 1962, NPG [*see illus.*] • photograph, repro. in *The Times* • photograph, repro. in *The Independent* • photographs, repro. in Bowler, *Danny Blanchflower*

Wealth at death £105,000: administration, 19 Jan 1994, *CGPLA Eng. & Wales*

Bland, Charles (*b.* **1802**, *d.* in or after **1834**). *See under* Bland, Maria Theresa (1769–1838).

Bland, Edith. *See* Nesbit, Edith (1858–1924).

Bland [*née* Fisher]**, Elizabeth** (*b. c.***1660**, *d.* in or after **1712**?), Hebraist, was the daughter and heir of Robert Fisher of Long Acre, Covent Garden, London, and his wife, who may have been named Marthare. She was born about the time of the Restoration and may have been baptized on 26 December 1660 at St Martin-in-the-Fields, Westminster. Her Hebrew teacher is said to have been Franciscus Mercurius van Helmont. On 26 April 1681 at the Savoy Chapel, off the Strand, she married Nathaniel Bland, then a merchant of London and freeman of the Glovers' Company. In 1692 Bland succeeded his father, Richard, as lord of the manor of Beeston, near Leeds, Yorkshire, to where the family now moved. Of their six children all but two, Joseph and Martha, died in infancy.

Elizabeth Bland is known only by a phylactery in Hebrew written at the request of the Yorkshire antiquary Ralph Thoresby for his *Musaeum Thoresbianum*, to which she also presented a 'Turkish commission'. Nehemiah Grew describes the phylactery as a scroll of parchment ¼ inch broad and 15 inches long, with four sentences of the law (Exodus 8: 7–11, 13–17; Deuteronomy 6: 3–10; and Deuteronomy 11: 13–19) 'most curiously written upon it in Hebrew' (Grew, 681). She taught Hebrew to her son and daughter. It appears from Thoresby's *Ducatus Leodiensis* that Bland was alive in 1712, but her precise death date is unknown. R. H. Brodie, *rev.* Philip Carter

Sources G. Ballard, *Memoirs of several ladies of Great Britain* (1752) • R. Thoresby, *Ducatus Leodiensis, or, The topography of … Leedes* (1715) • N. Grew, *Musaeum Regulis Societatis, or, A catalogue and description of the natural and artificial varieties belonging to the Royal Society* (1681) • *IGI*

Bland [*other married names* Hamilton, Sweeny]**, Esther** (*d.* **1787**), actress, is first recorded on 6 March 1742, when, as Mrs Bland, she played the part of Trusty in *The Provok'd Husband* by John Vanbrugh and Colley Cibber at Covent Garden, London. Her husband, George Bland, was a provincial actor who made his London début in 1751. Esther Bland was by then well established. With John Rich's Covent Garden company from 1742 to 1748, she had been trusted with increasingly important roles, most notably Regan in *King Lear*, Lady Anne in *Richard III*, and Emilia in *Othello* opposite David Garrick during his brief Covent Garden engagement in June 1746. Her career reached its peak, though, during the three seasons from 1748 to 1751, under Thomas Sheridan's management at the Smock Alley Theatre in Dublin. Ambitious and industrious, she played more than sixty roles for Sheridan, including Lady Macbeth, Cleopatra in John Dryden's *All for Love*, Constance in *King John*, Belvidera in Thomas Otway's *Venice Preserv'd*, and Millwood in George Lillo's *The London Merchant*. Dublin audiences were more accommodating than their London counterparts, and Esther Bland was probably no more than competent in tragedy. Having seen her as Lady Macbeth, the perceptive Mary Delany commented: 'a very handsome clever woman, acts with spirit, but wants judgment' (Sheldon, 164n). She was better in comedy: she played Beatrice in *Much Ado about Nothing*, Rosalind in *As You Like It*, and Portia in *The Merchant of Venice*, and cross-dressed as Sir Harry Wildair in George Farquhar's *The Constant Couple*. A poem in the *Dublin Journal* of 15–19 January 1751 celebrated simultaneously her quality and her industry:

> But of real Perfection no Mortal e'er tired,
> Bland is seen every Night, every Night is admired.

Demotion from leading roles is a serious blow to an actor's confidence. It would not be surprising, then, if Esther Bland's long decline began in the Dublin season of 1751–2, when Margaret (Peg) Woffington usurped her public favour. Resolved to return to London, and dissatisfied with the £7 per week offered to her by Garrick, she rejoined Rich at Covent Garden in September 1752 and remained with the company for the next ten years. George Bland died on 28 October 1753, after a fall from a horse, and on 15 June 1754 his widow married John Hamilton at St Martin-in-the-Fields, Westminster. What evidence we have suggests that, for her, it was an unfortunate marriage within which she was the only breadwinner. She remained, though, a reliable and respected member of the Covent Garden company until John Rich's death on 26 November 1761. The probability is that she then overplayed her hand with the new manager, John Beard, in the mistaken belief that her contract was secure. Beard cast her as Lady Wronglove in Cibber's *The Lady's Last Stake*, but she was determined to play her old part of Mrs Conquest. The quarrel resulted in her being dismissed at the end of the 1761–2 season, during which she had earned as much as £272. From then on, the story of her life, colourfully embellished by Tate Wilkinson in *The Wandering Patentee* (vol. 1, pp. 129–52), is all riches to rags. Forced into provincial touring, she was at the Theatre Royal, Bath, in 1762–3, where she again alienated the manager by her high-handedness. John Hamilton died in summer 1763, having swallowed much of his wife's remaining money in a failed attempt to establish a fashionable tea house in London, and his widow returned to the scene of her greatest triumphs, the Smock Alley Theatre in Dublin, now under the management of Henry Mossop. This was a period of cut-throat competition between Dublin's rival theatres at Crow Street and Smock Alley, and Mrs Hamilton had lost her appeal, except in her perennial role of Mrs Peachum in *The Beggar's Opera*.

Esther Hamilton's third marriage, to a much younger and wholly unprincipled Captain Sweeny, which was contracted somewhere in Ireland in summer 1764, was tainted by desperation on her side and financial greed on his. In increasingly reduced circumstances, she found work where she could. When Tate Wilkinson encountered her in 1771 she had been swindled and abandoned by her husband and was playing the Nurse in *Romeo and Juliet* with a company of strollers. It was out of compassion that he employed her at York in January 1772, but a humiliating accident with her false teeth led her to see that her acting career was over. She returned to London in abject poverty early in the summer of 1772. For the rest of her life she was effectively dependent on charity, and her appointment as dresser and wardrobe keeper at the summer theatre in Richmond through the 1780s was essentially honorary. Tate Wilkinson was confident that 'the true reason of the Theatrical Fund being established, was owing chiefly to the misfortunes of the late Mrs Sweeny' (Wilkinson, 1.151). The place of her death, Richmond, Surrey, and date, 27 November 1787, are known only from a reference in the notebook of the actor John Fawcett, now at the Folger Shakespeare Library, Washington, DC, USA.

PETER THOMSON

Sources Highfill, Burnim & Langhans, *BDA* • T. Wilkinson, *The wandering patentee, or, A history of the Yorkshire theatres from 1770 to the present time*, 4 vols. (1795) • E. K. Sheldon, *Thomas Sheridan of Smock-Alley: recording his life as actor and theater manager in both Dublin and London* (1967) • C. H. Hartmann, *Enchanting Bellamy* (1956) • J. C. Lucey, *Lovely Peggy* (1952) • *IGI*

Bland, Hubert (1855–1914), journalist and politician, was born on 3 January 1855 at 22 Wood Street, Woolwich, where his paternal grandfather had been a plumber and his maternal grandfather kept a public house. Hubert was the youngest of the four children of Henry Bland, a successful commercial clerk, and his wife Mary Anne. He was educated at various local schools, and from an early age showed a strong interest in the political ideas raised at social protest meetings, some of which were held locally. At the same time, growing up in Woolwich, with the strong military presence of the arsenal, barracks, and the Royal Military Academy, with its dashing gentleman cadets, he wanted to become an army officer, but after his father's death there was not enough money, and he was obliged to take a job as a bank clerk. Bland was tall, dark, and handsome—his friend George Bernard Shaw drew a vivid pen portrait of him as

> a man of fierce Norman exterior and huge physical strength … never seen without an irreproachable frock coat, tall hat, and a single eyeglass which infuriated everybody. He was pugnacious, powerful, a skilled pugilist, and had a shrill, thin voice reportedly like the scream of an eagle. Nobody dared be uncivil to him. (Shaw to Archibald Henderson, 3 Jan 1905, *Collected Letters*, ed. D. H. Laurence, 1972, 494)

Hubert wrote of himself, 'All who knew him liked him except those who hated him' (Briggs, 77). In later life he claimed to be descended from Yorkshire gentry, and he certainly looked the part.

At the bank Bland first met the young Edith *Nesbit (1858–1924), then engaged to one of his colleagues. They fell in love, though he failed to tell her that he had promised to marry his widowed mother's paid companion, Margaret (Maggie) Doran, with whom he already had an illegitimate son. Bland, giving a false address, married Edith Nesbit at the City of London register office on 22 April 1880, two months before the birth of their own son Paul. Bland did not tell his mother or Maggie that he was married, and continued to live half the week at home with

Hubert Bland (1855–1914), by Frederick Henry Evans

them (in the 1881 census he described himself as unmarried); it was only when he fell ill with smallpox in the summer of 1880 that Edith eventually found out about Maggie, though she quickly made friends with her. The small brush-making business he had begun collapsed when his partner absconded, and he took a job as secretary to a hydraulics company, but his real passion was for politics.

Bland had read widely, was an admirer of Browning and William Morris, and attended various 'advanced' societies devoted to arts, crafts, literature, and politics. In 1883 he became a member of Thomas Davidson's utopian Fellowship of the New Life, and on 4 January 1884 he chaired the meeting at which a number of members seceded, to regroup themselves as the (middle-class, socialist) Fabian Society. From its foundation until 1911 he was its honorary treasurer, and in May 1884 he recruited George Bernard Shaw. Bland attributed his own conversion to socialism to the influence of Henry George, William Morris, and especially to Henry Hyndman. In 1885 he belonged to the Social Democratic Federation, but later found its programme too inflammatory, though arguably he remained under the influence of Marxism. He also rejected republicanism.

Bland was an atypical Fabian, since he combined socialism with strongly conservative opinions that reflected his social background and his military sympathies. Shaw described him as a 'regular Blackheath Tory'. Bland was inclined to dismiss democracy as 'bumptious, unidealistic, disloyal … anti-national and vulgar' (*Essays*, 213). He was strongly imperialist, and thought the empire essential to British working men and the survival of the 'English race'. He was also strongly opposed to women's suffrage. At the same time he advocated collectivist socialism, wrote Fabian tracts, and lectured extensively on socialism. He consistently supported an independent socialist party and opposed the Webbs' policy of 'permeating' the Liberal Party. In 1886–7 he and his wife jointly edited the socialist periodical *To-Day*, and from 1887 until its demise in 1889 he was sole editor. In 1888 he helped Annie Besant organize the Bryant and May match girls' strike, and that same year he stood for the London school board for Finsbury, apparently being sharply disappointed when he was defeated; this was the only occasion on which he stood for a public office. In 1889 he contributed to the *Fabian Essays* (1889). In the 1890s he supported the Independent Labour Party on the one hand and the South African War on the other, writing in December 1899 that defeat in Africa would mean 'starvation in every city of Great Britain', while war would 'overcome national "flabbiness" and restore the "manhood" of the British people' (Wolfe, 95). No wonder some socialists saw him as reactionary.

Bland 'hated the Pharisees, the Prigs, the Puritans' (*Essays*, 284). He smoked, and claimed to be 'adventurous' with drugs, having taken 'opium in all its forms' (ibid., 206) as well as other drugs. Although in some respects conventional, he could not resist making love to women who attracted him, and was, in Shaw's phrase, 'an exceedingly unfaithful husband' (Briggs, xiv). Sexually vain, or perhaps just susceptible, he conducted a number of extramarital affairs, the most lasting of these being with Edith's friend Alice ('Mouse') Hoatson. When Alice became pregnant by him, she joined the Bland ménage as housekeeper, and Edith passed off Alice's daughter Rosamund, born in November 1886, as her own. Bland had three children with Edith: Paul, Iris (*b.* 1881), and Fabian (1885); and Alice had a son, John, born in 1899. Rosamund was said to be his favourite. His marriage to Edith was inevitably stormy at times—'scenes as usual', Shaw wrote after a visit (MacKenzie and MacKenzie, 100). But it was also a learning process for them both. At first Edith kept the household going by publishing poems and stories. During the 1880s she and Bland wrote two novels together, both on political themes, *The Prophet's Mantle* (1885) and *Something Wrong* (1886), which was serialized in the radical London newspaper the *Weekly Dispatch*. It was through her example and with her support that Bland became a journalist. As 'Hubert' he contributed a weekly column to the Manchester *Sunday Chronicle* from 1892 to his death, writing in a dry, man-of-the-world tone, and discussing a wide range of topics, from Hegel's theories of the state to the use of the powder-puff, from Kipling's fiction to the art of flirtation. He was an amusing, sharp-eyed, and pithy commentator on his times.

By 1899 Edith was on the brink of establishing her career as a famous writer for children, and Bland had become a well-known journalist. The family moved to Well Hall, Eltham, where their usual round of parties was tragically interrupted by the unexpected death of Fabian, following a minor operation at home, in October 1900. About the same time Bland became a Roman Catholic convert. He published selections of his essays and articles in *With the Eyes of a Man* (1905), *The Happy Moralist* (1907), and *Letters to a Daughter* (1907). By now he was a member of the 'old gang', the inner circle who controlled the Fabian Society. He sometimes disagreed with others in the group, and over the years he had been repeatedly outmanoeuvred and overruled by Shaw, Sidney Webb, and their supporters. In December 1906, doubtful about H. G. Wells's character and good intentions, he acted with other members of the 'old gang' to defeat Wells's attempt to take over and change the Fabian Society. In 1908 and 1910 he acted as a Fabian delegate at Labour Party conferences.

Wells remained Bland's personal friend despite the Fabian conflict until 1908, when he made a bid for Bland's daughter, the plump, attractive Rosamund, one of the 'Fabian nursery'. Apparently she and Wells tried to run away together, but Bland caught up with them at Paddington Station, punched Wells, and took Rosamund home. Both men were enraged. Bland referred to Wells as 'the little cad' (Briggs, 311) while Wells caricatured the Blands in *The New Machiavelli* (1911), where they appear as the Booles, parasitic imitators of the Baileys (the Webbs) and vindictive scandal-mongers. In his *Experiment in Autobiography*, Wells created another hostile, though recognizable, portrait of the Blands, and in the postscript to his autobiography, unpublished in his lifetime, he gave his own version of the Rosamund episode, claiming that Bland's attitude to Rosamund was 'unfatherly', even incestuous, while he himself had been motivated by 'a great disapproval of incest'.

For some years Bland had suffered from heart trouble, and in November 1910 he had a massive heart attack. In 1911 his sight, always poor, finally failed him. He gave up public lecturing and his post as treasurer of the Fabian Society, but continued reviewing and writing his weekly column, with Alice Hoatson as his amanuensis. As he was dictating to her at Well Hall, on the afternoon of 14 April 1914, he suddenly said that he felt giddy, lowered himself to the floor, and died of a heart attack in her arms a few minutes later. He was buried with Catholic rites on 18 April in the family plot at Woolwich cemetery. His wife survived him, remarried in 1917, and died in 1924.

The achievements of great journalists can be difficult to appreciate in retrospect: some of his contemporaries considered Bland the most powerful and influential columnist of his day. According to his friend Cecil Chesterton his articles represented 'almost the high-water mark of English journalism' (*Essays*, vii). Yet his writings are now forgotten, except by a few historians, whereas his wife's stories for children continue to be read and loved.

JULIA BRIGGS

Sources *DLB*, vol. 5 • J. Briggs, *A woman of passion: the life of E. Nesbit, 1858–1924* (1987) • W. Wolfe, 'Bland, Edith … and Bland, Hubert', *BDMBR*, vol. 3, pt 1 • N. MacKenzie and J. MacKenzie, *The first Fabians* (1977) • H. G. Wells, *Experiment in autobiography*, 2 (1969) • H. G. Wells, *H. G. Wells in love: postscript to an 'Experiment in autobiography'*, ed. G. P. Wells (1984) • *Essays by Hubert Bland: 'Hubert' of the 'Sunday Chronicle'*, ed. E. N. Bland (1914) • H. G. Wells, *The new Machiavelli* (1911) • M. Holroyd, *The first five lives of Annie Besant* (1961) • b. cert. • m. cert.

Archives BLPES, corresp. with Fabian society

Likenesses F. H. Evans, photograph, priv. coll. [*see illus.*] • photograph, repro. in Briggs, *Woman of passion*

Bland, Humphrey (1685/6–1763), army officer and author, was born in Ireland, of uncertain parentage, though to a Yorkshire gentry family settled there since the mid-1660s, in whose seat at Blandsfort, Queen's county, he himself later lived. On account of the loss of the Irish army's papers in the Four Courts fire of 1922, his early service is not known with certainty: he was first commissioned an ensign on 4 February 1704, made lieutenant on 1 June 1705, and promoted captain on 1 December 1706. Bland's treatise suggests that, as a subaltern and company commander, he saw service in the early campaigns of Marlborough's army in the Low Countries. He was promoted major in Sibourg's Huguenot regiment of foot on 19 July 1709, and was wounded at Almenara in 1710. Bland was reduced onto half pay in 1712 but returned to the army as a major in the 11th dragoons on 22 July 1715 and participated in operations against the Jacobites in the 1715 rising; he conducted prisoners—'gentlemen and noblemen of distinction taken at Preston' (*DNB*)—to London. On 5 August 1717 he was made major of the 1st dragoons, and on 26 March 1718 he was promoted lieutenant-colonel of the 2nd horse.

Devoted to his profession and aware that, by the mid-1720s, a new generation unused to the experience of modern war in Flanders from 1689 to 1712 had entered the officer corps, Bland published in April 1727 at London and Dublin his 360-page *Treatise of Military Discipline*, a second edition of which appeared later the same year. An intelligent, well-organized, and clearly written work of sound judgement, practical and not theoretical, it summarized at length the best of the army's contemporary practice, itself the fruit of its Flanders experience. The work described in detail the army's drill and training, together with all the duties of regimental officers in quarters, in garrison, in camp, and in the field. As much of its subject was not included in the army's regulations, the book was an immensely useful guide for young officers; and, as its influence spread, it helped to systematize routine throughout the army. Bland's treatise was easily the most successful and widely used military drillbook to appear in English during the century, and it remained valuable for over a quarter-century. Later editions (all printed in London, and all actually reprints of the first edition) appeared in 1734, 1740, 1743, 1746, and 1753. In 1759 an eighth, revised, edition appeared, the revisions the work of the tactician Sir William Fawcett; Fawcett's revision was reprinted as the ninth (and final) edition in 1762. Many shortened or simplified versions appeared, particularly in the American colonies, for provincials and militia.

Bland's book earned him royal favour and, later, the comradeship of the duke of Cumberland. On 27 June 1737 he was made colonel of an Irish corps, the 36th foot, from which he went on to the more valuable cavalry colonelcy of the 13th dragoons, another Irish corps, on 9 January 1741; and on 22 April 1742 he was made quartermaster-general of the forces on the British establishment, one of the most senior staff appointments, and one which he retained until his death. Made brigadier on 12 February 1743, he joined the army in Flanders shortly after, and was with it at Dettingen on 16 June 1743. Having been transferred to the colonelcy of the 3rd dragoons on 19 April 1744, Bland commanded a cavalry brigade in the army in the Low Countries in the campaigns of 1744 and 1745, where he was promoted major-general on 30 March 1745 and fought at Fontenoy on 30 April. At the outbreak of the Jacobite rising he returned with the troops to Britain and served with the main army in Scotland in 1745–6, commanding the cavalry and leading the pursuit immediately after Culloden; he was at the army's large Fort Augustus encampment formed that summer. When Cumberland departed Scotland in July 1746, Bland was left in command of one of the four military districts into which that country was then divided, running southwards from Stirling and including Edinburgh. He returned to the Low Countries the following April, for the 1747 campaign, where he served as second to Lieutenant-General Henry Hawley (who was general of horse) and was wounded at Lauffeldt on 21 June. Bland returned to Britain after the campaign and was made commander-in-chief in Scotland on 17 September 1747, following the earl of Albemarle (who had been commander-in-chief in Scotland since August 1746, but who had left for Flanders in March 1747). Promoted lieutenant-general on 12 September 1747, Bland arrived in his Edinburgh command on 31 October 1747, where he has been criticized for his rigour in the 'pacification' of the Highlands. Bland had obtained in 1743 the sinecure governorship of Fort William, a post which he held until rewarded for his Scottish services with the sinecure governorship of Edinburgh Castle on 6 February 1752; this position he retained until his death. He was made governor of Gibraltar on 7 March 1749, and was there in 1750–51, having been sent 'to redress the civil grievances of which the inhabitants … had complained' (*DNB*), and worked to regularize its government. He was given the colonelcy of the 1st dragoon guards on 8 July 1752. Bland had been replaced in the Edinburgh command by his second, Lieutenant-General George Churchill, who was appointed Scottish commander-in-chief on 23 December 1751; but following Churchill's death Bland was reappointed commander-in-chief in Scotland on 3 November 1753. He served actively again in Edinburgh until ill health obliged him in July 1756 to vacate the command, in which Lord George Beauclerk replaced him permanently that November.

Bland was married late in life, on 12 January 1755 at Edinburgh, to Elizabeth (1732–1816), the daughter of George Dalrymple of Dalmahoy, who was the brother of Field Marshal John *Dalrymple, second earl of Stair, and the eldest sister of John *Dalrymple, fifth earl. Bland had no children, but assisted the army careers of several nephews, one of whom, Thomas Bland, was his coheir. His last years were marred by the illness and infirmity that obliged him to leave Edinburgh, and he died in London on 8 May 1763, aged seventy-seven.

Bland was typical of the senior career soldiers who served under the first two Georges and the duke of Cumberland, a bluff, methodical, proficient general officer who took his duties seriously: 'you are quite unacquainted with my character, or you wou'd have been more punctual in several parts of your Duty', he advised a junior officer in 1749 (Taylor, 29). The blunt disciplinarian could strike some, even thorough, soldiers as the martinet: 'I am afraid General Bland is not quite so well-bred and polite as might be wished. He has a roughness about him that breaks out sometimes into ill-manners when he is in authority', said Lieutenant-Colonel James Wolfe, no less, in 1750 (F. H. Skrine, *Fontenoy*, 1906, 131); and a less thorough officer, John Mostyn, hoping in 1758 to succeed to Bland's colonelcy and hearing that he was dying, could even refer to him as a 'tedious old fool' (P. Mackesy, *The Coward of Minden*, 1979, 44). However, Lord George Sackville remarked in 1759 on 'the good old General, for whom I always had the greatest regard' (T. Hayter, *An Eighteenth-Century Secretary at War*, 1988, 287). The influence of the *Treatise* lasted into the late 1750s, by which time its drill had become obsolete, but Bland's name had become a byword in the army: when as late as August 1774 a youthful newly joined ensign proposed to reform the interior management and discipline of the 4th foot, at Boston, 'to his great amazement the boys only laughed at his schemes, and called him *Humphrey Bland* and *the young General*, and I am afraid have laughed him out of his plan of reforming the army' (G. D. Scull, *Memoir and Letters of Captain W. Glanville Evelyn*, 1879, 29–31).

J. A. Houlding

Sources J. A. Houlding, *Fit for service: the training of the British army, 1715–1795* (1981) • W. Taylor, *The military roads in Scotland* (1976) • army lists, PRO, WO 64/10, fols. 118–19 • notification books, PRO, WO 25/134–136 • commission books, PRO, WO 25/90–91 • *Scots Magazine*, 18 (1756), 366 • *Scots Magazine*, 18 (1756), 524 • *Scots Magazine*, 25 (1763), 302 • N. B. Leslie, *The succession of colonels of the British army from 1660 to the present day* (1974) • *Army List* (1754–63) • C. Dalton, *George the First's army, 1714–1727*, 2 vols. (1910–12) • orderly books, 1742–5, BL, Townshend MSS, Add. MSS 41144–41150 • orderly books, NAM, 6807-222; 6807-228-1,2,3 • order books, Royal Artillery Institution, MD-1001, 3/4, 4/4 • orderly books, Suffolk RO, Albemarle papers, HA67/461/99–103 • orderly books, Royal Arch., Cumberland papers, 4–7 • *DNB* • Burke, *Gen. GB* (1871)

Archives BL, account of governorship of Gibraltar, Lansdowne MS 1234 • NL Scot., letter-books and warrant book, MSS 304–306 | BL, letters to first Lord Hardwicke, Add. MSS 35448–35590, *passim* • BL, corresp. with duke of Newcastle, Add. MSS 32731–32888, *passim* • Bodl. Oxf., letters to George Burges • NA Scot., letters to Sir A. Grant, GD345/1159 • NL Scot., corresp. with Richard Coren

Bland, James (1798–1861). *See under* Bland, Maria Theresa (1769–1838).

Bland, John (*d.* 1555), protestant martyr, was born at Sedbergh, Yorkshire, and was educated by Roger Lupton, the provost of Eton College, before becoming a fellow of St John's College, Cambridge, where he took the degree of MA in 1536. According to John Foxe, Bland was at some point in his career the teacher of Edwin Sandys, a fellow Yorkshireman and alumnus of St John's, who went on to become archbishop of York. In 1537 Bland was presented to the living of Ospringe, Kent, which was in the gift of St John's. In Kent he came under the wing of Christopher Nevinson, the archbishop's commissary; in 1541 Bland received the substantial archiepiscopal living of Adisham, Kent, from Nevinson. Bland made his presence felt not only in his livings, but throughout the diocese. In the winter of 1542–3, in addition to stripping his church at Ospringe of images and furnishings, he preached in Faversham, Canterbury, and the surrounding area, denouncing images, fast days, prayer to saints, and other 'superstitious' practices. He also repeatedly preached that confession was unnecessary. At the same time, Bland was associating with protestant radicals, including some with direct ties to the Anabaptist Joan Bocher. (Significantly, when Bland was arrested a decade later, some Kentish freewillers would rally to his defence.)

How radical Bland's own views were is hard to determine. He was accused of making some statements in 1542–3 which pushed against the envelope of prevailing English protestant orthodoxy: that the mass was just a remembrance, 'that in the christening of children priests be murderers', and that the term *Trinitas* was not scriptural but was coined by Athanasius (Corpus Christi College, Cambridge, MS 128, pp. 67, 69, and 71). On the other hand, it is difficult to believe that Bland would have retained the support of both Nevinson and Archbishop Thomas Cranmer had his religious radicalism been too pronounced. The patronage of Cranmer and Nevinson, along with Bland's outspoken protestantism, made him a natural target for religious conservatives in Kent, and in the spring of 1543 his heresies were denounced to the king, as part of the conspiracy against Archbishop Cranmer which became known as the prebendaries' plot. Almost immediately the protestants in Cranmer's circle rallied round Bland. Nevinson resigned to him a prebend which he had held, and Rowland Taylor and Ralph Morrice, two zealous evangelicals closely associated with Cranmer, stood surety for the payment of first fruits for Bland's new living. Bland himself preached a defiant Palm Sunday sermon at Adisham, in which he denounced the hallowing of palms and other traditional ceremonies. In his sermon Bland also claimed that he had been commanded to preach on these topics by certain members of the privy council. Nevertheless, he was indicted for heresy on 27 September 1543, although the case against him disintegrated once it became clear that Cranmer retained Henry VIII's support.

Mary's accession, and Cranmer's consequent disgrace, left Bland dangerously isolated. On 3 September 1553 Bland got into a dispute with John Austen, one of his churchwardens; when Austen tried to remove the communion table from the church at Adisham, Bland, with the support of Edward Isaac, a stalwart protestant JP, instituted legal proceedings against him. On 26 October, Thomas Austen, another churchwarden, demanded that Bland rebuild the altar and pay for the restoration of a rood loft he had destroyed. Bland refused. The conservative faction in Adisham procured a priest from a neighbouring parish to celebrate mass. But on 28 December Bland disrupted the planned service and vehemently denounced the mass as an invention of Antichrist. He was assaulted by the churchwardens and then arrested, along with Laurence Ramsey, the former parish clerk of Adisham and a close ally of Bland's. (And perhaps significantly, Ramsey had been a freewiller as late as 1551.) Bland (who was also denounced as a married priest) and Ramsey were both taken to Canterbury, where they were released under bond.

If this had been merely a local dispute the matter might have ended here, but Bland's past came back to haunt him. In late February 1554, Sir Thomas Moyle, one of the former leaders of the prebendaries' plot, who had organized the accusations of heresy against Bland in 1543, ordered that Bland's bail be revoked. For the next year an elaborate cat and mouse game ensued as Bland was re-released on bail, then arraigned in an ecclesiastical court, then transferred to the county sessions, and finally transferred back to spiritual jurisdiction. The object of this manoeuvring was to keep Bland detained, so that he could face heresy charges the moment that the statute criminalizing heresy, which had been repealed in the previous reign, was re-enacted. Having been informally examined by Nicholas Harpsfield, the archdeacon of Canterbury, Bland was examined in the chapter house of Canterbury Cathedral on 21 May 1554. This remarkable session, which took place almost a year before Bland was actually tried for heresy, demonstrates the importance the diocesan authorities attached to this case. A particularly striking feature of this examination was that Cyriac Pettit, a layman (who had been deeply involved in the prebendaries' plot), took the lead in interrogating Bland. A little over a month after this ordeal, Bland was interrogated at the county sessions by Sir Thomas Moyle and Sir John Baker (another of the leaders of the prebendaries' plot).

In February 1555, with the heresy statute finally re-enacted, Bland was interrogated for a final time by Sir John Baker, and then transferred to spiritual jurisdiction. Richard Thornden, the suffragan bishop of Dover, and a long-standing adversary of Cranmer, took charge of Bland's protracted trial in the spring of 1555. Bland was condemned on 25 June 1555. He was burnt at Canterbury on 12 July, along with—in vivid, if not necessarily intentional, symbolism—another Edwardian cleric and two radical protestants. To a remarkable degree, Bland's career epitomizes the early Reformation in Kent. The staunch support and implacable enmity Bland attracted as a particularly active agent of evangelical reform are indications of the passions that would make Kent a burnt-over district, both literally and figuratively, by the end of Mary's reign. A belated but not insignificant sign of the changing of the old order in the county was a payment of 5*s.* made in the spring of 1576 by the chapter of Canterbury Cathedral to 'John Blande whose father was brent to help him withall' (Canterbury city and cathedral archives, misc. accounts, 40, fol. 451*r*). THOMAS S. FREEMAN

Sources J. Foxe, *Actes and monuments* (1563) • CCC Cam., MS 128, pp. 7–8, 14, 67–71, 105–7, 119, 135–6, 243–5, 255–6, 263, 267, 270 [*LPH*, 18/2, 291, 295, 311–12, 320–21, 323–4, 351–4, 357–9] • Bland to his 'sister', Emmanuel College, Cambridge, MS 261, fol. 62*r–v* • Venn, *Alum. Cant.* • Cranmer's register, LPL • exchequer, first fruits and tenths office, composition books, PRO, E 334/2, fols. 52*r*, 139*r* • C. Burrage, *The early English dissenters in the light of recent research (1550–1641)*, 2 vols. (1912) • Canterbury city and cathedral archives, misc. accounts, 40, fol. 451*r*

Bland, John (1702–1749), writing master and accountant, was born in Crutched Friars, London, on 17 August 1702, the son of a clerk in the custom house. He spent four years at Westminster School, where, according to William Massey, 'he principally formed his hand' (Massey, 2.26). After leaving this school in 1714 he was apprenticed to Charles Snell, the writing master at Sir John Johnson's Free Writing School in Foster Lane. It appears that Bland did not complete his full indenture with Snell; in 1717 he followed his father into the custom house, where he too worked as a clerk until 1726. In this profession he must have become familiar with all the standard forms of commercial documentation, such as bills of lading and invoices, that would eventually form the basis of his output as a writing master.

Bland's career as a penman did not begin until 1726, when he took up the post of writing master at Mr Watt's academy in Little Tower Street, where he taught for the next thirteen years. During that period he published his *Essay in Writing Exemplified in Forms of Business* (1730), which won him the reputation for specializing in utilitarian writing styles designed to facilitate communication in 'trade, and mercantile affairs' (Massey, 2.27). In 1739 he left Watt's establishment to set up his own academy in Bishopsgate Street, where he taught writing and accounts to youths destined for a mercantile career. He seems to have published only one copybook by himself; however, several examples of his calligraphy were included in compilations engraved by George Bickham, such as *Penmanship in its Utmost Beauty and Extent* (1731).

Bland died on 21 January 1749 at Cornhill, and was buried in St Martin's Outwich, Threadneedle Street. From Massey's account of his funeral we can surmise that Bland was a well-liked man: despite the frequent acrimony and competition between writing masters, Bland was carried to his grave by a number of his profession, as well as two of the teachers who worked at his academy.

LUCY PELTZ

Sources A. Heal, *The English writing-masters and their copy-books, 1570–1800* (1931) • A. Heal, 'The trade cards of engravers', *Print Collectors Quarterly*, 14 (1927), 219–50 • W. Massey, *The origin and progress of letters: an essay in two parts* (1763) • G. Meissner, ed., *Allgemeines Künstlerlexikon: die bildenden Künstler aller Zeiten und Völker*, [new edn, 34 vols.] (Leipzig and Munich, 1983–)

Bland, John (*d. c.*1788), barrister and writer, was the son of Nathaniel Bland, doctor of law, and judge of the prerogative court in Dublin. Although he does not appear to have been a graduate of Trinity College, he almost certainly enjoyed a classical education before entering King's Inns, Dublin, in Hilary term, 1741. At that date all candidates for the Irish bar were required to keep terms in one of the inns of court in London, and Bland was subsequently admitted to Lincoln's Inn on 16 January 1742. He was duly called to the Irish bar in Hilary term, 1754, and was called to the bar at Lincoln's Inn on 12 June 1752. The fact that he took ten years to be called at Lincoln's Inn, when the minimum interval for those without a university degree was seven years, in conjunction with his extraneous scholarly preoccupations might suggest that his commitment to a legal career was less than wholehearted. His absence from

Browne's General Law Lists in 1779 and 1787 implies that he was not practising in these years.

Bland is styled a gentleman on the title-page of his dramatic translation, in blank verse, of the Song of Solomon, his only contribution to literature, published in 1750. In his preface he claims to have completed a manuscript, now lost, entitled 'A treatise on the rhetorical power and use of the accent points of the Hebrew code, both in prose and verse' but, lacking 'proper Encouragement for the Publication thereof', he prepared this translation, and other pieces from the Old Testament, as a 'Specimen, to exemplify the Rules investigated and laid down in the said Treatise' (*A Grammatical Version, from the Original Hebrew, of the Song of Solomon*, sig. A2r). *The Song*'s meticulous, scholarly footnotes, elucidating major variations from other translations, clearly demonstrate the author's impressive erudition. Bland's gambit, to advertise the intrinsic merits of the 'Treatise' itself, was seemingly unsuccessful because his manuscript was never published.

The preface to *The Song*, signed on 10 February 1750 from Bland's house in Poorpool Lane, Gray's Inn Lane, concludes with an advertisement that the author is prepared to give lessons in the art of punctuation by Hebrew accents code. Evidence of further scholarly endeavour is revealed in an undated manuscript note in an edition of *Biographia dramatica* preserved in the British Library (11795 DF) which states that Bland translated Addison's tragedy *Cato* into Latin. Bland is said to have died at his house in Deptford about November 1788, although the reason why he chose to reside so far from the city, in an area which was then in decline owing to the gradual removal of naval dockyard facilities to Chatham, is unclear. There is no record of his burial in the parish churches of St Nicholas and St Paul which served the Deptford community at that date. JAMES WILLIAM KELLY

Sources register, St Paul's, Deptford, LMA [baptisms, June 1730–June 1788; marriages, July 1730–March 1754; burials, June 1730–June 1788] · St Paul's, Deptford, parish register of burials, July 1788–1812, Lewisham Local Studies Library · parish register, St Nicholas's, Deptford, April 1754–Jan 1764, LMA, Microfilm XO 86/132 [marriage] · *Browne's general law list* (1779), (1787) · St Nicholas's, Deptford, printed index of burials, Jan 1730–1837, LMA, Microfilm XO 102/46 · D. E. Baker, *Biographia dramatica, or, A companion to the playhouse*, rev. I. Reed, new edn, rev. S. Jones, 3 vols. in 4 (1812), vol. 1, p. 44 · J. Egerton, *Theatrical remembrancer* (1788) · Foster, *Alum. Oxon.* · T. Gilliland, *The dramatic mirror, containing the history of the stage from the earliest period, to the present time*, 1 (1808), 269 · E. Keane, P. Beryl Phair, and T. U. Sadleir, eds., *King's Inns admission papers, 1607–1867*, IMC (1982) · W. P. Baildon, ed., *The records of the Honorable Society of Lincoln's Inn: admissions*, 1 (1896) · W. P. Baildon, ed., *The records of the Honorable Society of Lincoln's Inn: the black books*, 3 (1899) · W. Oulton, *Barker's complete list of plays … to 1803, to which is added a continuation to the Theatrical remembrancer, designed to shew collectively each author's work* (1803), 302 · Venn, *Alum. Cant.*

Bland, John Otway Percy (1863–1945), writer and journalist, was born on 15 November 1863 in Malta, the second son of the ten children of Major-General Edward Loftus Bland (1829–1923) and Emma Frances Franks (*d.* 1894). Educated in Switzerland, and then at Victoria College, Jersey, he was a first-year undergraduate at Trinity College, Dublin, in 1883, aiming for the bar, when his father—then a colonel in the Royal Engineers—announced that family finances could no longer support him. Colonel Bland applied to Sir Robert Hart, inspector-general of the imperial Chinese maritime customs, for a position for his son. Hart, who packed the service with the progeny of his Ulster neighbours, took him on, and Bland sailed to China, arriving in July 1883.

China made, and unmade, John Otway Percy Bland. Until his departure for good in 1910 this talented but latterly bitter man worked actively in almost every sector of the non-official British establishment in China. He served in the customs, worked for settler imperialism through the Shanghai municipal council, and for finance imperialism through the British and Chinese Corporation. As a writer he did much to popularize the notion of the treaty port good life that was later to be lampooned so effectively by W. Somerset Maugham in *On a Chinese Screen* (1922). As a journalist who, in league with G. E. Morrison, was 'bent on stratagems and spoils for the glory of the Raj' (Bland, chap. 9, 12) and who also worked hand in glove with Valentine Chirol, latterly producing a series of angry and intemperate commentaries, Bland cast a long shadow over the public discourse of Anglo-Chinese relations. However, his career, for all this furious lobbying and action, and all this fluent and talented bluster, was in many ways a frustration and a disappointment.

A billet in the customs offered a good career path for those who kept their heads. Bland began as a fourth assistant A, rising slowly through the ranks and serving in Hankou (1884–6), Canton (Guangzhou) (1887), and Peking (Beijing) (1887–94), with a break in Shanghai (1888–9) occasioned by an indiscreet love affair in Peking. On 29 November 1889 in Shanghai, Bland married an American, Louisa Dearborn Nickels (*b. c.*1864), widow of M. C. Nickels and daughter of a Pacific Mail Line skipper, Captain H. C. Dearborn. These were halcyon days, bouts of ill health apart. Bland initially looked at China as exile, and the 'spiritual wilderness of the outports' (Bland, chap. 5, 1) was suffused for expatriate residents with an insular tedium enlivened only by drink, sex, or sport, and terminated through disgrace, illness, or death. Unlike many others Bland was not undone and he escaped the wilderness to positions in Shanghai and in Peking, where he served as Hart's private secretary in 1894–6. He also began penning light verse, publishing his first collection, *Lays of Far Cathay*, in 1890.

Promotion even for the talented Bland was slow, and in 1896 he joined the British-dominated Shanghai municipal council (SMC), which administered the international settlement at Shanghai, as assistant secretary. Shanghai was still, he later wrote, a 'happy hunting ground for taipans of the good old English school' (Bland, chap. 9, 1) and there was certainly happy hunting for a young Bland on the make. He speculated in land there, and in newly opened treaty ports and concessions, and launched a humorous periodical, *The Rattle*, which he co-owned and co-wrote. Shanghai was where Bland's imperialism and imagination were let loose. With little to do before the retirement of Robert Forrester Thorburn as secretary in 1897, Bland began working as Shanghai correspondent for *The Times*, and continued writing for the paper, latterly when in Peking as deputy to G. E. Morrison. As SMC secretary (1897–1906) Bland oversaw the massive expansion of the settlement from 1800 to 5500 acres in 1899, and lobbied hard for further increases. Bland was an activist secretary, energetic and driven, and his letters show how hard he worked to defend British interests in China—as he (often quite singularly) saw them—and to work for their extension. The SMC and the international settlement were 'the best British assets in the Yangtze Valley' he wrote to Morrison in July 1903 (Bland MSS, box 3). As well as working to protect the autonomy of the SMC from the Foreign Office and its agents in China—let alone from the Chinese—Bland was an active secretary of the Shanghai committee of the China Association, ever alert to London plots and to the lack of a firm British policy in China. He was one of the leading 'Shanghai insurgents' of 1905, who attacked the association's lack of gumption, as they saw it, in pressing the British government for an activist policy.

The 'insurgents' had been especially critical of Jardine Matheson & Co., and its chairman, William Keswick. But Bland switched sides in late 1905 and signed on at the behest of the Hongkong and Shanghai Bank's Charles Addis with the British and Chinese Corporation (BCC), formed largely by Keswick and by the bank in 1898, as its agent in China for conducting railway loan negotiations. Bland left the SMC from January 1906 for Peking although he continued there to lobby furiously on the council's behalf. He was however much more suited to Shanghai's insular settler politics. Bland was hardly a tactful negotiator with the Chinese, and his days 'In the house of Mammon' (Bland, chap. 12, title) were a disaster. Bland claimed that he was 'sacrificed to the Bank's German policy'. In fact he was, effectively, dismissed because his own vision of a specifically British-controlled railway, locked into a British loan, conflicted with the realities of rival imperialisms in China, let alone the rise of assertive Chinese popular nationalism, and adept official nationalism. Bland also alienated his partners, his superior Charles Addis, the BCC (which had misgivings about his relationship to Pauling & Co., which was seeking the construction contracts), and the Chinese. The leading Chinese statesman involved in the negotiations, Zhang Zhidang, eventually refused to conclude negotiations if Bland was at all connected to them. He was recalled to Britain in 1910 and his departure from the BCC hastily arranged through mutual consent. Addis went on to greater things; Bland counter-attacked through the pages of *The Times* in 1910—in collaboration with Valentine Chirol—lambasting the bank's pro-German bias, but it was miserable revenge for the humiliation of his recall, and effective and very public dismissal.

Bland now faced a second exile, this time from his professional *raison d'être*, China, and he faced other challenges to his reputation. Bland and Morrison had long fallen out, for Morrison could brook no rival, especially not the Peking Bland who wrote as 'Our Correspondent' in *The Times*. Morrison schemed against him on two fronts, at *The Times*—where he successfully forced the paper to choose between Bland and himself in mid-1911—and through Sir Edmund Backhouse, once Morrison's collaborator, now Bland's. Backhouse worked with Bland on two histories, *China under the Empress Dowager* (1910) and *Annals and Memoirs of the Court of Peking* (1914), but what was ever likely to be a problematic relationship—given Backhouse's enigmatic behaviour—was made much more difficult because of Morrison's intrigues.

Bland never held a China-related position again. He briefly worked as a clerk for the Cabinet Office during the First World War, published a volume entitled *Germany's Violations of the Laws of War* (1915), and worked as an agent for the National Party (*c.*1917). He toured South America, but he mostly turned to journalism and later to his farm in Aldeburgh. No longer Our Correspondent for *The Times*, Bland wrote commentaries (*Recent Events and Present Policies in China*, 1912; *China, Japan and Korea*, 1921) and light fiction, and his papers abound with plans and discussion for different works, or for film and theatrical versions of published material.

At some point, probably in 1910–11 when Bland lost China, the BCC, and *The Times*, he also finally lost his sense of humour. The effect on his reputation has been catastrophic. *China: the Pity of it* (1932) was a splenetic attack on Chinese nationalism, the republic, and the manifold changes which had occurred since the overthrow of the Qing dynasty in 1911–12. *Something Lighter* (1924) had softened its satire of legation mores and diplomatic inadequacies with irony and humour. His essay in *China*, 'The foreign office school of thought', was an angry denunciation of a changing world. Old partners in imperialism broke with him. From his retirement in Aldeburgh, Bland continued none the less to produce a steady stream of angry articles and letters until his death on 23 June 1945 in the Ipswich Nursing Home, 57 Fonnerean Road, Ipswich.

If his commentaries made him well known for an unpleasant racism, Bland's elegantly written histories left him remembered as unwitting dupe of one of the strangest British participants in the China scene, Sir Edmund Backhouse. *China under the Empress Dowager* (1910) and *Annals and Memoirs of the Court of Peking* (1914) were collaborations based on Backhouse's selection and translation of Chinese texts, and Bland's skills as a populist writer. Unfortunately Backhouse also forged or knowingly acquired forged documents, notably the so-called 'Diary of His Excellency Ching-Shan' which formed the centrepiece of the first work. To the end of his life Bland was still dealing with sceptical challenges to the authenticity of this diary (led, even before publication, by Morrison). The histories were popular, however, and served to introduce many (such as the historian C. P. Fitzgerald) to an exotic and excited reading of contemporary Chinese history, but Bland is now best remembered as Backhouse's patsy, and as an unreconstructed and bitter 'old China hand'. His personal misjudgements and temper have overshadowed his achievements: a small body of elegant light literature, histories which had a definite impact on the British popular imagination's conception of China, and his (unpublished and unfinished) 'Memoirs', an engaging account of the treaty port good life of the late nineteenth century. But the British advance into China that Bland worked so vigorously and wrote so furiously for turned into a full disengagement in the course of his lifetime. 'I mind my farm and let the East go hang' (Bland to Edmund Gilchrist, 24 July 1937, Bland MSS, box 7) he later wrote. It can hardly be said that Bland liked China itself, or that he saw it other than as a place for imperial advance, and for the advance of his own career. In its confusions and contradictions, and in its anger and sense of betrayal, Bland's relationship with that country tells us much about the failures of the British enterprise in China in the early twentieth century. ROBERT BICKERS

Sources J. O. P. Bland, 'Memoirs', *c.*1936, University of Toronto, Thomas Fisher Rare Book Library, Bland MSS, box 27 • R. A. Dayer, *Finance and empire: Sir Charles Addis, 1861–1945* (1988) • H. Trevor-Roper, *A hidden life: the enigma of Sir Edmund Backhouse* (1976); repr. as *Hermit of Peking: the hidden life of Sir Edmund Backhouse* (1978) • E. W. Edwards, *British diplomacy and finance in China, 1895–1914* (1987) • F. H. H. King, *The history of the Hongkong and Shanghai Banking Corporation*, 2 (1988) • N. A. Pelcovits, *Old China hands and the foreign office* (1948) • *CGPLA Eng. & Wales* (1945) • *WWW* • *Royal Engineers Journal*, new ser., 38 (1924), 141 [obit. of E. C. Bland] • *The Times* (24 June 1945)

Archives News Int. RO, corresp. • University of Toronto, Thomas Fisher Rare Book Library, journals and papers | Mitchell L., NSW, letters to G. E. Morrison • News Int. RO

Wealth at death £29,442 11*s.* 2*d.*: probate, 12 Dec 1945, *CGPLA Eng. & Wales*

Maria Theresa Bland (1769–1838), by Samuel De Wilde, 1805 [as Sally Shamrock in *The Shipwreck* by Samuel James Arnold]

Bland [*née* Romanzini], **Maria Theresa** (1769–1838), singer, was born of Italian-Jewish parents named Romanzini, who settled in London soon after her birth. In the spring of 1773 she was engaged at Hughes's Riding School, performing as Romanzini. She sang in the children's company at the opening of the Royal Circus on 7 November 1782, where she was also taught by the director, Charles Dibdin; she was then engaged by Richard Daly for the Theatre Royal, Dublin, where she sang with great success. In 1782 she went to Drury Lane to take the small parts known as 'singing chambermaids'. She performed at Sadler's Wells in 1786, and her first operatic appearance at Drury Lane was on 24 October that year, when she played the boy Antonio in an English version of Grétry's *Richard Coeur-de-Lion* adapted by Thomas Linley. In 1789 she sang in Liverpool with such success, both on the stage and in concerts, that she refused to return to Drury Lane unless her salary was raised. The management rejected her request, but she returned after a few weeks.

On 21 October 1790 Romanzini married George Bland, brother of Dorothea Jordan of Drury Lane and a minor actor. The marriage did not last, and Bland left her to go to America; she later had several illegitimate children. Although she also sang at the Haymarket from 1791 and at Vauxhall Gardens, she remained with the Drury Lane company for nearly forty years. Here she sang secondary roles in nearly all Storace's operas: Michael Kelly took Haydn and Pleyel to *The Cherokee* in 1794 and wrote of 'the great simplicity and truth' of her singing of 'A little bird sat on a spray'. Its success led to the belief that it was a genuine Welsh folk-song, and a setting for George Thomson's collection by Beethoven.

Mrs Bland's voice was a mezzo-soprano of very sweet quality, and, though her powers were limited, as a singer of English ballads she was free from any blemish of style or taste. In person she was short and dark, but her acting was very bright and vivacious. A deteriorating mental condition aggravated by the death of a child led to a breakdown after her last stage appearance in June 1822. A benefit at Drury Lane and a public subscription raised about £800; the money was passed to Lord Egremont, who allowed her an annuity of £80. She lived for the rest of her life with a family named Western, and died from apoplexy at their house, 11 Broadway, Westminster, on 15 January 1838. She was buried at St Margaret's, Westminster, on 25 January.

Her son **James Bland** (1798–1861) sang as a bass from 1826 at the Lyceum (English Opera House) and then at Drury Lane, and from 1831 at the Olympic Theatre in burlesque and extravaganzas. His success in these led to his performing kings and fathers in pantomimes by Planché and others. He died at the Strand Theatre on 17 July 1861. Another son, **Charles Bland** (*b.* 1802, *d.* in or after 1834), was a tenor who first appeared in 1824 as Don Carlos in Thomas Linley's *The Duenna*. He created the title role in Weber's *Oberon* under the composer at Covent Garden on 12 April 1826. Planché, the opera's librettist, thought him 'happily gifted with a voice which enabled him to execute at least respectably the airs assigned to the King of the Fairies', but Sir Julius Benedict wrote that he was 'a bad actor with an offensive voice', and he was not well received. His appearances outside London included Manchester in 1831; he then sang in London at the Olympic Theatre in 1831–2 and Astley's in 1833–4.

W. B. SQUIRE, *rev.* JOHN WARRACK

Sources S. Sadie, ed., *The new Grove dictionary of opera*, 4 vols. (1992) • Highfill, Burnim & Langhans, *BDA* • W. Van Lennep and others, eds., *The London stage, 1660–1800*, 5 pts in 11 vols. (1960–68) • R. Edgcumbe, *Musical reminiscences, containing an account of the Italian opera in England from 1773*, 4th edn (1834) • 'Memoirs of Mrs Bland', *Oxberry's Dramatic Biography*, 1/10 (1825), 161–7 • M. Kelly, *Reminiscences*, 2 vols. (1826) • J. R. Planché, *The recollections and reflections of J. R. Planché*, 2 vols. (1872) • J. Benedict, *Carl Maria von Weber* (1881) • T. J. Walsh, *Opera in Dublin, 1705–1797: the social scene* (1973) • *Annual Register* (1838), 197 • d. cert.
Likenesses S. De Wilde, engraving, 23 June 1795 • engraving, 1 Feb 1796 • Graham, engraving, 21 Jan 1797 • S. De Wilde, engraving, 1805 (as Sally Shamrock in *The shipwreck*), Garr. Club [*see illus.*] • colour engraving, 12 March 1805 • J. Condé, stipple, BM, NPG; repro. in *Thespian Magazine*, 1 (1 Aug 1792) • S. De Wilde, watercolours, Garr. Club • engraving (as Madelon in *The surrender of Calais*) • prints, Harvard TC

Bland, Miles (1786–1867), mathematician, was born at Sedbergh, Yorkshire, on 11 October 1786, the son of Thomas and Esther Bland. He was educated at Sedbergh School and at St John's College, Cambridge, where he graduated BA in 1808, as second wrangler and Smith's prizeman. He was afterwards elected fellow (5 April 1808) and tutor of his college, and acted as moderator (1814–16) and public examiner (1817–18) in mathematics. He has been described as a 'strong Tory, active in the University as well as his college' (Venn, *Alum. Cant.*). He was twice married: his first wife was Ann, daughter of T. Templeman of Ramsgate, and his second Emma, daughter of Claud Russell of Binfield, Berkshire; he had two sons and at least one daughter. He was ordained in 1810 and became rector of Lilley, Hertfordshire, in 1823 and a prebendary of Wells Cathedral in 1826, when he proceeded DD.

Bland wrote both mathematical works and biblical commentaries. His published mathematics consists mainly of textbooks and books of problems, for use at both school and university level. His *Algebraical Problems* (1812) was a very popular school textbook; a ninth edition was published in 1849. He also produced books of exercises in geometry, mechanics, and philosophy. His biblical studies resulted in the publication of commentaries on the gospels of St Matthew (1828) and St Mark (1829). He was a fellow of the Royal Society, of the Society of Antiquaries, and of the Royal Astronomical Society. He died on 27 December 1867 at 5 Royal Crescent, Ramsgate.

[ANON.], *rev.* JULIA TOMPSON

Sources *Men of the time* (1868) • *N&Q*, 6th ser., 9 (1884), 218 • Venn, *Alum. Cant.* • Boase, *Mod. Eng. biog.* • d. cert.
Archives St John Cam., notebooks and papers relating to mathematics, classics, and theology • U. Lpool, Sydney Jones Library, papers | RS, corresp. with Sir John Herschel
Wealth at death under £16,000: administration with will, 17 April 1868, *CGPLA Eng. & Wales*

Bland [*formerly* Crumpe], **Nathaniel** (1803–1865), Persian scholar, was born on 3 February 1803, the only son of Nathaniel Bland of Randalls Park, Leatherhead. His father's name was originally Crumpe, but after leaving Ireland and purchasing Randalls Park, in 1812 he took the surname of his mother, Dorothea, daughter of Dr Bland of Derriquin Castle, co. Kerry.

Bland entered Eton College in 1818, and matriculated from Christ Church, Oxford, on 16 October 1821, graduating BA in 1825. He was an elegant Persian scholar, and between 1843 and 1853 contributed several valuable papers to the *Journal of the Royal Asiatic Society*. The first, in the June issue of 1843 (vol. 7), was a notice of the *Atash Kada*, a collection of lives of poets. This and a supplementary article in volume 9 of the *Journal* became the standard texts for some time, but are now superseded by other translations. Bland contributed articles to the *Journal* on several other topics, including Persian chess and the Islamic science of the interpretation of dreams as well as one describing the Pole collection of oriental manuscripts in Eton College Library. Some of these articles were later published independently. In 1844 he edited Nizam's *Makhzun al-Asrar* for the Oriental Translation Fund, but unfortunately he did not finish this work. In the latter part of his life he took to gambling, had to sell Randalls Park, and eventually committed suicide at Hombourg-les-Bains in Belgium on 10 August 1865. His valuable collection of Persian and other manuscripts was sold through Bernard Quaritch in 1866 and purchased by the earl of Crawford. It subsequently formed part of the Bibliotheca Lindesiana.

HENRY BEVERIDGE, *rev.* PARVIN LOLOI

Sources *Journal of the Royal Asiatic Society of Great Britain and Ireland*, new ser., 2 (1866), iii–v • Foster, *Alum. Oxon.* • Boase, *Mod. Eng. biog.*
Archives BL, memoranda of oriental literature, Add. MSS 30378–30379

Bland, Richard (1710–1776), revolutionary politician in America, was born on 6 May 1710 in Williamsburg, Virginia, the eldest son of Richard Bland (1665–1720) and his second wife, Elizabeth Randolph (*d.* 1720). Sometimes known as 'the Antiquary' for his extensive knowledge of legal and constitutional history, Bland became the most active member of the Virginia house of burgesses in the final decades of the colonial period and penned some of the earliest and most forceful arguments for colonial sovereignty within the British empire.

Like most members of his generation Bland's success rested squarely on landed wealth, a good marriage, and a sound education. His 1000 acre Jordan's Point plantation in Prince George county, inherited from his father at the age of nine, provided a solid financial base; his marriage, on 21 March 1729, to Anne (1712–1758), daughter of Peter Poythress, connected him to an important local family. Though the details of his education are uncertain he probably studied under a private tutor at home; he did attend the College of William and Mary in the late 1720s. His education continued into adulthood with private study of the law; he qualified for the bar in 1746.

Bland moved beyond these traditional gentry footings, however, by acquiring more than 3000 additional acres in several counties as well 40,000 acres in the back country of Augusta county, Virginia, which he held in partnership with five other prominent Virginians. He invested in powder mills along the James River and maintained a home in Williamsburg, where he spent much of his time. The marriages of many of his twelve children reinforced his social connections, as did his own subsequent marriages: in 1758, to Martha, *née* Macon (1722–*c.*1760), widow of William Massie (*d.* 1749), and then, between 1760 and 1762, to Elizabeth (*c.*1710–1775), daughter of council president John Blair and widow of John Bolling (*d.* 1757).

Eighteenth-century political careers followed a well-worn path, and Bland's was no exception. As a young man he accepted appointments as a vestryman of his local Church of England parish, as an officer in the county militia (1738), and—most importantly—as a justice of the peace of Prince George county (1733). His most significant achievements built upon these local offices and sprang from thirty-five years in the legislative service of the Virginia house of burgesses (1741–76), all five Virginia revolutionary conventions (1774–6), the first meeting of the state house of delegates (1776), and the first and second continental congresses (1774–5).

First elected to the house of burgesses in 1741, Bland spent the next decade mastering the intricacies of legislative politics. Following the 1752 election he immediately assumed a more active role in the house, which included service on several major committees. By the 1760s he and six other burgesses routinely monopolized the chairmanship of all six standing committees. Few transactions of the house escaped his touch.

Bland's most significant contributions to Virginia and to the American independence movement came in a series of pamphlets which suggested that the good of the people is superior to the long-standing prerogatives of kings and governors; that the people's needs are best determined by an appropriately constituted representative body, such as the Virginia house of burgesses; and that sovereignty within the British empire is logically and historically divided between these local legislative bodies, which control internal affairs, and parliament, which regulates the broad external affairs of the empire.

Bland began to refine these principles in 1752, when he helped to draft a protest to the king for having disallowed ten acts passed by the previous Virginia assembly. The following year Bland went a step further and strongly objected to Governor Dinwiddie's imposition of a small 'pistole' fee on land patents. Bland noted that while governors of other colonies might collect such fees with the approval of their legislatures Virginians 'cannot be deprived of the least part of their property without [the] consent' of the people's representatives (Bland, *A Fragment on the Pistole Fee*, 37). Independent legislative action was again Bland's theme when he came to the defence of the controversial Two Penny Act of 1758. Because the act allowed fixed salaries to be paid at a rate of 2*d.* per pound of tobacco—which constituted a significant loss of income for parish ministers—the clergy protested to London and got the act disallowed. Bland rose in outrage against the disallowance with his *Letter to the Clergy of Virginia* (1760) and his satirical *The Colonel Dismounted* (1764), which argued for the exclusive right of provincial assemblies to pass internal laws best suited to the welfare of the people. Although Bland objected to the strongly worded stamp act resolves proposed by Patrick Henry in 1765 he none the less constructed *An Inquiry into the Rights of the British Colonies* (1766), in which he suggested not only that the act violated the divided sovereignty principle that he had articulated earlier but also that natural law allowed men to 'retire' from a government that no longer met their needs.

After 1774 Bland's arguments were echoed by many Americans and he turned his attention to ridding Virginia of its last royal governor and constructing a new state constitution. In addition he served in the first and second continental congresses, where he was respected for his great learning and logical mind. However, as Virginia and America accelerated toward independence, Bland showed some hesitancy to sever all ties with Britain and he was accused of disloyalty. Although he acquitted himself of all charges the ordeal probably exacerbated his declining health. He died of apoplexy at Williamsburg on 26 October 1776 and was buried at his Jordan's Point estate.

JOHN G. KOLP

Sources R. C. Daetweiler, *Richard Bland and the origins of the revolution in Virginia*, ed. E. M. Riley [1981] • R. C. Daetweiler, 'Richard Bland: conservator of self-government in eighteenth-century Virginia', PhD diss., University of Washington, 1968 • J. P. Greene, 'Society, ideology, and politics: an analysis of the political culture of mid-eighteenth-century Virginia', *Society, freedom, and conscience: the coming of the revolution in Virginia, Massachusetts, and New York*, ed. R. M. Jellison (1976), 14–76 • H. R. McIlwaine and J. P. Kennedy, eds., *Journals of the house of burgesses of Virginia, 1619–1776*, 13 vols. (1905–15) • *Executive journals of the council of colonial Virginia*, 4, ed. H. R. McIlwaine (1930); 5, ed. W. L. Hall (1945); 6, ed. B. J. Hillman (1956) • *The Bland papers: being a selection from the manuscripts of Colonel T. Bland*, ed. C. Campbell, 2 vols. (1840–43) • R. Bland, *An inquiry into the rights of the British colonies* (1766); repr. in W. J. van Schreeven and R. L. Scribner, eds., *Revolutionary Virginia: the road to independence*, 1: *Forming thunderclouds and the first convention, 1763-1774* ([Charlottesville, VA], 1973) • R. Bland, *The colonel dismounted, or, The rector vindicated* (1764); repr. in B. Bailyn, ed., *Pamphlets of the American Revolution, 1750–1776*, 1 (1965) • R. Bland, *A fragment on the pistole fee, claimed by the governor of Virginia, 1753*, ed. W. C. Ford (New York, 1891) • R. Bland, *A letter to the clergy of Virginia in which the conduct of the general-assembly is vindicated, against the reflections contained in a letter to the lords of trade and plantations, from the lord-bishop of London* (1760) • C. Rossiter, 'Richard Bland: the whig in America', *William and Mary Quarterly*, 10 (1953), 33–79 • *Virginia Gazette* (3 Jan 1777)

Wealth at death at least 1000 acres at Jordan's Point, Prince George county; thirty slaves; 100 cattle; fifty-six hogs; library: *Virginia Gazette*

Bland, Robert (1740–1816), man-midwife, was born at King's Lynn, Norfolk, the son of David Bland, an attorney in the town, and was educated at the London hospitals. He married some time about 1774; the classical scholar Robert *Bland (1779?–1825) and the politician William *Bland (1789–1868) were among his four children. Bland received the degree of MD from the University of St Andrews in 1778, and was admitted licentiate of the Royal College of Physicians on 30 September 1786. He was connected to the Westminster General Dispensary from 1774 until 1781. He obtained an extensive practice as an accoucheur in London, and his reputation was such that he was engaged to write all the articles on midwifery for Rees's *Cyclopaedia*. To the *Philosophical Transactions* (no. 71/1, 22, 35–72) he contributed in 1781 a paper entitled 'Some calculations of the number of accidents or deaths which happen from parturition; proportion of male and female children born; of twins, monstrosities … taken from the reports of the Westminster General Dispensary', and in the same year a 'Table of the chances of life from infancy to twenty-six years of age'. He published in 1794 *Observations on Human and Comparative Parturition*, and he was also the author of *Proverbs Chiefly Taken from the Adagia of Erasmus, with Explanations; and Illustrated by Examples from the Spanish, Italian, French, and English Languages* (2 vols., 1814). From 1796 until 1816 Bland was chairman of the Basingstoke Canal Navigation Company. He was described as being 'skilled in his profession and of extensive experience but eccentric in manner' (Vine, 46). He died at Leicester Square, London, on 29 June 1816. His library was sold later by Sothebys.

[Anon.], *rev.* Michael Bevan

Sources Munk, *Roll* • P. A. L. Vine, *London's lost route to Basingstoke: the story of the Basingstoke Canal* (1994) • A. Wilson, *The making of man-midwifery: childbirth in England, 1660–1770* (1995) • *GM*, 1st ser., 86/2 (1816), 186

Bland, Robert (1779?–1825), classical scholar, son of Robert *Bland (1740–1816), was educated at Harrow School and at Pembroke College, Cambridge, where he was admitted in 1797 and graduated BA in 1802. He entered holy orders in 1801, and was an assistant master at Harrow from 1802 until 1808, Byron being among his pupils. He was next a reader and preacher at some London chapels. Later he was appointed minister to the English church at Amsterdam, but 'the circumstances of the times not permitting him to fulfill the objects of his appointment' (*GM*, 1st ser., 95/1, 646), he returned to England. In 1811 Byron helped to extricate him from a duel with an officer in the guards who had made off with the mistress whom Bland shared with another literary clergyman in Byron's circle, Francis Hodgson. In 1813 he received the curacy of Prittlewell, Essex, exchanging this in 1816 for the curacy of Kenilworth. He combined his clerical duties with private tuition, preparing pupils for university entrance. In 1813 Bland married Eliza, daughter of Archdale Wilson Tayler; they had six children. He died at Leamington on 12 March 1825.

As a classical scholar and teacher Bland was much esteemed in his day. His *Elements of Latin Hexameters and Pentameters*, which reached its twenty-first edition in 1853, remained in use for decades. His *Translations, Chiefly from the Greek Anthology, with Tales and Miscellaneous Poems* (1806), in which he collaborated with J. H. Merivale, attracted considerable notice. In politics a whig, Bland was a member of the literary circle which included Francis Hodgson, his future brother-in-law. His poetry received a complimentary notice in Byron's *English Bards and Scottish Reviewers* (*Lord Byron: The Complete Poetical Works*, ed. J. J. McGann, 1, 1980, 415). Well versed in French and Italian, Bland translated, with Anna Plumptre, the *Memoirs of Baron de Grimm* and *Diderot* (2 vols., 1813).

A. H. Bullen, *rev.* M. C. Curthoys

Sources *GM*, 1st ser., 95/1 (1825), 379, 646 • Venn, *Alum. Cant.* • *N&Q*, 6th ser., 10 (1884), 199 • *Byron's letters and journals*, ed. L. A. Marchand, 2 (1973) • [J. T. Hodgson], *Memoir of the Rev. Francis Hodgson BD scholar, poet and divine*, 2 vols. (1878)

Bland, Tobias (*c*.1563–1605), Church of England clergyman, matriculated sizar from Pembroke College, Cambridge, in 1575 and proceeded BA in 1581, in which year he migrated to Corpus Christi College. Accused of publishing a satirical libel against the master of the college, Robert Norgate, which began 'In the name of the father, the sonn, and the old wiffe' and was set out in the form of a catechism, he admitted the offence and was ordered to sit in the stocks. Norgate became vice-chancellor soon after, so that Bland's reputation in Cambridge remained questionable; a petition to the university chancellor, Lord Burghley, signed by fifty members of senate, unsuccessfully attempted to prevent Bland's progression to MA in 1584. By this date he had been ordained deacon and he proceeded to priest's orders at Lincoln in December 1585.

Bland's early clerical career remains obscure, but by 1589 he had come under the patronage of Lord St John of Bletso, whose chaplain he was and to whom he dedicated *A Baite for Momus*, a sermon on 1 Timothy, 4: 1–2 delivered at Bedford and published in that year. The sermon appears to have aroused some controversy among the clergy of the area but is not notably partisan, though in it Bland refers to another, longer, work, apparently not published, which may have set out more contentious views. Through the influence of his patron he became, in 1589, rector of Ripton Abbots, Huntingdonshire, an office he held jointly with the mastership of St John's Hospital, Huntingdon, from 1599 until his death.

Meanwhile, Bland had also recovered his reputation at Cambridge, moving to Magdalene College and taking his BD in 1591, and a promising career beckoned on his appointment as sub-almoner to Queen Elizabeth in 1594. He was subsequently rector of the valuable Northamptonshire living of Brington from 1599 to 1601 before being collated to the first prebendal stall at Peterborough Cathedral on 29 October 1602. He died early in 1605 and was buried at St Sepulchre's, Cambridge, on 4 April that year.

William Joseph Sheils

Sources Venn, *Alum. Cant.* • T. Bland, *A baite for Momus, so called upon occasion of a sermon at Bedford, injuriously traduced by the factions* (1589) • H. I. Longden, *Northamptonshire and Rutland clergy from 1500*, ed. P. I. King and others, 16 vols. in 6, Northamptonshire RS (1938–52) • *DNB*

Bland, William (1789–1868), medical practitioner and politician in Australia, was born in London on 5 November

1789, the second son of Dr Robert *Bland (1740–1816). William was said to have attended the Merchant Taylors' School, but this has not been confirmed. Certainly, he was drawn to medicine and on 6 January 1809 qualified as a surgeon's mate in the navy, rising to naval surgeon in 1812. On 7 April 1813, while aboard the *Hesper* at Bombay, he killed the purser, Robert Case, in a duel and was sentenced to seven years' transportation.

Having arrived at Sydney on the *Frederick* on 14 July 1814, Bland was sent to the asylum at Castle Hill and served there until pardoned on 27 October 1815. He moved to Sydney, set up a successful medical practice, and on 17 April 1817 married Sarah (*b.* 1797), the eldest daughter of the missionary, William Henry. The couple separated and Sarah left the colony in 1818, after William accused her of infidelity and sued Richard Drake of the East India Company. On 24 September 1818, Bland was himself tried for lampooning Governor Macquarie and was sentenced to a year in Parramatta gaol. He did not again break the law and after release resumed his medical practice.

A highly successful surgeon, who performed demanding operations, Bland contributed articles to the *Australian Medical Journal* and became president of the Australian Medical Subscription Library in 1859. Earlier, in 1821, he had begun an involvement with the Benevolent Society that lasted until 1863. His concern for the health of the poor was further reflected in his work for the Sydney Dispensary between 1826 and 1845. He was also anxious to improve educational opportunities for the colonists, rich as well as poor. He helped establish the Sydney School of Arts and Mechanics Institute in 1833 and prepared a plan for the non-denominational Sydney College on 18 August 1828. The college offered a classical education and opened on 19 January 1835. Bland served as treasurer until 1844 and president from 1845 until 1853. His community work extended to patronage of the arts and financial support for the construction of a church at Ashfield.

Bland also became a substantial landowner, acquiring large properties at Prospect and Hunters Hill near Sydney and grazing runs at Yass and Gerringong on the south-western plains. He thus contributed to the growth of the pastoral industry, running cattle and sheep. His interest extended to horse racing, which was one of his enjoyments. All this helped identify him with the landed gentry and like many of their number he became involved in colonial politics. During the 1820s and 1830s he threw his weight behind the cause of reform, supporting the group known variously as the Emancipists, or more accurately, Botany Bay Whigs, who advocated representative government and trial by jury. When the Australian Patriotic Association was formed in 1835 to co-ordinate the group's efforts and strengthen links with a parliamentary agent in London, Bland was made chairman of the committee of correspondence. He played a leading role in the ensuing struggle for self-government and helped draft a constitution bill. In 1842 the legislative council was enlarged, its powers were increased, and provision was made for two-thirds of the members to be elected. Bland was returned as a representative for Sydney on 15 June 1843 and over the next five years was active in council affairs, taking a generally liberal stand. He lost his seat to Robert Lowe in 1848, but regained it in 1849 when Lowe resigned. A year later Bland left politics and did not return until 1858 when he was appointed to the new upper house. Refused an annuity in 1861 at the end of his term of office, he was also declared bankrupt.

Despite this misfortune, Bland stands out as one of the more constructive figures in early New South Wales. He possessed wide interests, contributed to numerous facets of colonial life, and published several writings. Colourful and outspoken, he was noted for his drive, progressive ideas, and professional skills. He died of pneumonia in Sydney on 21 July 1868, leaving his second wife, the coroner's widow, Elizabeth Smeathman, whom he had married on 5 February 1846, after himself being widowed. He left no children. He was buried on 23 July at Haslem Creek. BRIAN H. FLETCHER

Sources N. J. Dunlop, 'Dr William Bland', *Royal Australian Historical Society Journal and Proceedings*, 11 (1925–6), 321–51 • A. M. McIntosh, 'Life and times of William Bland', *Bulletin of the Post-Graduate Committee in Medicine* [University of Sydney], 10 (1954) • J. Cobley, 'William Bland', *AusDB*, 1.112–15 • Mitchell L., NSW, J. D. Lang MSS • W. Bland, 'Account of the duel between William Bland and Robert Case …', Mitchell L., NSW • W. Bland, *Papers of the Australian Patriotic Association* (1846) • W. Bland, *Letters to Charles Buller from the Australian Patriotic Association* (1849) • Mitchell L., NSW, Henry Parkes MSS, 40.59–63 • W. Bland, Memorandum Book, 1835, Mitchell L., NSW

Archives Mitchell L., NSW | Mitchell L., NSW, J. D. Lang MSS • Mitchell L., NSW, Henry Parkes corresp.

Likenesses portrait, 1840–60, Mitchell L., NSW • R. Read?, portrait, 1844–54, Mitchell L., NSW • G. Goodman, photograph, 14 Jan 1845, Mitchell L., NSW • watercolour, Mitchell L., NSW

Blandford, George Fielding (1829–1911), physician and psychiatrist, was born at Hindon, Wiltshire, on 7 March 1829, the only son of George Blandford (*bap.* 1796), a surgeon who practised successively at Hindon, Hadlow in Kent, and Rugby, and his wife, Mary Fielding (1794?–1852). Blandford was educated at Tonbridge School (1840–41) and Rugby School (1841–8), and matriculated from Wadham College, Oxford, on 10 May 1848, graduating BA in 1852 and MA in 1857. He started his medical studies at St George's Hospital, London, in October 1852 and in 1857 qualified BM and LSA, and MRCS in 1858. Throughout his life Blandford remained linked to St George's. In 1865 he gave his first lecture on insanity there, taking his DM in 1867, and remained lecturer on psychological medicine at the hospital until May 1909. On 31 March 1864 he married Louisa (1840/41–1937), only daughter of the Revd George Holloway, in Amersham, Buckinghamshire. They had two sons and two daughters.

Early in his career Blandford became friendly with Dr A. J. Sutherland, who was physician to St Luke's Hospital, but also had an extensive private practice in psychiatric medicine. He visited St Luke's with Sutherland, and provided holiday cover for the superintendent, Henry Stevens. In 1859 Sutherland appointed Blandford resident medical officer to one of his private asylums, Blacklands House, where he held the post until 1863.

Blandford then followed the career path of Sutherland,

and other earlier Victorian alienists such as George Man Burrows and Thomas Monro, by combining a private practice where he saw wealthier insane patients, with the ownership of, or a visiting physician role at, a private asylum. Like J. C. Bucknill, Henry Maudsley, and James Crichton-Browne he saw his primary reference group within the Royal College of Physicians rather than the Medico-Psychological Association (MPA). In 1863 Blandford set up in private practice in Clarges Street, moving successively to Grosvenor Street (1871) and Wimpole Street (1890). Competition was fierce, with five other doctors listed in Clarges Street and twenty-six in Grosvenor Street. While building his private practice Blandford acted as visiting physician to Blacklands House (and from 1891 its successor Newlands House) and its sister, Otto House, posts he held until his retirement in 1909. He was also visiting physician to Featherstone Hall, Southall (1891–1909), and Clarence Lodge, Clapham Park (1903–9), private asylums for ladies. From 1874 to 1895 he was the principal proprietor of Munster House, sharing the licence with a fellow doctor from St George's.

Blandford was typical of second-generation nineteenth-century psychiatrists who were inspired to apply more rigorous scientific methods to the study of insanity. His major work, *Insanity and its Treatment* (1871), was dedicated to Henry Maudsley, and posited a physical basis for insanity. He focused on the need to direct patients' thoughts away from introspection and towards more social habits. In that same year he produced a critical review of Maudsley's presidential address to the MPA, and increasingly came to dislike his degenerationist ideas. However, the concerted attack on Maudsley in 1877, in which his resignation from the MPA was debated during Blandford's presidency, owed more to the former's attacks on the private asylum system than to his materialism or degenerationist views. It may well have been Blandford who wrote several hostile reviews of Maudsley's publications which appeared in the *Journal of Mental Science*. Blandford's presidential address that year, delivered by special agreement of the MPA at the Royal College of Physicians, specifically addressed the proposed changes in the lunacy laws that threatened private asylum care.

Blandford had a typical Victorian attitude to women, who were generally perceived as less robust constitutionally and more liable to asocial behaviour. Blandford believed that no man or woman should marry after suffering from a mental illness. This got him into trouble in 1895 after he signed an 'urgency' order to incarcerate the socialist and feminist Edith Lanchester, who was living with a railway clerk against her family's wishes. Blandford argued that her opposition to conventional matrimony made her unfit to care for herself.

A very clubbable man, Blandford was an active member of the College of Physicians, becoming a member in 1860 and fellow in 1869. He gave the Lumleian lectures in 1895, and was a councillor from 1897 to 1899. He was president of the psychological section of the British Medical Association and gave an address on the prevention of insanity. From 1857 he was for forty-four years an active member of the MPA, being part of the educational and parliamentary committees that protected the interests of private asylum owners, as well as county asylum doctors.

As a young man Blandford was very athletic. He accompanied his father on horseback during his medical rounds and was a good cricketer, oarsman, and footballer. He also served in the 2nd (South) Middlesex volunteers for some years. Blandford had a lifelong interest in art, literature, and music, and from 1862 was a member of the Athenaeum, a club for authors and promoters of the fine arts. Blandford was an early purchaser of Whistler's etchings, and had a large collection of books and prints of old London. He was a member of the Western friendly club and Mayfair medical book club, and president of the Graphics Society of St George's Hospital. In later life he took up watercolour sketching. From 1898 until his death he took an active part in the After Care Association set up to help patients discharged from asylum care, and was also president of the Society for the Relief of the Widows and Orphans of Medical Men.

In 1909 Blandford retired to Woodlands, Camden Park, Tunbridge Wells, where he died of bronchopneumonia on 18 August 1911. He was buried in Tunbridge Wells on 23 August. D'A. POWER, *rev.* NICK HERVEY

Sources *The Lancet* (1911), 2.733 • *BMJ* (2 Sept 1911), 524 • A. Scull, *The most solitary of afflictions: madness and society in Britain, 1700–1900* (New Haven, CT, 1993), 254–5, 283 • E. Showalter, *The female malady: women, madness and English culture, 1830–1980* (New York, 1985) • W. Bynum, R. Porter, and M. Shepherd, eds., *The anatomy of madness: essays in the history of psychiatry*, 3: *The asylum and its psychiatry* (1988) • A. Scull, C. Mackenzie, and N. Hervey, *Masters of Bedlam: the transformation of the mad-doctoring trade* (Princeton, 1996), 224, 250, 271 • C. Mackenzie, *Psychiatry for the rich: a history of Ticehurst private asylum* (1992) • G. F. Blandford, 'Acquitted on the grounds of insanity (from a mad doctor's point of view)', *Cornhill Magazine*, 12 (1865), 426–40 • *IGI* • *Medical Directory* • m. cert. • d. cert. [Louisa Blandford] • *CGPLA Eng. & Wales* (1911)

Wealth at death £106,785 17*s*.: probate, 10 Oct 1911, *CGPLA Eng. & Wales*

Blandford, Thomas (1861–1899), co-operative movement activist, was born on 19 August 1861 in Curragh, co. Kildare, to a father of Scottish extraction and a mother of Irish descent. Blandford's parents are recorded in one source as strolling players and this is consistent with the limited record of his early life. The family settled in Newcastle upon Tyne where Blandford obtained employment in a warehouse. By 1881 he had moved to London, finding new opportunities both in employment—he became a foreman in a wholesale house—and in education. Blandford attended lectures at the Men's and Women's College, Queen Square, where his interest in economics was developed by James Bonar; such was his appetite for learning that he temporarily gave up his warehouse work to study in the British Museum.

Blandford's interest in labour conditions and co-operative production led him to join the Labour Association in 1885. This recently formed educational and propagandist body promoted principles of co-partnership including profit-sharing and worker participation in the ownership and administration of business. Blandford served as president of the association for two years and was vice-president at the time of his death. He was also involved in specific co-operative productive ventures, including the Co-operative Bookbinders and the London Productive Society. Blandford's perception of productive societies' need to display their output to potential customers led to involvement with the Co-operative Festivals Association which held its first annual event at Crystal Palace in 1888. Blandford also served on the Co-operative Congress Exhibitions committee which organized other festivals in northern and midland England and Scotland during the 1890s.

In 1894 Blandford took up a full-time post as the general secretary of the Co-operative Productive Federation, a group founded in 1882 and to which the Labour Association owed its origins. The federation aimed to assist producers' co-operatives, acting as a central agency providing capital and opening up markets for co-operative output. Initially its concrete achievements were few; under Blandford, however, the organization did begin to fulfil some of its original objectives. He established a loan department to assist the capitalization of producers' co-operatives, and had some success in reviving trade union support for such ventures. Blandford was also a relentless propagandist and spoke at over 200 trade union branches urging support for co-operative production. He was equally active in print, establishing *Labour Co-Partnership*, a monthly journal, in 1894 and producing the *Co-Operator's Year Book*. Producers' co-operation remained under-developed in Britain by comparison with the success of the consumers' movement. It did, however, undergo modest expansion in the later 1890s, with twenty new societies applying to join the Co-operative Productive Federation between 1896 and 1899. This revival of interest was at least in part associated with Blandford's charm, idealism, and energy in promoting the cause.

Blandford was involved in the international development of co-operation. By virtue of his birth he took an interest in the development of agricultural co-operation in Ireland. Blandford served as chairman of the trading relations committee of the International Co-operative Alliance and was delegated to attend congresses in Paris (1896) and Delft (1897). This, however, increased the strain on Blandford's health, and as early as 1897 friends expressed concerns about his physical well-being. He suffered from consumption and incipient heart disease, as well as the mental stress suffered by a private, contemplative man driven to a public role by a sense of duty. Blandford refused to curtail his work, and even while convalescing in Devon in 1899 visited trade union branches. He returned home to Camden Town while still far from recovered, and died there of influenza on 25 February 1899. He was buried in Highgate cemetery three days later. Blandford was unmarried; he was survived by a sister, also resident in London. On his death he was hailed as a martyr for co-operation, and his work was commemorated in the naming of the Blandford Congress Memorial Fund.

MARTIN PURVIS

Sources R. Halstead, *Thomas Blandford: hero and martyr of co-partnership* (1925) · J. Bellamy, 'Blandford, Thomas', *DLB*, vol. 1 · *Co-operative News* (4 March 1899) · E. O. Greening, *Report of the Co-operative Congress* (1899) · G. D. H. Cole, *A century of co-operation* (1945) · F. Hall and W. P. Watkins, *Co-operation: a survey of the history, principles, and organisation of the co-operative movement in Great Britain and Ireland*, new edn (1937) · minute book, Co-operative Production Federation, 1896–1901, U. Hull, Brynmor Jones L., DCF/1 · A. Bonner, *British co-operation: the history, principles, and organisation of the British co-operative movement*, rev. edn (1970)

Archives U. Hull, Co-operative Production Federation, minute book, DCF/1

Likenesses photograph, *c.*1890, repro. in Halstead, *Thomas Blandford*

Blandford, Walter (1615/16–1675), bishop of Worcester, was the son of Walter Blandford, and was born at Melbury Abbas, Dorset. He became a servitor of Christ Church, Oxford, in 1635, aged nineteen, was admitted scholar of Wadham College in 1638, graduated BA on 10 December 1639, and proceeded MA on 28 June 1642. In 1644 he was admitted as a fellow of Wadham. He was recorded as having been expelled by the parliamentary visitors on 14 July 1648, but it seems that he remained in his fellowship none the less.

There is no proof that Blandford took the solemn league and covenant. What evidence there is demonstrates Blandford's royalist sympathies. About this time he was appointed chaplain to the cavalier Lord Lovelace of Hurley. During the interregnum Blandford was a member of John Wilkins's royalist circle at Wadham. His election as warden of the college in 1659 (a post he held until 1665) demonstrated growing royalist confidence within the university. At the Restoration he was created DD in 1660 and became chaplain to Sir Edward Hyde, later earl of Clarendon, who obtained for him a prebend in Gloucester Cathedral on 6 August, and a chaplainship-in-ordinary to the king. In the same year he was made rector of Remeneham in Berkshire. Between 1662 and 1664 he was vice-chancellor of Oxford University and in 1665 he was made rector of Witney in Oxfordshire. That year he was consecrated bishop of Oxford and soon afterwards he was nominated dean of the Chapel Royal. About this time he seems to have been given a grant of arms.

Blandford's connections with the Hyde family survived the fall and death of Clarendon. According to the memoirs of James II on 30 March 1671 he was brought to attend the deathbed of the earl's daughter, Anne, duchess of York, by her brother Laurence Hyde. The duchess had requested her husband, James, to tell any bishops who came to attend her of her secret conversion to Rome; if they still insisted on seeing her they might come in provided they did not attempt to shift her faith. When the situation was explained to Blandford by the duke, the bishop

> said to him, He made no doubt but that she would do well (that was his expression) since she was fully convinced, and did it not out of any worldly end; and afterwards went into the room to her, and made her a short Christian exhortation suitable to the condition she was in, and then departed. (Clarke, 1.453)

Three months later Blandford was translated to the see

of Worcester, where he died at the bishop's house at Hartlebury, Worcestershire, on 9 or 16 July 1675. He was buried in the cathedral, where there is a memorial to him. In his will the bachelor Blandford left £100 towards the rebuilding of St Paul's Cathedral and £500 to renovate the house at Hartlebury. However, it appears that there were legal disputes over this bequest and it is unclear whether the money was ever spent on the house (there was a clause in the will which stated that if work was not begun within six months after his successor had been installed the money should be given instead to charitable causes). Blandford published nothing, though Nicholas Lloyd, also of Wadham College, dedicated his edition of Charles Estienne's *Dictionarium historicum* (1670) to him. There is a portrait of Blandford in Wadham and a copy of the painting in the bishop's house at Hartlebury.

EDWARD VALLANCE

Sources *DNB* • Foster, *Alum. Oxon.* • M. Burrows, ed., *The register of the visitors of the University of Oxford, from AD 1647 to AD 1658*, CS, new ser., 29 (1881), 162 • *Hist. U. Oxf.* 4: *17th-cent. Oxf.*, 766, 769, 809 • clauses from will and letter from Bishop Fell to Bishop Compton, Bodl. Oxf., MS Tanner 140, fols. 137, 148, 150 • Bishop Blandford to Bishop Ward, Bodl. Oxf., MS Tanner 42, fol. 123 • draft dedication to Walter Blandford prefixed by Nicholas Lloyd to *Dictionarium historicum*, Bodl. Oxf., MS Rawl. D. 32, fol. 10 • *Fasti Angl., 1541–1857*, [Ely] • letter of Edward Walker to Sir Richard Browne, BL, Add. MS 15858, fol. 186 • *The life of James the Second, king of England*, ed. J. S. Clarke, 1 (1816), vol. 1, pp. 452–3 • will, PRO, PROB 11/352, sig. 135
Archives Worcs. RO, letter-book
Likenesses oils, Wadham College, Oxford; version, Hartlebury Castle, Worcester
Wealth at death considerable; donated £600 in cash gifts: clauses from will and letter from Bishop Fell to Bishop Compton, Bodl. Oxf., MS Tanner 140, fols. 137, 148, 150

Blandie, William. *See* Blandy, William (*fl.* 1563–1581).

Blandy, Mary (1718/19–1752), murderer, was born in Henley-on-Thames, Oxfordshire, the only child of Francis Blandy (*c.*1689–1751) and Mary Stevens (*c.*1700–1749), parents so 'excessively fond' of her that they could 'scarce bear her out of their sight', and 'whose continual Study was to promote her Happiness' (*Genuine and Impartial Account*, 3; *Authentic Tryals*, 21). Francis Blandy, an attorney, whose 'whole thoughts were bent to settle her advantageously in the world', not only provided her with 'the most liberal Education' but, presumably in hopes of marrying her 'into Opulence', committed the 'pious fraud' that would ultimately prove the undoing of both father and child. Although Blandy's wealth was later discovered to amount to less than £3000, he 'gave out, or encouraged, or did not contradict, a Report, that he was a Man of £10,000 Fortune' (Roughead, 65; *Authentic Tryals*, 6; *London Evening Post*). Not surprisingly, Mary's reputed wealth, 'join'd to her Accomplishments'—for, although no beauty, Miss Blandy was described as having an 'agreeable' and 'genteel Person' and 'engaging' manners, as well as a 'Capacity as few Women are Blessed with'—attracted many suitors (*London Evening Post*; *Genuine and Impartial Account*, 3). Unfortunately, however, 'every Match … was broke off, because the Father would advance no Money with his Daughter but only promis'd that he would leave her his All at his Death'. In the view of many contemporaries, 'such frequent Disappointments of Miss's Expectations, and natural Desires, undoubtedly raised her Resentment' (*London Evening Post*).

In the summer of 1746 Captain William Henry *Cranstoun (*bap.* 1714, *d.* 1752), the younger son of a Scottish lord, began to pay his addresses to Miss Blandy, then in her late twenties and still unmarried. Cranstoun cut a less than dashing figure; he was more than twelve years Mary's senior and, in the words of one account, 'diminutive in Stature', 'of a very mean Aspect', and so 'disfigured by the Small Pox … as to have his Face all in Seams'. He was, however, possessed of sufficient 'Flattery and Complaisance' to insinuate himself into the daughter's good graces, while the fact that he was 'quality' was recommendation enough for the 'unhappy father', who was said to have cherished the hope of some day becoming 'grandfather to a lord' (*Genuine and Impartial Account*, 5, 4; *GM*). However, after learning that Cranstoun had a wife and child in Scotland, Francis Blandy actively discouraged the captain's suit. But the latter continued to correspond with Mary, whom he assured that the marriage was not legal. Beginning in June 1751, apparently at Cranstoun's urging, Mary laced her father's tea and later his water-gruel with arsenic—or, as Mary claimed to have believed, a 'love powder' which would induce her father to look more favourably upon their union. In early August Francis Blandy fell seriously ill; he lingered for over a week, finally expiring on 14 August 1751.

Mary Blandy, who had been seen tampering with her father's oatmeal and behaving suspiciously in general, was almost immediately apprehended for murder. While Mary had burnt her correspondence with Cranstoun, several fragments of a package containing arsenic were salvaged by the servants, and an apparently incriminating letter she had sent to her lover intercepted. More damning evidence emerged at her trial at the Oxford assizes on 3 March 1752, where servants testified that Mary had cursed her father for 'a rogue, a villain, a toothless old dog' whom she wished 'dead and at Hell', and was once heard to remark, 'who would grudge to send an old Father to Hell for £10,000?' (Roughead, 105; *Genuine Account*, 7). Perhaps the most moving testimony concerned the last interview between father and daughter, when the latter confessed to administering the 'love powder' to her father, but maintained she had done so only 'to make him love Cranstoun' (*Genuine and Impartial Account*, 7). When Mary begged her father not to curse her, the latter replied: 'my dear, how couldst thou think I could curse thee? No, I bless you, and hope God will bless thee and amend thy life'; he then instructed her to 'say no more', lest she say anything 'to her own prejudice' (Roughead, 93).

While it took less than five minutes for the jury to find Mary Blandy guilty, public opinion was sharply divided over the case. Many found it incredible that the accomplished Miss Blandy could have been so foolish as to mistake arsenic for an innocent 'love powder'; others—including, it seems, her own father—saw Blandy as the innocent dupe of that 'cruel Spoiler', Cranstoun: a 'poor lovesick girl' who would do anything for 'the man she love[ed]' (*Covent-Garden Journal*, 10 March 1752; *Genuine and Impartial Account*, 7). After all, even if 'she were, as common repute would have it, a woman of "superior Understanding" she was still a woman' (*Case of Miss Blandy*, 19). And if many characterized Blandy as a cold-blooded murderer who during her trial neither 'shew[ed] the least Remorse' nor 'shed a Tear' and who, shortly after receiving sentence of death, supped 'very heartily' on 'Mutton Chops' and 'Apple Pye' (*Authentic Tryals*, 14; *Genuine and Impartial Account*, 8, 10), it was this very 'coolness and courage', as well as the steadfastness with which Blandy maintained her innocence which, as Horace Walpole sourly remarked, 'made a kind of party in her favour; as if a woman who would not stick at Parricide would scruple a lie' (Walpole, 4.317).

Mary Blandy would maintain to the last not only her innocence but her resolution. On 6 April 1752 the 33-year-old 'Fair Parricide' went to the gallows 'with such serenity and composure … as greatly surprised and charmed many of the spectators', 'many of whom … shed tears'. A lady to the end, Blandy's last words before ascending the ladder at the place of execution were, 'Gentlemen, don't hang me high for the sake of decency'; and, shortly afterwards, a tremulous 'I am afraid I shall fall' (*London Magazine*, April 1752; *GM*). She was buried with her parents in Henley parish church. William Cranstoun, for many the real villain, died on 2 December 1752 of natural causes in France, where he had fled the previous year to avoid prosecution, leaving his small fortune to the wife and daughter whom he had once renounced. ANDREA MCKENZIE

Sources *A genuine and impartial account of the life of Miss Mary Blandy* (1752) • *A genuine account of the most horrid parricide committed by Mary Blandy, spinster, upon the body of her father* (1751) • *The authentic tryals of John Swan, and Elizabeth Jeffryes, for the murder of Mr. Joseph Jeffryes of Walthamstow in Essex: with the tryals of Miss Mary Blandy, for the murder of her own father* (1752) • W. Roughead, ed., *Trial of Mary Blandy* (1914) • *Miss Mary Blandy's own account of the affair between her and Mr. Cranstoun … published at her dying request* (1752) • *Execution of Miss Blandy, who was tried at the assizes, at Oxford, and suffered at the same place, April 6th, for poisoning her father* [1752] • *Memoirs of the life of William Henry Cranstoun, esq* (1752) • *The case of Miss Blandy, consider'd as a daughter, as a gentlewoman, and as a Christian … by an impartial hand* (1752) • *A letter from a clergyman to Miss Mary Blandy with her answer thereto … as also Miss Blandy's own narrative* (1752) • *London Evening Post* (5–7 March 1752) • *Covent-Garden Journal* (10 March 1752) • *Covent-Garden Journal* (14 April 1752) • *London Magazine*, 21 (1752), 127–33 • *London Magazine*, 21 (1752), 180–84, 186–7 • *GM*, 1st ser., 22 (1752), 109–17, 153–5 • *General Advertiser* (8 April 1752) • *Read's Weekly Journal, or, British Gazetteer* (11 April 1752) • *Read's Weekly Journal, or, British Gazetteer* (3 Feb 1753) • Walpole, *Corr.* • *Remarkable trials and interesting memoirs, of the most noted criminals*, 2 vols. (1765)

Likenesses B. Cole, line engraving, BM, NPG • T. Ryley, mezzotint (after F. Wilson), BM, NPG • portrait, repro. in *A genuine account of the most horrid parricide*, frontispiece • portrait, repro. in *A genuine and impartial account of the life of Miss Mary Blandy*, frontispiece • prints, BM • sepia drawing, repro. in Roughead, ed., *Trial of Mary Blandy*, frontispiece

Wealth at death approx. £2000–£3000: *London Evening Post*; *London Magazine*

Blandy [Blandie], **William** (*fl.* **1563–1581**), translator, was born in Newbury, Berkshire, the son of William Blandy. He was elected to a probationer fellowship at New College, Oxford, in 1563. Following his admission to a full fellowship on 8 June 1565, he graduated BA a year later, on 3 July 1566. A devoted Catholic, he was stripped of his degree and fellowship in the same year by the evangelical college visitor, Bishop Robert Horne. Blandy was 'removed for Popery' and left Oxford (Foster, *Alum. Oxon.*, 1.138). He moved to London, where he joined the Middle Temple in 1571.

Blandy's *The five books of the famous, learned and eloquent man, Hieronimo Osorius, contayning a discussion of civill and Christian nobilitie*, a translation into English of the work of Bishop Jeronimo Osorio da Fonseca, was published in London in 1576 and dedicated to the earl of Leicester as chancellor of Oxford University. In the preface Blandy spoke eloquently of his motivation to translate the work of a Catholic Portuguese bishop into English. He believed the interrelation between the nobility and the world of learning sketched by Osorio worthy of imitation by any Christian nobleman:

> It may appeare most manifeste, that neither Princes maye live cleare and knowen to posteritie wythoute the penne and helping hande of learneds Arte: neyther man excelling in learning would be eyther in lyfe reputed or spoken of after death, withoute the countenaunce, defence, and patronage of noble Peeres. (Blandy, *Five Books*, sig. A 3v)

In a later work, *The castle, or, Picture of pollicy, shewing forth most lively the face, body, and partes of a commonwealth, the duety of a perfect souldier, the martiall feates late done by our nation, under the conduct of J. Noris, generall of the army of the states in Friesland* (London, 1581), Blandy reflected on the accomplishments of the English troops in the Low Countries during the emergence of the Dutch republic. Although he was a believing Catholic, Blandy opted to support English interests in the Low Countries and so, paradoxically, played an active part in the eventual elimination of Catholic worship in the provinces of the Dutch union by spring 1580. His date of death is unknown.

J. ANDREAS LÖWE

Sources W. Blandy, *The five books of the famous, learned and eloquent man, Hieronimo Osorius* (1576) • W. Blandy, *The castle, or, Picture of pollicy* (1581) • Wood, *Ath. Oxon.*, new edn, 1.428 • Foster, *Alum. Oxon.* • *Reg. Oxf.*, 1.264

Blane, Sir Gilbert, first baronet (**1749–1834**), physician, the fourth son of Gilbert Blane, was born on 29 August 1749 at Blanefield, Ayrshire, in western Scotland; the Blanes were a wealthy merchant family. Gilbert was educated at Kirkoswald and Maybole schools in Ayrshire until the age of fourteen, before attending the University of Edinburgh with the intention of beginning a career in the church. However, after five years in the faculty of arts Blane then undertook another five years in the faculty of medicine. Never one to remain inconspicuous, he was elected as a president of the students' medical society and during his term of office had the prestigious duty of presenting a speech at the laying of a foundation stone of a new hall for the society in 1775 (*Authentic Memoirs*, 135–45).

Blane was extremely fortunate to be acquainted with

Sir Gilbert Blane, first baronet (1749–1834), by Sir Martin Archer Shee, in or before 1833

two of the most famous doctors of the late eighteenth century. Before he received his MD from the University of Glasgow on 28 August 1778, Blane studied under William Cullen who then introduced him to William Hunter in London. Blane's obvious ability quickly led to Hunter's recommendations, first to Lord Holdernesse and then to George Rodney (the future Admiral Rodney), that they should employ this young Scottish doctor as their own personal physician. It was in this capacity, rather than as a surgeon of the British navy, that Blane in 1779 sailed with Rodney to the West Indies on board the *Sandwich*. At the time Britain was embroiled in the American War of Independence and Blane was present at no fewer than six naval battles during which he acted far beyond his duties as a doctor—even to the point of relaying the admiral's orders to those manning the guns. In recognition of both Blane's personal bravery and his medical prowess, Rodney appointed him as physician to the West Indies fleet in 1780. Now officially recognized by the navy, Blane served in this role until the end of the war three years later. One of his first actions in his new position of authority was to compile and print at his own expense a small book entitled *A short account of the most effectual means of preserving the health of seamen, particularly in the Royal Navy* (1781?), which he then sent to all the surgeons who served in the fleet to use as a guideline in any provision of healthcare. He became a licentiate of the Royal College of Physicians in 1781.

At the request of Rodney, surgeons were required to collect detailed figures of morbidity and mortality on board each ship. Blane collated this information, compiled nosological tables, and then, in a manner which was to become typical for him, used statistics as a tool for justifying reforms in naval healthcare. For example, on 13 October 1781 he presented data to the Admiralty that demonstrated how one in seven men had died from disease on the West Indies station and suggested ameliorative measures including an improved diet that included fresh fruit in order to prevent scurvy, and strict sanitary measures. On 16 July 1782, less than a year after the reforms were instigated, Blane relayed the news that mortality levels were now only one in twenty. Other officers of the fleet recommended to the Admiralty that Blane should receive special recompense and he was subsequently awarded a pension in recognition of his excellent work in the West Indies fleet.

Blane's early experience at sea led him to the conclusion that prevention was better than cure, and in particular that 'cleanliness and discipline are the indispensable and fundamental means of health' (*Observations on the Diseases Incident to Seamen*, 1785, 251). He also asked much more from naval surgeons who were to take a new role in the prevention of ill health. This encouragement effectively extended the traditional domain of surgeons serving in the British navy, and may have served to improve their status. However, surgeons were generally regarded as inferior in rank to ship officers throughout this period. At every opportunity throughout his life Blane fought for the higher status of naval surgeons, whom he saw as pivotal for good health in the British navy.

Blane's work with the navy served to introduce him to powerful patrons who ensured his success as a physician in civilian life. Blane had met the duke of Clarence while serving in the navy and this led to his being appointed physician-extraordinary to the prince of Wales in 1785. Later he became physician-in-ordinary to the prince's household and was eventually physician to the king after George IV had acceded to the throne. Another factor in Blane's meteoric success was the excellent reference provided by Lord Rodney that led to his post of physician at St Thomas's Hospital, London, where, after a close-run contest, Blane was elected on 19 September 1783 by a majority of ninety-eight votes to eighty-four. However, while in the navy it was commendable that Blane appeared unflappable when under fire, this same air of detached coolness was not appreciated by his civilian medical colleagues. Astley Cooper remarked that Blane was 'a painstaking physician, but he was so cold in temperament, that we called him "Chilblane"' (Cooper, 306).

The revolutionary wars against France caused Blane to resign from St Thomas's in 1795 and resume his service in the navy, at the invitation of Lord Spencer, who was the first lord of the Admiralty. Blane was appointed a commissioner for sick and wounded seamen and held this powerful office until the peace of Amiens in 1802—seven strategically important years in the history of the Royal Navy. Britain was fighting for naval supremacy, upon which the empire depended. Any degree of mortality and morbidity within the navy exacerbated the perennial problem of a shortage of skilled and motivated men. Also, ships were at sea for long periods of time, covering long distances, and, when crews succumbed to tropical diseases or sickness such as scurvy, the efficiency of the ship necessarily deteriorated. During wartime this was particularly unsatisfactory. Blane's tactics to keep seamen healthy incorporated lessons he learned while serving in the West Indies fleet; his scientific approach to preserving the health of seamen was founded upon observation and statistical reporting. Every surgeon within the navy was encouraged to report the state of health for each ship by using standardized forms and medical logbooks. An estimated 634 surgeons served in the navy at the end of the eighteenth century, allowing Blane's love of statistics to be applied on a hitherto unknown scale (Pope, 131). The use of a scientific numerical approach to finding the best way to combat disease was not unknown during this period and other naval surgeons such as Robert Robertson (1742–1829) had taken the initiative of compiling statistics in an effort to find the answers to medical problems. Blane's important contribution to the growth of medical science was that he extended the quest for data and information to all naval surgeons. He also encouraged accountability on the part of surgeons for their actions, and this, coupled with new communications with the government board for the sick and wounded, meant that the gathering of data started to become an official and centralized procedure.

Alongside the recommendations of Thomas Trotter, who was physician to the Channel Fleet, Blane was also instrumental in the issuing of lemon juice to all seamen in order to combat the eighteenth century's constant threat of scurvy, the direct result of a deficiency of vitamin C in the diet. The anti-scorbutic power of lemons had been recognized for centuries by seafarers, and Dr James Lind (1716–1794) had attracted recognition for his curative experiments first noted in his *Treatise on the Scurvy* (1753). Blane's contribution came with his authorization in 1795 for lemon juice to be universally distributed throughout the navy.

Although the role of medical practitioners in curing scurvy might be more marginal than traditionally assumed (Rodger, 333–4), contemporaries of Blane deemed his pioneering measures to be highly successful, and as a result he became a figure of authority on the subject of healthcare. In 1799, when plague struck areas of the Mediterranean, an anxious British government along with merchants in the Turkey Company enlisted help from Blane and several other eminent physicians. It was under anti-plague regulations specifically dictated by Blane that the army was allowed to return from its active service in Egypt. The Home Office also consulted Blane on a number of public health matters relating to conditions inside prisons and convict ships. His recommendations of improved ventilation, of carrying fewer men, and of the provision of an adequate diet resulted in a dramatic reduction in the deaths of convicts on board the *Glatten* in 1802. The most striking testimony to Blane's medical expertise came when the government called upon him for advice over a medical fiasco at Walcheren. On this island off the Netherlands, troops lay totally devastated by disease. The army's medical board had performed ineptly and confidence in the army's ability to cope with the situation had evaporated. In 1810 Blane was sent out to make a report and was subsequently charged with supervising the return of the sick and wounded. He concluded that the expedition should be aborted. A baronetcy, awarded in 1812, marked the exceptional esteem placed on Blane's professional expertise.

Healthcare at sea continued to be a concern for Blane even though he had officially resigned from the navy in 1802. For example, he supported compulsory vaccination for all seamen in *Elements of Medical Logick* (1819), and encouraged academic study for naval surgeons. In 1829 he founded a prize medal (the Blane naval medical medal) for the best journal kept by surgeons of the Royal Navy and his express wish was that the medical knowledge of naval surgeons should be extended beyond the empirical. Using his own naval experience Blane wrote for medical journals such as the *Transactions of a Society for the Improvement of Medical and Chirurgical Knowledge*. Blane continued to be a conspicuous medical figure in intellectual society through his activities as a fellow of the Royal Society in both Edinburgh (1783) and London (1784), as a proprietor of the Royal Institution, and as a member of the Imperial Academy of Sciences at St Petersburg.

Blane's personal life centred round his long marriage to Elizabeth, the only daughter of Abraham Gardner. Married on 11 July 1786, they had six sons and three daughters and lived mostly at Culverlands in Berkshire. Blane outlived his wife, who died in the cholera epidemic of 1832, and also survived all his children with the exception of two sons: Hugh Seymour (1795–1869) (who inherited his father's title) and Charles Collins (*b.* 1799).

The latter years of Blane's life were beleaguered by ill health. From 1821 onwards, suffering from an irritating skin disease named prurigo senilis, he resorted to using large doses of opium. This in turn caused distressing symptoms and eventually Blane died, aged eighty-five, on 27 June 1834, in his house at 8 Sackville Street, Piccadilly, London. J. Wallace

Sources J. J. Keevil, J. Coulter, and C. Lloyd, *Medicine and the navy, 1200–1900*, 3–4 (1961–3) · *GM*, 2nd ser., 4 (1835), 93–4 · R. D. Leach, 'Sir Gilbert Blane MD, FRS', *Annals of the Royal College of Surgeons of England*, 62 (1980), 232–9 · *Authentic memoirs, biographical, critical, and literary, of the most eminent physicians and surgeons of Great Britain*, 2nd edn (1818), 135–45 · Munk, *Roll* · *The health of seamen: selections from the works of Dr. James Lind, Sir Gilbert Blane and Dr. Thomas Trotter*, ed. C. Lloyd, Navy RS, 107 (1965), 132–211 · E. Turner, 'Naval medical service, 1793–1815', *Mariner's Mirror*, 46 (1960), 119–33 · U. Tröhler, 'Quantification in British medicine and surgery, 1750–1830', PhD diss., U. Lond., 1978, 72–258 · M. C. Buer, *Health, wealth and population in the early days of the industrial revolution* (1926) · N. A. M. Rodger, 'Medicine and science in the British navy of the eighteenth century', *L'homme, la santé et la mer*, ed. C. Buchet (1997), 333–44 · B. B. Cooper, *The life of Sir Astley Cooper*, 1 (1843) · D. Pope, *Life in Nelson's navy* (1981) · G. B. Mundy, *The life and correspondence of the late Admiral Lord Rodney*, 2 vols. (1830) · Burke, *Peerage* (1857) · Boase, *Mod. Eng. biog.*

Archives Lpool RO, papers relating to French prisoners of war · NMM, corresp. and papers · Royal Medical Society, diss. | Hants. RO, letters to James Harris, first earl of Malmesbury · NL Scot.,

corresp. with Lord Melville • W. Sussex RO, letters to duke of Richmond
Likenesses M. A. Shee, oils, in or before 1833, RCP Lond. [*see illus.*] • Beynon & Co., lithograph, Wellcome L.

Blaneforde, Henry (*fl. c.*1324). *See under* Rishanger, William (*b.* 1249/50, *d.* after 1312).

Blanesburgh. For this title name *see* Younger, Robert, Baron Blanesburgh (1861–1946).

Blaney, Thomas (1823–1903), physician and philanthropist, was born at Caherconlish, Pallas Green, co. Limerick, Ireland, on 24 May 1823. Of humble origin, he went out to Bombay with his parents when only three. Ten years later, in 1836, he was apprenticed to the subordinate medical department of the East India Company. He served 'up country' for eight years but returned in 1847 to Bombay, where in 1851 he became a government student at the Grant medical college; he attended classes there for four years. After reaching the post of apothecary at the European general hospital, in 1860 he was invalided from the service. Soon afterwards he founded a large private practice among the European and Indian inhabitants of Bombay. In 1867 he published the pamphlet, *Fevers as Connected with the Sanitation of Bombay*, and during the famine in southern India in 1878 he identified a form of 'relapsing fever'. Blaney was equally concerned with cholera, which made frequent appearances in Bombay, and he was one of the foremost advocates of sanitary reform in the municipal commission. When plague arrived in 1896, he was among the first to recognize the gravity of the situation, which was greatly underestimated by the city's health department. Known as 'the Jury-wallah Doctor', because he served as coroner from 1876 to 1893, he was held in great local repute professionally, and grateful Indian patients often remembered him in their wills. Dr Honnusji, an Indian municipal commissioner, described Blaney as being to all intents and purposes a native of India. All Blaney's large earnings, except the small amount needed for his simple style of life, were given to the poor and to causes which won his sympathy. He made it a rule to take no professional fee from a widow. For many months he provided free tuition and a midday meal in his own home for children of poor white people. More than seventy children were cared for, and ultimately, under the name of Blaney School, the institution was taken over and maintained for a time by a representative committee.

In civic affairs Blaney first came to notice for the vigour with which he condemned in the local press, under the pseudonym of 'Q in the Corner', the wild financial speculation of 1861–5. In 1868 he was appointed to the bench of justices, which had restricted powers of municipal administration, and when a municipal corporation at Bombay was established in 1872 he was one of the original members; he retained office until his retirement from public life and was elected to the chair on four occasions between 1877 and 1893. A member for nine years of the municipality's statutory standing committee, which was responsible for civic expenditure, and its chairman from 1890 to 1894, he refused the fees payable for attendance, a sum which totalled about £1000. An eloquent speaker and an ardent but always fair fighter, he exercised a wise and beneficent influence on civic life. He successfully resisted the efforts of a powerful English syndicate to obtain control of the water supply, which was one of his special responsibilities as municipal commissioner. He was chairman of the joint schools committee, a member of the city improvement trust, and a fellow of the university. The government of India appointed him sheriff of Bombay in 1875 and 1888. He was created CIE in May 1894, and on 2 June of the same year a statue of him, for which upwards of Rs22,000 (£1460) was subscribed by his fellow citizens, was unveiled, opposite the Bombay municipal buildings. Four years later age compelled Blaney's retirement from both civic and professional work. His generosity had deprived him of means of support, but a few fellow townsmen provided for his needs. He died unmarried, in Bombay, on 1 April 1903, and was buried at Sewri cemetery on the following day. F. H. BROWN, *rev.* MARK HARRISON

Sources *Times of India* (2 April 1903) • *Bombay Gazette* (2 April 1903) • *Bombay Gazette* (19 Jan 1882) • *Bombay Gazette* (7 April 1882) • M. Harrison, *Public health in British India: Anglo-Indian preventive medicine, 1859–1914* (1994) • personal knowledge (1912)
Likenesses Valla, marble statue, 1894, near Bombay municipal buildings, India
Wealth at death gave away much of his fortune

Blanford, Henry Francis (1834–1893), meteorologist and geologist, was born on 3 June 1834 at 27 Bouverie Street, Whitefriars, London, where his father had a workshop manufacturing gilt mouldings, the son of William Blanford and his wife, Elizabeth Simpson. He was the younger brother of the geologist William Thomas *Blanford. He went to schools in Brighton and Brussels. After then studying for some time at the School of Design, first at Somerset House, then at Marlborough House, he entered the Royal School of Mines, London, in 1851. There he received the duke of Cornwall's scholarship. Afterwards he studied mining for a year at the Bergakademie, Freiberg, Saxony, and spent some time preparing *An Introduction to the Use of the Blowpipe* (1856; 3rd edn, 1875), an English translation of Carol Johann August Theodor Scheerer's work.

In 1855 Blanford and his brother William were appointed to the Geological Survey of India. Arriving at Calcutta in late September of that year, they spent their first field season (1855–6) surveying the Talchir coalfield in Orissa. There they identified the effects of ice action in the boulder bed now known as the Talchir tillite, thereby laying a foundation for the later conception of the Gondwana glaciation and of Gondwanaland as a great southern continent. From 1 December 1856 Blanford acted as first curator of the new Museum of Geology at Calcutta, and took charge of the office of the superintendent of the geological survey. He also delivered a course of lectures on geology at Presidency College, Calcutta, during that winter. In 1857 he was dispatched to Madras, where he spent three years determining the stratigraphy and palaeontology of the cretaceous rocks near Trichinopoly and Pondicherry. In December 1861, partly because his health was suffering, he resigned from the survey and returned to Europe. However, the following year he accepted a post as professor in the Bengal education department, lecturing in physics and chemistry at Presidency College, where he remained until 1872.

In August 1863 Blanford became one of the secretaries of the Asiatic Society of Bengal, and partly in consequence of his duties there he became interested in meteorology. In the following year Calcutta suffered from a devastating cyclone, of which Blanford published a detailed description in 1866, and the urgent requirement to establish a storm warning system for the port led the lieutenant-governor of Bengal to appoint Blanford as meteorological reporter for Bengal in 1867. In this post Blanford began to systematize the gathering of meteorological data in Bengal and made important observations concerning the origin of cyclones. His accounts, published annually as the *Report of the Meteorological Reporter*, were praised as 'model monograms of the subject' (*Nature*, 11, 1874–5, 146).

Blanford married Charlotte Mackenzie, daughter of George Ferguson Cockburn of the Bengal civil service, and granddaughter of Lord Justice Cockburn, on 20 June 1867. In 1874, at the recommendation of General Richard Strachey, he was appointed meteorological reporter to the government of India, with the object of organizing a comprehensive pan-Indian system of data gathering, analysis, and dissemination. One of his most important contributions during this time was his hypothesis that the 'varying extent and thickness of the Himalayan snows exercise a great and prolonged influence on the climatic conditions and weather of the plains of North West India' ('On the Connection of the Himalaya Snowfall with Dry Winds and Seasons of Drought in India', *Proceedings of the Royal Society*, 37, 1884, 3), the application of which enabled him correctly to forecast deficient summer monsoon rainfall over western India in 1885.

Blanford held the post of reporter until he retired in 1889, but during the final two years he was in England on furlough. From early 1892 failing health forced him to abandon scientific work, and he died of cancer at his home, 7 Ingles Road, Folkestone, on 23 January 1893. His wife, one son, and three daughters survived him.

Blanford was elected a fellow of the Geological Society in 1862, and of the Royal Society in 1880. In 1884–5 he was president of the Asiatic Society of Bengal. He was a versatile and prolific writer, publishing over eighty scientific papers. He made a number of important contributions to both geology and, more especially, to meteorology, but also wrote on malacology and archaeology. The majority of his papers appeared in *Nature*, the *Journal* and *Proceedings* of the Asiatic Society of Bengal, and the *Indian Meteorological Memoirs*, an important series which he instituted at Calcutta. Of his several independent works the most important were, perhaps, *The Indian Meteorologist's Vade Mecum* (1868; enlarged edn, 1877), which was described as a 'model handbook' (*Nature*, 19, 1878–79, 294); *A Practical Guide to the Climates and Weather of India, Ceylon, Burma, and the Storms of the Indian Seas* (1889); and the pedagogic work, *Rudiments of Physical Geography for the Use of Indian Schools* (1873; 6th edn, 1878). ANDREW GROUT

Sources W. T. B, *PRS*, 54 (1893), xii–xix · W. H. Hudleston, *Quarterly Journal of the Geological Society*, 49 (1893), 52–4 · *Nature*, 47 (1892–3), 322–3 · *Geological Magazine*, new ser., 3rd decade, 10 (1893), 191–2 · 'Despatches on the organization of a meteorological department in India', *Parl. papers* (1874), 48.25–55, no. 185 · L. Leigh Fermor, *First twenty-five years of the Geological Survey of India* (New Delhi, 1976) · *Catalogue of scientific papers*, Royal Society, 1 (1867), 418; 7 (1877), 190–01; 9 (1891), 258–9; 12 (1902), 86; 13 (1914), 595–6 · Boase, *Mod. Eng. biog.* · T. H. D. La Touche, *A bibliography of Indian geology and physical geography*, 5 vols. (1917–26) · private information (1901) · *DNB*
Likenesses photograph, repro. in *Report on the administration of the Indian Meteorological Department for 1924* (1925)
Wealth at death £9558 1s. 10d.: probate, 16 March 1893, *CGPLA Eng. & Wales*

Blanford, William Thomas (1832–1905), geologist and zoologist, was born on 7 October 1832, at 27 Bouverie Street, Whitefriars, London, the son of William Blanford, manufacturer, and his wife, Elizabeth Simpson; he was the brother of Henry Francis *Blanford. He attended a private school at Brighton until about 1846, and later studied in Paris (1848). He returned to England in 1851 and briefly joined the family business as a carver and gilder, while studying at the School of Design in Somerset House, London. He then abandoned this career and followed his brother to the Royal School of Mines, where he stayed from 1852 to 1854.

In 1854, after a short time at the Bergakademie or mining school of Freiberg, Saxony, Blanford obtained a post in the geological survey of India. His first assignment was to investigate the coalfield near Talchir, in Orissa. Apparently the coal was of limited value, but Blanford recognized the signs of ice action in a boulder bed in the coalfield—what is now known as the Talchir tillite. This important observation contributed to the recognition of a widespread Permian glaciation in the southern hemisphere (the Gondwana glaciation), for signs of ice action were later seen in rocks of comparable age in Australia, South Africa, and South America. As well as at Talchir, Blanford also worked on the Raniganj coalfield, and over the years maintained an interest in the fossil plants of the Permo-Triassic *Glossopteris* flora. The geological age of the Indian coal interested him and in his address to the British Association in 1884 he commented on the difficulty of determining its age.

In November 1860 Blanford was sent to Burma, where he investigated Puppadoung, an extinct volcano, near Pagan. While on home leave in 1862 he was promoted to deputy superintendent. He was later employed on a geological survey of the Bombay presidency (1862–6), where he worked on the Deccan traps, an enormous volcanic feature of southern India of Cretaceous to Eocene age. Late in 1867 he was attached to the military and scientific expedition to Abyssinia. He went to Magdala and made a natural history collection: the outcome was his *Observation on the Geology and Zoology of Abyssinia* (1870). A journey to Sikkim in the Himalayas in 1870 with the naturalist H. J. Elwes

(1846–1922) resulted in a paper in the *Proceedings of the Asiatic Society of Bengal* in which new bird species were described. Leave in England followed.

In 1871 Blanford was back in India; in the same year he began what was perhaps his most important surveying appointment—the India–Persia boundary commission. In connection with this work he visited Baluchistan, Tehran, the Alborz mountains, and the Caspian Sea. He returned to England through Russia and Moscow in September 1872. His extensive travels in the region resulted in his contribution on the geology and zoology in *An Account of the Journeys of the Persian Boundary Commission* (1876). The rigours of this survey left him weakened in health. In 1874 he was elected a fellow of the Royal Society.

Blanford returned to administrative duties in Calcutta in 1874, and with H. B. Medlicott wrote the *Manual of the Geology of India*, in which Blanford's treatment of the Miocene to Plio-Pleistocene fauna from the Sewalik hills reveals him to have been a most able palaeontologist. The *Manual* was important in understanding Indian geology and was still valuable well over 100 years after its publication. Duty took him next to the desert areas of Sind (1874–7). On his next leave in Europe, in 1881, he went to Bologna, Italy, for the International Geological Congress to represent Indian geology. He was back at Quetta in Baluchistan in 1881–2, but he was again ill and was finally compelled to retire on medical grounds in 1882. He settled in London. In 1883 he married Ida Gertrude Bellhouse; they had two sons and a daughter.

The Geological Society of London awarded Blanford the Wollaston medal in 1882, and he attended and chaired the geological section of the British Association meeting in Montreal in 1884; he was president of the Geological Society from 1888 to 1890. He visited the west coast of Canada in 1897. Apart from geology he devoted much of his retirement to his interests in the natural history, and particularly the zoology, of India; he was made companion of the Indian Empire in 1904. He died at his home, 72 Bedford Gardens, Campden Hill, London, on 23 June 1905. He was survived by his wife.

Blanford was a productive and indefatigable worker for all aspects of Indian geology, palaeontology, and zoology. The Royal Society's *Catalogue of Scientific Papers* notes some 115 of his articles, and the writer of his obituary in the society's *Proceedings* indicated that the total was nearer 175 papers. With his brother he wrote numerous papers on Indian malacology, and he worked with Dr John Anderson FRS on Burmese freshwater molluscs collected on the Yunnan expeditions. Without doubt, however, his greatest zoological work was the editing of the early volumes of the monumental *Fauna of British India* (1888–1943). He wrote in his own right on the mammals and birds, and was writing a contribution on the terrestrial and aquatic molluscs of India at the time of his death. He donated several natural history specimens to the British Museum, later in the Natural History Museum, London. D. T. MOORE

Sources T. G. B., *PRS*, 79B (1907), xxvii–xxxi • 'Eminent living geologists: William Thomas Blanford', *Geological Magazine*, new ser., 5th decade, 22 (1905), 1–15 • *The history of the collections contained in the natural history departments of the British Museum*, British Museum, 2 vols. (1904–12) • T. G. Vallance, 'The fuss about coal: troubled relations between palaeobotany and geology', *Plants and man in Australia*, ed. D. J. Carr and G. M. Carr (1981), 136–75 • personal knowledge (1912) [*DNB*] • private information (1912) • *CGPLA Eng. & Wales* (1905)
Archives BL OIOC | NHM, letters and corresp. with Albert Gunther and R. W. T. Gunther
Likenesses photograph, repro. in 'Eminent living geologists'
Wealth at death £9125 9*s*. 1*d*.: probate, 9 Sept 1905, *CGPLA Eng. & Wales*

Blankett, John (*c*.1740–1801), naval officer, is of unknown parentage. He served as a volunteer and midshipman in the *Somerset* with Captain Edward Hughes, and was present at the reduction of Louisbourg in 1758 and Quebec in 1759. On his return to England he presented a report to the Admiralty concerning the possible existence of a north-west passage to the Pacific. In 1761 he was made a lieutenant. Two years later he was condemned to death for murder by a court at Gibraltar, but he was later reprieved (PRO, ADM 1/384). After the peace in 1763 he obtained leave to go to Russia to gather information concerning recent discoveries on the east coast of Asia.

In 1770 Blankett served as lieutenant under Captain Barrington, and four years later he was granted leave to go to St Petersburg with a view to gathering information for a future voyage of exploration. Lord Sandwich, the first lord of the Admiralty, refused to make any firm commitments in support of these ventures (NMM, SAN V12, fol. 310). Some years later Sandwich was criticized in the press for not supporting Blankett and appointing others, notably James Cook, to undertake a number of the voyages Blankett had proposed (ibid., F36, fol. 24). Blankett distanced himself from these attacks but apparently harboured some ill feeling towards Sandwich. He was first lieutenant of the *Victory*, flagship of Admiral Keppel, in 1778 and was made a commander in 1779. He was then appointed to the sloop *Nymph* and sent to the East Indies to join Sir Edward Hughes. He was made a captain in the *Rippon* on 23 January 1780. This ship was shortly afterwards ordered home and Blankett held no further appointment during the American War of Independence.

On his return Blankett busied himself supplying the opposition press with information to discredit Lord Sandwich, and with Lord Shelburne and Captain Robert Tomlinson he assisted in producing lists and accounts on naval matters for the opposition speakers in parliament. After the peace in 1783 he commanded the frigate *Thetis* in the Mediterranean, where he came to the notice of the king of Naples, who accompanied him on a cruise and presented him with his portrait set in diamonds. In July 1790 he sailed for China in the *Leopard* in command of a convoy; on his return he was appointed to the *America* as commodore of a small squadron sent to the Cape of Good Hope. There, in August 1795, he was joined by the squadron under Sir George Elphinstone, under whom he served at the reduction of that settlement. In June 1798 he was appointed once again to the *Leopard*, with orders to proceed to India. On his arrival he was sent as senior officer to the Red Sea, where he commanded during the subsequent operations in Egypt, and about which he complained bitterly: 'The Red-Sea is a job no longer for anybody' (*The Spencer Papers*, ed. J. S. Corbett and H. W. Richmond, 4 vols., 1913–24, 4.228).

In February 1799 Blankett became rear-admiral. In August 1800 he went for a short time to Bombay; on passage he captured the *Clarisse*, a very active French privateer, which under the command of Robert Surcouf had been the terror of commerce of the Indian seas. By January he was back in the Red Sea, and from April to June in the Gulf of Suez. His health had already suffered and the terrible heat of the Red Sea summer proved fatal to him. He died on the *Leopard* near Mocha on 14 July 1801. He was described as an unusually good linguist, having a perfect mastery of French, Italian, and Portuguese. Seen by many as a good officer and an accomplished and amiable gentleman, he was criticized by others for his bad temper and eccentricity during his last days in the Red Sea.

J. K. LAUGHTON, *rev.* CLIVE WILKINSON

Sources W. James, *The naval history of Great Britain, from the declaration of war by France in 1793 to the accession of George IV*, [8th edn], 6 vols. (1902) • *The Tomlinson papers*, ed. J. G. Bullocke (1935) • N. A. M. Rodger, *The insatiable earl: a life of John Montagu, fourth earl of Sandwich* (1993)

Archives NA Scot., observations on the commerce of the Red Sea | BL, corresp. with Lord Liverpool, Add. MSS 38223–38234, 38310–38311, 38416 • BL, Wellesley MSS, Add. MS 13760 • BL, corresp. with William Windham, Add. MSS 37875–37880, *passim* • Bodl. Oxf., Petty MSS, MSS Film dep. 961–1005 • NMM, Howe MSS • NMM, letters to Lord Sandwich • priv. coll., letters to Lord Lansdowne

Blantyre. For this title name *see* Stewart, Walter, first Lord Blantyre (*d.* 1617); Stewart, Alexander, fifth Lord Blantyre (*d.* 1704).

Blaquiere, Edward (1779–1832), author and philhellene, was born in Ireland, the sixth of eight children of James Blaquiere (1726–1803), soldier and farmer. His father, a lieutenant-colonel in the 13th dragoons, was the brother of John Blaquiere, first Baron de Blaquiere (1732–1812), and both were among the nine children of Jean de Blaquiere (1675–1753), of Huguenot descent, who emigrated from France in 1685 following the revocation of the edict of Nantes, and who later established himself as a merchant in London. The family was descended from a French noble family, and James Blaquiere may have established the Irish line of the family. Nothing is known of Edward Blaquiere's mother, and she may well have died prior to his father's death in 1803.

Little is also known of Blaquiere's early years and education, though a number of his brothers attended Dublin University and, like him, followed naval careers. Blaquiere entered the navy on 12 July 1794, and received his first commission as a lieutenant on 20 July 1801. He served in the British navy throughout the Napoleonic wars on various ships and especially in the Mediterranean. His first book, *Letters from the Mediterranean*, published in two volumes in 1813, reflected his experiences and provided accounts of life and politics especially in Sicily, Tripoli, Tunis, and Malta. There was little indication of Blaquiere's radicalism in this early book.

At the same time Blaquiere became an enthusiastic disciple of the philosopher and reformer Jeremy Bentham (1748–1832), having read his *Traités de législation, civile et pénale* (1802), and met him on several occasions. Partly funded by Bentham, he set off for Spain in 1820 to witness 'a great people struggling for their liberties' (Blaquiere to Bentham, 4 May 1820, *Correspondence of Jeremy Bentham*, vol. 9.430). His main object was to collect materials for *An Historical Review of the Spanish Revolution* (1822), but he also used his newly established links with liberal politicians and journalists to arrange for the translation of Bentham's works and to encourage the Cortes to invite Bentham to draft new codes of law. During this period Blaquiere made friends with the youthful John Bowring (1792–1872), whom he introduced to Bentham in 1820. Bowring and Blaquiere worked together to advance Bentham's reputation as a liberal theoretician in Spain, Portugal, France, Greece, and Latin America.

When the liberal Spanish regime fell in 1823, Blaquiere and Bowring turned their attention to Greece, and formed the London Greek Committee early that spring with Bowring as secretary. Blaquiere journeyed to Greece in March 1823 with Andreas Louriottis, the agent of the fledgeling Greek government, who had been attempting to raise funds for the struggle for Greek independence first in Spain and then in London. Blaquiere stopped in Genoa to enlist the support of Lord Byron, who eventually served in Greece as the agent of the London Greek Committee. After presenting Bentham's commentary on the first Greek constitution (constitution of Epidaurus) to the Greek government, Blaquiere then returned to London in the autumn of 1823, where he published an enthusiastic report to the London Greek Committee on the prospects for the Greek struggle (*Report on the Present State of the Greek Confederation*, 1823) and subsequently a book (*The Greek Revolution*, 1824).

In the autumn of 1823 Blaquiere toured England to enlist the support of MPs and newspaper editors, in order to raise awareness and funds for the struggle in Greece. The money was used to finance the expedition led by Byron and Leicester Stanhope, later fifth earl of Harrington, to Missolonghi. When Blaquiere returned to Greece in 1824 with the first instalment of the Greek loan, he found himself at odds with Stanhope over the latter's attitude towards the Greeks and the arrangements for distributing the loan: if Stanhope thought that the Greeks should be treated as inferior 'natives', Blaquiere accepted them as Europeans, and gave strong support to their nationalist aspirations. For this reason, he was regarded as the most popular foreigner to have visited Greece. But the London Greek Committee, unmoved by modern nationalism, supported the views of Stanhope rather than those of Blaquiere. Though short of funds, he had difficulty obtaining his expenses from the committee, and was never given the credit he deserved for developing philhellenism in Britain. He continued to support the Greek cause in numerous publications (*Narrative of a Second Visit to Greece*,

1825; *Greece and her Claims*, 1826; *Letters from Greece*, 1828), and favoured the Greek deputies rather than his former friends on the committee during the Greek loan scandal of 1826. He also supported independence movements elsewhere in Europe and Latin America. He combined a strong sympathy with nationalism with support for early liberalism, and hoped to see an alliance of liberal forces throughout Europe to oppose the Holy Alliance. He died in early 1832 when an unseaworthy vessel sank during an expedition to the Azores in an attempt to establish a constitutional monarchy in Portugal under Dom Pedro IV. His wife, named Emma, of whom no further details have been discovered, died in 1847. F. ROSEN

Sources F. Rosen, *Bentham, Byron and Greece* (1992) · UCL, Huguenot Library, research files · *The works of Jeremy Bentham*, ed. J. Bowring, [new edn], 11 vols. (1843–59), vols. 10–11 · C. Gobbi, 'Edward Blaquiere: agente del liberalismo', *Cuadernos Hispano-Americanos*, 350 (1979), 306–25 · *The correspondence of Jeremy Bentham*, ed. T. Sprigge and others, [11 vols.] (1968–), in *The collected works of Jeremy Bentham*, vols. 8–10 · D. Syrett and R. L. DiNardo, *The commissioned sea officers of the Royal Navy, 1660–1815*, rev. edn, Occasional Publications of the Navy RS, 1 (1994) · *Navy List* · A. Palma, *Greece vindicated* (1826)

Archives John Murray, London | BL, Bentham MSS · National Library of Greece, London Greek Committee MSS · UCL, Bentham MSS

John Blaquiere, first Baron de Blaquiere (1732–1812), by James Heath, pubd 1811 (after John Comerford)

Blaquiere, John, first Baron de Blaquiere (1732–1812), politician, was born on 15 May 1732, the fifth son of Jean de Blaquiere (1675/6–1753), an émigré Huguenot merchant of Greenwich, Kent, and Mary Elizabeth, daughter of Pierre de Varennes, a Huguenot bookseller of the Strand, Westminster. His contemporaries describe him variously. James Caulfeild, first earl of Charlemont, contemptuously dismisses him as 'a man of low birth, no property and weak genius' (GEC, *Peerage*, 4.108n). According to John Lees, an astute commentator and former private secretary to the Irish viceroys, lords Townshend and Harcourt, he had a 'manly mind', but 'in other respects has all the vanity of a foolish boy of fifteen' (John Lees [to Auckland], 13 March [1798], Sneyd papers, PRO NIre., T/3229/2/29).

Blaquiere was employed in the counting-house of a London merchant before taking up a military career. He entered the army in an Irish regiment, becoming a major of the 18th dragoons in 1759, and a brevet lieutenant-colonel in 1762. In the following year he became a lieutenant-colonel in the 17th dragoons. In 1771 he was appointed secretary to Simon Harcourt, first Earl Harcourt, who was ambassador-extraordinary and minister-plenipotentiary to Paris. When Harcourt went to Ireland in 1772 as lord lieutenant, Blaquiere accompanied him as his chief secretary. In the same year he was sworn of the privy council. He retired from the army the following year because of his onerous official duties.

As Harcourt's 'ostensible Minister of the [Irish] House of Commons', Blaquiere was chiefly responsible for creating and maintaining a government majority in it (Harcourt to Rochford, 6 March 1774, *Calendar of Home Office Papers, 1773–1775*, 1899, 3.193). Indeed, W. Hunt states that he 'exercised an authority in the House of Commons which, combined with his tactical skill, was of the highest value on any critical occasion' (Hunt, xxvi). Remoteness from London often bedevilled the Irish administration's relations with the British government—official dispatches did not always communicate sufficient detail to British ministers. Consequently Blaquiere found it necessary to travel to London to discuss policy on sensitive issues. For example, during the summer and autumn of 1773 he canvassed support for a controversial tax on absentee landlords. This special mission was to act as a precedent for many more of the kind. In January 1775 he was in London again, this time seeking approval for Henry Flood's appointment as joint vice-treasurer of Ireland—a post traditionally bestowed on members of the British parliament. However, there were still difficulties, and on one occasion he complained to Harcourt that he had 'waited … three hours for the sake of three minutes conversation with Lord North [the British premier]' (Blaquiere to Harcourt, 25 Jan 1775, Harcourt, 9.296).

When Blaquiere left office in 1776, along with Harcourt, he continued to participate actively in Irish politics, and remained in residence in Ireland—the only chief secretary, it was generally remarked, known to have done so when the pay of that office ceased. In reward for his services to the Irish administration he was invested in 1774 with the Order of the Bath, and created a baronet ten years later. He represented a number of constituencies in the Irish parliament until its legislative union with the parliament of Great Britain in 1800: Old Leighlin, co. Carlow (1773–83); Carlingford, co. Louth (1783–90); Charleville, co. Cork (1790–97); and Newtownards, co. Down (1797–1800).

Blaquiere was a regular speaker in the Irish House of

Commons and made an important contribution to the debate on the regency issue in 1789, supporting the address calling on the prince of Wales to assume the regency of Ireland. Indeed, he won considerable praise from Charles Bingham, first earl of Lucan, who declared that 'Blaquiere deserves public thanks for cutting up the odious wretch [George Nugent-Temple-Grenville, first marquess of Buckingham, the Irish viceroy] as he did' (Lucan to Edmund Sexton Pery, 12 Feb 1789, *Buckinghamshire MSS*, 196). It was one of the few occasions in his political career that he did not follow the Irish administration's policy line. However, Buckingham was so unpopular on both sides of the Irish Sea that his opposition did not damage seriously his reputation as a stalwart government supporter.

Blaquiere was also at the centre of controversy when the issue of the legislative union was being contested. In return for his support he obtained an Irish peerage and became Baron de Blaquiere of Ardkill, co. Londonderry, on 30 July 1800. He had hoped to acquire a representative peerage, but the British government resisted strongly. However, Lord Castlereagh, then Irish chief secretary, was forced to offer him an alternative reward—an Irish pension of £1000 per annum for the lives of his wife and daughter, £700 to be put on the pension list from March 1802, and £300 from March 1803.

Although one of Blaquiere's first experiences on Irish soil was a duel, in 1773, with the reckless Beauchamp Bagenal, MP for co. Carlow, he enjoyed his time in Ireland. On 24 December 1775 he married Eleanor (1755/6–1833), daughter and heir of Robert Dobson of Anne's Grove, co. Cork, and his wife, Maria, coheir of Alexander Tompkins of Prehen, co. Londonderry, who brought him the Ardkill estate. They had four sons and three daughters. Apart from the chief secretaryship he held other Irish offices. He was appointed alnager of Ireland and bailiff of the Phoenix Park in 1775, a trustee of the linen board in 1784, and a commissioner of the Dublin paving board in 1786. He earned a reputation for being a jobber and pluralist, but he was popular with his peers and took great pleasure in entertaining them. Jonah Barrington comments:

> to his jobbing is that capital [Dublin] indebted for its wide streets, paving, lighting, and convenient fountains. He made as much as he could of these works, it is true; but every farthing he acquired in Ireland he expended in it. (Barrington, 1.188)

After the Union Blaquiere spent a good deal of his time in London. He represented the constituencies of Rye in Sussex (1801–2) and Downton in Wiltshire (1803–6) in the parliament of the United Kingdom. Initially he supported Addington's ministry, but later he wavered, favouring Pitt's return to power. He voted for the abolition of the slave trade, and opposed Catholic relief. Though well into his seventies, he continued to speak and vote regularly, and finished his parliamentary career in opposition to the ministry of all the talents. He was left without a seat at the dissolution in 1806. He died at Bray, co. Wicklow, aged eighty, on 27 August 1812. DAVID LAMMEY

Sources D. Lammey, 'A study of Anglo-Irish relations between 1772 and 1782, with particular reference to the "free trade" movement', PhD diss., Queen's University of Belfast, 1984 · E. W. Harcourt, ed., *The Harcourt papers*, 14 vols. (privately printed, London, [1880–1905]), vols. 3, 9–10 · Blaquiere papers, NL Ire., MS 877 · R. G. Thorne, 'Blaquiere, Sir John', HoP, *Commons, 1790–1820* · GEC, *Peerage* · H. Cavendish, 'Notes on the debates of the Irish House of Commons, 1776–89', PRO NIre., T 3435 and MIC 12 [transcript and microfilm of the Cavendish MSS, L. Cong.] · J. Barrington, *Personal sketches of his own times*, 3 vols. (1827–32) · J. Redington and R. A. Roberts, eds., *Calendar of home office papers of the reign of George III*, 4 vols., PRO (1878–99) · A. P. W. Malcomson, ed., *Eighteenth-century Irish official papers in Great Britain: private collections*, 2 (1990) · W. Hunt, *The Irish parliament, 1775* (1907) · J. Kelly, *Henry Flood: patriots and politics in eighteenth-century Ireland* (1998) · *The manuscripts of the earl of Buckinghamshire, the earl of Lindsey … and James Round*, HMC, 38 (1895) · *DNB*

Archives National University of Ireland, Galway, notebook on Irish MPs · NL Ire., corresp. relating to Irish affairs and national defence, MSS 877, 5932 | BL, corresp. with first earl of Liverpool, Add. MSS 38207–38310, *passim* · NL Ire., Harcourt papers, MSS 755, 5161 · Northants. RO, corresp. with E. Burke · TCD, letters to N. Clements and H. T. Clements

Likenesses J. Heath, engraving, pubd 1811 (after drawing by J. Comerford), NPG [*see illus.*]

Blaschko, Hugh [*formerly* Karl Felix Hermann] (1900–1993), biochemist and pharmacologist, was born on 4 January 1900 in Friedrichstrasse, Berlin, the only son and second of the three children of Alfred Blaschko (1858–1922), dermatologist and venereologist, and his wife, Johanna (1873–1943), daughter of Karl Litthauer, medical doctor. Surrounded in Berlin by many Jewish relations and by medical and socialist friends of his father, Hermann (or Hugh as he was known in England) developed an early interest in natural science and became an internationalist. An extraordinarily detailed and vivid account of this period is given in his posthumously published book *Memories of my Early Life* (1997). He was educated at a private school on the Landsberger Platz, Berlin (1906–9) and at the Prinz Heinrich Gymnasium, Berlin Schöneberg. With so much medicine in the family (father and both grandfathers), it was inevitable that he would then study medicine, first in Berlin (1917–19), then in Freiburg im Breisgau (1919–21), then back in Berlin for his clinical studies (1921–2). It was at Freiburg that he first met, as a fellow student, Hans Krebs, who was to join him at Oxford thirty-five years later. His first post was at the university clinic for internal medicine in Göttingen (1923), but it was his period with Otto Meyerhof (just awarded the Nobel prize) in Berlin and later Heidelberg (1925–32) that gave him an insight into scientific method and also introduced him to many of the leading biochemists of the time. Blaschko's warmth and sincerity led to lifelong friendships with many he met at this time. One of his outstanding qualities was the way in which he nurtured his friendships, however far away his friends lived.

Blaschko's first period in England was with Archibald Vivian Hill (who shared the Nobel prize with Meyerhof) at University College, London, in 1929–30. It was while he was with Hill that Blaschko carried out his first truly independent piece of research, perhaps reflecting the different attitude of British and continental professors to their young protégés. The visit to Hill was to be of great importance for another reason. After his return to Germany Blaschko suffered several recurrences of tuberculosis (which he first contracted in 1926), and one of these was in 1933, when the advent of the Nazi regime made him realize that he had no future in Germany. He was in hospital in Freiburg, being attended by Hans Krebs as physician, but while convalescing he worked in Krebs's laboratory to improve his skills in manometry—a technique crucial to several of his later discoveries. While he was still in hospital, a letter arrived from Hill inviting him to return to University College, London. He did not hesitate to accept: as he wrote later, his return 'felt more like a homecoming'. Instead of beginning independent research in Hill's laboratory, Blaschko had to continue his convalescence, and so spent most of his time helping Hill with the Academic Assistance Council. The society had been founded by Hill, Archbishop William Temple, A. D. Lindsay, and Sir William Beveridge to help refugee scholars. Blaschko's main job was to interview scholars from Germany and advise Hill about their needs. He later claimed to have learned from Hill that a scientist's duty does not end in the laboratory but extends to the support and care of the human being, something that his own life clearly demonstrated.

One of the most productive periods of Blaschko's scientific life followed his move to Cambridge in 1934; upon the advice of Hill and Krebs he went to Joseph Barcroft's physiological laboratory with a grant from the Society for the Protection of Science and Learning. It was in response to a question from Barcroft, who asked him how adrenalin was destroyed in the body, that he did the crucial experiments that led to the discovery in 1937 of the enzyme amine oxidase. Blaschko's grant only lasted for two years, and so he had to support himself by teaching at Cambridge—a somewhat precarious business, since he never knew until the beginning of each term whether he would have any students. He often used to recount the future careers of his Cambridge pupils. He told these stories at times when his young colleagues became despondent about the heavy teaching load they had to bear: 'Never mind, you never know whether one of your pupils will be another Sanger', he used to say (private information). (Frederick Sanger won the Nobel prize twice and was one of Blaschko's pupils.) In 1939 he proposed the sequence of reactions that led to the synthesis of adrenalin in the body; his idea had to wait ten years for convincing experimental proof.

The last and long-lasting flowering of Blaschko's scientific life occurred after he moved to Oxford in 1944 in response to an invitation from J. H. Burn to join the department of pharmacology. Blaschko had the great fortune to move from a department that was the mecca for physiologists to one that rapidly became the mecca for pharmacologists. There he discovered how the potent substance adrenalin was safely stored in the adrenal gland at very high concentration. This discovery paved the way for the understanding of how chemical transmitter substances are stored in, and released from, nerves throughout the body. Not only did Oxford give him his first and only permanent post (he retired in 1967), but there he met and, on 29 December 1944, married Mary Douglas Black (1908–2000), daughter of John Robert Black, of Yelverton, Devon. She was a Quaker and a teacher at the Dragon School, Oxford. The marriage was one of exceptional harmony, mutual support, and happiness, although childless. However, the Blaschkos made up for a lack of children by embracing all who came into their life, such that they had a remarkable extended family throughout the world. Their home at 24 Park Town became a haven for innumerable scientists of all ages. Blaschko kept up with his 'family' by correspondence and could remember the finest details of their lives. Indeed, one of his extraordinary attributes was a phenomenal memory, extending back into his childhood. In his relationships he was open-minded, thoughtful, and low-key. He found good in everyone, and had an impish sense of humour and a total lack of conceit. He was a most delightful person to be with.

In 1965 Blaschko became *ad hominem* reader in biochemical pharmacology in the department of pharmacology, University of Oxford, and a fellow of Linacre College, a college he helped to found. He retired in 1967, becoming emeritus reader and emeritus fellow of Linacre. For nearly half a century he was one of the great figures in Oxford science and in its community. His greatness was not flamboyant but lay in his ever-alert mind, his sense of curiosity and wonder, and his belief in, and encouragement of, others younger than himself. He was author of more than 200 scientific articles, was elected FRS in 1962, and was awarded many distinctions around the world, including the Purkinje medal (Prague, 1963), the Schmiedeberg Plakette of the German Pharmacological Society (1972), the first Thudicum medal of the Biochemical Society (1974), and the Wellcome gold medal of the British Pharmacological Society (1979). He was a member of the editorial boards of numerous journals, including *Pharmacological Reviews* and the *Journal of Physiology*. He died at his home in Oxford, following a sudden internal haemorrhage, on 18 April 1993. A commemoration was held on 22 May 1993 at the Friends' meeting-house, Oxford. His wife, who survived him, endowed the Blaschko visiting scholarship at the department of pharmacology, Oxford, and Linacre College (where there is a Blaschko Room), in order to continue the tradition that he began of bringing young scholars from Europe into his laboratory.

A. DAVID SMITH

Sources H. Blaschko, *Memories of my early life* (Oxford, 1997) [privately printed] · H. Blaschko, 'A biochemist's approach to autopharmacology', *Comprehensive Biochemistry*, 35 (1983), 189–231 [sel. topics in the history of biochemistry: personal recollections] · H. Blaschko, 'My path to pharmacology', *Annual Review of Pharmacology*, 20 (1980), 1–14 · G. V. R. Born and P. Banks, *Memoirs FRS*, 42 (1996), 41–60 · *The Guardian* (27 April 1993) · *The Independent* (27 April 1993) · *The Times* (28 April 1993) · *WWW*, 1991–5 · personal knowledge (2004) · private information (2004) · *CGPLA Eng. & Wales* (1993)

Archives Wellcome L., corresp., notes, lectures, PP/HKB | Bodl. Oxf., corresp. relating to Society for Protection of Science and Learning · CAC Cam., corresp. with A. V. Hill | FILM Biochemical

Society Archive, 59 Portland Place, London W1N 3AJ, video interview with Peter Banks

Likenesses black and white photograph, 1963, repro. in Born and Banks, *Memoirs FRS* · colour photograph, 1990, repro. in Blaschko, *Memories of my early life* · black and white photograph, repro. in Blaschko, 'My path to pharmacology' · colour photograph, repro. in B. Bell, ed., *Insight guide to Oxford* (1990), 188

Wealth at death £304,886: probate, 21 July 1993, *CGPLA Eng. & Wales*

Blashfield, John Marriott (1811–1882), terracotta manufacturer, was born on 1 November 1811 in the parish of St James, Westminster, one of at least two sons of John and Eleanor Blashfield. No further details are known of his background and his early life and education are similarly obscure. By 1841, and described as an artist, he was living at 1 Upper Stamford Street, Blackfriars, but he first comes to light two years earlier in 1839 laying a Venetian *pisé* (hard scagliola) floor at Deepdene in Surrey, the home of Henry Thomas Hope. Two years later he provided scagliola for Sir Charles Barry's Reform Club. At about that time he entered into partnership with the roman cement makers Wyatt, Parker & Co., and as a result of this he is personally credited with supplying the finest cement for the final phase of the Thames Tunnel (1835–42).

Blashfield had also been carrying out small scale terracotta experiments, but he was more interested in tessellated pavements, giving them as the reason for entering into the Wyatt Parker partnership. However, a patent taken out in 1840 by Richard Prosser of Birmingham, for making china buttons from hydraulically compressed dry clay, changed his line of thought. He saw in it possibilities for making mosaic tesserae, but unfortunately, Herbert Minton took a half share in Prosser's patent. This was a blow as from then on Blashfield had to use Minton's fired clay tesserae for his own work. In 1843 Blashfield and Minton jointly installed one of their earliest pavements in the Society of Arts at the Adelphi. Despite his dependence on Minton, Blashfield was given great credit by contemporaries for the development of tessellated pavements and for his associated work on encaustic tiles.

1843–7 saw an unfortunate and financially disastrous period in Blashfield's life. He entered the field of building speculation and attempted to undertake a major part of the development of Kensington Palace Gardens in London. The commissioners of woods and forests (forerunners of the crown estate commissioners) were offering ninety-nine year leases to build thirty-three houses on part of the former kitchen gardens of Kensington Palace. Blashfield tendered for twenty of them, offering a total rent rising to almost £2000 per annum. This was an extremely high rent and Blashfield made his first houses too large for their sites, and so he had difficulty in disposing of them. By 1847, with five houses under construction, he was in severe financial difficulty and was declared bankrupt on 14 May with losses estimated at over £40,000. It is difficult to see how he recovered from this blow. He had been able to direct Wyatt Parker money towards his building speculation, but his bankruptcy caused him to surrender his interests in tessellated pavements and encaustic tiles to Herbert Minton. It is likely that he also handed over premises, as from 1848 onwards Minton's is recorded as occupying a former Wyatt Parker address.

Whatever the other effects of his bankruptcy, Blashfield was able to continue his cement and scagliola business and in 1851 felt able to expand his Millwall factory into terracotta manufacture. He had a good artistic and technical grounding for this and, additionally, he had been developing valuable contacts over the previous decade with prominent and rising architects, designers, and sculptors. He went to some pains to prove to his peers and the general public the quality of his work. The colossal figures he supplied in 1853 for the resited Crystal Palace at Sydenham included *Australia* by John Bell, which at 9 feet tall was the largest single piece of terracotta ever fired; also from this period survives a huge Triton fountain in the courtyard of the Radcliffe Infirmary, Oxford (based on Bernini). Blashfield's works, largely in the classical tradition, began to appear in numerous country house gardens and on several buildings in London: for example, Hampton Court, Kew Gardens, Marlborough House, the duchy of Cornwall office (10 Buckingham Gate), the Sheepshanks Gallery (Victoria and Albert Museum), Chelsea Bridge, and Woolwich barracks. His *Catalogue of 500 Articles* (1855) and published catalogues of 1857 and 1868 show the range of his work.

In December 1858 Blashfield moved from London to Stamford in Lincolnshire to be nearer a good source of clay and save money on wages. By this time he was married, but he and his wife, Isabella Mary Ann, had no children. They adopted as son their nephew, Joseph Joiner, who came to work for Blashfield in the Stamford pottery. On coming to Stamford, Blashfield was able to lease an almost new factory from the marquess of Exeter and his kilns were ready for firing by March 1859. It is a measure of Blashfield's success in London that the sale of stock on quitting his Millwall factory brought in undreamed-of prices; this story was repeated two years later when he moved his London showroom.

The 1860s were Blashfield's most successful years. By 1861 he was employing sixty-five workers and during the decade he received his major commissions. He was an innovative manufacturer and in 1860 patented a muffle kiln that set new standards in terracotta production. He supplied a number of large vases to Buckingham Palace in 1862 and terracotta for the Duke of Cornwall Hotel, Plymouth (1863–5, architect, Charles Forster Hayward). Between 1865 and 1868 he received over £4500 for balustrading, urns, and statuary in Matthew Digby Wyatt's major garden works at Castle Ashby near Northampton, but his largest commission was the new Dulwich College (1866–70), designed by Charles Barry the younger. In 1870 he carried out further work for Digby Wyatt at Lady Alford's new house in Prince's Gate, London. Locally, he built facades for two Stamford buildings, and in 1871 constructed a large boathouse for the marquess of Exeter in Burghley Park. Blashfield also carried out much work abroad, including commissions in New Zealand and, by 1865, completion of the triumphal arch in the Victoria Gardens, Bombay (architects, Scott and McClelland). In the early 1870s he supplied terracotta for his most famous foreign building, the Museum of Fine Arts, Boston, Massachusetts (architects, Sturgis and Brigham, dem. *c.*1906). Illustrative of the sculptural work carried out at this time are twelve relief panels for the facade of the Wedgwood Institute, Burslem (1863–9), depicting the processes in ceramics manufacture, and a large statue of Prince Albert (1865) for a hospital in Bishop's Waltham.

Though successful artistically, Blashfield showed a remarkable lack of business acumen. Through a series of uneconomic contracts and a lack of capital, he ran into difficulties. Things came to a head in 1872 when he had to turn his pottery into a limited liability company to finance his Boston museum contract. He had been working for over two years to achieve this and the contract was signed and the prospectus for the new company issued within weeks of each other in July. It was a pyrrhic success: the contract was also uneconomic and by 1875 Blashfield went into voluntary liquidation. There was another reason for his downfall. Despite Blashfield's criticisms of the earlier schools of terracotta, he was a part of them and relied on complex clay recipes and extensive retooling after moulding and drying. Varying clay mixes meant shrinkage rates were not constant, causing much wastage. There was also a reaction against the ultra-fine finish of these terracottas in favour of something slightly less refined and more vigorous. During the 1860s the balance between the old and new schools tipped in favour of the latter. The rougher-textured terracotta, straight from the mould, using only single fire clays and grog to control shrinkage rates, found much favour and produced a considerable economy. With fashion and economics against it, the old school was doomed. Two seminal meetings at the Royal Institute of British Architects in 1868, and published in its *Transactions* for 1867/8 and 1868/9, are a microcosm of the contemporary debate and centre on the work of Barry and Blashfield at Dulwich College.

Because Blashfield's personal finances became mixed with those of his company his American debts remained outstanding after the failure of the company. As a result he was declared bankrupt for a second time in 1877. He left Stamford in the same year, returning to London. There, over the next few years, he dealt in terracotta in what must have been a very small way. He died on 15 December 1882 at his home, 17 Great College Street, Westminster, leaving just £52.

Blashfield was a strong-minded and resourceful entrepreneur, respected by his contemporaries. An 1871 photograph shows him to be a large man with receding hair and long half-beard. Though thwarted by circumstance in his original intention to produce tessellated pavements, he was highly successful in his second choice, terracotta. His importance lies in the link he provided between the eighteenth-century school of terracotta of Mrs Coade and the flourishing industry which developed from the 1870s to the 1930s. Blashfield was also indirectly responsible in part for its development in the United States; his nephew, adopted son, and works manager, Joseph Joiner, and senior foreman, James Taylor, both emigrated to the USA in the 1870s and became founding fathers of its terracotta industry.

JOHN F. H. SMITH

Sources M. Stratton, *The terracotta revival* (1993) • J. Davis, *Antique garden ornament* (1991) • C. Barry, 'Some descriptive memoranda on the works executed in terra cotta at New Alleyn's College, Dulwich, by Mr Blashfield … from the designs … of Charles Barry, architect', *Transactions of the Royal Institute of British Architects* (1867–8), 259–79 • 'Discussion on Mr C. Barry's paper', *Sessional Papers of the Royal Institute of British Architects* (1868–9), 15–29 • F. H. W. Sheppard, ed., *Northern Kensington*, Survey of London, 37 (1973), chap. 8 • J. M. Blashfield, *The history and manufacture of ancient and modern terra cotta* (1855) • J. M. Blashfield, *A catalogue of 500 articles made of patent terra cotta* (1855) • J. M. Blashfield, *A selection of vases, statues, busts, etc. from terra-cottas* (1857) • J. M. Blashfield, *Terra cotta and architectural pottery* (1868) [catalogue] • L. F. W. Jewitt, *The ceramic art of Great Britain, from pre-historic times*, new edn (1883); repr. (1985) • *Stamford Mercury* (18 Feb 1859) [Tour of works] • M. H. Floyd, 'A terra-cotta cornerstone for Copley Square: Museum of Fine Arts, Boston, 1870–1876', *Journal of the Society of Architectural Historians*, 32 (1973), 83–103 • parish register (baptisms), 1 March 1812, St James, Westminster, London • census returns for St George's Square, Stamford, Lincolnshire, 1861, 1871 • d. cert. • *Stamford Mercury* (22 Dec 1882) • *The Builder*, 43 (1882), 826 • *Journal of the Society of Arts*, 31 (1882–3), 136 • *CGPLA Eng. & Wales* (1883)

Archives crown estate office, London, relating to Kensington Palace gardens • Wedgwood Institute, Burslem, Staffordshire, panels depicting processes of ceramics manufacture

Likenesses group portrait, photograph, June 1871, Stamford Museum

Wealth at death £52: probate, 20 Feb 1883, *CGPLA Eng. & Wales*

Blatchford, Robert Peel Glanville (1851–1943), journalist and author, was born at Maidstone on 17 March 1851 and named after the Conservative prime minister who had died the year before. His English father, John Glanville Blatchford, and his half-Italian mother, Georgiana Louisa Corri, granddaughter of Domenico Corri, were both provincial actors. His father died before Robert was two years old and his mother continued acting for eight years in order to bring up her two children, Montagu, the elder, and Robert; but she hated the stage, determined to keep her sons off it, and had them both apprenticed to trades. Robert at fourteen was indentured for seven years to a brushmaker at Halifax; but when he was twenty he ran away, tramped from Yarmouth to London, starved there for some weeks, and finally enlisted in the 103rd regiment, an old 'John Company' corps newly back from India. He did well and in eighteen months was promoted sergeant; he also became a marksman. His army years powerfully influenced his later views; he finally left the service in 1878, having obtained a situation as a timekeeper at Northwich under the Weaver Navigation Company. His pay was 27*s.* a week, and on 1 May 1880, when it was 30*s.*, he married. His wife, Sarah Crossley, daughter of Nathan Crossley, machine maker, he had met thirteen years before at the Halifax brush shop; and their union, which was a very happy one, did much to shape the rest of his life.

Blatchford soon needed to earn more. His bent was towards art, but at Northwich he had nowhere to learn. So he turned to writing. He earned his first half-guinea in 1883 with a story in a paper called *The Yorkshireman*. In 1884

Robert Peel Glanville Blatchford (1851–1943), by unknown photographer

he came to know Alexander Mattock Thompson, thenceforward his lifelong friend and ally. Thompson was working at Manchester on the *Sporting Chronicle*, owned by the father of Edward Hulton; and when Hulton bought *Bell's Life in London* in 1885 and made it a daily, Thompson recommended Blatchford for a post. He was engaged at £4 a week, left Northwich for London, and became a professional journalist. In the same year Hulton started the *Sunday Chronicle* in Manchester, and Blatchford wrote its leaders from London. He adopted the pen-name 'Nunquam Dormio' ('I never sleep'), which he used from time to time throughout his life ('Nunquam' became his nickname). In 1887 he moved to Manchester, and then first became known as an individual writer. He began with soldier stories and sketches; next he went to Ireland to write up the land war; then he started writing about the Manchester slums. His experiences made him a socialist, and his socialism probably cost him, in 1891, his post on the *Sunday Chronicle*, in which he was earning £1000 a year. He helped to found the Manchester Fabian Society in 1890 and he had close connections with the local Social Democratic Federation; he soon found himself more in sympathy with the latter than the former. With his friend Thompson, his brother, Montagu, and another Hulton journalist, Edward Francis Fay, he started *The Clarion*, as a socialist weekly; they put up the £400 capital between them. The paper's first sale, on 12 December 1891, was 40,000, and the circulation remained for some years about 34,000. Despite its brilliance and the charm of its writing (not least E. F. Fay's), the paper stuck there. Then a series of articles on socialism by Blatchford was reprinted as a book, *Merrie England* (1893), and in the next year they issued a penny edition of it. This sold extremely well, helped to make socialism really well known in England for the first time, and sent *The Clarion*'s circulation to 60,000. Ultimately in Great Britain, in America, and through translations elsewhere, the book sold over two million copies. It was Blatchford's highest flight as a propagandist; he never surpassed it, and through it mainly he left his mark upon history.

The death of Fay in 1896 hit *The Clarion* hard, but it continued for another three years to be the chief popular organ of English socialism. It was indeed much else; it popularized a wide range of good literature and poetry; it 'sang to its readers', and with genial tolerance found space for almost any kind of forward-looking movement. Many organizations—cycling, hiking, singing, scouting—were founded by the Clarion movement. In its infectious enthusiasm it mirrored Blatchford himself, who was much more a crusader than a politician. Many attempts were made by admirers to get him on platforms or nominate him for parliament. But he was no orator, disliked party manoeuvring, and was never happy with the leaders of the then dominant Independent Labour Party, though he founded the Manchester branch on 14 May 1892. On the outbreak of the Second South African War this division became sharper because the party became pro-Boer, while Blatchford was pro-war. With the war's ending *The Clarion* entered calmer waters, or would have done if Blatchford had not stirred up new opposition by entering on a campaign against orthodox religion; this lost him many readers, but added more. As much could not be said of his warnings against Germany before the First World War; they were seen after the event to have been justified, but at the time alienated most English socialists, especially when he carried his views into the columns of the *Daily Mail*. This last episode began a connection with the Northcliffe press that lasted until the summer of 1916. Blatchford forswore the socialist movement in October 1914. He opposed conscription but ridiculed conscientious objectors, making himself a bogeyman of the left by his jingoistic speeches. After 1916 he wrote for Hulton in the *Sunday Chronicle* until 1924, for the *Sunday News* from 1924 until 1927, and then became a freelance. He kept *The Clarion* going for some years, but had, eventually, to abandon it. After his wife's death in 1921 he came to believe in spiritualism.

Blatchford published many books, of which *Britain for the British* (1902), *God and my Neighbour* (1903), and *The Sorcery Shop* (1907) were outstanding. Many of them were collections of short articles or stories; his short stories about soldiers were excellent, but his fiction was not otherwise remarkable. His essays in literary criticism showed his feeling for style; his favourite books were neither fiction nor poetry, but prose *belles-lettres* like those of Sir Thomas Browne. His controversial appeal, it has been said, was in inverse ratio to his reader's education; but he was vigorous and sincere, and at his best he wrote very pure English. Blatchford was a passionate critic of capitalism, but did not share the Labour Party's fondness for parliament. In 1931 he wrote: 'I was always a Tory Democrat' (Thompson, 230), and this was reflected in his protectionism and jingoism. In that year he published a vivid autobiography, *My Eighty Years*.

Blatchford had four sons, three of whom died in infancy, and two daughters; the loving care of the latter, Winifrid Norris and Dorothea Glanville Blatchford, made happy his last twenty-two years. In 1914, after living for many years in Norfolk, the Blatchford family moved to Horsham, Sussex, eventually settling at The Firs, King's Road, Horsham; there Blatchford died, from influenza, on 17 December 1943.

R. C. K. ENSOR, *rev.* H. C. G. MATTHEW

Sources L. Thompson, *Robert Blatchford* (1951) • L. S. A. Jones, *Robert Blatchford and the Clarion* (1986) • R. P. G. Blatchford, *My eighty years* (1931) • private information (1959) • *DLB* • *Manchester Guardian* (20 Dec 1943)

Archives W. Yorks. AS, Calderdale, articles, essays | BL, letters to John Burns, Add. MS 46287 • BL, corresp. with G. K. Chesterton, Add. MSS 73232 A, fol. 28; 73235, fols. 122–33; 73353 B, fols. 4–9 • BL, A. R. Wallace MSS • BLPES, corresp. with the Independent Labour Party • Man. CL, Manchester Archives and Local Studies, letters to William Palmer • Man. CL, Manchester Archives and Local Studies, letters to Alexander Thompson • Man. CL, *Clarion* newspaper MSS • NL NZ, Turnbull L., letters to William Ranstead • U. Lpool, corresp. with John and Katharine Bruce Glasier

Likenesses Palmer, ink, 1891, repro. in Blatchford, *My eighty years* • J. Simpson, chromolithograph, NPG • photogravure, NPG [*see illus.*]

Wealth at death £4593 1s. 11d.: probate, 26 April 1944, *CGPLA Eng. & Wales*

Blathwayt, Mary (1879–1961), suffragette, was born on 1 February 1879, the first of two children of Colonel Linley Blathwayt (1839–1919) and his wife, Emily *née* Rose (1852–1940). In 1882, when Colonel Blathwayt retired from active service in India, the family moved to live in Eagle House, Batheaston, a village on the outskirts of Bath. Mary was educated at Bath high school and then remained at home. Her brother, William, who was two years younger, trained as an electrical engineer and for a number of years taught English in Germany, returning to Batheaston on the eve of the First World War.

Before she became involved in the suffrage movement, Mary Blathwayt spent her time swimming, cycling, and attending lectures and concerts with her family and friends. She belonged to a number of literary and scientific groups, including the Bath Ladies' Microscopical Society, where she studied grubs and insects, an interest that she shared with her father, who had an expertise in entomology. Apart from her membership of the local rifle club, Mary's pursuits were typical of those of other provincial, middle-class young women. Her conventional way of life was to change, however, in 1906 when she attended her first women's suffrage meeting. It seems likely that she was introduced to the movement by local friends, the Tollemache family. Mrs Tollemache, the widow of a clergyman who had retired to Batheaston in 1894 after spending many years in the East, and her daughters Aethel, Grace, and Mrs Mary Everett all became enthusiastic suffrage campaigners.

Initially, Mary Blathwayt and her mother, Emily, took a general interest in the suffrage movement, attending local meetings of the Bath Women's Suffrage Society and subscribing to suffrage newspapers. After taking part in suffragette demonstrations in London, Mary became more interested in working for the militant group, the Women's Social and Political Union (WSPU), and in 1908 became treasurer of the Bath WSPU. Shortly afterwards she was persuaded by Annie Kenney, WSPU organizer for the west of England, to give a full-time commitment to suffrage propaganda. Between May 1908 and October 1909 Mary moved to Bristol to share lodgings with Annie Kenney. She carried out organizing and propaganda work all over the west country, frequently staying for up to a week in other towns. From being a shy, rather conventional young woman, Mary began to engage in activities which took place in the street rather than the drawing-room. She distributed leaflets, chalked pavements, made detailed arrangements for meetings, attended demonstrations, and carried out personal tasks for Annie Kenney, such as mending and washing her clothes, so that she would be freed for propaganda work. As Mary's own confidence grew she began to take the chair at meetings, and frequently encountered violence from the crowd.

Mary Blathwayt's parents also gave support to the WSPU. Emily Blathwayt organized garden parties in the grounds of Eagle House and provided hospitality for visiting speakers, who were collected from the station by Colonel Blathwayt in his motor car. In 1909 Linley Blathwayt began to take photographs of all the suffragettes who visited his home and they were encouraged to plant a tree in a part of the grounds which was known as Annie's arboretum. He also constructed a summer house in which suffragettes could rest after imprisonment, write speeches, and drink tea. Although most leaders of the WSPU visited Eagle House at some point, it was Annie Kenney who stayed most often to recuperate from her punishing speaking schedule.

Despite their admiration for the courage of imprisoned suffragettes, all of the Blathwayts were uncomfortable about acts which broke the law. Emily Blathwayt resigned from the WSPU in September 1909 after stones had been thrown at Asquith, the prime minister, but she was reluctant to criticize those who had been close friends and they were still welcome in her home. Mary Blathwayt continued to work for the union but returned to Eagle House in October 1909 suffering from exhaustion and from problems with her eyes. She now concentrated on propaganda work in Bath, which included helping to run the suffrage shop and preparing for public meetings. In 1912, as members of the WSPU became increasingly involved in large-scale destruction of property, there was a noticeable tailing off of her suffrage work and in May 1913 she too resigned from the union. Her parents joined the National Union of Women's Suffrage Societies in January 1914 when Mrs Fawcett was at last prepared to go against the Liberal Party, but there is no evidence that Mary Blathwayt did the same. She continued, however, to attend public meetings organized by the WSPU in Bath, took part in tax resistance sales, and frequently helped Aethel and Grace Tollemache in the suffragette shop. For example, she took photographs of suffragette parades and turned these into postcards which could be sold to raise money for the cause, and helped her friends in other ways, such as delivering letters or pricing goods for sale. Despite her continued interest in the suffrage campaign Mary Blathwayt was now on the sidelines rather than in the thick of the struggle, and clearly felt disappointed when Grace did not invite her to visit Aethel in Holloway in June 1914.

Once war was declared, Mary Blathwayt, along with her father, tried to support the war effort by sending subscriptions to groups such as the Queen's Fund for working women and the Red Cross Society, while the Tollemache sisters produced food for sale. Mary had to deal with family illnesses for the first few months of war, but then became more actively involved in the Bath branch of the Red Cross Society. The Blathwayt family continued to take an interest in the progress of women's suffrage as it was reported in the newspapers and remained in contact with Annie Kenney until she married in 1920.

Mary Blathwayt was typical of many young women who were inspired by the charismatic leaders of the WSPU to take political action for the first time. Although she was never imprisoned, Mary Blathwayt helped to further the militant cause through her organizational and propaganda work. The significance of her contribution, and that of her parents, might have gone unnoticed if Mary Blathwayt and her mother had not kept diaries on a daily basis which provide details of all their activities. For a brief period the suffrage movement took over Mary Blathwayt's life, but after her resignation from the WSPU she never took part in political work again. She returned to her previous interests, attending meetings of literary and scientific societies to which she subscribed, and lived quietly in Eagle House with her family until her death there on 25 June 1961. JUNE HANNAM

Sources M. Blathwayt and E. Blathwayt, MS diaries, 1906–20, Dyrham Park, Gloucestershire • B. M. W. Dobbie, *A nest of suffragettes in Somerset* (1979) • O. Banks, *The biographical dictionary of British feminists*, 1 (1985) • A. Kenney, *Memories of a militant* (1924) • d. cert. • Burke, *Gen. GB* (1937)

Archives Glos. RO, diaries and accounts • NRA, priv. coll., diaries and MSS

Likenesses photograph (as a young woman), repro. in Dobbie, *Nest of suffragettes*

Blathwayt, William (*bap.* 1650, *d.* 1717), government official, was baptized on 2 March 1650 at St Botolph, Aldersgate, London. He was the only son of William Blathwayt (1594–*c*.1650), barrister of the Middle Temple, and Anne (*b.* 1618?, *d.* in or after 1673), daughter of Justinian Povey, accountant-general to Anne of Denmark and auditor of the exchequer. Blathwayt's father died soon after he was born, leaving an estate 'extremely embroil'd and impaired' (Glos. RO, MS D1799/C9), and he was brought up by his uncle Thomas *Povey, a politician and successful, if sometimes inept, government and royal official of the Cromwellian and Restoration periods. In 1665 Blathwayt was admitted to the Middle Temple, London, and three years later, in 1668, Povey and Secretary of State Arlington induced Sir William Temple to employ the young Blathwayt as a clerk in the embassy at The Hague. His linguistic skill (he was the only official at the embassy who knew Dutch) rendered him a most useful member of the staff. After Temple's recall he returned to England (January 1672) in time to join the entourage of the duke of Richmond, who was departing on a diplomatic mission to Denmark. From there, Richmond sent him to Sweden and then to Germany; after Richmond's death Blathwayt continued to Italy on what had become a grand tour before returning to England in 1673.

With the help of the secretary of state Sir Joseph Williamson, Thomas Povey (himself an expert in colonial business), and Povey's friend Sir Robert Southwell, Blathwayt entered the plantations office in September 1675. The reorganization and expansion of plantation business in this period, combined with Blathwayt's capacity for hard work, facilitated his rapid rise; he became clerk-in-extraordinary of the privy council (July 1678) as a 'mark of … encouragement … for the pains he has taken in the plantation business' (*Ormonde MSS*, 4.444) and secretary to the lords of trade in December 1679. A reorganization of colonial finance in 1680 led to Blathwayt's appointment as surveyor and auditor-general of his majesty's revenues in America, a post which he held until his death, and from 1681 to 1683 he was under-secretary of state to Lord Conway in the northern department, transacting business with his customary efficiency. In 1683, with the permission of Charles II, who already had a particular 'kindness for him' (ibid., 4.449), he purchased the post of secretary at war. Royal favour from both Charles and his brother James significantly assisted Blathwayt in these years, and in 1686 he became clerk-in-ordinary of the privy council, although not without a struggle with another claimant to the vacancy, William Bridgeman. King James, reported Blathwayt importantly to his mentor Southwell, had been his 'Advocat & Champion' (Glos. RO, MS D1799/C8). John Evelyn's diary entry for 18 June 1687 summarizes the impression made on one discerning observer: 'I din'd this day at Mr. Blathwaites … [he] having raised himselfe by his Industry, from very moderate Circumstances: He is a very proper handsome person, and very dextrous in buisinesse, and has besids all this married a very greate fortune' (Evelyn, 554).

This last reference was to Mary Wynter (1650–1691), daughter and heiress to John Wynter of Dyrham Park, Gloucestershire. Blathwayt had initially considered her age uninviting (she was thirty-six) but soon claimed to be more interested in the person of the lady than in the size of the estate. The marriage contract was, however, constructed with that meticulous attention to financial detail which Blathwayt always displayed; the wedding took place on 23 December 1686. They had four sons, of whom two survived, William (1688–1742) and John (1690–1754), and a daughter, Anne (1691–1717), who married the son of Sir Robert Southwell.

Blathwayt negotiated the difficulties of the revolution of 1688 successfully, despite having served as the chief government witness at the notorious trial of the seven bishops and having, as secretary at war, accompanied James II on the march to Salisbury. His many posts were, he claimed, all 'places of pains or Experience' (Glos. RO, D1799/C8), and, as he never tired of pointing out to his correspondents, they were mainly held during good behaviour rather than at pleasure. Blathwayt was challenged only in his tenure of the secretaryship at war. Sir William Temple's son, John, was appointed to the post in April 1689, but collapsed under the strain and Blathwayt was promptly reappointed. This Dutch-speaking administrator was clearly too useful to be dispensed with; William III found him dull (as did others) but admitted that he had 'a good method' (Foxcroft, 226). From 1692 to 1701 Blathwayt accompanied William on campaign to Flanders as his acting secretary of state; the king also recognized his unrivalled knowledge of the colonies in appointing him to the newly formed Board of Trade in 1696.

However, the death of William and the accession of Anne signalled the decline of Blathwayt's career. In 1702 he told George Stepney that he had been 'no ways concern'd in Politicks a great while'; by 1706 he admitted to operating in a 'Lower Sphere' (Blathwayt papers, Box 21). He had been dismissed from the secretaryship at war in 1704; henceforth the post would be filled by a politician, not an administrator. In 1707 he lost his seat on the Board of Trade in a party purge; he had been blind to the implications of the rise of party and to the increased importance of parliament. He sat as MP for Newtown in the Isle of Wight on the government interest (1685–7), and for Bath (1693–1710) with the patronage of the duke of Beaufort. Although Stepney had once congratulated Blathwayt on having an 'unalterable' interest at Bath, the duke of Beaufort's belief that Blathwayt had voted against the high-church clergyman Dr Sacheverell in the impeachment proceedings of 1710 meant the end of Blathwayt's parliamentary career.

Blathwayt's correspondence reveals that he preferred a mode of government modelled on the French example, an army promptly paid and efficiently run, and an empire overseen by honest and effective governors acting in the royal interest. It was a vision which could never be fully realized, particularly by someone who feared to offend the 'great men' and whose patronage was limited, but he clung to it with tenacity throughout a career of almost fifty years. Together with other 'men of business' he helped to make the civil service more professional and worked to strengthen England's sinews of power. None the less, like his fellow administrators, he operated within the standards of the day; an acquisitive man, he took palpable delight in the 'tributes' that he received from grateful diplomats and colonial officials. Many of these gifts, such as the black walnut from Virginia, the cedar from Bermuda, and the deer from Germany, contributed to the stocking of Dyrham Park, rebuilt and refurnished by Blathwayt at vast expense, although in somewhat old-fashioned style, between 1692 and 1702. It was to Dyrham, its new façade supervised by the Huguenot architect Hauduroy, its east front designed by William Talman, comptroller of the royal works, its elaborate formal gardens, including the much admired fountains and 'cascade', laid out by the famous gardener George London, that Blathwayt rather reluctantly retired in the last years of his life. There he died, after what Horatio Walpole described as a 'desperate illness', on 26 August 1717; he was buried at Dyrham church on 30 August. His estate remained for many years in the possession of his descendants; the house and parkland are now in the hands of the National Trust.

BARBARA C. MURISON

Sources G. A. Jacobsen, *William Blathwayt: a late seventeenth century administrator* (1932) · B. C. Murison, 'William Blathwayt's empire: politics and administration in England and the Atlantic colonies, 1668–1710', PhD diss., University of Western Ontario, 1981 · W. Blathwayt, 'A schedule of my estate', 20 June 1717, Glos. RO, Blathwayt MS, D1799 · W. Blathwayt, letter, 1673, Glos. RO, Blathwayt MS, D2659/1 · P. Watson, 'Blathwayt, William', HoP, *Commons, 1660–90* · Blathwayt papers, Yale U., Beinecke L., Osborn collection · *Calendar of the manuscripts of the marquess of Ormonde*, new ser., 8 vols., HMC, 36 (1902–20), vol. 4 · Evelyn, *Diary*, vol. 4 · *The life and letters of Sir George Savile … first marquis of Halifax*, ed. H. C. Foxcroft, 2 (1898) · *DNB* · L. Stone, ed., *An imperial state at war* (1994) · parish register, London, St Botolph, Aldersgate, 2 March 1650 [baptism] · 'Blathwayt, William', HoP, *Commons, 1690–1715* [draft] · L. G. Wickham Legg, *Matthew Prior* (1921) · BL, Add. MS 38700, fol. 127 · H. A. C. Sturgess, ed., *Register of admissions to the Honourable Society of the Middle Temple, from the fifteenth century to the year 1944*, 1 (1949), 171 · Burke, *Gen. GB* (1898) · W. H. Godfrey and W. M. Marcham, *The parish of St Pancras*, ed. J. R. H. Roberts, 3, Survey of London, 21 (1949), 19, 33 · W. A. Shaw, ed., *Calendar of treasury books*, 32/2, PRO (1957), 321 · J. A. K.-B. [J. A. Kenworthy-Browne], *Dyrham Park, Gloucestershire: a property of the National Trust*, 6th edn (1980)

Archives BL, corresp. and papers, Add. MSS 9719–9764, 10452, 11759, 15572, 19771, 21486–21491, 21522, 22031, 22045, 24328, 34348–34357, 35105–35106, 37979–37982, 38694–38714, 39860, 41683, 46528–46530, 56239–56247, 57943; Egerton MSS 919–920, 2428 · Bodl. Oxf., diplomatic corresp.; diplomatic papers · Boston PL, corresp. · Colonial Williamsburg Foundation, Virginia, corresp. and papers relating to American and West Indian affairs · Glos. RO, corresp. and papers · Hunt. L., corresp. and papers · L. Cong., corresp. and papers relating to American affairs · PRO, letter-books, T64/88–90 · Rigsarkivet, Copenhagen, corresp. and papers relating to Denmark · U. Nott. L., diplomatic and other corresp. and papers · Yale U., Beinecke L., corresp. and papers | BL, letters to John Ellis, etc., Add. MSS 28877–28909, *passim* · BL, corresp. with Sir William Trumbull · BL, corresp. with James Vernon, Add. MSS 40771–40775 · Bodl. Oxf., Rawlinson and other MSS · CAC Cam., corresp. with Thomas Erle · CKS, corresp. with Alexander Stanhope · Dorset RO, letters to Sir John Trenchard · Hunt. L., letters to Lord Bridgewater · Leics. RO, corresp. with Lord Nottingham · Longleat House, Wiltshire, corresp. with Matthew Prior, librarian and archivist to the marquess of Bath · NMM, Phillipps-Southwell papers, corresp. and papers mainly relating to naval affairs · Northants. RO, corresp. with duke of Shrewsbury · NRA, priv. coll., letters to Lord Cutts · Princeton University, New Jersey, corresp. with Sir Paul Rycaut · PRO, state papers, Colonial Office papers, Treasury papers, and War Office papers · PRO, corresp. with George Stepney, SP 105/54, 58–60, 82 · TCD, corresp. with Sir George Clarke · University College, Cork, corresp. with Major-General Stewart · Yale U., Beinecke L., letters to Edmund Poley; letters to Laurence Hyde, first earl of Rochester

Likenesses M. Dahl, oils, Dyrham Park, Gloucestershire

Wealth at death approx. £31,500: Blaythwayt, 'A schedule'

Blaugdone, Barbara (*c.*1609–1704), Quaker preacher, was 'a Woman of good Parts and Education' (Besse, 2.37) and well connected. Her husband, about whom nothing is known, probably died young, leaving her a widow with a small income which she supplemented by teaching. She was converted to Quakerism in 1654 by John Audland and John Camm. Of her earlier life it is known only that she 'feared the Lord' and 'sought' him 'earnestly' (Blaugdone, 5). She may have been one of the Bristol Seekers from whom many Quakers at this time were recruited. After conversion, to 'subdue her body', she abstained for a year 'from all Flesh, Wine and Beer', drinking only water (ibid., 9). 'She became plain both in speech and habit', alienating her employers and losing her pupils (Sewel, 1.252).

For entering churches in Bristol 'to bear testimony against their formalities', Blaugdone was imprisoned for three months in 1654 (*DNB*). On leaving a meeting at a private house she was stabbed, narrowly escaping death. To gain the release from prison of two Quaker preachers, she went to Basingstoke. Denied access to them, she successfully pleaded their cause with the mayor. In 1656, when several Quakers were imprisoned in Ireland, she felt called to continue their mission and sailed for Cork. A storm forced her boat into Dublin, where she met the deputy, Henry Cromwell (second son of the lord protector), and cautioned him about his treatment of Quakers. She left him 'much troubled and … melancholy' (Besse, 2.459). In Cork her religious enthusiasm and the power of her preaching alarmed friends. She was accused of witchcraft and imprisoned. A letter to George Fox told of a call to Jerusalem, but she was dissuaded and on release went home. Shortly afterwards she was back in Dublin, exhorting judges in the court of justice to righteousness. Again imprisoned, 'she suffered much' (Sewel, 1.308). Only the intervention of powerful friends obtained her release. She went to Limerick, was imprisoned, and moved to Cork and Kinsale gaols before being released and banished.

In 1657 in Marlborough, Blaugdone attempted to speak in the church following the service, was attacked, brought before a magistrate, and imprisoned for six weeks, during which she fasted six days. On release she went to the mayor and so powerful were her reproaches that he 'acknowledged the truth of her doctrine' and henceforth attempted to protect Quakers (Brailsford, 169). She visited Molton, Barnstaple, and Bideford in the west country 'in all which places a Prison was her Lot' (Sewel, 1.253). For bearing witness in Great Torrington she was sent to Exeter prison, long detained before trial, and finally 'whipt till the Blood ran down my back' (Brailsford, 172). After the Restoration she remained active. The year 1681 found her in prison in Bristol for attending a Quaker meeting. Two years later in Ilchester, Somerset, she was again imprisoned, and in the same year she was fined £280 for failing to attend the local Anglican church. In 1686 she wrote to James II about the continued imprisonment of many Quakers. Her memoirs, published in 1691 but almost certainly circulated privately long before, end in 1657. In 1689 two other writings intended for publication were censored. She died in London in 1704.

BRIDGET HILL, *rev.*

Sources [B. Blaugdone], *An account of the travels, sufferings and persecutions of Barbara Blaugdone* (1691) • W. Sewel, *The history of the rise, increase, and progress of the Society of Friends*, 4 vols. (1833–4) • J. Besse, *A collection of the sufferings of the people called Quakers*, 2 vols. (1753) • W. C. Braithwaite, *The beginnings of Quakerism* (1912) • M. R. Brailsford, *Quaker women, 1650–1690* (1915)

Blavatsky, Helena Petrovna (1831–1891), founder of theosophy, was born at Ekaterinoslav (Dnepropetrovsk), Ukraine, at midnight on 30–31 July 1831, the daughter of Colonel Peter Hahn (*d.* 1873), descended from the counts Rotenstern-Hahn of Mecklenburg, and of his wife, Helena Pavolovna Fadeev. She was a petted, wayward, invalid child whose mother, a novelist who advocated women's emancipation, died when she was small. From girlhood onwards she was a beguiling story-teller. On 7 July 1848 she married an older man, General Nikifor Vasilievich Blavatsky, but separated from him in October 1848.

Early travels Helena Blavatsky's claims to have become an intrepid traveller seem partly authentic. She sailed for Constantinople in 1848 and toured Turkey, Greece, Egypt, and western Europe during 1849–50. Her curiosity having been aroused by Fenimore Cooper's Red Indian novels, she went to Canada in 1850–51, and then proceeded to investigate New Orleans voodoo. Afterwards she visited Texas, Mexico, and Latin America. She reached India in 1852, but failed in 1853 to enter Tibet, which was then closed to foreigners. Instead she visited Java and Singapore before proceeding to England. She crossed from New York to San Francisco in a covered wagon during 1853–4, proceeded to Japan in 1855, returned to India, and finally in 1856 supposedly entered Tibet, where she was initiated into Buddhism. Next she lived in France and Germany before returning to Russia (1858–63). During these years she 'claimed to have ridden bareback in a circus, toured Serbia as a concert pianist, opened an ink factory in Odessa, traded as an importer of ostrich feathers in Paris, and worked as interior decorator to the Empress Eugénie' (Washington, 31). Boase believed she 'kept a gambling hell in Tiflis about 1863' (Boase, 2.430).

Blavatsky travelled in Europe from 1863, and averred that as an adherent of Garibaldi she had sustained sabre and bullet wounds when the Italian patriot army was dispersed by French and papal troops at the battle of Mentana (1867). According to other statements, she was shipwrecked at Spetsai off the Greek coast in 1871. These excitements are far less momentous than her claim that after returning to Asia in 1867 she had re-entered Tibet, where she remained in spiritual seclusion studying esoteric mysteries until 1870. Credence that she was a solitary visitor in Tibet for a total of seven years and was initiated by Himalayan seers is not universal.

Blavatsky, who had intermittently practised spiritualism from 1863, established herself as a medium holding seances in Cairo (1870–72). According to her insistent recollections, she had met a dematerializing Tibetan, Master Morya, in visions some time before a corporeal meeting in London during 1851. She identified Morya as a Rajput prince who was a member of the Great White Brotherhood of Mahatmas (masters), sublime sages whose strict training and absolute purity vested them with esoteric powers. These masters (she represented) were in touch with the infinite, lived on a higher plane than the rest of humanity, could dematerialize, and were clairvoyant. It was they who had made her an adept in their arcane knowledge during her Tibetan seclusion. A lord of the world, living in the Gobi desert, headed their hierarchy. The brotherhood also numbered Buddha, Confucius, Plato, Abraham, Moses, Solomon, Lao Tzu, Cagliostro, Mesmer, Roger Bacon, and Francis Bacon among its number. Blavatsky proclaimed herself as the chosen messenger of this celestial brotherhood without explaining why she had been chosen; she acknowledged that dark forces often vilified the human intermediaries who transmitted the doctrines of the masters. Contact with the spirits of the dead, at which she was an adept, was of little importance compared with communion with the living masters, she later insisted.

In 1873 Blavatsky reached New York City in a condition of near destitution. Her prosperity began to revive after a meeting with Colonel Henry Olcott, whom she impressed with her powers as a medium. Although accused of fraud by another medium, Daniel Dunglas Home, she was undeterred. In 1875 she discovered that her masters could transmit their ideas through 'precipitated' letters which were communicated to her by automatic writing or mysteriously materialized in her own or other people's homes.

Blavatsky's name had been linked during the 1850s and 1860s with those of a German baron, a Polish prince, and a Hungarian or Serbian opera singer, Agardi Metrovich; but suggestions that she was a *grande horizontale* seem spurious. She enjoyed intrigue of every sort, as well as stormy rows; but her professed dislike of sexual activity seems sincere. Nevertheless, on 3 April 1875, supposedly after obtaining an American divorce, she married (perhaps bigamously) Michael C. Betanelly, an immigrant businessman from Russian Georgia. If they cohabited, it was only briefly.

The founding of theosophy Blavatsky was richly imaginative and an omnivorous, highly suggestible reader familiar with Asian theology, Masonic, Rosicrucian, and Templar rituals, and the occult romances of Bulwer Lytton. These sources were invaluable in 1875 when she founded, with the support of Olcott and William Q. Judge, the Theosophical Society. This society aimed to form a nucleus of the universal brotherhood of humanity without distinction of race, creed, sex, caste, or colour; to promote the study of comparative religion, philosophy, and science; and to investigate the mystic or occult powers latent in life and matter. Overall Blavatsky was unsympathetic to Christianity, neglectful of Islam and Judaism, and considered Hinduism and Buddhism as the conduits of religious discovery. She promised her votaries that theosophy could cure human anguish by enriching the spirit and rejecting sterile intellectualism, secularism, and materialist philosophy and psychology. From early on it was identified with the nascent movement for the cremation of corpses.

Having become high priestess of a new religious system (which, however, she insisted was a science), Blavatsky next produced its bible, *Isis Unveiled* (1877). This hectic survey of magic and mystery was supposedly the result of astral dictation or other interventions by the mahatmas (masters). Its extracts and paraphrases from ancient writings challenged the mechanical and materialist spirit of the age, and provided spiritual stimulation at a time when religious faith seemed to be weakened. The book's first section belabours David Hume, Charles Darwin, and Thomas Huxley for constricting scientific notions to demonstrable laws governing the material universe. Blavatsky insisted that other laws of nature, hitherto accessible only to occult wisdom, were indispensable for full scientific understanding. She was especially antagonistic to Darwin, and kept in her room a stuffed bespectacled baboon, dressed in wing collar, morning coat, and tie, with a copy of *The Origin of Species* tucked under its arm to express her contempt for evolution theory. The second part of *Isis Unveiled* contained Blavatsky's exposition of Buddhism and thoughts on comparative religion. The book excited the hopes and passions of credulous, earnest, and perhaps ill-educated readers who were undeterred by its hodgepodge of ideas, quotations, and huge spiritual projections.

Blavatsky became a US citizen in 1878 but never re-visited the country after sailing for India later that year. Arriving in Bombay in February 1879, she and Olcott started a magazine, *The Theosophist*, and became minor celebrities (viewed with deep suspicion, initially, by the imperial government). The Anglo-Indian journalist Alfred Sinnett was among those who found her sincere, brilliant, and life-enhancing. He became one of her most persuasive propagandists, but recognized her blunders:

> She was rugged and eccentric in appearance; she dressed anyhow—in loose wrappers—and smoked cigarettes incessantly. Worse than this, she was passionate and excitable, and often violent in her language. Namby-pamby conventionality shrank from her aghast—to her grim satisfaction, for she loathed it. She had a loud voice, that grew harsh in its tones when she felt irritated, and something or other would irritate her fifty times a day. (*Review of Reviews*, 3, 551)

Expansion of the society In India, from 1879, Blavatsky and Olcott converted many adherents to theosophy. In 1880 they both became nominal Buddhists in Ceylon where the Buddhist Theosophical Society subsequently built many schools and had a long-term progressive effect on Sri Lankan education. Subsequently, in 1882, they established the headquarters of the Theosophical Society at Adyar, near Madras. By 1885 121 lodges (on a Masonic model) had been chartered by the Theosophical Society, 106 of them in Burma, India, and Ceylon. Independent theosophical sections were formed in the USA (1886), UK (1888), India (1891), Australia and Sweden (1895), New Zealand (1896), the Netherlands (1897), and France (1899). The theosophical movement always lacked administrative and doctrinal cohesion; moreover, it attracted members whose interest in esoteric contact with rulers of the universe suggested neuroses or worse.

The frauds at seances perpetrated by Blavatsky became more reckless. She was an indiscreet woman who courted but could not control publicity. Eventually she was denounced as a fraud. Emma Coulomb, an unpleasant woman who had been involved with Blavatsky's Cairo seances of 1872, was unwisely employed as housekeeper at the society's headquarters. In 1884 she caused panic and indignation among theosophists by revealing the legerdemain behind some of Blavatsky's supernatural tricks: Richard Hodgson was dispatched by the Society for Psychical Research to Madras to investigate her allegations. Some months later in 1884 a Madras missionary magazine (which opposed theosophy for exalting those Oriental philosophies against which the Christians were working) obtained from Mrs Coulomb letters from Blavatsky betraying her as an impostor. The letters' authenticity was denied; but Hodgson decried her as a crafty, vulgar, and deceitful adventuress who should be shunned as a fraudulent medium rather than honoured as the chosen spokeswoman of hidden seers. A turbulent and destructive scandal ensued.

Blavatsky left India in 1885, almost overwhelmed by obloquy, although her devoted adherents considered these denunciations as signs of grace. After living quietly in Italy, Germany, and Belgium, she established her own esoteric Blavatsky Lodge in London (1887), together with a theosophical magazine, *Lucifer the Light-Bringer*. Her robust and captivating conversation impressed many in these final years. W. B. Yeats, who became a member of Blavatsky Lodge in 1888, likened her talk to Samuel Johnson's. She seemed to have:

> more human nature than anybody else … She sat there all evening, talking to whoever came—vast and shapeless of body, and perpetually rolling cigarettes—humorous and unfanatic, and displaying always … a mind that seemed to pass all others in her honesty. (Yeats, *Memoirs*, 24)

It was in this period that Blavatsky wrote her huge, complicated book *The Secret Doctrine* (1888). Supposedly derived from stanzas written in a language of Blavatsky's own invention, Senzar, it covers cosmic evolution, the origins of the universe, the history of humankind (derived from higher beings of lunar origins), reincarnation, and other incomprehensible matter.

Despite Blavatsky's huge, cumbersome bulk, she ran a heterogeneous community household of admirers and a busy volunteer staff. They were convinced that she was the visible agent of transcendent powers and individuals, and credited her with a stupendous revival of forgotten knowledge. She manipulated her followers, and thrived on strife, as Yeats noted in 1889 when she expelled three members for flirtation or gossiping:

> Madame Blavatsky is in high spirits. The society is like the 'happy family' that used to be exhibited around Charing Cross station—a cat in a cage full of canaries. The Russian cat is beginning to purr now and smoothen its fur again—The canary birds are less by three—The faithful will be more obedient than ever. (*Collected Letters of W. B. Yeats*, 1.162)

Reputation Blavatsky was a prolific correspondent whose own words near the end of life best describe her aims and self-assessment. She wrote in 1890:

> The Theosophical Society has been called the Royal Asiatic Society *plus* philanthropy. The theosophical movement was a necessity of the age [because] it appealed to certain human instincts and aspirations, and held up a certain lofty ideal of perfectibility … its strongest allies were the human yearnings for light upon the problem of life, and for a nobler conception of the origin, destiny and potentialities of the human being.

She was convinced that:

> morals, peace and prosperity will be promoted by the universal belief in a life after death (whether eternal or broken up by a series of incarnations on the same earth), and in man's possession of a higher, undying SELF, latent spiritual powers, and consciousness.

Theosophy and its leaders were the victims of 'sectarian bigotry … frenzied calumny and downright falsehood' (Blavatsky, 'Recent progress', 174–6).

Blavatsky was dishonest, rash, mischievous, and self-infatuated; but her intellect, physical powers, creative energy, and tenacity were exceptional. 'A very gifted and original woman', W. T. Stead rightly judged; 'a fiery, impulsive, passionate creature, full of failings, and personally the very reverse of beautiful' (W. T. Stead, 'Madame Blavatsky', *Review of Reviews*, 3.549). Latterly she was grossly overweight and was trundled about by her admirers in a wheelchair of eccentric design. Weakened by Bright's disease (kidney failure), she died of influenza on 8 May 1891 at her home, 19 Avenue Road, St John's Wood, and was cremated at Woking on 11 May. Her ashes were scattered at Madras. Her death precipitated further deep divisions in theosophy and the emergence of Annie Besant as one of its leaders. Besant, who in 1895 was confirmed as Blavatsky's *de facto* successor, considered that 'she was much more a man than a woman. Outspoken, decided, prompt, strong-willed, genial, humorous, free from pettiness, and without malignity, she was wholly different from the average female type' (*Review of Reviews*, 4, 41).

RICHARD DAVENPORT-HINES

Sources P. Washington, *Madame Blavatsky's baboon* (1993) · S. Cranston, *H. P. B.: the extraordinary life and influence of Helena Blavatsky* (1993) · M. Meade, *Madame Blavatsky* (1980) · M. Gomes, *The dawning of the theosophical movement* (1987) · J. Overton Fuller, *Blavatsky and her teachers* (1988) · J. Dixon, *Divine feminine* (2001) · M. Neff, *Personal memoirs of H. P. Blavatsky* (1937) · W. B. Yeats, *Memoirs*, ed. D. Donoghue (1972) · *The collected letters of W. B. Yeats*, 1, ed. J. Kelly and E. Domville (1986) · H. P. Blavatsky, 'Recent progress in theosophy', *North American Review*, 151 (Aug 1890), 173–86 · *Review of Reviews*, 3 (June 1891) · *Review of Reviews*, 4 (July 1891) · H. S. Olcott, *Old diary leaves*, 6 vols. (1895–1935) · W. Kingsland, *The real H. P. Blavatsky* (1928) · A. P. Sinnett, *Incidents in the life of Madame Blavatsky* (1886) · Boase, *Mod. Eng. biog.* · *The Times* (9 May 1891)

Archives Theosophical Society, Madras | BL, letters to A. P. Sinnett, Add. MSS 45287–45289

Likenesses photograph, *c*.1890, repro. in E. Longford, *Eminent Victorian women* (1981), 148 · Elliott & Fry, photograph, 1891, repro. in *Review of Reviews* (June 1891), 551

Blaxter, Sir Kenneth Lyon (1919–1991), animal nutritionist, was born at Egbert House, Wroxham Road, Sprowston, Norfolk, on 19 June 1919, the son of Gaspard Culling Blaxter, a handicraft teacher who ran a smallholding, and his wife, Charlotte Ellen, *née* Lyon. He was educated at the City of Norwich School and left at the age of fifteen to take up an appointment as a clerk with the Norwich Union Life Assurance Society. Drawn to agricultural science as a career, K. B. (as he was universally known) undertook an honours course in agricultural science at Reading University from 1936 to 1939. After graduation he was appointed as an assistant to Professor H. D. Kay, then director of the National Institute for Research in Dairying in Shinfield, Reading, and under Kay's direction he became closely involved in the national policy for feeding high yield dairy cows, investigating the use of iodinated casein for this purpose. After service in the Royal Artillery (1940–41) he returned to the institute and was then seconded to the Ministry of Agriculture and Fisheries' Veterinary Research Institute, Weybridge, and joined the team of Green and Alcroft in studies on the significance of trace elements such as copper and cobalt. His own studies on the toxicity of lead in feed for ruminant livestock were many years later still recognized as the outstanding papers on that subject. He obtained his PhD from Reading University in 1944 for a thesis, 'The maintenance of the winter milk supply in wartime'. On 23 February 1946 he married Edith Klara Goeritz (*b.* 1917/18), a scientific assistant at the Imperial Bureau of Dairy Science, and daughter of Siegfried Goeritz, a leather goods manufacturer. There were no children of the marriage, which ended in divorce in 1952.

In August 1946 Blaxter was awarded a Commonwealth fellowship to study under Professor H. H. Mitchell at Illinois University, USA. Mitchell was recognized throughout the world as one of the outstanding animal nutritionists of his time, with a particular interest in establishing the nutrient requirements of farm livestock on a scientific basis. It was at the Illinois campus at Urbana that Blaxter developed his subsequent interest in the dominant role played by energy in ruminant animals' metabolism, and its role in determining protein and other nutrient requirements in general. Mitchell's postgraduate taught courses in nutrition were immensely stimulating and Blaxter took an active part in these.

On returning to the UK in 1947 Blaxter was appointed to the headship of the nutrition department of the Hannah Dairy Research Institute, Ayr, and thus began his hands on research interest in energy metabolism of ruminant livestock. The wide range of related studies bore testimony to his tireless energy, his inquiring mind, and his ability to direct the research work of his nutrition department staff. Subjects for study ranged from nutritional disorders of calves, with particular reference to magnesium deficiency, to vitamin E and selenium and their significance in relation to muscular dystrophy of calves. These were additional to his major interest in the utilization of feed energy by ruminants, the environmental effects upon their energy requirements and feed energy utilization, and studies affecting feed intake by ruminants. For his energy studies Blaxter designed, constructed, and used four 24 hour respiration chambers for sheep and goats, and one for steers. Although Blaxter had had no formal training in mathematics he recognized the powerful contribution that appreciation of mathematical studies could make to the analysis of biological data, and was soon recognized as a world authority in its application to the data obtained at the Hannah Institute. In this he was greatly encouraged by Lord Rothschild, who was at that time chairman of the UK's Agricultural Research Council. Dr H. Ruben, a mathematician, was seconded to work at the Hannah Institute in the early days of Blaxter's headship.

On 12 October 1957 Blaxter married Mildred Lillington Hall (*b.* 1924/5), daughter of Robert Charlton Hall, a bank manager. She had a degree in English literature from Oxford and subsequently took a first-class honours degree in sociology at Aberdeen University. They had three children, all of whom entered the field of biology: Alison (the oldest) trained as a veterinary surgeon, Mark became a molecular biologist working in the field of medicine, and Piers a conservation officer in the outer islands of Scotland. Mildred was appointed to the Sociology Research Institute at Aberdeen University and became one of the most respected and active workers in the field of sociology research, a fact of which Blaxter was immensely proud.

At the Hannah, largely on the basis of work carried out by himself and his colleagues, Blaxter formulated the early developments of a feed evaluation system for ruminants which he greatly extended during his later work at the Rowett Research Institute, Bucksburn, Aberdeen, where he was appointed director in 1965 in succession to Sir David Cuthbertson. At that time the principal objective of the institute was to establish research aimed at providing the Scottish farmer with knowledge of direct assistance to him, with particular reference to the Scottish livestock industry. With great enthusiasm Blaxter took aboard this continuing objective of the Rowett. In this regard it is relevant to note that in addition to academic degrees he held national diplomas in agriculture (NDA) and in dairying (NDD); at the same time he realized the importance of maintaining and expanding basic research. Thus the programme under Blaxter was a wide-ranging one, including subjects as varied as branched chain fatty acids, interactions of trace elements, muscle protein and collagen syntheses, the biochemistry of cell walls, and (of major interest to Blaxter) continuing work on energy utilization by ruminants and feed evaluation. From the vastly increased knowledge concerning feed energy utilization Blaxter made further advances in his feed evaluation system. From a practical point of view he was also a great exponent of the red deer project—the farming for venison of red deer—which he considered was the first large ungulate of temperate regions to be domesticated for thousands of years. In conjunction with the Hill Farming Research Organisation he published a monograph on the progress made in this field.

Blaxter retired from the directorship of the Rowett

Research Institute in 1982 (becoming an honorary research associate) and he and his wife moved from Aberdeen, taking up residence at Stradbroke Hall, Stradbroke, near Eye, Suffolk. In 1982 he was appointed member and then chairman of the Individual Merit Promotion Panel responsible to the cabinet office, a post he held until the panel was disbanded in the early 1990s. During his retirement he became increasingly involved in the question of world food supply, and was very much in demand as a speaker. His immensely busy career is well reflected in the following facts: he published more than 300 original research papers, gave sixteen nominated lectures, published four textbooks, and was given eleven honours and awards in addition to being knighted in 1977. He was elected a fellow of the Royal Society of Edinburgh in 1965 (president from 1979 to 1982) and fellow of the Royal Society in 1967. He will always be remembered as one of the foremost world authorities in the field of animal nutrition. His influence extended far beyond the nutrition of man and animals, although underlying the ability to be so farsighted was his love of agriculture and the practical aspects of farming in the UK—a characteristic rare in so many agricultural scientists of his time. He died at his home, Stradbroke Hall, of a brain tumour on 18 April 1991, and was buried three days later. He was survived by his second wife and his three children. A memorial service was held in King's College chapel, Aberdeen University, on 30 September 1991. D. G. ARMSTRONG

Sources J. C. Waterlow and D. G. Armstrong, *Memoirs FRS*, 39 (1994), 37–58 • *The Times* (29 April 1991) • *The Times* (2 May 1991) • *The Independent* (25 April 1991) • *The Independent* (8 May 1991) • personal knowledge (2004) • private information (2004) • *WWW* • b. cert. • m. certs.

Archives Wellcome L., corresp. with Sir Ernst Chain

Likenesses photograph, repro. in Waterlow and Armstrong, *Memoirs FRS* • photograph, repro. in *The Times* (29 April 1991) • photograph, repro. in *The Independent* (25 April 1991)

Wealth at death £43,578: probate, 8 July 1991, *CGPLA Eng. & Wales*

Blaydes, Frederick Henry Marvell (1818–1908), classical scholar, was born at Hampton Court Green on 29 September 1818, the third son of Hugh Blaydes (1777–1829) of High Paull, Yorkshire, and Ranby Hall, Nottinghamshire, JP and high sheriff for the latter county; his mother was Delia Maria, second daughter of Colonel Richard Wood of Hollin Hall, Yorkshire. James Blaides of Hull, who on 25 March 1615 married Anne, sister of the poet Andrew Marvell, was a direct ancestor.

After his father's death in 1829, Blaydes was sent to a private school at Boulogne. He went on from there on 14 September 1831 to St Peter's School, York, where he became a free scholar in June 1832 and gained an exhibition before matriculating at Oxford on 20 October 1836 as a commoner of Christ Church where Thomas Gaisford was dean. In 1838 Blaydes was elected Hertford scholar and a student of Christ Church, and in Easter term 1840 was placed in the second class in *literae humaniores*. He graduated BA in 1840, proceeding MA in 1843.

In 1840–41, Blaydes went on a long tour (which he described in family letters) through France and Italy and on to Athens, via Malta and Corfu, returning to Oxford in August 1841. In 1842 he issued an edition of Aristophanes' *Birds* with short Latin notes. Ordained deacon the same year and priest in 1843, he vacated his studentship in February 1843 and accepted the college living of Harringworth, Northamptonshire. Harringworth was Blaydes's home for forty-three years (1843–86). A staunch protestant, on 10 December 1850 he joined the deputation from his university headed by the chancellor, the duke of Wellington, which presented an address to Queen Victoria against the 'papal aggression' (*The Times*, 11 Dec 1850).

On 17 June 1843 Blaydes married Fanny Maria, eldest daughter of Sir Edward George Thomas Page-Turner, fifth baronet, of Ambrosden, Oxfordshire, and Battlesden, Bedfordshire. They had three sons and four daughters. Blaydes managed his finances injudiciously. From the 1830s onwards he made repeated applications to Christ Church to defray repairs to his vicarage. All were unsuccessful, and by the 1870s debts forced him to sell many of his books. In 1874, however, on the death of her only brother, Sir Edward Henry Page-Turner, sixth baronet, his wife became a coheir to her father's estate. Her death in a carriage accident on 21 August 1884 finally gave Blaydes an ample fortune, of which he spent £30,000 on his library, curios, and the printing of his classical editions.

Blaydes was one of a generation of scholar-parsons in the days before the emergence of an academic career structure. His interest and ample leisure were mainly absorbed by classical study. In 1845 he published an edition of a second play of Aristophanes—the *Acharnians*. In 1859 he published in the Bibliotheca Classica three plays of Sophocles. The reception of the book was not altogether favourable, and a difference with the publishers (Bell and Daldy) led him to issue separately the four remaining plays with Williams and Norgate. He reckoned that he gave more than twenty years to Sophocles, and, with intervals, more than fifty to Aristophanes.

Having shown limited talents as a pastor, Blaydes resigned his benefice in 1886, and went to live at Brighton. In 1894 he married his second wife, Emma, daughter of H. R. Nichols. The marriage was not popular with his children, but it helped to make his retirement both highly contented and productive. He completed his work on Aristophanes' comedies in 1893, and subsequently brought out further editions of Aeschylus and Sophocles.

Scholarship meant for Blaydes what it had meant for Elmsley at Oxford, for Porson and Dobree at Cambridge. With the later and more literary school of Sir Richard Jebb in England and von Wilamowitz-Moellendorff in Germany he had small sympathy. He likewise considered the study of Chaucer and Shakespeare a waste of time. Verbal criticism and the discovery of corrupt passages mainly occupied him, and his fertile and venturesome habit of emendation exposed his work to disparagement (N. Wecklein in *Berliner philologische Wochenschrift*, 28/20, 1908). Yet a good many of his emendations have been approved by later editors, most recently by Sir Hugh Lloyd-Jones and N. G. Wilson in their *Sophocles* (Oxford

Classical Texts, 1990), in which many of Blaydes's proposals are either accepted in the text or thought worthy of mention in the *apparatus criticus*. Blaydes's own views on the editing of classical texts are to be found in the introduction to his *Sophocles* (vol. 1) and in the preface to *The Philoctetes of Sophocles* (1870). The University of Dublin made him an honorary LLD on 6 July 1892; he was also a PhD of Budapest, and a fellow of the Royal Society of Letters at Athens.

Blaydes made a hobby of homoeopathy and was summoned to Sandringham to advise when the prince of Wales fell ill with typhoid in 1870. He also delighted in music, being an accomplished baritone singer and naming his third son, George Frederick Handel, after the composer. To St Paul's School, where his eldest son was a pupil, he was a munificent benefactor. In 1901 he presented to it the greater part of his classical library, amounting to 1300 volumes. Blaydes died at his home, 19 St Edward's Road, Southsea, Hampshire, on 7 September 1908 and was buried in Brighton cemetery.

W. G. Field, *rev.* Nigel Aston

Sources *The Times* (8 Sept 1908) • *Morning Post* (8 Sept 1908) • *The Pauline* [magazine of St Paul's School, London], 26 (1908), 172–7 • *Oxford Magazine* (29 Oct 1908) • *Northampton Herald* (11 Sept 1908) • N. Aston, 'Frederick Blaydes of Harringworth: a Victorian scholar-parson and his family', *Northamptonshire Past and Present*, 9 (1994–7), 159–69 • Burke, *Gen. GB* • *CGPLA Eng. & Wales* (1908)
Archives Christ Church Oxf., MS estates • Northants. RO • Peterborough Cathedral, diocesan papers | Beds. & Luton ARS • priv. coll., Page-Turner MSS • U. Reading L., letters to his publisher, George Bell, concerning his edition of Sophocles
Likenesses two photographs, *c*.1850–1880, Harringworth Church, vestry • portrait, repro. in *The Pauline*
Wealth at death £3550 11*s*. 9*d*.: probate, 8 Oct 1908, *CGPLA Eng. & Wales*

Blaykling, Ann (*fl.* **1652–1708**), Quaker preacher, was probably born at Draw-well, near Sedbergh in Yorkshire, the daughter of Thomas Blaykling, of whom nothing is known except that he shared a substantial house with his son John (1625–1705). Another son, Richard, was a puritan minister. When George Fox visited Sedbergh in May 1652 he was taken to stay at the Blaykling's' house, and both John and Ann became Quakers as a result of hearing him preach. Believing that she had been called to the ministry, Ann Blaykling began travelling throughout England to spread the message. She was one of a group of early Quakers who came to be known as the First Publishers of Truth, and whose missionary activities frequently got them into trouble with the authorities. In 1654 she and another Quaker woman, Dorothy Benson, were imprisoned briefly in York for interrupting the service in a parish church. Later the same year she travelled to Cambridge, where she was charged with vagrancy and imprisoned for six months. Upon her release in 1655 she travelled to London, where in April she had an audience with Oliver Cromwell, then lord protector. Returning to Norfolk in June 1655 with three Quaker men, she was again arrested and charged with preaching to 'a great concourse of people … to the disturbance of the public peace'. When she was searched the justices found that she was carrying papers 'containing directions for travels into several counties and places in this commonwealth' (Vann, 10). She was committed to the house of correction in Swaffham as a dangerous vagabond.

In 1656 Blaykling was preaching in Cornwall. She was briefly imprisoned in Falmouth, and it was reported that a number of soldiers at Pendennis Castle became Quakers after hearing her. Later that year she returned to Suffolk, and in December was arrested at Haverhill for causing a disturbance at the parish church. According to the warrant issued by Sir Thomas Barnardiston committing her to the gaol in Bury St Edmunds, Blaykling had abused the parish priest, calling him 'hireling and deceiver, greedy dumb dog with many more words of the same nature' (Penney, *Extracts*, 20–21). In 1657 it seems that she was in Bedfordshire, where she disputed in public with the Baptist preacher John Bunyan. According to his scandalized account in *A Vindication of … Some Gospel Truths Opened* (1657), she accused him of using 'conjuration and witchcraft', and advised him to 'throw away the Scriptures' (*Miscellaneous Works*, 1.185).

It seems that about this time Blaykling may have temporarily separated from the Quakers. In his journal George Fox complained that she had 'run out and gathered a company to work on first days and not to pay taxes, but they must pay the impropriators tithes' (*Journal of George Fox*, 2.314). A Quaker account of her written in 1708 acknowledged that she had done good service in her years as a travelling evangelist, but reported that 'for want of watchfullness the enemy prevailed to lead her into singularity and whimsies in several things, by which she run out of unity with Friends for several years' (Penney, *First Publishers*, 252). The same account records that she subsequently returned to the fold, and married a Quaker from Sedbergh, where she was then living. Nothing more is known of Blaykling, but her brief career provides a vivid illustration of the impact made by the socially iconoclastic Quakers in the middle decades of the seventeenth century. Itinerant women Quakers were regarded with particular horror by the authorities; indeed the wife of a Cornish justice was so appalled at what she regarded as Blaykling's impudency that she declared her to be 'no woman but a man' (Reay, 58).

W. R. Owens

Sources N. Penney, ed., *'The first publishers of truth': being early records, now first printed, of the introduction of Quakerism into the counties of England and Wales* (1907) • W. C. Braithwaite, *The beginnings of Quakerism*, ed. H. J. Cadbury, 2nd edn (1955) • *The journal of George Fox*, ed. N. Penney, 2 vols. (1911); repr. (New York, 1973) • N. Penney, ed., *Extracts from state papers relating to Friends, 1654–1672* (1913) • R. T. Vann, *The social development of English Quakerism, 1655–1755* (1969) • B. Reay, *The Quakers and the English Revolution* (1985) • 'A vindication of some gospel-truths opened', in T. L. Underwood, *The miscellaneous works of John Bunyan*, ed. R. Sharrock, 1 (1980)

Blayney, Andrew Thomas, eleventh Baron Blayney (**1770–1834**), army officer, was born at Castle Blayney, co. Monaghan, on 30 November 1770. His father, Cadwallader Blayney, ninth Baron Blayney of Monaghan in the peerage of Ireland (1720–1775), a lieutenant-general in the army, was descended from an old Welsh family which had lived in Ireland since the reign of Elizabeth I. His mother was

Elizabeth Tipping (*d.* 1775), daughter of Thomas Tipping of Beaulieu, co. Louth. Educated at military academies in France and Germany, Blayney succeeded his brother as eleventh Baron Blayney on 2 April 1784 and entered the army as an ensign in the 32nd regiment on 25 November 1789. He became lieutenant in an independent company in 1791, and captain in the 38th on 28 February 1792. Having raised part of the new regiment in Ireland, he was gazetted major in the 89th foot on 3 December 1793 and served with it during the campaign in Flanders in 1794–5, gaining special mention after the action at Boxtel in September 1794. His regiment was then ordered to accompany Sir Ralph Abercromby to the West Indies; but the terrible storm, known as 'Christian's storm' from the name of the admiral, drove the transports back. On 3 May 1796 he became brevet lieutenant-colonel, purchasing that substantive rank in the 89th on 1 March 1798. On 5 July 1796 he married Lady Mabella Alexander (1775–1854), eldest daughter of James, first earl of Caledon. They had three children: Cadwallader Davis (*b.* 21 Feb 1803, *d.* 1874), Anne, and Charlotte Sophia.

In 1797–8 Blayney was actively engaged in subduing unrest in Ireland, culminating in defeat of the rebels at Vinegar Hill. In January 1799 the 89th was ordered to form part of the garrison of Minorca, which had just been captured by Sir Charles Stuart. Following Rear-Admiral Lord Nelson's recommendation that Sicily be protected from French attack, Blayney went on to Messina in command of the 89th, arriving on 18 March 1799. The regiment then joined reinforcements, who landed in St Paul's Bay, Malta, on 9 December 1799, to tighten the siege of French troops in Valletta. With little action likely, Blayney left for northern Italy, where he witnessed the exploits of General Suvorov's army, about which he sent home an admirable account; but he returned to Malta in time to plant the English flag on the ramparts of Ricasoli, on 4 September 1800. The 89th then took part in Abercromby's expedition to Egypt, being present, though not engaged, at the battle of Alexandria on 21 March 1801. The regiment advanced with the main body to capture Cairo and remain as part of its garrison until the British expeditionary force withdrew from the country. Blayney received the approbation of Lieutenant-General J. H. Hutchinson (commander after Abercromby's death) for his conduct during the campaign. The 89th landed at Cork on 28 January 1802. Following the peace of Amiens on 27 March, it was reduced to peacetime establishment and remained in Ireland for the next three years. When Lieutenant-Colonel William Stewart, his senior, left the regiment on 14 November 1802, Blayney formally obtained command.

Promoted colonel on 1 January 1805, Blayney sailed in November with the 89th (who became known as Blayney's Bloodhounds) to join Lord Cathcart's expedition to Hanover, arriving on the River Weser on 5 January 1806 to discover cancellation of the enterprise after Napoleon's victory at the battle of Austerlitz. *En route*, Blayney had left his troopship off the Thames to visit London, and he returned to find that it had resumed passage, which meant that he had to catch up in another vessel. After a short spell in England, on 14 September 1806 the 89th left Ramsgate for South America, but put into Portsmouth due to a serious outbreak of ophthalmia. It left again, on 29 February 1807, and arrived off Montevideo after Lieutenant-General John Whitelock had surrendered; it was, therefore, ordered to the Cape of Good Hope. Three ships became waterlogged and put into Saldanha Bay on the African coast, and Blayney had to march their troops 90 miles to Cape Town over arid wasteland in extreme heat. Survival of the bulk of the party was ascribed to Blayney's determined leadership. While he was away on active service Blayney, a strong Orangeman, was MP for Old Sarum (1806–7), the notorious burgage borough which his brother-in-law, the second earl of Caledon, had bought in 1802.

Blayney soon found that there was no fighting to be expected at the Cape; he returned to England and was sent to Cadiz, then under siege, in July 1810. He rapidly moved on to Gibraltar, where he found the 2nd battalion 89th regiment, and was promoted major-general on 25 July. He inspected it and reported unfavourably on its discipline. General Campbell, governor of Gibraltar, soon sent him—with a mixed force of 300 British (four companies of the 89th), 800 Spanish, and 500 German, Italian, and Polish deserters from the French army—to make a descent on Malaga. Blayney disembarked near Fuengirola on 14 October 1810, and was joined by a few Andalusian guerrillas. His force of 1400 men now spoke five languages but had no artillery. Nevertheless, in vain, he summoned the garrison of Fuengirola to surrender, as he learned of an approaching relief column under General Sebastini. Instead of re-embarking, he decided to engage Fuengirola again and to land artillery from the accompanying gunboats under cover of darkness before Sebastini could intervene. Two batteries were brought ashore during the night and, despite heavy infantry casualties the previous day, Blayney once more opened fire on Fuengirola. A sortie by the garrison on his left dispersed Spanish troops, who abandoned their artillery. He gathered the 89th successfully to retake the guns, recording: 'In advancing to the charge my horse was wounded, and soon after killed by a second shot, so I was obliged to charge on foot' (Cunliffe, 133). Thus dismounted, he could not verify reports that a body of Spanish had been seen. Belatedly, he realized that Sebastini had, in fact, arrived, and he promptly charged the enemy, though still on foot. Many of his former French troops redeserted, and he and several British survivors were captured. He recorded that he was roughly treated by Polish infantry ('they tore my cloaths, rifled my pockets, and attempted to pull off my epaulettes'; ibid.) until a French officer appeared. His conduct of the whole affair, however, was later condemned as foolhardy and impetuous.

Lord Blayney's passage as a prisoner of war through Spain, and his imprisonment in France at Verdun, Bitche, and Guéret, provided him with a novel experience. In his two-volume *Narrative of a forced journey through Spain and France as a prisoner of war in the years 1810 to 1814* (1814) he shows great powers of observation, describing vividly how the Spanish people lived while under French occupation. During his captivity he was entrusted with funds for the relief of the poorer English prisoners. His health was now impaired, however, and he saw no further military service, though he was promoted lieutenant-general on 12 August 1819. Blayney died suddenly at Bilton's Hotel, Sackville Street, Dublin, on 8 April 1834 and was buried at Castle Blayney, co. Monaghan. He had left the estate neglected, and it was sold to Henry Thomas Hope, Disraeli's friend and patron. His son became the twelfth baron, but never married, and at his death, on 18 January 1874, the barony became extinct. JOHN SWEETMAN

Sources *Army List* • M. Cunliffe, *The royal Irish fusiliers, 1793–1950* (1952) • Burke, *Peerage* (1857) • R. Brinckman, *Historical record of the eighty-ninth, Princess Victoria's regiment* (1988) • H. E. D. Harris, *The royal Irish fusiliers* (1972) • *Outline history of the royal Irish fusiliers (Princess Victoria's)* (1955) • GEC, *Peerage*, new edn • M. G. Hinton, 'Blayney, Andrew Thomas, 11th Baron Blayney [1] (1770–1834)', HoP, *Commons* • R. G. Thorne, 'Old Sarum, Wiltshire', HoP, *Commons* • *DNB*

Archives PRO NIre., letters to first and second earls of Caledon, D 2431–2433

Likenesses I. R. Havell, senior and R. Havell, junior, group portrait, aquatint etching, pubd 1823 (after J. P. Haverty; after J. R. Reilly, The public entry of George W. King of England into Dublin 17th August 1821)

Blayney, Benjamin (1727/8–1801), Hebraist and Church of England clergyman, may have been baptized at St Swithin's, Worcester, on 18 February 1727, and may have been the son of Thomas and Betty Blayney. He was educated at Worcester College, Oxford, where he matriculated aged eighteen on 1 July 1746; he graduated BA (1750) and MA (1753). Afterwards he became a fellow, and eventually vice-principal, of Hertford College, and took the degree of BD in 1768. He was employed by the university's Clarendon Press to prepare a corrected edition of the Authorized Version of the Bible. This appeared in 1769 and was widely praised for its accuracy. Unfortunately a large part of the impression was destroyed in a fire which took place at the bible warehouse in Paternoster Row, London, though copies can still be found in the Bodleian Library, Oxford, and the British Library, London. Blayney received much assistance in his Hebrew studies from the celebrated William Newcome, later archbishop of Armagh, also a fellow of Hertford, to whom he dedicated several of his works. In 1775 he published *A dissertation by way of inquiry into the true import and application of the vision related, Dan. ix. 24 to the end, usually called Daniel's prophecy of seventy weeks*. This work attracted considerable attention, and was translated into German by Johann David Michaelis. (A corrected edition was published by the author in 1797.) In 1784 Blayney published new translations of Jeremiah and Lamentations, and in 1786 and 1788 two sermons, *The Sign Given to Ahaz* and *Christ the Greater Glory of the Temple*. In 1787 he was appointed regius professor of Hebrew at Oxford, and in the same year was made a canon of Christ Church and received the degree of DD. In 1790 he published an edition of the Hebrew–Samaritan Pentateuch, transcribed in ordinary Hebrew characters, with critical notes. His last production was a new translation of the prophecy of Zechariah (1797).

Like his friend Archbishop Newcome, and many other eminent biblical scholars of the period in England, Blayney did not escape a reputation for heterodoxy, and was the object of several very acrimonious attacks, from which he defended himself with exemplary fairness and courtesy. He died at his rectory of Poulshot, Wiltshire, on 20 September 1801. By his will he directed that his unpublished writings, among them 'A new version of the Psalms', 'Critical comment on the Psalms', and 'Notes on Isaiah', after being submitted to the judgement of his friend and patron Shute Barrington, bishop of Durham, should be deposited in the archiepiscopal library at Lambeth. His will also requested that he be buried at Christ Church Cathedral, Oxford, with his late daughter from his marriage to Jane (*d.* before 1801) (will, PRO, PROB 11/1363).

HENRY BRADLEY, *rev.* PHILIP CARTER

Sources Foster, *Alum. Oxon.* • *GM*, 1st ser., 71 (1801), 1054 • *GM*, 1st ser., 73 (1803), 1108 • B. Blayney, *A dissertation by way of inquiry into the true import and application of the vision related, Dan. ix. 24 to the end, usually called Daniel's prophecy of seventy weeks* (1775), preface • *IGI* • PRO, PROB 11/1363, fols. 306*r*–309*v*

Archives LPL, papers | LPL, corresp. with Samuel Horsley [copies]

Blease, (Walter) Lyon (1884–1963), barrister and civic activist, was born on 30 May 1884 at 5 Beech Street, Fairfield, Liverpool, the second son and second of three children of Walter Blease (*c.*1853–1940), chartered accountant, and his wife, Mary Cecilia (*d.* 1936), daughter of James Harvey of Manchester and his wife, Anne. Lyon, as he was known, grew up in comfortable circumstances, a devoted son of affectionate parents. His father, whose family were Baptists, worked strenuously to expand an accounting firm established by his father and an uncle. Mrs Blease's family were Presbyterian and committed to temperance, free trade, and other Liberal causes. Both parents were active in charities. Mrs Blease served as a poor-law guardian.

Brought up a Presbyterian, Lyon Blease attended Parkfield School, Liverpool (*c.*1891–1899), and was then sent to Sedbergh School but soon returned home with a knee injury. He then went to Shrewsbury School (1900–02). An able student, he was made praeposter and head of house, but was ill at ease with his peers. Principled and prudish, he was treated with contempt. Devastated, he feigned illness, neglected his schoolwork, and contemplated suicide. Finally, his father agreed that he should not return to school. By then, however, Blease had acquired an enduring commitment to serious reading and self-study. History and literature were his favoured subjects, but he was also interested in the arts. Intensely high-minded, he was bent both on self-improvement and on preparing himself for public life. At a time when he was shifting to agnosticism, he found a sense of ethical purpose in the prospect of public service.

At his father's urging, Blease read for a law degree and the bar at the University of Liverpool, keeping terms at Lincoln's Inn. He received his LLB and was called to the bar in 1906. Awarded a studentship at the bar final examination (1906), he took an LLM at Liverpool in 1908. He practised as a Chancery lawyer in Liverpool, and in 1910 was appointed lecturer in the law and custom of the constitution at Liverpool University.

More drawn to politics and letters than the law, Blease campaigned on behalf of temperance, free trade, and other Liberal causes before the First World War and in the January 1910 general election unsuccessfully contested Lancashire's Chorley division for the Liberals. A strong suffragist, he was president of the Liverpool committee of the Men's League for Women's Suffrage from 1908. Together with his occasional writings, Blease's *The Emancipation of English Women* (1910) and *A Short History of English Liberalism* (1913) brought his views before a wider public. An exponent of the new Liberalism, he urged state welfare provision to enable individuals to develop their abilities and contribute to the common good.

During the First World War Blease served with hospital units in Serbia, Russia, and Romania. In Serbia he worked as a gentleman orderly in a medical mission led by the surgeon James Berry, co-authoring an account, *The Story of a Red Cross Unit in Serbia* (1916). Here Blease met his future wife, Harriott Davies (1884–1972), a spirited trained nurse. Both later served at the Anglo-Russian hospital in Petrograd. With Russia's military collapse, members of the staff travelled east to Japan.

Blease and Davies were married in Tokyo in 1918 and remained in Japan for a year. He worked as assistant editor of the *New East* and with Harriott's help prepared his study *Suvorof* (1920), using material gathered in Russia. The couple had three daughters, and Blease proved very solicitous for their education.

From 1919 to 1949 Blease was Queen Victoria professor of law at Liverpool University, serving twice as dean of the law faculty (1919–25 and 1942–5). He combined the appointment with practice at the bar. Consistently with the faculty's emphasis on professional training rather than on research, his legal scholarship was limited to textbooks on conveyancing. Eloquent and charming, he was public orator of the university from 1931 to 1949.

Throughout his life, Blease remained a tireless champion of humane and liberal causes. His concerns ranged from the university's ban on married women staff (which he vigorously opposed) to work for Jewish refugees. In the general elections of 1945 and 1950 he contested Liverpool's East Toxteth and Garston divisions for the Liberals, again unsuccessfully. An accomplished, many-sided man, he used his talents to enrich the life of his community. He lectured on literary and other subjects to diverse groups (including the Workers' Educational Association); participated in radio broadcasts and amateur theatricals; served as chairman of the Liverpool Philharmonic Society, the Merseyside Film Institute Society, and the Liverpool executive council of the National Health Service (1952–60).

Blease's distinction rested not on any one achievement but on many good works. Although the parliamentary career he dreamed of eluded him, his life lent substance to his liberal vision, linking self-development with civic virtue. He died of coronary thrombosis on 12 April 1963 at his home, 12 Eaton Road, Cressington Park, Liverpool, and was cremated in Liverpool.

JOYCE SENDERS PEDERSEN

Sources *WWW*, 1961–1970 • U. Lpool, W. Lyon Blease papers [incl. diary and autobiographical fragment transcript] • A. Allan, 'Biographical note and guide to W. Lyon Blease papers', U. Lpool • private information (2004) [Jill Webber, daughter; Alexander Webber, son-in-law; Jane MacLachlan (Mrs Jacken), daughter; Krista Cowman, department of history, University of York] • *The Times* (15 April 1963) • T. Kelly, *For advancement of learning: the University of Liverpool, 1881–1981* (1981) • *Centenary brochure, 1892–93–1992–93, faculty of law, University of Liverpool* [n.d.] • b. cert. • d. cert.

Archives British Red Cross Museum and Archives, Guildford, Surrey, letters, slides of Russia and Serbia and photograph negatives, and other memorabilia • U. Lpool L., papers, memorabilia, etc. | NAM, collection of pamphlets on the First World War • priv. coll., corresp. with his future wife | SOUND U. Lpool, recorded talks

Likenesses Lethsome & Sons, group portrait, photograph, 1908, U. Lpool • photograph, 1910, U. Lpool; repro. in *To the electors of the Chorley parliamentary division* [Blease election manifesto] • photograph, pubd 1945, U. Lpool; repro. in *Blease's election address to the constituents of East Toxteth* • F. T. Copnall?, oils, U. Lpool

Wealth at death £40,581 2s. 0d.: probate, 17 Sept 1963, *CGPLA Eng. & Wales*

Blech, Harry [*formerly* Hirsch] (**1909–1999**), conductor and violinist, was born in the East End of London in June 1909, the son of Henri Blech, provisions merchant and commercial traveller, and his wife, Sophie Stock. Shortly after he was born his father went to South America without registering the birth. On his return, to appear not to have broken the law, he registered it as 2 March 1910, the date which appears in most reference books. Harry Blech (as he was always known) went to school at the Central London Foundation and began to play the violin at the age of nine. Two years later he was awarded a scholarship to study with Sarah Fennings at Trinity College of Music, London. On her advice he attended two of Otakar Ševčík's courses at Pišek, Czechoslovakia. When he was eighteen, in 1927, he went to the Royal Manchester College of Music to study with Arthur Catterall. While there his performances of Beethoven's violin sonata in C minor, op. 30 no. 2, with Alan Rawsthorne as pianist, led the veteran cello professor Carl Fuchs to declare that 'they could play it anywhere' (Kennedy).

In 1929 Blech joined the Hallé Orchestra, and in the following year he became the youngest member of the first violins in the newly formed BBC Symphony Orchestra, which was led by his former teacher Catterall. He played in the orchestra for six years. During this period he formed his own spare-time string quartet in 1933 with David Martin (second violin), Frederick Riddle (viola), and Willem de Mont (cello). They gave their first Wigmore Hall concert in 1935. On 18 December in the same year he married Enid Marion Lessing (1913–1977), daughter of Rudolf Lessing, chemist. They had a son and two daughters.

After leaving the BBC orchestra in 1936, Blech formed a permanent quartet with Edward Silverman, Douglas Thompson, and William Pleeth. This ensemble rapidly became acknowledged as one of the best in Britain, along with the Griller Quartet, and gave first performances of works by Rawsthorne, Benjamin Frankel, and others. With the outbreak of the Second World War the quartet was disrupted. Silverman died of a heart condition, Thompson was killed learning to fly, and Pleeth joined the army. Blech went into the RAF, where he played in the RAF Symphony Orchestra at Uxbridge. Among his colleagues were David Martin (leader), Frederick Grinke and Leonard Hirsch (violins), Dennis Brain (horn), and Gareth Morris (flute). He kept the quartet in being with Max Salpeter, Keith Cummings, and Douglas Cameron.

Blech's conducting career began in 1942 when he took over at the last minute for one of the RAF concerts and was then invited by Myra Hess to present a series of serenades at her National Gallery concerts. He called on some of the wind players in the RAF orchestra, called them the London Wind Players, and had a sell-out success with Mozart's serenade in B♭ (K361). 'Even conductors wrote to me saying what a pleasure it was to hear a wind group play so beautifully in tune', he recalled. 'In those days there were no wind bands at all' (*The Independent*). In 1946 he formed the London Symphonic Players, comprising students from the colleges and some talented amateurs. Their first concert, at the Kingsway Hall, was another sell-out. His own violin playing became less frequent because of an ailment affecting the nerve-ends in his fingers which made it impossible for him to press down on the strings. He disbanded the Blech String Quartet in 1950 (the second violinist since 1946 having been Lionel Bentley).

In 1948 the pianist Dorothea Braus asked Blech to conduct some Mozart concertos with her at the Wigmore Hall. This led to the formation of the London Mozart Players, with Max Salpeter as leader. Its inaugural concert, a Mozart programme, was on 11 February 1949. To underwrite its activities, Blech formed the Haydn–Mozart Society as parent body. The London Mozart Players soon became an indispensable part of London's musical life, calling on soloists such as Dennis Brain, Archie Camden, Denis Matthews, and Nina Milkina. The orchestra took part in the first week of concerts at the new Royal Festival Hall in 1951. Later it transferred its concerts to the Queen Elizabeth Hall and became resident ensemble at the Fairfield Halls, Croydon. It gave 100 concerts a season and in 1956 made its first overseas tour. Blech's first marriage was by then foundering, and it ended in divorce in 1957. On 6 September in the same year he married Marion Rose Manley (*b.* 1931), pianist and daughter of Richard Manley, manager of a sewing machine company. They had a son and three daughters.

Blech was always looking for new talent and had a remarkable ear for it. Among his 'finds' were Barry Tuckwell (horn), Gervase de Peyer (clarinet), Christopher Hyde-Smith (flute), Rodney Friend and György Pauk (violins), Marisa Robles (harp), and Stephen Kovacevich and Imogen Cooper (pianists). He also encouraged young conductors, among them Andrew Davis, John Eliot Gardiner, and Roger Norrington, all later knighted. He conducted several recordings for HMV and Decca in the 1960s, including a classic account of Goldmark's violin concerto with Nathan Milstein. He also recorded Mozart's bassoon concerto with Archie Camden, and the *Sinfonia concertante* for violin and viola (K364) with Norbert Brainin and Peter Schidlof.

Blech retired as conductor of the London Mozart Players in 1984, becoming conductor laureate and handing over to Jane Glover. The orchestra celebrated his eightieth 'official' birthday at the Barbican in 1990, and he conducted

Harry Blech (1909–1999), by Elliott & Fry, 1958

for the last time at Croydon in 1992. Although frail, he attended the London Mozart Players' fiftieth anniversary concert at the Festival Hall in 1999. A big, ungainly man, he used a conducting style that was anything but elegant—Sir Adrian Boult once told him that he looked as if he was chasing a bus. But it was effective, thanks to his outstanding musicianship. His players, like his audiences, adored him. He remained a loyal friend to many of them, ever ready to help if they fell on hard times. He could laugh at himself, a rare trait among conductors, and was a splendid raconteur. He died of heart failure at 35A Arterberry Road, Wimbledon, on 9 May 1999 and was cremated at Golders Green on 14 May. He was survived by his second wife, Marion, their four children, and the three children of his first marriage. MICHAEL KENNEDY

Sources *The Times* (11 May 1999) • *Daily Telegraph* (11 May 1999) • *The Guardian* (12 May 1999) • *The Independent* (12 May 1999) • M. Kennedy, *The history of the Royal Manchester College of Music, 1893–1972* (1971) • *WWW* • personal knowledge (2004) • private information (2004) • b. cert. • m. certs. • d. cert.

Archives SOUND BL NSA, some London Mozart Players recordings

Likenesses Elliott & Fry, photograph, 1958, NPG [*see illus.*] • photograph, 1990, repro. in *Daily Telegraph* • photograph, repro. in *The Times* • photograph, repro. in *The Guardian* • photograph, repro. in *The Independent*

Wealth at death £1,006,743—gross; £1,001,438—net: probate, 22 Oct 1999, *CGPLA Eng. & Wales*

Bleddri (*d.* 1022/3), bishop in south-east Wales, was associated in later sources with Llandaff. Claims of his election as bishop by the kings, clergy, and people of Morgannwg, his investiture by Æthelred II, his consecration by Ælfric, archbishop of Canterbury, and the date assigned to it (983) are not reliable. The tale of English royal and ecclesiastical involvement is likely to have been produced at Llandaff at some later period, probably the early twelfth century, as part of that see's attempts to protect itself from the temporal and spiritual ambitions of St David's. Three important grants of land to the bishop of Llandaff are attributed to the time of his episcopate but cannot originally have been made to Bleddri. T. F. TOUT, *rev.* K. L. MAUND

Sources J. G. Evans and J. Rhys, eds., *The text of the Book of Llan Dâv reproduced from the Gwysaney manuscript* (1893) • W. Davies, 'The consecration of the bishops of Llandaff in the tenth and eleventh centuries', *BBCS*, 26 (1974–6), 53–73 • W. Davies, *The Llandaff Charters* (1979) • K. L. Maund, *Ireland, Wales, and England in the eleventh century* (1991)

Bleddyn ap Cynfyn (*d.* 1075), king of Gwynedd and of Powys, was the son of Cynfyn ap Gwerystan, probably a nobleman from Powys, and Angharad, daughter of *Maredudd ab Owain (*d.* 999), ruler of Deheubarth. According to English sources Edward the Confessor granted Bleddyn and his brother Rhiwallon ap Cynfyn [*see below*] the lands of their half-brother, *Gruffudd ap Llywelyn, after the latter's death as ruler of all Wales in August 1063, in return for promises of service and tribute. In the early years of his reign Bleddyn was probably challenged by Gruffudd ap Llywelyn's sons Maredudd and Ithel, for it was only after their deaths in 1069, as a result of the battle of Mechain (in which Rhiwallon was also killed), that, in the words of the Welsh chronicle *Brut y tywysogyon*, 'Bleddyn ap Cynfyn held Gwynedd and Powys' (*Brut: Hergest*, 27). In the meantime he had devastated English settlements in Archenfield (Ergyng) during Edward the Confessor's reign, while after the Norman conquest he joined Eadric the Wild in an attack on Herefordshire in 1067 and allied with earls Edwin and Morcar in their revolt against William I in 1068. After 1071 Bleddyn was the target of Norman aggression in north Wales, for Orderic Vitalis records that he was ambushed by Robert of Rhuddlan, who 'made him fly abandoning rich booty' (Ordericus Vitalis, *Eccl. hist.*, 4.145).

Bleddyn's rule ended in 1075 when he was killed by Rhys ab Owain, ruler of Deheubarth, as a result of, in the words of the *Brut*, 'the treachery of the evil-spirited rulers and chief men of Ystrad Tywi'. The same chronicle claims that Bleddyn had, like Gruffudd ap Llywelyn before him, ruled 'the whole kingdom of the Britons', and also praised him as 'the gentlest and most merciful of kings' (*Brut: Hergest*, 29). His posthumous reputation was also promoted by the medieval Welsh law books, for he is one of only two Welsh rulers to whom they attribute changes to the native law of Wales following its alleged reform by Hywel Dda (*fl.* 903–950). Bleddyn fathered five sons and up to four daughters with, according to later medieval pedigrees, four different partners, two of whom are identified as Haer, daughter of Gillyn, and an unnamed daughter of Brochwel ap Moelyn of Twrcelyn, Anglesey. The sons and grandsons of Bleddyn achieved a wide hegemony in late eleventh- and early twelfth-century Wales, and the dynasty he founded survived in Powys until the fourteenth century.

Rhiwallon ap Cynfyn (*d.* 1069) was the brother of Bleddyn ap Cynfyn, with whom he shared authority until his death in the battle of Mechain in 1069. Rhiwallon had two sons, one of whom, Meilyr, was killed at the battle of Mynydd Carn in 1081; one of his two daughters, Gwladus, married *Rhys ap Tewdwr, king of Deheubarth (*d.* 1093).

Cadwgan ap Bleddyn (*d.* 1111), son of Bleddyn ap Cynfyn and an unidentified mother, appears to have inherited a share of Powys after his father's death in 1075. Cadwgan first appears in the Welsh chronicles in 1088 when he joined his brothers Madog and Rhiryd in expelling Rhys ap Tewdwr from Deheubarth, but Rhys soon returned and defeated the sons of Bleddyn at Llech-y-crau; Madog and Rhiryd were killed but Cadwgan escaped and returned after Rhys's death to plunder Dyfed towards the beginning of May 1093. Cadwgan played a leading role in the Welsh revolt against the Normans which began in spring 1094, defeating a Norman army sent against Gwynedd. However, in 1098 Cadwgan was forced to flee to Ireland together with Gruffudd ap Cynan (*d.* 1137) in the face of an attack on Gwynedd and Anglesey led by the earls of Chester and Shrewsbury, and on his return the following year he made peace with the Normans and was granted a portion of Powys and also Ceredigion, presumably under the overlordship of Robert de Bellême, the new earl of Shrewsbury. Although Cadwgan, together with his brothers Iorwerth and Maredudd, supported Robert's revolt in 1102, he retained his lands in Powys and Ceredigion after the earl's fall and indeed increased his power following the imprisonment of both Maredudd and Iorwerth.

However, Cadwgan was unable to consolidate his position because of difficulties created by members of his family, especially his son Owain [*see below*]. After Cadwgan had held a great feast for the leading men of his land in Christmas 1109 (or perhaps 1108), Owain abducted Nest, wife of Gerald of Windsor. As a result, Cadwgan was expelled from his lands by his nephews Madog and Ithel ap Rhiryd at the instigation of Henry I's representative at Shrewsbury, Richard de Belmeis (*d.* 1127). Fleeing initially to an Irish ship in the Dyfi estuary Cadwgan then hid in Powys until he made peace with Henry I, who later allowed him to redeem Ceredigion for £100 on condition that he give no support to Owain. However, following Owain's killing of William of Brabant in 1110, Henry I dispossessed Cadwgan of Ceredigion and granted it to Gilbert de Clare (*d.* 1117). After the murder of Iorwerth ap Bleddyn in 1111 the king granted Powys to Cadwgan, but the latter was almost immediately killed by Madog ap Rhiryd at Welshpool.

Cadwgan had at least seven sons and possibly one daughter with at least five different partners, among whom were Gwenllian, daughter of Gruffudd ap Cynan, and a daughter of Picot of Sai, lord of Clun.

Sir Owain ap Cadwgan (*d.* 1116), son of Cadwgan ap Bleddyn and an unidentified mother, destroyed Gerald of Windsor's castle at Cenarth Bychan after Christmas 1109 (or 1108) and abducted Gerald's wife, *Nest (*b.* before 1092, *d.* *c.*1130), daughter of Rhys ap Tewdwr, with whom Owain subsequently had two sons. The immediate result of this action was the expulsion of Owain and his father from their lands and the flight of the former to Ireland, whence he returned in 1110 to Powys and raided Norman lands in alliance with his cousin, Madog ap Rhiryd, until they were expelled from Powys by their uncle, Iorwerth ap Bleddyn. Owain fled to Ireland again later that year after Henry I had confiscated Ceredigion from his father in reprisal for Owain's killing of the Flemish leader, William of Brabant, but was allowed to return and hold the greater part of Powys after the deaths of Iorwerth and Cadwgan in 1111. Two years later Owain blinded Madog ap Rhiryd and granted the latter's portion of Powys to Maredudd ap Bleddyn. Henry I's Welsh campaign of 1114 was directed partly against Owain, who was forced to submit to the king and accompanied him to Normandy, whence he returned, having been knighted, the following year. Owain's turbulent life ended in 1116, when he fell victim near Carmarthen to the vengeance of the Flemings of Rhos and Gerald of Windsor while campaigning at the king's behest against Gruffudd ap Rhys of Deheubarth (*d.* 1137).

Iorwerth ap Bleddyn (*d.* 1111), a son of Bleddyn ap Cynfyn and, according to later medieval pedigrees, a daughter of Brochwel, supported Robert de Bellême in his revolt against Henry I in 1102; however, during the siege of Bridgnorth later that year he was won over to Henry's side by gifts and by promises of the Welsh lands of Bellême and his brother, Arnulf of Montgomery. His defection played an important part in ending the revolt, after which he soon seized and imprisoned his brother Maredudd and then granted Ceredigion and a portion of Powys to his brother Cadwgan. However, Henry refused to grant Iorwerth the lands he had promised him in and around Dyfed and in 1103 had him tried at Shrewsbury and imprisoned. Iorwerth was released in 1110 and restored to his portion of Powys. The decision to free him was probably prompted by the threat posed by Owain ap Cadwgan, who had joined forces in Powys with his cousin, Madog ap Rhiryd: Iorwerth soon expelled Owain and Madog from his territory. In revenge Madog had Iorwerth killed in Caereinion in 1111 with the help of Llywarch ap Trahaearn of Arwystli.

Maredudd ap Bleddyn (*d.* 1132), king of Powys, was the son of Bleddyn ap Cynfyn and, according to later medieval pedigrees, Haer, daughter of Gillyn. After supporting Robert de Bellême's revolt in 1102, he was soon seized by his brother Iorwerth, who had him imprisoned. However, Maredudd escaped in 1107 and co-operated with his nephew Owain ap Cadwgan, after the latter received Iorwerth ap Bleddyn's share of Powys in 1111; two years later Maredudd captured Madog ap Rhiryd and received the latter's share of the kingdom from Owain. After Owain's death in 1116 Maredudd was the most prominent member of Bleddyn ap Cynfyn's line. Although forced to submit and pay a huge tribute of cattle to Henry I after the latter's campaign against him in 1121, Maredudd survived and exploited the feuding between his nephews—one of whom, Llywelyn ab Owain ap Cadwgan, he ordered to be blinded and castrated in 1130—so as to establish a hegemony over the whole of Powys by his death in 1132. He was succeeded by *Madog ap Maredudd (*d.* 1160), one of three sons he had with his wife, Hunydd, daughter of Einudd. In addition he had another son, Iorwerth Goch, with Cristin, daughter of Bledrus, and fathered up to four other children whose mothers are unknown. HUW PRYCE

Sources T. Jones, ed. and trans., *Brut y tywysogyon, or, The chronicle of the princes: Peniarth MS 20* (1952) • T. Jones, ed. and trans., *Brut y tywysogyon, or, The chronicle of the princes: Red Book of Hergest*, 2nd edn (1973) • J. Williams ab Ithel, ed., *Annales Cambriae*, Rolls Series, 20 (1860) • *ASC* • John of Worcester, *Chron.* • Ordericus Vitalis, *Eccl. hist.* • P. C. Bartrum, ed., *Welsh genealogies, AD 300–1400*, 8 vols. (1974) • J. E. Lloyd, 'Wales and the coming of the Normans (1039–1093)', *Transactions of the Honourable Society of Cymmrodorion* (1899–1900), 122–79 • J. E. Lloyd, *A history of Wales from the earliest times to the Edwardian conquest*, 3rd edn, 2 vols. (1939); repr. (1988) • R. R. Davies, *Conquest, coexistence, and change: Wales, 1063–1415*, History of Wales, 2 (1987) • K. L. Maund, *Ireland, Wales, and England in the eleventh century* (1991) • R. R. Davies, 'Henry I and Wales', *Studies in medieval history presented to R. H. C. Davis*, ed. H. Mayr-Harting and R. I. Moore (1985), 133–47

Bleddyn Fardd (*fl.* *c.*1220–*c.*1285). *See under* Gogynfeirdd (*act.* *c.*1080–1285).

Bleddyn [Blethin], **William** (*d.* 1590), bishop of Llandaff, was born at Shirenewton Court, Monmouthshire, the son of Griffith Bleddyn (*fl.* *c*.1510–*c*.1560), freeholder, a descendant of Hywel Dda, king of Deheubarth (900–950), and a distant relative of Morgan Bleddyn, abbot of Llantarnam. His mother was Elizabeth (*fl.* *c*.1510–*c*.1565), daughter of Thomas ab Ieuan Hywel. In 1559 he was appointed rector of Sunningwell, Berkshire, and, in 1560, non-resident rector of Rogiet, Monmouthshire, and canon of St Dubricius, Llandaff Cathedral. In 1562 he graduated BCL from New Inn Hall or Broadgates Hall, Oxford, and became prebendary of Osbaldwick in York Cathedral. His first wife was Anne (*d.* 1589), daughter of Robert Young of Pembrokeshire and niece of Thomas Young, bishop of St David's (1559–61) and archbishop of York (1561–8).

Bleddyn was licensed to preach and became resident rector of Rogiet (1563–70) and archdeacon of Brecon (collated on 25 or 27 July 1567). On 13 April 1575 he was elected bishop of Llandaff, confirmed on 16 April and consecrated on 17 April by Archbishop Parker. The temporalities of the see were restored to him on 2 May. Owing to the poverty of his diocese he retained his offices and preferments. As bishop, he attempted to reform the canons and vicars-choral of his cathedral and to protect its property. In a letter of 30 January 1576 Bleddyn severely admonished the prebendaries for seriously neglecting their duties. He reminded them of the ordinances and customs of Llandaff and declared that if the prebendaries had governed the church according to those rules its condition would not have been so critical. He sternly opposed Catholic recusancy, a major threat to the Elizabethan church, and attempted to suppress it with great vigour.

Although Bleddyn was an ardent reformer he was also eager to advance his own interests. He purchased the manor of Bisham, near Caer-went, made his sons Morgan and Philemon prebendaries of Llandaff, and installed Philemon as vicar of Caer-went and rector of Shirenewton. Bleddyn spoke Welsh and patronized the bards, tributes being paid to him and his wife by Dafydd Benwyn; he himself composed an *englyn* (stanza) praising Lewys Dwnn, the famous genealogist. Bleddyn's first wife died in 1589 and on 14 October of the same year he married his second wife, Anne, who survived him. He died on 15 October 1590 and was buried in the chancel in Matharn church, near the bishop's palace. His will was proved on 21 May 1591.

J. Gwynfor Jones

Sources Jesus College, Oxford, MSS 13; 21a; 75b; 112a; 238b · NL Wales, MS 5270, 98b · Wood, *Ath. Oxon.*, new edn, 2.827 · *Fasti Angl.* (Hardy), 1.311; 2.208, 252, 266 · will, PRO, PROB 11/77, sig. 42 · L. Thomas, *The Reformation in the old diocese of Llandaff* (1930), 132–53 · B. Willis, *A survey of the cathedral church of Llandaff* (1719), 65–6, 97 · J. Jones, ed., *Monmouthshire wills proved in the prerogative court of Canterbury, 1560–1601* (1997), 155–7 · J. A. Bradney, *A history of Monmouthshire*, 4/1 (1933); facs. edn (1994), 65–6 · J. A. Bradney, 'The speech of William Blethin, bishop of Llandaff, and the customs and ordinances of the church of Llandaff', *Y Cymmrodor*, 31 (1921), 240–64 · G. Williams, *Wales and the Reformation* (1997) · J. G. Jones, 'The Reformation bishops of Llandaff, 1558–1601', *Morgannwg*, 32 (1989), 38–69

Wealth at death approx. £600–£700

Bledisloe. For this title name *see* Bathurst, Charles, first Viscount Bledisloe (1867–1958).

Bledri Ddoeth. *See* Bleddri (*d.* 1022/3).

Bleeck, Arthur Henry (1829/30–1877), orientalist, was for some time in the British Museum, where his remarkable linguistic capacity rendered him very useful. He had a wide knowledge of both oriental and European languages. He afterwards went out to the East during the Crimean War, and until the conclusion of peace held a post in connection with the Land Transport Corps at Sinope on the Black Sea, where his co-author, William Burckhardt Barker, was also stationed.

Refused readmission to the British Museum on his return to England, Bleeck worked for several years for a prominent Parsi merchant, Muncherjee Hormusjee Cana, who employed him to prepare an English version of the Avesta, the religious books of the Parsis, who were Zoroastrians, from an existing German translation. He performed the task well, publishing the work in 1864 in three volumes.

Bleeck's other works are *A Practical Grammar of the Turkish Language* (with W. Burckhardt Barker, 1854), *A Concise Grammar of the Persian Language* (1857), and *Catalogue of the Napoleon Library in the Possession of Mr. Joshua Bates* (1858).

Bleeck died of alcoholism at his home, 56 Bevington Road, Kensington, on 27 January 1877. He left at least one daughter but nothing more is known of his private life.

Thompson Cooper, *rev.* Elizabeth Baigent

Sources Boase, *Mod. Eng. biog.* · Allibone, *Dict.* · *The Athenaeum* (3 Feb 1877), 157–8 · d. cert.

Bleek, Dorothea Frances (1873–1948). *See under* Bleek, Wilhelm Heinrich Immanuel (1827–1875).

Bleek, Wilhelm Heinrich Immanuel (1827–1875), philologist, was born at Berlin on 8 March 1827, the first of six sons and four daughters of Friedrich Bleek (1793–1859), professor of theology at Berlin University, and from 1829 at Bonn University, and his wife, Augusta Charlotte Marianne Henriette, *née* Sethe (*d.* 1873). He was educated in Bonn, and then studied theology at Bonn University from 1845 to 1848. When he went to study Hebrew at Berlin for two terms in 1848–9 he developed an interest in African languages. He returned to Bonn and until 1851 studied theology and philosophy. His doctoral thesis, 'De nominum generibus linguarum Africae australis, Copticae, Semiticarum aliarumque sexualium', dealt with grammatical gender, and attributed a north African provenance to Khoi (Hottentot). Also in 1851 he translated into German a work on the Akra language (1828) by Rasmus Rask. In 1852 he studied with the famous Egyptologist Professor Carl Richard Lepsius, and adopted his phonetic script. Late in 1852, in pursuit of African language studies, he was in Berlin, where Professor Wilhelm K. H. Peters (1815–1883), who had been in east Africa in 1842–8, gave him his African languages material to edit.

During a visit to England in 1853, or early 1854, Bleek

met Dr William Balfour Baikie RN, and joined his expedition up the Niger and Isadda, as linguist and ethnographer. They left from Liverpool in May 1854, but Bleek was obliged by an attack of fever to turn back at Fernando Po, and by August was again in London. There he was introduced to Sir George Grey, recently appointed governor of Cape Colony, and to J. W. Colenso, first bishop of Natal. In November Bleek accepted Colenso's offer of work on the completion of a Zulu grammar, and in May 1855 arrived with the bishop in Natal. There, as recorded in his diaries (1855–6), he used a small German grant to travel widely, learned Zulu (and later Xhosa), visited the Zulu king, Mpande, made first-hand studies of 'Kaffir' language and culture, and published *The Languages of Mozambique* (1856). He contributed articles to Peterman's *Geographische Mitteilungen* (1855–7) and edited the *Natal Witness* to earn money. He met several missionaries who had useful material on African languages. In Durban he met Archdeacon W. H. C. Lloyd, but probably did not meet his daughter, Jemima Charlotte Lloyd (1837–1909), until March 1861.

In 1856 Sir George Grey invited Bleek to become his official interpreter, and in November he moved to Cape Town. Sir George put him in charge of his valuable collection of books and manuscripts, mainly on philology and ethnography, which Bleek catalogued in *The Library of H. E. Sir George Grey* (vols. 1–2, 1858–9; vol. 3, 1862; vol. 4, 1867). When Grey was appointed to New Zealand in 1861, the new governor, Sir Philip Wodehouse, cancelled Bleek's post as interpreter. Fortunately, Sir George wrote from New Zealand, leaving his collection to the public library in Cape Town on condition that Bleek be made curator, a post he held from August 1862 until his death. This appointment, worth £250 per annum, enabled him on 22 November 1862 to marry Jemima Lloyd, and they set up house in Mowbray, a suburb of Cape Town. They had a son and six daughters, the son and one daughter dying in infancy. To raise money Bleek wrote ephemeral articles for the *Volksblad* of Cape Town. In 1863 he supported his friend Bishop Colenso in his celebrated trial for 'heresy'.

Ill health and financial worries prevented Bleek from undertaking the major African expeditions he had originally planned. Instead he produced his major work, *A Comparative Grammar of South African Languages* (pt 1, *Phonology*, 1862; pt 2, *The Concord*, section 1, *The Noun*, 1869). In this pioneering work he clearly distinguished the two language families of sub-Saharan Africa: on the one hand the Bantu or Bântu languages (a term he introduced), which extend in a vast swathe from west Africa through the Cameroons to south Africa, and on the other the Bushman (San) group, with their distinctive 'clicks', and the possibly related Hottentot (Khoi) group.

As early as 1857 Bleek visited Bushmen imprisoned on Robben Island and in the Cape Town gaol, where he tested a Bushman vocabulary he had received from a Dr Lichtenstein. The Bushmen, as hunter-gatherers, had come in conflict with the settlers and herdsmen, white and black, who encroached on their territories, killing game. When Bushmen retaliated by stealing or killing cattle, the settlers either shot them down or enslaved them. Governors of Cape Colony faced settler demands for punitive forays, or annexation, as opposed to Westminster's policy on human rights, and its aversion to costly campaigns and imperial adventures. Bleek sided with the pro-Bushman white missionaries who supplied him with valuable linguistic material, and in 1866 made further visits to Bushmen in prison.

Bleek's publications in the 1860s included *Reynard the Fox in South Africa, or, Hottentot Fables and Tales* (London, 1864; Weimar, 1870), based mainly on material from G. Kronlein. His brief work on the origin of language, *Über den Ursprung der Sprache*, had a Darwinian approach. This was first published privately in 1867 in Cape Town and Jena, and then with a preface by his cousin Ernst Haeckel in Weimar in 1868. It received an English translation in 1869 in New York.

In 1867 an economic depression in Cape Colony led to a 16 per cent reduction in Bleek's salary, and in addition to problems in funding and publishing his work he was still in poor health. This took him for a few months in 1869 to Europe, where he visited German relatives and was at the funeral of his brother Johann Friedrich. In England, through the influence of Sir George and other distinguished academics, he was awarded in 1870 a queen's civil-list pension of £150 p.a.

In 1870 Bleek visited twenty-eight North Cape /Xam Bushmen in Breakwater prison, and was allowed to install several of them in his home, including an older man, //Kabbo (Dream or Old Jantje; *d.* 1876), who had a wealth of Bushman stories. Bleek now concentrated increasingly on his Bushman studies, intent on recording this dying race, and in this he was helped increasingly by his sister-in-law Lucy Catherine Lloyd [*see below*], who had joined the household shortly after his marriage. He issued two reports: *Report of Dr. Bleek Concerning his Researches into the Bushman Language* (Cape of Good Hope, 1873) and *Second report concerning Bushman researches … presented to both houses of parliament of the Cape of Good Hope* (London and Cape Town, 1875). In the latter he refers to 7200 half-pages of Bushman literature and 11,000 entries to a Bushman–English English–Bushman dictionary. Bleek's numerous articles in the *Cape Monthly Magazine* included 'Scientific reasons for the study of the Bushman language' (new ser., 7, September 1873, 149–53). By 1874, when George William Stow, a trader and geologist, sent Bleek some of his copies of Bushman rock paintings, Bleek and Lloyd were fluent in their /Xam Bushmen's language, and, using these paintings as a talking point, deepened their understanding of Bushman stories and culture.

Early in 1875 Bleek was again unwell, but continued to work. He died suddenly at Charlton House, Mowbray, of a long-established disease of the lungs, on the morning of 17 August 1875, and was buried in the nearby Anglican cemetery at Wynberg.

Lucy Catherine Lloyd (1834–1914), philologist and folklorist, was born on 7 November 1834 at Norbury, Staffordshire, England, the second eldest daughter of William

Henry Cymric Lloyd, rector of St Peter's Church, and his wife, Lucy Anne, *née* Jeffreys. When Lucy was eight her mother died, and she and her three sisters went to live with their maternal aunt, Mrs Caroline Dundas, and were privately educated. When William Lloyd was appointed colonial chaplain for Natal in 1849 Lucy and her sisters accompanied him, along with his second wife and family, to Natal.

A short career as a schoolteacher was ended by ill health, and after her sister Jemima married Wilhelm Bleek in 1862, Lucy joined their household at Mowbray, Cape Town, and helped Bleek with his language studies. She proved an able pupil, and, with Bleek's ill health and increasing deafness, became indispensable in work with the Bushman informants. Some two-thirds of the Bushman transcripts are hers. In a codicil to his will, dated 30 June 1871, Bleek entrusted his posthumous papers to Lucy Lloyd, gratefully acknowledged her help in his literary labours, and asked her to continue their joint Bushman studies, 'in which her quicker ear, and great industry has been of so important help to science'. He urged his scientific colleagues to assist her financially.

After Bleek's death Lucy appealed to his associates in Europe for financial support in the expenses of Bushman research. She continued the work with the /Xam Bushmen informants, especially with //Kabbo's son-in-law, /Han≠kass'o, 'an excellent narrator of Bushmen lore' (Lloyd, *Short Account*, 3), studied Bushman music and drawings, and collected material on other Bushman languages, including !Kora and !Kung. She succeeded Bleek as curator of the Grey collection, but at half salary. She was secretary of the South African Folklore Society, and in 1879 helped to establish the *Folklore Journal*. When she was given her notice as curator in 1880, in favour of a professional, Dr J. T. Hahn, she sought legal remedy, but the case dragged on, and Hahn was appointed. When he had to resign in 1883, having proved ineffective, Lloyd was not reappointed. When G. W. Stow died in 1882 she bought his copies of rock paintings, but lacked the funds to publish them.

Overworked and in poor health, Lucy left south Africa about 1887, and, after some time at Rhyl in Wales, joined Jemima and her daughters, who had moved to Berlin. Her work is recorded in *A Short Account of Further Bushman Material Collected* (1889). In 1904 Jemima and her daughters returned to South Africa, where Lucy joined them about 1906 and resumed her work, assisted by her niece Dorothea Frances Bleek [*see below*]. Together with Dorothea's sister Edith, they saw through the press *Specimens of Bushman Folklore* (1911). This contained English translations of a selection of the Bushman stories, and the verbatim /Xam and !Kung transcripts as recorded between 1870 and 1884.

In 1913 Lucy Lloyd received an honorary doctorate of literature from the University of the Cape of Good Hope, the first woman in South Africa so to be honoured. She died on 31 August 1914 at Charlton House, Mowbray, Cape Town, and was buried in Wynberg cemetery.

Dorothea Frances Bleek (1873–1948), philologist and folklorist, was born on 26 March 1873, at The Hill, Mowbray, Cape Town, the sixth child of Wilhelm Heinrich Immanuel Bleek and Jemima Charlotte, *née* Lloyd (1837–1909). She was two and a half when her father died. In 1883 Jemima took her five daughters to Europe, where Dorothea attended schools in Germany and Switzerland. She then trained as a teacher in Berlin, took a course in African languages at Berlin University, and attended the school of oriental languages in London.

In 1904 Dorothea returned to Africa and taught at Rocklands Girls' High School in Cradock until 1907. With a colleague, Helen Tongue, she visited Bushman rock paintings, and Helen's copies were exhibited in London in 1908. Some of these paintings, with notes by Dorothea and her sister Edith, were published in 1909. Back in Africa, Dorothea devoted herself to further studies of Bushman life and languages, and assisted her aunt Lucy Lloyd until the latter's death. She then edited much of the research left by her father and Lucy. She made many expeditions to study Bushman dialects and rock art, and visited the Kalahari, Bechuanaland, Angola, and modern Tanzania, taking many photographs of shelter, weapons, and dress. In 1928 Dorothea visited the original sites of sixty of the seventy-four copies of rock paintings by Stow, which she had inherited from Lucy Lloyd, and published them with descriptive notes in 1930. Besides /Xam, she studied other Bushman languages.

From 1923 to 1948 Dorothea was honorary reader in Bushman languages at the University of Cape Town. She published her important collection of /Xam folk-tales, *The Mantis and his Friends* (1923, 1930), and articles on the customs and beliefs of the /Xam Bushmen in *Bantu Studies*, parts 1–8 (1931–6). In the introduction to *The Mantis* (a trickster deity) she writes:

> The Bushman is a good lover and a good hater, very loyal and very revengeful. He remains all his life a child, averse to work, fond of play, of painting, singing, dancing, dressing up and acting, above all things fond of hearing and telling stories.

Her *Bushman Dictionary* (published posthumously in 1956) incorporated the lexicon of her father and Lucy Lloyd.

In 1936 the University of the Witwatersrand wished to confer on Dorothea an honorary doctorate, but she declined, reputedly saying that there could be only one Dr Bleek. She died on 27 June 1948 at Plumstead, Cape Province. JOHN D. HAIGH

Sources *DSAB* • O. H. Spöhr, *Wilhelm Heinrich Immanuel Bleek: a bio-bibliographical sketch* (Cape Town, 1962) • *The Natal diaries of Dr W. H. I. Bleek, 1855–56*, ed. O. H. Spöhr (Cape Town, 1965) • J. Deacon and T. A. Dowson, eds., *Voices from the past: /Xam bushmen and the Bleek and Lloyd collection* (1996) • J. Deacon, 'The /Xam informants', *Voices from the past: /Xam bushmen and the Bleek and Lloyd collection*, ed. J. Deacon and T. A. Dowson (1996) • J. Deacon, 'A short note on Lloyd's !Kung informants', *Voices from the past: /Xam bushmen and the Bleek and Lloyd collection*, ed. J. Deacon and T. A. Dowson (1996) • S. Schmidt, 'Lucy Catherine Lloyd', *Voices from the past: /Xam bushmen and the Bleek and Lloyd collection*, ed. J. Deacon and T. A. Dowson (1996) • W. H. I. Bleek, *Report of Dr Bleek concerning his researches into the Bushman language* (Cape of Good Hope, 1873) • W. H. I. Bleek, *A brief account of Bushman folk-lore and other texts … second report concerning Bushman researches* (1875) [incl. letter of 1875 from L. Lloyd with quotation from codicil to Bleek's will] • W. H. I. Bleek, 'Scientific reasons for the study of the Bushman language', *Cape Monthly Magazine*, new ser., 7 (Sept 1873), 149–53; repr. in *Voices from the past*, ed. J. Deacon and T. A. Dowson (1996) • L. C. Lloyd, preface, *A short account of further Bushman material collected* (1889) • D. F. Bleek, introduction and notes, in G. W. Stow, *Rock-paintings in South Africa* (1930) • D. F. Bleek, ed., *The Mantis and his friends: Bushman folklore collected by the late Dr W. H. I. Bleek and the late Dr Lucy C. Lloyd* [1923] • A. H. Sayce, *The Academy* (2 Oct 1875), 357–8 • R. E. Asher and J. M. Y. Simpson, eds., *The encyclopedia of language and linguistics* (1994), 369–70 • L. van der Post and J. Taylor, *Testament to the Bushmen* (1984), 35, 38, 39–40, 94, 127–33, 146

Archives South African Museum, Cape Town, collection of San artefacts • University of Cape Town Library, Bleek and Lloyd collection, letters, manuscripts, notebooks, papers

Likenesses W. H. Schröder, portrait, 1875, National Library of South Africa, Cape Town • photograph, repro. in Deacon and Dowson, eds., *Voices from the past* • photograph, repro. in Spöhr, *Bleek* • portrait, University of Cape Town

Blegborough, Ralph (1769–1827), physician and man-midwife, was born on 3 April 1769 at Richmond, Yorkshire, where his father, Henry Blegborough, was a surgeon. He was educated at the grammar school of his native town, and, after acting for some time as apprentice to his father, continued his medical studies first at the University of Edinburgh, and then at Guy's and St Thomas's hospitals, London. Having become a member of the Company of Surgeons, London, he commenced in London as a general practitioner in Bridge Street, Blackfriars. He became MD of Aberdeen on 29 December 1804, and was admitted a licentiate of the Royal College of Physicians on 30 September 1805. About 1804 he entered into partnership with Thomas Walshman, a practitioner in midwifery, and from then on devoted himself exclusively to this branch of medicine, in which his reputation became so high that he was selected as a medical witness before the committee of the House of Peers on the question of the Gardner peerage. On 1 June 1812 he married Harriett Thresher, who predeceased him. Blegborough contributed several papers to the medical journals, and also published separately *Two Articles on the Air Pump, Extracted from the Medical and Physical Journal* (1802); *Facts and observations respecting the air pump and vapour bath in gout … and other diseases* (1803); and *Address to the Governors of the Surrey Dispensary* (1810). He devoted a large proportion of his time to unpaid practice among the poor, and died at Brixton Hill, Surrey, on 23 January 1827.

[Anon.], *rev.* Michael Bevan

Sources Munk, *Roll* • *GM*, 1st ser., 97/1 (1827), 92 • P. J. Wallis and R. V. Wallis, *Eighteenth century medics*, 2nd edn (1988) • *IGI*

Blencowe, John (*b.* 1609, *d.* in or after 1640), playwright and Church of England clergyman, was born on 29 January 1609 and baptized on 8 February following in St Bride's, Fleet Street, the son of John Blencowe, citizen of London. In 1620 he entered Merchant Taylors' School, where in June 1627 he was one of the 'nyne of the principall schollars who [did] pronounce orations … [and] were examined' (in his case successfully) for one of the vacant places on the school's fellowship (Vienken, 5). He matriculated from St John's College, Oxford, in 1629 and graduated BCL on 25 June 1633. He was subsequently elected to a fellowship at St John's. He wrote a Latin mythological drama, *Mercurius, sive, Literarum lucta*, which was performed at the college in the 1630s. He resigned his fellowship upon marriage in 1638, and he may be the same John Blencowe who was vicar of Abergwili, Carmarthenshire, in that year. In 1640 he published *Michaels Combat with the Divel, or, Moses his Funerall*, a typical anti-vice sermon which he dedicated to Sir Henry Martin.

Sidney Lee, *rev.* Sarah E. Trombley

Sources Foster, *Alum. Oxon., 1500–1714* [John Blencow] • *Mercurius, sive, Literarum lucta*, ed. H. Vienken (1981) • J. Blencowe, *Michaels combat with the divel, or, Moses his funerall* (1640) • *Walker rev.*

Blencowe, Sir John (1642–1726), judge and politician, was born on 30 November 1642 at Marston St Lawrence, on Northamptonshire's border with Oxfordshire, the eldest son of Thomas Blencowe (1602–1674) and his second wife, Mary (*c.*1618–1687), daughter of the Revd Dr Francis Savage of Ripple, Worcestershire. Blencowe's family had been lords of the manor of Marston since the mid-fifteenth century, before which time they had long been settled at Greystoke in Cumberland. On 24 May 1661 Blencowe matriculated as a student at Oriel College, Oxford, several earlier members of his family having been closely associated with the college, one as a benefactor and another, Anthony Blencowe, as its provost from 1572 to 1617.

Blencowe began his legal studies at the Inner Temple in November 1663 and was called to the bar in November 1670. On 23 December 1675 he married Anne (*d.* 1718), the eldest daughter of John Wallis, the eminent Savillian professor of geometry at Oxford whose outstanding ability at decoding intercepted messages and documents had rendered him invaluable to the post-Restoration government. The marriage subsequently produced three sons, one of whom was the cryptographer William *Blencowe, and four daughters. Blencowe established a solid reputation at the bar. In 1687 he was made a bencher of his inn of court, and in April 1689 he became serjeant-at-law. In 1690 Blencowe was elected to parliament for Brackley, a short distance from the family estate which he had inherited on his father's death in 1674. He naturally featured in Commons proceedings as a whig firmly attached to the court, but stood down at the 1695 election. John Wallis had for several years persistently badgered his contacts among senior government figures for his son-in-law's advancement to the judicial bench, though without success. In June 1696, however, Lord Keeper Somers proposed that he be appointed a baron of the exchequer; and in forwarding the recommendation to the king, the duke of Shrewsbury, secretary of state, commended Blencowe as 'an honest and able lawyer' who had given the government consistent support during his spell in the House of Commons. The appointment took effect from September, though Wallis complained to the new secretary of state, Sir William Trumbull, that he had wanted Blencowe to be a judge of the common pleas rather than the exchequer where the fees were paltry in comparison to his practice. In November 1697, however, Blencowe was transferred to the court of common pleas, and on 12 December he was knighted by the king at Kensington. When the chief judgeship of that court became vacant early in 1701, Wallis naturally pressed for Blencowe's promotion though Blencowe himself had avoided making an application for it, knowing that the lord chief justice, Sir John Holt, had it earmarked for Sir Thomas Trevor. Shortly after Queen Anne's accession there was some feeling that he might be removed, but he remained a puisne judge in common pleas and in fact was destined to progress no further on the judicial ladder. Some older authorities err in stating that he sat from this time in queen's bench.

Blencowe retained his post at George I's accession in 1715. He retired in June 1722 aged eighty, and as a mark of ministerial gratitude for many years' service he was granted a continuation of his official salary of £1000 in the form of an annuity. While still active as a judge, he became obsessed with discovering a way of determining longitude, although his ideas, which apparently filled several reams of paper, were not taken seriously. He was remembered for his honesty and blunt integrity, and a story illustrating his humane disposition relates how he refused his wife's plea to dismiss one of his labourers, an old man of ninety, and allow him to remain at home on his wage of 8*d*. a day. 'Let him spoil on', the judge is reported to have said, 'he has pleasure in thinking he earns his daily bread at fourscore years and ten; but if you turn him off he will soon die of grief' (Baker, 639). Dementia seems to have overtaken Blencowe in his last years when he was sometimes under an impression that he was already dead. He died on 6 May 1726 and was buried at Marston.

A. A. Hanham

Sources HoP, *Commons, 1690–1715* [draft] • G. Baker, *The history and antiquities of the county of Northamptonshire*, 2 vols. (1822–41), 1.639, 645 • Nichols, *Lit. anecdotes*, 9.273 • Foster, *Alum. Oxon.*

Likenesses G. Vertue, line engraving, 1713 (after A. Russell, 1713), BM, NPG

Blencowe, William (1683–1712), cryptographer, was born on 6 January 1683, the third son of Sir John *Blencowe (1642–1726), a judge and baron of the exchequer, and his wife, Anne, the eldest daughter of the mathematician and cryptographer John Wallis. He matriculated at Lincoln College, Oxford, in 1697 and moved later that year to Magdalen College, where he graduated BA in 1701. On the nomination of Archbishop Thomas Tenison he became a fellow of All Souls College on 21 December 1702, and he was made MA in 1704. He was instructed in the art of deciphering by his maternal grandfather, and for his encouragement received the survivorship of Wallis's pension of £100 p.a., following the latter's death on 28 October 1703. As a matter of course Blencowe succeeded Wallis as decipherer to the government; the statement of a survivor that he applied for the office 'unrecommended' cannot therefore be accepted as accurate. His eventual salary for the office was £200 per annum.

In 1709 Blencowe sought a dispensation to permit him to retain his fellowship at All Souls without his taking holy orders. This request was resisted by the warden, Bernard Gardiner, who tried to force Blencowe and Matthew Tindal, another college fellow, to take orders or resign. Following Queen Anne's intervention on Blencowe's behalf, the dispute led to the abolition of the warden's veto on dispensations; thereafter the non-residence of the fellows became a leading characteristic of All Souls College.

In his late twenties Blencowe fell ill with a violent fever, from which he was recovering, when, on 25 August 1712, he shot himself during temporary insanity caused by a relapse. He was buried in All Saints' Church, Northampton, where the monument to his memory records that he was a 'man studious of many kinds of learning, particularly of the common law, which he professed and practised with reputation; and of the art of deciphering letters wherein he excelled, and served the public for ten years'.

T. F. Henderson, *rev.* Philip Carter

Sources J. Granger, *A biographical history of England, from Egbert the Great to the revolution*, 2 vols. (1769); suppl. (1774) • *GM*, 1st ser., 58 (1788), 380–81, 479–80 • *GM*, 1st ser., 59 (1789), 787–8 • *GM*, 1st ser., 60 (1790), 521 • M. Burrows, *Worthies of All Souls* (1874) • J. Bridges, *The history and antiquities of Northamptonshire*, ed. P. Whalley, 2 vols. (1791) • *IGI*

Blenerhasset, Thomas (*c*.1550–1624), poet and writer on Ireland, was a younger son of William Blenerhasset of Horsford Park, near Norwich, who died in 1598. His eldest brother, Edward, who, like Thomas, had a successful career in Ireland, was knighted on 23 July 1603. Thomas was, according to his own account, educated at Cambridge without taking a degree. Thomas subsequently entered the army, and was stationed for some years as captain at Guernsey Castle from 1577 on.

At Guernsey Blenerhasset produced his most important literary work, an expansion of the *Mirrour for Magistrates*. He claims that he intended it for the private perusal of a friend, but during his absence 'beyond the seas' it was published in London in 1578 by Richard Webster under the title of *The Seconde Parte of the Mirrour for Magistrates*. An interesting letter was prefixed, which contained some autobiographical facts addressed by the author to the anonymous friend for whom the work was written. He describes the difficulties of his situation, without access to a library, and 'sittyng on a rock in the sea … in *Garnzie* Castle, where although there be learned men, yet none whiche spende their tyme so vainely as in poetrie' (*Parts Added*, 381–2).

The original *Mirrour for Magistrates*, which dealt with episodes in English history from the time of Richard II, had been issued in 1559, under the editorship of William Baldwin, and had been reprinted in 1563. In 1574 John Higgins wrote a new series of poems on legends drawn from far earlier history than that of which Baldwin's work treated. This book, bearing the title of *The First Parte of the Mirrour for Magistrates*, was reprinted in 1575. Blenerhasset's contribution to the *Mirrour* was a continuation of Higgins's book, 'from the conquest of Caesar unto the commyng of Duke William the Conqueror'. It dealt with the legends of 'Guidericus, Carassus, Queen Hellina, Vortiger, Uter Pendragon, Cadwallader, Sigebert, Lady Ebbe, Alurede,

Elgured, Edricus, and King Harolde'. Blenerhasset's contribution to the project marks a change in emphasis. Baldwin's original version used episodes from English history to reflect on the present, whereas Blenerhasset—like Higgins—simply tells patriotic stories of England's past. In 1610 ten of these poems of Blenerhasset were included in a complete reprint of the various parts of the *Mirrour for Magistrates* undertaken by Richard Niccols.

Blenerhasset's literary work also included—non-extant—a translation of Ovid's *De remedio amoris*, executed while at Cambridge but never printed, and a sophisticated poem called *A Revelation of the True Minerva*, a panegyric describing Queen Elizabeth's triumph over mutability printed in London in 1582, but of which only one copy, recently in the Heber collection, is known to be extant.

Blenerhasset notes in his dedication of the latter to Lady Leighton, one of the ladies of the queen's privy chamber, that he had taken part in long voyages into the Atlantic. He was named as one of Sir Edward Denny's discharged soldiers in Ireland on 10 April 1589. On 12 May of the same year he is recorded as a freeholder granted 6000 acres by Denny and as having numerous farmers, copyholders, and cottagers in his command. Denny appears to have used Blenerhasset as an intermediary in his feud with Sir William Herbert. It is likely that Blenerhasset remained in Ireland for much of the rest of his life, although he returned to Norfolk with his brother in 1605 or 1606 to deal with property affairs.

In 1610 Blenerhasset was one of the 'undertakers' for the plantation of Ulster, and wrote a brief pamphlet dedicated to Prince Henry, entitled *A Direction for the Plantation in Ulster*. Here he argued that fortified garrison towns would be required to help extirpate the recalcitrant Irish and make the plantation profitable and successful both for the settlers and the crown. In 1611 he received 2000 acres at Clancally in co. Fermanagh, and in 1612, with thirty-nine others, appealed to the lord deputy, Sir Arthur Chichester, to grant them jointly a part of Sligo, 60,000 acres in co. Fermanagh, and some neighbouring territory, on their undertaking to expend £40,000 on the land, and to settle upon it 1000 'able men furnished for all kinds of handiwork'. In his signature to this appeal Blenerhasset describes himself as being still of Horsford, Norfolk. In 1624 Blenerhasset was stated to own the barony of Lurge and two proportions of Eddernagh and Tullenageane in co. Fermanagh. Blenerhasset died on 11 March 1624, having just built a residence called Castlehasset on the shore of Lough Erne. His father's will proves him to have been married before 1598, and to have had several children. At least two, Lennard and Samuel, survived him. Sir Edward Blenerhasset, who shared with him several grants of Irish land, died in 1618, both having become substantial landowners in Ireland.

SIDNEY LEE, *rev.* ANDREW HADFIELD

Sources *Parts added to 'The mirror for magistrates'*, ed. L. B. Campbell (1938), 363–83 • *CSP Ire.*, *1586–92*; *1610–24* • T. Blenerhasset, *A revelation of the true Minerva* (1582) [with introduction by J. W. Bennett, 1941] • Venn, *Alum. Cant.* • *The whole works of Sir James Ware concerning Ireland*, ed. and trans. W. Harris, rev. edn, 2/2 (1764), 333 • H. Hackett, *Virgin mother, maiden queen: Elizabeth I and the cult of the Virgin Mary* (1995), 119–23 • G. Hill, *An historical account of the plantation in Ulster at the commencement of the seventeenth century, 1608–1620* (1877) • J. Bulwer, 'Hasset's House, Pockthorpe', *Norfolk Archaeology*, 7 (1872), 79–92, esp. 86–92 • T. Barrett-Lennard, 'Some account of the manor or castle of Horsford', *Norfolk Archaeology*, 15 (1903–4), 267–92

Blenkinsop, John (1783–1831), developer of the steam locomotive, was born near Leeds and became the principal agent of the Brandling family, who owned the extensive Middleton collieries in that district. On 10 April 1811 he obtained a patent for a new type of locomotive, developing some of the ideas embodied in the engine constructed by Richard Trevithick in 1803, but combining with them a new plan to overcome the presumed lack of adhesion between the engine wheels and smooth rails. This was effected by means of a racked or toothed rail, laid along one side of the road, into which the toothed wheel of the locomotive worked as pinions work into a rack. The boiler of Blenkinsop's locomotive was a plain cylinder of cast iron, with one flue—the fire being at one end and the chimney at the other. It was supported on a carriage resting without springs directly on two pairs of wheels and axles, which were unconnected with the working parts, and served merely to support the weight of the engine on the rails, traction being achieved by the cogwheel working into the toothed rack. The engine had two cylinders instead of one as in Trevithick's engine. The invention of the double cylinder was due to Matthew Murray, of the firm of Fenton, Murray, and Wood, one of the best mechanical engineers of his time; Blenkinsop, who was not himself a mechanic, consulted him about all the practical details. The connecting rods gave the motion to two pinions by cranks at right angles to each other. These pinions communicated the motion to the wheel which worked into the cogged rail.

The first experiment with Blenkinsop's engine was made on the afternoon of Wednesday 24 June 1812 when, according to a report in the *Leeds Mercury* (27 June 1812), the machine ran from the coal staithe to the top of Hunslet Moor, where six and afterwards eight wagons of coal, each weighing 3¼ tons, were hooked to the rear. This immense weight was subsequently augmented by about fifty spectators mounted on the wagons. The return journey, a distance of about a mile and a half, was performed in twenty-three minutes, without incident. The machine was stated to be capable, when lightly loaded, of moving at a speed of 10 miles per hour. A drawing and description of it with the official specification were given in the *Leeds Mercury* (18 July 1812).

Blenkinsop's locomotive has an undoubted claim to be considered the first commercially successful engine employed on any railway. By the end of 1813 three engines were at work at the Middleton collieries and it is a tribute to Blenkinsop's reputation that others were to be found at Orell colliery in Lancashire and at the Coxlodge and Fawdon wagon-ways near the Tyne. According to contemporary accounts these locomotives proved reliable and economical in service, at least as employed on the Middleton line where they operated until the early 1830s. Despite this evident commercial success, Blenkinsop's locomotives represented an engineering cul-de-sac and it was left to George Stephenson to prove the superiority of the smooth edge-rail over the rack-rail transmission.

Stephenson had observed one of the 'Leeds engines' at Coxlodge on 2 September 1813, and his first locomotive, *Blucher*, constructed at Killingworth, near Newcastle upon Tyne, was built to a large extent after the Blenkinsop pattern. Thereafter, however, Stephenson focused on the vital links between the weight of locomotives, their tractive effort, and the quality of the permanent way. The result, by 1820, was the practical demonstration of locomotive power reliant on the adhesion of flanged wheels running on smooth edge-rails.

Blenkinsop died at Leeds on 22 January 1831, after a long illness, aged forty-eight. A beautiful model of his engine of 1812 was exhibited at a *conversazione* of the Leeds Philosophical Society in December 1863, and a photograph of this model with explanatory notes was placed in the Leeds Philosophical Hall.

THOMAS SECCOMBE, *rev.* M. W. KIRBY

Sources W. W. Tomlinson, *The North Eastern railway: its rise and development* [1915]; repr. with new introduction by K. Hode (1967) • C. F. Dendy Marshall, *A history of railway locomotives down to the end of the year 1831* (1953) • R. W. Kidner, *The early history of the locomotive, 1804–1876* (1956) • W. G. Rimmer, 'Middleton colliery near Leeds (1770–1830)', *Yorkshire Bulletin of Economic and Social Research*, 7 (1955), 41–57 • C. E. Lee, 'The first steam railway: Brandling's colliery line between Leeds and Middleton', *Railway Magazine*, 81 (1937), 7–25 • S. Smiles, *Lives of the engineers*, 3 (1862) • *Leeds Mercury* (29 Jan 1831) • R. Welford, *Men of mark 'twixt Tyne and Tweed*, 3 vols. (1895) • R. V. Taylor, ed., *The biographia Leodiensis, or, Biographical sketches of the worthies of Leeds* (1865)

Blenkiron, William (1807?–1871), racehorse breeder, was born at Marrick, near Richmond, Yorkshire. His father was a Swaledale farmer but Blenkiron abandoned that pursuit and moved in 1834 to London, where he commenced business as a general agent in Wood Street, Cheapside. In 1845 he added a business manufacturing stocks and collars to his economic activities but three years later retired in favour of his son to devote his time to the breeding of racehorses.

In 1847, while living at Dalston, Middlesex, Blenkiron purchased a mare named Glance. A colt of hers, Young Beverlac, was raced with moderate success and was exchanged for three mares which formed the commencement of a stud destined to become the most celebrated in Europe. About 1852 Blenkiron, wishing to expand his breeding facilities, moved from Dalston to Middle Park Farm at Eltham in Kent. The establishment rapidly increased to more than two hundred of the highest-class mares and stallions that money and experience could produce. Kingston, Touchstone, Birdcatcher, and Newminster were the four cornerstones of Blenkiron's extensive stud, and it was to the first of these that he to a great extent owed his success as a breeder, for Kingston was the sire of Caractacus, perhaps the most sensational Derby winner on record.

William Blenkiron (1807?–1871), by unknown engraver, pubd 1871

Unlike many successful industrialists, Blenkiron did not abandon his business practices when he entered racing. He spent heavily but usually wisely. Among his purchases he gave 5000 guineas for Blink Bonny (one of only four fillies to have won both the Derby and the Oaks), 5800 guineas for Gladiateur (the first French horse to win the Derby), and 5000 guineas for Blair Athol (winner of the St Leger).

The first major sale of Middle Park bloodstock took place in June 1856, when thirteen lots brought £1447, an average of £111 each; at a sale in 1871, forty-six lots produced £14,525, the average price being £315. Middle Park was by then the largest breeding stud in the country. After 1866, the year in which Blenkiron purchased all Lord Zetland's brood mares, it became necessary to hold two annual sales to dispose of the increase in the stock.

Blenkiron bred Hermit, the Derby winner in 1867, and Gamos, which won the Oaks in 1870. This was unusual among the commercial studs as most classic winners still emanated from private breeders, to whom time and money were often no object. He died at Middle Park Farm on 25 September 1871, and was buried five days later in Eltham churchyard. His son sold the stud in 1872 for 124,620 guineas. G. C. BOASE, *rev.* WRAY VAMPLEW

Sources W. Vamplew, *The turf: a social and economic history of horse racing* (1976) • *The Field* (30 Sept 1871) • *The Sportsman* (26 Sept 1871) • Boase, *Mod. Eng. biog.* • S. Sidney, *The book of the horse (thorough-bred, half-bred, cart-bred), saddle and harness, British and foreign* (1875) •

J. Rice, *History of the British turf*, 2 vols. (1879) • [E. H. Thurston], ed., *British sport and sportsmen: breeding, agriculture, country-life pursuits* [n.d., *c.*1926] • J. Fairfax-Blakeborough, *Northern turf history* (1948)

Likenesses engraving, NPG; repro. in *ILN*, 59 (1871), 377 [*see illus.*] • portrait, repro. in *Illustrated Sporting and Dramatic News*, 1 (1874), 1811

Wealth at death under £120,000: resworn probate, Nov 1872, *CGPLA Eng. & Wales* (1871)

Blennerhasset, Harman (1764/5–1831), lawyer and settler in America, born in Hampshire on 8 October 1764 or 1765, was the youngest of the three sons of Conway Blennerhasset of Conway Castle, Killorglin, co. Kerry, Ireland, and his wife, the daughter of Major Thomas Lacy, the descendant of an old Anglo-Norman family. He was educated at Westminster School and Trinity College, Dublin, where he graduated BA in 1790 and LLB in the same year. Having, through the death of his elder brothers, succeeded to the family estates, he spent some time travelling in Europe. During this period he became a republican and resolved to settle in the United States of America. While in England he met and married Margaret Agnew (*d.* 1842), the daughter of the lieutenant-governor of the Isle of Man. After disposing of his lands to a relative, and supplying himself with an extensive library and scientific apparatus, he sailed for New York in 1796. In 1798 he purchased part of Blennerhasset Island on the Ohio, about 2 miles below Parkersburg, West Virginia, and there lived a retired and studious life. However, in 1806 he became implicated in the treasonable schemes of Aaron Burr without properly realizing their intent. In support of the views of Burr he published a series of papers in the *Ohio Gazette*, under the signature of Querist, and spent much of his fortune on boats, provisions, and arms for Burr's contemplated expedition against Mexico, then a territory of Spain, with which the USA was at peace. In the spring of 1807 he was arrested, and although he regained his liberty his fine house was destroyed and looted during his absence. He then turned successively to cotton growing in Mississippi (1807–19), legal practice in Montreal (1819–22), and an attempt to recover his lands in Ireland. Having failed in all three undertakings, he retired to Guernsey, where he died in 1831.

The involvement of Blennerhassett and his wife in the ill-fated schemes of Burr has inspired several novels, including those by William Venable (*A Dream of Empire*, 1901), Charles Pidgin (*Blennerhassett, or, The Decrees of Fate*, 1901), Edward Stanley (*The Rock Cried Out*, 1949), and Marie Wood (*None Called him Neighbour*, 1951), and a play by Pidgin (*Blennerhassett, or, The Irony of Fate*, 1901), as well as considerable interest in their house on Blennerhasset Island. He was a strikingly unsuccessful man, but his failures were romantic enough to inspire and sustain popular interest.

T. F. Henderson, *rev.* Elizabeth Baigent

Sources M. Hickson, *Selections from old Kerry records* (1872) • A. Burr, *Reports of the trials of Colonel Aaron Burr* (1808) • W. Safford, *The life of Harman Blennerhassett* (1850) • W. Safford, *The Blennerhassett papers* (1864) • R. R. Swick, *Harman Blennerhassett* (1971) • T. Blennerhassett-Adams, *The true story of Harman Blennerhassett* (1901) • *DNB*

Blennerhassett, Charlotte Julia, Lady Blennerhassett (1843–1917). *See under* Blennerhassett, Sir Rowland, fourth baronet (1839–1909).

Blennerhassett, Sir Rowland, fourth baronet (1839–1909), journalist and politician, born at Blennerville, co. Kerry, on 5 September 1839, was the only son of Sir Arthur Blennerhassett, third baronet (1794–1849), and his wife, Sarah, daughter of John Mahony. His only sister, Rosanna (*d.* 1907), became a Red Cross nurse. Both parents were Roman Catholics. Rowland succeeded to the baronetcy on the death of his father in 1849. After being educated first at Downside School, under the Benedictines, and then at Stonyhurst College, under the Jesuits, he matriculated in 1859 at Christ Church, Oxford, but left, without taking a degree, for the University of Louvain. There he took a doctor's degree in political and administrative science, 'with special distinction'. He afterwards, in 1864, studied at Munich, where he formed a lifelong friendship with J. J. I. von Döllinger. Finally he proceeded to Berlin, where he became acquainted with many leading politicians, including Bismarck. A frequent visitor to France, he came to know the chief figures of all parties under the Second Empire.

About 1862 Blennerhassett became intimate with Sir John Dalberg (afterwards Lord) Acton, with whose stand against later developments of ultramontanism he had a strong sympathy. The discontinuance by Acton in April 1864 of the *Home and Foreign Review*, a Roman Catholic organ of Liberal tendencies, suggested the possibility of establishing a journal the main objects of which should be political and literary; and Blennerhassett found the money for starting *The Chronicle*, a weekly newspaper, under the direction of T. F. Wetherell. Blennerhassett and Acton were of great service in searching for competent foreign correspondents. The first number appeared on 23 March 1867, and the last on 13 February 1868. As Gladstone predicted, it proved too Roman Catholic for Liberals, and too Liberal for Roman Catholics, and its early support of home rule for Ireland further prejudiced its chances of success. Save on ecclesiastical questions, the paper seldom expressed Blennerhassett's opinions. *The Chronicle* lacked sympathy with the reasoned imperialism which developed out of Blennerhassett's early admiration of Bismarck and engendered a faith in the superiority of German to British methods of progress. His early desire that Britain should learn from Germany passed into a strong desire that the country should prepare itself for the rivalry which the new German ambitions were making inevitable. Thus with him foreign policy grew to be an absorbing interest.

Meanwhile Blennerhassett took an active part in Irish politics. In 1865 he became Liberal MP for Galway City, a seat that he retained until 1874. But he lost the confidence of the priesthood, owing to his association with Döllinger and Acton (although he remained Roman Catholic) and his vote on the Irish University Bill of 1873. From 1880 to 1885 he represented County Kerry, his native county. (He should not be confused with his fellow member and cousin Rowland Ponsonby Blennerhassett.) In that interval his attitude on the home-rule controversy changed completely. A lukewarm supporter of home rule as a parliamentary movement under Butt and Shaw, he actively opposed it as a national movement under Parnell. Defeated in the Harbour division of Dublin city at the general election of November 1885, he did not re-enter the House of Commons.

During his parliamentary career Blennerhassett was mainly concerned with Irish university education and the Irish land question. His speeches on Fawcett's Irish University Bill in 1871, and on Gladstone's Irish University Bill of 1873, which he supported, showed an intimate knowledge of continental universities. He regretted Gladstone's exclusion of religiously divisive subjects, modern history and moral philosophy, from the curriculum, and pressed the system—borrowed from Germany—of two denominational faculties in the same university. In 1872 he moved the second reading of a bill for the purchase of Irish railways. In regard to the land question, he anticipated the legislation of 1903 in a confidential memorandum, dated April 1884 (afterwards printed), suggesting the appointment of a commission to convert large tracts of Irish land into peasant properties, by buying the estates of landlords willing to sell, at twenty-two years' purchase of the judicial rent.

After his retirement from the House of Commons Blennerhassett continued to play a part in Irish public life. He was a commissioner of national education and a member of the senate of the Royal University. From 1890 to 1897 he was an inspector of reformatory and industrial schools; from 1897 to 1904 he was president of Queen's College, Cork; and in 1905 he was sworn of the Irish privy council. During these years he constantly wrote on political subjects in *The Times*, the *Daily Telegraph*, the *Nineteenth Century*, the *Fortnightly Review*, the *Deutsche Rundschau*, and, especially at the end of his life, in the *National Review*. Blennerhassett published several of his speeches in parliament and his inaugural address on *University Education* at Queen's College, Cork, in 1898. He edited Ringhoffer's *Bernstorff Memoirs* in 1908. He deeply regretted the change to intransigence in papal policy on the election of Pius X, though he admitted the provocation given by the French legislation against the church, and the difference between the modernism of the 1900s and the liberal Catholicism of his youth. A ready talker as well as writer, Blennerhassett died on 22 March 1909 at 54 Rutland Gate, London, and was buried at Downside.

On 9 June 1870 Blennerhassett married Countess Charlotte von Leyden, daughter of Count von Leyden, of an old Bavarian family, whom he had first met in Rome four months earlier. **Charlotte Julia Blennerhassett**, Lady Blennerhassett (1843–1917), was a well-known historian and the author of several books, notably a life of Madame de Staël (1889). Like her husband, she had studied with Döllinger and enjoyed a close intellectual relationship with Acton, who recruited her as a contributor to the *Cambridge Modern History*, for which she wrote two articles on nineteenth-century Catholicism. The Blennerhassetts had two sons, of whom Arthur Charles Francis Bernard succeeded to the baronetcy; an only daughter, Marie Carola Franciska Roselyne, married Baron Raphael d'Erlanger.

D. C. Lathbury, *rev.* Josef L. Altholz

Sources *The Times* (23 March 1909), 13 · *WWW, 1916–28* · *Wellesley index*, 5.81–2 · *Lexicon der Frau* (1953), 1.451 · V. Conzemius, ed., *Ignaz von Döllinger: Briefwechsel mit Lady Blennerhassett* (1981) · *CGPLA Ire.* (1910)

Archives CUL, corresp. and papers | CUL, Acton MSS

Blessington. For this title name *see* Boyle, Murrough, first Viscount Blessington (1648–1718) [*see under* Boyle, Michael (1609/10–1702)]; Gardiner, Marguerite, countess of Blessington (1789–1849).

Blessington, Marguerite. *See* Gardiner, Marguerite, countess of Blessington (1789–1849).

Blethyn, William. *See* Bleddyn, William (*d.* 1590).

Blew, William John (1808–1894), liturgical scholar and hymn writer, the only son of William Blew of St James's, Westminster, was born in that parish on 13 April 1808, and educated with John Henry Newman at St Nicholas's School, Ealing, and at Oxford, where he matriculated from Wadham College in October 1825. He was elected Goodridge exhibitioner of Wadham in 1826, graduating BA on 13 May 1830 and MA on 13 June 1832. He was curate of Nuthurst, Sussex, from 1832 to 1840, being ordained deacon in 1832 and priest in 1834 by the bishop of Chichester. From 1840 to 1842 he was curate of St Anne's, Soho, and in 1842 became incumbent of St John's, Milton, near Gravesend, where he was free to give a Tractarian tone to the services. In 1850, owing to a difference with his bishop, George Murray (a critic of the Tractarians), he retired from active clerical work and devoted himself mainly to liturgical and theological studies. He had married after his father's death in 1845, and lived at his father's house, 6 Warwick Street, London, where he died on 27 December 1894.

Blew was a scholar of some repute. He published translations of the *Iliad* in 1831, Aeschylus's *Agamemnon* in 1855, and Euripides' *Medea* in English verse in 1887. He also edited two plays under the title *Queen Mary* (1876): *The Famous History of Sir Thomas Wyat* by Dekker and Webster and *If you Know not me, you Know Nobody, or, The Troubles of Queen Elizabeth* by Thomas Heywood. But his chief interest lay in ecclesiology, and probably his most solid work was his edition of the *Aberdeen Breviary* for the Bannatyne Club in 1854. In 1852 he published, with his friend Henry John Gauntlett, *The Church Hymn and Tune Book*, which reached a second edition in 1855. The hymns, which are chiefly translations from the Latin by Blew, 'are terse, vigorous, musical, and of great merit' (Julian). The volume also contains several original hymns by Blew. This was followed by *Hymns and Hymn Books* (1858) and in 1877 by an edition of the 1548 *Altar Service of the Church of England*.

A. F. Pollard, *rev.* H. C. G. Matthew

Sources *The Guardian* (9 Jan 1895) · *Church Times* (4 Jan 1895) · *The Times* (29 Dec 1894) · Crockford (1894) · Foster, *Alum. Oxon.* · H. J. Gauntlett, 'The Chapel Royal hymns, and hints for the history of

English hymnody', *N&Q*, 2nd ser., 7 (1859), 6–7 • J. Julian, ed., *A dictionary of hymnology* (1892)

Wealth at death £10,201 6*s*. 6*d*.: resworn probate, June 1895, *CGPLA Eng. & Wales*

Blewitt, Jonas (1757–1805), musician, was born on 9 September 1757 in Virginia Street, in the parish of St George-in-the-East, Middlesex, the son of John Blewitt, mariner, and his wife, Mary. He was baptized at the church of St George-in-the-East on 3 October. He was almost blind. In 1769 he was apprenticed to the Lambeth organist William Godfrey, and he also studied with Samuel Jarvis, organist of St Sepulchre, Holborn. He was appointed organist of St Katharine Coleman, Fenchurch Street, about November 1777, and about April 1783 he also became organist of the united parish of St Margaret Pattens and St Gabriel Fenchurch, holding both posts until his death. By 1780 Blewitt was composer to Spa Gardens, Bermondsey, and he also wrote music for Vauxhall Gardens, the Apollo Gardens, Astley's Amphitheatre, Covent Garden Theatre, the Lyceum, and the Royal Circus; he may have played the organ at these places. In the autumn of 1793 he played at the revival of the Eidophusikon at the Great Room, Spring Gardens, accompanying readings at the piano and playing the organ while panoramic scenes were displayed.

Blewitt's *Six Songs and a Cantata*, op. 1, was published about 1778, and *A Collection of Favourite Ballads*, op. 3, about 1785; other songs were issued individually. All his other published music was for the organ: two sets of *Ten Voluntaries* (op. 2, *c*.1780, and op. 5, 1796), *Twelve Easy and Familiar Movements*, op. 6 (*c*.1797), and *A Complete Treatise on the Organ*, op. 4 (1794?). The treatise is his most significant work, as it is one of the first English organ tutors and provides invaluable details of eighteenth-century performance practice; a 'Set of Explanatory Voluntaries' was appended. The work gives his address as Grange Road, Bermondsey, but Doane's *Musical Directory* for 1794 gives his address as Bermondsey Square. The *Treatise* was probably written a few years earlier, as the organist John Worgan (*d*. 1790) is described in it as 'now living'. Blewitt's son Jonathan *Blewitt (1782–1853) became a prominent musician, and Jonas's daughter Mary Ann Blewitt (*b*. 1784) succeeded her father as organist of St Katharine Coleman. C. Blewitt, singer at Spa Gardens (1785–8), may also have been related. Blewitt's death was reported on 10 April 1805. According to James Brown's *Biographical Dictionary of Musicians* (1886) he was a noted organist 'famed for his powerful and effective style' (Brown).

David Burchell

Sources D. Dawe, *Organists of the City of London, 1666–1850* (1983) • Highfill, Burnim & Langhans, *BDA* • *New Grove* • J. Doane, ed., *A musical directory for the year 1794* [1794] • J. D. Brown, *Biographical dictionary of musicians: with a bibliography of English writings on music* (1886) • P. Sawyer, 'A neglected late 18th century organ treatise', *Journal of the British Institute of Organ Studies*, 10 (1986), 76–87 • C. Kent, 'A revolution in registration—Marsh to Mendelssohn: a view of English organ music, 1788–1847', *Journal of the British Institute of Organ Studies*, 13 (1989), 25–44

Blewitt, Jonathan (1782–1853), composer, was born on 19 July 1782 in London, the son of the organist Jonas *Blewitt (1757–1805). He was educated by his father and his godfather, Jonathan Battishill (1738–1801), and he is also said to have received some instruction from Haydn. At the age of eleven he acted as deputy to his father, and thereafter held several appointments as an organist in London. He was also successively organist of Haverhill, Suffolk, and of Brecon, where he remained for three years. About 1808 he returned to London for the production of an opera he had written for Drury Lane, but the theatre burnt down in February 1809, before the work was produced. Blewitt next went to Sheffield, and from there proceeded in 1811 to Ireland, where he acted as private organist to Lord Cahir. His piano sonata *The Battle and Victory of Salamanca* appeared in 1812. He became organist of St Andrew's, Dublin, succeeded Tom Cooke in June 1813 as composer and director of the music at the Theatre Royal, Crow Street, and was appointed grand organist to the masonic body of Ireland by the duke of Leinster. An active conductor in Dublin, Blewitt also joined J. B. Logier when he introduced his system of music instruction into Ireland; he became a very successful teacher in his own right, and published in Dublin a treatise on singing and *An Epitome of the Logierian System of Harmony*. About 1825 he was back in London, and began the long series of pantomime compositions, musical plays, and light operas with which his name was connected for the rest of his life. For over twenty-five years he wrote music for most of the London theatres, and his last work, the pantomime *Harlequin Hudibras*, was brought out at Drury Lane on 27 December 1852. In 1828 and 1829 he was director of music at Sadler's Wells Theatre, and he was also, at different times, music director at Vauxhall and at the Tivoli Gardens, Margate, and pianist for the Vocal Entertainments run by the tenor John Templeton, with whom he revisited Ireland in 1849. He wrote hundreds of vocal pieces, most of them comic songs and ballads in the Irish style, which were particularly popular, the best-known at the time being *Barney Brallaghan* (a selective list of works is given in *New Grove*). In his latter years Blewitt sank into great poverty and suffered from a 'painful internal disease' (*MT*). He died on 4 September 1853 in London, and was buried at St Pancras. He left a widow and two daughters.

W. B. Squire, *rev.* David J. Golby

Sources *MT*, 5 (1852–4), 269 • E. F. Rimbault and A. Loewenberg, 'Blewitt, Jonathan', *New Grove* • [Clarke], *The Georgian era: memoirs of the most eminent persons*, 4 (1834), 550 • *GM*, 2nd ser., 40 (1853), 429 • T. J. Walsh, *Opera in Dublin, 1798–1820: Frederick Jones and the Crow Street Theatre* (1993)

Likenesses portrait, Harvard TC

Wealth at death none or very little

Blewitt, (John) Octavian (1810–1884), writer and literary administrator, was born on 3 October 1810 at St Helen's Place, Bishopsgate, London, the son of John Edwards Blewitt (*d*. 1860), merchant, and Caroline, daughter of Peter Symons, mayor of Plymouth. Much of his childhood was spent in Cornwall at Marazion House, the home of his great-uncle Hannibal Curnow Blewitt. He was educated at Plymouth grammar school, and then pursued a medical career, spending his five-year apprenticeship partly with his uncle Mr Dryden, assistant surgeon of the Devonport Dockyard, and partly with Mr Pollard of Torquay. He went to London in 1833 to continue his medical studies at St George's Infirmary, Hanover Square, but never qualified. After spending some time in tutoring Sir James Clark's son in classics he went with a patient to Madeira, staying at Funchal for eight months, and subsequently travelling in Egypt, Greece, Turkey, and other countries. In the latter part of 1837 and early 1838 he resided in Italy, an experience he put to good use writing two works in Murray's Handbooks for Travellers series, one about central Italy published in 1843, and the second, which came out a decade later, about southern Italy. He married Anne Roper Howard (*b.* 1811), a widow, daughter of David Edward Williams, on 12 September 1846 in London.

After repeated petitions Blewitt was elected in 1839 secretary of the Royal Literary Fund, a post he held until his death. It was the most influential position on the committee and through it he became an adviser to the governors of Charterhouse School. More significantly, the appointment meant that he was consulted by Gladstone and other prime ministers on civil-list pensions, and for forty-five years he was under-secretary for literary patronage. His staunch Anglicanism—he wrote *A Treatise on the Happiness Arising from the Exercise of the Christian Faith* at the age of twenty-two—was reflected in his stern moral attitude to applicants to the fund. During his term of office beneficiaries had to be of known good character, and no grant was given to an author's widow without the production of a marriage certificate. However, he was a kindly man, and he and his wife would occasionally receive and aid impoverished authors at their own door.

Blewitt's secretaryship came at a crucial time for the Royal Literary Fund, which had been criticized for its methods of accounting for and distributing its funds. He gained a reputation for diligence in the fund's affairs, keeping good accounts and careful records, and he recognized the importance of the fund's archives, spending many years getting them into good order. Yet he was dogged in his defence of the fund's ways which forced authors to write begging letters for meagre grants, and he refused to accept the case for reform put by Charles Dickens and Charles Wentworth Dilke between 1852 and 1858.

Probably the most influential of Blewitt's contributions to periodical magazines was an anonymous article in the *Quarterly Review* in April 1871 about the revision of the pension list. However, he was a regular contributor to many other periodicals, and for twenty-nine years edited the news section of *Gardiner's Chronicle*. He was a FRGS (1839) and was created knight of the order of Leopold by the king of the Belgians, who was a guest at the annual fund-raising dinner in 1872. Octavian Blewitt died on 4 November 1884 at his home, 133 Elgin Crescent, London, and was buried in Paddington cemetery on the 11th.

ALEXIS WEEDON

Sources N. Cross, *The common writer: life in nineteenth-century Grub Street* (1985) • N. Cross, *The Royal Literary Fund, 1790–1918: an introduction … with an index of applicants* (1984) • S. D. Mumm, 'Writing for their lives: women applicants to the Royal Literary Fund, 1840–1880', *Publishing History*, 27 (1990), 27–47 • C. W. Dilke, ed., *The papers of a critic: selected writings by Charles Wentworth Dilke*, 2 vols. (1875) • A. Trollope, *An autobiography*, ed. M. Sadleir and F. Page (1950); repr. (1980) • Boase & Courtney, *Bibl. Corn.* • [V. Bonham Carter], 'Royal Literary Fund', *TLS* (21 March 1968), 300 • *The Times* (7 Nov 1884) • *The Times* (11 Nov 1884) • *The Athenaeum* (15 Nov 1884), 626 • *Men of the time* (1884) • O. Blewitt, *The panorama of Torquay*, 2nd edn (1832) • O. Blewitt, *Italy, central including the papal states, Rome and the cities of Etruria*, Handbooks for Travellers (1843) • N. Cross, ed., *Archives of the Royal Literary Fund, 1790–1918* (1982–3) [microfilm] • m. cert. • *DNB* • O. Blewitt, *A treatise on the happiness arising from the exercise of the Christian faith* (1832) • census returns, 1881 • d. cert.

Archives BL, corresp. | BL, Royal Literary Fund MSS • Royal Literary Fund, London, archives • U. Aberdeen L., corresp. with Peter Buchan

Wealth at death £160: probate, 24 Nov 1884, *CGPLA Eng. & Wales*

Blicke, Sir Charles (1745–1815), surgeon, received his medical education at St Bartholomew's Hospital, London, where he was elected assistant surgeon in 1779; he succeeded Percivall Pott as surgeon 17 July 1787. Blicke was one of the court of assistants at Surgeons' Hall. In 1803 he became master of the Royal College of Surgeons; he was knighted in the same year.

In 1772, while living in Old Jewry, Blicke published his only work, *An essay on the biliou or yellow fever of Jamaica, collected from the manuscript of a late surgeon*. In the preface Blicke states that he has abridged the original work and simplified its style. The essayist, whose name is not preserved, advocates the treatment of the fever by bleeding, purging, warm baths, fresh air, and acid drinks. Some twenty authors are quoted to little purpose, and the only interesting contents of the composition are a few lines on the sufferings of the Carthagena expedition, in which the original writer had served, and the mention of the fact that the water of the Bristol hot wells was exported to Jamaica. Whatever he may have cut out, Blicke certainly added nothing. The essay was translated into Italian.

In 1779 Blicke, then living in Mildred Court, received John Abernethy as his apprentice in surgery.

> The tone in which he [Abernethy] usually spoke of Sir Charles's practice did not convey a very favourable idea of the nature of the impression which it had left on him. In relating a case he would say: 'Sir Charles was at his house in the country, where he was always on the look out for patients.' (Macilwain, 42)

Blicke died on 30 December 1815 in Bedford Place, Russell Square, London.

NORMAN MOORE, *rev.* MICHAEL BEVAN

Sources G. Macilwain, *Memoirs of John Abernethy*, 1 (1853) • Z. Cope, *The Royal College of Surgeons of England: a history* (1959) • *GM*, 1st ser., 86/1 (1816), 89, 177 • S. C. Lawrence, *Charitable knowledge: hospital pupils and practitioners in eighteenth-century London* (1996)

Bligh, Edward Vesey (1829–1908), Church of England clergyman, was born on 28 February 1829 at 37 Grosvenor Place, London. He was the second son of Edward Bligh, fifth earl of Darnley (1795–1835), and his wife, Emma (1804–1884), daughter of Henry *Parnell, first Baron Congleton. His mother was a strict Irvingite trembling on the edge of religious mania. Although Bligh's uncle and guardian, Longley, later archbishop of Canterbury, ensured that he was reared in the Church of England, a strain of ultra-protestantism was nevertheless grafted onto the boy. Bligh was educated at Eton College (1839–45), in Hanover and France (1845–6), and at Christ Church, Oxford (1848–50), where he chiefly hunted and raced. Leaving Oxford without taking a degree, he worked in the Foreign Office under Palmerston, and served as an attaché at Hanover (1850–51), Florence (1851–2), and Berlin (1852–3). His most important work in Florence was on behalf of Englishmen who had been insulted or arrested by the Austrian military authorities protecting the régime of Grand Duke Leopold; his intervention saved from execution the three Stratford brothers, sons of the fifth earl of Aldborough.

At this time Bligh fell in love with Lady Isabel Mary Frances Nevill (1831–1915), whose family at Eridge Castle were county neighbours of the Darnleys at Cobham Hall. As a precondition of their marriage her father, the fourth earl of Abergavenny, insisted that Bligh abandon diplomacy and settle in Kent. Yielding to this ultimatum, and committing vocational suicide, Bligh was married on 23 February 1854. The couple had two children, a son and a daughter. As a married undergraduate Bligh attended Downing College, Cambridge (MA 1854), before ordination (1855). He was a lieutenant in the West Kent yeomanry (1853–5), chaplain to that corps (1855–70), and curate at Snodland (1855–6); in 1856 was appointed to a living within Abergavenny's gift near Eridge at Rotherfield. Bligh, whose detestation of Roman Catholicism had increased in Tuscany, found that his congregation had been alienated by the sacerdotalism of the previous rector. As an evangelical who preached in the open air he won back some parishioners, but was so disheartened by the difficulties of his poor, sprawling parish that in 1863 he broke down. While recuperating he was impressed by the lay evangelical Sir Arthur Blackwood and henceforth allied himself with low-church reformers such as lords Radstock and Ebury. He was active in the Prayer Book Revision Society and from 1864 had numerous letters published in *The Times* and the *Daily Telegraph*. He controversially preached to the Countess of Huntingdon's Connexion in order to promote Anglican intercommunion with Reformation, rather than with what he regarded as ritualistic priest-ridden, churches.

In 1865 Bligh became vicar of Birling, a moribund parish in Abergavenny's gift, and initiated the Birling religious revival of 1866. Supported by lay evangelists he achieved some conversions and deathbed confessions but raised social unrest against the Abergavennys, who suppressed his zeal. He was relieved when his wife's inheritance enabled him to buy Fartherwell Hall, near West Malling, in 1874, and to resign his incumbency the following year. Although active as a Kentish magistrate, deputy lieutenant, and county alderman, Bligh was long oppressed by a sense of failure. After visiting Palestine in 1890 and publishing *Lord Ebury as a Church Reformer* (1891) he emerged from his depression to enjoy an affectionate and contented old age. Like most Blighs he was a talented cricketer (his grandson in 1887 was christened Harroweton after the match) and a superb game shot. He died of chronic gout and heart failure on 22 April 1908 at Fartherwell Hall, and was buried at Birling churchyard.

RICHARD DAVENPORT-HINES

Sources E. Wingfield-Stratford, *This was a man: the biography of the Honourable Edward Vesey Bligh, diplomat-parson-squire* (1949) • E. Cust and E. Pelham, *Edward, fifth earl of Darnley and Emma Parnell, his wife* (1913) • E. V. Bligh, *Lord Ebury as a church reformer* (1891) • *The Times* (23 April 1908)

Likenesses photographs, *c*.1854–1900, repro. in Wingfield-Stratford, *This was a man*, facing pp. 56, 88, 153, 217, 249, 264–5

Wealth at death £2432 18*s*. 1*d*.: probate, 22 May 1908, *CGPLA Eng. & Wales*

Bligh, Ivo Francis Walter, eighth earl of Darnley (1859–1927), cricketer and bequeather of the 'Ashes', born on 13 March 1859 at Bruton Street, London, was the second son of John Stuart Bligh, the sixth earl (1827–1896), who owned estates in Kent and co. Meath, and his wife, Lady Harriet Mary Pelham (1829–1905), daughter of Henry Thomas *Pelham, the third earl of Chichester. He was educated at Cheam preparatory school and Eton College, where he was in the eleven (1876–7). He was in residence at Trinity College, Cambridge, from 1877 to 1881 (BA 1882), and represented the university at racquets and tennis as well as winning four cricket blues (1878–81). In 1881, however, his health broke down and despite being captain, he made only three appearances. His best year proved to be 1880, when he appeared for the Gentlemen against the Players and scored 1013 runs (average 30.69).

Bligh is indelibly associated with the origin of the 'Ashes' in 1882. Australia's victory over England led to an 'obituary' in the *Sporting Times* 'in affectionate remembrance of English cricket which died at the Oval on 29 August 1882 … the body will be cremated and the Ashes taken to Australia' (*Sporting Times*, 2 Sept 1882). Bligh 'thought it would be very good fun' (*Cricket Field*, 30 June 1894, 233) to take a side to Australia and by September his party was at sea. The passengers included Florence Rose Morphy (*d*. 1944), companion to the wife of Sir William Clarke, Australia's first baronet and president of Melbourne Cricket Club. Bligh returned to Australia in 1884 and married Florence on 10 February that year. Their first married home was in Melbourne, where (in 1886) the future ninth earl was born. They would have another son and a daughter.

In welcoming the tourists at Melbourne, W. L. Murdoch hoped they would not take home 'those revered ashes' (*Melbourne Herald*, 28 Nov 1882). But, at the end of three matches, the *Sydney Morning Herald* (31 January 1883) reported they were in Mr Bligh's 'custody' though *Wisden* (1884) made no such reference. Nevertheless, the mythical 'Ashes' became a reality. At a 'social' match on Christmas eve 1882, at the Clarkes' home at Rupertswood, near Melbourne, Lady Clarke had a bail burnt and put in an urn as a personal gift to Bligh. He told the story in the *Cricket Field* in 1894 and bequeathed the urn to Lord's on his death. At a reception for the 1930 Australian tourists in London, the dowager Countess Darnley recounted the events at Rupertswood in detail (*The Times*, 27 June 1930).

While the 'Ashes' would be a lodestar for Anglo-

Australian cricket in the future, Bligh's own star was only briefly in the ascendant and after the tour of Australia he played very little. Expectations of him had always been greater than fulfilment, yet *Cricket* could write 'it would be difficult to name any English sportsman of any kind more deservedly popular … a very dangerous batsman if allowed to get set' (16 March 1883). But ill health continued to prevail and he began 'to despair of ever getting well' until taking up golf in 1889 (*Cricket Field*, 30 June 1894, 233).

Bligh was president of Kent County Cricket Club (1892 and 1902) and of the MCC in the year he inherited the earldom from his elder brother (1900). In 1905 he was elected a representative peer for Ireland and he was a deputy lieutenant and alderman for Kent. He died in his sleep at his home, Puckle Hill, Cobham, near Gravesend, Kent, on 10 April 1927 and was buried four days later in Cobham churchyard. Florence Darnley, who was made a DBE (1919) for her work for the arts, died on 30 August 1944.

GERALD M. D. HOWAT

Sources *The Times* (11 April 1927) • *Cricket* (16 March 1883), 17 • 'Chats on the cricket field', *Cricket Field* (30 June 1894), 233 • *Baily's Magazine*, 42 (1884), 389–90 • A. Haygarth, *Marylebone club cricket scores and biographies*, 13 (1880), 985 • A. Haygarth, *Arthur Haygarth's cricket scores and biographies*, 14 (1895), 107 • J. Munns, *Beyond reasonable doubt* (1994) • Lord Harris, ed., *The history of Kent county cricket* (1907) • *Wisden* (1877–84) • *Wisden* (1928) • *The Times* (31 Aug 1944) [obit. of Lady Darnley] • *Sydney Morning Herald* (31 Jan 1883) • *Melbourne Herald* (28 Nov 1882) • GEC, *Peerage* • Venn, *Alum. Cant.* • *CGPLA Eng. & Wales* (1927)

Archives Medway Archives and Local Studies Centre, Rochester, Kent, family MSS

Likenesses W. H. Harrison, photograph, *c.*1906, repro. in Harris, ed., *History of Kent county cricket* • J. Brown, photograph, repro. in *Baily's Magazine*, 42 (1884), 389 • Elliott & Fry, photograph, repro. in 'Chats on the cricket field' • Spy [L. Ward], cartoon, repro. in *Statesmen*, 766 (7 April 1904) • photo line drawing, repro. in *Cricket* (23 March 1883), 17

Wealth at death £237,030 9*s.* 3*d.*: probate, 15 Nov 1927, *CGPLA Eng. & Wales*

Bligh, Richard (1780–1838), barrister, was the second son of John Bligh of Abingdon Street, London, secretary of the Chelsea waterworks, and his wife, Lucy Shuter. He was educated at Westminster School and at Trinity College, Cambridge, where he graduated BA in 1803 and MA in 1806. On 29 November 1817, he married Harriet Maria, daughter of Vice-Admiral William *Bligh and a close relative. Bligh was called to the bar at Lincoln's Inn in November 1826 and became an equity draftsman at the chancery bar. He did not have a large practice, but was chiefly engaged in reporting at the House of Lords for several years. Several publications resulted, including *Reports of Cases Heard in the House of Lords, on Appeals and Errors of Writ* (1823, 1829). Bligh died of apoplexy in James Street, London, on 22 May 1838. JAMES MEW, *rev.* BETH F. WOOD

Sources Venn, *Alum. Cant.* • W. P. Baildon, ed., *The records of the Honorable Society of Lincoln's Inn: admissions*, 2 (1896), 121 • d. cert.

Bligh, Sir Richard Rodney (1737–1821), naval officer, was the second son of Lieutenant Richard Bligh (*b.* 1713), naval

Sir Richard Rodney Bligh (1737–1821), by William Ridley, pubd 1805 (after John Opie, *c.*1797)

officer, and his wife, Ann, *née* Page, and a third cousin of Vice-Admiral William Bligh. He was baptized in Holy Trinity Church, Gosport, on 8 November 1737, with George Bridges Rodney—the future Baron Rodney—as his godfather.

Bligh went to sea with Rodney in the *Rainbow* in 1750, and was a midshipman in the *Ramillies* with Admiral John Byng at the battle of Minorca in 1756. He was commissioned lieutenant in the *Nightingale* in 1757, and took part in Rodney's victorious West Indian campaign. Bligh was promoted commander by Rodney in 1762, and given command of the sloop *Virgin*. On 13 November 1765 he married Ann Worsley (1744/5–1797), daughter of Sir Edward Worsley. In 1777 he was made a post captain and appointed to the *Camel*. He took, as an acting lieutenant, Bartholomew James, who recorded that Bligh treated him with civility. Bligh seems to have been a humane commander; the punishments recorded in his logs are few and moderate.

In 1782 Bligh commanded the *Asia* (64 guns), under Lord Howe, at the relief of Gibraltar. He was appointed to the *Alexander* (74 guns) in 1794 and on 6 November, in company with the *Canada* (74 guns), met a French squadron of five line-of-battle ships, three frigates, and a brig. The *Alexander* engaged three line-of-battle ships for upwards of two hours, allowing the *Canada* to escape. With the ship in danger of sinking and two other enemy ships coming up, Bligh had to strike his colours and was taken to Brest a prisoner. He had been advanced to the rank of rear-admiral in October 1794, but had not been officially informed of it. On returning to England he was court martialled for the loss of the *Alexander* but most honourably acquitted, the court very highly approving of the conduct of all the ship's company.

From 1796 to 1799 Bligh was second in command at Jamaica. He infuriated the commander-in-chief, Sir Hyde Parker, over his conduct of a court martial arising from the *Hermione* mutiny, during which Captain Hugh Pigot and nine officers had been murdered. The acquittal of two defendants, one a boy of twelve, and the recommendation to mercy of a third, led Parker to write to the Admiralty accusing Bligh of 'supineness' and demanding his removal (28 May 1798, PRO, ADM 1/248).

Bligh became a vice-admiral in February 1799, and returned home in September. His wife had died on 7 July 1797 and on 28 July 1800 he married Mary Golightly (1745/6–1834). He was commander-in-chief at Leith from 1803 to 1804 and advanced to the rank of admiral in April 1804. He saw no further service afloat but was invested with the GCB in 1820. Bligh died on 30 April 1821 at Belle Vue, a mansion he had bought in Southampton. He was buried in the family vault at St Mary's, Alverstoke, Hampshire, on 9 May.

Bligh left a son and four daughters from his first marriage. His son, Captain George Miller Bligh, had served as a midshipman with him in the *Alexander* and as a lieutenant in the *Victory* at Trafalgar, where he was severely wounded. The daughters were Harriet Worsley, Ann Caroline, Elizabeth, and Sophia Holmes who married Charles Carter, who had served as a lieutenant in the *Alexander* and was later a vice-admiral.

J. K. LAUGHTON, *rev.* MADGE DARBY

Sources J. Ralfe, *The naval biography of Great Britain*, 4 vols. (1828), vol. 2, p. 517; vol. 4, p. 261 • G. Haddon, 'Bligh family tree', *Mariner's Mirror*, 85 (1999), 204 • *The journal of Rear-Admiral Bartholomew James, 1752–1828*, ed. J. Knox Laughton and J. Y. F. Sullivan, Navy RS, 6 (1896) • court martial for loss of the *Alexander*, 25 May 1795, PRO, ADM 1/5332 • D. Spinney, *Rodney* (1969) • D. Pope, *The black ship* (1963) • *GM*, 1st ser., 91/1 (1821), 468 • D. Syrett and R. L. DiNardo, *The commissioned sea officers of the Royal Navy, 1660–1815*, rev. edn, Occasional Publications of the Navy RS, 1 (1994) • ships' logs, PRO, ADM 51/1029; ADM 51/156; ADM 51/67 • muster books, PRO, ADM 36/2811; ADM 36/6461; ADM 36/6180; ADM 36/6993; ADM 36/8462; ADM 36/11264 • J. J. Colledge, *Ships of the Royal Navy: an historical index*, 1 (1969) • G. H. Williams, *The Bligh tomb at Alverstoke*, Gosport Society, Gosport Records, 7 (1973) • *Monumental inscriptions of St Mary, Alverstoke, Hampshire*, Hampshire Genealogical Society (1986) • will, PRO, PROB 11/1643, 10 July 1821 • parish register, Gosport, Holy Trinity, Portsmouth RO, 8 Nov 1737 [baptism] • parish register, Gatcombe, Isle of Wight, St Olave, Isle of Wight RO, 13 Nov 1765 [marriage: Ann Worsley] • parish register, Kingston upon Thames, All Saints, Surrey HC, 28 July 1800 [marriage: Mary Golightly] • parish register, Alverstoke, St Mary's, Portsmouth RO, 9 May 1821 [burial]

Archives NMM, letters to Lord Keith • PRO, logs of ships, ADM 51

Likenesses W. Ridley, stipple engraving, pubd 1805 (after J. Opie, *c.*1797), NPG [*see illus.*] • oils, priv. coll.

Wealth at death est. £30,000; left bequests of £21,000; plus mansion in Southampton and two properties in Gosport: will, PRO, PROB 11/1643

Bligh, Thomas (1685–1775), army officer and politician, was born on 15 January 1685, the second son of Thomas Bligh (*c.*1654–1710) of Rathmore, co. Meath, Ireland, and his wife, Elizabeth (*d.* 1737), the daughter of Colonel James Naper, of Longhcrew, co. Meath. His father, a grazier by origin who was granted lands under the Williamite confiscations of 1688, was MP for County Meath (1695–1710) and was made a privy councillor by James Butler, second duke of Ormond. His elder brother, John (1683–1727), who was in 1725 created earl of Darnley, was buried in Westminster Abbey. Thomas Bligh was often entitled 'honourable' by contemporary writers, as if he were the younger son of an earl. He was returned to the Irish parliament as member for Athboy, co. Meath, in 1715, and held the seat for sixty years.

In 1717 Bligh purchased a captaincy in the 6th Irish horse (later the 5th dragoon guards). His promotion to lieutenant-colonel of the regiment in October 1719 owed much to his uncle Lieutenant-General Robert Naper, colonel of the regiment. In 1737 he married Elizabeth (*d.* 1759), the daughter of John Bury of Shannon Grove, Limerick. Their only child died young. In 1740, having failed to secure the colonelcy of his regiment upon the death of his uncle, Bligh was appointed colonel of the 20th foot, which served in Flanders during the War of the Austrian Succession (1740–46). In 1745 he became brigadier-general, and commanded in a very sharp action at the causeway of Melle when marching to reinforce the garrison of Ghent. In 1746 he was transferred from the 20th foot to the 12th dragoons, in 1747 he became major-general, in December the same year he was transferred to the colonelcy of his old regiment, the 5th dragoon guards, which had then become the 2nd Irish horse, and in 1754 he became lieutenant-general.

In July 1758 preparations were made on an extensive scale for another descent on the French coast, to create a diversion in favour of the army under Prince Ferdinand of Brunswick in Germany. Against his better judgement, and under pressure from Pitt's government, Bligh (now aged seventy-three) accepted command of the expedition, in place of Lord George Sackville and the duke of Marlborough, who successfully lobbied to be sent with the British forces to Germany—a command Bligh had expected to fill upon his arrival in London. The fleet under Howe, with the troops under Bligh on board, left England at the beginning of August 1758, and in seven days arrived in Cherbourg Roads. The troops were landed and Cherbourg was captured, but Bligh and his staff showed themselves inadequate leaders of men. The harbour, piers, and forts of Cherbourg were destroyed as ordered, but the troops were allowed to plunder and pillage the surrounding area with devastating effect, and the plans for re-embarkation had to be drawn up and supervised by Howe. The troops took with them Cherbourg's brass ordnance as trophies. On 3 September Bligh landed his force at St Luniare in preparation for a siege of St Malo. While the infantry were being disembarked a reconnaissance revealed that the plan to force a passage across the River Rance was impracticable. A sudden change in the weather forced the fleet to weigh anchor with the artillery and horse still on board. It was then decided to march the infantry a short distance westwards to the Bay of St Cast, where the fleet would be waiting.

However, the march was poorly conducted, the condition and morale of the line regiments had deteriorated, and there were considerable losses from harrying French militia. The expedition reached Matignon, inland from St Cast, on 11 September and the fateful decision was taken to make camp rather than re-embark immediately. Intelligence was received during the night of an approaching French force under the command of the duc d'Aiguillon which was of similar size. Instead of slipping away quietly in the night, Bligh and his staff waited until break of day, announcing their plans to the enemy with the drumming of the reveille. The first troops were embarked at 9.00 a.m. By 11.00 a.m. three brigades of the line together with the wounded were on board when the French appeared on the heights above. They were met by the rear guard, now stranded on the beach, consisting of the Grenadier Guards and the grenadier companies of the line regiments, under the command of Major-General Alexander Dury. Despite inflicting severe casualties upon the French, the bulk of this force (approximately a thousand men) were either killed, wounded, or taken prisoner. Dury was among those who drowned in a desperate attempt to swim out to the boats.

Bligh was severely censured for his conduct in the affair. He was criticized by the commander-in-chief, John, Viscount Ligonier, for compromising the expedition's diversionary strategy by failing to land his artillery and horse and meet the French in battle. More recent commentators have pointed to the poor condition of his troops; his real failure was in not making a more rapid re-embarkation. Bligh was snubbed at court and, believing himself to have been made a scapegoat by Pitt, he resigned all his commissions and offices and retired to his property in Ireland.

The incident became the subject of a pamphlet war in London between supporters and opponents of Pitt's war policy. A rigid censorship was imposed and the military dispatches were never published. Bligh himself publicly disowned authorship of a pamphlet purporting to be *A Letter from the Honourable L—t G—l B—gh to the Rt. Hon. W—m P—t Esq.* (London, 1758), which set out a defence of his actions. However, this is believed to be founded on a genuine letter combining his own narrative with remarks by the anonymous pamphleteer.

It is also thought that the foolhardy decision to attack St Malo (the geographical difficulties were well known) was pressed upon Bligh by the court of George, prince of Wales (the future George III), at Leicester House. The prince's brother, Prince Edward, served as a volunteer in the fleet under Howe, and General Clark, Bligh's incompetent quartermaster-general, was close to the Leicester House faction. The ministry's treatment of Bligh was taken as a slight by this group, and it was the prince of Wales's adviser, John Stuart, third earl of Bute, who prevailed upon him to resign his offices. Notwithstanding his incapacity for this command, which age alone should have precluded and his better judgement attempted to resist, his subsequent treatment as a pawn of political faction was a sad end to what had been an honourable and brave, if somewhat modest, military career.

Some time after his retirement Bligh married again. His second wife, Frances, the daughter of Theophilus Jones, of Leitrim, had no children. He died at Brittas, near Dublin, on 15 September 1775, at the age of ninety, and was buried at Rathmore. His ample fortune of £100,000 he bequeathed to his younger brother, Robert Bligh (1703–1778), dean of Elphin.

H. M. CHICHESTER, *rev.* JONATHAN SPAIN

Sources 'Darnley', GEC, *Peerage*, new edn • Burke, *Peerage* (1999) [Darnley] • Burke, *Gen. Ire.* (1976) • Foster, *Alum. Oxon.* • C. Dalton, *George the First's army, 1714–1727*, 2 vols. (1910–12) • R. Whitworth, *Field Marshal Lord Ligonier: a story of the British army, 1702–1770* (1958) • F. W. Hamilton, *The origin and history of the first or grenadier guards*, 3 vols. (1874) • R. L. Pomeroy, ed., *The story of a regiment of horse, being the regimental history from 1685 to 1922 of the 5th Princess Charlotte of Wales' dragoon guards*, 2 vols. (1924) • B. Smyth, *History of the XXth regiment, 1688–1888* (1889) • Fortescue, *Brit. army* • R. Middleton, *The bells of victory: the Pitt–Newcastle ministry and the conduct of the Seven Years' War, 1757–1762* (1985) • M. Peters, *Pitt and popularity: the patriot minister and London opinion during the Seven Years' War* (1980) • J. S. Corbett, *England in the Seven Years' War; a study in combined strategy*, 1 (1907) • *A letter from the Honourable L—t G—l B—gh to the Rt. Hon. W—m P—t Esq.* (1758) • R. Cannon, ed., *Historical record of the fourth, or royal Irish dragoon guards* (1839)

Archives Medway Archives and Local Studies Centre, Rochester, Kent, family and estate MSS

Likenesses T. Gainsborough, oils, Metropolitan Museum of Art, New York

Wealth at death over £100,000: *Scotsman Magazine*, 37 (Sept 1775), 525

Bligh, William (1754–1817), naval officer and colonial governor, was born in Plymouth on 9 September 1754, the only son of Francis Bligh (1721–1780) and his wife, Jane Pearse, *née* Balsam (*d. c.*1770). The Bligh family had long resided at Tinten in Cornwall. Bligh's father was a customs officer at Plymouth; other family members had entered the army and the navy. William Bligh is recorded in the *Monmouth*'s muster book as 'Captain's Servant' in 1762, as able seaman in that of the *Hunter* in July 1770, and as midshipman (*Hunter*) from February 1771. In September 1771 he transferred to the *Crescent* (36 guns), then, in September 1775, to the *Ranger*, from which he gained his lieutenant's passing certificate on 1 May 1776. Bligh must have shown distinct ability in these postings, for in March 1776, preparing for his third voyage of exploration to the Pacific Ocean, Captain James Cook chose the still quite junior officer as master of the *Resolution*.

For three years Bligh oversaw the working of the ship, and assisted in the navigation and charting of this immense voyage (1776–80), which explored the islands and coastlines of the northern Pacific Ocean, and which saw Cook killed at Kealakekua Bay, Hawaii, in February 1779. Afterwards Bligh was bitter that Captain James King did not make what he considered to be proper acknowledgement of his contributions in King's *A Voyage to the Pacific Ocean* (1784):

> None of the Maps and Charts in this publication are from the original drawings of Lieutenant Henry Roberts; he did no more than copy the original ones from Captain Cook, who

William Bligh (1754–1817), by John Russell, 1791

besides myself was the only person that surveyed and laid the coast down, in the *Resolution*. Every plan & Chart from C. Cook's death are exact Copies of my Works. (marginalia in the copy in the Admiralty library)

After his return to England Bligh was promoted lieutenant (September 1781), and served in a number of line-of-battle ships in the North Sea and the Mediterranean. He went on half pay on 13 January 1783.

Bligh had married Elizabeth Betham (1754?–1812) at Douglas on the Isle of Man on 4 February 1781. The couple had three daughters in the next years, and three more subsequently. With the peace Bligh undertook a series of trading voyages to the West Indies in vessels owned by his wife's relative Duncan Campbell, the overseer of the convict hulks in the Thames. Fatefully, he took Fletcher *Christian with him on two of these, and the pair became friendly.

In mid-1787, as a consequence of Sir Joseph Banks's patronage, Bligh received the command of the *Bounty*, then being fitted to transport breadfruit and other plants from the islands of the central Pacific Ocean and from south-east Asia to the West Indies. This proposed plant transfer was part of an elaborate scheme to increase British trade with Asia: the mechanization of the spinning and weaving industry then beginning was creating the capacity for greatly expanded production; cotton goods might be manufactured in England, and exported to India and, especially, China; the growth of this trade would both give East India Company ships outward cargoes, and lessen the need for the British to find silver with which to purchase Chinese goods; for greater production of cotton goods, more raw supplies were needed; if plantation owners might feed slaves more cheaply, then large-scale cotton cultivation might become feasible in the West Indies; the breadfruit and other fruits and vegetables which grew in great abundance in the eastern tropics might become cheap staples for the slaves.

With a crew of forty-four, Fletcher Christian among them, the *Bounty* sailed in December 1787. After failing to enter the Pacific Ocean round Cape Horn, Bligh reached Tahiti at the end of October 1788. Laden with more than 1000 young breadfruit plants, he sailed again at the beginning of April 1789. In the early morning of 28 April 1789, when off the island of Tofua (Tonga), Fletcher Christian led part of the crew in mutiny.

Subsequent events, and their repeated evocation in literature and film, have made this mutiny the most famous in the history of the sea. The rebels set Bligh and eighteen men adrift in the ship's 23 foot long launch, with little food and only minimal navigational tools. Incredibly Bligh managed to reach Kupang in Timor two months later with the loss of only one man, after a harrowing 3500 mile voyage. The mutineers spent nine months ranging the central Pacific in search of a haven. In the end some chose to remain at Tahiti, where they were arrested by Captain Edward Edwards and subsequently tried at court martial. Others went with Christian and Polynesian companions to a bloody fate on Pitcairn, then mislocated on charts. The causes of the mutiny and the motives of the mutineers have been much debated. Bligh suggested that the rebels listened to Tahiti's siren song; Christian's supporters, on the other hand, argued that Bligh's harsh treatment had driven him mad. While puzzles remain, it is clear that Bligh and Christian became locked into a deeply ambivalent symbiosis that led to tragedy.

In 1791–3 Bligh returned to the Pacific with the *Providence* and the *Assistant*; and this time succeeded in bringing the breadfruit to the West Indies. On his return to England he found that his reputation had been much diminished by evidence presented at the trial of the captured *Bounty* mutineers. War with France having broken out, he returned to active service, taking command of the *Calcutta* (26 guns) in April 1795, then, as post captain, of the *Director* (64 guns) in January 1796. He participated in the battle of Camperdown under Admiral Adam Duncan (11 October 1797), and in the battle of Copenhagen under Nelson (2 April 1801), in both of which he acted courageously. In these years, though, he suffered the indignity of another mutiny, at the Nore, in May 1797 after which he strenuously protected his men and ensured that none were hanged for participation. After the Nore Bligh suffered a case of serious insubordination by Lieutenant John Frazier on the *Warrior* in 1804. In February 1805 the court martial brought by Frazier 'reprimanded' Bligh, and 'admonished' him to be 'in future more correct in his language' (Kennedy, *Mutinies*, 278).

In 1805 Sir Joseph Banks procured for Bligh the governorship of the New South Wales colony. After a voyage during which he and Captain Joseph Short argued incessantly, Bligh arrived in August 1806, to find the society deeply divided between the military and civilian officers and free settlers ('exclusives') on the one hand, and convicts and former convicts ('emancipists') on the other. Bligh took the part of the smallholders about the Hawkesbury River in their economic quarrels with the exclusives. Following a series of skirmishes the officers of the New South Wales Corps deposed him on 26 January 1808. After a weary exile on the *Porpoise*, mostly in the Derwent estuary outside Hobart, Bligh was superseded by Lachlan Macquarie in January 1810.

Bligh returned to England in October 1810. In May 1801 he had been elected FRS. He was promoted by seniority rear-admiral (July 1811), then vice-admiral (1814). His wife having died on 15 April 1812, Bligh relocated his family to Farningham in Kent. He died on 7 December 1817 in Bond Street, London, and was buried next to his wife at St Mary, Lambeth.

William Bligh was clearly a superior navigator; and danger, whether on an arduous ocean or in the heat of battle, brought out the best in him. But he was an abysmal leader otherwise, and this incapacity became more pronounced with age. A brief acquaintance showed Macquarie that '[Bligh] certainly is a most disagreeable Person to have any dealings, or Publick business to transact with; having no regard whatever to his promise or engagements however sacred, and his natural temper is uncommonly harsh, and tyrannical in the extreme' (Kennedy, *Mutinies*, 299).

It is important to note, however, that Bligh's 'violence' was habitually more verbal than physical (his cruel punishment of David Collins's young son on the *Porpoise* notwithstanding). Greg Dening has established that Bligh flogged less than any other British commander in the Pacific Ocean in the later eighteenth century. What most threw Bligh into 'those violent Tornados of temper' (Kennedy, *Mutinies*, 306), during which he gestured violently with his hands, was perceived dereliction of duty by officers and seamen's incompetence. When either of these occurred Bligh's invective could bruise men's egos as much as any lash their backs. After the *Bounty* left Tahiti, Bligh fretted excessively about the plants' welfare. When officers and crew offended he called them 'damn'd Infernal scoundrels, blackguard, liar, vile man, jesuit, thief, lubber, disgrace to the service, damn'd long pelt of a bitch'; he told them he would make them 'eat grass like cows'; he told the officers that he would make them jump overboard before they reached Torres Strait (Barney, 64, 69; *Journal of James Morrison*, 19). Interestingly, this 'bad language' was not obscene in the modern sense; rather, it was humiliating and dislocating. As Dening puts it, '[Bligh's language] was bad, not so much because it was intemperate or abusive, but because it was ambiguous, because men could not read in it a right relationship to his authority' (Dewing, 61). Bligh's great failing was that he was so unaware of the effect his mood swings and harsh criticisms had on those about him. The story of the *Bounty* proved popular with twentieth-century film-makers, most notably in Frank Lloyd's *Mutiny on the Bounty* (1935), in which Bligh was played by Charles Laughton, and in subsequent remakes in 1962 and 1984, when the role of the captain was taken by Trevor Howard and Anthony Hopkins respectively. In these depictions, Bligh appears as overbearing and cruel, and as significantly older than he was (at thirty-four he was only ten years older than Christian). ALAN FROST

Sources Mitchell L., NSW, Bligh MSS • E. Egan, *Guide to the papers of William Bligh and the Bligh family in the Mitchell Library, State Library of New South Wales* (1989) • MSS in admiralty files, PRO • MSS in admiralty files, NMM • F. M. Bladen, ed., *Historical records of New South Wales*, 6 (1898) • W. Bligh, *A voyage to the south sea* (1792) • [S. Barney], *Minutes of … the court-martial … on ten persons charged with mutiny on board his majesty's ship the 'Bounty'* (1794) • *The journal of James Morrison*, ed. O. Rutter (1935) • W. Bligh, *The log of the 'Bounty'*, ed. O. Rutter, 2 vols. (1937) • G. Kennedy, *Bligh* (1978) • G. Kennedy, *Captain Bligh: the man and his mutinies* (1989) • G. Dening, *Mr Bligh's bad language: passion, power and theatre on the Bounty* (1992) • *The Bligh notebook*, ed. J. Bach (1987) • G. Mackaness, *Bligh* (1951)

Archives BL, charts and MSS, RP 1927 [copies] • Mitchell L., NSW, corresp. and papers • NL Aus., MSS, notebook, and log • NMM, MSS • PRO, Admiralty collection, MSS • State Library of New South Wales, Sydney, Dixson Wing, log books and charts • State Library of Queensland, South Brisbane, logbooks | NL Aus., letters to Francis Bond • NMM, letters to Francis Bond • NRA, letters to Sir Joseph Banks

Likenesses R. Dodd, group portrait, engraving, 1790 (*The mutineers turning Lieut. Bligh and part of the officers and crew adrift from his majesty's Ship the Bounty*), London • J. Russell, pastel drawing, 1791, Captain Cook Memorial Museum, Whitby [*see illus.*] • G. Dance, pencil drawing, 1794, NPG • Bromley, group portrait, line engraving, pubd 1802 (*The hospitable behaviour of the governor of Timor to Lieutenant Bligh*; after Benezach), NPG • G. Noble and J. Parker, group portrait, line engraving, pubd 1803 (*Commemorating 11 October 1797*; after *Naval victories* by J. Smart), BM, NPG • J. Smart, pencil and watercolour drawing, *c.*1803, NPG • H. A. Barker, portrait, 1805, State Library of New South Wales, Sydney • M. Clark, statue, 1987, Circular Quay, Sydney • J. Condé, coloured stipple (after J. Russell), BM, NPG

Blight [Bright], **Ellen Eliza** [Helen] (**1833/4–1850**), lion tamer, was the daughter of John Blight (or Bright), a bugle player and bandleader with George Wombwell's menagerie, and his wife, Elizabeth, the daughter of Samuel Wombwell and so George Wombwell's sister. As a young child Ellen travelled with the menagerie and showed no fear of the animals, and frequently rode on the back of the Bengal tiger. In 1849 she succeeded Ellen Chapman as the 'Lion Queen' in the menagerie, and performed that year before Queen Victoria. On Friday 11 January 1850, while the menagerie was at Chatham, on the Military Road, some naval officers strolled in at about nine o'clock after the conclusion of the public performance, and asked to see the act. Ellen Blight complied, entered a cage containing a lion and a tiger, and rashly clipped the dozing tiger on the nose with her small whip. The animal jumped up, catching the Lion Queen by her dress. She fell; the tiger's claws stripped the flesh from her right leg, and then the animal caught her by the throat, mortally wounding her. The tiger was driven off with an iron bar, and Blight was removed, unconscious, to a living-van, and attended by a doctor who was present, but she died within minutes. Both her parents and a brother witnessed her death.

Ellen Blight, sometimes referred to as Ellen or Helen

Bright, was buried at Coventry on 15 January, in the grave of her cousin William Wombwell. The incident turned the public against the performances of Lion Queens. It was said that George Wombwell had always had a lurking fear of such an accident's happening to his niece, and banned any replacement. The tiger was retained, kept in a separate cage, and was later advertised as the animal which killed the Lion Queen. JOHN M. TURNER

Sources *Rochester, Chatham and Strood Gazette* (15 Jan 1850), 2 · *Dover Chronicle* (19 Jan 1850) · 'Frightful death of Mr Wombwell's Lion Queen', cutting of unknown origin, Chatham Public Library · *Coventry Standard* (15 Sept 1888) · *Coventry Standard* (31 Jan 1896) · W. S. Meadmore, *King Pole* (April–June 1935), 19 · C. H. Keeling, *Zoological Society of Greater Manchester*, 10/38 (1989–90), 16 · d. cert.

Blight, William (1785–1862), naval officer, entered the navy on 9 May 1793, as a volunteer on board the *Intrepid* (64 guns, Captain the Hon. Charles Carpenter). In that ship he continued as midshipman, master's mate, and acting lieutenant, most of the time in the East and West Indies, until confirmed as lieutenant on 15 April 1803, and appointed to the *Britannia* (100 guns) with Captain, afterwards Rear-Admiral, the earl of Northesk. In the *Britannia* he served at Trafalgar, and was sent to take possession of the French *Aigle* (74 guns), which was lost in the gale immediately after the battle. Blight, however, was rescued, and in the spring of 1806 followed Northesk into the *Dreadnought*. In August 1806 he was appointed to the *Néréide* (36 guns, Captain Corbet), and served in the attack on Buenos Aires in July 1807. The *Néréide* afterwards went to the East Indies; the crew mutinied, and in February 1809, when Captain Robert *Corbet was tried for cruelty in the suppression of the disorder, Blight, the first lieutenant, was the principal defence witness. He was afterwards (1812–14) agent for transports at Palermo; from 1819 to 1821 first lieutenant of the flagship *Queen Charlotte* at Portsmouth, and on 12 February 1821 was promoted to commander. In May 1828 he was appointed to the *Britannia*, carrying the flag of Lord Northesk as commander-in-chief at Plymouth; from there he was transferred to the *St Vincent*, and was posted from her on 22 July 1830. He held no further appointment in the navy; he retired as a captain on 1 October 1850, and was promoted retired rear-admiral on 27 September 1855. He died at East Stonehouse, Plymouth, on 22 July 1862, survived by his wife, Jane Money Blight. He had previously been married to Louisa, sister of Commander J. B. Howell RN.

Blight was a man of very humble origins who rose on merit to become a lieutenant in time of war and, through the earl of Northesk, acquired enough patronage for peacetime promotion to post rank. The *Néréide* mutiny was the one blemish on his career.

J. K. LAUGHTON, *rev.* ANDREW LAMBERT

Sources D. Syrett and R. L. DiNardo, *The commissioned sea officers of the Royal Navy, 1660–1815*, rev. edn, Occasional Publications of the Navy RS, 1 (1994) · *GM*, 3rd ser., 13 (1862), 238 · J. Marshall, *Royal naval biography*, 4 vols. (1823–35) [with 4 suppls.] · O'Byrne, *Naval biog. dict.* · Boase, *Mod. Eng. biog.* · *CGPLA Eng. & Wales* (1862)
Likenesses oils, NMM
Wealth at death under £2000: probate, 7 Aug 1862, *CGPLA Eng. & Wales*

Blincoe, Robert (*c.*1792–1860), factory apprentice, was a parish orphan who knew neither parent, did not know his place of birth, and was uncertain even about his name. Between the ages of four and seven he was brought up in St Pancras workhouse, London. Soon after his arrival there, a woman enquired about him under the name 'Saint'. Partly for this reason, and partly because there were rumours of his being the illegitimate child of a clergyman, he was called 'the Young Saint', and later 'Parson' or 'the Young Parson'. Yearning for freedom, he even thought that being apprenticed to a chimney sweep would be preferable, but he was too small to be selected.

About a year later, in August 1799, with eighty children from the workhouse who were also thought to be at least seven years old, he was bound apprentice until aged twenty-one to Messrs Lambert, cotton spinners, who owned Lowdham Mill near Nottingham. After about four years Parson was transferred to Ellice Needham's Litton Mill, near Tideswell, Derbyshire. By 1813, when his apprenticeship was completed, he had lost his left forefinger and his legs were crooked; his portrait was used by opponents of the factory system to illustrate its defects. At this point he discovered that he had been apprenticed as Robert Blincoe, a name he adopted thereafter, assuming that Blincoe had been his clergyman father. He then worked in several textile mills until 1817, by which time he had saved enough to set up as a cotton-waste dealer. He married a woman named Martha on 28 June 1819, and occupied a shop at 108 Bank Top, Manchester; then in 1824 he moved to 2 Edge Place, Salford. Blincoe had by then saved 'a few pounds' (evidence to Dr Hawkins, 'Second report', 1833) and became a cotton spinner, owning his own machinery and renting power and space in Ormrod's mill near Tib Street. Almost ruined by a fire at the mill, he was imprisoned before 1828 at Lancaster Castle for debt, but later returned to business. By 1830 he was dealing in cotton waste at 32 High Street and kept a shop at 407 Oldham Road.

Blincoe's historical importance lies in the memoir of him that was compiled from his discussions with John Brown, a journalist in Bolton; there William Smith, later editor of the *Bolton Chronicle*, was campaigning for factory reform. Brown was 'much pleased with his conversation'; he said that 'in his manners [Blincoe] appeared remarkably gentle; in his language, temperate; in his statements, cautious and consistent' (Brown, 7). The biography was first published in Richard Carlile's radical paper *The Lion* in five weekly instalments from 25 January to 22 February 1828, three years after Brown had killed himself, and without consulting Blincoe, who was at first angry but eventually acquiesced. Its aim was to stimulate public concern about the plight of factory children, and the movement to curb factory hours used it for this purpose. Propagandist in intent and highly emotive—even melodramatic—in tone, the memoir none the less provided chapter and verse on the guilty and their victims. Vividly and in often wearisome detail Brown portrayed the bad air, long hours, inadequate food, poor sanitation, brutal discipline, and dreadful injuries which the children experienced. He memorably described Blincoe's early attempt at escape and his recapture, and sought to throw contemporary humanitarians on the defensive by likening the children to the slaves who were then at the heart of humanitarian concern, though Blincoe's protests to magistrates late in his apprenticeship did have some effect.

The memoir was also published as a pamphlet, which the trade union leader and publisher John Doherty republished in 1832; there are close resemblances between it and Mrs Trollope's novel *The Life and Adventures of Michael Armstrong* (1839). Brown's memoir contains some truth, as other contemporary sources show. Indeed, without that, its contemporary impact would be difficult to explain. Yet by later standards these were years of brutal discipline for all children, and not only for those within factories. Furthermore, the memoir's propagandist function was distant indeed from scholarly objectivity. One historian has even branded it as 'written by a gullible sensationalist, whose statements must be treated with the utmost caution' (Chapman, 208–9).

In 1832 Blincoe was still dealing in cotton waste but also manufactured sheet wadding and kept a grocer's shop at 19 Turner Street, Manchester. In the same year he stood surety for Doherty when the latter was allowed bail in a libel case. In 1833 Blincoe gave evidence to Dr Hawkins for the select committee on the employment of children in manufactories; when asked whether he sent his three children to factories, Blincoe said 'I would rather have them transported' (evidence to Dr Hawkins). By 1833 his eldest child was at home helping her mother, but all three of his children had by then been or were still going to school, and a son graduated from Queens' College, Cambridge, in 1848 to become a clergyman. It was Doherty's pamphlet, 'describing my own life and sufferings', that he presented to the select committee (ibid.).

Blincoe continued dealing in cotton waste and manufacturing sheet wadding in Manchester until at least 1843. He died of bronchitis at his daughter's home in Gunco Lane, Sutton, Macclesfield, on 12 December 1860. Blincoe's name is commemorated by the street name Blinco Street, thus spelt, in Urmston, near Manchester, where Doherty's son Austin built three streets of houses named after episodes in his father's career. His memoir was republished by Caliban Books in 1977. BRIAN HARRISON

Sources 'Second report … inquiring into the employment of children in factories', *Parl. papers* (1833), 21.D3, 17–18, no. 519 [royal commission] · J. Brown, *A memoir of Robert Blincoe* (1832); republished (1977) · R. G. Kirby and A. E. Musson, *The voice of the people: John Doherty, 1798–1854, trade unionist, radical and factory reformer* (1975) · A. E. Musson, 'Robert Blincoe and the early factory system', in A. E. Musson, *Trade union and social history* (1974), 195–206 · S. D. Chapman, *The early factory masters: the transition to the factory system in the midlands textile industry* (1967), 203–9 · d. cert.

Likenesses woodcut, repro. in Brown, *Memoir of Robert Blincoe*, title page

Blind, Karl (1826–1907), political refugee and author, was born of middle-class parents in Mannheim, in the grand duchy of Baden, Germany, on 4 September 1826. He was educated at the Lyceum, Mannheim, and then at Karlsruhe, where he won gold and silver medals; he proceeded with a scholarship to Heidelberg University in 1845, and there studied jurisprudence, literature, archaeology, and philosophy. At Mannheim, the centre of the German radical movement, he imbibed revolutionary principles, and advocated the cause of a united Germany under a republican government. At Heidelberg he actively engaged in political agitation, helping to form democratic clubs among undergraduates, soldiers, and others, and contributing to the advanced nationalist press of Baden, Bavaria, and Prussia. For writing an article in 1846 in which he hotly denounced the punishment of a freethinking soldier, Blind was arrested on a charge of treason. He was acquitted on trial through the eloquence of his advocate, Friedrich Hecker, leader of the advanced liberal group in the Baden Reichstag. However, he was dismissed from Heidelberg University shortly afterwards, and lost his scholarship. He continued his studies at Bonn, and pursued his violent propaganda there. He repeatedly revisited Heidelberg in disguise to take part in political meetings of the students. For the secret distribution of a treasonable pamphlet entitled *Deutscher Hunger und deutsche Fürsten* at Dürkheim, near Neustadt, in 1847, he was arrested for the third time, and with the woman who became his wife he was imprisoned.

In 1848—a year of revolution throughout Europe—Blind took part in March in the democratic risings in Karlsruhe and other towns in Baden. He was present at Frankfurt during the meetings of the Vorparlament, the gathering of advanced liberals, and with Hecker, Gustav von Struve, and other leading republicans, agitated for the body's continuance as a permanent national assembly. He was wounded slightly in a riotous street conflict with the police, and in April joined Hecker in the republican rising near Lake Constance. Proscribed by the Baden government, he took refuge in Alsace, but was there accused of complicity in the June rising in Paris. Imprisoned at Strasbourg by order of General Cavaignac, he was taken in chains to the Swiss frontier. He re-entered Baden, and was prominent in the rising under Struve at Staufen (24 September 1848); with Struve he was taken prisoner at Wehr by some members of the 'city guard' soon afterwards. Sentenced to eight years' imprisonment, he was confined in the underground casements at Rostatt, and ultimately, in May 1849, transferred to Bruchsal, but released by a party of armed citizens as revolution spread there. The revolutionaries soon established at Offenburg under Brentano, on 1 June 1849, a provisional government for Baden and Rhenish Bavaria, and Blind was sent as its representative on a political mission to Paris. Implicated there in Ledru-Rollin's movement against Louis Napoleon, the president of the new French republic, he was arrested on 13 June, sentenced to perpetual exile from France, and, after arbitrary imprisonment for two months in La Force, was conducted to the Belgian frontier. He was there joined by his wife, Friederike Ettlinger, widow of a merchant named Cohen, whom he had married *c.*1849, together with their two children: Rudolph, later an artist, and Ottilie, who later married Charles Hancock, a barrister. In 1852 Blind was in turn exiled from Belgium, owing to pressure from Louis Napoleon's government, and after arriving in England, he settled with his family at Hampstead.

Blind, though never naturalized, thenceforth made England his permanent home, and for more than half a century devoted himself without respite to literary support of 'nationalism' and democratic progress in Germany and elsewhere. His house at Hampstead became a rendezvous for political refugees from Europe, and filled a prominent place in the history of all advanced political movements. He welcomed to England Mazzini, who became an intimate friend, and whom he introduced to Swinburne. At Garibaldi's reception in London in 1864 he spoke on behalf of the German community. He entertained Ledru-Rollin, Louis Blanc (with whom he worked on the *Morning Advertiser* in the 1850s), Marx, Kinkel, and Freiligrath. It was his particular aim to enlist and educate English public opinion on behalf of the German revolutionary cause. In 1863–4, as head of a London committee to promote the independence of Schleswig-Holstein, he acted as intermediary between the leaders of the Schleswig Diet and the British Foreign Office.

An ardent champion of Polish freedom, Blind was in communication with the revolutionary government at Warsaw during 1863, and in lectures that he delivered throughout England and Scotland denounced Russia's oppression of the Poles. He also produced writings in support of the north during the American Civil War, of Germany during the Franco-Prussian War of 1870–71, of Greece in her various disputes with Turkey, and of Japan in her war with Russia in 1904. For his services to Greece he was decorated by King George of Greece with the order of St Andrew. He also strenuously advocated the claims to independence of the Egyptian nationalists from 1882 onwards, and of the Transvaal Boers from 1878 until his death.

Apart from contemporary politics, Blind wrote much on history and on German and Indian mythology, and contributed to leading reviews in England, Germany, America, and Italy. Among his better-known articles were biographical studies of Freiligrath, Ledru-Rollin, and the Hungarian statesman Francis Deak, *Zur Geschichte der republikanischen Partei in England* (1873), and *Fire-Burial among our Germanic Forefathers* (1875), which were reprinted in pamphlet form. To his advocacy was due the foundation of a memorial to Feuerbach, the philosopher, at Landshut, and the erection of monuments to Hans Sachs, the cobbler bard of Nuremberg, and to Walther von der Vogelweide at Bozen (now Bolzano, Italy) in 1877.

Blind died at his home, 3 Winchester Road, Hampstead, on 31 May 1907 and was cremated at Golders Green. In addition to his own children, he had a stepdaughter and a stepson: Mathilde *Blind (1841–1896), a writer, and Ferdinand Cohen Blind, who attempted to assassinate Bismarck in Unter den Linden on 7 May 1866, and who later committed suicide in prison.

S. E. FRYER, *rev.* MATTHEW LEE

Sources *The Times* (1 June 1907) • *Illustrierte Zeitung* (6 Sept 1906) • *Men and women of the time* (1899) • E. Oswald, *Reminiscences of a busy life* (1911) • *Wellesley index* • G. Vapereau, *Dictionnaire universel des contemporains*, 6th edn (Paris, 1893) • K. Blind, 'In years of storm and stress', *Cornhill Magazine*, [3rd] ser., 5–8 (1898–1900) • M. Taylor, *The decline of British radicalism, 1847–1860* (1995) • *CGPLA Eng. & Wales* (1907)

Archives BL, corresp., Add. MSS 40123–40126 | Shetland Archives, Lerwick, letters to Arthur Laurenson relating to folklore

Likenesses bust, 1912, priv. coll. • portrait, repro. in *Illustrierte Zeitung*

Wealth at death £172 13*s*. 11*d*.: probate, 2 July 1907, *CGPLA Eng. & Wales*

Blind [*née* Cohen], **Mathilde** (**1841–1896**), poet and biographer, was born at Mannheim, Germany, on 21 March 1841, the elder of two children of a Jewish banker named Cohen and his second wife, Friederike Ettlinger. Cohen died in Mathilde's infancy and she subsequently adopted the name of her mother's second husband, Karl *Blind (1826–1907), a political writer who participated in the Baden insurrections of 1848–9. After the suppression of the revolutionary movement the Blinds took refuge in London, where their home in Hampstead became a meeting-place for other refugees from abroad, including Garibaldi and Mazzini. Mathilde Blind was more inspired by their political conversation than by the haphazard education she received at a series of girls' schools. Her own thoughts on poetry and on the education of women were reinforced by her reading of Elizabeth Barrett Browning's *Aurora Leigh*. In 1859 she visited Switzerland, where she went on a solitary walking tour of the Alps, was denied access to the lectures at Zürich University, studied philology, Latin, and other languages on her own, and passed much of her time with a group of dedicated revolutionaries. One acquaintance recalled Blind in her late teens as a dazzling beauty, full of the joy of life. She was profoundly affected, however, when in 1866 her younger brother, Ferdinand, failed in an attempt to assassinate Bismarck and then committed suicide in prison. In 1867 she published, under the pseudonym Claude Lake, a volume of *Poems* dedicated to Mazzini; her 'Recollections of Mazzini' eventually appeared in 1891, in an issue of the *Fortnightly Review*. Shelley was another of her heroes: she gave public lectures on his poetry, wrote an essay about him for the *Westminster Review* which appeared in 1870, and edited a selection of his poetry in 1872. She translated David Friedrich Strauss's *Der alte und der neue Glaube* (as *The Old Faith and the New*, 1873), and during the early 1870s she also contributed reviews of poetry to *The Examiner*.

At the age of thirty Blind, who never married, moved out of her parents' home to establish an independent life. She was one in a circle of women writers that included Mona Caird, Violet Paget (Vernon Lee), Amy Levy, Olive Schreiner, and Augusta Webster. She knew James Thomson (B.V.), William Sharp (Fiona Macleod), and Algernon Charles Swinburne, and she was particularly close to the William Michael Rossettis. In the early 1880s she lived in Manchester with the painter Ford Madox Brown and his wife, Emma; there were rumours, after Emma died, that Brown wished to marry her. Arthur Symons, who met

Mathilde Blind (1841–1896), by Harold Steward Rathbone, 1889

Blind when she was in her forties, described her face as 'the most emotional, but the most worn and haggard and furrowed I have ever seen' (*Selected Letters*, 42). Vernon Lee, who claimed to like Blind and admire her poetry, regarded her as 'amiable' but ugly and 'coarse … extremely like Ouida' (*Vernon Lee's Letters*, 64, 80, 91). Others who knew her described her as handsome, despite a disagreeable and strongly accented speaking voice. Although she was known for her animated conversation, she had no discernible sense of humour.

Blind travelled extensively in an attempt to improve her health and alleviate her frequent depressions. Visits to Scotland inspired *The Prophecy of St Oran* (1881), which narrates the mission of St Columba to the Hebrides, and *The Heather on Fire* (1886), a passionate denunciation of the highland clearances. She continued, in the 1880s, to give public lectures on Shelley, and in 1886 she edited the poems, letters, and journals of Byron. Her essay on Mary Wollstonecraft's educational theories was published in 1878 in the *New Quarterly Magazine*. She also wrote the first full-length biography of George Eliot (1883) and a biography of Madame Roland (1889). In her only novel, *Tarantella: a Romance* (1885), she develops a highly imaginative plot set, somewhat incongruously, against scenes of provincial realism more typical of George Eliot's fiction. She translated from French the controversial *Journal de Marie Bashkirtseff*; in the introduction she assailed the 'cut-and-dried theories [of men] as to what women are or ought to be' (*Journal of Marie Bashkirtseff*, trans. M. Blind, 1890, new edn, 1985, 695). Blind's most ambitious work, however, was *The Ascent of Man* (1889), a poetic epic based on Darwinian theories of evolution. Arthur Symons described this volume as 'a hymn of religious ecstasy; for the scientific teaching of Darwin … inflamed her with the ardour of a worshipper' (Symons, 'Introduction' to *Poetical Works*, v). Her next three volumes of poetry show the influence of her extensive travelling, which included a trip to Egypt in 1891. Ford Madox Brown contributed a frontispiece to *Dramas in Miniature*, which includes 'The Russian Student's Tale' and other poems illustrating the inequity between the sexes. *Songs and Sonnets* appeared in 1893, followed in 1895 by *Birds of Passage: Songs of the Orient and Occident*. Late in life Blind inherited a sizeable legacy from her half-brother, Max Cohen. She was living in Stratford upon Avon when she wrote her last poems, a group of sonnets inspired by Shakespeare. She died at her home, 96 Belgrave Road, London, on 26 November 1896 and was cremated; the remains were interred at a memorial erected in St Pancras cemetery, East Finchley. The bulk of her estate was bequeathed to Newnham College, Cambridge. In the year after her death Symons edited a collection entitled *The Poetical Works of Mathilde Blind*; this volume also includes a memoir by Richard Garnett, who quoted from Blind's unfinished autobiography.

Blind was regarded in her own lifetime as an author of some repute. Twentieth-century scholars have praised her biography of George Eliot for the extent and accuracy of its research, for its incisive critical analyses, and for its emphasis on Eliot's feminism. As for Blind's poetry, her contemporary readers, as well as those in the twentieth century, have tended to prefer her shorter and more lyrical efforts such as 'The Sower', 'Reapers', 'Lassitude', 'Manchester by Night', and 'The Dead'. Feminist critics have called attention also to the impressive sonnet 'Motherhood', which describes the pain of labour and childbirth. More recently, in *Victorian Poetry: Poetry, Poetics and Politics* (1993), Isobel Armstrong has re-evaluated the longer works, particularly *The Heather on Fire* and *The Ascent of Man*, in the context of 'a gendered tradition in women's poetry of the nineteenth century'. According to Armstrong, Blind, by reconfiguring 'a new myth of creativity and gender', demonstrates the best that this tradition can achieve in terms of social and political analysis (Armstrong, 374–6). PATRICIA SREBRNIK

Sources R. Garnett, 'Memoir', in *The poetical works of Mathilde Blind*, ed. A. Symons (1901) · *Arthur Symons: selected letters, 1880–1935*, ed. K. Beckson and J. M. Munro (1989) · *Selected letters of William Michael Rossetti*, ed. R. W. Peattie (1990) · F. M. Hueffer [F. M. Ford], *Ford Madox Brown: a record of his life and work* (1896) · I. Armstrong, *Victorian poetry: poetry, poetics, and politics* (1993) · *Vernon Lee's letters*, ed. I. C. Willis (privately printed, London, 1937) · R. Lhombreaud, *Arthur Symons: a critical biography* (1963) · H. R. Angeli, *Dante Gabriel Rossetti: his friends and enemies* (1949) · A. Symons, 'Introduction', in *The poetical works of Mathilde Blind*, ed. A. Symons (1901) · G. Handley, *State of the art: George Eliot, a guide through the critical maze* (1990) · C. Kaplan, ed., *Salt and bitter and good: three centuries of English women* *poets* (1975) • I. B. Nadel, *Biography: fiction, fact and form* (1984) • R. V. Redinger, *George Eliot: the emergent self* (1975) • K. Hickok, *Representations of women: nineteenth-century British women's poetry* (1984) • *CGPLA Eng. & Wales* (1897)

Archives BL, corresp. and papers, Add. MSS 61927–61930 • Bodl. Oxf., commonplace book | BL, corresp. with Richard Garnett, Add. MSS 61927–61929 • BL, letters to Thomas J. Wise, Ashley A.4140

Likenesses H. S. Rathbone, portrait, 1889; Christies, 11 July 1996, lot 88 [*see illus.*] • M. Brown, chalk • photograph, repro. in *Review of Reviews*, 1 (June 1890), 5

Wealth at death £2736 17*s*. 6*d*.: probate, 28 Jan 1897, *CGPLA Eng. & Wales*

Blind Jack of Knaresborough. *See* Metcalf, John (1717–1810).

Bliss, Sir Arthur Edward Drummond (1891–1975), composer, was born on 2 August 1891 at Hawthornden, Queen's Ride, Barnes Common, Barnes, Surrey, the eldest of three sons of Francis Edward Bliss (*d.* 1930), an American businessman from Massachusetts, and his second wife, Agnes Kennard Davis (1858–1895). There was one son from a previous marriage.

On his wife's death in 1895, Francis Bliss took over the upbringing of Bliss and his brothers Francis Kennard (1892–1916) and James Howard (1894–1977). Untypically for the period, he was not a remote figurehead, but an active and devoted parent. His response to the situation was characteristic of his New England sensibility, with its sense of duty and high thinking, qualities he passed on to his sons. From his father Bliss gained too a love of visual arts, theatre, classical history, and mythology, all of which would be manifest in his works. Bliss frequently drew inspiration from the technical processes of painting and sculpture; among his friends were Jacob Epstein and Paul Nash. Classical mythology is the inspiration behind Bliss's *Hymn to Apollo* (1926) as well as the *Pastoral* (1928); and the theatrical sense displayed in his film scores, ballets, and operas may be traced to his early enthusiasms.

In 1900 Bliss was sent to Bilton Grange, the preparatory school for Rugby School, which he attended from 1905 to 1910. He then went up to Pembroke College, Cambridge, with a classical exhibition, but also studied composition with Charles Wood and found a stimulating mentor in Edward Dent. He graduated BA and MusB in 1913, then spent a year at the Royal College of Music, London. Although he found his teacher, Charles Stanford, uninspiring, he was part of an outstanding generation of talented musicians including Herbert Howells, Ivor Gurney, Arthur Benjamin, and Eugene Goossens. At this time he also met Edward Elgar, who offered encouragement.

During the First World War Bliss served with distinction and gallantry in the 13th Royal Fusiliers (1914–17) and the Grenadier Guards (1917–19). He was wounded in 1916 during the battle of the Somme, gassed at Cambrai in 1918, and mentioned in dispatches in 1916. However, the death of his brother Kennard in action had a long-lasting effect on him, and the futility of war was engraved on his personality. Its deepest musical expression is the choral symphony *Morning Heroes* (1930); but it also surfaces in sudden shifts in his music to threatening, malevolent moods, for example in the interlude 'Through the Valley of the Shadow of Death' in *Meditations on a Theme by John Blow*

Sir Arthur Edward Drummond Bliss (1891–1975), by Mark Gertler, 1932

(1955). His abhorrence of time-wasting was a further result of his war years. He knew how fortunate he was to have survived, and was determined not to lose a moment's opportunity—as witnessed by contemporary descriptions of him immediately after the war which portray a forthright young man bursting with energy and purpose. These qualities are vividly evoked too in Wyndham Lewis's lithe pencil sketch of 1922. Bliss was received into the Roman Catholic church in 1918.

During the war a string quartet (*c*.1914) and piano quartet (1914–15) were performed and published, although Bliss subsequently withdrew them. It was with a series of original ensemble works, many of them with voice, that he established his name immediately after the war: *Madam Noy* (1918), *Rhapsody* (1919), *Conversations* (1920), *Rout* (1920), and incidental music for Viola Tree's production of *The Tempest* (1921). Influenced by Maurice Ravel and Igor Stravinsky and showing an allegiance to the French composers known as 'Les six', they startled the conservative critics of the day by their modernity, and gained Bliss considerable notoriety.

Bliss's first major orchestral work, *A Colour Symphony* (1921–2), commissioned by the 1922 Gloucester Three Choirs Festival at Elgar's instigation, consolidated his reputation as a major figure in British contemporary music. The work adumbrates the mature composer. In the ceremonial grandeur of its outer movements it hints at an embryonic master of the queen's music; the balletic scherzo looks forward to his dance scores; while the introspective slow movement points to the deeper, personal utterance of *Morning Heroes*. Stravinsky's influence has been absorbed in the frequent dissonance, as has the pomp and circumstance of Elgar.

In 1923 Bliss travelled to the USA with his father, who had remarried and wished to spend his last years in his homeland. They settled in Santa Barbara, California, where Bliss met Gertrude (Trudy) Hoffmann (*b*. 1904), later a writer and broadcaster, daughter of Ralph Hoffmann, director of the Natural History Museum at Santa Barbara. They married on 1 June 1925, and in his wife Bliss found the ideal partner who created for him a secure domestic happiness upon which his art could flourish. The couple had two daughters. Compositions from his USA sojourn include the song cycle *The Women of Yueh* (1923) and the suite for piano (1925).

Bliss returned to England with his wife shortly after their marriage. The two works he composed next had American links, since the *Introduction and Allegro* (1926) and *Hymn to Apollo* (1926) were conceived specifically for the Philadelphia and Boston orchestras and for their respective conductors Leopold Stokowski and Pierre Monteux. Performances by such orchestras and conductors bear witness to the reputation Bliss now commanded. In the next three major works that followed, the oboe quintet, commissioned by Elizabeth Sprague Coolidge (1927), the *Pastoral* (1928), and the *Serenade* (1929), Bliss reached maturity establishing a distinctive voice in which a more overt Romantic vein comes to the fore.

From 1929 to 1939 Bliss lived at East Heath Lodge, Hampstead. He and his wife were in the midst of an artistic community, and friendships developed with Barbara Hepworth, Ben Nicholson, Mark Gertler (whose portrait of Bliss is in the National Portrait Gallery, London), and J. B. Priestley. In 1934 they built a country house in Somerset, Pen Pits, which was designed by Peter Harland in the modern style influenced by the Bauhaus.

The 1930s were highly successful for Bliss. In *Morning Heroes* (1930) his war experiences and the pain of Kennard's death were translated into a profound choral symphony, in which he exorcised a horrific recurring dream of the trenches. The clarinet quintet (1932), viola sonata (1933), and *Music for Strings* (1935) showed his mastery of absolute forms. The quintet was conceived for the clarinettist Frederick Thurston, and the sonata for the viola player Lionel Tertis. Writing works for great artists such as these and collaborating with major figures in other art forms were to become hallmarks of Bliss's career. This is apparent in his next important commission: a score for Alexander Korda's film of H. G. Wells's *Things to Come* (1934–5), based on his novel *The Shape of Things to Come*. It remains one of the finest scores for the medium. The music showed a natural dramatic talent that was further evident in the ballet *Checkmate* (1937), with a scenario by Bliss based on one of his lifelong enthusiasms: chess. Ninette de Valois choreographed the ballet, which had designs by E. McKnight Kauffer; it was still a classic of the Royal Ballet's repertory at the end of the twentieth century. Bliss capped the decade with the piano concerto (1939), especially written for Solomon to perform at the New York World Fair in June 1939.

After the première Bliss and his family remained in the USA on holiday and were there when war was declared. On the advice of friends in England, Bliss initially remained in America, becoming a visiting professor at the University of California at Berkeley. There he composed two of his most personal works, the *Seven American Poems* (1940) and the first string quartet (1941). However, even though his family remained in the USA, he increasingly felt that he must return to England to help in the war effort. This he did in 1941 when he joined the BBC overseas music service, subsequently serving as the BBC's director of music from 1942 to 1944. The far-sighted vision of his 'Music policy statement' was influential and led to the founding of the Third Programme. Bliss and his family were reunited in November 1943. For the rest of the 1940s Bliss was occupied with theatrical projects: the ballets *Miracle in the Gorbals* (1944) and *Adam Zero* (1946), which were choreographed by Robert Helpmann (who also danced the leading roles), and the opera *The Olympians* (1948–9), with a libretto by J. B. Priestley. The latter was staged at Covent Garden in 1949, but did not prove a great success.

Bliss was knighted in 1950 and appointed master of the queen's music in 1953, a post he served diligently with distinction and which included composing the music for the investiture of the prince of Wales (1969). During his tenure Bliss was unstinting in his work for the music profession. Among many appointments he was president of the

Performing Right Society (1954–75), and in 1956 under the auspices of the British Council he led the first delegation by British musicians to the Soviet Union since the end of the Second World War. His outstanding public service was recognized by two further honours: KCVO (1969) and CH (1971). He received honorary degrees at Cambridge, London, and Edinburgh universities among others, and was gold medallist of the Royal Philharmonic Society (1963).

Several major works of the 1950s reflect again Bliss's association with great artists of the time: the second string quartet (1950), for the Griller quartet; a *scena*, *The Enchantress* (1951), for Kathleen Ferrier; the piano sonata (1952), for Noel Newton-Wood; and the violin concerto (1955), for Alfredo Campoli. In that decade he composed too the work that he felt was perhaps his finest and most personal achievement: the orchestral *Meditations on a Theme by John Blow* (1955). This was followed by a television opera, *Tobias and the Angel* (1959–60), with a libretto by Christopher Hassall. The early sixties produced three significant choral works: *The Beatitudes* (1961), commissioned for the reopening of Coventry Cathedral, and *Mary of Magdala* (1962), both of which were further collaborations with Hassall, and *The Golden Cantata* (1963), in which he set words by Kathleen Raine.

Bliss continued to compose vigorously into his seventies and eighties, producing the orchestral *Metamorphic Variations* (1972), the cello concerto (1970), premièred by Mstislav Rostropovich, and a cantata, *Shield of Faith* (1974). In his early career Bliss was a prolific writer about music, and he was also a fine conductor; he conducted the premières of *A Colour Symphony* and *Morning Heroes*, and formed a close association with the London Symphony Orchestra, serving as its president from 1958 to 1973. His autobiography, *As I Remember* (1970; reprinted, 1990), is a fascinating description of the composer's life and music. Bliss was an outstanding speaker and conversationalist, although he was reticent about discussing his music in depth, preferring that it spoke for itself. In 1955 Sir Arthur Bliss and his wife moved to 8 The Lane, Marlborough Place, St John's Wood, London, where he died from cancer on 27 March 1975; after cremation at Golders Green on Easter Saturday 1975, his ashes were interred in Mortlake Catholic cemetery. His wife survived him.

ANDREW BURN

Sources private information (2004) [Lady Bliss, widow] • A. Bliss, *As I remember* (1970) [autobiography] • G. Dannatt, introduction, *Catalogue of the complete works by Arthur Bliss* (1980) • *DNB* • *CGPLA Eng. & Wales* (1975)

Archives BBC WAC • CUL, MSS • IWM, MSS | BL, letters to E. Clark, Add. MS 52256 • CUL, letters to Ernest Newinson | FILM Granada Television, film footage, 1973–4 [material filmed for a planned documentary] | SOUND BL NSA, 'Bliss and the concerto', BBC Radio 3, 1 Feb 1972, M1935W

Likenesses Hoppe, photograph, 1921, priv. coll. • H. Lambert, photograph, *c*.1922, NPG • W. Lewis, pencil drawing, 1922, priv. coll. • M. Gertler, oils, 1932, NPG [*see illus.*] • Anthony, photograph, 1937, priv. coll. • W. Stoneman, photograph, 1952, NPG • W. Bird, photograph, 1963, NPG • L. Lyons, bronze bust, 1965, Royal College of Music, London • photograph, 1965, BBC Cardiff • M. Gerson, photograph, 1966, NPG • G. Macdomnic, photograph, 1966, priv. coll. • B. Glass, photograph, 1967, priv. coll. • R. Stone, chalk drawing, 1969–70, NPG • F. Goodwin, photograph, 1970, priv. coll.

Wealth at death £16,632: probate, 29 May 1975, *CGPLA Eng. & Wales*

Bliss, Douglas Percy (1900–1984), painter and printmaker, was born on 28 January 1900 at Karachi, then part of British India, the son of Joseph Bliss (1868–1936), pharmacist, and Isabel Douglas Percy (1868–1966). He was educated in Scotland, where he attended George Watson's College in Edinburgh from 1906 to 1917. After military service in the Highland light infantry, he studied English, history, and art history at Edinburgh University from 1919 to 1922. He moved to London to study painting from 1922 to 1925 at the Royal College of Art, where he knew the graphic artists and painters Eric Ravilious and Edward Bawden.

Bliss held printmaking in high regard alongside painting. He produced fantastic woodcut illustrations to his selection *Border Ballads*, published by Oxford University Press in 1925. His imagination was populated by flying devils and grotesque hags in vertiginous and stormy perspectives. Further dramatic illustrations followed. In 1926 J. M. Dent in London published Dr Johnson's *The History of Rasselas*, in which Bliss provided intense drama in small-scale wood-engravings. In 1927 he exhibited at the St George's Gallery, London, with Bawden and Ravilious, and his wood-engravings were published by Oxford University Press as illustrations to Cervantes' *The Spanish Lady* in 1928. That year he exhibited prints in Paris and Buenos Aires and wrote *A History of Wood Engraving*, published by J. M. Dent. He provided coloured wood-engravings to *The Palace of Pleasure* by William Painter, published by Cresset Press, London, in 1929, and he again exhibited at the St George's Gallery. He illustrated, and introduced, *The Devil in Scotland*, published by Maclehose, London, in 1934. A career in illustration seemed assured.

After Bliss married the portrait painter Phyllis Dodd (1899–1995) on 18 April 1928, they settled in Lambeth, London. His fearsome subjects mellowed and painting dominated his work. In 1934 he exhibited drawings at the Lefevre Gallery, London, and in 1937 he showed paintings there in a joint exhibition with Barbara Hepworth. He moved to Blackheath, London, in 1932 and taught at Blackheath School of Art and Hornsey College of Art. He also wrote for *The Scotsman* newspaper and illustrated Edgar Allan Poe's *Some Tales of Mystery and Imagination* for Penguin Books in 1938. His paintings frequently depicted gardens seen from a window, contrasted against wilder landscape beyond. Home was a secure base separated by the garden from the vicissitudes of the world beyond. These landscapes could be both intimate and panoramic in their balance of man and nature, even in the city gardens of Blackheath. Bliss was committed to conservation in the face of development and war. In 1937 he was a founder of the Blackheath Society for Amenity Conservation. But his house at Blackheath was bombed early in the war and in 1940 he and his family were evacuated to Shottle in Derbyshire. Here the landscape was certainly a refuge. He painted its image as an idyll of domestic peace and natural plenty where rural craftsmen worked with nature to produce their crops. He found industrialized agriculture as menacing as invasion. His direct contribution to the war effort was in the department of concealment and decoy of the Royal Air Force Volunteer Reserve from 1941 to 1945.

After the war Bliss returned to teaching at Hornsey College of Art and also taught at Harrow School of Art in 1945–6. He held a joint exhibition with Phyllis Dodd in Derby City Art Gallery in 1946. His appointment as director of the Glasgow School of Art took him back to Scotland until his retirement in 1964. His work and opinions were increasingly recognized. He exhibited watercolours at the Lefevre Gallery in 1948, wrote for *The Scotsman* and the *Glasgow Herald* newspapers, and in 1952 *Memoirs of Prince Alexy Haimatoff* by T. J. Hogg, with illustrations by Bliss, was published by the Folio Society, London. Bliss became a member of the Scottish Council of Industrial Design and in 1954 visited the USSR. He was invited by the Swedish and Danish governments to make official visits in 1956. In 1957 the Leverhulme Foundation funded a tour of northern Italy and the Italian government presented him with a medal for promoting Italian culture. A study tour of West Germany followed in 1963. Throughout this period Bliss tirelessly produced paintings. On his retirement in 1964 he was appointed governor of the Derby College of Art and was awarded an honorary DA (Diploma in Art and Design) at Manchester College of Art.

In 1978 Bliss was commissioned to write a biography of Edward Bawden which was published in 1979 by the Pendomer Press, Godalming, Surrey. That year he suffered a slight stroke after the visit of a BBC film unit to record his garden in Derbyshire, which was populated by his grotesque and imaginative sculptures. Yet the following year two exhibitions were held in London at which the Tate Gallery acquired examples of his work. A retrospective exhibition followed at the Hatton Gallery of the University of Newcastle upon Tyne in 1981, and a further exhibition was held in Derby that year. A second stroke led to Bliss's death at the hospital in Ashbourne, Derbyshire, on 11 March 1984. He was buried on 17 March in Turnditch parish church, near Belper, Derbyshire. A further retrospective exhibition was held at the Museum and Art Gallery, Derby, in 1996.

In both his art and his writing Bliss was an outspoken defender of the British cultural heritage, especially in Scotland where he was instrumental in preserving the designs and furniture of Charles Rennie Mackintosh, whose most celebrated building he occupied during his directorship of the Glasgow School of Art. The Ingram Street tea-rooms in Glasgow, designed by Mackintosh, owe their survival at least in part to Bliss. He was a sharp critic of artists, both past and present, who made their own importance a priority, and he lampooned their styles and self-esteem in a long series of watercolours. He was also charming in day-to-day life, however, and his articulate criticisms, when they came, found their recipients unguarded and defenceless. Public collections of Bliss's works are in the National Museum and Gallery of Wales, Cardiff; the Scottish National Gallery of Modern Art, Edinburgh; Glasgow Art Gallery and Museum; Royal Leamington Spa Art Gallery and Museum; Perth Museum and Art Gallery; the Tate collection; and the British Museum and Victoria and Albert Museum, London. His work was also acquired by the National Art Collections Fund and the Contemporary Art Society. JOHN MILNER

Sources *Douglas Percy Bliss: retrospective exhibition* (1996) [Museum and Art Gallery, Derby, exhibition leaflet] • private information (2004) [family, friends] • *D. P. Bliss* (1981) [exhibition catalogue, U. Newcastle, Hatton Gallery] • *Phyllis Dodd, 1899–1995: paintings and drawings* (1995) [exhibition catalogue, Museum and Art Gallery, Newport, Monmouthshire]

Archives Glasgow School of Art, artefacts and archive • priv. coll.

Likenesses P. Dodd, oils, 1927, priv. coll. • Fayer, photograph, 1946, priv. coll. • P. Dodd, oils, 1963, Glasgow School of Art

Wealth at death £30,755: probate, 24 July 1984, *CGPLA Eng. & Wales*

Bliss [*née* Moore], **Kathleen Mary Amelia** (1908–1989), religious administrator and university teacher, was born on 5 July 1908 in Fulham, London, the elder child and only daughter of Thomas Henry Moore, local government officer, and his wife, Ethel Steward. She was educated at Fulham county high school before winning a scholarship to Girton College, Cambridge, where she graduated second class (division two) in part one of the history tripos (1929) and first class in part one of the theology tripos (1931). She was also active in the Student Christian Movement (SCM), widening her Congregational inheritance. After temporary posts teaching religious education, in 1932 she married Rupert Geoffrey Bliss, marine engineer, the son of Arthur Harold Antonio Bliss, traveller and big-game hunter. Sixteen years later her husband inherited the Portuguese barony of de Barreto and in 1950 was ordained in the Church of England, but from 1932 to 1939 the young couple were missionaries with the London Missionary Society (mainly Congregational) in south India. Later Rupert Bliss became a teacher, administrator, and marriage consultant.

Kathleen Bliss's missionary experience developed her interest in education, in the problems of society at large, and in the possibilities of drawing Christians together in response to them. After a year's leave back in England she became assistant to J. H. Oldham, editor of the influential *Christian News Letter*. Her own contributions were recognized by her appointment as assistant editor (1942) and editor (1945), until the journal had to close in 1949, when the time had passed for its sophisticated discussion of Christian values amid wartime hatreds and post-war reconstruction. For four years from 1945 she also served on the staff of the British Council of Churches, organizing 'Religion and life' weeks and local councils of churches. Having moved into the Church of England, she was in 1948 a delegate to the first assembly of the World Council of Churches (WCC). In the WCC she made such a mark that she was entrusted with drafting (she originated the

Kathleen Mary Amelia Bliss (1908–1989), by unknown photographer

unforgotten phrase 'we intend to stay together'), was appointed the part-time secretary of a commission on women in the churches, and was elected to serve energetically on the central and executive committees in 1954. In 1949 the University of Aberdeen gave her an honorary DD. For five years from 1950 she was a producer with the BBC. The discussions which she organized for the Third Programme, between Christians of various shades and non-believers, broke the corporation's previous caution in presenting alternatives to Christianity. In 1958 she began her major work. In a time of optimism and new activity she was the first general secretary of the new board of education of the Church of England, charged with the co-ordination of work from primary schools through teacher training colleges to university chaplaincies, and from Sunday schools to the educational activities of the Mothers' Union. She resigned in 1966, exhausted and somewhat disillusioned. A less complicated job awaited her after a rest, and her time as senior lecturer in religious studies at the University of Sussex (1967–72) brought fulfilment to her academic gifts as well as yet another pioneering opportunity: to develop theological (not only Christian) interests in a university excitingly new and not ecclesiastical. She continued to be an active participant in, and commentator on, religious and ecological movements in her retirement to the countryside near Shaftesbury, Dorset, and then to London. The admiration of many for her abilities and energies meant that invitations to preach, speak, or advise continued throughout her life. She was, for example, a member of the Public Schools Commission (1967–70) and was select preacher at Cambridge University in 1967.

Kathleen Bliss's domestic background was unusual, but for her essential (she was thoroughly feminine) and fortunate. Her husband, a priest with independent means and part-time pastoral duties, was responsible for much of the upbringing of their three daughters, who like their mother were redheads with clear-cut features and opinions. (One of them, Deborah, became a distinguished surgeon.) A highly strung, incisively critical, often overworking intellectual, she could show the strain of her life when her wider commitments allowed her time at home, but from 1946 to 1974 she was supported by a Cambridge friend, Margaret Bryan, who lived with the family and was glad to absorb any outbursts. Family life was also helped by shared interests in music, reading, current affairs, and dressmaking.

Kathleen Bliss articulated and organized a phase in the ecumenical movement (for Christian renewal and reunion) when a definitely lay approach, which underplayed denominational customs, was not detached from academic standards or the routine of the churches. Being a perfectionist, she wrote fewer and shorter books than was to be expected and never completed her biography of her mentor, J. H. Oldham, but she was for many years a director of the SCM Press. Her own publications put on record her most passionate interests: *The Service and Status of Women in the Churches* (1952), arising out of the WCC; *We the People* (1963), about the Christian laity; and *The Future of Religion* (1969), about the response to secularization. She died of cancer on 13 September 1989 in the King Edward VII Hospital, Midhurst, Sussex.

DAVID L. EDWARDS, *rev.*

Sources S. Herzel, *A voice for women: the women's department of the World Council of Churches* (1981) • *The Times* (21 Sept 1989) • personal knowledge (1996) • private information (1996)
Likenesses photograph, News International Syndication, London [*see illus.*] • photograph, repro. in *The Times*
Wealth at death £27,452: probate, 11 May 1990, *CGPLA Eng. & Wales*

Bliss, Nathaniel (1700–1764), astronomer, was born on 28 November 1700, the son of Nathaniel Bliss, a clothier, of Bisley, Gloucestershire. He matriculated at Pembroke College, Oxford, in 1716, and graduated BA on 27 June 1720 and MA in 1723. He married shortly thereafter Elizabeth, the daughter of Thomas Hillman of Painswick and an eminent Oxford scholar; of their very numerous offspring, four survived him. He became rector of St Ebbe's, Oxford, in 1736.

Bliss attended James Bradley's lectures in the Old Ashmolean, and on the death of Edmond Halley his application for the Savilian professorship of geometry was supported by George Parker, second earl of Macclesfield, Martin Folkes, Bradley, and the professors of astronomy at Oxford and Cambridge, William Jones and Robert Smith. He was duly appointed on 18 February 1742 and was elected a fellow of the Royal Society the following May. A notice for his lectures advertised courses in arithmetic, algebra, and plane and spherical trigonometry, with the use of logarithms and surveying instruments. He accepted between six and ten students in each class; they had to attend three times a week, for not less than one hour daily. He charged 2 guineas for each course, which lasted about three months, another half guinea being payable for every month the course lasted thereafter. At this time Bliss established the fourth observatory in Oxford, fixing his instruments to a part of the city wall, which extended from his official house to the north-west angle of New College cloisters. His meridian mark was on the buildings of All Souls College. He sent Bradley his observations of Jupiter's satellites in 1742, and, despite the illness of his wife and several of his children at that time, data on a comet seen at the end of December 1743.

Bliss was a frequent guest of and scientific assistant to Macclesfield, who had established his own observatory at Shirburn Castle. On 12 February 1745 Bliss wrote asking Macclesfield to attempt a meridian observation of the brilliant comet then approaching the sun, which he did on two days at the end of the month. Bliss often assisted Bradley at Greenwich, and, Bradley being unwell, Bliss undertook the observations for the transit of Venus on 6 June 1761.

When Bradley died in 1762, Bliss applied successfully for the post of astronomer royal, to which he was appointed on 26 August 1762. With Thomas Hornsby and Antony Shepherd, then the professors of astronomy at Oxford and Cambridge respectively, he examined the instruments which Nevil Maskelyne and Charles Green took to St Helena for their longitude observations in 1763–4. He sent the Royal Society an account of Eustacio Zanotti's observations of the transit of 1761 as seen from Bologna, and of his own observation of an annular eclipse visible at Greenwich on 1 April 1764. He died suddenly, probably at Greenwich, on 2 September 1764, and was buried two days later at St Margaret's Church, Lee, in Kent.

Bliss died intestate and, the Greenwich observations being regarded as his widow's property, the Royal Society purchased them for 50 guineas. They were published long after his death, as a supplement to those of Bradley, in 1805. Mrs Bliss remained in Oxford, from where she issued a notice on 20 May 1765 announcing that the electrical experiments for the entertainment of ladies and others, given by Hornsby, would take place on 21 May in the Schools Tower, the tickets being priced at half a crown.

ANITA MCCONNELL

Sources G. L'E. Turner, 'The physical sciences', *Hist. U. Oxf.* 5: *18th-cent. Oxf.*, 659–81 • R. T. Gunther, *Early science in Oxford*, 2: *Astronomy*, OHS, 78 (1923), 86–7 • R. T. Gunther, *Early science in Oxford*, 11: *Oxford colleges and their men of science* (1937), 275–7 • *Miscellaneous works and correspondence of the Rev. James Bradley*, ed. [S. P. Rigaud] (1832), 58, 426–7, 431 • *Lady's Magazine* (1764), 144 • *GM*, 1st ser., 34 (1764), 450 • *GM*, 1st ser., 32 (1762), 343 • *N&Q*, 6th ser., 11 (1885), 235 • BL, Add. MS 35587, fol. 18*r* • BL, MS 38199, fol. 42*r* • private information (2004) • parish register (burial), St Margaret's, Lee, 4 Sept 1764

Archives CUL, papers

Likenesses sketch, repro. in Gunther, *Early science in Oxford*, 11

Bliss, Philip (1787–1857), antiquary and book collector, was the elder son of Philip Bliss (*d.* 1803), rector of Dodington and Frampton Cotterell, near Chipping Sodbury,

Philip Bliss (1787–1857), by J. Bridges

Gloucestershire, where Bliss was born on 21 December 1787. His mother was Anne, daughter of Thomas Michell, of Corsham, Wiltshire. Bliss was educated at the free grammar school at Chipping Sodbury, then at Merchant Taylors' School, London, from 1797 until 1806, when he went as a scholar to St John's College, Oxford, matriculating thence as a student of civil law. He became a fellow of St John's in 1809, and took the degrees of BCL in 1815 and DCL in 1820. He was ordained deacon in 1817 and priest in 1818; he briefly held a curacy at Newington, Oxfordshire, and in 1830 was made rector of Avening, Gloucestershire, but took little active interest in the parish. On 22 July 1823 he married Sophia, second daughter of Robert Barker Bell, formerly fellow of New College, and thereafter resided at 38 St Giles', Oxford; their son and daughter both died in childhood.

An antiquary and book collector from boyhood, Bliss was bibliographically precocious, writing for Sir Egerton Brydges' *Censura literaria* from 1805, and for other organs, including the *Oxford University and City Herald* from 1808 (he became a part proprietor of this newspaper in 1835); he also published historical reprints as small tracts in limited editions. In 1808 he became an assistant at the Bodleian Library, where he worked on the catalogue of the Rawlinson and Gough collections. His major publications started soon afterwards with an edition of John Earle's *Microcosmography* (1811), which carried a useful appendix listing English character books, a category strongly represented in Bliss's own library.

From 1809, following a proposal negotiated for him by Thomas Park with the London bookseller Joseph Harding, Bliss was engaged in editorial work on Anthony Wood's *Athenae Oxonienses*, published in four volumes (including the *Fasti*) between 1813 and 1820. A new edition was started by the Ecclesiastical History Society in 1848 but proceeded no further than a first volume containing the *Life of Wood*. Bliss's interleaved copy of the 1813 edition, with materials for the continuation, was bequeathed to the Bodleian (Bodl. Oxf., MSS top. Oxon. d. 8–13).

In 1813 appeared *Letters Written by Eminent Persons in the Seventeenth and Eighteenth Centuries, and Lives of Eminent Men by John Aubrey … from … the Bodleian*, notable for Bliss's editorial contribution of the first substantial (though inaccurate) publication of Aubrey's *Brief Lives*. *Reliquiae Hearnianae*, a selection from Thomas Hearne's voluminous diaries, was announced in a prospectus put out in 1816; 576 pages were printed in 1821–2, but work was broken off, presumably when Bliss's new administrative duties intervened, and publication was resumed only in 1857. Even then only 50 large-paper and 150 ordinary copies were published; another issue with additional matter followed in 1869. The proof sheets of the *Reliquiae*, as well as Bliss's own copy, are in the Bodleian.

In 1822 he was appointed, on second application, to the staff of the British Museum, but later that year was brought back to Oxford by his friend Bulkeley Bandinel to be the junior sub-librarian at the Bodleian. He held the post until 1828. (He had previously, in 1818–20, attempted unsuccessfully to obtain the librarianship of the Advocates' Library in Edinburgh.) Oxford proved ideally congenial for him, but his contribution was more to the university's administration than to its library.

From December 1824 until April 1853 (when he retired in advance of the University Reform Act of 1854 on a pension of £200) he was registrar of the university, and in 1826 (having eight years before failed to secure the appointment) he was elected unopposed to be keeper of the archives, a post in which his penchant for accumulation seems to have impeded administrative efficiency. He resigned his Bodleian sub-librarianship at the end of 1828 and held numerous offices in the university, notably that of principal of St Mary Hall, 1848–57, in succession to Bishop Hampden. His prominence and diligence in university business and his polished manners made him the embodiment of the traditions of *ancien régime* Oxford. He died at the principal's lodgings of St Mary Hall on 18 November 1857 and was buried in St Giles's churchyard on the 21st. His wife survived him.

Bliss assembled a substantial library, much of it related to his biographical and bibliographical researches and thus strong in books with Oxford connections, sixteenth- and seventeenth-century English poets, and works by 'royal and noble authors' (of which an earlier collection of his had been sold in London on 11 January 1811). His books bear the discreet ownership mark of a 'P' written before the printed signature 'B', with a two-digit year of purchase following. His library was sold by Sotheby and Wilkinson in two main groups beginning 28 June and 9 August 1858, which with supplementary sales produced a total of £5672 14*s*.; the Bodleian acquired 745 volumes of local importance. Bliss left instructions that his general correspondence should be offered to the British Museum, which purchased it from his widow in January 1858: it is now Add. MSS 34567–34582. ALAN BELL

Sources S. Gibson and C. J. Hindle, 'Philip Bliss, 1787–1857, editor and bibliographer', *Oxford Bibliographical Society Proceedings and Papers*, 3 (1933), 173–260 • H. H. E. Craster, *History of the Bodleian Library, 1845–1945* (1952) • Foster, *Alum. Oxon.* • *GM*, 3rd ser., 3 (1857), 677–8 • *GM*, 3rd ser., 4 (1858), 99–100 • J. Hunter, BL, Add. MS 36527, fol. 122*r–v*

Archives BL, academic and bibliographical corresp. and literary notes, Add. MSS 25100–25101, 34567–34582 • BL, annotated copies of various printed works • Bodl. Oxf., collections and official papers relating to Oxford University • Bodl. Oxf., corresp., notes, and papers • Bodl. Oxf., corresp. and papers relating to his edition of Wood's *Athenae*, incl. annotated authorial copy • Bodl. Oxf., legal corresp. and papers • Bodl. Oxf., literary corresp., annotated books, notebooks, and papers • Bodl. Oxf., notes on Gloucestershire and Oxfordshire • Bodl. Oxf., notes relating to books in the Bodleian • Bodl. Oxf., notes relating to medieval MSS • Bodl. Oxf., papers, incl. annotated copy of Earle's *Microcosmography* • Harvard U., Houghton L., papers, incl. notes from MSS in AM Oxf. • Magd. Oxf., corresp. and papers | BL, corresp. with Sir Frederic Madden, Egerton MSS 2837–2846, *passim* • Bodl. Oxf., letters to S. L. Giffard • Bodl. Oxf., letters to Richard Heber • Bodl. Oxf., corresp. with Sir Thomas Phillipps • Lpool RO, letters to fourteenth earl of Derby • U. Southampton L., letters to first duke of Wellington

Likenesses W. Rivière, oils, 1850, Oriel College, Oxford • J. Bridges, oils, Oriel College, Oxford [*see illus.*]

Wealth at death books sold for £5672 14*s*.

Blith, Walter (*bap.* **1605**, *d.* **1654**), writer on husbandry, was baptized on 7 August 1605 in Allesley, Warwickshire, the fourth and youngest son of John Blith (*d.* 1626), yeoman farmer, and Ann, daughter of Barnaby Holbeche of Birchley Hall, Fillongley. His father, a relatively prosperous cereal and dairy farmer, had moved to Hollyfax in Allesley from Coleshill, where his family had lived for centuries, some time between 1593 and 1597, and established himself on the fringes of the lesser gentry; Walter's elder brother Francis, who became a lawyer and married Mary, daughter of Sir Thomas Hesilrig of Noseley, Leicestershire, was deemed a gentleman.

Blith married Hannah, daughter of John Waker of Snitterfield, near Stratford upon Avon. They had three sons—Samuel, who eventually became heir to his uncle Francis Blith, John (*d.* 1679), who became a physician, and Nathaniel—and four daughters, of whom Mary and Hannah were still living in 1650.

Blith farmed his own land with diligence and care. Sir William Dugdale (1605–1686), historian of fen drainage, lived at Blythe Hall in Shustoke parish next door, and was a close friend of Walter's brother Francis. Walter became a captain in the parliamentary army during the civil war, was solicitor and sequestrator of royalist land in Warwickshire and Coventry, collector of rents from lands of the bishop and dean and chapter of Worcester, and in 1649 and 1650 was surveyor of confiscated crown lands in four

Walter Blith (*bap.* **1605**, *d.* **1654**), by unknown engraver, pubd 1653

counties, Bedfordshire, Cambridgeshire, Huntingdonshire, and Norfolk, making twenty-seven surveys and certificates. He bought confiscated crown land at Potterspury, in Whittlewood Forest, Northamptonshire, using debentures as payment. The conveyance describes him as a gentleman of Cotesbach, Leicestershire.

Blith wrote two books on husbandry which surpass all others of their time for their practical good sense, their evidence of his own and others' farming experience, the candour of the author's judgments and opinions, and the care given to describing new farming practices and making textual changes as time and improved knowledge permitted. His *The English Improver, or, A New Survey of Husbandry* (1649), offering six pieces of improvement, was dedicated to both houses of parliament and the 'ingenuous reader'. In the same year another edition appeared. A so-called third impression was 'much augmented' (1652) and was, in fact, a thoroughly revised work. It was entitled *The English Improver Improved, or, The Survey of Husbandry Surveyed*, and its second part contained 'Six Newer Pieces of Improvement'. It was dedicated to Cromwell, the council of state, nobility, gentry, soldiers, husbandmen, cottagers, labourers, and the meanest commoner and reflected new information concerning agricultural innovations, such as woad, clover, sainfoin, lucerne, hops, liquorice, rapeseed, and orchard and garden fruits. Another edition appeared in 1653. Blith intended a further work on animal husbandry, including goats and rabbits, but evidently did not complete it.

Blith deliberately wrote 'in our own natural country language and in our ordinary and usual home-spun terms' (2nd edn, 1649, 2). His works strongly urged agricultural improvement, but his enthusiasm for enclosure was always tempered by deep concern for poor men: enclosure should not cause depopulation, but obstruction by a few should be overruled by legislation. Blith's views were doubtless coloured by discussion with Joseph Lee, the celebrated pamphleteer who strongly advocated enclosure, and was rector of Cotesbach, where enclosure had caused turmoil in 1603 and made it a centre of the midland revolt in 1607. Blith in all his writing showed sympathy for the common man. He understood the aspirations of the Diggers, but did not think them realistic. He voiced in his first book (1649) deep reservations about fen drainage, but expressed a desire to know more. Somehow he later acquired that practical knowledge, for in the second book (1652, 1653) he praised the drainers, having learned especially to understand the role of an inspiring overseer who could capture the loyalty of his men.

When Blith made his will in 1650, he was living at Cotesbach, but an additional memorandum declares that he lived for four years from 1650 in Lincolnshire, so he may well have spent that time in the fenland. He died in Lincolnshire in 1654 leaving some £1900 in cash to his children, of which each received between £260 and £340 apiece, to be employed 'either in a way of grazing or merchandizing'. Blith was a member of Samuel Hartlib's circle, described by Hartlib as his 'very loving and experienced friend' (*Discourse of Husbandrie*, 2nd edn, 1652, 'To the Reader'), but his parliamentary sympathies precluded the republication of his work after 1660. In 1819 J. Harding, a London publisher, claimed to be 'nearly ready' to publish the 1652 edition, considering it 'not inapplicable to the present day' (advertisement in Thomas Radcliff, *A Report on Agriculture of Eastern and Western Flanders*, 1819), but it did not appear.

JOAN THIRSK

Sources J. Thirsk, 'Plough and pen: agricultural writers in the seventeenth century', *Social relations and ideas: essays in honour of R H Hilton*, ed. T. H. Aston and others (1983), 295–318, esp. 306–14 · L. C. Philpott, ed., 'Blithe of Allesley', 1974, Warks. CRO, B.All.Phi (p) [a genealogy] · W. Blith, *The English improver, or, A new survey of husbandry*, [2nd edn] (1649) · W. Blith, *The English improver improved, or, The survey of husbandry surveyed*, rev. edn (1652); another edn (1653) · PRO, PROB 11/235, fol. 142 [will of Walter Blith] · PRO, PROB 11/380, 1685, fol. 67 [will of Samuel Blith] · PRO, PROB 11/364, 1680, fol. 160 [will of Francis Blith] · Lichfield RO, Wills, 1626B [will of John Blith] · *CSP dom., addenda, 1625–41* · M. A. E. Green, ed., *Calendar of the proceedings of the committee for compounding … 1643–1660*, 5 vols., PRO (1889–92) · PRO, E121/1–4 [Blith's dealings in debentures] · S. Madge, *The domesday of crown lands* (1938) · PRO, E 134, 2 Jas. I, Easter 18 [Holbeach family in Allesley] · PRO, E 179/193/298 [Lay subsidy of 22 Jas. I for Allesley for John Blith, Walter's father]

Likenesses line engraving, BM; repro. in Blith, *The English improver improved* (1653) [*see illus.*]

Wealth at death approx. £1920: will, PRO, PROB 11/235, fol. 142

Blitheman, John (*c.*1525–1591), composer, is of unknown origins and parentage; the principal manuscripts of his music suggest he was born about 1525. Until 1980 works of reference, following Hawkins, usually gave his forename as William. This is indeed the form of his name in the Fitzwilliam virginal book, but other musical sources give the surname only. There is no doubt, however, that the composer of organ and vocal sacred music is identical with the John Blytheman who appears as a gentleman of the Chapel Royal in documents dating from 13 December 1558 (the burial of Queen Mary) until 1590, and it seems certain that he is also to be identified with the John Blytheman (variously spelt) whose presence at Christ Church, Oxford, is recorded in 1555–6 and at various times from December 1560 until 1578 (from 1563 as head of the lay clerks). The arrangements made for his service in the choir of Christ Church from 1560 onwards allow for his possible absence for extended periods, as would be expected of a member of the Chapel Royal. One further documentary reference is more doubtful. A John Blitheman was paid for a single quarter of the year 1548–9 as a junior vicar-choral of the cathedral of Wells, in which city there occur several contemporary references to a Bartholomew Blitheman, perhaps a kinsman.

Much of Blitheman's surviving music is for the Latin liturgy and would have been written during the reign of Queen Mary. His six organ compositions on the plainsong *Gloria tibi trinitas*, whether or not they were intended to serve a liturgical purpose, provide a demonstration of various techniques for setting a plainsong *cantus firmus*. His keyboard music survives mainly in the Mulliner book, copied by Thomas Mulliner. There are also two vocal compositions in the Gyffard partbooks (BL, Add. MSS 17802–17805), of which the compline responsory *In pace* is a particularly well-knit specimen of contrapuntal writing in the mid-Tudor style.

Blitheman died on 23 May (Whitsunday) 1591 and was buried at the parish church of St Nicholas Olave, London. His epitaph, recorded by Stow, describes him as an organist and teacher of John Bull. His will, made on 25 December 1590 and proved on 25 May 1591, includes bequests to his pupil John Bull, to his sister Elizabeth Taylor, widow, in Newcastle upon Tyne, to his sister Robinson, and to Robert Blytheman, vicar of Walgrave, near Henley-on-Thames. Monetary bequests total £49.

John Caldwell

Sources A. Ashbee, ed., *Records of English court music*, 6 (1992), 2, 6, 13, 17, 24, 33, 55; 8 (1995), 319 • J. Stow, *A survay of London*, rev. edn (1603); repr. with introduction by C. L. Kingsford as *A survey of London*, 2 vols. (1908), 4, 357 • Wood, *Ath. Oxon.: Fasti* (1815), 235 • E. F. Rimbault, ed., *The old cheque-book, or book of remembrance, of the Chapel Royal, from 1561 to 1744*, CS, new ser., 3 (1872), 5, 196 • *Act Book, 1541–1593, of the vicars choral of Wells*, ed. L. S. Colchester (1986) • communar's paper account book H, 1548/9, Chapter Library, Wells, fol. 2 • H. W. Shaw, *The succession of organists of the Chapel Royal and the cathedrals of England and Wales from c.1538* (1991), 3, 209 • chapter act book 'A', Christ Church Oxf. • D. Stevens, ed., *The Mulliner book*, Musica Britannica, 1 (1951) • J. Hawkins, *A general history of the science and practice of music*, 5 vols. (1776) • J. A. Fuller-Maitland and W. B. Squire, eds., *The Fitzwilliam virginal book* (1899) • *In pace*, ed. D. Stevens (1963) • D. Mateer, 'The "Gyffard" partbooks: composers, owners, date and provenance', *Royal Musical Association Research Chronicle*, 28 (1995), 21–50, esp. 24–5 • A. Ashbee and D. Lasocki, eds., *A biographical dictionary of English court musicians, 1485–1714*, 1 (1998), 159–60 • will, proved 25 May 1591, commissary court of London, GL, 9171/17, fol. 342*v*

Archives PRO, LC 2/4/2; E179/69/81, etc. | BL, Stow's MS draft of his survey, Harley MS 538

Wealth at death £49: will, commissary court of London, GL 9171/17, fol. 342*v*

Blixen [*née* Dinesen], **Karen Christenze** [*pseud.* Isak Dinesen] (**1885–1962**), autobiographer and short-story writer, was born on 17 April 1885 in Rungstedlund, near Copenhagen, Denmark, the second of five children of Wilhelm Adolph Dinesen (1845–1895) and his wife, Ingeborg Westenholz (1856–1940). Thomas, her younger brother, was her great confidant, especially during her later years in Africa. Her father came from a landowning family in Jutland in the north of Denmark and had been a soldier—in both the Danish and French armies—a writer, and a traveller, in Canada, North America, and Europe. Unlike his conservative family he was what the great Danish critic Georg Brandes called 'an aristocratic radical', and his book *Letters from the Hunt* has remained a minor Danish classic. Wilhelm later became an independent with liberal sympathies in the Danish parliament. He committed suicide in 1895, having been told that he had an incurable illness. Her mother was from an extremely wealthy family which also had land in Jutland, but they had made their fortunes through trade in corn and other commodities.

Educated initially at home, Karen Dinesen spent nine months at the École Benet in Lausanne, Switzerland. This was followed by further study at the Hillerød folk high school, at a private drawing school, and then at the Kongelige Danske Kunstakademi (Royal Academy of Fine Arts), Copenhagen. Despite opposition from her family, Karen became engaged in December 1912 to her Swedish cousin Baron Bror Blixen-Finecke (1896–1940), 'the rough, extroverted nobleman and remorseless prankster' (Thurman, 105). Bror's uncle Count Morgens Frijs encouraged them to escape from Denmark: 'Go to Kenya, you two' (ibid., 106). Bror Blixen went on ahead to buy land, and they were married in a civil ceremony at Mombasa on 14 January 1914.

The different strands of Karen's Danish background—her hero worship of her adventurous, radical, book-loving, aristocrat father Wilhelm, and her tense relationship with the members of her mother's wealthy bourgeois family, the Westenholzes—in some ways prepared her well for her life in British East Africa, and Kenya as it later became. The early twentieth-century fluidity of the region left her relatively unconstrained by conventional gender, class, and even racial roles. She was both insider and outsider, a European but a Dane, and a woman, and therefore on the edges of the dominant imperial and very masculine nexus of settler, hunter, administrator. Of striking appearance—her huge dark eyes were often remarked on—she was courageous, unorthodox, and (on the strength of her husband's title) an 'aristocrat'.

During the eighteen years following her marriage Blixen, or Tanne as she was familiarly known, managed a coffee estate of 6000 acres in the Ngong Hills, close to both Kikuyu and Maasai 'reserves' and near the town of Nairobi. It was owned by the Karen Coffee company, set up

Karen Christenze Blixen [Isak Dinesen] (**1885–1962**), by unknown photographer

largely by members of her family who were confident that coffee had a bright future. As it turned out, the land was a fraction too high for coffee and the soil too acidic. Her marriage was short-lived; Bror Blixen was regarded by contemporaries—along with her lover Denys Finch-*Hatton (1887–1931)—as the model of the African white hunter, and is said to have inspired the figure of Robert Wilson in Ernest Hemingway's *The Short, Happy Life of Francis Macomber*. He was, according to his friends, 'one of the most durable, congenial, promiscuous, prodigal creatures who ever lived' (Thurman, 112). As a husband he was a disaster, and in the first year of marriage passed on syphilis (of the spine, *tabes dorsalis*) to his young wife. She struggled with its blight all her life, often suffering intensely from its secret and violent assaults on her body, particularly in her last years. Yet the Blixen marriage was finally dissolved only in 1925, and her own response to this was typical of her attitude to fate and misfortune: she loved the dramatic, the mocking gesture in the face of a harsh blow from life, and many of her later stories reflected this austere, gallant, and defiant philosophy. In a letter to her brother Thomas, in September 1926, she wrote: 'my illness was not so terribly "repugnant" to me; many shauries [difficulties] that might seem completely intolerable to some people, to me are quite stimulating, such as the difficulties that my "pro-nativeness" land me in with the English' (Dinesen, *Letters from Africa*, 283).

Even before the Blixens parted in 1919 she had met and taken as her lover the Ariel-like hunter–scholar, the Honourable Denys Finch-Hatton, who was to be the great love of her African life. She and Finch-Hatton sometimes hunted together, and to a point he was her adviser and confidant, yet he visited only infrequently between safaris and journeys 'home' to England. Finch-Hatton brought Tanne intense happiness, representing a kind of ultimate challenge she had wanted all her life; he introduced her to a range of English and French poets and writers outside her own extensive reading of Spinoza, Voltaire, Nietzsche, John Stuart Mill, and the classic Danish authors such as A. G. Oehlenschlager, S. S. Blicher, and J. L. Heiberg, and also Hans Christian Andersen, all of whom she continued to read avidly while in Kenya. Yet Finch-Hatton refused any real commitment, and their last meeting before his fatal crash in his light aeroplane in May 1931 (a month before she herself left Kenya) may well have been the scene of a bitter quarrel arising from Blixen's jealousy.

In Nairobi Blixen became—in one way—part of the European colonial and settler community based around the young, ramshackle town with its bricolage of buildings ranging from ambitious colonial structures to bungalows, shacks of corrugated iron, and the flimsy structures of the Somali ghetto on its periphery. Among the European community of Nairobi, itself made up of a colourful variety of social types and nationalities, Baroness Blixen must have cut a bold and unconventional figure, walking down Government Street with her finely dressed and dignified Somali servant Faraah Aden a short distance behind her, carrying, usually, her shawl and a rifle. At other times she would be driven by him perhaps to a party at Government House, to the Muthaiga Club—known in the twenties as the Moulin Rouge of Africa and started by her friend Berkely Cole—or she would be seen *en route* to visit the 'flimsy Somali ghetto' on the Limuru Road (Thurman, 151).

Karen Blixen was a fine shot and an intrepid hunter, earning the name Lioness Blixen from some of the Africans who knew her; she had also, among the Kikuyu 'squatters' on her farm, a 'reputation as a great if quixotic doctor' (Thurman, 244). She was an extravagant hostess, who believed in grand menus perfectly executed; her second home, Mbogani House, was a magnet for outcasts and visiting dignitaries alike. These included the prince of Wales, who in 1928—after meeting Karen Blixen at Government House—asked to see an *ngoma* (a dance) on the farm. It was arranged with difficulty as it was the wrong time of the year for such harvest festivities, but the Kikuyu chiefs agreed, and it was a huge success. In the lesser-known of her two memoirs of Kenya, *Shadows in the Grass* (1960), Blixen describes how

> a stream of supple fiery young people of both sexes [arrived], set on dancing should it cost them their life. The small group of an old Chief and his aged counsellors in rich, heavy monkey skin cloaks, advanced in state, isolated from the

common crowd by ten feet of empty space before and after them. (Dinesen, *Shadows*, 42)

By the time she left Kenya, Baroness Blixen was a celebrity, not only among the circle around Government House, but also one who was known and respected by many Maasai, Kikuyu, and Somalis and by the Indian community. Her knowledge of Swahili, her fierce if hierarchic sense of justice, and her rare attitude of reciprocity towards other cultures, races, and religious beliefs (particularly Islam) marked her out from most other Europeans of the time. Her voluminous letters home (published in English as *Letters from Africa, 1914–1931*, in 1981), written largely to her mother, her Aunt Bess Westenholz, and her brother Thomas, show not only her love for Africa as a landscape, but also her clear understanding that both Africans and Indians would play their part in a future Kenyan state. She was, as she herself once put it, 'God's chosen snob' (Thurman, 205), but she wore her 'pro-native' label with a defiant pride.

Karen Blixen began drafting in English what later became her first collection of tales (*Seven Gothic Tales*, 1934) in the long lonely hours on the farm, and she began writing in earnest in 1926, when the collapse of the estate seemed near. The spare, beautifully written, and highly selective memoir of her life in Kenya *Out of Africa* (1937) was written in English and later translated by her into Danish. She had returned to Denmark in June 1931 to live with her mother, Ingeborg, in the old family home at Rungstedlund, next to the sea and looking across Öre Sund to Sweden. She was forty-six, the coffee estate had been sold, and the company was bankrupt. Blixen had lost her livelihood, her lover, and, perhaps most painful of all, any possibility of staying on in east Africa. For many years she exchanged letters with some of the people on the farm who had been a part of her Kenyan life, but she would never see them again.

The manuscript of her classic, yet unorthodox, account of settler experience in east Africa was written in 1936. By then she had begun to make a name for herself (as Isak Dinesen) through the success in 1934 first in America and then in Britain of *Seven Gothic Tales*. Blixen, encouraged by her brother Thomas and struggling to give her past in Africa some meaning in her life, worked partly from notes that she had begun on the Kenyan farm in 1926. She began writing at Rungstedlund and finally, needing solitude, moved to Skagen, on the northernmost tip of Jutland, and finished the manuscript there. As her biographer Judith Thurman states, *Out of Africa* is not in any sense documentary writing but rather an overview, 'a landscape from the air' with time and action 'compressed and telescoped' (Thurman, 325). In 1985 the book provided the title and narrative structure of a major feature film, starring Meryl Streep as Karen and Robert Redford as Denys Finch-Hatton.

Karen Blixen never returned to east Africa, however much she wished to do so. World events and her uncertain health made it impossible. When Denmark was occupied by the Germans in 1940, she remained at Rungstedlund, writing *Winter's Tales* first in English and then in Danish. The English version was sent to Random House, New York, in the Swedish diplomatic pouch, and was published in 1942 under the name Isak Dinesen. A small armed-services edition, able to fit snugly in a soldier's jacket, was also produced, and there is a copy in the British Library. At Rungstedlund Blixen became a magnet for a group of younger Danish writers including Bjorn Parlsen and Thorkild Bjornvig, who later became one of Denmark's leading poets. In the early 1950s she began regular work for radio and spoke on her seventieth birthday speech in 1955 of her pleasure 'to be a voice and not a piece of printed matter' (Thurman, 397). Radio, she felt, confirmed her identity as a storyteller, one of an 'ancient, wild and useless tribe', her roots in the oral tradition, drawing her power from a charged complicity with those who listened (ibid.).

Karen Blixen died at Rungstedlund on 7 September 1962 at the age of seventy-seven. The last pictures of her were taken by the photographer Cecil Beaton, whom she had met in France on one of her travels as a writer and celebrity (C. Beaton, *The Restless Years*, 1976, 159–61). By the end of her life Karen Blixen had carved a place for herself not only in Danish writing but also in British and postcolonial literature, where she remains a complex and unusual voice speaking from a particular moment in Britain's history of empire. LIZ GUNNER

Sources I. Dinesen, *Letters from Africa, 1914–1931*, ed. F. Lasson, trans. A. Born (1981) • J. Thurman, *Isak Dinesen: the life of Karen Blixen* (1982) • K. Blixen, *Out of Africa* (1937); repr. (1966) • I. Dinesen [K. Blixen], *Shadows on the grass* (1960) • E. Trzebinski, *Silence will speak: a study of the life of Denys Finch Hatton and his relationship with Karen Blixen* (1985) • E. Huxley, *Out in the midday sun: my Kenya* (1985) • *The Times* (8 Sept 1962) • E. Brundbjerg, *Isak Dinesen, Karen Blixen: woman, heretic and artist* (1997)

Archives Kongelige Bibliotek, Copenhagen, archives | BL, corresp. with Society of Authors, Add. MS 63214 • Random House Publishers, New York, corresp. with Robert Haas | FILM BFI NFTVA, *Arena*, BBC2, 11 March 1985 | SOUND BL NSA, performance recordings • BL NSA, 'The tale bearer', xx (1826900.1)

Likenesses photograph, 1908, Karen Blixen Museum, Rungstedlund • photograph, 1914, Karen Blixen Museum, Rungstedlund • photograph, 1915, repro. in Dinesen, *Letters from Africa* • double portrait, photograph, 1922 (with Thomas Dinesen), repro. in Dinesen, *Letters from Africa* • Søgaard, photograph, 1930, Kongelige Bibliotek, Copenhagen • double portrait, photograph, 1956–9 (with Clara Svendsen), Kongelige Bibliotek, Copenhagen, Karen Blixen archives • P. Beard, photograph, 1960, repro. in Thurman, *Isak Dinesen* • C. Beaton, photographs, repro. in C. Beaton, *The restless years* (1976), 159–61 • photograph, Kongelige Bibliotek, Copenhagen, Karen Blixen archives? [*see illus.*]

Blizard, Thomas (1772–1838), surgeon, was a pupil of Sir William *Blizard, who was both his brother-in-law and half-cousin through their grandfather John Blizard. Starting as a teacher of anatomy, he became surgeon to the London Hospital in 1795. He was a skilled lithotomist, and invented a special knife for the surgical removal of urinary calculus. He also had a large private practice in the city, earning a 'larger sum than is recorded of any medical practitioner' (*London Medical Gazette*, 475), but he published only two case studies. He was elected a fellow of the Royal Society in 1803.

In 1816 Blizard retired to the continent, where he cared for his unwell wife until she died in 1837. Blizard himself died at his home in Cumberland Terrace, Regent's Park, London, on 7 May 1838, leaving £100 to the Samaritan Society and £500 to the London Hospital.

G. T. BETTANY, *rev.* JEAN LOUDON

Sources *London Medical Gazette*, new ser., 2 (1837–8), 249, 301, 474–6 · *GM*, 2nd ser., 9 (1838), 666 · *British and Foreign Medical Review*, 6 (1838), 288 · *Transactions of the Provincial Medical and Surgical Association*, 8 (1840), 280 · S. C. Lawrence, *Charitable knowledge: hospital pupils and practitioners in eighteenth-century London* (1996) · private information (2004)

Wealth at death large contributor to Gloucester Infirmary, Brighton Hospital; £100 legacy to Samaritan Society, £500 to London Hospital: *London Medical Gazette*

Blizard, Sir William (*bap.* **1744**, *d.* **1835**), surgeon, the third of four sons and the fourth child of William Blizard and his wife, Elizabeth Robinson, was born in Barn Elms, Surrey, and baptized at St Mary's Church there on 26 February 1744. According to a biographical sketch in *The Lancet* written shortly before his death, Blizard 'was born in a little one-story, and now antique tenement, next door to the "Sun" public-house at Barnes, where his father carried on the business of a hair-dresser, bleeder, and tooth-drawer' (*The Lancet*, 18). A memoir written just after Blizard's death claimed that his father was an auctioneer (Cooke). Blizard was articled to a Mr Besley, a surgeon-apothecary at Mortlake, Surrey, before studying under Henry Thompson, surgeon at the London Hospital. Blizard attended lectures given by Percivall Pott, John and William Hunter, and assisted a surgeon who practised in Crutched Friars. He may have also been the 'occupier of a little shop in the "medical way" at Lambeth Butts' (*The Lancet*, 18).

As a young man Blizard involved himself in radical politics and became a supporter of John Wilkes. Writing under the name of Curtius he contributed to the Wilksite *Middlesex Journal, or, Chronicle of Liberty* and the *Freeholders' Magazine, or, Monthly Chronicle of Liberty*. The latter published a piece by him 'On the intent and end of government' in October 1769 (pp. 73–4). However, Blizard's radicalism did not endure and he became conservative in outlook and a strong supporter of Pitt. Blizard married Jane Blizard, sister of Thomas *Blizard.

Blizard was elected surgeon to the Magdalene Hospital and by 1778 was lecturing on anatomy and surgery with Robert Maclaurin at Thames Street, and then at 12 Mark Lane, Fenchurch Street, London. He later lectured with Thomas Blizard. In 1780 Blizard was appointed surgeon to the London Hospital after defeating George Vaux and John Andree in the election. During the same year he joined the Honourable Artillery Company and took part in the suppression of the Gordon riots. In 1781 he became surgeon to the company with whom he served until 1790. He was also at one time a lieutenant-colonel with the 6th regiment of London Loyal volunteers.

Blizard's most notable achievement was establishing the London Hospital medical school which, together with Robert Maclaurin, he founded in 1785. Blizard considered himself something of a poet, and to celebrate the opening of the operating theatre he composed an ode, which was set to music by Samuel Arnold, telling of 'how providence befriends this seat of commerce and benevolence' (Cooke, 7). As a lecturer Blizard digressed too much 'and allowed too much liberty to a discursive fancy and warm imagination' (Cooke, 8); as a surgeon he was discriminating, decisive, energetic, and skilful. He was also scrupulous about professional etiquette, particularly in regard to the use of language. On one occasion he asked a student what was happening in the operating theatre and was told, 'Mr Headington is operating in a case of strangulated hernia, but the gut is quite rotten'. Blizard replied, 'Pray sir, do not call it *gut*, or say that it is *rotten*, or you will be taken for a butcher; but call it *intestine*, and say that it is *gangrenous*' (Cooke, 11). In 1787 he was appointed professor of anatomy to the Company of Surgeons and elected a member of its court of assistants in 1796. Later he was master of the Royal College of Surgeons (1814), president in 1822–3, and three times Hunterian orator. He was a member of the court of examiners from 1810 until 1835 and was 'dreaded by the students, from his austerity and testiness of manner' (*The Lancet*, 18). He was elected a fellow of the Royal Society in 1787 and a fellow of the Royal Society of Edinburgh in 1799. He was knighted in 1802.

Although his early radicalism dimmed, Blizard involved himself in philanthropic activities. He founded the Samaritan Society in 1791, he knew Jonas Hanway, having worked with him in the Marine Society, and had interests in prison reform, and in ensuring the respectful treatment of dead bodies. His interest in the latter, which may have stemmed from his religious beliefs and from the experience of assisting in grave robbing as an apprentice, caused him to appear in full court dress when, as president of the Royal College of Surgeons, he received the bodies of executed criminals from the hangman at the college's house in Cock Lane. Blizard's formality on these occasions was seen by some as a sign of his pomposity; it is more likely that it was adopted out of respect for the corpse.

In 1827, at the age of eighty-three, Blizard carried out his final operation in public. In the same year he made a journey to Edinburgh, the longest he had ever taken. The only objects that interested him on the four-day journey were the local hospitals encountered on the way. In September 1834 he underwent a successful cataract operation but went into gradual decline not long after; he began to experience difficulty breathing and developed heart problems. Blizard died at his home at Brixton Hill, Surrey, on 27 August 1835 and was buried in a vault beneath Brixton church on 4 September. He was survived by his wife.

Tall with strongly marked features, Blizard had been prone to joke about his prominent nose. In addition to the posts already mentioned he held appointments at the Deaf and Dumb Asylum, Marine Society, Clergy Orphan Asylum, and the London Orphan Asylum. He was an earnest Anglican and a keen supporter of Sunday schools.

Among Blizard's writings were *Suggestions for the Improvement of Hospitals and other Charitable Institutions* (1796) and papers in the *London Medical Journal*, between 1789 and 1790. MICHAEL BEVAN

Sources W. Cooke, *A brief memoir of Sir William Blizard* (1835) · A. E. Clark-Kennedy, *The London: a study in the voluntary hospital system*, 2 vols. (1962–3) · S. C. Lawrence, *Charitable knowledge: hospital pupils and practitioners in eighteenth-century London* (1996) · *DNB* · 'Lancet Gallery of Medical Portraits: Sir William Blizard', *The Lancet* (30 March 1833), 17–18 · Z. Cope, *The Royal College of Surgeons of England: a history* (1959) · private information (2004) [Diana Self]
Archives Wellcome L., poetical compositions and memoir compiled by nephew T. B. Curling
Likenesses E. Edwards, etching, 1796, NPG · J. Opie, oils, exh. RA 1804, RCS Eng. · F. Chantrey, pencil drawing, *c*.1815, NPG · W. H. Clift, pencil drawing, *c*.1823, BM · R. Martin, lithograph, *c*.1830 (after J. K. Meadows), NPG · C. A. Rivers, wax bust, 1834, RCS Eng. · F. Chantrey, marble bust, RCS Eng.
Wealth at death not wealthy: Cooke, *Brief memoir*

Bloch, Denise Madeleine (1916–1945). *See under* Women agents on active service in France (*act.* 1942–1945).

Bloch, Martin (1883–1954), painter and graphic artist, was born on 16 November 1883 in Neisse, Upper Silesia, the younger of two children of Maximilian Bloch (1852–1932), a textile factory owner, and his wife, Margarete, *née* Mosse (*d.* 1942), who died in a concentration camp in Theresienstadt. Both parents were Jewish.

Bloch's earliest known drawings were of the Sudeten mountains. His parents opposed his wish to become a painter, hoping his gift for drawing could be used to design patterns for lace. As a compromise he studied architecture in Berlin from 1902; he went on to study history of art, aesthetics, and psychology in Munich in 1905, and returned to Berlin in 1907 to study classicism and the baroque under the art historian Heinrich Wölfflin. In Berlin Bloch also took drawing lessons from the German impressionist Lovis Corinth and from the landscape and portrait painter George Mosson. Largely self-taught as a painter Bloch studied old master techniques intensively. He joined the Berlin Sezession and, in 1909, rented his first studio. The Paul Cassirer Gallery, which played a major role in promoting artists from the Berlin Sezession, mounted Bloch's first solo exhibition in 1911 and a second in 1913. Between these exhibitions Bloch worked in Paris, where he belonged to a circle of artists who admired Henri Matisse. Here he learned to apply colour in clean, unadulterated masses. He drew inspiration from southern France, where he spent the first half of 1914, and, throughout the First World War, from Spain. He then returned to Berlin, where, in 1920, the Paul Cassirer Gallery organized his third and highly successful exhibition, of fifty-four paintings, almost all produced in Spain. His large triptych *Southern Light* (1914–20; Harvard U., Fogg Art Museum) surprisingly has survived; many of his works were lost or destroyed during the Nazi régime.

In 1920 Bloch married a journalist, Charlotte Dorothea, *née* Ruhemann (1886–1979), whose first married name was Reiss and whose second married name was Zavrel, with whom he had a daughter, Barbara Grant (*b.* 1922). In 1923 he founded the Berlin Bloch–Kerschbaumer school of painting with Anton Kerschbaumer. After Kerschbaumer's death in 1926 Karl Schmidt-Rottluff, a former member of the expressionist group Die Brücke, helped Bloch to run the school. During the 1920s and early 1930s Bloch took his students to Malcesine, Lago di Garda, Italy, each summer, where he gave them intensive individual tuition. In his art he interpreted elements of fauvism and expressionism in softened form. Although he lived in Berlin he was less interested in the social and political interests of the German expressionists and their harsh forms than in the high-keyed colour transpositions of the Fauves. He himself employed a green sky in *Casa Rigo: Lago di Garda* (1925; Tate collection), a painting that captures the atmosphere of a Lombard lake scene.

In 1932 Bloch became secretary of the Reichsverband Bildender Künstler Deutschlands. While he was hanging the 1933 winter exhibition Sturm Abteilung guards forced entry and removed paintings disapproved of by the Nazis. Bloch convened a meeting of protest and, as a result, was expelled from the Reichskammer der Bildenden Künste. Deprived of his rights as a painter, he and his wife and daughter emigrated to Britain, via Denmark, taking up an invitation from Karin Michaelis, the Danish novelist, who assisted many émigrés, including Bertolt Brecht. Bloch arrived in London in 1934 and opened the School of Contemporary Painting in association with the Australian artist Roy de Maistre. Bloch remained true to his aim, established in Germany, of fostering each student's individual style: 'Treat everybody as a potential artist, be tolerant, do not force any rubber stamped theory on the pupil. Encourage, try to discover his personal approach' (Bloch). He ran the school until 1939, teaching, among others, May Hillhouse, Heinz Koppel, and Harry Weinberger. In that year Bloch had his first solo show in Britain, at the Alex Reid and Lefèvre Gallery, London. In 1940, having failed to be naturalized owing to the outbreak of war (he received British citizenship in 1947), he was interned at Huyton, Lancashire, and at Sefton, Isle of Man. After his release in 1941 he returned to London and was given Ministry of Information clearance to record war damage in the City of London. The resulting works combine a sense of drama with a documentary purpose.

In the 1940s Bloch became friends with Josef Herman, with whom he shared a studio from 1943. Herman recalled Bloch thus:

> [He] was a methodical man, he got up in the morning, had a small breakfast, would light his pipe … He would choose a drawing and decide to translate it into painting, tense and excited, he would make an outline of the composition with charcoal … then start to underpaint the canvas. ('Conversations with Josef Herman', *Omnibus*, BBC television, 1983)

From 1943 Bloch regularly visited Wales, where he and Herman painted the miners and landscapes of north Wales; his *Down from the Bethesda Quarries* (1950–51) is in the National Gallery of Wales, Cardiff. After the war Bloch, aged sixty-five, travelled throughout North America, painting, for example, *The Mississippi at Minneapolis* (1948;

Tate collection), teaching at the Walker Art Center in Minneapolis, and exhibiting there, in Princeton, and in New Jersey. From 1949 until his death he taught painting at Camberwell School of Arts and Crafts, London. Bloch exhibited widely in Britain, including at the Ben Uri Gallery, London, in 1945, 1949, and 1953. He contributed to the Festival of Britain exhibition *60 Paintings for '51* and to exhibitions abroad, including a Canadian touring exhibition in 1952. He died, of a heart attack, in Fulham Hospital, London, on 19 June 1954 and was cremated at Golders Green crematorium. His *œuvre* comprises over 200 paintings and innumerable drawings, shown in retrospectives such as the 1957 Arts Council and the 1984 South London Art Gallery exhibitions. Bloch's great achievement was to convey his understanding of colour through his painting and teaching. Locations for his works in permanent collections include the Tate collection; Leeds City Art Gallery; the Cecil Higgins Art Gallery, Bedford; Leicestershire Museum and Art Gallery, Leicester; and the National Gallery of Canada, Ottawa. JUTTA VINZENT

Sources M. Bloch, 'Thoughts on art education', MS, Tate collection, 7817.11 • *Martin Bloch, 1883–1954: an exhibition of paintings and drawings* (1984) [exhibition catalogue, South London Art Gallery, 1984] • J. P. Hodin, introduction, *Martin Bloch: retrospective exhibition, 1883–1954* (1974) [exhibition catalogue, Crane Kalman Gallery, London, 8–26 Oct 1974] • R. Alley, 'Martin Bloch: re-assessed', *Studio International*, 179 (1970), 231–2 • S. Andrews, 'Martin Bloch', *The Studio*, 155 (1958), 40–43 • H. A. Strauss and W. Röder, eds., *Biographisches Handbuch der deutschsprachigen Emigration nach 1933 / International biographical dictionary of central European émigrés, 1933–1945*, 2 (1983), 121 • *Kunst im Exil in Großbritannien, 1933–1945*, Neue Gesellschaft für Bildende Kunst Berlin, ed. [H. Krug and M. Nungesser] (Berlin, 1986), 119 [exhibition catalogue, Orangerie des Schlosses Charlottenburg, Berlin, 10 Jan – 23 Feb 1986] • W. Schwab and J. Weiner, eds., *Jewish artists: the Ben Uri collection*, 2nd edn (1994), 25 [exhibition catalogue, Ben Uri Gallery, London] • G. Hassell, *Camberwell School of Arts and Crafts: its students and teachers, 1943–1960* (1995) • private information (2004) [B. Grant] • 'Conversations with Josef Herman', *Omnibus*, BBC television, 1983

Archives National Gallery of Art, Washington, DC • Tate collection, MSS, catalogues, photographs

Likenesses M. Bloch, self-portrait, oils, 1925, priv. coll. • M. Bloch, self-portrait, oils, 1942, priv. coll. • photograph, 1948, Hult. Arch.

Blochmann, Henry Ferdinand [*formerly* Heinrich Ferdinand] (**1838–1878**), orientalist, was born in Dresden, Germany, on 7 or 8 January 1838, the son of Ernest Ehrenfried Blochmann, printer, and nephew of Karl Justus Blochmann, a distinguished pupil of Johann Heinrich Pestalozzi. He was educated at the Kreuzschule in Dresden and the University of Leipzig (1855), where he studied oriental languages under H. L. Fleischer, and afterwards (1857) under Haase at Paris. In the following year he came to England. Eager to visit India and to study eastern languages further, he enlisted in the British army in 1858, and went out to India as a private soldier.

Blochmann's linguistic and other abilities became known on the voyage to India, however, and soon after his arrival in Calcutta he was set to do office work in Fort William College, and gave lessons in Persian. In the course of about a year he obtained his discharge, and for a time entered the service of the Peninsular and Oriental Company as an interpreter. He was befriended by the Arabic scholar William Nassau Lees of Calcutta, who had assisted in obtaining his discharge, and through whom he obtained, at the age of twenty-two, his first government appointment (1860), as assistant professor of Arabic and Persian in the Calcutta madrasa. In 1861 he graduated MA and LLD at the University of Calcutta, choosing Hebrew for the subject of his examination. In the following year he was appointed pro-rector and professor of mathematics at Doveton College. In 1865 he returned to the madrasa; he remained there for the rest of his life and was principal at his death.

Though Blochmann made some archaeological tours in India and British Burma, he generally lived quietly in Calcutta, worked hard at Persian and Arabic, and in 1868 became philological secretary to the Asiatic Society of Bengal. He contributed extensively to the society's *Journal* and *Proceedings*. He wrote competently on anything connected with the history of Islamic India, but the most elaborate and valuable of his papers were his 'Contributions to the history and geography of Bengal' (*Journal of the Asiatic Society of Bengal*, vols. 42, 43, 44, 1873–5). The work, however, on which his fame mainly rests is his translation of the *A'in-i-Akbari* of Abu'l-Fazl, the first attempt at a thorough translation of the original. Blochmann did not live to translate more than the first volume (Calcutta, 1873), and the work was completed by H. S. Jarrett. Blochmann's notes are full and accurate, and throw a flood of light on the emperor Akbar and his court, and on the administration of the Mughal empire. Prefixed to the translation is a life of Abu'l-Fazl. Another important work was *The Prosody of the Persians* (Calcutta, 1872). With all his learning, Blochmann was the most modest of men, and welcomed criticism and correction.

Overwork and the exhausting climate caused Blochmann's early death on 13 July 1878 in Calcutta. He was buried in the Circular Road cemetery, Calcutta. He married an Irishwoman, who survived him, and left three children. HENRY BEVERIDGE, *rev.* PARVIN LOLOI

Sources W. T. Blanford, *The Proceedings of the Asiatic Society of Bengal* (Aug 1878), 164 • H. Krone, *Zeitschrift der Deutschen Morgenländischen Gesellschaft*, 33 (1879), 335 • Boase, *Mod. Eng. biog.* • C. E. Buckland, *Dictionary of Indian biography* (1906)

Likenesses marble bust, Asiatic Society of Bengal, India

Bloet family (*per. c.*1080–*c.*1300), gentry, in the south-west and Welsh march, was first represented by **Ralph** [i] **Bloet** (*fl.* 1086–*c.*1112), chief tenant of the honour of Striguil at the time of the Domesday survey. He held lands totalling forty-three hides in Hampshire, Somerset, Wiltshire, and Gloucestershire in 1086. He granted the manor of Ruddle, Gloucestershire, to Gloucester Abbey before 1100, and confirmed the manor of Bulley, Gloucestershire, to the same abbey before 1112, grants that indicate that he had also obtained the Domesday lands of Walter Balistarius after the survey, but before the death of William II. The **Ralph** [ii] **Bloet** (*d.* in or before 1157) who appears as a prominent follower of Gilbert de Clare, earl of Pembroke (*d.* 1148), and his son Earl Richard de Clare (*d.* 1176)—successive lords of Striguil—may have been son or grandson of the first Ralph. Nothing much of Ralph [ii] is known, other than that he had died by 1157 and fathered a number of sons, some of whom founded cadet lines. One of these younger sons, Walter Bloet (who had died by 1199), founded a branch of the family at Raglan, Monmouthshire, which he had by grant of Earl Richard de Clare, and participated in the earl's conquest of Leinster. Another younger son, Sir Robert Bloet (*fl.* 1207), took a share of the Bloet lands at Daglingworth, Gloucestershire, and picked up Wiltshire estates based at Salthrop. Both the Raglan and Daglingworth branches survived and prospered into the fourteenth century.

Sir Ralph [iii] **Bloet** (*d.* 1199) inherited the bulk of the family lands, and also his father's leading position in the honour of Striguil. He accompanied his lord, Earl Richard de Clare, on the conquest of Leinster and is named by the 'Song of Dermot and the Earl' as one of the earl's council at Waterford in 1171. But neither he nor his brothers acquired any sizeable estates in Leinster as a result. On the earl's death Ralph and his younger brother William were granted wardship of the honour of Striguil and Chepstow Castle, which they jointly held until 1185, and Ralph alone thereafter until Michaelmas 1188. Ralph can be proved to have held all the lands that had been in the hands of Ralph [i] in 1086, and his considerable holdings within the honour are sufficient to explain his local prominence. After William (I) Marshal acquired the honour of Striguil by marriage to Countess Isabel de Clare (daughter of Earl Richard) the connection persisted, for Ralph [iii] witnessed the Marshal's charters in 1189. Ralph died early in 1199. His wife, Nest *Bloet (*d.* 1224/5), was a member of the Welsh royal dynasty of Caerleon, and had been a mistress of *Henry II during the early 1170s. Ralph [iii] brought up her illegitimate son by the king, Morgan Bloet, later provost of Beverley and bishop-elect of Durham (1213). She seems to have been responsible for the close connections between their many sons and the royal curia in the time of King John. Nest Bloet survived Ralph by many years and enjoyed a substantial dower settlement.

Their eldest son, **Sir Ralph** [iv] **Bloet** (*d.* 1241/2), continued the family's connection with the household of the lords of Striguil. He attested acts of William (I) Marshal, earl of Pembroke (*d.* 1219), and fought on his side during the wars of 1215–17. The connection was long-lasting; Ralph [iv] was suspected of supporting the rebellion of his lord, Richard Marshal, earl of Pembroke (*d.* 1234), against Henry III and had his English lands confiscated in 1233 as a result, although they were soon restored. He appears as a knight active across the several counties where he held land. He died at some time late in 1241 or early in 1242 leaving his sons minors. The result was a wardship agreement between Walter Marshal, earl of Pembroke, and Earl Simon de Montfort, by which Ralph [iv]'s lands, sons, and their marriages were granted to Montfort. The eldest, **Sir William Bloet** (*d.* 1287x1300), took the bulk of the lands but has no known later connection with the earl; however, William's younger brother, Ralph [v] Bloet of Hinton Blewitt, fought and died for Montfort at Evesham in 1265. William was of age in 1251 and had respites of knighthood, a status he was still avoiding in 1256, but to which he had succumbed by 1264, securing a lifetime exemption for juries in 1268. He was active in public affairs, investigating (as a knight of Hampshire) the abuses of Adam of Stratton on the Isle of Wight, and being summoned to a great council at Gloucester in 1287. He had died by 1300, when the family's lands had come to one John Bloet, who may well have been his son, although this is not certain.

The family of Bloet was a remarkable instance of continuity both of a magnate connection and prosperity over several generations. Four, or perhaps five, successive heads of the family were leading retainers of the lords of Striguil, a period spanning over 150 years. The continuity of the link may have had a lot to do with the size of the Bloet holding (some six large manors) within the honour, which was a significant proportion of the tenured lands, and which was referred to—exceptionally—as a *baronia* within it (rather like the *baroniae* of the honours of Glamorgan and Chester) in 1284. There is also the significance of the fact that the family had from the Clares (probably since the twelfth century) another large manor in Langstone, Monmouthshire, which tied them to the march and marcher interests. The family largely retained its original endowment: interests at Daglingworth and Hinton Blewitt were subinfeudated to cadet branches, and not alienated. Other cadets were endowed with acquisitions, some acquired through their own initiative (like Raglan) and others by marriage, like Liswerry and Salisbury, Monmouthshire, which came to William Bloet, son of Ralph [iii], from the marriage settlement of Nest, Ralph's wife. The family made some endowments of religious houses. Ralph [i] patronized Gloucester Abbey, and Ralph [iii] Godstow Abbey, where his sister became a nun. The use of Gloucestershire lands in both cases indicates that the family regarded its English centre as elsewhere: certainly Silchester, Hampshire, was its chief seat by the thirteenth century. The family's arms appear on William Bloet's seal (*c.*1250) and in St George's roll (*c.*1285) as or, two wings conjoined in fess gules. DAVID CROUCH

Sources A. Farley, ed., *Domesday Book*, 2 vols. (1783) • W. H. Hart, ed., *Historia et cartularium monasterii Sancti Petri Gloucestriae*, 3 vols., Rolls Series, 33 (1863–7) • A. Clark, ed., *The English register of Godstow nunnery*, 2 vols., EETS (1906–11) • PRO, E327/298; KB 26/131 m 8d; C 47/1/1 m 23; WARD2/28/94E/7, 61 • G. H. Orpen, ed. and trans., *The song of Dermot and the earl* (1892) • K. H. Rogers, ed., *Lacock Abbey charters*, Wilts RS, 34 (1979) • F. Barlow, ed., *Durham annals and documents of the thirteenth century*, SurtS, 155 (1945) • *Close rolls of the reign of Henry III*, 14 vols., PRO (1902–38), vols. 2, 6–7 • C. Moor, ed., *Knights of Edward I*, 5 vols., Harleian Society, 80–84 (1929–32)

Bloet, Nest [Nest of Wales, Nest the Welshwoman] (*d.* **1224/5**), royal mistress, was the daughter of Iorwerth ab Owain, lord of Caerleon, and Angharad, daughter of Uthred, bishop of Llandaff. She was also known as Nest of Wales or Nest the Welshwoman. She married before 1175 Ralph *Bloet (*d.* 1199) [*see under* Bloet family], the most substantial tenant of the honour of Striguil and her father's neighbour in Gwent.

The annals of Durham imply that Nest's affair with

*Henry II—which produced an illegitimate son, Morgan Bloet, later provost of Beverley and bishop-elect of Durham—occurred after her marriage to Ralph. The affair may have occurred during Henry II's visit to Gloucester in 1175, when he restored Caerleon to her father, although the king also met Iorwerth earlier, in 1172.

Nest became a widow in 1199, before 29 September, and immediately began litigation against her brother-in-law, Robert Bloet, and her brother Hywel ab Iorwerth, lord of Caerleon. She settled her claim against Hywel for land valued at £15 in the manor of Salisbury, east of Newport, apparently by means of the direct intervention of King John. There is evidence that Nest received a good deal of favour from John, including grants in Ireland and Pembrokeshire before he was king. Three of her sons (Thomas, Roland, and William) were prominent knights of King John's household, and her illegitimate son, Morgan, was nominated by the king to the see of Durham in 1213, although Innocent III suppressed his election after Morgan refused to deny his bastardy in the curia. This support for his father's former mistress and her children is an interesting sidelight on the character of John. Nest was alive at Michaelmas 1224 but had died before 26 August 1225 when custody of her lands in Ireland had been granted to John of Tew.

Nest Bloet's eldest son, Ralph *Bloet (*d.* 1241/2) [*see under* Bloet family], succeeded to the widespread paternal inheritance and was a Marshal adherent. Her son Thomas (*d.* 1211x15) was a follower of King John and made a career in Ireland. Another son, Roland, was also a knight of King John and was killed in battle with his cousin Morgan ap Hywel of Caerleon in 1217. The youngest son, William, received his mother's manor of Salisbury in Gwent by January 1226 and survived in royal service until at least 1261. A daughter, Petronilla, was married by her brother Thomas to Diarmait Mac Carthaig, king of Desmond.

DAVID CROUCH

Sources PRO, E 368/7 · PRO, E 159/8 · PRO, KB 26/146 · F. Barlow, ed., *Durham annals and documents of the thirteenth century*, SurtS, 155 (1945) · *Curia regis rolls preserved in the Public Record Office* (1922–) · T. D. Hardy, ed., *Rotuli litterarum clausarum*, 2 vols., RC (1833–4) · P. C. Bartrum, ed., *Welsh genealogies*, AD *1400–1500*, 18 vols. (1983)

Bloet, Ralph (*fl.* **1086–*c.*1112**). *See under* Bloet family (*per. c.*1080–*c.*1300).

Bloet, Ralph (*d.* in or before **1157**). *See under* Bloet family (*per. c.*1080–*c.*1300).

Bloet, Sir Ralph (*d.* **1199**). *See under* Bloet family (*per. c.*1080–*c.*1300).

Bloet, Sir Ralph (*d.* **1241/2**). *See under* Bloet family (*per. c.*1080–*c.*1300).

Bloet, Robert (*d.* **1123**), administrator and bishop of Lincoln, was Norman by birth, a member of the baronial family of Ivry. Hugues, bishop of Bayeux, and Jean, archbishop of Rouen, were his kinsmen. A chaplain of William I, in September 1087 Bloet was dispatched to England with William Rufus, carrying a letter to Archbishop Lanfranc, instructing the latter to crown Rufus as king. He flourished in the new reign: he was appointed chancellor by 27 January 1091, and held that office until about February 1094, when he became bishop of Lincoln. He had been nominated as bishop in the previous year, but his consecration was delayed when Archbishop Thomas of York (*d.* 1100) claimed that Lindsey, the northern half of Lincoln diocese, belonged to his own province and diocese. The difficulty was resolved by Rufus, who granted to Thomas the abbeys of Selby and St Oswald, Gloucester, and persuaded Robert to pay a sum variously reported as £3000 and £5000 to the king himself, so as to secure Lincoln's liberties. Bloet remained close to the king for the rest of Rufus's reign; one of the 'justiciars of England' recorded in 1096, he was probably a member of the council of regency left to govern England when the king went overseas in that year, and was present at the Whitsun court of 1099 when the new Westminster Hall housed its first royal feast.

Bloet remained at the centre of government for almost the whole of the rest of his life, serving Henry I as he had done William Rufus. In March 1101 he was one of the witnesses for the king in his treaty with Count Robert of Flanders, and in 1102 led the troops that besieged Tickhill, Yorkshire, held by the men of Henry's enemy, Robert de Bellême. In 1110 he was the first witness on the king's behalf to another treaty with Robert of Flanders, and in all witnessed 155 royal *acta* between 1100 and his death. In 1111 he was a member of the court sitting in the exchequer, and in 1119 was a justice in the *curia regis*. When the king went abroad, Bloet (who is only once, in 1114, reliably recorded as accompanying Henry I to Normandy) was one of the small group of administrators who stayed in England, wielding viceregal powers under the nominal direction of Queen Matilda or Prince William. He was probably also a shire justiciar in Lincolnshire, as well as exercising nationwide judicial authority as he had done in the previous reign; no doubt it was in the latter capacity that he acted as a judge at Brampton in 1116. William of Malmesbury understandably regarded him as second to none in his knowledge of secular business, though the chronicler was less impressed by Bloet's attention to ecclesiastical affairs.

In this William may have been somewhat unfair. Bloet found a new cathedral church which needed to be completed, furnished, and to some extent endowed, and he so far busied himself with this work as to double the number of prebends, from twenty-one to forty-two. His predecessor, Bishop Remigius, had refounded a pre-conquest house at Stow, north-west of Lincoln, probably intending that its monks should replace the cathedral canons; but Bloet transferred the monks to Eynsham, Oxfordshire, and took over their estates for the cathedral. He also retained the patronage of Eynsham for the bishopric, and it is noteworthy that after his death his viscera were buried there. He used his credit with the king to obtain numerous grants and confirmations of lands, churches, and privileges for himself and his see. The manors of Nettleham, Lincolnshire, and Tixover, Rutland, the king's vineyard at Lincoln, the right to take tolls at the fairs of Stow, leave to make a way through the city walls of Lincoln to reach his own house—these were just a few of the benefits of royal favour.

Bloet added the considerable Huntingdonshire manor of Spaldwick to the endowments of his see, though only at the cost of agreeing to the creation in 1109 of the see of Ely from the larger part of the Isle of Ely and county of Cambridgeshire, formerly belonging to the archdeaconry of Huntingdonshire. He was, indeed, thought by some to be a rather indecisive bishop, and his failure to persuade the abbot of St Albans to allow him to ordain clerks from the archdeaconries of Hertfordshire, Buckinghamshire, and Bedfordshire in the abbey church attracted much unfavourable comment, although the episode does also show him attempting to perform an important diocesan function. His few surviving episcopal *acta* show him to have been active in consecrating churches and in confirming gifts to religious houses. His problems with ordinations notwithstanding, he dedicated the abbey church at St Albans in 1115, and granted an indulgence of one day's remission of penance in every week for a year to penitents visiting St Albans. He himself founded the hospital of the Holy Sepulchre at Lincoln, and reportedly sent young clerks from his household to study under Bishop Ivo of Chartres, the most distinguished canonist of his time. At a national level Bloet attended Anselm's reforming council at Westminster in 1102, was present when the archbishop consecrated five bishops at Canterbury in 1107, and was among the bishops who came to the council at Westminster in 1115, which, though summoned by the king, was primarily devoted to ecclesiastical business.

The low regard in which Bloet was held by William of Malmesbury must have been largely due to the bishop's perceived coolness towards monks. Not only did he remove the monks from Stow to Eynsham, but he was twice, in 1114 and 1123, reported as opposing the choice of a monk to succeed to the archbishopric of Canterbury. In other respects, too, Bloet would have appeared an unduly worldly figure, and not only in monastic eyes. He had a son, Simon, conceived while he was still chancellor, who later became dean of Lincoln. His household, as remembered by the chronicler Henry 'of Huntingdon' (*d. c.*1157), who was brought up in it, was large and splendid—there was a train of noble youths, who included the king's illegitimate son Richard, as well as Gilbert of Sempringham, a future saint, whom Robert ordained to the priesthood. Bloet's appearance in the story of Christina of Markyate is less than creditable—he is alleged to have been bribed to give judgment against Christina's efforts to enter religion.

The end of Bloet's life was such as to give moralists much to savour. Although he continued to attend the court, he fell into Henry I's disfavour. Henry of Huntingdon tells of the bishop's dissolving in tears as he contemplated the lawsuits in which he became embroiled, the heavy fines that resulted, and his household now clad in woollens because he could no longer afford for them the splendid apparel of his great days. On 10 January 1123 Bloet went out hunting at Woodstock, in the company of Roger of Salisbury and Henry I himself, and as they were talking suddenly exclaimed 'Lord king, I am dying', and fell speechless to the ground. He died shortly afterwards, silent and unshriven. He was buried in Lincoln Cathedral, in front of St Mary's altar, at the southern entrance of the lesser cross aisle. DOROTHY M. OWEN

Sources John de Schalby, 'Lives of the bishops of Lincoln', *Gir. Camb. opera*, 7.193–216 • *The book of John de Schalby, canon of Lincoln, 1299–1333, concerning the bishops of Lincoln and their acts*, trans. J. H. Srawley (1949) • C. W. Foster and K. Major, eds., *The registrum antiquissimum of the cathedral church of Lincoln*, 1, Lincoln RS, 27 (1931), appx 1, pp. 267–76 • Henry, archdeacon of Huntingdon, *Historia Anglorum*, ed. D. E. Greenway, OMT (1996) • D. M. Smith, ed., *Lincoln, 1067–1185*, English Episcopal Acta, 1 (1980), 5–11 • D. M. Owen, ed., *A history of Lincoln Minster* (1994), 14–24, 112–63 • Ordericus Vitalis, *Eccl. hist.*, 5. 6 • *Willelmi Malmesbiriensis monachi de gestis pontificum Anglorum libri quinque*, ed. N. E. S. A. Hamilton, Rolls Series, 52 (1870) • *Reg. RAN*, vols. 1–2 • D. Whitelock, M. Brett, and C. N. L. Brooke, eds., *Councils and synods with other documents relating to the English church, 871–1204*, 2 (1981) • F. Barlow, *The English church, 1066–1154: a history of the Anglo-Norman church* (1979) • M. Brett, *The English church under Henry I* (1975) • F. Barlow, *William Rufus* (1983) • J. A. Green, *The government of England under Henry I* (1986) • D. Knowles, *The monastic order in England*, 2nd edn (1963) • D. M. Owen, *Church and society in medieval Lincolnshire*, History of Lincolnshire (1971) • R. W. Southern, *Medieval humanism and other studies* (1970), 206–33 • C. W. Hollister, *Monarchy, magnates, and institutions in the Anglo-Norman world* (1986), 223–45 • *ASC*

Bloet, Sir William (*d.* 1287x1300). *See under* Bloet family (*per. c.*1080–*c.*1300).

Blogg, Henry George (1876–1954), lifeboat coxswain, was born in Cromer on 6 February 1876, the son of Ellen Blogg. He was educated at the Goldsmiths' School, Cromer, where he proved quick at learning and revealed an unusually retentive memory. He took no part in games, failed to defend himself against bullying, and never learned to swim. When nearly twelve he began life as a longshore fisherman. In 1894 he joined the Cromer lifeboat crew, becoming second coxswain in 1902, and coxswain in 1909. His record of service was unique, and when he retired in 1947 Cromer's had long been the most famous of all lifeboats and Blogg himself an international character.

A silent, reticent man who neither smoked nor drank, he had a quiet kindliness and humour and remarkable qualities of personality and endurance. He inspired complete confidence in his lifeboat crew, who knew him as a superb seaman: quick and resolute in decision, unerring in judgement, fearless before danger. On 16 October 1901 Blogg married Annie Elizabeth (1877/8–1950), daughter of Henry Brackenbury, fisherman, of Cromer. Their only son died in infancy and their only daughter in her twenties.

During Blogg's fifty-three years with Cromer lifeboats 873 lives were saved and he was three times awarded the gold medal of the Royal National Lifeboat Institution. He won the first of these in 1917 for rescuing eleven men from the Swedish steamer *Fernebo*. His crew of ageing men had already been at sea for several hours and had taken sixteen men from a Greek steamer, *Pyrin*. When the call to

Henry George Blogg (1876–1954), by Thomas Cantrell Dugdale, 1942

the *Fernebo* came it proved impossible to launch the lifeboat against the mountainous seas. A second attempt was made after darkness fell, but when the boat was halfway to the wreck she was hit by a tremendous sea and, losing several oars, was forced back to the shore. Undaunted, Blogg seized his moment to make yet another attempt, which succeeded.

By 1927, when Blogg received his second gold medal (for rescuing fifteen men from the Dutch tanker *Georgia* after twenty hours at sea), he was using a motor lifeboat and the difficulties of launching had been overcome by the building of a slipway. In 1941 he was awarded his third gold medal and also the British Empire Medal for rescuing eighty-eight men from six steamers in convoy. He was four times awarded the Lifeboat Institution's silver medal, for rescuing thirty men from the Italian steamer *Monte Nevoso* (1932), two from the barge *Sepoy* of Dover (1933), twenty-nine from the Greek steamer *Mount Ida* (1939), and forty-four from the steamer *English Trader* (1941). He received the Empire Gallantry Medal in 1924 and the George Cross in 1941; in 1948 the new Cromer lifeboat was named the *Henry Blogg*. Blogg died in the Cromer and District Hospital, Cromer, on 13 June 1954. H. M. Palmer, *rev.*

Sources *The Life-Boat* (Sept 1954) • *Year Book of the Royal National Life-Boat Institution* (1955) • C. Jolly, *Henry Blogg of Cromer* (1958) • private information (1971) • *CGPLA Eng. & Wales* (1954) • m. cert. • d. cert.

Likenesses W. Dring, pastel drawing, 1942, IWM • T. C. Dugdale, oils, 1942, Royal National Lifeboat Institution, London [*see illus.*] • O. Edis, photograph, *c*.1942, NPG • J. Woodford, bronze bust, Cromer, Norfolk

Wealth at death £12,449 2*s*. 11*d*.: probate, 12 Aug 1954, *CGPLA Eng. & Wales*

Blois. For this title name *see* Adela, countess of Blois (*c*.1067–1137).

Blois, Henry de (*c*.**1096–1171**), bishop of Winchester, was the fourth and youngest son of Étienne, count of Blois, and *Adela, daughter of *William I.

Early career to 1135 The dates of birth of all the children of Étienne and Adela are uncertain, but Henry can be presumed to have been born either *c*.1096, shortly before his father left on the first crusade, or *c*.1100, soon after his father's return. He was professed a monk at Cluny in Burgundy, a house for which he retained a warm affection and frequently visited, but no details survive of the time he spent there. It is possible that he was briefly prior of the small Cluniac house at Montacute in Somerset; but more likely that he controlled it later in another capacity. He is first mentioned in 1126, when he was appointed abbot of Glastonbury by his uncle Henry I. He was an active abbot, vigorous in reclaiming property, as is attested by his own brief record (*libellus*) of his work, one of the earliest treatises on English estate management. Soon after appointment as abbot of Glastonbury Henry was nominated bishop of Winchester, and consecrated on 17 November 1129. He refused to resign the abbey of Glastonbury, holding it in plurality with the see of Winchester until his death. He was frequently at Henry I's court, including the meeting at Northampton in September 1131, when oaths were sworn by the leading laymen and churchmen to support the succession of Henry's daughter, the Empress Matilda. He may have crossed to Normandy with the court in summer 1133, for shortly thereafter he is known to have visited Cluny.

The king's brother, 1135–1140 Henry then appears at Westminster on 22 December 1135, when his brother *Stephen was crowned king of England. Stephen's accession was a coup in which Henry was heavily involved. It was Henry who brokered the deal by which Stephen was recognized as king in return for promises that he would act as a model ruler of the church; and Henry claimed a directive role in their implementation. The first bishopric vacant, that of Bath, was filled at Easter 1136 by one of Henry's nominees, Robert of Lewes (*d*. 1166), who previously had served as an administrator at Glastonbury. Henry was present shortly after this at the siege of Exeter, and when the garrison surrendered he was placed in charge of the castle and the surrounding area.

The death of William de Corbeil, archbishop of Canterbury, in August 1136 saw Henry take the episcopal estates in hand, and draw on his network of contacts in the hope of securing the appointment for himself. He was in Normandy in the winter of 1136–7, and remained there in the spring and summer of 1137, when he and Stephen were engaged in diplomacy with their brother Theobald, count of Blois, and the French king Louis VII. However, in December 1138, at a church council at Westminster presided over by the papal legate, Alberic of Ostia, Theobald, abbot of Bec (*d*. 1161), was elected archbishop of Canterbury. The story was later told that this was done covertly

Henry de Blois (*c.*1096–1171), seal [obverse]

while Henry of Winchester was absent at St Paul's ordaining clergy to the diaconate. Even if true, this can hardly be the whole story. As soon as Alberic returned to Rome in March 1139, Pope Innocent II (*r.* 1130–43) established Henry, not Theobald, as his legate within the English province. It is most likely that this deal was worked out in England.

The legation of Henry de Blois was confirmed as England descended into civil war. The enamel plaques made for Henry, now in the British Museum, describe him as the man on whom the difference between war and peace depended. This may be taken as his own text for his legation. The arrest of the bishops of Salisbury, Lincoln, and Ely at Oxford in June 1139, and the confiscation of their castles, was taken by Henry as a challenge to clerical liberties, a breach of the agreement of December 1135. He summoned at Winchester in late August 1139 a legatine council at which Stephen was required to defend his behaviour. There were precedents for the king's actions, and he escaped censure, but a rift between church and state had opened up. It was further widened when, a month later, the empress and Robert, earl of Gloucester (*d.* 1147), arrived in England, and sought refuge at Arundel with Henry I's widow, Queen Adeliza (*d.* 1151). Henry mediated agreements both with Robert of Gloucester and with the king that gave the empress a safe conduct to Bristol; and he then escorted her through his diocese. Henry here, though his actions were much criticized, was endeavouring to make peace, and in the following year he redoubled his efforts. He first convened a meeting of the two sides near Bath, in the summer of 1140, and then in September crossed to France for discussions with Louis VII and his own brother Theobald. The king's side rejected the terms proposed.

The crisis of 1141 Stephen's capture at the battle of Lincoln on 2 February 1141 forced Henry once more into the limelight. He made a deal with the empress that paralleled an earlier one he had made with Stephen in December 1135. The empress agreed to accept that Henry would continue to have a leading role, 'in all matters of chief account in England, notably in appointments to bishoprics' (Malmesbury, *Historia novella*, para. 45). In return she was recognized as *domina Anglorum* ('lady of the English'), received as such within Winchester, and confirmed by a further legatine council convened by Henry at Winchester on 7 April. Henry sought to go beyond this, and make a permanent peace. This would turn on the provision for Eustace, Stephen's elder son, the key to any agreement on the Blois side. The empress's inflexibility and her increasing military weakness drew Henry away from her. She was driven from Westminster by the Londoners in late June, after a plot in which Henry was rumoured to be involved. She then returned to Winchester on 31 July. As she rode in through one gate, so the story was told, Henry rode out through another. Henry helped rally the king's forces, and 'hired ordinary knights at very great expense' in his support (*Gesta Stephani*, 128–9). The empress was forced to retreat from Winchester, and in the retreat Robert of Gloucester was captured. Henry and Archbishop Theobald, 'the archbishop and the legate', then helped negotiate the exchange of Robert of Gloucester and the king, offering themselves as hostages for the performance of the terms agreed. Thereafter a further legatine council was summoned at Westminster in early December, at which the decisions made earlier in the year were reversed, and Stephen was restored to power.

The travails of civil war, 1142–1150 Henry's reputation never quite recovered from the events of 1141. The king's supporters reproached him for accepting the empress; the Angevins felt betrayed when he abandoned her. Their opprobrium fell not just on the legate but on the higher clergy in general. A fragment of Henry's correspondence with Brian fitz Count is highly revealing. The bishop produced one of his texts for the times, 'remember the wife of Lot, who when she looked back was turned into a pillar of salt' (Davis, 300–01). Brian brushed this text aside; he defended his own honour and consistency, and challenged the bishop to a duel; and he accused him of prolonging the civil war by his actions. This was the view also of some of the clergy. Henry, archdeacon of Huntingdon, called him 'a new kind of monster, composed part pure and part corrupt, I mean part monk and part knight' (Huntingdon, *Historia Anglorum*, 611). If Henry did not lead troops in battle, he procured and paid for them on numerous occasions, including the battle of Wilton on 1 July 1143.

On 24 September 1143 Innocent II died, and Henry of Winchester's legation lapsed. Henry tried desperately to secure its renewal, or alternatively to have Winchester made an archbishopric; but to no avail. He was embroiled at the same time in the disputed election to the see of York, where he had fostered the candidature of William Fitzherbert (*d.* 1154). Bernard of Clairvaux, in a letter to Pope Lucius II (*r.* 1144–5) wrote in vitriolic terms of Henry, 'that old deceiver of Winchester' (*Letters of St Bernard*, 276). Henry's reputation at the papal curia fell further when he was held responsible for Stephen's attempt to prevent the majority of the English episcopate from attending the Council of Rheims in 1148. Henry was threatened with suspension from office, and was required to appear in person at Rome to explain his actions. This he successfully did, and on his return he is found at Cluny, where he lent the abbey a large sum, the terms for its repayment carefully specified. The record of this, dated 1149, shows that Henry travelled with a large retinue, including his private secretaries and his personal chef. A little later, possibly after a further visit to Rome, he visited Santiago de Compostela.

Retreat and recovery, 1150–1161 Henry was in England in the early 1150s, and in 1153 he took a prominent role in negotiating the treaty of Winchester, in which Duke Henry of Normandy, the empress's son, was adopted as Stephen's heir. Stephen died on 25 October 1154. Henry de Blois attended Henry II's coronation at Westminster on 19 December 1154 and was at court early in the following year. As he observed the working out in practice of the agreements that he had negotiated in principle, he became increasingly concerned. At some time in 1155 Henry sent treasure to Cluny via its abbot, Peter the Venerable, whom he had brought to England to lend him prestige, and slipped after him. The castles he had fortified in the civil war, among them Meredon in Hursley, Hampshire, where he had imprisoned one of the knights of Brian fitz Count, and Downton, Hampshire, earlier the scene of much military activity, were destroyed. Henry was at Cluny for at least two years, and in one of them, it was said, he supported the whole convent for a full year from his own resources. Archbishop Theobald urged him to return; reproached him for neglecting his duties ('the decay of morals is far more lamentable than the decay of walls'; *Letters of John of Salisbury*, 1.67); reassured him as to the king's goodwill; and offered a personal safe conduct to the royal court. The pipe roll of Michaelmas 1158 shows that he had been restored to favour during the preceding year, and suggests he returned in the winter of 1157–8. Immediately after his return, in 1158, very likely in the king's presence, he reinterred the bodies of the early English kings in his cathedral church, emphasizing the continuity of the monarchy and the part played by his own city in its history.

Elder statesman, 1161–1171 The final decade of Henry's long life started with the death of Theobald of Canterbury in April 1161. Henry was then once again at Cluny, the last time he is recorded outside England. In May 1162 Thomas Becket was elected as the new archbishop; and Henry de Blois, as subdean of the province of Canterbury, presided over his election and his consecration. At this time, it was reported, he advised Becket to abandon his secular responsibilities. In the breakdown of Becket's relationship with Henry II, and in his subsequent exile, Henry of Winchester managed to retain the respect of both sides. At Northampton in October 1164—the last time he is recorded outside Winchester—Henry pronounced the judgment of the king's court, that Becket was guilty of failing to obey a royal summons, and thus should forfeit his possessions. He then looked for compromise, offering 2000 marks against Becket's alleged debts as chancellor, but the king refused. Some of the bishops wanted Becket to resign, but Henry advised against it: it would set a most dangerous precedent, and was clearly contrary to the canon law. In late June 1166 he was one of those who sealed the bishops' appeal against Becket's Vézelay excommunications.

In all this Henry's behaviour was quite consistent. He was primarily concerned with the liberty of the church; he saw himself as a diplomat, anxious to settle disputes by negotiation, happy to find cash to smooth the way; he would not support sanctions against diocesan bishops. Thereafter, though his messengers maintained to the end an active correspondence, Henry slipped from the public gaze. In 1166 he was appointed a papal judge-delegate in the case which the lay brothers brought against Gilbert of Sempringham (*d.* 1189); but he was too ill to serve. Increasingly frail, at the very end of his life he went blind; but his mind remained clear to the end. On 6 August 1171, on his deathbed, he was visited by Henry II, whom he reproached for the death of Becket in the previous year. The king then confirmed his last bequest to the monks of his cathedral priory, returning their estates but insisting on an annual audit. Two, or possibly three, days later Henry de Blois died, and was buried in his cathedral church.

Wealth and power Henry de Blois throughout his life had the independence and stature which come from great wealth, unquestioned authority, and a clear conscience. He was a speaker of great eloquence, 'greater than Cicero' in this regard according to the inscription on one of his enamel plaques, while Eugenius III's reported comment, that he could corrupt two nations by his tongue, makes the same point more critically. When his actions were criticized, as they often were in Stephen's reign, he replied politely and at length and held his ground. That he was singled-minded, reluctant to abandon a course of action when he had set himself to it, was the judgement of William of Malmesbury, the doyen of the historians of his day, who knew him well. His pursuit of the legatine commission showed this single-mindedness at its worst; the pursuit of peace the same qualities at their best. He was a man of simple certainties.

Domesday Book Henry could produce for visitors, and it was made, he told them, 'in order that every man may be content with his own rights, and not encroach unpunished on those of others' (*Dialogus*, 63). This may serve as text for his work at Glastonbury (in his *libellus*), at Winchester (where he made surveys of the city and the monastic estates), and at Cluny (where a survey of provisions and cash renders for the monastery, made *c.*1156, is stated to have been drawn up by his own hand). Many church estates which fell vacant between 1136 and 1141, when Henry's power was at its height, were brought under his direct control. Henry succeeded Roger of Salisbury as dean of the collegiate church of St Martin's-le-Grand, London, where the clerks of the royal household held prebends, serving from 1139 until *c.*1160. This was an active centre of royal administration. He founded the hospital of St Cross in Winchester, and he reformed the old collegiate church of Christchurch in Twinham, turning this, *c.*1150, into a house of Augustinian canons. His college at Marwell, south of Winchester, consisting of four priests praying for the souls of the kings of England and the bishops of Winchester, has many of the features of a later chantry. Everywhere he served, best practice was designed to secure a profit.

Henry de Blois was a man of legendary wealth. The valuation in Domesday Book of Glastonbury (the richest monastery in England), and the episcopal and monastic estates at Winchester, was only a little below £2500. This figure will have greatly underestimated his actual resources, particularly during Stephen's reign, when he took over the monastery of Hyde in Winchester, and controlled the port at Southampton. He was vigorous in pursuit of economic privileges: his first request of Henry I for Glastonbury was the confirmation of its fair; his first request of Henry II the extension of the St Giles fair at Winchester, during which time the bishop enjoyed regalian rights in the city. Henry's wealth set a gulf between him and his monks and clergy greater than he can have realized: his efforts to get his parochial clergy to use silver not pewter chalices, a story told to his credit by Gerald of Wales, can only seem patronizing and insensitive viewed from their side. A less equivocally creditable act, also described by Gerald, was his distribution before his death of almost all his wealth to charitable works.

The personality of the patron Henry used his wealth in all the ways expected in one of his status, and in some ways that were not. Among the latter may be noted his interest in relics and Roman antiquities. John of Salisbury in his memoirs of the papal court has a picture of Henry on one of his visits to Rome, 'conspicuous for his long beard and philosophical solemnity' (John of Salisbury, *Historia pontificalis*, 79), touring the antique shops and buying statues, which he shipped back to Winchester. He left to Winchester a rich treasure of gold and silver work, decorated hangings and vestments, and other artefacts, including some of these statues. He was remembered as a great builder both at Glastonbury, where the monastic buildings were largely rebuilt in his time, and at Winchester, where he built the palace of Wolvesey, and on his estates. At his palaces he built 'great lakes and ingenious watercourses' (*Gir. Camb. opera*, 7.45), and assembled collections of exotic birds and wild animals. He built a town house at Southwark, explaining that this was necessary because he had often to be in London, 'on royal affairs or other urgent business' (Franklin, no. 24).

Henry's buildings are largely destroyed, and most of his movable wealth dissipated, but a few artefacts survive to give a measure of this aspect of the man. The great font of Tournai marble which he gave to his cathedral church still remains there, showing St Ambrose active in his pastoral work, his beard carefully trimmed. The binding of the Winchester survey shows French influence, and may like the font be the work of French craftsmen. Surviving capitals from Wolvesey are seen to show the influence of St Denis. The great Winchester Bible was commissioned by Henry in the 1160s, and left unfinished on his death. Here, in a fine initial, Desiderius, wearing episcopal vestments, is clearly a portrait of Bishop Henry, with the Bible under his arm, talking with St Jerome on equal terms. Here is an image of the confidence of the ruling class of twelfth-century Europe. Henry de Blois was the last survivor, and in many ways the most able, of the grandchildren of William the Conqueror. EDMUND KING

Sources M. J. Franklin, ed., *Winchester, 1070–1204*, English Episcopal Acta, 8 (1993) • L. Voss, *Heinrich von Blois, Bishof von Winchester (1129–1171)* (Berlin, 1932) • *Reg. RAN*, vols. 2–3 • K. R. Potter and R. H. C. Davis, eds., *Gesta Stephani*, OMT (1976) • William of Malmesbury, *Historia novella: the contemporary history*, ed. E. King, trans. K. R. Potter, OMT (1998) • M. Biddle, ed., *Winchester in the early middle ages: an edition and discussion of the Winton Domesday*, Winchester Studies, 1 (1976) • D. Whitelock, M. Brett, and C. N. L. Brooke, eds., *Councils and synods with other documents relating to the English church, 871–1204*, 2 (1981) • H. W. C. Davis, 'Henry of Blois and Brian fitz-Count', *EngHR*, 25 (1910), 297–303 • John of Salisbury, *Historia pontificalis: John of Salisbury's memoirs of the papal court*, ed. and trans. M. Chibnall (1956) • *Vita S Remigii*, *Gir. Camb. opera*, 7.43–9 • D. Knowles, *The monastic order in England*, 2nd edn (1963) • F. Barlow, *Thomas Becket* (1986) • *The letters of John of Salisbury*, ed. and trans. H. E. Butler and W. J. Millor, rev. C. N. L. Brooke, 2 vols., OMT (1979–86) [Lat. orig. with parallel Eng. text] • J. Crook, ed., *Winchester Cathedral: nine hundred years, 1093–1993* (1993) • E. Bishop, 'Gifts of Bishop Henry of Blois, abbot of Glastonbury, to Winchester Cathedral', *Liturgica Historica: papers on the liturgy and religious life of the Western church* (1918), 392–401 • C. Donovan, *The Winchester Bible* (1993) • G. Zarnecki, 'Henry of Blois as a patron of sculpture', *Art and patronage in the English romanesque*, ed. S. Macready and F. H. Thompson, Society of Antiquaries of London Occasional Papers, new ser., 8 (1986), 159–72 • Henry, archdeacon of Huntingdon, *Historia Anglorum*, ed. D. E. Greenway, OMT (1996) • A. Bernard and A. Bruel, eds., *Receuil des chartes de l'abbaye de Cluny*, 5 (1894), 490–505 • Adam of Domerham, *Historia de rebus Glastoniensibus*, ed. T. Hearne, 2 vols. (1727) • G. Zarnecki, J. Holt, and T. Holland, eds., *English romanesque art, 1066–1200* (1984) [exhibition catalogue, Hayward Gallery, London, 5 April–8 July 1984] • *The letters of St Bernard of Clairvaux*, trans. B. S. James (1953) • R. Fitz Nigel [R. Fitzneale], *Dialogus de scaccario / The course of the exchequer*, ed. and trans. C. Johnson (1950) • *Fasti Angl., 1066–1300*, [Monastic cathedrals], 85 • D. Knowles, C. N. L. Brooke, and V. C. M. London, eds., *The heads of religious houses, England and Wales*, 1: *940–1216* (1972), 51

Likenesses Tournai, portrait on marble font, 1129–71 (as St Nicholas?), repro. in Crook, ed., *Winchester Cathedral*, fig. 9.1 • seal, 1129–71, Winchester College muniments • enamel plaque, 1135–54, BM • Master of the Genesis Initial, illuminated initial, 1160–69 (as Pope Desiderius), Winchester Cathedral, Winchester Bible, MS fol. 3 • seal, BL; Birch, *Seals*, 2241 [*see illus.*]

Wealth at death wealthy, although wealth depleted owing to charitable gifts two years before death: *Vita S Remigii*, 49

Blois, Peter of (1125x30–1212), letter writer and ecclesiastic, was born into a Breton family of minor nobility in or near Blois. Various nephews and other members of his family are mentioned in his letters, but only two are significant in his life: his brother, Guillaume, who became a monk and abbot in Sicily, and wrote plays and poems, and an uncle or cousin, Pierre de Blois, who was Peter's first tutor, wrote poetry, and became learned in Roman law.

His years in the schools, c.1140–1165 Since Blois was not a cathedral town in the twelfth century, it had no school that could provide education at an advanced level. So Peter, having briefly visited Paris ('Epistolae', ep. 240; *Later Letters*, ed. Revell, no. 5), went to the school attached to the cathedral at Tours in the early 1140s, probably with Pierre de Blois as his personal tutor. Here he studied under the great master Bernard Silvestris, who taught literature and the art of writing, particularly letter-writing. Peter records that Bernard required him to learn by heart the letters of Hildebert, archbishop of Tours (*d.* 1133), and advised him to avoid myths and fables and to concentrate on history ('Epistolae', ep. 101). His later works show that in the main he followed this advice. As part of his course Peter also studied poetry, and (according to his own account) wrote lascivious verses in his youth and poems on moral and contemporary issues in later life (ibid., ep. 57). None of his early, and only about ten of his later, poems have so far been satisfactorily identified, despite attempts to add to their number.

After his literary education in Tours, Peter went to Bologna, where he studied Roman law, having the later archbishop of Canterbury Baldwin (*d.* 1190) as his tutor, and Umberto Crivelli (afterwards Pope Urban III) as one of the masters whose lectures both he and Baldwin attended (*Later Letters*, ed. Revell, no. 10n.). During these years he developed a great admiration for Roman law; but, to judge from his description of himself as being violently attracted and mentally inebriated by 'the secular law, wantoning in its glorious panoply of words and its elegant urbanity of speech' ('Epistolae', ep. 26), he admired its verbal grandeur more than its legal doctrine. Consequently it is not surprising that when in 1186 his knowledge of Roman law was tested in the papal court, he was badly beaten, and this disappointment was one cause of the change in his outlook which will be examined later.

From the study of Roman law Peter turned to theology, and this caused him about 1155 to move from Bologna to Paris. On his arrival he wrote the letter to his former master mentioned above, regretting the change and adding that he still read his Roman-law texts for recreation. However, an emended version of this letter made about thirty years later mentions Roman law and lawyers with great acerbity.

Peter continued his studies in Paris until 1166, supporting himself (like many other advanced students) by taking pupils, among whom were two sons of Jocelin de Bohun, bishop of Salisbury ('Epistolae', ep. 51). One of these pupils, Reginald Fitzjocelin (*d.* 1191), after encountering opposition in which Peter played the part of sympathetic observer (ibid., ep. 30), was consecrated bishop of Bath in 1174.

Although Peter has left few details of his Parisian studies or of the masters under whom he studied, his later works show him to have been familiar with all three of the main styles of theological study current at Paris during these years—the allegorical interpretation in which Richard of St Victor was pre-eminent; the historical matter of the Old Testament, which Peter Comestor organized; and the systematic and analytical study of doctrine, in which Peter Lombard was supreme. The historical facts and allegorical interpretations of the Bible alone are conspicuous in Peter's works until the last decade of his life, when his letters show that he had preserved analytical theological notes of his Parisian years which he used in answering some of the questions of his correspondents (*Later Letters*, ed. Revell, no. 37). Overall, therefore, there is abundant evidence that Peter's studies at Tours, Bologna, and Paris embraced comprehensively the literary, legal, and theological sciences of his day. His only problem was to find employment commensurate with the long labour of laying the foundations.

Search for employment, 1165–1174 By 1165, while supporting himself by taking pupils, Peter was looking round for a career in the world of government. He had an uncle who was bishop of Perigord, whom he tried, without success, to interest in his future ('Epistolae', ep. 34). He also had hopes—which he never entirely abandoned—of getting a substantial canonry at Chartres. (He did in fact get canonries at both Rouen and Chartres but they provided little or no revenue; ibid., epp. 128, 130; *Later Letters*, ed. Revell, nos. 6, 13.) So, for a career, he had to look elsewhere, and his first serious opportunity arose in 1166 from the premature death of King William of Sicily, who left as his heir a young son aged twelve in the care of his widow, Margaret. She was a member of the family of the counts of Perche, and—surrounded as she was by Sicilian barons who had opposed her husband on several occasions and from whom she could hope for no support—she wrote to her French relatives, and particularly to Rotrou, archbishop of Rouen, for help. As a result of this appeal, a band of French adventurers and relatives was gathered to help the widowed queen in the government of Sicily and of course to promote their own interests. Peter and his brother Guillaume both joined them.

In the end no fewer than thirty-seven adventurers were collected, and they arrived in Sicily in September 1166 ready to take over the administration of a country with a unique combination of Arab, Norman, and Sicilian people, of whose habits and expectations the newcomers knew nothing. For a very short time all went well: Peter became tutor to the young king and keeper of the royal seal, and his brother became abbot of Santa Maria di Maniaci near Maletto ('Epistolae', epp. 46, 66, 93). But the whole enterprise had very frail foundations, and in the autumn of 1168 most of the newcomers were driven out by the local baronage. Peter was lucky to escape with his life on a ship which took him to Genoa, whence he made his way back to northern France determined never again to move if he could stay in his native land (ibid., ep. 90).

Despite its failure, this unlucky initiative proved to be the beginning of Peter's future career, for Archbishop Rotrou, who seems to have been the cause of his going to Sicily, began employing him to write letters. This brought him into the ambience of Angevin politics in the last stage of the conflict between Henry II and Archbishop Thomas Becket, which was largely conducted as a war of letters. Since this was Peter's speciality, he was soon engaged as a letter writer, first on behalf of Archbishop Rotrou, and then in association with his old pupil Reginald Fitzjocelin, who was one of Henry II's main agents in conducting his case against Thomas Becket, and who—as a result of royal influence—was elected bishop of Bath in April 1173. In view of his association with Henry II's campaign against Thomas Becket, Reginald had a very stormy passage in getting his election ratified ('Epistolae', ep. 30); but this was finally achieved, and shortly afterwards Peter got his first steady employment as chief letter writer and later chancellor in the household of Richard of Dover, Thomas Becket's successor in the archbishopric of Canterbury (elected June 1173 and consecrated April 1174). Peter would greatly have preferred to stay in France, but there were many more administrative posts available in England, so he had reluctantly to settle down in a country whose language he never managed to learn (ibid., ep. 160). Of course even his employment at Canterbury was only for the lifetime of the archbishop, but greater security came in 1182 when, a vacancy in the archdeaconry of Bath having occurred, Reginald Fitzjocelin made Peter his archdeacon. Thus, at the age of about fifty-five, Peter at last had a position that gave him security for life; and, while he was a member of the archbishop's staff, the archdeacon's work could be done by a deputy.

The decade of conspicuous achievement, 1174–1184 Peter now had a stimulating position at the heart of Angevin government, and it was a further satisfaction that, besides his skill in letter-writing, he had begun writing remarkably vivid treatises in which he brought the biblical teaching of the Parisian schools to audiences both of clergy and of laity. In particular his two short works on the conversion of St Paul and the transfiguration of Jesus sufficiently impressed the exceptionally literate Henry II for him to ask Peter to write something specially for him. Thereupon Peter wrote his *Compendium in Job*, in which—writing in his moments of leisure between (in his words) 'camps and courts'—he drew on Gregory the Great's *Moralia in Job* and the sermons of St Bernard to urge the king to bear his trials with fortitude in the confident expectation of a happy ending.

In many ways these were the happiest days of Peter's life. He was busy as the official eulogist of Angevin government after the disasters of the rebellion of the king's sons and the catastrophe of Thomas Becket's murder, and he started writing an account of Henry II's reign which he called *De praestigiis fortunae* ('The deceptions of fortune'), which he mentions more often than any of his other works. When he was writing this work he evidently thought that Henry II was going to triumph over his misfortunes and thus prove the deceptiveness of fortune. As will become evident, this hope was itself to prove deceptive as Henry collapsed under the weight of his misfortunes, and Peter's laudatory work has not survived.

Meanwhile, although he lamented the horrors of the itinerating court with its bad food, uncertain lodgings, and execrable drink ('Epistolae', ep. 14), Peter was basically content. He was twice at the papal court, in 1169 and 1179. On one of these occasions, probably in 1169, he wrote in the pope's name an *Instructio fidei catholicae* ('Instruction in the Catholic faith') for the Muslim sultan of Konia, which Matthew Paris a hundred years later thought a sufficiently important example of learning elegantly presented in the service of Christendom to be transcribed in full into his chronicle. His visit in 1179 gave him a rather different claim to fame: he borrowed money which he failed to repay and the pope's letter to the archbishop of Canterbury on behalf of the creditor found a permanent place in the code of canon law issued by Gregory IX in 1234 (*Liber Extra*, 3.22.3). In short, during the years 1174–84 Peter was at the centre of Angevin government in its most prosperous days, and he was in touch with the greatest men and events of his time.

In the full flood of his prosperity Peter wrote a letter, which can be dated between 1182 and 1184, to his namesake and old tutor, in his most grandiloquent style: 'I rejoice with all my heart in our identity of name … Our writings have carried our fame throughout the world so that neither flood nor fire nor any calamity nor the passage of time can obliterate our name' ('Epistolae', ep. 77). It is evident from this boastful effusion that Peter already looked on writing, and more particularly letter-writing, as the occupation most likely to bring the fame that he ardently desired, and this helps to explain his next enterprise.

The pivotal year, 1184 In February 1184 Archbishop Richard died, and Peter's future was once more uncertain, for—if the new archbishop did not employ him—he would have no excuse for not descending to the local duties of a rural archdeacon. So these were anxious months for him. According to his own account the king offered him the bishopric of Rochester, which was vacant from August 1184 to July 1185, but what he most dearly desired was fame, and he used the period of uncertainty and leisure between the death of the old and the appointment of a new archbishop to consolidate his claim to fame by making a collection of his letters which he dedicated to the king ('Epistolae', ep. 1).

Peter's collection was different from earlier letter collections of the eleventh and twelfth centuries in that it was made for general circulation by the writer himself in mid-career, and therefore it was available for the author's addition of new letters and changes in the texts of earlier letters in accordance with his changing views or aims. The aim of the collection was ostensibly to teach the art of letter-writing, but in fact, as is evident from his letter to his namesake mentioned above, his real aim was to make himself known to future generations. It is very likely that the first collection which he made in 1184 already contained many alterations in the texts that had actually been dispatched, and he went on correcting and making omissions or additions to the texts until about 1202, after which he seems to have lost interest in the collection amid other occupations.

In association with this collection, Peter wrote a brief manual on the art of letter-writing. Only one copy of this has survived (CUL, MS Dd.9.38) and its authenticity has often, though almost certainly wrongly, been denied. At all events, though the manual won few if any readers, the letter collection became one of the most widely distributed works of the twelfth century.

By the time the collection had been made and the short manual written, Peter's months of leisure were brought to an end by the appointment of the new archbishop in November 1184. From Peter's point of view the king's choice of an archbishop—and it was most emphatically the king's choice and not that of the Canterbury monks—could not have been happier for Peter: it was Baldwin, bishop of Worcester, who had been his friend and tutor in Bologna and who at once appointed Peter as his main legal adviser and letter writer. The position opened up more interesting prospects than ever before with—most unluckily as it turned out—more emphasis on his legal learning than his epistolary skill. Baldwin was a much more active man than his predecessor, and he at once undertook to build new headquarters near Canterbury for his staff. Moreover, with the death of Henry, the most rebellious of Henry II's sons, in 1183, it seemed as if a new order of governmental growth and peace was about to begin, with Peter at its hub, writing his triumphal account of Henry's reign. The reality however turned out to be very different.

The decade of failure and doubt, 1184–1194 For Peter and the new archbishop, as also for Henry II and western Europe generally, things began to go wrong almost at once. At the local level, it was necessary to get papal consent for the new archiepiscopal headquarters. The monks of Canterbury, who were enjoying unprecedented prosperity as a result of the offerings of the huge numbers of pilgrims to the tomb of their new martyr, Thomas Becket, were violently opposed to the archbishop's project as tending to the diminishment of their influence in his counsels. Moreover they could afford to employ an outstanding Roman lawyer, a certain Pillius, to conduct their case at the papal court. So, after protracted preliminary tussles between the archbishop and the monks, Peter was obliged to go to the papal court to answer the objections of the monks to the archbishop's plans, and he spent the months from March 1187 to January 1188 on this mission, travelling through northern Italy with the papal court.

These months are very fully documented in the letters that the monks' representatives at the papal court sent back to Canterbury (Stubbs, *Epistolae Cantuarienses*). They show Peter spending several weeks at Verona arguing the archbishop's case against Pillius, and being defeated all along the line. Then, when the papal court moved from Verona to Ferrara in October 1187, Peter rode with Pope Urban III, his old professor of Roman law, and tried a last plea, reminding the pope that he and Baldwin had been fellow students under him at Bologna ('Epistolae', ep. 152). This attempt at lobbying so incensed the pope that he had a heart attack and died next day. This of course delayed Peter's defeat, but he had never had any prospect of success. After the rapid election of a new pope, Gregory VIII, he had to spend a further three months itinerating with the papal court until at Pisa—shortly before Christmas—Pope Gregory also died. A new pope, Clement III, was then elected, and Peter spent a further month suffering the long ignominy of inevitable defeat before his return to England.

These tribulations helped to destroy Peter's earlier regard for Roman law. A small symptom of this can be seen in the alterations that he made in the old letter of thirty years earlier which he had written when he had just come from Bologna to study theology in Paris ('Epistolae', ep. 26; for the two versions, see Wahlgren, 72–80). In its original form it is full of praise for Roman law; but, as revised about 1190, praise has been replaced by recriminations against Roman lawyers. This change is symptomatic of a painful personal experience. But much more important, even for his own future, was the stream of news that arrived at the papal court while Peter was in attendance. First there was the news of the defeat of the crusading army at Hattin in July 1187, followed by the martyrdom of the French leader Renaud de Châtillon, and finally by the fall of Jerusalem on 2 October. In a brief businesslike letter, which he did not include in his letter collection, Peter reported the arrival of news of these disasters to Henry II, and Roger of Howden, who was at the royal court, put it in his chronicle.

These events destroyed Peter's confidence in the state of Western Christendom; and he was further shaken when he got back to France to find that the struggles of Henry II and his sons, which had seemed to have been successfully concluded ten years earlier, had now reached their fatal climax leading to the despair and death of Henry II on 6 July 1189.

This combination of disasters changed his whole picture of the safety and stability of western Europe and of Henry II as a successful ruler, and for the next few years he directed all his literary energies to new themes: a hagiographical work on the life of Renaud de Châtillon; a dialogue between the abbot of Bonneval and Henry II about the causes of the disasters of the time; and a passionate plea for a concentration of all the energies of Christendom on a new crusade. These themes fill most of Peter's writing in the period 1188–9; and they culminated in his setting out at the end of 1189, closely followed by the archbishop of Canterbury, among the first of the English contingent on the third crusade. They travelled with Richard I as far as Sicily, and then they pressed on to join the crusading army at Tyre while the king stayed in Sicily to await the arrival of his mother, Queen Eleanor, with his destined bride, Berengaria of Navarre.

Within a month of their arrival at Tyre, the archbishop

died, on 20 November 1190, and this left Peter no alternative but to find his own way back to England. He returned to Sicily, which he reached at about the same time as Eleanor of Aquitaine who had brought Richard's bride. The marriage took place on 12 May, and Queen Eleanor left Sicily at once. Peter probably travelled with her through Italy and France; then, while Eleanor stayed in France, he went on and arrived back in England in the autumn of 1191.

At first it seemed likely that Peter would continue as the principal member of the new archbishop's staff, for on 27 November his old friend and pupil Reginald Fitzjocelin was elected archbishop. This prospect, however, was destroyed by Reginald's death within a month of his election, and there was a long vacancy at Canterbury until December 1193 when Hubert Walter, the most efficient of the administrators available to Richard I, became archbishop of Canterbury. He sometimes consulted Peter on particular points during the next few years, but he never gave him a position in his household. Consequently, Peter was in danger of being reduced to the necessity of having to perform his duties as archdeacon, for which he had always employed a deputy ('Epistolae', ep. 157).

Peter seems to have sought employment with Queen Eleanor, for he wrote three letters in her name to the pope protesting against King Richard's imprisonment in Germany in violation of his immunity as a crusader; and two more on the same subject, one to the pope in the name of the archbishop of Rouen, and another in his own name to the archbishop of Mainz, with whom he had shared lodgings when they were students together in Paris, urging him also to write to the pope ('Epistolae', epp. 144–6, 64, 143). But if he hoped for employment with Queen Eleanor, his hopes were dashed, and he had to look elsewhere.

One possibility was Odo, bishop of Paris, to whom he wrote in 1197–8 seeking a position in his chapter ('Epistolae', epp. 127, 160). Another possibility was Geoffrey, an illegitimate son of Henry II and archbishop of York from 1191 to 1212, with whom he clearly had some short-lived position about 1199, and to whom he dedicated a life of St Wilfrid, which was seen in the sixteenth century by the antiquary John Leland but is now lost. Nothing came of this. So he had to face the fact that there was no further role for him in the world of politics, and he found solace in new intellectual and spiritual interests.

Peter's theological and spiritual works, 1195–1212 As a first step Peter seems to have contemplated making a revised edition of his letters with many theological additions culled largely from recent Parisian theology. Two contemporary manuscripts of his letter collection with these additions have survived which exemplify this ill-conceived plan (LPL, MS 421, and Milan, Biblioteca Ambrosiana, MS C. 103 sup.). But the additions clearly made the letters unreadable, and they have not been found in any other copies of the letter collection.

Much more successfully, Peter began to take a new interest in the spiritual life of the Cistercians and Carthusians and in theological and devotional questions. These interests led to a new series of works: 'On friendship', 'On penance', 'On confession', 'On faith', 'On the episcopal office'. In substance none of these works was original, but to all of them he brought a new style and new illustrative quotations. In particular, his *Tractatus de fide* ('On faith') was based on Archbishop Baldwin's *Liber de commendatione fidei*; and his treatise 'On friendship' was an elaboration of the work of the Cistercian Ailred of Rievaulx, to which Peter added many classical quotations. He also rewrote two ancient saints' lives: his life of St Wilfrid, already mentioned, and a life of St Guthlac of Crowland, giving both of them a modernity of style and spiritual outlook.

This whole body of work testifies to the changing direction of Peter's thoughts; but, so far as his immediate future was concerned, his most significant step was to dedicate his work 'On friendship' to an old acquaintance in the royal household, William de Sainte Mère-Église, who became bishop of London in 1199 (for the dedication, see *Later Letters*, ed. Revell, no. 78).

Whether as cause or effect, this dedication is associated with the new bishop's offering Peter the archdeaconry of London, which he accepted. This of course was not promotion, but it fitted well with his new range of interests by giving him a position in which he met a continuing flow of people who went to London on business and with whom he discussed many theological problems. The letters that he wrote as a result of these discussions generally have no merits as examples of epistolary style and he never added them to his letter collection; but they have a great interest in disclosing the extent to which the problems discussed in the schools had become part of the mental equipment of large numbers of clergy in every level of the ecclesiastical hierarchy. These new interests seem also to have stirred in him a search for a deeper religious experience, and he wrote three letters to Pope Innocent III protesting against the lack of warmth in the language of the mass (*Later Letters*, ed. Revell, nos. 1–3). So, even though he had now lost his position at the centre of government which had provided the opportunity for writing many of his earlier letters, he was fully occupied probing more deeply into theological and devotional problems as he sank into a quiet old age.

Like many clergy, Peter spent some time in France during the great interdict from 1208 to 1213 when the normal activities of the church were suspended and clergy in administrative positions were footloose. This seems once more to have renewed his hope of settling down at Chartres. He may even have died there for his death was recorded both at Chartres and at Rouen; but, wherever he died, his death was known in London in February 1212, and must have taken place shortly before this date.

Peter's life and work in modern scholarship: his prose works All Peter's works, whether letters, sermons, or treatises, had the same general purpose of bringing the learning of the schools to bear on religious and practical affairs of every description, and it is this that gives a lasting interest to nearly everything that he wrote.

Peter was certainly prodigiously fluent, and he had a

ready command of most areas of the scholastic learning of his day. As evidence of his fluency he claimed that he could, and at least sometimes did, write four letters simultaneously, dictating three and writing the fourth with his own hand. This of course is not impossible, but its literal truth is placed in doubt by its reflecting a skill possessed by Julius Caesar, as reported by Pliny and repeated by John of Salisbury (*Policraticus*, 5, chap. 8), from whom Peter, who never hesitated over appropriating other men's learning, probably borrowed it. After all, the great schools of the twelfth and thirteenth centuries came into existence to make the learning of the past available for the needs of the present; and, in being a great appropriator, Peter of Blois was carrying out this plan.

Peter's poetry The only direct evidence about Peter's poetry comes from three of his letters. In an early letter ('Epistolae', ep. 12) he asks a nephew to send him the *versus et ludicra* that he had written when he was (presumably as a student) at Tours. Thereafter no more is heard about his verses until, in a letter (ibid., ep. 57) in the second recension of the collection of about 1190, he writes to a friend who, having entered a religious order and suffered a good deal of boredom, asked Peter to send him some of his amatory poems. In his reply, Peter acknowledged that he had written such poems in his youth, but he attached to his letter only a few verses in his later, more mature style. A few years later, in revising his letter collection after his return from the crusade, as well as adding several new letters, he added to *epistola* 57 a few more poems of serious religious instruction or indignation at the captivity of Richard I on his return from the crusade ('Epistolae', 1127–36).

The existence of the poems attached to *epistola* 57 has naturally raised the question whether there are others that can be identified, and there are certainly a few. In particular two poems (published by Braunholtz in *Zeitschrift für Romanische Philologie*, 1927) in praise of wine may safely be added; and, most unexpectedly, there are a few lines ascribed to 'that excellent letter writer [*dictator*] Peter of Blois', in a German polemical work (*Chronica regia Coloniensis*) written in the neighbourhood of Cologne about 1206. Three poems in the *Carmina burana*, attributed to Peter of Blois by the editors in 1930 on grounds of similarity of language and style, may also be added as borderline cases.

So are there any more additions that can be made? This is a question that has occupied scholars for many years. The greatest stimulus in provoking a search for new poems was the publication in 1925 of the poems of Gautier of Châtillon, a contemporary of Peter of Blois and one of the great poets of the twelfth century, who in one of his poems mentions Peter of Blois as one of the four most accomplished poets of the time. But which Peter of Blois was he referring to—the letter writer or his namesake and tutor? The failure to answer this question properly is one reason why the additions suggested by various eminent scholars and finally and most lavishly of all by Peter Dronke are either certainly or probably not by the letter writer. It must however be added that the last named scholar has provided by far the best texts of some of the letter writer's authentic poems.

Posthumous reputation The interest in Peter of Blois after his death was almost entirely centred on his letters, which continued until the seventeenth century to have readers who appreciated their style, their widely ranging quotations from classical authors, and their vivacity. Through these claims on their attention, Peter's letters would have taught their readers skill in observing the prose rhythms which were required in correctly written letters. The papal curia was by far the most important source of authoritative letters at the time when Peter made his first collection of letters, and the stylistic rules for papal letters, including the elaboration of strict rules of prose rhythm known as the *cursus*, had been stabilized at the papal court at the time when Peter was writing his early letters. He outlined them in his treatise on letter-writing and he observed them in his letters. Indeed one reason for the lack of success of his very jejune theoretical work may have been that the rules could be learnt much better from his letters themselves, where, besides the rules of *cursus*, the reader would find examples of careful structure and the use of convincing authorities. In brief, while teaching the rules of letter-writing as an essential tool of government, Peter's letters also made interesting reading for times, such as meals, when short texts were called for; and many found in them pleasure as well as instruction. Even as late as the seventeenth century, when the practical utility of the medieval rules of letter-writing had become obsolete, the first serious editor of his letters, J. Busaeus, in 1601 in his preface recommended them 'for their vivacity of expression and their wealth of doctrine'; and their next editor, Pierre de Goussainville in 1667, echoed these words.

So, in the mid-seventeenth century, Peter of Blois's letters were still being read as living literature; but by its end, both the rules he exemplified and the subjects that made his letters interesting had lost their power of eliciting admiration, and the nineteenth-century scholars who re-edited or reprinted Peter's letters did so solely for their historical information, and they blamed them for not giving more.

It should be added that Peter was also an indefatigable writer of sermons. These too he collected, and they show his total recall of the text of the Bible. But they lack the variety of themes that made his letters famous, and they never had more than a very modest circulation.

R. W. Southern

Sources 'Petri Blesensis epistolae', *Patrologia Latina*, 207 (1855) · *The later letters of Peter of Blois*, ed. E. Revell (1993) · 'Libellus de arte dictandi rethorice magistri Petri Blesensis archidiaconi ecclesiae Bathoniensis', CUL, MS Dd.9.38 · Peter of Blois, 'Life of St Guthlac', *Nova legenda Anglie*, ed. John of Tynemouth, J. Capgrave, and others, 2, ed. C. Horstman [C. Horstmann] (1901), 89–97 · G. Waitz, ed., *Chronica regia Coloniensis* (*Annales maximi Colonienses*), MGH Scriptores Rerum Germanicarum, [18] (Hanover, 1880), 321 · E. Braunholtz, 'Die Streitgedichte Peters von Blois u. Roberts v. Beaufeu', *Zeitschrift für Romanische Philologie*, 47 (1927), 32sqq · *'L'Histoire Job': an Old French verse adaptation of Peter of Blois's 'Compendium in Job'*, ed. J. Gildea (1974) · P. Dronke, 'Peter of Blois and poetry at the court of Henry II', *Mediaeval Studies*, 37 (1975), 185–235 • E. Friedberg and A. Richter, eds., *Corpus iuris canonici*, [2nd edn], 2 (Leipzig, 1922) [*Decretales Gregorii p. IX*] • *Petri Blesensis opera omnia*, ed. [P. de Goussainville] (1667) • *Carmina burana*, ed. A. Hilka and O. Schumann, vols. 1 and 2 (1930), nos. 29, 30, 31 • C. R. Cheney and B. E. A. Jones, eds., *Canterbury, 1162–1190*, English Episcopal Acta, 2 (1986); repr. with corrections (1991) • C. R. Cheney and E. John, eds., *Canterbury, 1193–1205*, English Episcopal Acta, 3 (1986) • W. Stubbs, ed., *Gesta regis Henrici secundi Benedicti abbatis: the chronicle of the reigns of Henry II and Richard I, AD 1169–1192*, 2 vols., Rolls Series, 49 (1867), 2.15 [incl. Peter of Blois's letter to Henry II on the fall of Jerusalem] • W. Stubbs, ed., *Chronicles and memorials of the reign of Richard I, 2: Epistolae Cantuarienses*, Rolls Series, 38 (1865) • J. A. Robinson, *Somerset historical essays* (1921), 100–40 • E. S. Cohn, 'The manuscript evidence for the letters of Peter of Blois', *EngHR*, 41 (1926), 43–60 • R. W. Southern, 'Some new letters of Peter of Blois', *EngHR*, 53 (1938), 412–24 • R. W. Southern, *Medieval humanism and other studies* (1970), 113–32 • R. W. Southern, 'The necessity for two Peters of Blois', *Intellectual life in the middle ages: essays presented to Margaret Gibson* (1992), 103–18 • L. Wahlgren, *The letter collections of Peter of Blois: studies in the manuscript tradition*, 58 (1993)

Archives Biblioteca Ambrosiana, Milan, MS C.103 sup. • BL, Royal MSS, letters and MS works • Bodl. Oxf., letters • CUL, MS Dd.9.38 • LPL, MS 421

Blois, William de (*d.* 1236), bishop of Worcester, is of unknown parentage, though it is probable that he was related to William de Blois, bishop of Lincoln (1203–6), under whom he served as archdeacon of Buckingham; this position he retained until his own election to the see of Worcester. He seems to have gained little else in the way of ecclesiastical preferment during this period, holding only the prebend of Sutton by virtue of his position as archdeacon, and the church of Swallow, Norfolk, at the presentation of Sir Thomas de Lascelle. By 1218 he had obtained a university degree, although it is not clear whether he studied at Paris, where the elder William de Blois had taught, or at Oxford.

William's election in 1218 was not welcomed by the chapter of Worcester Cathedral priory, who declared that he had been forced upon them by the papal legate, Guala; and he was accepted only after the intervention of Stephen Langton, archbishop of Canterbury. On 28 October he was enthroned, and began an episcopate distinguished by his dedication to reform and by conflict with the monastic chapter. The years up to 1224 were marked by violent quarrels with the cathedral priory. In 1220 the bishop tried, unsuccessfully, to depose the prior, and throughout the following year there were complaints of numerous injuries inflicted upon the monks. The priory's claim to have papal letters stating that the prior could not be removed except through papal judges-delegate led to a hearing at Rome, and the suspension of Prior Simon, whom the bishop replaced with William Norman. Although Simon's suspension was lifted through the offices of the archbishop of Canterbury, William Norman remained as prior, and opposition to him grew. Hence, in 1224, an agreement was made between the bishop and the priory, and a new system for the appointment of the prior was established—one which was to last into the fifteenth century. The cathedral monks were to nominate seven candidates from among their own number, from whom the bishop would choose one. All eventualities, including the bishop's absence from the country, were provided for. This settlement marked the end of active antagonism between the two parties.

As bishop, William de Blois himself was absent from England only twice: once in 1222, when he is said to have journeyed to Rome, for the hearing caused by his attempted deposition of Prior Simon, and again when he attended the Cistercian general chapter in 1228. He seems to have had little interest in politics, dedicating himself to his episcopal duties. The rebuilding of the east end of Worcester Cathedral was begun during his episcopate, and although it is unclear how far he was involved in this personally, he was certainly responsible for the building of the chapel to St Thomas, a free-standing structure to the north of the cathedral. He demonstrated an enthusiasm for church reform: at least four diocesan synods were held during his episcopate, in 1219, 1220, 1229, and 1232, and on at least two of these occasions he issued diocesan statutes, laying down guidelines for the effective administration of the see. He also proved himself a determined monastic visitor. It is certain that he visited three monasteries—Worcester Priory itself, St Augustine's Abbey, Bristol, and Great Malvern. In the last instance he demonstrated his resolution by gaining admittance in 1233 despite the monks' opposition, and by returning the following year. William died on 17 August 1236, at the episcopal manor of Alvechurch, Worcestershire. A tomb monument, said to be his, remains in the lady chapel of Worcester Cathedral. PHILIPPA HOSKIN

Sources *Ann. mon.*, vol. 4 • PRO • Worcester Cathedral, Worcester Cathedral MSS • D. M. Smith, ed., *Lincoln, 1186–1206*, English Episcopal Acta, 4 (1986) • F. M. Powicke and C. R. Cheney, eds., *Councils and synods with other documents relating to the English church, 1205–1313*, 1 (1964) • S. Davies, 'The administration of the diocese of Worcester in the thirteenth century', PhD diss., U. Wales, 1971 • K. Major, ed., *Acta Stephani Langton*, CYS, 50 (1950) • B. Singleton, 'The remodelling of the east end of Worcester Cathedral in the earlier part of the thirteenth century', *Medieval art and architecture at Worcester Cathedral*, ed. [G. Popper], British Archaeological Association Conference Transactions, 1 (1978), 105–15

Archives Worcester Cathedral, Worcester Cathedral MSS

Likenesses monument, *c.*1236, Worcester Cathedral, tomb of William de Blois?

Blom, Eric Walter (1888–1959), music critic and lexicographer, was born on 20 August 1888 in Bern, Switzerland, the only son and eldest child of Frederick Walter Blom, bookseller and amateur singer of Danish origin, and his wife, Anna Elise Rosalie Wenger. He was educated privately and was always very reticent about his early years: he seems to have been largely self-taught in music. Blom settled in England shortly before the First World War, and after working for two music publishers—Breitkopf and Härtel in Bern and J. and W. Chester in London—he began to make his name in 1919 as a writer of programme notes for the Queen's Hall Promenade Concerts, being first invited to do so by Rosa Newmarch. His flair and knowledge led to his becoming London music critic of the *Manchester Guardian* in 1923; an appointment to the *Birmingham Post* followed in 1931; and from 1949 onwards he worked as music critic of *The Observer*. In all three tenures Blom

Eric Walter Blom (1888–1959), by Howard Coster, 1942

showed a wide range of musical sympathies and balanced judgements, and he wrote with fine style and sensitivity. Of his dozen books *Mozart* (1935) was by far the most successful. Written with insight and affection, for the Master Musicians series (of which he was editor), it remained in print for over fifty years. In 1923 he married Marjory Spencer (*d.* 1952), with whom he had a son and a daughter.

Blom's fluent command of languages was invaluable in his work as a lexicographer. His Everyman's *Dictionary of Music* (1946) revealed his gift for the systematic organization of a large quantity of material. Its success led at once to his appointment as editor of the fifth edition of *Grove's Dictionary of Music and Musicians*, a task that occupied him until 1954. The fourth edition of *Grove* appeared in 1940, comprising a revision of the five volumes of the third edition of 1927, with a sixth, supplementary, volume. But clearly by the late 1940s an entirely new approach was required, and Blom was given a free hand to bring everything as up to date as possible. Of the 8 million or more words to which the nine-volume fifth edition ultimately amounted, over half were entirely new articles or replacements of old ones, and nearly all else was revised. Though some of the original contributions by Sir George Grove were still retained, Blom was able to take account of the huge expansion of musical scholarship and history that had occurred during the preceding quarter of a century. In addition to planning and editing, he read the entire dictionary in proof, a prodigious task for one man. The result was the crown of his life's work and his lasting monument. In 1950, because of pressure of work on *Grove*, Blom gave up the important editorship of *Music and Letters*, which he had held since 1937. He resumed it in 1954 and continued as editor until his death. In this capacity his wisdom and tolerance gave much encouragement to young writers. A supplementary volume to the fifth edition of *Grove* was published in 1961, containing not only corrections but a number of important new articles.

Blom was a man of sterling character—modest, kindly, humorous, hospitable, and friendly: he hated pretentiousness in any form. Although preferring music by the classical masters, he was by no means hostile to contemporary music, the development of which he followed with interest. In 1955 he was appointed CBE and he was awarded a DLitt by the University of Birmingham. Blom died in the Princess Beatrice Hospital, London, on 11 April 1959. ALEC HYATT KING, *rev.* G. R. SEAMAN

Sources *New Grove* · personal knowledge (1993) · private information (1993) [C. Jennings] · *The Times* (13 April 1959) · *CGPLA Eng. & Wales* (1959)
Archives JRL, letters to the *Manchester Guardian*
Likenesses H. Coster, photograph, 1942, NPG [*see illus.*]
Wealth at death £11,942 17*s.* 7*d.*: probate, 10 Sept 1959, *CGPLA Eng. & Wales*

Blomberg, William Nicolas (1702/3–1750), biographer and Church of England clergyman, was the son of Charles John, Baron Blomberg, a nobleman of the duchy of Courland resident in the parish of St Martin-in-the-Fields, London, and his wife, Elizabeth, daughter of the physician Edmund *Dickinson. He was educated at Merton College, Oxford, where he matriculated on 16 May 1720, aged seventeen. Elected fellow of his college, he proceeded BA (1723) and MA (1726). He became vicar of Fulham in 1733, rector of that parish in 1734, and rector of Cliffe, Kent, in 1739. In the same year he published *An Account of the Life and Writings of Edmund Dickinson*, to which, in its second edition, he appended Dickinson's manuscript on the Grecian games. He died on 5 October 1750.

THOMPSON COOPER, *rev.* PHILIP CARTER

Sources *GM*, 1st ser., 20 (1750), 477 · Foster, *Alum. Oxon.* · T. Faulkner, *An historical and topographical account of Fulham* (1813) · D. Lysons, *The environs of London*, 4 vols. (1792–6) · E. Hasted, *The history and topographical survey of the county of Kent*, 4 vols. (1778–99)

Blome, Richard (*bap.* 1635?, *d.* 1705), cartographer and bookseller, may have been the son of Jacob Blome and his wife, Mary, baptized at St Ann Blackfriars, London, on 10 July 1635, especially if this Jacob was the bookseller of Knightrider Street of that name. Beginning his career as a heraldic painter, developing an expertise in arms-painting for funerals and other solemn occasions, Blome became a publisher and was among the first to use the advance subscription method to finance many projects. He had a shop in London between 1668 and 1679 and sold his own books at Mr Kid's at the corner of Lincoln's Inn Fields, where he lodged. In 1694 his address is given as New Weld Street near Clare-Market, according to Thomas

Chubb. Much of Blome's work was heraldic and geographical, specializing in topographical works.

With his more famous rival, the cartographer and mapseller John Ogilby, Blome has been given credit for inaugurating a new period of activity in English cartography, if not geography. Both men conceived of producing an English atlas containing county maps; Blome may even have preceded his rival in the idea, having entered his proposed work by title at Stationers' Hall on 28 July 1668, whereas Ogilby's proposal for a world atlas was issued in May 1669. In any case, Ogilby probably perceived Blome's less ambitious project as a threat to his own. After a series of delays the main fruit of the project, *Britannia* (arguably the most famous of Blome's publications), was not published until 1673. Although Blome listed about 800 subscriptions for this work it was not considered a success by the Royal Society and other contemporaries, who awaited Ogilby. A decade later Blome's *Cosmography and Geography* (1682), which included a translation of Varenius's *Geographia generalis* and 'A geographical description of the four parts of the world' taken from Nicholas Sanson (late geographer to the French king), marked an attempt to fill a gap in geographical theory for English readers; it also revealed Blome's environmental determinism.

Blome has been accused of lack of originality and of employing hack writers for a pittance. In 1696 the antiquary Bishop William Nicolson accused Blome of plagiarizing William Camden and John Speed for text and maps respectively in the compilation of *Britannia*, calling him the 'boldest Plagiary in the whole pack' (Nicolson, 15). He acted more as compiler or editor than as author of his best-known work outside of the cartographic field, *The Gentleman's Recreation* (1686), which treats the utility of the liberal arts and sciences, and includes some of the earliest illustrations published of British field sports. More credit for this work has been given to Nicholas Coxe and to prominent engravers employed in its production. Among Blome's other publications is *A Description of the Island of Jamaica* (1672), while his most intriguing secular study is a translation of Anthony le Grand's *Institutio philosophiae* entitled *An Entire Body of Philosophy* (1694), containing half-baked dissertations on demonology and other curious pieces. Blome also wrote on biblical themes.

By 1700 it appears that Blome's affairs generally and presumably his finances more particularly were in some disarray, although he continued to publish until near the time of his death. Already ill, he made his will on 7 May 1705, desiring to be buried in the church of Harlington, near Uxbridge. He left a total of 40 shillings to the poor of St Martin-in-the-Fields and Harlington, while the residue of his estate passed to Jane Hilton, with whom he lived for many years. His exact date of death is unknown, but as sole executor she proved the will on 22 October 1705. Recent reassessment of his work gives Blome an enigmatic reputation ranging from that of a farcical, petulant sycophant, to that of an opportunistic, business-like cultivator of both patronage and the mapmaker's art.

S. Mendyk

Sources S. L. C. Clapp, 'The subscription enterprises of John Ogilby and Richard Blome', *Modern Philology*, 30 (1932–3) • *BL cat.* • F. W. Steer and others, *Dictionary of land surveyors and local map-makers of Great Britain and Ireland, 1530–1850*, ed. P. Eden, 2nd edn, 1, ed. S. Bendall (1997) • R. A. Skelton, *County atlases of the British Isles, 1579–1830: a bibliography* (1970) • E. Arber, ed., *The term catalogues, 1668–1709*, 3 vols. (privately printed, London, 1903–6), vol. 1 • M. Bowen, *Empiricism and geographical thought: from Francis Bacon to Alexander von Humboldt* (1981) • W. Nicolson, *The English historical library*, pt 1 (1696) • D. Smith, *Antique maps of the British Isles* (1982) • G. Parry, *The trophies of time: English antiquarians of the seventeenth century* (1995) • T. Chubb, *The printed maps in the atlases of Great Britain and Ireland: a bibliography, 1579–1870* (1927) • S. Tyacke, 'Map-sellers and the London map trade, c.1650–1710', *My head is a map: essays and memoirs in honour of R. V. Tooley*, ed. H. Wallis and S. Tyacke (1973) • R. W. Shirley, *Printed maps of the British Isles, 1650–1750* (1988) • Y. Beresiner, *British county maps* (1983) • C. Moreland and D. Bannister, *Antique maps*, 3rd edn (1989) • *DNB*

Archives BL, description of Jamaica, Sloane MS 1394 • Bodl. Oxf., engraved armorial playing cards, MS Eng. misc., fol. 51 | Cumbria AS, Carlisle, letters to Sir Daniel Fleming

Likenesses mezzotint, NPG

Blomefield, Francis (1705–1752), topographical historian and Church of England clergyman, was born on 23 July 1705 at Fersfield, Norfolk, the eldest son of Henry Blomefield (1680–1732) and his wife, Alice Batch (*d.* 1730), daughter of Henry Batch of Lynn. He came from a family of yeomen farmers and was the first member to receive a university education. He began attending classes run by the rector of Diss, but about 1714 was sent to Thetford grammar school. In April 1724 he was admitted sizar to Gonville and Caius College, Cambridge, under the tuition of Sir James Burrough, the future master of the college; he graduated BA in 1727 and proceeded MA in 1728. In March 1728 he was ordained and became curate of Quidenham, and in July 1729 he was instituted into the rectory of Hargham, which he held only for six months on behalf of John Hare. In September 1729 he was instituted into the rectory of Fersfield, the next presentation of which had been purchased by his father in 1708. He also held the rectory of Brockdish (1739–52), the curacy of Poringland Magna (1736–50), and ministries in the Norwich parishes of St James and St Mary Coslany for periods during the 1740s. He married on 1 September 1732 Mary (*c.*1707–1796), the daughter of Lawrence Womack, rector of Buxton, Oxnead, and Caistor. They had three daughters, two of whom survived him.

From about 1719 the young Blomefield began recording monumental inscriptions from churches he visited in Norfolk, Suffolk, and later Cambridgeshire. While at Caius he started to keep genealogical and heraldic notes relating to local families, transcribed historical manuscripts in the library, and undertook some critical historical writing. Soon after leaving university he was actively collecting materials for a published account of the antiquities of Cambridgeshire, but in 1732 this project was deferred when another more promising opportunity presented itself.

In the spring of 1732 the course of Blomefield's career was determined when his friend Thomas Martin gave him virtually unrestricted access to an enormous collection of materials relating to the history of Norfolk. These had been amassed before his death in 1729 by Peter Le Neve, who had intended to publish a county history. Le Neve's collection included many original historical records, the notes and manuscripts of several previous Norfolk antiquaries and collectors, and transcripts, calendars, and indexes to local references in the public records. Le Neve had intended to leave them to a public repository, and appointed Thomas Martin and Thomas Tanner as his executors. However, the terms of his will were never carried out. Tanner was appointed to the see of St Asaph, and Martin married Le Neve's widow, Frances, in January 1732. The couple removed the collection to Martin's home at Palgrave, where they remained thereafter.

With Martin's encouragement and assistance Blomefield planned to use these materials as the basis of a county history, and issued proposals in June 1733 for *An Essay towards a Topographical History of Norfolk*. This was intended to comprise two quarto volumes, published in monthly parts over a two-year period beginning in March 1734. It was to be distributed to subscribers through local booksellers, or else by the author, his friends, or colleagues. The project excited sufficient interest to proceed, but Blomefield had no conception of the scale of task he was embarking upon, nor of the labour involved in collecting the additional materials required. His schedule was unrealistic, and publication did not commence until March 1736. By the time of his death sixteen years later Blomefield had almost completed three large folio volumes, but had only covered 40 per cent of the county. The years 1733 to 1735 were spent collecting additional materials, by means of tours through the county on horseback during the summer months, visits to libraries, record repositories, and country houses. However, the strain of travelling brought on a prolonged period of illness during the autumn of 1734. Blomefield was therefore compelled to collect materials through a detailed printed questionnaire—an idea he may have copied from his friend Francis Peck. This was sent to several hundred Norfolk incumbents during the early months of 1735, and much useful additional information was gained in this way. While convalescing in April 1735 Blomefield was granted access to the muniment room of William Paston, the second earl of Yarmouth, at Oxnead Hall. Here he discovered 'innumerable letters, of good consequence in history' (*Correspondence*, 85), which are now known as the 'Paston letters'. The means by which these and many associated manuscripts eventually found their way into his own and Thomas Martin's collections is obscure.

Blomefield recruited Charles Parkin, rector of Oxburgh, as a collaborator in July 1733, and Parkin took responsibility for the west of the county that was most remote from Blomefield's Fersfield rectory. Parkin therefore contributed the accounts of the hundreds of Grimeshoe and South Greenhoe published in Blomefield's lifetime. Other significant helpers in areas remote from Blomefield were Dr Henry Briggs, rector of Holt, John Holmes, master of the grammar school there, and Dr Edmund Newdigate, a physician from Walsingham. The antiquaries Sir Andrew Fountaine, Beaupré Bell, and James Baldwin also helped, as did Antony Norris of the Middle Temple, who had substantial collections for east Norfolk. Bishop Thomas Tanner also greatly encouraged the project, both by commenting upon Blomefield's manuscript for the first two hundreds, and subsequently by granting him permission in his will to use the detailed registers of Norfolk institutions, compiled while he was chancellor of the diocese. Thus while the Norfolk history is indeed a co-operative work incorporating the work of many earlier and contemporary antiquaries, there is no question that Blomefield was the prime mover in its publication and the work is deservedly associated with his name.

By the summer of 1735 Blomefield considered himself ready to embark upon publication of his work, although only about 10 per cent was ready for the press. He therefore looked for a suitable printer. Enquiries in Norwich persuaded him that no printer there would have the necessary materials, and he was deeply suspicious of London tradesmen, whom he felt would be likely to swindle him. As a result he set up his own press at Fersfield and employed a journeyman printer, named Nicholas Hussey, from Bury St Edmund's. The autumn and winter of 1735 were spent converting a barn and negotiating with tradesmen for the supply of the necessary equipment and materials, and also for the provision of engravings and woodcuts. His press was ready to begin operation by February 1736 and the first part was issued to subscribers the following month.

Within a fortnight of publication the original figure of 320 subscribers had doubled, and as news of the work spread, new subscribers continued to come forward. As a result Blomefield was forced to reprint his first number on two occasions, and also to appoint a London agent, thereby delaying progress with the second and subsequent parts. Thereafter the size of the edition remained at about 800 copies. The project was further delayed for two months the following November, when Blomefield was again taken seriously ill. However, progress continued through the southernmost hundreds during 1736 and 1737 at the rate of one part every seven weeks. The twenty-eight numbers of the first volume were eventually completed by March 1740.

During 1737 the author began to receive complaints from subscribers about the practices of many of his bookseller agents, who were seeking to enhance the meagre commission he paid by imposing delivery charges, or else lending out the work to others before delivery. As a result, after Michaelmas Blomefield dealt only with a limited number of booksellers in the large towns, and made use of a rider employed by him for the purpose of delivering them in the country. These employees are reputed to have created just as many distribution problems, and created as many opportunities for creaming off his profits, as the provincial booksellers. Indeed Blomefield appears to have been in dispute with, or cheated by, virtually every workman he ever employed.

The success of the publication also gave rise to jealousies among the antiquarian community in Norfolk, notably with Benjamin Mackerell, who had helped Peter Le

Neve collect materials and resented the unavailability of this collection to the public. Mackerell suggested to Blomefield that he should cover the urban areas of the county, leaving Blomefield to cover the rural. When the latter refused, Mackerell went ahead and published his *History and Antiquities of King's Lynn* (itself a plagiarism) late in 1737. Blomefield then published his account of Thetford both as part of the history of Norfolk, and also simultaneously in quarto as a discrete history of the town. More significantly, Mackerell was known to be working on a detailed history of Norwich, which was complete and ready for the press at the time of his death in March 1738. Mackerell's work was never published, but the existence of the manuscript caused Blomefield to alter his plans in 1739 and publish proposals for the second volume of the history of Norfolk, devoted to the city of Norwich. Blomefield's 900 folio page history of Norwich, published between April 1741 and May 1745, represents his crowning achievement, and was the part with which he had least assistance. His public claim to have access to the papers of the late Norwich historian John Kirkpatrick was denied in the press by the latter's brother Thomas, who threatened to publish his brother's work. However, there was an element of truth in Blomefield's claim in so far as John Kirkpatrick had supplied Le Neve with his rough notes once they had been transcribed. The account of Norwich was simultaneously published to subscribers as volume 2 of the history of Norfolk, and also as a separate publication. Production appears to have run smoothly, although after March 1743 there was disruption when the press was transferred from Fersfield to a house in Willow Lane, Norwich. The suggestion by Chambers that this was after a fire at his press has not been substantiated; it was more likely due to difficulties recruiting skilled workmen in the country, or the need to reside in the city to collect materials.

Volume 3 was also delayed owing to ill health and the lack of a workman, but the first part was eventually published by January 1747. Throughout the 1740s Blomefield had used any free capacity of the press to print his materials relating to Cambridgeshire, which were eventually published as a small quarto volume, entitled *Collectanea Cantabrigiensia*, in 1750. The volume had reached the twenty-third part by December 1751, when Blomefield went to London to visit the Rolls Chapel and present a paper to the Society of Antiquaries. He contracted smallpox, and died at his Fersfield rectory on 16 January 1752, having exhausted his health and bankrupted his family. He was buried on 18 January 1752 in his parish church, St Andrew's, where there is a memorial. At the instigation of Thomas Martin, Charles Parkin completed the history of Norfolk between 1755 and 1764, although not with anything like as much care or detail as Blomefield had expended. Parkin's completion was published posthumously between 1767 and 1775 by Whittingham of Lynn. The work was largely pirated in a history of the county published by Crouse and Booth of Norwich between 1778 and 1781, and then reprinted in its original form between 1805 and 1810.

Blomefield's reputation was shabbily treated in the *Dictionary of National Biography* by Walter Rye, who made scathing remarks concerning his work as a historian which do not stand up to detailed scrutiny, and spread unsubstantiated rumours about drinking and foxhunting. It is not difficult to find errors and misinterpretations in Blomefield's work, including his own genealogy, and the quality of the printing is poor. Yet given the period and circumstances in which he was at work, and the immensity of his task, his was a great achievement. His weakness was in underestimating what he had taken on. There has as yet been no other history of Norfolk on a comparable scale, and it remains the standard work. DAVID STOKER

Sources *The correspondence of the Reverend Francis Blomefield, 1705–52*, ed. D. Stoker, Norfolk RS, 55 (1992) · D. Stoker, 'Mr Parkin's magpie, the other Mr Whittingham, and the fate of Great Yarmouth', *The Library*, 6th ser., 12 (1990), 121–31 · D. Stoker, 'The genesis of *Collectanea Cantabrigiensia*', *Transactions of the Cambridge Bibliographical Society*, 9 (1986–90), 372–80 · [J. Chambers], *A general history of the county of Norfolk*, 2 (1829), 1156–7 · T. L. M. Hawes, 'Genealogy of the Reverend Francis Blomefield', *Norfolk Archaeology*, 38 (1981–3), 59–66 · S. W. Rix, 'Cursory notices of the Rev. Francis Blomefield', *Norfolk Archaeology*, 2 (1849), 201–24 · G. A. Stephen, 'Francis Blomefield's queries in preparation for his history of Norfolk', *Norfolk Archaeology*, 20 (1919–21), 1–9 · D. Stoker, 'Benjamin Mackerell, antiquary, librarian, and plagiarist', *Norfolk Archaeology*, 42 (1994–7), 1–12 · D. Stoker, 'Blomefield's History of Norfolk', *Factotum: Newsletter of the XVIIIth-Century Short Title Catalogue*, 26 (1988), 17–22 · D. Stoker, '"Innumerable letters of good consequence in history": the discovery and first publication of the Paston letters', *The Library*, 6th ser., 17 (1995), 107–55 · R. W. Ketton-Cremer, 'The rector of Fersfield', *Norfolk Archaeology*, 30 (1947–52), 365–9 · C. L. S. Linnell, 'Some notes on the Blomefield MSS in the Bodleian Library', *A miscellany*, ed. P. Millican, Norfolk RS, 22 (1951), 65–83 · *DNB*

Archives BL, topographical history of Norfolk, Add. MSS 23013–23023 · Bodl. Oxf., Cambridge and Norfolk antiquarian collections · Coll. Arms, church notes · CUL, Cambridgeshire and Suffolk collections · Norfolk RO, collections relating to Newton Flotman · Norfolk RO, collections for history of Norwich · Norfolk RO, letter-book, notes, papers, and collections · Norfolk RO, list of subscribers to his 'History of Norfolk', accounts · Norfolk RO, volume of Norfolk and Suffolk documents [transcripts] · Norfolk RO, journal and letter-book · Suffolk RO, Ipswich, MS notes relating to Suffolk churches and extracts from medieval documents

Wealth at death insolvent: will, Norfolk Archdeaconry, 1751/74

Blomefield [*formerly* Jenyns], **Leonard** (1800–1893), naturalist, was born on 25 May 1800 at 85 Pall Mall, London (his maternal grandfather's home). He was the youngest son of George Leonard Jenyns (1763–1848), canon of Ely and chairman of the board of agriculture, and his wife, Mary (1763–1832), a daughter of Dr William *Heberden (1710–1801) and a first cousin of Dr William Wollaston (1766–1828). On the death of his cousin Soame Jenyns in 1787, George Leonard Jenyns had inherited the Bottisham Hall property in Cambridgeshire. Jenyns's mother, as Mary Heberden, had had her portrait painted by Gainsborough.

In 1813 Jenyns was moved from a school at Putney to Eton College, where he remembered Edward and Philip Pusey as dull schoolfellows. He took no part in the school games, but was devoted to chemistry, and was introduced to Sir Joseph Banks in 1817 as 'the Eton boy who lit his

Leonard Blomefield [Jenyns] (1800–1893), by Lock & Whitfield

rooms with gas' (Blomefield, *Chapters in my Life*, 40). In 1818 he went to St John's College, Cambridge, and took a pass degree four years later. At Cambridge he came to the attention of J. S. Henslow (1796–1861). They worked together on natural history projects until Henslow's death, and in 1823 Henslow married Jenyns's sister, Harriet.

In 1823 Jenyns was ordained deacon by Bishop George Pelham of Lincoln in Old Marylebone Church, and next year was ordained priest in Christ's College by the master John Kaye (1783–1853), who was then also bishop of Bristol. After ordination he entered parish work immediately as curate of Swaffham Bulbeck, a parish of seven hundred souls adjoining the Bottisham estate in Cambridgeshire. During the years of his curacy he never saw his vicar. The latter resigned in 1827, and Jenyns was given the benefice by Bishop Sparke of Ely. He was the first resident vicar at Swaffham Bulbeck, but in the execution of the reforms that were necessary he observed the strictest moderation, and so gained the permanent goodwill of his parishioners. He reorganized a local charity school which had got into evil hands, enlarged the vicarage house, and planted a garden.

Cambridge was within an easy ride, and Jenyns was thus able to maintain regular communications with his fellow natural historians. He proceeded MA in 1825, the year in which he read his first paper, on the 'Ornithology of Cambridgeshire', to the Cambridge Philosophical Society. From about 1828 he began regularly to contribute pieces to both learned and popular publications, including *Loudon's Magazine of Natural History* and the *Annals and Magazine of Natural History*. His diary for 1831 records that he received an 'offer of accompanying Capt. Fitzroy, as Naturalist, in the Beagle, on his voyage to survey the coasts of S. America, afterwards going round the globe'. He 'declined the appointment w[h] was afterwards given to Charles-Darwin Esq. of Xts' College Cambridge'—he felt duty-bound to his parish and his health was not perfect.

In 1832 Jenyns joined the British Association for the Advancement of Science, which met that year in Oxford. He also attended (and read a paper at) the 1834 meeting at Edinburgh. In the following year, he published two works, *A Systematic Catalogue of British Vertebrate Animals* and *A Manual of British Vertebrate Animals*; the latter work was held in high estimation as a work of reference. Before he had completed it, at the request of Charles Darwin, he undertook to edit the monograph *Fishes* for *The Zoology of the Voyage of HMS Beagle*, published in 1840.

On 23 April 1844 Jenyns married Jane (1817–1860), eldest daughter of the Revd Andrew Edward Daubeny (1784–1877) and niece of Professor Charles Daubeny of Oxford (whom Jenyns subsequently visited often). In October 1849 the state of his wife's health compelled Jenyns's removal to Ventnor, and eventually his resignation of the vicarage at Swaffham Bulbeck in 1853, when his parishioners subscribed to a handsome testimonial for him. In the autumn of 1850 he settled at South Stoke, near Combe Down, Bath, but two years later moved to Swainswick, where for eight years he served the curacy of Woolley, and for a year or two of Langridge as well. On his wife's death in 1860 he settled finally in Bath. He was the founder (18 February 1855) and first president of the Bath Natural History and Antiquarian Field Club. In 1856 at the meeting of the British Association for the Advancement of Science at Cheltenham, he read a paper entitled 'The variation of species', a paper of which Darwin asked to be sent a copy. (Jenyns broadly supported the latter's ideas, subsequently published in *Origin of Species*.) In 1869 Jenyns was the donor of the Jenyns Library, a munificent gift of some 1200 volumes, which went to Bath's Royal Literary and Scientific Institution. He also donated to this institution his choice herbarium of British plants, consisting of more than forty folio and an equal number of quarto volumes, the result of his life work in this branch of science. He had originally extended his studies from zoology to botany under the influence of Henslow, and on his friend's death he wrote a masterly memoir of him, published in 1862 (the year in which, on 24 June, he married his second wife, Sarah (1819–1907/8), daughter of the Revd Robert Hawthorn of Stapleford). The *Proceedings* of the Bath Field Club abound with papers and addresses from his pen. Not the least valuable are those on the climate and meteorology of Bath. It was entirely at his instance that the small observatory was erected in the Institution gardens in 1865.

Towards the close of his career Jenyns was held in honour as the patriarch of natural history studies in Great Britain. He was elected a member of the Linnean Society in November 1822, and in the same year was elected into the Cambridge Philosophical Society. He was an original member of the Zoological (1826), Entomological (1834), and Ray (1844) societies. He had the greatest veneration for Gilbert White, whose *Selborne* he copied out while a boy at Eton, and knew almost by heart. He edited the *Natural History of Selborne* in 1843, and one of his latest interests was the welfare of the Selborne Society, before which on 14 May 1891 he read a delightful paper entitled 'The records of a rookery'.

In 1871, through Jenyns's connection with the Chappelow family (he was the great-grandson of Edward Chappelow of Diss and his wife, Elizabeth, the sister of Francis Blomefield, the historian of Norfolk) a considerable property worth some £7000 devolved on him, on the condition he adopted the name of Blomefield. In that same year, aged seventy-one, he ascended Snowdon, in a round trip of 12 miles from his lodgings at Llanberis. In 1888 the British Association for the Advancement of Science met in Bath; Blomefield was vice-president. Extremely methodical and regular in all his habits, he retained his mental vigour almost to the last. By 1891 he was suffering bronchial attacks and gout, but rallied sufficiently to give two lectures in that year. He died at his home, 19 Belmont, Bath, on 1 September 1893, aged ninety-three. He was buried in Lansdown cemetery, Bath, on 5 September.

Blomefield's attractive personality is revealed in his *Chapters in my Life* (privately printed at Bath in 1889), a short autobiography written with the greatest simplicity and directness. It contains interesting vignettes of Charles Darwin, Buckland, Heberden, Wollaston, Whewell, Daniel Clarke, and Leonard Chappelow, and nothing that he relates is second-hand.

In addition to the works mentioned above, Jenyns published, in 1846, a kind of supplement to White's *Natural History*, under the title *Observations in natural history: with an introduction on habits of observing, as connected with the study of that science. Also a calendar of periodic phenomena in natural history.* Almost all the material for this was collected by Jenyns over a period of twenty years and assembled while he was editing White's book, which he was scrupulously careful not to overload with notes. In 1858 appeared his *Observations on Meteorology*. At Bath, in 1885, he printed for private circulation some highly interesting *Reminiscences* of William Yarrell and of Prideaux John Selby. A large number (fifty-five) of scientific memoirs, contributed to the transactions of learned bodies, are enumerated at the end of his *Chapters in my Life*.

THOMAS SECCOMBE, *rev.* ROGER F. VAUGHAN

Sources L. Blomefield, *Chapters in my life*, enl. edn (privately printed, Bath, 1889) · L. Blomefield, 'About myself', MS, priv. coll. · L. Blomefield, *Reminiscences of William Yarrell* (privately printed, Bath, 1885) · L. Blomefield, *Reminiscences of Prideaux John Selby* (privately printed, Bath, 1885) [incl. notices on other naturalists] · *Letters from scientific men, to L. Jenyns*, MS (4 vols.), Bath Royal Literary and Scientific Institution · L. Jenyns [L. Blomefield], *Memoir of the Rev John Stevens Henslow* (1862) · *Bath Chronicle* (7 Sept 1893) · *The Times* (11 Sept 1893) · *ILN* (9 Sept 1893) · *ILN* (16 Sept 1893) · *The Guardian* (14 Sept 1893) · *IGI*

Archives Bath Royal Literary and Scientific Institution, Bath, corresp. and library · Cambs. AS · priv. coll. · U. Cam., department of plant sciences, his annotated copy of Relham's *Flora Cantabrigiensis* · U. Cam., Museum of Zoology, research notes and papers | CUL, corresp. with Darwin · CUL, Alfred Newton MSS · U. Cam., Museum of Zoology, letters to Prideaux Selby

Likenesses Lock & Whitfield, photograph, Linn. Soc. [*see illus.*] · carte-de-visite, repro. in Blomefield, *Chapters of my life* · portrait, repro. in *Proceedings of the Bath Natural History and Antiquarian Field Club* · portrait, repro. in *ILN* (9 Sept 1893) · portrait, repro. in *ILN* (16 Sept 1893)

Wealth at death £9233 18*s.* 5*d.*: probate, 20 Oct 1893, *CGPLA Eng. & Wales*

Blomefield, Miles. *See* Blomefylde, Myles (1525–1603).

Blomefield, Sir Thomas, first baronet (1744–1822), army officer, was born at Milton, Kent, on 16 June 1744, the only son of the Revd Thomas Blomefield (*c*.1691–1771), rector of Hartley and Chalk, Kent, and chaplain to the duke of Dorset, and his second wife, Mary, widow of William Branch and daughter of John Matthews. In September 1755 Blomefield was placed by his father as a midshipman in the *Cambridge* (eighty guns) but after expressing his preference for the army he was procured a cadetship at the Royal Military Academy, Woolwich, which he entered on 9 February 1758. His abilities in mathematics and chemistry drew the attention of John Muller (1699–1784), then professor of fortifications and artillery, and he passed out as a lieutenant-fireworker in the Royal Artillery on 1 January 1759. Blomefield's previous naval experience secured the command of a bomb (that is, mortar) ketch that year, when aged only fifteen, at the bombardment of Le Havre, and afterwards he joined the fleet blockading Quiberon, under Admiral Hawke. Henceforth he was to become a specialist in water-borne artillery. On 5 March 1762 he sailed from Portsmouth on a bomb vessel with Lord Albemarle's expedition against Havana. He took an active part in the siege, which lasted from early July until the capitulation on 10 August. Shortly before, on 1 August, Albemarle promoted him second lieutenant, to replace losses in the field, a promotion confirmed by the Board of Ordnance the following year.

Following the end of the Seven Years' War Blomefield served with the garrison artillery at Pensacola and Mobile. Despite widespread sickness among the troops he survived with his health intact and was promoted first lieutenant on 28 May 1766. Following his return to England he became aide-de-camp to General Conway, master-general of the ordnance, in 1771. As a staff officer he was closely involved in developments in the peacetime ordnance establishment at Woolwich—later to become the Royal Arsenal. He was promoted captain-lieutenant on 29 January 1773 and served as aide-de-camp to Lord Townshend on his succession as master-general. Much of his time was taken up with experiments in gunnery.

In the spring of 1776 Blomefield, at his own request, returned to active service, sailing with his company of the Royal Artillery to join General Burgoyne's army in Canada. On his arrival on 3 June he was given a staff appointment as major of brigade to Major-General Phillips, commander of the artillery. His principal task was to construct floating batteries on the Canadian lakes, which he had planned before he left England. With the army encamped for winter he returned to England in November with letters from Burgoyne and Phillips requesting further artillery and stores and his own return in the spring to assist Burgoyne's ill-fated expedition down the Hudson River. Back at Woolwich, at Burgoyne's request, he worked on a new gun and carriage designed for use on land and water. This he brought with him on his return to Canada the following year; eventually he rejoined the army at Ticonderoga on 23 July 1777.

Blomefield was reappointed major of brigade to Phillips until the latter's order of 14 September, returning Blomefield, again at his request, to regimental duties with the field artillery. He took an active part in the battle of Freeman's Farm (or Stillwater) on 19 September and served with Major William's battery at the battle of Bemis Heights on 7 October. Some twenty minutes after the attack began he was wounded in the face and took no further part. Baroness von Riedesel, who nursed him after the battle and upon the retreat to Saratoga, described how a bullet had passed through both cheeks, smashing his teeth and grazing his tongue:

> He could not keep anything in his mouth … We had some Rhine wine. I gave him a bottle, hoping that the acid would cleanse his wounds. He took a little in his mouth, and this alone had such a fortunate effect that his wounds healed entirely, and I gained another friend. (*Baroness von Riedesel*, 61)

Blomefield was included in the Saratoga convention and signed the Cambridge parole. Despite the failure of congress to abide by the terms of the convention and return Burgoyne's army *en masse* to England, during the course of 1778 a growing number of officers were exchanged privately under parole, apparently including Blomefield, who had returned to England by the spring of 1779. In June he was called by his former commanding officer, Burgoyne, to give supporting evidence before a parliamentary committee of inquiry into the strength and disposition of the artillery.

In 1779 Blomefield returned to his former post as aide-de-camp to Lord Townshend and on 19 January 1780 he was promoted to the rank of full captain of no. 8 company, 1st battalion of the Royal Artillery. However it was not on the field of battle but at the ordnance establishment at Woolwich that he now made a major contribution. There was then great need for stricter military supervision of armaments manufacture, and in particular the proofing of guns at Woolwich before their use in the field. In 1780 Blomefield was appointed to the new post of inspector of artillery and in his first year he condemned as many as 496 pieces of ordnance in proof. The widespread problem of 'bursting' led him to visit various foundries to examine the metals used, and to the consideration of instruments for better measuring the strength and accuracy of guns. The value of his efforts was quickly apparent and under a royal warrant of 24 January 1783 the whole department was reorganized; the artillery workshops, gun butts, and proof office were placed under Blomefield's entire control. His salary as inspector of artillery was raised to £350. His responsibilities included periodic surveys of the strength and condition of coastal artillery. Between 1779 and 1793 he produced a series of systematic and detailed reports on the military ordnance along the coasts of eastern and southern England.

On 27 July 1788 Blomefield married Elizabeth, second daughter of John Eardley *Wilmot (1709–1792), chief justice of the court of common pleas; they had one son, Thomas William, born on 23 March 1791. Blomefield was promoted major on 25 September 1793 and lieutenant-colonel on 5 December of the same year. From 20 April 1797 he took on the additional post of inspector of the royal brass foundry (in 1801 his combined salary was £441 5s.) and continued to hold both offices until his death. The administrative and technical changes that he introduced contributed greatly to the high quality of British cast iron and brass gun manufacture, which date from this period. Having been promoted full colonel on 12 November 1800 and major-general on 25 September 1803, on the creation of the 9th battalion of the Royal Artillery he was appointed its colonel-commandant on 1 June 1806.

In 1807 Blomefield was chosen to command the artillery in the expedition against Copenhagen, to enforce the surrender of the Danish fleet. The city was completely invested by 17 August and the bombardment began on 2 September. After 6000 shells had been fired into the city, setting it ablaze, on 5 September a flag of truce was flown, the bombardment was suspended, and the naval ships and stores were handed over. On 19 September Lord Chatham reported to Blomefield the king's intention to reward him 'as testimony of the sense entertained of your eminent services upon this occasion' (Duncan, 2.166). He also received the thanks of parliament and on 14 November 1807 was created a baronet. On 25 July 1810 he was promoted lieutenant-general, and on 19 July 1821 full general.

After an illness of three days Blomefield died at his home at Shooter's Hill in Kent on 24 August 1822, aged seventy-eight. He was survived by his only son, Sir Thomas William Blomefield, second baronet (1791–1858). His long association with the Royal Arsenal, from the early 1770s until his death, covered a period of profound change there. What had been a miscellaneous collection of small craft-based workshops had become by the early nineteenth century an institution of national importance with the beginnings of a modern factory-based system. The great improvement in the manufacture of military ordnance, and consequently of their strength and reliability in the field, that Blomefield oversaw was an integral part of this process. JONATHAN SPAIN

Sources Burke, *Peerage* (1999) · Foster, *Alum. Oxon.* · Venn, *Alum. Cant.*, 1/1 · J. Kane, *List of officers of the royal regiment of artillery from the year 1716 to the year 1899*, rev. W. H. Askwith, 4th edn (1900) · F. Duncan, ed., *History of the royal regiment of artillery*, 2 vols. (1872–3) · *GM*, 1st ser., 92/2 (1822), 370–72 · O. F. G. Hogg, *The Royal Arsenal: its background, origin, and subsequent history*, 2 vols. (1963) · Fortescue, *Brit. army*, vols. 2–3, 6 · A. E. Macrae, 'Surveys of the English coast, 1779–1793. From records of reports made by the inspector of royal artillery, on the coast defences of England', *Journal of the Royal Artillery*, 45 (1918), 73–86 • G. Howson, *Burgoyne of Saratoga: a biography* (1979) • H. Bird, *March to Saratoga: General Burgoyne and the American campaign, 1776* (1963) • *Baroness von Riedesel and the American Revolution: journal and correspondence of a tour of duty, 1776–83*, ed. and trans. M. L. Brown (1965) • *Hadden's journal and orderly book*, ed. H. Rodgers (Boston, 1972) • S. F. Batchelder, 'Burgoyne and his officers in Cambridge', *Cambridge Historical Society Publications*, 18 (1925), 17–80 • J. Burgoyne, *A state of the expedition from Canada* (1780)

Archives Royal Artillery Institution, Woolwich, London, papers, MD 206 | BL, corresp. with Sir R. Pearson, 1781, Add. MS 33116, fols. 35–41

Blomefylde [Blomefield], **Myles** (1525–1603), medical practitioner and alchemist, was born on 5 April 1525 in Bury St Edmunds, Suffolk, the son of John Blomefilde and his wife, Anne. He is said to have been a scholar at St John's College, Cambridge, but records show only that in 1552 the university awarded him a licence to practise medicine. His father died in 1549, leaving him and his mother as executors of a small estate. By 1559 he must have married and been resident in Bury, since his daughter Elizabeth was baptized in St Mary's Church on 16 September that year. Sometime in the 1560s he probably moved his medical practice to Chelmsford, Essex, though 1568 saw him in Venice. Certainly by 1572 he was securely established in Chelmsford; in the 1570s he often served as juror in manorial courts, and between 1582 and 1590 was a prominent churchwarden. In the 1591 survey of the manor of Chelmsford he is 'Myles Blomefielde, gent' (Essex RO, D/bnp1), holding a substantial house and 10 acres of land adjoining the churchyard, as a freehold of the manor.

For centuries after his death, Blomefylde's annotated collection of alchemical manuscripts led him to be mistakenly identified with an admired alchemist and probable kinsman, William *Blomfild. Myles himself was a 'cunning man' whose felonious activities—prophesying the recovery of a certain George Freeman's mare and showing in a looking-glass the stealer of one Sybil Brown's laundry—brought him before the Essex court of quarter sessions in 1578. The legal repercussions of his soothsaying are unknown, but the future churchwarden and 'gentleman' apparently incurred no enduring ill repute.

Blomefylde's importance lies mainly in his small but significant book collection. Beyond the alchemical manuscripts that he copied, illustrated, and annotated, he owned some unique late medieval dramatic manuscripts, the only complete copy of Medwall's *Fulgens and Lucres* (printed by J. Rastell, *c*.1513–19), and some twenty other volumes (devotional and polemical works, prose narratives, books on language, travel, history, mathematics, medicine, and surgery). Notes in his Sarum *horae* imply that he was once a devout Roman Catholic, and his possession of manuscript plays such as 'Mary Magdalen' may suggest, even during his years as an Anglican churchwarden, a continuing affection for the old faith. From his varied library and its characteristically flamboyant and self-referential marginalia, and from his circumstantial and sometimes pompous churchwarden's accounts, Blomefylde emerges as a person intellectually curious and self-concerned, rather smugly proud of his community, and quite pleased with his substantial place in it. He died at his home in Chelmsford in 1603 and was buried at the parish church there on 29 November 1603.

Robert M. Schuler

Sources D. C. Baker and J. L. Murphy, 'Myles Blomefylde, Elizabethan physician, alchemist and book collector: a sketch of a life', *Bodleian Library Record*, 11 (1982–5), 35–46 • D. C. Baker and J. L. Murphy, 'The books of Myles Blomefylde', *The Library*, 5th ser., 31 (1976), 377–85 • D. C. Baker, J. L. Murphy, and L. B. Hall, eds., *The late medieval religious plays of Bodleian MSS Digby 133 and E Museo 160*, EETS, 283 (1982), xii–xiii • I. Gray, 'Footnote to an alchemist', *Cambridge Review* (30 Nov 1946), 172–3 • D. C. Baker and W. B. Guthrie, 'Footnotes to an alchemist', *N&Q*, 223 (1978), 421–4 • H. Medwall, *Fulgens and Lucres*, ed. F. S. Boas and A. W. Reed (1926)

Archives CUL, department of manuscripts and university archives | BL, Harley MSS • Bodl. Oxf., MSS Digby

Wealth at death substantial house and 10 acres of land in Chelmsford, Essex, left to unnamed heirs

Blomfield, Sir Arthur William (1829–1899), architect, was born at Fulham Palace, Middlesex, on 6 March 1829, the fourth son of Charles James *Blomfield (1786–1857), bishop of London, and his wife, Dorothy (1795–1870), widow of the barrister Thomas Kent and daughter of the brewer Charles William Cox. He was educated at Rugby School and Trinity College, Cambridge, where he graduated BA in 1851 and MA in 1853. After university he was articled for three years to Philip Charles Hardwick (1822–1892), architect to the Bank of England and the son of Philip Hardwick; a continental tour with Frederick Pepys Cockerell (1833–1878) followed.

During 1856 Blomfield set up in independent practice at 8 Adelphi Terrace in London, where he rapidly developed a significant ecclesiastical practice through his family connections. He later relocated his office to Henrietta Street, at the corner of Cavendish Square, and then to 6 Montagu Place. His London houses were at 8 St Martin's Place and later 28 Montagu Square, and he also had a house at Broadway in Worcestershire. In 1860 he married Caroline Smith (1839/40–1882), the daughter of Charles Case Smith, and they had two sons—Charles James Blomfield (1863–1935) and Arthur Conran Blomfield (1863–1935)—who joined his architectural practice as partners in 1890. His first wife died in 1882 and in 1887 he married Sara Louisa Ryan [*see* Blomfield, Sara], the daughter of Matthew Ryan.

Blomfield was one of the last great Gothic revivalists. He was also a prolific architect, whose primary activity was church building and restoration. His favourite style was English Perpendicular, which he considered particularly suitable for church designs, though his variant of this style was not based on a slavish copying of architectural precedent, or on any search for eccentric originality. He was also open to the possibilities offered by modern materials, especially iron, which he used regularly, for instance in an iron screen at St Peter's Church, Eaton Square (1895), and for iron columns in St Mark's Church on the Marylebone Road (1871–2). His reputation was such that *The Builder* described his works as being 'distinguished both by knowledge and by refinement' (4 Nov 1899, 407). He was architect to the diocese of Winchester and, at various times, responsible for works on the cathedrals at Lincoln, Chichester, Canterbury, Peterborough, Salisbury, and Hereford. His ecclesiastical connections made him especially knowledgeable about nineteenth-century Anglican liturgical needs, and he was active in reordering existing churches so that they could be made appropriate to modern worship. His ecclesiastical output was considerable, and it was in such buildings, and others with an ecclesiastical connection, that he produced his best work, the most notable example being that concerned with the erection of a nave, south porch, and south transept for St Saviour's, Southwark (1890–97). His successful practice drew the attention of the young Thomas Hardy (1840–1928). Hardy's training as a Gothic draughtsman was a strong recommendation to Blomfield, in whose office he worked on his arrival in London in 1862.

Blomfield also received commissions from a number of wealthy patrons. Of particular note are: the work he did at St Mary Magdalene, Sandringham, for the prince of Wales (1890); the chapel he added to Tyntesfield, Somerset, for the Gibbs family (1875); Holy Trinity at Privett, Hampshire (1876–8), which he designed for the Nicholson family; St Mary's, Portsea, Hampshire (1887–9), for William Henry Smith; and Denton Manor, near Grantham, Lincolnshire, for Sir William Welby Gregory. Other important works included completion of the law courts in London (with A. E. Street) after the death of George Edmund Street (1824–1881), the law courts branch of the Bank of England (1886–8), which he designed in a classical style, and Church House in Dean's Yard, Westminster (from 1896). He was responsible for designing a number of colleges and schools, or for making additions to existing buildings, including: the Whitgift Hospital schools at Croydon (1869–71); King's School, Chester (*c*.1875–7); Bancroft's School, Woodford, Essex (1887–9), which was commissioned by the Drapers' Company; a headmaster's house at St Edmund's junior school, Canterbury (1897); Sion College Library on the Thames Embankment, London (1886); Queen's School and the lower chapel for Eton College (1889–91); a library and master's house at Trinity College, Cambridge (1876–8); a chapel and other buildings at Selwyn College, Cambridge (1882–9); chapels for Malvern College (*c*.1898) and for Queen Anne's School at Caversham, Berkshire; and the great hall for the relocated Charterhouse School at Godalming, Surrey (1885). In London the most notable buildings for which he was responsible included the Royal College of Music (1894), St John's Church, Wilton Road, St Barnabas's, Bell Street (1875), St Saviour's, Oxford Street, St James's, West Hampstead, and the rearrangement of St Peter's in Eaton Square (1873–5 and 1894).

Blomfield was also active overseas, and designed: St George's Cathedral, Georgetown, Demerara, which he designed to be built of timber on a concrete raft (1881); Christ Church Cathedral, Port Stanley, Falkland Islands (1890–92), for which most of the materials were exported from Britain; St George's Church, Cannes (1887); an English chapel at St Moritz; and St Alban's Church in Copenhagen (1885–7).

Blomfield was a member of the Architectural Association, and became its president in 1861. He was also an associate of the Royal Institute of British Architects, became a fellow in 1867, was made vice-president in 1886, and was awarded the institute's royal gold medal in 1891. He was elected honorary member of the Royal Academy of Fine Arts of Copenhagen, and received the third-class medal of the Dannebrog from the king of Denmark; both awards resulted from his designs for the English church in Copenhagen. At home he was a trustee to the Soane Museum, was appointed architect to the Bank of England in 1883, was elected an associate of the Royal Academy in 1888, and was knighted in 1889. He pursued an active social life. In his youth he was a rower, and occupied the bow seat in the Trinity College eight; somewhat later in life he became an amateur actor, and the president of the Westminster Abbey glee club. He died suddenly at the Royal Societies Club, 63 St James's Street, London, on 30 October 1899, and was buried at Broadway on 3 November. A memorial service was held at St Mary's, Bryanston Square, London. His second wife survived him.

PAUL WATERHOUSE, *rev.* JOHN ELLIOTT

Sources *The Builder*, 77 (1899), 407, 418–19, 433, 449 • *RIBA Journal*, 7 (1899–1900), 19–20 • A. E. Street, 'Sir Arthur Blomfield', *RIBA Journal*, 7 (1899–1900), 36–7 • *The Times* (1 Nov 1899), 7 • *ILN* (16 Dec 1899), 888 • biographical file, RIBA BAL • *Architect and Contract Reporter* (3 Nov 1899), 276–7 • J. M. Anderson and A. W. Blomfield, 'Presentation of the royal gold medal', *Journal of Proceedings of the Royal Institute of British Architects*, new ser., 7 (1890–91), 361–5 • *CGPLA Eng. & Wales* (1899) • F. E. Hardy, *The early life of Thomas Hardy, 1840–1891* (1928) • *Dir. Brit. archs.* • marriages index • *The Post Office directory* [annuals] • wills index

Archives Essex RO, Chelmsford, plans, etc. regarding work in Essex parish churches • Hants. RO, corresp., estimates, sketches, and accounts relating to rebuilding of Chawton church • RIBA, drawings collection and MSS | Leics. RO, corresp. with Hussey Packe relating to Prestwold church • NRA, priv. coll., letters to Lord Henry Scott relating to Palace House

Likenesses R. Robinson, photograph, NPG • portrait, RIBA BAL • portrait, repro. in *Building News* (3 Jan 1890), 12 • portrait, repro. in *ILN* (11 Nov 1899), 681 • portrait, repro. in *Year's Art* (1889), 248

Wealth at death £28,006 12*s*. 2*d*.: probate, 4 Dec 1899, *CGPLA Eng. & Wales*

Blomfield, Charles James (1786–1857), bishop of London, was born on 29 May 1786 at Bury St Edmunds, the eldest son among the six children of Charles Blomfield (1763–1831), a schoolmaster (as was Charles James's grandfather, James), JP, and chief alderman of Bury, and his wife, Hester (1765–1844), daughter of Edward Pawsey, a Bury grocer. Charles James began his formal education at the age of eight under Michael Thomas Becher at Bury grammar school, where he acquired the nickname 'Tit' Blomfield. He often rose at five o'clock in the morning to commence his studies and displayed a precocious ambition, boldly declaring that 'I mean to be a bishop'. In 1799 Blomfield was awarded a King's scholarship at Eton College, but his father refused to send him to the school.

University, classical scholarship, and early ecclesiastical career In 1804 Blomfield was admitted pensioner at Trinity College, Cambridge. He had been a sickly child, and his efforts as an undergraduate left him with an enduring

Charles James Blomfield (1786–1857), by William James Ward, pubd 1827 (after Samuel Lane)

nervous condition. For years after he suffered from disordered digestion and would experience nervous spasms when riding. None the less he showed great promise: in 1805 he gained a scholarship and won Browne's prize for a Latin ode, and the following year won a Craven scholarship and took Browne's prize for a Greek ode. Edward Maltby was sufficiently impressed to take Blomfield as a pupil without payment. Solitary by nature, Blomfield nevertheless counted as friends some promising contemporaries, including his brother Edward Valentine *Blomfield, James Henry Monk, and Thomas Rennell the younger; Frederick Pollock coached Blomfield when, from 1806, he decided to concentrate on his mathematical studies. Blomfield graduated BA as third wrangler in 1808, also winning the chancellor's medal and the member's prize for a Latin dissertation. In 1809 he was elected a fellow of Trinity. Blomfield was ordained deacon in March 1810 and priest in June by the master of Trinity, William Lort Mansel of Bristol, and, having declined the position of tutor to Lord Chesterfield's sons, accepted a curacy at Chesterford, Essex. In October 1810 he was presented to Quarrington, Lincolnshire, by Lord Bristol (a former pupil of Blomfield's grandfather and friend of his father). There being no parsonage at Quarrington, he continued to reside at Chesterford. In November 1810 Blomfield married Anna Maria (*b.* 1784/5, *d.* 1818), daughter of W. Heath of Hemblington, Norfolk. The couple had six children, of whom only one survived infancy.

In December 1811 Blomfield resigned Chesterford (retaining Quarrington until 1820) when the second Earl Spencer, impressed by his edition of *Prometheus vinctus* (1810), presented him to the rectory of Dunton, Buckinghamshire, where he resided until 1817. A parish of only seventy-two inhabitants, with only one non-communicant male, this, like his previous livings, afforded Blomfield the opportunity to take in pupils (including George Spencer and Lord Hervey) and pursue his classical studies. He soon established a considerable reputation, being among the most important of a group of scholars, including Maltby, Monk, and Peter Paul Dobree, who were pupils of Richard Porson and adopted his editorial principles. Blomfield's editions of *Septem contra Thebas* (1812), the *Persæ* (1814), *Agamemnon* (1820), and the *Choephoroe* (1824) were accurate and critical, if prosaic, and displayed his extensive learning. His 1815 edition of Callimachus was for some time the standard text; he also produced an edition of Euripides (1821), and contributed editions of fragments of Sappho, Alcaeus, and Stesichorus to Thomas Gaisford's *Poetæ minores Græci* (1823). When Edward Blomfield died in 1816 Charles completed his translation of Matthiae's Greek grammar. In 1813 he founded the important journal *Museum Criticum* with Monk, which published fragments and lesser-known authors rather than prize poems; he himself contributed many articles before it closed in 1822. Like the others in what Samuel Parr dubbed the 'critical gang' of Porsonians, however, Blomfield also sustained his teacher's academic feuds. His acerbic criticism of scholars associated with both Parr and Edward Valpy gave notice of the arrogant manner on which many later commented. From 1810 until 1815, when the overall tone of the journal led him to sever his connection, he wrote on classical subjects for the *Edinburgh Review*. His first review, of Samuel Butler's uncritical Aeschylus, provoked a fierce reply from Butler who thought Blomfield was 'showing himself off at my expense' and alienated Parr (Butler, 1.61). His criticism of Edmund Henry Barker's edition of Stephens's Greek thesaurus in the *Quarterly Review* of 1820 destroyed Barker's academic reputation, and elicited an equally outspoken response in *Aristarchus Anti-Blomfieldianus*. Blomfield came to regret at least some of these spats: he was reconciled with Butler by 1818, and he later secured George Burges, who had accused Blomfield of plagiarism, a pension from the civil list.

If clerical life at Dunton was relaxed, Blomfield was not simply a gentleman scholar. In 1813 he was appointed a JP. He was reading in patristics, and in 1817 and 1819 published on Jewish tradition and the understanding of scripture. More practically, he established a district depot at Aylesbury for the Society for Promoting Christian Knowledge (SPCK). In a visitation sermon for George Pretyman he called the clergy to pastoral responsibility and doctrinal orthodoxy, condemning both Calvinism and Socinianism. While in his preaching he was emerging as a high-churchman, he was widely regarded as a liberal on account of his support for Roman Catholic relief and his taking the *Morning Chronicle*. The apparent inconsistency was seized on by Barker, who suggested that the public contrast 'his Speech in the chapel of Trinity College on the character of William the Third, worthy of a man bearing the Christian names (*Charles James*) of Mr. Fox, with certain passages of his printed sermons, more worthy of the Tory and the High-Churchman' (Barker, 112).

Rector in London A new phase of Blomfield's life began a few years before 1820. His first wife died in 1818 and in the following year he married Dorothy (1795–1870), widow of the barrister Thomas Kent and daughter of a brewer, Charles William Cox, and his wife, Mary, *née* Munnings. The eleven offspring of this marriage proved healthier than those of Blomfield's first, only one dying in infancy: among their children were Lucy Elizabeth *Bather, the children's writer, and Arthur William *Blomfield, architect. His clerical career now rapidly advanced. In 1817 Lord Bristol presented Blomfield to the rectory and vicarage of Great and Little Chesterford and to the rectory of Tuddenham, Suffolk (resigned 1820); he was also appointed chaplain to Bishop Howley of London. In 1819, shortly after Bristol brought Blomfield to the attention of his brother-in-law Lord Liverpool, Howley presented him to St Botolph without Bishopsgate, London, a preferred candidate having refused it on discovering that the parsonage was frequented by the graveyard rats. With his new parish yielding some £1600 per annum net, Blomfield's financial position was secured. St Botolph's was a fashionable living (it was at the request of parishioners that in 1820 Blomfield added a DD to the BD acquired in 1818). It further contrasted with Blomfield's previous cures in having a population of over 10,000; Chesterford, which he retained and where he spent three months annually, became literally a rest-cure.

St Botolph's presented Blomfield with the pastoral challenge of the city. He reorganized the parish finances, visited his flock, promoted infant schools, and preached regularly in his straightforward style against heterodoxy and expounding basic doctrines. His classical publications were now supplemented by a catechism, sermons, occasional essays in church defence, an abandoned plan for a simplified Old Testament, and, perhaps surprisingly for a high-churchman, a *Manual of Family Prayers* in 1824. Pastoral experience softened his attitude to evangelicalism, for he gradually permitted the SPCK to distribute more evangelical tracts, and even proposed Charles Simeon as a member. As importantly, however, as an associate of Howley in London he was at the heart of the network of charitable and auxiliary societies of the orthodox high-church circle of the Hackney Phalanx, and his activity in both the SPCK and the National Society probably confirmed him in his own high-churchmanship.

The year 1822 brought further preferment when Howley appointed Blomfield archdeacon of Colchester (15 January 1822). His relish at his new authority was apparent in his primary charge, as George Biber described it exhibiting 'as much of the *os* as of the *oculus episcopi*' (Biber, 40). Only two years later Lord Liverpool offered him the see of Chester; he was consecrated on 20 June 1824. Lady Spencer urged him to accept exile to one of the largest, poorest, and most remote dioceses, astutely indicating the prospect of London should Howley be elevated to Canterbury: 'remember it is the step you must tread on to a richer one' (Blomfield, *Memoir*, 1.93). The pill was sugared with permission to retain St Botolph's.

Bishop of Chester, 1824–1828 Although often absent in London, at Chester Blomfield established himself as a reformer. Diocesan committees of the national church societies were reinvigorated or established. In 1827 the post of archdeacon of Richmond was restored to full activity; he himself visited the major manufacturing towns. Among Blomfield's chief concerns, however, was the clergy. If Liverpool was 'the most orthodox and *canonical* place that I have yet seen (Hackney always excepted)' (Bodl. Oxf., MS Eng. lett. c. 789, fol. 128*v*), the diocese as a whole was 'sadly relaxed' in discipline. He stressed rubrical observance, insisting on the gown in the pulpit, and deplored Wednesday evening lectures as undermining the proper services. The doctrine of the atonement was to be preached distinctly. Collections for non-diocesan charities and especially for pan-denominational causes were discouraged. A strict ordination policy was imposed to raise clerical standards, Blomfield rejecting former servicemen and reducing the number of non-graduates and Irishmen admitted. Clergy discipline brought out Blomfield's puritanical streak. He discouraged secular amusements, especially fox-hunting. Sydney Smith versified Blomfield's primary charge:

> Hunt not, fish not, shoot not;
> Dance not, fiddle not, flute not;
> But before all things, it's my particular desire;
> That once at least in every week, you take
> Your dinner with the squire.
> (Soloway, 320)

Blomfield could assume the last activity to be non-corrupting, given his attitude to lay pursuits. He was a life-long sabbatarian. At Chesterford he successfully demanded that the Newmarket races no longer commence on Monday so that the village was not swamped by racegoers on Sunday, just as later he opposed the Sunday opening of the Great Exhibition. He was also a temperance campaigner, serving as the first president of the London Temperance Association from 1831 and in 1830 promoting a licensing bill which would have regulated not only beer but also skittles.

Appointment as bishop of London, 1828 On 23 August 1828 Howley's promotion to Lambeth indeed saw Blomfield translated to London, and he was also appointed a privy councillor and dean of the chapels royal. He had earned his elevation not only in his diocesan activity, but in the House of Lords, where his first speech answered Lord Holland's attack on the church in the Catholic emancipation debates of 1825. Blomfield now spoke as an opponent of emancipation. He claimed that closer examination of the Roman church had changed his opinions; critics observed the change of patron away from the pro-emancipation Bristol and Spencer. If Blomfield was now clearly aligned with toryism, however, he did not slavishly support the government, voting against Wellington in a critical division on a corn bill on the eve of his elevation. Nor was he willing to defend every aspect of the confessional state, speaking against the profanity of test acts. Blomfield's parliamentary behaviour again attracted criticism during the debates over the Reform Bill. Blomfield supported the bill, fearing for the consequences if the church were seen to oppose reform. He absented himself from the crucial vote on the second Reform Bill of October 1831, however, on the grounds of the recent death of his father. His excuse would have carried more weight had he not spoken the following morning at the opening of King's College, London, and he was widely accused of cowardice. Lord Grey subsequently approached Blomfield and secured his vote in April 1832, as well as his assistance in rallying episcopal colleagues to support the bill.

Blomfield and social policy During the 1830s and 1840s Blomfield's participation in parliamentary debates extended beyond ecclesiastical matters. He often spoke on social questions, on which his position was modified in the light of experience (particularly of the metropolis itself). In 1826 he compromised his *laissez-faire* beliefs sufficiently to organize a committee to relieve distressed weavers in Chester and Spitalfields, urging Peel to intervene. By 1830, however, he seems to have lost his faith in intervention and charity, and instead looked to the moral education of the poor. This attitude underpinned his contribution when appointed by Althorp as chairman of the poor law commission, whose report led to the Poor Law Amendment Act in 1834. Blomfield was initially an enthusiastic advocate of the act, arguing that it would return the poor to robust independence. He engaged in a bitter exchange with Bishop Henry Phillpotts over the bastardy clauses when the latter complained that they victimized the mothers of illegitimate children, Blomfield arguing that the only relevant consideration was whether the clauses provided an effective check on immorality. Blomfield never publicly defended the act later, however, and this seems to reflect a return to a more interventionist approach. In 1842 he argued that the state should regulate collieries and urban life; in 1847 he backed the ten-hours movement. Blomfield came to acknowledge that improvement of the physical environment of the poor was probably a precondition of their evangelization. It was at his initiative that Edwin Chadwick and the poor law commissioners were instructed in 1839 to compile a *Report on the Sanitary Conditions of the Labouring Population*, and throughout the 1840s Blomfield supported associations and legislation to improve sanitation in urban slums. In 1848 he strongly backed Chadwick over the Public Health Act, and in 1854 fought unsuccessfully to preserve the Board of Health.

Ecclesiastical statesman As bishop of London Blomfield was at the heart of the nexus of church and state and was the most important and controversial ecclesiastical statesman of his generation. He was one of Peel's main advisers on church affairs, including appointments, but his energy and administrative ability were of value to all administrations while Howley remained at Canterbury. Blomfield's approach to ecclesiastical issues was, despite his high-churchmanship, essentially pragmatic. He sought the state's co-operation in efforts to equip the church to fulfil its national function (not least as 'instructress to the people') and so answer radical criticism of the church as part of 'old corruption'. To this end he was prepared to violate what many regarded as fundamental aspects of an episcopal church polity in the search for efficiency and the resources necessary to fund reform in the absence of direct state financial support. Thus, in the debates on whig Irish church legislation in 1833, Blomfield, while denouncing appropriation, welcomed the redistribution of the church's revenues. In his charge of 1834 Blomfield spoke of discarding 'ornamental parts' of the church if they stood 'in the way of improvements, calculated to enhance and give lustre to the true beauty of the Church—the beauty of its holy usefulness' (Blomfield, *Memoir*, 1.189). Other high-churchmen were appalled by so apparently utilitarian a conception of the church, and occasionally, as in the debates on the abortive centralizing church discipline bill of 1839, they effectively exposed the ecclesiological shortcomings of Blomfield's arguments.

Blomfield welcomed Lord Grey's royal commission on ecclesiastical revenues of 1832, on which he served. Its report, issued in 1835, provided the statistical basis for the work of the ecclesiastical commission, with which Blomfield was associated from the start. When Peel took office as prime minister in 1834 he consulted Blomfield, Howley, and Henry Goulburn concerning church reform, and it was from these discussions that the ecclesiastical duties and revenues commission emerged in 1835, being metamorphosed into the permanent ecclesiastical commission in 1836. Blomfield became the commission's driving force: as Edward Vernon Harcourt, archbishop of York, later ruefully observed, 'Till Blomfield comes, we all sit and mind our pens, and talk about the weather' (Blomfield, *Memoir*, 1.223). The commission produced radical proposals for diocesan reorganization, legislative action on pluralities and non-residence, reduction of the cathedral chapters, and centralized management and redistribution of church property. It was primarily Blomfield who championed the proposals in the House of Lords. The cathedral reforms in particular upset both dignitaries who thought them unwarranted violations of the principles of locality and the sanctity of property and high-churchmen who thought reform should reinvigorate the cathedrals' historic functions rather than redistribute their revenues to the parishes. The failure to include representatives of the lower clergy on the commission, and its reliance on bishops as instruments of reform, prompted accusations of an unmerited arrogation of power to the episcopate, particularly the commissioner bishops, and above all Blomfield, who was one of the most regular attenders and who also served on the church estates committee after 1850. Again Sydney Smith did not spare him, writing in his first 'Letter to Archdeacon Singleton' (1837): 'He will become the Commission, and when the Church of England is mentioned, it will only mean *Charles James, of*

London, who will enjoy a greater power than has ever been possessed by any Churchman since the days of Laud, and will become the *Church of England here upon earth*'. A spirited riposte came in the embittered Blomfield's finest parliamentary speech, putting the case for the Dean and Chapters Act on 30 July 1840. To justify his approach to church reform Blomfield contrasted the splendours of St Paul's Cathedral with the spiritual and moral destitution which surrounded it, and argued that if fear had been a motivation of the commissioners, it was not fear of public opinion but of being found 'unfaithful to our trust'. The proposals could be justified on the unanswerable ground of 'necessity'.

In other aspects of national ecclesiastical policy Blomfield's position was more typical of a pre-Tractarian high-churchman. Blomfield opposed the Catholic Relief Bill of 1844 and the Maynooth grant of 1845. He attached great importance to preserving the church's role in education. Blomfield was a leading figure in the foundation of King's College, London, in 1831 as a pointed riposte to the 'godless' University College. He contributed considerable sums to the project and sat on council, in 1853 proposing the motion which led to the dismissal of Frederick Denison Maurice on the grounds of his rejection of the doctrine of everlasting punishment. Blomfield was also a keen supporter of the National Society, not least in his own diocese, and a zealous opponent of the Central Society of Education. In 1839 he opposed the government scheme for state supervision of schooling through a committee of the privy council and a non-denominational normal school, and was one of the architects of the 'concordat' of 1840 in which a compromise on inspection enabled most churchmen to accept the new arrangements.

To the horror of the Tractarians, but along with other orthodox high-churchmen who welcomed the prospect of introducing the apostolical succession into the Prussian Lutheran church, Blomfield strongly supported the establishment of the Jerusalem bishopric in 1841. His involvement in this last project reflected his responsibility as bishop of London for Anglican clergy overseas without their own bishops. He was a convinced advocate of the need for an increase in the colonial episcopate, and a letter he published on the issue led to the foundation of the Colonial Bishoprics Fund in 1841, no fewer than fifteen dioceses being established during the following twelve years. Blomfield also took a prominent role in the national ecclesiastical controversies at the end of the 1840s. He led the thirteen bishops who publicly remonstrated with Lord John Russell over the elevation of Renn Dickson Hampden to the see of Hereford in 1847. In 1850 he dissented from the majority of the judicial committee of the privy council in the Gorham case, finding for Phillpotts; he had previously sponsored an unsuccessful bill to alter the composition of the final court of appeal in ecclesiastical causes, and did so again after the judgment.

The diocese of London: church extension and church party In his own diocese Blomfield set out to relieve the spiritual destitution of the metropolis through an ambitious programme of church extension and diocesan reform (including the revival of the diocese's rural deans in 1833 and ruridecanal chapters in 1844). In 1836 he founded the Metropolitan Church Building Society, which aimed to finance the building of fifty new churches through voluntary contributions (Blomfield's original suggestion of a levy on coal having been rejected). By the time of its incorporation into the Diocesan Church Building Society in 1854 £266,000 had been raised (£106,000 in the first year alone), although the target of fifty churches was not attained. A separate initiative to provide ten new churches for Bethnal Green, commenced in 1839, was complete by 1850, and Blomfield encouraged other localized and private initiatives, not least through his own munificent giving. In all some 200 churches were consecrated in the diocese during his episcopate. The difficulties of financing church extension led him to accept the necessity of pew-rents at a time when others were beginning to question them. Blomfield himself came to realize, however, that church extension in itself was not enough, even when accompanied by no less essential schools. If he never lost faith in the parochial ideal, by the mid-1840s he was reconciled to lay visiting and the use of unconsecrated buildings, and in the 1850s sought to close redundant city churches to facilitate provision elsewhere.

Blomfield's London episcopate coincided with the rise of Tractarianism, and he sympathized with some of its objectives. By 1839, however, he believed extreme high-churchmen to be 'corrupting the simplicity of the Gospel', and in 1842 resigned from the Camden Society and condemned Tract 90 in his charge. The same charge sought to chart a middle way, once again calling for rubrical observance. When Archdeacon Hale repeated the call in the following year evangelical clergy from Islington protested to the bishop, and Blomfield unwisely exempted them from his injunctions. This generated great controversy as others demanded similar concessions while those who had obeyed the bishop felt abandoned, not least as the bishop privately communicated to some his desire that they should disregard his own instructions. Blomfield's vacillations severely damaged his public reputation. Throughout his episcopate Blomfield's dealings with individual clergy were frequently difficult, his overbearing manner provoking much comment; he wrote to one correspondent citing ancient precedent that 'St Augustine was Bishop of Hippo, but you will be good enough to remember that I am bishop of London'. In the context of the papal aggression he took a firm line on what he regarded as the romanizing tendency of ritualism, and became involved in controversy over the ministry of William James Early Bennett at St Barnabas, Pimlico, which culminated in Blomfield's insistence on Bennett's resignation in November 1850. His previous tolerance of Bennett's activities again laid him open to the charge of irresolution.

Decline and death In 1847 an accident at Osborne left Blomfield with partial facial paralysis and slurred speech; in 1848 he was passed over for Canterbury. Together these two events marked a turning point. While Blomfield remained active, for example taking a prominent part in early proceedings of the revived convocation of Canterbury, he now ceded to Samuel Wilberforce something of his former pre-eminence among the episcopate. In 1855 his eyesight began to fail, and after a seizure he was paralysed on his left side. Early in 1856 he sought to resign his see, and his episcopate closed in controversy over the necessary legislation and its allocation of his continued use of Fulham Palace (on which he had lavished considerable expenditure) and a pension of £6000 in order to keep up his insurances on his resignation on 30 September 1856. Blomfield's health deteriorated further, and after two epileptic seizures he died at Fulham Palace on 5 August 1857. He was buried in the churchyard of All Saints, Fulham, on 11 August.

A controversial reputation Some 5 feet 8 inches tall, with small hands, a pale complexion, and an 'urgent walk', Blomfield's impetuosity, relentless administrative energy, self-confidence, and pomposity attracted caricature: not only from Sydney Smith but also Disraeli in *Tancred* (1847) and Anthony Trollope, who cast him as the eldest son of Archdeacon Grantly in *The Warden* (1855). His talents were more suited to his role as administrative reformer than to his efforts to uphold an orthodox high-church vision of the Anglican church as the rise of Tractarianism heightened party tensions. Fellow orthodox high-churchmen were worried by his cavalier way with ecclesiology in his reform initiatives and what they viewed as the unnecessary radicalism of his approach. Evangelicals resented the high-church tendency of his diocesan policy. Tractarians smarted under his criticism and were appalled by his easy relations with secular authority. His fiercest critics exploited the importance of classical scholarship and patronage to his career along with his haughty manner—his son suggested that he had 'inherited notions of authority … disappearing before the democratic progress of the age' (Blomfield, *Memoir*, 2.211)—to portray him as a relic of an outmoded, greedy, Erastian prelacy, an impression reinforced by the fuss over his retirement. In fact Blomfield approached his duties conscientiously and with integrity, and was extremely generous in his private philanthropy. Nevertheless, immediately posthumous assessments were generally at best lukewarm and often hostile, as in Harriet Martineau's *Biographical Sketches* (1869), dwelling on what were seen as the shortcomings of his diocesan management and the failings of his church reforms, a judgement long perpetuated in the predominantly Anglo-Catholic tradition of ecclesiastical historiography. Later historians have offered a more positive assessment, recognizing the centrality of Blomfield's contribution to the refashioning of the Victorian church and the importance of his role in the poor law commission, and paying less attention to party disputes in which he became embroiled. He has been presented as a modernizer rather than an archaism: a character symbolized in his being the first bishop to abandon his wig. His role in energizing the ecclesiastical commission, and the explicitly utilitarian approach to church reform this embodied, has come to be regarded as his outstanding achievement. Indeed the gradual rehabilitation of Blomfield's historical reputation has effectively fulfilled his own prediction to Archdeacon John Sinclair: 'They may blame me now for these measures, but they will hereafter confess that those very measures have been the saving of the Church' (Blomfield, *Memoir*, 1.227).

ARTHUR BURNS

Sources A. Blomfield, *A memoir of Charles James Blomfield, with selections from his correspondence*, 2 vols. (1863) • P. J. Welch, 'Bishop Blomfield', PhD diss., U. Lond., 1952 • G. E. Biber, *Bishop Blomfield and his times* (1857) • G. F. A. Best, *Temporal pillars: Queen Anne's bounty, the ecclesiastical commissioners, and the Church of England* (1964) • O. Brose, *Church and parliament* (1959) • C. O. Brink, *English classical scholarship: historical reflections on Bentley, Porson, and Housman* (1986) • M. L. Clarke, *Greek studies in England, 1700–1830* (1945) • R. A. Soloway, *Prelates and people: ecclesiastical social thought in England, 1783–1852* (1969) • O. Chadwick, *The Victorian church*, 3rd edn, 1 (1971) • P. J. Welch, 'Blomfield and Peel: a study in co-operation between church and state, 1841–6', *Journal of Ecclesiastical History*, 12 (1961), 71–84 • R. Blomfield, *A Suffolk family: being an account of the family of Blomfield in Suffolk* (1916) • S. Smith, 'First letter to Archdeacon Singleton on the ecclesiastical commission', in *The works of the Rev. Sydney Smith*, new edn (1869), 711–31 • S. Butler, *The life and letters of Dr Samuel Butler*, 2 vols. (1896) • E. H. Barker, *Aristarchus anti-Blomfieldianus, or, A reply to the notice of the New Greek thesaurus, inserted in the 44th number of The Quarterly Review* (1820) • H. Martineau, *Biographical sketches, 1852–1868*, 2nd edn (1869) • A. Burns, *The diocesan revival in the Church of England, c.1800–1870* (1999) • P. B. Nockles, *The Oxford Movement in context: Anglican high churchmanship, 1760–1857* (1994) • E. R. Norman, *Church and society in England, 1770–1970* (1976) • *Hansard* 3 (1840), 55.1133–55 • *The Times* (7 Aug 1857)

Archives Duke U., Perkins L., corresp. • Hunt. L., letters • LPL, letter-books, corresp., papers, and visitation returns; corresp. and papers; letters | Alnwick Castle, letters to Henry Drummond • BL, corresp. with Lord Aberdeen, Add. MS 43195 • BL, corresp. with Samuel Butler, Add. MSS 34584–34589 • BL, corresp. with W. E. Gladstone, Add. MSS 44354–44527 • BL, corresp. with Robert Peel, Add. MSS 40373–40600, *passim* • BL, letters to second Earl Spencer • Bodl. Oxf., letters to Samuel Wilberforce • CKS, corresp. with Lord Romney • Exeter Cathedral, letters to Henry Phillpotts • King's AC Cam., letters to R. B. Sheridan and Mrs Sheridan • Lancing College, letters to Nathaniel Woodard • LPL, corresp. with Charles Golightly • LPL, corresp. with Christopher Wordsworth • Lpool RO, letters to fourteenth earl of Derby • PRO, corresp. with Lord John Russell, PRO30/22 • Pusey Oxf., letters to Edward Pusey • Suffolk RO, Bury St Edmunds, letters to the marquess of Bristol • Trinity Cam., letters to J. H. Monk, bishop of Gloucester • Trinity Cam., letters to William Whewell • U. Durham L., archives and special collections, corresp. with second and third Earl Grey • U. Edin., New Coll. L., letters to Thomas Chalmers • UCL, corresp. with E. Chadwick • W. Sussex RO, letters to duke of Richmond

Likenesses S. Lane, oils, exh. RA 1826, bishop's house, Chester; version, Fulham Palace, London • C. S. Taylor, stipple, pubd 1826 (after C. Penny), BM, NPG • W. J. Ward, mezzotint, pubd 1827 (after Samuel Lane), NPG [*see illus.*] • C. R. Leslie, group portrait, oils, 1838 (*Queen Victoria receiving the sacrament after her coronation, 1838*), Royal Collection • J. Doyle, pen and pencil caricature, 1840, BM • J. S. Templeton, lithograph, pubd 1840, NPG • G. Richmond, group portrait, ink, pencil, and wash, 1840–45, NPG • C. R. Leslie, group portrait, oils, 1841 (*The christening of the princess royal, 10 February 1841*), Royal Collection • J. Doyle, pen and pencil caricature, 1842 (a scene from *Henry IV*), BM • J. Thomson, stipple, pubd 1847 (after G. Richmond), BM, NPG • G. Richmond, effigy, 1859–67, St Paul's Cathedral, London • W. Bell, engraving (after bust by Behnes), repro. in

Blomfield, *Memoir of Charles James Blomfield* · G. Hayter, group portrait, oils (*The christening of the prince of Wales, 1842*), Royal Collection

Wealth at death £60,000: PRO, death duty registers

Blomfield, Edward Valentine (1788–1816), classical scholar, was born on 14 February 1788, the second son of Charles Blomfield, a schoolmaster at Bury St Edmunds, and his wife, Hester Pawsey, and younger brother of Charles James *Blomfield, bishop of London. He was educated under Dr M. T. Becher (1764–1809) at the grammar school in Bury St Edmunds and proceeded from there to Gonville and Caius College, Cambridge, in 1807. In 1811 he took his BA degree as thirteenth wrangler. He had, however, obtained such classical distinctions as were then open to competition; he was Browne's medallist in 1809 and 1810, members' prizeman in 1812, and finally first chancellor's classical medallist. The fellowships in his own college being full, he was elected in 1813 to a classical lectureship and fellowship at Emmanuel, and was ordained in the same year. He died from a fever contracted in a long vacation tour in Switzerland in 1816. He managed, after being taken ill at Dover, to reach Cambridge where he died in his rooms at Emmanuel College on 9 October 1816, and was buried in Emmanuel College chapel.

Blomfield acquired a high reputation for learning and general accomplishments, being a good modern linguist and draughtsman, as well as a brilliant scholar. His chief work was a translation of the Greek grammar compiled by A. H. Matthiae. Completed in the spring of 1816, it was left for his brother Charles James to edit. Blomfield had met with Matthiae's book in the course of a tour in Germany, undertaken in 1813, as soon as the events of that year had opened the continent to English travellers. Another fruit of this tour was a paper in the *Museum Criticum* entitled 'The state of classical literature in Germany', a subject which had then become almost unknown in England. Besides a few other papers contributed to the *Museum* Blomfield had projected a Greek–English lexicon to take the place of the old Greek–Latin lexicons of Scapula and Hedericus, which gave needless difficulty to students and were neither full nor accurate. He published a specimen of his lexicon, which was well received, and his plans seem to have been rational and promising. Had Blomfield lived, some of the labours of H. G. Liddell and his fellow lexicographer Robert Scott might have been anticipated.

E. S. Shuckburgh, *rev.* M. C. Curthoys

Sources A. Blomfield, *A memoir of Charles James Blomfield, with selections from his correspondence*, 2 vols. (1863) · Venn, *Alum. Cant.* · *GM*, 1st ser., 86/2 (1816), 373 · J. H. Monk, 'A memoir of Edward Valentine Blomfield, M.A. fellow of Emmanuel College', *Museum Criticum*, 2/7 (1826), 520–28

Blomfield, Ezekiel (1778–1818), Independent minister and writer, was born on 28 October 1778 at North Walsham, Norfolk. His parents were very poor, and in 1783 he moved with them to Norwich. He read widely, but the book that determined his lifelong studies was Anna Letitia Barbauld's *Evenings at Home* (1792–6), which quickened his interest in the phenomena of nature. At about fifteen he became imbued with strong religious convictions and was placed under the care of a nonconformist minister, the Revd S. Newton of Norwich. Under his capable mastership he rapidly acquired Latin, Greek, and Hebrew. After combating old doubts, in 1796 he joined Newton's church, and, resolving to become a minister, attended the Independent Homerton Academy. After a year spent at Norwich in ill health he accepted a call to a congregation at Wymondham.

On 20 October 1800 Blomfield married Mary Fursnell of Hanworth, Norfolk. Soon after his marriage he delivered a course of lectures on history at Wymondham. As his family increased he eked out a slender income by hack work for Brightley, a printer at Bungay, and subsequently went into partnership with him. Pecuniary difficulties followed, and led to a move from Wymondham to Wortwell in 1809. Blomfield founded the Norfolk and Norwich Auxiliary British and Foreign Bible Society. In 1810 he projected a classical academy; he planned a history of education, and delivered a successful course of lectures on the philosophy of history from materials gathered in 1815 and 1816. He died on 14 July 1818 at Glemham, Suffolk, leaving his widow and young family of eight children totally unprovided for. His *Philosophy of History* was published in a fine quarto in 1819, with a memoir, to assist in their maintenance. It is somewhat fragmentary and commonplace. In 1807 had appeared, in two huge volumes, Blomfield's *A general view of the world, geographical, historical, and philosophical, on a plan entirely new*; this work shows wide but ill-digested reading.

A. B. Grosart, *rev.* K. D. Reynolds

Sources 'Memoir', E. Blomfield, *Philosophy of history* (1819) [preface] · *GM*, 1st ser., 88/2 (1818), 381

Likenesses etching, NPG

Blomfield, Sir Reginald Theodore (1856–1942), architect, was born at the vicarage, Bow, Devon, on 20 December 1856, the third son and one of the eleven children of the Revd George John Blomfield (*d.* 1900), who became vicar of Dartford in 1857, and his wife, a distant cousin, Isabella, second daughter of C. J. *Blomfield, bishop of London. In 1869 Blomfield entered Haileybury College and was awarded a leaving exhibition in 1875, when he also won a Stapledon scholarship at Exeter College, Oxford. He obtained a first class in *literae humaniores* in 1879. His academic success was complemented by his sporting prowess, but he also developed a keen interest in art. He thought of pursuing sculpture as a career, but a private income was necessary so he decided instead to channel his artistic interest into architecture, and entered the office of his maternal uncle Sir A. W. *Blomfield in 1881. The older man was a successful exponent of the Gothic revival style, who built mainly ecclesiastical buildings. His nephew was articled free of charge. Although Reginald found office life mundane, he was employed at a time when the practice was completing the Royal Courts of Justice, unfinished at G. E. Street's death. He attended the Royal Academy,

Sir Reginald Theodore Blomfield (1856–1942), by Sir James Jebusa Shannon, exh. RA 1915

where he won both junior and senior school prizes, but after two years he left his uncle's office, following a misunderstanding, and travelled in Europe, studying architecture in France and Spain.

Blomfield began his own practice in 1884, although it was some years before it became firmly established, and several of his earliest commissions came through family connections. He designed the Bradby memorial hall (1886) at his old school, Haileybury, restored some small churches, and extended and reordered a large house, Brooklands, at Weybridge for his cousin in 1889. During the lulls in practice he wrote and illustrated articles on historical architecture, beginning with 'Sussex foundries' for *The Portfolio* (1886), followed by a series on English Renaissance architects, also published in *The Portfolio*. These were the beginnings of a lifelong involvement in architectural research and writing.

Meanwhile, Blomfield had been introduced to the circle of young architects associated with Richard Norman Shaw, the leading practitioner of the day. They were prominent in the development of the arts and crafts movement, in particular the Art Workers' Guild, which Blomfield joined, rising to become secretary during William Morris's presidency. He was also involved with the Arts and Crafts Exhibition Society, and with a commercial venture, Kenton & Co., which sought to make furniture in accordance with artistic principles. However, he moved away from these activities as his practice expanded and as his views on architecture changed.

The publication of Blomfield's first book, *The Formal Garden in England* (1892), followed by *A History of Renaissance Architecture in England, 1500–1800* (2 vols., 1897), was significant in that the books represented a change in architectural fashion away from the 'bric à brac' style of the 1880s to the more ordered and consistent 'Wrenaissance' of the Edwardian period. These volumes—learned, admirably written, and well illustrated—introduced Blomfield to many owners of historic mansions who employed him as architect and garden designer. Among the houses reordered, restored, or enlarged between 1896 and 1909 were: Heathfield Park, Sussex, for William Alexander; Brocklesby Park, Lincolnshire, for Lord Yarborough; Chequers Court, Buckinghamshire—the prime minister's country house; La Manoire de la Trinité, Jersey; and Mellerstain, Roxburghshire, for Lord Binning. Blomfield also designed new houses, often (but not always) in the 'Wrenaissance' style, such as Moundsmere Manor, Hampshire (1908) for Wilfred Buckley. At the same time the number of public and commercial buildings that he undertook increased, varying from the remarkable warehouse in Greycoat Place, Westminster, for the Army and Navy Stores (1895) to Lady Margaret Hall, Oxford University (1896–1926), and the water tower at Lincoln (1910). During the first decade of the twentieth century his style became more urbane, as illustrated by the United University Club, London (1906; extended 1924, 1938). This change may have been due to his increasing admiration for French architecture, as he collected information for *A History of French Architecture, 1494 to 1774* (4 vols., 1911–21).

Blomfield was by now a family man, having married Anne Frances May, daughter of Henry Burra, a civil servant in India, in 1886. They had a daughter and two sons, one of whom became an architect and continued his father's practice until 1969. In 1892 Blomfield built a pair of houses in Frognal, Hampstead, and lived in one of them until his death. He also acquired and subsequently extended a cottage at Point Hill, Rye, as a country retreat.

Blomfield's country-house practice declined substantially after the First World War, but instead of contemplating retirement his career took a new turn. He was one of the principal architects appointed by the Imperial War Graves Commission to superintend the design of cemeteries in France and Belgium, and he also contributed a standard feature, the 'cross of sacrifice', which appeared in most commission sites. In addition, he was responsible for a memorial to the missing, the Menin gate at Ypres (1922). He also designed the Belgian war memorial (1917) and the RAF memorial (1921), both in London.

Before the war he had been thwarted in a golden opportunity to design in the 'grand manner', which he had championed in his collection of lectures, *The Mistress Art* (1908), when Edwin Lutyens appointed Herbert Baker assistant architect for New Delhi. However, from 1916 to 1926 Blomfield was able to complete the rebuilding of the Quadrant, Regent Street, left unfinished when Norman Shaw died. He made a suggestion for the redesign of the whole of Piccadilly Circus (not executed) and designed the elevational treatment of the Headrow commercial development in Leeds (1924–37).

A man of abounding energy, sincerity, self-assurance, and pugnacity, Blomfield was involved in architectural politics and controversy throughout his career. In 1891 he was one of the 'memorialists', artist-architects who resigned from the RIBA over the issue of professional registration. He was deeply involved in architectural education, becoming professor of architecture of the Royal Academy in 1906, and one of the original members of the newly founded board of architectural education. He rejoined the RIBA in 1906, was elected president in 1912, and received the royal gold medal for architecture in 1913. He was a member of the editorial committee of the *Architectural Review* and was also involved with the founding of the British School at Rome. In 1905 Blomfield became an associate of the Royal Academy, where he played an active part in committee work, and was elected a full member in 1914.

In the 1920s and 1930s Blomfield fought hard to prevent the proposed demolition of the London city churches and Waterloo Bridge, but working in conjunction with others he designed the new Lambeth Bridge, completed in 1932. His trenchant writings and his position as an *arbiter elegantiarum* were turned against him, however, when his design for a bulky office building in Carlton Gardens led to proposals for a scheme to replace the whole of Nash's Carlton House Terrace. Many influential people were ranged against him and, following a parliamentary debate, his scheme was not pursued, a defeat which led Blomfield to resign from the Royal Fine Arts Commission which had initially approved his design.

In his later years Blomfield was a doughty opponent of continental modernism, and his book *Modernismus* (1934) was a witty and slashing attack. Ironically, he was appointed by the Central Electricity Board to advise on the design of supply pylons—a modernist icon. He continued to publish, and among other works are his *Memoirs* (1932), and *Richard Norman Shaw, RA* (1940), a belated if slight tribute to an architect who was an early influence on Blomfield and his contemporaries but who was, by then, unfashionable.

Blomfield's phenomenal vitality continued to the very end of his life. A big and powerful man, he played most games well and some to a great age. He had also enlisted in the Inns of Court Volunteers in 1900 and again in the First World War. He was a genial figure in the billiard-room of the Athenaeum up to the last. He was elected honorary fellow of Exeter College, Oxford, in 1906, received the honorary degree of LittD from Liverpool University in 1920, and was knighted in 1919. He was also awarded several foreign decorations. He died at home at 51 Frognal, Hampstead, on 27 December 1942, leaving an estate valued at over £110,000. M. S. BRIGGS, *rev.* RICHARD A. FELLOWS

Sources R. T. Blomfield, *Memoirs of an architect* (1932) · R. A. Fellows, *Sir Reginald Blomfield* (1985) · C. H. Reilly, 'Sir Reginald Blomfield', *Representative British architects of the present day* (1931), 54–65 · M. S. Briggs, 'Voysey and Blomfield: a study in contrast', *The Builder*, 176 (1949), 39–42 · *The Times* (29 Dec 1942) · *Manchester Guardian* (29 Dec 1942) · A. E. Richardson, 'Sir Reginald Blomfield', *RIBA Journal*, 50 (1942–3), 65–7 · A. Blomfield, 'List of buildings designed by Sir Reginald Blomfield', *RIBA Journal*, 50 (1942–3), 88–9

Archives Commonwealth War Graves Commission, corresp. relating to Imperial War Graves Commission · Winchester College, archives, file of corresp. relating to windows at Winchester College | BL, corresp. with Macmillans, Add. MS 55234 · RIBA, Drawings Collection, topographical drawings, sketch and notebooks, perspective and orthographic drawings, detail drawings · U. Glas. L., letters to D. S. MacColl · UCL, letters to Sir Francis Galton

Likenesses J. J. Shannon, oils, exh. RA 1915, RIBA [*see illus.*] · W. R. Dick, bronze bust, 1927, NPG · W. Rothenstein, chalk drawing, NPG · J. Russell & Sons, photograph, NPG · W. Strang, etching, BM

Wealth at death £112,057 5*s*. 9*d*.: probate, 18 May 1943, *CGPLA Eng. & Wales*

Blomfield [*née* Ryan], **Sara Louisa** [Sitárih Khánum] (**1859–1939**), Bah'i promoter and philanthropist, was born in Knockaneven, near Limerick, the daughter of Matthew John Ryan. She received a convent education in England. On 21 April 1887 she married Arthur William *Blomfield (1829–1899), architect and son of Charles *Blomfield, bishop of London; they had two daughters, Mary and Rose. In 1889 Blomfield was knighted. After her husband's death in 1899 Lady Blomfield and her daughters left their London house in Montague Square for their country house at Broadway, Worcestershire, where she continued to entertain extensively for a time. Losing her enthusiasm for society, Lady Blomfield developed a deep respect for the Christianity taught by Basil Wilberforce, archdeacon of Westminster, who became a personal friend.

About 1907 Lady Blomfield visited Paris with her daughter Mary. There, at a reception at the house of Madame Lucien Monod, she was introduced to the Bah'i message by Bertha Herbert, who declared 'It is true! True! We have been taught to believe that a great Messenger would again be sent to the world. He would set forth to gather together all the peoples of good will in every race, nation, and religion on the earth. Now is the appointed time! He has come! He has come' (Blomfield, 1). She went on to say that there was a lady in Paris who had recently visited ʿAbd al-Bahaʾ, the son of the Bahaʾ Allah (the 'bearer of the message'), who was then a captive in the fortress prison of Acre, Palestine. A meeting with this lady, a Miss Rosenberg, and the scholar Hippolyte Dreyfus, who was the first French Bah'i, was arranged, and the Blomfields welcomed the Bahaʾi message.

In August 1911 Lady Blomfield (who took the name Sitárih Khánum) invited the recently released ʿAbd al-Bahaʾ to be her guest at her house, 97 Cadogan Gardens, London, and arranged a programme of events to introduce him to Britain. Within a week of his arrival on 4 September 1911 he made his first public appearance, addressing the congregation of the City Temple, Holborn: the minister, R. J. Campbell, was a friend of Lady Blomfield's and well-known for his liberal thought. She also arranged for ʿAbd al-Bahaʾ to address Archdeacon Wilberforce's congregation at St John's, Smith Square. When ʿAbd al-Bahaʾ left England for Paris in October, Lady Blomfield and her daughters followed him; they took notes of his talks,

Sara Louisa Blomfield (1859–1939), by unknown photographer

which they published as *Talks by Abdul Baha Given in Paris* (1912). (This work ran to many editions, forming an essential part of Baha'i writings.) Lady Blomfield placed her home at his disposal when he returned to England after a year spent in Egypt and North America, again organizing an intense programme of activities for him; he eventually returned to Haifa, Palestine, in December 1913.

When the First World War began the Blomfields were living in Geneva, but moved to Paris to work for the Red Cross before returning to London in March 1915. In the spring of 1918 Lady Blomfield learned that the life of ʿAbd al-Baha' was endangered by the Turks in Palestine, who were threatening to crucify him. She went at once to Lord Lamington, who alerted the foreign secretary, A. J. Balfour, who in turn instructed General Allenby to 'extend every protection and consideration to 'Abdu'l-Bahá, his family and his friends, when British march on Haifa'. When Allenby took Haifa, he telegraphed news of the safety of ʿAbd al-Baha'.

After the war Lady Blomfield made her home for part of each year in Geneva, where she met Eglantyne Jebb, the founder of the Save the Children Fund. Lady Blomfield set up an assisting fund, the Blomfield Fund, under the sponsorship of Lord Weardale in London, and was involved in lobbying to have Jebb's children's charter adopted by the League of Nations as the declaration of Geneva in 1924.

When the eldest grandson of ʿAbd al-Baha', Shoghi Efendi Rabbani, went to Oxford, he was befriended by Lady Blomfield; she accompanied him to Haifa in December 1921 when he learned of the death of his grandfather. She remained in the Holy Land for several months, assisting Shoghi Efendi as he assumed his new role as guardian of the Baha'i faith. She made a second journey to the Holy Land in 1930. Thereafter she lived with her daughter Mary and her daughter's husband, Basil Hall, in Hampstead. She remained dedicated to the service of her faith, serving for eight of the first eleven years on the National Spiritual Assembly of the Baha'is of the British Isles. She died on 31 December 1939 at 40 Belsize Grove, Hampstead, and was buried in Hampstead municipal cemetery. A volume of her reminiscences, *The Chosen Highway*, was published in 1940. PHILIP HAINSWORTH

Sources H. M. Balyuzi, *ʿAbdu'l-Bahá* (1971) • ʿAbd al-Baha' ibn Baha' Allah, *ʿAbdu'l-Bahá in London: addresses and notes of conversations* (1912) • S. L. Blomfield, *The chosen highway* (1940) • O. Z. Whitehead, *Some early Bahis of the west* (1977) • *Baháí World*, 8 (1939), 651–6 • m. cert. • M. B. Hall, 'Sitárih Khánum', BL NSA • private information (2004)

Archives National Baha'i Archives, London

Likenesses photograph, repro. in Blomfield, *Chosen highway* [*see illus.*] • photographs, priv. coll. • portrait, Baha'i World Centre, PO Box 155, Haifa 31001, Israel • portrait, National Spiritual Assembly of the Baha'is, 27 Rutland Gate, London • portrait, repro. in Blomfield, *Chosen highway*

Wealth at death £4308 15*s*. 3*d*.: probate, 25 April 1940, *CGPLA Eng. & Wales*

Blomfild [Blomefield], **William** (*fl.* **1529–1574**), alchemist and priest, was born in Bury St Edmunds. He was a Benedictine monk and priest at Bury in his youth. In 1529 he was questioned at London regarding certain protestant tenets (which he abjured) although he seems later in life to have gravitated towards Calvinism. In 1543, at which time he was living in London, he was imprisoned; subsequently, in 1546, he was arraigned as a conjuror, but apparently acquitted (PRO, SP 1/222, fol. 132). In 1557 he wrote his best-known work, *Bloomfield's Blossoms, or, The Campe of Philosophy*, an alchemical work in verse, first published by Elias Ashmole in 1652 in *Theatrum chemicum Britannicum* (pp. 305–23); numerous manuscript copies survive. The work consists of eighty-four stanzas in rhyme royal, and concludes with nine couplets.

Blomfild was made vicar of the parish of Sts Simon and Jude at Norwich in April 1569 by Bishop John Parkhurst, but was forced out in less than a year. In a dedicatory epistle to Queen Elizabeth prefixed to another alchemical work, *Blomefyld's Quintaessens, or, The Regiment of Lyfe* (written about 1574), he complains of being forced to 'forsake my lyvyng' by 'obstinat papistes' who 'troubled & molested me for religions sake' (Blomfild, fol. 1). These 'papistes' were presumably Anglicans who objected to Blomfild's puritanical tendencies and 'godly exercises' (Schuler, 'Blomfild', 80–85).

Blomfild has frequently been confused with Myles *Blomefylde (Blomefield) (1525–1603) who copied the *Quintaessens*. The authorship of *Bloomfield's Blossoms* has sometimes erroneously been attributed to Myles, but the initial letters of the first verses of each of the three sections of text spell out the name William Blomfild. Myles

Blomefylde appended a brief but valuable biographical note to what is now the Cambridge Library copy of *Quintaessens* in which he claims William was versed in many languages both ancient and modern, and 'in Alchimistri & Distillation he hath not left his lyke in this Nation'. It is probable that the two men were related (both having been born at Bury St Edmunds), as Ashmole suggested in *Theatrum chemicum*. Blomfild was well regarded as an alchemist through the seventeenth century, and at least seven brief tracts (besides the *Blossoms* and *Quintaessens*) are attributed to him. It is not known when he died, although the date 1585 has often been cited.

LAWRENCE M. PRINCIPE

Sources R. M. Schuler, 'William Blomfild, Elizabethan alchemist', *Ambix*, 20 (1973), 75–87 · R. M. Schuler, 'An alchemical poem: authorship and manuscripts', *The Library*, 5th ser., 28 (1973), 240–42 · E. Ashmole, ed., *Theatrum chemicum Britannicum* (1652) · W. Blomfild, 'Blomefyld's Quintaessens', c.1574, CUL, MS Dd. 3.83, art. 6 · Tanner, *Bibl. Brit.-Hib.*, 107

Blondel, James Augustus (1665/6–1734), physician, was born in Paris, the son of a legal counsellor. He matriculated at the University of Leiden on 28 April 1691. At Leiden he studied medicine as the classmate of the later renowned Hermann Boerhaave, and received his MD on 17 July 1692, having published his thesis, *Disputatio medica inauguralis de crisibus*, a work dedicated to Frederick Spanheim, his Leiden professor of theology. According to the *Dictionnaire historique de la médecine* (1828), Blondel was well versed in the dead languages, particularly Hebrew, and wrote many theological works, reputedly all published anonymously. Blondel established a practice in London, settling in 1700 with his wife, Marianne, in the parish of the French church on Threadneedle Street, the mother church of the Walloon and French congregations in England. They had two children, Marie (*b.* 1701) and Jacques (*b.* 1702).

Blondel was made a licentiate of London's Royal College of Physicians on 26 March 1711. In 1727 he published an anonymous work entitled *The strength of imagination in pregnant women examined; and the opinion that marks and deformities in children arise from thence, demonstrated to be a vulgar error*. He later claimed to have written this work in response to Mary Toft's delusion that her unfulfilled cravings for rabbit actually caused her to give birth to a litter of rabbits. However, another member of the college, Daniel Turner, deemed Blondel's work to be an attack on a chapter, 'Spots and marks of a diverse resemblance imprest upon the skin of the foetus, by the force of the mother's fancy', in his book, *De morbis cutaneis*, a work on skin disease, first published in 1714. In September 1729 Turner responded with a pamphlet addressing Blondel's work. Later that year, Blondel issued a second work, *The Power of the Mother's Imagination over the Foetus Examined*. Blondel presented the whole issue of the power of the mother's imagination as a vulgar error, scorning the credulity of the medical practitioners involved in the Toft case. He represented the belief of the 'imaginationists' as irrational and mathematically unsound, using a deductive Newtonian approach to sustain his hypothesis regarding the maternal imagination. Blondel and Turner, in polemical pamphleteering common to this period, both presented arguments which gained support for many years. Their influence spread beyond London, and Blondel's 1729 pamphlet was translated into French (1737), Dutch (1737), German (1756), and Italian (1760). The widespread contemporary interest in this dispute suggests that Blondel, together with Turner, raised the phenomenon of the maternal imagination from an issue of folk belief to a concern of eighteenth-century medicine.

Blondel died on 4 October 1734, and was buried 'Privately and with as little Ceremony' as possible at Stepney Causeway, near the area of London in which he had practised for many years.

PHILIP K. WILSON

Sources P. K. Wilson, '"Out of sight, out of mind?": the Turner–James Blondel dispute over the power of the maternal imagination', *Annals of Science*, 49 (1992), 63–85 · O. Dezeimeris and R.-D. Dezeimeris, *Dictionnaire historique de la médecine* (1828), vol. 1, p. 418 · S. Kottek, 'La force de l'imagination chez les femmes enceintes', *Revue d'Histoire de la Médecine Hebraïque*, 27 (1974), 43–8 · N. F. J. Eloy, *Dictionnaire historique de la médecine ancienne et moderne*, 4 vols. (Mons, 1778), vol. 1, p. 360 · A. Rees and others, *The cyclopaedia, or, Universal dictionary of arts, sciences, and literature*, 45 vols. (1819–20), vol. 4 · W. Minet and S. Minet, *Livre des témoignages, 1669–1719, de l'église de Threadneedle Street* (1909), 24 · *The registers of the French church, Threadneedle Street, London*, 3, ed. T. C. Colyer-Fergusson, Huguenot Society of London, 16 (1906), 208, 221 · W. A. Shaw, ed., *Letters of denization and acts of naturalization for aliens in England and Ireland, 1603–1700*, Huguenot Society of London, 18 (1911), 193 · PRO, Prob. 11/667 · Munk, *Roll*

Blondin. *See* Gravelet, Jean-François Émile (1824–1897).

Blood, Sir Bindon (1842–1940), army officer, was born on 7 November 1842 near Jedburgh, the third son of William Bindon Blood of Cranagher, co. Clare, civil engineer, and his second wife, Margaret, daughter of Robert Stewart of Hawick. He was a descendant of Colonel Thomas Blood, who attempted to seize the crown jewels in 1671. He was educated at the Royal School, Banagher, and Queen's College, Galway, and entered the East India Company's military college at Addiscombe in January 1860. In December 1860 he was commissioned from there by open competition as temporary lieutenant in the Royal Engineers. For the next ten years he specialized in signalling and pontoon bridging. He designed the boats which replaced the sausage system of pontoons, and became the first commander of the Royal Engineers telegraph troop formed in 1870. He embarked for India in 1871, and, except for short periods of active service in South Africa, served there for thirty-five years. In India he was posted to the Bengal Sappers and Miners at Roorkee, where he remained for the next few years enjoying sport and big-game shooting.

In 1873 Blood was promoted captain, and served on the committee under Sir Frederick Roberts that arranged for the ceremony to proclaim Queen Victoria empress of India in 1877. Towards the end of that year he commanded on the north-west frontier part of a punitive expedition against the Jowaki Afridis (1877–8).

In August 1878 Blood returned home on leave, but on the outbreak of the Anglo-Zulu War he went to Africa early in 1879 as commanding royal engineer, 1st division Zulu field

Sir Bindon Blood (1842–1940), by Bassano, 1898

force. He was made brevet major for his services there. In 1880 he served in the Second Anglo-Afghan War, but took little part in the fighting and returned to Roorkee towards the end of the year. He left India in 1882 and was posted to command the 26th field company, Royal Engineers, at Shorncliffe, but after only a few months was ordered to Egypt, where his sappers took part in the battle of Tell al-Kebir. This campaign brought him promotion to brevet lieutenant-colonel (1882).

Blood returned to England in 1883, and married on 12 July Charlotte Elizabeth (*d.* 10 May 1948), second daughter of Sir Auckland *Colvin. They had one son and two daughters. He succeeded in getting himself posted once more to India, rejoining the sappers and miners as commandant in Simla in 1885. Seven years later he was appointed brigadier-general and commanded Bundelkhand district, with headquarters at Agra. In 1895 he was made chief staff officer as acting major-general of the Chitral relief force. For these services he was appointed KCB. He returned to Agra in January 1896 but in July 1897 was appointed to command the Malakand field force, which he did with great success. Blood was responsible for the young Winston Churchill's participation in the campaign. He was promoted major-general in 1898.

On returning to India from short leave, Blood commanded the Meerut division for the next two years, but early in 1901 Kitchener asked for his services in South Africa, and as lieutenant-general he commanded the troops in the eastern Transvaal, with headquarters at Middelburg, and for some months was engaged on various anti-guerrilla operations. Late in 1901 he took up the important military command of the Punjab, which he held, having been promoted full general in 1906, until he retired in November 1907.

Blood then settled in London, continuing to lead a very active life. He was a popular man, with many friends. In 1909 he was appointed GCB and in 1914 colonel-commandant, Royal Engineers. For the next sixteen years his activities were largely concerned with the interests of the corps, and he also did recruiting work during the First World War. In 1932 he was appointed GCVO, and in 1936 was the first officer to fill the recreated post of chief royal engineer.

Blood's successes were due to his exceptional staff work and strategy, and his carefully acquired knowledge of opposing forces. He died at his residence, 59 Cadogan Square, London, on 16 May 1940, his name having appeared in the *Army List* for eighty years. His cremation took place at Golders Green crematorium.

C. V. OWEN, *rev.* JAMES LUNT

Sources *The Times* (17 May 1940) • *The Times* (21 May 1940) • B. Blood, *Four score years and ten* (1933) • J. R. E. C. and S. H. S., 'General Sir Bindon Blood', *Royal Engineers Journal*, new ser., 54 (1940), 321–31 • J. F. Maurice and M. H. Grant, eds., *History of the war in South Africa, 1899–1902*, 4 vols. (1906–10) • W. S. Churchill, *The story of the Malakand field force* (1898) • *WWW* • Burke, *Gen. Ire.* (1976) • H. M. Vibart, *Addiscombe: its heroes and men of note* (1894)

Archives BL OIOC, Sir George Stuart White papers, MSS Eur. F. 108

Likenesses Bassano, photograph, 1898, NPG [*see illus.*] • E. H. Neale, oils, 1910, Tidworth, Hampshire • W. Stoneman, photographs, 1917–32, NPG • E. H. Neale, oils, 1932, Royal Engineers, Chatham, Kent • portrait, repro. in R. S. Churchill, *Winston S. Churchill*, 1: *Youth, 1874–1900* (1966), facing p. 384

Wealth at death £1785 1*s.* 7*d.*: probate, 22 Nov 1940, *CGPLA Eng. & Wales*

Blood, Sir Hilary Rudolph Robert (1893–1967), colonial governor, was born in Glasgow on 28 May 1893, the eldest son of the Revd (later Canon) Alban Francis Blood, rector of Holy Trinity Church, Kilmarnock, and his wife, Adelaide Therèse Feldtmann. He was educated at the Irvine Royal Academy and at Glasgow University where he obtained his MA in 1914. In the First World War he served in the Royal Scots Fusiliers and was wounded in the Gallipoli campaign. In 1919 he married Alison Farie (*d.* 1972), youngest daughter of William Boyd Anderson, a lawyer in Glasgow; they had one son and two daughters.

In 1920 Blood entered the Ceylon civil service as a cadet, and served there for the next ten years. He was colonial secretary in Grenada (1930–34) and in Sierra Leone (1934–42). He was governor of the Gambia (1942–7), of Barbados (1947–9), and of Mauritius (1949–54). As a governor, Blood was highly regarded. He was a shrewd administrator, and his friendly nature, his genuine interest in people and their individual problems made him a sympathetic and popular ruler. He had the dignity and presence for ceremonial occasions but none of the vanity and pretence which sometimes afflict men in these elevated positions.

Perhaps the happiest moment in his career was in Barbados when he went into the commentator's box during a test match between the West Indies and the MCC and took over anonymously from the official commentator. He did it very well, and when the public learned that the new commentator was none other than their own governor, he became more popular than ever.

His wide experience in so many of the smaller territories in the British empire gave Blood a particular interest in the very difficult problem of their advance to some form of self-government or independence. In 1958 he wrote a pamphlet for the Conservative Commonwealth Council in which he tried to identify the complex factors, varying from colony to colony, which affected this advance and to put forward tentative solutions. He was able to give some practical shape to his ideas by service as a constitutional commissioner in British Honduras in 1959 and in Zanzibar in 1960. In the same year he became chairman of the constitutional commission for Malta. There his work was of great importance and in the opinion of good judges it facilitated a smooth transition from the period of direct rule to the grant of independence in 1964.

In his later years Blood was active in the service of the Royal Commonwealth Society, the Royal Commonwealth Society for the Blind (of which he was chairman from 1962 to 1965), and as chairman of the Royal Society of Arts from 1963 to 1965. During this period of active retirement he worked frequently for the civil service commission, both as a group chairman at the civil service selection board testing candidates for the administrative class of the home civil service and the senior branch of the foreign service, and as a member of the final selection boards in the same class of competition.

Blood was a burly man, standing about 6 feet tall, with broad brow, square jaw, and lively hazel eyes. He walked with a pronounced limp, the result of his wound in Gallipoli. To all his activities throughout his life he gave his undeflected attention and performed all his tasks with complete integrity. A deeply religious man, his chief distinction was his humanity and his sympathetic understanding of all those who worked for him and with him. His whole bearing, his friendly smiles, and the deep tones of his voice gave people, young and old, confidence in him and brought him innumerable friends and a devoted family.

Appointed CMG in 1934, Blood was advanced to KCMG in 1944 and appointed GBE in 1953. The honour which gave him the most pride and pleasure was the honorary LLD which his old university at Glasgow conferred on him in 1944. Blood died at the Ashford Hospital, Kent, on 20 June 1967. GEORGE MALLABY, *rev.*

Sources *The Times* (21 June 1967) · private information (1981) · personal knowledge (1981) · *Commonwealth Journal*, 10/4 (Aug 1967), 160 · *CGPLA Eng. & Wales* (1967)

Archives Bodl. RH, political papers

Wealth at death £14,165: probate, 18 Oct 1967, *CGPLA Eng. & Wales*

Blood, Holcroft (*c.*1657–1707), army officer and military engineer, the third son of Colonel Thomas *Blood (1617/18–1680) and his wife, Mary (*fl.* 1650–1670), the daughter of Lieutenant-Colonel John Holcroft of Holcroft, Lancashire, was born in Sarney, co. Meath, Ireland. In 1672, unknown to his father, he enlisted in the navy and served during the Third Dutch War. Later, under the false name Leture, he joined the French guards as a cadet and studied engineering.

In April 1676, at the request of his father, who was employed at court in spying on the king's enemies, Charles II granted Blood the offices of clerk of the crown and peace in co. Clare. The Blood family had originally settled in co. Clare in the 1590s, where they were now well established. Blood did not in fact take up this office, which was assigned to a deputy. In 1678 Charles II granted him a licence of absence on the grounds that 'he has been so absent by the King's command and has remained in England on the King's service' (*CSP dom.*, *1678*, 241).

Holcroft was now living in London and, it would appear, was closely connected with his father's intrigues. In 1686 he married Elizabeth Fowler, the daughter of Richard King, a barrister, at St Pancras Church. In 1688, as a result of the imminent threat of invasion, he was employed, together with Jacob Richards, in strengthening the fortifications at Sheerness. In early October, under orders from Lord Dartmouth, he was busy pressing a number of men employed on the works to serve in James II's hastily gathered fleet. Later that month, through family influence, he achieved his first important step, being appointed captain of the pioneers in James II's train of artillery; Elizabeth Blood's cousin Richard Biddulph secured Blood's appointment with Lord Dartmouth, master of the ordnance. Following the successful landing of William of Orange at Torbay, the train accompanied James's infantry under the command of Faversham down to Salisbury. In contrast to the widespread defections and disarray which affected other regiments, the train returned in good order to the Tower—much to the satisfaction of the newly convened council of peers.

Notwithstanding his service under the old regime, Blood remained on the establishment after William's accession. In May 1689 he was promoted second engineer on the train of artillery bound for Ireland, his salary raised from 5*s*. to 10*s*. per day. He served in all the major sieges and battles of the campaign in Ireland and was wounded at Cavan in February 1690. In 1693 he was in receipt of a Treasury payment for demolishing the fortifications at Cashel by the king's direct order.

During the mid-1690s Blood's relations with the Board of Ordnance deteriorated; he was not appointed to either of the two artillery trains sent to Flanders in 1692. However, it was still a widespread practice for regiments to appoint their own engineer officers, and Blood was promoted captain in Colonel John Foulkes's regiment, then serving in Flanders with King William. In 1693 he was accused of robbing the post boy of mails from Spain, but after a trial at the Old Bailey was acquitted. The incident worked out rather to his advantage, for the king, convinced of his innocence and having first-hand experience of his abilities as a siege engineer in Ireland, secured his rapid advancement. In October 1693 he was promoted major and in 1694 received a commission in Lord Cutts's regiment. After being promoted lieutenant-colonel in Sir George St George's regiment, he served as an engineer at the siege of Namur in 1695.

Blood continued to enjoy royal patronage. By warrant of January 1696 he was raised to the position of second engineer of England, passing over Jacob Richards, his senior, under whom he had served in Ireland. According to Porter the Board of Ordnance, much displeased with this royal interference with precedent, put off the appointment for as long as possible but was eventually forced to comply. In May of the same year Blood was paid £180 as reward for his part in apprehending the leaders of a conspiracy to assassinate the king. Later, in October, William moved to circumvent the functions of the board further by appointing Blood commander of the King's company of engineers, a little-known body under the monarch's direct control, paid by special warrant from the Treasury. Blood had twenty-eight engineers under his command, paid between 5*s.* and 10*s.* a day, although several were also on the establishment of the board at the same time. The company was active in the autumn of 1696, preparing fixed defensive lines in front of the British army's winter quarters near Bruges. On 18 October Blood wrote to the king with plans of his retrenchments, together with troop dispositions 'to cover Bruges from the insults of the French' (*CSP dom.*, *1696*, 418–19).

However, the war in Flanders was drawing to a close, and the evolution of an independent company of engineers was ended with the treaty of Ryswick (1697). While the army was rapidly disbanded, the Board of Ordnance moved to increase its establishment, and the first artillery train in peacetime was formed under Jacob Richards, although it soon fell foul of cries for economy. Similarly, in March 1700 the King's company of engineers was finally broken. Blood, however, remained on the establishment as second engineer of England with a salary of £250; he also retained his commission as a lieutenant-colonel, with a salary of £365.

The dispute between the board and Blood continued with the resumption of hostilities against France in 1702. When offered command of the train for Flanders he at first declined, on the grounds that the board's practice of granting short temporary commissions undermined the commander's authority when 'the confusion and disorder which always happens in new corps, seems in my humble opinion to require a greater power and authority to bring them into good order'. Blood's anticipation of the arguments for a permanent corps was not well received by the board, who wrote to the earl of Romney calling for his immediate discharge from 'the employment of the office' (correspondence, 16 April 1702, BL, Add. MS 61298, fols. 1–3). With the appointment of the duke of Marlborough as master of the ordnance in late June 1702 matters appear to have been resolved, for Blood did in fact take up the post of colonel of the train. He saw distinguished service in that capacity under the duke in the following years. At the siege of Venloo in September 1702 Lord Cutts led a foolhardy but successful assault on the fortifications, commending Blood in his dispatch; a party of 300 workmen and a number of engineers:

> under Colonel Blood who acted as First Engineer under Mr Coehorne and was to have made the lodgement continuous. When he saw that I had quitted that design he shew'd the part of a brave officer, charging with the men sword in hand and killing an officer of grenadiers who made a vigorous opposition with his party. (Porter, 1.111)

In July 1702 Blood was appointed lieutenant-colonel of Sir Matthew Bridge's regiment, and took over the regiment on Bridge's death the following year. The regiment saw service in Spain and Portugal, being present at Almanza in 1707 and at Saragossa and Brihuega in 1710. Blood remained in Flanders, and it was as colonel of the train during Marlborough's campaign of 1704 that he achieved his greatest feats of gunnery, engineering, and logistics. Transporting a train of thirty-eight field pieces and four howitzers a distance of 250 miles from the Meuse to the Danube in six weeks, partly by boat up the Rhine, then on foot through rolling country from Mainz to Heidelberg, and finally over the passes of the Jura mountains in continuous rain and deteriorating tracks, Blood arrived at the town of Donauwörth on 2 July. Here he was able to bring several batteries of guns immediately to bear on the slopes between the town and the fortified heights of the Schellenberg in support of a sudden and successful assault by Marlborough's infantry.

At Blenheim, Blood's artillery played an important role throughout the course of the battle. Arriving at dawn on the day of the battle, the combined allied artillery was positioned by Marlborough on the heights covering the Nebel Stream and surrounding marshes. In the morning the battle commenced as Blood's artillery directed its barrage on the opposing French cannon, in support of the advancing allied forces. Later Marlborough sent Blood forward with several batteries to stiffen the wavering assault by Holstein Beck's forces in the vicinity of Oberglau. At 4 o'clock in the afternoon Blood was ordered to bring a battery of nine field pieces across the marshes by pontoon bridge to support the allied advance in the centre. Under heavy fire he brought up the guns and proceeded to decimate the nine brigades of the French centre at close range with partridge shot before the main body of allied cavalry succeeded in cutting the French army in two. For his distinguished action during the battle Blood was promoted to brigadier-general.

The campaign of 1704 continued long into December in an attempt to maximize allied gains. Desiring to secure the lower Moselle before moving into winter quarters, and being delayed by sturdy resistance at Landau, on 22 October Marlborough sent Colonel Blood, with three regiments of foot, fourteen cannon, and four howitzers, ahead of the main column towards Homburg in preparation for an attack upon the fortress at Treves (Trier). After a rapid march through densely wooded hills, made possible by unseasonably good weather, Marlborough arrived with all his forces at Treves on 29 October. The advance enjoyed complete surprise, and the French garrison withdrew, offering no resistance. The subsequent siege of Trabach, which was opened on 4 November, was not so easy, however; Blood was kept busy with siege work until 20 December, when the garrison pleaded for terms.

Blood's military career had reached its zenith, yet professional success and public acclaim were accompanied by increasing turbulence in his private life. His relationship with his wife, Elizabeth, had deteriorated, largely as a consequence of sexual infidelity on his part—principally, but not solely, his long-standing affair with Mrs Mary Andrews, a chief witness for the defence at his trial for robbing the mails. Elizabeth left the marital home in 1700, together with a large quantity of household goods, having run up significant debts. In October Blood attempted a reconciliation which ended in a public brawl. Elizabeth's attempts to have warrants issued against him for assault were deflected by a combination of social influence and legal trickery—his brother Charles was a barrister. In 1702 Elizabeth turned to the consistory court of London with a suit for separation with alimony on grounds of cruelty and adultery. Her accusations appeared wild and uncorroborated, and Blood was able to call on friends of social standing for character witness. On account of his absences in the field the case dragged on until 1704. However, before judgment could be given Blood produced evidence of adultery on his wife's part and her suit was thrown out. Despite her refutation of this charge on appeal to the court of arches, Blood's public position and military career proved decisive. Separated from his independent and resourceful wife, he returned to Flanders in 1705.

Under Marlborough's command, artillery was playing an increasingly important role, and consequently trains of artillery were becoming bigger; in 1705 Blood commanded a train of forty-six guns, including twenty 24-pounders, in addition to sixty mortars. In 1706 he commanded a similar sized train at Ramillies, perhaps Marlborough's most decisive victory. Moreover, Blood's relations with the board appear to have improved. In early June the board thanked him for his report on the victory at Ramillies and later advances and again in September for his account of the siege of Menin, where Blood was in charge of the engineering works.

This was to prove the last action in which Blood served. The army shortly went into winter quarters. At the start of the campaign of 1707 he was lying ill in Brussels, where he died on 19 August 1707, aged fifty. He left an illegitimate son, Holcroft, of St Anne's, Soho, whose mother was Dorothy Cooke of Dort, Holland. The son died unmarried about 1724. Both were main beneficiaries of his will, which he made shortly before his death. His wife, Elizabeth, received a small payment.

In an age when artillery was heavy, cumbersome, slow, usually late to the battle and rather inaccurate, Blood's endeavours as commander of the train in Marlborough's campaigns appear herculean. It was an age when the commander of the train combined the demanding roles of gunnery officer, siege engineer, and logistical support. More particularly Blood's career reflects the transition in the use of artillery in warfare during the early eighteenth century: a movement away from the static, defensive encounters of the seventeenth century, with an emphasis on siege warfare and territorial occupation, towards the strategy of decisive offensive action through the destruction of the enemy's army on the battlefield. This required not only greater mobility in the movement of armies and supporting artillery but also mobility in terms of the tactical requirements of the battlefield. This was exemplified by Marlborough's campaign of 1704, in which Blood's artillery played such an important part.

JONATHAN SPAIN

Sources Burke, *Gen. Ire.* (1976) · Burke, *Gen. Ire.* (1912) · L. Stone, *Broken lives: separation and divorce in England, 1660–1857* (1993) · C. Dalton, ed., *English army lists and commission registers, 1661–1714*, 6 vols. (1892–1904) · G. Story, *A true and impartial history of the most material occurrences in the kingdom of Ireland* (1691) · N. Luttrell, *A brief historical relation of state affairs from September 1678 to April 1714*, 6 vols. (1857) · W. Porter, *History of the corps of royal engineers*, 1 (1889) · O. F. G. Hogg, *English artillery, 1326–1716* (1963) · D. Chandler, *The art of warfare in the age of Marlborough* (1976) · D. Chandler, *Marlborough as military commander* (1973) · I. P. Prielan, 'Marlborough as logistician', *Journal of the Society for Army Historical Research*, 68 (1990), 36–48, 103–19 · *The letters and dispatches of John Churchill, first duke of Marlborough, from 1702 to 1712*, ed. G. Murray, 1 (1845) · *The Marlborough–Godolphin correspondence*, ed. H. L. Snyder, 3 vols. (1975) · C. T. Atkinson, *Marlborough and the rise of the British army* (1921) · *The manuscripts of the earl of Dartmouth*, 3 vols., HMC, 20 (1887–96), vol. 1, pp. 146, 152, 178 · *CSP dom.*, *1678*, 38–9, 237, 241; *1696*, 418–19; *1696–7*, 147; *1689–92*, 1665 · will, PRO, PROB 11/503
Archives BL, John, first duke of Marlborough, corresp. and MSS, Add. MSS 61101–61143
Wealth at death £100 p.a. annuities to illegitimate son and latter's mother, Dorothy Cooke; £50 each to two sisters; all goods and chattels to Dorothy Cooke: will, PRO, PROB 11/503

Blood, Thomas (1617/18–1680), adventurer and spy, was born at Sarney, co. Meath. His early life is obscure, but it was later claimed that his father (who was possibly Neptune Blood) was a blacksmith and ironworker, 'serious, honest and of no inferior credit' (R. H., 219).

Landowner and army officer An Irish letter patent for Thomas Blood, gentleman, described various rented lands that he held in 1640, and in 1654–6 he was listed by the survey of Ireland as having owned some 220 acres of land at Sarney since 1640. In 1663 Blood was said to have possessed a small house and to have £100 a year in Dunboyne, which was of 'ancient inheritance', but all his lands were lost to him for his rebellious actions in that year (*CSP Ire.*, *1663–5*, 133).

Between 1641 and 1654 Blood fought in the civil wars of Ireland and England. The details are obscure. In 1671 he was described as a former captain in 'the old King's army under Sir Lewis Dyve' (BL, Add. MS 36916, fol. 233), a claim supported by the appearance of 'Captain Bludd' as captain to Dyves's quartermaster in the indigent officers' list of 1663. Another source reported that Blood had served in Ireland under George Monck (which might have been either in 1642–3 in Ormond's army or in 1647–9 in parliament's). When interviewed by the king in 1671 Blood claimed that he had fought in England as a royalist under

Thomas Blood (**1617/18–1680**), by unknown artist

Prince Rupert; indeed, the prince was said to remember Blood as a 'very stout bold fellow' (*Sixth Report*, HMC, 370; *CSP dom.*, *1671–2*, 373). There is, however, no firm evidence of this service, and Rupert may have been yet another person seduced by the Irishman's eloquence: John Evelyn later noted that Blood's speech was 'dangerously insinuating' (Evelyn, 3.567). In truth Blood may never have risen any higher than the rank of lieutenant in the course of the wars, though this did not prevent his regular self-promotion to captain, major, and finally colonel as he became ever more notorious.

In 1650 Blood, apparently having abandoned the royalist cause for that of parliament, was in Lancashire, where he married Mary Holcroft, daughter of Lieutenant-Colonel John Holcroft of Holcroft Hall, on 21 June. The couple had six children: Thomas junior (who became an accomplice of his father's but predeceased him), Holcroft *Blood (Marlborough's general of artillery), William, Charles (an informer for James, duke of York), Mary, and Elizabeth. By 1651 Blood and his wife had moved back to his lands in Ireland where he remained until at least 1660. According to a published account of his life, in these years Blood acted as both a good protestant and a defender of English rule in Ireland, receiving the favour of the lord deputy, Henry Cromwell. In turn he was alienated in the early 1660s by the Restoration settlement of Ireland: the 'hard usage' that he received at the hands of the court of claims, some of his lands being taken away from him, reinforced the dissatisfaction of an Irish protestant and former parliamentarian with the policies of the new regime. By 1662 Blood had begun his life as a conspirator, heavily involved in the plot that came to light in Dublin in May 1663.

The Dublin plot Blood acted as go-between and recruiter for the plot in Ireland. Those involved had connections with conspirators across the Irish Sea who were active in the north of England. According to the account that James Tanner later gave to the authorities, it was Blood's scheme that the Irish conspirators had intended to use in their attempt to seize both Dublin Castle, the seat of government, and James Butler, duke of Ormond, the lord lieutenant, in May 1663. Plotters disguised as 'handicraft' men waving petitions were initially to enter the castle to seize the duke. A raid on the castle itself was to follow while the guards would be distracted by a cartful of bread overturned at the castle gates; Blood and 100 men would rush the place. The scheme was betrayed by the government's paid informers, among them Philip Alden, one of the main conspirators. Blood allegedly urged that the plan should go ahead regardless. In the event, those not arrested promptly fled, Blood among them. He was said to have tried to rescue some of his captured friends, including his brother-in-law, from the scaffold, an attempt which put a price on his head. Blood was to see his subsequent escape from capture in miraculous terms as a blessing from God, and thereafter he tended to take all his daring escapades in this light: as assurance of God's providence in his life. At some point in the 1660s he wrote down all these 'deliverances' in a pocket book (Bodl. Oxf., MS Rawl. A. 185) that was taken from him upon his capture in 1671; the copy that came into the hands of Samuel Pepys provides a valuable source into both Blood's exploits and his mentality.

After fleeing from Dublin in 1663, Blood had various adventures and many close calls in the Irish countryside before he could escape to England. Of his arrogant courage there is little doubt: returning to Dublin to visit his wife, he dared to leave 'at the gates at noonday & through the streets' (Bodl. Oxf., MS Rawl. A. 185, fol. 473). In England a secret meeting with his mother-in-law in Lancashire nearly resulted in his capture; getting away, he wandered the north country, still in a state of disruption following the failure of the equally abortive northern plot.

Conspirator—and double agent? Blood gradually made his way to London where he met up with other conspirators—some drawn from the nonconformist community, others former Cromwellians, republicans, and rogues—who collectively and somewhat clumsily opposed the government of Charles II. Blood also visited the Netherlands at this time, before returning to London. Thereafter he was reported to be engaged in a number of intrigues against the regime, from organizing meetings in Coleman Street (a notorious den of nonconformity, both religious and political) to outwitting the government's 'trepanners', trying to stay one jump ahead of the authorities and, in 1665, the plague.

In 1666 Blood was recruited for a secret mission: he and his friend John Lockyer visited the republican regicide Edmund Ludlow to try to persuade him to leave his exile in

Switzerland and join with Algernon Sidney and others in a plan to overthrow the Restoration regime. The new plot was backed by the Dutch government, but in his fearful exile Ludlow chose to remain where he was and write his manuscript history of his times. Blood returned to England and in the following year was almost arrested on several occasions. He was almost certainly in London during the great fire in September 1666; in November he was on the edges of the failed Pentland rising in Scotland. Sojourns in Lancashire and Westmorland followed, but evidently tiring of these rebellious courses Blood and his family finally returned to London. Mary Blood and her family set up in Shoreditch, while the eldest son, Thomas, was apprenticed to an apothecary in Southwark (later taking to highway robbery under the alias Hunt). Blood himself, using the aliases Doctor Ayliffe and Doctor Allen, practised as a physician (despite lacking any qualifications) in semi-retirement from conspiracy.

Blood the conspirator in the 1660s was, however, not all he seemed. There is evidence that he had contacted the government at some point and may even have worked for them as a double agent spying on his friends. The papers of Joseph Williamson, under-secretary and the regime's security chief, appear to place Blood on the side of the regime at the very least in 1666, and possibly indicate his involvement in a scheme to capture Edmund Ludlow. This ambiguous role may explain how Blood managed to survive unscathed in this period and was even rewarded at his capture in 1671 following his attempt to steal the crown jewels.

In July 1667 Blood launched the first of a trio of daring adventures that made his name notorious. He helped rescue his friend, the plotter Captain John Mason, from an escort of soldiers who were taking him to York for his trial and probable execution. The ambush at Darrington, near Doncaster, during which five of Mason's guards were shot, was described by Edmund Ludlow as agreeable 'work for the Lord' (Bodl. Oxf., MS Eng. hist. c.487, 1265). Blood himself was badly wounded and recognized by an informer travelling with the party, but escaped. Three years later another ambush reinforced Blood's notoriety.

The attack on the duke of Ormond On the evening of 6 December 1670 five men led by 'Dr Allen' ambushed the carriage of the duke of Ormond as he was quietly returning to his residence at Clarence House. The raiders apparently intended either to murder the duke or to hold him for ransom for some 'ten or twenty thousand pounds' (*Eighth Report*, HMC, 155). The plan went badly wrong. The elderly Ormond fought back and brought down the horse, with its rider, on which the kidnappers were trying to place him. They then fired pistols at the prostrate Ormond as he was lying on the road—and missed. With signs of pursuit in the offing, 'Dr Allen' and his men promptly fled. A committee of the House of Lords was appointed to investigate the crime and soon discovered the names of the leading perpetrators: Thomas Blood (alias Dr Allen, Aylett, Aylofe, or Aleck), Thomas Blood junior (alias Hunt), and Richard Halliwell (alias Holloway). All three men and their dependants evaded the officers sent to seize them. A price of £1000 was set upon their heads by the government.

Blood had forgiven Ormond neither for the seizure of the lands nor for the imprisonment and execution of his friends in 1663. Indeed, according to one version, he intended to pay Ormond back in kind: the attackers were said to have dragged the duke to Tyburn and were attempting to string him up when he broke free. However, Blood may also have been sponsored in the kidnapping by Ormond's rivals at court. It was soon alleged that Blood had been prompted into the attack by none other than George Villiers, second duke of Buckingham. The duke assuredly had the connections with prominent dissidents, former Cromwellians, and republicans to stage such an affair: according to Roger North, he had at one time set himself up as 'one of the heads of that faction' (North, 1.68). His feuds at court were intense, occasionally violent, and he 'hated the Duke of Ormonde mortally' (Carte, 2.424). Blood was certainly later linked with Buckingham; that they were associated before 1671 is not unlikely, given Blood's connections with the nonconformist community. Blood, if no one else among the nonconformists, seems to have believed that Buckingham was their protector. Moreover a letter sent from Blood to his wife in November 1670 indicates that he was near to reaching some form of agreement with an important personage that very month. Ormond's son Thomas Butler, earl of Ossory, certainly believed that Buckingham was behind the attack on his father and openly threatened him should such an event happen again.

The theft of the crown jewels Six months after the attack on Ormond, on 9 May 1671, Blood engaged in the last daring escapade of this sequence: his attempt to steal the crown jewels from the Tower of London. This finally led to his capture and to a change in his fortunes in the world of conspiracy and espionage.

Security surrounding the jewels was under Talbot Edwards, an elderly former soldier who was assistant keeper of the jewels and lived with his family above the room in which they were kept in Martin Tower. Edwards was permitted to make some profit out of his charge by taking a fee from curious visitors to the Tower. In April 1671 he had two visitors to his home: Doctor Ayliffe and his wife. Ayliffe, dressed in the habit of a parson, was most interested in the jewels, but unfortunately his wife was taken ill. The obliging Edwards allowed the lady to recover in his own apartment where his wife and daughter tended her. Ayliffe was willing to express his gratitude at such Christian charity and became a frequent visitor to the Edwards household as a result. Keen to establish this burgeoning friendship on firmer ground, Ayliffe suggested a match between Edwards's daughter and his own nephew. By such means did Dr Ayliffe, alias Thomas Blood, gain frequent access to the Tower.

Terms for the match being agreed, the marriage day dawned on 9 May 1671. At about seven o'clock in the morning five men rode up to the Tower. One, William Smith, a fifth monarchist, remained outside with the horses. Blood (disguised as Ayliffe), his son Thomas (playing the part of the enamoured nephew), Captain Robert Perot, a former silk-dyer (later hanged for his part in Monmouth's rising), and Captain Richard Halliwell (one of Blood's accomplices in the attack on Ormond) made their way to the Martin Tower. All the men were armed with pocket-pistols, knives, and rapiers disguised as canes. There Edwards met them. Blood suggested that the regalia might be shown to his friends while they waited for his wife to arrive. Halliwell remained on guard while the others proceeded to the room on the lowest level of the tower where the jewels were kept. Once inside, and with the door closed, Edwards was overpowered and silenced by a plug of wood in his mouth. It was later claimed that he was told that if he remained quiet he would come to no harm, but the old man struggled so much that he was given several 'unkind knocks on the head'; he was also stabbed and threatened with knives.

With Edwards out of the way, the jewels were distributed among the three men. Blood held the crown and after crushing it put it inside his parson's cloak, and Perot put the orb in his loose breeches, while Blood's son prepared to file the sceptre in two and put it in a bag. It was at this point that providence took a hand: Edwards's son, who had been overseas for several years, chose this moment to return home. He went to see his mother and sister, having first been stopped by the waiting Halliwell, then to see his father. Forewarned by this time, Blood and the others had left the jewel house and were on their way to the horses. However, the elder Edwards regained consciousness, managed to escape, and gave warning; his son soon found him, also raised the alarm, and with Captain Martin Beckman led the chase. Halliwell and the younger Blood reached their horses and rode off, though the latter in his haste crashed into the pole of a cart that had turned in front of him and was subsequently arrested, dazed but unhurt. After a brief struggle, in which shots were exchanged, Blood and Perot were also taken. Blood seems to have been undaunted by the failure of his scheme and is alleged to have merrily told Beckman that 'It was a gallant attempt … [but] … it was for a crown' (BL, Harley MS 6859, fols. 1–17).

Pardon The capture of such a formidable set of outlaws did not provoke the consequences that everyone expected. Thomas Blood seems to have gloried in the deed, and when faced with examination in the Tower that he had so lately breached he demanded to see the king in person. To everyone's surprise, King Charles agreed. It is unlikely to have been simply idle curiosity on the king's part. Blood had great persons at court working on his behalf. One was undoubtedly Henry Bennet, earl of Arlington, the secretary of state, perhaps prompted by his right-hand man Joseph Williamson; Buckingham may have been another.

The king interviewed Blood on 12 May 1671. Details of what passed between the two men are sparse. It was later alleged that Blood admitted his involvement in the rescue of Mason and attack on Ormond, refused to name his fellow conspirators, lied about his age, and cheekily claimed that he had been engaged in a plot to kill Charles while the latter was bathing in the Thames but that 'his heart misgave him out of awe of His Majesty' (Carte, 2.422–3; *CSP Venice, 1671–2*, 49; *Fourth Report*, HMC, 370). Asked what he would do if his life were spared, Blood was alleged to have replied that he would endeavour to deserve it. After the interview Blood was returned to the Tower.

Blood's good fortune thereafter must not be found just in his native eloquence and persuasive manner, but in the regime's own plans for the declaration of indulgence that was issued on 15 March 1672. The offer of a form of religious toleration was intended to placate nonconformists on the eve of a new war with the Dutch, indeed to prevent elements of them from allying with the Dutch as many had done in the previous war. With these considerations in mind, the need for intelligence on the activities of the most militant members of the nonconformist community seems to have caused the regime to spare a man whom Edmund Ludlow described as 'having been acquainted with most of the secret passages that have been of late transacted in order to the reviving of the Lords witnesses' (Bodl. Oxf., MS Eng. hist. c.487, 1265).

The way was soon cleared for Blood's public rehabilitation. Arlington worked hard in making Blood's peace with the cynically amused Ormond; Blood even wrote an apologetic and ingratiating letter to the duke asking his forgiveness. On 18 July 1671 Arlington dined at the Tower, bringing with him the warrant for Blood's release. By 5 August a courtier noted Blood lounging in the precincts of Whitehall, free and dressed in a

> new suit and periwig … extraordinary pleasant and jocose: he has been at liberty this fortnight; he is nothing like the idea I have made to myself of him, for he is a tall rough-boned man, with small legs, a pock frecken[ed] face, with little hollow blue eyes. (*Sixth Report*, HMC, 370)

On 26 August Blood received a full pardon for all his previous crimes and a grant of Irish lands worth £500 per annum. While Joseph Williamson thought that such an open action rather devalued Blood as a secret agent for the regime, he was privately to claim that Blood was still worth 'ten times the value [of the] Crowne' (Bodl. Oxf., MS Eng. lett. d. 37, fol. 84).

Blood's fate was used as a spectacular display of royal mercy to reassure his still outlawed friends of the benefits that they could expect to receive should they make their peace. Arlington at least had no qualms about this, plainly telling the committee of foreign affairs on 22 October 1671 that 'upon the pardoning of Blood he went away among his brethren to bring in some of his friends on assurance of pardon' (PRO, SP 104/176, fol. 315). Soon afterwards a number of arrests were made of militants and former army officers, as Blood also named names. Others were indeed persuaded to come in to receive pardon. Blood was also soon being employed as a domestic intelligencer and mediator to several other parties, enabling him to spy on their activities. He provided Williamson with details of the movements, habits, and demands of the dissenters, information that was used to frame the declaration of indulgence. He intervened on behalf of the sectaries and acted as a channel between the court and certain presbyterian leaders. He was regarded, upon the publication of the declaration, as a man who could obtain—for a price—the necessary licences to worship. With the outbreak of war in 1672 Blood was occasionally sent abroad to spy on the Dutch and on those extremists who had not come in. Lastly Blood was used by many a court politician for their own purposes and rivalries, keeping in not only with Arlington and Williamson, but also with the duke of Lauderdale, the earl of Danby, and even the king's brother, the duke of York. From his daily resort at White's coffee house near the Royal Exchange Blood loudly proclaimed, 'It's no matter if one let[s] me fall, another takes me up. I'm the best tool they have' (*CSP dom.*, 1671–2, 46).

The Popish Plot When the allegations made by Titus Oates and others of a Popish Plot burst out in the autumn of 1678 Blood was swept ever further into a world of imaginary and sham plots. His actions are inevitably obscure, though the evidence suggests that his main role was as a spy and *agent provocateur* for the government. Little is known of Blood's dealings with Oates, though their names were occasionally linked by rumour at the height of the latter's fame. They may have met at the club of the whig magistrate Sir William Waller in Westminster Market Place, a club that both men patronized, though neither Blood nor Waller could have been considered allies of Oates and each regarded the other with contempt. According to one report Blood at one stage intended to damage Oates's credibility by planting treasonable letters in his papers to prove that he was the hireling of the presbyterian faction. This scheme, if it ever existed, failed to come off, though Blood was apparently never that sympathetic to either Oates or his confederate Israel Tonge, especially as the latter in his crazed ramblings was fond of blaming Blood for beginning the great fire of London.

When in January 1679 an Irish Catholic in the Marshalsea prison, James Netterville, revealed to a friend of Blood's, Arthur Bury, a scheme to turn the Popish Plot against the opposition and offered him a bribe of £500, Blood was in the background advising Bury to find out more about the plot. The information was passed on to Sir Joseph Williamson, though in the event Oates, William Bedloe, and Waller successfully intimidated Netterville, leaving Bury in the lurch. (This is Bury's version. Netterville's own account actually claimed that it was Blood himself rather than Bury whom he had spoken with and tried to bribe, only for Blood to tell all to Williamson.) Other schemes followed. Blood in these years was a useful agent of the secretariat, but his activities also put him in the public eye and made him a target for accusation. Blood certainly figured in the calculations of another informer, Thomas Dangerfield, author of the so-called Meal-Tub Plot (a Catholic attempt to undermine the advocates of the Popish Plot) who mentioned Blood as one of the major-generals in a possible rebel army. Blood subsequently investigated an alleged scheme for rebel commissions apparently engineered by Dangerfield to give his story credibility. In fact, during the course of the crisis of 1678–80, Blood seems to have cautiously placed himself on the side of the regime rather than with any of its whig opponents.

Downfall Blood had broken with Buckingham at some point in the late 1670s. The duke's reputation, both political and sexual, was already lavish in its indiscretions and in 1680 Blood became involved in a 'dirty tricks' plot, evidently at the behest of the king's fallen minister, Thomas Osborne, earl of Danby, to bring down the whig leader with a charge of sodomy. Blood and the earl's servant Edward Christian appear to have provided money to suborn witnesses to make the accusation. Two Irishmen, Philomen Coddan and Samuel Ryther, were to swear that the duke had committed sodomy on one Sarah Harwood and then sent her into France; further witnesses were found in Philip Le Mar and his mother, Frances Loveland. In the event the plot fell apart as the mud flew in all directions and the various parties attempted to make political capital out of the affair.

According to Coddan's version of events, he and another Irishman, Maurice Hickey (alias Higgins or Higges), had drawn Ryther into the conspiracy in exchange for copious amounts of drink and money, intending him to act as first witness to the charge with Coddan himself as second witness. When Ryther began to get frightened and uncooperative Thomas Curtis, who was working for Blood, entered the scheme, trying to stiffen Ryther's resolve with promises of money and the protection of great persons. At one of the many meetings that took place in the disreputable taverns and alehouses of London they were joined by Blood himself. Blood's association with many at court in the 1670s had given him links with the factions there as a special agent and 'gun for hire'. Despite his vociferous denials he was undoubtedly involved in the plot against Buckingham, apparently acting as a go-between for Edward Christian and the Irish witnesses. Taking Coddan to one side, Blood asked him what he would swear against the duke; anything they asked him to, came the reply. Blood used all the talents at persuasion which were so central to his *modus operandi*. He was cautious but affable to all, a trait he appears to have deliberately cultivated. In his intelligence work his preferred methods—the ones he thought would achieve the best results—seem to have been the quiet word, the delicate bribe, the drink, or the persuasive conversation rather than violence or the threat of violence.

Unfortunately for Blood the whole plot soon began to unravel. In the game of double bluff that followed Coddan and Ryther soon changed sides, revealing the plot to Buckingham's solicitor Mr Whitaker; Coddan reportedly said that 'we will do this rogue Blood's business for him and get enough to swear against him by [the] time Sir William Waller comes to town' (*The Narrative of the Design*, 14). On 20 January 1680 Waller sent for Blood. Neither man liked the other and Waller's over-zealous pursuit of the plot—including bribery and tampering with witnesses—was eventually to cost him his place on the bench. At the meeting Blood was faced by Waller, Coddan, and Ryther, Whitaker, and Francis Jenks, a Buckingham client and old enemy. Blood attempted to brazen the affair out; he also resisted arrest for a few days, but was eventually arrested and placed in the Gatehouse prison. The plotters were soon mopped up, and after a series of engineered delays on both sides Blood, Christian, Le Mar, Curtis, Hickey, and three others were tried at the king's bench on charges of blasphemy, confederacy, and subornation: all were found guilty, severely fined, and gaoled.

In prison Blood caught a fever and, eventually released in July 1680, left it a sick man. By 22 August, after making his will, Blood lapsed into a coma, and on 24 August 1680 he died at his home in Bowling Alley, Westminster, aged sixty-two. He was buried in Tothill Fields, Westminster. Even his death was regarded as some trickery; to quash the rumours the authorities were forced to exhume his body.

Assessment Thomas Blood was a strange mixture: deeply religious, a daring adventurer, a defender of nonconformity, and occasionally just plain greedy and untrustworthy. His career has few parallels in the period. Although his activities as plotter against, and then spy for, the regime of Charles II were not entirely untypical, his actions in the middle part of his life were quite unique. It was the trio of daring adventures between 1667 and 1671 that made Blood's name, yet his motivation remains obscure. He left no memoirs as such. His earliest biographer of 1680 appears to have had information either from Blood himself or from someone close to him; the work was signed by 'R. H.', possibly Richard Halliwell, Blood's accomplice in 1671. Blood's own correspondence is scarce, but the entries in the diary of deliverances seized in 1671 are very revealing. They are the products of nonconformist reflection and a belief in divine providence as it affected Blood's own life. Blood, a nonconformist who sought a Calvinist way to God, was more than just a one-dimensional adventurer: he was a man with a motive, a strong faith in God and in himself. This sustained him in his exploits, though even Thomas Blood was subject to self-doubt. He also possessed a strong streak of morality, claiming to avoid strong wine and drink, 'recreations, or pomps or execesse in apparele … quibling or jokeing … all obsene & scurulouse talke' (Bodl. Oxf., MS Rawl. A. 185, fol. 474). His double-sided morality is strikingly seen in his condemnation of the younger Thomas's activities as a highwayman for actions that the father had also used, but in another context. Common highway robbery was not, to Blood, at all like the conspiracy, treachery, kidnapping, possible murder, and violence in which he had engaged. Blood saw his own actions as a means to an end.

The raid on the crown jewels was thus not mere robbery, but possibly a slight against the monarchy by a republican rebel. Yet it was also rumoured that the act was merely mercenary, that Blood intended breaking up and selling the jewels. Edmund Ludlow was certainly puzzled by the affair and its result. The action did, however, raise Blood's reputation among his fellow nonconformists. They had, it was rumoured, disliked Blood's attack on Ormond: 'those congregations of nonconformists which … [Blood and his men] have formerly frequented abhor this fact, and would be glad to bring them to punishment if it were in their power' (Bodl. Oxf., MS Eng. hist. c.487, 1265). Blood may well have gambled that the spectacular seizure of the crown jewels would make him more acceptable to those he called 'God's people' (Bodl. Oxf., MS Rawl. A. 185, fol. 475). He may also have thought that the robbery would give him access to the king where he could plead both his and their cause. Blood was a man who thought on a grand scale.

Even so there was in Blood the element of the eccentric gambler. He was a man who delighted to perform deeds for their own sake: thus his frequent resort to tricks and elaborate disguises, the baroque planning of the schemes he became involved with. Ultimately Blood's motivation in such matters could well have been the delight of making 'a noise in the world' and to escape at the last minute with all the skill of an adventurer. This mix of elements therefore should be seen together to make up the motivation of this greatest of all seventeenth-century adventurers. ALAN MARSHALL

Sources R. H., 'Remarks on the life and death of the famed Mr. Blood', *A collection of scarce and valuable tracts … Lord Somers*, ed. W. Scott, 2nd edn, 8 (1812), 438–54 · *CSP Ire.*, *1663–5* · T. Blood, 'Deliverances since I was for the Lord's cause', Bodl. Oxf., MS Rawl. A. 185 · E. Ludlow, 'A voyce from the watch tower', Bodl. Oxf., MS Eng. hist. c. 487 · memoirs and narratives by Sir Gilbert Talbot, BL, Harley MS 6859, fols. 1–17 · Bodl. Oxf., MS Eng. lett. d. 37, fol. 84 · foreign entry book, PRO, SP 104/176, fol. 315 · *CSP dom.*, *1660–85* · *A true narrative of the late design of the papists to charge their horrid plot upon the protestants, by endeavouring to corrupt Captain Bury and Alderman Brooks of Dublin* (1679) · *The narrative of the design lately laid by Philip Le Mar and several others against his grace George, duke of Buckingham* (1680) · *True domestic intelligence* (1680) · W. C. Abbott, *Colonel Thomas Blood, crown stealer, 1618–1680* (1911) · M. Petherick, *Restoration rogues* (1951) · A. Marshall, *Intelligence and espionage in the reign of Charles II, 1660–1685* (1994) · *Reports on private collection no. 122*, NL Ire. [Blood Papers] · *Fourth report*, HMC, 3 (1874) · *Sixth report*, HMC, 5 (1877–8) · *Seventh report*, HMC, 6 (1879) · *Eighth report*, 3 vols. in 5, HMC, 7 (1881–1910) · *Ninth report*, 3 vols., HMC, 8 (1883–4) · *A list of officers claiming to the sixty thousand pounds granted by his sacred majesty, for the relief of the truly loyal and indigent party* (1663) · *The horrid conspiracie of such impenitent traytors as intended a new rebellion in the kingdom of Ireland: with a list of prisoners, and the particular manner of seizing Dublin-Castle by Ludlow, and his accomplices* (1663) · R. North, *The lives of … Francis North … Dudley North … and … John North*, ed. A. Jessopp, 3 vols. (1890) · T. Carte, *An history of the life of James, duke of Ormonde*, 3 vols. (1735–6) · *CSP Venice*, *1666–80* · Evelyn, *Diary* · will, PRO, PROB 11/364, fols. 123–4

Archives Bodl. Oxf., MS Rawl. A. 185

Likenesses attrib. G. Soest, oils, 1670–80, NPG · G. Scott, line engraving, pubd 1804 (after unknown artist), NPG · G. White, mezzotint, BM, NPG · G. White, mezzotint (modern impression), BM, NPG · chalk drawing, Magd. Cam., Pepys Library [*see illus.*] · prints, NPG · wash drawings, Magd. Cam., Pepys Library

Wealth at death 'small temporal estate'; he had been bailed from gaol at a considerable sum and seemed to lack funds; the references in will to goods and chattels are not specified further; presumed he was living in poverty towards end of his life: will, PRO, PROB 11/364, fols. 123–4

Bloodworth, James (*c.*1760–1804), architect in Australia, was probably born in Middlesex. Nothing is known of his childhood and early adulthood until in 1785, in his mid-twenties, he was convicted of an unknown felony at Kingston upon Thames and sentenced to seven years' transportation. He was then a master builder's assistant, and possessed of a thorough grounding in contemporary design and construction in brick, stone, and wood. He arrived in New South Wales aboard the *Charlotte* in the first convict fleet in January 1788. Governor Arthur Phillip, who had not been permitted to bring any free architect or builder with the expedition, asked Bloodworth to take charge of all the colony's architectural design and construction projects, giving him the title of master bricklayer to the settlement. Almost immediately Bloodworth began living with Sarah Bellamy (*b*. 1770), a convict from Worcester, who had arrived on the *Lady Penrhyn*. In the following month Bellamy gave birth to a son, Joseph, who had been fathered by a sailor on the ship, but the baby died nine days later. Her relationship with Bloodworth was to produce at least three daughters and a son.

After only two years of his sentence Bloodworth was pardoned by Phillip as a mark of gratitude for his architectural work. Although free to return to England, Bloodworth signed an agreement to serve the governor for a further two years in exchange for clothing, food, and other necessities.

Bloodworth designed the mass-produced wooden convict houses, the impressive neo-Palladian brick governor's mansion (occupied from 1789, but remaining only half-completed until its demolition in 1845), his own house next to the governor's mansion, the stone King's Warehouse, the wooden hospital, Surgeon-General White's residence, Major Ross's house, and other early Sydney buildings—but no church. Away from Sydney he designed the auxiliary government houses at Parramatta and Norfolk Island, again within the first two years of his arrival. Later, he oversaw further building work in Sydney, Parramatta, and Toongabbie, but twice declined to oversee construction for Lieutenant-Governor Collins at Port Dalrymple and the Derwent.

Bloodworth made good use of poor building materials, making mortar from burnt shells and mud, and structural timber out of the wattle tree. Most of his designs were simple but well proportioned. His work was not up to date with leading British designs, but his provincial neo-Palladianism can be compared with houses by James Paine and with contemporary North American designs. Unfortunately, all of his buildings have long since been destroyed. Bloodworth is also believed to have drawn the first great seal for New South Wales, which was however somewhat altered in London before being granted.

Phillip granted Bloodworth 50 acres on Petersham Hill, where he built himself a country house by 1795. He subsequently acquired a further 175 acres there (including 20 that Phillip granted to Sarah), and by 1802 35 acres were cleared and 10 acres were devoted to growing wheat and maize. In the same year Bloodworth was chosen by townspeople as a sergeant in the Sydney Loyal Association, a militia formed by free settlers and emancipated men to help combat French invasion or rebellion by disaffected Irish convicts.

Bloodworth also served as master and superintendent of bricklayers in the Sydney area until his resignation at the beginning of 1804 over pay levels, but in a few days he was reinstated. Shortly after, however, he caught pneumonia and died at his home, Bloodworth farm, Petersham Hill, in March 1804. The Sydney Loyal Association escorted Bloodworth's body to the town's cemetery, where he was buried with much pomp and full military honours. For some unknown reason Bloodworth died insolvent, so Sarah, whom he never married, moved to Sydney with their children, where she was last noted as living on Clarence Street in 1828. JOHN FITZHUGH MILLAR

Sources D. Chapman, *1788: the people of the first fleet* (1981) · J. F. Millar, *A handbook on the founding of Australia, 1788* (1988)

Wealth at death insolvent, in spite of 225-acre farm: Chapman, *1788*

Bloom, Ursula Harvey (1892–1984), writer, was born on 11 December 1892 in Springfield, Chelmsford, Essex, the only daughter of James Harvey Bloom, a Church of England clergyman, and Mary Gardner (*d*. *c*.1915), both from Norfolk families. Her mother, whom Ursula called Polly, left her philandering husband just before the First World War, moving Ursula and her younger brother, Joscelyn, from the rectory at Whitchurch near Stratford upon Avon, Warwickshire, to less comfortable circumstances at St Albans, Hertfordshire. Ursula was self-educated and at seven privately published her first book, *Tiger*. She was taught the piano and violin, and first worked as a cinema pianist to help support her family.

On 14 November 1916 Bloom married Captain Arthur Brownlow Denham-Cookes (*b*. 1890/91) of the 24th London regiment, who died in 1918 of influenza; they had one son, Philip. Her first novel was *The Great Beginning* (1924), and in the following year she began her normal output of two books annually. On 28 November 1925 she married Commander Charles Gower Robinson RN. In the 1930s she became a crime reporter for the *Empire News* and *Sunday Dispatch*, then a feature writer for the *Sunday Pictorial* and beauty editor of *Woman's Own*. She also wrote 'agony aunt' columns.

Bloom was disciplined in her writing, striving for 10,000 words a day, and in her life, neither smoking nor drinking, and in 1937 joining George Bernard Shaw to support Gymnosophist societies that promoted nudity. Bloom began to have migraines in the 1940s when living in Malta, where her husband was stationed, and spent considerable time in hospitals seeking a cure. This experience was recounted in *No Lady in Bed* (1944) and led to several hospital novels under the pseudonyms Sheila Burns and Rachel Harvey. She wrote four stage plays in the 1940s and several radio plays in the 1960s.

In all, Bloom published some 560 books (she was once in the *Guinness Book of Records* as the world's most prolific female writer). These were mostly atmospheric romances that were insignificant but inventive and well constructed with a fluent, readable style. She admitted to being not romantically inclined, and thought her romantic novels were silly and light. She wrote them variously under her real name and as Sheila Burns. Most novels had emotive titles, such as *Love is Everything* (1933), *The Tides of Spring Flow Fast* (1955), and *Perchance to Dream* (1971). As Mary Essex, Bloom wrote modern romances, and as Lozania Prole she produced historical novels beginning with *Our Dearest Emma* (1949), based on the life of Emma Hamilton. She also wrote two slightly inaccurate biographies of her parents, recounting her father's life in *Parson Extraordinary* (1963) and her mother's in *Price above Rubies* (1965). Her seven autobiographies and memoirs included *Mistress of None* (1933), *Rosemary for Stratford-on-Avon* (1966), *A Roof and Four Walls* (1967), and *Life is No Fairy Tale* (1976). Her non-fiction included biographies such as *Hitler's Eva* (1954) and *The Duke of Windsor* (1972), and books on various subjects like religion, careers, needlework (for which she was noted), cookery, and beauty.

Bloom's second husband died in 1979, the year in which she wrote her last novel: the optimistic *Sweet Spring of April*. She died on 29 October 1984 at the Winton Nursing Home, Nether Wallop, Hampshire. JOHN D. WRIGHT

Sources *Annual obituary, 1984* (1985) · *The Times* (31 Oct 1984) · *WWW, 1981–1990* (1991) · *The world who's who of women* (1978) · d. cert.
Archives BBC WAC, letters and radio scripts
Wealth at death £86,872: probate, 24 Jan 1985, *CGPLA Eng. & Wales*

Bloomer, Stephen (1874–1938), footballer, was born at Bridge Street, Cradley, Worcestershire, on 20 January 1874, the son of Caleb Bloomer, an iron puddler, and his wife, Merab Dunn. The family moved to Derby when Bloomer was five. He learned to play football at elementary school where, although not formally part of the curriculum, the game had been introduced by enthusiastic young teachers. He played local recreational football and was signed by Derby County, at a wage of 7*s*. 6*d*. a week, after scoring four goals in one match for their reserves. He was to be the club's leading scorer for fourteen seasons. Yet he did not look the part of the athlete. Harry Newbould, secretary of the Derby club in the 1890s, said that when Bloomer first turned out for them he was 'pale, thin, ghost-like, almost ill-looking' and some of the crowd laughed when they first saw him (Rippon, *Derbyshire Life*, 61). But he was strengthened by the regular training which the Derby club had recently introduced. In his second full season Bloomer's nineteen goals helped Derby to third place in the first division, the highest the club had achieved. By 1895 he was scoring spectacular goals for England.

Before 1914 football heroes were essentially local, their prized qualities loyalty, reliability, and steadiness. Professional footballers were part of the urban social fabric. The Football Association (FA) cup final drew the biggest crowds and it was the competition between clubs which fed parochial and civic pride and provided the players with some hard-won celebrity. Every town had its football team and every club its local heroes and Steve Bloomer was one of them. Although he spent four seasons late in his career with Middlesbrough, Bloomer was synonymous with Derby County, for whom he played from 1892 to 1906 and again from 1910 until his retirement at the age of forty in January 1914. He played 474 league games for Derby, scoring 293 goals, and 50 FA cup ties with another 38 goals.

Stephen Bloomer (1874–1938), by W. H. King, *c*.1905

He also scored 28 goals in 23 international appearances for England, a record which remained unbroken until 1956.

Contemporaries were particularly impressed by his speed off the mark, which was allied to a rare ability to shoot straight, with both feet and from any angle or distance and, crucially, with little backlift and using the boot close to the toe rather than the instep. It was this element of surprise which enabled Bloomer to get in shots at goal where others could not. He was not a great dribbler but an inside right who could not only bring his wing partner into the game but also provide the penetrative through pass for the centre forward. Ivan Sharpe, who played with him, thought he had 'rare judgement, inspired raiding and passing and sudden shooting' (Sharpe, 22).

Bloomer tended to be impatient with the faults of more ordinary footballers and would point out their shortcomings, both on the field and off, in blunt and pungent terms. That his professional life was not without its frustrations is also suggested by the number of times he was admonished by the Derby board of directors for insobriety and neglect of training. He was almost certainly one of those players who lost money when the maximum wage was introduced in 1901, which could hardly have improved his attitude.

In common with many other professional footballers of his era, Bloomer did not find life after football easy. It was his bad luck to have accepted the position of coach to the Britannia sports club in Berlin in 1914. He arrived three weeks before war broke out and stayed for another three and three-quarter years as an internee in the notorious Ruhleben camp, where he helped organize the sporting competitions which did so much to maintain morale among the inmates.

In the 1920s Bloomer coached briefly in Canada and Spain and had jobs with Derby County and British Celanese. He also did some football reporting for local newspapers. He and his wife had four daughters, two of whom died in early childhood. His wife died in 1935.

Bloomer's own health deteriorated in the 1930s, when he suffered from asthma and bronchitis. In 1938 a group of local sportsmen raised £500 to send him on a cruise. He died three weeks after his return, on 16 April 1938, at the Great Northern inn, Junction Street, Derby, the home of his daughter and son-in-law. His funeral on 20 April was spectacular, the cathedral packed with admirers from the world of football, and large crowds lined the route from there to the Nottingham Road cemetery.

Although his football career was spent mainly playing for Derby, where he lived for most of his life, Steve Bloomer was one of the first footballers to be recognized as a national sporting figure. In 1904 he had been selected for England for the twenty-first time, then a record. The FA presented him with a portrait of himself, in oils, to mark the occasion, a unique honour for a football player, although Bloomer might have preferred money. He was one of the small number of professional footballers to be included in Burke's *Who's Who in Sport* (1922). More recently, in 1994 his grandson sold nineteen of his international caps for £8050 in order to fund a commemorative plinth which now stands in the Fishmarket in Derby and marks the goal-scoring achievements of a man whose name will always be linked with the town.

TONY MASON

Sources A. Rippon and A. Ward, *The Derby County story, 1884–1991* (1991) • A. Rippon, 'Steve Bloomer', *Derbyshire Life and Countryside*, 49 (Sept 1984) • I. Sharpe, *40 years in football* (1952) • A. Mason, 'Our Stephen and our Harold: Edwardian footballers as local heroes', *European heroes: myth, identity, sport*, ed. R. Holt, J. A. Mangan, and P. Lanfranchi (1996) • minutes of meetings of the board of directors, Derby County FC, 1898–1902, Derby County football club • *Derby Evening Telegraph* (16 April 1938) • *Derby Evening Telegraph* (20 April 1938) • *Evening Telegraph* [Derby] (26 Oct 1994) • A. Gibson and W. Pickford, *Association football and the men who made it*, 4 vols. [1905–6], vol. 4 • J. Davidson Ketchum, *Ruhleben: a prison camp society* (1965) • b. cert. • d. cert. • P. Barnsley, 'Steve Bloomer', *The Blackcountryman*, 22/3 (1989), 25–31 • P. Barnsley, 'The Steve Bloomer memorial', *The Blackcountryman*, 30/2 (1997), 29–30

Likenesses W. H. King, photograph, *c.*1905, repro. in *Derby Evening Telegraph* [*see illus.*]

Bloomfield, Benjamin, **first Baron Bloomfield (1768–1846)**, army officer and courtier, the only son of John Bloomfield, of Newport, co. Tipperary, a lieutenant in the Grenadier Guards, and his wife, Anne (*d.* 1828), daughter of Samuel Waller, barrister, and sister of Sir Robert Waller, baronet, was born at Bloomfield Lodge, Newport, on 13 April 1768. He entered the Royal Military Academy, Woolwich, in 1779 and became second lieutenant in the Royal Artillery, at the age of thirteen, on 24 May 1781. Early in his military career he served in Newfoundland and at Gibraltar. He was one of the first officers appointed to the horse artillery. He also served on a gun-brig during the early part of the French Revolutionary War, and commanded some guns at Vinegar Hill during the Irish uprising of 1798. He married, on 7 September 1797, Harriott (*d.* 12 Sept 1868, aged ninety-two), the eldest daughter of John Douglas, of Grantham, Lincolnshire; they had one son, John Arthur Douglas *Bloomfield, diplomatist, and three daughters.

About 1806, when Bloomfield was serving as brevet major and captain of a troop of horse artillery with the 10th hussars at Brighton (and, according to his biographer, a poor man), his social and musical attainments attracted the prince of Wales, who in 1812 made him a gentleman attendant and afterwards, from 1812 to 1817, his chief equerry and clerk marshal. Earlier, when acting as the prince's spymaster against the princess of Wales in 1810, he was described by an enemy as 'a canting methodistical hypocrite, always talking religion and morality, but living, though a married man, in barefaced adultery with Lady Downshire' (HoP, *Commons*, 3.222). He was aide-de-camp from 1811 to 1814 and from 1812 to 1818 was MP for Plymouth, where the prince had electoral interest and a succession of 'Carlton House men' were returned. He supported the tory government, opposed Catholic relief, and in 1818 vacated his seat, presumably at the prince's command, to accommodate another of his favourites, Sir William Congreve, second baronet. In 1814 he was promoted major-general, and in 1815 he was made KCH. He was auditor and secretary of the duchy of Cornwall in 1816–17. From 1817 to 1822, as private secretary to the prince regent, he was the recognized confidant of the prince with considerable (some ministers thought unconstitutional) influence and power. He fell from favour in 1822 and resigned his appointments. His fall was attributed largely to the machinations of Sir William Knighton and the king's mistress, Lady Conyngham, though there was also talk of embezzlement from the privy purse. Cynical observers said he knew too much and, though his demands for a UK peerage were refused, he was generously compensated with a civil GCB (April 1822), a promise of an Irish peerage, a pension, two sinecures, and a diplomatic post. From 1822 to 1832 Bloomfield was minister-plenipotentiary to Stockholm, and while in Sweden he joined the Wesleyan connexion. In May 1825 he was raised to the Irish peerage as Baron Bloomfield of Oakhampton and Redwood, co. Tipperary. He commanded the garrison at Woolwich for some years, where his hospitality and benevolence made him popular, and where he founded the schools for the children of soldiers of the ordnance corps.

Following a lengthy, painful illness Bloomfield died at Portman Square, London, on 15 August 1846 and was buried at Loughton, King's county, on the 22nd. He was succeeded by his only son, John Arthur Douglas Bloomfield (1802–1879), a diplomat, who was in 1871 created Baron Bloomfield of Ciamhaltha in the UK peerage; at his death his peerages became extinct. His wife, Georgiana, published a two-volume *Memoir* (1884) of his father. In 1856 a tract was published, *A coronet laid at the feet of Jesus: as illustrated by the conversion of the late Lord Bloomfield*, by G. Scott, a Wesleyan minister.

H. M. CHICHESTER, *rev.* ROGER T. STEARN

Sources *Memoir of Benjamin Lord Bloomfield*, ed. G. Bloomfield, 2 vols. (1884) • HoP, *Commons* • *GM*, 2nd ser., 26 (1846), 422–4 • G. Scott, *A coronet laid at the feet of Jesus: as illustrated by the conversion of the late Lord Bloomfield* (1856) • *Army List* (1791–1838) • P. H. Fitzgerald, *The life of George the Fourth*, 2 vols. (1881) • GEC, *Peerage* • Burke, *Peerage* • d. cert.

Archives PRO, letter-books • Royal Armouries, The Waterfront, Leeds, court sword | BL, corresp. with J. W. Croker, Add. MSS 52470–52471, *passim* • BL, letters to Lord Hertford, Egerton MS 3262 • BL, corresp. with Prince Lieven, Add. MS 47258 • BL, corresp. with the earl of Liverpool, Add. MSS 38262–38290, 38565–38574, *passim* • BL, letters to earl of Liverpool, loan 72 • Cumbria AS, Carlisle, letters to first Earl Lonsdale • NRA Scotland, priv. coll., corresp. with William Adam • RA, corresp. with Thomas Lawrence • TCD, corresp. with Lord Donoughmore • U. Southampton L., corresp. with Palmerston

Likenesses C. Turner, mezzotint, pubd 1819 (after T. C. Thompson), BM • F. P. Stephanoff or J. Stephanoff, drawing, 19 July 1821, V&A • C. Turner, mezzotint, pubd 1829 (after T. Lawrence), BM • E. McInnes, mezzotint, pubd 1844 (after J. Lilley), BM

Bloomfield [*née* Liddell], **Georgiana**, **Lady Bloomfield** (**1822–1905**), courtier and author, born on 13 April 1822 at 51 Portland Place, Marylebone, Middlesex, was the sixteenth and youngest child of Thomas Henry Liddell, first Baron Ravensworth (1775–1885), and his wife, Maria Susannah (*c*.1773–1845), daughter of John Simpson of Bradley Hall, co. Durham. She was educated at home, and in December 1841 became maid of honour to Queen Victoria, resigning in July 1845 prior to her marriage on 4 September 1845 at Lamesley Chapel, co. Durham, to John Arthur Douglas *Bloomfield, second Baron Bloomfield. She accompanied her husband on his diplomatic missions, going to St Petersburg in the month following her marriage, and thence to Berlin (1851–60), and to Vienna (1861–71). There were no children of the marriage, and after her husband's death at his home, Ciamhaltha, Newport, co. Tipperary, in 1879, Lady Bloomfield settled at Shrivenham, in Berkshire, to be near her sister, Jane Elizabeth, widow of the sixth Viscount Barrington. When Lady Barrington died on 22 March 1883, Lady Bloomfield moved to Bramfield House, about 2 miles from Hertford. Here she exercised much hospitality and interested herself in the affairs of the village.

In 1883 she published *Reminiscences of Court and Diplomatic Life* (2 vols.), a lively account of her 'official' career, and in 1884 she edited a *Memoir of Benjamin, Lord Bloomfield*, her father-in-law, in two volumes. Her last work, *Gleanings of a Long Life* (1902), collected extracts from her favourite books. A *grande dame* of the old school, she was deeply religious, tolerant, and charitable. She founded in 1874 the Trained Nurses' Annuity Fund, and built and endowed almshouses on her husband's estate in co. Tipperary. She sketched well in water colours, and her sketches formed a sort of diary of her journeys. She was an accomplished musician, playing the organ; was a good billiard player; and an excellent gardener.

Lady Bloomfield died, after a long illness, at Bramfield House, Hertfordshire, on 21 May 1905, and was buried in the family mausoleum beside her husband in the churchyard of Borrisnafarney, King's county, Ireland.

ELIZABETH LEE, *rev.* K. D. REYNOLDS

Sources GEC, *Peerage* • Lady Bloomfield [G. Bloomfield], *Reminiscences of court and diplomatic life* (1883) • W. A. Lindsay, *The royal household* (1898) • *The Times* (23 May 1905)

Wealth at death £58,144 1*s*. 2*d*.: probate, 29 June 1905, *CGPLA Eng. & Wales*

Bloomfield, John Arthur Douglas, **second Baron Bloomfield and first Baron Bloomfield of Ciamhaltha** (**1802–1879**), diplomatist, was the son of Benjamin *Bloomfield, first Baron Bloomfield (1768–1846), army officer, and his wife, Harriott Douglas (1775/6–1868). He was born on 12 November 1802, and educated privately; at the early age of sixteen he became an attaché to the embassy at Vienna. Throughout his life he remained in the diplomatic service, and his history consists of little more than a list of the places where he served his country. He was paid attaché at Lisbon, from October 1824; secretary of legation at Stuttgart, from December 1825, and at Stockholm, from September 1826; and secretary of embassy at St Petersburg, from June 1839. He served as envoy-extraordinary and minister-plenipotentiary to the court of St Petersburg from 3 April 1844, and then moved in the same capacity to Berlin, on 28 April 1851. He was made ambassador-extraordinary and -plenipotentiary to the emperor of Austria on 22 November 1860, but resigned on 28 October 1871, when he retired on a pension and was created Baron Bloomfield of Ciamhaltha in the UK peerage.

Bloomfield married, on 4 September 1845, the Hon. Georgiana (1822–1905), sixteenth and youngest child of Thomas Henry Liddell, first Baron Ravensworth [*see* Bloomfield, Georgiana]. He succeeded his father as second Baron Bloomfield in the peerage of Ireland on 15 August 1846. He played no active role in politics, but was associated with the Liberals. He was made a CB in 1848, KCB in 1851, and GCB on 3 September 1858, and was sworn of the privy council on 17 December 1860. He died childless at his residence, Ciamhaltha, Newport, co. Tipperary, on 17 August 1879.

G. C. BOASE, *rev.* H. C. G. MATTHEW

Sources *FO List* (1879) • Boase, *Mod. Eng. biog.*

Archives PRO, corresp. and papers | BL, corresp. with Lord Aberdeen, Add. MS 43144 • BL, corresp. with Sir Austen Layard, Add. MSS 39102–39120, *passim* • BL, corresp. with Lord Westmorland, M/528/1, 516/1, 526/3 [microfilm] • Bodl. Oxf., corresp. with fourth earl of Clarendon • Bodl. Oxf., letters to Sir John Crampton • Bodl. Oxf., letters to Lord Kimberley • Hants. RO, corresp. with earl of Malmesbury • Notts. Arch., corresp. with John Saville • PRO, corresp. with Lord John Russell, PRO 30/22 • PRO, corresp. with Odo Russell, FO 918 • U. Nott. L., letters to Sir Andrew Buchanan • U. Southampton L., corresp. with Lord Palmerston

Likenesses T. Lawrence, oils, 1819, NPG • G. Cook, stipple, NPG • F. Sargent, pencil, NPG

Wealth at death under £70,000: probate, 4 Oct 1879, *CGPLA Eng. & Wales*

Bloomfield, Robert (**1766–1823**), poet, was born on 3 December 1766 at Honington, a village in Suffolk, the son of George Bloomfield (*d*. 1767), a village tailor, and Elizabeth Manby (*d*. 1803), schoolmistress at Honington. His father died of smallpox when Robert was a year old and left the family of three boys and three girls penniless. His mother augmented her earnings from her position as

Robert Bloomfield (1766–1823), by Henry Edridge, *c*.1805

schoolmistress by spinning wool, but the family struggled. It was mainly under his mother's tutelage that Bloomfield learned to read and write at an early age, though he did spend three months in 1772 learning to write from a Mr Rodwell of Ixworth. Bloomfield's early reading included Thomas Gray's *Elegy Written in a Country Churchyard* and Oliver Goldsmith's *The Deserted Village*, both of which were to influence him greatly in his own poetic compositions.

Before Bloomfield turned seven, his mother married a man named John Glover, and additional children appeared on the scene, crowding even further the already cramped house. In or about 1778 Bloomfield was sent to his mother's brother-in-law, William Austin of Sapiston, who worked a farm in the manor of the duke of Grafton, who would later become Bloomfield's patron. Though assuming the humble position of 'farmer's boy' on his uncle's farm, he was treated decently, and details of his uncle's benevolence, as well as nostalgia for this period of his life, in which he experienced his first intimacy with nature, are present in *The Farmer's Boy*. It became apparent by the time Bloomfield was fifteen, however, that, owing to his slight build (even in his maturity, Bloomfield was barely 5 feet tall), he was not cut out for the rigours of farm labour, and so Austin advised Bloomfield's mother to find him a situation more suited to his physical capabilities.

London Bloomfield's mother turned to her eldest sons, George and Nathaniel (the latter of whom, in a bid to capitalize on his younger brother's notoriety, also tried his hand at poetry, though with little success), then living in London, who offered to take their younger brother into their charge. It was decided that George, a shoemaker, would take in Robert and teach him the trade, while Nathaniel, a tailor, would provide the neophyte cobbler with clothing. Accordingly, on 29 June 1781, Bloomfield and his mother completed the stagecoach trip to London, where he was left in his brothers' keeping. Thus Bloomfield lived for a time with his brother George and four other cobblers in a small, low-rent garret (which also doubled as their workshop) at 7 Pitcher's Court, Bell Alley, Coleman Street. There he began learning to make shoes but earned his keep mainly by running errands and reading the newspaper aloud to the others while they worked. After he complained that he did not understand many of the words he was reading, George bought him a used dictionary, which greatly aided him in his mission to educate himself. He also enthusiastically attended the popular Sunday evening lectures of a dissenting minister, the Revd Mr Fawcet, who held forth weekly to standing room only audiences at a meeting-house in the Old Jewry.

About 1783, apparently unsettled by the epileptic fits of a new lodger at Pitcher's Court, Robert and George decamped and took up residence at Blue Hart Court, Bell Alley. Another lodger there, James Kay generously lent Robert a number of books, among them *Paradise Lost* and James Thomson's *The Seasons*, the latter of which became his favourite reading material. Over the years Bloomfield developed a prodigious memory for poetry and could recite any passage from *The Seasons* or Thomson's *The Castle of Indolence*, as well as large swathes of Burns.

In 1784, fearing prosecution by the Committee of the Lawful Crafts for illegally cobbling without having been officially apprenticed, Bloomfield fled back to the sanctuary of his uncle Austin's farm. During this period Bloomfield fell in love with a woman from Broadmere named Nancy Bantock, but the relationship did not work out, and Bantock eventually married a local man.

Despite ongoing legal difficulties Bloomfield returned to London after a two-month retreat and managed to finagle a quasi-legal standing as a cobbler by paying 5*s*. to John Dudbridge, who acted as his pro forma journey master. By 1786 Bloomfield was a skilled enough shoemaker to make his own way, and his brother George left London.

It was also about this time that the earliest evidence that Bloomfield was composing poetry surfaces. Poems that he had apparently composed in his mind while engaged in cobbling and later copied down were dispatched to the *London Magazine* for publication in the 'Poet's corner', but his earliest published poem, 'A Village Girl', appeared in Mary Say's *Gazetter* for 24 May 1786. Bloomfield also acquired a violin and a taste for music. In an act rich with symbolism for a nature poet living during the Romantic period, he also began hand-crafting aeolian harps, an avocation which eventually afforded him a small income. He actually once sold an aeolian harp of his own manufacture to James Montgomery.

Within four years, however, Bloomfield wrote to his brother George that he 'had sold his Fiddle and got a Wife' (Lofft, xiii). On 12 December 1790 Bloomfield married Mary-Anne Church, the daughter of a shipbuilder from Woolwich. Their first child, Hannah, was born on 25 October 1791. In the following year the Bloomfields took up residence at 14 Bell Alley, Coleman Street, where the growing family lived and struggled to make ends meet for the next seven years.

The Farmer's Boy In May 1796 Bloomfield began composing a poem that he at first intended only to be a present for his mother, but which eventually grew into *The Farmer's Boy*, the poem on which his reputation as a minor poet of the period chiefly rests. Like Thomson's *The Seasons*, *The Farmer's Boy* (nearly 1500 lines in heroic couplets) is divided into four parts, with each part corresponding to one of the seasons. It depicts the experiences of Giles, a young farm boy, as he does his chores and communes with nature. After three publishers in London had rejected the work (even when, after the first rejection, Bloomfield offered to underwrite the publication costs), Bloomfield gave up trying to get the poem published and presented the manuscript to his brother George for his personal enjoyment and that of his friends. In November 1798, however, George showed the manuscript to Capel Lofft, the radical editor and writer and a prominent figure in Suffolk society, who liked it well enough to make grammatical and orthographical amendments to the text and shepherd the poem into print along with his own evaluative preface. The publishers Vernor and Hood agreed to publish *The Farmer's Boy*, but it did not begin to appear in shops until March 1800. It was immediately popular and even achieved critical success, such as Bloomfield never managed to achieve with subsequent works. It brought him to the attention of Robert Southey, who gave the book a favourable review and who remained Bloomfield's greatest champion among the Romantics. Given his predominant themes of nature and the common man, it is also understandable that William Wordsworth and Samuel Taylor Coleridge initially reacted with plaudits (in 1802 Coleridge reckoned Bloomfield among the major contemporary poets), but this laudatory reception lapsed over the years into indifference. Other authors of the period, such as Lord Byron and Charles Lamb, were less than charitable in their assessments of his poetic worth. In any event, the success of *The Farmer's Boy* thrust the cobbler-poet into a limelight which proved to be simultaneously gratifying and irksome to a man who was by nature modest and retiring. Though he was initially circumspect about the income to be derived from the poem's publication, it was difficult for Bloomfield not to imagine that a better life for him and his family was at hand.

After a brief respite, however, Bloomfield continued to experience financial difficulties, exacerbated by the demands his celebrity placed on his time. Sitting for portraits, visiting in high society, and otherwise satisfying the public's curiosity about his person and poem detracted from the time he spent cobbling, which was still his main source of income. Though he contemplated other occupations, none of these came to fruition and by September 1801 he was forced to apply for an advance from his publishers. Luckily, however, Bloomfield had continued to write during this period, and though he was caught up in a messy quarrel between his then patron Capel Lofft and his publishers, and suffering from rheumatism and the recurrence of a stomach ailment, his financial prospects seemed excellent as his *Rural Tales, Ballads, and Songs* went to press in the autumn of 1801 and new editions of *The Farmer's Boy* continued to come out. *Rural Tales* contains shorter poems in various metres, mostly vignettes and lyrics depicting the joys and vicissitudes of rural life and the folk ways of villagers. The themes may be compared to those in the poems by George Crabbe or even Wordsworth, taking common folk and their lives for their subject matter. This was a trend Bloomfield continued in much of his other poetry.

In addition to his income from his two books, his cobbling, and his manufacture of aeolian harps, Bloomfield also began to receive an annuity of £15 from the duke of Grafton. Characteristically, Bloomfield generously shared his income with his brother George and his mother. Bloomfield's good financial fortunes seemed to wax even further when in late 1802 the duke of Grafton appointed him to the position of undersealer in the king's bench court. But Bloomfield, who always craved more peaceful surroundings, found the hustle and bustle of the court noxious and resolved in the spring of 1803 to resign his post at the seal office.

Bloomfield's mother died at the end of 1803, and Bloomfield's extraordinary generosity to her heirs and his stepfather, as well as expenditures on his mother's care in her decline and her funeral again landed him in financial difficulties. Bloomfield was also coping at this time with the illness of his son Charles, who had issued into the world about the same time as *The Farmer's Boy*. Charles had developed a swelling on his knee and suffered from convulsions, a condition that lingered over the following three years and left the boy disabled. His son's illness had a profound impact on Bloomfield and he resolved to do what he could to keep his family healthy. Bloomfield, who had befriended Dr Edward Jenner, had for some time been interested in Jenner's controversial smallpox vaccine. When his brother Nathaniel lost a third child in 1802 to the disease which had also killed their father, Bloomfield decided to have his family inoculated. He even championed Jenner's cause in a poem at once didactic and melodramatic called 'Good Tidings', which was published in 1804, but did not do well.

In 1806 Bloomfield published a new book of poems dedicated to his by then disabled son, entitled *Wild Flowers, or, Pastoral and Local Poetry*. Also published in the same year was a book of illustrations of Suffolk by the engravers Storer and Grieg, whose interest in the region was inspired by Bloomfield's poetry. In 1807 Bloomfield went on a rejuvenating ten-day tour along the Wye with Mr and Mrs Thomas J. Baker and others from Gloucestershire. Mightily impressed with the mountainous countryside and delighted with his companions, Bloomfield kept a poetical journal of his experiences during this expedition. He worked in fits and starts over the next three years polishing and expanding what he had begun in the journal and it was finally published in 1811 as *The Banks of the Wye: a Poem*.

Financial difficulties and final years Despite the cheer brought by the publication of *The Banks of the Wye* and its initial commercial success, in keeping with the pattern his life had taken on, Bloomfield was beset with other sadnesses and difficulties. First, there was the death of his patron the old duke of Grafton, who was succeeded by his son Lord Charles Fitzroy. The new duke of Grafton did not share his father's enthusiasm for cobbler-poets, and

Bloomfield had to enlist the services of Capel Lofft to petition the new duke for his £15 annuity, which Fitzroy eventually granted but was thereafter sometimes desultory in supplying. The second blow came when Mr Hood, the most active member of Bloomfield's publishers, died, and the business passed into the hands of another partner, named, appropriately enough, Sharpe. By 1812 Sharpe had brought the firm near to bankruptcy and decided to bail out. He sold 4500 copies of Bloomfield's books to another bookseller and although he received £509 and a line of credit for himself, he refused to give Bloomfield his due. The Bloomfield family, now consisting of five children, was forced to borrow money, leave the expensive city, and retire to Shefford in Bedfordshire. Bloomfield returned to London in October 1812 to attend to his business matters, and although he was eventually able to secure an advance from Crosby, the bookseller to whom Sharpe had sold Bloomfield's lot, Bloomfield was by this time disgusted with the publishing business; he wrote a letter saying as much to his family, and signed it 'Your cheated and bamboozled Father' (*Selections*, 55). Nor was London conducive to the production of poetry, for in another letter he complained, 'I can write only as Rabbits *S—t*, in little bits, for the cart wheels roar, and the waiters are noisy, and there is a chimney on fire within sight, and a brave crowd' (BL, Add. MS 28268, fols. 330–331).

Despite numerous journeys to London, efforts over the next few years to secure revenues from the sales and copyrights of his books were not very successful, and the Bloomfield family suffered for it. In 1814 Bloomfield's daughter Mary Anne died. In the next year, Bloomfield was forced to find Charles an apprenticeship and also placed Charlotte at a milliner's. The publication of a children's book, *The History of Little Davy's New Hat*, did not bring much relief, and the Bloomfields were forced to move to a less expensive house. By 1816 Bloomfield's health, never robust, was failing, and his financial distress so great that it prompted Sir Samuel Egerton Brydges and other supporters to issue a subscription on his behalf. This small income, along with what the duke of Grafton begrudgingly supplied, was augmented when in 1817 Bloomfield found Charles a position as a schoolmaster, and the Bloomfield family were able to pay off some debts. Bloomfield was thereby able to resume with renewed enthusiasm a project that he had begun years before and which culminated in the 1822 publication of *May-Day with the Muses*, the last of his books published while he was still alive. Hearing that George Crabbe had been handsomely paid by the publisher Murray for his *Tales*, Bloomfield tried in the spring of 1820 to place *May-Day* with Murray. Murray, however, declined to publish the book, and Bloomfield was forced to go with the publishers Baldwin, Cradock, and Joy.

Bloomfield was also contending in the last years of his life with attacks on his reputation. He had heard a report from Thomas Baker that rumours concerning his political and religious beliefs and his associates were in circulation—rumours which might estrange the poet's patrons and conservative audience. In short, he was rumoured to be 'Deistical and Republican' in outlook (BL, Add. MS 28268, fols. 415–416). Baker even went so far as to solicit from Bloomfield a direct and public denial of such charges, but Bloomfield's partly indignant, partly whimsical response asserted that although such accusations were groundless, no such denial would be forthcoming. Bloomfield further noted that political liberals had also attempted to besmirch his name; apparently William Cobbett had accused Bloomfield of following a governmental directive to avoid writing about commoners in an ennobling light. Bloomfield's last word on the topic came in the 'Preface' to the first edition of *May-Day*, where he obliquely denied the rumours about him: 'I have been reported to be dead; but I can assure the reader this, like many other reports, is not true' (p. viii).

Although Bloomfield found some happiness in the final year of his life through a reawakened interest in John Clare's poetry and by attempting to finish some poetical projects he had begun years before, his deteriorating health and financial situation made composition of new material difficult. Still, his chief anxieties were for his children, and for their sake he continued working until the very last months of his life. Bloomfield died on 19 August 1823 in Bloomfield House, Bedford Street, Shefford. Sadly, his family were left so destitute that they had to auction Bloomfield's books and even their household items to pay off debts. Bloomfield was buried in the country churchyard at Campton, Bedfordshire. The epitaph on his headstone read 'Let His Wild Native Wood Notes Tell the Rest'. DAVID KALOUSTIAN

Sources J. Lawson, *Robert Bloomfield* (1980) • W. Wickett and N. Duval, *The farmer's boy* (1971) • *Selections from the correspondence of Robert Bloomfield*, ed. W. H. Hart (1870) • C. Lofft, 'Preface', in R. Bloomfield, *The farmer's boy* (1800), i–xvi • J. Weston, ed., *The remains of Robert Bloomfield*, 2 vols. (1824) • E. W. Brayley, 'Memoir of Robert Bloomfield', in J. Storer and J. Grieg, *Views in Suffolk, Norfolk, and Northamptonshire* (1806) • J. Lawson, 'Introduction', in R. Bloomfield, *Collected poems by Robert Bloomfield* (Gainesville, Florida: Scholar's Facsimiles, 1971), vii–xv • D. H. Reiman, 'Introduction', *Robert Bloomfield and Nathaniel Bloomfield: the farmer's boy &c.* (1977), v–ix • W. Hone, *The Every-day Book and Table Book*, 3 vols. (1830), vol. 1, pp. 1125–27; vol. 2, pp. 801–5 • R. Gant, 'Introduction', in R. Bloomfield, *A selection of poems* (1947), 7–14 • R. Southey, *The lives of the uneducated poets* (1836), 163

Archives BL, Egerton MS 2245 • BL, corresp., diary, papers, and poems, Add. MSS 28265–28268, 29896, 30809 • BL, Add. MS 26265 • Moyse's Hall Museum, Bury St Edmunds, aeolian harp • Suffolk RO, Bury St Edmunds, copies of letters

Likenesses Brown, line engraving, pubd 1800 (after S. Polack), BM, NPG • H. Edridge, watercolour drawing, *c.*1805, NPG [*see illus.*] • J. Young, mezzotint, pubd 1805 (after J. Rising), BM, NPG • Young, mezzotint, pubd 1805 (after miniature by P. Violet), BM, NPG • H. Bone, miniature, watercolour and bodycolour on ivory (after miniature by R. Cosway, *c.*1800), NPG • R. Cosway, miniature, NPG • W. Ridley, stipple (after S. Drummond), BM, NPG; repro. in *Monthly Mirror* (1800) • J. Storer and J. Grieg, engraving, repro. in Brayley, 'Memoir' • engravings, repro. in Lawson, *Robert Bloomfield* • engravings, repro. in Wickett and Duval, *The farmer's boy*

Wealth at death almost destitute; valuable books, furniture, etc. auctioned: *A catalogue of … the property of the late Mr. R. Bloomfield, the poet* (1824)

Bloor, Joseph (*d.* 1846). *See under* Bloor, Robert (*d.* 1846).

Bloor, Robert (*d.* 1846), ceramicist, was probably born at Church Gresley, Derbyshire, where many of his family are buried. He worked as a clerk for the Old Derby China Works for several years before buying the firm for £5000 in 1811, from Michael Kean and the younger William Duesbury. Under his management sales increased and at its height the firm employed as many as fifty painters, as well as a great number of potters, burnishers, apprentices, and female staff. It is generally considered that the former high quality and finished decoration of the Derby ware deteriorated while he was proprietor. He organized large scale auctions of stock which had accumulated in the factory, some of it either old or faulty, which simultaneously flooded the market and lowered public perceptions of Derby ware. However, according to Geoffrey Godden and John Twitchett some fine painters were employed during this period and superb quality porcelains were produced. It was during Bloor's proprietorship that the 'Japan' or Imari pattern wares which are associated with Royal Crown Derby were first produced, often painted by women. Examples of work from the Bloor period are preserved at the Museum and Art Gallery, Derby, and the Royal Crown Derby Museum.

In 1828 Bloor suffered a mental breakdown from which he never recovered. James Thomason took over the running of the business until 1844. Robert Bloor died at Hathern in Leicestershire on 11 March 1846. The factory was taken over by his granddaughter, Mrs Thomas Clarke, who sold the concern to Samuel Boyle. The business failed and the Nottingham Road factory closed in 1848. **Joseph Bloor** (*d.* 1846) was the brother of Robert Bloor. He was engaged at the works in sundry capacities, mainly in mixing 'bodies' for the paste. He died in 1846.

AMANDA GIRLING-BUDD

Sources J. Haslem, *The old Derby china factory: the workmen and their productions* (1876) • G. A. Godden, *Encyclopaedia of British porcelain manufacturers* (1988) • J. Twitchett, *Derby porcelain* (1980) • F. A. Barrett and A. L. Thorpe, *Derby porcelain* (1971) • E. Cameron, *Encyclopaedia of pottery and porcelain, the nineteenth and twentieth centuries* (1986) • G. Meissner, ed., *Allgemeines Künstlerlexikon: die bildenden Künstler aller Zeiten und Völker*, [new edn, 34 vols.] (Leipzig and Munich, 1983–) • W. Chaffers, *Marks and monograms on pottery and porcelain*, 2nd edn (1866)

Archives Derby Central Library, corresp. and MSS of John Haslem

Blore, Edward (1787–1879), antiquarian artist and architect, the eldest child of Thomas *Blore (1764–1818), antiquary and topographer, and his first wife (his cousin), Margaret Blore (1761–1791), was born in All Saints' parish, Derby, on 13 September 1787 and baptized on 30 September at All Saints' Church, Derby. According to C. L. Eastlake, he was apprenticed to an engraver, but an acquaintance stated that 'He was brought up to no profession except that of an Artist' (Hunter, BL, Add. MS 36527, fol. 36*v*). As a youth he lived at Bakewell, Derbyshire, with his father and his second wife and subsequently at Stamford with his father, whom he assisted by drawing architectural illustrations for his *History of Rutland* (1811). 'In point of accuracy', his youthful sketches of church monuments, carefully outlined and shaded in Indian ink,

Edward Blore (1787–1879), by George Koberwein, 1868

'have been compared to photographs' (Eastlake, 138). He then helped to illustrate James Hall's *Essay on the Origin, History and Principles of Gothic Architecture* (1813). To Hunter at this period Blore 'appeared very prepossessing. There was a delicacy of frame, and a kind of trembling delicacy of spirit which interested agreeably', which he retained in later life (Hunter, BL, Add. MS 36527, fol. 36*v*).

The antiquarian artist In London before 1807 Blore had made the acquaintance of the future architect Thomas Rickman. Their correspondence from 1813 to 1822 shows that by the end of 1813 Blore was 'again in London', and some months later he was engaged by the topographer John Britton to illustrate his work on Peterborough Cathedral, followed by similar commissions for Durham and Winchester (published in 1817). As his father sank into lunacy (although he did not die until 1818), Edward Blore, his sole support, was 'driven by sheer necessity' (Hunter, BL, Add. MS 36527, fol. 36*v*) to draw such architectural illustrations for authors and booksellers, and also made detail drawings for architects. He contributed to R. Surtees's *Durham*, G. Baker's *Northamptonshire*, and R. Clutterbuck's *Hertfordshire*. But he told Hunter, whom he charged £367 for work on *Hallamshire*, that his profession was not a profitable one. Britton paid him partly in books for his twenty-six drawings of Winchester and seventeen of York, charged at 7 guineas each in 1816–17. His drawings of Althorp for T. F. Dibdin's *Aedes Althorpianae* (1822) brought him the acquaintance of the Spencer family, which was to prove of great value: the second Earl Spencer employed him to draw and restore the family tombs in Great Brington church; his younger son George

('Father Ignatius') told Blore in 1835 that 'I considered that you were my original friend' in matters of church architecture, and that 'many circumstances of ancient and happy recollection bind us together' (George Spencer to Edward Blore, 3 March 1835, CUL, Add. MS 8170). Lady Spencer, who showed his drawings among her friends, told the bishop of London in 1826 that Blore was 'a Man of deep learning, & of accurate information, as an Antiquarian, on all subjects related to Gothick Architecture, & joins to these essential & rare qualifications the most exquisite taste, & the most correct adherence to his estimates' (Howley MS 40, fol. 153). It was the Spencers' urging that secured him the restoration of Lambeth Palace; and Sir Francis Chantrey mentioned their high regard in recommending him for Weston, Warwickshire.

Liberated by his father's death, in 1819 Blore married Sarah Ann (or Anne; 1799?–1862), daughter of the Revd W. Hodges, vicar of Mattersey, Northamptonshire; they had five daughters and three sons. In 1820 Blore was established in 56 Welbeck Street, St Marylebone. Already, however, he was seeking to stretch his wings. His first known architectural designs were in November 1816, for enlarging Abbotsford, Sir Walter Scott's farmhouse. A London actor, Daniel Terry (a former pupil of the architect Samuel Wyatt), recommended Blore to Scott, who found him 'a very fine young man, modest, simple, and unaffected in his manners, as well as a most capital artist'. He provided 'a very handsome elevation' for the new rooms (*Letters of Sir Walter Scott*, 4.289). Scott found plans from William Atkinson superior, but for a time he preferred Blore's elevations as 'less Gothic & more in the old fashioned Scotch stile' (ibid., 333–40). Though supplanted, Blore remained in the Abbotsford circle. Scott subsequently recommended him to friends in the Scottish borders, and he managed the publication of Scott's *The Provincial Antiquities and Picturesque Scenery of Scotland* (2 vols., 1819–26), for which he also furnished the architectural drawings. Blore's diversification into supplying and fitting steam boilers was a short-lived enterprise of 1819, though in 1828 he designed Chantrey's bronze foundry and superintended its execution.

Early architectural commissions By 1824 Blore's architectural career was taking off: the Scottish judge George Cranstoun, a close friend of Sir Walter Scott, commissioned designs for a house at Corehouse, Lanarkshire, which became a model for small mansions in Tudor style; Lord Spencer wanted a new parsonage and cottages at Great Brington, Northamptonshire; at Canford, Dorset, the Hon. W. Ponsonby sought plans for a new house; while minor commissions brought in the odd 10 guineas. The following year Lord Ruthven (whose wife was another friend of Scott) wanted designs for Freeland House, Perthshire. Nevertheless, Blore, elected a fellow of the Society of Antiquaries in 1823, was still substantially engaged in the preparation of antiquarian drawings, including those for his own publication *Monumental remains of noble and eminent persons comprising the sepulchral antiquities of Great Britain*; this comprised fine engravings of medieval tombs and brasses with text by the Revd Philip Bliss, for which the publisher had demanded better and 'much more laborious' drawings than originally intended (Blore to Bliss, 23 March 1825, BL, Add. MS 34569). When the work finally appeared in 1826, it was not a success. Blore, however, was now busy with drawings for Canford (1826–36), for Sir George Philips's Weston, Warwickshire (1826–30; dem. 1932), and for improvements to the choir of Peterborough Cathedral (1828–32). Furthermore, inspired by Rickman's success, he sought work under the church building commission: he secured the appointment for St George's, Battersea (1827–8), and soon afterwards for churches at Plaistow, Essex, and Warrington, Lancashire. Thereafter, church work remained an important element in his practice, though country houses predominated.

One of the most notable of these, and one of only three designs Blore ever exhibited at the Royal Academy, was Goodrich Court, Herefordshire (1828–31), for Dr Samuel Rush Meyricke. Goodrich Court has evoked contrary opinions: unconvincing or stylistically authentic. Its authenticity, partly copied from Goodrich Castle, just across the River Wye, was diminished by adaptation for modern life. It had a dual function: at once country house and museum for displaying medieval armour. Its rooms were of different styles, mostly drawn from Blore's precise knowledge of period examples. The banqueting hall with arch-braced roof was one of the first revivals of this feature. Unexpected continental features, such as the conical spire, are attributable to Meyricke's German tour (1823); Blore himself did not visit the continent until the 1840s and 1850s.

Archbishop Howley's commission in 1829 to rebuild Lambeth Palace, the principal seat of the archbishops of Canterbury (1829–38; £58,000), marked Blore's arrival as a leading architect. It was in reference to Lambeth that Lady Gower designated Blore 'the cheap architect' (Leconfield and Gore, 156), a recommendation rather than a sneer, earned by Blore's uncommon facility for keeping within his estimates. This required a highly efficient office, with tight on-site controls through his clerk of works and frequent personal visits, and scrupulous record-keeping, as well as very careful preparation of designs and working drawings. Whenever possible, Blore preferred gross contracts (often with Locke and Nesham) to expensive daywork.

The successful country house architect Such efficiency, coupled with his old friendship with Lord Spencer's son Lord Althorp, then chancellor of the exchequer, secured Blore in 1831 the conspicuous appointment to complete Buckingham Palace (1831–8) after the dismissal of John Nash. About that time Blore moved to a 'handsome' house, 62 Welbeck Street, where an old employer, the Revd Joseph Hunter dined with him, the Revd Philip Bliss, the neurologist Sir Charles Bell, and their wives. 'The furnishing of the house had something of the superb about it', he noted (Hunter, BL, Add. MS 36527, fol. 37). Blore could well support such a lifestyle. In the 1830s his services were greatly sought after. Most of his clients were drawn from the parliamentary gentry or the peerage: whigs and tories in approximately equal numbers. He now had commissions for work at Norman Court, Hampshire (C. B. Wall, 1829); the Bishop's Palace, St Asaph (enlargement, 1830–31); Keele Hall, Staffordshire (stables and projected alterations to house for Ralph Sneyd, 1830–33); and a new house for the seventh marquess of Lothian at Mounteviot (*c*.1830; abandoned for lack of money after the office wing was built). There were subsequent commissions for country seats at Latimer, Hertfordshire (1832–7), for Lord Cavendish; Merton Hall, Norfolk (1832–5); Crom Castle, co. Fermanagh (1832–8), for Lord Erne at a cost of £26,600; Isleworth House, Middlesex (1833–4), for W. H. Cooper; and Orford Court, Shoreham, Kent (1833–9; dem. *c*.1955), for H. St J. Mildmay. Major work—new or rebuilding, remodelling, or enlargement—followed at Pull Court, Worcestershire (1834–9), for the Revd E. Dowdeswell; Crewe Hall, Cheshire (1837–43), for Lord Crewe, at a cost of £30,000; Capesthorne, Cheshire (1837–9), for Edward Davies Davenport, at a cost of £20,000; Ballydrain, co. Antrim (1837–8), for H. Montgomery; Ramsey Abbey (1838–40), for Edward Fellowes; the dramatically sited Merevale, Warwickshire (1838–44), for Sir W. Dugdale at a cost of £35,000; and Haveringland, Norfolk (1839–43; dem. 1946), for Edward Fellowes. The following decade rounded off his career with substantial works or new houses at Shadwell, Norfolk (*c*.1840–43) for Sir R. J. Buxton, bt; Worsley, Lancashire (1840–45; dem. 1945–6), for Lord F. Egerton, later earl of Ellesmere; Great Moreton, Cheshire (1841–6), for G. H. Ackers, a businessman, an unusual client (sometimes regarded as his best work, its great hall has a hammerbeam roof); Hatchford, Surrey (1842–3; dem.), for Lord F. Egerton; Castle Hill, Devon (1842–5), for Lord Fortescue; Crakaig, Sutherland (1845), for the duke of Sutherland; Kingston, Nottinghamshire (1843–5), for Lord Belper; Thicket Priory, Yorkshire (1844–7), for the Revd J. Dunnington-Jefferson; North Mimms, Hertfordshire (1845–6), for Fulke Greville; and The Frythe, Welwyn, Hertfordshire (1845–6), for William Wilshere. In all, Blore was responsible for major works at some thirty-eight houses.

All this activity demanded constant travel. Blore made, for instance, eight visits to Crom Castle in the 1830s, each of about eight days; in 1839–43 Worsley received sixty-one visits. In 1838 alone he inspected works at fifteen houses. Cranstoun of Corehouse feared in 1835 'that the extent of your engagements and the splendour of your reputation in the South' would have precluded his again working in Scotland (Cranstoun to Blore, CUL, Add. MS 8170, fol. 23); and his designs were in requisition in places as far distant as the Crimea and Sydney, New South Wales, where the governor's house (1837–45) was erected to his somewhat *retardataire* plans. The palace erected (1830?–40) at Alupka in the Crimea for Prince Vorontsov is one of the most original of Blore's buildings, and superbly exploits its rocky site. The principal block had a Jacobean entrance front and an 'Asiatic' or 'Saracenic' garden front: his client had prescribed one front in 'Oldentime' architecture that would recall his early connections with England, and for the other a style appropriate to the locality.

Blore was also employed by HM office of works to restore Hampton Court Palace, Middlesex, in 1838–48, to improve the royal apartments at Windsor Castle, Berkshire, in 1841–7, and to reconstruct the Military Knights' lodgings in the Lower Ward in 1840–47; also to complete Buckingham Palace by building an east front to provide private accommodation for the royal family in 1847–50, a much criticized and troubled work. On its completion he is said to have been offered, and to have refused, a knighthood. He also designed a half-timbered marine villa for the royal family at Osborne, Isle of Wight, but Prince Albert preferred his own Italianate scheme.

Ecclesiastical work Blore's later ecclesiastical work included restorations or alterations at Ripon Minster (1829–31) and at Norwich (*c*.1840), Ely (1840–41 and 1844), and Glasgow (from 1846) cathedrals; the chapels of Wadham (1831–2), Merton (1838–43), and St John's (1843) colleges, Oxford, and Trinity College, Cambridge (1831–2); Thorney (1840–41) and Ramsey (1843) abbeys; and several parish churches. He designed the new churches (many in a Norman revival style) at Waltham Cross, Hertfordshire (1831–2); Leytonstone, Essex (1832–3); Croft, Lancashire (1832–3); Stratford, Essex (1833–4); Potters Bar (1835); Vincent Square, Westminster (1836–7; dem. 1923); St Peter's, Stepney (1837–8); Christ Church, Chelsea (1838), and Christ Church, Hoxton (1839; bombed 1944)—dismissed by *The Ecclesiologist* as 'truly contemptible' (*The Ecclesiologist*, 13, 1842, 99); St Luke's, Soho (1838–9; dem. 1936); Lambeth, London (1838–9; bombed *c*.1941); Barkingside, Essex (1839–40); Latimer, Buckinghamshire (1841–2); St James the Great, Bethnal Green (1841–4; converted to flats *c*.1990); St Thomas's, Charterhouse Gardens, London (1841–2; dem. 1909); Windsor, Berkshire (1842–4; altered 1875); Bushley, Worcestershire (1842–3); and Cinderford, Gloucestershire (1843–4). Blore restored or designed stone altar screens at Peterborough Cathedral (*c*.1830; dem. *c*.1890), Ottery St Mary, Devon (*c*.1832), Bath Abbey (1835; dem. *c*.1860); began the restoration of the spire of St Mary the Virgin, Oxford (1848–50); and designed fonts and covers for the Savoy Chapel, London (1865), and St Thomas's, Worcester (1867). He also designed a number of monuments. As surveyor to Westminster Abbey (£10 p.a.), from 1827 to 1849, Blore rescued the thirteenth-century retable, installed a screen between nave and choir, remodelled the choir to provide more seating and designed new stalls (1843–8), and restored the cloister and the exterior of the north side of the nave (1849), though the Camdenian organ *The Ecclesiologist* condemned him as 'entirely unacquainted with the true spirit of Pointed Architecture; … manifestly unfit for the charge of any works in Westminster Abbey' (*The Ecclesiologist*, 3, 1844, 99). Eastlake, however, thought that his Westminster restorations 'though wanting in life and vigour, abound in careful detail' (Eastlake, 141).

Among secular public buildings Blore won the competition for new school buildings (1829) for the Harpur trust at Bedford (and used a similar design at Tavistock grammar school, for the duke of Bedford in 1837), but was unsuccessful in those for the houses of parliament (1835–6) and the Reform Club (by invitation, 1836). His first designs for the Pitt Press at Cambridge were chosen from a limited competition (1829), and a revised, Late Perpendicular design built in 1831–2 at a cost of £10,700. For the Oxford University Press Blore had already built a new wing in 1829. His large Romanesque residential teacher training college at Chelsea for the National Society for Promoting the Education of the Poor in the Principles of the Established Church (1840) included a free-standing chapel and an octagonal training school (1843). Extensive works for the new public school at Marlborough, Wiltshire, from 1844, included a large Decorated chapel (dem. 1884). He also designed a market house for the duke of Bedford at Woburn, and a public library in Perpendicular at Greenock (1835–7, 1846).

Architectural character Blore benefited from the increasing wealth and new living requirements of the aristocracy and gentry. His 'Old English' style, presented in delusively attractive drawings, implied length of ancestry, though its precise ingredients might range from late Gothic to Jacobean. Although Blore, together with W. Burn and A. Salvin, was a forerunner in reviving 'Jacobethan' styles, he failed to exploit the Elizabethan E and H plan; instead, his main house formed a rectangular block. Symmetry governed the principal fronts, though Blore, a child of the Picturesque, added interest by exploiting the device of approximate symmetry that became a Victorian architectural cliché, varying slightly elements on either side of the central axis. The lesser ranges are often built in a rougher stone or an older style, implying an aggregative history for the house, as at Merevale. His house, offices, and stables are frequently organized on a diagonal axis as at the Elizabethan Burghley House, Northamptonshire, but more loosely than would have been acceptable before the 1820s. While he placed the more noisome buildings—stables, brewhouse, washhouse—farthest from the main house, Blore did not develop the intensely organized hierarchy of service quarters that earned Burn his rosette. None the less, the result was, as Lord Erne, writing of Crom Castle, remarked, 'as comfortable a House as possible and admired by all Visitors for its compactness as well as the Handsome and convenient Arrangement of Rooms &c' (Erne to Blore, CUL, Add. MS 8170, fol. 43).

In silhouette Blore's houses display greater irregularity than the typical Late Georgian 'Oldentime' mansion, rising from a low stable block to higher offices to a yet higher main block overtopped by a tower, and crowned by chimney-stacks and spiky ornamental chimneys. Blore's vocabulary (often anticipated by Burn) included bays, usually canted, of two storeys, their windows mullioned and transomed; gables, frequently shaped rather than simple; a principal tower, turreted in the style of Burghley (very familiar from his life at Stamford), and a lesser tower (which might have a ventilating function), often octagonal, terminating in an ogee dome; emphatic external chimney-stacks (anticipating Pugin), rising from the ground or corbelled out at a higher level; with a balustrade at roof level; and for enrichment, strapwork, of which Blore was an early proponent. He designed Tudor or Elizabethan exteriors throughout his career, but at Pull Court (1834) he extended his repertory, with Jacobean (hitherto used only internally), perhaps inspired by his acquaintance with Keele. Thereafter he remodelled Jacobean Crewe Hall (1837–8) and subsequently designed similar Hatfield-inspired Jacobean fronts at Merevale (1838) and Capesthorne (1839). Like any competent Late Georgian architect, Blore also designed in the classical style, notably at stuccoed Isleworth (1832) and Grecian Haveringland, Norfolk (1839–43), and at Buckingham Palace.

Blore employed such modern refinements as gas lighting in the corridors (Worsley), steam heating, water-closets, and large panes of glass; and he used up-to-date techniques: iron girders to span wide spaces, copper casements in his windows, smooth and uniform machine-cut ashlar for facing, superbly constructed but leaving little freedom to the craftsman—thereby contributing to the habitual smoothness and thin, papery quality for which he has principally been criticized, though most of his clients evidently liked this. One who did not was Ralph Sneyd of Keele Hall, who after years of consideration rejected Blore's 'slightness and poverty of detail' (Sneyd MSS, University of Keele, S/RWV/RS, 300) in favour of Salvin's more massive style, more authentic proportions, and greater feeling for materials.

Retirement and family Blore received an Oxford DCL degree in 1834. A founder of the British Archaeological Association, he supported his friend Albert Way in the controversy of 1845 which led to the formation of the Royal Archaeological Institute: Way imported 'that delicious sparkling Moselle' for Blore's cheerful dinners (CUL, Add. MS 8170, fol. 87). Blore, a founder member also of the Institute of British Architects (1834), retired from practice in 1849, resigning his surveyorship of Westminster Abbey, but he continued to draw, as well as to lead an active social life for many years at 4 Manchester Square, London, where he had moved about 1839. He died there after 'a long and painful illness' (*The Builder*, 13 Sept 1879, 1019) on 4 September 1879, and was buried in Highgate cemetery, Middlesex, on 9 September. He collected his drawings, including 'almost every example of ancient castellated and domestic architecture remaining in England' (*Proceedings of the Society of Antiquaries*, 352), and views of his own houses, into forty-eight volumes (now in the British Library). He left an £80,000 estate among his four surviving children: Edward William (1828–1885), fellow of Trinity College, Cambridge; George John (1835–1916), headmaster of King's School, Canterbury; and his two daughters. His pupils included F. C. Penrose, Frederick Marrable, Henry Clutton, and William Burges. M. H. PORT

Sources J. Hunter, 'Biographical notices', BL, Add. MS 36527, fols. 35–36v • Blore drawings, BL, Add. MSS 42000–42047 [esp. *42027–42029, *42047] • working drawings, Thicket Priory, BL, Add. MS 47610 • letters from Rickman, 1813–22, BL, Add. MS 52587 • corresp. with Revd P. Bliss, BL, Add. MSS 34569, fols. 181–2; 34570, fol. 490; 34571, fol. 515; 34574, fols. 110, 202, 283, 325–7, 627; 34575, fols. 224, 256, 264, 476, 671–2 • letter to Brayley, 1832, BL, Add. MS 52481, fol. 20 • letters from clients, CUL, Add. MS 8170 • account books, 1818–49, CUL, Add. MSS 3954–3956 • works' accounts, CUL, Add. MSS 3922–3953 • MSS, LPL, 1726, fols. 1–4 • MSS, LPL, 2197, fols. 1–8 • MSS, LPL, 3563, fols. 25–7 • LPL, 3704–3705 [plans] • LPL, 2949 [watercolours, before and after restoration of palace] • LPL, 1561 [accounts] • LPL, Fulham MSS, Howley, 40, fols. 153–4 • PRO, Work 19 and Work 34 [Buckingham Palace] • drawings for houses, churches, etc., V&A, department of prints and drawings, A251–269, DD3 • census returns, 1841, PRO, HO 107/680/7; 1851, HO 107/1488/577; 1861, RG 9/75/50; 1871, RG 10/162 • *IGI* • St Marylebone baptismal registers, Westminster reference library • *Proceedings of the Society of Antiquaries of London*, 2nd ser., 8 (1879–81), 347–52 • *The Builder*, 37 (1879), 1019 • *The letters of Sir Walter Scott*, ed. H. J. C. Grierson and others, centenary edn, 12 vols. (1932–79), vol. 4, pp. 287–91, 327–9, 333–40, 388, 591–3; vol. 5, pp. 171, 196; vol. 6, p. 327 • W. Partington, *Sir Walter Scott's post-bag* (1932) • Colvin, *Archs.* • H. D. Meller, 'Blore's country houses', MA diss., Courtauld Inst., 1975 • J. M. Crook and M. H. Port, eds., *The history of the king's works*, 6 (1973) • *The Ecclesiologist*, 3 (1843–4), 97–101 • *The Ecclesiologist*, 8 (1847–8), 363–5 • *The Ecclesiologist*, 9 (1848–9), 316–18 • H. Meller, 'The architectural history of Goodrich Court, Herefordshire', *Transactions of the Woolhope Naturalists' Field Club*, 42 (1976–8), 175–85 • M. Girouard, 'Merevale Hall', *Country Life*, 145 (1969), 598–601, 662–5 • M. Girouard, *The Victorian country house* (1971) • C. L. Eastlake, *A history of the Gothic revival* (1872), 138–46 • J. Franklin, *The gentleman's country house and its plan, 1835–1914* (1981) • J. Allibone, *Anthony Salvin: pioneer of Gothic revival architecture* (1988) • *Three Howard sisters: selections from the writings of Lady Caroline Lascelles, Lady Dover, and Countess Gower, 1825 to 1833*, ed. Maud, Lady Leconfield, rev. J. Gore (1955), 156 • London Directories, 1822–8 [Pigot's, Kent's, Robson's, Post Office Guide] • *Country Life*, 65 (1929), 482–4, 515 [Hinchingbroke] • *Country Life*, 75 (17 March 1934), 272–7 • *Country Life* (24 March 1934), 300–5 [Castle Hill] • *Country Life*, 151 (1972), 513–17 [Aloupka] • *An apology for those who object to the lateral position of an organ in Winchester Cathedral* (1825) • E. Blore, *A report … to the dean of Winchester, on the proposed removal of the organ* (1828) • E. Blore, *Monumental remains of noble and eminent persons comprising the sepulchral antiquities of Great Britain* (1826) • *Annual Report* [Society for the Protection of Ancient Buildings], 25 (1902), 72 • Graves, *RA exhibitors* • T. F. Dibdin, *Aedes Althorpianae* (1822) • *The parish of St Mary, Lambeth*, 1 (1951), 99–102 • *VCH Oxfordshire*, 3.57 • *VCH Wiltshire*, 8.95 • W. Keane, *Beauties of Middlesex* (1850), 66 • T. G. Jackson, *Wadham College, Oxford* (1893), 125, 147, 156–7 • private information (2004) [Westminster Abbey librarian] • H. Meller, 'From engraver to architect', *Country Life*, 164 (1978), 1205–6 • C. Wainwright, *The romantic interior: the British collector at home, 1750–1850* (1989) • *CGPLA Eng. & Wales* (1879) • K. Thomson, *Turner and Sir Walter Scott: the provincial antiquities and picturesque scenery of Scotland* (1999) [exhibition catalogue, NG Scot., 17 Dec 1999 – 19 March 2000]

Archives CUL, account books • PRO, wk 34 • RIBA, account books • Royal Arch. | BL, letters to Philip Bliss, Add. MSS 34569–34580 • BL, letters to Lord Spencer, p8 • Durham RO, corresp. with James Raine • NL Scot., corresp. with Sir Walter Scott

Likenesses J. Ternouth, bust, 1845, Abbotsford, Roxburghshire • J. Ternouth, marble bust, 1845, Cambridge University Press • G. Koberwein, chalk drawing, 1868, NPG [*see illus.*] • photograph, *c*.1875, repro. in *Country Life* (14 Dec 1945), 1058 • attrib. W. Hilton, oils, Cambridge University Press; repro. in E. A. Crutchley, *History … of the Pitt Press* (1938) • wood-engraving, NPG; repro. in *ILN*, 75 (1879)

Wealth at death under £80,000: probate, 11 Oct 1879, *CGPLA Eng. & Wales*

Blore, Eric (1886–1959), actor and theatrical sketch writer, was born on 23 December 1886 at Elm Park Road, Church End, Finchley, Middlesex, one of two children of Henry Blore (*d*. 1914), a schoolmaster, and his wife, Mary Newton. After leaving school in Finchley, Blore began selling insurance, but in 1908 he went on the stage.

Although Blore became one of the most recognizable of film 'character actors'—usually as a (subversive) butler or valet—his early theatrical career was more varied. After touring Australia with a concert party, in 1910 Blore won a role in an English touring version of the popular musical comedy *The Arcadians* and became a protégé of the variety comic G. P. Huntley. By 1913, the year of his West End performing début in the Empire revue *All the Winners*, Blore's sketches and short plays, rich in absurd situations and wordplay, were being produced in London. These included *Alice up to Date* at the Pavilion (1913) and *A Burlington Arcadian* at the Coliseum (1914).

After the rise of intimate revue, Blore formed a partnership with composer Philip (Pa) Braham, placing songs—often flirtatious and faux-innocent—in such shows as *The Bing Boys are Here* (1916). During the First World War, Blore, a lieutenant in the South Wales Borderers, ran a concert party called 'The Welsh Wails'. He later said that his batman 'taught me the whole art' of being a gentleman's gentleman: 'He had a way of putting out my studs that made them look worth at least 2 guineas' (private information). On 29 October 1917 Blore married Violet Lydia Victoria, daughter of George Winter; she died, childless, on 19 February 1919, a victim of the influenza epidemic of late 1918.

In 1920 Blore contributed sketches to the André Charlot revue *Jumble Sale* and made his film début in *A Night Out and a Day In*. 1921 was the year of his collaboration with Inglis Allen and Austin Melford in creating the revue *Ring Up* for Jack Hulbert and Cicely Courtneidge; one of his wartime sketches, 'The Disorderly Room' (all the dialogue is set to the tunes of popular songs) was taken up by the aspiring variety performer Tommy Handley, who played it for twenty years, in a royal variety performance in 1924 as well as on record, film, radio, and television. A Blore song with Braham, 'How d'you do?', opened *Charlot's London Revue* in New York (1924).

Blore's onstage acting career had begun with roles portraying farcical 'dudes' with names such as Alsop Bibby and the Honourable H. Buff-Orpington. The second half of his career began in New York with another one, Bertie Bird, in *Little Miss Bluebeard* (1923). Bird was the first of a line of Blore's fops and clapped-out nobles on Broadway—Reggies and Basils and Roddys—stretching throughout the decade. Blore first played a butler in *Gentleman in Waiting* (1925). In 1926 he married the American actress Clara Macklin; they had one child and remained married until Blore's death. In the same year he was Lord Digby in the first film version of *The Great Gatsby*. After playing a waiter in Cole Porter's musical comedy *The Gay Divorce* on Broadway (1932) and in the West End (1933), Blore was summoned to RKO-Radio Pictures in Hollywood as Butterbass, a not quite head waiter who suffered seethingly under the prissy Franklin Pangborn, in *Flying Down to Rio* (1933), the first notable pairing of Fred Astaire and Ginger Rogers.

Four more Astaire–Rogers films followed, including *Top Hat* (1935), in which Blore created a multi-dimensional valet (introducing himself to his bumbling employer, Edward Everett Horton, as 'We are Bates, sir', he spoke one of the era's most memorable lines). After these films Blore was rarely at liberty. Never billed higher than third, he appeared in more than eighty films, earning as much as $3500 (then £750) per week. In *It's Love I'm after* (1937) he remarked, 'If I were not a gentleman's gentleman, I could be such a cad's cad.' In Laurel and Hardy's *Swiss Miss* (1938) he endured a contretemps with a stingy St Bernard. In the English film *A Gentleman's Gentleman* (1939) he took up blackmailing.

Blore's valets were rarely obsequious. Eyebrows arched, face twitching, nostrils flaring, he could switch instantly from innocence or impishness through wounded dignity to (usually comic) menace. Blore also developed a useful sideline in seedy tropical expatriates (*The Island of Lost Men*, 1939, *South of Suez*, 1940).

In his later years in California, Blore retained his English persona, peppering conversation with 'Good chap' and 'Don't y'know?' In 1940 Blore revisited his revue past, joining other expatriates in the Hollywood run of *André Charlot's War Relief Revue*. In 1944 Blore made a final Broadway appearance in a nostalgic revival of *The Ziegfeld Follies*. His was the manic voice of Toad in Disney's *The Wind in the Willows* (1949), a somehow fitting near-finale; early on, he had played an owl in a Liverpool panto. After a stroke in 1956 Blore retired from film. He died of a heart attack in the suburban Los Angeles Motion Picture Country Home Hospital on 1 March 1959; his ashes were inurned in the Chapel of the Pines, Forest Lawn.

JAMES ROSS MOORE

Sources *Los Angeles Times* (3 March 1959) · J. Parker, ed., *Who's who in the theatre*, 4th edn (1922) · T. Kavanagh, *Tommy Handley* (1949) · A. Croce, *The Fred Astaire and Ginger Rogers book* (1972) · C. Hirschhorn, *The Hollywood musical* (1981) · G. Bordman, *American theatre, 1914–1930* (1995) · G. Bordman, *American musical theatre*, 2nd edn (1992) · files and reviews, Theatre Museum, London · files and reviews, BFI · files and reviews, American Film Institute, Los Angeles · playscripts and commentary, BL, lord chamberlain's collection · b. cert. · m. cert. · d. cert. · K. Gänzl, *The British musical theatre*, 2 vols. (1986) · private information (2004) · A. Charlot, unpubd essays, Los Angeles

Likenesses photographs, Hult. Arch.

Blore, Robert (1810–1868), porcelain manufacturer, was born in Derby, the son of a monumental mason working in Bridge Gate. Blore served his apprenticeship at the Old Derby china works, but shortly afterwards left to work briefly at Minton's factory. In 1830 he returned to Derby, and set up a small establishment for himself in his father's yard. There he modelled porcelain vases and figures. In 1835 he returned to the potteries district, this time as an assistant at the factory of G. M. and C. J. Mason at Lane Delph. From there he went to Middlesbrough, Yorkshire, where he superintended the works of Isaac Wilson & Co., earthenware manufacturers.

Blore is best known for his work in biscuit porcelain which includes a *Sleeping Endymion* after the Canova original at Chatsworth. This and other figures can be seen at the City Museum and Art Gallery, Derby. He died in 1868.

W. H. TREGELLAS, *rev.* AMANDA GIRLING-BUDD

Sources J. Haslem, *The old Derby china factory: the workmen and their productions* (1876); repr. (1973) · E. Cameron, *Encyclopaedia of pottery and porcelain, the nineteenth and twentieth centuries* (1986) · J. Twitchett, *Derby porcelain* (1980) · F. A. Barrett and A. L. Thorpe, *Derby porcelain* (1971) · Boase, *Mod. Eng. biog.* · G. Meissner, ed., *Allgemeines Künstlerlexikon: die bildenden Künstler aller Zeiten und Völker*, [new edn, 34 vols.] (Leipzig and Munich, 1983–)

Wealth at death under £200: probate, 7 Aug 1868, *CGPLA Eng. & Wales*

Blore, Thomas (1764–1818), county historian, was born in Ashbourne, Derbyshire, on 1 December 1764, the son of John Blore and his wife, Elizabeth, and educated at Queen Elizabeth's Grammar School in Ashbourne. He married Margaret (1761–1791), daughter of John and Martha Blore, also of Ashbourne, on 16 July 1786. A son, Edward *Blore, antiquarian artist and architect, was born in Derby on 13 September 1787, but the couple later became estranged. Having first been employed as a solicitor in Derby, Blore went to Hopton Hall, Derbyshire, as agent to the owner, Philip Gell (*d.* 1795). After Gell's death, Blore married his widow, Dorothy, daughter of William Milnes of Chesterfield, in May 1798, and moved to London. The relationship was acrimonious and the couple separated formally in April 1802. Dorothy Blore died in April 1808. Blore entered the Middle Temple, but was never called to the bar.

From at least 1791 Blore was collecting materials for his intended history of Derbyshire. To encourage subscribers he published in that year his 'Proposals' and three examples of his work: histories of South Wingfield Manor and Manor House, Alderwasley, and Breadsall Priory. In the course of his researches he corresponded extensively with other local antiquaries, such as Daniel Dakeyne of Holt House, Darley Dale.

Blore transferred his attention to Hertfordshire while living at Benwick Hall, near Hertford, and collected historical notes which formed the nucleus of Robert Clutterbuck's history of the county, eventually published between 1815 and 1827. He then moved successively to Mansfield Woodhouse in Nottinghamshire; Burr House, near Bakewell, Derbyshire; Manton in Rutland; and Stamford in Lincolnshire. The pattern of ambitious plans partially realized, first seen in Derbyshire, was repeated in Rutland, for which only the second part of the first volume of Blore's projected *History and Antiquities of the County of Rutland* was published in 1811. For a short period he edited *Drakard's Stamford News* and he also produced an account of Stamford's charitable foundations in 1813, and a guide to Burghley House and its collections in 1815.

Thomas Blore died in London on 10 November 1818, and his memorial stone in Paddington church recorded that his 'days were embittered and [his] life was shortened by intense application'. He was a fellow of the Society of Antiquaries and all his historical writings are characterized by thoroughness and careful detail, a feature recognized by later antiquaries such as Llewellynn Jewitt (1816–1886), who regretted that Blore's projects had met with 'a lack of proper encouragement'. The bulk of Blore's papers are now in Cambridge University Library, although some survive in the Dakeyne and Gell collections in Derbyshire Record Office. MARGARET O'SULLIVAN

Sources *William Woolley's history of Derbyshire*, ed. C. Glover and P. Riden, Derbyshire RS, 6 (1981) • parish registers, St Oswald, Ashbourne, Derbys. RO

Archives CUL, collections on lawyers and relating to Derbyshire, Rutland, etc. • Leics. RO, historical and genealogical notes for his history of Rutland and for projected history of Derbyshire | Bodl. Oxf., Brooke MSS • Derbys. RO, Dakeyne MSS • Derbys. RO, Gell MSS • S. Antiquaries, Lond., letters to Hayman Rooke

Blouet, (Leon) Paul [*pseud.* Max O'Rell] **(1848–1903)**, humorist, born at Avranches in Normandy on 2 March 1848, was the son of the governor of the prison on Mont-St Michel. After some time studying the piano at the Paris Conservatoire, he was educated in Paris at the École Polytechnique, served as a cavalry officer in the Franco-Prussian War, was captured at Sedan, set at liberty early in 1871, and severely wounded in the second siege of Paris. He was retired on account of his wound, and in 1872 he went to England as correspondent to several French papers—having left France because his newspaper had been suppressed for its liberalism—and four years later became French master at St Paul's School, London. He taught French through speech rather than books; he wrote several manuals and edited texts. About this time he married Mary Bartlett of Devon; they had at least one child.

In 1887, under the pseudonym of Max O'Rell, which he permanently adopted, Blouet dedicated to John Bull his *John Bull et son île*, a vivacious picture of English eccentricities and racial characteristics, laced with a sometimes hard edge; 'few people have said more vitriolic things about England and the English than he' (Furniss, 159). It was translated by his wife and achieved such a rapid success that he determined to abandon his successful teaching career for one of popular writing and lecturing, mainly on British life and manners. In addition to *John Bull et son île*, he wrote *John Bull's Womankind* (1884), *Drat the Boys* (1886); in collaboration with Georges Petilleau *Jonathan and his Continent* (1889), *Woman and Artist* (1900; dedicated to his wife), *Her Royal Highness Woman* (1901; dedicated 'to the nicest little woman in the world'), and *Rambles in Womanland* (1903). All were written originally in French and produced almost simultaneously in English; many were translated into other languages. In 1887 and 1890 he lectured in the United States; and in 1893, with his wife and daughter, he toured the British colonies, his readiness as a speaker and lecturer ensuring him a welcome everywhere from people who enjoyed seeing their foibles presented in a humorous light. According to Harry Furniss, he was more popular in the United States than in Britain, and more popular in the north of England than in London. In 1902 he settled in the Champs-Élysées quarter of Paris as correspondent of the *New York Journal* and wrote in the French newspaper *Le Figaro* in support of the *entente cordiale* between England and France. He died of cancer of the stomach at 9 rue Freycinet on 24 May 1903 and was buried in the church of St Pierre de Chaillot, Paris. A tolerant, shrewd, and on the whole impartial observer, on lines inherited from Voltaire, Edmond About, Hippolyte Taine, and Jules Verne, Blouet mixed a good deal of flattery with his smart and witty banter, and with the leverage thus gained was able now and then to tell an unpalatable truth, not entirely without effect.

THOMAS SECCOMBE, *rev.* H. C. G. MATTHEW

Sources *The Times* (26 May 1903) • *ILN* (30 May 1903) • *The Pauline* [magazine of St Paul's School, London], 21 (1903), 120–24 • H. Furniss, *Harry Furniss at home* (1904), chap. 6 • *CGPLA Eng. & Wales* (1904)

Likenesses Barraud, photograph, NPG; repro. in *Men and Women of the Day*, 2 (1889) • H. Furniss, cartoon, repro. in Furniss, *Harry Furniss at home*

Wealth at death £7570 14*s.* 4*d.*: administration with will, 2 March 1904, *CGPLA Eng. & Wales*

Blount, Charles, fifth Baron Mountjoy (1516–1544), courtier and patron of learning, was the eldest son of William *Blount, fourth Baron Mountjoy (*c.*1478–1534), and his third wife, Alice Brown, *née* Kebel (or Keble; *d.* 1521). Charles was born on 28 June 1516 in Tournai, where his father was governor, and after William was recalled in 1517 to resume his role as chamberlain to Katherine of Aragon, his son was in due time made a page in her household. Charles's education was based on the most rigorous humanist standards and his tutors were remarkable for their learning. In 1522 Jan van der Cruyce, a graduate of the university at Louvain and a friend of Erasmus, travelled to England to become private tutor to Mountjoy's children. He remained in the household until 1527, when he returned to Louvain and was appointed a professor of Greek. Possibly on the recommendation of Erasmus, van der Cruyce was succeeded by Petrus Vulcanius of Bruges, also a graduate of Louvain, who remained in England until 1531. In 1531 Erasmus praised Charles Blount for his fine written style, but after Vulcanius's departure realized that the credit should have gone to the preceptor rather than the student. John Palsgrave, who composed *L'esclarcissement de la langue francoyse* (printed in 1530 and dedicated to Henry VIII) and was tutor to Henry Fitzroy, also gave tuition to the sons of several court noblemen, Charles Blount among them. One of his fellow schoolmates in this group was Thomas Howard, son of the second duke of Norfolk, whose own tutor at Lambeth had been John Leland. Leland in turn praised Charles's skill in Latin and presented a book along with commendatory verses to him. In 1523 Juan Luis Vives wrote a short educational treatise dedicated to Charles, *De ratione studii puerilis ad Carolum Montioium Guilielmi filium*. This served as a parallel to the tract on female education Vives had composed in the same year for the benefit of Mary Tudor. Erasmus added Charles's name to that of his father in the dedication to the 1528 edition of the *Adagia* and Charles was the dedicatee of the next two editions (1533, 1536) as well. Erasmus also dedicated his 1531 edition of Livy to him.

About August 1530 Charles Blount married Anne, daughter of Robert, second Baron Willoughby de Broke.

Her mother was Dorothy, daughter of Thomas Grey, fourth marquess of Dorset, who had become the fourth wife of Charles's father. Succeeding to the title after his father's death in 1534, Mountjoy was regular in his attendance in the House of Lords. In May 1537 he was one of the peers summoned for the trial of lords Darcy and Hussey and he was also on the panel of 3 December 1538 for the trial of Henry Pole, Lord Montague, and Henry Courtenay, marquess of Exeter, his own brother-in-law. His country house was at Apethorpe, Northamptonshire, and in London he lived in Silver Street.

After the dissolution of Syon Abbey in 1539 Mountjoy granted asylum at his London house to the pious, learned, and outspokenly conservative priest Richard Whitford, who had been patronized by his father. Whitford remained in the household until his death in 1542 and may have acted as tutor to Mountjoy's children. Like his father, Mountjoy was deeply interested in the humanist educational programme and he tried to engage the learned scholar and educationist Roger Ascham, then teaching at Cambridge, as a tutor to his eldest son and secretary to himself. Although Ascham did not take the position—and he also refused a similar offer from Margaret Roper—he admired Mountjoy and referred in flattering terms to his learning, likening his household for its patronage of learning to that of the Medici. Mountjoy left 40 marks in his will to provide lectures for the children of Westbury under the Plain, Wiltshire, for the succeeding two years.

Mountjoy drew up his will on 30 April 1544, just before embarking for France with the expeditionary force. In it he admonished his children to 'kepe themselfes worthye of so moche honour as to be called hereafter to dye for ther maister and countrey' (PRO, PROB 11/30, fol. 343). He also composed his own epitaph in English verse. Present with Henry VIII at the siege of Boulogne he died on 10 October of that year at Hooke, Dorset (formerly the home of his mother), probably from illness contracted on campaign. In his will he reckoned his assets, in money, goods, and debts owed to him, at nearly £2100. He was buried at St Mary Aldermary, London. His widow remarried and lived until 1582.

Mountjoy's heir was his eldest son, **James Blount**, sixth Baron Mountjoy (1532/3–1581), who was made a knight of the Bath in 1553 at the coronation of Queen Mary. On 26 May 1559 he became lord lieutenant of Dorset and he was a JP for Dorset and Wiltshire in 1562 and 1564. On 10 February 1564 he was admitted to Gray's Inn. In 1572 he took part in the treason trial of Thomas Howard, fourth duke of Norfolk. He married Catherine, daughter of Sir Thomas Leigh, and their sons William and Charles succeeded in turn to the title. In the dedicatory epistle to his *Lyues of M. Luther, J. Ecolampadius & H. Zuinglius* (1561) Henry Bennet situated Mountjoy within the tradition of good letters followed by his father and grandfather. Bennet also claimed that James had a zeal towards good religion and in the same year Jean Veron dedicated his antipapal tract *The Ouer Throw of the Iustification of Workes* to him. Apparently Mountjoy dabbled in alchemical studies and according to Sir Robert Naunton's *Fragmenta regalia*, written about 1630, he spent the family fortunes in pursuit of the philosopher's stone. He was also a shareholder in the Company of Mines Royal, and in his attempt to find a formula for the production of alum and copperas he fell badly into debt and was forced to mortgage several properties. He patronized a company of players from at least 1558 to 1578; they toured predominantly in the south-west. Mountjoy died on 20 October 1581 at Hooke, Dorset. He had two younger brothers, Francis and William, the former of whom later became a friend of John Dee. JAMES P. CARLEY

Sources GEC, *Peerage*, new edn, 9.341–3 · R. Naunton, *Fragmenta regalia, or, Observations on the late Queen Elizabeth, her times and favorits*, 3rd edn (1653); repr. (1870) · M. Dowling, *Humanism in the age of Henry VIII* (1986), 128, 145, 149, 176, 181, 191–2, 194, 202–3 · PRO, PROB 11/30, fols. 343–5 · *LP Henry VIII*, vols. 4–19

Wealth at death liquid assets, incl. debts, nearly £2100: will, PRO, PCC, PROB 11/30, fols. 343–5

Blount, Charles, eighth Baron Mountjoy and earl of Devonshire (1563–1606), soldier and administrator, was the second son of James *Blount, sixth Baron Mountjoy (1532/3–1581), nobleman [*see under* Blount, Charles, fifth Baron Mountjoy], and his wife, Catherine (*d.* 1576), daughter of Sir Thomas Leigh of St Oswald's, Yorkshire. He later claimed that he was, from an early age, acutely aware of his venerable family's declining reputation and worsening financial straits. In a childhood portrait he reputedly insisted on being painted holding a trowel with the motto *Ad reaedificandam antiquam domum*, or, 'To restore the family fortunes' (Jones, 21), written beneath the picture. He is said to have studied at Oxford, but failed to attain a degree. Instead he travelled to London to study law and entered Clifford's Inn, transferring to the Middle Temple on 20 June 1579. Blount's elder brother, William, had been living in London for some time and introduced his provincial brother to the ways of the court. On one occasion, about 1583, the handsome Charles caught the attention of Queen Elizabeth, who remarked to him 'faile you not to come to court, and I will bethinke my self, how to doe you good' (Naunton, 132). He availed himself of this rare opportunity for advancement and was instantly catapulted from obscurity to the centre of English social and political life.

The reluctant courtier Despite a retiring disposition and a proclivity to immerse himself in study Blount was a success as a courtier, but his rapid rise provoked the jealousy of Robert *Devereux, second earl of Essex, the queen's favourite. Following Blount's conspicuous display of a gift given to him by the queen, Essex quipped, 'now I perceive every foole must have a favour' (Naunton, 120). Hearing of this affront Blount challenged Essex to a duel, emerging unscathed while the latter suffered a flesh wound. His successful defence of his honour was a rite of passage that won him the respect of other courtiers, including the influential Essex. About this time Blount began his political career, representing St Ives, Cornwall, where his brother owned land, in the 1584 parliament. But parliamentary service proved too mundane a pursuit for Blount, who was eager to distinguish himself through military

Charles Blount, eighth Baron Mountjoy and earl of Devonshire (1563–1606), by Nicholas Hilliard, 1587

service. The opportunity came in 1585 when he accompanied Sir John Norris on a campaign in the Low Countries, serving as a captain. Norris had become something of a father figure to Blount, who devoted himself utterly to the respected general. In October 1585 he was wounded in a skirmish after rashly deserting his command to aid Norris. He returned to England, but resumed his command some months later and was present when Sir Philip Sidney received his fatal wound near Zutphen in September 1586. Following this he again returned to England and represented Bere Alston, Cornwall, in parliament in October 1586. But the lure of glory compelled him to return once again to the Low Countries, where he remained for much of 1587. Unhappy with his long absences from court the queen recalled him in October. He was knighted by the earl of Leicester prior to his return to England.

Not content with the monotony of court life Blount regularly absented himself from the queen's company to pursue his military career. The threat posed by the Armada in summer 1588 allowed him another opportunity to distinguish himself in combat. Like many of the younger nobility he rallied to England's defence and provided financial backing for the construction of ships. According to one historian he was given command of a London man-of-war, the *Lion*, against the invaders, although in another account he served as a volunteer aboard the *Rainbow*. The queen rewarded him by appointing him keeper of the New Forest in 1588 and one of the queen's gentlemen pensioners in 1589. He was also created MA at Oxford in 1589. His appointments were designed to dissuade him from pursuing his military ambitions but the desire to become a respected soldier and leader of men overrode other considerations. When in 1593 Blount's former company in the Low Countries and Norris were deployed against the Spanish in Brittany, he abandoned the court—and his duties as MP—to join them in secret. The queen had explicitly forbidden such behaviour and in a letter to Norris in June 1593 insisted that Blount be sent back to England. The queen, according to Naunton, scolded him upon his return, warning him, 'you shall go when I send you; in the mean time, see that you lodge in the court where you may follow your books, read, and discourse of warre' (Naunton, 59). Though confined to court he was left fully salaried as a captain and in nominal control of nearly a thousand men in Brittany. This punishment, cloaked in royal favour, was a humiliating setback for Blount. Events in 1594, however, allowed him to establish an identity independent of queen and court.

Eighth Baron Mountjoy The death of Henry Ratcliff, earl of Sussex, in December 1593 left the governorship of the town of Portsmouth vacant. The continued threat of an amphibious Spanish landing in southern England made Portsmouth a strategically important position while transforming its governorship into a prestigious appointment. The queen—sufficiently confident in his abilities—appointed Blount governor of Portsmouth in January 1594. On 27 June that year Blount's brother William, who had succeeded his father as Baron Mountjoy, died unexpectedly, so allowing Blount to inherit the title as eighth baron. Thus a prominent military appointment and his elevation to the peerage at last afforded Mountjoy a degree of independence from court and allowed him to re-establish his military reputation. At Portsmouth he vigorously put into practice many of the military strategies he had carefully studied: he oversaw the construction and renewal of fortifications and honed his naval skills. At an administrative level he became a parliamentary patron both at Bere Alston and at Portsmouth, where, as high steward, he nominated one of the two members of the 1597 parliament, in which he himself sat as Lord Mountjoy in the House of Lords. Yet Mountjoy's independence was far from complete: he was specifically forbidden to accompany Essex on his expedition to Cadiz in 1596. But in April 1597 he was created a knight of the Garter and, that summer, received the queen's permission to accompany Essex on an expedition to the Azores, where he was made lieutenant of the land forces. Though the Azores voyage ended in fiasco Mountjoy's reputation emerged unblemished.

Over the course of the expedition Mountjoy's friendship with Robert Cecil, the queen's secretary, had strengthened and, aware of his influence with the queen, he implored Cecil 'to continue his good opinion and not to repent the course he has hitherto held to advance her Majesty's gracious inclination toward him' (*Salisbury MSS*, 7.470). In affiliating himself with Cecil, however, Mountjoy risked alienating the opposing court faction led by his former rival, and recent commander, Essex, whose reputation had been dealt a crushing blow following the Azores débâcle. For Cecil, Mountjoy doubtless represented a potentially valuable ally: he was the queen's intelligent and capable favourite who lacked the domestic influence and pretensions of Essex. For two years Mountjoy managed to keep safely outside this dangerous rivalry without committing himself openly to either faction. In doing so, however, his rapid ascent faltered: he remained governor of Portsmouth, but without the backing of a court faction he was denied an appointment to the privy council and was thus deprived of any real power. This lull in his career, compounded by the stalemate at court, was ultimately broken by events in Ireland which, by August 1598, demanded immediate attention.

The rebellion by Hugh O'Neill, earl of Tyrone, posed the most serious threat yet faced by the Tudors in Ireland and required the swift dispatch of a strong deputy to crush the rebels and restore order. It was initially thought that Mountjoy would receive the appointment and in November 1598 he was actually nominated by the council; but it was inevitable that Essex—due as much to his political stature and military experience as his recent military failure and aggressiveness with the queen—would go to Ireland, where either redemption or ruin awaited. Essex's appointment did not, as expected, push Mountjoy towards the Cecil faction; rather their friendship grew stronger. In a letter written to Essex prior to his departure Mountjoy remarked, 'I fear not, since needs go you must, but that your virtue shall beget as great a necessity for your welcome home' (Jones, 46). He became increasingly involved in Essex's plan to force the queen to acknowledge King James of Scotland as her successor. In summer 1599 he dispatched a secret messenger to Scotland to inform James that Essex supported his succession to the English throne. The queen could not live for ever, and, for Mountjoy, an alliance with Essex and the future king would ensure a prominent position in the new administration. But Mountjoy was not a traitor. His loyalty to Essex and his desire to secure James's succession did not amount to a willingness to topple Elizabeth. Essex, however, had grown increasingly desperate following his manifest failure to defeat Tyrone and by October 1599 he was confined to court. Charles was subsequently offered the Irish deputyship; he accepted the post in November and was scheduled to depart within twenty days. In desperation Essex urged Mountjoy, who looked after his fortunes during his confinement, to employ his newly assembled army against the queen's councillors; but Mountjoy prevaricated and eventually departed for Ireland in February 1600 leaving Essex and his intrigues behind.

Lord deputy of Ireland The direction of the campaign against Tyrone had been decided prior to Mountjoy's arrival in Ireland. He was to oversee the reform of a demoralized army and open up new fronts against the rebels through the plantation of strongly defended garrisons deep within rebel territory; vital to this strategy was the plantation of two garrisons supported by sea behind Tyrone at Lough Foyle and Ballyshannon. The nature of Mountjoy's position, moreover, was to be fundamentally different from that of his predecessors: military power, formerly consolidated in the deputy, was immediately decentralized to avoid a scenario where one slow moving, unwieldy English force could be outmanoeuvred or counter-attacked by smaller Irish contingents. The plan's immediate implementation, however, was delayed due to shortages of victuals and money and Mountjoy's wrangling with the Irish council; in March the exasperated lord deputy wrote to Cecil, 'if I were aided by a council of Solomons, I think this Kingdom and this army, as they now are, would afford them matter enough to try their best wits' (PRO, SP 63/207(2)/28). Mountjoy, however, remained focused on the task at hand and by September his cautious and calculated implementation of his military objectives had taken their toll on Tyrone. His level temperament and careful attention to geographical detail—coupled with an inherent awareness of the dire consequences that one poorly judged march might bring—had denied Tyrone any opportunity to exploit the Irish terrain or English military conceit to his advantage. In an effort to undermine Tyrone's economic base Mountjoy ravaged the Irish countryside unsparingly, a tactic which he employed to its greatest limits with cold precision and fixity of purpose that amounted almost to a blind automatism (Jones, 78). Fynes Moryson, Mountjoy's secretary in Ireland, described the deputy as 'courtly, grave, and exceedingly comely'; he was 'of stature tall, and of very comely proportion, his skin faire, with little haire on his body …, and thinne on his head, where he wore it short, except a locke under his left eare, which he nourished the time of this warre', with good table manners, a man who 'tooke Tobacco abundantly', and favoured 'private retirednesse, with good fare, and some few choice friends' (Moryson, *Itinerary*, 2.261–3).

When word came of Essex's failed rebellion in early 1601 Mountjoy panicked and prepared a ship in which he planned to escape from Ireland to France. But despite his complicity in Essex's early plans to ensure James's accession he had suitably distanced himself from Essex prior to the rebellion and his role in the affair was overlooked. His favourable relationship with the queen was doubtless a factor in the suppression of evidence against him; but ultimately it was his success in Ireland that insulated him from the charges that claimed Essex and his fellow conspirators. Victory in Ireland, however, was far from certain and Mountjoy understood that both his career and reputation had become wholly dependent on a decisive victory over Tyrone. Yet drawing Tyrone into an open confrontation proved difficult; only the arrival of Spanish reinforcements commanded by Don Juan D'Águila in the coastal town of Kinsale in September 1601 prompted Tyrone to abandon his defensive position in Ulster and make the impossibly long march south to link up with the Spaniards. The long-awaited confrontation was imminent, but the arrival of about 3400 Spaniards was a worrying development for Mountjoy, who raced to dislodge them. He invested Kinsale in October as Tyrone began his southerly descent. But the Spaniards clung on stubbornly and by December Mountjoy's army was suffering from disease and shortages of food. A winter cessation of hostilities seemed likely, but Tyrone, who had assembled a force of some 6500 men, committed himself to open field combat outside Kinsale on 24 December. The Spaniards failed to counter-attack from Kinsale and Mountjoy's troops routed Tyrone's forces. Though he had gained the most spectacular victory of his career, effectively breaking any organized military resistance, he offered the rebels no quarter and doggedly pursued them as they limped back to Ulster. In September 1602 he destroyed the O'Neill inauguration stone at Tullaghoge to symbolize his victory over both Tyrone and the Gaelic order.

Tyrone submitted unconditionally in December 1602 and was received, in March 1603, at Mellifont, where he made his formal submission, on his knees, to Mountjoy, the queen's representative. The queen, however, had died nearly a week prior to Tyrone's submission; Mountjoy had concealed her death both to prevent Tyrone from holding out for more favourable terms and to safeguard Tyrone's interests from his enemies who might seek to renegotiate the submission under the new king. Mountjoy hoped to rehabilitate Tyrone and employ him as a stabilizing influence in an Ireland devastated from years of war. He acted, in the main, as a voice of reason among the vulture-like English adventurers who descended on Ireland in the wake of Tyrone's defeat, and set about laying the foundations of a new system of government. Following James I's accession, however, Mountjoy sought his immediate recall; he was made lord lieutenant of Ireland and a privy councillor in April 1603, which allowed him to return to England. Before he departed he was faced with serious rioting in Cork which spread to the other major towns. The towns—which had, crucially, remained staunchly loyal throughout the rebellion—bore the brunt of the economic collapse following Tyrone's defeat and were forced to maintain garrisons. The preponderantly Catholic townsmen, moreover, hoped that James's accession would herald a return to Catholicism; but in the meantime they produced ancient municipal charters to assert their independence and prevent Mountjoy's intervention in their affairs. Mountjoy, who, Moryson remarked, 'would cut King John's charter in pieces with King James' sword', acted quickly to suppress the potentially dangerous revolt and brought the towns to submission (Moryson, *History of Ireland*, 2.337). He then departed for England where, upon his arrival in June, he presented the 'arch-traitor' Tyrone to James I.

Earl of Devonshire, scandal, and death On 27 July 1603 an appreciative king created Mountjoy earl of Devonshire. To this distinction were added lucrative sinecures and substantial grants of land in both England and Ireland. In May 1604 he was appointed to a commission which negotiated a peace with Spain and in November of the following year a nervous James I nominated him to defend the crown against the insurrection which it was thought might follow the discovery of the Gunpowder Plot. Though an insurrection failed to materialize Devonshire presided over the investigation into the affair. In these later years he maintained an interest in learning and was a regular patron of poets: John Davies published a sonnet to him in his *Microcosmus* in 1603 and in 1605 Nicholas Breton dedicated to him 'The honour of valour'. Following his triumph in Ireland Devonshire had, it appeared, achieved the financial security, the respect, and the military distinction that he had sought so persistently in his youth. His scandalous involvement with a married woman, however, plagued him to his death and besmirched his otherwise impeccable reputation.

On 26 December 1605 Devonshire married Lady Penelope *Rich (1563–1607). Lady Penelope was the daughter of Walter *Devereux, first earl of Essex, and was sister of the late second earl of Essex. She had been Devonshire's lover from at least 1590 despite her marriage to Robert, Lord Rich, in 1581. All parties had overlooked their questionable relationship until Lord Rich obtained a divorce from Penelope in the ecclesiastical courts in November 1605. Devonshire then sought to legitimize their relationship, and their five children, by marrying Penelope, and, although an ecclesiastical divorce did not permit remarriage, he persuaded William Laud, his chaplain, to perform the rite. A scandal ensued. In his defence Devonshire wrote a tract, dedicated to the king, in which he appealed to scripture and to protestant divines to justify his reasons for marrying Penelope, but to no avail. The scandal—coupled with a falling out with Cecil in early 1606—made Devonshire a social pariah whose future was uncertain. In March 1606 he travelled to London to visit Cecil, but became stricken with a respiratory infection—doubtless aggravated by years of heavy smoking—and died at Savoy House in the Strand on 3 April 1606. According to Chamberlain he left this life 'soon and early for his years, but late enough for himself: happy had he been if he had gone two or three years since, before the world was weary of him, or that he had left his scandal behind him' (*Memorials of Affairs of State*, 2.206). He was buried in St Paul's chapel of Westminster Abbey on 7 May and in his honour John Ford wrote a poem entitled 'Fames memorial, or, The earle of Devonshire deceased' while Samuel Daniel composed 'A funeral poeme upon the death of the late noble earle of Devenshyre'.

As his marriage was unrecognized Devonshire's children were deemed illegitimate and his titles became extinct at his death. He provided generously for Penelope and his eldest son, Mountjoy *Blount, received a substantial inheritance. His other children, St John, Charles, Penelope, and Isabella also received an annual sum out of his vast estate. Devonshire had successfully reversed the financial decline of his noble house and had completed the transformation from a favoured Tudor courtier to a respected general and statesman, but his domestic misery and early death prevented him from becoming a figure of major importance. CHRISTOPHER MAGINN

Sources F. M. Jones, *Mountjoy, 1563–1606* (Dublin, 1958) • C. B. Falls, *Mountjoy: Elizabethan general* (1955) • *Calendar of the manuscripts of the most hon. the marquis of Salisbury*, 24 vols., HMC, 9 (1883–1976), vols. 7, 9 • *CSP dom.*, 1547–80 • PRO, SP 63 • Mountjoy's letter to James on his marriage, BL, Lansdowne MS 885 • will, Exeter College Library, Oxford • T. Stafford, *Pacata Hibernia, or, A history of the wars in Ireland, during the reign of Queen Elizabeth* (1633); repr. (1810) • J. S. Brewer and W. Bullen, eds., *Calendar of the Carew manuscripts*, 6 vols., PRO (1867–73) • *APC*, 1542–7 • *AFM* • R. Naunton, *Fragmenta regalia: memoirs of Elizabeth, her court and favourites* (1824) • F. Moryson, *An itinerary containing his ten yeeres travell through the twelve dominions*, 4 vols. (1907–8) • J. Ford, *Fames memorial, or, The earle of Devonshire deceased: with his honourable life peacefull end, and solemne funerell* (1606) • F. Moryson, *An history of Ireland from the year 1599 to 1603*, 2 vols. (1735) • *Memorials of affairs of state in the reigns of Q. Elizabeth and K. James I, collected (chiefly) from the original papers of … Sir Ralph Winwood*, ed. E. Sawyer, 3 vols. (1725) • W. B. Devereux, *Lives and letters of the Devereux, earls of Essex … 1540–1646*, 2 vols. (1853) • *The works of Francis Bacon*, ed. J. Spedding, R. L. Ellis, and D. D. Heath, 14 vols. (1857–74), vols. 2–3 • B. Burke, *A genealogical history of the dormant, abeyant, forfeited and* *extinct peerages of the British empire*, new edn (1883) · N. M. Sutherland, 'Blount, Charles', HoP, *Commons, 1558–1603* · *DNB* · GEC, *Peerage*, new edn

Archives BL, letter to James on his marriage, Lansdowne MS 885 · Bodl. Oxf., Tanner MSS, papers · LPL, letters to Sir George Carew · NRA, priv. coll., letters to earl of Essex

Likenesses N. Hilliard, miniature, 1587, Antony House [NT], Cornwall [*see illus.*] · oils, *c.*1597, Mapledurham House, Oxfordshire; version, Mapledurham House, Oxfordshire · group portrait, oils, 1604 (*The Somerset House conference*), NPG · V. Green, mezzotint, pubd 1775 (after portrait by P. Van Somer), NG Ire. · T. Cockson, print, BM · N. Hilliard, two miniatures, priv. coll. · engraving (after contemporary engraving), BL · engraving (after T. Cockson), BL · portraits, repro. in Jones, *Mountjoy*

Wealth at death over £20,000: will, Exeter College, Oxford

Blount, Charles (1654–1693), freethinker and author, was born at Upper Holloway, Islington, Middlesex, on 27 April 1654 and baptized at Highgate Chapel, Hornsey, on 10 May 1654, the fourth son of Sir Henry *Blount (1602–1682), traveller, of Tittenhanger, Hertfordshire, and his wife, Hester (*c.*1620–1678), daughter of Christopher Wase of Upper Holloway, Middlesex. He was clearly a precocious child 'endowed by nature with a great capacity, and with a strong propensity to learning' (Kippis, 2.380) and his father had him and his elder brother, Thomas Pope *Blount, educated at home, being opposed to 'sending youths to the universities' where 'they learnt … to be debaucht' (*Brief Lives*, 1.109). On 3 December 1672 at Westminster Abbey he married Eleanor (*c.*1654–1689), fourth daughter of Sir Timothy Tyrrell of Shotover, Oxfordshire, with whom he had three sons and three daughters. About the same time Blount inherited some lands in Islington and was also given the family estate of Blount's Hall, in Staffordshire, where he lived the life of a gentleman and man of letters.

Blount's first publication was the anonymous *Mr Dreyden Vindicated* (1673), a defence of John Dryden's play *The Conquest of Granada* (1672) against the criticisms of both Richard Leigh's *The Censure of the Rota* (1673) and *The Friendly Vindication* (1673) attributed to Robert Howard. In 1696 Dryden made a complimentary reference to him in his *The Life of Lucian* prefixed to the edition of *The Works of Lucian* (1711) partly translated by Blount himself. On 19 December 1678 Charles became a member of the Green Ribbon Club, a political group of whig activists and propagandists. In the same year he published anonymously the first of his major works, *Anima mundi*, with the false imprint 'Amsterdam, *Anno Mundi*. 00000', in the writing of which he probably had the assistance of his father, whose libertine ideas he inherited (see Sir Henry Blount's fragment 'De anima' in *The Oracles of Reason*, 1693). Relying mainly upon unorthodox authors such as Montaigne, *Anima mundi* is an essay on pagan doctrines about the nature of the human soul and its destiny in the afterlife. The author apparently argues in favour of the immortality of the soul on moral and psychological grounds but is purposely ambiguous and unconvincing throughout. The sceptical tone of the book raised a great clamour. The bishop of London ordered only 'the Bare Suppression of it', but 'Advantage was taken' (L'Estrange) and during the bishop's absence from London the book was burnt. Blount sent a copy of it to Hobbes with a letter, dated 1678, in which he expressed his preference for the religion of the Arians and gave a polemical description of the first Christian councils. The same sceptical conclusions on the nature of the soul reappeared in two letters that he sent in February 1680 to his libertine friend the earl of Rochester (printed in *The Oracles of Reason*).

In 1679, under the pseudonym Junius Brutus, Blount published a pamphlet of strong whig tendencies, entitled *An Appeal from the Country to the City*, defending the reality of the Popish Plot and describing the fate of London should the duke of York and the papists gain control of the city. Benjamin Harris, the printer of this work, was brought to trial and fined, while the pamphlet was condemned to be burnt by the common hangman. In the same year Blount, under the pseudonym Philopatris, addressed parliament with *A Just Vindication of Learning* (1679), asking that body to consider his arguments against the renewal of the Licensing Act, which was due to expire. Following the arguments of Milton's *Areopagitica*, Blount stressed the importance of freedom of the press for the achievement of liberty and condemned censorship as the greatest affront to learning. Soon after Hobbes's death in 1679 he edited anonymously *The Last Sayings, or Dying Legacy of Mr Thomas Hobbs* (1680), a broadsheet chiefly consisting of extracts from *Leviathan* whose ambiguous nature concealed the real intentions of the author.

The influence of Thomas Hobbes and Edward Herbert, Lord Herbert of Cherbury, is strongly evident in Blount's next two works, published in 1680: *Great is Diana of the Ephesians*, published anonymously with the false imprint 'Cosmopoli', and *The Two First Books of Philostratus*. The former, mixing the libertine criticism of positive religions with analysis of the origin and decline of the rational creed, is an open attack upon heathen sacrifices concealing a harsh polemic against Christianity. The latter is an English translation of the life of Apollonius Tyaneus by Philostratus with long discursive annotations partly taken from the anonymous manuscript 'Dialogue between a tutor and his pupil'. The text, a biography of the neo-Pythagorean philosopher Apollonius, whose life offered an ironic surrogate for that of Christ, was later condemned in 1693.

In 1683 Blount published anonymously *Miracles, No Violations of the Laws of Nature*, a set of quotations (without acknowledgement) from Thomas Burnet, Hobbes, and Spinoza proving the groundlessness of any pretended miracles. The text drawn from Spinoza was Blount's translation of the sixth chapter of *Tractatus theologico-politicus*, the first English translation of any of Spinoza's writings. In the same year Blount published *Religio laici*, a deistic tract chiefly taken from Herbert's 'Religio laici' (first published in 1933) and *Dialogue between a Tutor and His Pupil*. Expressing his adherence to the five Herbertian principles of any natural religion and to the concept of reason as the only foundation of faith, Blount thus answered Dryden's criticism against deists contained in a poem with the same title published in 1682.

Ten years later, in January 1693, Blount issued anonymously *King William and Queen Mary Conquerors*, a tract which claimed that both sovereigns came to the throne in 1689 by right of conquest and, following Hobbes and Grotius, that subjects should submit to any rulers who could protect them, even if conquerors. The pamphlet was, however, moderate, arguing that only certain circumstances could justify conquest, and that a conqueror could not legitimately claim absolute power. It was licensed by Edmund Bohun, the tory licenser of the press, who agreed with its political theory. It was probably not, as previously thought, deliberately written to discredit Bohun and had only a small role in the demise of the Licensing Act, which was renewed in 1693 but expired in 1695. Its argument, however, proved highly controversial. Many whigs agreed with its moderate conquest doctrine but it also found both whig and tory opponents in the House of Commons, which after a heated debate, concluded that it was 'highly injurious to their Majesties; and inconsistent with the Principles on which this Government is founded' (*JHC*, 10.788). On 23 January the book was condemned to be burnt by the common hangman, and the following day Bohun was dismissed from office. No action against the author is recorded. Soon after that, a pamphlet was published under the initials J. M.—*Reasons Humbly Offered for the Liberty of Unlicens'd Printing* (1693). Another adaptation of *Areopagitica* against the futility of licensing acts and the inadequacies of Edmund Bohun, this was generally presumed at the time to be by Blount, but in fact it is unlikely that he wrote it. Just before his death Blount published *The Oracles of Reason* (1693), a collection of miscellaneous tracts and letters written by himself, his friend Charles Gildon, and other freethinkers from 1678 to 1693. The volume questioned or denied the validity of 'many strongly held beliefs, by raising doubts over Genesis, denying revelation, doubting miracles, and even venturing the eternity of a plurality of worlds' (Redwood, 497).

Blount's wife had died in 1689, and he and his deceased wife's sister fell in love, but both knew that a marriage between persons so connected was illegal. On 8 March 1693 Blount wrote a letter to his friend Gildon 'to Justifie the Marrying of two Sisters, the one after the other' (*Oracles of Reason*, 135) and also petitioned the archbishop of Canterbury, but to no avail. Having long laboured in vain to convince her that she might marry him anyway, at last, whether in a deliberate attempt to kill himself or in the hope of touching her heart, Blount committed suicide. After languishing for about a month he finally died in Catherine Street, London, at the end of August 1693, and was buried in the family vault at Ridge, Tittenhanger. His freethinking is confirmed in his will of 11 February 1693, in which he resigned his 'soul into the universal spirit whereof she [*sic*] is a particle', and submitted himself 'to the allwise and great God's disposall not distrusting his divine providence in the next world who hath been so good and gracious to me in this' (will). He also sent his 'prayers to the great and only supream mind for his blessing upon my poor children' (ibid.). Concerning his books he instructed that if his heirs had 'any vallue for my memory they will never sell or dispose of that study and theire collection which I have with soe much charge and trouble gathered together' (ibid.). He left his estate to his five children and earnestly requested that if his executors carried out only one of his instructions it would be to bury him next to his wife, 'my dearest Nelly the best woman that ever lived' (ibid.). Perhaps because of difficulties over the manner of his death, the will was not proved until 18 June 1697, by his eldest son, Henry. In 1695 Charles Gildon published *The Miscellaneous Works of Charles Blount* with a preface by himself containing a defence of suicide. Wrongly considered a plagiarist by some, Blount was rather author, compiler, and propagator of important freethinking works, widely circulated and criticized.

DARIO PFANNER

Sources K.-J. Walber, *Charles Blount (1654–1693), Frühaufklärer* (1988) • U. Bonanate, *Charles Blount: libertinismo e deismo nel Seicento inglese* (1972) • A. Kippis, 'Blount, Charles', *Biographia Britannica, or, The lives of the most eminent persons who have flourished in Great Britain and Ireland*, ed. A. Kippis and others, 2 (1780) • P. Harth, *Contexts of Dryden's thought* (1968), 73–94 • M. Goldie, 'Charles Blount's intention in writing *King William and Queen Mary conquerors* (1693)', *N&Q*, 223 (1978), 527–32 • J. A. Redwood, 'Charles Blount (1654–93), deism and English free thought', *Journal of the History of Ideas*, 35 (1974), 490–98 • J. S. L. Gilmour, 'Some uncollected authors XVII', *Book Collector*, 7 (1958), 182–7 • *DNB* • *Brief lives, chiefly of contemporaries, set down by John Aubrey, between the years 1669 and 1696*, ed. A. Clark, 1 (1898), 108–11 • R. L'Estrange, *The Observator*, 1/290 (1684) • *JHC*, 10 (1688–93), 784–8 • P. Bayle, *Dictionnaire historique et critique*, 2 (1820), 188–96 • *The correspondence of Thomas Hobbes*, ed. N. Malcolm, pbk edn, 2 (1997), 790–95 • BL, Add. MS 36242 • will, PRO, PROB 11/438, fols. 177–9 • A. Collins, *The English baronetage*, 3 (1741)

Archives Athenaeum Club, London, Blount's miscellanea MS, casemark 100Ab • U. Aberdeen L., discussion of *Oracles of reason* | BL, Harley MS 7315, fols. 146–9 • BL, tracts on religion, 873.b3 • Bodl. Oxf., MS Firth, c.16, fols. 130–34

Wealth at death see will, PRO, PROB 11/438, fols. 177–9

Blount, Sir Christopher (1555/6–1601), soldier and conspirator, was the second son of Thomas Blount (*b.* before 1523, *d.* 1568) of Kidderminster, Worcestershire. Blount's early life was profoundly shaped by two key influences: devout Catholicism (especially on the part of his mother, Margery, *née* Poley, who was listed as a confirmed recusant in 1577); and his family's tradition of service to the Dudley family. Blount's paternal grandfather, Edward (*d.* 1558), had served John Dudley, duke of Northumberland (executed 1553), being a first cousin of the duke's wife. In his turn Blount's father had become comptroller to Northumberland and then a steward to the latter's son, Robert Dudley, earl of Leicester. Blount's elder brother, Edward (*c.*1554–1630), continued the tradition and carried a banderole at Leicester's funeral in 1588. Unlike his brother, however, who inherited substantial land around Kidderminster, Christopher needed to make his fortune through service to Leicester. He became gentleman of the horse to Leicester, who was himself master of the horse to the queen, by October 1584.

Blount's Catholic heritage was reflected in his schooling. As a boy he was tutored by William Allen (later cardinal) at Louvain. He may have been the English student who fell sick there in 1562 and who was tended by Allen until he himself became ill. In 1572 Blount, aged sixteen, and his brother matriculated at Hart Hall, Oxford. He did not take a degree but instead went overseas to the Catholic college at Douai (*c*.1575–1576). At the end of 1576, when the college was forced to leave Douai, Lady Blount sent a servant to bring Christopher home. He and a Mr Throckmorton instead travelled to Paris, where they mixed with supporters of Mary, queen of Scots, including Thomas Morgan.

By October 1577 the English ambassador, Sir Amias Paulet, was sufficiently alarmed by these contacts to warn Blount against Morgan's company and report them to Leicester and Sir Francis Walsingham. Morgan later claimed that he cultivated Blount's friendship in the hope that his attachment to Leicester might one day benefit Mary's cause. This opportunity seemed to have arrived in early 1585, when Mary was moved to confinement at Tutbury. Aware of Blount's necessary association with the nearby stud for the queen's horses, Morgan asked Blount to assist Mary by arranging some secret means for her to communicate with her supporters abroad. Blount responded by sending Robert Poley (probably a kinsman) to assure Morgan of his loyalty to Mary and the Catholic cause. In fact Poley had been an agent working against Mary for some time. Blount's success in convincing Morgan to trust Poley must be seen as a calculated endeavour by Blount to profit from his Catholic upbringing by betraying his old friends and associates to Leicester and Walsingham. It is unclear whether his motives were entirely materialistic or partly intended to protect his mother, brother, and other relatives from religious persecution. Blount claimed to Walsingham in 1588 that he himself had forsaken Catholicism. Whatever the motivation Blount and Poley ensured that communications with Mary in 1585 were exposed to her enemies, foreshadowing the process by which other agents would monitor Mary's messages after her removal to Chartley and reveal her complicity in the Babington plot during 1586.

In December 1585, when Leicester led an army to the Netherlands, Blount accompanied his master overseas and became a cavalry officer. At the battle of Zutphen in September 1586 he rescued Sir Francis Vere after the latter's horse had been killed. After serving as lieutenant to Sir Thomas Perrot he assumed the captaincy of Leicester's company of lancers. When the earl handed over command in the Low Countries to Lord Willoughby, Blount remained with the army. In 1588 he was maimed in one hand at Berke. He was later knighted by Willoughby, who described him as 'cousin'. In January 1589 he returned home to recuperate from his wound. In April Blount joined the Portugal expedition as a companion of Leicester's stepson, Robert Devereux, second earl of Essex.

Blount's participation in this expedition was driven by his sudden marriage to Essex's mother and Leicester's widow, Lettice, *née* Knollys [*see* Dudley, Lettice (*b.* after 1540, *d.* 1634)]. News of this sensational match had reached Paris by the beginning of May and the wedding itself probably occurred in March or April. The marriage apparently sprang from the countess's need for male support in her struggle over Leicester's heavily indebted estate, though she and Blount had known each other for some years and proved to be a genuinely happy couple. Fifteen or sixteen years his senior, Lady Leicester brought the tall and black-haired Blount undreamed-of wealth, a tangled web of legal problems, and association with Essex, the queen's new favourite. Blount spent the rest of his life seeking to banish Essex's initial uncertainty about this 'unhappy' match (BL, Lansdowne MS 62, fol. 78*r*). Described in private letters as the countess's 'best friend', Blount vowed himself to 'faythfully honor and … ever trewlly serve' Essex 'tyll after I be dead' (Warks. CRO, TD 69/6, Blount to Essex, 26 June 1597). Blount soon plunged into property transactions which sought to settle the countess's huge debts with the crown and other legal liabilities. In doing so he sold most of her jewels and 'choptte and chainged awaye' her jointure (BL, Harley MS 304, fol. 88*r–v*).

Essex's backing ensured that Blount was elected knight of the shire for Staffordshire in the 1593 and 1597 parliaments and that he acted as a virtual deputy lieutenant for the county. Blount served as colonel of a regiment in Essex's expedition to Spain in 1596 and became campmaster for the army after Sir John Wingfield was killed during the storming of Cadiz. Blount and his troops later acted as Essex's vanguard for the attack on Faeroe. In 1597 Blount helped to train the army being prepared for Essex's new expedition, joining the earl's council of war as second-in-command of the infantry under his distant cousin Lord Mountjoy. When the expedition was converted into a voyage to the Azores he joined with Sir Gelly Meyrick and other partisans of Essex to accuse Sir Walter Ralegh of committing a capital offence by his landing at Fayal. Essex ultimately dismissed these charges, but they underlined the growing divide between the earl's friends and opponents. Blount's factional adherence to Essex resulted in his creation as an MA of Oxford on 10 July 1598 in company with several other friends of the earl.

Partisan politics also lay behind the unwelcome suggestion in April or May that Blount should be appointed lord deputy of Ireland but, like several others, he refused the post. Blount was full of misgivings when Essex agreed to become lord lieutenant of Ireland later in the year. Ironically Essex's eagerness to appoint him marshal of the army in Ireland made the reluctant Blount an object of contention between the earl and the queen. Elizabeth agreed to his appointment as marshal in March 1599, but refused to let him join the council of Ireland. Blount accompanied Essex on his campaign in the southern counties, before being badly wounded in the legs in King's county. Essex released him from service in late August, though he was paid as marshal until 30 September. Blount's wound was so severe that he feared for his life and turned again to the Church of Rome, encouraged by two Catholic priests in Dublin. Blount later secretly converted Sir John Davies to Catholicism. Before his return to England, Blount was visited by Essex and the earl of Southampton, who were soon to march north against the Irish leader Tyrone. Essex raised the prospect of returning to England with an army. Blount and Southampton opposed the idea, suggesting instead that he take only a few picked officers as a bodyguard. Essex later returned to England in great haste and was arrested. During 1600 Blount unsuccessfully urged Essex to consider escaping from imprisonment and going into exile abroad.

Blount's influence with the earl now seems to have been overshadowed by that of the more bellicose Southampton, with whom he enjoyed rather strained relations. When he joined Essex and his friends in London in late January 1601 Blount found the two earls already committed to action, but confused in their planning. Called upon to aid his stepson in the forthcoming *coup*, Blount was more earnest than enthusiastic. According to an abortive plan for seizing the court, Blount would have been entrusted with securing the gate. When Essex and his partisans were panicked into action on Saturday 7 February, Blount was clearly unhappy with the decision to enter the City on foot. As a cavalryman, he preferred the use of horses. Nevertheless he played a vigorous role in Essex's insurrection on 8 February, seizing weapons from a London armourer, laying hands upon a messenger from the queen, and leading the attack at Ludgate, where he repeatedly hacked at the defenders' pikes with his sword before being bludgeoned to the ground by blows to the head.

When Blount fell, Essex's force lost heart and retreated in disorder. Badly wounded, Blount was imprisoned in the nearby house of a London tailor, Richard Newsome. When he was arraigned and condemned at Westminster Hall on 5 March, he had to be carried there on a litter. Although he wrote begging for mercy and reminded the authorities of his service fifteen years earlier, the only mercy Blount received was death by beheading. He was executed on Tower Hill on 18 March 1601, openly professing his Catholicism on the scaffold, and he was probably buried at the Tower on the same day. PAUL E. J. HAMMER

Sources PRO, SP classes 12 (Eliz. domestic), 63 (Ireland), 84 (Holland) · *State trials*, vol. 1 · A. J. Perrett, 'The Blounts of Kidderminster', *Transactions of the Worcestershire Archaeological Society*, new ser., 19 (1942), 10–18 · *Calendar of the manuscripts of the most hon. the marquis of Salisbury*, 24 vols., HMC, 9 (1883–1976), vols. 3–14, esp. vol. 9 · Warks. CRO, TD 69/6 (ii) · T. F. Knox and others, eds., *The first and second diaries of the English College, Douay* (1878) · *A collection of state papers … left by William Cecill, Lord Burghley*, ed. W. Murdin, 2 (1759) · S. Adams, ed., *Household accounts and disbursement books of Robert Dudley, earl of Leicester, 1558–1561, 1584–1586*, CS, 6 (1995) · BL, Lansdowne MSS 62, 78, 243 · BL, Harley MSS 304, 6996 · *Reg. Oxf.*, 2/1–4 · Folger, Bagot papers, L.a.1–1078 · *The letters of John Chamberlain*, ed. N. E. McClure, 2 vols. (1939) · PRO, E351/238, 240 · *Report on the manuscripts of the earl of Ancaster*, HMC, 66 (1907) · *APC, 1596–1604* · *VCH Worcestershire*, vol. 3 · W. A. Shaw, *The knights of England*, 2 (1906) · G. L. Craik, *The romance of the peerage*, 2 vols. (1848–50), 1.1–339 · LPL, MS 647, fol. 247 · Wood, *Ath. Oxon.: Fasti* (1815), 280 · W. Camden, *The history of the most renowned and victorious Princess Elizabeth*, 4th edn (1688), 618 · W. Hervey, *The visitation of Suffolk, 1561*, ed. J. Corder, 1, Harleian Society, new ser., 2 (1981), 123–4 · M. A. S. Hume, ed., *Calendar of letters and state papers relating to English affairs, preserved principally in the archives of Simancas*, 4, PRO (1899), 1587–1603

Archives priv. coll., letters to the earl of Essex · Warks. CRO, Finch-Knightley of Packington Hall MSS, TD 69/6 (ii)

Wealth at death total estate valued at approx. £8000: PRO, SP 12/279/45, fols. 60r–62v

Blount [Blunt], **Edward** (*bap.* **1562**, *d.* in or before **1632**), bookseller and translator, was baptized on 31 January 1562 in the parish of St Laurence Pountney, London, probably the sixth of eight known children of Ralph (Rafe) Blount (Blunt or Blonte; *d.* 1571), merchant tailor. Ralph, freed of his apprenticeship in 1548, was reasonably prosperous, but never became a member of the Merchant Taylors' Company. Edward's unknown mother must have died when he was quite young; his father remarried in 1566. Edward's stepmother, Margaret Roberdine Blount, was buried on 5 August 1571, followed by his father on 9 September. His father's will, written just four days before, divides his estate equally between his six surviving 'welbelovde children' (Guildhall Library, MS 9171, fol. 77r).

Born into the urban middle class, orphaned at a young age, Edward lived seventy years in London, a tradesman like his father, but unlike most small shopkeepers he had a profound impact on English cultural life. He had an unparalleled gift for recognizing new works that would eventually become classics: he was more consistently successful in anticipating the cultural consensus of the future than Daniel, Sidney, Jonson, or any other early modern critic. This achievement was made possible by his father's most important legacy: a literary education. The son of a merchant tailor, Edward almost certainly attended—as did his two elder brothers—the Merchant Taylors' School, founded in 1561. There, with Edmund Spenser and Lancelot Andrewes among others, he would have been taught by the famous schoolmaster, humanist intellectual, and educational theorist Richard Mulcaster. Blount read and wrote Latin and Italian, and an early aptitude and interest in reading may explain why, on 24 June 1578, he began an association with the Stationers' Company that lasted fifty-four years. Having been apprenticed on 24 June 1578 and freed on 25 June 1588, he acquired his own first apprentice in 1595, rose to the company's livery on 10 May 1611, was elected an assistant on 25 October 1625, and served on the court of assistants until December 1630. During most and perhaps all of that time, he lived and worked in St Paul's Churchyard, the centre of the retail book trade, first as an apprentice at the Bishop's Head, later in his own shop at the Black Bear (1609–27). His friends were other booksellers: in 1600 Thomas Thorpe dedicated Marlowe's translation of Lucan to 'his kind and true friend, Edward Blount', and Thorpe and Blount were still drinking partners in the 1620s (*Lucans First Book*, sig. A2r). Even his wife was the widow of another stationer: Elizabeth Royden married Richard Banckworth in 1595, and was granted administration of his estate on 11 April 1614. Blount married her before 1618.

Blount had been apprenticed for ten years (not the usual seven) to William Ponsonby, described by McKerrow as 'the most important publisher of the Elizabethan period' (McKerrow, 39). Ponsonby published almost all the work of Edmund Spenser and Sir Philip Sidney; he pioneered commercial exploitation of a developing market for contemporary vernacular literature, and Blount—the most important publisher of the early seventeenth century—followed in his master's footsteps. But Blount did not inherit Ponsonby's shop, or his priorities. By contrast with most early modern stationers (including Ponsonby), Blount was a remarkably secular bookseller. For instance, until he formed a business partnership with William Barrett (1609–13), he did not publish a single sermon, although that genre was popular and profitable.

The first book Blount published did not appear until six years after he was freed of his apprenticeship: Josuah Sylvester's *The Profit of Imprisonment* (1594), a French poem translated by an English merchant living in the Low Countries. (Sylvester was then unknown; his translations of Du Bartas, in part published by Blount, would eventually make him one of the English writers most admired by his contemporaries.) Blount's second publication was Charles Tessier's *Le premier livre de chansons* (1597), a book of French and Italian songs; his third was John Florio's Italian–English dictionary, *A Worlde of Wordes* (1598). The cosmopolitan ambition of these first three books was characteristic of Blount's career: he published European histories and European travel books; dictionaries of Italian, Spanish, and Latin; and works translated out of French, Italian, Spanish, Dutch, Greek, Latin, and neo-Latin.

Blount also developed relationships with English ambassadors abroad. Between 27 October 1613 and 25 January 1620, the name Ned Blunt appears repeatedly in John Chamberlain's letters to Sir Dudley Carleton, ambassador to Venice (1610–15) and The Hague (1616–25). Three documents, signed by Blount between 15 June 1614 and 23 June 1615, show him involved in Carleton's efforts to deliver Italian works of art for the collection of his new patron, Robert Carr. The Blount–Carleton connection links the book trade with international commercial networks in art objects, currencies, cloth, seeds, and foodstuffs. More interesting as human documents are Blount's five surviving letters, written between 15 June 1621 and 9 May 1623, to William Trumbull, English agent in Brussels. They establish that Blount also sold manuscripts and banned books, and document his 'neerenesse of freindship' with his fellow stationer John Bill (Sir Thomas Bodley's agent in acquiring books printed abroad) and at least two authors whose work he published, the Italophile Sir Robert Dallington and the Hispanophile James Mabbe (BL, Add. MS 72361/116). Another of his authors, Leonard Digges, was sending a package 'to Ned Blounte' in a letter from Oxford written on 30 January 1631 (BL, Lansdowne MS 841, fol. 30*v*).

Blount was the chief publisher—listed on the title-page alongside the printer Isaac Jaggard—of the first folio edition of Shakespeare's *Comedies, Histories, and Tragedies* (with commendatory verses by his friends Mabbe and Digges). He also published Shakespeare's 'The Phoenix and the Turtle', Marlowe's *Hero and Leander*, and the first essays of Thomas Hobbes; the first (and still most admired) English translations of Montaigne's essays, Cervantes' *Don Quixote*, and Matteo Aleman's picaresque classic *Guzman de Alfarache*, as well as *Naturall and Morall Historie of the East and West Indies*, after the original by José de Acosta, 'the most original and influential of all histories of the New World' (Grafton, 207), and *Of Wisdom*, a translation of Pierre Charron's banned 'scandalous book', one of the foundational texts of post-Christian philosophical atheism (Gregory, 87); significant literary texts by George Chapman, John Earle, Joseph Hall, Ben Jonson, and John Lyly; and Samuel Daniel's *Defence of Rhyme*, the most important work of English literary criticism written between Sidney's *Apology* and Dryden's *Of Drammatick Poesie*.

Blount probably translated the works that he published and dedicated as Tomasso Garzoni's *Hospitall of Incurable Fooles* (1600) and Lorenzo Ducci's *Ars aulica, or, The Courtier's Arte* (1607). He also signed prefaces to nine other books, including *Hero and Leander* (1598), in which he called Christopher Marlowe his 'friend' and described himself as 'executor' of Marlowe's 'intellectual will' (sig. A3*r*), and *Sixe Court Comedies* (1632), which praises the wit and originality of John Lyly—'The *Lyre* he played on, had no borrowed strings' (sig. A3*v*). This last preface acknowledges that Blount himself is 'no executor, yet I presume to distribute the Goods of the Dead' (ibid.).

Blount's own goods were soon to be so distributed. By October 1632 he was dead, and on 3 October 1636 his widow sold his remaining copyrights to Andrew Crooke. But his real heirs were the two seventeenth-century publishers who, from Blount, took up the task of shaping the English literary canon: Humphrey Moseley and Jacob Tonson. GARY TAYLOR

Sources index of freemen, Merchant Taylors' Company, GL · parish register, St Laurence Pountney, 31 Jan 1562 [baptism] · parish register, St Stephen Coleman Street, London [marriage] · will, commissary court of London, GL, MS 9171, fols. 76*v*–77*v* [Ralph Blount, father] · administration, commissary court of London, GL, MS 9168, fol. 25 · J. Brownbill, 'Edward Blount's wife', *TLS* (7 June 1923), 388 · PRO, SP 14/80/89, 115a, 117 · BL, Lansdowne MS 841, fol. 30*v* · BL, Trumbull Miscellaneous Correspondence, Add. MS 72361/11, 116; Add. MS 72364/152; Add. MS 72365/46, 55 · Mrs E. P. Hart, ed., *Merchant Taylors' School register, 1561–1934*, 2 vols. (1936) · *STC, 1475–1640* · Arber, *Regs. Stationers* · P. W. M. Blayney, *The bookshops in Paul's Cross churchyard* (1990), 17, 26–7 · W. A. Jackson, ed., *Records of the court of the Stationers' Company, 1602 to 1640* (1957) · H. R. Plomer, *Abstracts from the wills of English printers and stationers from 1492 to 1630* (1903) · *The letters of John Chamberlain*, ed. N. E. McClure, 2 vols. (1939) · D. F. McKenzie, ed., *Stationers' Company apprentices*, [2]: *1641–1700* (1974) · H. G. Aldis and others, *A dictionary of printers and booksellers in England, Scotland and Ireland, and of foreign printers of English books, 1557–1640*, ed. R. B. McKerrow (1910) · A. Grafton, *New worlds, ancient texts: the power of tradition and the shock of discovery* (1992), 207 · T. Gregory, 'Pierre Charron's "Scandalous Book"', *Atheism from the Reformation to the Enlightenment*, ed. M. Hunter and D. Wootton (1992), 87–110 · *Lucans first book*, trans. C. Marlowe (1600)

Blount, Edward (1769–1843), campaigner for Roman Catholic civil rights, was born on 18 July 1769, the second of the three children of Sir Walter Blount, sixth baronet (*d.* 1785), of Sodington, and his wife, Mary Aston, daughter of James, fifth Lord Aston of Forfar. Blount belonged to an

English Catholic gentry family which had held estates at Sodington, Worcestershire, since the Norman conquest. He was educated at the Catholic seminary at Douai (1782–6), and married Frances, daughter and coheir of Francis Wright of Fitzwalters, Essex, on 20 April 1803. They had five sons, including the banker and railway promoter Sir Edward Charles *Blount, and five daughters. He first came to prominence as a parliamentary reformer, being a founder member of the Hampden Club in 1811; but it was in the campaign for Catholic emancipation that he made his mark.

In 1822 Blount became secretary of the largely aristocratic pressure group the Catholic Board, and a year later assumed the same office in the British Catholic Association. By the dissemination of propaganda this newly established body aimed to reassure the protestant majority that the extension of civil rights to Catholics would pose no threat to church and state, a campaign which Blount thought indistinguishable from 'the general cause of civil liberty', and he attempted to make common cause with dissenters. But his pluralist, gradualist approach did not find universal favour with his fellow Catholics. In November 1828 a damaging rupture occurred with Daniel O'Connell, the Irish Catholic leader, over Blount's readiness to welcome partial measures of legislative relief. Dissension, underfunding, and apathy caused him to threaten to resign on several occasions, and in facing down a vote of no confidence in January 1829 he belied his description in the *Catholic Miscellany* as 'one of the most dispassionate looking men living' by mounting a robust defence of his record. The British Catholic Association was dissolved on the passage of emancipation in April. Charles Butler, a leading member, conceded in his *Memoir of the Catholic Relief Bill* (1829) that their Irish counterparts had acted 'with much greater boldness and effect' to bring this about, but praised the endeavours of Blount, 'the soul of all the proceedings' on the British side, to create a favourable climate of opinion.

Blount entered parliament at the general election in 1830 for Steyning, a pocket borough of the Catholic twelfth duke of Norfolk, to whom he acted as personal auditor. He supported the whig-led Grey ministry, and spoke occasionally, chiefly on matters pertaining to remaining Catholic grievances. He was re-elected in 1831, but his seat was abolished by the Reform Act, for which he had voted. An unsuccessful candidate for Horsham in the 1832 general election, he was afterwards active in supporting reform of the Church of Ireland and religious provision for Catholic convicts in Australia. He became chairman of the Bank of Australasia in 1833 and was a partner in a Paris bank, but his business ventures evidently ended calamitously: when he died in Brussels 'on or about' 20 March 1843, he left a personalty of only £50. An early example of a pressure group politician, Blount played an important supporting role in the struggle for Catholic equality in the early nineteenth century.

H. J. Spencer

Sources B. N. Ward, *The eve of Catholic emancipation*, 3 vols. (1911–12), vol. 3 · *Catholic Miscellany*, 1–9 (1822–8) · 'The special meeting of the British Catholic Association', *Catholic Miscellany*, new ser., 2 (1829), 139–44, esp. 142–3 · C. Butler, *A memoir of the Catholic Relief Bill* (1829) · J. Kirk, *Biographies of English Catholics in the eighteenth century*, ed. J. H. Pollen and E. Burton (1909), 29 · E. Blount, *Petition vs. corporation and test acts … adopted at the open meeting of the British Catholic Association*, ed. J. H. Pollen and E. Burton (1828) · J. A. Hone, *For the cause of truth: radicalism in London, 1796–1821* (1982), 206, 208, 210 · W. Albery, *A parliamentary history of Horsham* (1927), 269–86 · [W. Pare], *A full and authentic report of the great Catholic meeting … in the town hall, Birmingham … 1835* (1835) · R. Therry, *Reminiscences of thirty years' residence in New South Wales and Victoria*, 2nd edn (1863), 148–50 · S. J. Butlin, *Australia and New Zealand Bank: the Bank of Australasia and the Union Bank of Australia Limited, 1828–1951* (1961); 2nd edn (1963), 23 · *GM*, 2nd ser., 19 (1843), 558–9

Archives Arundel Castle archives, material on Blount as auditor to the twelfth duke of Norfolk | Horsham Museum, 1832 election material

Likenesses portrait, Loxley Hall, Staffordshire; repro. in Ward, *Eve of Catholic emancipation*, facing p. 244

Wealth at death under £50—estate at Shabbington, Buckinghamshire, to son: administration, PRO, PROB 6/221/25; *VCH Buckinghamshire*, 4.103

Blount, Sir Edward Charles (1809–1905), banker and railway promoter, was born on 16 March 1809 at Bellamour, near Rugeley, Staffordshire, the second son of Edward *Blount (1769–1843), banker and politician, and his wife, Frances (*d.* 1859), daughter of Francis Wright of Fitzwalters, Essex. The Blount family was a staunchly Catholic house of ancient lineage. Edward Blount senior was active in the agitation for Catholic emancipation and was secretary of the Catholic Association. He joined with Daniel O'Connell in founding the Provincial Bank of Ireland, a 'Catholic' bank, and was whig MP for Steyning, Sussex, in the unreformed parliaments of 1830 and 1831.

At home, at the family seat of Bellamour, the young Edward gained a useful knowledge of French from Father Malvoisin, an *émigré* priest. He was then educated at the neighbouring grammar school in Rugeley, before attending the Catholic college of St Mary's at Oscott, near Birmingham, from 1819 to 1827. In the summer of 1827 he joined the London office of the Provincial Bank of Ireland. He was appointed to the Home Office during George Canning's short-lived ministry and often went to the House of Commons, developing an interest in Catholic emancipation. He was subsequently employed by his father as an assistant to the Catholic Association and was introduced to many leading liberal politicians at Holland House.

In the autumn of 1829 Blount was appointed to the British embassy in Paris and served as an attaché under Lord Granville. In the summer of 1830 he transferred to the Rome consulate, where he met Cardinal Weld, Lord Shrewsbury, and the future Napoleon III. Such diplomatic and political connections proved invaluable during his banking career. He returned to Paris in 1831 and abandoned diplomacy to establish a fortune of his own.

To begin with Blount lived on a family allowance and dabbled in journalism, writing for the first railway newspaper, *The Railway Chronicle*, before joining Callaghan & Co., a Paris bank that was agent for the Catholic bank of Wright, Selby & Co., of London. He then set up his own bank with his father's financial backing: Edward Blount, Père et Fils. On 18 November 1834 he married Gertrude

Frances Jerningham (*d.* 1907), daughter of William Charles Jerningham. They had two sons and three daughters.

The bank prospered with deposits from wealthy British expatriates. Blount soon formed a partnership with Charles Laffitte, nephew of Jacques Laffitte, a famous financier and politician. From 1836 Laffitte, Blount & Cie became a tireless promoter of French railways. France then had only 25 miles of railroads (England had 2000). Blount was surprised by French investors' lack of interest and, after parliament excluded state financing for the railways in 1838, he offered to finance and build a line from Paris to Rouen. He easily raised 15 million French francs in London, Liverpool, and Manchester, and this encouraged French investors to subscribe the same amount. The French government lent the project 14 million francs and authorized the line on 15 July 1840.

A company, the Chemins de Fer de l'Ouest, was formed by Blount, who became the first chairman. The board of directors was half French and half English, and those who backed the venture included Baron James de Rothschild, Lord Overstone. The line, which was designed by the English civil engineer Joseph Locke, with Thomas Brassey as contractor, was opened on 9 May 1843. To gain a thorough knowledge of railway management, Blount learned engine driving, spending four months on the London and North Western Railway (LNWR). Mr Buddicom, the locomotive manager of the LNWR at Liverpool, brought over fifty British train drivers for the French railway, which prospered from the start.

Laffitte, Blount & Cie subsequently promoted the construction of the expanding French railway network, in collaboration with Baron James de Rothschild and others. After the failure of the bank following the 1848 revolution, Blount, having paid its creditors in full, resumed business in 1852 as Edward Blount & Co., with the help of Thomas Brassey and other wealthy friends. Between 1838 and 1870 Blount helped to finance the Rouen–Le Havre, Amiens–Boulogne, Nord–Dieppe–Fécamp, Creil–Saint-Quentin, Lyons–Avignon, and Lyons–Geneva railways. When these were absorbed into regional networks, Blount joined the board of the new companies, acting as director of the Compagnie du Nord, director and vice-chairman of the famous Paris–Lyons–Mediterranean railways, and chairman of the Chemins de Fer de l'Ouest until 1894.

Blount also promoted Swiss, Austrian, Portuguese, and Middle Eastern railways, such as the Fell Railway over Mont-Cenis; and he financed other major engineering projects, becoming chairman of the Compagnie des Eaux. Attracted by the technical challenge he also invested in the Compagnie des Polders de l'Ouest, which turned marshes into farmland, and the Channel Tunnel Company; he lost money in both ventures.

To raise money for these projects Blount joined the Réunion Financière in 1856, a coalition of private bankers set up by James de Rothschild to counteract the rise of the Pereires' Credit Mobilier. In 1864 Blount was a founding member of Société Générale de Paris. In 1870 he transferred his business to this limited-liability bank and became its chairman. In 1901 he was made honorary chairman, remaining the bank's London agent. He also took directorships in the London Joint-Stock Bank and the General Credit and Finance Company (later the Union Discount Company of London Ltd).

Blount's memoirs, which were published in 1902, depict the political and economic developments of France in the nineteenth century. Blount was acquainted with leading French and British liberal politicians and engineers. As a staunch supporter of liberalism and free trade he felt closer to the regime of Louis-Philippe than to the empire of Napoleon III, though he approved of the regime's 'liberalization' in the 1860s. He witnessed the 1848 revolution and made a small contribution to the restoration of order after the popular uprising in June, riding a train to Amiens on behalf of General Cavaignac to collect French troops.

On the outbreak of the revolution in Paris on 4 September 1870, Blount wound up the affairs of his bank and transferred the business to the Société Générale de Paris, of which he became president. When the Prussians threatened to besiege Paris, he sent his wife and family to England but remained in the capital with his son Aston through the siege. His letters to his wife give a vivid picture of its horrors. Lord Lyons, the British ambassador, left for Tours on 17 November and in the absence of all the officials of the English embassy Blount took charge of British interests; on 24 January 1871 he was formally appointed British consul. During the siege, and especially at its close, he with Richard Wallace and Dr Alan Herbert distributed the money and food contributed in England to relieve the besieged. He dined with Bismarck at Versailles after the fall of the city, and left for London at the end of March 1871. He was convinced that England should have come to the rescue of France, and he expressed his views with frankness, when on his arrival in England he breakfasted with W. E. Gladstone, the prime minister; Lord Granville, the foreign minister, was a fellow guest. For his services Blount was made CB on 13 March 1871, and KCB on 2 June 1878. He was also a commander of the Légion d'honneur.

Blount founded and chaired the British chamber of commerce in Paris. He also belonged to the Paris Cercle de l'Union, the French Jockey Club, and the Reform Club in London. Additionally, he acted as banker to the papal government. After the war of Italian independence of 1859, and the annexation of the Papal States to the new kingdom of Italy, he had the delicate task of arranging the transfer of the financial liabilities of the Papal States to the new Italian government, and the conversion of the papal debt. A benefactor of the Roman Catholic church in Britain, Blount built a school near Birmingham, and a church at East Grinstead. Devoted to the turf, he was a patron of the stable of the Comte de Lagrange; and following the latter's death in 1883 he kept a small stable of his own.

Blount died at his home, Imberhorne, East Grinstead, Sussex, on 15 March 1905, aged ninety-six; he was survived by his wife. ISABELLE LESCENT-GILES

Sources *Memoirs of Sir Edward Blount*, ed. S. J. Reid (1902) • *The Times* (16 March 1905) • *The Times* (21 March 1905) • *FO List* (1905) • *WWW* • B. Gille, *La banque en France au XIXe siècle* (1970) • B. Gille, *La banque et le crédit en France de 1815 à 1848* (1959) • M. Levy-Leboyer, *Les banques Européennes et l'industrialisation internationale* (1964) • Y. Leclercq, *Le réseau impossible, 1820–1852* (1987) • G. Ribeill, *La révolution ferroviaire* (1993) • F. Caron, *Histoire de l'exploitation d'un grand réseau* (1973) • S. D. Chapman, *The rise of merchant banking* (1984) • *The Railway Times* (18 March 1905) • *The Railway News* (18 March 1905) • *DNB* • d. cert. • *CGPLA Eng. & Wales* (1905)

Likenesses portrait, repro. in Reid, ed., *Memoirs of Sir Edward Blount*

Wealth at death £160,147 12s. 9d.: probate, 15 April 1905, *CGPLA Eng. & Wales*

Blount [*married names* Tailboys, Fiennes de Clinton], **Elizabeth** (*c*.**1500–1539x41**), royal mistress, was the second daughter of John Blount of Kinlet (1484–1531) and his wife, Katherine (1483–1540), heir of Sir Hugh Peshall of Knightley and his wife, Isabel Stanley of Elford. Her early childhood was probably spent in Shropshire. The Blount family's links with Prince Arthur's court at Ludlow, in particular their kinship with Sir Richard Croft, the steward of the prince's household, were no doubt instrumental in securing Elizabeth's acceptance as a maid of honour to Katherine of Aragon from 25 March 1512. Reported by John Barlow, dean of Westbury, as more beautiful than Anne Boleyn, her possession of a volume of poetry by John Gower (BL, Egerton MS 1991) suggests she was also well educated. Renowned for her skill in music and dancing, she was a frequent player in court masques. At the new year revels of 1514 she was partnered by *Henry VIII (1491–1547). However, the lack of any concurrent references suggests that their subsequent affair was short-lived. Perhaps it was occasioned by Katherine's pregnancy in 1518—Elizabeth's last recorded appearance at court was on 3 October that year, at celebrations to mark the betrothal of Princess Mary.

The king's child Henry *Fitzroy (1519–1536), later duke of Richmond, was probably born in June 1519 and by September that year Elizabeth Blount had married Gilbert *Tailboys (*c*.1500–1530) [*see under* Tailboys, Sir William], heir of George, Lord Tailboys of Kyme, and his wife, Elizabeth Gascoigne. Since Gilbert had become a ward of the crown after his father was declared lunatic in 1517, the match was clearly envisioned by the king as a reward to his former mistress. The statute 14 & 15 Hen. VIII c. 34 granted Elizabeth property worth £200 p.a. out of Tailboys lands for her life. The couple settled in Lincolnshire and they had three children, Elizabeth (described as aged twenty-two in June 1542), George, and Robert. She continued to enjoy the king's favour throughout her life, receiving a series of grants between 18 June 1522 and 9 January 1539. In 1532 her new year's gift from Henry was a gilt goblet with a cover weighing over 35 ounces. Her role in the life of her royal son is less well documented, although her relatives were employed in Richmond's service, and a 1531 inventory of his goods records her gifts of a doublet and two horses. A letter of 1529 to her from John Palsgrave, Richmond's tutor, suggests that her involvement in the duke's upbringing was greater than has been generally allowed. After the death of Gilbert Tailboys on 15 April 1530 the opportunity of legitimizing Richmond by subsequent marriage was apparently not even considered by a king already fully decided on repudiating Katherine in favour of Anne Boleyn.

Elizabeth was unsuccessfully courted by Lord Leonard Grey in 1532; her second husband, to whom she was married by 12 February 1535, was Edward Fiennes de *Clinton, ninth Baron Clinton and Saye (1512–1585), who later became first earl of Lincoln. This union produced three daughters, Bridget, Katherine, and Margaret. Elizabeth died some time between January 1539, when a grant of monastic lands was made to her and her husband, and June 1541, when Lord Clinton is referred to as remarried. She was not buried with either husband. Her only known likeness is a stylized brass from St Mary and All Saints Church, South Kyme, Lincolnshire.

Beverley A. Murphy

Sources B. A. Murphy, 'The life and political significance of Henry Fitzroy, duke of Richmond, 1525–1536', PhD diss., U. Wales, 1997 • statute 14 & 15 Hen. VIII c. 34 • M. Newton, *South Kyme* (1995) • BM, PS221297 • W. S. Childe-Pemberton, *Elizabeth Blount and Henry VIII: with some account of her surroundings* (1913) • *LP Henry VIII*, vols. 4–16 • inventory of the wardrobe of Henry Fitzroy, duke of Richmond, 1531, [17], Historical Manuscripts Commission, London, Longleat miscellaneous MSS, microfilm, reel 2 • *Hall's chronicle*, ed. H. Ellis (1809) • BL, Egerton MS 1991 • BL, Add. MS 28585, fol. 43 • exchequer, king's remembrancer, accounts various, PRO, E101/420/15 • state papers, general series, Henry VIII, PRO, SP1/55, p. 14 • exchequer, treasury of receipt, miscellaneous books, PRO, E36/215, fol. 250 • A. Craik, *Annals of our ancestors* (1924) • palatinate of Durham chancery court, cursitor's records, PRO, DURH3/177, no. 155

Archives Derbys. RO, family MSS • Shrops. RRC, family MSS • Staffs. RO, family MSS

Likenesses funeral brass, BM, PS 221297

Wealth at death granted £200 of lands by statute in 1529, incl. £40 annuity, subsequent small gifts and grants

Blount, Elizabeth Anne Mould de Sodington [*née* Elizabeth Anne Mould Williams; *other married name* Elizabeth Anne Mould Morgan], **Lady de Sodington Blount** (**1850–1935**), pamphlet writer and social activist, was born on 7 May 1850 at 82 Upper Stamford Street near Waterloo, Lambeth, London, the daughter of James Zacharias Williams, who was originally from Cadair Idris, Wales, and his wife, Elizabeth Anne Mould. Educated privately and probably encouraged by her father, who was an active participant in several London clubs and societies, she developed a strong sense of social responsibility. Having wide interests including social reform, religion, science, literature, music, and art, she was increasingly active even as a young woman in London's social and intellectual life.

On 16 May 1874 Elizabeth Williams married Sir Walter de Sodington Blount, ninth baronet (1833–1915). They had two sons and two daughters. As a married woman, she divided her time between a London town house in Marylebone and her husband's family estate, Mawley Hall, Cleobury Mortimer, Shropshire. She became a fellow of the Royal Society of Literature as well as a fellow of the Society of Antiquaries, but her social energies were increasingly focused on religious and racial issues.

Lady de Sodington Blount served for a period as president of the Universal Zetetic Society, a group founded by the physician Samuel Birley Rowbotham (1816–1884) to promote his philosophical system, which included the contention that the earth was not a globe. Modelled on the London Dialectical Society, the Universal Zetetic Society fostered debates on moral and philosophical issues. In 1881, for example, George Bernard Shaw addressed a meeting on the virtues of capital punishment over life imprisonment, a talk which Blount may have heard, for women were expected to participate in the society's debates. Despite its fundamentalist tendencies, the society insisted upon uncensored speech on all social, political, and philosophical subjects, and it was the practice to examine speakers at the conclusion of their papers; lively discussions, which might even include heckling, were strongly encouraged.

Zetetic Society members regularly referred to Bible passages to substantiate their belief that the earth was flat, and made extensive efforts to reinforce their claim by purportedly scientific observations of bodies of water. In 1888 Lady de Sodington Blount and her husband undertook a series of experiments on Old Bedford Level Canal, and concluded that indeed the earth had no curvature. Among her pamphlets was an investigation entitled *Magnetism as a Curative Agency* (1905). After her husband's death in October 1915, she divided her time between London and Bognor, where during the course of religious work she met Stephen Morgan, a master builder and naval pensioner, the son of Isaiah Morgan, a bricklayer. In a civil ceremony on 28 August 1923 she married the much younger Morgan, who shared her evangelical interests; she was seventy-three and he was forty. She continued to divide her time between London and a house in the country, eventually moving to Hayling Island.

Focusing her energies on racial problems, Elizabeth Morgan joined the Society for the Protection of the Dark Races in England. She served as its president in the early 1930s, and continued to speak and write extensively on scientific and evangelical subjects, publishing numerous articles in *The Earth*, the journal of the Universal Zetetic Society, which she edited at this time. She died of cancer on 2 January 1935 at her home, Top House, New Cut, North Hayling, leaving only a small estate, having apparently given away most of her considerable wealth to charities associated with the causes she had worked for throughout her life. CAROLINE ZILBOORG

Sources Burke, *Peerage* (1939) · *The Earth* [journal of the Universal Zetetic Society] (1930–39) · *The women's who's who, 1934–5: an annual record of the careers and activities of the leading women of the day* (1934) · b. cert. · m. certs. · d. cert. · M. Holroyd, *Bernard Shaw*, 1 (1988), 127, 129, 172 · M. Oliver, *Los Angeles Times* (25 March 2001) [obituary for Charles Johnson, leader of the Flat Earth Society] · Boase, *Mod. Eng. biog.* [Samuel Birley Rowbotham]

Wealth at death £49 6*s*. 0*d*.: administration, 26 Jan 1935, *CGPLA Eng. & Wales*

Blount, Sir Henry (1602–1682), traveller, was born at Tittenhanger, Hertfordshire, on 15 December 1602 and baptized at Ridge, Hertfordshire, on 22 December, son of Thomas (later Sir Thomas) Blount (1556–1639) and Frances Pigot (*c*.1564–1619). He went to the free school at St Albans and on 30 June 1615 matriculated as a gentleman commoner from Trinity College, Oxford; he graduated BA on 18 June 1618. In 1620 he was admitted to Gray's Inn. According to John Aubrey 'he was pretty wild when young, especially addicted to common wenches' (*Brief Lives*, 25–7). In early 1629 he wrote a commendatory poem to William D'Avenant's *The Tragedy of Albovine, King of the Lombards*, and on 23 September of that year he and William Blount, an Oxfordshire gentleman, were given passes to travel for three years to Spain, France, and Italy. Later he alluded to this first journey in the preface to his account of his 1634 travels in the Levant, *A Voyage into the Levant* (1636).

Sir Henry Blount (1602–1682), by Sir Peter Lely

Blount began his account of this journey in Venice, from where he sailed on 7 May 1634 down the Adriatic coast, and then travelled inland into the Balkans. He reached Constantinople and after spending only a few days he crossed to Egypt via Rhodes in the Turkish fleet and docked in Alexandria. He visited the great pyramid in Giza, wandered around the Faiyûm, and in November embarked for Palermo, Naples, and finally Venice, having travelled above 6000 miles in eleven months. In the preface Blount declared that his purpose in travelling had been Baconian: to gain knowledge by means of personal—'ocular'—experience without the constraints of national and religious history. He travelled alone to the Middle East because he wanted to describe Islam and the world of the Ottomans in an 'empirical rather than religious frame of reference' (MacLean, 94). He was eager to see and learn from the non-Christian world, and realized that no people were more suitable for study than the 'Turkes, who are the only moderne people, great in action'. Blount praised them for their military discipline and social organization, emphasizing their importance for English trade and marvelling at the diversity of religious communities that lived among them. He established such good rapport that he was invited by the coffee drinking pasha to 'serve under them going against the Polacke'. Blount declined the offer but declared that King Charles I would have encouraged him because the latter had 'a League with the Gran Signior, [and] continually held an Embassadour at his Court, esteeming him the greatest Monarch in the World' (Blount, 15). Blount was fully aware how attractive the Ottoman world must have seemed to potential Christian converts seeking employment and advancement. *The Voyage* shows a sharp and iconoclastic mind. 'By your eyes', wrote Bishop Henry King in commendation of the accuracy and detail of the book,

> I here have made my full discoveries;
> And all your countries so exactly seen,
> As in the voyage I had sharer been.

Soon after his return to England, and the publication of his travels, which won recognition from the king, Blount became a gentleman pensioner to Charles I and was knighted on 21 March 1639. He committed himself to the royalist cause and attended the king at York and took part in the battle of Edgehill. He stayed with the king in Oxford, but then went to London, where after entering Westminster Hall with his sword on his side he was questioned by the House of Commons for his apparent royalism. In 1647 he married Hester (*c.*1620–1678), daughter of Christopher Wase of Upper Holloway, Middlesex, and widow of Sir William Mainwaring of Chester. However, he continued to indulge himself: Henry Neville anonymously published in that year a pamphlet entitled *The Parliament of Ladies* in which Blount states that it is 'cheaper and safer to lye with common wenches than with ladies of quality'. Aubrey recounts some episodes about Blount's frequenting of bordellos which support that claim while Wood describes him as 'a great banterer' (Wood, *Ath. Oxon.*, 4.54).

At the beginning of the interregnum Blount changed sides and in January 1652 Cromwell appointed him to serve on the Hales commission for the reformation of the criminal code. He opposed tithes and urged that no minister of the church be paid more than £100 per annum for 'administering the Gospel'. In May 1654 he served as a juror at the trial of the brother of the Portuguese ambassador, Pantaleon Sa, along with three others and an English boy, all of whom were accused of murder in the New Exchange. In November 1655 he was appointed to the trade and navigation committee to 'regulate and improve trade, and receive propositions for the benefit thereof' (*CSP dom.: Commonwealth*, 2). Two years later he wrote a foreword to Walter Rumsey's *Organon salutis*, the first detailed account in English of coffee, that 'physick' which the Turks use for preventing 'Consumption' and 'Lethargie', 'Rickets in Children', and 'Stone and Gout'. Judge Rumsey, whose letter to Blount appeared in the dedication, credited Blount with popularizing coffee in the country: 'your discovery in your excellent Book of Travels, hath brought the use of the Turkes Physick, of Cophie in great request in England'. Blount, who was known to drink only water, became an inveterate drinker of coffee, frequenting numerous coffee houses in London. John Evelyn, who met him in 1659, described him as the 'famous traveller and water-drinker'. Blount declaimed against drunkenness, and against the universities, which in his view corrupted the youth. But he also had his humorous side: Aubrey thought him 'a great shammer', telling falsities for the pleasure of it all. He was known not to urge his servants to church, preferring them to attend executions at Tyburn, 'which work more upon them than all the oratory in the sermons'.

At the Restoration, Blount supported the new king and in 1661 he became sheriff of Hertfordshire. He remained in Tittenhanger, where Nathaniel Vincent served him as chaplain, spending his time in book collecting and writing. In November 1678 his wife died, and in September 1682, while on a visit to London, he became ill; he returned to Tittenhanger, where he died on the morning of 9 October 1682. He was buried two days later. Four of his children survived him: Thomas (later Sir Thomas) Pope *Blount (1649–1697), Charles *Blount (1654–1693), Frances (1648–1699), and Ulysses (1664–1704). NABIL MATAR

Sources *APC*, *1629–30*, 138 • *Aubrey's Brief lives*, ed. O. L. Dick (1949), 25–7 • H. Blount, *A voyage into the Levant* (1636) • M. Cotterell, 'Interregnum law reform: the Hale commission of 1652', *EngHR*, 83 (1968), 689–704 • W. D'Avenant, *The tragedy of Albovine, king of the Lombards* (1629) • *The diary of John Evelyn*, ed. W. Bray, new edn, 1 (1907); rev. edn (1952); repr. (1966), 337 • Foster, *Alum. Oxon.* • W. B. Johnson, *Companion into Hertfordshire* (1952), 182–3 • H. King, *Poems* (1657) • G. MacLean, 'Ottomanism before Orientalism?', *Travel knowledge*, ed. I. Kamps and J. G. Singh (New York, 2001), 75–97 • H. Neville, *The parliament of ladies* (1647) • T. Warton, *The life of Sir Thomas Pope, founder of Trinity College, Oxford*, 2nd edn (1780), 206–7 • Wood, *Ath. Oxon.*, new edn • *IGI* [Ridge parish register] • N. Matar, *Islam in Britain, 1558–1685* (1998)

Likenesses D. Loggan, line engraving, 1679, BM, NPG • P. Lely, oils, NPG [*see illus.*]

Blount, Sir James (*d.* 1492). *See under* Blount, Walter, first Baron Mountjoy (*d.* 1474).

Blount, James, sixth Baron Mountjoy (1532/3–1581). *See under* Blount, Charles, fifth Baron Mountjoy (1516–1544).

Blount, Sir John (*d.* 1418). *See under* Blount, Sir Walter (*d.* 1403).

Blount, John, third Baron Mountjoy (*d.* 1485). *See under* Blount, Walter, first Baron Mountjoy (*d.* 1474).

Blount, Martha (1690–1763), Roman Catholic gentlewoman, was born on 15 June 1690 at the family estate of Mapledurham, Berkshire, the third child (but second eldest surviving) of six born to Lister Blount (1654–1710) and his wife, Martha (*d.* 1743), daughter of Anthony Englefield of Whiteknights, near Reading. She was known to family and friends as Patty, and her mother was known as Pax. Her sister **Teresa Maria Blount** (1688–1759), born on 15 October 1688 in Paris, was the eldest of the surviving children. Both sisters were educated principally at the English Benedictine convent in Paris. Their father's death

Martha Blount (1690–1763), by Charles Jervas, 1716 [left, with her sister Teresa Blount]

in 1710 revealed that the estate was in financial crisis, and resources were concentrated on the heir, their younger brother Michael. On his marriage in 1715 they and their mother left Mapledurham for accommodation in London. Although they received letters of elaborately teasing gallantry from other members of the young Catholic élite (Teresa as Zephalinda and Martha as Parthenissa), the loss of their financial prospects effectively disqualified them from marriage.

The sisters had met Pope about 1707 through their grandfather Anthony Englefield. They constituted Pope's most intimate link with the Roman Catholic high society which provided the subject of *The Rape of the Lock*: Martha's godfather, John Caryll, commissioned the poem to smooth over the cutting of Arabella Fermor's hair by his ward, Lord Petre. Lord Petre himself had been commended to the sisters, if only in jest, as an object of matrimonial pursuit; and Arabella, on whose final match with a country gentleman Teresa wrote a caustic commentary, was their cousin. In 1716 Charles Jervas painted them as 'a Couplet', calling them 'Pope's Favorites' and evoking in the balances and contrasts of the image something of the fascination that the sisters held for Pope: Martha, blonde, blue-eyed, and retiring, looks across at her sister, while Teresa, darker and more assertive, boldly confronts the viewer's gaze (*Correspondence of Alexander Pope*, 1.332).

The vivacious and sharp-tongued Teresa seems at first to have been the more attractive to Pope: she was probably addressed in 'You Know Where' (1710), and was certainly the addressee of 'Epistle to Miss Blount, with the Works of Voiture' (1710) and 'Epistle to Miss Blount, on her Leaving the Town, after the Coronation' (1714). (Martha had missed the coronation because she had smallpox.) 'Verses Sent to Mrs. T. B. with his Works' (1718) suggest that Teresa was increasingly irritated by his attentions; and in the same year she took offence at his settling on her an annuity of £40. Several letters suggest that he was on difficult terms with both sisters: he declared in a letter jointly addressed to both:

> I have some times found myself inclined to be in love with you: and as I have reason to know from your Temper & Conduct how miserably I should be used in that circumstance, it is worth my while to avoid it. (*Correspondence of Alexander Pope*, 1.456)

Another letter, refusing an invitation to visit, suggests that one of the sisters had rebuffed his advances: 'You will please to consider that my Coming or not is a thing Indifferent to both of you. But God knows, it is far otherwise to me, with respect to One of you' (ibid., 1.460). The 'One' may have been Teresa, but she may equally, by this stage, have been Martha; for in listing his complaints against Teresa he accuses her of betraying his confidence by 'telling the party concern'd, it was all butt an Amusement occasiond by my Loss of another Lady' (ibid., 1.468). By the 1720s Pope and Teresa were irreconcilable: Pope claimed that she was having an affair with a married man, slandering him and Martha, and subjecting her mother to physical abuse.

In 1715 Pope had inscribed 'To a Lady with the Temple of Fame' in Martha's presentation copy of *The Temple of Fame*, and in 1716 he hinted that she had asked him to delete a tribute to her which had originally formed the conclusion of *Eloisa to Abelard*. Martha enjoyed romances, evinced a 'Romantic' response to landscape, disliked dressing formally, and was very shy: she found it very difficult to assert herself, and tended to confide ill usage to Pope rather than directly confronting those responsible. Increasingly Pope idealized her quieter and more introspective qualities. He encouraged her friendship with Henrietta Howard, countess of Suffolk, the king's mistress (although in later years his friendship for Lady Suffolk cooled, and Martha increasingly cultivated the Roman Catholic widow Elizabeth, Lady Gerard). Martha was often ill, and although Pope blamed this on domestic tension which he attributed to scandalous and violent behaviour on Teresa's part, Martha persistently refused to give in to his entreaties that she would set up house on her own. Martha's weakness (as he saw it) in staying with her family exasperated him, but stemmed from the same virtues of humility and loyalty which qualified her in his eyes as a properly good woman. Unlike the more obviously striking and articulate Teresa, this sensitive, retiring, but intensely loyal woman evoked his lifelong devotion.

In 1723 his verses on Martha's birthday implicitly offered himself as 'a Friend' (*Twickenham Edition*, 6.244–7). She and Pope denied persistent rumours that she had become his mistress, fiancée, or secret bride. In 1729 Caryll seems to have offered Pope a dowry for her, but he declared that 'I have no tie to your God-daughter but a good opinion, which has grown into a friendship with experience that she deserved it' (*Correspondence of Alexander Pope*, 3.74–5). His *Epistle to a Lady: on the Characters of Women* (1735) contains his most substantial tribute to the qualities he found in her: she, though unnamed, is the 'Friend' to whom Apollo has given 'Sense, Good-humour, and a Poet'. She may also have been the tantalizing beloved of 'The First Ode of the Fourth Book of Horace' (1737).

In later years some of Pope's newer friends resented Martha's long-established intimacy, and the feeling may have been mutual. A quarrel in 1743 at the home of Ralph Allen, a recent but crucial addition to Pope's circle, pitted Martha against the Allens and Pope's new protégé William Warburton, and she wrote to Pope in bitter terms:

> I hope you are well. I am not. My spirits are quite down, tho they should not. for these people deserve so much to be dispised, one should do nothing but Laugh … Mr Warburton takes no notice of me. tis most wonderfull. they have not one of èm named your name, nor drank your health since you went. they talk to one another without putting me at all in the conversation. (*Correspondence of Alexander Pope*, 4.462)

Pope returned an agitated letter commiserating over 'such monstrous Treatment', and ended by declaring 'W. is a sneaking Parson, & I told him he flatterd' (*Correspondence of Alexander Pope*, 4.463–4). Warburton remained her enemy and circulated various anecdotes impugning her integrity, particularly through the materials he provided for Owen Ruffhead's *The Life of Alexander Pope* (1769).

In 1743 Pope arranged to buy a twenty-six-year lease on a house in Berkeley Street (or Row) for Martha. His last letter to her is a somewhat awkward attempt to explain his reconciliation with the Allens without making light of her anger. He pleads:

> Would to God you would Quicken your haste to settle, by reflecting what a pleasure it would be to me, just to see it, and to see you at ease; & then I could contentedly leave you to the Providence of God, in this Life, & resign my Self to it in the other! (*Correspondence of Alexander Pope*, 4.511)

He closes by assuring her that 'I love you upon unalterable Principles, which makes me feel my heart the same to you as if I saw you every hour.' He died in May 1744, and in his will, dated 12 December 1743, left her £1000, his goods and chattels, and the income from his estate for life, which enraged his half-sister Magdalen Rackett, who later became another source of derogatory anecdotes about Martha.

Martha was now comfortably provided for and presided over a household of her own for the first time in her life, although she continued to lend Teresa small sums of money. In 1749 she spoke affectionately about Pope to Joseph Spence, who added a substantial group of her reminiscences to his collection of anecdotes. Horace Walpole, recognizing her in later life in the street on a rainy day 'with her petticoats tucked up like a sempstress' and 'nothing remaining of her immortal charms but her *blue eyes*', was content to dismiss her as 'red-faced, fat, and by no means pretty' (Walpole, *Corr.*, 33.511).

Teresa died on 7 October 1759 after a long illness, and was buried in the churchyard of St Pancras in London (that is, Old St Pancras, a customary burial site for Catholics). Her estate was administered by her nephew Michael Blount of Mapledurham. Martha died suddenly at her Berkeley Street home on 12 July 1763 and was buried beside her sister. Apart from a few small legacies she left everything to her nephew Michael, father of her goddaughter Martha ('Little Patty'). VALERIE RUMBOLD

Sources V. Rumbold, *Women's place in Pope's world* (1989) · priv. coll., Blount archives · *The correspondence of Alexander Pope*, ed. G. Sherburn, 5 vols. (1956) · J. Spence, *Observations, anecdotes, and characters, of books and men*, ed. J. M. Osborn, new edn, 2 vols. (1966) · *The Twickenham edition of the poems of Alexander Pope*, ed. J. Butt and others, 11 vols. in 12 (1939–69) · *The prose works of Alexander Pope*, ed. N. Ault and R. Cowler, 2 vols. (1936–86) · N. Ault, *New light on Pope, with some additions to his poetry hitherto unknown* (1949) · O. Ruffhead, *The life of Alexander Pope, esq., compiled from original manuscripts, with a critical essay on his writings and genius* (1769) · G. Sherburn, 'New anecdotes about Alexander Pope', *N&Q*, 203 (1958), 343–9 · *Reminiscences written by Mr Horace Walpole in 1788*, ed. P. Toynbee (1924)

Archives BL, Suffolk MSS, corresp., Add. MSS 22626–22627 · NRA, priv. coll., archives

Likenesses G. Kneller, oils, *c.*1712 (Teresa Blount), repro. in M. Mack, *Alexander Pope: a life* (1985), pl. 32 · J. J., oils, 1713, priv. coll. · C. Jervas, double portrait, oils, 1716, priv. coll. [*see illus.*] · C. Jervas, double portrait, oils, second version (Martha and Teresa Blount), FM Cam. · G. Kneller?, oils (as Mary Magdalen), repro. in M. Mack, *Alexander Pope: a life* (1985), pl. 74 · pair of oils (Martha and Teresa Blount as children), repro. in M. Mack, *Alexander Pope: a life* (1985), pl. 28–9 · pastels (in later life), repro. in Rumbold, *Women's place in Pope's world*, pl. 5

Wealth at death approx. £300 in legacies and 'All the wordly Goods and Effects I die possest of' to nephew: will, 13 Dec 1762, priv. coll., Blount archives

Blount, Mountjoy, first earl of Newport (*c.*1597–1666), courtier and politician, was the eldest of three illegitimate sons of Charles *Blount, earl of Devonshire (1563–1606), and Lady Penelope *Rich (1563–1607), daughter of Walter Devereux, first earl of Essex; his parents were eventually to marry, contrary to canon law, in 1605. He was the half-brother of Henry *Rich, first earl of Holland (*bap.* 1590, *d.* 1649), and Robert *Rich, second earl of Warwick (1587–1658). When his father died in April 1606, he left him considerable estates at Wanstead, Essex, and elsewhere, worth at that time an estimated total of £3000 to £4000 a year; Clarendon later observed that he possessed 'a very plentiful revenue' (Clarendon, *Hist. rebellion*, 1.78).

Early years and success as a courtier Blount quickly established himself as a favourite at court and was created Lord Mountjoy, baron of Mountjoy Fort in the Irish peerage, in January 1618. He went overseas at the end of that year, where his travels took him to, among other places, Turin and Venice. On 8 January 1621 he acted in a masque before King James and the French ambassador at Essex House, and in April the following year he was in Prince Charles's company at a tilt. During 1622 he also travelled with Colonel Edward Cecil to the Low Countries, where it was falsely reported that they had been slain. On 21 February 1623 Mountjoy accompanied the earl of Carlisle on a visit to the French court to request that Prince Charles might pass through Paris in disguise, on his way to Spain, without kissing the king's hand. After this, Mountjoy rode on to Spain, where he caught tertian fever. After his return he attended the Spanish ambassador, Mendoza, in London

Mountjoy Blount, first earl of Newport (*c*.1597–1666), by Sir Anthony Van Dyck, *c*.1637–8

the following November. In April 1625 he was granted a pass to the United Provinces for himself or his deputy to take 100 men to serve there as horsemen.

Further evidence of Charles's favour came on 5 June 1627 when he created Mountjoy Baron Mountjoy of Thurveston (Derbyshire) in the English peerage, with a special clause giving him precedence over barons created since 20 May of that year. Following objections from the only two barons affected, Lord Fauconberg and Lord Lovelace, the Lords' committee for privileges ruled in April 1628 that this grant of precedence was illegal. Accordingly, on 27 July 1628 Charles created Mountjoy earl of Newport (in the Isle of Wight) in the English peerage and the following month appointed him to a command in the expedition for the relief of La Rochelle. However, Buckingham's assassination delayed the expedition's departure until October, and Newport was appointed rear-admiral of the fleet. Throughout 1629 and 1630 he petitioned for payment for his services, and a warrant for payment was finally issued on 12 May 1631. He was granted the reversion to the custodianship of Hyde Park in June 1630.

On 7 February 1627 Newport had married Anne Boteler (*d*. 1669), daughter of Sir John Boteler, bt (later first Baron Boteler), and Elizabeth Villiers. In 1637 Lady Newport created a sensation by converting to Catholicism. Her husband begged Laud's assistance in securing the punishment of those whom he held responsible, including Walter Montagu and Sir Toby Matthew, and the archbishop's attempts to do so led him into a major row with Queen Henrietta Maria, who vigorously defended her co-religionists. The queen successfully frustrated attempts to regulate access to her chapel, and she summoned Lady Newport and a number of other recent converts to attend mass there on Christmas day 1637. It is possible that these events help to explain Newport's subsequent alienation from the court and his association (albeit temporary) with some of the crown's leading critics in the early 1640s.

On 31 August 1634 Newport had been appointed master of the ordnance for life. Over the next five years he was actively involved with the ordnance office and succeeded in making large profits for himself. He was appointed a privy councillor in September 1638, and was one of the lords of the council at York who took the oath of allegiance to the king in April 1639. He became colonel of a regiment of foot the following month, and later general of the artillery in the king's army in the north. In September 1639 he sold gunpowder to the Spanish ambassador, Cardenas, for the Spanish fleet that was attacking the Dutch in the channel, at an inflated price. Arguing that 'the King of Spain is very rich, and it is of no importance to him how much he gives for the powder of which he is so greatly in need' (S. R. Gardiner, *History of England from the Accession of James I to the Outbreak of the Civil War, 1603–1642*, 10 vols., 1883–4, 9.61), Newport struck a deal whereby Charles received £5000 above the value of the powder, and he himself £1000. The following month he bargained with Cardenas to convey Spanish soldiers from the fleet to Dunkirk at 30*s*. a head, contrary to Charles's instruction that England remain strictly neutral in the conflict between Spain and the Dutch.

The coming of civil war In the Short Parliament and the opening months of the Long Parliament, Newport aligned himself with the king's critics in the Lords. On 29 April 1640 he voted with the minority of peers in supporting the Commons' resolution that redress of grievances should precede supply, although he later tried to excuse his conduct to the king by claiming that in the heat of the moment he was so agitated that he had voted the wrong way by mistake. In April 1641 George Goring leaked intelligence of the first army plot to Newport (possibly with royal approval). The earl at once took him to see Bedford and Mandeville, who passed the news on to Pym. In an attempt to conciliate him, Charles promptly appointed Newport constable of the Tower on 6 May; however, any possible benefits to the king that might have come from this gesture were lost amid the revelations of the army plot. After the Lords had passed the bill for Strafford's attainder, and while Charles was hesitating over whether to accept it, Newport gave his assurance that in his new capacity as constable of the Tower he would ensure that Strafford was put to death even if the king refused his assent. In June Charles ordered Newport to proceed to York to safeguard munitions in the north, and on 25 June the Lords petitioned the king to permit him still to be paid as constable of the Tower in the meantime. On 18 August the houses ordered Newport to take up residence in the Tower and to make sure that it was safely guarded.

During the autumn of 1641 Newport continued to be identified among the more radical members of the Lords. On 9 September he was one of a minority of peers who voted against the Lords' order that 'the divine service be performed as it is appointed by the Acts of Parliament' (*JHL*, 4, 1628–42, 395). When the Lords further resolved to publish this order before conferring with the Commons, Newport recorded his protest, together with Bedford, Warwick, Clare, Wharton, and Mandeville. The king's suspicion of him was reinforced by a report that while Charles had been in Scotland in August 1641 Newport had allegedly informed a gathering at Kensington which included Essex, Saye and Sele, Wharton, Nathaniel Fiennes, and John Pym that if it turned out that the king was hatching a plot, then 'here are his wife and children; insinuating the same to signify that the person of Her Majesty and her children should be seized upon'. When Charles later confronted Newport with this story the earl denied it, whereupon the king replied dismissively 'I am sorry for your lordship's memory' (*JHL*, 4, 1628–42, 490, 493).

Charles's growing suspicion of Newport was apparent towards the end of December 1641, when the Commons, disturbed by the king's appointment of Sir Thomas Lunsford as lieutenant of the Tower, repeated their request that Newport take up residence there. Charles's immediate response was to dismiss Newport from the constableship. At about the same time, on 27 December, Newport raised the matter of the Kensington rumours in the Lords, and the next day both houses submitted a joint petition asking the king to name his informant. On 30 December Charles replied, stating that he 'neither did nor do give credit to any such rumour' (*JHL*, 4, 1628–42, 498). It is indeed possible that Charles had not entirely lost personal trust in Newport for that same day he gave him the keys of Whitehall Palace.

Newport's royalism and its consequences The likeliest explanation of Newport's behaviour is that he was trying to retain credit with both the king and his critics within the houses. These attempts led the royalist Sir Philip Warwick to brand Newport 'a very weak and faithless person' (Warwick, 131). During the opening months of 1642 there were clear signs that Newport was attempting to rebuild his bridges with the king. On 5 January he accompanied Charles, together with Essex, Hamilton, and his own half-brother Holland, to the City of London in search of the five members. The following April, he allegedly advised the king to go to Hull, and was with Charles when Sir John Hotham denied him entry to the garrison. On 11 May the Lords ordered Newport to attend the house 'as a delinquent' (*JHL*, 5, 1642–3, 59), but apparently he did not comply. On 15 June he was among the king's supporters at York who signed a declaration pledging Charles's commitment to 'the firm and constant settlement of the true Protestant religion, the just privileges of Parliament, the liberty of the subject, [and] the law, peace, and prosperity of this kingdom' (Clarendon, *Hist. rebellion*, 2.185–6). By December 1642 he was the earl of Newcastle's lieutenant-general, but his forces arrived too late to assist the royalist assault on Tadcaster, a failure that Newcastle's wife attributed to 'neglect or treachery' (*Life of William Cavendish*, 16). Newport was also defeated in an engagement with Sir Hugh Cholmley in north Yorkshire in January 1643, and the following month he quarrelled with Newcastle over the latter's desire to employ Catholics in his army. That same month Newcastle attempted to arrest him at Pontefract following allegations that Newport had plotted to seize the queen on her return from the Netherlands. There is, however, no evidence to support these accusations, and the fact that he immediately afterwards fled back to the king may suggest that they were groundless.

The cost of royalism In the event parliamentarian troops captured Newport before he reached Charles: in mid-March 1643 it was reported that he was 'stayed at Coventry' and the Lords ordered that he be brought to London (*JHL*, 5, 1642–3, 649). On 28 March Newport surrendered himself and was committed to the custody of the gentleman usher of the Lords; on 4 April he was granted 'liberty to go abroad, and take the air for his health', provided that the gentleman usher accompanied him (ibid., 692). On 11 June the Commons ordered Newport's saddle and horse-arms, and other property left in the Tower from when he had been constable, to be handed over to Sir Thomas Myddleton.

Newport was apparently released during the summer of 1643, and he was with the king at Oxford by November. In May 1644 he was one of Prince Rupert's commissioners at Shrewsbury, and the following month he visited Weymouth, where he went aboard the ship of his half-brother Warwick, the parliamentarian admiral. Newport was apparently present at the second battle of Newbury (27 October 1644) and marched with the king to Bath on the night after the battle. By the end of 1645 he was with the king's forces in Devon, and was taken prisoner at the fall of Dartmouth Castle on 23 January 1646. Fairfax sent him in custody to London, where he was again entrusted to the gentleman usher of the Lords. On 11 February Newport petitioned the Lords requesting 'leave to be confined to some private place' where his maintenance would cost him 'a more easier charge' (*JHL*, 8, 1645–6, 162). The Lords accepted a recognizance of £2000 from Newport on 17 February, on condition that he would 'be a true prisoner, and not go out of the precincts of the liberties of the parishes of St Martin's-in-the-Fields and the Covent Garden' (ibid., 171). It seems that about this time Newport was also attempting to curry favour with the houses by suborning a lieutenant of the prince of Wales's guard to convey the prince to Westminster (although nothing came of this and the prince departed for the Isles of Scilly on 2 March 1646). On 23 March Newport was granted 'liberty to go abroad, and take the air, within four or five miles from London, for his health's sake'. He entered into a new recognizance, again for £2000, on condition that he would be 'a true prisoner to this House, and shall go no further than five miles from the lines of communication about London' (ibid., 226). He was later 'released from his bail' on 22 July 1646 (ibid., 437).

On 30 April 1646 Newport begged to compound for his delinquency at the rate of one-tenth, equivalent to the value of two years' income from his estate. His composition fine was initially set at £4579, and shortly afterwards reduced to £4179 following the settlement of a debt. On 4 October 1647 the Lords accepted Newport's request that allowance be made for his loss of the office of master of the ordnance, and recommended to the Commons that his composition fine be further reduced accordingly. However, after a lengthy review his fine was confirmed at £4179 on 11 April 1650. Newport's estate was apparently then discharged in 1652 upon payment of the fine.

The interregnum and Restoration Newport's activities during the interregnum remain relatively obscure. In December 1653 he presented a petition to the council of state. Two months later he and Lord Vaux were summoned before the council, having 'been apprehended on a warrant touching challenge' (*CSP dom.*, *1653–4*, 404). In February 1655 he was reportedly one of Clarendon's chief correspondents. It is likely that the courier was the countess, who was travelling regularly between England and the Low Countries during the mid-1650s. In June 1655, in the wake of Penruddock's rising, Newport was briefly committed to the Tower on suspicion of treason, and in June 1657 the Cromwellian agent Colonel Bampfield urged that the countess be sent for and examined. In November of that year Newport attended the marriage of his great-nephew Robert Rich, grandson of the earl of Warwick, to Cromwell's daughter Frances, and reportedly 'danced with her Highness' (*Fifth Report*, HMC, 177).

After the Restoration, on 24 June 1660 Newport was formally discharged from the office of master of the ordnance, and appointed instead as a gentleman of the bedchamber. On 10 November 1662 he was granted a pension of £1000 a year from this office, subsequently backdated to 24 June 1660. He died 'of the stone' (GEC, *Peerage*, 9.552) on 12 February 1666 at St Aldate's, Oxford, having gone there from London to avoid the plague. He was buried three days later on 15 February in the south aisle of Christ Church Cathedral. The following year his widow married Thomas Weston, fourth earl of Portland. She died on 26 May 1669, at Newport House in St Martin-in-the-Fields, and was privately buried, as a Catholic, in the chapel at Somerset House.

Assessment The overall impression of Newport's character and career is of someone who failed to live up to his early promise. Royal favour, allied to good fortune and high connections, helped him to achieve prominence at court at a notably young age. However, both before and during the civil wars he seems to have been guided principally by a wish to protect his own interests, and he apparently lacked firm political convictions. In the early 1640s he tried to maintain his links with both the king and leading parliamentarians for as long as possible, with the result that he eventually aroused suspicion on all sides. Increasingly perceived as untrustworthy, and lacking either the ability or the ambition to attain high office, his political influence was gradually eclipsed and he declined into relative obscurity from the later 1640s onwards.

DAVID L. SMITH

Sources *JHL*, 4–11 (1628–66) · GEC, *Peerage*, new edn, 9.549–52 · M. A. E. Green, ed., *Calendar of the proceedings of the committee for compounding … 1643–1660*, 1, PRO (1889), 1244–6 · P. R. Newman, *Royalist officers in England and Wales, 1642–1660: a biographical dictionary* (1981) · state papers domestic, Charles I, PRO, SP 16 · state papers domestic, interregnum, PRO, SP 18 · Clarendon, *Hist. rebellion* · P. Warwick, *Memoires of the reigne of King Charles I* (1701) · *The life of William Cavendish, duke of Newcastle … by Margaret, duchess of Newcastle*, ed. C. H. Firth (1907) · *Fifth report*, HMC, 4 (1876) · Thurloe, *State papers* · R. Scrope and T. Monkhouse, eds., *State papers collected by Edward, earl of Clarendon*, 3 vols. (1767–86) · *DNB* · *IGI*

Archives Yale U., Beinecke L., letters to William Legge

Likenesses A. Van Dyck, oils, *c.*1635–1640 (with Baron Goring), Petworth House, West Sussex; copy (with minor variations), Knole, Kent; *see illus. in* Goring, George, Baron Goring (1608–1657) · A. Van Dyck, oils, *c.*1637–1638, Yale U. CBA [*see illus.*] · M. Droeshout, portrait (at an early age) · Hollar, portrait · A. Van Dyck, oils, second version, Weston Park, Shropshire · oils (after D. Mytens), Lennoxlove, Lothian region

Blount, Richard (*c.*1565–1638), Jesuit, probably the son of William Blount and Frances Blount (*née* Love or Pope), was the younger brother of Sir Thomas Pope Blount, of Osbaston, Leicestershire, and Tittenhanger, Hertfordshire, and grandson of Walter, son of John Blount, of Blunt's Hall, Staffordshire. Born in Osbaston, Leicestershire, Blount matriculated at Balliol College, Oxford, in 1581. Awarded a BA on 29 November 1582, he was ejected shortly thereafter apparently for religious reasons. His aunt Elizabeth, Lady Paulet, granted Blount a fellowship at Trinity College, Oxford, founded by her late husband, Sir Thomas Pope. He held it for a few weeks before leaving England for the continent. He arrived at the English College in Rheims on 22 July 1583; by 15 April 1584 he was at the English College in Rome where he was ordained priest on 1 April 1589. In October he was at the recently founded English College in Valladolid, moving to Seville in early 1591. With eleven others Blount left Seville for England on 1 April 1591. To facilitate their return Robert Persons devised a wonderful masquerade. Appropriately dressed, they were presented as English sailors captured during the earl of Essex's expedition against Spain and now duly released. William, Lord Howard of Effingham, lord admiral, examined Blount upon his arrival: after two or three days of examination he was rewarded and released. He was placed at Scotney Castle, Sussex, home of the Darell family.

Blount entered the Jesuits in England in September of 1596. He was a Jesuit novice when he made his celebrated escape from government agents at Scotney Castle in either 1597 or 1598. He completed his noviceship on 7 September 1598. Some time after his escape Blount moved to

London. In 1609 he ministered to Thomas Howard, earl of Arundel; his mother, Anne (Dacre) Howard, countess of Arundel; Elizabeth (Hastings) Somerset, countess of Worcester, and her family; Anne (Rivett) Windsor, Lady Windsor; and others. Father Morris cited a report that George Abbot, archbishop of Canterbury, knew Blount's residence but refused to disclose it in memory of their time together in Oxford, and because of the archbishop's respect for Blount's hostess (Morris, 192–3). Most likely his London base was a house belonging to the Arundels. In London, perhaps at the same residence, he pronounced his final vows on 1 May 1609.

On 17 April 1619 Blount succeeded Michael Walpole as superior of Jesuits in England. Three months later, on 6 July 1619, he was named vice-provincial of the recently established Jesuit vice-province of England that included England, Wales, and English Jesuit foundations in the Spanish Netherlands. England was elevated to full provincial status on 21 January 1623 with Blount as provincial, a position he retained until the summer of 1635.

During his term the province thrived: from 242 members, 138 of whom worked in England and Wales, in 1623, it grew to 359 Jesuits, 188 working in the kingdom, in 1636, with a new mission to Maryland established in 1633 and proposals for new colleges on the continent (Osnabrück). The growth was subsidized by generous benefactions from patrons such as the countess of Arundel; George Talbot, earl of Shrewsbury; Henry Somerset, earl and later marquess of Worcester; William, Lord Petre; and Thomas Sackville, younger son of Thomas Sackville, earl of Dorset, whom Blount reconciled to the Roman church shortly before the earl's death. Blount guided the society through various crises, including a prolonged theological battle with secular clergy over the rights and prerogatives of Richard Smith, bishop of Chalcedon, John Gerard's controversial support for Mary Ward and her revolutionary 'English Ladies', and the dismissal (albeit temporary) from the society of Thomas Poulton because of offensive remarks against Cardinal Richelieu.

Some time after the completion of his term Blount petitioned Charles I that as a Roman Catholic priest he should be imprisoned, and recommended that he be confined at his brother's house at Tittenhanger. It is uncertain whether his request was granted. On Passion Sunday in 1638 he suffered an apoplectic seizure that left him partially paralysed. He died in London on Pentecost, 13 May 1638, and was buried in Queen Henrietta Maria's Catholic chapel at Somerset House. Robert Catesby once said of him: 'Here comes Father Blount, who is everybody's favourite, and has no favourites himself' (Morris, 204). Of many compliments paid to him, at least one is incontestably true: an unsigned evaluation compiled prior to Blount's final profession sang his praises. Among his many gifts, 'he is fit for government and for all the duties of the Society' (Morris, 205). THOMAS M. MCCOOG

Sources G. Anstruther, *The seminary priests*, 1 (1969), 41 · T. F. Knox and others, eds., *The first and second diaries of the English College, Douay* (1878), 197 · T. M. McCoog, ed., *Monumenta Angliae*, 2: *English and Welsh Jesuits, catalogues, 1630–1640* (1992), 238 · Foster, *Alum. Oxon.* · W. Kelly, ed., *Liber ruber venerabilis collegii Anglorum de urbe*, 1, Catholic RS, 37 (1940), 48–9 · E. Henson, ed., *The registers of the English College at Valladolid, 1589–1862*, Catholic RS, 30 (1930) · H. Foley, ed., *Records of the English province of the Society of Jesus*, 3 (1878), 481; 7/2 (1883), 892 · J. Morris, ed., *The troubles of our Catholic forefathers related by themselves*, 1 (1872), 189, 202–6 · P. Williams, 'Elizabethan Oxford: state, church and university', *Hist. U. Oxf.* 3: *Colleg. univ.*, 397–440 · R. Persons, 'Annals of the English College, Seville', ed. J. H. Pollen, *Miscellanea, IX*, Catholic RS, 14 (1914), 1–24, esp. 15 · T. M. McCoog, *English and Welsh Jesuits, 1555–1650*, 2 vols., Catholic RS, 74–5 (1994–5) · T. M. McCoog, 'The Society of Jesus in England, 1623–1688: an institutional study', PhD diss., University of Warwick, 1984 · B. Basset, *The English Jesuits, from Campion to Martindale* (1967) · *VCH Hertfordshire*, vol. 2 · *IGI* · Archives of the British Province of the Society of Jesus, London, Collectanea M, extracts and summaries of correspondence, fols. 95–101

Archives Archives of the British Province of the Society of Jesus, London, Collectanea M, extracts and summaries of corresp., fols. 95–101 · Archivum Romanum Societatis Iesu, Rome, extracts and summaries of corresp., Anglia 37, fols. 102*r*–109*r*

Likenesses portrait, repro. in H. More, *Historia provinciae Anglicanae Societatis Iesu* (1660), frontispiece

Blount, Teresa Maria (1688–1759). *See under* Blount, Martha (1690–1763).

Blount, Sir Thomas (*b.* after 1348, *d.* 1400), knight, was the first son of Sir Thomas Blount (*c.*1321–*c.*1407), of Compton Valence, Dorset, and Kingston Blount, Oxfordshire. Blount's mother, Joan, was the daughter of Sir Edmund Hakluyt of Longford, Herefordshire, and widow of Reynold Fitzherbert of Midsomer Norton, Somerset. His other principal estate was at Laverstock, Wiltshire.

Blount was knighted before 1374, probably for service overseas, although he failed in his undertaking to cross the channel in the retinue of John, duke of Brittany. He joined the household of Richard II, who made him a personal gift of 20 marks in May 1383, and paid him 40 marks a year later for escorting a French ambassador from Berkhamsted Castle to Scotland and then via London to Calais. As a knight of the chamber Blount took part in Richard's expedition to Scotland in 1385, following which he was granted a wardship as he 'had scanty means of support'. However, he soon surrendered this in exchange for a life annuity of £40. In March 1386 he received £20 for additional services to the king, and was then employed on the defence of Calais under Sir Thomas Percy (afterwards earl of Worcester).

In 1387 Blount secured the hand of Isabel, daughter of John, second Lord Botetourt, and widow of Sir Hugh *Seagrave, the former treasurer of England, but although this was a prestigious match it did not bring him much in the way of material benefits. Blount was expelled from court by the lords appellant in January 1388, but escaped the harsh judgments meted out by the Merciless Parliament on several of his colleagues, and was reinstated in the chamber as soon as the king regained the political initiative. In 1391 he was sent to Paris as Richard's personal messenger to Charles VI, and in 1394 he took part in the royal expedition to Ireland. Along with the king's councillor, Sir Henry Green, he was returned for Wiltshire to the parliament of September 1397, which brought to fruition Richard's plans for revenge on his enemies. Yet although his election may have been the outcome of a deliberate policy to secure seats in this parliament for the king's supporters, Blount was qualified to represent the county through property brought by his second marriage (which had taken place by October 1394), to Joan (*b. c.*1344), niece and heir of John Tudworth of Laverstock, and widow of Sir Hugh Cheyne of Rolleston, Leicestershire.

Blount's annuity was confirmed by Henry IV in November 1399, but he never accepted the deposition of Richard II, to whom he remained devoted, and joined the conspirators headed by the earls of Kent, Salisbury, and Huntingdon, who on 17 December at the abbey house in Westminster plotted to seize the new king while he was at Windsor for the feast of Epiphany. The plot miscarried and the traitors were forced to flee to Cirencester. There, after a fight, Blount was arrested. He was taken to Oxford for trial in the marshal's court, and sentenced to execution on 12 January. The most graphic contemporary account of his death, in which, after suffering hanging and evisceration, he responded to the taunts of Sir Thomas Erpingham with a declaration of his willingness to die in the service of his sovereign lord, Richard II, should be discounted as an untrustworthy source. Similarly, the chroniclers' descriptions of him as 'un sage baron' ('a wise lord') or 'un bon chevalier' ('a good knight') perhaps reveal more about their own bias than about Blount himself. His estates were forfeited to the crown, but not for long, for the manor of Blatchington, Sussex, which he had held for life since 1393 soon reverted to the heirs of his half-brother Sir Edmund Fitzherbert, and that of Kingston Blount, which he had leased from his father for £20 p.a., returned to the latter. His widow reclaimed her property in 1401 after her third marriage, to Thomas Linford. Blount died childless; his heir was his brother, Hugh. LINDA CLARK

Sources HoP, *Commons* • *Miscellanea Genealogica et Heraldica*, 5th ser., 7 (1929–31), 73–83, 319–20 • B. Williams, ed., *Chronicque de la traïson et mort de Richart Deux, roy Dengleterre*, EHS, 9 (1846), 90–91 • J. J. N. Palmer, 'The authorship, date and historical value of the French chronicles on the Lancastrian revolution', *Bulletin of the John Rylands University Library*, 61 (1978–9), 145–81; 398–421, esp. 408 • inquisition post mortem, PRO, C 137/14/59 • Pleas of Marshalsea Court, PRO, E37

Wealth at death at least £30 p.a. from land; annuity of £40: PRO, C 137/14/59

Blount, Sir Thomas (*c.*1383–1456). *See under* Blount, Sir Walter (*d.* 1403).

Blount, Thomas (1605/6–1678), landowner and local politician, was the second son of the six sons and two daughters born to Edward Blount (1559–1618), lawyer and landowner, and his second wife, Fortune, daughter of the London merchant Sir William Garway (Garraway). The Blount family held the manor and 280 acres of Wricklemarsh, near Charlton, Kent, and as his elder brother predeceased their father Thomas inherited Wricklemarsh. He matriculated from Brasenose College, Oxford, on 5 December 1623, aged seventeen; the following year he was admitted to Gray's Inn but did not proceed to the bar. By 1629 he was giving legal advice to the vestrymen of Greenwich. From 1636 until 1660 he was an active JP in his corner of north-west Kent and assiduously attended assizes up to the mid-1650s and rather more infrequently thereafter. On 4 February 1629 or 1630 at St Peter-le-Poer, London, he married Sarah, the daughter of Captain Anthony Wood of Rotherhithe, Surrey. They are known to have had four sons—of whom the eldest was Thomas, (*b.* 1636/7)—and three daughters.

Blount was present at the meetings at Maidstone of county gentry, including Sir Edward Dering and Sir Roger Twysden, which resulted in the getting up of the royalist Kentish petition at the assizes of March 1642; he reported the matter at the bar of the House of Commons and was an organizer of the pro-parliamentarian counter-petition. With the coming of war he was appointed colonel of a Kentish regiment, and he was one of two men excepted from the royal pardons offered to Kent in November and December 1642. He became a leading figure on the county committees, an ally of Sir Anthony Weldon in overriding local interests in the cause of parliament. Indeed, he was one of only eight men to sit on the chief committee continuously throughout the period 1643–60 (out of a total of 274 who served on it at some point in those years), as the more established and politically moderate county leaders gave way to minor gentry more ruthless in doing parliament's bidding. Socially Blount—a man of some substance but from a family only recently settled in the county—was an intermediate figure between these two groups; politically his inclinations were very much with the latter. Sir Roger Twysden, who was at the receiving end of Blount's duties as a sequestration commissioner, remarked that he was 'a great stickler for the two houses of parliament' ('Sir Roger Twysden's journal', 202n.). In January 1645 Blount shielded the Antinomian John Saltmarsh from a local crowd when he tried to preach at Westerham. In April that year he was active in suppressing a royalist rising in the county, when he 'caused to be beaten an alarm on the top of his own house, and summoned in the country all about' (Everitt, 216). A few months later he engineered a less serious combat: to appease the local population for the loss of their May day games he staged a mock battle on Blackheath, with two infantry regiments acting as cavaliers and roundheads.

In 1649 Blount was nominated to sit on the high court of justice to try Charles I, but he failed to attend any of its sessions. In 1652 he was a radical presence on the commission for law reform (the so-called Hale commission) set up by the Rump Parliament. The following year he was summoned to sit in Barebone's parliament, having been nominated by the gathered churches of Kent. There he showed 'mildly radical leanings in both … religion … and … politics' (Woolrych, 119). He sat on a dozen committees, including some which reflected his religious preoccupations (those for tithes and for the advancement of learning) and some his legal (for civil marriage, for abolishing the court of chancery, and for suppressing highwaymen). To judge by the divisions for which he served as teller, he shared the radical hostility to tithes and lay patronage.

In the early 1650s Blount extended his estate by the purchase of crown lands on the Isle of Sheppey and in Lewisham, Kidbrooke, and Charlton. In 1656 he transferred his interest in the Wricklemarsh property to his son Thomas, recently married to Anne Oldfield, although he continued to occupy the main house. In 1657 he provided both men and arms to suppress Thomas Venner's Fifth Monarchist rising and two years later opposed a royalist rising in Kent. At the Restoration he was removed from the bench and became an object of suspicion to the new regime. In 1661 he attended services at St Margaret, Lee, Kent, where the clergymen (both shortly to be ejected for their failure to conform) were more congenial to him than the incumbent who now presided at St Luke, Charlton. His action was reported by spies, and he was arrested, charged with sedition, and imprisoned for conspiracy. However, the testimony of friends and his own exculpatory statements secured his release after two months. He claimed that during the war he had refused a commission which was worded as coming from parliament alone rather than from king and parliament; he had treated kindly the duke of Richmond and other royal servants; and he had given the Greenwich bellringers 20s. to ring the peal celebrating the Restoration. The following year the former magistrate suffered the indignity of being himself the victim of highway robbery.

During the 1650s Blount was friendly with Robert Boyle and John Wilkins, two of the circle who later founded the Royal Society, to which Blount was elected in February 1665. His first encounter with John Evelyn was in 1652 when Evelyn had been robbed and tied up while on his way from Tunbridge Wells to London. On freeing himself, Evelyn went to the nearby Wricklemarsh House, from where Blount immediately sent out hue and cry to search for the robbers. They were not found, but the episode led to Evelyn and Blount becoming friends. In 1655 Evelyn was shown Blount's subterranean rabbit warren and drank the wine from his vineyard, which he noted in his diary as 'good for little' (Evelyn, *Diary*, 3.161); in 1656 Boyle and other virtuosi, having dined with Evelyn, called afterwards on Blount to see his new plough and in the following year he saw the odometer which Blount had affixed to his carriage, activated by the turning wheel, so as to count the miles travelled. In 1659 Evelyn met at Wricklemarsh Sir Henry *Blount (1602–1682), Blount's kinsman and Levant traveller.

Samuel Pepys was another acquaintance; on 1 May 1665 he met Lord Brouncker and others going to Blount's for dinner, and was persuaded to join them, finding Blount's house 'a very stately seat for its situation and brave plantations; and among others, a vineyard, the first that ever I did see' (Pepys has forgotten his visit to the Hatfield House vineyard in 1661):

> after dinner to the tryall of some experiments about making of coaches easy. And several we tried, but one did prove mighty easy (not here for me to describe, but the whole body of that coach lays upon one long spring and we all, one after another, rid in it; and it is very fine and likely to take. (Pepys, 6.94)

In September, 'after dinner comes Colonel Blount in his new chariott made with springs, as that was of wicker, wherein a while since we rode at his house'. This held one passenger and the driver sat in a sprung saddle. Pepys tried it for comfort, 'and found it pretty well but not so easy as he pretends' (Pepys, 6.213). The following January Brouncker, Wilkins, Pepys, and Robert Hooke again met at Blount's to discuss coaches. This was one of a series of trials of new chariots, in competition with similar French designs. A report was made to the Royal Society on 14 March.

In November 1666 Blount presented the Royal Society with two sorts of English wine, new and old, some black salsify, which he said might be propagated in England much as parsnips, a type of pea, said to be extremely fertile, and some spirit of cherry wine, of singular strength. He withdrew from the society in 1668, perhaps offended by the society's declared preference in 1667 for William Croune's chariot, and died ten years later. He was buried at St Luke, Charlton, on 2 December 1678.

ANITA MCCONNELL and TIM WALES

Sources N. Rhind, *Blackheath village and environs, 1790–1970*, 2 vols. (1976–83), vol. 2, pp. 2–9 • L. M. Day, *Charlton, near Woolwich, Kent, monumental inscriptions: St Luke, Charlton* (1908) • 'Sir Roger Twysden's journal from the Royden Hall MS', *Archaeologia Cantiana*, 1 (1858), 184–214 • Evelyn, *Diary*, vol. 3 • Pepys, *Diary*, 6.94, 213; 7.20 • E. Hasted, *The history and topographical survey of the county of Kent*, 1 (1778), 36 • W. Berry, *Pedigrees of the families of the county of Kent* (1830), 417 • Foster, *Alum. Oxon.* • A. Everitt, *The community of Kent and the great rebellion, 1640–60* (1966) • A. Woolrych, *Commonwealth to protectorate* (1982) • M. de L. Landon, 'Blount (or Blunt), Thomas', Greaves & Zaller, *BDBR*, 76–7 • *CSP dom.*, 1636–61 • G. J. Armytage, ed., *A visitation of the county of Kent, begun … 1663, finished … 1668*, Harleian Society, 54 (1906), 16 • J. S. Cockburn, ed., *Calendar of assize records: Kent indictments, Charles I* (1995) • J. S. Cockburn, ed., *Calendar of assize records: Kent indictments, 1649–1659* (1989) • J. S. Cockburn, ed., *Calendar of assize records: Kent indictments, 1660–1675* (1995) • I. Gentles, 'The debentures market and military purchases of crown land, 1649–1660', PhD diss., London, 1969 • *IGI* • *Charlton parish register, 1653–1753* (1977) [published by Local History Library, Blackheath]

Blount, Thomas (1618–1679), antiquary and lexicographer, was born at Bordesley Park, Worcestershire, the eldest of the three sons and five daughters of Miles Blount (*c.*1585–1663), gentleman, and his wife, Anne (*d.* 1669), daughter of William Bustard of Adderbury. Both his parents were from strongly Catholic families and his adherence to the religion was to affect his life profoundly. It is not known where he was first educated, but he did not attend a university, and his choice of a legal training—he entered the Inner Temple in 1639 and was called to the bar in 1648—qualified him for a profession which his religion prevented him from practising. The sequestrations of his father's estate in 1646 and 1649 also strained the family income, and it was probably in the hope of financial gain that Blount first turned to writing to supplement his modest income from conveyancing.

Neither of Blount's first two books—*The Art of Making Devises* (1646) and *The Academie of Eloquence* (1654)—made an important contribution to scholarship, the former being a translation of a French work, and the latter a book of demonstration letters for young people largely copied from earlier examples; both, however, were popular. His third book was a much greater achievement. *Glossographia, or, A dictionary interpreting all such hard words, of whatsoever language, now used in our refined English tongue*, which appeared in 1656, was only the fourth monolingual English dictionary, and the first attempted on such a scale. It was also the first dictionary to give sources for definitions (albeit only in a minority of cases), and to attempt etymologies. Within a year it was heavily plundered by Edward Phillips for his *New World of English Words*.

Meanwhile, at some date between July 1650 and February 1652 Blount had married Anne (1616/17–1697), daughter of Edmund Church of East Maldon, Essex, and his wife, Anne, daughter of Edward Atlsow of Eversholt, Bedfordshire, a family as firmly Catholic as his own, Atlsow and Church both having been imprisoned for recusant activities. In 1658 Blount ventured to publish, under the name of Grass and Hay Withers, *The Lamps of the Law and Lights of the Gospel*, a satirical look at contemporary radical protestant writing. It was not until the Restoration, however, that he felt he could write in favour of his own religion and its recent martyrs. Then—and for the next four years—he published nothing which did not further the Catholic cause. First among these works was *A catalogue of the lords, knights and gentlemen (of the Catholick religion) that were slain in the late warr* (1660), a work demonstrating the loyalty of the Catholics in England, reprinted many times in works by him as well as others. In the same year he published *Boscobel, or, The history of his sacred majesties most miraculous preservation after the battle of Worcester*, in which he again stressed the part played by the Catholics in the defence of the king's person. Far from being mere propaganda, this work was compiled from eyewitness accounts obtained from the individuals involved, and approved by the king, who ordered Blount to continue it, although *Boscobel, the Second Part, with the Addition of Claustrum regale reseratum* did not appear until 1681. In 1661 he published *Calendarium Catholicum*, the first edition of his Catholic almanac which he produced annually under various titles for four years.

In 1666 Blount tackled a different subject with *Booker Rebuked*, a critique of John Booker's almanac of the previous year; in the later 1660s he returned to the subject of lexicography. In 1667 he published a new edition of *Les termes de la ley*, an alphabetical dictionary of legal terms first published in 1527. In this he attempted to eradicate antiquated expressions, and add new ones; but it was soon made redundant by the appearance in 1670 of his own *Nomolexikon: a Law-Dictionary*. This work, which has been described as his most important, seems largely to have been based on John Cowell's *The Interpreter*, but it was much more than a mere modernization. Indeed, it was so well received that it was not long before it was, like *Glossographia*, plundered, plagiarized, and published under a different name. Within a matter of months Blount was writing to Anthony Wood that it was 'at the presse surreptitiously, being transcribd and mutilated, and disguisd with som new title, and this by a beggarly halfwitted schollar hird for the purpose' (Bodl. Oxf., MS Wood F.40, fols. 89–90). The halfwitted scholar in this instance was Thomas Manley, and the new book, *Nomothetēs*, appeared in 1671. The publication in the same year of a new edition of *The New World of Words*, which had been copied from *Glossographia*, caused Blount scrupulously to write *A World of Errors Discovered in 'The New World of Words'* (1673). Refusing to let the plagiarists deter him, he continued to make notes for a second edition of *Nomolexikon*, which was published posthumously in 1691.

Although Blount deserves notice both for his dictionaries and for *Boscobel*, it is primarily as an antiquary that he is remembered today. However, it was only in the last ten years of his life that he turned his attention to this field; his only antiquarian publication before 1670 was his edition (the third, 1661) of Henry Peacham's *The Compleat Gentleman*, to which he added one chapter and a genealogy of his own family. Several factors may have provoked this change: the death of his mother in 1669 and the subsequent benefit of her estates, and his recent friendship with William Dugdale and Anthony Wood were probably the most important, but the catalyst seems to have been the publication in 1670 of the fifth edition of Sir Richard Baker's popular *Chronicle of the Kings of England*, a work to which Blount was probably already highly indisposed after a continuation had been published by Edward Phillips, the plagiarist of *Glossographia*, in the third edition (1660). In 1671 he proposed to Wood that they collaborate on a *Chronological History of England*, and on being turned down, turned for help to his cousin, the Catholic writer John Belson. The work, which was not published, disappeared until parts were rediscovered by Theo Bongaerts among the Barrett-Belson family papers. Blount's *Animadversions upon Sir Richard Baker's Chronicle* was published, however, in 1672, with Wood's help. The following year Blount composed a similar *Animadversions on Blome's Britannia*, although it seems that this was not published.

In the mid-1670s, after a brief foray into merchant law with *A Collection of Statutes Concerning Bankrupts* (1670) and *The Several Forms of Instruments Relating to the Affairs of Merchants and Traders* (1674), Blount began to write what would prove his most significant book—a history of Herefordshire. In the months when John Belson was unable to work due to ill health, Blount collected material, making use of printed chronicles as well as manuscripts, in London as well as in Herefordshire. He also visited a large number of churches, and about 1677 compiled the history in two volumes, arranged alphabetically by parish. Although never published, it has been used by every subsequent historian of the county. The first volume, relating to parishes A–K, was unfortunately lost in the mid-eighteenth century, having been lent to Sir Robert Cornewall, but not before William Brome, Richard Walwyn, and James Hill had used it; the second volume was acquired by Hereford City Library in 1956.

Blount's last work, *Fragmenta antiquitatis, Antient Tenures of Land, and Jocular Customs of some Manors*, was published in 1679. The book, made up of snippets from legal manuscripts found while he had been researching *Nomolexikon*, was intended both to be amusing and instructive, and indeed shows more than any other publication his sense of humour. As to its instructiveness, Sir William Holdsworth spoke highly in its favour. At the same time as it appeared, however, the wave of anti-Catholic sentiment in the wake of the Popish Plot threatened Blount, and on 28 April 1679 he wrote to Wood that he was sick with 'a spice of the palsey, from what occasion you may conjecture' and that he had 'quitted all books except of devotion' (Bodl. Oxf., MS Wood F.40, fol. 230). He died at Orleton Manor, Herefordshire, on 26 December of that year, and was buried two days later in the chancel of the parish church. His widow, who erected a memorial to him, still extant, died on 4 March 1697, aged eighty. They had one daughter, Elizabeth (*b.* before 1663, *d.* 1724), who married Richard Griffin of Brickmarsh, Warwickshire.

IAN MORTIMER

Sources *The correspondence of Thomas Blount (1618–1679): a recusant antiquary*, ed. T. Bongaerts (1978) • C. R. J. Currie and C. P. Lewis, eds., *English county histories: a guide* (1994) • Wood, *Ath. Oxon.*, new edn • *DNB* • Gillow, *Lit. biog. hist.* • R. C. Alston, *A bibliography of the English language from the invention of printing to the year 1800*, 10 vols. in 1 [1965–73]; repr. with corrections (1974) • *N&Q*, 8 (1853), 286 • Bodl. Oxf., MS Wood F. 40

Archives BL, political and civil observations, Add. MS 27320 | Bodl. Oxf., letters to Anthony Wood, MSS F.40, 45

Wealth at death Orleton Manor, 'a fair and plentiful estate'; widow died eighteen years after him, leaving goods worth £800: Wood, *Ath. Oxon.*

Blount, Sir Thomas Pope, first baronet (1649–1697), politician and writer, was born on 12 September 1649 at Upper Holloway, Middlesex, the eldest son of Sir Henry *Blount (1602–1682), traveller, and his wife, Hester (*c.*1620–1678), first daughter and coheir of Christopher Wase of Upper Holloway and widow of Sir William Mainwaring of Chester. The Hertfordshire Blounts have been linked to the distinguished medieval Staffordshire family, but their connection to the county can be taken back no further than the early Tudor period. It was from Sir Thomas Pope (1507?–1559), the founder of Trinity College, Oxford, who had an acquisitive hand in the suppression of the monasteries under Henry VIII, that the family inherited the manor of Tittenhanger, the former residence of the abbots of St Albans. This house Sir Henry entirely rebuilt, probably but not certainly in the final years of the Commonwealth. Blount was educated under his father's supervision, and acquired a reputation as a learned and accomplished young man, but did not go to university. He entered Lincoln's Inn on 1 December 1668.

On 22 July 1669, at St Olave's, Hart Street, London, Blount married Jane Caesar (1650–1726), only daughter of Sir Henry Caesar, of Benington Place, Hertfordshire, and Elizabeth Angel. They had five sons and nine daughters. In 1678, on his mother's death, and within his father's lifetime, he succeeded to the seat at Tittenhanger, Sir Henry having settled the manor on his wife four years earlier. Blount succeeded to the remainder of the family's estates, in Hertfordshire, Middlesex, and Essex, on his father's death in October 1682. He was created a baronet by letters patent on 27 January 1680. For this dignity he was belatedly compelled to pay; although he disputed the debt, judgment went against him, and on 2 June 1686 he paid the exchequer £1095.

A loyal whig (like his father and his younger brother Charles *Blount he was a member of the Green Ribbon Club), he was returned to the House of Commons as member for St Albans for three parliaments between 1679 and 1681, and subsequently for one of the two Hertfordshire county seats for three further parliaments from 1689 until his death. His political career began quietly. 'Totally inactive in committee in 1679, he spoke only to explain how he had come to deliver to the Speaker a letter from a madman, which seemed designed to interrupt the business of the House' (HoP, *Commons, 1660–90*, 1.669–70). He held a number of local offices, however (commissioner for assessment for Hertfordshire, 1673–80, for St Albans, 1679–80, 1689, and for Hertfordshire and Middlesex, 1689–90, deputy lieutenant of Hertfordshire, 1687–97, and justice of the peace for the same county, 1690–96), before being appointed in 1694, and then reappointed until his death, one of the commissioners for public accounts.

Blount's literary activities appeared in print in the final decade of the century. His first publication was *Censura celebriorum authorum* (1690), a volume, he explains in the preface, he had originally compiled for his own use and which he published only 'at the request of persons of distinguished learning', and with the hope that it 'might promote letters' (*Biographia Britannica*, 2.833, where a translation is provided). The work, a handsomely printed folio, is a biographical and bibliographical dictionary of the most eminent literary and scientific writers, collated from the opinions of fellow writers and reproduced in the several languages of those sources. The entries are arranged chronologically. They begin with Hermes Trismegistus, the writer 'thought to have been coæval with Moses' (*Biographia Britannica*, 2.833), and conclude with contemporaries of Thomas Hobbes, including in well over 500 entries many historians, physicians, philosophers, astronomers and mathematicians, theologians and churchmen, as well as smaller numbers of, for instance, geographers, printers, and antiquaries. Poets are also well represented, but Blount omits most modern English writers (Chaucer is included, Shakespeare is not), as well as later scientists of all lands. Subsequent editions were published in Geneva: a second in 1694, in which, for the sake of a uniform text, all the passages in modern languages were translated by the anonymous editor into Latin, and a third in 1696. Subsequent works adapt this model.

In *A Natural History* (1693) Blount collected observations from 'the Best Modern Writers' (title-page) on various phenomena (amber, coral, tea and coffee, silver, diamonds, glow-worms, spiders, volcanoes, and the like), and in *De re poetica* (1694) he offered a compendium of literary thought 'Extracted out of the Best and Choicest Criticks' (title-page) on poetry in general, on the different genres, and on poetry in Italian, Spanish, and French, to which he appended 'Characters and Censures', a biographical and critical account of sixty-seven writers, ancient and modern, including those English poets (Donne, Jonson, Milton, and Spenser, for example) not included in the *Censura*. His only original work was a collection of *Essays on Several Subjects* (1691; 2nd edn, 1692), 'writ in my idle hours, for my own Entertainment' (1691, sig. A2*v*). In seven short pieces, he treats of self-interest; the mischiefs of learning; education and custom; a tempered respect for antiquity; the virtues of modern men; passion; and the uncertainty of human knowledge. An eighth essay, added to a third, expanded edition (1697), concerns religion. In domestic metaphors and plain prose, Blount reveals himself to be sceptical, cynical, cheerfully optimistic, possessed of a dry wit, and warmly anti-Catholic. 'To infer the truth of a Religion, from the Number of its Professors', he comments on a characteristic concern, characteristically expressed, 'is falsely to conclude the fineness of the Cloth from the largeness of the Measure' (1697, 140).

Blount was well regarded in his lifetime as a cultivated and retiring man. He died of apoplexy at Tittenhanger on 30 June 1697, and was buried in the family vault at Ridge, Hertfordshire, on 8 July 1697. He was forty-seven.

Jonathan Pritchard

Sources H. P. Blount, 'Manuscripts of Sir Harry Pope Blount by which he made out the pedigree of the Blount family', BL, Add. MS 36242 · H. P. Blount, 'Pedigree of the Blounts of Tittenhanger in com Hertford, extracted from wills, evidences, church registers, visitation books in the heralds' offices, &c', 1735, BL, Add. MS 36274b · R. Clutterbuck, ed., *The history and antiquities of the county of Hertford*, 1 (1815), 209–12 · HoP, *Commons*, 1660–90, 1.268–9, 271–2, 669–70 · *Biographia Britannica, or, The lives of the most eminent persons who have flourished in Great Britain and Ireland*, 2 (1748), 833–5 · J. Burke and J. B. Burke, *A genealogical and heraldic history of the extinct and dormant baronetcies of England, Ireland and Scotland*, 2nd edn (1841); repr. (1844), 67–8 · GEC, *Baronetage*, 4.113 · W. A. Shaw, ed., *Calendar of treasury books*, 8, PRO (1923), 335, 762, 768–9, 1981–3; 10 (1935), 722 · A. Grey, ed., *Debates of the House of Commons, from the year 1667 to the year 1694*, 7 (1763), 236–7 · *CSP dom., Jan 1686–May 1687*, 156, *June 1687–Feb 1689*, 123 · J. R. Jones, 'The Green Ribbon Club', *Durham University Journal*, 49 (1956–7), 17–20 · H. A. Tipping, 'Tyttenhanger, Hertfordshire, the seat of the earl of Caledon [pt 1]', *Country Life*, 46 (1919), 424–32 · H. A. Tipping, 'Tyttenhanger, Hertfordshire, the seat of the earl of Caledon [pt 2]', *Country Life*, 46 (1919), 454–62 · N. Luttrell, *A brief historical relation of state affairs from September 1678 to April 1714*, 1 (1857), 376 · W. J. Hardy, ed., *Notes and extracts from the sessions rolls, 1581 to 1698* (1905), 416–17 · W. P. Baildon, ed., *The records of the Honorable Society of Lincoln's Inn: admissions*, 1 (1896), 303 · W. Le Hardy, ed., *Calendar to the sessions books … 1658 to 1700* (1930), 519

Archives BL, Hardwicke MSS, corresp., Add. MS 36242, vol. 894; Add. MS 36274b

Blount, Sir Walter (*d.* 1403), soldier and diplomat, of Barton Blount, Derbyshire, was the third son of Sir John Blount (*d.* 1358) of Sodington, Worcestershire, and of his first wife, Iseult, daughter and heir of Thomas Mountjoy of Gayton, Staffordshire. Immortalized by Shakespeare as one of the three knights who gave their lives by impersonating Henry IV at the battle of Shrewsbury, Sir Walter was indeed a devoted supporter of the house of Lancaster, to which he owed his advancement, wealth, and influence. He was still a young man when, in 1367, he accompanied John of Gaunt, duke of Lancaster, on the first of six military expeditions overseas. Five years later he joined the ducal household (of which he became chamberlain in 1392), while also assuming a prominent place in the management of his patron's north midland estates, as constable of Tutbury Castle, Staffordshire, and master forester of Needwood Chase in the same county. So highly did Gaunt value his services that his income as a Lancastrian retainer eventually exceeded £176 a year, thereby enabling him to purchase the Bakepus family's extensive Derbyshire and Leicestershire estates. These gave him a strong territorial base, and augmented the relatively modest possessions which, as a younger son, were all he could hope to inherit.

Blount's marriage, by 1374, to Sancha de Ayála, a daughter of Diego Gomez, principal secretary of the province of Toledo, and his wife, Inez de Ayála, a favourite lady in waiting of Gaunt's second duchess (herself the elder daughter of Pedro the Cruel, king of Castile), cemented the bond between him and the duke. It also gave him a vested interest in Gaunt's claim to the throne of Castile, and made him an obvious choice as diplomatic envoy to the Iberian peninsula. He undertook two long missions to Castile, in 1378 and 1393, evidently acquitting himself well, despite the overwhelming odds against success; and he later served as an ambassador to Portugal and Aragon for Gaunt's son, the newly crowned Henry IV, in 1400. Further evidence of Blount's negotiating skills may be found in his presence, in 1383, as ducal representative at peace talks on the Scottish border. Blount had to draw upon his military and diplomatic experience nearer home, for the gentry of the north midlands resented Gaunt's intervention in local issues. His position as the duke's leading retainer in Derbyshire and Staffordshire, where he also sat on the bench in the 1380s, was fraught with difficulties, but he continued to enjoy every mark of confidence from his patron. Gaunt made him an executor of his will, and left him a personal bequest of 100 marks. His trust was not misplaced: when Henry Bolingbroke landed at Ravenspur, in July 1399, to recover the confiscated duchy of Lancaster from Richard II, Blount welcomed him with one of the largest private retinues then marshalled by his supporters.

A mainstay of the new regime, Blount represented Derbyshire in the first parliament of Henry's reign. He was entrusted with the care and tutelage of the young Prince Thomas, who, in 1402, became lieutenant of Ireland. In death, as in life, Blount honoured the ties of good lordship, asking in his will of 1401 to be buried at the Lancastrian foundation of St Mary in the Newarke, Leicester. This wish was fulfilled after the battle of Shrewsbury, where he was killed. Sancha Blount survived until 1418 or 1419 as a pensioner of the crown, and was buried beside him. They had five sons, the most celebrated of whom, **Sir John Blount** (*d.* 1418), became a knight of the Garter and fell at the siege of Rouen. His younger brother, **Sir Thomas Blount** (*c.*1383–1456), who had been intended for the church, in turn assumed the Lancastrian livery, and rose high in royal service to be made treasurer of Normandy. In recognition of two generations of unstinting loyalty, Prince Thomas set aside 1000 marks for the erection of a splendid Blount family chantry at St Mary's.

CAROLE RAWCLIFFE

Sources HoP, *Commons* • N. H. Nicolas, ed., *The Scrope and Grosvenor controversy*, 2 vols. (privately printed, London, 1832) • S. Walker, *The Lancastrian affinity, 1361–1399* (1990) • A. Croke, *The genealogical history of the Croke family*, 2 vols. (1823) • R. Somerville, *History of the duchy of Lancaster, 1265–1603* (1953) • *Chancery records*

Blount, Walter, first Baron Mountjoy (*d.* **1474**), administrator, was the eldest son of Sir Thomas *Blount (*c.*1383–1456) [*see under* Blount, Sir Walter (*d.* 1403)] and Margaret Gresley, and was probably born at Barton Blount, Derbyshire. Walter and his brother Thomas were in the service of Henry VI in the early 1450s, but by 1454 were associated with Richard, duke of York, and his ally Richard Neville, earl of Warwick. When in May 1454 Nicholas Longford sacked Walter's house at Elvaston as part of a violent feud with the Blounts, the damage included the slashing of a tapestry bearing Blount's arms 'for that the said Walter Blount was gone to serve traitors, therefore his arms shall be thus quartered' (Storey, 154). Blount escaped attainder at the Coventry parliament of November 1459, receiving a pardon for his treasons in December, but his offices were confiscated. During the Yorkist ascendancy after the battle of Northampton he was made treasurer of Calais, where his patron Warwick was captain. In March 1461 he fought on the Yorkist side at Towton. He was made knight of the Bath at Edward IV's coronation, and in June was reappointed treasurer of Calais, a post which he held until November 1464, when he surrendered it to his brother Thomas on being made treasurer of England. On 20 June 1465 he was created Baron Mountjoy. In August 1467 he received two grants of forfeited land in the south-west, perhaps as compensation for yielding the treasurership to the king's father-in-law, Earl Rivers, in the previous year. In September 1468 he indented to lead troops to Brittany for six months to aid the duke of Brittany against Louis XI of France, but the expedition was cancelled, and Blount, who had by then been paid for his retinue, served instead at sea under Anthony, Lord Scales, for rather less than three months and was allowed to pocket the difference, which may have been some compensation for the money he was still owed by the crown for his service at Calais.

Walter Blount's first wife, whom he married in or before 1442, was Ellen, the daughter of Sir John Byron of Clayton, Lancashire. By November 1467 he had married as his second wife Anne, daughter of Ralph, earl of Westmorland, and widow of Humphrey Stafford, duke of Buckingham (*d.* 1460). Blount died on 1 August 1474 and was buried in the Apostles' Chapel in the Greyfriars Church, London, although he also made major bequests to the church of Elvaston, where his first wife was buried, and to the hospital of St Leonard near Alkmonton, Derbyshire, a family foundation. His eldest son, **William Blount** (*d.* 1471), had died at Barnet on 14 April 1471, from wounds received in the battle, after sharing Edward IV's exile. Walter's heir was thus William's son, Edward, whose custody was granted in January 1475 to his stepfather, John Elrington, the treasurer of the king's household, who had married William's widow, Margaret Echingham (*d.* 1481). Edward died on 1 December 1476 and was succeeded by his uncle, Walter's second son, John, who had licence to enter his father's lands on 15 January 1476, back-dated to 2 January.

John Blount, third Baron Mountjoy (*d.* 1485), was knighted at the marriage of Richard, duke of York, in January 1478. He had been lieutenant of Hammes since 6 April 1470, but after being made constable of Guînes by Richard III seems to have left Hammes to his younger brother, James, who had been granted the office jointly with him in May 1476. By 14 August 1484 John was seriously ill and Sir Thomas Montgomery (who was later to marry his widow) was authorized to act as his deputy. Blount made his will on 6 October 1485, in which he prayed his sons 'to live rightwisely and never to take the state of baron upon them if they may leave it from them, nor to desire to be great about princes for it is dangerous' (GEC, *Peerage*, 9.338, n. f). He died on 12 October. With his wife, Lora, the daughter of Sir Edward Berkeley of Beverstone, Gloucestershire, he had two sons, William and Rowland, and a daughter, Constantyne, all of whom were under age at his death. In 1488 the wardship of his heir, William *Blount, was granted to his brother James, the third son of Walter, Lord Mountjoy.

Sir James Blount (*d.* 1492), soldier, had been an esquire of the body of Richard III and as constable of Hammes was gaoler of the imprisoned Lancastrian John de Vere, earl of Oxford. At the beginning of November 1484 Blount freed his prisoner and went with him to join Henry Tudor in France. He accompanied Tudor's invasion of England in 1485 and was knighted by him at his landing at Milford Haven. He was subsequently rewarded with land forfeited by Richard's allies 'for services rendered at great bodily risk and expense in favouring the king's title' (*CPR, 1485–94*, 230). He married Elizabeth, one of the two daughters and coheirs of John Delves, who died with his father on the Lancastrian side at Tewkesbury. The Delves's land was thereby forfeited, although Edward IV granted Blount their manor of Apedale in Staffordshire in June 1475. Blount was later to find himself in dispute with John Delves's brother Ralph over the descent of other family property. Blount made his will on 24 July 1492, naming the earl of Oxford supervisor, and died on 29 July. He willed burial with his father and brothers in the London Greyfriars.

ROSEMARY HORROX

Sources *Chancery records* • PRO, Prerogative court of Canterbury [wills], Prob 11 • *RotP* • GEC, *Peerage* • R. Horrox and P. W. Hammond, eds., *British Library Harleian manuscript 433*, 4 vols. (1979–83) • 'Register of the sepulchral inscriptions existing temp. Hen. VIII in the church of the Grey Friars, London', *Collectanea Topographica et Genealogica*, 5 (1838), 274–90 • R. L. Storey, *The end of the house of Lancaster* (1966) • C. L. Scofield, *The life and reign of Edward the Fourth*, 2 vols. (1923) • R. Horrox, *Richard III, a study of service*, Cambridge Studies in Medieval Life and Thought, 4th ser., 11 (1989) • S. M. Wright, *The Derbyshire gentry in the fifteenth century*, Derbyshire RS, 8 (1983) • G. Ormerod, *The history of the county palatine and city of Chester*, 2nd edn, ed. T. Helsby, 3 (1882), 522

Blount, William (*d.* 1471). *See under* Blount, Walter, first Baron Mountjoy (*d.* 1474).

Blount, William, **fourth Baron Mountjoy** (*c.*1478–1534), courtier and literary patron, was born in the parish of Barton Blount, Derbyshire. His father, John *Blount, third Baron Mountjoy [*see under* Blount, Walter, first Baron Mountjoy], died in 1485 and William succeeded to the title as a minor. His uncle Sir James Blount was granted the custody of his lands and marriage and he did not enter into his inheritance until 31 January 1500. After his father's death his mother, Lora Berkeley (*d.* 1501), married first Sir Thomas Montgomery (*d.* 1495) and then Thomas Butler, seventh earl of Ormond (*d.* 1515), who was a grandfather of Thomas Boleyn.

It is unlikely that Mountjoy went to Paris as early as 1496, as tradition relates. In 1497 he was involved in the suppression of the Cornish uprising and about Easter that year he married Elizabeth Say, daughter and coheir of Sir William Say of Essenden, Hertfordshire. She was probably too young to begin living with him and did not go with him to Paris in 1498. He was, however, accompanied by Richard Whitford, a fellow of Queens' College, Cambridge, who would later become his chaplain and to whom he would act as a supporter throughout his life. In Paris he made the acquaintance of Erasmus, who had been acting as tutor to Thomas Grey and sharing accommodation with him. Erasmus became Mountjoy's tutor in turn and when Mountjoy returned to England in 1499 he asked Erasmus to join him. Erasmus, who stated himself willing to follow Mountjoy even to the lower world itself, complied and soon established himself in his patron's household, which was generally perceived as a haven to scholars. Although his father had in his will specifically warned his sons of the dangers of desiring 'to be grete about princes', Mountjoy became a *socius studiorum* to Prince Henry at this time, perhaps through the influence of his stepfather Ormond, who was chamberlain to Queen Elizabeth of York, and Elizabeth seems to have had the primary responsibility for her son's education. In the dedicatory epistle to Charles Blount of his 1531 edition of Livy, written some thirty years later, Erasmus would recall that the principal subject studied by the young men had been history. Mountjoy arranged for both Erasmus and Thomas More to visit the royal nursery at Eltham in 1499, and in later years Erasmus claimed that the reason Henry's written style was similar to his own was because Mountjoy encouraged Henry to read his works at an early age. With Mountjoy's encouragement Erasmus began compiling his *Adagia*, which was first published after his return to Paris in 1500 and dedicated to his pupil. In 1499 Mountjoy requested Erasmus to produce an expanded form of *De conscribendis epistolis*, which had been written for his pupils in Paris, and the new version was dedicated to him.

In 1500 Mountjoy was in Calais with Henry VII and in 1501 he was present at Prince Arthur's marriage to Katherine of Aragon. In 1504, through the mediation of their mutual acquaintance John Colet, Erasmus let it be known that he would welcome renewed patronage from Mountjoy. Mountjoy duly invited him back to England and provided him with an annuity of 100 crowns. Although Erasmus's stay in England was brief, from late 1505 until June 1506, his praises for Mountjoy were renewed and he claimed that 'the sun never shone on a truer friend of scholars' (Mynors and others, ep. 186). Before 1507 Mountjoy was a member of Henry VII's council and Henry visited him in 1508. His first wife died before 21 July 1506 and was buried at Essenden.

At the coronation of Henry VIII on 23 June 1509 Mountjoy was created a knight of the Bath and on 9 July he was made master of the mint. Before the end of July he married Agnes de Vanegas, who had been one of the attendants of Katherine of Aragon as princess of Wales. Henry wrote to Ferdinand II of Aragon supporting her claim to a legacy from Queen Isabella. On 6 October Mountjoy was appointed lieutenant of the castle of Hammes, near Calais, for twenty years and thereafter during pleasure, a position his father had occupied before him. Mountjoy was keenly enthusiastic about the new dispensation under Henry and his most famous letter to Erasmus, dated 27 May 1509 (and probably composed by Andrea Ammonio who was acting as his secretary), is a panegyric to the king: 'Heaven smiles, earth rejoices; all is milk and honey and nectar. Tight-fistedness is well and truly banished. Generosity scatters wealth with unstinting hand' (Mynors and others, ep. 215). Erasmus did in fact return to England soon afterwards as Mountjoy had hoped, but Mountjoy himself was much occupied on the continent during this period. In late 1511 Erasmus wrote to Ammonio and Colet from Cambridge to enquire about Mountjoy's whereabouts, but even after Mountjoy came back to England in November Erasmus avoided his household because of the presence of 'Cerberus', perhaps the French poet Bernard André, to whom he owed money.

By May 1512 Mountjoy had succeeded Ormond as Katherine of Aragon's chamberlain, and in that office received an annuity of £66 13*s.* 4*d.* In March of the following year he was at the court of Spain. He was then put in charge of transport for the war against France and in September departed for Calais with a force of 500 men. After the capture of Tournai he was made acting lieutenant, bailiff, and, in January 1515, governor of the city. In that capacity he was responsible for the beginnings of works on a citadel within the town, intended to provide a separate stronghold for the English garrison there. Unfinished when Mountjoy was replaced, it was never fully completed. Erasmus visited Mountjoy in Tournai in the spring of 1515 *en route* for England. Richard Sampson, Wolsey's vicar-general in Tournai, became involved with Mountjoy in an attempt to secure a prebend for Erasmus at this time, although the plan did not succeed. Once he reached London, Erasmus wrote to Cardinal Domenico Grimani complaining that 'the oldest patron of my studies, has been so overwhelmed by the burdens of war that his help fell short of his affection' (Mynors and others, ep. 334). In 1516 Mountjoy informed Wolsey that he would like to be replaced as governor, but this did not occur until January 1517 and he returned to England in that year.

It is not known when his second wife died, but by February 1515 Mountjoy had married Alice (*d.* 1521), daughter of Henry Keble of St Mary Aldermary, and widow of William Brown; among their children was Charles *Blount, courtier and patron of learning. She was with Mountjoy in the entourage of Katherine of Aragon at the Field of Cloth of Gold in 1520. In May 1521 he was one of the peers who tried the third duke of Buckingham and in August he was at Bruges for the meeting of Wolsey with the emperor Charles. In 1521 Henry VIII was much involved in the Lutheran controversy and Mountjoy wrote to Erasmus asking him to declare his own position on Luther. Alice died on 8 June 1521 and was buried in the church of the London Greyfriars. The next year Mountjoy was present at Henry's meeting with Charles at Canterbury.

In 1523 Mountjoy accompanied Charles Brandon, duke of Suffolk, on his invasion of France. On 30 January 1523 Erasmus wrote to Johann von Botzheim, noting that his panegyric on marriage much impressed Mountjoy as a young man—'He has been married three times, and is now a widower; but perhaps he will marry a fourth time—so easy is it to push the wagon on the way it already wants to go' (Mynors and others, ep. 1341a)—and before 29 July 1523 he married Dorothy, widow of Robert, Lord Willoughby, and daughter of Thomas Grey, marquess of Dorset, Erasmus's former pupil in Paris. She outlived him and did not die until 1553. In 1525 Mountjoy solicited a treatise on the subject of marriage from Erasmus on Queen Katherine's behalf. Erasmus complied, and in 1526 published the *Christiani matrimonii institutio*, dedicated to Katherine. The presentation copy survives in Emmanuel College, Cambridge. In 1526 Mountjoy was elected a knight of the Garter and in the subsidy of 1527 he was rated at £1000. About 1529 he was elected steward of Cambridge University. After his twenty-year appointment as lieutenant of Hammes was completed in 1529, Henry permitted him to sell the office to William, Lord Grey of Wilton, and he surrendered his patent in May 1531.

Although Mountjoy was one of the lords signing the open letter to Pope Clement VII urging the divorce in 1530 he remained Katherine's chamberlain. Chapuys wrote in April 1533 that he had been ordered to stay with Katherine to prevent her escaping from England. In July he was head of the delegation that went to see Katherine at Ampthill to persuade her to submit to the consequences of the king's new marriage and acknowledge herself dowager princess. Katherine spurned all their conditions, and Cromwell later declared to Chapuys that if Katherine had been a man she would have surpassed all the heroes of history. After this failed mission, no doubt repugnant to him, Mountjoy requested to be replaced as chamberlain and on 10 October 1533 he wrote to Cromwell that 'hit is not my parte, nor for me this often to vexe or unquyet her whom the kynges grace cawsed to be sworne unto and truly to serve her to my power' (*State Papers, Henry VIII*, 1.408). After his death he was not replaced in that office.

In July 1534 Mountjoy was on the panel of lords at the treason trial of William, Lord Dacre. He died on 8 November following at Sutton on the Hill, near Barton Blount, Derbyshire, and was buried at his own request at Barton Blount. In his will, dated 14 October 1534, he asked patience of his creditors, considering that he had impoverished himself to provide for his son and that he had often been called abroad in service of the king to whom he had been a 'slender suter' (PRO, PROB 11/25, fol. 243*v*). His house in London was on Silver Street.

The mother of Mountjoy's daughter Gertrude was his first wife Elizabeth Say. Gertrude married on 25 October 1519 Henry Courtenay, who was created marquess of Exeter on 18 June 1525 and executed in 1539. She was close to Princess Mary and when the latter came to the throne she was rehabilitated and made a lady-in-waiting. The mother of his eldest son and heir, Charles, and his daughter Catherine (later Champernown and Berkeley) was Mountjoy's third wife, Alice Keble. His fourth wife, Dorothy Grey, was the mother of his son John, who was her principal beneficiary, and his daughters Dorothy (later Blewett) and Mary (later Dennys). Henry VIII's mistress Elizabeth Blount, who had been a lady-in-waiting to Katherine and who was the mother of Henry Fitzroy, was Mountjoy's cousin. JAMES P. CARLEY

Sources GEC, *Peerage*, new edn, 9.338–41 • P. G. Bietenholz and T. B. Deutscher, eds., *Contemporaries of Erasmus: a biographical register*, 1 (1985), 154–6 • H. Miller, *Henry VIII and the English nobility* (1986), 18–19, 64, 82, 90, 94, 103–6, 111, 122, 136n., 146, 176–7, 183–4, 208 • M. Dowling, *Humanism in the age of Henry VIII* (1987), 13, 228 • *The correspondence of Erasmus*, ed. and trans. R. A. B. Mynors and others, 22 vols. (1974–94) • J. K. McConica, *English humanists and Reformation politics under Henry VIII and Edward VI* (1965), 60, 156–7 • will, PRO, PROB 11/25, fol. 243*r–v* • *State papers published under … Henry VIII*, 11 vols. (1830–52), vol. 1 • H. M. Colvin and others, eds., *The history of the king's works*, 3 (1975)

Wealth at death asked creditors to be lenient: will, PRO, PROB 11/25, fol. 243*r–v*

Blow, Detmar Jellings (1867–1939), architect, was born on 24 November 1867 at the Two Ashes, Forest Hill, Sydenham, Kent, the third of five children of Jellings Blow (*d.* 1898) and his German-born wife, Johanna Antoinette Finke (*d.* after 1910). His father was a merchant in the City of London and the family later moved to 96 Cheyne Row in Chelsea; his mother was taught to play the piano by Clara Schumann. Blow went to Hawtreys School before beginning his architectural education in 1883 at the South Kensington School of Art, where he met Edwin Lutyens. Articled for a four-year period to the firm of Wieson, Son, and Aldwinckle, Blow attended the Architectural Association evening classes from 1887. In June 1888 he was awarded the Architectural Association travelling studentship and, in November, first prize in the class of design.

On commencing his travelling studentship in France, Blow met John Ruskin by chance on 25 June 1888 at the Tête de Bœuf in Abbeville. As a direct result Blow put off his studies at Beauvais Cathedral, and spent the next six months travelling with Ruskin, an experience that was to shape the rest of his career. Soon after his return he met William Morris and Philip Webb, whose principles as inculcated through the Society for the Protection of

Ancient Buildings (SPAB) instilled in Blow the belief that architecture had to be undertaken at first hand, through a direct involvement in the building process. Like Morris, he considered architecture an art rather than a profession. Later he attended the master's deathbed in 1896. Decking a yellow harvest wagon with willow boughs and vine leaves, he drove Morris's coffin to the grave in a waggoner's smock.

In 1892 Blow won the Royal Institute of British Architects' Pugin scholarship with his drawings of Beauvais Cathedral and Barfreston church in Kent. Before this Webb had introduced him to his first client, Hugh Fairfax-Cholmeley, for whom he built Mill Hill (1891), a small house in Brandsby, Yorkshire. Under Webb's guidance Blow had determined to forsake the conventional architect's office for an itinerant lifestyle and he lived on site throughout much of the construction period, thus embarking on the first and perhaps most significant period of his career, as a wandering architect.

Webb introduced Blow to work on site for the SPAB also, as a result of which he repaired the church tower at East Knoyle, Wiltshire (1892). His involvement in other SPAB projects included the rescue of the Old Post Office (1896), a small medieval manor house in Tintagel, Cornwall (now belonging to the National Trust). He worked on site at Lake House, Wiltshire (1897), and on other church towers at Clare, Suffolk (1898–9), and Amesbury, Wiltshire (1901). Blow's early clients included Lord Antrobus at Amesbury Abbey and he was on hand when one of the trilithons at nearby Stonehenge fell in a gale on the last day of 1900. Antrobus, then the owner of Stonehenge, worked in conjunction with Blow, the SPAB, and the Society of Antiquaries and, although the fallen stone was not re-erected until 1958, Blow straightened an adjacent leaning stone, all that remained standing of the largest of the trilithons, in 1901.

Detmar Blow's work as a wandering architect encompassed new work as well as old. Sharing a London base from 1897 with Alfred Powell—another itinerant SPAB architect to emerge from under the wing of Philip Webb—the two men worked on Long Copse, Ewhurst, Surrey, from 1895, with Powell taking the lead. From 1897 Blow worked in association with another of their friends, the architect and furniture designer Ernest Gimson. He built three cottages in the Charnwood Forest near Leicester to Gimson's designs. A larger-scaled product of their association, the flint-walled and thatch-roofed Happisburgh Manor, Norfolk (1900), is attributed solely to Blow.

Throughout this period Blow worked with a band of itinerant masons, two of whom—Frank Green and James Neale—had been with him from the start at East Knoyle and taught him their trade. Indeed both men continued to work for Blow into the twentieth century, Green being on site at Wilsford Manor (1904) near Salisbury and Neale at Little Ridge, later extended and known as Fonthill House, near Tisbury, Wiltshire (also 1904; dem. 1972). These new houses represent the culmination of Blow's wandering career: hand-built by craftsmen, they were made of local materials and by local building techniques. Both incorporated materials from earlier houses.

Blow's timeless way of working was swamped by demand. His meteoric rise as a society architect followed, and partnership with the Frenchman Fernand Billerey in 1905 added a fashionable *beaux-arts* dimension to the practice's output. Together they undertook an enormous number of commissions in the years leading up to the First World War, rivalling Lutyens in the country house market. Typical of the practice's output were the enlargement and alteration of Breccles Hall, Norfolk (1907; later altered again by Lutyens); Heale House, near Salisbury, Wiltshire (*c*.1910); and Broome Park, Kent (from 1911), for Lord Kitchener. New houses included Horwood, Buckinghamshire (1911). Blow and Billerey worked on many London houses too: their interior at 10 Carlton House Terrace and the enlargement of 34 Queen Anne's Gate both attracted attention.

On 5 November 1910 Blow married Winifred Gertrude, the second daughter of the Hon. Hamilton Tollemache, in St Paul's Cathedral. His itinerant mason friends were given pride of place in the front pews and the house Blow built from 1913 for his growing family (eventually consisting of two sons and two daughters) at Hilles, near Painswick, Gloucestershire, harks back to his earlier style. During the Edwardian years Blow became increasingly friendly with the maverick second duke of Westminster, freeholder of the Grosvenor estate in London. This led to considerable work for Blow and Billerey, including Mimizan, a hunting-lodge outside Bordeaux for the duke himself (1911), and buildings on his Mayfair estate. The commission for Government House, Salisbury, Rhodesia (1911), also came through the duke. During the First World War, Blow at first worked for Kitchener in France, but following the latter's death in 1916 he accepted a post as the duke of Westminster's private secretary, with an undefined overview of his London estates. This led to friction with the Grosvenor estate's surveyor, Edmund Wimperis. When Wimperis resigned in 1928, Blow succeeded him. Although he had given up architecture himself, he used his influence with the duke to promote Lutyens and his former partner Billerey as consultants for major development schemes on the Mayfair estate, notably the rebuilding of Grosvenor Square. In March 1933, however, Blow was abruptly dismissed, following unproven allegations of dishonesty. He retired with impaired health to Hilles, where he died from coronary thrombosis on 7 February 1939. Like Morris, he was carried to his hillside grave near by, overlooking Gloucester, on a farm cart.

MICHAEL DRURY

Sources M. Drury, *Wandering architects: in pursuit of an arts and crafts ideal* (2000) • N. Lytton, 'The art of Detmar Blow', *English Life* (June 1925), 58 • S. Blow, *The ghost walks on Friday* (1935) • M. Comino, *Gimson and the Barnsleys* (1980) • 'The work of Mr Detmar Blow and Mr Fernand Billerey', *Country Life*, 32 (1912), suppl., v–xxvi, esp. xvi • 'Wilsford Manor, Wiltshire', *Country Life*, 20 (1906), 450–55 • 'Little Ridge, Fonthill, Wiltshire', *Country Life*, 32 (1912), 566–74 • C. Hussey, 'Horwood House, Winslow, Bucks', *Country Life*, 54 (1923), 644–51 • S. Blow, 'Blow by Blow', *The Guardian* (24 Feb 1979) •

S. Blow, 'A Blow by Blow account of a duke's desertion', *The Spectator* (25 Jan 1986) • N. Lytton, *The English country gentleman* (1925) • b. cert. • m. cert. • d. cert.

Archives NRA, priv. coll.

Likenesses N. Lytton, pencil drawing, 1910? • A. John, drawing, repro. in C. Aslett, *The last country houses* (1982) • A. John, drawing

Wealth at death £23,570 1s. 2d.: probate, 22 May 1939, *CGPLA Eng. & Wales*

Blow [Blaw], **James** (1676–1759), printer and bookseller, was born on 29 July 1676, the youngest of nine children of John Blaw (*d.* 1709) of Culross, Perthshire, Scotland, and his first wife, Elizabeth Wilson. The Blaw family had owned Castlehill estate in Culross parish at least since 1543, and James was the first in the family to change the surname to Blow, this spelling subsequently being adopted by the Belfast branch of the family.

James Blow achieved a long career as printer and bookseller. In 1694 he arrived in Belfast as assistant to Patrick *Neill, who set up the first printing press in the town at the request of the sovereign (mayor) of Belfast, William Craford; James married Patrick's sister Abigail, and in 1688 his own sister Agnes had married Patrick. The first Belfast printed book was an edition of *The Confession of Faith* (1694). James took over the printing establishment from Patrick Neill about 1705, the earliest surviving example from his own press being James Kirkpatrick's sermon *The Saint's Life and Death* (1706). Many of the earliest books that Blow produced omitted details of author, printer, and location, since they were printed without permission of the religious authorities. The first important work printed by James Blow was Kirkpatrick's *An Historical Essay upon the Loyalty of Presbyterians* in 1713, which is the first printed work to mention contemporary Belfast citizens, and provides a picture of the political and social position of Presbyterians in Belfast. In these pages the justification for the Blow press can be seen in the defence of printing Presbyterian books, which in Dr William Tisdall's castigating phrase 'corrupts the principles of the people' (Kirkpatrick, 523). In 1714 Blow printed *The Experienced Huntsman* by Arthur Stringer, the first secular work by a local author originally printed in Belfast. In 1722 he printed *The Church Catechism in Irish* by Francis Hutchinson, bishop of Down and Connor, in which Hutchinson strenuously supported the use of roman characters for the Irish language in print, and presented his Raghlin alphabet (named after Rathlin Island where he began his evangelizing mission). The personal autograph of James Blow can be seen in several copies of I. Watts's *A Guide to Prayer* (1738) and W. Guthrie's *A Christian's Great Interest* (1743) in the inscription at the end of the printed presentation: 'This Practical Piece of Piety, being a great help to Devotion, is with a religious Respect Recommended to my worthy friend By'.

The least understood aspect of James Blow's printing history is his production of bibles. Blow's Bible is dated 1751 and has the imprint 'Belfast: Printed by and for James Blow'. In several copies of the edition it can be clearly seen that this title-page is a replacement. A second version, the 'Genesis reprint', is just the first two gatherings reprinted from the 1751 Bible to replace the first two gatherings in various older bibles of a similar size. The two surviving copies of the so-called Blow 1702 Bible are in fact 1751 Blow bibles with the roman numeral date defaced to read 1702. A group of bibles and New Testaments variously imprinted 'James Blow', 'George Grierson', '1745', '1755', and '1768' all have a common source. A Bible printed by James Blow in 1725 claims on the title-page to have been printed in London in 1684. The so-called Sin-on-more Bible was printed with an unfortunate typesetting transposition for 'Sin no more' and required replacement of the relevant sheet in 'upwards of 8000 copies' but the exact edition has not been identified (Hodgson, 76). It was claimed in his obituary that James Blow printed the first English edition of the Bible in Ireland, and this is repeated by his son Daniel in 1806, although no Blow Bible has yet been identified that is earlier than a 1714 Dublin Bible.

Blow died in Belfast; the charity board from the old parish church there recorded that 'Mr James Blow dyed the 16th August 1759' and left £40 10s. 0d. to the poor of the parish. He was succeeded by his son Daniel, after whose death in 1810 the original wooden press was reportedly still in use in Youghal, co. Cork, as late as 1824. James Blow's daughter Jane married the king's printer in Dublin, George Grierson, who was in turn succeeded by her son Hugh Boulter Grierson. ANTHONY S. DRENNAN

Sources G. Benn, *A history of the town of Belfast* (1877), 425–36 • C. N. Johnston, *John Blaw of Castlehill: Jacobite and criminal* (1916), 142–5 • J. R. H. Greeves, 'Two Irish printing families', *Proceedings of the Belfast Natural History and Philosophical Society*, 2nd ser., 4 (1950–55), 38–44 • A. S. Drennan, 'On the identification of the first Belfast printed book', *The Library*, 7th ser., 1 (2000), 193–6 • [J. Kirkpatrick], *An historical essay upon the loyalty of Presbyterians* (1713) • J. Hodgson, 'Antiquarian notes and queries', *Ulster Journal of Archaeology*, 3 (1855), 76–7 • J. Anderson, ed., *Catalogue of early Belfast printed books, 1694 to 1830*, new edn (1890) [incl. app. on Blow's Bible] • *Faulkner's Dublin Journal* (25 Aug 1759) • D. Blow, letter, *Belfast News-Letter* (12 Sept 1806) • *IGI* • charity board from Old Belfast church, Clifton House, Belfast

Wealth at death left £40 10s. 0d. to the poor of Belfast parish church: charity board from Old Belfast Church, Clifton House, Belfast

Blow, John (1648?–1708), musician and composer, was baptized at St Mary Magdalene, Newark-on-Trent, Nottinghamshire, on 23 February 1649. The record of his doctorate at Lambeth Palace confirms the identification; the age on his marriage allegation suggests that he was born in 1648. He was the second of three children of Henry Blow, who in 1646 married Katherine Langwith, a widow, at Newark, where other members of the family are also recorded. John Blow's recruitment into the Chapel Royal points to early musical training, perhaps under John Hinton, the master of Thomas Magnus's song school in Newark.

Blow may have been one of five boys from Newark and Lincoln for whose procurement Henry Cooke, the master of the children of the Chapel Royal, was reimbursed under a warrant of 4 July 1661. An entry of 1665 in the accounts of the treasurer of the chamber describes the education of Chapel Royal boys, which included Latin, writing, and playing on instruments. Blow's memorial at

John Blow (1648?–1708), by Robert White, pubd 1700

Westminster Abbey states that he was a pupil of Christopher Gibbons, who at the Restoration became an organist of the Chapel Royal and organist of Westminster Abbey (where he was also master of the choristers, 1664–6); Hawkins adds that Blow was first a pupil of the court musician John Hingeston, formerly Cromwell's organist and master of music. Blow was clearly an apt scholar, for James Clifford's *Divine Services and Anthems* (1664) contains the words of three of his anthems, and he joined two other boys, Pelham Humfrey and William Turner, in composing 'I will alway give thanks'.

Blow's voice broke towards the end of 1664, payments for his maintenance after dismissal from the chapel being authorized from 25 December. His voice had not recovered by 21 August 1667, when with another of Cooke's boys he visited Samuel Pepys, who noted their 'extraordinary skill', notwithstanding which 'to hear them sing with their broken voices, which they could not command to keep in tune, would make a man mad, so bad it was' (*DNB*).

Early career, 1668–1680 Blow evidently continued his musical studies, and in 1668 was appointed organist of Westminster Abbey, succeeding Albertus Bryne, who had become organist in 1666 when Gibbons vacated both his abbey posts. Blow's oath on appointment was taken on 3 December, though the abbey's accounts misleadingly record his payment from the previous Michaelmas.

Blow also obtained posts at court. He was admitted as a musician for the virginals from 25 March 1669, although there is no sign of the appointment's confirmation until 30 October 1674, when payment was ordered in consideration of his liveries for 1669–73. A warrant listing musicians of the Chapel Royal and string players who attended the king at Windsor from May to July 1671 includes Blow as organist; possibly he held an extraordinary post in the chapel, since the cheque book says he was sworn in as a gentleman (but not yet as an organist) on 16 March 1674. The large-scale anthem 'When Israel came out of Egypt' appears to have resulted from the new appointment. Further offices came Blow's way with the death on 14 July 1674 of Pelham Humfrey, who had followed Cooke as master of the children and to whose role Blow now succeeded. A warrant for his admission, dated 23 July, also granted him Humfrey's post of composer for voices in the king's private music.

Besides his now extensive official duties, Blow was active in the Corporation of Musick, a society of court musicians on which a royal charter conferred unrealistically wide powers over other professionals. His signature occurs frequently in the corporation's minute book from 1673 to 1679; on 26 June 1673 he was elected one of two wardens for the ensuing year, and he was again a warden in 1676–7.

In 1674 Blow married Elizabeth Braddock (*d.* 1683) at St Paul's, Covent Garden: on 4 September according to the parish register, though the marriage allegation (giving his age as about twenty-six, hers as about twenty) is dated 23 September. Elizabeth's father, Edward Braddock, was master of the choristers of Westminster Abbey, and a gentleman of the Chapel Royal and clerk of the cheque. By 1683 the Blows lived in Great Sanctuary, where Braddock already lived, and Blow remained there for the rest of his life.

Marmaduke Alford states that Blow became one of the organists of the Chapel Royal following Gibbons's death on 20 October 1676. Just over a year later, on 10 December 1677, Blow was created a doctor of music by the dean and chapter of Canterbury Cathedral (the archbishopric being vacant). Some two years after that he relinquished his post as organist of the abbey, perhaps because of his other duties, or because Henry Purcell, whom Blow's memorial and Henry Hall's verse in *Amphion Anglicanus* describe as his pupil, was ready for the post. The abbey's annual accounts for the year ending Michaelmas 1679 record payments to Blow, and the next set names Purcell as organist; as with Blow's appointment, this may be misleading and Purcell may have taken over in the course of 1679–80.

Official records contain much evidence of Blow's presence as a liveried musician at court, though they also show that, like other servants of the king, he often experienced long delays in payments due to him. As master of the children Blow was charged with seeing that the choristers were housed, fed, clothed, and cared for when sick, and with seeking new boys for the chapel. Their academic and musical training was his responsibility, a by-product of which may be his treatise on thorough bass (BL, Add. MS 34072). Testimony to Blow's effectiveness as a teacher is found in the careers of William Croft, Jeremiah Clarke, and others among his pupils.

Blow's industry as a composer was great, and a document detailing his music copied for the Chapel Royal in the period 1670–76 lists two services, a Benedicite and Te Deum, and nine anthems. In fact, by 1680 he had written over thirty anthems, many with instrumental accompaniments such as Charles II favoured, though his output decreased markedly once Purcell started to share the burden. The stamp of Blow's personality is firmly impressed on his early sacred music, despite the initial influence of Matthew Locke and Humfrey. His anthems contain much of his finest work, skilfully incorporating a variety of styles, and while unevenness must be admitted, a breadth of conception is undeniable. Blow's compositions for special occasions began with 'O Lord, I have sinned' for General Monck's abbey funeral in 1670. Almost every year from 1678 to the end of the century he provided a court ode marking the new year, and he wrote seven further odes celebrating royal birthdays; these contain fine moments but betray a sense of duty and only fitful engagement.

Blow's early work as a songwriter is represented in the second book of *Choice Ayres & Songs* (1679), one of more than a dozen song collections to include his music during his lifetime. Blow's duties as a performer are revealed only in part by his extant compositions for keyboard, and while many of his organ and harpsichord pieces presumably date from his early years, most are found in later sources.

Years of maturity, 1681–1700 Blow's *Venus and Adonis* may have been performed before the court at Oxford in 1681. It reflects Blow's knowledge of Lully's stage works, and notwithstanding its small scale may be accounted the first true English opera; the passionate dialogue in act III is among Blow's finest achievements. He never attempted another piece of the kind, and its natural successor is Purcell's *Dido and Aeneas*.

In mid-1682 Blow and Nicholas Staggins, the master of the king's musick, jointly obtained a post 'for the composition and practize of the violins'. In April 1683 they petitioned the king for a licence permitting them to set up an 'Academy or Opera of Musick' where their compositions might be performed, but it seems that action was stayed. While Staggins was responsible for music in the secular sphere, it is clear that Blow by now had overall charge of the chapel's music. Although he was the junior organist until Purcell replaced Edward Lowe in 1682, his other senior colleague, William Child, was elderly, and it was to Blow that Staggins was instructed in 1683 to send the instrumental musicians required for practising anthems.

On 29 October 1683 Elizabeth Blow died in childbirth, aged about thirty, and she was buried two days later in the abbey's north cloister. She had borne five children, all of whom were buried at the abbey. Four died unmarried: Henry (*d.* 1676), John (*d.* 1693), Catherine (*d.* 1730), and Mary (*d.* 1738), who was buried in her father's grave. The wills of Catherine and Mary are extant; the latter's legatees include her cousin Elizabeth Blow of Theobald's Park, Hertfordshire. Another daughter, Elizabeth, died in 1719, four months after marrying William Edgeworth at St Anne's, Soho; during her brief marriage she wrote her name in a book (Brussels conservatory, MS 15418) into which, about 1700, her father had copied German keyboard music (reflecting his lifelong interest in the work of other composers), she herself adding part of one of his grounds.

Blow was still comparatively young and continued to work with vigour. In 1684 he composed *Begin the Song*, his first ode for the Musical Society's annual celebration of St Cecilia's day; others followed in 1691, 1695 (when he also supplied a Te Deum and Jubilate, with trumpets and strings), and 1700. In 1684, too, Blow and Purcell joined in demonstrating an organ built for the Temple Church by Bernard Smith, in competition with Renatus Harris—a contest not decided in Smith's favour until the winter of 1687–8. Smith and Blow were to share the post of tuner of the royal instruments, which fell vacant when Purcell died in 1695. In 1708 it became Blow's alone, following Smith's death.

Blow and Purcell worked closely together on music for James II's coronation in 1685, though Blow's three anthems, including the broadly conceived 'God spake sometime in visions', were the largest contribution by any composer. In a review of court posts conducted in the new reign, Blow kept his places in the Chapel Royal, and a composer's place in the private musick; that of virginalist went to Purcell, but Blow regained it after Purcell's death. In 1687 Blow assumed another responsibility with the death of Michael Wise, almoner and master of the choristers at St Paul's since the choir's reconstitution in Wren's unfinished building. Blow took Wise's place, in 1697 producing the instrumental anthem 'I was glad' for the consecration of the chancel, and, to celebrate the peace of Ryswick during the same service, 'Praise the Lord, O my soul' with organ accompaniment only. He remained in the post until 1703. On 28 November that year the dean and chapter resolved that Jeremiah Clarke should replace Blow, who was to surrender his patent; Clarke's indenture is dated 11 January 1704.

Compared with James II's coronation service, that of William III in 1689 was musically less demanding, and Blow's principal work, 'The Lord God is a sun', is accordingly modest. William's visit to the Netherlands in 1691, accompanied by a group of musicians, was the only occasion on which Blow and Purcell are known to have left England. Purcell's death in 1695 meant that composition for state occasions fell mainly to Blow; but he still found time for other activities. In 1698 he was a steward of the Festival of the Sons of the Clergy, supplying the somewhat dry 'Blessed is the man that feareth the Lord'; in 1702 he reused part of this in the notably fresh 'O sing unto the Lord a new song', for a charitable concert at Stationers' Hall. Purcell's death also left vacant the organist's post at Westminster Abbey, to which Blow was immediately recalled. Purcell died on 21 November, and a week later the *Post Boy* reported Blow's reappointment. In March 1700 he was admitted to a new post of composer for the Chapel

Royal (the cheque book's '1699' is clarified by Bodl. Oxf., MS Mus. E. 17).

Final years Blow's long series of odes ended in 1700 with *Appear, Appear in All thy Pomp* for the new year and *Come, Bring the Song* for Princess Anne's birthday. When Anne was crowned in 1702 Blow seems merely to have adapted two earlier coronation anthems. Although many of his late anthems are short, sober, polyphonic pieces for full choir (perhaps a response to King James's institution of a Catholic chapel with its own musicians, and to a direction of 1691 that the Chapel Royal should have 'solemn musick like a collegiate church'), the years 1703–7 saw the composition for official functions of six elaborate instrumental anthems with florid vocal solos. While tonal planning was never Blow's strongest point, these pieces manifest a well-developed architectural sense despite their relatively independent movements.

Towards the end of his life Blow prepared some of his music for publication. *Amphion Anglicanus* (1700), 'for one, two, three and four voices, with several accompagnements', is modelled on *Orpheus Britannicus* (1698), a posthumous collection of Purcell's songs; but while Blow shared Purcell's musical ideals and often his manner, his work frequently suffers by comparison. Blow's songs too often lack harmonic and melodic certainty; yet a few, such as 'The Self-Banished', have worn well, and a genuinely rich vein of expression is found in pieces like the deeply felt *Ode on the Death of Mr. Henry Purcell*.

Blow's harpsichord pieces appeared in several anthologies, starting with *The Second Part of Musicks Hand-Maid* (1689), but he may himself have planned *A Choice Collection of Lessons* (1698), where he is the only composer represented. His suites show familiarity with French harpsichord music and a wish to emulate the Italian musicians living in London. They share the weaknesses of his songs, but nevertheless contain much that is interesting and attractive. Blow's organ music remained unpublished in his lifetime, except for his settings of psalm tunes (printed in 1703, though the surviving copy is a reprint of *c.*1730). The body of Blow's organ works is larger than that of any of his contemporaries; while rooted in the tradition handed on by Gibbons and Locke, his pieces reveal a keen awareness of developments abroad (three in fact quote from Frescobaldi).

The best of Blow's music is to be found in his sacred works, where he appears as a composer of considerable stature, both imaginative and innovative, as the short 'Cry aloud, and spare not' demonstrates. A number of such pieces survive in autograph copies (listed by Shaw), but his intention of publishing some, expressed in the dedication of *Amphion Anglicanus*, remained unfulfilled. Blow's memorial rightly focuses attention on his church music as his principal legacy. Even Charles Burney, who failed to recognize Blow's historical position and whose condemnation of 'Dr. Blow's crudities' was excessive, acknowledged that 'Some of his choral productions are doubtless in a very bold and grand style'. Despite Blow's shortcomings, attributable in part to his intensive labours over more than thirty years, he was second only to Purcell among English composers of his day.

Glimpses of Blow's friendships with colleagues are afforded by their wills. He received mourning rings under those of John Harding (1684) and John Twiss (1687). He witnessed the will of Richard Hart in 1689, and in 1702 was an overseer of the will of Moses Snow, who bequeathed him a guinea piece of gold. Blow made his own will on 3 January 1708, observing that he was sick. His father-in-law, Edward Braddock, who still held his posts at the abbey and in the Chapel Royal, died on 12 June. Blow himself did not die until 1 October 1708; he is presumed to have died at his home in Great Sanctuary, Westminster. The words 'in the 60th year of his age' on his memorial must mean 'aged sixty'. The abbey's register states that he was buried in the north aisle on 8 October, 'against the door going up to the organ'. His will was proved on 14 October by his daughters, to whom he left most of his property, including several leases and a copyhold estate at Hampton in Middlesex.

Hawkins, who probably heard it from those who remembered Blow, said he was 'a very handsome man in his person, and remarkable for a gravity and decency in his deportment'. Robert White's engraving in *Amphion Anglicanus* was drawn from life, and incorporates the arms adopted by Blow. Of the other pictures said to portray Blow (all in private collections), probably only a half-length by John Riley has a claim to authenticity; a small head attributed to Lely or Riley and an oval head and shoulders attributed to Closterman are reportedly spurious.

JOHN HARLEY

Sources parish register, Newark-on-Trent, St Mary Magdalene, Notts. Arch. [baptism] · Lord Chamberlain's papers, PRO, LC5 · treasurer of the chamber's accounts, PRO, E351 · state papers, PRO, SP44/55; calendared in A. Ashbee, *Records of English court music* (1986–96) · Archive of her majesty's Chapel Royal, St James's Palace: the cheque books; ed. A. Ashbee and J. Harley, *The cheque books of the Chapel Royal* (2000) · PRO, MS RG8/110 [containing notes by Marmaduke Alford]; ed. A. Ashbee and J. Harley, *The cheque books of the Chapel Royal* (2000) · J. L. Chester and G. J. Armytage, eds., *Allegations for marriage licences issued by the dean and chapter of Westminster, 1558 to 1699; also, for those issued by the vicar-general of the archbishop of Canterbury, 1660 to 1679*, Harleian Society, 23 (1886) · W. H. Hunt, ed., *The registers of St Paul's Church, Covent Garden, London*, 5 vols., Harleian Society, 33–7 (1906–9) · overseers' accounts, parish of St Margaret, 1675–1708, City Westm. AC, E188–E221 · faculty office muniment book, 1669–79, LPL · minute book of the Corporation of Musick, BL, Harley MS 1911; ed. A. Ashbee, *Records of English court music* (1986–96) · Pepys, *Diary* · Westminster Abbey muniments, 33702, 33703, 33714, 33729, 61228A · J. L. Chester, ed., *The marriage, baptismal, and burial registers of the collegiate church or abbey of St Peter, Westminster*, Harleian Society, 10 (1876) · St Paul's Cathedral, dean's register, GL, MS 25630/5 · St Paul's Cathedral, minute book, GL, MS 25738/3 · J. Hawkins, *A general history of the science and practice of music*, 5 vols. (1776) · Burney, *Hist. mus.* · will, PRO, PROB 11/504, sig. 228 [3 Jan 1708, proved 14 Oct 1708] · B. Wood, 'Blow, John', *New Grove*, 2nd edn, 3.718–27 [incl. list of works] · W. Shaw, 'The autographs of John Blow (1649–1708)', *Music Review*, 25 (1964), 85–95 · J. Clifford, *The divine services and anthems usually sung in his majesties chappell, and in all cathedrals and collegiate choires in England and Ireland: the second edition* (1664) · will, City Westm. AC, dean and chapter Westminster, 29 March 1736, proved 23 Nov 1738 [will of Mary Blow] · will, City Westm. AC, dean and chapter Westminster, original will no. 802, 23 Sept 1684, proved 27 Nov 1684 [will of John

Harding] • will, City Westm. AC, dean and chapter Westminster, original will no. 922, 26 Dec 1689, proved 25 Feb 1690 [will of Richard Hart] • will of Catherine Blow, 8 July 1728, proved 1 June 1730, PRO, PROB 11/638, sig. 147 • will, PRO, PROB 11/468 sig. 39, 12 Dec 1702, proved 11 Feb 1703 [will of Moses Snow] • will, PRO, PROB 11/397, sig. 69, 14 April 1687, proved 4 May 1687 [will of John Twiss] • A. Ashbee and D. Lasocki, eds., *A biographical dictionary of English court musicians, 1485–1714*, 2 vols. (1998)

Archives BL, autograph copies of music, Add. MSS 30382, 30931–30933, 31403–31404, 31444–31446, 31452, 31455, 31457–31460, 31462, 31465, 31468, 31559 • Christ Church Oxf., autograph copies of music

Likenesses attrib. Closterman, portrait, probably priv. coll. • attrib. Lely or Riley, small head, probably priv. coll. • probably J. Riley, portrait, repro. in Grove, *Dict. mus.*, 3rd edn, pl. XX; priv. coll. • R. White, line engraving, BM, NPG; repro. in J. Blow, *Amphion Anglicanus* (1700), frontispiece [*see illus.*] • process block (after J. Closterman), BM, NPG

Wealth at death copyhold estate at Hampton, Middlesex; leases of eight messuages (incl. two in Great Sanctuary, Westminster, two in Orchard Street, Westminster, three in Duck Lane); £220 in bequests: will, PRO, PROB 11/504, sig. 228

Blower, Samuel (*d.* **1701**), clergyman and ejected minister, was born at Loughborough, Leicestershire. Little is known of his background and family, but Blower later in life used to boast that he and his fellow nonconformist minister John Howe were both born in the same town and had attended the same school, by which he probably meant Winwick grammar school in Lancashire. He matriculated from Magdalen College, Oxford, on 20 February 1649, graduating BA in 1652 and MA in 1654, and being incorporated at Cambridge in 1656. He was a fellow of Magdalen from 1652 to 1660 and its senior dean of arts in 1658–9. On 8 April 1657 he was admitted by the committee for plundered ministers lecturer at Woodstock, Oxfordshire, and later that year, on 29 September, was appointed an assistant to the Oxfordshire triers.

In 1660 Blower was ejected both from his fellowship at Magdalen, on the grounds of slight nonconformity, and his lectureship at Woodstock. He found a place as chaplain to Samuel Dunch of North Baddesley, Hampshire, who in 1667 left him £20 per annum for life, for his 'great paines for the spirituall good of both me and my Family' (Cliffe, 48). In 1672 Blower was licensed as a congregationalist preacher at Sudbury in Suffolk, where he seems to have had family connections, but finally settled at Northampton in 1674 or early 1675 after an invitation to serve as pastor to the presbyterian Castle Hill congregation. In 1692 he was one of those ministers who condemned the evangelizing activities of the Northamptonshire Independent pastor Richard Davis with its echoes of an earlier, more radical phase of dissent. In 1689 Blower is also found serving a congregation at Coventry. In 1694 he retired from his ministry at Northampton and moved to Abingdon.

Blower's will, made at Abingdon on 16 June 1699, reveals the existence of a wife, Elizabeth, but does not mention any children. He held property at Eynsham, some of which had been conveyed to him through their marriage settlement, and elsewhere in Oxfordshire. A cousin was to preserve his books, writings, and papers 'except some English authors which his wife desires to have for her own use' (Gasquoin and others, 90). Blower died in 1701 and was buried on 13 October at St Helen's Church, Abingdon. Edmund Calamy had a good opinion of him, describing him as 'of a meek temper, peaceable principles, and a godly life', one who was 'very desirable as a friend; for he was free and communicative, candid in the last degree, of a very sympathising spirit'. Calamy recorded that 'scripture revelation in scripture language' was a favourite subject for his discourses and that 'he affected not a pompous way of preaching' (Calamy, *Continuation*, 2.717). Blower's only published work was a funeral sermon for Mrs Elizabeth Tub on Psalm 18: 46 (1697).

CAROLINE L. LEACHMAN

Sources Greaves & Zaller, *BDBR*, 77–8 • *Calamy rev.*, 61–2 • E. Calamy, *A continuation of the account of the ministers … who were ejected and silenced after the Restoration in 1660*, 2 vols. (1727), vol. 2, pp. 717–18 • T. Gasquoin and others, *A history of Northampton Castle Hill Church* (1896) • *The nonconformist's memorial … originally written by … Edmund Calamy*, ed. S. Palmer, 2 (1775), 312–13 • A. Gordon, ed., *Freedom after ejection: a review (1690–1692) of presbyterian and congregational nonconformity in England and Wales* (1917) • *IGI* • J. T. Cliffe, *The puritan gentry besieged, 1650–1700* (1993) • Venn, *Alum. Cant.* • will and inventory, Berks. RO, D/A1/48/93

Wealth at death £202 0s. 9*d.*—also property at Eynsham and elsewhere in Oxfordshire: will and inventory, Berks. RO, D/A1/48/93; *Calamy rev.*, 62

Blowitz, Henri Georges Stephan Adolphe Opper de (**1825–1903**), journalist, was born at Blovice in the Plzeň district of Bohemia, on 28 December 1825, the elder son of Marc Opper or Oppert, a tradesman, and Anne Hartmann. The exact circumstances of his early life are uncertain; the account that he dictated for his posthumously published *Memoirs* (1903) was deliberately designed to hide his humble origins. Government records confirm that in 1847 he was living in France where, for twelve years, he taught German at various lycées. He did not become a naturalized French citizen until 1870. In 1859 he married a rich widow, Anne-Amélie Bethfort (1814–1893), daughter of a naval paymaster, distantly related through her mother to the royal house of Bourbon. To make himself appear more acceptable to his wife's family, Blowitz abandoned Judaism for Roman Catholicism and added his birthplace to his surname. His wife was tall and handsome; Blowitz was extremely short and corpulent. His large, bald head he complemented with extravagant thickets of side-whiskers and moustaches; his singular appearance was further exaggerated by an ostentatious taste in clothes. *Tout ensemble*, Blowitz inspired humour more readily than thoughts of romance, yet he enjoyed a considerable reputation as a *coureur*. He admitted, in his fractured English: 'All women fell to me for love' (Giles, 27), but he never wavered in his admiration for his 'madonna', Anne-Amélie. They made an incongruous-looking couple, but theirs was a remarkably happy marriage; their only child, Stephan Lauzanne, was adopted.

Blowitz's first essay into journalism was in the local *Gazette de Midi* in 1866. The permanent change from idle *rentier* to journalist was prompted by events in the winter of 1870–71. How exactly he became a friend of Louis Thiers remains a mystery, but it was the politician probably who recommended Blowitz as an assistant to *The Times*'s Paris

Henri Georges Stephan Adolphe Opper de Blowitz (1825–1903), by Henri Dochy

correspondent. Within four years, the diminutive, audacious opportunist had succeeded to *The Times*'s most prestigious foreign posting. Reservations about Blowitz's suitability had been totally disarmed by his interview of Alfonso XII of Spain, described by J. T. Delane, the editor, as a 'really masterly stroke' (Blowitz, 99). Blowitz gathered news assiduously, always with an eye to his readers' pleasure. This delighted J. C. MacDonald, manager of *The Times*, who particularly valued the little man's talent for blurring the distinction between authorized and unauthorized, real and fictitious, and the glittering style that converted the dullest official communiqué into the stuff of Ruritanian romance. Blowitz became part of the history he chronicled with inexhaustible fluency. As a contemporary *aperçu* acknowledged: 'Il n'y a décidément que deux hommes en Europe, Bismarck et Blowitz'.

In his *Memoirs* Blowitz stated that, in 1875, he had prevented war between Germany and France. This is an example of his imagination overtaking accuracy. He liked to place himself at the centre of important events, a foible so widely recognized that *Punch* dubbed him 'Blowitz-own-Trumpet'. The 1878 Berlin Congress was, however, an undoubted personal triumph. To London he sent a stream of stories about the personalities and the progress of events, and by an amazing coup succeeded in telegraphing the exact terms of the treaty to *The Times* to appear on the day it was signed in Berlin. For services rendered, Blowitz received from France advancement in the Légion d'honneur from chevalier to officier; from Germany, a decoration, third class. But the honour Blowitz valued most was an interview with Bismarck; thereafter he referred frequently to his supposed intimacy with the Iron Chancellor. Often reminiscing in print: 'Let me recall what Prince Bismarck said to me …', Blowitz was denigrated in the controlled German press as a troublemaker, and his reports dismissed as 'Munchausen stories', the 'crazy inventions of a scandal monger'. Blowitz did nothing to dissuade Bismarck that 'Herr Oppert aus Blowitz' was entirely responsible for how *The Times* viewed European affairs. Indeed, throughout the 1880s Blowitz effectively was a one-man foreign department. His regular European-wide surveys he based on information supplied by friends and contacts in every European capital. His privilege was to write when and what he pleased knowing that he would always have the support of his editor.

Blowitz was a generous host. His Paris apartment was invariably crowded with distinguished guests drawn from all walks of life. An informed, brilliant conversationalist, he was welcomed in every leading Paris salon. A polished *boulevardier*, he was the essential constituent of any significant social, literary, or theatrical gathering. No important private view, première, or reception was complete without the *ambassadeur du Times*. Blowitz insisted that the endless whirl of his social life was essential grist to his journalistic mill. To profession and employers alike, he always showed the highest degree of fidelity. He was not without faults as a journalist; he could be touchy, impudent, vulgar, and pushing. But he was never a moral coward, and any cause in which he believed, no matter how unpopular, he advocated fearlessly and consistently. He was a doughty Dreyfusard and a tireless, lifelong supporter of the house of Orléans. He was obliged to write his dispatches in French, but if his grasp of English was always uncertain, no one was a greater Anglophile.

From J. C. MacDonald's death in 1889, Blowitz's influence at *The Times* slowly declined, a process hastened by Sir Donald Mackenzie Wallace's appointment to lead a newly constituted foreign department. Wallace, sober of demeanour and conservative of taste, a diplomat rather than a journalist, intensely disliked Blowitz's sensationalism. In September 1895 he wrote to the Paris correspondent: 'Your great journalistic talent … unfortunately … does not easily accommodate itself to … the style of *The Times* … in which each worker strives to sink his own personality in the collective personality of the paper' (*History of The Times*, 3.139). Wallace might as well have expected a peacock to masquerade as a sparrow as to suppose that Blowitz might modify his style. Instead, copy from Blowitz was altered, reduced, even ignored, without reference to the author. His coups were dismissed variously as 'too credulous', 'indiscreet', or, '*jeux d'esprit* of questionable taste' (ibid., 3.136). Wallace's all-important ally in muzzling Blowitz was C. F. Moberly Bell. Both men were convinced that the Blowitz style of journalism was outdated. Nevertheless, the old man stubbornly clung to his post until increasing frailty finally undermined his resolve and, most unwillingly, he accepted retirement at the end of 1902. Blowitz was spared the final indignity of seeing William Lavino replace him as Paris correspondent, that post for which he still supposed himself uniquely best fitted. On 18 January 1903, he died from peritonitis, at 2 rue Greuze, Paris; he was buried at Boulogne-sur-Seine. No journalist had been more written about in his lifetime by fellow journalists. His coups inspired awe, but also spite and professional jealousy. At his death, the world's press united to compliment the little correspondent who had towered over his profession. *The Times* declared him 'unique'; *Punch* extolled him as 'a prince of correspondents' who was 'without peer'. 'The king of interviewers', pronounced the *Journal de Bruxelles*; and none disagreed with the *New York Evening Post*'s accolade that Blowitz had been 'the last of the great correspondents of the old school' (Giles, preface). Blowitz was all these things, and more. He was a legend in his own lifetime.

A. J. A. MORRIS

Sources F. Giles, *A prince of journalists: the life and times of de Blowitz* (1962) • H. G. S. de Blowitz, *My memoirs* (1903) • [S. Morison and others], *The history of The Times*, 3 (1947) • E. T. S. Dugdale, ed. and trans., *German diplomatic documents* (1928), 1.186–8, 193
Archives News Int. RO, papers | Newspaper Library, Colindale, London, *The Times* file
Likenesses W. H. Thomson, miniature, exh. RA 1900, unknown collection • Ape [Carlo Pellegrini], caricatures, NPG; repro. in *VF* (1885), (1889) • H. Dochy, engraving, NPG [*see illus.*] • H. Furniss, pen and ink drawing, NPG
Wealth at death £187 10s.: administration with will, 12 Jan 1904, *CGPLA Eng. & Wales*

Bloxam, Andrew (1801–1878), naturalist, was born at Rugby on 21 September 1801, the fourth son of the Revd Richard Rouse Bloxam, a master at Rugby School. Bloxam himself entered Rugby in 1809, leaving in 1819 for St John's College, Cambridge, where he matriculated on 5 March. In 1820 he moved to Worcester College, Oxford, where he later became a fellow.

After graduating in 1824, Bloxam accepted the position of naturalist on HMS *Blonde*, on which his eldest brother was chaplain. The ship transported the bodies of the king and queen of the Hawaiian Islands, who had died in England, back to their homeland, a voyage lasting eighteen months. During it a large collection of natural history specimens was made which was deposited in the British Museum on the *Blonde's* return in 1826. The same year Bloxam, with his captain, George Anson, Lord Byron, published an account of the voyage.

Soon after his return, Bloxam took holy orders. From 1839 to 1871 he served as priest in charge of Twycross, Leicestershire, and from 1871 to 1878 was rector of Harborough Magna, Warwickshire, where he died on 2 February 1878 at the age of seventy-six. He was survived by his wife, Ann, daughter of the Revd J. Roby of Congerstone. It is not known when they married, but they had a large family.

Bloxam has been described as an all-round naturalist, although he himself claimed to be no more than a 'holiday botanist'. His works are not numerous but he contributed to several regional natural histories of the midlands and he was a corresponding member of the Birmingham Natural History and Microscopical Society.

B. D. JACKSON, *rev.* GILES HUDSON

Sources M. J. Berkeley, *Midland Naturalist*, 1 (1878), 88–90 • *Journal of Botany, British and Foreign*, 16 (1878), 96 • Desmond, *Botanists*, rev. edn • Venn, *Alum. Cant.*
Archives Leics. RO, corresp. and papers • NHM, natural history notes made on the voyage of HMS *Blonde*, rough diary of voyage and letters | Leics. RO, Flora Leicesterensis • MHS Oxf., corresp. with William Buckland • RBG Kew, letters to Sir William Hooke
Likenesses T. Laurence, portrait; formerly National Gallery, 1885 • J. M. W. Turner, group portrait, watercolour (*The funeral of Sir Thomas Lawrence, January 1830*); formerly National Gallery, 1885
Wealth at death under £800: probate, 13 March 1878, *CGPLA Eng. & Wales*

Bloxam, Charles Loudon (1831–1887), chemist, was born on 23 March 1831 at Meriden, Warwickshire, the third son of William Bloxam, surgeon. The family subsequently moved to 28 Duke Street, London. He attended King's College School in 1842–3, and from 1845 trained in chemistry under A. W. Hofmann at the Royal College of Chemistry, London, becoming full assistant in 1849. In 1852 he became a full-time private tutor and chemical analyst at 28 Duke Street, London. With Frederick Abel he published *A Handbook of Chemistry* in 1854. In the same year he became demonstrator in chemistry in King's College, London. In 1856 he succeeded J. E. Bowman as professor of practical chemistry there, becoming full professor on the death of W. A. Miller in 1870. Simultaneously, he was lecturer in chemistry at the Royal Military Academy, Woolwich (1855–82), and the Royal Artillery College, Woolwich (1864–87). In 1882, he resigned from the Royal Military Academy following gross indiscipline of the cadets and poor teaching conditions, an incident which highlighted the unsatisfactory arrangements for science teaching in military establishments at this time.

Bloxam's earliest researches were on the determination and qualitative separation of tin, antimony, and arsenic, and such analytical investigations, including his electrolytic test for arsenic, constituted most of his research during 1852–87, published mainly in the *Journal of the Chemical Society* and *Chemical News*. His outstanding contribution was to the teaching of chemistry, to which end he published *Chemistry, Inorganic and Organic* (11 edns, 1867–1923) and *Laboratory Teaching* (6 edns, 1869–93). He also revised J. E. Bowman's *Practical Chemistry* to 1885 and his *Medical Chemistry* to 1862. These were outstanding and durable student texts.

In early life, Bloxam kept detailed diaries. These are still extant, and form an interesting historical source. He was an indefatigable lecturer to medical, applied science, analytical, evening, and occasional students of chemistry at King's College, and to military academy cadets. He also trained his brother, Thomas Bloxam (1836–1872), who assisted him in his post at King's College before becoming assistant to Dr George Wilson at the Industrial Museum of Scotland in 1855.

On 17 July 1856 Bloxam married Frederica Louisa (*d.* 1901), daughter of John Leopold Abel, a musician, and sister of Frederick Abel. They had four daughters and four sons, one of whom, Arthur George Bloxam (1866–1940), was sometime head of the chemical department at Goldsmiths' Institute, London. Bloxam, who was suffering from emphysema, died on 28 November 1887, at 16 Endsleigh Gardens, Euston Square, following bronchitis, and was buried in Charlton cemetery, London, on 1 December 1887.

Bloxam's nephew, **William Popplewell Bloxam** (1860–1913), chemist, was born on 9 January 1860 at 21 Mount Street, Grosvenor Square, London, the son of William Bloxam, surgeon, and his wife, Emma Caroline Kite. He was trained by his uncle at King's College. He became demonstrator in chemistry under Heinrich Debus (1824–1915) at the Royal Naval College, Greenwich, researching especially sulphur compounds. He was briefly professor of chemistry in Madras, and he subsequently conducted research into improving the efficiency of indigo extraction from natural sources. He continued these and other colour chemistry researches at the Clothworkers' Research Laboratory, Leeds University, under A. G. Perkin, from 1904.

On 6 August 1885 William Popplewell Bloxam married Jessie Christian, daughter of Edwin Low, a solicitor. He died, following a cerebral haemorrhage, in Guy's Hospital, London, on 26 December 1913. ROBIN J. SPRING

Sources D. I. Davies, D. C. Lyon, and R. J. Spring, 'C. L. Bloxam', *Ambix*, 33 (1986), 11–32 • R. J. Spring, 'The development of chemistry in London in the nineteenth century', PhD diss., U. Lond., 1979 • *JCS*, 53 (1888), 508–9 • R. J. Spring, 'The electrolytic test for the detection of arsenic alone and in the presence of other metals', *Talanta*, 29 (1982), 883–5 • King's Lond., Bloxam MSS • *JCS*, 26 (1873), 773–4 • A. G. Perkin, *JCS*, 105 (1914), 1195–1200 [obit. of William Popplewell Bloxam] • F. R. Miles, ed., *King's College School: a register of pupils in the school … 1831–1866* (1974) • m. cert. • d. cert. • b. cert. [William Popplewell Bloxam] • m. cert. [William Popplewell Bloxam] • d. cert. [William Popplewell Bloxam] • London borough of Greenwich burial records

Archives King's Lond., corresp., diaries, and working papers [photocopies] • priv. coll., apparatus formerly belonging to Charles Loudon Bloxam, F.C.S.

Likenesses photograph, King's Lond., department of chemistry

Wealth at death £9083 1s. 7d.: probate, 5 Jan 1888, *CGPLA Eng. & Wales*

Bloxam, John Rouse (1807–1891), antiquary, was born at Rugby on 25 April 1807, the sixth son of Richard Rouse Bloxam DD (*d.* 1840), under-master of Rugby School for thirty-eight years, and rector of Brinklow and vicar of Bulkington, both in Warwickshire, and his wife, Anne, sister of Sir Thomas Lawrence. Bloxam and his five brothers, who included Andrew *Bloxam and Matthew Holbeche *Bloxam, were all foundationers at Rugby School. In 1826 Bloxam proceeded to Worcester College, Oxford, where he held a Bible clerkship. From 1830 to 1835 he held a demyship at Magdalen College, Oxford, obtaining an honorary fourth class in classics in 1831 and graduating BA in 1832. He was ordained deacon by the bishop of Oxford in 1832 and priest in 1833, and took the further degrees of MA in 1835, BD in 1843, and DD in 1847.

In July 1832 Bloxam became chaplain and classical master in the private school at Wyke House, near Brentford, of which Dr Alexander Jamieson was principal, and from 1833 to 1836 he was second master at Bromsgrove School. In 1836 he returned to Magdalen, having been elected a probationer fellow, and resided there until 1862. Among the college offices he held were bursar, vice-president, and librarian (1851–62), though he was never a tutor. In 1837 he succeeded Isaac Williams as curate to J. H. Newman at Littlemore, where he had the opportunity to promote the cause closest to his heart, the revival of ceremonial in the Church of England. Peter Maurice (1803/4–1878), the evangelical chaplain of New College, attacked Bloxam's alterations in church decoration and ritual after a visit to Littlemore (P. Maurice, *Popery of Oxford*, 1837). One of the most zealous followers of the Tractarians, Bloxam caused a scandal in 1839 when it was reported that he had bowed to the host during the celebration of mass during a visit to Alton Towers, the seat of the Roman Catholic earl of Shrewsbury. He resigned the Littlemore curacy in the following year. A carriage accident in a Leicestershire lane introduced him to Ambrose Phillipps De Lisle. They corresponded in 1841 and 1842 on a possible reunion of the Anglican and Roman churches. In 1842 he privately printed an incomplete *Book of Fragments*, giving a series of extracts from authorities on ecclesiastical rites. Further publication was halted on the appearance of a similar volume, *Hierugia Anglicana*, under the auspices of the Cambridge Camden Society. Bloxam was an early member of the Oxford Society for Promoting the Study of Gothic Architecture, founded in 1839, and became a friend and patron of A. W. Pugin, securing for him the commission for a new gateway to Magdalen College, which was built in 1844. On Christmas eve 1845 he resisted Newman's entreaties to join the Roman communion, but they maintained a regular correspondence and close friendship until Newman's death.

At Magdalen, Bloxam was considered the 'incarnation of all that was ideal in the College, its mediaevalism, sentiment, piety' (W. Tuckwell, *Reminiscences of Oxford*, 2nd edn, 1907, 165). At the centre of his room, which was hung with religious icons, was a model of the tomb of the college founder, William Waynflete (*Oxford Magazine*, 25 May 1906, 389–90). He edited for the Caxton Society the *Memorial of Bishop Waynflete, by Dr Peter Heylyn* (1851) and later collected the series of documents *Magdalen College and James II* (Oxford Historical Society, 1886), showing the college's earlier successful resistance to the depredations of the monarch. He particularly cherished the college's choral tradition, and claimed to have been responsible for ensuring, from 1844, a more reverential celebration of the May day custom of singing a Latin hymn on Magdalen College tower (and was a prominent figure in Holman Hunt's depiction of the ceremony, first exhibited in 1891). Although doubt attaches both to his version of the origins of the custom, and how far its celebration altered after 1844, he did succeed in making the ceremony a self-conscious occasion. His subsequent antiquarian labours, inspired by the example of Dr Routh, the college president, were devoted to compiling a biographical register of members of the college; he rose daily at 5.30 in the morning for the purpose. Seven volumes appeared between 1853 and 1881. The venture was continued by W. D. Macray. Bloxam also compiled a bibliography of the works published by members of the college, partly, it was said, to refute Edward Gibbon's aspersions about the idleness of the Magdalen fellows.

In February 1862 Bloxam was appointed by his college to the vicarage of Upper Beeding, near Steyning in Sussex, vacating his fellowship in the following year. He was acknowledged in later life as 'the Grandfather of all ritualists' (Frederic Rogers, Lord Blachford, to Bloxam, 1 Nov 1884, Magd. Oxf., MS 304). By then revivals pioneered by Bloxam, such as the wearing of a black stole by priests and the adornment of altars with elaborately decorated cloths, had become widely adopted within the Church of England. Conspicuous in his Oxford days as 'a striking figure, spare and erect, with reverent dignity' (*DNB*), he enjoyed excellent health almost to the end of his life. Bloxam, who never married, died at The Priory, Upper Beeding, on 21 January 1891 and was buried in Beeding churchyard. M. C. CURTHOYS

Sources J. R. Bloxam, *A register of the presidents, fellows … of Saint Mary Magdalen College*, 8 vols. (1853–85), vol. 7 • W. D. Macray, *A register of the members of St Mary Magdalen College, Oxford*, 6 (1909) • R. D. Middleton, *Magdalen studies* (1936), chap. 2 • R. D. Middleton, *Newman and Bloxam* (1947) • R. Judge, 'May morning and Magdalen College Oxford', *Folklore*, 97 (1986), 15–40 • W. A. Pantin, 'The Oxford Architectural and Historical Society, 1839–1939', *Oxoniensia*, 4 (1939), 174–94 • Magd. Oxf. • *DNB*

Archives Bodl. Oxf., letters and papers mainly relating to antiquarian matters • Magd. Oxf., corresp. and papers | Birmingham Oratory, letters to J. H. Newman • BL, letters to Philip Bliss, Add. MSS 34577–34581, *passim* • Bodl. Oxf., corresp. with Sir Thomas Phillips • Bodl. Oxf., letters to Gibbes Rigaud • Pusey Oxf., corresp. with J. H. Newman • U. St Andr. L., letters to Wilfrid Ward

Likenesses photograph, *c*.1850, Magd. Oxf. • W. H. Hunt, group portrait, oils, 1891 (*May morning on Magdalen Tower*), Birmingham Museums and Art Gallery • S. Laurence, crayon drawing, Rugby School • J. M. W. Turner, group portrait, watercolour (*The funeral of Sir Thomas Lawrence, January 1830*), BM

Wealth at death £1949 8*s*. 9*d*.: resworn probate, Sept 1891, *CGPLA Eng. & Wales*

Bloxam, Matthew Holbeche (1805–1888), architectural historian, was born at midnight on 12 May 1805 in a boarding-house at the corner of Lawrence Sheriff Street and Sheep Street, Rugby, opposite Rugby School, where his father was an assistant master. Matt, as he was known, was the eighth of the ten children of Richard Rouse Bloxam (1765–1840), later rector of Brinklow and vicar of Bulkington, Warwickshire, and his wife, Anne Lawrence (1767–1835), sister of the painter Sir Thomas Lawrence. All six Bloxam boys became foundationers at Rugby School, Matt joining in the second term of 1813 at the age of eight, and leaving in 1821 after an undistinguished academic career to become articled to George Harris, a Rugby solicitor. In 1827 he travelled to London to be admitted to practice in the courts of law and equity. During his subsequent long career as a solicitor in Rugby, Bloxam held several local offices: he was clerk of the Rugby petty sessions from 1831 to 1871, sometimes officiated as deputy registrar of the county court, was a member of the local board from 1855 to 1863, and audited the Rugby Union accounts from 1836 until the appointment of district auditors.

However, as Bloxam himself admitted, although the legal profession assured his financial stability, his passions lay elsewhere. From an early age he had been fascinated by archaeology, a pursuit probably fostered by his

Matthew Holbeche Bloxam (1805–1888), by E. H. Speight, *c*.1880

father, and as a clerk he visited countless churches and found the time to read John Carter's antiquarian articles in the *Gentleman's Magazine*. A natural talent for draughtsmanship (which could be attributed to his maternal side) allowed him to record the visual details of buildings, which, together with his methodical character, discriminative observation, and prodigious memory for detail, combined to produce an ideal antiquary. His first book, *The Principles of Gothic Architecture*, was published in 1829, a slim volume of seventy-nine pages, presented in question and answer form. Under the title *The Principles of Gothic Ecclesiastical Architecture* the book was added to and improved in subsequent editions and the catechetical arrangement was replaced by narrative. Sir George Gilbert Scott persuaded Bloxam to publish the eleventh, final, and definitive version in 1882, consisting of three volumes concerning the development of Gothic architecture, the internal arrangement of churches prior to and following the Reformation, and a *Companion* volume addressing the subject of church vestments. A copy of this edition was presented to Cardinal Newman by Bloxam's younger brother, the Revd John Rouse *Bloxam (1807–1891). The popularity of the book, of which 17,000 copies had been sold before the 1882 publication, was due to its pocket size, cheapness, clear, concise, and comprehensive text, and good woodcut illustrations, the latter being the work of Thomas Orlando Sheldon Jewitt (1799–1869), based on his own and Bloxam's drawings.

In 1834 *A glimpse at the monumental architecture and sculpture of Great Britain, from the earliest period to the eighteenth century* was published, and read by Thomas Rickman (1776–1841), who felt compelled to write to Bloxam personally requesting the removal of 'the very puzzling and absurd term *Florid* in speaking of the latest gothic work' (Payne Smith, xxvii). Although Bloxam perhaps complicated matters by introducing transitional categories of architectural style, his works are eminently readable, factual, informative, well structured, and certainly less opinionated than those of many of his contemporaries. Bloxam also wrote about 200 articles, based on his knowledge of over 1000 churches and his particular interest in effigies and costume. These appeared in *Archaeologia Cambrensis*, the *Archaeological Journal*, the *British Critic*, the *Gentleman's Magazine*, the *Rugby Almanack*, and numerous architectural and archaeological society transactions and periodicals.

A member of the Oxford Architectural Society, and honorary member of the Ecclesiological Society, Bloxam was elected fellow of the Society of Antiquaries in 1863, and belonged to many regional associations. His advice on ecclesiastical architectural matters was frequently sought and freely given.

Identifying closely with Rugby, Bloxam became the historian of both town and school. His writings on the latter were collated by W. H. Payne Smith and published posthumously as *Rugby: the School and the Neighbourhood* (1889). Bloxam regularly attended the Sunday afternoon chapel services, gave athletics prizes for the younger boys, presented gifts annually on the occasion of his birthday, read papers to the Natural History Society, contributed articles to the school magazines *Meteor* and *Leaflet*, and encouraged any boys who evinced interest in archaeology. He bequeathed his library of rare books and manuscripts and his collection of antiquities to the school.

Described in an obituary as 'the most amiable and, at the same time, the most modest of men' (*Proceedings*, 387), photographs portray Bloxam as a studious-looking individual with small round-rimmed glasses perched on the bridge of his nose, the long face accentuated by a high, domed forehead and Piccadilly weepers. In 1843 Bloxam built himself a three-storey house with basement in St Matthew's Place, within sight of Rugby School, and lived there with his unmarried sister Mary Isabella until his death. The only idiosyncrasy in this practical, spacious, yet unpretentious house was a fourth-storey turret from which Bloxam probably studied the stars through his Dolland telescope.

Scrupulous in his search for truth, Bloxam had no qualms in demystifying popular legends. He asserted that Godiva's nude canter through Coventry was pure invention, and told a dismayed audience at Lutterworth that their objects of veneration associated with John Wyclif were fakes. It is therefore surprising that, without bothering to corroborate his facts, he perpetuated the myth that the game of rugby originated with William Webb Ellis handling the ball during a Rugby School match in 1823. Correspondence in *The Standard* in 1876 concerning the interest in rugby football initially prompted Bloxam to declare that the game was entirely different when he left the school in 1821. However, probably influenced by fellow Rugbeians and pride in his alma mater, he retracted the statement, having 'ascertained' that a foundationer had run with the ball, and by 1880 was successfully embellishing his story with authentic detail.

Bloxam never married. He enjoyed a healthy constitution until weakened by bronchitis late in 1887. On 18 January and 5 March 1888 he suffered paralytic seizures and died on 24 April in his home town. Rugby School and the parish church lowered their flags to half-mast, tradesmen closed their shops, and blinds were drawn in most homes on Friday 27 April 1888 when Bloxam was buried, at his own request, near a yew tree in the churchyard of St Michael and All Angels, Brownsover, near Rugby.

Libby Horner

Sources H. T. Kirby, Warks. CRO, CR1001 and CR1168 · M. H. Bloxam, *Rugby: the school and the neighbourhood*, ed. W. H. Payne Smith (1889) · P. B. Chatwin, *Incidents in the life of Matthew Holbeche Bloxam*, Dugdale Society, 13 (1959) · *Rugby Advertiser* (28 April 1888) · *Proceedings of the Society of Antiquaries of London*, 2nd ser., 12 (1887–9), 387 · *Meteor* (12 May 1888) · E. L. Barnwell, 'Biographical notice: Matthew Holbeche Bloxam', *Archaeologia Cambrensis*, 4th ser., 14 (1883), 84–8 · 'Manuals of Gothic architecture', *Archaeological Journal*, 3 (1846), 379–92 · 'Notices of archaeological publications', *Archaeological Journal*, 39 (1882), 473–7 · J. Summerson, ed., *Concerning architecture: essays on architectural writers and writing presented to Nikolaus Pevsner* (1968) · M. Aldrich, 'Gothic architecture illustrated: the drawings of Thomas Rickman in New York', *Antiquaries Journal*, 65 (1985), 427–33 · W. J. Baker, 'William Webb Ellis and the origins of rugby football: the life and death of a Victorian myth', *Albion*, 13 (1981), 117–30 · H. T. Kirby, 'Some notes on Bloxam's principles', *ArchR*, 103 (1948) · parish register, St Mary de Castro, Leics. RO, 8D59/85 · d. cert. · census returns for Rugby, 1841, 1851, 1861, 1871, 1881

Archives Birm. CL, Cat. no. 36 3386; Cat. no. 36 3388 · Rugby School, Warwickshire, antiquarian corresp. · Warks. CRO, corresp. and papers, CR 1001; CR 1168 · Warks. CRO, notes on antiquarian subjects | Leics. RO, 8D59/85 (St Mary de Castro)

Likenesses S. Howell, oils, 1830; formerly in possession of George Mitchell · photograph, *c*.1830, Warks. CRO · W. A. Delamotte, pencil drawing, 1838, Rugby Public Library · photograph, *c*.1870, Rugby Public Library · S. Howell, oils, 1873, Rugby School · C. Ridgway, engraving, 1880 (after E. H. Speight), Warks. CRO · E. H. Speight, photograph, *c*.1880, Rugby Public Library [*see illus.*] · J. M. W. Turner, group portrait, watercolour (*The funeral of Sir Thomas Lawrence, January 1830*), BM · statue, Rugby Museum

Wealth at death £8110 12*s*. 11*d*.: probate, 6 June 1888, *CGPLA Eng. & Wales*

Bloxam, William Popplewell (1860–1913). *See under* Bloxam, Charles Loudon (1831–1887).

Bloxham, John (*d*. 1334/5), Carmelite reformer, joined that order in Chester, and later studied at Oxford University. Evidently his talents impressed his superiors, for while only a BTh he was granted a royal safe conduct on 4 April 1325 to travel to Ireland as vicar of the prior-general, and to conduct a visitation of the Irish Carmelite houses there. He is presumed to have presided at the Irish provincial chapter held at Ardee later that year, and to have introduced reforms into the province following the new constitutions that had been issued by the general chapter the previous year. As a result of his activities a house of studies was established at Dublin for the Irish Carmelite students. Bloxham continued to study and lecture at Oxford, and he incepted as DTh some time before 1333. In that year he was elected provincial of the English province, at a provincial chapter held in Lincoln. In the following year, 1334, he was nominated for a second time as vicar-general, this time to conduct a visitation of the Scottish Carmelites. He presided over the English provincial chapter at Gloucester the same year, but then, after only two and a half years in office, he died in late 1334 or 1335 and was buried in the Carmelite house at Oxford. He wrote a number of works of which John Bale preserves the titles of three in an early notebook: a commentary on the *Sentences* of Peter Lombard, an index to Henry Cossey's book on the Apocalypse, and a collection of 186 letters. Later, Bale added statutes for Ireland, and the usual collections of questions and sermons. A short extract from one of his questions on the *Sentences* is preserved in Bodl. Oxf., MS Bodley 73, fol. 45v.

RICHARD COPSEY

Sources J. Bale, Bodl. Oxf., MS Bodley 73 (SC 27635), fols. 39v, 45, 80, 119, 133v, 197 • J. Bale, Bodl. Oxf., MS Selden supra 41, fols. 160v, 166v • *CPR, 1324–7*, 113 • *CEPR letters*, 2.113 • J. Bale, BL, Harley MS 3838, fols. 43v, 66–66v, 170v • P. O'Dwyer, *Irish Carmelites* (1988), 11, 20 • Bale, *Cat.*, 1.398–9 • Emden, *Oxf.* • J. Bale, *Illustrium Maioris Britannie scriptorum … summarium* (1548), fol. 249v • *Commentarii de scriptoribus Britannicis, auctore Joanne Lelando*, ed. A. Hall, 2 (1709), 403
Archives Bodl. Oxf., MS Bodley 73, fol. 45v

Bloxham, John [Geffrei] (*c.*1340–1387), theologian and college head, evidently came from Bloxham, Oxfordshire. He was elected fellow of Merton in 1361, and spent his whole life thereafter at the college, as bursar in 1365–7, and as warden from 16 October 1375 until his death. He studied theology as a fellow, and having completed all the requirements for the doctorate by October 1375 qualified as an inceptor in theology; but, presumably omitting to perform his necessary lectures as a regent master, he did not graduate as a doctor. He benefited from the ecclesiastical patronage of his college, becoming vicar of Embleton, Northumberland (1369–72) and rector of the free chapel of Kibworth Harcourt, Leicestershire (1385–7). He was also made archdeacon of Winchester by Bishop William Wykeham (1382–7), though no other connection between Wykeham and Bloxham can now be traced. He served in various university capacities, acting as one of the arbitrators appointed to settle both the contentions in Queen's College in 1379, and the disputed election to the provostship of Oriel College in 1386. He seems not to have shared the sympathy for John Wyclif (*d.* 1384) and his radical colleagues felt by several fellows of Merton, including John Aston, Robert Rygge (lately fellow and afterwards chancellor), and William James; indeed he sat with the council of theologians and canon lawyers convoked by Archbishop William Courtenay (*d.* 1396) at Blackfriars, London, in May 1382, in which the teaching of Wyclif was condemned, and before which at least two fellows or former fellows of Merton, Aston and Rygge, were arraigned. As warden Bloxham was active in forwarding college building: although the completion of Mob Quad by the building of the library was initiated in 1371, before he was elected, he travelled with William Humberville, the architect, who had worked at Windsor Castle, to inspect other buildings, notably the library of the Blackfriars in London. The work was completed by 1379. As executor of William Rede, bishop of Chichester (*d.* 1385), he effected the bishop's great bequest of about a hundred books to Merton; he left two theological books of his own, a repertory of theological questions, and the commentary of the Franciscan William of Nottingham (*d.* 1254) on the gospels. The works ascribed to his authorship by Pits and Tanner are based on confusion with an earlier John Bloxham, a Carmelite who died in 1335. Bloxham died shortly before July 1387. There is a memorial brass in Merton College chapel.

JEREMY CATTO

Sources Merton Oxf., Records, 492, 495, 614–15, 617, 2630, 2942, 2953, 2986, 3011, 3054, 3696–9, 3700–3, 3706, 3791b, 4174, 4175b, *Catalogus vetus* • William of Nottingham, gospel commentary, Merton Oxf., MS 156 • William of Nottingham, theological *quaestiones*, Merton Oxf., MS 284 • *CClR, 1381–5*, 452; *1385–9*, 660 • *CPR, 1377–81*, 420; *1385–8*, 160 • [T. Netter], *Fasciculi zizaniorum magistri Johannis Wyclif cum tritico*, ed. W. W. Shirley, Rolls Series, 5 (1858), 287 • J. Pits, *Relationum historicarum de rebus Anglicis*, ed. [W. Bishop] (Paris, 1619), 559–60 • Tanner, *Bibl. Brit.-Hib.* • H. W. Garrod, 'Merton College', *VCH Oxfordshire*, 3.95–106, esp. 101–2 • Emden, *Oxf.*
Archives Merton Oxf., records
Likenesses memorial brass, Merton Oxf.

Blueskin. *See* Blake, Joseph (*c.*1700–1724).

Blumenfeld, Ralph David (1864–1948), newspaper editor, was born at Watertown, Wisconsin, USA, on 7 April 1864. He was the fourth son of the seven children of David Blumenfeld and his wife, Nancy, *née* Levensen. A former professor of literature and history at Nuremberg, David Blumenfeld had migrated to America in 1848. There he founded and edited *Der Weltbürger*, one of the first German-language newspapers in the mid-west.

R. D. Blumenfeld wanted to become an editor, like his father. He was rejected several times by the *New York Herald* before, in 1884, joining the *Chicago Herald*. He made his first visit to London in 1887, reporting Victoria's jubilee for United Press. After his return to New York his dramatic account of a fire, published in Albert Pulitzer's *Morning Journal*, so impressed Pulitzer's rival newspaper tycoon, James Gordon Bennett jun., that he immediately offered Blumenfeld a job with his *New York Herald*.

The association of the tyro correspondent and the enigmatic, capricious newspaper proprietor powerfully influenced Blumenfeld's career. Rapidly and deservedly he earned distinction as a special correspondent. He wrote with verve and a commendable brevity and simplicity. 'No one ever had a keener nose for news' (Dark, 15). Bennett required Blumenfeld to undertake an unusual variety of demanding managerial, supervisory, and editorial tasks. Eventually Blumenfeld bridled at Bennett's whimsical arbitrariness in switching him from one post to another.

Ralph David Blumenfeld (1864–1948), by Howard Coster, 1929

There were sharp differences about news values and Blumenfeld refused to return to New York from London. He resigned, his rebellion the braver if not the wiser since in 1892 he had married his second cousin Teresa (Daisie; *d.* 1957), daughter of Louis Blumfeld. Their long and happy marriage produced two daughters and two sons, the younger of whom, having changed his name by deed poll, was the railway manager Sir John *Elliot (1898–1988).

For the next six years Blumenfeld made and sold linotype machines. Though his business was a success it never brought the satisfaction he had derived from journalism. It was during this period that he was offered both *The Observer* and the *Sunday Times*, 'lock, stock and barrel for £5,000'. He was not tempted. 'The two high-brow heavies … [were] … always in deep financial distress. There was … not much lock, very little stock, and you could not see the barrel' (Blumenfeld, *Press*, 159–60).

When in the mood Blumenfeld could be expansive and exuberantly loquacious. It was after experiencing a Blumenfeld verbal torrent that Harmsworth told a colleague, 'If he performs at journalism as well as he talks about it, we must have him' (Fyfe, 94). In September 1900 Harmsworth told Blumenfeld to 'throw over [his] stupid machines and come back to journalism' (Clarke, 83). Offered the news editorship of the *Daily Mail*, Blumenfeld accepted with alacrity. Within a month he was Harmsworth's chosen intermediary in an unsuccessful attempt to buy *The Times*.

The *Daily Express* had been founded in 1900 by C. Arthur Pearson, as the *Daily Mail*'s direct competitor for the halfpenny popular daily market. In 1902 Pearson persuaded Blumenfeld to cross Fleet Street and join the *Express*, where he was soon effectively the editor. A keen proponent of protectionism, Blumenfeld introduced Pearson to Joseph Chamberlain and thereby recruited the *Daily Express* to the tariff reform cause. It was Blumenfeld who coined the ubiquitous campaign slogan, 'Tariff Reform means work for all'.

Not until 1912 did Pearson finally withdraw altogether from involvement with the *Express*. Blumenfeld had become a director of the *Express* company in 1908, pledging his own money. He found himself burdened by out-of-date machinery and debts to his newsprint supplier that he could not meet. He was reluctant to accept help from the Conservative central office, but on the recommendation of his friend Andrew Bonar Law accepted a personal loan of £25,000 from Max Aitken. The circulation of the *Daily Express* remained stagnant at less than 200,000 and finances remained a problem. Aitken's shares in the *Express* he held as a commissioned trustee for the Conservative Party. Gradually Aitken, now ennobled as Lord Beaverbrook, established personal control over the newspaper that was complete by 1917.

Blumenfeld was considered irreplaceable at the *Express*, and as editor appreciated the degree of independence his proprietor allowed him. The two men shared many political ideas. Where they differed Blumenfeld was not afraid to express himself forcibly. But increasingly editorial comment reflected Beaverbrook's political priorities and predilections. It suited Beaverbrook's purpose, when sniping at the Conservative Party, to hide behind his editor. And Blumenfeld, after consulting with Beaverbrook, happily fielded the brickbats from central office. 'I would not remain Editor of this paper for one hour if I had to become the servant of any political organisation' (Blumenfeld to Sir George Younger, 28 Feb 1919, in Koss, 2.356). While Beaverbrook's enemies attributed anything in the *Daily Express* they disliked to proprietorial interference, Blumenfeld's friends bemoaned 'the many things for which he has been criticised but was not responsible' (Dark, 16). Taffy Gwynne was not the only former editorial ally of R. D. B. to observe 'The *Express* has got more masters than one just now' (Koss, 265). Blumenfeld remained editor of the *Daily Express* until 1929, and was titular chairman of the company until his death. But from Beaverbrook's arrival it was always only a question of time before Blumenfeld was elbowed aside and kicked upstairs.

Blumenfeld gave shape and form to the *Daily Express*. By adopting the American pattern of using the front page for news instead of advertisements, and by using banner headlines and other typographical initiatives, Blumenfeld could claim to be an architect of modern, popular journalism. But by 1914 he presented the news in such a way as to make the whizz-kid of the 1880s seem increasingly *passé*. He retained the respect of Fleet Street but in the post-war world he seemed a little 'staid and old fashioned in his writings, perhaps also too exclusively political' (Taylor, 173).

The master of his craft, Blumenfeld as an editor was impatient of incompetence but quick to help, and generous in his appreciation. He was an inveterate, persistent prankster who took a small boy's delight in making jokes at inappropriate moments. This facetiousness explained his lifelong over-fondness for punning headlines. His waggish sense of humour belied the subtlety of his thinking, just as the languid manner he affected disguised an uncommon energy. A great clubman, he was the first journalist to be elected a member of the Carlton. There he first met Stanley Baldwin, with whom he enjoyed a very close friendship for many years, untroubled by Baldwin's fierce quarrel and put-down of Beaverbrook and other overmighty press magnates. Blumenfeld became a naturalized British subject in 1907. He declined the knighthood he was offered by the Conservative Party for political services. With the passing of the years he became ever more English, *plus royaliste que le roi*.

Blumenfeld retired from Fleet Street in 1932, having been editor-in-chief of the *Daily Express* from 1924. He was president of the Institute of Journalists (1928), master of the Company of Newspaper Makers (1931–3), and deputy master of the Worshipful Company of Stationers and Newspaper Makers (1931–5). He was also chairman of Essex Rural Community Council (1934–7). He wrote two short books about journalism—*What is a Journalist* (1930) and *The Press in my Time* (1933)—and several autobiographical sketches, of which the most complete is *Home Town* (1944).

Illness in 1936 severely physically incapacitated Blumenfeld, who died at his home, Muscombs, Great Easton, Dunmow, Essex, on 17 July 1948.

A. J. A. MORRIS

Sources *DNB* • private information (2004) [librarian/archivist, *Daily Express*] • R. D. Blumenfeld, *The Pick Axe Club* (1885) • R. D. Blumenfeld, *Exiled in England* (1896) • R. D. Blumenfeld, *R.D.B.'s diary, 1887–1914* (1930) • R. D. Blumenfeld, *All in a lifetime* (1931) • R. D. Blumenfeld, *R.D.B.'s procession* (1935) • R. D. Blumenfeld, *Home town* (1944) • R. D. Blumenfeld, *The press in my time* (1933) • A. J. P. Taylor, *Beaverbrook* (1972) • K. Middlemas and J. Barnes, *Baldwin: a biography* (1969) • S. Dark, *Mainly about people* (1925) • T. Clarke, *Northcliffe in history* (1950) • H. Fyfe, *Sixty years of Fleet Street* (1949) • S. E. Koss, *The rise and fall of the political press in Britain*, 2 (1984) • *CGPLA Eng. & Wales* (1948) • *WW* (1930)

Archives HLRO, corresp. and MSS • Watertown Historical Society, Watertown, Wisconsin, letters | BLPES, corresp. with E. D. Morel • HLRO, corresp. with Lord Beaverbrook • NA Scot., corresp. with Lord Elibank

Likenesses N. Lewis, oils, 1927, Stationers' and Newspaper Makers' Company, London • H. Coster, photographs, 1929, NPG [*see illus.*] • P. Larkin, oils, Daily Express, London • F. K. Sage, oils, Stationers' and Newspaper Makers' Company, London • photograph, repro. in Blumenfeld, *R.D.B.'s diary*, frontispiece

Wealth at death £41,947 6*s*. 4*d*.: probate, 11 Dec 1948, *CGPLA Eng. & Wales*

Blumenthal, Jacques [Jacob] (**1829–1908**), composer and pianist, was born at Hamburg on 4 October 1829, the son of Abraham Lucas Blumenthal. Destined from youth for the musical profession, he studied under F. W. Grund in Hamburg and with C. M. von Bocklet and Simon Sechter in Vienna. He entered the Paris conservatory in 1846, studying the piano as a pupil of Henri Herz and Jacques Halévy. In 1848 he settled in London, becoming pianist to Queen Victoria and a fashionable teacher, and was naturalized as a British subject. He married Léonie Souvoroff Gore in 1868; they had no children. Blumenthal published numerous short piano pieces and a very large number of songs, some of which, such as 'The Message' and 'The Requital' (1864) and 'We Two' (1879), achieved a lasting popularity. His more ambitious attempts at composition were less successful. A piano trio and a *Morceau de concert* for piano, both early works, were published, but perhaps his albums of songs are most representative of his *œuvre*.

Blumenthal died on 17 May 1908 at his home at Queen's House, Cheyne Walk, Chelsea, leaving an estate, which included a home in Switzerland, valued at more than £60,000. In accordance with his wishes, his widow assigned the valuable copyrights of his songs to the Royal Society of Musicians. His portrait, painted in 1878 by G. F. Watts RA, was presented by his widow to the Royal College of Music. FREDERICK CORDER, *rev*. DAVID J. GOLBY

Sources A. Maczewsky, 'Blumenthal, Jacques (Jacob)', Grove, *Dict. mus.* (1954) • J. D. Brown, *Biographical dictionary of musicians: with a bibliography of English writings on music* (1886), 101 • *Musical World* (June 1908) • *MT*, 49 (1908), 406

Likenesses J. M. Cameron, photograph, *c*.1867, U. Texas, Gernsheim collection • G. F. Watts, oils, 1878, Royal College of Music

Wealth at death £62,387 8*s*. 6*d*.: probate, 17 June 1908, *CGPLA Eng. & Wales*

Blumlein, Alan Dower (**1903–1942**), electronics engineer, was born on 29 June 1903 at 31 Netherhall Gardens, Hampstead, London, the only son and the second of two children of Semmy Joseph Blumlein (1863–1914), a German mining businessman and naturalized British subject, and his wife, Jessie Edward Dower, daughter of the Revd William Dower, a Scottish missionary, and his wife.

Blumlein, possibly the greatest British electronics engineer of the twentieth century, was a remarkably versatile, prolific, and creative engineer. His 128 patents, which were produced in a working lifetime of just eighteen years, embrace the fields of telephony, electrical measurements, sound recording and sound reproduction (both monophonic and stereophonic), high-definition television, radar, and electronics generally.

Blumlein was educated at various schools, including Highgate School, Middlesex (1918–21), and at the City and Guilds College, London (1921–3). He graduated with a first-class honours degree in electrical engineering in 1923, and was then appointed an assistant demonstrator (1923–4). With Professor Mallett, Blumlein devised a new method of high-frequency resistance measurement. Their joint paper was awarded a premium by the Institution of Electrical Engineers in 1925.

Blumlein joined the International Western Electric Company in September 1924. His endeavours, in the field of telephony, on loading coils, and the reduction of cross-talk and electrical interference, were appreciated by the company and led to Blumlein's being given a bonus of a

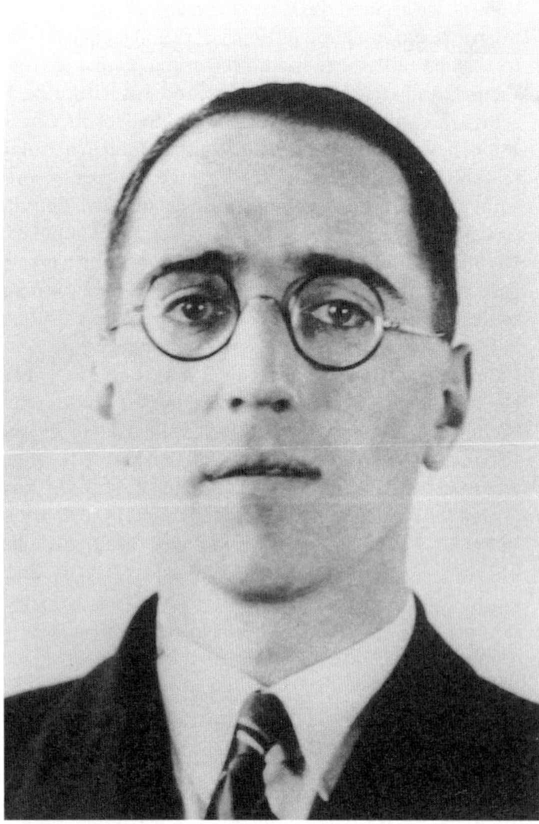

Alan Dower Blumlein (1903–1942), by unknown photographer

year's salary. Later, during an investigation of capacity unbalance, he invented the widely used transformer ratio arm bridge. In 1929 he was appointed by the Columbia Graphophone Company to engage in work on monophonic sound recording and reproduction, primarily to circumvent the Western Electric patents on electrical recording. He was eminently successful in his task and engineered a superior system.

About 1930–31 Blumlein became interested in stereophonic recording and reproduction. His extensive investigations resulted in one of the classic patents of the electrical recording literature. Such was the profusion of his ideas that the patent contains no fewer than seventy claims. However, his work was twenty-five years in advance of the recording art, and its significance was recognized only in 1958, when a citation was awarded posthumously to him by the Audio Engineering Society of the USA.

Following the formation in 1931 of EMI, Blumlein made sterling contributions to the realization of the world's first, public, all-electronic, high-definition television service. His patents on camera tubes, camera mosaics, wide-band amplifiers of all types, modulators, pulse circuits, power supplies, transmission lines, antennas, test equipment, and electronic circuits generally, constitute a set which illustrates the manifold ideas and the intellectual power of Blumlein's genius. With E. C. Cork he designed the wide-band cable which was utilized during the televising of the 1937 coronation. In 1938 he invented slot antennas, and, with H. Kallman and W. S. Percival, the transversal filter.

The threat of war caused Blumlein and E. L. C. White to design and demonstrate in 1939 a 60 MHz radar. This was a private venture of EMI and was conceived when government radar work was a closely guarded secret. When the Second World War began Blumlein applied his binaural concepts to the problem of the sound location of enemy aircraft, and his transformer ratio arm principles to the design of a low-level altimeter for the RAF.

Of great importance was Blumlein's work, with White, on air interception (AI) radar. Their solution to the minimum range problem and their development of a new modulator–transmitter (which became part of the AI Mark IV radar) contributed substantially to the defeat, from the beginning of 1941, of the German night bomber offensive over England. An improved version, AI Mark VI, was engineered by Blumlein and White for single-seater fighters.

Blumlein's work on the navigation radar H_2S and its adaptation, known as air surface vessel (ASV) radar, for locating enemy U-boats, was invaluable. These radars had a dramatic effect on the battle of the Atlantic and on the allies' long-range strategic bombing of Germany. His delay-line circuits, automatic strobe-following concepts, and diverse electronic circuits found application in other types of radar, including GL Mark III—a gun-laying radar which played a significant role in the anti-aircraft gunnery defence of the United Kingdom.

On 22 April 1933 Blumlein married Doreen Lane (1908–1989), daughter of W. H. Lane, auctioneer and estate agent of Penzance, and his wife, and settled in Ealing, London. Their sons, Simon and David, were born in 1936 and 1939 respectively.

Blumlein was killed, aged thirty-eight, on 7 June 1942, while flight testing, over the Wye valley, a version of the H_2S radar. He was cremated on 13 June at Golders Green crematorium. Of Blumlein's life's work, Isaac Shoenberg, director of research at EMI, said: 'There was not a single subject to which he turned his mind that he did not enrich extensively' (J. D. McGee, 'Contributions to television', *British Kinematography, Sound and Television Journal*, July 1968). R. W. Burns

Sources R. W. Burns, 'A. D. Blumlein', *Engineering, Science and Education Journal*, 1 (1992), 19–33 · R. W. Burns, *The life and times of A. D. Blumlein* (1999) · A. C. Lynch, 'Blumlein's transformer bridge network', *Engineering, Science and Education Journal*, 2 (1993), 117–20 · J. A. Lodge, 'Blumlein and audio engineering', *Engineering, Science and Education Journal*, 2 (1993), 121–4 · E. L. C. White, 'Blumlein and television', *Engineering, Science and Education Journal*, 2 (1993), 125–8 · K. R. Thrower, 'Blumlein's contribution to electronics', *Engineering, Science and Education Journal*, 2 (1993), 129–32 · R. M. Trim, 'Blumlein and radar', *Engineering, Science and Education Journal*, 2 (1993), 133–6 · R. W. Burns, 'Introduction', *Engineering, Science and Education Journal*, 2 (1993), 115–16 · personal collection of R. W. Burns [patents, letters, tape recordings, learned society papers, internal reports, recollections, and sundry gleanings] · d. cert.

Archives Central Research Laboratories, Hayes, Middlesex, EMI Music Archives, papers · priv. coll., internal reports, letters, patents, and memoranda | FILM EMI Archives, a very short film of Blumlein conducting experiments on stereophony | SOUND BL NSA, taped recollections of Blumlein made by his wife, his son Simon, and his closest friend, J. B. Kaye

Likenesses photograph, priv. coll. [*see illus.*] · photographs, priv. coll.

Wealth at death £2893 2*s.* 1*d.*: probate, 28 July 1942, *CGPLA Eng. & Wales*

Blund, John (*c.*1175–1248), ecclesiastic, is first recorded as one of a group of scholars lecturing on the liberal arts in the schools of Oxford at the end of the twelfth century. The only source for his early career is a Latin verse panegyric written by Henry d'Avranches in 1232 in support of Blund's election to the see of Canterbury. From this it is known that he studied arts, probably at Paris, and returned to Oxford to lecture on the arts in the last years of the twelfth century. Possibly this phase of his career was terminated by the suspension of the Oxford schools in 1209 after the summary hanging of two clerks by the city authorities. He returned to Paris to study theology and after twelve years he incepted and taught as a doctor of theology. He again suffered displacement by the 'great dispersal' of the University of Paris in 1229, a protest at the violent repression by the provost of Paris of student disorder. Matthew Paris names Blund as one of five famous English masters who returned home at this time, perhaps in response to an open invitation made by Henry III to the aggrieved scholars of Paris. Four of them, including Blund, were promptly rewarded with royal notice and patronage—though with John Blund it is necessary, but not always easy, to distinguish him from a contemporary of the same name, a royal clerk and canon of Lichfield, who died in 1239.

Master John Blund had acquired a prebend in Chichester Cathedral at some time before 1232, and besides this he obtained the parish livings of Horsley in Derbyshire and Barton in Cambridgeshire, which he held in plurality. He stood high in the favour of the king and the king's mentor, Peter des Roches, the bishop of Winchester. Consequently, on 27 August 1232 he was elected archbishop, by the monks of Canterbury, to succeed Richard Grant, who had died in Italy in the preceding year. The royal assent was promptly signified on 30 August, and on 10 September Blund embarked for Rome with a party from the Canterbury chapter. At the curia, however, Pope Gregory IX, acting on the advice of Simon Langton, the archdeacon of Canterbury, quashed the election. It was alleged that Blund's case failed because he was found to be a pluralist, holding two benefices involving cure of souls, without the requisite dispensations. This is implausible as he was immediately granted the necessary dispensations and received an indult allowing him to be elected to any other bishopric. He was more likely to have been compromised by the support of Peter des Roches, whose political activities were regarded with suspicion at the curia. Returning home, he continued to be favoured with gifts from the king. In 1234 he was appointed chancellor of York Cathedral by Archbishop Walter de Gray, a position he held until his death in 1248.

Blund wrote a treatise on the soul, the only work of his known to survive. A typical scholastic dissertation, disputatious in form, it is probably a product of his Oxford lectures in arts. The fact that Alexander Neckham borrowed from it indicates that it was composed in the years 1197–1204. Although the author's analysis of cognition and the powers of the soul shows familiarity with the *Physics* and the other *libri naturales* of Aristotle, his major source of inspiration is the *De anima* of the Muslim philosopher Avicenna (Ibn Sina; *d.* 1037). His work thus demonstrates the absorption by the schools of Paris and Oxford at the beginning of the thirteenth century of Arabic science as well as of the newly translated scientific books of Aristotle.

C. H. LAWRENCE

Sources *The shorter Latin poems of Master Henry of Avranches relating to England*, ed. J. C. Russell and J. P. Heironimus (1935) · Paris, *Chron.*, vol. 3 · *Ann. mon.* · *Chancery records* · *CEPR letters*, vol. 1 · J. Raine, ed., *The register or rolls of Walter Gray, lord archbishop of York*, SurtS, 56 (1872) · *Hist. U. Oxf.* 1: *Early Oxf. schools* · R. W. Hunt, *John Blund: Tractatus de anima*, ed. D. A. Callus (1970) · D. A. Callus, 'The introduction of Aristotelian learning to Oxford', *Proc. of the British Academy*, 29 (1943), 229–81 · D. A. Callus, 'The treatise of John Blund on the soul', *Autour d'Aristote: recueil d'études de philosophie ancienne et médiévale offert à Mgr. A. Mansion* (1955), 471–95

Blund, Nicholas le (*d.* 1305), bishop of Down, apparently of English or Anglo-Irish birth, was, at the death of his predecessor, Thomas Lidell, treasurer of Ulster and prior of St Patrick's, Downpatrick. The king's licence to elect a bishop was granted to the chapter of Down by Edward I on 20 February 1277, and the writ investing Nicholas with the temporalities of the see was issued on 29 March 1277. In 1279 the archbishop of Armagh was ordered to appear before the pope to explain why the diocese of Down had been visited without need. In 1284 Nicholas was excommunicated by the archbishop; he was amerced 100 marks, and his temporalities were taken into the king's hands. In March 1288–9 he had a suit against the abbot of St Mary of York concerning some land. He was restored to his see and in 1291 joined the other bishops of Ireland in swearing to resist pressure from the lay power.

In 1297 Blund was tried on a *quo warranto* for the following offences. It was alleged that he had entered into a combination with Nicholas Mac Maol Íosa (*d.* 1303), archbishop of Armagh, and agreed on certain constitutions which excluded clergy born in England from the monasteries in their dioceses. This he denied. He was further charged with assuming the administration of justice on his church lands, and following Irish law, by taking *eiric*, a ransom-fine, in commutation of the felony of killing an Englishman. He pleaded that such administration had from time immemorial been the privilege of his predecessors in the see, but the plea was disallowed. In the same year, 1297, the place of abbot of St John's, Downpatrick, was voided by the cession of William Rede. The prior and convent obtained the king's licence to elect a successor. Nicholas broke into the monastery, took forcible possession of the licence, and himself appointed an abbot. He maintained his hold of his diocese until his death in 1305.

ALEXANDER GORDON, *rev.* B. SMITH

Sources *CEPR letters* • H. S. Sweetman and G. F. Handcock, eds., *Calendar of documents relating to Ireland*, 5 vols., PRO (1875–86), vol. 5

Blundell, Francis Nicholas Joseph (1880–1936), politician and farmer, was born on 16 October 1880 at Altmouth, Alt Road, Hightown, near Liverpool, the first of the three children of Francis Nicholas Blundell (1853–1884), land agent, and his wife, Mary (Polly) Sweetman (1859–1930). Blundell was a prominent public figure between the wars whose main interests were agriculture and Roman Catholic causes. His father died when he was three and he was brought up with his two sisters by his mother, a successful author who wrote some fifty novels and plays under the name M. E. Francis. He was educated at Stonyhurst College, Lancashire, from 1893, and the Oratory School in Birmingham from 1896. He then read law at Merton College, Oxford, graduating in 1904.

In October 1909 Blundell came into the Crosby estate near Liverpool, where he had been brought up, on the death of his uncle William Blundell. The village of Little Crosby had remained Catholic despite the English Reformation and Blundell devoted himself to maintaining that tradition, of which he was intensely proud, with its claim that Little Crosby had within its borders 'neither protestant pub nor pauper'. At the same time he was a progressive landowner and active in the county. He joined the Lancashire Farmers Association, of which he was later president, and stumped the county to form the Lancashire Federation of Rural Friendly Societies to protect the interests of small rural societies. He became a magistrate in 1912, a member of Lancashire county council in 1913 and a deputy lieutenant in 1925.

He served in France during the First World War with the Lancashire hussars yeomanry and from April 1918 was aide-de-camp to General Hunter-Weston. In 1919 he was mentioned in dispatches. On 25 July 1918 Blundell married Theresa (Tetta) Victoria Ward (1891–1979), the second daughter of Wilfrid *Ward (the biographer of his father, William George *Ward, and of Cardinal Newman). His wife's elder sister was Maisie *Ward (1889–1975), the co-founder of the Catholic publishing firm Sheed and Ward. Blundell and his wife had two sons and a daughter.

After the armistice Blundell took up farming and specialized in the outdoor rearing of pigs, of which he became fond, insisting that they were clean animals. He stood for parliament as a Conservative and won Ormskirk in the 1922 general election. He held the seat in December 1923 and again in October 1924. Blundell spoke mostly on agriculture but his lasting achievement was the passing of the Roman Catholic Relief Act of 1926 which abolished almost all the obsolete laws affecting Catholics. There were three acts and sixteen sections of other acts aimed at Catholics, such as a section of the Relief Act of 1829 which made a person becoming a member of a Catholic religious order liable to banishment for life. The bill aroused considerable opposition in and out of parliament but, thanks to Blundell's perseverance, became law on 15 December 1926.

In the 1929 general election Blundell lost his seat, partly owing to a local cry of 'no popery'. He remained active in public life: on the Imperial Economic Committee; on Lancashire county council (as alderman in 1931); on the court of Liverpool University; as a papal chamberlain; as chairman of the Catholic Education Council; and on a number of other bodies. He wrote two books, *The Agricultural Problem* (1928) and *A New Policy for Agriculture* (1931), and sat on several government agricultural committees.

Blundell died on 28 October 1936 of a coronary thrombosis at the Hotel Rembrandt, Thurloe Place, London, and was buried two days later in St Mary's churchyard at Little Crosby. He was admired by all who knew him. He was devoted to his church, his family, and to the people of Little Crosby, who erected a wayside shrine in his memory. The author of a letter to *The Observer* wrote that his loss was

> irreparable for he occupied a place to which scarcely a parallel remains within England. The parish of which his ancestral home of Crosby Hall is the centre was left virtually untouched by the Reformation; and Francis Blundell was squire of an estate like none other … his relations with his people were as nearly perfect as such human relations can be. (1 Nov 1936)

Brian Whitlock Blundell

Sources Lancs. RO, Blundell of Little Crosby papers, DDBL • parish registers, Little Crosby, Merseyside • priv. coll. • private information (2004) • *CGPLA Eng. & Wales* (1937) • *WWBMP*, vol. 3 • *WWW* • d. cert.
Archives Lancs. RO, corresp.; corresp. and political papers
Likenesses photographs, *c*.1899–*c*.1918, Crosby Hall, Liverpool • Soame, photograph, *c*.1902, Crosby Hall, Liverpool • Elliott & Fry, photograph, *c*.1922, Crosby Hall, Liverpool
Wealth at death £65,129 11*s*. 6*d*.: probate, 1937, limited to settled land • former grant, 1937, 'D.R.'

Blundell, Henry (1724–1810), art collector, was born at Ince Blundell, Lancashire, the son of Robert Blundell (*d.* 1773) and his wife, Katharine, daughter of Sir Stanley Rowland, bt, of Hooton, Chester. Like many Catholics he received his education abroad, first at the college of the English Jesuits at St Omer, and then at the English College at Douai, where he remained until 1745. He then travelled to Paris where he was placed under the care of Dr Joseph Holden, president of the St Gregory's English seminary. He returned to England by 1750, and in 1760 married Elizabeth (1733/4–1767), daughter of Sir George Mostyn, bt, of Talacre, Flintshire, with whom he had a son, Charles Robert, and two daughters, Katherine and Elizabeth. The year following Henry's marriage his father settled the family estates on him, and retired to Liverpool with his second wife, Margaret Anderton, whom he had married in 1752. It was a marriage that was to prove providential to Henry. The family's modest income was dramatically increased with the death in 1760 of Sir Francis Anderton without male heir. His estates of Lostock and Lydigate then passed to the Blundell family. Henry's wealth increased further with the deaths in 1767 and 1773, respectively, of his wife and father, his wife's income and that from his mother's estates devolving to him. With this substantial change in his financial fortunes, and the loss of much of his immediate family, Blundell devoted himself to improving the house and estate at Ince.

Blundell's collection began modestly in the 1760s, with the limited patronage of leading artists of his generation. He commissioned a portrait of his wife from Joshua Reynolds, and, on Edward Penny's advice, employed Richard Wilson to paint four pieces (*c.*1763–7) for the dining room at Ince Blundell Hall. Blundell paid 70 guineas for the paintings, although Wilson asked only 50, for what were mainly studio works. This was not the only example of Blundell's generosity: he also paid Antonio Canova 100 zecchini more than the agreed price for a sculpture, *Psyche*, commissioned in 1790. In the 1770s Blundell began to buy old masters, eventually amassing a collection of over 300 works which included paintings by and after Poussin, Ruisdael, Breughel, Jacopo Bassano, Veronese, and Andrea del Sarto. He purchased some of these paintings on visits to Paris, including a copy of Veronese's *Marriage at Cana*. However, many works were bought in Italy, where he also patronized the painters Gavin Hamilton and Anton Raphael Mengs, and acquired most of the classical antiquities for which his collection was, and is, renowned.

Blundell was probably encouraged to start collecting at the age of fifty-three not only by his new-found wealth, but also by his Catholic friend and neighbour Charles Townley, who had already formed a significant collection. In 1776 Blundell set out for Italy with the intention of joining Townley there. Travelling via Milan, Venice, and Ancona, he arrived in Rome in February 1777 before making a brief tour to Naples with his neighbour. Townley, who was well connected with those involved in the excavation and sale of antiquities in Rome, introduced Blundell to the dealer Thomas Jenkins. It was through Jenkins that Blundell made his first purchases of antiquities: a seated philosopher and eighty pieces from the Villa Mattei. This latter purchase included not only busts and statues but also urns and inscriptions, and represented what remained of a large collection from which 'the very best pieces had already been extracted', those items still in Jenkins's hands being 'heavily, and often, very imaginatively, restored' (Vaughan, 14).

Initially Blundell was not a highly discriminating collector, and his wholesale acquisition of antiquities continued with a group from Villa Borrioni (probably also in 1777); again the best pieces had already been dispersed. He was happy to buy works he knew to have been imaginatively restored, purchasing a number of pieces from the restorers and dealers Bartolomeo Cavaceppi and Giovanni Volpato. He was also content for his collection to include modern copies, to which end he bought from Giuseppi Angelini and Carlo Albacini. Blundell may simply have been 'interested in the sculptures for the classical ideas that they represented … and not unduly worried initially whether a piece was ancient or not' (Southworth). This opinion is further encouraged by Blundell's treatment of the statue *Sleeping Hermaphrodite*, which he purchased in 1801 from Lord Bessborough's sale. He had the subject's male genitalia and the genii that surrounded the figure removed, in order to recast the subject as a sleeping Venus.

Blundell made three further visits to Italy; he was in Rome in 1782–3, 1786, and 1790, when he also revisited Naples. He had grown to distrust Jenkins, and on the last two visits relied principally on Father John Thorpe (whom he had probably first met at St Omer) to assist him as his agent. However, it was through Jenkins that he purchased, in 1786, the statue of Minerva from Palazzo Lante. This was an important acquisition and, as an antique of the finest quality, marked a new phase in the sort of works Blundell sought to acquire. For example, he purchased twelve pieces from Villa d'Este including a *Theseus* that Townley regarded as the 'best specimen in Blundell's collection' (Vaughan, 16). In addition he bought significantly more marbles—Townley observed 39 pieces in 1786 and 325 in 1793 (ibid.). However, the Napoleonic wars halted the expansion of his collection, for a time anyway.

In England, Blundell paused in his collecting mania and built a garden temple to house his collection. However, in the early 1800s, perhaps having come into further money, he began to collect again. Advised by Townley, he bought at the sales of the collections of Lord Cawdor (1800) and Lord Bessborough (1801). The extent of Blundell's increased wealth may be exemplified by his purchase of a sarcophagus relief, *Phaeton before Helios*, at Christies. The work had been recovered in May 1800 from a French cargo ship *en route* for Paris from Italy, where it had previously been in the papal collection. Blundell had earlier bought this work soon after it was uncovered at Villa d'Este, for £10. After cleaning, its fame had spread and Blundell obliged Pope Pius VI's desire for it to enter the papal collection. Blundell had to pay 260 guineas for the same piece in 1801, but as he proclaimed in a letter to his brother-in-law that same year, 'You may think me extravagant … but if I lay out 1000 pounds it is no great affair to me: the money is no object' (Fejfer and Southworth, 12).

In 1801 Blundell began work on the construction of a pantheon in the grounds of Ince Blundell Hall, also to house his growing collection. He evidently received many visitors, for he found it necessary to limit the number of days he made the collection available to the public. In 1803 he published *An account of the statues, busts, bass-relieves, cinerary urns, and other ancient marbles, and paintings at Ince. Collected by H.B.* which was 'written with the sole view of serving as a kind of interpreter, in order to obviate the daily questions of those visitors who are not much versed in history, or heathen mythology' (frontispiece). This publication listed 553 items, but by the time of the next published account in 1809–10 there were 599 items in the collection, then the largest private collection of antiquities in Britain. It was on the advice and with the assistance of Townley that he published in 1809 *Engravings and etchings of the principal statues, busts, bass-reliefs, sepulchral monuments, cinerary urns etc. in the collection of Henry Blundell, esq., at Ince*, a two-volume collection of 150 engravings.

Although, as a Catholic, Blundell could not hold public office, he was a well-known figure in Liverpool society. He was involved with the early exhibitions held in Liverpool and was the first patron of the Liverpool Academy in 1810. In November 1808 Joseph Farington recorded that Blundell was nearly blind (Farington, *Diary*, 10 Nov 1808). He died on 28 August 1810 at Ince Blundell and was interred in the family vault at Sefton church in Lancashire. The funeral procession was reputed to have extended nearly half a mile (*GM*, 385).

The relationship between Blundell and his son was unhappy. Charles was unsociable and refused to marry. Consequently, to preserve the family succession, Blundell left the Lostock estate to his daughters and only Ince Blundell to his son. The will was contested, but sustained. When Charles died in 1837 he left the estate to a cousin, Thomas Weld of Lulworth, on the condition he took the Blundell name; again following litigation the will was upheld. Despite these problems with inheritance, Charles kept the collection intact, adding a significant number of old master drawings. In 1959, with the sale of the estate, the Ince Blundell collection of antiquities was offered as an unconditional gift to the city of Liverpool; it is now part of the collection of the National Museums and Galleries on Merseyside, housed in the Walker Art Gallery, Liverpool. It is the largest collection of antiquities in Britain outside the British Museum. The pictures, bronzes, and modern sculptures remained with the family for many years, although most of the pictures were dispersed at Christies in 1980 (12, 18 December), 1991 (12, 19 April), and 1992 (3 April). DEBORAH GRAHAM-VERNON

Sources G. Vaughan, 'Henry Blundell's sculpture collection at Ince Hall', *Patronage and practice: sculpture on Merseyside*, ed. P. Curtis (1989), 13–21 • J. Fejfer and E. Southworth, *The Ince Blundell collection of classical sculpture* (1991), vol. 1, pt 1 • J. Fejfer, *The Ince Blundell collection of classical sculpture* (1997), vol. 1, pt 2 • E. Southworth, 'The Ince Blundell collection: collecting behaviour in the eighteenth century', *Journal of the History of Collecting*, 3/2 (1991), 219–34 • *DNB* • J. Ingamells, ed., *A dictionary of British and Irish travellers in Italy, 1701–1800* (1997) • X. Brooke, *Mantegna to Rubens: the Weld-Blundell drawings collection* (1998) • C. Waagen, *Treasures of art in Great Britain*, 3, 242–60 • H. B. [H. Blundell], *An account of the statues, busts, bass-relieves, cinerary urns, and other ancient marbles, and paintings at Ince. Collected by H. B.* (1803) • H. Blundell, *Engravings and etchings of the principal statues, busts, bass-reliefs, sepulchral monuments, cinerary urns, etc. in the collection of Henry Blundell, esq., at Ince*, 2 vols. (1809) • Farington, *Diary* • *GM*, 1st ser., 80 (1810), 290, 385 • *Pictures from Ince Blundell Hall* (1960) [exhibition catalogue, Walker Art Gallery, Liverpool, 1960] • B. Ashmole, *A catalogue of the ancient marbles at Ince Blundell Hall* (1929)

Likenesses M. Brown, portrait, *c.*1800 (as an old man) • J. Gibson, statue on monument, 1813, Sefton church, Merseyside • G. Bullock, bust, Liverpool Corporation

Blundell, James (1790–1878), physician and physiologist, was born in London on 27 December 1790. Educated first by the Revd Thomas Thomason, and then at the United Borough Hospitals by his maternal uncle, the physiologist John Haighton, he graduated MD at Edinburgh in 1813. Haighton proved to be a great influence on his nephew, who lived with him for some time. From 1814 Blundell lectured in London on midwifery in conjunction with his uncle, and soon after began to lecture on physiology. In 1818 he succeeded his uncle as lecturer in midwifery and as lecturer in physiology at Guy's Hospital. As professor of obstetricy and lecturer on the diseases of women he was reputed to have the largest classes in midwifery in London. He was the author of *Researches Physiological and Pathological* (1824) and two papers on abdominal surgery and blood transfusion, edited by S. Ashwell, and published in 1828; the *British Medical Journal* considered him to be the father of the operation of transfusion in Britain. He also published *Principles and Practice of Obstetricy* (1834) and *Observations on some of the More Important Diseases of Women* (1837). He was considered to be in advance of other obstetric practitioners, not least in using the uterine sound for diagnostic purposes.

Blundell left Guy's in 1834 following a dispute with the hospital's treasurer. He became a fellow of the Royal College of Physicians in 1838. Blundell, who retained an interest in the classics from his days with Thomason, published his *Hexametrical experiments, or, A version of four of Virgil's pastorals … with hints to explain the method of reading, and a slight essay on the laws of metre* in the same year. With a large private practice and significant bequests, he amassed a fortune estimated variously at between a third of and half a million pounds, and was thus able to retire from full-time practice in 1847. During his later years he never rose until around noon, saw patients during the afternoon, dined, and commenced visits at 8 or 9 pm. He always carried books with him on his rounds, reading them by means of a light specially installed in his carriage.

Blundell died on 15 January 1878 at his home at 80 Piccadilly, London. [ANON.], *rev.* ANNE DIGBY

Sources *BMJ* (9 March 1878), 351–2 • H. C. Cameron, *Mr Guy's Hospital, 1726–1948* (1954) • Munk, *Roll* • J. H. Young, 'James Blundell (1790–1878): experimental physiologist and obstetrician', *Medical History*, 8 (1964), 159–69 • B. A. Myhre, 'James Blundell: pioneer transfusionist', *Transfusion*, 35/1 (1995), 74–8 • *CGPLA Eng. & Wales* (1878)

Archives Wellcome L., transcripts of physiology lectures

Likenesses J. Cochran, line and stipple engraving, pubd 1847 (after H. Room), NPG, Wellcome L. • Beynon & Co., portrait (*The past surgeons and physicians at Guy's Hospital, Southwark*; after M. Hanhart), Wellcome L. • portrait, repro. in Young, 'James Blundell'

Wealth at death under £350,000: probate, 29 Jan 1878, *CGPLA Eng. & Wales*

Blundell, Sir Michael (1907–1993), farmer and politician in Kenya, was born on 7 April 1907 at 33 Campden House Court, Kensington, London, the third of four sons of Alfred Herbert Blundell, a London solicitor, and his wife, Amelia Woodward Richardson. His father's family came from Appletreewick in the Yorkshire dales. He was educated at Wellington College from 1921 to 1925, and was destined to go to Magdalen College, Oxford, but the school had an offer from an old Wellingtonian in Kenya to take on an assistant on his farm. Fired by a visit to the Empire Exhibition at Wembley in 1924, Blundell decided to take up the offer.

Blundell arrived in Mombasa in October 1925 with two tin trunks, a shotgun, and £100. The farm was in Kipkarren in western Kenya, an area of European settlement set up for ex-soldiers after the First World War. Blundell's role as a trainee was to manage the African farmworkers and

Sir Michael Blundell (1907–1993), by Barker, 1962

to drive a tractor which had replaced the ox-teams for ploughing. He shot regularly for the pot and for sport and went on hunting safaris, mainly on foot. It was a pioneering life which brought him into close contact with Africans, whom he quickly learned to respect. In 1927 he moved to manage a farm at Solai, near Nakuru in the Rift valley. He later bought the farm in partnership with his elder brother Jack, who was killed in the Second World War. Blundell played the piano and sang well. He found friends with whom he could indulge in his love of music, and in 1936 visited Austria to study singing and became absorbed in the great lieder cycles, but soon returned to Kenya. Farming in Africa remained the formative influence of his life.

A burly figure, with strong features, Blundell had prodigious energy, both physical and mental. He was fascinated by the new challenges posed by Africa and studied his environment in depth. His mastery of botany enabled him to write a popular book, *The Wild Flowers of Kenya*, published in 1982. This was revised and enlarged as *The Wild Flowers of East Africa* and published as a definitive guide by Collins in 1987. Above all, Blundell was a natural leader, not afraid of making forthright statements even if they offended older settlers in the small European community of Kenya. The Rift valley became the platform for his move from full-time farming to the political arena, which he chronicled in two books of memoirs, *So Rough a Wind*, published in 1964, and *A Love Affair with the Sun*, published posthumously in 1994.

Following the onset of the Second World War, Blundell was drafted in 1940 to command a battalion of pioneers, recruited largely from western Kenya. They took part in the Abyssinian campaign, fighting through to the capture of Addis Ababa, the assault on Gondar, and the defeat of the Italian forces. He was made an MBE in 1943. The battalion was afterwards upgraded to a royal engineer unit and sent to the Fourteenth Army, working mainly in Ceylon and India until the war ended, when they all returned to Kenya. Close comradeship with his soldiers made Blundell aware of African aspirations for political advance. Before leaving the army he was promoted colonel to an organization preparing for the reintegration of troops to civilian life.

In 1946 Blundell married and returned to his farm in Solai, bringing with him his wife, Geraldine Lötte Robarts (*d.* 1983), previously the wife of an army officer. Just before the war he had been singled out to serve the farming community as a member of the coffee board of Kenya. Now the government appointed him a commissioner in charge of settlement schemes for European ex-soldiers, over 300 of whom had come to the highlands. This was an important step intended to increase agricultural production. Although he gave up this job after a year, Blundell later used his political clout to press the rights of these farmers—who had been led to believe that Kenya would remain a British colony—to fair compensation from the British government. He was already involved in government and deputized briefly for the Rift Valley member of the legislative council in 1947. The following year, in the general election, he stood for the seat and defeated Lord Francis Scott, a doyen of settler politics, to embark upon his own political career.

In a country of 5 million people, the resident European community of about 35,000 had been the dominant group in the political life of Kenya since the 1920s. They acted as an opposition to the government officials and nominees who held power. Their policy priorities were simple: European leadership, the sanctity of the 'white highlands', a communal electoral roll, and separate education for the races. Blundell stood firmly on this platform. He was the epitome of the younger breed of settlers embarking on modern farming methods and growing cash crops. In 1948 he sold his land in Solai and moved to a higher farm at Subukia, east of Nakuru, where he grew pyrethrum and built a new house. A year later he was appointed chairman of the pyrethrum board of Kenya, a post he held for four years. He was re-elected unopposed in the 1952 election and soon became leader of the European elected members. However, there was a growing rift between the older members, who wanted to maintain the status quo, and those who saw the need for political change.

The testing time came with the declaration of Mau Mau emergency in 1952. This uprising, mainly among the Kikuyu and their cousin tribes in the central province, shook the governments in Nairobi and London. Blundell was in the thick of political developments. Faced with attacks on farms and murders of loyal Kikuyu, the European members were strongly critical of the conduct of what had become a limited war. Blundell showered the new governor, Sir Evelyn Baring, with advice, and proposed strengthening the administration of Kikuyu areas. He was at Government House when a mob of angry Europeans demonstrated outside. Baring sent him out with some of his colleagues to address and ultimately disperse them. On a visit to London, Blundell was invited to explain his views to ministers and to the media. In 1954 he became minister without portfolio in the Kenya government and a member of the war council. With the arrival of British troops and expanded administrative and police forces the violence was controlled. The focus turned to intensive development of agriculture in the African areas. Blundell threw himself into this as minister for agriculture, animal husbandry, and water resources (1955–9). He promoted the 'Swynnerton plan' to extend the planting of cash crops by African farmers and directed a revolution in land tenure to give them freehold land titles.

Meanwhile there had been a change in political alignments. Blundell and some of his colleagues broke away in 1954 to form the United Country Party (UCP). This grouping with liberal and multiracial aims aroused the opposition of many Europeans. Blundell considered that this polarization was a mistake and the UCP was wound up three years later. He resigned from the government in 1959 and became leader of the New Kenya Group, now as a specially elected member. He was determined to create a nation of all races under African majority leadership, and spoke widely—and to African audiences in Swahili—in preparation for the conference on the future of Kenya which was to be held early in 1960.

Blundell now played a key role in negotiating the constitutional developments leading to Kenya's independence. He was trusted by the political leaders in the Conservative Party, though not implicitly by the colonial secretary, Iain Macleod. The result of the Lancaster House conference in January 1960, when it became clear that the British government would accept majority rule based on universal suffrage, was a shock to European opinion in Kenya. Blundell himself was alarmed by the speed of change to African rule, but he had to bear the opprobrium. On arrival at Nairobi airport he was met by cheering Africans, and by angry Europeans who threw thirty coins at his feet, declaring 'Judas, you have betrayed and left us' (Blundell, *So Rough a Wind*, 283). Though ostracized by the bulk of the white community, he worked on in politics, returning to his old job at the agriculture ministry in 1961 after being re-elected with strong African support. His energies were applied to implementing settlement schemes for landless Africans. He was made a KBE in 1962, and in 1963 finally retired from active politics, just before Kenya gained independence. However, this was not the end of his service to the country of which he proudly became a citizen. He devoted himself to the running of Egerton Agricultural College (later a university), and was chairman of its board in 1962. He took great pride in funding the building of a rural school in the area from which most of his troops in the Abyssinian campaign had come. His skills were also sought in commercial boardrooms. He was chairman of East African Breweries from 1964 to 1977, a major job which he carried out with conspicuous success.

In his later years Blundell became a doyen of Kenya politics, respected and consulted by presidents and senior visitors. Ironically, he was looked upon as an advocate with the government by the Europeans in Kenya, coming forward in this capacity in 1990, at the age of eighty-three, to give evidence to the Kenya electoral review committee. His greatest joy was to sit on the veranda of his final home, Ridgeway, in Kiambu district, near Nairobi, and look out over the garden which he had created. After the death of his wife in 1983 he lived at Ridgeway with his daughter and his two granddaughters, and died there on 1 February 1993. He was cremated, and his ashes interred at St Paul's Church in Kiambu.

Blundell served two homelands, Britain and Kenya, with distinction. His major achievement was to pave the way for white Kenyans to come to terms with majority rule; but first and foremost he saw himself as an African.

JOHN JOHNSON

Sources M. Blundell, *So rough a wind* (1964) · M. Blundell, *A love affair with the sun* (1994) · Bodl. RH, Sir M. Blundell MSS, MS Afr.s.746 · *The Times* (3 Feb 1993) · *The Guardian* (11 Feb 1993) · *The origins and growth of Mau Mau*, Kenya sessional paper (1959–60), no. 5 · P. Mitchell, *African afterthoughts* (1954) · b. cert. · *WW* · personal knowledge (2004) · private information (2004)

Archives Bodl. RH, corresp. and papers | Bodl. RH, corresp. with Sir R. R. Welensky | FILM BFI NFTVA, documentary footage · IWM FVA, documentary footage | SOUND BL NSA, current affairs recording

Likenesses Barker, photograph, 1962, News International Syndication, London [*see illus.*] · photograph, 1991, priv. coll. · oils, Nairobi, Kenya

Blundell, Nicholas (1669–1737), diarist and landowner, was born on 1 September 1669 at Little Crosby Hall, Lancashire, the son of William Blundell (1645–1702) and his wife, Mary (*d.* 1707), daughter of Rowland Eyre of Hassop in Derbyshire. The eldest of fourteen children, he was educated at home by his grandfather William Blundell but was later sent to the Jesuit college at St Omer in Flanders. His grandfather died in 1698 and his father only four years later, on 2 August 1702, when Nicholas inherited the estate, which included the manors of Little Crosby and Ditton (near Widnes) and property in several neighbouring townships.

Blundell was thirty-two years old and his first dynastic task was to find a well-connected Catholic wife. Why he eventually chose the seventeen-year-old Frances Langdale (*b.* 1686), younger daughter of the third Lord Langdale, is now quite unclear, but they were married at her home, Heythrop in Oxfordshire, on 17 June 1703. The marriage was not a success. Frances Blundell, a difficult and temperamental woman, was unhappy in Lancashire and had a poor relationship not only with her husband's female relatives but also with the servants, who often left after only a few days. She and Nicholas had two daughters, Mary (1704–1734) and Frances (*b.* 1706), but although the parents consulted many medical experts they were unable to produce a male heir, a matter of intense disappointment.

Blundell was an obsessive record keeper. He wrote a detailed entry in his diary every day from 27 July 1702 until 20 January 1728. His recipe book included numerous medical prescriptions and receipts, from which he regularly made his own remedies for administration to friends and family, and his joke book was filled with anecdotes, after-dinner stories, and details of card tricks. The account books, letter-books, lease books, and other estate papers were meticulously maintained. But it is the diaries which are his greatest achievement, for in them he recorded almost every aspect of his life to give an unrivalled picture of estate management, social intercourse, the role of the squire in the community, business dealings of the estate, the weather, natural events, illnesses and treatments given, the pastimes and entertainments of the family, and the comings and goings of visitors, friends, and tenants.

Blundell had a prominent public role as squire and, like other leading Lancashire Catholics, his faith did not prevent his enjoying excellent relations with neighbouring protestant gentry and clergy—he served as churchwarden of Sefton parish on several occasions. He was a strict but just landlord, with a deep concern for the welfare of his tenants, presiding at their Michaelmas goose feast, taking them food and medicines at times of illness, and regarding himself as a counsellor to those in difficulties. He was intensely interested in estate management, taking an active personal role in agricultural work, directing drainage operations and building projects, and showing a particular expertise in horticulture and fruit growing, in which he innovated and experimented, importing new strains of flowers and vegetables and undertaking extensive trials in forcing and overwintering plants.

During the Jacobite rising of 1715 Blundell fell under government suspicion because of his recusancy. His diary confirms that at Little Crosby he gave shelter to individuals, presumably priests or refugees, and the house was searched on several occasions. In November 1715 he and his wife went to London whence, in March 1716, they travelled into voluntary exile in Flanders. The estate was not sequestrated and no formal legal action was taken against him—that he had not borne arms in support of the Jacobites was in his favour—but the couple did not return to Little Crosby until August 1717.

In his old age Blundell suffered the sudden death in 1734 of his beloved elder daughter, Mary, wife of John Coppinger of Barrismore, co. Cork, but his last years were heartened by the birth in 1735 of a son, Christopher, to his younger daughter, Frances, and her husband, Henry Peppard, a Liverpool Irish merchant. Blundell died at Little Crosby Hall on 21 April 1737, aged sixty-seven, and was buried on 23 April at Sefton parish church. His wealth at death was a little over £630. His voluminous papers are in the Lancashire Record Office and his diaries, published by the Record Society of Lancashire and Cheshire, are an exceptionally useful source for historians not only of the region but also of the period. ALAN G. CROSBY

Sources *The great diurnal of Nicholas Blundell of Little Crosby, Lancashire*, ed. F. Tyrer and J. J. Bagley, 3 vols., Lancashire and Cheshire RS, 110, 112, 114 [1968–72] • parish register, Sefton, Lancashire, 1737 • probate inventory, Lancs. RO, DDB1/54/24
Archives Lancs. RO, MSS incl. those of other members of his family
Likenesses portrait, repro. in Tyer and Bagley, eds., *Great diurnall* (1968), frontispiece; priv. coll.
Wealth at death £631 5*s.* 2*d.*: probate inventory, Lancs. RO

Blundell, Peter (*c.*1520–1601), clothier and philanthropist, was born in Tiverton, Devon, of humble parentage. As a boy he saw the little community freed from the dominance of the Courtenay earls of Devon, and he lived to see it, untrammelled by either civic or industrial regulation, and somewhat encouraged by the protestant ethic, enter a period of considerable growth and prosperity based on the manufacture of kerseys, the woollen cloths in which the town and its immediate hinterland specialized. Whether the young Blundell himself learned any of the necessary industrial skills is not apparent. He was essentially an industrial entrepreneur—still a rarity in late sixteenth-century Devon—but it was his ability to find a market in London for the lightweight and inexpensive west-country product that enabled him to prosper so exceedingly. There is no evidence that he was ever a freeman of the City of London or a member of any of its guilds, but when he made his will in 1599 he left £150 to each of the twelve great livery companies, part of the income of which was to be given to poor inmates of the city's various penal institutions. He left more sizeable sums to each of the three great London hospitals (St Bartholomew's, St Thomas's, and Christ's Hospital) and to some of his London business friends. Ann Whitmore, a merchant's widow living in the parish of St Michael Paternoster Royal, was generously provided for by the elderly bachelor, as were each of her nine children (one of them a future lord mayor) and several of her servants, suggesting that Blundell had lodged with the family when he was in London; and indeed it was in this parish that he was assessed for tax in 1581. It was on no less a person than his friend Sir John Popham, the lord chief justice and a fellow west-countryman, that he placed the main burden of carrying out his multifarious wishes.

The bulk of Blundell's considerable fortune went to a wide circle of fellow clothiers, their widows and children, many of them also his relations, in and around Tiverton, with a few in the city of Exeter. His many employees also benefited—even his carrier, William Wood, receiving £50. His only brother, James, having predeceased him, his heir presumptive was his nephew John, who, with his infant son Peter, received rather less than another nephew, Robert Chilcott, his clerk. Blundell's residuary legatees were the five men he named as his executors, two of them London merchants and the other three Tiverton cousins. He created several charitable trusts, including one enabling four Tiverton boys a year under the age of fifteen to be apprenticed to husbandry—a new idea in 1599, reflecting Blundell's appreciation of the need for a healthy rural economy. Others to benefit were the ten inhabitants of

Tiverton most heavily assessed for the subsidy. In all, Blundell provided for cash disposals amounting to the amazing sum of over £32,000. This included £2400 to build premises for what was to be his lasting memorial, a free grammar school in Tiverton, the running costs to be met from his estate. His extraordinary will, which he claimed to have written in his own hand, contained the most detailed particulars regarding the school's construction, the choice of pupils, and the provision of staff. Finally, for the increase of preachers of the gospel, he provided scholarships to support six former pupils at the universities of Oxford and Cambridge. Blundell died, possibly on 18 April 1601, in the London parish of St Michael Paternoster Royal, his second home. The parish register for 9 May 1601 lists the burial of 'P er Blunden', but this may be a copyist's error. JOYCE YOUINGS

Sources J. Prince, *Danmonii orientales illustres, or, The worthies of Devon* (1701), 89 • M. Dunsford, *Historical memoirs of the town and parish of Tiverton* (1790) • B. Incledon, *Donations of Peter Blundell to the free grammar school at Tiverton* (1792) • will, 1601, PRO, PROB 11/98, sig. 50 • T. L. Stoate, ed., *Devon taxes, 1581–1660* (1988) • R. G. Lang, ed., *Two Tudor subsidy assessment rolls for the city of London, 1541 and 1581*, London RS, 29 (1993), 292 • parish register, St Michael Paternoster Royal, 1558–1653, GL, MS 5142

Likenesses portrait; formerly, in possession of Whitmore family; [reportedly lost, 1694]

Wealth at death £35,000–£40,000—bequests of over £32,000, plus land: will, PRO, PROB 11/98, sig. 50

Blundell, William (1560–1638), antiquary, was the elder of two sons of Richard Blundell (*d*. 1591/2) and his wife, Anne, of Little Crosby, in the parish of Sefton, near Liverpool. The family, who had been landowners in the area since the thirteenth century, resisted the Reformation and suffered persecution throughout the late sixteenth and seventeenth centuries. Following the regular family practice of education abroad, in 1580 William went to Douai, while his brother, Richard, became a priest.

Richard Blundell the elder died a prisoner in Lancaster Castle in 1591 or early 1592, accused of harbouring a priest. William was imprisoned at the same time, and subsequently spent two years in prison in London. A search of his home late in the 1590s forced William to flee; his wife, Amelia or Emilia Norris (*d*. 1631), was also committed to prison in Chester and released only on the intercession of friends at court. Both Blundells received pardons at the accession of James, but this did not mitigate the persecutions of protestant neighbours and shrieval officials, who through the next three decades conducted frequent raids on his cattle and searches of the hall, culminating in the sequestration of the estate during the civil wars.

In addition to collecting a number of family records and several pro-Catholic 'ditties', William Blundell recorded a particularly significant archaeological discovery, a large trove of Anglo-Saxon coins found by accident in 1611, a few months after he had secretly established a cemetery for local Catholics on his own land, because the local puritan minister had refused Catholics the right of burial at Sefton church. The site of the cemetery was known as the Harkirke because oral tradition suggested that a church had once stood there. Blundell's cemetery endured for over a century, though an attempt by the sheriff of Lancashire, Sir Ralph Assheton, to destroy the graveyard in 1624 was met with resistance by Little Crosby's residents. The riot on that occasion resulted in an action against Blundell and his tenants in Star Chamber, and he was fined £2000 by the court in 1629, though this was eventually reduced.

Blundell took the discovery of the coins as a sign of divine favour of his family's endurance in the face of persecution, and he immediately turned some of his trove into a silver pyx and chalice; the pyx still survives at Little Crosby church. Blundell penned two accounts of his coins, using various medieval and contemporary scholarly and historical sources to identify them. He also had a copperplate reproduction of several of them executed, and this circulated throughout the seventeenth century. The coins themselves were sent to relatives in Wales during the civil wars for safety and were lost soon after. Blundell's account of his coins demonstrates a surprisingly good grasp of Anglo-Saxon history and numismatics.

Blundell died at Crosby Hall, Little Crosby, on 2 July 1638. He was buried in Little Crosby. His wife, Amelia, and their son, Nicholas, had both died in 1631, while his daughter, Margaret, had entered, under the name of Winifred, the English Augustinian house at Louvain. Blundell was succeeded by Nicholas's son, also William *Blundell (1620–1698). D. R. WOOLF

Sources F. Tyrer, 'A star chamber case: Assheton v. Blundell, 1624–31', *Transactions of the Historic Society of Lancashire and Cheshire*, 118 (1966), 19–37 • D. R. Woolf, 'Little Crosby and the horizons of early modern historical culture', *The historical imagination in early modern Britain*, ed. D. R. Kelley and D. M. Sacks (1997), 93–132 • W. Blundell and others, 'The Great Hodge Podge', Lancs. RO, DDBl. Acc. 6121 • Gillow, *Lit. biog. hist.*, 1.248–50 • W. Blundell, *Crosby records: a cavalier's notebook*, ed. T. E. Gibson (1880) • T. E. Gibson, ed., *Crosby records: a chapter of Lancashire recusancy*, Chetham Society, new ser., 12 (1887) • PRO, STAC 9/1/2 • A. Hamilton, ed., *The chronicle of the English Augustinian canonesses regular of the Lateran*, 1 (1904), 153

Archives Lancs. RO, Blundell of Little Crosby

Wealth at death £665 19*s*. 11*d*.: inventory, 6 July 1638, Lancs. RO, DDBl 24/13

Blundell, William (1620–1698), royalist landowner and topographer, was born on 15 July 1620 at Crosby Hall, Little Crosby, Lancashire, the second son of Nicholas Blundell (*c*.1590–1631) and Jane (*d*. 1640), daughter of Roger Bradshaigh of Haigh, near Wigan. In 1635 at the age of fifteen he married, in Scotland, Anne (*c*.1620–1685), daughter of Sir Thomas Haggerston. On the death of his grandfather, also William Blundell, in July 1638, he succeeded to the family estates. As a Roman Catholic he did not attend university, but as a youth he had a taste both for learning and travel, and visited Dublin in 1639.

On 22 December 1642 Blundell was commissioned at Leigh, Lancashire, as a captain in Thomas Tildesley's dragoon regiment. Made a prisoner at Preston on 9 February 1643, he was released in time to march to Lancaster, where on 18 March 1643 his thigh was shattered by a musket shot. So serious was this that early in 1644 an attempt was made to take Blundell to Chester for proper medical care, and he continually petitioned Sir Thomas Fairfax and the local parliamentary leader John Moore about this. Time spent hiding in north Wales between 1644 and 1646 apparently did not help: Blundell commented that 'after I was lamed in the war, tho' I could not use a sword, I was 4 times made a prisoner and payd my ransom twice' (Baines, 216–17). In addition he claimed that his wound cost him 3 inches in height. In February 1651 Blundell, who dubbed himself Halt-Will, described in a letter to his sister-in-law his 'gross full body of an ell or more in the waist, with an old peruke clapped on a bald pate' (*Cavalier*, 39).

As a Catholic delinquent Blundell could not compound for his estate, and all his real property was seized by the sequestration commissioners for nine or ten years. In the late 1640s, in order to escape further notice, he resorted to the use of the pseudonym Cicely Burton in signing his letters. On 12 May 1648 his estate was used to finance part of the £10,000 paid to compensate Liverpool for war damage. In 1653, however, he was able to repurchase the estate at a cost of £1340.

Blundell's experiences weighed heavily on him. He later wrote that after the repurchase 'I was so overcharged with care, debts, business and imprisonments, that I took no exact account of the value of any goods until the yeare 1658' (*Cavalier*, 40). None the less, he was possessed of a lively, inquisitive mind, and made the most of his travels. In 1646 and again in 1648 he had sailed to the Isle of Man, and his second stay produced the first extensive study of the island. The manuscript work is divided into three books. The first deals with topography and economic geography, the second covers politics, history and the law, and the last discusses Manx customs, society, and religion. The scope of the work makes it a prime source for the history of Man in the seventeenth century and its study of Manx agriculture is deemed to be especially valuable.

Blundell also wrote 'A short treatise on the penal laws'. He made copious notes on many subjects in two small quarto volumes of 1200 manuscript pages each entitled 'Historia' and 'Adversaria', as well as in a large quarto 'Hodge Podge'. None of these is dated. Extracts were published by T. E. Gibson in 1880.

Blundell remained a marked man throughout the Interregnum, being listed as a royalist suspect in 1655 and a holder of a commission in 1658, in which year he visited Rouen. He was also in Breda in 1660 prior to Charles II's departure for England, having taken his youngest son, Thomas, for education at St Omer. With the Restoration his fortunes improved and, after paying a further £1202 5*s*. 8*d*. to clear rent arrears to the crown, he was eventually able to settle his estates in 1662.

Much later, in the charged atmosphere following the revolution of 1688, Blundell was again imprisoned, this time at Manchester. He was not arrested in 1694 as he was clearly peripheral to the Lancashire Jacobite plot of that year. Blundell, who had fathered five sons and seven daughters, several of whom had entered convents abroad, died on 24 May 1698 at Crosby Hall and was buried in the family chapel at Sefton parish church three days later.

MALCOLM GRATTON

Sources T. E. Gibson, ed., *A cavalier's note book, being notes, anecdotes, and observations of William Blundell* (1880) · *Cavalier: letters of William Blundell to his friends, 1620–1698*, ed. M. Blundell (1933) · W. Blundell, *A history of the Isle of Man*, ed. W. Harrison, 2 vols., Manx Society, 25, 27 (1876–7) · Lancs. RO, Blundell deeds, DDB1 2/1, 52/4 · Lpool RO, Moore deeds, MD 1228 · G. Ormerod, ed., *Tracts relating to military proceedings in Lancashire during the great civil war*, Chetham Society, 2 (1844) · *The great diurnal of Nicholas Blundell of Little Crosby, Lancashire*, ed. F. Tyrer and J. J. Bayley, 1, Lancashire and Cheshire RS, 110 (1968) · E. L. Lonsdale, 'John Lunt and the Lancashire plot, 1694', *Transactions of the Historic Society of Lancashire and Cheshire*, 115 (1963), 91–106 · E. Baines and W. R. Whatton, *The history of the county palatine and duchy of Lancaster*, 4 vols. (1836) · J. H. Stanning and J. Brownbill, eds., *The royalist composition papers*, 1, ed. J. H. Stanning, Lancashire and Cheshire RS, 24 (1891) · *DNB* · list of royalist suspects, 1655, BL, Add. MSS 34013, fols. 2–55 · R. Whitley, notebook, 1658–9, Bodl. Oxf., MS Eng. hist e. 309 · C. F. Russell, ed., 'The parish registers of Sefton, 1597–1783', *Lancashire Parish Registers Society*, 86 (1947), 254

Archives Crosby Hall, Lancashire, history of Isle of Man · Crosby Hall, Lancashire, letters · Crosby Hall, Lancashire, 'A short treatise on the penal laws', 'Historia', 'Adversaria', 'Hodge podge' · Lancs. RO, MSS

Likenesses portrait, Crosby Hall, Lancashire; repro. in Blundell, ed., *Cavalier*, frontispiece

Wealth at death annuities to be paid to children; two thirds of residue to wife; one third to son; remainder to help poor of Sefton parish, especially Little Crosby: Lancs. RO, DDB1 (Blundell deeds) 2/1, 52/4

Blunden, Anna Elizabeth (1829–1915). *See under* Women artists in Ruskin's circle (*act.* 1850s–1900s).

Blunden, Edmund Charles (1896–1974), poet and university teacher, was born on 1 November 1896 at 54A Tottenham Court Road, London, the eldest of the nine children (five sons and four daughters) of Charles Edmund Blunden (1871–1951) and his wife, Georgina Margaret (1868–1967), daughter of Henry Tyler and his wife, Georgina. Both parents were schoolteachers. When Edmund was four the family moved to Yalding in Kent, where he discovered the love of rural life and natural history that pervaded his whole career as a writer. He was a clever child with precocious literary tastes and ambitions. He attended Cleave's Grammar School in Yalding for two years and then in 1909 won a scholarship to Christ's Hospital, Horsham, Sussex, a public school which had been founded in the sixteenth century to provide an education for poor boys. Throughout his life Blunden was devoted to the school, and to the writers who had attended it, such as Charles Lamb, Leigh Hunt, and S. T. Coleridge. His final year there was overshadowed by the First World War.

In August 1915 Blunden was commissioned as a second lieutenant in the Royal Sussex regiment. Early in 1916 he was sent to Flanders, where he saw violent action in the trenches and on the battlefield and was awarded the Military Cross. Very much against the odds for a young infantry officer, Blunden survived nearly two years in the front line without a scratch. In mind and spirit, though, he was indelibly affected by the death and destruction he witnessed so early in his life. Blunden is remembered as one of the finest poets of the First World War, though many of his war poems were written afterwards, contemplating events in retrospect. He was affected not only by the loss of

Edmund Charles Blunden (1896–1974), by Ralph Hodgson, 1921

human life, including several of his friends, but by the brutal destruction of a countryside that, in its natural state, was very like the rural England that he loved. These memories haunted him and reappeared in his dreams and his poetry until the end of his life. 'When the events were not yet ended' (Blunden, *Undertones of War*, 1928, vii) Blunden wrote a prose account of his experiences, *De bello germanico*, but he was not satisfied with it. It was not published until 1930, and then only in a limited edition.

After returning to England in 1918 Blunden was serving at a camp in Suffolk when he met and married, on 1 June 1918, a young local woman, Mary Daines (1900–1957). He left the army in 1919 and launched himself on a literary career, meeting Siegfried Sassoon, who became a lifelong friend (and, on occasion, a source of financial support). The Blundens' first child, Joy, was born in July 1919, but died when only a few weeks old; Blunden grieved for her all his life. There were two more children of the marriage. While still at school Blunden had been awarded a scholarship to Oxford, and in October 1919 went up to Queen's College. He made friends among the aspiring writers in the university, many of them ex-servicemen like himself, but he found it hard to settle to academic work and in 1920 he left Oxford to take up a part-time editorial post at *The Athenaeum*, later incorporated in *The Nation*. In that year he published a collection of poems, *The Waggoner*, and co-edited the poems of John Clare, a countryman poet to whom he felt a great devotion. Blunden's next book of poems, *The Shepherd*, was awarded the Hawthornden prize, and he was recognized as a young writer of great promise. He was a fluent but thoughtful reviewer; his copious literary journalism reflected wide reading in the poets and prose writers of the Romantic era and their eighteenth-century antecedents. Despite his productive career as an editor, journalist, critic, and biographer, Blunden always regarded himself as essentially a poet, and a poet in the Romantic tradition. He was not influenced by the modernist literary revolution, but his poetry was admired by its adherents, such as T. S. Eliot. Blunden was a true nature poet, but in his work nature is menacing as well as consoling, as in such well-known poems as 'The Pike' and 'Midnight Skaters'. And his evocations of nature are often clouded by memories of war.

Sassoon, though ten years his senior, greatly admired Blunden; in 1922 he wrote in his diary that 'he brings with him his aura of enthusiasm for literature. He creates a special atmosphere which inspires me with certainty that I am a privileged person sharing the mysteries of the noble craft of letters' (*Siegfried Sassoon Diaries*, 161). Less reverentially, Sassoon wrote of Blunden 'perching' on a bed: 'he always reminds me of a bird' (ibid., 170). It was a widespread response to his small stature, sharp features, and rapid, darting movements (though when he was in the army his commanding officer referred to him as Rabbit).

Despite Blunden's growing fame, his poetry and literary journalism were not sufficiently lucrative to support a family. In 1924 he struck out on a new path by accepting the post of professor of English at the Imperial University of Tokyo. He came to love Japan, which brought him new friends and fresh subjects for poetry. While there he made another attempt at a prose account of his war experiences. The result was *Undertones of War*. Written without any documentation other than maps, it represents an extraordinary feat of memory and is Blunden's greatest contribution to the literature of war.

Blunden returned to England in 1927, and in 1928 *Undertones* was published. His wife had refused to accompany him to Japan, and the marriage ended in divorce in August 1931. Blunden resumed his connection with *The Nation* and was literary editor for a year; in 1931 he went back to Oxford as fellow and tutor in English literature at Merton College. On 5 July 1933 he married Sylva Norman (1901/2–1971), *née* Nahabedian, a young novelist and critic.

At Merton, Blunden was highly regarded as a tutor; his students included the famous Canadian critic Northrop Frye and the poet Keith Douglas, who was killed in action in 1944. During his years in Oxford, Blunden published several collections of poetry, and studies of Charles Lamb, the Keats circle, and Thomas Hardy. His *Cricket Country* (1944) reflects his abiding passion for the game. Eventually he came to feel restricted by academic life; he returned to full-time writing in 1944, and in the following year became assistant editor of the *Times Literary Supplement*. In May 1945 his second marriage, which was childless, was dissolved, and he married on 29 May 1945 Claire Margaret Poynting (*b*. 1918), a teacher, who had been one of his students; they had four daughters. Blunden's highly praised life of Shelley appeared in 1946, and in the following year he returned to Japan as a member of the United Kingdom liaison mission in Tokyo; he lectured widely on English literature and renewed some of his old acquaintance from the 1920s. Blunden was back in England from 1950 to 1953 and then accepted the post of professor of English literature at the University of Hong Kong. Here, as previously in Japan, he made many friends and admirers among his students.

Blunden retired in 1964 and settled in Suffolk, where he had lived in the 1920s; for almost the first time in his adult life he had a permanent home. His achievements were publicly recognized: he became a CBE in 1951, received the queen's gold medal for poetry in 1956, and in 1962 was made a companion of the Royal Society of Literature. In 1966 he was nominated for the Oxford professorship of poetry and reluctantly agreed to stand. Blunden was elected by a large majority over the other candidate, the American poet Robert Lowell (who warmly admired his work), but he found electioneering dispiriting. In the words of his biographer:

> For his Oxford lectures Edmund clung to the familiar themes of Romantic poetry, war poets, and Thomas Hardy, but found it increasingly difficult to order his thoughts or even to engage in any sustained reading. His nervousness and fear of public failure brought him almost to a state of collapse. (Webb, 318)

After two years he resigned from the post because of ill health. He died of a heart attack at his home, Hall Mill, Long Melford, Suffolk, on 20 January 1974; he was buried at Holy Trinity Church, Long Melford, on 25 January 1974. His wife, Claire Margaret, survived him.

BERNARD BERGONZI

Sources B. Webb, *Edmund Blunden: a biography* (1990) • *DNB* • A. M. Hardie, *Edmund Blunden*, 2nd edn (1971) • *Siegfried Sassoon diaries, 1920–22*, ed. R. Hart-Davis (1981) • *More than a brother: correspondence between Edmund Blunden and Hector Buck, 1917–1967*, ed. C. Z. Rothkopf and B. Webb (1996) • B. Kirkpatrick, *A bibliography of Edmund Blunden* (1979) • S. S. K. Fung and G. H. L. Chu, *Edmund Blunden: a bibliography of criticism* (1983)

Archives Col. U., corresp. and papers • Ransom HRC, corresp., literary MSS, and papers • Royal Society of Literature, letters • University of Iowa Libraries, corresp. and literary MSS | BL, corresp. with Society of Authors, Add. MS 63215 • BL, corresp. with Marie Stopes, Add. MS 58501 • Bodl. Oxf., letters to W. G. Bebbington • Bodl. Oxf., letters to A. H. Buck • Bodl. Oxf., letters to J. L. Hammond • Bodl. Oxf., corresp. with Graham Pollard • Bodl. Oxf., corresp. with Sidgwick and Jackson • Commonwealth War Graves Commission, Maidenhead, corresp. and papers relating to work for Imperial War Graves Commission • CUL, letters to Geoffrey Keynes • Gloucester Public Library, letters to G. Finzi • IWM, letters to H. M. Tomlinson and poems • Keats House, Hampstead, London, letters to Dorothy Hewlett • King's Cam., letters and postcards to G. H. W. Rylands • King's Lond., Liddell Hart C., corresp. with Basil Liddell Hart • NL Scot., letters to Agnes Ethel Mackay • U. Aberdeen L., letters to J. B. Chapman • U. Leeds, Brotherton L., letters to Edmund Gosse • U. Leeds, Brotherton L., letters to Thomas Moult • U. Oxf., letters to Harold Owen • U. Oxf., letters to Susan Owen • U. Reading L., letters to Joy Finzi • U. Reading L., letters to Richard Wheeler • U. Sussex, corresp. with Leonard Woolf • W. Sussex RO, letters to Robert Gittings • Wightwick Manor, Wolverhampton, letters to Lady Rosalie Mander • Yale U., Beinecke L., letters to W. F. Stead | SOUND BL NSA

Likenesses R. Hodgson, pencil drawing, 1921, NPG [*see illus.*] • W. Rothenstein, drawing, 1922, NPG • J. Finzi, pencil drawing, 1952, U. Reading L.; repro. in Webb, *Edmund Blunden* • J. Finzi, pencil drawing, 1953, U. Reading L.; repro. in Webb, *Edmund Blunden* • D. Bland, oils, 1957, University of Hong Kong • J. Finzi, pencil drawing, 1960–64, U. Reading L.; repro. in Webb, *Edmund Blunden* • Y. Carter, drawing, repro. in Rothkopf and Webb, eds., *More than a brother*

Wealth at death £35,381: probate, 15 Aug 1974, *CGPLA Eng. & Wales*

Blunden, Humphrey (*b.* 1609, *d.* in or after 1654), publisher and bookseller, was born on 12 November 1609, the son of Richard Blunden (*d.* 1621?), gentleman, of Chelton, Shropshire. He was bound apprentice on 4 September 1626 to Philemon Stephens, bookseller, and made free of the London Stationers' Company on 22 June 1635. Richard Baxter fondly recalled his acquaintance with Blunden, remarking that he was 'a sober godly, understanding Apprentice' (*Reliquiae Baxterianae*, 1.11). In April 1636 Blunden took out a loan from his company, doubtless using the money to help finance a publishing venture. In the following year he paid for the copyright of his first two publications, James Day's *A New Spring for Divine Poetry* (1637) and *Colloquii inter praecipuos aliquot Germaniae theologos, de conciliandis ecclesiarum evangelicarum dissidiis. Anno MDCXXXI* (1637). Blunden's shop was at The Castle in Cornhill near the Royal Exchange and all his known future imprints bore a variation of this address.

By October 1638 Blunden had been admitted to the yeomanry of the Stationers and in the coming years he became actively involved in company politics. In January 1642 Blunden published one issue of *A Continuation of the True Diurnall of Passages in Parliament* (printed for 'Humphry Blunden' in *Cornhill*). The events surrounding the outbreak of civil war saw his productivity soar and in August 1642 he published *Certain Information from Devon and Dorset: concerning the Commission of Array* (printed for 'H. Blunden', 1642) and the third number of *Speciall Passages and Certain Informations from Severall Places* (printed for 'H. Blunden', 1642); one writer mockingly termed the latter newsbook 'Blunden's Passages' (*Mercurius Civicus*, 25, 1 May–8 June 1643, 40). On 19 August 1644 Blunden signed the Stationers' Company petition to the House of Commons protesting at the 'monopolies' held by royal patent to print English bibles and 'sundry Bookes of generall use' (Stationers' Company, Liber A: letter-book of the Stationers' Company, fol. 149*r*).

During the latter half of the 1640s Blunden entered into partnership with the bookseller John Partridge (*d.* 1649) and the printer Thomas Brudnell to issue the writings of the astrologer William Lilly. On Partridge's death Brudnell presented his executors, the booksellers Philemon Stephens and Luke Fawne, with a bill for £368 18*s.* 0*d.* This included a schedule of expenses incurred in the printing of Lilly's almanac *Merlini Anglici Ephemeris* (13,500 copies in 1646, 17,000 copies in 1647, and 18,500 copies in 1648). The last edition of Lilly's almanac issued by Blunden was for the year 1655. Blunden also published six works by Thomas Vaughan, and may be the H. B. who appended an encomium to 'his ever honour'd' friend's *Magia Adamica, or, The Antiquity of Magick* (1650). Blunden himself was accounted 'an extraordinary Chymist' (*Reliquiae*

Baxterianae, 1.11). He was probably the Mr. Blunden familiar to Samuel Hartlib, who 'hath gotten an Instrument for curing of deafnes from Glauber which hee purposed to apply to his wife, but hee was faine to pay for it 5 lib.' (Sheffield University, Hartlib papers, 31/22/4A), and was doubtless the same Blunden who queried 'some passages' in Johann Glauber's books (Sheffield University, Hartlib papers, 'Ephemerides', Jan–June 1648, 60/3/6A). Baxter, moreover, noted that it was Blunden who 'got Jacob Behmen his Books translated and printed' (*Reliquiae Baxterianae*, 1.11). Indeed, such was Blunden's enthusiasm for that 'deep illuminated man of God' that he 'furnished' Durand Hotham with material for the latter's brief memoir of the German mystic (J. Boehme, *Four Tables of Divine Revelation*, trans. H. B., 1654, sig.H3; D. Hotham, *The Life of Jacob Behmen*, 1654, sig.B2). In all Blunden published ten works by or derived from the writings of Jacob Boehme, several in association with the printer Matthew Simmons. He is most likely the H. Blunden who supplied a prefatory epistle to Boehme's *Four Tables of Divine Revelation* (1654), a work rendered into English by H. B.—either Blunden, a namesake licensed to practise medicine, or Humphrey Blundell (educated in Shropshire and a former pupil of Charles Hotham's) may be identified with this translator's monogram.

In his ephemeris for 1654 Hartlib noted that the servant of one White, a stationer near Aldgate, was 'very active' and 'comes to dwel in Blundens-shop' (Sheffield University, Hartlib papers, 'Ephemerides', 1 Jan–24 April 1654, 29/4/6A). Little else is known of Blunden's activities, though in March 1657 Johann Moriaen, a former minister at Cologne with interests in Helmontian medicine and chemistry, informed Hartlib that Blunden had corresponded with Petrus Serrarius, a millenarian resident in Amsterdam and an enthusiastic student of iatrochemistry and mystical theology. In October 1671 a Mrs Blunden, widow, began receiving money from the Stationers' Company poor fund. Richard Baxter 'very much loved' Blunden, 'who by his Consolotary Letters and Directions for Books, did afterwards do me the Offices of an useful Friend' (*Reliquiae Baxterianae*, 1.11). ARIEL HESSAYON

Sources A. Hessayon, *'Gold tried in the fire': the prophet Theaurau John Tany and the puritan revolution* [forthcoming] · *Reliquiae Baxterianae, or, Mr Richard Baxter's narrative of the most memorable passages of his life and times*, ed. M. Sylvester, 1 vol. in 3 pts (1696) · Sheffield University, Hartlib papers 31/22/4A; 60/3/6A Ephemerides, Jan–June 1648; 29/4/6A Ephemerides, Jan–Apr 1654

Blundevill [Blundeville], **Randulph de**. *See* Ranulf (III), sixth earl of Chester and first earl of Lincoln (1170–1232).

Blundeville, Ranulf de. *See* Ranulf (III), sixth earl of Chester and first earl of Lincoln (1170–1232).

Blundeville, Thomas de (*d.* 1236), bishop of Norwich, was a member of a minor gentry family who held small estates of the honour of Hockering at Deopham and Newton Flotman in Norfolk. His uncle was Hubert de Burgh, the justiciar, and his older brother William served as constable of Corfe Castle. He himself became an exchequer clerk, and by 1225 was constable of the Tower of London. In September 1226 he was appointed dean of the royal free chapel of Tettenhall in Staffordshire, but within a month he was granted custody of the bishopric of Norwich, to which he was elected in October; the temporalities were restored on 21 November, and he was consecrated on 20 December, the day after he was ordained priest. In September 1227 he was one of those sent to Antwerp to meet the imperial ambassadors, but after his elevation, apart from attendance at great councils such as Merton in January 1236, there is little evidence of continued service to the crown outside East Anglia where, for example, he was custodian of Norwich Castle until September 1228.

Within his diocese, the main evidence for Blundeville's activities is provided by a collection of almost a hundred *acta*. He obtained various grants for the bishopric and church of Norwich from Henry III, and was himself generous to the monks of the cathedral priory, who commemorated him as a benefactor. He conducted a visitation of his diocese in 1233, after the papal mandate to the English bishops so to do, and he acted on various occasions as papal judge-delegate. The main themes that emerge from his *acta* include his support of small new Augustinian houses such as Kersey in Suffolk and Spinney in Cambridgeshire; his insistence on the establishment of vicarages in parish churches appropriated to religious communities; and a campaign to extend the ecclesiastical patronage of the bishop by insisting, in return for financial concessions, that monastic patrons should allow him and his successors to choose the parochial clergy nominally presented by the religious. His episcopate saw another round of the long struggle between the diocesan and the men of Bishop's Lynn, this time in 1234 over the making of the mayor. He also battled with the priors of the Norfolk Benedictine houses of Binham and Wymondham over the extent of the obedience and reverence owed by daughter houses of exempt St Albans, and over the respective rights of bishop and priors in parish churches; this was settled amicably by papal judges-delegate. There is some evidence in the records of the king's courts of conflict between royal and ecclesiastical jurisdictions; the bishop's officers were frequently cited to appear at the *curia regis* to answer why they had heard cases in the court Christian which were beyond its competence according to the common law and after a writ of prohibition. In 1234 Blundeville claimed that the local sheriff was releasing to chancery excommunicates, who had been imprisoned on Blundeville's signification, before they had made satisfaction to the church.

Of Blundeville's personality and relationships there is little evidence. His career was obviously fostered by his uncle; his withdrawal from secular government, despite his earlier career in administration, may be explained either by Hubert de Burgh's loss of royal favour from late 1229, or by the opposition of the episcopate in general to the justiciar; but it was to Bishop Thomas's house at Terling in Essex (rather than, as some sources state, Brentwood) that Hubert fled, and whence he was dragged from the altar in September 1232. Some indication of

Blundeville's religious sentiments is provided by his statement in a charter for Christ Church, Canterbury, of his devotion to St Thomas, and even more by his counter-seal, showing a bishop kneeling before the Virgin and Child with the legend *Est Thome signum Virgo*. He died on 16 August 1236 and was buried in his cathedral church.

CHRISTOPHER HARPER-BILL

Sources C. Harper-Bill, ed., *Norwich, 1215–1243*, English Episcopal Acta, 21 (2000) • *Chancery records* • *Curia regis rolls preserved in the Public Record Office* (1922–) • H. W. Saunders, ed., *The first register of Norwich Cathedral priory*, Norfolk RS, 11 (1939)

Likenesses seal, Canterbury Cathedral Archives

Blundeville, Thomas (1522?–1606?), author and translator, was the eldest son of Edward Blundeville (1492/3–1568), of Newton Flotman, Norfolk, and Elizabeth, daughter of Thomas Godsalve. His brother was Jeremy Blundeville of Toft Monks. Suggestions that he was educated at Cambridge remain unsubstantiated; it is possible that he entered Gray's Inn in 1541. Blundeville apparently lived in London for some years before returning to live in Norfolk on the death of his father, aged seventy-five, in 1568, when he inherited the family estate at Newton Flotman. He married twice, first Rose Puttenham in 1554 and second Margaret Johnson of Woodnorton (*d.* 1617) in 1581. With his first wife he had a son, born in 1555 (probably named Anthony although sometimes referred to as Andrew), who was apparently killed in the Low Countries and died unmarried. He had two daughters from his second marriage: Elizabeth (*bap.* 1584) in 1610 married Rowland Meyrick of Gladestry, Radnorshire, son of Sir Gelly Meyrick, and had, among others, one son named Blundeville Meyrick, probably also born in 1610; Patience (*bap.* 1585, *d.* 1639) in 1605 married Robert King of Culpho, Suffolk (who later styled himself Robert King Blundeville).

Thomas Blundeville was the author of a number of works covering matters as diverse as horsemanship, astronomy, and the study of history. Most of his writings are prose, except the *Three Morall Treatises* (1561), which includes two pieces in verse. Two of his works deal directly with horsemanship. *The Fower Chiefyst Offices Belonging to Horsemanshippe* (1565–6) is a substantial and wide-ranging work, discussing such matters as horse breaking, the art of riding, the diet and diseases of horses, and the various offices of the rider, the breeder, and the farrier. It also includes a number of engravings of horse bits and shoes.

Among Blundeville's other interests were mathematics and navigation. He had been a mathematics tutor in the households of Sir Nicholas Bacon and Justice Francis Wyndham for a time, and among his friends were some of the leading mathematicians of the age, including John Dee and Henry Briggs. His navigational writings were principally directed towards young gentlemen, providing instruction on astronomy, maps, and instruments. In *The Theoriques of the Planets* (1602) he describes (with diagrams) the motions of the planets as well as lunar and solar eclipses. In this treatise he also discusses the measurement of latitude and provides engravings of various navigational instruments. Likewise, his *M. Blundevile his Exercises, Containing Sixe Treatises* (1594) considers arithmetic, cosmology, the elements of the earth, and navigation.

Blundeville's other works include a treatise entitled *The True Order and Methode of Wryting and Reading Hystories* (1574). This is the first separately printed English work to deal with the study of history. It not only explains sixteenth-century notions of history, but also anticipates more recent historical views, for instance the relationship between man and the environment. Several of Blundeville's other works were translations—he had, apparently, travelled in Italy, and was able to translate accurately. In *A Very Briefe and Profitable Treatise* (1570) he translated from Italian a treatise originally written in Spanish by Federigo Furio, which had been translated into Italian by Alfonso d'Ulloa. He also translated into English a Latin work by John Sturmius, under the title *A Ritch Storehouse, or, Treasurie for Nobilitye and Gentlemen* (1570).

In 1571 Blundeville erected a monument to his family at the church in Newton Flotman, with effigies of his great-grandfather, his grandfather, and his father, and with a place for his two wives and two daughters. He, too, is buried there, under an effigy representing him in armour, kneeling at a faldstool, on which are lying a book and helmet. Blundeville's will is dated 1605, and it is believed that he died in 1606. He left the bulk of his estate to his wife, Margaret, while his elder daughter, Elizabeth, was to be paid her portion provided she married with her mother's consent. Her bequest was to be made up to £100 when her mother thought this was suitable. Blundeville also left charitable bequests to twenty households in Newton Flotman and Swainthorpe, and £5 to his lawyer and friend Robert Redmayne. He stipulated that pieces of furniture, armour, books, and astronomical instruments were to be left in the house for the use of future generations. A series of suits in chancery show that the implementation of Blundeville's will proved a matter of some contention. It appears that he had initially intended Elizabeth to marry Robert King, but that Elizabeth jilted him and instead married Rowland Meyrick. Blundeville, as a result, permitted King to marry his younger daughter, Patience, and (according to King) granted him the right to bear the name of Blundeville. The contents of the household were fought over for some time, but it appears that Robert King finally established his title to the manor of Newton Flotman; in 1646 he sold the estate to John Burman of Norwich.

TESSA BEVERLEY

Sources A. Campling, 'Thomas Blundeville of Newton Flotman, co. Norfolk, 1522–1606, author and poet', *Norfolk Archaeology*, 21 (1921–3), 336–60 • Cooper, *Ath. Cantab.*, 2.342–4; 3.131 • F. Blomefield and C. Parkin, *An essay towards a topographical history of the county of Norfolk*, [2nd edn], 11 vols. (1805–10), vol. 5, pp. 64–70 • M. A. Farrow and T. F. Barton, eds., *Index of wills proved in the consistory court of Norwich, 1604–1680*, Norfolk RS, 28 (1958), 31 • H. G. Dick, 'Thomas Blundeville's *The true order and methode of wryting and reading hystories, 1574*', *Huntington Library Quarterly*, 3 (1939–40), 149–70 • *IGI* • W. T. Lowndes, *The bibliographer's manual of English literature*, ed. H. G. Bohn, [new edn], 1 (1864), 222–3 • *DNB* • Allibone, *Dict.* •

J. Ames, T. F. Dibdin, and W. Herbert, eds., *Typographical antiquities, or, The history of printing in England, Scotland and Ireland*, 4 vols. (1810–19), vol. 4, 204–5, 221 • W. Rye, ed., *The visitacion of Norffolk … 1563 … 1613*, Harleian Society, 32 (1891), 40–41 • *STC, 1475–1640*, nos. 3142–61, 11488 • E. G. R. Taylor, *The mathematical practitioners of Tudor and Stuart England* (1954); repr. (1984)

Likenesses effigy on family tomb, 1571, probably Newton Flotman church, Norfolk

Wealth at death bulk of estate to second wife; left daughter sum of money, which Blundeville hoped his wife would make up to £100, when she thinks 'most meete'; £5 to friend and lawyer Robert Redmayne; 8*d.* charity to twenty households in Newton Flotman and Swainsthorpe: will, 1 Nov 1605, Campling, 'Thomas Blundeville'

Blunt. *See also* Blount.

Blunt, Alfred Walter Frank (1879–1957), bishop of Bradford, was born in St Malo, France, on 24 September 1879, son of Francis Theophilus Blunt (1837–1881) of the colonial service and his wife, Emily Ellen Hobart Rainsford (*d.* 1911). The second of two sons, with three older half-siblings from a previous marriage, he was educated by his mother after his father's death in 1881, and then at Church Hill preparatory school at Crondall, near Farnham. In 1893 he went to Marlborough College, and then studied classics at Exeter College, Oxford (1897–1901). He studied education for a term before teaching at Wellington College (1902) and taking up a classical fellowship and tutorship at Exeter College. He attended Cuddesdon Theological College, where he was ordained in 1904, and took up a curacy at St John the Evangelist, Carrington, Nottingham, in 1907. Here he ministered energetically to an industrial parish, distinguished himself as an accomplished preacher, and arrived at the conviction, which he held for the rest of his life, that 'The Gospel is intended both for individual redemption and for social amelioration' (Peart-Binns, 50), a statement which explains both his Christian socialism and his willingness to support controversial causes such as women's suffrage. At Carrington, too, under the influence of his bishop, Edwyn Hoskyns, he acquired an enduring sense of the catholicity of the church, and of its relevance to every aspect of individual and social life, and began to publish his first books on the New Testament. On 20 October 1909 he married Margaret (Maggie) Catherine Duke, the daughter of a doctor in the Indian Medical Service.

In 1917 Blunt was appointed vicar of St Werburgh's, Derby, another industrial slum parish. He was offered the bishopric of Worcester in 1930, and after a lively correspondence with the then prime minister, Ramsay MacDonald, about the episcopal residence, Hartlebury Castle, which he regarded as 'a white elephant' (Binns, 83), he refused the offer for private reasons and was appointed bishop of Bradford in 1931. As bishop he appealed to a broad Anglicanism which was both traditionalist and progressive, even-handedly encouraging the Anglo-Catholics in the diocese and reversing some of the strictness of his evangelical predecessor, acting as president of an Anglo-Catholic congress in Bradford in 1934. He continued to

Alfred Walter Frank Blunt (1879–1957), by Walter Scott, 1932

prefer ministry in the slums and youth work to convocation or church assembly meetings. A member of the Christian Social Union since 1907, and a member of the Labour Party since the general strike (1926), Blunt paid unofficial visits to factories and preached widely on unemployment, presiding over clergy conferences on the subject in 1933. He told the diocesan conference in 1936 that 'The Church must preach to the rich of the "deceitfulness of riches"' (Peart-Binns, 178–9), arousing a chorus of protests from tory MPs. Blunt was the author of a number of books. Works such as *The Faith of the Catholic Church* (1936), *Our Need of God* (1937), and *What the Church Teaches* (1942) embodied his social and religious concerns.

The rejection of the 1928 prayer book affected him deeply, confirming his belief in the spiritual autonomy of the church and convincing him of the virtues of disestablishment. It was this conviction which made him the centre of controversy, when, on 1 December 1936, he addressed the Bradford diocesan conference on the coronation of Edward VIII. Bishop Barnes of Birmingham had suggested that there should be no communion service at the coronation in order to allow nonconformists to participate; Blunt argued

> To allow such another measure of covert piecemeal disestablishment is to make the worst of both worlds—to retain the invidiousness, such as it is, of the name of establishment, while losing one by one every item of reality which the term connotes, and abandoning without defence

> any claim which we may make to have a contribution of spiritual grace to offer to the acts of the State. (Peart-Binns, 275)

He added that the sacramental effectiveness of the coronation depended, among other things,

> on the faith, prayer and self-dedication of the King himself; and on that it would be improper for me to say anything except to commend him … to God's grace … We hope that he is aware of his need. Some of us wish that he gave more positive signs of such awareness. (ibid., 277)

Blunt's speech was a plea for the church to accept the spiritual responsibilities, rather than merely the privileges, conferred upon it by establishment at a time when 'Our civilization is in a tottering and unstable condition' (ibid., 278), but his statement unfortunately coincided with revelations in the press about the king's affair with Mrs Simpson, and was widely interpreted as a veiled allusion to it. The king himself regarded Blunt's statement as 'the spark that caused the explosion' (duke of Windsor, 349).

When Sir Richard Acland proposed to the Malvern conference (which brought together 400 Anglican priests and laity in 1941) that the church should condemn 'the present form of private ownership as a stumbling block to the Christian way of life', Blunt was vocal in his support, and when the Beveridge report was published in 1943, he urged the convocation of York to welcome it as a positive solution to problems of poverty and unemployment. In answer to those who accused him of meddling in politics, he responded

> that in the last two centuries the churches in England (and elsewhere) have largely been content to preach only part of the gospel of Christ. They have preached conversion to individuals; they have not preached the Kingdom of God to society. Christ preached both. (Peart-Binns, 187)

He had continued to move to the left politically, advocating communism in wartime, while being deeply critical of the Russian variety of it, leading the *Church Times* editor, Sydney Dark, to praise him as the 'most courageous Churchman of our time', while arousing the indignation of Lord Vansittart. A firm opponent of appeasement and an advocate of British rearmament during the late 1930s, Blunt rejected pacifism, but was also rigidly opposed to the hate campaigns of Vansittartism. In response to a series of broadcasts by Vansittart, later published as *Black Record*, he remarked, 'It would be easy to write a similar Black Record of Britain which would prove that our policy had been sympathetically one of economic grab and exploitation, and that, if the Germans are "butcher birds", the British are harpies' (ibid., 204).

From 1931 onwards Blunt suffered from a series of nervous illnesses which led him to proclaim that 'Life is crucifixion' (Peart-Binns, 242). The perfectionism with which he regarded preaching and liturgy, combined with the constant controversy engendered by his political activism, both took their toll. In 1955 he was compelled to retire after a stroke. His health continued to decline and he died in York on 2 June 1957 and was buried at Calverley. He was survived by his wife. His ministry had been marked by a sincerity which at times made his surname seem singularly appropriate, and while this may have cost him ecclesiastical preferment, it was also true that his faith was thoroughly in keeping with his rebellious nature: 'It is not supreme law which we worship, but God. It is not the Christian character which we imitate, but Christ. And it is in relation to this fact that Christianity justifies itself' (ibid., 66). GILES C. WATSON

Sources J. S. Peart-Binns, *Blunt* (1969) • *CGPLA Eng. & Wales* (1957) • Duke of Windsor, *A king's story: the memoirs of HRH the duke of Windsor* (1951)

Likenesses W. Scott, photograph, 1932, NPG [*see illus.*] • photograph, repro. in Peart-Binns, *Blunt*

Wealth at death £11,626 10*s*. 8*d*.: probate, 27 Aug 1957, *CGPLA Eng. & Wales*

Blunt [*née* King], **Anne Isabella Noel**, *suo jure* **Baroness Wentworth** (**1837–1917**), traveller and breeder of Arab horses, was born on 22 September 1837 in London, the second of the three children, and the only daughter, of William King, first earl of Lovelace (1805–1893) and his wife, Ada King [*see* Byron, (Augusta) Ada (1815–1852)], the only child of the poet Lord Byron and his wife, Anne Isabella Milbanke. Educated privately, Lady Anne, an accomplished linguist, was taught the violin by Joachim and drawing by John Ruskin.

Lady Lovelace, who worked with Charles Babbage on the development of his difference engine, a prototype of the computer, spent little time with her children. Lady Anne was only fifteen when her mother died, and she was brought up mainly under the spartan rule of her grandmother Anne *Noel, Lady Byron. Her austere father took her on continental travels, where she absorbed four languages. During further European travel she met, in Florence, her future husband, Wilfrid Scawen *Blunt (1840–1922), who was then in the diplomatic service. They married on 8 June 1869 and had four children, only one of whom survived, Judith Anne Dorothea (1873–1957), later Baroness Wentworth. Marriage to the erratic Blunt transformed Lady Anne's somewhat sombre life to a hectic tempo: despite his charm and talents, her husband was extremely difficult to live with. His imperious ways and constant infidelities gave her much anguish and eventually led, in 1906, to their separation.

In 1872 Blunt inherited family estates in Sussex. He and Lady Anne designed and rebuilt the house at Crabbet Park, which remains a monument to their talents. With Blunt she travelled extensively in the Middle East: her scientific interests are manifest in the mass of aneroid readings, barometric pressures, and compass bearings in her journal entries of their travels in the Arabian deserts. There she found happiness, and her numerous journals give a fascinating account of their experiences. Written simply as a private daily record, they provide frank insights into every aspect of her life, including her views on the political events in which her husband was involved. They also reveal a woman of remarkable courage and endurance. She converted to Roman Catholicism as a result of a vision experienced when Blunt lay seriously ill in a remote spot during a journey in 1879. She was one of very few women of her time to travel into the heart of the desert. The

Blunts undertook three long journeys, on horseback, taking only a few Arab servants with camels. Her artistic talent is evident in her sketches: whether of desert scenes, Arabs and their animals, town dwellings, or ruined forts, they were executed meticulously. Her superb watercolours capture the spirit of the desert, and exhibitions of her paintings were held in Saudi Arabia and London in 1993; her journals, which are housed in the British Library, were displayed there in 1977.

Lady Anne was heir to a considerable fortune, inherited from the Milbanke family, and it was largely her money that funded the Blunts' travels and the stud they started in 1878. That year, through the British consul in Aleppo, they met Arab sheikhs of famed horse-breeding tribes, and decided to buy Arabian stallions and mares to found a stud in England. This brought an important new dimension into their lives. Their Crabbet Arabian stud, gradually enlarged over the next decade with more desert-bred horses and, later, with the remnants of the famous Abbas Pasha collection in Egypt, became one of the greatest private studs, destined to influence Arabian horse breeding worldwide. The stud survived for nearly a century under the ongoing expertise of Judith, Lady Wentworth, after her mother's death.

In 1882 the Blunts purchased a 37 acre walled garden outside Cairo named Shaykh ʿUbayd, after the saint whose tomb stood in the grounds. They made it their winter home, establishing a second stud there. Lady Anne became fluent in Arabic, and the insights she gained into the people and their customs ensured an encyclopaedic knowledge of the Bedouin and their horses. She also translated original Arab texts, two of which were put into verse by Blunt and published in England. She spent many years compiling a book on Arabian horses, but died just before its completion; happily much of this work is incorporated in the classic work by her daughter, Judith, Lady Wentworth, *The Authentic Arabian Horse* (1945). Two travel books, *The Bedouin Tribes of the Euphrates* (2 vols., 1879) and *Pilgrimage to Nejd* (2 vols., 1881), despite appearing under Lady Anne's name, were not written by her. Purporting to be extracts from her journals, whole sections describing their travels were rewritten by Blunt.

After Lady Anne's separation from her husband in 1906, she rented a house near Crabbet Park, where Judith and her husband, the Hon. Neville Lytton, then lived with their three children. She wintered at Shaykh ʿUbayd where, with a few faithful servants and friends, she felt truly at home, the East having become an integral part of her life. She became Baroness Wentworth on 18 June 1917, having inherited the barony from her niece. Lady Anne died in the Anglo-American Hospital, Cairo, on 15 December 1917, and was buried in the Nun's burial-ground at the Jebel Ahmar. She was held in honour by her many Arab friends, to whom she was 'the noble lady of the horses'.

ROSEMARY ARCHER

Sources *Lady Anne Blunt: journals and correspondence, 1878–1917*, ed. R. Archer and J. Fleming (1986) · R. Archer, C. Pearson, and C. Covey, *The Crabbet Arabian stud: its history and influence* (1978) · E. Longford [E. H. Pakenham, countess of Longford], *A pilgrimage of passion: the life of Wilfrid Scawen Blunt* (1979) · D. L. Moore, *Ada, countess of Lovelace* (1977) · BL, Wentworth Bequest · GEC, *Peerage*

Archives BL, diaries, sketchbooks, and papers, Add. MSS 53817–54155 · Bodl. Oxf., corresp. | Bodl. Oxf., Noel MSS

Likenesses photograph, FM Cam. [*see illus.*]

Blunt, Anthony Frederick (1907–1983), art historian and spy, was born at Holy Trinity vicarage, Bournemouth, Hampshire, on 26 September 1907, the third and youngest son (there were no daughters) of the Revd (Arthur) Stanley Vaughan Blunt (1870–1929) and his wife, Hilda Violet (1880–1969), daughter of Henry Master of the Madras civil service. His brothers, Wilfrid Jasper Walter *Blunt (1901–1987) and Christopher Evelyn *Blunt (1904–1987), were a teacher of art and a numismatist respectively. Blunt's father was a kinsman of the poet, anti-imperialist, and libertine Wilfrid Scawen Blunt, while his mother's family

Anne Isabella Noel Blunt, *suo jure* Baroness Wentworth (1837–1917), by unknown photographer [with Kassida]

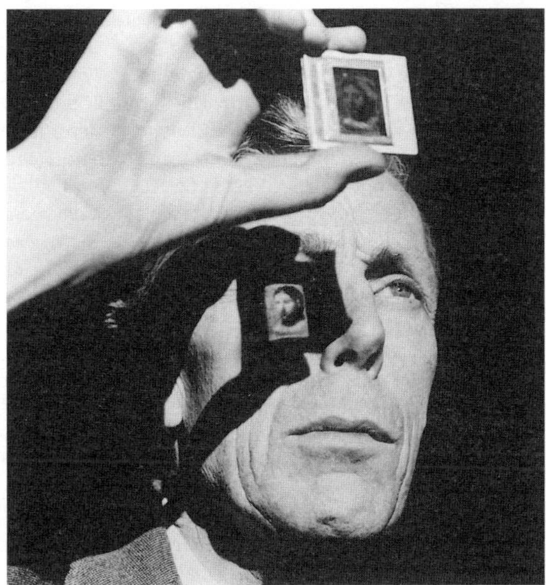

Anthony Frederick Blunt (1907–1983), by Snowdon, 1963

were acquaintances of the future Queen Mary: both these connections were to have a curious significance for Blunt's future career. As a child in Paris, where his father was the British embassy chaplain, Blunt acquired a lasting enthusiasm for French art and architecture, a passion encouraged by his eldest brother, Wilfrid, a future art master at Eton College. By the age of sixteen, at Marlborough College (where with his best friend Louis MacNeice he was part of a group of rebellious young aesthetes), he was producing precociously fluent defences of modern art, much to the infuriation of the deeply conservative art teacher—an early indication of his academic talent and his instinctive contrariness.

Cambridge and the NKVD In 1926 Blunt won a scholarship to Trinity College, Cambridge, graduating there with a second in part one of the mathematical tripos (1927) and a first in both parts (1928 and 1930) of the modern languages tripos (French and German). In 1932 he was elected a fellow of the college on the strength of a dissertation on artistic theory in Italy and France during the Renaissance and seventeenth century; he remained there until 1937. By 1932 he was already writing for the *Cambridge Review* and within a year had become *The Spectator's* regular art critic, a position he held until 1938.

While still an undergraduate, Blunt was invited to join the Apostles. The significance of Blunt's membership of this secret, all-male Cambridge debating society has generally been overstressed. In 1928 its main attraction for him lay in its strong links with Bloomsbury, then at its height as the self-styled cutting edge of avant-garde art and liberal social mores. At school Blunt had adopted Roger Fry's and Clive Bell's ideas on modern art; now through the Apostles he took on Bloomsbury values, which have been summed up as the cult of the intellect for its own sake, belief in freedom of thought and expression irrespective of the conclusions to which this freedom might lead, and the denial of all moral restraints other than loyalty to friends. An influential minority of the society's members were, moreover, like Blunt himself, homosexual at a time when homosexual acts were still illegal in Britain.

In 1933–4 Blunt—hitherto the image of an elegant, apolitical, social young academic—began to take an interest in Marxism under the influence of his friend the charming, scandalous Guy Burgess, a fellow Apostle, who had recently converted to communism. Blunt's move to the left can be plotted in his art reviews, in which he turned from a Bloomsbury acolyte into an increasingly dogmatic defender of social realism. He eventually came to attack even his favourite contemporary artist, Picasso, for the painting *Guernica*'s insufficient incorporation of communism.

According to documents in the Russian intelligence archives, it was just at this time, spring 1937, that Burgess introduced Blunt to the Hungarian former priest Theo Maly, an agent of the NKVD, the precursor of the KGB. Blunt was asked to become a 'talent spotter'—that is, to find students who might be willing to work clandestinely for communism. He recruited two young men, Michael Straight and Leo Long, and sized up a third, John Cairncross, before the entire NKVD London residence was recalled to Moscow and caught up in Stalin's purges in summer 1937.

Blunt's work for the NKVD has sometimes been put down to a sexual passion for Burgess. Certainly he was fascinated by Burgess's outrageousness, which was the antithesis of his own reserved self-discipline, and they may have had a brief sexual affair at the beginning of their long friendship. However, Blunt's attraction to spying was more complex. He possessed a streak of unexorcised rebelliousness. His initial commitment to the left in the 1930s was sincere, though this was combined with an undeniable pleasure in the potential for secrecy and intrigue of his position. In 1939, when the Soviet–Nazi pact destroyed the USSR's claims to champion antifascism, he seems to have suffered no obvious pangs of conscience.

London and MI5 In summer 1937 Blunt left Cambridge to work at the Warburg Institute in London, where he met a generation of Jewish émigré academics who greatly influenced his art history. He performed no further services for Moscow until the NKVD's London resident re-established contact in December 1940 and was amazed to discover that Blunt had joined MI5. With the new demands wartime placed on it, MI5 was drafting in clever academics; Blunt was hired on the recommendation of his old Cambridge friend Victor Rothschild. His main task was to gather information about foreign embassies by planting agents—usually in the guise of domestic servants—and clandestinely opening diplomatic bags. He also worked directly for MI5's most influential officer, Guy Liddell, overhauled its surveillance system, and ran liaison with other secret departments. This brought him into contact with British intelligence's most sensitive secret, Ultra, the information produced at Bletchley Park from the breaking of German military codes.

The question of whether Blunt's actions led to deaths is hard to answer. As MI5's remit was internal security, most of the information to which he had access related to espionage on British soil. On the other hand, for six months before the Nazi invasion of the Soviet Union in June 1941, the USSR was allied to Germany and thus not only an enemy of Britain, but also potentially handing Blunt's information to the Germans, though there is no evidence that they did. Moreover, Blunt was a diligent spy—he brought to it the same conscientiousness that made him a good art historian—and went out of his way to know every area of MI5's work and to pass on everything he came across. The KGB archives have over 1000 documents which he passed, though this hardly compares with the other Cambridge spies: between mid-1944 and the end of the war Burgess passed over 4000 documents. Whether the Soviets took advantage of the material is another complicated question. The KGB (as the NKVD was renamed in 1954) was so inefficient that much material was never translated, and so sure that the Soviet embassy was being watched by MI5 that it took Blunt's accurate assertions to the contrary as lies. It also disapproved of the fact that Blunt and Burgess shared a flat in Bentinck Street famous for its lively parties. Indeed between 1942 and 1944 Russian intelligence became so suspicious of Blunt, Burgess, and Philby that it seriously considered having them assassinated. At the end of the war Blunt left MI5. Thereafter he had few secrets to impart, though he passed gossip from his former MI5 colleagues and documents from Burgess, until the defection of Burgess and Maclean in 1951. Yuri Modin, his controller, tried to persuade Blunt to flee too, but he refused.

Surveyor of the king's pictures and director of the Courtauld Institute of Art All through the war Blunt had continued with his art history; even his Soviet controllers noted that it was the only subject by which he seemed to be really excited. Already before the war he saw that the refugee scholars at the Warburg Institute had brought with them from Hamburg both an intellectual rigour and a soundly based historical method that were new to the study of the art of the past in Britain. In 1937–9 he published scholarly articles in the Warburg *Journal* on diverse topics, including 'The Hypnerotomachia Poliphili in 17th-century France' and Blake's *Ancient of Days*, and began his great work on the seventeenth-century French painter Nicolas Poussin, characteristically with an article showing that Poussin's 'Notes on painting' were not original but were largely copied from obscure ancient and Renaissance literary sources. Blunt also helped to establish friendly relations between the Warburg and Courtauld institutes, becoming deputy director of the latter in 1939. In 1940 most of his fellowship dissertation was published as *Artistic Theory in Italy, 1450–1600*; written with his customary lucidity and stylistic grace, it remains a useful introduction to its subject. During the Second World War he wrote further articles in periodicals and a book on the French architect François Mansart (1941); in 1945 he published a catalogue of the French drawings in the Royal Collection at Windsor Castle.

In the same year, 1945, to the puzzlement of his friends, who knew of his political sympathies though not of his activities as a spy, Blunt accepted appointment as surveyor of the king's (after 1952 the queen's) pictures (a role that later inspired Alan Bennett's play *A Question of Attribution*, 1988). One motive for taking the job may have been to deflect suspicion if one of his fellow spies had been caught: who would suspect a senior royal servant? He also enjoyed being in charge of such an extraordinary collection, and was responsible for professionalizing its care, bringing in restorers and academics to contribute their services, often on a tiny budget. In 1962 he oversaw the opening of the Queen's Gallery. He remained surveyor until 1972, when his deputy, Oliver Millar, who had been doing most of the day-to-day work for many years, took over.

Blunt's appointment has caused much lurid speculation, some of it stemming from a series of trips he made between 1945 and 1947 to Westphalia and Hesse in Germany and Haus Doorn in the Netherlands, to recover a number of objects which the king did not want to fall into occupying hands, American or Soviet. These included the crown jewels of Hanover. The rumour that Blunt rescued from Hesse a series of letters proving the duke of Windsor had made a deal with the Nazis seems quite unfounded.

In 1947 Blunt became director of the Courtauld Institute of Art and professor of the history of art in the University of London. Thenceforth the institute was his home (he had a flat at the top of the building, designed by Robert Adam, in Portman Square) and the centre of his life. In almost every sense he was a superb director. He had a natural authority, an infectious enthusiasm for his subject, and a winning way with students and younger colleagues. Teaching more by example than by precept, he inspired those around him to give of their best. Under him the Courtauld became the principal centre for training art historians in Britain, with a worldwide reputation for excellence. The first phase of Blunt's scholarly career was crowned by a masterly survey in the Pelican History of Art series: *Art and Architecture in France, 1500–1700* (1953). Lucid, penetrating, and comprehensive, this is still the best study of its subject and is perhaps Blunt's single most successful book.

The next dozen years, spent mainly working on Poussin, culminated in the exhibition Blunt curated at the Louvre in 1960 and by his monograph (1967) on the artist, but were marred by his bitter dispute with the art historian Sir Denis Mahon. Mahon claimed, not without some justice, that Blunt had mistaken the chronology of Poussin's paintings and had overstressed the artist's intellectual, at the expense of his visual, qualities. Blunt took this hard, not least because in some sense he identified with Poussin, seeing in the artist qualities which he valued in himself: clarity, scepticism in religious matters, subordination of emotion to reason. At the height of the dispute he appears to have deliberately blocked the reattribution of a lost Poussin that Mahon owned which turned out to be authentic. Nevertheless, Blunt's book, which concentrates on the intellectual content and context of Poussin's work, is still a landmark in modern writing on the artist. His numerous other publications ranged in subject from William Blake to Picasso to baroque architecture, the passion of his later years.

His commitment to his work impelled Blunt to take on more roles: in 1948 he became the National Trust's first picture adviser, put on exhibitions at the Royal Academy, went on foreign lecture tours, edited numerous books, and sat on every influential art committee. He was knighted in 1956, appointed to the Légion d'honneur in 1958, and received a series of honorary fellowships, before retiring in 1974.

Exposure and death Yet all this time Blunt was at risk of exposure as a former spy. He was interrogated frequently by the security services during the 1950s but gave away nothing. Outwardly he seemed utterly in control, ever the composed academic, but his secret took its toll: in 1945 he was hospitalized with exhaustion; from the 1950s he took large doses of seconal and drank a bottle of spirits a day; in 1953 the strain brought on an attack of Bell's palsy which left one side of his face paralysed for several years. Before the war he had been known as an expansive and charming party giver. Now he turned inward, concentrating on his work and the Courtauld. Although those in his field were often surprised by his generosity and kindness, he kept intruders at bay with a practised coldness and those outside his circle could find him unpredictable and arrogant. Despite his acknowledged skills as a lecturer he rejected all invitations to introduce himself to a wider audience through radio and television as Kenneth Clark was to do.

In 1964 Michael Straight confessed to the American Federal Bureau of Investigation that he had been recruited to Soviet intelligence and said he was prepared to testify against Blunt. MI5 offered Blunt immunity from prosecution in return for a full confession. In the later 1970s the pressure mounted again, as a result of investigations by independent writers on espionage relying on information leaked by former security officers. On 15 November 1979 the prime minister, Margaret Thatcher, confirmed in the House of Commons that Blunt had been an agent of, and talent spotter for, Russian intelligence before and during the Second World War, although she added that there was insufficient evidence on which criminal charges could be brought. His knighthood was annulled, as was the honorary fellowship he had held at Trinity College since 1967. He resigned from the Society of Antiquaries at their behest, but a row erupted within the British Academy over his continued membership, many members threatening their own resignation if he was not expelled and many if he was. Its council voted narrowly in favour of his expulsion but the members avoided a vote at the academy's annual general meeting, after which Blunt resigned. The press, radio, and television began a campaign of vilification. Wild rumours accused him of spying for the Germans, of authenticating fakes, of salting away a fortune abroad; he was caricatured as snobbish, imperious, sexually predatory. Blunt outwardly remained cool, completing one book on baroque Rome and starting another on Pietro da Cortona. But the London flat to which he had retired near the Courtauld was besieged by journalists for months. His long-term partner, (William) John Gaskin (1919–1988), attempted suicide. When asked after his exposure how he had managed to survive the strains, Blunt answered, pointing to a glass of whisky, 'With this, and more work and more work' (Margot Wittkower, Interview Transcript, p. 125, Interviews with Art Historians, Getty Research Institute, Research Library 94109).

Undoubtedly some of the agitation was motivated by Blunt's intellectuality and homosexuality as well as by class hatred. It is a striking fact that both Blunt's own actions and the treatment of him not only by the public but also by officials were pervaded at every turn by the class divisions in British society. His career can perhaps best be explained by the fatal conjunction in him of outstanding gifts and a desire to be at once part of the establishment and against it; or, as Sir Isaiah Berlin put it, 'The trouble with Anthony was that he wanted both to run with the hare and hunt with the hounds.' He died of a heart attack at his home, 45 Portsea Hall, Portsea Place, Westminster, London, on 26 March 1983 and was cremated on 30 March at Roehampton, London.

MICHAEL KITSON, *rev.* MIRANDA CARTER

Sources A. Blunt, 'From Bloomsbury to Marxism', *Studio International*, 186/960 (Nov 1973), 164–8 · M. Carter, *Anthony Blunt: his lives* (2001) · L. MacNeice, *The strings are false* (1965) · B. Penrose and S. Freeman, *Conspiracy of silence* (1986) · N. West and O. Tsarev, *The crown jewels* (1998) · C. Andrew and O. Gordievsky, *KGB: the inside story of its foreign operations, from Lenin to Gorbachev* (1990) · P. Wright, *Spycatcher* (1987) · J. Costello, *Mask of treachery* (1988) · E. Waterhouse, introduction, *Studies in Renaissance and baroque art presented to Anthony Blunt* (1967), ix–xi · P. Kidson, 'The recent transformation of art history', lecture, 10 Nov 1995, Courtauld Inst. · N. Annan, 'Et tu Anthony', *New York Review of Books* (Oct 1987), 3–4 · W. Blunt, *Married to a single life* (1985) · W. Blunt, *Slow on the feather* (1986) · *The Times* (28 March 1983) · private information (2004) · d. cert. · *Daily Mail* (31 March 1983) · K. Dover, *Marginal comment: a memoir* (1994) · b. cert. · d. cert. [William John Gaskin]

Archives Courtauld Inst., corresp. and papers | Tate collection, corresp. with Lord Clark | SOUND BBC Sound Archives, Caversham, recordings of art lectures, *c.*1937–*c.*1960

Likenesses photograph, *c.*1925, King's Cam., 'Dadie' Rylands papers · photographs, 1962–80, Hult. Arch. · Snowdon, photograph, 1963, priv. coll. [*see illus.*]

Wealth at death £862,521: probate, 13 Jan 1984, *CGPLA Eng. & Wales* (1984)

Blunt, Christopher Evelyn (1904–1987), merchant banker and numismatist, was born on 16 July 1904 at the vicarage, Ham Common, London, the second of the three sons (there were no daughters) of the Revd (Arthur) Stanley Vaughan Blunt (1870–1929) and his wife, Hilda Violet (1880–1969), daughter of (John) Henry Master of Montrose House, Petersham, London. He was educated at Marlborough College, but, unlike his brothers, Wilfrid Jasper Walter *Blunt, writer and artist, and Anthony Frederick *Blunt, art historian and Soviet agent—both of whom were destined for academic careers—he did not go to university. After a year in Germany and Spain and two years as a trainee accountant, in 1924 he joined the small banking house of Higginson & Co. in London, which later became part of Hill Samuel. There he ultimately became head of corporate finance. Tall, fair, and patrician, he was a distinguished figure in the City for many years. In 1930 he married Elisabeth Rachel (*d.* 1980), daughter of Gardner Sebastian Bazley, barrister, of Hatherop Castle, Gloucestershire; they had a son and two daughters. The family moved from London to Hungerford, Berkshire, in 1944, and in 1952 to Ramsbury Hill, near Marlborough. For most of the war Blunt had worked for Supreme Headquarters, Allied Expeditionary Force, being mentioned in dispatches for his liaison work in the evacuation from Bordeaux in 1940, and he was later engaged in preparations for the Normandy invasion. He was demobilized as colonel, and in 1945 was appointed OBE and the American Legion of Merit.

While at Marlborough, Blunt had met John Shirley-Fox, a leading student of medieval English coins, a subject to which Blunt himself was to devote the greater part of his leisure for the rest of his life. In 1935 he became director of the British Numismatic Society and from 1946 to 1950 was its president. The society, which had acrimoniously spun off in 1903 from the Royal Numismatic Society in order to give more attention to British coins, had lost momentum. Under his leadership its finances were strengthened, its membership increased, and its academic standing established.

From 1956 to 1961 Blunt served as president of the Royal Numismatic Society, finally laying to rest the lingering tensions between the two societies. In 1965 he was elected a fellow of the British Academy—an exceptional distinction for an amateur scholar who had no formal education after his schooling, and one that recognized his leading role in establishing the Sylloge of Coins of the British Isles, a project for publishing fully illustrated catalogues of English coins in major collections in Britain and abroad. A committee was set up in 1953 with Sir Frank Stenton as chairman, the first volume appeared in 1958, and when Blunt died the fortieth was in course of preparation.

Blunt's early numismatic work was devoted to the later middle ages, but after the Second World War his interests turned towards the Anglo-Saxon series, largely neglected in the previous generation. Although increased responsibility in the City and his editorial duties with the *British Numismatic Journal* and the sylloge left relatively little time for his own research, in conjunction with R. H. (Michael) Dolley, appointed to the British Museum coin room in 1951, Blunt soon brought about a fundamental reappraisal of early English coinage. After retirement from Hill Samuel in 1964, he remained a director of Eucalyptus Pulp Mills Ltd and as chairman guided it through the difficulties of the political revolution in Portugal. But he was now able to devote most of his time to numismatics, moving on from the Heptarchic period between Offa and Alfred, on which he had previously concentrated, to the tenth century, during which previously fragmented English coinage gradually became unified. This work culminated in three seminal publications: a magisterial monograph on Æthelstan (1974); for the British Museum, *Athelstan to the Reform of Edgar* (with Marion M. Archibald, 1986), volume five of *Anglo-Saxon Coins*; and *Coinage in Tenth-Century England* (with B. H. I. H. Stewart and C. S. S. Lyon, 1989). Blunt's contribution to English numismatics was exceptional. In addition to his own scholarly achievement, his judgement and diligence as editor had a pervasive influence on the standards of English numismatic literature for half a century. Through hospitality at Ramsbury and extensive correspondence he was able to provide a focus and continuity for a subject in which professional scholars have always been in a minority. Although distressed by revelations about his brother Anthony in 1979 and by the death of his wife, Elisabeth, in 1980, he continued to work productively until a few weeks before his own death at his home at Ramsbury Hill, on 20 November 1987. He was buried at Ramsbury. With the needs of future students in mind, one of his last acts was to provide for his magnificent coin collection (incorporating that of Shirley-Fox, which he inherited in 1939) to be offered to the Fitzwilliam Museum, Cambridge, in lieu of estate duty.

STEWARTBY, *rev.*

Sources D. F. Allen, *British Numismatic Journal*, 42 (1974), 1–9 · H. E. Pagan, *Numismatic Circular* (1988), 3–4 · I. Stewart, 'Christopher Evelyn Blunt, 1904–1987', *PBA*, 76 (1990), 347–82
Archives FM Cam., coin collection
Likenesses A. Eley, medal, 1984
Wealth at death £1,237,944: probate, 6 June 1988, *CGPLA Eng. & Wales*

Blunt, Henry (1794–1843), Church of England clergyman and writer, the son of Henry Blunt and Mary, *née* Atkinson, was born at Dulwich on 12 August 1794 and baptized at the chapel of Dulwich College on the 20th. He was educated at Merchant Taylors' School, London, from 1806, and went to Pembroke College, Cambridge, as Parkin exhibitioner, in 1813. He took his BA degree as ninth wrangler in 1817, and became fellow of his college. He was ordained on his fellowship by William Howley, bishop of London, receiving deacon's orders on 5 July 1818 and priest's orders on 20 December of the same year. After filling preacherships at the Philanthropic Institution, at Park Chapel, Chelsea, and at Grosvenor Chapel, in 1820 he was appointed vicar of Clare in Suffolk, and on 21 December of that year married Julia Ann, *née* Nailer, one of the six daughters of a merchant living in Chelsea. At Clare, in addition to his parochial duties, Blunt took private pupils.

In 1824 G. V. Wellesley (a brother of the first duke of Wellington), then rector of Chelsea, persuaded Blunt to resign his country living to become his curate. This post he filled for six years with steadily increasing fame as a preacher, and when Trinity Church was built in Sloane Street, London, in 1830, he was appointed its first incumbent, becoming a rector on 15 June 1832. So high was the estimation in which Blunt was held that, on Wellesley's resignation in 1832, he was offered by Lord Cadogan, the patron, the mother church of St Luke's, with the understanding that he was to hold the two livings together, with a sufficient staff of curates. This offer Blunt unhesitatingly declined.

In 1835 he was presented by the duke of Bedford to the rectory of Streatham, Surrey. Blunt's health, always delicate, had by that time been completely undermined by the demands of a large London parish, and pulmonary weakness compelled him to pass successive winters at various health resorts, including Rome, Pau, and Torquay. He died in his rectory at Streatham on 20 July 1843, and was buried at Streatham.

Blunt's chief work as a preacher and a writer was done at Chelsea. Here the influence he exerted, especially over the propertied classes, was very great, while the clearness and simplicity of his style made him also acceptable to the labouring classes. Blunt was a staunch evangelical, strongly, but not narrowly, opposed to Tractarianism. His was 'perhaps the most influential congregation in London' (Balleine, 156), but he did not favour interdenominational co-operation. The most popular of his published works were the courses of lectures delivered in successive Lents at Chelsea to crowded audiences on the lives of various leading persons in the Old and New testaments. These were published between 1823 and 1839, and went through many editions. He also published a life of Christ (3 vols., 1834–6), a book on the articles (1835), selected sermons (1837 and 1838), and an *Exposition of the Pentateuch* (3 vols.) for family reading. Three volumes of sermons were published posthumously under the editorship of his old friend the Revd John Brown, of Cheltenham, and passed through a number of editions.

Despite frequent ill health, Blunt was a hard-working parish priest. He started the first Sunday school in Chelsea at the Clock House, and also, amid much ridicule and determined opposition, introduced Bible and communicants' classes. He published the first parish magazine, called the *Poor Churchman's Evening Companion*.

EDMUND VENABLES, *rev.* H. C. G. MATTHEW

Sources Venn, *Alum. Cant.* • G. J. Davies, *Successful preachers* (1884) • D. Lewis, *Lighten their darkness* (1986) • G. R. Balleine, *A history of the evangelical party in the Church of England*, new edn (1933)

Likenesses J. Brown, stipple and line engraving (after R. Fadanza), NPG

Blunt, Sir John, first baronet (*bap.* **1665**, *d.* **1733**), financier and a founder of the South Sea Company, son of Thomas Blunt, a Baptist shoemaker of Rochester, Kent, and Isabella, daughter of Thomas Blacke, yeoman, was baptized at St Nicholas's Church, Rochester, on 24 July 1665. He became free of the Merchant Taylors' Company on 5 March 1689 by apprenticeship to Daniel Richards, scrivener of Holborn. On 16 July 1689 he married Elizabeth Court (*d.* 1708) with whom he had five sons and two daughters. He later married Susannah Tudman, *née* Cradock, daughter of the governor of Bengal (22 December 1713); the couple had no children.

In 1693 and again in 1702 Blunt proposed to the Treasury a new method of public accounting. In 1703 he became secretary of the Sword Blade Bank, originally a chartered stock company for the manufacture of swords, now dealing in forfeited estates, enabling it to become a major creditor of the government. This was a challenge to the Bank of England's near monopoly in funding the national debt.

In 1710 Robert Harley, the new lord treasurer, eager to end the War of the Spanish Succession and to become less dependent on the Bank of England, sought new ways of funding the national debt. His government negotiated with the Sword Blade directors and the result was the founding of the South Sea Company, in which the credit supporting factor (equivalent of the forfeited estates in the Sword Blade) was the Asiento clause in the proposed peace settlement, according to which Britain would be permitted to trade with the Spanish Indies. Blunt and several other Sword Blade partners were in key positions to guide the new company.

The operation, seen by Jonathan Swift as 'the Restoration and Establishment of the Kingdom's Credit' (*Examiner*, 7 June 1711), was successful in the short term: the armed forces were paid without aid from the Bank of England, the war ended, and the company survived the fall of the tories, and the change of dynasty after the death of Queen Anne in August 1714. Yet the Asiento clause had amounted to next to nothing in practice. The company had raised credit but failed in trade.

These moves may be seen as a development of the financial revolution initiated by the Bank of England after its founding in 1694 and displayed more recently by the policies of John Law in Paris. The revolution was the realization that credit, if raised in proportion to accessible wealth and if guaranteed by government, could release the inherent economic resources of a nation. A debt did not necessarily have to be paid in kind or coin, but in stock. As more politicians came to understand this Blunt's competitive eyes were drawn to Paris, where John Law had gained almost complete control of the French economy and national debt. 'As Mr. LAW had taken his pattern from him,' Blunt declared, 'he would now improve upon what was done in France, and out-do Mr. LAW' ('Secret history', 1.406–7). Blunt's proposal in 1719 was apparently that the Bank of England, the East India Company, and the South Sea Company should join in issuing stock to fund the national debt, with control of the Africa trade, Nova Scotia, and part of St Kitts 'as solid supports to the Stock' (Blunt, 18, 20). Discussion with ministers and in parliament reduced Blunt's proposal to a dangerous auction between the South Sea Company and the bank to fund the remaining national debt. The company prevailed at the cost of offering the administration the fantastic sum of £7½ million.

Without the credit likely to have accrued from institutional concurrence, and with no 'solid supports to the Stock', nothing remained but for Blunt to rely on what he did best: short-term manipulation. The '*advancing by all means the price of the stock*', he insisted, 'was the *only way to promote the good of the Company*' ('Secret history', 423). This he achieved by alternating money subscriptions and loans. With the failure of John Law in Paris, the speculators' market moved to London, and between March and August 1720 Blunt successfully carried out this manoeuvre three times, driving the price of the stock up. By 4 August the conversion of the national debt into stock was completed. A rage for speculation had the moneyed part of the country in its grip, but Blunt, who on 17 June had been made a baronet 'for extraordinary services in raising public credit to a height not known before', was less confident than he seemed (ibid., 443; Carswell, 130). Cool customers were starting to sell. On 25 June, Blunt and a few Sword Blade partners formed a new bank into which they paid a large sum. On 13 July Blunt began to buy land. Two days later, even before the final conversion of the debt, the stock began to fall. This was the bursting of the South Sea bubble. A fourth subscription failed to check the trend. As the price of stock plunged widespread loss amounted to a national disaster. In the wake of the crisis Robert Walpole moved forward to power with several well-publicized solutions.

The House of Commons now set up a committee of secrecy to investigate the whole affair. On 23 January 1721 Blunt was taken into custody. To the horror of many he now became a willing key witness to all that had occurred. 'The examination is very strict,' he told a colleague, 'and nothing but the truth will do' (Cobbett, *Parl. hist.*, 7.720). The committee wanted to reward Blunt for his disclosures, but Walpole singled him out for punishment. *The Inventory of Sir John Blunt* showed him to be worth £183,349 10*s.* 8¾*d.* (abstract, p. 3); of this he was allowed to keep £1000, later raised to £5000. In his *True State of the South-Sea Scheme* Blunt defended his record, blamed the Bank of England in driving the company to exploit speculators, and finally accused 'THE DISTEMPER OF THE TIMES, which captivated the Reason of Mankind in General, not only in *England* … who leaving the usual Methods of Labour and Industry … were all tainted with the fond Opinion of being rich at once' (ibid., 41).

Blunt's will, dated 13 February 1732, refers to 'my Estate of above two hundred thousand pounds … most unjustly taken from me by a cruel & unjust Act of parliament'. Nevertheless able to bequeath £13,000 to his family, Blunt died on 21 January 1733 at Bath.

Despite his high-handed methods and 'prophetick stile' Blunt is usually considered an imitative figure by comparison with the great John Law. Each, however, sought to apply the example of the Bank of England in new situations, and each was defeated by 'the distemper of the times'. HOWARD ERSKINE-HILL

Sources J. Blunt, *A true state of the South-Sea-Scheme* (1722) • *The particular and inventory of Sir John Blunt, Bart., one of the late directors of the South-Sea Company* (1721) • T. Janssen (?), 'The secret history of the South-Sea scheme', *A collection of several pieces of Mr John Toland* (1726), 404–47 • J. Redington, ed., *Calendar of Treasury papers*, 3, PRO (1874), 80.4 • 'Wardmote Inquest Book of Cornhill', GL, MS 4069/2, fol. 420 • J. Swift, *The history of the four last years of the queen*, ed. H. Davis and H. Williams (1951) • GEC, *Baronetage* • J. Carswell, *The South Sea Bubble*, rev. edn (1993) • H. Erskine-Hill, *The social milieu of Alexander Pope: lives, example, and the poetic response* (1975) • P. G. M. Dickson, *The financial revolution in England: a study in the development of public credit, 1688–1756* (1967) • will, PRO • *IGI*

Likenesses portrait, BM; repro. in Carswell, *The South Sea Bubble*, pl. 4

Wealth at death £13,000: will, PRO

Blunt, John Henry (1823–1884), ecclesiastical historian and theological writer, was born at Chelsea on 25 August 1823, where he was educated in a private school. For some years after leaving school he was a manufacturing chemist, but in 1850 he entered University College, Durham, intending ordination in the Church of England. In 1852 he became licentiate in theology; he was ordained deacon in 1852 and priest in 1855. In 1855 he became an MA of Durham. After filling a number of curacies he was appointed in 1868 vicar of Kennington, near Oxford, by the warden and fellows of All Souls College. In 1873 he was presented by W. E. Gladstone with the crown living of Beverston in Gloucestershire, which he retained until his death. In June 1882 his university made him a doctor of divinity.

In his earlier years Blunt was a constant contributor to church reviews and magazines, and the author of many pamphlets and sermons. In 1855 his first volume, *Atonement*, was published. He afterwards became a voluminous writer in the fields of theology and ecclesiastical history. His theological dictionaries collected much valuable matter in a convenient form. His *Annotated Book of Common Prayer*, which went through many editions, is still of some value. *The Reformation of the Church of England* (1868) was republished in a variety of formats. It reflects his high-church views. His *Directorium pastorale* (1864) and his *Book of Church Law* (1872) were both standard works for the late Victorian church.

Blunt was a man of great mental and physical energy, and his passion for literary work in all probability hastened his death. He died rather suddenly at 47 St Stephen's Avenue, Shepherd's Bush, London, on 11 April 1884 (Good Friday), and was buried in St Mary's church cemetery, Battersea. At the time of his death he was working on *Cyclopaedia of Religion*, published posthumously (1884), and a dictionary of religion, completed by William Bentham (1887). T. F. TOUT, *rev.* H. C. G. MATTHEW

Sources private information (1885) • Crockford (1884) • *CGPLA Eng. & Wales* (1884) • B. Heeney, *A different kind of gentleman: parish clergy as professional men in early and mid-Victorian England* (1976) • Gladstone, *Diaries*

Archives Bodl. Oxf., copy of *Reformation of the Church of England* with his copious MS additions and corrections, and notes for an article on Wolsey

Wealth at death £532 13*s.* 9*d.*: probate, 22 July 1884, *CGPLA Eng. & Wales*

Blunt, John James (1794–1855), Church of England clergyman and theological writer, was born at Newcastle under Lyme, Staffordshire, in 1794 and baptized on 29 June, the son of the Revd John Blunt (1765/6–1843), master of the local grammar school. No details are known of his mother. He was educated by his father, a former fellow of St John's College, Cambridge, and was admitted a pensioner there in 1812, afterwards securing a scholarship. In 1813 he became first Bell's scholar in the university and was awarded the Browne medal for a Latin ode in the year following, and members' prizes for a Latin essay in 1817 and 1818. His degrees were BA 1816 (fifteenth wrangler),

MA 1819, and BD 1826. St John's elected him to a fellowship in 1816, which he held for twenty years until his marriage. Having been awarded a Worts travelling bachelorship in 1818 Blunt visited Italy and Sicily; since he was required to write an account in Latin to the vice-chancellor of foreign customs and rarities he was fortunate to meet a peasant who related to him anecdotes of Napoleon at the battle of Waterloo. This expedition and further tours in 1820–21 provided materials for *Vestiges of Ancient Manners and Customs Discoverable in Modern Italy and Sicily* (1823), which was translated into German but was not republished.

After his ordination Blunt obtained the curacy at Hodnet in Shropshire under Reginald Heber, and after Heber's appointment to the bishopric of Calcutta in 1822 he remained there for some years under his successor. He later held the curacy of Chetwynd in Shropshire. During these years of parish work he began to write long miscellaneous review articles for the *Quarterly Review* on Heber, Paley, Parr, Milton, Gibbon, and other subjects. He is said to have known Butler's *Analogy* and *Paradise Lost* almost by heart. Academic scholarship was not neglected; he gave the Hulsean lectures at Cambridge in 1831 and 1832, which were published. He held Great Oakley, a rich college living in Essex, between 1834 and 1839, where he rebuilt the parsonage and established the parish school. At Barlaston, Staffordshire, on 14 June 1836, he married Elizabeth Roylance Child, youngest daughter of Baddeley Child of that place; they had two daughters before his wife's early death on 12 April 1841. On 13 January 1852 at Uttoxeter, he married Harriet (1810–1889), second daughter of Thomas Sneyd-Kynnersley of Loxley Park, Staffordshire; they had no children. On 9 May 1839 Blunt was elected to the Lady Margaret chair of divinity at Cambridge and worked conscientiously in that post. Lord Aberdeen, who preferred moderate, uncontroversial churchmen in the House of Lords, offered more than once to appoint him bishop of Salisbury in 1854 but he declined. Joseph Romilly, the university registrary, commented 'Blunt is now looked on as a prodigy by all Clergymen: he is not 60, but considers himself too old for a Bishop'. In truth Blunt's health had begun to fail, and he died of erysipelas at Cambridge on 17 June 1855. He was buried with his first wife at Barlaston on 23 June.

Blunt's publications were successful and widely read for a generation. His most popular book, *A Sketch of the Reformation in England* (1832), went through many editions and was translated into French and German; it was followed in 1837 by *A Sketch of the Church of the First Two Centuries after Christ*, which like much of his work was revised from material originally given in sermons or lectures. His principal series of books on related themes was at the same time old-fashioned and novel, an attempt to widen the application of William Paley's interpretation of scripture on the basis of 'undesigned coincidences'. It underlay his *Veracity of the Gospels and Acts of the Apostles* (1828) and works with a similar theme on the Pentateuch and other Old Testament scripture. They were brought together and revised as *Undesigned Coincidences* in 1847, which reached a sixth edition in 1859 but did not survive the new biblical criticism that was then in the ascendant. For Blunt, 'the truth of Christianity depends upon the truth of its leading facts' (*Essays Contributed to the 'Quarterly Review'*, 1860, 147). His Cambridge lectures on the early fathers appeared in 1840 and 1843, and were reprinted together soon after his death, as were other unpublished lectures, *On the Right Use of the Early Fathers* (1857) and *A History of the Christian Church during the First Three Centuries* (1856). His pieces in the *Quarterly Review* were collected in one volume in 1860.

As early as 1832 Blunt had published on the role and duties of the Anglican clergy and this subject was considered in *Acquirements and Principal Obligations and Duties of the Parish Priest* (1856), which was based on his Cambridge lectures. Although he could draw on wide experience for this work it soon became obsolete, not simply because of its donnish tone but because the book presupposed a readership of university-educated country clergy (it recommended extensive reading for the preparation of sermons), whose parishioners were mostly agricultural workers: the industrial revolution and problems of the church in large cities might not have existed. Yet the Cambridge authorities during Blunt's time as professor were more aware than before of the need for a formalized training of the Anglican clergy, and (although he disliked the compulsory element enforced towards the end of his life) his teaching was well thought of. His schedule of lectures from 1840 appears in *Two Introductory Lectures* (1856 edn, xiii–xiv). An obituarist wrote that 'It was by his lectures that he was principally known; and by their means the influence of a sound judgment and reasonable allegiance to the Church of England were spread through the land' (*Clerical Journal*). At second-hand Blunt's influence was carried through the empire. A moderate high-churchman, he eschewed overt theological controversy and, while his studies of the early church did not lead him to adopt Tractarian views, nor did they bring him to understate the place of tradition in its usages. Yet his writings and teachings were essentially polemical, since they expressed a conviction that the English church of the Reformation was consonant with early Christianity and that the contemporary church should seek to emulate both. In academic life he was conservative and voted against attempts to admit dissenters to Cambridge degrees. Writing in 1854 E. H. Browne detected a falling off in Blunt's influence, 'perhaps that he is older … but more it may be, because he is not quite up the age. The theology of the day is not the theology of fifteen years ago' (Kitchin, 228–9).

JOHN D. PICKLES

Sources W. Selwyn, 'Memoir', in J. J. Blunt, *Two introductory lectures on the study of the early fathers*, 2nd edn (1856), v–xii • review, *QR*, 104 (1858), 151–70 • G. J. Davies, *Successful preachers* (1884) • G. W. Kitchin, *Edward Harold Browne* (1895), 169, 228–9 • *Clerical Journal* (23 July 1855), 329 • *Cambridge Chronicle and Journal* (17 April 1841) • *Cambridge Chronicle* (23 June 1855) • notes about J. J. Blunt, St John Cam. • J. A. Jeremie, *A sermon [on 1 Peter v. 2, 3] preached … on Sunday, July 1st on the occasion of the death of the Rev. J. J. Blunt* (1855) • *N&Q*, 3rd ser., 2 (1862), 109 • *Romilly's Cambridge diary, 1848–1864*, ed. M. E. Bury and J. D. Pickles (2000) • *Christian Remembrancer*, 5 (1823), 229–33 • *IGI* •

GM, 2nd ser., 20 (1843), 327 · Burke, *Gen. GB* (1952) · *The Guardian* (16 Jan 1889)

Archives CUL, commentary on Tertullian · LPL, lecture notes
Likenesses J. A. Vinter, lithograph, NPG

Blunt, Wilfrid Jasper Walter (1901–1987), teacher of art and writer, was born on 19 July 1901 at the vicarage, Ham (near Richmond, Surrey), the eldest of the three sons of the Revd (Arthur) Stanley Vaughan Blunt (1870–1929) and his wife, Hilda Violet Master (1880–1969). One brother, Christopher Evelyn *Blunt (1904–1987), achieved distinction as a numismatist, the other, Anthony Frederick *Blunt (1907–1983), as an art historian and spy. All three gained scholarships to Marlborough College. Wilfrid was a pupil from 1914 to 1920, in his opinion five years of imprisonment; he had an aversion to athletics. He entered Worcester College, Oxford, in 1920 but in March 1921 gladly forsook Oxford to become an art student at the Atelier Moderne in Paris. In January 1922 he became a student at the engraving school of the Royal College of Art, London, gaining the degree of associate of the Royal College of Art (ARCA) in 1923. Despite the much appreciated kindness and hospitality of Sir William Rothenstein, in whose home he met many distinguished people, Blunt did not enjoy the college very much; he preferred to spend his time in the Victoria and Albert Museum, and he painted as a hobby.

In August 1923 Blunt was invited, much to his surprise, to become art master at Haileybury College, Hertfordshire. He stayed there fifteen years, introducing pottery as a school subject. Music became an avocation; he had a fine baritone voice and often sang publicly. In 1933, he was granted a year's leave of absence to train as an opera singer in Munich and visit Italy. Although he gave a song recital at the Wigmore Hall, London, he decided that he was 'ill suited, both by temperament and by my total incompetence as an actor, to the operatic stage' (Blunt, *Married*, 274). Nevertheless this year in Germany and Italy enriched him intellectually. He returned to the security of teaching at Haileybury but found conditions by no means so pleasant and congenial as before: the somewhat tyrannical Canon E. F. Bonhote had replaced the easy-going John Talbot as master of Haileybury. His autobiography *Married to a Single Life, 1901–1938* (1983) describes this Haileybury period.

In 1937 an aunt, who knew a retired Eton housemaster, told Blunt that the post of second drawing master at Eton College was about to become vacant. He wrote to the headmaster, Claude Elliott, and got the job. Thus began a happy and creative period which extended beyond his retirement in 1959. He enjoyed teaching boys at Eton as at Haileybury, a consequence, as he admitted frankly, of a homosexual tendency scrupulously and firmly controlled and sublimated, and he found much friendship there, even though he has been described as being at both schools 'a gangling, eccentric misfit, protected only by his amiability and his sense of the absurd' (*The Independent*). The second volume of his autobiography, *Slow on the Feather … 1938–1959* (1986), describes this Eton period. When asked by a friend about this odd title, Blunt explained that 'it means "rowing badly" or, more generally, totally incompetent at every form of sport, me in a nutshell' (personal knowledge).

At Haileybury, having become interested in the architect William Wilkins (1778–1865), who had designed the college in 1806, Blunt published privately in 1938 *The Haileybury Buildings*. Of this he later wrote: 'I had no illusions about it; it was very badly written, for nobody had taught me to write' (Blunt, *Married*, 293), despite a Marlborough education. This deficiency he overcame so successfully that from the early 1940s onwards writing had become a passion and by 1959, the year of his retirement, he had published eight books. One, the very successful *Art of Botanical Illustration* (1950, new edition 1994), had an odd beginning. An editor of the New Naturalist series asked Blunt to write such a book, another asked W. T. Stearn. Neither author then knew the other. However, their collaboration resulted in a better, more balanced reference book than either could have achieved alone. It also began another of Blunt's lasting friendships.

Ultimately, between 1947 and 1989, Blunt published twenty-seven books, all entertaining, light-hearted, well-written, and meticulously researched. They were products of extensive reading and much travel, for he enjoyed both composition and ferreting out information. He became ever on the look-out for a subject about which he could write a book and his interests were certainly wide. His biographies dealt with people as diverse as ʿAbd al-Kader (*Desert Hawk*, 1947), Mawlay Ismaʿil (*Black Sunrise*, 1951), John Christie (*John Christie of Glynbourne*, 1968), Ludwig II of Bavaria (*The Dream King*, 1970), Carl Linnaeus (*The Compleat Naturalist*, 1971), and Felix Mendelssohn (*On Wings of Song*, 1974). His eastern travels resulted in *A Persian Spring* (1957), *Isfahan, Pearl of Persia* (1966), *The Golden Road to Samarkand* (1973), and *Splendours of Islam* (1976). Nearer home are *The Ark in the Park* (1976), on the London Zoo, and *In for a Penny* (1978), on the Royal Botanic Gardens, Kew, both essentially anecdotal like his other books. At Eton he promoted italic handwriting, on which he published *Sweet Roman Hand* (1952). Two sumptuously illustrated folio works are *Captain Cook's Florilegium* (1973) and *The Australian Flower Paintings of Ferdinand Bauer* (1976), both in collaboration with W. T. Stearn. *The Illustrated Herbal* (1979) was the joint work of Blunt and Sandra Raphael. His one excursion into fiction, *Of Flowers and a Village, an Entertainment for Flower Lovers* (1963), purports to be gossipy letters, mostly on botanical odds and ends, from one godfather Wilfrid Sharp to his god-daughter Flora.

On retiring from Eton in 1959 Blunt had the good fortune to be appointed curator of the Watts Gallery, Compton, near Guildford, Surrey. This involved little curatorial work and gave him ample leisure for the pleasure of writing. He loved flowers and gardens, provided somebody else tended them; he disliked such physical exertion. He retired in 1983 but the trustees permitted him to continue to live in the curator's house until his death. He died of cancer in the Royal Surrey County Hospital, Guildford, on 8 January 1987.

Wilfrid Blunt was a tall, good-looking man, lanky in

youth but portly with age, genial and witty, with a mischievous sense of humour, throughout his life well liked by pupils, colleagues, and friends, of whom he had many. He never married. WILLIAM T. STEARN

Sources W. Blunt, *Married to a single life: an autobiography, 1901–1938* (1983) · W. Blunt, *Slow on the feather: further autobiography, 1938–1959* (1986) · *WWW* · *The Times* (12 Jan 1987) · *The Independent* (13 Jan 1987) · *Daily Telegraph* (11 Jan 1987) · personal knowledge (2004) · b. cert.

Likenesses photograph, repro. in Blunt, *Married to a single life*, frontispiece · photographs, repro. in Blunt, *Slow on the feather*, frontispiece, 192, 243, 254

Wealth at death £427,135: probate, 3 April 1987, *CGPLA Eng. & Wales*

Blunt, Wilfrid Scawen (1840–1922), hedonist, poet, and breeder of Arab horses, was born at Petworth House, Sussex, on 17 August 1840, the second son of the three children of Francis Scawen Blunt (1790–1842) of Crabbet Park, Poundhill, and Newbuildings Place, Southwater, Sussex, and his wife, Mary (1806–1855), daughter of John Chandler, squire and rector of Shipley, Surrey. The Blunts had been Sussex landowners for 300 years, and what Wilfrid called the 'manly' side of his nature came from his Sussex background ('Secret memoirs'). His widowed mother sent Wilfrid and his elder brother, Francis, aged seven and eight, away to Twyford preparatory school, where they were always hungry, scavenging for nuts and orange peel on the downs. Why did they not complain? Like all 'oppressed peoples', Wilfrid wrote, they did not realize that their misery could be alleviated by radical change. For the rest of his life Wilfrid knew which side he was on—that of the weak.

In 1851 Blunt's mother joined the Roman Catholic church, taking her children with her. She died of tuberculosis when Wilfrid was fifteen. During his education at Stonyhurst and Oscott colleges, Blunt spent his holidays in Surrey with Henry Currie, the banker—his guardian and great-uncle—or in London with his other guardian, Lady Leconfield, and his fashionable Wyndham cousins. If his world politics were to be radical, his domestic creed was always tory.

Blunt entered the diplomatic service in 1858, serving for eleven years in Europe and South America as secretary of legation. At Athens (1859) he bought an ancient white stallion and galloped about, feeling himself a Byronic hero (his father had fagged for Byron at Harrow School). At Frankfurt (1860) the young attachés argued over the problems of Charles Darwin and his evolutionary theories, rather than Schleswig-Holstein, and Blunt's religious faith was shaken. At Madrid (1862) he took a mistress, Lola, who encouraged him to practise bull fighting, and in Paris (1864) he nearly captured the ambassador's daughter. In Lisbon (1865) he became close friends with Robert Lytton, the future governor-general of India, but on holiday in Bordeaux he 'enjoyed the least decent period' of his life ('Secret memoirs') as the young lover of Catherine *Walters, the notorious courtesan Skittles. They revelled in each other's beauty; Wilfrid had chestnut hair and dark, flashing eyes. This affair led to a variety of romances, some of them celebrated in Blunt's poetry (Skittles was

Wilfrid Scawen Blunt (1840–1922), by Elliott & Fry

Esther in his *Sonnets and Songs by Proteus*, 1875). A critic whom John Murray, Byron's publishers, consulted about publishing Blunt reported that his poetry was of a vintage 'truly of the grape, not of the gooseberry' (Longford, 104). In Buenos Aires (1867) Blunt had a half-Indian mistress, Anita, and at Bern (1869) it was the wife of a prominent English resident who seemed to be his long-sought ideal love. He was to become a self-confessed hedonist, writing in old age,

Pleasure is duty, duty pleasure
In equal measure.
(*Poetical Works*, 2.8)

But though he declared that love was to him what a dram was to a drinker, he later pursued only liaisons that were compatible with his social position. That meant no more Lolas or Anitas, but was to involve, embarrassingly, several of his relatives.

In 1869 Blunt began a *vita nova*, and on 8 June married Byron's granddaughter, Lady Anne Isabella Noel King (1837–1917) [*see* Blunt, Lady Anne Isabella Noel, *suo jure* Baroness Wentworth] daughter of William, first earl of Lovelace, and Ada Byron. Now a rich man, Blunt left the diplomatic service, his marriage seeming to underline the Byronic traits in his character. The death of his brother and beloved sister Alice from tuberculosis in 1872 destroyed his last vestiges of religious faith, but left him squire of Crabbet Park and Newbuildings. Next year the Blunts' only surviving child was born, Judith Anne Dorothea. Soon afterwards the couple departed on the desert travels that were to build their joint reputations for courage and expertise. After riding through Turkey, Algeria, Egypt, Palestine, Syria, and Arabia, with a visit to the Lyttons at Simla, they founded their admired Crabbet Arabian stud, having purchased in Aleppo in 1878 the purebred Arab stallion, Kars, for £69. In the same year Blunt published *Proteus and Amadeus*, a religious dialogue in which Proteus (Blunt) asked, 'Has God got a smell?' His publisher changed 'smell' to 'scent'.

At forty Blunt had entered full manhood—according to his analysis, youth being for feeling, age for meditation, and manhood for battle. In England he began another *vita nova*, this time in active politics, his aim being to make England liberate and regenerate Islam. He met the prime minister, W. E. Gladstone, whom he tried to interest in an Arabian, instead of an Ottoman, caliphate. When next in Cairo in 1881, the Blunts bought the exquisite little estate of Shaykh ʿUbayd, and when the Egyptian nationalist leader, Arabi Pasha, seized the khedive Tawfiq's palace in a bloodless revolution against the Turks, the Blunts and their Irish friend Lady Gregory returned to London to put Arabi Pasha's case. Blunt was able to use his diplomatic contacts and his friendship with E. W. Hamilton, Gladstone's private secretary, to gain access to the prime minister. Initially he had considerable success in persuading Gladstone to pursue the goal of 'Egypt for the Egyptians', but other forces prevailed; by May 1882 Hamilton felt that 'Blunt and all his enthusiasm for the "National" party in Egypt has been shown up' (Gladstone, *Diaries*, 10.lxviii, n.). Blunt became *persona non grata* in Downing Street, Alexandria was bombarded, Egypt occupied, and Arabi exiled. But rarely has an anti-imperialist come so close to preventing an imperialist act. When Blunt denounced European imperialism, he was in turn denounced as only another Arabi in a frock coat. Banned from Egypt, Blunt retaliated by publishing *The Wind and the Whirlwind* (1883), a poem that depicted the British empire's fall:

> Thou hast thy foot upon the weak. The weakest
> With his bruised head shall strike thee on the heel.

Blunt revisited India in 1883–4, writing *Ideas about India* (1885) and preaching reform; but an Arab horse he bought and called Reformer died. Also in 1885 he stood for parliament as a tory democrat supporting Irish home rule, and was defeated in Camberwell North. His vanquisher, wrote Blunt, would do no good but simply show off as an MP among his 'fellow grocers' ('Secret memoirs'). He fought Kidderminster for the Liberal home-rulers in 1886, but lost by 285 votes. He even dared to take the chair at a political meeting in Sussex for a Liberal, thereby causing tory friends to boycott his literary Crabbet Club and annual tennis weekend. On 25 October 1887 he chaired an anti-eviction meeting in Woodford, co. Galway, that had been expressly banned by Arthur Balfour, the Irish chief secretary, whose new Crimes Bill was designed to crush home rule. Blunt was arrested, tried, and imprisoned, first in Galway gaol then in Kilmainham, Dublin, from 3 January to 6 March 1888. Meanwhile he stood as an anti-coercion candidate for Deptford, losing by 275 votes. In 1889 he published a prison sonnet sequence called *In vinculis* ('In chains').

Blunt's friend Oscar Wilde said that Balfour's act had changed Blunt from a clever rhymer into a deep-thinking poet. Wilde and George Curzon both attended the Crabbet Club weekend in 1891, conducting a ferocious verbal duel after dinner. At dawn the younger guests dived into the lake before playing nude tennis, Blunt, sitting cross-legged and dressed in pink and green pyjamas, watching impassively from Anne's bedroom balcony. Blunt took his revenge on Balfour when, in an exotic seduction in the desert, he made his cousin Mary Elcho [*see* Charteris, Mary Constance], Balfour's Egeria, his 'Bedouin wife' when she visited Blunt at Shaykh ʿUbayd ('Secret memoirs'). As a result, Mary had a daughter by Blunt, Mary Pamela Madeline Sybell Charteris (1895–1991), and a son by her unfaithful husband, in consecutive years. The nineties saw Blunt's hedonism in its last and most extravagant phase, when he could name as the objects of his romance women such as Lady Gregory, the virginal Margot Asquith, Lady Blanche Hozier (though Blunt was not the father of Clementine Hozier, later Churchill), Lady Margaret Sackville, and Dorothy Carleton (Percy Wyndham's niece).

Blunt kept a diary for much of his adult life, parts of which he published in *The Secret Occupation of Egypt* (1907), *India under Lord Ripon* (1909), *Gordon at Khartoum* (1911), and *My Diaries* (2 vols., 1919–20). The diary, which itemizes Blunt's sexual exploits in considerable detail, including the names of his conquests, was deposited in the Fitzwilliam Museum, Cambridge; it was opened in 1972, fifty years after his death, and forms a chief source for *A Pilgrimage of Passion* (1979) by Elizabeth Longford.

Old age and the new century brought ill health rather than meditation. In 1906, after Blunt installed his nurse, Miss Lawrence, at the head of his table and adopted Dorothy Carleton as his 'niece', his long-suffering wife, Anne, left him and the stud was divided. In 1910 he refused a prostate operation, influenced by Bernard Shaw's *Doctor's Dilemma*. An invalid throughout his last twelve years, he counted among his friends the Bellocs, the Winston Churchills, Roger Casement, St John Philby (father of Kim), the Meynells, the dying Francis Thompson, Father Vincent McNabb, and a group of important young poets. On 18 January 1914 a peacock was culled from the Newbuildings flock for roasting and Blunt was entertained in his famous Arab robes at the Peacock Dinner (lunch) by, among others, W. B. Yeats, Ezra Pound, and Richard Aldington. Blunt was the first poet, they agreed, to relate poetry to real life; Pound wrote of his 'unconquered flame' (Longford, 406).

Lady Anne died in Egypt of dysentery on 15 December 1917, having (by his account) been reconciled with Wilfrid in May. But her will was disputed; a bitter lawsuit followed over the stud's ownership, which Blunt lost to his daughter, Judith, and her children, Anthony, Anne, and Winifred Lytton, in 1920. Wilfrid and Judith made peace a month before his death at Newbuildings Place on 10 September 1922. Buried in his own Sussex woods, he was acclaimed by E. M. Forster for *My Diaries* as 'an English gentleman of genius' and '*enfant terrible*' of politics (Longford, 418).

Blunt had struck reverberating blows against imperialism. His most memorable line of poetry on the subject comes from *Satan Absolved* (1899), where a cynical devil explains to the Almighty that, 'The white man's burden, Lord, is the burden of his cash' (*Poetical Works*, 2.254). Blunt thus stands Rudyard Kipling's familiar concept on its head, arguing that the imperialists' burden is not their moral responsibility for the colonized peoples, but their urge to make money out of them.

ELIZABETH LONGFORD

Sources W. S. Blunt, 'Secret memoirs', FM Cam. • E. Longford [E. H. Pakenham, countess of Longford], *A pilgrimage of passion: the life of Wilfrid Scawen Blunt* (1979) • Earl of Lytton, *Wilfrid Scawen Blunt: a memoir* (1961) • E. Finch, *Wilfrid Scawen Blunt, 1840–1922* (1938) • W. S. Blunt, *My diaries: being a personal narrative of events, 1888–1914*, 2 vols. (1919–20) • W. S. Blunt, *The poetical works of Wilfrid Scawen Blunt: complete edition*, 2 vols. (1914) • W. S. Blunt, *The land war in Ireland: being a personal narrative of events* (1912) • N. Lytton, *The English country gentleman* (1925) • M. Egremont, *The cousins: the friendship, opinions and activities of Wilfrid Scawen Blunt and George Wyndham* (1977) • J. Wentworth, *The authentic Arabian horse* (1945) • Gladstone, *Diaries* • d. cert. • personal knowledge (2004)

Archives BL, corresp. and papers, Add. MSS 53817–54155 • FM Cam., corresp. and papers • PRO, corresp. relating to Egypt, FO 633 • W. Sussex RO, corresp. and papers • W. Sussex RO, family and estate papers | BL, letters to T. H. S. Escott, Add. MS 58775 • BL, corresp. with W. E. Gladstone, Add. MS 44110 • BL, letters to Sir Edward Walter Hamilton, Add. MS 48619 • Bodl. Oxf., corresp. with Lord and Lady Anne Blunt • Bodl. Oxf., letters to Sir William Harcourt • Bodl. Oxf., letters to Gilbert Murray • Castle Howard, Yorkshire, letters to the ninth countess of Carlisle • Cumbria AS, Carlisle, letters to Lord Howard of Penrith • Dartmouth College, Hanover, New Hampshire, letters to R. B. Cunninghame Graham • Harvard U., Houghton L., letters to Wilfred Meynell • Herts. ALS, letters to earl of Lytton • NL Ire., corresp. with John Redmond • PRO, corresp. with Lord Cromer, FO 633 • St Ant. Oxf., Middle East Centre, letters to Philby and memo relating to Mesopotamia • TCD, corresp. with John Dillon • U. Reading L., letters to Sophie Singleton

Likenesses Bassano, carte-de-visite, *c.*1870, NPG • Maull & Fox, carte-de-visite, *c.*1870, NPG • Lady Anne Blunt, portrait, 1881, priv. coll.; repro. in Longford, *Pilgrimage of passion* • T. Ellis, etching, 1883, NPG • H. Holiday, pencil sketch, 1887, NG Ire. • photograph, 1888, FM Cam.; repro. in Longford, *Pilgrimage of passion* • photograph, 1914, FM Cam.; repro. in Longford, *Pilgrimage of passion* • Ape [C. Pellegrini], chromolithograph caricature, NPG; repro. in *VF* (31 Jan 1885) • Elliott & Fry, two photographs, NPG [*see illus.*] • E. Walker, photograph (after carte-de-visite), NPG • sepia photograph, NPG

Wealth at death £78,364 4*s*. 8*d*.: probate, 7 Feb 1923, *CGPLA Eng. & Wales*

Blyden, Edward Wilmot (1832–1912), advocate of pan-Africanism, was born on 3 August 1832 on the island of St Thomas (then under Danish rule) in the West Indies. He was the third of the seven children of Romeo Blyden, a tailor, and his wife, Judith, a schoolteacher. He later

Edward Wilmot Blyden (1832–1912), by unknown photographer

claimed that his background was of 'pure Negro' parentage from the Igbo people of eastern Nigeria (Lynch, 3). Edward Blyden was, however, brought up in a largely Jewish and English-speaking community, and with his family attended services of the integrated Dutch Reformed church. In 1842 the Blydens moved to Venezuela, returning about 1845. Influenced by the Revd John P. Knox and his wife, Edward Blyden applied in 1850 to Rutgers Theological College, USA, but was rejected because of his colour; but he remained in the USA with the Knoxes. He met a number of religious leaders involved in the African Colonization Society. Encouraged by them, he went to Monrovia, in recently independent Liberia. There he became a lay preacher in 1853, and soon after a tutor at Alexander high school.

In 1856 Blyden published his first pamphlet, *A Voice from Bleeding Africa*, and married Sarah Yates, the mixed-race niece of G. P. Yates, vice-president of Liberia. The marriage was not happy, Blyden blaming this on his wife's loyalty to the mixed-race community, of which he became a 'fanatical opponent' (Lynch, 39); there may also have been other sources of discord. The Blydens had three children. Blyden was ordained a Presbyterian minister in 1858, being promoted at the same time to be principal of the high school. He conducted a considerable correspondence with prominent people in English-speaking countries, among them W. E. Gladstone, who advised him on classical studies and sent him books on Homer. In 1861 Blyden was appointed Liberian educational commissioner, travelling to the USA and Britain on a tour to lecture, fund-raise, and encourage African-Americans to emigrate to Liberia. In Britain he met Gladstone and other prominent persons, Gladstone offering to support him at a British university. Blyden turned down the offer and on his return to Liberia taught classics at Liberia College. He served as secretary of state from 1864 to 1866, but in 1871 left Liberia for Sierra Leone after a quarrel with Edward James Roye, the new president and hitherto his friend, over an expensive British loan to Liberia (Blyden was declared innocent of the charge of adultery with Roye's wife). He was able after Roye's death to return to Liberia again to head the high school, and from 1877 to 1879 was Liberian minister in

London. He was disappointed at his failure to gain financial support for his country. He was minister of the interior in 1880–82 and again president of Liberia College in 1880–84. Once more in exile in Sierra Leone, he ran unsuccessfully for the presidency of Liberia in 1885. He was again minister in London in 1892, and was special envoy in Paris and London in 1905. From 1906 to 1910 he was director of Muslim education in Sierra Leone. His health deteriorating, he was operated on for an aneurysm of the knee in the Royal Southern Hospital, Liverpool, in 1909. The Colonial Office arranged a pension of £25 in 1910 (subscribed by the governments of Sierra Leone, Lagos, and the Gold Coast). Blyden died in Sierra Leone, at his home in Rawden Street, Freetown, on 12 February 1912; his coffin was carried by Muslims to the graveyard at Freetown racecourse, where he was given a Christian burial.

Throughout his life Blyden published widely on race and pan-Africanism. In the Liberian context his views were highly controversial because his concept of the 'negro' largely excluded people of mixed heritage. His hope was that 'pure negroes' would return to Africa and provide an educated élite to lead the continent to freedom. He encouraged Christian–Muslim understanding in Africa. Disappointed by the failure of African-Americans to return to west Africa to provide leadership, he came to see European expansionism as a necessary phase in African development. He consequently supported British expansionism in west Africa, hoping that Sierra Leone would develop into a major west African state. He preferred Britain's localist approach to government in Africa, and strongly opposed the French policy of seeing African territory as an integral part of French government and culture. Blyden worked with Mary Kingsley to encourage a better British understanding of African social systems. He was himself a strong defender, in principle as well as practice, of polygamy. From 1876 he lived with Anna Erskine (a black schoolteacher from Louisiana), though still married and spasmodically living with Sarah, from whom he never formally separated; this probably prompted his resignation from the Presbyterian church in 1886.

Blyden's collected articles, *Christianity, Islam and the Negro Race* (1886), with an introduction by Sir Samuel Lewis, created a considerable impact, being published just after the Berlin conference which arranged the partition. In all he published some twenty-nine books and pamphlets. Blyden was important in Africa as a person articulating many of its future concerns, both accepting the imperial phase and already looking past it. In Britain he represented African intelligence of a high order, with an imposing physical presence, at a time when a sense of racial superiority was in danger of becoming instinctive.

H. C. G. Matthew

Sources H. R. Lynch, *Edward Wilmot Blyden* (1970) • A. Deniza, *Blyden* (1923) • J. O. Cole, *Edward Wilmot Blyden* (1935) • W. Moses, *The golden age of black nationalism, 1850–1925* (1978) • Gladstone, *Diaries* • W. Azikiwe, *Liberia in world politics* (1934) • J. D. Hargreaves, *Life of Sir Samuel Lewis* (1958) • K. Welch, 'Blyden, Edward Wilmot', *ANB*

Archives BL, corresp. with W. E. Gladstone, Add. MSS 44393–44450

Likenesses photograph, National Archives of Nigeria, Ibadan [*see illus.*] • photographs, repro. in Lynch, *Edward Wilmot Blyden*

Blyenberch, Abraham van (1575/6–1624), painter, was born in the Spanish Netherlands, the son of Noë van Blyenberch and Margriet Fredericx. He married Catharina Peeters before 13 November 1615 (the date of their will). On 29 December 1617 he acquired Antwerp citizenship but was never registered as a student or master painter in the Sint-Lucasgilde (the professional painters' association) of Antwerp.

From about 1617 to 1621 or 1622 van Blyenberch worked as a painter in London, living in the parish of St Martin-in-the-Fields. Like his neighbours Paul van Somer and Daniel Mytens, van Blyenberch was 'tried out' as a portrait painter by the lord chamberlain, the earl of Pembroke, who commissioned portraits of himself from them all, but evidently preferred Mytens's work to van Blyenberch's (*William Herbert, Third Earl of Pembroke*, 1617; Powis Castle; exh. Tate Gallery, London, 1995). However, van Blyenberch painted portraits of other art collectors at James I's court: *Robert Ker, later First Earl of Ancrum* (1618; Newbattle Abbey collection, Midlothian; Lothian Trustees); and *The Prince of Wales, later Charles I* (*c.*1617–20; NPG). He also painted *Count Gondomar, the Spanish Ambassador* (*c.*1622; Royal Collection). Van Blyenberch's most famous portrait is, however, not that of an aristocrat, but *Ben Jonson*, the English poet and dramatist (*c.*1626; engraved by Robert Vaughan by 1627). The version in the National Portrait Gallery may have been inventoried in the duke of Buckingham's collection in 1635. Van Blyenberch also executed the history painting *Jacob and Esau* (sold from the Royal Collection in 1650; Millar, *Tudor, Stuart Pictures*).

Sir Theodore Turquet de Mayerne recorded van Blyenberch's advice on how to match colours when executing or repairing paintings in distemper on canvas in his *Pictoria sculptoria et quae subalternarum artium* (1620; repr. Lyons, 1977). Such expertise in distemper painting suggests that van Blyenberch probably executed cartoons for Mortlake tapestries, or wall-hangings. (See J. A. van de Graaf, *Het de Mayerne Manuscript*, 1958, 191–92, entry no. 123.) Sir Theodore also described the painter's palette: of 'white' (white-painted?) iron, with small depressions to hold colours. Like a modern watercolourist's palette, its use would have made it easier to judge colours precisely. Van Blyenberch's portraits reveal that he indeed relied on colour and chiaroscuro (rather than line) to create an illusion of three-dimensional form, and to establish mood. The resulting naturalism and emphasis on character in his portraiture, and that of other Anglo-Netherlandish painters in Stuart London, was an important contribution to the development of British art.

In 1621 or 1622 van Blyenberch returned to Antwerp. According to a document he signed there on 11 April 1624, the painter Theodore (Dierik) van Thulden studied in his studio in 1621–2. Van Blyenberch was buried in Antwerp on the third Sunday in Advent (December) 1624, as 'Abraham van Blyenberch, schilder' (painter).

Anne Thackray

Sources O. Millar, 'Blyenberch, Abraham van', *The dictionary of art*, ed. J. Turner (1996) • E. Duverger, 'Abraham van Blyenberch leermeester van Dierik van Thulden', *Gentse bijdragen tut de kunstgeschiedenis en oudheidkunde* [University of Ghent], 30 (1998), 228–31 • M. K. Talley, *Portrait painting in England: studies in the technical literature before 1700* (1981) • O. Millar, *The Tudor, Stuart and early Georgian pictures in the collection of her majesty the queen*, 2 vols. (1963), vol. 1, p. 83 • K. Hearn, ed., *Dynasties: painting in Tudor and Jacobean England, 1530–1630* (1995), 83 [exhibition catalogue, Tate Gallery, London, 12 Oct 1995 – 7 Jan 1996] • O. Millar, *The age of Charles I: painting in England, 1620–1649* (1972), 20 [exhibition catalogue, Tate Gallery, London, 15 Nov 1972 – 14 Jan 1973]
Archives Stadtsarchief Antwerpen, *Antwerpen pooters-breken*, Antwerp 2.d., dl. V, p. 53 • Stadtsarchief Antwerpen, notaris Michiel van Couwenberghe, N478 (1624), fols. 78*v*–79

Blyke, Richard (*d.* **1775**), antiquary, was the son of Theophilus Blyke (*d.* 1718), deputy secretary at war. He may have been a native of Hereford but a Richard Blyke was baptized on 26 June 1716 at St Bride's, Fleet Street, London, whose parents were Theophilus and Mary Blyke. On his father's death his mother married a Gloucestershire clergyman. Blyke was deputy auditor of the office of the imprest, and was a member of the committee appointed to prepare the rolls of parliament for the press. In 1767 he was elected a fellow of the Society of Antiquaries; he was also a fellow of the Royal Society. In 1775 he edited Sergeant Glanville's *Reports of Determinations on Contested Elections* in collaboration with John Topham FRS. He gathered together an extensive manuscript collection, in twenty-two volumes, in preparation for the publication of a topographical history of Herefordshire, but his death in 1775 prevented him from achieving this. The collection was purchased by Charles Howard, earl of Surrey, later tenth duke of Norfolk, with the hope of encouraging someone else to undertake this work. It was later used by John Duncombe in his own history of the county. Blyke was buried in the churchyard at Isleworth, Middlesex, where his father was also buried.

THOMPSON COOPER, *rev.* J. A. MARCHAND

Sources Nichols, *Lit. anecdotes*, 3.206–7, 743 • G. J. Aungier, *The history and antiquities of Syon Monastery, the parish of Isleworth, and the chapelry of Hounslow* (1840), 171 • register of fellows, S. Antiquaries, Lond. • *IGI*
Archives BL, transcript for 'Rotuli parliamentarium', Add. MS 4631

Blysse, John (*d.* **1530**), physician, was born in the diocese of Bath and Wells. He graduated BA at Oxford in June 1507 and was elected a probationary fellow of Merton College in 1509, having the character of 'an excellent disputant in philosophy' (Brodrick, 248). In 1510 he was selected by the university to dispute with a Spaniard from the University of Montpellier. He proceeded in arts, and applied himself to the study of medicine. He was appointed guardian of the Danvers chest in 1513, and had to replace 53*s*. deficient when he left the office in July 1515. Blysse married, and moved to London, where he was practising in 1525; he became a fellow of the College of Physicians in 1529. He proceeded DM in February 1528. Being an astronomer as well as a physician he left certain astronomical tables at Merton, which disappeared long ago. He died a Dominican in April 1530 and was buried in the church of the Blackfriars' convent at London. Blysse's will mentions his 'wellbeloved wife Alice'.

[ANON.], *rev.* PATRICK WALLIS

Sources Foster, *Alum. Oxon.* • Munk, *Roll* • Wood, *Ath. Oxon.* • G. C. Brodrick, *Memorials of Merton College*, OHS, 4 (1885) • *Reg. Oxf.* • will, PRO, PROB 11/23, sig. 19

Blyth, Sir Arthur (**1823–1891**), politician in Australia, was born at Birmingham on 19 March 1823, the third of the four sons of William Blyth (1788–1855), a wholesale merchant of Birmingham, and his wife, Sarah (*c.*1797–1861), the daughter of the Revd William Wilkins of Bourton on the Water, Gloucestershire. He was educated at King Edward VI Grammar School, Birmingham, before emigrating with his parents to Adelaide in 1839. Having worked in his family's business for two years, Arthur established a successful ironmonger's business with his brother Neville. They also invested heavily in land, and became wealthy, with several directorships of major local companies. On 5 March 1850 Arthur married Jessie Ann (*c.*1827–1891), the daughter of Edward Forrest of Birmingham. They had five children, two of whom died soon after birth.

Blyth was elected to the South Australian legislative council in 1855 for the seat of Yatala, before moving in 1857 to the house of assembly, where he represented Gumeracha. He held this seat until 1868—when he travelled to England for two years on account of his wife's ill health—and then again from 1870 to 1875. He represented North Adelaide from 1875 to 1877, in which year he was knighted.

From 1861 Blyth relinquished all direct involvement in his business interests and devoted himself entirely to politics. In an unstable political era, he held the positions of commissioner for public works, commissioner for crown lands and immigration, treasurer, and chief secretary, on numerous occasions in various ministries in the period 1857 to 1876. Blyth was first elected to the position of premier on 4 August 1864, his ministry lasting until March the next year. A 'convinced free trader' (*The Times*), he was widely respected in political circles, and by the public, for the hard work and efficiency he demonstrated in all roles he was given. He was chosen as premier on a further two occasions—November 1871 to January 1872, and then for almost two years from July 1873 to June 1875.

A 'leading Anglican layman … well known for his commitment to religious equality' (Elford, 315), Blyth was also an early proponent of the revision of marriage practices in his state. In 1856, after a local furore erupted over the acceptability of applying church laws to marriage arrangements, he proposed a bill to make 'the ceremony of marriage merely a civil contract' (ibid.). His political views generally were characterized as 'practical, liberal, and moderate' (*The Times*), although his 'nervous temperament' (Bowes) was less well regarded, since it was thought to weaken his decisiveness and abilities as a political leader. A contemporary judgement was that he 'originated no measure of first-rate importance' (ibid.).

On his retirement from parliament, Blyth was appointed South Australian agent-general in London. He held this post from February 1877 until 1891. He died on 7 December 1891 at his home, Sunnydene, Grassington Road, Eastbourne, Sussex. His wife, Jessie, survived him by only a fortnight. MARC BRODIE

Sources *The Times* (8 Dec 1891), 9 · K. Bowes, 'Blyth, Sir Arthur', *AusDB*, vol. 3 · K. Elford, 'Marriage and divorce', *The Flinders history of South Australia: social history*, ed. E. Richards (Netley, SA, 1986) · S. Brookes, Blyth family tree, www.netspace.net.au/~sashab/FFAMILY/FT301.html · *IGI* · H. Coxon, J. Playford, and R. Reid, *Biographical register of the South Australian parliament, 1857–1957* (Netley, SA, 1985) · *DNB* · *CGPLA Eng. & Wales* (1892) · d. cert.

Archives Mitchell L., NSW, MSS · State Library of South Australia, Adelaide, Mortlock Library of South Australiana, South Australian archives, letters | Mitchell L., NSW, Parkes MSS; Walcot MSS · State Library of South Australia, Adelaide, Mortlock Library of South Australiana, South Australian archives, Hart MSS

Wealth at death £6763 14*s*. 3*d*.: probate, 30 Jan 1892, *CGPLA Eng. & Wales*

Blyth, Edward [*pseuds.* Zoophilus, Z] (**1810–1873**), zoologist, was born on 23 December 1810 at 9 Ironmongers Lane, City of London, the son of Clare Blyth (1749–1821) from Norfolk, clothier, and his second wife, Catharine Saunders. After his father's death he was educated at Robert Fennel's gentlemen's boarding-school in Wimbledon, Surrey. His industry and prodigious memory were remarkable, as was his inclination to truancy to pursue natural history. He was originally intended for the church but Fennel suggested that he study chemistry, so he was apprenticed to Mr Thomas Keating, druggist, of Keating & Co., 79 St Paul's Churchyard, City of London. He bought a druggist's business in Lower Tooting, London, around 1832 but neglected it, which led to its failure in 1837.

From a young age Blyth devoted himself to zoology, and became a leading ornithologist. He published several hundred natural history contributions and conducted a voluminous correspondence with fellow naturalists throughout his adult life. His early, mainly ornithological, work appeared in Rennie's *Field Naturalist*, Loudon's *Magazine of Natural History* (later *Annals and Magazine of Natural History*), Wood's *The Naturalist* and *The Analyst*, and the proceedings of the Ornithological and Zoological societies of London. He published an edition of White's *Natural History of Selborne* (1836). He moved to Brixton, Surrey, by May 1837, and, though unsuccessful in seeking employment in the British Museum, in 1838 he was appointed curator (possibly honorary) of the Ornithological Society of London's new museum.

In 1840 Blyth edited and enlarged the mammals, birds, and reptiles sections for a single-volume English edition of Cuvier's *Regne animal*, further establishing his scientific credentials, and marking his interest in larger mammals, including sheep, hyenas, and horses, on which he wrote lengthy papers. In 1841 he was recruited by Horace Hayman Wilson, librarian of the India House Museum, as the curator of the Asiatic Society of Bengal's museum. He arrived in Calcutta in September 1841, and remained curator effectively until 1862. During his curatorship he greatly increased the range and volume of the museum's natural history collections by establishing an extensive network of correspondents and donors, including hunters, travellers, foreign curators, and local animal enthusiasts. The society's collection was purchased by the crown in 1865, and formed the national Indian Museum.

Blyth's contribution to Asiatic zoology was substantial. Around 140 items, including monographs (on ungulates, birds, felines, primates, and others), notes, and curatorial reports, appeared in the *Journal of the Asiatic Society*. He also encouraged and advised the work of field collectors such as Brian Houghton Hodgson, Allan Octavian Hume, Thomas Caverhill Jerdon, and Arthur Purves Phayre. His failures as a curator stemmed partly from his difficult personality, which caused conflict with society members and senior officials. Although generous and unfailingly helpful to all who sought assistance, he tended to underrate field naturalists (treating their claims to priority carelessly), resented authority, and relied overmuch on the patronage of the nobility. In 1847 he was severely censured by the Asiatic Society and denied a long-sought pay rise. Despite this stringent criticism (partly resulting from past conflicts and prejudice against his lack of formal qualifications), he retained his position. Some of the museum's problems were caused less by incompetence than by a severely limited establishment. He supplemented an inadequate salary with live-animal dealing and writing pseudonymously for the *Indian Sporting Review* (later the *Indian Field*) and the *Calcutta Review*.

Blyth married Elizabeth Mary Turner Hodges (1825–1857), widow, and daughter of James Sutton, on 20 February 1854. The shock of her sudden death from hepatitis in December 1857 caused Blyth's near-fatal physical collapse. Despite restorative field trips to Burma, this led eventually to his departure from Calcutta in November 1862 and retirement finally in 1863, on a belatedly awarded pension of £150. From at least 1865 until the end of his life he suffered recurring ill health, of possibly psychological origin, sometimes with mania and paranoid tendencies, and exacerbated by alcohol abuse. In 1866 he was briefly placed in an asylum. Nevertheless, he continued to write prolifically, usually as Zoophilus or Z. Lengthy pieces on domesticated animals (mostly based on previously published work), correspondence, and an anonymous column on new arrivals at London Zoo appeared in *Land & Water* (1866–9). Numerous notes, letters, and articles, including a series of papers on the animals of Burma and a monograph on cranes, appeared in *The Field* (1869–73). He also published in *The Ibis*.

From 1855 Blyth was one of Charles Darwin's most indefatigable correspondents and a major source of information on domestication and sexual differences in birds and animals. Mistakenly identified by Eiseley as the inspiration for Darwin's theory of natural selection, he was actually a conservative zoologist, unusually interested in locality and ecology. His attention to detail and encyclopaedic knowledge gave his work continuing value but often delayed his papers, to the frustration of his employers and the regret of his obituarists. He became an enthusiastic Darwinist after the publication of *On the Origin of Species* (1859).

In 1872 Blyth again became ill, probably with the heart disease from which he died on 27 December 1873, at his sister's residence, 11 Regent's Park Terrace, London. He was buried at St James's cemetery, Highgate, on 2 January 1874. His *Catalogue of the Mammals and Birds of Burma* was published posthumously in 1875.

CHRISTINE BRANDON-JONES

Sources A. Grote, 'Memoir', *Journal of the Asiatic Society of Bengal*, [43] pt 2/August (1875) [whole issue, *Catalogue of mammals and birds of Burma (1875) by the late E. Blyth*] · *The correspondence of Charles Darwin*, ed. F. Burkhardt and S. Smith, 1–8 (1985–93) · C. Brandon-Jones, 'Long gone and forgotten: reassessing the life and career of Edward Blyth, zoologist', *Archives of Natural History*, 22 (1995), 91–5 · letters from E. Blyth, NHM, Gould MSS · E. Blyth, letters, CUL, Newton MSS · E. Blyth, letters, CUL, Darwin MSS · *Quarterly Ecclesiastical Returns of Marriages for the Archdeaconry of Calcutta*, 85 (1854), 126 · *Quarterly Ecclesiastical Returns for Burials for the Archdeaconry of Calcutta*, 92 (1857), 935 · parish register, London, St Martin Pomeroy, GL [baptism] · L. Eiseley, 'Charles Darwin, Edward Blyth and the theory of natural selection', *Proceedings of the American Philosophical Society*, 103 (1959), 94–158 · d. cert. · parish register, St James's cemetery, Highgate, London, Holborn Local History Library, London [burial]

Archives American Philosophical Society Library, Philadelphia, letters | CUL, letters to Charles Darwin · CUL, Newton MSS · NHM, Gould MSS · Royal Museum, Edinburgh, letters to Sir William Jardine

Likenesses daguerreotype, NHM, Owen MSS; repro. in Blyth, 'Catalogue of mammals and birds'

Blyth, Francis [*alias* Francis Courtney; *name in religion* Simon Stock of the Blessed Trinity] (*c*.**1705–1772**), Carmelite friar, was born to protestant parents and raised in their beliefs. He converted to Catholicism when a youth and in 1723 entered the noviciate of the Discalced Carmelites in Modena, Italy, taking in religion the name Simon Stock of the Blessed Trinity. After receiving a dispensation from irregularity due to defective vision he proceeded to Malta to study for the priesthood, and was ordained there. He returned to England in 1730, working first on the mission in Wiltshire and then in the London district under the alias Francis Courtney. He was a noted preacher and in 1740 he published a pastoral letter entitled *A Caution Against Prejudice* and the sermon *Eternal Misery the Necessary Consequence of Infinite Mercy Abused* (repr. 1742, 1745). In the same year a new chapel was built at the Portuguese embassy, and in 1741 Blyth was appointed assistant chaplain, a position which usually demanded a fine singing voice. The ambassador at this time was Dom Sebastião-José de Carvalho e Mello, the future marqués de Pombal, and Blyth was later to deny having aided him in his anti-Jesuit machinations.

Blyth was vicar provincial of the English Carmelites from 1742 to 1755, years which saw such bitter dissension between monastic and secular missioners that Pope Benedict XIV issued a brief on the matter in 1745, and on 30 May 1753 the bull *Apostolicum ministerium*, delineating the respective rights and privileges of the religious and the seculars. In 1756 Blyth became chaplain major at the Portuguese embassy in London, remaining in that post until his death at the embassy on 11 December 1772. He was buried in the cemetery of St Pancras. In his will, drawn up on 20 June 1760, he made the midwife Jane Chevalier his residuary legatee, 'that I may to the last discharge with Fidelity the great Trust of honour and humanity I took upon me for the protection of injured Virtue', after other bequests including 'the small beginnings' of a literary collection, left to the British Museum (PRO, PROB 11/984/22).

During his chaplaincy at the embassy Blyth published several sermons and discourses, the most famous of his works being the *Devout Paraphrase on the Seven Penitential Psalms* (1741; repr. 1742, 1749, 1751, 1873) and *Sermons for every Sunday in the Year* (4 vols., 1742–3). *The Passion of our Lord and Saviour Jesus Christ: a Sermon on Good Friday* was published posthumously in 1775.

The priest Francis Blyth was a close relation of the printer of the same name (*d.* 1787), part proprietor of the *Public Ledger*, a daily morning newspaper, and of the *London Packet*, a thrice-weekly evening paper.

PAUL ARBLASTER

Sources B. Zimmermann, 'Blyth, Francis', *The Catholic encyclopedia*, ed. C. G. Herbermann and others, 2 (1907) · Gillow, *Lit. biog. hist.*, 1.252 · F. Blom and others, *English Catholic books, 1701–1800: a bibliography* (1996), 31–2 · G. Scott, *Gothic rage undone: English monks in the age of Enlightenment* (1992) · P. Guilday, *The English Catholic refugees on the continent, 1558–1795* (1914) · will, PRO, PROB 11/984/22

Wealth at death see will, PRO, PROB 11/984/22

Blyth, Geoffrey (*c*.**1470–1530**), bishop of Coventry and Lichfield, born at Norton, Derbyshire, was the second son of William Blyth of Leeds, Yorkshire. His mother was the sister (name unknown) of Thomas Rotherham, archbishop of York. His brother John *Blyth became bishop of Salisbury and master of the rolls. Geoffrey Blyth was educated at Eton College and at King's College, Cambridge, graduating BA in 1487 and MA in 1490. Ordained priest on 4 April 1495, he incepted as a doctor of theology in 1497–8; a papal dispensation of 1498 still referred to him as a bachelor of theology, but papal letters when he became a bishop in 1503 describe him as master of theology, confirming that he had proceeded to the doctorate. In 1498 or 1499 he became warden of the King's Hall, a position he retained until 1528.

A successful pluralist, Blyth held prebends in Beverley and York minsters in the diocese of York, and became rector of Hedon, Nottinghamshire. He also became rector of Corfe Castle, Dorset, and was collated to prebends in Salisbury Cathedral and St Paul's Cathedral. On 9 May 1493 his uncle Archbishop Rotherham collated him to the archdeaconry of Cleveland, a position he vacated in 1498, when he became archdeacon of Gloucester, while his brother John collated him first (1 November 1494) to the treasurership, and then (22 August 1499) to the archdeaconry, of Salisbury. He was also elected dean of York (26 January 1497). All those benefices which he still held he resigned when he became a bishop. He probably owed his elevation to his serving Henry VII as an ambassador; on 27 May 1502 he was sent on an embassy to Ladislas II, king of Hungary and Bohemia, and he went on many subsequent, though less important, diplomatic missions.

Blyth was provided to the see of Coventry and Lichfield on 5 May 1503. The temporalities were released on 26 September, and he was consecrated on the following day by Richard Fox, bishop of Winchester. As bishop, Blyth seems to have been unable to avoid controversy. He was hampered by the independence enjoyed by the dean and chapter, which exempted them from taking an oath of obedience, but still performed a small number of ordination ceremonies and carried out the occasional visitation of religious houses (where he appears to have found fewer serious problems than his contemporaries on the bench, and those more financial than doctrinal). Early in 1509 he found it expedient to obtain a pardon, to cover his financial responsibilities as executor of the wills of both uncle and brother, while between 1510 and 1513 he was drawn into the testamentary jurisdiction disputes between Bishop Fox and Archbishop Warham (supporting Fox).

In 1512 Blyth was appointed lord president of the council in Wales, an office he held until 1524; on taking up office he set up a commission to investigate 'insurrection, rebellions and Lollardy' in south Wales and the counties of the Welsh march (Hudson, 34), but it is not known if any action followed, and Blyth usually seems to have been something of a figurehead as president. Meanwhile, an inquest held on 15 June 1513, following the death of Sir Ralph Langford, leaving a minor as his heir, found that Langford and Blyth had conspired in January 1511 to convey the title to lands and manors in Derbyshire, Nottinghamshire, and Lincolnshire to Anthony Fitzherbert, so as to defraud the king of his wardship. Then in 1523 Blyth faced a charge of treason, accused by an unknown Welshman; the background to the affair remains obscure (it may have arisen from ill will within the Lichfield chapter), and Blyth was eventually cleared following examination by a committee of peers, but only after three months in custody.

Despite his troubles, Blyth seems to have dealt seriously with his episcopal responsibilities. He acted vigorously against heresy, trying to halt the spread of Lollard literature, and taking some forty abjurations in person between January and February 1512. In the famous case of Richard Hunne, a suspected London heretic who died in the bishop's prison in suspicious circumstances following his arrest in 1514, Blyth was called upon to examine Hunne's annotated copy of the Bible, and his observations were central in several of the articles Bishop Fitzjames later objected against Hunne, as well as being useful in the anti-heresy campaigns of other bishops. Personal difficulties persisted, however, and, on 11 July 1530, following Wolsey's downfall, a *praemunire* information was filed in king's bench against Blyth and thirteen other clerics. The basis of the information appears to have been his having abetted Wolsey's papal legacy by having granted him a third of his annual income through a negotiated composition. Although this might have been related to the dropped treason charge of 1523, he was none the less guilty of *praemunire* by association. Little seems to have come of it, however, and Blyth died in London soon afterwards.

Blyth was buried in Lichfield Cathedral before the image of St Ceadda (Chad), where a monument (long since destroyed) was erected to his memory. He had secured offices and benefices in his diocese for a number of his relations. In his will, dated 28 April 1530 and proved on 1 March 1531, he bequeathed legacies to his cathedrals, to the churches of St Chad in Shrewsbury and Norton, to Eton College, and to King's College and King's Hall, Cambridge. To Eton and King's College he left great standing cups, both gilt with covers. A notable builder, in his lifetime he built houses for the choristers of Lichfield and a chapel at Norton (in which he erected an alabaster tomb for his parents), also establishing a chantry there. He gave King's College a gilt mitre for the boy-bishop in 1510, a pair of great organs worth £40 in 1512, a rochet of the best cloth for the boy-bishop in 1518, and a fair banner representing the assumption of the Virgin in 1519. He also collected all the statutes of Lichfield, and had these confirmed by Cardinal Wolsey, in his capacity of legate, in 1526. ANDREW A. CHIBI

Sources P. Heath, 'The treason of Geoffrey Blythe, bishop of Coventry and Lichfield, 1503–31', *BIHR*, 42 (1969), 101–9 · P. Heath, ed., *Bishop Geoffrey Blythe's Visitations, c.1515–1525*, Staffordshire RS, 4th ser., 7 (1973) · P. Heath, 'Supplements to Bishop Blythe's Visitations', Staffordshire RS, 4th ser., 13 (1988), 47–56 · *LP Henry VIII*, vols. 1–4 · T. N. Cooper, 'Oligarchy and conflict: Lichfield Cathedral clergy in the early sixteenth century', *Midland History*, 19 (1994), 40–57 · J. J. Scarisbrick, 'The conservative episcopate in England: 1529–1535', PhD diss., U. Cam., 1963 · A. A. Chibi, *Henry VIII's bishops: administrators, scholars and shepherds* [forthcoming] · Rymer, *Foedera* · S. Thompson, 'The pastoral work of the English and Welsh bishops, 1500–58', DPhil diss., U. Oxf., 1984 · A. Ogle, *The tragedy of the Lollard's tower* [1949] · [H. Wharton], ed., *Anglia sacra*, 2 vols. (1691) · W. Beresford, *Lichfield* [1889] · Emden, *Cam.*, 67–8 · J. Fines, 'Heresy trials in the diocese of Coventry and Lichfield, 1511–12', *Journal of Ecclesiastical History*, 14 (1963), 160–74 · S. M. Leathes, ed., *Grace book A* (1897) · M. Bateson, ed., *Grace book B*, 1 (1903) · E. E. Barker, ed., *The register of Thomas Rotherham … 1480–1500*, CYS, 69 (1976) · R. Thoroton, *The antiquities of Nottinghamshire*, rev. J. Throsby, 2nd edn, 3 vols. (1790–96), vol. 3, p. 147 · A. Hudson, *The premature reformation: Wycliffite texts and Lollard history* (1988) · *DNB* · A. A. Chibi, 'The social and regional origins of the Henrician episcopal bench', *Sixteenth Century Journal*, 29 (1998), 955–73 · A. B. Cobban, *The King's Hall within the University of Cambridge in the later middle ages*, Cambridge Studies in Medieval Life and Thought, 3rd ser., 1 (1969), 289

Archives Lichfield Joint RO, B/A/1/14 (Reg. Blythe) · Lichfield Joint RO, B/A/1/14ii · PRO, SP 1/53, fols. 241–42 · PRO, SP 1/54, fol. 34 · PRO, SP 1/56, fol. 209 · Lichfield dean and chapter MS, Acta capitularia | PRO, state papers domestic, Henry VIII, SP 1/50, fol. 165

Blyth, George Francis Popham (1832–1914), bishop of Jerusalem and the East, second son (of ten children) of the Revd George Blanchard Blyth and his wife, Mary Frances Ann Popham, was born on 25 April 1832 at Old North Bar House, Beverley, Yorkshire. He was educated at St Paul's School, London, and Lincoln College, Oxford, graduating as BA in 1854 and MA in 1858. In 1887 he became honorary DD. Blyth was ordained deacon in 1855, and priest in the following year. He acted as curate of Westport St Mary, Wiltshire, from 1855 to 1861, and at Sigglesthorne, Yorkshire, in 1861; he was domestic chaplain to the earl of Kimberley in 1863.

In 1866 Blyth left for India and served as chaplain at

Allahabad in Uttar Pradesh, and then as chaplain to the bishop of Calcutta in 1867. He was subsequently chaplain at Barrackpore in West Bengal (1868–74), at Nainital in Uttar Pradesh (1874–7), and at Fort St Williams in West Bengal (1877–8). In 1879 he was appointed archdeacon of the diocese of Rangoon in Burma, serving in that role until 1886. In India he married Mary Anne Crommelin, eldest daughter of Colonel James Arden Crommelin, at Barrackpore on 14 February 1870. Mary died on 6 June 1908 after a short illness on her way from Palestine to England, and was buried at sea in the Strait of Messina. The Blyths had one son, Reginald, who was killed in action in June 1915, and five daughters: Estelle, Nina, Grace, Evelyn, and Elinor.

In 1887, after returning to England via Palestine and Egypt, Blyth was offered the episcopate in Jerusalem by the archbishop of Canterbury. Four decades earlier (1841) Britain and Prussia had established the joint protestant bishopric in Jerusalem with the aim of improving the condition of protestants in the Holy Land. The first bishop was the converted rabbi Michael Solomon Alexander (1799–1845), a member of the London Society for Promoting Christianity amongst the Jews. After his death in 1845 Alexander was succeeded by the Swiss missionary Samuel Gobat (1799–1879), a member of the Church Missionary Society, who served from 1846 to 1879. The third bishop, from 1880 to 1881, was Joseph Barclay (1831–1881), another missionary of the London Society for Promoting Christianity amongst the Jews. After his death the bishopric in Jerusalem was vacant for six years. Germany, whose status in Europe as well as in Palestine grew in forty years of co-operation, decided to cease her support of the joint bishopric. In 1887 the bishopric was terminated and Germany established a bishopric of its own in Jerusalem. The archbishop of Canterbury was determined to continue financing an Anglican bishop by British means with only the support of the London Society for Promoting Christianity amongst the Jews and the Church Missionary Society.

After some hesitation Blyth accepted the nomination and was consecrated on 25 March 1887 in Lambeth Palace as the Anglican bishop of Jerusalem and the East. The bishop was in charge of the congregations and interests of the Anglican church in Palestine, Syria, Egypt, Cyprus, and Abyssinia. He left England in April and arrived in Jerusalem in mid-May 1887 with well-defined missionary conceptions of working among all the people in Palestine, Christian-Arabs, Muslims, and Jews alike. He found that the majority of the English clergy in the Holy Land were employed by the two missionary societies, which conducted the local mission affairs from their London offices, which conflicted with his vision of a united Anglican endeavour in the East. He soon began an attempt to subject the London Society for Promoting Christianity among the Jews and the Church Missionary Society institution to his own authority, but the societies' strong opposition led him in 1890 to establish a separate institution of his own, the Jerusalem and the East Mission. Its object was 'the establishment and maintenance of mission work amongst the Jews in Bible Lands, and the furtherance of such work by the provision of Church privileges for English speaking people resident in those lands'.

On account of the contributions that Blyth managed to collect in Europe, his institute, now the official representative of the Church of England in the East, developed very quickly. During his twenty-seven years in Palestine he established numerous institutions including a church, a hospital, boys' and girls' schools in Jerusalem, and a mission house in Haifa; boys' and girls' schools, a church, and a mission house in Cairo; as well as mission posts in Beirut, Alexandria, and Suez. But his most renowned enterprise was St George's College in Jerusalem. The complex comprised a collegiate church, a residence for the bishop, a college, a clergy house, and a library, schools for boys and girls, and the medical institution of St Helen. The church was consecrated by the bishop of Salisbury on St Luke's day, 18 October 1898. From that date Blyth acted as dean of the collegiate church. St George's College is situated half a mile north of the old city walls of Jerusalem and still functions as the residence for the Anglican bishop in Jerusalem.

After his eighty-second birthday Blyth decided to retire and left Palestine via Egypt for England on 21 July 1914. He died at his home, 97 Comeragh Road, Fulham, London, on 5 November 1914 and was buried in Hammersmith cemetery two days later. YARON PERRY

Sources E. Blyth, *When we lived in Jerusalem* (1927) · Y. Perry, *British mission to the Jews in nineteenth-century Palestine* (2002) · St Ant. Oxf., Middle East Centre, Estelle Blyth MSS, GB 165-0031 [papers relating to her father] · papers, 1841–1970x79, St Ant. Oxf., Middle East Centre, Jerusalem and the East Mission, GB 165-0161 · Blyth papers, 1887–1914, LPL, MSS 2227–2237 · Jerusalem and the East Mission Fund papers, 1844–1936, LPL, MSS 2327–2341 · *Bible Lands: Quarterly Papers of the Jerusalem and the East Mission* (1877–1916) · *Jerusalem and the East Mission Fund Annual Report* (1884–1914) · *The primary charge of the Right Reverend George Francis Popham Blyth* (1890) · *The second triennial charge* (1893) · *The third triennial charge* (1896) · *CGPLA Eng. & Wales* (1914) · d. cert.

Archives LPL, corresp. and papers, incl. notes on his life and work by his daughter Estelle, MSS 2227–2237, 2327–2341, 2551, 3212 · St Ant. Oxf., Middle East Centre, corresp. and papers · U. Durham L., corresp. relating to Egypt and Sudan | LPL, corresp. with Benson · LPL, letters to Athelstan Riley · LPL, letters to John Wordsworth · U. Durham L., corresp. with Sir Reginald Wingate

Likenesses photograph, 1913, repro. in Blyth, *When we lived*

Wealth at death £3675: probate, 7 April 1915, *CGPLA Eng. & Wales*

Blyth, John (*c.*1450–1499), bishop of Salisbury, was the son of William Blyth of Norton, on the Derbyshire–Yorkshire border, and of a sister of Thomas Rotherham, archbishop of York (*d.* 1500). His younger brother Geoffrey Blyth (*d.* 1530) became bishop of Coventry and Lichfield. A fellow from 1476–7, and warden from 1488 to 1498, of the King's Hall in the University of Cambridge, John Blyth was created a DCL in 1485 and served as chancellor of the university from 1494, probably until his death. Rotherham, while bishop of Lincoln, gave him the archdeaconry of Stow in 1477, and then the archdeaconry of Huntingdon in 1478, which he held until 1494; he also held a canonry in Lincoln Cathedral with the prebend of Leighton Ecclesia

(1482–5). Benefiting further from Rotherham's patronage after his uncle's translation to York, Blyth was a canon of York Minster, with the very valuable prebend of Masham, 1484–94, and held the important office of archdeacon of Richmond (1485–94). Henry VII promoted him to the bishopric of Salisbury by papal provision on 13 November 1493, and he was consecrated on 23 February 1494.

From March to August 1499 Blyth presided over a series of heresy trials at Reading, Sonning, and Ramsbury. Otherwise he left little impression on his see, retaining the officials of his predecessor and employing a suffragan to celebrate ordinations on all but two occasions (in 1498). He was installed in his cathedral church by proxy, and his first recorded presence in the diocese was in August 1494. He resided chiefly at the episcopal manors at Ramsbury and Sonning. He advanced his brother Geoffrey, to whom he gave several benefices including—on the day before he died—the archdeaconry of Sarum. In 1496 the islands of Jersey and Guernsey were taken from the see of Coutances and added to that of Salisbury, but in 1499 they were incorporated in Winchester diocese.

On 5 May 1492 Blyth was appointed keeper (or master) of the rolls. This was an office several times given to trained civilians who afterwards became bishops in the later middle ages, and like other such holders Blyth resigned it when he was consecrated to his see. The appointment suggests involvement in government at this time, as does the fact that he was appointed to commissions of the peace for fifteen counties in the midlands in May 1493; however, from November 1494 he served only on the commissions for Berkshire, Dorset, and Wiltshire (that is, for the counties in his diocese), and for the town of Cambridge. He died on 23 August 1499 in Ramsbury, apparently suddenly, and was buried behind the high altar of his cathedral church, beneath the confessional chair, being laid north and south, in a tomb which, according to Leland, was constructed but not used by Bishop Richard Beauchamp (*d.* 1481). Blyth's will, made on the day of his death and proved one month later, does not survive.

D. P. Wright

Sources Emden, *Cam.* • J. Blyth, bishop's register, 1494–9, Wilts. & Swindon RO • *CPR, 1485–94* • *The itinerary of John Leland in or about the years 1535–1543*, ed. L. Toulmin Smith, 5 vols. (1906–10); repr. with introduction by T. Kendrick (1964) • Sainty, *Judges*
Archives Wilts. & Swindon RO, register

Blyth, Phoebe (1816–1898), educationist and philanthropist, was born at Gray Street, Newington, in Edinburgh, on 5 April 1816, the daughter of Robert Brittain Blyth, a metal merchant, and his wife, Barbara Cooper. Phoebe had a brother, the Revd Robert Blyth, who was an ardent supporter of Scottish sabbath schools. The family were active members of the Church of Scotland. Sundays consisted of two sermons, morning and afternoon, and the evening was spent reading religious books. She was privately educated at Mr Andrews's school, which was considered to be one of the best private schools for girls in Edinburgh in the early nineteenth century. She became accomplished in geography, elocution, French, drawing, music, and dancing. Her grandmother also taught her the art of housekeeping and nursing.

Phoebe Blyth was one of the early pioneers in the women's movement in mid-Victorian Scotland. She was a leading campaigner for opening up opportunities for women in professional employment. In 1860 she was a founder member of the Edinburgh Society for Promoting the Employment of Women, a counterpart to the London society founded in the previous year by Jessie Boucheret, Bessie Parkes, and Adelaide Proctor. A register was set up and potential employees and employers paid a fee, and this prepared the pathway for providing women with remunerative employment. In the first three years of its operation, the registry list included teachers in every department of schools, families, or private instruction, as well as companions, female missionaries, Bible women, sick nurses, seamstresses, shop assistants, and domestic servants.

Phoebe Blyth, along with her brother, Robert, were members of the National Association for the Promotion of Social Science, which was formed in 1857. In 1863 the association held its conference in Edinburgh and Phoebe Blyth gave a paper in which she strongly advocated that girls should be educated for employment and receive a practical training in household management. She referred to many young girls aged between sixteen and eighteen who signed the register for paid employment but who were ignorant of household management.

In 1873 Phoebe Blyth was elected with Flora Stevenson a member of the first Edinburgh school board. By this time, both women had established formidable reputations in Edinburgh public life. They were both active in the movement for the opening of the medical profession and university education to women. Phoebe supported women's suffrage, though she was not a campaigner in the movement. Both women played a prominent role in the local administration and implementation of the Education (Scotland) Act passed in 1872.

Miss Blyth served on the Edinburgh board for eight years and retired in 1881. She promoted the teaching of cookery and household management for schoolgirls and was convenor of the committee of domestic economy in 1881. This task involved persuading the Edinburgh ratepayers of the educational value of the teaching of domestic economy for girls in board schools.

Throughout her public life Blyth was committed to philanthropic work in her capacity as a visitor of public board schools in Edinburgh. She also was engaged in missionary activities and was convenor of the ladies' African committee of the Church of Scotland. Phoebe Blyth died on 12 February 1898 at her home, 27 Mansion House Road, Edinburgh, and was buried three days later at the Grange cemetery in Edinburgh.

Helen Corr

Sources Boase, *Mod. Eng. biog.* • *The Scotsman* (14 Feb 1898) • C. C. Stopes, 'The education of Scotch girls during the first half of the century', *Englishwoman's Review*, 29 (1898), 158–64 • Edinburgh school board minutes, Edinburgh Central Library • *Transactions of*

the National Association for the Promotion of Social Science: Edinburgh meeting, 1863 (1863) • b. cert. • d. cert.
Wealth at death £3690 1s. 11d.: confirmation, 26 May 1898, *CGPLA Eng. & Wales*

Blythe, Colin [Charlie] (**1879–1917**), cricketer, was born on 30 May 1879 at 78 Evelyn Street, Deptford, Kent, the son of Walter Blythe, engine fitter, and his wife, Elizabeth Dready. His cricketing talent was first recognized by Captain William McCanlis (1840–1925), the Kent coach, who saw Blythe, a spectator at a Kent county match at Deptford, bowling on the ground before the game and was impressed by his action. McCanlis later acknowledged the luck involved in this discovery, since Deptford was not an area where the county club normally sent its scouts (*Wisden*, 1907, xcvi–xcviii). Following a trial, he was taken on at the cricket 'nursery' at Tonbridge, founded in 1897 by Kent to develop young professional cricketers for the county game.

Charlie Blythe made his professional début for Kent against Yorkshire at Tonbridge on 21 August 1899 and marked the occasion by clean bowling F. Mitchell with his first ball in first-class cricket. He played fifteen full seasons for Kent (1900–14), taking a total in all his first-class cricket of 2503 wickets (average 16.81) with his slow left-arm spin bowling. Deceptive in flight and graceful in style, he made full use of his height and was able to deliver a faster ball which went with the arm. On dry or crumbly wickets he was virtually unplayable. His best season was 1909, when he took 215 wickets; he failed to take 100 wickets in a season for Kent only once, in 1901, when, hampered by ill health, he captured ninety-three victims. His best performance for Kent was in 1907, against Northamptonshire, when he took ten for 30 and seven for 18 in a single day. He was *Wisden* cricketer of the year in 1904.

Blythe represented England on nineteen occasions, including four overseas tours (with A. C. MacLaren to Australia 1901–2, MCC to Australia 1907–8, and MCC to South Africa 1905–6 and 1909–10). His best test-match performance came in the 1909 series against Australia, when his haul of eleven for 102 helped England to a ten-wicket victory. He is the only player to have taken fifteen wickets in a test match against South Africa (eight for 59 and seven for 40 at Leeds in 1907). He was a sufferer from epilepsy which, together with a nervous and highly strung temperament, curtailed his test-match career. He also vied for international selection with the other great left-arm spinner of the Edwardian period, Wilfred Rhodes. As a county player, however, there was no doubt of his importance, and he was the mainstay of the Kent side which won the county championship four times (1906, 1909, 1910, and 1913) in nine years.

Blythe enlisted as soon as war broke out in 1914. He served in the Kent Fortress Volunteers, attached to the King's Own Yorkshire light infantry, holding the rank of sergeant. His last cricket match was at Lord's in August 1917, for the army and navy against the Australians and South Africans. He was killed in action near Passchendaele in Belgium on 8 November 1917, leaving a widow, Janett Gertrude Blythe. He was buried at Oxford Road cemetery in Belgium. *Wisden* (1918, 172) called his loss 'the most serious' that cricket sustained during the war. The war memorial at the St Lawrence ground, Canterbury, was erected originally in his sole memory.

GLENYS WILLIAMS

Sources B. Croudy, *Colin Blythe: his record innings by innings* (1995) • C. Martin-Jenkins, *World cricketers: a biographical dictionary* (1996) • P. Bailey, P. Thorn, and P. Wynne-Thomas, *Who's who of cricketers*, rev. edn (1993) • B. Green, ed., *The Wisden book of obituaries* (1986) • Commonwealth War Graves Commission, Maidenhead
Archives St Lawrence ground, Canterbury, war memorial
Likenesses A. C. Tayler, portrait, 1906, Kent county cricket club • C. Blythe, A. Fielder, and E. Humphreys, postcard, Marylebone cricket club • B. C. Flemons or Mockering, photographs, Kent county cricket club • Spy [L. Ward], cartoon (*Charlie*), Kent county cricket club; repro. in *VF* (3 Aug 1910) • photographs, George Beldam collection
Wealth at death £2828 13s. 8d.: probate, 6 March 1918, *CGPLA Eng. & Wales*

Blythe, Ernest [Earnán de Blaghd] (**1889–1975**), politician and theatre director, was born on 13 April 1889 in Magheragall, Lisburn, co. Antrim, the eldest child of James and Agnes Blythe. He came from a Church of Ireland and staunchly Orange background and was a most unlikely convert to Irish nationalism. Educated at the local Molgaberry and Ballycarrickmaddy national schools, he joined the civil service in 1905 and was placed in the department of agriculture and technical instruction in Dublin. He became friendly with the labour activist (and later playwright) Sean O'Casey, who swore him into the Irish Republican Brotherhood (IRB) in 1906. Blythe also joined the Gaelic League and became convinced of the need to restore the Irish language to widespread and general use if Irish independence were to have any real meaning.

Blythe turned to journalism, and in 1909 took a job with the *North Down Herald*, a Unionist weekly published in Bangor. He acted as an organizer for the IRB in Ulster. As Unionist resistance to the 1912 Home Rule Bill hardened in the province he kept his conversion to Irish nationalism secret. In 1913 he went to live in Corca Dhuibhne in Irish-speaking west Kerry to acquire fluency in the language. He made a living by working as a farmhand for the family of Thomas Ashe, a nationalist who later died while on hunger strike in prison. Other nationalists with whom he became friendly in west Kerry were Desmond FitzGerald and The O'Rahilly. Blythe became an organizer for the Irish Volunteers in 1914 and was ordered to leave the country by government edict in July 1915. Arrested a month before the 1916 rising for not complying he was imprisoned in Brixton, where one of his fellow inmates was Sir Roger Casement.

After 1916 Blythe continued to organize the volunteers and was arrested and imprisoned in Cork and then in Belfast. Although he was the author of the much publicized 'ruthless warfare' in *An tÓglach* (the Irish Volunteer organ) during 1918, which advocated that all collaborators with the 'foreign invader' be killed without mercy, he had private misgivings about the shooting of policemen during the Anglo-Irish war of 1919–21. He was elected to the Sinn

Ernest Blythe (1889–1975), by unknown photographer, 1922

Féin executive in 1918 and to the Dáil at the end of that year for the constituency of North Monaghan, which he continued to represent until 1933. He was appointed director of trade and industry in the first Dáil in April 1919. Later that year, on 13 November, he married Annie McHugh. They had one child, Earnán (*b.* 1925).

Ernest Blythe supported the Anglo-Irish treaty that was signed on 6 December 1921. He was minister for finance (1922–32), minister for posts and telegraphs (1927–32), and vice-president of the executive council (that is, deputy prime minister) (1927–32). A conservative in economic matters he believed firmly in balancing budgets and took a very strict attitude to public expenditure. He is still remembered in Irish political folklore for reducing the old-age pension in his 1924 budget. His grant of £1000 to the Abbey Theatre is less well remembered, but it made the Abbey one of the first state-sponsored theatres in the world.

The Irish language was an abiding passion and Blythe supported it in many ways as minister for finance. Among his initiatives were the setting up of An Gúm, the official Irish-language publishing company; the provision of special assistance to all Irish schools; the establishment of state-aided courses in Irish-speaking areas (the Gaeltacht), and the introduction of housing grants and other measures to benefit these parts of the country. He did not agree that the state's revival effort should have no element of compulsion and remained blunt and uncompromising in this attitude.

Blythe lost his Dáil seat in 1933. He was an enthusiastic supporter of the Blueshirt movement, which, as he saw it, possessed the party organization which Cumann na nGaedheal lacked. From late 1932 he was advocating the merger of Cumann na nGaedheal, the Blueshirts, and the Centre Party, which came to pass in September 1933 in the form of the Fine Gael party. He was a party official in Fine Gael from 1933 to 1936 and a member of the Irish senate from 1934 to 1936. He thereupon retired completely from politics and was secretary of Clondalkin Paper Mills from 1937 to 1941. An ordinary member of the board of the Abbey Theatre (1935–41) he was managing director of the theatre from 1941 until 1967. He guided the Abbey through the difficult years after the disastrous fire of 1951, and was concerned with developing a bilingual acting tradition in the process. Many of his decisions as managing director were strongly criticized on artistic grounds by the literary establishment of the time.

Blythe's Ulster protestant background gave him a special insight into the problem of the partition of Ireland. In August 1920 he expressed strong opposition to the proposed 'Belfast boycott' in the Dáil; two years later he produced a policy document for the provisional government in which he criticized Collins's covert armed action against the northern government. In 1955 he published *Briseadh na teorann* ('Obliterating the border'). He accepted that partition was there at the wish of northern protestants rather than that of the British government. The only way to end it, he argued, was to persuade a few hundred thousand protestants to vote for its abolition and he urged friendship and contacts with unionism. He linked the failure of the majority tradition to assimilate the Ulster planter tradition, as it had assimilated other foreign traditions, to the decline in Irish culture and language and especially to the failure of nineteenth-century nationalist leaders to appreciate the importance of cultural tradition. His views on partition proved unpopular at the time he expressed them but have since become commonplace in Irish nationalist attitudes.

Ernest Blythe was never afraid to court unpopularity. His decision to go against his ethnic progenitors is probably the most conclusive evidence of this facet of his character, but instances can be found throughout his life. As early as 1922 he was advocating the conciliation of Ulster Unionists, something that was not seriously considered by nationalist Ireland for another fifty years. His austere financial policies in the 1920s won him little popularity with the Irish people in general but he remained an unwavering disciple of fiscal rectitude. He was almost unique in his party for his opposition to the Irish electoral system of proportional representation by the single transferable vote, believing that it militated against the formation of stable governments. When Fine Gael proposed to abolish compulsory Irish he did not hesitate to express openly his disagreement with his erstwhile colleagues.

Ernest Blythe died at his home, 50 Kenilworth Square, Rathmines, Dublin, on 23 February 1975. Three volumes of autobiography were published: *Trasna na Bóinne* ('Across the Boyne') in 1957, *Slán le hUltaibh* ('Farewell to Ulster') in 1970, and *Gaeil Á Múscailt* ('Arousing the Irish') in 1973.

BRIAN MAYE

Sources E. de Blaghd, *Trasna na Bóinne* ('Across the Boyne') (1957) • E. de Blaghd, *Slán le hUltaibh* ('Farewell to Ulster') (1970) • E. de Blaghd, *Gaeil Á Múscailt* ('Arousing the Irish') (1973) • University College, Dublin, Ernest Blythe MSS • B. Maye, *Fine Gael, 1923–1987* (1993) • Nollaig Ó Gadhra, 'Earnán de Blaghd, 1889–1975', *Éire-Ireland*, 11/33 (1976), 93–105 • M. McInerney, 'Ernest Blythe: a political profile', *Irish Times* (30 Dec 1974–3 Jan 1975) • H. Boylan, *A dictionary of Irish biography*, 3rd edn (1998)

Archives NL Ire., corresp. • University College, Dublin, corresp. and papers | NA Ire., cabinet papers for Cumann na nGaedheal governments • TCD, corresp. with Thomas Bodkin

Likenesses photograph, 1922, Hult. Arch. [*see illus.*] • portrait, Abbey Theatre, Lower Abbey Street, Dublin

Blythe, Geoffrey. *See* Blyth, Geoffrey (*c.*1470–1530).

Blythe, Geoffrey (**1496/7–1542**), clergyman, was the son of Thomas Blythe of Barnby, Yorkshire, where he was born. He was probably the nephew of Geoffrey Blythe, bishop of Lichfield, and of John Blythe, bishop of Salisbury; presumably it was the former who arranged for his younger namesake to be educated at Eton College, having himself been a schoolboy there. A king's scholar at Eton, in 1515 the younger Geoffrey Blythe, now aged eighteen, was elected to King's College, Cambridge, where he was a fellow between 1518 and 1524, and where he graduated BA in 1520 and proceeded MA in 1523. Between these degrees he was collated successively to the prebends in Lichfield Cathedral of Pipa Minor (1520) and Tervin (1521). He also went to Louvain, travelling in 1521 with Nicholas Daryngton (later prebendary of Lichfield and diocesan visitor), who noted that Blythe was seriously ill at the time, and matriculating at the university there on 6 December 1522. In 1528 he was appointed warden of the King's Hall, Cambridge, as both his likely uncles had been before him, and was vicar of Chesterton from then until 1534. In 1529 he was admitted to the degree of DCL at Cambridge.

Probably in 1529 Blythe became archdeacon of Stafford, but resigned following his collation to the treasurership of Lichfield on 6 June 1530. It may have been in 1529 that he was one of the 'swarme' of divines recorded by Foxe as 'preachyng … and barking' at Cambridge against Hugh Latimer (Foxe, 2.1735). In 1541 he resigned his wardenship of the King's Hall, and he died in the following year, presumably in Cambridge, being buried in All Saints' Church there on 8 March 1542.

D. G. NEWCOMBE

Sources Venn, *Alum. Cant.*, 1/1.171 • *Fasti Angl., 1300–1541*, [Coventry] • J. Foxe, *Actes and monuments*, 4th edn, 2 vols. (1583) • W. Sterry, ed., *The Eton College register, 1441–1698* (1943) • T. Harwood, *Alumni Etonenses, or, A catalogue of the provosts and fellows of Eton College and King's College, Cambridge, from the foundation in 1443 to the year 1797* (1797) • P. S. Allen, ed., 'Some letters of masters and scholars, 1500–1530', *EngHR*, 22 (1907), 740–54 • P. Heath, ed., *Bishop Geoffrey Blythe's Visitations, c.1515–1525*, Staffordshire RS, 4th ser., 7 (1973)

Blythe, John. *See* Blyth, John (*c.*1450–1499).

Blythe, John Dean (**1842–1869**), writer, son of Peter Dean Blythe and his wife, Elizabeth, was born at Ashton under Lyne, Lancashire, on 12 April 1842. His grandfather James Blythe was a notable Scottish schoolmaster at the village of Limekilns, about 15 miles from Edinburgh. After a brief stay at the Ryecroft British School, he worked in a factory. He then obtained a post on a local paper as a reporter, and afterwards entered a firm in Manchester, in whose employment he remained until his death. He attended evening classes and studied on his own. He learned Latin, French, and Spanish, and read English literature, and his retentive memory enabled him to recall an immense number of passages, especially from Shakespeare. On one occasion he supplied the references to fifty-seven out of sixty passages selected to test him. His literary efforts were encouraged by the Revd Joseph Rayner Stephens and John Critchley Prince. A contribution to *Punch* and some verses in the Ashton newspapers are the only pieces known to have been printed during his lifetime.

In his politics Blythe was a philosophical radical. For the greater part of his life he taught at the Sunday school of the Methodist New Connexion in Stamford Street, Manchester. He also edited a manuscript magazine which circulated among the members of a self-improvement society. On 5 February 1869 he was killed by the accidental discharge of a revolver in the hands of a friend. He left behind him a considerable amount of manuscript, and a small memorial volume entitled *A Sketch of the Life, and a Selection from the Writings, of John Dean Blythe* was issued in 1870.

W. E. A. AXON, *rev.* NILANJANA BANERJI

Sources [T. W.], *A sketch of the life, and a selection from the writings, of John Dean Blythe* (1870)

Blythswood. For this title name *see* Campbell, Archibald Campbell, first Baron Blythswood (1835–1908).

Blyton [*married names* Pollock, Darrell Waters], **Enid Mary** (**1897–1968**), children's writer, was born on 11 August 1897 at 354 Lordship Lane, East Dulwich, London, the eldest child of Thomas Carey Blyton (1870–1920), a salesman, and his wife, Theresa Mary, *née* Harrison (1874–1950). There were two younger brothers, Hanly (*b.* 1899), and Carey (*b.* 1902), who were born after the family had moved to the neighbouring suburb of Beckenham. Enid Blyton was very close to her father, who encouraged her musical talents and inspired her lifelong interest in natural history. The fact that he left the family for another woman in 1910 affected her deeply. From 1907 to 1915 Enid Blyton attended St Christopher's School for Girls in Beckenham. It had been intended that she should pursue a musical career and attend the Guildhall School of Music. However, her gift for story-telling was already apparent and, convinced that she was unsuited to a career in music and that she needed to leave home, she went to stay with the Hunt family on their farm near Woodbridge in Suffolk. Ida Hunt taught at Ipswich high school, which included a kindergarten where teachers were trained. Recognizing that Enid Blyton had an obvious flair for handling young children, she encouraged her to think of teaching as a possible career and Enid Blyton embarked on a training course at the high school in September 1916. In January 1919 she began teaching at Bickley Park, a small independent school for boys in Kent, and a year later became a nursery

Enid Mary Blyton (1897–1968), by John Gay, 1949 [right, with her daughter Imogen Pollock]

governess to the four Thompson boys in Surbiton. It was while she was there that she had her first success as a writer. After contributing poems, stories, and articles to various magazines, her first book, *Child Whispers*, a collection of poems, was published in 1922. During the 1920s much of her work had an educational bias, and she became a regular contributor to *Teachers' World*, establishing a favourable reputation among teachers. In 1923 five of her poems were used in a special issue, which also included work by John Drinkwater, John Masefield, Walter de la Mare, and Rudyard Kipling.

On 28 August 1924 Enid Blyton married Major Hugh Alexander Pollock DSO (1888–1971), editor of the book department in the publishing firm of George Newnes, which published two of her books that year. Hugh Pollock had been married before but his first wife had left him during the war and they divorced in 1924. After her marriage, she devoted herself to the writing, which was by then providing a steady income, estimated at over £500 in 1924. Hugh and Enid Pollock began married life in a Chelsea flat, moved to Elfin Cottage in Beckenham in 1926, and to Old Thatch, Bourne End, Buckinghamshire in 1929. They had two daughters: Gillian, born on 15 July 1931 and later the wife of Donald *Baverstock, the television producer, and Imogen Mary, born on 27 October 1935. In 1938 the family moved to Green Hedges in Beaconsfield, an address that was to become familiar to English-speaking children around the world as the home of their favourite author.

However, life in reality was very different from the ideal portrayed by Enid Blyton in her letters to readers. By 1939 her marriage to Hugh Pollock was in difficulties, and in 1941 she met Kenneth Fraser Darrell Waters (1892–1967), a London surgeon, with whom she began a friendship which quickly developed into something deeper. After each had dissolved their marriage, on 20 October 1943 they married at the City of Westminster register office, and she subsequently changed the surname of her two daughters to Darrell Waters. Hugh Pollock remarried and had little contact with his daughters thereafter. Enid Blyton's second marriage was very happy and, as far as her public was concerned, she moved smoothly into her role as a devoted doctor's wife, living with him and her two daughters at Green Hedges.

As a writer, Enid Blyton was both controversial and a phenomenon. In 1974 she was the fourth most translated author in the world. She produced so much work that her total output can only be estimated as being between 600 and 700 books. The publication that first established her reputation as a children's writer was the magazine *Sunny Stories*, which she began to edit for Newnes in 1926. Until 1937 this consisted mainly of retellings of traditional stories and informative articles, but then the title was changed to *Enid Blyton's Sunny Stories* and it took a new direction. The emphasis shifted to original fiction and many of Enid Blyton's most famous books first appeared as serials in its pages. In April 1942 the magazine became a fortnightly publication, initially, perhaps, because of wartime paper shortages, and in June the title changed back to *Sunny Stories*, the last issue of which appeared in February 1953. A month later *Enid Blyton's Magazine*, also a fortnightly magazine in a similar format, was launched and ran for six and a half years until September 1959.

Producing material for a regular magazine undoubtedly influenced Enid Blyton's style, as she had to make the content attractive enough to encourage the child or adult guardian to buy the next issue. The serials, in particular, required each instalment to end on a note of suspense, and even when she wrote fiction that was not destined for serial publication, the habit of providing cliff-hanging chapter endings often prevailed. Each issue of the magazine normally contained an editor's letter, a chapter of a serial, three short stories, a poem, and a picture-strip story for younger children. Favourite characters such as Amelia Jane, a doll, and Mister Meddle, a pixie who cannot mind his own business, made regular appearances in short stories, later gathered together to make a book, while tales of Brer Rabbit, based on Joel Chandler Harris's retellings of traditional tales from the American south, were retold in language which made them comprehensible to young children.

The first serial story, *Adventures of the Wishing Chair*, published as Enid Blyton's first full-length story-book in 1937, and *The Enchanted Wood* (1939), which introduced the magic Faraway Tree, are both fantasies that reflect the influence of the Norse myths she enjoyed as a child. In *The Secret Island* (1938) four children live a Robinson Crusoe type of existence on an island in a lake. *The Naughtiest Girl in the School* (1940), her first school story, is unusual in that it is set in a co-educational, somewhat progressive, boarding-school. *The Adventurous Four* (1941), one of her few books set firmly in time and place, is a wartime adventure about children involved with German ships secretly hidden off an island on the Scottish coast. *Shadow the Sheep Dog* (1942) is written from the animal's viewpoint. These early books illustrate the wide range of genres in which Blyton wrote and represent some of her best work.

The series for which Enid Blyton is most famous now began to appear. The first book about the Famous Five, *Five on a Treasure Island* (1942), introduced Julian, Dick, and Anne, their cousin Georgina, always known as George, and George's dog, Timmy, characters so popular with readers that they appeared in twenty further titles. These books are the most filmed and televised, with adaptations by the Children's Film Foundation (1957, 1964), Southern Television (1978, 1979), and Zenith Films (1995, 1997). There was a stage play based on a Famous Five adventure in 1955 and, to celebrate Blyton's centenary in 1997, a musical. Another series of mystery and adventure began with *The Island of Adventure* (1944); this is more complex in terms of plot and characterization. Younger children were catered for by *The Secret Seven* (1949) and the other stories in this series in which adventure and mystery are set in a more domestic environment. *Little Noddy Goes to Toyland* (1949), a picture story-book for even younger children, and its successors owe much of their popularity to the coloured illustrations by the Dutch artist Harmsen van der Beek, with whom Blyton worked closely. Noddy inspired a major industry, with many spin-offs in clothing, toys, games, soft furnishings, nursery equipment, television programmes, and videos. Meanwhile *First Term at Malory Towers* (1946) had introduced Darrell Rivers, a schoolgirl whose name is clearly based on that of Enid Blyton's second husband. Her progress through six books, from new girl to head girl, has been keenly followed by several generations of schoolgirls.

Although Enid Blyton was business-like in her contacts with publishers, her income was so great that by 1950 it was necessary to establish a company, Darrell Waters Ltd, to deal with her business affairs. Her work became controversial in the 1950s, by which time she was writing for children of all ages. Three factors led to reassessment of her writing. First, with the end of the Second World War with its restrictions on publishing, the number of books for children increased and new writers emerged. Second, teachers, librarians, and parents began to take a more critical look at what children were actually reading in their leisure time; and, third, children's public libraries and school libraries were developing and, since money was limited, decisions about how to spend it to the best advantage had to be taken. Children's librarians faced the problem of balancing the demand for Blyton's books against the need to provide a wide range of authors. The fact that they limited the number of Blyton titles or did not buy any eventually became widely known in 1964 when there were well publicized cases of 'banning Blyton' at Nottingham and St Pancras (London) libraries. By the early 1960s it was nearly impossible to find any journalist who did not know the name of Enid Blyton and stories of her being criticized were exploited by the press, not only in Britain but in Australia, New Zealand, and South Africa.

Criticism of Enid Blyton's work at first focused upon what was seen as her impoverished style and vocabulary, lack of imagination, stereotyped characterization, snobbery, and xenophobia. Later, as Britain became more of a multicultural society, she was condemned for her racism, and, with the coming of the feminist movement, her sexism. Colin Welch, in an article in *Encounter* (1958), commented, 'It is hard to see how a diet of Miss Blyton could help with the 11-plus or even with the Cambridge English Tripos' (Welch). In 1973 Margery Fisher, a leading critic of children's literature, described Blyton's work as 'slow poison' (Fisher).

Enid Blyton wrote very simply, aware of the needs and abilities of her audience; to her, the story was all-important and she possessed an undoubted talent for making readers turn over the page to find out what happens next. There are many tributes to the part played by her books in creating readers. Some of her attitudes are outdated, but they were shared by many of her contemporaries; the problem is that her work survived, although some titles have been edited to make them politically correct.

Afflicted by presenile dementia, Enid Blyton was moved into a nursing home three months before her death; she died at the Greenways Nursing Home, 11 Fellows Road, Hampstead, London, on 28 November 1968, and was cremated at Golders Green. Photographs taken of her at the peak of her career show a woman of above average height, with dark curly hair, often portrayed with children and animals. Through the magazines that she wrote and edited, she encouraged her readers to raise money for animal and children's charities. In 1985 the National Library for the Handicapped Child was set up by the Enid Blyton Trust for Children to provide a source of information and advice. In 1996 Darrell Waters Ltd was sold to the Trocadero, which set up a subsidiary, Enid Blyton Ltd, to handle the vast business, including reprints, new editions, audiotapes, videos, and films, that her work had generated. In her centenary year, Enid Blyton was as widely read and as popular as she had ever been; a set of British postage stamps depicted her most famous series: Noddy, the Famous Five, the Secret Seven, the Faraway Tree, and Malory Towers. SHEILA RAY

Sources B. Stoney, *Enid Blyton: a biography* (1974); rev. edn (1992); 2nd edn (1997) · S. Ray, *The Blyton phenomenon* (1982) · I. Smallwood, *A childhood at Green Hedges* (1989) · T. Summerfield, *A comprehensive bibliography of the books of Enid Blyton, 1922–1970* (1997) · E. Blyton, *The story of my life* (1952) · D. Rudd, *Enid Blyton and the mystery of children's literature* (2000) · d. cert. · C. Welch, 'Dear little Noddy', *Encounter*, 10/1 (1958), 18–22 · M. Fisher, review, *Growing Point*, 12 (1973), 2230–31

Archives NRA, corresp. | FILM BFI NFTVA, *Bookmark*, BBC2, 26 Dec 1996 · BFI NFTVA, *Secret lives*, Channel 4, 16 Dec 1996 · BL NSA, *Secret lives*, Channel 4, 16 Dec 1996, V3852/4 | SOUND BL NSA, 'Enid Blyton', BBC Radio 4, T5067R · BL NSA, performance recordings

Likenesses photographs, *c*.1945–1962, Hult. Arch. · J. Gay, double portrait, photograph, 1949, NPG [*see illus.*] · T. Adams, portrait (after photograph); Sothebys, 29 Oct 1997 • D. Houston, oils, priv. coll. • photographs, repro. in Stoney, *Enid Blyton* • photographs, repro. in Smallwood, *Childhood at Green Hedges* • photographs, repro. in Blyton, *Story of my life*

Boaden, James (1762–1839), biographer and playwright, was born on 23 May 1762 in Whitehaven, Cumberland, the only son of William Boaden (1735?–1790) and his wife, Elizabeth. His father (originally from Penryn, Cornwall), a merchant in the Russian trade, took the family to London, where Boaden was educated for a mercantile career. But after a period in a counting-house he turned to journalism, and in 1789 was installed editor of *The Oracle*, a newly founded literary newspaper. On 12 June 1793 he was admitted as a student of the Middle Temple. Though he remained in membership for almost thirty-three years, until early 1826, he was not called to the bar.

Boaden's first dramatic work, the musical romance *Ozmyn and Daraxa* (songs published 1793), earned him £100. More significant are the melodramas *Fontainville Forest* (1794, described in the prologue as being '[c]aught from the Gothic treasures of Romance', and acted fifteen times in 1794–5) and *The Italian Monk* (1797)—both adapted from Mrs Radcliffe—and *Aurelio and Miranda* (1798; published 1799), based on Lewis's *The Monk*. In *Cambro-Britons* (1798), set in the time of Llewelyn and Edward I, Boaden gothicizes Celtic myth, drawing partly on Gray's ode *The Bard*. His last plays, *The Voice of Nature* (adapted from Caigniez) and *The Maid of Bristol* (both 1803), are in more sentimental vein. His one poem, *A Rainy Day* (1801), celebrates in blank verse the 'salubrity' of Brighton's air and its 'very excellent' theatrical company and library.

Boaden published nothing after 1803 for twenty-one years. Of independent means, he none the less acted as an army agent during 1805 (possibly longer) and from at least 1812 was associated with the Whitehall firm Donaldson and Boaden. Late in life, however, the catastrophic failure of his private income in 1824 projected him into a new career as theatrical biographer. In the *Quarterly Review*, Sir Walter Scott described his *Life of John Philip Kemble* (2 vols., 1825) as 'grave, critical, full and laudably accurate', if stylistically somewhat 'too Gibbonian' (Scott, 203, 241), and the *Gentleman's Magazine* (95/1, 1825, 334) praised its learning and 'manly … tone of feeling'. His *Life of Mrs Siddons* (2 vols., 1827) (sold for £100 including copyright) was preferred for its vibrancy and authoritativeness over Thomas Campbell's version (1834). His memoir of Mrs Jordan (2 vols., 1831) more accurately balanced her stage career and private life than previous attempts, and the memoir of Mrs Inchbald (2 vols., 1833), based on her letters, introduced important new material. Boaden also edited Garrick's correspondence (1831). His quasi-novels from the same period—the pseudonymous *Man of Two Lives* (1828), on metempsychosis, and the moralistic *Doom of Giallo* (1835), inspired by an idea in Beckford—are literary curiosities, but Boaden's biographies, founded mostly on personal acquaintance with his subjects, remain standard works, valued for their vivid detail and descriptions of acting styles and performances of the period.

Boaden was fascinated by literary puzzles, but his premature endorsement of *Vortigern* and the other so-called Shakespearian discoveries of William Ireland (*The Oracle*, Feb–April, 1795) was unequivocally retracted in his *Letter to George Steevens, Esq.* (1796). From this lifelong interest in Shakespeare, mainly antiquarian rather than critical, came two late essays: his discussion of the authenticity of Shakespeare's iconography (1824) and his influential theory (*GM*, 1832; published in a longer version 1837), devised some twenty years previously, that identified William Herbert, earl of Pembroke, as addressee of the *Sonnets*. Since his time Boaden's contributions to the Shakespearian debate have gone largely unrecognized, but Schoenbaum (*Shakespeare's Lives*, 1991) redresses the balance with a detailed discussion of Boaden's theories and a graceful tribute to his scholarship.

Repeated applications to the Royal Literary Fund from 1831 reveal Boaden's grievous financial state as new work became increasingly difficult to place. Publishers, he lamented in his last letter to the Fund (24 March 1838), seemed interested only in 'the writings of the whimsical "Boz"'. Although his distinguished record ensured him assistance to a total, over eight years, of £140, creditors forced him to surrender the family's residence (60 Warren Street, Fitzroy Square, London) in late 1831, and for three months during 1835 to seek refuge in the Fleet gaol. Remarkably, destitution compromised neither his scholarly integrity nor instinct as a gentleman.

Valued for his intellect and fund of anecdote, Boaden had a range of literary and theatrical friends. Deafness aside, he enjoyed good health almost to the end. He died of dropsy in lodgings at 36 Waterloo Bridge Road, London, on 16 February 1839, and was buried at Kensal Green with his wife, Sarah (1763/4–1838), who had died as a result of dysentery on 1 August the preceding year. Of their nine children, John *Boaden was an artist and Caroline (*fl.* 1825–1839) wrote at least nine plays and some short fiction for the *Lady's Magazine*. JOHN RUSSELL STEPHENS

Sources *GM*, 2nd ser., 11 (1839), 436–8 • Royal Literary Fund, archives, file no. 698 [Caroline Boaden], 833 • D. E. Baker, *Biographia dramatica, or, A companion to the playhouse*, rev. I. Reed, new edn, rev. S. Jones, 1 (1812), 44 • [W. Scott], review, *QR*, 34 (1826), 196–248 • *GM*, 1st ser., 95/1 (1825), 232–5, 332–4 • student ledgers, Honourable Society of the Middle Temple • BL, Add. MS 27781, fols. 5, 73, 77, 91 • BL, Add. MS 39196, fols. 43, 69, 71, 85 • BL, Add. MS 40371, fols. 16, 18 • BL, Add. MS 40372, fol. 283 • BL, Add. MS 40374, fol. 217 • BL, Add. MS 46611, fol. 302 • S. Schoenbaum, *Shakespeare's lives*, new edn (1991) • A. Nicoll, *Late eighteenth century drama, 1750–1800*, 2nd edn (1952), vol. 3 of *A history of English drama, 1660–1900* (1952–9) [bibliography of plays] • A. Nicoll, *Early nineteenth century drama, 1800–1850*, 2nd edn (1955), vol. 4 of *A history of English drama, 1660–1900* (1952–9) [bibliography of plays] • C. B. Hogan, ed., *The London stage, 1660–1800*, pt 5: *1776–1800* (1968) • J. Shattock, ed., *The Cambridge bibliography of English literature*, 3rd edn, 4 (1999) • Cumbria AS • d. cert. [Sarah Boaden] • d. cert.

Archives BL, letters, publisher's agreements | BL, corresp. with Sir Robert Peel, Add. MSS 40371–40374 • Hunt. L., Larpent MSS • Royal Literary Fund, archives • V&A, letters to Colburn, publisher

Likenesses E. Bell, mezzotint, 1801 (after J. Opie), BM • J. Opie, mezzotint, pubd 1801 (after E. Bell), BM, NPG • G. H. Harlow, black and red chalk drawing, 1814, NG Ire. • S. De Wilde, pencil and black chalk and watercolour drawing, 1815 (with his daughter Caroline?), AM, Oxford • G. H. Harlow, mezzotint chalk drawing, NG Ire. • Ridley, stipple (after J. Opie), NPG • engraving, repro. in *Monthly Mirror* (1803), 361

Boaden, John (1792/3–1839), portrait and figure painter, was one of the nine children of James *Boaden (1762–1839), the dramatist and critic, and his wife, Sarah (1763/4–1838). Boaden exhibited at the Royal Academy from 1810 to 1833, at the British Institution from 1810 to 1839, and at the Society of British Artists from 1827 to 1840. Boaden's sitters included many theatrical figures, such as the celebrated actress Fanny Kemble (1809–1893) (ex Sothebys, 25 November 1998). He often portrayed actors and actresses in their stage roles, and his dramatic sketches of John Philip Kemble in eight of his principal characters (exh. British Institution, 1818) were seen by Kemble himself, who 'thought the whole of them exceedingly like him' (Lane, 1). They were later lithographed by Richard Lane. Boaden assisted with illustrations for his father's book entitled *An inquiry into the authenticity of various pictures and prints, which from the decease of the poet to our own times have been offered to the public as portraits of Shakespeare* (1824). According to Mark Haworth-Booth, Boaden's portrait of the poet the Revd C. H. Townshend (exh. RA, 1828; Victoria and Albert Museum, London, Townshend bequest) captures an early 'Byronic and Pushkinian splendour' which predates the sitter's melancholy decline (Haworth-Booth, 12). He also painted rustic peasant figures, set in landscape and often in regional or national costume, notably Constantine Soferes (Victoria and Albert Museum, London, Townshend bequest), a youth in Albanian costume.

Boaden's style was compared to Sir Thomas Lawrence and Harlow (Seguier, 21), but his work, according to Redgrave, 'although pleasing, did not rise above mediocrity' (Redgrave, 45). Boaden died, unmarried, at his home, 58 Newman Street, Oxford Street, London, on 4 April 1839. He was buried at Kensal Green. REBECCA VIRÁG

Sources R. J. Lane, *Illustrations of the late John Philip Kemble, drawn on stone by Richard J. Lane from pictures painted in his life-time by John Boaden* (1826) • J. Boaden, *An inquiry into the authenticity of various pictures and prints, which from the decease of the poet to our own times have been offered to the public as portraits of Shakespeare* (1824) • F. P. Seguier, *A critical and commercial dictionary of the works of painters* (1870) • M. Haworth-Booth, 'The dawning of an age: Chauncey Hare Townshend: eyewitness', *The golden age of British photography, 1839–1900*, ed. M. Haworth-Booth (1984), 11–21 [exhibition catalogue, V&A, 1984] • R. Parkinson, ed., *Catalogue of British oil paintings, 1820–1860* (1990) [catalogue of V&A] • *DNB* • Redgrave, *Artists* • Graves, *RA exhibitors* • Graves, *Brit. Inst.* • J. Johnson, ed., *Works exhibited at the Royal Society of British Artists, 1824–1893, and the New English Art Club, 1888–1917*, 2 vols. (1975) • Graves, *Artists* • B. Stewart and M. Cutten, *The dictionary of portrait painters in Britain up to 1920* (1997) • d. cert. • will, PRO, PROB 6/215, fol. 224r

Archives Courtauld Inst., Witt Library, photographs and other sales and exhibition catalogues

Wealth at death £300: administration, PRO, PROB 6/215, fol. 224r

Boadicea. *See* Boudicca (*d*. AD 60/61).

Boag, John (1775–1863), lexicographer, was born at Highgate in the parish of Beith, Ayrshire, on 7 January 1775. He matriculated at the University of Glasgow in 1797, and completed his course with a view to taking orders in the Church of Scotland. However, he joined the body of Independents or Congregationalists who in 1812 formed themselves into the Congregational Union of Scotland. He acted for many years as an evangelist, and not infrequently in the open air or by the wayside. He had small charges in the Isle of Man and Helensburgh. Ultimately he accepted the appointment of pastor over a very small Independent congregation in the village of Blackburn, Linlithgowshire, from which, it is believed, he never received more than £25–30 a year. He married Agnes Hamilton on 19 June 1798; they had six sons and three daughters. One of his sons was Sir Robert Boag, mayor of Belfast.

Boag kept a day school on his own account, and it was in this humble position that he compiled his *magnum opus*, the *Imperial Lexicon*. His aim was to combine etymology, pronunciation, and explanations of scientific terms and others used in art and literature. He wished also to incorporate new words that had emerged since Dr Johnson's dictionary, and to include modifications and other changes of meaning. He began this arduous undertaking after he had entered his seventieth year. Within three years his manuscript was ready for the press. It was printed and published by the Edinburgh Printing and Publishing Company. Unfortunately this company speedily became bankrupt. About 1847 Messrs Fullarton & Co. became proprietors of the *Imperial Lexicon* and issued it in parts or numbers, constituting two massive volumes. The work had an enormous sale and held its own until the publication of John Ogilvie's *Imperial Dictionary of the English Language*, which drew on it. Prefixed was a 'Popular grammar of the English language' by R. Whyte.

Besides his *Imperial Lexicon*, Boag was the author of a number of pamphlets on questions of the day, and was a frequent contributor to contemporary religious periodicals. He died at Craigton House, Linlithgowshire—the residence of a daughter-in-law, with whom he had lived in his later years—on 15 September 1863, in his eighty-ninth year. A. B. GROSART, *rev.* ROBERT BROWN

Sources private information (1885) • Allibone, *Dict.*, suppl. • Boase, *Mod. Eng. biog.* • T. McArthur, ed., *The Oxford companion to the English language* (1992)

Boaks, William George (1904–1986), road safety campaigner and parliamentary candidate, was born on 25 May 1904 at 104 Warner Road, Walthamstow, Essex, the son of William Robert Boaks, a vegetable salesman's cashier, and his wife, Annie Edith, *née* Palmer. Educated in elementary schools, he entered the Royal Navy as an ordinary seaman during the First World War, perhaps aged only twelve. Boaks enjoyed a varied and distinguished naval career, rising through the ranks to retire in 1949 as a lieutenant-commander. During the Second World War he was gunnery officer on HMS *Rodney* in the engagement with the *Bismarck* and commanded HMS *Basilisk*, a corvette, at Dunkirk, for which he was awarded the DSC. He married Ivy June Collier (1909–1997) in 1930 and they had three children.

On leaving the navy Boaks settled in south London, took

a job in local government, and embarked upon his eccentric campaigning career. Standing as an independent, he mistakenly contested Walthamstow East in the general election of 1951, having intended to oppose Clement Attlee in the west division; Boaks received just 174 votes in a poll of over 40,000. In 1956 he fought Walthamstow West when Attlee retired. Throughout his political career he campaigned for better road safety. Rather than canvass, or issue leaflets, he painted his car as a zebra crossing and decorated it with placards bearing slogans, a mast and sail, and loudspeakers. Later he devised a reinforced bicycle laden with placards for the same purpose.

Boaks's early campaigning activities led him to become a regular visitor to the law courts in the 1950s and 1960s. He was fined once in 1952 and twice in 1953 for using his car as an advertisement. In 1955 he was convicted of obstructing the highway by stopping his car in the middle of London's Kilburn High Road when traffic was heading away from a major football international at Wembley stadium, and again at Cambridge Circus in the city centre. Later that year he blocked up the Strand and broadcast his argument with a policeman over his car's loudspeakers to the gathering crowd. This led to a period in custody when a magistrate requested an assessment of Boaks's state of mind, but he was eventually given a conditional discharge. He sued the magistrate involved for wrongful imprisonment and took his case to the House of Lords but received no satisfaction.

In 1959 Boaks failed in an attempt to summons Lady Attlee for causing death by dangerous driving following a serious road accident in which she had been involved. Undaunted, he tried again in 1960 after Lady Attlee was involved in another crash, and in 1964 he unsuccessfully sought the summons of the queen and the duke of Edinburgh for the same reason. Boaks himself was reprimanded in court in 1963 for helping to cause a crash in which a girl was injured after he stopped for her to cross at traffic lights which were green.

Boaks championed other causes as well as the rights of pedestrians. In his early election contests he demanded equal pay for women and tax-free allowances for children. These ideas later became part of the political mainstream, although others were more unusual. He was an enthusiast for helicopters and asked for planning permission for a heliport in his own garden. He wanted inland airports closed and replaced by coastal heliports instead. Opposition to immigration also became a theme of his campaigns. Allowed six words of description on ballot papers after 1970 he chose 'Public Safety Democratic Monarchist White Residents' but he would have liked many more.

Throughout the 1960s his intentions to stand for election came to nothing, but after 1970 Boaks became a regular feature in parliamentary elections throughout the country. He fought Clapham in 1970 and three London seats in the general election of February 1974, achieving the best result of his career—240 votes—in Wimbledon, his home constituency. Between 1976 and 1982 he contested eighteen by-elections, polling only five votes in Glasgow Hillhead in 1982, the lowest poll of any parliamentary candidate in modern times.

Boaks was involved in a road accident in November 1982 and never fully recovered from the head injuries he suffered. He died on 4 April 1986 in St George's Hospital, Tooting, of pneumonia and heart failure. Boaks's long-standing interest in road safety was widely admired and the transport minister, Peter Bottomley, attended his funeral. He was buried at sea, in the naval graveyard outside Portsmouth harbour, with full honours.

A maverick political campaigner, who enlivened the political scene for many years, Boaks differed from other perennial by-election candidates in the earnestness with which he held his views and the lengths to which he was prepared to go to publicize them. Rather than demean politics, he demonstrated how anyone unprepared to conform with mainstream views could put them before the electorate for judgement, although at a cost; he lost over £3000 in deposits. He was sure that, in his case, the line between success and utter failure was thin. After his triple defeat in February 1974 he declared: 'If I had been elected I would have been the next Prime Minister' (*The Times*, 3 March 1974).

ROBERT INGHAM

Sources private information (2004) · N. Hamilton, *Great political eccentrics* (1999), 187–95 · *The Times guide to the House of Commons* (1951); (1970); (Feb 1974); (Oct 1974); (1979); (1983) · *The Times* (6 Sept 1952), 2f; (11 Aug 1953), 3a; (5 Sept 1953), 3d; (13 July 1955), 11a; (12 June 1956), 12c; (13 June 1956), 5c; (28 Nov 1956), 5d; (14 Feb 1957), 12g; (17 April 1957), 6e; (15 Dec 1959), 6d; (19 Dec 1959), 2e; (6 July 1960), 7b; (30 Jan 1963), 15f; (19 June 1963), 9e; (4 July 1964), 6f; (8 Jan 1966), 8a; (30 March 1967), 12c; (14 June 1967), 11c; (27 Oct 1967), 14d; (14 Feb 1968), 4g; (19 Feb 1974), 6a; (3 March 1974), 3b; (21 April 1979), 10c · *Wimbledon and Mitcham News* (11 April 1986), 2 · *Evening News* [London] (18 March 1966) · b. cert. · d. cert.

Likenesses photograph, repro. in *The Times* (30 March 1967)

Wealth at death £13,079: probate, 13 Aug 1986, *CGPLA Eng. & Wales*

Board, Lillian Barbara (1948–1970), athlete, was born in Addington Hospital, Durban, South Africa, on 13 December 1948, the second of the three children of George Board, a builder, and his wife, Frances Eleanor. She had a twin sister, Irene, born fifteen minutes after her. Her parents had emigrated from Manchester to South Africa, but the family became homesick and returned to England in 1950, initially to Manchester, where Lillian started primary school at St Paul's School, Wilmslow Road, Withington. When she was seven they moved to Ealing, west London, where she attended Drayton Green primary school, before going on to Grange Secondary Modern Girls' School. She began to show great promise as an athlete and, encouraged by her physical education teacher at school and her father, she joined the London Olympiades club. By the age of thirteen she had secured a place in the club's junior relay team and competed in the 100 yards, while also trying the long jump. Her natural ability and physical fitness, developed by her father (who was her trainer throughout her career), ensured that she became a fine long jumper: she won the event in the English schools championships in July 1963 and the junior event in the

Lillian Barbara Board (1948–1970), by unknown photographer, 1968

southern inter-counties championships in September 1963.

Over the next couple of years, however, Board gave up the long jump to concentrate on the sprints; her training regime, fixed by her father, became very serious and intense. The dedicated training paid off and in the 1964 season she found herself competing against, and beating, the best intermediate runners in the country at 100 and 220 yards. By the end of the season she competed in and won her first ever 880 yards, an event that she was to make her own as a senior. Young, strong, and 'a natural', Board was recognized as a possible successor to another of Britain's great female athletes, Mary Rand. Rand, the Olympic gold medallist and an inspiration and model for Lillian, tipped her to become an international athlete. 'Just watch her', Rand told the press, 'and in a couple of years she's going to be the greatest' (Emery, 29). She had meanwhile left school and after taking a secretarial course at Chiswick Polytechnic worked as a typist in between carrying out her rigorous athletics training regime.

Board's international career began in 1966, when she ran in the 440 yards for England in the Commonwealth games at Kingston, Jamaica (8 August 1966); she was just seventeen. But it was a match between the USA and the Commonwealth at Los Angeles in 1967 that transformed her from a fine national athlete to a world-class sprinter. She surged from the back of the field on the final bend to come first in the 400 metres (9 July 1967), setting a European junior record of 52.8 seconds. The race was televised live and her performance gained her overnight fame. The press dubbed her Golden Girl, Princess of Pace, Golden Goddess, and Queen of the Quarter (Emery, 53). Later that year she won the 400 metres at the European cup final in Kiev (15 September 1967), the only British winner in the competition.

In 1968 Board went to the Mexico Olympics, heavily tipped to win the 400 metres. Leading into the home straight, she was pipped for first by the relatively unknown French athlete Colette Besson. Of her second place Board said: 'It's lovely to win a silver medal, but I feel hurt when some people think I let the country down by not getting the gold. But I didn't really let them down. Colette was better than me on the day' (*Daily Mirror*, 28 Dec 1970, 19). This pragmatic and refreshing attitude must have been difficult to maintain since she now found the weight of the country's expectations on her shoulders each time she ran. The British press and public adopted Board as something of a national icon. With her blonde good looks and 'fresh, friendly personality' (*The Times*, 28 Dec 1970), she represented the 'feminine' side of athletics; her interest in fashion later led to her being taken on as a designer for a sportswear manufacturer. At the European championships in Athens she won two gold medals, for the 800 metres and the 4 x 400 metres relay (18 and 20 September 1969). Here she exacted some kind of 'revenge' over Colette Besson, whom she overtook during the final leg of the relay. Typically, her reaction to the victory was to run over and embrace Besson, telling reporters that 'I knew she felt just as I felt when she beat me in Mexico' (ibid.).

In the 1970 new year's honours list Board's achievements were recognized with the appointment as MBE, an award that she said she treasured more than any Olympic medal. Her last race was on 20 June 1970, when she came third in the 800 metres at the women's Amateur Athletic Association championships. She had not been well for some time, but felt compelled to run. Her condition deteriorated and following an exploratory operation her 'severe back pains' were diagnosed as intestinal cancer. In November 1970 she travelled to Germany, choosing to fight the disease by the natural methods practised by Dr Josef Issels at his Ringberg cancer clinic at Rottach-Egern in Bavaria. She was unable to recover and died in a Munich hospital on 26 December 1970. Her death at the age of twenty-two was not only a tragedy for her family and friends but also a heavy blow to women's athletics in Britain. She was cremated at Putney and a memorial service was held in St Paul's Cathedral. Her fiancé, David Emery, published her biography the following year.

RACHEL CUTLER

Sources D. Emery, *Lillian* (1971) • *The Times* (28 Dec 1970) • *Daily Mirror* (28 Dec 1970) • J. Huntington-Whiteley, ed., *The book of British sporting heroes* (1998), 46–7 [exhibition catalogue, NPG, 16 Oct 1998 – 24 Jan 1999] • *CGPLA Eng. & Wales* (1971)

Archives SOUND BBC WAC

Likenesses photographs, *c*.1966–1970, Hult. Arch. • photograph, 1967, repro. in Huntington-Whiteley, *The book of British sporting heroes*, 47 • photograph, 1968, Empics Sports Photo Agency, Nottingham [*see illus.*] • photographs, repro. in Emery, *Lillian*

Wealth at death £1341: administration, 30 March 1971, *CGPLA Eng. & Wales*

Boardman, Andrew (*d*. in or after **1595**), Church of England clergyman, was a native of Lancashire. He was admitted a scholar of St John's College, Cambridge, on 9 November 1568, matriculating as a pensioner three days later. He graduated BA in early 1572, and was admitted fellow on

Lady Margaret's foundation on 12 March 1573, the same day as his friend Everard Digby, to whose *Theoria analytica* (1579) he contributed some prefatory Greek verses. Having proceeded MA in 1575, on 5 September 1580 he was appointed Greek lecturer at St John's, and was elected one of the college preachers some days later, at Michaelmas. He was made junior bursar on 27 January 1582, and, proceeding BD shortly afterwards, was that year appointed minister of St Mary, Bury St Edmunds, where his house was identified in the feoffees' accounts for 1586 as 'next St. James steple'.

Boardman left Bury in 1586, moving to the benefice then known as Allchurch, near Warwick. On 11 January 1591 he was appointed by the town corporation to the vicarage of the collegiate church of St Mary, Warwick. Here he clashed with the presbyterian Thomas Cartwright, master of Leycester's Hospital, who claimed that Boardman welcomed into his pulpit preachers who issued 'whole sermons invective' against him (Pearson, 451). Cartwright's imprisonment during the Star Chamber trials of 1590–91 left him vulnerable, and in January 1592 he wrote to Lord Burghley that Boardman, already possessed of a living worth £100 per annum, had designs on the hospital. If so, Boardman did not succeed, and Cartwright remained in possession.

In 1594 Boardman was granted the degree of DD at Cambridge, but in 1595 Thomas Hull succeeded to the vicarage of St Mary, and after this date nothing further is known of Boardman. Although he has been identified as the writer of some English commendatory verses, subscribed A. B., prefixed to Thomas Morley's *Plaine and Easie Introduction to Practicall Musicke* (1597), the attribution seems highly unlikely. ARTHUR H. GRANT, *rev.* STEPHEN WRIGHT

Sources Cooper, *Ath. Cantab.*, 2.238–9 • Venn, *Alum. Cant.*, 1/1.181 • *VCH Warwickshire*, 8.522–9; 2.308 • A. F. S. Pearson, *Thomas Cartwright and Elizabethan puritanism, 1535–1603* (1925) • W. Dugdale, *The antiquities of Warwickshire illustrated*, rev. W. Thomas, 2nd edn, 2 vols. (1730) • S. Tymms, *An architectural and historical account of the church of St. Mary, Bury St. Edmunds* (1854) • T. Baker, *History of the college of St John the Evangelist, Cambridge*, ed. J. E. B. Mayor, 2 vols. (1869)

Boardman, Peter David (1950–1982), mountaineer and author, was born on 25 December 1950 at 19 Ack Lane, Bramhall, Cheshire, the second of two sons of Alan Howe Boardman (1920–1979), engineering executive, and his wife, Dorothy Griffiths (*b.* 1923), lecturer. From 1956 to 1969 he attended Stockport junior school and Stockport grammar school, and he subsequently went on to Nottingham University, where he graduated BA in English studies in 1972. He gained a PGCE in English and outdoor pursuits, with distinction, from University College of Wales, Bangor, in 1973.

Boardman's professional life was as a mountain guide. In 1973 he became an instructor at Glenmore Lodge in the Cairngorms, where he met his wife, Hilary Eve Collins (*b.* 1951), a teacher specializing in outdoor pursuits and in teaching children with learning disabilities; they were married at her home town, Chester-le-Street, co. Durham, on 25 August 1980. In 1975 he became national officer of

Peter David Boardman (1950–1982), by Terry Tullis

the British Mountaineering Association, based in Manchester. In 1978, after Dougal Haston's death, he was appointed director of the International School of Mountaineering in Leysin, Switzerland. Elected president of the British Association of Mountain Guides in 1979, he played an important role in that organization's entry into the Union Internationale des Associations des Guides de Montagne. A testament to his versatile skills comes from an elderly member of a trekking party in Nepal in 1980 (the only trekking party he ever led):

> I shall cherish the memory of a supremely gentle giant with panther-like tread, who led his motley flock (twelve of us) with patient humour and whose dreaming eyes, usually scanning the far horizon, still managed to keep an unobtrusive watch on the heads of the elderly. (private information)

Boardman began climbing while at school. After joining Stockport's Mynydd climbing club in 1966 he quickly became a proficient rock-climber on the traditional forcing ground of Derbyshire gritstone, as well as in the mountains of Snowdonia and the Lake District. He first went to the Alps in 1970, and rapidly established himself as one of the leading alpinists of the day, with a particular passion for the unfrequented big mixed routes of the Bernese Oberland. As well as climbing the north face of the Matterhorn he made first British ascents of the north face direct on the Olan, the Gervasutti route on the north face of the Breithorn, the north face of the Nesthorn, and the north face direct on the Lauterbrunnen Breithorn.

Boardman's first visit to the greater ranges came with the 1972 Nottingham University Hindu Kush expedition, which made first ascents of five minor summits and climbed five new routes. Particularly noteworthy were alpine-style ascents of the north faces of the Koh-i-Khaaik and Koh-i-Mondi (also a first ascent of the peak). In 1974 a trip to Alaska with Roger O'Donovan yielded a first ascent of the south face of Mount Dan Beard. A trip to the Caucasus followed in early 1975.

These early expeditions led to an invitation to join Chris Bonington's 1975 expedition to the south-west face of Everest. The military organization of the traditionally run expedition (which Boardman described in his diary as 'one of the last great Imperial experiences that life can offer') was a new experience for a climber specializing in fast alpine ascents, but he adapted well and was selected as a member of the second ascent team. On 26 September, two days after Doug Scott and Dougal Haston reached the summit, he left Camp 6 with Sherpa Pertemba, the expedition sirdar, Martin Boysen, and Mick Burke. Boysen soon turned back, but Pertemba and Boardman reached the summit at 1.10 p.m. While descending they met Burke heading upwards 30 metres below the summit. They waited for over an hour on the south summit for Burke, before blizzard conditions forced them to descend. Mick Burke was never seen again. Boardman and Pertemba only made it back to Camp 6 by the skin of their teeth.

The following year Boardman teamed up with **Thomas Joseph** [Joe] **Tasker** (1948–1982), whom he had first met in 1971 on the north-east spur of the Droites. This was the beginning of one of the best-known and most successful climbing partnerships in recent British climbing history. Tasker was born at 3 Lee Smith Street, Hull, on 12 May 1948, the eldest son in the family of ten children of Thomas William Tasker, painter and decorator, and his wife, Elizabeth Duffy. At the age of thirteen he was sent to Ushaw College, a Jesuit seminary, where he was encouraged in his climbing by one of the priests. On discovering, at the age of twenty, that he had no vocation for the priesthood, he left Ushaw and went on to study at Manchester University, where he graduated in sociology in 1973.

Joe Tasker climbed extensively in the Alps with Dick Renshaw from 1971 to 1975, with an impressive string of ascents that included the north face of the Eiger (in summer in 1973 and then in winter in 1974) and the east face of the Grandes Jorasses (which he considered one of his most memorable alpine climbs). In 1975 he and Renshaw made a pioneering and epic alpine-style ascent of the south ridge of Dunagiri (7066 metres) in the Garhwal Himalaya.

The ascent by Boardman and Tasker in 1976 of the west wall of Changabang (6864 metres) in the Garhwal Himalaya (India) over a total of forty days is widely recognized as a major breakthrough in lightweight expedition climbing in the Himalayas. Boardman's account of the expedition, *The Shining Mountain* (1978), was an immediate success in the climbing world and won the 1979 John Llewelyn Rhys memorial prize. In 1978 both men joined a small expedition led by Chris Bonington to the west ridge of K2 (8611 metres). The expedition was abandoned after Nick Estcourt was killed by an avalanche. In 1979 Boardman and Tasker teamed up with Doug Scott and Georges Bettembourg for another pioneering oxygen-free ascent of the north ridge of Kanchenjunga (8598 metres). The three British climbers all reached the summit, despite the fact that Boardman broke his ankle on the approach march.

Boardman and Tasker went back to K2 in 1979 with Doug Scott and Dick Renshaw, but were beaten back by avalanches and bad weather. In 1980 Boardman made another fine alpine-style ascent of the west ridge of Gauri Sankar (7134 metres) in Nepal with John Barry, Tim Leach, and Guy Neidhardt. That winter Tasker joined an unsuccessful expedition to the west ridge of Everest, which led to his first book, *Everest, the Cruel Way* (1981). In 1981 both men joined Al Rouse and Chris Bonington to climb Kongur (7719 metres) in China's Xinjiang province.

Boardman's final expedition, and Tasker's, was to the north-east ridge of Mount Everest in the 1982 pre-monsoon season. The expedition was a small one: the other climbing members were Dick Renshaw and Chris Bonington. On their fourth foray onto the ridge the two men disappeared while attempting to climb the series of pinnacles below the junction of the north-east ridge with the original north ridge route. They were last seen alive on 17 May 1982, moving upwards at approximately 8200 metres on the north-east ridge of Mount Everest, some 600 metres short of the summit. Bonington wrote: 'Pete Boardman and Joe Tasker lost their lives on a climb they were superbly qualified to attempt and which they both deeply and maturely wanted to achieve' (*Alpine Journal*, 1983, 286). Boardman's wife survived him. Tasker was unmarried. Both men wrote acclaimed books which were posthumously published: Peter Boardman's *Sacred Summits* (1982) and Joe Tasker's *Savage Arena* (1982). An appeal after their deaths led to the establishment of the annual Boardman–Tasker award for mountaineering literature—a fitting tribute to two of Britain's leading mountaineers and authors. JOSÉ LUIS BERMÚDEZ

Sources C. Clarke, 'In memoriam: Peter D. Boardman', *Alpine Journal*, 88 (1983), 265–9 · D. Renshaw, *Alpine Journal*, 88 (1983), 270–74 · C. Bonington, *Mountain*, 87 (1982), 36–7 · C. Bonington and C. Clarke, *Everest: the unclimbed ridge* (1983) · C. Bonington, *Everest the hard way* (1976) · b. certs. · m. cert. [Boardman] · private information (2004) · *CGPLA Eng. & Wales* (1982) [Peter David Boardman and Thomas Joseph Tasker]

Likenesses C. Bonington, photograph, repro. in C. Bonington, *The climbers* (1992), 239 · T. Tullis, photograph, Alpine Club, London [*see illus.*]

Wealth at death £23,083: administration, 1982, *CGPLA Eng. & Wales*

Boase, Alan Martin (1902–1982), French scholar, was born in Rathalpin, St Andrews, on 23 June 1902, the son of William Norman Boase (1870–1938), the owner of a linen mill, and his wife, Mabel Margaret, the daughter of John Leadbetter of Broughty Ferry. His father gained distinction in Scotland for his entrepreneurship in manufacturing and for his service as chairman of the Royal and Ancient Golf Club at St Andrews. Boase was educated at Eton College and New College, Oxford, where he took a first in French in 1924, and then undertook postgraduate research at Trinity College, Cambridge, and the University of Paris, gaining his Cambridge PhD in 1930. His privileged background did not preclude sympathy for the left-wing values enshrined for that generation in the Spanish Civil War. On 19 March 1931, in the Chapel of the Savoy, London, he married Elizabeth Grizelle (1911–1977), the eldest daughter of Edward Seymour Forster, professor of Greek at the University of Sheffield. Her tragic death in a car accident affected him deeply. They had four sons.

Boase began his academic career in 1929 as a lecturer in French at the University of Sheffield. In 1936 he was appointed professor of French in the University College of Southampton; a year later, he was appointed to the Marshall chair of French at Glasgow (established in 1917), a post he held with distinction until his early retirement in 1965. Under his leadership, the department of French in Glasgow became the largest and one of the most dynamic in the UK, the launching pad for many distinguished academic careers.

With Leavisite aesthetic values, Boase imported the tutorial system from Oxford and Cambridge, which he combined with a traditional lecturing system. The syllabus reflected the Oxbridge breadth and rigour, even for students embarking on the three-year MA ordinary degree. Staff were expected to be able to emulate his cultural depth and erudition by taking on, at a moment's notice, lectures on any aspect of French literature. His business acumen and aesthetic interests were well deployed in the refurbishment of the modern languages building. This characterless 1950s construction was, at his insistence, equipped with a theatre and adorned by numerous reproductions of old masters and, notably, a rare nineteenth-century map of Paris. Fittingly, the French artist Marc Chagall honoured Boase with a wash drawing for the frontispiece of the collection of essays presented to him to mark his retirement. On the lighter side, Boase offered horticultural produce from his extensive estate in Bowling, both for sale to the college club and as rewards for secretarial services provided by colleagues.

Boase's international reputation as a scholar was achieved largely through his work on Renaissance French literature. His monograph *The Fortunes of Montaigne: a History of the Essays in France, 1580–1669* (1935) and his critical edition (with Arthur Tilley) of Montaigne's *Selected Essays* (1934, revised, with a new preface, in 1954) made him a leading authority on one of France's most enigmatic writers. However, his most original contribution to French scholarship was his discovery of one of Montaigne's contemporaries, the poet Jean de Sponde. Boase joined pioneers in English criticism such as Sir Herbert Grierson and T. S. Eliot, who had rediscovered the metaphysical and religious poets John Donne, George Herbert, and Henry Vaughan. Eliot's Clark lectures on 'The Varieties of Metaphysical Poetry' at Trinity College in Cambridge in 1926 no doubt had a formative influence on Boase, whose seminal article in Eliot's *Criterion* five years later, in 1931, 'Then Came Malherbe', posed the now celebrated question: 'Where are the French metaphysical poets?' Boase published the poems of Sponde in four scholarly volumes, a biography of the poet (*La vie de Jean de Sponde*), and what is likely to be the definitive edition of the *Œuvres littéraires* (1978).

Boase's acute sensitivity to poetry was also reflected in a landmark series of four anthologies, *The Poetry of France: an Anthology* (1964–73), designed to make French poetry from its origins to the present day accessible to students and general readers. The volumes, a fixed point on the Glasgow syllabus, became academic best-sellers.

His enthusiasm for all aspects of French culture equipped Boase to engage with leading French writers, critics, and academicians, making him an ideal contributor to the *Companion to French Studies* (ed. R. L. Graeme Ritchie, 1937). His love of theatre, evident in his edition of Cocteau's *La machine infernale* (1944), extended to practical (including acting) support for Glasgow's French department dramatic society, founded in 1952.

Boase's international stature was enhanced by his visiting professorships in the universities of California at Berkeley (1962) and Monash in Australia (1969). Made an honorary fellow at the Collège de France in 1974, he was invited to serve as president of the Association of Professors of French, and was appointed to chair the consultative committee of the French Institute in Scotland. His outstanding contribution to French culture was recognized by the title of officier of the Légion d'honneur and the grand prix du rayonnement français of the Académie française. He died from heart failure at his home in Edinburgh, 39 Inverleith Place, on 7 November 1982.

NOËL PEACOCK

Sources D. R. Haggis and others, *The French Renaissance and its heritage: essays presented to Alan M. Boase by colleagues, pupils and friends* (1968) · *The Times* (16 Nov 1982) · A. Steele, *French Studies*, 38 (1984), 118–19 · *The Scotsman* (8 Nov 1982) · b. cert. · m. cert. · d. cert. · *WWW* · private information (2004)

Wealth at death £403,542.79: confirmation, 17 Feb 1983, *CCI*

Boase, Charles William (1828–1895), historian and antiquary, born in Chapel Street, Penzance, on 6 July 1828, was the eldest child of John Josias Arthur Boase JP (1801–1896) and Charlotte (1802–1873), second daughter of Robert Sholl of Truro, who had married at St Clement, near Truro, on 4 July 1827 (*The Times*, 12 Sept 1896, 9). George Clement *Boase (1829–1897) and Frederic *Boase (1843–1916) were younger brothers.

Charles Boase was sent to Penzance grammar school to 1841, and to Truro grammar school from that date to 1846. At Truro he gained several medals and prizes, and during four years (1846–9) he held from it an Elliot scholarship at Exeter College, Oxford, where he matriculated on 4 June 1846. From 1847 to 1850 he combined with it an open scholarship at his college, and on 18 May 1850 he graduated BA with a second class in classics. He was elected to a Cornish fellowship on 30 June 1850, proceeded MA in 1853, and was ordained deacon at Cuddesdon by Bishop Wilberforce on 4 March 1855.

From the day of his matriculation to that of his death Boase lived at Exeter College. He witnessed its rebuilding, and took an especial interest in the construction and fitting of its library buildings. He was assistant tutor 1853–5, tutor 1855–84, lecturer in Hebrew 1859–69, lecturer in modern history 1855–94, and librarian from 1868. Between 1857 and 1875 he examined in various schools, and he was appointed in 1884 the university reader in foreign history. He resigned this last appointment and his college lectureship in modern history (which he held for nearly forty years) in the summer of 1894, but retained the place of librarian. He died in his rooms at Exeter College on 11 March 1895, and was buried in St Sepulchre's cemetery, Oxford, on 13 March.

Boase had acquired vast stores of knowledge, which

were given ungrudgingly to others, and was endowed with much quiet humour. He had long studied the history of Exeter College and its alumni, and in 1879 two hundred copies were printed for private circulation of his annotated *Register of the Rectors, Fellows, Scholars … of Exeter College*, with a historical introduction. A second edition, but without the introduction, came out in 1893–4, and a third edition, with the introduction revised and greatly expanded, forms volume 27 of the publications of the Oxford Historical Society, the cost of the printing, a sum exceeding £200, being defrayed by the author. The second part of the college register, containing a similar list of the commoners, being 'all names other than those in the previous volume', was issued by him in 1894. He contributed the article on Exeter College to Andrew Clark's *Colleges of Oxford*.

On the formation of the Oxford Historical Society in 1884 Boase was one of the honorary secretaries, and he acted on the committee to 1 June 1892. Much of its success was due to his judgement and energy, and its first publication consisted of the *Register of the University of Oxford, 1449–63, 1505–71* (1885–9), which he compiled and edited. He also wrote the preface to J. E. T. Rogers's *Oxford City Documents … 1268–1665*, which the society issued in 1891. *Oxford*, published by Longmans as part of their Historic Towns series in 1887, was written by Boase, but much of the information which he had collected was omitted.

Boase edited, with G. W. Kitchin (afterwards dean of Durham), the *History of England*, the translation in six volumes of the work by Leopold von Ranke, published in 1895, and was entirely responsible for the rendering of the first volume. In conjunction with his two brothers he compiled an *Account of the Families of Boase or Bowes*, tracing his ancestors back in west Cornwall to the end of the sixteenth century (1876; 2nd edn, 1893). He contributed to the *Literary Churchman*, *The Academy*, and *English Historical Review*, wrote the article on the Macedonian empire in the *Encyclopaedia Britannica* (9th edn), and the lives of the Cornish saints in W. Smith and H. Wace, *Dictionary of Christian Biography* (1877–87). An account of the deeds and writs (1306–1836) in the Dawson collection was compiled by him for the *Catalogue of … Penzance Public Library* (1874; pp. 336–43).

Boase was a noted bibliophile and the possessor of large collections of Cornish genealogies. The bulk of his library, of which he kept a full record, was catalogued and sold by Blackwells booksellers after his death. Some of the most valuable items, however, passed to his college, including a now famous fourteenth-century manuscript of Suetonius' *Twelve Caesars*, later recognized to have been owned and annotated by Petrarch. His own working methods were somewhat disorderly, and the books which he wrote are often inadequately referenced by modern standards. His main claim to fame, beyond his local distinction as the historian of Exeter College, lies in his position as a mainstay of the Oxford history school during the decades of its first flourishing. As his surviving tutorial notebooks testify, he taught widely and conscientiously, though without any great originality of mind, and he was a popular figure in his college and university:

> He had a quick way of talking, altogether without the least air of pretension or even consciousness that he was pouring forth an amount of knowledge, skilfully and humorously compounded, which would have made the reputation of many a professed conversationalist … His friends will speak of his geniality, his cheery good nature, his unfailing kindness, which in a moment made children feel at home with the most human of old bachelors. (*The Athenaeum*)

W. P. Courtney, *rev.* J. R. Maddicott

Sources C. W. Boase, *Register of the … members on the foundation of Exeter College, Oxford* (1879) · C. W. Boase, G. C. Boase, and F. Boase, *An account of the families of Boase or Bowes* (1876) · *The Athenaeum* (16 March 1895), 345–6 · *The Athenaeum* (23 March 1895), 378 [correction] · F. C. Conybeare, *The Academy* (16 March 1895), 237 · *Oxford Magazine* (13 March 1895) · *Oxford Magazine* (1 May 1895) · P. R. H. Slee, *Learning and a liberal education: the study of modern history in the universities of Oxford, Cambridge and Manchester, 1800–1914* (1986) · *EdinR*, 152 (1880), 344–79

Archives Exeter College, Oxford, boxes J. I. 1–15, L. III. 3–5

Likenesses photograph, *c.*1885, Exeter College, Oxford

Wealth at death £14,907 4*s.* 5*d.*: resworn probate, June 1895, *CGPLA Eng. & Wales*

Boase, Frederic (1843–1916), lawyer and biographer, was born on 7 October 1843 in Larrigan, near Penzance, the youngest in the family of four sons and two daughters of John Josias Arthur Boase (1801–1896), banker, and his wife, Charlotte (1802–1873), daughter of Robert Sholl. He was educated at Penzance and Bromsgrove grammar schools from 1855 to 1859, and in 1861 was articled to Thomas Cornish, a solicitor in Penzance. He passed his law finals in London in 1867 and was admitted attorney and solicitor in that year. Until 1868 he worked as a solicitor in Exmouth after which he moved to London to a post as a conveyancing clerk, which he held until 1872. In 1877 he was appointed librarian of the Incorporated Law Society. He was an original member of the Library Association.

In 1891 Boase published a *Catalogue of Printed Books in the Library of the Incorporated Law Society*, which was reprinted in 1906, and in 1892 he published the first volume of his *Modern English Biography*, which contains many thousands of concise memoirs of people who had died since the year 1850. This was printed privately in a limited edition of 250 copies, and in its preface the author expressed his gratitude to his father and to his eldest brother, Charles William *Boase, 'for their great kindness in conjointly defraying the cost of printing this work which I claim to be an important contribution to the English biography of the nineteenth century'. Boase explained that for twenty years he had made a collection of notes relating to English persons deceased since 1850, and that in compiling his work he had kept in mind the dictum of James Anthony Froude, 'we want the biographies of common people', so that many hundreds of the thousands of entries included in his compilation related to persons who had not been eminent but had led interesting lives, accounts of which could not be found in any other book.

The second and third volumes of *Modern English Biography* were published (also in limited editions) in 1897 and 1901. In 1903 Boase retired from his post of librarian of the

Law Society and devoted the rest of his life to his biographical work. Volume 4 was issued in 1908, volume 5 in 1912, and volume 6 in 1921 (by which time the author had been dead for five years). In 1965 all six volumes were republished with a new preface written by Anna Kate Rance. The full six volumes of Boase's *magnum opus* contain 30,000 entries, a stupendous achievement to come from the pen of one author. The work remains an essential tool for historical research into the period covered. The indexes are of exceptional usefulness and Boase set new standards in the use of sources. He developed a curious relationship to the *Dictionary of National Biography*, which he both contributed to and plundered.

From 1868 Boase lived in London with his brother, George Clement *Boase, bibliographer, who, up to the time of his death in 1897, assisted his younger brother with his biographical studies. Charles William Boase, the Oxford historian, together with George Clement and Frederic, all collaborated in the preparation of *An account of the families of Boase or Bowes, originally residing at Paul or Madron in Cornwall*. This was printed as a limited edition of seventy-five copies for private circulation in 1876, and a second edition limited to 100 copies appeared in 1893.

Frederic Boase never married. He died in St Leonards on 23 December 1916.

H. F. Oxbury, *rev.* Myfanwy Lloyd

Sources C. W. Boase and others, *An account of the families of Boase or Bowes* (1893) • Boase, *Mod. Eng. biog.*, prefaces
Wealth at death £8876 19*s.* 3*d.*: probate, 27 Jan 1917, *CGPLA Eng. & Wales*

Boase, George Clement (1829–1897), bibliographer, born at Chapel Street, Penzance, on 20 October 1829, was the second son of John Josias Arthur Boase (1801–1896), a banker, and his wife, Charlotte (1802–1873), daughter of Robert Sholl of Truro. Charles William *Boase and Frederic *Boase were his brothers. He was educated at Regent House Academy and the grammar school at Penzance, and for a short time in 1844 at Bellevue House Academy, Penryn. From that year to 1846 he was in a local bank at Penzance; from 1847 to 1850 he was with Nehemiah Griffiths, ship and insurance broker, at 2 White Hart Court, Lombard Street, London; and from 1850 to 1854 he was a clerk with Ransom & Co., bankers, at 1 Pall Mall East.

Boase sailed for Australia on 29 April 1854. He became corrector of the press on the *Melbourne Age*. He went on to become a gold-digger at Simpson's ranges, and then worked in a general store. During 1855–64 he was tutor with the Darchy family on the Murrumbidgee River, New South Wales, and on Lachlan River, and was also correspondent of the *Sydney Morning Herald*. In 1864 he returned to Britain, and managed the business of Whitehead & Co., provision merchants, from 1865 to 1874, when he retired and occupied himself in biographical and antiquarian literature. During his retirement years he lived in London, successively at 15 Queen Anne's Gate and at 36 James Street (later 28 Buckingham Gate), where he collected a unique library illustrative of the biography of the nineteenth century.

George Clement Boase (1829–1897), by J. Howie, pubd 1897

Boase was the joint author, with W. P. Courtney, of the *Bibliotheca Cornubiensis* (1874–82), and the sole author of a kindred volume, *Collectanea Cornubiensia* (1890). With his brothers Charles William and Frederic, he compiled *An Account of the Families of Boase or Bowes* (1876), helped in the compilation of the works on Exeter College, Oxford, by his elder brother, Charles William, and the magnificent compilation *Modern English Biography* (1892–1901) by his youngest brother, Frederic. He compiled with W. P. Courtney, for Walter William Skeat, the Cornish portion of *A Bibliographical List of the Works … Illustrative of the Various Dialects of English* (English Dialect Society, 1877), and he assisted John Ingle Dredge in his tracts on Devon bibliography. He was a frequent contributor to *Notes and Queries* and the *Western Antiquary*. He supplied 723 memoirs to the *Dictionary of National Biography*. Boase died at 13 Granville Park, Lewisham, London, on 1 October 1897, and was buried at Ladywell cemetery on 5 October 1897.

W. P. Courtney, *rev.* Nilanjana Banerji

Sources *The Times* (5 Oct 1897) • C. W. Boase, G. C. Boase, and F. Boase, *An account of the families of Boase or Bowes*, 2nd edn (privately printed, Truro, 1893) • *N&Q*, 8th ser., 12 (1897), 301–2 • personal knowledge (1901) • *CGPLA Eng. & Wales* (1897)
Likenesses J. Howie, photograph, pubd 1897, NPG [*see illus.*]
Wealth at death £16,044 18*s.* 10*d.*: probate, 4 Nov 1897, *CGPLA Eng. & Wales*

Boase, Henry (1763–1827), banker and writer on finance, was born at Madron, Cornwall, on 3 June 1763, the fourth son of Arthur Boase (*d.* 1780) and Jane, daughter of Henry Lugg. He was educated privately in classical languages and French, and in 1779 became a clerk in the office of a relative, Stephen Luke, of Penzance. In 1785 Boase went from Penzance to Roscoff, in Brittany, in a fishing boat, and resided for a time at Morlaix, where he perfected his knowledge of French.

In 1788, not finding any business opening in Cornwall, he obtained a situation in London, as corresponding clerk in the West End banking house of Ransom, Morland, and Hammersley. This house had an extensive continental connection, and after the flight of Louis XVI in 1791 a large part of the funds for the support of the emigrant clergy and nobility passed through its hands. Boase prospered in this position, being promoted to chief clerk in 1792. Seven years later he became the managing partner. On 26 October 1794, Boase married Anne, only child of Matthew and Anne Craige, of Walsall, at St Andrew's Church, Holborn, London. They had a large family, consisting of eight daughters and five sons, including Henry Samuel *Boase, geologist and chemist.

During his residence in London, Boase moved in philanthropic and reforming circles and was acquainted with Granville Sharp and Robert Owen. He was a leading member of the London Missionary Society, and played a considerable part in the foundation of the British and Foreign Bible Society, in conjunction with the Revd Thomas Charles, of Bala. He was also much interested in the formation of schools on the new monitorial system of Joseph Lancaster.

Boase wrote a number of works on financial questions, including, in 1802, a discussion of the Bank Restriction Bill, as well as various proposals for the reform of the currency. In 1804 he went to Scotland to examine the affairs of the Dundee New Bank. This led to its reconstruction under new proprietors, including two of Boase's own sons.

Boase's health was seriously affected by the severe winters in London, and in 1809 he retired from his business interests in the City, and went to live at Penzance. There he became a partner in the banking house of Batten, Oxham, and Carne, from 1810 until 1823, when, with the copper manufacturers George Grenfell and Pascoe Grenfell as partners, Boase took over the Penzance Union Bank. A prominent figure in the town, Boase served as a magistrate before becoming mayor of Penzance in 1816.

Scientific and literary pursuits flourished in Cornwall early in the nineteenth century, and Boase found time for both. He played an active role in 1814, along with Dr John Paris and Ashhurst Majendie, in the foundation of the Royal Geological Society of Cornwall: he contributed to its *Transactions*, and his eldest son, Dr Henry S. Boase, served as its secretary. He also helped promote the Penzance Public Library. In 1821 Boase was elected a fellow of the Royal Society of Literature.

Boase died at Alverton, Penzance, on 8 April 1827. He was survived by his wife and twelve of his children, and was buried at St Mary's Church, Penzance. His wife died in 1863 at the age of eighty-eight. Boase's sons were also important Cornish figures, and extended their father's banking and intellectual pursuits.

G. C. Boase, *rev.* Robert Brown

Sources C. W. Boase, G. C. Boase, and F. Boase, *An account of the families of Boase or Bowes*, 2nd edn (privately printed, Truro, 1893) · J. Carne, *Letters, 1813–1837* (1885), 187, 114 · D. Gilbert, *The parochial history of Cornwall: founded on the manuscript histories of Mr Hals and Mr Tonkin*, 3 (1838), 95 · C. W. Boase, *A century of banking in Dundee*, 2nd edn (1867) · Boase & Courtney, *Bibl. Corn.* · J. Owen, *The history of the origin and first ten years of the British and Foreign Bible Society* (1816)
Likenesses portrait, repro. in Boase, Boase, and Boase, *An account of the families of Boase or Bowes*

Boase, Henry Samuel (1799–1883), geologist and chemist, was born at 6 Knightsbridge, London, on 2 September 1799, the third child of Henry *Boase (1763–1827), a banker, and his wife, Anne, daughter of Matthew Craige. He came from an extensive Cornish family; three of his nephews, C. W. Boase, G. C. Boase, and Frederic Boase, were noted for their historical and biographical work. He first attended school in Sloane Street, and in 1809 went to Blundell's School, Tiverton. He showed an early interest in chemistry, and in 1815 his father, after consulting members of another Cornish family, the Davys, decided that he should go to the Royal Cork Institution to be taught by Edmund Davy, and to work in his chemical laboratory. By 1816 Boase had decided that he wished to study medicine; he therefore left Cork against the advice of Davy, and in September 1817 started at the University of Edinburgh. He graduated in 1821 with an MD.

After graduation Boase returned to Penzance, where his family now lived, and in February 1822 was appointed physician to the Penzance Dispensary. He held this post for less than four years, and did not practise again, having found medicine a most unattractive profession. In 1824 he married Elizabeth Valentina (1799–1876), daughter of William Stoddard of Dorset; there were ten children from this marriage. In the same year he joined his father as a partner in the Penzance Union Bank, and in a company of tin smelters, Grenfell and Boase. He began to show an interest in geology, and in 1822 was appointed secretary to the Royal Geological Society of Cornwall, a post which he held until 1827 and again from 1833 to 1837. During this time he delivered two series of lectures on chemistry and read twenty-five papers on geological subjects, four of which were published in the society's *Transactions*. In 1827, he resigned his position as secretary in order to devote time to an extensive study of Cornish geology, with the intention of completing a geological map of that county. He claimed to have walked more than 2500 miles in the course of his investigations. The map was published in 1834 in the fourth volume of the *Transactions of the Royal Geological Society of Cornwall*, together with a long paper, 'Contributions towards a knowledge of the geology of Cornwall'. The map was, however, based on Boase's conviction that granites were stratified and of the same age as the surrounding rocks, a theory which was becoming discredited, and it did not contain any information on mineral deposits, so important to Cornwall. It was therefore of little value, and only five years later was superseded by the larger scale and more detailed maps of the Geological Survey. In 1834 Boase published *A Treatise on Primary Geology*, intending to present his theory on the formation of granites before the meeting of the British Association for the Advancement of Science at Edinburgh (1834), at which he was to deliver a paper. His ideas, which were closer to those of Werner than to Hutton, were forcefully criticized by the established geologists, Sedgwick, Buckland, and Lyell. He argued that mineral veins were formed at the same time as the surrounding rocks, and that all had been formed by the action of water.

While in Cornwall, Boase served on the committee of

the Royal Cornwall Polytechnic Society, and as president of the Penzance Literary and Scientific Institution. In 1837 he moved to London, hoping to be appointed to a post at one of the colleges of the new university, but was disappointed. He was elected a fellow of the Geological Society in April 1837, and was a member of its council in 1838–9. In May 1837 he was elected a fellow of the Royal Society. In 1838 he moved to Dundee, a town with which his family had banking connections. His chemical researches into dyeing and bleaching products had brought him into contact with the Scottish textile industry and he became a partner in the textile bleaching firm of Turnbull & Co. In 1846 he became managing director of the same company, which then took the name of Boase & Co. In this capacity he continued his chemical researches, and in 1855 he took out a patent relating to 'the process of drying organic substances' (*DNB*). While resident in Dundee, Boase published several books on the nature of science, including *The Philosophy of Nature* (1860), in which he argued that all phenomena are the consequences of two opposed causes, and that all natural bodies are dualisms of powers, attractive and repulsive. This book attracted little notice. In a sequel, *An Essay on Human Nature* (1865), he discussed human will and the necessity of revealed religion, and made clear his opposition to the evolutionary ideas of Darwin. He retired from his textile business in 1870. He died on 4 May 1883 at his home, Seafield House, 5 Magdalen Place, Dundee, and was buried at the western cemetery, Dundee.

DENISE CROOK

Sources C. W. Boase, G. C. Boase, and F. Boase, *An account of the families of Boase or Bowes*, 2nd edn (privately printed, Truro, 1893) · Boase & Courtney, *Bibl. Corn.* · J. Morrell and A. Thackray, *Gentlemen of science: early years of the British Association for the Advancement of Science* (1981), 461 · 'Obituary of Dr. H. S. Boase', *Annual Report of the Royal Geological Society of Cornwall*, 70 (1883), cxcv · *DNB* · Boase, *Mod. Eng. biog.* · d. cert.

Likenesses group portrait, silhouette, *c.*1825 (with his family), repro. in Boase, Boase, and Boase, *Account of the families*, facing p. 3

Wealth at death £36,560 8*s.* 2*d.*: confirmation, 23 June 1883, *CCI*

Boase, Thomas Sherrer Ross (1898–1974), art historian and university teacher, was born in Dundee on 31 August 1898, the only son and elder child of Charles Millet Boase, the manager and part owner of a bleaching mill at Claverhouse outside Dundee, and his wife, Anne Malcolm, daughter of Thomas Sherrer Ross, a merchant of the same city. Books abounded in his home and he read widely from an early age. Moving from a local preparatory school to Rugby School in 1912, he long believed himself at a disadvantage because he was so bad at ball games. However, he became head of his house, and won a prize essay contest on the subject of Lorenzo de' Medici and then an exhibition to enter Magdalen College, Oxford. From 1917 to 1919 he was with the Oxford and Buckinghamshire light infantry and for the last year of the war fought on the front between St Quentin and Cambrai. He was awarded the MC. His Oxford education had already begun, the cadet battalion which he joined on leaving Rugby being housed in Wadham College. At this time he first met F. F. (Sligger) Urquhart of Balliol, whose style and standards were to influence him profoundly. He returned in 1919 to read modern history at Magdalen, took a second class degree in 1921, and was elected to a fellowship at Hertford College in 1922.

Boase rapidly became an effective teacher. He lectured on both medieval and modern themes, a breadth of view reflected thirty years later in his equal concern for medieval and Victorian art. An interest in Italy developed into his first book, *Boniface VIII* (1933), and his study *St. Francis of Assisi* (1936). He was at the same time immersed in Oxford activities academic and social. As treasurer of the Oxford University Dramatic Society he made the acquaintance of the finest theatrical talent of the day; for the rest of his life he delighted to take pupils to the theatre, and patronized drama. He also turned his attention to the visual arts. The 1930 exhibition of Italian art at the Royal Academy deeply impressed him, and he learnt much from his friendship with Kenneth Clark and Lord Balniel (later earl of Crawford and Balcarres), who helped to mount the exhibition. Beside his frequent visits to Urquhart's chalet in the French Alps, constant travel in western Europe and the Near East was meanwhile making him an experienced viewer of pictures, monuments, and buildings.

In 1936 these interests brought Boase to the attention of those who were involved with the problems of the Courtauld Institute, founded in 1932 for the study of art history. Following the resignation of W. G. Constable as director, the committee of management selected Boase for the post in 1937 (he also held the London University chair in the history of art from 1937 to 1947), although he seemed to some art historians, critics, and students an amateur not properly qualified to succeed Constable. In taking up this challenge Boase enjoyed one advantage. Maintaining old friendships in Berlin and Frankfurt, participating in the World Council of Churches with its concern for events in Germany under Hitler, he was the better prepared to collaborate with scholars who had moved with the Warburg Library and Institute to London, and to learn from them. The Courtauld discovered that, although he did not satisfy everybody, the new director was able to give it an improved syllabus and greater stability. The two foundations were brought closer together; the first of his own numerous contributions to the *Journal of the Warburg and Courtauld Institutes*, 'The arts in the Latin kingdom of Jerusalem', appeared in 1939. Later Boase contributed the notice of Samuel Courtauld to the *Dictionary of National Biography*.

Immediately on the outbreak of the Second World War, Boase went to the Government Code and Cypher School at Bletchley, and from there to Cairo, where he worked for the Royal Air Force for nearly two years. From the end of 1943 he was once again based in Cairo, in charge of British Council activities in the Middle East. He travelled widely, made many friends both Arab and Jewish, enriched his old passion for the history of the crusades, and in 1945 returned to the Courtauld 'with resilience a little dulled for the taking up of a former life' (Boase). Aided principally by Anthony Blunt, he contributed to the revival and expansion of art-historical studies in post-war London, but in 1947 accepted the presidency of his old college,

Magdalen. It was quickly evident there that the new president's deft style of management, combined with a splendid talent for getting to know large numbers of undergraduates, would leave its mark. He remained vigorously in control for a dozen years, until tenure of the vice-chancellorship of the university (1958–60) and less robust health led to a phase of diminished activity. He retired in 1968.

All this time Boase gave equal attention to his work for the arts. His main undertaking was the *Oxford History of English Art*, as general editor and author of two out of eleven volumes. *English Art, 1100–1216* (1953) and *English Art, 1800–1870* (1959) offer sturdy summaries of modern knowledge; in the first illuminated manuscripts, and in the second minor rather than major artists, were the topics on which he wrote most effectively. Meanwhile he contributed many articles to books of reference, and generous introductions to work by other scholars. He served as trustee or adviser for the National Gallery (1947–53), the British Museum (1950–69), the Victoria and Albert Museum (1947–70), the Shakespeare Memorial Theatre, the Gulbenkian Foundation, and other institutions. He received several honorary degrees (including that of DCL of Oxford in 1960) and was a fellow of the British Academy (1961).

Boase died at his home at 6 Atherton Drive, Wimbledon, London, on 14 April 1974, having completed his contribution for a history of the Cilician kingdom of Armenia (published in 1978) and a study of Vasari (published in 1979). He was always energetic, a bachelor who organized his time with great precision and worked rapidly. He was an excellent speaker; collected good pictures; and disliked extravagance. Brought up in the Scottish Episcopal church, he remained a firm Christian, a great supporter of his college choir and chapel. His portrait by Anthony Devas, emphasizing a characteristic gesture of his hands, hangs in the hall of Magdalen. JOHN STOYE, *rev.*

Sources *The Times* (15 April 1974) · *The Times* (20 April 1974) · T. S. R. Boase, autobiographical memoir, 1972–3, Magd. Oxf. · C. Bailey, *Francis Fortescue Urquhart* (1936) · *Burlington Magazine*, 71 (1937), 107–8, 188–9, 237–8 · G. Zarnecki, *Burlington Magazine*, 117 (1975), 809 · personal knowledge (1986) · private information (1986) · *CGPLA Eng. & Wales* (1974)

Archives Courtauld Inst., papers · Magd. Oxf., corresp. and papers | Bodl. Oxf., corresp. relating to Society for Protection of Science and Learning · LUL, corresp. with Duckworth & Co. · Tate collection, corresp. with Lord Clark

Likenesses A. Devas, portrait, Magd. Oxf.

Wealth at death £154,716: probate, 29 July 1974, *CGPLA Eng. & Wales*

Boat Memory (1809/10–1830). *See under* Exotic visitors (*act. c.*1500–*c.*1855).

Boate, Arnold (1606–1653), biblical scholar and writer on natural history, was born in Gorinchem in the Netherlands, a younger son of Godefroy de Boot (*c.*1570–1625), knight, and Christina van Loon (*fl.* 1600–1630). With his elder brother Gerard *Boate he studied arts and medicine at the University of Leiden, graduating as a doctor in 1630. In the same year the two brothers moved to London to practise as physicians, and they were subsequently involved in some disputes with the College of Physicians. Arnold Boate was, however, lucky enough to be appointed personal physician to Robert Sidney, earl of Leicester, then viceroy in Ireland. As a result of this, and possibly owing to scholarly contacts with James Ussher, archbishop of Armagh, Boate moved to Ireland in 1636, where he became physician to Ussher and to Lord Deputy Wentworth. Ussher acted as Boate's patron in Dublin and it was to him and Robert Sidney, Boate's initial patron, that Arnold and Gerard dedicated their attack on the Aristotelian system, *Philosophia naturalis reformata* (1641). Through Ussher's influence Boate was appointed as surgeon-general for Ireland, an experience that encouraged him to write *A Remonstrance of Divers Remarkable Passages … of our Army in … Ireland* (1642).

Boate's marriage to Margaret Dongan or Dungan (*d.* 1651), daughter of Thomas Dungan, justice of the court of common pleas at Dublin, on Christmas day 1642 strengthened his links with the protestant Dublin gentry. They had three children: the elder daughter died on 2 October 1647 aged three and her brother died on 15 May 1649, aged seven months; the younger daughter, Maria Anna Boot, born on 13 September 1646, later married Marcus Beyerman. On the death of his wife, due to complications in pregnancy, on 17 April 1651 Boate wrote a very affecting memoir of his marriage to her, *The character of a trulie vertuous and pious woman, as it hath been acted by Mistris Margaret Dungan* (1651).

The aftermath of the Irish rising of 1641 had forced Boate to leave Ireland in 1644. He initially stayed with his brother in London from May to October, but he then moved to Paris, which became his base for the rest of his life. It is this period that saw Boate's involvement in scholarly disputes with Louis Capel, French Calvinist theologian at Saumur. Boate had already published at Leiden a work, in conjunction with Francis Taylor, in 1636 entitled *Examen Praefationis Morini in Biblia Graeca de textus Ebraici corruptione et Graeci authoritate*. In 1644 Boate published at London a further treatise concerned with the Hebrew text of the Old Testament, *Animadversiones sacrae ad textum Hebraicum veteris testamenti*, which evoked a reply from Capel. A pamphlet war ensued that not only involved Boate and Capel but also J. Morin, Capel's editor, and John Buxtorf, who rejected some of Capel's conclusions. Boate was also successful in involving Ussher in his dispute with Capel, as is demonstrated by his 1650 publication at Paris, *De textus Hebraici veteris testamenti certitudine et authoritate contra Ludovici Capelli criticam epistola Arnoldi Bootii ad reverendissimum Jacobum Usserium archiepiscoporum Armachanum*. Boate's last printed work, *Arnoldi Bootii vindiciae, seu, Apodixis apologetica pro Hebraica veritate* (1653), containing a dedication to Gisbert Voet, professor of theology at the University of Utrecht, was also concerned with the Capel dispute.

However, Boate's interest extended beyond Hebraic studies, as is demonstrated by his *Observationes medicinae* (1649) and even more significantly by the vital role that he played in the consolidation of an Irish wing of the Hartlib circle, a wide-ranging group of scholars who corresponded on scientific, religious, and political issues with Samuel Hartlib. Even after he departed from Ireland Boate continued to act as a conduit between Ussher and Hartlib, exchanging letters, books, and news of scholarly advances and disputes between the two. He played a major role in the development of one of the major publications of the Hartlib circle concerning Ireland, Gerard Boate's *Irelands Naturall History* (1652), which had prefaces by Hartlib and Arnold Boate. The latter's preface indicates not only his millenarian preoccupations, but also the fact that much of *Irelands Naturall History* was based on his own recollections of his journeys in Ireland, particularly in the provinces of Leinster and Ulster, as his brother had never actually been there. The 1652 edition of *Irelands Naturall History* included only the first part of the work, illustrating the essentially Baconian empirical approach of the Hartlib circle. The initial project had, however, encompassed a far wider endeavour, covering areas such as Irish flora and fauna, but all the time aiming at a consolidated approach to colonization. Hartlib was already aware of Boate's own interest in the natural history of Ireland for Boate had written a commentary on Hartlib's own 'Legacie of husbandry' in 1652. He therefore wanted Arnold to finish the entire project, but Boate's death in Paris in 1653 prevented him from doing so. ELIZABETHANNE BORAN

Sources P. C. Molhuysen and P. J. Blok, eds., *Nieuw Nederlandsch biografisch woordenboek*, 4 (Leiden, 1918), 211 · T. Barnard, 'The Hartlib circle and the origins of the Dublin Philosophical Society', *Irish Historical Studies*, 19 (1974–5), 56–71 · P. Coughlan, 'Natural history and historical nature: the project for a natural history of Ireland', *Samuel Hartlib and universal reformation: studies in intellectual communication*, ed. M. Greengrass, M. Leslie, and T. Raylor (1994), 298–317 · *The whole works of … James Ussher*, ed. C. R. Elrington and J. H. Todd, 17 vols. (1847–64), vol. 16 · *DNB* · A. Boate, *The character of a trulie vertuous and pious woman* (1651) · Sheffield University, Hartlib MSS database · K. T. Hoppen, *The common scientist in the seventeenth century: a study of the Dublin Philosophical Society, 1683–1708* (1970), 12 · Wing, *STC* · *British Museum general catalogue of printed books … to 1955*, BM, vol. 3 (*c*.1967) · T. C. Barnard, *Cromwellian Ireland: English government and reform in Ireland, 1649–1660* (1975), 214, 225, 235 · G. Clark and A. M. Cooke, *A history of the Royal College of Physicians of London*, 1 (1964), 262

Archives University of Sheffield, Hartlib MSS database

Boate, Gerard [*formerly* Gerrit Boot] (**1604–1650**), physician and natural historian, was born in Gorinchem, the Netherlands, one of five children born to Godefroy de Boot (*c*.1570–1625), soldier and author, and Christina van Loon (*fl.* 1600–1630). He entered the University of Leiden, possibly first as a student of letters, but certainly as a medical student, on 21 June 1628. He graduated DM on 3 July 1628. In 1630 he published the well-received *Vrolycke uuren* (*Horae jucundae*), a book of Low German and Latin poems. About 1630 Boate and his younger brother Arnold *Boate, also a medical student from Leiden, went to England to join their mother and sisters. Boate settled in London, where he was appointed physician to the king. In 1631 he married Katherine Menning.

Most of what we know of Boate and his brother stems from their close association with the Boyle family and other Anglo-Irish politicians, and with Samuel Hartlib. They were men of science, Baconian empiricists, protestants, and improvers. Webster suggests that they were part of Boyle's Invisible College and they were certainly involved in Hartlib's Office of Address for Communications for the dissemination of useful learning. The brothers turned their reforming pens first to philosophy and in 1641 published a treatise critical of Aristotelian philosophy, an event referred to by Samuel Beckett in his poem 'Whoroscope': but Gerard is remembered mainly for his natural history of Ireland. This was a project of some importance to the Hartlibians. When he wrote his natural history Boate had never visited the country. He relied on information from his brother, who had spent eight years travelling and practising medicine there, and from Sir William Parsons, surveyor-general of Ireland, his son Richard, and other families who had been driven from their large Irish estates by the civil war. Boate apparently completed his natural history by 1645, having begun work in 1644 when Arnold sent information, but it was not published immediately.

Boate was admitted a licentiate of the College of Physicians on 6 November 1646 and his London practice throve. On 17 July 1647 Boate's Irish connections secured him appointment as physician to the army in Ireland, but the disturbances there delayed his arrival until towards the end of 1649 and he died in Dublin in January 1650.

Boate's papers were acquired by Hartlib after his death. They included medical papers, particularly Boate's 'choicest secrets', namely '1. Receipt against the Consumption Cough for which he was mainly cryed up. 2. Receipt against the stone. 3. Receipt of his Purge which the old Archbishop Abbot hugely commended because the next day the body was not costive or bound which was a great inconveniency in all other purges' (Hartlib MSS, Ephemerides 1653, pt 2 28/2/57A). They also included his natural history, which Hartlib, with the agreement of Arnold Boate, who was then in Paris and who edited the text, published as *Ireland's naturall history … conducing to the advancement of navigation, husbandry, and other profitable arts and professions … published … for the common good of Ireland, and more especially for the benefit of the adventurers and planters there* (1652). The dedication to Oliver Cromwell and Charles Fleetwood, commander-in-chief in Ireland, apparently by Hartlib but in fact by John Dury, is a fine piece of religious writing. He expresses the hope that Ireland will be settled by Adventurers and perhaps exiled Bohemians and other protestants. Boate's text itself is described by Webster as 'a major development in economic geography' (Webster, 429). In a break with the chorographic tradition of Camden which emphasized antiquities and local curiosities, Boate describes natural resources plainly and systematically to produce a coherent regional geography. There is little topographic information and there are no maps, but his scientific education is evident from his descriptions of geology and processes such as glass making. His aim was systematic description as a prelude to improvement by and for protestant settlers: consequently the natural features of the country are described with enthusiasm to interest new settlers, but the Irish are reproached for their failure to improve the land and for their unruliness and disorderliness. This might well reflect the influence of William Parsons who was fiercely anti-Catholic and bitter towards the Irish. In a letter to Hartlib prefixed to the volume Arnold Boate stated that his brother had contemplated three further books on the flora, fauna, and people of Ireland respectively. A French translation was published in 1666 and further versions were published in Dublin in 1726, 1755, and 1860. Hartlib prevailed unsuccessfully on several others to complete the work of producing a natural history of Ireland: Arnold Boate contributed an *interrogatory* or questionnaire about Ireland to Hartlib's *Reformed Spiritual Husbandman* of 1652. Further progress was made by Robert Wood and Miles Symner but the impetus for scientific reform in Ireland passed to the surveying and mapping of Petty and others, and Gerard Boate's contribution remained the most important part of the natural history project.

Boate and his wife are listed among the Adventurers who financed the English suppression of the Irish rising of 1641, and in repayment Boate's widow Katherine obtained under certificate dated 15 November 1667 more than 1000 acres of land in co. Tipperary. Boate's sons Gerard, Godefroy, and Gerson, became respectively a lawyer, a Treasury secretary, and a preacher to the German congregation in Dublin. Other descendants played a distinguished part in the history of Irish medicine into the twentieth century.

ELIZABETH BAIGENT

Sources C. Webster, *The great instauration: science, medicine and reform, 1626–1660* (1975) • P. Coughlan, 'Natural history and historical nature: the project for a natural history of Ireland', *Samuel Hartlib and universal reformation: studies in intellectual communication*, ed. M. Greengrass, M. Leslie, and T. Raylor (1994), 298–317 • Y. M. Goblet, *La transformation de la géographie politique de l'Irlande au XVIIe siècle* (1930) • *The Hartlib papers*, ed. J. Crawford and others (1995) [CD-ROM] • Munk, *Roll* • 'Boate, Gerard', *Nieuw Nederlandsch biografisch woordenboek*, ed. P. C. Molhuysen and P. J. Blok, 1 (Leiden, 1911) • *DNB*

Archives University of Sheffield, Hartlib MSS

Bobart [Bobert], **Jacob, the elder** (*c.*1599–1680), botanist and gardener, was born at Brunswick. After a period as a soldier, during which he added a working knowledge of English and Latin to his native tongue, he settled in Oxford, possibly as an innkeeper, before being appointed superintendent of the university's new physic garden, apparently shortly before 1641, by its founder, the earl of Danby. Danby's estate was subsequently sequestrated and for at least seven years Bobart went unpaid, but he must have continued to work assiduously, for in 1648 the 64-page *Catalogus plantarum horti medici Oxoniensis*, which though anonymous is credited to him on the testimony of Dillenius, boasted an impressive 1600 '*stirpes*' (many of them now known to be mere horticultural varieties), among which Canadian plants feature prominently. An improved edition (1658) was issued in conjunction with his son and two others. By then admiring tributes to the beauty and richness in species he had effected in the garden had long been coming from its visitors, who included Evelyn, Ashmole, Pepys, the grand duke of Tuscany, and the prince of Orange (with whom he conversed in Dutch).

Thomas Baskerville knew Bobart as a stocky, square-set man, tall and strong, and recorded how one Whitsuntide he tagged his waist-length beard with silver and drew a crowd to the garden as a result. A later writer in the *Gardeners' Chronicle* (1885, 208) was to remark on the patently strong character caught in a portrait of him, that of someone who 'could hold his own among the dons of the University'.

Bobart's two sons, from his first marriage, to Mary (*d.* 1655), also became professional gardeners, the elder, Jacob *Bobart the younger, succeeding to his physic garden post. His second wife, Ann, outlived him, and died in 1696. Bobart died in office on 4 February 1680 and was buried in the church of St Peter-in-the-East, Oxford, where a tablet to his memory describes him as 'a man of great integrity'. His will, made three years earlier, reveals him as the owner of considerable local property: an inn was left to his elder surviving son, some houses to the younger one, and a further house to one of his six daughters. *Bobartia*, a genus of South African members of the iris family, was named by Linnaeus in honour of him and his elder son jointly; though he himself invariably spelt his name Bobert, his elder son changed this to Bobart, which has traditionally been used for both.

D. E. ALLEN

Sources S. H. Vines and G. C. Druce, *An account of the Morisonian herbarium in the possession of the University of Oxford* (1914), xv–xxii • 'Thomas Baskerville's account of Oxford *c.* 1670–1700', ed. H. Baskerville, *Collectanea: fourth series*, OHS, 47 (1905), 175–225 • G. C. Druce, 'The foundation of the Oxford Botanic Garden and its tercentenary', *Report of the Botanical Society and Exchange Club of the British Isles*, 7 (1923–5), 335–6 • H. T. Bobart, *A biographical sketch of Jacob Bobart* (privately printed, Leicester, 1884) • G. C. Druce, *The flora of Oxfordshire* (1886), 373–4 • B. Henrey, *British botanical and horticultural literature before 1800*, 1 (1975), 96 • *Extracts from the literary and scientific correspondence of Richard Richardson*, ed. D. Turner (1835), 9–11 nn. • *N&Q*, 7 (1853), 578 • *N&Q*, 8 (1853), 37, 344 • *Gardeners' Chronicle*, new ser., 24 (1885), 208 • will, 2 Nov 1677, U. Oxf.

Likenesses M. Burghers, line print (after D. Loggan), BM • M. Burghers, oils (after D. Loggan), BM • line print, NPG • oils, NPG

Bobart, Jacob, the younger (1641–1719), botanist, was born in Oxford on 2 August 1641, the elder of the two sons of Jacob *Bobart the elder (*c.*1599–1680) and his first wife, Mary (*d.* 1655). After a schooling which imparted a graceful literary style but a poor command of Latin he worked under his father in the Oxford Physic Garden until the age of nearly forty. Though Thomas Baskerville may merely have been referring to their respective sizes in saying the son was but a shrimp compared to the father, the forceful personality suggested by the father's portrait could have produced a diffident son.

In contrast to the elder Bobart, who remained essentially a gardener, the younger displayed more scholarly inclinations. At about the age of twenty he started a personal herbarium, which grew to fill twelve folio volumes with some 2000 named specimens, most presumably from the garden; although not documented further, it is of lasting value for tracing the history of old horticultural varieties. A record contributed to Merret's *Pinax* (1666) shows that he was also studying the local wild flora by then, to such effect that he impressed John Ray by producing from his herbarium a British species new to Ray. A short list of his finds in Ray's 1691 *Synopsis* includes four plants new to Britain and shows that, besides extensive fieldwork around Oxford, he had ranged as far as Somerset. He also botanized in the Netherlands, Flanders, and the Jura before his marriage to Anna (*d*. 1718), about 1673.

On his father's death in 1680 Bobart succeeded him as superintendent. Only three years later he lost his scientific mentor too, with the untimely death of the professor of botany, Robert Morison, in an accident, and was asked to take over the latter's lecturing. This caused many of his contemporaries to assume he had also succeeded to Morison's post, but that was precluded by his never being a member of the university. The elevation nevertheless led to his contributing to the proceedings of the Philosophical Society of Oxford and, more important, to being entrusted by the University Press with the editing and completion of Morison's *Plantarum historiae universalis Oxoniensis*, of which only the second of three projected parts had been published. Bobart necessarily had to neglect his garden work for much of the thirteen years this massive undertaking took. The first part proved irretrievable, but with much help from William Dale of Queen's College he substantially wrote *Pars tertia*—as it is traditionally known—and greatly extended it to include very many plants unknown to Morison, in the research for which he was much assisted by the young William Sherard. External events, however, led the press to lose interest for five years and, demoralized, Bobart talked about leaving Oxford for a position elsewhere, preferably at Chelsea. Fortunately at that point, in 1691, the project was revived and concluded, but Bobart's key role was not adequately acknowledged and for a century afterwards botanical authors denied him the credit he deserved.

Bobart published nothing further in his lifetime, reserving his energies for manual work in the garden and further enrichment of its collections by exchanging seeds, plants, and dried specimens with a wide range of fellow enthusiasts, especially with Petiver, with whom he was on particularly friendly terms. Hence, expecting a fellow learned gentleman, Zacharias von Uffenbach was shocked, on paying a visit in 1710, to find a *praefectus horti* not at all as he had imagined. Instead, he was confronted with:

> an unusually pointed and very long nose, small eyes deeply set in his head, a wry mouth with scarcely any upper lip, a large and deep scar on one cheek, and his whole face and hands as black and coarse as those of the meanest gardener or labourer,

dressed in clothes that were 'very bad' (*Merkwürdige Reisen*, 3, 1754, 163).

In 1717 illness caused Bobart to place the garden temporarily in the care of his brother, Tilleman, who substantially exceeded its approved budget. The vice-chancellor declared the university would rather have no garden than pay as much as £100 a year for its upkeep, and Bobart was required to resign as a result. His family and friends denounced this as callous, but he was allowed to stay on in the Garden House. Only a few months later, though, on 28 December 1719, he died. He was buried two or three days later in the church of St Peter-in-the-East, Oxford, alongside his parents and his wife of forty-five years, who predeceased him by just over a year. His personal stock of plants, seeds, and tools, extensive library, papers, and the two herbaria he had formed (one, the so-called 'Morisonian herbarium', designed to illustrate the *Historia*) were left to the university; he also bequeathed a field for the use of the poor of the parish. A year later his twelve-page *Historiae naturalis sciographia*, of high interest as the sole complete exposition of Morison's classificatory system, was published anonymously. Apart from the genus *Bobartia*, which Linnaeus named in honour of father and son jointly, he is commemorated in a colour form of the knotted figwort, *Scrophularia nodosa*.

D. E. ALLEN

Sources H. M. Clokie, *An account of the herbaria of the department of botany in the University of Oxford* (1964), 3, 13–17, 54–8, 134 · S. H. Vines and G. C. Druce, *An account of the Morisonian herbarium in the possession of the University of Oxford* (1914), lii–lxv · G. C. Druce, *The flora of Berkshire* (1897), cxxi–cxxv · H. T. Bobart, *A biographical sketch of Jacob Bobart* (privately printed, Leicester, 1884) · *Extracts from the literary and scientific correspondence of Richard Richardson*, ed. D. Turner (1835), 10–11, 152 · J. Britten and J. E. Dandy, eds., *The Sloane herbarium* (1958), 91–2 · G. C. Druce, *The flora of Oxfordshire*, 2nd edn, 2 (1927), lxxx–lxxxii · E. J. Whittaker, *Thomas Lawson, 1630–1691* (1986) · R. T. Gunther, *Early science in Oxford*, 4 (1925); 12 (1939); 14 (1945) · C. E. Raven, *John Ray, naturalist: his life and works* (1942) · G. C. Druce, 'The foundation of the Oxford Botanic Garden and its tercentenary', *Report of the Botanical Society and Exchange Club of the British Isles*, 7 (1923–5), 335–6 · will, PRO, PROB 11/575, sig. 188 · C. Webster, 'The medical faculty and the physic garden', *Hist. U. Oxf.* 5: *18th-cent. Oxf.*, 683–723

Archives BL, corresp., Sloane MSS 3321–3322, 4036–4038, 4040–4041, 4043–4044, 4064 · Bodl. Oxf., botanical notebooks and MSS; memoirs · U. Oxf., department of plant sciences, the Morisonian herbarium, herbarium; MSS | RS, letters to William Sherard

Likenesses engraving, repro. in A. Evans, 'Vertumnus', *Oxford Almanac* (1719), frontispiece · oils (of Bobart?), Botanic Garden Library, Oxford; repro. in Vines and Druce, *Account of the Morisonian herbarium*, lvii

Wealth at death see will, proved 2 Jan 1720, archives of the chancellor's court

Bobath [*née* Busse], **Berta Ottilie** (1907–1991), physiotherapist, was born in Berlin on 5 December 1907, the daughter of Hermann Busse, a Jewish manufacturer of dresses. She trained as a remedial gymnast in Germany, and married Kurt Roehl, from whom she later obtained a divorce. In 1938 she left Germany as a refugee and arrived in Britain, where she met another refugee, the psychiatrist Dr **Karel Bobath** (1905–1991). Bobath was the Berlin-born son of Hynak Bobath, a merchant from an Orthodox Jewish family in Prague, and was working in casualty at Willesden General Hospital when he married Berta on 23 April 1941. They had one son.

Berta Bobath had worked in Germany with children suffering from cerebral palsy, and in 1944 she set up a unit for children affected by the condition at the Princess Louise Hospital, London. After the Second World War she was asked to treat the society portrait painter Simon Elwes, who had suffered a severe stroke, and with her help he learned to walk again and to paint with his left hand. This success led her to work on rehabilitating other stroke patients. She took the diploma of the Chartered Society of Physiotherapy in 1950, and was awarded a fellowship of the society in 1954 for her thesis 'A study of abnormal postural reflex activity in patients with lesions of the central nervous system', which was published in 1975 as an illustrated monograph as *Motor Development in the Different Types of Cerebral Palsy*. In 1951 she started a private clinic, which became the Western Cerebral Palsy Centre, a registered charity, in 1957. Karel Bobath was honorary consultant physician of the charity. He had been an assistant psychiatrist at Brookwood Hospital, Woking, and went on to work with Dr Alex Shapiro at Harperbury Hospital in St Albans, where he set up the first unit for children with physical disabilities in a hospital for the mentally handicapped in England.

Berta Bobath did not believe that spasticity was untreatable, and at her clinic she was able to develop her neurological approach to treating children with cerebral palsy, based on the idea that such children were not born with abnormal patterns of posture and movement but developed them through their own activity, and that these could therefore be improved through correct positioning and handling. She believed in the importance of very early diagnosis and treatment, devising individual plans which included teaching parents how to handle their children at home. Her object was to counteract abnormal patterns of movement and avoid further deterioration, and thus help the child reach their full potential and to function as normally as possible. In treating adult stroke patients she concentrated on retraining the affected side through physiotherapy, rather than through allowing the patient to neglect the hemiplegic side and confine themselves to using the unaffected side. Her treatment was based on real-life situations, so that what the patient learned would be part of their daily routine, and not just a series of exercises divorced from daily life. She strongly believed that the more 'normal' a patient could be, the easier it would be to readjust to family and social life. In all this she was greatly helped by her husband, from 1960 medical director of the cerebral palsy unit at Harperbury, who developed the theoretical basis to support her ideas.

The Bobaths developed postgraduate courses at the centre to train physiotherapists, occupational and speech therapists, and doctors in the Bobath approach to the treatment of neurological disorders. They went on lecture tours abroad, and addressed international conferences, developing a world-wide following. In 1975 the centre moved to larger premises in Hampstead, London, and was renamed the Bobath Centre. Berta Bobath was appointed MBE in 1978, and in 1981 she received an honorary doctorate from Boston University. She and her husband won the Harding award for 'outstanding work of benefit to the disabled'. She published *Abnormal Postural Reflex Activity Caused by Brain Lesions* (1965; 3rd edn 1985) and *Adult Hemiplegia: Evaluation and Treatment* (1970; 3rd edn 1990).

Berta and Karel Bobath were both suffering from heart disease when they took drug overdoses and died together on 20 January 1991 at their home, 36C Arkwright Road, Camden. As a result of a memorial appeal, a new purpose-built Bobath Centre for Cerebral Palsy was opened in East Finchley in 1993. ANNE PIMLOTT BAKER

Sources J. Barclay, *In good hands: the history of the Chartered Society of Physiotherapists, 1894–1994* (1994) • S. Levitt, *Treatment of cerebral palsy and motor delay*, 3rd edn (1995), 23–4 • *The Times* (25 Jan 1991) • *Physiotherapy* (Feb 1991) • *The Independent* (25 Jan 1991) • *The Guardian* (14 Feb 1991) • *Daily Telegraph* (30 Jan 1991) • m. cert. • d. cert. • d. cert. [Karel Bobath]

Likenesses P. Weedon, double portrait, photograph (with Karel Bobath), repro. in *Physiotherapy*, 99 • photograph, repro. in Barclay, *In good hands*, 289

Wealth at death £494,015: probate, 18 April 1991, *CGPLA Eng. & Wales* • £9500: probate, 30 July 1991, *CGPLA Eng. & Wales* • £165,196—Karel Bobath: probate, 18 April 1991, *CGPLA Eng. & Wales* • £4750—Karel Bobath: probate, 30 July 1991, *CGPLA Eng. & Wales*

Bobath, Karel (1905–1991). *See under* Bobath, Berta Ottilie (1907–1991).

Bobbin, Tim. *See* Collier, John (1708–1786).

Bocfeld, Adam. *See* Bockenfield, Adam of (*d.* 1279x92).

Bocher, Joan (*d.* 1550), religious radical, also known as Joan Knell and Joan of Kent, is of unknown origins, but Bocher and Knell families are found either side of the rim of Romney Marsh. Her religious history is also obscure. The earliest that is known for certain is that she was much in favour in reforming circles in Canterbury in the late 1530s and early 1540s. After being denounced for words against the sacrament of the altar she was imprisoned for a period, before being released largely on the initiative of Cranmer's commissary Christopher Nevinson. The failure properly to prosecute Joan at this time was one of the charges made against Cranmer in the prebendaries' plot of 1543. Her opponents alleged that she had previously abjured in Colchester, a charge which has led to her being identified with the 'mother Bocher' and 'Joan Bocher, widow' named in Bishop Cuthbert Tunstall's 1528 investigations in Essex. There is no record, however, that this Bocher abjured, although one who did abjure was a William Bocher of Steeple Bumpstead, a man with a family history of heresy. It is possible therefore that Joan Bocher had a Lollard background, a possibility also raised by some of the accusations against her, for instance that she had declared 'that matins and evensong was no better than rumbling of tubs' (Davis, 229). However, the execution for treason in 1538 of William Knell, head of the Kentish Knell family, may point to religious conservatism elsewhere in her family.

In the years after 1543 Bocher's beliefs took an Anabaptist turn. She became convinced of the theory of Christ's celestial flesh—that Christ did not derive his physical body from his mother but that it was a divine distillation. Such views were unusual in England. Although they had been heard from exiled Dutch Anabaptists in the mid-1530s, it is more likely—as Martin Micron, himself Flemish born, hinted—that she picked them up from the influx of refugees early in the reign of Edward VI. She was arrested, probably in 1548, and convicted of heresy in April 1549. She was then imprisoned for more than a year, for some of the time in the house of Lord Chancellor Rich, while great efforts were made to persuade her back to Edwardian orthodoxy, led by Archbishop Cranmer and Bishop Ridley of London. When she remained adamant in her opinions, the privy council decided to proceed with her execution by burning, despite the lack of a statute under which to proceed. Although there are difficulties with Foxe's account of Cranmer's browbeating the reluctant Edward VI into signing the death warrant, it is likely that the archbishop did indeed have some role in bringing Joan Bocher to the stake. She was burnt at Smithfield on 2 May 1550, still upbraiding those attempting to convert her, and maintaining that just as in time they had come to her views on the sacrament of the altar, so they would see she had been right about the person of Christ. She also asserted that there were a thousand Anabaptists living in the diocese of London.

Immediately after Bocher's death attempts were made to discredit her: there were sermons from Hugh Latimer, an academic refutation from Roger Hutchinson, and doggerel verse from Edmund Beck. Her views were described by Latimer and others as 'Arian', that is, heretical in denying the full divinity of Christ, which they were not, having far more in common with those of extreme opponents of Arius. Her death led to Joan's being much cited by opponents of the Elizabethan church. She was adopted by separatists for whom her fate exposed the true nature of established episcopal church government; and her execution was also used by Catholics responding to charges of cruelty in the Marian persecutions. The Catholic apologist Robert Persons, writing in 1599, is the first to record three interesting stories about her which are otherwise unattested: that she took part in the smuggling operations to bring Tyndale's New Testament to England; that she smuggled books to the Henrician court hidden under her skirts; and that she was a close friend of Anne Askew. All are possible and although the stories are late, Persons claims to have spoken to someone present at her trial. It was not for her views however, which despite the fears of the Edwardian establishment never became popular, but as a victim of intolerance that Joan Bocher was to be remembered—and by none more eloquently than William Wordsworth in whose sonnet to her she is described as condemned by 'mandates nature doth disown' (*Poetical Works*, 343).

ANDREW HOPE

Sources J. Strype, *Memorials of the most reverend father in God Thomas Cranmer*, 3 vols. in 4 (1848–54) • R. Persons, *A temperate wardword, to the turbulent and seditious wach-word of Sir Francis Hastinges knight* (1599) • *The works of Roger Hutchinson*, Parker Society, 4 (1842) • E. Beck, *A brefe confutacion of this most detestable, & Anabaptistical opinion, that Christ did not take hys flesh of the blessed Vyrgyn Mary nor any corporal substaunce of her body, for the maintenaunce whereof Jhone Bucher otherwise called Jhone of Kent most obstinantly suffered and was burned in Smythfyelde, the .ii. day of May* (1550) • *Sermons and remains of Hugh Latimer*, ed. G. E. Corrie, Parker Society, 20 (1845) • *The acts and monuments of John Foxe*, ed. J. Pratt, [new edn], 8 vols. in 16 (1853–70), vols. 5, 7 • *APC*, 1550–52 • J. Strype, *Ecclesiastical memorials*, 3 vols. (1822), vols. 1–2 • J. Davis, 'Joan of Kent, Lollardy and the English Reformation', *Journal of Ecclesiastical History*, 33 (1982), 225–33 • *LP Henry VIII*, vols. 4, 13, 18/2 • H. Robinson, ed. and trans., *Original letters relative to the English Reformation*, 1 vol. in 2, Parker Society, [26] (1846–7) • J. Ridley, *Thomas Cranmer* (1962) • M. Huggarde, *The displaying of the protestantes* (1556) • *The works of John Knox*, ed. D. Laing, 6 vols., Wodrow Society, 12 (1846–64), vol. 5 • *Life and letters of Thomas Cromwell*, ed. R. B. Merriman, 2 vols. (1902) • *The poetical works of William Wordsworth*, ed. E. de Selincourt and T. Hutchinson, new edn (1904); repr. (1936) • G. R. Elton, *Policy and police* (1972), 294–5 • *The chronicle and political papers of King Edward VI*, ed. W. K. Jordan (1966) • S. Brigden, *London and the Reformation* (1989) • D. MacCulloch, *Thomas Cranmer: a life* (1996)

Bock, Eberhard Otto Georg von, Baron von Bock in the Hanoverian nobility (1755–1814), army officer, was born on the family estate at Elze, north of Hanover. His military career started in 1774, when he joined the Hanoverian 5th infantry regiment. He later moved to the 13th infantry regiment, and in 1779 he transferred to the mounted life guards as a second lieutenant, rising to captain in 1783, major in 1794, and lieutenant-colonel in 1799. After joining the newly founded 'King's German Legion' after the collapse of the Hanoverian army in 1803 he was appointed colonel of the legion's 1st heavy dragoon regiment on 21 April 1804. From 1806 onwards he was permitted to use the title baron.

In 1805 Bock took part in the expedition to north Germany, which, though unsuccessful, gained many new recruits for the legion; some of these recruits helped to form the legion's 2nd heavy dragoon regiment. Bock was promoted major-general on 25 July 1810, and in 1811 took command of the brigade formed by the two heavy dragoon regiments. In 1812, after five and a half years' service in Ireland, his brigade was sent to the Iberian peninsula, where Bock won the army gold medal (Salamanca) for the unparalleled achievement of his men in riding down and taking prisoner three battalions of French infantry at Garcia Hernandez on 23 July 1812. Before leading the charge, the short-sighted Bock had to ask Lieutenant-Colonel May to point the enemy out to him. He then briefly replaced the wounded General Stapleton Cotton as commander of the British cavalry in the Peninsula. He fought with distinction at Vitoria on 21 June 1813 and received a clasp to his army gold medal. While returning to England on the transport *Bellona*, he was caught in a storm in the Bay of Biscay and struck the Tulbest Rocks, near Pleubian, France, on 21 January 1814. Bock drowned together with his son, Ludwig, a captain in the 2nd hussars of the King's German Legion. His body was washed ashore at the Breton village of Pleubian, where he was buried on 24 January.

PETER HOFSCHRÖER

Sources B. von Schwertfeger, *Geschichte der königlichen deutschen Legion, 1803–1816*, 2 vols. (1907) • B. von Poten, 'Die Generale der königlichen hannoverschen Armee und ihrer Stammtruppen', *Militär-Wochenblatt*, suppl., 7 (1903) • N. L. Beamish, *Geschichte der königlich deutschen Legion*, 2 vols. (Hanover, 1832–7) • B. von Poten, 'Des königs deutschen Legion, 1803 bis 1816', *Militär-Wochenblatt*, suppl. 11 (1905) [whole issue] • *The dispatches of … the duke of Wellington … from 1799 to 1818*, ed. J. Gurwood, new edn, 9: *Peninsula, 1790–1813* (1838) • P. Hofschröer, *The Hanoverian army of the Napoleonic wars*

(1989) • C. Oman, 'A dragoon of the legion', *Blackwood*, 193 (1913), 293–309

Bockenfield [Bocfeld, Buckfield], **Adam of** (*d.* 1279x92), commentator on Aristotle, was born at Bockenfield near Morpeth in Northumberland, on lands he eventually inherited from his father, Robert of Graunteleye. Since Adam's name differs from his father's, the supposition is that his name is toponymic. Adam's position as a landowner led him into several judicial actions between 1255 and 1278. However, his name first appears in 1238, when he was among those arrested in an Oxford riot. Owing to the efforts of Robert Grosseteste, then bishop of Lincoln (*d.* 1253), the king ordered that Adam de Bokingfeld and three others were to be allowed to leave Oxford, should they so wish. In 1243, now styled master, Bockenfield was presented by the prior and convent of Durham to the church of West Rounton in Yorkshire, and in 1249 was granted the living of Iver in Buckinghamshire by Grosseteste. For the latter appointment Adam enjoyed the strong support of Adam Marsh (*d.* 1259), an Oxford friend and colleague, who wrote that 'his profession of the sacred scriptures [*divinorum eloquiorum*] as well as humane letters renders him worthy of commendation' (*Monumenta Franciscana*, 165). By 1263 he was a canon of Lincoln Cathedral, and in that capacity installed a new abbess of Little Marlow, Buckinghamshire, in 1264. By order of the pope, moreover, Adam and the archdeacon of Lincoln were appointed in 1267 to collect the papal tithe in the diocese. Before 1276 he had resigned the West Rounton living, and by late 1278 his name is omitted from a listing of the canons of Lincoln. Since his will was proved during the archbishopric of John Peckham, it is assumed that he died between 1279 and 1292, probably some years after he retired from active teaching.

Bockenfield's contribution to the discipline he professed was as commentator on all of the treatises that constituted the *corpus vetustius* of Aristotle, as well as three falsely ascribed works. Several of these have two or three recensions, so that a total of at least twenty-two works issued from his hand. Of these only a part of the commentary on the *Metaphysics* and the commentary on the *De anima* have been edited; an edition of the commentary on the *De vegetabilibus*, which incorporates most of Alfred of Shareshill's glosses on the same work, is in preparation. The impressive number of manuscripts containing some or all of Adam's commentaries—fifty-eight at the latest count—testifies to the vogue these works enjoyed, especially on the continent, where most of the copies are found. At the same time, the fact that they stopped being copied at a relatively early date (virtually by the end of the thirteenth century) most probably means that the kind of glossing they represented, namely a literal exposition and analysis in the manner of Averroes's middle commentaries, had by then passed out of fashion. In the middle decades of the century, however, and before the new translations of Aristotle began to make their appearance in the 1260s, Adam was by every measure the most influential English commentator on that philosopher.

R. James Long

Sources H. Powell, 'The life and writings of Adam of Buckfield with special reference to his commentary on the *De anima* of Aristotle', BLitt diss., U. Oxf., 1964 • C. H. Lohr, 'Medieval Latin Aristotle commentaries', *Traditio*, 23 (1967), 314–413, esp. 317–23 • F. Pelster, 'Adam von Bocfeld (Bockingfeld), ein Oxforder Erklärer des Aristoteles um die Mitte des 13. Jahrhunderts', *Scholastik*, 11 (1936), 196–224 • S. H. Thomson, 'The works of Magister Adam of Bocfield (Bouchermefort)', *Medievalia et Humanistica*, 2 (1944), 55–87 • Emden, *Oxf.*, vol. 1 • A. Maurer, 'Adam of Buckfield, *Sententia super secundum metaphysicae*', *Nine mediaeval thinkers*, ed. J. R. O'Donnell (1955), 99–144 • R. J. Long, 'The reception and interpretation of the pseudo-Aristotelian *De plantis* at Oxford in the thirteenth century', *Knowledge and the sciences in medieval philosophy: proceedings of the eighth international congress of medieval philosophy* [Helsinki 1987], ed. R. Työrinoja, A. Lehtinen, and D. Føllesdal, 3 (1990), 111–23 • M. Grabmann, 'Die lateinische Averroismus des 13. Jahrhunderts und seine Stellung zur christlichen Weltanschauung', *Sitzungsberichte d. Bayerischen Akademie* (1931), 33 • M. Grabmann, 'Die Aristoteleskommentatoren Adam von Bocfeld und Adam von Bouchermefort: die Anfänge der Erklärung des "neuen Aristotel" in England', *Mittelalterliches Geistesleben* (1936), 138–82, 613–16 • M. Grabmann, 'Mitteilungen über Werke des Adam v. Bocfeld aus MS Lat. Quart. 906 der Preussischen Staatsbibliothek in Berlin', *Divus Thomas*, 17 (1939), 3–25 • S. H. Thomson, 'A further note on Master Adam of Bocfeld', *Medievalia et Humanistica*, 12 (1958), 23–32 • D. A. Callus, 'Two early Oxford masters on the plurality of forms', *Revue Neo-Scholastique de Philosophie*, 42 (1939), 411–45 • L. J. Bataillon, 'Adam of Bocfeld: further manuscripts', *Medievalia et Humanistica*, 13 (1960), 35–39 • R. J. Long, 'Adam of Buckfield and John Sackville: some notes on Philadelphia Free Library MS Lewis European 53', *Traditio*, 45 (1989–90), 364–7 • D. A. Callus, 'Introduction of Aristotelian learning to Oxford', *PBA*, 29 (1943), 229–81, esp. 255–6 • Paris, *Chron.*, vol. 3 • *Commentarii de scriptoribus Britannicis, auctore Joanne Lelando*, ed. A. Hall, 2 (1709), 269 • Bale, *Cat.*, 2.45–6 • J. S. Brewer, ed., *Monumenta Franciscana*, 1, Rolls Series, 4 (1858), 165 • T. B. Noone, 'Evidence for the use of Adam of Buckfield's writings at Paris', *Mediaeval Studies*, 54 (1992), 308–16

Bocking, Edward (*d.* 1534), Benedictine monk, may have been a relation of the Bocking family settled at Ash Bocking, Suffolk. The church there was appropriated to Canterbury Cathedral priory, where Edward was professed a monk in 1500. In 1504 he was admitted a scholar to Canterbury College, Oxford, where he became warden in 1510. In 1512 he supplicated for the degree of BTh, to which he was admitted on 16 June 1513. He proceeded DTh in June 1518 and resigned his wardenship in the same year, a step doubtless accounted for by his becoming cellarer at Canterbury, also in 1518. In 1526 he was a member of the commission appointed by Archbishop William Warham to investigate the divine revelations allegedly received by Elizabeth *Barton, a servant of Thomas Cobb, the steward of the archiepiscopal manor of Aldington, Kent. The commissioners judged Barton to be genuinely inspired. Soon afterwards she left Aldington to become a nun of St Sepulchre's, Canterbury, and Bocking became her confessor and spiritual adviser.

By October 1528 Barton had turned to politics, agitating against Henry VIII's plan to annul his marriage to Katherine of Aragon, and from the beginning of these activities Bocking was her closest confidant. His most important role, however, was as a publicist for Barton. He was often accused, both by Henry VIII's government and by later historians, of having concocted rather than merely disseminated her revelations. It is impossible to tell whether there is substance in the charge but it has the appearance of misogyny, and certainly the government benefited greatly by using it to undermine the commonplace assumption that Barton's revelations must have been holy because a woman could not normally have had the wits to invent them on her own.

Bocking is known to have spread word of Barton's vision that Henry VIII would lose his crown if he married Anne Boleyn, describing the vision in person to the prior of Leeds, the prior of Monks Horton, and a number of priests and merchants in Kent. He also wrote in his own hand a 'great book' of Barton's revelations, a compendium of her visions that later became the principal evidence on which Barton and her associates were attainted of treason; on several occasions he is known to have lent out portions of this manuscript, one quire at a time, for scribal reproduction. In 1533 a fair copy of Bocking's manuscript was made by Thomas Laurence of Canterbury, and 700 copies of the book were issued by the printer John Skot, who supplied 500 copies to Bocking. The government's crackdown on the Barton circle prevented distribution of the book, however, and all copies were apparently confiscated and destroyed; none exists today. There does survive in Bocking's hand a single-page manuscript entitled *Elizabethae virginis spiritualis gratiae libri secundi prologus*, which may have been part of another book about Barton (PRO, SP 1/80, fol. 140).

Bocking had been arrested by 25 September 1533 and was imprisoned in the Tower. Denounced for his involvement with Barton he was among her associates who shared her public penance and humiliation first at Paul's Cross on 23 November and then in Canterbury on 7 December. Sent back to the Tower at the end of March 1534 he was attainted of treason under the statute 25 Hen. VIII. c. 12, and hanged at Tyburn on 20 April along with Barton herself and four other of her associates. His head was set on one of the city gates, but his other remains were interred in the cemetery of the London Blackfriars. These deaths were the first Catholic 'martyrdoms' of the English Reformation. The most detailed sources for Bocking's career—the act of attainder and the Paul's Cross sermon preached against Barton on 23 November 1533—were composed as propaganda by Bocking's enemies in an effort to discredit him and his allies. These sources have in the past been taken at face value by many scholars, who have thus suggested that Bocking encouraged Barton to fake her revelations, that he coerced her into opposing the crown, and that the two were sexual partners. Such stories are almost certainly slanderous, and letters written to Bocking in the early 1530s suggest that he was widely respected by his associates not only for his principled opposition to the royal divorce but also for his holiness. ETHAN H. SHAGAN

Sources L. E. Whatmore, ed., 'The sermon against the Holy Maid of Kent and her adherents … 1533', *EngHR*, 58 (1943), 463–75 • A. Luders and others, eds., *Statutes of the realm*, 11 vols. in 12, RC (1810–28), vol. 3, pp. 446–51 • various MSS, PRO, SP 1 (State Papers, Henry VIII, esp. SP 1/77, 79, 80 [calendared in *LPH*, vols. 6, 7] • W. A. Pantin, *Canterbury College, Oxford*, 4 vols., OHS, new ser., 6–8, 30 (1947–85) • D. Watt, 'Reconstructing the word: the political prophecies of Elizabeth Barton (1506–1534)', *Renaissance Quarterly*, 50 (1997), 136–63 • D. Watt, *Secretaries of God: women prophets in late medieval and early modern England* (1997) • E. J. Devereux, 'Elizabeth Barton and Tudor censorship', *Bulletin of the John Rylands Library*, 49 (1966–7), 91–106 • R. Rex, 'The execution of the Holy Maid of Kent', *Historical Research*, 64 (1991), 216–20 • S. L. Jansen, *Dangerous talk and strange behaviour: women and popular resistance to the reforms of Henry VIII* (1996) • A. Neame, *The Holy Maid of Kent: the life of Elizabeth Barton, 1506–1534* (1971) • Emden, *Oxf.*, 4.54

Archives PRO, State Papers, Henry VIII, SP 1

Bocking, Ralph (*d.* after **1272**), Dominican friar and hagiographer, wrote a life of St Richard of Wyche, bishop of Chichester, whom he had known as a friend and served as confessor. Nothing is known of Bocking other than what he relates himself in the life of St Richard, which, as is shown by internal evidence, was composed in the years 1268–72. He states that he wrote it on the instructions of Robert Kilwardby (*d.* 1279), then prior provincial of the English Dominicans and later archbishop of Canterbury, and at the request of Isabella d'Aubigny, countess of Arundel, known from other sources to have been an enthusiast for hagiographical literature. He based it upon his own memories of Richard and the dossier of the saint's canonization process, to which he evidently had access. From his knowledge of patristics it is apparent that he was a theologian who had been trained in the schools. Despite the oleaginous rhetoric of his style, which sometimes obscures his meaning, he is sparing and sober in his evocation of the miraculous. Some years later (*c.*1276–93), the life was translated into Anglo-Norman verse by Master Peter of Fetcham or Peckham (*d.* 1293).

C. H. LAWRENCE

Sources 'Vita s. Ricardi episcopi', *Acta sanctorum: Aprilis*, 1 (Antwerp, 1675), 282–318 • D. Jones, *St Richard of Chichester: sources for his life*, Sussex RS, 79 (1995) • D. Jones, 'The medieval lives of St Richard of Chichester', *Analecta Bollandiana*, 105 (1987), 105–29

Bockman, Gerhard (**1686–1773**), portrait painter and engraver, is believed to have been born in the Netherlands, at Amsterdam. He worked in Britain from at least 1711 until his death, painting and copying portraits, and engraving portraits in mezzotint after both his own work and that of others. Notable among his own works are a life-size, half-length portrait, *Admiral Russell* (date unknown; Maritime Hospital, Greenwich), the *Coningsby Family* (date unknown), and *St Dunstan Holding the Devil by the Nose with a Pair of Tongs*. His engraving of this last is signed with his name, with the addition 'pinx.et sculp 1743' (impression in the British Museum department of prints and drawings). As many as nine copies by Bockman after Kneller are in the Royal Collection at Hampton Court Palace. He engraved over twenty portraits, mostly after other artists including Van Dyck, Van Loo, and Michael Dahl, four being after James Worsdale. Portraits engraved after his own work include the *Duke of Cumberland* (1746, impression in the British Museum department of prints and drawings). Most of Bockman's engravings were commissioned. He published only three mezzotints himself: *Sir Thomas Reeve*, after Jacopo Amigoni (*c.*1737), *Charles, Lord Talbot* (*c.*1737, impression in the British Museum department of prints and drawings), and the *Children of Frederick, Prince of Wales*, after Enoch Seeman (date unknown, impression in the British Museum department of prints and drawings).

Bockman's portraiture is notable for its similarity to Kneller's treatment of faces and his arrangement of poses. Although his obituarist recorded that he was 'the last surviving disciple of Sir Godfrey Kneller' (*London Magazine*), suggestions that he was a pupil of Kneller appear to be unfounded, and nothing is known about his education. It is possible that the two had a close association before or not long after 1711, when the Academy of Drawing and Painting in Great Queen Street, London, was founded, with Kneller as its president, and Bockman, spelt Borman by Vertue in his list of members, as one of its students, aged twenty-five. Bockman was also listed by Vertue as a member of the Rose and Crown Club in 1724. Previous biographical outlines of Bockman have been uncertain as to whether his initial was C, G, or R (his prints show it clearly to be G), and by Redgrave's incorrect statement that Bockman's widow applied for relief to the Society of Artists in 1769. Very little is known of Bockman's personal life. The identities of his parents are not known, and there is no evidence he was married or had children. He is not recorded as having left a will. He lived in London at Great Russell Street, Bloomsbury (about 1737), and King Street, Covent Garden (in the 1740s). He died on 2 April 1773 'at his home in Tash Street, Gray's Inn Lane' (ibid.).

NICHOLAS GRINDLE

Sources *DNB* · *London Magazine*, 42 (1773), 205 · J. C. Smith, *British mezzotinto portraits*, 4 vols. in 5 (1878–84) · I. Bignamini, 'George Vertue, art historian, and art institutions in London, 1689–1768', *Walpole Society*, 54 (1988), 1–148 · *Engraved Brit. ports.* · archive material, Courtauld Inst., Witt Library · J. D. Stewart, *Sir Godfrey Kneller and the English baroque portrait* (1983) · Lord Killanin, *Sir Godfrey Kneller* (1948) · Redgrave, *Artists* · J. Kerslake, *National Portrait Gallery: early Georgian portraits*, 2 vols. (1977), 1

Bocland, Geoffrey of. *See* Buckland, Geoffrey of (*d*. 1225).

Bocland, Hugh of. *See* Buckland, Hugh of (*d*. 1116x19).

Bodda Pyne, Louisa Fanny. *See* Pyne, Louisa Fanny (1828?–1904).

Boddington, George (1646–1719), merchant and Independent lay leader, was born on 15 October 1646, the first surviving son of George Boddington (1611–1671), packer, of St Margaret, Lothbury, London, and Hannah, daughter of Thomas Adams, of Philpot Lane, St Clement, Eastcheap, London. He was educated at various schools in London. Acquiring a zeal for trade from his father, Boddington also absorbed the piety of a puritan mother, who instilled good principles of religion and morals in all her children. He came of age in the late 1660s, at a time of great uncertainty caused by the conjunction of plague, fire, and war and the persecution of protestant nonconformists. Dating his spiritual conversion to the plague-time renewal of visible dissenting ministry, Boddington was admitted to the congregation of Thomas Vincent, which by the end of the decade worshipped in a purpose-built meeting-house. In 1669 the elder George Boddington was chosen for the common council of the corporation as the dissenting civic élite of the protectorate re-established their presence in London affairs. In 1670 the younger Boddington's pastor was among those dissenting clergy whose convictions under a new Conventicle Act prompted street confrontations in the City. Boddington's marriage on 19 December 1671 also indicated the political and religious milieu of the family. His wife, Mary Steele, who brought him a portion of £2000, was the daughter of William *Steele, radical lawyer, Independent recorder of London (1649–55), lord chief baron of the exchequer (1655–6), and lord chancellor of Ireland (1656–60).

Despite these early indications of outspoken dissent, Boddington seems always to have preferred his trade and family to a public life. Admitted freeman of the Levant Company in 1666, he was comfortably established by his father in the Turkey trade, despite the latter's considerable fire losses. The young merchant also entered the Clothworkers' Company and learned the Baltic trade as bookkeeper to an Eastland merchant. After his first wife, Mary, died in childbirth in 1673, Boddington married on 2 July 1674 Hannah (*d*. 1699), daughter of John Cope, Cannon Street haberdasher, who brought him another significant portion and with whom he had fourteen children. By 1677 he had settled in the parish of St Helen's, Bishopsgate, where he remained throughout his career. In 1678, when Thomas Vincent's successor compromised the congregational order of Boddington's church, he left for the Lime Street meeting, in which he remained active thereafter.

Like many other prominent City dissenters, Boddington signed the London petition of May 1679 intended to encourage parliamentary consideration of exclusion. His brother James (1652–1731), a packer, signed a subsequent London whig petition; but George Boddington is not known to have taken any further part in London politics during the exclusion era. He was, nevertheless, one of more than 300 Londoners temporarily incarcerated in 1685 at the time of Monmouth's rebellion.

The London port books for the 1680s and 1690s show Boddington importing silk, mohair, and cotton from Iskenderun, Leghorn, and Smyrna and exporting cloth to the Mediterranean and the Levant, to the Baltic, and to Hudson's Bay and New England. The volume of his trade was considerable, but not exceptional.

The revolution of 1688 and the financial developments that followed the establishment of the Bank of England in 1694 found Boddington at the zenith of his career. Like many other City nonconformists grateful for the Toleration Act, he subscribed to the post-1689 corporation of London loans to the new government of William and Mary. In 1694 his subscription of £2000 to the bank brought him election to its first court of directors. Finding that the bank took up too much of his time, however, he disposed of his stock. He was similarly diffident about political office. Although repeatedly nominated for the London common council by the vestry of his parish between 1688 and 1692, he refused to take the sacramental test when actually chosen for 1689/90. Whether Boddington had changed his mind about the test by the time of his return to parliament, as a whig, representing Wilton,

Wiltshire, in July 1702 is unknown. In any case he was unseated by the Commons; and the tory uproar about dissenting activism in Wilton in this election was instrumental in launching the first Occasional Conformity Bill under Queen Anne. In the meantime Boddington had served his parish, as churchwarden, and his congregation, as an officer of two funds for the support of the dissenting clergy: the short-lived Common Fund (1690–93) of Presbyterians and Independents and the subsequently established Congregational Fund. He was also Greenland Company governor (1693), Levant Company assistant (1695, 1701, 1703), and Clothworkers' Company master (1705).

Reflecting upon his career near its conclusion, Boddington dwelt upon none of this recognition but rather upon the providential preservation of his eldest son, George, and much of his trading stock in the Smyrna fleet disaster of 1693. But his final years were troubled by family misfortunes. He rescued his bankrupt brother; and he blamed personal losses upon the mismanagement of his son George, his Turkish factor, and a Smyrna consul, who also married a Roman Catholic. The career of a promising son-in-law, Robert Wakeman, a marine insurer, was clipped by the West Indies fleet loss of 1703 and closed by a premature death as consul in Cyprus.

Boddington died at his house in the parish of St Helen's in London on 10 May 1719, mentioning in his will almost £20,000 in previous or new bequests and several City properties. He had invested the family future not in land, as did some successful mercantile contemporaries, but rather in three sons (Thomas, Isaac, and Benjamin), who succeeded him in the Levant trade. Still embarrassed by the public extravagance of his first wedding, he ordered a 'private and frugall' night burial. GARY S. DE KREY

Sources GL, Boddington Family MSS, MS 10823/1 · will, PRO, PROB 11/569, sig. 99 [proved, June 1719] · D. W. Hayton, 'Boddington, George', HoP, *Commons* [draft] · G. S. De Krey, *A fractured society: the politics of London in the first age of party, 1688–1715* (1985), 92–3, 108, 130–31 · S. P. Anderson, *An English consul in Turkey: Paul Rycaut at Smyrna, 1667–1678* (1989) · G. S. Holmes, *British politics in the age of Anne* (1967), 100–01, 474 n. 78 · CLRO, Alchin MS 33, piece 15, fol. 10 · minute book, 1684/5–1687, CLRO, London Lieutenancy Court, fols. 32–3 · Congregational Fund board, minutes, DWL [vol. 1] · A. Gordon, ed., *Freedom after ejection: a review (1690–1692) of presbyterian and congregational nonconformity in England and Wales* (1917) · church book of the meeting-house in Lime Street, GL, MS 557 · Lime Street Meeting births and baptisms, PRO, RG 4/4410 · London port books, PRO, E 190/102/1, 190/134/1, 190/144/1 · D. W. Jones, 'London overseas merchant groups at the end of the seventeenth century, and the move against the East India Company', DPhil diss., U. Oxf., 1971, 391, 474, 482 · vestry minutes, St Helen's, Bishopsgate, GL, MS 6846/1 · [S. Lee], *A collection of the names of the merchants living in and about the City of London* (1677); repr. as *The London directory of 1677* (1878)

Archives GL, commonplace book; family MSS, MS 10823

Wealth at death £19,070 legacies mentioned in will; plus an unevaluated 'Talley or order of Survivorship'; properties, incl. London 'mansion house' in St Helen's Bishopsgate Within, with outhouses and warehouses; several houses in St Margaret Lothbury, incl. his childhood home (total rental value of at least £100 p.a.); the Sun Tavern and leasehold fish shops in New Fish Street; tenements at Enfield Green, Middlesex; 'great part' of estate described as being 'in foreign parts': will, PRO, PROB 11/569, sig. 99

Boddington, Henry John (1811–1865), landscape painter, was born in the Marylebone district of London, as Henry John Williams, second son of the painter Edward ('Moonlight') *Williams (1781–1855) and his wife, Ann Hildebrandt (*bap.* 1780, *d.* 1851), who was of German-Jewish extraction. Edward Williams was a nephew of the painter James Ward. In 1832, Henry John married Clarissa Eliza Boddington (1812–1905), and at once adopted her maiden name, in order to distinguish his work from that of his five brothers, all of whom also became landscape painters: Edward Charles Williams (1807–1881), George Augustus Williams (1814–1901), and Alfred Walter Williams (1824–1905) retained the family name, but Sidney Richard *Percy (1821–1886) and Arthur Gilbert (1819–1895) worked under their last forenames.

Boddington, who trained in his father's studio, developed a style clearly derived from the Dutch landscape tradition of Ruisdael and Hobbema, but characterized by greater naturalism and a more vivid use of colour. This air of modernity soon made his green and leafy landscapes very popular with the public. His name was well established by 1842 when he was elected a full member of the Society of British Artists, with whom he had exhibited since 1837 and where he displayed a total of 244 works.

Boddington was also a regular exhibitor with the Royal Academy and other London art associations, as well as provincial bodies such as the Royal Liverpool Academy. His bright style greatly appealed to the wealthy manufacturing classes who were the new art patrons, and he was a popular choice with Art Union prize winners. The front page of the *Illustrated London News* for 6 March 1847 showed a wood-engraving of *The Village Church*, exhibited at the British Institution in that year and described in the accompanying text as 'a genuine scene of English life'. Sketching tours of Devon, Yorkshire, and the Lake District had broadened his scope. A first visit to north Wales in 1846 made a still deeper impact, and he later returned many times to the Merioneth area to produce some of his most admired and frequent subjects. *On the Hills, North Wales* (exh. Society of British Artists, 1860) won a lyrical description from a critic for the *Art Journal*, who wrote 'The mountains are melting in vapoury sunlight … the artist is a master of this effect' (*Art Journal*, 22, 1860, 143).

Boddington's only child, Edwin Henry (1836–*c.*1905), painted in the manner of his father, but with less talent, disappearing from the exhibiting scene about 1870, and later from the family circle when he emigrated to Australia. H. J. Boddington always lived in the London area, finally in 1854 setting up a handsome establishment at 1 Lonsdale Villas, Barnes, where his father and brothers were already in neighbouring houses. Boddington was known as a kind and cheerful man, much respected by fellow artists. His last years were marred by failing eyesight and the crippling effects of a brain tumour, which led to his death, at his home, in mid-career, at the age of fifty-three, on 11 April 1865. He was buried in the Old Barnes cemetery; his grave is near those of Edward Williams, George Augustus Williams, and several other members of the family. An obituary in the *Fine Arts Quarterly Review* noted that 'He was an artist, who if he fell into mannerism, had yet during a hard working life, painted pictures not only large, but sometimes grand. His landscapes of mountain, lake and river had scenic breadth and power' (p. 371).

The paintings of H. J. Boddington are now considered the most aesthetically pleasing of those produced by the Williams family, but they do not command such high prices as those of S. R. Percy. Works are held in the Victoria and Albert Museum, London; the National Museum and Gallery of Wales, Cardiff; the Glasgow Art Gallery; the City Art Gallery, Blackburn; the Harris Museum and Art Gallery, Preston; the Graves Art Gallery, Sheffield; the City Art Gallery, York; and the Museum of Fine Arts, Boston, USA.

JAN REYNOLDS

Sources J. Reynolds, *The Williams family of painters* (1975) • *DNB* • *Art Journal*, 27 (1865), 191 • *Fine Arts Quarterly Review*, 3 (1865), 371 • Graves, *Brit. Inst.*, 51–2 • Graves, *RA exhibitors* • J. Johnson, ed., *Works exhibited at the Royal Society of British Artists, 1824–1893, and the New English Art Club, 1888–1917*, 2 vols. (1975) • *London Art Union Prize Annual* (1845), 4–8 • Wood, *Vic. painters*, 2nd edn • d. cert. [Edward Williams] • census returns [Edward Williams] • parish registers (baptism), St Mary, Whitechapel, 14 July 1780 • headstone, Barnes [Ann Hildebrandt] • d. cert. [Clarissa Eliza Boddington] • headstone, Old Barnes cemetery

Wealth at death under £3000: probate, 11 May 1865, *CGPLA Eng. & Wales*

Bode, John Ernest (1816–1874), Church of England clergyman and poet, was the son of William Bode, who worked for the Post Office, and his wife, Mary, only daughter of the Revd T. Lloyd of Peterly House, Oxfordshire. He was educated at Eton College and Charterhouse School, 1830–34, where he became a scholar on the foundation. From Charterhouse he proceeded to Christ Church, Oxford, and was the first winner, in 1835, of the Hertford scholarship, instituted the year before. He took his BA degree in 1837, with a first class in *literae humaniores*, and his MA in 1840. He became a student and a tutor of his college, 1841–7, of which he was appointed censor in 1844, and acted as one of the public examiners in *literae humaniores* for the years 1846–8. He was ordained deacon in 1841, and priest in 1843. In 1847 he was presented by his college to the rectory of Westwell, Oxfordshire, and on 22 July in the same year was married to Hester Charlotte, *née* Lodge, of St Nicholas, Guildford.

In 1848 Bode was appointed one of the select preachers in the university, and on 12 December 1850, being founder's day, preached a sermon at the Charterhouse chapel, which was afterwards published as *Our Schoolboy Days Viewed through the Glass of Religion* (1850). In 1855 he preached the Bampton lectures before the University of Oxford, published as *The absence of precision in the formularies of the Church of England, scriptural and favourable to a state of probation* (1855). In 1857 Bode was defeated by Matthew Arnold in the election for the chair of poetry at Oxford; his claims rested mainly on a volume of poems suggested by a course of reading of the old English and Scottish ballads from 1841, published as *Ballads from Herodotus, with an Introductory Poem* (1853; 2nd edn with four additional poems, 1854). Bode also published *Short Occasional Poems* (1858), and a smaller volume entitled *Hymns from the Gospel of the Day* (1860). In 1860 Bode was presented by the governors of Charterhouse to the living of Castle Camps, Cambridgeshire, at the rectory of which he died suddenly, at the age of fifty-eight, on 6 October 1874; he was survived by his wife.

ARTHUR H. GRANT, *rev.* H. C. G. MATTHEW

Sources Foster, *Alum. Oxon.* • Crockford (1870) • *English Churchman and Clerical Journal* (15 Oct 1874) • *Sussex Advertiser* (27 July 1847) • *CGPLA Eng. & Wales* (1874)

Wealth at death under £6000: probate, 24 Nov 1874, *CGPLA Eng. & Wales*

Bode, Mary de [*née* Mary Kynnersley], **Baroness de Bode in the nobility of the Holy Roman empire** (*d.* 1812), letter writer, was born into the English gentry, the fourth daughter of Thomas Kynnersley (*d.* 1755), landowner, of Loxley Park, Staffordshire, the place of her birth. In her youth she made a trip to France, where she met Charles Auguste Louis Frederick de Bode, Baron de Bode (*d.* 1797), whom she married at the church of St Marylebone on 21 October 1775. Her husband was a soldier of German birth in the service of Louis XVI. As the grandson of a privy counsellor to emperor Charles VI and a relative of the princes of Creuz and Gavres, the courts of Europe were open to him, but he had little private wealth. On 23 April 1777 Mary gave birth to Clement, the first of eleven children to be born to the couple over the next fourteen years, of whom eight survived to adulthood.

After living at Saarbrücken for some years Mary de Bode travelled to her native country in 1781, where she was presented to George III. In 1782, amid mounting debts, the family moved to Bergzabern on the Franco-German border. Philanthropic and resourceful by nature, Mary announced her intention to open a 'copperous' works on her estate, and corresponded with Josiah Wedgwood and Matthew Boulton on the subject (Childe-Pemberton, 43); she also found time to set up a lace-making manufactory to provide work and moral instruction for poor girls.

Shortly after his and Mary's ninth child was born Charles secured the fief of Soultz, a wealthy living in Alsace, at which point Mary became a naturalized French subject. In December 1788 she and Charles ceremoniously took up residence in their fiefdom and Mary recorded with relish the promise of riches to come: ''Tis a land flowing with Corn and oil and wine … If God has sent us a quantity of children, He has also sent us plentifully to provide for them!' (Childe-Pemberton, 68). Political events were soon to overtake them, however. In the aftermath of the French Revolution the baroness's hopes that Alsace would be saved from political turmoil were soon confounded. During Christmas 1793–4, at the height of the terror, the de Bodes fled to Germany. There they moved from one court to another under the protection of patrons before making an ill-fated attempt to return to Soultz. Husband and wife made a dramatic escape with two of their children through the Vosges mountains in the face of certain death at the hands of the national guard. They were forced to leave behind five of their smallest children, with whom they were later reunited, but lost almost all of their material possessions. As Mary wrote to her niece Maryanne:

> Think! All that charming furniture, all our music, our fine Pianofortes … all our charming Collection of books … about twenty sheets of flowers that I had painted—a whole summer's work … two carriages, waggons … in short, I can hardly tell you what we have lost. (ibid., 160)

The family took refuge with the baron's sister, the abbess of Altenburg. In 1794 Mary undertook a perilous 2000 mile journey to the court of St Petersburg to petition for refuge. After protracted diplomatic representations the family made an unsuccessful attempt to settle in the Crimea, where the baron died in 1797. Mary and her children eventually made their home near Narva, on the Gulf of Finland.

An early portrait of Mary shows a stately rather than a handsome woman, with dark flowing hair. She was fluent in several European languages, including French, German, and Italian, and wrote an autobiography, which was never published. She quoted Voltaire, Shakespeare, and Gothic novels in her correspondence; she also took an interest in natural history. Though her husband was a Catholic she herself remained a lifelong member of the Church of England 'because I have not yet found a religion that I think better' (Childe-Pemberton, 168). Her letters to her family in England form a valuable account of the private world of German princelings and French aristocrats in the dying years of the *ancien régime*. Her correspondence reflects the experience of members of her own class, an indifference to political events in France, and the futile hope that the old order would soon be restored.

Mary de Bode died in Moscow early in 1812, shortly before the city fell to Napoleon. Her son Clement, a British citizen, later took out a famous lawsuit that lasted forty years, in which he made a futile attempt to gain compensation from parliament for the loss of his French estates.

HELEN BERRY

Sources W. S. Childe-Pemberton, *The Baroness de Bode, 1775–1803* (1900) · T. Brettell, *The case of the Baron de Bode* (1854)
Archives priv. coll., letters
Likenesses W. L. Colls?, oils (in youth), priv. coll.; repro. in Childe-Pemberton, *The baroness de Bode* · oils? (in old age), priv. coll.; repro. in Childe-Pemberton, *The Baroness de Bode* · two plate illustrations, repro. in Childe-Pemberton, *The Baroness de Bode*

Boden, Joseph (*d.* **1811**), army officer in the East India Company and benefactor, details of whose birth and parentage are unknown, was appointed lieutenant in the Bombay native infantry on 24 November 1781. He became captain on 25 October 1796, major on 12 October 1802, and lieutenant-colonel on 21 May 1806. His name was borne at various times on the rolls of the 3rd, 5th, 6th, 8th, and 9th native infantry, and he held successively the offices of judge-advocate, aide-de-camp to the governor, quartermaster-general, and member of the military board at Bombay. He retired from the service in 1807, and died at Lisbon on 21 November 1811, where he had gone for the benefit of his health.

Following the death of his daughter Elizabeth (29 August 1827), Boden's property went to the University of Oxford, under conditions recorded on a tablet placed by his executors in Trinity Church, Cheltenham. This set out Boden's plan that his estate, said to be valued at about £25,000 in 1827, be presented to the university for the creation of a chair in Sanskrit language as a means 'of enabling my countrymen to proceed in the conversion of the natives of India in the Christian religion, by disseminating a knowledge of the Sacred scriptures among them, more effectually than by all other means whatever'.

The offer was accepted by the university in convocation on 9 November 1827, and the first election took place in 1832, when Professor Horace Hayman Wilson was appointed to the chair. Four Sanskrit scholarships in connection with the same endowment were founded by decrees of the court of chancery in 1830 and 1860. Boden was not himself a Sanskrit scholar. The Boden professorship and the Boden prize remain important features of Sanskrit teaching at Oxford.

H. M. CHICHESTER, *rev.* PHILIP CARTER

Sources *N&Q*, 5th ser., 5 (1876), 414, 458 · *GM*, 1st ser., 81/2 (1811), 589 · R. F. Gombrich, *On being Sanskritic: a plea for civilized study and the study of civilization* (1978) [inaugural lecture, University of Oxford, 14 Oct 1977]
Wealth at death approx. £25,000 in 1827

Bodenham [Bodnam], **John** (*c.***1559–1610**), literary patron and grocer, was born in London, perhaps in the parish of St Stephen Walbrook. He was the eldest son in a family of five children of William Bodnam (*d.* 1580), grocer, and his wife, Katherine Wanton (*d.* in or before 1598), eldest daughter of Thomas Wanton of York. On 3 December 1570 he was admitted to the Merchant Taylors' School, London, and was also educated by a tutor, a 'Mr Thackam'. Bodenham was admitted to the Grocers' Company in 1580, of which both his father and paternal grandfather, John, were free, his father having been elected junior warden in 1563 and senior warden in 1570. Bodenham attained his majority in 1580, and having been left a substantial paternal inheritance, he apparently was not very active in the Grocers' Company. He owned income-producing property in the grocery colony in the parish of St Mary Woolchurch and in Bucklersbury, in the parish of St Stephen Walbrook, including a dwelling at the latter known as The Woolsack, the family home; a tenement called The Lamb; and a warehouse. Bodenham may have obtained the coat of arms depicted in the front matter of *Belvedere* (1600) and of *Englands Helicon* (1600), though this may have been fabricated to honour him as the books' patron.

Bodenham's historical importance is as the initiator, projector, and patron of a series of five printed prose and poetical commonplace books, material for which he gathered from his extensive reading before handing it over to others for final arranging and editing. Three of the five are dedicated to Bodenham: *Politeuphuia, Wits Commonwealth* (1597), edited by Nicholas Ling; *Belvedere, or, The Garden of the Muses* (1600), a collection of 4482 one- or two-line poetical citations arranged, like the prose compilations, under commonplace headings, edited by Anthony Munday and dedicated to Bodenham, who is called:

> Arts lover, Learnings friend,
> First causer and collectour of these floures

and *Englands Helicon* (1600), edited by Nicholas Ling, with a dedicatory poem by A. B. (possibly the editor), 'To his loving kinde friend, Maister John Bodenham', that praises Bodenham for collecting the poetry and projecting the previous works. Francis Meres's *Palladis tamia, Wits Treasury* (1598) was dedicated to Thomas Eliot, but, Rollins points out (Rollins, 47–8), it was conceived as the second of a series of three prose compilations projected by Bodenham. The fifth text, *Wits Theater of the Little World* (1599), was edited by Robert Allott and published by Ling.

Politeuphuia and *Wits Theater* are commonplace-book compilations of prose aphorisms, sententiae, and reading notes, representing a practice widespread in manuscript culture, the material arranged under set headings facilitating their subsequent use in speech and writing. To this end, as Crawford has shown (Crawford, 199), the compiler, presumably Bodenham, rewrote some poetical selections as prose to fit the general format. These popular publications went through many editions through the next century. In *Belvedere* the one- and two-line pentameter excerpts are arranged under commonplace headings—many prose excerpts actually being reformulated as verse. Its ballad-writing editor (Anthony Munday), the patron, and the collection itself are mocked in the contemporary Cambridge satiric comedy *The Second Part of the Return from Parnassus* (I.ii.173–335). A reprint of *Belvedere* was published in 1875 by the Spenser Society.

Englands Helicon, perhaps the finest of the Elizabethan poetical miscellanies, is a rich collection including such authors as Breton, Barnfield, Chettle, Drayton, Dyer, Greene, Lodge (Bodenham's relative through his mother's family), Marlowe, Munday, Peele, Ralegh, Sidney, Spenser, Surrey, Watson, and Young. It prints for the first time Marlowe's 'The Passionate Shepherd to his Love', with Ralegh's reply. This pastoral anthology contains some non-pastoral pieces modified to give them a pastoral flavour or setting. A second edition, with an additional nine poems, was published in 1614, and a modern critical edition was produced in 1935 by Rollins. At his death on 16 July 1610 Bodenham was unmarried and childless; he bequeathed his estate to his sister Mary, the financially distressed widow of the grocer Thomas Vesey.

ARTHUR F. MAROTTI

Sources H. Rollins, ed., *England's Helicon, 1600, 1614* (1935), 1.184–6, 2.41–70 • F. Williams, 'John Bodenham, "Art's lover, learning's friend"', *Studies in Philology*, 31 (1934), 198–214 • C. Crawford, *Englands Parnassus* (1913) • J. B. Leishman, ed., *Three Parnassus plays (1598–1601)* (1949), 230–47 • C. T. Wright, 'Anthony Mundy and the Bodenham miscellanies', *Philological Quarterly*, 40 (1961), 449–61 • C. Crawford, 'Belvedere, or, The garden of the muses', *Englische Studien*, 43 (1910–11), 198–228 • C. T. Wright, 'Young Anthony Mundy again', *Studies in Philology*, 56 (1959), 150–68, esp. 165–7 • M. T. Crane, *Framing authority: sayings, self, and society in sixteenth-century England* (1993), 183–56 • M. A. Shaaber, 'The third edition of *Wits commonwealth*', *Library Chronicle, University of Pennsylvania*, 15/2 (summer 1949), 56–8

Bodi [Bode], **John** (*fl.* 1357), Benedictine monk and scholastic writer, graduated doctor of divinity at Oxford University. His institutional affiliation is not known, but he might have been attached to Gloucester College, which was established for monks of his order. His personal circumstances are known only from an incident in which a friar was ordered by the university to make a public apology for having made insulting references to him in a lecture of 20 December 1357. The following January Bodi witnessed a disclaimer made by the Augustinian friars of Oxford in St Mary's Church. However, he is known chiefly from a work in the best fourteenth-century Oxford tradition of applying logical techniques to the analysis of problems that were superficially physical. There were at Oxford at this time disputations based on sophisms, intended as an aid to learning logic. Those who took part were the more advanced students—who thus became known as *sophistae*. The disputations could be held outside the schools, but were supervised by masters, or possibly bachelors. Although the physics was not usually introduced for its own sake so much as for the sake of disputation, the activity was occasionally the source of useful new physical concepts, and the resulting Oxford literature brought the 'calculators' a certain European reputation for ingenuity.

Bodi's only known work (beginning *A est unum calidum*) is a collection of twenty-two sophisms in this tradition. Of three known copies of the text, one is ascribed to John Bodi (that in Vatican City, Biblioteca Apostolica Vaticana, MS Vat. lat. 4447). It is of some interest for its treatment of infinite series, which in the two previous decades had given rise to much activity centred on what were seen as paradoxical arguments. The series were handled intelligently, by the rearrangement and manipulation of terms. They were not regarded as a part of an abstract mathematics, however, but as part of a calculus of qualities—in particular degrees of heat, which were typically reckoned to be only eight in number. Bodi's work, on the other hand, cannot be considered as a contribution to a physical theory of heat, for it dealt only with imaginary problems, without any empirical basis. It was probably without much influence, by comparison with the work of his mid-fourteenth-century contemporaries Richard Swineshead and William Heytesbury. Pierre Duhem was under the impression that *A est unum calidum* was written under the influence of the ideas of Nicole Oresme (*d.* 1382), but Anneliese Maier—who first identified Bodi as the author of the collection—showed that this was not the case.

Nothing is known of Bodi's later career or death. A John Body who was fellow of Merton College in 1338, possibly already by 1334, and about whom it seems nothing else is known, was fairly certainly not the Benedictine of that name.

J. D. NORTH

Sources Emden, *Oxf.* • H. L. L. Busard, 'Unendliche Reihen in *A est unum calidum*', *Archive for History of Exact Sciences*, 2 (1962–6), 387–97 • A. Maier, *An der Grenze von Scholastik und Naturwissenschaft* (Essen, 1943), 267, 355 • P. Duhem, *Études sur Léonard de Vinci*, 3 (Paris, 1913), 474–7 • P. Duhem, *Le système du monde: histoire des doctrines cosmologiques de Platon à Copernic*, 10 vols. (Paris, 1913–59), vol. 7, pp. 648–50

Archives Biblioteca Apostolica Vaticana, Vatican City, MS Vat. lat. 4447

Bodichon, Barbara Leigh Smith (1827–1891), artist and women's activist, was born on 8 April 1827 in Whatlington, near Robertsbridge, Sussex, the eldest of the five children of the radical MP Benjamin *Smith (1783–1860) [*see under* Smith, William (1756–1835)] and Anne Longden (1801–1834), a milliner. The Smiths were a Liberal reforming dynasty, members of the nineteenth-century 'intellectual aristocracy'. Barbara Bodichon's paternal grandfather was MP for Norwich and, together with William Wilberforce and Thomas Clarkson, played a significant role in bringing about the abolition of slavery. He was also the leading spokesman in parliament for protestant dissenters. Ben Smith believed that the laws of England were inimical to justice for women and gave that as a reason for not marrying Barbara's mother, Anne Longden. It seems likely that the liaison started in 1826 when Ben Smith met her on a visit to his sister, Fanny Nightingale, at her home, Lea Hurst, in Derbyshire. Anne Longden was the daughter of a corn miller in Alfreton, about 6 miles from the Nightingale home. After the death of Anne Longden from tuberculosis in 1834, despite advice from some sections of his family to have the children discreetly brought up abroad, their father brought them up himself, first at Pelham Crescent, Hastings, and later at his London home, 5 Blandford Square, Marylebone. As the Leigh Smith children were illegitimate they were not acknowledged by many of their Smith relations, including their aunt Fanny Nightingale and their first cousin, Florence Nightingale. Barbara's ambiguous social position paradoxically allowed her unusual social mobility.

Education and youth In her early youth Barbara's education was largely supplied by a governess, Catherine Spooner, and a private tutor, Harry Porter. Ben Smith employed James Buchanan, a Swedenborgian who had originally been the teacher in Robert Owen's experimental school in New Lanarkshire, in Westminster infant school, which he supported. Ben sometimes sent Buchanan down to Sussex to teach the Leigh Smiths, where he principally read aloud to them from the Bible, the Arabian Nights, and Swedenborg, and took them on long walks, talking to them about the harmony of nature. Barbara's secondary education was at the Unitarian Misses Wood's School for Girls in Upper Clapton, London, where the rote learning struck her as dull compared with Buchanan's imaginative and child-centred teaching. In 1848, when her brother, Benjamin Leigh *Smith, went to Cambridge University, Barbara studied political economy at home with a private tutor, Philip Kingsford, engaged by her father from the College of Preceptors.

Although the majority of the Smith relatives refused to recognize the 'tabooed family' when they were young, nevertheless Barbara's aunts Julia Smith, on her father's side, and Dorothy Longden, on her mother's side, befriended them. Several 'motherly' women also had great significance in her youth. These were Elizabeth Parkes (the granddaughter of Joseph Priestley), the writer Mary Howitt, and the art critic and historian Anna Jameson. The last two women also provided models of professional women earning their own living.

Barbara Leigh Smith Bodichon (1827–1891), by André Adolphe Eugène Disderi

In 1848, on reaching her majority, Barbara's father gave her a portfolio of shares and property, which yielded an independent income of between £250 and £300 per annum. This independent income put Barbara Leigh Smith in a very rare position for a young woman of her time. She was able to study and to enact her ambitions to become a professional artist and to embody her social reforming theories. The closest friends of her youth were Bessie Rayner Parkes (later Belloc), the poet and writer, Anna Mary Howitt, the Pre-Raphaelite painter, and Joanna Samworth, a painter of landscapes and flower studies. In the early 1850s she met Marian Evans (George Eliot), who regarded Barbara as her 'first friend' (*George Eliot Letters*, 3.63), and Elizabeth Blackwell, the first woman doctor, whom Barbara encouraged to move from America in order to open up the medical profession to women in England.

Early career and marriage Barbara's first public statements were under the pen-name of Esculapius in the *Hastings and St Leonards News*. Early pieces included an attack on the foolishness of feminine fashion, especially the injurious habit of tight-lacing stays, and a plea for the education of women. In 1854 she adopted the initials B. B. to write two letters to *The Leader* on the subject of prostitution, advocating the provision of training and work opportunities for women as the way to 'cure' prostitution rather than Magdalen hospitals. She regarded prostitution as essentially an economic matter, and was never interested in quasi-spiritual cant about purity.

Barbara was an extremely striking young woman, tall, with vivid expression and golden-red hair. She had several suitors, but in 1855 both her personal attractions and her wealth attracted the attention of John Chapman, editor of the *Westminster Review*. He proposed a 'free-love' relationship with her, and she was deeply tempted despite his being already married. She withdrew from his influence after her father revealed that Chapman was feckless with both women and money. In the winter of 1856, owing to the ill health of one of her sisters, Isabella, Ben Smith took his three daughters to Algiers. There Barbara met Eugène Bodichon (1810–1885), a French physician, ethnographer, and scholar whom, despite the misgivings of some family members, she married on 2 July 1857 at Little Portland Street Unitarian Chapel, London. Her father's wedding gift was his house in Blandford Square, which had been his political base and was to serve Barbara similarly. As a consequence of her marriage she spent half of each year in Algiers with her husband concentrating on her artistic career and half the year in England involved with social reform. In 1859 she bought a Moorish-style house on Mustapha Supérieure, overlooking the Bay of Algiers, which she named Campagne du Pavillon. It became a centre for English and French artistic and literary visitors to Algiers, including Matilda Betham-Edwards, Eliza Bridell-Fox, Sophia, Lady Dunbar, Gertrude Jekyll, and Frederick Walker. As her husband hated London, in 1863 she built another house, Scalands Gate, on the Glottenham estate, Robertsbridge, Sussex, which her brother Benjamin Leigh Smith had inherited from their father. Her husband was an eccentric man who neither learned English nor made much effort to endear himself to her family or friends. More positively, he accepted his wife's commitment to her career as an artist and her work as a social reformer. Towards the end of their lives there were a few sad years when he was too ill to travel to England and she was too ill to travel to Algeria; they did not meet after 1880 and he died in 1885.

Artistic career Barbara's ambition to be a professional landscape painter was formed at an early age. In Hastings she was taught by W. Collingwood Smith and Cornelius Varley, and was advised by William Henry Hunt. In 1849 she attended art classes taught by Francis Cary at the newly opened Bedford Ladies' College, London; she left Bedford College £1000 in her will. In 1850 Barbara made an unchaperoned trip across Europe with her friend Bessie Rayner Parkes to visit two artist friends, Anna Mary Howitt and Jane Benham (Hay), who had gone to study with Wilhelm von Kaulbach in Munich because the Royal Academy Schools were not open to women. While there Barbara formed a plan for an art-sisterhood of writers and painters, which Anna Mary Howitt described in *An Art Student in Munich* (1853). Barbara was at the forefront of campaigns to enable aspiring women artists to become professional. She helped to establish the Society for Female Artists in 1857 and in 1859 organized a petition to persuade the Royal Academy to admit women students.

Through her friendship with Anna Mary Howitt she came into the orbit of the Pre-Raphaelite group and was especially friendly with Dante Gabriel Rossetti and Elizabeth Siddal. They formed an art club called The Folio, in which they contributed paintings or drawings monthly, loosely based on a particular theme, and gave each other critical feedback. In 1864 she studied in Corot's studio in Paris and became a great friend of Charles-François Daubigny of the Barbizon school. In the 1860s she formed a fast friendship with Hercules Brabazon Brabazon, and they painted together whenever he was in England. Having no children she was free to travel widely and her landscapes included—as well as Sussex, the Isle of Wight, the Lake District, Cornwall, and Wales—France, Spain, Italy, North America, and north Africa. She exhibited her landscape paintings steadily all her working life (1850–81), and her greatest critical successes were probably her solo exhibitions at Gambart's French Gallery in Pall Mall, London (1859, 1861, and 1864), where her oriental landscapes were extremely successful. In 1875 she bought the poorhouse in Zennor, Cornwall, as a base for painting for herself and her many artist friends. At her death this house was left to Gertrude Jekyll, the garden designer and craftswoman.

Leader of Langham Place group Barbara's network of friends was the rock on which her feminist campaigns were built. As leader of the Langham Place group she was at the heart of feminist agitation in England and led four great campaigns: for married women to be granted legal recognition, and for women's right to work, to vote, and to have access to education. Perhaps partly as a result of her parents' unorthodox relationship Barbara was especially concerned with the legal and civil rights of women. Her earliest political act was to write and publish a pamphlet, *A brief summary of the laws in England concerning women: together with a few observations thereon* (1854). This was largely a précis of J. J. S. Wharton's *An Exposition of the Laws Relating to the Women of England* (1853), although she also took advice from a family friend, Matthew Davenport Hill, the recorder of Birmingham. The *Summary* was widely circulated and read, and in 1856 a second edition was published. Davenport Hill brought the *Summary* to the attention of the Law Amendment Society, founded by Lord Brougham in 1844, which was dedicated to reforming outdated laws. It was decided by the Law Amendment Society to introduce a Married Women's Property Bill in order to safeguard the property and earnings of married women. Barbara formed a committee to collect signatures for seventy petitions in support of the measure, and by a chain-letter system they collected 26,000 signatures altogether. A women-only petition was presented in parliament on 14 March 1856 by Lord Brougham in the Lords and by Sir Erskine Perry in the Commons. In February

1857 Lord Brougham introduced a bill in parliament which aimed to establish a married woman in the same position as an unmarried woman with respect to property. It took persistent campaigning until 1882 to achieve this significant change in the law. Property law reform was a prerequisite for a change in the suffrage to include women. Representation in parliament was dependent upon two things: a property qualification and a gender qualification. If married women could not own property, even were the gender qualification removed, they could not vote. There was also an assumption that their interests were represented by their husbands, and that therefore they could not possibly need direct representation. Marian Evans immediately recognized that Barbara's first campaign was merely 'one rung of a long ladder stretching far beyond our lives' (*George Eliot Letters*, 2.227).

Barbara had a sophisticated grasp of the importance of the press in influencing public opinion; her uncle, Octavius Smith, was a major shareholder in the *Westminster Review*. Subsequently she became the major shareholder in the *English Woman's Journal* (1858–64), founded primarily by herself and Bessie Rayner Parkes, for which she wrote many articles, continuing Smith family tradition by writing a series of abolitionist articles protesting against slavery in the southern states of North America, which she had visited in 1857–8. In an article published in a feminist journal called the *Waverley*, and subsequently reprinted as a pamphlet entitled *Women and Work* (1857), Barbara argued that middle-class women must not be denied meaningful work. The offices of the *English Woman's Journal* in Langham Place became a centre for a wide variety of feminist enterprises. These included a women's reading-room and dining club, offices for the Society for Promoting the Employment of Women, and offices for training law copiers. In conjunction with these activities Emily Faithfull set up the Victoria Press, which trained and employed female compositors. Barbara also helped Maria Rye set up the Female Emigration Society to help women (especially governesses) who could not find work in England to emigrate to the colonies. In 1863 Barbara appointed Emily Davies as temporary editor of the *English Woman's Journal* when Bessie needed a break. This was the start of an important partnership which continued after the close of the journal in 1864.

Suffrage campaigns Barbara was an equal-rights feminist and her political endgame was always to achieve full citizenship for women. She took every opportunity to increase women's participation in social reform and persuaded Lord Brougham to invite women to participate in the Social Science Association. From its foundation in 1857 the association acted as a powerful pressure group on government policy and offered one of the very few places where women could make their contribution to social policy. In the spring of 1865 Barbara led the members of the Langham Place group in supporting the election campaign of John Stuart Mill, who had committed himself to female suffrage in his election addresses. In May 1865 Barbara was a founding member of a fifty-strong women-only discussion group called the Kensington Society. It was there that Barbara made contact with John Stuart Mill's stepdaughter, Helen Taylor (1831–1907), who provided a significant link to Mill himself. After consulting Helen Taylor, in May 1866 Barbara formed a committee to gather signatures for a petition to parliament. On 7 June 1866 Mill presented the petition of 'Barbara L. S. Bodichon and others' which protested the anomaly that 'some holders of property are allowed to use this right, while others, forming no less a constituent part of the nation, and equally qualified by law to hold property, are not able to exercise this privilege.' This petition contained the signatures of 1499 women. Her Kensington Society paper, slightly revised and entitled *Reasons for the Enfranchisement of Women*, was read at the Social Science Association meeting held in Manchester in October 1866, where it attracted the attention of Lydia Becker (1827–1890), who then went on to form the Manchester Women's Suffrage Committee early in 1867. The Manchester group asked for 3000 copies of Barbara's pamphlet to encourage another wave of petitioning. In response to hostile articles in the press Barbara wrote *Objections to the Enfranchisement of Women Considered* (1866). Ten thousand of each of Barbara's pamphlets were circulated in order to encourage further petitioning campaigns. A general petition of 3559 signatures of men and women sympathetic to female enfranchisement was presented in parliament on 28 March 1867 and another petition with the signatures of 1605 'women householders' was presented on 8 April 1867. On 20 May 1867 John Stuart Mill moved an amendment on Disraeli's Representation of the People Bill (clause 4) to leave out the word 'men' in order to insert the word 'person' instead. Although the amendment was defeated by a majority of 123, Mill gained 79 favourable votes. This was as much as Barbara had hoped for on this occasion. Helen Taylor insisted that a women-only suffrage committee should be formed. Barbara disagreed with this strategy, believing that the loss of politically experienced men from their committee might cost them ten years, and she attempted, but failed, to change Helen Taylor's mind. As a consequence Barbara resigned from the general suffrage committee (envisioned as permanent) in June 1867. However, her two articles were combined and published once again in 1869 and 1872 as *Reasons for and against the Enfranchisement of Women*, so she continued to influence public opinion.

Girton College and Emily Davies Barbara inherited her father's interest in educational experiments. She founded Portman Hall School in Paddington in 1854, a secular co-educational school, which she financed until 1863. Her experience at Bedford College, which had been founded by Julia Smith's friend Elizabeth Reid, was important because it had revealed to her the inadequacies of the education provided for middle-class girls. She wrote a paper about these inadequacies for the Social Science Association entitled 'Female education in the middle classes', which was reprinted in the *English Woman's Journal* of June 1858. Barbara had dreamed of a university college for women since first reading Tennyson's *The Princess* at about the same time as her brother, Ben, went to Cambridge. In

1862 a small group of members of the Social Science Association who were committed to the higher education of women formed a committee which included Barbara and Emily Davies. In the spring of 1867 an executive committee to establish a university college for women was set up by Emily Davies which omitted Barbara's name because she was so publicly associated with 'strong-minded' women's rights campaigners. Nevertheless both women were involved in planning the campaign during 1867. Barbara had caught typhoid in Algeria and was convalescing at Scalands Gate, so Emily spent August with her planning. Barbara promised £1000 to build the college, although she made three conditions: one, that the college should be set up as a secular educational institution; second, that Elizabeth Blackwell should be appointed as professor of hygiene; and third, the college should be in the heart of Cambridge. Emily did not keep faith with Barbara on any of the three issues. Nevertheless, following her father's maxim *bis dat qui cito dat* ('he gives twice who gives early'), Barbara put down the first £1000 and chaired the building committee to raise money for permanent buildings. Barbara formally joined the executive committee in February 1869 to help organize the entrance examination for students at her Blandford Square home. Barbara was antagonistic to beginning the college in rented accommodation, which she regarded as a waste of resources; nevertheless Emily persuaded the executive committee to begin in a rented house at Hitchin. They began with only five students and Cambridge dons having to travel by train to Hitchin. In the summer term of 1872 Barbara briefly took the role of acting mistress.

Emily and Barbara continued to argue over the issue of the location of the permanent college. At length a compromise was reached and 50 acres of land was purchased at Girton, 2 miles from the centre of Cambridge. The architect Alfred Waterhouse was commissioned to design dignified but relatively inexpensive buildings. Barbara was involved in all the details of building the college, and sent up furniture and books to help furnish it. She was a frequent and enthusiastic visitor and gave holidays to the early students at Scalands Gate. She remained on the executive committee of Girton College until 1877, when she suffered a stroke which reduced her to semi-invalidism. In 1884 Barbara gave Girton College another £5000 to help it expand. In 1891 she donated all of her pictures that she had lent over the years and in her will she left another £10,000, thus helping to secure the college's establishment without debt in its early years.

Last years After her stroke in 1877, when Barbara could no longer travel to Algeria, she asked Gertrude Jekyll to design a reading-room as an addition to her Sussex home. This served as a night school for local young men who could not read and write. Her old friend William Ransom, erstwhile editor of the *Hastings and St Leonards News*, taught in it during the winter months. During the six summer months Barbara's husband joined her in England until he himself became too ill to travel.

Barbara was disappointed not to have children of her own, but one happy result of her involvement with Girton College was that she met a young Jewish woman called Hertha Marks (1854–1923) [*see* Ayrton, (Phoebe) Sarah], who virtually became a daughter to her. Barbara encouraged Hertha to apply for a scholarship at Girton, and when she did not succeed organized what amounted to a personal scholarship fund so Hertha could go up to Girton in 1876. Barbara died at Scalands Gate on 11 June 1891 and was buried four days later in Brightling church at a funeral attended by family and friends and a long line of her night-school 'boys'. There is a memorial plaque at her Hastings home. In her will Barbara left enough money for Hertha to resume her studies in electrical engineering. Hertha named her daughter Barbara Bodichon after her benefactress. This 'granddaughter', Barbara Bodichon Gould (1886–1950), entered parliament as a Labour member in 1945, thereby embodying and fulfilling Barbara Bodichon's dream of women taking up their full roles as citizens. PAM HIRSCH

Sources P. Hirsch, *Barbara Leigh Smith Bodichon: feminist, artist and rebel* (1998) · S. Herstein, *A mid-Victorian feminist, Barbara Leigh Smith Bodichon* (1985) · H. Burton, *Barbara Bodichon, 1827–1891* (1949) · *The George Eliot letters*, ed. G. S. Haight, 9 vols. (1954–78) · A. M. Howitt, *An art student in Munich*, 2 vols. (1853) · N. G. Annan, 'The intellectual aristocracy', *Studies in social history: a tribute to G. M. Trevelyan*, ed. J. H. Plumb (1955), 241–87 · private information (2004) · m. cert.

Archives Girton Cam., corresp. and papers · Women's Library, London, letters | BLPES, Mill-Taylor corresp. · Claydon House, Buckinghamshire, Nightingale MSS · CUL, William Smith family MSS · Girton Cam., Blackburn collection · Girton Cam., Emily Davies MSS · Girton Cam., Moore family MSS · Girton Cam., corresp. with Bessie Rayner Parkes and others · Hants. RO, Bonham Carter MSS · NRA, priv. coll., corresp. with Sir Norman and Amy (Leigh Smith) Moore

Likenesses photograph, *c*.1853, priv. coll. · Holmes of New York, photograph, 1858, NPG · S. Laurence, crayon drawing, 1861, Girton Cam. · S. Laurence, oils, 1861, Girton Cam. · E. M. Osborn, ink on thin board, 1884, Girton Cam. · E. M. Osborn, oils, 1884, Girton Cam. · G. Jekyll, photograph, *c*.1885, U. Cal. · A. A. E. Disderi, photograph, Girton Cam. [*see illus.*] · E. M. Osborn, oils, Girton Cam. · lithograph (after oil painting by S. Laurence, 1861), NPG · photograph, NPG

Wealth at death £28,603 18*s*. 7*d*.: resworn probate, June 1892, *CGPLA Eng. & Wales* (1891)

Bodie, Walford [*real name* Samuel Murphy Bodie] (**1869–1939**), music-hall entertainer, was born on 11 June 1869 at 33 George Street, Aberdeen, the son of William Bodie, journeyman baker, and his wife, Margaret, *née* Murphy. Educated at Robert Gordon College, Aberdeen, he joined the National Telephone Company as an electrician in the mid-1880s. He reputedly made his stage début demonstrating electricity in an amateur show at Stonehaven in 1886, but his subsequent early career is hard to document, not least because of the variously embroidered accounts he later offered. In 1897 he began work as assistant manager of a Norwich music-hall run by his brother-in-law, H. Werner Walford, before briefly managing a hall at Macclesfield. As Dr Walford Bodie (he may have obtained an American qualification of dubious provenance) he then founded the Royal Magnets Variety Company, quickly establishing a reputation in Scotland and the English provinces. He probably made his London début at the Britannia, Hoxton, in 1903 and for the next few years was one of the biggest attractions ever seen on the British variety stage.

Tall, with piercing eyes and a large, dramatically pointed moustache, Bodie had tremendous stage presence. His act contained a number of elements of greater or lesser importance at different stages of his career. A renowned ventriloquist, he was also a highly gifted hypnotist, specializing in the physical and mental manipulation of his assistants and popularizing the hypnosis and subsequent embarrassment of audience members. Yet another element involved the carrying out of electrical exhibitions and experiments, often involving the passage of supposedly lethal doses of electricity through his body and that of volunteers. An endlessly inventive self-publicist, happy to refer to himself in his posters as the Most Remarkable Man on the Earth, his stunts included hypnotizing animals in Dundee Zoo in 1904 and exhibiting the original electric chair in the 1920s.

Walford Bodie's box-office success, however, was ultimately built upon his reputation as a healer through the deployment of what he termed 'bloodless surgery'. More than 76,000 people were reputed to have seen his shows during a three-week run at the Bristol People's Palace music-hall in 1904, at which he claimed to have cured some fifty patients 'discharged as hopeless and incurable cases from the Royal Infirmary and the general Hospital' (*Era*, 7 July 1904). Bloodless surgery involved an amalgam of hypnotism, muscular manipulation, faith-healing, and what he termed 'Bodie-force', the intuitive direction of electrical currents via his hands and feet to the relevant parts of the patient's body. Whatever its validity and for whatever reason, his treatment clearly benefited some individuals. Unsurprisingly, Bodie was a constant target for the medical profession. Medical students heckled his performances while senior practitioners attacked him in the press: even a visit to his home town in 1904 was thus marked. Bodie deliberately courted the publicity that ensued, teasingly dedicating his 'textbook' *The Bodie Book* (1905) to British doctors 'in the hope that it may lead them to a fuller understanding of the finer forces of which it treats'. However, in November 1909, during the course of a successful court action brought against Bodie by a former assistant, many of his stage secrets, including selective choice of patients and the exaggeration of their symptoms, were exposed. His next engagement at the Glasgow Coliseum was disrupted for several nights by medical students and finally closed by a virtual riot on 12 November. Further demonstrations and an attack on his business premises followed the next week in London. Although Bodie remained an attraction—his company's dramatic escape from the torpedoed SS *Arabia* on return from an Indian tour in 1916 gave valuable publicity—he concentrated far less on healing and found it increasingly difficult to obtain bookings in leading halls.

Bodie invested his not inconsiderable earnings in a number of business ventures, owning a hotel, shops, and houses in Macduff, Banffshire, by 1903. He also ran the Bodie Electric Drug Company in London, which produced 'electric liniment' and 'electric life pills'. He wrote a body of literature to support his act and created the fictional detective Harley the hypnotist, with a book-length treatment published in 1910 enjoying some commercial success. In 1890 he married the eldest daughter of David Henry, a road surveyor from Macduff. As Princess Rubie, illusionist and thought-reader, she worked with him until her retirement in 1930. Four of her sisters also had spells with his company, as did his sister Marie Walford, who appeared as Mystic Marie, the Electric-Magnetic Floating Lady. In 1903, the Bodies built the Manor House, Macduff, with Bodie happily playing the role of local laird and enjoying golf and masonic activity. They were badly affected by the early deaths of their daughter, Jeannie, who worked in the family show, and son Albert who had managed his father for a period. A third child, Samuel, survived both parents.

On 15 February 1932, a year after the death of his first wife, Bodie married Florence Joan (Florrie) Robertshaw (*b.* 1909/10), a 22-year-old, Leeds-born dancer who worked in his show as La Tesla. He was taken ill while performing at the Blackpool Olympia in October 1939 and died in Blackpool Victoria Hospital on 19 October, six days after an unsuccessful operation on a perforated ulcer. He was buried in Macduff five days later. His obituarist declared: 'Whatever he was, he was an exquisite showman' (*Aberdeen Evening Express*, 20 Oct 1939); Bodie personified the diversity of twentieth-century variety and skilfully exploited the tensions between popular belief and scientific–medical knowledge. DAVE RUSSELL

Sources R. Jay, *Learned pigs and fireproof women* (1987) · W. Bodie, *The Bodie book* (1905) · R. Busby, *British music hall: an illustrated who's who from 1850 to the present day* (1976) · *The Era* (7 July 1904) · *The Times* (2 Nov 1909) · *The Times* (5 Nov 1909) · *The Times* (13 Nov 1909) · *The Times* (16 Nov 1909) · *Aberdeen Evening Express* (20 Oct 1939) · *Performer* (26 Oct 1939) · *Performer* (28 Jan 1931) · *Yorkshire Observer* (21 Oct 1939) · b. cert. · d. cert.

Archives Ransom HRC, corresp. with Harry Houdini

Likenesses advertising still, repro. in *The Era*, 35 · photographs, repro. in Bodie, *The Bodie book*, frontispiece, 104, 120

Bodington, Sir Nathan (1848–1911), university administrator, born at Aston, Birmingham, on 29 May 1848, was the only son in a family of one son and one daughter of Jonathan Bodington (1794–1875), miller, and his wife, Anne Redfern (1818–1894). He entered King Edward's School, Birmingham, in 1860, and proceeded thence to Oxford as a scholar of Wadham College in 1867. He won the Hody exhibition for Greek in 1870, and in the following year a first class in the final classical school. But a fellowship was slow in coming, and for three years he held successively assistant masterships at Manchester grammar school and Westminster School. In 1875 he was elected fellow and tutor of Lincoln College, Oxford. His activities as one of the reforming party, his membership of A. H. D. Acland's circle, and his social gifts made him prominent in Oxford society. But his tenure at Lincoln became uncertain after the successful defence by Christopher Wordsworth in 1881 of the clerical restrictions attached to the college's fellowships. Although professing himself a churchman, Bodington was unwilling to take holy orders, and his fellowship lapsed in 1885.

Like others of his generation, he was attracted to educational work in industrial cities, leaving Oxford in 1881 to become the first professor of Greek at Mason College, Birmingham. He retained the chair for only one session, being appointed in 1882 professor of Greek and principal of the Yorkshire College, Leeds, on the recommendation of his Oxford friend, Arthur Rücker. In his early years at Leeds the inadequacy of his stipend, from which he supported his widowed mother and unmarried sister, caused him to seek other educational appointments in Britain and abroad. He remained at Leeds, however, and his life was thenceforth identified with the steady growth of the Yorkshire College. Founded in 1874, the college was exclusively concerned with science until 1878, when an arts course was added to the curriculum and the college became a place of education in all branches. In 1884 it was united with the Leeds school of medicine, and in 1887 was admitted as a constituent member of the Victoria University, a federation of Owens College, Manchester, and University College, Liverpool, which had been established in 1880. From 1896 to 1900 Bodington served as vice-chancellor of the Victoria University and, supported by Acland, he opposed the breakup of the federal university in 1901. When in 1903 Manchester and Liverpool obtained charters for separate universities, he actively promoted the foundation of an independent University of Leeds. With the help of Lord Ripon, afterwards first chancellor of the university, he was successful in raising a fund of over £100,000, which it was stipulated should be subscribed before the royal charter was granted.

On the inauguration of the newly constituted university (18 August 1904) Bodington resigned his chair of Greek, and was nominated vice-chancellor. In this capacity he did much to bring the university into touch with the typical industries of Leeds, by providing the appropriate scientific and technical instruction. At the same time he always strove hard to secure a wider appreciation of art and literature as an integral part of the university course of study. His administrative ability was generally recognized in the county, and he took an active interest in the educational development of the West Riding. He had a particular interest in archaeology. He was an enthusiastic member of the Territorial Army Association, a magistrate of the West Riding from 1906, and president of the Leeds Literary and Philosophical Society (1898–1900). Victoria University conferred on him the honorary degree of LittD in 1895, and Aberdeen that of LLD in 1906. Edward VII opened the new university buildings at Leeds in June 1908, and in the following November conferred a knighthood on him. Bodington married on 8 August 1907 Eliza, daughter of Sir John Barran, first baronet, of Chapel Allerton Hall, Leeds. He died, after a short illness, at Woodbourne, North Hill Road, Headingley, Leeds, on 12 May 1911, and was buried at Headingley. His wife survived him without issue. G. S. WOODS, *rev.* M. C. CURTHOYS

Sources W. H. Draper, *Sir Nathan Bodington: a memoir* (1912) • P. H. J. H. Gosden and A. J. Taylor, eds., *Studies in the history of a university, 1874–1974: to commemorate the centenary of the University of Leeds* (1975) • *The Times* (13 May 1911) • *Yorkshire Post* (13 May 1911)
Likenesses A. Hacker, oils, U. Leeds
Wealth at death £6895 4*s*. 11*d*.: probate, 8 July 1911, *CGPLA Eng. & Wales*

Bodkin, Sir Archibald Henry (1862–1957), lawyer, was born in Highgate on 1 April 1862, the youngest of the eight children of William Peter Bodkin (1814–1900) and his wife, Elisabeth, daughter of William Clowser, of Hampstead. He came from a family of lawyers: his grandfather was Sir William Henry *Bodkin, chairman of Middlesex quarter sessions and a prolific writer on criminal law, and his father for forty-four years chaired the Highgate bench. There were plans after 'Archie' left Highgate School to send him to South Africa to join one of his brothers on a farm, and he actually spent a year on a farm at Barnsley; but his interests were already fixed on the criminal bar, and when the South Africa scheme fell through he was without delay entered at the Inner Temple. He was called in 1885, and became a pupil of E. T. E. Besley, then the busiest junior of the day, where he was later joined by Travers Humphreys.

From the first Bodkin was a tremendous worker, meticulous in detail, and specializing in drafting indictments which, before the passing of the Indictments Act of 1915, was a highly technical accomplishment. His style as a prosecuting advocate, at north London and Middlesex sessions, and at the Old Bailey, was formed early on: simple and direct in manner, he scorned the dramatic mannerisms popular in his day, and although he possessed a bubbling if somewhat heavy sense of humour, he never allowed it to get out of hand. He relied on accurate and detailed knowledge of the facts and law contained in his brief, and a strong mind directed to the task in hand: the conviction of the accused, in which he had an extremely high success rate. Yet, powerful advocate that he became, he never pressed a case beyond its merits.

Bodkin's innate ability and sheer hard work were soon recognized. He took only brief and infrequent holidays, and save for a game of billiards allowed himself few other interests than the law. And the law for him meant criminal prosecutions, for his defence briefs were rare. He built up a large licensing practice, but as brewster sessions, when most of the work was done, were then held in August, these briefs did not clash with his work at the Old Bailey. He was already saving money, and on 8 July 1891, only six years after call, was able to marry Maud Beatrice, daughter of Robert Wheler Bush, rector of St Alfege, London Wall, a marriage of great contentment which ended only with his death. They had one son.

In 1892 Bodkin was appointed junior Treasury counsel at the Old Bailey, and rapidly built up a reputation which he shared with Horace Avory, Charles Gill, and Richard Muir as one of the four leading criminal advocates of the day. In 1908 he was appointed senior Treasury counsel. By now he had joined the chambers of his uncle Sir Harry Bodkin Poland at 5 Paper Buildings, and in time became head of them. In 1901 he succeeded Poland as recorder of Dover, and although he had to resign in 1920 on becoming director of public prosecutions, he was reappointed in 1931 and did not resign until 1947, when he was eighty-five.

Tall and lean, Bodkin had a magnificent physique, and was a considerable athlete as a young man. Although well able to afford it he never drove a car and preferred to walk long distances from court to court; at an advanced age he was quite content with public transport. In the First World War Bodkin was largely concerned with the prosecution of spies, where his knowledge of the law, great industry, and ability to marshal and direct a mass of deadly detail were of the greatest value. He was responsible for the prosecution of Carl Hans Lody, and built up the complex case against Sir Roger Casement for the attorney-general. Perhaps his greatest murder prosecution was that known as the 'Brides in the bath' (G. J. Smith) in 1915, in which he called 112 witnesses for the crown.

In the troubled post-war period it was essential to appoint a strong man to succeed Sir Charles Mathews as director of public prosecutions and in 1920 Bodkin began the most strenuous ten years of his life. He would personally examine some 2000 sets of papers a year, and here his industry was at times a defect, for he was unwilling to delegate responsibility. Day after day he would be first at his office at Richmond Terrace, personally drafting indictments which should have been left to junior Treasury counsel, and always taking work home at the weekend. The legend in Temple that one Christmas evening he was seen leaving his chambers with a bundle of papers is probably true. Here, too, his understanding of contemporary thought and habit were narrowed by the limited range of his own private life. In the application of the criminal law he sought only to reflect the public's wishes, but he was unaware of important developments in society at large—especially in the world of art and literature—and his vigorous forays into the sphere of public morals were open to criticism. In 1922 he was a driving force behind the ban on James Joyce's *Ulysses*, the passages dealing with Molly Bloom's orgasms being enough to convince him of the book's obscenity. The ban was strictly enforced until it collapsed in 1936. And he was also instrumental in the suppression in 1928 of Radclyffe Hall's *The Well of Loneliness*, which dealt with lesbianism. The book was defended by many eminent figures, among them the writer and critic Desmond MacCarthy and the lawyer Norman Birkett, and the ban prompted the future lord of appeal Cyril Asquith to call for a review of the obscenity law. The book remained banned until 1948.

Famous cases to which Bodkin gave the whole of his attention included those arising from the Irish Republican Army troubles in Ireland, the prosecution of Horatio Bottomley, Herbert Armstrong (1922), Jean-Pierre Vaquier (1924), Patrick Mahon (1924), John Thorne (1925), Frederick Guy Browne and William Henry Kennedy (1928) for murder, and that of the fraudster Clarence Hatry and his associates. The closest that he came to political controversy was in July 1924 when he instigated the prosecution of John Campbell, acting editor of the communist *Workers' Weekly*, under the 1797 Incitement to Mutiny Act. The subsequent withdrawal of the prosecution led to the downfall of the first Labour government, but criticism of the handling of the Campbell case was mostly levelled at the attorney-general (Sir Patrick Hastings), who accepted responsibility.

Over the Savidge case in 1928, however, Bodkin was directly in the line of fire. The arrest and subsequent acquittal at a magistrate's court of Sir Leo Chiozza Money, and a young unmarried woman named Irene Savidge, on charges of indecent behaviour, obliged Bodkin to investigate for perjury the arresting officers. But under his guidance the police inquiry seemed concerned with establishing the guilt of Money and Savidge for the offence with which they had earlier been acquitted, rather than with uncovering evidence of perjury on the part of their police accusers. On 15 May Savidge was subjected to a 'third degree' interrogation at New Scotland Yard which, according to *The Times*, 'would have been a legal procedure under "Dora", but … is utterly illegal at common law' (*The Times*, 19 May 1928, 15b). The home secretary responded to parliamentary questions on the matter with a tribunal of inquiry that exonerated the police and the director of public prosecutions from any blame, while raising important questions about their respective powers. In the opinion of one contemporary Bodkin was fixated with securing convictions, when his responsibility was rather to see if there were grounds for prosecution, and because of this his influence 'was not altogether fortunate' (Biron, 121). In March 1930 he suddenly announced his resignation, leaving his office the same afternoon.

Bodkin was knighted in 1917 and was appointed KCB in 1924. In 1930 he went to live in Sidmouth, where he became a noted gardener. But he soon found new employment in the field of criminal law as chairman of Devon quarter sessions, where he sat until 1947. As a judge he loved a legal argument, and insisted, with some pedantry, on the meticulous proof of every fact in dispute. With failing powers he finally relinquished his various appointments and retired to live with his wife and son at their home, Beechers Croft, at Rogate, Sussex. There, at the age of ninety-five, a wealthy man from the savings of his hard-earned income, he died on 31 December 1957.

CHRISTMAS HUMPHREYS, *rev.* MARK POTTLE

Sources *The Times* (18 May 1928), 8c–8d · *The Times* (19 May 1928), 15b · *The Times* (7 June 1928) · *The Times* (14 July 1928), 15b · *The Times* (21 July 1928), 7d–7e, 8a–8b · *The Times* (14 Aug 1928), 11b–11c · *The Times* (10 Nov 1928), 9b · *The Times* (21 Nov 1928), 15e · *The Times* (14 Dec 1928), 4d · *The Times* (15 March 1930) · *The Times* (3 Jan 1958), 11a–11b · R. Jackson, *Case for the prosecution* (1962) · D. G. Browne, *Sir Travers Humphreys* (1960) · C. Biron, *Without prejudice: impressions of life and law* (1936) · J. Rosenberg, *The case for the crown: the inside story*

of the director of public prosecutions (1987) · H. Montgomery Hyde, *Norman Birkett* (1965) · personal knowledge (1971) · private information (1971)
Likenesses photograph, repro. in *The Times* (15 March 1930), 16
Wealth at death £124,385 6s. 1d.: probate, 28 July 1958, *CGPLA Eng. & Wales*

Bodkin, Thomas Patrick (1887–1961), museum director and art critic, was born in Dublin on 21 July 1887, the eldest of the family of two sons and four daughters of Matthias McDonnell Bodkin, a journalist who was later county court judge of Clare and MP for North Roscommon, and his wife, Arabella, daughter of Francis Norman, of Dublin. He was educated at Belvedere College, Clongowes Wood College, and the Royal University of Ireland, from which he graduated in 1908, having won medals and prizes for oratory, among them the lord chancellor's prize. He was called to the bar (King's Inns) in 1911 and practised for five years. He was a fluent speaker and a ready wit, a man who enjoyed debate and argument; these characteristics, perhaps exaggerated by his legal training, affected his attitudes in the very different career he was later to adopt.

Bodkin had a great love of beautiful things. He began to collect for himself early in life and a major influence on his development in this and other respects was the art collector Sir Hugh Lane. His fastidious care for personal appearance in both himself and others, his conviction that taste and flair were more important than scholarship, perhaps even his addiction to playing bridge, all owed something to Lane's example. Bodkin came to know him well and in one of the codicils to Lane's controversial will the wish is expressed that he should advise on setting up a gallery of modern art in Dublin. The disputes over interpreting the will following Lane's death in the sinking of the *Lusitania* in 1915, and the consequent legal uncertainties, were well set out by Bodkin in *Hugh Lane and his Pictures* (1932).

On 2 February 1917 Bodkin married Aileen Patricia, third daughter of Joseph Richard Cox, nationalist MP for North Clare. They had five daughters. On leaving the bar he became increasingly involved in public affairs. He acted as commissioner and secretary to the commission of charitable donations and bequests in the Irish Free State. In 1926 he served on the commission to advise the Irish government on coinage design, being mainly responsible for choosing animal and bird designs by Percy Metcalfe. His appointment to succeed Lucius O'Callaghan as director of the National Gallery of Ireland followed in 1927. During his term of office perhaps the most notable acquisition was the Perugino *Pietà* once in the celebrated Orléans collection.

In 1935 Bodkin left Ireland to take up the dual appointment as director of the newly founded Barber Institute and professor of fine arts in the University of Birmingham. At that time the funds of the institute compared favourably even with those of some national museums, and Bodkin was given an enviable opportunity to build up a major new public collection. The Barber Trust required that all works of art purchased on its behalf should be among the best of their kind. It would have been impossible for any director to live up to this demand consistently, but Bodkin began well, his early acquisitions ranging from Egyptian, Greek, and Chinese sculpture, medieval ivories, and Italian Renaissance bronzes, to paintings by Simone Martini, Mabuse, Poussin, and Gainsborough. Perhaps with Lane in mind, and perhaps instinctively, he bought as if for his own private enjoyment and thereby gave the gallery the stamp of a connoisseur's collection which it still retains. This character was emphasized even in the design of the picture galleries—each having a succession of bays which create a semi-private atmosphere for the group of paintings they contain. Bodkin was proud of having influenced the plans of the architect, Robert Atkinson.

Bodkin became a colourful if sometimes disputatious personality in the University of Birmingham, for some years acting as public orator, an office well suited to his gifts and temperament. He also responded to the rapidly developing media of radio and television. His Irish voice and bearded features, not unlike those of George Bernard Shaw, became popular in such programmes as *Animal, Vegetable, and Mineral*. This, however, was not quite the true Bodkin. There was a more serious and basically simple side to him which is best appreciated in his writings, in particular *The Approach to Painting* (1927), a book which has always 'told' with the young, and in personal reminiscences like *My Uncle Frank* (1941), a spontaneous piece of unabashed and natural writing. His other books include *May it Please your Lordships* (1917), which contains his translations of modern French poetry, *Four Irish Landscape Painters* (1920), and *Dismembered Masterpieces* (1945).

Bodkin could never quite appreciate the fact that the English are not very Irish, a failure of understanding which frequently landed him and others in situations of embarrassment and sometimes fury. He was quite unlike any other museum director in Britain. In many ways he belonged to the generation just before his own, the silk and velvet world of the Edwardian dealer and private collector, and as a midnight raconteur he evoked this society with complete success. He received honorary degrees from the National University of Ireland and the University of Dublin, was a trustee of the National Library of Ireland, a governor and guardian of the National Gallery of Ireland, and honorary professor of the history of fine arts at Trinity College, Dublin. He was an honorary associate of the Royal Institute of Architects, an officer of the Légion d'honneur, and a knight of St Gregory to the Holy See. He died at his home, 259 Hagley Road, Birmingham, on 24 April 1961. KENNETH GARLICK, *rev.*

Sources A. Denson, *Thomas Bodkin: a bio-bibliographical survey* (1966) · *The Times* (25 April 1961) · *Birmingham Post* (25 April 1961) · personal knowledge (1981) · A. Kelly, 'Thomas Bodkin at the National Gallery of Ireland', *Irish Arts Review Yearbook*, 8 (1991–2), 171–80 · *CGPLA Eng. & Wales* (1962) · m. cert. · d. cert.
Archives TCD, corresp. and papers · U. Birm. L., personal papers | NL Ire., letters to Frank Gallagher · Tate collection, corresp. with Lord Clark · TCD, letters to Thomas McGreevy · U. Glas. L., letters to D. S. MacColl

Likenesses J. Keating, group portrait, oils, *c*.1919 (*Homage to Hugh Lane*), Hugh Lane Gallery of Modern Art, Dublin • J. Sleator, portrait, 1949, priv. coll. • B. Fleetwood-Walker, oils, 1955, Birmingham Museums and Art Gallery • C. Wheeler, terracotta bust, 1955, NPG • C. W. Heath, photographs, 1961, NPG • H. Coster, photographs, NPG • S. O'Sullivan, drawing, NG Ire. • J. Sleator, oils, NG Ire. • C. Wheeler, bronze bust, Barber Institute of Fine Arts, Birmingham

Wealth at death £55,481 8*s*. 0*d*. in England: probate, 19 April 1962, *CGPLA Eng. & Wales*

Bodkin, Sir William Henry (1791–1874), legal writer, the son of Peter Bodkin, descended from a well-established family in the county of Galway, was born at Islington on 4 August 1791. His mother was Sarah Gilbert of Lichfield. He was educated at the Islington Academy. In 1812 he married Sarah Sophia Poland (*d*. 1848), the eldest daughter of Peter Raymond Poland of Winchester Hall, Highgate. He was called to the bar in 1824 by Gray's Inn, of which society he became a bencher in 1826. For several years he worked on the home circuit. He practised in criminal law at the Middlesex, Westminster, and Kent sessions, and at the central criminal court, and was made recorder of Dover in 1832.

In 1821 Bodkin became honorary secretary to the Society for the Suppression of Mendicity; in the same year he published *Brief observations on the bill now pending in parliament to amend the laws relative to the relief of the poor in England*. His interest in poor-law reform probably influenced his decision to enter politics. At the general election in 1841 he was returned to parliament as a Conservative at Rochester, as the colleague of James Stoddart Douglas, defeating Lord Melgund by two votes. He supported Peel over free trade in 1846, and was defeated easily in 1847. He did not stand in 1852, but was defeated at a by-election for Rochester in 1856. He was responsible for the passage of a statute stipulating that confirmed paupers should be chargeable to the common funds of the unions. Bodkin's act was passed for one year only; but it was continued and extended.

In 1859 Bodkin was appointed assistant judge of the Middlesex sessions. He married again on 25 March 1865, his second wife being Sarah Constance Miles, the daughter of Joseph Johnson Miles JP of Highgate. On 3 August 1867 he received a knighthood. He was for many years counsel to the Treasury, and the president of the Society of Arts, of which he was one of the earliest and most enthusiastic members. Bodkin was also a deputy lieutenant of Middlesex and chairman of the Metropolitan assessment sessions. An attack of cancer in the cheek led him to resign his office some weeks before his death, on 26 March 1874, at his house, on West Hill, Highgate. He was buried in Highgate cemetery. He had one son and one daughter.

JAMES MEW, *rev.* NILANJANA BANERJI

Sources *The Times* (28 March 1874) • *Men of the time* (1872) • *Hampstead and Highgate Express* (28 March 1874) • *WWBMP* • *Debrett's Illustrated House of Commons and the Judicial Bench* (1872) • m. cert. • d. cert. • *CGPLA Eng. & Wales* (1874)

Archives BL, minutes of the Society for Suppression of Mendicity, Add. MS 50136, *passim*

Likenesses J. P. Knight, oils, exh. RA 1864, Guildhall, Westminster, London • wood-engraving, NPG; repro. in *ILN* (1859) • wood-engraving, NPG; repro. in *ILN* (1874)

Wealth at death under £40,000: probate, 11 May 1874, *CGPLA Eng. & Wales*

Bodley, George Frederick (1827–1907), architect and designer, was born at his parents' home, 4 Albion Street, Hull, on 14 March 1827, the sixth child and youngest son of William Hulme Bodley MD (1781–1855) of Edinburgh, physician of the Hull Royal Infirmary, and his wife, Mary Ann (1790/91–1883), daughter of the Revd Frederick Hamilton of Brighton. After his enthusiasm for architecture had been aroused by reading M. H. Bloxam's *Principles of Gothic Ecclesiastical Architecture* (1829), he was encouraged to take up the subject as a career by the architect George Gilbert *Scott (1811–1878), whose brother Samuel was married to Bodley's sister Georgina. Following five years as the first pupil in Scott's office, from 1845 to 1850, Bodley set up in practice at his family home in Furze Hill, Brighton, his father having retired to the town in 1837. After his father's death in 1855, Bodley moved to London and lived first in Wimpole Street and from 1861 in Harley Street.

Gothic architecture was then undergoing a remarkable creative renewal. Among the leaders of the avant-garde were two of Bodley's slightly older colleagues from Scott's office, George Edmund Street and William White. Like these friends, he turned away from Scott's reliance on English late thirteenth-century models towards a new synthesis intended to develop Gothic into a modern style. Inspiration was drawn from early Gothic models, which were as often continental as English, partly thanks to the writings of Ruskin, a lifelong influence on Bodley. The success of this new style, known to twentieth-century historians as High Victorian, was made publicly apparent in the 1856 competition for the Crimea Memorial Church at Constantinople, in which Bodley, not yet thirty, was placed third, after William Burges and Street. By then he had completed his first church, at Longgrove in Herefordshire (1854–6), and was busy with commissions in the Cotswolds from the Tractarian clergy associated with Thomas Keble, vicar of Bisley. These included a new church at Selsley in Gloucestershire (1859–62), which is the finest achievement of his early years: its mighty saddleback tower magnificently exploits its site on a high ridge to the south-west of Stroud. Family friendships helped bring him his first major town churches: St Michael's, Brighton, designed in 1858, and St Martin's, Scarborough, designed in 1860–61. These buildings, with Selsley and St Stephen's, Guernsey (1861–5), are best-known for their stained glass and decoration by Morris, Marshall, Faulkner & Co. Bodley's acquaintance with the firm's partners went back to 1856, when William Morris had spent a year as a pupil in Street's office. So important were Bodley's commissions for the fledgeling firm that it was suggested he might become a partner, although it is unlikely that he felt entirely at home in Morris's robustly bohemian circle. However, the new ideas he encountered there helped give shape to an abrupt departure in his architecture.

In 1860 Bodley was given the commission for rebuilding All Saints', Cambridge. His first design was in the bold

George Frederick Bodley (1827–1907), by unknown photographer, 1899

early French style of his former churches, but when this had to be abandoned for reasons of cost, he produced in 1862 the radically different proposal which, with modifications, was finally built. In some ways a throwback to Scott and even Pugin, its purely English forms were a reaction against what Morris and others felt to be the coarseness of contemporary architecture. In the later 1860s Bodley evolved an alternative style based not on development, but on the creative use of a paradigm—English Decorated Gothic of the first half of the fourteenth century. The first churches that resulted, such as St Salvador's, Dundee (1865–74), and St John's, Tue Brook, Liverpool (1867–70), were for the most part designed for a clergy who used ritual to convey a controversial emphasis on the sacraments and the real presence. Bodley's striving for beauty and grace in architecture was directed to the same end. Yet it reflected a new aesthetic ideal seen also in his domestic designs of the 1860s. These pioneering exercises in a neo-Georgian style based on the vernacular of his native Sussex had profound influence on the Queen Anne revival in the 1870s.

An increasing workload led Bodley to collaborate with Thomas *Garner, a former pupil of Scott, who in October 1867 abandoned his modest Warwickshire practice to move to London. A serious illness in 1868–9, which left Bodley badly lame, prompted him to take Garner into an informal partnership. On 5 September 1872 Bodley married Minna Frances Henrietta Reavely (1851–1933), a daughter of Thomas Reavely of Kinnersley Castle, Herefordshire, with whom he had one son, George. Their first home was at 24 Church Row, the beautiful street of Georgian houses which leads to the parish church at Hampstead. Garner and Scott's eldest son, George Gilbert Scott jun., lived at nos. 20 and 26 respectively, and the three architects met daily to discuss ideas.

This was the background to the two contrasting buildings of the early 1870s which are Bodley and Garner's best-known churches. St Augustine's, Pendlebury, designed in 1870 for an industrial suburb of Manchester, is a sublimely tall, nobly proportioned church, which unites nave and chancel in a single vessel. Its sheer walls and enormous, uninterrupted interior space, achieved by internal buttresses, make an overwhelming impact. In 1872 the partners designed Holy Angels', Hoar Cross, for an idyllic situation in the park of a Staffordshire country house. In the widowed Emily Meynell Ingram, who commissioned the church to serve as her husband's mausoleum, the partners had a patron whose exacting perfectionism matched their own. The result was a highly wrought work of art, in which the rich furnishings, sculpture, and stained glass are held together by the power of the architectural forms. Yet their most influential churches were less idiosyncratic than either of these masterpieces. In St Michael and All Angels, Folkestone, designed in 1870 (dem. 1953), St Michael's, Camden Town, begun in 1879, and St German's, Cardiff, begun in 1882, Bodley and Garner created the type of town church to which they remained loyal for the rest of their careers. Tall, and often clerestory-less, they have high, widely spaced arcades, and the division between nave and chancel is made as transparent as possible, to allow the congregation an uninterrupted view of the liturgy.

The practice was not exclusively ecclesiastical. Its office building for the London school board (1872–6; dem. 1929), in a Franco-Flemish Renaissance style, marked the abandonment of Gothic for secular buildings. Garner alone seems to have been responsible for the firm's few substantial domestic commissions, and he probably had the larger part to play in its collegiate work, which included St Swithun's Quadrangle at Magdalen College, Oxford (1879–84). Bodley designed few houses after 1868, but he became a specialist in the restoration of old ones, notably Ham House at Richmond, Surrey (1889–90), and Powis Castle, Montgomeryshire (1901–7). He also took an interest in garden design.

Bodley alone was responsible for the most celebrated of the partnership's later churches. These include the chapel at Clumber Park in Nottinghamshire (1886–9) for the youthful and ardently Anglo-Catholic seventh duke of Newcastle. This was said to be Bodley's favourite project; he certainly bitterly resented his dismissal after a row about overspending. A happier commission was the magnificent parish church at Eccleston in Cheshire (1894–1900), for the first duke of Westminster, which houses the duke's monument (1901). Bodley's numerous works of church restoration, extension, and furnishing included such major projects as the new chancel at St Helen's,

Brant Broughton, Lincolnshire (1874–6), a new Gothic interior for the eighteenth-century St Giles's, Wimborne St Giles, Dorset (1886–7; burnt 1908), and the tower of Holy Trinity, Long Melford, Suffolk (1898–1903).

Bodley's exceptional talent for decorative detail, especially flat-pattern design for painted decoration, textiles, and wallpaper, was perhaps unexpected in an architect who—unlike Garner—was not a fluent draughtsman. His approach to design was the antithesis of the arts and crafts movement: he believed in subsuming the identity of the craftsman into the architect's controlling vision, and he strove to ensure that nothing would disturb the integrated harmony of his buildings. To achieve this, in the early 1870s he abandoned Morris in favour of craftsmen he could control more tightly. These included Burlison and Grylls for stained glass and Watts & Co.—a firm he founded with Garner and Scott in 1874—for wallpaper, textiles, and furniture.

The dissolution of the partnership in 1897, as a result of Garner's conversion to Roman Catholicism the year before, had no effect on Bodley, who continued to design with unflagging energy to the end of his long life. Although he remained loyal to the English Decorated idiom evolved in the 1860s and 1870s, its application was rarely mechanical. Always responsive to the specific requirements of a commission, his late designs range from the sturdiness of the Eton Mission Church at Hackney Wick, London, begun in 1889, to the cerebral abstractions of the chapel for the Cowley Fathers in Oxford (1894–1904) and the *fin de siècle* attenuation of Holy Trinity, Prince Consort Road, London (1901–6). Perhaps the greatest disappointment of Bodley's life was the failure in 1879 to win the competition to design Truro Cathedral, but in 1906 he was asked to design new cathedrals for the American Episcopal church at Washington, DC, and San Francisco. The latter was not built, although the designs were complete at Bodley's death, but the eastern parts of the former cathedral are close to what he intended. In 1903 he was an assessor, with Richard Norman Shaw, in the second competition for Liverpool's Anglican cathedral (a design by Bodley and Garner had been unsuccessful in the abortive 1885–6 first competition). Following the decision to adopt a design by Giles Gilbert Scott, Bodley was appointed joint architect, since Scott was then only twenty-one. Inevitably, perhaps, the collaboration was not happy, but Bodley's influence on the first part of the cathedral to be built, the lady chapel (1906–10), was significant.

In 1882 Bodley was appointed architect to York Minster, and by the end of his life he was also consultant architect at Peterborough, Exeter, and Manchester cathedrals, as well as diocesan architect for Leicester. He was British representative on the jury for the 1899 competition to design a church in Vienna to commemorate the emperor Franz Josef's jubilee. Bodley largely remained aloof from the workings of his profession, but in 1899 he was awarded the Royal Institute of British Architects (RIBA) gold medal and he served for two years on the institute's council. This probably meant less to him than his election as Royal Academician in 1902 (he had been made ARA in 1882). He received the honorary degree of DCL from Oxford University in 1907.

Notoriously unbusinesslike in his affairs—he covered his cheque book with architectural sketches and ignored unwelcome correspondence—Bodley relied on the support of an excellent office, which after his marriage moved from Harley Street to Gray's Inn. His assistants and pupils included C. R. Ashbee, Sir Ninian Comper, F. C. Eden, Professor F. M. Simpson, Sir Walter Tapper, F. Inigo Thomas, Henry Vaughan, and Edward Warren. Sir Robert Rowand Anderson and Sir Robert Lorimer also spent brief periods in the office. The records of Bodley's practice, which was inherited by Cecil Hare (1875–1933), a favourite pupil whom he took into partnership shortly before his death, were destroyed after a bomb damaged the offices in March 1941. However, unusually for a Victorian church architect, all but a few of his major buildings survived intact through the twentieth century.

In 1886 Bodley and his family moved from Hampstead to 26 Park Crescent, and five years later to 41 Gloucester Place. About 1895 he acquired a country house, the beautiful Queen Anne Bridgefoot House at Iver, Buckinghamshire, but in 1906 he moved again, to the Elizabethan manor house on the Cherwell at Water Eaton, Oxfordshire, where he died on 21 October 1907. He was buried in St James's churchyard at Kinnersley on 25 October.

Bodley was survived by his wife, who remarried, and his son, who died a bachelor in 1938, since when no family papers have come to light. As a result, Bodley's personality, especially as a young man, remains elusive. He had a lifelong love of music and poetry: in his youth he played the organ at St Paul's, Brighton, and to the end of his life he entertained dinner guests with improvised piano playing. In 1899 he published a modest volume of verse. Just as the word 'refinement' which is invariably applied by historians to his later buildings overlooks a challengingly hard-edged quality in his designs, so the dreamy character portrayed by his obituarists is belied by an occasional perceptive insight: to Walburga, Lady Paget, who introduced him to Oscar Wilde in 1894, Bodley was 'spiritually a porcupine' (W. Paget, *In my Tower*, 1924, 1.66).

Unquestionably the most influential architect at work in the Anglican church during the last third of the nineteenth century, Bodley played a leading part in creating the high architectural and aesthetic standards which the Church of England absorbed from Anglo-Catholicism. His Gothic-revival visual legacy has been remarkably resilient: despite the challenges of modernism in architecture and liturgy, every member of the Church of England will at some time have worshipped in a building which aspires to the example he set. MICHAEL HALL

Sources F. M. Simpson, 'George Frederick Bodley', *RIBA Journal*, 15 (1907–8), 145–58 • E. Warren, 'The life and work of George Frederick Bodley', *RIBA Journal*, 17 (1909–10), 305–36 • D. Verey, 'George

Frederick Bodley climax of the Gothic revival', *Seven Victorian architects*, ed. J. Fawcett (1976) • *CGPLA Eng. & Wales* (1907) • J. A. R. Bickford and M. E. Bickford, *The medical profession in Hull* (1983)

Archives Hove Central Library, Sussex, letters to Viscount and Lady Wolseley • Staffs. RO, corresp. and accounts relating to Hoar Cross church

Likenesses photograph, 1899, RIBA BAL [*see illus.*] • photograph, *c*.1902, priv. coll.; copy, NPG • T. Murphy, marble effigy on a monument, 1911, Holy Trinity, Prince Consort Road, London • T. Murphy, plaster bust, 1911, Bodl. Oxf. • wood-engraving, NPG; repro. in *ILN* (29 April 1882)

Wealth at death £22,265 18*s*. 3*d*.: probate, 27 Dec 1907, *CGPLA Eng. & Wales*

Bodley, John (*c*.1520–1591), religious radical and publisher, was born in St Stephen's parish, Exeter, the son of the merchant John Bodley (*d*. 1527), of Exeter, and Alice Gale (*d*. 1558), of Dartmouth. About 1543 he married Joan (*d*. 1586), the daughter of the prominent merchant Robert Hone of Ottery St Mary. Bodley and his kin were some of the leading merchants of Exeter and, perhaps because of their trade links with Bristol, London, and other centres of religious radicalism, were at the forefront of the burgeoning protestant movement in that city, one of the few in the south-west in which protestantism found popular support in the first half of the sixteenth century. During the 1549 rebellion against Edward VI's new prayer book, Bodley and his stepfather, Thomas Prestwood, and brother-in-law John Periam provided the funds required to finance Lord John Russell's lifting of the siege of Exeter, and his eventual suppression of the revolt. It was probably also at this time that Bodley met Miles Coverdale, then chaplain to Lord Russell, who was to remain a close colleague during their various travels over the following several years.

The presence of Coverdale as bishop of Exeter from 1551 no doubt further encouraged Bodley in his support of the protestant cause, and to his own peril he maintained his activities even after the accession of Mary I. He appears to have been one of the few people in the south-west involved in Sir Peter Carew's abortive uprising in 1554, and the Exeter chronicler John Hooker recounts how Bodley and John Periam were the special targets of William Smith, mayor of Exeter in 1553–4 and 'an enemy to all such as were known or suspected to be true professors of the gospel' (J. Hooker, commonplace book, Devon RO, book 51, fol. 350). Sir Thomas *Bodley in his autobiography writes,

> my Father in the time of Queen Mary, being noted and knowne to be an enemy to Popery, was so cruelly threatened, and so narrowly observed, by those that maliced his Religion, that for the safeguard of himselfe and my Mother, who was wholly affected as my Father, he knew no way so secure, as to fly into Germany; where after a while he found meanes to call over my Mother, with all his children and family. (*Life*, 1–2)

Bodley probably left England in 1555 (it has been suggested with Coverdale) and settled first in the English colony in Wesel, subsequently moving on to Frankfurt. There he was of the party opposed to the use of the English prayer book, and eventually left for Geneva, arriving in that city in May 1557. He served as elder for the English congregation there from December 1557 until his return to England. In 1558 he was made a citizen of Geneva, and established a printing press to produce William Whittingham's and Miles Coverdale's English translation of the Bible, known as the Geneva Bible. Bodley provided the principal financial backing behind the Geneva Bible and, after returning to England in September 1559, he was granted on 8 January 1561 a licence from Elizabeth I to have sole rights of publishing and importing the Bible for a period of seven years. Editions of this Bible were produced and imported from Geneva, presumably under Bodley's licence, in 1560, 1562, and 1570. In 1565–6 Bodley tried to have this licence renewed for a further twelve years, but appears to have dropped his suit, in objection to Archbishop Parker's condition that the bishops examine and approve of the translation and its strongly Calvinist marginal annotations.

According to Thomas Bodley, his father settled in London upon his return to England from exile, 'within the first [year] of the Queen' (*Life*, 3), and certainly by 1568 he was living at 'the Three Cranes' in the London parish of St Michael Paternoster Royal, also the parish of his old friend Coverdale. Throughout this period in London he actively maintained his connections and involvement in the international Calvinist cause. He served as an elder in the French and Walloon refugee church in London from 1571, or perhaps earlier, until his death. In 1583–4 he acted as the conduit through which money collected nationally for the relief of Geneva was directed to that city. Thomas Sampson, a leading puritan divine, relied on him to bear his letters to Burleigh and other officials, and to act as his spokesman before them. He was closely aligned with the *Culverwell family, another Devon family who were principal figures among the 'godly' in Elizabethan London. He was an overseer for the wills of the brothers Nicholas and Richard Culverwell; an executor for Nicholas's widow, Elizabeth; and in his own will gave generous privileges to his son-in-law Anthony *Culverwell [*see under* Culverwell family (*per. c*.1545–*c*.1640)], nephew of Richard and Nicholas, who had married Bodley's daughter Sybil in 1582. Moreover he was a patron and protector of the artist Nicholas Hilliard, also from Exeter, who as a youth had been part of his household in Geneva.

Bodley was also a prominent merchant in London. He was a freeman of the Drapers' Company from 1575, a merchant adventurer, and a founding member of the Eastland Company. Through trade, and perhaps secondarily through publishing, he was very wealthy, assessed at £160 for the 1577 lay subsidy and able to contribute £200 for the defence of London during the Armada scare of 1588. In his will of 7 July 1591 he left small charitable bequests to the poor in his parish, in the French church, and in the hospitals and prisons of London, but gave the bulk of his large fortune (his bequests amounted to £2425) to his numerous children: £1000 to his eldest son, Thomas, £500 and his house at Three Cranes to another son, Sir Josias *Bodley, and £100 to each of his other children—Laurence *Bodley and Miles Bodley, and his married daughters Prothesia

(Prothesy) Bogan, Alice Helman, Sybil Culverwell, Elizabeth Willis, and Susan Shute. John Bodley died shortly after making this will, and was buried on 14 October 1591 in the parish of St Michael Paternoster Royal.

CHARLES G. D. LITTLETON

Sources F. B. Rose-Troup, *Sir Thomas Bodley's father and kindred* [1903] • B. Usher, 'The silent community: early puritans and the patronage of the arts', *The church and the arts*, ed. D. Wood, SCH, 28 (1992), 287–302 • C. Martin, *Les protestants anglais réfugiés à Genève au temps de Calvin, 1555–1560* (Geneva, 1915) • C. H. Garrett, *The Marian exiles: a study in the origins of Elizabethan puritanism* (1938) • J. S. Burn, *Livre des Anglois, à Genève* (1846) • R. Whiting, *The blind devotion of the people: popular religion and the English Reformation* (1989) • *The life of Sir Thomas Bodley, written by himself* (1647) • D. Trim, 'Sir Thomas Bodley and the international protestant cause', *Bodleian Library Record*, 16 (1997–9), 314–40 • will, PRO, PROB 11/78, sig. 90 • parish register, St Michael Paternoster, 1558–1653, GL, MS 5142 • A. M. Oakley, ed., *Actes du consistoire de l'église française de Threadneedle Street, Londres*, 2, Huguenot Society of London, 48 (1969) • J. Vowell [J. Hooker], *The description of the citie of Excester*, ed. W. J. Harte, J. W. Schopp, and H. Tapley-Soper, 3 pts in 1, Devon and Cornwall RS (1919–47) • F. F. Bruce, *The English Bible: a history of translations from the earliest English versions to the new English Bible*, rev. edn (1970)

Wealth at death £2425—total monetary bequests excl. residue which was to go to Thomas and Josias Bodley; estate also included: 'fee simple of the howse wherein I nowe dwell and the two tenements adjoyninge … which I purchased of the president and fellows of Saint Johns his Colledge in Oxford'; 'certayne land lyinge in Morton Hampstead' with a rent of £10 p.a.; revenue from his 'lease of the Cathedrall church of the Cittie of Exeter of the Sheaffe of Wall in Cornwall': will, PRO, PROB 11/78, fols. 275–6

John Edward Courtenay Bodley (1853–1925), by Robert Kastor, 1903

Bodley, John Edward Courtenay (1853–1925), writer on France, was born on 6 June 1853 at King Street, Hanley, Staffordshire, the son of Edward Fisher Bodley, commercial traveller, and later a wealthy pottery owner, and his second wife, Mary Ridgway. Bodley was educated at Mill Hill School, London, and in 1873 matriculated at Balliol College, Oxford; his friends at Oxford included Oscar Wilde and Cecil Rhodes. He took a pass degree in 1877 (MA 1879). Called to the bar by the Inner Temple in 1874, he practised as a barrister on the Oxford circuit, and then in June 1880 became political secretary to Sir Charles Dilke. His father was so disappointed at his abandoning law that he was disinherited in favour of a younger brother. In 1884 Dilke appointed Bodley as secretary of the royal commission on the housing of the working classes. Bodley wrote three reports on housing for England, Scotland, and Ireland, but his political hopes were dashed when Dilke was ruined by a divorce scandal in 1885.

Bodley visited South Africa in 1887–8 and the United States and Canada in 1888–9, meeting senior officials, politicians, and churchmen, and in 1890 he settled in France. The following year he married Evelyn Frances Bell, the daughter of John Bell of Rushpool Hall, Yorkshire; they had two sons (one of whom became a soldier and the other a painter) and a daughter, Ava, who married Ralph Follett *Wigram. Bodley's marriage ended in divorce in 1908.

Bodley began his literary career in France with the publication of *France* (1898), on French political institutions, which displayed an encyclopaedic knowledge of French local custom and tradition. It was followed by *L'anglomanie et les traditions françaises* (1899) and the publication in 1906 of two lectures on the separation of church and state. *The Romance of the Battle-Line in France* (1919) recounted the historic associations of the departments ravaged in the First World War. Bodley was a corresponding member of the Institut de France (Académie des Sciences Morales et Politiques), and contributed to the *Encyclopaedia Britannica* articles on the history of the Third Republic. He knew France so well that Charles Maurras once described him as almost a Frenchman.

Cardinal H. E. Manning intended Bodley to be his biographer, but Bodley was absent in France when Manning died, and Edmund Sheridan Purcell guilefully secured the job for himself. Bodley drew Manning's portrait in *Cardinal Manning and other Essays* (1912), and wrote by royal command the official record of Edward VII's coronation (published 1903). The king personally rewarded him with the Royal Victorian Order, fourth class, but broke off relations when the disgruntled recipient returned it the following day.

In 1920 Bodley married Phyllis Helen Lomax, the daughter of the Revd Henry Joshua Lomax of Stoke Golding. He died at The Chestnuts, Haywards Heath, Sussex, on 28 May 1925; his wife survived him.

Bodley's life was one of disappointments, over Dilke's disgrace, the Manning biography, the coronation record, and the lack of English official acknowledgement of his work for Anglo-French relations. He failed to make a wholly satisfactory career.

SHERIDAN GILLEY, *rev.*

Sources *The Times* (29 May 1925) • S. Leslie, *Memoir of John Edward Courtenay Bodley* (1930) • *CGPLA Eng. & Wales* (1925)

Archives Balliol Oxf., corresp., journal of South African tour · Bodl. Oxf., corresp., journals, and notes | NL Scot., letters to Blackwoods · U. St Andr. L., letters to Wilfrid Ward

Likenesses R. Kastor, pen-and-ink drawing, 1903, NPG [*see illus.*] · photograph, repro. in Leslie, *Memoir of John Edward Courtenay Bodley* · photograph, repro. in *The Times*

Wealth at death £17,428 1*s*. 11*d*.: administration, 11 Aug 1925, *CGPLA Eng. & Wales*

Bodley, Sir Josias (*c*.1550–1617), soldier and military engineer, was born in Exeter, the fifth and youngest son of John *Bodley (*c*.1520–1591), merchant and later publisher, and his wife, Joan, *née* Hone (*d*. 1586). His brothers included the more celebrated Sir Thomas *Bodley (1545–1613), founder of the Bodleian Library, Oxford, and Laurence *Bodley (1547/8–1615), Church of England clergyman. During the Marian persecution the family fled to Wesel and Geneva, where Josias received his early education and may have been influenced by such renowned teachers as Calvin and Beza, and certainly by Drusius who corresponded with him and his brothers. After his return to England he studied, but briefly, at Merton College, Oxford. For a long interval he remains obscure. He seems to have been employed in commerce in Danzig, Poland, where the English ambassador noticed him as the son of John Bodley in 1581 (*CSP for.*, 15.582). Later, in his 'Journey to Lecale', he wrote about Polish and Irish drinking habits which he participated in and closely observed.

Bodley chose the soldier's life and by 1615 he could boast of having had three apprenticeships in the army, all of which included continental service. Of his early military career little is known, but he was with Leicester's expeditionary forces in the Netherlands at Leiden in 1586. When Hugh O'Neill, second earl of Tyrone, was in the ascendant with his victory at the Yellow Ford in August 1598, Bodley was one of the captains sent with a large force under Sir Samuel Bagenal from the Netherlands to Ireland. Apart from desultory visits to England he spent the remainder of his life and busy career there as soldier, engineer, surveyor, and map maker. He was first stationed at Newry and later at Mountnorris, the new fort erected by Mountjoy in his strategy of encircling Ulster with garrisons and forts; but Bodley was also active with Mountjoy's mobile field army in 1601–2. He won Mountjoy's praise for bravery in skirmishes at Carlingford and particularly for his imaginative attack with Captain Edward Blaney on the island fortress of Loghrorcan near Newry on 6 April 1601 when he had arrows tipped with wildfire shot into the fort, which the defendants deserted leaving much pillage of cattle, sheep, and stores to Bodley's men. At the Spanish landfall at Kinsale on 2 October 1601, Bodley's company moved south to join Mountjoy and Carew. He is much mentioned in the whole Kinsale campaign of both siege and battle there and especially, as trenchmaster-general, in advising Mountjoy on trench plans, and as chief engineer in the erection of siege forts at a stipend of 10*s*. per diem. After Kinsale, Bodley was at the neighbouring sieges of Baltimore, Berehaven, and Castlehaven, co. Cork. In January 1602 he travelled to England with a strong recommendation from Mountjoy to the privy council to support his undisclosed ambitions. It is likely that on that visit he donated a quadrant, an astronomical sphere, and other brass instruments, all signs of his mathematical and engineering skills, to the Bodleian Library in Oxford. He is favourably mentioned in the queen's letter to Mountjoy and the Dublin council of 17 June 1602 on the question of what places to fortify in Ireland.

On his return to Ireland, Bodley was briefly governor of an Armagh garrison, probably Mountnorris in Ulster, but the following year he was transferred to work on the fortifications at Waterford, where Sir Richard Moryson was governor. Bodley was knighted by Mountjoy on 25 March 1604 and from then until 1606 he held the command of the nearby fort of Duncannon. In these years he was also engaged in coastal fortifications in Munster especially at Cork and in Limerick where his engineering skills were much in demand. The Dutch engineer Levan de Rosa and Sir Arthur Chichester, the future lord deputy and driving force in the Ulster plantation, worked with Bodley in selecting sites, drawing up plans which he presented to King James on his next visit to England. He returned with orders to build St Patrick's Fort at Waterford and another at Cork, and he appears to have had a hand in the building of Mountjoy Fort in Ulster, but all on condition of resigning his post at Duncannon and relinquishing his band of foot soldiers for which he gained a pension. In April 1606 Bodley was again in London promoting his own interests and to get arrears of pay. Sir Arthur Chichester urgently wanted him back in Ireland to complete his work on fortifications. In 1607 Bodley was appointed superintendent of castles in Ireland at 20*s*. per diem and by the end of that year he was the agent of the English privy council to oversee the forts at Cork, Limerick, Waterford, and Kinsale; it was not a patented post but paid out of the annual Irish establishment list which caused him to run into large debts. His reports of his inspections of fortifications accompanied by Levan de Rosa, by another Dutch engineer, Joyes Everard, and by Sir Henry Danvers, the president of Munster, show him travelling over 700 miles by December 1608. For the improvements to such important forts as Elizabeth Fort, Cork, and St Augustine's, Galway, and to Limerick Castle, Bodley was paid about £6700 in the years 1607 to 1609.

Not much is known of Bodley's further activities until his involvement with surveying for the Ulster plantations, except that Sir Francis Bacon in writing his 'Certain considerations touching plantation in Ireland' in the summer of 1608 mentioned that a Mr Jones (was it Inigo?) wished to introduce Sir Josias Bodley to him. It is most likely that Bacon had seen Bodley's reports and may have wanted his advice on forts in the plantations. Part of his professional duties was the surveying of land and in 1609 he helped William Parsons, surveyor-general, survey the six escheated counties of Ulster—Tyrone, Armagh, Coleraine, Fermanagh, Cavan, and Donegal—but he took full honours for himself and his assistants in the production of a coloured set of maps within sixty-seven days. In 1611 he petitioned for 'some competent allowance during the few days that he has to live' but in the same breath offered to survey all the fortifications in Ireland (*CSP Ire.*, *1611–14*,

154–5). In 1612 he covered Ulster again with the help of John Ball, making a survey of the progress of the new plantations which apparently so pleased King James that in January 1613 Bodley finally got a patent to be director-general and overseer of the fortifications and buildings in Ireland, for life and at his former salary. In March 1613 he attended the funeral of his brother Sir Thomas, who left him £100, leaseholds in London, and a release from debts due to loans. Sir Josias was still in London in November 1613 when Sir Arthur Chichester asked him to report to the privy council on sites and plans for defence works left incomplete at Cork and Waterford. Maybe because Cecil held the patronage of conferring patents of forfeited Ulster lands, Bodley failed in his application to get a grant on account of the family's friendship with the earl of Essex: he complained bitterly of this not only to Michael Hicks, Cecil's secretary, but, more successfully, to Sir Ralph Winwood (the secretary of state, who married his brother Thomas's stepdaughter), for the latter ordered that arrears of his allowance be paid. Under Chichester's direction Bodley surveyed the plantations of the London Companies in Londonderry; once again he presented his report to the king who was angered at the defects found in the non-fulfilment of the plantations' conditions and, while thanking Bodley, wanted him to extend his investigations into other Ulster plantations in 1616. In the last year of his service in Ireland he surveyed 16,500 acres in co. Wexford for a new plantation there using the improved technique of the surveyor's chain. He was succeeded in his office of director-general of fortifications by the joint appointment of Sir Nicholas Pynnar and Sir Thomas Rotheram.

Apart from his reports, letters, surveys, and maps Sir Josias Bodley wrote a light-hearted description in colloquial Latin of his journey to and a party at Lecale in co. Down in 1602, in which he extols the delights of hard drinking and the taking of tobacco. (One of several transcripts is published by Falkiner, 1904.) He has perhaps been underestimated as a military engineer and surveyor at a time when military geography was institutionalized in Ireland by the creation of the office of overseer of fortifications, the responsibilities of which he fulfilled with little profit to himself. Bodley was unmarried and died intestate on 22 August 1617, probably in Dublin. He was buried on 26 August in Christ Church, Dublin, where he has a memorial tablet. J. J. N. McGurk

Sources *CSP Ire., 1603–25* • 'Letter-book of Sir Arthur Chichester, 1612–1614', ed. R. D. Edwards, *Analecta Hibernica*, 8 (1938), 3–177, esp. 141–2, 151 • 'Bodley's visit to Lecale, county of Down', *Ulster Journal of Archaeology*, 2 (1854), 73–99 • 'Notes and queries', *Ulster Journal of Archaeology*, new ser., 15 (1909), 185 • J. Buckley, 'Report of Sir Josias Bodley on some Ulster fortresses in 1608', *Ulster Journal of Archaeology*, new ser., 16 (1910), 61–4 • *Calendar of the manuscripts of the most hon. the marquess of Salisbury*, 18, HMC, 9 (1940); 21 (1970) • *Report on the manuscripts of his grace the duke of Buccleuch and Queensberry … preserved at Montagu House*, 3 vols. in 4, HMC, 45 (1899–1926), vol. 1 • F. Moryson, *An itinerary containing his ten yeeres travell through the twelve dominions*, 2–3 (1907–8) • *Report on the manuscripts of the late Reginald Rawdon Hastings*, 4 vols., HMC, 78 (1928–47), vol. 4 • R. Bagwell, *Ireland under the Stuarts*, 1 (1909) • J. S. Brewer and W. Bullen, eds., *Calendar of the Carew manuscripts*, 4: *1601–1603*, PRO (1870) • J. S. Brewer and W. Bullen, eds., *Calendar of the Carew manuscripts*, 6: *Miscellaneous papers*, PRO (1873) • T. W. Moody, *The Londonderry plantation, 1609–41* (1939) • T. Stafford, *Pacata Hibernia*, 2 vols. (1633); repr. (1810) • A. Kippis and others, eds., *Biographia Britannica, or, The lives of the most eminent persons who have flourished in Great Britain and Ireland*, 2nd edn, 2 (1780), 393 • R. C. Strong and J. A. van Dorsten, *Leicester's triumph* (1964) • J. Prince, *Danmonii orientales illustres, or, The worthies of Devon* (1701); 2nd edn (1810) • *VCH Devon* • J. Finlayson, *Inscriptions on the monuments … in Christ Church Cathedral, Dublin* (1878) • R. Loeber, *A biographical dictionary of architects in Ireland, 1600–1720* (1981) • *The letters and life of Francis Bacon*, ed. J. Spedding, 7 vols. (1861–74), vol. 4, pp. 66, 110 • J. H. Andrews, 'The maps of the escheated counties of Ulster, 1609–1610', *Proceedings of the Royal Irish Academy*, 74C (1974) • G. Hill, *An historical account of the plantation in Ulster* (1877); facs. edn (1970), chap. 6 • C. L. Falkiner, *Illustrations of Irish history and topography* (1904) • *DNB* • Wood, *Ath. Oxon.*, 1st edn, 1.96, 122; 2.127, 678

Archives BL, Lecale journey, Add. MS 4784 [transcript] • BL, report on the forts and garrisons in the north of Ireland, Lansdowne MS 156, fols. 335–336*v* • LPL, survey of the Munster forts, incl. a letter to Carew, MS 629, fols. 146–7 • PRO, letters, SP 63 (Ireland) • PRO, payments to him, AO 1/288/1082; 289/1085; 290/1088, 1090 • W. Yorks. AS, Bradford, Spencer Stanhope MSS, account of Lecale journey, Latin copy, Sp St/11/5/4/1, fols. 38*r*–42*r*

Wealth at death letters often told of money problems; there are begging letters to Sir Ralph Winwood, secretary of state; brother left him £100 and leaseholds in London, and released him from debts

Bodley, Laurence (1547/8–1615), Church of England clergyman, was the son of John *Bodley (*c.*1520–1591), an Exeter merchant, and his wife, Joan, *née* Hone (*d.* 1586). Laurence was the brother of Sir Thomas *Bodley, founder of the Bodleian Library, and of the soldier Sir Josias *Bodley. Their father, a man of strongly protestant convictions, helped finance the government's suppression of the western rebellion of 1549, and during the reign of Mary took his family to Frankfurt, and then to Geneva, where he opened a printing office and late in 1557 became an elder of the exiles' church. The records of those taking refuge in the city mention the young Laurence.

The Bodley family returned to England in 1559, settling in London, though Laurence soon left for Oxford. He became a student at Christ Church in 1561, graduating BA in 1566 and MA in 1568. By 1575 he was back in the Swiss confederation as a student of the University of Basel. His talent and his commitment to Calvinistic church discipline were already well developed, for on 13 March 1576, William Barlow (probably the future archdeacon of Salisbury who had been at Oxford with Bodley) wrote to Zürich a letter of introduction on his behalf, trusting that the pastor, Joseph Simler, would treat him kindly: 'He is a man of small stature, but of distinguished erudition and probity, and exceedingly partial to your church' (Robinson, 270). It seems, however, that Bodley did not stay long; before 24 August he had returned to England with a letter from Rodolph Gualter which he delivered to Archbishop Parker.

Bodley's religious sympathies did not prevent his becoming a notable pluralist. On 27 October 1579 he was instituted to the rectory of Hinton St George, Somerset, on the presentation of Amias Paulet. On 21 March 1580 he compounded for the first fruits of the rectory of Sampford Peverill, Devon, and on 10 August 1580 for those of the canonry of Worminster (not to be confused with Warminster) in the diocese of Bath and Wells. He also held Seavington St Michael, resigning in 1580, and on 17 April 1581 he compounded for the first fruits of the rectory of Seavenhampton, Gloucestershire. The yearly value of these livings in 1581 was more than £50. But Bodley continued to accrue ecclesiastical preferments. He was admitted to the crown living of Shobrook, Devon, on 25 September 1582, and is thought to have built the rectory there. In 1585 he was occupying a house in the cathedral close at Exeter, having been instituted to a canonry. In 1602 the dean and chapter gave eighty-one early manuscripts which were then in the keeping of Exeter Cathedral Library to the library newly founded at Oxford by Thomas Bodley. Outstanding among them was the Leofric missal (now MS Bodley 579), a composite volume of materials from the ninth to the eleventh centuries notable for containing what are probably the earliest English examples of drawings in coloured line. The gift may very well have been inspired by Laurence Bodley, who himself in 1610 gave the large sum of £20 to his brother's library.

On 30 May 1613 Bodley was admitted DD at Christ Church, Oxford, to which college he donated books. Perhaps it was for the pursuit of his studies that he bought 'my best cristall spectacles which alone cost mee fifteene shillings' (PRO, PROB 11/125, fol. 465*v*). In his later years Bodley and a fellow canon named Leach were rewarded by Exeter city chamber with sugar loaves, 'in approbation of their pains in the morning lecture at St Peters' (Rose-Troup, 724). He also inherited both money and property from his brother Sir Thomas in 1613. Unmarried, he was able to bequeath substantial sums to brothers, sisters, and other members of his family. Bodley left books on divinity to Exeter Cathedral Library and provided £400 for the purchase of land to fund a third lectureship for the city. The lecturer was to be chosen by the mayor and corporation, but should be 'allowed for his sufficiencie and conformitie accordinge to the lawes of the Realme either by the Lord Bishop of the diocesse or by the Lord Archbishop of Canterburie' (PRO, PROB 11/125, fol. 466). The subsequent choice of John Hazard to be the first lecturer led to much contention between the bishop and the town. Bodley died on 19 April 1615, aged sixty-seven, and was buried in Exeter Cathedral close on 9 May. STEPHEN WRIGHT

Sources F. Rose-Troup, 'The pedigree of Sir Thomas Bodley', *Report and Transactions of the Devonshire Association*, 35 (1903), 713–45 • *Reg. Oxf.*, 2.11, 12 • H. Robinson, ed. and trans., *The Zurich letters, comprising the correspondence of several English bishops and others with some of the Helvetian reformers, during the early part of the reign of Queen Elizabeth*, 2, Parker Society, 8 (1845) • *Fasti Angl.*, *1541–1857*, [Bath and Wells] • A. F. S. Pearson, *Thomas Cartwright and Elizabethan puritanism, 1535–1603* (1925) • P. S. Seaver, *The puritan lectureships: the politics of religious dissent, 1560–1662* (1970) • W. T. MacCaffrey, *Exeter, 1540–1640: the growth of an English county town* (1958) • H. J. Cowell, *The sixteenth-century English-speaking refugee churches at Geneva and Frankfort* (1939) • J. Loach, 'Pamphlets and politics, 1553–8', *BIHR*, 48 (1975), 31–44 • W. D. Macray, *Annals of the Bodleian Library, Oxford*, 2nd edn (1890), 402–18 • will, PRO, PROB 11/125, fols. 465*v*–466*v* • R. Deshman, 'The Leofric missal and tenth-century English art', ed. P. Clemoes, *Anglo-Saxon England*, 6 (1977), 145–73

Wealth at death approx. £1000: will, PRO, PROB 11/125, fols. 465*v*–466*v*

Bodley, Sir Thomas (1545–1613), scholar, diplomat, and founder of the Bodleian Library, Oxford, was born on 2 March 1545 in a house on the corner of High Street and Gandy Street, Exeter, the eldest son of John *Bodley (*c.*1520–1591), religious radical and publisher, of Exeter, and his wife, Joan (*d.* 1586), daughter of Robert Hone of Ottery St Mary, Devon. His brothers included Laurence *Bodley (1547/8–1615) and Sir Josias *Bodley (*c.*1550–1617). The family was related to the Bodleys of Dunscombe.

Marian exile and education in Geneva, 1555–1559 Being identified with protestant reform during Mary I's reign, 'so cruelly threatned, and so narrowly observed' (Bodley, *Life*, 1), John Bodley departed, probably in 1555, to exile in Europe, and was followed by his family. They resided for a short time at Wesel before moving to Frankfurt, where Bodley was involved in the controversy over the prayer book and ritual which split that congregation. When the party led by John Knox moved to Geneva in September 1556, the Bodley family followed, arriving there in May of the following year. With Bodley were his wife, his brother Nicholas, his sons Thomas, Josias, and Laurence, his daughter Prothesia (Prothesy), and three servants. Also in the party was Nicholas Hilliard (1547?–1619), then aged nine, who had been placed with the Bodley family by his father. John Bodley came to occupy an important place in the English congregation at Geneva.

It was in Jean Calvin's Hieropolis, meeting place of English and continental religious and intellectual life, that Thomas Bodley received his early education. He was lodged in the house of Philibert Sarrasin, a French physician and schoolmaster. The curriculum included Latin and Hebrew, and he read Homer with the lexicographer Robert Constantin. Although his name does not appear in the register of students, he followed courses in the Geneva Academy from June 1559, when it was founded, to September, when his family left the city. Thus he is able to describe himself as an 'auditor of Chevalerius [Antoine Chevalier] for Hebrew, of Beroaldus [François Bérault] in Greek, of Calvin and [Theodore] Beza in Divinity' (Bodley, *Life*, 2). After Mary's death, John Bodley returned with his family on 5 September 1559 to London, where he settled and became a freeman of the Drapers' Company later that year.

Education and academic career at Oxford, 1559–1576 Thomas Bodley matriculated at Magdalen College, Oxford, in 1559. He entered as a commoner and was placed under the tuition of Laurence Humphrey, also a Marian exile and leader of the Calvinists at Oxford. He graduated BA in 1563, and in that year was accepted as a probationer fellow of Merton College, being admitted as a fellow in 1564. His academic career was distinguished by the diversity of his talents and interests. Merton led Oxford at this time in teaching beyond the curriculum, and in 1565 Bodley was appointed its first lecturer in Greek. He served three times as bursar, and was also for a time garden-master.

Bodley's interest in Hebrew developed, enabling him to

Sir Thomas Bodley (1545–1613), by unknown artist

translate inscriptions in college deeds and bringing him into close association with Joannes Drusius in the promotion of Hebrew studies in the college, when the latter resided there between 1572 and 1576. His linguistic versatility is shown further by his contribution to the appendix of Humphrey's *Ioannis Iuelli … vita & mors* (1572) of a Hebrew poem. This poem shows a level of competence in Hebrew that was unusual in Oxford at this time. He also became known outside the college. After taking the MA in 1566 he read natural philosophy in the schools; in 1569 he was elected junior proctor; and for some years he deputized for the public orator, Arthur Atye. In view of his later achievement, the most significant outcome of Bodley's time at Merton was the lifelong friendship established with Sir Henry Savile, who became his principal adviser in the refoundation of the university library.

Diplomatic career, 1576–1604 Bodley left Oxford in 1576, for 'I waxed desirous to travell beyond the Seas, for attaining to the knowledge of some speciall moderne tongues, and for the encrease of my experience in the managing of affaires' (Bodley, *Life*, 4). In September 1576 he was given leave by the college to travel. Initially, he went to France before spending the next four years in Germany and Italy, achieving proficiency in Italian, French, and Spanish. On his return he continued to reside at Merton, being senior fellow for three years before his resignation in 1586. However, Bodley was frequently absent because he was increasingly involved in state affairs, under the patronage of Robert Dudley, earl of Leicester, and Sir Francis Walsingham, principal secretary. About 1583 he became a gentleman usher to Elizabeth I and in 1584 was returned as MP for Portsmouth, Hampshire, preferring that seat to Hythe, Kent, which was offered on the recommendation of William Brooke, tenth Baron Cobham, lord warden of the Cinque Ports. In the next parliament he was returned for St Germans, Cornwall. He was not a very active parliamentarian.

During his European travels Bodley became engaged in the foreign affairs which were to be the chief concern of his political career. In October 1579 his presence in Paris was confirmed by the English special ambassador, Edward Stafford, in reply to a letter from Leicester's secretary, Atye. The resident ambassador, Sir Henry Cobham, entrusted to him, because of his knowledge of their language, negotiations with a group of expatriate Italians in July 1580. Bodley's first major diplomatic mission took place from April to July 1585, when he was dispatched by the queen to Denmark and Brunswick. This was a fruitless attempt to bring together Frederick II of Denmark with the duke of Brunswick, William (IV) Hesse-Kassel, landgrave of Hesse, and other adherents of the Augsburg confession, in a conference which was intended to lead to an alliance in favour of Henri of Navarre and the French protestants. In May 1588 he was sent, unaccompanied and bearing letters in Elizabeth's own hand (in which he is described as 'confidant et sage et secret'), on a mission to Henri III at the time when the French king was forced to flee from Paris by Henri Guise-Lorraine, prince de Joinville and third duc de Guise (*CSP for., 1588*, 611, 629). Bodley claimed that the mission was one of great benefit to the French protestants, and that it contributed to the fall of Guise in September. In August 1588 he was dispatched on an urgent mission to the king of Denmark and the merchants at Hamburg, urging them not to offer assistance to the Spanish Armada (*APC, 1588*, 225, 229).

Between these missions, Bodley married Ann (1564–1611), daughter of Richard Cary of Bristol, on 19 July 1586. She was the widow of Nicholas Ball, a wealthy fish merchant and mayor of Totnes, Devon. It was largely his wife's fortune, inherited from her father, a wealthy merchant (augmented in 1591 by £1000 inherited from his own father), that laid the foundation of Bodley's subsequent career. They had no children.

Not long after his return from the second embassy to France, Bodley was dispatched upon the most important of his missions, as Elizabeth's ambassador to the United Provinces. His formal status was as one of the two members of the council of state she was entitled to appoint under the treaty of Nonsuch. He was resident at The Hague from December 1588 until early 1597, apart from absences in 1591, when he was granted leave to settle his financial affairs on the death of his father, and again, after the death of his brother Miles, in 1595. On 24 May 1589 a safe conduct was issued for Ann Bodley to take ship to the United Provinces, but it is not clear whether, or for how long, she resided at The Hague.

Bodley's principal instructions concerned Elizabeth's

relations with the United Provinces. Among other things he was to ensure their acceptance of a revised treaty; to require them to give military assistance to her campaign against Spain and to pay the expenses of the English auxiliary forces; and above all to repay her considerable loans, largely borrowed at usurious rates from Sir Horatio Palavicino. In the last matter in particular Bodley was perpetually frustrated. Effective power lay not with the council of state but with the states general, its secret committees, and the advocate-general Johan van Oldenbarnevelt, 'by whom they are strangely ruled and overruled' (*CSP for.*, 1592, 51). The states, increasingly prosperous in trade, and under the efficient military leadership of Maurice, count of Nassau, saw little reason to bend to Elizabeth's will, and found endless procedural excuses to delay decisions about repayment. This was a principal reason for Bodley's disillusion and eventual demission from an office he found irksome throughout, and in which he often incurred the queen's displeasure. In May 1595 he wrote to Anthony Bacon that 'I hear for my comfort, that the Queen on Monday last did wish I had been hanged' (T. Birch, *Memoirs of the Reign of Queen Elizabeth*, 2 vols., 1754, 1.244). He asked frequently to be recalled. In October 1592 he wrote to Sir Robert Sidney 'I would I were departing together with your Lordship, being wonderfully weary of this Hage, and this Soile, and this paltrie kinde of People' (A. Collins, ed., *Letters and Memorials of State*, 2 vols., 1746, 1.340). He finally returned to England, disillusioned and ill, in 1597, and resigned from all public service. Bodley seemed naturally destined for higher office, but his ambitions were compromised in the rivalry between the Cecil family and Robert Devereux, second earl of Essex, each faction seeking to associate the possibility of his preferment to the secretaryship with their own political aims. Eventually his disenchantment with this 'throng of Court contentions' led him to take his 'full farewell of State imployments' (Bodley, *Life*, 12, 14). His reputation remained high: William Camden gave him much credit for the eventual settlement with the United Provinces. He was proposed in 1598 and 1601 for embassies to France and in 1602 for a resumption of his mission to the United Provinces. In 1604 Robert Cecil, Viscount Cranborne, supported him again for the secretaryship.

The foundation of the Bodleian Library, 1598–1613 All these proposals were rejected by Bodley, because by now he was completely immersed in the project which was to occupy the last fifteen years of his life: the restoration of the former university library at Oxford. A celebrated passage in the *Life* relates how:

> I concluded at the last to set up my Staffe at the Library doore in *Oxford*; being throughly perswaded, that in my solitude and surcease from the Common-wealth affaires, I could not busy my selfe to better purpose, then by reducing that place (which then in every part lay ruined and wast) to the publique use of Students. (*Life*, 14–15)

He felt qualified to carry out this task because of his linguistic and scholarly background, wealth, and influential connections. These qualities are implicit in the letter which he wrote on 23 February 1598 to Thomas Singleton, the vice-chancellor, announcing his momentous offer to restore the library at his own expense and 'to stirre up other mens benevolence, to helpe to furnish it with bookes' (*Letters … to the University*, 4). After acceptance by convocation of this offer matters moved rapidly. Bodley's letter of 19 March recommended that a delegacy be set up to consider a design which Savile and he would bring before them at Easter. He had already ordered the construction materials, including the timber (a gift from Merton), and arranged for its sawing and seasoning. The shelves were modelled on those in the west wing of Merton College library, which were based on the continental plan introduced for the first time in England in 1589. The delegacy was set up immediately and, since Bodley lived in London, was vital in seeing through the project, as was Savile, who was consulted on all matters of design. In the statutes, which Bodley wrote as early as 1605, and which were accepted by convocation on 12 June 1610, the delegacy was replaced by a body of curators headed by John King, the vice-chancellor.

Refurbishment was well under way by December 1599 when Bodley wrote to Thomas James, the first keeper of the library, that this phase of the operation would be finished within two or three months. The letters to James which followed, throughout the rest of Bodley's life, deal with every aspect of the library: acquisitions; cataloguing and classification; binding; preservation; cleaning; the receiving of visitors. They constitute a manual of library management, and a uniquely detailed account, from its founder's point of view, of the birth of a great library. In June 1602 Bodley wrote to the vice-chancellor that, the construction work being completed, he had begun to busy himself and his friends about 'gathering in Bookes'. His flair for public relations and 'understanding of the psychology of giving' (*Hist. U. Oxf.* 4: *17th-cent. Oxf.*, 137) ensured that the library was famous from its inception. Already in March 1598 Dudley Carleton reported that 'every man bethinks himself how, by some good book or other, he may be written in the scroll of benefactors' (*CSP dom.*, *1598*, 35). And those who were inscribed in the register, which Bodley saw as a vital part of his fund-raising, demonstrate the extent of his network of well-wishers, including leading courtiers, family, and friends. The first gift reported to George Abbot, the vice-chancellor, in June 1600 was the large number of books taken by Essex in 1596 from the episcopal library in Faro.

Several London antiquaries, including Camden and Sir Robert Cotton, were benefactors; these, together with a number of academics, such as Thomas Allen and Thomas James, were important in obtaining many manuscripts alienated from monastic libraries, then beginning to find their way through private collections into public access. Many of the gifts were of money and, together with Bodley's own resources, enabled the founder to pursue an extraordinarily adventurous acquisition policy. In this Bodley exercised his own choices, but depended also on the judgement of the booksellers who worked for him: John Norton, who imported twice yearly from the Frankfurt fair; and his apprentice John Bill, who between 1602 and 1604 made several book-buying excursions to Paris and Frankfurt, to a number of towns in Italy, and even to Seville. Bodley's vision extended beyond European languages, and he built up an impressive collection of Hebrew material, and through benefactors such as Paul Pindar, consul of the Aleppo Merchants, works in or on Syriac, Arabic, Turkish, and Persian. Chinese books, regarded by other collectors as curiosities, were acquired by Bodley as early as 1604.

Bodley insisted that the library should have a respectable collection of books before being opened, and after several delays it was finally inaugurated, in his absence, with about 2000 volumes, on 8 November 1602. It rapidly became internationally renowned. In the first two years of the library's existence twenty-two foreign readers were admitted. It grew rapidly, and a main concern of Bodley's letters was now with the arrangement of the books and with cataloguing. He saw the catalogue as an important feature of the library's first royal visit. James I had already become a patron of the library. On 18 April 1604 he knighted Bodley, and on 20 June issued letters patent granting licence for the library to be endowed with lands in mortmain, declaring that it should be known as 'Bibliotheca ex fundatione Thomae Bodley Militis' (Macray, 31). The king visited the library on 20 August 1605, being presented with a copy of the catalogue. He also made an offer, later rescinded, that Bodley should receive such works as he might select from the royal library. The culmination of Bodley's activities in the acquisition of books came in December 1610 when the Stationers' Company entered into an agreement to supply a free copy of every book registered at Stationers' Hall, ultimately the foundation of legal deposit in Britain. Bodley feared that this source might introduce into the library 'idle books, and riffe raffes', and was anxious about 'the harm that the scandal will bring unto the Librarie, when it shalbe given out, that we stuffe it full of baggage books' (*Letters … to Thomas James*, 219, 222). It was perhaps the prospect of the influx of London books which led to a change in the design of the first extension of the library, already proposed as early as 1609, built between 1610 and 1612. Here, for what has generally been agreed to be the first time in England, is to be found wall shelving with a gallery offering accommodation for the increasing numbers of books of smaller format which could not be chained.

Last years and reputation From the outset Bodley was concerned with sound finance and endowment for the library, which until his death he funded personally. In 1609 he purchased from Francis Norris, second Baron Norris, the manor of Hindon, Wiltshire, and tenements in Distaff Lane, London, and in his will bequeathed these to the university, ensuring from the rents annual incomes of £90 10*s.* and £40 respectively. He was intent on further extension. On 5 November 1611 he wrote to the vice-chancellor outlining an ingenious scheme by which funds might be raised to provide an eastern expansion of the library, which he intended to finance himself. This addition was constructed, as part of the schools quadrangle, under Savile's supervision, after Bodley's death.

Bodley suffered from increasing ill health during his final years. He long suffered from the stone, and John Chamberlain reported in July 1612 that he was now also afflicted with scurvy and dropsy. Although he seems to have recovered sufficiently to visit Oxford, presumably to see the arts end extension, in August, it seems unlikely that he could have left London thereafter, and he died there, at his house adjacent to St Bartholomew's Hospital, on 29 January 1613. Lady Bodley had died in 1611, and had been buried on 12 June in St Bartholomew-the-Less, where she is commemorated by a monument on which her husband wrote of the twenty-four years of their happy married life. He was buried with much ceremony on 29 March in Merton College chapel, having left £666 13*s.* 4*d.* for this purpose. Two volumes of commemorative verse were published (*Bodleiomeneme*, by members of Merton, and *Iusta funebra Ptolemae Oxoniensis Thomae Bodleii*), as well as sermons by John Hales and the public orator, Sir Isaac Wake. His will includes a large number of legacies, amounting to about £1500, to individuals, as well as annual grants to poor people in Oxford and elsewhere. By far the greater part of his fortune was left to the university, and Chamberlain, who computed its value at £7000, recorded the disappointment of many friends and relatives, and complaints of Bodley's being 'so drunk with the applause and vanitie of his librarie, that he made no conscience to rob Peter to pay Paul' (*CSP dom., 1613*, 187). The will was indeed contested, by Bodley's brother Laurence and his niece Elizabeth Willis, who were left £200 and £210 respectively, but judgment was given in favour of the executors.

A question open to interpretation is that of Bodley's intention in restoring the library. It was asserted first by Thomas Hearne that 'the original design of the library [was] chiefly for books against the Roman Catholicks' (T. Hearne, *Remarks and Collections*, Oxford Historical Society, 11 vols., 1885–1921, 8.262), a view often supported, most recently by D. Trim. However, his coolness towards Thomas James's anti-papist intention in collations of the fathers, his trust in members of Gloucester Hall (then reputedly a home of recusancy), the Catholic connections and sympathies of many of the early donors, and the very universality of the collections argue against so narrow an interpretation.

Any estimate of Bodley's character and motives should take into account his autobiography of 1608, printed in 1647. This has some claim to be considered the first English autobiography in which an author writes 'a skilfully structured apologia for his career' (Wooden, 62–75). Where the record might suggest a largely frustrated diplomatic career, Bodley claimed one of independence and success marred only by faction; where some of his contemporaries saw ambition and vanity, the *Life* proposed a disinterested ideal of 'duty towards God' exemplified in 'the true part of a profitable member of the State', who 'need not be the publisher of the dignity and worth of mine owne Institution' (*Life*, 14–16). His coat of arms incorporates three crowns. The most plausible interpretation of his motto *Quarta perennis* is that it derives from an aphorism of Rabbi Schimeon in which the three crowns, of learning, priesthood, and kingship, are surpassed by a fourth, congenial to the Renaissance mind, that of a good name. Posterity will doubtless agree that Bodley's breadth of vision and his single-minded assiduity in the use of his talents and fortune have ensured his renown as the greatest benefactor of Oxford University of his time.

W. H. CLENNELL

Sources T. Bodley, *The life of Sir Thomas Bodley, the honourable founder of the publique library in the University of Oxford, written by himselfe* (1647) • *Letters of Sir Thomas Bodley to Thomas James, first keeper of the Bodleian Library*, ed. G. W. Wheeler (1926) • *DNB* • *Letters of Sir Thomas Bodley to the University of Oxford, 1598–1611*, ed. G. W. Wheeler (1927) • W. D. Macray, *Annals of the Bodleian Library, Oxford, with a note of the earlier library of the university*, 1st edn (1868); 2nd edn (1890) • I. Philip, *The Bodleian Library in the seventeenth and eighteenth centuries* (1983) • F. Rose-Troup, *Sir Thomas Bodley's father and kindred* (1903) • *Pietas Oxoniensis: in memory of Sir Thomas Bodley, knt, and the foundation of the Bodleian Library* (1902) • *The letters of John Chamberlain*, ed. N. E. McClure, 2 vols. (1939) • C. Roth, 'Sir Thomas Bodley—hebraist', *Bodleian Library Record*, 7 (1966), 242–51 • HoP, *Commons, 1558–1603* • *CSP for.*, *1578–80; 1584–6; 1588; 1591–3* • *CSP dom.*, *1581–90; 1598–1603; 1611–18* • *Hist. U. Oxf.* 4: *17th-cent. Oxf.* • D. Trim, 'Sir Thomas Bodley and the international protestant cause', *Bodleian Library Record*, 16 (1999), 314–40 • W. W. Wooden, 'Sir Thomas Bodley's *Life of himself* and the epideictic strategies of encomia', *Studies in Philology*, 83 (1986), 62–75 • plaque, Gandy Street and High Street, Exeter • will, Bodl. Oxf., MS A. 186

Archives BL, autobiography, Sloane MS 1786 • Bodl. Oxf., account of negotiations in the Netherlands • Bodl. Oxf., autobiography • Hunt. L., account of embassy to Netherlands • LPL, letters | BL, corresp. and papers, Harley MSS • BL, corresp. and papers, Cotton MSS • CKS, letters to earl of Leicester

Likenesses school of N. Hilliard, watercolour miniature, 1598, Bodl. Oxf. • marble bust in niche, 1605, Bodl. Oxf. • oils, 1636–7, Bodl. Oxf. • N. Stone, effigy, Merton Oxf. • J. Varin, medal sculpture, BM • oils, Bodl. Oxf. [*see illus.*]

Bodley Scott, Sir Ronald. *See* Scott, Sir Ronald Bodley (1906–1982).

Bodrugan [Trenowith], **Sir Henry** (*c*.1426–1487x1503), landowner and rebel, sometimes called Henry Trenowith, was the son and heir of Sir William Bodrugan of Newham, Cornwall (*c*.1398–1441), and of Philippa, daughter of Sir John Arundel of Lanherne, Cornwall (*fl.* 1426–1450). He was descended through his paternal great-grandmother, Joan, wife of Ralph Trenowith, from an ancient knightly family. He married in 1454 Joan, widow of William Beaumont of Devon, whose illegitimate son he may have fathered. She died between 1466 and 1475; his second marriage, by 1475, to Margaret, youngest daughter of William, Lord Herbert, and widow of Thomas Talbot, Viscount Lisle, was childless.

A ward of Thomas *Courtenay, earl of Devon, from 1441 to 1447 (Devon paid the earl of Suffolk and other royal servants for the privilege), Bodrugan grew up during years of developing warfare between Devon and William, Lord Bonville. Described as 'scheff reulere of Cornwayle' (Warkworth, 27), he was regularly commissioned between 1454 and 1486 as JP, commissioner of array, and to investigate piracy. He befriended, by 1454, Devon's dissident cousins the Courtenays of Powderham, evidently following them into the Yorkist camp (he was ordered to be brought before the privy council in 1460 following a parliamentary petition, and the spate of commissions to him ceased between 1458 and 1460, resuming on 28 March 1461). While his mother held valuable dower lands at least until 1450, his estate possibly deteriorated under Devon's guardianship. He was in financial (and perhaps political) difficulties between 1450 and 1458: it was alleged that he sold, then fraudulently repossessed, timber, and that, immediately after Edward IV's accession, he forcibly repossessed lands that he had earlier quitclaimed. His own counter-petitions generally disputed landownership. He was charged in 1473 to besiege John de Vere, earl of Oxford, in St Michael's Mount. Deprived of commanding the siege, allegedly for double-dealing with Oxford, he subsequently retained some of Oxford's men, and was attainted in 1474. The commission to carry out the attainder was cancelled, following his petition in parliament. Unlike the Powderham Courtenays he did not support Clarence, taking no part in the readeption and becoming a consistent peace commissioner only after the duke's fall in 1478. Almost certainly knighted in 1475, he was a knight of the body of Richard III, and possibly present at Bosworth. His Ricardian stance gained him two manors; but helping Richard III ultimately seems to have proved expensive. In 1485 he mortgaged several manors held by his family since 1389.

From *c*.1456 to 1478 Bodrugan was repeatedly accused in chancery, privy council, and parliament of a range of violent, extortionary, and piratical offences. Detailed petitions suggest his practised expertise in extortion, but are hardly disinterested and may also reflect a hairbreadth medieval distinction between lawful provincial administration and the unjustified use of force. The statement that he 'manned twoo Karvels to the See' (*RotP*, 6.138) implies piracy, but could easily be redefined as legitimate privateering whenever international alliances shifted. Accused of forcibly repossessing a tin mine, he claimed that his warrant as JP was to protect the original developer's interests. Charles Ross's statement that 'half the gentry of Cornwall' petitioned against him in the 1473 parliament (Ross, 410) is exaggerated; of five petitioners, Bodrugan had pre-existing land disputes with at least two. Contemporary allegations that the petitioners' lives were at risk if they pursued cases at common law must be read warily. It was not unusual, in any appeal to equity, to claim that for such reasons common-law justice was unattainable. However, the accusation that Bodrugan illegally altered wills and proved testaments to his own advantage is unusual enough to warrant suspicion, though no known supporting evidence of such misdeeds survives. Finally, the picturesque story that in 1484 he systematically persecuted Sir Richard Edgcumbe, who retaliated in 1487 by pursuing him so hotly that he escaped only by leaping over a cliff to a waiting boat, though possibly based on tradition, apparently stems from persistently over-imaginative readings of Richard Carew's *Survey of Cornwall* (1602).

Though named on one Tudor commission, Bodrugan early supported Lambert Simnel. On 8 February 1487 a commission was issued to arrest him and his putative son as rebels. Both attended Simnel's 'coronation' in Dublin that May, and though not listed as fighting at the battle of Stoke in June, were attainted on 11 November 1487. Bodrugan died in exile between then and 1503, when his next heirs petitioned the king for reversal of his attainder. Though often thought to typify fifteenth-century aristocratic lawlessness and prodigality, he may be better understood in the light of undoubted political (and, at least between 1450 and 1458, financial) constraints, and of fifteenth-century administrative realities.

PHILIPPA C. MADDERN

Sources *RotP*, vol. 6 • early chancery proceedings, PRO, C1 16/474, 27/338, 28/388, 32/168, 34/47, 48/81, 53/56, 55/42–44, 58/342, 59/283, 76/32, 76/48–49, 116/14, 173/47–48, 305/40–41 • Star Chamber proceedings, Henry VIII, PRO, vol. 16, fol. 181 STAC2/16; vol. 23, fol. 305 STAC2/23 • *CPR, 1422–1509* • *CClR, 1422–61, 1483–5* • J. Warkworth, *A chronicle of the first thirteen years of the reign of King Edward the Fourth*, ed. J. O. Halliwell, CS, old ser., 10 (1839) • R. Horrox and P. W. Hammond, eds., *British Library Harleian manuscript 433*, 4 vols. (1979–83) • HoP, *Commons, 1386–1421*, vols. 1–2 • A. L. Rowse, 'The turbulent career of Sir Henry Bodrugan', *The little land of Cornwall* (1986), 178–90 • C. Ross, *Edward IV*, new edn (1975) • J. Whetter, *The Bodrugans: a study of a Cornish medieval knightly family* (1995) [to be used with caution] • ancient correspondence of chancery and exchequer, PRO, SC 1, vol. 50, nos. 142, 162 • ancient petitions, PRO, SC8, file 344 no. E1281 • *The register of Edmund Lacy, bishop of Exeter*, ed. G. R. Dunstan, 5 vols., CYS, 60–63, 66 (1963–72), vol. 3 • copy of inquisition post mortem for Sir Richard Edgcumbe, Royal Institution of Cornwall, Henderson MSS, vol. 25, p. 36 • D. Gilbert, *The parochial history of Cornwall: founded on the manuscript histories of Mr Hals and Mr Tonkin*, 4 vols. (1838) • R. Carew, *The survey of Cornwall* (1602); facs. edn (1969) • M. J. Bennett, *The battle of Bosworth* (1985) • GEC, *Peerage* • *CIPM, Henry VII*, 2 • W. E. Hampton, *Memorials of the Wars of the Roses: a biographical guide* (1979)

Wealth at death approx. £100 p.a. in 1487 at attainder, based partly on value (£67 p.a. in 1489) of nine estates passing to Sir Richard Edgcumbe; technically devoid of real estate after attainder: copy of inquisition post mortem for Sir Richard Edgcumbe, Royal Institution of Cornwall, Henderson MSS, vol. 25, p. 36; *RotP*, 6.400

Bodvoc (*fl.* AD 15–20). *See under* Roman Britain, British leaders in (*act.* 55 BC–AD 84).

Bodwill, Thomas. *See* Canes, Vincent (1608–1672).

Bodwrda, William (1592/3–1660), Church of England clergyman and manuscript copyist, was the second son and one of thirteen children of Huw Gwyn Bodwrda (*c*.1573–1622), landowner, of Bodwrda, Aberdaron, Caernarvonshire, and Elsbeth Gwyn (*d.* 1637) of Berth-ddu in the Conwy valley. The family home was enlarged with the addition of two brick extensions to an earlier building on the same site in 1621. This small mansion was a cultural haven, visited by contemporary Welsh poets. The herald Lewys Dwnn and the scholar and transcriber Sir Thomas Wiliems are also known to have visited the house in 1588 and 1602 respectively.

Little is known of Bodwrda's schooling but he matriculated at Hart Hall, Oxford, on 7 April 1609, aged sixteen, gaining his BA in 1612. He then moved to St John's College, Cambridge, in 1614 where his maternal uncle, Owen Gwyn, was master. After gaining his MA in 1616, he was elected a college fellow, being ordained in 1621 and attaining his BD in 1623. He served as senior bursar between 1635 and 1638, when a new library was built with the patronage of Archbishop John Williams of Cochwillan, an uncle by marriage and one whom Bodwrda served as a personal chaplain.

Bodwrda's fortune changed during the civil war. His property was sequestered and he and other college officials were ejected in 1644, a year after Cromwell captured Cambridge. Bodwrda returned to Wales and served as rector of Aberdaron between 1651 and 1659, a living held by St John's College, Cambridge. From 1644 until his death he spent long hours transcribing Welsh poetry and prose. He would visit his sister Gwen and her husband, Sir Gruffydd Williams of Penrhyn, a man of like interests.

Bodwrda died in 1660, some time between 15 January, when he signed his will, and 9 August, when it was proved at London. In the will eight folio manuscripts are listed, lettered A to H. Six of these can be identified by using the transcriber's index in NL Wales, Llanfair and Brynnodol MS 2 (namely BL, Add. MS 14966, NL Wales, Mostyn 145, and NL Wales, Llanstephan 122–125). Twenty-three of his manuscripts are known to have survived, while two folio manuscripts have been lost.

Bodwrda is a prime example of a Welshman who adapted his humanistic ideals to serve Welsh scholarship and culture. He safeguarded a body of literature which affords us a survey of the poetic traditions of an earlier era, but also provides a store of contemporary poetry and information on the social life of Llŷn and Eifionydd during the first half of the seventeenth century.

DAFYDD IFANS

Sources R. G. Gruffydd, 'Llawysgrifau Wiliam Bodwrda o Aberdaron (a briodolwyd i John Price o Fellteyrn)', *National Library of Wales Journal*, 8 (1953–4), 349–50 • D. Ifans, 'Wiliam Bodwrda (1593–1660)', *National Library of Wales Journal*, 19 (1975–6), 88–102, 300–10 • D. Ifans, 'Bywyd a Gwaith Wiliam Bodwrda (1593–1660) o Aberdaron', MA diss., U. Wales, Aberystwyth, 1974 • Venn, *Alum. Cant.* • Foster, *Alum. Oxon.* • will, PRO, PROB 10/931

Archives BL, Add. MSS 14892, 14966 | Bodl. Oxf., Welsh MSS e.2–3 • Harvard U., Welsh MS 8 • NL Wales, MSS 16B, 560B, 1559B, 2030–1B, 3048D; Brogyntyn MS 4; Cwrt-mawr MS 25A; Iolo Aneirin Williams MS 5 (section 9); John Glyn Davies MS 2; Llanfair and Brynnodol MS 2; Llanstephan MSS 122–125, 187; Wynnstay MS 2 • St John Cam., bursar's records, etc. • U. Wales, Bangor, Bangor (Mostyn) MS 9

Wealth at death bequeathed £6 2*s.* 6*d.*; two gold rings and eight folio MSS: will, PRO, PROB 10/931, proved at London, 1660

Body, (Mary) Agnes (1866–1952), headmistress, was born at Sandyfields, Cotwall End, Sedgley, Staffordshire, on 29 April 1866, the third of the seven children of George *Body (1840–1911), clergyman, who was serving as curate of Sedgley, and his wife, Louisa Jane (*b. c*.1837), daughter of William Lewis, vicar of Sedgley. Following her father's appointment as rector of Kirby Misperton in 1870, Agnes spent most of her childhood in Yorkshire and was educated at home by a governess before attending the school where she was confirmed as a member of the Church of England. In 1883, when her father was appointed canon-missioner of Durham Cathedral, she moved to Durham.

In September 1886, at the age of twenty, Agnes Body entered Cheltenham Ladies' College, boarding at St Hilda's College, which catered for women wishing to train as secondary-school teachers or pursue university studies. She proved her academic abilities with a grade one result in the Cambridge higher local examination in July 1887 for which she was awarded the Lowman prize. The following year she trained as a teacher and sat her Cambridge teacher's certificate, gaining honours in both theory and practice.

After declining a teaching post at Alice Ottley's School in Worcester in 1888, Body joined the staff of Cheltenham and, under the influence of her headmistress, Dorothea Beale, came to view her chosen profession as a 'sacred ministry' to which she had been 'called by her Lord' (George Body to Beale, 5 Aug 1890, Cheltenham Ladies' College archives). Although only an assistant mistress at Cheltenham, her talents were so highly regarded that, when she finally left the school in 1893, she left not as a novice teacher, but as the headmistress of Lincoln Christ's Hospital Girls' High School (LHS), a new girls' school which opened in September that year.

Despite beginning with little more than 'two dozen pencils' (*Queen Margaret's School Magazine*, 1952, 8), Agnes Body built the school up into one of the most respected girls' schools in the country and in 1899 was invited to found a new girls' school under the direction of the Woodard corporation. Although reluctant to abandon her 'dear friends and children', Agnes felt 'called' to this new challenge and left Lincoln in June 1900 (*LHS Magazine*, 5, Easter 1900, 4–5). From there she went to Scarborough, where she established Queen Margaret's School (QMS) in May 1901 and, with the help of a small band of Lincoln staff and pupils, transformed it into a successful day and boarding-school, which became widely known simply as Miss Body's School (*QMS Magazine*, 14, Christmas 1913, 3).

Combining high-church ideals with a strong sense of missionary endeavour, Body was a woman of great earnestness; her strength and determination belied her small, slender frame. Despite being a strict disciplinarian, her calm, gentle manner, simple humility, and extraordinary memory enabled her to relate to people on a uniquely individual level. Blessed with a 'superb carriage, a striking dignity and a beautiful, warm voice' (*LHS Magazine*, 107, summer 1952, 9), which was at its most powerful when delivering one of her Sunday night addresses at Queen Margaret's, she inspired great devotion and loyalty in her staff and pupils who, it was claimed, 'would have gone through fire and water for her' (ibid.).

However, the demanding nature of her work took its toll and in June 1913 Body was forced to resign because of ill health. Although reluctant to abandon her 'beloved' school, she accepted her retirement as an opportunity for pursuing her interest in mission work—work to which she had felt 'increasingly drawn' and which, she hoped, would involve 'less physical and mental strain' (*QMS Magazine*, 13, June 1913, 1). Accordingly, in November 1913 she went to Truro to train as a missionary at the Home of the Epiphany, a religious community where her father had once been warden.

After another bout of illness in 1914, Body was forced to abandon her missionary career but the following year travelled to New Zealand to lecture and inspect schools. While there she visited the Auckland Diocesan High School and was welcomed in April 1915 as the school's 'grandmother' (*Diocesan High School Chronicle*, 17, April 1915, 15), as she had trained four of its staff at Lincoln.

Returning to England as a Roman Catholic in 1920, Body settled in Bishop's Stortford, before moving to Torquay ten years later to live with a friend, Miss Kirkman-Finlay. Although crippled by rheumatism in her later years, she kept in touch with both her schools until she died from the combined effects of coronary thrombosis, arterial sclerosis, and hypertension at her home, 6 Rowley Road, St Marychurch, Torquay, Devon, on 31 March 1952. Her funeral was held at the church of Our Lady and St Denis, St Marychurch, and she was buried in Torquay cemetery on 4 April 1952. MARGARET A. E. HAMMER

Sources *Lincoln Christ's Hospital Girls' High School Magazine*, 107 (summer 1952), 1, 5–12 • *Queen Margaret's School Magazine*, 13 (June 1913) • *Queen Margaret's School Magazine*, 14 (1913) [Christmas 1913] • *Queen Margaret's School Magazine*, 16 (1914) [Christmas 1914] • *Queen Margaret's School Magazine* (June 1952?) • *Lincoln Christ's Hospital Girls' High School Magazine*, 1, 2, 4, 5, 6, 9 (1898–summer 1901) [Christmas 1898–midsummer 1901] • George Body's letters to Dorothea Beale, 27 April 1888; 2 July 1888; 14 Nov 1888; 5 Aug 1890; 12 July 1893, Cheltenham Ladies' College archives, Cheltenham • pupil register and college magazine, Cheltenham Ladies' College archives, Cheltenham • 'Body, George', *DNB* • J. Skinner, ed., *Lincoln Christ's Hospital School: a 900 year heritage* (1990), 9–11 • L. Cowie and E. Cowie, *That one idea: Nathaniel Woodard and his schools* (1991), 115–17 • b. cert. • d. cert. • minutes of the governors of Lincoln Christ's Hospital Girls' High School, 11 July 1893, 15 Dec 1899, and 4 April 1900, Lincoln Central Library, Lincoln • census returns for Kirby Misperton rectory, Yorkshire, 1881 • *Diocesan High School Chronicle*, 17 (April 1915), 5, 15 • private information (2004) [reference department, Torquay Central Library; Torquay cemetery]

Likenesses photograph, repro. in *Lincoln Christ's Hospital Girls' High School Magazine*, 107 (summer 1952)

Wealth at death £315 0s. 8*d*.: probate, 4 June 1952, *CGPLA Eng. & Wales*

Body, George (1840–1911), Church of England clergyman, born at Cheriton Fitzpaine, Devon, on 7 January 1840, was the son of Josiah Body, surgeon, and his wife, Mary Snell. He was educated at Blundell's School, Tiverton, from 1849 to 1857, and subsequently entered St Augustine's Missionary College, Canterbury. His intention of undertaking missionary work abroad had to be abandoned because of ill health. In 1859 he matriculated from St John's College, Cambridge, graduating BA in 1862 and proceeding MA in 1876. Subsequently he received from Durham University the degree of MA *ad eundem* (1884) and an honorary DD (1885). On 25 September 1864 he married Louisa Jane (*b.* *c.*1837), daughter of William Lewis of Sedgley.

Body was ordained deacon in 1863 and priest the following year. He served successively as curate of St James, Wednesbury (1863–5), Sedgley (1865–7), and Christ Church, Wolverhampton (1867–70). Like other 'slum priests', such as Charles Lowder and G. R. Prynne, he sought to bring the teaching and practices of the Oxford Movement to the working classes, combining evangelical fervour with Tractarian principles. Nominated rector of Kirby Misperton, Yorkshire, in 1870 he took an active part in the parochial mission movement. In 1883 he was appointed canon-missioner of Durham by Bishop Lightfoot, and for twenty-eight years carried on successful mission work among Durham miners. He had a fine reputation as a mission preacher: his sermons were remarkable for their directness and sincerity, an appeal enhanced by a west country burr which he retained to the end of his life.

Body's varied activities covered a wide area. He was proctor in convocation for Cleveland from 1880 to 1885, and for Durham in 1906, and vice-president of the Society for the Propagation of the Gospel (1890), and succeeded his friend Bishop G. H. Wilkinson as warden of the Sisterhood of the Epiphany, Truro, in 1891. He was select preacher at Cambridge (1892–6 and 1900–06) and lecturer in pastoral theology at King's College, London, in 1909. He also acted as examining chaplain to the bishop of St Andrews from 1893 to 1908. Although he was a member of the English Church Union his sympathies were broad, and his conciliatory attitude during the ritualist crisis of 1898–9 exercised a moderating influence on the militant section of the high-church party. He published many sermons and devotional works.

Body died at The College, Durham, on 5 June 1911. He was survived by his wife and his three sons and four daughters, among whom was (Mary) Agnes *Body (1866–1952). A memorial fund was raised after his death for the maintenance of the diocesan mission house and a home for mission workers among the Durham miners.

G. S. Woods, *rev.* G. Martin Murphy

Sources *The Times* (6 June 1911), 11 • *The Guardian* (9 June 1911) • *Blundellian* (June 1911) • *Men and women of the time* (1899) • *CGPLA Eng. & Wales* (1911)

Likenesses S. A. Walker, photograph, *c.*1889, NPG • Mrs Boyd, miniature, priv. coll. • J. Lindsey, black and white drawing, priv. coll.

Wealth at death £6378 18*s.* 8*d.*: probate, 16 June 1911, *CGPLA Eng. & Wales*

Boece [Boethius], **Hector** (*c.*1465–1536), historian and college head, was born in Dundee into the Boyis or Bois family of Panbride in Angus (Forfarshire): Boethius is a Latinized version of the original name and Boece a retranslation. His father was probably Alexander Boyis (*fl.* 1460–1500), a burgess of Dundee, whose name appears in the register of the great seal between 1481 and 1487.

Family background and education According to Boece his great-grandfather Hugh had received the lands at Panbride in 1332 through marriage with an heiress, as recognition of his father's death at Dupplin that year, fighting for David II. Boece, however, consistently refers to himself as Deidonanus and refers to Dundee as his *patria*, suggesting that his own family was a cadet branch. His father was none the less wealthy enough to put at least three sons through advanced schooling and to send two for further study in Paris; among Hector's colleagues at King's College in Aberdeen was his brother Arthur, a scholar of civil law, and nearby was another brother, Walter, the priest at St Mary's ad Nives, the parish church of Old Aberdeen. There may well have been other brothers, since other Boises appear in the records in the early years of the sixteenth century; without doubt, the family were important members of Dundee society.

After his initial education, probably at Dundee grammar school, Boece went to the University of Paris, specifically to the Collège de Montaigu, probably not later than 1485. Montaigu was then under the leadership of Jan Standonc, a native of Malines in Brabant and an austere man, who ran the college under the rules of poverty and discipline. There, as well as following the traditional arts course, Boece met many men who were to make their own mark on Scottish affairs, as he commemorates in his description of his time in Paris in his own *Vitae episcoporum Aberdonensium et Murthlacensium*. They included John Mair, the scholastic philosopher and fellow historiographer, Patrick Paniter, private secretary to James IV, and George Dundas, later the master of the knights of St John of Jerusalem in Scotland. In addition he also met and struck up a friendship with the great humanist Desiderius Erasmus, receiving from him the dedication of Erasmus's only volume of poetry (1495). Through his acquaintance with Erasmus it is possible that Boece gained an introduction to some of the humanist circles in Paris, including that of Robert Gaguin, who was both a historian of France and a translator of Julius Caesar. After he returned to Scotland, Boece seems not to have maintained any degree of intimacy with Erasmus, though he wrote to him in 1528 when the Dutch humanist had been condemned by the Sorbonne, commending one of his books and assuring him of his esteem. While there was little enough that Boece could do for his old acquaintance, doubtless Erasmus was pleased by any show of support.

Aberdeen Boece completed his MA in 1492, when he is likely to have been in his late twenties, and thereafter remained at Montaigu as a regent while studying for his degree in theology. Then in 1497 William Elphinstone, bishop of Aberdeen, invited Boece to come to Aberdeen to teach liberal arts at the recently founded King's College. Elphinstone's university was designed to serve the north-east of Scotland and also to provide education for laymen as well as those intending to go into the church. In choosing Boece and his associates as the first teachers Elphinstone was aligning King's College both with humanist study of the arts and also with an austere and orthodox position in religion, an alignment which was evident in the teaching of liberal arts, more particularly of theology, within the college. Once Elphinstone had obtained the foundation charter for King's College, granted on 17 September 1505, he nominated Boece as first principal of the university. The appointment could not have been made previously, since one of the requirements of the principal was that he should hold a master's degree, or at the very least a bachelor's degree, in theology, a qualification Boece could have attained only a little earlier. As principal Boece received a substantial salary, with board and lodging, in return for wide-ranging duties which included administering the finances and the practical running of the college, monitoring the behaviour of teachers and students alike as well as the quality of the lectures. He also acted as the first librarian, an office not laid down in the foundation charters but evident from Boece's signatures and comments on many of the early volumes currently belonging to Aberdeen University Library. He was responsible for teaching theology and arts, and for preaching publicly in the vernacular six times a year. Boece seems to have performed these duties well, keeping the college together after Elphinstone's death in 1514, and furthering its development under Gavin Dunbar, bishop of Aberdeen from 1518 to 1532. As well as being principal Boece was a canon of the cathedral, rector of Tyrie from at least 1509, vicar of Tullynessle by 1528, and chaplain of the altar of St Ninian in the town's kirk of Aberdeen.

Minor writings Despite being committed to all these positions Boece continued his own intellectual development. Shortly after gaining his first qualification in theology he also finished his bachelorship in medicine, for he describes himself as a medical graduate in a document dated 1 October 1506. There is only one anecdote of his practising medicine, dating from 1535, late in his life, when he was summoned to the bedside of Thomas Crystall, abbot of Kinloss. Unfortunately Crystall was dying, and Boece was unable to do more than note his condition and ease his passing. Boece's interest in medicine is, however, evident in his writings, where there are some professional considerations of disease and causes of death; his library contained Galen's *Thegnis, seu, Ars medica* and Pliny the elder's *Historia naturalis*, two standard medical textbooks of the period. Boece also continued his studies in theology, becoming a doctor in the subject in 1528. More famously he also undertook several literary projects. His first book, on logic, was *Explicatio quorundam vocabulorum ad cognitionem dialecticos conducentium opera*, and was printed probably in Paris, in 1519; only one copy, in Glasgow University Library, seems to survive. It has been described as an undergraduate textbook, sound in its approach and particularly strong in the area of inference. That Boece should publish on logic demonstrates that no matter how enthusiastic he was in his devotion to the *studia humanitatis*, his thinking was none the less deeply imbued with scholastic modes of thinking, particularly in philosophy and theology.

Boece's other works are better known and clearly aspire to humanist models of historiography. The first, *Vitae episcoporum Aberdonensium et Murthlacensium*, was printed in Paris in 1522 by Jodocus Badius Ascensius, a printer from the Low Countries who seems to have been a favourite among Scottish writers. Possibly modelled on Bartolomeo Platina's *Lives of the Popes*, a copy of which Boece owned, Boece's *Lives of the Bishops of Aberdeen* is primarily a biography of Bishop Elphinstone, whose life takes up nearly half the volume. While the tone of Boece's account tends towards the hagiographic, it nevertheless provides detailed information on the foundation of King's College and on Elphinstone's actions as bishop. The discussion of Elphinstone and King's College was also designed as a goad to Gavin Dunbar, bishop of Aberdeen when the work was published, since it highlights works still to be completed or even undertaken for the benefit of the university. The lives of the earlier bishops are treated more cursorily, though there is more detail as the account approaches Boece's own time. The work demonstrates several of the concerns which were to underwrite Boece's second historiographical work, the *Scotorum historia*, namely the use of antiquity, the relationship of church and state, the importance of morality for rulers, and finally humanist style.

The *Scotorum historia*: purpose and reception Boece's greater work is *Scotorum historiae a prima gentis origine libri xvii*. Published in Paris at the author's expense in 1527, again by Ascensius, the *Scotorum historia* (as it is generally known) is an account of the Scottish people from their very earliest origins and the foundation of the Scottish realm in Scotland in 330 BC until the death of James I and the capture and punishment of his murderers in 1438. In seventeen books, it takes the form of a dramatic narrative, with speeches before battle, councils, and embassies, in its style emulating classical historiography as exemplified by Livy and thus also contemporary humanist practice as seen in the writings of such men as Marcantonio Sabellico and Paolo Emilio. Boece also makes use of the latest in humanist learning in presenting the recently rediscovered *Agricola* and *Annales* of Tacitus as a source. With some help from Tacitus, Boece presents the Scots as a people of antique virtue and unyielding independence, notably through an unbroken line of kings. Throughout the narrative Boece draws attention to the connection he perceives between the austere virtue and devotion to duty of the ruler and good government. That poor rulers, especially in the earlier books, are frequently punished and deposed for their failures and misdeeds does not necessarily mean that Boece himself was a republican or a particularly radical republican, even though that was the interpretation applied to his work by George Buchanan; rather it falls into the category of more general 'advice to princes', common in Scottish literature and historiography, and with an awareness of conciliarist arguments.

The *Scotorum historia* is dedicated to James V, to whom Boece presented a copy at its first publication. In return the king rewarded Boece with an annual pension of £50 Scots, which was afterwards doubled, and he also commissioned John Bellenden to make the first translation of the work into Scots. When searching for an account of the Scots to inform his new queen, Madeleine, James seems also to have chosen the *Scotorum historia* as the basis of a French version. The king's enthusiasm for Boece's account was repeated elsewhere. The Latin edition was reprinted in 1574 and again in 1575 in Lausanne, though circulated from Paris, under the guidance of Giovanni Ferrerio, who met Boece while he was resident at Kinloss Abbey. The later editions contain two further books, 18 and 19, which brought the account up to the death of James III. Ferrerio explains that the additional books remained incomplete at Boece's death, and himself completes the account of James III with a brief annal. Although the additional books are slight there is no reason to doubt that they are of Boece's composition. Narrative sources for the second half of the fifteenth century seem to have been scarce, and perhaps Boece's age disinclined him for extensive research. Polydore Vergil used the *Scotorum historia* as an occasional source for his *Historia Anglica* (1534), while both John Lesley's *De origine, moribus et rebus gestis Scotorum* (1578) and George Buchanan's *Rerum Scoticarum historia* (1582) depended heavily upon it.

The *Scotorum historia* proved just as popular in the vernacular. After completing his first translation of the work for James V, Bellenden embarked on a second, printed in Edinburgh around 1535 to 1540 and allegedly corrected by Boece himself. It is unclear whether this assertion is in fact true, since Bellenden did not translate the additional books, nor do the alterations made for the second translation appear to move the translation closer to the original Latin. However, Bellenden's printed text circulated quite widely, not least to the compilers of Holinshed's *Chronicles*, and hence to Shakespeare. There are two further translations of the *Scotorum historia*, both nearly contemporary with Bellenden's versions. The first, in pentameter couplets, was composed by William Stewart, a courtier of James V; the second, written in prose, is known as the Mar Lodge Translation, since the manuscript in which it appears does not contain the name of the author. There are also at least two continuations, one by John Lesley and the other by Robert Lindsay of Pitscottie, suggesting that they at least perceived the *Scotorum historia* as the standard account of the Scottish past.

The *Scotorum historia*: critics and commentators Despite the popularity and immense influence of the *Scotorum historia* in its various forms, it has always had its critics. On its first publication, other historiographers, particularly those from England such as John Leland and John Bale, criticized its presentation of Arthur and the Brutus myth, crucial to their own versions of the English past. More recent critics have remarked upon Boece's style and approach, contrasting it unfavourably with that of his contemporary at the Collège de Montaigu, John Mair. In his *Historia majoris Britanniae, tam Angliae quam Scotiae* (1521), Mair eschews ornate oratory, dismisses the origin myths of both England and Scotland, and applies his logic to arguing his case for the union of the crowns; so great is the difference between the two works that it has been suggested that the *Scotorum historia* was written with the particular purpose of answering the arguments in *Historia majoris Britanniae*. However, references to the *Scotorum historia* in Boece's *Lives* demonstrate that the author was composing his *Scotorum historia* before the publication of *Historia majoris Britanniae*, and moreover that the two works—both published by Ascensius—seem designed to serve different functions: Mair's argues a strongly held political cause, while Boece's belongs to the humanist fashion for historiography on a grand scale to affirm national identity.

The most serious criticism of the *Scotorum historia* has always been focused on Boece's identification of his sources for his account of the early history of the Scots, among whom he cites Elphinstone as well as Veremundus, Cornelius Hibernicus, and John Campbell. No writings by men of these last three names survive, and it is common to question whether such material ever existed independently of Boece. Forgery of this kind was not unknown in the period, and Boece's line of forty kings neatly fills the gap left by his predecessors John Fordun and Walter Bower. It is also clear that the continuous kingship of the Scots underpins Boece's presentation of Scottish identity. Queries about the nature of Veremundus and the others first appear in the sixteenth century, particularly around Buchanan's use of Boece's early narrative. Some commentators, such as Humphrey Lhuyd, were still enthusiastic supporters of the Brutus myth, but others, such as John Twyne, raised serious questions about the authority and nature of Boece's sources.

The first detailed analysis of Boece's history was undertaken by Thomas Innes in *A Critical Essay on the Ancient Inhabitants of the Northern Parts of Britain or Scotland* (1729). As a Jacobite, Innes also had a political agenda to meet, but as a scholar he identified the major deficiencies of Boece's narrative: that there is no corroboration for the sources (later references by David Chambres in his *Histoire abregée* are unreliable, since most of the information on the Scottish past is taken from the *Scotorum historia*); that Boece used the genealogies contained in Fordun's *Chronica* and turned them into king-lists; and that some of Boece's material contradicts Roman accounts and other versions of events. Innes believed that Boece's intention was to convince his audience that the deposition of unsatisfactory monarchs had always been part of Scottish government, and that he had invented authorities and manipulated his material to prove it. Innes's view that Boece's sources could not be what he claimed them to be prevailed for the next two centuries, though opinion was divided as to whether Boece had fabricated his authorities as Innes claimed, or whether he had been deceived by a forgery. In the nineteenth century only William Skene considered the possibility of Veremundus's existence. Recent study, however, both of early Scottish historiography and of Boece himself, has suggested that Boece may have been neither a forger nor a dupe.

Since the first edition of the *Scotorum historia* stopped its account in 1438, and since the later books in the second edition are so curtailed, the work is a disappointing witness for events in Scotland during Boece's lifetime. There are some interesting anecdotes, such as how Boece's ancestors came to Angus, the action of Katherine Douglas in trying to protect James I by using her arm as a door-bar, and an unexpectedly positive summary of James III in the catalogue of kings at the beginning of the narrative, but nothing more substantial. Boece's *Vitae*, however, is different, being a major source for the life of Elphinstone. Although designed to praise rather than to criticize, this work does offer some insights into Scottish affairs in the late fifteenth and early sixteenth centuries, particularly as they affected Aberdeen. Otherwise Boece's principal contribution to modern understanding of his own time is to be found in his expression of the nature of good government and his presentation of national identity.

Personality and likenesses As well as being respected for his literary and administrative achievements Boece seems to have been well liked. He was accompanied to Aberdeen by two of his brothers, and by his schoolfriend William Hay, who succeeded him as principal at King's College. He is also recorded as acting as defence in a case in Dundee in 1522, though his advocacy appears to have been unsuccessful. On 5 September 1528 Aberdeen town council awarded him a present of either a tun of wine or else £20 to buy bonnets. Elphinstone evidently made a good choice in the first principal of his new university. There survive two likenesses identified as Boece. One came into the possession of King's College in the early nineteenth century and is reproduced as the frontispiece to the collective volume published in 1937 as *Quatercentenary of the Death of Hector Boece*; it represents a cleric dressed in the garments of the seventeenth century, and is unlikely to be Boece. The other, also in the possession of the University of Aberdeen, is older and is more likely, though not definitely, the principal. The last mention of Boece in the surviving records was made in 1532, when he witnessed the marriage settlement of Isabella Boyiss, assumed to be a niece. He had died by November 1536, when the king awarded the rectory of Tyrie to another man. He was buried in King's College chapel, where his tombstone is still visible. On the outside of the chapel is his coat of arms together with his initials and a notice of his date of death—*ob.* 1536.

NICOLA ROYAN

Sources H. Boece, *Vitae episcoporum Aberdonensium et Murthlacensium* (Paris, 1522) · *Hectoris Boetii murthlacensium et aberdonensium episcoporum vitae*, ed. and trans. J. Moir, New Spalding Club, 12 (1894) · H. Boece, *Scotorum historiae a prima gentis origine* (Paris, 1527) · *APS*, *1424–1567* · G. Neilson and H. Paton, eds., *Acts of the lords of council in civil causes, 1496–1501*, 2 (1918) · G. Burnett and others, eds., *The exchequer rolls of Scotland*, 11 (1888) · G. Burnett and others, eds., *The exchequer rolls of Scotland*, 16 (1897) · J. Stuart, ed., *Extracts from the council register of the burgh of Aberdeen*, 1: *1398–1570*, Spalding Club, 12 (1844) · J. M. Thomson and others, eds., *Registrum magni sigilli regum Scotorum / The register of the great seal of Scotland*, 11 vols. (1882–1914), vols. 2–3 · M. Livingstone, D. Hay Fleming, and others, eds., *Registrum secreti sigilli regum Scotorum / The register of the privy seal of Scotland*, 1 (1908) · M. Livingstone, D. Hay Fleming, and others, eds., *Registrum secreti sigilli regum Scotorum / The register of the privy seal of Scotland*, 2 (1921) · *Opus epistolarum Des. Erasmi Roterodami*, ed. P. S. Allen and others, 12 vols. (1906–58); repr. (1992), nos. 47, 1996, 2283 · J. B. Black, 'Boece's *Scotorum historiae*', *The quatercentenary of the death of Hector Boece* (1937), 30–53 · A. Broadie, *The circle of John Mair* (1985) · D. Broun, 'The birth of Scottish history', *SHR*, 76 (1997), 4–22 · J. Durkan, 'Early humanism and King's College', *Aberdeen University Review*, 48 (1979–80), 259–79 · *Johannis de Fordun Chronica gentis Scotorum / John of Fordun's Chronicle of the Scottish nation*, ed. W. F. Skene, trans. F. J. H. Skene, 2 vols. (1871–2) · T. Innes, *A critical essay on the ancient inhabitants of the northern parts of Britain, or Scotland*, 2 vols. (1729); repr. in 1 vol. (1885) · T. D. Kendrick, *British antiquity* (1950) · L. J. Macfarlane, *William Elphinstone and the kingdom of Scotland, 1431–1514: the struggle for order*, quincentenary edn (1995) · N. R. Royan, 'The *Scotorum historia* of Hector Boece: a study', DPhil diss., U. Oxf., 1996 · N. R. Royan, 'The relationship between the *Scotorum historia* of Hector Boece and John Bellenden's *Chronicles of Scotland*', *The rose and the thistle: essays on the culture of late medieval and Renaissance Scotland*, ed. S. Mapstone and J. Wood (1998), 136–57 · W. D. Simpson, 'Hector Boece', *The quatercentenary of the death of Hector Boece* (1937), 7–29 · tombstone, King's College chapel, U. Aberdeen

Likenesses oils (Hector Boece?), U. Aberdeen, King's College; repro. in Simpson, 'Hector Boece' · oils, U. Aberdeen, King's College

Boehm, Anthony William [*formerly* Anton Wilhelm Böhme] **(1673–1722)**, Lutheran minister and religious writer, was born on 1 June 1673 at Ösdorf in the county of Waldeck, Germany, the fifth son of Anton Böhme (1623/4–1679), pastor, and Anna Catharina Oynhausen (1640/41–1717). Educated at the newly founded University of Halle from 1693 to 1698 Boehm was the leading representative in England of Halle pietism, a 'new Reformation' within the Lutheran church of Germany, which sought to revive the practice of Christianity through inward and personal spiritual renewal. In Halle, Boehm was influenced by August Hermann Francke, the organizational mastermind and charismatic promoter of Halle pietism. A brief stint as a court tutor in Arolsen, Germany, ended in controversy because of Boehm's uncompromising pietist beliefs. He then moved to London to establish a school for German children; however, his frail, asthmatic constitution curtailed his ability to teach and he lived for years in poverty. His fortunes changed in 1705 when Prince George of Denmark invited him to become his court chaplain at the German Lutheran chapel at St James's, where he remained until his death.

Boehm's legacy is threefold. First, as the prince's chaplain he carried on an active pastoral ministry even though he was never ordained. His primary role was preaching and Prince George held it in such esteem that he appointed a second chaplain to administer the sacraments. Boehm made weekly visits to the prisons and became a significant figure in their reform. His introduction to the Society for Promoting Christian Knowledge (SPCK) resulted from a shared interest in prison reform. Known for his concern for the destitute he was eulogized as 'a Hearty Friend to the Poor at Home' by the secretary of the SPCK (Newman). However, his dominant pastoral concern as a pietist was for the salvation of individual souls. Not only was Boehm engaged in the pastoral care of Germans in London but he also reached out to the thousands of German Palatine emigrants who arrived in London between 1708 and 1710, seeking passage to the New World. By procuring large shipments of bibles and devotional writings he hoped primarily to care for their spiritual well-being. Indeed Boehm and future Lutheran chaplains adopted an unofficial mothering role toward their 'daughter' churches in the colonies, thereby influencing the rise of American Lutheranism.

Second, Boehm was remembered for his involvement in the SPCK. A newly founded voluntary society, its main *modus operandi* was education, made evident by its co-ordination of the fledgeling charity school movement and by its distribution of Christian publications. After taking a tour of charity schools Boehm decided to translate and publish Francke's account of the rise of the orphanage in Halle. *Pietas Hallensis* appeared in 1705, helping to further the charity school movement and to encourage the SPCK. On 7 September 1710 the society, following Boehm's proposal, decided to lend its support to the East India mission. Principally at Boehm's instigation the SPCK became increasingly entwined in international operations that overshadowed its domestic interests for the next thirty years. Most unusually, in the East India mission an Anglican society supported a royal Danish mission in sending German Lutheran pietist missionaries from Halle to southern India. As a non-Anglican SPCK member Boehm prodded the SPCK to sustain its participation. At one point he found himself mediating in a brewing conflict within the society (initiated by Archbishop Thomas Tenison) over the use of non-episcopally ordained missionaries in an Anglican-supported enterprise. The society considered him the 'grand cement' that held together this remarkable effort in pragmatic ecumenism (Henry Newman to William Wake, Middle Temple, 28 May 1722, Christ Church Library, Oxford, Wake MS 24.121). The worldwide focus of the society intensified in 1720; Boehm was the mainspring in persuading the SPCK to take on its most ambitious publishing venture to date, the preparation of an Arabic psalter, New Testament, and catechism.

Finally, Boehm's legacy is seen in his publishing activity. From 1709 to 1721 he kept the East India mission before the English public with updated editions of *Propagation of the Gospel in the East*. Among his English translations of German works, he translated and edited various works by Francke, including two Latin pieces by which he hoped to contribute to theological study in England. The most influential of Francke's works was *Nicodemus, or, A Treatise Against the Fear of Man*, which John Wesley later abridged and published. The most important author to Boehm, however, was Johann Arndt, whose *True Christianity*, in the early seventeenth century, revived an emphasis on piety lost since the Reformation. Boehm placed high hopes on his translations into both Latin and English of *True Christianity*; this work best represented his own desire to spread a common, non-sectarian Christianity that would rise above party differences. Many of Boehm's own works were also published, including sermons, catechisms, and his major treatise *Enchiridion precum* (1715), which consisted of prayers and extracts in over fifty categories. Most of his published sermons were collected in *Several Discourses and Tracts for Promoting the Common Interest of True Christianity* (1717). From 1705 scarcely a year passed in which Boehm did not publish at least one work. Through his literary output he influenced many Anglicans, nonconformists, and evangelicals; he was one of the few 'respectable' non-Anglican writers who promoted neglected Reformation ideals in the period between puritanism and the evangelical revival. Boehm died, unmarried, on 27 May 1722 in Greenwich, at the country home of his friend Dr Frederick Slare. Isaac Watts wrote of him: 'I fear there are but few such Men in the Ministry, British or German, Episcopal or Presbyterian, etc. I am sorry the World and the Church has sustained so heavy a Stroke' (Isaac Watts to [J. C. Jacobi], Rambach, 40). Boehm was buried at Greenwich on 30 May 1722. DANIEL L. BRUNNER

Sources D. L. Brunner, *Halle pietists in England: Anthony William Boehm and the Society for Promoting Christian Knowledge* (1993) • G. F. Nuttall, 'Continental pietism and the evangelical movement in Britain', *Pietismus und Reveil* [Zeist, 1974], ed. J. van der Berg and J. P. van Dooren (Leiden, 1978), 207–36 • A. Sames, *Anton Wilhelm Böhme, 1673–1722: Studien zum ökumenischen Denken und Handeln eines halleschen Pietisten* (Göttingen, 1989) • J. D. Walsh, 'Origins of the evangelical revival', *Essays in modern English church history: in memory of Norman Sykes*, ed. G. V. Bennett and J. D. Walsh (1966), 132–62 • J. G. Rambach, *Memoirs of the life and death of the late Reverend Mr. Anthony William Boehm*, trans. J. C. Jacobi (1735) • *Anton Wilhelm Böhmens weiland Sr. Königl. … erbauliche Briefe* (Altona and Flensburg, 1737) • W. R. Ward, 'Power and piety: the origins of religious revival in the early eighteenth century', *Bulletin of the John Rylands University Library*, 63 (1980–81), 231–52 • L. Curtze, 'Nachrichten über Gelehrte, Schriftsteller und Künstler der Fürstenthümer Waldeck und Pyrmont von der Reformation an bis auf die Gegenwart', *Beiträge zur Geschichte der Fürstenthümer Waldeck und Pyrmont*, ed. L. Curtze and A. Hahn, 4 vols. (Arolsen, 1866–72), vol. 2, pp. 189–92 • *DNB* • [H. Newman], 'Epitaph on Mr Boehm', 1722, Bodl. Oxf., MS Rawl. C. 743, 98

Archives Society for Promoting Christian Knowledge, London • Universitäts- und Landesbibliothek Sachsen-Anhalt, Halle, Archiv und Missionsarchiv | Bodl. Oxf., Rawlinson MSS • Staatsbibliothek, Berlin, Nachlass A. H. Francke, K30

Likenesses portrait, repro. in *Der Königlich-Dänischen Missionarien aus Ost-Indien eingesandten Ausführlichen Berichte*, 8 (Halle, 1765), frontispiece

Boehm, Sir (Joseph) Edgar [*formerly* Josef Erasmus Böhm], **baronet (1834–1890)**, sculptor, was born on 4 July 1834 in Vienna, the youngest son of Josef Daniel Böhm (1794–1865), court medallist, engraver, and director of the imperial mint at Vienna, and his wife, Maria Aloysia Lussman (1797–1839), daughter of Dominic Lussman. Josef Daniel Böhm was a Hungarian who settled in Vienna in 1813 and formed a major art collection which served as a basis for his son's education. From 1848 to 1851 the younger Boehm attended Leigh's art academy (later Heatherley's) in London and then returned to Vienna, where he studied medal design and modelling at the Akademie der Bildenden Künste. After visiting Italy he worked in Paris from 1859 to 1862, where he was influenced by contemporary realist practice.

Boehm's marriage in 1860 to (Louisa) Frances (Fanny) Boteler (*c*.1835/6–1890) was one reason for his decision to settle in London in 1862. Another was the dreary and insular state of English sculpture. Boehm could capitalize on his recent Parisian experience and thus increase his impact. In his sculpture he avoided anachronistic classical idealism. He believed that art which is 'not of its time is failing in the all essential element of common sense' (Meynell, 336). He was equally confident whether carving in marble or modelling in terracotta, a material more common in French sculpture than in English. From the outset critical opinion was divided about Boehm. Francis Turner Palgrave, for example, commented that his 'showy work delighted the vulgar' (Stocker, 'Sculpture', 92), a sentiment echoed by Thomas Woolner, who used his influence to delay Boehm's election to the Royal Academy.

Boehm's first work to attract major interest was a statuette of William Makepeace Thackeray (1864, National Portrait Gallery, London). Its success led to an edition of seventy plaster casts. Anthony Trollope admired Boehm's rendition of 'the figure of the man exactly as he used to stand before us' (Stocker, *Royalist and Realist*, 63). Thackeray's waistcoat, watch strap and glasses, and his inelegant pose—with hands in pockets—immediately distinguished Boehm's realism from the neo-classical mainstream. Boehm also sculpted equestrian statuettes, a genre which as a passionate horseman naturally attracted him. His eye for a horse is evident in bronzes of racehorses and hunters, for example *Johnny Armstrong* (1863, National Horseracing Museum, Newmarket). Sporting sculpture has been so neglected by art historians that Boehm's introduction of it, under the influence of the French *animalier* Pierre-Jules Mène, has passed virtually unnoticed. It was, however, admired by contemporary critics, including Edmund Gosse, who noted 'the refinement and delicacy' of his horses (ibid., 307).

Portrait busts form the majority of Boehm's works. In their quantity and quality they reveal how he effectively cornered the market of the famous and the fashionable. His sitters included James Whistler, John Ruskin, Thomas Huxley, Herbert Spencer, and Franz Liszt. His busts reflect his diversity, ranging from the vivid alertness of *W. E. Gladstone* (1879, plaster, Victoria and Albert Museum, London) to the sensuously neo-rococo *Adeline, Countess of Cardigan* (1869, marble, Deene Park, Northamptonshire). Adeline reappeared as a loving widow in Boehm's monument to James Thomas Brudenell, seventh earl of Cardigan (1868–70, St Peter's, Deene, Northamptonshire). Some of Boehm's fifty-seven documented church monuments, such as those in Westminster Abbey to Benjamin Disraeli (1881–3) and Arthur Stanley (1882–4), are highly convincing as portraiture. He collaborated with Philip Webb and Edward Burne-Jones in the charming, lyrical relief commemorating Charles and Mary Howard (1879–81, Lanercost Priory, Cumberland).

Boehm's work attracted Queen Victoria's attention in 1869. His talents, together with her regard for his 'very gentleman-like, clever and excessively modest' personality (Stocker, *Royalist and Realist*, 80), led to an association which lasted until his death in 1890. In all, he received over forty royal commissions, and he gave lessons to Princess Louise, Queen Victoria's daughter. In 1880 he was appointed sculptor-in-ordinary to the queen and in 1889 was created a baronet. Royal patronage made other sculptors jealous but it was a mixed blessing for Boehm. Some commissions were straightforward, such as the life-sized marble figure of the queen's collie, *Noble* (1884, the Royal Collection). Queen Victoria's main concern with more ambitious sculptures was for precise renderings of uniform, costume, and likeness. Gosse's gibe that Boehm 'sacrificed humanity to buttons' thus rings true (ibid., 239). His talent for creating what his patrons wanted, his efficiency in delivering the goods, and his gentlemanly inability to refuse a commission meant that he sacrificed imaginative creativity. Among his finest works for Queen Victoria are the effigies of her father, the duke of Kent (1872–4), and her daughter Princess Alice (1878–80), both in the Royal Mausoleum, Frogmore, Windsor. The former is swathed in an impressive marble cloak, while the latter pays moving tribute to Alice's maternal affection.

Boehm's most famous work is his life-sized statue of Thomas Carlyle (1875; bronze version of 1882, Chelsea Embankment Gardens, London). A close friendship arose

Sir (Joseph) Edgar Boehm, baronet (1834–1890), by J. P. Mayall, pubd 1884

between sculptor and sitter, which led to Boehm's undertaking research for Carlyle on portraits of John Knox. There are close links between the *Carlyle* and Jean-Antoine Houdon's *Voltaire* (1778, Comédie-Française, Paris), a work which Boehm greatly admired. In the portrait Boehm fulfils his belief in treating modern dress *con amore*, while his truthfulness to life and dislike of classical affectation made him the perfect artist for Carlyle. The statue was unanimously praised at the 1875 Royal Academy show and won a silver medal at the Paris Universal Exhibition in 1878.

Other notable examples of Boehm's fifty-seven known public monuments include the craggy bronze of Field Marshal Sir John Fox Burgoyne (1877, Waterloo Place, London) and the carefully researched historical portraits of John Bunyan (1872–4, St Peter's Green, Bedford) and Sir Francis Drake (1882–3, Tavistock, Devon; 1882–4, The Hoe, Plymouth). One of his most ambitious monuments, to the duke of Wellington (1884–8, Hyde Park Corner, London), was less successful. The central group of Wellington and his mount, Copenhagen, fails to cohere with the corner figures of Napoleonic war veterans, added by the memorial committee as an afterthought. Even less satisfactory was his effigy of Queen Victoria for the jubilee coinage (1887). During its protracted history, changes in design were repeatedly made but the outcome pleased no one, least of all Boehm. With its small crown threatening to slip from the queen's head, the effigy was ridiculed by cartoonists and public alike and was soon replaced.

These failures lowered Boehm's reputation, and his consequent distress probably hastened his death. His late work, however, did not necessarily deteriorate in quality. An example is *Cupid and the Mermaid* (1889), which exists in two versions at Woburn Abbey, Bedfordshire—a large outdoor statue and a bronze statuette. The latter, a lithe, lively work, beautifully cast by the Compagnie des Bronzes in Brussels, shows Boehm's willingness to learn from the New Sculpture movement of Alfred Gilbert and Edward Onslow Ford. Like much of the New Sculpture, it was also influenced by Italian Renaissance bronzes.

Boehm died suddenly on 12 December 1890 at his home, The Avenue, 76 Fulham Road, London, and was buried on 20 December in St Paul's Cathedral. Frances Boehm had died four months earlier. Boehm was survived by three daughters and a natural son. Princess Louise's presence in Boehm's studio when he died provoked press gossip and subsequent, unsubstantiated speculation upon their possible sexual relationship. All accounts agree about Alfred Gilbert's central role in comforting Princess Louise in her distress. What followed was significant: the rapid advancement of Gilbert's career as a sculptor of royalty and the destruction of almost all Boehm's papers.

Boehm's talented studio assistants included Gilbert, Alfred Drury, Édouard Lantéri, and Robert Glassby. Even allowing for their role, they cannot fully account for the huge total of 360 different works documented in Boehm's name. A collection of 156 letters addressed to Boehm (Getty Research Institute, Los Angeles) which escaped destruction reflects his significance in the Victorian art world. He was frequently consulted by his friend Frederic Leighton, and also by George Frederic Watts, for help with their respective sculptural projects. In turn, he took advice from Gilbert about themes, interpretations, and techniques. Boehm admired Auguste Rodin, another correspondent, and helped secure acceptance of *The Age of Bronze* at the 1884 Royal Academy show. Despite his delayed election as an associate member of the academy (1878), Boehm was loyal to the institution and lectured there as well as serving as a visitor at the schools. He was elected to full membership in 1881. In addition, he was elected to the Rome and Florence academies in 1880 and 1881 respectively, and to the Akademie der Bildenden Künste in Vienna in 1890.

Boehm's art-historical neglect was caused by factors beyond the critical unfashionability of Victorian sculpture. The more innovative talents behind the New Sculpture obscured his own achievements. He was the victim of his own success and consistency. Burne-Jones noted how 'it sickened him to let … life go by and be so little of what he could have been as an artist' (Stocker, *Royalist and Realist*, 281). When Boehm did attempt imaginative, large-scale works, they were less convincing than his portraiture. Gosse observed that *St George and the Dragon* (1885, Swanston Street, Melbourne, Australia) lacked 'not size, for it is enormous, but largeness, which is quite another thing' (ibid., 290). In his important essay 'The New Sculpture, 1879–1894' Gosse portrayed Boehm as a dominating personality who sought to monopolize prestigious sculptural commissions and to exclude rivals. This, however, is contradicted by his kindness towards and encouragement of other, younger sculptors. An example was his role in securing Gilbert the commission for the Shaftesbury memorial (1886–93) in Piccadilly Circus, London. While he cannot be given the traditional art-historical accolade of a 'genius', Boehm was the most popular, prolific, and successful sculptor of late nineteenth-century England. Examples of his work are in the Royal Collection; the Tate collection; the National Portrait Gallery and the Victoria and Albert Museum, London; St George's Chapel, Windsor; and Westminster Abbey and St Paul's Cathedral, London.

MARK STOCKER

Sources M. Stocker, *Royalist and realist: the life and work of Sir Joseph Edgar Boehm* (1988) · M. Stocker, 'Boehm, Joseph Edgar', *The dictionary of art*, ed. J. Turner (1996) · M. Stocker, 'Sir Edgar Boehm's sculpture', *Antique Collector*, 59 (1988), 92–7 · M. Stocker, 'The church monuments of Joseph Edgar Boehm', *Church Monuments*, 2 (1988), 61–75 · W. Meynell, 'Our living artists: Joseph Edgar Boehm', *Magazine of Art*, 3 (1879–80), 333–8 · C. Eaglestone, 'A memoir of Sir Edgar Boehm', *Blackwood*, 149 (1891), 345–51 · E. Gosse, 'Living English sculptors II', *Century Magazine*, 31 (1886), 39–50 · B. Read, *Victorian sculpture* (1982) · R. Dorment, *Alfred Gilbert* (1985) · E. Gosse, 'The New Sculpture, 1879–1894 [pt 4]', *Art Journal*, new ser., 14 (1894), 306–11, esp. 308–10 · *DNB* · *CGPLA Eng. & Wales* (1891) · J. Wake, *Princess Louise: Queen Victoria's unconventional daughter* (1988) · E. Longford, ed., *Darling Loosy: letters to Princess Louise, 1856–1939* (1991) · Graves, *RA exhibitors*, 1 (1905), 218–20

Archives Bedford estates archives, London · Getty Research Institute, Los Angeles, Special Coll. #86-A1315 · NL Scot., letters · priv. coll., Colin Easden collection · RA, letters to Royal Academy · Royal Arch. | Hunt. L., letters to Grenville family · NL Scot., corresp. with Thomas Carlyle

Likenesses photograph, *c.*1880, NPG · T. B. Wirgman, pen-and-ink and pencil, 1882, NPG · J. Pettie, oils, 1883, Aberdeen Art Gallery, MacDonald collection · J. P. Mayall, photogravure, pubd 1884, NPG [*see illus.*] · Walery, photograph, *c.*1890, NPG · É. Lantéri, cast bronze medal, 1891, NPG · H. J. Brooks, group portrait, oils (*Private view of the Old Masters Exhibition, Royal Academy, 1888*), NPG · R. Glassby, marble bust, Royal Collection · J. M. Johnstone, woodcut (after photograph), BM, NPG; repro. in *Magazine of Art* · Lock and Whitfield, woodburytype photograph, NPG; repro. in *Men of mark* (1883) · R. W. Robinson, photograph, NPG; repro. in *Members and associates of the Royal Academy of Arts, 1891* · Spy [L. Ward], cartoon, repro. in *VF* (22 Jan 1881) · G. J. Stodart, stipple engravings (after H. T. Wells), NPG · woodcut, BM

Wealth at death £67,372 6*s.* 10*d.*: resworn probate, Dec 1891, *CGPLA Eng. & Wales*

Boevey [Bovey; *née* Riches], **Catherina** [Catharina] (*bap.* **1670**, *d.* **1726**), benefactor, was baptized on 1 May 1670 in the parish of St Laurence Pountney, London, the first child of John Riches (1628–1718), a merchant and landowner, and his wife, Anne, daughter of Thomas Davall (1619–1663), a merchant, and Anne Potts (1620–1700), daughter of Thomas Potts, gentleman. Catherina's father was a naturalized Dutchman, originally from Amsterdam. The most notable member of her mother's family was Catherina's uncle, the MP Sir Thomas Davall. Catherina had one sister, Anne (Hannah; 1671–1689), and one brother, John Riches (*d.* 1676).

As a child, Catherina Riches lived in St Laurence Pountney, the London parish in which her father was active and to which she was assigned the grant and demise of the rectory, tithes, advowson, and hereditaments in 1704 (Crawley-Boevey, 70). In 1685, aged only fifteen (though officially claiming to be 'about eighteen'), she married William Boevey (1657–1692), merchant, son of James *Boevey (1622–1696), an Anglo-Dutch merchant and lawyer, and his wife, Izabella de Visscher. Thereafter Catherina lived out her life on William's estate at Flaxley Abbey, Gloucestershire, while also keeping a town house in Duke Street, Westminster.

Little is known of Boevey's brief married life. The couple had at least two servants, Rachel Vergo and Matthew Stephens. A female friend of Richard Steele claimed that Catherina suffered her husband's 'excesses both in debauch and ill-humour like a martyr, cheerful under her very feelings' (Manley, 3.209). In 1692, when Catherina was twenty-two, William died of dropsy. In the inscription on his tomb in Flaxley church, Catherina described him as 'a man most distinguished for faithfulness and good repute; not sparing of aught that was his own; not covetous of aught that was another's; known to no one by wrong done, known to countless persons by kindness wrought'. They had no children.

The sole heir to her father's considerable wealth, and left £1000 in trust by her step-grandfather, the military engineer Sir Bernard de Gomme, in 1685, Boevey inherited on her husband's death the Flaxley estate, despite the fact that her father-in-law, James Boevey, contested the will. When her own father died in 1718 Catherina also inherited his 'real and personal estate in the counties of Kent, Surrey, London, and Middlesex'.

Although well acquainted with one of her neighbours, John Kyrle (Pope's 'Man of Ross'), and often courted, Catherina never remarried. Instead she devoted her life to charitable work and so 'in every minute particular fulfilled the character of a woman of nice honour and strict virtue' (Manley). She was the centre of a circle of female philanthropic friends, such as Mrs Cowling, Margaret Barrow, Grace Butler, and in particular Mary Pope of Twickenham, with whom Boevey had agreed to be buried in the same vault after their deaths. Other members of her circle included Dorothy Bayley (*d.* 1727), of Fretherne, Gloucestershire, and Susanna Lloyd, wife of John (friends of Catherina's distant relation Bishop Thomas Ken), who was godmother to Marie Renouard, wife of Colonel St Pierre of the Royal dragoon guards.

Boevey's charity extended from lending money to those in distress to inviting six poor children to her house every Sunday for dinner and religious instruction. By 1695 her philanthropic activities had involved her with the Society for Promoting Christian Knowledge (SPCK) founded by Thomas Bray. Like Bishop Ken, she founded and maintained one of the earliest catechetical schools in the parish of Flaxley. With Bishop Robert Frampton she helped the mission of the Revd John Talbot and the Revd George Keith in New England, including the endowment of St Mary's Church at Burlington, New Jersey. The silver chalice Boevey presented to the church in 1708 was still in use in 1876. In addition she contributed a subscription of £500 to a college established to train missionaries in the Bermudas, following Dean Berkeley's *Proposal for the better supplying of churches in our foreign plantations, and for converting the savages to Christianity* (1724). This sum was originally donated by 'a Lady who desires to be unknown' (Anderson, 3.476), and the identity of the benefactor was only disclosed by Mary Pope after Boevey's death. Her religious sympathies lay with the nonjuring bishops of the Church of England, like Thomas Ken. Two who accepted her offer of shelter at Flaxley Abbey were Frampton and George Hickes, the titular bishop of Thetford, whose *Linguarum septentrionalium thesaurus* (1705) was written with Boevey's financial support. Other beneficiaries included the Three Choirs Festival, of which she was a founder, held at Hereford, Worcester, and Gloucester from 1715.

Boevey's philanthropy and widowhood went hand in hand with a love of fashionable clothes. Her female servant, who was also her milliner and mantua maker, claimed that 'Mrs Boevey frequently called for her charity account book to see if it kept pace with her expenses in dress, which was always very handsome' (Crawley-Boevey, 113–14). Certainly she was well known for her fine appearance and beauty. Hickes, for example, described her as the 'Christian Hypatia of our England' (Hickes, 1.xlvii). To Delarivier Manley she was Portia in the third volume of her *The New Atalantis: Memoirs of Europe towards the Close of the Eighth Century*. Manley saw her as:

> one of those lofty black and lasting beauties that strikes with reverence, and yet delight. There is no feature in her face, nor anything in her person, her air and manner, that could be exchanged for any others, and she not prove a loser. Then as to her mind and conduct, her judgment, her sense, her

> stedfastness, her reading, her wit, and conversation, they are admirable, so much above what is lovely in the sex; shut but your eyes, and allow for the music of her voice, your mind would be charmed as thinking yourself conversing with the most knowing, the most refined of ours. Free from all levity and superficialness her sense is solid and perspicuous. She is so neat, so perfect an economist, that in taking all the greater beauties of life she does not disdain to stoop to the most inferior. In short, she knows all that a man can know without despising what as a woman she should not be ignorant of. (quoted in Crawley-Boevey, 86)

Richard Steele likewise praised her:

> aspect and mien which draw the attention and expectation of all who converse with you, and a wit and good sense which surmount the great conceptions your person raises in your beholders, [yet] those perfections are enjoyed by you like gifts of common acceptation; that lovely and affable air expresses only the humility of a great and generous heart; and the most shining accomplishments, used by others to attract vulgar admiration, are serviceable to you only as they adorn piety and charity. (*Lady's Library*, vol. 2, 21 July 1714, dedication)

Three years earlier Boevey's combination of virtue, piety, and beauty had placed her at the centre of a series of articles about Platonic love which appeared in Steele's and Addison's *The Spectator* (nos. 113, 115, 118, 517). According to Arthur W. Crawley-Boevey, Catherina was the inspiration for the character of the 'perverse widow'—beautiful, confident, but inaccessible—sought by the lovelorn Sir Roger de Coverley.

In the words of Mary Pope's half-sister, Margaret Barrow, Boevey was taken 'with a most violent colick' on 18 January 1726 (Fosbrooke, 2.179). She died between 11 a.m. and noon on 21 January 1726 from, according to her servant Rachel Vergo, a bowel complaint (Crawley-Boevey, 115). She was buried on 23 January at Flaxley church alongside her friend Mrs Cowling (*d.* 1719), and later her friends Grace Butler (*d.* 1763) and Mary Pope (*d.* 1747). A few years after Catherina's death Mary Pope had a monument, designed by James Gibbs, erected to her in Westminster Abbey; this formed the backdrop to Sir Elton John's rendition of 'Goodbye England's Rose' at the funeral of Diana, princess of Wales, in September 1997. M. H. PORTER

Sources *DNB* · A. W. C. Crawley-Boevey, *The 'perverse widow': being passages from the life of Catharina, wife of William Boevey* (1898) · [D. Manley], *Secret memoirs and manners of several persons of quality of both sexes, from the New Atalantis*, 7th edn, 4 vols. (1736) · J. Kip, *Britannia illustrata, or, Views of several of the queen's palaces* (1708) · G. M. Hills, *History of the church in Burlington, New Jersey* (1876) · J. S. M. Anderson, *The history of the Church of England in the colonies and foreign dependencies of the British empire*, 3 vols. (1845–56) · G. Hickes, *Linguarum*, 2 vols. (1705) · *N&Q*, 7th ser., 2 (1886), 47 · T. D. Fosbrooke, *Abstracts of records and manuscripts respecting the county of Gloucester, formed into a history*, 2 vols. (1807)

Archives Glos. RO, diaries

Likenesses portrait?, repro. in Crawley-Boevey, *The 'perverse widow'*, frontispiece

Boevey, James (1622–1696), merchant and philosopher, was born at 6 a.m. on 7 May 1622 at Mincing Lane, in the parish of St Dunstan-in-the-East, London, the first of two children of Andreas Boevey (1566?–1625), financier and elder of the Dutch church at Austin Friars, and his second wife, Joanna (*d.* 1644), daughter of Peter de Wilde. Boevey's parents were both of Dutch Huguenot descent, the Boevey family having fled to London in the 1570s after the invasion of the Low Countries by the duke of Alva. Boevey's father had eleven children in all, nine with his first wife, Esther Fenn. James was his youngest son. In 1628, three years after the death of Boevey's father, his mother married Johnnes van Abeele, a widower from the Dutch community in Norwich. Boevey was educated at the Mercers' School, where he was tutored by one Mr Augur, before being sent to the Netherlands in 1631 where he apparently perfected his Latin and Greek. In 1635 his mother set up a household in Little Chelsea, on the corner of Lover's Lane and Fulham Road (it was later sold to the physician Baldwin Hamey in 1665 and then to the earl of Shaftesbury). In 1636 Boevey was sent on the grand tour.

Boevey was married three times: his first wife was Susannah de Weyer (*d.* 1649), the niece of Jan de Monchy, an elder of the Dutch church at Austin Friars. Their two children were Margaret (*bap.* 1639) and Hesther (*bap.* 1640). About 1653 Boevey married Izabella (*d.* in or before 1669), daughter of William de Visscher, an émigré merchant from Emden; they had a son, William, and a daughter, Cornelia, and Izabella died some time before 16 September 1669, when her will was proved. Boevey's third marriage, to Margaret Cresset (1638–1714), was childless.

Boevey's early career involved his working for the prominent Dutch financier Sir William Courten, as 'cashier' for the banker Dierik Hoste, and for the Spanish ambassador in London; he was also responsible for the funds of the king of Spain's 'assentisters', and was 'Cash-Keeper' for Sir Theodore Mayerne, a Chelsea neighbour. Boevey became a merchant and made a number of unsuccessful attempts at naturalization. In 1660 he retired from his mercantile activities and on 10 June was admitted to the Inner Temple. Although he does not appear to have been called to the bar, it is this period in his life to which he owes his reputation for litigiousness. Much of the rest of his life was spent in litigation, with his family over property in Chelsea, Gloucester, and the United Provinces, and in particular with the residents of Exmoor. His dealings in the United Provinces twice landed him in prison, the first time for three years, the second time for eighteen months between 1672 and 1674.

Boevey was familiar with prominent figures in Restoration London such as Elias Ashmole, John Aubrey, and John Evelyn. After once dining with Boevey, Pepys described him as 'a solicitor and a lawyer and a merchant altogether who hath travelled very much; did talk some things well, only he is a Sir Positive; but talk of travel over the Alps very fine' (Pepys, 9.206). A list of the books on magic which Boevey had in his library, written in Elias Ashmole's hand, reveals the interest he shared with Ashmole in the occult (BL, Add. MS 36674, fols. 123*r*–129*v*). In 1642 Boevey visited Florence, where he made 'what inquiry he could after [Machiavelli's] reputation, and found that he left a good name behind him, as of a pious, charitable, sincere, good man, as any in that city'. Boevey wrote a manuscript entitled 'The vindication of that hero of political learning, Nicholas Machiavel; the second Tacitus' (*Harleian Miscellany*, vol. 7, 1810). In 1692 Boevey presented the Bodleian Library with a table of exchange rates entitled 'The secret algebraick key to treasure, parallel to the philosopher's stone' (Bodl. Oxf., MS Bodley 947). The Boevey family had long been at the heart of the Dutch mercantile community in London and Norwich and the manuscript is a curious monument to the Dutch finance involved in the establishment of the Bank of England in 1694.

At only 5 feet tall and slenderly built, with extremely black hair curled at the ends, an equally black beard, and the darkest of eyebrows hovering above dark but sprightly hazel eyes, Boevey was, according to Aubrey, 'a person of great temperance, and deepe thoughts, and a working head, never idle'—'Ever a great lover of Natural Philosophie'—'from 14 [Boevey] had a candle burning by him all night, with pen, inke, and paper, to write downe thoughts as they came into his head; so that he might not loose a thought' (*Brief Lives*, 1.114).

Boevey's writings eventually culminated in a series of manuscripts which he referred to as representing his 'Active Philosophy'. They were never published, but circulated among some friends and acquaintances. Bishop Moore's daughter, Rose More, certainly read them, as did Aubrey. Aubrey even asked Boevey to donate those writings to the library of the Royal Society. Although only a few of his manuscripts have survived, about 1677 Boevey sent John Aubrey a list of the works that made up his 'Active Philosophy' (Bodl. Oxf., MS Aubrey 7, fol. 13*v*), what Aubrey described as 'all the Art and Tricks practised in Negotiation, and how they were to be ballanced by counter-prudentiall rules … a thing not donne before'. Those that are still extant are all dated 1665 or 1666. They are 'The art of building a man, or, Education', 'The government of action', 'The government of friendshipp', 'The government of enmities', 'The government of law-suites', 'The government of amor conjugalis', 'The causes of the diseases of the mind', 'The cures of the mind', 'The art of discerning men', and 'The art of man's selfe'. Those that have disappeared are: 'The characters, or, Index rerum: in four tomes', 'The introduction to active philosophy', 'The art of conversation', 'The art of complyance', 'The art of governing the tongue', 'The art of governing the penn', 'The government of resolution', 'The government of reputation', 'The government of power', 'The government of servients', 'The government of subserviency', 'The art of gaining wealth with the family', 'The art of buying and selling', 'The art of preserving wealth', 'The art of expending wealth', 'The government of secrecy', 'Of amor concupiscentiae', 'The government of felicity', 'The laws of Atticus', 'Religion from reason', 'The Life of Cum-fu-zu, Soe Farr Wrote by J. B.', and 'The life of Mahomet, wrote by Sir W. R.'s papers, with some small addition for methodizing the same'.

In 1642 Boevey joined his half-brother William in the joint purchase of Flaxley Abbey in Gloucestershire. In 1653 Boevey purchased the freehold of the Forest of Exmoor from the parliamentary commission appointed to dispose of the assets of Charles I; he built a house there at Simonsbath in 1654. Some time about 1670 he moved to Cheam, Surrey. There is a tradition which claims that he used a mysterious vault under his house in Cheam to coin his own money. This may stem from his success with algebraic accounting, or from the anti-Dutchness in Rochester's and Oldham's 1682 satirical references to Boevey. Pepys certainly thought him an 'intolerable boaster'. Twenty years after Boevey's death, the literary critic John Dennis ('On the deceitfulness of rumour' [1715?]) wrote of 'that ugly Beau Bovey' who personified 'the credulity of people' to 'the Poison of false Praise [which] has more than once grown epidemically contagious, by the Error and Imbecility of a fear, and the conspiracy of a false Report'. In the algebraic manuscript which Boevey dedicated to 'Pro Gloria Anglicana', he himself wrote: 'My good Countrymen, Thus you may see, how I Dare to Love you, even with the Hazard of my Reputation' (Bodl. Oxf., MS Bodley 947). He died at his home, the Vault House, 5 Malden Road, Cheam, on 8 January 1696, and was buried on 13 January at Lumley church, Cheam (where his wife, too, was later buried). M. H. Porter

Sources A. W. C. Crawley-Boevey, *The 'perverse widow': being passages from the life of Catharina, wife of William Boevey* (1898) • J. H. Hessels, ed., *Register of the attestations or certificates of membership, confessions of guilt, certificates of marriages, betrothals, publications of banns, &c, &c* (1892) • A. H. McDermott, *A history of Exmoor Forest* (1973) • *Brief lives, chiefly of contemporaries, set down by John Aubrey, between the years 1669 and 1696*, ed. A. Clark, 1 (1898) • O. P. Grell, *Dutch Calvinists in early Stuart London* (1989) • T. Crofton Coker, *A walk from London to Fulham* (1860) • O. Manning and W. Bray, eds., *The history and antiquities of Surrey*, 2 (1974) • J. Lindeboom, *Austin Friars: history of the Dutch Reformed churches in London* (1950) • B. Thorns, *A brief history of the parish of Cheam* (1919) • W. J. C. Moers, ed., *The marriage, baptism and burial registers, 1571 to 1874, and monumental transcriptions of the Dutch Reformed church, Austin Friars, London* (1884) • Pepys, *Diary* • Bodl. Oxf., MS Rawl. C. 791

Archives BL, MSS • Bodl. Oxf., MSS • CUL, MSS • Flaxley Abbey, Gloucestershire, MSS • U. Cal., Los Angeles, William Andrews Clark Memorial Library, MSS • Wellcome L., MSS

Likenesses oils, 1635? (possibly James Boevey), Flaxley Abbey, Gloucestershire

Bogan, Zachary (1625–1659), classical and biblical scholar, was born about 24 June 1625 at Gatcombe House, Little Hempston, Devon, the third son of William Bogan (*bap.* 1582, *d.* 1658), gentleman, and his wife, Joane Irish, daughter of Zachary Irish. His paternal grandmother was Prothesia (Prothesy) Bodley, sister of Sir Thomas Bodley; the Bogans were originally merchants from Totnes. Having been 'excellently grounded in Grammar, and the Classick Authors' by an eminent local schoolmaster, Mr Batten (Prince, 118), Bogan became a commoner of St Alban Hall, Oxford, in Michaelmas term 1640, matriculating on 13 November, and was tutored by the puritan Ralph Button. On 26 November 1641 he entered Corpus Christi College as a scholar but a year later, the city having become a royalist garrison, he retired to his parents' home. After parliament captured Oxford in 1646 he returned and graduated BA on 21 October. He was elected a probationary fellow of Corpus Christi College in 1647.

When summoned by the parliamentary visitors on 9

May 1648, most college members objected on legal grounds. Bogan answered, 'When I shal be satisfied in conscience that I may lawfully doe it, I will readily submitt', and was listed for expulsion with the rest (Burrows, 62). He escaped on account of illness: James Metford, one of those expelled, recalled that Bogan was 'consumptive and his death daily expected'; the visitors left him 'by their Charity' as one whom 'twas plain inhumanity to drive out' (Fowler, 217). He was formally readmitted as a fellow on 2 November 1648, and is named in the visitors' register for 1649 and 1651. He became MA on 19 November 1650. Wood described him as 'a retired and religious Student, and much noted in the University for his admirable skill in the Tongues'; he mentioned him with Edward Pococke for excellence in Hebrew and the oriental languages (Wood, *Ath. Oxon.*, 2.237, 160). Bogan was an outstanding tutor, whose students included Daniel Agas, to whom he left his library, and the antiquary William Fulman. After years of ill health, he died on 1 September 1659 at Corpus Christi College and was buried to the south of the college chapel. He had inherited £1500 from his father, and in his will, dated 1 August 1659, he left most of it to his elder brother William. He bequeathed £500 to sponsor apprenticeships in five Oxford parishes, in appreciation of which his portrait, 'drawn more to the Death, than to the Life (so wan and pale it looks)' (Prince, 121), hangs in the city council chamber.

Bogan greatly enlarged Francis Rous's *Archaeologia Attica*, a popular companion to Greek studies. His additions (published in 1649 and acknowledged by Bogan in 1654) deal with 'customes in Marriages, Burialls, Feastings, Divinations &c.' A postscript apologizes for this product of 'my *Tyrocinium*' (first attempt) written 'to divert my humor of Melancholy' but impeded by illness and want of time. In 1652 he recalls being 'in a manner buried alive in melancholy', for months unable to read and for years to remember what he had read. That is in the dedication 'To my honoured father' (sig. *3r) of *A View of the Threats and Punishments Recorded in the Scriptures, Alphabetically Composed* (1653), drafted with surprising energy 'in very little more than a fortnight's time' (sig. A2r). Bogan had already written *Meditations of the Mirth of a Christian Life* (1653): not his own experience ('whole yeares altogether in *Sadnesse*') but what 'other Christians better than I am, *may* have', and definitely not '*carnall merriment*', which he would have castigated at greater length but for 'a troublesome, and dangerous sicknesse' ('To my honoured mother'; sig. ¶2r–v). In 1655 Bogan contributed to Edmund Dickinson's *Delphi Phoenicizantes*, a Latin dissertation that connects the giants in Job 26: 5 with Hesiod's Typhon. This line of speculation led to his *Homerus Hebraizōn, sive, Comparatio Homeri cum scriptoribus sacris quoad normam loquendi* (1658). Structured as a commentary on Homer, this substantial Latin discourse accumulated comparable expressions from the Old Testament and also the New. Bogan wrote it for pleasure when illness forced him to discontinue a treatise on Greek particles. He never finished that book, or another on the use of the poets. His last publication was posthumous, edited by Daniel Agas: *A Help to Prayer, both Extempore, and by a Set Forme* (1660). This was another collection of scriptural texts similar to *Threats and Punishments*, unpublishable when written in 1651 on account of its impressively open-minded preface in which Bogan compared the old forms of his childhood worship with the extempore prayer that he now found more affecting. HUGH DE QUEHEN

Sources J. Prince, *Danmonii orientales illustres, or, The worthies of Devon* (1701) • T. Fowler, *The history of Corpus Christi College*, OHS, 25 (1893) • Wood, *Ath. Oxon.*, 2nd edn • M. Burrows, ed., *The register of the visitors of the University of Oxford, from AD 1647 to AD 1658*, CS, new ser., 29 (1881) • F. Madan, *Oxford books: a bibliography of printed works*, 2–3 (1912–31) • F. Rose-Troup, 'The pedigree of Sir Thomas Bodley', *Report and Transactions of the Devonshire Association*, 35 (1903), 713–45 • Foster, *Alum. Oxon.* • *Walker rev.* • Mrs R. Lane Poole, ed., *Catalogue of portraits in the possession of the university, colleges, city and county of Oxford*, 3 vols. (1912–25), vol. 1 • PRO, PROB 11/300, quire 163, fols. 22v–23r

Likenesses Shorter, oils, 1660, Oxford town hall

Wealth at death approx. £1500: Prince, *Danmonii orientales illustres*

Bogarde, Sir Dirk [*real name* Derek Niven van den Bogaerde] **(1921–1999)**, actor and author, was born on 28 March 1921 in a taxi in Hampstead, the son of Ulric van den Bogaerde (*d.* 1973), the Dutch-born arts editor of *The Times*, and Margaret Niven (*d.* 1981), a Scottish actress whose father, Forrest, had also acted. Raised largely by his nanny, Lally, he began acting out little scenarios as a boy and made his stage bow in an amateur production of *Alf's Button*. However he was sent at thirteen to live with impoverished relatives in Glasgow, where the misery of being bullied at Allan Glen's School was relieved only by a bit part in a courtroom drama starring his godmother, Yvonne Arnaud.

Bogaerde returned to London in 1936 to attend University College School, and went on to study commercial art under Henry Moore and Graham Sutherland at Chelsea Polytechnic. Throughout this period he painted backdrops for various theatre companies and took occasional roles as Derek Bogaerde, although one poster listed him as Birk Gocart. In 1939 he ventured into films as an extra in the George Formby vehicle *Come on, George*; this was followed later in the same year with his first professional stage appearance in J. B. Priestley's *When we are Married*, at the Q Theatre, Kew. However, director Basil Dearden was less than impressed by the débutant, lamenting, 'Oh Christ, I know there's a war on now, they're rationing the talent' (Morley, 20).

Having graduated to the West End in Priestley's *Cornelius* (1940), Bogaerde spent a season with Amersham Repertory, where he met his lifelong companion and business manager, Anthony Forwood (*d.* 1988). Conscription meant that his stint with the Entertainments National Service Association proved even shorter, and he joined the army intelligence photographic unit as an interpreter of aerial reconnaissance pictures. He took part in the battle for Normandy and the liberation of the Bergen-Belsen concentration camp, later recording his recollections in *Snakes and Ladders* (1978) and *Cleared for Take-off* (1995). He also served in India and Singapore, making copious

Sir Dirk Bogarde (1921–1999), by George Courtney Ward, 1959

sketches, some of which are held in the British and Imperial War museums. However, his war ended on a tragic note when the jeep he was driving through Calcutta on VJ-day skidded in the monsoon rain and killed two deserters in a prisoner escort. He was exonerated, but never drove again.

Within days of his demob Bogaerde was informed that he had been overpaid by £800, and as a consequence he accepted the role of a modern-dress Jesus in a BBC television play. This led on to a live production of *Rope*, which saw him billed for the first time as Dirk Bogarde. But his big break came in February 1947, when he was ushered into the wrong audition room and ended up co-starring alongside Kenneth More in Michael Clayton-Hutton's *Power without Glory* at the New Lindsay Theatre. Against the express wishes of a new friend, Noël Coward, he followed his first featured movie role, in *Dancing with Crime* (1947), with the caddish male lead in *Esther Waters* (1947) and landed himself a £30 a week contract with the Rank Organisation. However, he did reject an offer to go to Hollywood, learn Spanish, and be repackaged as a 'Latin lover'. Instead he became typecast as Rank's rogue on the run, most notably in *The Blue Lamp* (1949) and *Hunted* (1952). He sought to prove himself capable of weightier material by returning to the stage in Jean Anouilh's *Point of Departure* (1950) and Coward's revival of *The Vortex* (1952), both at the Lyric, Hammersmith. However, similar attempts to demonstrate his screen versatility backfired, and after the disastrous comedy *Penny Princess* (1952) he resumed his life of crime in *The Gentle Gunman* (1952).

Despite Bogarde's modest box-office success in *Appointment in London*, Rank supremo Earl St John was unconvinced of his worth, and he only narrowly survived the struggling studio's drastic economy drive of 1953. Producer Betty Box, however, was convinced of his potential, and cast him as Simon Sparrow in her adaptation of Richard Gordon's novel *Doctor in the House* (1954). It was a runaway success and Bogarde was suddenly a matinée icon; he reprised the role in *Doctor at Sea* (1955), *Doctor at Large* (1957), and *Doctor in Distress* (1963). But another of his assignments in 1954 had a more lasting impact on his career, as the psychological melodrama *The Sleeping Tiger* brought him into contact with Joseph Losey, the blacklisted Hollywood director who set him on the road to art-house respectability in the early 1960s.

In the meantime Bogarde endured a series of glossy but unrewarding outings, including *The Spanish Gardener* (1956), *Ill Met by Moonlight* (1957), and *A Tale of Two Cities* (1958). Such was his new-found status at Rank that sets were designed to accommodate his preferred left profile. But he quickly became bored with what *Daily Express* critic Derek Monsey called 'those taut, truculent, antipathetic parts which he plays with beautiful precision' (Morley, 65). Indeed, he had much sympathy with playwright John Osborne's comments in the *Evening Standard*:

> For years he has been Britain's most popular screen actor during which time he has never appeared in a good film. This is an interesting phenomenon and it could be deduced that his enormous public actually prefer to see him in mediocre films. However, as they have never been given the opportunity to see him in anything else it is impossible to prove it. (Morley, 75)

It was not for lack of trying, however, as Rank denied Bogarde the chance to join the generation of angry young men in screen versions of Osborne's *Look Back in Anger* and Alan Sillitoe's novel *Saturday Night and Sunday Morning*. Similarly it blocked a loan to MGM for *Gigi*, and baled out of Anthony Asquith's biopic of Lawrence of Arabia. Even when Columbia did secure Bogarde's services, as Liszt in *Song without Love* (1960), it proved a demoralizing experience, particularly after he had responded so positively to the challenge of playing three roles in Asquith's *Libel* (1959). Sensing that his time as the 'idol of the Odeon' was ebbing, he boldly tackled the still-taboo subject of homosexuality in Dearden's *Victim* (1961) and took the risk of buying out his Rank contract for £10,000. Ironically, Betty Box lured him back for such mainstream items as *Hot Enough for June* (1964), which gave him the latitude to pursue more personal projects like Judy Garland's final film, *I could Go on Singing* (1962), for which he did some uncredited rewrites.

However, it was Bogarde's association with Losey that finally allowed him to express his gift for 'painful anguish and quiet torment'. He earned a British Academy award for *The Servant* (1963), which he partly directed while Losey was stricken with pneumonia. Having attacked the class system, the pair turned to military justice in *King and Country* (1964) and bounced back from the disappointment of *Modesty Blaise* (1966) to team up with screenwriter Harold

Pinter for *Accident* (1967), a darkly unflattering study of academe. In between times Bogarde drew another British Academy award for John Schlesinger's snapshot of the swinging sixties, *Darling* (1965). Artistic fulfilment came at a price, however, and in 1968 he was forced to accept work on a commercial for Italian sunglasses. Fortunately, it was seen by director Luchino Visconti, who cast him in both *The Damned* (1969) and *Death in Venice* (1971), a masterly adaptation of Thomas Mann's *roman à clef* about Gustav Mahler's final days. As Bogarde wrote:

> For me, *Death in Venice* is the peak and the end of my career. Oh, I shall go on working to earn money, or if a project interests me, but I can never hope to give a better performance in a better film. (Morley, 148)

These proved prophetic words. Bogarde's cameo as Boy Browning in *A Bridge Too Far* (1977) was denounced by Arnhem veterans, while the *New Yorker*'s famously vitriolic critic, Pauline Kael—who had once unflatteringly described him as Britain's answer to Robert Wagner—savaged his performance in Liliana Cavani's *The Night Porter* (1974): 'Bogarde is now just overexposed. We know all his neurasthenic tricks—the semaphoric eyebrows, the twitching mouth, the sneak vindictive gleam, the pinch of suffering are all warmed-over from earlier performances' (Morley, 153). Disappointed with both Alain Resnais's *Providence* (1977) and Rainer Werner Fassbinder's *Despair* (1978), Bogarde withdrew from films for twelve years, returning only for Bertrand Tavernier's *Daddy Nostalgie*, in 1990. Now resident in Provence, the fiercely private actor concentrated on writing, although he did star in his own teleplay adaptation of Graham Greene's *May we Borrow your Husband?* (1986). In addition to seven volumes of autobiography and six novels, the first of which was *A Gentle Occupation* (1980), he also began reviewing books for the *Sunday Telegraph* after his return to London in 1986.

Bogarde was knighted in 1992, the year in which he received a lifetime achievement award from the British Academy. Having survived strokes in 1987 and 1996, the latter of which left him confined to a wheelchair, he died at his flat at 2 Cadogan Gardens, Chelsea, on 8 May 1999. Increasingly reclusive in his later years, especially after Anthony Forwood's death in 1988, Bogarde became an active vice-president of the Voluntary Euthanasia Society in 1991. As he completed each volume of his autobiography, he destroyed the original material on which it was based, determined to control his reputation with posterity. Yet he disclaimed any wish to be remembered, saying he wanted no funeral or memorial service; 'just forget me' (quoted in *Sunday Times*, 9 May 1999).

DAVID PARKINSON

Sources S. Morley, *Dirk Bogarde: rank outsider* (1999) · D. Bogarde, *A postillion struck by lightning* (1977) · D. Bogarde, *Snakes and ladders* (1978) · D. Bogarde, *An orderly man* (1983) · D. Bogarde, *Backcloth* (1986) · D. Bogarde, *A particular friendship* (1989) · D. Bogarde, *A short walk from Harrods* (1991) · D. Bogarde, *Cleared for take-off* (1997) · *The Times* (10 May 1999) · *The Guardian* (10 May 1999) · *Daily Telegraph* (10 May 1999) · *The Independent* (10 May 1999) · b. cert. · d. cert. · *Sunday Times* (9 May 1999) · *Sunday Telegraph* (9 May 1999)

Archives Boston University, Mugar Memorial Library, corresp. and papers | BFI, corresp. with Joseph Losey

Likenesses G. C. Ward, photograph, 1959, NPG [*see illus.*] · portraits, Pinewood Archive · portraits, Huntley Collection · portraits, Kobal Collection · portraits, Ronald Grant Collection

Bogdani, Jacob (1658–1724), still-life and bird painter, was born on 6 May 1658 in Eperjes, upper Hungary, the son of Lucas Bogdani (*fl.* 1656–1684), painter, and his wife, Susanna. He was educated at the Felsőmagyarországi Evangélikusok Kollégiuma, Eperjes, and probably became his father's pupil. By 1684 he was in Amsterdam—an obvious refuge at that date for a young protestant with artistic ambitions—and is documented as still being there in the company of the still-life painter Ernst Stuven (1660–1712) in 1686. By the spring of 1688 he had moved to England and was living in Tower Street, St Giles-in-the-Fields, the area of London in which he probably remained for the rest of his life. In 1693 (on or after 29 November) he married Elizabeth Hemmings (*d.* 1722), and two of their five children survived infancy. According to Vertue, 'he was always a mild gentle temper'd man, courteous & civil' (Vertue, *Note books*, 1.127). He was at first known only as 'the Hungarian' but within a short time had 'gain'd great applause & was much employd by people of Quality, in whose possessions are many of his peices [*sic*] to be seen' (ibid.). One of his early commissions was a set of flower pieces for Queen Mary's 'Looking Glasse Closett in the Thames Gallery' at Hampton Court (1694), and he also supplied paintings for William III's palace at Dieren in the Netherlands (1700). Other patrons included the first duke of Devonshire, Edward Harley, the second earl of Oxford, Matthew Prior, Sir Robert Walpole, the first earl of Albemarle, and Queen Anne 'who was pleas'd with his performances & encourag'd him much' (ibid.).

Both contemporary comment and pictorial evidence indicate that initially Bogdani painted mainly flower and fruit still-lifes in the Dutch manner and that the bird paintings for which he is probably better known today were a later addition to his *œuvre*. Clearly influenced by Melchior de Hondecoeter (1636–1695) though lacking his more ferocious elements, Bogdani's exotic and English birds, poultry, game, and occasionally small animals, somewhat improbably grouped in park or landscape settings, are more civilized and restful. They are also meticulously and accurately represented, and richly colourful and decorative—qualities greatly valued by his aristocratic patrons. Some of Bogdani's earliest bird paintings, a unique record of the rare birds in the famous Windsor aviary of the duke of Marlborough's brother Admiral George Churchill, were acquired by Queen Anne after the admiral's death.

Bogdani's surviving works, all oil paintings on canvas, are never dated but usually signed 'J. Bogdani'. Occasionally, probably prior to his naturalization in 1700, he signed 'J. v Bogdane' or added the inscription 'Hungarus'. His prolific output and exact repetitions of his more successful images suggest a reliance on sketches and the use of assistants. His son William Bogdani (1699–1771), a distinguished civil servant who 'formerly painted in his father's manner' (Walpole, 143), and his son-in-law, the Transylvanian painter Tobias Stranover (1684–1756), are thought to have been his pupils. They inherited his 'Modells' (probably sketches) and Stranover often adopted motifs from Bogdani's paintings. Many public and private collections contain examples of his work, including the Royal Collection; Chatsworth House, Derbyshire; the Victoria and Albert Museum, London; the Fitzwilliam Museum, Cambridge; the Yale Center for British Art, New Haven, Connecticut; and the National Gallery of Hungary, Budapest. By the end of his life Bogdani 'had gain'd by his industry a pretty fortune' (Vertue, *Note books*, 1.127) and owned property in Finchley, Spalding, and Hitchin where he was lord of the manor, a position also enjoyed by his son and grandson. He died 'at his house, the sign of the Golden Eagle, in Great Queen Street', Lincoln's Inn Fields, London (Walpole, 3.143), and was buried on 11 February 1724 at St Mary's, Finchley, Middlesex. After his death his work was largely forgotten until Hungarian interest *c.*1900 aroused international attention that continued to increase throughout the twentieth century. DIANA BROOKS

Sources M. Rajnai, *Jacob Bogdani, c. 1660–1724* (1989) [exhibition catalogue, Richard Green Gallery, London] • notification of birth, Štátny Oblastný archív, Prešov, c.863/2, s.150 • register of town taxpayers, Prešov, 1655–94, Štátny Oblastný archív, Prešov, no. 1144 • marriage licence, 28 Nov 1693, LPL, 'Faculty Office marriage allegations, 8/1691–12/1694', FMI/13 • parish register (baptism), St Paul's, Covent Garden, 1696, 1698, 1699 • parish register (burial), St Paul's, Covent Garden, 1697, 1698 • parish register (baptism), St Giles-in-the-Fields, 1701 • parish register (death), St Mary, Finchley, 1724 • will, PRO, PROB 11/595, sig. 23 • M. Rajnai, 'Jacob Bogdani's working practices, his own account, 1691', *Acta Historiae Artium*, 36 (1993), 87–94 • Vertue, *Note books*, 1.127 • O. Millar, *The Tudor, Stuart and early Georgian pictures in the collection of her majesty the queen*, 2 vols. (1963), vol. 1, pp. 164–6 • H. Walpole, *Anecdotes of painting in England … collected by the late George Vertue, and now digested and published*, 3 (1763), 143 • M. Rajnai, 'Bogdány Jakab munkásságának néhány kérdése', *Művészettörténeti Értesítő*, 3–4 (1988), 186–93 ['Jacob Bogdani: some aspects of his work'] • I. Varga, *A magyarországi protestáns iskolai színjátszás forrásai és irodalma* (1988), 117, 127 ['Sources and bibliography of dramatic performances in Hungarian protestant schools'] • I. Gál, 'Bogdány Jakab angliai pályakezdete', *Művészet* (July 1971), 9 ['The beginnings of Jacob Bogdani's career']

Wealth at death bequests to family, friends, charities, poor of Finchley parish: will, PRO, PROB 11/595, sig. 23

Boghurst, William (1630/31–1685), apothecary, of St Giles-in-the-Fields, London, was the son of William Boghurst of Ditton, Kent, and served his apprenticeship with a London apothecary, Francis Drury. During the great plague of 1665 his medical practice expanded and he made his name. He stayed in the city throughout the epidemic, treating by his own account '40, 50 or 60 patients a day' (*Intelligencer*, 7 Aug 1665) and advertising his medicines and services in *The Intelligencer*. By the end of the year his reputation was sufficient to attract offers from the corporation of Norwich, which tried to employ him when the infection reached there.

Boghurst described the symptoms of the disease, and remedies for it, in 'Loimographia, or, An experimentall relation of the plague' (1666, BL, Sloane MS 349). This manuscript, which was clearly intended for publication, reflects his personal observation as well as drawing on the published literature (in Latin as well as English) on the disease. Boghurst was critical of the established practice of quarantining infected households—a policy 'oft enough tried and always found ineffectual'—and was in general doubtful about the conclusions drawn from theories of contagion. He also criticized the standard treatments of bleeding and purging and the practice of fumigating houses, though he sensibly warned against using the linen and bedding of sick patients. He described the symptoms of the disease with great accuracy, and correctly predicted its gradual decline in 1666, since 'the plague hath a long tail, … going backwards and forwards in little increases and decreases till it be quite gone'. His work is both a testimony to the critical acumen of a seventeenth-century general practitioner and the most reliable eyewitness account of bubonic plague in 1665.

Boghurst also wrote a poem in praise of London, 'Londinologia, sive, Londini encomium' (1666, BL, Sloane MS 904, fols. 53–68), estimating its population at one million (double the actual figure), celebrating the antiquity of St Paul's (on the eve of its destruction in the great fire), and welcoming the growth of the West End over the past forty years:

> so large, so beautiful, so fair and strait
> both streets and houses uniform and neat.

Little is known about Boghurst's family or personal circumstances. According to an epitaph, 'he was an honest, just man, skilful in his profession, and in the Greek and Latin tongue, delighting in the study of antiquity; and played exceeding well upon the lute, which he took naturally. He left a sorrowful widow and six children, to whom he afforded commendable breeding' (BL, Sloane MS 904, fol. 68*r*). In later life, however, his fortunes appear to have declined: he could not afford the livery of his company in 1682. He died in London on 2 September 1685 and was buried in Ditton. PAUL SLACK

Sources P. Slack, *The impact of plague in Tudor and Stuart England* (1985), 276 • C. Wall, *A history of the Worshipful Society of Apothecaries of London*, ed. H. C. Cameron and E. A. Underwood (1963), 112, 352 • BL, Sloane MS 904, fols. 53–68

Wealth at death could not afford livery of his company in 1682: BL, Sloane MS 904, fol. 68*r*

Bogle, George (1700–1784), merchant, was born in Glasgow, the son of Robert Bogle, a prosperous local trader, who resided at the estate of Daldowie, near Bothwell, Lanarkshire, which George inherited in 1720. He had more than the usual mercantile education, matriculating at the University of Glasgow in 1723 into the class under Alexander Ross, professor of humanity. He was sent in 1725 to the continent for an extended period of travel and residence which included two years of study at Leiden, then popular with students from Scotland; this experience confirmed a personal taste for history rather than for the law. His reading was wide: T. M. Devine has noted that his library contained books by French, Dutch, and Latin authors. Though Bogle showed an aptitude for business, he was always studious, unlike many of his contemporaries. In later life he was four times lord rector of Glasgow University (1737–8,

1743–4, 1747–8, and 1757), and was no ceremonial figurehead; rather, he took an active part in shaping the college's affairs, and a particular interest in the library.

Bogle's mercantile career from the later 1720s was focused on the colonial trades of sugar and tobacco. He was already heavily committed in 1729 when he found himself in some financial difficulty over customs dues, but he weathered this and other difficulties, and was able to diversify into a range of other activities. These included the Easter Sugarhouse, the Glasgow Cudbear Company, which supplied dyestuffs for the area's growing textile industry, and the Smithfield Iron Company, which exported heavily to the American and Caribbean markets. While not directly involved, as other leading tobacco merchants were, in the promotion of new banks at Glasgow, he was active in a range of transactions in the capital market, both borrowing from and lending to local landowners and merchants.

In 1732 Bogle married Anne (*d.* 1752), daughter of Sir John Sinclair, bt, of Stevenson, and Martha Lockhart; the marriage brought with it the estate of Whiteinch, near Glasgow. The couple had nine children, of whom the third son, George *Bogle, later achieved fame as a diplomat in India. The family's fortunes, which were considerable, survived the stress of the financial crisis of the early 1770s, when their estates were temporarily put into trust, and the shock of the American War of Independence, which brought the tobacco trade to an abrupt end. It appears that Bogle, suffering from gout, largely withdrew from active business. He died on 29 January 1784 at Daldowie. His son Robert Bogle inherited the family estates, and the dynasty continued in the mercantile world.

ALASTAIR J. DURIE

Sources Mitchell L., Glas., Bogle MSS • J. Coutts, *A history of the University of Glasgow* (1909) • T. M. Devine, *The tobacco lords: a study of the tobacco merchants of Glasgow and their trading activities, c.1740–1790* (1975) • U. Glas., Archives and Business Records Centre, MS GUA 30290 • J. O. Mitchell, *Old Glasgow essays* (1905) • *Scots Magazine*, 46 (1784)

Archives Mitchell L., Glas., MSS • U. Glas., Archives and Business Records Centre, MSS

Bogle, George (1746–1781), diplomatist, was born on 26 November 1746 at Daldowie, near Bothwell, Lanarkshire, the third son and youngest of nine children born to George *Bogle (1700–1784), merchant and rector of Glasgow University, and his wife, Anne (*d.* 1752), daughter of Sir John Sinclair, fourth baronet (*d.* 1726), of Stevenson, Haddingtonshire, and his wife, Martha Lockhart. He received his early education in Haddington and Glasgow, and after attending the University of Edinburgh from November 1760 to April 1761, he was sent to a private school at Enfield for three years. After six months' travel on the continent, in June 1765 he entered as clerk the counting house of Bogle and Scott in London, of which his eldest brother, Robert, was the head. In 1769 his friends obtained for him an appointment in the East India Company, and the following January he sailed on the *Vansittart* for Calcutta, arriving there on 19 August. His first letters home provide a vivid description of a devastating famine in Bengal. While serving first as writer with the select committee that had charge of political matters, he quickly learnt Persian. On 10 October 1772 he was appointed assistant secretary to the board of revenue and in that capacity accompanied the governor of Bengal (and future governor-general), Warren Hastings, on a tour to Cossimbazar. On 9 March 1773 he was made registrar of the court of appeals (*diwani adalat*) and soon after secretary to the select committee, holding the two posts simultaneously. To save the family home at Daldowie from being sold to meet the debts of his brother Robert, he began from this time to send nearly all his savings to his father.

For the respect and loyalty he showed to Warren Hastings, already caught in a web of factional strife, Bogle was rewarded by appointment as envoy to the third Panchen Lama of Tibet, Lobsang Palden Yeshé (1738–1780). The lama, a broad-minded scholar-statesman who maintained close contact with many Asian courts, had interceded with Hastings on behalf of the Bhutanese in a border conflict. The governor was quick to exploit this overture, not only with the aim of securing the free flow of British goods across the Himalayas into Tibet but also to satisfy his scientific and scholarly interests. Hastings was exceptionally well served by Bogle, whose qualities of good humour and warm tolerance were matched by diligence and efficiency. After a protracted delay in Bhutan for four months, he and his companion Alexander Hamilton entered Tibet on 23 October 1774, the first Britons ever to reach that country. They were the guests of the Panchen Lama, first for a month at an isolated monastery where he had gone to escape from a smallpox epidemic, and then for five months at his principal seat of Tashilhunpo at Shigatse. The mission returned to India in June 1775 after a further two months in Bhutan. Owing to opposition from the Chinese in this period of the Qing ascendancy in Tibet, Bogle won only temporary and limited commercial gains for the British. However, the very genuine friendship that developed between him and the lama opened the door to further contacts between the British and the Tibetans.

It is difficult to think of anyone who fits the colonial stereotype less than Bogle. As he admitted, 'I always like to do at Rome as they do at Rome' (Markham, 88). He was quick to adopt Tibetan dress and to master colloquial Tibetan, enjoying many opportunities to indulge in 'merriment' as he feasted with his Tibetan hosts, hunted with the lama's nephews, played chess with Kalmyk merchants, and, it can be assumed, pursued amorous dalliance (see below). Yet he was no profligate, taking his duties very seriously in the course of complex negotiations with many interested parties at Tashilhunpo. The lively prose of his surviving correspondence (preserved at the Mitchell Library, Glasgow) and mission journal (not published until 1876, a hundred years after the mission) reveals a warm, cultivated humanity dedicated to friendship, intellectual curiosity, and the pleasures of life.

Bogle found himself unemployed on his return to India because the powerful factions opposed to his patron, Hastings, were blocking all nominations. However, in November 1776, after the governor-general had again secured a majority in council, Bogle was appointed both to oversee the renewal of the leases of the company's provinces and to serve as commissioner of lawsuits. In April 1779 Hastings asked him to lead a second mission to Tibet, but this was abandoned when it was learnt that the Panchen Lama had left for Peking (Beijing), where he later died. In September of that year Bogle was appointed collector of Rangpur, where he established an annual trade fair for merchants from Bhutan. In January 1781 he was recalled by Hastings to serve on a new committee of revenue in Calcutta. There he was taken ill and died on 3 April. His tomb lies in the South Park Street cemetery.

Although Bogle's papers appear to have been censored by his family, it is clear that he fathered at least five children during his career in the east. Two daughters, Martha and Mary, were sent after his death to the care of his family at Daldowie, both later marrying Scotsmen. Their descendants asserted that the girls' mother had been a Tibetan lady called Tichan (Dechen, a common Tibetan name properly romanized as bDe-chen), describing her as 'sister of the Teshoo [Panchen] Lama' (Richardson, 76). She was more probably a niece or other more distant relative of the lama and may perhaps be identified with the Beebee Bogle who was still being paid a pension in Calcutta from Bogle's estate fifty-seven years after his death. Alternatively, that lady may have been the mother, probably a Bengali, of yet another daughter of Bogle, also called Mary, whom he had sent to the care of a friend in London in 1780. Bogle also had two, possibly three, sons, one of whom died on 31 April 1782, and another, George, who was baptized in Calcutta on 10 February 1784 on the same occasion as (his true sisters?) Martha and Mary, who were sent to Scotland. MICHAEL ARIS

Sources C. R. Markham, 'Biographical sketch of George Bogle, Bengal civil service', *Narratives of the mission of George Bogle to Tibet and of the journey of Thomas Manning to Lhasa*, ed. C. R. Markham (1876) • H. Richardson, 'George Bogle and his children', *Scottish Genealogist*, 29 (1982), 73–83 • L. Petech, 'The missions of Bogle and Turner according to the Tibetan texts', *T'oung Pao*, 34 (1950), 330–46 • J. Stewart, 'An account of the kingdom of Tibet in a letter from John Stewart … to Sir John Pringle', *PTRS*, 67 (1777), 465–88 • P. Bishop, 'Tibet discovered, 1773–92', *The myth of Shangri-la: Tibet, travel writing, and the Western creation of sacred landscape* (1989), 25–64 • T. Moore, 'The little grand lama', *Fables for the Holy Alliance* (1823)
Archives BL, narrative of mission to Tibet, Add. MSS 19283, 16261 • BL OIOC, corresp. and papers, MS Eur. E 226 • Mitchell L., Glas., letter-books, letters, MSS relating to India, Tibet, etc. | BL, corresp. with David Anderson, Add. MS 45421 • BL, corresp. with Warren Hastings, Add. MSS 29117, 29134, 29144–29146
Likenesses T. Kettle, oils, *c*.1775, Royal Collection; repro. in M. Archer, *India and British portraiture, 1770–1825* (1979) • miniature, repro. in F. Younghusband, *India and Tibet* (1910)

Bogue, David (1750–1825), Independent minister, was born on 18 February 1750 at Dowlaw, in the parish of Coldingham, Berwickshire, the sixth of the twelve children of John Bogue (*bap.* 1713, *d.* 1786), who became laird and farmer at Hallydown, and Margaret Swanston (*d.* 1805). He was educated at the parish school of Eyemouth and Duns grammar school, whence he proceeded in 1762 to the University of Edinburgh. He studied for the ministry of the Church of Scotland, and received licence as a preacher.

Bogue's father, however, refused on principle to ask the patron of the Coldingham living, Lord Marchmont, to present him, and instead advised him to seek work in London. Thus in 1771 Bogue taught in schools in Edmonton, Hampstead, and finally Chelsea, with the Revd William Smith, whom he assisted also in his ministerial duties. In 1777 he became minister of an Independent or Congregational chapel at Gosport in Hampshire, and played a key role in the formation of the Hampshire Association of Independent Churches. He provided some tuition for students, and from 1789 was able to develop the Gosport Academy for the education of young men destined for the Independent ministry. On 28 August 1787 he married Charlotte Uffington (*d.* 1824).

Early in 1792 Bogue emerged as a pioneer in the cause of protestant missions overseas, expressing his concern forcefully in *A sermon preached at Salters-Hall, March 30th, 1792, before the Society in Scotland for Propagating Christian Knowledge in the Highlands and Islands* (1793). Thereafter he took a leading part in the foundation of the London Missionary Society, notably through his influential appeal published in the *Evangelical Magazine* for September 1794 and the consultations which it stimulated. He preached the closing sermon at the society's inauguration in 1795, hailing its interdenominational principle as 'the funeral of bigotry' (*Sermons Preached in London at the Formation of the Missionary Society, September 22, 23, 24, 1795*, 1795, 130), and was one of the society's original directors. In 1796 he and his friend Robert Haldane of Airthrey planned to go to India themselves as missionaries, but the East India Company refused to sanction the scheme. Bogue's major contribution to the society instead became the education of its missionaries. Most of its directors at first considered this unnecessary, but Bogue convinced them otherwise, especially for those who would work amid the ancient civilizations of Asia; so, from 1800, prospective missionaries were trained at the Gosport Academy with Bogue as their tutor. He retained this position for the rest of his long life, providing a course centred on divinity but not neglecting other subjects. Bogue also took an active part in founding the Religious Tract Society (1799), to which he contributed the first of a series of long-popular tracts, and also—though less conspicuously—the British and Foreign Bible Society (1804).

In 1790 Bogue had published *Reasons for Seeking a Repeal of the Corporation and Test Acts*. He argued consistently that religious freedom was dependent on civil liberty: initially he hailed the French Revolution with enthusiasm, seeing in it the overthrow of a Roman Catholic tyranny oppressive to protestants. In 1802 he published an *Essay on the Divine Authority of the New Testament*, which was quickly translated into French and other languages, and appeared as the preface to a French edition of the New Testament. During the brief peace of 1802 he visited France. His pacifist principles are clear in his *On Universal Peace, being Extracts from a Discourse Delivered in October 1813*, published as tract 6 of the Society for the Promotion of Permanent and Universal Peace in 1819.

Bogue's address at the foundation of Mill Hill School, published as *The Nature and Importance of a Good Education* (1808), demonstrated his concern for a broad Christian and liberal education. His 'Proposal for establishing a university for dissenters' (*London Christian Instructor*, May 1820) contributed to the subsequent foundation of University College, London.

Bogue's major scholarly work was his *History of Dissenters from the Revolution in 1688 to the Year 1808* (4 vols., 1808–12), prepared in association with Dr James Bennett. A second edition in two volumes was issued in 1833: painstakingly researched, it was for long a standard work. It contains material which remains of value, especially on the dissenting academies and the careers of notable individuals. Written from the standpoint of moderate Calvinist evangelicals, it is polemical in places, for example in its critique of the Arminian Wesley. A major theme is concern for religious liberty—that peaceable citizens should have the right to form churches 'which the state should neither establish nor oppress, but protect' (1.xxvi). This commitment to toleration is attested by the authors' condemnation of persecution even by regimes of which they approve, such as the reformers of Edward VI's reign, while the religious policy of William and Mary and of the early Hanoverian kings is warmly commended. Other publications included numerous sermons, his theological lectures, and articles in the *Evangelical Magazine* and other periodicals. In 1815 Yale College, Connecticut, conferred upon Bogue the degree of doctor of divinity.

Charlotte Bogue died on 26 February 1824; four of their seven children also predeceased him. Bogue himself died at Brighton during the course of a preaching tour on behalf of the London Missionary Society, on 25 October 1825. He was buried at Alverstoke parish church, Gosport, on 2 November.

Bogue was a moderate Calvinist, but relatively undogmatic as a teacher. His learning was extensive rather than profound. As a preacher he was rational—even dry—rather than emotional. Energetic and industrious, firm without being domineering, he was an impressive, indeed patriarchal, figure: one of the most influential Congregationalists of his time. MICHAEL LAIRD

Sources J. Bennett, *Memoir of the life of the Rev. David Bogue, D.D.* (1827) · C. Terpstra, 'David Bogue, DD, 1750–1825: pioneer and missionary educator', PhD diss., U. Edin., 1959 · J. Morison, *The fathers and founders of the London Missionary Society*, 2 vols. [1840]; new edn [1844] · R. Lovett, *The history of the London Missionary Society, 1795–1895*, 1 (1899), 1 · S. Piggin, *Making evangelical missionaries, 1789–1858* (1984) · N. Gunson, *Messengers of grace* (1978) · J. Griffin, *A sermon occasioned by the death of the Rev. David Bogue, D.D.* (1825) · 'Memoir of the Rev. David Bogue', *Congregational Magazine*, 9 (1826), 1–5, 57–65 · J. Bennett, *The translation of Elijah: a funeral sermon for the late Rev. David Bogue, D.D.* (1825) · *DNB* · *IGI*

Archives SOAS, London Missionary Society archives · U. Edin., New Coll. L., papers, diary, sermons, and lecture notes | DWL, New College collection, J. Lownes MSS, MS L14

Likenesses Thomson, stipple, pubd 1826, NPG · Blood, engraving (after drawing by Wageman), United Reformed church, Bury Road, Gosport, Hampshire; repro. in Bennett, *Memoir* · Freeman, stipple (after Orme), NPG; repro. in *Evangelical Magazine* (1794) · stipple, NPG; repro. in *Evangelical Magazine*

Bogue, David (1807/8–1856), publisher and bookseller, was probably born and raised in Scotland. He worked as an assistant to the Edinburgh bookseller Thomas Ireland before moving to London in 1836. He then entered the shop of Charles *Tilt (1797–1861), publisher and bookseller, at 86 Fleet Street. The corner shopfront had large multi-paned windows in which Tilt could display his stock of illustrated works. He 'had a genius for making money' (Vizetelly, 1.108). He imported French lithographic sheets that yielded over £100 a week and also published and sold children's books, reprints of novels, and scrapbooks and annuals embellished with steel engravings. After the stamp duty on almanacs was repealed in 1834, Tilt did a thriving trade in all sorts of almanacs, including one that would fit into a top hat (Browning, 296). He was a principal publisher of George Cruikshank's works—several short-lived periodicals, brief illustrated stories, and the *Comic Almanack* (1835–53), which began bravely with a circulation of 20,000 but lost customers to *Punch's Almanack* and other rivals by the late 1840s.

In 1840 Tilt, passing over his three senior employees, invited the youngest and newest clerk to join him as partner for a limited period, and then to buy him out. Bogue, a 'kindly and tolerant' man (Patten, 2.151), was flabbergasted to receive the offer, but he none the less accepted and devoted himself even more concertedly to justifying Tilt's faith in him. Three years later Tilt decided that the substantial assets he had amassed allowed him to retire from business and to travel. Bogue was able to purchase the firm for approximately £50,000 because Tilt made generous provisions for the long-term buy-out of his interest. Within a few years Bogue also bought shares in the *Illustrated Times*. He married and had five children, including a son, David, who went into publishing as well, although he did not thrive, took bankruptcy in 1885, and was found dead on the beach at Folkestone in 1897.

Bogue initiated a European Library of classics reprinted in an inexpensive format and sold for 3*s*. 6*d*. a volume; in it he published historical biographies by Alexandre Dumas and John Galt, among others, and works by François Mignet, William Hazlitt, and Jules Michelet. The success of this enterprise prompted Henry Bohn, who dealt on a large scale with remainders and inexpensive series, to set up a rival Standard Library collection in 1846. Among other purchases Bohn bought up the stock of an illustrated book on Lorenzo de' Medici; at that time copyright in illustrations travelled with the owner of the copyright in the book for which the plates were supplied. When Bogue reprinted these illustrations in William Roscoe's *Life of Lorenzo de' Medici*, Bohn sued. Bogue lost in the court of chancery, and within a few years Bohn purchased Bogue's European Library, folding it into the Standard Library, which eventually reached 150 titles.

Bogue's fortunes declined after the mid-1840s. Although one of his assets was Cruikshank, their various publishing ventures failed. The graphic temperance series *The Bottle* (1847) was 'a positive flop' (Cruikshank to C. P. Pitt, Patten,

2.251); so was its sequel, *The Drunkard's Children* (1848), whose failure led Cruikshank to lament to his publisher 'that England is not California', then in the grip of gold-rush fever (ibid., 2.269). No more successful were comic novels written by Henry and Augustus Mayhew and illustrated by Cruikshank, including *1851*, a story intended to capitalize on the Great Exhibition. Bogue experimented with multi-volume compendia (*Comic Natural History*, 17 vols., *Manuals of Utility*, 8 vols., and *Books for the Race, Road and Fireside*, all 1847), and *Traveller's Guides* (to Belgium and the Rhine, Paris and its environs, Switzerland and Savoy, as well as the *Traveller's Dictionary*, 1852–3). Bogue, who wrote children's stories anonymously, expanded the list of publications for the nursery: for example, eight Little Mary's Books (1847–50, co-published with Joseph Cundall) and Cruikshank's Fairy Library (1853–4), which died after Dickens savaged Cruikshank's temperance slant in a review, 'Frauds on the fairies' (*Household Words*, 1 Oct 1853). Bogue also tried to combine strengths in his list, for instance by melding art with travel and landscape. William Makepeace Thackeray's *Sketches after English Landscape Painters* (1850) was written to accompany reproductive engravings by his Parisian friend Louis Marvy, exiled by the French revolution of 1848. Another expedient Bogue attempted was to introduce the immensely popular French *Physiologies* to Britain; Albert Smith wrote the 'phenomenally successful' first in a projected series of 'social zoologies', on 'gents', but when Bogue's printer Henry Vizetelly asked Thackeray to write as many of these little volumes as he pleased he declined because he did not want to be associated with Smith.

Having suffered from heart disease, Bogue died at his home, 76 Camden Road Villas, Camden Town, London, on 19 November 1856, aged forty-eight. Charles Tilt resumed control of the firm and negotiated with numerous creditors. W. Kent succeeded to the stock and copyrights, but many of the profitable ventures had already been imitated or bought out by Bohn. George Bell of Bell and Daldy negotiated the sale of Cruikshank's temperance prints to W. Tweedie, and in September 1862 Frederick Arnold bought Cruikshankiana held by Bogue's executors against the artist's significant debts to the firm.

ROBERT L. PATTEN

Sources R. L. Patten, *George Cruikshank's life, times, and art*, 2 (1996) • D. B. Mock, 'David Bogue/Tilt and Bogue', *British literary publishing houses, 1820–1880*, ed. P. J. Anderson and J. Rose, DLitB, 106 (1991), 57–8 • L. D. Browning, 'Charles Tilt/Tilt and Bogue', *British literary publishing houses, 1820–1880*, ed. P. J. Anderson and J. Rose, DLitB, 106 (1991), 296–8 • H. Vizetelly, *Glances back through seventy years*, 2 vols. (1893) • *The letters and private papers of William Makepeace Thackeray*, ed. G. N. Ray, 4 vols. (1945–6) • Boase, *Mod. Eng. biog.* • L. Melville, *William Makepeace Thackeray* (1927) • J. Buchanan-Brown, *The book illustrations of George Cruikshank* (1980) • S. Low, ed., *English catalogue of books* (1864) • R. McLean, *Joseph Cundall: a Victorian publisher* (1976) • d. cert.
Archives U. Reading, George Bell & Sons archive

Bogue, Richard (1783–1813), army officer, was the son of John Bogue MD (*d.* 1811) of Fareham, Hampshire, and his wife (*d.* 1806), the eldest daughter of Richard Bargus JP of Fareham. He entered the Royal Military Academy, Woolwich, on 31 January 1797, passing out as a second lieutenant, Royal Artillery, in July 1798, and becoming a captain in March 1806. In June 1813 he went to north Germany with artillery detachments, which were united under his command as a rocket brigade (later the 2nd rocket troop, Royal Artillery), using Congreve rockets. The brigade, the only British unit there, while attached to the army of Bernadotte, the prince royal of Sweden, served at the battle around Leipzig on 16–19 October 1813. On 18 October, while supporting Bulow's corps, which formed the extreme left of Bernadotte's forces, the rocket brigade bombarded the French-held village of Paunsdorff and the enemy, confused, began to retreat. Bogue charged them with his brigade's cavalry escort, a squadron of dragoons. Over 2000 enemy soldiers surrendered. When the rocket brigade then attacked another village and came under heavy fire, Bogue was shot through the head. He was buried next day in the village of Taucha, about 4 miles north-east of Leipzig. He left a widow, the eldest daughter of John Hanson of Great Bromley Hall and of the Rookery, Woodford, Essex, and two infant children. He was awarded, posthumously, the Swedish order of the Sword. His memorial, erected in 1815, is still in Taucha cemetery.

H. M. CHICHESTER, *rev.* ROGER T. STEARN

Sources *GM*, 1st ser., 83/2 (1813), 507 • F. A. Whinyates, 'Captain Bogue and the rocket brigade', *Minutes of the Proceedings of the Royal Artillery Institution*, 24 (1897), 131–6 • F. Duncan, ed., *History of the royal regiment of artillery*, 3rd edn, 2 vols. (1879), vol. 1, pp. 394, 404; vol. 2, p. 290 • marquess of Londonderry [C. S. H. Vane-Tempest-Stewart], *Narrative of the war in Germany and France, in 1813 and 1814* (1830) • W. D. Jones, *Records of the Royal Military Academy (1741–1840)* (1851) • R. Dowling, 'The Richard Bogue monument: a tribute to an early British rocketeer', *Journal of the British Interplanetary Society*, 45 (1992), 285–8 • F. H. Winter, *The first golden age of rocketry* (1990)
Archives Royal Artillery Institution, Woolwich, London, papers
Likenesses portrait, repro. in Dowling, 'The Richard Bogue monument', 285

Bohee, James Douglass (1844–1897), musician, was born in Indiantown, Saint John, New Brunswick, Canada, on 1 December 1844, the second son in the family of seven or eight children of James Bohee, teamster, and his wife, Isabella. Both parents were born in New Brunswick. Bohee's sister Laura (*fl.* 1870–1890) and brother George (*b.* 1856, *d.* after 1905) also became entertainers. St John's black population had its origins in the Caribbean and the USA (those who sided with Britain in the American War of Independence having relocated to Canada) and the Bohee family moved to Boston by 1859; in 1860 James Bohee was listed as a sailor.

Boston was the centre for banjo manufacturing, and James and George Bohee took up that popular instrument. They toured the United States from 1876—from 1878 in Jack Haverley's Genuine Colored Minstrels. By May 1880 they had reached Canada, where James Bohee was reported as the drum major in the troupe's street parades. They opened at Her Majesty's Theatre, London, on 30 July 1880. There were over sixty performers in the troupe, which toured Britain and returned to America in 1882.

James Bohee remained in Britain, owning a minstrel

show that toured theatres and halls for several months each year. As the banjo craze spread across Britain, he provided banjo lessons at his London studio. Among his pupils were Edward, prince of Wales, later Edward VII, and his wife, Alexandra. Edward's louche associates (the bane of his mother, Queen Victoria) were seldom musical, yet through his wife he was involved in the development of the Royal College of Music at this time. James and George Bohee also owned the Gardenia Club in Leicester Square from about 1882, selling it to William Dudley Ward, later MP for Southampton.

The publicity for a short season at the Free Trade Hall, Manchester, in May 1889 described the brothers as 'The famous royal Bohee Bros, banjoists and entertainers to T. R. H. the Prince and Princess of Wales'. This programme stated that James D. Bohee was the world's champion banjo player. As well as singing, George Bohee danced to his brother's banjo and played a banjo duet with him. James provided solos. The brothers, with or without colleagues, 'can be engaged for Private Parties', and banjos 'manufactured by the Messrs. Bohee, and played by them nightly, may be purchased from them … Lessons given' (Lotz, 41, 45). No doubt the banjos were manufactured in Boston and branded with the Bohee name.

James and George Bohee were London institutions by 1890. They often appeared at the Pavilion Theatre. They kept in contact with America, introducing songs and providing employment opportunities. 'Home Sweet Home' and 'A Boy's Best Friend is his Mother' are examples of the sentimental compositions that made them famous. Black Americans who associated with them in England included composer James Bland; actress Amy Height (who remained in England); opera soprano Marie Selika and her husband, baritone Sampson Williams; and the Black Swan Trio.

The Bohees presented a highly musical act, visually attractive, for they played and danced at the same time. Their new songs were widely copied, with one newspaper reporting in 1897 that 'I'll meet her when the sun goes down' was played on every street barrel organ. James Bohee's last public performance on the banjo was in Merthyr Tudful on 1 December 1897, and his death, from pneumonia, was at nearby Ebbw Vale on 8 December. He was buried on 11 December 1897 in Brompton cemetery, London, where his grave is among those of other entertainers. He was married, and his wife survived him. The Bohee brothers had never visited Germany yet Bohee's death was reported in *Der Artist* eleven days after his death. This report described him as 'one of the first of the clever banjo players to visit England' and said that the brothers 'were considered the best banjoists in the world' (*Der Artist*, 19 Dec 1897).

George Bohee went on to work as a solo performer, made recordings (as he and James may have done about 1891), and toured on the new Empire Theatre circuit. His death has been variously dated from 1915 to the 1930s. Had James survived a dozen years the Bohee Brothers would probably have made disc recordings and topped the bill at major British theatres. All those who knew Bohee praised his skills. He was a musical pioneer, an adept instrumentalist, a successful promoter, and active in many aspects of Britain's entertainment world between 1880 and 1897. Obviously of African descent, although light in complexion (in a census of 1860 his father was described as mulatto, his mother as black), he was among the most prominent of the black musical entertainers active in Britain at a time when the larger society associated people of colour with empire and slavery.

JEFFREY GREEN and RAINER E. LOTZ

Sources R. E. Lotz, *Black people: entertainers of African descent in Europe and Germany* (1997) [with audio CD] · R. E. Lotz, 'The Bohee brothers: the 19th century world wide odyssey of two pioneering Afro-Canadian banjoists', *78 Quarterly*, 1/7 (1992) · P. F. Gura and J. F. Bollman, *America's instrument: the banjo in the nineteenth century* (Chapel Hill, 1999) · J. Green, 'British newspapers as source material: the case of James Douglass Bohee (1844–1897)', *Black Music Research Bulletin*, 7/1 (1984) · N. V. Rosenberg, 'Canadian newspapers as source material: further notes on James Douglass Bohee (1844–1897)', *Black Music Research Bulletin*, 10/2 (1987) · E. LeRoy Rice, *Monarchs of minstrelsy* (New York, 1911) · E. Southern, *Biographical dictionary of Afro-American and African musicians* (Westport, 1982) · private information (2004)

Likenesses photographs, repro. in Lotz, *Black people*, pp. 36, 38

Boheme, Anna Maria. *See* Seymour, Anna Maria (*c*.1692–1723).

Boheme, Anthony (*d.* 1732). *See under* Seymour, Anna Maria (*c*.1692–1723).

Boheme [Bohemus], **Mauritius** (*fl.* 1646–1662), clergyman and ejected minister, was born at Kolberg, Pomerania. In a rare reference to Boheme's early life, Simon Ford, minister at Reading, states that 'being a pilgrim in this land, [he hath] by the gracious providence of God been transplanted from his native soil, to labour in Christ's vineyard within this nation', which may encourage the speculation that the family's drastic move was occasioned by zeal or persecution (Bohemus, preface). Certainly Mauritius was the nephew of Johannes Bergius (1587–1658), chaplain to the elector of Brandenburg, but as to the date of his arrival in England it is known only that his parents emigrated some time after the birth in 1628 of Mauritius's younger brother, George (*d.* 1711), later vicar of New Sleaford, Lincolnshire, who after the Restoration was a schoolmaster at Walcot, Lincolnshire.

Boheme became rector of Hallaton, Leicestershire, some time between the death of a previous incumbent, Edward Shield, who was buried on 16 February 1644, and an incident during the last days of the civil war. On 5 April 1646, the county committee was informed, a band of troopers, having deserted the Leicester garrison in search of plunder, arrived in Medbourne and attacked some of its inhabitants. They then plundered the vicarage, where the minister, Mr Doughty, was entertaining Mr Bohemus, minister of neighbouring Hallaton, and both men were fortunate to escape through a side door.

It seems likely that at first Boheme's legal status in the parish was insecure or uncertain; John Walker records that his successor had been sequestered, and Boheme compounded for the south portion of the rectory on 3 September 1651. Boheme was married at least three times, first to Jane, who was buried at Hallaton on 14 December 1647. His second wife, Eizabeth, gave birth to a daughter, Ann, baptized on 12 March 1652, but also died at an early age and was buried on 10 July 1654. On 27 February 1656 Boheme married Hannah Vowe, who gave birth to a son, Samuel, on 15 December 1656.

Mauritius Boheme served as assistant to the Leicestershire and Rutland commission for approving parish ministers in 1654. In that year, he issued *A Christian's Delight, or, Morning Meditations*, with a Latin epistle, dedicating the work to Sir Arthur Heselrige. Evidently the godly ministers of London were anxious to encourage him, for as a second preface by Thomas Jacombe, minister of St Martin Ludgate, reports, several of his brethren in the city, having read the manuscript, 'do unanimously judge this treatise to be sound, wholesome, savouring a spirit of piety'. The following year Boheme issued a translation, dedicated to Cromwell, of an eirenic work by his uncle, Bergius, under the title *A Pearle of Peace and Concorde*. Walker reports that Boheme was ejected by act of parliament in 1660, and it appears that his successor was instituted to the rectory on 10 October in that year. The Leicestershire antiquary John Nichols, however, asserts that a loose parchment in the parish register maintains that Boheme was ousted from Hallaton only in 1662. All authorities are agreed that not long after his ejection Boheme returned to Germany, but nothing is known of his further activities.

STEPHEN WRIGHT

Sources J. Nichols, *The history and antiquities of the county of Leicester*, 2/2 (1798) • *Calamy rev.* • J. Walker, *An attempt towards recovering an account of the numbers and sufferings of the clergy of the Church of England*, 2 pts in 1 (1714) • M. Bohemus, *A Christian's delight, or, Morning meditations* (1654) [with preface by S. Ford] • P. A. Scaysbrook, *The civil war in Leicester and Rutland* (1977)

Bohler, John (1797–1872), botanist, was born at South Wingfield, near Alfreton, Derbyshire, on 31 December 1797. He began work as a stocking-weaver, but his early interest led him to gather plants and he became a collector of medicinal plants for doctors. His expanding knowledge and experience (and perhaps the extirpation of rare saleable plants) permitted him to forgo the patronage of doctors in favour of more scientific pursuits. He became an expert field botanist and microscopist, traversing England, Ireland, and Wales. In time he became acquainted with almost all the indigenous plants, as well as with many fellow botanists.

In 1835–7 Bohler published *Lichenes Britannici, or, Specimens of the Lichens of Britain*, containing sixteen fasciculi, each of eight actual specimens, collected and mounted by him, with original descriptions. About 1860 he explored Snowdon and the adjacent mountains and hills under the auspices of a botanical committee of the British Association. As well as papers in scientific journals, his publications include a list of the plants of Roche Abbey in an appendix to Dr Aveling's *Roche Abbey, Yorkshire* (1870), and a description of the flora of Sherwood Forest in Robert White's *Nottinghamshire* (1875). Later in life he became a great collector of rare fungi, gathered from widely scattered localities throughout the land. He died at Sheffield on 24 September 1872.

JOHN WESTBY-GIBSON, *rev.* P. E. KELL

Sources R. White, *Nottinghamshire: Worksop, the Dukery, and Sherwood Forest* (1875) • J. Holland, 'Cheap Tommy', *The Reliquary*, 11 (1870), 212–13 • B. D. Jackson, *Guide to the literature of botany* (1881) • G. A. Pritzel, ed., *Thesaurus literaturae botanicae omnium gentium* (Leipzig, 1851)

Bohm, David Joseph (1917–1992), physicist and philosopher, was born on 20 December 1917 in Wilkes-Barre, Pennsylvania, USA, the son of Samuel Bohm, proprietor of a furniture store, and his wife, Freda. Both parents were immigrants from Europe, his father being born in the Ukraine. Bohm graduated from Pennsylvania State College in 1939 and after a period at the California Institute of Technology moved to Berkeley where he studied for his PhD on proton–deuteron scattering under Robert Oppenheimer. He then began work on plasmas and established his reputation as a theoretical physicist developing important theoretical techniques to describe collective oscillations of plasmas and deriving a formula for what has become known as the Bohm diffusion coefficient. After moving to Princeton in 1947, working with his research student, David Pines, Bohm was able to extend these ideas to the description of electrons in metals, laying the foundations of our understanding of the collective behaviour of electrons in metals. Problems in the interpretation of quantum theory fascinated him and he set out to write a book which would make the widely accepted Copenhagen interpretation of quantum theory, with its inherent randomness and observer dependence, as clear as possible. His *Quantum Theory* (1951) has become a classic in the field and is remarkable for its clarity and physical insight; his formulation of the Einstein–Podolsky–Rosen experiment formed the basis of important experimental tests of quantum theory and his discussion of the theory of measurement became the standard. Not satisfied with the Copenhagen interpretation, Bohm developed a causal interpretation of quantum theory, which he published in the *Physical Review* in 1952. Similar ideas had been published previously by Louis de Broglie and the interpretation became known as the de Broglie–Bohm interpretation. This interpretation brought out the revolutionary features of quantum theory in a clear and accessible way, without the postulate of inherent randomness in nature. Bohm's approach made clear the essential unity of quantum phenomena manifested in his approach through a non-local connection of distant events. Difficulties with the House Un-American Activities Committee led to Bohm's being suspended from Princeton, but supported by both Einstein and Oppenheimer he obtained a professorship at the University of São Paulo in 1951.

In 1955 Bohm moved to the Technion-Israel Institute of Technology in Haifa where he met Saral (Sarah) Woolfson, the daughter of an English doctor; they were married in March 1956 and had no children. They moved to England in 1957 and Bohm took up a fellowship at Bristol University where, with Yakir Aharonov, he published a paper on the magnetic vector potential describing an effect now known as the Aharonov–Bohm effect. In 1961 Bohm was appointed to the newly created chair of theoretical physics at Birkbeck College, where he remained until his retirement in 1983. Bohm believed that the problems faced by modern physics could not be solved in a truly satisfactory manner within the usual Cartesian conceptual framework and sought to construct a description based on the notion of primitive processes out of which space, time, and matter would emerge. Working with Basil Hiley, he investigated the use of algebraic structures to describe such primitive processes. A renewed interest in his interpretation of quantum theory was stimulated in the late 1970s when his research students began to use computational techniques to calculate quantum particle trajectories in order to demonstrate exactly how the theory worked. After years of neglect Bohm's interpretation is now widely accepted as a viable alternative to Bohr's Copenhagen interpretation.

In concert with Bohm's work in physics he maintained a deep interest in wider philosophical issues; he explored notions of wholeness and fragmentation across a wide spectrum of thought, and his insight was valued in diverse disciplines. Many of his general ideas on language and thought arose from his friendship and collaboration with Jiddo Krishnamurti, an Indian philosopher and teacher. Their formal dialogues, held in Switzerland, California, and England, were recorded and some were published. Bohm was for some years a trustee of Krishnamurti's foundation school in Hampshire. Bohm was elected fellow of the Royal Society in 1990 and was awarded the Franklin Institute's Elliott Cresson medal in 1991. He died in Edgware General Hospital on 27 October 1992. CHRIS DEWDNEY

Sources B. J. Hiley, *Memoirs FRS*, 43 (1997), 107–31 • D. F. Peat, *Infinite potential* (1996) • *WWW* • B. J. Hiley, *The Independent* (30 Oct 1992) • *The Times* (9 Dec 1992) • *New York Times* (29 Oct 1992) • *Nature*, 360 (12 Nov 1992), 107 • d. cert. • *CGPLA Eng. & Wales* (1993)

Archives Birkbeck College, London, corresp. and papers

Wealth at death £68,918: probate, 6 Aug 1993, *CGPLA Eng. & Wales*

Bohn, Henry George (1796–1884), translator and publisher, was born on 4 January 1796 and baptized in London on 7 February, the first of four sons of John Henry Martin Bohn (*c*.1757–1843), of Münster, Westphalia, Germany, and Elizabeth Watt, niece of James Watt, inventor of the steam engine; one of his brothers was the bookseller James *Bohn. Bohn was educated at George III's expense, his father being the court bookseller. When he left school he joined his father's second-hand bookselling business. After a disagreement with him, he spent a short but successful period working in the City, before being persuaded to return to the family business. At an early age Bohn was entrusted by his father with the purchase of rare books. He travelled to the chief continental centres of the book trade and was one of the few bidders at a book fair at Leipzig on the day of the battle of Waterloo. While working for his father, he began his career as a translator, largely of German authors, although he was also fluent in French. His translations of Schiller and Humboldt afterwards appeared in his Foreign Classics series. He also gained experience of antiquarian books by cataloguing his father's acquisitions and by compiling a list of the library of Samuel Parr, which his father and J. Mawman published in 1827. Later, he assisted William Beckford and the duke of Hamilton in the acquisition of their libraries, being employed by the latter to compile a handlist of his collection.

Henry George Bohn (1796–1884), by Mayall

Bohn, however, began to perceive that there was little hope of a partnership, and so, with the experience in his father's business behind him and a starting capital of £2000, he set up his own firm at 4 York Street, Covent Garden, London, in 1831, subsequently expanding to take over the neighbouring two houses. In the same year he married Elizabeth Lamb Simpkin (*c*.1802–1890), only child of the bookseller William Simpkin. They had three sons and one daughter.

His father let Bohn have some remainders at cost price and enabled him to buy stock on the continent before he started up on his own. In 1841, after ten further years of quiet progress, he astounded the book world with his guinea catalogue, so called because of its price. It cost Bohn upwards of £2000 to make and was famous not only for its size—it contained over 23,000 articles and, with a list of remainders 152 pages long, was the largest of its day—but also for its descriptions of the works for sale. It became a collector's item in its own right and made Bohn's reputation as a second-hand bookseller.

In 1843 Bohn's father died and his brother James went bankrupt. Family tensions developed, and, possibly unaware that his father had left instructions that his book stock was to be divided and sold at different auction houses, Bohn sought to dispose of the stock himself. His brothers disputed his right to do so and brought an injunction against him. The matter was resolved and James put back on his feet with the help of his brother John and three investors.

Shortly after this, Bohn turned to the remainder trade, reissuing dependable and instructive works in cheap formats. The stimulus for this was a dispute with David Bogue of Fleet Street who had published in his European Library series a life of Lorenzo de' Medici containing illustrations for which Bohn owned the copyright. Bohn brought an injunction against Bogue, and started a cheaper, rival series, his Standard Library. When Bogue went out of business, Bohn added the European Library to his own series. The Standard Library was soon followed by the Scientific and the Antiquarian (1847), Classical (1848), Illustrated (1849), Shilling (1850), Ecclesiastical (1851), Philological (1852), and British Classics (1853) series, together with further Collegiate, Historical, and Uniform series—over 600 volumes in all. The libraries represented one of the boldest and most successful experiments in publishing serious works at low prices—initially the Standard Library retailed at 3*s.* 6*d.* per volume, while later additions were priced at 5*s.* The libraries were successful largely because of Bohn's personal commitment to the project. He was a practical and shrewd man in business, an energetic worker, and tireless promoter of his libraries. He wrote, edited, translated, and indexed works he believed would enhance the series and selected the best of his remaindered copyrights for the purpose. The *Gentleman's Magazine* commented that these cheap editions 'established the habit in middle-class life, of purchasing books instead of obtaining them from a library' (*GM*, 5th ser., 257, 1884, 413), and Ralph Waldo Emerson said that Bohn had done 'as much for literature as railroads have done for internal intercourse' (Mumby, 400).

Bohn sold many of his works overseas and was all too aware of the problems of international copyright. On one occasion, Bohn's publication of Washington Irving's work, to which John Murray claimed the British rights, brought into public debate the issue of the protection of American copyright in Britain. His strong feelings on the issue led Bohn to publish a report of a public meeting held on 1 July 1851 on the question and he later claimed that he had been 'a main instigator and abettor in overthrowing American and other foreign pretences of copyright in this country' (Bohn, 6). Bohn was also an advocate of free trade in books and in 1852 campaigned as a member of the booksellers' committee against restrictions on their sale. The free traders won their point by the majority of a single vote and the Booksellers' Association was disbanded. Eight years later he objected to the abolition of paper duty, believing it would not lead to the fall of paper prices but to increased foreign competition in the manufacture and export of books to the colonial market. This time the political tide was against him and the paper duty was abolished.

When it became evident that his sons did not wish to follow him into the business, Bohn decided to retire and sell his various enterprises. In 1864 he sold the stock, copyrights, and stereotypes of the libraries and some other works to Bell and Daldy for £40,000 and they moved into his York Street premises. They continued to publish the libraries, adding their own series including the Reference (1875), Novel (1876), Artists (1877), Economics (1881), Select (1888), and Sports and Games (1891) libraries. In 1921 the last new title was added to Bohn libraries. In January 1875 Bohn sold the remainder of his publishing business to Chatto and Windus for about £20,000.

Bohn withheld two favourite works from this deal: his *Dictionary of Quotations* (1867), into which he introduced a few verses from his own manuscript poems, and George Gordon's *Pinetum* (1875), to which he added an index and a list of plates from three earlier nineteenth-century botanical works. His friendship with the author encouraged him in his own enthusiasm for gardening at his home at North End House, Twickenham, Middlesex, which he had bought in 1850. His remarkable collection of conifers, rare shrubs, and roses was displayed in annual entertainments attended by Charles Dickens, George Cruikshank, and others, and his plants frequently figured in illustrated gardening journals.

After the sale of his publishing business Bohn catalogued his general second-hand stock which he kept in several Covent Garden warehouses, and secured temporary premises at his father's former business address in Henrietta Street. His contribution to bibliography resides largely in his enlargement and revision of W. T. Lowndes's *Bibliographer's Manual* (1864) carried out between 1857 and 1858, which is based on the knowledge he had gained through his acquisitions. The auction of Bohn's collection in 1872 contained many rare and valuable books including some volumes from the library of Horace Walpole. It raised above £13,500.

Many of Bohn's original works testify to his practical involvement in the projects he endorsed. For instance, he published a working plan to create a catalogue of the library of the British Museum, and played an important role in the Great Exhibition in 1851 and in the subsequent Crystal Palace Company. He also wrote for the Philobiblon Society on the progress of printing and contributed a *Biography and Bibliography of Shakespeare* (1864), drawing on his revised edition of Lowndes. Through his participation and regular attendance at meetings and debates, he played a valuable part in the life of the societies of which he was a member. These included the Society of Antiquaries, and the Royal Horticultural, Linnean, and the Royal Geographical societies.

One of the works Bohn contributed to his libraries was a guide to the collection of pottery, which grew out of his own interest in and knowledge of the subject. He had begun collecting seriously in the mid-1830s, accumulating a historical collection of rare and curious examples of pottery including some fifty pieces of so-called Lowestoft porcelain and earthenware, some bought from descendants of workers. Between 1875 and 1878 he sold this collection together with his china, porcelain, and ivories, raising nearly £25,000. After the sale, and with more room in his house, he turned his mind to pictures and in his eighties he compiled a catalogue raisonné. He revised the proof just before his death and his daughter, Elizabeth Munton, finalized the catalogue. Speculating on the size of her father's collections his daughter estimated he 'must have bought about a dozen [pictures or virtu] a month for 50 consecutive years' (*The Times*, 1 April 1885). The final part of his art collection was sold in March 1885 raising about a further £20,000. Bohn died on 22 August 1884 at his home, North End House. ALEXIS WEEDON

Sources F. A. Mumby, *The romance of bookselling* (1910) · E. Bell, *George Bell, publisher: a brief memoir* (1924) · D. Mock, 'H. G. Bohn', *British literary publishing houses, 1820–1880*, ed. P. J. Anderson and J. Rose, DLitB, 106 (1991), 59–62 · *The Bookseller* (4 Sept 1884) · *Publishers' Circular* (1 Sept 1884) · *The Garden* (30 Aug 1884) · H. G. Bohn, *The paper duty* (1860) · reports of auctions, *The Times* (2 June 1870) · reports of auctions, *The Times* (18 July 1872) · reports of auctions, *The Times* (15–16 March 1875) · reports of auctions, *The Times* (20 March 1875) · reports of auctions, *The Times* (21 June 1875) · reports of auctions, *The Times* (28 March 1876) · *The Times* (25 Aug 1884) · report of auctions, *The Times* (27 Dec 1884) · reports of auctions, *The Times* (1 April 1885) · reports of auctions, *The Times* (15–16 Oct 1890) · *IGI* · Desmond, *Botanists*
Archives Bodl. Oxf., corresp. with William Beckford · Bodl. Oxf., letters and bills to Sir Thomas Phillipps · NRA Scotland, priv. coll., letters to the duke of Hamilton · U. Edin., corresp. with James Halliwell-Phillipps · U. Reading, George Bell & Sons archive
Likenesses Mayall, photograph, NPG [*see illus.*]
Wealth at death £34,150 12*s*. 6*d*.: probate, 4 Sept 1884, *CGPLA Eng. & Wales*

Bohn, James George Stuart Burges (1803–1880), bookseller and bibliographer, was born on 20 December 1803 in London, the son of (John) Henry Martin Bohn (*c*.1757–1843), bookseller of London, and his wife, Elizabeth, niece of James Watt. The translator and publisher Henry George *Bohn (1796–1884) was his brother. He was educated at Winchester College, and was also sent to Göttingen to study German and French.

Bohn assisted in his father's business for some years, and in February 1834 began bookselling on his own account at 12 King William Street, Strand, London, where his knowledge of literature and bibliography soon attracted customers. Bohn's shop became a meeting place for a number of distinguished scholars and Bohn published catalogues in 1834 and 1837. Then in 1840 he produced a substantial catalogue which became a reference source for bibliographers; it included nearly complete lists of the works of Gilbert Burnet, Daniel Defoe, Thomas Hearne, and Joseph Ritson. Despite these accomplishments, or perhaps because they were unprofitable, this first shop failed as a business.

Bohn's second bookselling venture lasted from 1845 until 1847, this time at 66 St James's Street, London. Here he published an eight-volume edition of Sir William Dugdale's *Monasticon Anglicanum* (1846). After this second business failed in 1847 he made his living by writing. Bohn's work included contributions to the *Family Herald* and service as assistant editor on *The Reader*. In 1857 he prepared another scholarly catalogue, this time of theological books in foreign languages, for the bookseller David Nutt. In later years he was employed to compile catalogues of foreign-language books for his friend Nicholas Trübner, the bookseller. James Bohn died at Peckham, London, on 4 January 1880.

G. C. BOASE, *rev.* LESLIE HOWSAM

Sources *The Bookseller* (3 Feb 1880), 105–6 · *IGI*

Bohun, Edmund (1645–1699), writer and press licenser, was born on 12 March 1645 at Ringsfield, Suffolk, the only son of Baxter Bohun (*bap*. 1616, *d*. 1658) and his wife, Margaret Lawrence (*d*. 1687). Edmund's father and grandfather, also Edmund, both died in 1658, leaving the thirteen-year-old boy the family's estates in Suffolk. On 11 February 1662 Edmund was admitted as a fellow-commoner to Queens' College, Cambridge, but he left in 1666 without a degree, apparently having been driven out by the plague. On 26 July 1669 he married Mary Brampton (*d*. 1719), and the following year they settled at Westhall Hall, near Halesworth. He became a Suffolk justice of the peace in 1675. From 1677 Bohun wrote a diary intermittently which charted his struggle with debts, deafness, and the damage wrought by his abrasive personality. In his first published work, *An Address to the Free-Men and Free-holders of the Nation*, which appeared in three parts in 1682–3, he recalled that he had been 'bred a dissenter … and taught betimes to fear Monarchy', but as JP and writer he assailed religious diversity and disloyalty to *jure divino* kingship (*Address*, 3). An adversary called him 'as furious a Prosecutor of Protestant Dissenters as was to be found in England', although John Dunton praised him for 'a wit so pregnant and prompt' (Blount, 17; *Diary*, 100).

In 1684 Bohun moved with his wife to London, aiming to write to 'earn my bread' and hoping for preferment from acquaintances including Archbishop William Sancroft (*Diary*, 77). In 1684 he wrote *A Defence of Sir Robert Filmer* against Algernon Sidney's scaffold speech, and in 1685 he published and prefaced an edition of Filmer's *Patriarcha*, based on a manuscript supplied by Sancroft. In 1688 Bohun witnessed William of Orange's entry into London and argued against continued support for James II, with the result that 'by the end of February, I had not one friend left' (ibid., 83). His *History of the Desertion*, published in April 1689, provided one of the first narratives of the 'Stupendious Revolution' (p. 13), while the apparent volte-face on his part was discountenanced by *The doctrine of non-resistance or passive obedience no way concerned in the controversies now depending between the Williamites and the Jacobites* (1689). His acceptance of William alienated his Jacobite acquaintances but he was also a target for the whigs, both generally for his tory views and because of allegedly pro-James changes made without his knowledge to a second edition of his 1688 *Geographical Dictionary*.

Despite this unpopularity, in August 1692 Bohun was recommended for the post of licenser of the press by John

Moore, bishop of Norwich, assisted by a manuscript defence he wrote of the 1662 Licensing Act. He took up the post on 7 September, at £200 a year, and 'thought myself the happiest man alive' (*Diary*, 98). The happiness was short-lived. On 2 December he heard that his son Humphrey, the eldest of six children surviving childhood, had died at Cambridge (ibid.). Then on 11 January 1693 Bohun licensed an anonymous tract attributed to Charles Blount, *King William and Queen Mary conquerors, or, A discourse endeavouring to prove that their majesties have, on their side against the late king, the principal reasons that make conquest a good title*. Bohun, who had used conquest arguments in his *History*, said he read the book 'with incredible satisfaction'. However, when it was published a few days later, 'the title alone offended almost everybody' (ibid., 103). The Commons ordered Bohun's arrest, burnt the book, and declared that asserting William and Mary to be king and queen by conquest undermined their rightful title and the rights of the English people. On 28 January Bohun was removed from his post. The episode suggested the unworkability of the licensing system and within two years the Licensing Act lapsed, ending pre-publication censorship. A traditional view held that Bohun's endorsement of conquest theory was so singular that the book was a satire intended to trap him, but more recently Bohun's own claim that the subject had 'been treated of very often before' has been largely confirmed (ibid.). In the *History*, a manuscript account, and the *Diary* Bohun deployed a *jus gentium* argument derived from Grotius to insist that William's and Mary's title was not founded on *de facto* conquest 'but upon her majesty's hereditary title, brought into present possession by the vanquishing of King James in a just war, and his deserting the kingdom' (ibid., 119–20). Bohun protested that his dismissal was based not only on a failure to read the book but to read the full title, which indicated that the conquest was of James, not of the nation.

Bohun saw the affair as a plot to remove him, evidenced by the publication by an 'outrageous whig' of *The Just and True Character of Edmund Bohun*, appended to a tract against licensing (*Diary*, 100). He returned to Suffolk but complained of being ejected as a JP 'by the republican party'. In 1698 Bohun left England to become chief justice of South Carolina, where his son Edmund was a merchant. Letters indicate that he managed to antagonize several settlers before falling victim to a fever epidemic. He died on 5 October 1699. Bohun's eight-volume collection of printed and manuscript tracts and papers, covering 1675–92, is in Cambridge University Library. GEOFF KEMP

Sources *The diary and autobiography of Edmund Bohun, esq.*, ed. S. Wilton Rix (New York, 1975) · [C. Blount], *Reasons humbly offered for the liberty of unlicens'd printing, to which is subjoin'd, The just and true character of Edmund Bohun* (1693) · Wood, *Ath. Oxon.*, new edn [Degorie Whear] · T. B. Macaulay, *The history of England from the accession of James II*, abridged edn, 2 (1889), 409–16 · M. Goldie, 'Edmund Bohun and *jus gentium* in the revolution debate, 1689–1693', *HJ*, 20 (1977), 569–86 · *An account of Mr. Blunts late book, entituled, 'King William and Queen Mary conquerors', now under the censure of the parliament* (1693) · [E. Bohun], *An address to the free-men and freeholders of the nation*, 3 pts (1682–3) · CUL, Bohun collection, Sel. 3.238 (344), Sel. 3.238 (359) · *IGI* · Venn, *Alum. Cant.*

Archives Bodl. Oxf., corresp. · CUL, collection, Sel. 3.230–3.238

Wealth at death see will repro. in *Diary and autobiography*, ed. Wilton Rix, xxx–xxxi

Bohun, Henry de, first earl of Hereford (1176–1220), magnate, was the son of Humphrey (III) de *Bohun (*d.* 1181) and Margaret (*d.* 1201), daughter of Henry of Scotland and widow of Conan (IV), duke of Brittany. He was identified in 1185 as a minor in the custody of his grandmother, Margaret de Bohun (*d.* 1187), daughter of Miles of Gloucester, earl of Hereford. She was administering his estates in 1187, but he had been given control of his own lands by 1190. He attested a number of her charters and accounted for relief for her lands in 1197. The elder Margaret brought to the Bohuns her family's claims to a royal constableship and to the earldom of Hereford. The office of constable had been granted to her son, Humphrey (III) de Bohun by 1174 and was inherited by Henry de Bohun, who styled himself 'Henry the constable' in a number of his early charters. Despite his youth he occasionally attested charters of Richard I and was one of the king's sureties in negotiations with the count of Flanders in 1197. He married Maud or Matilda, the daughter of Geoffrey fitz Peter, earl of Essex. Charters issued to Llanthony Priory by Henry, as earl of Hereford, indicate that their son, Humphrey (IV) de *Bohun, was born after 28 April 1199.

King John created Bohun earl of Hereford by charter on 28 April 1199, explicitly prohibiting him, with Bohun's acquiescence, from making any claims by virtue of a charter issued by Henry II to his ancestor Roger, earl of Hereford. His grandmother's determination was a factor in this process of restitution, but his political significance also owed much to the fact that his mother was a granddaughter of *David I, king of Scots, and that, in 1199, the king of Scots was his uncle, *William the Lion. Between 1204 and 1211 he was engaged in a long dispute to establish his claim to part of his mother's dower lands, the estates and twenty fees of the lordship of Ratho, Edinburghshire. Relations between King John and Earl Henry deteriorated in 1212 when William (I) Longespée, earl of Salisbury, laid claim to Bohun's honour of Trowbridge. The king assumed control of the honour, but allowed Earl William's agents to levy scutage from its tenants. In protest Bohun joined the rebels against the king, and was one of the twenty-five barons appointed to ensure that Magna Carta was observed. His lands were seized by the crown in June 1215, and he secured the restoration of his honour, although not of Trowbridge Castle, later in the year.

On John's death Earl Henry remained loyal to Louis of France, and was taken prisoner at the battle of Lincoln on 20 May 1217. He made peace with the new government, attending the court of the young Henry III, receiving the third penny of Herefordshire, and accounting for scutage. He died on pilgrimage to the Holy Land on 1 June 1220; the transfer to his son, Humphrey, of his responsibilities and eventually his lands was in hand before Michaelmas 1221.

DAVID WALKER

Sources *Calendar of the fine rolls*, 22 vols., PRO (1911–62) • L. Landon, *The itinerary of King Richard I*, PRSoc., new ser., 13 (1935) • L. Landon, ed., *The cartae antiquae: rolls 1–10, printed from the original in the custody of the master of the rolls*, PRSoc., 55, new ser., 17 (1939) • D. Walker, ed., 'Charters of the earldom of Hereford, 1095–1201', *Camden miscellany, XXII*, CS, 4th ser., 1 (1964), 1–75 • W. Farrer and others, eds., *Early Yorkshire charters*, 12 vols. (1914–65), vol. 4 • G. W. S. Barrow, ed., *Regesta regum Scottorum*, 2 (1971) • W. H. Hart, ed., *Historia et cartularium monasterii Sancti Petri Gloucestriae*, 3 vols., Rolls Series, 33 (1863–7) • D. M. Stenton, ed., *Pleas before the king or his justices, 1198–1212*, 3, SeldS, 83 (1967) • T. D. Hardy, ed., *Rotuli chartarum in Turri Londinensi asservati*, RC, 36 (1837) • *The historical works of Gervase of Canterbury*, ed. W. Stubbs, 2 vols., Rolls Series, 73 (1879–80) • *Chronica magistri Rogeri de Hovedene*, ed. W. Stubbs, 4 vols., Rolls Series, 51 (1868–71) • Paris, *Chron.* • J. C. Holt, *Magna Carta* (1965), appx 7 • GEC, *Peerage*
Archives Bodl. Oxf., MS Dugdale 17

Bohun, Humphrey (II) de (*d.* **1164/5**). *See under* Bohun, Humphrey (III) de (*b.* before 1144, *d.* 1181).

Bohun, Humphrey (III) de (*b.* before **1144**, *d.* **1181**), constable to Henry II, was the son and heir of Humphrey (II) de Bohun [*see below*] and his wife, Margaret (*d.* 1187), the eldest daughter of Miles of *Gloucester, earl of Hereford. The family name was derived from St Georges de Bohon in the Cotentin, from where Humphrey (III)'s great-grandfather, Humphrey 'with the beard', came to England with William the Conqueror. During William Rufus's reign this Humphrey's son, normally described as Humphrey (I) de Bohun, married Maud, the daughter of Edward of Salisbury, and as a result acquired estates based on Trowbridge, Wiltshire. He died *c.*1123, leaving **Humphrey (II) de Bohun** (*d.* 1164/5), who with his mother, Maud, founded the Cluniac priory at Monkton Farleigh, Wiltshire, evidently in fulfilment of his father's wishes. In 1130 Humphrey (II) de Bohun still owed relief for his father's land, plus 400 marks for the purchase of a royal stewardship. As steward he witnessed charters of Henry I towards the end of his reign, and also King Stephen's Oxford charter of liberties in 1136. However, he deserted to the Empress Matilda on her arrival in England in 1139 and successfully defended his castle at Trowbridge against the king. In 1144 he received from the empress confirmation of his lands and of his 'stewardship in England and Normandy', with a grant of other estates. He was loyal to the Angevins in the civil war, witnessing as steward both for the empress in the 1140s and for Henry II, before and after his accession as king, between 1153 and 1157. However, during the year 1158 he was deprived of former royal demesne which he was holding in Wiltshire. None of the royal charters he attested can with certainty be dated to 1158 or later, and it may be that he fell out of the king's favour. On the other hand he was present at the promulgation of the constitutions of Clarendon in January 1164. He was dead by Michaelmas 1165, when his son Humphrey (III) de Bohun owed 300 marks as relief. In the following year his widow, Margaret, who had become coheir to Miles of Gloucester following the deaths of her brothers, answered for the knights' fees which formed her share of the inheritance, and which passed to Humphrey (III) de Bohun along with the Bohun lands in Wiltshire.

Humphrey (III) de Bohun attested several of Henry II's charters as constable, an office previously held by Miles of Gloucester, and distinguished himself on the king's side in the war of 1173–4. He was in the royal army at Breteuil in August 1173, and with the justiciar Richard de Lucy later sacked Berwick and led troops into Lothian against William the Lion, king of Scots, before having to return south to deal with rebellion in England. In October 1173 he featured prominently in the defeat and capture of the earl of Leicester and others at Fornham near Bury St Edmunds. He witnessed the treaty of Falaise between Henry II and the king of Scots at the close of 1174. Through his marriage, which took place between February 1171 and Easter 1175, to Margaret (*d.* 1201), daughter of Henry of Scotland, earl of Northumberland (*d.* 1152), and widow of Conan (IV), duke of Brittany (*d.* 1171), he became brother-in-law to the king of Scots. He died while a member of the army led into France towards the end of 1181 by Henry II's sons to assist Philippe II against the count of Flanders, and was buried at Llanthony (Secunda) Priory, Gloucestershire. He left a daughter, Matilda, and a son, Henry de *Bohun, who in 1187 was a minor in the custody of Margaret de Bohun, the widow of Humphrey (II) de Bohun.

GRAEME WHITE

Sources Dugdale, *Monasticon*, new edn, vols. 5–6 • R. Howlett, ed., *Chronicles of the reigns of Stephen, Henry II, and Richard I*, 3–4, Rolls Series, 82 (1886–9) • K. R. Potter and R. H. C. Davis, eds., *Gesta Stephani*, OMT (1976) • *Reg. RAN*, vols. 2–3 • W. Stubbs, ed., *Gesta regis Henrici secundi Benedicti abbatis: the chronicle of the reigns of Henry II and Richard I*, AD *1169–1192*, 2 vols., Rolls Series, 49 (1867), vol. 1 • R. W. Eyton, *Court, household, and itinerary of King Henry II* (1878) • J. H. Round, ed., *Calendar of documents preserved in France, illustrative of the history of Great Britain and Ireland* (1899) • *Pipe rolls* • GEC, *Peerage* • I. J. Sanders, *English baronies: a study of their origin and descent, 1086–1327* (1960) • *VCH Wiltshire* • L. C. Loyd, *The origins of some Anglo-Norman families*, ed. C. T. Clay and D. C. Douglas, Harleian Society, 103 (1951) • K. Major, ed., *Acta Stephani Langton*, CYS, 50 (1950) • L. F. Salzman, *The Wiltshire, Devonshire and Dorsetshire portion of the Lewes chartulary*, ed. W. Budgen (1943) • *Materials for the history of Thomas Becket, archbishop of Canterbury*, 5, ed. J. C. Robertson, Rolls Series, 67 (1881)

Bohun, Humphrey (IV) de, second earl of Hereford and seventh earl of Essex (*d.* **1275**), magnate, was the eldest son of Henry de *Bohun, first earl of Hereford, and Matilda or Maud, daughter of Geoffrey fitz Peter, earl of Essex, and sister and heir of William de Mandeville, earl of Essex. His father (the first Bohun earl of Hereford) died in June 1220, and in June the following year, at the petition of King Alexander of Scotland and the barons of England, Humphrey was permitted to succeed to the family estates, concentrated for the most part in the Welsh marches and in Wiltshire, including the castle of Caldicot in Monmouthshire and a share of the honour of Trowbridge. Through the marriage of Humphrey's grandfather to Margaret, sister of King William of Scotland, the Bohuns also controlled a considerable estate in Scotland. In February 1225 Humphrey de Bohun witnessed the reissue of Magna Carta as earl of Hereford, and his title to the third penny of the county of Hereford was confirmed in October 1225, presumably at the same time that he was belted as earl. William de Mandeville died in 1227, leaving Bohun's mother as countess of Essex for the remainder of her life. Following her death in August 1236 Bohun succeeded to her title, and to the honour and castle of Pleshey in Essex. Earl Humphrey married twice. His first wife was Matilda, daughter of Raoul de Lusignan, count of Eu (*d.* 1219), whom he had married by 1238 and who brought her husband various lands in Kent. She died on 14 August 1241 and was buried at Llanthony. He married second Matilda of Avebury, who died on 8 October 1273 at Sorges in the Dordogne.

In 1227 Bohun joined the earls of Cornwall, Chester, and Pembroke in their brief confederation against the king, but he served on the king's expedition to Brittany in 1230, and, at the coronation of Queen Eleanor in 1236, carried out the ceremonial duties of marshal of the king's household. In 1237 he made a pilgrimage to Santiago de Compostela, and in 1239 he was one of the sponsors at the baptism of Edward, the king's first-born son. From 1239 until 1241 he was sheriff of Kent and constable of Dover. He took part in the king's expedition to Poitou in 1242, and in 1244 assisted the repression of a Welsh rising on the marches. However, later that same year the Welsh rose again, angered, it was said, by Bohun's retention of the dower lands of Isabella de Briouze, his son's sister-in-law and the wife of Dafydd, son of the Welsh prince Llywelyn ab Iorwerth (*d.* 1240). In 1246 Bohun was among the English barons who wrote to the pope in defence of the liberties of the church in England. In 1250 he took vows as a crusader, but seems not to have gone on crusade. Two years later he was one of the barons who spoke in defence of Simon de Montfort against the king. In 1253 he joined the king's expedition to Gascony, but took offence at the actions of the king's Lusignan half-brothers who had inflicted summary punishment upon various Welsh mercenaries, without referring the case to the court over which Bohun presided as hereditary constable of the king's army. As a result he returned to England together with various other leading barons. In 1257 he was one of those set to defend the marches against attacks from the Welsh.

Humphrey de Bohun joined the confederation of the barons in 1258, and was appointed to enforce the sentence of banishment imposed upon the king's Lusignan kinsmen. Under the provisions of Oxford, he was elected to the baronial council of fifteen and in 1260 was nominated as justice on eyre for the counties of Gloucester, Worcester, and Hereford. Thereafter, however, he broke with the party of Simon de Montfort, and renewed his support for the king, receiving custody of the Welsh lands of the honour of Gloucester between July 1262 and August 1263. He was one of the royalists captured at the battle of Lewes in May 1264, in which his son, Humphrey (V) de Bohun (known as Humphrey the younger), took the side of the barons. Humphrey the younger was himself taken prisoner during the royalist victory at Evesham in 1265, after which Earl Humphrey obtained the reversion of his son's lands. In October 1265 he served as royalist keeper of the city of London, and in 1266 was one of the arbiters appointed to administer the dictum of Kenilworth. He died on 24 September 1275 and was buried at Llanthony (Prima) Priory, in Monmouthshire.

Shortly before his death Bohun had conveyed the honour of Pleshey to his younger son, Henry de Bohun. The remainder of his estate passed to his grandson, Humphrey (VI) de *Bohun (*d.* 1298), son and heir of Humphrey the younger, who had died in captivity on 27 October 1265, at Beeston Castle, near Chester. Besides his son Humphrey, Bohun had other sons named Henry, John, and Savaric, and at least four daughters, including Matilda, the wife of Anselm Marshal, earl of Pembroke (*d.* 1245). He was a regular though not lavish patron of the religious orders, granting and confirming lands to Llanthony, to the Mandeville abbey of Walden in Essex, and shortly before his death to the nuns of Lacock in Wiltshire. Despite his supposed hostility to the king's alien courtiers, it is intriguing to note the Poitevin and Gascon connections of both of his wives. NICHOLAS VINCENT

Sources chancery rolls • GEC, *Peerage* • Paris, *Chron.* • *Ann. mon.* • Dugdale, *Monasticon*, new edn, 6.135 • K. H. Rogers, ed., *Lacock Abbey charters*, Wilts RS, 34 (1979) • obituary notice, Llanthony Priory
Archives PRO, chancery rolls

Bohun, Humphrey (VI) de, third earl of Hereford and eighth earl of Essex (*c.*1249–1298), magnate, was the son of Humphrey (V) de Bohun (*d.* 1265) and Eleanor, daughter and coheir of William (V) de Briouze (*d.* 1230) and his wife, Eva, one of the daughters and coheirs of William (II) *Marshal. Humphrey inherited his titles and paternal lands, centred in Essex and Wiltshire, directly from his grandfather, Humphrey (IV) de *Bohun, on the latter's death in 1275. Through his mother Humphrey (VI) gained a significant stake in the march of Wales, consequently playing a leading role in the Welsh wars as well as in the politics of Edward I's reign.

Humphrey (VI) de Bohun's father was wounded and captured at the battle of Evesham in 1264 and died in captivity the following year. His son was only sixteen, so the Briouze lands were taken into royal custody. Henry III granted the marcher lordship of Brecon to Gilbert de Clare, earl of Gloucester, along with the heir's marriage. Bohun inherited his mother's lands when he came of age in 1270, and promised Gloucester £1000 for his marriage, but Brecon was controlled by Llywelyn ap Gruffudd, who had conquered much of the Welsh marches in 1262–3. Indeed, Bohun had earlier joined his father in the struggle against Llywelyn.

During the 1270s Humphrey de Bohun fought to regain his inheritance, attacking Llywelyn's men in Brecon. By 1275 the venture had largely succeeded, and in 1276 Bohun was among those lords in the king's council who gave judgment against Llywelyn. He served with Edward I in Wales in 1276 and again in 1277, and, when the campaign ended, he received protection from the king to go on pilgrimage to Santiago de Compostela.

Bohun fought in Wales throughout the 1280s, when his relations with neighbouring lords degenerated into private warfare. In 1284 Edward awarded possession of Iscennen, which bordered on Brecon, and which Bohun felt belonged to him by right of conquest, to John Giffard. Bohun raided on Giffard's lands and men, but a royal court supported Giffard, and Edward confirmed his grant of Iscennen to Giffard in 1289. Irritation between Bohun and the earl of Gloucester had also been building. The latter claimed that Bohun had not fully paid his marriage fine, while Bohun chafed at being ordered to serve under Gloucester in 1282, as well as at Gloucester's appointment as captain of the army in Brecon in 1287. More dangerous was Gloucester's construction of a castle at Morlais, on the border between the lordships of Brecon and Glamorgan. Bohun was in an awkward position. His Welsh holdings were not as substantial as those of other lords were, he had never fully subdued the Welsh in Brecon, and now he was confronted by two assertive neighbours interested in enlarging their territories. In 1289–90 Bohun appealed to the king for aid against Gloucester, thereby breaking with marcher custom, but Gloucester seized the initiative and raided Brecon in February 1290, justifying his attack by citing those same customs. After two more raids and counter-attacks Edward asserted his authority and ordered the antagonists to appear before a royal tribunal. The final sentences, handed down in parliament in January 1292, condemned both to prison and declared Glamorgan and Brecon forfeit, though Bohun gained his freedom with a fine of 1000 marks and recovered Brecon on 15 July.

Bohun was punctilious in upholding the dignity of his position. In 1277 he proffered the military service that he owed as hereditary constable of England, and throughout the subsequent campaigns in Wales he consistently served without pay. His request in 1282 for his wartime profits as constable prompted a search of exchequer records to ascertain the extent of his rights. In the previous year, when summoned to answer a complaint about unjust distresses, he asserted that the king's statutes had no place in his lands and refused to appear, at which the king marvelled greatly. Bohun's claim to the custody of the manors of the bishop of St David's in Brecon resulted in armed conflict during a vacancy in 1280, and was pointedly overruled by the king in parliament in 1293. Four years later Edward sent royal commissioners to hear complaints by the men of Brecon against Bohun and to take them into the king's peace, directly undermining the earl's lordship.

Bohun's sensitivity about his rights, and the rebuffs that he received at Edward's hands, explain why he became such a staunch opponent of the king during the crisis of 1297. Edward's wartime demands had produced widespread resentment. When in parliament in February 1297, he asked the magnates to serve with him in Gascony, Roger (IV) Bigod, earl of Norfolk and marshal of England, refused. Edward went ahead and summoned an army, but when it was to be mustered, both the constable and the marshal refused to perform their duties. In July, at a meeting between the king's representatives and the barons near London, Bohun gave a lengthy speech summarizing the causes of complaint and demanding remedy. This formed the basis of the Remonstrances, the written articles submitted by the barons. Edward also tried desperately to raise money, but Bohun and Bigod appeared at the exchequer in August with an armed force to prevent the collection of any taxes. The danger passed when the Scots invaded England and Edward made concessions to the opposition in the documents known as the *De tallagio* and the *Confirmatio cartarum*. Both Bohun and Bigod received pardons, and then marched off to Scotland to defend the realm.

Bohun married Maud, daughter of Enguerrand de Fiennes, in 1275. Their son Humphrey (VII) de *Bohun (*d.* 1322) inherited the family estates on his father's death. Humphrey (VI) died at Pleshey on 31 December 1298, and was buried at Walden Priory, Essex. The Bohuns had long been patrons of Walden, and Humphrey (VI) de Bohun was remembered there as one who 'did much good to our monastery' (Dugdale, *Monasticon*, 4.141). His benefactions included licensing the monks to accept lands given or sold to them by his tenants. SCOTT L. WAUGH

Sources GEC, *Peerage*, new edn, 6.463–6 • F. Palgrave, ed., *The parliamentary writs and writs of military summons*, 2 vols. in 4 (1827–34) • *RotP*, vol. 1 • *Chancery records* • Rymer, *Foedera*, new edn, vol. 4 • J. G. Edwards, *Calendar of ancient correspondence concerning Wales* (1935) • W. Rees, ed., *Calendar of ancient petitions relating to Wales* (1975) • *The chronicle of Walter of Guisborough*, ed. H. Rothwell, CS, 3rd ser., 89 (1957) • M. Prestwich, ed., *Documents illustrating the crisis of 1297–98 in England*, CS, 4th ser., 24 (1980) • Dugdale, *Monasticon*, new edn, 4.141; 6.135 • I. J. Sanders, *English baronies: a study of their origin and descent, 1086–1327* (1960), 8, 57, 72, 92 • M. Prestwich, *Edward I* (1988), 58, 174, 189, 204, 223, 262, 339, 348–52, 413, 416, 419, 421–2, 424–7, 429–30, 433, 435, 461, 467, 478, 481–3, 511, 518, 562 • R. R. Davies, *Lordship and society in the march of Wales, 1282–1400* (1978), 225, 252, 255, 256, 258, 259–60, 261, 262, 265–9, 290 • J. E. Morris, *The Welsh wars of Edward I* (1901), 21, 25, 39, 48, 58, 59–62, 112, 123, 126, 155, 158, 170, 178, 179, 194, 201, 206, 211, 222–4, 236, 242, 247, 252, 256, 261, 274–7, 280–83, 285, 290–92, 296 • M. Altschul, *A baronial family in medieval England: the Clares, 1217–1314* (1965), 132–3, 140, 144, 146–53, 272, 274 • S. Wood, *English monasteries and their patrons in the thirteenth century* (1955)

Bohun, Humphrey (VII) de, fourth earl of Hereford and ninth earl of Essex (*c.*1276–1322), magnate and administrator, was the son and heir of Humphrey (VI) de *Bohun, third earl of Hereford and eighth earl of Essex (*c.*1249–1298), constable of England, and his wife, Maud de Fiennes, daughter of Enguerrand, seigneur de Fiennes. Edward I received his homage and granted livery of his father's lands on 16 February 1298. Bohun attended the marriage of Edward I to Margaret of France at Canterbury on 10 September 1299. In 1300 he was present at the siege of Caerlaverock, and in the following year he was among those barons who sealed a letter of grievances to the pope. He married Elizabeth, youngest daughter of *Edward I, and widow of John, count of Holland, in 1302; among their children was William de *Bohun, first earl of Northampton. Before the marriage he surrendered all of his lands and rights as both earl and constable to the king. They were regranted jointly to the earl and his wife after the wedding took place. In October 1304 he was to have accompanied the prince of Wales to Amiens to perform homage on his father's behalf for Aquitaine, but the journey was not undertaken. In 1306 he and his wife were granted Lochmaben Castle and all the lands of Robert Bruce in Annandale. He participated at the knighting of Edward of Caernarfon (the future Edward II) on 22 May 1306, fastening one of the prince's spurs. Later, in the Scottish campaign, he served with Thomas of Lancaster, investing the castle at Kildrummy.

Early on in Edward II's reign, Bohun seems to have been well disposed to the new king. He witnessed the grant of the earldom of Cornwall to Edward's Gascon favourite, Piers Gaveston, in August, he dined with the king in August and September, and he was present at court in October and November 1307. He attended the Wallingford tournament in December, when Gaveston defeated a party including himself and the earls of Arundel and Surrey. When he accompanied the king to France for his marriage to Isabella in January 1308, however, he appears to have entered the baronial opposition that was beginning to develop. He sealed the so-called Boulogne agreement which foreshadowed the opposition that was to emerge, led by the earl of Lincoln, at the parliament of April 1308. Nevertheless, at the coronation of Edward II he bore the sceptre with the cross, and throughout 1308–9 he was frequently present at court, as his presence as a witness in the charter rolls attests. In 1310 he was elected as one of the *lords ordainer, appointed to reform the king's household and government. According to the *Vita Edwardi secundi* he refused to accompany the king on the Scottish campaign of 1310–11 because of his hatred of Gaveston. Edward II stripped him of the constableship, but restored him to the office on 28 August 1311. When Gaveston returned from his third and final exile early in 1312, Bohun was among the magnates who organized opposition to the king and his favourite. He was charged with protecting Essex and the east while others hunted Gaveston down. Following Gaveston's capture Bohun was present at Warwick and participated in the deliberations that resulted in Gaveston's execution on 19 June. Indeed, on 18 June letters were sealed by the earls of Lancaster and Warwick guaranteeing Bohun against any losses he might suffer as a consequence of this act. He was active in the subsequent peace negotiations with the king, and was among those pardoned by Edward in October 1313. In the following year he fought at Bannockburn and was taken prisoner. According to the *Vita Edwardi secundi* a dispute between Bohun, constable of England, and the young earl of Gloucester over who should have precedence in the line of attack was a major factor in the English failure. Bohun was subsequently exchanged for Elizabeth de Burgh, wife of Robert I.

From 1315 until 1320 Bohun was regularly present at court, where he is constantly found as a witness in the charter rolls, eclipsed in the frequency of his attendance only by the Despensers. The full nature of his reconciliation with the king is clearly indicated by his presence at Kings Langley on 3 January 1315 for the long-delayed burial of Gaveston. On 11 February 1316 he was appointed captain of the English forces being raised to suppress the revolt of Llywelyn Bren in Glamorgan, and in this he was successful. Later in the year he was appointed to the committee established to reform the king's household and kingdom, but by 1317 he had entered an indenture of service with the king on very favourable terms. He was present at the negotiation of the treaty of Leake in 1318, and he was appointed to the new council that resulted. In 1318–19 he served in the war with Scotland.

Throughout this period, however, the power and influence of the Despensers had grown inordinately. As an important marcher lord Bohun was the natural leader of the opposition to the younger Despenser's territorial aggrandizement. On 30 January 1321 he was sent a royal order not to attend or assent to an illegal assembly that he was about to hold with other magnates, including the earls of Arundel and Surrey. It is likely that soon after this he met with Lancaster to form an alliance. On 16 March the king occupied Bohun's castle at Builth for the latter's failure to appear at a conference with the earl marshal. Further warnings from the king and denunciations of the favourites by the marchers led to an escalation of tensions but no settlement. On 4 May Bohun and the marchers began the destruction of the Despenser estates. In the short term the marchers' objectives were achieved and the Despensers were driven into exile. But the king soon recalled them and showed an unwonted zeal in prosecuting a counter-offensive against his baronial foes in the autumn of 1321. Bohun occupied Gloucester in December, and burned Bridgnorth and destroyed its bridge. Forced to go as far north as Shrewsbury, Edward crossed the Severn on 14 January, after which many of the marchers, including the Mortimers, surrendered. Bohun withdrew to Pontefract, and on 23 January the king ordered the confiscation of his goods. Edward consolidated his grip on the south before turning north for a final confrontation with Bohun and the earl of Lancaster. This came on 16 March 1322 at Boroughbridge, where Bohun was killed in battle. He was buried at the Dominican house in York.

Described in the Caerlaverock roll as 'a rich and elegant young man', Bohun's fluid political loyalties characterize the problems of Edward II's tumultuous reign. He was succeeded by the second of his six sons, John. Another son, Humphrey, succeeded John as sixth earl in 1335.

J. S. Hamilton

Sources J. R. Maddicott, *Thomas of Lancaster, 1307–1322: a study in the reign of Edward II* (1970) • J. R. S. Phillips, *Aymer de Valence, earl of Pembroke, 1307–1324: baronial politics in the reign of Edward II* (1972) • N. Fryde, *The tyranny and fall of Edward II, 1321–1326* (1979) • *Calendar of the charter rolls*, 6 vols., PRO (1903–27) [PRO C53] • GEC, *Peerage* • *CPR* • *CClR* • N. Denholm-Young, ed. and trans., *Vita Edwardi secundi* (1957) • *CIPM*, 2, no. 552

Archives PRO, C53

Bohun, Jocelin de (1105x1110?–1184), bishop of Salisbury, was born into the Sussex branch of the Bohun family, probably between about 1105 and 1110. His uncle (*patruus*) was Engelger de Bohun (*d.* 1175), and he was a close relative, perhaps first cousin once removed, of Savaric Fitzgeldewin, bishop of Bath (*d.* 1205). He was somehow related to the earls of Gloucester, Earl William (*d.* 1183) calling him his kinsman (*cognatus*). His brother, Richard, became bishop of Coutances, and his illegitimate son, *Reginald fitz Jocelin (*d.* 1191), was successively bishop of Bath and archbishop-elect of Canterbury. Bohun's early life and education are obscure, but, since Pope Alexander III (*r.* 1159–81) later claimed him as an old friend, and his son was known as the Lombard, it is likely that he studied in north Italy, where his son was born, possibly of a Lombard mother. The first certain context for him is the household of Henry de Blois, bishop of Winchester (*d.* 1171), who appointed him archdeacon of Winchester before 1139. His election as bishop of Salisbury in 1141 or 1142 was the unforeseen outcome of a dispute over the filling of the see between King Stephen and Henry de Blois, who was by then papal legate. After the preferred candidates of both sides had been mutually rejected, and following Stephen's capture in February 1141, Henry supported Bohun's nomination, although his election by the chapter was not unanimous, being opposed particularly by Dean Azo. He was consecrated by Archbishop Theobald (*d.* 1161) in 1142. He attended Henry II's coronation at Westminster on 19 December 1154, and assisted at Archbishop Thomas Becket's consecration at Canterbury on 3 June 1162.

Bohun played a significant part in the ensuing conflict between Becket and the king, but one dictated more by circumstance than by conviction or principle. When the quarrel began he was out of favour with Henry, possibly owing to differences between them over his reluctant quitclaim of Devizes Castle in 1157, and moreover he had recently followed the archbishop's advice on the treatment of criminous clerks. At the Council of Clarendon in January 1164 it was partly Henry's enmity towards Bohun and William Turbe, bishop of Norwich (*d.* 1174), that induced Becket reluctantly to accept Henry's demands. When Becket and the bishops eventually swore to observe the realm's ancient customs, Bohun hesitated and sought guidance from the archbishop, who told him to swear with the others. During Becket's trial at Northampton in October 1164 Bohun was one of two bishops who attempted to console him, while also joining other bishops later in advising him to resign.

Bohun was turned into an enemy of Becket by an episode subsidiary to the main dispute. In May 1165 John of Oxford (*d.* 1200) was one of the king's emissaries in discussions with the antipope Paschal III's party at the imperial diet of Würzburg. As a reward Henry put pressure on Bohun to have John elected to the vacant deanery of Salisbury. Bohun, mindful no doubt of his recent troubles with the king, and despite prohibitions from Alexander III and Becket, complied. He was accordingly suspended by the archbishop in 1166. He appealed against his sentence to the pope and wrote to Becket justifying his action, asserting that the new dean had been canonically elected by a unanimous chapter. Nevertheless, although John of Salisbury and others interceded on Bohun's behalf, Becket insisted on the quashing of John of Oxford's appointment before the suspension could be lifted. This Bohun would not accept. He was driven to seek support from Gilbert Foliot, bishop of London (*d.* 1187), one of Becket's bitterest opponents, with whom he was closely associated thereafter, becoming increasingly identified with the king's party. In November 1167 he was among the bishops who met the papal legates at Argentan, where he joined Foliot in appealing to the pope on behalf of the English bishops against Becket. In 1168 Alexander III conditionally lifted Bohun's suspension but, after Foliot's fresh appeal to Rome in 1169, both bishops were excommunicated by Becket on Palm Sunday. They were absolved by the pope early in 1170 but, after assisting Archbishop Roger of York at the coronation of Henry the Young King at Westminster on 14 June 1170, their excommunication and suspension were renewed in September by papal letters dispatched to Becket for use at his discretion. From Wissant, Becket sent the letters across the channel to the three prelates waiting at Dover to cross to the king in Normandy. It was their bitter complaints to Henry that set in train the events that culminated in the archbishop's assassination on 29 December. In the aftermath of the murder the pope, evidently anxious not to prolong Bohun's and Foliot's excommunication, conditionally absolved them in April 1171, but their suspension was maintained until March 1172.

Bohun was probably more at home in the administration of his diocese than in the great quarrel which engulfed him. He ruled for forty-two years, the longest pontificate of any twelfth-century English bishop. His surviving charters (numbering over 100) reveal him as a conscientious diocesan. He exerted his authority within the diocese, being active in the appointment of parochial clergy and in settling disputes over churches and tithes. Despite problems at Cerne and Sherborne abbeys in the 1140s and clashes with Malmesbury over its claim to exemption, he appears on the whole to have maintained amicable relations with religious houses, issuing general confirmations to a number of individual monasteries and helping to promote the cult of St James's hand at Reading. At the cathedral of Old Sarum he consolidated and enlarged the prebendal system, developed the full complement of dignities, and built up the common fund. He was occasionally employed as a papal judge-delegate in the first half of his pontificate, most notably in the important settlement of 1157 between York Minster and Gloucester Abbey over certain Gloucestershire manors. Despite the doubts voiced by David Knowles about Bohun's legal learning, Archbishop Theobald clearly felt his opinion worth having; he was, for example, one of the bishops whose advice Theobald followed in handling the difficult case of Osbert the archdeacon in 1155. His son Reginald became archdeacon of Wiltshire and his kinsman Savaric treasurer of the cathedral, but Bohun did not otherwise promote his family at Salisbury. He attended Archbishop Richard's provincial council at Westminster in May 1175, and a royal council at Woodstock in July. In 1184 he resigned his bishopric to become a monk at the Cistercian abbey of Forde, where he died on 18 November. He was buried at Old Sarum, whence his remains were moved on 14 June 1226 to the new cathedral at Salisbury.

B. R. Kemp

Sources J. C. Robertson and J. B. Sheppard, eds., *Materials for the history of Thomas Becket, archbishop of Canterbury*, 7 vols., Rolls Series, 67 (1875–85) • D. Knowles, *The episcopal colleagues of Archbishop Thomas Becket* (1951) • *Fasti Angl., 1066–1300*, [Salisbury] • D. Whitelock, M. Brett, and C. N. L. Brooke, eds., *Councils and synods with other documents relating to the English church, 871–1204*, 2 (1981) • W. H. Rich Jones, ed., *Vetus registrum sarisberiense alias dictum registrum S. Osmundi episcopi: the register of St Osmund*, 2 vols., Rolls Series, 78 (1883–4) • A. Saltman, *Theobald, archbishop of Canterbury* (1956) • F. Barlow, *Thomas Becket* (1986) • *Letters and charters of Gilbert Foliot*, ed. A. Morey and others (1967) • A. Morey and C. N. L. Brooke, *Gilbert Foliot and his letters* (1965) • M. Howell, *Regalian right in medieval England* (1962) • B. R. Kemp, ed., *Salisbury, 1078–1217*, English Episcopal Acta, 18 (1999)
Archives Salisbury Cathedral, charters

Bohun, Ralph (*bap.* 1639, *d.* 1716), Church of England clergyman, was born at Coundon, Warwickshire, and baptized on 13 July 1639 at Holy Trinity, Coventry, eldest of the numerous children born to Abraham Bohun (*b.* 1617), rector of Elmedon and vicar of Foleshill, Warwickshire, and his wife, Elizabeth, daughter of George Bathurst of Hothorp, Northamptonshire. In 1655 Bohun entered Winchester College as a founder's kin scholar through his mother's line. (about 1836 this claim was found to be flawed: Bohun and several other families were not related as had been supposed.) Bohun entered New College, Oxford, where he matriculated on 8 December 1658; as founder's kin he was entitled to a fellowship on entry. He graduated BCL in 1665 and DCL in 1685.

In 1666 Bohun succeeded Edward Phillips as resident tutor to John Evelyn's son John (*b.* 1655), and continued to tutor him when he went at a very young age to Oxford in 1667. The youth was expected to read Aristotle in Greek, as Bohun explained to his father:

> I begin with the philosophy of the schooles, which though I make it not my creed, and have often declared to yourselfe how insufficient I believe the peripatetic hypothesis to solve the phaenomenas of nature, with any tolerable consistency to itselfe, yet … its almost impossible, as things stand, to be either divine, physician, or lawyer, without him. (*Hist. U. Oxf.*, 4.401)

He further explained that if Evelyn's son spoke out against Aristotle, it would be because he had read him, not because Aristotle was out of vogue at the Royal Society. This lack of bias was not universal: Bohun was scornful of Cressy Dymmock, who arrived in Oxford in 1667 and offered a condensed course in experimental philosophy where he decried Aristotle.

After five years in Evelyn's household, 'having well and faithfully performed his charge' (Evelyn, 4.566), Bohun went to reside in New College, and published in Oxford his *Discourse concerning the origine and properties of wind: with an historical account of hurricanes, and other tempestuous winds* (1671). 'By reason of my residence in a place principally concerned in naval affairs' (Preface), presumably a reference to Evelyn's interests and his house at Deptford, Bohun was enabled to compare the observations of ships' captains with the writings of classical philosophers, whose experience never compassed the distant East and West Indies now so familiar. Of the moderns, Isaac Vossius seemed reliable. Bohun then discusses both the regular, meaning trade winds and monsoons, and tempestuous winds, among which he includes waterspouts, tornadoes, and hurricanes, devoting space to individual accounts of such devastating events. Dismissing predictions based on superstition, he notes that an acquaintance living near the sea can foretell storms several hours before they arrive from the action of his barometer. His only other known writing is the commendatory poem prefixed to the second and subsequent editions of Evelyn's *Sylva*.

Bohun became rector of West Kington, Wiltshire, in 1674. When the living of Wotton, which was in the gift of Evelyn, became vacant in 1701, he gave it to Bohun, who took up residence there. He maintained a friendly relationship with Evelyn, whose *Diary* reports many of his sermons delivered in London and elsewhere. However, harsh words were exchanged in 1703, when Bohun preached against the pride and luxury of apparel on an occasion when, apart from the well-dressed Evelyn family, only the humble of the parish were in church. In 1701 he was made a prebend of Salisbury Cathedral. In 1704 he inherited a legacy and one third of the library of his uncle, Dr Ralph Bathurst, president of Trinity College, Oxford, and dean of Wells.

Bohun died at Wotton, Surrey, on 12 July 1716 and was buried at the church of St John the Evangelist, Wotton, on 16 July. In his will he named Evelyn as his principal executor, and he dispersed his estate and library, by bequests of money and books to the same value, to Evelyn, to several cousins, and to officials of Winchester and New colleges.

Anita McConnell

Sources *Hist. U. Oxf.* 4: *17th-cent. Oxf.* • *N&Q*, 12th ser., 2 (1916), 321–2 • Evelyn, *Diary*, vols. 1, 3–4 • Foster, *Alum. Oxon.* • T. F. Kirby, *Winchester scholars: a list of the wardens, fellows, and scholars of … Winchester College* (1888), 188 • parish register, Holy Trinity, Coventry, Warwickshire, 13 July 1639 [baptism] • parish register, St John the Evangelist, Wotton, Surrey, 16 July 1716 [burial] • W. H. Rylands, ed., *The visitation of the county of Warwick … 1682 … 1683*, Harleian Society, 62 (1911), 38–41 • PRO, PROB 11/557, sig. 70 • Wood, *Ath. Oxon.*, new edn, 4.549

Bohun, William de, first earl of Northampton (*c.*1312–1360), magnate, was the fifth son of Humphrey (VII) de *Bohun, fourth earl of Hereford and ninth earl of Essex (*c.*1276–1322), and Elizabeth (1282–1316), daughter of *Edward I. He and his twin brother, Edward (*d.* 1334), were close personal associates of the young Edward III and took part in the ambush and arrest of Roger (V) Mortimer, earl of March, at Nottingham Castle in 1330. In November 1335, when a papal dispensation was granted for his marriage to Elizabeth, *née* Badlesmere, the widow of Mortimer's recently deceased heir, it was stated that the alliance had been arranged specifically to heal the enmity between the two families. Bohun quickly established himself as a prominent figure in the king's household and participated actively in Edward III's Scottish wars. He fought in Scotland in 1333 and, as a knight-banneret of the household, led a contingent of sixty mounted archers on the Roxburgh campaign of 1334–5. He served on the summer expedition of 1335 with forty-three men at arms and eighty mounted archers, and was campaigning in Scotland again in 1336 when he was also appointed to negotiate an Anglo-Scottish truce.

Such service was handsomely rewarded. Already in 1332 Bohun had been granted a series of manors formerly held by Thomas of Brotherton, earl of Norfolk; his wife, Elizabeth, not only brought to Bohun her dower from the Mortimer marriage but was also coheir to the estates of Giles Badlesmere. On 16 March 1337 Bohun was created earl of Northampton and was granted, in expectation, the lordships of Stamford, Fotheringhay, Grantham, and Oakham, together with a life interest in the shrievalty of Rutland; until he came into these rights, and to ensure that he maintained the income of £1000 deemed appropriate to his new estate, he was granted annuities from the customs revenues and the farms of London and Essex. In the 1350s Bohun added further to his landed base through purchases, particularly around the lordship of Brecon and in Essex.

Bohun's promotion, like that of the other five earls appointed in March 1337, was intended to replenish the ranks of the military aristocracy in preparation for the impending war with France. In the winter of 1337–8 he was employed in negotiation with the French; and in the following year he represented the king in discussions with prospective allies in Brabant and Flanders and accompanied Edward on his journey to Koblenz. Having been sent back to England to treat with the council at the end of 1338, he spent 1339 in the Low Countries and participated in Edward III's campaign in the Cambrésis and the Thiérache. After travelling to England with the king for the spring parliament of 1340 he returned to the continent, and took part in the battle of Sluys on 24 June 1340. The loan of £800 to Edward III on the eve of this campaign was a mark not only of Bohun's loyalty but also of the king's desperate shortage of cash; ironically, in July, Bohun was temporarily arrested in Brussels as a hostage for the debts owed by Edward in the Low Countries, and he only escaped further victimization by absconding from the city of Ghent with the king in November and fleeing to England.

Bohun played some part in Edward III's subsequent hostile attack on the domestic administration led by Archbishop John Stratford. He was present at the Tower of London when the chancellor, Robert Stratford, was forced to resign the great seal on 1 December 1340. He also acted as the king's spokesman in discussion with the archbishop when the latter was excluded from parliament in the spring of 1341, and was among the peers later appointed to hear the charges made against Stratford. But the reconciliation between king and archbishop in October allowed the aristocracy to turn its attention back to war, and on 20 July 1342 Bohun was appointed as Edward III's lieutenant in the duchy of Brittany. He raised the siege of Brest, defeated Philippe VI's candidate for the duchy, Charles de Blois, at Morlaix in September, and laid siege to Nantes. Although he gave up the lieutenancy on 2 April 1343 and spent most of the following two years in England planning an ultimately abortive diplomatic mission to Avignon, he was the obvious choice of commander for the new offensive planned against Brittany by Edward III in 1345, and was reappointed as king's lieutenant there on 24 April 1345. He joined in Edward III's invasion of Normandy in 1346, fought at Crécy, and participated in the early stages of the siege of Calais; but his replacement as lieutenant of Brittany on 10 January 1347 signified his return to diplomacy, and between 1347 and 1349 he was occupied in negotiations with the Flemings and the French.

The early 1350s saw another change of focus, as Bohun was deployed as warden of the Scottish marches, admiral of the fleet in the north, and commander of Carlisle; he was present at Roxburgh in January 1356 when Edward Balliol surrendered his claims to the Scottish throne to Edward III. He accompanied the king to Calais in 1355, took part in the French campaign of 1359–60, and was one of the English witnesses to the treaty of Brétigny (8 May 1360). He died on 16 September 1360 and was buried on the north side of the presbytery at the Benedictine abbey at Walden, Essex. His wife, who had died in June 1356, was buried at the London Blackfriars.

Despite his busy military career, Bohun took part in the political and cultural life of the English court. He was a frequent witness to royal charters and, when in England, a regular participant in the council. He was present at tournaments held at Dunstable in 1334 and 1342. Although not a founder member of the Order of the Garter, he was quickly recruited into its ranks to fill the stall left vacant by the death of Sir Hugh Courtenay in September 1349. His friendship with Edward III probably facilitated the rehabilitation of his stepson, Roger (VI) Mortimer. As cousins to the king Bohun and his brothers enjoyed a particularly exalted status, and Edward III provided the gilt cloth used at the earl's funeral. W. M. Ormrod

Sources GEC, *Peerage* • G. A. Holmes, *The estates of the higher nobility in fourteenth-century England* (1957) • J. Sumption, *The Hundred Years War*, 1 (1990) • G. L. Harriss, *King, parliament and public finance in medieval England to 1369* (1975) • M. Jones, 'Edward III's captains in Brittany', *England in the fourteenth century* [Harlaxton 1985], ed. W. M. Ormrod (1986), 99–118 • J. Vale, *Edward III and chivalry: chivalric society and its context, 1270–1350* (1982) • R. Nicholson, *Edward III and the Scots: the formative years of a military career, 1327–1335* (1965) • *Chancery records* • *Calendar of papal registers* • PRO • *The wardrobe book of William de Norwell*, ed. M. Lyon and others (1983) • *Adae Murimuth continuatio chronicarum. Robertus de Avesbury de gestis mirabilibus regis Edwardi tertii*, ed. E. M. Thompson, Rolls Series, 93 (1889) • *CIPM*, 10, no. 639

Wealth at death very wealthy

Boileau, Sir John Peter (1794–1869), antiquary, was born at Hertford Street, London, on 2 September 1794, the eldest son of the John Peter Boileau (1747–1837) and his wife, Henrietta (*d.* 1817), the daughter of the Revd George Pollen of Little Bookham, Surrey. His father, who had been a member of the council at Masulipatam, had returned to England in 1785 and invested his Indian earnings in the Tacolneston estate in Norfolk. The family was descended from Charles Boileau, baron of Castelnau and St Croix, a

Sir John Peter Boileau (**1794–1869**), by Sir Martin Archer Shee, exh. RA 1834

Languedoc Huguenot immigrant to England in 1691, and his French aristocratic origin, even more than his recent nabob inheritance, gave Boileau a taste for heraldry, genealogy, and antiquities, and a decidedly masterful streak of personality.

Boileau was educated at Merton College, Oxford (he matriculated in 1811 but did not take a degree), and at Edinburgh University. He was commissioned into the rifle brigade on 9 September 1813, and served under Lynedoch in the Netherlands, where he was present at the capture of Bergen-op-Zoom. On 14 November 1825 he married Lady Catherine Sarah Elliot (*d.* 1862), the third daughter of the first earl of Minto. He acquired Thursford Hall, near Fakenham, and then in 1836 the Ketteringham estate, where he built a spacious Gothic hall and resided from 1841. On 24 July 1838 he was created a baronet in the coronation honours. A prominent whig, Boileau was a county magistrate and a deputy lieutenant; he was high sheriff of Norfolk in 1844.

In London Boileau was connected with many learned and charitable organizations and at various times served as a vice-president of, among others, the Archaeological Institute, the British Association, the Royal Institution, the Society of Arts, the Statistical Society, and the Zoological Society. He was elected FRS on 1 June 1843.

Wealthy and civilized, Boileau was a learned antiquary with a keen interest in local, especially Roman, history. His estates included the site of the large Roman fort Garianonum, at Burgh Castle, just over the Suffolk border, near Great Yarmouth. He was a founding vice-president of the Norfolk and Norwich Archaeological Society, and its president from 1849. He published a number of papers in *Norfolk Archaeology* (volumes 5 and 7), and commissioned from Joseph Hunter a monograph on Ketteringham published in the same journal (3, 1852, 245–314) and reprinted for private distribution. He was elected a fellow of the Society of Antiquaries on 9 December 1852, and served two four-year terms as a vice-president of the society between 1858 and 1867.

Boileau's diligent local service and cultivated metropolitan activity are reflected in his diary, now in the Norwich City Library. This was skilfully drawn on in 1960 by Owen Chadwick, whose *Victorian Miniature* portrays a strong personality of pious disposition and a high sense of pastoral responsibility to his rural tenantry. By way of contrast Chadwick also had the use of the diary (in private hands) of William Wayte Andrew, the evangelical vicar of Ketteringham. Andrew was as proud-spirited a minister to his flock as his squire was a paternal governor of his broad acres. The contrasting journals provide an unusually detailed vignette of acrimonious relations between mansion and parsonage, but one which nevertheless confirms Boileau's high contemporary reputation in antiquarian circles.

Boileau, who died at Torquay on 9 March 1869, was buried at Ketteringham. He had four sons and five daughters; his second son, Francis George Manningham Boileau, succeeded him in the baronetcy and estates. ALAN BELL

Sources O. Chadwick, *Victorian miniature* (1960) • J. Hunter, 'The history and topography of Ketteringham', *Norfolk Archaeology*, 3 (1852), 245–314 • *CGPLA Eng. & Wales* (1869)

Archives NL Scot., European travel journals • Norfolk RO, corresp., diary, and family journal | NL Scot., letters from him and Lady Boileau to second earl of Minto

Likenesses M. A. Shee, portrait, exh. RA 1834; Sothebys, 22 March 1995, lot 21 [*see illus.*] • T. H. Maguire, lithograph, 1851, BM, NPG

Wealth at death under £90,000: probate, 24 May 1869, *CGPLA Eng. & Wales*

Bois, du, family (*per. c.***1071–1313**), barons, were important tenants and retainers of the earls of Leicester. For seven generations each head of the family bore the name Arnold, which became a component of the place names of their principal residences. Substantial earthworks next to the church at Thorpe Arnold are all that remains of the du Bois manor house there. There is also mention of a residence at Bois-Ernault in Normandy.

Arnold (I) du Bois [Arnold fitz Popelina] (*fl.* 1071–1094) was a leading tenant of the honour of Breteuil in Normandy, with lands in ten surrounding settlements. He also held Pullay of the duke of Normandy. He was one of ten knights taken prisoner during a baronial conflict at Ivry in Normandy in 1094 and subsequently gaoled. **Arnold (II) du Bois** (*fl.* 1100–1125) was the castellan of Lyre in Normandy when it was attacked by Henry I in 1119. Arnold, like the majority of the tenants of Breteuil, had revolted after the imposition upon the honour of a royal nominee, the Breton baron Ralph de Gael. In 1121 the honour passed by marriage to Robert (II), earl of Leicester (*d.* 1168), whose lordship Arnold accepted and in return received a substantial grant of lands in Leicestershire.

Arnold (III) du Bois (*fl.* 1130–1160) acquired further

estates in Gloucestershire and Warwickshire through marriage to Isabel de Waterville, heir of another Leicester tenant. He served the earl throughout the troubled reign of Stephen, as constable and *de facto* deputy in Normandy in 1138–9 and as steward and constant attendant in England from 1140 onwards. He appears as a witness to charters of Stephen and of Henry Plantagenet, as duke of Normandy and subsequently as king of England, on most occasions in the company of his lord the earl, who supported Stephen and Henry in turn. In 1147 Arnold founded the Cistercian monastery at Biddlesden in Buckinghamshire, a daughter house of Garendon, Leicestershire, on land to which he had dubious title. He also made substantial grants to Leicester Abbey; and like his father and grandfather he was a patron of Lyre Abbey in Normandy.

The relationship between **Arnold (IV) du Bois** (*d.* 1205) and Robert (III) de Breteuil, earl of Leicester (*d.* 1190), was perhaps not as close as that which had existed between their respective fathers, although Arnold appears to have supported the earl in his revolt against Henry II in 1173 and afterwards served as his steward. Arnold accompanied Robert (IV) de Breteuil, earl of Leicester (*d.* 1204), on the third crusade, and was one of the party led by the earl that successfully routed a band of Turks outside Ramlah in late 1191. On his return from the Holy Land he was impleaded for debt by the moneylender Elias fitz Aaron of Lincoln. He married Emma, daughter and coheir of Payn of Houghton, Northamptonshire, acquiring through her lands in Northamptonshire and Lincolnshire. His brother Robert du Bois (*fl.* 1154–1190) was rector of Claybrooke, Leicestershire, and a household clerk of the earls of Leicester. **Arnold (V) du Bois** (1186?–1222) was a minor at his father's death in 1205, and was placed in the wardship of Roger of Basingham. He reached his majority in 1207 but his inheritance was much reduced, both in extent and prestige. The loss of Normandy to the Capetians in 1204 had irrevocably deprived the family of its ancestral lands, and the division of the earldom of Leicester after 1204 extinguished the du Bois stewardship. The division also left Arnold with two overlords for the lands formerly held of the earldom, Saer (IV) de Quincy (*d.* 1219) and Simon de Montfort (*d.* 1218). In the civil war of 1216 Arnold fought against the king, and he was briefly deprived of his lands as a result. He married Alice, heir of Henry of Tubney, steward of the earl of Warwick and lord of Tubney, Berkshire.

Arnold (VI) du Bois (*d.* 1255) was one of the knights who mustered at Portsmouth in late 1229 for an abortive royal expedition to Brittany. He was custodian of Nottingham Castle and acting sheriff of Nottinghamshire and Derbyshire for part of 1239, and in 1253 he was appointed justice of the forests south of the Trent. He was an adherent of Simon de Montfort, earl of Leicester (*d.* 1265), and his sister Joan du Bois married Montfort's steward Thomas Astley. His brother William du Bois (*fl.* 1235–1260) was a household knight of Roger de Quincy, constable of Scotland. Arnold married Joan Beauchamp, coheir of John Beauchamp of Ashington, Suffolk. Matthew Paris gave his arms as argent, two bars and a canton gules. The heraldic seal of one of Arnold's charters shows two bars, on a canton or quarter a lion passant. He died on 6 February 1255 and was buried in Biddlesden Abbey. **Arnold (VII) du Bois** (*d.* 1277) was obliged to mortgage his manor of Ashington to the bishop of Norwich in order to raise money in 1259. He also supported Montfort, but a fortuitous illness precluded his participation in the baronial wars of 1264–5, and he did not suffer for his earlier allegiance. His eldest son, Arnold, died in his lifetime and, on his death on 1 April 1277, he was succeeded by his second son, **John du Bois**, Lord du Bois (1253–1290), who was born on 29 June 1253. John had a summons to the Shrewsbury parliament of 1283. He married, but there were no children of the union, and on his death before 6 February 1290 his heir was his younger brother Master William du Bois, a cleric. After William's death, before 6 March 1313, the bulk of the du Bois lands passed to his niece Maud Lovell and her husband, William de la *Zouche, first Lord Zouche [*see under* Zouche family]. RICHARD DACE

Sources Biddlesden cartulary, BL, Harley MS 4714 • Lyre cartulary, Château de Semilly, collection du marquis de Mathan • *Pipe rolls* • *Chancery records* • D. Crouch, *The Beaumont twins: the roots and branches of power in the twelfth century*, Cambridge Studies in Medieval Life and Thought, 4th ser., 1 (1986) • Ordericus Vitalis, *Eccl. hist.* • Ambroise, *L'estoire de la guerre sainte* (Paris, 1897) • Paris, *Chron.* • BL, Harley charters, 84, H55 • GEC, *Peerage*, new edn
Archives BL, Harley charters, 84, H55 • BL, Harley MS 4714

Bois, Arnold (I) du (*fl.* **1071–1094**). *See under* Bois, du, family (*per. c.*1071–1313).

Bois, Arnold (II) du (*fl.* **1100–1125**). *See under* Bois, du, family (*per. c.*1071–1313).

Bois, Arnold (III) du (*fl.* **1130–1160**). *See under* Bois, du, family (*per. c.*1071–1313).

Bois, Arnold (IV) du (*d.* **1205**). *See under* Bois, du, family (*per. c.*1071–1313).

Bois, Arnold (V) du (**1186?–1222**). *See under* Bois, du, family (*per. c.*1071–1313).

Bois, Arnold (VI) du (*d.* **1255**). *See under* Bois, du, family (*per. c.*1071–1313).

Bois, Arnold (VII) du (*d.* **1277**). *See under* Bois, du, family (*per. c.*1071–1313).

Bois, John du, Lord du Bois (**1253–1290**). *See under* Bois, du, family (*per. c.*1071–1313).

Bois, John (**1561–1644**), biblical translator, was born on 3 January 1561 at Nettlestead, Suffolk, the only child to live to adulthood of William Bois (1513?–1591), rector of West Stow, Suffolk, and his wife, Mirabel, *née* Pooley (*c.*1513–*c.*1601). William Bois, an early protestant and a scholar (he was a foundation fellow of Trinity College, Cambridge), who originated in Yorkshire, gave his son an ideal start as a Bible scholar. By five John Bois had read his Bible through, by six he could write Hebrew, and he learnt Greek. Home education was supplemented by the grammar school at Hadleigh, Suffolk, whose master, John Still, was also master of St John's College, Cambridge. Still was probably influential in Bois's being admitted to St John's aged fourteen. Bois records that he was admitted on 12 November 1575, but also that his parents sent him to Cambridge on 27 February, presumably 1576, and that he was admitted on 1 March; he had matriculated in the Easter term of 1575. Andrew Downes, fellow of the college and regius professor of Greek, delighted in his knowledge of Greek and gave him special tuition in the most demanding Greek authors. After six months Bois was chosen as a scholar, and he it was who composed Greek epistles for various college occasions. He graduated BA early in 1579, and in 1581, aged twenty, he was elected fellow. Though he had smallpox at the time, Downes and his tutor carried Bois in his sickbed to be admitted, almost costing him his life but ensuring he lost no seniority. He proceeded MA in 1582.

Bois thought of studying medicine but, imagining he had every disease of which he read, gave it up. Yet his constitution was strong. He often walked the 20 miles from college to his mother's house for dinner, reading as he walked if he fell in with tedious company. Throughout his life he was careful of his health. He picked and rubbed his teeth so assiduously that, in his biographer Anthony Walker's phrase, 'he carried to his grave almost an Hebrew alphabet of teeth' (Allen, 147), that is, about two-thirds of his teeth. He ate only dinner and supper, with nothing in between except occasional aqua vitae and sugar for wind, and would allow an hour or more for digestion, either sitting or walking. Following three precepts for health from William Whittaker, a master of St John's for whom he wrote a funeral oration, he always studied standing, never studied in a window, and never went to bed with cold feet.

If health was a fetish, study was a passion. Bois frequently worked from four in the morning until eight at night in the university library; even in old age he studied eight hours a day. Elected lecturer (praelector) on 2 January 1582 and Greek lecturer on 4 November 1588 (re-elected 1590, 1593, and 1595), he proceeded BTh in 1590 and was appointed principal lecturer on 4 July 1595. He supplemented normal teaching with a voluntary 4 a.m. lecture in his chambers. He became a thoroughly dutiful senior dean (appointed on 11 December 1593), and when a senior fellow (from 11 June 1593) he initiated the practice of moderating after set speeches. The college gave him £100 when he left for a life in the church and marriage.

Bois's career in the church was, like the man, modest. He was ordained deacon at Norwich on Friday 21 June 1588, and priest by dispensation the following day. When his father died in 1591, his mother wished to stay at West Stow, so, through the patronage of her brother, Bois took the living, but resigned it when she went to live with the brother. By this time one Holt, rector of Boxworth, some 6 miles from Cambridge, had died, providing a dowry and a spouse for one of his daughters (her name is lost). He gave her the patronage of the living, and requested some friends that, 'if it might be by them procured, Mr Bois of St John's might become his successor by the marriage of his daughter' (Allen, 137). Bois and Miss Holt, it seems, had not met. Bois was instituted to the living on 13 October 1596 and married Holt's daughter on 7 February 1597 or 1598.

Bois's exemplary conduct as rector and from 25 August 1615 as a prebend of Ely is fully described by Walker. He prayed that he might live only so long as he could preach, and serve God and his people as minister. Taking nothing but his Bible into the pulpit, his ambition was always to be understood by all. Although he published nothing of his own, he remained a scholar and a teacher. At Boxworth he established a weekly study circle with eleven or twelve other ministers. He usually kept a scholar to help with his children's education and that of the poorer local children, and he took in children of gentlemen as boarders and students.

Bois's lasting claim to fame is that he alone of the men who worked on the King James Bible made notes on some of the discussions. Though some of the Cambridge fellows were jealous, thinking they needed no help from the country, Bois was appointed in 1604 to the second Cambridge company to work on the Apocrypha. His old mentor, Downes, was also a member. Walker, who had his information from Bois but is not wholly reliable, thought parts were done individually. Bois, he writes, 'showed me the very copy he translated by', and adds, 'but, to my grief, I know not which part' (Allen, 139). At this time Bois spent six days a week at St John's and one in his parish. He undertook a second part, presumably of the Apocrypha, this time having commons in another college. By the end of 1608 James I was hurrying the work to a conclusion. The Cambridge, Oxford, and Westminster companies each sent a copy of their work to London, and their delegates reviewed the work. Bois and Downes went from Cambridge, probably as representatives of the Apocrypha group, though Walker writes that they were the only two to go from Cambridge and that they met with 'four fellow labourers'. Bois's priceless notes were long thought lost, but a copy was discovered in Corpus Christi College Library (MS CCC 312, Fulman collection). A second copy was found in the British Library (Harley MS 750); this, though in some ways inferior because of weaknesses of the copyist, appears to be a copy of Bois's original, and shows that the Fulman manuscript was a copy of a copy.

Bois was always a note taker and maker. After hearing a sermon, for instance, he would note the date, text, and preacher and much of the content. His notes of the discussions have the same qualities and are personal memoranda on nearly 500 points in the epistles and Revelation: the text at issue is recorded and the discussion of it summarized with occasional references to his own views if they differed from those of his colleagues. They reveal the highly scholarly nature of discussions which characteristically focused on the meaning of the original. His interest is always in the problem rather than the eventual solution adopted for the English of the 1611 Bible.

The notes contain frequent references to St John Chrysostom. Both Bois and Downes contributed extensively to Sir Henry Savile's multi-volume edition of Chrysostom, and the page references in the notes show that they were made after the publication of the 1610 volume and before the publication of the 1611 volume. Sadly, the work on Chrysostom led to an estrangement between Downes and Bois. Downes, by now a cantankerous old man, thought Savile preferred Bois's work to his own and remained unreconciled with his former pupil at his death.

In 1628 Bois moved to Ely, though he retained the living of Boxworth until 1636. The following year he became rector of Thorpe Parva. His marriage was not always smooth. Bois left money matters to his wife and unawares found himself in debt. To clear this, he sold at great loss 'his darling', his library. Perhaps because of this there was strife between the two of them and he was rumoured to have thought of going overseas. Although his wife's temper was not always the best, things mended, and at her death on 16 May 1642 Bois described her as his 'dearest wife, with whom, in blameless marriage, I have lived five and forty years and more'. They had four sons and three daughters; the second son, John, and oldest daughter he saw married, the latter, Mary (*bap.* 1599, *d.* 1638), to William Walker, father of Anthony *Walker (*bap.* 1622, *d.* 1692).

Bois's inclination for fame was as slight as his learning was great. In his will of 6 June 1643 (copied in Walker's manuscript) he was most careful of his books and papers. Some borrowed books were to be returned with his apologies for having filled their margins with annotations. His own books and papers were to be 'skilfully regarded & duely looked unto'. Among the papers was an incomplete collation of commentaries intended to have covered the whole New Testament, eventually published in 1655 as *Veteris interpretis cum Beza aliisque recentioribus collatio in quatuor evangeliis, & Apostolorum Actis*. Of sums totalling £244 in his will, £80 went to the poor of Boxworth and Ely, and £20 to reparation of the church at Boxworth. Bois's youngest daughter, Anne, already had £500 following her mother's death. Bois died at Ely on 14 January 1644 and was buried there on 6 February. Of his children, only John and Anne survived him. DAVID NORTON

Sources A. Walker, 'The life and death of Mr John Bois batchellour in divinity', BL, Harley MS 7053, 94–129 / fols. 37r–54v • A. Walker, 'The life of that famous Grecian Mr John Bois, S.T.B., one of the translators of the Bible, *temp. Jac. I.* and senior prebendary of Ely, who died 14 Jan 1643', *Desiderata curiosa*, ed. F. Peck, new edn, 2 vols. in 1 (1779), 325–42; repr. in W. Allen, ed. and trans., *Translating for King James* (1969), 127–52 • Venn, *Alum. Cant.* • W. Allen, ed. and trans., *Translating for King James: being a true copy of the only notes made by a translator of King James's Bible* (1969) • D. Norton, 'John Bois's notes on the revision of the King James Bible New Testament: a new manuscript', *The Library*, 6th ser., 18 (1996), 328–46 • T. Baker, *History of the college of St John the Evangelist, Cambridge*, ed. J. E. B. Mayor, 1 (1869), 290, 326 • Cooper, *Ath. Cantab.*, 2.101 • *Walker rev.*, 264

Archives CUL, diaries | BL, Harley MS 750, fols. 3r–16r • CCC Oxf., Fulman collection, untitled notes from the work on the Authorized Version made by Bois, MS 312, fols. 61r–80r

Wealth at death £244; and estate

Boisil [St Boisil] (*d.* *c.*661), prior of Melrose, is reliably recorded only in the pages of Bede. He was celebrated among his contemporaries as a learned and holy priest and spiritual guide, and in 651 his reputation attracted Cuthbert to his community, in which Boisil held office under Abbot Eata, and he became the future saint's spiritual director. As well as teaching his pupil the scriptures, he inculcated in him by personal example the duty of going out to visit and preach to the inhabitants of neighbouring villages. When *c.*659 Eata and Cuthbert were summoned south by Aldfrith, son of King Oswiu of Northumbria, to establish a monastery at Ripon, Boisil remained at Melrose. He died of plague about 661. Cuthbert, who had by then returned from Ripon, attended him during the last week of his life, and according to Bede received prophecies about his future career and elevation to the episcopate. In later life Cuthbert spoke with great affection of Boisil, and reputedly, although reluctant, accepted episcopal office as the fulfilment of his dying master's words.

Boisil is known to have inspired a similar affection in, and to have exercised similar posthumous influence over, at least one other pupil, a companion in Ireland of the Northumbrian *peregrinus* and bishop, Ecgberht. When Ecgberht was planning a missionary visit to Germany *c.*716, Boisil appeared to this man in two visions to forbid the proposed expedition and command Ecgberht to go to Iona instead. His injunctions were obeyed and eventually resulted in the conversion of Iona to the generally observed method of calculating Easter.

Bede reports that Cuthbert spoke of Boisil as a saint. An eighth-century stone reliquary-coffin, fragments of which survive at Jedburgh and which perhaps originated at Melrose, may be his shrine, but the identification is far from certain. His remains were allegedly translated to Durham by Alfred Westou *c.*1120, together with those of other saints associated with Cuthbert, and placed next to Cuthbert's shrine. Boisil's cult is commemorated by the place name St Boswells, Roxburghshire, and in the dedication of the church at Tweedmouth. His cult spread in Scotland and England in the middle ages, and he is commemorated in calendars on 23 February, 7 July, and 9 September. ALAN THACKER

Sources Bede, *Hist. eccl.*, 4.27–8; 5.9 • Bede, 'Vita sancti Cuthberti', *Two lives of St Cuthbert*, ed. and trans. B. Colgrave (1940), chaps. 6, 9, 22 • Symeon of Durham, *Libellus de exordio atque procursu istius, hoc est Dunhelmensis, ecclesie / Tract on the origins and progress of this the church of Durham*, ed. and trans. D. W. Rollason, OMT (2000), 3.7, pp. 164–5 • 'De situ Dunelmi et de sanctorum reliquiis', Symeon of Durham, *Opera*, 1.221–2 • *Venerabilis Baedae opera historica*, ed. C. Plummer, 2 (1896), 266 • C. A. Ralegh Radford, 'Two Scottish shrines: Jedburgh and St Andrews', *Archaeological Journal*, 112 (1955), 43–60

Boissier, George Richard (1790/91–1858), Church of England clergyman, was the son of Robert Boissier of Penshurst, Kent, and his wife, Barbara Goring. He was educated at a school at Kirby Hill, Yorkshire, and matriculated at Magdalene College, Cambridge, in 1824. He graduated BA in 1828, the same year in which he published anonymously *Notes on the Cambridgeshire Churches*. Drawing its terminology from Thomas Rickman's *An Attempt to Discriminate the Styles of Architecture in England* (1817), it was an unusually early work of ecclesiology. Boissier's comments concerning unsuitable later additions to medieval churches, such as singing galleries, anticipated the arguments of the Ecclesiological Society, as did too the central message of his preface. Here he complained that the churches of Cambridgeshire and other counties were sadly neglected, describing them rather colourfully as 'cold, comfortless, unhealthy; the haunts of colds, catarrhs, and rheumatism; the receptacle frequently for filth, and the abode of toads and reptiles' (Boissier, *Notes*, 13).

Boissier was ordained deacon on 2 March 1828, and priest on 14 June 1829. He was curate of Chiddingstone, Kent, in 1828, and subsequently became the priest-in-charge of Oakfield, Penshurst. He died at Penshurst on 23 June 1858. ROSEMARY MITCHELL

Sources Venn, *Alum. Cant.* • *GM*, 3rd ser., 5 (1858), 199 • J. P. Anderson, *The book of British topography: a classified catalogue of the topographical works in the library of the British Museum relating to Great Britain and Ireland* (1881), 58 • *CGPLA Eng. & Wales* (1858) • S. Halkett and J. Laing, *Dictionary of anonymous and pseudonymous English literature*, ed. J. Kennedy and others, new edn, 4 (1928), 203

Archives CKS, papers

Wealth at death under £300: probate, 31 Aug 1858, *CGPLA Eng. & Wales*

Boit, Charles (1662–1727), miniature painter, was born on 10 August 1662 in Stockholm, the son of Charles Boit, a French silk merchant and salt manufacturer, and his wife, Marie, daughter of Noak Creveleur of Calais, France. Boit served an apprenticeship to a goldsmith in Stockholm from 1677 to 1682 and then spent three months in Paris before heading to Göteborg. There he married his first wife, *née* Flitzberg, with whom he had a daughter who died in infancy.

By the time that Boit had returned to Stockholm, in 1685, he had become fully versed in the French art of enamelling. Reynolds suggests exposure to the work of Jean Petitot and Jacques Bordier in Paris and a previous connection with Pierre Signac, a French enamellist working at the Swedish court, as important early influences. Boit came to England in 1687 and soon became the protégé of the Swedish artist Michael Dahl, some of whose portraits, like those of Godfrey Kneller, he copied in miniature. He also worked from life and appears to have travelled around the country at this early stage of his career in search of work. Two of his earliest miniatures, of Sir Gervase and Lady Scrope (1693), were painted in Lincoln. He also worked in Coventry at about this time teaching drawing to Humfrey Wanley, library-keeper to Robert Harley, earl of Oxford, one of Boit's most influential patrons. The hallmark of his style, already distinctive at this early stage, was the application of rich colours to the enamel with very smoothly blended brushstrokes which became invisible on firing. He usually signed his work on the reverse 'C. Boit pinxit' and often with the initials C. B. in monogram on the obverse. Boit's life was beset by crises and Walpole records the anecdote that, during his travels, he was unjustly imprisoned for conducting an affair with one of his pupils. This does not seem to have impeded his success for on his return to London he was appointed court enameller to William III (1696).

Boit left England to visit the Netherlands (1699), Düsseldorf (1700), and Vienna (1700–03). In Vienna he produced his most impressive work to date, a huge enamel of Emperor Leopold I and his family, measuring 38 cm by 46 (Kunsthistorisches Museum, Vienna). Though this miniature was flawed by severe cracks Boit undertook an even more ambitious commission for Queen Anne on his return to England in 1703: an allegorical enamel, measuring approximately 60 cm by 40, commemorating the battle of Blenheim. Boit's assistant, Otto Peterson, gave Vertue a detailed account of the technical and financial difficulties that dogged the project over almost ten years. Eventually, in 1714, Boit was asked to return the money that had been invested in the failed scheme and he was subsequently forced to flee in debt to France. He visited Dresden in 1719–20 but settled in Paris and at first appears to have prospered, receiving a salary of £250 per annum and lodgings from the king according to Vertue. He was made an *agrée* of the Académie Royale and enjoyed the patronage of Peter the Great, tsar of Russia, whom he had first encountered in London in 1698, and of the regent, the duke of Orléans. However, he was once again in debt by the time of his death, at his lodgings in the rue de la Petit-Bourbon, quartier du Luxembourg, Paris, on 6 February 1727. He left three children by his second marriage, to Anne-Marguerite Williart, who predeceased him: Alexandre (*b.* *c.*1712), Anne (*b.* *c.*1714), and Charlotte (*b.* *c.*1720).

Examples of Boit's English work can be seen in the Victoria and Albert Museum and the National Portrait Gallery, London, and in the Ashmolean Museum, Oxford. Of his largest surviving enamels one represents Queen Anne and Prince George of Denmark (1706; Royal Collection), another John Manners, second duke of Rutland (*c.*1714; Fitzwilliam Museum, Cambridge). Examples of Boit's work in France can be seen in the Musée du Louvre, Paris, and in the Musée Condé, Chantilly; other enamels are in the National Museum, Stockholm, and the Rijksmuseum, Amsterdam. A portrait of Boit, engraved by A. Bannerman, was published in Walpole's *Anecdotes of Painting in England* (1763). His career was important not only for the transcendence that it gave enamel painting in England over the more traditional method of painting miniatures in watercolour on vellum but also for the transmission of the enamelling skills he had learned to his pupils Otto Peterson, John Milward, and Christian Frederick Zincke.

V. REMINGTON

Sources Vertue, *Note books*, 1.33, 84, 129; 2.20–21, 77–8; 3.25, 150 • G. W. Lundberg, *Charles Boit, 1662–1727, émailleur-miniaturiste suédois: biographie et catalogue critique* (Nogent-le-Rotrou and Paris, 1987) • G. W. Lundberg, *Emaljmålaren Charles Boit, 1662–1727* (Stockholm, 1933) • W. Nisser, *Michael Dahl and the contemporary Swedish school of painting in England* (1927), 135–63 • J. Guiffrey, 'Scellés et inventaires d'artistes', *Nouvelles Archives de l'Art de France*, 2nd ser., 4 (1883), 286–91 • R. W. Goulding, 'The Welbeck Abbey miniatures', *Walpole Society*, 4 (1914–15), esp. 17–19 [whole issue] • H. Walpole, *Anecdotes of painting in England: with some account of the principal artists*, ed. J. Dallaway, [rev. and enl. edn], 3 (1827), 290–93 • G. Reynolds, *English portrait miniatures* (1952); rev. edn (1988), 87–91 • B. S. Long, *British miniaturists* (1929), 35–6 • G. Cavalli-Björkman, *Svenskt miniatyrmaleri: en konstbok fran Nationalmuseum* (Stockholm, 1981), 38–46 • E. Speel, *Dictionary of enamelling* (1998)

Likenesses A. Bannerman, print, 1762, BM, NPG · A. Bannerman, double portrait, line engraving (with J. Baker), BM, NPG; repro. in Walpole, *Anecdotes of painting in England*, 3.290

Boitard, Louis-Philippe (*fl.* 1733–1767), engraver and designer, was the son of François Boitard (1667–1719), designer. Louis-Philippe Boitard's place of birth is unknown although he was generally considered to be a Frenchman: his father, born in France, was based in London from at least 1709 to 1712 but probably died in Amsterdam. François Boitard was employed by Jacob Tonson to illustrate his editions of Shakespeare and the plays of Beaumont and Fletcher. He drew in the style of Raymond Lafage and, according to Horace Walpole, he made frequent trips to Holland to buy curiosities for the renowned collector Richard Mead. Louis-Philippe Boitard first attracted notice from George Vertue in 1742: 'Boitard engraver, lately come from Paris—some merit—good stock of assurance &c' (Vertue, *Note books*). In fact Louis Boitard's earliest known work, 'drawn from the Life at London April 1733', was a print of an 8-foot German, so it would appear that he had been working in London for some years before Vertue noticed his presence. Six plates that he had engraved after Canaletto for the fan painter Joseph Baudin were published in April 1736; he designed the frontispiece to George Lillo's *London Merchant* in 1737, and he engraved and published the *Inside of the Pantheon*, after a painting by Pannini in the collection of Lord James Cavendish, in 1738. Shortly after this Boitard visited France: in 1742 several sets of prints of birds, animals, hunting scenes, and Turkish ambassadors that he had engraved were published in Paris by the printseller Michel Odieuvre. It would seem that George Vertue first noticed him on his return. In 1744 Boitard advertised in the *Mercure de France* and it seems that he may have envisaged a cosmopolitan career like his father's. However, most of his work was done in London. During the 1740s he worked as a journeyman in the studio of the engraver William Henry Toms, where the hard-working John Boydell remarked disdainfully that 'Boitard had such a habit of *taking snuff* that He was perpetually having recourse to His Box and actually lost Hours every day from the indulgence of this practice' (Farington, *Diary*, 4.1415). In 1747, however, Boitard supplied forty-one large plates for Joseph Spence's *Polymetis*. He had also established himself by then as a designer (more rarely engraver) of satirical prints, illustrations to books, topical and theatrical portraits, watch-papers, and anatomical prints. A number of political satires, including several mocking the duke of Cumberland, have also been attributed to his hand. He worked on John and Paul Knapton's English edition of Albinus (1747–) and Walpole says that he was also employed by Dr Woodward and Dr Douglas on other anatomical figures. Walpole further reveals that he married an Englishwoman and that they had a son and a daughter. In 1753–4 he supplied designs, which were engraved by Robert Hancock, to the Battersea enamel factory, and his designs were also transferred to Worcester porcelain. He engraved the illustrations to Paltock's *Peter Wilkins* (1750), the *Scribleriad* of Richard Owen Cambridge (1751), and Cambridge's *Description of Ranelagh Rotundo and Gardens* (1762). His social satires are lively and interesting, preoccupied with a critique of luxury, the consumption of French goods, and the riotous confrontation of poverty with affluence. A number of surviving sketches and drawings record his observant fascination with the street life of the metropolis. For Robert Sayer he produced *The cries of London, for the year 1766, being a collection of humorous characters in 86 prints, done under the direction of Mr. Boitard*. His last recorded work was for James Anderson's *The Constitutions of the Antient and Honourable Fraternity of Free and Accepted Masons* (1767). His illustrations to two earlier books on freemasonry suggest that he might possibly have been a mason himself. The date of Boitard's death is unknown.

TIMOTHY CLAYTON and ANITA MCCONNELL

Sources M. Blondel, 'Boitard, Louis Philippe', Thieme & Becker, *Allgemeines Lexikon*, 12.332–3 · Vertue, *Note books*, 3.88, 109; 6.197–8, 202 · H. Walpole, *A catalogue of engravers, who have been born, or resided in England* (1763), 111 · F. G. Stephens and M. D. George, eds., *Catalogue of prints and drawings in the British Museum, division 1: political and personal satires*, 1–4 (1870–83) · F. G. Stephens and E. Hawkins, eds., *Catalogue of political and personal satires preserved in the department of prints and drawings*, 3 (1877), 100–01, 157, 665, 722–3, 747–9, 790–91, 796–9, 814, 968–70, 1117–18; 4 (1883), 288–9, 412–13 · M. Roux and others, eds., *Inventaire du fonds français: graveurs du dix-huitième siècle*, 3 (1934), 116–20 · J. Döring, *Eine Kunstgeschichte der frühen englischen Karikatur* (Hildesheim, 1991), 156–68 · H. Hammelmann, *Book illustrators in eighteenth-century England*, ed. T. S. R. Boase (1975), 18–19 · H. Hammelmann, 'Portrayer of 18th-century cockneys', *Country Life*, 126 (1959), 356–7 · C. Cook, 'Early prints on old Worcester porcelain', *Apollo*, 50 (1949), 49–52 · C. Cook, 'Louis-Philippe Boitard and his designs on Battersea enamels', *Apollo*, 57 (1953), 72–5 · *Sayer and Bennett's enlarged catalogue of new and valuable prints* (1775); repr. (1970), 79, 85 · D. Alexander, 'Canaletto and the English print market', *Canaletto and England*, ed. M. Liversidge and J. Farrington (1993), 39–40 [exhibition catalogue, Birmingham Gas Hall Exhibition Gallery, Birmingham, 14 Oct 1993 – 9 Jan 1994] · Farington, *Diary*, 4.1415

Bokenham, Osbern (*b.* 1392/3, *d.* in or after 1464), poet and Augustinian friar, was born on 6 October 1393, or possibly 1392. He was a friar at the convent of Stoke by Clare in Suffolk. Most of the little that is known about his life is derived from his best-known and most substantial work, *Legendys of Hooly Wummen*. There he ends his life of St Faith by remarking that he was born on her feast day, and in the life of St Margaret of Antioch (begun on 7 September 1443) he says that his mortal thread has lasted 'ful yerys fyfty'. His birthplace was, he says, 'even by' an 'old priory of black canons': it was most probably Old Buckenham (Bokenham) in Norfolk, just north of the Suffolk border. He says himself that he was an Augustinian friar, and that he brought his translation of the life of St Margaret back to Clare. The *explicit* in the manuscript of the *Legendys* describes the translator as 'a doctor of dyuinite clepyd Osbern Bokenham frere austin of the convent of Stoke-clare' (and a later hand has added 'a suffolk man'). His degree of DTh may have been obtained at Cambridge. He seems to take a quiet pride in being 'a Suffolk man'—he ends an apology for his lack of rhetorical skill with the words:

þerfore spekyn & wrytyn I wyl pleynly
Aftyr þe language of Suthfolk speche;

And who-so-euere lyke not þer-by,
Whereeuyr he lyst he bettyr do seche.
(Bokenham, *Legendys*, 111, ll.4063–6)

Yet he was something of a traveller, it seems. He was in Italy at least twice. In 1423 he was granted permission to visit by the prior-general, and he was there again in 1438—the date is established by his remark in the prologue (begun in September 1443) that five years earlier he had been in Venice. On this occasion ('the laste tyme I was in Itayle') he learned the story of St Margaret and her relics. On his way back from Rome he was delayed by heavy rain at Montefiascone ('Mownt Flask'), where he visited the virgin. (Relics of St Margaret had been brought from the East to this part of Italy in the twelfth century, and were later taken to Venice.) Elsewhere in the *Legendys* he tells us that he went on pilgrimage to Santiago de Compostela (1445). That his name continues to appear in the registers of the order in 1461, 1463, and 1464, twice as one of the vicars-general for the provincial chapter, disproves the earlier belief that he died in 1447. Bokenham seems to have been widely read, especially in hagiographical literature. He refers in passing (usually in asseverations of his lack of eloquence) to a few ancient authors, and several times expresses admiration for the work of Chaucer and Gower, 'and now' Lydgate. He also mentions John Capgrave's *St Katharine*.

Legendys of Hooly Wummen survives in one manuscript, BL, Arundel MS 327 (copied in Cambridge in 1447 on the instructions of his 'son' Friar Thomas Burgh, probably a member of the convent at Cambridge), which was composed between 7 September 1443 and 1447. It is an ambitious work of 10,616 lines, and relates thirteen legends (adapted from various Latin sources), a number of them dedicated to a special friend and patron, usually from the area around Clare: St Margaret (written at the request of Thomas Burgh); St Anne (for Katherine Denston and her husband, John, of Melford, who had a daughter of that name); St Christina; the 11,000 virgins; St Faith; St Agnes; St Dorothy (for John Hunt and his wife, Isabel); St Mary Magdalen (at the request—on twelfth night 1445—of Lady Isabel Bourchier, countess of Eu, the sister of the duke of York); St Katherine (for Katherine Howard, probably the wife of John Howard of Stoke Neyland near Clare, who later became duke of Norfolk); St Cecilia; St Agatha (for Agatha Flegge); St Lucy; and St Elizabeth (at the request of Lady Elizabeth de Vere, countess of Oxford, who was related to John Howard). The poem shows that Bokenham was a noted local writer and offers a glimpse into East Anglian patronage of devotional literature, and it has other points of interest—as a collection of the lives of women saints (although it is not clear that it was consciously planned as such), as an example of translation and adaptation of sources, and as a hagiographical work. In general literary historians have not rated it highly, except for its interesting and attractive personal passages. However it is an eloquent work, which often does justice to the marvels of the legends.

A number of other works can be attributed to Bokenham with some confidence. The *Mappula Angliae* (probably composed before 1445, surviving in BL, Harley MS 4011) is a prose translation of the section on England in Higden's *Polychronicon*. The initial letters of the chapters spell out Bokenham's name. He is probably the author of a translation into long unrhymed lines of part of Claudian's *De consulatu Stilichonis* (BL, Add. MS 11814) made at Clare in 1445, and dedicated to the duke of York. A dialogue 'betwix a Seculer … and a Frere', which demonstrates 'the lyneal descent of the lordis of the honoure of Clare' from 1248 to 1456, a genealogy of the house of York in both Latin and English verse preserved by Dugdale (Dugdale, *Monasticon*, 6.1600) has been attributed to him on stylistic grounds, and would again suggest strongly Yorkist connections. If he is the Bokenhamus of the Latin *Liber de angelis, annuli characteribus et imaginibus planetarum*, a tract on astrology in CUL, MS Dd.9.45, it would indicate that he also had a scientific interest. There are two clear references to works that have been lost. In the *Mappula Angliae* he speaks of 'the englishe boke the which I have compiled of legenda aurea and of other famous legendes at the instaunce of my specialle frendis' (mentioning specifically Ceadda, Felix, Edward, Oswald, and 'many oþer seyntis of Englond' (*Mappula*, ed. Horstmann, 6) to which his translation is to provide a geographical guide. It has been claimed that a remark in his legend of St Anne indicates that he wrote a Latin poem in praise of the Virgin Mary. He refers the reader to Lydgate's English *Life of Our Lady* and to a Latin work in ten books 'Of þe Weddynge Dytees', although he does not there claim that as his. But at the end of the legend he does speak of a Latin poem he had composed: he remarks that Anne had three daughters all called Mary:

but wheþer be oon husbonde or ellys be thre,
At þis tyme I wil not determyne,
For in þis mater what best plesyth me
I haue as I can declaryd in latyn
In balaade-ryme.
(Bokenham, *Legendys*, 57, ll. 2078–82)

This could have been a poem on the childhood of Mary or a life of St Anne. DOUGLAS GRAY

Sources N. Toner, 'Augustinian spiritual writers of the English province in the 15th and 16th centuries', *Sanctus Augustinus*, 2 (1956), 496–504 · Emden, *Cam.*, 69–70 · O. Bokenham, *Legendys of hooly wummen*, ed. M. S. Serjeantson, EETS, orig. ser., 206 (1938) · '*Mappula Angliae*, von Osbern Bokenham', ed. C. Horstmann, *Englische Studien*, 10 (1886–7), 1–34 · E. Flügel, 'Eine mittelenglische Claudian-Übersetzung', *Anglia*, 28 (1905), 255–99, 421–38 · Dugdale, *Monasticon*, new edn, 1600–02 · S. Moore, 'Patrons of letters in Norfolk and Suffolk, *c*.1430', *Publications of the Modern Language Association of America*, 27 (1912), 188–207; 28 (1913), 79–105

Archives BL, Add. MS 11814 · BL, Arundel MS 327 · BL, Harley MS 4011 · CUL, MS Dd. 9.45

Bokyngham, John. *See* Buckingham, John (*c*.1320–1399).

Bolam, Silvester (1905–1953), newspaper editor, was born on 23 October 1905 at 84 George Street, Willington Quay, Tynemouth, Northumberland, the son of Thomas Bolam, a foreman blacksmith, and his wife, Amelia English. He was educated at Tynemouth Municipal High School and Armstrong College, Newcastle (then part of Durham University), graduating in economics in 1926. On 21 April 1934

Bolam married Annabel Cecilia (*b.* 1906), daughter of John Scorer, coal fitter; they were to have two children.

Initially destined for a business career, on graduating Bolam instead took a job on the *Newcastle Journal*. After making his mark amid the ferocious newspaper competition of the late 1920s, he moved to Manchester to work for the *News Chronicle*, then in 1936 joined the *Daily Mirror* as a sub-editor. Leaving in 1938 to rejoin the *News Chronicle*, he was told by H. G. Bartholomew, editorial director of the *Mirror*, 'you'll be back' (Griffiths, 118). Within ten months he was, as joint night editor beginning a rise through the *Mirror's* executive ranks. His success was built on 'disciplined habits of work and an imperturbability rare among newspaper executives' (*Manchester Guardian*, 28 April 1953). A gifted newspaper technician, he was noted for skill in making heavy subjects accessible and had a close working relationship with the cantankerous, wayward Bartholomew, whom he praised for 'the sense of purpose he created in the young men around him' (Griffiths, 118).

In July 1948 Bolam succeeded Cecil Thomas as editor. His four and a half years in charge were to see the *Mirror* displace the *Daily Express* as Britain's best-selling daily paper. Soon after he became editor Bolam memorably expressed his credo:

> Sensationalism does not mean distorting the truth. It means the vivid and dramatic presentation of events so as to give them a forceful impact in the mind of the reader. It means big headlines, vigorous writing, simplification into everyday language and the wide use of illustration by cartoons and photographs. (Cudlipp, *Walking on the Water*, 174)

Bolam is mainly remembered for his imprisonment in March 1949, for contempt of court. He admitted an error of judgement in printing a story in the *Daily Mirror* which might prejudice the trial of John Haigh, who was subsequently executed for murder. However, Lord Goddard, the lord chief justice (clearly aware of Bolam's editorial stance), chose to interpret it as 'a matter of policy, pandering to sensationalism for the purpose of increasing the circulation of this paper' (*World's Press News*, 31 March 1949). Bolam was sent to Brixton gaol for three months, the first national newspaper editor gaoled for reasons relating to his paper since 1901.

Bolam was philosophical about his imprisonment: 'Most executive journalists never get the chance to think. If you have 18 hours a day by yourself for three months you have a valuable opportunity for reaching objectivity, for clearing your mind, for setting your sights' (Griffiths, 118). Nevertheless, his *Mirror* colleague W. N. Connor (better known as Cassandra) believed it 'may well have been solid claustrophobic hell for a man whose hobby happened to be mountaineering' (*Daily Mirror*, 1 May 1953).

In July 1949 Bolam returned to the paper, edited in his absence by Alex Little, a former classmate at Tynemouth Municipal High School. He remained editor for a further three and a half years. However, the period was not entirely happy. In 1951, recognizing that the behaviour of his mentor, Bartholomew, had become impossibly erratic, he cast the decisive vote in a board-room coup against him. His relations with Bartholomew's successor Cecil King, who found him far too earnest, were poor, and in January 1953 he left the post, resigning ostensibly because of a disagreement with the management (*World's Press News*, 30 Jan 1953), although the history of the *Daily Mirror* describes him as 'a deferential editor sacked for disagreeing with his superiors' (Edelman, 156).

Bolam was a serious-minded man, a slight figure with a goatee beard and 'the mild manner of a professor of languages' (*Newcastle Journal*, 28 April 1953), whose dedicated Christianity earned him the nickname Bish. His *Mirror* colleague Hugh Cudlipp recalled him as a 'friendly, wiry bird with a dozen interests—books, art, music, the countryside' (Cudlipp, *Publish and be Damned!*, 251–2).

He died suddenly on 27 April 1953 at his home, Lincoln House, West Road, Guildford, his wife surviving him. He was cremated on 30 April at St John's crematorium, Woking, Surrey. HUW RICHARDS

Sources D. Griffiths, ed., *The encyclopedia of the British press, 1422–1992* (1992) · H. Cudlipp, *Publish and be damned! The astonishing story of the 'Daily Mirror'* (1953) · M. Edelman, *The Mirror: a political history* (1966) · H. Cudlipp, *Walking on the water* (1962) · *World's Press News* (2 Dec 1948) · *World's Press News* (24 March 1949) · *World's Press News* (31 March 1949) · *World's Press News* (30 Jan 1953) · *World's Press News* (1 May 1953) · *World's Press News* (7 July 1949) · *Newcastle Journal* (28 April 1953) · *Manchester Guardian* (28 April 1953) · *Daily Mirror* (3–4 March 1949) · *News Chronicle* (28 April 1953) · *Daily Mirror* (1 May 1953) · *CGPLA Eng. & Wales* (1953) · b. cert. · m. cert. · d. cert.

Likenesses photograph, repro. in Cudlipp, *Publish and be damned!*

Wealth at death £18,568 3*s*. 10*d*.: administration, 27 June 1953, *CGPLA Eng. & Wales*

Bolan, Marc [*real name* Mark Feld] (**1947–1977**), musician and poet, was born on 30 September 1947 in Hackney, London, the second child of Simeon Feld, cosmetics salesman (1920–1991), and his wife, Phyllis Winifred, *née* Atkins (1927–1991). The energy of 1950s rock'n'roll captivated the young Mark Feld, prompting him to take up the guitar. He left school at fourteen, worked as a model, and wrote reams of prose and poetry in his characteristic dyslexic hand. He released several solo records in the mid-1960s, changed his name to Marc Bolan, and joined the group John's Children for a short spell. Their hit single 'Desdemona' (1967) was banned by the BBC for what were regarded at the time as risqué lyrics. When the band broke up shortly afterwards, Bolan found himself adrift in London with no musical equipment.

During the 'summer of love' of 1967 Bolan formed an acoustic duo, called Tyrannosaurus Rex, with **Steve** [Peregrine] **Took** [*real name* Stephen Ross Porter] (1949–1980) on bongoes, percussion, and backing vocals. Took was born in Eltham, London, on 28 July 1949, the son of Leonard Henry Porter, bakery manager, and Betty George. They recorded three albums, *My People were Fair and had Sky in their Hair* (1968), *Prophets, Seers, and Sages* (1968), and *Unicorn* (1969), all produced by Tony Visconti. With the help of the disc jockey John Peel, Tyrannosaurus Rex became a successful 'underground' act. Bolan's other vital support was his wife, June Ellen Child (1943/4–1995), a record company receptionist, whom he married on 30 January 1970. She

Marc Bolan (1947–1977), by Keith Morris, 1972

provided vital organization and a stable domestic life where the creativity of the less firmly grounded Bolan could flourish.

The acoustic, whimsical songs of Tyrannosaurus Rex (T. Rex) contrasted with much of 1968's high-volume rock-blues and revolutionary stances; at their best, these albums have a childlike innocence. Sung with an inimitable vibrato and steeped in a Tolkienesque mythology, Bolan's songs evoked a gentler pastoral world of wizards, queens, fauns, and unicorns. This mythology also shaped *The Warlock of Love* (1969), a best-selling collection of poetry, and other writings published posthumously. Bolan's verse shows a lack of literary awareness, yet demonstrates an instinctive sensitivity to rhyme and rhythm, and the romanticized imagery which made his song lyrics original.

A Beard of Stars (1969) saw Mickey Finn (1947–2003) replace the increasingly unreliable Steve Took, who went on to join the Pink Fairies and Shagrat. Took died, after choking on a cherry stone, on 27 October 1980. Much of his music was unreleased at his death, but has since gained a cult following. On *A Beard of Stars* Bolan introduced electric guitars into the music and, like Bob Dylan before him, faced cries of 'sell-out' from part of his audience. Dreaming of mainstream success, Bolan spent the summer of 1970 listening to old rock'n'roll records and recorded *T. Rex* (1970), an evocative and distinctly English-sounding record that struck an excellent balance between the acoustic and electric elements.

These sessions produced his first hit, 'Ride a white swan', which spent five months in the UK top forty, and reached number two. In March 1971 the follow-up 'Hot love' went to number one for six weeks. Steve Currie (bass) and Bill Legend (drums) were hired to make T. Rex a functioning rock quartet. Once glimpsed on television, Bolan's androgynous beauty, wild corkscrew hair, lurex jackets, and glitter make-up seized the imagination of a generation of post-1960s teenagers looking for a figurehead. Along with David Bowie, Bolan was the epitome of the 'glam rock' phenomenon. A third single, 'Get it on', went to number one for four weeks. T. Rex embarked on an autumn UK tour to promote *Electric Warrior*, one of the best-selling albums of 1971. 'Jeepster', released as a single against Bolan's wishes, went to number two, his fourth hit of the year. The music press heralded a new 'Beatlemania'. Bolan had taken elements of 1950s rock'n'roll but filtered them through a 1960s post-Dylan, post-Hendrix sensibility. It was as though Chuck Berry had collided with *Lord of the Rings*. Sexy, commercial, yet imaginative, T. Rex seemed a breath of fresh air in the otherwise over-serious 'progressive' music scene. As a guitarist and song-writer, Bolan was self-taught and had a limited technique and no knowledge of theory. But T. Rex records of 1970–72 are full of simple but elegant lead guitar, and fine rhythm guitar playing.

Now a teenage idol, Bolan signed with EMI, set up his own label—the T. Rex Wax Company—and had four more hits in 1972: 'Telegram Sam', 'Metal guru' (both number ones), 'Children of the revolution', and 'Solid gold easy action'. *The Slider* was a patchy but strong album overall, and Bolan's biggest ever UK gigs came with two shows in March at the Wembley Empire Pool (later Wembley Arena). These were filmed by Ringo Starr and given a cinema release as *Born to Boogie*.

By the end of 1972 Bolan had passed his commercial and artistic peak. The music became formulaic, and stardom brought the usual problems of ego-inflation and drug abuse. Much to his frustration, America stubbornly refused to find any virtue in T. Rex, with only 'Get it on' managing to be a moderate hit, while in the UK he was eclipsed by Slade, David Bowie, and Roxy Music. By 1973 Bolan had parted from his wife June (though apparently they never divorced), and became estranged from supporters such as John Peel and his fellow disc jockey Bob Harris. Later T. Rex albums such as *Tanx* (1973) are not without some good songs, but pretentious arrangements often overwhelm simple ideas. In 1976 Bolan regained some credibility by re-positioning himself as the 'godfather of punk' and showcasing new bands on a Granada television series entitled *Marc*.

On 16 September 1977, just before his thirtieth birthday, Bolan was killed when the Mini driven by his girlfriend, the singer Gloria Jones (*b.* 1947), crashed into a tree on Barnes Common, west London. Despite filling his songs with references to cars, Bolan never learned to drive, believing that like Eddie Cochran he would die in one.

Bolan was survived by Rolan (*b.* 1975), the son he had with Jones. He was cremated on 20 September at Golders Green, London.

Along with David Bowie, Marc Bolan is remembered as the leading light of early 1970s popular music in the UK, revitalizing the singles charts with records that paid homage to and successfully updated 1950s rock'n'roll.

RIKKY ROOKSBY

Sources M. Paytress, *Twentieth-century boy* (1992) • P. du Moyer, 'The man who would be king', *Mojo*, 47 (Oct 1997), 33–48 • T. Dicks and P. Platz, eds., *Marc Bolan: a tribute* (1978) • D. Regenold, www.primenet.com/~regenold/marc/marc.html [Marc Bolan information page] • B. Hoskyns, *Glam! Bowie, Bolan and the glitter rock revolution* (1998) • b. cert. • m. cert. • d. cert. • 'Steve Took's domain', www.steve-took.co.uk • *CGPLA Eng. & Wales* (1978) • b. cert. [Steve Took] • d. cert. [Steve Took]

Archives FILM BFI NFTVA, *Night network*, 3 Sept 1987 • BFI NFTVA, 'Marc Bolan: the legendary years', 16 Sept 1992 • BFI NFTVA, 'Marc Bolan: dandy in the underworld', 16 Sept 1997 • BFI NFTVA, documentary footage • BFI NFTVA, performance footage | SOUND BL NSA, 'Marc Bolan', V2278/1 • BL NSA, 'The story of Marc Bolan', V2318/1 • BL NSA, documentary recordings • BL NSA, performance recordings

Likenesses K. Morris, photograph, 1972, NPG [*see illus.*] • P. Sanders, photographs, repro. in T. Rex, *Beard of stars* (1970), cover • photographs, Hult. Arch.

Wealth at death £30,870: administration with will, 17 Nov 1978, *CGPLA Eng. & Wales*

Boland, Gerald (1885–1973). *See under* Boland, Henry James (1887–1922).

Boland, Henry James [Harry] (1887–1922), tailor's cutter and Irish revolutionary, was born on 27 April 1887 at 6 Dalymount Terrace, Phibsborough Road, north Dublin, the third of five children of James Henry Boland (1856–1895), paving overseer for the Dublin corporation, and Catherine (*c.*1861–1932), daughter of Philip Woods. Both James and Kate were Mancunians, their own parents being immigrants to England from Roscommon, Galway, and Louth. Like many embittered products of the Lancashire Irish they roved the urban world in search of work and vengeance upon England. Having met in Manchester they had married in Dublin on 21 October 1882 and produced children in both America and Lancashire before settling in Dublin in 1885. In each country Jim Boland plotted with the most 'advanced' republicans, manufacturing bombs, intimidating hostile factions, supporting Parnell in the split, and becoming Leinster's delegate to the supreme council of the Irish Republican Brotherhood (IRB). His presidency of the Dublin county board of the Gaelic Athletic Association (GAA) was a tribute to his conspiratorial rather than his sporting prowess. His close associates included some of the Invincibles responsible for the Phoenix Park murders in 1882; and his death from a brain cyst, when only thirty-eight, was ascribed to a battle with anti-Parnellites, three years earlier, for possession of the *United Irishman*'s office.

Making of a revolutionary The manner of Jim Boland's life and death were critical influences upon Harry's revolutionary development. The family was shielded from destitution by public subscriptions raised after the funeral,

Henry James Boland (1887–1922), by unknown photographer, 1919

which was a massive gathering of Parnellites, conspirators, and sportsmen. Kate was able to secure a south-side tobacconist's shop in Wexford Street before moving to nearby Lennox Street in 1907, and north to 15 Marino Crescent (the Clontarf birthplace of Bram Stoker) in 1914. After a turbulent period with the Christian Brothers' school at Synge Street, Dublin, Harry was accepted as a boarder by the De La Salle Retreat at Castletown, Queen's county, with the prospect of a noviciate. Lacking both money and a vocation he left school at the turn of the century, working briefly in Manchester before becoming a tailor's cutter in Todd, Burns & Co. of Mary Street, then one of Dublin's largest department stores. Radical and conspiratorial politics were rampant among Dublin's artisans, and he soon emulated his father by joining the IRB and GAA, as well as the radical Keating branch of the Gaelic League. His Irish remained rudimentary, but his hurling was proficient enough to earn him a place in Dublin's team for an all-Ireland final in 1909. He proved even more adept as a sporting administrator, securing his father's former post as Dublin county chairman in 1911. By November 1913, when he became a founder member of the Irish Volunteers, Boland was already an influential 'insider' in Dublin's republican underground. He supported the volunteers' provisional committee when it repudiated Redmond's leadership in October 1914, and continued to drill with the 2nd battalion, Dublin brigade. Known to the public only as a hurler, he was an activist but not a leader until the Easter rising of 1916. In these respects, as in many others, he resembled Michael Collins, whom he is said to have introduced to the IRB when visiting London in 1909.

The Easter rising In 1916 Harry Boland was still living with his mother and his surviving sister (Kathleen) in Marino Crescent, his brothers Gerald (1885–1973) [*see below*] and Edmund (1893–1928) having left home. All three brothers were involved in the rising, Edmund avoiding arrest after Pearse's surrender and Gerald being interned along with Michael Collins, whom he disliked and distrusted. After some initial sorties around Fairview, Harry entered the General Post Office (GPO) on Easter Tuesday evening, being one of the last to escape the bombardment three days later after gallantly disabling unused bombs in the basement. Though neither an officer nor a noteworthy combatant in the rising he was court-martialled and sentenced to ten years' penal servitude, having been pointed out by a machine-gun instructor whom he had incarcerated in the GPO. This fortuitous promotion from the ranks gave Boland the opportunity to demonstrate his finesse as an organizer to emerging leaders such as Eamon de Valera, his fellow prisoner at Dartmoor, Lewes, and Maidstone. With his hearty good humour, robust self-confidence, and ingenuity in devising torments for the warders he was quickly identified as a ringleader by the authorities and a likely lad by nationalists.

Republican organizer Following the general amnesty of June 1917 Boland rapidly reasserted his influence in the republican fraternities, while using the cachet of the freedom fighter to infatuate a procession of women. Though one found him 'a bluff hearty fellow' who was 'a wee bit rough' (PRO, CO 904/214/405), others such as Kitty Kiernan of Granard, co. Longford, were entranced by his fashionable attire, boisterous antics, fervent singing, and dramatic stories. His chief partner in both republican and sexual politics was Collins, who usually excelled Boland in both pursuits and thus gained an ascendancy that turned sour only in 1921. Both were elected to the executive of Sinn Féin when it was reconstituted in October 1917, so promoting IRB influence over that vast and unwieldy popular movement. Whereas Collins antagonized the 'politicians' and soon redirected his energy to the volunteers, Boland became a key figure in drafting propaganda, organizing electoral campaigns, and maintaining morale at headquarters in 6 Harcourt Street. After the arrest of de Valera and most other leading republicans in May 1918 those shrewd enough to evade arrest consolidated their power. While Collins and Mulcahy prepared the volunteers for armed resistance against conscription Boland became joint honorary secretary of Sinn Féin and an architect of its electoral triumph after the armistice. Mildly socialist by inclination, and egalitarian in manner, he managed to win the confidence of labour leaders and manoeuvre them into withdrawing from the election and collaborating with Dáil Éireann, the republican assembly inaugurated in January 1919. Boland secured election for South Roscommon, outpolling by 10,685 votes to 4233 his constitutionalist opponent who had mocked him as 'only a tramp tailor' (de Valera MSS, University College, Dublin, archives department, P150/96).

Boland's growing political influence was still underpinned by his fraternal and conspiratorial connections. He remained active in administering and politicizing the GAA, which repaid his investment in November 1917 by organizing a benefit hurling match at Croke Park, so helping Boland to set up his own tailoring business at 64 Middle Abbey Street. The arrest of Seán McGarry in May 1918 allowed Boland to join the IRB's supreme council, of which he was soon elected president (and therefore, according to its then constitution, president of the republic). Its treasurer was Collins, with whom Boland continued to consort, wrestle, hurl, and tipple while on the run. They collaborated in the spectacular rescue of de Valera from Lincoln gaol in February 1919, a bloodless triumph of ingenuity and improvisation. It was evidently at de Valera's bidding that Boland was sent to the United States, three months later, as a 'special envoy' of the Dáil.

Mission to America Boland's mission was conducted on many levels, illuminating the shadowy connections among the administrative, political, military, and conspiratorial strands of the Irish revolution. Throughout de Valera's own period in America (from June 1919 to December 1920) Boland acted as his private secretary, tour organizer, bagman, political adviser, butler, and personal entertainer. With difficulty he managed to offload responsibility for the promotion and sale of republican 'bonds', which presented daunting managerial and technical problems beyond his competence. Charged with restoring unity among the squabbling factions of Irish-American activists he ultimately did more than most to foster disunity. After impassioned, sustained, but futile attempts to reconcile the Friends of Irish Freedom and Clan na Gael to de Valera's Irish-centred political strategy Boland disavowed both organizations in late 1920, organizing rival bodies under his own dictatorial management. The creation of a tame American Association for the Recognition of the Irish Republic was widely publicized; but the reorganization of the Clan na Gael, as a subsidiary body to the home organization, was a clandestine undertaking that horrified the latter and exasperated even Collins. Boland's ruthless campaign against John Devoy and Daniel Cohalan alienated many old supporters of the Irish cause in America; but his team of organizers and propagandists mobilized hundreds of thousands of Americans, many without Irish antecedents, behind the demand for self-determination. The strategy of confrontation was de Valera's, but Boland was largely responsible for its execution.

Still deeper motives lay behind Boland's presence in America through most of the Irish revolution. He co-ordinated an ambitious programme for procuring arms and smuggling them to Ireland, which required him to recruit and manipulate an intricate network of agents and contacts. Though ostensibly subject to Cathal Brugha's authority as minister for defence, these operations were conducted through the IRB and its American affiliates, leading to bitter conflict between Brugha and

Boland (as well as Collins) over funding and supervision. Boland's reputation as a master gun-runner was shattered, in June 1921, by the capture in Hoboken of 495 Thompson sub-machine guns, an expensive consignment of the latest model which embodied the last hope of military success for the insurgents in Ireland. Boland made his second trip home in August 1921 to attend the second Dáil (to which he had been elected unopposed) and also to vindicate his conduct, returning to America with enhanced 'diplomatic' credentials. In addition to securing weapons capable of transforming the Irish Volunteers into an army, he had the still more startling ambition of building up a worldwide network of conspirators ready to attack British targets overseas. This scheme, concocted with Collins in 1919 but still in gestation in 1921, was suspended during the truce and never tested.

Opposition to the treaty and death Before returning to America Boland had resumed his role as de Valera's faithful messenger, acting as an intermediary with Lloyd George at Gairloch in September 1921. His eventual decision to follow the Chief in opposing the treaty settlement, though presented as an independent expression of political principle, was influenced by both loyalty to de Valera and growing animosity towards Collins. In Boland's absence, Collins had taken charge not only of the IRB but of Kitty Kiernan, the republican belle from Granard who had been intermittently pursued by both men since 1917. Boland arrived back in Ireland on 5 January 1922, in time to vote with the minority of deputies against the treaty. More strongly than Collins he continued to believe that fraternal solidarity could surmount all divisions, and spent the first half of 1922 seeking a reconciliation between Collins and de Valera. Ever optimistic and cheerful, he imagined that goodwill and belief in the cause of freedom could prevail against sectional and personal animosities. He was a key figure in negotiating the abortive pact preceding the election of June 1922, in which he was again elected without opposition to the Dáil.

At the outbreak of civil war, for the first time since the rising, Boland took arms against the government (as did both brothers). Briefly quartermaster-general for the irregulars, he was prominent in the occupation and abandonment of Blessington. After a period on the run in Dublin, and the capture of his letter soliciting money and guns from the Clan na Gael, Boland was surprised and shot by a raiding party in the Grand Hotel, Skerries, dying in St Vincent's Hospital, Dublin, on 1 August 1922. His personal estate amounted to only £657 in cash and insurance policies, his tailoring business having collapsed during his absence in America. Harry Boland's funeral at Glasnevin cemetery, where he was buried on 4 August, though unreported because of censorship, attracted vast crowds to mourn one of the most genial, attractive, yet impenetrable of Irish revolutionaries. The event was recorded by Jack Yeats in two striking paintings which convey the general dismay occasioned by his loss. Loyal and sincere, intimate with the leaders of both factions, he epitomized in his death the failure of the revolutionary ideal.

Gerald Boland (1885–1973), Harry's elder brother, was born at 33 Francis Street, Manchester, on 25 May 1885. After training as an engine fitter and civil engineer he married Annie Keating, a farmer's daughter, on 8 September 1915. Their seven children included Kevin (*b.* 1917), who held several ministries under Fianna Fáil after 1957 before breaking with the party in 1970 and founding an ineffectual rival, Aontacht Éireann. By contrast with Harry, Gerald's experience in the rising (as an officer at Jacob's factory) led him to repudiate the conspiratorial approach of Collins and the IRB. After internment at Knutsford and Fron-goch he resumed drilling with the volunteers and spent much of 1918 in Belfast gaol, afterwards serving the Dublin corporation as an engineer. Before the truce he commanded the 7th battalion, Dublin brigade, leading the 3rd battalion of Dublin irregulars in the first weeks of the civil war until his arrest and internment (July 1922 to July 1924). In 1925 he accompanied Seán Russell to the Soviet Union in an apparently vain attempt to secure arms and money for the IRA. Soon afterwards he followed de Valera into Fianna Fáil and repudiated the subversive strategy, becoming with Seán Lemass the party's key organizer and eventually its chief whip. De Valera rewarded him with the ministries of posts and telegraphs (1933–6), lands (1936–9), and justice (1939–48, 1951–4). As minister for justice he introduced the Emergency Powers Act of 1940, resulting in the imprisonment, internment, execution, and death on hunger strike of many former colleagues. More introspective and uncertain than Harry, Gerald treasured his younger brother's memory and convictions until his own death in Clontarf on 5 January 1973. DAVID FITZPATRICK

Sources J. Maher, *Harry Boland: a biography* (1998) • H. Boland, diaries, 1919–22, University College, Dublin, de Valera MSS • H. Boland, correspondence, University College, Dublin, de Valera MSS • H. Boland and G. Boland, correspondence, notebooks, etc., priv. coll. • NL Ire., J. M'Garrity MSS • NL Ire., J. Devoy MSS • American Irish Historical Society, New York, D. Cohalan MSS • NYPL, Humanities and Social Sciences Library, F. P. Walsh MSS, manuscripts and archives division • Villanova University, Philadelphia, Falvey Memorial Library, J. M'Garrity MSS • earl of Longford and T. P. O'Neill, *Eamon de Valera* (1970) • T. P. Coogan, *De Valera: long fellow, long shadow* (1993) • L. Ó Broin, *In great haste: the letters of Michael Collins and Kitty Kiernan* (1983) • M. M'Inerney, 'Gerry Boland's story', *Irish Times* (8–19 Oct 1968) • PRO, CO 904/214/405

Archives priv. coll., MSS | American Irish Historical Society, New York, D. Cohalan MSS • NL Ire., J. Devoy MSS • NL Ire., J. M'Garrity MSS • NYPL, F. P. Walsh MSS • University College, Dublin, de Valera MSS, diaries and corresp.

Likenesses International Feature Service, photograph, 1 July 1919, Hult. Arch. [*see illus.*] • photograph, *c.*1920, repro. in Maher, *Harry Boland*, cover • Walshe, group portrait, photograph, 21 Feb 1922, Hult. Arch. • L. Whelan, oils, 1922?, priv. coll. • J. B. Yeats, group portrait, oils, 1922 (*The funeral of Harry Boland*), Sligo County Museum • photographs, priv. coll.

Wealth at death £657 7*s.* 1*d.*—gross, personal estate • £627 7*s.* 1*d.*—net, personal estate • £15,716: probate, 1973, Ireland

Boland, John Pius (1870–1958), politician and tennis player, son of Patrick Boland (1840–1877), businessman, and his wife, Mary Donnelly, was born at 135 Capel Street, Dublin, on 16 September 1870. His father, the wealthy proprietor of the largest bakery in Ireland, died in 1877, and his mother in 1882, leaving their seven children under the guardianship of Mrs Boland's half-brother Nicholas Donnelly, auxiliary bishop of Dublin. John Pius Boland owed his second name, which caused him some embarrassment in youth, to the fact that his baptism followed shortly after Pope Pius IX's loss of temporal power upon the capture of Rome by Victor Emmanuel. He was educated by the Marist Fathers at the Catholic University School, Lower Leeson Street, Dublin, and then from 1881 to 1890 at the Oratory School, Birmingham, where he was a contemporary of Hilaire Belloc. In 1890, after a semester at the University of Bonn, he proceeded to London University, where he graduated BA in 1892. In January 1893 he matriculated at the University of Oxford from Christ Church, where he read jurisprudence, and graduated BA with fourth-class honours in 1896 (he proceeded MA in 1901).

At Oxford, Boland was a prominent sportsman and debater. In the spring of 1896 he travelled to Athens at the invitation of Constantine Thrasybulos Mano (1869–1913), a Greek undergraduate at Balliol during 1894–5, who was involved in the organization of the first Olympic games of the modern era. On the spur of the moment Boland entered the singles and doubles in lawn tennis; he was paired in the doubles by Fritz Traun of Germany, and despite having to play in leather-soled shoes and with 'a tennis bat of sorts, secured at the Panhellenic Bazaar' (journal, fol. 103, 10 April 1896), he emerged victorious in the finals (11 April 1896) of both events. Boland thus ranks as Ireland's, and Britain's, first Olympic champion.

On his holidays in the south-west of Ireland Boland was disturbed by the illiteracy prevailing in districts where lessons were taught in a language—English—which the children did not speak. He now committed himself to the twin causes of home rule and the Irish language. Though called to the bar from the Inner Temple in 1897, he never practised. He was elected MP for South Kerry in 1900 and held the seat for the next eighteen years. In 1902 he married Eileen (1876–1937), daughter of Dr Patrick Moloney, a wealthy Australian, and with her had one son and five daughters.

Appointed a nationalist party whip in 1906, Boland soon became adept at manipulating the rules of parliamentary procedure, turning unlikely subjects such as the Maltese language question in an Irish direction. A vice-president of the Irish Industrial Development Association, he was active in promoting Irish trade, and it was due to his efforts that an Irish trade mark was patented in 1906. His main speciality, however, was education, the cause for which he had entered politics. After the passage of the Irish Universities Bill in 1908, he was appointed as one of the ten commissioners charged with the establishment of the new university based in Dublin, which at his suggestion was named the National University of Ireland. As a lawyer he was much involved in drafting the statutes, and he brought to the commission a broad experience of three universities. It was on his insistence that competence in the Irish language was made a condition of matriculation.

In 1918 Boland became acting chief whip of the Irish party, but later that year lost his seat in the general election which brought Sinn Féin a majority of Irish seats. In recognition of his work for education he received a papal knighthood. Disillusioned by the turn of events in Ireland, he retired from political life and settled in London, where from 1926 to 1947 he served as secretary of the Catholic Truth Society. In his memoir, *Irishman's Day: a Day in the Life of an Irish MP* (1944), he evoked the camaraderie of the Irish Parliamentary Party in its final phase under the leadership of John Redmond. His contribution to Irish university education was honoured in June 1950, when the National University conferred on him an honorary doctorate in laws.

Boland died at his London home, 40 St George's Square, Westminster, on 17 March (St Patrick's day) 1958. One of his daughters, Mrs Honor Crowley, represented his old constituency of South Kerry in the Dáil for some years as a Fianna Fáil deputy. Another daughter, the novelist and playwright Bridget Boland, paid an affectionate tribute to her parents in her memoir *At my Mother's Knee* (1978).

G. Martin Murphy

Sources C. White, 'John Pius Boland', *UCD News* [international edn] (1986) • C. White, 'The 80th anniversary of the National University of Ireland', *UCD News* (1988) • J. P. Boland, *Irishman's day* (1944) • B. Boland, *At my mother's knee* (1978) • *The Tablet* (22 March 1958) • *WWW, 1951–60* • F. C. Burnand, ed., *The Catholic who's who and yearbook* (1910) • I. Burnahan, *British Olympians* (1991) • *WWBMP* • J. P. Boland, journal, British Olympic Association, London

Archives British Olympic Association, London, journal | NL Ire., letters to John Redmond, MS 15171

Likenesses photograph, c.1907, repro. in Boland, *At my mother's knee*

Wealth at death £6886 8s. 3d.: probate, 23 June 1958, *CGPLA Eng. & Wales*

Bolckow, Henry William Ferdinand (1806–1878), ironmaster, was born at Sulten, Mecklenburg, Germany, on 8 December 1806, the son of Heinrich Bölckow, of Varchow, Mecklenburg, and his wife, Caroline Dussher. He had at least five sisters and a brother. About 1821 his parents placed him in a merchant's office at Rostock. He made the acquaintance there of Christian Allhusen, who soon migrated to Newcastle upon Tyne, where, in 1827, Bolckow joined him in a corn merchant's business. After twelve years of dealings Bolckow had accumulated more than £40,000; he then severed his partnership in Newcastle, and instead entered into one with a practical ironmaker, John Vaughan. Bolckow became naturalized in 1841, and that year he and Vaughan opened an iron and engineering works on the Tees at the small coal-shipping port of Middlesbrough. In 1846 they started blast furnaces to produce iron at Witton Park in co. Durham, and in 1850 Vaughan began to exploit the Cleveland ironstone near to Middlesbrough. By 1855 the partners had a dozen blast furnaces making iron on Teesside and the spectacular growth of the district's industry and population was proceeding: from 8000 in 1851, the population of Middlesbrough increased to 40,000 in 1871.

The success of the partners' business enabled them to multiply their possessions: besides ironworks, they acquired collieries, limestone quarries, additional ironstone workings, and brickfields. Middlesbrough received a charter of incorporation in 1853 and Bolckow was elected the first mayor. He married Miriam Hay *née* Poole, widow of C. Hay, about 1840, but she died in 1842. In 1851 he married Harriet, the only daughter of James Farrar of Halifax. She died on 13 August 1890.

In 1864 the partnership of Bolckow and Vaughan was formed into a limited liability company with a capital of £2,500,000, Bolckow becoming chairman of the company on 1 January 1865. In 1868 he presented to the inhabitants of Middlesbrough the Albert Park, at a cost of more than £20,000. In the following year he spent £7000 in the erection of the St Hilda's schools. When the town was granted parliamentary representation Bolckow was unopposedly elected the first member on 16 November 1868, and held that position until his death. In the election of 1874, when he was returned as a Liberal, he was opposed.

Bolckow built up a fine collection of pictures, mainly by contemporary artists. A JP, and sometime deputy lieutenant for the North Riding of Yorkshire, he was also a knight of the order of the Wendish Crown. He died at Ramsgate, Kent, on 18 June 1878, and was buried in Marton churchyard, near Middlesbrough, on 22 June. He left an estate valued at under £800,000. The major part of this passed to a nephew, Carl F. H. Bolckow, who assumed the chairmanship of Bolckow, Vaughan & Co. Ltd. One of his sisters, who predeceased him, was the wife of the Teesside ironmaster W. R. I. Hopkins.

G. C. Boase, *rev.* J. K. Almond

Sources R. Gott, *Henry Bolckow, founder of Teesside* (1968) • J. S. Jeans, *Pioneers of the Cleveland iron trade* (1875), 47–77 • *Journal of the Iron and Steel Institute*, 1 (1878), 288–90 • J. K. Almond, 'Bolckow, Henry William Ferdinand', *DBB* • W. H. Burnett, *Old Cleveland … local writers and local worthies* (1886), 94–9 • *The Times* (19 June 1878) • *ILN* (29 June 1878), 613 • *CGPLA Eng. & Wales* (1878) • d. cert.

Likenesses W. D. Stevenson, bronze statue, 1881, Exchange Place, Middlesbrough • portrait, Middlesbrough municipal buildings

Wealth at death under £800,000: probate, 27 July 1878, *CGPLA Eng. & Wales*

Bold, Henry (*d.* 1677). *See under* Bold, Henry (1627–1683).

Bold, Henry (1627–1683), poet, was born in Hampshire, the fourth son of Captain William Bold of Newstead in Hampshire, a descendant of the ancient Lancashire family of Bold of Bold Hall. He was educated at Winchester College, before proceeding to New College, Oxford, where he was elected a probationer fellow in or about 1645. From this position he was removed three years later by the parliamentary visitors, later settling in London and becoming a member of the examiner's office in the court of chancery.

Wit a Sporting in a Pleasant Grove of New Fancies (1657) was the first work to appear under Bold's initials but the volume is a comprehensive piracy. The portrait placed before the title-page, for example, professes to represent Bold but in fact depicts Christian Ravus, or Ravius, whose likeness had originally prefixed his *Discourse of the Oriental Tongues* (1649). The text itself also appropriates the work of others. Much of the first fifty pages is taken *verbatim*, but in a reordered sequence, from the secular section of Thomas Beedome's *Poems Divine and Humane* (1641); Robert Herrick's *Hesperides* (1648) is the source for many more items scattered throughout the rest of the volume. In making those poems his own, Bold regularizes Beedome's spelling and changes the names of the addressees (and, thus, the titles), lineation, and even the wording of Herrick's verse.

Bold's second collection was *Poems Lyrique, Macaronique, Heroique, &c.* (1664), dedicated to Colonel the Hon. Henry Wallop, of Farley Wallop in Hampshire. The first half is devoted to lyric verse self-consciously Cavalier in its idiom

(Tush! Love or say thou *wilt not*
I'me *content!*
'Tis, but an *hour*, idely *spent.*)
('Song XXVIII', p. 38)

The second half contains a more various selection of occasional verse and longer poems, as well as a number of epitaphs, elegies, and translations from Latin, and, further, a series of poems on the Restoration first published as separate pamphlets or single sheets and including 'To his Sacred Majesty Charles the Second, at his Happy Return' (1660), 'On the Thunder Happening after the Solemnity of the Coronation' (1661), and 'Satyr on the Adulterate Coyn Inscribed the Common-Wealth, &c.' (1661). The volume concludes with the words 'Expect the second Part' (p. 236), but no second part is known; the final title to be published under Bold's name was *Latine Songs, with their English, and Poems* (1685), a posthumous gathering of the poet's papers collated by his brother William. The collection offers Latin versions of a number of English songs in facing-page translations, including a spirited run through 'Chevy Chace' composed at the request of the bishop of London, and an elegant rendering of Suckling's song 'Why so pale and wan, fond lover?'. The contents of the rest of the volume are similar in both matter and manner to the work Bold published during the Restoration. 'Song XXIV: an Ode', for instance, is a simple statement of first principles:

The Royal line,
Heaven doth dispose of. 'Tis not theirs or mine,
But his by whom Kings Rule, and are Divine.
(p. 108)

Bold died in Chancery Lane on 23 October 1683 and was buried at West Twyford, near Acton.

Another **Henry Bold** (*d.* 1677) graduated BD from Christ Church, Oxford, on 5 July 1664, while chaplain to the earl of Arlington, by whose influence he subsequently became a fellow of Eton College and chanter in Exeter Cathedral. Wood reports that he died at Montpellier in late September or early October 1677.

Jonathan Pritchard

Sources Wood, *Ath. Oxon.*, new edn, 4.116 • T. Corser, *Collectanea Anglo-poetica, or, A … catalogue of a … collection of early English poetry*, 2, Chetham Society, 55 (1861), 310–18 • H. Bold, *Latine songs, with their English, and poems*, ed. W. Bold (1685), sigs. A4r–A8r • H. Bold, *Poems lyrique, macaronique, heroique, &c.* (1664), 228, 236 • *DNB*

Bold, John (1679–1751), Church of England clergyman, was born at Laughton, near Welford, Leicestershire, the son of John Bold, also an Anglican clergyman. Educated first of all at a school in Kibworth Beauchamp, he entered St John's College, Cambridge, in 1695, and received his BA in 1699. He returned to Leicestershire and was master of a small school at Hinckley from 1698 to 1732 (which brought him an annual salary of £10). He was ordained deacon in 1701, became a priest in 1703, and was curate of Stoney Stanton, near Hinckley (£30 p.a.), from May 1702 until his death.

Bold wholly devoted himself to the religious welfare of his parishioners, and, although without private means, lived frugally and was able out of his small income to help parishioners in need, and to make several charitable bequests at his death.

Bold was the author of three pious works: *The Sin and Danger of Neglecting the Public Service of the Church*, which appeared in 1745, and was frequently reissued by SPCK; *Religion the most Delightful Employment*; and another which praised the pleasures of holy living, *The Duty of Worthy Communicating Recommended and Explained*. Bold died on 29 October 1751, and was buried in the churchyard at Stoney Stanton. SIDNEY LEE, *rev.* ROBERT BROWN

Sources W. F. Hook, *An ecclesiastical biography*, 8 vols. (1845–52) · Venn, *Alum. Cant.* · Nichols, *Illustrations*, 5.130–42

Bold, Samuel (1648x52–1737), Church of England clergyman, is of obscure origins. He was brought up and educated in Chester by William Cook (1611/12–1684), curate of St Michael's parish there. Cook was ejected in 1662 and served as nonconformist minister in the city thereafter. Bold later paid tribute to Cook's widow, Mary, for her 'great love' and 'motherly affection' from his infancy through childhood and youth (Bold, *Man's Great Duty*, sig. A2r). A Samuel Bold, according to the university register, matriculated from Jesus College, Oxford, on 3 November 1671, aged nineteen; if this is our subject, he was the son of Edward Bold (1603/4–1654/5), rector of Hawarden, Flintshire, and was born in 1651 or 1652 rather than 1648 or 1649, the dates derived from his reported age at death. However, Bold's name does not appear in the college's admission records, and there is no evidence of his graduation in either the college or university archives. Bold is notable principally on three counts: as an advocate of religious toleration, for his defence of John Locke, and for his later views on human nature and immortality.

In 1674 Bold was instituted vicar of Shapwick in Dorset, from which pulpit in March 1682, following the required reading of a brief on behalf of persecuted protestants in France, he preached against intolerance and persecution, in support of the French protestants in particular and condemning persecution in general. He decried both the repulsive nature of persecution and its perpetrators with equal clarity and zeal. The sermon was shortly published as *A Sermon Against Persecution*, specifically for 'the consideration of violent and headstrong men' (Bold, *Sermon*, title-page). It aroused much local indignation, particularly in view of Bold's defence of dissenters personally known to him as men 'of great learning, exemplary piety, strict devotion, and extraordinary loyalty' and his denunciation of those responsible for persecution as the 'devil's agents' (ibid., sig. A2v, 4) inflicting on the church 'unspeakable injury' (ibid., 23, 28) and who, having 'a great affection for Popery, are hastening towards Rome as fast as they can' (ibid., 6). Given the political climate—of the failure to exclude the Catholic James, duke of York, from the succession and the intensified persecution of dissenters during the tory reaction—it was, to say the least, injudicious.

Bold sought to justify his position and avert retribution with *A Plea for Moderation towards Dissenters* (1682) but the damage had already been done. He only succeeded in further alienating popular and ecclesiastical opinion. *A Plea for Moderation*, although couched initially in more conciliatory language, deploring 'mutual animosities and contentions' and pleading for 'mutual forbearance', did so in view of the perceived papal threat and the fear 'that Hannibal [Rome] is at our gates' (Bold, *Plea*, 5, 6). Bold concluded by protesting again at the 'immoderate heat and peevishness of those fatuous and headstrong bigots' who attacked dissenters (ibid., 36). At a time when English gaols, particularly in the west country, were filled with dissenters on account of the efforts of local informers and magistrates it was more than the authorities, civil and ecclesiastical, could take. Bold was presented to the assizes in Sherborne in August 1682 and shortly afterwards to the court of William Gulston, bishop of Bristol, accused of 'scandalous libel' and sedition. The civil court imposed fines, and Bold was imprisoned for seven weeks until the fines were fully paid. The ecclesiastical prosecution was terminated following Gulston's sudden death.

Bold resigned from Shapwick later that year, possibly on account of the furore raised by his defence of dissenters, but probably also because he had already accepted the more comfortable living at Steeple in the Isle of Purbeck. To the chagrin of his successor at Shapwick, Obadiah Beane, Bold remained popular with former parishioners and was frequently requested to officiate at marriages and baptisms. Beane recorded such events in the parish registers as married or baptized 'by an unlawful priest' (Sparkes, 19). Bold's views on sovereignty and allegiance and his advocacy of toleration may all have derived from his early association with William Cook, a 'zealous royalist' who before coming to Chester about 1651 had been deprived of the living of Ashby-de-la-Zouch for refusing to take the engagement, thereby withholding his allegiance from the Commonwealth, and had been charged with treason in 1659 for his support of Sir George Booth's royalist rising, only at the Restoration to become a victim of persecution under the so-called Clarendon code (*Nonconformist's Memorial*, 1.327). 'Besides[,] many of those you prosecute', Bold reminded his audience:

> have given greater demonstrations of their loyalty, having suffered more in the late times of usurpation, for the king, than many, if not all of you have, and contributed much more to the bringing of him back to his crown and his just right. (Bold, *Sermon*, 27)

In 1688 Bold published anonymously *A brief account of the*

first rise of the name protestant … by a professed enemy to persecution, a tract urging protestant unity in the face of the popish threat perceived in the policies of James II. In 1690 Bold took issue with Thomas Comber in *An Examination of Dr. Comber's Scholasticall History* which he perceived, probably mistakenly, had been written to justify persecution of dissenters.

Bold was installed as rector at Steeple, also in Dorset (from 1721, Steeple-cum-Tyneham), in April 1682, through the influence of William Churchill. It was from there, in 1697, that he commenced the work for which he is chiefly remembered, his defence of John Locke. Locke's *The Reasonableness of Christianity* had appeared in 1695 and was immediately attacked as Socinian by the Calvinist John Edwards in *Socinianism Unmasked* (1696). Locke's own *Vindication* (1695) and *Second Vindication* (1697) of the *Reasonableness of Christianity* against Edwards were supported by Bold who, in 1697, entered the field with *A Short Discourse of the True Knowledge of Christ Jesus* in which he contended with Locke that Christ and the apostles considered it sufficient for a Christian to believe that Jesus was the Christ. Bold published two further works in that year, contra Edwards, in defence of Locke and his own *Short Discourse*, and in 1698 added *Observations on the animadversions … on a late book entituled, the Reasonableness of Christianity*, again in defence of Locke.

In 1699 Bold turned his attention to the vindication of Locke's other great work, the *Essay Concerning Humane Understanding* (1690) which by then was already in a second edition but which had attracted unfavourable comment. Bold's *Some considerations on the principal objections and arguments … against Mr. Locke's essay of humane understanding* (1699), together with his earlier work in support of *The Reasonableness of Christianity* drew the comment that Bold was 'one of the ablest advocates of Mr. Locke' (Hutchins, 1.612), as well as Locke's own unstinted gratitude. Bold was frequently mentioned in Locke's correspondence with great regard and Locke wrote to him in 1699 'everything must be welcome to me that comes from your pen' (*N&Q*, 137), although in 1703 when Bold visited Locke at Otes (or Oates) he was dissuaded by Locke from further publication.

In 1706, however, after Locke's death, Bold's earlier publications in defence of Locke were republished, together with some of his more recent works, in *A collection of tracts publish'd in vindication of Mr. Locke's Reasonableness of Christianity*. One of these later works, *A Discourse Concerning the Resurrection of the Same Body* (1705), seems to have been generated by Bold's assimilation of Locke's views on human existence, resulting in a major shift in Bold's own thinking regarding the nature and destiny of man. In 1696 Bold had published *Meditations Concerning Death* in which he had upheld the traditional view of the soul's immortality and immediate felicity in heaven after death. 'We have immortal souls', he had declared. Death is 'the departure or separation of the immortal soul from the body' to receive either eternal 'happiness or misery' (Bold, *Meditations Concerning Death*, 4, 6).

But there are already hints of a move away from this traditional eschatology in the *Observations* of 1698 and *Some Considerations* of 1699, where in defending Locke's mortalist views Bold asserts that 'the truth of the case' is that immortality, lost by all through Adam's transgression, is restored by Christ 'in that he will raise them all from death' (Bold, *Observations on the Animadversions*, 86), and that 'after the Resurrection man will be immortal' (Bold, *Some Considerations*, 25). In the 1705 *Discourse Concerning the Resurrection*, contra Daniel Whitby and Samuel Parker, who had opposed Locke's view of human nature, contending that death means only the death of the body, Bold predicated a more defined mortalist view, arguing that death 'happeneth to the [whole] man' rather than to the body alone, and confessing that the belief that after death 'man is not dead' was beyond his comprehension. Bold otherwise appears to have been doctrinally orthodox, despite later inclusion in Wallace's *Antitrinitarian Biography* where the author concedes that there was 'no ground for suspecting his orthodoxy' concerning the Trinity (Wallace, 315).

Most of Bold's more than twenty published works appeared during his years at Steeple and in addition to his appeals for tolerance, his defence of Locke, and his own modified theology of the soul and immortality, included a number of sermons and devotional pieces, notably *Man's Great Duty* (1693), *The Duty of Christians* (1717), and *Help to Devotion* (1736), the latter containing a short prayer on every chapter in the New Testament. Bold died at Steeple in August 1737 after a ministry there of more than fifty-five years, aged eighty-eight, and greatly respected.

BRYAN W. BALL

Sources 'Neglected biography, no. 1: some account of the writings, correspondence and persecution of Rev. Samuel Bold, rector of Steeple, in the county of Dorset', *The Christian Reformer* (Aug 1860), 466–78 • G. D. Squibb, *Dorset incumbents, 1542–1731* (c.1946) • J. Hutchins, *The history and antiquities of the county of Dorset*, 4 vols. (1861–70), vol. 1 • *N&Q*, 11 (1855), 137–9 • *DNB* • R. Wallace, *Antitrinitarian biography, or, Sketches of the lives and writings of distinguished antitrinitarians*, 3 vols. (1850), vol. 3 • Foster, *Alum. Oxon.* • *The nonconformist's memorial … originally written by … Edmund Calamy*, ed. S. Palmer, [3rd edn], 1 (1802) • S. Sparkes, *St. Bartholomew's Church, Shapwick* (1996) • J. Gorton, *A general biographical dictionary* (1841) • J. Watkins, *The universal biographical dictionary* (1821) • Watt, *Bibl. Brit.* • [C. B. Heberden], ed., *Brasenose College register, 1509–1909*, 2 vols., OHS, 55 (1909) • S. Bold, *Man's great duty* (1693) • S. Bold, *A sermon against persecution* (1682) • S. Bold, *A plea for moderation towards dissenters* (1682)

Boldero, Edmund (1609–1679), college head, was born at Bury St Edmunds, Suffolk, the seventh of the eleven children of John Boldero and his wife, Mary, daughter of Raygnall Tillot of Rougham. He was educated at Ipswich School and at Cambridge University, where he matriculated from Pembroke College in 1626, graduated BA in 1629, was awarded a fellowship on 4 February 1631, and proceeded MA in 1632. He became a curate of St Lawrence, Ipswich, and rector of Westerfield, Suffolk, in 1643.

During the civil war Boldero strove to defend the established church. Besides challenging William Dowsing's iconoclasm in Pembroke College chapel (unsuccessfully), he co-authored with John Barwick, Peter Gunning, William Lacy, Isaac Barrow, Seth Ward, and William Quarles a tract against the solemn league and covenant, *Certain Disquisitions and Considerations Representing to the Conscience* (1644). He was ejected from his fellowship in 1644. John Walker, in the *Sufferings of the Clergy* (1714), claimed that Boldero was sent in captivity to London, where he was 'detained under a long and chargeable confinement' (p. 162). The committee for plundered ministers sequestered him, as rector of Westerfield, for drunkenness on 1 July 1647. He was also charged from St Lawrence, at an unspecified date, with scandalous living and doctrinal misdemeanours which consisted of administering the sacrament only at the rails and obliterating from the church wall the final clause of 1 Corinthians 3: 17, which specified the temple of God to be situated in people, rather than buildings.

According to Boldero's later claim, he then became a chaplain in Scotland under the marquess of Montrose and subsequently 'was released from prison only by banishment' (*CSP dom., 1660–61*, 117). Roger North, whose brother was a colleague of Boldero's in the 1660s, suggested that 'between the ladder and the rope, [Boldero] had narrowly escaped hanging' (*The Lives of … the Norths*, 1826, 3.278–9).

In 1661 Boldero was created DD at Cambridge by royal mandate. He was restored to Westerfield in 1662. Bishop Wren of Ely, to whom he was chaplain, presented him to the Suffolk rectories of Glemsford, on 15 February 1662, and of Harkstead. He was successfully nominated by Wren master of Jesus College, Cambridge, and admitted on 27 May 1663; he left Harkstead when Wren also presented him to the rectory of Snailwell, Cambridgeshire, on 13 July 1663. Life at Jesus under Boldero was generally undistinguished, but he seems to have transformed the college library. He was vice-chancellor of the university in 1668 and 1674. Boldero died at Cambridge on 5 July 1679, and was buried in Jesus College chapel. Most of his goods were bequeathed to his niece Jane Colman and his kinsman Daniel Boldero, and all his books went to Jesus Library.

S. L. SADLER

Sources BL, Add. MS 19077, fols. 222, 307b, 308, 322a • petition of Edmund Boldero, 11 July 1660, PRO, SP 29/7, fol. 9 • *CSP dom., 1660–61*, 117; *1661–2*, 325 • will, CUL, CUR, university wills, bundle 18, 1679 • W. C. Metcalfe, ed., *The visitations of Suffolk* (1882), 115 • [J. Barwick], *Querela Cantabrigiensis* (1647), 25, 26 • Venn, *Alum. Cant.*, 1/1.174; 1/3.105 • P. Barwick, *The life of … Dr John Barwick*, ed. and trans. H. Bedford (1724), 38–9 • *Walker rev.*, 328, 338 • J. B. Mullinger, *The University of Cambridge*, 3 (1911), 268, 287–8, 291, 620 • J. Twigg, *The University of Cambridge and the English Revolution, 1625–1688* (1990), 96, 199, 249, 269, 273, 290, 291, 294 • A. Gray and F. Brittain, *A history of Jesus College, Cambridge*, rev. edn (1988)

Wealth at death £73 in cash and two 40*s.* rings; also unspecified number of 20*s.* rings; goods and chattels in houses at Snailwell, Glemsford, and Jesus College: Edmund Boldero's will, CUL, CUR, university wills, bundle 18, 1679 • will, PRO, PROB 11/360, fols. 299–299*v*

Boldero, Sir Harold Esmond Arnison (1889–1960), physician and medical administrator, was born in Maida Vale, London, on 20 August 1889, the elder son of John Boldero, company director, and his wife, Clara Arnison, of Penrith, Cumberland. Boldero was educated at Charterhouse School and at Trinity College, Oxford, where he obtained a third class in physiology in 1912. He was an outstanding sportsman, representing Oxford in both athletics and hockey. Having qualified MRCS, LRCP from the Middlesex Hospital, London, in 1915, he served in France as a regimental medical officer in a field ambulance and as deputy assistant director of medical services, and was twice mentioned in dispatches. In 1917 he married Margery Florence (*d.* 1950), elder daughter of Arthur Tempest Blakiston Dunn, the founder and later headmaster of Ludgrove preparatory school, Barnet. They had two sons.

Boldero returned to the Middlesex in 1919 and took his Oxford BM, BCh in 1920 and his DM in 1925. While holding junior posts at the Middlesex he became interested in paediatrics and, after a period as clinical assistant at the Hospital for Sick Children, Great Ormond Street, in 1921, he was appointed to the staff of the Evelina Hospital for Children, London (1921–34); in 1922 he was also elected an assistant physician at the Middlesex, where at that time the junior physician looked after the children. This appealed to Boldero who had a flair for dealing with children and entering into their way of thinking.

In 1934 Boldero became dean of the Middlesex Hospital medical school, an appointment which largely determined his subsequent career. He proved a most able administrator and served the hospital with distinction as dean until he retired in 1954. At first he was concerned with the integration of clinical medicine, teaching, and research, and he was also responsible with A. E. Webb-Johnson for the concept of the Courtauld research wards, to which patients would be admitted for investigation under the joint care of a member of the staff of the hospital and a professor of one of the basic sciences in the school. As soon as the building of the new wards was completed, Boldero drew up plans for the rebuilding of the medical school; however, only the first phase, which included the construction of an administrative block, was completed before war broke out in 1939. Like other medical deans Boldero had been involved in plans for the continuation of the work of the school and hospital in the event of war, and he now became a sector officer in the Emergency Medical Service. He maintained the running of the school and its teaching through two evacuations, to Bristol and Leeds; and when the hospital building in London was damaged he was responsible for ensuring that repairs and reconstruction were carried out, so that medical staff could return to a hospital ready not only to carry on but, as it rapidly turned out, to expand. Boldero's work as an educationist included membership of the senate of the University of London, and for many years he was chairman of its board of advanced medical studies.

The Second World War also saw the beginning of a new phase in Boldero's career. Sir Charles Wilson (later Lord Moran) became president of the Royal College of Physicians of London in 1941, and was looking for a capable administrator to help in the work of the college. He chose Boldero, who had been elected FRCP in 1933, first to be treasurer (1941) and then to be registrar (1942–60). Consequently Boldero became closely involved in the development of British medicine during the planning and establishment of the National Health Service. He represented his college in the negotiations between the medical profession and the government, which eventuated in the National Health Service Act, and he was also on the joint consultants' committee, which was subsequently accepted by the Ministry of Health as the consultants' representative body. There were stormy times when disputes between the profession and the government on questions of remuneration led to threats of withdrawal from the service. Boldero was by nature conservative and strongly attached to traditional ideas and practices, but he recognized the need for change and saw that on the whole more was to be gained from co-operation with the government than from opposition to it. His counsel in committee was always shrewd and often quietly humorous. He helped to maintain the influence of the college and gave wise guidance to the profession in difficult times. He spoke also as someone with much practical experience, since he was a member of the North-West Metropolitan Regional Hospital Board and of the council of the Medical Protection Society. He also served on the General Medical Council. For six years before his death he was chairman of the council of the Chartered Society of Physiotherapy. He was knighted in 1950. Boldero died in London on 30 November 1960. BRAIN, *rev.*

Sources *BMJ* (10 Dec 1960) • personal knowledge (1971) • private information (1971)
Likenesses W. Stoneman, photograph, *c.*1950, NPG • H. Knight, oils, 1957, Middlesex Hospital, London; copy, RCP Lond.
Wealth at death £91,859 11*s.* 9*d.*: probate, 6 March 1961, *CGPLA Eng. & Wales*

Boldon, Uthred [John] (*c.*1320–1397), prior of Finchale and theologian, was born at Boldon, co. Durham, and resident there until September 1331, though in a document of 1342 he is called Uthredus de Bamburgh, and the Franciscan Richard Trevytlam in an Oxford satire castigates him as of Scottish origin. No other evidence connects him either with north Northumberland or with the distinguished East Riding family of Ughtred; whether his forename was Uthred, as Durham documents use it, or John, as he is named in the *Eulogium historiarum*, is also uncertain. He lived at Newark from 1331 to September 1334, and in London until February 1338, when he went up to Oxford as a secular scholar. He became a monk of the Durham Benedictine community on 26 August 1341, and was ordained priest there on 29 May 1344. He resided at Stamford Priory, a dependency of Durham, in 1344. He went up to Durham College, Oxford, in Michaelmas term 1347 to read theology; he was warden of the college from 1350 to 1367, bachelor of theology in 1355, and incepted as doctor on 13 October 1357.

Boldon's lectures on the *Sentences*, given about 1355–6, were cited by contemporaries but do not survive; they cannot be identified with those of the Monachus Niger (the Black Monk) much cited by contemporary theologians. During this period he must have participated in the widespread debate, on the nature of human dominion and its origin in the state of innocence before the fall, which had been inaugurated by Archbishop Richard Fitzralph (*d.* 1360) in 1356; Boldon's opinion, recorded in a Worcester monk's notebook of about 1365, that every human being enjoyed at death a 'clear vision' of God, was seized on by William Jordan, a Dominican defender of the friars against Fitzralph's and his Benedictine allies' strictures, as evidence of heresy, and publicly denounced. Uthred's robust reply was delated to the archbishop of Canterbury, Simon Langham, who censured his views on the 'clear vision' and other matters, together with some of Jordan's views, on 9 November 1368, though neither protagonist was mentioned by name. By then Boldon had become prior of Finchale, a dependency of Durham, an office he held in 1367–8, 1375–81, and 1386–97, alternating it with the sub-priorship of Durham (1368–73, 1381–6) and spending therefore most of his time in or near Durham.

However, Boldon continued to play a part in the corporate affairs of the English Benedictine monks, partly as a polemicist, but primarily as one of the monks who worked to define the nature of monastic life and to clarify its rules. He attended provincial chapters of the black monks in 1360, 1363, and 1366, was called on by the English government to give his views on the papal demand for a clerical subsidy, probably in 1373, and was one of the envoys to the pope at Avignon to negotiate the question from 25 July 1373 to 20 February 1374. During this journey he was captured and imprisoned for a time at Chambéry by a band of freebooters. His Oxford lectures in defence of ecclesiastical endowments may have been given to refute the case made by the friars consulted by the government on this occasion; they were answered by John Wyclif (*d.* 1384) in lectures of 1377–8. He developed his views on the office of kings and that of priests in a further tract of perhaps 1379, and attacked Wyclif's opinions on transubstantiation in another of about 1383. Many of these works were only known in Durham, and his principal literary activity seems to have been writing tracts on the monastic life which arose from his work as a monastic visitor and legislator, and perhaps for the instruction of novices. His defence of monasticism as a state deeply rooted in human rationality, essentially not one of external observance but of interior disposition, allowed him to relate it to spiritual life in the world, the ideal of the 'mixed life' set out by Walter Hilton (*d.* 1396). Boldon's *Meditatio devota*, unlike his monastic and polemical tracts, circulated outside monastic communities as an item of devotional literature for the laity, a burgeoning genre in his later years. His view of the monastic life was summarized in a saying recorded by Prior John Wessington of Durham (*d.* 1451), that one should not lose sight of the substance of it, which was celebrating and hearing mass, keeping the monastic hours and maintaining monastic charity, while learning and teaching were secondary. Boldon died on 28 January 1397, and was buried at the entry to the choir at Finchale.

All the works of Uthred Boldon are listed by W. A. Pantin, but only two of them have been published, his riposte to Jordan's attack by M. E. Marcett (1938), and his *Meditatio devota* by D. H. Farmer (1958). His later responses to the friars on endowment were transcribed, and his tract on kingship and priesthood summarized, by C. H.

Thompson in his thesis of 1936. Uthred's two most substantial treatises on the monastic life were summarized by Pantin, while his censured opinions have been edited by M. D. Knowles. JEREMY CATTO

Sources 'Select documents, II: a medieval biography', *BIHR*, 3 (1925–6), 46 • Durham Cath. CL, polemical tracts, MS A. IV. 33 • 'Pro monachis veris', Durham Cath. CL, MS B. IV. 26 • Durham Cath. CL, monastic works, MS B. IV. 34 • Jesus College, Cambridge, monastic works, MS 41 • 'Contra fratrum mendicitatem', Bibliothèque Nationale, Paris, MS Lat. 3183 • J. T. Fowler, ed., *Extracts from the account rolls of the abbey of Durham*, 3 vols., SurtS, 99–100, 103 (1898–1901) • H. E. D. Blakiston, ed., 'Some Durham College rolls', *Collectanea: third series*, ed. M. Burrows, OHS, 32 (1896), 1–76 • [J. Raine], ed., *The priory of Finchale*, SurtS, 6 (1837) • W. A. Pantin, ed., *Documents illustrating the activities of the general and provincial chapters of the English black monks*, 3, CS, 3rd ser., 54 (1937), 318 • F. S. Haydon, ed., *Eulogium historiarum sive temporis*, 3 vols., Rolls Series, 9 (1858), vol. 3, p. 337 • *Commentarii de scriptoribus Britannicis, auctore Joanne Lelando*, ed. A. Hall, 2 (1709), 392–3 • Bale, *Index*, 462–3 • Bale, *Cat.*, 1.482–3 • M. E. Marcett, *Uthred de Boldon, Fr. William Jordan and Piers Plowman* (1938) • C. H. Thompson, 'Uthred of Boldon, a study in fourteenth-century political theory', PhD diss., University of Manchester, 1936 • W. A. Pantin, 'Two treatises of Uthred of Boldon on the monastic life', *Studies in medieval history presented to Frederick Maurice Powicke*, ed. R. W. Hunt and others (1948), 363–85 • M. D. Knowles, 'The censured opinions of Uthred of Boldon', *PBA*, 37 (1951), 306–42 • Emden, *Oxf.*, 1.212–13 • 'The *Meditatio devota* of Uthred of Boldon', *Analecta monastica: textes et études sur la vie des moines au moyen âge*, ed. R. Foreville and others, 5 (Rome, 1958), 187–206

Archives Bibliothèque Nationale, Paris, MS Lat. 3183 • Durham Cath. CL, MS B.IV.34; MS A.IV.33; MS B.IV.26 • Jesus College, Cambridge, MS 41

Boldrewood, Rolf. *See* Browne, Thomas Alexander (1826–1915).

Bolebec, Isabel de, countess of Oxford (*c*.1164–1245), magnate and monastic patron, was the eldest daughter of Hugh de Bolebec (*d. c*.1165), lord of Whitchurch, Buckinghamshire, and a patron of the order of Friars Preacher in England. She appears first in the records as the widow of Henry de Nonant (*d.* 1206), lord of Totnes, Devon, her first husband. In 1207 she petitioned the crown for the right to marry whom she wished. The first instalment of her fine was paid by Robert de *Vere, earl of Oxford (*d.* 1221), her second husband, who had made his own fine to marry Isabel if she consented. At the time of her remarriage she was coheir of her niece Isabel de Bolebec, countess of Oxford and Robert de Vere's former sister-in-law (with whom she is frequently confused). By *c*.1225 Isabel had inherited all of the Bolebec honour of thirty knights' fees in Buckinghamshire.

Isabel bore her only known child, Hugh de Vere, late in her reproductive years. She purchased his wardship and the guardianship of his inheritance upon her husband's death in 1221 for £2228 (6000 marks), and travelled with him on pilgrimage 'beyond the seas' in 1237 (*CPR*, *1237–42*, 175). A generally successful suitor at court, she engaged in a long-running dispute with Woburn Abbey.

The countess was the chief benefactor of the Dominican order in Oxford. The friars sent to England in 1221 were assisted in their search for quarters in the Oxford Jewry by Isabel, who took a Dominican as her confessor and financed their oratory to the east of St Aldate's Street *c*.1227. When the friars decided to expand, she bought land to the south of Oxford for them. On her death on 3 February 1245 her body was temporarily entombed in their oratory, then transported to the newly consecrated Dominican priory church in St Ebbe's for burial. A monument proclaimed Isabel their 'foundress'. Her other known charitable grants were to the hospital of St Mary Magdalene, Crowmarsh, Oxfordshire, and to Woburn Abbey, Bedfordshire (a Bolebec foundation). RAGENA C. DEARAGON

Sources *Sixth report*, HMC, 5 (1877–8) • *Curia regis rolls preserved in the Public Record Office* (1922–) • *Pipe rolls* • *The memoranda roll*, PRSoc. • *CPR* • *Feet of fines, Buckinghamshire* • *Close rolls of the reign of Henry III*, 14 vols., PRO (1902–38) • *Calendar of the charter rolls*, 6 vols., PRO (1903–27) • Paris, *Chron.* • GEC, *Peerage* • W. G. D. Fletcher, *The black friars of Oxford* (1882) • A. Wood, *Survey of the antiquities of the city of Oxford*, ed. A. Clark, 2, OHS, 17 (1890)

Likenesses seal; [Birch, *Seals*, vol. 2, p. 378]

Wealth at death possessed paternal inheritance of thirty knights' fees; also dowries from two husbands

Boles, Abigail. *See* Watson, Abigail (1685–1752).

Boleyn, George, Viscount Rochford (*c*.1504–1536), courtier and diplomat, was the only son of Thomas *Boleyn, earl of Wiltshire (1476/7–1539), and Elizabeth Howard (*d.* 1538), eldest daughter of Thomas *Howard, earl of Surrey and later second duke of Norfolk (1443–1524). He first appears in the public record participating in the Christmas revels of 1514, and he signalled his father's success when he became a royal page in 1516. His earliest recorded grants resulted from his father's service to the crown and his sister Mary's relationship with the king. With his father in 1522, he was granted various offices at Tonbridge, which had belonged to the fallen duke of Buckingham. He received the manor of Grimston, Norfolk, in 1524 and was admitted to the king's privy chamber, perhaps about the same time.

Early in 1526 Cardinal Thomas Wolsey pushed through the Eltham ordinances, designed to reduce the size of the king's household and to reduce the privy chamber's potential as a source of political opposition to his ascendancy. George Boleyn was one of the gentlemen removed by Wolsey, who recognized that the Boleyns had become his most serious rivals at court. Boleyn suffered little personal damage from Wolsey's actions. Shortly after his dismissal he married Jane Parker (*d.* 1542) [*see* Boleyn, Jane, Viscountess Rochford], a daughter of Henry, Lord Morley and Monteagle, and Alice St John of Bledsoe, herself a maternal half-niece of Henry VIII's grandmother the countess of Richmond. The king granted Boleyn an annuity of £20 to support the newly wed couple at court. As his sister *Anne became firmly established as Henry's favourite, Boleyn's career accelerated rapidly. By 1528 Henry was actively seeking to divorce Katherine of Aragon, and the Boleyns were entrenching themselves at court.

In September 1528 Wolsey, trying to placate his powerful new challengers, helped George Boleyn secure an income of 50 marks, payable by the chief butler of England out of the prizes for wines. On 26 September he was appointed esquire of the body (Ives, 128n.; *LP Henry VIII*, 4, no. 4779). The next year proved particularly lucrative for him. Wolsey's situation had deteriorated further, and Thomas Cromwell, the cardinal's chief lieutenant now in control of his patronage, arranged for Boleyn an annuity of £200 from the lands of the bishopric of Winchester and another 200 marks from the temporalities of St Albans. Also in 1529 Boleyn secured the chief stewardship of the honour of Beaulieu, Essex, and the office of the New Park there. In addition he was appointed to the office of master of the buckhounds and to the governorship of the hospital of St Mary of Bethlehem, near Bishopsgate, London.

In the autumn of 1529 Boleyn was knighted and began his diplomatic career, heading an embassy to France. It was well understood that the ambassadorial appointment of such an inexperienced young man reflected the new realities of power. This point was amplified when his father was promoted to the earldoms of Wiltshire and Ormond, and George Boleyn became Viscount Rochford. He carried out further diplomatic missions in France in 1530 and 1532, but seemed primarily concerned to secure favourable opinions about the divorce. By 1533, having acquired some ambassadorial experience, Rochford was sent to the court of François I to tell him about Henry's marriage to his sister and to secure the French king's support in the struggle against papal denunciation of the divorce. He was accused of bragging and ignoring proper diplomatic forms, but these charges came primarily from defeated opponents of the Boleyn marriage and the religious reform carried in its train.

More embassies to France followed in 1533 and 1534. Rochford spent much time trying to plan a meeting between François and Henry that neither monarch wanted. Diplomatic service, however, promoted valuable rewards. In June 1534 Rochford was made warden of the Cinque Ports, and in April 1535 the crown granted him the manor of South, in Kent, formerly held by Sir Thomas More. Rochford then served on the commission that tried and condemned More on 26 June 1535.

Under his sister's factional leadership Rochford played an important role on behalf of religious reform in England. Eustache Chapuys, the imperial ambassador, characterized Rochford as a Lutheran, a charge with some merit. His advocacy of reform was particularly open. He worked with other crown officials in 1531 in support of Henry's claim to be supreme head of the Church of England and was charged to argue the crown's position in convocation. He was widely regarded as one of the king's principal advisers in backing efforts to secure the submission of the clergy, and he served as a member of the group of leading councillors and courtiers who met with the upper house of convocation to handle the final stages of the submission.

Rochford's motivation for reform carried beyond loyalty to his sister's cause. His interest in reformed religion was a guiding light in his life. About 1534 he gave two manuscript texts, written by French reformers, to Anne. He commissioned the translations of these books, both deeply committed to putting scripture in the hands of laymen. His final public utterances spoke to his devotion 'to the true word of God' and his hope that listeners would both observe and set it forth. He desired that his audience would trust in God especially and not in the vanities of the world, and blamed his own travails on his lack of perfect understanding of this important lesson.

Rochford's eclipse might have been signalled as early as the spring of 1536. On 23 April, St George's day, he and Sir Nicholas Carew were competing candidates to fill a vacancy among the knights of the Garter. Henry had already promised François I that he would promote Carew at the earliest opportunity; nevertheless, when Carew was selected, many interpreted the king's choice as a defeat for the Boleyns.

As Anne began losing her grip on the king's affections, Rochford too inevitably began to slip. Opponents of the Boleyn faction at this point realized that any attempt to overthrow Anne Boleyn had to destroy her brother as well. Rochford had ability and energy and could be expected to mount a vigorous defence of his sister if left free. The plot was developed accordingly, and, it is said, with the active involvement of Jane Parker, his wife. Lady Rochford, according to Chapuys, was the source for the story that Henry's declining sexual capacities had become a matter of discussion in the queen's household. Even more damaging was the charge, raised by Bishop Burnet, that Lady Rochford had intimated that there was an incestuous familiarity between George and Anne.

The trap was sprung on 1 May 1536. Rochford participated in a royal tournament in Greenwich from which the king precipitately withdrew. The next day he was arrested and imprisoned in the Tower, accused with four other men of having committed adultery with Queen Anne Boleyn, his sister, an act 'most detestable against the law of God and nature also', and of conspiring to cause the king's death. No one has ever suggested that the charges against Rochford were sustainable. He was formally accused on one occasion of spending a long time in Anne's room and on another of claiming that the king was not Elizabeth's father. Rochford defended himself at his trial with energy and eloquence, blaming his wife for the accusation of incest. He denied all the articles brought against him, and his demeanour drew praise from many. People on the streets, it is said, offered long odds against his conviction. It was, however, a foregone political conclusion.

Rochford was tried and convicted on 15 May 1536 and beheaded at Tower Hill two days later. Before he died he was allowed to speak. He did not say anything about the specific charges, but submitted himself to the law and the king's will. In a loud voice, it was reported, he said, 'I am come hither not to preach and make a sermon, but to die.' This he did, and his remains were buried, probably on the same day, in the chapel of St Peter ad Vincula at the Tower. JOSEPH S. BLOCK

Sources *LP Henry VIII* · P. Friedmann, *Anne Boleyn: a chapter of English history, 1527–1536*, 2 vols. (1884) · C. Wriothesley, *A chronicle of England*, ed. W. D. Hamilton, 2 vols. (1875–7) · GEC, *Peerage*, new edn · R. Warnicke, *The rise and fall of Anne Boleyn* (1989) · E. W. Ives, *Anne Boleyn* (1986) · D. Starkey, *The reign of Henry VIII* (1985); repr.

(1991) • '"Her moost loving and fryndely brother sendeth greeting": Anne Boleyn's manuscripts and their sources', *Illuminating the book … essays in honour of Janet Backhouse*, ed. M. P. Brown and S. McKendrick (1998)

Boleyn, George (*d.* 1603), dean of Lichfield, is often said to have been the son of Jane *Boleyn, *née* Parker (*d.* 1542), and George *Boleyn, Viscount Rochford, executed in 1536 on a charge of incest with his sister, Queen Anne Boleyn. In his will of 1603, George Boleyn refers to Sir William Knollys, grandson of Mary Boleyn, Queen Anne's sister, as his kinsman, but the fact that Rochford's inquisition post-mortem names Mary, rather than George, as his heir throws doubt on the supposition that George was his son, or at any rate on George's legitimacy. Considering the Boleyn family's difficult political position in the years after the queen's execution, it is perhaps not surprising that George's ancestry should have remained unacknowledged, and that he seems to have been bitter about the loss of his inheritance.

George Boleyn may have been born in London; he matriculated at Cambridge in November 1544. That he was a sizar suggests an impoverished background. A member of Trinity Hall, he graduated BA in 1552, proceeding MA in 1560, BTh in 1567, and DTh in 1576. On 29 September 1559 he obtained his first significant ecclesiastical appointment, being presented to the prebend of Ulleskelf, in York Minster. He was subsequently named rector of Kempston, Nottinghamshire, and was installed as a prebendary of Canterbury Cathedral on 21 December 1566. Here his career was marred by his 'chollerick' nature and his admitted tendency to swear when provoked. In 1573 he was charged with threatening to nail the dean to the wall, thrashing a lawyer, and attempting to strike a fellow canon, Anthony Rushe. Two years later he attacked one of the six preachers with a dagger and was suspended for four months, against which sentence he appealed to the queen. Nevertheless the dean and chapter presented him to the rectory of St Dionis Backchurch, London, in February 1575. He resigned this living in 1592, and in 1595, not without difficulty, was appointed to the rectory of Bangor, Caernarvonshire.

On 22 December 1576 Boleyn had been installed as dean of Lichfield. He remained a prebendary of both Canterbury (where, although non-resident, he attempted to secure a better house for himself) and of York. Always argumentative, he became involved in a dispute with the bishop of Coventry and Lichfield, William Overton, who was said to have been poor and 'laboured all he could to supply himself from his clergy' (Strype, *Whitgift*, 1.201). Boleyn resisted Overton's demands, eventually appealing to the privy council, which asked the archbishop of Canterbury to resolve the matter, and also writing to Lord Burghley for assistance. Boleyn was clearly concerned about his own emoluments. In addition to his stipend as dean of Lichfield, he continued to receive about £40 a year from Canterbury and £34 from York. A schedule of fees payable at Lichfield adopted during his tenure shows that he was to be paid £20 on the occasion of the burial of a bishop and £10 for the burial of a residentiary canon. But the surviving records suggest that he did not make a great impact on the cathedral establishment. The fact that there is no continuous chapter act book for his years as dean may imply inefficiency or lack of concern about record keeping.

At court Boleyn attempted, sometimes wittily, to use his relationship with the queen to secure a bishopric. It was later said that she offered to appoint him bishop of Worcester, but that he declined. In an engaging letter to Burghley, dated 10 June 1589, Boleyn asked for help in persuading John Still, master of Trinity College, Cambridge, to grant a scholarship to a poor boy whom Boleyn had befriended and educated. Both the Martin Marprelate tracts and John Manningham's diary contain references to Boleyn's dog, which accompanied him to church and occasionally interrupted the services.

It is disappointment and anxiety, however, rather than cheerfulness and wit, which are principally conveyed by Boleyn's will, drawn up on 12 January 1603 (PRO, PROB 11/101, fol. 1*r*). He names seven men and women as his executors, including Archbishop Whitgift, 'because that he onely spake for me to her maiestie to give me my preferments'; Sir Thomas Egerton and Lord Hunsdon, because they had helped him retain his living of Bangor when he had looked likely to lose it; and Sir John Fortescue, because he had prevented 'the ruine and downfall of this our church of Lichfield'. Later in his will Boleyn refers darkly to 'machivils' who 'make more accompte of private gaine then of the good of the church'. But the most remarkable of his proposed executors is the first, Queen Elizabeth herself, 'because that her maiestie gave me all that ever I have and subiectes gave me nothing and therefore knowe no cause wherefore I should be beholden to anie of them'. It was in keeping with this resentful frame of mind that Boleyn should have made no individual bequests whatever—all his movable goods were to be distributed among his menservants. He had died, in Lichfield, by 25 January 1603 and was buried in Lichfield Cathedral. STANFORD LEHMBERG

Sources P. Collinson and others, eds., *A history of Canterbury Cathedral, 598–1982* (1995) • G. E. Aylmer and R. Cant, eds., *A history of York Minster* (1977) • T. Harwood, *History and antiquities of the church and city of Lichfield* (1806) • dean and chapter of Lichfield, act book V, Lichfield Joint RO • miscellaneous accounts, Canterbury Cathedral Library, esp. M. A. 40 • J. Strype, *The life and acts of John Whitgift*, new edn, 3 vols. (1822), vol. 1 • J. Strype, *Annals of the Reformation and establishment of religion … during Queen Elizabeth's happy reign*, new edn, 3 (1824) • Cooper, *Ath. Cantab.*, 2.341 • *Fasti Angl.*, 1541–1857, [Canterbury] • *Fasti Angl.*, 1541–1857, [York] • B. Willis, *A survey of the cathedrals*, 3 vols. (1742) • BL, Lansdowne MS 45, fol. 152 • will, PRO, PROB 11/101, sig. 1 • PRO, Chancery, C 115, box M117 • *Diary of John Manningham*, ed. J. Bruce, CS, old ser., 99 (1868) • *The protestatyon of Martin Marprelat* (1589) • E. W. Ives, *Anne Boleyn* (1986)

Likenesses monument, Lichfield Cathedral

Boleyn [*née* Parker], **Jane, Viscountess Rochford** (*d.* 1542), courtier, was the daughter of Henry *Parker, tenth Baron Morley (1480/81–1556), gentleman usher to Henry VIII, and his wife, Alice (1486–1552), daughter of Sir John St John of Bletsoe. Her elder sister Margaret (*fl.* 1530–1536) married

Sir John Shelton of Shelton near Norwich [*see under* Shelton family]. Throughout her life Jane was active at court, starting about 1522, when she played the part of Constancy in the pageant of the assault on the Château Vert which Henry VIII laid on to impress imperial ambassadors. Elaborate white and gold hose 'for masking' would later be recorded among her belongings, along with sleeves and apparel made of rich fabrics, plate, and jewellery, indicating her high status and fashionable tastes. In 1526 she married George *Boleyn (*c.*1504–1536), who became in 1529 Viscount Rochford; they had no acknowledged children, although George *Boleyn (*d.* 1603) was supposed to have been their son. There is no evidence that she shared either her husband's evangelical leanings or her father's literary interests and Catholic piety, though two books were listed among her possessions in 1536. During Henry VIII's visit to Calais in 1532 Lady Rochford appeared alongside Anne Boleyn in the masked dance staged for François I. But as the new royal marriage grew strained, Lady Rochford, who was lady of the bedchamber to the queen, was implicated: she was dismissed for conspiring with Anne to procure the withdrawal from court of 'the young lady whom the king has been accustomed to serve' (*LP Henry VIII*, 7, no. 1257). Later, however, she turned against Anne, taking part in a demonstration against her by London citizens' wives in the summer of 1535, for which she and Lady William Howard were briefly sent to the Tower. She may even have been the source of the rumours of incest between Anne and her brother Lord Rochford, and also of the king's impotence, which were used as evidence in their trials. These stories suggest that sexual jealousy might have poisoned her relationships with the Boleyns. Although she wrote to assure him that she would 'humbly suit' to the king on his behalf, her husband was executed on 17 May 1536.

Lady Rochford's return to court was surprisingly rapid, and a letter which she wrote to Cromwell might point to the latter's influence in bringing this about. Her husband's death caused her financial loss, and she put pressure through Cromwell on her father-in-law, the earl of Wiltshire, to increase her allowance, to which he grudgingly agreed, despite her childlessness. She was lady of the bedchamber to the next three queens, and bore Princess Mary's train at Jane Seymour's funeral on 12 November 1537. When Anne of Cleves described her eventless nights with the king, she expostulated, 'Madam, there must be more than this, or it will be long ere we have a Duke of York!' (*LP Henry VIII*, 15, no. 850/14)—critical evidence for the king's subsequent divorce, which she witnessed on 11 July 1540.

Remaining lady of the bedchamber, Lady Rochford quickly became the chief confidante of Katherine Howard, whom Henry VIII had married on 28 July 1540, and colluded with her in encouraging the advances of Thomas Culpeper. Katherine Tylney and Margaret Morton later described carrying messages between the three and being sworn to secrecy, and Culpeper blamed her for 'having provoked him much to love the queen' (*LP Henry VIII*, 16, no. 1339). Katherine Howard entreated Culpeper to come and see her specifically when Lady Rochford was present, 'for then I shall be latest at leisure to be at your commandment' (*LP Henry VIII*, 16, no. 1134). Her skill in arranging clandestine meetings was particularly evident during the royal progress to the north in 1541. When the queen's adultery came to light, in November that year, Lady Rochford made only feeble protestations of ignorance, and eventually she admitted the affair. When it was clear that she was to die, under an act of attainder which contemptuously described her as 'that bawd, the Lady Jane Rocheford' (*LP Henry VIII*, 17, no. 28), she broke down, and the king sent his own physicians to ensure that she was well enough to die as an example. The French ambassador commented that 'all her life [she] had the name to esteem her honour little and thus in her old age hath shown little amendment' (*LP Henry VIII*, 16, no. 1336). She was executed on Tower Green on 13 February 1542, after making a conventional speech of confession and prayer for the king's welfare, and was buried in the nearby church of St Peter ad Vincula. CATHARINE DAVIES

Sources *LP Henry VIII*, vols. 4–17 · L. B. Smith, *A Tudor tragedy: the life and times of Catherine Howard* (1961) · E. W. Ives, *Anne Boleyn* (1986) · J. G. Nichols, ed., *The chronicle of the grey friars of London*, CS, 53 (1852) · GEC, *Peerage*, new edn, 10.142 · *DNB*

Archives BL, state papers relating to Henry VIII · PRO, state papers relating to Henry VIII

Boleyn, Mary. *See* Stafford, Mary (*c.*1499–1543).

Boleyn, Thomas, earl of Wiltshire and earl of Ormond (1476/7–1539), courtier and nobleman, was probably born at Blickling, Norfolk. The second son of Sir William Boleyn (*c.*1451–1505), landowner, of Blickling, and his wife, Margaret (*d.* 1539/40), second daughter and coheir of Thomas Butler, he described himself as aged fifty-two in 1529. The MP James Boleyn, seventh earl of Ormond (*d.* 1561), was his younger brother. His grandfather Sir Geoffrey Boleyn had been lord mayor of London in 1457. In 1497, aged twenty, Thomas was in arms with his father against the Cornish rebels and in 1501 he attended the wedding of Prince Arthur and Katherine of Aragon. Two years later he accompanied Margaret Tudor to Scotland.

Early career By 1500 Boleyn had married Elizabeth (*d.* 1538), first daughter of Thomas *Howard, second duke of Norfolk (1443–1524), and his first wife, Elizabeth. The couple had three children, *Anne (*c.*1500–1536), queen of England, Mary *Stafford (*c.*1499–1543), and George *Boleyn, Viscount Rochford (*c.*1504–1536). Eager for court advancement and expecting to inherit half the Ormond fortune, Boleyn had to exist on an annuity of £50 and the occupancy of Hever Castle in Kent in the meantime. His father's death gave him a landed base in Norfolk as well as Kent—he was sheriff of the latter county from 1510 to 1511 and from 1517 to 1518.

Already Henry VIII's squire of the body, Boleyn was made a knight of the Bath at the coronation of 23 June 1509. He was also appointed keeper of the exchange at Calais and the foreign exchange in England. In the early years of Henry's reign he was one of the sympathizers with the ambitions of the young warlike king against the more cautious counsel of Henry VII's bureaucrats. He also was a valued participant in royal entertainments, especially tournaments. He was the king's opponent at Greenwich Palace in May 1510 and among his answerers at the great Westminster Palace challenge of February 1511, appearing in the guise of a pilgrim from Santiago de Compostela. At Christmas 1514 he was involved in a fancy dress dance and indoor mêlée, and at Princess Mary's baptism on 20 February 1516 he was one of a select group holding the canopy. With his linguistic skills, his charm, and his knowledge of horses, hawks, and bowls, Boleyn made an ideal courtier.

Diplomatic service Boleyn was of most service to the king as an outstanding diplomat, chosen as an English pioneer of the resident, rather than extraordinary, ambassador. A sophisticated and cultivated man, he was employed for his fluency in French. He spent a year from 1512 to 1513 with Dr John Young, Sir Richard Wingfield, and Sir Edward Poynings at the court of Margaret of Savoy, regent of the Low Countries, and on 5 April 1513 concluded an enlargement of the anti-French holy league to include the empire. Boleyn found favour with the regent as a quick and incisive negotiator, and won a courser from her by concluding the league negotiations within ten days. He joined in the invasion of France in summer 1513 with a retinue of 100 men.

From early 1519 Boleyn spent a year in France as resident ambassador to François I, arranging the interview at the Field of Cloth of Gold and discussing a marriage for Princess Mary. In June 1520 he returned to France to attend the Field of the Cloth of Gold and Henry's subsequent meeting with Charles V at Gravelines. He was involved in the Franco-imperial conferences organized by Cardinal Thomas Wolsey in 1521. In 1522 he was assigned to accompany the king to meet the emperor at Canterbury in May and in October was sent with Richard Sampson to Spain on a further mission promoting an offensive alliance against France, from which he returned in May 1523. Boleyn was one of ten English pensioners of Charles. On 18 June 1525 at Bridewell Palace he was elevated to the peerage as Viscount Rochford. He went again to France in May 1527 as a commissioner with Sir Anthony Browne to receive François's oath to a new treaty with Henry, and was rewarded with a French pension. Back in England at the end of June, he assisted in discussions pursuing the project of Mary's French marriage. In 1530 Henry said that there was no skilled negotiator to equal him.

Henry's high opinion of Boleyn encouraged hopes of substantial reward. He promised him the comptrollership of the household, but during his French embassy in 1519 Wolsey informed him he would not have it, instead extending the prospect of the higher household office of treasurer on the anticipated ennoblement of Sir Edward Poynings. Boleyn, having enquired whether the cardinal perceived some fault in him, was ostensibly reassured. It has been debated whether he held a grudge against Wolsey from this point, but he was apparently comptroller in September 1520 and then, some time between October 1521 and April 1522, treasurer. Reliability was assumed by his presence on the special commission of 1521 that indicted Edward Stafford, third duke of Buckingham. Meanwhile, Henry also sought to induce Piers Butler, who claimed the earldom of Ormond as heir male, to surrender it to Boleyn. Boleyn's brother-in-law Thomas *Howard, earl of Surrey (1473–1554), then lord lieutenant of Ireland, suggested that the dispute could be resolved by marrying Butler's son to Anne Boleyn, but Butler probably baulked. Both Surrey and the king had to strike a balance, as Butler was useful and in fact succeeded Surrey as lord deputy.

The king's Great Matter There is no doubt that Boleyn advanced in royal favour when he unleashed his precocious daughters, Mary and Anne, on Henry's court. In 1513 he had secured from Margaret of Savoy an invitation for Anne to join the schoolroom of her four wards, the grandchildren of Maximilian I. Anne wrote to him from Brussels professing her love and obedience and promising to become fluent in French. Next year the two girls went to the French court; Anne acted as interpreter for Henry's sister Mary Tudor and then remained for seven years in the household of François's queen, Claude, the most exclusive finishing-school for young ladies in Europe. By 1522 both of Boleyn's daughters were at the English court. Mary was soon the king's mistress, assisting Boleyn's elevation to the peerage as Viscount Rochford in 1525; he had already been made knight of the Garter (and was falsely reported a baron) in 1523. The ambitious father was, however, to benefit yet further when it looked as if Anne, maid of honour to Katherine of Aragon, might come to replace the queen.

There was a more intellectual side to Rochford the courtier, if one not unconnected to his ambitions. He read Latin and owned a printed copy of Martial's *Epigrams*. He employed a humanist scholar, Gerard Phrysius, who commissioned on his behalf from Desiderius Erasmus three works which established the Boleyn family's humanist and pietistic credentials: *Enarratio triplex in psalmum xxiii* (Basel, 1530), *Dilucida et pia explanatio symboli* (Basel, 1533), and *De praeparatione ad mortem* (Basel, 1534). The last ironically was used to fortify Katherine of Aragon on her deathbed, but her supporters criticized Erasmus for his dedications. In further partisan humanist patronage Rochford took up the Hebraist Robert Wakefield once he had abandoned his support for Katherine, and housed Thomas Cranmer and John Baker, a fellow of Corpus Christi College, Oxford, much engaged with the question of the royal divorce.

The imperial ambassador Eustache Chapuys claimed in 1531 that Anne and her father were more Lutheran than the Lutherans, and a year later he said both were considered true apostles of the new sect. Chapuys was probably concerned with their anti-clericalism, not with solifidian theology. John Foxe too was of the opinion that Wolsey feared the king's marriage to Anne as she and her family would exert their influence to abolish the whole power of the papacy.

The marriage of Henry and Anne initially seemed, not only to the king but also to Rochford, most likely to be brought about through Wolsey. However, once it was obvious that the cardinal was failing to make headway with Clement VII, Rochford's resentments and the increasing power of his family contributed to Wolsey's fall in June 1529. In 1527 it was reported to Wolsey that the king usually took supper with Surrey (now duke of Norfolk), Charles Brandon, first duke of Suffolk, and Rochford. Foreign ambassadors made clear that in the period just before and after Wolsey's dismissal Rochford, unlike the other two, was in constant attendance on the king. Jean du Bellay, the French ambassador, indeed accused him of seeking a monopoly of influence and of leading 'the dance against the dukes and Wolsey' (*LP Henry VIII*, 4, no. 2665). The newly arrived Chapuys too thought Rochford's influence was dominant; the viscount also participated in framing the parliamentary charges against the cardinal. Soon after Wolsey's death in November 1530 Rochford had a tasteless farce of the cardinal's descent into hell performed for the French ambassadors.

Rochford's profits included a grant of the revenues of the see of Durham and Durham House in London; it was now clear that he was one of Henry's small inner ring of councillors and that his daughter was Henry's intended queen. On 8 December 1529 he was promoted earl of Wiltshire and earl of Ormond. Piers Butler had been forced to resign the latter title, to which the Boleyn claim as representing only the younger of two sisters was hardly strong. On 24 January 1530 the new earl replaced Cuthbert Tunstall, bishop of Durham, as lord privy seal as part of a significant laicization of the great offices of state brought about by Henry's impatience with clerical restraint on his personal power. Following the example of Wolsey, Norfolk, and Suffolk, Wiltshire was named to every commission of the peace. Whitehall Palace was rebuilt for Anne, and in 1531 her father was allocated a set of rooms there.

Thanks to Anne, Wiltshire had risen faster than Sir William Fitzwilliam, another courtier–diplomat who became earl of Southampton in 1537. Unlike Fitzwilliam, Wiltshire was still used as a diplomat after his promotion. Selected in 1530, with Cranmer, for a tour of Germany, Italy, and France to canvass academic opinion on Henry's divorce, he represented in his own person, being Anne's father, the king's commitment to the policy. Wiltshire also found Charles at Bologna, for his coronation by Clement, and raised the embarrassing question of Henry's divorcing his aunt. Reportedly, Charles told him 'that he was not to be believed in this case, as he was a party, and several other things' (*LP Henry VIII*, 4, no. 2827). According to Foxe, Wiltshire declined to pay the pope the accustomed reverence of kissing his toe—an affront perhaps premature when diplomatic channels for the divorce had not yet been exhausted, but a testimony to the family's subsequent anti-clerical reputation. When Cranmer was appointed archbishop of Canterbury in 1533 the king told him he had Anne to thank.

Father of the queen and final years Wiltshire naturally became an outspoken supporter of the divorce and the Henrician Reformation. In the parliament of 1532 he was one of the first to declare that neither pope nor prelate had the right to make laws and pursued his attack on ecclesiastical jurisdiction by visiting convocation with Norfolk to browbeat the clergy into submission after the supplication against the ordinaries. He canvassed for the bill in restraint of appeals (24 Hen. VIII c.12), reportedly hectoring Thomas Manners, first earl of Rutland, until he voted for it. In 1534 he was sent to Mary to seek an acknowledgement of her own illegitimacy, but without actually threatening her with death by proffering the oath of succession. On the death of Katherine of Aragon in January 1536 Wiltshire showed his self-seeking ruthless nature by remarking that it was a pity Mary had not died too. However, his and his daughter's influence was already being overshadowed by that of Thomas Cromwell. In 1534, for instance, the reliance of Gerald Fitzgerald, ninth earl of Kildare, on Wiltshire to maintain him as lord deputy of Ireland—both wanted to keep out Piers Butler—was unavailing in the face of Cromwell's inclination to 'reform' the government.

Once Anne fell in 1536 the whole Boleyn family followed. There is no evidence that Wiltshire tried to communicate with his daughter in the Tower of London; he was named to the commission of oyer and terminer to try several of her alleged lovers, Mark Smeaton, Henry Norris, Sir Francis Weston, and William Brereton. Anne and her brother George Boleyn, Viscount Rochford, were executed in May; on 29 June their father lost the office of lord privy seal to Cromwell, agent of their fall, thus becoming the only nobleman dismissed from one of the great offices of state 'by the mature Henry VIII apart from those who were also condemned as traitors' (Miller, 178). He was removed from the commission of the peace even in his native Norfolk and retained only in Kent, and was forced to provide annuities from estates given him by the crown (as late as April 1536) for new favourites. Wiltshire attended Prince Edward's baptism on 15 October 1537, but this did not represent sufficient rehabilitation to end his troubles. Piers Butler reasserted himself, and by early 1538 he had been recognized as earl of Ormond. Wiltshire supposedly sought comfort in the claim that there might be two earls of Ormond as there were two lords Dacre in England. The countess of Wiltshire died at the London residence of Hugh Faringdon, abbot of Reading, on 3 April and was buried on 7 April 1538 in Lambeth church. Whether or not Wiltshire's own service as well as his daughter's rise had helped secure his remarkable gains, all but his English earldom (now without an heir) were irretrievably lost before he died at Hever Castle on 12 March 1539 and was buried in St Peter's Church there. A papal report of 1538 might well call him 'wise' but 'of little power' (*LP Henry VIII*, 13/2, no. 280). Cranmer stood by him in his last, broken years and attempted to untangle his affairs, but disputes over Wiltshire's estates continued until the archbishop's arrest in 1553.

JONATHAN HUGHES

Sources P. Gwyn, *The king's cardinal: the rise and fall of Thomas Wolsey* (1990) • E. W. Ives, *Anne Boleyn* (1986) • *LP Henry VIII* • M. Dowling, *Humanism in the age of Henry VIII* (1986) • D. MacCulloch, *Thomas Cranmer: a life* (Yale, Connecticut, 1995) • R. M. Warnicke, *The rise* *and fall of Anne Boleyn* (1989) • D. Loades, *The politics of marriage: Henry VIII and his queens* (1994) • N. Williams, *Henry VIII and his court* (1971) • D. Hoak, *Tudor political culture* (1995) • GEC, *Peerage* • H. Miller, *Henry VIII and the English nobility* (1986) • S. G. Ellis, *Ireland in the age of the Tudors* (1998)

Archives BL, Cotton MSS, letters to Thomas Wolsey and misc. papers

Likenesses brass monumental effigy, Hever church, Kent; repro. in Ives, *Anne Boleyn*, pl. 41 • line engraving (after effigy), NPG • portrait, Royal Collection; repro. in Williams, *Henry VIII and his court*, 104

Bolingbroke. For this title name *see* St John, Oliver, first earl of Bolingbroke (*c*.1584–1646); St John, Henry, styled first Viscount Bolingbroke (1678–1751).

Bolingbroke, Henry (**1785–1855**), author, was born at Norwich on 25 February 1785, the son of Nathaniel Bolingbroke. He sailed for Demerara, in British Guiana, on 28 November 1798, returned to England on 21 October 1805, but set out for Surinam, in Dutch Guiana, on 3 March 1807 to become deputy vendue master, with charge of public sales and auctions, for six years. He returned to Plymouth on 25 June 1813. On 7 October 1815 he married Ann Browne of Norton. Latterly he was in business in Norwich, where he died on 11 February 1855. He published *A Voyage to the Demerary* (1807), revised and edited by William Taylor (1765–1836), of Norwich. The book went to two editions and contained a statistical account of the settlements on the Demerara and other rivers of Guiana, a little-known area. ALEXANDER GORDON, *rev.* ELIZABETH BAIGENT

Sources Boase, *Mod. Eng. biog.* • [J. Watkins and F. Shoberl], *A biographical dictionary of the living authors of Great Britain and Ireland* (1816) • J. W. Robberds, *A memoir of the late William Taylor of Norwich*, 2 (1843), 254 • private information (1885)

Bolitho, (Henry) Hector (**1897–1974**), writer, was born at Britannia Boarding-House, Vincent Street, Auckland, New Zealand, on 28 May 1897, the elder of the two sons (there were no daughters) of Henry Bolitho (1868–1945), hairdresser, born in Ballarat, whose father emigrated from Cornwall to Australia during the gold rush, and his wife, Etheldred Frances Bushe (1875–1958), the daughter of a New Zealand schoolmaster, Michael Francis (Frank) Bushe.

Hector Bolitho often told friends he believed himself to be of partly Maori descent. He wrote that his maternal grandmother Catherine Bushe, *née* Bregman, 'had been under fire when the Maoris stormed the Waiuku stockade and, in some earlier battle, she had seen the head of a white man impaled on a native spear'. Later she became an interpreter between the English and native leaders. She spoke their language perfectly and translated the Psalms into Maori.

In 1898 Bolitho's father designed and printed the world's first airmail stamps, for a pigeon-carrier letter service operating between Auckland and the Great Barrier Island. As a sensitive boy of ten, on his great-uncle's farm at Waiau Pa, Hector Bolitho was horrified by the sight of a shepherd castrating lambs with his teeth. His autocratic Methodist mother wanted him to become a doctor, but at Seddon Memorial College, Auckland, his teacher, Ronald Algie, later New Zealand's minister of education, inspired in him a love of English literature. Without his parents' permission, he left school at fifteen to join the staff of the *New Zealand Herald*, moving in 1915 to the *Auckland Star* as shipping reporter. In 1916 he became a corporal in the New Zealand army, in which he served for the last two years of the First World War. When the war ended, he went to stay on a small island in Auckland's outer harbour which became the subject of his first book, *The Island of Kawau* (1919), which he sold to a New Zealand publisher for £20. With the proceeds, he sailed to the south seas, where he wrote a book about Fiji, Samoa, and Tonga, *The Islands of Wonder* (1920), for which he received £30. In April 1920 the prince of Wales, later Edward VIII, arrived in New Zealand on an official visit. Bolitho was invited to travel on the royal train to report the tour. This provided material for a third book, *With the Prince in New Zealand* (1920).

Homosexual, but obliged to conceal his true nature, Bolitho was never at ease in the then homophobic atmosphere of New Zealand society. In May 1920 his boyhood mentor Charles Ewing Mackay (1875–1929), mayor of Wanganui, was arrested and imprisoned for seriously wounding a man to whom he had made homosexual advances. Shaken by this scandal, in 1921 Bolitho left New Zealand for Australia, where he became editor of the *Shakespearean Quarterly* and literary editor and drama critic of the Sydney *Evening News*.

In 1923 Bolitho arrived in London, where he began work as a freelance journalist, writing articles for *The Spectator*, the *Daily Mail*, and the *Financial Times*. In 1925 he went to Johannesburg to edit the *South African Pictorial*, but resigned after only seven months because of his refusal to accept South African racialism. After his return to England, he published two novels, *Solemn Boy* (1927) and *Judith Silver* (1929), both with manifestly autobiographical New Zealand backgrounds. His prose style was graceful, but neither book was commercially successful. With his third novel, *The Flame on Ethirdova* (1930), Bolitho 'went through the strange and unprofitable sensation of being "remaindered"'.

Already in 1926, however, the course of Bolitho's career had been decisively influenced when the dean of Windsor, Albert Victor Baillie, invited him to go to live in the cloisters of Windsor Castle, where he remained for eight years, helping the dean to edit two volumes of *Letters of Lady Augusta Stanley* (1927–9), Queen Victoria's lady-in-waiting. Bolitho was almost expelled from Windsor by George V for contracting German measles while the royal family was in residence.

Bolitho's unrestricted access to the Royal Archives, and his discovery, in Coburg, of unpublished letters written by Prince Albert, consort of Queen Victoria, led to his first international bestseller, *Albert the Good* (1932), widely regarded as the most important royal biography since (Giles) Lytton Strachey's *Queen Victoria*.

In 1934 Bolitho worked with Terence Rattigan on the play *Grey Farm*, but their collaboration ended in acrimony, and when it was staged in New York six years later, the play ran for only thirty-five performances. Bolitho's volume of sinister supernatural short stories, *The House in Half*

Moon Street (1935), showed vivid stylistic flair. In 1936 he was chosen as the official biographer of Rudyard Kipling, but found the conditions imposed by Kipling's daughter unacceptable. Instead he wrote *King Edward VIII: his Life and Reign* (1937). Published three months after the abdication, it was severely critical of the former monarch and provoked scathing condemnation of the author by Winston Leonard Spencer-Churchill and (Edward Montague) Compton Mackenzie.

In 1938 the British Broadcasting Corporation produced Bolitho's radio play *Victoria and Disraeli*, with the role of the queen-empress played by the celebrated actress Marie Tempest, whose tyrannical character Bolitho had amusingly portrayed in an unintentionally revealing biography, *Marie Tempest* (1936). Bolitho made a major contribution to historical scholarship as the editor of *Further Letters of Queen Victoria* (1938).

Bolitho became a life fellow of the Royal Society of Arts in 1937, and a fellow of the Royal Society of Literature in 1940. On the outbreak of the Second World War, he joined the Royal Air Force Volunteer Reserve as an intelligence officer with the rank of squadron leader, editing the *Royal Air Force Weekly Bulletin*, which in 1941 became the *Royal Air Force Journal*. In 1942 he was appointed editor of the *Coastal Command Intelligence Review*.

In 1946 Bolitho wrote a second anthology of short stories, *No Humour in my Love*. His deep, resonant voice and commanding presence launched him on a highly successful tour of the United States in 1947, during which he delivered more than 130 lectures.

In 1949 Bolitho began the most important relationship of his life when he met a former public schoolboy and army officer, Captain Derek Wilmot Douglas Peel, born on 25 February 1924, who had been educated at Wellington College and wounded while serving in no. 9 commando. They collaborated on a book, *Without the City Wall* (1952), and lived together for the rest of Bolitho's life.

Jinnah, Creator of Pakistan (1954), Bolitho's biography of Mohamed Ali Jinnah, provoked intense controversy in Pakistan over the propriety of the book's being written by a non-Muslim. Bolitho almost abandoned the project, but persevered. On publication the biography received international acclaim.

At the age of sixty-five Bolitho made an avuncular chairman to a panel of teenagers in the television series, *The Young Elizabethans* (1962), but was not at ease in the medium. He raised substantial sums of money for polio research as chairman of the Committee for Writing and Reading Aids for the Paralysed. His autobiography, *My Restless Years* (1962), revealed a not entirely happy personality. In 1963 he wrote to a friend:

> I am weary, weary, weary. Weary of the written word. I would not write another if it weren't that I like my good food and must pay for it. Like my escapes on long voyages, and must pay for them.

In 1964 Bolitho's biography of Prince Albert was revised and reissued as *Albert, Prince Consort*, with interesting comparisons with the role, as consort, of Prince Philip, duke of Edinburgh. A member of the Athenaeum, Bolitho liked to sit in its drawing-room, looking at Charles Meryon's etchings of his native New Zealand. Though sixteen of his fifty-nine books were devoted to the subject of monarchy, Bolitho always considered himself 'left wing' and a rebel at heart. He enjoyed debunking his somewhat portentous public image. In private, his favourite pastime was playing 'Home Sweet Home' on the piano with his nose.

In 1965 Bolitho suffered the first of several strokes. His last book, *The Drummonds of Charing Cross* (1967), was completed in collaboration with Derek Peel, who did most of the research and writing. Through the onset of arteriosclerosis, Bolitho's health rapidly declined, and Peel wrote all the articles and book reviews that appeared under Bolitho's name in the *Washington Star* and other publications during the last years of his life. Hector Bolitho died on 12 September 1974 at Lee House Nursing Home, 61 Dyke Road, Brighton, the town in which he and Peel had lived since 1956. He was cremated on 18 September at Downs crematorium, Bear Road, Brighton, at a private service attended only by Derek Peel and their housekeeper. After Bolitho's death, Derek Peel succumbed to alcoholism and was found dead on 28 April 1979.

MICHAEL THORNTON

Sources H. Bolitho, *My restless years* (1962) • H. Bolitho, *Older people* (1935) • H. Bolitho, *A penguin in the eyrie* (1955) • H. Bolitho and D. Peel, *Without the city wall* (1952) • W. Reyburn, *Gilbert Harding: a candid portrayal* (1978) • *Contemporary Authors: Permanent Series*, 1 (1975) • S. J. Kunitz and H. Haycraft, eds., *Twentieth century authors: a biographical dictionary of modern literature* (1942) • S. J. Kunitz and V. Colby, eds., *Twentieth-century authors: a biographical dictionary of modern literature, first supplement* (1955) • R. Goring, ed., *Larousse dictionary of writers* (1994) • *WWW* • Burke, *Gen. GB* • *The Times* (21 Sept 1974) • *The Times* (30 Sept 1974) • H. Bolitho and D. Peel, letters to Michael Thornton, 1958–75, priv. coll. • b. cert. • m. cert. [Henry Bolitho and Etheldred Frances Bushe] • d. cert. • personal knowledge (2004)

Archives Auckland Public Library, diaries, typescripts, research files, letters, photographs, NZMS 986 | priv. coll., private corresp. with Michael Thornton and between Derek Peel and Michael Thornton • priv. coll., scrapbooks and other material relating to Hector Bolitho and Derek Peel | SOUND BBC Sound Archives, Room G067, Broadcasting House, Portland Place, London, *Victoria and Disraeli*, radio play by Hector Bolitho, broadcast on 25 Sept 1938, starring (Dame) Marie Tempest as Queen Victoria • BBC Sound Archives, Room G067, Broadcasting House, Portland Place, London, Hector Bolitho on (Dame) Marie Tempest, Woman's Hour, 15 Jan 1954 • BBC Sound Archives, Room G067, Broadcasting House, Portland Place, London, Hector Bolitho on Queen Salote of Tonga, BBC Home Sevice, 5 Jan 1966

Likenesses R. Whistler, drawing, *c.*1927, repro. in Bolitho, *My restless years*, frontispiece • H. Coster, photographs, *c.*1937, NPG • W. Bird, photograph, Auckland City Libraries, Auckland, New Zealand, Hector Bolitho MSS • photographs, Auckland City Libraries, Auckland, New Zealand, Hector Bolitho MSS

Wealth at death £31,624: probate, 8 Nov 1974, *CGPLA Eng. & Wales*

Bolland, James (*c.*1727–1772), sheriff's officer and forger, was probably born in the parish of St Olave, Southwark, reputedly the son of a butcher, who, according to *A True and Genuine Account of the Life* (1772), died while Bolland was a child; his mother, who survived her husband, supported herself and Bolland through her work as a toymaker, chandler, and moneylender. Bolland pursued a lucrative career that established him as the archetypal corrupt bailiff. 'He was a personable man … [who] knew all the quirks of the law, and had no restraint from conscience against committing the most villainous acts which the law could not reach' (*GM*). The primary source for his life, on which other accounts are largely based, is the anonymous *Memoirs of James Bolland* (two editions, 1772).

In his youth Bolland was brought up to become a butcher. About 1749 he married the daughter of the publican of the Nine Bells in St Saviour's churchyard, Southwark, and set up a butcher's shop at the corner of Falcon Court. Bolland's addiction to gaming and the racetrack undermined his business and he began to engage in dishonest practices, such as defrauding St Thomas's Hospital through the use of a false weight. At the time that Bolland's fraud was exposed, his apprentice nephew was found hanged, probably at the hands of Bolland's journeyman, though Bolland was believed to be a party to the crime.

Forced to abandon the butcher's trade, Bolland was bonded a sheriff's officer for Surrey, keeping a 'villainous spunging-house' (*Middlesex Journal*, 21–4 March 1772, 2) at the bottom of Falcon Court. There he hid debtors fearful of incarceration in Newgate gaol, from whom he extorted cash and valuables. At this time, despite the fact his first wife was still living, Bolland apparently married for a second time. Needing, however, 'a larger field … to display his talents in' (*Memoirs*, 7), Bolland commenced as sheriff's officer in the county of Middlesex, setting up another 'spunging-house' in London in the Savoy. When some of his schemes failed and creditors threatened legal action against him he obtained a certificate of bankruptcy and moved himself to Fleet prison until released by an act of insolvency. In the 'college of the Fleet' (*A True … Account*, 7), he 'improved his extraordinary genius for roguery' (*Memoirs*, 16).

Lacking the customary iron bars of a sponging-house, the house Bolland took in Great Shire Lane (a street long noted for its associations with fences and corrupt sheriff's officers) soon 'groaned with its load of ill-got wealth' (*Memoirs*, 30). His schemes, for which he employed unscrupulous persons and indigent tradesmen who had fallen into his clutches, included horse dealing, bill discounting, swearing of false debts, sham bail, and illegal seizure of property. An inveterate womanizer, Bolland engineered the imprisonment of two women with whom he had been intimate. One secured her release; the other died in Fleet prison. Bolland tempted fate with his favourite toast, 'May hemp bind those whom honour won't' (*Annual Register*, 15.59).

The post of City marshal falling vacant, Bolland successfully bid £2400 at auction for the position but was rejected by the court of aldermen. One factor in their decision was a public letter denouncing Bolland (*A Letter to the Citizens of London, on a Very Interesting Subject*, 1771) by Robert Holloway, who had been Bolland's 'bed-fellow' (*Memoirs*, 11) in the Fleet, and 'with whom he was sometime since engaged in a paper war, to the no small diversion and information of the public, who thereby were let into many secrets of great advantage to be known' (*A True … Account*, 6). Learning that Bolland's purchase money lay in the chamberlain's office, his creditors attached it, and Bolland found himself 'quite in the suds' (*Memoirs*, 48). Indeed 'his character in the city was become so notorious that his recommendation would not have got a man credit for a roll and cheese' (*Memoirs*, 47).

Shortly afterwards, in October 1771, Bolland scraped all but the *B* of his name off the back of a promissory note for £100 drawn by Thomas Bradshaw on horse dealer Samuel Pritchard, substituting *anks* to make the name *Banks*. This action, and his refusal to own the truth of it when confronted by Francis Lewis Cardineaux, then holder of the note, led to his arrest for forgery. Examined and committed for trial by the magistrate Sir John Fielding, Bolland was indicted, tried, and found guilty at the Old Bailey on 19 February 1772. In his defence Bolland stated, 'I never in my life forged with intent to cheat or defraud any person in the world … I must leave the rest to my council; I don't understand the case' (*Whole Proceedings*, 133).

Petitions addressed on his behalf to George III, Queen Charlotte, and members of both houses of parliament failed to bring a reprieve. Aged about forty-five, Bolland was hanged at Tyburn on 18 March 1772, and his body interred in Bunhill Fields, London, five days later. It was reported that at 4 a.m. on the morning after his execution Bolland's first wife died at Bermondsey workhouse, Rotherhithe. In July 1772, however, a woman named Sarah Bolland, identified as his widow, was granted administration of his effects. In addition to his one or possibly two legal wives, Bolland was connected with several other women: a Southwark fish woman, Sarah Blake (who may have been Bolland's 'widow' in 1772); an unnamed prostitute who, according to the *Annual Register*, became Bolland's mistress after the death of his first wife; and an unknown wealthy widow whom Bolland was said to have married in a Fleet ceremony.

With Bolland's execution City officials were rid of one of London's most infamous 'buccaneers and hussars of law' (Holloway, 13). Bolland's case fuelled spirited and often droll exchanges between supporters and opponents of Sheriff John Wilkes in newspapers such as *The Gazetteer* and the *Middlesex Journal*. It was alleged that Bolland, on the scaffold, had passed a letter to Wilkes. A fictitious, satirical copy of this letter was published in *The Gazetteer* (21 March 1772). PAGE LIFE

Sources *Memoirs of James Bolland, formerly a butcher in the borough, then officer to the sheriff of Surry, afterwards officer to the sheriff of Middlesex, and lately a candidate for the place of city marshal; executed at Tyburn, March 18, 1772, for forgery*, 2nd edn (1772) · *A true and genuine account of the life, trial and execution of James Bolland, late officer to the sheriff of Middlesex, who was executed at Tyburn, March 18, 1772, for forgery*, 2nd edn (1772) · *The whole proceedings on the king's commission of the peace, oyer and terminer, and gaol-delivery for the City of London; and also the gaol-delivery for the county of Middlesex, held at the justice-hall in the Old-Bailey on Wednesday the 19th … February 1772 … the third session in the mayoralty of the right honourable William Nash, esq., lord-mayor of the City of London. Number III. Part II* (1772) · *Annual Register* (1772), 54–61, 83–4, 175–8 · *Annual Register* (1773), 101 · *Middlesex Journal, or,*

Chronicle of Liberty (Jan–March 1772) • *Gazetteer and New Daily Advertiser* (25 Feb–31 March 1772) • *The Craftsman, or, Say's Weekly Journal* (21–8 March 1772) • *GM*, 1st ser., 42 (1772), 148 • R. Holloway, *A letter to John Wilkes, esq; sheriff of London and Middlesex* (1771) • *LondG* (16–19 Nov 1771) • PRO, PROB 6/148, fol. 161 [29 July 1772] • A. Knapp and W. Baldwin, *The new Newgate calendar*, 5 vols. (1826) [British Biographical Archive, microfiche edn, 1.123, fiches 1–28] • J. L. Rayner and G. T. Crook, eds., *The complete Newgate calendar*, 4 (privately printed, London, 1926), 77–86 • C. Pelham, *The chronicles of crime*, 2 vols. (1886), 1.229–34 • L. O. Pike, *A history of crime in England*, 2 vols. (1876), 2.394–5 • A. B. Beaven, ed., *The aldermen of the City of London, temp. Henry III–[1912]*, 2 vols. (1908–13), vol. 2

Likenesses line engraving, *c*.1772, repro. in *Memoirs of James Bolland*, frontispiece • line engraving, *c*.1772, BL

Wealth at death 'a few shillings': *Gazetteer*, 19 March 1772, 4; PRO, PROB 6/148, fol. 161

Bolland, Sir William (1771/2–1840), lawyer and book collector, was the eldest son of James Bolland of Southwark. He was educated under Dr Valpy at Reading School where he wrote several prologues and epilogues for the school's annual dramatic performances. He then went to Trinity College, Cambridge, matriculating on 26 September 1789 at the age of seventeen. He graduated BA in 1794, proceeded to his MA in 1797, and won the Seatonian prize for poems on miracles (1797), the Epiphany (1798), and St Paul at Athens (1799). These prize-winning poems were printed separately, as well as being published in the *Seatonian Prize Poems* (1808).

After leaving Cambridge, Bolland trained as a lawyer, and was called to the bar by the Middle Temple on 24 April 1801. He practised at the Old Bailey with great success, built up a good commercial practice, and was one of the four city pleaders (1804–29). On 1 August 1810 he married his cousin Elizabeth, the third daughter of John Bolland of Clapham, Surrey.

From April 1817 until he was raised to the bench Bolland was recorder of Reading. He was a candidate for the common serjeantcy (or office of circuit judge of the criminal court) of the City of London in 1822, but was defeated by Lord Denman. In November 1829 he was created a baron of the exchequer, resigning in January 1839 on grounds of ill health.

In 1800 Bolland issued an anonymous satire, *The Campaign, to his Royal Highness the Duke of York, Britannia in the Year 1800 to C. J. Fox*, which was circulated privately among his friends. Although he did not publish much, he was an enthusiast for early English literature and assembled an impressive library. Called 'Hortensius' by his friends, Bolland was remembered for his dinner parties as well as his scholarship. It was at one such party at the Adelphi Terrace that the Roxburghe Club was formed. Its first publication was *Certain bokes of Virgiles Aenaeis turned into English meter. By the right honorable lorde, Henry, earl of Surrey*, reprinted in 1814 (though the dedication was signed 17 June 1815), which presented the 1557 translation (held at Dulwich College) of books II and IV of the *Aenaeis* to a wider public. Bolland died at Hyde Park Terrace, London, on 14 May 1840. His library, which included some three thousand volumes, was sold for a total of about £3000.

W. P. Courtney, *rev.* Hugh Mooney

Sources *GM*, 2nd ser., 14 (1840), 433–4 • Foss, *Judges* • T. F. Dibdin, *The bibliographical decameron*, 3 (1817), 27–8 • T. F. Dibdin, *Bibliomania, or, Book madness: a bibliographical romance*, new edn (1876), 132–3, 588–91 • *Reminiscences*, 1, 368–9

Likenesses J. Lonsdale, oils, *c*.1830, NPG • R. W. Sievier, marble bust, 1830, Trinity Cam. • T. Bridgford, lithograph, 1840, NPG • R. J. Lane, lithograph, 1840, NPG

Bollard, Nicholas (*fl.* 1427), Dominican friar and writer on botany, was assigned by a provincial chapter after 1427 to Oxford convent as a *friar ministerialis*. He was the author of a work on arboriculture headed 'A tretee of Nicholas Bollard departid in 3 parties: of gendrying of trees; 2 of graffynge; the third forsooth of altracions', of which several copies are known. A treatise entitled 'Experimenta naturalis', seen by Dr John Bale at the house of Thomas Caius at Oxford and attributed to Bollard, is now lost.

Sidney Lee, *rev.* Anita McConnell

Sources R. Thoresby, 'Musaeum Thoresbyanum', *Ducatus Leodiensis, or, The topography of … Leedes*, ed. T. D. Whitaker, 2nd edn (1816), 83 • Emden, *Oxf.* • J. K. Floyer, ed., *Catalogue of manuscripts preserved in … Worcester Cathedral*, rev. S. G. Hamilton, Worcestershire Historical Society (1905), 192 • Bale, *Cat.*, 2.88

Archives BL, MS [copy] • CUL, MS [copy]

Bolling, Robert (1738–1775), poet and essayist, was born in Chesterfield, Virginia, on 17 August 1738, the son of Major John Bolling (1700–1757), a planter, and his wife, Mary Elizabeth Blair (1709–1775). The Bollings were descended from an Essex family which had settled in Virginia during the seventeenth century, and from Pocahontas and John Rolfe. Prominent landowners and elected officials, the Bollings were linked by ties of kinship, friendship, and patronage to most of colonial Virginia's wealthiest and most socially élite families.

Bolling was educated at Wakefield School in Yorkshire, England, where he excelled at the study of languages, learning to write 'equally well in Latin, French, and Italian' (Scribner, 3.307). On his return to Virginia in 1756 he briefly studied law with Benjamin Waller in Williamsburg, then established himself as a planter at Chellow, in the newly incorporated Buckingham county. From 1761 to 1765 he served in the house of burgesses as representative for Buckingham county, subsequently becoming that county's sheriff and a justice of the peace. On 5 June 1763 he married Mary Burton, who died in childbirth the following year; he married his second wife, Susan Watson, on 31 May 1765. In 1775 he was selected to be a delegate to the third Virginia convention in Richmond, which met in order to discuss the issue of resistance to British imperial control.

From 1756 until his death Bolling was Virginia's most prolific writer and poet, publishing frequently in American and English literary periodicals. While courting Anne Miller in 1760 he produced a journal-epistle, 'A circumstantial account of certain transactions, that once greatly interested the writer …', in which he detailed his ultimately unsuccessful wooing of Miller against the backdrop of the social and political milieu of pre-revolutionary Virginia. His comic narrative poem 'Neanthe' offered a bawdy and grotesque view of the backwoods gentry of Virginia, and is a precursor of the genre of southern folk humour. He also composed letters, pamphlets, and articles on the subject of viticulture, urging Virginians to produce their own wines in order that 'we shall become a more hardy and manly Race of People, when our Constitutions are no longer jaundiced nor our Juices vitiated by abominable West Indian Distillations' (Scribner, 3.307).

Although much of his poetry and prose concerned itself with the social and economic life of colonial Virginia, Bolling's education at an élite English public school and his resulting encyclopaedic knowledge of Romance languages and literatures encouraged him to produce poetry which was strongly influenced, in its language and subjects, by classical and Renaissance writers. In verses such as 'The Satyr's Imprecation' (published in *Imperial Magazine*, June 1761) and 'With all my heart,—his Lordship may' (ibid., August 1762), Bolling consciously imitated the style and substance of writers such as Virgil, Horace, Ovid, Ariosto, and Tasso, 'suggest[ing] an affinity for Italian writers unmatched in the colonies' (C. Mulford, review of Lemay, *Robert Bolling Woos Anne Miller*, *Early American Literature*, 26, 1991, 211). Even in the deliberately lewd and vulgar 'Neanthe', which 'portrays the crudeness, savagery, and grotesqueness of backcountry life on Virginia's Eastern Shore' (Lemay, 'Grotesque', 108), Bolling draws on classical allusions and traditional Renaissance literary forms. Here, as throughout his *oeuvre*, Bolling combined European and colonial elements in order to create a distinctively new American literary voice.

Bolling died suddenly on 21 July 1775, in the course of his service as a delegate to the Virginia convention in Richmond. Manuscript volumes of his verse are on deposit at the University of Virginia Library and the Henry E. Huntington Library. NATALIE ZACEK

Sources J. A. Lemay, ed., *Robert Bolling woos Anne Miller: love and courtship in colonial Virginia, 1760* (Charlottesville, 1990) · J. A. Lemay, ed., 'Southern colonial grotesque: Robert Bolling's "Neanthe"', *Mississippi Quarterly*, 35 (1982), 97–126 · J. A. Lemay, *A calendar of American poetry*, American Antiquarian Society (1972) · R. L. Scribner, ed., *Revolutionary Virginia*, 3 (Charlottesville, 1977)

Bolnest, Edward (*fl.* **1666–1675**), medical practitioner, practised medicine in London, residing on Jewen or Jewin Street (near Cripplegate) in 1665, and on Queen Street (near Guildhall) in 1672; few details of his life are known. Along with several other advocates of the 'chymical' approach to medicine, he contributed to the boisterous seventeenth-century opposition to traditional Galenic medicine, and as such could reasonably be described as a Paracelsian. His first work, *Medicina instaurata* (1665), assailed medical authorities and promoted a rigidly spagyric approach to pharmacy, maintaining that the efficacy of medicines was impeded by 'dross and impurity' which 'choaks and overpowers' the operative principles, and proposed the separation, purification, and reconstitution of materia medica into purer and more potent forms. Marchamont Needham supplied a prefatory epistle for the work. Bolnest was a member of the 'Society of Chymical Physicians' formed partly in opposition to the established College of Physicians, and was one of those who endeavoured to prove the superiority of chemical medicines by remaining active in London during the great plague of 1665.

Bolnest was involved in a dispute with the alchemist and philosopher Thomas Vaughan (Eugenius Philalethes). According to Vaughan's deposition, Bolnest approached him about 1656–7 offering to pay £300 for instruction in 'naturall philosophy and Chimicall physicke' (18 May 1661, PRO, C7/354/45) but paid only £20 to £30 and then brought soldiers to plunder Vaughan's house and arrest him (Vaughan later claimed that Bolnest was a soldier for Cromwell). Vaughan offered a bond from which Bolnest offered release for 'a certain physicall receipt of great value', to which Vaughan assented. Later Bolnest sued Vaughan for £150, whereupon Vaughan subpoenaed Bolnest. Bolnest denied Vaughan's charges, claiming he lent Vaughan £250 to make the philosophers' stone, which he later found he could not do. The resolution of the case is unknown.

Bolnest's notions were derivative of Paracelsus and van Helmont. *Medicina instaurata*'s postscript promised an *Aurora chymica*, which eventually appeared in 1672 (Latin edn, 1675), containing receipts for chemical medicines. A further work, *Fontina salutis*, was promised in a postscript to *Aurora*, but never appeared. The failure of this work to appear may suggest Bolnest's death in the mid- or late 1670s. LAWRENCE M. PRINCIPE

Sources J. R. Partington, *A history of chemistry*, 2 (1961), 181–2 · H. Thomas, 'The Society of Chymical Physitians: an echo of the great plague of London, 1665', *Science, medicine and history*, ed. E. A. Underwood, 2 (1953), 56–71 · *The works of Thomas Vaughan*, ed. A. Rudrum (1984), 17–21 · J. Ferguson, ed., *Bibliotheca chemica*, 2 (1906), 114 · PRO, C7/354/45

Bolron, Robert (*fl.* **1665–1682**), informer and perjurer, was born in Newcastle upon Tyne. Apprenticed to a jeweller in London, he left after a year to become a foot soldier at Tynemouth Castle. During the Second Anglo-Dutch War (1665–7) he served on a frigate. In 1674 Sir Thomas Gascoigne of Barmbow Hall, Yorkshire, appointed Bolron manager of his colliery. Bolron wed Mary Baker, Gascoigne's former servant, in July 1675, and leased the farm of Shippon Hall (in Barwick in Elmet) from him. Retrospectively depicting himself as a gentleman in 1680, Bolron then claimed to have an annual income of £30 from a coal farm, £10 from a lime kiln, and £7 from his farm. He embezzled £240 from Gascoigne and falsified his accounts, for which Sir Thomas dismissed him in 1678 and obtained bonds for repayment of some of the money. Bolron allegedly endeavoured to persuade one of Gascoigne's servants to steal the bonds as well as his money, but without success. Sir Thomas ejected Bolron from Shippon Hall in June 1678 when his rent was in arrears.

Seeking revenge as well as relief from his debts, Bolron, inspired by the tales of the Popish Plot, went to a local cleric and then a justice of the peace with accusations that Gascoigne had schemed to assassinate Charles II. Bolron repeated his story to Sir Robert Clayton on 3 July 1679 and the earl of Shaftesbury the following day. On 30 May of that year, he claimed, the priest William Rushton and Sir

Thomas had tried to enlist him in their plot, promising him £1000. For material considerations, he averred, he had converted to Catholicism in 1675 and had often attended Catholic meetings at which Sir Thomas insisted that the Catholics were resolved to overthrow Charles. Around early 1676, Bolron charged, Gascoigne had sent £3000 to Jesuits in London and £50 to Catholics on the continent. He also accused Sir Thomas of holding a meeting at his house in the spring of 1677 to establish a nunnery near Ripley in preparation for the reconversion of England to Catholicism. Bolron implicated numerous priests as well as such laity as Sir Miles Stapleton and Viscount Molyneux. The council dispatched Bolron and several messengers to Yorkshire to arrest some of the accused. For the necessary second witness Bolron recruited Lawrence Mowbray, who had been dismissed as Sir Thomas's servant after allegedly stealing from his daughter, Lady Tempest. Both men testified at the trial of Gascoigne, now deaf and unwell, in February 1680, but their credibility was successfully impugned and the jury acquitted Sir Thomas.

Bolron publicized his accusations in a narrative the same year and, with the approval of the House of Commons, in a sensational account of an oath to murder Charles and root out protestantism in England, reputedly administered to Bolron in February 1677 by Rushton. Bolron's testimony against Stapleton and Lady Tempest was also insufficient to procure convictions, but the priest Thomas Thwing was not so fortunate, and was executed in October 1680. In the pay of Titus Oates and the whig attorney Aaron Smith, Bolron testified on behalf of Stephen College in August 1681. He also accused the JP Edmund Warcup of attempting to suborn him to accuse leading whig peers of having solicited him to charge the duke of York and the queen with complicity in the Popish Plot.

By 1 September 1681 Bolron had placed his services at the disposal of the tories after being charged with falsely accusing the crown witnesses Warcup and John 'narrative' Smith of subornation, the latter in College's trial. He now accused assorted whigs of attempting to suborn him, including Aaron Smith, Peter Norrice, John Ayloffe, Edward Norton, Edmund Everard, and Robert Murray. As a crown witness, Bolron received an allowance of 40s. per week, but when this ceased in the latter part of 1682, Lawrence Mowbray charged that Bolron was claiming the court had urged him falsely to accuse Shaftesbury and his supporters of conspiracy. No more is known of him after 1682. Described by Sir Robert Southwell in 1679 as 'a young yeomanlike fellow' (*Ormonde MSS*, 4.530), Bolron had learned from Oates, whom he personally knew, how to profit by selling his inventive, malicious tales.

Richard L. Greaves

Sources *The narrative of Robert Bolron, of Shippon-Hall, gent.: concerning the late horrid popish plot and conspiracy for the destruction of his majesty and the protestant religion* (1680) • *State trials*, 7.959–1044; 8.652–4, 675, 677 • PRO, state papers, 29/412–13, 415–18, 421 • [R. Bolron], *The papists bloody oath of secrecy and letany* (1680) • [R. Bolron], *Animadvertions on the papists most wicked bloody oath of secrecy* (1681) • *CSP dom., 1680–81, 1682* • W. A. Shaw, ed., *Calendar of treasury books*, 7/1, PRO (1916), 206, 572–3; 8 (1923), 1377, 1414 • D. C. Greene, ed., *Diaries of the Popish Plot* (1977) • R. L. Greaves, *Secrets of the kingdom: British radicals from the Popish Plot to the revolution of 1688–89* (1992) • J. Kenyon, *The Popish Plot* (1972) • *Calendar of the manuscripts of the marquess of Ormonde*, new ser., 8 vols., HMC, 36 (1902–20)
Archives PRO, state papers, 29/412–13, 415–18, 421

Bols, Sir Louis Jean (1867–1930), army officer, was born on 23 November 1867, the second son of Louis Guillaume Bols, of the Belgian consular service, and his wife, Mary Wilhelmina, daughter of William Davidson, of Killyleigh, co. Down. Before entering Lancing College, Louis Bols had already been with his parents in Cape Town, Sydney, Budapest, and Quebec. He was commissioned in 1887 to the Devonshire regiment and entered upon what proved to be eleven years of routine work which included service in Burma (1891–2) and Chitral (1895). Bols married in 1897 Augusta Blanche, younger daughter of Captain Walter Cecil Strickland; they had two sons.

Having been promoted captain in 1897, Bols was sent to India on a station staff appointment in 1898, but the change was not altogether to his liking, and he much preferred the adjutancy at Aldershot (1899) of the 2nd battalion of his regiment. On the outbreak of the Second South African War in October 1899 he sailed with this unit for South Africa, where he came under the influence of General Sir Henry Hildyard. Bols developed very quickly as a result, with the valuable additional experience of the battles of Colenso and Spion Kop and the operations leading up to the relief of Ladysmith. He was thrice mentioned in dispatches, and was awarded the DSO and the queen's and king's medals. He studied deeply, and after passing through the Staff College, Camberley, in 1905, was given the command of a company of cadets at the Royal Military College, Sandhurst. In 1907 he was appointed brigade major, a post he held for just over two years during which he attended the German army manoeuvres. A soldier whose name was to become famous a few years later, General Von Mackensen, was the subject of a special report by Bols to the War Office.

In 1910 Bols received an appointment at the Staff College under Sir Henry Wilson and Sir William Robertson. There he quickly became very popular. The spring of 1914 found him at Belfast as lieutenant-colonel in command of the 1st battalion of the Dorset regiment. After proceeding with his regiment to France on the outbreak of the First World War, he took part in the field-fighting at the battles of Mons, Le Cateau, the Marne, and the Aisne. He was soon offered a staff appointment, but his corps commander refused to spare him, and he was still commanding the Dorsetshires at the battles of Givenchy and La Bassée. In November 1914 he was wounded and captured, but escaped back to his own lines, and by December he was again in the field commanding the 15th, 13th, and 84th brigades in turn. While in the Ypres salient with the last-named brigade his rare spirit did much to keep up the hearts of those who fought with him in face of the dreadful losses incurred—some 5600 out of a total strength of 7000 under his command. He was created CB in 1915. A high appointment on the staff of the 12th corps (brigadier-general, general staff) was followed in the same year (1915) by a still higher post with the Third Army (major-general,

general staff), where he served under General Allenby. In this appointment Bols was responsible for the plans of operations for the battles of the Somme and Arras. Promoted to the substantive rank of major-general in 1917, he was given command of the 24th division, and with that division took a prominent part in the battle of Messines Ridge in June. Then followed his most important appointment and most conspicuous achievement. Accompanying General Allenby to Palestine as his chief of staff in June 1917, Bols showed his profound knowledge of the handling of troops, their limitations, and their skilful use, which enabled him to effect one of the most brilliant feats of the war: the capture of Jerusalem (9 December 1917) and the final defeat of the Turks in Syria. In 1918 he was created KCMG at the hands of the duke of Connaught in Jerusalem, and in the following year he was promoted KCB. He had been twelve times mentioned in dispatches, and besides his two military knighthoods had received many decorations from the allied powers.

Bols attended the peace conference in Paris in 1919 (January–March) and returned to Palestine later that year as chief administrator of the province (still a military appointment). Despite great hopes of what he could achieve, he felt stymied by the Zionist commission, which he described as an administration within the administration (Segev, 95). A civil administration led by Herbert Samuel took over from Bols and the military in 1920. However, before transferring power the latter was forced to sign 'one of the most quoted documents in Zionist history'. This read: 'Received from Major-General Sir Louis J. Bols K.C.B.—One Palestine, complete' (ibid., 155). Samuel described the event in his *Memoirs* (1945).

In 1920 Bols was appointed to command the 43rd Wessex division and the south-west area, and in 1921 he became colonel of his own (the Dorset) regiment and of the 12th London regiment (the Rangers). Seven years later he was appointed governor and commander-in-chief of Bermuda. As an executive officer he had few equals in the service, and carried out the plans of others when that was his duty with the same enthusiasm and efficiency as he devoted to his own. He was of a kindly and sympathetic disposition, and the possessor of a keen sense of humour, these attributes attracting the admiration and affection of his comrades. Bols died at 8 Upper Church Street, Bath, on 13 September 1930. He was survived by his wife.

C. V. OWEN, *rev.*

Sources *The Times* (15 Sept 1930) • J. F. Maurice and M. H. Grant, eds., *History of the war in South Africa, 1899–1902*, 4 vols. (1906–10) • G. MacMunn and C. Falls, *Military operations: Egypt and Palestine*, 3 vols., History of the Great War (1928–30) • T. Segev, *Yamei ha-kalaniyot / One Palestine, complete: Jews and Arabs under the British mandate*, trans. H. Watzman (2000) • T. Pakenham, *The Boer War* (1979) • O'M. Creagh and E. M. Humphris, *The V.C. and D.S.O.: a complete record*, 3 vols. [1920–24] • *CGPLA Eng. & Wales* (1930)

Archives FILM BFI NFTVA, documentary footage • IWM FVA, actuality footage • IWM FVA, news footage

Likenesses W. Stoneman, photograph, 1919, NPG

Wealth at death £998 8*s*. 1*d*.: probate, 6 Dec 1930, *CGPLA Eng. & Wales*

Bolt, Robert Oxton [Bob] (1924–1995), scriptwriter and playwright, was born on 15 August 1924 at Sale, Manchester, Lancashire, the second of the two children of Ralph Bolt and Leah Binyon. Ralph ran a glassware and furniture shop, and Leah, a socialist feminist, was a teacher. Theirs was a northern Methodist household, guided by a firm moral code but enlivened by the vigorous argument of nonconformist politics.

Robert followed Sydney, his elder brother by four years, from Sale prep school to Sale high school and Manchester grammar school but not to Cambridge University: Bob, as he was known, was a disappointment at school and was caught shoplifting. He left school aged sixteen for the rigours of office life, which he found so boring that he determined to cram for university entrance. In 1943 he entered Manchester University, where he studied economics and joined the Communist Party. Academic life was foreshortened by the call-up, to the Royal Air Force. In 1944 he transferred to the army and a commission as a lieutenant. He finished his training in South Africa and was sent to the Gold Coast as part of the Royal West African frontier force until 1946, when he was able to return to Manchester University. He switched to history and graduated BA in 1949 with upper second-class honours.

Bolt left the Communist Party in 1947 and dallied with various forms of mysticism. At the same time he began seeing Celia Ann Roberts (*b*. 1929), known as Jo, a student at the neighbouring Manchester School of Art who was later known as a novelist. She became pregnant and they married on 6 November 1948 in a Moss Side church. Their daughter Sally Virginia was born the following year; she was to die later in a car crash—Bolt believed it to be suicide, though other family members disagreed. After swapping the grimy north-west for rural Devon, when Bolt took up a teaching diploma course at Exeter University (1949–50), they had a son, Benedict (Ben), born in 1952, and another daughter, Joanna (known as JoJo), born in 1958. Bolt became a primary school teacher in the village of Bishopsteignton in Devon, and, two years later, in 1952, an English teacher at the public school Millfield in Somerset, where he stayed for six years. He had written since childhood but had not tried writing plays until in his first term at the village school he was asked to write a nativity play. He then turned to radio plays and children's stories for television, and subsequently to plays that were performed on stage.

The change in Bolt's fortune as a playwright came about when a BBC radio producer introduced him to a newly established play agent, Peggy Ramsay (1908–1991), who agreed to represent him and became his demanding mentor. She managed to sell to the Oxford Playhouse his play *The Critic and the Heart*, which he had modelled on Somerset Maugham's carefully crafted *The Circle*. Remarkably, before it had opened, she had sold his next and more imaginative play, *Flowering Cherry*, to the distinguished director Frith Banbury, who, at her persuasion, took the play to the most powerful theatrical management of the day, H. M. Tennent Ltd. The play, which drew on Bolt's office experiences, told of an insurance salesman who dreams

Robert Oxton Bolt (1924–1995), by Stephen Hyde, 1985

of owning an orchard in the west country, and was an immediate West End hit. Its success proved crucial to both the survival of Ramsay's agency and Bolt's playwriting career: he won the 1957 *Evening Standard* award for most promising playwright, and left teaching to become a full-time writer.

In 1961 Bolt scored his greatest triumph in the theatre with *A Man for All Seasons*, which had begun life as a radio play and for which Bolt and Paul Scofield, who played Thomas More, won several prizes. Characteristically, the quarrel between Henry VIII and his chancellor More over the king's divorce not only provided meaty acting roles but, in an accommodation of certain Brechtian techniques, offered intellectual debate linking the personal to the political in accessible language that did not threaten the audience. This literate, epic style was to mark his later achievements in the cinema. On the strength of this play, Bolt was recommended to the film producer Sam Spiegel, who needed a speedy rewrite of a screenplay about T. E. Lawrence, which was being shot by David Lean.

Bolt spent a year on the film, and developed his taste for the high life aboard the movie mogul's luxury yacht. The celebrity of *Lawrence of Arabia*, which won seven Oscars, though not one for Bolt, came at a personal cost. Unpleasant wrangling over credit for Michael Wilson, the once blacklisted original screenwriter, was not satisfactorily resolved until after Wilson's death. Furthermore, production of the film itself was threatened when Bolt was arrested, along with two-thirds of the anti-nuclear Committee of 100 of which he was a founder, in a clumsy attempt by the police to thwart an impending demonstration. Bolt, like his comrades, refused to be bound over, and was sent to an open prison in Staffordshire. He ignored Spiegel's blandishments to recant until the producer drove to the prison in his Rolls-Royce and face to face persuaded Bolt to abandon gaol in order to finish the script. Bolt never forgave himself for this compromise—the very opposite of the steadfastness displayed by Thomas More—and found himself for ever thereafter uncomfortably caught between the moral and the material world.

International fame and the lifestyle that went with it also took its toll, and Jo told Bolt in 1964 that their marriage was over. In 1966 he began to live with the actress Sarah Miles (*b*. 1941), and history repeated itself. She became pregnant and they married, at Woking register office, on 25 February 1967; their one child, Thomas (after More, known as Tom), was born that October and was later, through drug addiction, another cause of unhappiness for Bolt the father. By the time Bolt and Miles separated in 1973, he had been the highest-paid screenwriter in Hollywood, with four more films to his credit and two Academy awards: the Oscar-winning *Doctor Zhivago* (1965), directed by Lean, and *A Man for All Seasons* (1966), directed by Fred Zinnemann, *Ryan's Daughter* (1970), a reworking of *Madame Bovary* for Miles and directed by Lean again, and *Lady Caroline Lamb* (1972), which Bolt wrote for Miles but directed himself. He had kept up a presence in the theatre through his most experimental but flawed play *Gentle Jack* (1963), a children's play *The Thwarting of Baron Bolligrew* (1965), *Brother and Sister* (1967; revised 1968), and *Vivat! Vivat regina!* (1970), another script written for Miles, this time playing Mary, queen of Scots. His last play to be staged was *State of Revolution* (1977, National Theatre).

Life as a tax exile took Bolt to Tahiti to work on a script about HMS *Bounty* for Lean, but in 1979 he suffered a heart attack, followed shortly by a triple bypass operation, a stroke, which left him paralysed down one side of his body, and yet another heart attack. Following a brief marriage on 31 May 1980 to an old friend, the actress Ann Zane (*b*. 1928/9), known also as Lady Queensberry, he eventually remarried Sarah Miles, on 27 February 1988. She looked after him as he learned to use new technology to overcome his disabilities, and he regained powers of speech, even if conversation was slow, tiring, and punctuated by expletives of exasperation that shook his sturdy frame. Earlier scripts, *The Bounty* (1984) and *The Mission* (1986), were filmed during this period, as well as a new television film, *Thumbs up: the James Brady Story* (1991), about Ronald Reagan's press secretary who was shot and had a stroke. In all Bolt wrote eighteen broadcast radio plays, nine performed stage plays, seven film scripts that were made, two uncredited screenplays, two television films, and numerous unrealized screen- and teleplays. He was made a CBE in 1972. He died at his home, Chithurst Manor, Chithurst, Trotton, Sussex, on 20 February 1995, and was buried in the grounds of the house three days later. Sarah Miles survived him. COLIN CHAMBERS

Sources A. Turner, *Robert Bolt: scenes from two lives* (1998) · C. Chambers, *Peggy: the life of Margaret Ramsay, play agent* (1997) · S. Miles, *A right royal bastard* (1993) · S. Miles, *Serves me right* (1994) · S. Miles, *Bolt from the blue* (1996) · R. Hayman, *Robert Bolt* (1969) · C. Smith, 'Robert Bolt', *International dictionary of theatre*, 2: *Playwrights* (1994) · K. Brownlow, *David Lean* (1996) · A. Turner, *The making of 'Lawrence of Arabia'* (1994) · C. Duff, *The lost summer: the heyday of the West End* (1995) · F. Zinnemann, *An autobiography* (1992) · P. Hall, *Diaries: the story of a dramatic battle*, ed. J. Goodwin (1983) · P. Hall, *Making an exhibition of myself* (1993) · S. Fay, *Power play: the life and times of Peter*

Hall (1995) • A. Wesker, *As much as I dare* (1994) • K. Williams, *Diaries*, ed. R. Davies (1994) • K. Williams, *Letters*, ed. R. Davies (1995) • V. Redgrave, *An autobiography* (1992) • *The Times* (23 Feb 1995) • *The Independent* (23 Feb 1995) • personal knowledge (2004)

Archives BBC WAC, papers relating to radio plays • Millfield School, Somerset, corresp. • NRA, corresp. and literary papers • priv. coll., MSS | Ted Turner Broadcasting Corporation, Atlanta, Georgia, MGM legal documents • U. Cal., Los Angeles, cinema and theater arts department, Michael Wilson papers • U. Reading, Barbara Cole collection of corresp. • U. Reading L., corresp. with Edward Thompson of Heinemann • U. Texas, Frith Banbury collection

Likenesses S. Hyde, photograph, 1985, NPG [*see illus.*]

Wealth at death £673,345: probate, 14 June 1995, *CGPLA Eng. & Wales*

Bolton. For this title name *see* Paulet, Charles, first duke of Bolton (1630/31–1699); Paulet, Charles, second duke of Bolton (*c.*1661–1722); Powlett, Charles, third duke of Bolton (1685–1754); Fenton, Lavinia, duchess of Bolton (1710–1760); Powlett, Harry, sixth duke of Bolton (1720–1794); Powlett, Thomas Orde-, first Baron Bolton (1746–1807).

Bolton, Arthur Thomas (1864–1945), architect and architectural historian, was born on 14 April 1864 at 37 Westbourne Park, Bayswater, London, the second son in a family of five sons and three daughters of Thomas Bolton (1819–1895), solicitor, and his wife, Emily Wildman (1831–1906), of Chilham Castle, Kent. He was educated at Dr Huntingford's Preparatory School, Wimbledon, and Haileybury College, before entering University College, London, in 1882. In 1884 he was articled for three years to the architect Robert Edis. He studied at the Architectural Association from 1885 to 1888 and from 1888 to 1889 acted as clerk of works to Ewan Christian before setting up his own architectural practice in 1890. He was elected an associate of the Royal Institute of British Architects (RIBA) in 1888 and a fellow in 1909. In 1893 Bolton won the Soane medallion for his 'Design for a railway terminus', and in 1895, having become increasingly interested in the history of architecture, he won the RIBA's silver medal for an essay, 'The influence of literature on architecture'.

On 26 January 1897 Bolton married, in London, Harriet Barnes (1863–1944), daughter of Samuel Fall of Carolina. They had three sons and two daughters. In 1901 Bolton was appointed first headmaster of the new day school at the Architectural Association. His first major commission was a factory and offices in Limehouse for the Sanitas Company (1900). He built for himself a house, Larkscliff, on the cliffs at Birchington, Kent (1906). His most important commission was to complete the offices for the Hamburg-Amerika Linie in Cockspur Street, London (1906–8). Subsequently Bolton built a house in the country for a wealthy barrister (Hurtwood in Sussex) and another in the Usk valley (Colomendy), where he also displayed a talent for garden design (1912–14). However, most of the work he was doing at this time was of a minor nature.

Having moved his family back to London in 1913, Bolton was in 1917 appointed curator of Sir John Soane's Museum in succession to Walter L. Spiers. He remained in this post until his death. He opened up the museum to scholars and architectural historians by writing many articles on Soane and his collections for the architectural press in the 1920s and also embarked on a series of publications about Soane: *The Works of Sir John Soane* (1924), an edition of Soane's Royal Academy *Lectures on Architecture* (1929), and *The Portrait of Sir John Soane* (1927), as well as a number of pamphlets. During the 1920s he campaigned tirelessly to stop the destruction of Soane's Bank of England by Sir Herbert Baker. Besides his work on Soane, Bolton became a great authority on the Adam brothers and wrote a two-volume work, *The Architecture of Robert and James Adam* (1922), still regarded as a major source of reference on the subject. This led to work at several Adam buildings and to an invitation from Sir Lawrence Weaver to design an Adam room for the British Empire Exhibition at Wembley in 1925.

Bolton was elected a fellow of the Society of Antiquaries in 1914 and served on the council of the London Topographical Society (1918–27). From 1923 until his death he was joint editor with H. Duncan Hendry of the Wren Society volumes, which aimed to publish all the drawings, documents, and facts relating to Wren's life and works; the twentieth and final volume was published a few days before Bolton's death in January 1945. In the 1930s he carried out extensive research on the work of Sir Charles Barry and was working on a study of Barry's diaries at the time of his death. Bolton enjoyed only modest success as an architect, although he was greatly respected; but as a scholar he excelled. He died of a heart attack in London on 17 January 1945, having collapsed on the platform of Queensway tube station on his way to a meeting of the trustees of Sir John Soane's Museum.

PETER THORNTON, *rev.* SUSAN PALMER

Sources Arthur Thomas Bolton, curatorial and personal papers, Sir John Soane's Museum, London • correspondence between Dr Robert Bolton [son] and the curator of Sir John Soane's Museum, 1990–99, Sir John Soane's Museum, London • J. Lever, 'A. T. Bolton, architect', *Architectural History*, 27 (1984), 429–37 • *The Times* (18 Jan 1945) • W. Godfrey and H. W. Hobbiss, *RIBA Journal*, 3rd ser., 52 (1944–5), 115–16 • *Architectural Association Journal*, 60 (1945) • A. T. Bolton, *Chilham Castle, Canterbury, Kent* (privately printed, 1912) • G. Mitchell, *The Wren Society 1923–45: an appreciation* (1990) • E. Harris, 'Bolton's Adam room at Wembley', *Furniture History*, 29 (1993), 201–4 • A. Stuart Gray, *Edwardian architecture: a biographical directory* (1985)

Archives RIBA, MSS, incl. reviews, notes, and cuttings relating to Wren Society • Sir John Soane's Museum, London, curatorial and personal MSS

Likenesses photograph, Sir John Soane's Museum, London

Wealth at death £18,083 8*s.* 11*d.*: probate, 15 Aug 1945, *CGPLA Eng. & Wales*

Bolton [Boulton], **Edmund Mary** (*b.* **1574/5**, *d.* in or after **1634**), antiquary and historian, was born in 1574 or 1575, according to an impress in his own hand styled 'Edmundus Maria Boltonus, aetatis 47, 1622' (BL, MS Harl. 6521, fol. 152). His parentage is unknown, but he speaks of himself as having descended from the Basset family. Elsewhere he refers to himself as a poor kinsman of George Villiers, duke of Buckingham, so it may be speculated that his family originated in the north midlands, perhaps even in Leicestershire.

Like several antiquaries of the early seventeenth century, Bolton was a practising Roman Catholic, having been raised in that religion from birth. He took the name Mary as a middle name, and although he did not suffer persecution until near the end of his life, Bolton's adherence to Rome undoubtedly had a negative effect on his literary career and prosperity. Bolton's early education is unclear, but autobiographical details in his surviving letter-book (MS Harl. 6521) record that he lived for several years at Trinity Hall, Cambridge, as a free commoner. He is known to have matriculated—presumably disguising his Catholicism—in 1589 (Venn, *Alum. Cant.*; MS Harl. 6521, fol. 247) before moving on, about 1600, to the Inner Temple in London. In one of his earliest works, *The Elements of Armories* (1610), a dialogue on the conventions of heraldry, the character of Sir Amias, who may represent the author himself, also refers to university life. It was probably while at Cambridge and then the Inner Temple that he began to make the many acquaintances mentioned in his letter-book, for instance the great antiquary John Selden. Bolton married, about 1606, Margaret Porter, the sister of Endymion Porter, future servant to the duke of Buckingham and Caroline courtier; a letter of 1625 to Secretary Sir Edward Conway refers to Bolton's 'wife and family', but the names of any surviving children are unknown.

Bolton first appears as a public figure near the end of Elizabeth I's reign, when he joined Sir Walter Ralegh and other poets in contributing to the anthology *Englands Helicon* (1600). He also penned Latin verses prefixed to Camden's *Britannia* (1600), Thomas Andrewe's *Unmasking of a Feminine Machiavell* (1604), and Ben Jonson's *Volpone* (1605). In addition, Bolton may previously have been the 'E. B.' who wrote a sonnet to Lucy, countess of Bedford, printed in Michael Drayton's *Mortimeriados* (1596), though this has not been verified.

Bolton's true vocation, however, lay not in verse but in history (especially English and ancient Roman history), and in antiquarian and philological erudition. Although somewhat exaggerated claims for his stature have been made by earlier biographers, he was certainly an important English antiquary of the second rank, well acquainted with William Camden, John Selden, Sir Robert Cotton, Henry Howard, earl of Northampton, and the London historian John Speed. A lifelong friend was the future secretary of state, Sir John Coke. There is no evidence that Bolton was directly connected with the Elizabethan Society of Antiquaries that met, off and on, from 1586 to 1614, but his participation in that body cannot be ruled out since he was known to many of its members, and his interests in antiquities, numismatics, genealogy, and heraldry reflect the subjects covered in the society's extant discourses. Bolton's first full-length work to be published, *The Elements of Armories*, is among the several works to be produced in late Elizabethan and Jacobean times dealing with heraldry and coats of arms, a subject in which the gentry of the period had a fervent interest; the book appeared in the same year as the better known *Display of Heraldrie* by John Guillim.

His various writings, and his largely unsuccessful career, reveal Bolton to have been a man of great ambition but scant financial means, who pressed his causes on his friends and prospective patrons with a persistence that sometimes caused ill will. Among his earliest supporters was the antiquary and manuscript collector Cotton, whose great library was the central meeting-place of antiquaries throughout the first third of the seventeenth century. In 1608 Bolton attempted to secure the patronage of Robert Cecil, earl of Salisbury, for a 'litle Latin work', without success. Through Cotton, he then approached the earl of Northampton, who as a Catholic may have been more sympathetic; even Northampton, however, soon grew weary of Bolton's apparently endless requests for assistance and told him henceforth to contact him only indirectly, through Cotton. It must have been a severe disappointment to Bolton when, in 1614, Northampton died and left him nothing.

It must also be said, however, that Bolton was equally indefatigable in promoting the interests of less fortunate friends and relatives, without reference to creed. In 1610 he asked Northampton, through Cotton, to provide an impoverished cousin with some appointment, in lieu of such a reward to Bolton himself who, as a Catholic, was unable to hold public office. In 1617 he again sought help for the same cousin, this time at the hands of Edward Alleyn, the famous actor.

About the same time that Bolton published his *Elements*, Cotton found him employment as a kind of research assistant to the tailor turned historian John Speed, himself a client of Fulke Greville. Speed was at this point compiling materials for his *History of Great Britaine* (1611) and the accompanying volume of maps, *The Theatre of the Empire of Great Britaine*. Although Speed wrote most of this himself, he made extensive use of the researches of others. Bolton provided the life of Henry II, but on review it was found to be too favourable to Thomas Becket, and Bolton's work was replaced by a piece by John Barcham or Barkham, prebendary of St Paul's. It was probably about this time that Bolton conceived one of his lifelong ambitions, the writing of a new, scholarly history of England that went beyond both the Elizabethan chroniclers, such as John Stow, and Speed's own patchwork history.

Bolton set off on his own plans again in 1617, when he approached the rising favourite, Buckingham, to enlist his support in the establishment of an 'academ roial'. Unlike France, England had no official learned or literary body, outside the universities, and several schemes were afoot to remedy that in the early seventeenth century. Bolton's went beyond the usual goal of setting up a finishing school for gentry and nobility; his academy was to be dedicated to the study of history, antiquities, heraldry, and literature in general. More than simply a revived Society of Antiquaries, however, this was to be an elaborate, tripartite structure chartered and endowed by the crown with £200 per annum. Its members were to be tutelaries (knights of the Garter, the lord chancellor, and the two university chancellors); auxiliaries (select members of the aristocracy); and essentials, the heart of the body, leading gentlemen of prominent families, of independent means, and of scholarly interests. Upon the academ were to fall great privileges and the role of cultural police, licensing non-theological books and reviewing translations of learned works. The names that Bolton selected for the original membership of eighty-four included some of the leading poets and scholars of the period—his friends prominent among them—including John Selden, Sir Henry Spelman, Sir Kenelm Digby, Sir Edward Coke, Endymion Porter, Sir Henry Wotton, Sir Robert Cotton, Ben Jonson, and Michael Drayton. Various versions of Bolton's proposal survive, and the scheme continued to enjoy Buckingham's support until 1624, but appears to have died with James I in the following year.

Bolton was at the same time developing the groundwork for the writing of a new history of England, and as a prolegomenon to this he authored one of his best-known works, an essay entitled *Hypercritica, or, A Rule of Judgement, for Writing or Reading our Histories*. Although this has often been dated as early as 1610, he began it no earlier than 1618, and it is referred to in a translation of the Roman historian Lucius Florus that Bolton published the following year, when William Camden also saw it. It cannot have been finished before 1621, since it refers to Francis Bacon by the title of Viscount St Albans. Unpublished in his lifetime, the *Hypercritica*, in contrast to other *artes historicae* ('arts of history') of the period, stressed the writing rather than the reading of history. In particular, it emphasized the need to found any new history of England on rolls, manuscripts, and other materials to be found in the Tower and other archives as well as the more traditional chronicle sources. Although he was not nearly as dismissive of medieval chroniclers as his older contemporary Sir Henry Savile, Bolton was also among the principal exponents of the view that the chronicle was an outdated genre; he distinguished, however, between the value that medieval chroniclers retained as sources and the unsatisfactory character of Elizabethan historians (such as Raphael Holinshed or Richard Grafton) and their 'vast vulgar tomes'. Like his contemporary Francis Bacon, and many French writers, he believed that proper scholarship would produce a perfect history of the kingdom that would eventually need no further revision, a definitive *Corpus rerum Anglicarum*. The manuscripts to the *Hypercritica* also shed light on Bolton's flexibility: an early version refers to a work by Fulke Greville, *Mustapha*, as 'impious'; by 1621, when he may have been in receipt of some assistance from Greville, he had changed that word to 'matchless' (Bodl. Oxf., MS Wood F.9, fols. 37, 29; MS Rawl., D.1, fol. 15).

Roman history was another of Bolton's preoccupations, and he did his most original work in this field, admiring Polybius above all other ancient authors. In addition to the above-mentioned translation of Florus, and a work, which has not survived except in notes, on the reign of Tiberius, Bolton made a special study of the sources for the reign of Nero Caesar, and this became the subject of a full-length history, *Nero Caesar, or, Monarchie Depraved*, first published in 1624. This may have been produced in haste, since at many points blank spots appear where images of coins were intended to be placed, a fault remedied in the second edition of 1627. *Nero Caesar* appears on the one hand to be a shamelessly sycophantic plea for patronage from Buckingham and Charles I, stressing the virtues of strong rule. Bolton's purpose, however, was not to apologize for Nero's reign but to compare its severity with the benefits of Stuart government, and to argue that even the most despotic rule must not be resisted by rebellion; the consequences of Nero's deposition, monster though he may have been, were endless successive rebellions and depositions throughout the remainder of Roman imperial history. The language of the preface suggests that the work was encouraged by James I himself, perhaps through Buckingham, and Bolton may have intended it as a working out of some of the king's own ideas on monarchy. The real originality of *Nero Caesar*, however, lies less in what it says than in its use of sources. Unlike many contemporaries, Bolton adduced non-literary evidence such as coins and inscriptions (published in collections by Camden and by European scholars such as Janus Gruter and Jacopo de Strada) in proof of his assertions and as a corrective to the accounts of the ancients themselves. It is thus one of the earliest English attempts to synthesize humanist narrative history with advanced philological and antiquarian scholarship.

Bolton's livelihood was never secure—he complained, as many authors, of the rapacious character of booksellers and did not grow wealthy from his publications. The last of these was *The Citties Advocate* (1629), an enquiry into the question of whether commercial activity, and especially apprenticeship, extinguished gentility. This turn of interest reflects the close connection with the London city élite that Bolton developed in his last years, a shift away from the intellectual aristocracy he had cultivated in the years of the 'academ roial' scheme. In part this turn to a municipal patron arose from necessity. By 1628 Buckingham had abandoned Bolton—as early as 1623 the duke had failed to appoint his impecunious client to an unnamed educational post, perhaps the vacant provostship of Eton College.

Meanwhile, the new king, Charles I, had embarked upon a more vigorous persecution of Catholics than his father. In 1628 Bolton was fined as a recusant and, being unable to pay, confined to Fleet prison, whence he was moved to the Marshalsea, probably within a year or so. Requests to friends and relatives for assistance produced little: Endymion Porter tore his brother-in-law's letter up in disgust. As a means of reducing his debts, he proposed to the London aldermen that he undertake a complete chronological history of London, with maps, entitled the *Vindiciae Britannicae*. This was to be published in Latin and English, and was intended to improve on John Stow's 1598 *Survay of London*, which Bolton thought reliable but badly written. Several months of work on the project and some encouragement from the city led to profound disappointment when the aldermen, faced with his estimate of £3000 to £4000 pounds as the cost of publishing the book, backed out of the project and refused to reimburse him for expenses incurred. In an early example of an appeal to academic referees, Bolton suggested that his manuscript be sent out to learned readers such as Ben Jonson, John Selden, Sir Henry Wotton, Kenelm Digby, Sir Edward Coke, Sir Dudley Digges, and Degory Whear, the Camden professor of ancient history at Oxford (and fellow student of both Lucius Florus and the *ars historica*). There is no evidence that this occurred, but in 1632 Bolton gave the manuscript of the *Vindiciae*, which has not survived, to Selden, his long-time neighbour in Whitefriars, for delivery to the aldermen. Unknown to Bolton, the city had already contracted with the better known Jonson to provide a more modest chronology at no charge. In 1634 Bolton contacted his old friend Sir John Coke, sending him the unpublished life of Tiberius that he had written as a companion to *Nero*. Since this is his last known letter, it may be presumed that Bolton died at Marshalsea soon thereafter. D. R. WOOLF

Sources D. R. Woolf, *The idea of history in early Stuart England* (1990) • D. R. Woolf, 'Edmund Bolton, Francis Bacon and the making of the *Hypercritica*, 1618–21', *Bodleian Library Record*, 11 (1982–5), 162–8 • Bolton's note and letter-book, BL, Harley MS 6521 • Venn, *Alum. Cant.* • J. Hunter, 'Chorus vatum Anglicanorum', BL, MS Add. 24488, fols. 113–45 • R. W. Caudill, 'Some literary evidence of the development of English virtuoso interests in the seventeenth century', DPhil diss., U. Oxf., 1975 • E. M. Portal, 'The "Academ Roial" of King James I', *PBA*, [7] (1915–16), 189–208

Archives BL, Harley MS 6521 • Folger, MS 916.1:x.c.8 | BL, Cotton MS Julius C.III, fols. 28, 30, 32 • BL, Hicks MSS, MS Lans XC, fol. 180 • Bodl. Oxf., Rawlinson MSS D.1; Wood F.9

Bolton, Sir Francis John (1831–1887), army officer and electrical engineer, was the son of Dr Thomas Wilson Bolton, surgeon, of London and Manchester. He enlisted in the Royal Artillery and soon became a non-commissioned officer. He was commissioned ensign in the Gold Coast artillery corps on 4 September 1857, and served in the expedition against the Crobboes in 1858, being promoted lieutenant on 9 November. In 1859 he was adjutant in the successful expedition against the Dounquah rebels.

On his return to England Bolton was transferred to the 12th (East Suffolk) regiment, and promoted captain on 21 September 1860. For several years he co-operated with Captain P. H. Colomb RN, in developing a system of visual signalling, which was adopted by the authorities. He also invented an oxy-calcium light for night signalling. The *Army and Navy Signal Book* was compiled by Bolton and Colomb, assisted by an officer of the Royal Engineers, and was used effectively during the Abyssinian expedition. Bolton married in 1866 Julia Maria, second daughter of R. Mathews of Oatlands Park, Surrey; she survived him.

From 1867 to 1869 Bolton was deputy assistant quartermaster-general and assistant instructor in visual signalling at the School of Military Engineering, Chatham, under Captain Richard Hugh Stotherd, instructor in telegraphy. He was promoted on 8 July 1868 to an unattached majority for his services to army signalling.

Bolton was largely instrumental in 1871 in founding the Society of Telegraph Engineers and Electricians, of which he became honorary secretary. He edited the journal of the society, and was afterwards vice-president. In 1871 he was appointed by the Board of Trade under the Metropolis Water Act as water examiner to the metropolis, and in 1884 he published *London Water Supply*. He was promoted lieutenant-colonel on 15 June 1877, and retired from the army with the honorary rank of colonel on 1 July 1881. He was knighted in 1884.

Bolton interested himself in electrical matters, and a beautiful display of coloured fountains and electric lights at the exhibitions at South Kensington from 1883 to 1886 were designed by him and operated from the central tower under his personal superintendence. Bolton died on 5 January 1887 at the Royal Bath Hotel, Bournemouth, Hampshire. R. H. VETCH, *rev.* JAMES LUNT

Sources *The Times* (7 Jan 1887) • *Royal Engineers Journal* (Feb 1887) • *Hart's Army List* • *Annual Register* (1887)

Likenesses wood-engraving (after photograph by W. & D. Downey), NPG; repro. in *ILN* (19 Jan 1884)

Wealth at death £85,978 17*s*. 7*d*.: probate, 11 May 1887, *CGPLA Eng. & Wales*

Bolton, Sir George (*fl.* 1790–1799), tutor and inventor of gun-locks, of unknown parentage and early life, was schooled in military tactics and mathematics preparatory to a career in the army, but was instead appointed instructor to the royal princesses in writing, geography, and arithmetic. Being of independent means, he indulged his interest in firearms by seeking to improve the musket gun-lock, which in both military and sporting firearms was so defective that accidents were frequently caused by guns going off at half-cock in the heat of battle or when forging through dense vegetation. The self-acting and detached bolting lock that he designed was constructed by mathematical instrument makers (whom he found more obedient to his orders than the gun makers), and patented in 1795 (no. 2041). The Board of Ordnance had several examples made for trial at Woolwich, but although their performance was deemed admirable, cost ruled out their general adoption. Bolton designed a simpler version, both models being described in his *Remarks on the present defective state of fire-arms, with an explanation of a newly invented patented gun-lock* (1795); the locks were obtainable from the gunsmith Fisher of High Holborn. In March 1799 Bolton let it be known in court circles that he was about to depart for the West Indies and would be much assisted in his intended business (which was not disclosed) by a knighthood. George III duly knighted him on 3 April 1799. His later life is obscure; it is thought that he may have died about 1807. ANITA MCCONNELL

Sources G. Bolton, *Remarks on the present defective state of fire-arms* (1795) • *The later correspondence of George III*, ed. A. Aspinall, 5 vols. (1962–70), vol. 3, p. 201 • F. Townsend, *Calendar of knights … from 1760 to the present time* (1828), 8 • Watt, *Bibl. Brit.*

Bolton, Sir George Lewis French (1900–1982), banker, was born on 16 October 1900 at 1 Lawley Street, Lower Clapton, Hackney, east London, the son of William George Lewis Bolton, a shipping clerk, and his wife, Beatrice Louise, *née* French. He was educated at Leyton county high school before joining the London branch of the Société Générale de Paris at the age of sixteen to be trained as an exchange dealer. He can be regarded as a leading influence behind the rebirth of London as the world's leading international financial centre from the 1950s.

Bolton's successful career as an exchange dealer was well-suited to his intellectually agile and highly individualistic character. After working with Société Générale he was employed by the merchant bank Helbert Wagg in 1920, where he remained for twelve years, developing an extensive foreign exchange business. This expertise brought him to the attention of the governor of the Bank of England, Montagu Norman. Following the pound's dramatic departure from the gold standard in 1931, the Bank of England had become involved in the management of the sterling exchange rate. Bolton joined the Bank of England in 1933, became deputy principal of the foreign exchange section in 1934, and served as principal between 1936 and 1941.

At the Bank of England, Bolton exercised a considerable influence on international monetary policy. During the late 1930s he undertook secret preparations for a structure of wartime exchange control plans, which were duly implemented following the outbreak of war. He was appointed adviser to the Bank of England on exchange and monetary policy in 1941, and following his appointment as external director of the bank in March 1948, Bolton exercised a personal ascendancy on most questions of external financial policy. Few officials could challenge his forceful and powerful arguments, even though they were sometimes erratic.

The problems of sterling, undermined by Britain's deteriorating economy, were a central concern. In a speech in 1956 Bolton predicted that the loss of international confidence in sterling would lead to 'a collapse of civilisation as we know it over a very large area of the world' (Fry, 43), but his solutions to the difficulties which beset the British currency in the post-war world were idiosyncratic. He was one of the chief proponents of a radical scheme (code-named ROBOT) in 1952 for a floating rate of exchange for sterling and for the full convertibility of the currency subject to the funding of 80 per cent of the sterling balances held by non-dollar countries. After a bitter controversy, the ROBOT scheme was finally rejected by the prime minister, Winston Churchill. In retrospect, it is widely believed that if the scheme had been adopted it would have had politically and economically disastrous consequences for Britain.

In 1957 Bolton was persuaded to become chairman of the Bank of London and South America (Bolsa), the descendant of more than half a dozen British overseas banks which had established branches in Latin America in the nineteenth century. In the 1950s the bank's prospects did not look good in the face of growing economic nationalism, while its management lacked vigour, a situation which its main shareholder since the inter-war years, Lloyds Bank, showed little interest in improving.

Bolton's period as chairman of Bolsa between 1957 and 1970 was of major significance both for the bank and for London's financial community more generally. Bolton had finally become convinced that sterling's role as a world reserve currency was doomed, but he firmly believed that the City of London could none the less be reborn as a dynamic financial centre. He argued that the key to this rebirth was the removal of tight government restrictions, and the existence of a liberal regulatory framework which would enable London to flourish as a financial entrepôt. He was one of the first to see the potential of London as a location for new global financial markets. On appointment as chairman of Bolsa he set up a foreign exchange department, with the dealers instructed to look for deposits in foreign currencies. Bolsa thereby became one of the first movers in the new eurodollar markets, whose location in London was to provide such a major impetus behind the City's renewal.

During the 1960s Bolton was extensively engaged in a series of schemes to reorganize Britain's overseas banking interests. In 1965 Mellon National Bank acquired a 15 per cent shareholding in Bolsa. Subsequently Bolton sought to build on the Mellon connection by uniting all the overseas banking operations of Lloyds and Barclays to create a global Anglo-American multinational bank which would have had branches spanning Latin America, Europe, Africa, and Asia. However it never proved possible to secure such a fusion in the face of vested interests.

Bolton's vision of an Anglo-American multinational bank reflected his attachment to the United States. He was disconcerted by, and distrustful of, the European Common Market, formed in 1958. He strongly opposed British membership, fearing that the Common Market would lead to a political union with a written constitution and a common currency and legal system, which he considered would be intolerable for Britain. In place of ties with continental Europe, Bolton favoured the formation of a north Atlantic free trade association including Britain, the United States, and Canada.

During the 1970s Bolton pursued a wide range of international business and other interests. In 1973 he became deputy chairman of Lonrho, the controversial British conglomerate active in Africa, and he served as chairman of the Commonwealth Development Finance Company (1968–80) and Premier Consolidated Oilfields (1974–6). He was chairman of the influential Bolton inquiry in 1971 on the financial problems facing small firms. In addition, he served as sheriff of London in 1952 and 1961, governor of the London School of Economics from 1961, and was a member of the council of Benenden Girls' School in Kent.

Bolton had an impressive physical appearance. He was well over 6 feet tall, had reddish hair, light blue eyes, a cheerful countenance, and a deep and seductive voice. Combined with his imagination, ebullience, and conviction, it was not surprising that his ideas often carried the day. He was a man of strong principles, which he pursued stubbornly and with candour, qualities which made him enemies as well as friends.

Bolton married, on 3 March 1928, in Bayswater, London, May, daughter of Charles Colley Howcroft, a designer;

with her he had one son and two daughters. He was created KCMG in 1950, and received decorations from Argentina in 1960 and Chile in 1965. He died on 2 September 1982, at 61 St George's Square, Westminster, survived by his wife. G. JONES

Sources R. Fry, ed., *A banker's world: the revival of the City, 1957–70* (1970) • R. P. T. Davenport-Hines, 'Bolton, Sir George Lewis French', *DBB* • J. Fforde, *The Bank of England and public policy, 1941–1958* (1992) • G. Jones, *British multinational banking, 1830–1990: a history* (1993) • *The Times* (3 Sept 1982) • d. cert. • *CGPLA Eng. & Wales* (1982) • b. cert.
Archives Bank of England, London | Lloyds TSB, London, archives
Likenesses portrait, Lloyds Bank archives
Wealth at death £454,497: probate, 15 Nov 1982, *CGPLA Eng. & Wales*

Bolton, James (*bap.* **1735**, *d.* **1799**), natural history artist and mycologist, was baptized on 23 November 1735; he was probably born on a farm in the Calder valley, Yorkshire. He was the younger son of a weaver, William Bolton (or Boulton). His elder brother, Thomas (1722?–1778), was also a competent botanist, and this has frequently given rise to confusion in attributing their respective or joint role in botanical recording. It is not known if James received any formal education; a self-taught artist, he acquired some of his techniques indirectly, or perhaps directly, from Georg Ehret, whom he may well have met through their mutual patron, the duchess of Portland. Bolton was employed in his early adult life as a weaver but later became a respected art teacher, as well as an author and illustrator of works on plants, fungi, and birds; in the late 1790s he became the landlord of a public house in or near Luddenden Foot. In 1768 he married Sarah Blackburn (or Blakeburn; *b.* 1749), who probably predeceased him; they had three sons, Virgil, Thomas, and John, and probably a daughter, Sally, who died in childhood.

Bolton was one of the foremost eighteenth-century mycologists. His talent as a botanical artist and portrayer of taxonomic detail, and as author of the first British book devoted to fungi, is widely recognized. His role in natural history recording is less widely understood, but his illustrations show his prowess in field observation, and manuscript material exists which shows that he made numerous field records, often noting important ecological details. The published catalogue of plants in John Watson's *The History and Antiquities of the Parish of Halifax in Yorkshire* (1775), often attributed to him, was in part compiled by his brother Thomas and probably other local naturalists.

Bolton lived for his entire life in the Halifax area, which provided a rich source of material, particularly fungi, for his drawings, but he also travelled and collected in the Craven district of Yorkshire, neighbouring counties, and north Wales. He communicated with key botanists of his day, including Jean Bulliard, James Dickson, John Lightfoot, and Carl Willdenow, but it is not clear if mentions by other important correspondents and visitors to 'Bolton' refer to him or to his brother. He was elected an honorary member of the Natural History Society of Edinburgh, and in 1788 the genus *Boltonia* (Compositae) was named by Charles L'Heritier de Brutelle in his honour.

Bolton is best remembered as the author of three major works, *Filices Britannicae* (2 vols., 1785–90), *An History of Fungusses Growing about Halifax* (3 vols., 1788–90; supplement, 1791), and *Harmonia ruralis* (2 vols., 1794–6), the illustrations to all of which he drew and etched himself. His *History of Fungusses* was republished in German in four volumes, with inferior plates, as *Geschichte der Merkwürdigsten* (1795–1820). He also provided the illustrations for Richard Relhan's *Flora Cantabrigiensis* (1785).

Bolton died in Yorkshire on 7 January 1799. His estate (paintings, microscope, printing equipment, and personal effects) was auctioned in the following June.

MARK SEAWARD

Sources J. Edmondson, *James Bolton of Halifax* (1995) • R. Watling and M. R. D. Seaward, 'James Bolton: mycological pioneer', *Archives of Natural History*, 10 (1981–2), 89–110 • C. Crossland, *An eighteenth century naturalist* (1995) • J. Edmondson, 'New insights into James Bolton of Halifax', *Mycologist*, 9 (1995), 174–8 • Desmond, *Botanists*, rev. edn • B. Henrey, *British botanical and horticultural literature before 1800*, 3 vols. (1975) • J. Webster and D. Moore, *Brief biographies of British mycologists*, ed. G. C. Ainsworth (British Mycological Society, Stourbridge, 1996) • C. Crossland, 'The study of fungi in Yorkshire', *The Naturalist* (March 1908), 81–96 • M. Blackwell, 'Links with past Yorkshire naturalists', *The Naturalist* (April–June 1961), 53–66 • W. B. Crump and C. Crossland, *The flora of the parish of Halifax* (1904) • E. C. Nelson, 'James Bolton's botanical paintings and illustrations, and his association with Georg Ehret', *The Naturalist*, 106 (1981), 141–7 • W. B. Crump, 'James and Thomas Bolton of Halifax', *The Naturalist* (April 1940), 105–6
Archives NHM • Royal Horticultural Society, London, Lindley Library • United States department of agriculture, Beltsville, Maryland • W. Yorks. AS, Calderdale | Bodl. Oxf., Gough MSS • Knowsley Hall, Lancashire, library of the earl of Derbyshire • Milton House, Dunbartonshire, Sir Peter Hutchinson's collection

Bolton, James Jay (1824–1863), Church of England clergyman, was born on 11 February 1824 at Southdown College, near Weymouth, the fifth son of Robert Bolton, nonconformist minister, and his wife, a daughter of the Revd William Jay of Bath. His early years were spent at Henley-on-Thames, where his father was a minister. At the age of twelve he went with his parents to America, where circumstances placed his father in charge of an episcopal congregation at Christ Church, Pelham, New York. He was educated at Dr Muhlenburg's, College Point, New York, after staying for some time at Brook Farm, New Rochelle, and Pelham. He returned to England, and entered Corpus Christi College, Cambridge, in 1844. He obtained a scholarship in his first year, and took a BA degree in 1848. After taking orders in 1848 he was curate of Saffron Walden from 1849 to 1851, and of St Michael's, Chester Square, Pimlico, from 1851 to 1852. In 1853 he was appointed to the incumbency of St Paul's Episcopal Chapel, Kilburn, where he remained until his death. On 30 June 1853 he married Lydia Louisa, third daughter of the Revd W. W. Pym, rector of Willian, Hertfordshire.

Bolton's faith was strongly evangelical, and he excelled as a children's preacher. His brother, W. J. Bolton, arranged and published two series of his *Selected Sermons* in 1863 and 1866. Bolton also contributed extensively to the *Family Treasury*, the *Sunday Scholars and Teachers' Magazine*, and similar children's publications. He published several other religious works, not all for children. Among the most significant were *Fragments of the Great Diamond Set for Young People: being Addresses to Children* (1856) and *Life Lessons, or, Scriptural Truths Illustrated* (1862). Bolton died at the parsonage, Kilburn, on 8 April 1863.

JAMES MEW, *rev.* I. T. FOSTER

Sources Venn, *Alum. Cant.* • Allibone, *Dict.* • Boase, *Mod. Eng. biog.* • *Record* (10 April 1863)

Bolton, Sir John Brown (1902–1980), politician in the Isle of Man and accountant, was born on 20 January 1902 in Methwold, Norfolk, the eldest of four sons of the Revd Richard Bolton (1867–1951), Primitive Methodist minister, and his wife, Charlotte, *née* Brown (1865–1962). Although he was born in Norfolk, his family ties were primarily with Yorkshire and he was educated at Hull grammar school followed by Keighley trade and grammar school. On leaving school in 1918 he started training as an accountant in Keighley, but in 1919, when his father was transferred to Ramsey in the Isle of Man, he and his three brothers followed their father to the island.

On arriving in the Isle of Man, Bolton took up articles in Douglas with Mr B. Sugden and qualified as an incorporated accountant in 1924. After qualifying, he continued to work at Sugden's, where he met Mary Smith (1902–1993), whom he married on 18 June 1930, having established his own accountancy practice in Athol Street, Douglas, in 1928. They had two children, Douglas and Kathleen, and lived in Douglas throughout their married life.

Bolton had been brought up as a Primitive Methodist and for some time during his first years in the Isle of Man he was a local preacher for that church while training as an accountant. In 1925 he became organist in St Andrew's Presbyterian Church in Douglas. He was a regular churchgoer throughout his life, and continued as organist at St Andrew's for the next twenty-one years. His move to the Presbyterian church was due only to his position as organist rather than to any shift in religious belief.

Bolton's long career in Manx public service began in 1940 when he was co-opted to Douglas corporation. He served the town as councillor until he was elected to the House of Keys in 1946 as a member of the Manx People's Political Association, which stood for the promotion of private enterprise on the island. He held his seat for North Douglas and later West Douglas for a further fifteen years. He was a courageous politician with an acute sense of humour who stood with the strength of his convictions, never currying favour where it meant going against his beliefs or backing down in the face of criticism or even, on occasion, the threats which accompany public life. It was this strong-minded attitude which may have lost him his seat in the House of Keys in 1962 but which resulted in his joining the legislative council as governor's appointee in the same year; he remained there (from 1970 as an elected member) until his retirement in 1979. He wore many hats during his forty years in Manx politics: chairman of the finance board from 1966 to 1976, member of the executive council from 1951 to 1962 and again from 1966 to 1979, chairman of the income tax commission, member of the Common Market and common purse arrangement committees and the standing committee on the common interests of the Isle of Man and the UK, vice-chairman of the local government board, member of the boards of agriculture, health services, assessment, and police, and chairman of the highway board. Despite throwing himself fully into this varied career in politics, he maintained a successful accountancy practice and helped and advised in the early days of a number of companies which later became household names on the island.

Bolton's greatest political achievements were perhaps the abolition of surtaxes in 1962 when he was chancellor of the island's exchequer, and the brokering of a special relationship between the Isle of Man and the EEC in 1971–2. His contribution to the development of a climate which allowed the island's financial sector to flourish was enormous, and was criticized by some, on the grounds that this development would lead to a weakening in Manx culture, with an influx of new residents and businesses. He responded by pointing out that, as well as the money and employment generated by the financial sector, 'it is not going to interfere with the environment, like factories with big chimneys' (*Isle of Man Courier*, 7 Dec 1979).

Bolton's role in the development of the Isle of Man was recognized in 1973 with his appointment as OBE in the new year's honours list, and again in 1977 when he was knighted in the queen's silver jubilee and birthday honours list 'for public services in the Isle of Man'. Although not Manx-born, when called a 'comeover' by a member of the House of Keys he replied with good humour that he had come over before that member was born—and had, in fact, attended his christening. His impact on the Isle of Man's constitution and economy and the dedication that he showed through forty years of public service were immense. His political career spanned enormous changes in the island's constitution and prosperity. He had little time for reactionaries, and when nearing retirement in 1979 spoke of Tynwald as he had found it in 1946 in far from nostalgic terms: 'There was no health service, no social security, no Executive Council, the Government Secretary was also the Government Treasurer and the Governor was the Government. It was reckoned that the House of Keys was the official opposition in 1946' (*Isle of Man Courier*, 7 Dec 1979).

Bolton was a keen motorcyclist, golfer, and horseman. He contributed his energy and organizational abilities to these activities too, serving as president of the Peveril Motor Cycle and Light Car Club, Douglas Golf Club, and the Scooter Club. He was proud of the fact that he had achieved what few golfers ever do—a hole in one. He also had a great interest in the study of social history. He died at the Nobles Hospital, Douglas, on 11 September 1980, of cancer and heart disease, just a year after retiring from public office, and was buried in Douglas municipal cemetery. He was survived by his wife and their two children.

Perhaps his greatest legacy was the thriving financial sector found on the Isle of Man within a few years of his death. SUSIE ALEGRE

Sources *Isle of Man Weekly Times* · *Isle of Man Examiner* · *Isle of Man Courier* · *Manx Independent* · *WWW* · private information (2004) · personal knowledge (2004)
Likenesses photographs, 1920–80, priv. coll.
Wealth at death £245,000: *Isle of Man Courier* (3 Oct 1980), 5

Bolton, John Gatenby (1922–1993), astronomer, was born on 5 June 1922 at 3 Clarkehouse Road, Broomhall, Sheffield, Yorkshire, the elder of two children of John Gatenby Bolton (*d.* 1952), schoolmaster, of Skelton, Cleveland, and his wife, Ethel, *née* Kettlewell (*d.* 1942), schoolteacher of Goole, Yorkshire. He was educated at King Edward VII School, Sheffield, from which he won a state scholarship to Trinity College, Cambridge, in 1940. The exigencies of war led to a shortened course and in 1942 he was awarded the degree of BA with honours in physics.

In 1942 he obtained a reserve commission in the Royal Navy and after a short course in electronics and radar he was sent to the Telecommunications Research Establishment in Malvern, Worcestershire, to assist in the installation in naval fighter aircraft of the 1½ metre air interception radar already developed for the Royal Air Force night fighters. After D-day he was appointed radio officer to HMS *Unicorn* of the East Indies fleet. At the end of the war in Sydney he was seconded to the Royal Australian Navy and then to the army, who demobilized him. He remained in Australia for the greater part of the remainder of his life, marrying, in 1948, Letty, daughter of Edward and Ruby Pearl Burke, of Mandurama, New South Wales, and widow of E. T. Leslie, a navigator in Coastal Command who had been killed in action during the Second World War. There were two sons of her first marriage, Brian and Peter, whom Bolton adopted.

In the light of his qualifications, Bolton was advised to meet E. G. Bowen, one of the pioneers in the development of radar in England, who had joined the radiophysics laboratory of the Council for Scientific and Industrial Research (later the Commonwealth Scientific and Industrial Research Organisation (CSIRO)) in Sydney in 1944. When Bolton joined the radiophysics division in 1946 Bowen was abroad and J. L. Pawsey was in charge. It was this circumstance that determined Bolton's subsequent research on the radio waves arriving on earth from outer space—a subject soon to be known as radio astronomy. Pawsey's interest was in the recently discovered emission of intense bursts of radio waves by the sun. In February 1942 J. S. Hey of the army operational research group had discovered, during a secret investigation of the enemy jamming of British radars, that bursts of radio waves were emitted by sunspots and solar flares. It was this phenomenon that Bolton was asked to investigate. He built the appropriate metre wave radio receiver and installed it at Dover Heights, an ex-wartime station near a cliff edge. He did not observe any radio bursts from the sun and decided to direct his aerials over the sea in the hope of observing the radio waves emanating from the Milky Way. When Pawsey discovered this he ordered Bolton to return to the radiophysics laboratory and so this initial excursion to Dover Heights ended. At that stage Bolton joined Gordon Stanley and built equipment to observe the solar radio emission during an eclipse in Brazil, but the equipment was not ready before the last ship, which Pawsey had intended to take to Brazil, had sailed.

This misfortune led to one of the historic events in astronomy. Instructed by Pawsey to find some other use for this radio equipment, in March 1947 Bolton and Stanley returned to Dover Heights and soon they observed the radio emission from a giant sunspot on three widely separated radio frequencies. Their interpretation of these observations formed the subject of their first scientific publication. It was soon realized that on this cliff site, radio waves from the sun or other object reached the aerial through two paths, one direct and the other after reflection from the surface of the sea. From the interference pattern so generated it was possible to locate the source of the emission (in one dimension) to an accuracy of a few minutes of arc. This was the radio analogue of the Lloyd's mirror interferometer in optics.

Bolton and Stanley then searched for sources of extraterrestrial radio emission. In his survey of the extragalactic radio emission J. S. Hey had discovered a localized source of emission in the constellation of Cygnus. He observed that the intensity was fluctuating and concluded that the source of the emission must have small angular dimensions. Bolton and Stanley found that, as this source in Cygnus rose, the chart records of the intensity of the emission showed a maximum and minimum (a fringe pattern) from which it was possible to set an upper limit to the angular size of 8 minutes of arc. The variation in intensity observed by Hey was subsequently discovered to be a consequence of the passage of the radio waves through the earth's ionosphere and was not inherent to the source. By chance Hey had reached the right conclusion for the wrong reason.

Three other extragalactic radio sources of small angular diameter were discovered. There was no obvious optical identification and in order to make possible a search with the large optical telescopes a more precise position for the radio sources had to be determined. Bolton and Stanley moved their interferometer to New Zealand, and by measurements from a number of appropriate cliff sites they were able to place close enough limits on the position of these radio sources to facilitate a search for the optical counterparts by the large American telescopes. These searches with the 200 inch Palomar telescope, particularly by Walter Baade and Rudolph Minkowski, revealed that one of the radio sources was the supernova remnant of the Crab nebula in the Milky Way. The other two, in Virgo and Centaurus, were shown to be objects of large red shift, that is extragalactic, soon to be accepted as typical of a new class of objects to be known as radio galaxies. Thereby began the radio study of the universe and the mapping of many radio galaxies—faint optically but emitting radio waves of an intensity observable by the relatively crude radio equipment of that epoch.

By 1953 the system at Dover Heights could no longer

compete with superior equipment evolving elsewhere for the radio studies of the universe. Pawsey would not agree with Bolton's plans for the future development of his own group, and that prompted Bowen (then head of the radiophysics division) in August 1953 to persuade Bolton to join his cloud physics research. For eighteen months Bolton worked on cloud physics, then in January 1955 took leave of absence from CSIRO to initiate research in radio studies of the universe at the California Institute of Technology (Caltech), where he was appointed a senior research fellow. In 1956 he was appointed professor of radio astronomy at Caltech and resigned his position with CSIRO.

Bolton spent six years at Caltech, during which he created the Owens Valley Radio Observatory. He built an interferometer consisting of two 90 foot diameter steerable paraboloids, on railway tracks so that they could be separated up to 1600 feet either in a north–south or east–west direction. The system, operated at higher radio frequencies than previously, and the location of radio galaxies and their identification using the large optical telescopes, flourished. This equipment measured the accurate right ascension of the radio source known as 3C48, interest in which had been stimulated by the angular diameter measurements at Jodrell Bank, which implied that it could be the most distant object yet known. The subsequent search by the 200 inch Palomar telescope revealed a hitherto unknown type of blue object without a measurable red shift. This result, first presented at the December 1960 meeting of the American Astronomical Society, was the first step towards the conclusion, two years later, that a hitherto unknown class of distant galaxies had been discovered—soon to be known as quasars.

During Bolton's stay at Caltech, Bowen had begun the construction of the 210 foot diameter steerable radio telescope at Parkes, New South Wales. Late in 1960 Bolton left Caltech to supervise the final stages in the construction of this telescope. The Parkes telescope was commissioned in late 1961, and Bolton became the director of this Australian national radio observatory. Under his direction the telescope had widespread use in many radio astronomical researches. His own major interest remained in the discovery and identification of the extragalactic radio sources, and the Parkes catalogue soon extended to many thousands of these sources. In particular he was involved with Cyril Hazard in the precise measurement of the position of the source known as 3C273, by means of lunar occultation. This led to the conclusive discovery that, like 3C48, this was one of the new class of nebulae (quasars) with very high red shifts and hence at great distances in the universe. The catalogue of some 8000 radio sources assembled under Bolton's direction, and the search for the optical identifications, remained his primary interest. With his Australian and American collaborators he found identifications for about 1000 radio sources; this work was published in more than forty papers from 1965 to 1982, and through it he gained considerable experience with the large American optical telescopes. This led to his association with the planning and commissioning of the 4 metre Anglo-Australian optical telescope at Siding Springs.

Bolton was involved on a number of occasions with the NASA space programmes; the signals from Neil Armstrong's landing on the moon in 1969 came via the Parkes telescope, as did the transmissions during the drama of the endangered Apollo 13 mission. He retired as director of the Parkes telescope during the changes of 1971–2, when Bowen retired as chief of the radiophysics division, but he continued to work at Parkes and elsewhere as astronomer-at-large. In 1979 he suffered a severe heart attack but recovered sufficiently to continue the analysis with his colleagues of the Parkes data. In 1981 he retired to Buderim, a coastal resort in Queensland.

Bolton was a keen sportsman; an avid cricketer, he also enjoyed competitive games of golf, table tennis, and billiards. He received many honours and awards, being appointed CBE in 1982. He was elected a fellow of the Royal Society in 1973 and a fellow of the Australian Academy of Sciences in 1969. In 1977 he was awarded the gold medal of the Royal Astronomical Society and in 1988 the Bruce medal of the Astronomical Society of the Pacific. He died at his home in Buderim after a final attack of pneumonia, following persistent heart trouble, on 6 July 1993. He was survived by his wife. BERNARD LOVELL

Sources J. P. Wild and V. Radhakrishnan, *Memoirs FRS*, 41 (1995), 73–86 · V. Radhakrishnan, 'John Bolton, astronomer extraordinary', *Astronomy and Astrophysics*, 14 (1993), 115–20 · K. I. Kellerman, 'John Gatenby Bolton, 1922–1993', *Publications of the Astronomical Society of the Pacific*, 108 (1996), 729–37 · R. Bhathan, *Australian astronomers* (1996), 104–16 · *Australian Journal of Physics*, 47/5 (1994) [John Bolton issue, *Pioneering a new astronomy*, ed. D. E. Goddard and R. F. Haynes] · *The Independent* (29 July 1993) · personal knowledge (2004) · private information (2004) [Mrs L. Bolton, Mrs P. J. Wheatley] · b. cert.

Likenesses photograph, repro. in *The Independent* · photograph, repro. in Wild and Radhakrishnan, *Memoirs FRS*, 72

Bolton, Sir Richard (*d.* 1648), lawyer and politician, was the son of John Bolton of Fenton, Staffordshire. Having attended the Inner Temple in London, he practised for a time as a barrister in England. It is possible that he married his first wife, Frances, daughter of Richard Walter of Stafford, with whom he had one son and several daughters, before he left for Ireland with the object, it has been alleged, of avoiding the results of a censure passed on him by the court of Star Chamber. At the close of 1604 he obtained employment as temporary recorder of Dublin. In the following year he was appointed recorder of that city—'during good behaviour'—at an annual salary of £25. As counsel in the famous case of tanistry, Bolton defended the ancient Gaelic custom of partible inheritance, a key obstacle to the legal assimilation of Ulster into the English imperium in Ireland. He was dispatched in 1608 to London as law agent to the municipality of Dublin in connection with suits relating to its customs and privileges. Sir Arthur Chichester, lord deputy of Ireland, in a letter dated 15 October 1608, commended Bolton to the earl of Salisbury.

Bolton was admitted to the Society of King's Inns, Dublin, in 1610. Through government influence he was elected on 27 April 1613, in opposition to the Roman Catholic candidate, one of the representatives of the city of Dublin in the parliament of which Sir John Davies became the speaker. He resigned the recordership of Dublin in the same year. He received a knighthood on 4 July 1618 from Sir Oliver St John, lord deputy of Ireland. Under privy seal dated Westminster 31 December 1618, and patent of the 10th of the following February, Bolton was appointed solicitor-general for Ireland. In 1621 he published at Dublin, in a folio volume, a selection of statutes passed in parliaments held in Ireland, dedicated to his benefactor, Sir Oliver St John, who had encouraged him to undertake it.

Bolton became attorney-general to the court of wards at Dublin in 1622, and was appointed chief baron of the exchequer in Ireland by privy seals dated 13 April and 29 May, and patent dated 29 June 1625. To his printed volume of the statutes an addition containing those of the tenth and eleventh years of Charles I was published in 1635. Bolton published in 1638, at Dublin, a folio volume entitled *A Justice of the Peace for Ireland*, setting out the duties of JPs out of session and detailing the form of their proceedings during sessions. By this time he was closely associated with Richard Boyle, earl of Cork. However, he aligned himself with Wentworth and played a leading role in the lord deputy's commission for defective titles. By privy seal dated at Westminster 6 December 1639, and a patent given at Dublin on 15 January 1640, Bolton was appointed to the chancellorship of Ireland, in place of Sir Adam Loftus, with a moiety of the profits derivable from chancery writs, together with £500 per annum, during his tenure of office. As chancellor he presided in the parliament which began at Dublin in March 1640. On 11 February 1641 the House of Lords acquitted him from a charge of having endeavoured to prevent the continuance of the existing parliament. With a letter dated 18 February Bolton transmitted to the committee of the house attending the king in England a schedule of grievances of Ireland voted by the lords at Dublin on the same day. He was regarded as a chief adviser of Strafford in his attempts to introduce arbitrary government. On 27 February 1641 a committee was appointed by the House of Commons in Ireland to draw up charges against the chancellor, Bolton, and against Bramhall, bishop of Derry, Sir Gerard Lowther, chief justice of the common pleas, and Sir George Radcliffe, to impeach them of high treason. The chancellor, as chairman of the house, had to receive the articles against himself. The wrath of his accusers was heightened when he suggested that Poynings' Law restricted the Irish parliament's powers of impeachment. On 1 March 1641 the house ordered that the lord chancellor should enter into recognizances to appear when the articles should be exhibited. After some further debate the peers left it to the lords justices to do as they saw fit, as there were no precedents. They further declared 'the sense of the house that the lord chancellor was not fit to execute that place, nor to sit at the council board, and that they desired a new speaker'. Sir William Ryves, justice of the king's bench, appointed by letters patent speaker of the House of Lords in Ireland, during pleasure, in the absence of the chancellor, took office on 11 May 1641. In the following July the lords justices communicated to the House of Commons the king's desire that they should forbear proceeding further with the impeachment. The ensuing struggle to continue with the prosecution was of great constitutional significance, giving rise to the debates from whence transpired Darcy's 'Argument' in assertion of Irish independence under English law.

Bolton, as member of the privy council at Dublin, signed the dispatch of 25 October 1641 announcing to the earl of Leicester, the lord lieutenant, then in England, the start of hostile movements in Ireland. He took part in the preparation of an elaborate statement, transmitted to the House of Lords in London in November 1641, in relation to the English administrative system in Ireland. By a resolution of 21 June 1642, that no members should sit or vote until they had taken the oath of supremacy, the House of Commons excluded the Roman Catholic representatives, among whom were those who had been most active in the proceedings against Bolton and his associates. On the same day Bolton and Lowther petitioned the house, and it was unanimously resolved to proceed no further upon the articles of accusation against them. On the following day Bolton was restored by the Lords to his place as chancellor, and on 2 August 1642 resumed his position in their house.

Bolton was actively engaged in negotiations connected with the cessation of hostilities between England and the Irish in 1643. In 1643–4 he was a principal counsellor of the lord lieutenant, Ormond, in negotiating with the Irish confederation concerning peace. His name appears first among those of the privy council who signed the proclamation issued at Dublin on 30 July 1646 announcing the conclusion of a treaty of peace between Charles I and his Roman Catholic subjects in Ireland. In writings condemnatory of the terms of that peace Bolton was represented as more devoted to the parliament of England than to the king, and much opposed to concessions to the Roman Catholics of Ireland. A contemporary answer to some of the allegations against Bolton is extant in an unpublished manuscript in the British Library. Bolton signed the instructions on 26 September 1646 to those who were commissioned to treat with the English parliament for succours after the peace had been rejected by the Irish. He joined in the statement on the condition of Ireland of 19 February 1647 submitted by Ormond to Charles I, and preserved in the twentieth volume of the Carte papers in the Bodleian Library.

Bolton died in November 1648. His second wife, whom he married at an unknown date, was Margaret (*d.* in or after 1663), daughter of Sir Patrick Barnewall. In 1661 the peers at Dublin ordered that the books of their house for 1640 and 1641 should be expunged 'where they contained anything that did intrench upon the honor of the late Earl of Strafford, the late Bishop [Bramhall] of Derry, the lord chancellor Bolton, and several others'. In the archives at Kilkenny Castle is a petition in which Lady Bolton, widow of Sir Richard Bolton, applied in 1663 to the duke of

Ormond, then viceroy, for the arrears due to her late husband. Bolton's son Edward succeeded him as solicitor-general in Ireland in 1622, and as chief baron in 1640. On the death of Charles I, Edward Bolton was by Charles II reappointed chief baron. He was removed from that office by the parliamentarian government, which, however, employed him in 1651 as commissioner for the administration of justice in Ireland.

J. T. GILBERT, *rev.* SEAN KELSEY

Sources R. Lascelles, ed., *Liber munerum publicorum Hiberniae … or, The establishments of Ireland*, 2 vols. [1824–30] • H. Kearney, *Strafford in Ireland, 1633–41* (1959) • A. Clarke, *The Old English in Ireland, 1625–1642* (1966), 143 • T. W. Moody and others, eds., *A new history of Ireland*, 3: *Early modern Ireland, 1534–1691* (1976) • H. Pawlisch, *Sir John Davies and the conquest of Ireland: a study in legal imperialism* (1985), 77 • W. A. Shaw, *The knights of England*, 2 vols. (1906) • W. H. Cooke, ed., *Students admitted to the Inner Temple, 1547–1660* [1878] • A. Vicars, ed., *Index to the prerogative wills of Ireland, 1536–1810* (1967), 42

Wealth at death see will, Vicars, ed., *Index*

Bolton, Robert (1572–1631), Church of England clergyman, was born at Blackburn, Lancashire, on Whitsunday, 25 May 1572, the sixth son of Adam Bolton (*d.* 1593) of Brookhouse, Blackburn, a yeoman and governor of the free grammar school there in 1567, and his wife, Elizabeth (*d.* 1610). Much of what is known about him is to be found in the 'Life and death of Mr. Bolton' prefixed to various editions of Bolton's works by Edward Bagshawe, who, having been one of his first students at Oxford, became a lifelong friend. His parents, finding in their young son 'a great towardliness for learning, destinated him to be a scholar, and struggled with their estate to furnish him with necessaries in that kind' (Bagshawe, 5–6); he studied at Blackburn School under its master, Yates (perhaps Lawrence Yates), becoming 'the best scholler in the schoole' (ibid.).

Oxford In 1592 Bolton was admitted to Lincoln College, Oxford, where his tutor was John Randall. Here Bolton's school work, and comparative maturity, gave him an advantage over others in his cohort, and he progressed well in the study of logic and philosophy. Within a few months, however, the death of his father (himself a younger son) reduced him to penury. From the need to return books borrowed from his tutor and others he learned the habit of summarizing them extensively in notebooks. He became especially expert in Greek, and, according to Anthony Wood, could write it better than English or Latin.

Bolton transferred to Brasenose, perhaps hoping to resolve his financial difficulties by securing a fellowship, and graduated BA there on 2 December 1596. By 2 December 1597 he held a Nowell scholarship, a foundation designed for the support of Lancashire men. Yet lacking well-placed friends and connections a fellowship initially eluded him; it seems possible that his religious outlook may have been a factor. During this difficult period he depended greatly upon another Greek scholar, Dr Richard Brett, of Lincoln College, 'most bountifully to contribute to his relief' (Bagshawe, 10). Eventually in 1602 he became

Robert Bolton (1572–1631), by John Payne, 1632

a fellow of Brasenose and proceeded MA on 8 July. Appointed lecturer in logic and moral and natural philosophy, he was subsequently chosen by George Abbot, then vice-chancellor, to hold a dispute before the king on natural philosophy on the occasion of James's visit to the university in 1605.

Throughout his university career up to this point, according to Bagshawe, Bolton had been exceptionally hard-working yet he had developed sympathies with Roman Catholicism, a fault akin to atheism: 'he was a very mean scholar in the school of Christ, he drew no religious breath from the soil he came'. Having travelled to Cambridge to hear William Perkins, possibly the most eminent puritan of his generation, Bolton rejected his plain style of speaking and its content, calling the great man 'a barren empty fellow, and a passing mean scholar' (Bagshawe, 11, 13). Bagshawe, himself a zealous puritan, tells us that Bolton also enjoyed 'stage plays, cards and dice, he was a horrible swearer and sabbath breaker, and boon-companion', a character which may have been coloured to contrast with his subject's later piety (Bagshawe, 12). An attempt by the Jesuit Lawrence Anderton, formerly of Blackburn School and then of Christ's College, Cambridge, to persuade Bolton to take ship for a seminary in Flanders failed when Anderton did not himself appear at the rendezvous. Bolton shortly afterwards returned to Brasenose, where he proceeded BD on 14 December 1609, and where the vice-president, Thomas Peacock, was instrumental in his conversion to the austere form of protestantism which he was to follow for the rest of his life. Bolton soon decided to become a minister, for, as he explained, he observed in the university 'many reverend and learned men, full of the light of divine truth, and of the water of life, able gloriously and comfortably to enlighten many dark places and dry souls in the bosom of this their famous nurse, not brought up by her to die at her breasts', but ready instead 'to enlarge Christ's kingdom abroad, and to oppose with all their power, against the bloody torrent of popery and rage of antichrist' (Bolton, *Discourse*, sig. A3).

Rector of Broughton On 12 February 1610 Bolton was inducted to the rectory of Broughton, Northamptonshire, on the presentation of Sir Augustine Nicols, sergeant in the household of Prince Henry, and on 22 June he was granted a preaching licence. He resigned his fellowship on 2 March 1611 and soon afterwards married Anne or Anna, the youngest daughter of Thomas Boyse of Eythorne, Kent. Their first child was buried, unbaptized, at Broughton on 21 March 1612.

Bagshawe describes the vigorous programme of daily prayer and spiritual reflection followed by Bolton and his growing family. His mental outlook was transformed by the pains of his spiritual rebirth, in which God came 'not by any soft and still voice, but in terrible tempests and thunder, the Lord running upon him as a giant, taking him by the neck and shaking him to pieces as he did Job; beating him to the very ground, as he did Paul, by laying before him the ugly visage of his sins' (Bagshawe, 15–16). From many months of temptations and suffering Bolton emerged with unshakeable convictions, but he never forgot the torment his conscience had suffered. Thus it was that 'though in his preaching he was a *son of thunder*, yet unto bruised reeds and those that mourned in spirit, he was as sweet a son of consolation as ever I heard' (ibid., 20). Indeed, conceded Anthony Wood, 'he was sought to far and near, and divers beyond the seas' came to him for relief from the doubts that afflicted their consciences (Wood, *Ath. Oxon.*, 2.515). Several of Bolton's works reflect a deep preoccupation with the inner life of the saint, not least in their titles: *Some General Directions for a Comfortable Walking with God*; *Instructions for a Right Comforting Afflicted Consciences*; *A Cordiall for Christians in the Time of Affliction*. There is no doubt that Bolton's ministry was directed at a minority of that minority who conventionally saw themselves as good people in the sight of God: there was 'no hope for the drunkard, the swearer, the liar, the usurer, the unclean person, the sabbath breaker, the sacrilegious, simonical, and sinners of such infamous rank', though he spoke with grief rather than anger of the sins of his flock. Yet 'many thousands' of others falsely supposed that, being free 'from gross and notorious sins', and having 'civil honesty, a formal profession of Christianity, outward performances of religious seriousness, that then their case is good enough for heaven, though there be wanting the … saving power of inward sanctification, and the truth of a sound conversion'. And he pointed instead to 'a paradise of Christian comforts, a royal peculiar, a victorious simplicity, a neglected innocency, a marvellous light, an invisible kingdom, an heaven upon earth; which I call the state of grace' (Bolton, *Discourse*, sig. A3). Such a standpoint was perhaps not best calculated to strengthen the religious unity of the people of Broughton.

Public morality Bolton was a patriotic puritan minister, remarking upon 'the mighty workings of King James his works upon the adversaries' (R. Bolton, *Instructions for a Right Comforting Afflicted Consciences*, 1631, 4). The vigour and frequency of his diatribes against popery probably reflect Bolton's still unquiet conscience about his own record. He makes much of Catholic encouragement to 'furious assassins and incendiaries, for murdering of princes, butcheries of people, and fiering of states', stressing that in English protestantism, there was no warrant for the popular deposition of kings (R. Bolton, *Two Sermons Preached at Northampton*, 29). Here and in other such passages the Gunpowder Plot figures largely, and in his will Bolton provided that his bequest to the poor of Broughton should be paid on 5 November following his death and on that date in two subsequent years. His works are often prefaced by dedications to leading gentlemen of Northamptonshire such as Edward Montague and Erasmus Dryden.

Bolton favoured a magistracy which would deal firmly with evil-doers (including usurers and enclosers), but saw popery and profanity as its chief enemies, and the godly preaching ministers as its chief allies. He attacked on the one side the 'negligent and unconscionable minister, which never goes about to stir the devil in the ignorant, profane and those that hate to be reformed' and on the other, 'the idle justice, that only hunts after plausibleness and popularity, and for the good word of all the good fellows about him' (R. Bolton, *Two Sermons Preached at Northampton*, 56). There was 'no more notorious villany' than for

> an ingenious and free people … to have a magistrate set over them, which adding craft to his power and skill, welds them all three to work his own ends, and practise his private revenge from time to time upon his supposed opposites.

Justices should be 'men of truth', 'true hearted Nathaniels in their private and personal conversation; let them prize and prefer the truth … Before gold or friend, favourite, or richest favour' (ibid., 63).

Bolton's most prominent public platform was the celebrated, and officially sanctioned, lecture at Kettering. 'His doctrine was never drawn into question either for error or schism' (Bagshawe, 27), and he did not urge reform in church or state, but he repeatedly demanded that both should operate in a more godly fashion. He was extremely and repeatedly outspoken in condemning corruption. In 1621—in a sermon before the assize at Northampton—Bolton took as his text 'When the righteous are in authority, the people rejoice: but when the wicked beareth rule, the people mourn'. He pointedly asked whether

> this gangrene of going into offices, benefices, and high rooms by corruption, is not unhappily crept into this famous and flourishing state; which if it should, it will eat into the

> hearts and sinews of the state, that no wit of man can foresee, into what baseness and degenerations this noble kingdom would fall in the next age. (R. Bolton, *Two Sermons Preached at Northampton*, 3)

On simony he was even less restrained, contrasting his deceased patron's integrity in disposing of livings with 'the practice of the times', attacking openly those among his auditory, who

> for a little bloody gain put upon them an ignorant, idle, dissolute, non-resident, or some way unfaithful minister … And what a vexing cry in the ears of all sacrilegious church robbers will that be of a damned wretch in hell; when he shall complain everlastingly that his soul had been saved, if such a man had not been simoniacal. (*Works*, 1.161–2)

Bolton came to believe that many among the governing classes of England were becoming more selfish and arrogant, less godly and less humane; he attacked the 'degenerations of our gentility', in which gentlemen

> think to bear down all before them with an artificial affected impetuousness, as it were, of countenance; a disdainful neglect and contemptuousness in their carriage, with a kind of outbraving and brow beating of their brethren, as though brave apparel and a big look were demonstrations of a noble spirit. (*Works*, 1.167)

He thought that when a 'patriot which in some high place like a strong pillar opposes the corruptions and popery of the times; or any faithfull pastor … is taken away' then people should prepare 'against an evil day', and he feared 'some heavy thing is preparing for us', for the sins of England were 'ripe for His revenging hand' (*Works*, 1.157). In 1629, in what was surely taken as a comment on recent developments in religion, he pointed to the danger of 'unrighteous ruling' by means of 'tampering with our articles of religion … by labouring to put false glosses upon them, and talking of some reconcilement of our church to the Romish synagogue' (R. Bolton, *Two Sermons Preached at Northampton*, 76). It may be that he also became more aware of and unhappy at the sale of offices. In 1630 he attacked the practice in a sermon before justices of assize Sir Richard Hutton and Sir George Croke, quoting Tacitus, 'Never came any to an high room wrongfully, and unworthily: but he exercised his power and authority wickedly and unjustly' (*Works*, 1.188).

Bolton's biographer claimed that his zeal 'was always tempered with discretion' (Bagshawe, 27), but this had limits. He corresponded with Arthur Hildersham, a veteran of the Elizabethan puritan movement, and was friendly with John Preston. His sympathies were with the reformed churches abroad: 'for his charity, he was ever universally bountiful, but especially he exceeded in those public distresses of Germany, France, Bohemia etc and to those that stood in true need' (Bagshawe, 28). Bolton knew from his training that the word 'puritan' meant sympathy with the teachings of the heretic Novatius. Before his conversion he was not above deploying it as a mere insult, but later he sought to correct the misuse of the term, to rebut the sort of sneering attacks which he himself had once mounted, and to identify with the people thus stigmatized. In 1610 he could note that 'The world is come to that wretched pass, and height of profaneness, that even honesty and sanctification, is many times odiously branded by the nick-name of puritan' (Bolton, *Discourse*, 132). Almost two decades later he thought it had become commonplace: 'Nowadays, every Nimrod, impure drunkard, and self-guilty wretch, is ready with great rage' to impute puritanism to anyone of religion and integrity, thus striking 'at Gods best servants, and the kings best subjects' (R. Bolton, *Two Sermons Preached at Northampton*, 84). Ironically, through its abuse the name had become synonymous with honesty in public life:

> We are coming to a strange pass, that it should be holden a puritanical point, to condemn all corrupt coming into places of preferment, and public charge, since even politic pagans, and barbarous nations, out of light of reason, and ordinary notions of nature, did abhor it. (ibid., 92)

Bolton took his family and pastoral responsibilities with the utmost seriousness, and undoubtedly acted and appeared in a demeanour calculated to encourage respect. His portrait depicts a well-built, handsome, grave man of nearly sixty, with long white hair and impressive beard. It would be unwise to dismiss out of hand as an invention of puritan hagiography the story that Bolton, when 'walking in the streets, was so much cloathed with majesty' that people would stop their levity, for fear of attracting his disapproval or censure (Bolton and Bolton, 227). He acquired a reputation far outside Northamptonshire. For Anthony Wood, a historian rarely generous to men of Bolton's stripe, he was 'a most religious and learned puritan', and 'a painful and constant preacher, a person of great zeal for god, charitable and bountiful' (Wood, *Ath. Oxon.*, 2.513, 515). After enduring for over three months a 'quartan ague' (characterized by the recurrence of fits every four days), Robert Bolton died on 17 December 1631. His funeral sermon was preached two days later at St Andrew's, Broughton, by Nicholas Estwick and was published in 1635. Bolton was buried in the chancel, where in an alcove was set a half-length figure of the rector at prayer, his arms resting on an open bible. He was survived by his wife, Anne, son Samuel (*d.* 1669), and daughters Hannah, Mary, Elizabeth, and Sara. STEPHEN WRIGHT

Sources E. B. [E. Bagshawe], 'The life and death of the author', in *The works of … Robert Bolton*, ed. E. B. [E. Bagshawe] (1641) • *The works of … Robert Bolton*, 3 vols. (1638–41) • Wood, *Ath. Oxon.*, new edn, vol. 2 • H. C. Bolton and R. P. Bolton, *The family of Bolton, in England and America, 1100–1894: a study in genealogy* (privately printed, New York, 1895) • P. Collinson, *Godly people: essays on English protestantism and puritanism* (1983) • R. Hovenden, ed., *The visitation of Kent, taken in the years 1619–1621*, Harleian Society, 42 (1898) • W. Abram, *History of Blackburn* (1877) • T. Webster, *Godly clergy in early Stuart England: the Caroline puritan movement, c.1620–1643* (1997) • R. Bolton, *A discourse about the state of true happinesse, delivered in certaine sermones in Oxford and in St. Paul's Crosse, 1611* (1612) • H. I. Longden, *Northamptonshire and Rutland clergy from 1500*, ed. P. I. King and others, 16 vols. in 6, Northamptonshire RS (1938–52) • [C. B. Heberden], ed., *Brasenose College register, 1509–1909*, 2 vols., OHS, 55 (1909) • J. Garstang, *History of the Blackburn School* (1897) • will, PRO, PROB 11/161, sig. 59

Likenesses J. Payne, line engraving, 1632, BM, NPG; repro. in E. B. [E. Bagshawe], ed., *Mr. Bolton's last … worke of the Foure last things* (1632) [*see illus.*]

Wealth at death moderate: will, PRO, PROB 11/161, sig. 59; Bolton and Bolton, *The family*

Bolton, Robert (1697–1763), dean of Carlisle, was born in April 1697 in London, the son of John Bolton (*d.* *c.*1699), a merchant of Lambeth. His early education was in Kensington, after which he went to Wadham College, Oxford, in 1712, where he became a scholar in 1713, graduated BA in 1715, and proceeded MA in 1718. He was awarded the Lambeth degree of LLD in 1735. At Wadham, Bolton had hoped to be 'elected fellow in his turn; but in this he was disappointed, and appealed without success' to the college visitor, George Hooper, bishop of Bath and Wells (Coates, 118). By 20 December 1719, when he was ordained deacon in St Paul's Cathedral by John Robinson, bishop of London, Bolton had transferred to Hart Hall, Oxford; but he served his title in Stepney. Robinson ordained him priest in Fulham Chapel on 11 April 1721.

Bolton stayed with the bishop for two years, perhaps as chaplain. In 1722 he joined Dulwich College, and lived there. Though he was not elected first fellow (or preacher) until March 1725, there is clear evidence of his activity in the college as early as March 1723. After resigning the fellowship in May 1725 he moved to Kensington where he lived off his private income. Here he became friendly with William Whiston, the mathematician and rationalist, who had lost his Cambridge mathematical professorship on account of his Arian views. Whiston introduced Bolton to Sir Joseph Jekyll, master of the rolls, and Philip Yorke who, as earl of Hardwicke, became lord chief justice and then lord chancellor. Whiston's son John later claimed Bolton shared his father's views, but this did not stop him subscribing to the Thirty-Nine Articles.

In 1729 Jekyll nominated Bolton preacher at the Rolls Chapel in succession to Joseph Butler, later bishop of Durham. Doubtless it was through Hardwicke's patronage that Bolton was appointed dean of Carlisle; he was installed by proxy in February 1735. Though eventually he bequeathed money to support poor clergy in the diocese, Carlisle records reveal him as totally non-resident there. He showed more interest in his parish of St Mary's, Reading, where he became vicar in 1738. This was another crown appointment which he held concurrently with the deanery. Despite having a curate he was present at five of the eight triennial visitations and preached at two; and in July 1763, only four months before his death in London on 26 November, he was present at the primary visitation by John Gilbert, bishop of Salisbury. Certainly a sermon after his death describes him as 'constantly almost residing in this place … he held forth to all by his daily example and pressed upon [his parishioners] by his weekly instruction and exhortation' (Wray, 27–8). The same sermon described him as 'an excellent scholar, as well as a most pious Christian, as exemplary in his life as instructive in his writings' (ibid., 33). He was buried in the church porch at St Mary's, Reading.

Bolton's publications were mainly tracts and sermons, and included pieces such as *An answer to the question—Where are your arguments against what you call lewdness, if you make no use of the Bible* (1755), with references to Greek and Roman authors; and a curious work about Duke Ernest I of Saxe-Gotha (1601–1675), entitled *The ghost of Ernest, great-grandfather of HRH the princess dowager of Wales, with some account of his life* (1757). WILLIAM MARSHALL

Sources *Fasti Angl.* (Hardy) • Foster, *Alum. Oxon.* • ordination register, GL, MS 9535/3 • ordination papers, GL, MS 10326/49 • Sarum episcopal registers, Wilts. & Swindon RO, D 1/2/26, D 1/2/27 • Sarum clergy book, Wilts. & Swindon RO, D 1/2/26 • dean and chapter registers, Carlisle, Cumbria AS, Carlisle, 1/10, 11 • W. Young, *The history of Dulwich College* (1889) • C. Coates, *The history and antiquities of Reading* (1802) • H. C. Bolton and R. P. Bolton, *The family of Bolton, in England and America, 1100–1894: a study in genealogy* (privately printed, New York, 1895) • Dulwich College, Dulwich, archives • W. V. Wray, *Sermon on the text of Numbers 23: 10* (1764) • *DNB*

Archives BL, letters to first Lord Hardwicke and Charles Yorke

Bolton, Samuel (1605/6–1654), Church of England clergyman and college head, was the son of William Bolton of Lancashire. Educated at Manchester School, he matriculated as a pensioner at Christ's College in 1625, graduated BA in 1629, and proceeded MA in 1632. In 1633 he married Elianor Little, and in 1634 was curate of Harrow, Middlesex. For three years from about 1638 he was minister of St Martin Ludgate, London, and then for seven years minister of St Saviour's, Southwark. In 1641 he was also appointed as a lecturer at St Anne and St Agnes, Aldersgate.

Highly regarded both as a preacher and as a pastor, in 1642 Bolton was appointed to the Westminster assembly. His first publication was a set of fast sermons, *A Tossed Ship Making to Safe Harbor, or, A Word in Season to a Sinking Kingdome* (1644). In *The Guard of the Tree of Life* (1645), dedicated to his 'beloved friends' the congregation at Southwark, he described his work and that of his fellow minister in encouraging a right attitude to the Lord's supper. Pastoral concern and an essentially moderate stance characterize both this volume and his *The True Bounds of Christian Freedome* of the same year, dedicated to the earl of Manchester.

In 1645 Bolton was chosen as master of Christ's College, Cambridge, but 'his desire to win souls to Christ by preaching was so great' (Calamy, 25) that he continued to give regular sermons in London, especially at St Andrew's, Holborn. He was still described as the minister of St Saviour's in *The Arraignment of Error* (1646), dedicated to John, 'Lord Roberts' (Robartes). Despite its title the work stressed the need to avoid unnecessary controversy and seek happy accommodation; the pastoral use of synods and the power of the civil magistrate, 'a nursing father to the church' (p. 317) were necessary, but both should be limited and clearly defined. On 29 July 1646, choosing as his texts verses on waiting in hope and the blessedness of peacemakers, he gave a fast sermon to the Lords, subsequently published as *Deliverance in a Birth* (1647). He was probably the Mr Bolton who, on 9 March 1649, attended the failed peacemaker, the earl of Holland, on the scaffold.

Bolton did not neglect Cambridge, serving as vice-chancellor of the university from 1650 to 1652. In December 1650 he was one of six college heads who, in response to the parliamentary visitors' demands for subscription to the engagement, petitioned 'protesting as we had

Samuel Bolton (1605/6–1654), by William Faithorne the elder, pubd 1657

adhered to the parliament, soe we would live peaceably not disturbing the present government, desireing this might be accepted for our subscription' (Twigg, 156). In 1654 he was nominated as an assistant to the committee of ejectors in Cambridgeshire, Huntingdonshire, and the Isle of Ely, but by this time he had succumbed to a 'long, tedious and costly sickness': his diseases, according to Edmund Calamy, who visited him, were 'many, very many' (Calamy, 26).

Bolton died on 15 October 1654, aged forty-eight, and was buried four days later. His funeral sermon, preached by Calamy at St Martin Ludgate, was published both as *The Saint's Transfiguration* (1655), an official version dedicated to the earl of Warwick and acknowledging the deceased as 'very dear to Lady Lucy Roberts', and also as *The Doctrine of the Bodies Fragility* (1655), a surreptitious version—the duplication a testament to Bolton's standing among the godly. 'He was', asserted Calamy, 'a shining light in this our Israel … a workman that needed not to be ashamed … [whose] life was an excellent commentary upon his sermons' (Calamy, 24). Two years later a series of Bolton's treatises 'prepared for the press in the author's lifetime' were published as *The Dead Saint Speaking*. Dedicated by his widow, Elianor, to the earl and countess of Warwick, these were largely devotional in character, but in 'The wonderful workings of God for his church and people' Bolton exhibited continuing public, political concerns: 'the Grounds of hope from the Church of God, the good of most other reformed Churches in the Christian world doth depend upon the welfare of England'.

VIVIENNE LARMINIE

Sources E. Calamy, *The saint's transfiguration* (1655) · B. Brook, *The lives of the puritans*, 3 (1813), 223–4 · Venn, *Alum. Cant.* · P. S. Seaver, *The puritan lectureships: the politics of religious dissent, 1560–1662* (1970), 268–9 · B. Whitelocke, *Memorials of English affairs*, new edn, 4 vols. (1853), vol. 2, pp. 549–50 · J. Twigg, *The University of Cambridge and the English Revolution, 1625–1688* (1990) · *BL cat.*

Likenesses W. Faithorne the elder, line engraving, BM, NPG; repro. in S. Bolton, *The dead saint speaking to saints and sinners* (1657) [*see illus.*] · oils, Christ's College, Cambridge

Bolton, Theophilus (**1677/8–1744**), Church of Ireland archbishop of Cashel, was born in co. Mayo, Ireland. Nothing is known of his parentage or schooling but by 1695 he was a scholar of Trinity College, Dublin, from where he graduated BA in 1698 and MA in 1701. He was ordained deacon in the diocese of Dublin in 1702 and was priested in the following year. His first known ecclesiastical preferment was to the prebend of Monmahenock in St Patrick's Cathedral, Dublin, in 1707, which he resigned later in the same year for the prebend of Stagonil, and he remained in St Patrick's until 1722, exchanging his prebendal stall in 1714 for that of the chancellor, a position which he held together with the rectory of St Werburgh's, Dublin.

While in St Patrick's Bolton continued his studies in Trinity College; he obtained the degrees of BD and DD in 1716. His growing reputation as a canon lawyer caused antagonism between him and the dean of St Patrick's, Jonathan Swift, who in 1717 wrote that Bolton 'has taken every opportunity of opposing me, in the most unkind and unnecessary manner' (*Correspondence*, 3.393). However, his abilities were recognized by William King, archbishop of Dublin, who made Bolton his vicar-general in 1721, appointed him precentor of Christ Church Cathedral in 1722, and was instrumental in securing for him the bishopric of Clonfert, for which Bolton was consecrated on 30 September 1722 in St Patrick's Cathedral, Dublin. Unusually for the times, Bolton chose to reside in his diocese and while in Clonfert he seems to have made his peace with Swift, who visited him in 1723: the dean's report that 'the Bishop has made, in four months, twelve miles of ditches from his house to the Shannon' (ibid., 3.173) was the first indication of Bolton as an improver.

Bolton's period in Clonfert, however, was short, for in April 1724 he was translated to Elphin and in January 1730 was appointed archbishop of Cashel, despite the earlier opposition of the primate, Hugh Boulter, who in 1727 had advised that Bolton's translation to Cashel would be against the English interest. Bolton had opposed the government in 1724, when it sought to discover the identity of the author of the *Drapier's Letters*, and he was to do so again in 1728, when he organized opposition to a bill to prevent abuse of the parliamentary privilege of immunity from arrest. He was a protégé and long-time friend of William Conolly, the influential speaker of the Irish House of Commons, who favoured the appointment of Irishmen to Irish offices, and was suspected by Boulter of seeking to establish himself as the head of an Irish interest in parliament. His appointment to Cashel was not due to a lessening of Boulter's suspicion of him but to the happy coincidence of the sees of Dublin and Cashel being vacant at the same time, so allowing Bolton's translation to Cashel in return for the acceptance of the appointment of an Englishman, John Hoadley, to Dublin.

In Cashel, Bolton built a new palace, drained the extensive swamps to the west of the city, provided a public water supply, improved the way to the cathedral, and announced his intention to lay out £1000 in repairing the fabric. However, his most enduring legacy to Cashel was the creation of the library, which still bears his name. Following the death of Archbishop King in 1729 he had acquired about 6000 volumes from King's collection. These, with his own books, formed the nucleus of the library, which he housed in a two-storey building beside his palace. The collection is rich in law and theology, reflecting Bolton's academic background, but, despite his intellectual training and the convenience of a library, he published only a few sermons. By May 1735 his energies seemed exhausted and he wrote to Swift that 'a good bishop has nothing more to do than to eat, drink, grow fat, rich and die; which laudable example, I propose for the remainder of my life to follow' (*Correspondence*, 5.173); thereafter little was heard of him. Bolton died on 31 January 1744, aged sixty-six, and was buried in St Werburgh's Church, Dublin, on 2 February. In his will he bequeathed his library for the use of the archbishop of Cashel and the clergy of the diocese for ever. RAYMOND REFAUSSÉ

Sources [R. W. Jackson], 'Diocesan worthies: Archbishop Theophilus Bolton, of Cashel', *United dioceses of Cashel and Emly Waterford and Lismore … Year Book* (1948) • D. Woodworth, *Cashel's museum of printing and early books: a short history of the GPA-Bolton library* (1994) • I. Ehrenpreis, *Swift: the man, his works and the age*, 3 vols. (1962–83) • *The correspondence of Jonathan Swift*, ed. F. E. Ball, 6 vols. (1910–14) • H. Cotton, *Fasti ecclesiae Hibernicae*, 2nd edn, 1 (1851) • J. B. Leslie, 'Fasti of Christ Church Cathedral, Dublin', Representative Church Body Library, Dublin, MS 61/2/2 • H. J. Lawlor, *The fasti of St Patrick's, Dublin* (1930) • M. Tallon, *Church of Ireland diocesan libraries* (1959) • *Letters written by … Hugh Boulter … to several ministers of state*, ed. [A. Philips and G. Faulkner], 2 vols. (1769–70); repr. (1770) • W. King, letter-books, TCD, MS 750 • Burtchaell & Sadleir, *Alum. Dubl.*, 2nd edn • S. C. Hughes, *The church of S. Werburgh, Dublin* (1889) • J. Loveday, *Diary of a tour in 1732 through parts of England, Wales, Ireland and Scotland*, ed. J. E. T. Loveday, Roxburghe Club, 121 (privately printed, Edinburgh, 1890) • R. E. Burns, *Irish parliamentary politics in the eighteenth century*, 1 (1989) • *GM*, 1st ser., 14 (1744), 108 • F. M. Powicke and E. B. Fryde, eds., *Handbook of British chronology*, 2nd edn, Royal Historical Society Guides and Handbooks, 2 (1961)

Archives GPA-Bolton Library, Cashel, Bolton's collection of printed books • PRO NIre., corresp. and papers | TCD, corresp. with William King

Bolton, William (*d.* **1532**), prior of St Bartholomew's, West Smithfield, London, and royal administrator, was of unknown parentage. A canon of the Augustinian order, his talents permitted him to rise to a degree of prominence. Between 1501 and 1503 he attended the Augustinian foundation of St Mary's College, Oxford. Entries in the register of the chancellor of the university naming him as proxy for a lawyer from the court of arches suggest that he already had wealthy London connections. His election as prior of St Bartholomew's in West Smithfield, London, was given royal assent on 21 August 1505 and confirmed by the bishop of London on 27 August. In 1509 Bolton was named in the will of Henry VII as master of the king's works; it is probable that he had taken over these responsibilities in 1504. He oversaw building work at Henry VII's chapel and the monument to Lady Margaret Beaufort (in 1511) in Westminster Abbey, supervised small works at Hampton Court, and, from 1517, controlled the major rebuilding of New Hall, Boreham, Essex. Between 1513 and 1517 Bolton also initiated major reconstruction at St Bartholomew's Priory, where the oriel window in the nave of the church of St Bartholomew-the-Great remains as evidence, as well as at the priory's manor of Canonbury, Islington. Bolton's rebus, a barrel (tun) pierced by a crossbow bolt, was carved on both these buildings, although it was not until 1530 that he received the formal grant of arms of a shield *gules*, a vessel in the manner of a tun *argent* pierced by a bolt *or*, feathered *argent*. In 1518 he was fined by the general chapter of his order for overlooking visitation duties.

Henry VIII presented Bolton to the prebend of Bullinghope belonging to Hereford Cathedral on 7 July 1516 but, two years later, refused him promotion to the see of St Asaph, remarking that promotion depended not solely upon building skills but also on additional qualities such as profound learning. This drew the comment from Richard Pace, the king's secretary, in a letter to Cardinal Wolsey that the newly appointed bishop was not to be compared to the prior. The prior is listed among distinguished members of Gray's Inn, to which he seems to have been admitted some time before 1520. On 23 September 1522 Bolton received preferment as rector of Harrow on the Hill, Middlesex. In 1527 he became very ill and it appears that thereafter lameness rendered him immobile. He died on 5 April 1532 in London and was buried before the high altar of the priory church. JUDITH ETHERTON

Sources W. T. Mitchell, ed., *Registrum cancellarii, 1498–1506*, OHS, new ser., 27 (1980), 92, 161, 163 • bishops of London registers (Stokesley), GL, MS 9531/11, rebound pagination 100r • *CPR, 1494–1509*, 429 • *LP Henry VIII*, 2/2, no. 4083; 4/2, no. 3334 • J. Foster, *The register of admissions to Gray's Inn, 1521–1889, together with the register of marriages in Gray's Inn chapel, 1695–1754* (privately printed, London, 1889), 1 • BL, Arundel MS 26, new foliation 72v • *The diary of Henry Machyn, citizen and merchant-taylor of London, from AD 1550 to AD 1563*, ed. J. G. Nichols, CS, 42 (1848), 174 • E. A. Webb, *The records of St Bartholomew's Priory and of the church and parish of St Bartholomew the Great, West Smithfield*, 2 vols. (1921) • H. M. Colvin and others, eds., *The history of the king's works*, 6 vols. (1963–82), vol. 3, pp. 213–14; vol. 4, pp. 128, 172 • *Fasti Angl., 1300–1541*, [Hereford] • *VCH Middlesex*, 8.55 • *Hist. U. Oxf.* 2: *Late med. Oxf.*, 554

Bolts, William [*formerly* Willem Bolst] (**1739–1808**), merchant and speculator, was born on 7 February 1739 on the continent, probably in Germany. However, as a child he lived in Britain, and he became an apprentice in a London merchant house. He was acting in a commercial capacity in Lisbon by the time of the great earthquake of 1755 which devastated that city.

Following his return to Britain, Bolts was appointed as a factor in the service of the East India Company in November 1759 and he arrived in Bengal the following summer. By acquiring a working knowledge of Bengali, and by drawing on his previous experience as a merchant, he was able to develop his own private trading activities while working for the company, and he soon entered into a partnership with two members of the council at Fort William (Calcutta), John Johnstone and William Hay. The partners engaged in a wide range of speculative activities, the nature of which drew them into conflict with both the company and the Indian authorities. Bolts acquired a reputation as an unscrupulous and untrustworthy figure and he was repeatedly censured by the company for his misconduct.

Bolts married Ann Aston (*d.* 1821) in Calcutta on 11 February 1764. In 1765 he was recalled to Fort William from Benares, where he was then serving as second in council, but events were then given a remarkable twist when he was appointed as alderman of the mayor's court of Calcutta in August 1766. Further disputes with the company, however, led to his resignation three months later. Bolts was ordered to return to Britain by the next available ship, but he repeatedly delayed his departure from Bengal in order that he could seek further to extend his business interests in the region. This brought him into conflict with the new governor of Bengal, Harry Verelst, who was making a vigorous effort to implement the company's policy of curbing private trade in the territories under its control. Bolts's position was further undermined by the fact that he was suspected of intriguing with the Dutch and French, and after many warnings he was arrested on 23 September 1768, and deported to Britain a week later.

On reaching Britain in April 1769 he at once appealed to the court of directors, who would have nothing to do with him and declared him a 'very unprofitable and unworthy servant', and in 1771 commenced a lawsuit against him. In 1772 he published the first volume of his *Considerations on India Affairs*, in which he attacked the whole system of British government in Bengal, and complained of the arbitrary power exercised by the authorities, and of his own deportation by Verelst. The volume caused some excitement and was at once answered by Verelst himself in *A View of the Rise, Progress, and Present State of the English Government in Bengal* (1772), which Bolts attacked in a second volume of *Considerations* in 1775. This vigorous exchange of views developed into a bitter controversy and played an important part in fuelling the extensive public debate that was taking place on the subject of the East India Company's operations in India.

Bolts's lawsuits with the company and the cost of publishing his books bankrupted him in the autumn of 1773 for, owing to his deportation, he had not been able to realize more than £30,000 out of the fortune of £90,000 which he had accumulated in India.

Thus, following a visit to Vienna in 1775, he was glad to accept an offer from the empress Maria Theresa to enter the Austrian service. He was made a lieutenant-colonel and sent out to India to establish factories for the Imperial East India Company of Trieste. After arriving in Surat in September 1777 as commander of the *Joseph and Theresa*, he founded a number of factories, including three on the Malabar coast, much to the annoyance of the British. He was well on the way towards making another personal fortune when the project failed because of poor relations with his partners in Antwerp. The Imperial Company went bankrupt in 1784 and Bolts then unsuccessfully floated ambitious trading schemes with the French and Swedish governments. He lived in France during the 1790s, returned briefly to Britain in 1800–01, and then established himself in Lisbon once more. Finally, he moved to Paris in 1808 where, a ruined man, he died in hospital later the same year. H. V. Bowen

Sources N. L. Hallward, *William Bolts: a Dutch adventurer under John Company* (1920) • A. Holden Furber, 'In the footsteps of a German "nabob": William Boltts in the Swedish archives', *Indian Archives*, 12 (1958), 7–18 • 1808, PRO, PROB 11/1485, sig. 710 • W. Bolts, *Considerations on India affairs, particularly respecting the present state of Bengal and its dependencies* (1772) • W. Bolts, *Considerations on India affairs, particularly respecting the present state of Bengal and its dependencies*, 2nd edn, 3 vols. (1772–5) • H. Verelst, *A view of the rise, progress, and present state of the English government in Bengal, including a reply to the misrepresentations of Mr Bolts and other writers* (1772)

Archives BL OIOC • Riksarkivet, Stockholm, Handel och Sjöfart, 193

Wealth at death died in poverty; few possessions apart from library: will, PRO, PROB 11/1485, sig. 710

Bomberg, David Garshen (1890–1957), painter, was born in Birmingham on 5 December 1890, the fifth of the eleven children of Abraham Bomberg, a Polish immigrant leather-worker, and his wife, Rebecca, whose family kept an inn and reared horses. In 1895 the family moved to Whitechapel, London, and Bomberg attended Old Castle Street School, off Aldgate High Street. About 1906 he was apprenticed to the German immigrant lithographer Paul Fischer in Islington. But far more important to his future development as a painter were the evening classes at the Westminster School given by Walter Sickert, which he attended from 1908 to 1910. Then, fortified by a visit to Roger Fry's 'Manet and the post-impressionists' exhibition at the Grafton Galleries, London (1910), where he saw Cézanne's work for the first time, Bomberg entered the Slade School of Fine Art in London with the help of a much-needed loan from the Jewish Education Aid Society.

During his time at the Slade (1911–13), Bomberg proved himself a precocious and innovative student. One of an exceptional Slade generation, which included Mark Gertler, Paul Nash, William Roberts, Stanley Spencer, and Edward Wadsworth, he rapidly gained a reputation as a forceful member of the avant-garde. The artist and critic Percy Wyndham Lewis visited Bomberg at his Tenter Buildings studio in 1912, and in 1913 he travelled to Paris with the sculptor Jacob Epstein to select work for the Jewish section of an important exhibition 'Twentieth century

David Garshen Bomberg (1890–1957), self-portrait, 1931

art' at the Whitechapel Art Gallery (1914). After leaving the Slade, Bomberg had a short and stormy affiliation with the Omega workshops of Roger Fry before exhibiting six works in the 'cubist room' section of 'The Camden Town Group and others' exhibition (December 1913), a major survey of the British avant-garde held at Brighton City Art Galleries.

But 1914 was the *annus mirabilis* of Bomberg's early career. Having exhibited five works as a founder member of the London Group, including a frenetic and impressively organized canvas called *In the Hold* (1913–14; Tate collection), he asserted his independence from Wyndham Lewis's newly formed vorticist group [*see* Vorticists]. Bomberg's first one-man show at the Chenil Gallery, Chelsea (July 1914), established him as a remarkably powerful cubo-futurist. In a youthful masterpiece entitled *The Mud Bath* (1914; Tate collection), he presented a vision of his local Whitechapel steam baths as a stark arena where harsh, clear-cut figures, an amalgam of human and machine forms, hurled themselves around and into the pool.

Bomberg shared the vorticists' involvement with the machine-age dynamism of modern urban life. In 1915 he exhibited six works in the 'invited to show' non-members' section of the first vorticist exhibition, held at the Doré Galleries in London. By November, however, he had enlisted in the Royal Engineers, from which he later transferred to the 18th King's Royal Rifles. In 1916 Bomberg married Alice, daughter of John Burton Mayes, a London wholesale stationer, and divorced wife of Jack Richardson. In March that year he was sent to the front line in France.

Although the First World War prevented Bomberg from painting, he did receive an important commission in 1917 from the Canadian War Memorials Fund. The subject was *Sappers at Work* and the first version (1918; Tate collection) was rejected. The second, more representational version (1919; National Gallery of Canada, Ottawa) was accepted. During the 1920s Bomberg underwent an irrevocable loss of faith in machine-age abstraction. He turned instead to a more traditional style rooted in his response to landscape. After journeying to Jerusalem in 1923 with funds provided by the Palestine Foundation Fund, he painted surprisingly naturalistic views of the city and countryside. Then, having returned to London in 1927 and left his wife, he held an exhibition of Palestine and Petra paintings at the Leicester Galleries (1928).

In 1929 Bomberg made his first trip to Spain, where the city of Toledo inspired him to achieve a greater breadth and expressiveness in his landscapes. He returned to London early in 1930, but only displayed his Spanish paintings in a 1932 one-man show at the Bloomsbury Gallery. These were the years when Bomberg's reputation faltered, and during his brief affiliation with the Communist Party he visited Russia in 1933. Lack of success then drove him back to Spain, where his best work was painted at Ronda in Andalusia. By the time Bomberg applied for a war artist's commission in 1939 he was a sadly neglected figure. After several rejections the War Artists' Advisory Committee grudgingly asked him to paint an underground bomb store near Burton upon Trent in 1942. It inspired some of his finest work, but the committee only accepted three bomb-store drawings. In 1941 he married the painter Lilian Mendelson, divorced wife of Jacob Mendelson, an art dealer. She was the daughter of Oliver Oswald Holt, civil servant. They had one daughter, Diana, born in 1935.

Bomberg suffered continual rejection during the Second World War. The last one-man show he ever held in London was staged at the Leger Gallery (1943), and the only art school to accept him as a teacher was the Borough Polytechnic, London, where he taught part-time from 1945 to 1953. Although the classes were small, he became a legendary teacher. Among his students were Frank Auerbach, Dennis Creffield, Leon Kossoff, and Gustav Metzger, and the Borough period coincided with his most fruitful post-war painting expeditions: Cornwall in August 1947, and Cyprus in the summer of the following year. The heat and light of the Mediterranean inspired him to paint his most exuberant and expressive landscapes, but they remained largely unseen.

Bomberg returned to Ronda in 1954. There, after an abortive attempt to establish a school of painting at the Villa Paz, he executed his final landscapes and figure paintings. A new turbulence enters his freely handled work, and the *Last Self-Portrait* (1956) reveals the extent of his despair. In 1957 Bomberg became seriously ill and was moved to hospital in Gibraltar, and later to England. He died at St Thomas's Hospital, London, on 19 August 1957.

RICHARD CORK, *rev.*

Sources R. Cork, *David Bomberg* (1987) · R. Cork, *David Bomberg* (1988) [exhibition catalogue, Tate Gallery, London, 17 Feb – 8 May, 1988] · Tate collection, David Bomberg archive · private information (1993) · *DNB*

Archives Tate collection, corresp. and papers | Tate collection, MSS relating to him and collected by his sister Kitty Newmark and her husband James Newmark

Likenesses D. G. Bomberg, self-portrait, chalk drawing, *c.*1913–1914, NPG · D. G. Bomberg, self-portrait, charcoal-and-wash drawing, 1931, NPG [*see illus.*] · D. G. Bomberg, self-portrait, oils, 1937, U. Lond., Slade School of Art · D. G. Bomberg, self-portrait, oils, 1937, Birmingham Museums and Art Gallery · D. G. Bomberg, self-portraits, oils on millboard, *c.*1937, NPG · F. Man, photograph, 1943 (with Joseph Bard), Hult. Arch.

Bomelius, Eliseus (*d.* 1579), physician and astrologer, born in Wesel, Westphalia, was probably the son of Henry Bomelius (*d.* 1570), a native of Bommel (now Zaltbommel) in the Netherlands, who from 1540 to 1559 was Lutheran preacher at Wesel, and the author of several religious and historical books of wide repute. The *Summa der godliker scrifturen*, published in England as *The Summe of the Holye Scripture and Ordynary of the Christen Teachyng* (1548), is attributed to him. Henry Bomelius's friend Bishop Bale lived for some time at Wesel: he contributed Latin verses in the author's praise to Bale's *Illustrium maioris Britanniae … summarium* (1548), and to his *Scriptorum … catalogus* (1557).

It was probably on Bale's advice that Eliseus Bomelius was educated at Cambridge, which is probably what Jerome Horsey meant by writing that Bomelius was 'brought up' there. He proceeded to the degree of doctor of medicine. Well received by the English reformers, he contributed an 'epigramma' in Latin elegiacs to an edition of Thomas Becon's early works (1560). Henry Bennet of Calais, in dedicating his life of Oecolampadius to James Blount, sixth Baron Mountjoy, praises Mountjoy for entertaining with 'zealous affection Heliseus Bomelius, a German, who readeth unto your honour the liberal sciences, and whom Phillip Melancthon hath in familiar letters praysed highly for erudicion and godlynes' (Bennet). Although Bennet refers to Bomelius's 'learned works published' (ibid.), no such piece has been identified. Bomelius married Jane Richards, of St Stephen Walbrook, London, on 18 July 1564. In 1567 he was said to be living in Lord Lumley's house (presumably, his London residence, near Tower Hill); his last known domicile in London was in St Michael-le-Querne parish.

As a physician and astrologer, Bomelius rapidly made a high reputation in London. An astrological discussion made in 1570 for the prospective marriage of Queen Elizabeth, and found among William Cecil's papers, has been attributed to Bomelius (or to Sir Thomas Smith (1513–1577)). *An almanacke and pronostication of master Elis Bomelius for ye yere of Our Lorde God 1567 autorysshed by my lorde of London* [Edmund Grindal] was published in London in 1567. Prescriptions—not identified—in Gervase Markham's *The English Hus-Wife* were claimed to have been 'gathered together' by Dr Bomelius and 'Dr Burket' (Burchard Kranich) (Markham, 5). A few Latin letters Bomelius wrote survive in the Public Record Office (state papers, domestic) and the British Library.

In 1567 Bomelius was arrested at the instance of Thomas Francis, president of the College of Physicians, for practising medicine without licence of the college, and was imprisoned in the Wood Street Compter. On 27 May 1567 he wrote to Cecil, praying for an opportunity to expose Francis's ignorance of astronomy and Latin, and on 3 May 1568 he supplicated at Oxford for incorporation, as a doctor of medicine of Cambridge.

Early in 1569 Bomelius's wife stated before the censors' committee of the College of Physicians that her husband had given due satisfaction for his offence, and petitioned for his liberation. The censors demanded payment of a £20 fine and £15 costs, which Bomelius was unable to pay. (In a letter to Cecil, of February 1568, he said that while living in London he had expended over £100 but received only £12.) On 2 June 1569 the committee appears to have offered Bomelius his release on condition of his giving a bond of £100 to abstain from practice. Before Easter 1570 he was 'an open prisoner' of the king's bench.

On 3 April 1570 Archbishop Matthew Parker wrote to Cecil about Bomelius: 'Whether any practitioner hath resorted to him (as many have a wonderful confidence in him and in his magic) I know not'. What he did know, however, was that, 'last term', Bomelius had deliberately holed the bottom of Parker's 'poor barge' on the Thames, and he feared 'some conspiracy' (*Correspondence*, 363–5). He enclosed a letter of Bomelius's, concerning England's imminent peril: accordingly, Cecil wrote to Bomelius, to find that the 'conspiracy' was merely an astrological forecast.

In early May 1570 Bomelius sent a Latin letter to Cecil, claiming: 'In about a month hence I shall be enabled … to devote my services … to Her Royal Majesty, and point out a way whereby these intestine evils may be healed, without any effusion of blood'. However, he observed that 'the Russian Ambassador sends messengers to me daily, and does not expect to obtain my services without a large stipend' (Leigh). As Cecil treated Bomelius's announcements with deserved contempt, Bomelius resolved to live in Muscovy. The English government did not hinder his departure, and late in 1570 Bomelius, who had promised to supply Cecil with political information, was settled in Russia. During his travels in that country (1572), Sir Jerome Horsey frequently met Bomelius, then living in great pomp at the court of Ivan IV, in high favour with the tsar as a magician, and holding an official position in the household of the tsar's son. He was said to have amassed great wealth, which he transmitted by way of England to his native town of Wesel; and by his astrological calculations, to have encouraged the tsar to persist in an absurd scheme of marrying Queen Elizabeth, falsely represented as a young girl. Charged with intriguing with the kings of Poland and Sweden against the tsar, Bomelius was arrested with others and racked. After being roasted at a stake, he was put into a loathsome dungeon where he died, in 1579. Horsey, who gives a full description of his death, characterizes him as 'a skilful mathematician, a wicked man, and practiser of much mischief'. Like his preacher father, he was a protestant, and when near his end, under torture, 'cast up his eyes, naming Christ'. Only in 1583 could Sir Jerome Bowes obtain leave for the widow, Jane, to leave Russia and return to England. No will or administration of Bomelius's has been noticed, but a marriage licence of 29 October 1586 shows Jane, widow of Eliseus Bomelius, late of St Michael-le-Querne, MD, about to marry Thomas Wennington, gentleman, of St Margaret Pattens parish, London. JOHN BENNELL

Sources J. Strype, *Annals of the Reformation and establishment of religion … during Queen Elizabeth's happy reign*, new edn, 2/1 (1824), 22–3 • *Correspondence of Matthew Parker*, ed. J. Bruce and T. T. Perowne, Parker Society, 42 (1853), 363–5 • H. Bennet, *A famous and godly history…* (1561), sigs. I.iv, ivv • *CSP dom.*, 1547–80 • J. von Hamel, *England and Russia: comprising the voyages of John Tradescant the Elder, Sir Hugh Willoughby, Richard Chancellor, Nelson, and others to the White Sea*, trans. J. S. Leigh (1854), 202–6, 420–21 • 'The travels of Sir Jerome Horsey', *Russia at the close of the sixteenth century*, ed. E. A. Bond, Hakluyt Society, 20 (1856), 168, 173, 187 • R. Hakluyt, *The principal navigations, voyages, traffiques and discoveries of the English nation*, 3, Hakluyt Society, extra ser., 3 (1903), 324 • J. L. Chester and G. J. Armytage, eds., *Allegations for marriage licences issued by the bishop of London*, 1, Harleian Society, 25 (1887), 28, 155 • *Reg. Oxf.*, 1.270 • W. B. Bannerman and W. B. Bannerman, jun., eds., *The registers of St Stephen's, Walbrook, and of St Benet Sherehog, London*, 1, Harleian Society, register section, 49 (1919), 52 • *The early works of Thomas Becon*, ed. J. Ayre, Parker Society, 2 (1843), 33 • G. Markham, *Countrey contentments, in two books … the second intituled, The English hus-wife* (1615); repr. in G. M. [G. Markham], *A way to get wealth* (1631), pt 5

Bompas, Henry Mason (1836–1909). *See under* Bompas, William Carpenter (1834–1906).

Bompas, William Carpenter (1834–1906), bishop of Selkirk, Canada, was born on 20 January 1834 at 11 Park Road, Regent's Park, London. He was the fourth son of Charles Carpenter Bompas and his wife, Mary Steele Tomkins, of Broughton, Hampshire. His father, a serjeant-at-law and leader of the western circuit, was said to have been the original of Dickens's Mr Serjeant Buzfuz; he died suddenly on 29 February 1844, leaving his widow with five sons and three daughters in difficult circumstances. Educated privately, Bompas was brought up a strict Baptist, like his parents. On 7 July 1850 he was publicly baptized by immersion at John Street Chapel by the Baptist preacher and poet Roden Berkeley Wriothesley Noel. In 1852 he joined his brother George Cox Bompas at a London firm of solicitors, but within five years a spiritual crisis prompted him to abandon the law and join the Church of England.

Bompas was confirmed an Anglican in 1858; ordained deacon in 1859; and licensed to curacies at Sutton in the Marsh (1859–62), New Radford, Nottingham (1862–3), Holy Trinity, Louth, Lincolnshire (1863–4), and Alford (1864–5). He then volunteered his services to the Church Missionary Society to relieve the ailing missionary Robert McDonald (afterwards archdeacon), of the North West America mission. Bompas was accepted on 1 May 1865 and was ordained priest in St Paul's, Covent Garden, London,

William Carpenter Bompas (1834–1906), by unknown photographer, 1905

on 25 June 1865, by Robert Machray, who had been consecrated bishop of Rupert's Land the day before.

After a journey of 177 days Bompas reached Fort Simpson, on the Mackenzie River, on Christmas morning 1865. Meanwhile Robert McDonald had recovered, so Bompas was assigned duties as a travelling missionary. He began a ceaseless round of journeys from station to station—Forts Norman, Rae, Vermilion, Chipewyan, Simpson, and Yukon—learning the local languages, teaching adults and children, and baptizing and preaching. In 1872 Bishop Machray created three new sees out of Rupert's Land. Bompas was consecrated bishop of one of them, Athabasca, in Lambeth parish church on 3 May 1874, by Archbishop Archibald Tait. On 7 May 1874 Bompas married his first cousin, Charlotte Selina (1830–1917), daughter of Joseph Cox MD of Fishponds, Bristol, and she worked as his partner in the mission. They had no children of their own and adopted two Native American girls, but both of them died in childhood.

On 4 September 1876 Bompas held a synod of his new diocese which consisted of one archdeacon, two other clergymen, two catechists, and an employee of the Hudson's Bay Company. In 1884 there was a further subdivision of Bompas's diocese into Athabasca in the south, and Mackenzie River in the north, to which Bompas was appointed. In August 1886 he held the first synod of his new diocese at Fort Simpson. Once more, in 1891, there was a division of Bompas's diocese, the new diocese of Selkirk (later Yukon) being created out of the western portion. Bompas established his headquarters as its first bishop at Forty Mile on the Yukon River.

The discovery of gold on the Klondike and the arrival of large numbers of non-native settlers after 1898 changed the character of the see. Bompas, who preferred travelling among Native Americans, moved his mission in 1901 to Carcross, where he ran a school for the indigenous children and built a church which he consecrated on 8 August

1904. In 1905 he resigned his bishopric and inaugurated his successor, I. O. Stringer.

Declining a pension, Bompas intended to start a mission on Little Salmon River, but on 9 June 1906 he died suddenly at Carcross, where he was also buried. With the exception of his visit to England for consecration in 1874 and a trip to Winnipeg, Manitoba, in 1904, he remained continuously in the far north for more than forty years.

Bompas was the author of *The Diocese of Mackenzie River* (1888) and *Northern Lights on the Bible* (1892). He also published a number of translations of portions of the Bible, the Book of Common Prayer, and hymns and prayers—into Slavey (for people in the Mackenzie River area), in Chipewyan, Beaver (for those living near the Peace River), and in 'Tukudh' (for the Gwich'in or Loucheux people). These were published by the SPCK and the Bible Society.

Henry Mason Bompas (1836–1909), county court judge, the bishop's youngest brother, was born on 6 April 1836. He studied at University College, London (BA, London University, 1855; MA 1857; mathematical gold medal; LLB, 1862), and at St John's College, Cambridge, and was called to the bar by the Inner Temple in 1863. He was a bencher in 1881, and treasurer in 1905. On 20 September 1867 he married Rachel Henrietta, eldest daughter of the Revd Edward White. They had three sons and four daughters.

Like his father Bompas joined the western circuit, and he became recorder of Poole in 1882 and of Plymouth and Devonport in 1884. In 1891 he was appointed commissioner of assize for south Wales, and in 1896 county court judge (circuit no. 11), with his centre at Bradford. He resigned shortly before his death in London on 5 March 1909. Judge Bompas, who was for many years an active volunteer, remained a Baptist all his life and took a keen part in denominational affairs.

E. H. Pearce, *rev.* Kerry M. Abel

Sources H. A. Cody, *An apostle of the north: memoirs of the Right Reverend William Carpenter Bompas* (1908) • North West America Mission corresp., NA Canada, Church Missionary Society Archival Collection [microfilm] • T. C. B. Boon, *The Anglican church from the bay to the Rockies: a history of the ecclesiastical province of Rupert's Land and its dioceses from 1820 to 1950* (1962) • *Register of missionaries … from 1804 to 1904*, Church Missionary Society, 2 vols. in 1 [1896] • E. Stock, *The history of the Church Missionary Society: its environment, its men and its work*, 4 vols. (1899–1916) • *Montreal Daily Star* (11 June 1906) • *Toronto News* (11 June 1906) • S. A. Archer, ed., *A heroine of the north: memoirs of Charlotte Selina Bompas* (1929) • K. M. Abel, 'Bishop Bompas and the Canadian church', *The Anglican church and the world of western Canada, 1820–70*, ed. B. Ferguson (1991), 113–25 • K. S. Coates, 'Send only those who rise a peg: Anglican clergy in the Yukon, 1858–1932', *Journal of the Canadian Church Historical Society*, 28 (1986), 3–18 • Provincial Archives of Alberta, Edmonton, records of the diocese of Mackenzie River, records of diocese of Athabasca • A. H. Sovereign, *In journeyings often: glimpses of the life of Bishop Bompas* [n.d., 1916?] • K. Abel, 'Bompas, William Carpenter', *DCB*, vol. 13

Archives Church Missionary Society, London, North West America Mission MSS • Provincial Archives of Alberta, Edmonton, diocese of Mackenzie River records • Provincial Archives of Alberta, Edmonton, diocese of Athabasca records • Provincial Archives of Manitoba, Winnipeg, Hudson's Bay Company Archives, John Christian Schultz MSS • Provincial Archives of Manitoba, Winnipeg, Hudson's Bay Company Archives, Augusta Morris MSS • Yukon Territorial Archives, Whitehorse, Anglican church collection

Likenesses photograph, 1905, NPG [*see illus.*] • photograph, repro. in Cody, *Apostle of the north* • photographs, Provincial Archives of Alberta, Edmonton, Alberta, Canada

Wealth at death £1778 14*s*.: probate, 25 July 1906, *CGPLA Eng. & Wales*

Bon, Christoph Rudolph (1921–1999). *See under* Chamberlin, Peter Hugh Girard (1919–1978).

Bonar, Andrew Alexander (1810–1892), Free Church of Scotland minister, was born at Paterson's Court, Edinburgh, on 29 May 1810, the seventh son of James *Bonar (1757–1821), solicitor of excise, and Marjory Maitland (*d.* 1854), daughter of James Pyott, bailie of Montrose. He was educated at Edinburgh high school, where he was dux, before studying at Edinburgh University. Although he intended to follow his elder brothers Horatius *Bonar and John James Bonar [*see below*] into the ministry, he did not undergo a conversion experience until October 1830. He began his divinity studies the following year and was licensed by the presbytery of Jedburgh in July 1835. He worked as an assistant in Jedburgh until in November 1836 Robert Smith Candlish offered him a position as missionary in St George's parish, Edinburgh. He was ordained assistant and successor to the parish of Collace, Perthshire, in September 1838.

The early years of Bonar's ministry were distinguished by his friendship with Robert Murray McCheyne. Their circle also included William Chalmers Burns and Alexander Somerville. In 1839 he accompanied McCheyne, with Alexander Black and Alexander Keith, to the Holy Land. Bonar's description of their journey appeared in 1842 as *Narrative of a Mission of Inquiry to the Jews*. This book was hugely popular and would itself have assured him of lasting influence, even had it not been followed by the still more popular *Memoir and Remains of the Rev Robert Murray McCheyne* (1844). Bonar published numerous other works, chief among which were *A Commentary on the Book of Leviticus* (1846) and his edition of Samuel Rutherford's *Letters* (1848).

After the Disruption of 1843, in which controversy he joined as a pamphleteer, Bonar remained in Collace as minister of the Free Church congregation. He married on 4 April 1848 Isabella Dickson (*d.* 1864), with whom he had four daughters and two sons, including James *Bonar (1852–1941), civil servant and economist. In December 1856 he transferred to a new congregation at Finnieston, in Glasgow, where he remained for the rest of his life. His later publications included *Christ and his Church in the Book of Psalms* (1859). He received the degree of DD from Edinburgh in 1874 and was elected moderator of the Free Church general assembly in 1878. It was also in that year that his congregation moved to a larger building near the West End Park, Glasgow. He died, after a short illness, at his home, 20 India Street, on 30 December 1892 and was buried in Sighthill cemetery on 4 January 1893. His diary and letters were collected and published by his daughter.

Invariably described as saintly, one obituary described

Bonar as 'an Evangelical of the Evangelicals' (*Glasgow Herald*, 2 Jan 1893). He was little interested in church courts and accepted the moderatorship with reluctance; his interest lay in evangelism and revival, and he latterly worked closely with the American Dwight L. Moody. While staunchly conservative in matters of doctrine he held some unfashionable views, for example on prophecy and millennialism, which he had formed under the influence of Edward Irving. As a preacher he was notable for his unusual sing-song delivery, and for the stamina that allowed him to preach three or four times a Sunday until almost the end of his life.

His elder brother **John James Bonar** (1803–1891), Free Church of Scotland minister, was born in Edinburgh on 25 March 1803. Educated at the high school and Edinburgh University, he was licensed by the presbytery of Edinburgh in April 1827. He served as assistant at Scoonie, Fife, before succeeding William Cunningham as assistant to Dr John Scott of the Middle parish church, Greenock, in January 1834. A year later, a dispute led to the withdrawal of a portion of the congregation with Bonar as their pastor. He was ordained minister of St Andrew's Chapel, West Stewart Street, Greenock, in August 1835. After the Disruption of 1843 Bonar and his congregation adhered to the Free Church and, unusually, were able to retain their building. Bonar remained in St Andrew's Free Church for the rest of his long ministry.

The least well known, though possibly the most genial of the three brothers, Bonar shared many of their gifts. Like them he was an evangelical who combined the covenanting spirit of the seventeenth century with the literary cultivation of the nineteenth. An outstanding preacher, he was also a contributor to the *Presbyterian Review* and the *Quarterly Journal of Prophecy*. He was for fifty years secretary of the Greenock branch of the Bible Society. Bonar married on 17 July 1838 Isabella Watt (*d*. 1875), with whom he had five sons, two of whom died in infancy. In 1883 he was honoured with the degree of DD from Edinburgh University. He died at his home in Greenock on 7 July 1891, and was buried in the town cemetery.

LIONEL ALEXANDER RITCHIE

Sources *Andrew A. Bonar … diary and letters*, ed. M. Bonar (1894) • *Reminiscences of Andrew A. Bonar*, ed. M. Bonar (1895) • F. Ferguson, *The life of the Rev. Dr. Andrew A. Bonar* (1893) • *Fasti Scot.* • J. A. Wylie, *Disruption worthies: a memorial of 1843*, ed. J. B. Gillies, new edn (1881), 31–8 • W. R. Nicoll, *Princes of the church* (1921), 55–61 • *Glasgow Herald* (8 July 1891) • *Glasgow Herald* (2 Jan 1893) • *Free Church of Scotland Monthly* (Oct 1891), 309–10 • *The Bailie* (22 May 1878) • *DSCHT* • *DNB*

Archives NL Scot. • U. Edin., New Coll. L., letters

Likenesses caricature, repro. in *The Bailie* • photograph (aged eighty), repro. in Bonar, *Reminiscences of Andrew A. Bonar*, facing frontispiece • photograph, repro. in Ferguson, *The life of the Rev. Dr. Andrew A. Bonar*, facing frontispiece • two photographs (aged thirty-five and in old age), repro. in Bonar, *Andrew A. Bonar … diary and letters*, frontispiece, facing p. 120

Wealth at death £2419 12*s*. 7*d*.: confirmation, 28 Feb 1893, *CCI* • £5864 6*s*. 5*d*.—John James Bonar: confirmation, 29 Oct 1891, *CCI*

Bonar, Archibald (1753–1816), Church of Scotland minister, was the fifth son of John *Bonar (1721–1761), minister, and Christian Currier (1724–1771). His elder brother, John *Bonar, later became the first solicitor of excise in Scotland. He was born at Cockpen, Edinburghshire, on 23 February 1753, and was educated at Edinburgh high school and the University of Edinburgh. He was licensed to preach on 29 October 1777, ordained minister of the parish of Newburn, Fife, on 31 March 1779, and was transferred to the North-West Church, Glasgow, on 17 July 1783. As a young man Bonar had been influenced by George Whitefield's evangelicalism and remained a proponent of 'vital religion' in his ministries. On 15 August 1782 he had married Bridget (*d*. 1787), eldest daughter of the Revd Mr Black, minister of Perth. Bonar's health compelled him to resign his charge, and on 19 April 1785 he settled in the parish of Cramond, near Edinburgh. After his wife's death on 4 January 1787 he married, on 16 August 1792, Ann, daughter of Andrew Bonar; they had two sons and three daughters. While at Cramond he published his *Genuine Religion* (1796) which was reprinted at Boston (1807) and at Middlebury, Vermont (1810), and *Sermons, Chiefly on Devotional Subjects* (1815–17). The second volume, published after his death at Cramond on 8 April 1816, includes a memoir by his brother James *Bonar.

HORATIUS BONAR, *rev.* MARY CATHERINE MORAN

Sources *Fasti Scot.*, 1.135 • J. Bonar, 'Memoir of the Rev. Archibald Bonar, minister of Cramond', in A. Bonar, *Sermons, chiefly on devotional subjects*, 2 (1817), xvli–lv, vol. 2 • *DSCHT*

Archives U. Edin. L., special collections division • U. Edin. L., corresp. | U. Edin. L., Laing MSS, corresp. with R. Balfour; Alexander Bonar; J. Campbell; T. Davidson; R. S. Moncrieff; M. E. Ruthven; J. Snodgrass; Lady Torphicen, La. 11/509 • U. Edin. L., letters to Mr Tawse, and the secretary of the Royal Patriotic Society

Bonar, Horatius (1808–1889), Free Church of Scotland minister and hymn writer, was born at Edinburgh on 19 December 1808. He was the sixth son of James Bonar, the second solicitor of excise at Edinburgh, and his wife, Marjory Maitland (*d*. 1854), the daughter of James Pyott, bailie of Montrose. Bonar was educated at the high school and the University of Edinburgh, where his contemporaries included Robert Murray McCheyne (1813–1843). After attending the Divinity Hall, Edinburgh, he was licensed as a preacher and did mission work at Leith.

In November 1837 Bonar settled at Kelso as the minister of the new North Church, founded as a part of Thomas Chalmers's church extension scheme. He became a prominent evangelist and a popular preacher. He anticipated the methods of the Evangelical Alliance by arranging for eight or more days of united prayer, and instituted special meetings once a month for children. He also produced many pamphlets, editing a series of religious tracts known as the Kelso Tracts, and published evangelical works of considerable popularity, such as *The Night of Weeping* (1846), which sold 59,000 copies. The influence on Bonar of Edward Irving's lectures in 1828–30 on the Apocalypse was evident in *Prophetic Landmarks* (1847) and *The Coming and Kingdom of Our Lord Jesus Christ* (1849). While he was still at Leith he had begun to write the hymns for which he is best known, a practice which he continued at Kelso. On 16 August 1843 he married Jane Catherine (*d*.

Horatius Bonar (1808–1889), by David Octavius Hill and Robert Adamson

1884), the third daughter of Robert Lundie, a former minister at Kelso. They had three sons and six daughters. Jane was sympathetic to his work, and seems to have written religious verse herself. She died in December 1884.

At the Disruption in 1843 Bonar and his congregation joined the Free Church of Scotland. Some years later, however, the North Church reverted to the Church of Scotland, and Bonar was obliged to hold services first in a hired room and later in a church lent by the burgh council. This hardship was not his to endure for any length of time: in June 1866 he was appointed minister of the Thomas Chalmers Memorial Church in Edinburgh. His reputation continued to grow during this ministry: his congregation followed suit, increasing from 61 in October 1866 to 805 in July 1888. He continued to hold children's services, established a mission at Causewayside in the poorer part of his parish, and preached frequently in the open air in addition to his usual Sunday duties. In 1874 he shared a platform with the American evangelist Dwight Moody. Bonar continued his literary activities: in 1862 he published *God's Way of Peace: a Book for the Anxious*, which was translated into French, German, and Gaelic, and sold more than 285,000 copies during his lifetime. He was the editor of several religious journals, including the *Christian Treasury* and the *Presbyterian Review*. Several events varied his ministerial and literary activities. In 1856 he visited Palestine, a journey which resulted in the publication of *The Desert of Sinai* (1856) and *The Land of Promise* (1858). He is said to have composed hymns even as he crossed the Sinai Desert on a camel. In May 1883 he became moderator of the general assembly of the Free Church of Scotland. He died in Edinburgh on 31 July 1889, survived by only four of his children.

Bonar was (and is) best known for such famous hymns as 'I heard the voice of Jesus say' (1846). His verses are spontaneous and essentially lyrical; he composed them quickly and rarely revised his work, which explains the retention of some very poor lines. He wrote more than 600 hymns, which appeared in publications such as *The Bible Hymn Book* (1845) and *Hymns of Faith and Hope*, published in three series between 1857 and 1866. In *The Scottish Hymnary*, a work widely used by Scottish and Irish Presbyterians, eighteen of his hymns were included. J. Julian's *Dictionary of Hymnology* (1907) reported that 110 of his hymns were in common use at the time of its publication, but their popularity later declined, possibly because Bonar's premillenarian sentiments were less and less favoured. It is a sad irony that Bonar, one of the few Scottish hymn writers to gain an international audience for his work, never heard his hymns sung in his own church in Edinburgh, since his was one of the Free Church congregations which opposed the introduction of hymns.

ROSEMARY MITCHELL

Sources *Horatius Bonar, DD: a memorial* (1889) · G. L. Gibb, *Horatius Bonar and his hymns* (1989) · *Fasti Scot.*, 2.74–5 · *The Scotsman* (1 Aug 1889) · *DSCHT* · D. M. Lewis, ed., *The Blackwell dictionary of evangelical biography, 1730–1860*, 2 vols. (1995) · Boase, *Mod. Eng. biog.*
Archives NL Scot., hymns, poems, and sermons · U. Edin., New Coll. L., hymns, papers, sermons | NL Scot., letters to J. J. Bonar
Likenesses D. O. Hill, photograph, repro. in *Memories of Dr. Horatius Bonar by relatives & public men* (1909) · D. O. Hill and R. Adamson, photograph, NPG [*see illus.*]
Wealth at death £15,010 12*s.* 10*d.*: probate, 1 Nov 1889, *CCI* · £453 0*s.* 9*d.*: additional estate, 23 Dec 1889, *CCI*

Bonar, James (1757–1821), Greek scholar and writer, was born on 29 September 1757, the eighth son of the ten children of John *Bonar (1721–1761), minister of Cockpen and Perth, and Christian Currier (1724–1771). He was educated at Edinburgh high school and at the University of Edinburgh. Bonar entered the office of the solicitor of excise where his elder brother John *Bonar was employed; John later became the first solicitor of excise in Scotland. James, by contrast, is better known for his scholarship. On 9 December 1777 he was admitted as a member of the Speculative Society of Edinburgh University (of which John Bonar was a co-founder) and was elected an extraordinary member on 24 December 1781. For several years he was treasurer of the Royal Society of Edinburgh. He was one of the original promoters of the Astronomical Institution, and a founder of the Edinburgh Subscription Library in 1794. In March 1797 he married Marjory Maitland (*d.* 1854), daughter of James Pyott, bailie of Montrose.

Bonar contributed the article 'Posts' in *Encyclopaedia Britannica* (1794) and the entries, among others, 'Alphabet characters', 'Etymology', 'Excise', and 'Hieroglyphics', for the *Edinburgh Encyclopaedia* (1808–18). He wrote *Disquisition on the Origin and Radical Sense of the Greek Prepositions* (1804), edited a new edition of *Ewing's Greek Grammar*, and published an English edition of Hans Holbein's *The Dance of Death* in 1788. A regular contributor to the *Edinburgh Magazine*, *Missionary Magazine*, and *Scottish Register* in the period 1790–95, Bonar also wrote the memoir of his brother Archibald *Bonar (1753–1816), which is prefixed to the second volume of the latter's *Sermons, Chiefly on Devotional Subjects* (1815–17). James Bonar died on 25 March 1821. He was survived by his wife and eight children including John James *Bonar (1803–1891) [*see under* Bonar, Andrew Alexander], Horatius *Bonar (1808–1889), and Andrew Alexander *Bonar (1810–1892). PHILIP CARTER

Sources *DNB* · *Fasti Scot.*, new edn · NA Scot., Bonar of Kilgraston, MS GD 194/8 · *History of the Speculative Society* (1845)
Archives NL Scot., biography · NL Scot., shorthand diary | NA Scot., Bonar of Kilgraston MSS

Bonar, James (1852–1941), civil servant and economist, was born in the manse at Collace, Perthshire, on 27 September 1852, the elder son and second of the six children of the Revd Andrew Alexander *Bonar (1810–1892), a Free Church minister, after whom the politician Andrew Bonar Law was named, and his wife, Isabella (*d.* 1864), younger daughter of James Dickson, an Edinburgh stationer. James *Bonar (1757–1821) was his grandfather and Horatius Bonar, the hymn writer, was his uncle. His father having become minister of Finnieston, Glasgow, James was educated at Glasgow Academy from the age of ten to fifteen. He then joined Glasgow University, where he graduated MA in 1874 with first-class honours in mental philosophy and gained an impressive range of prizes and awards, which he affected to dismiss as no more than 'sweeties' for good behaviour.

Bonar spent short periods at the universities of Edinburgh, Leipzig, and Tübingen, before proceeding with a Snell exhibition to Balliol College, Oxford, where he matriculated in October 1873. There he took up fencing and skating, and in 1877 obtained a first-class degree in Greats. Influenced by Arnold Toynbee and by Alfred Milner, his Balliol contemporary, he then became a university extension lecturer in political economy in the East End of London, where he founded an Adam Smith club to debate economic subjects. In 1881, after a year as a private tutor in Oxford, he was appointed a junior examiner in the civil service commission, and fourteen years later he became a senior examiner. In 1883 he married Mary Mewburn (*d.* 1908), daughter of George Sparston Miller, a Liverpool shipbroker, and Caroline, daughter of Francis Mewburn, solicitor to the Stockton and Darlington Railway. They had two sons, one of whom died in infancy, and two daughters. In 1885 he formed a bookbinders' co-operative society in Bloomsbury, an early experiment in profit sharing which continued until within a few years of his death.

Bonar early developed an enthusiasm for the writings of Malthus; a brief monograph was followed by a longer study, *Malthus and his Work* (1885), which ranked its subject as a theorist at least equal to Ricardo. For a while, his was the definitive work on Malthus, and throughout the rest of his life he was engaged on a full-scale intellectual biography of the man. However, as new information and changing perceptions of Malthus emerged, the value of Bonar's contribution clearly diminished, and the biography remained unpublished. Bonar also edited two volumes of Ricardo's correspondence (1887–9), which contained some dating errors and were later superseded by Piero Sraffa's complete edition of the letters (1951–73). In 1894 Bonar compiled a handsomely printed *Catalogue of Adam Smith's Library*.

Bonar contributed over eighty articles and reviews to the *Economic Journal* and seventy entries to Palgrave's *Dictionary of Political Economy* (1894–9), to which he also gave editorial help. He also wrote about the economics of John Stuart Mill in the *Journal of Political Economy* (November 1911), and was one of the first to introduce the work of the Austrian school of economists to English-speakers. His *Philosophy and Political Economy* (1893) is one of the more enduring of his works, particularly in the discussion of utilitarianism.

Bonar was very active as a public figure. In 1890 he was one of the founders of what became the Royal Economic Society, which in 1930 elected him as a vice-president. In 1898 he was president of the economics section of the British Association. An honorary member of the Political Economy Club, he served numerous terms of office as vice-president of the Royal Statistical Society. In 1907 he accepted the post of deputy master of the Ottawa branch of the Royal Mint. Although his wife died the following year, he stayed in Canada, and his useful role in the First World War included emergency arrangements for the coinage of South African gold at short notice. In 1919 he returned to London, where he resumed his manifold activities.

In 1929 Bonar delivered the Newmarch lectures at the University of London, published in 1931 as *Theories of Population from Raleigh to Arthur Young*. He was elected FBA in 1930 and a foreign member of the Reale Accademia dei Lincei in 1932. Having been granted the honorary degree of LLD in 1887 at the early age of thirty-four, he was made honorary LittD of the University of Cambridge in 1935 as part of the centenary celebrations of Malthus, a Cambridge graduate.

Bonar had a great gift for friendship, and took walks near his Hampstead home with F. Y. Edgeworth until his friend's death in 1926, and with James Ramsay MacDonald while his fellow Scot was living there. His enthusiasms were boyish and artistic rather than frivolous. As a child in the manse, he had been laughed out of learning the piano but he took up the cello at fifty and kept it up to an advanced age. He learned to ski in Canada, and on the continent of Europe was a great mountaineer; in 1913 he climbed the 12,000 feet peak of the Wetterhorn, with remarkably little effort for a sixty-year-old. He remained very agile physically and mentally until mid-1939, when his powers began to decline. He died in his sleep at his home, 13 Redington Road, Hampstead, on 18 January 1941. T. A. B. CORLEY

Sources *DNB* • G. F. Shirras, 'James Bonar, 1852–1941', *PBA*, 27 (1941), 359–76 • J. Eatwell, M. Milgate, and P. Newman, eds., *The new Palgrave: a dictionary of economics*, 4 vols. (1987) • T. W. Hutchison, *A review of economic doctrines, 1870–1929* (1953), 430 • J. M. Keynes, *Essays in biography*, rev. edn, ed. G. Keynes (1951); repr. (1961), 81–124 • J. A. Schumpeter, *History of economic analysis*, ed. E. B. Schumpeter (1954) • Boase, *Mod. Eng. biog.* • *IGI*

Archives BLPES, corresp. and papers relating to Royal Economic Society • BLPES, history of Royal Statistical Society • NA Canada, diaries • U. Glas. L., corresp. and papers; notebooks; notes on Edward Caird's lectures on moral philosophy • University of Illinois, Urbana-Champaign, life of Malthus | BLPES, letters to Edwin Cannon • King's AC Cam., corresp. with John Maynard Keynes • U. Glas. L., corresp. with G. F. Shirras • UCL, letters to Sir Francis Galton • University of Toronto, Thomas Fisher Rare Book Library, letters to James Mavor

Likenesses photograph, *c.*1920, repro. in Shirras, 'James Bonar', facing p. 359 • W. Stoneman, photograph, *c.*1932, NPG

Wealth at death £21,430 14*s.* 0*d.*: administration with will, 9 May 1941, *CGPLA Eng. & Wales*

Bonar, John (1721–1761), Church of Scotland minister, was born at Clackmannan on 4 November 1721, the eldest son of John Bonar (1696–1752), then a tutor in the family of Colonel Bruce at Kennet, and Jean Smith (*b.* 1695), daughter of William Smith of Alloa, Clackmannanshire. Following his father's ordination as minister of Fetlar and North Yell in Shetland in 1729 he was sent for his primary education to the parish school at Torphichen, Linlithgowshire, where his grandfather, John Bonar (1671–1747), was the minister, and then to the University of Edinburgh, where he graduated MA on 27 April 1742. Bonar of Torphichen was a prominent evangelical leader who preached at the famous Cambuslang revival in 1742, and his grandson is said to have left behind manuscript accounts of two visits that he made there. He completed the divinity course at Edinburgh and was licensed to preach the gospel by the presbytery of Glasgow on 5 June 1745. On 29 January 1746 he was presented by Archibald Cockburn of Cockpen to the little parish of Cockpen in Edinburghshire, where he was ordained on 22 August. Three months later he married, on 18 November 1746, Christian (1724–1771), daughter of Andrew Currier of Edinburgh, writer to the signet. They had a large family, with eight children who survived infancy, including John *Bonar (1747–1807), a solicitor of the excise who was among the six co-founders of the Speculative Society at the University of Edinburgh; Archibald *Bonar (1753–1816), minister of Cramond; and James *Bonar (1757–1821), also a solicitor of the excise, whose life of Archibald, in the second volume of the latter's *Sermons* (1815–17), is not always reliable as a source of information about their father.

John Bonar was allied with the orthodox or popular party in ecclesiastical affairs, but was well versed in secular as well as scriptural learning. His first publication, a pamphlet entitled *Observations on the Conduct and Character of Judas Iscariot*, appeared in 1750, went to a second edition in 1752, and was reprinted with a memoir of the author in 1822. Said to be 'one of the most popular preachers in the Church' (Somerville, 169), he was invited to preach the annual sermon before the Society in Scotland for Propagating Christian Knowledge on 6 January 1752, published one month later as *The Nature and Necessity of a Religious Education*. In its passionate affirmation of 'useful knowledge' in association with religious knowledge, the sermon prefigures Bonar's later work on behalf of educational academies. Another passage asserts that magistrates must use their authority to restrain 'open immoralities,—a contempt of religion,—and the immoderate use of public diversions' (pp. 6–9, 22), anticipating another important theme in Bonar's career. On 26 May 1755 he published an anonymous pamphlet, *An analysis of the moral and religious sentiments contained in the writings of Sopho and David Hume, esq.*, designed to persuade the members of the general assembly of that year to take action against

> the public attack which in this country has of late been made on the great principles and duties of natural and revealed religion, in the works of David Hume; and in the essays of an author who has been distinguished by the name of Sopho [Lord Kames]. (p. 2)

Bonar may have acquired his zeal for purifying the kirk from his grandfather, who wrote in a work published in 1743 of the need to 'shun the company of such as are either of unsound Principles or unsuitable Conversations' (Bonar and Willison, 31). Shortly after the campaign against Hume and Kames failed in the general assembly Bonar was involved in an attempt, successful in his presbytery but eventually overturned in the synod, to censure Alexander Carlyle for attending a performance of the tragedy of *Douglas* in December 1756. Even Carlyle, however, acknowledged that Bonar 'was a man of sense—an excellent preacher; he was temperate in his opposition' (*Autobiography*, ed. Burton, 247).

In January 1756 Bonar was presented to Jedburgh through the influence of the fourth marquess of Lothian, but he was never translated due to opposition from the parishioners, who had already committed themselves to Thomas Boston. Bonar was soon called to the second charge at Perth (later the West Church), where he was translated and admitted on 29 July 1756. On 16 April 1760 he preached a sermon before the synod of Perth and Stirling, 'The nature and tendency of the ecclesiastic constitution in Scotland', which was published later that year and was also in the first volume of *The Scotch Preacher* (1775); it praised the presbyterian system of the Church of Scotland for its tendency to support ecclesiastical and civil liberty and order, as well as doctrinal purity. The following year Bonar wrote his 'Memorial relative to the academy in Perth', dated 11 November 1761, which argued warmly against an educational system based on 'the Grammatical knowledge of Dead Languages and a skill in Metaphysical Subtiltys' and in favour of an alternative system grounded in practical scientific applications tending towards 'the Improvement of the Merchant, Mechanick and Farmer in their respective Arts'. Although never published it was an important expression of the philosophy of practical education that helped to define the pedagogical policy and curriculum of Perth Academy and similar institutions.

Scarcely one month later, on 21 December 1761, Bonar died at the age of forty from what his son James called 'an inflammatory fever' (Bonar, xxv). His surviving manuscripts include several sermons and an unfinished book, 'History of Tyre', intended to show that 'national punishment has been, and ever must be the Consequence of National Guilt'. RICHARD B. SHER

Sources J. Bonar and J. Willison, *The duty and advantage of religious societies, proven from scripture and reason … In two letters one by John Willison of Dundee and one by Bonar of Torphichen* (1743) · J. Bonar, 'Memoir of the Rev. Archibald Bonar, minister of Cramond', in A. Bonar, *Sermons, chiefly on devotional subjects*, 2 (1817), xvli–lv · *The autobiography of Dr Alexander Carlyle of Inveresk, 1722–1805*, ed. J. H. Burton (1910); facs. edn with introduction by R. B. Sher (1990) · A. Fawcett, *The Cambuslang revival: the Scottish evangelical revival of the eighteenth century* (1971) · J. R. McIntosh, *Church and theology in Enlightenment Scotland: the popular party, 1740–1800* (1998) · *DNB* · 'Letters from John Bonar to William Creech concerning the formation of the Speculative Society', ed. H. Paton, *Book of the Old Edinburgh Club*, 5 (1912), 163–90 · *Fasti Scot.*, new edn, 1.12–13, 231, 307; 4.235; 7.296 · R. B. Sher, *Church and university in the Scottish Enlightenment: the moderate literati of Edinburgh* (1985) · T. Somerville, *My own life and times, 1741–1814*, ed. W. Lee (1861); repr. with new introduction by R. B. Sher (1996) · D. J. Withrington, 'Education and society in the eighteenth century', *Scotland in the age of improvement*, ed. N. T. Phillipson and R. Mitchison (1970), 169–99 · D. Allan, 'Protestantism, presbyterianism and national identity in eighteenth-century Scottish history', *Protestantism and national identity: Britain and Ireland, c.1650–c.1850*, ed. T. Claydon and I. McBride (1998), 182–205 · *Edinburgh Evening Courant* (26 May 1755)
Archives NA Scot., 'Memorial relative to the academy in Perth', in *Register of the proceedings of the managers appointed by the magistrates and town council of the burgh of Perth for superintending the affairs of the academy there*, 11 Nov 1761, B59/22/34 · U. Edin., New Coll. L., MS of 'History of Tyre' and sermons, X156 1/5, boxes 27–8

Bonar, John (1747–1807), lawyer, was born on 22 or 24 August 1747 at Cockpen, near Dalkeith, the eldest of the ten children of John *Bonar (1721–1761), Church of Scotland minister, and his wife, Christian Currier (1724–1771), daughter of Andrew Currier, writer to the signet, of Edinburgh. He was educated at the high school, Edinburgh, and between 1763 and 1769 at the University of Edinburgh. There in November 1764, together with William Creech, John Bruce, Henry Mackenzie, and Mr Belcher of Invermay, he co-founded the Speculative Society, and from 1764 until 1771 acted as secretary and treasurer of this debating society. In 1767 he published *Considerations on the proposed application to his majesty and parliament for the establishment of a licensed theatre in Edinburgh*, expressing strong moral hostility to the plan. It had been intended that Bonar should follow his father into the ministry but by 1766 he had begun to work as a temporary clerk in the office of the solicitor of excise in Scotland. He was appointed a deputy solicitor in 1767 and pursued this career for the rest of his life, eventually becoming first solicitor of excise. He was considered to be skilled in leading evidence from reluctant witnesses and expert in knowledge of the revenue laws. He helped to produce the parliamentary report on Scottish distilleries in 1798. He married Janet Palmer, but they separated; they had no children. Bonar died on 3 April 1807 at Worcester, while returning from an extended visit to Bath, taken for the sake of his health. He was buried in Greyfriars churchyard in Edinburgh on 18 April 1807. EMMA VINCENT MACLEOD

Sources NA Scot., Bonar of Kilgraston MSS, GD 194/8 · *DNB* · *Scots Magazine and Edinburgh Literary Miscellany*, 69 (1807), 319 · *History of the Speculative Society of Edinburgh* (1845) · A. Bower, *The history of the University of Edinburgh*, 3 (1830), 211–12 · *Fasti Scot.*, new edn · parish registers, General Register Office for Scotland, Edinburgh · 'Letters from John Bonar to William Creech concerning the formation of the Speculative Society', ed. H. Paton, *Book of the Old Edinburgh Club*, 5 (1912), 163–90 · *History of the Speculative Society* (1968) · W. Anderson, *The Scottish nation*, 9 vols. (1865–7), vol. 9, p. 688
Archives NA Scot., MSS, GD 194/8

Bonar, John James (1803–1891). *See under* Bonar, Andrew Alexander (1810–1892).

Bonaventura. *See* Ó hEodhasa, Giolla Brighde (*c.*1570–1614).

Bonaventure, Richard (*fl.* 1250–1260). *See under* Moneyers (*act. c.*1180–*c.*1500).

Bonaventure, Thomasine. *See* Percyvale, Thomasine (*d.* 1512).

Bond, Capel (*bap.* 1730, *d.* 1790), musician, was baptized at St Mary de Lode, Gloucester, on 14 December 1730, the son of William Bond, a bookseller in the city, and his wife, who was probably Mary Duks. The painter and japanner Daniel *Bond (*bap.* 1725, *d.* 1803) was his elder brother. His uncle, the Revd Daniel Bond, presided over the Crypt School, where he is likely to have received his early education. At the age of twelve he was apprenticed to Martin Smith, the cathedral organist at Gloucester, for £2 10*s*. He moved in 1749 to Coventry, where he was appointed organist at St Michael and All Angels (later Coventry Cathedral) and, from Easter 1752, Holy Trinity. Bond held these high-profile appointments until his death. He rose to the challenge, and some measure of his success can be seen in the payment of £10 per annum, in addition to his £30 Holy Trinity salary, that he was awarded from 1770. He married Ann Spooner on 21 September 1768 at Holy Trinity, Coventry.

Bond's influence spread beyond his church activities. Through his subscription concerts, his direction of the Coventry Musical Society, and the role he played in helping to found and directing in the first Birmingham festival (1768), he 'did much to develop musical life in the Midlands' (Edwards and Holman). His promotion of oratorio in midland towns formed another part of his enduring legacy: this began with the Coventry festival of 1760, where Bond presented Handel's *Messiah* and *Samson*, using professional musicians from Worcester and Gloucester.

Bond's *Six Concertos in Seven Parts*, published in London in 1766, were an interesting and attractive contribution to the concerto repertory, and one of the most accomplished sets by an English provincial composer. Subscriptions came from midlands musicians and music societies, and performances at the Concerts of Ancient Music continued into the following century. They are mainly retrospective in style and scoring, although the first and last of the set, for trumpet and bassoon respectively, are, as published wind concertos, more individual (they were reissued in the twentieth century in an edition by Gerald Finzi). Bond's trumpet concerto is said to be closely related to that of a fellow midlands composer, Richard Mudge, which formed part of a set published in 1749, and the *galant* bassoon concerto is said to show a debt to William Boyce's writing for the instrument. Bond's other known published works, which appeared in 1769, are six anthems of some quality. They received numerous reprints and appeared in later collections. Bond died in Coventry on 14 February 1790. DAVID J. GOLBY

Sources O. Edwards and P. Holman, 'Bond, Capel', *New Grove*, 2nd edn, 3.850 • W. Weber, *The rise of musical classics in eighteenth-century England* (1992) • H. D. Johnstone and R. Fiske, eds., *Music in Britain: the eighteenth century* (1990), 210 • *IGI*

Bond, Charles John (1856–1939), surgeon and advocate of voluntary euthanasia, was born at Bittesby, in the Lutterworth area of Leicestershire, on 27 October 1856, the son of George Bond, a farmer and grazier, and his wife, Elizabeth Higginson. He was educated at Repton School. Having spent a year in agriculture he was a pupil at Leicester Royal Infirmary from February to October 1875, when he entered University College, London, as a medical student. He won gold medals in anatomy and physiology and silver medals in surgery, midwifery, and medical jurisprudence, and later served as assistant demonstrator of anatomy. Having qualified in 1879 he became house surgeon at Bedford General Infirmary, and in 1882 he was elected FRCS. In 1886 he was appointed honorary assistant surgeon to Leicester Royal Infirmary and shortly afterwards became honorary surgeon, a position he held for the following twenty-six years. Along with Sir Charles Hayes Marriott he was responsible for introducing aseptic surgery into the hospital. On retirement from the active staff of the infirmary in 1912 he was elected successively honorary consulting surgeon, vice-president, and vice-chairman of the governors.

In 1912 Bond was appointed to the newly formed national health insurance committee and from 1913 to 1920 he served on the Leicester health insurance committee. During the First World War he was consulting surgeon to the northern command, and he represented the Medical Research Council on the inter-allied commission on the treatment of war wounds in Paris in 1916–18. In 1917 he was created CMG. For two years he was a member of Leicester city council, and he was twice (1901–2, 1935–6) president of the Leicester Literary and Philosophical Society.

Bond was much in demand as a committee man and on official inquiries. He was vice-chairman of the Ministry of Health's medical consultative council, and for eight years was a member of the Medical Research Council of the privy council. He was a member of the departmental commissions on the cause and prevention of blindness, and on cancer, and of Lord Trevethin's committee on the prevention of venereal disease. He was also deputy chairman of the Industrial Fatigue Research Board, president of the Society for the Study of Inebriety, vice-president of a number of temperance societies, an original member of the Sociological Society, and of the Genetical Society. He received life membership from the British Association for the Advancement of Science. In 1924 he became a fellow of University College, London, and was subsequently made a life fellow. In 1925 he received the freedom of the city of Leicester.

Bond's recreational activities included sociology and research into heredity. He was famed for conducting numerous genetic experiments in his garden and poultry yard. His keen interest in eugenics was translated into practical measures in his own city of Leicester. The national health committee of Leicestershire introduced a eugenic consultative committee that provided advice to individuals on the prospects of their offspring. He was also involved in establishing the Bureau of Human Heredity as an international centre for documents and information. He was active in the Eugenics Society and was elected vice-president in May 1930. He was a vocal advocate of sterilization for 'mental defectives' and for the 'ignorant, careless, and irresponsible' (Bond to C. P. Blacker, 2 July 1936, Wellcome L., CMAC/SA/EUG/C.32, II) individuals who did not use contraception. He served on the National Birth Control Council and allegedly persuaded a group of blind men to undergo sterilization.

During Bond's retirement, along with Dr Charles Killick Millard he founded in 1935 the Voluntary Euthanasia Legalisation Society and served as chairman until his death. He was rather more outspoken and radical than his colleague, suggesting on several occasions that once the principle of voluntary euthanasia for incurable and painful disease had been established, it would be extended to other cases including the mentally defective. He believed that one should measure the 'value of human life' in terms of the 'capacity for happiness, joy, self-development and service to others' (*Leicester Evening Mail*, 13 Nov 1937).

Bond was a prolific writer, producing 157 essays and memoirs between 1878 and 1939, covering such diverse subjects as surgery, sociology, genetics, haematology, and eugenics. A collection of his works, *Essays and Addresses: Sociological, Biological, and Psychological*, was published in 1930. He died at his home, Fernshaw, 10 Springfield Road, Leicester, on 23 November 1939, leaving a widow, Edith, daughter of George Simpson JP, of Hazelbrow, Derbyshire, with whom he had a son and a daughter. Despite the failure of the movement between the wars to legalize voluntary euthanasia, Bond helped to bring this and a host of contentious socio-medical issues into the forum of public discussion. N. D. A. KEMP

Sources *BMJ* (2 Dec 1939) • *The Lancet* (2 Dec 1939) • *WWW* • *Eugenics Review* (1939), 215–16 • b. cert. • *CGPLA Eng. & Wales* (1940)
Archives NRA, priv. coll., photographic collection | CUL, corresp. with C. C. Hurst • Wellcome L., Eugenics and Voluntary Euthanasia Society MSS
Wealth at death £59,787 7s. 3d.: probate, 1 Feb 1940, *CGPLA Eng. & Wales*

Bond, Daniel (*bap.* 1725, *d.* 1803), painter and japanner, sometimes called John Daniel Bond, was baptized on 6 July 1725 at Stroud, Gloucestershire, the son of William Bond, bookseller and bookbinder, and probably Mary Duks; he was the elder brother of Capel *Bond (*bap.* 1730, *d.* 1790), composer. His uncle the Revd Daniel Bond was usher of the Crypt School in Gloucester, and it is likely that he was educated there. Nothing is known of Bond's early career until 1761, when under the name Daniel Bond he exhibited a landscape drawing after Vernet at the Society of Artists in London.

From 1762 to 1769 Bond exhibited over thirty landscape paintings at the Free Society of Artists in London, winning the second premium prize for landscape in 1764. His work was described as highly finished, with figures, in the style of George Lambert and Gaspar Poussin. It is possible that during this period he taught drawing; in 1763 James Butler exhibited *A Drawing of a Landscape after Mr. Bond of Birmingham* at the Free Society of Artists. Bond exhibited only twice after 1769, showing one painting in 1775 and two in 1780, both at the Free Society of Artists. He also provided nine illustrations for William Shenstone's *Works in Verse and Prose* (1764) and the tailpiece for the fourth edition of Robert Dodsley's *Cleone: a Tragedy* (1765), all engraved by Charles Grignion. Besides painting on canvas, Bond was employed decorating japanned wares for the papier mâché producer Henry Clay in Birmingham. The dates of his employment here are not known. He became a freeman of the city of Gloucester on 2 February 1789, when he was described as a painter and japanner of Birmingham.

Bond was married; it is possible his wife was Susannah Hodgetts (*fl.* 1758–1803), to whom a Daniel Bond was married on 1 October 1758 at St Philip's, Birmingham, and who together had three daughters. Bond's personal circles were noted by contemporaries as 'confined' (*GM*, 1803). He does not appear to have had any contact with influential groups in Birmingham concerned with the manufacture of wares, such as the Lunar Society. He died on 18 December 1803 at his home, at Hagley Row, Edgbaston, Birmingham. In the months following his death there was a small flurry of interest in the paintings owned by his widow in the *Gentleman's Magazine*, although no record of a public sale has been traced. A large landscape by Bond is in Aston Hall, Birmingham. NICHOLAS GRINDLE

Sources private information (2004) • *GM*, 1st ser., 73 (1803), 1259 • *GM*, 1st ser., 74 (1804) • H. Hammelmann, *Book illustrators in eighteenth-century England*, ed. T. S. R. Boase (1975) • G. Meissner, ed., *Allgemeines Künstlerlexikon: die bildenden Künstler aller Zeiten und Völker*, [new edn, 34 vols.] (Leipzig and Munich, 1983–) • *IGI* • Graves, *Soc. Artists* • 'Lunar Society correspondence', *The Boulton and Watt archive and the Matthew Boulton papers from Birmingham Central Library*, Birmingham Central Library (1993), ser. 1 of *Industrial revolution: a documentary history* • V. Skipp, *A history of Greater Birmingham, down to 1830* (privately printed, Birmingham, 1980) • archive material, Courtauld Inst., Witt Library • O. Edwards, 'Bond, Capel', *New Grove*

Archives Aston Hall Gallery, Birmingham • BL • Courtauld Inst., Witt Library

Wealth at death property in Hagley Row, Edgbaston, Birmingham

Bond, Denis (1588–1658), merchant and politician, was born on 30 August 1588, the eldest son of John Bond (1556–1633) of Lutton, in the Isle of Purbeck, Dorset, merchant and four times mayor of Weymouth, and his wife, Margaret (*d.* 1631), daughter of Richard Pitt of Weymouth. John Bond was an apprentice in France at the time of the St Bartholomew's day massacre (1572) and his son, in turn, travelled abroad in connection with the family's trading interests, journeying to St Malo in 1603 and spending the years 1605–7 in Cadiz. He appears to have moved to Dorchester in 1610, when he married Joane (1588–1620), daughter of John Gould, a director of the Dorchester Company; they had two sons—John *Bond (1612–1676), MP for Melcombe Regis from 1645 and vice-chancellor of Cambridge University in 1658–60, and William (*d.* 1669)—and three daughters. Two years after Joane's death Bond married Lucy (*d.* 1651), daughter of William Lawrence of Winterbourne Steepleton, Dorset; they had four sons, including Samuel (MP for Poole and Melcombe Regis) and Nathaniel *Bond, lawyer and politician, and two daughters.

Bond set himself up as a clothier in Dorchester, becoming a large employer by 1630, and expanding through purchase his inherited property, which included the Lutton estate. Family resources may have been insufficient for him to acquire a formal education but he built up a library, largely theological, and, over the course of several years, compiled a 'chronology' of local, national, and international events, including political events from the 1640s and 1650s, and collected genealogical information, registering a family pedigree which placed his ancestors in Somerset. He established a local political career in Dorchester, securing office as constable (1619), capital burgess (1621), bailiff (1630), lord mayor (1635), and alderman (1636), and winning the friendship of the prominent local minister and puritan colonizer John White. In 1640 he was elected a Dorchester MP in both the Short and Long parliaments, in the latter of which he served on 263 committees. He retained his local power base, sitting on the county committee for Dorset in 1643–50 and being appointed a militia commissioner in 1648.

On the radical parliamentarian wing throughout the 1640s, Bond supported the 'war party' drive for army reorganization in 1643. He also proved himself unremitting towards opponents of the cause, civil or religious. Along with several other MPs he ransacked the chapel of the queen's Capuchins at Somerset House in February 1643 and spoke against allowing William Laud to defend himself during the archbishop's impeachment. A member of the committee for compounding with delinquents from September 1643, he consistently opposed the granting of generous terms to parliament's opponents; in one debate in 1648 on the exception from pardon of named royalists he stated that he hoped 'to see the day when we may have power to hang the greatest lord of them all (if he deserves it) without trial by his peers' (*Mercurius Pragmaticus*, 10–17 Oct 1648). Even so, when named as a judge for the trial of Charles I he did not attend any sessions of the proceedings and did not sign the royal death warrant. Nor did he attend parliament between Pride's Purge in December 1648 and the execution of the king the following January.

Bond did, however, return to political activity under the Rump regime, actively participating from November 1649 as a member of the Rump's first council of state; he would be elected to all five councils of state during the Commonwealth years, and was to serve two monthly stints (1652 and 1653) as council president. He served on the council's admiralty committee from 1650 and became a recognized expert on naval affairs. In foreign policy he seems to have acted in association with Bulstrode Whitelocke: in January 1652 both men may have been involved in an attempt to secure Dunkirk for England, as well as participating in negotiations with the Dutch. In May, Bond and Cromwell were empowered to investigate the clash between the Dutch and English fleets which would prompt the First Anglo-Dutch War. The experience seems to have inclined Cromwell towards support of the war, and perhaps the same is true of Bond. Over the summer of 1652 both men were engaged with Colonel William Purefoy in discussing the possible movement of troops to Dover for coastal defence, but already it was being reported that Bond, like Cromwell, was willing to countenance moves towards peace. He also served on several parliamentary committees on law reform, though he opposed reform 'at critical moments' (Worden, 116), and on the Hale commission on legal reform of 1652. He was one of four commissioners appointed in December 1652 to inspect and reorganize the treasuries, retaining that post until May 1653.

With the fall of the Commonwealth, Bond has been seen as having 'apparently abandoned political ambitions and accepted the semi-sinecure office of Clerk of the Pells and Treasurer's Clerk in the Lower Exchequer' (Aylmer, 118); he already held the office of master of the Savoy Hospital, granted in 1645. He was, however, appointed to Cromwell's council for trade in July 1655, and was elected to the protectorate parliaments of 1654 (Weymouth) and 1656–8 (Melcombe Regis). According to Thomas Burton's parliamentary diary, Bond made at least fifty speeches in the 1656/7 session and spoke sixty-six times in the 1657/8 session. He criticized members who absented themselves to attend to personal affairs and opposed lifetime clerical appointments. Still hostile to religious toleration, he favoured the execution of the Quaker radical James Naylor in 1656. He seems to have supported Cromwell's plans to nominate members of an upper house in 1657, and was sufficiently trusted by the lord protector to be one of the commission appointed in 1658 to tender an oath of loyalty to prospective MPs.

Bond died in London on 30 August 1658 just a few days before Cromwell's death, a coincidence often cited by royalists. He was buried in September at Westminster Abbey, only to have his remains exhumed in 1661, like those of other parliamentarian leaders, and removed to a common grave at St Margaret's, Westminster.

DANIEL WEBSTER HOLLIS, III

Sources J. Hutchins, *The history and antiquities of the county of Dorset*, 3rd edn, ed. W. Shipp and J. W. Hodson, 4 vols. (1861–74) • *Diary of Thomas Burton*, ed. J. T. Rutt, 4 vols. (1828) • *The writings and speeches of Oliver Cromwell*, ed. W. C. Abbott and C. D. Crane, 4 vols. (1937–47) • *JHC*, 6–7 (1648–59) • *CSP dom.*, 1649–53 • C. H. Mayo, ed., *Municipal records of the borough of Dorchester, Dorset* (1908) • Burke, *Gen. GB* (1969) • G. E. Aylmer, *The state's servants: the civil service of the English republic, 1649–1660* (1973) • A. R. Bayley, *The great civil war in Dorset, 1642–1660* (1910) • B. Whitelocke, *Memorials of English affairs*, new edn, 4 vols. (1853) • D. Brunton and D. H. Pennington, *Members of the Long Parliament* (1954) • K. Sharpe, *The personal rule of Charles I* (1992) • D. Underdown, *Fire from heaven: the life of an English town in the seventeenth century* (1992) • B. Worden, *The Rump Parliament, 1648–1653* (1974) • S. C. A. Pincus, *Protestantism and patriotism: ideologies and the making of English foreign policy, 1600–1668* (1996)

Bond, Sir Edward Augustus (1815–1898), librarian, was born on 31 December 1815 at Hanwell, the son of the Revd John Bond, who conducted a large private school there, and Sophia Bond. He was admitted to Merchant Taylors' School in December 1830. In 1833 he was appointed assistant at the Record Office under the supervision of Sir Thomas Duffus Hardy and the Revd Joseph Hunter. In 1838 he was appointed assistant in the British Museum manuscripts department, where he rapidly earned the respect and affection of the keeper, Sir Frederic Madden, for his expertise and industry. He married in 1847 Caroline Frances, a relative, daughter of the Revd Richard Harris *Barham, author of the *Ingoldsby Legends*. They had five daughters.

At the British Museum, Bond became indispensable as a channel for conducting the manuscripts department's business with Sir Antony Panizzi, the principal librarian, with whom Madden was not on speaking terms, and it says much for Bond's tact and integrity that he was trusted by both these imperious and exigent officers. Madden praised Bond warmly to the royal commission on the British Museum in 1848, and his good opinion even survived Bond's appointment by the trustees as Egerton librarian in 1852, nominally in charge of the Bridgewater bequest of manuscripts. The earl of Bridgewater had provided capital for a stipend of £227 to be paid to the holder of this post, and in 1832 the trustees decided that it should be paid to the librarians of the manuscripts department. It was in practice paid to the keeper of manuscripts, but his salary was reduced by the same amount, a violation of the terms of the Bridgewater bequest for which the trustees were censured in the royal commission report of 1850. Their response was to separate the Egerton librarianship from the keepership of manuscripts for the first and last time, so that Madden could no longer complain that he had the office without the salary. This was a meaningless ploy, as he was still responsible for the custody of the Egerton manuscripts as head of the department, and it was a tribute to the value that Madden placed on Bond's services that their friendship outlasted what he called 'a pitiful and unworthy trick to take away the money from me to augment Bond's salary' (Madden, journal, 8 May 1852).

Bond succeeded John Holmes as assistant keeper on the latter's death in 1854. Madden delegated much routine administration to him and when he succeeded him as keeper in 1866 he was virtually running the department. He at once addressed its most pressing problem, the twelve years' arrears of cataloguing. He gave priority, however, to the creation of the class catalogue of manuscripts. Descriptions of manuscripts were cut out of published catalogues, arranged in subject order, and laid down in folio volumes; a subject index was provided, and

Sir Edward Augustus Bond (1815–1898), by unknown engraver, pubd 1879

descriptions were added when new catalogues were published. This invaluable unpublished research tool made it possible for the first time to learn what the department held on particular subjects. Catalogues of additions between 1854 and 1875, published in 1875–7, cleared the cataloguing arrears, and further special catalogues were produced, notably the *Facsimiles of Ancient Charters* (1873–8) and the *Catalogue of Spanish Manuscripts* (1875–93). He advocated the creation of a separate department of oriental manuscripts, which was established in 1867.

In August 1878 to the surprise of many, including himself, Bond was appointed principal librarian upon the resignation of John Winter Jones, the post having been unexpectedly declined by the heir apparent, Sir Charles Thomas Newton. He immediately set about making the museum more welcoming and useful to the public. Almost his first act was to install electric light in the reading-room, an innovation attended with some misgiving in view of the primitive and hazardous circuitry and apparatus. It was, however, an inestimable boon for readers: the room was now open until 8 p.m. instead of having to be shut upon the failure of natural light, which often happened in the mornings when winter fogs descended. The period when the reading-room was closed for cleaning was cut from eighteen to eight days. The galleries were opened to the public every day instead of three and a half days a week, and the ban on babes in arms was ended. The public restaurant was improved. Accommodation for books was greatly increased at modest expense by the installation of sliding presses suspended from the gridiron floors of the bookstacks, modelled on those in use at the Bethnal Green Free Library. Improved accommodation for manuscripts, newspapers, prints, and drawings was provided by the completion of the White wing to the east of the colonnade in 1884, built with the legacy of £72,000 from William White, bequeathed in 1823 but subject to a life interest which did not expire until 1879. The delicate business of transferring the natural history collections to the new museum in South Kensington was successfully accomplished in 1880.

Bond also speedily addressed the intractable problem of the printed books catalogue, which then consisted of manuscript title slips prepared by transcribers and laid down in folio volumes. As the slips grew in number, the volumes were continually being broken down and rebound; between 1850 and 1875 their number had swollen from 150 to 2250. The situation was out of control and the expense of the endless relaying and rebinding brought repeated rebukes from the Treasury. Bond capitalized on the Treasury's alarm and in 1880 negotiated its consent to the printing of all new accession titles and the publication of the existing manuscript volumes. The *General Catalogue of Printed Books* took twenty years to complete, and with its supplement, published in 1905, it described the library as it was on the last day of the nineteenth century. The British Museum Library was the first library of its size to make its contents known to all the world through a comprehensive printed catalogue, to the inestimable benefit of literature and scholarship.

Bond's personal contributions to scholarship were substantial. For the Hakluyt Society he edited Giles Fletcher's *Of the Russe Common Wealth* and the Russian travels of Sir Jerome Horsley (1856). He edited the *Speeches … in the Trial of Warren Hastings* (4 vols., 1859–61), and for the Rolls Series the *Chronica abbatiae de Melsa* (3 vols., 1866–8). In 1873 he founded the Palaeographical Society with his assistant keeper, Edward Maunde Thompson, which did much to develop palaeography as a scientific discipline, and he began publication of the invaluable *Facsimiles of Ancient Manuscripts* (5 vols., 1873–88). Also with Thompson, he published *The Utrecht Psalter* (1874). He was elected FSA in 1880 and retired as principal librarian in 1888. Bond's colleague Richard Garnett wrote of him that 'beneath a cold and reserved exterior' he had 'a most kind heart and truly elevated mind, far above every petty consideration and delighting to dwell in a purely intellectual sphere' (Garnett, 338). He managed to remain aloof from the professional jealousies, feuds, and intrigues rife in the museum for much of his career, and he was entirely without self-importance; he was always receptive to new ideas for the improvement of the museum from whatever quarter, and having accepted them, he would immediately put them into practice. A photograph of *c.*1880 hints at his benevolent disposition: a broad, open face, generous mouth, and penetrating but kindly eyes.

Official recognition of Bond's great service to the museum was tardy; although he was appointed CB in 1885, he was made KCB only shortly before he died at his house, 64 Prince's Square, Bayswater, on 2 January 1898. His wife survived him. MICHAEL BORRIE

Sources A. Esdaile, *The British Museum Library: a short history and survey* (1946) · E. Miller, *That noble cabinet: a history of the British Museum* (1973) · R. Garnett, 'The late Sir Edward A. Bond, KCB', *Essays in librarianship and bibliography* (1899) · F. Madden, journal,

Bodl. Oxf., MSS Eng. hist. c. 140–182 • B. McCrimmon, *Power, politics and print: the publication of the British Museum catalogue, 1881–1900* (1981) • *WW* • *WWW*

Archives BL, letters to W. C. Hazlitt and others • Bodl. Oxf., corresp. with Sir Thomas Phillipps • NHM, corresp. with Richard Owen and William Clift

Likenesses photograph, c.1880, BL • Mrs J. A. Platt, oils, c.1891, BM • wood-engraving, NPG; repro. in *ILN* (8 Feb 1879) [*see illus.*]

Wealth at death £15,033 19*s*. 4*d*.: probate, 3 Feb 1898, *CGPLA Eng. & Wales*

Bond, Frederick Bligh (1864–1945), architect, author, and psychical researcher, was born on 30 June 1864 at Marlborough, Wiltshire, the third son of the Revd Frederick Hookey Bond, headmaster of Marlborough Royal Free Grammar School, and of his wife, Mary Isabella Dela Fosse. He was educated at Bath College, where his father had taken up a post, and in 1882 was articled to the Bristol architect Charles F. Hansom. In 1887 he went into partnership with Hansom, working with him and, after Hansom's death in 1891, with his son Edward, on Clifton College and on the buildings of the University College, Bristol.

From 1900 Bond practised alone, built a solid reputation as both an ecclesiastical and domestic architect (his most important building is the public hall in the Bristol suburb of Shirehampton), and gained his FRIBA. In 1909 he cemented his reputation with the publication of his first book, *Roodscreens and Roodlofts*, written jointly with Bede Camm, and with his appointment as consulting architect to Malvern Priory church. Shortly before this Bond had become director of excavations at Glastonbury Abbey, which in 1908 had been purchased by the Church of England and was administered by the Bath and Wells Diocesan Trust. Bond's fascination with Glastonbury, which rapidly became an obsession, had begun in 1907 and provided him not only with a mission, but also with solace for an unhappy marriage.

In 1894 he had married Mary Louise Mills, and their only child—Mary Theodora St Vincent Bligh Bond—was born the following year. The marriage rapidly failed, and by 1898 Bond and his wife were legally separated; bitter legal battles over custody of his daughter continued for many years. It was, perhaps, symptomatic of Bond's growing enthusiasm for esoteric subjects, and especially with what was later termed 'sacred geometry', that he should name his daughter after the masonic lodge, St Vincent, no. 1404, at Bristol, of which he was then the master. His enthusiasm also carried over into his work at Glastonbury.

From the outset Bond saw himself as a pioneer, describing himself as the 'first in applying psychical research methods to archaeological work' (*WWW*, 4.119). He was not the active agent in these controversial methods, that role being taken by Captain John Allen Bartlett ('John Alleyne'), a west country poet and folklorist. At Bond's direction Bartlett produced, by automatic writing, a long series of scripts about the history of Glastonbury Abbey, together with sketch plans of the site. On the basis of these Bond excavated and uncovered the foundations of two previously unknown structures, the Edgar and Loretto chapels. The story of their discovery was publicized in Bond's book *The Gate of Remembrance* (1918), and alleged messages from medieval monks were published in two further books, *The Hill of Vision* (1919) and *The Company of Avalon* (1924), and in a long series of pamphlets, *The Glastonbury Scripts* (1921–5).

Bond's research was highly controversial and the diocesan trust, uneasy over his methods—despite his successes—and unhappy with the publicity, dismissed him from his post as director of excavations in 1922. He was no longer practising as an architect, and relied increasingly on his writing and research for an income. From 1921 to 1926 he edited the journal *Psychic Science*, and, with the Revd T. S. Lea, published works on the Greek cabbala. This was an application of symbolic word numbers to the symbolic interpretation of the Greek text of the New Testament and to the true interpretation of geometrical forms. But such works as *The Apostolic Gnosis* (1919–21) had a limited appeal and did little to provide an income. Far more successful were books purporting to reveal hitherto unknown gospels, but they were not destined to bring success to Bond. While acting as editor of *Psychic Science*, Bond had been associated with the automatic writing of Geraldine Cummins, but when in 1926 he attempted to publish and to claim copyright in her *Chronicle of Cleophas*, on the grounds that his presence and influence had been essential to its production, she brought a successful legal action against him. When the book appeared in 1928, it was in her name and to her sole financial advantage.

Bond then took up a series of lecture tours in the USA, encouraged by his friend and fellow architect Ralph Adams Cram. During one of these he met Archbishop W. H. F. Brothers of an American branch of the Old Catholic church and felt a calling to the priesthood. In 1932 Bond was ordained by Archbishop Brothers and in the following year consecrated as a bishop. He had, however, neither parish nor diocese, and after he returned to England in 1937 ceased to use the title the Right Revd Monsignor Bond OSB. This clerical phase was the last in his curious career; his attempts to excavate at Glastonbury once again came to nothing and he settled for retirement. From 1938 to 1942 Bond lived with his married daughter at Wimbledon, and then moved to Dolgellau in north Wales, where he died, at the Cottage Hospital, on 8 March 1945. He was buried in Llanelltyd churchyard, Dolgellau.

Bond had left a respectable legacy as an architect, but his real achievement was to set Glastonbury firmly in the English psyche and to link it inseparably to the sacred geometry which he had helped to formulate.

R. A. GILBERT

Sources W. W. Kenawell, *The quest at Glastonbury: a biographical study of Frederick Bligh Bond* (New York, 1965) • P. Benham, *The Avalonians* (1993) • S. Whittingham, 'Mind of an architect', *Nonesuch* [Bristol University alumni magazine], 7/1 (autumn 1996), 34–7 • A. Gomme, M. Jenner, and B. Little, *Bristol, an architectural history* (1979) • P. F. Anson, *Bishops at large* (1964) • *WWW, 1941–50* • private information (2004) [Dr M. Crossley-Evans, University of Bristol] • *CGPLA Eng. & Wales* (1945)

Archives priv. coll., MSS • Som. ARS, papers relating to his excavations at Glastonbury Abbey

Likenesses photograph, c.1920, repro. in Benham, *The Avalonians* • photograph, 1933, repro. in Benham, *The Avalonians*

Wealth at death £1762 13s. 4d.: probate, 18 Oct 1945, *CGPLA Eng. & Wales* • £50: further grant, 29 Aug 1946, *CGPLA Eng. & Wales*

Bond, George (1750–1796), lawyer, was the younger son of George Bond (*d*. 1792), of Farnham, Surrey. His mother was a daughter of Sir Thomas Chitty (*d*. 1792). He and his elder brother, Thomas, were both called to the bar on 12 February 1779 at the Middle Temple.

Bond became famous as a counsel in criminal cases, and obtained a large practice at the Surrey sessions. He often played on his local associations, referring to 'my native county', which rarely failed to sway Surrey juries, who were enthralled by his coarse and vulgar humour. A common verdict at the Surrey sessions was: 'We finds for Serjeant Bond and costs' (Polson, 207). He was made a serjeant in 1786, and a king's serjeant in 1795. He married Kitty Cooke on 1 April 1793 at St George's, Hanover Square, London. His wife was a granddaughter of one of the protonotaries of the common pleas and they had two children. Bond died on 19 March 1796, aged only forty-six, from a rheumatic fever. He was survived by his wife.

J. M. RIGG, *rev.* ROBERT BROWN

Sources *GM*, 1st ser., 66 (1796), 261–2 • *European Magazine and London Review*, 29 (1796), 215 • A. Polson, *Law and lawyers, or, Sketches and illustrations of legal history and biography*, 2 vols. (1840), vol. 1, pp. 206–7 • H. A. C. Sturgess, ed., *Register of admissions to the Honourable Society of the Middle Temple, from the fifteenth century to the year 1944*, 3 vols. (1949) • J. Hutchinson, ed., *A catalogue of notable Middle Templars: with brief biographical notices* (1902) • will, PRO, PROB 11/1273, sig. 165

Bond, Graham John Clifton (1937–1974), jazz and rock musician, was born in the area of Romford, Essex, on 28 October 1937 of unknown parentage. He was adopted from a Dr Barnardo's children's home in early 1938 by Edwin Bond, a civil servant, and his wife, Edith. He began to learn piano at the age of six and was educated from 1948 at Royal Liberty School, Romford, where he played oboe and cello in the school orchestra. In 1953 he formed a traditional jazz band, the Modernaires, and took up the alto saxophone. He later formed a band with the drummer Terry Lovelock under the name Terry Graham Trio, which nominally played modern jazz but primarily provided music for local dances. He also played clarinet in a local traditional jazz band. In summer 1957 he worked as a solo pianist in Majorca, then returned to London early in 1958, where he rejoined Lovelock and worked as a sales manager, as well as filling various freelance musical engagements. He married Diane Eaton on 26 March 1960. In April 1961 he joined Don Rendell's Quintet, with which he first made records, playing alto saxophone in a style influenced by Sonny Rollins and Eric Dolphy. He continued to work in bop-based jazz groups, including Live New Departures, accompanying the poets Pete Brown and Michael Horowitz, and from September 1962 to mid-1963 with the John Burch Octet, but he was becoming interested in reaching a wider public with rhythm and blues piano. In November 1962 he left Rendell and joined Alexis Korner's Blues Incorporated. Shortly after this he took up the Hammond organ, which he played in a trio with Blues Incorporated's bassist and drummer (Jack Bruce and Ginger Baker), who were also fellow members of John Burch's group. In spring 1963 this trio severed connections with Korner and with the addition of other players became the Graham Bond Organization, playing an aggressive blues-based fusion of jazz and rock, often featuring Bond's own compositions. The band appeared in the film *Gonks Go Beat* (1965), recorded extensively, and toured widely before effectively disbanding in September 1967 with the departure of two of its key members, the saxophonist Dick Heckstall-Smith and the drummer Jon Hiseman, who had replaced Baker after June 1966. Bond tried to keep the band going with a shifting personnel, but by this time his first marriage had ended in divorce (1966) and he was struggling with a severe drug problem. He had also become committed to the occult beliefs of Aleister Crowley and convinced himself that he was Crowley's son. About this time he began a relationship with the singer and dancer Diane Stewart. He was hired as the musical director of a rock band called The Fool, with which he travelled to the USA, where he worked during 1968–9 and published some compositions under the pseudonym Billy Gamble. On his return to Britain he formed a new band, Initiation. Despite Bond's being arrested in London at its début on 18 September 1969 at the Country Club, Hampstead, for non-payment of maintenance to his ex-wife, the group played a 'welcome back' concert at the Albert Hall, London, in October 1969 and endured until summer 1970, by which time Bond was also playing with Ginger Baker's Airforce. In May 1970 he married Diane Stewart, who had become a regular member of his bands. In August 1970 he formed Holy Magick to record an album celebrating his occult involvements, and from September 1971 worked with the jazz group Jack Bruce & Friends. In December 1971 he formed a new band, Bond and Brown, with Pete Brown, which lasted until November 1972. His second marriage failed in 1972. Early in the following year he was briefly involved with a folk-rock band, Magus, led by Carolanne Pegg, but his deteriorating mental health led to hospitalization in February 1974 after he had sought sanctuary with the police from a dispute with drug dealers. He died under a train at Finsbury Park underground station, London, on 8 May 1974, an apparent suicide. His ashes were scattered at Tintagel, Cornwall.

HOWARD RYE

Sources H. Shapiro, *Graham Bond: the mighty shadow* (1992) • J. Chilton, *Who's who of British jazz* (1997) • H. Shapiro, *Alexis Korner: the biography* (1996) • C. Larkin, ed., *The Virgin encyclopedia of popular music*, concise edn (1999)
Archives FILM BFI NFTVA, performance footage | SOUND BL NSA, performance recordings
Likenesses photographs, repro. in Shapiro, *Graham Bond*

Bond, Henry John Hayles (1801–1883), physician, younger son of the Revd William Bond (1745–1832), fellow of Gonville and Caius College, Cambridge, and rector of Wheatacre, Norfolk, and his wife, Martha Hayles, was born in Wheatacre on 22 December 1801. He was educated at Norwich grammar school under Edward Valpy. He studied medicine at Cambridge, London, Edinburgh, and Paris, and graduated MB at Corpus Christi, Cambridge, in 1825, and MD in 1831.

By 1831 Bond had settled in Cambridge, where he soon

established a large practice. On 11 December 1834 he married Mary, daughter of William Carpenter, of Toft Marks, Norfolk, and niece of Sir Edward Berry, bt.; they had a large family. In 1835 he was elected a fellow of the Royal College of Physicians, and in 1851 he was appointed regius professor of physic at Cambridge in succession to John Haviland. From 1858 to 1863 he was a member of the General Medical Council. He resigned his professorship in 1872, having largely retired from practice some time before.

Bond published nothing except an excellent syllabus of his lectures, but his tenure of office was contemporary with a great rise in the reputation of the medical school at Cambridge. He was a man of great integrity and ability, but was shy and retiring, and an enemy of ostentation. He died at his home, 4 Regent Street, Cambridge, on 3 September 1883, and was buried in Cambridge cemetery. He was survived by his wife.

E. S. Shuckburgh, *rev.* Patrick Wallis

Sources Venn, *Alum. Cant.* • Munk, *Roll* • *BMJ* (15 Sept 1883), 553 • *The Lancet* (15 Sept 1883) • private information (1885) • *CGPLA Eng. & Wales* (1883)

Wealth at death £27,501 3*s*. 11*d*.: resworn probate, May 1884, *CGPLA Eng. & Wales* (1883)

Bond, Sir (Charles) Hubert (1870–1945), psychiatrist and mental health administrator, was born at the vicarage, Ogbourne St George, Wiltshire, on 6 September 1870, the elder son of the Revd Alfred Bond, who became chaplain to the Worcester County Asylum, and his wife, Frances Elizabeth, daughter of Charles Smallridge, clerk of the peace for Gloucester. Bond's younger brother, Sir Reginald Bond (1872–1955), became medical director-general of the Royal Navy and honorary physician to the king. At Edinburgh University, Bond graduated MB in 1892, BSc in public health in 1893, MD in 1895, and DSc in 1898. On 12 May 1900 he married Janet Constance (*b*. 1872/3), daughter of Frederic Robert Laurie, bank manager, of Worcester, and they had one daughter. He entered on his long psychiatric career by taking a junior appointment at Morningside Asylum in Edinburgh of which Thomas Clouston was the outstanding head. Subsequent posts at Wakefield, Banstead, and Bexley led to his appointment as first medical superintendent of Ewell Colony for Epileptics in 1903; after four years he became medical superintendent of a new London county council mental hospital at Long Grove. During the next five years he established a reputation as an administrator and gathered round him a group of able young men who were to become leaders of this branch of medicine in the period between the two world wars.

In 1912 Bond was appointed a commissioner in lunacy, and in 1914 he became a commissioner at the Board of Control which was set up under new legislation. In 1930 he was promoted one of the four senior commissioners who, with the chairman, constituted the board. The duties of this post were exactly suited to his temperament and gifts. He enjoyed the visits to mental hospitals, where his clinical interests, his regard for young doctors beginning their careers in the speciality, and his humane concern for the patients' well-being could all find satisfaction. He did his best to raise the level of medical work in mental hospitals, and was eager to cement links between psychological medicine and branches of physical medicine. This emphasis led to his supporting focal sepsis theory which was subsequently discredited. Bond combined his commissionership with a great deal of lecturing, examining, and administrative work.

Bond had far-sighted views about the future of mental hospitals and the legislation needed to give them their due place in the health services of the community. These views he expressed in a lengthy address to the Royal Medico-Psychological Association in 1921. Like an earlier commissioner, Samuel Gaskell, he pressed for the voluntary admission of mentally ill patients rather than their certification, as the means of obtaining treatment in a mental hospital. It was not, however, until 1930 that the Mental Treatment Act made this change possible. In the meantime Bond experienced a painful set-back to his career: a patient whom he had interviewed sued him and another doctor in 1924 for wrongful detention. The jury found for the plaintiff and awarded very heavy damages of £25,000. The Court of Appeal (later confirmed by the House of Lords) set the verdict aside and ordered a retrial, but this did not take place as the plaintiff accepted £250 paid into court. Bond's misfortune undoubtedly had a considerable effect in bringing about changes in the law which were recommended by the royal commission on lunacy in 1926 and embodied in the act of 1930.

Bond contributed little to the literature of psychological medicine, but his early papers on the need for systematically collecting accurate data reflect a precise mind. He lectured for twenty years at the Maudsley Hospital to successive classes of young psychiatrists on mental illness and the law. In both world wars he gave much help in adapting mental hospitals to provide for psychologically traumatized soldiers. For many years he was also consultant in neurology and mental disorders to the Royal Navy. Although of slight build, Bond was of distinguished appearance and had a somewhat foreign air, largely due to his Vandyke beard. He was appointed CBE in 1920 and advanced to KBE in 1929. He died on 18 April 1945 at 383 North Drive, St Annes, Lancashire, less than a month after retiring from his post at the Board of Control. He was survived by his wife.

Aubrey Lewis, *rev.* Nick Hervey

Sources *The Lancet* (5 May 1945), 579–80 • *The Lancet* (12 May 1945), 613 • *BMJ* (28 April 1945), 612 • b. cert. • m. cert. • d. cert. • personal knowledge (1959)

Likenesses W. Stoneman, photograph, 1932, NPG

Wealth at death £14,199 16*s*. 10*d*.: probate, 28 Sept 1945, *CGPLA Eng. & Wales*

Bond, John (*c*.1550–1612), physician and classical scholar, is of unknown parentage. He was associated for the greater part of his life with Taunton, Somerset. He may have been related to George Bond of Trull, 2 miles south of Taunton, who became lord mayor of London in 1588. However, as MP for Taunton in 1601 he described himself as 'a

Devonshire man' (Townshend, 306). He was 'educated in grammaticals' at Winchester College, and from there proceeded to New College, Oxford, in 1569, 'about the nineteenth year of his age'. He gained the degree of BA on 4 February 1574, 'being either one of the clerks or chaplains of New coll. and much noted for his proficiency in academical learning' (Wood, *Ath. Oxon.*: *Fasti*, 1.115). On 6 July 1579 he received the MA and later in the same year he took up the mastership of the grammar school at Taunton, a post which lay within the gift of the warden and fellows of New College.

For the next twenty-two years Bond was engaged in the Sisyphean labour of schoolteaching, as he characterizes it in the opening words of the preface to his edition of Horace's works: 'While I was undertaking the task of educating the young, a stone that I rolled for twenty years and more' (Horace, sig. A4*v*). But his efforts, however arduous, were crowned with considerable success, since 'he did exercise such an admirable way of teaching, that many departed thence so excellently well grounded in humane learning, that they proved afterwards eminent either in church or state' (Wood, *Ath. Oxon.*: *Fasti*, 1.115). During his years as a schoolmaster Bond also took up the study of medicine, eventually becoming well known as a physician: 'at length being in a manner worn out with the drudgery of a school, he did for diversion, I cannot say profit, practise physic, tho' he had taken no degree in that faculty … and became at length eminent therein' (ibid.). When he entered parliament in 1601 it was as a physician rather than as a classical scholar that he was known to his fellow MPs.

Bond's first intervention in the House of Commons occurred during the debate on a bill designed to increase attendance at church on Sundays. He argued that the bill would place excessive power in the hands of JPs. By speaking of the 'luxuriant authority' of JPs he caused grave offence to certain prominent members, including the puritan Sir Francis Hastings, MP for Bridgwater, Somerset, the promoter of the bill. Hastings accused him of making 'dangerous and seditious' speeches, described his strictures on JPs as 'insolent', and demanded that he be called to the bar of the house (Townshend, 277–8). Bond apologized, but on the third reading of the bill again declared his opposition, calling it 'altogether needless' (ibid., 317). When the bill was defeated by a single vote Sir William Knollys, comptroller of the household, delivered the following rebuke: 'We have been often troubled by a Physician (meaning Mr. *Bond*) … He troubled us with *Aristotle* and other books; if he had stayed there, it had been well: … it is a most intolerable disorder' (ibid., 321). During the first parliament of James I's reign Bond proved to be an ardent advocate of union between England and Scotland. His last recorded intervention came on 2 May 1610, when his speech provoked 'much hissing and spitting' (*JHC*, 1.423).

Bond left no writings on medicine. As a Latinist, however, he enjoyed a lasting reputation, based on his editions of Horace, first printed in 1606 and dedicated to Henry, prince of Wales, and of Persius, published posthumously in 1614. His notes, the fruit of his experience as a schoolmaster, are concise and to the point. For Horace much of his material is derived from the commentary of Lambinus, but Bond concentrates on the essentials, giving the sense of the passage where Horace's poetic expression is not immediately clear and explaining geographical, historical, and mythological references as briefly as possible. His edition very quickly gained the approval of writers on education. In the year of his death John Brinsley, the author of *Ludus literarius: or, The Grammar Schoole*, recommended 'M. Bonde upon Horace; who hath by his paines made that difficult Poet so easie, that a very childe which hath been well entred, and hath read the former Schoole Authors in any good manner may go thorough it with facilitie, except in very few places' (Brinsley, 122). Bond wrote the preface to his edition of Persius in 1610, but died before it could be published, and it was seen through the press by his son-in-law Roger Prowse, who was married to his daughter Elizabeth. Little is known about his wife, Anstice, who survived him. Wood states that his commentaries were used at free-schools and universities and frequently printed abroad. At least twenty separate editions of Bond's Horace were printed, fifteen of them outside Britain. The most eloquent tribute to his achievement as a scholar was paid by the Parisian publisher Nicolas-Louis Achaintre, who in 1806 produced a new edition of Horace with Bond's annotations. Achaintre's preface sets Bond above every other commentator on Horace.

In his will Bond stated that he had made provision for the construction of a hospital in Magdalene Lane, Taunton. His wife received his house in Taunton and most of his goods. He died on 2 August 1612 and was buried in the chancel of the church of St Mary Magdalene in the town.

S. F. RYLE

Sources *Quinti Horatii Flacci Poemata*, ed. J. Bond (1606) · H. Townshend, *Historical collections, or, An exact account of the proceedings of the four last parliaments of Queen Elizabeth* (1680), 277–8, 317, 321 · *JHC*, 1 (1547–1628), 266, 278, 282, 298, 423 · Wood, *Ath. Oxon.*: *Fasti* (1815), 115 · HoP, *Commons, 1558–1603* · *DNB* · J. Brinsley, *Ludus literarius, or, The grammar schoole* (1612), 122 · *Auli Persi Flacci satyrae sex, cum posthumis commentariis Joannis Bond*, ed. J. Bond (1614) · N.-L. Achaintre, ed., *Quinti Horatii Flacci Opera* (1806), v–x · W. Notestein, *The House of Commons, 1604–1610* (1971), 3, 4, 184, 202, 217–18, 527 n. 7, 548 n. 9 · F. Watson, *The English grammar schools to 1660* (1908), 360 · J. W. Binns, *Intellectual culture in Elizabethan and Jacobean England: the Latin writings of the age* (1990), 194 · Fuller, *Worthies* (1662) · will, PRO, PROB 11/120, fol. 333*v*

Wealth at death see will, PRO, PROB 11/120, fol. 333*v*

Bond, John (1612–1676), college head, was born on 12 April 1612, the son of Denis *Bond (1588–1658), clothier of Dorchester, Dorset, and later MP for Lutton in the same county, and his wife, Joane (1588–1620), daughter of John Gould, a director of the Dorchester Company. Nathaniel *Bond was his youngest half-brother. He was educated first by John White, rector of Dorchester, and then at St Catharine's College, Cambridge. There he matriculated at Michaelmas 1628, graduated BA in 1632 and proceeded MA in 1635. He appears never to have married. Bond was for long, and understandably, confused with an Exeter minister of the same name, born in Dorset about the same time, who also had a connection with John White, succeeding him as master of the Savoy.

Following the issue of a writ on 25 September 1645, Bond and William Sydenham were admitted as the two MPs for Melcombe Regis, Dorset. Bond was already a member of the county committee and on 18 October he was admitted to the post of recorder of Weymouth and Melcombe Regis; he retained the position until 23 April 1649 when he was replaced by Samuel Bond (who was perhaps his half-brother). In 1646, in a controversial appointment, Bond became master of Trinity Hall, Cambridge, vacant through the death of Thomas Eden. After the mastership was declined by John Selden, on 28 October 1645 the fellows elected Dr Robert King. King, however, was politically unacceptable to parliament, which on 7 March following appointed Bond to the position. He appeared at Trinity Hall and was admitted on the 11th of that month; about the same time he was admitted to the degree of doctor of civil law. On 26 March 1646 the Commons' journal reported the house's approval of the appointment to the college of 'John Bond, DCL, a member of this House' (*JHC*, 4, 1644–6, 489).

On 5 June 1646 Bond was named to a parliamentary commission for the exclusion of 'notorious offenders' from the sacrament, and the following May he was appointed a commissioner for appeals from the visitors of the University of Oxford. On 29 August 1648 he was named to a committee of both houses to judge scandalous offences, but he was one of those secluded at Pride's Purge a few weeks later. On 4 May the following year he was appointed professor of law in Gresham College in the place of Dr Thomas Leonard. He was also appointed as a master in chancery on 22 May 1650, holding the office until 3 May 1655. He was admitted as member of the Inner Temple on 20 January 1651 and on 1 February was called as an associate of its bench.

Bond continued as master of Trinity—on 20 November 1655 he was paid £53, the arrears due to him for the augmentation earlier granted to his position—and also acted as vice-chancellor of Cambridge University in 1658–9. He was one of the members readmitted to the Rump Parliament by Monck in 1660, and was named as one of the militia commissioners of Dorset in the act of 12 March 1660. However, Bond lost his preferments later that same year; he left Trinity Hall before the reappointment of Robert King on 3 August and resigned his Gresham professorship on 23 October. He retired to Dorset and died in 1676; he was buried at Steeple, Dorset, on 30 July of that year.

STEPHEN WRIGHT

Sources *Calamy rev.* • J. Hutchins, *The history and antiquities of the county of Dorset*, 3rd edn, ed. W. Shipp and J. W. Hodson, 4 vols. (1861–74) • H. C., 'Dr John Bond', *N&Q*, 9th ser., 10 (1902), 165–7 • Venn, *Alum. Cant.* • J. Ward, *The lives of the professors of Gresham College* (1740) • C. Crawley, *Trinity Hall: the history of a Cambridge college, 1350–1975* (1976) • C. H. Firth and R. S. Rait, eds., *Acts and ordinances of the interregnum, 1642–1660*, 3 vols. (1911) • F. A. Inderwick and R. A. Roberts, eds., *A calendar of the Inner Temple records*, 2 (1898) • F. J. Varley, *Cambridge during the civil war, 1642–1646* (1935) • A. R. Bayley, *The great civil war in Dorset, 1642–1660* (1910) • *JHC*, 4 (1644–6), 285, 489 • *Fifth report*, HMC, 4 (1876), 587–8

Bond, John James (1819–1883), archivist, was born on 9 December 1819, the son of William Andrew Bond of Ashford, Kent. In 1841 he entered the public service as a clerk, assisting Henry *Cole, his brother-in-law, in the arrangement of the public records when they were transferred from Whitehall to the Royal Riding School of Carlton House. Bond became an assistant keeper in 1855 and in August 1862 he was appointed superintendent of the literary search room. In 1866 he published a *Handy Book of Rules and Tables for Verifying Dates of Historical Events*. This work was well regarded but Bond never rose above the rank of assistant keeper because of his 'oddness', which by 1883 had reached the point where it could be called mental instability. He was convinced that he was an illegitimate son of the duke of Sussex, a belief that his colleagues regarded as delusionary. He died on 9 December 1883 at his home, 96 Philbeach Gardens, Earls Court, London, where he had lived with his sister, Marian Fairman Cole.

THOMPSON COOPER, *rev.* JOANNE POTIER

Sources Boase, *Mod. Eng. biog.* • *Annual Register* (1883) • *The Times* (11 Dec 1883), 6 • Allibone, *Dict.* • J. D. Cantwell, *The Public Record Office, 1838–1958* (1991) • *CGPLA Eng. & Wales* (1884)

Wealth at death £497 8*s*. 2*d*.: administration, 15 Jan 1884, *CGPLA Eng. & Wales*

Bond, John Linnell (1764–1837), architect, was born on 14 September 1764. Of his parents nothing is known. Though described as having been taught architectural drawing by James Malton, it is more probable that it was from Thomas Malton junior that he received instruction, for when exhibiting his first design, for the inside of a banqueting room, at the Royal Academy in 1782, his address was given as Mr Malton's, Carlisle Street, Soho. In the same year Thomas Malton junior exhibited a design for the front of a banqueting house, when his address was given as 8 Carlisle Street, Soho. Bond entered the Royal Academy Schools in 1783, aged nineteen, and won a silver medal in 1784, and a gold medal in 1786 with a design for a mausoleum. His architectural drawings and designs, which he continued to exhibit at the Royal Academy until 1814, included views of the temples of Jupiter and Minerva, as well as Tintern Abbey, Raglan Castle, and other Gothic ruins. His varied designs included an anatomical theatre for J. Brooks in Blenheim (now Ramillies) Street, a cast-iron bridge over the Thames near the Adelphi at the Strand (eventually built by John Rennie to his own designs), a naval obelisk, an altar, an Egyptian hall, a 'Gothic villa' and several villas at Wimbledon, Bushey, and in Kent. Of his exhibited designs, those which include further reference to construction include 'a room erected at Southampton Castle for the Marquis of Lansdowne after the manner of the Moorish architecture at Granada' (Papworth, 1.108), and a shop-front 'lately erected' to Messrs Tatham and Bailey's premises, 13–14 Mount Street, Grosvenor Square, London. His most important work appears to have been that commissioned by Sir Gerard Noel MP, for whom Bond built the nucleus of Exton Hall, Rutland (1811), and the neo-classical Stamford Hotel at Stamford, Lincolnshire (*c*.1810–1829).

In 1818 Bond travelled to Italy and Greece; he returned

in 1821, after which date he appears to have ceased practising as an architect, although he continued to contribute several papers on architectural subjects to the *Literary Gazette*. In 1833 he exhibited at the Society (later Royal Society) of British Artists, Suffolk Street, *The interior of the Temple of Jupiter at Olympia, designed from the description of it in the 5th book of Pausanias*, and in 1834 *The interior of the Temple of Apollo at Delphi, designed from the description of it in the 10th book of Pausanias*, together with *The interior of the Parthenon at Athens, attempted to be restored from the description of it in the 1st book of Pausanias, in Pliny, and in other authors* (Johnson, 1.47). A noted classical scholar, William Gifford, editor of the *Quarterly Review*, gave Bond a copy of his translation of Juvenal for comment. It was suggested by a contemporary that:

> his retired habits and the modesty of his disposition rendered him averse to appear before his public, and that he preferred to confine his labours to the gratification and service of the few friends who had discernment enough to appreciate his merits. (Colvin, *Archs.*, 136)

He died, apparently unmarried, at his home, 87 Newman Street, London, on 6 November 1837, leaving in manuscript a translation of Vitruvius on which he had worked for more than twenty years.

[ANON.], *rev.* ANNETTE PEACH

Sources Colvin, *Archs.* • *GM*, 2nd ser., 8 (1837), 655 • S. C. Hutchison, 'The Royal Academy Schools, 1768–1830', *Walpole Society*, 38 (1960–62), 123–91 • *The exhibition of the Royal Academy* (1782) [exhibition catalogue] • Graves, *RA exhibitors* • [W. Papworth], ed., *The dictionary of architecture*, 11 vols. (1853–92) • J. Johnson, ed., *Works exhibited at the Royal Society of British Artists, 1824–1893, and the New English Art Club, 1888–1917*, 2 vols. (1975)

Archives BL, drawings of Henry VII's chapel, 1807, Add. MS 15529

Likenesses H. Singleton, oils, RIBA

Bond, Martin (1558?–1643), merchant, was the third or fourth son of **William Bond** (*d.* 1576), an alderman of London and merchant adventurer, who was sheriff in 1567. It is unclear whether he was the Martin Bond who, in 1572, was admitted to St Alban Hall, Oxford. Like his father he joined the Haberdashers' Company, obtaining his freedom in 1580. During the 1588 Armada campaign he served as a captain in the London militia, and was apparently among the forces assembled at Tilbury to meet the Spanish invasion. He subsequently travelled to Stade, in northern Germany, where, as a merchant adventurer, he traded in cloth for a short period before returning to England. His cloth business prospered, and during the Jacobean period he invested in the Spanish, Virginia, and Somers Island companies.

Settling in Aldgate ward, London, in a house leased from the corporation, Bond soon became a member of common council, and in 1606 was sufficiently trusted to be included in the small committee named to oversee the preparations for the visit to London of James I and his brother-in-law, the king of Denmark. But though he twice served as a London auditor, was briefly deputy governor of the Irish Society (1613–14), and rose to the rank of deputy alderman (by 1626), he never attained the highest City offices, failing in several elections during the 1620s to unseat Cornelius Fish as chamberlain. His talents in the field of bookkeeping were nevertheless well regarded, for after two years' service as an auditor of St Bartholomew's Hospital, he was appointed its treasurer, which post he held for twenty-two years until his resignation in 1642 due to ill health. He also served as master of the Haberdashers' Company in 1624–5, and was the first president of the Honourable Artillery Company (1616–18). In addition he twice represented London in parliament (in 1624 and 1625), where he spoke in defence of the monopoly of the merchant adventurers against the criticisms of the outports. His financial expertise undoubtedly explains why he was named as one of the eight treasurers of the subsidies voted by parliament in 1624.

Dying unmarried, Bond was buried on 11 May 1643 in St Helen's Church, Bishopsgate, where his father lay interred, rather than in his own parish church, St Katharine Cree. He remained wealthy enough to make generous bequests to both the Haberdashers' Company and St Bartholomew's Hospital. His nephew William erected an impressive stone monument over his tomb to his 'piety, prudence and honesty', in which Bond was depicted as a young captain at Tilbury, sitting in armour in a tent, outside which a servant holds his horse and two sentries are on guard with matchlocks. His portrait in oils, by an unknown artist, has been preserved in the hospital, with a pewter inkstand bearing his arms.

ANDREW THRUSH

Sources A. Thrush, HoP, *Commons, 1604–29* [draft] • J. E. Cox, ed., *The annals of St Helen's, Bishopsgate, London* (1876) • A. B. Beaven, ed., *The aldermen of the City of London, temp. Henry III–[1912]*, 1 (1908) • N. Moore, *The history of St Bartholomew's Hospital*, 2 (1918) • I. W. Archer, *The history of the Haberdashers' Company* (1991) • W. R. Baumann, *The merchant adventurers and the continental cloth trade, 1560s–1620s* (1990) • GL, MS 15,873, fol. 30*r* • GL, MS 15,866/1, 494–5 • GL, MS 15,842/1 • GL, MS 15,857/1, fol. 118*r* • M. Bond, letter-books and journals, CLRO • CLRO, City's cash accounts, 1/1–1/3 • *The manuscripts of the Right Honourable F. J. Savile Foljambe, of Osberton*, HMC, 41 (1897), 39 • W. B. Bannerman, ed., *The registers of St Helen's, Bishopsgate, London*, Harleian Society, register section, 31 (1904), 295 • V. A. Ives, ed., *The Rich papers: letters from Bermuda, 1615–1646* (1984) • PRO, C193/12/2, fol. 90*r* • GL, HB5/1, fol. 55 • GL, HA1/4, fols. 269*r* – 270 • E. A. Fry, ed., *Abstracts of inquisitiones post mortem relating to the City of London*, 3: 1577–1603, British RS, 36 (1908), 133–4 • P. Croft, *The Spanish Company*, London RS, 9 (1973) • Foster, *Alum. Oxon., 1500–1714* • S. M. Kingsbury, ed., *The records of the Virginia Company of London*, 4 (1935) • Edward Nicholas's parliamentary diary, PRO, SP 14/166 • will, PRO, PROB 11/201, sig. 168

Likenesses portrait, *c.*1602, St Bartholomew's Hospital, London • effigy on monument, St Helen's Church, Bishopsgate, London

Bond, Nathaniel (1634–1707), lawyer, was born on 14 June 1634 at Dorchester, Dorset, the fourth son of one of the town's puritan leaders, Denis *Bond (1588–1658), a linen draper, and his second wife, Lucy (*d.* 1651), daughter of William Lawrence of Winterbourne Steepleton, Dorset, and widow of John Fley, vicar of Buckerell, Devon. John *Bond was one of his half-brothers. In 1648 the parliamentary visitors at Oxford University awarded Nathaniel Bond a fellowship at All Souls College. He matriculated from Wadham College in 1650, graduating as bachelor of civil law after four years' study, and proceeded to the Inner Temple, where he was called to the bar in 1661. With only a legacy of £500 under his father's will he must have drawn upon his professional earnings to purchase Lutton, the ancestral home of the Bond family, from his elder brothers. On 21 December 1667 he married Elizabeth Churchill (*b.* 1648/9), daughter and coheir of John Churchill, rector of Steeple in Dorset. She died without issue on 18 December 1674, and Bond's second marriage, on 3 August 1675, marked a decisive advance in social status. Mary (1641/2–1728), with whom he had two sons, was the daughter of Lewis Williams of Shitterton and the widow of Thomas Browne of Frampton; both families ranked among the established Dorset gentry and both had supported parliament in the civil war. With a dowry of £2000 and a jointure of two large farms on the Frampton estate she was well provided for.

Bond succeeded his brother Samuel as recorder of Weymouth in 1673. He was elected as a whig for Corfe Castle in 1679 and for his father's old constituency of Dorchester in 1681. But he never showed much interest in parliament. Upon Churchill's death in 1682, Bond presented to Steeple the controversial Samuel Bold, whose sermon against persecution was published by Awnsham Churchill in the same year. In consequence the grand jury at the winter assizes of 1684 found a true bill against him for seditious practices. Like Bold, Bond was a strong supporter of James II's policy of toleration in 1687–8, with its repeal of Roman Catholic as well as protestant nonconformist disabilities. He became a bencher of the Inner Temple in 1687 and was recommended as court candidate for Weymouth; but as one of James's whig collaborators, he failed to find a seat in the Convention Parliament, though he accepted the somewhat empty dignity of serjeant-at-law in May 1689. By the purchase of Creech Grange in 1691 he took the decisive step that propelled the family into county magnate status. He was advanced to king's serjeant and, according to family tradition, refused a judgeship from love of solitude. Regaining his Dorchester seat in 1695, he was one of the few whigs to scruple at the attainder of Sir John Fenwick. In 1699 he was made recorder of Poole. He retired from his profession on the accession of Anne and the return to power of the tories, and died at Creech Grange on 31 August 1707. He was buried at Steeple the following day. A portrait of his widow, who survived him for more than twenty years, remains with his descendants, but no likeness of Bond himself survives.

JOHN FERRIS

Sources J. Hutchins, *The history and antiquities of the county of Dorset*, 3rd edn, ed. W. Shipp and J. W. Hodson, 1 (1861), 602–4, 607 • HoP, *Commons, 1660–90* • H. J. Moule, *Documents of Weymouth* (1883), 221 • Browne–Williams marriage settlement, 1658, Dorset RO, D1/7579 • G. D. Squibb, 'Dorset incumbents, 1542–1731: part 5', *Proceedings of the Dorset Natural History and Archaeological Society*, 74 (1953), 60–78 • HoP, *Commons, 1690–1715* [draft] • private information (2004) [M. Bond] • R. Morrice, 'Ent'ring book', DWL, Morrice MS P, 432–3 • G. Duckett, ed., *Penal laws and Test Act*, 2 (1883), 222, 242 • Baker, *Serjeants* • H. W. Woolrych, *Lives of eminent serjeants-at-law of the English bar*, 2 vols. (1869)

Bond, Nathaniel (1754–1823), politician, was born on 1 November 1754 at Creech Grange, Isle of Purbeck, the second surviving of seven children, including four sons, of John Bond (1717–1784), landowner and politician, and his wife, Mary (1717–1787), daughter of Edmund Dummer of Swaythling, Hampshire. He was educated together with his elder brother John at Winchester College (from in or before 1766), Magdalene College, Cambridge, (from 1771), and the Inner Temple (1773), where Nathaniel was called to the bar in 1779. He served as recorder of Dorchester from 1781 to 1806 and enjoyed a king's bench and western circuit practice; he became KC in 1795, and held the offices of bencher, reader, and treasurer of his inn (1795–1801). He was about to retire from the law but his friend Joseph Jekyll dissuaded him, recommending 'bustle' to his 'bilious, nervous' colleague, on 22 December 1800 (Dorset RO, Bond MSS, D367). John Bond opportunely vacated the family's parliamentary seat for Corfe Castle when Pitt resigned, and Nathaniel was elected at the subsequent by-election on 25 February 1801.

Bond's prospects seemed good, for his school friend Henry Addington was then premier, and in March he was seated at the Treasury board. He declined the Irish chief secretaryship in February 1802, pleading illness: he feared overwork. His maiden speech, on 14 May, eulogized the Amiens peace treaty. He part-framed and defended the Nottingham election and police bills in debate in 1803, and rumour designated him secretary at war. In reality he was sworn of the privy council on 23 November 1803, and was again offered the Irish chief secretaryship, which he again declined in January 1804. He became vice-president of the Board of Trade on 8 February, but lost office in June after Pitt's restoration.

Like Addington, Bond opposed Pitt, who courted him in October 1804 after George III, having met Bond at Weymouth, suggested him as the next judge-advocate-general. Bond demurred until Addington, by now Lord Sidmouth, rejoined Pitt and solicited for him. He anticipated becoming judge-advocate until the reconciliation between Pitt and Sidmouth faltered. Changing tack, he supported criminal inquiry into naval maladministration on 2 May 1805, but opposed Lord Melville's impeachment; his successful amendment on 12 June for prosecution by the attorney-general, was, however, subsequently overthrown. Pitt's refusal to place Bond, who waived office, and Hiley Addington, brother of the former prime minister, on 27 June ruptured the merger. Bond reluctantly became judge-advocate in Grenville's ministry on 8 March 1806, after he had defended Lord Chancellor Ellenborough's cabinet seat in debate on 3 March. Daunted by William Windham's War Office memorandum awarding the duke of York, commander-in-chief, sole access to the king on all courts martial, Bond offered to resign in June. When a participatory role for him was concocted, he capitulated on 24 July, despite suffering from deteriorating eyesight.

Bond did not seek re-election in 1807. In November he resigned from office, overwrought and aware that his likely successor, Richard Ryder, had royal approval. He retired to East Holme, Dorset, which he had inherited from his uncle Nathaniel. In better health, he occasionally contacted Sidmouth to discuss current political issues. He died at East Holme, unmarried, on 8 October 1823 and was buried at Steeple, Dorset, on 15 October. He left East Holme to his namesake nephew. ROLAND THORNE

Sources R. G. Thorne, 'Bond, Nathaniel', HoP, *Commons* · Dorset RO, Bond papers [(D367) and (D413, box 1)] · *GM*, 1st ser., 93/2 (1823), 469 · Devon RO, Sidmouth papers · *Pedigree of the family of Bond of the Isle of Purbeck* (1858) · Cobbett, *Parl. hist.*, vol. 36 · Venn, *Alum. Cant.*

Archives Dorset RO, corresp. and papers, D367, D413, box 1 | BL, Hardwicke MSS, Add. MSS 35701, 35704, 35712 · Devon RO, letters to Lord Sidmouth

Wealth at death under £35,000: PRO, death duty registers, IR 26/944

Bond, Nicholas (1540–1608), college head, was from Lincolnshire. He matriculated as a pensioner at St John's College, Cambridge, on 27 May 1559 and was elected Lady Margaret scholar on 27 June, graduating BA in 1563/4. In 1565 he was admitted a fellow of Magdalen College, Oxford, taking his MA in that university on 17 October 1567. In 1574 he was admitted to the rectory of Bourton on the Water, Gloucestershire, on presentation of the crown, and resigned his fellowship of Magdalen College the following year. On 15 July 1580 he was awarded a doctorate of divinity for a thesis concerning the question 'Is God's will immutable?'. On 1 March 1582 Bond was presented by Queen Elizabeth to the fifth prebendal stall of Westminster Abbey, and later in that year he was named as one of those qualified to confer with captured Jesuits. In or before 1584 he was appointed a chaplain-in-ordinary to the queen, and a chaplain of the Savoy. But his further progress was not smooth.

On the death of Richard Alvey, the master of the Temple, a protracted struggle developed over the succession to his post, not least because one of the candidates was the presbyterian Walter Travers. In August 1584 Whitgift, the new archbishop of Canterbury, wrote to the queen strongly opposing Travers and recommending instead 'Dr Bond', a man 'very fit for that office, and willing also to take pains therein'. Nevertheless, Bond's candidature was rejected. Burghley, the lord treasurer, seems with many reservations to have favoured the other man for the mastership. The lawyers' preference may also have played a role in Bond's failure. Burghley considered Bond 'one well learned and honest', but believed that 'if he came not to the place with some applause of the company he should be weary thereof' (Strype, *Whitgift*, 1.343). Whitgift could not secure the victory of his protégé, but he was able to block Travers: in the end a compromise candidate, Richard Hooker, was installed.

Bond appears to have carried out his duties as a canon of Westminster more conscientiously than many, for as Dean Goodman reported in April 1586, he was one of those 'most commonly present' in midsummer quarter and was ranked among 'such as preach and come to divine service in their habits being present' (Strype, *Annals*, 3, pt ii, 415–16). Further preferments followed. On 3 May 1586 Bond acquired the rectory of Britwell, Oxfordshire, and in 1590 that of Alresford, Hampshire. In 1586 he was proposed by Whitgift for the deanery of Worcester, but was unsuccessful, despite the sympathy of Burghley.

In 1589 Bond's ambition, and the strength of his connections and influence, was subjected to a most exacting test. Lawrence Humphrey, the president of Magdalen College, was a Calvinist scholar whose alleged laxity in government and religion had nevertheless for some years aroused puritan disapproval. Humphrey's death on 1 February 1589 gave rise to a division as to the choice of his successor. The name of Ralph Smith was canvassed among the 'precise party', notably by the college vice-president, John Harding. Within days, however, the fellows received from the queen a letter which brooked no argument: 'we will and command you, and every one of you, immediately upon receipt hereof … to nominate and elect unto the place of your president the said Doctor Bond' (Harriss, 19). The privy council was also moved to write in Bond's favour. Such heavy pressure probably owed much to the continuing patronage of Archbishop Whitgift, determined as ever to resist puritan advances. In the college, however, the ranks of Bond's more precise opponents were swelled by those who resented royal and governmental interference. Others were unimpressed by his performance in the roles of dean of arts in 1570, bursar in 1571–2, and vice-president in 1572, recalling his 'lightness in behaviour and small skill or care of matters in our House' (ibid.). On the day of the senior fellows' decision, Ralph Smith emerged with eight votes, but it seems that some of Bond's supporters, sensing defeat, had planned a means to evade it: 'before the scrutiny could be announced, Swithin Stroud, one of Bond's voters, snatched away the papers from the scrutator, and rushing out of the chapel with his friends, contrived to delay the election beyond the statutable time' (Cooper, *Ath. Cantab.*, 2.466). Feeling ran very high and the official candidate was dubbed the 'bond of iniquity' by Smith's partisans. But their loud protests at the frustration of the majority will were to no avail: since the election had not been valid under the statutes, the right of presentation lapsed to the queen under the royal prerogative. On 4 April 1589 Elizabeth signed letters patent appointing Bond to the presidency.

Very soon after, on 16 July 1589, Bond was appointed vice-chancellor of Oxford University, probably on the urging of his old patron, Whitgift, and of Sir Christopher Hatton, the chancellor. Hatton seems to have expected rapid progress in enforcing regulations more rigorously and in imposing upon the advanced protestant party the oath of subscription to Whitgift's three articles. On 8 July 1590 he ordered the vice-chancellor to read out before congregation a catalogue of the university's supposed failings in such matters. Bond refused, protesting in a letter to Richard Bancroft that the charges were unjust and tended to his own disgrace. Regulations, he asserted, were taken seriously: at Magdalen, for example, the 'scholars dare not presume to speak any other language than Latin' (Wilson, 135–6). A few days later, on 16 July 1590, Bond resigned the vice-chancellorship.

Bond served a second term for the year from 13 July 1592; in September, the queen visited Oxford and was feasted at Magdalen. Here, Bond's influence was considerable. Support for puritanism dwindled during his presidency, though it was to revive under his successor, John Harding. It is indeed ironic that as an executor of the will of the countess of Sussex, Bond played a role in the foundation in 1596 of the puritan stronghold of Sidney Sussex College, Cambridge. But at Magdalen his regime was not one of rooted traditionalism; purchase for the library of books by theologians of the reformed churches increased considerably during his presidency, and there were important reforms and improvements. In December 1591 Bond instructed that the 'poor scholars' were to attend the grammar school. The students of logic and sophistry were divided into classes with lecturers appointed for each; efforts were made to require bachelors to make more determined efforts to improve themselves. Meanwhile, the college prospered. By the mid-1590s the accounts showed a growing surplus which was used for repairs and a new organ for the chapel.

For half a century after the Reformation in England, the independent spirit of Magdalen College had often inconvenienced governments. The election of Bond marked something of a watershed. When Hatton died on 20 November 1591, there was pressure from the advanced protestant party for the appointment of the earl of Essex to the university chancellorship, a proposal strenuously opposed by the court and by Whitgift. It was Bond, more than any other individual in the university, who worked for and secured the election of Thomas Sackville, Lord Buckhurst. Generally, 'Elizabeth had confidence in Bond, not least for his ability to keep the puritan element under control and he did much to strengthen ties with the court' (Harriss, 21). A tradition of independence survived, however, in the college. In 1602 Bond found it expedient to write to Burghley, explaining that his own strong recommendation for a fellowship for a court nominee, Edward Othen, had been insufficient to prevent the Magdalen fellows rejecting him in favour of John Burrows.

On the death of Queen Elizabeth, Bond published Latin verses in her honour. He continued in his position after the accession of the new king. It was during his presidency that on 28 August 1605 Prince Henry matriculated at Magdalen, and with King James was entertained at the college; extensive renovation was carried out in advance of the royal visit. Bond died on 8 February 1608. He was a benefactor of the college library and the Bodleian. His own collection must have been very extensive, since it was valued at £290. Among the more unusual bequests were the two globes and mathematical instruments granted to his servant, George Neighbour, whom he had long permitted to use them. Bond was buried in the chapel of Magdalen College, Oxford, where there is an inscription in his memory. STEPHEN WRIGHT

Sources G. Harriss, 'A loyal but troublesome college, 1458–1672', *Magdalen College and the crown: essays for the tercentenary of the restoration of the college, 1688*, ed. L. Brockliss, G. Harriss, and A. Macintyre (1988), 9–30 • H. A. Wilson, *Magdalen College* (1899) • J. Strype, *The life and acts of John Whitgift*, new edn, 3 vols. (1822) • C. M. Dent, *Protestant reformers in Elizabethan Oxford* (1983) • P. Williams, 'Elizabethan Oxford: state, church and university', *Hist. U. Oxf.* 3: *Colleg. univ.*, 397–440 • N. R. Ker, 'The provision of books', *Hist. U. Oxf.* 3: *Colleg. univ.*, 441–77 • Foster, *Alum. Oxon.* • Cooper, *Ath. Cantab.* • J. Strype, *Annals of the Reformation and establishment of religion … during Queen Elizabeth's happy reign*, new edn, 4 vols. (1824) • will of Nicholas Bond, PRO, PROB 11/111, sig. 16, fols. 124v–125v • R. Somerville, *The Savoy: manor, hospital, chapel* (1960) • Venn, *Alum. Cant.* • Wood, *Ath. Oxon.*

Wealth at death books valued at £290: will, PRO, PROB 11/111, sig. 16, fols. 124v–125v

Bond, Oliver (1760/61–1798), woollen merchant and Irish nationalist, was born at St Johnstown, co. Donegal, the son of a dissenting minister. His full name may have been Oliver Cromwell Bond, as this was used in contemporary reports of his radical activities. After serving an apprenticeship in Londonderry he moved about 1783 to Dublin, where he worked as a woollen draper, initially at Pill Lane and, from 1786, in larger premises at 13 Lower Bridge Street. In June 1791 he married Eleanor Jackson (*d.* 1849), daughter of Henry Jackson, iron founder and later a senior United Irish figure; they had four children.

Bond joined the Dublin Society of United Irishmen at its inception in 1791. William James MacNeven later commented that 'He was one of the earliest in planning and promoting the union of Irishmen … His feelings were truly Irish, his principles those of an enlightened republican' (Madden, 4.166). Bond was closely involved in attempts during late 1792 to establish a new radical volunteer force in Dublin, styled the National Guard. On 1 March 1793 he and Simon Butler, as secretary and president of the Dublin Society of United Irishmen, were arrested on account of an allegedly libellous paper that had criticized the secret committee of the Irish House of Lords. Bond denied signing the paper but admitted that it had been printed on his authority. Both men were sentenced to six months' imprisonment in Dublin's Newgate gaol and fined £500.

During the later 1790s Bond became a central member of the militant United Irishmen, who frequently used his home at Bridge Street as a meeting place. In 1797 Lady Lucy Fitzgerald described him as 'a great merchant, one of the handsomest and most delightful men to all appearances there ever was' (Maher, 102). R. R. Madden suggested that by 1797 Bond was a member of both the northern executive and the Leinster directory. On 12 March 1798 the Leinster delegates met at Bond's house but the organization had been betrayed to the government by one of its members, Thomas Reynolds, and all those present were arrested. Bond was again imprisoned at Newgate until his trial for high treason on 23 July. On this occasion the attorney-general characterized him as 'a man of strong mind and body, and of talents which, if perverted to the purposes of mischief, are formidable indeed' (*The Trial of Oliver Bond*, 3). The key prosecution witness was Thomas Reynolds. Despite the searching cross-examination of Reynolds carried out by John Philpot Curran, Bond was quickly found guilty and sentenced to death. The execution was initially scheduled for 27 July but was postponed for two days. In the interim the United Irish state prisoners and the Cornwallis administration reached an agreement that saved the lives of Bond and the remaining prisoners. The latter agreed to provide a detailed statement concerning the United Irish conspiracy in return for their lives and voluntary exile.

Bond died suddenly in prison a few months later, on 6 September 1798. Despite allegations of suspicious circumstances the official report suggested an apoplectic seizure as the cause. He was buried in the churchyard of St Michan's, Dublin. His wife, also a sworn United Irish activist, continued the family business until 1809, when she moved with her family to Baltimore, USA, where she died on 15 September 1849. LIAM CHAMBERS

Sources R. R. Madden, *The United Irishmen: their lives and times*, 2nd edn, 4 vols. (1857–60) • M. Maher, 'Oliver Bond', *Dublin Historical Record*, 11/4 (1949–50), 97–115 • *The trial of Oliver Bond, esq. for high treason* (1798) • R. B. McDowell, ed., *Proceedings of the Dublin Society of United Irishmen*, IMC (1998) • N. J. Curtin, *The United Irishmen: popular politics in Ulster and Dublin, 1791–1798* (1994) • W. T. W. Tone, *Life of Theobald Wolfe Tone*, ed. T. Bartlett (1998) • M. Elliott, *Partners in revolution: the United Irishmen and France* (1982) • R. O'Donnell, *1798 diary* (1998) • tombstone, St Michan's, Dublin
Archives NA Ire., rebellion papers
Likenesses portrait, repro. in O'Donnell, *1798 diary*
Wealth at death approx. £30,000: Madden, *United Irishmen*

Bond, Sir Robert (1857–1927), politician in Newfoundland, was born on 25 February 1857 in St John's, Newfoundland, the second son of John Bond (1804–1872), a merchant of Torquay, Devon, and his wife, Elizabeth (1818–1900). John Bond entered the Newfoundland trade in the late 1820s, and became the local agent for William Hounsell & Co. of Bridport. The family was sufficiently wealthy for Robert to be educated at Queen's College, Taunton.

On his return to Newfoundland, Bond began to train for a legal career, but decided not to pursue this, ostensibly on the grounds of poor health, and instead devoted his career to politics. This was unusual in a colony where politicians invariably combined public life with a business or professional occupation, and was made possible by an inheritance from his father, who had died in 1872.

Bond entered politics in 1882 as the protégé and electoral partner of the then premier, Sir William Whiteway, and was elected to the house of assembly as a member for Trinity Bay. A major political upheaval in 1885 saw him serve briefly as speaker and finish the year as leader of a small Whitewayite opposition group, Whiteway himself having been temporarily squeezed out of public life. In 1889, however, Whiteway led his Liberal Party to victory in a general election, and Bond joined the executive as colonial secretary.

By this time Bond's political views and priorities had become clear. He was a Newfoundland nationalist who stressed the colony's equality of status with Canada, and opposed suggestions that it join the confederation. He keenly supported the completion of a railway across the island (started in 1881) which would, he was convinced, make valuable natural resources accessible and break the colony's almost total dependence on the cod fisheries. He also advocated the development of close economic ties with the USA. The imperial government he viewed with suspicion, mainly as a result of its handling of the French shore question: the complex web of disputes which surrounded the French right, deriving from the treaty of Utrecht, to fish on the Newfoundland coast between Cape St John and Cape Ray. Bond believed that Britain had been and remained all too ready to sacrifice the colony's interests for the sake of good relations with France.

The French question was a major preoccupation of the Liberal government. The specific issue in contention was whether the French had the right to catch and process lobsters on the treaty shore. Pending a final decision, an Anglo-French *modus vivendi* allowing a French lobster fishery to continue was settled early in 1890, without colonial assent to the final version. This precipitated a political crisis. Bond was a member of a delegation, led by Whiteway, which went to London that summer in an unsuccessful attempt to find a solution to the lobster question and other related issues—among them the need for new legislation to enforce French fishing rights, previous statutes having expired. However, the colony was given permission to explore the possibility of a trade agreement with the United States.

Bond visited Washington twice during the autumn of 1890 and managed to settle a draft convention with James Blaine, the secretary of state. However, the Canadian government protested so vigorously that the British government refused to carry the matter forward. There was great resentment in Newfoundland at this development, and Bond himself was outraged—indeed, he seems to have felt personally humiliated, and angrily denounced the Canadian and imperial governments. He persuaded the colonial government to retaliate by denying Canadian fishing vessels access to bait, an action which led to a short tariff war in 1891–2, and he did what he could to exacerbate the difficulties of the French issue.

The central problem now was the enactment of enforcement legislation. When the colony refused to act, the imperial government introduced a bill in the House of Lords. The legislature immediately dispatched a delegation to London led by Whiteway, which left Bond in charge of government business in St John's. The delegation proposed a compromise, but Bond apparently felt it should have been fighting obdurately, even if this meant 'imperial coercion'. It was only with great difficulty, therefore, that the legislature was persuaded in May 1891 to accept an agreement worked out by the delegation, of which one element was the negotiation of permanent enforcement legislation to be passed in Newfoundland. When Whiteway introduced the necessary bill in May 1892, Bond deserted him and ensured its overwhelming defeat. Relations between the two men became distant and embittered.

However, both Bond and Whiteway were members of a delegation which met Canadian government representatives at Halifax, Nova Scotia, the following November. Very little was achieved on the major issues in dispute, since the Newfoundlanders refused to discuss confederation and the Canadians refused to withdraw their veto on the Bond–Blaine convention.

For all the Liberal government's difficulties, external and internal, it was re-elected in 1893. The tories then counter-attacked by filing election petitions against seventeen Liberals, including Bond, alleging corrupt practice. All of them lost their seats, and the government its majority. This sensational manoeuvre created understandable fears about the stability of the colony's finances and economy, and was a major factor in precipitating the sudden and permanent closure of the two local banks in December 1894, which in turn brought the colony to the verge of bankruptcy. The tories resigned, and by early February 1895 the former government was back in office, Bond with a temporary seat in the legislative council.

It was at this juncture that Bond began to make his political reputation. Since Whiteway was ill, Bond led a delegation to Ottawa to negotiate terms of union with Canada. When the attempt failed, Bond set out to try and negotiate loans to prop up both the government and its savings bank. Against all predictions he succeeded, his personal guarantee forming part of the security for the savings bank loan. He had in fact managed to prevent a default on the public debt, an action which cemented his reputation as a selfless patriot. In local folklore he became the man who had pledged his fortune to save his country.

Though Bond was personally in the ascendant, the government was disintegrating, and was defeated in the 1897 election. Bond, then member for Twillingate, became leader of the opposition. The major issue was the future of the newly completed railway. The new tory government proposed to transfer it to the contractor who had built it, Robert G. Reid, together with (among other things) the dry dock, the government telegraphs, and the coastal steamer service. In addition, Reid would be entitled to 4 million acres in land grants. The privatization was designed to save public money and promote both efficiency and economic development.

Some Liberals accepted this rationale, their main spokesman being Edward P. Morris. But Bond mounted a patriotic opposition to the contract, arguing that it was an immoral sell-out to a Canadian monopolist and an abdication of control and responsibility. Though the contract passed the legislature, the effectiveness of the campaign against it by Bond (who became Liberal Party leader in 1899) and his allies helped destabilize the government, which collapsed in March 1900 after Bond and Morris joined forces to carry a vote of no confidence. Bond formed his first administration (he was both premier and colonial secretary), and won a convincing majority in an election held that autumn on an anti-Reid platform. But since his party contained supporters of the Reid contract, Bond could seek only its modification, not its repeal. The result was a new, more limited contract settled in 1901 which satisfied neither side.

In domestic affairs, the main achievement of Bond's first term in office was a contract with the Harmsworths to build a large newsprint mill at Grand Falls. In external affairs, Bond was closely involved in the talks which culminated in the Anglo-French fisheries convention of 1904, part of the *entente cordiale*, which effectively ended the French presence on the Newfoundland coast. He also returned to his central obsession, reciprocity with the USA. After the 1902 Colonial Conference, where Bond voiced his opposition to imperial preference, he went once again to Washington and negotiated a draft convention. This time the opposition came not from Canada, whose objections had been overruled, but from American fishing interests.

The issue was to dominate Bond's second term in office, which followed his landslide victory in the 1904 election. It became clear in 1905 that the United States senate would not accept the convention. Sir Robert—he was made KCMG in 1901—retaliated by harassing the valuable herring fishery carried on by Americans on Newfoundland's west coast, and by adopting a strict and contentious interpretation of the 1818 convention which defined American rights in Canadian and Newfoundland waters. If Bond hoped that these actions would change the senate's mind, he was badly mistaken; and the British government, unwilling to allow the dispute to disrupt friendly relations with the United States, intervened forcefully to contain the damage. Humiliated once again, Bond stubbornly raged against the imperial government, and put his case to the 1907 Colonial Conference. It was to no avail. He had to withdraw the sanctions imposed on American fishermen, and agree to an arbitration at The Hague.

This episode made Bond unpopular in London and Ottawa, and won him few votes at home, where his political supremacy was no longer secure. The Reid family had decided by 1905 that Bond was so hostile to their interests that they would work to remove him from power. Assured of their financial support, Morris resigned from the government in 1907 and formed a new opposition party in time for the 1908 election. The result was a tie. Bond asked the governor to dissolve the legislature immediately it convened. When this advice was refused he resigned in February 1909. Morris then formed a government; unable to elect a speaker, he was granted a dissolution and a second election took place in May. Bond's Liberal Party was soundly defeated. Though the Liberal government had administered the colony competently and with financial caution, it had been dominated by Bond, who was in turn obsessed by the American issue and tended to neglect the vital small change of local politics. The electorate was in the mood for something more exciting.

Bond was an unenthusiastic leader of the opposition, and in 1913 faced what was to him the unpleasant necessity of coming to terms with the Fishermen's Protective Union, which planned to run candidates in several Liberal districts. When the election gave the Liberals fewer seats than the union, Bond retired from politics. Attempts to bring him back into public life failed, and he lived the rest of his bachelor life in seclusion at Whitbourne, some 60 miles from St John's, where he had a small estate and farm. He died there on 16 March 1927, and was buried there on 21 March.

It was not long before the myth of Bond as the great

Newfoundland statesman began to emerge. It grew out of a mood of contempt for contemporary politicians generated by economic depression, financial difficulties, and evidence of widespread patronage and petty corruption. In retrospect and in contrast, Bond appeared to be a model of probity and disinterested patriotism. In many respects the exaggerations of the myth were based on reality. Bond was intelligent, well-read, honest, hard-working, and a good administrator; he possessed real talents, was devoted to his country, and had a clear vision of what it might become. But he lacked detachment and objectivity, and would have achieved more had he been less certain of the correctness of his opinions, less inflexible and dictatorial, and a better political tactician. Nevertheless, Bond stands out as one of the colony's more effective and imaginative premiers, and the last one to take a serious interest in Newfoundland's status and position in the empire. JAMES K. HILLER

Sources J. K. Hiller, 'The political career of Robert Bond', *Twentieth-century Newfoundland: explorations*, ed. J. K. Hiller and P. Neary (1994), 11–45 • S. J. R. Noel, *Politics in Newfoundland* (1971) • J. K. Hiller, 'A history of Newfoundland, 1874–1901', PhD diss., U. Cam., 1971 • W. G. Reeves, 'Our Yankee cousins: modernization and the Newfoundland–American relationship, 1898–1910', PhD diss., University of Maine, 1987 • I. MacDonald, *'To each his own': William Coaker and the Fishermen's Protective Union in Newfoundland politics, 1908–1925* (1987) • *St John's Evening Telegram* [St John's, Newfoundland] (1882–1909) • *Daily News* [St John's, Newfoundland] (1894–1909) • *Free Press* [St John's, Newfoundland] (1903–8)
Archives priv. coll. | PRO, CO 194
Wealth at death £92,750 in Newfoundland: probate division, supreme court of Newfoundland

Bond, Thomas (1765–1837), topographer, was born at East Looe, Cornwall, in February 1765, the son of Thomas Bond, JP, and his wife, Philippa, daughter of John Chubb of East Looe (said to be the first discoverer of fossils in Cornwall). Bond was by training a lawyer, and practised as a solicitor in East Looe; his legal knowledge was considered extensive. In 1789 he was appointed town clerk of the two parliamentary boroughs of West and East Looe, to which latter his father had been elected mayor. Both boroughs were controlled by the Buller family of nearby Morval, and East Looe was 'managed' by Bond's cousin Davies Giddy (later Gilbert). In 1823, while still in office, Bond published *Topographical and historical sketches of the boroughs of East and West Looe, in the county of Cornwall*, which was illustrated by his relative Mrs Davies Gilbert. This work, written 'for private amusement', was published for the benefit of 'travellers, strangers and residents'. Bond also contributed to the *Journal of the Royal Institution of Cornwall*. He died, unmarried, at East Looe on 18 December 1837, and left most of his property to Davies Gilbert. He was buried in the churchyard of St Martin by Looe on 23 December.

JOHN WESTBY-GIBSON, *rev.* CHRISTINE NORTH

Sources Boase & Courtney, *Bibl. Corn.*, 1.32, 1019 [Bond family] • G. C. Boase, *Collectanea Cornubiensia: a collection of biographical and topographical notes relating to the county of Cornwall* (1890) • *GM*, 2nd ser., 9 (1838), 667 • HoP, *Commons, 1790–1820*, 2.70
Archives Cornwall RO, East Looe and West Looe borough archives • Cornwall RO, Davies Gilbert MSS

Bond, William (*d.* 1576). *See under* Bond, Martin (1558?–1643).

Bond, William (*c.*1675–1735), journalist and poet, was, in adulthood, said to be of Bury St Edmunds, Suffolk. His parentage is uncertain, but he claimed to be related to Sir Henry Bond (*d.* 1721), a Roman Catholic Jacobite, and to Thomas, Viscount Gage (*d.* 1754) (Bond, 389; 'Dedication', *The Spectator*, 9). Another Suffolk aristocrat, John Hervey, first earl of Bristol (1665–1751), acknowledged Bond as his 'cousin' (*Letter-Books*, iv). It has been argued (Baine, 171–2) that Bond was the youngest son of Sir Henry Bond's younger brother Thomas, who was very distantly related to Viscount Gage, but Bond's dedications in 1723 and 1732 to Thomas's children, Henry Jermyn Bond and Judith Bond, do not imply that he was their sibling; also Bond's reputed age at death makes it virtually impossible that he was a legitimate son of Thomas.

Nothing is known of Bond's upbringing and education except that his writings imply that he once lived in France. He may be the William Bond, 'a Protestant', who was given a pass to travel to Holland in 1697 (*CSP dom.*, 1697, 206). He was certainly in England by 1715, when he emerged in print as something between a gentleman amateur and a hack. He wrote in the *Weekly Journal* and was the editor and chief author of a spurious continuation of Steele and Addison's *Spectator*, twice a week from January to August 1715. He and Thomas Willis, a fellow contributor to *The Spectator* continuation, were said to be Jacobite plotters in 1718, when it was also claimed that Bond had used his pen in the Jacobite cause in 1715 (*Stuart Papers*, 287), but his identifiable early writings seem politically unexceptionable. By 1720 he was publishing stridently loyal Hanoverian verse.

Bond was the proprietor and probably part author of the *Weekly Medley* from July 1718 to January 1720, and he was co-author with Aaron Hill of the better-known *Plain Dealer* from March 1724 to May 1725. Richard Savage called Hill and Bond 'the two contending Powers of Light and Darkness' because, as Johnson explained, the character of the *Plain Dealer* rose with Hill's essays and fell with Bond's, but this is hardly noticed by an impartial reader (Johnson, 25n). Bond published translations of two books of Tasso's *Jerusalem Delivered* (1719, 1732), a poor edition of Edward Jones's translation of George Buchanan's *History of Scotland* (1722), and other editions and translations. Between 1720 and 1730 he addressed several complimentary poems to royalty and aristocracy. Some of his verse appeared under the pen-name H. Stanhope and was published by Edmund Curll. With Martha Fowke Sansom (1689–1736) Bond wrote *The Epistles of Clio and Strephon* (1720), a fictional courtship in the form of Ovidian love poems with occasional prose letters.

Bond lodged for a while with the deaf mute fortune-teller Duncan Campbell (*d.* 1730) and wrote the well-known anonymous *Life* of Campbell (1720), once thought to be by Defoe even though it was reissued as *The Supernatural Philosopher* (1728) under Bond's name. Bond also wrote a verse address to Campbell, 'The Parallel', much of which consisted of an attack on Alexander Pope. It first appeared in *Mr Campbell's Packet* (1720) and was reprinted by Curll as the title-poem in an anti-Pope collection, *The Progress of Dulness* (1728), at which point Pope responded by naming Bond as a hitherto nameless dunce in notes to the *Dunciad variorum* (1729, 2.118, 3.151). Happily, Pope seems to have been unaware that Campbell later accused Bond of causing dissension in his family and of ruining honest men by inveigling them into dubious business ventures: all the more deplorable because he was 'a Man of good Family' (Campbell, 26).

The Tuscan Treaty, or, Tarquin's Overthrow, a blank-verse tragedy, 'written by a gentleman lately deceased' (title-page), revised and altered by Bond, with prologue and epilogue by Aaron Hill, was acted twice at Covent Garden in August 1733 and printed in the same year. Hill gave more substantial help when he allowed his own new tragedy *Zara* to be staged by amateurs in the York Buildings for the benefit of Bond, who, according to the playbill, 'has lain ill of the Gout, and Rheumatism, upwards of Four Years' (Scouten, 496). Bond played Lusignan, father of the heroine, on the first night, 29 May 1735, but fainted on the stage and was carried home, where he died the following morning, aged about sixty. It is not known if Bond was ever married: his works contain scattered references to unhappy marriages. In his *Spectator* essays (1715) he repeatedly describes himself as old, but not too old for love.

JAMES SAMBROOK

Sources R. M. Baine, *Daniel Defoe and the supernatural* (1968), 137–80 • D. Campbell, *Secret memoirs of the late Mr Duncan Campbell, the famous deaf and dumb gentleman* (1732), 26–32 • W. Bond, *Weekly Medley* (10–17 Oct 1719), 389 • A. Hill, *The Prompter*, 60 (6 June 1735), 1–2 • *The Spectator*, 9 (1721) • *London Magazine*, 4 (1735), 334 • *Calendar of the Stuart papers belonging to his majesty the king, preserved at Windsor Castle*, 7 vols., HMC, 56 (1902–23), vol. 7, p. 287 • A. H. Scouten, ed., *The London stage, 1660–1800*, pt 3: *1729–1747* (1961), 311–12, 496–7 • *Letter-books of John Hervey, first earl of Bristol*, ed. S. H. A. H. [S. H. A. Hervey], 3 (1894), 129 • *CSP dom., 1697*, 206 • [E. Curll], *The Curliad* (privately printed, Edinburgh, 1729), 24–5 • *Clio: the autobiography of Martha Fowke Sansom, 1689–1736*, ed. P. J. Guskin (1997) • *GM*, 1st ser., 40 (1770), 406, 513 • A. Pope, *The Dunciad*, ed. J. Sutherland (1943), vol. 5 of *The Twickenham edition of the poems of Alexander Pope*, ed. J. Butt (1939–69); 3rd edn [in 1 vol.] (1963); repr. (1965), 430 • GEC, *Baronetage*, 3 (1903), 20 • S. Johnson, *Life of Savage*, ed. C. Tracy (1971), 25

Bond, William Bennett (1815–1906), archbishop of Montreal, born at Truro on 15 September 1815, was the son of John Bond, grocer, of that town, and his wife, Nanny Bennett. He received his early education at Truro and in London. Subsequently he emigrated to Newfoundland and became a lay reader there, and after studying at Bishop's College, Lennoxville, he was ordained deacon at Quebec in 1840 and priest in 1841. In the latter year he married Eliza Langley (*d.* 1879) of St John's, Newfoundland. For two years he acted as a travelling missionary in the region between the southern shores of the St Lawrence and the American frontier, his headquarters being at Russeltown Flats and at Napierville. Under instructions from George Mountain, bishop of Quebec, he organized missions in the district, and founded schools in connection with the Newfoundland School Society. He settled as a missionary at Lachine in 1842 and in 1848 he was appointed curate of St George's, Montreal.

Bond's connection with this church remained unbroken for thirty years. He succeeded to the rectory in 1860, and during his incumbency the church buildings in Dominion Square were erected together with the school house and rectory. He played a prominent part in the inauguration of Christ Church Cathedral chapter and in the diocesan synod. In 1863 he was nominated rural dean and in 1866 canon of Christ Church. During the campaigns of 1866 and 1870 against the Fenian raiders Bond served as chaplain to the 1st Prince of Wales's rifles. He became archdeacon of Hochelaga in 1870, and dean of Montreal in 1872. In 1878 the synod, recognizing his organizing capability, elected him bishop of Montreal in succession to Ashton Oxenden. Bond waived his claim to the title of metropolitan of Canada, which had previously been associated with the bishopric. The higher rank passed with his assent to the senior bishop, John Medley, of Fredericton. In 1901 Bond's bishopric was raised to the dignity of an archbishopric, and he then assumed the title of metropolitan of Canada. In 1904, on the death of Robert Machray, archbishop of Ruperts Land, he became primate of all Canada.

Bond lived to see a rapid expansion of the Anglican church in Canada, and during his long episcopate seven new bishoprics were created. In his dealings with his clergy he showed broad sympathies and sound business qualities. Without learning or eloquence he rose to eminence through sheer force of character. A pronounced low-churchman, he actively co-operated with nonconformists, but his conscientious devotion to evangelical principles did not prevent his living on cordial terms with the Roman Catholic population. Good relations with other denominations were fostered by his strenuous advocacy of temperance. In Montreal he strongly supported the cause of municipal reform and helped to found the Citizens' League. He served as secretary of the Colonial and Continental Church Society schools in Ontario (from 1848 to 1872) and was active in promoting the welfare of the Montreal Diocesan College. He was also president of Bishop's College, Lennoxville, which conferred upon him the honorary degree of MA in 1854 and subsequently those of DD and DCL. He was made LLD of McGill University in 1870. He retained his vigour until the end, and died at Bishop's Court, Montreal, on 9 October 1906. He was buried there in the Mount Royal cemetery, leaving one son, Colonel Frank Bond, and a daughter; his wife, two sons, and one daughter had predeceased him. In his memory the Archbishop Bond chair of New Testament literature was endowed at Montreal Diocesan College.

G. S. WOODS, *rev.* H. C. G. MATTHEW

Sources *The Times* (10 Oct 1906), 7 • *The Gazette* [Montreal] (10 Oct 1906), 5 • *Montreal Daily Witness* (9 Oct 1906) • W. B. Heeney, ed., *Leaders of the Canadian church* (1918) • F. S. A. Lowndes, *Bishops of the* *day: a biographical dictionary of the archbishops and bishops of the Church of England* (1897)

Likenesses R. Harris, oils, 1890, Montreal Diocesan College, Montreal, Canada • E. Dyonnet, oils, 1892; in possession of Verdun protestant hospital, France, 1912 • photograph, NPG

Bonde, William (*d.* 1530), Bridgettine monk and author, came from Northumberland and was educated at Cambridge University, where he taught before entering the Bridgettine monastery of Syon Abbey, Middlesex. At Cambridge he obtained his BA in 1500–01 and MA in 1503–4. In that year he became a fellow of Queens' College, and also *lector philosophiae*. In 1506–7 he transferred to Pembroke College, where he was junior treasurer in 1507–9. A contemporary fellow was John Fewterer, who later became confessor-general at Syon. In 1509–10 Bonde was appointed university preacher while studying for a higher degree, which was unfinished when he entered religion.

Syon Abbey, the only English house of the order founded by St Bridget of Sweden in 1370, was a centre of religious reform from its foundation in 1415, and later of orthodox opposition to the Reformation. Bonde joined a dynamic group of highly educated priest brethren dedicated to serving the sacramental needs of a larger body of sisters, and to evangelizing through preaching and spiritual direction. Their aims were furthered by the use of the new medium of printing to disseminate a range of devotional books and pamphlets. Written in English, not Latin, these were aimed at an audience of educated lay people, and the religious, especially women. Bonde's two books contributed to the collective reputation of the house. The first, *The Directory of Conscience* (1527; *A Devote Treatyse*, 1534), was aimed at those in the early stages of religious life, and was also suitable for devout lay people. It addressed the problem of scrupulosity, over-anxious adherence to regulations through fear of God, common among the religious, and also melancholy, or depression. It offered clear guidance and practical remedies. The use of the holy name of Jesus, simple prayers, and meditations on his passion, were characteristic of the *devotio moderna*. The skill with which information was structured, the use of standard frames of reference, such as the seven deadly sins and examples from scripture and saints' lives, made it suitable for oral transmission, as well as private reading. The text itself contained numerous references to the Bible and writings of the doctors of the church, including more recent authorities Gerson and Nidar.

Bonde's *The Pylgrimage of Perfection* (1526; 2nd edn, 1531) was likewise heavily referenced and illustrated with devotional woodcuts. A far more complex work, it was written primarily for those with pastoral responsibility for others. It covered the same topics as elementary catechisms, but in great detail, including expositions of basic prayers, the mass, and the passion of Christ. In anticipation of St Ignatius, the Christian journey was divided into seven days, symbolic of spiritual progression. Bonde was concerned to describe methodically the path from the active religious life to the contemplative, which was reached on the sixth day. On the seventh day extracts from St Bernard and Herphius conveyed something of the joy of contemplation. In its orthodoxy and lack of innovation it refuted Lutheran heresies, and has been described as a '*summa* of late medieval teachings on the religious life' (Rhodes, 22).

Bonde's written works contain all that is known of him as a personality. They reveal a man of great intellectual ability and deep knowledge of the Bible and church doctors, an advanced spiritual practitioner, compassionate, and with an astute understanding of human psychology. The clarity with which he conveyed information attests to his vocation as preacher and teacher. Most of the twenty-nine works he bequeathed to the Syon brothers' library were by Thomas Aquinas, or were bibles and Bible commentaries. They show a somewhat old-fashioned orthodoxy, although the emphasis on biblical scholarship, advocated by St Bridget, was also fundamental to protestant Christianity. Bonde died at Syon Abbey on 18 July 1530 (and was buried there), before the abbey's stand against the English Reformation. VIRGINIA R. BAINBRIDGE

Sources [W. Bonde], [*The directory of conscience: a pr*]*ofytable* [*treatise for su*]*che that be tymorous and ferfull in conscyence* [1527] • W. Bonde, *A devote treatyse to them that ben tymorouse and fearefull in conscience*, [2nd edn] (1534) • W. Bonde, *The pylgrimage of perfection* (1526); [2nd edn] (1531) • Emden, *Cam.*, 72 • J. T. Rhodes, 'Syon Abbey and its religious publications in the sixteenth century', *Journal of Ecclesiastical History*, 44 (1993), 11–25 • M. B. Tait, 'The Brigittine monastery of Syon (Middlesex) with special reference to its monastic usages', DPhil diss., U. Oxf., 1975 • M. Bateson, ed., *Catalogue of the library of Syon Monastery, Isleworth* (1898) • G. J. Aungier, *The history and antiquities of Syon Monastery, the parish of Isleworth, and the chapelry of Hounslow* (1840) • 'Martiloge of Syon Abbey', BL, Add. MS 22285, fols. 47r, 189r

Bondfield, Margaret Grace (1873–1953), trade unionist, campaigner for women's interests, and politician, was born on 17 March 1873 at Chard, Somerset, the tenth of eleven children and third of four daughters of William Bondfield (1814–1901), foreman laceworker, and his wife, Anne Taylor (1827?–1911). After elementary school and a year as a pupil teacher, she became a shop assistant at the age of fourteen, working first in Brighton and from 1894 in London. Her parents gave her a nonconformist faith and ethic, a strong sense of the dignity of work, and a belief in an active female role, while contact with philanthropists and preachers encouraged her to read widely about social, ethical, and spiritual issues. Repelled by the long hours and poor pay of shop work and by the moral unhealthiness and the oppressions of its prevailing 'living-in' requirement, she joined the National Union of Shop Assistants, Warehousemen, and Clerks (NUSAWC), and using the name Grace Dare contributed to its journal, *Shop Assistant*. In 1896 she was recruited by the Women's Industrial Council (WIC) for covert social investigation, working in a series of West End shops to collect information for campaigns for shop work reform. She presented evidence on shop work in the *Economic Journal* (9, 1899), and before the 1901 House of Lords select committee on early closing of shops and the 1908 departmental committee on the Truck Acts.

With WIC help, Bondfield's union appointed her assistant secretary in 1898. Feeling 'no vocation for wifehood or

Margaret Grace Bondfield (1873–1953), by Bassano, 1922

motherhood', she thereafter 'just lived for the Trade Union Movement' with a 'concentration … undisturbed by love affairs' (Bondfield, 36–7). She was also prominent in securing recognition of women's interests within the labour movement. As a Women's Trade Union League (WTUL) executive member, she recommended Mary Macarthur as organizer and in 1906 they established the first women's general union, the National Federation of Women Workers (NFWW). With Macarthur, Bondfield formed her most important partnership: 'from ardent disciple [Macarthur] grew into my chief' (*The Woman Worker*, February 1921). Already an Independent Labour Party (ILP) member, at the 1899 trades union congress (TUC) she spoke for the creation of the Labour Representation Committee. She became a leader of the Adult Suffrage Society, and in 1906 helped found the Women's Labour League (WLL).

Bondfield retired from her NUSAWC post in 1908 to develop these widening commitments. She also returned to social investigation, for the WIC on married women's employment, and for the Women's Co-operative Guild on maternity and child welfare. The introduction of state maternity benefit, and improved medical care for mothers and infants from 1914, owed much to this work. As an ILP administrative committee member (1913–21) Bondfield criticized the government's war policies, while helping Macarthur organize and protect women absorbed into war work. In 1915 she resumed full-time union office as the NFWW's organizing secretary.

Bondfield's work for women's interests sought less a distinctive female position than equal status with men. Believing this well advanced by 1918, she accepted the WLL's and WTUL's conversion into women's sections of the Labour Party and the TUC, and the NFWW's merger with what became the National Union of General and Municipal Workers (NUGMW), of which Bondfield was appointed chief women's officer on Macarthur's death. She supported equal adult—rather than limited female—suffrage, and considered it mistaken 'to argue the specific woman point of view in connection with political questions' (Harrison, 145). Welcoming wider female choice, she nevertheless believed domestic service, home-making, and motherhood deserved as much respect, efficient organization, and communal support as other work. Her socialism was more ethical than economic, seeking to raise living standards but also to elevate character, promote mutual service, and advance 'the reign of God on earth'. An active Congregationalist, she preached for the YWCA and Brotherhood and Sisterhood movements. Physically short and stout, she impressed with sparkling eyes, a firm, brisk manner, and effective, sometimes inspired, public speaking.

As the leading woman trade unionist of the 1920s, Bondfield established a series of female 'firsts'. She was the first woman elected to the TUC executive (1918–24, 1925–9), and to its chairmanship (1923). She became prominent in the international labour movement, notably as delegate to the International Labour Organization at Washington (1919) and Geneva (1921–4, 1926–7). A member of the 1920 TUC–Labour Party mission to Russia, she returned an opponent of both Western intervention and British communism. She was unsuccessful as parliamentary candidate at Northampton in 1920 and 1922, but on her election for the constituency in 1923 she became one of the first three women Labour MPs. When the first Labour government was formed in January 1924, she became the first woman minister, as parliamentary secretary to the Ministry of Labour. Defeated in the 1924 election, she returned to parliament at the Wallsend by-election of July 1926. After her party's 1929 election victory, her appointment as minister of labour made her the first woman cabinet member and privy councillor.

Bondfield's ministerial career turned upon the issue of unemployment insurance. While official Labour Party–TUC policy was to fund more generous benefits from general taxation, she believed in contributory insurance on moral and financial grounds, and in a properly solvent insurance fund. Her signature of the 1927 Blanesburgh committee report, which sought these aims with some restrictions of benefit, attracted much criticism from the Labour Party and the TUC. As minister of labour during the increased unemployment of 1930–31, her attempts to contain the fund's deficit brought still fiercer criticism, while its increased borrowing provoked attacks from the Conservative and Liberal parties and Treasury officials. Her task was impossible, and her determination in trying to match incompatible pressures often appeared as political insensitivity. Her autobiography faithfully echoes the subsequent condemnation of MacDonald by the labour movement; yet the proposed cut in benefit rates which fatally split the Labour cabinet in August 1931 had been her policy since February, and she assured MacDonald of her 'deep sympathy in and admiration for' his decision to lead the National Government (Bondfield to MacDonald, 24 Aug 1931, J. R. MacDonald MSS). Had she been asked she might have remained in office. But her political reputation had now collapsed: following Labour into opposition, she was defeated at Wallsend in the 1931 election and again in 1935, and failed to regain election to the TUC general council.

Bondfield returned to her NUGMW post until her retirement in 1938. Between 1941 and 1943 she undertook speaking tours for the British Information Service in North America. Other wartime tasks included co-ordination of the voluntary services as chairman of the Women's Group on Public Welfare from 1939 to 1949 and vice-president of the National Council of Social Service. She was a JP for London from 1920, and was appointed CH in 1948. She died unmarried at Verecroft Nursing Home, Sanderstead, Surrey, on 16 June 1953, and was cremated at Golders Green crematorium. PHILIP WILLIAMSON

Sources M. Miliband, 'Bondfield, Margaret Grace', *DLB* [incl. bibliography of her writings], vol. 2 • F. Hunter, 'Bondfield, Margaret', *BDMBR*, vol. 3, pt 1 • M. G. Bondfield, *A life's work* [1948] • M. A. Hamilton, *Margaret Bondfield* (1924) • *The Times* (18 June 1953) • *The Times* (22 June 1953) • *The Times* (9 July 1953) • S. Lewenhak, *Women and trade unions: an outline history of women in the British trade union movement* (1977) • R. Lowe, *Adjusting to democracy: the role of the ministry of labour in British politics, 1916–1939* (1986) • R. Skidelsky, *Politicians and the slump: the labour government of 1929–1931* (1967) • B. Harrison, *Prudent revolutionaries: portraits of British feminists between the wars* (1987)

Archives BLPES, corresp. with the independent labour party • Labour History Archive and Study Centre, Manchester, letters • London Metropolitan University, TUC collections • PRO, Ministry of Labour MSS • U. Warwick Mod. RC, National Union of General and Municipal Workers MSS; TUC MSS • Vassar College, Poughkeepsie, New York, corresp., diaries, and papers | PRO, J. R. MacDonald MSS | FILM BFI NFTVA, news footage

Likenesses Bassano, photograph, 1922, NPG [*see illus.*] • W. Stoneman, photograph, 1930, NPG • W. M. Knight, miniature, 1937, NPG • C. Gill, black chalk drawing, Man. City Gall.

Wealth at death £6063 16*s*. 4*d*.: probate, 23 Sept 1953, *CGPLA Eng. & Wales*

Bondington, William of (*d*. 1258), bishop of Glasgow, was probably of Scottish birth, his family name coming from one of the several (now) Bonningtons in Scotland; that in Peeblesshire has been particularly favoured because his first preferment was as parson of Eddleston. He seems not to have attended a university, and first appears as clerk of two chancellors of Alexander II between 1226 and 1231, an office to which he was himself appointed in 1231. He may have been archdeacon of Lothian briefly before he was elected to the see of Glasgow at some time between April and June 1233 and consecrated at Glasgow on 11 September of that year.

The cathedral in which the ceremony took place had been dedicated in 1197, but under Bishop Walter (1207–32) a new and enlarged nave had been begun. This work was now halted and Bondington began rebuilding the eastern arm on a new spacious plan, containing a larger choir and presbytery, with a square ambulatory and eastern chapels, but supported on a lower church or crypt of superb quality, the finest structure of its kind from thirteenth-century Britain. It includes carved heads of old and boy kings, placing its construction in the years around 1249. An Aberdeen synodal decree of 1242 solicited contributions from the faithful every year during Lent for the work on the fabric—and this may have been copied from Glasgow and imitated in other dioceses.

Bondington was generous to his chapter, enlarging its common property, providing the archdeacon of Glasgow with a prebend, conceding free election of the dean, and only four days before his death granting to it the liberties and customs of Salisbury, a repetition of the grant of Bishop Herbert (*d*. 1164) which still left the canons puzzled as to what rights they had acquired; but the bishop's goodwill is undoubted. He also divided the diocese into two archdeaconries in 1238, a move which the parish clergy may not have welcomed. It must have been Bondington and his chapter who had brought the Dominicans to Glasgow by 1246.

Although he did not go to the Council of Lyons in 1245, Bondington had gone in 1240–41 to attend the abortive church council summoned to Rome and he then obtained from the abbot of Cluny the right of Paisley Abbey to elect its own abbot. He took a close interest in the affairs of this abbey, whose west front is also of this period. It had escaped being converted into a Cistercian house, and the endowments of the abortive Gilbertine foundation of Dalmilling went to it in 1238. This was balanced by Bondington's resolution in 1244 of a dispute whereby he required Paisley to build a monastery at Crossraguel. Although no synodalia can be attributed to him, he appears in the records as a caring, active, even proactive, bishop.

It is the more remarkable, therefore, that Bondington retained the chancellorship until at least 8 February 1247, evidently by association with the powerful Comyn family, and thereby secured promotion for his friends. His influence was then eclipsed until the Comyns seized power in 1251; the bishop subsequently secured the see of St Andrews for his protégé, Gamelin. Both were ousted in the coup of September 1255, when Bondington was already an unfit man. He died at his manor of Ancrum on 10 November 1258 and was buried in Melrose Abbey, though he had no close association with it. A. A. M. DUNCAN

Sources J. Dowden, *The bishops of Scotland … prior to the Reformation*, ed. J. M. Thomson (1912), 302–3 • N. F. Shead, 'The administration of the diocese of Glasgow in the twelfth and thirteenth centuries', *SHR*, 55 (1976), 127–50 • A. O. Anderson, ed. and trans., *Early sources of Scottish history*, AD *500 to 1286*, 2 (1922), 268–351 • I. B. Cowan and D. E. Easson, *Medieval religious houses: Scotland*, 2nd edn (1976), 64–5 • A. O. Anderson and M. O. Anderson, eds., *The chronicle of Melrose* (1936)

Likenesses Melrose charter, Laing cast, NA Scot. • seal, U. Durham L., Durham dean and chapter archives

Bone, Henry (1755–1834), miniature and enamel painter, was born at Truro on 6 February 1755, the son of Henry Bone, a cabinet-maker and carver, who took his family to Plymouth, where Bone learned to paint on hard paste china for the Cookworthy factory. He continued his

Henry Bone (1755–1834), by John Opie, 1799

apprenticeship with Richard Champion in Bristol until the firm went bankrupt in 1779, whereupon he moved to London with 1 guinea in his pocket and £5 borrowed from a friend. Here he worked on jewellery design and enamelling watches and fans. Dr Wolcot (better known as Peter Pindar), also a Truro man, is said to have advised him to return to Cornwall to paint miniatures on ivory and make copies in enamel; but he finally decided to remain in London and began to exhibit miniatures at the Royal Academy in 1781. One of his first portraits was a miniature on ivory, painted in 1779, of Elizabeth Van der Meulen (*d. c.*1830), a descendant of Philip Van der Meulen, battle-painter to William III, whom he married on 24 January 1780 (Victoria and Albert Museum, London; copy in Bristol Art Gallery). They had many children, of whom five, including Henry Pierce *Bone, and also two grandchildren, became miniaturists and helped in the production of an enormous corpus of enamels, mainly copies of well-known portraits and old masters, usually signed with the monograms 'HB', 'WB', and 'HPB', and lavishly inscribed in purple paint on the counter-enamels.

The Bone technique was first to visit a private collection, Woburn Abbey for instance, and laboriously copy the chosen picture on to squared paper. Occasionally the picture might be borrowed from the artist or owner and copied in his studio in Berners Street (Farington, *Diary*, 7.4295). The drawings were in pencil, the exact size of the intended enamel, and could be used for several enamels of various sizes. The paper was notched to allow accurate alignment, laid over another paper coated with red chalk, and traced through to the prepared enamel plaque, usually copper or brass, which was then fired to fix the chalk outline. Sometimes the outline was traced in ink on to transparent paper. The drawings, bound into three large albums and copiously annotated by Bone's sons, are in the National Portrait Gallery library. The number of firings varied from six or seven to twelve or more, and could take as long as three years to complete. Benjamin Haydon described Bone's nervous twitch and creaking voice, 'as if he was always watching a bit of Ivory in a furnace for fear it should crack!' (*Diary*, ed. Pope, 3.121–3). And 'Rainy Day' Smith believed that the value of Bone's work lay in the preservation of an artist's colours, especially in portraits by Sir Joshua Reynolds where 'much of the interest is annually lessened by the fading of his colours' (Smith, 223–4).

The pictures chosen for enamel copies, usually commissioned by the owners, reflect the popular taste of the time. The majority were religious and mythological subjects, in frequency order by Titian, Guido Reni, Correggio, Annibale Carracci, Raphael, and Rembrandt. Most of them were medium sized (about the average postcard today), but Bone was ambitious and some were much larger. His enamel copy of Leonardo's *Madonna of the Rocks*, then belonging to the earl of Suffolk, now in the National Gallery, measures 16¼ in. x 10 in.; it was begun in 1806 and finished in 1808. An even larger enamel, a copy of Titian's *Bacchus and Ariadne*, then belonging to Lord Kinnaird and now also in the National Gallery, begun in 1808 and finished in 1811, was exhibited in Bone's studio and visited by several thousand admirers. It was sold to a keen enamel collector, George Bowles, for 2200 guineas, and it is reported that Bone cashed the cheque on his way home, in the nick of time, before Fauntleroy's Bank crashed the next day (Rogers, 292).

Bone was an immensely prolific artist and towards the end of his life two major projects occupied his energies and were available to the public during May to July 1822. The first was a series of portraits of the Russell family, commissioned by the duke of Bedford and copied from portraits at Woburn Abbey, mostly in 1823 and 1824. They are still at Woburn Abbey. The second was an eighty-five strong series 'Portraits of illustrious characters in the reign of Queen Elizabeth'. Bone's collections were valued at £10,000 and the offer to the nation for £4000 was declined. They were exhibited in his studio at 15 Berners Street after his death in 1834, and again at the British Institution where they were sold by Christies in April and June 1836. Most were sold for between 5 and 30 guineas each. The highest price was 124 guineas for lot 62, the Hatfield portrait of Queen Elizabeth. A group of forty kings and queens from Edward III to Charles II, by Henry Bone and his son Henry Pierce Bone, was acquired for the Royal Collection, and many more were bought by William Bankes for his Dorset house, Kingston Lacy, where they still hang in a row in the drawing-room.

Bone was appointed enamel painter to the prince of Wales in 1800, and thereafter to George III, George IV, and William IV. He was elected an associate of the Royal Academy in 1801, and Royal Academician in 1811, his diploma work, which is still at Burlington House, being an enamel *Nymph and Cupid* (exh. Royal Academy, 1963). He died of paralysis in Clarendon Square, Somerstown, London, on 17 December 1834. Likenesses of him by Andrew Plimer (*c*.1790), G. F. Joseph (1798), John Opie (1799; National Portrait Gallery, London), R. Jean (1803), his son H. P. Bone (1805), Peter Rouw (1808), John Jackson (*c*.1814; National Portrait Gallery, London), George Harlow (*c*.1818; Woburn Abbey), Sir Francis Chantrey (1816–20; Burlington House), and by another son William, holding glasses and with the 'Elizabethan gallery' in the background (1828; National Portrait Gallery, London), are all discussed in R. Walker's *Regency Portraits* (1985). R. J. B. Walker

Sources *Annual Biography and Obituary*, 20 (1836), 40–49 · J. J. Rogers, 'Notice of Henry Bone, RA, and his works, together with those of his son, Henry Pierce Bone, and of other members of the family', *Journal of the Royal Institution of Cornwall*, 6 (1878–81), 287–318 · W. H. Tregellas, *Cornish worthies*, 2 vols. (1884), vol. 1, p.163 · R. Walker, 'Henry Bone drawings in the National Portrait Gallery', *Walpole Society*, 61 (1999), 305–67 · D. Foskett, *Miniatures: dictionary and guide* (1987), 303–6, 495 · E. Speel, 'Henry Bone and the technique of enamel painting', *Glass on Metal*, 7 (Feb 1988), 12–16 · R. Walker, *National Portrait Gallery: Regency portraits*, 1 (1985), 55–7 · R. Walker, *The eighteenth and early nineteenth century miniatures in the collection of her majesty the queen* (1992), 269–315 · Farington, *Diary* · J. T. Smith, *Nollekens and his times*, 2 (1828), 223–4 · *The memoirs of Susan Sibbald (1783–1812)*, ed. F. P. Hett (1926) · *The diary of Benjamin Robert Haydon*, ed. W. B. Pope, 5 vols. (1960–63) · *European Magazine and London Review*, 81 (1822), 293–4 · *Literary Gazette* (8 June 1822), 362 · H. Owen, *Two centuries of ceramic art in Bristol* (1873), 235

Archives City Westm. AC, corresp. and papers · Cornish Studies Library, Redruth, obituary and numerous articles in print · U. Edin. L., corresp.

Likenesses G. F. Joseph, miniature, exh. RA 1798 · J. Opie, oils, 1799, NPG [*see illus.*] · R. Jean, miniature, exh. RA 1803 · J. Jackson, pencil and watercolour drawing, *c*.1814, NPG · F. Chantrey, pencil drawing, *c*.1816, NPG · F. Chantrey, marble bust, 1816–20, RA · G. H. Harlow, oil on wood, *c*.1818, Woburn Abbey, Bedfordshire · F. C. Lewis, mezzotint, pubd 1824 (after G. H. Harlow), BM, NPG · W. Bone, miniature on ivory, 1828, NPG · H. Bone, self-portrait, enamel on copper, 1830 (after J. Opie), NG Ire. · R. T. Bone, miniature, exh. 1831 · W. Bone, double portrait, enamel on copper, 1842 (Henry Bone with Elizabeth Bone), NG Ire. · W. Bone, miniature, exh. RA 1842 · H. P. Bone, oils, Musée d'Ixelles, Brussels, Belgium · A. Plimer, miniature, priv. coll.

Bone, Henry Pierce (1779–1855), miniature and enamel painter, was born in Islington, London, on 6 November 1779, the eldest son and pupil of the enamel painter Henry *Bone (1755–1834) and his wife, Elizabeth, *née* Van der Meulen (*d*. *c*.1830). He went to school in Tooting, Surrey, then trained under his father, learning to paint in oils and watercolour and in the art of enamelling. He entered the Royal Academy Schools on 17 March 1796, aged sixteen, but does not seem to have been too diligent a student; he had to be reprimanded for the late delivery of a life school drawing (Farington, *Diary*, 4.1315–1316). Three years later he began to exhibit at the Royal Academy, first portraits in oils, then subject pictures from the classics, Shakespeare, and the Bible. In 1833 his father became seriously ill (he died the following year) and, exploiting his early training, he turned to enamels, often of a size slightly larger than his father's. His first enamel exhibits were a copy of the *Virgin and Child* by Carlo Maratti, the *Infant Saviour* after

Henry Pierce Bone (1779–1855), self-portrait, 1847

Murillo, and portraits of the duchess of Kent, William IV, Georgiana, Lady Spencer, and Lavinia, Lady Spencer. He continued year after year, producing a stream of enamel copies of portraits by Holbein, Rubens, Van Dyck, Kneller, Reynolds, Benjamin West, Beechey, and Winterhalter, interspersed with several painted *ad vivum* by himself. The quality of his work may not have the delicate finish of his father's but the drawing is good and the colouring rich and faithful to the originals. He nearly always signed with his initials, 'HPB', and copiously annotated the counter-enamels with informative details. A substantial collection of his enamels, mostly historical portraits, are in the Royal Collection. Examples of his work are also in the Victoria and Albert Museum, London: *Charles I* (1825) after Van Dyck, *Rubens's Self-Portrait* (1834), *Sarah Duchess of Marlborough* (1843) after Kneller, *Isaac Newton* (1847) after Vanderbank; in the National Portrait Gallery, London: *Nelson* (1840) after Lemuel Abbott, and *Wellington* (1845) after Lawrence; in the Fitzwilliam Museum, Cambridge: *George IV*, one of many also copied by Henry Bone, after Lawrence; in the Ashmolean Museum, Oxford: *Prince Albert* (1842) after Winterhalter; and in the Wallace Collection: *Lady Cockburn and her Three Eldest Sons* (1842) after the Reynolds now in the National Gallery, London. He was a prolific artist and many other enamels are in various museums and galleries, and private collections. He succeeded his father as enamel painter to Queen Adelaide, the duchess of Kent, and later Queen Victoria and Prince Albert, but in spite of several attempts at election he never became an associate of the Royal Academy. The whole Bone family was closely involved with the art community in London. In October 1805 Bone married Anna Maria, the daughter of a watchmaker, John Long, of Clerkenwell. They had three daughters, Louisa, Elizabeth, and Maria. Farington describes a dinner at which Mr and Mrs Henry Bone, Mr and Mrs Henry Pierce Bone, and one of the daughters entertained the painters Edmund Garvey, Thomas Stothard, Beechey, West, John Yenn, William Owen, Samuel Woodforde, Turner, and Callcott (Farington, *Diary*, 11.3881).

Bone died at his home, 22 Percy Street, Bedford Square,

London, on 21 October 1855. There was a sale of his enamels at Christies, on 13–14 March 1856, when 172 of his best works fetched substantial prices. 'On the back of each enamel is indelibly recorded its history' (Christies sale catalogue), a practice which is of considerable value and interest to the historian and collector, especially in relation to the provenance of old masters.

Bone's brother, **Robert Trewick Bone** (1790–c.1840), was born on 24 September 1790, and was taught to paint by his father. He also studied at the Royal Academy Schools which he entered on 19 January 1809. He gained the academy's silver medal in 1811 and exhibited at the Royal Academy and British Institution from 1813 to 1841. An enamel portrait of him, copied by his brother William from a portrait by their father, is in the National Gallery, Dublin.

Another brother, William Bone (1792–1846), also exhibited at the Royal Academy from 1815. His work included an enamel portrait of their father copied from an oil by John Opie, which are both in the National Portrait Gallery, London. Henry Bone's sons, and possibly a grandson, William, helped to produce an invaluable collection of their father's preliminary drawings, bound into three quarto albums in the National Portrait Gallery library, London.

R. J. B. Walker

Sources J. J. Rogers, 'Notice of Henry Bone, RA, and his works, together with those of his son, Henry Pierce Bone, and of other members of the family', *Journal of the Royal Institution of Cornwall*, 6 (1878–81), 287–318 • G. C. Boase, *Collectanea Cornubiensia: a collection of biographical and topographical notes relating to the county of Cornwall* (1890) • Farington, *Diary* • D. Foskett, *Miniatures: dictionary and guide* (1987) • *The exhibition of the Royal Academy* (1799–1855) [exhibition catalogues] • R. Walker, 'Henry Bone drawings in the National Portrait Gallery', *Walpole Society*, 61 (1999), 305–67 • S. C. Hutchison, 'The Royal Academy Schools, 1768–1830', *Walpole Society*, 38 (1960–62), 123–91, esp. 165

Archives Cornish Studies Library, Redruth, printed materials

Likenesses H. P. Bone, self-portrait, enamel, 1847; Christies, 4 March 1992, lot 61 [*see illus.*] • H. P. Bone, self-portrait; Christies, 9 Nov 1965, lot 72 • H. P. Bone, self-portrait; Christies, 31 March 1981, lot 72

Bone, James (1872–1962), journalist, was born in Glasgow on 16 May 1872, the second (but first surviving) of the six sons among the eight children of the journalist David Drummond Bone (1841–1911) and his wife, Elizabeth Millar Crawford (1847–1886). Among his brothers were Sir Muirhead *Bone, artist, Sir David Bone, of the Anchor Line, and Alex Bone, writer of seafaring reminiscences. 'We were born', said James Bone, 'with a pencil in our mouths'. Bone, like his brothers, left school in Glasgow early. At the age of fourteen he went to work in the waterfront office of the Laird Line until he could join the *North British Daily Mail*, the paper his father served. By the time it closed in 1901 Bone's gifts as a descriptive writer were well developed. He and a young lawyer, later a professor, Archibald Hamilton Charteris (1874–1940), wrote the text, under the pseudonym James Hamilton Muir, for a book, *Glasgow in 1901* (1901), which was illustrated by his brother Muirhead. While freelancing Bone met a man from the *Manchester Guardian* and in 1902 its editor, C. P. Scott, was persuaded to give him a trial at the London office. His appointment was confirmed at what was then a respectable salary of £280 a year, and he married in 1903 Anne (*d.* 1950), daughter of John McGavigan, of Lenzie; there were no children.

At the *Manchester Guardian* Bone served under two London editors, J. B. Atkins and R. H. Gretton. In 1912, after ten years' service, Bone was made London editor. However, command was incomplete, for he was not given charge of the parliamentary lobby work. Scott told him: 'You have no great political knowledge or interest'—which was true. Bone, although fanatically loyal to the paper and its Liberal policies, was conservative by temperament and not radical; nor was he an intellectual, but rather an artist with a painter's vision and a poetic pen.

Indeed Bone was a very good art critic, and if he could not bring himself to accept the post-impressionist revolution when Roger Fry presented it to London in 1910, he grappled hard with the problem. He was not blind to the decorative charm of Gauguin and of Van Gogh's irises. Of the latter he wrote: 'They are painted with a fierce, arid skill which seems to rob the iris of its floweriness. In one way the identity of the iris is heightened … but the flower, all the same, has been wronged'.

Bone's life's work was the London letter of the *Manchester Guardian*, headed: 'Our London correspondence, by private wire'. Most provincial morning papers carried a London letter and the *Guardian*'s was acknowledged to be easily the best of them. Bone inherited a letter which had been much improved by Atkins and strengthened by contributions from G. W. E. Russell, a former secretary of Gladstone. The feature was supposed to be a letter to the editor who was addressed, sometimes to the mystification of the reader, as 'you'. To preserve the atmosphere of a letter all titles were informal. Clergymen, for example, were always 'Mr' and never 'the Reverend'. The letter could describe events in home and foreign politics as they were seen from London (sometimes important news was buried in it). Most of the paragraphs were written by Bone, two general reporters, and their colleagues on the political staff. A miscellany of paragraphs told of sales and exhibitions of paintings and sculptures, the arrival of interesting visitors from abroad, what was happening at court, buildings going up and coming down, the fashions, new Christmas party games, and even the weather. Bone excelled at writing what was known as 'the mood paragraph' which might be about a political scandal, a strike inconveniencing the capital, or a spell of exceptional weather. Stuck for a lead paragraph, Bone would write, 'People are saying tonight that …', and the inspiration would come. The letter was the only collectively written feature in the paper. Bone sub-edited severely but creatively, and made the copy, as it were, his own.

He drew on a number of outside contributors, a band of scholarly, decayed gentlemen, who eked out their private incomes by hawking around the London offices of provincial papers erudite paragraphs about coins, stamps, curios, and visiting Ruritanian royalty. Bone's London letter, never sour or malicious, was invested with his own blithe spirit and unquenchable Victorian optimism. He filled the London office with his own zest for the event of the hour, be it a test match, an abdication, or a fog. He would invent a series of paragraphs prescribing mottoes for London clubs or telling 'short, short' stories: '"Drive me to the Caledonian Club"; the cabby's face fell'.

Yet admirable miniaturist though Bone was, he was still better on a broader canvas, writing glowing descriptive pieces about royal occasions, or going to the Derby, in the news columns of the paper where the London editor enjoyed the exclusive title of 'Our London correspondent'. On 31 December each year he published his 'Londoner's retrospect', a social history of the past year. But Bone was best of all when his frame was a book containing his brother's illustrations. His *The London Perambulator* (1925) is a small masterpiece, a description and an obituary of the London of the first twenty-five years of the twentieth century, the London that had lost Nash's Regent Street and Rennie's Waterloo Bridge. Anyone who read the chapter on Portland stone saw London with new eyes. That, and a chapter in *The Perambulator in Edinburgh* (1926) on the 'lands', the decayed and elegant mansions where the aristocracy lived when Edinburgh was indeed a capital, was Bone's writing at its best.

Yet what Bone did was in his day perhaps less important than what Bone was. He moved in a group which might be described as 'the higher Bohemia'—a circle of writers and painters with style, wit, and a fondness of one another's society. Bone—plump, dapper, in dark suit, bow-tie, and bowler hat—would appear each night in three or four Fleet Street taverns, staying for fifteen minutes only and having one small drink. He was a good listener but his Glasgow accent and a slight stammer handicapped his stories in a noisy environment. His rooms in the Temple and his cat, Arthur, were known to writers in many parts of the English-speaking world. When his home in King's Bench Walk was bombed in the Second World War he settled into the Strand Palace Hotel to keep an eye on wartime London. Bone also became well known in Mencken's Baltimore. The *Baltimore Sun* employed the *Guardian* editorial service and Bone took its London correspondents into his pastoral care.

Bone's wife died in 1950, and yet she might well have survived him, for in December 1940 Bone was returning from the United States on the *Western Prince* when it was torpedoed. He was then sixty-eight and had undergone an operation in Baltimore. Nevertheless, he survived hours in an open boat and, on landing, filed a long descriptive piece. 'The line between wives and widows', he wrote, 'was very close that Saturday night'. He was made a Companion of Honour in 1947, after he had retired from the London editorship of the *Manchester Guardian* in 1945. For a while he continued as one of its directors, which he had become in 1919. He was made an honorary associate of the Royal Institute of British Architects (1927). Bone lived to celebrate his ninetieth birthday and received messages from the queen, President Kennedy, the prime minister, and Hugh Gaitskell. He died at his home, Abbots Holt, Tilford, Farnham, Surrey, a few months later, on 23 November 1962.

John Beavan, *rev.*

Sources D. Ayerst, *Guardian: biography of a newspaper* (1971) • *The Times* (24 Nov 1962) • private information (1981) • personal knowledge (1981) • *CGPLA Eng. & Wales* (1962)

Archives JRL, corresp. and MSS | NL Scot., corresp. with James Miller • U. Glas. L., letters to D. S. MacColl

Wealth at death £6336 12*s.* 3*d.*—save and except settled land: probate, 18 March 1963, *CGPLA Eng. & Wales* • £6750—limited to settled land: probate, 20 May 1963, *CGPLA Eng. & Wales*

Bone, Sir Muirhead (1876–1953), printmaker and draughtsman, was born on 23 March 1876 at 1A Hamilton Terrace West, Partick, Glasgow, the fourth of eight children of David Drummond Bone (1841–1911), journalist, and his wife, Elizabeth Millar Crawford (1847–1886), the daughter of a tailor. His parents were both Scottish and he was educated in the Glasgow City Schools, which he left at the age of fourteen; there he made friends with Francis Dodd, whose sister he later married. From 1891 to 1894 he served an apprenticeship in a small Glasgow architect's office; at the same time he attended Archibald Kay's evening classes at the Glasgow School of Art, later moving on to those of Francis Newbery. Bone gave up the idea of a career in architecture, however, and in 1897 took a small studio, joined the Glasgow Art Club, began to experiment with lithography, and first visited London. Two of his drawings of Glasgow were published by John Lane in the final volume of the *Yellow Book* (1897), following an introduction to Lane by John Buchan. The following year he acquired a printing press from D. Y. Cameron and learned etching.

Bone returned to London in 1899, taking a set of his first published prints, *Six Etchings of Glasgow*, with him and staying for a month. The set included *Shipbuilders*, *Whiteinch*, and *The Old Jail*, an impression of which was exhibited at the New English Art Club, lent by William Rothenstein. Bone contributed both illustrations and much of the text to the classic portrait of the city, *Glasgow in 1901*, written with his brother, James *Bone, and Archibald Hamilton Charteris. Published under the *nom de plume* James Hamilton Muir, this proved to be Bone's farewell to Glasgow: later that year he moved permanently to London.

Bone's first London exhibition was mounted by Oscar Wilde's executor, Robert Ross, at his Carfax Gallery in Ryder Street in 1902. It included etchings, drawings, and oil paintings, one of which—*Snowy Morning, Queen Margaret College, Glasgow* (1897)—is now in the Tate collection. Bone had lodgings in the Temple near Newgate prison, which was about to be demolished, and the Strand, which was then being relaid for the coronation procession: he made a series of drawings of both subjects, by night. The following summer he toured country towns, producing a portfolio of *Ten Drypoints* which was published by Obach & Co. in 1904; it included *Old and New Gaiety Theatres, Southampton* and *Chiswick*. An advance of £70 enabled him in 1903, after a five-year engagement, to marry the writer Gertrude Helena Dodd (1876–1962), daughter of Benjamin

Sir Muirhead Bone (1876–1953), self-portrait, 1908

Dodd, a Methodist minister; they moved to Thamescote, Chiswick Mall. They had two sons, the painter Stephen *Bone (1904–1958) who married the mural artist Mary Adshead (1904–1995), and Gavin Bone (1907–1942) who was also an artist. Neither was able to emulate their father's success.

This period also saw the foundation of the Society of Twelve, dedicated to promoting prints and drawings, of which Bone was secretary. The group included Augustus John, Edward Gordon Craig, David Young Cameron, William Nicholson, and William Strang. Later, William Orpen and Walter Sickert showed in the society's seven exhibitions which were held at Obach & Co. between 1904 and 1915. By this time Bone had established himself in London and he hit his stride with a succession of magnificent drypoints, on which his artistic reputation is built: *The Shot Tower* (1904), *Somerset House* (1905), *Demolition of St James's Hall, Interior* and *The Great Gantry, Charing Cross Station* (1906), and *The Ballantrae Road* (1907). A visit to Scotland produced his masterpiece, *Ayr Prison* (1905), a building at the end of Wellington Square, where he had had a studio in 1900. Such was Bone's standing that, in 1909, a catalogue of his 225 etchings and drypoints done between 1898 and 1907, compiled by Campbell Dodgson, keeper of prints and drawings at the British Museum, was published. Dodgson's continuation of the catalogue to 1916 was published in the *Print Collector's Quarterly* in 1922, and he maintained a manuscript list of the remainder of Bone's output.

Bone continued to travel, visiting Italy in 1910 and Holland in 1913. His most important drypoints of this period were *Rainy Night in Rome* (1913) and *Piccadilly Circus* (1915), both dramatically lit night scenes. A grimmer excursion followed: in 1916 William Rothenstein, a fellow member of the Society of Twelve, proposed a scheme for sending artists to the Front to record the First World War and Bone was the first to be appointed. He was sent to France in August 1916, and later joined the fleet. His drawings were published in ten issues of the *Western Front*, each described by C. E. Montague. Bone was a moving spirit behind the foundation of the Imperial War Museum and was appointed a trustee in 1920. He gave the museum 400 of his own drawings and watercolours, and set up a fund of £2000 to buy works by younger artists with the proceeds of his own sales.

By 1916 Muirhead Bone had made 356 etchings and drypoints, and although he continued to make memorable prints in the inter-war period, his output was reduced. He became a trustee of the Tate Gallery in 1920, and served until 1927. On a voyage to America in 1923 he met Joseph Conrad and made three drypoint portraits of him. His most important prints of this period, however, were *A Manhattan Excavation*, *Stockholm* (1923), and *A Spanish Good Friday* (1925). He illustrated a book by his brother James, *The London Perambulator* (1925), and travelled abroad extensively with his wife. They collaborated on several books, including *Children's Children* (1908), *Old Spain* (1936), and *Days in Old Spain* (1938). Bone made his final drypoint in 1939: the last phase of his work in printmaking saw two major works, *Windy Night Stockholm* (1935) and *Railway Sheds, Marseilles* (1937).

Bone became an important and perceptive patron, and an early buyer of work by Stanley Spencer and Mark Gertler. He was a supporter of Jacob Epstein and made drawings for the installation of his controversial sculpture *Rima* in Hyde Park: both Spencer and Epstein made portraits of Bone. He also gave David Bomberg the money to travel to Palestine in 1923. He continued to practise draughtsmanship, and in 1930 and 1931 had two large exhibitions of drawings of Spain at Colnaghi's. When the Second World War broke out, Bone was again the first war artist to be appointed. He worked principally for the Admiralty, but his most important work is the huge chalk and ink drawing *St Bride's and the City after the Fire, 29th December 1940* (Imperial War Museum, London) which measures 198 by 112 cm. He was also made a trustee of the National Gallery (1941–8) and reappointed to the Tate Gallery (1942–6).

In total, Bone made 478 etchings and drypoints, as well as a number of lithographs and thousands of drawings and watercolours. The most important collections of his work are those in the British Museum, the Hunterian Art Gallery, Glasgow (the Leonard Gow collection), the Imperial War Museum, the Tate collection, and the Boston Public Library, Massachusetts. During the 1920s he was an established and successful artist, and he grew wealthy during the etching boom which lasted until 1929. Kenneth Clark, who admired him both as a man and an artist, described him as 'one of the most honest, warm-hearted and unselfish men I have ever known' (*Another Part of the Wood: a Self-Portrait*, 1974, 59). He was among the greatest

British draughtsmen, and his images of cities, particularly buildings being built or demolished, display extraordinary technical skill.

Bone was knighted in 1937, and received honorary degrees from the universities of Oxford (DLitt), Glasgow, St Andrews, and Liverpool (LLD). He died of leukaemia at Grayflete, Ferry Hinksey, Oxford, on 21 October 1953, and was buried in Whitegate church, near Northwich, Cheshire. There is a memorial tablet to him in the crypt of St Paul's Cathedral. GORDON COOKE

Sources *The Times* (23 Oct 1953) · *DNB* · C. Dodgson, *Etchings and dry points by Muirhead Bone: a catalogue*, 1 (1909) · C. Dodgson, 'The later drypoints of Muirhead Bone (1908–1916)', *Print Collector's Quarterly*, 9 (1922), 173–200 · C. Dodgson, 'Etchings of Muirhead Bone, 1917–1939', MS, 1948, BM · private information (2004) · M. Bone, 'From Glasgow to London', *Artwork*, 5 (1929), 145–60 · P. Trowles, *Muirhead Bone: portrait of the artist* (1986) [exhibition catalogue, Crawford Centre for the Arts] · R. Ingleby, *Muirhead Bone, 1876–1953* (1990) [exhibition catalogue, Fine Art Society] · [G. Cooke], *Muirhead Bone, 1876–1953* (1984) [exhibition catalogue, Garton & Cooke, London, and C. & J. Goodfriend, New York] · K. M. Guichard, *British etchers, 1850–1940* (1977) · M. Harries and S. Harries, *The war artists* (1983) · b. cert. · m. cert. · d. cert. · *WWW, 1951–60*

Archives BL, corresp. with Sir Sydney Cockerell, Add. MS 52707 · Bodl. Oxf., corresp. with Gilbert Murray · Harvard U., Houghton L., letters to Sir William Rothenstein · NL Scot., letters to Richard Curle · NL Scot., corresp. with James Millar · Tate collection, corresp. with Lord Clark · U. Glas. L., letters to D. S. MacColl

Likenesses F. Dodd, ink drawing, 1907, Scot. NPG · M. Bone, self-portrait, drypoint, 1908, Hunterian Art Gallery, Glasgow [*see illus.*] · F. Dodd, drypoint, 1908, Hunterian Art Gallery, Glasgow · J. Epstein, bronze bust, 1916, Dundee Museum and Art Gallery · S. Bone, oils, *c*.1931, Dundee Museum and Art Gallery · F. Dodd, chalk drawing, 1931, NPG · F. Dodd, etchings, NPG · S. Spencer, pencil drawing, NPG

Wealth at death £10,341 8*s*. 6*d*.: probate, 26 Jan 1954, *CGPLA Eng. & Wales*

Bone, Robert Trewick (1790–*c*.1840). *See under* Bone, Henry Pierce (1779–1855).

Bone, Stephen (1904–1958), artist, writer, and broadcaster, was born on 13 November 1904 in Chiswick, Middlesex, the first of two sons of the engraver Sir Muirhead *Bone (1876–1953) and of Gertrude Helena Dodd (1876–1962), writer. His Scottish father's successful career as an engraver brought rigour rather than comfort to Stephen's childhood, which was overshadowed by his mother's staunch Methodist principles (he later considered himself simply a non-practising Christian). Presents, entertaining, and alcohol were banished; pencil and paper for drawing were deemed sufficient diversion at the house, Byways, Steep, near Petersfield, to which the family moved in 1913, when Stephen enrolled at Bedales School, a nearby progressive co-educational school. His relationship with his father was, and remained, of great importance to him. He encouraged Stephen's early artistic talent and brought Stanley Spencer to lodge at the house and teach him drawing. After leaving school in 1920 Bone travelled extensively with his father on the continent and then entered the Slade School of Fine Art in 1922. He left in 1924, disenchanted with the dry emphasis on draughtsmanship, and moved into his father's flat at 1 Knightsbridge, London. He illustrated books for his mother with wood-engravings (such as *Of the Western Isles*, which won a gold medal at the 1925 Paris Universal Exhibition) as well as the work of other writers. In 1926 he exhibited, jointly with Robin Guthrie and Rodney Burn, at the Goupil Gallery, and in 1928 he painted a mural decoration for Piccadilly Circus underground station.

Bone was a striking and conversationally gifted young man, very tall, at 6 feet 4 inches, with deep-set eyes and well-boned features. In 1927 he met Elisabet Waldenström, whose wealthy Swedish family became good patrons and established contacts for him in Sweden, which resulted in a large exhibition in Stockholm in 1937. His friendship with Elisabet was lifelong and affectionate; nevertheless it was (Sylvia) Mary *Adshead (1904–1995), a mural painter and Slade contemporary, whom he married in 1929. After their marriage they travelled extensively in the British Isles (Cornwall, Ireland, and Scotland) and on the continent (Greece, France, and Italy). Bone painted outdoors in all weathers on small panels. His bright, fresh, painterly landscapes sold easily at the exhibitions of the New English Art Club (where he was made a member in 1932) and at the Royal Academy, as well as at his solo exhibitions at the Redfern Gallery, London (1935); Heffers, Cambridge (1938); Victor Waddington, Dublin (1940); and the Leicester Galleries, London (1943). In 1939 he published *Albion, an Artist's Britain*, a travelogue illustrated with his own work.

In 1930 Stephen and Mary Bone moved to 43 Haverstock Hill, Hampstead, and seven years later moved further up the hill to no. 140. The first of their three children was born in 1931. With the outbreak of war Bone joined the camouflage organization, as an officer, in 1940 and moved with his family to 26 Portland Place, Leamington Spa, until 1946. In 1943 he was appointed official war artist attached to the Royal Navy. His work at this period (especially where he captured the dramatic effects of combat during the Normandy landings) is among his best and is now in the collection of the Imperial War Museum, London.

In 1945 Bone's career as a painter received a drastic setback when the Leicester Galleries declined to exhibit his work again. Feeling his style out of step with recent trends he made little attempt to show again elsewhere but, increasingly depressed, continued to paint, filling up his studio with unsold work. He moved back to 140 Haverstock Hill in 1946 and turned to journalism (he was art critic for the *Manchester Guardian* from 1948 and provided humorous work for the *Glasgow Herald* under the name of Luggage McLuggage). His fluency and versatility made him a natural broadcaster; he participated in BBC radio's *The Brains Trust* and *The Critics*, as well as the long-running television quiz programme *Animal, Vegetable or Mineral*. He also wrote and illustrated children's books with his wife. His later canvases were larger and sombre in tone and, in the main, painted in the studio. Bone died of cancer on 15 September 1958 at St Bartholomew's Hospital, London.

Examples of his work are in the Tate collection, the National Portrait Gallery, the City of London Museum, the Imperial War Museum, Graves Art Gallery, Sheffield, Tenby Museum, and the Government Art Collection.

SALLY HUNTER

Sources private information (2004) [son] · MSS, Bedales School archive · MSS, Slade School of Fine Art archive · unpublished material, Sally Hunter Fine Art, London · *CGPLA Eng. & Wales* (1959) · *DNB*

Archives BL, corresp. with Society of Authors, Add. MS 63214 | FILM BBC television archives, *Animal, vegetable or mineral* | SOUND BBC sound archives, broadcasts on radio and television during 1950s

Likenesses F. Dodd, oils, 1918, priv. coll. · M. Adshead, oils, *c.*1930, priv. coll.; repro. in *Stephen Bone* (1986) [exhibition catalogue, Sally Hunter and Patrick Seale Fine Art, London, 8–31 Oct 1986] · R. Shephard, oils, 1930, priv. coll. · S. Bone, self-portrait, oils, 1957, priv. coll.

Wealth at death £14,567 17*s.* 7*d.*: probate, 25 March 1959, *CGPLA Eng. & Wales*

Bone, William Arthur (1871–1938), chemist and fuel technologist, was born at Stockton-on-Tees on 19 March 1871, the eldest son of Christopher Bone, tea merchant, of Stockton, and his wife, Mary Elizabeth Hutchinson. He was educated at Middlesbrough high school, and subsequently at the Friends' school at Ackworth and Stockton high school, where the science master was a particularly inspiring teacher. As a boy, Bone spent much of his spare time at the Skinningrove ironworks, of which his uncle, T. C. Hutchinson, was manager. These two influences led him towards a scientific career.

Bone spent a year at the Leys School, Cambridge, before entering Owens College in the Victoria University, Manchester, in 1888. After graduating in chemistry three years later, he continued to work in Harold Baily Dixon's laboratory at Victoria University and his first paper, entitled 'The behaviour of ethylene on explosion with less than its volume of oxygen', was published in 1892 in the *Journal of the Chemical Society*, 61, 873–88. In the same year he won a scholarship and went to study for a year in Victor Meyer's laboratory at Heidelberg, where he worked on the indoxazen derivatives (1892–3). On his return to England he joined the staff of Battersea Polytechnic and eventually became head of the chemistry department for two years (1896–8). In 1898 he returned to Owens College as lecturer in chemistry and metallurgy and worked with W. H. Perkin (1860–1925) on various carboxylic acids. During the next ten years Bone continued researches in organic chemistry and published a number of papers with collaborators. In recognition of this work, he was elected a fellow of the Royal Society in 1905. However, his early interests then drew him back to study the chemistry of combustion, which became his life's work.

Bone was twice married. In 1893 he married Kate (*d.* 1914), daughter of Richard Hind, JP, who was twice mayor of Stockton; they had one son and two daughters. In 1916 he married Mabel Isabel (*d.* 1922), daughter of John Edward Liddiard, civil engineer, of Swindon. In 1906 Bone was appointed professor of fuel and metallurgy, and in 1910 first Livesey professor of coal, gas, and fuel industries at the University of Leeds. After six years of activity, he moved to London in 1912 to establish a department of fuel technology at the Royal College of Science, South Kensington, and became professor of chemical technology in the University of London. He made his home at St Albans, Hertfordshire. He was a fine experimentalist and founded a flourishing school of fuel technology at the Imperial College of Science and Technology. Most of his work was published with collaborators in the *Philosophical Transactions* and *Proceedings* of the Royal Society and the *Journal of the Chemical Society*. He summarized the main content of his research career in a lecture delivered to the Society of Chemical Industry in 1933: his early interests in iron smelting combined with the influence of Dixon at Victoria University enabled him to envisage combustion from both the technical and the scientific points of view.

Bone's early work on combustion was in support of some long neglected experiments of John Dalton which showed that in hydrocarbon combustion the hydrogen was not burned preferentially: during this work he investigated the explosive combustion of ethylene, acetylene, cyanogen, hydrogen, and pentane. His most important research was probably that on the slow combustion of the hydrocarbons, which began in 1902 and continued until the end of his career. As a result of these researches, he formulated a hypothesis, known as the hydroxylation theory of hydrocarbon combustion. Although later work on the reactions of hydrocarbons and oxygen showed that the theory was not completely representative, it was nevertheless a useful guide in the pioneering work which he carried out in the field, and he staunchly defended it.

While he was at Leeds, Bone carried his researches on gaseous combustion to high pressures and he continued this work at South Kensington in collaboration with D. M. Newitt and D. T. A. Townend; they eventually reached initial pressures of 750 atmospheres and explosion pressures as high as 7000 atmospheres. The combustion of carbon monoxide and the influence of water on its combustion became the subject of an elaborate series of investigations which illustrated Bone's exceptional pertinacity. He eventually proved that carbon monoxide could be burned without the intervention of any water vapour.

Quite early in his career Bone set about studying the catalytic combustion at surfaces of various kinds. At one period of this work (1908–12), along with C. D. McCourt, he developed the incandescent surface combustion process (to which the name Bonecourt was given). The process was adapted to crucible and muffle furnaces, to steam raising in multi-tubular boilers, and to other practical uses. He was also known for improvements which he introduced in methods for the accurate analysis of gases. From about 1930 onwards Bone and R. P. Fraser carried out the most remarkable series of photographic investigations of flame propagation which had been made up to that date. During the First World War Bone had carried out various investigations in chemical and fuel problems, and helped to train skilled chemists for munitions factories, but his pacifist ideals prevented him from doing any work on the use of poison gases.

Bone's early interest in blast furnace technology culminated in studies with his assistant, H. L. Saunders, on the chemical reactions within the blast furnace. He had a very wide knowledge of coal and its treatment and his advice was widely sought by industry. In 1919 he began to publish his researches on the constitution of coal. He proved that the benzenoid constituents increase with the maturity of the coal. His last book, written jointly with G. W. Himus, was entitled *Coal, its Constitution and Uses* (1936).

Bone was fiercely independent and forceful in expression. Rugged in appearance and taller than average, he had a positive and dominant personality which inevitably led him into controversies; nevertheless many of those who disagreed with him admired his character. He had wide interests and a memory richly stocked with knowledge. He was a staunch supporter of free trade.

Bone retired in 1936 but continued his supervision of the research on blast furnace reactions at Imperial College for some months. He received the Melchett medal of the Institute of Fuel in 1931, the medal of the Society of Chemical Industry in 1933, and was awarded the Davy medal of the Royal Society in the year of his retirement. His work was interrupted by illness towards the end of that year, and, after undergoing several operations, he died in a London hospital on 11 June 1938.

A. C. EGERTON, *rev.* K. D. WATSON

Sources G. I. Finch and A. C. Egerton, *Obits. FRS*, 2 (1936–8), 587–611 · *Nature*, 142 (1938), 62–3 · *The Times* (13 June 1938), 16d
Archives ICL, papers · priv. coll., letters
Likenesses photograph, repro. in Finch and Egerton, *Obits. FRS*
Wealth at death £43,400 2*s.* 2*d.*: probate, 2 Aug 1938, *CGPLA Eng. & Wales*

Boner, Charles (1815–1870), poet and journalist, was born at Weston, near Bath, on 29 April 1815, the second child and only son of Charles Antonius Boner (1759–1833), and his wife, Maria. Boner was educated at Bath from 1825 to 1827, and then at Tiverton grammar school from 1827 to 1829. From 1831 to 1837 he was tutor to the two elder sons of John Constable, the painter. Boner became a close friend of the Constables, organizing the painter's private affairs, and helping him research and write his lectures on landscape painting.

After his mother's death in 1839, Boner accepted an invitation to join Baron August Doernberg in Germany. The following spring he accompanied the baron to Regensburg, where he accepted the offer of a post in the family of the Prince Thurn und Taxis. Boner, who shared the prince's passion for art and literature, spent twenty years in the family of Thurn und Taxis, and became intimate with a large number of the prince's friends.

Boner travelled widely throughout Germany and Austria, and devoted himself to the study of the German language. In 1844 he was contracted by the London *Literary Gazette* for a series of articles on the German poets. Boner's facility in the language of his adopted country was widely admired, and his translations into English, notably of the German versions of Hans Christian Andersen's tales, *A Danish Story Book* (1846) and *The Dream of Little Tuck* (1848), were held to be remarkably faithful and idiomatic. In August 1845 Boner was introduced to Mary Russell Mitford, and the two writers embarked on a literary correspondence that was to last for a decade. A number of Mitford's letters to Boner, many offering constructive criticisms of Boner's work, are printed in Rosa Kettle's *Memoirs and Letters of Charles Boner* (1871).

While in the service of Thurn und Taxis, Boner came to love the forests and mountains of Bavaria, and his experiences as a naturalist and huntsman are recorded in *Chamois Hunting in the Mountains of Bavaria* (1853). Boner's *Memoirs* reveal that *Chamois Hunting* was scrutinized in manuscript by Mary Russell Mitford. In 1855 Boner composed the letterpress to *English Landscape Scenery*, a collection of engravings by John Constable. In the same year he translated Professor Masius's work from the German as *Studies of Nature*. Boner also turned his hand to verse, publishing *Cain* in 1855, *The New Dance of Death and other Poems* in 1857, and *Verses* in 1858.

Boner left Regensburg in 1860 and settled in Munich. In 1863 he travelled through Transylvania. A detailed account of his studies there, *Transylvania, its Products and People*, was published in 1865, and later translated into German. On 27 February 1865 Boner's daughter Marie married Professor Theodor Horschelt (1829–1871), the Munich painter who twelve years earlier had supplied the illustrations for *Chamois Hunting*. In September 1865 Boner left Munich for Vienna as special correspondent of the London *Daily News*. While in Vienna, he contributed articles to a number of other newspapers, including the *New York Tribune*. In 1867 he went to Salzburg to be present at the meeting of Napoleon III and the emperor of Austria, and wrote a very graphic description of the scene. He later attended the funeral in Trieste of the emperor Maximilian, of whom he compiled a memoir. Boner died in Professor Horschelt's house at Louisenstrasse 5, Munich, on 9 April 1870.

CHARLES BRAYNE

Sources *Memoirs and letters of Charles Boner*, ed. R. M. Kettle, 2 vols. (1871)

Bonfiglioli, Kyril Emanuel George [Cyril] (1928–1985), art dealer and writer, was born on 29 May 1928 at 9 Upperton Road, Eastbourne, the second among the three children of Emanuel Bonfiglioli (1886–1961), and his wife, Dorothy Annie Pallett (*c.*1900–1943). His father was an Italo-Slovene, born in Carniola, his mother English. A natural history specialist in antiquarian books, his father was a gifted linguist and a hard taskmaster. Cyril's habits of observation, wide-ranging interests, and visual and factual memory—so useful in art dealing, so entertaining in his writing—began in a home crowded with books, pictures, aquariums, vivariums, terrariums, and plants. Just before his fifteenth birthday in 1943 the death of his mother and only brother in an air raid caused lifelong emotional damage. His father's grief suggested that the 'wrong brother' had died. Survivor's guilt, vulnerability, and a sense of the sudden arbitrariness of events can be traced in Bonfiglioli's letters and fiction. Wit, humour, practical jokes, and a zest for knowledge and convivial company often masked this inner loss.

Educated first at elementary school, at eleven Cyril went to Eastbourne College and was evacuated with the school to Hitchin, where he and his sister were billeted separately. Cyril's schoolboy writing displays exotic vocabulary and Kiplingesque satire. At sixteen he went to work in London with a travel agent until in 1947 national service took him into the Royal Army Educational Corps and then to west Africa. During this period he met Elizabeth Mary Smith (*b.* 1924/5), a nurse in a London hospital. They married at Marylebone register office on 16 June 1950. Bonfiglioli re-enlisted in the regular army to support his wife, now living in Aberdeen, where their two sons, Aeneas and Roderick, were born. Elizabeth died in 1953 not long after Roderick's birth. Anxiously juggling child-care with army duties, Bonfiglioli moved nearer his father in Eastbourne, temporarily fostering out his boys.

In 1955, on the basis of formidable reading and study of languages, Bonfiglioli was accepted by Balliol College, Oxford, to read English. At this point Cyril became Kyril, his foreign name no longer a disadvantage. A new life began for him and his boys, first in a single room then sharing a small house in Cranham Street with Antony Harris, a journalist. Bon, as he was widely known, loved Balliol, cooking for and entertaining his new friends at home or in the pub next door. In his third year he met Margaret Ann Elizabeth Slater (*b.* 1935), a postgraduate student. Without a grant his hopes of doing research after obtaining his second-class honours degree in 1958 were dashed. Instead he collated and identified slides at the Ashmolean Museum for Professor Edgar Wind. He had been paying for groceries and booze through his finds among junk-shop paintings, cleaning them and selling them on at a profit. Enhanced knowledge and contacts already made helped him evolve into a picture dealer. In 1958 his first gallery opened in a Little Clarendon Street basement. He married Margaret Slater in 1959. Ten years of intensely varied activity and increasing responsibilities followed. Three children, Christopher, Catriona, and Amanda, were born.

Without capital himself, Bonfiglioli persuaded others to invest in his talents and opened a gallery at 13 Turl Street, Oxford, later becoming manager of Sanders of Oxford and the Drawda Hall bookshop. Opening nights of his regular exhibitions of old English watercolours caused queues along the Turl, and he sometimes sold a third of the stock at the private view. He authenticated works of art and gave valuable advice to purchasers. Exhibitions encouraging local artists and of Japanese prints and west African carvings and masks attracted press reviews. In Workers' Educational Association lectures in Abingdon he discussed and identified antiques, anticipating the BBC *Antiques Road Show*, and attracted more than 100 students. He also wrote for local papers on allied topics. In 1962 the family moved to 18 Norham Gardens, a house big enough to show large oil paintings of Dante's *Inferno* by Uttermohlen, astonishing cabinets and screens, large less saleable cases of stuffed birds, and to accommodate twelve lodgers. A freeze-up, a flood, and two house fires added to a sometimes chaotic domestic life: 'You married me for insecurity', he told Margaret.

Bonfiglioli's writing career began in 1964 when he became editor of the semi-defunct magazine *Science Fantasy*. As its circulation increased, editorials explored the genre with fans and writers; he discovered new authors and drew contributions from known ones such as Brian Aldiss. 'Blastoff', his first short story, written to fill a space, was anthologized by the American Judith Merril in *England Swings SF* (1968). Margaret's appreciation of a first chapter of what became *Don't Point that Thing at Me* encouraged him to continue his first novel. In the same year a Tintoretto *Resurrection* bought at a country sale, authenticated and sold to Colnaghis for £4000, was the peak of all finds and added another story to the many about him. This money offered new hope but was swallowed up in paying off loans. He nevertheless bought an ancient Rolls Royce. Divorced from Margaret in 1969, he moved with Judith Tod (*b.* 1936) to Yewbarrow, Lancashire, in 1970. *Don't Point that Thing at Me* contains a prophetic vignette: 'Lights were burning up at Yewbarrow and a strain of New Orleans jazz filtered down through the trees—old Bon would be settling down to an all-night poker and whisky session' (Bonfiglioli, 224).

Now that Bonfiglioli was cut off from Oxford sources of income, writing became a more urgent necessity. Work continued on *Don't Point that Thing at Me*, in which his new-minted protagonist, the Hon. Charlie Mortdecai, explores all aspects, from aristocratic to base, of being 'a proper Charlie'. He is a seasoned coward, ever quick of mind and foot, sometimes lustful, as he faces assaults from all directions probable and improbable. Charlie's rich, exotic, and dazzling wife Johanna is 'the leading enthusiast in torrid but comic sex scenes' (Bonfiglioli, 182), while his constant companion and trusty brother-in-arms, the much-loved Jock, is, as protector, rescuer, and cook, an anti-Jeeves: 'the best thug that money can buy' (ibid., 128).

In 1973 Bonfiglioli left the bailiffs of Lancashire and was living with Antony Harris in London when *Don't Point that Thing at Me* was published. By 1974, when it won the John Creasey memorial prize, he had moved to Jersey. There he wrote stories and letters to local papers and, as assistant editor of the Anglican *Jersey Pilot*, reviewed church services, signing himself Karl Bellamy. He considered Jersey an economical place for a drinker, but Ireland gave a tax-free welcome to writers. In Shercock, co. Cavan, he was developing an Irish voice when *Something Nasty in the Woodshed*, his second Mortdecai black comedy thriller, richly flavoured with Jersey culture and folklore, appeared in 1976. The *Irish Press* took his succinct and witty reviews (the funniest about a Barbara Cartland cookery book) and also short stories including 'The Gombeen Man'. This sombre moral fable of famine times appeared again in *New Irish Writing* edited by David Marcus. Poolbeg Press included 'As Simple as That' in the anthology *Visitor's Book* (1979).

From a somewhat isolated and cash-poor life among kind neighbours came spirited and affectionate letters to his children, to Tom Rosenthal and John Blackwell of Secker and Warburg, and to fellow writers, particularly Christopher Priest. Friends in England conspired to get Bonfiglioli an Arts Council grant. His first historical novel of the high seas—*All the Tea in China* (1978)—provides Charlie Mortdecai with Karli, a Dutch-Jewish ancestor whose narrative voice is reminiscent of Emanuel Bonfiglioli. Unheroic Charlie Mortdecai's misadventures pick up again in *After you with the Pistol* in 1979, completing a trilogy in the rueful Chandler-Wodehouse manner of the first two novels. After a brief visit to California, where he posed as a count, Bonfiglioli decided to leave damp Ireland and settle finally in Jersey. Compact and of medium height, he had a high forehead and brown hair and eyes. Mustachioed as a sergeant, clean-shaven as an art dealer, with an eyebrow quizzically raised and modulations of his voice he could express a wide variety of moods. Never a team player but quick on his feet, he prided himself on having been sabre champion of Scotland in his army days. Increasingly in poor health, changing addresses, and labouring to finish another Mortdecai novel, he finally found a home with a widowed friend, Barbara Cox, and was able to organize his papers.

Bonfiglioli left tantalizing fragments and notes for future books, including a Kiplingesque historical novel set in Afghanistan and *Lord Mortdecai, or, Cross my Art*, intended to complete the Mortdecai family tree by introducing Charlie's father, Bernard, first Baron Mortdecai, a man 'humourless to the point of mental deformity', and Charlie's hated inheriting brother Robin. A scintillating first chapter remains in which Charlie, now a lord, extracts the memoirs of his dead relatives from a booby-trapped safe.

On 3 March 1985 Kyril Bonfiglioli died in hospital in Jersey of cirrhosis of the liver and was cremated on 12 March. Members of his family along with Barbara Cox scattered his ashes in Bonne Nuit Bay, Jersey. In 1991 Blackspring Press published *The Mortdecai Trilogy* in paperback: 'you couldn't snuggle under the duvet with anything more disreputable and delightful', wrote Stephen Fry (cover blurb). Charlie returned to Oxford in Bonfiglioli's posthumous novel *The Great Mortdecai Moustache Mystery* (1999), its missing penultimate chapter supplied by Craig Brown.

MARGARET BONFIGLIOLI

Sources personal knowledge (2004) • private information (2004) • M. Bonfiglioli, *The Mortdecai ABC: Bonfiglioli reader* (2001) • b. cert. • m. cert. [Elizabeth Mary Smith]
Archives U. Reading L., papers | U. Reading L., Secker and Warburg papers | SOUND 'Something nasty in the bookshop', BBC Radio 3, 12 October 1997
Likenesses T. Heinman, photographs, U. Reading L.
Wealth at death left books, MSS, and pictures

Bonham, Francis Robert (1785–1863), political party agent, was born in London on 6 September 1785, he and an older sister Susan being the only surviving children (two sons and a daughter having died in infancy) of Francis Warren Bonham, landowner of Ballintaggart, co. Kildare, who settled in England, and his second wife, Dorothea Sophia Herbert, of Muckross, co. Kerry. After private tutoring Bonham went to Corpus Christi College, Oxford, where he took his BA in 1807. In 1808 he entered Lincoln's Inn; he was called to the bar in 1814 though he never practised.

In 1830 Bonham was elected for the government borough of Rye and the following year was active as tory assistant whip. Though defeated at Rye in 1831 he took part in the management of the 1832 general election. From 1832 he replaced William Holmes, who was out of the House of Commons from 1832 to 1837, as the Conservative Party's chief electoral expert. When Sir Robert Peel formed his first ministry in 1834 he appointed Bonham storekeeper of the ordnance. Bonham sat in the 1835–7 parliament as member for Harwich and assistant whip, losing his seat at the next general election. Though making no attempt to stand for parliament in 1841, he was again appointed storekeeper of the ordnance in Peel's second ministry. He resigned this post in 1845 as a result of a parliamentary inquiry into alleged improper acquisition of railway shares. He continued nevertheless to act as unpaid organizer and adviser to the Peelites up to 1852. In 1853, through the good offices of W. E. Gladstone and other Peelites in Lord Aberdeen's government, he was rescued from penury by an appointment as commissioner of income tax; he retired through ill health some time before his death.

Bonham was a founder-member of the Carlton Club, from where he carried out most of his work. His detailed and systematic accumulation of electoral information provided him with an unsurpassed knowledge of constituencies and candidates and greatly contributed to the efficient Conservative organization which triumphed in 1841. Modest, discreet, industrious, and loyal, Bonham enjoyed the friendship, affection, and trust not only of Peel but of many other leading members of the party. His career marks an important stage in the development of party management in the post-1832 era, when legal registration of voters constituted a new factor in electoral calculations.

Bonham died unmarried on 26 April 1863 at 13 Albert Terrace, the Knightsbridge home he shared with his sister, and was buried on 2 May 1863 at Brompton cemetery. His voluminous political correspondence was purchased from her by Peel's literary executors, the fifth Earl Stanhope and Edward, Viscount Cardwell, and destroyed except for the two volumes incorporated in the Peel papers, now in the British Library, and letters of his own retained by Lord Stanhope.

NORMAN GASH, *rev.*

Sources N. Gash, 'F. R. Bonham: Conservative "political secretary", 1832–47', *EngHR*, 63 (1948), 502–22 • N. Gash, 'Bonham and the conservative party', *Pillars of government and other essays on state and society, c.1770 – c.1880* (1986), 108–35 • N. Gash, *Politics in the age of Peel*, 2nd edn (1977) • Gladstone, *Diaries* • d. cert.
Archives BL, political corresp., Add. MSS 40399–40429, *passim*; 40485–40603, *passim*; 40616–40617 | BL, corresp. with W. E. Gladstone, Add. MS 44110 • BL, Peel MSS • St Deiniol's Library, letters to duke of Newcastle
Wealth at death under £600: probate, 1 June 1863, *CGPLA Eng. & Wales*

Bonham, Sir (Samuel) George, first baronet (1803–1863), colonial governor, was born at Faversham, Kent, on 7 September 1803, the son of Captain George Bonham (*d.* 1810) of the naval service of the East India Company and his second wife, Isabella Baines (*d.* 1852), only daughter of Robert Woodgate of Dedham, Essex. He had one sister, Isabella, who married Ferdinand, count d'Oultremont, of Belgium. On 16 June 1846 he married Ellen Emelia (*d.* 1859), eldest daughter of Thomas Barnard of the East India Company; they had one son.

In 1837, after a period of service with the East India Company, Bonham was appointed governor of the incorporated settlement of Prince of Wales Island, Singapore, and Malacca. He held this post for ten years, during which he acquired a measure of knowledge of the Chinese language, customs, and habits; later in his career he was said to prefer officials who had not learned the language, believing that the 'study of Chinese warped the intellect and undermined the judgement' (Coates, 83). On 20 March 1848 he was appointed by Palmerston to succeed Sir John Davis as governor of Hong Kong and her majesty's plenipotentiary and superintendent of trade in China.

The issue of British entry into Canton (Guangzhou) had not been resolved during Davis's governorship and was to dominate Bonham's time in office. Davis had reached an agreement with the imperial commissioner at Canton, Qiying, for the British to be given admittance to Canton in 1849; however, Qiying had been replaced in 1848 by the ferociously anti-foreign Xu Guangjin, who rebuffed Bonham's attempts to negotiate the preliminary arrangements for British entry. The British government was unwilling to force the issue at this time, and Palmerston's instructions to Bonham to let the matter stand in abeyance were taken by the Chinese as a sign of their victory in the matter. Warnings to the emperor's court that British actions were taken from a position of strength, not weakness, were greeted with derision in Peking (Beijing).

In Hong Kong itself Bonham's governorship met with mixed reviews. The German missionary and official Ernst Johann Eitel (1838–1908) considered him a 'model Governor, the first really popular and successful one of the Colony's rulers' (Eitel, 287), while recognizing that there were those in the Hong Kong community who viewed him as 'a useless governor, purely ornamental, highly decorated and extravagantly paid' (ibid., 286). His relationships with his subordinates were seldom easy, as he had a tendency to bully them: with Rutherford Alcock and his own eventual successor, John Bowring, then consul in Canton, his relations were particularly tense. In 1851 he was made a KCB for his services in China, and the following year was created a baronet. In April 1853 he led the first foreign mission to meet the Taiping insurgents, securing from them rights for foreigners to enter their territory and trade there; he recommended that the British government maintain a position of neutrality towards the rebels, rather than support the Manchu government, as was being urged in some quarters.

Bonham retired from his appointments in China on 12 April 1854 and returned to England, where he died at the Great Western Railway Hotel, Paddington, on 8 October 1863. His son, George Francis, of the diplomatic service, succeeded to the baronetcy. K. D. REYNOLDS

Sources I. C. Y. Hsü, *The rise of modern China*, 5th edn (1995) • P. D. Coates, *The China consuls: British consular officers, 1843–1943* (1988) • E. J. Eitel, *Europe in China* (1895); repr. (1983) • C. Hibbert, *The dragon wakes: China and the West, 1793–1911* (1970) • Burke, *Peerage* (1939) • *FO List* (1860)

Archives U. Durham, Grey MSS

Wealth at death under £120,000: will with a codicil, 12 Nov 1863, *CGPLA Eng. & Wales*

Bonham, John Henry (1948–1980), musician, was born at 84 Birchfield Road, Redditch, Worcestershire, on 31 May 1948, the eldest son of John Henry (Jack) Bonham and his wife, Joan Isobel Sargent. Bonham had a younger brother, Michael, and a sister, Debbie. Bonham's early attraction to percussion proved hard for his parents to ignore: they bought him a snare drum when he was ten, and a full, second-hand kit when fifteen. He took pride in teaching himself to drum, influenced initially by American soul records and later by the Who's Keith Moon and by Ginger Baker, later of the band Cream. Leaving school at sixteen, he initially worked with his father as a builder, but despite parental misgivings he soon turned to drumming and joined a succession of bands including the Crawling King Snakes, whose singer was Robert Plant. In 1965 he met Pat (*née* Phillips), whom he married on 19 February 1966. In 1967 he briefly played for Plant's new group, Band of Joy. Bonham, often known by his nickname Bonzo, was earning a reputation as the strongest, loudest drummer on the circuit, hitting his drums with such intensity that the skins frequently broke.

By 1968 Bonham was earning a decent wage drumming for the American folk-singer Tim Rose. That summer he received several offers of work, but the most persuasive was that of his friend Plant, who had himself just agreed to be vocalist in a group being assembled by the highly regarded guitarist Jimmy Page. Page's previous band, the innovative Yardbirds, had recently split up. The ensemble was completed by bass player John Paul Jones, and managed by the Yardbirds' most recent manager, Peter Grant. Since the Yardbirds were still contracted to play several gigs, the New Yardbirds set off immediately to play in Scandinavia. The band quickly realized that they needed a new name, and most sources agree that 'going down like a lead zeppelin' had originally been the predicted fate of an earlier, abortive band, though conflicting stories credit the joke first either to Keith Moon or to the Who's bass player, John Entwhistle.

Led Zeppelin recorded their first, eponymous, album at the Olympic Studios in Barnes, London, in November 1968. Produced, like all the band's recordings, by Page, it covered several American blues tunes, newly arranged. Seven more studio albums followed: *Led Zeppelin II*, released in October 1969; *Led Zeppelin III*, released in October 1970; a fourth, untitled, album, released in November 1971; *Houses of the Holy*, released in March 1973 (on which Bonham was credited as primary writer of 'The ocean'); *Physical Graffiti*, released in February 1975; *Presence*, released in March 1976; and *In Through the Out Door*, released in August 1979. There was also a live album, *The Song Remains the Same*, recorded live at Madison Square Garden, New York, in July and August 1973, and released in September 1976. Most of the recordings were made in various studios in the USA, Britain, and Europe, but from 1970 the band often used mobile recording facilities at the Hampshire mansion Headley Grange.

Led Zeppelin became one of the most successful rock bands of the era, earning huge sums thanks partly to the then uniquely favourable contract that Peter Grant had negotiated for them with Atlantic Records in 1968. In 1974 the band launched their own label, Swan Song, as an offshoot of Atlantic. Led Zeppelin came to define a 'heavy' style of rock (its many imitators were often known as 'heavy metal'), an essential element of which was the driving rhythm provided by Bonham, using the heaviest sticks (or 'trees') on his Ludwig drum kits. Perhaps the finest examples of his style were the solo on *Led Zeppelin II*'s 'Moby Dick' and the crushing beat recorded through a single microphone on a brand new kit set up in the great hall of Headley Grange, which opens 'When the levee breaks', the traditional blues number that concluded the fourth album. The latter has been frequently sampled for use on later recordings.

Led Zeppelin's reputation rested at least as much on their lavish live performances as on their records. Between December 1968 and July 1980 the group made eleven tours of the USA, four of Europe, two of Japan, and one of Australasia. The decadent lifestyle of rock musicians in this era, later something of a cliché, was always bound to appeal to a gutsy character like Bonham. The band's antics, especially on the road, were the stuff of rumour and, ultimately, legend: tales of drug and alcohol abuse, sexual experimentation, and occult interests followed them around as intently as the girls who swarmed around them after every concert. While the wilder stories depend wholly on the traditional mystique surrounding artistic prowess, charisma, and wealth, it has been widely recounted that Led Zeppelin binged on the stimulants that came with success, egged on by the group's archetypally boisterous road manager Richard Cole, with whom Bonham shared a taste for knockabout humour and fisticuffs. When hotel rooms were wrecked, Bonham and the road crew were generally the perpetrators.

But Bonham had a split personality. Its more settled side was represented by his wife and their two children: Jason, born in 1968, and Zoë, born in 1975. Bonham forwent the tax exile of the other band members to be present at Zoë's birth. The family lived in bucolic comfort at Old Hyde Farm, Worcestershire; there Bonham kept his growing collection of cars, which already numbered twenty-one by the end of 1970. In the bosom of his family, Bonham was the genial country squire; away from them, however, and especially during Led Zeppelin's long sojourns in California, his fragile personality proved unable to cope with the sheer indulgence allowed him, and he used drink and drugs to excess. In February 1978 he received a fine and suspended sentence for his part in a violent incident at a concert in Oakland, California, in the previous July. In the mean time, tax exile and a series of mishaps and tragedies, culminating in the death of Robert Plant's son from a viral infection in July 1977, were robbing Led Zeppelin of their momentum. At a concert in Nuremberg on 27 June 1980 Bonham collapsed: officially this was put down to exhaustion, but it is known that he was using heroin by this time. The band gathered for a rehearsal for a forthcoming European tour at Page's new mansion at Mill Lane, Berkshire, on 24 September 1980. Bonham drank steadily throughout the day until he passed out and was put to bed, where he was found dead the next day. His funeral was held at Rushock, Worcestershire, on 10 October and he was cremated; his wife survived him.

Marios Costambeys

Sources S. Davis, *Hammer of the gods: the Led Zeppelin saga* (1985) · R. Yorke, *Led Zeppelin: the definitive biography* (1993) · R. Cole and R. Trubo, *Stairway to heaven: Led Zeppelin uncensored* (1992) · D. Lewis, *Led Zeppelin: a celebration* (1991) · m. cert. [John Henry Bonham and Joan Isobel Sargent] · m. cert.

Archives FILM BFI NFTVA, performance footage | SOUND BL NSA, documentary recordings · BL NSA, performance recording

Likenesses photographs, 1970–79, Hult. Arch.

Wealth at death £856,498: administration, 18 May 1981, *CGPLA Eng. & Wales*

Bonham, Thomas (*c.*1564–*c.*1628), physician and surgeon, about whose early life nothing is known, matriculated at St John's College, Cambridge, during the Easter term of 1581, which places his birth probably between 1563 and 1565. As a sizar, he most likely came from a relatively humble family. In 1584 he earned a bachelor's degree (which he took the trouble to incorporate at Oxford in the same year), and continued for the master's degree, which he completed in 1588. He apparently also earned a medical doctorate at Cambridge, for his later claim to one was never disputed; he therefore probably graduated in medicine in the middle to later 1590s, and certainly before he signed himself 'in Medic: Doct.' in 1602, at the end of a laudatory Latin poem prefaced to a treatise on the king's evil by the surgeon William Clowes the elder.

Despite being a physician, Bonham took the side of the London surgeons in their disputes with the College of Physicians. His poem celebrated the work of one of the most prominent surgeons of London; in early 1605 he signed the unsuccessful parliamentary petition of the Barber–Surgeons' Company asking for the right to administer internal remedies. But with the strengthening of the College of Physicians in the same years, Bonham presented himself to its censors on 6 December 1605 for the examination required for membership of that body. For whatever reason, he failed to answer the censors' questions to their satisfaction. Bonham underwent examination again on 14 April 1606, but this time his replies to questions were declared 'not pertinent'. The censors went further in making an example of his disobedience: because he had practised without membership in or licence of the college, the censors fined Bonham £5, and threatened him with imprisonment if he did not obey them. Bonham refused. On 3 October the censors recorded that Bonham had several times ignored their summons to appear before them to answer charges that he was continuing to practise without their permission, and that he would be arrested and fined £10. On 7 November Bonham and his lawyer, Dr Smith, appeared before the censors. When asked by the college's president, Henry Atkins, if he had come to be re-examined or to make satisfaction, Bonham defiantly put on his hat and said that he practised and would continue to practise without seeking the permission of the college and without obeying the president, since they had no power over graduates of the universities. Standing on recently reiterated legal precedent, the president and censors sent Bonham to Newgate prison for contempt, to be held at their pleasure.

Bonham's lawyer managed to free him from Newgate by entering a writ of habeas corpus before the court of common pleas on 13 November. After some delays due to other business, the college officers met on 1 May 1607, at the home of Lord Chancellor Ellesmere, with a committee of royal judges, which unanimously supported a rigorous interpretation of the college's statutes. The censors also gathered further evidence of Bonham's continuing practice in London, including his work with one Mrs Paine of Aldersgate Street. Subsequently, in Trinity term of 1608, the censors sued Bonham for twelve months' illicit practice (or a total of £60), with Attorney-General Hobart pleading their case before the court of king's bench. Bonham in turn returned to common pleas in the Michaelmas term of 1608, asking for £100 damages against the college for trespass against his person and wrongful imprisonment. About 3 February 1609 king's bench found Bonham guilty of illicit practice, imposed the fine, and sent him to prison. (One month later his alleged accomplice, Mrs Paine, was also fined £10 by the college and imprisoned.) Bonham nevertheless managed to become a member of the Barber–Surgeons' Company and got Archbishop Bancroft to write a letter on 3 October 1609 strongly desiring the college to release him. The college replied that it would let Bonham out only if he acknowledged its authority and dropped his suit. He did not.

Bonham's suit in common pleas against the college was finally decided in late February 1610. The decision of the justices set Bonham free, and fined the college £40. Chief Justice Edward Coke declared that because the College of Physicians was both judge and prosecuting body in cases brought before it, the parliamentary acts confirming the powers granted to it by charter were void:

> it appears in our books, that in many cases, the common law will controul Acts of Parliament … for when an Act of Parliament is against common right and reason, or repugnant, or impossible to be performed, the common law will controul it, and adjudge such Act to be void.

Coke may have intended only to overturn the college's royal patent, but his language allowed eighteenth-century Americans to interpret his words as giving the courts jurisdiction over parliament, helping to create the idea of a powerful supreme court. Lord Chancellor Ellesmere, Sir Francis Bacon, and King James were all furious with Coke's decision.

On 9 July 1611 Bonham incorporated his MD at Oxford, and on 8 August 1614 he entered Gray's Inn. As late as 1617 a page of the queen, Michael Silvester, was requesting the half of Bonham's fine due to the king. Thomas Bretnor dedicated his translation and enlargement of Angelo Sala's *Opiologia, or, A Treatise Concerning … Opium* (1618), a work advocating chemical preparations, to Bonham (and also to Nicholas Carter). Bonham continued to practise medicine in London, signed a parliamentary petition of the surgeons against a new charter for the College of Physicians in 1621, served as an assistant in the Barber–Surgeons' Company, and apparently sponsored surgical experiments in his home. Bonham died in the late 1620s; his servant in medicine and surgery, Edward Poeton, edited and published Bonham's well-regarded papers on medicines as *The Chyrurgians Closet, or, An Antidotarie Chyrurgicall* (1630), dedicated both to Frances, countess of Exeter, and to the London Barber–Surgeons' Company. Bonham's will, made on 16 July 1625, mentions his wife, Dorothy, and their son and daughter.

HAROLD J. COOK

Sources annals, RCP Lond. • RCP Lond., archives • *Dr Bonham's case* (1610), 8 Coke Report 107a, 77 ER 638 • *College of Physicians' case* (1609), 2 Brownlow and Goldesborough 255, 123 ER 928 • *CSP dom.*, 1611–18 • W. Clowes, *A right frutefull and approoved treatise, for the artificiall cure of that malady called in Latin struma, and in English the evill, cured by the kinges and queenes of England* (1602) • C. Goodall, *The Royal College of Physicians of London founded and established by law* (1684) • A. Sala, *Opiologia, or, A treatise concerning the nature, properties, true preparation and safe use and administration of opium*, trans. T. Bretnor (1618) • Foster, *Alum. Oxon.* • Venn, *Alum. Cant.* • J. Foster, *The register of admissions to Gray's Inn, 1521–1889, together with the register of marriages in Gray's Inn chapel, 1695–1754* (privately printed, London, 1889) • R. Berger, 'Doctor Bonham's case: statutory construction or constitutional theory', *University of Pennsylvania Law Review*, 117 (1969), 521–45 • H. J. Cook, 'Against common right and reason: the College of Physicians versus Dr Thomas Bonham', *American Journal of Legal History*, 29 (1985), 301–22 • C. M. Gray, 'Bonham's case reviewed', *Proceedings of the American Philosophical Society*, 116 (1972), 35–58 • T. F. T. Plucknett, 'Bonham's case and judicial review', *Harvard Law Review*, 40 (1926), 30–70 • S. E. Thorne, '*Dr Bonham's case*', *Law Quarterly Review*, 54 (1938), 543–52 • will, GL, MS 9051/6, fol. 194v

Bonham-Carter. For this title name *see* Carter, Mark Raymond Bonham, Baron Bonham-Carter (1922–1994).

Bonhôte [*née* Mapes], **Elizabeth** (1744–1818), writer, was born at Earsham Street, Bungay, Suffolk, and baptized on 11 April 1744 in St Mary's Church, Bungay, the elder of two surviving children of James Mapes (*bap.* 1714, *d.* 1794), baker and grocer of Bungay, and his wife, Elizabeth, *née* Galliard (*d.* 1789). Her first work, a novel entitled *Hortensia, or, The Distressed Wife*, was published anonymously in 1769. On 13 October 1772 she married Daniel Bonhôte (1748/9–1804), a solicitor of Bungay, later an under-sheriff of Suffolk and captain of the 2nd company of Bungay Volunteers. In that same year she published her second novel *The Rambles of Mr Frankly, Published by his Sister* (2 vols.). A moralizing tale influenced by Laurence Sterne's *Sentimental Journey* (1768), it describes how Frankly learns contentment from observing the lives of various classes of people during strolls in Hyde Park. Immediately popular, it was translated into German at Leipzig, later published in Dublin and Paris, and reprinted with additions by the Minerva Press in 1797. Illness following the birth of her three children between 1773 and 1777 prevented further publications from appearing until *Olivia, or, The Deserted Bride* in 1787. Her next work, and another best-seller, was an educational guide, *The Parental Monitor* (2 vols. published by subscription, 1788): it consists of a series of short, moral essays addressed to children, and enlivened by quotations and illustrative stories. It ran to three editions, and was published in Dublin and posthumously in the USA.

In total, Elizabeth Bonhôte published seven fictional works, all of which reflected the contemporary taste for novels of sentiment and sensibility, combining 'a reaction against coarseness, preoccupation with conventional morality and a strong bent towards emotionalism' (MacCarthy, 31–64). They appealed to a growing female readership catered for by the circulating libraries. In particular *Darnley Vale, or, Emelia Fitzroy* (1789) and *Ellen Woodley* (1790) were favourably noticed in the *Monthly Review* (February 1790, 223; July 1790, 351). In 1791 her husband purchased the site of Bungay Castle. Its ruined grandeur and fabled history appealed to her imagination and inspired her final novel, a Gothic romance entitled *Bungay Castle* (1796). Featuring the popular ingredients of a handsome hero imprisoned in a dungeon, a fair heroine of acute sensibility, secret passages, and ghostly hauntings, it confirmed her position as one of the Minerva Press's best-selling authors. In 1804 her husband died during a residence at Bury. Throughout her life she had published occasional verse and her last production was the anonymous *Feeling, or, Sketches from Life: a Desultory Poem* (1810). She died at Bungay on 11 June 1818 aged seventy-four. Her generous will left dwelling houses, a baking office, and shop in Bungay, and approximately £3500 in cash and annuities. No portrait of her is known, and little has been recorded about her appearance or personality; but her husband in his will dated 1792 referred to the 'excellency of her head and heart', a tribute which seems justly confirmed by her writings. CHRISTOPHER REEVE

Sources E. Mann, *Old Bungay* (1934); repr. (1984), 139–40, 214–15 · E. A. Goodwyn, *Elegance and poverty: Bungay in the eighteenth century* (1989), 90–98 · C. Reeve, 'When Bungay Castle was a stronghold', *Suffolk Fair* (April 1985), 48–9ff. · D. Blakey, *The Minerva Press, 1790–1820* (1939) · L. Orr, *A catalogue checklist of English prose fiction, 1750–1800* (1979) · B. G. MacCarthy, *The later women novelists, 1744–1818* (1947), 31–64 · J. M. S. Tompkins, *The popular novel in England, 1770–1800* (1932); repr. (1969), 51, 121, 139, 163, 225, 228 · Blain, Clements & Grundy, *Feminist comp.* · review of *The parental monitor, Monthly Review*, 79 (1788), 173 · review of *Darnley Vale, Monthly Review*, new ser., 1 (1790), 223 · review of *Ellen Woodley, Monthly Review*, new ser., 2 (1790), 351 · *GM*, 1st ser., 74 (1804), 1246 [obit. of Daniel Bonhôte] · *GM*, 1st ser., 88/2 (1818), 88 · parish registers, St Mary's, Bungay · parish registers, Holy Trinity, Bungay · parish register (burial), St Mary's, Thwaite

Wealth at death approx. £5000–£6000; £3500 in cash and annuities; dwelling-houses, baking office, and shop in Bungay; cottage and baking office in Earsham, Norfolk: will, Canterbury, Ledger 33, fol. 3, 680

Boniface [St Boniface] (**672x5?–754**), archbishop of Mainz, missionary, and martyr, is unusually well documented for a man of the early eighth century. One life was written about him by Willibald in Mainz before 769, and other lives followed in the course of the eighth and ninth centuries. He was also the major figure in the lives of numerous of his followers, notably in those of Sturm of Fulda and Gregory of Utrecht. More important for an in-depth understanding of the saint is that a large number of letters written by, to, and about him were gathered together, apparently at the behest of his pupil and successor at Mainz, Archbishop Lul. Among other works left by Boniface are a grammatical treatise and some riddles, while he is also known to have written a treatise on metrics. In addition, canons of several church councils in which he played a leading role have also survived. These sources are not without difficulties, since Boniface was a controversial figure, and some of the evidence relating to his career is undoubtedly skewed by the propaganda of both his supporters and his detractors. Moreover, even among his supporters there were differences of opinion, since rival factions, notably in Mainz, Fulda, and Utrecht, tried to claim Boniface as their own, as is apparent from the surviving hagiography relating to the martyr and his disciples. Nevertheless, the sum total of the evidence for Boniface makes him more accessible as an object of study than most other figures of the early middle ages.

Boniface's correspondence The collections which include the letters of Boniface shed light not just on the martyr himself, but also on a wide range of aspects of Anglo-Saxon and continental society in the late seventh and eighth centuries. The letters are essentially preserved in three manuscripts of the eighth and ninth centuries. Study of these collections suggests that there was once a *Collectio pontificia*, a collection of papal letters addressed to and from Boniface, as well as a separate *Collectio communis*, a more general collection of the saint's correspondence. To these were added a further collection of letters associated with Boniface's disciple Lul, as well as other miscellaneous letters from Anglo-Saxon England, several of them written by or sent to Aldhelm of Malmesbury.

Altogether there are 150 letters, of which 38 were written by Boniface, 32 were addressed to him, and a further 14 were written in support of him. In addition there are 15 letters by Lul and 24 written to him. Of obvious importance for reconstructing Boniface's career are the 15 papal letters (including 2 forgeries) written to him, and the 12 letters written on his behalf, by popes Gregory II (*r.* 715–31), Gregory III (*r.* 731–41), Zacharias (*r.* 741–52), and Stephen II (*r.* 752–7), as well as the 4 letters which Boniface himself addressed to popes Zacharias and Stephen. Equally interesting, however, is the correspondence of Boniface and Lul with other Anglo-Saxons. These letters reveal a network of family and professional connections and shed considerable light on the English church of the early eighth century, most notably on the piety and intellectual and cultural achievements of a number of Anglo-Saxon nunneries. There are 8 letters to Anglo-Saxon abbesses and nuns, and a further 4 from them. More specifically there are letters to and from Abbess Eadburh of

Thanet, from whom Boniface requested a copy of the epistles of St Peter written in gold; from Abbess Eangyth, and to and from the latter's daughter Bugga; and above all to and from the missionary's relative Leoba, who was to follow Boniface to the continent, where she became first abbess of the saint's foundation of Tauberbischofsheim. According to Rudolf of Fulda, who wrote the life of Leoba in the 830s, Boniface wanted the abbess to be buried in the same tomb as himself. In the event, Leoba was buried initially at Fulda, although not in the same tomb as the martyr, but was later translated to nearby Petersberg.

Early life to 716 Boniface's early years are known only from hagiography. He was probably born between 672 and 675 and apparently in the neighbourhood of Exeter: later medieval tradition named his birthplace more precisely, and apparently without justification, as Crediton. His original name was Wynfreth. After an early illness he was placed, according to his earliest hagiographer, on his own insistence and despite paternal opposition, as a *puer oblatus* ('child oblate') in the monastery of Ad-Escancastre (Exeter), which was then ruled by Abbot Wulfhard. Subsequently he transferred to the monastery of Nhutscelle (Nursling), near Southampton, where Wynberht was abbot, and where he completed his education in grammar, rhetoric, and the scriptures. Thereafter he was appointed head of the monastic school and his teaching there is presumably reflected in his treatise on grammar. On reaching the age of thirty, the traditional age for ordination, he also became a priest. Following a rebellion in Wessex, Wynfreth was sent as an envoy to Archbishop Berhtwald by a synod held, probably at Brentford in 705, by King Ine and his leading churchmen.

First years on the continent, 716–722 Despite his intellectual and diplomatic successes Wynfreth resolved to become a missionary on the continent. In making such a choice he may have known of the work of evangelization which had already been carried out in Frisia by Bishop Wilfrid of York, and of the mission to the same region begun in 690 by another Anglo-Saxon, Willibrord. Wynfreth left for Frisia in 716. The year was not a propitious one, for, in the aftermath of the death of the Frankish mayor of the palace, Pippin II, in 714, war had broken out between Pippin's son and successor, the eponymous founder of the Carolingian dynasty, Charles Martel, and the Frisian king, Radbod. As a result of this Radbod had turned against Christian communities in his kingdom, and against Willibrord, who had come to be closely associated with Charles. Although Wynfreth did manage to make contact with Radbod, he realized that he would achieve little in the circumstances, and returned to Nursling. There, on the death of Wynberht, he was elected abbot, but he refused the appointment and instead set off for Rome in 718, with a letter of introduction from Bishop Daniel of Winchester, who found an alternative abbot of Nursling in the person of Stephen. Wynfreth was to continue to turn to Daniel for advice, even when he was himself on the continent.

Wynfreth was not the first Anglo-Saxon missionary to travel to Rome: both Wilfrid and Willibrord had done so, the latter specifically to obtain approval for his work of evangelization. Nevertheless, Wynfreth was to develop a particularly close link with the Holy See, and especially with popes Gregory II and Gregory III. Having reached Rome in 719 he was examined by Gregory II; and on 15 May 719 the pope granted him a commission to preach to the pagans. It seems that on the previous day the pope had conferred on Wynfreth the name of Boniface, from Boniface, the martyr of Tarsus, whose relics had been brought to Rome. Thereupon, as Boniface, Wynfreth travelled north, via the court of the Lombard king, Liutprand (*r.* 712–44), to Bavaria, and thence to Thuringia and on to Frisia, much of which had been taken over by Charles Martel following the death of Radbod in 719. Boniface now joined forces with Willibrord in Utrecht, working in the neighbouring region for the following two years. In 721, however, when Willibrord offered to make him *chorepiscopus* (a suffragan bishop, with no diocesan centre, working in a rural, often missionary, zone), Boniface declined and resolved to carry out the commission conferred on him by Gregory II. He set off—via the nunnery of Pfalzel outside Trier, if traditions relating to the childhood of Gregory of Utrecht are to be believed—for Amöneburg in the Lahngau. There he preached with some success against the supposedly syncretist Christianity of the local rulers Dettic and Devrulf, and of their followers.

In 722 Boniface sent his companion Bynnan to Rome, and on receiving an invitation to the Holy See from the pope he set off, via Francia and Burgundy, on his second visit to the papacy. On his arrival he was again examined by Gregory II; and on St Andrew's day (30 November) he was raised to the episcopate, becoming a missionary bishop with no fixed diocese—an unusual, but by no means unprecedented, appointment, which was well suited to the needs of the church in an area which had as yet not been subjected to a diocesan structure. Thereafter he returned north, with letters of recommendation from the pope addressed to Charles Martel and to the leaders of Thuringia.

Missionary work in Germany, 723–741 Having paid his compliments to Charles, Boniface travelled on to Hesse, where he is said to have felled a great oak associated, according to Willibald, with the Roman god Jove (and presumably to be equated with the Germanic deity Thor), at Gaismar, near Fritzlar. Subsequently he turned his attention to Thuringia, where Christianity had supposedly collapsed during the period of rule of Theobald and Heden in the face of aggression from the pagan Saxons. Among Boniface's bases at this time was his monastery of Ohrdruf, near Gotha. In assessing the strength of paganism in Hesse and Thuringia it is, however, important to recognize two points: first, that these regions had been Christianized before Boniface's arrival (and here it must be remembered that early medieval clerics made very little distinction between pastoral work among imperfect Christians and mission to the outright heathen—they were adjacent points on the spectrum of sin); and, second, that the references to a resurgence of paganism in these areas may have had more than a little to do with the propaganda of Charles Martel and his apologists. For instance, Heden is known to have been a supporter of Willibrord's monastery of Echternach, while an inscription, now lost, showed Theobald to be a church founder. Their poor reputations are probably to be associated not with their religious positions, but with their opposition to Charles Martel.

In 731 Gregory II died, to be succeeded in the Holy See by Gregory III. A year later the new pope sent Boniface the pallium, thus conferring on him archiepiscopal status and considerable authority east of the Rhine—but Boniface still lacked a fixed diocese. Meanwhile, he continued to found monasteries in Hesse and the region of the Main, notably at Fritzlar, Tauberbischofsheim, Ochsenfurt, and Kitzingen. At some point before 736 he was invited to Bavaria, by Duke Hugobert, and it was then that he probably first became acquainted with his disciple Sturmi. Having reached Bavaria, however, Boniface travelled on south, to make his third visit to Rome. There, in 738, he received further support from Gregory III.

Meanwhile Boniface began to turn his attention northwards once again, not least because in 738 Charles Martel launched a major campaign against the continental Saxons. The evangelization of these peoples had always been very dear to Boniface's heart: indeed, like Willibrord's teacher, the Anglo-Saxon Ecgberht of Rathmelsigi, before him, he was particularly concerned to Christianize the continental cousins of the English. Although he had always kept in touch with relatives and clerics in England, hopeful that Charles would open up the possibility of a mission to the Saxons, Boniface now penned a number of well-known letters to his insular contacts, seeking help in the Christianization of Saxony. Taken out of the very specific context to which they belong, these letters have led to a certain overemphasis on the extent to which Boniface was involved in missionary activity among pagans. In the event, however, Charles's failure to press home his military advantage meant that Boniface's hopes came to nothing—although in the wake of his appeal for help he did attract a number of notable Englishmen to him, including Willibald, who had been living as a monk in Monte Cassino.

Instead of working as a missionary in Saxony, Boniface returned in 739 to Bavaria, whose duke was now Odilo. Here he reformed the ecclesiastical structure of the region, dividing it into four dioceses, Passau, Salzburg, Regensburg, and Freising. In fact these dioceses were not totally new creations: Vivilo, bishop of Passau, had already been consecrated by Gregory III, while Salzburg had had a bishop, Rupert, as early as the late seventh century; and in the generation before Boniface's work of reform, Regensburg and Freising had been the respective centres for Emmeranus and Corbinian. Further, the man chosen as bishop of Freising by Boniface, Erembert, was actually Corbinian's brother. Boniface's work in Bavaria was thus one of reorganization, rather than the creation of a Bavarian church.

Reformer of the Frankish church, 741–742 The deaths of two major figures in 741 affected Boniface's position radically. First, Charles Martel died on 22 October, leaving his power to be divided between his sons Pippin III and Carlomann, to the exclusion of Gripho, a third son from another marriage. Although he had backed Boniface when necessary, Charles had never been an enthusiastic supporter of the Anglo-Saxon missionary, preferring rather to cultivate the leading clergy of the Frankish kingdoms, on whom he depended for much political support. Carlomann and Pippin were to prove much more supportive of Boniface and his reforming ideals than their father had been. Second, on 29 November Gregory III died. Boniface had had consistently good relations with the two Gregorys, who had been never less than supportive. The new pope, Zacharias, appears not to have been on such cordial terms with the Anglo-Saxon, although he continued to approve his work, albeit sometimes rather reluctantly.

For Boniface the new regime in Francia quickly brought benefits. In 742 Carlomann, despite local opposition, conceded territory in the forest of Buchonia, along the banks of the River Fulda, for the foundation of what was to prove to be Boniface's greatest monastery, itself named after the river. The site had been discovered by Sturmi and Boniface appointed him the monastery's first abbot. After 747–8, when Sturmi spent a year in Rome and Monte Cassino, Fulda became a major centre for the transmission of the Benedictine rule. In 751 Boniface obtained a papal privilege for his foundation; and after his martyrdom Fulda became the main focus for his cult.

Meanwhile, since his father's death in 741, Carlomann had backed Boniface in his establishment of dioceses east of the Rhine. Boniface had already appointed the Anglo-Saxon Burchard to the see of Würzburg in 741; in the following year he raised Willibald (not to be confused with Boniface's hagiographer) to the see of Erfurt; and during the same period he appointed a third Englishman, Hwita, to be bishop of Büraburg, near Fritzlar. The creation of all three dioceses he announced in a letter of 742 congratulating Pope Zacharias on his elevation to the papacy. Replying in a letter of 743, the pope confirmed the new creations, despite some scepticism as to whether they were based in appropriately populous centres. The see of Erfurt did soon have to be abandoned, and Willibald was appointed to a new bishopric of Eichstätt in 745.

Church councils, 742–745 In 742 Carlomann had authorized the first of a number of reforming councils, held under the leadership of Boniface, which were to have a major impact on the Frankish church, and which were to end a long period (sixty or seventy years, according to Boniface, although rather less than that in reality) in which no church council had been held in the Frankish kingdom. The Concilium Germanicum, so called because its place of meeting is unknown, recognized Boniface as leader of the churchmen within Carlomann's domains (chiefly the eastern Frankish kingdom of Austrasia) and as papal legate, although as yet he had no diocese of his own. Thereafter the council turned to the abuses of the Frankish church, to the promotion of the rule of St Benedict, and also to the existence of semi-pagan beliefs. These were listed in greater detail in a short work known as the *Indiculus superstitionum et paganiarum*, which must, therefore, have originated in Bonifatian circles.

The council of 742 was followed on 1 March 743 by a second Austrasian council, which was held at Les Estinnes, near Lobbes, on the River Sambre, in present-day Belgium. Again the council dealt with ecclesiastical abuses and prescribed the use of the Benedictine rule. It also tried to regulate the development of precarial tenure in such a way that it did not impoverish monasteries. The leasing out of monastic estates was a long-standing practice, which had become a significant way of providing warriors with landed property. It had been abused under Charles Martel, but was too useful to subsequent rulers for it to be abolished completely, despite the complaints of Boniface and other reformers.

In March 744 Carlomann's brother Pippin III, prompted by Boniface, called a council at Soissons, which dealt with abuses similar to those which had been discussed at the Austrasian councils and also with the heresy of a bishop, Gallic by birth, called Adalbert. He was a charismatic, regarded by many as a wonder-worker, who treated his own hair and fingernails as relics. He refused, however, to recant, following the council, and was therefore sent for judgement to Pope Zacharias, along with a second heretical bishop, the Irishman Clemens, who rejected teachings of the church fathers. In a council held in Rome in 745 both men were stripped of their episcopal office: Adalbert was made to do penance and was threatened with excommunication, while Clemens was excommunicated.

Meanwhile, in 744, Boniface elevated three Neustrian clerics, Grimo of Rouen, Abel of Rheims, and Hartbert of Sens, to archiepiscopal status; and in a letter of 22 June 744 Pope Zacharias confirmed the appointments. Within months, however, Pippin revoked his support for the elevation of Abel and Hartbert, probably because of local Frankish opposition to them—a change of mind which angered the pope. Despite the setback caused by Pippin's second thoughts, Boniface was able to press on with his reforms, and at a general council of the whole Frankish church, held with the joint support of Pippin and Carlomann, one of the leaders of the old guard, Bishop Gewilib of Mainz, was deposed. At the same time the council decided to confer on Boniface the diocese of Cologne, which was elevated to the status of a metropolitan see. These decisions were approved by Zacharias in a letter of 31 October 745, in which the sentences on Adalbert and Clemens were also announced.

Secular and ecclesiastical disputes and debates, 746–751 In the event the planned transfer of the diocese of Cologne to Boniface did not take place. Instead he received Gewilib's old diocese of Mainz in 746, where he appointed his disciple Lul as his archdeacon. This new distribution of dioceses, however, was soon to lead to considerable conflict between Mainz and Cologne over their jurisdiction east of the Rhine and over their missionary interests, particularly in Frisia.

Also in 746–7 Boniface turned his attention to the English church and more particularly to the behaviour of the Mercian king, Æthelbald (*r.* 716–57), who was reputed to have been sleeping with nuns and to have violated the privileges of churches and monasteries. Together with seven other Anglo-Saxon bishops who had Frankish dioceses (Wera of Utrecht, Burchard of Würzburg, Werberht, Abel of Rheims, Willibald of Eichstätt, Hwita of Büraburg, and Leofwine), Boniface wrote a letter of admonition, which he sent first to Archbishop Ecgberht of York, for correction. Boniface's intervention in the affairs of the Mercian church was to bear fruit, first in the 747 Council of 'Clofesho', whose canons show close dependence on those of the Concilium Germanicum and on various letters of Boniface, and subsequently on the grant of ecclesiastical privileges made by Æthelbald at the Council of Gumley in 749, which regulated the scale of the obligations owed by the church to the king.

Although Boniface's prestige was apparently unchallenged in England, the same could not be said in Bavaria. Already in 746 the Irishman Virgilius, then abbot of St Peter's, Salzburg, and Sidonius, later bishop of Passau, wrote to the pope, complaining of the high-handed way in which Boniface had insisted on rebaptism in a case where a priest had made grammatical mistakes in the baptismal liturgy. Zacharias upheld Virgilius's point of view, arguing that grammatical errors did not invalidate the baptism and that rebaptism in itself was heretical. Virgilius continued to be a thorn in Boniface's side. In 747 he was put in charge of the diocese of Salzburg, by Duke Odilo, following the death of Boniface's appointee, John. The next year Virgilius was making open criticism of Boniface, while the latter held the Irishman guilty of such heretical thoughts as that there were other men beneath the world. Not that Virgilius was either a heretic or an opponent of church reform. In fact he was, like Boniface, a man of considerable missionary interests, and he was to play a major role in the Christianization of Carinthia. Indeed, it is possible to regard him as being more successful in the missionary field than his Anglo-Saxon contemporary.

Meanwhile, 747 saw another significant political development on the continent. Carlomann decided to retire from the office of mayor of the palace and become a monk at Monte Cassino, leaving his position to his son Drogo. In the event, Pippin was to take over rule of the whole Frankish kingdom, much to his brother's fury. As yet, however, Pippin, like his father and grandfather before him, could only lay claim to mayoral office and was not in a position to claim the Frankish throne, which was still occupied by a member of the Merovingian dynasty, Childeric III (*r.* 743–51). Before he could depose Childeric, Pippin had first to deal with his own half-brother, Gripho, who took advantage of Carlomann's retirement and the death of Odilo of Bavaria to seize the duchy of Bavaria in 748. It was not until the following year that Pippin could dislodge him, and only in 750 did he send Bishop Burchard of Würzburg and Abbot Fulrad of St Denis to ask Pope Zacharias whether it was right for him to take the crown of the kingdom of the Franks. Zacharias concurred and Pippin III was anointed king, perhaps by Boniface, in 751.

Final years, 752–754 By the late 740s Boniface himself was beginning to look to the future, when he would no longer be archbishop of Mainz. In 752 he sought the help of Fulrad, to ensure the protection of his followers after his death. He also wished to secure the appointment of Lul as his successor. This he wanted to arrange during his own lifetime, not least because he was intent on resigning his see and returning to missionary work. His concern was all the greater because of growing disagreement between himself and Bishop Hildegar of Cologne. What was at stake was the missionary legacy of Willibrord at Utrecht, where, on Carlomann's orders, Boniface had appointed a new bishop. Hildegar, however, laid claim to Utrecht on the grounds that King Dagobert I (*r.* 623–39) had given the place to Cologne as a missionary base from which to convert the Frisians. As Boniface pointed out, since the bishops of Cologne had not carried out missionary work, their claim to Utrecht had lapsed. All this Boniface set out in his last surviving letter addressed to a pope, the newly elected Stephen II. Stephen's reply does not survive, but in the event Boniface took matters into his own hands.

Hildegar died on campaign against the Saxons in 753. Meanwhile Boniface himself set off to work in Frisia, in other words in what he claimed to be the missionary field of Utrecht. In the summer of 754 he reached northern Frisia and on 5 June he and a number of companions, including a suffragan bishop, Eoban, were attacked, supposedly by thieves, while waiting to confirm those who had recently been baptized in the neighbourhood of Dokkum (in the province of Friesland in the modern Netherlands). The whole missionary party was massacred, Boniface himself dying, according to tradition, while trying to ward off blows with a copy of the gospels. Their belongings were ransacked, but the thieves found nothing they deemed to be of value, leaving the manuscripts which the missionaries had brought with them lying in the mud.

Legacy and assessment The bodies of Boniface and his companions were then taken by boat to Utrecht. There most of the party were buried, but the body of Boniface himself was taken on to Mainz, and then to Fulda, where, in July, he was buried in accordance with his own wishes. According to Eigil, the biographer of Abbot Sturm of Fulda, Bishop Lul intended to keep the martyr's body at Mainz, but was unable to do so. Other evidence, however, does not suggest that Lul attempted to prevent Boniface's burial in his monastic foundation. More important, from the moment of the arrival of the cortège, Fulda received enormous prestige as the resting-place of a martyr.

Fulda was to be developed into a northern equivalent of the shrine of St Peter in Rome. Indeed, beginning in 791, Ratgar, first as architect and then as abbot, embarked on rebuilding the main church at Fulda as a copy of St Peter's, which itself commemorated the greatest martyr of the western church. Boniface was, therefore, to be seen as the martyred apostle of the Germans. The building project, however, was to prove too costly. Among other relics of the martyrdom which the church of Fulda still claims to possess is the manuscript with which Boniface tried to protect himself—but far from being a gospel book, the manuscript in question is a copy of Isidore of Seville's *Synonyma*.

The manner of Boniface's death, and the development of the image of him as the apostle of Germany, buried in such a way as to make him the equivalent of St Peter in Rome, tends to stress the saint's importance as a missionary figure. It is certainly true that he spent time at the beginning and end of his continental career working among the pagans of Frisia. It is also true that he always longed to be an active missionary, particularly among the continental Saxons, whom he regarded as cousins of the English, and that he sought help, especially from England, for a mission to the Saxons, most notably around the time of Charles Martel's campaign in Saxony in 738. Nevertheless, he did not manage to work among the Saxons and his missionary career in Frisia was shortlived. Despite the lack of any clear line between mission and pastoral care, Boniface's continental career was above all that of a reformer and organizer. Even in Thuringia and Hesse, where he undoubtedly came across paganism, syncretism, and heresy, his major achievement lay in the foundation of monasteries and bishoprics and in the creation of a diocesan system. In Bavaria, where churches were well established, it was again in ecclesiastical appointments and diocesan organization that he was to play a crucial role. In this respect there is no sharp division between his work east of the Rhine and his reform of the Frankish church, which was to dominate his life in the 740s when he had the backing of Carlomann and subsequently of Pippin III.

What was new after Charles Martel's death in 741 was that at last Boniface had support to reform the church of the Frankish heartlands. This Charles had been unwilling to agree to, for he had relied too much on the support of the ecclesiastical old guard, in order to establish himself, to be able to turn against them *en masse*. Boniface knew only too well that he could do nothing without the help of, first, Charles, and, later, Carlomann and Pippin; and Charles, at least, gave him little aid, except where it was to his own advantage—in the peripheral regions of the Frankish kingdom, which had been most opposed to Carolingian rule. The lack of Frankish support during his early years on the continent, however, enhanced the significance for Boniface of his outside contacts, with England and the papacy. Not surprisingly, he came to play an important role in strengthening links between the Franks and the Holy See.

Boniface has, therefore, to be seen first and foremost as a reformer, and one aspect of that is his promotion of monasticism, and especially of the rule of St Benedict, which played an increasing role both at Fulda and in other monastic foundations like Heidenheim, where Winnebald, brother of Bishop Willibald of Eichstätt, was abbot. He packed his monasteries and the episcopal sees he created with like-minded individuals, many of them relatives or contacts from Anglo-Saxon England, and both men and women, like Leoba, abbess of Tauberbischofsheim. Moreover, through his English connections Boniface played a major role in bringing English learning and insular culture to the continent. Although Bede seems not to have heard of Boniface, making no reference to him in his *Historia ecclesiastica gentis Anglorum*, Boniface came to hear of Bede, and several of his letters to England are requests for copies of Bede's works. Further, Boniface's continuing links with England enabled him to involve himself in the reform of the English church, particularly in Mercia, where his attack on Æthelbald seems to have led directly to the reforms of the Council of 'Clofesho' in 747. Although the drama of his martyrdom has caused Boniface to be remembered as a martyr and a missionary, his achievements lay primarily in his reform and organization of the church across much of north-west Europe.

I. N. Wood

Sources Willibald, 'Vita Bonifatii', *Vita sancti Bonifatii archiepiscopi Moguntini*, ed. W. Levison, MGH Scriptores Rerum Germanicarum, [57] (Hanover, 1905) · 'Vita altera Bonifatii', *Vitae sancti Bonifatii archiepiscopi Moguntini*, ed. W. Levison, MGH Scriptores Rerum Germanicarum, [57] (Hanover, 1905) · Eigil, *Vita Sturmi, Die vita Sturmi des Eigil von Fulda*, ed. P. Engelbert (1968) · Liudger, 'Vita Gregorii abbatis Traiectensis', [*Supplementa tomorum I–XII, pars III*], ed. O. Holder-Egger, MGH Scriptores [folio], 15/1 (Stuttgart, 1887), 66–79 · M. Tangl, ed., *Die Briefe des heiligen Bonifatius und Lullus*, MGH Epistolae Selectae, 1 (Berlin, 1916) · A. Werminghoff, ed., *Concilia aevi Karolini*, MGH Concilia, 2/2 (Hanover, 1908) · A. Dierkens, 'Indiculus superstitionum et paganiarum: superstitions, christianisme, et paganisme à la fin de l'époque Mérovingienne', *Magie, sorcellerie, parapsychologie*, ed. H. Hasquin (Brussels, 1984), 9–26 · R. Rau, ed., *Briefe des Bonifatius: Willibalds Leben des Bonifatius* (1968) · [Hugeburc], 'Vita Willibaldi episcopi Eichstetensis', ed. O. Holder-Egger, [*Supplementa tomorum I–XII, pars III*], ed. G. Waitz, MGH Scriptores [folio], 15/1 (Hanover, 1887), 86–106 · [Hugeburc], 'Vita Wynnebaldi abbatis Heidenheimensis', ed. O. Holder-Egger, [*Supplementa tomorum I–XII, pars III*], ed. G. Waitz, MGH Scriptores [folio], 15/1 (Hanover, 1887), 106–17 · T. Schieffer, *Winfrid-Bonifatius* (1954) · T. Reuter, ed., *The greatest Englishman: essays on St Boniface and the church at Crediton* (1980) · W. Levison, *England and the continent in the eighth century* (1946) · J. M. Wallace-Hadrill, *The Frankish church* (1983)

Boniface of Savoy. *See* Savoy, Boniface of (1206/7–1270).

Bonington, Richard Parkes (1802–1828), landscape painter, was born on 25 October 1802 in Arnold, near Nottingham, and baptized there at High Pavement Unitarian Chapel on 28 November, the only child of Richard Bonington (1768–1835) and Eleanor Parkes (*d.* 1838). His father inherited the post of governor of Nottingham gaol in 1789, but eight years later resigned that sinecure under duress to become a drawing master and portrait painter. He would exhibit landscapes and watercolours at the Royal Academy in London in 1797 and 1808 and at the Liverpool Academy in 1811 and 1813. His posthumous and justly deserved reputation as an opportunist and exploiter of his progeny's fame has perhaps overshadowed the fact that he was a reasonably competent artist whose industry satisfied a variety of cultural needs in the provinces. He conducted weekly drawing lessons at the Jennings circulating library in Sheffield, for instance. In 1801 the senior

Richard Parkes Bonington (1802–1828), self-portrait

Bonington married Eleanor Parkes, an educated woman with prior experience tutoring children, and together they managed in Nottingham until 1813 a finishing school for girls and a 'repository of arts' that stocked artists' supplies and the latest graphic arts from London. The nearly 3000 old master and modern prints auctioned by his estate (Sothebys, 24 February 1838) would have figured prominently in the earliest artistic instruction of his son, for which he was unquestionably responsible.

Early years Economic stagnation during the second decade of the century devastated Nottingham, and in a distressed financial state the Boningtons moved in the autumn of 1817 to Calais, where the father had established a lace-making business in partnership with two other expatriate Nottinghamshire businessmen. The younger Bonington's earliest known works of art date from after his arrival in France. Although initially discouraged by his parents, he refined his skills as a painter of marine watercolours under the tutelage of the Anglo-French artist Louis Francia, who, after many successful years in London as a watercolourist, had returned to Calais only months before the Boningtons' arrival. The impact of Francia's style is actually less apparent in Bonington's earliest watercolours than in those of 1823, when the two artists again worked in close association in Paris.

Following the dissolution of the Calais partnership in October 1818, the family moved to Paris in the spring and opened a retail lace business at 22 rue des Moulins. They would subsequently occupy premises at 27 rue Michel le Comte and 16 rue des Mauvaises-Paroles. The younger Bonington began copying Dutch and Flemish paintings in the Musée du Louvre, where he met Eugène Delacroix. On the recommendation of the English artist James Roberts, whom he also met in the Louvre, Bonington was enrolled in April 1819 in the studio of Baron Antoine-Jean Gros, France's pre-eminent painter of historical subjects. Gros's studio, located in the Institut de France, was the most prestigious in Paris. Among the fellow pupils whom Bonington would befriend at this time were Eugène Lami, Camille Roqueplan, Paul Huet, and Henri Monnier. However, large-scale, academic figure painting was anathema to Bonington, and he eventually renounced formal training for a regimen of self-tuition in naturalistic landscape painting. Late in 1821 he made the first of several tours of Normandy, journeying to Rouen and then along the coast from Caen to Abbeville. Two watercolours from this trip, *Vue prise à Lillebonne* and *Vue prise au Havre*, received favourable critical notice when exhibited at the 1822 Paris Salon and were acquired by the Société des Amis des Arts. Watercolour painting was considered a British speciality and was not much practised at this time in France, but Bonington's bravura technique soon attracted both private collectors and numerous imitators. These early topographical watercolours, exhibited in the gallery of Madame Hulin and Claude Schroth at 18 rue de la Paix, Paris, Camille Corot later acknowledged as the inspiration for his becoming a painter.

Early commissions Until 1823 Bonington painted exclusively in watercolours, both for the middle-class cognoscenti and for publishers of illustrated topographical and antiquarian books. His first topographical commission was to copy in watercolours a sketch by the comte de Forbin for J. F. d'Ostervald's *Voyage pittoresque en Sicile* (1822–6), a *tour de force* of British printmaking technology, for which the Swiss-born publisher employed a battery of English watercolourists and aquatint etchers, including the entire Fielding family. With the proceeds of his watercolour sales, Bonington visited Belgium in 1823 and again toured Normandy, gathering material to illustrate Ostervald's *Excursions sur les côtes et dans les ports de France*, and for his own set of lithographic views of Gothic architectural monuments, *Restes et fragmens [sic] d'architecture du moyen âge*, also called *La petite Normandie*. Despite their great beauty as drawings, the last portfolio was a commercial failure owing to printing problems and the lack of any descriptive text. *Restes et fragmens* would appear in 1824, as would his most innovative lithographic contributions to Baron Taylor's voluminous *Voyages pittoresques et romantiques dans l'ancienne France*. Like most artists of his generation, Bonington admired the enchanting blend of historical pageantry and exacting archaeological research that typified the novels of Sir Walter Scott, and his 'instinctive predilection for historical reminiscences' (Roberts) is evidenced in these scrupulously observed antiquarian prints, as well as in his later genre lithographs *Cahier de six sujets* (1826) and the pseudo-Gothic illuminations for Ferdinand Langlé's *Contes du gay sçavoir* (1827).

Marine oil paintings The year 1824 was one of tremendous ferment in the arts. In the spring, two of the titans of romanticism died tragically—Théodore Géricault in Paris and Lord Byron in Missolonghi. Jacques-Louis David's principal disciple, Anne-Louis Girodet, would also not survive the year. In February Bonington and the artist Alexandre-Marie Colin left Paris for the coastal town of Dunkirk. This sketching tour, planned to last but a few weeks, developed into a self-imposed exile of nearly one year's duration. It was during this sojourn, which the artist described as the 'happiest year of my life', that Bonington concentrated on the marine oil paintings that would trumpet his arrival as a serious artist at the Paris Salon in August. The 1824 Salon was the most passionately contested cultural event in France of the 1820s, pitting the academic painters of David's school against the younger generation of artists, like Delacroix, who identified themselves as romantics. British artists were also invited to exhibit, and Bonington shared in the notoriety accorded such celebrities as Sir Thomas Lawrence and John Constable. With its vivacious brushwork and its serene expansiveness, *A Fishmarket, Near Boulogne* (Yale U. CBA), for which Bonington was awarded a gold medal, was a brilliant exercise in Anglo-Dutch naturalism without parallel in contemporary French practice. Altogether Bonington exhibited under his own name four marine oils, a watercolour view of Abbeville, and an impression of his *Rue de Grosse-Horloge, Rouen*, which remains one of the signal images of early lithography. Under Ostervald's name appeared an unspecified number of Bonington's watercolours related to various topographical publications. The success of the Salon pictures thrust the diffident artist to the forefront of the French romantic movement. His work, with that of John Constable, would influence the course of French landscape painting for the next decade.

Visit to England Inspired by what they had seen of British art at the Salon, Bonington and numerous French colleagues, including Colin, Delacroix, Hippolyte Poterlet, Édouard Bertin, and Augustin Enfantin, travelled to London in summer 1825. While in England, Bonington developed close ties to Delacroix and Eugène Isabey, working with the former at Westminster and at the collection of the antiquarian Dr Samuel Meyrick, and with the latter on the Normandy coast at the conclusion of their trip. Through the offices of the engravers Abraham Raimbach and William Cooke, he probably visited the superb old master and modern paintings collections of Sir Walter Fawkes, Sir John Leicester, and the marquess of Stafford, where he would have discovered the extraordinary range and power of J. M. W. Turner's art. In response to Constable and Turner, Bonington began painting oil sketches *en plein air* using a commercially prepared millboard that was readily available in London, and he enlarged his repertory of subjects to include a variety of landscape types, especially river scenes at twilight.

Major works After a sketching tour with Paul Huet along the Seine in autumn 1825, Bonington moved into Delacroix's Paris studio in the rue Jacob. Through Delacroix he was introduced to the most progressive French literati, including Prosper Mérimée, Honoré de Balzac, Charles Nodier, Victor Hugo, and Amédée Pichot, for whom he illustrated *Vues pittoresques de l'Écosse* (1825–6). While Delacroix and his circle persuaded Bonington to expand the scope of his ambitions to include historical subjects in oils, the earliest of which is *Anne Page and Slender* (Wallace Collection, London), Bonington's seminal influence on Delacroix is sensed, as Théophile Gautier first observed, in the new éclat of colouring and the more assured handling of paint that is evident in the French artist's pictures of 1826, in particular, his *Combat of the Giaour and Hassan* (Art Institute of Chicago) and the *Execution of the Doge Marino Faliero* (Wallace Collection, London). The clarity and dazzling execution of Bonington's style also inspired Delacroix and other French painters, like Alexandre Decamps, Charles Gleyre, Isabey, and Huet, to explore watercolour painting with renewed commitment.

In February 1826 the critic for the *London Literary Gazette* asked in his review of the annual exhibition of contemporary art at the British Institution, 'Who is R. P. Bonington?' The two oil paintings, *French Coast Scenery* and *French Coast with Fishermen* (both priv. coll.), that the artist had sent from Paris for inclusion in the exhibition had astounded his British compatriots who were seeing his work for the first time. In the spring, Bonington moved to his own studio at 11 rue des Martyrs, a building owned by Jules-Robert Auguste, an amateur artist and former friend of Géricault. Shortly thereafter he commenced a tour of northern Italy and Switzerland in the company of a friend and pupil, the future Baron Charles Rivet. Delacroix was meant to accompany them but at the last minute withdrew. Since it was the Italy of Shakespeare and Byron that fascinated Bonington, he spent most of his time in Venice, where he produced a substantial number of graphite, watercolour, and oil sketches of the principal monuments and views. These furnished him with studies for major exhibition pictures that he would send to the Salon and to the Royal Academy in 1828. As one of the earliest nineteenth-century artists to depict Venice in its faded splendour, Bonington appears to have influenced the way many French writers, including Chateaubriand, perceived the city. Antoine Claude Pasquin (M. Valéry), who was travelling in Italy at the same time, would write that:

> Bonington, a British artist of melancholy cast, has painted some new views of Venice in which is most perfectly sketched its present desolation; when compared with those of the Venetian painter Canaletto, they resemble a woman still beautiful but worn down by age and misfortune. (*Voyages historiques et littéraires en Italie*, 1831, 143)

The experience of Venetian Renaissance painting was also important to Bonington's increasingly comprehensive artistic interests, and, on resettling in Paris, he would become preoccupied once again with genre subjects.

After leaving Venice at the end of May, Bonington travelled to Padua, Florence, Pisa, Sarzana, Lerici, Spezzia, Genoa, and Turin. It has been assumed on the evidence of Rivet's correspondence that the two friends were back in Paris by 20 June; however, extant drawings from Staubbach, Thun, Bern, and Basel suggest that Bonington possibly separated from his companion and returned to France by way of Switzerland, thus extending his journey by perhaps several weeks.

Later years The last two years of Bonington's life were marked by astounding popular success both in England and in France. The development of his painting technique was breathtaking and experimental. By the summer of 1827 there was little but scale to distinguish visually between his work in oils and his work in watercolours. The denser texture of oil paint is simulated with gouache in the watercolours, while the limpidity of translucent watercolours has its analogue in the oil glazes that begin to dominate in his canvases. Although he continued to paint marines, including the radiant *On the Côte d'Opale, Picardy* (priv. coll.), exhibited at the Royal Academy in 1827, his primary subject interests were now views of Venice and illustrations to medieval and Renaissance history or the literary works of Scott and Goethe. In his genre paintings he was much influenced by the emerging science of modern historiography, with its demand for archaeological exactitude, and by the type of intimate historical painting known in France as the Troubadour style, of which Jean-Auguste-Dominique Ingres was then the foremost exponent. But, unlike Ingres, Bonington was also enamoured of the expressive techniques and colouring of Venetian painting, which he endeavoured to translate into his own stylistic idiom. His final master-works in this genre are *Quentin Durward at Liège* (Nottingham Castle Museum), which was commissioned by the duchesse de Berri, *Henri IV and the Spanish Ambassador*, and *Henri III of France* (both Wallace Collection, London).

At the end of 1827 Bonington moved his studio for the final time to 32 rue St Lazare and sent to the Salon two oil paintings, the *Ducal Palace* (Tate collection) and *Rouen Cathedral*, together with a watercolour and several lithographic interpretations of drawings by Maurice Rugendas for *Voyages pittoresques en Brésil* (1827). He again travelled to London in January 1828, where he met Sir Thomas Lawrence and exhibited *The Piazzetta, Venice* and *View of the Ducal Palace, Venice* (both Tate collection) at the British Institution. In February he exhibited, at the second Salon instalment, *Francis I and the Queen of Navarre* (untraced), *Henri IV and the Spanish Ambassador* (Wallace Collection, London) and *Entrance to the Grand Canal* (priv. coll.), a large picture commissioned by the publisher James Carpenter. To the Royal Academy, in May, he sent *Henri III* (Wallace Collection, London), Carpenter's *Grand Canal*, and a coast scene. Within a month of that exhibition, Bonington collapsed from either sunstroke or nervous exhaustion, and, in a weakened state, succumbed to tuberculosis. In an effort to save him, his parents took him to London in August, but treatment proved futile, and he died on 23 September at 29 Tottenham Street, the home of the publisher John Barnett. During his final illness he was attended by Thomas Shotter Boys, who helped him produce his only etching, *Bologna: the Leaning Towers*. He was buried in London, on 29 September 1828, at St James's Chapel, Pentonville, and later reinterred, at Kensal Green cemetery, in 1837. In a letter to his spouse, the engraver

George Cooke described the funeral and its many mourners, among whom were some of the first names in British painting: Sir Thomas Lawrence, Henry William Pickersgill, Clarkson Stanfield, John Frederick Lewis, and George Fennel Robson (J. Munday, *Edward William Cooke*, 1996, 44).

The little that we know of Bonington's character and appearance comes from two sources—a manuscript recollection written by James Roberts, probably in response to Allen Cunningham's flawed biographical notice of 1832, and a letter from Eugène Delacroix to Théophile Thoré (Noon, *On the Pleasure of Painting*, 12), composed decades after Bonington's death. Roberts had only recently preceded Bonington to Paris in 1817, and he recalled meeting him in the Louvre copying a picture by Gérard Dou. It was Roberts who alleged that there occurred a breach in the relationship between Bonington and Gros, which resulted in his unjust expulsion from the studio. Roberts also noted that:

> Bonington's appearance at that time was particularly boyish owing to his round plump cheeks … yet [one] would observe in his eyes unequivocal marks of intelligence. Although he was never noisy or boisterous like his comrades of the atelier he was fond of mirth. (Roberts)

Rivet, in his correspondence from Italy, described his companion as moody, obsessively self-critical, and addicted to his studies (Dubuisson and Hughes). Delacroix, on the other hand, wrote, 'I knew him well and loved him much. His British composure, which was imperturbable, in no way diminished those qualities that make life enjoyable'. His assessment of Bonington's merits was extremely apt:

> To my mind, one can find in other modern artists qualities of strength and of precision in rendering that are superior to those in Bonington's pictures, but no one in this modern school, and perhaps even before, has possessed that lightness of touch which, especially in the watercolours, makes his work a type of diamond that flatters and ravishes the eye. (Noon, *On the Pleasure of Painting*, 12)

Reputation After his death Bonington's reputation grew prodigiously. Lawrence, who owned several of his pictures including *A Seated Turk* (Yale U. CBA) and the resplendent *Lerici* (priv. coll.), actively promoted his reputation in England. In France his legacy was even more zealously defended. For writers and critics from Flaubert and Sainte-Beuve to Baudelaire and Thoré, Bonington was not only the equal of Turner and Constable, but also, with Delacroix and Géricault, one of the pillars of modern sensibility—an exquisite colourist and technician whose affinity with nature made his works emotional as well as painterly statements of the highest calibre. Bonington never sought, like Turner or Géricault or Delacroix, to depict the sublime events of nature and history, and he had little interest in the theoretical, but his vision was no less seminal to the development of modern art.

Despite the persistent high reputation of the artist through the nineteenth and twentieth centuries, there have been surprisingly few exhibitions of Bonington's work. The first retrospective was organized by Paul Oppé for the Burlington Fine Arts Club in 1937. The Nottingham Castle Museum exhibition of 1965 was the largest, while the 1991 exhibition in New Haven and Paris (Yale Center for British Art and Petit Palais) focused on defining a corpus of authentic masterworks from the plethora of imitations and forgeries that began flooding the markets as early as 1830. The most impressive single collection of Bonington's works is in the Wallace Collection, London, the benefaction of the most resolute of the artist's collectors, Sir Richard Wallace. At the first studio sale of 1829, the marquess of Lansdowne purchased a significant collection of architectural and Venetian drawings, which are now at Bowood House, Wiltshire. In Bonington's adoptive city, the Bibliothèque Nationale houses the Atherton Curtis bequest of drawings and prints and a number of Bonington's manuscript letters. The Musée du Louvre has several notable oils. Other important groups of works are in the British Museum and the Nottingham Castle Museum. During the twentieth century there has been only one tenacious collector, Paul Mellon, who donated eleven oil paintings to the Yale Center for British Art.

PATRICK NOON

Sources 'Biography: R. P. Bonington', *Literary Gazette* (27 Sept 1828), 619–20 · [E. Bertin?], 'Bonington', *Journal des Débats* (28 Sept 1828) · A. Jal, 'Bonington, peintre de genre', *Le Globe* (5 Oct 1828), 745–6 · J. D. Harding, *A series of subjects from the works of the late Richard Parkes Bonington* (1829–30) · 'Memoir of Richard Parkes Bonington', *Library of the Fine Arts*, 3 (1832), 201–9 · A. Cunningham, 'Richard Parkes Bonington', *The lives of the most eminent British painters, sculptors, and architects*, 5 (1832), 245–58 · 'On the genius of Bonington and his works', *Arnold's Magazine of the Fine Arts*, 1 (1833), 29–34, 144–51 · T. Thoré [W. Burger], 'Bonington', in C. Blanc, *Histoire des peintures de toutes les écoles* (1867), 1–14 · T. Gautier, *Histoire du romantisme* (1874), 212 · P. Mantz, 'Bonington', *Gazette des Beaux-Arts*, 2nd ser., 14 (1876), 288–306 · L. Rosenthal, *La peinture romantique* (c.1900) · A. Dubuisson, 'Influence de Bonington et de l'école anglaise sur la peinture de paysage en France', *Walpole Society*, 2 (1912–13), 111–26 · C. E. Hughes, 'Notes on Bonington's parents', *Walpole Society*, 3 (1913–14), 99–112 · A. Dubuisson and C. E. Hughes, *Richard Parkes Bonington: his life and work* (1924) · A. Dubuisson, *Bonington* (1927) · Burlington Fine Arts Club, *R. P. Bonington and his circle* (1937) · A. Curtis, *Catalogue de l'œuvre lithographié et gravé* (Paris, 1939) · A. Shirley, *Bonington* (1940) · S. Race, *Notes on the Boningtons: Richard Bonington the elder (1730–1803); Richard Bonington the younger (1768–1835); Richard Parkes Bonington (1801 [sic]–1828)* (1950) · M. Spencer, *R. P. Bonington* (1965) · M. Kemp, 'Scott and Delacroix, with some assistance from Hugo and Bonington', *Scott bicentenary essays* (1973), 213–27 · J. Ingamells, *Richard Parkes Bonington* (1979) · P. Noon, 'Bonington and Boys: some unpublished documents at Yale', *Burlington Magazine*, 123 (1981), 294–300 · M. Pointon, *The Bonington circle: English watercolour and Anglo-French landscape, 1790–1855* (1985) · P. Noon, 'Richard Parkes Bonington: *A fishmarket, near Boulogne*', *Essays in honor of Paul Mellon* (1986), 239–54 · P. Noon, *Richard Parkes Bonington: on the pleasure of painting* (1991) [exhibition catalogue, Yale U. CBA and the Petit Palais, Paris] · P. Noon, 'Bonington: un romantique anglais au Louvre', *Revue du Louvre* (Oct 1994), 48–63 · J. Roberts, 'Bonington's biography', c.1832, Bibliothèque Nationale, Paris, cabinet des dessins, réserve, Bonington dossier, MS 18445

Archives Bibliothèque Nationale, Paris, cabinet des dessins, réserve, J. Roberts, 'Bonington's biography', MS 18445

Likenesses R. P. Bonington?, self-portrait?, oils, c.1814–1815, Castle Museum, Nottingham · L. Boilly, group portrait, chalk, 1820, Musée Carnavalet, Paris, France · R. P. Bonington, watercolour drawing, c.1820–1825, NPG · watercolour, c.1822, Musée des Beaux Arts, Besançon, France · A. Colin, graphite head, 1824,

Musée Carnavalet, Paris, France • A. Colin, lithograph, *c*.1824, priv. coll. • E. Delacroix, charcoal drawing, *c*.1825, priv. coll. • T. Barber, oils, *c*.1827; Sothebys, 15 June 2000, lot 157 • M. Carpenter, oils, *c*.1827, NPG; copy, Castle Museum, Nottingham • A. M. Colin, pencil drawing, 1829, AM Oxf. • M. Carpenter, mezzotint, pubd 1831 (after J. P. Quilley), BM, NPG • watercolour drawing, 1834 (after M. Carpenter, *c*.1827), Castle Museum, Nottingham • F. W. Pomeroy, marble statue, exh. RA 1910, Nottingham School of Art • R. P. Bonington, self-portrait, watercolour, BM [*see illus.*] • Damour, aquatint print (after R. P. Bonington, *c*.1820), BM, NPG • J. D. Harding, lithograph (after chalk drawing by M. Carpenter), repro. in Harding, *Series of subjects*, frontispiece • E. Scriven, stipple (after A. Shaw), repro. in 'Memoir of Richard Parkes Bonington' • F. Villot, etching (after R. P. Bonington, *c*.1825)

Wealth at death several thousand pounds—studio sales, Sothebys (29 June 1829); Christies (23 May 1834); Sothebys (10 Feb 1838)

Bonn, Leopold Bernhard (1850–1929), banker and philanthropist, was born on 3 August 1850 in Frankfurt am Main, Germany, the ninth child of Baruch Bonn, a prominent Jewish banker. He was privately educated. After the annexation of Frankfurt by Prussia in 1866, Bonn applied for denaturalization and moved to Paris, where he became secretary to S. Kann, a banker and friend of his father. Following the outbreak of the Franco-Prussian War in 1870 Bonn moved to London and joined the firm of G. and A. Worms. He was appointed manager of the German Bank in 1871, and in 1877 joined Speyer Brothers, a London bank, which provided most of the finance for the Metropolitan District Railway Company. In 1880 Bonn married Ida Amalie Eltzbacher: they had one son and two daughters. While with Speyers, Bonn was elected a director of the German Bank, and he was also a director of the London and Liverpool Bank of Commerce from 1886 to 1913, and of the Union of London and Smith's Bank from 1900 to 1913. He left Speyers in 1895 to found the Bonn Bank with his nephew, Max Bonn. The Bonn Bank continued in business until after the First World War, when it amalgamated with Herbert Wagg & Co.

Bonn became deaf late in life, and while spending a season in Brighton in 1910 was recommended to go to Mary Hare, a teacher of lip-reading, for lessons. Mary Hare, who founded Deane Hollow School (later the Mary Hare Grammar School for the Deaf) in 1916, put him in touch with Arthur John Story, headmaster of the Mount Blind and Deaf School in Stoke-on-Trent, who had for some years been urging the need to establish a national organization to promote the interests of deaf people. In the *Quarterly Review of Deaf Mute Education* in 1898 he had outlined a scheme to bring together the many national and local societies, schools, and missions concerned with the education and welfare of deaf people. It was estimated in 1911 that there were more than 140 of these associations, including the British Deaf and Dumb Association, the National Association of Teachers of the Deaf, and the London Association for the Deaf and Dumb, but although much work was being done for deaf people, the lack of contact between the organizations was a severe obstacle to progress, as no one knew what anyone else was doing. What was needed was a central organization to co-ordinate activity, on the lines of the Volta Bureau, founded in the United States by Alexander Graham Bell in

Leopold Bernhard Bonn (1850–1929), by Lienhard & Salzborn

the 1880s, but to set up such an organization would take funds. Bonn became interested in the project and agreed to provide financial backing for the first two years. He called an inaugural meeting of the National Bureau for Promoting the General Welfare of the Deaf on 9 June 1911 at his London home, 22 Upper Brook Street, Mayfair. It was attended by over 100 people, and he was elected chairman and president, with Max Bonn as vice-chairman. Members of the council included representatives of the leading deaf charities and schools, and a number of influential people agreed to be vice-presidents, including Sir Edgar Speyer, Lord George Hamilton, and the Hon. Rupert Guinness. The aims of the bureau were centralization (to promote co-operation between existing agencies for deaf people); information (to collect, classify, and disseminate information relating to deaf people); and investigation (to make special studies of problems affecting deaf people). An office was opened at 28–9 Gwydir Chambers, 104 High Holborn, in October 1911, with a part-time secretary, W. Carey Roe, a teacher of deaf people. Once the bureau was established Bonn endowed it in December 1912 with £5000 to fund it for the next five years. He worked hard during the early years, setting up committees, raising subscriptions from his friends, and attending meetings. Early projects included compiling a directory of deaf organizations, establishing a library, organizing a deputation to the Home Office concerning the employment of deaf people, and a series of lectures by the Glasgow surgeon J. Kerr Love, later published as *The Causes and Prevention of Deafness* (1913). The bureau was particularly concerned about the Mental Deficiency Act (1913), and about the danger of deafness being mistaken for mental deficiency, and the parliamentary committee worked on this. During the First World War the bureau went into decline, although it continued to act as a clearing-house for information relating to deaf people. Bonn resigned as chairman in 1915 in favour of Max Bonn, but agreed to remain president. In 1924, with the help of the British Deaf and Dumb Association, and with Arthur John Story as its first full-time salaried secretary, the bureau was reconstituted as the National Institute for the Deaf (from 1961 to 1992 the Royal National Institute for the Deaf, and from 1992 the Royal National Institute for Deaf People); virtually all organizations concerned with deaf people affiliated themselves to it. Bonn agreed to transfer his endowment to the new body, and continued to take an active interest in its activities.

Bonn bought a country estate, Newbold Revel, near Rugby, Warwickshire, in 1911, and spent his last years as a country gentleman, particularly enjoying riding to hounds. He died on 28 November 1929 at Newbold Revel and was buried at Monks Kirby parish church, Warwickshire, on 2 December. He was survived by his wife.

Anne Pimlott Baker

Sources B. Grant, *The deaf advance: a history of the British Deaf Association, 1890–1990* (1990) · P. W. Jackson, *Britain's deaf heritage* (1990), 189, 385 · Royal National Institute for the Deaf, *RNID, 1911–1971: sixty years of service to the deaf* (1971) · annual reports of the National Bureau for Promoting the General Welfare of the Deaf, 1912–16 · *Teacher of the Deaf*, 28 (Feb 1930) · *Deaf Quarterly News*, 100 (1930) · *The Times* (2 Dec 1929) · *WWW* · private information (2004)
Likenesses Lienhard & Salzborn, photograph, Royal National Institute for the Deaf, London [*see illus.*]
Wealth at death £220,779 0s. 6d.: probate, 10 Feb 1930, *CGPLA Eng. & Wales*

Bonnar, George William. *See* Bonner, George Wilmot (1796–1836).

Bonnar, William (1800–1853), painter, was born in Edinburgh, the son of a house-painter. He showed artistic talent at an early age and was apprenticed to one of the leading decorative artists of the day; after some time he became foreman of the business. When George IV visited Edinburgh in 1822 Bonnar helped David Roberts to decorate the Assembly Rooms in George Street for the state ball. Shortly after this Captain Basil Hall recognized the quality of his work, having seen some signboards that Bonnar had painted, and encouraged Bonnar to become a professional artist. This he did in 1824, when he exhibited *The Tinkers* at Waterloo Place. This painting was well received and five years later Bonnar was elected a member of the Royal Scottish Academy, which had been founded the previous year, in 1828. He was also presented with the Hope and Cockburn award.

Bonnar specialized in rural scenes, pictures of children, and humorous subjects that show the influence of David Wilkie, such as *Showing the New Dress* (1829), *The Blessing* (1832), and *The Orphans* (1838). He was often inspired by Scottish literary sources such as the life and works of Robert Burns, as in *The Cottar's Saturday Night* (1839), Allan Ramsay, as in *The Gentle Shepherd*, and the works of Sir Walter Scott, as in *Jessie Deans in the Robber's Barn* (1836), *Kilmeny's Return* (1838), and *Caleb Balderstone Burnishing the Pewter Flagon* (1840). He also painted historical subjects including *The First Sermon of John Knox, in the Castle of St Andrews* and *King Robert Bruce and the Spider* (1840). Bonnar was a popular and prolific artist and many of his paintings were engraved. Latterly he concentrated on painting portraits, many of which were engraved by his sons. These include *Portrait of John Blackie Senior* (Glasgow Art Gallery), *Thomas Chalmers*, *William Cunningham*, *George Kemp*, and *Isabella Begg* (all Scot. NPG), and a self-portrait (NG Scot.).

Bonnar died in London Street, Edinburgh, on 27 January 1853. His son William Bonnar junior (*fl.* 1849) also became a painter.

Ernest Radford, *rev.* Jennifer Melville

Sources P. J. M. McEwan, *Dictionary of Scottish art and architecture* (1994) · J. L. Caw, *Scottish painting past and present, 1620–1908* (1908), 279–80 · J. Halsby, *Scottish watercolours, 1740–1940* (1986), 70, 126, 241 · W. Hardie, *Scottish painting, 1837–1939* (1976), 66, 78, 79
Likenesses W. Bonnar, self-portrait, oils, exh. 1853, NG Scot.

Bonneau, Jacob (*d.* 1786), painter, moved to England about 1741, with his father, an engraver, who worked in London for booksellers during the mid-eighteenth century. Probably trained by his father, Bonneau also worked for booksellers, for whom he engraved the heads prefixed to the *History of the American Buccaneers* published in London in 1741. Whitley noted that on the retirement of Alexander Cozens in 1754 the

> artists of London petitioned the Governors of Christ's Hospital to give the post [of drawing master] to Jacob Bonneau, afterwards one of the drawing masters to the Royal Family, who, although his reputation as a painter was small, received some support when a candidate for the Associateship of the Royal Academy twenty years later. Bonneau must have been extremely popular among his brother artists, for the petition, drawn up by Joseph Highmore, is signed by nearly all the important painters, sculptors and engravers of the time including Hogarth, Reynolds—then a young man not long returned from Italy—and Roubiliac. (Whitley, 316–17)

Bonneau was described in the petition, which is cited by Whitley in full, as 'being a person in every way qualified for that Trust' (ibid., 317). In the ballot he failed to obtain the post, losing by 15 votes to 40 to an artist named Bisse. From 1765 to 1778 Bonneau exhibited landscapes at the Society of British Artists, of which he was a member. From 1770 to 1781 he exhibited seven landscape paintings and the watercolour drawing *St John* at the Royal Academy. Bonneau worked chiefly in watercolour, and his principal occupation was that of a teacher of drawing and perspective. He died at Kentish Town, London, on 18 March 1786.

Walter Hepworth, *rev.* Asia Haut

Sources Redgrave, *Artists* · Mallalieu, *Watercolour artists* · M. H. Grant, *A dictionary of British landscape painters, from the 16th century to the early 20th century* (1952) · exhibition catalogue [Society of British Artists] · *The exhibition of the Royal Academy* [exhibition catalogues] · Bryan, *Painters* · W. T. Whitley, *Artists and their friends in England, 1700–1799*, 2 (1928), 316–17

Bonnell, James (1653–1699), government official, was born in Genoa on 14 November 1653, the son of Samuel Bonnell, a merchant and ardent royalist (*d.* 1663), and his wife, Rebecca Sayer (*d. c.*1691), daughter of Thomas Sayer of Norwich. John *Strype, the ecclesiastical historian, was James's cousin and close friend. Samuel himself was the grandson of the protestant refugee Thomas Bonnell, originally 'a gentleman of good family near Ypres' (Hamilton, 1), who had fled Spanish persecutions and settled in Norwich, where he became mayor. Samuel made a promising beginning to his career. Apprenticed to the great London merchant Sir William Courteen he eventually settled at Leghorn, and by 1649 was said to be worth £10,000. However, commercial misfortunes and generous subsidies to the exiled Charles II greatly reduced his circumstances, and in 1655 he returned to England. A belated recompense came in 1662 in the form of a grant of the office of accountant-general of Ireland, worth some £800 a year, jointly to himself and his son. After Samuel's death in March 1663 the office was regranted to James Bonnell and Robert Wood. The benefits of the patent were enjoyed only until 1669: after the removal of the duke of Ormond from the viceroyalty a new Irish establishment was issued in which all remuneration for the accountant-generalship was effectively suspended.

By this time James Bonnell was at Cambridge, where he had been sent, as he put it, 'by the Duke of Ormond's orders' (Hamilton, 1). His mother, 'a woman of singular piety and prudence', had taken great care in his upbringing to 'give a right tincture to his mind, and season it with the love of virtue and religion' (Hamilton, 3). After early education in Dublin he had been sent to school at Trim, co. Meath, under the care of Richard Tennison, later bishop of Meath, who remembered him as 'a child of a most innocent and genteel behaviour, never inclined to any vice, but strictly religious, and extraordinarily ingenious' (Hamilton, 4); one who 'had the greatest sense of religion that ever I knew any boy in my life' (NL Ire., Smythe of Barbavilla MSS, P.C. 435, Tennison to Mrs Jane Bonnell, 21 April 1705). He then proceeded, about 1667, to a nonconformist academy at Nettlebed, Oxfordshire, run by Thomas Cole, former principal of St Mary's Hall, Oxford. The general atmosphere, and in particular the behaviour of his fellow pupils, was not conducive to piety, and he seems to have felt distinctly uncomfortable there. While refusing to find fault with Cole he admitted that the school possessed 'all the dangers and vices of the university without the advantages' (Hamilton, 11).

At St Catharine's College, Cambridge, where he was admitted pensioner in July 1669 and matriculated in 1672, his situation greatly improved: he was taught by Benjamin Calamy, son of the prominent nonconformist Edmund Calamy sen. and was surrounded by like-minded undergraduates, including Calamy's brother James, who became his particular friend, and Offspring Blackall, future bishop of Exeter. In this atmosphere of intense religiosity 'his advancement in learning kept equal pace with his improvements in piety' (Hamilton, 12). He formed habits of personal introspection, prayer, and devotional practice which stayed with him throughout his life, especially the frequent reception of holy communion, and regular observance of fast days. Having graduated BA in 1673, and proceeded MA three years later, he obtained a post as tutor to the young Ralph Freman, son of Ralph Freman of Aspenden in Hertfordshire and later tory MP for the county. Having failed in an application to the crown for an ecclesiastical appointment he accompanied his young charge to the continent in 1678 on a prolonged grand tour to the United Provinces, France, and Italy; and this despite chronic ill health, which he endured with fortitude. They were at Nijmegen in 1678 during the negotiation of the treaty, where Bonnell made a favourable impression on the English diplomat Sir Leoline Jenkins. He eventually returned to Ireland in 1684.

In the meantime his office had been re-established as 'comptroller- and accountant-general': Bonnell held first a half-share and then the whole patent until he was replaced in 1691. Even then he acted as his successor's deputy for more than three years. At some point he ceased to pursue actively his ambition of taking holy orders, declining an offer from his former pupil Freman to purchase an advowson for him, but in essence he remained a priest *manqué*, and always regretted having followed a secular path.

Bonnell remained at his post throughout the revolution of 1688 and the ensuing war, but was subsequently critical of his own passivity, especially when contrasted with the more vigorous opposition to the Jacobites made by his friend William King, later bishop of Derry. At the time his prayers and meditations show not only a deep concern for the protestant cause in Ireland but sorrow for the sins which, he felt, had brought down this providential judgment. His joy and relief at the Williamite victory were tinged with anxiety for the security of the revolution settlement: this, he felt, required not only radical political measures, if possible an incorporating union between England and Ireland, but a thorough reformation in the religious and moral life of protestant Ireland, to propitiate divine providence.

Bonnell's Anglicanism was of a comprehensionist kind, as befitted a former associate of the Calamys, and although he was proud of the traditions of the established church, he was also conscious of the spiritual weaknesses of both clergy and laity. He helped to promote the religious societies which flourished in Dublin in the 1690s, bringing together pious young men to pray, sing psalms, and organize charity for the poor; and the societies for the reformation of manners, which sought to enforce the public observance of Christian precepts, notably sabbath observance (something always close to Bonnell's heart), and the rejection of blasphemy and sexual incontinence. In this work he was greatly encouraged by his marriage, in 1693, to Jane (*d.* in or before 1754), daughter of Sir Albert Conyngham of Mount Charles, co. Donegal, who was both pious and exceedingly well connected (one of her sisters married William Conolly, a future speaker of the Irish House of Commons). She brought him unexpected domestic happiness relatively late in life, bore him a son and a daughter, and subsequently devoted herself to fostering his posthumous reputation. Bonnell left the accountant-general's office in March 1695 to take on the secretaryship of the revived forfeitures commission, and when, a year later, the commission was wound up and its functions transferred to the Irish revenue commission, a place was found for him under the revenue commission as registrar of forfeitures.

Bonnell died of a fever in April 1699 and was buried in St John's Church, Dublin, on 29 April. His funeral sermon, preached by one of his many episcopal friends and admirers, Edward Wetenhall of Kilmore, offered his life as 'a pattern of most universal virtue' (Wetenhall, 30–31), and suggested that in earlier ages he would have been regarded as a saint. Another bishop, William King, composed the inscription for his funerary monument, and, in a somewhat proprietorial manner, proposed writing his life, but the formidable Mrs Bonnell arranged for this honour to pass instead to Archdeacon William Hamilton of Armagh. Published in 1703, the *Life* went through at least seven editions, the last in 1852. Bonnell himself studied and wrote extensively, leaving behind a corpus of manuscript meditations. His favourite authors, not surprisingly, were Thomas à Kempis and Richard Hooker. One work, *The Harmony of the Holy Gospels Digested into one History*, was published posthumously in 1705.

D. W. Hayton

Sources W. Hamilton, *The life and character of James Bonnell, Esq.* (1801) · Venn, *Alum. Cant.*, 1/1.178 · E. Wetenhall, *Of the intermediate state of blessed souls: a sermon preached at the funeral of James Bonnell Esq.* (1703) · J. Bonnell and J. Bonnell, letters to John Strype, CUL, Add. MSS 1–2 · Bonnell's memorials, BL, Lansdowne MS 354 · correspondence of Jane Bonnell, NL Ire., Smythe of Barbavilla MSS, P.C. 435 · W. A. Shaw, ed., *Calendar of treasury books*, 7–14, PRO (1916–34) · *CSP dom.*, *1677–8*; *1682*; *1686–7* · R. Lascelles, ed., *Liber munerum publicorum Hiberniae … or, The establishments of Ireland*, 2 vols. [1824–30] · *The manuscripts of his grace the duke of Portland*, 10 vols., HMC, 29 (1891–1931), vol. 3, pp. 476–81 · *Report on the manuscripts of the marquis of Downshire*, 6 vols. in 7, HMC, 75 (1924–95), vol. 1, p. 155 · A. Vicars, ed., *Index to the prerogative wills of Ireland, 1536–1810* (1897) · T. C. Barnard, 'Reforming Irish manners: the religious societies in Dublin during the 1690s', *HJ*, 35 (1992), 805–38

Archives BL, Lansdowne MS 354 · BL, Strype corresp., Add. MSS 4297, 5853, 38856; Stowe MS 746 · CUL, Strype corresp., Add. MSS 1–2 · NL Ire., Smythe of Barbavilla MSS, P.C. 435 · TCD, corresp. with William King and other material

Likenesses J. Nutting, line engraving (after portrait), NG Ire.; repro. in W. Hamilton, *The life and character of James Bonnell* (1703) · R. White, line engraving, NPG · bas-relief bust, St John's Church, Dublin · line engraving (after bas-relief bust), BM, NPG

Wealth at death see will, Vicars, *Index*, 43

Bonnell, Sara. *See* Talbot, Sara (1888–1993).

Bonner, Edmund (*d.* 1569), bishop of London, was probably born in Hanley, Worcestershire. He was the son of Elizabeth Frodsham, later the wife of Edmund Bonner, sawyer, but most contemporary records suggest that he was the natural son of George Savage, the rector of Davenham, Cheshire [*see* Savage family (*per.* *c.*1369–1528)]. Strype, however, suggests that the allegation of illegitimacy may be false, on the evidence of Sir Nicholas Lechmere, the great-grandson of a great friend of Bonner. If the allegations are indeed false, they may have stemmed from the kindnesses done to the youthful Bonner by John Savage, rector of Quatt in Shropshire, who was later rewarded with a licence to hold additional benefices after Bonner's appointment as bishop.

Early life: study and diplomacy Bonner was admitted to Broadgates Hall in Oxford about 1512. For seven years he studied civil and canon law, and was admitted to the degrees of bachelor of civil law and canon law on consecutive days in July 1519. In July 1526 he received his doctorate in civil law, and in October that year was admitted to the College of Advocates in London. His diplomatic career began in the following March, when he was sent on a mission to the Netherlands. By 1529 he was a chaplain to Cardinal Wolsey, and in August was sent on an embassy to the king of France. Wolsey's downfall in 1530 did not arrest Bonner's progress, and he became a loyal servant of Thomas Cromwell. He was often employed abroad, and during this period became well known for his anti-papal sentiments, expressed clearly in his preface to Stephen Gardiner's *De vera obedientia*. It was only after Cromwell's fall in 1540 that he became more clearly associated with the conservative elements of the Henrician reforms. In the meantime he amassed a number of benefices, which supported his work abroad on behalf of the state. He became archdeacon of Leicester in 1535, and two years later was appointed to a canonry at St Paul's in London, and prebend of Chiswick. Also in 1537 he became a chaplain to the king, receiving a licence to be non-resident and to hold benefices to the value of £500.

In January 1532 Bonner was sent to Rome by the king to protest against his citation there by the pope. He returned to England for a briefing in February 1533, returning to Rome in March. After Henry had been excommunicated Bonner followed the pope on his way to meet François I at Marseilles, where he made known the king's intention to appeal to a general council. In 1536 he was sent to negotiate with the protestants of Denmark and northern Germany. Two years later he was again sent abroad to make contact with the emperor with regard to the calling of a general council. He was transferred from that mission to the court of François I in July 1538, where he remained as ambassador until February 1540. While in Paris he promoted the printing of the Great Bible. It was during this time that the bishopric of Hereford became vacant through the untimely death of Edward Fox, and it was little surprise to find Bonner nominated to that see on 5 October 1538; formal election followed on the 26th.

Conservative prelate Bonner spent much of his time as bishop of Hereford on diplomatic missions abroad, and as a result he had still not received episcopal consecration when, after the death of John Stokesley, he was promoted to be bishop of London. Elected on 20 October 1539, he received royal assent on 7 November and had his temporalities on the 18th. Having returned from his embassy in France in February, Bonner was consecrated bishop on 4 April 1540. Soon afterwards, in September, he ordered a general procession to be held weekly in the city of London, to pray for the ending of the pestilence caused by that year's hot, dry summer. Bonner's enthronement as bishop of London took place in his cathedral church of St Paul on 16 April 1541. His concern with the prevention of the spread of heresy first showed itself when in December 1541 he issued an injunction requiring Alexander Nowell and William Tolwin, rector of St Antholin, Watling Street, to make a public recantation at Paul's Cross of their erroneous opinions regarding free will and good works. Soon after this he was again sent on an embassy, this time to the emperor Charles V, from February 1542 to November 1543. On Whit Sunday 1546 (13 June) Bonner took part in the public celebration of thanksgiving for the peace with France. He presided at a solemn Te Deum after high mass in the cathedral, sitting next to the lord mayor of London, then carried the sacrament in procession, with all the parish churches of London taking part. On the Friday following (18 June) he sat in the Guildhall with Nicholas Heath in the trial of Anne Askew and others for heresy. While the three men before them were persuaded (by Bonner, Heath, and others) to recant on the following day, Askew refused and was sent to the Tower where she was racked in order to obtain a confession (and probably to induce her to implicate Queen Katherine Parr, a known sympathizer with the new religion).

Despite his diplomatic contacts with continental protestantism Bonner remained broadly conservative in doctrine. When matters of religion took a turn towards reform on the accession of Edward VI, Bonner soon found himself in difficulties for his opinions. He was present at the coronation of the new king on 13 February 1547, and two days later attended the funeral of Henry VIII; he was one of a number of bishops who met the corpse at Syon and Windsor on its way to burial. Bonner appears to have given some offence to members of the council, to the extent that on 1 March the bishop of Winchester, Stephen Gardiner, found it necessary to write on his behalf to Sir William Paget. He seems to have kept a low profile in the first year of the young king's reign, and appears at the very least to have failed to encourage the progress of the reform that the new regime was promoting so vigorously. This lack of progress led the king to write to the bishop on 2 August 1549, not long after the first Book of Common Prayer came into force, of the negligence of many in his diocese who neglected to attend church and the holy communion. This was put down to Bonner's 'evil example and slackness'; although he used to preach frequently, and at least on all principal feasts, he now preached very rarely indeed. The king, as supreme head of the church, ordered Bonner to reform, and commanded him, in his next sermon at St Paul's, to preach strongly against rebellion and resistance to temporal authority, and in support of obedience in the use of the rites of the church as established by law. A week later the king sent further injunctions to the bishop (delivered to him on 10 August), requiring him to celebrate communion in St Paul's a week from the following Sunday, and to declare in his sermon that despite his youth the present king's authority was no less than that of any of his predecessors; he was also to preach God's displeasure at rebellion.

Instead of obeying these orders, however, Bonner preached in support of the doctrine of transubstantiation, and omitted to emphasize the authority of the king. His failure to observe the king's clear instructions was discussed by the council on 8 September, and a commission for his deprivation was appointed. He was committed to

Edmund Bonner (*d.* **1569**), by unknown engraver, pubd 1563 [seated, right]

the Marshalsea, and after inquiry by two royal commissions was deprived of his bishopric on 1 October. He returned to prison where he was to remain at the king's pleasure. His removal was well received by many of the reforming party. In a letter to Heinrich Bullinger of 7 November 1549 John Hooper wrote of the confinement and deposition of 'the most bitter enemy of the gospel', with whom he had had a 'sharp and dangerous contest' at Paul's Cross and in the council. Prophetically, he added 'Should he be again restored to his office and episcopal function, I shall, I doubt not, be restored to my country and my Father which is in heaven' (Robinson, 69–70). The author of the grey friars' chronicle relates how on 8 January 1550 Bonner had his bed removed by the keeper of the prison, and for eight days had only straw and a coverlet to lie on, for refusing to pay his gaoler the sum of £10. Bonner's appeal against his sentence was heard on 6 February 1550, when he was taken from the Marshalsea to the council, sitting in Star Chamber at Westminster. He was informed that his appeal had been considered and dismissed by eight privy councillors. His deprivation by the archbishop and other commissioners stood, and his sentence was confirmed. He remained confined in the Marshalsea, without allowance for food or clothing, for the remainder of Edward VI's reign.

Catholic restoration Edward VI died on 6 July 1553, and on Saturday 5 August a pardon was sent from Queen Mary to Bonner in the Marshalsea, under the great seal of England. Bonner was effectively immediately reinstated as bishop of London, and went straight to his house at St Paul's on that evening. He was greeted with great joy by the people, who rang the bells of the cathedral. There is evidence, however, that Bonner's release was not greeted with universal acclaim. On Sunday 13 August he was present at Paul's Cross for a sermon by the leading conservative preacher (later bishop of Bath and Wells) Gilbert Bourne, who included in his bidding prayer an intercession for the souls departed, and in his sermon declared that Bonner had been wrongfully imprisoned. A serious commotion ensued, and a dagger was thrown at Bourne, missing him but hitting the post of the pulpit. The mayor and aldermen dispersed the crowd only with some difficulty, and Bonner had to be led through St Paul's to safety.

Bonner was formally restored to his bishopric on 22 August. The altars of his cathedral had been torn down in the previous reign, and he immediately set about having them restored. He sang mass in St Paul's on 17 September, then on 7 October, at the beginning of the convocation held there, sang the mass of the Holy Ghost at the high altar in full pontificals, the first mass to be celebrated there after it had been set up again. Bonner enjoyed the royal favour from the outset, and in January 1554 he was sent as one of the queen's ambassadors to meet Philip of Spain at Portsmouth. On 13 March he was appointed one of the commissioners for the examination of those bishops who had contracted marriage in the previous reign, and two days later to the commission for the deprivation of several of them. To fill the vacancies thus created he assisted Stephen Gardiner in consecrating six new bishops on 1 April. There was, however, much resistance to the restoration of Catholicism of which these consecrations were an important part. On 8 April a cat, made to look like a priest saying mass, was found hanged in Cheapside. It was taken to Bonner, who had it displayed at Paul's Cross during sermon time. Despite the offer of a reward by the lord mayor, no one was ever brought to account for this action. On 25 July Bonner was present at the marriage of Philip and Mary in Winchester Cathedral. In the following month he was in St Paul's, with the lord mayor and nine other bishops, for high mass, Te Deum, and procession, to give thanks for the queen's (mistaken) pregnancy, and to pray for her safe delivery.

Bonner commenced a visitation of his diocese on 3 September, ending on 8 October 1555. Undertaken under his own authority as bishop, rather than by virtue of the royal supremacy as had been the case for the previous twenty years, Bonner's visitation was a model of thoroughness in its inquiries into the morals, beliefs, and practices of the people of his diocese. He visited in person, preaching everywhere he went, while his articles formed the basis for those of a number of later visitations by other bishops, including those of Cardinal Pole's metropolitical visitation of 1556. On 28 October he consecrated John Hopton as bishop of Norwich, then on 18 November consecrated Ralph Baynes to Coventry and Lichfield, and John Holyman to Bristol. He also conducted personally about a quarter of the ordination ceremonies held in the diocese throughout the reign of Mary, many of which seem to have included large numbers of candidates for minor orders, perhaps as a way of validating the orders of those who had been ordained using the Edwardine ordinals, then generally considered deficient. On Advent Sunday (2 December) he and the lord chancellor (Gardiner) received Cardinal Pole at St Paul's. In Christmas week Bonner ordered that the feast of St Thomas of Canterbury (29 December) be kept as a holy day throughout his diocese. In September the following year he undertook three more episcopal consecrations, and after the death of Gardiner on 13 November conducted his funeral rites.

On his release Bonner had returned to him the control of all the estates that he had held as bishop when he was first summoned to trial in 1549. The restored estates included manors at Braintree and Southminster and lands at Hackney which had been given away by Nicholas Ridley during his tenure of the London diocese. The manors had been intended for the endowment of the short-lived diocese of Westminster, and Bonner was also allowed to retain the lands that had been granted to Ridley in exchange for them. He found it difficult, however, to draw any revenue from these properties; no income from them is recorded in his accounts for 1557, while in 1558 he appealed to Pole for help in securing Southminster. Much of his concern for his lands stemmed from his desire to provide financial support for his relatives, members of the Mongey family, to whom he gave leases of diocesan estates for sixty or seventy years, and also his mother, sister, and niece.

The attack on heresy: 'Bloody Bonner'? It was during the Marian years that Bonner gained a reputation for fierceness in his prosecution of heresy, earning him the title Bloody Bonner. His diocese had a long history of Lollardy, and the capital tended also to draw to itself those most active in promoting new ideas, in religion as in anything else. It was not surprising that new ideas had taken root there more securely than elsewhere under Edward VI, and it was also the place where they would be most obvious to those in government who were concerned with the restoration of Catholic orthodoxy. However, in the early years of the reign Bonner was reluctant to proceed in this matter with much vigour. In 1555 he was warned by the council for his slackness, as two months had passed without any convictions. His image as a bloody persecutor of the godly derived from his later actions, after his earlier misgivings had been overcome by pressure from government and the goading of obstinate heretics. His active campaign began in earnest soon after this, when on 25 May he sat with the lord mayor in St Paul's, and condemned a number of individuals for their opinions against the sacrament of the altar. Of 282 burnings recorded in episcopal registers for the period, 232 took place in the dioceses of London, Canterbury, Norwich, and Chichester; half the burnings in these four dioceses took place in Bonner's see of London.

It was not only in the eradication of heretics that Bonner and the other bishops sought to restore Catholicism and eliminate heresy. In 1554 Queen Mary's articles had required of each diocesan bishop that the people should be compelled to attend church and to receive instruction. To enable this to happen the bishops were to set forth a uniform order by homilies or other means for the teaching of the people. Bonner's response to this was to publish in 1555 his treatise *A Profitable and Necessary Doctrine with Certain Homilies Adjoined Thereto*. The treatise was modelled on the King's Book of 1543, thus retaining both continuity with the recent past and a link with a work that had been a focus for traditionalists in the reign of Edward VI. He was sent to Oxford in February 1556, where he carried out with Thomas Thirlby the solemn degradation of Cranmer, after which the former archbishop, now reduced to the lay state, could be handed over to the civil powers for burning (though Foxe's account of the incident, contrasting Bonner's fierceness with the reluctance and gentleness of Cranmer's old friend Thirlby, may have been exaggerated). The execution took place on 21 March, and on the following day Cardinal Pole was consecrated as archbishop, Bonner being one of those who assisted in this rite. He was also one of the bishops who received Pole at Bow church in London for mass on the feast of the Annunciation (25 March). On 30 June he took part in a procession at St Paul's for the patronal feast, while in July he and other royal commissioners set out a new order for processions. On 29 December 1556 (the feast of St Thomas of Canterbury) the council appointed him to a commission to seek out heretical books and writings. When a commission to inquire concerning heresy was set up on 8 February 1557, Bonner was one of the two bishops appointed to it, along with Thomas Thirlby, then bishop of Ely. It was little surprise to find these two acting together, as both were trained in civil and canon law, and each had a diocese containing a number of major centres of heresy—London in Bonner's case, and Cambridge in Thirlby's.

An important part of the Catholic restoration was the attempt to reverse the dissolution of the monasteries, both by refounding dissolved institutions and (more rarely) by setting up new foundations. As a part of this process on 1 August 1557 Bonner carried out the perpetual enclosure of a community of nuns of Syon. The late summer of 1557 found Bonner associated with the funeral rites of a number of important people, including those for Anne of Cleves, the duchess of Norfolk, and the countess of Arundel. On 21 November 1557 he consecrated John Christopherson as bishop of Chichester. His activity against heretics continued through the final year of Mary's reign, and on 21 March 1558 he examined three heretics from his diocese, who were condemned to death by him, and handed over to the civil arm to be burnt. A report of Nicholas Sander, dating from about 1561, on the change of religion in England which took place in 1558–9 after the death of Queen Mary, includes both an evaluation of Bonner the man, and a rationale of his severe approach to the prosecution of heresy. Stressing Bonner's 'greatness of mind', Sander notes how even some Catholics considered he had been too zealous in his persecution, having condemned more heretics than all the other Marian bishops together. Bonner's usual reply to this charge was that one death, by which many lives would be saved, was full of mercy, and that in matters of state the individual was of less concern than the whole body of citizens.

Deprivation, imprisonment, and death The reputation of Bonner as a persecutor of heretics was widespread in the reign of Elizabeth I, and he was said by a contemporary commentator to have been in danger of his life whenever he ventured out, and that if any of the Marian bishops were executed, he would be the first to lose his life. There is a story that when the bishops were presented to the new queen after her accession she declined to offer him her hand to be kissed on account of his actions in the previous reign. He continued to be used on diplomatic business to the end, and on 23 May 1559 he entertained the French ambassadors, who stayed with him in his palace until 28 May. He was offered the oath of supremacy on 30 May, which he refused, and he was deprived of his bishopric, though allowed to remain at liberty. On 20 April 1560 he was again imprisoned in the Marshalsea, though it would appear under less restraint than during his previous confinement ten years before. He was held there under the jurisdiction of the bishop of Winchester, Robert Horne, for the rest of his life. In April 1564 he was taken from the prison by Horne and offered the oath of supremacy. Bonner had already once refused the oath, and to refuse a second time was a capital offence. At this point Bonner's legal training and forty years in the service of the state came into their own. When Horne presented the certificate of Bonner's refusal to the court of queen's bench, Bonner argued that it was without legal force as it named Horne as bishop of Winchester, and that under English law Horne's consecration was invalid, having been carried out by Matthew Parker whose own consecration as archbishop of Canterbury in 1559 had not been performed in accordance with the law then in force. Rather than test this argument in court the government chose not to proceed with the case. An act retrospectively validating all consecrations carried out since the beginning of Elizabeth's reign was passed in 1567, but Bonner was not again troubled with the oath. He died, still a prisoner in the Marshalsea, on 5 September 1569, and was buried at midnight in the churchyard of St George's, Southwark, on the order of Bishop Grindal of London, who feared that the occasion might otherwise lead to serious disturbances.

The image of Bonner as a cruel, even sadistic, man is drawn largely from Foxe's interpretation of his actions. While it is true that he could be short-tempered, insolent, and tactless (Cromwell had more than once to protect him from the consequences of his own actions), he was also an able lawyer, quick-witted in argument. He seems to have become more violent as he grew older, perhaps as a result of his harsh confinement in the early 1550s; even so, it is possible that some of his reported excesses of behaviour were intended to frighten heretics into recantation and so to save them from the flames. Although clearly a difficult personality, it is none the less unfortunate that his reputation for cruelty has come to overshadow many years of valued service to both church and state.

KENNETH CARLETON

Sources Emden, *Oxf.*, 4.57–9 • W. Stubbs, *Registrum sacrum Anglicanum*, 2nd edn (1897) • *Fasti Angl., 1300–1541*, [Lincoln] • *Fasti Angl., 1300–1541*, [Hereford] • *Fasti Angl., 1300–1541*, [St Paul's, London] • W. M. Brady, *The episcopal succession in England, Scotland, and Ireland, AD 1400 to 1875*, 2 (1876) • C. Wriothesley, *A chronicle of England during the reigns of the Tudors from AD 1485 to 1559*, ed. W. D. Hamilton, 2 vols., CS, new ser., 11, 20 (1875–7) • *The diary of Henry Machyn, citizen and merchant-taylor of London, from AD 1550 to AD 1563*, ed. J. G. Nichols, CS, 42 (1848) • J. G. Nichols, ed., *The chronicle of Queen Jane, and of two years of Queen Mary*, CS, old ser., 48 (1850) • J. G. Nichols, ed., *The chronicle of the grey friars of London*, CS, 53 (1852) • *APC*, 1547–50 • *CSP dom.*, 1547–80 • H. Robinson, ed. and trans., *Original letters relative to the English Reformation*, 1 vol. in 2, Parker Society, [26] (1846–7) • J. Strype, *Annals of the Reformation and establishment of religion … during Queen Elizabeth's happy reign*, new edn, 1/2 (1824) • J. H. Pollen, ed., 'Dr Nicholas Sander's report to Cardinal Moroni', *Miscellanea, I*, Catholic RS, 1 (1905), 1–47 [from a transcript of Archivio segreto vaticano, Armaria 64:28, fols. 252r–274r] • K. Carleton, *Bishops and reform in the English church, 1520–1559* (2001) • S. Brigden, *London and the Reformation* (1989) • F. Heal, *Of prelates and princes: a study of the economic and social position of the Tudor episcopate* (1980) • G. Alexander, 'Bonner and the Marian persecutions', *History*, new ser., 60 (1975), 374–91

Archives BL, corresp. and papers, Harley MSS • BL, papers relating to his mission to Lubeck, Add. MS 48036 • GL, episcopal registers, London, MS 9531/12, part 1 • GL, episcopal registers, London, MS 9531/12, part 2, fols. 323–483 • Inner Temple Library, London, corresp. and papers | BL, letters to Henry VIII and papers, Cotton MSS

Likenesses woodcut, pubd 1563, BM, NPG [*see illus.*]

Bonner, George Wilmot [George William] (**1796–1836**), wood-engraver, was born on 24 May 1796 at Devizes, Wiltshire. Having been educated at Bath, he was apprenticed first to an uncle, Allen Robert Branston, a wood-engraver in London, and later to James Henry Vizetelly, of Vizetelly and Branston. He became a proficient draughtsman and engraver, employing the white-line style of engraving, popularized by Thomas Bewick, in a competent if pedestrian way. His greatest skill was his ability to produce a gradation of tints by using a combination of blocks.

Bonner was also a good instructor, and several of his apprentices became important engravers. Most notably he trained William James Linton (from 1828), who lived with him for some time at 12 Canterbury Row, Kennington (Bonner's address in trade journals between 1832 and 1836). Linton described Bonner as 'a clever artist, and a good master' (Linton, 191–2), and recalled how his master had taught him all the processes of wood-engraving from the cutting of woodblocks to the most delicate graver work, and had encouraged him to sketch from nature (including from animals at London Zoo) to avoid becoming a mechanical copyist. Another talented apprentice of Bonner was W. H. Powis. By contrast, Henry Vizetelly, who came to Bonner around 1835, dismissed him as a 'second-rate wood engraver, who intensified in his woodcuts the conventional mannerisms of the bold watercolour drawings which he was somewhat adept at producing' (Vizetelly, 119–20). He finished his training elsewhere, on account of Bonner's unexpected death on 3 January 1836, which Vizetelly ascribed to brain fever. Bonner was apparently unmarried.

One of Bonner's first engravings was a frontispiece designed by Robert Cruikshank for John Cumberland's British Theatre and Minor Theatre series (1820 onwards). Another was his engraving of W. H. Brooke's painting *Mercy* (inspired by William Collins's 'An Ode on Mercy'), which was printed in colour in William Savage's *Practical Hints on Decorative Printing* (1822), a milestone in the history of chromoxylography. In its preface Savage noted that he had used engravers who would 'show what the art is capable of producing at the present day in England' (p. v).

Above all, Bonner excelled in his portrayal of animals. He produced plates for William Pickering's edition of Izaak Walton and Charles Cotton's *The Compleat Angler* (1825); engraved numerous vignettes after William Harvey's designs for James Northcote's *Fables* (1828; second series 1833); and provided wood-engravings for two zoological publications by Edward Turner Bennett: *The Tower Menagerie* (1829) and *Zoological Gardens* (1835). Quite frequently, too, he produced landscapes and topographical views. Many vignettes were commissioned by William Kidd for his guidebooks, including *Picturesque Pocket Companion to Margate, Ramsgate, Broadstairs* (1831) and *Kidd's New Guide to the 'Lions' of London* (1832), while numerous views by Bonner enlivened Arthur Freeling's *Picturesque Excursions* (1839).

Possibly the best-known publication on which Bonner worked was Francis Douce's *The Dance of Death*, printed at the Chiswick Press in 1833. Douce pointed out in the preface that the facsimile designs from the Lyons edition of 1547 had been 'executed with consummate skill and fidelity by Messrs Bonner and Byfield, two of our best artists in the line of wood engraving. They may very justly be regarded as scarcely distinguishable from their fine originals' (pp. v–vi). Certainly these engravings were far superior to most available at the time. Bonner signed his work in a spidery hand: G. W. Bonner; G. Bonner, SC; Bonner; G. B.; G. B. Sc; G. W. B.

SUSANNA AVERY-QUASH

Sources W. J. Linton, *The masters of wood-engraving* (1889), 99, 134, 171, 191–3, 201–2, 204 • H. Vizetelly, *Glances back through seventy years: autobiographical and other reminiscences*, 1 (1893), 119–24 • L. Binyon, *Catalogue of drawings by British artists and artists of foreign origin working in Great Britain*, 4 vols. (1898–1907) • R. K. Engen, *Dictionary of Victorian engravers, print publishers and their works* (1979) • *DNB* • Redgrave, *Artists* • R. Russell, *Guide to British topographical prints* (1979), 146 • R. McLean, *Victorian book design and colour printing*, rev. edn (1972), 34, 171 • Bryan, *Painters* (1903–5) • Thieme & Becker, *Allgemeines Lexikon* • Bénézit, *Dict.* • P. Muir, *Victorian illustrated books* (1971), 36–7
Archives BM, proofs

Bonner, Hypatia Bradlaugh (1858–1935), freethinker and radical, was born in London on 30 March 1858 at 3 Hedger's Terrace, Hackney, the second child of Charles *Bradlaugh (1833–1891), politician and freethinker, and Susannah Lamb Hooper (*d.* 1877). Her elder sister, **Alice Bradlaugh** (1856–1888), who was born on 30 April 1856 at 4 West Street, Bethnal Green, shared many of her early experiences and interests. They received a basic education at private schools in London, but learnt French from political refugees and in 1872 attended school briefly in Paris. However, after their parents' separation in 1870 most of their time was spent at their grandparents' home in Midhurst, Sussex, with their mother who suffered from alcoholism.

After Susannah Bradlaugh's death in 1877 the girls moved back to London to keep house for their father at 20 Circus Road, St John's Wood. He and Annie Besant were involved in the 'Knowlton pamphlet' obscenity trial, and the daughters were kept fully occupied in his support, though they resented Mrs Besant's presumptuous attitude towards their father. During the early 1880s their principal contribution to secularism was at the Old Street Hall of Science, where Edward Aveling ran the secularists' school. Alice studied chemistry and animal physiology, and subsequently taught French and botany; Hypatia taught chemistry and mathematics, four of her lectures being published in 1882 as *Chemistry of Home*. In 1881 both sisters were recognized as teachers by the Department of Science and Art, and Hypatia subsequently passed the matriculation examinations for London University. Educational progress, though, was halted by prejudice. In 1877 the sisters had attended J. H. Levy's political economy classes at the City of London College, only for the college to close its doors to female students, and in 1883 Alice, along with Annie Besant, was refused admittance to botany classes at University College.

Among Hypatia's pupils at the Hall of Science was Arthur Bonner (1861–1939), the son of a radical nonconformist minister. Following their engagement in January 1884 he was employed as Bradlaugh's printer, and they married at Marylebone register office on 18 June 1885. Shortly afterwards they took rooms with Annie Besant at 19 Avenue Road, Regent's Park, where Hypatia met many of the leading radical intellectuals of the day. A son, Kenneth, was born on 3 April 1886 but died on 22 September. Both Alice and Hypatia were active as freethought lecturers and contributors to the *National Reformer*, and in 1883 were elected vice-presidents of the National Secular Society. Hypatia also wrote for Annie Besant's *Our Corner* (1883–8), some of her children's stories there being published separately in 1886. Alice's only published lecture was *Mind Considered as a Bodily Function* (1884), though she left several manuscripts of lectures. She died of meningitis and typhoid on 2 December 1888 at her sister's home and was buried at Brookwood necropolis, Woking, on 5 December.

Hypatia moved back to 20 Circus Road where a second son, Charles, was born on 28 April 1890. She acted as her father's secretary until his death in 1891 and then moved to 30 Victoria Road, Clapham Common, and again, in 1894 or 1895, to 23 Streathbourne Road, which was to be their final home. The months immediately after her father's death were spent arranging his papers, defending his reputation, and writing her two-volume *Charles Bradlaugh: a Record of his Life and Work* (1894). Arthur Bonner continued to manage the printing and publishing business in partnership with Hypatia, who inherited the plant and titles, including the *National Reformer*, to which she contributed regularly until declining circulation forced its closure in 1893.

Politically Hypatia was an advanced Liberal, advocating women's suffrage but later opposing the violence of the suffragettes. From March 1897 she edited her own monthly paper, *The Reformer*, but falling circulation during the Second South African War forced its closure in 1904. She lectured widely and served on the executives of the Women's National Liberal Federation, the International Arbitration and Peace League, and the Humanitarian League, for which she wrote an attack on the death penalty in 1905. She was, however, increasingly dissatisfied with G. W. Foote at the National Secular Society and in 1905 became a Rationalist Press Association lecturer, joining the board in 1916. In 1910 she was founder chair of the Rationalist Peace Society and also campaigned against the blasphemy laws, of which she wrote a history, *Penalties upon Opinion*, in 1912.

Hypatia remained a popular lecturer in Liberal and rationalist circles until 1924, when her voice failed. Despite the fact that she had suffered ill health since she was a child, she showed remarkable vigour through a long public career and remained active into old age, continuing to write and serving as a London magistrate from 1921 until 1934. She died at 23 Streathbourne Road, London, after an abdominal operation for cancer, on 25 August 1935 and was cremated at Golders Green on 28 August. Her ashes were then buried in her father's grave at Brookwood. She was a daughter worthy of her formidable father, whose reputation she tenaciously defended. Her own role in public affairs has been underestimated, not least because she expressed her radicalism and belief in equal status for women from within Liberalism rather than through the more publicized suffragette movement.

EDWARD ROYLE

Sources A. Bonner and C. B. Bonner, *Hypatia Bradlaugh Bonner: the story of her life* (1942) · H. B. Bonner and J. M. Robertson, *Charles Bradlaugh: a record of his life and work … with an account of his parliamentary struggle, politics and teachings, by John M. Robertson*, 2 vols. (1894) · J. F. Rayner, 'The Bradlaugh Bonner family', *Truth Seeker* (Jan 1896), 1–3 · *Literary Guide* (Oct 1935), 179–82 · 'Mrs Bonner's last farewell', *Literary Guide* (Oct 1935), 182 · E. Royle, *Radicals, secularists and republicans: popular freethought in Britain, 1866–1915* (1980) · E. Royle, ed., *The Bradlaugh papers* (1975), x–xi · b. cert. · m. cert. · d. cert. · b. cert. [Alice Bradlaugh]
Archives Bishopsgate Institute, London, Bradlaugh MSS
Likenesses Beethoven of London, photograph, 1890, repro. in Bonner and Bonner, *Hypatia Bradlaugh Bonner*, facing p. 41 · Elliott & Fry, two photographs, repro. in Bonner and Bonner, *Hypatia Bradlaugh Bonner*, facing pp. 41, 102 · Lafayette & Co., photograph (in old age), repro. in Bonner and Bonner, *Hypatia Bradlaugh Bonner*, frontispiece · group portrait, photograph (with husband Arthur and son Charles), repro. in Rayner, 'The Bradlaugh Bonner family', 1
Wealth at death £2115 7s. 4d.: probate, 23 Dec 1935, *CGPLA Eng. & Wales*

Bonner, Richard (*fl.* 1541–1548), religious controversialist, was incumbent of St Tricat in Calais, appointed by Cranmer on 6 June 1541. Little more is known of him except the treatise published in his name in 1548, *A treatyse of the ryght honourynge and wourshyppyng of our saviour Jesus Christe in the sacrament of breade and wyne*. This work was dedicated to Cranmer, from 'your obedyent Diocesan and dayly orator, Rycharde Bonner', the dedication dated 14 November. The treatise discussed eucharistic doctrine, concerning which Bonner had recently been in correspondence with Martin Bucer, whose reply to Bonner dated 4 September 1548 survives. It expressed a view on how the sacrament should be honoured which incorporated much unacknowledged quotation from Bucer's own work. Bonner emphasized that outward signs of respect were appropriate, 'as with the uncoveryng of our headdes, wyth the knelyng and bowyng downe of our bodyes, and with the praysyng of hys goodnes therein with oure tounges' (Bonner, sig. Avv). However, such outward reverence was to be preceded by a spiritual honouring, and true faith and trust in Christ's passion and resurrection. He condemned practices such as the reservation of the host, or non-communicating, 'private' masses.

It seems likely that Bonner's primary purpose in writing this work may have been to deploy the views of Bucer and Cranmer at a precarious stage in the implementation of reformed eucharistic doctrine. Certainly in the preface Bonner stated that he had been 'constrayned to wryte of thys so weyghty a matter' (Bonner, sig. Aiiv). It is notable that ideas and actual phrases from the treatise can be found in the Book of Common Prayer of 1549 and 1552. The coincidence that the author bore the same surname as the conservative bishop Edmund Bonner may also have enhanced his suitability as a controversialist at this time. All this may suggest that Bonner was a relatively minor figure being used by Cranmer at a delicate stage of the Edwardian Reformation. And yet he was in correspondence with Bucer, a major reforming figure, which suggests another possibility, that he was one of the network of agents discreetly employed by Cranmer, a role in which his benefice in Calais would have been an asset. This would explain why so little about his life and work is known.

L. E. C. WOODING

Sources R. Bonner, *A treatyse of the ryght honourynge and wourshyppyng of our saviour Jesus Christe in the sacrament of breade and wyne* (1548) · D. MacCulloch, *Thomas Cranmer: a life* (1996), 372n., 399–403, 463 · D. MacCulloch, *Tudor church militant: Edward VI and the protestant Reformation* (1999), 234 · CCC Cam., MS 113, pp. 315–24 · Cranmer's register, LPL, fol. 380v
Archives CCC Cam., MS 113, pp. 315–24 · LPL, Cranmer's register, fol. 380v

Bonnerjee, Woomes Chunder (1844–1906), lawyer and politician, was born on 29 December 1844 at his paternal grandfather's country house at Sonai, Kidderpore, Bengal, the second but eldest surviving son of Girish Chunder Bonnerjee (1823–1868), an attorney, and his wife, Saraswati Devi. The family were Hindu, Bengali brahmins; they claimed descent from Bhattanarayan who went to Bengal in the reign of Adisur in the eleventh century. W. C. Bonnerjee's paternal grandfather, Pitambar Bonnerjee (1781–1853), was a banian (legal clerk) to British solicitors of the Calcutta supreme court. His eldest son, Girish Chunder Bonnerjee, was a successful attorney of the Calcutta high court, called 'the prince of attorneys' (Bonnerjee, 8), and died of diabetes. When W. C. Bonnerjee was a boy his family lived at 28 (later 15) Noyan Chand Dutt's Street in the Simla area of Calcutta. He was educated at the Oriental Seminary and the Hindu School, Calcutta. About 1859, when he was fifteen, he was married to Srimati Hemangini Devi, daughter of Nilmoni Motilal; they had four sons (one died aged eleven) and four daughters. Concerned at his negligence, his father removed him from school and in 1861 articled him to a local British solicitor. He worked hard, and also helped his friend Girish Chandra Ghosh found *The Bengalee*.

Bonnerjee won a government scholarship to study law in England and, knowing he would lose caste by crossing the ocean and that his father would not agree, left secretly without telling him. Though his father disapproved, he did not break with him but sent him money. Bonnerjee lodged at 108 Denbigh Street, St George's Road, London SW. He was admitted a student of the Middle Temple on 19 November 1864 and was called to the bar on 11 June 1867. He was a founder and secretary of the London Indian Society, and advocated representative and responsible government in India. He also travelled on the continent. England was apparently a formative experience. He wrote in August 1865 to his uncle that he was 'an altered man' and had 'discarded all ideas of caste', that India was then 'so degraded' and that he hated 'all the demoralising practices of our countrymen' (Bonnerjee, 14–15). Although he was 'inordinately proud' (ibid., 100) that he was a brahmin, he became Anglophile and largely Anglicized. According to his biographer, 'many have regretted that he should have so completely given up the habits of his countrymen' (ibid., 99).

Bonnerjee left England in November 1868, and on 12 November was enrolled an advocate of the Calcutta high court, the fourth Indian barrister there. He was outstandingly successful, building up a wide and lucrative practice. His successes included the Burdwan libel case, in which he defended Robert Knight, editor of *The Statesman*. He was the first Indian to act as standing counsel. He declined a judgeship, earning far more as a barrister. He was considered one of the greatest Indian lawyers. His legal eminence led to involvement with Calcutta University. He was a member of its syndicate, president of its faculty of law (1884), and its first representative on the legislative council (1894–5).

In 1883 Bonnerjee defended, allegedly feebly, Surendranath Banerjea, who had made untrue and defamatory criticism of Justice Norris of the Calcutta high court. Bonnerjee's effigy was burnt by Calcutta students for having defended Banerjea unsatisfactorily. In December 1885 in Bombay, Bonnerjee was a founder and, proposed by Allan Octavian Hume (1829–1912), was unanimously elected the first president of the Indian National Congress. Claiming to represent the people of India, the Congress was then not a political party but a pressure group; it was little more than an annual conference of loyal, western-educated moderates, largely Bengalis, Hindus—disproportionately brahmin—and lawyers, whose aim was not the destruction of the raj but fuller participation in it, with Indianization and representative institutions. Bonnerjee valued British political institutions, and spoke at Congress of 'England the land of political freedom' (Argov, 43). Like other Congressmen then, he looked to British Liberals to introduce the desired changes in India, and hoped to penetrate and influence the Liberal Party. Gladstone was his political hero, and he was proud that he and Gladstone had the same birthday. In 1888 Bonnerjee visited England and, under Liberal auspices, spoke at public meetings on India, in August at Northampton with Charles Bradlaugh. Bonnerjee was one of the small oligarchy who dominated and virtually controlled late-nineteenth-century Congress. In 1892 he was again president. While personally opposed to child marriage and the dowry system, he argued that Congress should confine itself to political issues, leaving social issues to the different religious communities. He also attempted to reassure Muslims that representative institutions would not be contrary to their interests. He and Pherozeshah Mehta controlled the 1901 Congress, ending the Indian Congress Committee, alleging that 'young and comparatively inexperienced members' (Argov, 90) were assuming unjustified responsibility. Bonnerjee and his associates were accused of despotism and the Punjabi delegates threatened to secede. Bonnerjee helped to subsidize Congress activity in India and England, including its British committee and journal *India*. He wrote in 1905 that he keenly sympathized with the Swadeshi movement.

Wealthy from the bar, Bonnerjee about 1890 bought a large house, 8 Bedford Park, Croydon, Surrey, which he named Kidderpore and where he 'lived in great affluence, mixed with the best English society' (Bonnerjee, 103). His children were educated mostly in England. His three surviving sons attended Rugby School and Oxford, and became lawyers: his daughters attended Newnham and Girton colleges, Cambridge. Bonnerjee lived partly in England and partly in India until 1902, thereafter living mostly at Croydon and practising before the judicial committee of the privy council. In 1895 he unsuccessfully contested Barrow in Furness as a Liberal candidate. Shortly before his death he was Liberal candidate for Walthamstow, east London, but withdrew through ill health. He had an attack of diabetes in 1888, and after it his health deteriorated. In his last years he suffered from diabetes (for which there was then no known cure or effective treatment) and Bright's disease. From 1904 his eyesight deteriorated and he became blind. Nevertheless he continued working, and conducted his last case before the privy council about three weeks before his death. He came to think in English, and valued English culture, Shakespeare and Dickens being his favourite authors. A tolerant man, he accepted the conversion to Christianity of one son and two daughters, and the marriage to British persons of two of his children. He died at his home, Kidderpore, on 21 July 1906 and was cremated, the urn being buried at his Croydon residence. His wife survived him. At a memorial meeting in London, Gokhale praised Bonnerjee as an 'ardent patriot' and said that 'in a self-governing country he would, without doubt, have attained the position of Prime Minister' (Bonnerjee, 117–18).

ROGER T. STEARN

Sources S. Bonnerjee, *Life of W. C. Bonnerjee: first president of the Indian National Congress* (1944) • H. A. C. Sturgess, ed., *Register of admissions to the Honourable Society of the Middle Temple, from the fifteenth century to the year 1944*, 2 (1949) • J. Foster, *Men-at-the-bar: a biographical hand-list of the members of the various inns of court*, 2nd edn (1885) • D. Argov, *Moderates and extremists in the Indian nationalist movement, 1883–1920* (1967) • B. R. Nanda, *Gokhale: the Indian moderates and the British raj* (1977) • V. Lovett, *A history of the Indian nationalist movement* (1921) • J. M. Brown, *Modern India: the origins of an Asian democracy* (1994) • P. Moon, *The British conquest and dominion of India* (1989) • R. J. Moore, *Liberalism and Indian politics, 1872–1922* (1966) • *Kelly's London suburban directory*, 1888, 1892, 1903 • F. W. S. Craig, *British parliamentary election results, 1885–1918* (1974) • *CGPLA Eng. & Wales* (1906)

Wealth at death £8884 15*s*. 4*d*.: probate, 17 Aug 1906, *CGPLA Eng. & Wales*

Bonnet, Stede (*d*. 1718), pirate, may have been a soldier as he was given the title of major during his trial, where he was also treated as an educated gentleman by the officers of the court. The most that can at present be said about his family is that he is probably the Stede Bonnet who married Mary Allumbey in the parish of St Michael's, Barbados, on 21 November 1709; they had at least one son, baptized in the same parish in September 1714.

Perhaps in an attempt to escape a bad marriage or to

recapture his more adventurous youth Bonnet took to the sea, buying and outfitting the ship *Revenge* of ten guns and 70 tons. In 1717 the *Revenge* appeared off Virginia and then sailed to Charles Town, South Carolina, where Bonnet captured two ships. Next he appeared on the Honduran coast, where he met the notorious Edward Teach or Blackbeard. Bonnet's men apparently doubted his ability as a captain, as did Teach, who removed Bonnet from command of the *Revenge* and replaced him with one of his own men. Bonnet was taken on board Blackbeard's ship where he was reported variously as a prisoner or a happy student learning a new trade. At a time when the buccaneers were leaving the Caribbean because of better Spanish defences and had turned to attacking the trade of the prosperous North American colonies, Blackbeard's small fleet sailed to the Carolina coast where they blockaded Charles Town and held its commerce to ransom. They then sailed to North Carolina where, on hearing of a general pardon for pirates offered by the crown, they took the pardon from Governor Eden. Bonnet took this opportunity to leave Blackbeard and regain control of the *Revenge*, now renamed the *Royal James*.

Bonnet was cleared to sail to the Danish island of St Thomas, where he hoped to obtain a privateering commission permitting him to attack the Spanish. Short on supplies for the voyage he took what he needed from some local ships before going to the Cape Fear area to refit his ship. On 26 September 1718 he was cornered by Colonel William Rhett of South Carolina. The South Carolina authorities, enraged by the ease with which pirates blockaded Charles Town and despoiled their trade, had determined to go on the attack. They had raised the funds to send out two ships under the command of Rhett to hunt for their antagonists. After a prolonged fight Bonnet was captured and he and his crew were taken to Charles Town for trial. The capture of Bonnet and his men was a sensation there and became even more so when Bonnet and David Harriot escaped from confinement in the home of the provost marshal, Nathaniel Partridge, and fled the city leaving rumours that they had had help in escaping. Meanwhile the provincial assembly had met and passed an anti-piracy law so as to enable the trial to proceed. On 28 October the trial of Bonnet's crew got under way with a ferocious and biased speech by the judge, Nicholas Trott. With some of the colony's leading citizens participating, the trial proceeded swiftly. On 5 November, twenty-nine were found guilty and sentenced to death, of whom twenty-two were executed three days later.

Bonnet had escaped on 25 October, but Rhett discovered him on Sullivan Island, where Harriot was killed and Bonnet taken. Bonnet was finally brought to trial on 10 November, when he elicited a great deal of sympathy from the audience in the court for his dignified bearing before the overbearing Trott. He maintained during the trial that his men forced him to take the ships and that there were three gentlemen who could testify to that effect. Judge Trott denied him a hearing on this evidence and after the prosecution presented their case Bonnet was found guilty and on 12 November sentenced to death. Prior to his execution on 10 December Bonnet wrote letters to the authorities proclaiming his innocence and continuing to claim that his men made him commit the piracies for which he was charged. These were ignored although he was given a great deal of time to compose himself before his execution.

Bonnet is among the most enigmatic of pirates. In an era when brutes such as Blackbeard terrorized shipping Bonnet's reasons for entering the trade were never adequately explained and he apparently threw away a life of privilege in order to become a pirate. ROBERT C. RITCHIE

Sources *The tryals of Major Stede Bonnet and other pirates* (1719) · *State trials*, vol. 15 · S. C. Hughson, *The Carolina pirates and colonial commerce, 1670–1740* (1894), 86–127 · *CSP col.* · *IGI*

Archives PRO, Colonial Office 5 | South Carolina Archives and History Center, Columbia, South Carolina court records, Books A and B

Bonney, Henry Kaye (1780–1862), dean of Stamford, was the son of Henry Kaye (or Key) Bonney, rector of King's Cliffe and prebendary of Lincoln, and was born on 22 May 1780 at Tansor, Northamptonshire, of which parish his father was then rector. His father's family friend Lord Westmorland procured for him a foundation scholarship at Charterhouse School, where he obtained an exhibition, and he went to Emmanuel College, Cambridge, in 1798. Having been elected to a Tancred divinity studentship, he migrated to Christ's College in December 1798. He graduated BA in 1802, MA in 1805, and DD in 1824. He was ordained deacon in 1803 and priest in 1804, with a charge at Thirlby, in Lincolnshire. After a few months he went to live with his parents at King's Cliffe, and undertook the parishes of Ketton and Tixover with Duddington. He was collated by Bishop Tomline on 8 January 1807 to the prebend of Nassington in Lincoln Cathedral.

Bonney was presented by the earl of Westmorland to the rectory of King's Cliffe in succession to his father, who died of paralysis on 20 March 1810. He published in 1815, with a dedication to the earl of Westmorland, the *Life of the Right Reverend Father in God, Jeremy Taylor, DD*. In 1821 Bonney dedicated to Lady Cicely Georgiana Fane his *Historic Notices in Reference to Fotheringay. Illustrated by Engravings* (done by his own hand). In 1820 he was appointed examining chaplain to George Pelham, the new bishop of Lincoln, and was collated by the same prelate on 10 December 1821 to the archdeaconry of Bedford. (An order in council, dated 19 April 1837, transferred the archdeaconry from the diocese of Lincoln to the diocese of Ely.) Bonney published the *Sermons and charges by the Right Reverend Father in God, Thomas Fanshaw Middleton, DD, late lord bishop of Calcutta. With memoirs of his life* in 1824. On 15 May 1827 he married Charlotte, the fourth daughter of John Perry, of Blackwall and of Moor Hall, Essex.

In 1827 Bonney was appointed to the deanery of Stamford by his close friend John Kaye, then recently translated from the see of Bristol to that of Lincoln, and was advanced by him, on 22 February 1845, from the archdeaconry of Bedford to that of Lincoln. Soon after his appointment he made a parochial visitation, recording each church's affairs and showing a nice sense of a visitation's purpose (see N. S. Harding, ed., *Bonney's Church Notes*, 1937). He shared Kaye's high-church sympathies. As an archdeacon Bonney was indefatigable. In the early part of 1858 he was seized with paralysis, and never entirely recovered. He died at the rectory, King's Cliffe, on 24 December 1862, and was buried in the churchyard of King's Cliffe with his wife, who had died childless on 26 December 1850 at King's Cliffe. Shortly before his death he had contributed £500 to the restoration of the church at King's Cliffe.

Bonney published his charges to the clergy of the archdeaconry of Bedford for the years 1823, 1843, and 1844, and the various charges delivered to the clergy and churchwardens of the archdeaconry of Lincoln at the visitations of 1850, 1854, and 1856. He also contributed a sermon to the third volume of *Practical sermons by dignitaries and other clergymen of the united church of England and Ireland* (1846). ARTHUR H. GRANT, *rev.* H. C. G. MATTHEW

Sources *Lincoln Gazette* (27 Dec 1862) · *Morning Post* (29 Dec 1862) · *Stamford Mercury* (26 Dec 1862) · *Stamford Mercury* (2 Jan 1863) · Venn, *Alum. Cant.* · W. F. J. Kaye, *A sermon … after the funeral of H. K. Bonney, with a short memoir of his life* (1863)

Wealth at death under £14,000: probate, 28 Jan 1863, *CGPLA Eng. & Wales*

Bonney, Thomas George (1833–1923), geologist, was born at Rugeley, Staffordshire, on 27 July 1833, the eldest of the ten children of the Revd Thomas Bonney, headmaster of Rugeley grammar school, and his wife, Eliza Ellen, daughter of Edward Smith of Rugeley. The family was of Huguenot origin and in comfortable circumstances. After attending Uppingham School, where he was head boy, Bonney went up to St John's College, Cambridge, in 1852. He became twelfth wrangler in 1856 and obtained a second class in classics. His health deteriorated after graduation, but he recuperated in the Alps and took up a position at Westminster School in 1857, teaching mathematics. He also studied for holy orders, being ordained deacon in 1857 and priest in 1858.

In 1859 Bonney was elected to a fellowship at St John's, and in 1861 he returned to his college as junior dean, becoming a tutor in 1868. He never studied geology formally, though he had a strong interest in the subject from his schooldays and attended some of Adam Sedgwick's lectures. In 1868 he began to teach the subject at St John's and was appointed college lecturer in geology in 1869, thereby initiating the notable association of that college with geology. In 1877 he was appointed to the Yates-Goldsmit chair of geology at University College, London, a position which he occupied concurrently with that at St John's. However, in 1881 he left Cambridge for Hampstead to enable him to give time to his work as assistant general secretary of the British Association for the Advancement of Science. While living in Hampstead, Bonney also wrote regularly for *The Standard*. In 1901 he retired from his London chair; he returned in 1905 to Cambridge, where he chose to continue teaching geology on a semi-formal basis.

Bonney joined the Geological Society in 1860, was secretary (1878–84) and president (1884–6). He received the society's Wollaston medal in 1889. He was president of the Mineralogical Society (1884–6), of the Alpine Club (1883), of Section C of the British Association (1886), and of the association itself for its Sheffield meeting (1910). He was elected FRS in 1878, served on the society's council on three occasions, and was vice-president from 1898 to 1899. He held the ScD degree of Cambridge University, honorary DScs from Dublin and Sheffield University, and an honorary LLD from Montreal University.

Bonney's geological work was undertaken in many branches of the science, but most significantly in mineralogy, petrology, and studies of glaciation. At Cambridge, from about 1870, Bonney learned, and then taught, the techniques of preparing rocks in thin sections and examining them microscopically. With this as his forte, he engaged in numerous geological controversies, sometimes pitting the results of laboratory investigation against field mapping. He emphasized the importance of fieldwork, but his work was largely based on traverses and sections, and he was not skilled at mapping or elucidating geological structures by the interpretation of geological maps. Bonney recorded that he drifted into microscopical petrologic studies because of his dissatisfaction with the state of geological theory and practice.

In his petrologic work Bonney was particularly interested in ultrabasic rocks, and their conversion to serpentines, which he studied particularly at the Lizard, Cornwall. The conversions were deduced by examination of mineral 'ghosts', detectable in thin sections. The study of metamorphism, more generally, captured Bonney's attention, challenging the suggestion that granite might be metamorphic in origin. While mostly contending against the German tradition of linking rock types with age, he was inclined to view crystalline schists and other similar rocks as being nearly always exceedingly ancient. In work at Charnwood Forest, Leicestershire, he had come to regard the rocks there, mapped by the Geological Survey as Cambrian, as Precambrian. This notion of British Precambrian was extended to other localities such as Pembrokeshire, north Wales, and the north-west highlands of Scotland, and so Bonney became a protagonist in the so-called 'Archaean controversy'—between certain 'amateur' geologists and the 'professionals' of the survey. In this controversy personal relations between Bonney and Archibald Geikie, director-general of the survey, deteriorated significantly.

Bonney was a considerable alpine climber, and not surprisingly he gave much attention to glacial phenomena. In his geomorphological investigations he emphasized the prime importance of fitting observations and theory, and contended against Andrew Ramsay (1814–1891) and others that many observations in Switzerland and elsewhere were incompatible with the theory that glaciers could gouge out rock basins, and hence give rise to lakes. Bonney's theory, derived from the earlier suggestions of Charles Lyell (1797–1875), was that many glacial markings could be ascribed to the rasping action of floating icebergs. While Bonney supported James Croll's astronomical theory of the ultimate cause of epochs of glaciation, he had no adequate theory for the formation of rock basins. Bonney was much interested in volcanoes as well as ice, and at one time argued that the extinct volcanoes of central France had been active as recently as AD 500. He also contributed to the publication of the important work of the Australian geologist Edgeworth David and William Sollas on the Pacific atoll of Funafuti, which supported Darwin's theory of the origin of coral reefs.

Bonney was a man with considerable artistic gifts and his rooms at St John's were adorned with his work. He had the reputation of being a hard teacher, but also a generous man. He gave financial support to the *Geological Magazine*, when it was in difficulties in its early years. He performed innumerable investigations of thin sections for other geologists, both at home and abroad, and he taught—with the help of popular field trips—in such a way as to be greatly admired by his pupils, many of whom became leading geologists.

Bonney was a prolific author, with publications ranging from technical papers, through popular books, to newspaper articles. His books included *The Story of our Planet* (1893), *Ice-Work* (1896), *Volcanoes* (1899), *Charles Lyell and Modern Geology* (1905), and *The Building of the Alps* (1913). He was no less active as a theologian, writing several collections of sermons. He was preacher at the Chapel Royal, Whitehall (1876–8); gave the Boyle lectures in 1890 ('Old truths in modern lights') and 1891 ('Christian doctrine in modern thought'); was Hulsean lecturer for 1884, yielding *The Influence of Science on Theology* the following year; Rede lecturer for 1892 ('The microscope's contribution to the earth's physical history'); and honorary canon of Manchester. His *Present Relations of Science and Religion* appeared in 1913.

Considering the relations between science and theology, Bonney maintained (not altogether consistently) that the essential Christian doctrines were not susceptible to scientific enquiry; that both revealed religion and science faced philosophical problems; that the claims of revelation should be subject to scientific and historical scrutiny; that in consequence theological doctrines may require modification from time to time; and that science can usefully influence theology by teaching theologians how to reason. Thus Bonney would have the theologian reason as rigorously as the mathematician and somewhat according to the manner of the scientist.

Though said to be of indifferent health at times, Bonney was a very active alpine mountaineer and carried out numerous field investigations, even into old age. He died at his home, 9 Scroope Terrace, Cambridge, unmarried, on 9 December 1923. His autobiography, *Memories of a Long Life* (1921), says little about Bonney's geological work, but records his impressive alpine achievements, gives fascinating insights into Cambridge life in the nineteenth century, and reveals the author as a tremendous trencherman with a seemingly inordinate interest in food.

DAVID OLDROYD

Sources T. G. Bonney, *Memories of a long life* (1921) • W. W. W. [W. W. Watts], *PRS*, 99B (1925–6), xvii–xxvii • 'Eminent living geologists: the Rev. Professor T. G. Bonney', *Geological Magazine*, new ser., 4th decade, 8 (1901), 385–400 • P. Lake, 'The Rev. Prof. Thomas George Bonney', *GJ*, 63 (1924), 366–8 • J. E. M. [J. E. Marr] and R. H. R. [R. H. Rastall], *Quarterly Journal of the Geological Society*, 80 (1924), xlviii–li • *Geological Magazine*, 61 (1924), 49–51 • L. J. Spencer, *Mineralogical Magazine*, 20 (1923–5), 255–6 • *The Times* (11 Dec 1923) • W. E. Heitland, *The Eagle*, 43 (1923–4), 262–4 • *CGPLA Eng. & Wales* (1924)

Archives LPL, letters and papers on geology manual • U. Cam., Sedgwick Museum of Earth Sciences, field notes | BL, corresp. with Sir Sydney Cockerell, Add. MS 52707 • Bodl. Oxf., corresp. with British Association • CUL, letters to Sir George Stokes • GS Lond., corresp. with Geological Society • UCL, letters to William Sollas

Likenesses T. Haddon, oils, 1895?, UCL; repro. in W. W. W., *PRS* • group portrait, photograph, 1912, St John Cam. • Scott and Wilkinson, photograph, St John Cam. • photograph, repro. in 'Eminent living geologists'

Wealth at death £22,061 16*s*. 6*d*.: resworn probate, 6 May 1924, *CGPLA Eng. & Wales*

Bonney, (William Francis) Victor (1872–1953), gynaecologist, was born in Chelsea, London, on 17 December 1872, the son of William Augustus Bonney, surgeon, and his wife, Anna Maria Alice Polixène Poulain. Educated privately, he studied medicine at St Bartholomew's Hospital, London, before transferring to the Middlesex Hospital, qualifying MB, BS (London) (1906); he had already gained his MD (1898), MS and FRCS (1899), and BSc, with first-class honours (1904). His original intention was to become a physician. In 1905 he was appointed obstetric tutor to the Middlesex Hospital and concomitantly held a research post. In the same year Bonney married Annie Oliver (1868/9–1963), daughter of Dr James Appleyard of Tasmania; the fact that they had no children may have encouraged his interest in treating infertility. In 1908 he was elected to the honorary staff as assistant gynaecological surgeon and in 1930 he succeeded Sir Comyns Berkeley as senior gynaecological surgeon. During the First World War he was surgeon to the military branch of the Middlesex Hospital at Clacton-on-Sea, Essex. He also gave his services to the Chelsea Hospital for Women, the Royal Masonic Hospital, the Miller Hospital, and Queen Alexandra's Military Hospital, and was visiting gynaecologist to the Royal Postgraduate Medical School. He retired from hospital practice in 1937.

When Bonney was appointed to the Middlesex, gynaecology was regarded askance by the profession, even though it formed a third part of the qualifying examination for medical students. With his acute surgical acumen Bonney was not slow to recognize that gynaecologists should be acknowledged as coequals with their surgical colleagues and he devoted all his great energy towards this end, raising gynaecology from its medical obscurity into the important position it came to hold as a major branch of surgery. Regarding himself as a general surgeon who specialized in the pelvis, Bonney opposed the formation of the College of Obstetricians and Gynaecologists. His stance offended some of his contemporaries and it was only with his election as an honorary fellow of the college in 1946 that a reconciliation was made.

Bonney was the pioneer of the operation of

myomectomy, that is, the removal of fibroid tumours from the womb without the removal of the womb itself; and with Berkeley he extended and perfected the operation for cancer of the neck of the womb. He devised a superb operative technique which was emulated by countless pupils. He was a stimulating and invigorating teacher who had cultivated a leisurely and affable manner and who never appeared to be hurried. He could be a severe critic, but always of the method, never of the individual.

A prolific writer, Bonney wrote many of his books with Sir Comyns Berkeley; the best-known is *A Textbook of Gynaecological Surgery* which was first published in 1911 and reached a sixth edition in 1952. The illustrations in Bonney's books, drawn by himself, point to the artist in him, as do his watercolours. Like other ready writers he was an avid reader. A great admirer as well as a friend of Rudyard Kipling, Bonney became vice-president of the Kipling Society. In early days a useful tennis player, in later life he became a keen fisherman, owning a long stretch of water on the River Wye.

Bonney's spiritual home was the Royal College of Surgeons where he was the first gynaecologist to secure a seat by open election on the council, on which he served for twenty years; he was three times Hunterian lecturer, Bradshaw lecturer (1934), and Hunterian orator (1943). In 1946 he was elected an honorary fellow of the Royal College of Obstetricians and Gynaecologists, and he was the first gynaecologist to be elected an honorary fellow of the Royal Australasian College of Surgeons (1928).

Bonney died in the Middlesex Hospital, London, on 4 July 1953. The Victor Bonney prize was founded in 1963 with a bequest of £3000 under the will of Mrs A. O. Bonney, to be awarded triennially for meritorious written work in gynaecological surgery or a closely related subject. The administration of the award was transferred from the Royal College of Surgeons to the Royal College of Obstetricians and Gynaecologists in 1994.

F. W. ROQUES, *rev.* MICHAEL BEVAN

Sources J. Peel, *The lives of the fellows of the Royal College of Obstetricians and Gynaecologists, 1929–1969* (1976) • R. H. O. B. Robinson and W. R. Le Fanu, *Lives of the fellows of the Royal College of Surgeons of England, 1952–1964* (1970) • private information (1971) • personal knowledge (1971) • *CGPLA Eng. & Wales* (1953)

Likenesses O. Birley, oils, 1926, RCS Eng. • M. Ayoub, group portrait, oils (*Council of College of Surgeons, 1926–7*), RCS Eng. • bronze bust, RCS Eng.

Wealth at death £31,357 8*s.* 1*d.*: probate, 3 Oct 1953, *CGPLA Eng. & Wales*

Bonnie Dundee. *See* Graham, John, first viscount of Dundee (1648?–1689).

Bonnor, Charles (*d.* 1829?), actor and civil servant, was the son of a distiller in Bristol. After commencing his working life as apprentice to a coachmaker, he appeared on the Bath stage on 4 October 1777 as Belcour, in Richard Cumberland's comedy *The West Indian*. He remained at Bath until the close of the 1782–3 season, playing such characters as Charles Surface in *The School for Scandal*, Ranger in Benjamin Hoadley's *The Suspicious Husband*, and Touchstone in *As You Like It*. He also made his first attempts at writing, and supplied successful prologues, epilogues, and occasional addresses. On 7 July 1783 he appeared for his farewell benefit as Mercutio in *Romeo and Juliet* and Puff in *The Critic*, and announced his forthcoming departure for London. He made his début there on 19 September 1783 at Covent Garden, as Brazen in *The Recruiting Officer*. In London, as in Bath, his reception was favourable.

In 1784 Bonnor was sent by Thomas Harris, the manager of Covent Garden, to Paris to establish an English theatre there. Initially it seemed as if the mission would be successful, and a theatre in the Tuileries was taken. However, when the queen of France withdrew her patronage the scheme failed, and all Bonnor and the others realized was an opportunity to perform in Paris for a while. On his return from France, Bonnor produced for his benefit, at Covent Garden on 6 May 1785, an interlude called *The Manager in Spite of himself*, translated by Bonnor himself from Dorvigny's *La fête de campagne*, in which he played all but one of the characters in the play. Meanwhile he also performed a variety of other parts, including Petulant in Congreve's *The Way of the World*, Lovelace in Arthur Murphy's *Three Weeks after Marriage*, and the title role in *The Marriage of Figaro*. Bonnor's last appearance at Covent Garden was in May 1785, as Lord Sparkle in *Which is the Man?* and Robin in *The Contrivances*. His only other connection with this theatre was in December 1790, when his pantomime adapted from the French, *Picture of Paris*, was produced there. Neither of Bonnor's plays was ever printed.

Soon afterwards John Palmer, the owner of the Bath theatre, and the first proprietor of mail coaches, who had been appointed comptroller-general, of the Post Office, availed himself of Bonnor's organizational abilities in his scheme for the establishment of a mail-coach service. This led to Bonnor's appointment as deputy comptroller of the Post Office, and his consequent retirement from the stage. In 1788 he became resident surveyor, as well as deputy surveyor and comptroller-general, of the General Post Office. When Palmer became involved in a dispute with the postmaster-general and vacated his post in 1793, Bonnor displayed his political astuteness by dissociating himself from his erstwhile benefactor and getting himself appointed to the comptrollership of the inland department of the Post Office. This position he held for two years. Changes were then made in the Post Office, the comptrollership was abolished, and Bonnor retired on a pension. Between 1797 and 1800 he published three pamphlets in connection with Palmer's claims. He was apparently still living in 1827, and was very possibly the Charles Bonnor of Gloucester whose death the *Gentleman's Magazine* recorded in August 1829.

JOSEPH KNIGHT, *rev.* NILANJANA BANERJI

Sources Highfill, Burnim & Langhans, *BDA*, vol. 2 • D. E. Baker, *Biographia dramatica, or, A companion to the playhouse*, rev. I. Reed, new edn, rev. S. Jones, 3 vols. in 4 (1812) • Adams, *Drama* • [J. Watkins and F. Shoberl], *A biographical dictionary of the living authors of Great Britain and Ireland* (1816) • *GM*, 1st ser., 99/1 (1829), 651 • *N&Q*, 6th ser., 12 (1885), 28, 94 • Genest, *Eng. stage*

Bonnor, Thomas (*c*.1743–1807x12), draughtsman and engraver, was probably born in Gloucestershire. He was apprenticed in 1758 to Henry Roberts, engraver, for a 20 guinea premium. In 1763 he was awarded a premium by the Society of Arts for a landscape by an artist aged under twenty-one, and in the same year his drawing of the comedian Richard Yates as Launce was engraved and published by Roberts. Working chiefly for magazines, he designed and engraved a number of portraits of actors such as Ann Catley and Spranger Barry, in character, and he also designed illustrations to the works of Richardson, Smollett, and Fielding. In 1773 he exhibited drawings, including a design for the Gloucestershire Society, at the Society of Artists, together with a proof of a landscape after Adriaen Boudewijns and Pieter Bout. This was published later that year.

Bonnor, however, failed as an engraver–publisher and in 1781 he was imprisoned in the king's bench prison as an insolvent debtor. Whether his work for Nash's *Collections for the History of Worcestershire* (1781–2) had landed him in debt or helped to get him out of it, his later career was devoted chiefly to topographical illustration. He drew and engraved country houses, churches, and monuments for John Collinson's *The History and Antiquities of the County of Somerset* (1791), Ralph Bigland's *Historical, Monumental, and Genealogical Collections Relative to the County of Gloucester* (1791–2), and Richard Polwhele's *The History of Devonshire* (1793–1806). By 1799 he had published four numbers of a proposed *New Copperplate Perspective Itinerary*, containing views of Gloucester Cathedral and Goodrich Castle, for which he also wrote the text. He exhibited some drawings of architectural ruins at the Royal Academy in 1807, and he died between that date and 1812.

TIMOTHY CLAYTON

Sources I. Maxted, ed., *The British book trades, 1710–1777: an index of the masters and their apprentices* (1983) • T. Clayton and R. Sharp, 'Catalogue of theatrical prints, 1740–80', priv. coll. • R. G. [R. Gough], *British topography*, [new edn], 2 vols. (1780) [Gough's annotated copy, Bodl. Oxf., MSS Gough] • I. Maxted, *The London book trades, 1775–1800: a topographical guide* (privately printed, Exeter, 1980) • Thieme & Becker, *Allgemeines Lexikon* • Graves, *Soc. Artists*

Bonny, Anne (1698–1782), pirate, was born near Cork in Ireland. Evidence from her descendants suggests that she was the illegitimate daughter of William Cormac, lawyer, and his maidservant. Cormac, who raised his daughter as a boy, found his legal practice so affected by his affair that he decided to go abroad. Taking Anne and the maid with him, he sailed to South Carolina, where he became a successful merchant and purchased a plantation.

Anne grew up to be a fierce-tempered and headstrong young woman. In 1718 she married a penniless sailor called James Bonny; this so upset her father that he turned her out of his house. Bonny and Anne made their way to the island of New Providence in the Bahamas, where they hoped to find employment. There Anne was courted by the pirate John *Rackam (*d*. 1720), a bold and reckless character whose colourful clothes had earned him the nickname Calico Jack. Rackam had arrived in the Bahamas in 1719 in order to take advantage of the royal pardon which had been extended to pirates. He persuaded Anne to leave her sailor husband and go to sea with him. When she became pregnant he took her to Cuba, where she gave birth to their child. Soon afterwards he sent for her and she rejoined his crew, dressed as usual in men's clothing. Rackam had resumed his life as a pirate and Anne took part in a series of attacks on shipping in the Caribbean.

Around this time another female sailor, Mary *Read (*c*.1695–1721), joined Rackam's crew. She too had been brought up as a boy, had spent some years as a soldier in Flanders, and after her husband's death had joined a merchant ship bound for the West Indies. Bonny and Read became close friends and, according to witnesses at their subsequent trial, were the fiercest members of the crew: 'they were both very profligate, cursing and swearing much and ready and willing to do any thing on board' (PRO, CO 137/14). On 5 September 1720 Captain Woodes Rogers, the governor of the Bahamas, issued a proclamation, printed in the *Boston Gazette*, which announced that Rackam and twelve others, 'including two women, by name Anne Fulford alias Bonny, & Mary Read', had stolen the *William*, a 12-ton sloop armed with six guns, from Providence roads and had committed several acts of robbery and piracy. Within a few weeks Rackam's ship was intercepted and captured off Negril Point, Jamaica, by a heavily armed privateer commanded by Captain Jonathan Barnet. The pirates were taken ashore and confined in the gaol at Spanish Town.

On 16 November 1720, at an Admiralty court presided over by Sir Nicholas Lawes, governor of Jamaica, Rackam and the ten men in his crew were found guilty of piracy. They were hanged a few days later. Bonny and Read were tried by the same court on 28 November and were also found guilty and condemned to death. However, they revealed that they were both pregnant and were reprieved. Mary Read died in gaol and was buried on 28 April 1721. Evidence provided by the descendants of Anne Bonny suggests that her father managed to secure her release from gaol and bring her back to Charles Town, South Carolina, where she gave birth to Rackam's second child. On 21 December 1721 she married a local man, Joseph Burleigh, and they had eight children. She died in South Carolina, a respectable woman, at the age of eighty-four and was buried on 25 April 1782.

DAVID CORDINGLY

Sources C. Johnson, *A general history of the robberies and murders of the most notorious pyrates* (1724) • *The tryals of Captain John Rackam and other pirates*, PRO, CO 137/14 [transcript of trial printed in Jamaica by Robert Baldwin, 1721] • *The Boston Gazette* (10–17 Dec 1720) • D. Cordingly, *Life among the pirates: the romance and the reality* (1995) • M. Rediker, 'Liberty beneath the Jolly Roger', *Iron men, wooden women, gender and seafaring in the Atlantic world, 1700–1920*, ed. M. Creighton and L. Norling (1996), 1–33
Likenesses engravings, repro. in Johnson, *General history*

Bonny, William (*bap*. 1657, *d*. 1719), printer and bookseller, was baptized on 22 June 1657 at Bath Abbey, the son of John Bonny, barber, and his wife, Alice. He was apprenticed to William Bowtell, draper of London, for seven years from 5 August 1674 and became a freeman of the

Drapers' Company (although he was later described in 1685 as a blacksmith). Nevertheless, in 1683 his name appears on the imprint of the fourth edition of Richard Baxter's *Directions and Perswasions to a Sound Conversion* as its printer. He also published *The Bloody Duke*, a pamphlet attack on James II, in 1690. About 1687 Bonny appears to have married Elizabeth Webster, widow of Richard Webster (buried 19 November 1686), a member of the Stationers' Company. Thus, while not a freeman stationer, Bonny was employed by the company to print *News from the Stars, or, An Ephemeris for the Year 1690* together with other almanacs, as well as a number of other works for London stationers; he was later in dispute with the company, and ceased printing for it. In 1690 the Drapers' Company noted that he was living in Little Britain; and between 1689 and 1694 he and his wife baptized four children in the local parish of St Botolph, Aldersgate.

John Dunton, who employed William Bonny to print several titles, testified to his generous and friendly character but indicated that he made great losses in trade in London and 'good fortune seemed to forget him' (Dunton, 329). Therefore, with the patronage of John Cary, a prosperous local merchant, Bonny petitioned the common council of Bristol in 1695 to move his press to that city, taking advantage of the final lapse of the restrictive 1662 licensing act in that same year. Bristol council lifted their by-law restricting trade to their own citizens on 24 April 1695, but specifically forbade Bonny to work as a bookseller or practise any trade other than that of printer.

Bonny acquired premises in Tower Lane, Bristol, where he printed John Cary's *Essay on the State of England in Relation to its Trade, its Poor, and its Taxes* in 1695, and his *Essay on the Coyn and Credit of England* in 1696, followed by a succession of other small works. By 1699 Bonny was also apparently operating as a bookseller in spite of the council's earlier prohibition, and later advertised other grocery wares for sale. This change may have coincided with a move to new premises in Small Street, 'near the Tolzey'. In November 1702 he also founded and edited the *Bristol Post-Boy*, probably the second English provincial newspaper after Francis Burges's *Norwich Post*. By 1704 he had moved again, to Corn Street, where he seems to have remained.

When John Dunton wrote his autobiography about 1703, he described Bonny as being 'stark blind'; nevertheless Bonny's press and the *Bristol Post-Boy* continued to operate in Bristol until December 1715 (Dunton, 329). The newspaper may ultimately have been a victim of the introduction of newspaper stamp duties in August 1712 or competition from *Sam Farley's Bristol Postman*, from 1713 onwards, which was printed in a format designed to avoid most of the duty. William Bonny died in May 1719, probably at Corn Street, Bristol; an inventory of his effects was compiled and letters of administration were granted on 14 May to his son Charles, who is recorded on a single surviving imprint as a Bristol printer in 1722.

David Stoker

Sources F. Hyett, 'Notes on the first Bristol and Gloucestershire printers', *Transactions of the Bristol and Gloucestershire Archaeological Society*, 20 (1895–7), 38–51 · H. R. Plomer and others, *A dictionary of the printers and booksellers who were at work in England, Scotland, and Ireland from 1668 to 1725* (1922); repr. (1968) · J. Dunton, *The life and errors of John Dunton … written by himself* (1705) · C. Blagden, *The Stationers' Company: a history, 1403–1959* (1960) · F. A. Hyett and R. Austin, *Supplement to the bibliographer's manual of Gloucestershire literature*, 2 vols. (1915–16) · *ESTC* · J. Latimer, *The annals of Bristol in the eighteenth century* (1893), 21, 48–50 · J. Latimer, *The annals of Bristol in the seventeenth century* (1900), 471, 474–5, 479–84 · G. A. Cranfield, *The development of the provincial newspaper press, 1700–1760* (1962) · W. Merton, 'A new Bristol pamphlet', *The Library*, 3rd ser., 8 (1917), 162–4 · J. Penny, *All the news that's fit to print: a short history of Bristol's newspapers since 1702* (2001) · K. T. Winkler, *Handwerk und Markt: Druckerhandwerk, Betriebswesen und Tagesschriftum in London, 1695–1750* (Stuttgart, 1993), 700–01 · will, PRO, PROB 6/95, fol. 85*r* · A. H. Johnson, *The history of the Worshipful Company of the Drapers of London* (1914–22), 4.355 · CLRO, CF1/11/12 · *IGI* · D. F. McKenzie, 'Dealers in books outside the Stationers' Company, *circa* 1685', *Factotum: Newsletter of the XVIIIth-Century Short Title Catalogue*, 8 (April 1980), 12–13 · court books, Stationers' Company, London · private information (2004) [M. Treadwell]

Wealth at death see probate administration, PRO, PROB 6/95, fol. 85*r*, 1719

Bonnycastle, John (*c.*1760–1821), mathematician, was born at Whitchurch, in Buckinghamshire. His parents, though not affluent, managed to provide him with a reasonable basic education. At an early age he went to London 'to seek his fortune' (*GM*), and afterwards kept an academy at Hackney. On the title-pages of the earlier editions of his first work (*The Scholar's Guide to Arithmetic*) he is described as a 'private teacher of mathematics', and was at one time private tutor to the sons of the earl of Pomfret, during which time he lived at Easton Neston in Northamptonshire. In October 1782 he became a mathematics master at the Royal Military Academy, Woolwich, and in July 1807 succeeded Charles Hutton as professor of mathematics.

Bonnycastle was a prolific and successful writer of textbooks. Of his chief works, *The Scholar's Guide to Arithmetic* first appeared in 1780 and ran to an eighteenth edition in 1851. *An Introduction to Algebra* followed in 1782. (A thirteenth edition appeared in 1824, 'with addenda by Charles Bonnycastle', the author's son.) His *Introduction to Astronomy* (1786), intended as a popular introduction to astronomy rather than as an elementary treatise, was one of the best-selling books on the subject for many years. An edition of Euclid's *Elements*, with notes (1789), and *An Introduction to Mensuration and Practical Geometry* (1782; 18th edn, 1840) were both translated into Turkish. Other works included *A Treatise on Plane and Spherical Trigonometry* (1806) and *A Treatise on Algebra* (2 vols., 1813). Besides elementary mathematical books, Bonnycastle was in early life a frequent contributor to the *London Magazine*. He also wrote the introduction to a translation (by T. O. Churchill) of Bossut's *Histoire des mathématiques* (1803) and a 'chronological table of the most eminent mathematicians from the earliest times' for the end of the book.

Bonnycastle married twice. His first wife, a Miss Rolt, whom he married when he was nineteen, died young. His second wife, Bridget Johnstone, survived him, as did three sons, including Sir Richard Henry *Bonnycastle, army officer, and one daughter. He seems to have been a man of considerable classical and general literary culture. He was strongly associated with the military, since many of the artillery officers had been his students, and he also seems to have been a popular tutor for children of the aristocracy. Leigh Hunt, who used to meet him in company with the Swiss painter Fuseli, of whom Bonnycastle was a great friend, left a description of him in his book *Lord Byron and Some of his Contemporaries*. He describes him as 'a good fellow … passionately fond of quoting Shakespeare and of telling stories'; he suggests that Bonnycastle may have 'thought a little more highly of his talents than the amount of them strictly warranted', but that 'the delusion was not only pardonable but desirable' in this case, given his strong sense of duty and his common humanity. Bonnycastle died at Woolwich Common, after a 'long and tedious illness' (*GM*), on 15 May 1821, and was interred, during a semi-military funeral, in a purpose-built vault at Charlton, Kent.

THOMAS WHITTAKER, *rev.* ADRIAN RICE

Sources *GM*, 1st ser., 91/1 (1821), 471–2, 482 • L. Hunt, *Lord Byron and some of his contemporaries*, 2 (1828), 203–7 • [J. Watkins and F. Shoberl], *A biographical dictionary of the living authors of Great Britain and Ireland* (1816) • A. De Morgan, *Arithmetical books from the invention of printing to the present time* (1847), 76 • H. D. Buchanan-Dunlop, ed., *Records of the Royal Military Academy, 1741–1892* (1895)

Bonnycastle, Sir Richard Henry (1791–1847), army officer, born on 30 September 1791 at Woolwich, was the son of Professor John *Bonnycastle and his second wife, Bridget, *née* Johnstone. He studied at the Royal Military Academy, Woolwich, passing out as second lieutenant Royal Engineers on 28 September 1808, and becoming first lieutenant in 1809. He served at the siege of Flushing in 1809 in the Netherlands campaign, and in the Anglo-American War of 1812–14, during which he was present at the capture of Fort Castine and the occupation of Maine east of the Penobscot, and was commanding engineer at the construction of the extensive works on the Castine peninsula. In 1814 he became captain, and in the same year married Frances, daughter of Captain W. Johnstone. They had two sons and three daughters. Subsequently he served with the army of occupation in France.

After service at home Bonnycastle was sent in 1826 to Upper Canada, serving at Fort George and at Kingston until 1832, when he was posted to York, in Toronto. He was keenly interested in colonial development, did original research in geology and mineralogy, and was a freemason and amateur artist. In 1837 he completed the construction of Fort Henry. As commanding royal engineer in Upper Canada he rendered crucial services during the uprising in 1837–9, particularly in February 1838 when, at the head of an *ad hoc* force of militia, volunteers, sailors, and Mohawks—in the absence of regular troops—he defeated the attempt of the insurgents at Napanee, and of the brigands at Hickory Island, near Gananoque, to attack Kingston. For these services he was knighted in March 1840.

Bonnycastle was afterwards commanding engineer in Newfoundland. He became a brevet major in 1837 and a regimental lieutenant-colonel in 1840, and retired in 1847. His publications included *The Canadas in 1841* (2 vols., 1842), *Newfoundland in 1842* (2 vols., 1842), *Canada and the Canadians in 1846* (2 vols., 1846), and the posthumous *Canada as it was, is and may be* (2 vols., 1852). These were competent and informative, and helped attract immigrants and capital to Canada.

Bonnycastle died on 3 November 1847 at Kingston, in Canada. Liked and esteemed by Canadians, Bonnycastle was a fine example of a 'constructive imperial military officer' (*DCB*). H. M. CHICHESTER, *rev.* JAMES LUNT

Sources G. K. Raudzens, 'Bonnycastle, Sir Richard Henry', *DCB*, vol. 7 • *Hart's Army List* • *The Times* (4 Dec 1847)

Bonomi, Ignatius Richard Frederick Nemesius (1787–1870), architect, was born on 31 October 1787 at 76 Great Titchfield Street, London, the fourth but eldest surviving child of Joseph *Bonomi (1739–1808), architect, and his wife, Rosa Florini (1755–1812). He was baptized in the Sardinian chapel on 27 December 1787, when his godparents were some of his father's important patrons, the fourth earl of Aylesford, the seventh Viscount Fitzwilliam, Mrs Elizabeth Montagu, and the engraver Francesco Bartolozzi.

It is not known where Bonomi was at school. About 1803 he started his architectural training in his father's office. Bonomi was twenty-one when his father died in 1808. Wishing to gain experience, he applied for a draughtsman's post in Sir John Soane's office, but was unsuccessful. Instead, he completed some of his father's commissions, notably Rosneath, Dunbartonshire, for the fifth duke of Argyll. The prospect of employment by his father's patrons, the Lambtons of Lambton Castle, co. Durham, and John Wharton of Skelton Castle, North Riding of Yorkshire, induced Bonomi to move to Durham *c.*1809. In 1811 he received the commission to complete the new Durham assize courts, after Francis Sandys and George Moneypenny had been dismissed for incompetence, and in 1813 he was appointed county bridge surveyor for Durham. Thus established with a comfortable salary, he made Durham his home for the next forty years. The county post was no sinecure, but required regular reports to the magistrates, which in turn demanded tours of inspection of bridges, often at the worst times of year, when bad weather had damaged them. Several of Bonomi's bridges were handsome structures, particularly Shincliffe Bridge, south of Durham, rebuilt in 1824–6.

Bonomi built up a considerable private practice in co. Durham and north Yorkshire. Further north, in Newcastle, his only professional colleague in the region, John Dobson, held sway. Bonomi produced the typical output of a provincial architect: inexpensive Gothic churches, suburban villas, and small country houses. His major country house commissions were at Lambton Hall, which he transformed (*c.*1820–1828) into Lambton Castle for John G. Lambton, later first earl of Durham, and two neoclassical houses, Burn Hall, near Durham (*c.*1821–1834), for Bryan Salvin, and Windlestone Hall (also *c.*1821–1834), for

Ignatius Richard Frederick Nemesius Bonomi (1787–1870), by Nicolas Bouet, 1833

Sir Robert Eden. Bonomi was surveyor to the dean and chapter of Durham (1827–40), and supervised the restoration of parts of the cathedral, especially the Nine Altars Chapel at the east end. His experience in bridge building recommended him to the Stockton and Darlington Railway Company, and in 1824 he designed the railway bridge over the River Skerne at Darlington. He was for some years architect to the London Lead Company, and designed houses for the company's agents at Long Marton, Westmorland, and Stanhope and Middleton in Teesdale, co. Durham. In the 1820s he favoured the Perpendicular style for church building, and his earliest church, at Redcar, North Riding of Yorkshire (1823–9), is perhaps his best. At Brough Hall, North Riding of Yorkshire, he built in 1834–7 a Roman Catholic chapel for Sir William Lawson, an accurate reproduction of the archbishop's chapel at York; but Lawson had the idea, and John Brown, historian of York Minster, provided the details: Bonomi translated this into workable reality. In the 1830s his churches were mostly in the Early English or lancet style, and rather plain and uninspired; a few, such as Hutton in Berwickshire and Upleatham in the North Riding of Yorkshire (both *c*.1834), were neo-Norman and more attractive.

Bonomi at first lived and had his office in Old Elvet, but in the late 1820s he bought land south of Durham city and in 1827–9 built a house for himself, Elvet Hill. The details were Perpendicular Gothic, but the overall effect was what a local writer called 'Italianate Tudor' (M. Apperley, *History of Elvet Hill*, 1913), referring to its flat roofs and picturesque grouping of the two blocks. In one block Bonomi had his drawing office, and in the other he planned to live with his sisters Mary Anne, Agnes, and Justina. Mary Anne married Dr George Goldie of York in 1828, and the other sisters preferred to live at York. Elvet Hill was too large, and perhaps too remote from the town to attract clients, and after about a year Bonomi let it and moved back into the city. It was later sold and its appearance was changed by the addition of a pitched roof. A somewhat similar, flat-roofed house was created out of the Tudor Gothic gatehouse of St Mary's Abbey, York, which Bonomi designed as a house for Professor John Phillips in 1839. Bonomi had several assistants who became minor architects, and also John Loughborough Pearson, architect, who was his pupil, and later his assistant, from 1831. Pearson left Bonomi in 1842, when it became clear that Bonomi was to enter into partnership with John Augustus Cory (1819–1887), a pupil of J. J. Scoles and a friend of Bonomi's brother Joseph. Cory, who was at Emmanuel College, Cambridge (1839–41), can be assumed to have been influenced architecturally by the Cambridge Camden Society, and he was probably responsible for the change in style in ecclesiastical architecture which is discernible in the output of the partnership after 1842.

Bonomi married on 27 December 1837, at the age of fifty, Charlotte Fielding (1799–1860), daughter of Israel Fielding of Startforth, near Barnard Castle. She was an Anglican, apparently of evangelical leanings. At some unknown time Bonomi renounced his Roman Catholicism and joined the Church of England. He was a churchwarden of St Mary-le-Bow, Durham, in the 1840s. His friendship with Canon William Gilly, historian of the Waldensians, led to his providing designs for Waldensian churches in Piedmont in the late 1840s and early 1850s, one of which was built to a somewhat modified design in the Waldensian capital, Torre Pellice. Charlotte Bonomi wrote a religious and moralizing novel, *Agnes Grey, or, Ten Years Ago*, published in 1861, in which the perceived errors of Roman Catholicism were contrasted with the protestantism of the Church of England and especially the Waldensian church. It was translated into Italian as *Lucia: storia d'una famiglia inglese nel 1849*, and published in Florence in 1861.

Bonomi retired from practice in 1850, and left Durham to live in London in 1856. In that year John Cory was appointed county bridge surveyor for Cumberland. Charlotte Bonomi died in 1860, and Bonomi, after an extended visit to his sister Justina in Genoa in 1861–2, lived with his brother Joseph and Joseph's young family at 36 Blandford Square, London, and later purchased land in Prince's Road, Wimbledon Park, Surrey. There in 1865–6 he designed The Camels as a family home, a curious house devised by Joseph Bonomi, who was an Egyptologist, with a frieze on the main façade showing camels as part of the train of life. It was bombed in the First World War and demolished. In 1868 Bonomi assisted Wyatt Papworth in preparing a memoir of Bonomi's father for the Royal Institute of British Architects. Bonomi died at home at The

Camels on 2 January 1870, aged eighty-two, and was buried with his wife in Paddington cemetery. His business was ultimately profitable, and his personal estate was sworn under £20,000. Most of his wealth was left to his brother Joseph and Joseph's family.

PETER MEADOWS

Sources Colvin, *Archs.* • CUL, Joseph Bonomi MSS, MS Add. 9389 • P. Meadows, 'Ignatius Bonomi: an architect in Cleveland', *Bulletin* [Cleveland and Teesside Local History Society], 50 (1986) • P. Meadows, 'Palatinate patronage', *Country Life* (14 Dec 1989), 64–9 • I. Curry, *Sense and sensitivity: Durham Cathedral and its architects* (1985) • A. F. Sealey and D. Walters, 'The first railway architects', *ArchR*, 135 (1964), 364–6 • A. Quiney, *John Loughborough Pearson* (1979) • C. Burlison, *The early life of Clement Burlison* (1897) • R. Bounous and M. Lecchi, *I templi delle valli valdesi* (1988) • J. Crosby, *Ignatius Bonomi of Durham, architect* (1987) • m. cert. • d. cert. • baptismal cert. • census returns • land tax returns • burial cert., Paddington cemetery, London [Charlotte Bonomi]

Archives N. Yorks. CRO, letters and plans • N. Yorks. CRO, Chaytor MSS | Cleveland Archives, Middlesbrough, Ward-Jackson diaries • Durham RO, corresp. with Lord Londonderry • Durham RO, letters to W. E. Salvin, plans and elevations for portico, Croxdale Hall • Lambton estate office, Lambton Park, Chester-le-Street, co. Durham, letters regarding Lambton Castle, plans, etc. • Normanby Hall, Lincolnshire, Ward-Jackson MSS • Northumbd RO, Newcastle upon Tyne, letters with sketch-plans, etc.

Likenesses P. Hoare, pencil sketch, *c.*1815, priv. coll.; repro. in P. Meadows, *Joseph Bonomi architect* (1988) • N. Bouet, pencil sketch, 1833, U. Durham L. [*see illus.*] • C. Martin, oils, 1861, priv. coll.; copies, photographs, priv. coll.

Wealth at death under £20,000

Bonomi, Joseph [*formerly* Giuseppe] (1739–1808), architect, was born on 19 January 1739 in Rome, the eldest of five children of Giovanni Giacomo Bonomi (*d.* 1750), agent to some of the Roman nobility, and his wife, Teresa Corbi. He studied at the Collegio Romano, and, according to his son Ignatius, writing in 1808, having as a child 'employed himself … in endeavouring to solve architectural problems' (I. Bonomi to Lord Buchan, May 1808, U. Glas. L., MS Murray, 502/41/3), he was placed under Antonio Asprucci (1723–1808), architect to Prince Borghese. He studied also with Girolamo Teodoli (1677–1766) and possibly received tuition in drawing from Charles-Louis Clérisseau. About 1763 James Adam, then on his grand tour in Rome, saw some of Bonomi's work, including drawings in competition for a gold medal in architecture, and engaged him to work exclusively for the Adam brothers in drawing Roman antiquities.

In 1767 Robert and James Adam invited Bonomi to Britain, where he worked as a draughtsman in their London office until 1781. His skill as a perspectivist makes it highly probable that some of the finest architectural drawings of the Adam office, especially interior views for the Adam brothers' publication *The Works in Architecture* (1778–9), were done by Bonomi. His only known independent design of this period, for the sacristy intended by Pope Pius VI for St Peter's, Rome (1776), must have been produced surreptitiously, since the Adams forbade their employees to engage in private work, under threat of a heavy financial penalty. In 1775 Bonomi married Rosa Florini (1755–1812), cousin and ward of the artist Angelica

Joseph Bonomi (1739–1808), by William Daniell (after George Dance, 1793)

Kauffman. Rosa Florini had come to Britain in 1767 with Angelica's father; Angelica herself married Bonomi's friend and erstwhile colleague in the Adam office, the artist Antonio Zucchi, in 1781. The Bonomis' first children, twins Angelica (*d.* 1792) and Luigi (*d.* 1784), were born in 1779.

Bonomi left the Adams in 1781 and set up as an independent architect. He prepared designs dated 1782, all apparently unexecuted, for several clients, including his later patrons the bluestocking Elizabeth Montagu and the fourth earl of Aylesford. In 1783 he was induced, probably by Angelica Kauffman, to return to Italy. His younger brother Giovanni Carlo Bonomi (1743–1801), professor of theology at the *propaganda fide* in Rome, possibly also held out the prospect of work. Bonomi was elected a member of the Accademia di Belle Arti at Bologna, and the Accademia di San Luca at Rome, and made a tour of southern Italy, examining among other sites the Greek Doric temples of Paestum. Success in Italy eluded him, however, and in 1784 he returned to London, practising there until his death. In Britain he received commissions almost immediately, and with some of his patrons his relations were close and long-lasting, particularly with Heneage Finch, fourth earl of Aylesford, to whom he acted as tutor and drawing-master as well as architect.

Bonomi exhibited regularly at the Royal Academy from 1783. In 1789, after several attempts, he was elected an associate on the casting vote of the president, Sir Joshua Reynolds. Reynolds proposed Bonomi as a full academician and professor of perspective in 1790, but Henry Fuseli was elected instead; regular attempts to promote

Bonomi were made until 1806, but he was consistently opposed by a group in the academy which included Joseph Farington. In 1800 Bonomi was appointed architect to the king of Naples, but was unable to take up the post because of political conditions in Italy. In 1804 he received the honorary title of architect to St Peter's, Rome. Bonomi's Royal Academy exhibits, many of which are now in the Royal Institute of British Architects drawings collection in London, showed a firm handling of perspective and a feeling for light and shade; there is an unsubstantiated family tradition that the young J. M. W. Turner painted the landscapes in some of Bonomi's exhibits. Bonomi's design for Elizabeth Montagu's Great Room in Portman Square, London (exhibited 1790), is especially fine. The Great Room excited much admiration when it was finished in 1791, and was inspected by Queen Charlotte, but it did not lead to any other commissions on so grand a scale.

In his designs Bonomi turned away from the Adam brothers' elaborate delicacy, producing stronger and more chaste designs which possibly reflect the influence of James Wyatt (with whom he occasionally collaborated) and Henry Holland. Bonomi's exteriors, however, were often blockish and severe, unless enlivened by a bold feature, such as a *porte-cochère* (at Longford Hall, Shropshire, built in 1789–92 for Ralph Leake, and Laverstoke Park, Hampshire, built in 1796 for Henry Portal) or an open colonnaded belvedere on the roof (as at Rosneath, Dunbartonshire, 1803–8; dem. 1961, for the fifth duke of Argyll). Other forceful features used by Bonomi were a double, superimposed portico—employed at Barrells House, Henley in Arden, Warwickshire (1792–4), for Robert Knight, and Stansted House, Sussex (1786–91), for Richard Barwell—and ground-floor wings linked to the *piano nobile* of the main house by descending quadrant passages, at Eastwell Park, Kent (1793–9), for George Finch Hatton.

Bonomi remodelled the interiors of Lord Aylesford's Packington Hall, Warwickshire, over many years. His work at Packington culminated in two extraordinary designs, the Pompeian Gallery (1787) and Packington church (1789–90). The source for the gallery, Nicolas Ponce's *Description des bains de Titus* (1786), may have been suggested by Aylesford, a connoisseur of architecture. Aylesford possibly also inspired the design of Packington church, a remarkable neo-classical building with a Greek-cross plan, vaulting derived from the Roman baths of Diocletian, and Greek Doric columns; Bonomi translated this eclectic material into solid form, producing a startlingly original building without parallel in English church architecture. His sources were mainly Roman: the pyramid of Caius Cestius in Rome inspired his pyramidal mausoleum (1793) at Blickling Park, Norfolk, for the second earl of Buckinghamshire. As a Roman Catholic he was at that time excluded from public commissions, but he designed two Catholic embassy chapels in London, the Bavarian chapel in Warwick Street (1789–90) and the Spanish chapel in Manchester Square (1793–6). Bonomi had no affection for the Gothic style, which he felt had totally corrupted architecture, but he produced a few unexecuted Gothic designs, for a gateway and a castellated summer house.

Bonomi died at home at 76 Great Titchfield Street, London, on 9 March 1808, and was buried in Marylebone churchyard. His grave no longer exists, but the Latin inscription on his gravestone was published in the second volume of the second edition of Daniel Lysons's *Environs of London* (1811). A son, Peter, died in 1792, and another son, John James (1782–1803), was killed at the battle of Assaye in India. His six surviving children were: Ignatius *Bonomi (1787–1870), also an architect; Charles (1789–1826), a soldier; Agnes (1792–1874); Joseph *Bonomi (1796–1878) and his twin sister, Mary Anne (1796–1872), mother of George Goldie, another architect; and Justina (1801–1890). PETER MEADOWS

Sources W. Papworth, 'Memoir of Joseph Bonomi', *Sessional Papers of the Royal Institute of British Architects* (1868–9), 123–34 · P. Meadows, *Joseph Bonomi: architect* (1988) · M. Binney, 'A pioneer work of neo-classicism', *Country Life*, 150 (1971), 110–15 · D. Fitzgerald, 'A gallery after the antique: some reflections on "The age of neo-classicism"', *The Connoisseur*, 181 (1972), 2–13 · P. Meadows, 'Drawn to entice', *Country Life* (28 April 1988), 128–33 · P. Meadows and J. Cornforth, 'Draughtsman decorator', *Country Life* (19 April 1990), 164–8 · J. Cornforth, 'Longford Hall, Shropshire', *Country Life*, 132 (1962), 354–8 · M. Binney, 'Packington Hall, Warwickshire [pts 1–3]', *Country Life*, 148 (1970), 102–6, 162–6, 226–9 · S. F. D. Rigaud, 'Facts and recollections of the XVIIIth century in a memoir of John Francis Rigaud', ed. W. L. Pressly, *Walpole Society*, 50 (1984), 1–164 · I. Bonomi to Lord Buchan, May 1808, U. Glas. L., MS Murray, 502/41/3 · b. cert. · *The exhibition of the Royal Academy* [exhibition catalogues]

Archives RIBA, accounts for Barrells House, Warwickshire; design drawings for various houses incl. Rosneath | Norfolk RO, letters and papers relating to Blickling mausoleum · NRA Scotland, priv. coll., plans and notes for Rosneath

Likenesses G. Dance, pencil drawing, 1793, RA; repro. in Meadows, *Joseph Bonomi* · J. F. Rigaud, oils, 1794, RA · W. Daniell, drawing (after G. Dance, 1793), NPG [*see illus.*] · A. Wivell, etching, BM

Bonomi, Joseph (1796–1878), sculptor and Egyptologist, and his twin sister, Mary Anne Bonomi (1796–1872), were born at 76 Great Titchfield Street, London, on 9 October 1796, the eighth and ninth but fourth and fifth surviving children of Joseph (Giuseppe) *Bonomi (1739–1808), architect, and Rosa Florini (1755–1812). Bonomi was baptized four days later in the Venetian Chapel in London, when his sponsors (by proxy) were Giovanni Carlo Bonomi, his uncle, and Angelica *Kauffman, his mother's cousin. Bonomi's parents died when he was young but comfortable provision was made for the children. He attended school at Carshalton, Surrey. By 1815, when the Society of Arts awarded him a silver medal for a bas-relief in plaster, Bonomi's thoughts were turning to sculpture, and in 1816 he joined the Royal Academy Schools, where the sculptor John Flaxman was his teacher; he won silver medals there in 1817 and 1818. About 1818 he became the pupil of Joseph Nollekens and in 1819 executed a monument to Captain Showers for Calcutta Cathedral. He eventually tired of the discipline of assisting the elderly Nollekens and in 1822 decided to go to Rome to study under Antonio Canova, who, however, died before his arrival.

In Rome, Bonomi soon became part of the British artistic community, meeting among other artists Charles Eastlake, John Gibson, Joseph John Scoles, and Frederick Catherwood. In an echo of his father's early career he turned aside from his sculptor's training and in 1824 joined Robert Hay's expedition to Egypt as a salaried artist. In 1825 Hay made a journey up the Nile to Abu Simbel, Philae, and Thebes, and on this trip Bonomi produced numerous drawings and helped to make casts at Kalabsha, the largest of which are in the British Museum. On a second visit to Thebes in 1826 Hay and Bonomi saw the temple of Hermopolis just before it was demolished. Bonomi quarrelled with Hay over ownership of his drawings and parted from him in the summer of 1826. He spent 1827–8 in Cairo producing engravings for James Burton's *Excerpta hieroglyphica*; he lived for a time in Thebes and formed a great friendship with the Italian traveller Rosselini; in 1830–31 he travelled in Egypt with two French artists, Linant and Dupuy; and in 1832 he was reconciled with Hay and worked with the architectural draughtsman and painter Francis *Arundale. In a letter dated 9 August 1832 from Thebes, Arundale noted that 'Bonomi and I live in the same tomb' (Vialla, 114), an abode he recorded in a letter and sketch (14 August 1832) of which he stated that 'the person entering the door is Bonomi in his habitual dress' (ibid., 115–16). While in Egypt, Bonomi formed a liaison with a woman called Fatima, with whom he had two children. In August 1833 Bonomi toured Palestine and Syria with Arundale and the draughtsman and printmaker Frederick Catherwood. Bonomi, mistaken for a native, having adopted Eastern dress, assumed Eastern manners, and learned Arabic, was one of the first Europeans to visit the Dome of the Rock (or the mosque of Omar), but Catherwood, posing as a military engineer, entered soon after, and both claimed credit for producing the detailed drawings which James Fergusson used in his *Essay on the Ancient Topography of Jerusalem* (1847) when he asserted that the Dome of the Rock covered the holy sepulchre (an assertion demolished by Robert Willis in his treatise on the holy sepulchre in 1849).

Bonomi returned to England some time after 1834 and was employed in illustrating the Egyptian works of John Gardner Wilkinson and Samuel Birch, and in helping to arrange the Egyptian exhibits in the British Museum, but he failed to find the regular employment which his family hoped would be his. In 1838 he went to Rome to copy the hieroglyphics and obelisks there. In 1842 he was asked to provide designs for an Egyptian façade for John Marshall's Temple Mills at Leeds. This monumental façade, based on the temple of Edfu, might have established Bonomi's architectural reputation. (Indeed, his designs for the mill later formed his chief claim to be an architect.) He decided, however, to join the Prussian government's expedition to Egypt led by Dr Karl Richard Lepsius. The invitation was the result of a chance meeting with the Prussian crown prince, Alexander von Humboldt, the Prussian ambassador Baron von Bunsen, and Lepsius in the British Museum, and Bonomi had only two days to prepare to sail, leaving Ignatius, his more prudent brother, to negotiate the details of his contract and remuneration. Bonomi spent two years in Egypt, measuring and drawing, and returned to England in 1844. In 1850 he went into partnership with Henry Warren and James Fahey and made a series of drawings which Warren and Fahey painted as a *Grand Moving Panorama of the Nile*, which was at first profitable but which finally ran into financial difficulties from which Bonomi was extricated with Ignatius Bonomi's help.

In 1845 Bonomi married Jessie Martin (1825–1859), daughter of the artist John Martin, with whom he had four children: Joseph Menes (*b*. 1846), Cautley (*b*. 1847), Jessie (*b*. 1849), and John (*b*. 1851); but in a devastating week in April 1852 all four died of whooping cough. Four more children followed: Isabella (*b*. 1853), Cecilia Nefeeseh (1855–1944), Joseph Ignatius (1857–1930), and Marion (1859–1887); but in 1859 Jessie Bonomi died, aged thirty-four. Thereafter Jessie's sister Isabella Mary Martin kept house for Bonomi and helped to raise his family.

In 1853 Bonomi had a notable success in assisting Owen Jones in the arrangement of the Egyptian court at the Crystal Palace; much of the modelling was executed by Bonomi himself. Among those whom he advised on their collections of Egyptian and other antiquities were John Lee of Hartwell House, Buckinghamshire, Henry Abbott, the earl of Ashburnham, the marquess of Northampton, and, notably, the duke of Northumberland, who as Lord Prudhoe had been one of the group of Egyptological enthusiasts in the 1820s and 1830s. In 1861 the curatorship of Sir John Soane's Museum in Lincoln's Inn Fields in London fell vacant. A practising architect had to be appointed; and after fierce struggle and controversy Bonomi, who, but for the work which he had done for John Marshall in Leeds, would have found it impossible to prove his qualification for the post, overcame his critics and was elected. The curatorship at last gave him a permanent salary, and he and his brother Ignatius purchased land at Wimbledon Park, Surrey, and built a house in Princes Road, The Camels, which Joseph adorned with a frieze of a caravan, representing the path of life. In 1864 he published remarkably detailed drawings of the Soane Museum's 'Belzoni sarcophagus' of Oimenepthah I, king of Egypt, with descriptions by Samuel Sharpe. In 1867 he designed the first hieroglyphic font to be produced in England, for the illustration of Birch's hieroglyphic dictionary. The Soane Museum post suited him, and he remained there until his death at The Camels on 3 March 1878. He was buried with his wife and first family in the Brompton cemetery, London, 'beneath a guardian Anubis' (Tillett).

Bonomi's scholarship was shown in articles on Egypt which he contributed to the principal publications of the time, especially the *Transactions of the Royal Society of Literature*; and his artistry was expressed in his illustrations for other people's works. One of the foremost hieroglyphic draughtsmen of his day, his work can be found in the *Transactions of the Syro-Egyptian Society*; the *Gallery of Antiquities Selected from the British Museum*, by Francis Arundale and Bonomi (1842–3), with descriptions by Samuel Birch; his catalogues of Robert Hay's collection; and John Lee's collection in the Hartwell House Museum. Bonomi frequently collaborated with Samuel Sharpe especially, illustrating most of Sharpe's books; in many cases it would be more correct to say that Sharpe supplied the text explaining Bonomi's drawings. Bonomi's major publication was *Nineveh and its Palaces*, a popular and scholarly work which regarded the city from the artistic and scriptural points of view and illustrated and discussed in depth the chief sculptures, reliefs, and inscriptions then known of that city; the work ran through several editions from 1852. Bonomi also invented a machine for measuring the proportions of the body and wrote a treatise on the proportions of the human figure. Samuel Birch, Egyptologist and keeper of oriental antiquities at the British Museum:

> praised his abilities … considering him to have greater knowledge of Egypt than anyone else of the period save Wilkinson; the number of works and projects he contributed to after 1830 was enormous and exceeded that of any other artist, so that although not an Egyptologist he yet made greater contributions than most. (Dawson and Uphill, 54)

PETER MEADOWS

Sources W. Simpson, 'Memoir of Joseph Bonomi, FRAS, FRSL', *Transactions of the Society for Biblical Archaeology*, 6/2 (1879), 560–73 · S. Tillett, *Egypt itself: the career of Robert Hay* (1984) · R. Gunnis, *Dictionary of British sculptors, 1660–1851*, new edn (1968) · W. H. Bartlett, *Walks about the city and environs of Jerusalem* (1844) · O. Jones and J. Bonomi, *Description of the Egyptian court erected in the Crystal Palace* (1854) · W. H. Smythe, *Aedes Hartwellianae* (1851) · D. Linstrum, *West Yorkshire: architects and architecture* (1978) · W. R. Dawson and E. P. Uphill, *Who was who in Egyptology*, 3rd edn, rev. M. L. Bierbrier (1995) · *CGPLA Eng. & Wales* (1878) · CUL, Bonomi MSS, Add. MS 9389 · J. Vialla, *Les Pickersgill-Arundale: une famille de peintres anglais au XIXe siècle* (Paris, 1983)

Archives BL, papers relating to Egypt, Add. MSS 25651, 25663, fols. 42–107, 29812–29860 · CUL, corresp. and papers · RAS, papers relating to Spain · U. Oxf., Griffith Institute, drawings, watercolours, and sketches made in Egypt, Nubia, Palestine, and elsewhere | BL, letters to Robert Hay, Add. MSS 38094, 38510 · Bucks. RLSS, corresp. with John Lee · U. Durham L., letters to John Lee

Likenesses J. Bonomi, self-portrait, pencil and ink sketch, 1845, BL; repro. in Tillett, *Egypt itself* · M. Sharpe, oils, 1868, NPG · print, 1878, NPG; repro. in *ILN* · photograph, repro. in J. Bonomi, *The proportions of the human figure*, 5th edn (1880)

Wealth at death under £8000: probate, 1 May 1878, *CGPLA Eng. & Wales*

Bononcini, Giovanni (1670–1747), composer, was born on 8 July (18 July NS) 1670 at Modena, the fifth of the eight children of Giovanni Maria Bononcini (*bap.* 1642, *d.* 1678), composer and chapel master at the cathedral, and his first wife, Anna Maria Prezii (1641/2–1677), whom he married in 1662. Anna Maria died after giving birth to Antonio Maria (1677–1726), and Giovanni Maria died a year later. Giovanni and Antonio Maria studied in Bologna with Giovanni Paolo Colonna, chapel master at San Petronio. In 1685–91 Giovanni published six instrumental and two vocal collections, was elected to the Accademia Filarmonica, played violoncello at San Petronio, was appointed chapel master at San Giovanni in Monte, and composed three oratorios. In 1692–8 he lived in Rome, where he served Filippo and Lorenza Colonna, joined the Accademia di Santa Cecilia and the 'chorus' in the Arcadian Academy, and composed six serenatas, five operas, and one oratorio, all to texts by the Roman librettist Silvio Stampiglia. *Il trionfo di Camilla* (Naples, 1696) had the greatest success; in 1698–1710 it was adapted for productions in nineteen other Italian cities, and in 1706–28 it was performed 111 times in London, where an attempt was made in 1707 to attract Bononcini himself. *Camilla* is a touchstone of Italian taste between 1696 and 1710 because its captivating melodies serve as a postscript to the seventeenth-century *bel canto* and a prelude to the eighteenth-century *galant* styles. Greater complexities are found in Bononcini's 300 cantatas, which exemplify 'no little *bizzaria*, beauty, harmony, artful study, and fanciful invention' (F. Gasparini, *L'armonico pratico al cimbalo*, 1708, 110; trans. F. S. Stillings, 1963, 94). Complexities abound in his *Duetti da camera*, op. 8 (1691), which are dedicated to Emperor Leopold I. From 1698 to 1712 he served Leopold I (*d.* 1705) and Joseph I (*d.* 1711) in Vienna, and he was clearly Joseph's favourite composer. After Joseph's death he served Johann Wenzel, Count Gallas, Charles VI's ambassador to Rome (*d.* 1719).

In the summer of 1719 Bononcini was invited to compose for the new Royal Academy of Music in London. The fifty-year-old arrived in mid-October 1720, and his first two seasons were outstandingly successful. Five of his operas (including one for which he set only act II) accounted for 82 of the 120 performances given by the academy, and he profited from engraved editions of his *Cantate e duetti* (which had 238 subscribers) and *Divertimenti da camera*. In 1721–2 his operas led the academy to its only profitable season. He then received commissions from Francis Atterbury, dean of Westminster, to write the anthem for the duke of Marlborough's funeral and from Katharine Sheffield, duchess of Buckingham, to set the choruses in *Marcus Brutus*, written by her late husband.

The duchess was a notorious Jacobite, and Atterbury was imprisoned for treasonous Jacobite activities in August 1722. By October the academy had terminated its employment of both Bononcini and the librettist Rolli, who were Italian Catholics, were associated with Jacobites, and would not accept significantly reduced salaries. During the 1722–3 season their *Erminia* was nevertheless produced, presumably as a rehearsal for its scheduled performance at Paris in July 1723. Bononcini had long been regarded in Paris as the sole 'modèle pour le gracieux' (F. Raguenet, *Défense du parallèle des Italiens et des Français*, 1705, 44). One negotiator for the July production was Luigi Riccoboni, the director of the Italian comedians in Paris and the husband of Elena Balletti, whose sister Margherita (*b. c.*1685, *d.* after 1738) had married Bononcini, perhaps by 1706. Although the July production was cancelled, Bononcini performed at Paris with various singers during the summers of 1723–4 and was offered employment there by the marquise de Prie, mistress of the duke of Bourbon, first minister of France. But he instead accepted a lifelong stipend of £500 per annum, offered by Henrietta Godolphin, duchess of Marlborough, on 14 May 1724. In return for this sum he organized her private concerts. In 1727 he did compose one more opera for the Royal Academy, but its performances were increasingly marred by catcalls blown by partisans of the rival prima donnas.

Bononcini and Handel likewise had their partisans, and in May 1725 John Byrom wittily ridiculed them at the end of a six-line epigram:

> Strange all this Difference should be
> 'Twixt Tweedle-dum and Tweedle-dee!
> (Deutsch, 180)

Bononcini's best friend in London was Giuseppe Riva, the secretary for Modena (1718–29), with whom he often resided in Suffolk Street. Riva's pamphlet, *Advice to the Composers and Performers of Vocal Musick* (1727), offers 'advice' to Handel. Bononcini's recitative, clearly superior to Handel's, was 'marked with great exactness and propriety' (J. Hawkins, *A General History of the Science and Practice of Music*, 5 vols., 1776, 5.281), and, 'both in writing and utterance, was universally allowed to be the best of the time, and in the true genius of the Italian language' (C. Burney, 'Bononcini', in Rees, *Cyclopaedia*, 1819, vol. 4). Hawkins aptly noted that 'Bononcini's genius was adapted to the expression of tender and pathetic sentiments. His melodies, the richest and sweetest that we know of, are in a style peculiarly his own; his harmonies are original, and at the same time natural'. But Bononcini's arias rarely convey the power that typifies those by Handel. As Burney noted, 'his melody was, perhaps, more polished and vocal, though not so new as that of his powerful Saxon rival; … as a correct, powerful, and inventive composer, he was an infant compared with Handel'. Bononcini's are instead 'agreeable and easie' (J. E. Galliard, *Six English Cantatas after the Italian Manner*, 1716, preface). They served from 1690 onwards as a 'modèle pour le gracieux', but by 1730 their 'too great Simplicity' troubled many listeners (*The Craftsman*, 10 June 1727).

Beginning in 1726 Bononcini was an active member of the newly formed Academy of (Ancient) Vocal Music. About 1728 his friend Maurice Greene introduced an unsigned manuscript of a madrigal, which Bononcini reportedly claimed to have composed. In 1731 Bernard Gates presented the same work, drawn from a 1705 publication by Antonio Lotti. A flagrant example of someone's unacknowledged borrowing had been uncovered, and several academicians vengefully discredited Bononcini and Greene by obtaining and publishing attestations from Lotti and his Venetian associates. Bononcini then ended his dozen years in London unwisely, in that he cast his lot with the infamous Count Ughi (a disguised Discalced Carmelite), left his generous patroness, and dedicated a work of 1732 to her chief antagonist, her own mother, Sarah, dowager duchess of Marlborough.

By November 1732 Bononcini had departed for Paris, where he composed and published works in 1733. He was in Madrid in December 1733 and in Lisbon by August 1735. In mid-1736 he returned to Vienna, where he composed two operas and an oratorio for productions of 1737. He was presumably unaware that Handel's *Serse* (London, 1738) revivifies much from his Roman *Xerse* of 1694 and thus contains flagrant examples of unacknowledged borrowing. He presented Empress Maria Theresa with a Te Deum in 1741, and in 1742 she increased his small pension to an amount that allowed him to spend his final five years in comfortable frugality. It is not known if his wife was with him after 1733, but their 22-year-old daughter, Theresia, died at Vienna on 10 May 1743; Bononcini died there, at a house called Al Luccio Azzurro in the rione Wieden, on 9 July 1747. LOWELL LINDGREN

Sources L. Lindgren, 'Bononcini, Giovanni', *New Grove*, 2nd edn • O. E. Deutsch, *Handel: a documentary biography* (1955) • G. E. Dorris, *Paolo Rolli and the Italian circle in London, 1715–44* (1967) • L. Lindgren, 'Musicians and librettists in the correspondence of Gio. Giacomo Zamboni (Oxford, Bodleian Library, MSS Rawlinson Letters 116–138)', *Royal Musical Association Research Chronicle*, 24 (1991) • L. Lindgren, 'Parisian patronage of performers from the Royal Academy of Musick (1719–28)', *Music and Letters*, 58 (1977), 4–28 • L. Lindgren, 'The three great noises "fatal to the interests of Bononcini"', *Musical Quarterly*, 61 (1975), 560–83 • L. Lindgren, '*Camilla* and *The beggar's opera*', *Philological Quarterly*, 59 (1980), 44–61 • H. S. Powers, '*Il Serse* trasformato', *Musical Quarterly*, 47 (1961), 481–92; 48 (1962), 73–92 • K. Hueber, 'Gli ultimi anni di Giovanni Bononcini: notizie e documenti inediti', *Atti e Memorie dell'Accademia di Scienze, Lettere e Arti di Modena*, 5th ser., 12 (1954), 153–71 • G. Roncaglia, 'Di insigni musicisti modenesi (documenti inediti), II: su la famiglia dei Bononcini', *Atti e Memorie della R. Deputazione di Storia Patria per le Provincie Modenesi*, 7th ser., 6 (1930), 13–18 • C. Sartori, *Bibliografia della musica strumentale Italiana stampata in Italia fino al 1700* (Florence, 1952), nos. 1685d–f, 1686c, 1687d–e • La Mara, *Musikerbriefe aus fünf Jahrhunderten*, 1 (1886), 119–20 • L. Lindgren, 'Vienna, the "natural centro" for Giovanni Bononcini', *Il teatro musicale italiano nel Sacro Romano Impero nei secoli XVII e XVIII* [Loveno di Menaggio 1997], ed. A. Colzani, N. Dubowy, A. Luppi, and M. Padoan (Como, 1999), 383–420 [Atti del VII Convegno internazionale sulla musica italiana nei secoli XVII–XVIII, Loveno di Menaggio, 15–17 July 1997] • L. Lindgren, 'To be a bee in 18th-century England, as exemplified by Handel's *Xerxes*', *Göttinger Händel-Beiträge*, 7 (1998), 57–72

Likenesses portrait, 1690–99, Civico Museo Bibliografico Musicale, Bologna, Italy • P. L. Ghezzi, caricature, 1720, Biblioteca Apostolica Vaticana, Vatican City • B. Dandridge, portrait, *c.*1730, Royal College of Music, London • J. Caldwall, engraving, repro. in J. Hawkins, *A general history of the science and practice of music*, 2nd edn, 1853 (1776) • portrait, Cambridge, H. R. Beard collection

Wealth at death virtual poverty: Hueber, 'Gli ultimi anni'

Bonsor, Sir (Henry) Cosmo Orme, first baronet (1848–1929), brewer and railway manager, was born on 2 September 1848 at Great Bookham, near Dorking, Surrey. He was the son of Joseph Bonsor (1807–1873) of Polesden Lacey, Surrey, a partner from 1852 in the London brewing firm of Combe, Delafield & Co. (later Combe & Co.), and his wife, Eliza Denne, *née* Orme. In 1865, after an education at Eton College, Cosmo joined the family brewing firm (his father was by this time the senior partner). He quickly established himself as a competent manager, orchestrating the company's expansion through the purchase of public houses and smaller breweries, and emphasizing the retailing and marketing functions of the business. He was also the driving force behind the incorporation and amalgamation of important brewing interests in London. He joined the board of Watney & Co. when it became a limited company in 1885, and in 1888 became a director of his own firm on its incorporation.

In 1898 the interests of Combe, Watney, and a third company, Reid's Brewery, were merged as Watney, Combe, Reid & Co., and Bonsor became its first chairman, a post he retained for thirty years. Capitalized at £15 million, it was not only the largest brewing company of its day, but also the biggest company in British manufacturing. However, with its evident over-capitalization and high gearing, the new giant was a daunting prospect for any manager. It says much for Bonsor's tenacity and financial acumen that he stayed on to pull the company round from the bad times (no dividend was paid on the deferred ordinary shares, 1908–16) to comparative security in the 1920s. The written-down capital was restored in 1922–5, and the company was strong enough to embark on a fresh wave of merger activity, acquiring the Cobham, Isleworth, Higgins, and London and Burton breweries in 1923–9. Bonsor was also a strong supporter of the brewing lobbies, serving as chairman and treasurer of the National Trade Defence Association from its establishment in 1888 to 1895. He was master of the Brewers' Company in 1881 and a vice-president of the Institute of Brewing from 1904.

Bonsor was also for many years manager of another controversial large corporation—the South Eastern and Chatham Railway. Elected chairman of the South Eastern Railway in 1898, and thereby inheriting the dubious legacy of the recently retired Sir Edward Watkin (1819–1901), Bonsor did much to restore stability between that company and its long-term rival, the London, Chatham, and Dover Railway. In 1899 he organized a 'working union' of the two companies, in the form of a merger which fell short of a full financial amalgamation. Bonsor acted as chairman of the South Eastern and Chatham managing committee, until the merged companies were themselves amalgamated into the Southern Railway in 1923. During his tenure of office the two railways, once the butt of music-hall jokes, became models of technical advance, efficiency, and competent management, although the price of rationalization was high, resulting in the addition of £9 million to the capital account between 1899 and 1912.

Bonsor also had other business interests. He was a director of the Bank of England for forty-four years (1885–1929), and of the Northern Assurance Company, and was for thirty-nine years chairman of the income tax commissioners for the City of London (1886–1925). He was also treasurer of Guy's Hospital and Conservative MP for Wimbledon from 1885 to 1900. He was created a baronet in 1925, and was a JP and deputy lieutenant for Surrey and a deputy lieutenant and alderman of the City of London. He was also an officer of the Légion d'honneur. In 1872 he married Emily Gertrude, *née* Fellowes, of Dorset; they had three sons and four daughters. After his wife's death in 1882 he married Mabel Brand of Croydon.

Frank, open, likeable, and a good talker, Bonsor had an excellent grasp of financial affairs, and was supported by solid political connections. He also had the gift of choosing competent subordinates. His memorable achievement was to take five of Britain's problematic companies and fuse them into rationalized, more efficient units—a model others would have done well to follow. Bonsor died on 4 December 1929 at boulevard Carabacel in Nice.

TERRY GOURVISH

Sources T. Corran, 'Bonsor, Sir Henry Cosmo Orme', *DBB* • *WWW* • W. P. Serocold, *The story of Watneys* (1949) • H. H. Janes, *The red barrel: a history of Watney Mann* [1963] • T. R. Gourvish and R. G. Wilson, *The British brewing industry, 1830–1980* (1994) • *Brewing Trade Review* (Jan 1930) • *Brewing Trade Review* (Feb 1930) • *Brewers' Journal* (15 Dec 1929) • *Brewers' Gazette* (19 Dec 1929) • T. R. Gourvish, 'The performance of British railway management after 1860: the railways of Watkin and Forbes', *Business History*, 20 (1978), 186–200 • P. L. Payne, 'The emergence of the large-scale company in Great Britain, 1870–1914', *Economic History Review*, 2nd ser., 20 (1967), 519–42 • P. S. Bagwell, 'The rivalry and working union of the South Eastern and London, Chatham and Dover railways', *Journal of Transport History*, 2 (1955–6), 65–79 • R. Roberts and D. Kynaston, *The Bank of England* (1995)

Likenesses photograph, repro. in *Brewing Trade Review* (1 Jan 1930), 54 • photograph, repro. in Serocold, *Story of Watneys*, 95 • photograph, repro. in Janes, *Red barrel* • photograph, Brewers and Licensed Retailers Association

Wealth at death £717,528 1s. 5d.: probate, 18 Jan 1930, *CGPLA Eng. & Wales*

Bonville [Boville; *alias* Terill], **Anthony** (1623–1676), Jesuit and theologian, was born at Canford in Dorset either on 20 February or on 2 March 1623, the son of Humphrey Bonville, esquire, and his wife, Mary. Both his parents were Roman Catholics, although, according to a later account by Anthony, his father 'was much estranged from the Catholic faith' (Kenny, 468). As a result the parents followed the not unusual procedure of raising their six sons as protestants, while their daughter was brought up as a Roman Catholic.

Owing to the missionary activities of the Jesuit Thomas Blackfan (or Bennett), Anthony and three of his brothers converted to Catholicism. At the age of fourteen Anthony went to Flanders and studied at the Jesuit college at Ypres for three years, after which he travelled to Rome to become a priest. He entered the English College at Rome on 4 December 1640 and received minor orders in 1642. Unwilling to subscribe to the usual college oath (which bound students to return to the English mission as soon as they had been ordained) he became a convictor, which meant that he had to pay for his own board and lodging. His ordination took place at St John Lateran on 16 March 1647 and on 20 June of the same year he entered the Society of Jesus at St Andrew's noviciate, Rome. In the following years he went through the various stages of higher Jesuit studies which he completed by being professed of the four vows on 25 March 1658 at Parma.

During these years Bonville also functioned as one of the penitentiaries at Loreto, taught philosophy at Florence, and completed his dissertation, *Conclusiones philosophicae rationibus illustratur* (1657). About this time the University of Parma appointed him professor of philosophy and subsequently professor of scholastic divinity.

In 1660 Bonville brought out a short treatise on mathematics, *Problema mathematico-philosophicum tripartitum*. Shortly afterwards he transferred to the English province of the Society of Jesus and was sent to the English Jesuit college at Liège where he stayed for the rest of his life, working as a professor of theology and mathematics and, from 1661 to 1674, as rector. At Liège he wrote his two most important works, *Fundamentum totius theologia moralis, seu, Tractatus de conscientia probabili* (1668) and the posthumously published *Regula morum, sive, Tractatus bipartitus de sufficienti ad conscientiam rite formandam regula* (1677). These two works established Bonville's reputation as one of the most systematical expounders of the seventeenth-century moral-theological doctrine of probabilism, whose central tenet was that when faced with a choice between two courses of action, neither of which has been explicitly condemned by the church, it is permissible to choose one course of action even though it is probable that the other course of action is morally safer. In his *Florus Anglo-Bavaricus* (1685) John Keynes had high praise for Bonville's intelligence, erudition, and personal charm. Bonville died at the Jesuit college at Liège on 11 October 1676.

J. Blom and F. Blom

Sources T. M. McCoog, *English and Welsh Jesuits, 1555–1650*, 1, Catholic RS, 74 (1994) • Gillow, *Lit. biog. hist.*, 1.279 • H. Foley, ed., *Records of the English province of the Society of Jesus*, 3 (1878), 420–21; 5 (1879), 413; 6 (1880), 352–3, 379 • W. Kelly, ed., *Liber ruber venerabilis collegii Anglorum de urbe*, 2, Catholic RS, 40 (1943), 23 • [J. Keynes and T. Stapleton], *Florus Anglo-Bavaricus* (Liège, 1685); facs. edn with new introduction by T. A. Birrell (1970) • G. Holt, *St Omers and Bruges colleges, 1593–1773: a biographical dictionary*, Catholic RS, 69 (1979) • A. de Backer and others, *Bibliothèque de la Compagnie de Jésus*, new edn, 7, ed. C. Sommervogel (Brussels, 1896), 1930 • G. Anstruther, *The seminary priests*, 2 (1975), 33 • A. Kenny, ed., *The responsa scholarum of the English College, Rome*, 2, Catholic RS, 55 (1963), 468–9

Bonville, William, first Baron Bonville (1392–1461), administrator and landowner, was probably born at Shute, near Axminster, Devon, the son of John Bonville (*d.* 1396) and his wife, Elizabeth Fitzroger (*b.* *c.*1370, *d.* in or before 1421), and heir to both his father and grandfather, Sir William Bonville (*d.* 1408). He was married twice, first in 1414 to Margaret, daughter of Reynold *Grey, third Baron Grey of Ruthin, and second, by 1430, to Elizabeth (*d.* 1471), daughter of Edward Courtenay, eleventh earl of Devon, and widow of John, Lord Harington (*d.* 1418). Her tomb at Porlock, Somerset, survives. William Bonville's son and grandson were both killed in 1460, and his estates passed on his death to his infant granddaughter, Cicely, who later married Thomas *Grey, marquess of Dorset (*d.* 1501).

Bonville's grandfather and namesake had been among the most prominent west-country gentry in the late fourteenth century, serving as MP for Devon and Somerset on ten and seven occasions respectively, and receiving a large number of local offices and commissions. He was a liveried retainer of the leading regional magnate, Edward Courtenay, earl of Devon, a close political and family bond that was destined to be violently sundered in the mid-fifteenth century.

The elder Sir William's two marriages, and that of his son, John, brought substantial property with them, and this, together with many purchases and inheritances, ensured that William, Lord Bonville, enjoyed one of the most valuable estates in the south-west, valued in 1435 at about £900 net per annum—a figure not far short of that enjoyed by the fifteenth-century earls of Devon themselves. Bonville's estates included outliers in many counties, but were concentrated in south-east Devon (where Shute was his principal seat) and mid-Somerset (including Chewton Mendip).

Bonville entered most of his estates in 1414 (their keeping during his minority having been entrusted to Edward, duke of York) and cut his teeth in military service in 1415 under Henry V's brother, Thomas, duke of Clarence, one of whose executors he became. He was active in west-country administration from the early 1420s. While his extensive and complex inheritances led to some violent disputes with neighbours during these years, these were on nothing like the scale of disorder that was to characterize Bonville's notorious conflict with the Courtenays during the 1440s and 1450s.

This power struggle was triggered by the appointment of Bonville in 1437 as royal steward in Cornwall for life. This was seen by the young Thomas *Courtenay, thirteenth earl of Devon, recently come of age and in possession of a severely reduced inheritance, as a serious challenge to his own regional authority. The bitterness of the strife that grew from this was symptomatic of a change in the local balance of power and wealth that had over a generation tilted against the Courtenay earls (the traditional leaders of west-country society) in favour of a small group of powerful gentry among whom Bonville was pre-eminent.

Violence reached an alarming level during the summers of 1439 and 1440, and the situation was worsened by a serious blunder on the part of the government—the appointment of the earl to the stewardship of the duchy of Cornwall, a post so similar to that held by Bonville as to be hardly distinguishable from it. Urgent attempts at even-handedness and arbitration failed, and the dispute was only temporarily resolved by the appointment of Bonville as seneschal of Gascony in December 1442, thereby removing him temporarily from the scene (he sailed from Plymouth in March 1443 but was back in Devon by April 1445). Even though the government, coming increasingly under the influence of the duke of Suffolk, was careful not to antagonize the earl of Devon, the latter was clearly seen to be the principal culprit. Bonville's connection with Suffolk grew stronger. He was a member of Suffolk's entourage at Margaret of Anjou's betrothal ceremonies at Rouen in May 1444, and married his daughter Elizabeth to one of Suffolk's henchmen, Sir William Tailboys. This development culminated in the parliament of 1449, when Bonville was raised to the peerage as Baron Bonville of Chewton.

Antagonisms hardened after the fall of Suffolk in 1450. The earl of Devon attached himself to the duke of York, and felt confident enough in the summer of 1451 to risk an encounter in the field with Bonville (and his ally, James Butler, earl of Wiltshire). Despite much plunder and violence, a major showdown was avoided when York's unexpected arrival in the west country persuaded the earl of

Devon to lift the siege of Taunton Castle, which Bonville had made his headquarters. Although temporarily imprisoned (as were Devon and the other principal malcontents), Bonville was soon able to exploit the dramatically changed political situation that followed the humiliating submission of York and Devon to the king at Dartford on 3 March 1452.

Between 1452 and 1455 Bonville became the dominant force in west-country politics. It was he who was made responsible for bringing Devon and his adherents to justice, and the king personally reinforced his position by staying at Bonville's house at Shute on his progress through the west country in the summer of 1452. Bonville was confirmed as steward of the duchy of Cornwall in 1452 (the post that had triggered the violence in 1439), and appointed constable of Exeter Castle in 1453, both posts to be held for life. He was active at sea as well as on land—he had been appointed again as seneschal of Gascony in September 1453 but did not take up the post—and his maritime activities were energetic enough to bring forth complaints of piracy from the duke of Burgundy.

These partisan appointments of Bonville to positions within the earl of Devon's traditional zone of influence forced the earl to take increasingly desperate measures, especially as the marriage of Bonville's grandson about 1455 to Katherine, a daughter of Richard *Neville, earl of Salisbury, further entrenched him within the dominant Yorkist circle. On 23 October 1455 Devon's son and other retainers murdered Nicholas Radford, one of Bonville's senior councillors, and embarked on a campaign of violence which this time did culminate in battle, at Clyst on 13 December. Bonville fared the worse but escaped; after a short period of incarceration Courtenay resumed his campaign of violence against Bonville which lasted well into 1456.

While the level of local violence appears to have abated thereafter, the enmities that had grown over more than twenty years proved irresolvable. The death in 1458 of Bonville's old adversary afforded him little comfort. The new earl of Devon—another Thomas Courtenay, the killer of Radford—quickly gained favour with Queen Margaret, and this presented enormous risks for Bonville and his family. Bonville was probably present at the parliament of 1460 that recognized York's right of succession to the throne, and both his son and grandson were caught up with York's ill-judged march north and perished at the battle of Wakefield on 31 December 1460. Bonville himself, while consolidating his west-country alliances, remained about the court. Aged nearly seventy, he, with Sir Thomas Kyriell, was given custody of the king's person when the Yorkist forces under the earl of Warwick met those of the Lancastrians at the second battle of St Albans on 17 February 1461. The Yorkists were defeated and the king's guardians were captured. The earl of Devon had been present, too, and at his and the queen's instigation, two days after the battle, a mock trial was held before the young prince of Wales, and on 19 February 1461 Bonville and Kyriell were executed. MARTIN CHERRY

Sources J. Prince, *Danmonii orientales illustres, or, The worthies of Devon* (1701) · R. L. Storey, *The end of the house of Lancaster*, new edn (1986) · M. Cherry, 'The struggle for power in mid-fifteenth-century Devonshire', *Patronage, the crown and the provinces*, ed. R. A. Griffiths (1981), 123–44 · M. Cherry, 'The Courtenay earls of Devon: the formation and disintegration of a late medieval aristocratic affinity', *Southern History*, 1 (1979), 71–97 · R. A. Griffiths, *The reign of King Henry VI: the exercise of royal authority, 1422–1461* (1981) · P. A. Johnson, *Duke Richard of York, 1411–1460* (1988) · GEC, *Peerage*, new edn, 2.218–19 · King's bench ancient indictments, PRO, KB9 · Chancery, inquisitions post mortem, PRO, C136, C137, C140 · additional charters, BL · court rolls, Devon RO · Exeter city receivers' accounts, Devon RO · *The register of Edmund Lacy, bishop of Exeter*, ed. G. R. Dunstan, 5 vols., CYS, 60–63, 66 (1963–72), vol. 3 · *RotP*, vol. 5 · *Chancery records* · 'William Gregory's chronicle of London', *The historical collections of a citizen of London in the fifteenth century*, ed. J. Gairdner, CS, new ser., 17 (1876), 55–239 · 'John Benet's chronicle for the years 1400 to 1462', ed. G. L. Harriss, *Camden miscellany, XXIV*, CS, 4th ser., 9 (1972) · J. S. Davies, ed., *An English chronicle of the reigns of Richard II, Henry IV, Henry V, and Henry VI*, CS, 64 (1856)

Wealth at death approx. £900 p.a.: Prince, *Danmonii orientales illustres*, 72–4

Bonvisi, Antonio [Anthony] (1470x75–1558), merchant, was born in England between 1470 and 1475, possibly the son of Louis Bonvisi. He belonged to an ancient family from Lucca, north Italy, which was descended from a councillor of the emperor Otto III in the tenth century, and had become merchants and bankers. He established himself in the family business, which he further extended by introducing a new method of spinning into the Devonshire cloth trade. By 1513 he was already a thriving merchant, and laying the foundation of the great wealth for which he was famous. In that year he received from Henry VIII a remission of customs for five years in repayment of a loan to the crown. He dealt largely in fine woollen cloth, and also imported jewels and other foreign articles, for which Cardinal Wolsey was one of his principal customers. He acted as banker for the government, transmitting money and letters to ambassadors in France, Italy, and elsewhere. Henry VIII personally contacted Cardinal Campeggi in Rome, requesting his favour towards Bonvisi in a lawsuit (1526). He was proctor-general for Silvestro Gigli, the absentee bishop of Worcester and the government's personal agent at the papal court. Sometimes through his correspondents he succeeded in obtaining earlier news of foreign events than the government did. In March 1528 Stephen Vaughan, agent to Thomas Cromwell, sent the latter news of the French invasion of Naples, which he had learned from Bonvisi.

Bonvisi was a patron and friend of a number of learned men. Thomas Starkey, Thomas Winter, Florence Volusenus, and others expressed their obligations to him, and he knew Sir Thomas More especially well. From the late 1490s, he regularly entertained More in his house. Their conversations probably had an influence on the content of More's *Utopia* (1516), which delighted Bonvisi. In 1524 he helped clarify More's thoughts on heresy and the papal primacy. He was godfather to one of More's grandsons, and in 1524 he purchased from More the lease of Crosby Place in Bishopsgate Street, London. When More was sent to the Tower in 1534, Bonvisi supplied him with meat and wine and provided a silk camlet gown for him to wear to his execution. In one of his last letters from the Tower, written with a coal, More speaks of himself as having been for nearly forty years 'not a guest, but a continual nurseling' in Bonvisi's house, and calls him 'the apple of mine eye' (*Correspondence*, letter 217). Bonvisi's friendship was also extended to Fisher, bishop of Rochester, imprisoned with More in the Tower, to whom he sent each day a quart of French wine, stewed meat, and jellies. His attitude to Henry VIII's divorce is demonstrated by the courageous help he gave to Friar Peto, who had fled to the Low Countries after preaching a violent sermon against the king.

Bonvisi spent late 1535 and most of 1536 in Lyons, in Lucca, and in other parts of north Italy. From Europe he wrote a series of letters to Thomas Cromwell which formed the government's main source of news about troop movements, the political situation, and rumours concerning the French and imperialists, battling for control of Italy. The last years of Henry VIII's reign show Bonvisi still in a position to command respect. In 1544 he was twice given a licence to trade with France, despite a general prohibition. But his well-known aversion to the principles of the Reformation (Wriothesley called him 'a rank papist') gave him a sense of insecurity in England as the Reformation advanced under Edward VI. The introduction of the first Act of Uniformity (1549) hastened his choice between conformity or exile. On 22 June 1547 he had obtained a licence to convey Crosby Place to Richard Heywood, in trust for himself, and about the same time he procured a quittance for all sums of money paid to him by the crown since 1544. Having thus settled his affairs, he fled to Louvain on 25 September 1549. His house was seized by the sheriffs of London on 7 February 1550.

Bonvisi's house in Louvain became a refuge for religious exiles, especially More's relations and friends. That his leadership of the exiled Catholics there was recognized by the English government is shown by his exclusion, together with others of his household at Louvain, from the general pardon of 1553. Although Mary's accession enabled him to regain his English property (10 May 1554), he was probably too old to contemplate returning. But the esteem in which he was held by the Marian regime is shown in an address by Cardinal Pole to an assembly of Londoners after the formal reconciliation with Rome (November 1554). He called Bonvisi 'a special benefactor to all Catholic and good persons … I doubt not but his name is in the Book of Life' (quoted in Ford, 235). Bonvisi died in Louvain on 7 December 1558, and was buried there, leaving Benedict Bonvisi, the son of his brother Martin, to inherit his English property.

C. T. MARTIN, *rev.* BASIL MORGAN

Sources *LP Henry VIII* • C. D. Ford, 'Good Master Bonvisi', *The Clergy Review*, new ser., 27 (1947), 228–35 • *CSP dom.*, 1547–53 • C. Wriothesley, *A chronicle of England during the reigns of the Tudors from AD 1485 to 1559*, ed. W. D. Hamilton, 2, CS, new ser., 20 (1877) • G. S. Fry, ed., *Abstracts of inquisitiones post mortem relating to the City of London*, 1: 1485–1561, British RS, 15 (1896) • *CPR*, 1547–53 • *The correspondence of Sir Thomas More*, ed. E. F. Rogers (1947) • R. J. Shoeck, 'Anthony Bonvisi, the Heywoods and the Ropers', *N&Q*, 197 (1952), 178–9 • W. H. Hutton, *Sir Thomas More* (1895) • A. Fox, *Thomas More* (1982) • T. F. Mayer, *Thomas Starkey and the commonweal: humanist politics and religion in the reign of Henry VIII* (1989)

Wealth at death assessed in 1548(?) at £1334 for light horses, etc., from the City of London: *CSP dom.*

Bonwick, James (1817–1906), educationist and historian, was born on 8 July 1817 at Lingfield, Surrey, the eldest son of James Bonwick, a former small farmer who had left the land to become a carpenter, and his wife, Mary *née* Preston. Educated at the Borough Road School, Southwark, he became a schoolteacher in 1833 and taught at Hemel Hempstead, Bexley, and Liverpool, before returning to London in 1838. In May 1841, he and his wife, Esther Anne (daughter of Barnabus Beddow, a Baptist minister in Exeter) whom he had married on 17 April 1840, left for Hobart where he had been selected to manage the new model school. He arrived in Van Diemen's Land on 10 October 1841, introduced new methods of teaching, wrote a school textbook, and in 1843 founded a boarding-school. He was active in the temperance movement and at the Hobart Mechanics' Institute, and was concerned for the plight of the Aborigines. A zealous nonconformist since 1837, his religious views broadened after he was introduced to freemasonry and mysticism.

Bonwick left Hobart in February 1850, disappointed at failing to gain appointment as inspector of schools, and moved to Adelaide where he opened a school. Heavy debts drove him to the Victorian goldfields and from there he went to Melbourne where he became involved in radical politics and the temperance movement and found employment as a newspaper proprietor, land agent, and teacher. From June 1856 he was stationed at Ballarat as inspector for the regional denominational school board, but, following a coaching accident, he returned to England in November 1859. Back in Melbourne in July 1862, he opened a school at St Kilda. This flourished while he was present, but encountered difficulties during his absence in England in 1869; and it was sold in August 1875 after Bonwick had again been overseas.

A prolific writer of school texts, educational tracts, and pamphlets on temperance and other current issues, Bonwick also had a strong interest in Australian history. In 1856 he published the *Discovery and Settlement of Port Phillip*, together with two books on Van Diemen's Land bushrangers. Over the coming decades he maintained a steady output, producing some sixty history books. While in London during the 1880s, working on *The First Twenty Years of Australia* (1882) and *Port Phillip Settlement* (1883), he became aware of vast quantities of untapped research material. Anxious to stay in England to be near his son, he awoke to the possibility of transcribing material on commission for use in Australia. He worked successively in this capacity for the Queensland and South Australian governments, the Melbourne Public Library, and Tasmania. His principal achievement, however, was to copy documents for the New South Wales Public Library. Appointed in April 1887, originally to provide material for Henry Parkes's commemorative National Palace, Bonwick laboured incessantly until 1902. Helped only by a part-time assistant, he worked principally in the Colonial Office and the Public

Record Office, combating advancing age and poor physical conditions with great fortitude. The voluminous collection of documents which he dispatched to Sydney enabled a start to be made on a centenary history of New South Wales. They were also published in the *Historical Records of New South Wales* and formed the basis for the pre-1830 volumes of the later *Historical Records of Australia*. Their availability opened the way to the rewriting of early Australian history.

Bonwick was a versatile man who, despite a varied and unsettled career, made an important contribution to Australian cultural life. Tribute was paid to him by the Royal Geographical Society and the Anthropological Institute which elected him fellow in 1865 and 1869 respectively. His writings were of a general nature, but by making original sources available he helped place Australian historiography on a new empirical footing. He died at Melbourne, South View Road, Southwick, near Brighton in Sussex, on 6 February 1906. Of his seven children, two died in infancy, one son predeceased him, and two sons and two daughters survived him.

BRIAN H. FLETCHER

Sources J. Bonwick, *An octogenarian's reminiscences* (1902) • E. E. Pescott, *James Bonwick* (1939) • G. Featherstone, 'The life and times of James Bonwick', MA diss., Melbourne University, 1968 • R. F. Doust, 'James Bonwick "Archivist of New South Wales"', *Journal of the Archives Section of the Library Association of Australia*, 8 (1969), 9–15 • G. Powell, 'The origin of the Australian Joint Copying Project', *Journal of the Archives Section of the Library Association of Australia*, 4 (1971), 9–24 • J. Cobley, 'Bonwick, James', *AusDB*, vol. 3 • G. Mackaness, 'Bibliography of James Bonwick, 1817–1906', *Royal Australian Historical Society Journal and Proceedings*, 23 (1927), 355–6 • B. H. Fletcher, *The 1888 centenary celebrations and new developments in the writing of Australian history* (1988) • Mitchell L., NSW, Parkes, Bonwick MSS • NPL, Mitchell Library archives • B. H. Fletcher, *Australian history in New South Wales, 1888–1938* (1993)

Archives Mitchell L., NSW, MSS | Mitchell L., NSW, Parkes MSS

Likenesses T. Bock?, watercolour, *c.*1845, Tasmanian Museum and Art Gallery, Hobart • photographs, 1870–1879?, Royal Historical Society, Victorian collection

Wealth at death £279 4*s.* 2*d.*: resworn administration with will, 27 April 1906, *CGPLA Eng. & Wales*

Bonwick, Theodora Ellen (1876–1928), educationist and women's rights activist, was born on 27 December 1876 at 60 Coningham Road, Shepherd's Bush, London, the daughter of William Priessnitz Bonwick, a schoolteacher, and his wife, Sarah, formerly Beddow, an executive member of the Women's Liberal Federation, and a member of the National Union of Women's Suffrage Societies. Like her mother, Theodora undertook temperance work and Sunday school teaching, which she gave up for the suffrage cause. She trained at Stockwell College and obtained a BA degree from the University of London. She taught in London elementary schools and was headteacher of Enfield Road School for Girls in Hackney before the First World War; in the 1920s she became headteacher of York Way Girls' School in King's Cross. Joining the Women's Social and Political Union (WSPU) in 1905, she was a popular speaker—she spoke at the Woman's Sunday demonstration in Hyde Park on 21 June 1908 and became the secretary of Hornsey WSPU. She was an active campaigner for women's rights in the London Teachers' Association, and was particularly prominent in the movement before the war for equal pay. Even her opponents respected her powers of oratory. The National Union of Teachers (NUT) paper, *The Schoolmaster*, declared that her strong speech for equal pay, which was endorsed at a packed meeting in the Royal Albert Hall in 1913, was 'undoubtedly the speech of the day' (*The Schoolmaster*, 1913, 710).

Theodora Bonwick joined the London-based Women Teachers' Franchise Union (WTFU) and became its president in 1914. She encouraged the affiliation of teachers' organizations to the Labour Party when the NUT was conducting a referendum on the question, believing that sex distinction was as invidious as class distinction. Like many contemporary feminists and humanitarians, Theodora Bonwick became a theosophist and joined the central London lodge in 1909. A member of the Association for Moral and Social Hygiene, she became a strong advocate of sex education in schools and gained the support of parents to teach this as a class subject in her Enfield Road School. This was the only school in the London county council (LCC) area which undertook such teaching as a class topic. But when she advocated that this subject should be taught throughout LCC schools in her presentation to the LCC inquiry on the teaching of sex hygiene, it was rejected. Believing that sex education was necessary to safeguard the moral and physical health of the nation, she continued to give talks on sexual and moral conduct, particularly to the Women's Suffrage Federation in London's East End. She argued that if young people were given knowledge this would prevent them from being 'poisoned by ignorance or impurely minded persons'. In common with the anti-regulationist strand of the social hygiene movement she argued for 'self protection' rather than tighter laws. In the 1920s she developed her interest in educating children in moral behaviour through her work as organizer of the cinema group of the London unit of the National Union of Women Teachers (NUWT). She was the only British representative at the second European film conference in The Hague in 1928 and led a deputation to the Cinematograph Exhibitors' Association to encourage the making of healthy, wholesome, amusing, and instructive films for children (*Woman Teacher*, 2 Jan 1928, 75).

Theodora Bonwick supported progressive ideas in education, opposing a competitive spirit in lessons and sports, and introduced the Dalton plan, a form of independent resource-based learning for older pupils, in her York Way school. Although the school's inspector, Dr Hayward, described her as 'an enterprising and devoted headteacher', he was critical of such methods (PRO, Ed 21/57031, 1926). She opposed the teaching of domestic science to girls, since this encouraged a feeling of inferiority and trained a girl 'to be a household drudge and to spend herself submissively attending to the needs of the menfolk' (*Woman's Dreadnought*, 71). By the 1920s Theodora, like many other feminists, had left the London Teachers' Association and joined the NUWT. She was a member of its central council from 1925 and the incumbent president of the London unit on her death. Friends believed that her early death from heart failure on 10 November 1928 at Woodlands, Crouch End Hill, London, was attributable to a nervous breakdown caused by exhaustion from her political activities. At her request the flowers donated at her cremation at Golders Green crematorium were given to an infirmary, a workhouse, and Holloway prison, the site of suffragette imprisonment.

Theodora Bonwick was a committed schoolteacher who brought her feminist and progressive beliefs to bear upon her work with children in the classroom. Her support for equal rights for women was articulated in her trade union, suffrage, and professional activities.

HILDA KEAN

Sources U. Lond., Institute of Education, National Union of Women Teachers archive • H. Kean, *Deeds not words: the lives of suffragette teachers* (1990) • H. Kean, 'State education policy', PhD diss., King's Lond., 1988, 332–3 • *Woman Teacher* (23 Nov 1928), 50 • *Woman Teacher* (2 Jan 1927), 75 • *Woman Teacher* (May 1951), 131 • Report of the education committee on the teaching of sex hygiene, LCC 1914 • PRO, Ed 21/57031, 1926 • *Annual Report* [Women Teachers' Franchise Union] (1915) • *Annual Report* [Women Teachers' Franchise Union] (1917) • *The Schoolmaster* (18 Oct 1913), 710 • *The Schoolmaster* (25 March 1916) [letter] • *Woman's Dreadnought* (18 July 1914), 71 • *Theosophical Society register*, 9 (1909–12), 111 • A. J. R., ed., *The suffrage annual and women's who's who* (1913) • b. cert. • d. cert. • *CGPLA Eng. & Wales* (1928)

Archives U. Lond., Institute of Education, National Union of Women Teachers archives

Wealth at death £1823 15s. 9d.: probate, 21 Dec 1928, *CGPLA Eng. & Wales*

Bonwicke, Ambrose (1652–1722), nonjuring Church of England clergyman and schoolmaster, son of the Revd John Bonwicke BD (1622–1698), later rector of East Horsley and of Mickleham in Surrey, was born on 29 April 1652 at East Horsley. On 11 September 1663 he entered Merchant Taylors' School, where the headmaster was John Goad, later dismissed for his sympathy towards the Roman Catholic church. Bonwicke matriculated at St John's College, Oxford, on 2 May 1668 and was elected fellow in 1669, graduating BA in 1673 and proceeding MA in 1676 (incorporated at Cambridge in 1678) and BD in 1682. His time as an undergraduate was vividly described by Bonwicke in a series of letters written to his father, many of which were later published with notes by John Nichols in his edition of the printer William Bowyer's *Miscellaneous Tracts* (1785). These letters make frequent allusion to acute shortage of money, a problem which was allayed when Bonwicke became tutor to Lord Stawell through the interest of Dr Peter Mews, president of St John's College from 1667 to 1673.

Having been ordained deacon in 1676 and priest in 1680, Bonwicke retained his fellowship at St John's until 1686, when, after the Merchant Taylors' Company had successfully resisted an attempt by James II to intrude his own nominee, Mr Lee, he was appointed to the headmastership of Merchant Taylors' School. Bonwicke proved a successful schoolmaster, and his pupils at this time included two future archbishops: Hugh Boulter (Armagh) and Sir William Dawes (York). In these years he married Elizabeth (*d.* 1722), daughter of Philip Stubbs, citizen and vintner of London, and sister of Philip *Stubbs, later a prominent high-churchman and noted supporter of Henry Sacheverell at the time of his trial in 1710. Ambrose and Elizabeth had twelve children, of whom their eldest son, Ambrose *Bonwicke the younger, was born on 30 September 1691.

Unwilling to take the oath of allegiance to William and Mary, Bonwicke was dismissed from his post as a nonjuror on 5 August 1691. His letters at this time to Richard Blechynden, a prebendary of Peterborough Cathedral and fellow of St John's College, who had conformed to the new regime, provide a concise statement of nonjuring scruples, echoing the doctrine of the *Oxford Decrees* (1683) and *The Whole Duty of Man*:

> I suppose … that King *James* had a right to my allegiance, and that secured by an oath; and unless he has given away this right or forfeited it, it is still in him. Now to me it does not appear that he has done either, therefore I dare not give it to another. (Bonwicke to Blechynden, 11 Aug 1691, cited in Mayor, 131)

> I am to consider how I am to behave myself under a king that has possession and not right … if it were barely submitting to him in power, I suppose we should have no great dispute. (20 Aug 1691, ibid., 132)

> The sons of the Church of England (by their general defection) have brought an indelible scandal upon her; and it is not to be wiped off by the constancy of a small party … if every man must be the judge of the actions of his prince, and quit his allegiance whenever he thinks the coronation oath broken, there can be no such thing as peace. (16 Sept 1691, ibid., 135)

Following deprivation Bonwicke opened a private school at Headley, near his father's parish of Mickleham in Surrey. The poet Elijah Fenton served as usher there for a brief period during Queen Anne's reign, and the younger William Bowyer, a pupil *c.*1711–1716, recalled Bonwicke's teaching ability and personal generosity with affection (Nichols, *Lit. anecdotes*, 1.63–6). Following the death of his eldest son, Ambrose, in 1714 Bonwicke was persuaded to write an anonymous account of his life by Bowyer's father, William the elder. In this memoir, published posthumously in 1729 as *A Pattern for Young Students in the University*, Bonwicke movingly presented his son as an exemplar of devotion and conscience.

Bonwicke died on 20 October 1722, and was buried six days later in the chancel of the parish church at Mickleham. In his will, dated 26 July 1722, he left personal bequests amounting to more than £3000. His wife died soon afterwards, on 3 December 1722.

RICHARD SHARP

Sources J. E. B. Mayor, ed., *The life of Ambrose Bonwicke: by his father* (1870) • H. B. Wilson, *The history of Merchant-Taylors' School*, 2 vols. (1814) • J. H. Overton, *The nonjurors: their lives, principles, and writings* (1902) • *Miscellaneous tracts, by the later William Bowyer*, ed. J. Nichols (1785) • Nichols, *Lit. anecdotes*, 1.40, 63–6 • A. R. Bax, 'On a ledger to the memory of James Bonwicke, esq.', *Surrey Archaeological Collections*, 13 (1897), 111–29 • Foster, *Alum. Oxon.* • C. J. Robinson, ed., *A register of the scholars admitted into Merchant Taylors' School, from AD 1562 to 1874*, 2 vols. (1882–3) • *DNB* • Venn, *Alum. Cant.* • will, PRO, PROB 11/589, sig. 3

Wealth at death over £3000: will, PRO, PROB 11/589, sig. 3

Bonwicke, Ambrose (1691–1714), nonjuror, eldest son of Ambrose *Bonwicke (1652–1722) and his wife, Elizabeth, *née* Stubbs (*d.* 1722), was born in the Schoolmaster's house, Merchant Taylors' School, London, on 30 September 1691. He grew up in Headley, Surrey, and in 1703 entered the Merchant Taylors' School in London, where his father had been headmaster. He spent more than seven years there, and, having reached the head form, was eligible for election to St John's College, Oxford. However, his refusal to read the prayer for Queen Anne and the house of Hanover deprived him of this advantage and compelled him to seek admission to St John's College, Cambridge, which had gained a reputation as a nonjuror stronghold.

Having entered St John's, Cambridge, in August 1710, Bonwicke's exemplary conduct and acquirements quickly procured him a scholarship, the enjoyment of which was somewhat marred by the scruples of an oversensitive conscience. The statutes, to his mind, not only enjoined personal obedience but implied some control over others. 'Am I', he asked his father, 'by the words "faciam ab aliis observari", which are part of the oath, obliged to tell lads continually their duty as far as I know it, and also to inform against transgressors?' (Bonwicke, 30). Happily his mind was set at ease on this point and he was able to continue in college, enthusiastically devoting himself to study and to religious exercises. 'His temperance was always very great, and his fasting and abstinence rather more than his weak constitution could well bear' (ibid., 32). Further reports may also suggest that Bonwicke suffered from tuberculosis. He died, unmarried, on the evening of 5 May 1714 in his college study, his favourite devotional works by Robert Nelson and Edward Lake beside him. He was buried four days later at All Saints' churchyard, Cambridge.

Bonwicke's father, at the suggestion of the printer William Bowyer, drew up an account of his son's life but desired that its authorship should be concealed. Bowyer edited the memoir after the death of Bonwicke the elder, and in 1729 published *A Pattern for Young Students in the University, Set Forth in the Life of Mr. Ambrose Bonwicke* with the intent to present 'the virtues of a private life' for general 'imitation' (Bonwicke, 1). It is interesting not merely as a picture of college life and reading habits in the early eighteenth century, but also because it depicts the nature and development of the scrupulous conscience which made both father and son nonjurors.

C. J. Robinson, *rev.* Christoph v. Ehrenstein

Sources [A. Bonwicke], *A pattern for young students in the university, set forth in the life of Mr. Ambrose Bonwicke, sometime scholar of St. John's College in Cambridge* (1729) • Nichols, *Lit. anecdotes*, vol. 1 • *IGI* • Venn, *Alum. Cant.*, 1/1 • C. J. Robinson, ed., *A register of the scholars admitted into Merchant Taylors' School, from AD 1562 to 1874*, 2 vols. (1882–3) • Mrs E. P. Hart, ed., *Merchant Taylors' School register, 1561–1934*, 2 vols. (1936) • J. B. Mullinger, *St John's College* (1901)

Bonython, Charles (*c.*1649–1705), lawyer, was the son and heir of John Bonython (*b.* 1618, *d.* after 1680) of Bonython, Cornwall, and Anne (*d.* 1723), daughter of Hugh Trevanion of Tregulan, Cornwall. He was admitted as a student at Gray's Inn on 26 October 1671, and was called to the bar on 12 June 1678. From surviving deeds it would seem that in 1680 he married Mary Livesay (*bap.* 1661), probably the daughter of William Livesay of Staple Inn. They had three sons and two daughters. Bonython was very active in pleading before the court of king's bench in 1680, and he appeared for the crown in some of the Popish Plot cases, notably in that against Lord Castlemaine. In April 1683 he was appointed deputy steward of Westminster, an office which no doubt paved the way for his election as MP for Westminster in 1685. He lost his deputy steward's post in February 1687, presumably because of his opposition to James II's religious policies, but he regained the office on 7 October 1688 when the king attempted to shore up his deteriorating position by re-employing his former tory supporters.

Bonython's position as steward, which he held until his death, gave him a political base in the city. He stood unsuccessfully for Westminster at the election for the Convention Parliament in 1688, and again on the 'pure Tory interest' (*Letters of Lady Rachel Russell*, 292) in a by-election in 1691. He was appointed a serjeant-at-law in April 1692. Bonython threatened to stand again for the city of Westminster in the 1698 election, although he did not go to a poll. In the following general election, in January 1701, he finished bottom of the poll. Amid another election campaign, on 30 April 1705, Bonython 'shot himself through the body with a pistol' (Luttrell, 5.545), although another report had it that he 'shot himself through the head' (*Ormonde MSS*, new ser., 8.152). John Evelyn commented that he 'hanged himself' (Evelyn, 5.593). His two surviving sons were educated at Gray's Inn: the eldest, Richard, on 8 June 1717, burnt down his chambers in Gray's Inn, stabbed himself, and then threw himself out of the window.

Stuart Handley

Sources HoP, *Commons, 1660–90*, 1.676–7 • 'Westminster', HoP, *Commons, 1690–1715* [draft], 202, 500 • Baker, *Serjeants* • E. G. Bonython, *History of the families of Bonython of Bonython and Bonython of Carclew* (1966), 51–6 • H. F. Burke, *History of the family of Bonython of Bonython* (1926), 13–15 • *IGI* • J. Polsue, *A complete parochial history of the county of Cornwall*, 1 (1867), 287 • *State trials*, 7.1069 • N. Luttrell, *A brief historical relation of state affairs from September 1678 to April 1714*, 1 (1857), 255; 5 (1857), 545 • *The historical register*, 2 (1717), 26 • *Letters of Lady Rachel Russell* (1819) • Evelyn, *Diary* • *Calendar of the manuscripts of the marquess of Ormonde*, new ser., 8 vols., HMC, 36 (1902–20), vol. 8

Bonython, Richard (*bap.* 1580, *d.* 1647x54), soldier and planter in America, was baptized on 8 April 1580 at St Columb Major, Cornwall, a younger son and one of eight children of John Bonython and his wife, Eleanor Myleinton. Nothing else is known of his early life. He married by 1607 Lucretia Leigh, daughter of William Leigh and Philippa Prest of St Thomas by Launceston, Cornwall. They had two sons and three daughters, of whom one son and two daughters lived to adulthood and married. On 29 February 1630 the Council for New England granted to 'Thomas Lewis and Capt. Ric[hard] Bonighton' a substantial tract of land between Cape Elizabeth and Cape Porpoise on the coast of New England (*York Deeds*, 2.110). Lewis had travelled to New England in 1628, and settled there permanently in 1631, but no record of Bonython is found in New England prior to 25 March 1636, when he served as a magistrate at Saco court. Bonython continued to serve in the various governments of the region which became Maine, holding office as councillor under Thomas Gorges in 1639 and 1640, and assistant in 1646. In 1645 he was made colonel-general of the militia in Saco.

Bonython was frequently associated with Sir Ferdinando Gorges, the leading promoter of New England colonization. In 1639 he was appointed to the council established by Gorges for his territory in New England, and in 1641 he attested to the earlier military service of Gorges. Bonython adhered to the Church of England, and opposed developing a New England church government. He died between 14 July 1647, when he was last recorded alive, and 29 June 1654, when his son John acted in his stead. The large tract of land granted to Lewis and Bonython in 1630 was in 1681 divided among the heirs of these two men, including representatives of the three children of Bonython. ROBERT CHARLES ANDERSON

Sources R. C. Anderson, G. F. Sanborn jun., and M. L. Sanborn, *The great migration: immigrants to New England, 1634–1635*, 1 (1999), 343–4 · parish register, St Columb Major, Cornwall [baptism] · parish register, Breage, Cornwall · [C. T. Libby], ed., *Province and court records of Maine*, 1 (1928) · *York deeds*, 18 vols. (1887–1910), vol. 1, pt 1, pp. 140, 152; vol. 2, p. 110; vol. 4, p. 22; vol. 8, pp. 30, 242; vol. 12, pp. 160, 173; vol. 13, p. 137 · *The Winthrop papers*, ed. W. C. Ford and others, 6 vols. (1929–92), vol. 4, pp. 308, 320; vol. 5, p. 15 · E. G. Bonython, *History of the families of Bonython of Bonython and Bonython of Carclew* (1966)

Booker, John (1602–1667), astrologer, was born at Manchester on 23 March 1602 and was later described as being of 'good parentage'; his father died on 23 March 1621. He received a sound schooling which gave him a lasting proficiency in Latin, and his writings show that he read widely. He moved to London in August 1616 and the following April was bound apprentice to a haberdasher of small wares in Laurence Lane. However, instead of pursuing that trade he taught for a time as a writing-master at a school in Hadley, near Barnet, Middlesex, and worked as a clerk for the London aldermen Sir Hugh Hammersley and Sir Christopher Clitheroe (both of whom served as mayor). According to William Lilly 'he served with great Credit and Estimation; and by that means became not only well known, but as well respected of the most eminent Citizens of London, even to his dying Day' (Lilly, 27).

Booker was drawn to astrology from an early age, poring over almanacs as a child, and he came to enjoy an extensive astrological practice in London. His friend the parson–astrologer William Bredon, formerly chaplain to Sir Christopher Heydon, may have been his mentor. Booker's casebooks for the years 1648–65, written in shorthand, survive among the Ashmolean manuscripts in the Bodleian Library; they cover roughly 16,500 enquiries from clients who ranged from peers through merchants and artisans to domestic servants. Lilly called him 'an excellent Proficient, … a very honest Man, abhorred any Deceit in the Art he studied; had a curious Fancy in judging of Thefts, and as successful in resolving Love-Questions' (Lilly, 27–8). His astrological practice flourished right up to his death.

Booker's wider fame rested on the series of almanacs he published annually from 1631 to his death. He used a variety of titles, including *Bowker: a New Almanack*, *Mercurius Coelicus*, *Uranoscopia*, *Celestiall Observations*, and, in his final years, *Telescopium Uranicum*. In the 1630s he was recognized as the leading astrologer of his day. His fame was secured by a hint in his almanac for September 1632 that Saturn and Jupiter in opposition threatened the death of kings, a 'prophecy' seen as fulfilled by the death of the conquering king of Sweden, Gustavus Adolphus, two months later. Booker was the most outspoken compiler of the 1630s. In 1632 he complained of pervasive 'bribery, oppression, extortion' (*New Almanack*, 1632, sig. C5v), and in 1633 made a provocative prediction of 'wonderful change in the church' (*New Almanack*, 1633, sig. C2). As a result he was arrested by the high commission in 1634, gaoled eight weeks in the Gatehouse, fined £500, and suspended from writing. The case prompted an order that henceforth all almanacs must be licensed by the archbishop of Canterbury or bishop of London. Booker did not publish in 1635, and his almanacs for the later 1630s were heavily censored; he later complained that he had been tempted to abandon writing them altogether.

In the 1640s Booker quickly emerged as a militant parliamentarian, and became so famous that his almanacs were pirated and counterfeited. In June 1643 he and the reader of mathematics at Gresham College were appointed by parliament as joint licensers of mathematical books (which included almanacs), a position he retained until 1660. His almanacs predicted the downfall of popery and sweeping reforms in religion, though he criticized separatists and was pained by the rift between Presbyterians and Independents. In 1644 he savaged the king for associating with the bloodthirsty Irish papists who in 1641 had 'cut the throats of 200,000 Israelites, I mean Protestants in Ireland' (*No Mercurius aquaticus*, 1644, 5). His political stance led to fierce quarrels in print with the royalist astrologer George Wharton, whom Booker attacked in *Mercurius Coelius* (1644) and who replied with *Mercurio-Coelico-Mastix, or, An anti-caveat to all such, as have (heretofore) had the misfortune to be cheated and deluded by that grand and traiterous impostor of this rebellious age, John Booker* (1644), and with the versifier turned royalist propagandist, John Taylor, whom Booker attacked in his vigorous *No Mercurius aquaticus, but a Cable Rope Twisted for John Tayler, the Water-Poet* (1644). None the less Booker continued to stand for a limited monarchy and he was shocked by the extremism he found in the first almanac submitted by William Lilly, which he licensed only after insisting on substantial changes. Lilly rapidly overtook him as the leading parliamentary astrologer, but they became friendly colleagues. Booker greatly admired Lilly's *Christian Astrology* (1647), and sometimes sought his professional advice. In 1647 they were both invited to the army's headquarters at Windsor, where General Fairfax tried to convince them of the justice of its cause. During the second civil war in 1648 they were summoned to Colchester to encourage the besieging forces with predictions of a speedy triumph, which quickly followed. Booker's importance in shaping public opinion is confirmed by the counterfeit astrological judgement issued in his name in 1649 by his rival Henry Walker, which claimed that the stars indicated the failure of Cromwell's expedition to Ireland.

After the king's execution Booker adopted a more radical political and religious stance. He now damned Presbyterianism as well as prelacy and popery, and predicted in 1651 that monarchy would soon disappear throughout Europe. He interpreted 'black Monday', the solar eclipse of 29 March 1652, as heralding the fall of kings as well as popery. His clients included several radicals, and he wrote a verse lamenting the death of John Lilburne, whose wife was a frequent visitor. During the 1650s Booker's almanacs gave warm support to the Commonwealth and protectorate, with dire warnings to royalists, Scots, Dutch, French, and Spaniards. In his almanac for 1660 he dismissed the failed rising of Sir George Booth as the 'gripings and wringings of Antichrist' (*Telescopium Uranicum*, sig. C5). The Restoration, which he had totally failed to anticipate, therefore demanded some nimble footwork. Henceforth Booker heaped praise on Charles II and his generous amnesty and poured fierce invective on the regicides. His political prophecies were now very cautious, and sales dwindled; his fee from the Company of Stationers accordingly halved from £40 to £20. The approach of 1666 rekindled something of his old anti-popery, however, and he prophesied that the year would prove fatal to the popish Antichrist.

Though Booker published little outside the field of astrology, he seems to have had some involvement in both iatrochemistry and natural magic. Lilly described him as very competent in physic, and he sometimes described himself as physician (and mathematician) as well as astrologer. He 'was a great Admirer of the Antimonial Cup', Lilly remarked, and 'not unlearned in Chymistry' (Lilly, 28). He was one of the friends who supplied Elias Ashmole with materials for his *Theatrum chemicum Britannicum* (1652). In 1650 he published *The Dutch Fortune-Teller … Brought into England by John Booker*, which set out a system of divination based on letters, words, and numbers and employing dice, 'wheels', and 'globes'. Egyptian in origin, it had been carried to Germany by an Ottoman ambassador and translated into German. Booker complained that many treated it merely as a jest; he stopped short of endorsing it, but suggested it might be seen as a form of natural magic, and similar to some of the writings of Dr Robert Fludd. Booker was also 'no mean Proficient in Astronomy' (Lilly, 28), vigorously supporting the system of Tycho Brahe against its Copernican rival. In 1639 he published an updated edition of William Rastall's concordance of years.

Booker married his wife, Joan, in June 1638; they had several children. One daughter, Victoria, born in 1644, was named after the victory at Marston Moor. In 1662 Booker sent an agitated note begging Lilly to help trace his son Samuel, who had run away from home on the eve of being bound apprentice, adding that he had sent another troublesome son (John) to Barbados; 'never was any man so vexed with his children', he complained (Bodl. Oxf., MS Ashmole 180, fol. 112). Gadbury's later comment that Booker possessed 'a competent share of Choler' (Gadbury, 181) may provide a clue to his domestic problems. Booker was still living at Hadley, at the house of Francis Atkinson, as late as 1633. By 1646 he had a house in Cree-Church Lane, near Duke's Place; from 1662 he gave his address as near St James's Church in Duke's Place. (The minister of St James's, William Harrison, was a client.) Booker died in Duke's Place on 8 April 1667, after three years of dysentery had 'at last consumed him to nothing' (Lilly, 28). He had also been diabetic. He was survived by his wife, two sons, and two daughters; Joan sold his collection of astrological books to Elias Ashmole for £140, which Lilly thought far more than they were worth. Ashmole, a client and friend since 1646, was the dedicatee of Booker's last almanac, and paid for a marble slab to be placed over his grave in St James's Church. No likeness of Booker is known to exist—perhaps a mercy, for a contemporary jibed that his face would 'fright a razor' (J. B., *A Faire in Spittle Fields*, 1652, 7). Lilly, summing up his career, said that he had always 'lived an honest Man, his Fame not questioned at his Death' (Lilly, 28). BERNARD CAPP

Sources B. S. Capp, *Astrology and the popular press: English almanacs, 1500–1800* (1979) • K. V. Thomas, *Religion and the decline of magic* (1971) • W. Lilly, *Mr William Lilly's history of his life and times: from the year 1602, to 1681*, 2nd edn (1715); repr. with introduction by K. M. Briggs (1974) • Bodl. Oxf., MS Ashmole 243, fol. 54–55; MS Ashmole 180, fol. 112 • *Elias Ashmole (1617–1692): his autobiographical and historical notes*, ed. C. H. Josten, 5 vols. (1966 [i.e. 1967]) • G. Wharton, *Mercurio-Coelico-Mastix* (1644) • J. Gadbury, *Collectio geniturarum, or, A collection of nativities* (1662) • H. G. Rusche, 'Merlini Anglici: astrology and propaganda from 1644 to 1651', *EngHR*, 80 (1965), 322–33 • Wood, *Ath. Oxon.*

Archives Bodl. Oxf., MSS Ashmole, case books and corresp.

Booker, Luke (1762–1835), Church of England clergyman and author, was born at Nottingham on 20 October 1762, the son of a schoolmaster who had been married four times and had thirteen children; he gave the names of the evangelists to his four sons. Educated at home, Booker was ordained in 1785 by Bishop Cornwallis of Lichfield and Coventry. He was soon afterwards appointed lecturer for the collegiate church of Wolverhampton. He also held the curacy of Old Swinford, Worcestershire, before accepting the incumbency of St Edmund's chapel of ease, Dudley. In 1806 he was presented by his brother-in-law, Richard Blakemore, to the rectory of Tedstone Delamere, Herefordshire. In addition he was presented by William, third Viscount Dudley, to the vicarage of Dudley in 1812. Booker soon found himself in difficulties: the historic church of St Thomas, Dudley, was demolished in 1816 in the face of much opposition, and Booker was subsequently satirized in the poem *The Procession and the Bells, or, The Rival Poets* (1817), reputedly by W. T. of Wantage.

Booker was a popular preacher of charity sermons, of which he was said to have delivered 173, raising nearly £9000. His poetry—which included *Malvern, a Descriptive and Historical Poem* (1798), *Calista, or, A Picture of Modern Life* (1803), and *The Springs of Plynlimmon* (1834)—was less successful. He also published *A Moral Review of the Conduct and Case of Mary Ashford* (1818), in which, extrapolating from the case of a twenty-year-old local girl murdered in 1817, he exposed the evils of promiscuous dancing assemblies. The pamphlet attracted much attention, as Booker assumed the guilt of Abraham Thornton who was, in fact, acquitted of the crime. Booker has been wrongly suggested as the author of *The Mysterious Murder* (1817?), a melodrama also based on the Ashford case, which was written by George Ludlam of the Theatre Royal, Birmingham. Additional works by Booker included numerous single sermons and *Select Psalms and Hymns for the Use of Churches* (1796). His most significant work, however, was his *Description and Historical Account of Dudley Castle* (1825), which was only superseded by Charles Twamley's history of the same edifice in 1867.

Booker was a JP for Worcester, Hereford, and Stafford, and a sternly orthodox opponent of atheists, Unitarians, and Roman Catholics alike. Like his father, he was married four times; he lost his eldest son, at the age of thirteen, in 1810. He died at Bower Ashton, near Bristol, on 1 October 1835.

ALEXANDER GORDON, *rev.* MARI G. ELLIS

Sources *Annual Register* (1835), 237 · *GM*, 2nd ser., 5 (1836), 93–4 · *N&Q*, 2nd ser., 11 (1861), 431 · C. F. G. Clark, ed., *The curiosities of Dudley and the Black Country, from 1800 to 1860* (1881)

Likenesses W. Say, mezzotint, pubd 1828 (after W. J. Pringle), BM; NPG

Boolde [Bolde], **William** (*d.* 1489x92), Benedictine monk, was professed at Christ Church Cathedral priory, Canterbury, on 25 March 1443, and ordained priest six years later. The only office he is known to have occupied within the monastery is that of keeper of the shrine (*magister tumbe*) of Thomas Becket, which he held shortly before his death. He owned a manuscript (now Bodl. Oxf., MS Bodley 648), which had previously belonged to Prior William Molasshe (*r.* 1428–38); Boolde's name on folio 6 is preceded by the word *constat*, implying possession, and followed by the year 1468, presumably the date he acquired it. This volume contains treatises on medicine, astrology, and doctrine, together with lists of popes, archbishops, religious houses, and castles in England and Scotland, and a brief chronicle. Tanner attributes to him the compilation of the lists and the chronicle, but evidence for this is lacking.

Boolde may have been a relative of Master William Bolde, a notary, who was mayor of Canterbury in 1457. His death occurred probably on 4 February in a year between 1489 and 1492. JOAN GREATREX

Sources Canterbury Cathedral, MS Lit. D. 12 · CCC Cam., MS 298 · Bodl. Oxf., MS Bodley 648 · register of Archbishop Stafford, LPL · W. G. Searle, ed., *Christ Church, Canterbury*, 2: *List of the deans, priors, and monks of Christ Church Monastery*, Cambridge Antiquarian RS, 34 (1902) · W. G. Searle, ed., *Christ Church, Canterbury*, 1: *The chronicle of John Stone, monk of Christ Church*, Cambridge Antiquarian RS, 34 (1902) · BL, MS Arundel 68 · Tanner, *Bibl. Brit.-Hib.*

Boole, George (1815–1864), mathematician and logician, was born on 2 November 1815 in Lincoln, the eldest of four children of a local tradesman, John Boole (1777–1848), and his wife, Mary Ann (1780–1854). He adopted a love of learning from his father, who was active in the local mechanics' institute, to such an extent that in his teens he was

George Boole (1815–1864), by unknown artist, 1847

employed as a teacher at schools in Lincoln and nearby; in his twentieth year he opened his own school. He also learned classical and modern languages and wrote poetry, and taught himself mathematics to a level which permitted him to engage in research. He began publishing in 1841, first and frequently in the *Cambridge Mathematical Journal*, founded two years earlier by D. F. Gregory, his initial mathematical mentor and inspiration.

Although his contributions quickly gained attention, Boole continued as a private teacher until the Queen's University in Ireland was set up in 1845. After delays caused by the potato famine, he took up appointment in 1849 as founder professor of mathematics at Queen's College, Cork, a post which he filled for the rest of his life. Often he spent the summer vacations in England, at Lincoln and studying in London libraries. While he was unable to generate a school of research students at Cork, his work was recognized by honorary doctorates from Trinity College, Dublin, in 1851 and Oxford University eight years later, and by fellowship of the Royal Society in 1857, although he was not elected to the Royal Irish Academy. Among other duties, between 1847 and at least 1852 he was an examiner of mathematics for the College of Preceptors, which was founded in 1846 as an institution to raise the reputation and calibre of the profession of school teachers.

Marriage and family On 11 September 1855 Boole married Mary Everest (1832–1916) [*see* Boole, Mary], daughter of the Revd Thomas Everest and niece of Sir George Everest of mountain fame. Brought up in France, she became greatly interested in mathematics; she had met Boole in 1850 when she was visiting her uncle John Ryall, vice-president of Queen's College. She assisted her husband with his two textbooks, as the first reader for intelligibility and also as checker of some of the exercises. After his death she moved her family to London, where Frederick Denison Maurice found her a post at his Queen's College in Harley Street. Later she was secretary to the philosopher James Hinton, and became interested in Judaism, and also in psychical research. She continued to proselytize Boole's philosophy, especially its application to educational questions, both in discourse and extensively in print. She gained a reputation as a crank, but her understanding of his ideas on logic and education were basically sound. She presented the bulk of his manuscripts to the Royal Society in 1873.

George and Mary produced five daughters with repetitive two-year regularity. Mary Ellen Boole (*b.* 1856) married the mathematician Charles Howard Hinton, the eldest son of James Hinton. Margaret Boole (1858–1935) married Edward Ingram Taylor, an artist; their son Geoffrey Ingram *Taylor (1886–1975) was to become one of the finest British mathematical physicists of the twentieth century. Alicia *Stott, *née* Boole (1860–1940) [*see under* Boole, Mary], was led into mathematics by her brother-in-law Charles Hinton, and produced fine work in solid geometry (a startling contrast to her father's totally algebraic style). From 1889 to 1896 she worked with friends on organizing her father's manuscripts, with an intention (not realized) of producing a new edition of *Laws*. Lucy Everest *Boole (1862–1904) [*see under* Boole, Mary] made a career in chemistry, teaching at the London School of Medicine for Women. She was the first woman professor of chemistry in Britain. Ethel Lilian Boole (1864–1960) [*see* Voynich, Ethel Lilian] studied in Germany in her teens, and became associated with revolutionary causes in central Europe. She became a radical socialist and freethinker, and consorted with the activist W. M. Voynich, whom she married in 1906; however, within four years she ran away with the remarkable spy Sydney Reilly. In 1897 she produced a novel called *The Gadfly*, seemingly based upon Reilly, which was to become very well known in the Soviet Union.

Contributions to mathematics Boole's contributions to mathematics were both characteristic of and important for the development of English mathematics in his time, for they were entirely guided by algebras of new kinds. His earliest work extended the notion of the invariant, which was to become a major English industry in the hands of Arthur Cayley and J. J. Sylvester. His own main effort was directed to the algebraic form of the differential and integral calculus. Born at the start of the century out of certain ideas of J. L. Lagrange, it had been taken up in England from the 1810s by Charles Babbage and especially John Herschel. Taking much inspiration from Gregory, Boole specialized in differential operators, in which the operation of differentiation of a mathematical function was represented by the letter 'D', and an algebra constructed in which second differentiation was given by the power D^2, the inverse operation of integration was D^{-1}, and so on. He became a leading practitioner of this theory for solving differential and difference equations, and summing series. His main paper, 'On a general method in analysis', was submitted to the Royal Society; after initial rejection, it was published in the *Philosophical Transactions* in 1844, and Boole later received the society's gold medal. This operator algebra became the largest single concern of English mathematicians in Boole's time, and his contributions gained him most of his attention. He examined operator functions F and G which did not commute ($FG \neq GF$), and applied his methods and solutions especially to linear differential equations. He also wrote two well-received general textbooks: *A Treatise on Differential Equations* (1859) and *A Treatise on the Calculus of Finite Differences* (1860).

The algebra of differential operators has a close bearing upon Boole's contributions to logic, which was then only an intriguing curiosity to his contemporaries but for which he is best remembered today. A dispute developed in the mid-1840s between the Scottish philosopher Sir William Hamilton and the English mathematician Augustus De Morgan over a certain extension of syllogistic logic which became called 'quantification of the predicate'; it inspired Boole to write up his ideas on logic in a short book entitled *The Mathematical Analysis of Logic* (1847). Seven years later, he presented a much longer account as *An Investigation of the Laws of Thought*; today it is recognized as the more authoritative and substantial book, but at the time it gained even less attention than had his *Analysis*.

Boole's logic Boole's logic was much more revolutionary relative to syllogistic logic than De Morgan's algebraic treatment; although they corresponded regularly, they communicated their respective ideas more than discussed them. However, Boole seems not to have recognized the full consequences of his own ideas when writing the *Analysis*, in that he referred there frequently to syllogistic logic. By the time of the *Laws*, however, it was treated only in the last of the fifteen chapters on logic.

Boole's basic method may be explained as follows, using the version in *Laws* where Boole gave prime place to classes, rather than the psychological interpretation concerning mental acts ('elective symbols') of choosing properties, which he preferred in *Analysis*. From a given universal class 1 (of men, say) the mind picks out some class x (of Englishmen, say), leaving the complementary class $(1 - x)$ of non-English men. The basic laws of these classes, which grounded his algebra of logic, imitated as closely as possible the laws that he had found for differential operators in the 1844 paper: commutativity, distributivity in both theories, and a third law which he called in each case the 'index law'. For differential operators the index law followed the usual property of powers, $D^mD^n = D^{n+m}$, but in logic it asserted that $x^2 = x$, that is, that the class x taken together with the class x gives the class x (or that to choose the property x and to choose x again is the same as choosing x once). This law distinguished this algebra from all others of his time. As consequences of it he formed equations expressing the laws of contradiction and of excluded middle, which were taken as basic assumptions in traditional logics.

To the operations of subtraction and multiplication Boole appended that of addition, where two classes were adjoined as long as they had no parts in common. He also worked with 0, denoting 'Nothing'—but none too clearly, since it was a class of some sort.

One main purpose of Boole's algebra was to take one or several propositions as premisses, express them as algebraic equations, and then to use various expansion theorems and processes of elimination of letters to relate a selected class to the others as derived equations; sometimes further equations arose which stipulated conditions (of no parts in common, say) on the classes in hand in order that any solution be found at all. As logic, these new equations expressed logical consequences of the premisses; syllogistic logic provided many cases, but only of special kinds. However, Boole's methods often did not find special solutions, and he did not always distinguish some of the modes used in quantification of the predicate.

Boole always understood his algebra of logic 'to investigate the fundamental laws of those operations of the mind by which reasoning is performed', as he put it in the opening of *Laws*, but he changed position on the philosophical foundations of his theory. The preference of classes over mental acts between the *Analysis* and *Laws* arose from a rejection of syllogistic logic as a foundation in favour of a different tradition stemming from John Locke and continued by the Scottish common-sense philosophers in some ways. In this view signs were taken as the primary cognitive notion, with language as an essential means of expressing them. In Boole's hands, nouns and adjectives were principal components, denoting classes: thus, say, 'men' were formed from a universe of humans, and 'good men' similarly from 'men'; taking 'good good men' made no difference by the index law. Prepositions expressed the means of combination: 'and' for conjunction, exclusive 'or' for disjunction, and 'except' for subtraction.

Boole tried several times to write a successor to the *Laws* which would explain its principles and philosophy in a general manner, but he never succeeded. His manuscripts show that he tried to ground his logic in a philosophical procedure of his time, though he paid better attention than normal to the difference between a mental act and its product. For him the act of conception by the mind produced a concept, such as 'man' (or the class of them); then the act of judgement of the copresence of concepts produced a proposition, such as 'this is a wise man'; finally, the act of reasoning produced a conclusion, perhaps 'wise men are …', as delivered by his algebra of logic. However, he still found no commensurably comprehensive philosophy of mathematics to explain how his logic had its mathematical basis.

Both in logic and in his educational theory, Boole thought that the mind was capable of original action, such as grasping general laws from particular cases. He would have hated the modern association of his logic with computing, and he had no particular congress with Babbage or concern to apply his logic to calculating machines. The religious aspects were also important; his 'universe 1' corresponded to the ecumenism of his day, in that it stood over and above the factions into which the Christian church was split. He was especially admiring of F. D. Maurice, who advocated ecumenism with great force in mid-century and so was dismissed from his chair at King's College, London: in his last years Boole attended Maurice's services when researching in London. He discreetly revealed his adherence right at the end of the *Laws*, with a reference to 'the Father of Lights'.

Chapters 16 to 21 of *Laws* were concerned with probability theory. One of Boole's main insights was to interpret compound events as Boolean combinations of simple ones. He also considered probabilistic inference, and in estimating probability values of logical consequences he manipulated inequalities in ways which place him among the precursors of linear programming. He also queried subjective interpretations of inverse probability (that is, given some event, calculating the probability of the circumstances which could have caused it to happen). After *Laws* he produced important papers in this area; one won the Keith prize of the Royal Society of Edinburgh in 1857. Later his principles and calculations were criticized by Jevons, among others.

Character and reputation Boole comes over as honest and straightforward, even naïve (as when he told people in the street about the birth of his first daughter). He was also rather serious, showing little sign of a sense of humour. The circumstances of his upbringing and career isolated him from the mathematical and scientific communities; perhaps in compensation he corresponded quite intensively, having substantial exchanges with William Thomson on operator methods and with De Morgan on algebra and logic. He was also on good terms with fellow mathematicians such as Arthur Cayley and Robert Harley.

Boole died from pleuro-pneumonia, the result of foolishly walking the 3 miles from home to university without proper protection from a rain storm—so probable an event in Cork. He died at his home, Lichfield Cottage, Ballintemple, on 8 December 1864, with Maurice's portrait set by his bedside at his request, and was buried at St Michael's Church of Ireland, Blackrock, on 12 December.

After Boole's death, his reputation declined for some decades. Differential operator methods became generally eclipsed by other techniques in the calculus, although his textbooks of differential and difference equations, which contained all basic techniques, continued to be well used after his death and are still in print. His work on logic remained marginal; John Venn was to remain its sole close adherent. Shortly after his death the chemist Benjamin Collins Brodie unsuccessfully tried to develop a similar algebra for chemical combination. The psychological and religious aspects of his logic disappeared completely, and the development of mathematical logic by men such as Giuseppe Peano and Bertrand Russell drew on quite different principles. His work on probability also made little impact.

The main single issue for followers of Boole's logic was his restriction of $(x+y)$ to classes with no parts in common. His arguments for this were not convincing, least of all to his first serious reader, Stanley Jevons, who declared that

+ should be definable for all classes. Jevons outlined his position in his book *Pure Logic* (1864), and corresponded at the time with Boole. Their test case was the expression $(x+x)$; for Jevons $(x+x)=x$, whereas for Boole it could not be 'interpreted', although when expanded the premiss $(x+x)=0$ led to the consequence $x=0$. A few years later the American logician C. S. Peirce came independently to the same modification; it altered Boole's algebra in quite a substantial way, which distanced it from the algebraic logic to come later in the century. The modern 'Boolean algebra' has $x^2=x$ among its axioms, but in technical and philosophical ways it differs from Boole's algebra of logic.

Boolean logic is the basis for the design of all modern computers since the ultimate components of these devices were capable of storing just two values (equated with true and false) and their circuitry calculates the basic Boolean operators over these two values. These domains of application have added to the importance of Boole's work already evident in the relationship between logic and mathematics. I. GRATTAN-GUINNESS

Sources D. MacHale, *George Boole: his life and work* (1985) • M. Panteki, 'Relationships between algebra, logic and differential equations in England, 1800–1860', PhD diss., Middlesex University (CNAA), 1992 • G. Boole, *The mathematical analysis of logic* (1847) • G. Boole, *An investigation of the laws of thought* (1854) • G. Boole, *A treatise on differential equations* (1859) • G. Boole, *A treatise on the calculus of finite differences* (1860) • G. Boole, *Studies in logic and probability*, ed. R. Rhees (1952) • M. E. Boole, *Collected works*, 4 vols. (1931) • T. Hailperin, *Boole's logic and probability*, 2nd edn (1986) • S. Neil, 'Modern logicians: the late George Boole', *British Controversialist*, 3rd ser., 14 (1865), 81–94, 161–74 • I. Grattan-Guinness, 'The correspondence between George Boole and Stanley Jevons', *History and Philosophy of Logic*, 12 (1991), 15–35 • *George Boole: selected manuscripts on logic and its philosophy*, ed. I. Grattan-Guinness and G. Bornet (1997) • L. M. Laita, 'Boolean algebra and its extra-logical sources', *History and Philosophy of Logic*, 1 (1980), 37–60

Archives RS, scientific MSS • TCD, MSS on symbolic logic • University College, Cork, corresp. and papers | CUL, letters to Lord Kelvin; letters to Sir George Stokes; letters to W. Thomson • U. Glas. L., letters to W. Thomson • UCL, corresp. with Augustus De Morgan

Likenesses pencil drawing, 1847, NPG [*see illus.*] • stained-glass window, University College, Cork • wood-engraving (after photograph), NPG; repro. in *ILN* (21 Jan 1865)

Wealth at death under £3000: probate, 15 Feb 1865, *CGPLA Ire.*

Boole, Lucy Everest (1862–1904). *See under* Boole, Mary (1832–1916).

Boole [*née* Everest]**, Mary** (1832–1916), scholar and educationist, was born at Wickwar, Gloucestershire, the elder of the two children of the Revd Thomas Roupell Everest (*d.* 1855), rector of Wickwar, and his wife, Mary (*d.* 1895), daughter of Isaac Ryall, surgeon at the Marine Infirmary, Plymouth. One of her uncles was Sir George Everest, the surveyor-general of India after whom Mount Everest is named. From 1837 until 1843 she lived in France, the family having moved so that Thomas Everest might receive treatment from the homoeopathic doctor Samuel Hahnemann. She was brought up strictly on Hahnemannian principles. Taught by French tutors, she became bilingual. After returning to England she spent some time at a boarding-school and also studied with her father. Algebra and arithmetic were special interests and she read avidly, particularly works on religion and the ancient occult sciences. Teaching in Sunday school and visiting the parish's elderly also occupied her.

In 1850, while visiting her uncle John Ryall, vice-president of Queen's College, Mary Everest met George *Boole (1815–1864), mathematics professor at Queen's College, Cork. They were married on 11 September 1855, shortly after the publication of Boole's book *The Laws of Thought*, one of the classics of nineteenth-century mathematics. Despite a seventeen-year age difference the marriage was happy; between 1856 and 1864 five daughters were born. Boole shared his interests with his wife, including his religious searchings and his ideas about the central role of mathematical processes in all human reasoning. Encouraged to study, she attended some of his lectures, and indeed was the guinea pig on which sections of his textbook *Differential Equations* (1859) were tried out until simplified to the required level.

In 1864 Mary Boole was left a widow, her youngest child only six months old. She had a heartfelt purpose, however: to explain and develop what she saw as the fundamental significance of her husband's work—the use of mathematical methods, developed in *Laws of Thought*, to reveal deeper spiritual and philosophical truths. Placing several of her children with relatives, she returned to England in 1865 and contacted the theologian and educationist F. D. Maurice, a man admired by her husband. She accepted Maurice's offer of a position as librarian at Queen's College, London, England's first college of higher education for women. She also ran a student residence, and offered a series of Sunday evening 'true logic' classes, in which she discussed religion, psychology, spiritualism, and mathematics. Her exposition *The Message of Psychic Science to Mothers and Nurses* (1883), an early book on mental health, was written at about this time, as was a work on her husband. Publication of the latter, hardly an interpretation of Boole's work likely to enhance his reputation as a mathematician, was at the time blocked by Maurice.

By 1873 Mary Boole had come to be regarded by the college administration as somewhat unstable and had had to leave. She then became secretary to James Hinton, writer on philosophy, psychology, and science, and she came to confuse the eccentric Hinton's disordered views about mental processes with her husband's work in logic. Her London home became a meeting-place for antivivisectionists, vegetarians, unconventional educational psychologists, and fringe religious groups. From the late 1870s she published a remarkable number of articles and books; Hebrew ritual and Indian philosophy interested her and she contributed to Jewish and Indian periodicals. On medical topics, although she took homoeopathic theories to extremes, she frequently offered sound advice. She was convinced of the equality of the sexes, but had little enthusiasm for the women's suffrage movement. Her *Symbolical Methods of Study* (1884) presented an introduction to psychic science; her treatise *The Mathematical Psychology of Gratry and Boole* (1897) attempted a psychological interpretation of Boole's work in relation to the thought of the French mystic August Gratry.

About the turn of the century Mary Boole joined the then very active progressive movement in education, speaking at meetings of the Parents' National Educational Union, contributing to the *Parents' Review*, and contacting progressive schools. In her books *Lectures on the Logic of Arithmetic* (1903) and *The Preparation of the Child for Science* (1904) she demonstrated how psychology can contribute to better teaching of elementary science and mathematics; her understanding of a child's unconscious assimilation of abstract concepts was well ahead of her time. Both works were influential, and the former, largely practical lesson notes emphasizing play methods and self-discovery, was pioneering. Her Boole Curve Sewing Cards (forerunner of the pins and metal-wire art form), devised for constructing such geometric notions as envelopes of lines, were sold commercially.

Mary Boole's *Collected Works*, published posthumously in 1931, is a remarkable mixture of insight, educational innovation, tedious banality, and an incomprehensible confusion of mathematics, religion, and philosophy. However, although undoubtedly an eccentric and unorthodox in many ways, she had a vision of early mathematical education that remains relevant, and her ideas on educational psychology deserve a wider audience. She died of heart failure at her home, 16 Ladbroke Road, Notting Hill, London, on 17 May 1916, and was buried three days later.

Through her five daughters, four of whom survived her, Mary Boole passed on the remarkable Boole genes. The eldest, Mary Ellen (*b.* 1856), married Charles Howard Hinton, son of James Hinton; their grandson was Howard Everest Hinton (1912–1977), a noted entomologist and head of the department of zoology at University College, Bristol. The second daughter, Margaret (1858–1935), married the artist Edward Ingram Taylor; the mathematical physicist Geoffrey Ingram *Taylor (1886–1975) was their son. The fifth and youngest daughter was Ethel Lilian *Voynich (1864–1960), the novelist.

The third daughter, **Alicia Stott** [*née* Boole] (1860–1940), geometer, was born on 8 June 1860 in Blackrock, near Cork. Her interest in geometry started in her late teens when she began to experiment with a large collection of cubes. Although poverty and family circumstances had severely limited her education, she developed a remarkably clear understanding of four-dimensional geometry. She discovered for herself that there are six regular polytopes (convex regular solids) of dimension four, and, using purely Euclidean ruler-and-compass methods, built cardboard models of their three-dimensional cross-sections—startlingly original work for a young person. Indeed, 'Alicia Boole had all the hallmarks of an extremely talented and creative pure mathematician' (MacHale, 261).

Alicia Boole married Walter Stott, an actuary, in 1890. About 1900 Stott drew her attention to publications by the Dutch mathematician Peiter Schoute on four-dimensional polytopes. She contacted Schoute and began a collaboration which lasted until Schoute's death in 1913, her exceptional powers of geometrical visualization complementing his more conventional methods. Her results appeared in two papers (1900, 1910). In 1914 she received an honorary doctorate from the University of Groningen. She resumed mathematical work in 1930, collaborating with the geometer H. S. M. Coxeter; her contributions were incorporated, with acknowledgements, into Coxeter's publications. The only one of George Boole's children to directly inherit her father's mathematical genius, Alicia Stott died at 12 Hornsey Lane, Highgate, Middlesex, on 17 December 1940.

The fourth daughter, **Lucy Everest Boole** (1862–1904), pharmaceutical chemist, was born on 5 August 1862 in Blackrock, near Cork. Despite little formal education, she was the second woman to pass the London School of Pharmacy's major examination (1888). Taking a post as assistant to W. R. Dunstan, professor of chemistry to the Pharmaceutical Society, she became the first woman in Britain to formally undertake research in pharmaceutical chemistry. Her procedure for analysis of tartar emetic (proposed in an 1889 joint paper with Dunstan) became the official method of assay, retained until 1963. She became lecturer in chemistry at the London School of Medicine for Women, was elected a fellow of the Institute of Chemistry, and continued research in the Pharmaceutical Society's laboratory for some years. Never marrying, she shared her mother's London house (not always harmoniously), and died there on 5 December 1904.

MARY R. S. CREESE

Sources D. MacHale, *George Boole: his life and work* (1985) · *Mary Everest Boole: collected works*, ed. E. M. Cobham, 4 vols. (1931) · *Mary Everest Boole: a memoir with some letters*, ed. E. M. Cobham (1951) · *A Boolean anthology: selected writings of Mary Boole on mathematical education*, ed. D. G. Tahta (1972) · E. Kaye, *A history of Queen's College, London, 1848–1972* (1972) · M. Boole, 'George Boole's philosophy', *The Athenaeum* (23 Aug 1884), 237–9 · H. S. M. Coxeter, 'Alicia Boole Stott, 1860–1940', *Women of mathematics: a bibliographic sourcebook*, ed. L. S. Grinstein and P. J. Campbell (1987), 220–24 · E. J. Shellard, 'Some early women research workers in British pharmacy, 1866–1912', *Pharmaceutical Historian: Newsletter for the British Society for the History of Pharmacy*, 12 (1982), 2–3 · *The Times* (19 May 1916) · *The Times* (18 Dec 1940) · *The Times* (8 Dec 1904) · d. cert. · *CGPLA Eng. & Wales* (1916) · *CGPLA Eng. & Wales* (1941)

Likenesses F. Hollyer, photograph (Alicia Stott, *née* Boole), priv. coll. · Window & Grove, photograph (Lucy Everest Boole), repro. in MacHale, *George Boole*, 266 · group portrait, photograph (with Alicia Stott, *née* Boole and Lucy Everest Boole), Lincoln City Libraries, Museum and Art Galleries · photograph, repro. in MacHale, *George Boole*, 239

Wealth at death £5789 0s. 8d.—M. Boole: probate, 19 June 1916, *CGPLA Eng. & Wales* · £681 6s. 1d.—Lucy Everest Boole: probate, 8 July 1905, *CGPLA Eng. & Wales* · £6848 14s.—Alicia Stott (*neé* Boole): probate, 3 March 1941, *CGPLA Eng. & Wales*

Boon, Alan Wheatley (1913–2000), publisher and editor, was born on 28 September 1913 at 264 Worple Road, Wimbledon, the second of the four children of Charles *Boon (1877–1943), publisher, and Mary Alice Cowpe (*b.* 1877). Their third child, **John Trevor Boon** (1916–1996), publisher, was born on 21 December 1916 in Kings Langley, Hertfordshire. Charles Boon was co-founder and editor of Mills and Boon Ltd, a small general publishing company founded in 1908 with his partner Gerald Rusgrove *Mills (1877–1928). Both Alan and John Boon were educated at Felsted School in Essex. Alan then played rugby for the Wasps, and joined his older brother Charles in their father's firm. He did so reluctantly: 'I remember my father saying, "Since you can't get jobs elsewhere, you might as well join the firm"' (private information).

At the time of Alan's arrival at Mills and Boon the publishing house was in some difficulty. A small general publisher, it could not compete with larger firms such as Hodder and Stoughton, and Hutchinson. After Gerald Mills's death in 1928, Charles Boon decided to concentrate on escapist romance, a genre growing in popularity among the female patrons of lending libraries. Alan worked in the editorial department where he acquired knowledge of the 'Mills and Boon romance', which was financially rewarding, if intellectually inferior. He thought it easier to run a specialized publishing house, although he worried about concentrating on one product. He later remarked to a literary agent that he would have to turn down a Shakespeare if he sent one along.

John went on to Trinity Hall, Cambridge, where he attained a double first in history and earned a blue in rugby. On graduation in 1938 he joined his two brothers at Mills and Boon. Like Alan, he did so unwillingly: 'I was dogsbody', he recalled:

> I did petty cash extremely badly. My father wanted me to develop a direct mail operation. And the way to do that was to look through the London telephone directory and pick out a name and send a card and catalogues. It wasted my time. (private information)

This personal attention to readers, however, became a trade mark of Mills and Boon's marketing style.

With the outbreak of the Second World War, both brothers enlisted. As commander of B company of the South Wales Borderers, Major John Boon led his battalion on D-day, landing at Hable de Heurot and participating in the capture of Bayeux. He married Felicity Ann (*b.* 1917/18), daughter of Samuel Stewart Logan, bank manager, on 4 September 1943; they had four sons. Alan Boon served in the Royal Navy where he met Olivia Rose Luck (*b.* 1920/21), daughter of Richard Samuel Luck, a taxi proprietor; they were married on 20 December 1946.

Alan left the navy when his father died in 1943 and assumed control over the editorial department. John, who rejoined the firm after the war, was general manager. With little publishing experience between them, the Boon brothers emerged as a perfect team, building Mills and Boon into the market leader in romantic fiction. John applied his natural skills as a leader and organizer to the financial side of the firm, while Alan, who was a born publisher and editor, oversaw the editorial process for forty years, shepherding hundreds of novels and authors. John Boon embraced the publishing world wholeheartedly and defended Mills and Boon against critics:

> We never despised our product. A lot of people who publish romantic novels call them 'funny little books' that make a bit of profit. We never did that. We never said this was the greatest form of literature, but we did say that of this form of literature, we were going to publish the best. (private information)

Alan Boon thought escapism was the basic appeal of Mills and Boon romances, likening their effects to Valium. From the beginning the firm imposed strict rules for its romantic novels, toning down the passion so as not to offend readers. The basic elements of the 'formula' remained into the twenty-first century: the heroine is a sympathetic Cinderella figure (young, clever, and often an orphan). The hero, usually the heroine's employer, is an 'Alphaman', as Boon himself called him, older than the heroine, mysterious and rough-edged. Settings range from an English village to an African desert. There is always a happy ending, usually a wedding, or if the couple is already married, a reconciliation. In the 1950s 'taboo' subjects were dealt with carefully: it was thought that one story featuring a divorcee would offend Irish readers, so the author was asked to think of a way around it. The closest physical contact between hero and heroine was hand-holding, an occasional kiss on the cheek, or the more intense 'punishing kiss'. Boon asked another author if she could possibly 'write out the Lesbian angle and the V.D. references' from her manuscript (letter from Alan Boon to Hilda Nickson, 1965, Mills and Boon archives).

Charles Boon had instilled in his son the importance of editorial control and personal attention to authors, some of whom wrote twelve novels every year. For hundreds of Mills and Boon authors, Alan Boon personified their romantic hero: he was the archetypal English gentleman, tall, handsome, wealthy, and charming. Different from most publishers, he became good friends with his authors, taking them to lunch at the Ritz, and sending them flowers, chocolates, and congratulatory telegrams. Some authors wrote to Boon four times a day, and he answered every letter.

In the 1950s John Boon revived the firm's non-fiction list as competition from other publishers intensified. Cookery books and other practical 'books for women' complemented the fiction list. In 1961 Mills and Boon acquired Allman & Sons Ltd, one of the oldest publishing houses in England, with an established list strong in domestic science, revision notes, and English grammar. With the assistance of academic friends at Cambridge, Boon launched a new school textbook series, which proved very profitable.

Always mindful of sales, Alan Boon strove to update the Mills and Boon romance to reflect the changes in sexual mores in the 1960s. There was now sex before marriage, although the couple usually married at the end. Boon commented that 'our books have always represented, as we thought it, morality at the time' (private information). Mills and Boon made the transition to paperbacks and the mass market in the 1960s, and sales soared around the world. John Boon struck up a friendship with the Bonnycastle family of Canada, founders of Harlequin Books, a small publisher of paperback books. This initiated an experiment in paperback distribution in North America that struck gold, and led to the eventual sale of Mills and Boon to Harlequin in 1971. Harlequin itself was acquired by the Torstar Corporation in 1975. Alan Boon acted as a mentor to a new generation of editors and authors until his retirement in the late 1980s. John Boon remained active on the boards and in the operations of the company until his death.

Alan reflected on the future of the romantic novel in 1986:

> 'The Mills & Boon Romance' is not something that is static. We shall continue to be successful if we believe in what we publish, sell books at a reasonable price, packaged nicely, and which answer in an attractive way the requirements of women's biological instincts. Our books must be romantically exciting, the dialogue must be alive, the background must be appealing, but always the hero must be 'the Alpha male', maybe camouflaged. (private information)

The romances continued to be enormously popular: at the beginning of the twenty-first century one in four women read Mills and Boon romances, and one of their books was sold every two seconds. John Boon was an active member of several book trade organizations. As president of the Publishers Association from 1961 to 1963, he mounted a successful defence in court of the net book agreement. He was president of the International Publishers Association from 1972 to 1976, and was invited to be an honorary life member. In 1968 he was awarded the CBE for his services to the publishing industry. Asked of his legacy, Boon replied, 'an efficient, well-run company with very good personal relations' (private information).

Alan Boon had a passion for horse-racing, and owned and bred racehorses. He retired to a village in Leicestershire, and died in Leicester on 29 July 2000. A former member of the Wasps with his brother Alan, John Boon remained a fan of rugby. He was a member of the Wine Society and sat on its management committee. John Boon lived in London, where he died, at his home at 7 Cambridge Square, on 12 July 1996. JOSEPH MCALEER

Sources J. McAleer, *Passion's fortune: the story of Mills and Boon* (1999) · J. McAleer, *Popular reading and publishing in Britain, 1914–1950* (1992) · private information (2004) · m. cert. · b. cert. · b. cert. [John Trevor Boon] · m. cert. [John Trevor Boon] · d. cert. [John Trevor Boon]

Archives Harlequin–Mills and Boon Ltd, Richmond, Surrey, archives

Likenesses photographs, Harlequin–Mills and Boon Ltd, Richmond, Surrey, archives · photographs, repro. in McAleer, *Passion's fortune*

Boon, Charles (1877–1943), publisher, was born on 9 May 1877 at 42 Castle Street, Westminster, London, eldest among the six children of Charles Boon, brewer's servant, and Margaret, *née* Wheatley. His childhood was deprived: the family lived in Seven Dials, above a brewery where Charles's father worked. On his father's death Charles, then twelve, left school and took a series of odd jobs, including work in the brewery and a boot factory. He was also influenced by early jobs in a bookshop and Mudie's circulating library, gaining insight into sales, distribution, and popular authors. In 1893 Charles Boon joined Methuen & Co., publishers, in London, as an office boy and warehouse clerk. In ten years he rose to become sales manager and general manager. There he met Gerald Rusgrove *Mills (1877–1928), who joined the firm in 1903 as educational manager. Methuen was an excellent training ground for the future publishing partners, and a number of authors on the Methuen fiction list, including Harold Begbie, E. F. Benson, and Jack London were later published by Mills and Boon. Methuen was also a successful educational publisher, and several authors of Methuen textbooks were also later published by Mills and Boon.

Boon and Mills decided to strike out on their own in 1908, registering their company, Mills and Boon, on 28 November (Mills provided most of the initial investment of £1000, which entitled him to put his name before Boon's). The firm, known today as a purveyor of light romantic fiction, was in the beginning a small, diversified, but profitable publisher. Boon oversaw the fiction list and marketing; Mills, the educational and non-fiction lists. Boon, who was charming and energetic, had a gift for finding new talent, and his literary discoveries, particularly women authors, including Ethel Stevana (E. S.) Stevens, Ida Alexa Ray (I. A. R.) Wylie, Beatrice Grimshaw, and Victor Bridges, generated much publicity. But perhaps Mills and Boon's biggest coup as a young publishing house was signing up Jack London, then at the height of his worldwide success, in 1911.

On 1 June 1911 Boon married Mary Alice Cowpe (*b.* 1877) of Burnley, Lancashire, daughter of Thomas Cowpe, cotton manufacturer. They had four children: Charles, Alan Wheatley *Boon (1913–2000), John Trevor *Boon (1916–1996) [*see under* Boon, Alan Wheatley], and Dinah. In the 1930s all three sons joined Mills and Boon: Charles worked in production, Alan on the editorial side, and John in finances. Of the three John and Alan emerged as natural publishers and carried on their father's legacy after the Second World War.

During the First World War Boon served in the Royal Navy, assigned to the hydrophone service as a radio operator. In the 1920s Mills and Boon's prosperity waned as competition intensified from larger and more established publishers such as Methuen, Macmillan, Collins, and Hodder and Stoughton, who were all expanding their fiction lists. But the economic circumstances of this period also allowed a denser exploitation of the publishing market, due in part to rising living standards and a growth in leisure time. The social and political changes created by the war revealed for publishers a vast, untapped market: the female reader. Larger lists of simply designed, popular fiction were produced to increase revenues and offset spiralling production costs, and to appeal to middle- and working-class women, who patronized the biggest growth market, the circulating libraries. Charles Boon, recognizing the potential of this trend, nurtured a section of his fiction list which was selling quite well: romantic fiction.

Gerald Mills's unexpected death on 23 September 1928

was a devastating blow for the firm. In financial difficulties, Boon nevertheless resisted a merger with or takeover by another publishing house. He found a new partner in-house, Joseph W. Henley, who worked in book production. Boon became the dominant shareholder, and from now on shaped the direction of Mills and Boon. He remade his company in the 1930s, setting it on a new and irreversible course as a single-genre publishing house, concentrating on romantic fiction. With commercial libraries opening across the country, particularly during the depression, publishing as a 'library house' was safe and profitable. In the 1930s the modern Mills and Boon publication emerged as a formulaic romantic novel with a distinctive look: bold and colourful jackets, brown bindings, expressive blurbs, flashy advertising. These branding techniques, credited to Charles Boon, were imitated by other publishers.

Commercial publishing relied on volume, a large list of titles that could be reissued many times in cheaper editions, and Boon encouraged his authors, who were all women, to be as prolific as possible; some wrote as many as eight novels in a single year. On average in the 1930s between 6000 and 8000 copies of each title were printed, and Mills and Boon issued two to four new titles every fortnight. Authors promoted their books at libraries and women's institutes to court their loyal fans. Ida Cook, who as Mary Burchell wrote 150 romances in fifty years, recalled that Charles Boon would urge her, 'never pass a Boots shop in Eastbourne, anywhere you are, without going in and making yourself known'; this was the 'personal touch' (private information).

In the 1930s Charles Boon brought to fullest fruition this 'personal touch', a marketing tool which promoted sales by encouraging close contact, even a sense of kinship, with readers. The end-pages of each Mills and Boon romance, which listed the complete catalogue, opened with a full-page notice headed 'To Fiction Readers: Why you should choose a Mills & Boon novel'. Boon was determined that each reader feel extra-special:

> Mills & Boon issue a strictly limited Fiction List, and the novels they publish all possess real story-telling qualities of an enduring nature. It is not necessary for Fiction readers to make a choice from a Mills & Boon new Fiction List. They can rest assured that each novel has been carefully chosen, and is worth reading. Therefore ask your bookseller or librarian to put on your list every novel published by Mills & Boon. (Mills and Boon catalogue, *c.*1938)

Readers did, and by the Second World War Mills and Boon enjoyed unprecedented prosperity, if little critical acclaim. Charles Boon had shaped a genre and a marketing style which exist to this day. Readers learned to ask for 'Another Mills and Boon, please', rather than a specific author, a triumph of branding. The Mills and Boon romance came with a 'guarantee' of an escapist romance with an obligatory happy-ever-after ending. Wartime enhanced this demand for escape, although paper rationing limited production, and profits.

Charles Boon, who had few interests outside publishing, died on 2 December 1943 from a cerebral haemorrhage at his home, 42 Aylmer Road, Hornsey, London. On their return from the war Boon's sons ran Mills and Boon and steered the firm to even greater heights of prosperity. JOSEPH MCALEER

Sources J. McAleer, *Passion's fortune: the story of Mills & Boon* (1999) • J. McAleer, *Popular reading and publishing in Britain, 1914–1950* (1992) • b. cert. • m. cert. • d. cert. • private information (2004)
Archives Harlequin–Mills and Boon Ltd, Richmond, Surrey, archives
Likenesses portrait, Harlequin-Mills and Boon Ltd, Richmond, Surrey, archives; repro. in McAleer, *Passion's fortune*
Wealth at death £28,798 8*s*. 5*d*.: probate, 28 April 1944, *CGPLA Eng. & Wales*

Boon, John Trevor (1916–1996). *See under* Boon, Alan Wheatley (1913–2000).

Boone, James Shergold (1798–1859), writer, born on 30 June 1798 at Sunbury, Middlesex, and baptized on 8 August 1798 there, was the second son of Thomas Boone (*b.* 22 July 1760), a surgeon, and his wife, Rose Ann, *née* Shergold, who died on 11 July 1798, shortly after her son's birth. He was educated from June 1812 to April 1816 at Charterhouse School, where he won composition prizes in 1814 and 1816, and then at Christ Church, Oxford, where he matriculated as a commoner on 30 May 1816 and was promoted to a studentship in 1818. In 1817 he won a Craven scholarship, as well as both the chancellor's Latin verse prize and the Newdigate English verse prize. While an undergraduate he published *The Oxford Spy*, an anonymous verse satire on university life critical of Oxford's curriculum and examinations, which caused a sensation. The first four dialogues and an appendix appeared in 1818, the fifth and last dialogue in 1819. In 1820 he won the chancellor's Latin essay prize. In keeping with his criticisms, however, Boone disdained an honours degree and took an ordinary BA on 24 May 1820. He took his MA on 4 March 1823.

In 1820 Boone published, again anonymously, *The Welcome of Isis*, a verse tribute to the duke of Wellington on the occasion of his expected, but postponed, visit to Oxford. He then returned to the subject of university reform with the publication of *An Essay on the Study of Modern History* (1821), urging the addition of the subject to the Oxford curriculum. One account states that after leaving Oxford Boone was offered a parliamentary seat by a patron impressed by his early promise (Mozley, 2.203). He declined, turning to literary pursuits in London and lecturing on such subjects as the mutual relations of art and science. *The Council of Ten*, a monthly periodical of which he was editor and virtually sole contributor, appeared in June 1822 but lasted only twelve numbers. He then published *Men and Things in 1823: a Poem in Three Epistles, with Notes* (1823), a survey of European politics in which he expressed high admiration for Canning.

On 24 April 1824 Boone married Ellen Cotterill, of Totteridge, Hertfordshire, relinquishing his Christ Church studentship in the same year. Ordained deacon in 1826 and priest in 1827, he returned to Charterhouse as a master in the latter year. Having stood unsuccessfully for the schoolmastership of Charterhouse in 1832, he accepted in

June the incumbency of the newly consecrated St John's, Paddington.

Boone's continued interest in educational matters found expression in *National Education: a Sermon* (1833) and *The Educational Economy of England* (1838), in which he railed against ideas of state control. Also of interest is *One, Manifold, or, System* (1848), a philosophical work prompted by European revolution. His most important literary undertaking, however, was the editorship from January 1834 of the *British Critic*, a high-church literary and theological quarterly controlled by the Hackney Phalanx; this is the clearest indication of his own churchmanship. After January 1836, however, when John Henry Newman struck an agreement to provide the *British Critic* with a fixed number of reviews written by his Tractarian coterie, Boone came under increasing pressure to suppress views uncongenial to the Oxford Movement. Newman's manoeuvres to wrest editorial control eventually undermined Boone's position and he resigned late in 1837, ultimately to be succeeded by Newman himself.

Boone's wife, Ellen, died on 11 April 1840, and he married Julia Maria, daughter of William Cox, of London, on 11 January 1842. There were no children by either marriage. Boone remained at St John's, Paddington, until his death aged sixty, after two years of illness, at 2 Stanhope Street (now Terrace), Hyde Park Gardens, on 24 March 1859. A brass erected to his memory remains in the chancel at St John's. Boone enjoyed some reputation as a preacher. He was appointed select preacher at Oxford in 1859, but illness prevented him from fulfilling the office. Various of his individual sermons as well as a collection, *Sermons on Various Subjects and Occasions* (1853), were published, while his *Sermons Chiefly on the Theory of Belief* (1860) was posthumously edited. S. A. SKINNER

Sources R. L. Arrowsmith, ed., *Charterhouse register, 1769–1872* (1974) · Foster, *Alum. Oxon.* · Crockford (1858) · *GM*, 1st ser., 68 (1798), 636 · *GM*, 2nd ser., 13 (1840), 553 · *GM*, 2nd ser., 17 (1842), 322 · *GM*, 3rd ser., 6 (1859), 545 · *N&Q*, 3rd ser., 3 (1863), 510 · *N&Q*, 3rd ser., 4 (1863), 35, 98, 138, 153–5, 299 · S. A. Skinner, '"Giant of a former age": a final note on James Shergold Boone?', *N&Q*, 242 (1997), 336–8 · T. Mozley, *Reminiscences, chiefly of Oriel College and the Oxford Movement*, 2 (1882), 200–04 · E. R. Houghton and J. L. Altholz, '*The British Critic*, 1824–1843', *Victorian Periodicals Review*, 24 (1991), 111–18 · *IGI* · *The Guardian* (30 March 1859), 278 · J. S. Boone, *Sermons chiefly on the theory of belief* (1860), vi

Archives Pusey Oxf., British Critic MSS | BL, Ripon MSS · Bodl. Oxf., Wilberforce MSS

Likenesses E. Cocking, lithograph, pubd 1852 (after a photograph by R. Hogg), NPG · photograph, St John's, Paddington, London

Wealth at death under £10,000: probate, 24 May 1859, *CGPLA Eng. & Wales*

Boone, Thomas (1730/31–1812), colonial governor and public official, was born in England, the son of Charles Boone (*d.* 1735), member of parliament and governor of Bombay, and his second wife, Mary, *née* Garth, the widow of George Evelyn. Boone attended Eton College, and Trinity College, Cambridge (1746). During the 1750s he lived in South Carolina securing property inherited from his uncle, Joseph Boone, a prominent planter and politician. Appointed royal governor of New Jersey in January 1760, Boone served until October 1761, when he was promoted to the royal governorship of South Carolina.

His administration in New Jersey was relatively uneventful, but his term in South Carolina proved disastrous. He arrived in Charles Town in December 1761, only three months after the end of the hard-fought Cherokee War (1759–61), which brought a shaky peace with South Carolina's most powerful native neighbours. To minimize the abuses of white traders that often led to conflict, Boone advocated a governmental monopoly of the American Indian trade; to curb the American Indians in the event of hostilities, he advocated taking and even shooting hostages. British officials, however, opened the trade to all who obtained licences and turned to the royally appointed and British-salaried superintendents of Indian affairs to regulate it.

Meanwhile Boone's attempt to reform the local election laws failed when he challenged the long-standing right of the South Carolina Commons house of assembly to determine the qualifications of its own members. During the ensuing dispute over the election of Christopher Gadsden, the house on 16 December 1762 refused to do further business with the governor until he apologized and accepted its position. Boone countered by ordering local newspapers to publish nothing derogatory about the government and attempting to seduce his opponents with land grants along the Altamaha River, an area acquired from Spain in the treaty of 1763 but claimed by Georgia as well as South Carolina. When these measures failed, he unceremoniously sailed for England in May 1764, taking with him the wife of a prominent local merchant, Sarah Tatnall Peronneau whom he married at some time after the death of her husband, Samuel, in 1768 and before the report of the marriage in the *South Carolina Gazette* on 8 August 1771. It seems to have been a happy union that produced at least two daughters and one son who became a lieutenant-colonel in the army. More immediately, however, authorities in London observed that Boone had pursued the dispute with the lower house with 'more Zeal than prudence … actuated by a degree of Passion and Resentment inconsistent with good Policy' (Greene, 488). And the South Carolina Commons house did indeed emerge from the controversy more determined to maintain its rights and more self-confident than ever before.

Boone's career nevertheless survived the setback, perhaps because his brother Charles was a well-connected member of parliament and a strong supporter of the North administration. The crown demanded that the legislature pay the arrears of his salary, which it had withheld, and, partly because Boone had lobbied for repeal of the Stamp Act in March 1766, the house complied. In December 1769 Boone also received an appointment at £1200 per year as a commissioner of the British customs service, an office which he held until his resignation in 1805. Until the American War of Independence he also had income from his rice plantations in South Carolina, which totalled approximately 8815 acres with 184 working hands, most of them slaves. But his attempt to evacuate his slaves as British forces abandoned Charles Town in 1782 failed when an American privateer captured their vessel. After the legislature confiscated his South Carolina lands that same year, Boone estimated his losses at more than £41,207; the British Loyalist Claims Commission established by the British government awarded him £22,533 8s. in compensation.

Boone died on 25 September 1812 at his family home, Lee Place, Kent. His rash and counterproductive behaviour in South Carolina appears to have been something of an aberration, since contemporaries in New Jersey considered him to be a genial man. Certainly his instructions for his own funeral and burial at Godstone, Surrey, do not suggest that he was an abrasively assertive individual. The ceremony was to be 'as private as possible consistent with my station in life' (will). ROBERT M. WEIR

Sources will, PRO, PROB 11/1537, sig. 445, fols. 289–90 · loyalist claim, PRO, AO12/47/317 · loyalist claim, PRO, AO12/109/82 · transcripts of records relating to South Carolina in the British Public Record Office, South Carolina Archives and History Center, Columbia, · F. Gilbert, ed., 'Letters of Francis Kinloch to Thomas Boone, 1782–1788', *Journal of Southern History*, 8 (1942), 87–105 · L. B. Namier, 'Charles Garth and his connexions', *EngHR*, 54 (1939), 443–70 · J. P. Greene, 'The Gadsden election controversy and the revolutionary movement in South Carolina', *Mississippi Valley Historical Review*, 46 (1959), 469–92 · R. M. Weir, *Colonial South Carolina: a history*, pbk edn (1997) · L. R. Gerlach, *Prologue to independence: New Jersey in the coming of the American Revolution* (1976) · D. L. Kemmerer, *Path to freedom: the struggle for self-government in colonial New Jersey, 1703–1776* (1940); repr. (1968) · HoP, *Commons, 1715–54* · E. E. Hoon, *The organization of the English customs system, 1696–1786* (1968) · R. Beatson, *A political index to the histories of Great Britain and Ireland*, 3 vols. (1806)

Boorde, Andrew (*c.*1490–1549), physician and author, was born at Borde Hill near Cuckfield, Sussex. Like many others in the field of healing he began his career as a monk. He was brought up at Oxford and admitted under age, in 1515, into the Carthusian order at the London Charterhouse. His precocity within the order was rewarded while he was still in his twenties by nomination as suffragan bishop of Chichester. In 1517, however, he was accused of being 'conversant with women', and was dismissed from his post by papal bull in 1521 before he could exercise any of its prerogatives. Uncomfortable with the abstemious, vegetarian lifestyle of the cloistered Carthusians, Boorde wrote in 1528 to John Batmanson, then prior of Hinton Charterhouse in Somerset, asking for release from his vows. Although some technical difficulties remained, Boorde received his dispensation and went abroad to study medicine at as many universities as he could. He returned to England in 1530 and, while staying with Sir Robert Drewry, ministered to Thomas Howard, duke of Norfolk. Boorde recorded that at Norfolk's request he attended Henry VIII, but no report of payment is recorded in the king's privy purse expenses.

Boorde was travelling again in 1532, conferring with medical men in Orléans, Poitiers, Toulouse, Wittenberg,

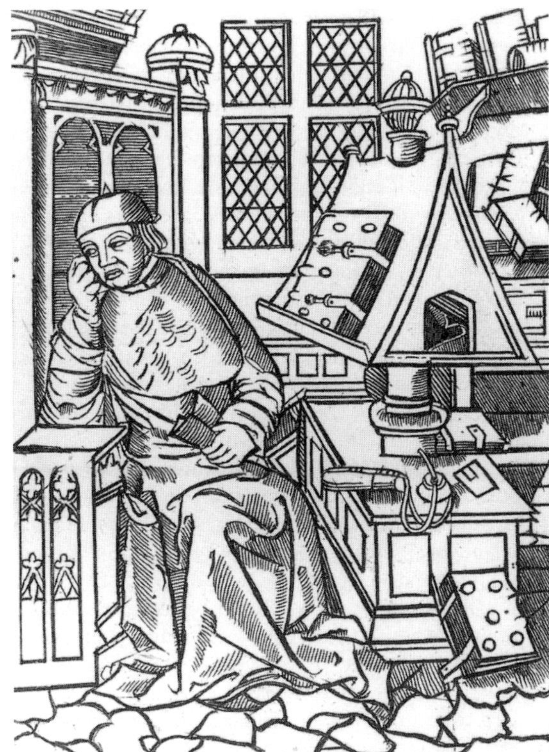

Andrew Boorde (*c.*1490–1549), by unknown artist [original, 1547]

and Rome. He also made a pilgrimage to Santiago de Compostela in Galicia and met surgeons at the university there. Back in England, on 29 May 1534, Boorde took the oath of conformity, perhaps influenced by a brief confinement in the London Charterhouse. Upon his release he spent some time with Thomas Cromwell in Hampshire.

Recognizing Boorde's usefulness as an itinerant physician Cromwell sent him abroad in 1535 to test continental opinion of the divorced king. Boorde travelled extensively through France, Spain, and Portugal. He corresponded with Cromwell on 20 June 1535 from Bordeaux, where he bemoaned England's lack of sympathetic allies in Europe excepting the French. Later that summer Boorde sent rhubarb seeds from Barbary to Cromwell with directions for their cultivation, noting that the plant was greatly prized in Spain (Boorde, *Introduction and Dyetary*, 56). Boorde's journey in 1535 was the most extensive he had yet undertaken, and he described it in *The Itinerary of Europe*, a diary describing each region, which he lent to Cromwell. Cromwell evidently lost the volume, but part of it may have been re-worked into *The Peregrination or Itinerary of England*, printed in 1735 (ibid., 23–4). *Peregrination* lists market towns, castles in England and Wales, and adjacent islands for the armchair traveller, and includes information on bridges, rivers, and highways into the shires from London.

By April 1536 Boorde was practising medicine in Glasgow, still writing regularly to Cromwell with information about the Scots, whom he did not like and who, he reported, did not like the English. After a year's residence in Scotland, Boorde was again briefly in England in 1537, spending some time in Yorkshire, Cambridge, and London, where he oversaw production of his *Almanake and Pronostication for 1537*. He experienced some trouble in the capital, and wrote to Cromwell asking for help in recovering horses stolen from him and sizeable debts owed him by individuals who called him 'appostata', and 'all-to-nowght' (good-for-nothing). Late in 1537, or after the dissolution of the religious houses in early 1538, Boorde left for Jerusalem to see the holy sepulchre, travelling for several years on a journey of remarkable range that took him east via Venice and back to the west through Naples and Rome. In 1540 a little treatise usually associated with Boorde, *Book for to Lerne a Man to by Wyse in Buyldyng his Howse for the Helth of his Body*, appeared anonymously in London. For a while Boorde settled in Montpellier, site of his favourite university, purportedly accumulating amusing stories that were ascribed to him and later published as *Scogin's Jests*, 'a preservative against melancholy' (John Scogin, *Scogin's Jests*, 1680). This comedic book and *Merry Tales of the Mad Men of Gotham*, traditionally attributed to Boorde, have led to the popular notion that he was the original Merry Andrew. In Montpellier in 1542 he wrote his *Pryncyples of Astronamye* and completed *The Compendious Regiment, or, Dyetary of Helth*, dedicated to Norfolk, which included the earlier *Book for to Lerne*. That same year he penned *The First Book of the Introduction of Knowledge*. Intended as a medical treatise, the *Introduction* was illustrated with woodcuts and records Boorde's good-natured observations made on a lengthy clockwise tour of Europe beginning at Calais. Using rhyme, dialect, and other amusing techniques Boorde provided delightful details about the fashions, foods, costumes, weather, and business of dozens of continental regions from Norway to Greece. Dedicated to the Princess Mary, the *Introduction* contained numbers, monetary information, and key foreign phrases including the first printed specimen of the Romani language. Boorde's lost *Boke of Berdes* appeared at about the same time, and satirist Milton Barnes, through whose work we can detect Boorde's, retorted that Boorde blamed his own drunken stench on his facial hair (Barnes, *Treatyse Answering the Book of Berdes*, 1543). Boorde's *A Breviary of Health*, a self-help book of remedies and preventives gleaned from his travels, followed in 1547. Written in a popular and confident style, the *Breviary* suggests oil of radish for ringing in the ears, green ginger for indigestion, and garlic for worms. Boorde returned to England later in 1547 to guide the *Dyetary*, the *Breviary*, and the *Introduction* through publication. It is likely that he lived for a while in the house of the master of the hospital of St Giles-in-the-Fields. Barnes acknowledged, however grudgingly, that Boorde had many patients in London.

Boorde took up residence in Winchester. Charged by John Ponet, later bishop of Winchester, with keeping three prostitutes in his chamber Boorde was put in Fleet prison in 1547; his old patrons dead or powerless, Boorde did not leave prison alive. His will was drawn up in the Fleet on 9 April 1549 and was proved on 25 April. He left two houses in Lynn given to him by Recorder Conysby; tenements in Pevensey, Sussex, that he had inherited from his brother; and diverse properties in and around Winchester. No record exists about his burial.

ELIZABETH LANE FURDELL

Sources [A. Boorde], *The fyrst book of the introduction … dyetary of helth*, ed. F. J. Furnivall (1906) • *DNB* • H. E. Poole, ed., *The wisdom of Andrew Boorde* (1936) • will, PRO, PROB 11/32, fols. 217–18 • M. Barnes, *Treatyse answering the Book of berdes* (1543) • A. Boorde, 'The peregrination of Doctor Boorde', in T. Hearne, *Benedictus, abbas Petroburgensis, de vita gestis Henrici II et Ricardi I* (1735), 764–804
Likenesses W. B. Rye, etching, 1853, Wellcome L. • Clamp, stipple (after 'Holbein'), Wellcome L. • line engraving (after 'Holbein'), Wellcome L. • woodcut (after original, 1547), NPG [*see illus.*]
Wealth at death see will, PRO, PROB 11/32, fols. 217–18

Boosey, Leslie Arthur (1887–1979), music publisher, was born in Bromley, Kent, on 26 July 1887, the eldest of five children (three sons and two daughters) of Arthur Boosey, music publisher, and his wife, Lucy Ashton. After some years at Malvern College he chose, instead of going to a university, to work for a time in the music publishing house of Durand in Paris, before joining the family business, a conservative and rather old-fashioned one largely associated at that time with the Boosey Ballad Concerts in the Albert Hall.

In 1908 Boosey joined the 22nd London regiment (the Queen's) as a territorial officer, and during the First World War served with it in France (1915–18). Captured, as a major, in the March offensive of 1918, he was put up against a wall to be shot for refusing to give information to the enemy: at the last moment, however, the German officer changed his mind: 'All right', he said, 'you can go back; you're a gentleman'. Boosey was recommended for appointment to the DSO, but the recommendation miscarried—the first but not the last occasion on which deserved recognition, sponsored by responsible people, was not forthcoming. He was, however, appointed a chevalier of the Légion d'honneur. On 28 April 1921 Boosey married Ethel Torfrida (*b.* 1898/9), daughter of Frank Marchant, paper maker; they had three sons and a daughter.

When he got back to the publishing business in 1920, Boosey had to adapt himself to conditions very different from those of 1914. Recording and radio transmission had created new problems and possibilities, and Boosey met the challenge by establishing firm friendships with many leading composers. A merger with the firm of Hawkes, completed in 1930, led to important developments in the manufacture of musical instruments and increased publishing activity, especially in the American market. The culmination of this vigorous expansion came with the acquisition in 1947 of the Koussevitsky catalogue, which added the names of Prokofiev, Rakhmaninov, and Stravinsky to a list that already included those of Strauss, Bartók, Copland, and Britten. By this time the firm of Boosey and Hawkes, in its own field, was one of the most influential in the world.

Leslie Boosey was an adventurous and shrewd publisher, but he was also a very scrupulous one. His weakness, if weakness it was, lay in his readiness to trust everybody and to believe that people would not do to him the things he would never do to them: he lived to learn that this was over-optimistic. In the later years of his publishing career he began to find himself involved in circumstances that were distasteful; and in 1963, after some years of increasing discomfort, he severed his connection with the firm whose prosperity he had done so much to create and sustain.

Boosey retained until the end of his life a great influence in the Performing Right Society, which he had joined in 1926, and whose chairman he became in 1929. This office he held with distinction until 1954, when he gave up the post to Sir Arthur Bliss. During his period of office he attended all the great international conferences, where he was respected by publishers, authors, and composers alike. In 1976 he was awarded the International Society's gold medal. He was also honoured by the Royal Philharmonic Society of London, with which he was closely associated during most of his life.

Boosey should be remembered, if for nothing else, for the fact that in 1944, by his personal initiative, he saved the Royal Opera House from becoming a Mecca dance-hall. He had learnt that a lease was about to be signed which would produce that very result, and he acted quickly. With his partner Ralph Hawkes, having been to Washington to gain the support of Lord Keynes, he secured the lease for the firm of Boosey and Hawkes and the Covent Garden Opera Company. It was an achievement of great importance at the time and for the future.

A casual observer, meeting Leslie Boosey, might have taken him for a typically urbane and conventional businessman; it would have been a mistake, for beneath the polished surface there lay a different reality. Experience in the trenches, which included the death of a loved brother and many friends, had led him to examine and reject most of the comfortable beliefs learned at home and at school, and to search for more dependable convictions. His mind was naturally sceptical and critical; he read widely in philosophy, theology, history, and science, and wrote a great deal, though not for publication. He was always ready to submit his views to criticism and discussion. And these studies, continued until the onset of his last illness, were undertaken not as an intellectual pastime, but in order to discover a way of life. That he was successful in this endeavour is suggested by the fact that he was able to accept without bitterness the realization that a long and helpful career had passed without public recognition—a source of surprise and regret to those who knew his work. His gaiety, his lively mind, and his amused observation of the world and its ways, made him a sought-after companion in the Savile Club and elsewhere. To those fortunate enough to know him better he was a great deal more than that.

Leslie Boosey died at his home, Meadowlands, Hambledon Road, Denmead, Hampshire, on 5 September 1979.

THOMAS ARMSTRONG, *rev.*

Sources personal knowledge (1986) • *WWW* • m. cert. • d. cert. • *CGPLA Eng. & Wales* (1979)
Archives FILM BFI NFTVA, news footage
Wealth at death £185,194: probate, 5 Dec 1979, *CGPLA Eng. & Wales*

Boot [*née* Rowe], **Florence Annie**, **Lady Trent** (1863–1952), businesswoman and benefactor, was born at 5 Grove Place, St Helier, Jersey, on 29 July 1863, the second daughter of William Henry Rowe and his wife, Margaret Agnes, *née* Campbell, who conducted a flourishing business as booksellers and stationers in Queen Street, St Helier. As a young woman she assisted in the shop, and later stated that she knew well what shop life was as she could never remember a time when she was not in one, learning from her father that all labour was dignified, that to be courteous and obliging was a great asset in business, and that life in a shop could be a high calling.

Jesse *Boot (1850–1931) went to the island to convalesce in 1886, having suffered a physical breakdown as a result of overwork. He was of a staunch Methodist family and it is believed that Florence met him at one of the nonconformist chapels of St Helier. They were married at St Helier's parish church on 30 August 1886 and, when his health improved, returned together to Nottingham to develop Boot's flourishing business. In 1896 a branch of Boots the Chemist opened in St Helier in premises adjacent to the Rowe's shop, and eventually the businesses were united—thus, under Florence Boot's influence, combining the sale of stationery and fancy goods with the original pharmaceutical trade.

The service which Boot provided to the nation by the provision of cheap and pure remedies through his chain of chemist's shops and his role as a benefactor were recognized in 1909 by the award of a knighthood and in 1928 by his elevation to the peerage as Baron Trent of Nottingham. His wife shared fully in his business interests, taking a particular interest in 'no. 2 department' (stationery, books, fancy goods, and so on), staff relations, and establishing social clubs and activities in the factories and larger branches.

By 1928 Baron Trent was severely disabled by arthritis and he and his wife retired to Jersey to spend the last years of his life at Villa Millbrook, near the sea-front of St Aubin's Bay. Their benefactions to the island were many. Lord Trent created the Florence Boot (F. B.) Fields for the promotion of sport among the youth, paid for the complete rebuilding of one of the town schools, and built three estates of houses for rental at reasonable prices to respectable working-class families. After his death in 1931, Lady Trent continued his philanthropic work. She created a well-appointed public park near her residence, naming it the Coronation Park in honour of the coronation of George VI, with which its completion coincided. In memory of her husband she totally refurbished the local village church, furnishing and embellishing it with unique glass designed and made by Réné Lalique. A bequest of £2 million was also made towards the establishment of the University of Nottingham.

In old age Lady Trent was a familiar figure in Jersey, being driven sedately in her green Rolls Royce by her green-liveried chauffeur, or waiting in the car outside 'her shop' while goods were brought out for her inspection. She died at St Lawrence, Jersey, in her ninetieth year, on 15 June 1952, and was buried in the family vault which she had created for Baron Trent on a hillside overlooking St Brelade's Bay. Their son, John Campbell *Boot, second (and last) Baron Trent (1889–1956), continued the generous family tradition, donating land at Beauport to the people of the island, thereby giving public access to one of Jersey's most beautiful small bays. Their two daughters, Dorothy Florence and Margery Amy, also retained homes in the island, to which they were frequent visitors.

F. L. M. Corbet

Sources personal knowledge (2004) • *The Times* (18 June 1952) • *Evening Post* [Jersey] (17 June 1952) • *The Boots Co. centenary report and accounts* (1977) • *100 years of shopping at Boots* (1977) • *Sunday Times* (13 March 1977) • *Sunday Times Magazine* (27 Feb 1977) • Société Jersiaise Library, Jersey, Boot MSS • *Evening Post* [Jersey] (14 June 1928) • *Evening Post* [Jersey] (2 June 1964) • F. L. M. Corbet and others, *A biographical dictionary of Jersey*, [2] (1998), vol. 2 • Burke, *Peerage*

Boot, Henry Albert Howard [Harry] (**1917–1983**), physicist, was born on 29 July 1917 in Hall Green, Birmingham, the elder child and only son of Henry James Boot, electrical engineer at the firm of Bellings, and his wife, Ruby May Beeson. Always known as Harry he was educated at King Edward's High School, Birmingham, and at Birmingham University, where he studied physics and graduated BSc in 1938. He had begun work for his PhD (which he obtained in 1941) when war broke out.

Mark Oliphant, professor of physics at Birmingham University, had recently been to Stanford University where he had encountered the klystron, an electron tube which could generate microwave radiation for use in radar. He put Boot, J. T. Randall, and James Sayers to work on the problem of developing microwave generators (centimetric wave transmitters). Boot and Randall used the magnetron, a thermionic valve capable of producing high power oscillations in the microwave region. By late February 1940 they had constructed a new type of cavity magnetron, with a radiation wavelength of 9.8 cm. By May 1940 an experimental radar set using a pulsed 10 cm cavity magnetron had been built at the Telecommunications Research Laboratory, Swanage, and by September 1940 a submarine periscope could be detected at a range of 7 miles.

The cavity magnetron—later improved by James Sayers—crucially influenced the outcome of the war, for centimetric radar enabled a precise radar beam and small lightweight radar transmitters to be used. At first Bomber Command aircraft used the transmitters in night raids, and soon anti-aircraft units, convoy escorts, and night fighters all carried the equipment. Thousands of cavity magnetrons had been manufactured by the end of the Second World War. Boot and Randall were given a prize of £50 from the Royal Society of Arts 'for improving the safety of life at sea' in 1945; when they applied to the royal commission for awards to inventors in 1949 they and James Sayers received £36,000.

In 1943 the Birmingham physics department returned to the study of atomic physics (for atomic bombs) and Boot moved for a time to British Thomson-Houston at Rugby to continue the development of very high power magnetrons. He rejoined the Birmingham department (to help build the cyclotron) in 1945 as a Nuffield research fellow. In 1948 he entered government service as a principal scientific officer with the Royal Naval Scientific Service in the Services Electronics Research Laboratories (SERL) at Baldock in Hertfordshire, and in the same year married Penelope May, daughter of Luke Herrington, an engineer; they had two sons. Boot was appointed senior principal scientific officer in 1954 and remained at Baldock until his retirement in 1977.

During his latter years in Birmingham and at Baldock, Boot continued his work on microwaves and magnetrons and further researched on plasma physics, controlled thermonuclear fusion, lasers, masers, and infrared viewing devices. He had exceptional success in designing, constructing, and operating powerful electrical devices, beginning as a schoolboy with generators of X-rays and of high voltages. He was awarded the John Price Wetherill medal of the Franklin Institute (1958) and the John Scott award (with J. T. Randall, 1959).

Boot and his wife lived for thirty years in a thatched cottage at Rushden, Hertfordshire, with 5 acres of land (although Boot disliked gardening) and a garage full of fifty assorted magnetrons. His great love was sailing; he kept two boats at Salcombe in Devon. He was a quiet, modest, and tactful man, neat in his dress and habits of work. He had a friendly and discerning manner, together with a mildly sardonic sense of humour. Boot died on 8 February 1983 in the Hope Nursing Home, Cambridge. He was survived by his wife. One of the prototype cavity magnetrons built by GEC went to the Institution of Electrical Engineers and several from Boot's own collection were given to Hatfield Polytechnic.

C. S. Nicholls, *rev.*

Sources H. A. H. Boot and J. T. Randall, 'Historical notes on the cavity magnetron', *Institute of Electrical and Electronics Engineers, Transactions on Electron Devices*, ED-23/7 (July 1976) • H. A. H. Boot and A. L. Norberg, interview, 1979, U. Cal., Berkeley, Bancroft Library • private information (1990) [P. B. Moon; M. H. F. Wilkins; P. Boot, widow] • *The Times* (15 Feb 1983), 14f • *New Scientist* (3 March 1983), 602–3 • *CGPLA Eng. & Wales* (1983)

Archives Inst. EE, archives, papers, with J. T. Randall, relating to development of cavity magnetron

Likenesses photograph, repro. in *New Scientist*

Wealth at death £65,071: probate, 11 May 1983, *CGPLA Eng. & Wales*

Boot, Jesse, **first Baron Trent** (**1850–1931**), retail and manufacturing chemist, was born in Nottingham on 2 June 1850, the only son of John Boot (1815–1860), a medical herbalist newly arrived from the country, and his second wife, Mary, daughter of Benjamin Wills of Nottingham. John Boot was a dedicated Wesleyan preacher, but his interest in popular medicine stemmed from the Thomsonians in America rather than from John Wesley's

Jesse Boot, first Baron Trent (1850–1931), by unknown artist

Primitive Physic. However, he brought an evangelistic passion from Wesleyanism into his business, using his itinerant lay ministry as a vehicle for bringing his herbal prescriptions to the poor, and passing his sense of mission and his evangelical nonconformity on to his son.

Boot was only ten when his father died and he shortly had to leave Nottingham high school to work long hours in the little herbalist shop, serving his working-class customers. The masses were now transferring their allegiance to well-advertised patent medicines, so the survival of the business demanded a fresh policy. Boot decided to expand his small proprietary medicine interests and, lacking capital to launch a remedy of his own, hit on the solution of selling a range of others' products at cut prices. Financed by two or three local tradesmen, he launched an advertising campaign in the *Nottingham Daily Express* in February 1877. His boldness caused a minor sensation in the town and increased his weekly takings from £20 to £100.

This campaign launched Boot into the first rank of his branch of retail trade, and established the cardinal points of his business policy for the rest of his long career: old-fashioned retailers, high turnover with small profit margins, and regular attempts to establish his own proprietary lines. He won the steadfast support of a circle of friends and employees, but also provoked bitter hostility and recurrent difficulties with those who had vested interests. After building attractive premises in Nottingham in 1883, he began to replicate his successful formula by opening branches in Lincoln, Sheffield, and other towns within a short train journey. He had always manufactured some of his own remedies, and in 1885 began to lease space in various factories near Nottingham's Midland Station. However, the most important development at this time came when Boot incorporated his rapidly growing business. A legal action that went all the way to the House of Lords, *Pharmaceutical Society* v. *The London and Provincial Supply Association Ltd*, produced the far-reaching decision that limited-liability companies could employ qualified pharmacists. Boot grasped the opportunity to move into dispensing and, more importantly, to recruit a corps of educated men with the ability to manage his retail branches. Always enthusiastic about shop display, advertising, and packaging, Boot established his own building, shopfitting, and printing departments, to give rapid form to his endless flow of ideas. A trip to America in 1889 further enlarged his ambitions.

Boot worked so hard to build up his business that in 1886 he suffered a nervous breakdown. He went for the first holiday of his life to Jersey, where he fell in love with Florence Annie Rowe [*see* Boot, Florence Annie (1863–1952)], who worked for her father, William Rowe, in a small bookshop in St Helier. After their marriage on 30 August 1886, Florence maintained her business interests by building up 'no. 2 department' (stationery, books, fancy goods, pictures, and so forth) within Boot's shops. She also acted as personnel manager for all the women employed in the company's shops, warehouses, and factories.

Boot's retail expansion now seemed to be hemmed in by the vigorous growth of Taylor's Drug Stores, which spread out from Leeds, and Day's Drug Stores, which dominated the metropolitan area, and he was threatened by other growing chains based on Bristol and Portsmouth. Seeking allies to conquer new territories, Boot first went into partnership with Alderman (later Sir) James Duckworth (1840–1915) of Rochdale, a Methodist tea dealer who had built up a grocery chain; together they colonized much of Lancashire. Boot's greatest retail coup came in 1901 when he acquired Day's companies in London and the south of England—sixty-five shops and two warehouses. He now began to advertise in the national press as well as leading provincial dailies. His acquisitions increased his drive for more outlets; the number of branches rose from 251 in 1901 to 560 in 1914, and he was constantly refitting and extending his existing premises. In 1903 one of the Nottingham shops was demolished to build a prestige departmental store in the then fashionable Gothic style, and the successful experiment was soon repeated in a sequence of other large towns. Boot's urge to build was complemented by his wife's passion for interior décor and ornamentation. In historic towns they restored, or created, new shop frontages in medieval style, while the seal of good taste was conferred by Mrs Boot's Booklovers' Library and tearooms in the larger branches.

The phenomenal growth of Boots was not achieved without stiff opposition, partly from the Pharmaceutical Society, but more particularly from a militant association of small retail chemists which called itself the Proprietary Articles Trade Association (PATA). It united the private chemists to force selected manufacturers to adopt resale price maintenance. Boot attacked the PATA by advertisements in the press and in his shops, and by lobbying in parliament. He formed the Drug Companies' Association to collect support, but the overall effect of the opposition was to restrain him, especially when the PATA began stirring up the Pharmaceutical Society. Attempts were made to introduce legislation to prevent companies employing pharmacists (1903–8), all without success, but the personal toll on Jesse Boot's health was heavy.

The First World War gave Boots the opportunity to embark upon the manufacture of fine chemicals, but otherwise did not change the basic structure of the business. Now gripped by chronic arthritis, Boot struggled on to the end of the war, when failing health finally forced him to retire. He had no faith in his only son, John Campbell *Boot, so in 1920 he sold his controlling interest in the business to Louis K. Liggett, chief of the Rexall group of chemists in America. The business continued trading as Boots the Chemists and by the end of the twentieth century was one of the most important retail chains in Britain, with an outlet in most towns of any size in the country.

Boot retired to Jersey, wondering how to spend the £2.275 million proceeds from the sale; his wife, son, and two daughters were extravagant, and he wanted to invest in something durable. He gave large sums to his native city to provide parks, boulevards, and hospital wards, but the main beneficiary was University College, Nottingham, which was rebuilt on a palatial scale on a green-field site outside the town. After the building was opened by King George V in 1928, Boot, a knight since 1909 and baronet since 1916 (thanks to his gifts to the Liberal Party), was created Baron Trent of Nottingham. He died at Vallée, on the island of Jersey, on 13 June 1931, his wife surviving him.

S. D. Chapman

Sources S. D. Chapman, *Jesse Boot of Boots the Chemists* (1974) • S. D. Chapman, 'Jesse Boot: a postscript', *Boots News* (7 July 1976) [house magazine] • J. E. Greenwood, *A cap for Boots: an autobiography* (1977) • *The Times* (15 June 1931) • S. D. Chapman, 'Boot, Jesse', *DBB* • *DNB* • d. cert.

Archives U. Nott. | Bodl. Oxf., corresp. with Asquith relating to the *Nottingham Daily Express* • Boots Company plc Library | SOUND BL NSA, documentary recording

Likenesses C. L. J. Doman, bust, U. Nott. • portrait, Boots Company plc, Nottingham [*see illus.*]

Wealth at death £222,317: administration with will, 31 Aug 1931, *CGPLA Eng. & Wales*

Boot, John Campbell, second Baron Trent (1889–1956), retail and manufacturing chemist, was born on 19 January 1889 in Nottingham, the only son of Jesse *Boot (1850–1931), the founder of Boots retail chain and manufacturing chemists. His mother, Florence Annie *Boot, *née* Rowe (1863–1952), being as absorbed in the business as his father, young John was brought up alongside their day-long attention to the continued development of Boots shops.

Boot was educated at the Leys School, Cambridge, and then spent a year at Jesus College, Cambridge, but was no scholar and greatly disappointed his father. He was employed in trivial work in the business until the First World War, when he was commissioned in the Sherwood Foresters, but served without distinction. In 1914 he married Margaret Joyce Pyman, the daughter of a shipowner. Jesse Boot's opinion of his son was so low that in 1920, following a period of ill health, he sold his controlling interest in Boots to an American group, the L. K. Liggett Company.

One of the few conditions attaching to the sale was that Liggetts should find jobs for Boot and the young finance director, J. E. Greenwood. To the elder Boot's surprise, the two were made directors, and took the lead as the first Boots executives to visit the US, where they studied efficient management practice and devised a new system to replace the autocracy left by the founder. Boot deeply resented his father's sell-out and took a sequence of initiatives to increase the company's independence, beginning with the sale of 25 per cent of the shares and flotation of a public company in 1923. This commitment to British control climaxed in the autumn of 1932, when the American owners became insolvent and were forced to sell. Boot placed himself at the head of a financial consortium which succeeded in driving off a more powerful syndicate in which Liggett allied himself with Philip Hill, the property tycoon and chairman of Beechams Pills, Taylors Cash Chemists (a northern retail chain), Timothy Whites (a southern chain), and a clutch of proprietary medicine companies. Boot's father had died the previous year and the new Lord Trent inherited not only his title but also, after the twelve years of American interregnum, his personal authority in the firm.

Despite their personal differences, Trent's interests within the business proved strikingly similar to those of his father. He made himself an undisputed authority on Boots shops and retail trade generally, and developed an almost instinctive sense of the efficiency of any branch he entered. But he was not so interested in manufacturing, which consequently continued to be the Cinderella of the business. Export sales were no more than a spillover from the firm's domestic retail operations. He calculated the strength of the business by the number of retail branches and regarded the closure of a shop as a defeat. In the 1920s the head of his estates department was opening a shop nearly every week; almost all of them were small pharmacies carrying traditional chemists' lines, as Trent believed that these were still the most profitable form of retailing in his sector of trade. The overall effect of this concentration on small shops was to reduce the importance of Boots departmental stores; by 1936 non-chemists' merchandise was down to a mere 13 per cent of turnover. The concentration on new retail outlets was challenged by Greenwood but Trent's policy prevailed until his retirement in 1954; he proudly opened the thousandth shop in 1933, and by the outbreak of war in 1939 another two hundred had been added. Probably the only divergence between Trent and his father on retail policy was that the former consciously strove to avoid the model of the popular American drug store. His aim was to raise Boots from a chain of cut-price medicine stores to well-appointed shops that offered value for money with variety, quality, and courteous service.

Trent's style of living was in total contrast to that of his father. He pursued to the full the life of a rich and distinguished businessman and public figure. He enjoyed hunting, shooting, fishing, and farming, indulging his passion at the 45,000 acre estate at Glenborrodale that his mother bought for him soon after his father's death. He liked to tour agricultural shows, exhibit pedigree animals, and distribute prizes. He was always immaculately dressed, owned a yacht and a fleet of cars, and entertained lavishly through the autumn at Glenborrodale and at Christmas at Lenton House, Nottingham. He was passionate about Scotland, prided himself on the Scottish line in his ancestry (commemorated in his name, John Campbell Boot), and loved to be a laird, wear a kilt, and retain his own piper. He fed this romantic streak by spending hours reading about Scotland and its history.

Trent inherited something of his parents' benevolent interest in the labour force, and the prosperity of Boots in the 1930s encouraged him to allow a substantial welfare dividend to factory workers. They in turn offered him their personal loyalty, as they had to his father. He toured the factories each Christmas to greet hundreds of staff and provide a direct personal connection. The opening of the first model factory at Beeston, Nottingham, in May 1932 not only introduced more pleasant working conditions for 1140 staff, but also led to an appreciable increase in productivity which allowed the company to reduce the working week from 47.5 to 42.5 hours per week and inaugurate the five-day week in 1934. A second factory was built on the Beeston site in two stages in 1936 and 1938, allowing the transfer of 'dry goods' from the jumble of buildings in the city centre. A general pension fund for all male staff over twenty-one and female staff over thirty-five was launched in 1935, and a new building for Boots College, a day continuation college for the youngest employees, was built in 1938. These attractive innovations placed Boots in the forefront of progress in workers' welfare in Britain. Trent was as proud to demonstrate his achievements for his workers as any manorial lord was to show off his model estates.

During the Second World War Trent became civil commissioner for the east midlands region, effectively leaving J. P. Savage in charge of Boots. He was made KBE in 1946. The war years took their toll on Trent's health and in 1951 he suffered the first of a series of illnesses which forced him to retire in 1953. There were no major initiatives in Boots in the early post-war years, except that falling profitability compelled Trent to appoint a bright young accountant, Arthur Cockfield, whose policies laid the foundation of the later resurgence of the firm. Trent died at his home, The Grove, St Lawrence, Jersey, on 8 March 1956, after a long period of ill health. He had four daughters but no heir in the business, so that control passed out of family hands when his son-in-law, W. R. Norman, retired from the chairmanship in 1975.

S. D. CHAPMAN

Sources S. D. Chapman, *Jesse Boot of Boots the Chemists* (1974) • J. E. Greenwood, *A cap for Boots: an autobiography* (1977) • J. M. Keyworth, *Cabbages and things: the background and story of the Covent Garden property companies to 1970* (privately published, 1990) • private information (2004) • m. cert. • *WWW* • Burke, *Peerage* • *CGPLA Eng. & Wales* (1956)

Archives Boots Company plc, Nottingham | U. Nott., Boots archives

Likenesses portraits, Boots Company plc, Nottingham • portraits, U. Nott.

Wealth at death £7806 5*s*. 5*d*. effects in England: probate, 25 June 1956, *CGPLA Eng. & Wales*

Booth, Abraham (1734–1806), Particular Baptist minister and author, was born at Blackwell, near Alfreton, Derbyshire, on 20 May 1734, the son of Robert Booth (*bap.* 1700) and Elizabeth Bradley. While an infant his parents moved to Annesley Woodhouse, Nottinghamshire, where his father had taken a small farm as a tenant of the duke of Portland. As the eldest of a large family he assisted them until his sixteenth year, during which time he was never at school for longer than six months, but on leaving farm labour for the stocking-frame trade he was able to support himself and get some further elementary education. On reaching his twenty-fourth year he married Elizabeth Bowmar (*d. c.*1804), a farmer's daughter, and soon afterwards he opened a school at Sutton in Ashfield, Nottinghamshire.

Early in life the preaching of some evangelical General Baptists awakened in Booth a sense of religion, and in 1755 he was baptized by immersion and began preaching in the east midlands. In 1760 he became superintendent of the Kirkby Woodhouse congregation, but declined to be their pastor. Up to this point he had been a strenuous advocate of Arminian doctrines and, when twenty years old, had written a poem on 'Absolute Predestination', but he now changed his views to the Calvinistic doctrines held by the Particular Baptists, and accordingly seceded. This change took place at the same time as he was in contact with ministers from the Northamptonshire Association such as Sutcliff, Fuller, Ryland, and the younger Hall. Soon after he began to preach on Sundays at Sutton in Ashfield, Chesterfield, and other east midland towns and villages, and kept his school, which was his only source of income, during the rest of the week. At this period he composed *The Reign of Grace* (1768; 2nd edn, 1771). Henry Venn, author of the *Complete Duty of Man*, read this work in manuscript and as a consequence travelled to Nottinghamshire to see him, a meeting which resulted in a lifelong friendship. Venn wrote the prefaces to both the first and second editions. Soon after its publication, the Particular Baptist church of Little Prescot Street, Goodman's Fields, London, invited Booth to be their pastor. He accepted the call and was ordained on 16 February 1769.

In 1770 Booth published *The Death of Legal Hope, the Life of Evangelical Obedience* as a supplement to *The Reign of Grace*, which was directed against the extremes of Arminianism and antinomianism. Theologically he was closer to the hyper-Calvinists than to Andrew Fuller, the leading Particular Baptist theologian of the day, whom he accused of abandoning true Calvinism. The hyper-Calvinists adhered to a theological system that emphasized the sovereignty of God in the work of salvation, yet ignored or denied man's responsibility. He was nevertheless a fervent and loyal supporter of the Baptist Missionary Society, one of the few London ministers to be so. He was active also in believing the gospel contained a complete warrant for the ungodly to believe in Jesus Christ, and this was the theme of his *Glad Tidings to Perishing Sinners* (1796). A strong opponent of infant baptism and open communion, his *Paedobaptism Examined* (1784), written as an answer to the posthumous work of the celebrated Matthew Henry, brought him into conflict with Edward Williams (1750–1813).

Booth died in London on 27 January 1806 aged seventy-one, having been a minister for fifty years. He was buried in the Maze Pond church burial-ground, London, and a marble tablet was erected to his memory in the Little Prescot Street church. His wife had died about four years before him, and he was survived by several children. Booth was a man of strong muscular frame and of sound constitution, whose private life was distinguished by purity and kindness. A female member of his church once left him a handsome legacy but, on finding that there were poor relations of hers still living, he went to the Bank of England and transferred the whole amount to them. Unostentatious and a man of simple tastes, he hated flattery and deceit. He was a firm believer in religious liberty, though somewhat dogmatic in stating his own view, particularly in later years. His early experiences gave him a sound understanding of men and affairs, but his eager mind was always handicapped by his lack of real education. This gave him a concern for ministerial education, which in turn led to the formation of the Baptist Education Society in 1804. This interest he pursued vigorously with help from William Newman, the pastor of a church in Bow, and two of his own deacons, William Taylor and Joseph Gutteridge. After his death the Education Society became the Stepney Academy and, later still, moved to Oxford, where it became Regent's Park College.

JOHN WESTBY-GIBSON, *rev.* E. F. CLIPSHAM

Sources J. Rippon, *A short memoir of the Rev. Abraham Booth* (1806) · W. Jones, *An essay on the life and writings of Mr Abraham Booth* (1808) · A. Taylor, *History of the English General Baptists*, 2: *The new connection of General Baptists* (1818) · A. C. Underwood, *A history of the English Baptists* (1947) · 'Mr. Booth's address to the missionaries', *Baptist Magazine*, 1 (1809), 267–72, 308–12 · 'Letter of the late Mr. Booth on the Arian scheme', *Baptist Magazine*, 2 (1810), 62–6, 95–100 · *IGI* · E. A. Payne, 'Abraham Booth and some of his descendants', *Baptist Quarterly*, 16 (1955–6), 196–9

Archives Regent's Park College, Oxford, Angus Library, family letters and MSS

Likenesses J. Collyer, stipple, pubd 1806 (after J. Robinson), NPG · MacKenzie, engraving, repro. in Jones, *An essay on the life and writings of Mr Abraham Booth* · Ridley and Hall, engraving, repro. in A. Booth, *The reign of grace*, rev. edn (1819), frontispiece

Booth, Alfred (1834–1914), merchant and shipowner, was born on 3 September 1834 in Liverpool, the eldest son of Charles Booth (1799–1860) of the same city and Emily Fletcher (1803–1853). His father's family ran a corn-factoring business and his mother's side was descended from West Indies merchants. He was educated at Edgbaston proprietary school and at the Liverpool Mechanics' Institute. In 1867 he married Lydia Allen Butler; they raised six children, two sons and four daughters.

Booth did not enter the family business but from 1850 worked for Lamport and Holt, shipping agents. His younger brother Charles *Booth (1840–1916), subsequently famous for his pioneering social investigations, joined him, but Alfred Booth left in 1857 for a brief appointment with Rathbones in New York, where he gained valuable experience in transatlantic trading. In 1860 he formed a partnership with Charles, and an American named Walden, to act as commission agents. More by chance than design they found themselves exporting skins to the United States, a small specialist business which exploited Booth's detailed knowledge and contacts but which did not compete with established trading. On Walden's retirement in 1863, the partnership was reconstituted as Alfred Booth & Co. of Liverpool and Booth & Co. of New York, with the brothers as principals, Alfred in the United States and Charles in Britain. Although supplemented by agency work and produce handling, the business was slow to prosper. Commission work brought only modest returns and the usual problems of price and seasonal fluctuations and the remittance of funds dogged the enterprise. However, improving American prospects after the civil war and investment in leather manufacturing on both sides of the Atlantic did increase profitability.

Encouraged perhaps by Charles Booth's fascination with steam shipping at a time when the compound engine was revolutionizing cargo traffic, and drawing upon their experience with Lamport and Holt, the brothers formed a shipping company to trade with northern Brazil. This market avoided competition with the established carriers to the east coast of Latin America but the new company could not afford a prolonged clash with R. Singlehurst & Co., which was already exploiting the Amazon business. Since cargo volumes were still small and sailing ships undercut steamers, profits eluded the Booths until they created commercial stability through agreements with their competitors. Booths integrated leather and shipping into mutually supportive activities as Brazilian skins were exchanged for American produce, with the parent firm acting as a holding company. By 1914 Booths dominated the Amazon trade, operating one of Liverpool's largest fleets, and owned the Surpass Tanning Company in America, which obtained international status in kid leather.

Booth's contribution to the success of the firm which bore his name is hard to evaluate. He certainly possessed qualities crucial for business success—sound judgement, an inability to suffer fools gladly, composure during commercial crises, and a methodical approach to administration. His tactical awareness complemented his brother's longer-term strategic sense. But Booth regarded business as a means to secure the financial independence required for the pursuit of life as a country gentleman, in complete contrast to his brother. He retired early, in 1887, before the firm's conspicuous success. Moreover, his experience and sources of funds, even the survival of the business in moments of crisis, owed much to the family alliances with the pillars of Liverpool's commercial élite, the Holts, the Lamports, and the Rathbones. Luck, hard work, and adaptability enabled Booth to learn from past mistakes and to seize opportunities when they arose.

In his private life Booth, though reserved, inspired loyalty and affection. In the best traditions of Liverpool merchants he gave generously of his time and money to public and philanthropic activities, both as a magistrate and as a devout Unitarian. Politically, he supported the Liberal cause. He died at his home, 46 Ullet Road, Toxteth Park, Liverpool, on 2 November 1914, of pneumonia and heart failure. ROBERT G. GREENHILL

Sources R. Greenhill, 'Booth, Alfred', *DBB* • A. H. John, *A Liverpool merchant house: being the history of Alfred Booth and Company, 1863–1958* (1959) • H. A. Whitting, *Alfred Booth: some memories, letters and other family records* (privately printed, Liverpool, 1917) • T. S. Simey and M. B. Simey, *Charles Booth: social scientist* (1960) • *Liverpool Courier* (3 Nov 1914) • *The Times* (3 Nov 1914) • G. Chandler, *Liverpool shipping* (1960) • d. cert. • *CGPLA Eng. & Wales* (1915) • *Alfred Booth, 1834–1914: a biographical sketch*

Likenesses portrait, repro. in John, *Liverpool merchant house* • portrait, repro. in Whitting, *Alfred Booth*

Wealth at death £43,753 2s. 1d.: probate, 14 Jan 1915, *CGPLA Eng. & Wales*

Booth, Bartholomew (*bap.* 1732, *d.* 1785), Church of England clergyman and schoolmaster, was born at Mellor, Derbyshire, where he was baptized in the village chapel on 7 October 1732, the son of Bartholomew Booth (*d.* 1750), the village schoolmaster. His family appears to have belonged to a cadet branch of the Booth family of Dunham Massey, Cheshire, earls of Warrington and barons Delamer. Taught initially by his father, Booth continued his education at Manchester grammar school from 1750 to 1752 before taking up a temporary post as usher to the schoolmaster at Marple, Cheshire. He married Mary Chatterton (*d.* 1789) of Marple on 6 March 1753, and from 1754 was a student at Brasenose College, Oxford, which he left in 1756 without taking a degree.

Appointed master of the charity school at Disley, Cheshire, in 1756, Booth served as a deacon at Disley before his ordination as a priest at Chester on 2 July 1758 and his appointment in 1760 as curate of Marple chapel. When his wife's growing mental instability intensified shortly thereafter, he separated from her and took custody of William and Robert, the elder two of their three sons. After a series of brief curacies in Derbyshire—at St Alkmund's, Derby, in 1762 and Brassington in 1764—and an equally brief period as second master of Derby grammar school in 1763–4, he moved to Liverpool, where he opened a private academy on the waterfront in 1765. There he quickly gained the patronage of two wealthy sisters, Mary Valens (1740–1810), who thereafter became his 'constant companion', and Anne Bardsley (1732–1781), a young widow. With their assistance, both financial and domestic, Booth opened in 1766 Woolton Academy, a boarding-school located at Woolton Hall, near Liverpool. There he and his assistant master, Peter Newby (1745–1827), offered an unusually wide and enlightened curriculum, comprising English grammar, Latin, Greek, French, German, writing, arithmetic, merchants' accounts, geography, navigation, astronomy, surveying, mathematics, drawing, perspective, music, dancing, and fencing. This type of education, which echoed much of Benjamin Franklin's educational philosophy, attracted the sons of the landed and mercantile classes from all parts of England and from North America, among whom were the future bibliophile George Hibbert (1757–1837) and the future general and MP Isaac Gascoyne (*c.*1760–1841).

After selling Woolton Hall in 1772, Booth moved his academy briefly to High Beach in Essex, before emigrating to Maryland with his two sons and two patronesses in the summer of 1773 to begin a new life away from the 'mean repinings' (Newby, 51) of his wife. Again with the financial assistance of his two female companions Booth purchased a substantial tract of land called the Forest of Needwood, near Frederick, in western Maryland, where he planned to spend the rest of his days quietly as a planter. Unusually for an Anglican clergyman, Booth identified with the republican cause at the outbreak of the American War of Independence in 1776. Following considerable pressure from certain of the American leaders who were aware of his sound reputation as a schoolmaster in England, he sought and eventually obtained extraordinary permission from the Maryland legislature to open at the Forest of Needwood an academy which operated from 1778 until 1785. To this school, which was one of the few in the emerging United States to exist without interruption throughout the war, significant numbers of prominent Americans sent their sons. Booth's patrons included General Benedict Arnold, Dr James Craik, Richard Henry Lee, Robert Morris, the financier of the revolution, Dr William Shippen, and George Washington, whose nephew and heir Bushrod Washington was Booth's student.

Despite his close and unwavering identification with the republican cause, Booth, as a recent English immigrant, was viewed with suspicion by the local populace in western Maryland. He was eventually forced to move his academy in 1783 to a new estate in Maryland, close to modern Hagerstown, to which he gave the name Delamer. There his educational work continued until an unspecified illness led to his untimely death on or about 10 September 1785; he was buried on his estate a few days later.

Booth's two elder sons perished at sea in the winter of 1785 *en route* from Maryland for Britain on a visit to their estranged mother and their younger brother, John. The latter emigrated to the United States in 1786 to claim his inheritance, but a considerable part of the schoolmaster's large estate, valued at £8445 in Maryland currency, reverted on his death to Mary Valens, who in 1786 married Booth's close friend and confidant General Horatio *Gates (1727?–1806).

Bartholomew Booth owed his success as an educator to a number of factors. His ability to combine skilfully all that was best in the classical tradition with the most useful elements of a 'modern' curriculum appealed greatly to enlightened parents on both sides of the Atlantic; and the substantial financial support of his two patronesses, combined with the continued support of a tightly knit, transatlantic, and largely masonic network of educational patrons, helped to give his work a prominence that it might not otherwise have enjoyed. MAURICE WHITEHEAD

Sources M. Whitehead, *The academies of the Reverend Bartholomew Booth in Georgian England and revolutionary America* (1996) · P. N. [P. Newby], *Six pastorals* (1773) · parish register, Mellor chapel, Derbyshire [baptism], 7 Oct 1732 · parish register, Stockport [burial of Bartholomew Booth the elder], 10 Jan 1750 · Manchester grammar school register · Brasenose College register · parish register, Cheadle, St Mary's [marriage], 6 March 1753 · parish register, Marple chapel [death of Mary Booth], 24 Sept 1789 · parish register, Liverpool, St George's [birth of Mary Valens], 23 Dec 1740 · burial register, New York city, Trinity Church, 1810 [burial of Mary Valens] · *Maryland Journal and Baltimore Advertiser* (16 Sept 1785)

Archives Maryland Diocesan Archives, Baltimore, collection · Maryland State Archives, Annapolis, papers · Washington County Museum of Fine Arts, Hagerstown, Maryland, papers | Maryland Historical Society, Baltimore, Horsey collection · NYPL, Astor, Lenox, and Tilden foundations, files

Likenesses oils, *c.*1760, Washington County Museum of Fine Arts, Hagerstown, Maryland

Wealth at death £8445 [Maryland currency]; incl. £2286 inventory; also £6159 owing to estate: inventory, 12 Nov 1785, Maryland State Archives, Annapolis, Washington County (Inventories), A#2, fols. 33–9, will, 19 Sept 1785, Washington County Wills, T.S. no. 1, fols. 208–10

Booth, Barton (1681–1733), actor, was the youngest of the three sons of John Booth, a Lancashire squire and a member of the extended family of the earls of Warrington. His family moved to London in 1684 after their estate became impaired. He was sent to Westminster School, then under the headmastership of Dr Richard Busby, where he developed a taste for both poetry and performance. He made his first acting appearance there as Pamphilus in a school production of Terence's *Andria*. Although arrangements had been made for him to attend Trinity College, Cambridge, in order later to pursue a clerical career, Booth instead sought to join the acting profession. Following an unsuccessful application to Thomas Betterton at the playhouse in Lincoln's Inn Fields, in June 1698 he set off to Dublin to act for Joseph Ashbury at the Smock Alley Theatre. He gave his first professional performance there, in 'blackface' as Oroonoko, earning himself 5 guineas. This initial success ensured his engagement for the 1698–9 season in Dublin, and he was entrusted with key roles in three of George Etherege's comedies: *The Comical Revenge*, *The Man of Mode*, and *She Would if she Could*.

Booth was back in London in 1700 and, with a letter of introduction from Lord Fitzhardinge and the recommendation of the actor John Boman (or Bowman), was accepted by Betterton at Lincoln's Inn Fields. He gave his first performance there late in 1700 as Maximus in John Fletcher's *Valentinian*, and was sufficiently impressive to be offered that December the role of Artaban in the first play by his former schoolfriend Nicholas Rowe, *The Ambitious Stepmother*. In January 1701 he appeared as Gratiano in Lord Lansdowne's *The Jew of Venice*, typical of the secondary roles he was to continue playing for the next decade. In 1704 he married Frances (*d.* 1710), the second daughter of Sir William Barkham, third baronet, of Norfolk.

Betterton moved to the newly erected Queen's Theatre in the Haymarket on 17 April 1705, taking Booth with him. Booth continued to play supporting characters, but slowly developed a firm reputation for serious roles. His annual salary of £100 was not as substantial as those paid to his seniors, Betterton, Robert Wilks, John Mills, and George Powell; his talents were clearly being ignored by Wilks, who had considerable say in the casting of productions and who would invariably favour his friend, the less capable John Mills. However, Booth was an ambitious and hard-working actor; his persistence paid off, winning him better roles over the years, including Hotspur in *1 Henry IV* and Laertes in *Hamlet*, both in 1707. The company moved during the 1707–8 season to Christopher Rich's Drury Lane Theatre, where Booth appeared for the first time as the Ghost in *Hamlet*, a role in which he was considered to be unrivalled. This was to be a key step in building his reputation as a formidable player of weighty and tragic roles.

The lord chamberlain closed Drury Lane in June 1709 following actors' complaints that Rich maintained a tyrannical regime there. It opened again for the 1709–10 season with Aaron Hill as manager, and with Booth as its leading player, giving performances as Othello, Brutus in *Julius Caesar*, Valentine in William Congreve's *Love for Love*, and Horatio in *Hamlet*. The change in management, however, had not brought an end to the turbulence of the theatre's internal politics, and the actors complained that Hill did not involve them enough in casting decisions. When Hill withdrew a joint management agreement involving eight actors, including Booth, the season was brought to a close with an effective mutiny. With Hill out of London, a group of actors led by Booth, Powell, Theophilus Keene, and John Bickerstaff refused to take to the stage and threatened to make off with a collection of costumes. The situation turned nasty, and ended with a sword being held to Hill's throat. Booth and his fellow rebels were suspended until the end of the season. Repercussions from the incident perhaps manifested themselves during 1710–11, when Booth had to revert to playing some of his secondary roles and to sharing leads with Powell. At the end of this season Booth regained status under the new management of Colley Cibber, Wilks, and Thomas Doggett.

Booth's performance on 17 March 1712 as Pyrrhus in Ambrose Philips's *The Distressed Mother* was much lauded. His achievement was consolidated a year later by his original portrayal of the title role in Joseph Addison's *Cato* (14 April 1713); the critical and financial success of this production brought him to the forefront of his profession, establishing him firmly as an actor of significance, and also served to further his ambition to be admitted to the management of the theatre. A letter to the lord chamberlain (dated 16 December 1712), and the patronage of Lord Bolingbroke, resulted in Cibber, Wilks, and Doggett's receiving the command of Queen Anne to share the management with Booth, causing no small resentment. Booth's key position at the theatre, coupled with his recent accolades, gave him the chance to tackle roles he had long coveted. In the following seasons he gave performances as Timon of Athens, King Lear, Banquo in *Macbeth*, Jaffier in Thomas Otway's *Venice Preserv'd*, Bajazet in Rowe's *Tamerlane*, and Melantius in Beaumont and Fletcher's *The Maid's Tragedy*. He was also an able poet, and published his masque *The Death of Dido* following its performance with music by John Christopher Pepusch at Drury Lane on 17 April 1716.

Booth married his second wife, the actress and dancer Hester Santlow [*see* Booth, Hester (*c*.1690–1773)], on 3 August 1719, at Chipping Ongar, Essex. They enjoyed a successful, loving marriage; his poems on her were affectionate, and in his will he named her as the sole inheritor of his estate. She, in turn, erected a memorial to him in Westminster Abbey forty-five years after his death. There were no children of either marriage.

Though past his prime, Booth continued treading the boards, adding only occasionally to his repertory, for example, with Anthony in John Dryden's *All for Love* and Fainfall in Congreve's *The Way of the World* in 1718. He continued to work hard and regularly, but was often said to perform without any true conviction unless his enthusiasm could be sufficiently mustered. He worked at a steady and reliable pace throughout the 1720s, burdened somewhat by his administrative duties, until September 1726, when he suffered a fever that lasted forty-six days. This effectively kept him from the stage until January 1727. The following season he was to play the part of Julio in Lewis Theobald's *The Double Falsehood*, but was taken ill on the opening night (13 December 1727) and had to be replaced by his understudy. He managed to resume his role on the fifth night, but after his performance on 9 January 1728 Booth walked off the stage for the last time, conceding to an illness which was eventually diagnosed as jaundice.

Booth spent the rest of his life in pursuit of good health. In 1728 he stayed for three months in Bath and a further three weeks in Belgium in search of medical cure and advice. He died back in London, at his home, 4 Charles Square, Covent Garden, on 10 May 1733, following six months of recurring colic and a foolish attempt at a cure which prescribed the daily ingestion of mercury. He was buried, according to his wishes, at the parish church of St Laurence, Cowley, near Uxbridge, on 17 May 1733.

As an actor Booth earned the admiration of his contemporaries. Thomas Davies said he was 'an actor of genius' (Davies, 279), and Theophilus Cibber considered him to have a natural talent, praised his voice and articulation, and commented warmly on his ability in roles of dignity and majesty, particularly Hotspur and Lothario. Aaron Hill spoke of his 'gestures', of his 'particular grace', his 'elegant negligence', and his 'talent of discovering the passions where they lay hid in some celebrated parts by the injudicious practice of other actors' (Russell, 56).

MARK BATTY

Sources D. E. Baker, *Biographia dramatica, or, A companion to the playhouse*, rev. I. Reed, new edn, rev. S. Jones, 2 (1812) • Genest, *Eng. stage* • T. Davies, *Dramatic miscellanies*, 3 vols. (1784) • B. Victor, *Memoirs of the life of Barton Booth* (1733) • Highfill, Burnim & Langhans, *BDA* • W. C. Russell, *Representative actors* [1888] • *IGI*

Likenesses J. Vanderbank, oils, 1733, Garr. Club • G. van der Gaucht, line engraving (after J. Vanderbank), BM, NPG; repro. in Victor, *Memoirs* • G. White, mezzotint (after unknown artist), NPG

Booth, Benjamin (*fl.* **1746–1789**), haberdasher and writer on book-keeping, originated in New England and was born before 1746, possibly the son of Benjamin and grandson of Ebenezer Booth (*d.* 1732), of Stratford, Massachusetts. He began work as a clerk in a New York store about 1759, eventually becoming chief clerk, when he first implemented his own book-keeping system. He subsequently conducted his own haberdashery business for several years, until, apparently, the outbreak of the War of Independence brought it to a close.

Booth then moved to England, where he advertised that he had been in business in New York for thirty years. He endeavoured to publicize his system, which he considered superior to those in general use, by means of his book, *A complete system of bookkeeping … by an improved mode of double entry … [with] … a new method of stating factorage accounts, adapted particularly to the trade of the British colonies* published in London in 1789. The sample invoices shown in the book revealed both humour and literary interest, citing imaginary dealings with Lemuel Gulliver, Peter Pindar, and Tristram Shandy. John Ramsay McCulloch listed Booth's book in his *Literature of Political Economy* (1845), with the erroneous date of 1799 (McCulloch, 139).

No further details of Booth's life are known and he may have returned to America after the book was published. No record of his death has been found.

JOHN BRUNTON

Sources B. Booth, *A complete system of bookkeeping* (1789) • J. N. Booth, *Booths in history* (1982) • P. L. Jacobus, *Genealogy of the Booth family* (1952) • J. Savage, *A genealogical dictionary of the first settlers of New England*, 4 vols. (1860–62), vol. 1 • J. R. McCulloch, *The literature of political economy: a classified catalogue* (1845), 139

Booth, (William) Bramwell (**1856–1929**), Salvation Army officer, was born at Halifax, Yorkshire, on 8 March 1856, the eldest son of William *Booth (1829–1912) and his wife, Catherine *Booth, *née* Mumford (1829–1890), the founders of the Salvation Army. He had two brothers and five sisters, including Catherine Booth-*Clibborn; all the children shared their parents' itinerant lifestyle until the family settled in London in 1865. Bramwell Booth saw the army grow from an obscure Christian mission, established in Whitechapel, into an international organization with numerous and varied social activities. He was educated at home and, briefly, a preparatory school and at the City of London School, where he was bullied. Known to his family as Willie, his health was poor, with digestive ailments, and he had a slight hearing loss. William and Catherine Booth set high standards for their children and Bramwell, as the eldest, found the weight of parental expectation particularly heavy. He was often responsible for his younger siblings, and both parents, William more than Catherine, took young Bramwell into their confidence. In 1870 he went to help in the management of his father's mission and in the cheap food kitchens established in its early days. It was as a teenager that the course of Bramwell's life was set; his parents were totally committed to their work and Bramwell, despite his early wishes to study medicine and his fear of public speaking, became William Booth's amanuensis, adviser, and administrator.

On 12 October 1882 Bramwell married Florence Soper [**Florence Eleanor Booth** (1861–1957)], eldest daughter of Dr Soper, a medical practitioner of Blaenau, Monmouthshire. Florence had joined the Salvation Army in 1880 and worked in France with Bramwell's sister Catherine. After her marriage she took charge of the women's social work. All of their seven children (five daughters and two sons) became active workers in the army.

Bramwell Booth was chief of staff of the Salvation Army from 1881 until his father's death in August 1912. Through Booth's guidance the right to hold open-air meetings—an issue which had brought the army into conflict with many local authorities—was firmly established. In 1885 he was associated with William Thomas Stead (1849–1912) in an attempt to publicize the traffic in young girls, which resulted in the spectacular July 1885 'Maiden tribute of modern Babylon' revelations in Stead's *Pall Mall Gazette* and the passing of the Criminal Law Amendment Act of 1885 raising the age of consent to sixteen years. Owing to Stead's bungling and a technical breach of the law in the collecting of evidence, Booth, Stead, and Rebecca Jarrett, a converted brothel-keeper who assisted them, were arrested and tried at the Old Bailey. Booth was acquitted but the others served prison terms.

William Booth appointed Bramwell his successor. Like his father, Bramwell ruled autocratically, and expected complete obedience. However, what officers would tolerate from William (already glorified as 'The Founder') they would not take from Bramwell. Bramwell was enough of his father's son to stamp down on perceived insubordination and he summarily retired officers with little cause, but seemed to lack his father's willingness to forgive (and reappoint) former objects of his wrath. Allegedly he gave his children posts for which others were better qualified. Discontent simmered among senior officers, including some of Bramwell's brothers and sisters. In his last years he increasingly handed control to his wife, who was given power of attorney when he was away travelling. She had acted as the army's 'first lady' since his mother died in 1890, and she started several army organizations including the Home League, Girl Guards, and League of Mercy.

As chief executive officer Booth was responsible for the preparation of *Orders and Regulations for Officers and Soldiers* and for the direction of the army's propaganda and operations. He wrote *Echoes and Memories* (1925), *These Fifty Years* (1929), and other books, as well as many articles on Bible studies and social problems, and frequent contributions to the press on prison reform, vagrancy, the homeless poor, and emigration. Bramwell did much to develop foreign missions, both as chief of staff and as general of the army. During his generalship the army made rapid progress, and he travelled extensively on its behalf.

The early years of Bramwell's generalship were complicated by the First World War, which threatened the international character of the Salvation Army. Bramwell was able to steer a course that neither offended German salvationists nor outraged British public opinion. As time wore on, senior officers, including Bramwell's sister Evangeline (1845–1950), began to question his leadership. In May 1928 Bramwell's health began to deteriorate, and by September he was suffering from insomnia and depression. His poor health offered those in the army who were dissatisfied with his leadership an opportunity to act, and in January 1929 the army's high council of leading officers was summoned to adjudicate on his fitness for duty. He was relieved of the generalship in February 1929 and a successor elected by the high council.

Bramwell Booth bore a strong facial likeness to his mother. Like both of his parents, Bramwell suffered much from poor health and adopted a vegetarian diet as a means of maintaining his rather fragile constitution. On the platform he presented a striking contrast to his father: the latter played on his hearers' emotions, his son relied on calm and reasoned argument. He was something of a mystic; none the less he inherited his father's flair with finance and property. Although mild and sensitive, he had inherited enough of his father's inflexibility and his mother's didacticism to preclude easy relations with his brothers and sisters and other senior officers; his loyalty to the Salvation Army was unquestionable and lifelong. He was 'promoted to Glory' on 16 June 1929 at his home, The Homestead, Hadley Wood, near Barnet, Hertfordshire, and was buried near his parents in Abney Park cemetery, Stoke Newington, London. Huge numbers attended his funeral. He was commemorated by the Bramwell Booth Memorial Hall, Queen Victoria Street, London. He was survived by his wife, who died on 10 June 1957.

D. C. Lamb, *rev.* L. E. Lauer

Sources C. Bramwell-Booth, *Bramwell Booth* (1933) • R. Hattersley, *Blood and fire* (1999) • B. Booth, *Echoes and memories* (1925) • B. Booth, *These fifty years* (1929) • F. A. Mackenzie, *The clash of the cymbals* (1929) • personal knowledge (1937) • private information (1937) • *CGPLA Eng. & Wales* (1929) • Bramwell Booth personnel file, Salvation Army International Heritage Centre, London

Archives BL, Add. MS 71574 • Salvation Army International Heritage Centre, London, corresp. and addresses • Salvation Army International Heritage Centre, London, Florence Booth papers | BL, corresp. with his wife, Add. MSS 64799–64806 • CAC Cam., letters to W. T. Stead • Georgetown University, Washington, DC, Lauinger Library, letters to Richard Wilson • LPL, corresp. with Edward Benson • NL Aus., corresp. with Alfred Deakin

Likenesses J. Collier, oils, 1924, International HQ of the Salvation Army, 101 Queen Victoria Street, London • E. H. Mills, double portrait, photogravure (with his wife), NPG; repro. in *ILN* • photographs, Salvation Army International Heritage Centre, London • print, NPG

Wealth at death £913 7*s*.: probate, 6 July 1929, *CGPLA Eng. & Wales*

Booth [*née* Mumford], **Catherine** (**1829–1890**), evangelist and writer, was born on 17 January 1829 at Ashbourne, Derbyshire, the fourth of five children. Only she and her younger brother, John, survived. Her father, John Mumford (1804–1879), was a coach builder and wheelwright,

Catherine Booth (1829–1890), by unknown photographer

and for some years a Wesleyan Methodist lay preacher. Her mother, Sarah Milward Mumford (1802–1869), was a devout Methodist. Catherine Mumford was educated by her mother and soon came to share her mother's serious faith. By the time she was twelve she had read the Bible from cover to cover eight times, as well as works by John Wesley, John William Fletcher, and Charles Finney. She spent much of her childhood at home, partly because she suffered from a curvature of the spine and consumption but also because her mother feared that she would meet others who might not share her serious religious convictions. Catherine Mumford's childhood was marked by her father's difficulties. John Mumford broke with the Methodists and took to drink in the early 1840s. His subsequent irregular employment caused his family considerable economic difficulty. The Mumfords' only son emigrated to America in 1849 and occasional references in letters between Catherine and Mrs Mumford make clear that he did not share their religious convictions.

The Mumfords moved to the London area in 1845 and settled in Brixton. Catherine Mumford was a member of the Wesleyan chapel until her ticket of membership was denied over a controversy within the connection. She was loosely associated with a group of Methodists expelled during the 'fly sheets' controversy of 1849. This group sought both greater connectional democracy and openness and the pursuit of a more zealous, evangelistic faith. Catherine began to attend services with the Reformers. She soon met William *Booth (1829–1912), a pawnbroker's assistant and lay preacher already noticed for his energy and devotion. Catherine and William were engaged to be married in 1852.

From 1852 to 1855 Catherine Mumford continued to live in Brixton with her mother. She taught Sunday school, read widely, and assisted her mother with lodgers and other efforts to make ends meet. She carried on an extensive correspondence with her fiancé (now in the British Library manuscripts collection). William began his career in ministry. After several years as a circuit preacher for the Reformers and a short period studying with the Independents, he joined the Methodist New Connexion in 1854 and began to study and preach in preparation for ordination. On 16 June 1855 Catherine and William Booth were married at Stockwell New Chapel in London by an Independent minister, the Revd David Thomas. For the next two years William worked as an itinerant evangelist for the Methodist New Connexion. A regular circuit was the usual assignment, but the Connexion regarded William Booth as an especially gifted evangelist. The Booths were deeply committed to revivalist work in the tradition of Americans James Caughey and Charles Finney, and they were very happy with the success of William's labours. Catherine's first child, (William) Bramwell *Booth (1856–1929), was born in 1856 and the baby accompanied them on their travels.

In 1857 William was assigned to his first Methodist New Connexion circuit at Brighouse, Yorkshire, and Catherine gave birth to her second child, Ballington. In 1858 William was ordained and assigned to Gateshead, where the Booths remained until 1860. They were a great success and more than doubled the congregation. Catherine gave birth to two more children, another Catherine in 1858 [*see* Clibborn, Catherine Booth-] and Emma in 1860. During these years she also published an influential pamphlet on female ministry and began her own preaching career. Her pamphlet was occasioned by the 1859 evangelistic tour of England by the American holiness speaker and writer Mrs Phoebe Palmer (1807–1874). During her tour the Revd A. A. Rees, minister of the Bethesda Free Church in Sunderland, wrote a pamphlet, *Reasons for not Cooperating in the Alleged 'Sunderland Revivals'*, to encourage others to shun Palmer's meetings. Rees asserted that the injunctions of St Paul against female teaching were universal and women were to remain in private under subjugation to men. Catherine then realized her long-standing ambition to write about female preaching. Her pamphlet, *Female teaching, or, The Rev. A. A. Rees versus Mrs Palmer, being a reply to the above gentleman on the Sunderland revival*, was published in December 1859, just days before the birth of her daughter Emma.

Catherine's argument rested on what she termed a common-sense reading of scripture. Passages were considered in light of the particular verse as well as within the context of the chapter and the whole Bible. The historical context was also considered. She argued, for example, that Paul's command 'let your women keep silence in the church' was a charge to the women of Corinth, not to women in all times and places, and it should therefore be read with an earlier passage in which Paul directed women to cover their heads when they prayed or prophesied. She also pointed to the women preachers and prophets in the Old and New testaments, and the passage in Joel; 'your sons and daughters shall prophesy'. Her pamphlet was not hermeneutically original. She drew heavily on the writing of the Methodist Adam Clarke and other nonconformist theologians. Her argument was significant, however, because she made no distinctions between a man's and a woman's call to preach. She argued that any woman called to ministry had the 'right to preach' without any 'man-made restrictions'. She did not believe women's preaching heralded the last days, like many nineteenth-century prophetic figures, nor did she claim women to be the weak, the foolish, or the low. Rather, she asserted that the church must be committed to vigorous soul-saving and that women were essential to that mission. This argument distinguished her from most of her contemporaries, who thought women could preach only with an extraordinary call and when their authority did not extend to other areas of church life. Her pamphlet was widely read and a second edition was printed in 1861. It was substantially revised and reprinted by the Salvation Army in 1870 as *Female Ministry, or, Women's Right to Preach the Gospel*, then much reprinted, anthologized, and quoted.

In 1857 Catherine began to speak in public, addressing female temperance audiences and Band of Hope meetings. She also began to speak on occasional Sundays after her husband's sermon. In 1860 this work became a necessity when her husband fell ill and left Gateshead to recover at a clinic. She took his place in the pulpit while continuing to run her household and care for her four children. She wrote to her husband, 'I must try to posses my soul in patience and do all in the kitchen as well as in the Pulpit to the Glory of God' (C. Booth to W. Booth [1860], BL, Add. MS 64802, fol. 145). This unusual circumstance was accepted by the Connexion and the chapel and her preaching was both acclaimed and condemned in the local press. One newspaper claimed she wore her husband's clothes when she preached. She enjoyed preaching and wrote to her mother, 'I felt quite at home on the platform—far more than I do in the kitchen' (C. Booth to parents, 23 Dec 1857, BL, Add. MS 64804, fol. 63).

In 1861 the Booths left the Methodist New Connexion when the conference refused to consider William's request to devote all his time to evangelism and assigned him to a regular circuit. The Booths began a series of independent revivals in Cornwall, Wales, the midlands, and the north over the following four years. Their work met with resistance from Methodists and other nonconformists. Some objected to itinerant evangelists, particularly to the Booths' revivalism, while others forbade female preaching. Still, during these years the Booths established a number of significant connections across the country that were important to the development of the Salvation Army. Catherine became a prominent independent preacher and received many invitations to address congregations. Their son Herbert was born in 1862 and daughter Marion in 1864. In February 1865 Catherine was invited to conduct a revival for the Free Methodists in London. In July William joined her in London and began to preach in the East End, with the support of the editors of the evangelical weekly newspaper *The Revival*. London offered both a wide range of opportunities for evangelistic work for the Booths and a settled home for their family, and they decided to remain there. Catherine gave birth to her seventh child, Eva, later called Evangeline, in December 1865. She continued to work as an independent revivalist, speaking in chapels and halls in London and elsewhere. Her last child, Lucy, was born in 1868. In 1865 William established the East London Christian Mission. He preached in the streets and in rented halls with the assistance of a number of well-established London evangelicals. Catherine's work supported her family during these early years and also raised funds to support the Mission, although the financial position of neither her family nor the Mission was ever secure.

The Mission adopted a structure of class meetings, circuits, and annual conferences loosely based on the Methodists. Catherine served on the several committees, attended the annual conferences, and preached frequently at Mission meetings. The Christian Mission grew to seventy-two mission stations in England and Wales by 1879 and it employed 127 evangelists. That year it transformed its structure and adopted a new name, the Salvation Army. This structure gave William Booth, as general superintendent for life, authority over the Mission's property and budget, and the power to establish and close mission stations and to hire and appoint evangelists. Uniforms were adopted, a series of ranks, each with its own duties and responsibilities, was developed, and military vocabulary was coined to describe the work. The Army soon opened corps in Europe and throughout the British empire.

Catherine Booth never held an official title but came to be known as the Army Mother. Her influence was felt in the Army's theology and practice, particularly in relation to women. Holiness was crucial to the Salvation Army's theology, and Catherine wrote and preached extensively on this doctrine. Holiness theologians taught that all believers must renounce sin, and that when infused with the Holy Spirit their hearts, minds, and wills would become the very likeness of God. Holiness was the most important requirement for office in the Salvation Army. This doctrine allowed for women's enhanced authority, because women and men could equally attain it, and the significance of other differences between men and women was therefore diminished. The Salvation Army institutionalized women's right to preach the gospel and thousands of women were local corps officers, divisional officers, and leaders in the Salvation Army's social services beginning in the mid-1880s. Catherine was the most important force in establishing women's position in the Army and a powerful example to the Army's new converts. She frequently addressed Salvation Army meetings and large audiences in halls throughout Great Britain and published extensively in Salvationist newspapers.

The prominence of Catherine Booth and other Salvationist women distinguished the Army from most other

Victorian Christian denominations. Many Christians insisted that women's preaching was unscriptural and brought women out of their rightful private sphere. It was considered by many a particular disgrace for a mother to appear in public and encourage other young women. Others admired Catherine Booth's preaching. The *Primitive Methodist Quarterly Review* (new ser., 7, 1885, 441) declared that she 'combined a facility of speech, a profound acquaintanceship with the spiritual power of the Cross and a knowledge of the subtle movements of the heart'.

In addition to preaching Mrs Booth was the author of many books, including *Practical Religion* (1878), *Aggressive Christianity* (1880), *Holiness* (1881), *Mrs Booth on Recent Criticisms of the Salvation Army* (1882), *The Salvation Army in Relation to Church and State* (1883), and *Popular Christianity* (1887), all published by the Salvation Army. She was active in the social purity campaigns—against prostitution and other vice—of the 1880s and, along with other leading Salvationists, was involved in W. T. Stead's 1885 crusade to raise the age of consent.

Catherine Booth was diagnosed with breast cancer in 1888 and in that year she ceased all public activity. She died on 4 October 1890 in Clacton. Over 30,000 people lined the streets of London to watch her funeral procession on 14 October, and she was buried in Abney Park cemetery, London. The *Bible Christian Magazine* called her the 'most famous and influential Christian woman of the generation', and the London and provincial press eulogized her as a preacher, writer, and social purity activist.

PAMELA J. WALKER

Sources *DNB* • P. J. Walker, 'A chaste and fervid eloquence: Catherine Booth and the ministry of women in the Salvation Army', *Women preachers and prophets through two millennia of Christianity*, ed. B. M. Kienzle and P. J. Walker (1998) • P. J. Walker, *Pulling the devil's kingdom down: the Salvation Army in Victorian Britain* (2001) • S. Ervine, *God's soldier: General William Booth*, 2 vols. (1934) • F. Booth-Tucker, *The life of Catherine Booth: the mother of the Salvation Army*, 2 vols. (1892) • R. Sandall and others, *The history of the Salvation Army*, 6 vols. (1979) • *East London Evangelist* (1868–9) • *Christian Mission Magazine* (1870–78) • *The Salvationist* (1879) • *War Cry* (1879) [and subsequent years] • b. cert. • d. cert. • BL, Catherine Mumford Booth and William Booth MSS, Add. MSS 64799–64806 • *Bible Christian Magazine*, 69 (1890), 710 • R. J. Green, *Catherine Booth: a biography of the cofounder of the Salvation Army* (1996)

Archives BL, corresp. and papers, mainly family corresp., Add. MSS 64799–64806 • Salvation Army Heritage Centre, 117 Judd Street, London, papers

Likenesses J. Earle-Morrell, oils, 1886, Salvation Army international headquarters, London • G. Wade, statue, 1929, William Booth Memorial Training College, London • mixed-method engraving (after daguerreotype), NPG • photograph, Salvation Army International Heritage Centre [*see illus.*] • photographs, Salvation Army International Heritage Centre, 117 Judd Street, London; repro. in C. Bramwell-Booth, *Catherine Booth* (1970)

Booth, Catherine Bramwell- (1883–1987), Salvation Army officer, was born on 20 July 1883 at Hadley Wood, Middlesex, the eldest in the family of two sons and five daughters of (William) Bramwell *Booth (1856–1929), Salvation Army general, and his wife, Florence Eleanor *Booth, *née* Soper (1861–1957) [*see under* Booth, (William) Bramwell]. Bramwell was the eldest son of Catherine *Booth and General William *Booth (1829–1912), the

Catherine Bramwell-Booth (1883–1987), by Snowdon, 1979

founder of the Salvation Army, and both he and his wife became Salvation Army leaders. Catherine spent all her childhood at Hadley Wood, which was 'so perfect that I have never written about it, as no-one would believe me'. Her mother disapproved of outside influences acting on the tender minds of her children and taught them all herself for two hours every morning.

At the age of eighteen Catherine Booth left her idyllic family life to become a full-time Salvation Army officer, an occupation she never left until her retirement. She added her father's forename to her surname. Following a period of study at the Salvation Army Training College, her first posting, in 1904, was as a captain in Bath. The pay was 7*s*. 6*d*. a week and the duties, which started at 6 a.m., meant providing some counter-attraction to the pubs and gin houses every night of the week. She then held appointments in a number of important provincial centres, in charge of the Salvation Army's evangelical work, before commencing, in 1907, a period of ten years assisting with the training of women officers at the army's International Training College in Clapton, London. In 1913 she preached in tsarist Russia and in 1917 made headlines when she led a rescue team into the area devastated by the Silvertown munitions factory explosion in West Ham, London, in which sixty people were killed. Later she was involved with relief work in Europe after both world wars. She vacated her post at the International Training College in 1917 to assume responsibility as international secretary for Salvation Army work in Europe, attached to the international headquarters in London. She was subsequently (1926–46) in charge of the movement's social work among women in Great Britain. In 1927 she was appointed a commissioner, concerned with all the Salvation Army's social welfare activities, meeting the needs of all types of people, from orphaned children to the elderly residents of

Salvation Army eventide homes. From 1946 she was international secretary for Europe until she retired in 1948.

Catherine Bramwell-Booth was nominated three times for the generalship of the Salvation Army. On each occasion, in 1934, 1939, and 1946, the election resulted in one of the other candidates assuming the mantle of international leader. Possibly it was felt that the movement, at that stage, should not appear to be dependent on the Booth 'dynasty'. Certainly Commissioner Catherine, as she became affectionately known, was firmly in the Booth mould of charismatic leadership. Throughout her life she remained true to the evangelical driving force of her parents and grandparents. Everyone confronted by her, from local tradesmen to distinguished national journalists, could expect a fearless cross-examination of their spiritual state and a presentation of the claims of her beloved Jesus Christ. She was a Salvation Army officer who never strayed from her roots and never lost her pioneering zeal. She had a keen analytical mind and a fund of knowledge which made her public addresses dynamic and inspiring, as well as informative.

Catherine Bramwell-Booth wrote several books, her best being a biography of her grandmother, *Catherine Booth: the Story of her Loves* (1970). This book brought her public recognition late in life, which resulted in her becoming something of a media personality, with a chirpy, engaging manner. During the last decade of her life she made frequent appearances as a stimulating guest on many radio and television programmes. In 1971 she was appointed CBE. Six years later, at the age of ninety-three, she received the Guild of Professional Toastmasters best speaker award—to her own amusement, because she was a lifelong teetotaller. In 1983 she was honoured with the Salvation Army's order of the Founder. She died, unmarried, at the age of 104 on 4 October 1987 at her home, North Court, in Finchampstead, Berkshire, where she lived with two of her sisters. EVA BURROWS, *rev.*

Sources M. Batchelor, *Catherine Bramwell-Booth* (1987) · C. Bramwell-Booth and T. Harrison, *Commissioner Catherine* (1983) · *CGPLA Eng. & Wales* (1988) · personal knowledge (1996)
Likenesses Snowdon, photograph, 1979, NPG [*see illus.*]
Wealth at death £249,218: probate, 14 Jan 1988, *CGPLA Eng. & Wales*

Booth, Charles (*d.* 1535), bishop of Hereford, is of uncertain parentage, but was undoubtedly a member of the noted Booth family of Barton, Lancashire. It has been thought that he was the son of Sir Robert Booth and therefore of a junior branch of the family. It is certainly true that he was closely related to Lawrence Booth and William Booth, archbishops of York in the second half of the fifteenth century, and to John Booth, bishop of Exeter between 1465 and 1478.

Charles Booth seems to have been educated at Cambridge, studying civil law at Pembroke College, and received the degree of BCL in 1485, but the grace book references are not conclusive. His likely uncles, William and Lawrence, had been members of Pembroke, so it is hardly surprising to find Charles Booth also associated with that college, of which he was later a benefactor. After Cambridge it is certain that he studied at Bologna, where he received the degree of DCL in 1493. In 1505–6 he was granted a grace of incorporation at Cambridge.

Leaving Bologna in 1493 Booth was an advocate at the court of Canterbury for two years, leaving in 1495 to become treasurer of the diocese of Lichfield under Bishop William Smith, a position he held until 1516. Although he had been rector of Normanton-on-Soar, Nottinghamshire, from 1493 (vacated in 1499), his career flowered after his association with Smith. In addition to the treasurership of Lichfield he was named canon of Auckland, co. Durham, and prebendary of St Helens. In 1499 he became rector of St James Garlickhythe, London. In 1501 he followed Smith to Lincoln, where he served as chancellor and commissary-general until 1506. In the same year he was collated canon of Lincoln and prebendary of Clifton (later exchanged for the prebend of Farendon). From 1505 until 1516 he was archdeacon of Buckingham and held various other positions including canon of St Paul's and prebendary of Reculverland (1516), until he became bishop of Hereford in 1516.

Booth's friendship with Smith in 1501 led him into the circle of advisers to Prince Arthur. Most sources claim that he served as chaplain and chancellor of the council of the marches of Wales in 1502 but it seems that that council did not have a position as chancellor, an error that seems to have originated in Francis Godwin's *Catalogue of the Bishops of England*. Booth appears to have been an active member of this council, working alongside Smith, whom he also supported in his efforts to defend the knights of St John. He continued his work after the death of the prince in 1502, being named as one of the 'lordys marchers in Wales', as late as 1531 (*LP Henry VIII*, 5, no. 390).

On 22 April 1516 Booth was nominated to the see of Hereford. Custody of the temporalities was granted on 17 May. Papal provision followed on 21 July, and he was consecrated on 30 November. In 1518 he was summoned by Wolsey to attend the council for the reformation of the clergy and subsequently organized a synod within his diocese to discuss the results of that council. It was undoubtedly while he was serving on the council of the marches of Wales that he made the acquaintance of Prince Arthur's wife, Katherine of Aragon. This relationship continued after the death of Arthur and her subsequent marriage to Henry VIII. He was one of the bishops invited to be present when the future Charles V visited England on his way to be crowned emperor at Aachen in 1520. He was also one of three bishops who attended the queen at the Field of Cloth of Gold, the others being Fisher of Rochester and Athequa of Llandaff (formerly her confessor). Although there is little firsthand evidence of Booth's position on the annulment he is thought to have been a strong supporter of the queen. His attitude at the convocation of 1529 certainly appears to have irritated the king, who instructed Cromwell in 1531 'to make processe and to prosecute against Charles, busshop of Hereford, according to the lawes, with all spede, if he do not agree' (*LP Henry VIII*, no. 394). Booth's advocacy of the queen stopped well short of the lengths to which others were prepared to go, and the king's warning seems to have had an effect. However strongly he may have felt about the issue he appears to have responded to the king's shot across his bows, for no further action was taken against him.

Once the proceedings for the annulment had been completed and the king remarried, Booth concentrated on his diocese. He was unreceptive to reforming ideas, and his register testifies to his conservative turn of mind. Archbishop Warham's instructions to his bishops of 1526 to collect and burn all translations of the New Testament are reproduced in their entirety in Booth's register, as is his letter in response claiming, with some pride, that there were no copies surrendered to him in Hereford. He appears to have conducted the business of the diocese with some care. There were, however, internal diocesan problems that seem to have been beyond his capabilities, for Cranmer wrote to him at one point hoping that he would not have to intervene in a dispute. Booth was also criticized for incurring too great a cost for his diocese in the repair of his house in London. During his episcopate the north porch of Hereford Cathedral was built.

Booth died on 5 May 1535, leaving all his books not already bequeathed elsewhere to the library at Hereford. He was buried in Hereford Cathedral, in the north aisle of the nave. D. G. NEWCOMBE

Sources A. L. Attwater, *Pembroke College, Cambridge: a short history*, ed. S. C. Roberts (1936) · A. T. Bannister, ed., *Registrum Caroli Bothe, episcopi Herefordensis*, CYS, 28 (1921) · R. Churton, *Life of Bishop Smyth* (1800) · *Miscellaneous writings and letters of Thomas Cranmer*, ed. J. E. Cox, Parker Society, [18] (1846) · Emden, *Cam.*, 77 · *LP Henry VIII*, vols. 1–9 · F. Godwin, *A catalogue of the bishops of England, since the first planting of Christian religion in this island*, 2nd edn (1615) · F. T. Havergal, *Fasti Herefordenses* (1869) · S. M. Leathes, ed., *Grace book A* (1897) · *Fasti Angl., 1300–1541*, [Lincoln] · *Fasti Angl., 1300–1541*, [Hereford] · *Fasti Angl., 1300–1541*, [St Paul's, London] · *Fasti Angl., 1300–1541*, [Coventry] · R. J. Mitchell, 'English law students at Bologna in the fifteenth century', *EngHR*, 51 (1936), 270–87 · W. G. Searle, ed., *Grace book Γ* (1908) · C. A. J. Skeel, *The council in the marches of Wales: a study in local government during the 16th and 17th centuries* (1904) · Venn, *Alum. Cant.* · *The Anglica historia of Polydore Vergil, AD 1485–1537*, ed. and trans. D. Hay, CS, 3rd ser., 74 (1950)

Booth, Charles (1840–1916), shipowner and social investigator, was born on 30 March 1840 at 27 Bedford North Street, Liverpool. He was the third son of Charles Booth (1799–1860), a prosperous corn merchant, and his first wife, Emily Fletcher (1803–1853). Both his parents were Unitarians, and had wide connections among the commercial, dissenting, and philanthropic 'aristocracy' of Liverpool (the Gurneys, Holts, Pilkingtons, Cromptons, and many others). Booth received his education at Liverpool's Royal Institution School (1850–56), where he distinguished himself only at arithmetic. This arithmetical bent persuaded his father that, rather than proceeding to university, he 'had better go into business', so at sixteen Charles was apprenticed to the shipping firm of Lamport and Holt, where he was given 'a sound business training' (Norman-Butler, 31–2). Six years later he set up a partnership with his eldest brother, Alfred *Booth, from which evolved the Booth Steamship Company, which specialized in commerce with Latin America.

Charles Booth (1840–1916), by George Frederic Watts, *c.*1901

Nevertheless, in both temperament and intellectual interests Charles Booth was in many ways unusual among the late Victorian business community. Of strikingly handsome physical appearance, he was prone throughout his adult life to chronic ill health, nervous depression, and undiagnosed digestive maladies that forced him to take long periods of rest and foreign travel. He had a strong though undeveloped artistic bent that found expression in sketching, painting in watercolours, composing dramatic sketches, and an admiration for John Ruskin. He was deeply interested in current religious and philosophical debates, although lack of serious intellectual training and a curious inability to absorb ideas from books meant that his grasp of such issues was often eclectic and derivative. The controversy that followed the publication of Darwin's *The Origin of Species* in 1859 left him feeling that although 'he would dearly have loved to go on believing in the Almighty he had been brought up to revere … science had as clearly disproved His existence as Galileo had demonstrated the correct solar system' (Norman-Butler, 36). He expressed similar disenchantment about the philanthropic traditions of the Liverpool bourgeoisie, dismissing them as 'the useless shell of an old world society' (Simey and Simey, 37). Although as a young man he shared many of the beliefs of radical Liberalism, the experience of electioneering in Toxteth in the 1860s left him with a lifelong distaste for organized democratic politics.

An alternative to this religious and political vacuum that presented itself to many confused intellectuals in the 1860s and 1870s was August Comte's 'Religion of Humanity'. Several of Booth's kinsfolk (Albert Crompton, Henry Crompton, and Ernest Beesly) were active members of the positivist movement, and although Booth himself felt unable to join the organized 'Church of Humanity', the philosophy of positivism was to have a lifelong impact upon his beliefs. He became convinced that the clue to intellectual truth and human betterment lay not in theology but in a new 'scientific' understanding of both the natural world and human and social relationships. 'No compromise is possible between the old world and the new,' he wrote in 1870. 'Science must lay down afresh the laws of life … I feel assured that the principles of Positivism will lead us on till we find the true solution of the problem of government' (Simey and Simey, 48–9).

Booth's rejection of Liverpool nonconformity led to some degree of estrangement from other members of the Booth family—an estrangement reinforced by his marriage on 29 April 1871 to Mary Catherine Macaulay (1847–1939) [*see* Booth, Mary Catherine], daughter of Charles Zachary Macaulay, a senior Whitehall official, and niece of Lord Macaulay. Mary was renowned as one of the cleverest and most widely read women of her day, and the marriage brought Booth into the orbit of a cosmopolitan intellectual aristocracy quite different in outlook from the business classes of Liverpool. Whether the pressures of such a marriage reinforced or assuaged Booth's depressive streak must be a matter of speculation; but certainly pressure from Mary encouraged him to engage in some form of intellectual challenge other than the running of a family business.

Precisely why Booth came to focus upon analysis of the condition of the London poor remains unclear, but such a subject brought together many of his earlier talents and interests—his arithmetical skills, his discontent with philanthropy, his hopes of developing a more 'scientific' approach to the study of society, his strong sense of personal and civic duty. His concern was also stimulated by the deep-seated social crisis of the 1880s. Most historians now reject the view that Booth embarked on his survey specifically to correct the exaggerated estimates of urban poverty advanced by H. M. Hyndman; but there can be no doubt that, both as a businessman and as a citizen, Booth was deeply perturbed by the confounding of earlier assumptions of progress. His interest in precise measurement led him to engage the services of a powerful network of young men and women, based on Toynbee Hall, the Charity Organization Society, and the Royal Statistical Society, who were dedicated to solving 'the social problem'. Many of these young investigators were themselves to become major figures in the development of social science and reformist public administration—among them Hubert Llewellyn Smith, Ernest Aves, Gerald Duckworth, David Schloss, Clara Collet, and Booth's cousin by marriage Beatrice Potter.

Booth's investigation, which began with his pilot survey of Tower Hamlets in 1887, was to last for fifteen years, and was eventually to be published in a gathered form as *Life and Labour of the People in London* in seventeen volumes (1902). It was based on information from a great variety of sources: interviews, questionnaires, reports from London school board visitors, house-to-house visitation. It focused upon three separate aspects of London life—poverty, industry, and religious influences. For purposes of analysis it divided the population into eight horizontal classes, ranging from class H (the upper middle class) through to class B (the casual poor) and class A (the savages and criminals). Its most famous finding was that approximately one third of the inhabitants of London were living in some degree of poverty; poverty caused partly by drink, but far more extensively by structural factors such as industrial depression, competition, and low wages. The industry volumes focused upon the problem of casual labour, and suggested that a great deal of urban distress was linked to chronic disorganization in the market for labour. The religious volumes came to no very clear conclusion, but uncovered an extraordinary patchwork of teeming religious pluralism, ranging from Roman Catholicism and high Anglicanism to extreme evangelical protestantism, from exaggerated enthusiasm and piety to indifference and irreverence, from monotheistic 'orthodoxy' through to an immense variety of idiosyncratic cults.

The significance of Booth's survey was hotly debated at the time, and continues to be so a century later. Some have claimed him as one of the founding fathers of sociology or of empirical social science, whereas others have suggested that, despite its huge accumulation of facts, the survey had little or no explanatory validity. Some have portrayed Booth's poverty findings as a crucial influence on the growth of the welfare state; whereas others have concluded that Booth's practical influence on social policy was negligible. Many have regretted the lack of a historical dimension; and Booth's own manuscripts reveal that he was himself troubled about his survey's rather static quality, and by the fact that it said little about whether conditions were deteriorating or improving. Current research on Booth has moved away from this type of question, and has concentrated less upon the survey's scientific strengths and deficiencies and more on its status as a unique historical archive; as a documentary periscope into the assumptions, beliefs, and anxieties of one of the major protagonists of the late Victorian era (O'Day and Englander, 1993; Englander and O'Day, 1995).

Booth himself, however, was ambitious to use his social inquiries to influence opinion and policy, as can be seen in his activities in a number of spheres, such as tariffs, industrial structure, and promotion of old age pensions. At all times his central concern was to defend and improve the position of the efficient, 'industrious' working class against 'unfair competition' in both foreign and domestic markets. Evidence of the adverse effect on London trades of unlimited foreign competition confirmed his view that free trade was no longer a viable policy for Britain, and led in 1903 to his active involvement in Joseph Chamberlain's campaign for tariff reform.

Likewise, at an early stage of his poverty inquiry Booth had concluded that the 'crux of the social problem' lay in the treatment of the parasitic group whom he had labelled as class B. This was the group, just above the savage outcasts of class A, who nevertheless performed no real economic or social function, but survived on the fringes of society as parasites upon the prosperity of the classes above them. This class was fostered by the structural phenomenon of casual labour, which enabled inefficient workers to eke out an occasional livelihood by undercutting the wages of the more efficient classes above them. Booth's policy solution, spelt out in a series of public inquiries from the select committees on distress from want of employment (1894–5) to the royal commission on the poor laws (1905–9), was the widespread regularization and 'decasualization' of employment, which would concentrate regular work on the efficient majority, and make it possible to apply remedial treatment to the inefficient 'residuum'. Such treatment might consist of compulsory retraining and education; or, *in extremis*, of permanent confinement in labour colonies sealed off from the rest of society. A similar outlook informed Booth's proposals on the poor law and old age pensions. In Booth's view, proper use of the poor law was being impeded by the fact that by far the largest pauper group were old people no longer capable of work, whom public opinion quite properly regarded as honourable and deserving. In Booth's view, if the old were removed from poor relief by payment of universal old age pensions, then the poor law could revert to its proper task of disciplining and deterring the small minority whose destitution was more or less 'voluntary'. Concerns of this kind led to his appointment to the royal commission on the poor laws in 1905, although a severe recurrence of his earlier ill health meant that Booth's membership of this great classic public inquiry was largely inactive. However, his contribution to the old age pensions movement was an important strand in the debate that led up to the first Old Age Pensions Act (as was acknowledged in an illuminated address presented to Booth by the National Committee of Organised Labour in 1909).

Throughout his life Booth's investigative and reformist interests were funded by his successful business management. He remained an active working chairman of the steamship company for more than forty years, and travelled annually to New York to develop his firm's North American connections. Despite his recurrent depressions his marriage appears to have been a happy one, producing three sons and four daughters. His fourth child, George Macaulay Booth, businessman, was a founder of the unit trust movement in Britain. Lloyd George brought him into Whitehall during the First World War to impress business methods upon public administration. Booth's public services were recognized by a long list of distinctions; he was elected president of the Royal Statistical Society (1892–4) and fellow of the Royal Society (1899), and sworn of the privy council in 1904. He was awarded honorary doctorates by the universities of Oxford, Cambridge, and Liverpool. He died on 23 November 1916 at his Leicestershire country home, Gracedieu Manor, and was buried at neighbouring Thringstone. A memorial tablet designed by Sir Charles Nicholson, bt, was erected in St Paul's Cathedral in 1920. JOSE HARRIS

Sources M. Booth, *Charles Booth: a memoir* (1918) · B. Webb, *My apprenticeship*, 2 vols. (1938) · T. S. Simey and M. B. Simey, *Charles Booth: social scientist* (1960) · B. Norman-Butler, *Victorian aspirations: the life and labour of Charles and Mary Booth* (1972) · R. O'Day and D. Englander, *Mr Charles Booth's inquiry: 'Life and labour of the people in London' reconsidered* (1993) · D. Englander and R. O'Day, *Retrieved riches: social investigation in Britain, 1840–1914* (1995) · m. cert. · R. P. T. Davenport-Hines, 'Booth, George Macaulay', *DBB* · *CGPLA Eng. & Wales* (1917)

Archives BL · BLPES, corresp. relating to Royal Economic Society · BLPES, papers relating to 'Life and Labour' · LUL, corresp. and papers · Royal Statistical Society, London, MS of statistics from census returns · U. Lpool, papers relating to 'Life and Labour' | HLRO, letters to Herbert Samuel

Likenesses G. F. Watts, oils, *c*.1901, NPG [*see illus.*] · W. Rothenstein, oils, 1908, U. Lpool · W. Rothenstein, pencil drawing, 1910, NPG · C. Nicholson, tablet, St Paul's Cathedral, London

Wealth at death £150,938 8*s*. 11*d*.: probate, 16 Feb 1917, *CGPLA Eng. & Wales*

Booth, David (1766–1846), lexicographer and writer, was born at Kinnettles, Forfarshire, on 9 February 1766. He was almost entirely self-taught, the whole amount paid by his father for his instruction being 18*d*. for one quarter at the parish school. In early life he was engaged in business, and for some years was manager of a brewery at Woodside, near Newburgh, Fife. Although the undertaking was not unsuccessful, his intellectual interests and love of literature led him to retire from it to become a schoolmaster at Newburgh.

Shortly before 1820 Booth moved to London, where, besides his involvement in general literary work, for several years he saw through the press the publications of the Society for the Diffusion of Useful Knowledge (SDUK). In 1818 he published *Tables of Simple Interest on a New Plan of Arrangement*, and in 1821 *The tradesman, merchant, and accountant's assistant, being tables for business in general on a new plan of arrangement*. He also turned to account his practical knowledge of brewing by writing for the SDUK *The Art of Brewing* (1829) and *The art of wine-making in all its branches, to which is added an appendix concerning cider and perry* (1834). The latter volume contains a description of the brewer's saccharometer, a device to which he had added a considerable number of refinements.

In 1806 Booth had published *An Introduction to an Analytical Dictionary of the English Language*. He was unable for some years to proceed further with the work, and the first volume of the dictionary, the only one published, appeared in 1830. Its special characteristics, as stated on the title-page, are that:

> the words are explained in the order of their natural affinity, independent of alphabetical arrangement; and the signification of each is traced from its etymology, the present meaning being accounted for when it differs from its former acceptation: the whole exhibiting, in one continual narrative, the origin, history, and modern usage of the existing vocabulary of the English tongue.

An idea of Booth's idiosyncratic method of arrangement, which is not easy to follow, may be gathered from the following list of the first twelve words in their order of succession: microcosm, man, wife, woman, male, female, masculine, feminine, human, baron, virility, virtue. In its reductive ideas on etymology and word relationship

Booth's work, like that of his contemporary Charles Richardson, shows the unfortunate influence of Horne Tooke, but lacking Richardson's mass of quotations had less value and little influence.

In 1831 Booth published *Principles of English Composition*, chapters 2–4 being reprinted from the *Introduction to an Analytical Dictionary*, and in 1837 *Principles of English Grammar*. His other works include *Observations on the English Jury Laws in Criminal Cases* (1833), strongly condemnatory of the 'unanimous verdict' system; *A letter to Rev. T. R. Malthus, being an answer to his criticism of Mr. Godwin's work on population* (1823); and *Eura and Zephyra, a Classical Tale, with Poetical Pieces* (1832). Dr Robert Blakey, who met Booth in October 1832 in Bloomsbury, recorded: 'He is one of the most extraordinary personages I have met for some time. He is not, I believe, five feet high, of very dark visage, eyes very red and watery, and presenting altogether an impish look'. Blakey accepted Booth's invitation to have tea with him, and was somewhat shocked by his system 'of complete scepticism' and his arguments against the Christian religion (*Memoirs*, 75–7).

Booth received a grant of £50 from the Royal Bounty Fund, and was also assisted by the Literary Fund Society. He died at the house of his son-in-law, Mr J. G. Stuart, at Balgonie Mills, Fife, on 5 December 1846. He left a widow, one son, and two daughters.

T. F. HENDERSON, *rev.* JOHN D. HAIGH

Sources M. F. Conolly, *Biographical dictionary of eminent men of Fife* (1866), 70 • *GM*, 2nd ser., 27 (1847), 322–3 • *Memoirs of Dr. Robert Blakey*, ed. H. Miller (1879), 75–77 • D. Booth, 'To the public', *An analytical dictionary of the English language*, 1 (1835), ii–iv • F. J. Hausmann and others, eds., *Wörterbücher: ein internationales Handbuch zur Lexikographie / Dictionaries: an international encyclopedia of lexicography*, 2 (Berlin, 1989), 1957–8 • J. Green, *Chasing the sun: dictionary-makers and the dictionaries they made* (1996), 292

Archives NL Scot., corresp. • UCL, corresp. | UCL, letters to the Society for the Diffusion of Useful Knowledge

Booth [*alias* Barlow], **Edward** (**1638–1719**), Roman Catholic priest and clockmaker, was the son of Richard Booth (*d.* 1673), a Catholic, of Woolston-cum-Poulton, near Warrington, Lancashire, and was baptized on 15 December 1639, his godfather being Edward Ambrose *Barlow OSB (*bap.* 1585, *d.* 1641), later martyr. Booth entered the English College at Lisbon on 28 September 1659 already well educated in Latin, Greek, Hebrew, and the humanities, studied philosophy under John Williams, and defended his thesis in 1663. He then began a course on theology but postponed it for three years. Booth had taken minor orders in 1663 and was ordained priest in September 1664. He taught humanities at Lisbon until 1667, took the missionary oath in 1670, and was sent to England, where he adopted the alias of Barlow and lived with Lord Langdale in Yorkshire. In 1672 he moved to Park Hall, a seat of the Houghton family, where he was vicar-general of the Lancashire district.

At Park Hall, Barlow attended to the poor of the neighbourhood, conforming to them in habit and dress. He also applied himself to clockmaking, perhaps collaborating with William and Richard Houghton—the latter was in the Clockmakers' Company. Prior to 1676 Barlow devised a rack and snail mechanism for a repeating clock—one which by pulling a cord or moving a knob would strike the previous hour again—a useful way to tell the time in the hours of darkness. Barlow's arrangement was more complicated than the earlier count wheel but had the advantage that the strike of each hour was independent of any possible earlier mis-strikes due to mechanical slip. It was adopted by the London clockmaker Thomas Tompion in 1676, who, according to Dodd, paid Barlow £200 for the rights. The rack and snail was adapted to a repeating watch and Barlow sought a patent for this in 1686, but was opposed by Daniel Quare, another London clockmaker, who had earlier devised a similar but simpler repeating watch. The Clockmakers' Company petitioned James II in support of Quare, and at the hearing in February 1688 Barlow's application was refused. Barlow also invented the cylinder escapement, which was patented under the name of Booth, with William Houghton and Tompion (no. 344 of 1695).

In 1715 Barlow published his *Meteorological essays concerning the origins of springs, generation of rain, and production of wind: with an account of the tide*, drawing on his knowledge of springs in Lancashire and, for the tides, where he took issue with Descartes, on seafarers' accounts of tides in distant seas. The same book, but with a longer title and dedicated to Robert, earl of Oxford and Mortimer, was published in 1717 and again in 1722, after his death; this time it contained the description of an engine for draining water, for which, as Edward Booth, he had been granted patent no. 359 of 1698. Barlow died at Park Hall in 1719.

THOMPSON COOPER, *rev.* ANITA MCCONNELL

Sources F. J. Britten, *Old clocks and watches and their makers*, 3rd edn (1911); repr. with corrections (1977), 218 • M. Sharratt, ed., *Lisbon College register, 1628–1813*, Catholic RS, 72 (1991), 16–17 • J. S. Hansom and J. Gillow, eds., 'A list of convicted recusants in the reign of Charles II', *Miscellanea, V*, Catholic RS, 6 (1909), 75–326, esp. 224 • *N&Q*, 6 (1852), 439–40 • Gillow, *Lit. biog. hist.*, 1.267–9 • S. E. Atkins and W. H. Overall, *Some account of the Worshipful Company of Clockmakers of the City of London* (privately printed, London, 1881), 170, 243–4

Booth, Edwin Thomas (**1833–1893**), actor, was born on 13 November 1833 near Bel Air, Maryland, fifth of the ten children of the actor Junius Brutus *Booth (1796–1852) and his second wife, Mary Ann Holmes (1802–1885) of London, whom he married in 1851. Three brothers and two sisters survived childhood. In 1847 Edwin persuaded the manager of the Holliday Street Theatre, Baltimore, to let him appear, but nervousness spoilt his performance. The same year he began touring as his father's dresser. His official début was as Tressel in Cibber's version of Shakespeare's *Richard III*, at the Boston Museum Theatre on 10 September 1849. After his father's death in 1852, he performed in California, Australia, and Hawaii. In 1857 he made his first tour of the United States as a star, playing melodrama heroes and villains and Shakespearian tragic leads. Although it was considered highly promising, his work was often criticized for unevenness and threatened by his tendency to drink. Short and slight with dark eyes, long dark hair, romantic good looks, and a warm, musical

Edwin Thomas Booth (1833–1893), by London Stereoscopic Co., *c.*1861

voice, Booth was attractive to women. In 1860 he married Mary Devlin (1840–1863), and in 1861–2 they travelled to England, where Booth appeared at the Haymarket and his daughter Edwina was born.

In Manchester Henry Irving played secondary roles to Booth's leads and was influenced by Booth's Hamlet in conceiving his own. England reported Booth 'a sound and sensible actor'. From earlier blood-and-thunder playing, he had begun to develop a quiet, intellectual, lyrical style favoured by cultured audiences. In 1863, devastated by his wife's death, he gave up drink. In 1864–5, at the Winter Garden, New York, he played a 100-night run as Hamlet. The assassination of Abraham Lincoln at Ford's Theatre, Washington, by his brother John Wilkes Booth in April 1865 led to his brief retirement. In 1869 he opened Booth's Theatre in New York as a 'temple to Shakespeare', where he mounted lavish productions, and the same year he married Mary McVicker (1848–1881). Their son Edgar died at birth, and the marriage was strained by Mary's growing mental illness. Booth considered leasing the Lyceum Theatre, London, and alternating between it and Booth's Theatre, but lost the option. He went bankrupt in 1874 and resumed national touring. In 1880–81 he revisited England, and appeared at the Princess's Theatre, London, with inadequate scenery and cast. Aspects of his technique struck English critics as old-fashioned, his gestures and facial expression as excessive, and sometimes he appeared to lack passion. But his elocution and grace were considered exemplary. Henry Irving invited him to the Lyceum, where they alternated Othello and Iago with huge success. Booth's cool, polished Iago was particularly praised (a contemporary rhyme contrasts him with Irving as 'the smooth Mr Booth').

Booth's second wife died in 1881, and in 1882–3 he travelled again to Europe. He opened in London at the Adelphi, then toured cities throughout the British Isles. His Hamlet, Richelieu, Iago, Othello, and King Lear were acclaimed in England and in Germany and Austria, where he acted in English with German-speaking companies. From 1886 until retiring in 1891 he worked with Lawrence Barrett in touring management. A champion of actors' social status, he founded The Players in New York, where actors could associate with leaders in other fields. Although he was shy, and often melancholy, his huge correspondence reveals a high-spirited lover of fun, especially word play. His recording of Othello's speech to the senate is intimate, warm, personable, almost colloquial. He contributed perceptive notes to the Furness Variorum Edition of Shakespeare, wrote short memoirs of Edmund Kean and Junius Brutus Booth, and, with William Winter, published his acting versions of Shakespeare's plays. He died on 7 June 1893, after a stroke, and was buried in Mount Auburn cemetery near Boston. Well into the twentieth century he was reputed America's greatest tragedian and foremost exponent of Hamlet.

ARTHUR KINCAID

Sources L. T. Oggel, *Edwin Booth: a biobibliography* (1992) • *Between actor and critic: selected letters of Edwin Booth and William Winter*, ed. D. Watermeier (1971) • E. B. Grossmann, *Edwin Booth: recollections by his daughter* (1894) • A. C. Sprague, *Shakespearean players and performances* (1953) • L. Irving, *Henry Irving: the actor and his world* [1951] • E. H. House, 'Edwin Booth in London', *Century Magazine*, 55 (1897), 269–79 • A. Badeau, 'Edwin Booth, on and off the stage', *McClure's Magazine* (1893), 255–67 • C. H. Shattuck, *Shakespeare on the American stage*, 2 vols. (1976–87) • C. H. Shattuck, *The Hamlet of Edwin Booth* (1969) • A. B. Clarke, *The elder and the younger Booth* (1881) • K. Goodale, *Behind the scenes with Edwin Booth* (1931) • S. Kimmel, *The mad Booths of Maryland* (1940) • I. M. Gibson, 'In my portrait gallery: Edwin Thomas Booth', *Woman Beautiful*, 2 (Feb 1909), 20–27 [Edwin Booth to Revd Dr Lidell, 12 Dec 1880]

Archives Folger • Harvard TC • Players Club, New York, Hampden–Booth Library | Maryland Historical Society, Baltimore, Alonzo May MS • University of Tulsa, Oklahoma, Henneke collection | SOUND archives of The Players, New York, recording made 1890 on wax cylinder of 'To be or not to be' and Othello's speech to the senate

Likenesses E. V. Valentine, bust, 1858, Valentine Museum, Richmond, Virginia • London Stereoscopic Co., photograph, *c.*1861, NPG [*see illus.*] • N. Sarony, photographs, *c.*1870, The Players, New York • J. C. Collier, oils, 1881, The Players, New York • O. I. Lay, oils, 1887, The Players, New York; copy, Royal Shakespeare Company Gallery, Stratford-upon-Avon, Warwickshire • J. S. Sargent, oils, 1890, The Players, New York • E. T. Quinn, statue, 1918, Gramercy Park, New York • B. Partridge, pen-and-ink drawing (as Othello), NPG • B. Partridge, pen-and-ink drawing (as Iago in *Othello*), NPG

Booth, Eva Selina Gore- (1870–1926), suffragist and poet, was born on 22 May 1870 at Lissadell, co. Sligo, Ireland, the second of three daughters and the third of the five children of Sir Henry William Gore-Booth, fifth baronet (1843–1900), Anglo-Irish landlord and Arctic explorer, and his wife, Georgina Mary (*d.* 1927), only daughter of Colonel Charles Hill of Tickhill Castle, Yorkshire. Of these five children two others also gave up their privileged positions in society to promote a new order in Ireland. The eldest, Josslyn, introduced co-operatives to Sligo and became the first landlord in Ireland to sell his land to his tenants after the 1903 Land Act. Constance [*see* Markievicz, Constance Georgine, Countess Markievicz in the Polish nobility (1868–1927)] became the 'rebel countess' of the 1916 Easter rising.

Eva was educated at home by a governess, Miss Noel, who had studied at Cambridge and who grounded her in Latin, Greek, and Italian. She was antipathetic to her mother and was strongly influenced by her devout grandmother Lady Frances Lumley. Studious and introspective, she was quite different from her flamboyant and more robust elder sister Constance. In appearance she was willowy and frail, and she attracted attention with her fair hair and eager expression. The poet W. B. Yeats was thoroughly charmed by her when he stayed at Lissadell in 1894, when they talked of each other's poetry. The west of Ireland was not a suitable climate for Eva's poor constitution: an illness, suspected consumption, led her to travel to Italy in search of health in 1896. At the home of George MacDonald in Bordighera she met Esther Roper, an organizer for the North of England Society for Women's Suffrage. This society was a branch of the national union organized by Mrs Fawcett, who was Esther Roper's mentor.

For the first time Eva was able to talk to a kindred spirit. Captivated by the woman and her cause, she impulsively decided to leave Ireland and join Esther in the suffrage cause in Manchester. At first under Esther's influence she devoted herself to trade unionism and suffrage, but then on her own account became involved in adult education for women, working with the Manchester University Settlement and the Lancashire and Cheshire Women Textile and Other Workers' Representation Committee. She became the mentor of the young Christabel Pankhurst in 1901, but after three years Christabel became irritated by Eva's gentle gradualism and pacifism and abandoned her friendship and guidance for militancy. Later Christabel quite unjustly damned Eva's character as 'temperament without direction' (Lewis, 97). It was clear to most contemporaries that Eva's work was thorough and painstaking, and maintained over years of campaigning. Roper and Gore-Booth were names prominent in campaigns on behalf of pit-brow workers, flower sellers, and barmaids, but their greatest success was in attracting large numbers of women from the working class to the suffrage movement. In 1901, when the membership of the National Union of Women's Suffrage Societies (NUWSS) was about 10,000, they organized a suffrage petition with 30,000 signatures.

As a relief from her work Eva wrote a great deal, recording her dreams, and incorporating some of them into her verse and plays. She published ten volumes of poetry, including *Unseen Kings* (1904) and *The Death of Fionavar* (1916). Her best-known poem, found in many anthologies of Irish verse, was 'The Little Waves of Breffny'. Her poems, from the first volume of 1898, in the publication of which she was encouraged by W. B. Yeats, dwelled on constant themes: Christian mysticism, love of nature, distaste for the 'iron fort' of materialism, and for the militaristic urge to dominate and control. Horrified by the outbreak of the First World War, she was among the pacifist seceders from the NUWSS, which supported the war effort, and she worked tirelessly as a representative of the No-Conscription Fellowship for conscientious objectors at their trials by tribunal, and for the Women's Peace Crusade; this involved travelling all over Britain.

In the aftermath of the Easter uprising in Dublin in 1916 Eva was instrumental in organizing the reprieve of the death sentence meted out to her sister Constance as one of the leaders of the uprising, but her campaign with Alice Stopford Green and others to prevent the hanging of Roger Casement failed. After the war her health broke down and she retired, with Esther, to Hampstead. During the last years of her life she was the leader of a group—concerned to reform sexual behaviour and discard gender stereotyping—that published the journal *Urania* from 1916.

Eva Gore-Booth died from cancer on 30 June 1926 at her home, 14 Frognal Gardens, Hampstead, London. In her obituary in *The Times*, Evelyn Underhill claimed that Eva Gore-Booth would be remembered chiefly as a mystical poet, but on the contrary the dominant reminder of her is by W. B. Yeats in his 'In Memory of Eva Gore Booth and Constance Markievicz', written in October 1927. Here he unjustly commemorated her 'dreaming' of a 'vague Utopia', her body and life wasted by politics. She was buried on 3 July 1926 in St John's, Hampstead, where she lies in a joint grave with Esther Roper under a headstone with an interlaced Celtic cross. GIFFORD LEWIS

Sources *Poems of Eva Gore-Booth*, ed. E. Roper (1929) [incl. biographical essay] · *Prison letters of Countess Markievicz (Constance Gore-Booth)* (1934) · NRA, priv. coll., Gore-Booth MSS · Man. CL, Suffrage collection · G. Lewis, *Eva Gore Booth and Esther Roper: a biography* (1988) · Burke, *Peerage* (1939) · d. cert.

Archives NL Ire., corresp. · NRA, priv. coll., literary MSS, papers, sketchpads, journal, corresp., etc. · Sligo Public Library, books and miscellanea · University of Pennsylvania, Philadelphia, Van Pett Library, corresp., literary MSS, and papers | Pennsylvania State University, historical collections, labor archive

Likenesses S. Purser, oils, 1881, Lissadell House, co. Sligo · photograph, *c.*1897, Lissadell House, co. Sligo · photograph, 1926, NRA, priv. coll., Gore-Booth MSS

Wealth at death £4262 12*s.* 0*d.*: probate, 21 Jan 1927, *CGPLA Eng. & Wales*

Booth, Sir Felix, first baronet (1775–1850), distiller and promoter of Arctic exploration, was the youngest son of Philip Booth, a distiller of 55 Turnmill Street, Clerkenwell, London, and his wife, Elizabeth Wallis, who had in all three sons and three daughters. Felix was the most energetic and able of his family, many of whom were distillers and wine merchants in London. When he entered the business he rebuilt the existing Clerkenwell distillery, built a second at Brentford, and took over other brewing and distilling concerns. Eventually he became the owner of the biggest distilling business in England, making principally gin, but also cognac, at his Regent's Park distillery. He used his considerable wealth to enter other businesses, such as gas lighting and banking.

Booth became interested in polar exploration, particularly the search for the north-west passage, and was a close friend of the explorer John Ross. Ross was unable to get official support to search for the north-west passage after the controversy and ill feeling which attended his earlier expedition and alleged discovery of mountains which were found to have been a mirage. He turned for financial backing to Booth, who initially declined to help, fearing that he would be thought to have been motivated by the government reward offered for the discovery of the passage. In 1828, however, the government offer was withdrawn and Booth, on condition of secrecy, provided £17,000, which largely financed Ross's expedition in the *Victory* (1829–33). During the four years the ship was away Booth anonymously sent weekly allowances to the sailors' wives. Ross's party finally returned to great acclaim. The north-west passage remained undiscovered, but they had surveyed very considerable areas and discovered the magnetic pole. Ross immortalized Booth in many land and sea features, such as the Gulf of Boothia, Felix Harbour, and Cape Felix. Sheriff's Harbour commemorated Booth's election in 1828 as sheriff of London and Middlesex, and other place names commemorated his sisters and his country houses. Booth's involvement in the voyage was made public, and he was rewarded with election to the fellowship of the Royal Society and on 27 March 1835 with a baronetcy.

In 1850 Booth helped finance John Ross's last voyage, when in the *Felix* he went unsuccessfully in search of Franklin. On 25 January the same year Booth died very suddenly, probably of a heart attack, at the Royal York Hotel, Brighton, Sussex. He was buried in the family vault at the church in Stanstead Abbots, Hertfordshire. As he was unmarried and childless his title passed to his nephew J. Williamson Booth. The title is now extinct. Booth's gin is still widely drunk, but the company is no longer in family ownership. ELIZABETH BAIGENT

Sources E. S. Dodge, *The polar Rosses* (1973) • A. G. E. Jones, 'The voyage of the "Felix", Captain Sir John Ross RN, 1850–51', *Fram*, 2/1 (1985), 275–89 • M. J. Ross, *Polar pioneers* (1995) • P. Balfour, Baron Kinross, *The kindred spirit: a history of gin and the house of Booth* (1959) • *Brighton Guardian* (1850)

Likenesses W. Bradley, oils, repro. in Balfour, *Kindred spirit*, 39 • T. Lawrence, oils, Booth's distillers • bust on memorial, Eventide House, Stanstead Abbots, Hertfordshire • engraving (after oil painting by W. Bradley), repro. in Balfour, *Kindred spirit*, 39

Booth, Florence Eleanor (1861–1957). *See under* Booth, (William) Bramwell (1856–1929).

Booth, George, first Baron Delamer [Delamere] (**1622–1684**), politician, was born on 18 December 1622, the second son of William Booth (*d.* 1636), and his wife, Vere (*d.* 1629), third daughter and coheir of Sir Thomas Egerton, son of Viscount Brackley, lord chancellor of England. He was descended from a younger branch of the Booths of Barton, Lancashire, which since 1433 had been settled at Dunham Massey, Cheshire. When his father died in 1636 Booth became the ward of his grandfather Sir George Booth, first baronet. He was educated at the Inner Temple in 1637. Booth is said to have quarrelled with his guardian late in 1639 or early in 1640, and to have fled to France. The quarrel had something to do with Booth's marriage on 30 November 1639 to Lady Katherine (*d.* 1643), daughter of Theophilus Clinton, fourth earl of Lincoln—a union which produced a daughter.

By the outbreak of the civil war Booth had returned to England and followed his grandfather in being one of the chief supporters of the parliamentary party in Cheshire. Thereafter, they were also in the van of the opposition to the putative parliamentarian leader in the county, Sir William Brereton. The Booths were 'more moderate religiously and politically' than Brereton (Dore, 14). Booth's wife, Lady Katherine, was buried at Bowden, Chester, on 5 August 1643 and, by a licence of 14 December 1644, Booth cemented his position within the parliamentarian élite by marrying Lady Elizabeth (1621/2–1691), daughter of Henry *Grey, first earl of Stamford. They had seven sons, two of whom died before Booth, and five daughters. Early in 1645 Booth was in London spreading anti-Brereton propaganda, and attempting to promote a petition against him in parliament in April. By the autumn of that year he was back in Cheshire taking a leading part in the siege of Chester. In 1646 he resigned his commission as a colonel in the Cheshire forces and was recruited to the county's vacant parliamentary seat, thanks largely to canvassing on his behalf by his grandfather, and probably in an attempt to counter Brereton's influence at Westminster. It was certainly suspected that Brereton, if he could, would obstruct Booth's election.

Booth was secluded at the purge in December 1648, his way into the Commons chamber barred on the 7th by soldiers under the direct instruction of his brother-in-law Thomas *Grey, Lord Grey of Groby. Booth signed a protest got up by several of his fellow sufferers that day, explaining to his Cheshire constituents that he and they had been kept out of the Commons because they had 'stickled for the privilege of Parliament, and restoration of their members, then in hold, the day before' (Underdown, 152). On his grandfather's death on 24 October 1652, Booth succeeded to the baronetcy. He sat for Cheshire in the first Cromwellian parliament in 1654, and was appointed to head the new militia commission in Cheshire established in the aftermath of John Penruddock's royalist revolt, and in anticipation of the settlement of the major-generals. However, suspicions arose that he had actually been intended as the commander of an insurrection in Cheshire and north Wales in 1655, and in 1656 he was excluded from taking his seat at Westminster in the second protectorate parliament.

In September 1658 General George Monck recommended to the new protector, Richard Cromwell, that he trust in Sir George Booth and men like him, in order to reassure and encourage the conservative gentry that the objective of 'healing and settling' the nation was still a priority, and that religious zealots would receive short shrift. Booth was subsequently returned to sit for Lancashire in the parliament which met in 1659 (having succeeded as lord of the manor of Warrington at the death of his father in 1636). On account of his grandfather's memory, Booth was, according to Clarendon, 'of absolute power with the presbyterians' (Helms, Hampson, and Henning). When the rump of the Long Parliament was restored later in 1659 Booth was chosen one of the committee of fourteen who were appointed by the members secluded in 1648 to attempt to obtain readmittance. After their repulse he joined the plot for an armed insurrection, receiving a commission from Charles II to command in Lancashire, Cheshire, and north Wales. The acquisition of arms and ammunition was conducted under cover of supposed fears of some kind of popular uprising, the possibility of which may have been lent some substance by John Bradshaw's victory at the polls in Cheshire in 1658 with the tumultuous support of freeholders and Quakers, a victory which repudiated utterly the social and electoral dominance of traditional élites in the region. However, the plot of 1659 failed at least partly because moderates were fearful of 'his Majesty's restoration by tumult', in the earl of Manchester's words (Underdown, 351).

Booth was the only would-be insurgent who enjoyed any success. On 5 August 1659, totally ignorant of how matters had gone in other parts of the country, Booth, along with the earl of Derby, Colonel Egerton, and others, at the head of four thousand men, seized the city of Chester, where they were shortly joined by Sir Thomas Middleton from Wales. A proclamation was issued from which the name of the king was omitted, but asserting 'the freedom of parliament, of the known laws, liberty and property, and of the good people of this kingdom, groaning under uncomfortable taxes' (*DNB*). Leaving a sufficient force to besiege Chester Castle, which held out against them, Booth and Middleton split up, the latter heading for south Wales, while Booth marched towards York. *En route* he learned of the disaster which had befallen the planned general rising, and that Major-General John Lambert was marching for Cheshire to extinguish the solitary spark of revolt. The two forces clashed at Northwich on 19 August. The skirmish was not bloody, but it was wholly decisive. Booth fled, and at some point on his way to London, whence he hoped to take ship for the continent, he put on female clothing. The disguise was penetrated at Newport Pagnell on 24 August, whereupon Booth was apprehended and conveyed to the Tower. He was interrogated by Sir Arthur Hesilrige and Sir Henry Vane the younger, then was retained to be dealt with by the council of state. He was set at liberty on bail of £5000 shortly after the readmission to the Commons of the secluded members in February 1660. In March he was restored to the Cheshire militia commission.

That spring Booth was elected, probably unopposed, to represent the same county in the Convention Parliament. He was the first of the twelve members chosen on 7 May 1660 to convey to Charles II the reply of the Commons to the declaration of Breda. Marked as a friend on Lord Wharton's list he was teller for the majority which voted that no more than twenty offenders should be excepted from the Bill for Indemnity and Oblivion. He opposed excepting Bulstrode Whitelocke from the provisions of the Indemnity Bill, personally submitted Oliver St John's plea for mercy, and spoke in favour of Sir Arthur Hesilrige and even his old foe, John Lambert. He also brought in two papers drawn up by his late brother-in-law, Thomas, Lord Grey of Groby, testifying to 'his penitence for his former being against the king' (Helms, Hampson, and Henning), and persuaded the house to remove him from the list of those denied the benefit of the bill, presumably in order to save Groby's estate from forfeiture. On 30 July, 'as a mark of respect for his eminent services and great sufferings for the public' (ibid.), the Convention granted Booth £10,000 out of excise revenues, which he offered to forgo in return for passage of a bill he had introduced that day permitting him to lease and sell lands in order that he might clear debts and provide portions for his younger children. The house evidently declined, the Lords' concurrence to the proposed gift was obtained, and order given to the excise commissioners that they make payment accordingly. In the second session of the Convention, Booth told for the minority who supported giving a second reading to the bill for establishment of a modified episcopacy.

On 20 April 1661 Booth was raised to the peerage as Lord Delamer, one of six barons created at the coronation of Charles II. He was apparently also granted the liberty of nominating six gentlemen for knighthoods, and he was made *custos rotulorum* of Cheshire. Reward for his services in promoting the Stuart restoration could not, however, ensure his loyalty to the new regime. Having supported in 1660 the case for cleansing episcopacy of its Laudian, high-church imperfections, Delamer came increasingly to distrust elements of the Restoration ecclesiastical settlement. In an undated letter to the Anglican Lord Bruce, probably written about the time of the debates on the Conventicle Bill in 1664, Delamer begged him to be 'merciful to us Presbiterians and at least give us leave to play innocently at bowls' (Swatland, 148). As the reign wore on and the cause of comprehension slowly died he was probably among those presbyterian peers who came to favour toleration. Delamer was also suspicious of the parameters within which the royal prerogative began to reassert itself in the immediate aftermath of Restoration. He appears to have believed that restraint on the import of Irish cattle, contrary to the wishes of the king and the lord lieutenant, was a matter of the utmost importance for 'the good of England' (Seaward, 297), although his economic self-interest was plainly involved at a time of depressed rent receipts and a decline in the profitability of farming.

By the time of Lord Treasurer Danby's ministry in the mid-1670s Delamer was firmly in the country party camp, and in 1677 was sympathetic to the duke of Buckingham's attempt, which was opposed by the court as encroaching on the royal prerogative, to secure the dissolution of the Cavalier Parliament. His opposition to government interests carried over during the exclusion crisis, during which he was one of the adverse or whig party in the Lords. In December 1679 he was one of the sixteen peers who signed and presented a petition to the king urging that he summon parliament to meet the following month, in an attempt to keep the threat of the Popish Plot firmly in the public eye, and hence sustain the pressure for the exclusion of the Catholic duke of York from the succession. He voted for the second Exclusion Bill in November 1680.

Delamer died at Dunham Massey on 8 August 1684, and was buried on 9 September at Bowdon in Cheshire. Lady

Elizabeth survived him—she died on 4 January 1691. Delamer was succeeded by his son Henry *Booth, the future first earl of Warrington. SEAN KELSEY

Sources *DNB* • GEC, *Peerage*, new edn • R. N. Dore, 'The Cheshire rising of 1659', *Transactions of the Lancashire and Cheshire Archaeological Society*, 69 (1959) • D. Underdown, *Pride's Purge: politics in the puritan revolution* (1971) • M. W. Helms, G. Hampson, and B. D. Henning, 'Booth, Sir George, 2nd bt', HoP, *Commons, 1660–90* • J. Morrill, *Cheshire, 1630–1660* (1974) • *The letter books of Sir William Brereton*, ed. R. N. Dore, 2 vols., Lancashire and Cheshire RS, 123, 128 (1984–90) • P. Seaward, *The Cavalier Parliament and the reconstruction of the old regime, 1661–1667* (1989) • A. Swatland, *The House of Lords in the reign of Charles II* (1996) • *IGI*
Archives JRL, papers
Likenesses W. N. Gardiner, wash drawing, AM Oxf.

Booth, George, second earl of Warrington (1675–1758), writer on divorce, second son of Henry *Booth, first earl of Warrington (1652–1694), and his wife, Mary (1652–1691), daughter of Sir James Langham of Cottesbrooke, Northamptonshire, was born on 2 May 1675 at Merehall, Cheshire. His elder brother having died young, George inherited the family estates centred on Dunham Massey, Cheshire, on his father's death in 1694. He found the estate heavily in debt and in bad repair. Warrington attributed this to his family's support for the protestant cause, and the generous portions allotted in his father's will to his sisters and younger brothers. The strain of these bequests on the estate finances led Warrington to try to suppress the will, but his siblings challenged him in the House of Lords and a trust was set up to pay the portions. The situation was compounded because his mother's marriage portion of £20,000 was never paid in full. In 1698 after his mother's death he brought a chancery suit for the recovery of the rest of his mother's portion against his grandfather. Although an out-of-court settlement was agreed the sum was never paid in full.

Warrington's aim on inheriting the estate was to clear it of debt. He could do this by borrowing money, selling land, or making a good marriage. Indebtedness was against his principles so part of the estate was sold and a search started for a rich bride. His name was linked with a Welsh heiress possessing £4000 per annum, and with Madam Offley, the daughter of Lord Crew, but in 1701 his uncle George Booth negotiated a marriage settlement between Warrington and Mary Oldbury (*d.* 1740) the eldest daughter of John Oldbury, a London merchant. Her fortune was rumoured to be £40,000 but was in reality £24,000. They married in 1702.

The marriage was not felicitous. Warrington accused his wife of financial profligacy, and contemporaries noted their incompatibility. After the birth of their only child, Mary (1704–1772), the couple lived in the same house but apart, and in 1739 Warrington published an anonymous pamphlet, *Considerations upon the Institution of Marriage*. The pamphlet advocated allowing divorce on the ground of incompatibility of temper. The obligations of a marriage contract in a landed family included the assurance that in the event of a wife's outliving her husband, her widow's jointure would be the first call on the estate. This particularly exercised Warrington although it did not happen in his case; his wife died the following year. Through Warrington's efforts the estate was put back on to a sound financial footing, and the family home at Dunham Massey was remodelled in the 1730s. Another pamphlet by Warrington, 'Letter to the writer of the "Present state of the republic of letters"', vindicated his father against reflections against him in Burnet's *History of our Time*, claiming that his debts were due to his imprisonment for high treason after the Monmouth rebellion. Although a conscientious whig, Warrington was not above taking a bribe from the tory earl of Oxford to vote in favour of the Malt Tax Bill in 1713. His growing cynicism with politics led to his withdrawal from political life, and the demise of the whig influence in Cheshire.

Warrington died at Dunham Massey on 2 August 1758 and was buried at Bowdon, Cheshire. His daughter married Henry Grey, fourth earl of Stamford, and the Dunham Massey estate passed to the Grey family. E. LORD

Sources Dunham Massey Hall, Grey MSS, earls of Stamford • Dunham Massey MSS, EGR1/8/11, 1/8/10/4a • [G. Booth, earl of Warrington], *Considerations upon the institution of marriage* (1739) • *Letters to and from Henrietta countess of Suffolk*, ed. J. W. Croker, 2 vols. (1824) • J. V. Beckett and C. Jones, 'Financial improvidence and political independence in the early eighteenth century: George Booth, second earl of Warrington', *Bulletin of the John Rylands University Library*, 65 (1982–3), 1–35 • J. Swarbrick, 'Dunham Massey Hall', *Transactions of the Lancashire and Cheshire Antiquarian Society*, 42 (1925), 53–78 • *DNB*
Archives JRL, corresp. and papers • priv. coll., family MSS | BL, corresp. with duke of Newcastle, Add. MSS 32709–32876, *passim*
Likenesses M. Dahl, oils, Tatton Park, Cheshire • attrib. G. Kneller, oils, Lanhydrock, Cornwall
Wealth at death £25,580: will, 1754, Dunham Massey MSS, EGR1/8/11, 1/8/10/4a

Booth, George (1791–1859), Latin scholar, was born on 12 November 1791 at Masborough House, Rotherham, the youngest son of William Booth of Ecclesfield. After attending Eton he went to Trinity College, Cambridge, in 1809, but left because of poor health. He moved to Lincoln College, Oxford, in 1811, and took his BA in 1813 and his MA in 1816. In 1823 he was created bachelor of divinity. He was ordained deacon as curate of Nether Hoyland, in the diocese of York, in 1815, and priest the following year. In 1816 Booth was elected to a fellowship of Magdalen College, Oxford, which he retained until 1834, and was made vice-president of the college in 1830, and dean of divinity in 1832. In 1833 he became vicar of Findon, Sussex, a post he held until his death, which occurred at Findon on 21 June 1859. He was married; his wife's name was Mary Ann. He was an accomplished Latin scholar and wrote two volumes of Latin verse, *Nugae canorae*, which he published pseudonymously as Etoniensis in 1826, and *Sicut lilium* (1854), a collection of choral songs. His other works include essays on Eton and the national debt.

C. W. SUTTON, *rev.* SARAH BROLLY

Sources Boase, *Mod. Eng. biog.* • *GM*, 3rd ser., 7 (1859), 196 • Foster, *Alum. Oxon.* • Venn, *Alum. Cant.* • *CGPLA Eng. & Wales* (1859)
Archives Magd. Oxf., papers
Wealth at death under £1500: probate, 30 July 1859, *CGPLA Eng. & Wales*

Booth, George Sclater-, first Baron Basing (1826–1894), politician, was born in London on 19 May 1826, the son of William Lutley Sclater (1789–1885) of Hoddington House, Odiham, Hampshire, and his wife, Anna Maria (*d.* 1879), daughter of William Bowyer. Descended from Richard Sclater (*b.* 1712), alderman of London, he was educated at Winchester College where he won the gold medal for Latin verse, and at Balliol College, Oxford, where he graduated BA in 1847 with a second class. He rowed as an undergraduate and was thought an excellent oar. A younger brother, the zoologist Philip Lutley *Sclater, was a student at Corpus Christi College, Oxford, at this time. George was called to the bar at the Inner Temple in 1851 and joined the western circuit, but never made much effort to secure a practice.

1857 was an important year for Sclater. He benefited from the will of his relative Anna Maria Booth and in accordance with it added Booth to his name. On 8 December he married Lydia Caroline (*d.* July 1881), daughter of Major George Birch of Clare Park, Hampshire. They had five sons and four daughters. Earlier that year, at the general election in April, he won North Hampshire as a Conservative and held it until 1886, his only contests being in 1865 and 1885. Sclater-Booth was a man the tory aristocrats liked to mock, and Disraeli thought him 'a boor' (Shannon, 226), but his virtues of reliability, competence, effective service on committees, and mastery of financial detail were important in a still weak tory party.

In March 1867 Sclater-Booth became secretary to the poor-law board in Disraeli's short administration, and in March 1868 was promoted to be financial secretary to the Treasury, but went out of office in December. During the six years of Gladstone's first government he served as chairman of the committee on public accounts. On 2 March 1874 he returned to office as president of the Local Government Board but, unlike his Liberal predecessor, was not included in the cabinet, a curious decision by Disraeli, given the significance of the office to the government's domestic objectives.

With R. A. Cross, Sclater-Booth was responsible for taking forward the Disraeli government's plans for urban reform, flamboyantly proclaimed in the slogan *sanitas sanitatum*. This he did with considerable initial effect. In 1875 he brought forward three important measures. The chief was the Public Health Act which took further the plans of the previous government; it remained the chief statute for sixty years. Sclater-Booth also saw through the Sale of Food and Drugs Act. His attempt to deal with river pollution, however, provoked strong opposition from manufacturers and was withdrawn; in 1876 a weaker bill was passed. On medical questions, Sclater-Booth was 'very much dominated' by Sir John Lambert, his permanent secretary, and the advice of medical experts was set aside, leading to the resignation of Sir John *Simon in May 1876 (Smith, 226). Sclater-Booth's measures were permissive rather than compulsory, and their effect in practice was less than they promised. They constituted, even so, an important moment in the history of British Conservatism, and the bills he passed remained points of reference for Conservative electoral candidates for half a century. Sclater-Booth did not maintain his burst of reform beyond 1876, though he tried to consolidate and compensate for the permissive character of the legislation already passed and in 1877 he attempted a plan of elective boards, which Derby thought 'a most confused & clumsy production' (*Diaries of E. H. Stanley*, 450). In 1880 he was appointed chairman of the grand committees in the Commons; he was knighted the same year.

In his own county, as a magistrate and man of business, Sclater-Booth's reputation was high, and he showed much tact in dealing with public meetings. He succeeded to the Hoddington estates in 1886, and on 7 July 1887 was raised to the peerage as Baron Basing of Basing and Byflete. In 1888 he was chosen chairman of the first county council of Hampshire, and he was also official verderer of the New Forest. A keen shot and competent amateur artist, Sclater-Booth was a privy councillor, LLD, and FRS. He died at Hoddington House on 22 October 1894 and was buried at Upton Grey, Hampshire. H. C. G. MATTHEW

Sources *The Times* (23 Oct 1894) • GEC, *Peerage* • *Dod's Parliamentary Companion* • P. Smith, *Disraelian Conservatism and social reform* (1967) • R. Shannon, *The age of Disraeli, 1868–1881: the rise of tory democracy* (1992) • *The diaries of E. H. Stanley, 15th earl of Derby, 1869–1878*, CS, 5th series, 4 (1994)
Archives Bodl. Oxf., letters to Disraeli • Hants. RO, letters to William Wickham
Likenesses Ape [C. Pellegrini], lithograph, NPG; repro. in *VF* (8 Aug 1874), pl. 181 • Faustin, caricature, BM • photograph, repro. in T. Cooper, *Men of mark: a gallery of contemporary portraits*, 3 (1878), p. 17 • woodburytype, NPG
Wealth at death £49,147 16*s*. 4*d*.: probate, 22 Nov 1894, *CGPLA Eng. & Wales*

Booth, Henry, first earl of Warrington (1652–1694), politician, was born on 13 January 1652, probably at Dunham Massey Hall, Cheshire. He was the eldest surviving son of George *Booth, second baronet and first Baron Delamer (1622–1684), politician and military leader, and Lady Elizabeth Grey (1621/2–1691), his second wife and the eldest daughter of Henry, first earl of Stamford. One of a dozen children Booth became heir apparent to the barony upon the death of his older brother William in 1662. He was well educated in preparation for the responsibilities of family and position he would assume, but he matriculated neither at Cambridge nor Oxford, nor was he admitted to one of the inns of court as his father had been. Booth succeeded to the title of Baron Delamer [Delamere] on 8 August 1684, the name by which he was best known both to contemporaries and subsequent students of history, and was created earl of Warrington on 17 April 1690.

On 7 July 1670 Booth married Mary Langham (1652–1691), the only child to survive from the several marriages of Sir James Langham, second baronet, of Cottesbrooke, Northamptonshire. The ceremony took place at St Helen's, Bishopsgate, London, a reflection of the long-standing Langham business interests and political ties in the city. Mary had also been baptized there, on 10 March 1653; she died on 23 March 1691 and was buried in the Booth family vault at Bowdon, Cheshire. Their first born son, James, died an infant. The surviving children included three other sons—George *Booth, later the second earl, Langham, and Henry, and two daughters—Elizabeth and Mary.

Exclusion politics Booth's public career began in 1673 at the age of twenty-one when his father resigned as *custos rotulorum* for Cheshire in his favour. The task of presiding over the commission of the peace was combined in many counties with the traditional military duties of the lord lieutenant, but since the lieutenancies of both Cheshire and Lancashire were firmly in the grasp of the earl of Derby, the separation of functions in the former had provided Charles II with a convenient way to recognize the very considerable influence of the Booths without giving substantial offence to the Stanleys. It was a position that Henry Booth learned to use to good advantage as a vehicle for advancing both personal and public goals. Among surviving examples of the charges he delivered to grand juries at the opening of quarter sessions are forceful pleas for the reformation of manners—he inveighs frequently against 'Swearing and Drinking' and 'the Horrible Profanation of God's name'—as well as cogent analyses of various national issues from a decidedly whig point of view. There is in these speeches, as well as in a number of essays he penned, evidence of a widely read man of strong intellect. They also give clear evidence of his presbyterian upbringing, although he himself conformed to the externals of Anglican practice, and of a degree of self-righteousness that has discomforted historians from Burnet to Macaulay.

In a 1678 by-election Booth was returned unopposed to the House of Commons as a member for Cheshire and as an open and ardent opponent of the court. He was then re-elected to all three Exclusion parliaments, the first two times apparently without contest and to the Oxford parliament with an overwhelming majority despite some local effort to stay the whig juggernaut. While in the Commons, Booth advocated frequent meetings of parliament and spoke out strongly against those members of the lower house who accepted pensions or other perquisites from the king—a stand that would come back to haunt him after the revolution of 1688 when he joined those on the receiving end of such favours. He also agitated for reform of the judiciary. In particular he singled out for stinging criticism Sir George Jeffreys, then (1680) chief justice of Chester, accusing him of heavy drinking, dereliction of duty and generally behaving 'himself more like a Jack-Pudding, than with that gravity that beseems a Judge' (Booth, 143). An early and passionate supporter of exclusion Booth took the position that the duke of York had no absolute right to the crown given the fact that the succession had been altered in the past when circumstances necessitated. As political passions mounted, however, he was careful to temper his rhetoric in an effort to reassure the county community that he was not trying to undermine the institution of monarchy and to quiet fears 'That 80, & 81 is become 40, & 41' (Booth, 627).

Even after the dissolution of the Oxford parliament Booth continued to offend in Stuart eyes. He was, for instance, one of a half dozen individuals prominently identified in the entourage that accompanied the duke of Monmouth on a trip into the north-west in the summer of 1682 likened by some to a royal progress. Then he directed the Cheshire grand jury at the October quarter sessions not to indict protestant dissenters on the grounds that the applicable Elizabethan legislation had really been enacted only for use against Catholics. By the end of the year Booth was removed as *custos rotulorum* and from the commission of the peace, and with the discovery of the Rye House plot in the summer of 1683 he suddenly found himself taken up with a dozen or more other radical whig activists, including lords Grey, Lovelace, and Russell, and imprisoned in the Tower of London on a charge of treason. In his case Charles II was particularly suspicious, perhaps because the rising that Booth's father had led in 1659—royalist in inspiration though it was—still lingered in memory as an example of the family's ability to command a significant popular following especially among protestant nonconformists. In any event Booth was closely examined by the privy council, and Dunham Massey Hall was carefully searched, as were the homes of surrounding tenants on the theory that weaponry might already have been put in their hands. Several months later he was finally released on bail since nothing could be proved against him.

Trial for treason His father having died the year before, Booth took his seat in the House of Lords as second Baron Delamer when parliament assembled shortly after James II ascended the throne in 1685. Then in July, while a prorogation was in effect, he was again arrested on a charge of high treason. Suspected of complicity in the Monmouth rebellion, he was essentially held incommunicado and without formal indictment for several months on the government's expectation that sufficient evidence would come to hand to warrant a trial and secure the conviction he had managed to side-step two years earlier. In truth, Delamer had been incautious in his contacts with agents of the duke of Monmouth, but there is no reliable evidence that he was actually prepared to take up arms even though several individuals were ready to implicate him in order to save their own necks. In any event, there followed some complicated legal manoeuvring. First Delamer petitioned the House of Lords to consider the grounds for his incarceration, arguing that it was a violation of his privilege as a peer and member of parliament. Despite efforts by both the earl of Devonshire and the marquess of Halifax to interest the upper house in the question, the matter was swept aside by a vote to adjourn that brought the session to an end. Delamer next sought and briefly secured his freedom under the terms of the Habeas Corpus Act. He was soon back in the Tower, however, this time with a bill of particulars specified and a trial date set for 14 January 1686.

Because parliament was not in session jurisdiction in this case fell to a special court presided over by a lord high steward appointed for the occasion by the crown and the lord triers, a panel of peers acting as a jury. The intent, obviously, was to make an example of Delamer. Lord Jeffreys—Delamer's Cheshire 'jack-pudding' of 1680 and now the most powerful judge in the land—was put in charge of the proceedings and he, in turn, picked a jury of thirty, of whom Macaulay reports fifteen were commanders of regiments who held their jobs at pleasure, another fifteen were court dependants, and all thirty were tories by political conviction. Heneage Finch, solicitor-general, did his best to make a case for conviction but was able to produce only one direct witness, whose testimony was doubtful at best, and circumstantial evidence that Delamer rebutted with relative ease. At the end of the trial, one by one, each of the twenty-seven lord triers then present declared him not guilty, although Ailesbury reported that the earl of Peterborough, groom of the stole, whispered into the ear of his neighbour just afterwards, 'Guilty by God' (*Memoirs*, 1.135). In fact, the case became something of a *cause célèbre* that caught the attention of the entire political spectrum from Lady Rachel Russell, widow of the whig martyr, to a high-church Oxford tory like Anthony Wood who spent 2*s*. 6*d*. to buy a copy of the pamphlet describing the trial. Certainly Wood and most other loyalists would have agreed with Peterborough's private view of the matter; but the patent unfairness of the proceeding, the trammelling of aristocratic privilege, and perhaps some element of disquiet growing out of the savage revenge visited upon even the most humble followers of Monmouth combined to save Delamer from the axe.

The revolution of 1688 Within the week Delamer was admitted to kiss the king's hand and to be lectured about his future conduct. Thereafter he dropped out of sight for the next few years, except when he agreed in 1687 (with others) to stand surety for the earl of Devonshire who was forced to give the king a bond for £30,000 as a guarantee of good behaviour. Although the circumstances of the case were vastly different, to Delamer it was another instance in which privilege of parliament was being unfairly denied to the accused. Certainly Delamer's name appears on the various lists of peers opposed to James II and his policies drawn up during this period, but he was not admitted to the carefully orchestrated contacts and correspondence that ultimately led to the dispatch of the invitation to William of Orange at the end of June 1688. During that summer, however, he was finally brought into the conspiracy, and evidence survives of meetings with the earl of Devonshire and the bishop of London as plans were developed for risings centred on Nottingham and York to coincide with William's expected arrival along the northern coast. Although he worried about the fate of his family, particularly because the children were so young, Delamer was absolutely confident in his decision to participate. He subsequently elaborated on his reasons for engaging, but at bottom strong religious conviction, pride of class, and a well-developed sense of personal grievance were the key motivators.

While the prince of Orange's descent at Torbay temporarily disrupted the plans of the northern conspirators, Delamer was in motion within less than a week, rallying friends and political associates among the Cheshire gentry and then reaching out for support from his tenantry and others willing to take up arms. Certainly he and the earl of Devonshire and, in turn, Devonshire and the earl of Danby, had to settle on a new timetable for action. But while the others moved cautiously at first Delamer was absolutely forthright about his intentions. On paper and then publicly at Manchester and on Bowdon Downs, where volunteers had been directed to assemble, he declared openly for William rather than taking cover under a call for a free parliament and, as well, made no secret of the planned rendezvous at Nottingham or of the names of the other principals associated in the project. Delamer understood the psychology of the situation. He fully expected that news of his taking up arms would encourage others to do likewise and that it would also complicate planning in London about how to deal with the larger situation at hand. Had there been a body of reliable troops available the force Delamer assembled might easily have been dispersed. However, he and the earl of Derby, recently restored to the lieutenancies of both Cheshire and Lancashire, had agreed that the latter would sit on his hands; and the one band of regular soldiers Delamer encountered at Manchester, a troop under the command of his neighbour Captain Richard Leigh, had yet to receive a supply of arms and, in fact, proved fertile recruiting ground for the rebel side.

On 18 November, Delamer and a few hundred mounted followers rode out from Bowdon Downs, going first to Newcastle under Lyme and then to Derby before reaching Nottingham on the 21st. Newsletters of the day quickly spread word about Delamer's movements, some of them embellishing their reports with tales of plunder, Catholic chapels despoiled, and other violations of the rules of knight errantry. One concluded with some accuracy that 'of all the men that have appeared in Armes & declared for the P[rince] none have done more zealously than those who began the Dance in Cheshire who gather weight like a Snow-Ball' (BL, Add. MS 4194, fol. 426). In fact, a basic difference in strategy if not in ultimate goals became quickly apparent after Delamer arrived at Nottingham. He remained intent on marching south to join William almost immediately, while the earl of Devonshire wanted to play a more cautious game and wait for other associates to come in and for additional troops to be raised and organized. Even the matter of securing agreement about the terms of a public declaration was apparently problematic, with the document that finally appeared focusing on a catalogue of grievances and looking to a freely elected parliament as the sole remedy to the national dilemma. The prince of Orange was not even mentioned, although at the Saturday market just before he left the city, Delamer remedied that lack with a crowd pleasing speech that emphasized the hand of providence in William's arrival to save protestantism and traditional English liberties.

Delamer's departure on 25 November brought with it a switch of partners. Lord Cholmondeley who had accompanied him from Cheshire stayed behind while the earl of Stamford, one of the first peers to join Devonshire, left with his cousin and long-time political associate. They took with them a troop of about 300 horse and set out to the west and then south—through Derby, Lichfield, Worcester, and Tewkesbury—on a line of march intended to avoid contact with any royal forces. Reaching Gloucester at the end of the month Delamer and Stamford freed Lord Lovelace from the castle where he had been held under arrest since making his own abortive attempt to reach the prince. They then moved on to Bristol and remained there until directed by William to join him at Hungerford on 7 December, by which time the focus of attention had shifted rapidly from the military to the political arena. The immediate and pressing problem was what to do about James II now that he had retreated from the contest, and Delamer numbered among the nineteen peers William summoned to consider the question at a meeting at Windsor ten days later. Joined by Lord Mordant, his cousin Stamford, and the earl of Shrewsbury, Delamer urged incarceration in the Tower, a plan the majority of the group wisely eschewed in favour of simply encouraging the king to flee England. That was advice William found to his liking, and he selected Delamer, Halifax, and Shrewsbury to deliver the message, a task by subsequent report that Delamer handled with greater sensitivity than might have been expected. Thereafter, however, he became an outspoken supporter of declaring the throne vacant. As Clarendon records in his diary for 31 January 1689:

> Lord Delamer said, it was long since he thought himself absolved from his allegiance to King James; that he owed him none and never would pay him any; and if King James came again, he was resolved to fight against him, and would die single with his sword in his hand, rather than pay him any obedience. (Singer, 2.257)

After the revolution Whatever good feelings Delamer had about the beginning of the reign of William and Mary soon dissipated, despite substantial rewards recognizing his role in bringing them to the throne. Almost immediately (14 February 1689) he was made a member of the privy council, and later that spring he was appointed chancellor of the exchequer (28 March 1689) and one of the commissioners of the Treasury (5 April 1689). William also restored him to the position of *custos rotulorum* of Cheshire and named him to the lieutenancy, a step taken with some reluctance perhaps because of the bitter quarrel that had erupted between Delamer and the earl of Derby about the latter's failure to act more forcefully during the revolution, but an appointment on which Delamer insisted saying 'he would not value all the K[ing] could give him, except hee might have that' (Foxcroft, 2.209). Other tokens of favour and emoluments followed, including long-term leases on former Jesuit properties in several counties, but appointment to one of the great offices of state eluded him, and Delamer soon came to feel that his advice on major issues confronting the government was ignored. For William, too, the working relationship was less than successful. Tory influence had increased substantially in the parliament elected to replace the Convention, and he needed financial managers able to persuade parliament to pay the bills for his military campaigns and other needs. Accordingly, Delamer and his two whig associates at the Treasury, Henry Capel and the earl of Monmouth, were all removed from their posts in the spring of 1690. To soften the blow Delamer was created earl of Warrington on 17 April of the same year and granted a pension of £2000 payable annually, but frequently paid in arrears.

The decision to push Delamer to the sidelines was wise, given his temperament. 'Actuated with a sense of Honour and Justice, not afraid to declare his Opinion, not willing to conceal his Sentiments, which he seldom found reason to alter', even his eulogist felt constrained to allude to his inflexibility, a rigidity of character simply unsuited for a major governmental post (Wroe, 19). However, Macaulay's characterization of him: 'A restless malecontent even when preferred' (Macaulay, 3.1797), misses the essence of the man and, rather unfairly, relies on the satirical and Jacobite inspired depiction of Delamer in Arthur Mainwaring's poem, *King of Hearts* (1690), from which the line is taken. The truth is that he was something of a throwback to an old-fashioned puritanism. It made him a very difficult man to deal with at close quarters; but it fed a public personality that many protestant dissenters and those to whom the label puritan low-churchmen has been applied found powerfully attractive. It was also the vein he tapped into when he returned to Cheshire in triumph as lord lieutenant in the early summer of 1689, escorted on his way out of London by as many as 500 horse; but at the same time it represented a view of the world that simply did not fit in the delicate balance of party politics that emerged after the revolution. As a consequence Warrington figured ever less importantly in that history, although he continued active in both local politics and parliament. Then late in 1693 he caught a cold at the Middle Temple Hall while listening to legal arguments growing out of a dispute between two peers. Characteristically, he insisted on continuing to attend sessions at the House of Lords, developed a fever and died in London, probably of pneumonia, on 2 January following. He was buried in the family vault at Bowdon twelve days later.

DAVID HOSFORD

Sources H. Booth, Lord Delamer and earl of Warrington, *Works* (1694) · R. Wroe, *Sermon at the funeral of the earl of Warrington* (1694) · *State trials*, vol. 11 · *Memoirs of Thomas, earl of Ailesbury*, ed. W. E. Buckley, 1, Roxburghe Club, 122 (1890) · *The manuscripts of Lord Kenyon*, HMC, 35 (1894) · *The manuscripts of S. H. Le Fleming*, HMC, 25 (1890) · *Seventh report*, HMC, 6 (1879) [Sir Frederick Graham] · *The manuscripts of the House of Lords*, 4 vols., HMC, 17 (1887–94), vol. 3 · *The manuscripts of his grace the duke of Portland*, 10 vols., HMC, 29 (1891–1931), vol. 3 · *The life and times of Anthony Wood*, ed. A. Clark, 5 vols., OHS, 19, 21, 26, 30, 40 (1891–1900) · *CSP dom.*, 1677–95 · W. A. Shaw, ed., *Calendar of treasury books*, [33 vols. in 64], PRO (1904–69), esp. vols. 9 and 17 · J. Redington, ed., *Calendar of Treasury papers*, 1, PRO (1868) · N. Luttrell, *A brief historical relation of state affairs from September 1678 to April 1714*, 1–2 (1857) · *The correspondence of Henry Hyde, earl of Clarendon, and of his brother Lawrence Hyde, earl of Rochester*, ed. S. W. Singer, 2 (1828) · *Bishop Burnet's History of his own time*, ed. G. Burnet and T. Burnet, 2 vols. (1724–34) · Ford, Lord Grey, *The secret history of the Rye-House plot: and of Monmouth's rebellion* (1754) · J. E. T. Rogers, ed., *A complete collection of the protests of the Lords*, 2 (1875) · G. Ormerod, *The history of the county palatine and city of Chester*, 2nd edn, ed. T. Helsby, 1 (1882) · T. B. Macaulay, *The history of England from the accession of James II*, new edn, ed. C. H. Firth, 6 vols.

(1913–15), vols. 2–3 · *The life and letters of Sir George Savile … first marquis of Halifax*, ed. H. C. Foxcroft, 2 vols. (1898) · D. H. Hosford, *Nottingham, nobles and the north: aspects of the revolution of 1688* (1976) · D. R. Lacey, *Dissent and parliamentary politics in England, 1661–1689* (1969) · GEC, *Peerage*

Archives JRL, papers | BL, Ellis newsletters, Add. MS 4194 · BL, Middleton papers, Add. MS 41805 · BL, War Office corresp., Add. MS 38695 · Bodl. Oxf., Le Fleming newsletters, donated MSS C/38, C/39 · DWL, entering book, Roger Morrice MS Q

Likenesses G. Kneller, oils, 1689, Gov. Art Coll. · J. Smith, engraving (after G. Kneller)

Booth, Henry (1789–1869), railway projector and manager, was born at 34 Rodney Street, Liverpool, on 4 April 1789, the son of Thomas Booth (1749–1832), a corn merchant, and his wife, Esther, *née* Noble (*d.* 1826), of Lancaster. He was privately educated at the Revd Shepherd's boarding-school, Gateacre, near Liverpool, and then employed in his father's office, before going into business on his own account as a corn merchant, but with no great success. On 27 August 1812 he married Ellen Crompton (1789–1871), eldest daughter of Abraham Crompton of Chorley Hall; they had three daughters and one son. In 1822 a committee of Liverpool merchants was established to promote the construction of a railway between Liverpool and Manchester. Thomas Booth was a member of the committee, and Henry became an early supporter of the scheme, visiting the Stockton and Darlington Railway in 1824, and organizing and writing in support of the Liverpool and Manchester line. His energy, his administrative abilities, and his gift for public relations were quickly recognized by the committee; he became a member and was appointed secretary after his father stood down in 1824. It was Henry Booth who wrote the Liverpool and Manchester Railway's lengthy and detailed prospectus, dated 29 October 1829, which was the company's first major public announcement. In early 1825 a bill for the construction of the railway came before parliament. It was thrown out after a costly struggle. In the following year a second bill was introduced, and was carried, and Booth was appointed company secretary and treasurer at £500 a year, and as effective managing director of the railway, took an active part in the construction of the line, which was begun in June 1826 and finished in 1830.

Booth was a consistent supporter of George Stephenson as principal engineer of the line, and an enthusiastic promoter of the use of steam locomotive power on the railway, in opposition to those directors who favoured horse-drawn vehicles or stationary steam engines. When the board of directors announced the holding of a series of competitive trials at Rainhill to test the capabilities of different locomotives, Booth and Robert Stephenson jointly constructed and entered the successful *Rocket*. Booth certainly had a remarkable mechanical talent; he suggested the multitubular boiler, which gave a very large and effective heating surface, increasing the locomotive's efficiency; he also invented the first screw coupling, sprung buffers, and an artificial lubricant for carriage axles.

In August 1845 the Liverpool and Manchester was absorbed into the Grand Junction Railway, for which Booth served as secretary for a year, until it in turn became part of the London and North Western Railway (LNWR) in 1846. Booth was appointed secretary for the northern section of the LNWR, and in October 1848 he became a director. He retired from office on 18 May 1859, after being presented with 5000 guineas by the company as a token of gratitude for valuable and faithful service. He spent the remainder of his life in his native town, where for some years he acted as a borough magistrate.

In religion Booth was a Unitarian, and in politics a moderate Liberal. Contemporary accounts of him give the impression of a grave, reserved, reticent man, utterly dependable and trustworthy, rigorously honest, and a thorough and indefatigable worker. He was a tireless writer and pamphleteer for much of his life, publishing books, papers, and articles on technical and scientific subjects, social questions, taxation, politics, and the economy. His *Account of the Liverpool and Manchester Railway* (1830) remains an indispensable starting point for serious study of the early history of that line. His works on politics, notably *A Reformed Parliament* (1833), reflect his moderate Liberalism, and his studies of economic questions, most importantly *Free Trade as it Affects the People* (1833), express his firm but pragmatic belief in *laissez-faire* principles. As a prominent railway manager later in life he was not a dogmatic opponent of government regulation of the railways—in which his brother James *Booth (1796/7–1880) was involved—but defended them against what he saw as unfair financial burdens, particularly in the case of the compensation payments they were required to make to the victims of railway accidents under Lord Campbell's Act of 1846; *A Letter to Lord Campbell on the 9th and 10th Vict., Cap. 93* (1854) is an important summary of the railway companies' position on this issue. He died at his residence, Eastbourne, Lodge Lane, Princes Park, Liverpool, on 28 March 1869, and was buried on 1 April at Toxteth Chapel.

FRANCIS WATT, *rev.* RALPH HARRINGTON

Sources H. Booth, *Henry Booth: inventor, partner in the 'Rocket' and the father of railway management* (1980) · R. Smiles, *Memoir of the late Henry Booth* (1869) · R. E. Carlson, *The Liverpool and Manchester railway project, 1821–1823* (1969) · E. Rideout, 'Rodney Street, Liverpool', *Transactions of the Historic Society of Lancashire and Cheshire*, 83 (1931), 61–95 · *Liverpool Daily Post* (30 March 1869) [suppl.] · d. cert.

Likenesses bust, *c.*1850, Sci. Mus. · W. Theed, statue, *c.*1870, St George's Hall, Liverpool · oils, repro. in Booth, *Henry Booth*, facing p. 128

Wealth at death under £35,000: probate, 20 April 1869, *CGPLA Eng. & Wales*

Booth [*née* Santlow], **Hester** (*c.*1690–1773), actress and dancer, was born about 1690. Very little is known about her parents and family background, although her mother, Jane (or Joanna), died in April 1724. She was apprenticed to the dancing-master René Cherrier, probably in 1704, and made her début as a dancer at Drury Lane on 28 February 1706. Her dancing attracted attention immediately, and in 1707 she danced in Mr Isaac's *The Union*, performed before Queen Anne and at Drury Lane to celebrate the Act of Union between England and Scotland. The dance was published in notation. Hester Santlow first appeared as an actress at Drury Lane on 3 December 1709, playing Prue in

Hester Booth (*c.*1690–1773), by John Ellys

William Congreve's *Love for Love*. In 1710 she achieved notable success in the title role of Charles Shadwell's *The Fair Quaker of Deal*. A visitor to London, Zacharias Conrad von Uffenbach, wrote of her at this time as 'universally admired for her beauty, matchless figure and the unusual elegance of her dancing and acting' (*London in 1710*, 30–31). Between the seasons of 1707–8 and 1711–12 she added a variety of roles to her repertory, including Ophelia in Shakespeare's *Hamlet*, Miranda in Susannah Centlivre's *The Busy Body*, Gatty in George Etherege's *She Would if She Could*, and Harriet in Etherege's *The Man of Mode*.

Hester Santlow was absent from the stage for most of the 1712–13 season, for she gave birth to a daughter, fathered by James *Craggs the younger (1686–1721), about February 1713. Her relationship with Craggs probably began about 1711, after his return from diplomatic duties abroad, and seems to have lasted until at least 1717. Their daughter, Harriot Craggs (*d.* 1769), married her first husband, Richard Eliot of Port Eliot, in 1726. Their son Edward Eliot became first Baron Eliot of St Germans; Harriot married her second husband, John Hamilton, in 1749; their son, John James Hamilton, became ninth earl and first marquess of Abercorn.

Hester Santlow resumed her acting and dancing career at Drury Lane in the 1713–14 season, and in the following few seasons she extended her repertory with Angelica in George Farquhar's *The Constant Couple*, Angelina in Colley Cibber's *Love Makes a Man*, Cordelia in Nahum Tate's adaptation of *King Lear*, Harriet in Richard Steele's *The Funeral*, Desdemona in Shakespeare's *Othello*, Celia in Ben Jonson's *Volpone*, and Selima in Nicholas Rowe's *Tamerlane*. On 3 August 1719 she married the actor Barton *Booth (1681–1733) in the parish church at Chipping Ongar, Essex. After her marriage she continued to work, and in the ensuing seasons she gained such new roles as Helena in Aphra Behn's *The Rover*, Elvira in John Dryden's *The Spanish Fryar*, and Lucinda in Steele's *The Conscious Lovers* (a role she created). A feature of her earlier career had been her appearances in 'boy's clothes', and she added several such roles to her repertory in the 1720s, among them the page Dowglass in John Banks's *The Albion Queens* and Fidelia in William Wycherley's *The Plain Dealer*.

Mrs Booth danced regularly in the entr'actes. Her solo *Harlequin Dance* was a particular favourite, but her varied repertory included a *Hussar* duet, a solo *Flute chacone*, and the group dance *Lads and Lasses*. Four of her serious dances, choreographed by Anthony L'Abbé, were published in notation in the 1720s in *A New Collection of Dances*. She was John Weaver's leading dancer, for she created the roles of Venus in his innovative *The Loves of Mars and Venus* (1717), Eurydice in *Orpheus and Eurydice* (1718), and Helen of Troy in his final work, *The Judgment of Paris* (1733). In 1721 Weaver wrote in the preface to his *Anatomical and Mechanical Lectures upon Dancing*:

> we have a Dancer in the Person of Mrs. *Booth*, where Art and Nature have combin'd to produce a beautiful Figure, allow'd by all Judges in our Art to be the most graceful, most agreeable, and most correct Performer in the World. (Weaver, x)

Mrs Booth also danced in the Drury Lane pantomimes of the 1720s: she appeared as Diana in John Thurmond's *Harlequin Doctor Faustus* (1723), as Daphne in his *Apollo and Daphne* (1725), and as Andromeda in Roger and Weaver's *Perseus and Andromeda* (1728).

The last years of Hester Booth's stage career were marked by her husband's illness. He was obliged to retire from the stage in 1728 and, although she went on working, she cared for him until he died on 10 May 1733. After his death she sold her share in the theatre's patent to the actor Henry Giffard, and her retirement from the stage was announced in the *Universal Spectator* for 22 September 1733. Thomas Davies assessed her abilities as an actress in *Dramatic Miscellanies* (1784):

> She was well suited, by the agreeableness of her person, her voice, and manner of speaking, to several of the soft and gentle females … She was rather a cold actress in tragedy; in comedy she displayed a pleasing vivacity and elegant deportment, that charmed the public long. (Davies, 2.275–6)

In 1772 Hester Booth had a monument to her husband erected in Westminster Abbey. She died on 15 January 1773 at her house in Great Russell Street, Bloomsbury, London, and was buried on 21 January alongside her mother and her husband in the parish church of St Laurence, Cowley, near Uxbridge. In her will she left the residue of her considerable estate to her grandchildren Harriot Neale, John Eliot, Ann Bonfoy, and Catherine Eliot. Moira Goff

Sources S. J. Cohen, 'Theory and practice of theatrical dancing: III Hester Santlow', *Famed for dance*, ed. I. K. Fletcher, S. J. Cohen, and R. Lonsdale (1960), 49–58 • E. L. Avery, ed., *The London stage, 1660–1800*, pt 2: 1700–1729 (1960) • A. H. Scouten, ed., *The London*

stage, 1660–1800, pt 3: *1729–1747* (1961) • A. L'Abbé, *A new collection of dances* (c.1725); facs. edn (1991) • Mr Isaac, *The union: a … dance … writt down in characters by J. Weaver* (1707) • *London in 1710: from the travels of Zacharias Conrad von Uffenbach*, ed. and trans. W. H. Quarrell and M. Mare (1934) • *Genealogical memoranda relating to the families of Eliot of Port Eliot and Craggs of Wyserley* (privately printed, 1868) • C. Cibber, *An apology for the life of Mr. Colley Cibber*, new edn, 1, ed. R. W. Lowe (1889), 76–8; 2 (1889), 94–6 • D. E. Baker, *Biographia dramatica, or, A companion to the playhouse*, rev. I. Reed, new edn, 1 (1782), 33 • J. Weaver, *Anatomical and mechanical lectures upon dancing* (1721), x • *Universal Spectator* (22 Sept 1733) • T. Davies, *Dramatic miscellanies*, 2 (1784), 275–6 • J. Milhous and R. D. Hume, eds., *Vice Chamberlain Coke's theatrical papers, 1706–1715* (1982) • B. Victor, *The history of the theatres of London and Dublin*, 1 (1761), 10 • parish register, Cowley, St Laurence's, 21 Jan 1773 [burial]

Likenesses J. Ellys, oils, c.1720–1725, Theatre Museum, London; copy, Port Eliot, Cornwall • J. Ellys, oils, c.1734, Port Eliot, Cornwall • possibly by J. Ellys, oils, Port Eliot, Cornwall • J. Ellys, oils, priv. coll. [*see illus.*]

Wealth at death over £600—legacies: will, PRO, PROB 10/2608, 93

Booth, Hubert Cecil (1871–1955), civil engineer, was born on 4 July 1871 in Gloucester, the sixth child of Abraham Booth (*d.* after 1903), timber importer, and his wife, Elizabeth Ann Watts. Educated at the College School, Gloucester, and at Gloucester county school, he entered the City and Guilds Central Institution in 1889, where he took a three-year course in civil and mechanical engineering. He obtained the associateship of the City and Guilds Institute, having distinguished himself in his academic studies. He became an associate member and, later, a member of the Institution of Civil Engineers, and was elected a fellow of the City and Guilds Institute.

Booth's first employment was with Maudslay, Sons, and Field, at that time the leading marine engine builders in the country, where he was first employed as a draughtsman attached to a group designing the engines for two new battleships for the Royal Navy. In 1894 he was chosen by W. B. Bassett (a director of Maudslays, who had floated a company for the construction and operation of 'great wheels') to assist with the correction of faulty techniques which had complicated the erection of the great wheel then being built at Earls Court. He was then commissioned by Bassett to design, plan, and control the erection of three similar structures at Blackpool, Vienna, and Paris. The Paris example was 300 feet in diameter, and remained a familiar landmark until it was dismantled in the 1920s. The great wheel in Vienna continued to be much patronized and became one of the best-known images of the city, featuring famously in the film, *The Third Man* (1949). The interest of these three huge wheels, designed by Booth between the age of twenty-four and twenty-six, lies in their being the first major structures into which a degree of flexibility was deliberately introduced in a mathematically controlled manner.

In 1901 Booth started his own business in London as a consulting engineer. He continued in active practice for the next forty years, apart from a break in 1902–3 when he took complete charge of the erection of the railway bridge at Connel Ferry in Argyll. At that time the bridge was about one-quarter built, and its construction was behind schedule. He returned to London when this task had been successfully completed. On 24 January 1903 he married Charlotte Mary (*d.* 1948), eldest daughter of Francis Tring Pearce, of Gloucester, and they raised two sons.

After seeing the demonstration of an American machine for blowing dust from carpets, Booth was inspired to invent the vacuum cleaner in 1901; his British Vacuum Cleaner Company was founded the same year and he continued as its chairman until his retirement at the age of eighty-one. When Booth's machine cleaned the carpet in Westminster Abbey before the coronation of Edward VII, the king asked for it to be demonstrated at Buckingham Palace, and subsequently machines were installed there and at Windsor. Booth's rights to the invention were challenged, and several years passed before he was able to have them established by the High Court. The early machines were large fixed or semi-fixed devices; the domestic vacuum cleaner of later years was, to Booth's mind, a mere toy, although he appreciated its value as a labour-saving device. He was particularly interested in the use of vacuum cleaning to promote hygiene, both in the home and workplace, and to reduce discomfort and disease in industrial processes.

Booth was gifted with a remarkable insight into the elements of any technological or intellectual problem he was called on to solve, and he was meticulous in his attention to detail. Consequently his work, much of it original, was rarely susceptible of improvement, save through the development of improved manufacturing techniques. His personal qualities of charm and integrity won him the affection and respect of a wide circle of friends in all walks of life. When young he was a keen amateur boxer. In later years his recreations lay in the field of philosophical speculation of an intuitive but realistic kind, and in good talk generally.

At the time of his death, which occurred at 2 Sydenham Road, Croydon, on 14 January 1955, Booth was living at Amberley, 107 Foxley Lane, Purley, Surrey.

MUIR JOHNSTON, *rev.* ANITA MCCONNELL

Sources private information (1971) • *Bulletin* [Association Suisse des Électriciens], 16 (1972), 63 • *The Times* (15 Jan 1955), 8f • *DNB* • m. cert. • d. cert.

Likenesses D. Jagger, portrait, priv. coll.

Wealth at death £80,935 13*s.* 3*d.*: probate, 1 March 1955, *CGPLA Eng. & Wales*

Booth, James (1707–1778), lawyer, was born at St Germain-en-Laye, France, one of four sons and a daughter of James Booth, formerly of Theobalds, Hertfordshire. His father, who was a Roman Catholic and a Jacobite, resided at the Stuart court. Roman Catholics were prevented by the statute 7 and 8 William III c. 24 from practising at the bar. Booth, who adhered to the faith in which he had been educated, nevertheless took out a licence to practise as a conveyancer, and soon acquired a considerable amount of business, owing partly to his own skill and ingenuity, and partly to the advantage which, in consequence of the various penal laws then in force, the Roman Catholics of that day derived from consulting a member of their own faith.

On the death of Nathaniel Pigott, the most eminent conveyancer of his day, and also a Roman Catholic, Booth succeeded to this position. His conveyances enjoyed the highest possible repute in the profession, and being often copied and used as precedents by lesser practitioners, they set the fashion in conveyancing for a great part of the eighteenth century. In one respect, however, they contrasted very unfavourably with those of his predecessor Pigott. Whereas Pigott's deeds had been models of conciseness, Booth's were remarkably prolix. This, while merely inconvenient to his wealthy clients, occasioned unnecessary expense to those whose advisers needlessly followed his example. He wrote no treatise on the subject, nor did he publish a collection of precedents, but his written opinions circulated within the profession, and several were printed. His knowledge of the 1536 Statute of Uses, a fundamental plank of his professional skill, was profound. He was said to have been consulted by the duke of Cumberland as to whether he could recover a legacy left to him by his father, George II, the new king having torn up the will, and to have advised that 'a king of England has by the common law no power of bequeathing personal property' (Polson, 2.84). He is also said to have drafted George III's will. He was for some years a friend of Lord Mansfield. Booth was admitted to the Middle Temple on 28 November 1772.

In politics Booth was a tory. Rather late in life he married Mary, the granddaughter of John Sharp, archbishop of York (1691–1714), from whom he was subsequently separated. In his later years he suffered considerably from cataracts. He died on 15 January 1778 at Old Boswell Court, London. He was survived by his wife.

J. M. Rigg, *rev.* Andrew D. E. Lewis

Sources C. Butler, *Historical memoirs of the English, Irish, and Scottish Catholics since the Reformation*, 3rd edn, 4 (1822), 360 • C. Butler, *Reminiscences*, 4th edn, 2 (1827), 274 • *GM*, 1st ser., 55 (1785), 243, 340 • [A. Polson (?)], *Law and lawyers*, 2 vols. (1840), 2.84 • T. Sharp, *The life of John Sharp D.D.*, 2 vols. (1825), 2.312 • Gillow, *Lit. biog. hist.*, vol. 1 • J. Hutchinson, ed., *A catalogue of notable Middle Templars: with brief biographical notices* (1902) • J. D. Holliday, *Life of Lord Mansfield* (1797), 32–3 • *GM*, 1st ser., 48 (1778), 46

Archives Ushaw College, Durham, opinions

Booth, James (1796/7–1880), civil servant, was the youngest of the four sons and two daughters of Thomas Booth (1749–1832), a prosperous merchant of Toxteth Lodge, Liverpool, and his wife, Esther Noble (*d.* 1826). Henry *Booth, the railway manager, was his elder brother. The family were Unitarians and prominent in the reform movement in Liverpool. James and his brothers campaigned for Lord Sefton, who stood against Canning in the general election of June 1818. He was admitted at Lincoln's Inn on 7 November 1818, when his age was given as twenty-one, and matriculated from St John's College, Cambridge, in Lent 1819, but did not graduate. He was called to the bar in February 1824, building up a successful practice in the chancery courts. In 1827 he married a cousin, Jane Noble (*d.* 1872). He was among the remarkable group of lawyers and philosophic radicals who attended John Austin's lectures at University College, London, during 1828–30. Subsequently he became a member of the council of University College, and framed its constitution.

In July 1833 Booth was appointed by the whig government as a member of the royal commission to inquire into municipal corporations; he and Charles Austin, brother of the jurist, investigated corporations in south and central Wales. In 1838 the speaker of the House of Commons, James Abercromby, appointed him to a temporary position preparing synopses ('breviates') conveying the substance of private bills for the use of select committees. He was appointed counsel to the speaker and examiner of recognizances in 1839 by Abercromby's successor, Charles Shaw Lefevre. He established general principles for the form of private bills and, in collaboration with Robert John Palk, drew up outline bills, known as model bills, for all the more important classes of bills. These were the basis for his most important achievement, the Clauses Consolidation Acts of 1845 and 1847, which brought together the provisions common to all bills relating to compulsory land purchase, railway schemes, and company formations. As a result, individual railway bills were shortened by about 90 per cent, and select committees could very rapidly assess in which respects an individual bill deviated from general principles and raised questions of public policy. Booth's acts enabled parliament to deal with the great volume of bills generated by the railway boom of 1844–6, and made procedures cheaper and more convenient for railway promoters (who included his brother). In 1850 he assisted his friend Sir John Romilly, the attorney-general, in preparing the act to regulate the court of chancery in Ireland.

Booth's post came under the scrutiny of a select committee on expenditure in 1848, and in 1850, fearing charges of sinecurism, Lord John Russell decided to abolish it (in the following year it was revived). On 10 October 1850 Booth accepted the office of secretary to the Board of Trade, in succession to Sir Denis Le Marchant, for which his experience of railway bills made him well qualified. During the long presidencies of Lord Stanley of Alderley (1852–8) and Thomas Milner-Gibson (1859–66), Booth and the other permanent officials decided most of the day-to-day issues which arose in the department. He retired from the secretaryship on 30 September 1865 and was created a CB on 6 July 1866.

As an experienced official, Booth was appointed a member of the royal commission on trade unions in February 1867. He was in close sympathy with the chairman, Sir William Erle, also a whig lawyer, and Erle entrusted to him the drafting of the commission's final report. Booth's draft, which restated the classical economic objections to trade unions, advocated a labour market free from artificial restrictions; he saw combinations as a form of protection, at variance with the commercial policy of free trade. His conclusions formed the basis for the report of the majority of the commission in 1869. He published in 1871 a utilitarian critique of organized religion, *The problem of the world and the church reconsidered, in three letters to a friend by a septuagenarian* (3rd edn, 1879), which argued that the church and its doctrines stood in the way of improving the material condition of mankind. Booth died at his home, 2 Princes Gardens, Knightsbridge, London, on 11 May 1880. He was survived by a son, George Booth (1829–1892).

M. C. CURTHOYS

Sources *Law Times* (22 May 1880), 71 • Venn, *Alum. Cant.* • O. C. Williams, *The historical development of private bill procedure and standing orders in the House of Commons*, 2 vols. (1948–9) • H. H. Bellot, *University College, London, 1826–1926* (1929) • H. Parris, *Government and the railways in nineteenth-century Britain* (1965) • H. Parris, *Constitutional bureaucracy* (1969) • H. Booth, *Henry Booth: inventor, partner in the 'Rocket' and the father of railway management* (1980) • J. C. Sainty, ed., *Officials of the board of trade, 1660–1870* (1974)

Wealth at death under £45,000: probate, 24 May 1880, *CGPLA Eng. & Wales*

Booth, James (1806–1878), mathematician and educationist, was born on 25 August 1806, the first of the three children of John and Ellen Booth of Lavagh, co. Leitrim. The Booths owned a small property and belonged to the Church of Ireland community of Annaduff parish. James obtained his early education in the small school of 'Parson Kane' at Drumsna, and was admitted to Trinity College, Dublin, in 1825. He graduated BA in 1833, and was awarded the Berkeley medal for Greek in 1834. He took fellowship examinations four times but though highly placed was not awarded a fellowship.

Booth left Ireland in 1840 and became principal of Bristol College. The college failed chiefly on account of clerical opposition to its secular curriculum. In 1843 he became vice principal of the newly founded Liverpool Collegiate Institution, under the principalship of Dr W. J. Conybeare. There he joined the Liverpool Philosophical Society, becoming its president in 1846. Elected FRS that year on the strength of published papers mainly on the geometry of conics and curved surfaces, Booth was regarded as inventor of the tangential co-ordinates (the 'Boothian co-ordinates'); however, he later discovered that Professor J. Plücker of Halle University had already published on the subject. Throughout his life Booth continued mathematical work, republishing his papers with some new material in *A Treatise on some New Geometrical Methods* in two volumes, one in 1873 and the other in 1878.

Booth was ordained in the Church of England in 1842, served as curate for a time in Bristol, and was then appointed vicar of St Anne's, Wandsworth, in 1854. On 28 September of the same year he married Mary Watney, daughter of Daniel Watney the brewer. The couple had three children, John William Watney, Elinor, and another son. Booth established on the site of the present South Thames College the Wandsworth Trade School, first of its kind in the country, where among others Professor Henry Moseley and J. C. Buckmaster taught classes. The school failed through lack of funds, but Moseley took the idea to Bristol when he became residentiary canon of the cathedral, and founded the Bristol Trade and Mining School, eventually part of Merchant Venturers' College. Booth also assisted in founding St Anne's elementary school. In 1859 he was presented to the living of St John, Stone, Buckinghamshire, by the Royal Astronomical Society (to which the advowsons had been transferred by Dr John Lee, ecclesiastical lawyer, landowner, and amateur astronomer), and was also admitted fellow of the Royal Astronomical Society. He persuaded Lee to found in Bishopstone a small school for the teaching of agricultural subjects, but it failed.

Booth was noted as a preacher and had several of his sermons published. His chief object as theologian was to reconcile the Bible with new scientific knowledge, arguing that science reveals physical truths, the Bible axiomatic moral truths. His most important work, however, was the promotion of scientific and technical education, mainly through the agency of the Society of Arts, of which he became a fellow in 1852. It was on his suggestion that the society (today the Royal Society of Arts) founded its journal. He quickly rose to become its treasurer and in 1855–6 he was chairman of council. He was again chairman in 1857, but resigned his office late in the year, owing to serious disagreements with other members of council.

The cause of the disagreement has been misunderstood and misreported in the society's histories. Most of Booth's energies at this time were absorbed into the society's examination project. Harry Chester, an official from the education committee of the privy council and chairman of the society in 1853, moved the original resolution in favour of an examination scheme. Accordingly, society historians allocated to him the credit of creating it. It was not so. Booth had in 1846 and 1847 published two influential pamphlets, the first in favour of industrial education and the other, *Education the Province of the State*, advocating state-run examination for all candidates for public, industrial, and commercial service. In 1853 he chaired and wrote the report of a committee of the society proposing examinations, and urging the government to spend money on industrial education. However Chester and Booth disliked one another. Booth therefore had no hand in the design of the first examination scheme, launched in 1855. Only one candidate appeared and the scheme was a failure. From then on Booth was put completely in charge, becoming chairman of the examination committee and an active promoter of a workable scheme. His first examination, in thirteen subjects, was held in June 1856 and attracted fifty-six candidates. Its success encouraged the society to extend its efforts and in 1857 examinations were held in London and Huddersfield, attracting 220 candidates who worked 546 papers.

Booth was then re-elected chairman of council. He wished to have more centres, and called for the examinations to be placed on an independent, professional footing, with their own office, funds, and paid examiners. However in this he over-reached the intentions of the society and met with opposition, led by Chester, who also objected to inclusion in the examinations of a viva voce element. The examination committee and the council failed to support Booth: an impatient and irascible man, he forthwith resigned.

Nevertheless, a national pattern of common examining now existed. In 1857 Oxford University imitated the society by setting up 'locals' for schools. Two years later the

Department of Science and Art launched its 'payment-on-results' examination scheme, taking over most of the society's science examinations. Booth left London and did not return to the society, to some of whose members he had become *persona non grata*. His wife, Mary, died in 1874 and he died at St John's vicarage, Stone, on 15 April 1878. He was buried at Stone.

C. W. SUTTON, *rev.* FRANK FODEN

Sources *Monthly Notices of the Royal Astronomical Society*, 39 (1878–9), 219–25 · F. Foden, *The examiner: James Booth and the origin of common examinations* (1989) · m. cert. · d. cert. · parish register (burials), Buckinghamshire, Stone, St John's, April 1878
Likenesses photograph, *c*.1868, RS; repro. in Foden, *The examiner* · sepia photograph, repro. in J. Booth, *A treatise on some new geometrical methods* (1873), frontispiece
Wealth at death under £800: probate, 6 May 1878, *CGPLA Eng. & Wales*

Booth, John (*bap.* **1584**, *d.* **1659**), genealogist, was baptized on 10 July 1584 at Swettenham, Cheshire, the eldest child of John Booth of Twemlowe, and his wife, Isabella, daughter of Richard Lowndes of Smallwood. His ancestors had long been landowners in Cheshire, and he succeeded his father at Twemlowe Hall. He occupied his time in researching the pedigrees of Cheshire families, relying on visitations but also on original research in charters, as is apparent from his surviving notebooks. His collections for Cheshire, now largely preserved in the Chester archives, were consulted by heralds and antiquaries such as Dodsworth. Sir Peter Leycester frequently acknowledged his indebtedness to the work of Booth, whom he addressed as 'cousin' (Thacker, 75). He died unmarried in 1659 and was buried on 25 November at Goostrey, Cheshire.

T. F. HENDERSON, *rev.* PETER SHERLOCK

Sources G. Ormerod, *The history of the county palatine and city of Chester*, 1 (1819), xxxviii–ix; 3 (1819), 137 · A. T. Thacker, 'Cheshire', *English county histories: a guide*, ed. C. R. J. Currie and C. P. Lewis (1994), 71–84
Archives BL, genealogical notes and extracts, Add. MS 5798 · Ches. & Chester ALSS, collections relating to Cheshire, incl. MSS and pedigrees, CR63/2/23–32 · U. Lpool, notebook of extracts from charters and other records relating to Cheshire | Bodl. Oxf., MSS Dodsworth 61, 63, 82, 154 · Coll. Arms, Vincent MS 120, fols. 388–91

Booth, John (**1779–1857**). *See under* Booth, Thomas (*c*.1755–1835).

Booth, Junius Brutus (**1796–1852**), actor, was born on 1 May 1796 near Tottenham Court Road, London, eldest of the three children of Richard Booth, a lawyer, and Jane Elizabeth Game. He had a brother who died in childhood and a sister. His mother claimed kinship with the radical politician John Wilkes. In his youth, Richard Booth had left England intending to fight for American independence, and America remained his mecca. Junius was classically educated, and, after trying painting, printing, the navy, law, and sculpture, settled on acting. He first appeared with an amateur company, then joined the Penley and Jonas management, and made his professional début as Campillo in *The Honey Moon* on 13 December 1813 in Deptford. The next year he toured the Netherlands with the company. Reputedly cited in adolescence in two paternity suits, he eloped with his Belgian landlady's daughter, Marie Christine Adelaide Delannoy (1792–1858), and married her in London in 1815. They had two children.

Booth made his début at Covent Garden as Silvius in *As You Like It* on 19 February 1816, but, seeing small chance of promotion, went to the Brighton and Worthing theatres, and on 25 September 1816 won notice substituting for Edmund Kean as Sir Giles Overreach. He was 5 feet 3 inches tall, slight, though muscular, with classical features, a pale complexion, brown wavy hair, and blue eyes, and resembled Kean in both physique and style; critics disagreed about whether he imitated Kean or both imitated nature. He returned to Covent Garden as Richard III—Kean's most famous role—but salary negotiations broke down, and he accepted Kean's invitation to join him at Drury Lane. He played Iago to Kean's Othello on 20 February 1817. Although he was outshone by Kean, young Booth's performance was applauded, and Hazlitt in *The Examiner* called it the best support of Kean he had seen. Finding that Kean intended to confine him to subordinate roles, Booth returned to Covent Garden, which claimed legal right to his services and now offered him a salary equalling that at Drury Lane. Offended at his defection, audiences at first refused to hear him when he appeared on stage. At the season's end he toured the provinces. Tired of acting, he considered joining the army, and his frustration showed itself in excessive drinking by 1818, when Keats referred to his inebriation. At Covent Garden in 1820 he played King Lear for the first time since George III's madness had caused the play to be banned. According to Hazlitt he played it with life, spirit, and human interest, his acting 'animated, vigorous, and pathetic throughout' (*Complete Works*, 18.328).

In 1821 Booth eloped with Mary Ann Holmes (1802–1885), the daughter of a Lambeth seed merchant, and, having settled £50 a year on his wife, left England. They landed in Norfolk, Virginia, on 30 June, and Booth appeared in Richmond on 6 July as Richard III, winning acclaim for the last two acts, in which, William Winter said, he always displayed 'a prodigious force and an impetuous, fiery, terrible passion', appearing 'like a whirlwind' in the battle (Winter, 99). He settled the question of imitation by performing one night in his own style, the next in Kean's. After playing at the Park Theatre, New York, in October, he toured the south. Always drawn to seek seclusion, Booth applied for the post of Cape Hatteras lighthouse keeper, but settled for a farm outside Bel Air, Maryland, which he alternated—between tours—with residences in Baltimore for the rest of his life. He wrote a verse melodrama, *Ugolino*, which was produced in his lifetime and revived by his sons.

For the 1825 season, Booth returned to England, where, to counteract scandal, he had his portrait painted with his wife and son. However, unfavourable economic conditions and newspaper hostility, combined with his refusing curtain calls, worked against his popularity. After touring the provinces and Amsterdam he returned to the

United States. During the 1827–8 season, while stage manager at the St Charles Theatre, New Orleans, Booth played Oreste in Racine's *Andromache* in French. Although drink and mental instability began to interfere with his work, and though sometimes he failed to appear when announced, he was repeatedly forgiven by both managers and audiences. In 1836–7 he was again in England, but continued to suffer comparisons with Kean, and now also with W. C. Macready and the American tragedian Edwin Forrest, also in England at this time.

When his sister and her large family joined him in America, Booth was under increased financial pressure, and his drinking and mental aberrations increased. During fits he twice attempted suicide, and once broke his nose, damaging his voice; although he restored it through exercises, it remained somewhat nasal. He began taking his children with him as attendants on the road: Junius Brutus Booth Jr, Richard Junius Booth (his son by his Belgian wife), and, finally, Edwin Thomas *Booth. His wife pursued him to America in 1846 and in April 1851 obtained a divorce. The next month Booth married Mary Ann, with whom he had produced ten children and enjoyed for many years what appeared a perfect marriage. He designed for his farm a stately residence, Tudor Hall (still standing), before travelling to California to act under his son Junius's management. On the way home he contracted a fever, and died on 30 November 1852. His body was shipped home and buried in Baltimore cemetery. In 1858 Edwin moved it to a family plot in Green Mount cemetery, Baltimore, where he erected a monument to 'matchless Booth'.

Shy and unassuming, Booth was a gentle, devoted husband and father, happiest digging his garden, selling his vegetables, or giving small boys pony rides. He held all life sacred, and would not allow meat to be eaten in his house or animals to be killed on his farm. His public demonstrations for animal rights were notorious: he tried to arrange a funeral for slaughtered pigeons, and invited neighbours to the burial of his horse. He refused to own slaves. He attended both an Episcopal church and the Baltimore dockside sailors' chapel and reverenced all religions, seeing Christianity as 'a beautiful type of Man's approach to perfection' but Hinduism as nearer that ideal. He was proficient in classical languages, spoke French fluently, and knew German, Italian, Spanish, Dutch, Hebrew, and some Arabic. Three sons followed him as starring tragedians, and both Edwin and John Wilkes achieved noteworthy reputations. His daughter Asia Booth Clarke wrote several books, including three memoirs of him. The distortions of the Kean–Booth controversy, John Wilkes Booth's assassination of Abraham Lincoln, and the wide geographical spread of his reviews caused his fame after death to be eclipsed. He seems, however, to have been a theatrical genius, a founder of the Romantic style. He acted by inspiration, thrilled by magnetism. He was an expert fencer, notorious for chasing opponents off the stage. He was renowned for the beauty and variety of his voice, the excellence of his consonantal elocution, his use of silences and pauses. While watching Kean was like reading Shakespeare by flashes of lighting, Booth illuminated his text consistently. He was famed for villains—Iago, Overreach, and Richard III—remembered for such heroes as John Howard Payne's Brutus, and even succeeded in farce. He was remarkable for making his characters distinct individuals, and for electrifying audiences with conflicting emotion, terror, remorse, despair, scorn, hatred, and fury. In the dream scene of *Richard III*, the anonymous author of *The Actor* recalls, 'He rushed to the footlights with face ashen and limbs trembling, eyes rolling and gleaming and face and form convulsed in excitement' (*The Actor*, 105). James Murdoch said that he 'displayed the most wonderful combination of intellectual beauty and force with consummate skill which was ever exhibited in modern times' (Murdoch, 175). And, for Walt Whitman, 'The words, fire, energy, *abandon*, found in him unprecedented meanings' (Whitman, 2.597). ARTHUR KINCAID

Sources A. B. Clarke, *The elder and the younger Booth* (1881) · [A. B. Clarke], *Passages, incidents and anecdotes in the life of Junius Brutus Booth* (1866) · [A. B. Clarke], *Personal recollections of the elder Booth* (privately printed, London, [1902]) · E. Booth, 'Some words about my father', *Kean and Booth and their contemporaries*, ed. B. Mathews and L. Hutton (1900), 93–103 · [J. T. Vail], *The actor* (1846) · *Oxberry's Dramatic Biography*, 4/59 (1826) · *The complete works of William Hazlitt*, ed. P. P. Howe, 21 vols. (1930–34), vols. 5, 18 · R. H. Ball, *The amazing career of Sir Giles Overreach* (1939) · J. Murdoch, *The stage* (1880) · W. Winter, *Shakespeare on the stage* (1912) · W. Whitman, *Prose works, 1892*, ed. F. Stovall, 2 (1964) · S. M. Archer, *Junius Brutus Booth, theatrical Prometheus* (1992) · *The Press* [Philadelphia, PA] (9 Aug 1891) · *New York Dramatic News*, 33 (1 Aug 1891) · d. cert. [Mary Ann (Holmes) Booth]

Archives Folger · Harvard TC · Players Club, New York | Maryland Historical Society, Baltimore, Alonzo May MS

Likenesses J. Neagle, oils, 1827, Museum of the City of New York, New York; copy, Garr. Club · R. Sully, oils, 1830–39, Valentine Museum, Richmond, Virginia · J. Ames, oils (as Richard III), Harvard U. · M. Brady, photograph, L. Cong. · T. Le Clear, oils (as Brutus in *The fall of Tarquin*), Garr. Club · R. Sully, oils, Art Institute of Chicago, Chicago · T. Sully, oils, Harvard U. · oils (as Iago in *Othello*), Harvard U. · prints, NPG

Wealth at death $4728.99, excl. Bel Air farm: Harvard TC unidentified newspaper clipping, 'The tomb of the Booths' (26 July 1891)

Booth [Bothe], **Laurence** (*c*.1420–1480), bishop of Durham and archbishop of York, was the illegitimate and probably youngest son of John Booth of Barton in Eccles, Lancashire (*d*. 1422). His mother is unknown. He was educated at Pembroke College, Cambridge, from which he took degrees in both civil and canon law by 1448. In 1442 he received papal dispensation as a son of unmarried parents for promotion to holy orders, and was duly ordained priest in 1446. By then he had already been presented to the rectory of Cottenham, near Cambridge. In 1450, although not a fellow, he was admitted master of Pembroke, which he remained until his death. He was rarely resident; indeed in January 1450 he was living in London as a residentiary canon of St Paul's.

Booth rose rapidly in the train of his elder brother William *Booth (*d*. 1464), bishop of Coventry and Lichfield since 1447 and archbishop of York from 1452, to whom he owed most of his early promotion. He succeeded William as chancellor to Queen Margaret on 7 March 1451, and rapidly acquired benefices, receiving licence to hold with the archdeaconry of Stow (which he held only briefly in 1452) any three incompatible benefices up to the value of £100. While holding a series of prebends in London, and a prebend in Lichfield, he also, after William's provision to York, received the valuable prebend of Wistow in York Minster, became a canon of Beverley (and provost in 1457), and was archdeacon of Richmond from 17 August 1454. For two years (1456–8) he was also chancellor of the University of Cambridge. His income from the diocese of York alone was well in excess of £200 a year.

Booth's political career advanced swiftly, matching his rapid ecclesiastical promotion. Service in the household of Queen Margaret led directly to his appointment as keeper of the privy seal on 24 September 1456 following the death of Thomas Lisieux, whom he also succeeded as dean of St Paul's. Booth's promotion was the preliminary step to a bid for power that Queen Margaret made at a general council meeting at Coventry in October. For the next four years he was closely linked with the resurgent court faction led by the queen, becoming a councillor of the prince of Wales and being found from time to time in the midlands where the queen concentrated her strength. However, Booth's principal service was to lie in the north following his provision to the bishopric of Durham on 22 August 1457. He was consecrated by his brother on 25 September, and received the temporalities on 18 October.

Booth's promotion to Durham has usually been interpreted as entirely partisan. To an extent it was. He was able to bring to the support of the queen's cause the political authority of the palatinate and, at the same time, by succeeding Robert Neville, remove one of the props of the Yorkist cause in the north. Yet there was a long and respected tradition of promoting the keeper of the privy seal to this key northern diocese in the royal interest. In times less fraught the provision would not have been controversial. Indeed, there is some indication that at first Booth sought to retain the goodwill of Richard Neville, earl of Salisbury, whose handsome annuity from the revenues of the bishopric he continued to pay, and several of whose servants he kept in office. Yet, as the kingdom drifted towards civil war, it was almost inevitable that Booth would promote members of the family of Salisbury's enemy, the earl of Westmorland, and their servants to positions of authority, as well as committing the resources of his palatinate to the Lancastrian cause. He took immediate advantage of the rout of Ludford (13 October 1459) to seize possession of Barnard Castle, the lordship of Richard Neville, earl of Warwick, to which the bishops of Durham had ancient claims, claims confirmed subsequently in a proviso to the earl's attainder.

Not surprisingly Booth was removed from the privy seal following the Yorkist victory at Northampton (10 July 1460), but following the comprehensive defeat of the Lancastrians at Towton (29 March 1461) he submitted to the victorious Edward IV, was received into his grace, and became his confessor. He was forced, however, to surrender Barnard Castle to Warwick. He remained loyal to his new master, rallying the men of the palatinate to defeat a Lancastrian incursion in June. Commissioned to treat with the Scots in 1462, he was rewarded by the king with the grant of the alien priory and manor of Tooting Bec in Surrey. Yet in December, when Edward IV was in Durham to counter a combined Lancastrian and Scottish incursion, he was stripped of his temporalities (that is to say the palatinate and episcopal estates) and removed to Pembroke College where he was obliged, for the only time during his tenure, to be its resident master. Booth was no doubt suspected of collusion with Margaret of Anjou, and since the episcopal castle of Norham was the only fortress then in English hands in the far north-east, the sequestration was, perhaps, a wise precaution. Yet there is no direct evidence of treason. It is as likely that he was the victim of Neville vindictiveness and resentment, for the Kingmaker and his brother, Lord Montagu, were the chief beneficiaries of his fall from favour.

Booth was released in April 1464 and the temporalities restored shortly before peace was made with the Scots. But he was obliged to continue to accept Montagu (created earl of Northumberland in this year) as his lay steward, and it would appear that for the rest of the decade the palatinate remained under unwelcome Neville oversight. Warwick's flight in the spring of 1470 gave Booth the opportunity to recover his freedom of action, and Barnard Castle was restored to him. He survived the readeption of Henry VI to emerge a key figure in Edward IV's regime after 1471, becoming once again the councillor of an infant prince of Wales and being rewarded with the manor of Battersea. Admittedly he failed to hold on to Barnard Castle, which, after a complex tussle with rival claimants, was granted to the king's brother, Richard, duke of Gloucester, in 1474. He was prominent in Anglo-Scottish negotiations culminating in the treaty of Edinburgh of 26 October 1474, and served as chancellor of the realm from 27 July 1473 to 27 May 1474, resigning, it was said, because he became weary and tired by the endless task of managing parliamentary business. But he remained a royal councillor, being nominated to the body that ruled England during the king's expedition to France in 1475. He was rewarded with translation to York on 31 July 1476.

Booth's four years at York were uneventful, noted more for the favour shown to his kinsmen than for any ecclesiastical acts. His nephew Ralph was appointed archdeacon of York soon after his translation and also became his clerk; a second nephew, Thomas, was collated to the prebend of Ampleforth in 1478; and a great-nephew, Robert, rose swiftly to be dean of York in 1477 and was collated to the lucrative prebend of Wetwang. Laurence died at Southwell on 19 May 1480, possibly after a long illness, for he drew up his will on 28 September 1479; he was buried alongside his brother in the chantry chapel dedicated to St John the Baptist which he had founded there, and which his executors were to complete. His tomb is now in the south aisle of the minster. He is credited with initiating the building of a new arts and canon-law school when he was chancellor of Cambridge, and he rebuilt the gate and adjoining buildings of the episcopal residence of Auckland Palace when bishop of Durham. He founded a chantry in Eccles parish church, Lancashire, and was a benefactor of Pembroke College.

Booth's career is enigmatic. A great pluralist in his early years, he subsequently became, perhaps following the example of Pope Sixtus IV, a great nepotist, for which he has been much criticized. He has also been dismissed as a time-serving partisan. But this underestimates him. He was a stickler for the rights and prerogatives of every benefice he held. As early as 1455, as archdeacon of Richmond, he challenged the claim of St Mary's, York, to exemption from visitation in its appropriated churches within the archdeaconry. At Durham he soon came into conflict with the cathedral priory, over its similar claims to archidiaconal jurisdiction over appropriated churches, and his insistence on exercising his feudal prerogatives over its estates. The same obsession with feudal prerogative led to his assertion of the title of the bishop, as the successor of St Cuthbert, over Barnard Castle. It is not surprising that he made powerful enemies of the earl of Warwick and his brother George, archbishop of York, to whom the Durham monks appealed for support. Yet Booth stood by his principles, and after 1471 he was supreme in his palatinate. To him can be credited a reform of the administration that brought it more directly under the control of his officers, and also a brief revival of its mint. Perhaps not quite a latter-day Antony Bek, he was determined to be his own man in his palatinate. In this he was not discouraged by Edward IV, for whom ultimately, if only for a short while, he performed the traditional role of the bishop of Durham as the king's right-hand man in the far north. A. J. POLLARD

Sources U. Durham L., archives and special collections, Durham Church Commission records, estate accounts • *Durham Chancery Records*, PRO, Durh 3 • *Chancery records* • [J. Raine], ed., *Testamenta Eboracensia*, 3, SurtS, 45 (1865), 248–50 • N. Pronay and J. Cox, eds., *The Crowland chronicle continuations, 1459–1486* (1986) • A. R. Myers, 'The household of Queen Margaret of Anjou, 1452–3', *Bulletin of the John Rylands University Library*, 40 (1957–8), 79–113, 391–431 • Emden, *Cam.*, 78–9 • E. Axon, 'The family of Bothe (Booth) and the church in the 15th and 16th centuries', *Transactions of the Lancashire and Cheshire Antiquarian Society*, 53 (1943), 32–82 • A. C. Reeves, 'Lawrence Booth: bishop of Durham (1457–76), archbishop of York (1476–80)', *Estrangement, enterprise and education in fifteenth-century England*, ed. S. D. Michalove and A. C. Reeves (1998), 63–88 • A. J. Pollard, *North-eastern England during the Wars of the Roses: lay society, war and politics, 1450–1500* (1990) • A. J. Pollard, 'The crown and the county palatine of Durham, 1437–1494', *The north of England in the age of Richard III*, ed. A. J. Pollard (1996), 67–87 • R. L. Storey, 'The north of England', *Fifteenth-century England*, ed. S. B. Chrimes and others (1974), 138–42 • R. B. Dobson, 'The later middle ages, 1215–1500', *A history of York Minster*, ed. G. E. Aylmer and R. Cant (1977), 44–110 • R. B. Dobson, 'Richard III and the church of York', *Kings and nobles in the later middle ages*, ed. R. A. Griffiths and J. Sherbourne (1986), 130–54 • R. A. Griffiths, *The reign of King Henry VI: the exercise of royal authority, 1422–1461* (1981) • J. L. Watts, *Henry VI and the politics of kingship* (1996) • E. B. Fryde and others, eds., *Handbook of British chronology*, 3rd edn, Royal Historical Society Guides and Handbooks, 2 (1986)

Booth [*née* Macaulay], **Mary Catherine** (1847–1939), social reformer and philanthropist, was born on 4 November 1847 at Clifton, Bristol, the second of the three children and only daughter of Charles Zachary Macaulay (1816–1886), civil servant, and Mary, *née* Potter (daughter of Richard *Potter [*see under* Potter, Thomas Bayley], known as Radical Dick). Her father was serving abroad as colonial secretary in Mauritius and her mother, Mary, and older brother, Thomas, were living in her grandfather Richard Potter's home in Manchester. Hers was, to say the least, an unorthodox upbringing. She was reading Plutarch's *Lives* at the age of three. Her father, married to an unstable wife, was devoted to, and became emotionally dependent upon, his only daughter.

Mary attended Hyde Park College, London, and Miss Marshall's boarding-school, Kensington. During her holidays she was entertained alongside her several Potter girl cousins at Standish, Gloucestershire. She left school at the age of sixteen and took over the housekeeping, but continued her self-education.

After a lengthy courtship, on 29 April 1871 at East Teignmouth Mary married Charles *Booth (1840–1916), a partner in the Liverpool-based Booth Steamship Company, who was to become renowned as a social investigator. In Liverpool she was unhappy among hostile Booth relatives. In 1873 Mary gave birth to the first of seven children, Antonia Mary (known always as Dodo). At this point Charles took his family to Europe for his health, and from there went with Mary to Brazil on business. On their return to England Charles set up an office of the company in London, and social relations with most of his family were severed. This stage of the Booth family life was spent at 6 Grenville Place, South Kensington.

In 1878 Charles effectively took command of the family business and split his time between London, Liverpool, and America. Because of these long separations Mary's relationship with Charles was frequently expressed in lengthy correspondence. As her granddaughter wrote: 'She was a partner in business in all but name, weighing every decision, and giving sensible advice' (Norman-Butler, 49). Diminutive in stature, she was ever large in personality. The two shared a great mutual respect and understanding and achieved a remarkable partnership.

Mary's own concern for the social problems of the age seems to have been inspired by a visit to Samuel and Henrietta Barnett at St Jude's, Whitechapel, in 1878. 'Boy, Boy, I must do something, put out a hand to help in all this misery. I do so long for strength and health', she wrote to Charles (letter, 1878, Booth correspondence). Her friendship with the Potter sisters, and especially Beatrice, was nurtured at least in part by a common interest in philanthropy. Few have noted how important Mary's help was in furthering and sustaining Booth's major works in the field of social investigation. This was not simply the support of a helpmeet (support which she certainly afforded in plenty), but an active intellectual and practical contribution. During the 1880s and 1890s there is ample evidence that Mary was reading widely and drawing to Charles's attention a number of important books—for example, the works of Marx. Associates and friends, such as Alfred and Mary Paley Marshall and the Barnetts, became valued visitors at the Booth table. In January 1892 the first evidence of her active involvement in Booth's work occurs: she interviewed J. A. Spender, author of *The State v. Pensions in Old Age*, in connection with the Booth's *Pauperism: a Picture*, and *The Endowment of Old Age: an Argument*. Her diary for this period is full of references to her work on the book. So close was Mary to Booth's social investigative work that she and Jesse Argyle saw this work on the pauper through proof and press. But it was in connection with the third and final series of Life and Labour of the People in London, the Religious Influences series, that Mary's role is best documented: she played a major critical role during the authorship of the Religious Influences books and was left holding the ultimate responsibility for publication of the Star volume. Her children recognized her literary style in parts of the work.

Mary's philanthropic work was notable. She spent a good deal of her time helping the families of local miners through the difficult times of a strike in the mid-1890s and a pit accident in 1897. The Booths had founded clubs for the women and men of Thringstone, near Gracedieu Cottage, Whitwick, Leicestershire, which was their home for many years. They also established a district nurse scheme. From her Macaulay income she financed from 1910 onwards the St Andrew's Home for invalid children.

During the years after her husband's death Mary made an important contribution to keeping his memory and that of his great work alive, publishing in 1918 the retrospective *Memoir*. The friendships she had built with Charlie dwindled as she retreated into the life of a Leicestershire lady and grandmother. She died on 25 September 1939. ROSEMARY O'DAY

Sources B. Norman-Butler, *Victorian aspirations: the life and labour of Charles and Mary Booth* (1972) • R. O'Day and D. Englander, *Mr Charles Booth's inquiry: 'Life and labour of the people in London' reconsidered* (1993) • BLPES, Booth collection [esp. A32–A57] • Goldsmiths' College, London, Booth correspondence • priv. coll, Mary Booth's diary • b. cert. • m. cert. • *CGPLA Eng. & Wales* (1939)

Archives BLPES, Booth collection • LUL, Goldsmith's Library of Economic Literature, corresp. • LUL, corresp., writings, and papers • NRA, priv. coll., diary

Likenesses photographs, priv. coll.; repro. in Norman-Butler, *Victorian aspirations*, facing pp. 32, 48, 49, 192

Wealth at death £13,619 6*s*. 10*d*.: probate, 18 Nov 1939, *CGPLA Eng. & Wales*

Booth, Paul Henry Gore-, **Baron Gore-Booth of Maltby** (**1909–1984**), diplomatist, was born on 3 February 1909 at Doncaster, Yorkshire, the elder son of Mordaunt Gore-Booth (1878–1958), of 37 Hall Gate, Doncaster, second son of Sir Henry Gore-Booth, fifth baronet, and manager of the Vickers Tyre Mill at Doncaster, and his wife, Evelyn Mary (*d*. 1963), daughter of Robert Stanley Scholfield, of Sandhall, Howden, East Riding of Yorkshire. The second of their three children, a daughter, died in infancy. He was educated as a King's scholar at Eton College, whence he won an open scholarship to Balliol College, Oxford, in 1928. He obtained second classes in *literae humaniores* (1931) and philosophy, politics, and economics (1932). An active Christian Scientist from boyhood and a lifelong teetotaller, he came from families known in public life in Ireland and in Yorkshire. One aunt, Constance *Markievicz, the Irish nationalist leader, was the first woman elected to Westminster; another, Eva Gore-*Booth, was a prominent suffragist. From his family Gore-Booth inherited musical and literary talent, an engaging streak of eccentricity, and a keen sense of duty.

In 1933 Gore-Booth entered the diplomatic service with the rank of third secretary. Having served in the Foreign Office and in Vienna he was promoted to second secretary in 1938 and moved to Tokyo. On 21 September 1940 he married, in Tokyo, Patricia Mary, daughter of Montague Ellerton, company secretary, originally from Adelaide, South Australia, but then residing in Kobe, Japan. They had twin sons and two daughters.

In December 1941 Gore-Booth was the senior official resident at the British embassy in Tokyo, and was the recipient of Japan's declaration of war. He was then immediately interned for nine months. On his release, in August 1942, he joined the highly talented team assembled in the British embassy in Washington, with the rank of first secretary. There he participated in several major conferences at which post-war reconstruction was being planned and which culminated in the San Francisco conference of 1945 which established the United Nations. He then served as secretary to the British delegation at the first meeting of the United Nations, in January 1946.

From 1945 to 1949 Gore-Booth was engaged in political and economic work in the Foreign Office as head successively of the United Nations (economic and social) and the European recovery departments. In 1949 he was appointed CMG. In the same year he came for the first time into the public eye. His appointment as director of the British Information Services in the USA was initially questioned by the British press, on the grounds that the post should be filled by a more senior figure, and one with more experience of dealing with the press. Despite the difficult background of declining British power he was successful and retained the respect of the press for the remainder of his career.

In 1953 Gore-Booth was sent as ambassador to Burma, where he and his wife made a particularly strong impression at a difficult time. In later years the Gore-Booths gave a home to the daughter of Aung San, the murdered Burmese leader, while she studied in Oxford. Daw Aung San Sun Kyi subsequently became leader of the opposition to the military regime in Burma, and was awarded the Nobel peace prize in 1992. For his services in Burma, Gore-Booth was promoted KCMG in 1957.

In 1956 Gore-Booth returned to London as deputy under-secretary in charge of economic affairs—a newly created post. His arrival coincided with the Suez crisis. Consistent with his character he was not silent in his opposition to government policy, and he was the prime mover behind a departmental 'round-robin' protesting at the government's actions. He later declared that he had come near to resignation over Suez. For the next four years he was prominently involved in the unsuccessful negotiations to reconcile the conflicting views of the United Kingdom and the continental powers on the economic development of

Europe. His own disappointment in the failure was diminished by his personal role as one of the 'three wise men' (the others being Warren Randolph Burgess of the USA and Bernard Clappier of France) whose report led to the transformation in 1960 of the Organization for European Economic Co-operation into the Organization for Economic Co-operation and Development, which included the USA and Canada.

In 1960 Gore-Booth was chosen, unusually for a diplomatic service officer, for the Commonwealth post of high commissioner in India at Delhi. This was at a time when relations between the United Kingdom and India were particularly sensitive. During his appointment Delhi was frequently the scene of great diplomatic activity involving Pakistan, Kashmir, China, and Congo. Gore-Booth was characteristically active and was well liked by the Indians for his frankness. During his time in India, he was appointed KCVO in 1961, and he was advanced to GCMG in 1965.

In February 1965 Gore-Booth was recalled to the Foreign Office to succeed Lord Caccia as permanent under-secretary, from May that year. This was a surprise to him and others who thought his talents suited him better for another important post abroad. But political factors had intervened. Gore-Booth, who had never been closely associated with Conservative policies, had been chosen the previous year by the new Labour foreign secretary, Patrick Gordon Walker. Gordon Walker failed to secure a parliamentary seat and was succeeded in January 1965 by Michael Stewart, who worked smoothly with Gore-Booth, describing him in his autobiography as 'wise and urbane' (Stewart, 207). In August 1966 conflicts in the cabinet led to George Brown's becoming foreign secretary. There was nothing in common between Brown and Gore-Booth, who found it a hard task to adjust himself and his department to the foreign secretary's flamboyant, provocative, and often brutal style. In spite of this he was scrupulously—some said unduly—loyal to his chief. Nevertheless, he was relieved when Stewart once again became foreign secretary in March 1968.

In February 1969 Gore-Booth (who had also become head of the diplomatic service in 1968) retired. His four years of office had been particularly anxious. The economic situation of the country hampered an international role when ministers wished to show a high profile. The atmosphere was poisoned by the Vietnam War, fighting in the Middle East, the Nigerian civil war, and the beginning of trouble in Rhodesia. In addition, there were jealousies in the cabinet. The diplomatic service itself had been thrown off balance by the Duncan report proposing internal changes and by the abrupt amalgamation with the Commonwealth Office. Few contested the logic of the amalgamation but not everyone was prepared for its effect on their own careers. Gore-Booth oversaw the inevitable reductions of senior posts with fairness. His sympathy was sincere but it was not his nature to parade it. No one could impugn his integrity or his intense devotion to the public service.

Following his retirement, Gore-Booth was made a life peer in 1969 and became a regular attender at the House of Lords where he spoke elegantly from the cross-benches on a wide variety of subjects. After a successful operation for cataract in both eyes, he was an active chairman of Save the Children Fund (1970–76), chairman of the board of governors of the School of Oriental and African Studies (1975–80), and chairman of the disasters emergency committee (1974–7). From 1967 to 1979 he was president of the Sherlock Holmes Society which in the words of an observer permitted him, 'suitably attired and giant eyebrows bristling, to play the lead in a reconstruction on the spot of his hero's dramatic end' (*The Times*). His autobiography, *With Great Truth and Respect*, appeared in 1974, and he edited the fifth edition of *Satow's Guide to Diplomatic Practice* (1979). He died at Westminster on 29 June 1984. A memorial service was held in his honour at St Margaret's, Westminster, on 25 October. GREENHILL OF HARROW, *rev.*

Sources *The Times* (3 July 1984) • P. Gore-Booth, *With great truth and respect* (1974) • personal knowledge (1990) • private information (1990, 2004) • J. Dickie, *Inside the Foreign Office* (1992) • M. Stewart, *Life and Labour: an autobiography* (1980) • *CGPLA Eng. & Wales* (1984)
Archives Bodl. Oxf., papers | Bodl. Oxf., William Clark MSS
Likenesses photographs, repro. in Gore-Booth, *With great truth*
Wealth at death £45,285: probate, 23 Aug 1984, *CGPLA Eng. & Wales*

Booth, Peniston (1679–1765), dean of Windsor, was baptized at Lusby, Lincolnshire, on 5 August 1679, one of at least two sons of Thomas Booth and his wife, Elizabeth. (Elizabeth's first husband was Anthony Penyston, whose daughter married Francis, sixth earl of Lincoln.)

Booth was educated first in Lincoln and then at Magdalene College, Cambridge (1698–1701); he received a BA in 1701 and an MA in 1705. Ordained deacon in 1703, he became a priest in 1707. He was a perpetual curate of Apley, Lincolnshire, and rector of Hanworth from 1717. His only published work, a sermon entitled *Of Baptism*, appeared in 1718. He was prebendary of Lincoln (1719–1746).

On 9 May 1722 Booth was appointed a canon of St George's Chapel, Windsor; on 26 April 1729 he was installed dean, an office which he held until his death. In addition on 23 July 1733 he was collated chancellor of London. Booth married Catherine Jones on 20 January 1729 in St George's Chapel. The couple had at least one daughter. By 1749 he had made many improvements in the deanery; and a detailed history of St George's Chapel was included in Joseph Pote's *History and Antiquities of Windsor* (1749). Two of the plates in this work were inscribed to him and his canons. Booth died on 21 September 1765. His wife predeceased him.

JENNETT HUMPHREYS, *rev.* ROBERT BROWN

Sources J. Pote, *History and antiquities of Windsor Castle, and the Royal College, and chapel of St George* (1749) • Venn, *Alum. Cant.* • S. L. Ollard, *Fasti Wyndesorienses: the deans and canons of Windsor* (privately printed, Windsor, 1950) • J. Cooke, *The preacher's assistant* (1783) • GEC, *Peerage* • *Fasti Angl.* (Hardy) • *GM*, 1st ser., 35 (1765), 443 • will, PRO, PROB 11/912, sig. 362 • *IGI*
Likenesses portrait, repro. in Ollard, *Fasti Wyndesorienses*, facing p. 95

Booth, Richard (1788–1864). *See under* Booth, Thomas (*c.*1755–1835).

Booth, Robert (*d.* **1657**), translator and Church of England clergyman, was probably born in Mixenden, Yorkshire, the son of the Revd George Booth (*d. c.*1636), vicar of South Kirkby, near Halifax, and his wife, Mary, daughter of Thomas Lister of Shibden. He was admitted sizar to Trinity College, Cambridge, in 1603, graduated BA in 1607, became a fellow of Emmanuel College in 1609, and proceeded MA in 1610. At Cambridge, he developed pretensions of becoming a scholar. In April 1611, his translation into English of a work by Jean Barclay on the spiritual and temporal powers of the papacy, while apparently approved by the king and several bishops, brought trouble with the authorities. A compendium, 'Synopsis totius philosophiae', was dedicated to his master at Trinity College, Dr Thomas Neville. In 1614 he translated the *Mercurius Gallo-Belgicus*, which documented the Jülich–Cleves succession dispute.

The same year Booth was ordained deacon and priest in Peterborough and about 1615 he was elected curate at Sowerby Bridge, near Halifax. There he became a prominent nonconformist, under the patronage of John Favour, vicar of Halifax, and followed Favour in neglecting church ceremonies. During the next thirty years he helped consolidate the reputation of the Halifax area as a godly stronghold. In 1620 he completed *Encomium Heroum*, a medical work dedicated to Francis Bacon. On 25 July that year, he married Sarah Cocecrofte who survived him, at Halifax; the couple remained at Sowerby Bridge until 1648. He then moved to nearby Skircoate and became preacher at Halifax, where he was buried on 28 July 1657.

S. J. Guscott

Sources R. Marchant, *The puritans and the church courts in the diocese of York, 1560–1642* (1960), 31–2, 230–31 • Venn, *Alum. Cant.* • 'Abstracts of Yorkshire wills', *Yorkshire Archaeological and Topographical Association*, 9 (1890), 109–10 • J. Watson, *The history and antiquities of the parish of Halifax, in Yorkshire* (1775); repr. (1973), 370, 461 • *CSP dom.*, 1611–18, 22 • *DNB* • will, PRO, PROB 11/267, sig. 335 • W. J. Walker, *Chapters on the early registers of Halifax parish church* (1885), 27–8 • *The history of Halifax gibbet law* (1708)

Booth, Sir Robert (*bap.* **1626**, *d.* **1681**), judge, was baptized on 2 July 1626 at the collegiate church, Manchester, Lancashire, the son of Robert Booth (*d.* in or before 1637) of Salford in the same county, and Ann (*d.* 1696), daughter of Oswald Mosley of Manchester. Following his father's death his mother married, in August 1637, Thomas Case, a puritan preacher in Salford. After attending Manchester grammar school Booth entered Gray's Inn in 1642, before matriculating from St John's College, Cambridge, as a fellow-commoner on 20 September 1644. He was called to the bar in November 1649 and practised in London. About 1651 he married Mary (*d.* 1660), daughter of Spencer Potts of Chargrove, Bedfordshire. The couple had at least one child, a son Benjamin, who died aged eleven.

Booth next appears in Ireland in 1657 upon becoming a member of King's Inns. His wife, Mary, died in 1660 and was buried in St Michan's, Dublin, on 7 September. On 1 December Booth became third judge of the Irish court of common pleas on the recommendation of Lord Chancellor Eustace. He was knighted at Whitehall on 15 May 1668 and made chief justice of common pleas on 30 January 1669. His second wife, Susanna, daughter of Sir Henry Oxenden of Deane in Kent, whom he married at an unknown date, died on 27 October 1669; the couple had four daughters.

In 1673 Booth's nonconformist sympathies caused the king to veto his appointment as chief justice of king's bench. However, within six years the turmoil caused by the Popish Plot had made his religious convictions an asset to the beleaguered monarch, who promoted him to the post on 26 March 1679. Having inherited a large estate from his father Booth was able to add to it with purchases in Ireland. Although regarded as the ablest man in his profession in Ireland he was frequently ill with gout or absent in England. He died in January 1681 and was buried on 2 March in Salford.

Sidney Lee, *rev.* Terry Clavin

Sources R. Lascelles, ed., *Liber munerum publicorum Hiberniae … or, The establishments of Ireland*, later edn, 2 vols. in 7 pts (1852), vol. 2, pp. 31, 36, 38 • *CSP Ire.*, *1660–62*, 113; *1669–70*, 69, 83 • *Calendar of the manuscripts of the marquess of Ormonde*, new ser., 8 vols., HMC, 36 (1902–20), vol. 3, p. 395 • Bodl. Oxf., MS Carte 146, fol. 168 • *Letters written by his excellency, Arthur Capel, earl of Essex, lord lieutenant of Ireland in the year 1675* (1770), 132–3 • 'Notes and queries', *Manchester Courier*, 6th ser., 10, 130–32 • F. E. Ball, *Some notes on the Irish judiciary in the reign of Charles II, 1660–85*, 1 vol. in 6 pts (1901–3), 10–12 • F. E. Ball, *The judges in Ireland, 1221–1921*, 2 vols. (1926), 1.349–50 • *IGI* • *Corrections and additions to the Dictionary of National Biography*, Institute of Historical Research (1966)

Booth, Sarah [Sally] (**1789x94–1867**), actress, was born in Birmingham of unknown parentage. Her father died when she was an infant, leaving a large family of which she was the youngest of three daughters. She claimed descent from the seventeenth-century actor Barton Booth but denied any connection with her contemporary, Junius Brutus Booth, whom she later tried to persuade to add an 'e' to his name to prevent misunderstanding. Her recorded career began in Manchester, where, about 1804, Sally and her sister Sophia appeared as dancers. She remained there under the management of the elder Macready, whose multiplicity of financial affairs soon proved embarrassing, but who promoted her to the performance of characters such as Prince Arthur in *King John* and the Little Girl in *Children of the Wood*. Her lack of education was said to have been rectified by the welcome she received as a visitor among several respectable families within the circuit of the Macready company. She subsequently went to Doncaster as a member of Tate Wilkinson's company and successfully took over the part of Alexina in Reynolds's *The Exile* when Mrs Stephen Kemble (*née* Elizabeth Satchell) dislocated a shoulder. R. W. Elliston, who was then managing the Surrey Theatre (formerly the Royal Circus), invited her to appear there in 1810 as Cherry in a burletta based on Farquhar's *The Beaux' Stratagem*, in which he himself played Archer. In November of that year she performed for the first time at Covent Garden, as Amanthis in *The Child of Nature*, an adaptation from the French by Elizabeth Inchbald. She achieved some popularity: a poem 'To Miss S. Booth' appeared in the *Theatrical Inquisitor*, written

Sarah Booth (1789x94–1867), by Henry Hoppner Meyer, pubd 1813 (after Henry William Pickersgill)

by one J. G. of Edinburgh, who had seen this performance. She remained at Covent Garden in various trivial pieces and was occasionally allowed to assume a major character such as Juliet. However, the rising fame of Eliza O'Neill wrested from her the hope of distinction in tragic roles, and she left Covent Garden until her rival had retired. Elliston remarked that she performed melodrama to perfection but added that she 'was for several seasons the heroine of that multitudinous succession of trash … the Covent Garden managers delighted to insult the taste of the town with' (Raymond). She then appeared at the Olympic, Drury Lane, the Haymarket, and the Adelphi, as well as touring widely in the provinces, where, it was said, she visited 'every tolerable place in England' along with her sister, playing a few nights in each for a share of the house, and taking her benefit, which led to the accumulation of a substantial fortune. She retired from the stage about 1828 and last appeared in a benefit at the Marylebone Theatre in 1841.

Sally Booth was a strict observer of her religious duties and a constant attender at church wherever she was performing. On one occasion a clergyman took advantage of her presence to criticize the stage, which reduced her to tears at the time but subsequently led to an increase in her local audiences. She was petite and pretty and was rumoured to wear false hair. Her dancing was her special attraction, and was described as full of grace, agility, and sylph-like lightness. She had a wide circle of friends, including Camilla Dufour Crosland, who in her *Landmarks of a Literary Life* (1893) described visiting Sally Booth's dressing-room as a child, while she made up for the stage, and recalled her home in Bloomsbury Square. She lived in a cottage retreat in Highgate during her retirement, and died on 30 December 1867.

JOSEPH KNIGHT, *rev.* J. GILLILAND

Sources *Oxberry's Dramatic Biography*, 4/52 (1826) • Mrs C. Baron-Wilson, *Our actresses*, 2 vols. (1844) • Mrs N. Crosland [C. Toulmin], *Landmarks of a literary life, 1820–1892* (1893) • *Theatrical Inquisitor* • *The biography of the British stage, being correct narratives of the lives of all the principal actors and actresses* (1824) • [J. Roach], *Authentic memoirs of the green-room* [1814] • Genest, *Eng. stage* • G. Raymond, *Memoirs of R. W. Elliston* (1857) • *Dictionary of national portraiture* (1979) • Hall, *Dramatic ports.* • Adams, *Drama* • Boase, *Mod. Eng. biog.*

Likenesses H. H. Meyer, mezzotint, pubd 1813 (after H. W. Pickersgill), BM, NPG [*see illus.*] • oils (as Juliet), Royal Shakespeare Memorial Museum, Stratford upon Avon, Warwickshire • portrait, Harvard TC • portrait (as Letitia Hardy), repro. in *Oxberry's Dramatic Biography* • portrait, repro. in *Biography of the British stage* • portrait, repro. in *Theatrical Inquisitor* • portrait (as Juliet); in possession of Dramatic College, Maybury, Surrey, 1893 • prints, BM, NPG

Booth, Thomas (*fl.* **1594–1616**), Church of England clergyman, was educated at Trinity College, Cambridge, where he entered as a sizar in 1594, and graduated BA in 1598, MA in 1601, and BD in 1609. He became rector of Langdon Hills in Essex in 1611 and a prebendary of Lichfield Cathedral in 1615. The dates when his successors were appointed to both positions imply that he died in 1616. In 1611 he published (under his initials) *Concio ad clerum jamdudum Cantabrigiae habita in Luc. cap. 5 ver. 10*. No copy of this sermon is known to survive in any major library.

THOMPSON COOPER, *rev.* TIM WALES

Sources Venn, *Alum. Cant.* • Cooper, *Ath. Cantab.*, 3.57 • *Fasti Angl.* (Hardy), 1.625 • R. Newcourt, *Repertorium ecclesiasticum parochiale Londinense*, 2 (1710), 359 • H. Smith, 'Some omissions in Newcourt's *Repertorium*', *Transactions of the Essex Archaeological Society*, new ser., 17 (1923–5), 23–7, esp. 25 • *STC, 1475–1640*

Booth, Thomas (*c.*1755–1835), stock breeder, was the owner and farmer of the estate of Killerby, near Catterick, Yorkshire, but little is known about his origins. In 1790 he turned his attention to the breeding of shorthorn cattle, selecting his cows from Mr Broader of Fairholme, and the bulls from the stock of Robert and Charles Colling. His aim was to raise animals that would be suitable for both beef and milk production. In breeding them he tried to reduce the bone of the animal, especially the length and coarseness of the legs, the prominence of the hips, the heavy bones of the shoulders, and the shoulder points, which previously were great defects in the unimproved shorthorns. Booth was very successful, and for many years his cows and bulls carried away the top prizes at the chief exhibitions of stock. By 1814 he was considered to be the best cattle breeder in the area.

Booth moved to Warlaby, Yorkshire, in 1819, and gave up the Killerby estate and part of the shorthorn herd to his eldest son, John Booth; he took the remainder with him to Warlaby, where he died in 1835. He and his wife, formerly Miss Bower, had two sons, also well known as cattle breeders.

John Booth (1779–1857), the eldest son of Thomas Booth, had his own ideas about breeding stock, and in the pastures near Richmond, Yorkshire, he found fresh crosses for his cattle. He also ran horses at Catterick, and his dog, Nips, won the Wensleydale cup in a coursing contest at Leyburn. For three seasons he was master of the Bedale hunt, and a constant attendant at the meets. Much of his time was occupied in acting as a judge at exhibitions of livestock. All his own stock were sold off on 21 September 1852, when forty-four lots averaged £48 12*s.* 8*d.* Booth married Miss Wright in 1819 and they had several sons. He died at Killerby on 7 July 1857, and was buried nearby, at Ainderby. Shortly afterwards a window to his memory was erected in Catterick church.

Richard Booth (1788–1864), the second son of Thomas Booth, in 1814 moved a few miles south of his father to Studley Farm, which he soon stocked with shorthorns. He was a great believer in inbreeding, and by 1834 his best cows were fine animals in direct descent from his own bull, Twin Brother, to Ben, a bull bred by his father in 1790. He gave up Studley Farm in 1834, and sold off the whole of his herd except Isabella by Pilot, and retired to Sharrow, near Ripon. On the death of his father in the following year he succeeded to the estate and the shorthorn herd at Warlaby, and again turned his attention to breeding. The judges of those days had not yet learned to distinguish between flesh and fat, and although the Booth cattle did not always carry away the prizes, they made the best carcass meat. When the royal cattle shows began in 1844, though not approving of such exhibitions, Richard Booth felt obliged to exhibit; and although at first the quality of his cattle was not understood, it was not very long before his name was often found in the lists of those receiving medals and other rewards. He died at Warlaby on 31 October 1864. G. C. BOASE, *rev.* ANNE PIMLOTT BAKER

Sources W. Carr, *The history of the rise and progress of the Killerby, Studley, and Warlaby herds of shorthorns* (1867) • J. Thirsk, ed., *The agrarian history of England and Wales*, 6, ed. G. E. Mingay (1989) • The Druid [H. H. Dixon], *Saddle and sirloin, or, English farm and sporting worthies* (1870), 195–207

Wealth at death under £16,000—Richard Booth: will, 1865

Booth [Bothe], **William** (*d.* **1464**), archbishop of York, was possibly born in Eccles, Lancashire, a younger son of Sir John Booth of Barton-on-Irwell and his wife, Joan, daughter of Sir Henry Trafford. Details of his birth date and early education are lacking. His was a large and close family; especially his half-brother, Laurence *Booth, followed closely in his wake—he too occupied the archbishopric and was buried in the same church—and both helped their nephew John considerably in his career towards the bishopric of Exeter, which he held from 1465 to 1478. William Booth studied common law at Gray's Inn, the only fifteenth-century bishop to do so. In 1416 he was admitted to the prebend of Oxton and Cropwell in Southwell, Nottinghamshire, and perhaps already had the rectory of Wilmslow, Cheshire, which he resigned in July 1418. He secured the prebend of Dunham and Newport in Lincoln Cathedral on 10 October 1420. Shortly afterwards he began a long association with the London diocese as canon residentiary and prebendary of Consumpta-per-Mare in St Paul's from 28 May 1421, and archdeacon of Middlesex, from May 1429 to about November 1441, besides other local parish preferment. With a papal dispensation for plurality he collected useful supplementary preferment around the country. At St Paul's he found the chapter's estate administration in disarray; by 1447 he held almost every manor himself and even procured life leases on his promotion to bishop, an abuse that it took the chapter five years to undo. He had profited energetically from his tenure but had at least restored the manors—and indeed the chapter's economy as a whole—to stability and financial health.

In the early 1440s Booth attracted the patronage of William de la Pole, earl (later duke) of Suffolk (*d.* 1450), the emerging power at the king's side. In 1445 he was made chancellor to the newly arrived Margaret of Anjou. When the see of Coventry and Lichfield fell vacant in March 1447, both king and queen wrote to Pope Nicholas V (*r.* 1447–55) to recommend Booth; he was duly provided on 26 April and consecrated in St Paul's on 9 July. He continued to serve Margaret as chancellor, most notably in her foundation of Queen's (later Queens') College, Cambridge. He was, as a result, often absent from his diocese, but his register shows him as an efficient administrator with able deputies.

In May 1450 Suffolk, impeached and widely hated, was murdered on his way into exile. Booth, like others, was tainted by association, his reputation smeared in satirical verses, and even his life threatened during Cade's revolt in May–July 1450. In November the parliamentary Commons demanded his expulsion from the king's court, along with some thirty others. Like these, Booth was not sacrificed by the crown; although no longer her chancellor (Laurence Booth now held the post), he was supported by the queen and by Edmund Beaufort, duke of Somerset (*d.* 1455), the new power at court. On 21 July 1452 he was even translated to the archbishopric of York, such was the government's recovery of confidence, though he was not formally enthroned until 4 September 1453. Thomas Gascoigne (*d.* 1458), the vitriolic theologian and commentator—and himself a Yorkshireman—condemned such a promotion as a grave disservice to God, but he often made such statements. In fact Booth seems to have been effective enough, if along conventional lines rather than by the preaching missions that the high-minded Gascoigne demanded (and, to be fair, practised). His York register shows that he was resident for two-thirds of the time, and otherwise attended on the affairs of the realm only as his status demanded. He chose able staff; three successive archdeacons of Richmond went on to become bishops themselves.

From the summer of 1453 national affairs became permanently and dangerously factional, not least around York where the Nevilles and Percys took to violence. Booth, his fingers already singed by events in 1450–51, took care to steer a prudent path; in spring 1454 he was at Westminster when there was rebellion in Yorkshire against Richard of York's protectorate, and again in the autumn when the two local magnate families clashed once more; on 22 May 1455 he was in his diocese when York attacked and killed his enemies around the king at St

Albans. Despite old loyalties he seems to have been cautious about joining Queen Margaret in her uncompromising revival of the Lancastrian regime in the following years. A week before she defeated and killed York and the earl of Salisbury at Wakefield on 30 December 1460 Booth was further south, at Southwell in Nottinghamshire; afterwards he still did not join her, and was indeed in London among her opponents, if not actively of them, by 27 January 1461, evidently not participating in her own invasion south to rescue her husband. There he remained until the final swing of the pendulum ended in Edward IV's victory at Towton in Yorkshire on 29 March.

Booth returned to his diocese in late April and ordered his clergy to help prepare the defence against a Scottish invasion on Henry VI's behalf. On 28 June he joined Archbishop Thomas Bourchier of Canterbury (*d.* 1486) in crowning Edward IV in Westminster Abbey, and in November participated fully in the king's first parliament. Over the next three years he was included in many royal commissions in his province and twice, in 1462 and 1463, prepared his clergy once more against invasion. He attended parliament at Westminster in April–June 1463, then twice acted on the king's behalf to prorogue intended sessions at York, in February and May 1464, as intended major campaigns by the king against Lancastrian resistance in the north and Scotland came to nothing. On 10 August 1464 Booth received an exemption for life from attendance at councils or parliaments because of his age and frailty.

Booth made his will on 26 August 1464 at his favourite residence, Southwell. It was not complicated. He and all the Booth family had established a notable collective chantry to St Katherine in Eccles church in 1450, and another there to Jesus and St Mary the Virgin (the patron saint) in 1460. Now the archbishop made further financial bequests to both and provided for a house to be built for the chantry priests. He left his pastoral staff and mitre to York Minster but little else. He died at Southwell on 12 September 1464 and was buried there, as he requested, in the chapel of St John the Baptist in the collegiate church. No trace now remains of a tomb. All his life he was a quietly efficient and talented administrator, for a while notorious and abused only because his patrons were; but he was not a factious politician and, even in the heat of civil war, this came finally to be recognized. A. C. Reeves

Sources A. C. Reeves, *Lancastrian Englishmen* (1981) [with extensive references] • A. Hamilton Thompson, 'Booth, William', *Dictionnaire d'histoire et de géographie ecclésiastiques*, ed. A. Baudrillart and others, 9 (Paris, 1937) • J. C. Bates, 'The episcopate of William Booth, bishop of Coventry and Lichfield (1447–52) with an edition of his register', MPhil diss., Nottingham, 1981 • E. Axon, 'The family of Bothe (Booth) and the church in the 15th and 16th centuries', *Transactions of the Lancashire and Cheshire Antiquarian Society*, 53 (1943), 32–82 • F. R. Raines, *A history of the chantries within the county palatine of Lancaster*, 2 vols., Chetham Society, 59–60 (1862) • J. Raine, ed., *The historians of the church of York and its archbishops*, 2, Rolls Series, 71 (1886), 435 • *Letters of Queen Margaret of Anjou and Bishop Beckington and others written in the reigns of Henry V and Henry VI*, ed. C. Monro, CS, 86 (1863) • A. C. Reeves, 'William Booth, bishop of Coventry and Lichfield (1447–52)', *Midland History*, 3 (1975–6), 11–29 • C. N. L. Brooke, 'The earliest times to 1485', *A history of St Paul's Cathedral and the men associated with it*, ed. W. R. Matthews and W. M. Atkins (1957), 63, 91 • [J. Raine], ed., *Testamenta Eboracensia*, 2, SurtS, 30 (1855), 264–7 • Borth. Inst., Reg. 20 Booth • PRO

Archives Borth. Inst., Reg. 20 Booth • Joint RO, Lichfield, register, MS B/A/1/10

Booth, Sir William (*bap.* **1657**, *d.* **1703**), naval officer, was baptized on 5 July 1657, the only son of Edward Booth (*d.* 1680), maltster and alderman of Pontefract, and his wife, Edith Kellam (*d.* 1662). He entered the navy, serving as a midshipman under Sir Roger Strickland in 1672 and being promoted rapidly, and at a remarkably young age, to command the fireship *Pearl* in June 1673 through the patronage of Prince Rupert; the ship was expended during the battle of the Texel on 11 August 1673. Booth commanded the fireship *Eagle* from 1675 to 1678 and, briefly, the *Richmond* in May 1678. His command of the *Adventure*, chiefly in the Mediterranean, from July 1678 to January 1683 was the making of his naval career. He married Rosamond Harrison, *née* Littleton (*d.* 1718) of Stepney on 14 May 1685. She and their sons Edward and William and daughters Mary and Elizabeth survived him; two other children, John and Dorothy, died in 1693.

Booth fought several single-ship actions with larger corsair vessels, capturing the *Golden Horse* of Algiers after a ferocious fight on 8 April 1681. Booth subsequently became involved in an acrimonious dispute over the prize claim to the *Golden Horse* with Captain Wheeler of the *Nonsuch*, which had come to his assistance. Following his return to England Booth was knighted by the king on 12 November 1682. He was flag captain to George Legge, Lord Dartmouth, aboard the *Grafton* in 1683–4, when Dartmouth took a fleet to evacuate and demolish England's short-lived colony at Tangier. During this time Booth became a confidant of Samuel Pepys and provided him with much information about the alleged corruption and perversions of the previous admiral commanding in the Mediterranean, Arthur Herbert, earl of Torrington. Dartmouth thought Booth 'a very knowing and active seaman and brave fellow', and Booth claimed that he had slept on deck for three years 'with nothing over him but a tarpaulin, that his seamen might be the better contented to do as he did' (Chappell, 135, 219).

Appointed a commissioner of the navy in February 1688, Booth became controller of the storekeeper's accounts when the Navy Board was reorganized on 12 October. He took command of the third-rate *Pendennis* on 25 September 1688 during the mobilization prompted by the invasion of William of Orange, but the success of the invasion—and of his enemy Herbert—made Booth consider the desperate expedient of defecting to France with his own ship and the *Warspite*. In conversation with Captain Wilford of the fireship *Eagle* on 16 March 1689 Booth claimed 'that he had thought of it 24 hours … let us push at our fortunes', and that no one would question his putting Wilford into the command of the *Warspite* because 'I am a commissioner of the navy, and who will dispute it?' (PRO, ADM 1/5253, fol. 132). On being rebuffed, Booth snapped 'damn if you won't, I'll go up and trim' (ibid.), but he was unable to conceal his intended treason and was forced to flee to France. He attempted to return to England in 1696, and despite problems over his bail and willingness to take the oaths of allegiance and supremacy, he was living in London again by 1697, subsequently corresponding with the Jacobite Colonel James Graham and commissioning an artist to draw his old friend Pepys. Booth had also acquired a plantation on Barbados and seems to have spent at least part of his time there between 1689 and his death at Greenwich in February 1703. He was buried at Greenwich on 18 February 1703. J. D. Davies

Sources 'Dugdale visitation of Yorkshire', *The Genealogist*, new ser., 27 (1910–11), 28–39, esp. 38–9 • PRO, ADM 1/5253, fols. 129–32 • PRO, ADM 10/15, p. 17 • PRO, PROB 11/469, fols. 14–15 • *The Tangier papers of Samuel Pepys*, ed. E. Chappell, Navy RS, 73 (1935) • *Report on the manuscripts of his grace the duke of Buccleuch and Queensberry … preserved at Montagu House*, 3 vols. in 4, HMC, 45 (1899–1926), vol. 2, pp. 334–5, 339, 353 • *The manuscripts of the earl of Westmorland*, HMC, 13 (1885); repr. (1906), 333–4 • *Report on the manuscripts of Allan George Finch*, 5 vols., HMC, 71 (1913–2003), vol. 2 • P. Le Fevre, 'The dispute over the *Golden Horse* of Algiers', *Mariner's Mirror*, 73 (1987), 313–17 • J. M. Collinge, *Navy Board officials, 1660–1832* (1978), 87 • J. D. Davies, *Gentlemen and tarpaulins: the officers and men of the Restoration navy* (1991) • C. Dalton, ed., *English army lists and commission registers, 1661–1714*, 1 (1892), 329 • *CSP dom.*, 1673, 349

Archives Magd. Cam. • PRO, ADM MSS

Wealth at death over £3000 bequests; plus estate in Barbados: PRO, PROB 11/469, fols. 14–15

Booth, William (1829–1912), founder of the Salvation Army, was born at Sneinton, a suburb of Nottingham, on 10 April 1829, one of five children of Samuel Booth (1775–1842), a speculative builder, and his second wife, Mary Moss (*b.* 1791). He was sent to Biddulph's School, Nottingham, but it failed to turn him into either a gentleman or a scholar; at thirteen, because of family poverty, he was apprenticed to a pawnbroker in a squalid part of Nottingham. Although he proved an able assistant to his employer, he spoke of this experience in later life with bitterness. Soon after his apprenticeship began his father, whose business affairs had gone from bad to worse, died; the family, struggling to make ends meet, moved into a shop. Booth's 'blighted childhood', as he always called it, left a powerful impression on his mind.

Booth drifted out of the Church of England, but there was little to suggest any marked change in his religious thinking before his father's death. He seems to have been stirred politically by the oratory of Chartist leader Feargus O'Connor (1796–1855), who visited Nottingham during the election of 1842. Deeply affected by the daily spectacle of ragged children crying for bread in the streets, Booth ranged himself on the side of the Chartists. A frequent attendant at Nottingham's Wesley Chapel, he was also coming under the sway of Methodism; in 1844, with his conscience tortured by a piece of sharp practice in which he had overreached some of his fellow assistants at the pawnbroker's shop, he made public confession of his sin and underwent conversion. Had it not been for his conscience, and the effect of confession, he might have become a radical. As it was, religion made him, from a political point of view, a die-hard conservative.

William Booth (1829–1912), by Olive Edis and Katherine Edis, 1902

The impressionable teenager came under the spellbinding oratory of the American Methodist James Caughey, who visited Nottingham in 1846. Booth joined a group of revivalists who conducted religious services in the streets of the city. He was then seventeen and distinguished by his height, pale face, black hair, and eloquence. In 1849 he moved to London in search of better paid work, but failing to find it he was obliged to go as assistant to a pawnbroker in Walworth. He took at this time several religious vows, which reveal an uncompromising spiritual intention, and almost starved himself in order to send money back to his mother and sisters. He devoted his leisure to religion and began to attract the attention of local Methodists, one of whom, E. J. Rabbits, a rich boot manufacturer, persuaded him to become a lay preacher. It was this boot manufacturer who introduced him into the family of a carriage builder living in Clapham, where he met the woman who was so powerfully to influence his subsequent career.

Catherine Mumford (1829–1890) [*see* Booth, Catherine], the daughter of the carriage builder, was an invalid who spent most of her time on a sofa. She had a cultivated mind to a degree unusual among people in suburban circles: while she admired Booth's character, she deplored his lack of culture. A child of the dissenting chapel, her religion was respectable, if not conventional. She criticized Booth's sermons, gave him devotional books, and tried to steady his religious ardour. He admitted his lack of learning, but not even her persuasions could tame his 'love for souls', which was the master passion of his life. In return, Booth gave her a wider outlook and gradually weaned her mind from its subservience to convention: the suburban bluestocking took fire from the provincial ignoramus. When Booth became an itinerant Methodist preacher in 1852 he consulted her about his sermons, sent her his clothes for mending, and exhorted her to approve of revivalist methods. They married on 16 June 1855. All of their children, three sons and four daughters, the eldest of whom was the preacher Catherine Booth-*Clibborn (1858–1955), were caught in the whirl of evangelicalism.

By the time of his marriage Booth had established something of a reputation as a travelling preacher of Methodism, but his unorthodox practices and violent rhetoric in the pulpit had made him enemies. At the end of nine years in the ministry, rather than submit to the authority of his church, he broke with Methodism and launched out as an independent revivalist. His wife joined in this work, and it was at her suggestion that he went to London in 1865 and started the Christian Mission in Whitechapel. It was largely by accident that the institution changed its name to the Salvation Army. The phrase 'a volunteer army' as a description for the mission came under discussion in 1878, and, under pressure from his son (William) Bramwell *Booth (1856–1929), William Booth altered it in favour of 'a salvation army'. The new name, complete with the definite article, appeared for the first time in the *Christian Mission Magazine* for September 1878.

The change of name was fortuitous, for as a result of it came the military titles and uniforms that transformed what was just another parochial city mission into a worldwide engine of revivalism. Booth himself initially resisted the army trappings, but an institution which soon became identified with authority, regulation, and family control was well suited to his autocratic temperament. A secret of the movement's success was the use of working-class officers to invade working-class districts. This practice, which had been used by other London charities, most notably the Ranyard Mission, proved highly effective for the Salvation Army. By the end of the nineteenth century there were 100,000 soldiers in Britain, mostly in urban areas. As the movement spread abroad, Booth followed the army flag—including tours of the United States in 1886 and India in 1892—and received the hospitality of kings and ambassadors.

Booth always held that you cannot make a man clean by washing his shirt, and his social work was largely an excuse for converting souls. (In a time when medicine could do so little for the body, the needs of the soul demanded more attention.) He had an unusual degree of social pity and admitted the influence of the environment on individual cases of distress, but he genuinely believed that eternal punishment was the fate of all those who died without conversion. A stern millenarian, his aim was to convert the masses. He did so with little reference to religious doctrine, of which he was himself largely ignorant: his was a brash, Bible-based, open-air Christianity, suited to the realities of slum life. Under the influence of his wife the Salvation Army adopted a non-sacramental form of worship. By banning the eucharist Booth may have alienated the orthodox, but he attracted the multitude.

Booth entertained an almost savage prejudice against science and philosophy. In everything intellectual he was an obscurantist of the most pronounced type, and in everything religious a 'Hebraist' of uncompromising narrowness. He condemned cricket and football as sharply as card-playing and horse-racing. Further, there was something of the casuist in his nature which enabled him, with no shock to his conscience, to conciliate mammon in the interest of his philanthropy. He had warm friends among bookmakers, commercial millionaires, and the aristocracy. Once he made Cecil Rhodes kneel down and pray with him in a railway carriage. He took tea with Gladstone at Hawarden in 1896 and had an interview with Edward VII, whom he greatly admired, in 1904. The king asked what the churches now thought of him: he replied with a dour humour, 'Sir, they imitate me' (Begbie, 1.113).

Booth was the champion of the degraded poor of the great cities and his work illustrated that the religious instincts of the public were not much changed since Wesley's day. He beat his showman's drum in what he believed to be God's service. As a consequence he became the target of ridicule, while some of the army's more exuberant practices, particularly the marches and band playing, became a cause of rioting. Assaults on Salvationists were common and several were 'promoted to Glory' by stones or beatings. It was partly because of his wife's influence that the army's rescue work among prostitutes was undertaken solely by women and that the movement encouraged a degree of female equality that was unusual among religious organizations of the day. Characteristically Booth hung back from a crusade for sexual purity which his son Bramwell persuaded William T. Stead (1849–1912) to undertake in the *Pall Mall Gazette*. In spite of all his platform outspokenness, he was a timorous administrator. Disdainful of balance sheets, he used his authority chiefly to safeguard the army's spiritual activities. Bramwell was the real organizer: Booth called him his Melanchthon.

Deeper acquaintance with the distresses of the urban poor led Booth to become a social reformer. In 1890 he published *In Darkest England and the Way Out*, a classic in the literature of poverty. With its proposals for the relief of unemployment and homelessness, it contained more practical advice than the earlier surveys of urban deprivation carried out by Henry Mayhew (1812–1887) or the Revd Andrew Mearns (1837–1925). Though written largely by Stead, it was full of Booth's inventive ideas, including city colonies, co-operative farms, the poor man's lawyer, and an emigration scheme, complete with an emigration bureau. It created a sensation, contributing to a wider knowledge of social ills and reminding the churches of their social responsibilities.

Though dismissed by intellectuals and attacked by T. H. Huxley (1825–1895), Booth received liberal financial support from the British public for many of his schemes. What distinguished him as a social reformer was a willingness to cope from day to day with an awesome level of endemic disease, unemployment, and other social ills, which were then less well understood. As he put it, he had nothing against utopianism, collectivist or individualist, but 'here in our Shelters last night were a thousand hungry, workless people. … It is in the meantime that the people must be fed, that their life's work must be done or left undone forever' (Booth, 79–80).

It is worth noting that Booth, despite his vehemence and striking physical presence, was of a singularly delicate constitution. He had a physical horror of dirt, even of shabbiness, and from his youth was noticeable for a meticulous attention to personal cleanliness. Noxious smells made him ill. The sight of suffering children brought tears to his eyes: it was this extreme sensitivity to suffering which made him so effective in unveiling society's darker corners. He saw sharply what others scarcely noticed at all, and he felt as an outrage what others considered to be natural. William James, the psychologist, cites Booth as an authority for the doctrine 'that the first vital step in saving outcasts consists in making them feel that some decent human being cares enough for them to take an interest in the question whether they are to rise or sink' (W. James, *The Varieties of Religious Experience*, new edn, 1985, 203).

Restless, harsh, and with a gift for self-advertisement Booth had the temperament of a prophet, and like other prophets he had a tendency to scowl and to spend other people's money. Booth himself described his explosive temper as 'Booth blood'. Family secessions and his wife's sufferings, which ended with her death from cancer in 1890, clouded his later life. Though frail in old age and suffering from blindness, he became widely venerated in Britain as a patriarch. He died on 20 August 1912, after an operation for cataract, at his home Rookstone, Lancaster Avenue, Hadley Wood, Middlesex. Some 35,000 people attended Booth's memorial service at Olympia, and he was buried on 29 August next to his wife in Abney Park cemetery, Stamford Hill, London. (William) Bramwell Booth succeeded his father as general; Evangeline Booth (1865–1950), his sister, organized the army in Canada before taking up the post of national commander for the United States in 1904.

If he did not leave 'Darkest England' much lighter than he found it, General Booth probably changed as many lives for the better as any philanthropist of his day. A great propagandist, he inspired an organization with worldwide ramifications. Unlike most Victorian charities, the Salvation Army—godly, uniformed, and family centred—remains recognizably the institution of its founder.

FRANK PROCHASKA

Sources H. Begbie, *Life of William Booth*, 2 vols. (1920) · G. K. Horridge, *The Salvation Army: origins and early days, 1865–1900* (1993) · *The Times* (21 Aug 1912) · W. Booth, *In darkest England and the way out* (1890) · F. Coutts, *No discharge in this war* (1975) · R. Hattersley, *Blood and fire: the story of William and Catherine Booth and their Salvation Army* (1999) · *War Cry* (1879–1912) · F. de L. Booth-Tucker, *The life of Catherine Booth*, 3 vols. (1893) · *DNB*

Archives BL, corresp., mainly family corresp., Add. MSS 64799–64806 · Salvation Army Archives, corresp., diary, and papers | Georgetown University, Washington, DC, Lauinger Library, letters to Richard Wilson | FILM BFI NFTVA, actuality footage

Likenesses J. Earle-Morrell, oils, 1887, William Booth Memorial Training College, London · H. von Herkomer, oils, 1897, William Booth Memorial Training College, London · bust, *c*.1900, NPG · O. & K. Edis, photograph, 1902, NPG [*see illus.*] · H. F. Joyce, photograph, 1906, NPG · S. Reid, pen-and-ink caricature, 1906, NPG · G. Wade, statue, 1929, William Booth Memorial Training College, London · C. Campbell, pen-and-ink caricature, NPG · N. D. Davis, oils, Castle Art Gallery, Nottingham · F. Dodd, pen-and-ink caricature, BM; copy, reverse etching, NPG · S. P. Hall, pencil drawing, NPG · H. Hampton, bronze panel, Victoria Memorial, Lancaster · H. Hampton, bust, Salvation Army International Headquarters, London · D. N. Ingles, oils, NPG; loan no 25 · E. H. Mills, photogravure photograph, NPG; repro. in *ILN* [supplement] · O. Scholderer, pastel drawing, Castle Art Gallery, Nottingham · lithograph, NPG · photographs, Salvation Army International Headquarters, London

Wealth at death £2181 5*s*. 10*d*.: probate, 28 Aug 1912, *CGPLA Eng. & Wales*

Boothby, Sir Brooke, seventh baronet (1744–1824), poet and writer, was born on 3 June 1744 at Ashbourne Hall, Derbyshire, the eldest son of Sir Brooke Boothby of Ashbourne Hall and Phoeby Hollings. In 1752 the family moved to Stafford, where Boothby attended the free school. They returned to Ashbourne Hall in 1761 and on 19 June that year Boothby was admitted as a pensioner to St John's College, Cambridge, but left without taking a degree. Boothby's father had wanted his son to follow a career in the law. Brooke, however, had set his heart on joining the army and was therefore sent to a military academy at Caen, Normandy. After completing his studies he was bought a commission in the Irish regiment of 18th light dragoons. Boothby accompanied Lord Hertford to Dublin and France and in 1767 joined the regiment at Irish county quarters. He retired from the army on half pay in 1772 and settled in his house in Lichfield. He joined the literary circle at Lichfield to which Anna Seward, Erasmus Darwin, Thomas Day, and the Edgeworths belonged, and was a member of a botanical society which Erasmus Darwin started there. One of Seward's odes and several of her printed letters are addressed to him.

Boothby wrote that:

> From the age of thirty to that of forty my life was dedicated to the *beau monde* at home & abroad. A member of the ladies club, of Brookes, the summers at Brighton, Cheltenham &c. & the opera and fine assembl[i]es – ten years of vanity and folly! (Mosley, 6)

In 1775 he travelled in Italy, visiting Turin, Florence, Rome, and Naples, and returning via Venice, the Tyrol, Strasbourg, and Paris. During his stay in Paris, Boothby called on Jean-Jacques Rousseau to renew a friendship that had begun when the latter had stayed at Wootton Hall, near Ashbourne, between 1766 and 1767. Boothby expressed his admiration for Rousseau in a letter to Lord Harcourt: 'During the six weeks that I was in Paris I passed much of my time with this *divine man*, & my love & respect are grown into absolute adoration' (ibid., 1). The well-known portrait of Boothby by Joseph Wright of Derby shows him holding a volume of Rousseau. In 1780, two years after Rousseau's death, Boothby published *Rousseau juge de Jean Jacques: dialogue*.

Boothby's period of vanity and folly ended with his marriage on 15 July 1784 to Susanna (1751/2–1822), daughter of Robert Bristowe or Bristoe of Micheldever, Hampshire. The only child of this marriage, Penelope (*b*. 1785), died on

13 March 1791 at the age of only six years, and was interred in Ashbourne church, where a monument by Thomas Banks RA was erected to her memory. It is said that Penelope's death caused Boothby and his wife to separate, never to be reconciled. In his daughter's honour Boothby published *Sorrows Sacred to the Memory of Penelope* (1796).

Boothby had succeeded to the baronetcy on the death of his father on 9 April 1789. In the next year he published *A Letter to the Right Honourable Edmund Burke*, a reply to Burke's *Reflections on the Revolution in France*. Boothby followed this with his *Observations on the Appeal from the New to the Old Whigs* (1792), in which he makes an earnest defence of Rousseau. Some time about 1794 he left England after suffering, as he put it in a letter to Lord Wellesley in 1806, 'pecuniary indiscretions which I have more cause to lament than be ashamed of', indiscretions which had caused him to be 'a solitary wanderer on the continent ever since' (Mosley, 2). Boothby's wanderings took him to Hamburg, Frankfurt, and Weimar, where, in 1804, he met Goethe, who recalled that 'His health was not good: he complained of our cold winters, disliked silk stockings, and could ride better than he danced' (ibid., 5). The winter of 1803–4 Boothby passed alone in a château on the banks of the Mein. His translation of Racine's *Britannicus* appeared in 1803. Boothby was in Dresden in 1806 and in Edinburgh two years later. Another translation, *Fables and Satires, with a Preface on the Esopean Fable*, was published in 1809. According to Robert Pearse Gillies 'Sir Brooke's habits were insulated and secluded—in his own phrase, he had done with the world, and his best philosophy seemed to consist in forgetting it altogether' (ibid., 5). He lived according to a routine he had adopted in Weimar: rising between four and five, dining at two, then, after finishing his writing, spending time on his watercolour drawings. At the end of the Napoleonic wars Boothby left Edinburgh for Brussels where he began to work on his memoirs. His wife died in Dover in 1822. Boothby lived on for another two years, dying on 23 January 1824, at Boulogne according to some sources, at Brussels according to others (ibid., 3). His corpse was returned to Ashbourne where it was buried in the church on Friday 13 February. REBECCA MILLS

Sources J. Mosley, 'Sir Brooke Boothby, bt., 1744–1824' [unpubd notes] • W. Playfair, *British family antiquity*, 6 (1811), 464–5 • [D. Rivers], *Literary memoirs of living authors of Great Britain*, 1 (1798), 61 • D. E. Baker, *Biographia dramatica, or, A companion to the playhouse*, rev. I. Reed, new edn, rev. S. Jones, 1/1 (1812), 50; 2 (1812), 68 • Watt, *Bibl. Brit.*, 1.134 • *The history and topography of Ashbourne, the valley of the Dove, and the adjacent villages* (1839), 35–8 • *The autobiography and correspondence of Mary Granville, Mrs Delany*, ed. Lady Llanover, 1st ser., 3 vols. (1861) • A. Seward, *Memoirs of the life of Dr Darwin* (1804), 78 • *Letters of Anna Seward: written between the years 1784 and 1807*, ed. A. Constable, 6 vols. (1811) • Venn, *Alum. Cant.*

Archives NRA Scotland, priv. coll., letters to Sir George Sinclair

Likenesses J. Wright, oils, 1781, Tate collection • J. Reynolds, oils, 1784, Detroit Institute of Arts • attrib. R. Cosway, miniature, Fonmon Castle, Barry, Glamorgan • A. Plimer, miniature, FM Cam. • A. Plimer, miniature, V&A

Boothby, Frances (*fl.* 1669–1670), playwright, was the first woman to have an original play professionally staged in London: her tragicomedy, *Marcelia, or, The Treacherous Friend*, was performed by the King's Company early in 1669 and published in 1670. The imminent performance of *Marcelia* was noticed in a letter from Elizabeth Cottington to Walter Aston, written in January 1669. 'I shall tremble for the poor woman exposed among the crittiks' (Clifford, *Letters*, 2.60), she continued, with well justified fears: Boothby's only other known work, a poem lamenting the play's failure, is also preserved in the papers of the Aston family. *Marcelia* is a conservative work, showing the defeat of upstarts and the triumph of aristocratic values. In portraying the fall of an ambitious favourite, it perhaps alludes to the recent fall of Clarendon, and in depicting a king who is (temporarily) false in love, it contributes to the widespread, but as yet tactful, theatrical criticism of the king's morals.

Boothby's identity is a mystery: even her forename is known only because it is preserved by Gerard Langbaine (Langbaine, 26–7), and almost the only certainty is that she was not (as has been suggested in Bell, Parfitt, and Shepherd, 31), the Frances Boothby, *née* Milward, who married Sir William Boothby in 1653, for this Frances died the following year. The only clues are the two relatives to whom she addresses her works: *Marcelia* is dedicated to Lady Yate, the most prominent recusant of Worcestershire, and the poem is addressed to her 'Cosen' Anne Somerset, a daughter of Walter Aston (Clifford, *Poetry*, 228–9). The Yates and Astons were linked by marriages with the Gage family of Firle Place, Sussex.

Although Sir William Boothby's first wife cannot be the author, his family is the only one of that name likely to have the exalted connections which Frances mentions. Lady Yate and Sir William's uncle Richard Boothby of Potters Marston did, indeed, have a common ancestor in Ralph Sacheverell of Morley, Derbyshire. Another relative of Sir William, the prosperous merchant Walter Boothby of Tottenham, had a daughter named Frances, born in the mid-1630s and still alive in 1690. DEREK HUGHES

Sources F. Boothby, *Marcelia, or, The treacherous friend* (1670) • L. Bazely, *The family of Boothby* (1915) • A. Clifford, ed., *Tixall poetry* (1813) • A. Clifford, ed., *Tixall letters*, 2 vols. (1815) • M. Bell, G. Parfitt, and S. Shepherd, *A biographical dictionary of English women writers, 1580–1720* (1990) • G. Langbaine, *An account of the English dramatick poets* (1691)

Boothby, Guy Newell (1867–1905), novelist, was born on 13 October 1867 at Glenosmond, Adelaide, South Australia, the eldest of the three sons of Thomas Wilde Boothby (1839–1885), member of the South Australian house of assembly, and his wife, Mary Agnes (1843–1907), daughter of Edward Hodding of Odstock, Salisbury, Wiltshire. His grandfather, Benjamin Boothby (1803–1868), a native of Doncaster, emigrated with his family to South Australia in 1853 on being appointed second judge of the supreme court of South Australia, and was removed from office in 1867 by the South Australian parliament owing to his objections to the Real Property (Torrens) Act. His uncle, Josiah Boothby CMG, born at Nottingham, was permanent under-secretary for the government of South Australia from 1868 to 1880. About 1874 Guy Newell Boothby went with his mother and brothers to England, and received his education at the Priory School, Salisbury.

In 1883 Boothby returned to South Australia, and in 1890 became private secretary to the mayor of Adelaide. During this period he devoted himself to writing plays, which were largely unsuccessful. In October 1888 he produced a melodrama at the Albert Hall, Adelaide, entitled *Falsely Accused*, and in August 1891 at the Theatre Royal *The Jonquille*, a piece set during the French Revolution. Of a roving disposition, Boothby travelled across Australia from north to south in 1891–2, and in 1894 he published *On the Wallaby*, in which he described his journey in a lively style. In the same year he settled in England, marrying Rose Alice, the third daughter of William Bristowe, on 8 October 1895. The couple first lived in William Bristowe's home at Champion Hill, and afterwards settled near Bournemouth, where Boothby devoted himself to novel writing and occupied his leisure in collecting live fish and breeding horses, cattle, and prize dogs.

The many stories which Boothby wrote at an exceptionally rapid rate during the last ten years of his life were sensational and dramatic; they enjoyed a wide vogue, but he had small faculty for characterization or literary style. He produced in all fifty-five volumes. He was at his best in his earlier studies of Australian life in *A Lost Endeavour* (1895), *Bushigrams* (1897), and *Billy Binks, Hero, and other Stories* (1898). His best-known novel, *A Bid for Fortune, or, Dr. Nikola's Vendetta* (1895; 2nd edn 1900), first appeared as a serial in the *Windsor Magazine*. Its success led Boothby to prolong his hero's mysterious adventures through many subsequent volumes, including *Dr. Nikola* (1896), *Dr. Nikola's Experiment* (1899), and *Farewell Nikola* (1901).

Boothby died unexpectedly, of pneumonia, at his house in Boscombe, near Bournemouth, Hampshire, on 26 February 1905, and was buried in Bournemouth cemetery. He was survived by his wife and their two daughters and one son. G. S. Woods, *rev.* M. Clare Loughlin-Chow

Sources *The Times* (28 Feb 1905) • *The Athenaeum* (4 March 1905) • *Adelaide Chronicle* (4 March 1905) • *The Advertiser* [Adelaide] (28 March 1905) • *Bournemouth Guardian* (4 March 1905) • private information (1912) [GSW] • P. Depasquale, *Guy Boothby: his life and work* (1982) • *ANB* • d. cert.

Archives NRA, letters | U. Leeds, letters to Bram Stoker

Boothby, Hill (1708–1756), friend of Samuel Johnson, was born on 27 October 1708 at Ashbourne, Derbyshire, the only daughter of Brooke Boothby (*d.* 1727) of Ashbourne Hall, Derbyshire, and his second wife, Elizabeth Fitzherbert, daughter of John Fitzherbert of Somersall-Herbert, Derbyshire. A woman of considerable ability, she made the acquaintance of Samuel Johnson in 1739 when he stayed in Ashbourne with John Taylor. She became reacquainted with Johnson in 1753, a year after his wife died. In March 1753 Miss Boothby's close friend Mary Meynell, wife of William Fitzherbert, died. As her executor Miss Boothby undertook the management of Fitzherbert's household and six children. On Easter Sunday 1753 Johnson wrote in his diary that he would 'try on Monday to seek a new wife'. Scholars believe the woman he had in mind was almost certainly Hill Boothby, but her duties in the Fitzherbert household prevented any serious thoughts of marriage. They did, however, correspond regularly. Johnson addresses her as 'my sweet angel' and 'dearest dearest madam', and writes, 'You know Des Cartes's argument, "I think therefore I am" It is as good a consequence … "I am alive therefore I love Miss Boothby"' (*Letters of Samuel Johnson*, 1.118). When she was near death Johnson wrote: 'I love you and honour you, and am very unwilling to lose you'. In the same letter he included a remedy for 'indigestion and lubricity of the bowels' (ibid., 1.120–21), dried orange peel taken with wine, thus disclosing the mystery of the orange peel, which Boswell asked for in vain (Boswell, *Life*, 1 April 1775). When Miss Boothby died on 16 January 1756 Johnson 'was almost distracted with his grief' (Piozzi, 114). Her letters (thirty-three are extant) were collected and published by Richard Wright, of Lichfield, in 1805, in *An Account of the Life of Dr. Samuel Johnson*. Kathryn M. Burton

Sources W. J. Bate, *Samuel Johnson* (1977) • *The letters of Samuel Johnson*, ed. B. Redford, 1 (1992) • S. Johnson, *Diaries, prayers, and annals*, ed. E. L. McAdam jr, 1 (1958) • H. L. Piozzi, *Anecdotes of the late Samuel Johnson*, ed. A. Sherbo (1974) • *DNB* • GEC, *Baronetage*, 2.83

Boothby, Louisa Cranstoun. *See* Nisbett, Louisa Cranstoun (1812–1858).

Boothby, Robert John Graham, Baron Boothby (1900–1986), politician, was born on 12 February 1900 at 5 Ainslie Place, Edinburgh, the only child of Sir Robert Tuite Boothby (1871–1941), manager of the Scottish Provident Institution and a director of the Royal Bank of Scotland, and his wife, Mabel Augusta (*d.* 1948), daughter of Henry Hill Lancaster, Edinburgh advocate. Robert, known throughout his life as Bob, was educated at Eton College and Magdalen College, Oxford, where he enjoyed himself and made many friends, but secured only a pass degree in modern history (1921). Between Eton and Oxford he trained as a guards officer, but was too young to take an active part in the First World War.

In 1923 Boothby contested Orkney and Shetland on behalf of the Conservative Party, whose new leader, Stanley Baldwin, was a friend of his father. Although he did not win there, his campaign provided ample evidence of his political assets, which included dark and dramatic looks, a lively and independent mind, an easy way with people, and the ability to make compelling speeches enhanced by humour, wit, and a voice well described as 'of golden gravel'. He was soon selected as the Conservative candidate for another seat, East Aberdeenshire, which he won in 1924 and held for nearly thirty-four years, until he left of his own accord. He gave his constituents, mainly fishermen and farmers, superb service as their MP, and they showed their gratitude by backing him loyally through the many vicissitudes of his career.

In parliament Boothby at once made his mark with a successful maiden speech and was soon regarded as a rising star. But some of his views were unorthodox, notably on economics—he was an early Keynesian—and his sympathies, personal and political, were by no means confined to his own party. He was quick to denounce the decision by the chancellor of the exchequer, Winston Churchill, to return Britain to the gold standard at the pre-war parity. Nevertheless, Churchill chose him as his parliamentary private secretary in 1926, and he held the post until the government fell at the next election, in 1929. Over the years his relations with Churchill, though intermittently close, were scarred by differences of opinion, for instance on India and the abdication of Edward VIII, and above all by Boothby's natural incapacity to be a disciple or courtier.

From his position on the left of the party Boothby contributed to the publication *Industry and the State, a Conservative View* (R. Boothby and others, 1927), to which another contributor was Harold Macmillan, his closest associate in politics. In 1929 he began an affair with Macmillan's wife, Lady Dorothy Evelyn, *née* Cavendish (1900–1966), which lasted on and off until her death. The affair was soon well known in political circles and was used by Boothby's enemies to discredit him, though Macmillan himself remained ostensibly friendly. Lady Dorothy claimed that Boothby was the father of one of her daughters, Sarah, but there are grounds for doubting this; she may have been making the claim in the vain hope of provoking Macmillan into divorcing her. Boothby himself was doubtful, but nevertheless accepted responsibility and treated Sarah with much kindness and affection.

The liaison with Dorothy Macmillan caused some colleagues to regard Boothby as a rackety character, while his attempts to make money in the City, necessitated by his extravagant and generous habits, earned him the reputation of a gambler, which was equally damaging to him politically. Yet he deserved to be taken seriously, not least because he was one of the very few MPs with a consistent anti-appeasement record in the 1930s. He took a stronger line than Churchill on Hitler's reoccupation of the Rhineland and on the Hoare–Laval pact, and he was among the thirty Conservatives, including Churchill, who refused to support the government over Munich. In May 1940 he was among the forty-one who voted against the government at the end of the Norway debate, with the result that Neville Chamberlain resigned and Churchill came to power. In the coalition then formed he was appointed under-secretary at the Ministry of Food. Since the minister, the first earl of Woolton, was in the House of Lords, Boothby was spokesman for the department in the House of Commons.

Boothby proved an excellent minister. The national milk scheme that he worked out was widely praised, and he reacted imaginatively to the problems created by the blitz. His regular broadcasts were practical and inspiring. He gained Woolton's warm confidence. Then suddenly, in October 1940, he was suspended from his duties while a select committee investigated his activities the previous year in connection with émigré Czech financial claims. When the committee reported that his conduct had been 'contrary to the usage and derogatory to the dignity of the House', he resigned. The verdict of Sir Robert Rhodes James, after careful analysis of the committee's report, was that it was 'heavily, and unfairly, loaded against Boothby' (James, 281). Though he was not quite blameless in the matter, the penalty he paid was out of all proportion to his offence. After delivering a resignation speech (January 1941), which won him much support, he served for a time as a junior staff officer with RAF Bomber Command. Later in the war he worked with the Free French, and after it his services to France were recognized by his appointment as a chevalier of the Légion d'honneur (1950).

In the late 1940s Boothby worked enthusiastically in Churchill's movement for a United Europe, but when Churchill became prime minister again in 1951 there was no post for him. He had to be content with his appointment as KBE in the coronation honours (1953). From 1949 to 1957 he was a British delegate to the consultative assembly of the Council of Europe, and from 1952 to 1956 vice-chairman of the committee on economic affairs. He opposed the Suez adventure in 1956, though he was a fervent Zionist. Macmillan's advent to the premiership brought him no office, perhaps understandably, but when a heart attack forced him to give up his seat, Macmillan recommended him, in 1958, for a life peerage. In the House of Lords he sat on the cross-benches and was a frequent contributor to debates.

Meanwhile, in the 1950s, Boothby's appearances in current affairs programmes on television and radio had made him a household name, which did not endear him to colleagues lacking his eloquence and engaging personality. At the end of the decade he was elected rector of St Andrews University, a post he held from 1958 to 1961; he was immensely popular with the students. Music played a great part in his life; he was chairman of the Royal Philharmonic Orchestra (1961–3) and a founder member of the Royal Philharmonic Orchestra Society.

In July 1964 the *Sunday Mirror* ran a story linking Boothby with the gangster Ronald Kray. A photograph was published of the two men together at Boothby's flat, and the police were said to be investigating a homosexual relationship between them. Scotland Yard issued a denial, and Boothby wrote a powerful letter to *The Times*, in which he denied being a homosexual but admitted having met Kray three times at his flat to discuss a business proposal which he had turned down. He denied having any knowledge of the criminal activities for which Kray and his brother were later imprisoned. The *Mirror* management apologized unreservedly and made Boothby a voluntary payment of £40,000 as compensation. After his death, however, further evidence suggested that his *Times* letter had not been wholly candid. Boothby was, in fact, bisexual, and his connection with Kray may well have involved some homosexual activity (then still criminal) with youths procured by Kray. Another photograph suggests this, but there is no evidence of any more sinister involvement.

Boothby published a volume of autobiography, *I Fight to Live*, in 1947, and another, *Boothby, Recollections of a Rebel*, in 1978. He also published *The New Economy* in 1943, and a collection of articles and speeches, *My Yesterday, your Tomorrow*, in 1962. His ambition was insufficiently concentrated, and his temperament too reckless, for complete worldly success. Yet he was right on most of the major issues of his career, and showed outstanding promise during his brief innings as a minister. He was also, as Queen Elizabeth the queen mother said, '*such* a jolly man'.

Boothby was twice married. On 21 March 1935 he married Diana (1909–1992), fourth daughter of Lord Richard Frederick Cavendish, landowner and former politician. The marriage ended in amicable divorce in 1937. In 1967 he married Wanda, daughter of Giuseppe Sanna, a Sardinian import-export wholesaler. She gave him nearly twenty years of comfort and security at the end of his life. There were no children of either marriage. Boothby died in Westminster Hospital, London, on 16 July 1986, following a heart attack, and his ashes were scattered at sea off the coast of his old constituency. JOHN GRIGG, *rev.*

Sources R. R. James, *Bob Boothby: a portrait* (1991) · R. Boothby, *I fight to live* (1947) · R. Boothby, *Boothby, recollections of a rebel* (1978) · *The Times* (18 July 1986) · *The Times* (24 July 1986) · personal knowledge (1996) · private information (1996) · *WWW, 1981–90* · Burke, *Peerage*

Archives priv. coll., papers | HLRO, corresp. with Lord Beaverbrook · HLRO, letters to David Lloyd George · King's Lond., Liddell Hart C., corresp. with Basil Liddell Hart · McMaster University Library, Hamilton, Ontario, corresp. with Bertrand Russell

Likenesses photographs, *c.*1930–1971, Hult. Arch. · F. Topolski, portrait, NPG

Wealth at death £140,259: probate, 4 Dec 1986, *CGPLA Eng. & Wales*

Boothby, Sir William, first baronet (*bap.* **1637**, *d.* **1707**), book collector, was baptized on 9 November 1637 at Broadlow Ashe, the son of the landowner and royalist Henry Boothby (*d.* 1648), of Clater Close, Oxfordshire, who was nominated first baronet during the civil war in 1644 but whose patent never passed the great seal, and his wife, Mary Hayes. Boothby inherited his father's estate in 1648, but little else is known of his early years. He was created baronet by Charles II, by letters patent dated 13 July 1660, and led an active life as a notable figure among the Derbyshire landed gentry, serving as county sheriff in 1661–2 and on the grand jury in the assizes of 1682. In 1671 he bought Ashbourne Hall, Derbyshire, and the manor of Ashbourne from the poet Sir Aston Cokayne (1608–1684). Boothby married twice, his first wife, Frances Milward, whom he married in 1653, dying a year later after presenting him with a son, Francis (Frank; *d.* 1684). In 1657 he married Hill Brooke (1640–1704), the second daughter and eventually sole heir of Sir William Brooke, the nephew and heir of Henry Brooke, eleventh Lord Cobham. She was the object of his great affection, as is clear from his later diary comments on what a 'Jewell' and 'Treasure' she was, whose 'sweet and good society' he enjoyed for so long. They had nine children over the next thirteen years.

Boothby would be remembered no more than any other midland landowner, gentleman farmer, and local dignitary of his time but for a series of his diaries and letter-books, written between 1676 and 1689, which came fully to light in the 1990s among the muniments of Fonmon Castle, Glamorgan, whither later generations of the Boothby family migrated through marriage into the Jones family. Besides documenting something of his relationship with his neighbour (8 miles away), the poet and translator Charles Cotton (1630–1687), and providing a glimpse of the provincial literary community to which they belonged, these four manuscript volumes (acquired in 1995 by the British Library) reveal in vivid and extensive detail, possibly unique of its kind, the predominant intellectual and recreational passion of Boothby's life, which was book collecting. 'My Books are the great joy of my life', he declared in a letter to Cotton on 21 July 1685. The result was years of book buying from a series of dealers, both in London and the midlands—his regular suppliers including Michael Johnson (1656–1731) in Lichfield and Richard Chiswell (1639–1711) in London—whom he frequently harangued for more information about current publications and whose attentions to his demands he often found woefully inadequate. He was a religious man and his tastes inclined especially to theology and ecclesiastical debate, but incorporated a wide spectrum of other categories, including literature, politics, science, medicine, history, travel, law, and rhetoric, as well as bibliography itself, books on miscellaneous social topics (such as marriage), and a variety of prints, maps, atlases, and dictionaries. He gave specific instructions for the binding he wanted on his books, and his frequent dissatisfaction with the results adds to the impression that dealers found him at times a difficult and perhaps cantankerous client. Boothby died at Ashbourne Hall on 24 March 1707, and was buried three days later at St Oswald's Church, Ashbourne. He was succeeded by his grandson Sir Henry Boothby (1682–1710).

The ultimate result of Boothby's bibliomania was a library which, according to his memorial, numbered at his death 'near six Thousand Books'. This library, which occupied at least 122 shelves, is, in fact, extensively listed by subject in 'A catalogue of all the books in the inner library at Ashburne-Hall, collected by Sr Willm: Boothby K^t: and baronet … 1715', a 57-leaf folio manuscript still preserved at Fonmon Castle. Apart from compiling this catalogue, his son Brooke Boothby (1670–1727), who erected a grand monument to him in St Oswald's Church, Ashbourne, is not known to have inherited his father's passion, but it seems that his grandson, another Brooke Boothby, the fifth baronet (1710–1789), did so, ordering (according to Samuel Pegge) '*every* book that was published to be sent to him' (J. Nichols, *The History and Antiquities of the County of Leicester*, 4, 1807, 179). A tribute to this later, expanded library appears in Ellis Farneworth's preface to *The Life of Pope Sixtus the Fifth … Translated from … Gregorio Leti* (1754). Nevertheless, it seems that the Boothby library was sold before the year 1776 and was subsequently dispersed. Several dozen books bearing Boothby's signature ('Will: Boothby'), with occasional pressmarks or notes on prices paid for binding, sometimes in his original characteristic bindings of calf with lion's paw crest in gilt, have come to light (in the British Library, the Folger Shakespeare Library, the Huntington Library, the Beinecke Library, Yale

University, the Humanities Research Center, University of Texas at Austin, the University Library, Durham, and elsewhere), and no doubt more will do so in the future.

PETER BEAL

Sources BL, Add. MSS 71689–71692 · P. Beal, '"My books are the great joy of my life": Sir William Boothby, seventeenth-century bibliophile', *Book Collector*, 46 (1997), 350–78 · M. Bartley, P. Beal, I. Doyle, and E. Havens, *Book Collector*, 46 (1997), 566–8 · M. Bartley, P. Beal, and I. Doyle, 'Bibliographical notes and queries', *Book Collector*, 47 (1998), 577–80 [see also p. 127] · E. Havens, 'Bibliographical notes and queries', *Book Collector*, 48 (1999), 286–91 · GEC, *Peerage* · Burke, *Peerage* · M. Evans, ed., *A catalogue of the library at Fonmon Castle, Glamorgan* (1969), 5 · MS catalogue, Fonmon Castle, Glamorgan · diary and letter-books, BL, Add. MSS 71689–71692
Archives BL, diary and letter-books, Add. MSS 71689–71692

Boothman, Sir John Nelson (1901–1957), air force officer and aviator, was born at Napier Road, Wembley, Middlesex, on 19 February 1901, the son of Thomas John Boothman, a railway clerk, and his wife, Mary, *née* Burgess. Educated at Harrow county school he was, in January 1918, too young to enlist in the British forces, so he joined the French Red Cross as a motor ambulance driver. After driving in the Balkan convoys, he was awarded the bronze star of the Croix de Guerre for 'more than a year's zeal and devotion in the evacuation of French wounded despite enemy bombardment'.

On his return to Wembley in October 1919 Boothman took flying lessons at Hendon airfield, was awarded a private pilot's licence (no. 691), and joined the Royal Aero Club in 1923. He was commissioned into the Royal Air Force in 1921 and married Gertrude (1895–1979), a secretary and the daughter of Herbert F. Andrews of Addiscombe, on 4 September 1922. Later that month he took part in flying operations with 4 squadron, equipped with Bristol F.2B MK. IIIa aircraft, at Constantinople during the Chanak crisis. At the Central Flying School at Upavon he qualified as a flying instructor and, as 'the best pilot on the course', was retained as an instructor until September 1926, winning the duke of York's cup at that year's Hendon air display. He then flew with nos. 55 and 30 (bomber) squadrons in Iraq, where his proficiency as a pilot was assessed as 'exceptional', as it was when he flew Siskin fighters in 32 squadron in 1930. He was then posted to the high speed flight of the Marine Aircraft Experimental Establishment (seaplanes) at Felixtowe, where he flew seventy-one flights in high-speed aircraft.

From the flying boat base at Calshot, near Southampton, on 13 September 1931 Boothman won the Schneider trophy outright in the Vickers Supermarine Rolls-Royce S.6B S1595, recording in his log book: 'Good trip. Average speed 340 mph, 100 Km record 342.9 mph.' He was awarded the AFC and, in November 1931, moved to 22 squadron at Martlesham Heath, Norfolk, by which time he had flown seventy-four different aircraft types. In 1934, as 'A' flight commander of the performance testing section of the Aircraft and Armament Experimental Establishment at Martlesham, he was again assessed as an exceptional pilot.

Boothman spent 1935 at the Staff College before serving

Sir John Nelson Boothman (1901–1957), by Walter Stoneman, 1946

as a squadron leader at headquarters, Far East, in Singapore. In February 1939, as wing commander, he returned to England to command 44 squadron at Waddington, Lincolnshire, flying Hampden bombers. In December 1939 he was posted to the Air Ministry (fighter operations), and in July 1940 he went to headquarters, Bomber Command—but these staff postings did not stop him from flying. At the ministry he managed to fly Hurricane, Spitfire, Manchester, and Beaufighter aircraft and even an ME 109E, while at Bomber Command he flew American aircraft types and, on 19 October 1940, a Hampden on a six-hour bombing raid on Hamburg. In March 1941 he was appointed station commander at Waddington, and in October that year he piloted a Tiger Moth with his son Patrick, who then made his first solo flight. In an eight-week goodwill and flight-testing tour of the United States and Canada he flew the latest American aircraft, including, in one day, three bomber and five fighter types.

Boothman returned to England to command RAF Finningley. Then, after further staff duties (operational requirements) at the Air Ministry, he was posted to Benson, Oxfordshire, in June 1943 to command 106 wing (later group), flying photographic reconnaissance missions over the continental beaches in preparation for the D-day invasion. For '14 missions over enemy territory [by] one of the oldest officers to engage in high altitude flying operations against the enemy' in 1944 he was awarded the American DFC and the DFC and appointed CB. Three weeks after D-day he was appointed to command the Aircraft and Armament Experimental Establishment at Boscombe Down. His son Patrick was awarded the DFC in 1945, and both father and son received their awards at the same investiture. Patrick was killed in a flying accident in 1946, the year in which Boothman was promoted air vice-marshal.

At the end of the war Boothman spent three years as assistant chief of the air staff (technical requirements) before being appointed air officer commanding, Iraq, where he made light of the illness that now troubled him. In September 1950 he was appointed controller (air) at the Ministry of Supply, where he calmly oversaw the rapid expansion in the production of aircraft and equipment during the rearmament period of the Korean War. In 1953 he dealt equally calmly with the problems of running down that rearmament effort. He was made KBE in 1951 and KCB in 1954. Boothman took up his final appointment as commander-in-chief, Coastal Command, in 1953 and held it, together with the relevant NATO appointments, for three years. Promoted air chief marshal in 1954, he retired in 1956. Boothman, who was one of the few former test pilots to achieve air rank, died, of an aneurysm, in Westminster Hospital, London, on 29 December 1957.

ROBIN WOOLVEN

Sources *The Times* (31 Dec 1957) • *The Times* (13 Jan 1958) • *The Times* (23 Jan 1958) • *DNB* • RAF Museum, Hendon, Boothman papers [mostly RAF flying log books etc. plus correspondence] • private information (2004), Martin Boothman; Gp Capt. Philip Baldwin; archivist, Old Gaytonians Association; Peter Elliot, archivist, RAF Museum, Hendon • Royal Aero Club obit., 1958 [in family possession] • *Royal Air Force Lists* (1919–56) • b. cert. • m. cert. • d. cert. • *CGPLA Eng. & Wales* (1958)

Archives Royal Air Force Museum, Hendon, papers, flying log-books, etc.

Likenesses photographs, 1931–45 • stained-glass window, 1933, Gayton School, Middlesex • W. Stoneman, photograph, 1946, NPG [*see illus.*] • N. Heppell, portrait (destroyed by fire, 1960s) • portrait (after photograph; after N. Heppell)

Wealth at death £12,272 4*s*. 11*d*.: probate, 21 April 1958, *CGPLA Eng. & Wales*

Boothroyd, Benjamin (1768–1836), Independent minister and Hebrew scholar, was born at Warley, in the parish of Halifax, Yorkshire, on 10 October 1768, the son of a poor shoemaker there. He was sent to the village school, and left it when six years old, able to read the Old and New testaments. He helped his father to make shoes for a time, but when about fourteen years old he ran away with only a few pence in his pocket. Making for Lancashire, he found work with a Methodist, who treated him very kindly. Boothroyd stayed with him until, hearing things were not well with his parents, he returned to Warley to superintend his father's business. About 1785 he vowed to devote himself to religion: he attended and spoke at prayer meetings and read Doddridge's works. Eventually he was admitted as a student at the dissenting college at Northowram, where he immediately made a favourable impression. In 1790 he was chosen minister at Pontefract, and after being ordained there he attracted so large a congregation that a new chapel had to be built.

At this time Boothroyd found that all that was left of his income, after paying expenses, was £20 a year, and he opened a shop as a bookseller and printer. In 1801 he was financially secure enough to marry a Miss Hurst (*d*. 1832) of Pontefract, with whom he had four daughters and four sons. In 1807, having received notes for a history of the town from a Richard Hepworth, he added to them and brought out, at his own press, his *History of the Ancient Borough of Pontefract*. His next project was the production of a new Hebrew Bible. He mastered the language and printed the work himself, while his wife helped him in correcting the proofs. It was brought out in quarterly parts, the issue beginning in 1810 and finishing in 1813 under the title of *Biblia Hebraica*, and finally formed two volumes. Seven years were spent over this undertaking. At the same time Boothroyd preached diligently and published several excellent standard works, besides many sermons of his own.

In 1818 Boothroyd (who had accepted the degree of LLD) became co-pastor at Highfield Chapel, Huddersfield, with William Moorhouse. In the same year he completed his *New Family Bible and Improved Version*, in three volumes. He printed many copies of this book at his own press. The University of Glasgow conferred on Boothroyd the degree of DD in 1824. In 1835 Boothroyd completed an octavo edition of his *Family Bible*. On 10 January 1836 he became ill; he died on 8 September and was buried at Huddersfield.

JENNETT HUMPHREYS, *rev*. J. M. V. QUINN

Sources 'Memoir of the Rev. Benjamin Boothroyd', *Evangelical Magazine and Missionary Chronicle*, new ser., 15 (1837), 105–10; 373–4 • *GM*, 2nd ser., 6 (1836), 445 • J. Darling, *Cyclopaedia bibliographica: a library manual of theological and general literature*, 1 (1854), cols. 287, 369 • Allibone, *Dict.*

Archives Leeds Leisure Services, MS history of Pontefract

Likenesses stipple, NPG

Boott, Francis (1792–1863), physician and botanist, was born on 26 September 1792 in Boston, Massachusetts, the third son of Kirk Boott (1755–1817), merchant, and his wife, Mary, *née* Love. Kirk Boott was English and had emigrated with his Scottish wife from Derby to Boston in 1783. Boott attended Harvard College (1806–10), where he was contemporary with Jacob Bigelow and Edward Everett. For several years he journeyed between England and America pursuing his interests in art, literature, and botany, and in 1816 was persuaded to look after the family's business affairs in England. Unfortunately, having fraudulent advisers, Boott lost £200,000 of assets. Although the business eventually recovered, Boott was criticized by other family members and decided to settle in Britain.

In 1820 Boott married Mary Hardcastle of Derby and they had a son and three daughters. To support his growing family Boott studied medicine with Dr John Armstrong, physician and teacher at the Webb Street School, Southwark, London. Boott graduated MD from Edinburgh (1824) and studied medicine and botany in Paris before returning to London and becoming a licentiate of the Royal College of Physicians in 1825. He rejoined the Webb

Street School and after Armstrong's death in 1829 he wrote Armstrong's memoir to which he appended *An enquiry into the facts connected with those forms of fever attributed to malaria or marsh effluvium* (2 vols., 1833–4) and so became known as an authority on fevers. His practice of using fresh air as a treatment drew strong criticism as nineteenth-century medical practice favoured restricting the patient to a hot and close room. In 1832 an inheritance provided Boott with enough financial security to retire from practice. He was elected to the council of University College in 1833 and in 1836 joined the senate, remaining a member until his death.

Boott is remembered primarily as a botanist and his major contribution was to the knowledge and organization of botany in Britain. His principal study was of sedges, the genus *Carex*, a large and complex family of plants. Over a period of thirty years Boott studied about 600 varieties of sedges which were distributed worldwide and he published his results in *Illustrations of the Genus Carex* (4 vols., 1858–67; 2nd edn, 1968). These were entirely self-financed publications and were acclaimed by contemporaries as outstanding advances in botanical knowledge. Boott's association with the Linnean Society began when Bigelow arranged for an introduction to Sir James Smith, physician and one of the founders of the society and its first president in 1788. Boott was elected fellow of the society in 1819 and became its secretary (1832–9), treasurer (1856–61) and vice-president (1861–3). Throughout his long association with the society he was an active and influential member instigating many reforms.

Boott retained strong links with his native country and was a member of many literary and scientific societies in London and Massachusetts. It is no surprise therefore that in 1846, after the first experiments with the inhalation of ether had taken place in Boston, both Bigelow (then professor of the medical school at Harvard) and Everett (then president of Harvard) wrote to Boott of these developments. Boott lost no time in informing the London medical world. He sent Bigelow's letter to *The Lancet* and also to Robert Liston, professor of clinical surgery at University College Hospital. On 19 December 1846 Boott witnessed the first use of ether in Britain in his own home in Gower Street. It was administered by James Robinson, a dentist, for a tooth extraction, and two days later Liston used ether at University College. The early introduction of ether to London owes much to Boott's enthusiasm and interest in scientific advances.

Boott had an abiding interest in literature and art and gathered a substantial library and a notable collection of paintings. Henry Crabb Robinson, writer, was the closest of his literary friends and Boott was also an admirer of the poet Henry Kirke White, although he never met him. In 1819 Boott paid for a memorial to be placed above White's grave in All Saints' Church, Cambridge. The church was later demolished and the memorial moved to the chapel of St John's College, Cambridge.

Boott was tall and thin and became well known in the 1830s for abandoning the traditional medical outfit of black coat, white neckcloth, knee breeches, and black silk stockings for the then fashionable outfit of a blue coat with brass buttons and yellow waistcoat. However, 'by outliving the fashion, as he had forestalled it, he came to be as well known in 1860 as he had been in 1830' (*Medical Times and Gazette*, 16 Jan 1864).

Boott never enjoyed robust health. In 1839 he suffered two attacks of pneumonia, mainly in his left lung, and afterwards suffered recurrent chest trouble. In June 1863 his right lung was struck by pneumonia from which he never fully recovered. Boott's final months were spent working on the last volume of *Illustrations* at his home, 24 Gower Street, London, until his death there on 25 December 1863. G. C. BOASE, *rev.* STEPHANIE J. SNOW

Sources R. H. Ellis, 'The introduction of ether anaesthesia to Great Britain', *Anaesthesia*, 32 (1977), 197–208 • *Proceedings of the Linnean Society of London*, 8 (1864), 23–7 • *BMJ* (1864), 102 • *The Lancet* (23 Jan 1864), 113 • *Medical Times and Gazette* (16 Jan 1864), 77 • F. Boott, 'Surgical operations performed during insensibility', *The Lancet*, 1 (1864), 5 • P. Paxon, 'Boott, Kirk', *ANB* • *CGPLA Eng. & Wales* (1864)

Archives Carnegie Mellon University, Pittsburgh, Hunt Institute for Botanical Documentation, journals • RBG Kew, corresp., journals, papers • UCL, corresp. | DWL, letters to Henry Crabb Robinson • Harvard U., Arnold Arboretum, letters to Ada Gray • Linn. Soc., corresp. with Sir James E. Smith • Linn. Soc., Pleasance, Lady Smith MSS

Likenesses black and bronze bust on unglazed porcelain, 1830–39, RBG Kew • E. U. Eddis, oils, 1840, RCP Lond. • Gambardella, oils, 1840–49, Linn. Soc. • photograph, 1840–49, RBG Kew

Wealth at death under £4000: probate, 11 Jan 1864, *CGPLA Eng. & Wales*

Boraston, Sir John (1851–1920), political organizer, was born at 163 Hockley Hill, Birmingham, on 24 June 1851, son of John Boraston, a tea merchant from a Worcestershire family, and his wife, Elizabeth Palmer. He trained as a solicitor and took an early interest in politics. Aged only twenty-three he acted as Liberal agent for Southampton in the general election of 1874, and subsequently he worked in the same capacity in Liskeard, though continuing to practise as a solicitor. He married on 13 May 1876 Louisa Jane, daughter of William Henry Lewis, an engineer, with whom he had a son and three daughters.

A strong unionist on Irish issues, Boraston became assistant secretary of the new Liberal Unionist Party organization in 1887. Initially he ran the machine for London, but from 1891 he was Liberal Unionist chief agent for the whole country. His close collaboration with the Conservatives' Captain Middleton brought Unionist electoral machinery to a legendary pitch of effectiveness in the 1890s, when during actual campaigns Boraston took charge of the parties' efforts in Ireland. He collaborated actively with the party's parliamentary figures, but worked most closely with Joseph Chamberlain who, among the Liberal Unionist leaders, was the most fascinated by organizational matters. Boraston helped to ensure that the Liberal Unionist council backed Chamberlain's tariff crusade from 1903. Thereafter, party divisions hampered electoral effectiveness, but when the Unionist organization committee reviewed the situation in 1911, witnesses contrasted Boraston's efficiency for the Liberal Unionists with the slacker approach at Conservative central office.

When the two parties finally merged in 1912, Boraston became principal agent for the combined party, and seems to have won the trust of the former Conservatives. For he was, wrote the *Morning Post*, 'a very tactful and genial man, and quickly gained the regard of those with whom his duties brought him into contact'. Thereafter, under the party chairman Arthur Steel-Maitland, he spruced up the party machine between 1912 and 1914. All this effort was rewarded with a clutch of by-election victories which steadily eroded the Liberals' parliamentary strength, and with progress in the annual registration courts that promised a more favourable register for a national contest. Boraston wrote in 1914 that fusion of the parties had been 'a sound investment and, although Unionist stock has appreciated greatly since the new issue, nobody has the slightest intention of selling out' (Ramsden, 93).

This seemed to presage well for the election due in 1915, but because of war no election was held. It was characteristic of the 'business as usual' manner in which Edwardian Britain went to war that its party machines were turned over to the war effort. Boraston became honorary secretary to the parliamentary recruiting committee, which conducted propaganda for voluntary enlistment through his usual repertory of leaflets, posters, and public meetings, and took personal charge of organizing meetings. The success of the campaign was indicated in the large number of volunteers, enabling Britain to avoid conscription until 1916; his work was recognized by the award of a knighthood in that year. When conscription did come about he was redeployed to similar campaigns for war savings and national service. His only son, John Herbert Boraston, was Douglas Haig's secretary at general headquarters during the war.

With Boraston so involved in war work, he had less time for central office, and his assistant was promoted to joint principal agent. On the return of peacetime politics, old party certainties had vanished and his health was poor, but he soldiered on, holding the post of principal agent until his death; he died of cancer of the colon on 18 April 1920 at the Greta Nursing Home, Blyth Road, Bromley, Kent. He was buried on 22 April at St Paul's, Beckenham. *The Times* noted the passing of 'a great political organiser', and the *Daily Telegraph* reported that 'the Unionist Party has suffered a heavy loss', for Boraston had been 'an admirable type of the British party official, dignified, reserved, discreet, and keen, but scrupulously fair in his methods'. JOHN RAMSDEN

Sources *WWW* · *Morning Post* (20 April 1920) · *Daily Telegraph* (20 April 1920) · *The Times* (20 April 1920) · J. Ramsden, *The age of Balfour and Baldwin, 1902–1940* (1978) · R. Douglas, 'Voluntary enlistment in the First World War and the work of the parliamentary recruiting committee', *Journal of Modern History*, 42 (1970), 564–85 · b. cert. · m. cert. · d. cert. · H. Cox, *Who's who in Kent, Surrey and Sussex* (1911)
Archives U. Birm. L., corresp. with J. Chamberlain
Wealth at death £6192 19s. 4d.: probate, 23 June 1920, *CGPLA Eng. & Wales*

Boraston [Burneston], **Simon** (*fl.* 1311–1338), Dominican friar and writer, may have been born at Boraston in Shropshire. It is not known when or where he became a Dominican, but the only house with which he is definitely linked is Oxford, in 1337–8; such an affiliation would explain his friendship with bishops John Grandison of Exeter (*d.* 1369) and Ralph Shrewsbury of Wells (*d.* 1363), and is compatible with his being presented to the bishop of Lincoln in 1318 for a licence to hear confessions. He is occasionally called *magister* or doctor, and later sources claim that he was a DD of Cambridge; Tanner conjectured that he was a DD of Oxford, but it is uncertain if he was a doctor at all. He is first heard of on 31 March 1311, when he was present at the process against the templars in London.

There is documentary evidence between 1328 and 1333 that Boraston was provincial of the English Dominicans, so he must have been elected in 1327, after the general chapter absolved the previous provincial, and he was no doubt the provincial absolved in 1336. The Dominicans had been keen supporters of Edward II, and in 1330 some of them were evidently still vociferous against the new regime, as the general chapter ordered such friars to be incarcerated. This gives credence to the report that the Dominican and Carmelite provincials were banished, presumably after the revolt of Edmund of Kent in that year. The Carmelite provincial, John Baconthorpe (*d.* 1346), was in Paris for a time in 1330, but nothing is known of Boraston's movements. He was in good standing again by 1333, as on 10 August of that year he received a royal command to remove all Scottish friars from Berwick.

Boraston's writings include a collection of sermons *de tempore*, preserved in one manuscript (Merton Oxf., MS 216), and a collection of *distinctiones* which circulated on the continent as well as in England. In 1337 he produced two treatises—*De unitate et ordine ecclesiasticae potestatis* and *De mutabilitate mundi*—in defence of the mendicants' privileges, which were evidently being attacked, especially their right to hear confessions and to grant burial in their cemeteries to anyone who requested it; only one non-English manuscript is known of either of these works. In 1338 he wrote *De ordine judiciario circa crimina corrigenda* on the legal procedures involved in the correction of erring friars, and this circulated quite widely, probably because the topic was on the agenda of the general chapter of 1339 and the English provincial went to it equipped with Boraston's treatise. SIMON TUGWELL

Sources S. L. Forte, 'Simon of Boraston O.P.: life and writings', *Archivum Fratrum Praedicatorum*, 22 (1952), 321–45 · Emden, *Oxf.* · T. Kaeppeli, *Scriptores ordinis praedicatorum medii aevi*, 3 (Rome, 1980), 343 · J. B. Schneyer, *Repertorium der lateinischen Sermones des Mittelalters: für die Zeit von 1150–1350*, 5 (Münster, 1974), 449–59 · A. B. Emden, 'Dominican confessors and preachers licensed by medieval English bishops', *Archivum Fratrum Praedicatorum*, 32 (1962), 180–210, esp. 182, 194, 196 · C. F. R. Palmer, 'Fasti ordinis fratrum praedicatorum: the provincials of the friar-preachers, or Black friars, of England', *Archaeological Journal*, 35 (1878), 134–65, esp. 150 · B. Jarrett, *The English Dominicans* (1921), 113 · Tanner, *Bibl.*

Brit.-Hib., 143, xxxix • J. Quétif and J. Echard, *Scriptores ordinis praedicatorum recensiti*, 1 (Paris, 1719), 594a
Archives Merton Oxf., MS 216

Borchardt, Louis (**1816/17–1883**), paediatrician, was born at Landesberg an der Warthe, in Brandenburg, East Prussia, of Jewish parents. He was educated at schools in his native town and at Berlin University. After graduating MD in 1838 he practised in Zörbich and subsequently in Breslau. He married Julia (*b.* 1815/16). When sent as a royal commissioner to Upper Silesia to combat a serious typhus epidemic in 1845, Borchardt is said to have acted with distinction.

After his return to Breslau, Borchardt, a keen liberal, became involved in the political opposition to the government. Following the revolution of 1848 he was arrested, tried, and imprisoned for two years in the fortress at Glatz. On his release, prohibited by official action from practising his profession, he tried to settle first in the Netherlands and then in Belgium. Unable to find a professional opening, he moved to Bradford, Yorkshire, with a letter of introduction to an old schoolfellow, and there made the acquaintance of H. M. Steinthal, a German merchant. When Steinthal, a Unitarian, relocated to Manchester in 1852, Borchardt followed with his wife and children. He settled successfully in practice in Manchester, and had two more children. In 1853 he obtained a post as honorary physician at the Children's Dispensary, a small institution, which largely through his efforts developed in 1855 into the General Hospital and Dispensary for Sick Children, one of the first children's hospitals in Britain.

Borchardt published little but was active in various medical organizations. From 1857 he was on the committee of the Manchester Medico-Ethical Association and he was its treasurer from 1862 to 1876. He was on the committee of council of the British Medical Association and at the time of his death was president of the association's Lancashire and Cheshire branch. He was a member, and president, of the Manchester Medical Society, a keen supporter of the Provident Dispensaries Association, and on the executive committee of the Manchester Nurse-Training Institution from its foundation in 1866.

An assimilated Jew, Borchardt was part of the 'substantial group which hovered between faith and apostasy' (Williams, 197). He was active in Liberal politics, president of the Withington branch of the South East Lancashire Liberal Association and chairman of the St Ann's branch of the Manchester Liberal Association. He was active in the German nationalist Deutscher National Verein, and in 1860 he was first chairman of the Manchester Schiller Anstalt, an Anglo-German gentleman's club whose members included a number of political exiles, among them Friedrich Engels. Karl Marx also knew Borchardt, who is mentioned, sometimes unflatteringly, in the Engels–Marx correspondence. In addition Borchardt was a supporter of female emancipation. It was at his home that the Manchester Women's Suffrage Committee, the first body of its kind in Britain, first met, in 1866. A decade later he spoke out in favour of the entry of women into the medical profession, a move most doctors opposed.

Borchardt played a large role in plans to move the in-patient accommodation of the General Hospital and Dispensary for Sick Children to a healthier rural site at Pendlebury, while retaining the dispensary in the city centre. In 1876, when the new hospital, now the Royal Manchester Children's Hospital, was nearing completion, he asked to retire but was persuaded to continue until the entire building was opened. Two years later his twenty-five years' service was marked by naming one of the pavilions the Borchardt ward; a marble bust of him was placed in the hospital and his wife was given a replica. Borchardt was presented with £1000 and appointed as consultant. In 1880 the high respect in which he was held was marred by a well-publicized staff dispute, during which he was accused of autocratic behaviour.

In 1882 Borchardt went to Karlsbad for his health and returned apparently improved. He died at his Manchester home, Swinton House, Fallowfield, on 15 November 1883, after suffering from obstruction of the bowel. He was buried on 20 November 1883 in the noncomformist section of Manchester southern cemetery. The funeral service was conducted by the Revd S. A. Steinthal.

JOAN MOTTRAM

Sources *Manchester Guardian* (16 Nov 1883) • *Manchester Guardian* (21 Nov 1883) • *BMJ* (24 Nov 1883), 1047 • *The Lancet* (24 Nov 1883), 931 • census returns for Chorlton, Chorlton-on-Medlock, 1861, PRO, RG 9/2878 • *London and Provincial Medical Directory* (1852–83) • B. Williams, *The making of Manchester Jewry, 1740–1875* (1976) • *Annual Reports* [Manchester Medico-Ethical Association] (1856–83) • *Jahres-Bericht* [Manchester Schiller-Anstalt] (1860–61) • *Annual Reports* [Manchester Nurse-Training Institution] (1866–83) • *Annual Reports* [General Hospital and Dispensary for Sick Children, Manchester] • W. O. Henderson, *The life of Friedrich Engels*, 1 (1976) • R. Fulford, *Votes for women: the story of a struggle* (1957), 55
Archives JRL, biographical material
Likenesses P. Ball, marble bust, 1879, Royal Manchester Children's Hospital, Pendlebury, Manchester • photograph (after bust), JRL
Wealth at death £3140 4*s.* 6*d.*: administration, 10 Dec 1883, *CGPLA Eng. & Wales*

Borden, Mary [May; *married names* Mary Turner; Mary Spears, Lady Spears; *pseud.* Bridget Maclagan] (**1886–1968**), writer, was born on 15 May 1886 in Chicago, USA, the second of the three children of William Borden (*d.* 1904), a wealthy milk magnate, and his socialite wife, Mary Whiting. Her early childhood was idyllic until her mother converted to fundamentalist Christianity and her easy-going father died. But after attending Vassar College (1904–7) May, as she was called, dispatched on a chaperoned world tour, met 'a gentle Scottish lay-missionary called George Douglas Turner' (Hart-Davis, 65) and was married in Lausanne, Switzerland, in 1908. He was described by E. M. Forster in India as 'the only Englishman I have met who seems to care for the people' (*Selected Letters*, 156), a remark anticipating Fielding in *A Passage to India*. A daughter was born in Maine in 1909 and a second in Kashmir in 1910.

In London, while her husband was abroad and turning his interests towards social reform, May had an affair with Percy Wyndham *Lewis, who saw in her 'the attractive freshness of the New World' (Egremont, 17). Using the pseudonym Bridget Maclagan she published two novels,

Mary Borden (1886–1968), by Howard Coster, 1931

The Mistress of Kingdoms (1912) and *Collision* (1913): these were autobiographical with feminist undertones (she had earlier taken part in a suffragette raid). In 1914 Turner enlisted, and May, pausing only to have a third daughter in London in 1915, went to Dunkirk to work in a typhoid hospital; she remained in France, running (at her own expense) a mobile hospital at the front. In recognition of her services she received the Croix de Guerre and was made a member of the Légion d'honneur. In 1916, on the Somme, she met Edward Louis *Spears (1886–1974), soldier and Anglo-French liaison officer; they fell in love and she asked Turner for a divorce. There was much gossip: that Spears was only marrying her for her money (which was in part true) and that he had broken up a happy home (also partly true). But like the heroine of her novel *Sarah Gay* (1931) May felt the war 'meant freedom, exhilarating activity and romance' (p. 17) and Spears was a symbol of this. They were married on 31 March 1918 during the bombardment of Paris.

Meanwhile, May had published *The Romantic Woman* (1916) under the name Bridget Maclagan—Mary Borden-Turner. It was her first novel to be successful in both Britain and America (where it appeared in 1920) and was about an American girl encountering English bohemia. In 1917 four poems about the war were published in the *English Review*: these are classics of the genre and possibly her best work. From 1918 to 1921 she played the part of society hostess: 'the French army had adopted Spears as a brother-in-arms and Paris had followed suit and opened its doors' (Borden, *Journey*, 11). May would later look back on these as the happiest days of her life for soon afterwards Spears had a row with the War Office in London; there was a custody battle with Turner; the birth of her son Michael in 1921 was difficult; and her life became increasingly blighted by her domineering husband's blatant devotion to his mistress. He was abusive, and his cruelty was noted: May would later remark about Elizabeth von Arnim's *Vera* (1921) that 'the feeling behind this bitter story had more than a little to do with her wish to save me' (Borden, 'Personal experiences', 90).

But Spears settled down to life as an MP and May to her writing, publishing twenty-one more books (under her maiden name) in the years up to 1956. Her theme of the impact of the New World on the old prompted comparisons with Edith Wharton: *Jane: our Stranger* (1923) was the best-known novel; *Flamingo* (1927) 'is a love story which should live as long as any woman believes in love' (Lawrence, 211). Mary Borden's most enduring book is *The Forbidden Zone* (1929), sketches and poems written with a bleak realism that make this one of the greatest of all wartime books by a woman. Her comparative poverty after the slump of 1929–30, a condition she bore with great dignity, drove her to write popular novels with a Christian background such as *The King of the Jews* (1935) as well as many articles and short stories. She also wrote non-fiction books: *The Technique of Marriage* (1933), containing chapters such as 'His honeymoon' and 'The right to divorce', caused a mild sensation; *Passport for a Girl* (1939) is a perceptive account of English attitudes to the rise of Nazism.

In 1933 May's daughter Comfort married the publisher Rupert Hart-Davis and went on to have three children; but a year later her younger daughter Joyce took her own life, while her son Michael (*d.* 1969), who suffered from ill health, failed to fulfil his parents' enormous expectations. 'Conservative, retiring, and extremely reserved … She has, both in life and in her writing, a distaste for emotionalism and for lack of self-control' (Kunitz and Haycraft) was a comment made in 1942. During the Second World War Lady Spears, as she became after her husband's creation as baronet in 1942, ran a mobile field hospital in the Middle East (Spears was British envoy in the Free French Levant) and wrote about this in *Journey Down a Blind Alley* (1946). *For the Record* (1950) is an account of the psychology of a secret agent, and *Martin Merriedew* (1952) describes a pacifist tried for treason; published in America as *You, the Jury*, it was a Book of the Month Club choice. In the 1950s May often travelled to the United States, partly in order to visit her beloved nephew Adlai Stevenson. The appearance of this very short (5 feet 3 inches) woman now 'could be disconcerting … alarmingly thin … the eyes were still huge, fixing people with a gaze of stern fascination' (Egremont, 288). Mary Borden died of heart failure on 2 December 1968 at her home, St Michael's Grange, Warfield, Berkshire. Her ashes were buried on 3 May 1969 in the cemetery of Warfield parish church.

NICOLA BEAUMAN

Sources M. Egremont, *Under two flags: the life of Major-General Sir Edward Spears* (1997) · S. J. Kunitz and H. Haycraft, eds., *Twentieth century authors: a biographical dictionary of modern literature* (1942) · R. Hart-Davis, *The power of chance* (1991) · *The Times* (3 Dec 1968) ·

Daily Telegraph (3 Dec 1968) · M. Borden, 'Personal experiences and the art of fiction', *Essays by Divers Hands, being the Transactions of the Royal Society of Literature of the United Kingdom*, new ser., 29 (1958), 87–96 · M. Borden, *Journey down a blind alley* (1946) · M. Lawrence, *We write as women* (1937) · private information (2004) [family; Mugar Memorial Library, Boston University] · D. Goldman, ed., *Women and World War I* (1993) · N. Beauman, *A very great profession* (1983) · S. Jameson, 'Mary Borden', *The borzoi, 1925: being a sort of record of ten years of publishing*, ed. [A. A. Knopf] (1925), 108–12 · *Selected letters of E. M. Forster*, ed. M. Lago and P. N. Furbank, 1 (1983) · J. Montefiore, *Men and women writers of the 1930s* (1996) · d. cert.

Archives Boston University, Mugar Memorial Library · priv. coll. | BL, corresp. with Society of Authors, Add. MS 63330 · CAC Cam., Spears MSS · Cornell University, New York, Wyndham Lewis collection · King's Lond., Spears MSS · St Ant. Oxf., Spears MSS

Likenesses photograph, 1915, repro. in Egremont, *Under two flags*, following p. 210 · photograph, *c.*1919, repro. in A. A. Knopf, ed., *The borzoi, 1920: being a sort of record of five years of publishing* (1920), facing p. 72 · H. Coster, photographs, 1931, NPG [*see illus.*] · photograph, repro. in Kunitz and Haycraft, *Twentieth-century authors*

Wealth at death £70,289: probate

Borden, Sir Robert Laird (1854–1937), lawyer and prime minister of Canada, was born in Grand Pré, in the Annapolis valley, Nova Scotia, on 26 June 1854, the eldest son of Andrew Borden (1816–1900), a farmer and railway station master, and his wife, Eunice Jane (*d.* 1915), the daughter of John Laird, a classical scholar and mathematician and sometime schoolmaster in Grand Pré. In 1638 an ancestor, Richard Borden, had left Headcorn, Kent, to settle in Portsmouth, Rhode Island. A descendant of his, Samuel Borden, was commissioned by the Nova Scotia government to survey the lands vacated after the expulsion of the Acadians from the Annapolis valley (1755–63). His son, Perry Borden, Robert's great-grandfather, took a land grant in the valley in 1760. Andrew Borden, Robert's father, first married Catherine Fuller, and they had two children before her death in 1847. In 1850 he married Eunice Jane, whose family had migrated to Nova Scotia from Scotland late in the eighteenth century: there were four children from this marriage.

Education and early professional life Borden's early education was at the Grand Pré Presbyterian Sunday school, where he was introduced to the shorter catechism and the confession of faith, and from the village schoolmaster. In 1863 he was enrolled in the community's private academy, Acacia Villa Seminary, where he learned Greek and Latin together with grammar, mathematics, literature, geography, and natural history. His formal schooling ended in the spring of 1869, when he was appointed assistant master of classical studies to fill a sudden vacancy at the seminary. In the autumn of 1873 he left Nova Scotia to become professor of classics and mathematics at a private academy, the Glenwood Institute, in Matawan, New Jersey. A year later he returned to Nova Scotia and was apprenticed to the firm of Weatherbe and Graham in Halifax to study law. He passed his bar examinations in 1877 and was admitted to the Nova Scotia bar in 1878. After a brief practice in Kentville, another Annapolis valley community, Borden returned to Halifax in 1881 to join the Graham firm, together with J. S. D. Thompson and Charles Hibbert Tupper. In 1888 Thompson, then minister of justice in the government of Canada, offered Borden the deputy ministership of his department, but Borden chose to remain in active practice. In 1889 he formed his own firm, and on 25 September that year married Laura Bond, the daughter of the deceased Thomas Henry Bond, a successful Halifax hardware merchant. There were no children of this marriage.

Sir Robert Laird Borden (1854–1937), by Sir William Orpen, 1919

Borden continued to practise law until March 1905. His Halifax firm was very successful. His own work was mostly at the appellate level, arguing cases on referral before the supreme court of Canada in Ottawa. He was appointed queen's counsel in 1891 and in 1893 argued his first of two cases before the judicial committee of the privy council in London, *Municipality of Pictou* v. *Geldert*. He was president of the Nova Scotia Barristers' Society from 1896 to 1901, and during the first year of his term the society initiated the founding meeting of the Canadian Bar Association in Montreal.

Entry into politics and leadership of the Conservative opposition In 1896 Borden accepted the invitation of Sir Charles Tupper, then prime minister of Canada, to stand for the Conservative Party for the dual seat of Halifax City and County in the dominion general election. He had had no significant involvement in politics up to that time, but was regarded by some Halifax Conservatives as a Liberal because in the 1882 general election he had spoken for his cousin, Fred Borden, Liberal MP for King's county, Nova Scotia. However, all the partners he had chosen for his law firm were Conservatives, and the firm had strong connections with the Conservative government in Ottawa and two of its ministers, Thompson and Charles Hibbert Tupper. Borden won his seat, one of the few Conservatives who did in 1896 when the Liberals, led by Wilfrid Laurier, won a commanding majority. In 1901 Sir Charles Tupper resigned as leader of the Conservative Party and, together with his son, Sir Charles Hibbert, persuaded a reluctant caucus to accept Borden, with only one term of parliamentary experience, as the new party leader, a position which he retained until 1920.

Unlike previous leaders of his party, Borden came to the leadership after a successful career outside politics and only a brief political apprenticeship. He frequently looked upon his political career with a sense of detachment and scepticism unknown to career politicians, and approached political life as a duty to be performed in the public interest. He found public speaking and debate physically and emotionally upsetting, and often longed to return to the quiet life and financial security of his profession. Throughout his career he was more interested in issues and policies than the exercise of political power. Influenced by currents of progressive thought in British and American politics in the period, he saw himself as a reformer. His 1907 Halifax platform advocated civil service reform, which was finally achieved by his Union government in 1918. The platform also set forth his belief in an active role for government in society, a conviction that government should do more than enforce law and maintain order; rather it had the responsibility to guide, regulate, and control economic activity in the national interest. In economic enterprises such as telephones, telegraphs, and railways, which he regarded as 'national franchises' (Brown, 'Robert Borden', 92), Borden believed in state ownership and operation. In 1904 he argued that the transcontinental railway chartered by Laurier's government should have been state owned. In 1917, during the crisis precipitated by the First World War, his own government nationalized the Canadian Northern Railway as the initial step in the creation of the state-owned and -operated Canadian National Railway system.

During the opposition years, from 1901 to 1911, Borden's ideas and policies frequently clashed with those of many of his parliamentary colleagues. The decade was marked by factional in-fighting in the Conservative Party and fierce quarrels, which Borden was seldom able to resolve, between its French- and English-Canadian members. Borden's own priorities on national issues were often shaped more by his legal experience and perspective than by the necessities and the thrust and parry of party politics. He was a very intense, reserved man who confided in only a few trusted friends in the party, many of them outside parliament. His relationship with his parliamentary colleagues, while always courteous, was aloof and sometimes imperious. On an occasion in 1913, after having had to reprimand a colleague, he recorded in his diary: 'Wrote Currie consoling letter. He wept. Geo. Lafontaine also wept today when I spoke kindly to him' (Brown, 'Robert Borden', 101).

Borden attempted to make the Conservative Party more democratic by establishing a strong, locally based, elected national organization: but he was continually thwarted by parliamentary colleagues who were, in the absence of a national organization, the focus of party power and influence. Most difficult was his troubled relationship with the French-Canadian Conservatives and their leader, his sometime Quebec 'lieutenant', Frederick Monk. On issue after issue, his views clashed with theirs. In 1905, during the heated debate over the schools' question for the new provinces of Alberta and Saskatchewan, Borden angered them when he refused to support their position. A dismayed Monk said that Borden's stand set the Conservative cause back fifteen years in Quebec. In 1910 Borden countered Laurier's proposal to establish a Canadian navy by advocating a financial contribution from Canada to build two dreadnoughts for the imperial navy. His policy was warmly applauded by English-Canadian party members and adamantly opposed by Monk and several other French-Canadian Conservative MPs. The crisis within the parliamentary party swelled into a potential revolt against his leadership that was put down only with his own threat of resignation.

Laurier's Liberal government, at the peak of its power and popularity, easily won the 1904 general election. In 1908 Borden's Conservatives fought a bitter campaign against corruption in the Laurier government and again lost. Then, in January 1911, the Laurier government announced that it had concluded a broad-based reciprocal trade agreement with the United States. At first downcast at the prospect of another defeat, Borden, urged on by anti-reciprocity interests, rallied his forces. Laurier was forced to abandon the bill implementing the agreement and call a general election. By skilful negotiation, much of it unknown to most of his parliamentary colleagues, Borden brought together a coalition of anti-Laurier groups including Liberal business interests opposed to reciprocity, French-Canadian *nationalistes* led by Henri Bourassa and supported by Monk who were opposed to Laurier's Naval Service Act of 1910, his parliamentary party, and the powerful Conservative administrations of the provinces of Ontario, Manitoba, British Columbia, and New Brunswick. The Conservatives and their *nationaliste* allies won, and on 10 October 1911 Borden became prime minister of Canada. He held office until his resignation in July 1920. He was appointed an imperial privy counsellor in 1912 and made knight grand cross in the Order of St Michael and St George in 1914.

Prime minister Borden's pre-war administration was marked by disappointment. It accomplished modest reforms in agricultural policy and the administration of government, but a Liberal-dominated senate rejected key government reforms in tariff policy and dominion–provincial financial arrangements. A renewed naval crisis in Britain resulted in the abandonment of Laurier's naval programme and led to Borden's 1913 Emergency Naval Aid Bill, which proposed spending $35 million for capital ships for the imperial navy. Again several French-Canadian members of his party bolted, and the bill was fiercely denounced by the Liberal opposition. It was forced through the House of Commons by closure and finally rejected by the senate. In 1914 plans for an early general election on a platform of senate reform were cancelled with the outbreak of war.

Borden's government passed an Emergency War Measures Act in September 1914, giving it extraordinary powers to conduct the war. Laurier's Liberal Party supported this and other war measures of the Borden government during the first years of war, including the build-up of industries and agriculture to support the war effort and a 1916 extension of the life of the parliament beyond its statutory five-year term. The Borden government introduced the first measures of direct taxation with a business war profits tax in 1916 and an 'emergency' personal income tax in 1917. It nationalized the grain trade in 1917, and a year later introduced a number of boards and regulatory agencies to control hydroelectric power, fuels, and food. It enforced rigorous censorship of the press and, in the last days of the war, passed a number of measures to restrict or ban the activities of left-wing organizations thought to be potentially subversive.

The most controversial war issue was military manpower. Borden made an unconditional commitment to send men overseas for service in the Canadian expeditionary force, and he promised that there would be no conscription to meet this commitment. But as the war dragged on, industrial and agricultural expansion created a buoyant demand for labour, and, as ever-growing casualty lists filled the columns of city dailies and rural weeklies, voluntary enlistment for overseas service dried up, just as the Canadian corps in Europe desperately needed replacements. By late 1916 and early 1917 English-Canadian demands for conscription were as intense and persistent as was the opposition of French Canadians. In May 1917 Borden returned from the first meetings of the imperial war cabinet in London and visits to the front to introduce conscription for overseas service in the Military Service Act. To gain support for conscription in the forthcoming general election, especially in Quebec, Borden asked Laurier to join him in a reconstructed coalition government. Laurier refused: but several conscriptionist Liberals, mainly outside the parliamentary party, did not. In October 1917, following the passage of the Wartime Elections Act and the Military Voters Act, which disgracefully manipulated the franchise before the election, Borden announced a new Union government made up of Conservatives and conscriptionist Liberals. Its pledges to enforce conscription and introduce political reforms earned the Unionists a huge victory in English Canada in December 1917. Conscription began in January 1918, and by Armistice day 100,000 men had been enrolled and about 20,000 had reached the front.

The political consequences of Union government and the bitter 1917 election were severe for both parties. The Unionists won only three of sixty-five seats in Quebec and the Liberals took only eight of eighty-two seats in Ontario and two of fifty-seven in western Canada. The Union government, which some hoped would evolve into a new, progressive political party, was short-lived. It enfranchised women in national elections and reformed the civil service, but it lacked leadership, as Borden spent most of his time in 1918 and 1919 in London and Paris, at meetings of the imperial war cabinet, and with the British delegation at the Paris peace conference. Winning the war had been the government's primary objective, and once that was done it broke into quarrelling factions. Borden, exhausted by wartime leadership and his efforts to reform the imperial relationship, took little interest in reviving the Unionists. After extended vacations in late 1919 and early 1920 to recover his health, he retired as prime minister in July 1920.

Imperial–dominion relations The First World War gave Borden and the British prime minister, David Lloyd George, the opportunity dramatically to change imperial relations. Like Laurier, Borden was convinced that the key to maintaining the imperial relationship was self-government, the autonomy of dominions. Laurier had consolidated dominion autonomy in domestic affairs and the substance of Canadian–American relations by 1911: but relations with other countries and the great issues of war and peace remained firmly in the control of the British government. During the early years of the war the British government conducted the war with scarcely any consultation with or heed to the interests of the dominions. 'Procrastination, indecision, inertia, doubt, hesitation', Borden complained in 1915, were the characteristics of British war leadership (Brown, *Borden: a Biography*, 2.34).

The imperial war cabinet, David Lloyd George's inspiration, opened the door to reform. At its meetings in 1917 and 1918 the dominions, led by Borden, won increasing influence over the conduct of the war and the planning for peace. At the Imperial Conference of 1917 Borden's Resolution IX laid the foundations for the emerging Commonwealth of Nations based upon 'full recognition of the Dominions as autonomous nations' which were entitled to 'an adequate voice in foreign policy and in foreign relations' and 'effective arrangements for continuous consultation in all important matters of common Imperial concern' (Brown, *Borden: a Biography*, 2.81). If Canada did not have 'that voice in the foreign relations of the Empire as a whole', Borden wrote a year later, 'she would before long have an independent voice in her own foreign relations outside the Empire' (Brown, 'Sir Robert Borden', 221).

In October 1918 Borden's government demanded participation in the forthcoming peace conference. 'New conditions', he remarked, 'must be met by new precedents' (Brown, *Borden: a Biography*, 2.145–6). At Paris, in the spring of 1919, having achieved membership of the new League of Nations, Borden persuaded Lloyd George, Woodrow Wilson, and Clemenceau that representatives of the self-governing dominions of the British empire might be selected or named as members of the League of Nations council. And he was instrumental in achieving separate signatures to the peace treaties and ratification of the treaties by the dominion governments. Finally, full recognition of the dominions as autonomous nation states was realized in the spring of 1920, when Britain and the United States agreed to the establishment of separate diplomatic representation for Canada in Washington. The theme of all of this work, Borden later observed, was that 'the assumption of national status within the Commonwealth carried with it national responsibility for the Commonwealth's security' (Brown, 'Sir Robert Borden', 204). That, he believed, was what his governments had done in the First World War and that was Canada's mandate for the future.

Retirement and death Borden led an active life as senior statesman in retirement. He represented Canada in the British empire delegation to the Washington Disarmament Conference in 1921 and led the Canadian delegation to the League of Nations in 1930. He was chancellor of McGill University and later of Queen's University, Kingston. In the late 1920s he began a new career in business as the president of the Crown Life Insurance Company and of Barclay's Bank, Canada, and in 1932, with New York partners, he established the Canadian Investment Fund, the first mutual fund in Canada. He was a popular lecturer, and his Marfleet lectures at the University of Toronto in 1922 and his Rhodes lectures at Oxford in 1927 were published as books. *Canadian Constitutional Studies* and *Canada in the Commonwealth* recorded his views on Canada's constitutional development and his role as an architect of the Commonwealth of Nations. Two other important books, his *Memoirs* and *Letters to Limbo*, were edited and published after his death.

After a brief illness Borden died, of heart failure, at his home, Glensmere, 201 Wurtenberg Street, Ottawa, on 10 June 1937, survived by his wife. On 12 June he was given a state funeral at All Saints' Church, with a procession flanked by a thousand veterans of the First World War, and buried in Beechwood cemetery, Ottawa.

ROBERT CRAIG BROWN

Sources *Robert Laird Borden: his memoirs*, ed. H. Borden, 2 vols. (1938) • R. C. Brown, *Robert Laird Borden: a biography, 1854–1937*, 2 vols. (1975–80) • [R. L. Borden], *Letters to Limbo*, ed. H. Borden (1971) • J. English, *The decline of politics: the Conservatives and the party system, 1901–20* (1977) • J. English, *Borden: his life and his world* (1977) • R. C. Brown, 'Robert Borden', *Les idées politiques de Baldwin et de LaFontaine / The political ideas of the prime ministers of Canada*, ed. M. Hamelin (Ottawa, 1969) • R. C. Brown, 'Sir Robert Borden, the Great War and Anglo-Canadian relations', *Character and circumstance: essays in honour of Donald Grant Creighton*, ed. J. S. Moir (1970), 201–24 • R. C. Brown and R. Bothwell, 'The "Canadian Resolution"', *Policy by other means: essays in honour of C. P. Stacey*, ed. M. Cross and R. Bothwell (Toronto, 1972) • P. G. Wigley, *Canada and the transition to Commonwealth: British-Canadian relations, 1917–1926* (1977) • J. L. Granatstein and J. M. Hitsman, *Broken promises: a history of conscription in Canada* (1977)

Archives Bodl. Oxf., corresp. with Herbert Asquith • Bodl. Oxf., letters to James Bryce • Bodl. Oxf., letters to Lewis Harcourt • HLRO, corresp. with Lord Beaverbrook • HLRO, corresp. with Andrew Bonar Law • HLRO, letters to David Lloyd George • NA Canada, Henri Bourassa MSS • NA Canada, Loring C. Christie MSS • NA Canada, Sir Wilfrid Laurier MSS • NA Canada, Sir Clifford Sifton MSS • NA Scot., corresp. with Lord Balfour • NA Scot., corresp. with Lord Lothian • NL Scot., corresp. with Lord Haldane | FILM BFI NFTVA, news footage • NA Canada | SOUND NA Canada

Likenesses A. John, portrait, 1919, National Gallery of Canada, Ottawa • W. Orpen, oils, 1919, NA Canada [*see illus.*] • D. Vicagi, oils, 1925, Law Courts, Halifax, Canada • J. Guthrie, group portrait, oils (*Statesmen of World War I*), NPG • J. Guthrie, oil sketch, Scot. NPG • J. Macgillivray, Acadia University, Wolfville, Canada • W. Stoneman, photographs, NPG

Bordley, John Beale (1727–1804), lawyer and agricultural improver in America, was born on 11 February 1727 in Annapolis, Maryland, the posthumous child of Thomas *Bordley (*c.*1683–1726), lawyer and government official, and his second wife, Ariana, *née* Vanderheyden (1690–1741), the widow of James Frisby. Bordley had two older brothers; four half-brothers and three half-sisters by his father's first marriage to Rachel Beard; three half-sisters by his mother's first marriage; and three half-brothers and one half-sister by his mother's third marriage to Edmund Jennings. In 1737 Bordley's mother moved to England with her husband, leaving the ten-year-old child in the care of her sister Francina and brother-in-law, Colonel Charles Hynson, of Kent county. Bordley studied for about two years during his residence in Kent at the Chestertown school of the Revd Charles Peale, father of the artist Charles Willson Peale. Aged seventeen, Bordley returned to Annapolis to read law with his half-brother, Stephen Bordley, from 1744 to 1749. Bordley completed his general education through reading Stephen's extensive library.

Bordley practised law for a few years, pursued a mercantile career briefly in the early 1750s, and then returned to the law. In 1751 he married Margaret (*d.* 1773), daughter of Samuel Chew and his wife, Henrietta Maria Lloyd. Within two years the couple moved to property Bordley owned outside Joppa town, seat of Baltimore county. In November 1753 he received an appointment as clerk of the county court, a position he held until his designation in 1768 as a member of the governor's council. Bordley also served as a judge of the provincial court from 1766 to 1776 and a judge of the Admiralty court between 1767 and 1776.

In 1770 Margaret Bordley's brother, Philemon Lloyd Chew, devised his estate on Wye Island in Queen Anne's county jointly to Margaret and her sister Mary, wife of William Paca. The two families divided the 2800 acre island between them, with the Bordleys taking the western half. This property, known as The Vineyards, became Bordley's primary residence (he had also inherited the family home in Annapolis from Stephen in 1764). It served as the focal point for the next twenty years of Bordley's interest in agricultural reform, an interest influenced both by English critics, such as Arthur Young, and by his own observation of local practices.

Bordley abandoned the cultivation of tobacco in favour of wheat as his primary staple crop, and advocated a system of crop rotation and manuring to restore soil fertility. He experimented with a variety of other market crops, including grapes, pomegranates, rice, palma christi, madder, hops, and almonds. He instituted a careful livestock breeding programme, raising cattle, horses, sheep, pigs, pigeons, and bees, and experimenting with deer, hares, partridges, and wild turkeys. Bordley's policy to improve the quality and independence of his farming operations extended to operating a brickyard, rope walk, windmill, brewhouse, saltworks, and gunpowder manufactory, as well as producing cloth for slave clothing. In recognition of his work the American Philosophical Society elected Bordley to membership in 1783. Two years later he became a founding member and the first vice-president of the Philadelphia Society for Promoting Agriculture. Bordley published a number of treatises promoting agricultural reform as well as books and pamphlets covering a range of other topics. Although a large slaveholder, he opposed the institution on philosophical, moral, and practical grounds—as inimical to good agricultural practice—and arranged for the eventual manumission of many of his slaves.

Bordley's wife, Margaret, died on 11 November 1773, leaving three children: Matthias, John, and Henrietta Maria. A fourth child, Thomas, had died in 1771 while a student at Eton College. On 8 October 1776 Bordley married Sarah, *née* Fishbourne (1733–1816), the widow of John Mifflin of Philadelphia and the mother of two sons. The couple had two daughters, Elizabeth and Margaret Chew, but only Elizabeth survived to adulthood. In 1791 the family moved to Philadelphia, when President George Washington appointed Bordley a commissioner for receiving subscriptions for the Bank of the United States, though he appears to have attended few meetings. Bordley died in Philadelphia on 26 January 1804, after several years of poor health, and was buried there at St Peter's Church.

JEAN B. RUSSO

Sources E. C. Papenfuse and others, eds., *A biographical dictionary of the Maryland legislature, 1635–1789*, 1 (1985) • E. B. Gibson, *Biographical sketches of the Bordley family, of Maryland, and their descendants* (1865) • O. M. Gambrill, 'Thomas Bordley: a study in the political life of provincial Maryland', Maryland State Archives, Alice Moore Bowerman Collection, SC952 • G. Stiverson, 'John Beale Bordley: patriot farmer', research files, Historic Annapolis Foundation • A. C. T[rue], 'Bordley, John Beale', *DAB* • F. Emory, *Queen Anne's county, Maryland: its early history and development* (1950)

Archives Maryland Historical Society, Baltimore, Bordley MSS, MS 64 • University of Pennsylvania, Philadelphia | Maryland Historical Society, Baltimore, Stephen Bordley letter-books, MS 81

Likenesses A. Hamilton, ink and wash, 1748–1755?, Maryland Historical Society, Baltimore, MS 854 • A. Hamilton, ink and wash, 1748–1755?, Maryland Historical Society, Baltimore, MS 1265 • C. W. Peale, oils, 1770, National Gallery of Art, Washington, DC

Wealth at death at least 1500 acres in Maryland; land in Pennsylvania; lots in Annapolis and Baltimore; stable and house in Philadelphia: Papenfuse and others, eds., *A biographical dictionary*, 145

Bordley, Thomas (*c*.1683–1726), lawyer and politician in America, was born in the parish of St Hilda, South Shields, co. Durham, the youngest son among the four children of the Revd Stephen Bordley (*d*. 1695), vicar of St Hilda's, and his wife, Mary. In 1689 the Bordleys moved to Newington Butts, Surrey, where the Revd Bordley became vicar of St Mary's parish. After the death of their father in August 1695, Bordley and his brother Stephen emigrated to Maryland in 1697. Thomas lived with his brother in Kent county, where Stephen served as rector of St Paul's parish, until he moved across the Chesapeake Bay to the colony's capital, Annapolis.

Bordley arrived in Annapolis no later than spring 1703, for he became clerk of the Anne Arundel county court in June of that year. In September 1703 he took the oath of office as clerk of the secretary's office and of the provincial court. By 1709 he had been admitted to practise in both the Anne Arundel and provincial courts. At that time he held the clerkship of the prerogative office, having been dismissed in 1708 from his Anne Arundel post and having resigned the secretary's office clerkship. In December 1708 Bordley married his first wife, Rachel (*d*. 1722), daughter of Richard Beard (*c*.1648–1703) of Annapolis; the couple had five children who survived infancy, four sons and a daughter.

Bordley represented Annapolis voters in the lower house from 1708 until 1711 and served as delegate from Anne Arundel or Annapolis from 1715 until his appointment to the upper house in 1720. He received considerable patronage from Governor John Hart, who assumed his post in 1715 and who appointed Bordley surveyor-general of the western shore (1717–18), commissary-general and surveyor-general (both 1718–21), and member of the governor's council (1720–21). During these years Bordley was also one of the colony's leading lawyers, frequently finding himself arguing one side of a case against his closest rival, the elder Daniel Dulany (1685–1753).

Bordley enjoyed less cordial relations with Hart's successor, Captain Charles Calvert, a cousin of the proprietor, the fifth Baron Baltimore, who dismissed Bordley from his positions in September 1721 for having given 'Counsel of pernicious Consequence' (*Archives of Maryland*, 34.277). After his dismissal from the proprietary offices Bordley returned to the lower house, where in the early 1720s he and Dulany led the popular opposition against the proprietary establishment.

Hostility to the proprietor's powers crystallized around efforts by the lower house to improve the finances of tobacco planters through repeal of legislation regulating the quality of exported tobacco. The refusal of consent by the upper house (the governor's council) initiated a period of attack and counter-attack in which the lower house sought to cast the upper house and proprietary officials as self-serving and themselves as defenders of the country's interest. Bordley edited the debates and proceedings of three sessions of the legislature for publication in Philadelphia in 1725 and was instrumental in bringing the printer William Parks to Annapolis in 1726 to further public awareness of the issues.

Following the death of his first wife in 1722, Bordley married, on 1 September 1723, Ariana (1690–1741), daughter of Matthias Vanderheyden and widow of James Frisby (1684–1719). The marriage added three young stepdaughters to Bordley's household. He and Ariana themselves had three sons. In 1726 Bordley travelled to London, where he died on 11 October during surgery (probably intended to remove a kidney stone). Bordley was survived by his wife, who gave birth to their third son, John Beale *Bordley, after his death, as well as by seven children, and two sisters living in Newcastle upon Tyne. He left a personal estate of £3179 14*s*. 8*d*. sterling and £1964 17*s*. 3*d*. current money of Maryland (including nineteen slaves, six servants, and 100 law books), over 7500 acres of land, and at least nine lots in Annapolis. EDWARD C. PAPENFUSE

Sources E. C. Papenfuse and others, eds., *A biographical dictionary of the Maryland legislature, 1635–1789*, 1 (1979) [pt of the Maryland State Archives biography project] · E. B. Gibson, *Biographical sketches of the Bordley family, of Maryland, and their descendants* (1865) · O. M. Gambrill, 'Thomas Bordley: a study in the political life of provincial Maryland', Alice Moore Bowerman Collection, Maryland State Archives, SC952 · A. Day, *A social study of lawyers in Maryland* (1989) · A. C. Land, *Colonial Maryland—a history* (1981) · R. J. Brugger, *Maryland: a middle temperament* (1988) · C. C. Hall, ed., *Proceedings and acts of the general assembly of Maryland, October 11, 1720 – October 26, 1723*, Archives of Maryland, 34 (1914)

Archives Maryland Historical Society, Baltimore, papers | Maryland Historical Society, Baltimore, Stephen Bordley letter-books

Likenesses G. Hesselius, oils, *c*.1715, Maryland Historical Society, Baltimore

Wealth at death £3179 14*s*. 8*d*. sterling; plus £1964 17*s*. 3*d*. current money of Maryland (incl. nineteen slaves, six servants, and 100 law books); also over 7500 acres of land: Papenfuse and others, eds., *Biographical dictionary*, vol. 1, p. 148

Bordon, John (*fl.* 1624–1659), army officer in the Swedish service, was born in Scotland. He was a descendant of the Scottish house of Burdon of Feddall or Pitfoddell, but his parents' identity remains uncertain. Bordon, like many Scotsmen at the time, entered Swedish military service during campaigns of the Thirty Years' War in Germany, serving in James MacDougal's regiment from 1629 to 1630 and as a lieutenant in Donald Mackay's regiment in 1632. Information is lacking on his whereabouts for the following ten years. It is unclear to whom and when Bordon was married, not least because Swedish sources have often confused him with Colonel John Gordon. He is known to have had three sons and one daughter, and two of his sons, Gustaf and Johan, also entered Swedish military service. Moreover Bordon had obviously become well-integrated in Sweden as in 1643 he was ennobled and introduced to the Swedish house of nobility.

During the Swedo-Danish War, which ended in 1645, Bordon served as the commandant of the Hammerhus garrison on Bornholm. The following year he became a lieutenant-colonel of a conscripted Dalregiment. In 1651 he became a full colonel of the same regiment; he retained this rank until his retirement. Bordon played a major role in the defence of Sweden during its wars with Denmark–Norway and Russia. In 1657 he helped defend the Swedish copper supply from Danish–Norwegian attack, thereby ensuring continued Swedish trade and finances. In the following year Bordon's regiment in Riga served under Field Marshal Robert Douglas's command during Sweden's war with Russia over Baltic dominion states. His favour with the Swedish crown was demonstrated when he received a grant of land from Karl X upon his decision to retire from military service in 1659. Neither his date of death nor anything else about him is known after this period. A. N. L. GROSJEAN

Sources G. Elgenstierna, *Den introducerade svenska adelns ättartavlor med tillägg och rättelser*, 9 vols. (1925–36), vol. 1 · 'Svenska sändebuds till utländska hof och deras sändebud till Sverige', 1841, Riksarkivet, Stockholm · Katalog öfver sköldebref, Riddarhusarkivet, Stockholm, Sweden · military muster rolls, Krigsarkivet, Stockholm, 1629/22–24, 1630/34, 37, 38, 1632/28, 1646/3, 1647/4, 1648/3, 1649/3, 17, 18, 1650/5, 1651/3, 1654/3, 1655/3, 5, 8, 9, 1656/5–7, 1657/2, 5, 1658/4, 1659/5 · N. A. Kullberg, S. Bergh, and P. Sondén, eds., *Svenska riksrådets protokoll*, 18 vols. (Stockholm, 1878–1959) · S. Bergh and B. Taube, eds., *Sveriges ridderskaps och adels riksdags-protokoll*, 17 vols. (1871) · J. Kleberg, *Krigskollegii historia biografiska anteckningar, 1630–1865* (1930)

Bordwine, Joseph (*d.* 1835), army officer and instructor, was born in America, and on 8 January 1801 he was appointed ensign in the 55th regiment, having previously served in the Canadian Volunteers. He was promoted lieutenant in the Royal Staff Corps on 22 December 1803 and transferred to the 88th regiment in October 1806. He served for some time under General Whitlock, but was deprived of his commission (a majority) in consequence of his having issued a pamphlet in which he criticized that general's conduct. He was made professor of fortification at Addiscombe College, Surrey, in 1811, having been assistant professor since 1809.

In 1803 Bordwine was appointed an assistant in the quartermaster-general's department, and attached to the staff of the western district. A French invasion was expected, and Bordwine drew up a sketch of a new circular system of fortification for the defence of the country. He continued the work at intervals, and at last in 1809 published the *Sketch*, which apparently attracted very little attention at the time. He was, however, prompted by friends to take the subject up again in 1830, resulting in the large *Memoir of a Proposed New System of Permanent Fortification* (1834). He retired from Addiscombe on account of ill health on 4 February 1835, and died at Croydon on 21 February 1835. B. C. SKOTTOWE, *rev.* JAMES LUNT

Sources J. Bordwine, *Memoir of a proposed new system of permanent fortification* (1834) · H. M. Vibart, *Addiscombe: its heroes and men of note* (1894) · *GM*, 2nd ser., 4 (1835)

Boreel, (Edith) Wendela (1895–1985). *See under* Sickert, Walter, pupils (*act.* 1890–1939).

Boreham, Hervey of (*b.* before 1228?, *d.* 1277), administrator and justice, was probably born some time before 1228 in the village of Boreham in Essex, the son of Ralph, son of William of Boreham, a minor landowner. He had at least one brother, named John. His first appearance in surviving records appears to be late in 1249, when he was appointed the abbot of Westminster's attorney for litigation in the common bench. He may already by then have become the abbot's steward, a position he is known to have held in 1254, and apparently retained until 1259. In that year he passed into the service of Richard de Clare, earl of Gloucester (*d.* 1262), as his steward, and went round the earl's estates hearing complaints against the earl's officials.

Although an ordained cleric, Boreham is said by the contemporary chronicler William of Rishanger to have been one of two standard-bearers of the men of London at the battle of Lewes in 1264. After the victory of Simon de Montfort, earl of Leicester (*d.* 1265), he became a king's clerk, and for a few months was one of those in day-to-day control of the royal administration. In Michaelmas term

1264 he was appointed a junior justice of the common bench, and remained a justice of the court until the end of Trinity term 1265. He may not, however, have sat in the final term as he was under sentence of excommunication, possibly for his part in the battle of Lewes.

Boreham's retention of the custody of a number of escheated royal honours in Essex and of Hadleigh Castle (originally granted to him in July 1264) until the end of 1265 or beginning of 1266, and his subsequent association with John de Burgh in June 1266 in the keeping of the peace in the counties of Essex and Hertfordshire, indicate that he successfully negotiated the transition from Montfortian rule to royalist restoration after the battle of Evesham. He may already have been linked by this date with Earl Richard's son, Gilbert, earl of Gloucester (*d.* 1295). He was certainly in the earl's service by 1267, when he was one of those who advised him to occupy London in support of the claims of the disinherited, and was given a safe conduct to bring a message from the earl to the king.

Boreham re-entered the king's service in the last month of Henry III's life and in early November 1272 was appointed a baron of the exchequer. In the final years of his life he achieved high office in the church. By 1272 he had become precentor of Hereford Cathedral and a canon of St Paul's; in 1274 he became dean of St Paul's. In 1275 he is said to have been a serious rival to the saintly Thomas de Cantilupe (*d.* 1282) for the see of Hereford. Boreham probably died a few days before 7 February 1277.

PAUL BRAND, *rev.*

Sources Court of King's Bench, Curia Regis Rolls, PRO, KB 26 • exchequer, king's remembrancer's memoranda rolls, PRO, E 159/47, m.2d • chancery, liberate rolls, PRO, C62/49, mm 2, 3 • BL, Harley charters 46. I. 40 • BL, Cotton MS Tiberius C ix, fols. 241r, 253r • *Ninth report*, 1, HMC, 8 (1883), 35, 41 • *Chancery records* • *CIPM*, 2, nos. 214–15 • *Fasti Angl., 1066–1300*, [St Paul's, London]

Boreham, Sir (Arthur) John (1925–1994), statistician and civil servant, was born on 30 July 1925 at Noddon, Beacon Hill, Hindhead, Surrey, the second surviving son of the Ven. Frederick Boreham (1888–1966), Church of England clergyman, and his wife, Caroline Mildred, *née* Slater (1890–1943). His father was canon of York (1941–7), then of Truro (1947–65), archdeacon of Cornwall (1949–65), and honorary chaplain to George VI (1941–52) and Elizabeth II (1952–66). Boreham was educated at Marlborough College (1939–43) and, after service in the RAF, at Trinity College, Oxford (1947–50). He graduated with a second-class degree in philosophy, politics, and economics, statistics being only an optional extra. Meanwhile, on 9 July 1948, he married Heather (*b.* 1927), daughter of Harold Edwin Horth, architect. They had three sons and a daughter.

After a brief spell at the Agricultural Economics Research Institute in Oxford, Boreham joined the civil service in 1951 as a professional statistician. He served in the Ministry of Food (1951–2), the Ministry of Agriculture (1952–5), the General Register Office (1955–8), and the central statistical office (1958–63), before becoming chief statistician at the General Register Office (1963–7), where his special interest in demographic and social statistics found a niche. He was then director of economics and statistics at the Ministry of Technology (1967–71). Next he served as assistant (1971–2) and then deputy director (1972–8) of the central statistical office (CSO). From 1978 to 1985 he was director of the CSO and head of the government statistical service. During his period with the CSO he contributed significantly to social and economic policy making. After 1979 he had to implement the Thatcher administration's economies in the provision of official statistics, and he showed leadership capacity in preserving the broad statistical framework while reducing staff by about a quarter. He was appointed CB in 1974 and advanced to KCB in 1980. He retired from government service in 1985.

Boreham was president of the Institute of Statisticians from 1984 to 1992, and of the Association of Social Research Organizations from 1990, and a visiting fellow of Nuffield College, Oxford, between 1981 and 1988. Almost equally at home in French as in English, he was chairman for two years of the Conference of European Statisticians. For a time he was—to his great enjoyment—regional co-ordinator of statistical training in the Caribbean, and, as in everything else, made sure that his proposals had practical results. He also worked for a year at Nassau, Bahamas, helping to reorganize the office of statistics there.

Boreham had rare personal qualities. He was full of warmth, passion, and human caring, and interested in using statistics to improve the human lot. He was described by Sir Claus Moses as 'unconventional, original, and independent in action and spirit' (*Independent*). In retirement he edited his father's voluminous diaries, and played the piano more than he had ever had time for before. He followed cricket assiduously and never tired of golf. He was playing golf at Knole Park, Sevenoaks, when he died of a heart attack on 8 June 1994. Boreham was buried at Putney Vale cemetery. He was survived by his wife and their four children.

ARTHUR GREEN

Sources *The Times* (15 June 1994) • *The Independent* (15 June 1994) • *WWW* • private information (2004) [Heather, Lady Boreham, widow] • b. cert. • m. cert. • d. cert.

Likenesses photograph, repro. in *The Times* • photograph, repro. in *The Independent*

Boreman, Richard (*c.*1485x90–*c.*1558), abbot of St Albans, was probably born in Hertfordshire. He must have entered the Benedictine community at St Albans no later than *c.*1505 because he was established as a monk-student at Gloucester College, Oxford, by 1509. Ordained a priest in 1517, he graduated as bachelor of theology in 1521 and returned to St Albans, where by 1524 he was almoner. He was still there in 1528, when he was named among the creditors of William Hope, but shortly afterwards he was appointed prior of the dependency at Hatfield Peverel. It is unclear how long he remained there, but he had certainly returned to the abbey by 1536.

Following his return Boreman became involved in the work of John Herford, a printer who had established a press within the abbey precincts. Boreman acted as patron for a number of Herford's editions, including *An Introduction for to Lerne to Reken with the Pen* (*STC*, 14117.7, A.3) and

An Epistle Agaynste the Enemies of Poor People and *A Godlye Disputation between Justus and Peccator and Senex and Iuvenis* attributed to Dionysius de Leeuwis, of which only fragments survive, and he may also have assisted in the printing of the St Albans breviary (*STC*, 15793.5) in 1535. Evidently Boreman was interested in promoting traditional intellectual and spiritual values, but he also turned his association with Herford towards more controversial ends. In 1536, under Boreman's patronage, Herford published *The Confutacyon of the Fyrst Parte of Frythes Boke with a Disputaycon before whether it be Possyble for any Heretike to Know that Hymselfe is one or not and also an other whether it be Wors to Denye Directly More or Less of the Fayth* (*STC*, 12557), a response to John Frith's rejection of the doctrine of transubstantiation. The text was the work of John Gwynneth, a secular priest then living at the abbey, but it was perhaps completed by Boreman himself, since Gwynneth had left St Albans before it was printed. Boreman may have collaborated with Herford on a similar treatise in 1539. The anonymous text *A Very Declaracyon of the Bond and Free Wyll of Man the Obedyence of the Gospell and what the Very Gospell Meneth* (*STC*, 6456.5) was certainly the product of Herford's press and is identical to their earlier books.

By the mid-1530s deep divisions had emerged within the abbey community. Abbot Catton had alienated many of the monks by making frequent concessions to Thomas Cromwell and his commissioners. Boreman, who had already risen to the defence of traditional religion with Gwynneth's *Confutacyon*, emerged as the leader of the dissidents. In April 1536 he presented a petition on their behalf to Sir Francis Bryan, one of the abbey's patrons, begging him to intervene against Catton, who he claimed was poised to 'waste or destroy our monastery' (PRO, SP 1/103/106). No intervention was forthcoming and by the end of 1537 Catton was ready to surrender the abbey. In early 1538, however, his negotiations with Cromwell for a personal settlement collapsed and he was deprived. Cromwell struggled to find a suitable successor, but before the end of April 1538 he was compelled to install Boreman, who at the least had the support of the monks.

Boreman's abbacy lasted only twenty months and was fraught with difficulties. He faced heavy financial demands and on one occasion was held in custody for failing to pay first fruits. In April 1539, after a few days of hesitation, he joined the parliamentary debates on the six articles. In his writings he had adopted a moderate reformist approach on some issues, and he followed a similar line now, supporting the notion of clerical marriage. He finally surrendered the abbey on 5 December 1539. It is a measure of his reputation as an abbot that no fewer than forty monks remained with him in the community at the end.

Granted a pension of £266 13*s.* 4*d.*, Boreman returned to Oxford, where he completed his doctorate in theology in 1541. After leaving university he may have spent some time in London, where he had acquired property, or Norfolk, where he held a benefice. However, towards the end of the 1540s he settled again at St Albans. In 1549 he secured a licence to establish a grammar school in the town, acquiring first a former guild chapel for this purpose and then in 1551 the former abbey's lady chapel. Shortly after Mary's accession in 1553 he appears to have planned the re-foundation of the abbey itself. In December 1556 the queen granted Boreman the abbey church together with the remaining conventual buildings, 'with intent to restore the abbey again' (PRO, C54/526 m. 3). The townspeople supported the project, and throughout 1557 and 1558 testators made significant bequests to the revival of the house. It remains unclear whether Boreman and a community of monks did return to the abbey buildings. The early seventeenth-century memoirs of Robert Shrimpton, an Elizabethan mayor of St Albans, imply that some form of monastic life had resumed, recalling that 'when the news of Queen Marie's death arrived at St Albans, the then abbot, for grief, took his chamber and dyd within a fortnight' (Bodl. Oxf., MS Rawl. B 165, fol. 102*v*). However, nothing further is known for certain of Boreman. JAMES G. CLARK

Sources J. G. Clark, 'Reformation and reaction at St Albans Abbey, 1530–58', *EngHR*, 115 (2000), 297–328 · Emden, *Oxf.*, 4.540 · *VCH Hertfordshire*, 2.56–8; 4.410–14 · *LP Henry VIII* · PRO, E36/120/68; SP1/103/106; E135/5/8; C66/675/32; C66/676/23; E322/208; SP1/154/17–18 · Bodl. Oxf., MS Jesus College, fol. 322*v* · D. S. Chambers, ed., *Faculty office registers, 1534–1549* (1966), 202 · Bodl. Oxf., MS Rawl. B. 165 · chancery close rolls, PRO, C 54/526

Wealth at death in receipt of pension of £266 13*s.* 4*d.* until shortly before death

Boreman, Robert (*d.* 1675), Church of England clergyman, was the son of William Boreman (*c.*1564–1646) of East Greenwich, a servant in the royal household under Elizabeth, James I, and Charles I, and probably of his wife, Jane (*d.* after 1646). The date and place of his birth are unknown, but he had at least four sisters and three brothers, one of whom, Sir William Boreman (*c.*1614–1686), was clerk of the greencloth to Charles II. Robert Boreman was educated at Westminster School; he matriculated as a pensioner at Trinity College, Cambridge, in Michaelmas 1627. He was elected scholar in 1628, and received the degrees of BA in 1632, MA in 1635, and BD in 1643. In 1633 he was elected fellow of Trinity College, was a tutor 1636–41, and for some time college lecturer in Hebrew. He was ordained priest at Peterborough on 18 February 1638.

Boreman was ejected from his fellowship by the parliamentary visitors, but seems to have remained in the vicinity of Cambridge during the 1650s. Whether he held any living is unknown. At this period he published several polemical tracts on topical issues, defending tithes in *The Country-Mans Catechisme* (1652), and the necessity of a university-educated ministry in *Paideia-thriambos: the Triumph of Learning over Ignorance* (1653). The latter work had originally been delivered at Swavesey, near Cambridge, where his opponents, said Boreman, yielded to his arguments 'with thankfull acknowledgments' (sig. A4*r*). Also with political overtones was his warmly eulogistic funeral sermon for the ejected master of Trinity College, Thomas Comber, published as *The Triumph of Faith over Death* (1654).

A Mirrour of Mercy and Judgement (1655) recounts the repentance and death of Freeman Sondes, a young man condemned to execution for the murder of his elder brother, to whom Boreman had ministered while on a visit to Kent.

In 1660 Boreman was restored to his fellowship and created DD by royal mandate. On 15 October in that year he was admitted to the rectory of Blisworth, Northamptonshire, a living to which he was apparently again admitted on 31 July 1662. Further tracts and sermons published by Boreman after the Restoration include *Autokatakritos, or, Hypocrisie Unvail'd* (1662), an attack on Richard Baxter, whom he notoriously accused of having slain 'a man with your own hand in cold blood' (15). Boreman claimed that his 'honest censures' were sincerely intended for Baxter's good, but Baxter, who was pursued by the accusation for many years, attributed the work rather to Boreman's ambition for preferment (*Reliquiae Baxterianae*, *Calendar*, 2.28, 26).

Preferment did follow, and on 18 November 1663 Boreman was appointed rector of the crown living of St Giles-in-the-Fields, Westminster, which he held until his death, having resigned the rectory of Blisworth. As rector of St Giles he knew Pepys, who heard him give 'an account of two papists, women, lately converted' (Pepys, *Diary*, 8.99); and his parishioners were to include Richard Baxter, and Alice, Duchess Dudley, whose funeral sermon he published as *A Mirrour of Christianity* (1669). Although Boreman showed courage in remaining at work in his parish during the plague of 1665, he was not popular with members of his vestry, and in 1670 brought an unsuccessful case against them in the court of exchequer over the right to elect a churchwarden. On 19 December 1667 he was installed as prebendary of Westminster Abbey. He never married but, according to Anthony Wood, 'spent his time in celibacy' (2.55). Robert Boreman died at Greenwich on 15 November 1675 and was buried there on 18 November. The administration of his estate was granted on 20 December 1675 to his brother Sir William Boreman.

JULIA J. SMITH

Sources Venn, *Alum. Cant.* • *Hasted's history of Kent: corrected, enlarged, and continued to the present time*, ed. H. H. Drake (1886) • *Calendar of the correspondence of Richard Baxter*, ed. N. H. Keeble and G. F. Nuttall, 2 vols. (1991) • will of W. Boareman the elder, proved 30 July 1646, PRO, PROB 11/197, sig. 104 • will of Sir W. Boreman, proved 21 July 1686, PRO, PROB 11/384, sig. 91 • administration, granted 20 Dec 1675, PRO, PROB 6/50, fol. 149v • W. Kennett, *A register and chronicle ecclesiastical and civil* (1728) • Evelyn, *Diary* • Wood, *Ath. Oxon.: Fasti* (1820), 55 • W. W. Rouse Ball and J. A. Venn, eds., *Admissions to Trinity College, Cambridge*, 2 (1913) • H. I. Longden, *Northamptonshire and Rutland clergy from 1500*, ed. P. I. King and others, 16 vols. in 6, Northamptonshire RS (1938–52) • G. Hennessy, *Novum repertorium ecclesiasticum parochiale Londinense, or, London diocesan clergy succession from the earliest time to the year 1898* (1898) • A. T. Hart, *The life and times of John Sharp, archbishop of York* (1949)

Boreman, Thomas (*fl.* 1730–1743), publisher, was the first professional publisher to cater primarily for juvenile readers, thereby antedating the work of John Newbery in London and Isaiah Thomas in Boston and Worcester, Massachusetts. Information about Boreman resides only in his publications; he maintained bookstalls at several different London locations: the corner of St Clement's Lane without Temple-Bar, Ludgate Hill at the Boot and Crown, Ludgate Hill at the Sign of the Cock, near Child's Coffee House in St Paul's Churchyard, and near the Guildhall.

Co-published with Richard Ware and Thomas Game in 1730, Boreman's *A Description of Three Hundred Animals* was 'the first work on natural history written for children' (Lisney, 86). His address to the reader makes clear his intention to 'entertain' rather than 'cloy' young readers, 'with short descriptions of animals, and pictures fairly drawn (which last Experience shews them to be much delighted with) to engage their Attention' (p. A2). Borrowing from Edward Topsell's *Historie of Foure-Footed Beastes* (1607), itself derived from Konrad von Gesner's sixteenth-century *Historia animalium*, the enumerated, illustrated collection of beasts, birds, fish, serpents, and insects proved so popular that Boreman alone produced two supplements: *A Description of a Great Variety of Animals* (1736) and *A Description of Some Curious and Uncommon Creatures, Omitted in the Description of Three Hundred Animals* (1739). By the end of the nineteenth century *A Description of Three Hundred Animals* had gone through thirty-eight editions; an advertisement in *Times Telescope* (1817) mistakenly attributed the authorship of a 1799 Edinburgh edition of the *Description* to 'one Mr. McQuin' (Gladstone, 446). Boreman's work is credited with influencing Comte Georges Louis Leclerc de Buffon's thirty-six-volume *Histoire naturelle* (1749–88) and Thomas Bewick's engravings (Lisney, 86). In addition to the precise detail of the illustrations, Boreman's earliest *Description* contained such exotic features as a triple-page fold-out depiction of the Greenland Whale Fishery, along with comments on the observed mating practices of male and female whales and some spirited disagreement that Jonah could possibly have been swallowed by and contained in the belly of a whale, whose 'throat can hardly take in the arm of a man' (p. 153).

The ten miniature volumes comprising Boreman's *Gigantick Histories of the Curiosities of London* (1740–43), with formats measuring 2.5 by 1.8 inches, define Boreman's innovations in the emerging field of publishing for children. Each tiny illustrated volume of more than 100 pages of verse and prose, bound in Dutch flowery embossed paper, published a list of juvenile subscribers. This 'crowning stroke' (Stone, 10) for a format previously associated only with biblical material, as in John Weever's *Agnus Dei* (1601) and John Taylor's *Verbum sempiternum* (1614), engaged an eager urban readership by following the formula announced in *The Curiosities in the Tower of London* (2 vols., 1741) that:

> That author, doubtless,
> aims aright,
> Who joins instruction
> with delight.

Moreover, Boreman involved his young subscribers in the continued success of the series, soliciting the set price of 6*d.* a set for the planned three volumes on the history of

Westminster Abbey (1743). In addition to including the Guildhall giants Gogmagog and Corineus as subscribers, his published lists of subscribers identified such prominent London youth as the son of the lord mayor, Thomas Abney, and children from Portugal, East India, and America, among them the grandson of Cotton Mather and the nieces and nephews of the governor of Massachusetts Bay, Thomas Hutchinson. Narrating the curious histories of the Guildhall giants, the Tower of London, St Paul's Cathedral, Westminster Abbey, and the contemporary Swedish giant Cajanus, Boreman was adept at puffery and promotion. Not only did he refer to himself as Master Tommy, he also ghost-wrote the praise of the 'well wisher A. Z', prefacing the two volumes of *Curiosities in the Tower of London* (1741), which disparages 'such ill conceited / artless lyes' as Tom Thumb and Jack the Giant Killer in favour of Boreman's *Gigantick* works offering 'something to please / and form the mind'. 'Jackey Heatherly' eulogized Master Tommy, in the two-volume *History and Description of the Famous Cathedral of St Paul's* (1741), noting that:

the Books you write
Give me much pastime
and delight.

Boreman also informed by inculcating obedience to authority. The 'crimes which 'prentice Boys commit sometimes' lead to their confinement in 'that terrible place call'd Little Ease' in the basement of the Guildhall, 'among rats, mice, and other vermin', where the apprentices' refusal to 'pardon beg' and 'promise on … bended knees no more … to displease' the masters, who are compared to 'fond' parents, may result in a sentence to Bridewell. His warning is blunt and monosyllabic: 'so take great heed / that you keep out' (*The Gigantick History of the Two Famous Giants*, 85–90). After the opening of John Newbery's bookshop in 1744, no record of Boreman exists.

PATRICIA DEMERS

Sources W. Macey Stone, *The gigantick histories of Thomas Boreman* (Portland, Maine, 1933) • A. A. Lisney, *A bibliography of British lepidoptera, 1608–1799* (1960) • H. S. Gladstone, 'Natural history', *N&Q*, 150 (1926), 446

Borenius, (Carl) Tancred (1885–1948), art historian, was born in Vipuri (Wiborg), Finland (now Vyborg, Russia), in 1885, the younger son of Carl Borenius, timber merchant and parliamentarian, and Olga Alfthan; he was of part north Italian descent on his mother's side. He was often taken as a boy to St Petersburg, where he assiduously studied the Hermitage collections. Educated at the Svenska Klassiska Lyceum, Helsinki, Borenius entered Helsinki University in 1902 and studied art history under Professor T. J. Tikkanen.

After graduation Borenius spent six months in Berlin, then went to Rome, where he worked under Professor Haseloff at the Prussian Institute and studied in the Vatican Library. Highly proficient in Italian (he eventually spoke nine languages fluently), he travelled extensively in Italy. He published his doctoral thesis in English as *The Painters of Vicenza, 1480–1550* (1909), a pioneering monograph. A staunch Anglophile, Borenius went to England in 1906, and through his friendship with Roger Fry, whom he had met in Venice, was introduced to the London art world. The publisher John Murray asked Borenius to complete a revised edition of Crowe's and Cavalcaselle's *History of Painting in North Italy* (1871), published in 1912; and in 1914 he revised volumes 5 and 6 of their *History of Painting in Italy* (1864–6).

In 1909 Borenius married his boyhood sweetheart, Anne-Marie Runeberg (*b.* *c.*1885), granddaughter of Finland's national poet Johan Ludwig Runeberg, and they settled at 29 Mecklenburgh Square, London; they had one son and two daughters. In 1914 Borenius succeeded Fry as lecturer in fine art at University College, London; he became the first Durning-Lawrence professor of the history of art there in 1922, retiring in 1947. A man of considerable charm, Borenius was welcomed into the Burlington Fine Arts Club, meeting the artistic establishment of the day. He was invited to catalogue the Cook collection at Doughty House, Richmond (1913), initiating a series of catalogues of private collections which also covered the Christ Church Picture Gallery, Oxford (1916), and the collections of Northwick Park (with Lionel Cust, 1921), Lord Lee of Fareham (2 vols., 1923, now Courtauld Inst.), the earl of Harewood (1936), and Lord Methuen (1939), as well as three collections of Italian maiolica, including the Leverton Harris (1931, now FM Cam.).

Borenius flourished when the professional art historian was an exotic rarity in England; he brought a European breadth to the subject (he admired the cultural historian Jacob Burckhardt), ranging widely over medieval to eighteenth-century art. He also admired French nineteenth-century artists as diverse as Ingres and Cézanne, and took an informed interest in the contemporary artists of his adopted country.

Finland declared itself independent of Russia after the Bolshevik Revolution of 1917, and Borenius became secretary to a diplomatic mission to secure recognition from Great Britain, France, Belgium, Spain, Italy, and the Holy See; in 1919 he was Finland's temporary diplomatic representative in London. In 1940, when Finland was at war with the USSR, he broadcast an appeal for help on the BBC's Finnish service; he also published a biography of Field Marshal Mannerheim (1940).

Borenius succeeded C. F. Bell as expert adviser on old-master prints at Sothebys in 1923 (until 1945). The earl of Harewood bought Titian's *Death of Actaeon* (National Gallery, London) and Paris Bordone's *Knight and Page* (Metropolitan Museum of Art, New York) on his recommendation.

On the consultative board of the *Burlington Magazine* from 1916, Borenius helped to found the more eclectic magazine *Apollo* in 1925, and contributed prolifically to both; and from 1940 to 1945 he was honorary acting editor and managing director of the *Burlington*, where his journalistic flair saw the magazine through difficult times.

Borenius wrote in collaboration with Professor E. W. Tristram *English Medieval Painting* (1927), one of the most comprehensive surveys of its day; he also edited a series of monographs on English medieval art, and in 1932 published *St Thomas Becket in Art*, a major survey of the iconography of that saint. Borenius's innate romanticism spurred him to begin excavations at Clarendon Palace, Salisbury, Wiltshire, in 1933, and his interim report, with John Charlton, to the Society of Antiquaries (of which he was a fellow) of 1936 contains an outline history of the medieval palace based on archival and archaeological evidence.

Borenius was described as 'a dark stocky man—"a rather massive cherub" … with lively manners' (*The Times*, 4 Sept 1948), but he became more reclusive in the 1940s, seeking solace in his library of 30,000 books at his home in Kensington Gate, London. He retired to Stocksbridge Cottage, Coombe Bissett, near Salisbury, Wiltshire, and died in a nursing home, Laverstock House, near Salisbury, after a long illness on 2 September 1948. A memorial service was held at the Swedish church, Harcourt Street, London, on 14 September 1948.

Borenius received many foreign decorations, including membership of the order of the White Rose of Finland (1930), and the papal order of St Gregory the Great (1918), a distinction rarely bestowed on a protestant. He was a DLit of London University. DENNIS FARR

Sources *The Times* (4 Sept 1948), 6 • *The Times* (15 Sept 1948), 6 • *Burlington Magazine*, 548/90 (Nov 1948), 327–8 • D. Sutton, 'Tancred Borenius: connoisseur and clubman', *Apollo*, 107 (April 1978), 294–309 • D. Sutton, 'Borenius', *Dictionary of art*, 4 (1996), 402–3 • K. Lindmann-Strafford, 'Tancred Borenius europé och viborgare', *Finländska Gestalter*, 11 (1976) • *WWW*, *1941–50* • d. cert. • *CGPLA Eng. & Wales* (1948) • F. Herrman, *Sotheby's: portrait of an auction house* (1980)

Archives S. Antiquaries, Lond., lecture notes relating to excavations at Clarendon Palace, MS 826 • UCL, lecture notes, MS Add. 173 • papers, *Burlington Magazine* | TCD, corresp. with Thomas Bodkin, MSS 6910–7079

Wealth at death £14,865 19*s.* 8*d.*: probate, 8 Nov 1948, *CGPLA Eng. & Wales*

Borgard, Albert [Albrecht Borgaard or Borregaard] (**1659–1751**), artillery officer, was born at Holbæk, Jutland, on 10 November 1659 of unknown parents. He is generally referred to as Albert Borgard in English sources and Albrecht Borgaard or Borregaard in Danish. He joined the Danish army in the Queen's regiment of foot in 1675 during the war between Sweden and Denmark, when he saw much active service on land and sea. He was made a gunner in 1676 and was promoted *fyrværker* or fireworker, a junior officer rank, in 1678. Described as one of 'de Conducteurer der forstaar Geometri' (cited in Rockstroh), that is, a land surveyor with a knowledge of trigonometrical surveying techniques, he spent 1680–81 as a land surveyor in Zealand. In 1680 he described in his memoir how he 'was ordered to Berlin in exchange of two Brandenburgher Fireworkers sent to Denmark to learn the difference of each Nations work, relating to all sorts of warlike and pleasant fireworks' (Hine, 130, from Borgard's memoir (fair copy), damaged by enemy action in 1940, remains preserved at Woolwich arsenal). He studied fortification in Strasbourg in 1681 and then returned as a lieutenant to his original regiment of foot. He served in 1683 at the relief of Vienna from the Turkish siege. He helped construct the fortifications at Christiansburg and then went on to serve at the battle of Gran and the siege of Buda.

In 1688 Borgard left the Danish army and fled abroad. The reasons for his flight are not clear. In his memoir he states the reason to have been 'some Injustice done me in my promotion' (Hine, 131). *Dansk biografisk leksikon*, however, mentions that he had been implicated in a treasonable matter and also the threat of a duel, which resulted from his having been passed over in promotion (Rockstroh). Whatever the reason, the result was that between 1686 and 1692 he made his way round Europe fighting in various armies. He first went to Poland as a volunteer, but later accepted a commission in the Prussian guards, with whom he served on the Rhine and at the siege of Bonn. In 1692 he left the Prussian army with a commission to raise a regiment for the emperor, but failing in this he joined the army of Louis XIV and distinguished himself in the attack on Namur. He declined a commission in the French army, not least because of his resolute protestantism, and joined the English artillery.

Though only thirty-three years old when he joined the English service, Borgard was one of the most experienced artillery and engineer officers in the world, having both theoretical and practical experience of all aspects of artillery, engineering, and surveying work. He was made a firemaster in the English service in 1693 and, having that year sought in vain to return to the Danish service, served thereafter with the English. He was made captain and adjutant of the artillery in Flanders in 1695 and saw action at the battles of Steenkerke and Landen and at the sieges of Huy and Namur. At the peace of 1697 he was one of only two foreigners retained by the English artillery. He went to England and in 1698 was made an engineer. In 1702 he helped to take the forts of St Catherine, Matagorda, and Durand. Having returned to England, he married in 1703 Barbara Bradshaw (*d.* 1714); they had several children including George (*bap.* 1704) and Albert (*bap.* 1706).

After serving in Flanders, Borgard was gazetted lieutenant-colonel of artillery in 1706 and sent to command the artillery in Spain and Portugal in the army of Lord Galway. He took Valencia de Alcántara, Ciudad Rodrigo, and Alcántara, and enabled Galway to advance into Spain. He superintended the reduction of the castle of San Felipe in Minorca. He was present with Stanhope at the battles of Almanza, Almanar, and Saragossa, where he was wounded, and at Villa Viciosa, where he was wounded, left for dead, and taken prisoner. On being exchanged he returned to England, and was appointed chief firemaster on 9 August 1712. On 7 July 1713 he 'made pleasure fireworks which was burnt on the River Thames in the Month of August over against Whitehall on the thanksgiving day for the Peace made at Utrecht' (Hine, 135). In 1715 he married Cathrine (*d.* 1754), daughter of Georg Mikkelsen (*d.* 1665), merchant and head of the Danish church in London, and his wife, Maria Bradshaw. Their children included Thomas Michael (*bap.* 1717), Cathrine (*bap.* 1718), Katharine Ambrosia (*bap.* 1727), Frederick (*bap.*

1728), and Elizabeth (*bap.* 1730). Borgard's will shows the complete confidence and trust he placed in his wife.

In 1715 Borgard commanded the artillery train sent to the duke of Argyll in Scotland. In 1716 he was badly injured at Moorfields when metal from captured French guns which were being recast before a distinguished invited audience flew out of control, killing seventeen people and wounding others. In 1716 the Office of Ordnance was reorganized: to reduce expenditure a large number of obsolete posts and ranks were abolished while fighting capacity was enhanced. Individuals whose posts had disappeared were put on the sinking establishment until they could be assigned new duties. Starting in May 1716 Borgard was paid on the sinking establishment until in April 1718 he was made assistant surveyor of the ordnance. From 1717 to 1718 Borgard planned in very considerable detail the needs of the artillery in terms of *matériel* and its laboratory, on which he had always laid particular emphasis. His object was to equip the artillery for all kinds of land and sea actions, and his planning led directly to the formation of the regiment of Royal Artillery, which is widely regarded as his greatest service to the English artillery. In 1719 he commanded the artillery in the expedition to Vigo, the success of which particularly pleased him and was in large part due to his plans and preparations.

Borgard became the first colonel of the Royal Artillery regiment on 1 April 1722. He was promoted major-general in 1735 and lieutenant-general in 1739. He died at Woolwich, where he was living, on 7 February 1751 and was buried in the Danish church in Marine Square, near the Tower of London. (The date of 15 March 1750 for the proving of his will seems to be an error for 15 March 1751.) He had been a loyal member of the church, a considerable benefactor, and from 1704 a member of the church council. At his death Borgard left one of the finest corps of artillery in the world. It had benefited from his practical experience throughout Europe, but also from his considerable powers of organization, his understanding of the science of fortification, and his dedication to duty and to the education and training of the junior officers of whom he had charge. His legacy lies in the regiment itself, in some installations built to his specifications at Woolwich, and in papers of his at Woolwich and at the British Museum, which cast considerable light on the functioning of the artillery during his lifetime. ELIZABETH BAIGENT

Sources K. C. Rockstroh, 'Borgaard, Albrecht', *Dansk biografisk leksikon*, ed. C. F. Bricka and others, 3rd edn, ed. S. Cedergreen Bech (Copenhagen, 1979–84) · O. F. G. Hogg, *English artillery, 1326–1716* (1963) · O. F. G. Hogg, *The Royal Arsenal: its background, origin, and subsequent history*, 2 vols. (1963) · F. Duncan, ed., *History of the royal regiment of artillery*, 2 vols. (1872–3) · *IGI* · *GM*, 1st ser., 19 (1749), 202 · H. W. L. Hine, 'An account of the battels, sieges, &c wherein Lieut-General Albert Borgard hath served. With remarks', *Minutes of the Proceedings of the Royal Artillery Institution*, 13 (1885), 129–58 · O. N. von Olsen, *Generallieutenant Albert Borgaards Levnet og Bedrifter* (Copenhagen, 1839) · will, PRO, PROB 11/786/72, fols. 173v–174 [PCC [1751] 72 Busby]

Archives BM, map, royal maps, and plans, fol. xvii, no. 25d · Royal Artillery Institution, Woolwich, London, papers, models, technical drawings, etc.

Likenesses C. Henckel, lithograph, repro. in Duncan, *History*, vol. 1, frontispiece · G. Kneller, oils, priv. coll.; repro. in Hine, 'An account', facing p. 129 · E. Walker, engraving (after G. Kneller), Royal Artillery Mess, Woolwich, London

Borgarucci, Giulio [*known as* Dr Julio] (*d.* 1581), physician, came from Urbino, being one of four sons of Carlo Borgarucci, and his wife, Caliope: the heraldic *Visitation of London* (Rawlins, 101–2), which describes Giulio's armorial bearings, identifies earlier generations. The other sons were Borgaruccio, the eldest; Prospero, the youngest, born in Canziano, who became professor of anatomy at Padua in 1564; and Bernardino, a jurisconsult. Giulio came to England as a protestant refugee, and was a member of the Italian church in London. In 1569, on a visit to Gravesend, his life was endangered by a Spaniard and two Italians, for religion. He obtained denization in 1562. The following year he was sent to 'Newhaven' (Le Havre), to aid Ambrose Dudley's besieged garrison, which was suffering from plague; but, becoming ill, he soon returned.

Back in London, Borgarucci successfully treated the plague epidemic by blood-letting, and advocated the use of a balsamic ball (*pomo*) for countering the effects of foul air. He lived in Wood Street, London, being assessed there for subsidy in St Alban's parish in 1564 on £70 and in 1572 on £50; by 1576 he had removed to St Botolph without Bishopsgate, where he was assessed on £60. In 1567 he was incorporated MD (as of Padua) in the University of Cambridge. He was paid for attendance on, and medication (some specified) used for, Sir Henry Sidney's family during 1568–75. From Spa, Christopher Hatton wrote to the queen (1573), saying, 'My dear Lady, I amend: some proof thereof hath Julio sent unto you' (Nicholas, 30). However, his chief patron was then the earl of Leicester (presumably, on his brother Ambrose's recommendation), who was alleged (Peck, 116) to have made malevolent use of Borgarucci's knowledge of poisons: hence, John Webster's *White Devil* (1612) has a poisoner named 'Julio, a doctor'. By patent of 21 September 1573 he was made physician to the royal household for life, replacing the deceased Dr Bentley, with a fee of £50 per annum.

Borgarucci married Alice, daughter of Thomas Nosworthy, of Chichester, but in October 1573 he wrote to Lord Burghley complaining that Sir William Cordell, master of the rolls, had for five months detained his wife in his house, nourishing her in his 'popish superstitions'. As late as 1576 Borgarucci wrote to Leicester, saying that 'the Archbishop of Canterbury [Grindal] had sworn I should never obtain this gentlewoman I have married' (Peck, 275). The latter was, presumably, his second wife, Eleanor (*d.* 1581): in 1578 and 1579 both Dr Julio and Mrs Julio exchanged new year's gifts with the queen.

In June 1578 the Spanish ambassador reported on 'a certain Julio' thought to be 'plotting some villainy' against Spain: bent, and 'of the colour of a Morisco … he usually looks on the ground … as he walks'. The fact that 'He speaks eight or nine languages beautifully and is closeted for hours every day with Leicester and Walsingham and sometimes with the queen' (Hume, nos. 502, 505) argues strongly that this was Borgarucci, who, his brother Prospero said, was *huomo ueramente de nostri tempi* (Borgarucci, 59).

In 1578 Giulio and Eleanor obtained a mansion with garden and orchard, part of the site of the dissolved St Mary Spital: they doubtless then occupied the property, as did Eleanor after Giulio's death. John Banister's *The Historie of Man* contains Borgarucci's commendatory Latin epistle; and letters he wrote survive in the Public Record Office (SP 46.44, fol. 53) and the British Library.

Borgarucci died on 7 January 1581, and was buried that day at St Botolph without Bishopsgate. By his will, begun on 26 December and completed on 30 December 1580, he bequeathed sums of money to his brother Bernardino's daughters Alicia and Isabella (in Venice, with their father), and to the poor prisoners in London; the residue was left to his wife Eleanor, who was executrix; the overseer was Giovanni Battista Castiglione. Probate was granted on 31 January 1581. Eleanor died on 10 August, and, as 'Mrs Elinor Julie', was buried with her late husband on 11 August 1581. JOHN BENNELL

Sources R. Cooke, *Visitation of London, 1568*, ed. H. Stanford London and S. W. Rawlins, [new edn], 2 vols. in one, Harleian Society, 109–10 (1963), 101–2 · E. A. Fry, ed., *Abstracts of inquisitiones post mortem relating to the City of London, 3: 1577–1603*, British RS, 36 (1908), 32–6 · D. C. Peck, ed., *Leicester's commonwealth: the copy of a letter written by a master of art of Cambridge (1584) and related documents* (1985), 116, 275 · M. A. S. Hume, *Calendar of letters and state papers relating to English affairs, preserved principally in the archives of Simancas*, 2, PRO (1894), 1568–79, nos. 502, 505 · *Report on the manuscripts of Lord De L'Isle and Dudley*, 1, HMC, 77 (1925), 244, 264, 427 · will, 1581, PRO, PROB 11.63/3 · Cooper, *Ath. Cantab.*, 1.450 · *CPR*, 1560–63; 1572–5 · P. Borgarucci, *Trattato di peste* (1565), 59, 105 · A. G. C. A. Bonet-Maury, *Early sources of English unitarian Christianity*, trans. E. P. Hall (1884), 133–4 · J. Strype, *The history of the life and acts of the most reverend father in God Edmund Grindal*, new edn (1821), 334–5 · *CSP for.*, 1563 · J. Nichols, *The progresses and public processions of Queen Elizabeth*, new edn, 2 (1823), 77–8, 88–9, 260, 270–71 · *DNB* · R. E. G. Kirk and E. F. Kirk, eds., *Returns of aliens dwelling in the city and suburbs of London, from the reign of Henry VIII to that of James I*, Huguenot Society of London, 10/1 (1900), 306; 10/2 (1902), 195 · N. H. Nicolas, *Memoirs of the life and times of Sir Christopher Hatton* (1847), 30 · GL, MS 2942, 1572, fol. 13 · A. W. C. Hallen, ed., *The registers of St Botolph, Bishopsgate, London*, 1 (1889), 286

Borland, James (1774–1863), army physician, was born at Ayr, Scotland, in April 1774. He joined the army medical department as a hospital assistant on 20 December 1790, becoming surgeon's mate in the Royal Highland regiment in 1792, and took part in the duke of York's disastrous campaign in Flanders in 1793–5, during which general hospitals were established in addition to regimental hospitals. Borland emphasized the adverse effect of this development on regimental medical officers, who resented the appointment of civilian physicians and staff surgeons over their heads to run the general hospitals. He also rejected as 'fallacious and mischievous … the argument that civilian doctors were better educated' (Cantlie, 228). On 2 April 1794 he was appointed surgeon to the 23rd foot and sailed with the regiment to the West Indies, leaving it in September 1795 to act as staff surgeon on San Domingo until British troops withdrew in 1798. In 1799 he accompanied the expedition to The Helder in the Netherlands, and after its failure was sent by the duke of York to the headquarters of the French general Brune, with a flag of truce, to arrange for the exchange of the wounded. For this service he was promoted, on 5 December 1799, to the newly constituted rank of deputy inspector of army hospitals. He then became attached to Russian troops, who had co-operated with the British in the northern Netherlands and had been ordered to winter in the Channel Islands until the breaking up of the ice in the Baltic Sea allowed them to return home. His work was rendered more onerous by an outbreak of malignant fever in Guernsey, and, for his efforts, he received the thanks of the tsar. However, he declined an invitation to enter the imperial service.

Borland was chief medical officer of the army in the southern counties, under the command of Sir David Dundas, at the time of the threatened French invasion. He became inspector-general of hospitals on 22 January 1807 and served at headquarters in London at a time when many improvements in army hospital organization were planned. During the ill-fated expedition to the Scheldt in 1809, he volunteered for the duty of enquiring into the causes of the sicknesses and deaths at Walcheren, being associated with Dr Lempriere, one of the physicians to the army, and Sir Gilbert Blane, who had then left the navy and was in practice in London. The report of these commissioners, on whose recommendation the fever-ridden troops were finally withdrawn, was ordered by the House of Commons to be printed among *Accounts and Papers for 1810* as *Papers Relating to the Scheldt Expedition* (fol. 2, no. 104).

From 1810 to 1816 Borland was principal medical officer in the Mediterranean, responsible for organizing the hospitals of the Anglo-Sicilian contingent, the efficiency and unprecedented economy of which prompted a special official minute on the disbandment of the force. His services during an outbreak of plague at Malta also received praise from Admiral Lord Exmouth. He accompanied the force sent to assist the Austrians to expel Joachim Murat from Naples, and the troops which held Marseilles and blockaded Toulon at the time of the Waterloo campaign. On 25 May 1816 he retired on half pay, was appointed honorary physician to the duke of Kent, and received the order of SS Maurizio e Lazzaro of Savoy. For many years he lived at Teddington, Middlesex, where his sterling character and many kindly deeds won general esteem. He died at Bridgeman House, Teddington, on 22 February 1863, aged eighty-eight. He was survived by his wife, Susannah Frances, and son, Robert Spencer Borland.

H. M. CHICHESTER, *rev.* JOHN SWEETMAN

Sources *Army List* · N. Cantlie, *A history of the army medical department*, 1 (1974) · Boase, *Mod. Eng. biog.* · *CGPLA Eng. & Wales* (1863)

Wealth at death under £12,000: resworn probate, Feb 1864, *CGPLA Eng. & Wales*

Borlase, Edmund (*c.*1620–1682), historian and physician, was one of three sons of Sir John *Borlase (*c.*1576–1648), a Cornishman who was appointed master-general of the ordnance in Ireland in 1634 and served as joint lord justice there from 1641 to 1644, and his wife, Alice. By his own account, Edmund Borlase was a member of Trinity College, Dublin, during the provostship of William Chappell (1634–40), but he is not known to have graduated. It is likely that he became a member of the Irish parliament which convened in March 1640: though his return is not recorded, Edmund Borlase was appointed to committees on ten occasions between 27 February 1641 and 9 April 1644. He is said to have been awarded the degree of doctor of physic at Leiden in 1650. He was incorporated as a doctor of medicine of Oxford in August 1660 and set up practice in Chester where Charles Stanley, eighth earl of Derby, was among his patients.

In 1670 Derby was acknowledged in the dedication as the 'rise and original' of Borlase's first publication, an account of Latham Spaw in Lancaster, which was situated on Derby's estate. His second book, *The Reduction of Ireland to the Crown of England*, which was dedicated to Derby's widow and included an account of the provosts of Trinity, was a 'catalogue' of the governors of Ireland from the conquest to 1672 compiled from published works. It contained a brief vindication of the integrity of his father's government and this theme was developed extensively, though impersonally, in his next book, *The history of the execrable Irish rebellion, trac'd from many preceding acts to the grand eruption, the 23 of October, 1641, and thence pursued to the Act of Settlement, 1662*. This work, published anonymously after severe cuts had been made by the licenser to the press, Sir Roger L'Estrange, was dated 1680, but it was in print by August 1679.

In December 1679 Robert Clavell, who had published the two earlier works, reported a generally unfavourable reaction to the *History*, from the archbishop of Canterbury among others, specifying in particular complaints about 'the style and long parentheses of the book, and that in the end you leave people dissatisfyed': booksellers were already returning unsold copies and Clavell now regretted his investment (BL, Sloane MS 1008, fol. 239). The earlier part of the *History*, though turgid and syntactically odd, is thorough and usefully documented, and benefited both from personal knowledge and from access to the collection of depositions made by Dr Henry Jones in the 1640s. However, Borlase simplified the task of dealing with the later period, of which he seems to have had no direct knowledge. As he acknowledged in his introduction, he had met 'with a Manuscript, whence I was supplied with much of the latter part of this History'. Though the evidence suggests that Borlase was unaware of its authorship, this was the work of the earl of Clarendon, published in 1720 as *The History of the Rebellion and Civil War in Ireland*. Despite his parliamentarian sympathies, Borlase incorporated it in his text with such telling minor changes as the substitution of 'Parliament of England' for 'English rebels' and with omissions, since 'a part of it was so weaved, as if justice could not have been done to some, without mutchthing of others, which we had reason to wave'. In 1682 John Nalson identified the source, described Borlase as having 'very artfully blended it with his own rough and unpolished Heap of Matter', and denounced him as a 'Plagiary' (Nalson, 2.viii). Borlase had already prepared a second edition, undoing the 'very many and large eradications and interpolations of the then corrector of the press', revising the text, and adding further documents. This remained unpublished and is now in the British Library (Stowe MS 82; quotation from flyleaf).

Borlase had also become involved in the dispute between the earl of Anglesey and the duke of Ormond which had been triggered by the publication of the *Memoirs* of the earl of Castlehaven in 1680 and Anglesey's anonymous reply, *A Letter from a Person of Honour in the Country*, a year later. At Anglesey's instigation, Borlase wrote his *Brief Reflections on the Earl of Castlehaven's Memoirs*, which was dedicated to the king over the initials E. B. and published posthumously in 1682. Although Borlase had commended Anglesey's *Letter*, he was not included in the English council's condemnation of the works of Castlehaven and Anglesey as scandalous libels. Borlase died at Chester on 5 January 1682 and was buried in the church of St John the Baptist in Chester.

AIDAN CLARKE

Sources papers relating to the Irish rising of 1641, BL, Sloane MS 1008 • revised version of *History of the rebellion*, BL, Stowe MS 82 • *N&Q*, 162 (1932), 368 • J. Nalson, *An impartial collection of the great affairs of state*, 2 vols. (1682–3) • R. MacGillivray, 'Edmund Borlase, historian of the Irish rebellion', *Studia Hibernica*, 9 (1969), 86–92 • *JHC* • Wood, *Ath. Oxon.*, new edn, 4.185 • *Eighth report*, 3, HMC, 7 (1881), 39 • Foster, *Alum. Oxon.* • B. McGrath, 'A biographical dictionary of the membership of the Irish House of Commons, 1640–1641', PhD diss., University of Dublin, 1997

Archives BL, corresp. and papers mainly relating to Irish rising, Sloane MSS 1008, 1015

Borlase, Henry (1806–1835), Plymouth Brother, eldest son of Henry and Ann Borlase, was born at Helston, Cornwall, on 15 February 1806, and educated by Dr Warren at Ottery St Mary, Devon, and at Trinity College, Cambridge, graduating BA in 1828. After taking orders he became curate at St Keyne, near Liskeard, about December 1830. At the end of 1832 he resigned his curacy and left the Church of England, explaining his actions in *Reasons for Withdrawing from the Ministry of the Church of England*, a pamphlet published in 1833. On taking up his residence in Plymouth he joined the newly formed Plymouth Brethren. He was a great friend and close associate of Benjamin Wills Newton, one of the originators of the movement. Borlase considered that the established church, as a human institution, had fallen into apostasy, and that separation from apostasy was no schism. In 1834 he became the editor of the *Christian Witness*, the first Brethren magazine. At the beginning of 1834 he broke a blood-vessel, and was subsequently in very precarious health. He died on 13 November 1835 at Plymstock, near Plymouth, having married Caroline Pridham. His contributions to the *Christian Witness* were published as *Papers by the Late Henry Borlase, Connected with the Present State of the Church* (1836).

ALEXANDER GORDON, *rev.* K. D. REYNOLDS

Sources H. H. Rowden, *The origins of the Brethren, 1825–1850* (1967) • Venn, *Alum. Cant.* • *N&Q*, 3rd ser., 5 (1864), 203 • private information (1885) • *IGI*

Borlase, Sir John (*c.*1576–1648), army officer and politician, was born in Cornwall, the eldest son of Edward Borlase of London, mercer, and Suzannah Isham. He matriculated as a pensioner from King's College, Cambridge, about 1591 but did not graduate, being admitted to the Middle Temple on 19 October 1595. Pursuing a military career, he fought with distinction in the Low Countries before the 1608 truce, having been knighted in 1606. Thereafter he was frequently on the continent on various missions. In 1620 he was second in command of the expedition sent to the Palatinate and in 1624–5 was made commander of an English regiment serving in the Low Countries. After returning to England in early 1627 he was a military adviser to the government, residing at Medmenham, Buckinghamshire. He married Alice Ravis (*d.* in or after 1649), widow of Thomas Ravis (*d.* 1609), bishop of London. They had three sons, the second being the historian Edmund *Borlase.

In June 1634 Borlase became master-general of the ordnance in Ireland after buying out the previous incumbent for £3000 with the encouragement of the lord deputy, Thomas Wentworth, who held him in high regard. His brief was to reform the Irish army, half of which would be in Dublin at any one time to exercise twice a week under him. His contacts in the Low Countries were also useful in purchasing arms and munitions there. He became an Irish privy councillor in 1638 and was MP for Enniskillen in 1634–5 and Belturbet in 1640–41. On the death of the lord deputy, Christopher Wandesford, he was made a lord justice of Ireland along with Sir William Parsons on 31 December 1640. The king had originally appointed Lord Dillon but as a close ally of Wentworth he was unacceptable to the English parliament. Borlase's appointment was more satisfactory for although he remained loyal to his fallen patron, testifying on his behalf during his trial in London in the spring of 1641, he was viewed as being more malleable. Although well versed in military matters, Borlase was no statesman and was frequently ill. Hence Parsons, a parliamentarian, was *de facto* governor until he was replaced by the royalist Sir Henry Tichbourne in April 1643. Borlase remained lord justice with Tichbourne until the earl of Ormond's appointment as lord lieutenant in January 1644.

Borlase appeared in London in the summer of 1645, petitioning parliament for a composition, which was granted on 4 October. From the summer of 1646 he advised parliament on Irish military matters. Towards the end of his life he was in financial difficulties, having borrowed money on his own account for the royal forces during his lord justiceship. He died in London on 15 March 1648 and was buried in the church of St Bartholomew-the-Great. His estate in Ireland had suffered so greatly during the rebellion that his wife was forced to petition parliament in 1649 for the cost of the funeral and for her own support.

TERRY CLAVIN

Sources R. Lascelles, ed., *Liber munerum publicorum Hiberniae … or, The establishments of Ireland*, later edn, 2 vols. in 7 pts (1852), vol. 2, pp. 7, 102 • *CSP dom.*, *1603–10*, 631; *1611–18*, 79; *1619–23*, 152; *1623–5*, 251, 267; *1626–7*, 113, 216, 507; *1627–8*, 113 • *CSP Ire.*, *1633–47*, 55–6, 164, 181, 248, 304, 462, 465; *1647–60*, 6, 21, 48, 766–7, 771; *1669–70*, 377 • Venn, *Alum. Cant.* • *Report on the manuscripts of the earl of Egmont*, 2 vols. in 3, HMC, 63 (1905–9), vol. 1, pt. 2, pp. 132, 256, 353 • *Calendar of the manuscripts of the marquess of Ormonde*, new ser., 8 vols., HMC, 36 (1902–20), vol. 1, p. 46 • B. Whitelocke, *Memorials of the English affairs*, new edn (1732), 47, 90, 175, 179, 289 • G. Radcliffe, *The earl of Strafforde's letters and dispatches, with an essay towards his life*, ed. W. Knowler, 2 vols. (1739), vol. 1, pp. 113–14, 165, 196–7, 217; vol. 2, p. 251 • J. Anderson, *A genealogical history of the house of Yvery*, 2 vols. (1742), vol. 2, pp. 186, 285 • W. C. Borlase, *The descent, name and arms of Borlase of Borlase in the county of Cornwall* (1888), 94–117 • *History of the Irish confederation and the war in Ireland … by Richard Bellings*, ed. J. T. Gilbert, 7 vols. (1882–91), vol. 1, pp. 8–10; vol. 2, pp. 172, 187, 190 • B. McGrath, 'A biographical dictionary of the membership of the Irish House of Commons, 1640–1', PhD diss., University of Dublin, 1997, 73–4 • *DNB*

Likenesses M. J. van Miereveldt, oils, 1625, NPG

Wealth at death ended life in financial difficulties; widow had to petition parliament for the cost of funeral and for her own support

Borlase, William (1696–1772), antiquary and naturalist, was born on 2 February 1696, the second son of John Borlase (1666–1755), landowner and twice MP for St Ives, and his wife, Lydia (*c.*1671–1725), youngest daughter of Christopher Harris of Hayne, Devon, at their home, Pendeen House, in the parish of St Just, Cornwall. The Borlases were said to be the descendants of a Norman family who had settled in Cornwall. He was sent to Christopher Pender's school in Penzance until 1709, when he started attending the Revd Mr Bedford's school in Plymouth. In March 1713 he entered Exeter College, Oxford, where he graduated BA in 1716 and proceeded MA in 1719. He was admitted into deacon's orders by Lancelot, bishop of Exeter, in 1719, and was ordained the following year. His father purchased for him the right of presentation to the rectory of Ludgvan, Cornwall, and, after some problems resolved with the assistance of Sir John Hobart, later the earl of Buckingham, he was presented to his living on 22 April 1722. He would spend the rest of his long life at the rectory at Ludgvan, also holding from 1732 the living of St Just. On 28 July 1724 at Illogan, Cornwall, he married Anne (1703–1769), eldest surviving daughter of the Revd W. M. Smith, rector of Camborne and Illogan, and his wife, Mary Farthing. They had six children, all boys, two of whom died in infancy.

As well as having interests in 'gardening and planting' (*GM*, 1115) and reading the classics, Borlase began collecting minerals and fossils. The copperworks of Lord Godolphin were in Ludgvan parish, and Borlase had access 'with the greatest ease' (ibid.) to such material. Friends to whom he sent various specimens

> encouraged him now first to think of studying the natural history of his native county, and look more narrowly into the structure and properties of the so much commended fossils, as well as trace the other, though less interesting bounties of nature. (ibid.)

These interests also stimulated a fascination with the 'many monuments of remote antiquity' (ibid.) which abounded in the region and which, he found, had either been overlooked or under-rated by previous examiners and writers. He became particularly interested in 'the study of the Druid learning; with the religion and customs of the ancient Britons before their conversion to Christianity, intending to describe and explain the several unknown, or hitherto ill understood, remains in Cornwall' (ibid.). He was assisted early on in these projects by his friend the Revd Edward Collins, the vicar of St Erth, as well as by his wife, who helped in the collecting and recording of samples. On antiquarian matters he corresponded with his friend Francis Wise, a fellow of Trinity College, Oxford, and later first Radcliffe librarian. Though Borlase was a good draughtsman and recognized the importance of making drawings and measurements of antiquities he was, however, mistaken in identifying natural rock basins as sacred structures built by the druids.

Borlase sent samples of the minerals he found, including tin, copper, iron, and lead ores, to his friend John Andrew, an Oxford physician, who in 1735 went to Leiden to study under Herman Boerhaave. Andrew passed on samples to Boerhaave, Carl Linnaeus, and J. F. Gronovius, and Borlase entered into a correspondence with the last. Andrew returned to Britain in 1738 with a copy of Linnaeus's *System of Botany* for Borlase. Through the introduction by their mutual friend William Oliver of Bath, in 1739 and 1740 Borlase also supplied samples of Cornish minerals to the poet Alexander Pope, who used them to decorate the grotto in his garden at Twickenham. Pope erected an inscription to Borlase in the grotto, and sent him a copy of his works as thanks.

Borlase's studies were hampered, as he realized, by his distance from the centres of learning of London and Oxford, a problem he could never fully overcome. In 1740 he proposed to the archdeacon of Cornwall the establishment of a library at Truro for the use of clergy and gentry, but this suggestion would not be realized until 1792. In 1748 he met and made friends with the Revd Dr Charles Lyttelton and Jeremiah Milles, who were both influential fellows of the Society of Antiquaries of London. They assisted and encouraged him in the undertaking of his work on Cornish natural history and antiquities. In the same year he began a correspondence with Emanuel Mendes da Costa FRS, a naturalist and mineralogist from London of Portuguese Jewish descent, who visited him in 1749 to study mines and geology. In 1750 da Costa successfully proposed him for fellowship of the Royal Society in recognition of his essay 'Spar and sparry productions, called Cornish diamonds', which was published in the society's *Philosophical Transactions*. Da Costa also put Borlase in touch with the antiquarian William Stukeley, who shared a similar fascination with ancient religion and druids, but their correspondence was only short-lived.

Borlase spent the months between July 1753 and January 1754 in Oxford, supervising the printing and publication of his *Observations on the antiquities historical and monumental, of the county of Cornwall. Consisting of several essays on the first inhabitants, Druid-superstition, and remains of the most remote antiquity, in Britain, and the British Isles* (1754; 2nd edn, 1769). This work was the first chronological account of the antiquities of the county, and the first book to describe, illustrate, and classify a significant number of them. It was divided into four sections: the early history of Britain with special reference to Cornwall; the rites and practices of the druids; the prehistoric monuments of Cornwall; and the Roman and later antiquities. An index included an English–Cornish vocabulary.

In 1752 Borlase travelled with his friend Henry Usticke to the Isles of Scilly, where they measured and recorded barrows, stone circles, and rock basins. His account of the islands was published in the *Philosophical Transactions* (vol. 48, 1758, p. 55), and enlarged into a book, *Observations on the Ancient and Present State of the Islands of Scilly* (1756). This volume was praised by Samuel Johnson as 'one of the most pleasing and elegant pieces of local enquiry that our country has produced' (*Literary Magazine*, 1/2, 1756, 91). Between 1738 and 1751 Borlase took the sons of local gentry into his home to educate, and many of these retained a close affection for their tutor. In the summers of 1744 and 1745 he came into conflict with John Wesley, who was successfully recruiting many of Borlase's parishioners to Methodism, and in his capacity as a magistrate he summoned Wesley before the local court.

Between 1752 and 1757 (with the exception of 1754) Borlase made tours around central and eastern Cornwall gathering material for his next book. He had hoped to publish a topographical survey of the county, but this ambition was beyond the capacity of one man, by then in his sixties, and he abandoned the plan in 1757. But *The Natural History of Cornwall* was published at Oxford in 1758, following which he donated his collection of fossils, minerals, and antiquities to the Ashmolean Museum. In acknowledgement of this gift, and in recognition of his achievements in literature and antiquarianism, on 23 March 1766 the university conferred upon him by diploma the degree of doctor of law. After this date Borlase devoted his time to more sedentary pastimes such as painting, and though a second edition of *Antiquities* was published in London in 1769, he abandoned the publication of his 'Private thoughts concerning the creation and the deluge' (a reconciliation of the Mosaic account with the fossil record) while it was at the press.

Borlase died at home in Ludgvan following a long illness on 31 August 1772, and was buried in the chancel of his church at Ludgvan on 3 September 1772. An obituary, probably written by his brother Walter, recorded that William

> was remarkably attentive to the affairs of his parish, and the regularity of his parishioners, was affable and easy of access … Though he was not admired as a preacher, yet several specimens he has left in manuscript, not unworthy of publication, prove that his studies were not confined to Antiquities or Natural History. (Walter Borlase MSS)

His wife predeceased him, and only two of his six sons survived him: the Revd John Borlase and the Revd George Borlase, casuistical professor and registrar of the University of Cambridge. DAVID BOYD HAYCOCK

Sources P. A. S. Pool, *William Borlase* (1986) · *GM*, 1st ser., 73 (1803), 114–17 [autobiography] · Penzance Library, Cornwall, Walter Borlase MSS · *DNB* · Nichols, *Lit. anecdotes*, 3.78, 689; 5.291–303 · Nichols, *Illustrations*, 4.227, 445, 460, 468

Archives BL, parochial memoranda relating to Cornwall, Eg. MS 2657 · Cornwall RO, Penzance, memoranda on the Cornish

tongue; addenda to his *Antiquities* and *Natural history of Cornwall* · Morrab Library, Penzance, corresp.; journal of tour to Scilly Isles; description of Ludgvan, etc. · Royal Institution of Cornwall, Truro, accounts, notes, collections, etc.; family papers | BL, letters to C. Lyttelton, Stowe MS 752 · BL, corresp. with E. M. da Costa, Add. MS 28535, fols. 1–176 · Bodl. Oxf., Ashmolean MSS; Gough maps 3; MS Don.; MS Eng. Misc. E557; MS Eng. Th. E151; MS Montagu; MS Top. Gen. B53 7; MS Top. Gen. D2 · JRL, Baker MSS · Linn. Soc., corresp. with John Ellis · Warks. CRO, letters to Thomas Pennant
Likenesses A. Ramsay, oils, County Museum, Truro, Royal Institution of Cornwall · oils, priv. coll.; repro. in Pool, *William Borlase*, pl. 4
Wealth at death approx. £700—£341 to two sons; plus approx. £200 value of MSS and library: Pool, *William Borlase*, 270–71

Born, Max (1882–1970), physicist, was born on 11 December 1882 at Wallstrasse 8, Breslau, then part of Germany (later Wrocław, Poland), the elder of the two children of Gustav Jakob Born (1851–1900), a professor of anatomy at the University of Breslau, and his first wife, Margarethe Kaufmann (1856–1886). The family home was cultured and musical (Born was an accomplished pianist), with a strongly scientific atmosphere. He attended the König Wilhelm Gymnasium, Breslau, from about 1889 to 1901. In the course of his subsequent university studies in Breslau, Heidelberg, and Zürich, Born became increasingly engaged in mathematics and physics, travelling to the centre of German mathematics at the University of Göttingen in 1904. There he met the mathematical luminaries David Hilbert and Hermann Minkowski, participating in a 1905 seminar they led in electrodynamics (an expression of their interest in current physics), and took courses with Voigt in optics and Schwarzschild in astronomy. Hilbert made Born his assistant, responsible for helping to prepare his lectures and writing them up for the mathematical reading room. Born also impressed Felix Klein, the doyen of German mathematics, with a report on the stability of the elastic line, but incurred his wrath by at first declining to enter the philosophical faculty prize competition Klein set on the topic. In order to rescue himself from the consequences of alienating Germany's most powerful mathematician, Born subsequently submitted this work both for the prize (successfully) and his doctoral dissertation.

Born then spent six months in Cambridge in 1907. Despite finding himself unprepared for the rigours of the experimental courses of the Cavendish professor of physics and recent Nobel laureate J. J. Thomson, and unable to understand the Irish dialect of the mathematical physicist Joseph Larmor, Born reported that he returned to the continent with a wish to become a 'real physicist' (Born, 121). After an unsuccessful flirtation with experimental work in Breslau, the inspiration of Einstein's 1905 paper on relativity prompted his first research contributions. Born returned to Göttingen to work with Minkowski shortly before the latter's unexpected death in 1909, and he employed Minkowski's four-dimensional formulation of relativity in an ambitious but flawed attempt to build a relativistic rigid body theory of the electron. In 1912 he turned to the second major theoretical breakthrough of the early twentieth century, following Einstein's lead to apply quantum theory to the specific heat of solids. Here Born and Theodor von Kármán developed a much more fundamental approach than the simultaneous and more rapidly assimilated work of Debye. From the strengths of his mathematical education Born drew a commitment to axiomatic approaches in physics (which he combined with atomism). He typically approached a problem in all its complexity, devising a mathematical formulation of appropriate generality before descending to more tractable specifics. A readiness to employ elegant but unfamiliar mathematical techniques often made Born's work initially inaccessible to other physicists.

Born and von Kármán's derivation of specific heats was one aspect of a broad programme to derive all crystal properties from the assumption of a lattice whose particles could be displaced under the action of internal forces. Born was to pursue this enquiry into the structure of matter throughout the rest of his career, largely alone through to the First World War and later often in collaboration with students and others. His contributions were foundational for the theory of crystal lattices and for solid-state physics. In addition to many path-breaking papers, his monographs and textbooks, *Dynamik der Kristallgitter* (1915), *Atomtheorie des festen Zustandes* (1923), and (with Huang) *Dynamical Theory of Crystal Lattices* (1954), were quickly recognized as landmarks in the field. Born's skill in writing technical textbooks was also reflected in theoretical optics, where his books *Optik* (1933) and (with Wolf) *Principles of Optics* (1959) became standard works. As an undergraduate text *Atomic Physics* (1935) enjoyed unrivalled popularity in the English-speaking world, with eight editions by 1969.

In 1913 Born married Hedwig Ehrenberg (1891–1972), the daughter of a Göttingen law professor. They had two daughters and one son, Gustav, who became professor of pharmacology. At the outbreak of the First World War Born was called to his first professorship in theoretical physics at the University of Berlin. There began a long friendship between the Borns and Einstein. Their correspondence provides a fascinating commentary on the extraordinary scientific and political events in which they participated, and drew forth some of Einstein's most famous sayings: it was to Born that Einstein first remarked that 'God doesn't play dice' (*Born–Einstein Letters*, 127).

After the war Born moved to Frankfurt (1919) and then Göttingen (1921), where he soon turned his attention to addressing the difficulties of the quantum theory of the atom, the second field in which his contributions were fundamental. As director of the Institute for Theoretical Physics, Born was responsible for Göttingen becoming one of the most important international centres of the new 'quantum mechanics' which he named in 1924. In 1925 Born recognized that a new formulation his former assistant Heisenberg had proposed could be expressed in terms of matrix operations, leading to the development of matrix mechanics by Heisenberg, Born, and Jordan (another of Born's impressive group of students and assistants). Then in 1926 Born initiated the statistical interpretation of Schrödinger's wave function—which he immediately saw to contradict the determinism of classical physics. It was for this work especially that Born was honoured with the Nobel prize in physics in 1954. Born's description of particle scattering, which became known as the Born approximation, has become important in high energy physics.

In 1933 antisemitic civil service laws stripped Born of his post in Göttingen and resulted in his emigration to Britain, where he was for three years Stokes lecturer in Cambridge. Searching for a more permanent position he spent six months at the Indian Institute of Physics in Bangalore, but was then appointed Tait professor of natural philosophy at the University of Edinburgh, which he held from 1936 until his retirement in 1953. There he gradually built a school of research physicists, concentrating in particular on the physics of the solid and liquid states. Many of his students and collaborators came from outside Britain, including a number of refugees from the continent. Among those who worked with Born in Edinburgh were Klaus Fuchs (later notorious for passing atomic weapon secrets to the Soviets), Fürth, Lonsdale, Bradburn, Peng, H. S. Green, Cheng, Yang, Huang, and Wolf, with the collaborations with Fuchs and Green (on the statistical mechanics of condensed systems) being particularly important.

In 1954 Born and his wife returned to the small town of Bad Pyrmont near Göttingen. The award of the Nobel prize gave something of a forum for Born's views on science in the cold-war period. Throughout his life he had exhibited a strong interest in the philosophical dimensions of physics, most fully expressed in lectures on the *Natural Philosophy of Cause and Chance* (1949) and articles collected in *Physics in my Generation* (1969). His equally deep concern with the place of science in culture was reflected in the thorough and imaginative pedagogy of his popularizations *Einstein's Theory of Relativity* (with three German editions between 1920 and 1922 and an English edition in 1924) and, on quantum theory, *The Restless Universe* (1936). Following the events of the Second World War, the dropping of the atomic bomb, and the cold war, Born was led to the pessimistic view that science and technology had destroyed the ethical basis of traditional society. He was passionate in his emphasis on the importance of scientific thinking, but also on the necessity for understanding the limits within which it was appropriate, and for acknowledging the responsibility of the scientist, particularly in relation to the development of nuclear weapons. Born participated in the founding of the Pugwash movement (1955) and his forthright views were expressed in, among other books, *Physics and Politics* (1962) and *My Life and my Views* (1968). He died in a Göttingen hospital on 5 January 1970.

Among other honours Born was awarded the Stokes medal of Cambridge University (1936), the Max Planck medal of the German Physical Society (1948), and the Hughes medal of the Royal Society (1950). He received nine honorary doctorates and was a member of scientific academies in several countries. RICHARD STALEY

Sources M. Born, *My life* (1978) · N. Kemmer and R. Schlapp, *Memoirs FRS*, 17 (1971), 17–52 · A. Hermann, 'Born, Max', *DSB* · R. Staley, 'Max Born and the German physics community: the education of a physicist', PhD diss., U. Cam., 1992 · *Albert Einstein, Hedwig und Max Born: Briefwechsel, 1916–1955*, ed. M. Born (Munich, 1969); trans. I. Born, *The Born–Einstein letters* (1971) · 'Born, Gustav Jakob', *Deutsche biographische Enzyklopädie*, ed. W. Killy and others (Munich, 1995–9)

Archives Staatsbibliothek, Berlin · University of Copenhagen, Niels Bohr Institute for Astronomy, Physics, and Geophysics | Archive for the History of Quantum Physics · Bodl. Oxf., Society for Protection of Science and Learning file · Bodl. Oxf., corresp. with C. A. Coulson · ICL, corresp. with Herbert Dingle · ICL, corresp. with Dennis Gabor · McMaster University, Hamilton, Ontario, corresp. with Bertrand Russell · Nuffield Oxf., corresp. with Lord Cherwell · Rijksmuseum voor de Geschiedenis der Naturwestenschappen, Leiden, Netherlands, corresp. with Ehrenfest · University of Copenhagen, Niels Bohr Institute for Astronomy, Physics, and Geophysics | SOUND Archive for the History of Quantum Physics, interview conducted by P. P. Ewald, T. S. Kuhn and F. Hund (1960, 1962) [51pp transcript held at Imperial College and Science Museum Library]

Likenesses Lotte-Meitner-Graf, photograph, repro. in Kemmer and Schlapp, *Memoirs FRS*

Borosky, Charles George (*d.* 1682). *See under* Königsmark, Karl Johann, Count Königsmark in the Swedish nobility (1659–1686).

Borough, Christopher (*fl.* 1579–1587), merchant, was the son of Stephen *Borough (1525–1584), a mariner, of Northam, Devon. Stephen and his brother William *Borough (*bap.* 1536, *d.* 1598) were both experienced navigators in European Arctic waters. Christopher acted as Russian interpreter for the sixth Muscovy Company trading venture, led by Arthur Edwards, which left Gravesend on 19 June 1579. The fleet arrived at St Nicholas (near the present port of Archangel) in the White Sea on 22 July and transferred to small craft for the journey up the northern Dvina and Sukhona rivers to Vologda. A short overland trek brought them to the Volga at Yaroslavl, where they again took ship. A month later, on 16 October, they reached Astrakhan, at the head of the delta, where they wintered. Leaving Edwards in charge at Astrakhan, Borough and his party embarked on 1 May 1580 on an English-built vessel headed into the Caspian Sea for the voyage south, making for Derbent, the chief emporium of that region. They were carried too far by adverse winds and stopped briefly near Baku before returning to Derbent, where they traded from 22 June to 3 October.

As his descriptions of Derbent and Baku show, Borough was fully aware of the growth of Turkish power at the expense of the former Persian domination on the shores of the Caspian Sea, a region then hardly known to Englishmen. His nautical training under his father and uncle led him to take a series of observations for latitude during his travels—probably the earliest made with reasonable accuracy by Europeans in these parts.

At the end of the season the party picked up stragglers between Derbent and Baku, including two Spaniards who had escaped from captivity near Tunis, and returned to Astrakhan on 4 December. They wintered there, left the following April, and reached St Nicholas on 16 July 1581. The merchandise which they had acquired was embarked on the *William and John*, which arrived in the Thames on 25 September 1581. Borough's account of the venture, compiled from various letters and reports sent to the Muscovy Company and to his uncle, was published by Hakluyt in the first volume of his *Voyages* in 1582.

Borough remained in Russia when Edwards's party left, and he continued to visit the company's houses between St Nicholas and Astrakhan. He was certainly there in 1584, when he carried letters from Moscow to Yaroslavl, but probably went home soon afterwards, for a letter written in March 1586 by Queen Elizabeth to Tsar Feodor states that he was then in England.

It is likely that Borough returned again to Russia, as in 1587 he submitted a lengthy report to the Muscovy Company regarding their affairs, and particularly exposing the devious policy of Sir Jerome Horsey in Moscow, who was busy making his private fortune at the company's expense. Borough also spoke of Horsey's harsh treatment of J. Peacock and other agents sent by the company in 1585 to investigate these matters. He ended his report by recommending that the company should close its houses in Moscow and elsewhere and transfer all business and traffic to the house at St Nicholas, in order to prevent private trading and political intrigue.

Borough's linguistic expertise is shown by two manuscripts in the Bodleian Library, Oxford, which he brought back and had elegantly bound in England, perhaps for presentation to Queen Elizabeth. MS Seld. superius III is an orthodox catechism, which includes elements of Church Slavonic Russian. MS Laud misc. 45 is a sixteenth-century copy of the pseudo-Aristotelian *Secret of Secrets*, written in Great Russian and signed twice by Borough, who may also have been the copyist. It is paginated with Europeanized arabic numerals and uses oriental arabic numerals in the text. Both manuscripts employ hyphens where words break at the ends of lines, and catch-words. These features were unknown in contemporary Russian scribal practice.

Borough had travelled with Persian merchants and lodged with them at Astrakhan. He had also recognized, and commented on, an Armenian inscription seen on the way to Astrakhan, and his writing reveals his general interest in languages and customs. The Bodleian manuscripts show that Borough was able to distinguish Church Slavonic and Great Russian from West Russian and Ukrainian. Nothing is known of Borough's later years, nor of the circumstances of his death.

ANITA MCCONNELL

Sources A. E. Pennington, 'A sixteenth-century English Slavist', *Modern Language Review*, 62 (1967), 680–86 · BL, Lansdowne MS 52, no. 37 · [C. Burrough], 'Advertisements and reports of the sixt voyage into the partes of Persia and Media, for the Company of English Merchants', *Early voyages and travels to Russia and Persia*, ed. E. D. Morgan and C. H. Coote, 2, Hakluyt Society, 73 (1886)
Archives Bodl. Oxf., orthodox catechism imported by Borough, MS Seld. superius III (SC 323) · Bodl. Oxf., copy of the 'Secret of secrets', signed and perhaps copied by Borough, MS Laud misc. 45 (SC 550)

Borough, John. *See* Burgh, John (*fl.* 1370–1398).

Borough, John (*c.*1494–1570), seaman, son of Stephen Borough (*c.*1474–1548), was born at Northam Burrows, Northam, Devon, the eldest of four brothers brought up there. Early seagoing experience off the treacherous north Devon and Cornish shores prepared him well for more challenging tasks with the vice-admiral Arthur Plantagenet, Viscount Lisle, later warden of Calais. Their naval association can be traced from February 1513 when Plantagenet was captain of the *Nicholas of Hampton*, and Borough was in charge of fitting out *Henry Imperial* following her launch, being ranked as her master until she was commissioned as the flagship *Henri Grace a Dieu*. By 1531 legal evidence shows that Borough had acted as master of Arthur Plantagenet's own ship, the *Mary Plantagenet*, on many voyages from Bideford, Topsham, Southampton, and Bristol to Sicily, Candia (Crete), and the Levant.

During 1533 Borough conducted an admiralty court suit for serious professional losses against the purser of the *Michael of Barnstaple*, John Andrews. A deposition field at Messina in 1533 alleged that Andrews had absconded with gold (consigned by John Semer of Messina to William Ballard in Bristol) and with valuable navigational aids from his sea chest including two Castilian texts, four compasses, a chart, a cross-staff and a quadrant, a rutter written in Castilian and two others, including one in English on which he had worked for over a year. He also sought compensation for a lute, 'a map in glass which cost vis viiid' and a chart 'for all Levaunt' (PRO, HCA, 24/7, fols. 116–18). He was thus in the vanguard of English users of new Iberian navigational technology.

After Charles V failed to win control of the north African shore in 1534–6 and counter a Franco-Turkish naval alliance, Borough concentrated on Newcastle's short-sea trade in unfinished cloths to the wool staple at Calais. Thereafter he helped Stephen *Borough (1525–1584) and William *Borough (*bap.* 1536, *d.* 1598), the sons of his own brother Walter, into successful seagoing careers in London, but none of the children born to his own wife, Christian, between 1523 and 1527—Peter, David, and Thomazin—nor Agnes, born well after September 1540, left Northam.

In 1538 Borough participated in coastal surveys in south Cornwall and Devon with his nephew Stephen, both learning thereby about new fortification theories through working alongside military engineers like Thomas Pettyt and Stefan von Hashenperg. The resultant plans (BL, Cotton MSS Augustus I.i.35, 36, 38, and 39) commissioned by Henry VIII in 1538 helped to transform the defensibility of Penzance, Falmouth, Plymouth, Dartmouth, Torbay, Teignmouth, and Exmouth and Topsham. The survey of Fowey and Falmouth in 1538 commissioned by his erstwhile employer the vice-admiral resulted in the new curviform forts at Pendennis and St Mawes anticipated on the map in the British Library (Cotton MS Augustus I.i.38), being completed during 1540 at a cost of £5614 and £5018 respectively.

In October 1539 Borough was chosen to survey possible sea passages to be taken by Henry VIII's future queen,

Anne of Cleves, in her journey from the Zuider Zee to London. The resultant rutter, the earliest in English to include coastal views and navigational directions, is now kept at Hatfield House. In March 1540 his letter from Antwerp to Thomas Cromwell details passages from Middleburg to Dover or Portsmouth but stresses that greater skill was needed to progress further west. In the event Anne took sail just from Calais to Dover. In 1541, with Richard Cavendish and John Bartelot, Borough signed plans to improve Dover harbour (BL, Cotton MS Augustus I.i.26). His proposals of the mid-1540s to fortify Alderney and improve Jersey's Orgueil fort and harbour would cost £9212 and £736 respectively to implement. As the naval commander-in-chief, Sir Thomas Cotton was instructed on 15 May 1549 to take to 'John Aborough on Alderney 42 sakers and halfsakers', plus shot and powder. In August 1549 while William Wynter's ships were unloading this ordnance beneath Borough's fortifications they had to beat off a French attack led by Leo Strozzi's flotilla of Genoese galleys.

Devon's lay subsidy rolls for 1524–7 and 1543–5 show Borough's assessment in Northam rising from £8 to £20 for he had acquired further land there in 1544. He died in January 1570 and was buried, as he had wished, at St Mary's Church, Northam. His wife had predeceased him. Protestant convictions are apparent in his will, made in Northam on 14 September 1556 and proved on 16 February 1570. Among his bequests were £20 to his brother Walter's children (not specified by name although in 1556 they were both exploring Muscovy's northern shores) and a similar sum for his brother Thomas's children. Most of his estate including his home passed to Agnes (*d.* 1620), who later married Thomas Leigh (*d.* 1609), a local landowner and shipowner. Both lived in the family home where David Borough, another shipowner, died in 1576, and where Peter Borough died in December 1586. Then John and Thomazin Hearneman, who were almost excluded by John's will, inherited most of Peter's estate under a will proved in January 1587. R. C. D. Baldwin

Sources J. F. Chanter, 'Borough or Burrough (Northam) and its inhabitants', *Report and Transactions of the Devonshire Association*, 58 (1926), 193–208 • BL, Cotton MSS Augustus I.ii.29, 26, 64; Cotton MS Galba Bx.106 [maps] • Hatfield House, Cecil papers, CP/223/1 • PRO, HCA 24/5, John Borough *contra* John Andrews &c; HCA 24/7 fols. 116–18 • state papers of Henry VIII, PRO, SP 3/9/66 • state papers of Edward VI, PRO, SP 10/14/26, SP 10/15/11, SP 10/7/12 • A. Ruddock, 'The earliest English seaman's rutter and pilot's chart', *Journal of the Institute of Navigation*, 14 (1961), 409–31 • J. Vanes, 'Documents illustrating the overseas trade of Bristol in the sixteenth century', *Bristol Record Society*, 21 (1979), 159–60 • E. G. R. Taylor, *The mathematical practitioners of Tudor and Stuart England* (1954); repr. (1970), 167 • A. H. W. Robinson, *Marine cartography in Britain* (1962), 21–2, 152, 161 • will, PRO, PROB 11/53, sig. 4 • parish register, St Mary, Northam, North Devon Record Office, Barnstaple • D. M. Loades, *The Tudor navy* (1992), 148

Wealth at death see will, PRO, PROB 11/53, sig. 4

Borough, Sir John (*d.* 1643), antiquary and herald, was the son of John Borough of Sandwich, Kent, and his wife, a daughter of Robert Denne of Dennehill, Kent, who inherited land in The Hague. His grandfather William Borough was apparently married to a Dutchwoman, and his father was described by contemporaries as a Dutch gardener or brewer. He should not be confused with Sir John Burrough, a professional soldier, who was killed at La Rochelle in September 1627.

In 1611–12 Borough was a student at Gray's Inn, the inn of Sir Francis Bacon. He had a position in Bacon's household before 1618 and served Bacon in the Lord Chancellor's Office. Borough also held office as keeper of the ancient records in the Tower of London, a position amenable to his antiquarian interests. In this capacity, with the prominent lawyer and antiquary John Selden, Borough assisted the disgraced Bacon with archival research for his *History of the Reign of Henry VII*.

Borough sat in the parliament of 1621 as MP for Sandwich. He was accused in the session of accepting bribes along with his employer, Bacon, but escaped censure when Thomas Howard, earl of Arundel and earl marshal of England, called upon him to assist the countess of Arundel, who was then in Europe. Arundel joined them the next year as ambassador to Venice with Borough serving as his secretary. Arundel himself had a strong antiquarian interest and patronized Selden and Borough's cousin, Sir Robert Cotton, for whom Borough purchased books and manuscripts in Venice.

In 1623, presumably in connection with his stewardship of the records in the Tower and reputation for knowledge of historical precedents, Borough was appointed one of the extraordinary clerks of the privy council. Arundel brought Borough into the College of Arms as Mowbray herald-extraordinary that same year, and by June 1624 Borough had advanced to Norroy king of arms; he was knighted in July of that year. Borough sat in the parliaments of 1624, 1625, and 1626 as MP for Horsham, Sussex, on Arundel's interest. Although a relatively inactive member of the House of Commons he kept detailed notes of the proceedings in these parliaments, an activity in line with his antiquarian interests.

Borough's expertise led crown officials to consult him on virtually all matters that might have historical precedents: in 1631 on the office of lord admiral, in 1634 on coat and conduct money, and also on ship money and other financial measures of the personal rule. Borough dabbled in writing verse, but his only published work resulted from his ship money research, *The Soveraignty of the British Seas*, written in 1633 although not printed until 1651. Borough accompanied Charles I on his coronation trip to Scotland in 1633 and the following year became Garter king of arms, the principal herald of the College of Arms and principal officer of arms to the chivalric Order of the Garter. He took a leave of absence from the college to serve in Arundel's embassy to the holy Roman emperor in 1636, and achieved unpopularity with his fellow heralds when he obtained a grant from the king maintaining his income from the office and suspending all heraldic visitations while he was away. In 1639 Arundel as earl marshal convened a court of inquiry into charges of corruption brought by Borough against Norroy and the Somerset herald, whom Arundel subsequently dismissed from the college.

The name of Borough's wife is unknown, but he was said to have had two sons and two daughters. One son, perhaps named Cassius, accompanied him in the 1636 embassy. The son travelled also in Italy with a son of the principal secretary of state, Sir Francis Windebank. It was presumably the same son who accompanied Borough and two of Windebank's sons in the bishops' war of 1639 against the Scots. Borough was in the king's entourage in his capacity as chief herald, but was also called on to clerk for the privy council when Sir Thomas Meautys fell ill. Borough reported to Secretary Windebank that he himself was ill and in any case had been excluded from all council meetings concerning military matters. The war came calling on Borough, however, when his tent in the king's camp was shot through twice. Despite his claim of having been excluded from proceedings, it was Borough who recorded for posterity most of the important negotiations in the bishops' wars, for example the pacification of Berwick and the treaty of Ripon. Borough was also consulted by the secretaries of state on how to call and hold a great council of peers, which he attended at York in September 1640, once again providing detailed notes of its proceedings.

Borough was a faithful royalist who followed the king in the civil war. At the royalist headquarters of Oxford he was created a doctor of civil law of the university in August 1643, and died there the following October. He was buried in the divinity chapel adjoining the choir of Christ Church. In the same month his post of keeper of the ancient records in the Tower was awarded by the Long Parliament to Selden. Borough's eldest son, John, was a lawyer in the court of chancery. He was knighted by Charles II, but lost his legal practice with the passage of the Test Act. S. A. Baron

Sources *The letters of John Chamberlain*, ed. N. E. McClure, 2 vols. (1939) • *CSP dom.* • Foster, *Alum. Oxon.*, *1500–1714*, vol. 1 • PRO, SP14, SP16 • D. Woolf, 'John Selden, John Borough, and Francis Bacon's *History of Henry VII*, 1621', *Huntington Library Quarterly*, 47 (1984), 47–53 • M. F. S. Hervey, *The life, correspondence and collections of Thomas Howard, earl of Arundel* (1921) • J. Haydn, *The book of dignities: containing lists of the official personages of the British empire*, ed. H. Ockerby, 3rd edn (1894) • *DNB*

Wealth at death received £50 p.a. as Garter king of arms; fees as clerk extraordinary to the council; presumably also small salary as keeper of records in the Tower of London

Borough, Stephen (1525–1584), explorer and naval administrator, was born on 25 September 1525 at Borough House, Northam Burrows, Northam, Devon, the elder son of Walter Borough (1494–1548) and Mary Dough; his younger brother was William *Borough (*d.* 1598).

Education and first voyages With his uncle, John *Borough (*d.* 1570), Stephen probably participated in the first measured surveys of south Devon and Cornwall in 1538; these survive in the British Library. The greatest influence on his childhood was undoubtedly John Borough, who until the late 1530s (when he began to undertake surveying tasks for Henry VIII) had sailed regularly from Bideford, Topsham, and Bristol to trade in Sicily, Crete, and the Levant. Stephen learned thereby to master a wide range of navigational and pilotage skills as a child, while his uncle must also have taught him useful linguistic skills using a Castilian Bible, a Castilian rutter (or book of sailing instructions), and another compiled in Portuguese. As a youth Stephen Borough also gained firsthand knowledge of the hazards of the Bay of Biscay; writing in 1563 of ships lost on voyages to Andalusia he noted that:

> some were lost on the coast, others have perished upon cape Finisterre in Galizia and also others upon the strymes and coast of Brittaine. The chiefest of these losses (as I am able to approve) hath happened throughe ignoraunce of the Arte [of navigation] and the presumption of the unskyllful. (BL, Lansdowne MS 116, fol. 7)

In consequence Borough matched his navigational skills with a speaking knowledge of Spanish, which later fitted him well for the first Muscovy voyages to which Sebastian Cabot brought the best of long-distance navigational and organizational practice from Seville.

On 20 May 1553 Stephen Borough sailed in the expedition that Cabot had prepared as master of the *Edward Bonaventure* (160 tons) under John Dee's talented tutee, Richard Chancellor, who had been appointed pilot-general of the fleet of three ships, including the ill-fated *Bona Esperanza* (120 tons), which under Sir Hugh Willoughby's command was trapped in the ice along with the *Bona Confidentia* (60 tons). So it was Borough's ship alone that was ready to open trade past the North Cape and through St Nicholas (Archangel). Chancellor journeyed overland to Moscow to formalize relations before both pilots sailed her back the next spring through the Kara Sea and past the fishing settlements at the mouth of the Dvina River. In 1589 Richard Hakluyt published Borough's exploratory voyage of 1556–7 as *The Navigation and Discoverie towards the River Ob*. Borough had bravely taken the pinnace *Searchthrift* as far as the Kola River, having been escorted by the Russian ketch *Pechora* until 15 July 1556. On 31 July Novaya Zemlya and the treacherous 35 mile wide Viagatz Strait were sighted. Borough stayed there until 23 August (with the result that it was named the Burrough Strait on admiralty charts until the late nineteenth century), recording with Richard Johnson's and William Borough's assistance the hostile icy environs of the Viagatz Strait in the late summer of 1556 before returning to Kholmogory on 11 September where Borough wisely chose to winter. Hakluyt records that Borough started his homeward voyage on 23 May 1557, travelling via Ribachi (Fisher Island, Finland), where he encountered Norwegian vessels with Dutch crews trading strong beer for stockfish. At Dronten (Trondheim) he learned of the loss of the *Bona Confidentia* and of the recovery of her sails by the town's mayor, and of the alleged loss of the *Philip and Mary*, although she had safely arrived in the Thames in April 1557. The real loss was of his colleague, Richard Chancellor, captain of the *Edward Bonaventure*, which had foundered in Pitsligo Bay, Scotland, on 10 November 1556.

Seville, 1558 In 1557–8 Dee and Borough worked on the technical problems of preparing a chart of the far northern waters explored by the latter in 1556. Later Dee compared Mercator's maps with 'my friend Stephen Borough, his platt' (BL, Cotton MS Vitellus C.vii, fol. 60*v*). Stephen

Borough's specialist navigational knowledge acquired on that route meant that he was ideally placed to go to Seville in 1558, in response to covert diplomatic arrangements made by Philip and Mary; his knowledge of the near Arctic was to be exchanged for an insight into the training of Spanish pilots. He later described to Hakluyt the organization of navigational training in Seville as he witnessed it in 1558. Hakluyt's dedication to *Divers voyages* (1582) asserts that Borough was treated with great honour by the Spaniards, and presented with a pair of perfumed gloves worth 5 or 6 ducats.

These gloves were the symbols of qualification and office to which the examined pilots were admitted. Borough was present there despite the formal prohibition on foreigners made at the instance of Charles V in 1547. When Borough arrived in Seville, Sebastian Cabot had only just died, although Alonso de Chaves had succeeded to his former office as pilot-major in 1552. This unique chance to be treated on a par with Cabot as an expert on Arctic waters was not lost on Borough, who wisely restricted himself to interest in the theoretical and scientific content of Martin Cortés's training manual *Breve compendio del arte de navegar*, completed in 1545 but not published until 1551. Borough clearly thought that Cortés's manual was a model document, and on his return to England ensured that the manual was made available to generations of English seamen, instrument makers, and hydrographers through translation by Richard Eden and publication by the queen's printer, Richard Jugge, as *The Arte of Navigation* in 1561. Stephen Borough's wisdom and achievements are commended in Eden's preface, written in 1561:

> he is neither malicious nor envious of his arte and science, in that he desireth the same for the common profite to be common to al men: And for the same intent was the first that moved certain worshipful of your company, as Syr William Garrerd, Maister William Merrick, Maister Blase Sanders, and Maister Edward Castlen to have this work translated into the English tongue.

Eden adds in praise of Borough's initiative that:

> whereas the same hath ben discovered unto you even to the mighty Ryver Ob, that falleth into the Scithian Ocean … A voyage of such difficultie, and in maner impossibilitie, that consyderyng the infinite dangiours thereof (as I have learned by th information of Steven a Burrugh, that was then the Chiefe Pilot of the same Voyage) that it may seme impossible that they should ever have escaped, excepte the mightye hand of God by the expert skilfulnesse of so excellent a pilot had delivered them from those daungers.

The Arctic trade With a right, as an assistant adventurer mentioned in the charter of 1555, to carry on personal trade within the Muscovy Company, Borough served as chief pilot in the *Swallow* in May 1560, taking a cargo of broadcloth, kerseys, salt, sack, and raisins, plus a pipe of sherry for Tsar Ivan IV marked by two round compasses on the bung. He returned from St Nicholas with Anthony Jenkinson after his epic overland journey into central Asia. He was back in Russian waters in May 1561, carrying Jenkinson as Queen Elizabeth's ambassador to Persia. His trips were part of a complex strategy to expand trade without operating in conflict with Spanish naval ambitions. While Lord Admiral Fiennes de Clinton and the privy council considered how to reorganize the navy following the loss of Calais in 1558 and Le Havre in 1562, Borough petitioned Queen Elizabeth to replicate the organization of the Casa de Contratacíon in Seville. Dated 1562, Borough's first draft set out both the form of his own experience and the need for change (BL, Lansdowne MS 116, fols. 3–7). This was followed by a later draft for the grant of the office of pilot-major to Borough, dated January 1564. Borough's clear appreciation of the value of the Casa's practice comes through. Although his case for the office of pilot-major was never accepted, he was soon afterwards made one of four keepers of the queen's ships on the Medway.

Hostility towards Stephen Borough's interests in the Arctic trade gradually emerged during the 1560s, with resentment growing inside the Muscovy Company that he, along with three other pilots, was allowed to undertake personal trade. The king's remembrancer's customs accounts for 1564 and later port books record the beginning of the controversy, which was created by Borough's embarking with private trade as chief pilot on voyages via the North Cape route in 1564, 1565, 1567, and 1568. Drapers' Company accounts show that in 1569 he shipped a private cargo of fourteen chests of 'brimstone' (saltpetre) in the *Swallow* of London. In 1571 his private adventure on the voyage to St Nicholas consisted of the export of seventy-two broadcloths, worth about £2000. John Hoddesdon's petition over prosecution for his own trade in furs in 1586–7 brought adverse if posthumous comparison of Borough's legitimate private trade, alongside more censorious criticism of the private trade of William Borough and Christopher *Borough, Stephen's son who had made six trips to Russia by 1579.

Master of Trinity House In 1574 Michael Lok reported that Stephen Borough was one of three members of the Muscovy Company appointed to treat in London with Martin Frobisher, Lok, and Christopher Hall about near polar voyaging to Cathay. Meanwhile he had found a safer career that allowed him to refocus on his domestic life at Chatham. He had unexpectedly lost his first wife, Elinor (*née* Smith), in 1562. On 26 March 1563 he married Johanna Overy (*d.* 1604), a widow, in St Dunstan and All Saints, Stepney. His children included Christopher, Judith, and two other much younger daughters, Anne and Elizabeth, mentioned in his brother's will of 1598. From 1563 until his death Stephen took on naval duties which increasingly tied him to work on the king's ships moored on the Medway between Rochester and Gillingham, and on the new dockyard facilities at Chatham, especially following a disastrous waterfront fire there on 4 August 1576. While this job overlapped with the formal duties of the elder brethren of Trinity House, any implicit conflict was amicably resolved with his election as a much respected master of Trinity House in 1572. Improvements he saw effected at Chatham included the acquisition of Upnor Castle for the specialized local storage of naval ordnance in 1568, the acquisition of land, plus the planning and construction of a massive store finished in 1580 with a new wharf alongside and a ropery 380 feet long completed in 1586. Fear that the complex was vulnerable to naval raids led to the insertion of defensive stakes in St Mary's Channel in 1574 and to the planning of a heavy chain barrier costing £250 deployed over two huge wheels, five lighters, and some smaller pinnaces, which had cost a further £360 to commission by January 1586. His responsibilities for twenty-nine berths for warships and the associated dockyard facilities all appear on an anonymous map of Chatham, perhaps drawn by him in 1584 (BL, Cotton MS Augustus I.i.52), showing the moorings for the whole fleet in ordinary.

Stephen Borough's advancement in 1572 to be master of Trinity House marks the point whereat his brother took over the responsibilities of the Muscovy Company's chief pilot, notably for shipping on the dangerous North Cape route. Stephen's duties at Trinity House entailed responsibility for organizing coastal pilotage and giving advice about which ships to accept into naval service. His status there conferred opportunities to promote improvements in navigational instruction with Richard Hakluyt. Hakluyt published his advice, along with more from Dee, about the conduct of voyages past the North Cape in *Principall Navigations* in 1589, and Borough's 'Instructions given to the masters and mariners of the ships of the Muscovie Companie, sayling towards the Bay of St Nicholas' of 3 May 1557 in the 1598 edition of *Principal Navigations*. Closely derived from Borough's experience is BL, Harley MS 167/2, mostly in one hand, comprising navigational instruction and diagrams, English translations made in 1578 of Spanish rutters for routes to Brazil, the Caribbean, and Mediterranean ports, and 'Borough's rules' for the passage from Orfordness, past the North Cape, to Russia's northernmost seaports.

Death and burial Borough died on 12 July 1584 at Chatham where he was buried the following day at St Mary's. An engraved Elizabethan brass placed on his tomb in the chancel reads thus:

> He in his lifetime discovered Moscovia, by the northern sea pasage to St Nicholas, in the yere 1553. At his setting forth of England he was accompanied in his ship by Sir Hugh Willoughbie, being Admirell of the fleete, who, with all the company of the said two shippes, were frozen to death in Lappia the same winter. After his discoverie of Roosia and the costes adjoyning to wit Lappia, Nova Zembla, and the cuntry of Samoyeda etc: he frequented the trade to St Nicholas yearlie, as chief pilot for the voyages, until he was chosen one of the four principal Masters in ordinarie of the Queen's Majesties royall Navy, where in he continued in charge of sundrie sea services till time of his death. (memorial brass)

R. C. D. Baldwin

Sources R. Hakluyt, *The principall navigations, voiages and discoveries of the English nation* (1589), 265–90, 311–33, 385–97, 406–7 • R. Hakluyt, *The principal navigations, voyages, traffiques and discoveries of the English nation*, 2nd edn, 1 (1598), 230, 232, 267, 283, 295 • J. Thorpe, ed., *Registrum Roffense, or, A collection of antient records, charters and instruments … illustrating the ecclesiastical history and antiquities of the diocese and cathedral church of Rochester* (1769), 731 • will, PRO, PROB 11/92, sig. 89 [William Borough] • administration, PRO, PROB 6/1, fol. 58 [Elinor Borough] • J. Dee, 'Of riche and famous discoveries', BL, Cotton MS Vitellus C.vii, fol. 60v • PRO, E190/2/1; 4/1; 5/1; E190 90/11; E190/4/2; E190/5/1 • rent book, 1580–84, Drapers' Company, London, fol. 72 • preface, M. Cortés, *The arte of navigation*, trans. R. Eden (1561) • R. W. Cotton, 'Stephen Borough the navigator', *Report and Transactions of the Devonshire Association*, 12 (1880), 332–60 [see also note in vol. 13 (1881), p. 76] • W. Pengelly, 'Prince's *Worthies of Devon* and the *Dictionary of National Biography*', *Report and Transactions of the Devonshire Association*, 18 (1886), 269–369, esp. 337–40 • R. W. Cotton, 'Stephen Borough (1525–1584)', *Report and Transactions of the Devonshire Association*, 25 (1893), 87–9 • J. F. Chanter, 'Borough, or Burrough, in Northam and its inhabitants', *Report and Transactions of the Devonshire Association*, 58 (1926), 195–208 • D. W. Waters, *The art of navigation in England in Elizabethan and early Stuart times* (1958) • A. H. W. Robinson, *Marine cartography in Britain: a history of the sea chart to 1855* (1962) • J. L. Chester and G. J. Armytage, eds., *Allegations for marriage licences issued by the bishop of London*, 1, Harleian Society, 25 (1887), 26, 156 • T. S. Willan, *The early history of the Russia Company, 1553–1603* (1956), 166–73, 175–7, 179, 196–7, 200–01, 218, 220, 244, 251, 253, 260 • T. S. Willan, *The Muscovy merchants of 1555* (1953), 13, 32, 82 • M. Oppenheim, *A history of the administration of the Royal Navy* (1896) • *CSP col.*, 2.3, 12, 13, 266, 288 • G. G. Harris, *The Trinity House of Deptford, 1514–1660* (1969) • A. H. Johnson, *The history of the Worshipful Company of the Drapers of London*, 5 vols. (1914–22), vol. 2 • C. R. B. Barrett, *The Trinity House of Deptford Strond* (1893) • D. M. Loades, *The Tudor navy* (1992) • E. G. R. Taylor, *The mathematical practitioners of Tudor and Stuart England* (1954); repr. (1970) • E. G. R. Taylor, *The haven finding art: a history of navigation from Odysseus to Captain Cook*, new edn (1971) • PRO, SP 11/7/39 • memorial brass, St Mary's Church, Chatham, Kent

Archives BL, Cotton MS, Aug I.i.3 and I.i.52 • BL, Cotton MS, Otho EVIII, fols. 10–16 and 42 • BL, Harley MS 167/2 • BL, Lansdowne MSS 11/37 and 116, fols. 3–10

Borough, William (*bap.* **1536**, *d.* **1598**), explorer and naval administrator, was born at Borough House, Northam Burrows, Northam, Devon, to Walter Borough (1494–1548) and Mary (*née* Dough) and baptized on 18 August 1536 in St Mary's, Northam. His childhood experiences included voyages made with his elder brother, Stephen *Borough (1525–1584), under the command of their uncle John *Borough (*d.* 1570). William later wrote that 'my mind earnestly bent to the knowledge of Navigation and Hydrography from my youth'. Next he claimed that in May 1553:

> I was in the first voyage for discoverie of the partes of Russia, which began in Anno 1553 (being then sixteen yeeres of age). Also in yeere 1556 when the coasts of Samoed, and Novaya Zemlya with the straights of Viagatz were found out; and the yeere 1557 when the coast of Lappia and the Bay of St Nicholas were more perfectly discovered. (Hakluyt, 1598, 1.418)

The earliest extant chart signed 'W. Borough' is of the north-east Atlantic and dates from 1558, but only part of it survives in an atlas at Trinity College, Dublin (MS 1209/23). In the early 1560s John Dee taught Borough to draw and use 'paradoxall compasses' or circumpolar charts. Borough showed he had mastered this in drafting 'Necessary rules for a voyage to Pecharia, Bass Indiae and Cataye' for an expedition planned by the Muscovy Company for 1568. By 1568 he had produced at least two more charts of the Norwegian and Russian shores for atlases assembled by William Cecil. One is in BL, Royal MS 10 D3, fol. 124; the other is bound into a Saxton atlas at Hatfield. William succeeded his brother as chief pilot from 1572 to 1582. In 1580 he took a major part with Dee and Cecil in the briefing of Arthur Pet and Charles Jackman for their attempt on the north-east passage.

While his brother Stephen had persevered until 1571 with the North Cape route, William Borough exploited his increasing familiarity with an alternative route through the Baltic to Narva where the Eastland Company (unlike the Muscovy Company) allowed him to trade; in 1566 he adventured eleven numbered long cloths, two chests packed with haberdashery, and two barrels of sweet oil in the *Harry* of London. The same Drapers' Company records show he also carried a private adventure that way for Anthony Jenkinson in 1566. The dangerous passage along the Gulf of Finland past 'Lyfland' (Estonia) appears on his signed chart of the North Sea and Baltic (NMM, MS G215.1/5). His mission of 1574–5 had required him to set down alternative ways to and from Moscow from Narva and St Nicholas and 'with great care and diligence, true observations and notes and descriptions of countreys, Islands, coastes of the sea, and other things requisite to the artes of Navigation and Hydrographie' (Hakluyt, 1598, 1.418). Hakluyt adds an account of Borough's beating off six Danske (Danish) pirate ships near the Tuttee in the gulf, and the capture of their leader, Hans Snarke. Borough made a short deposition to the Muscovy Company, which was passed first to the privy council, about alderman William Bond's illicit trade to Narva in 1576. Hakluyt used it in the 1589 edition of *Principall Navigations* alongside Borough's advice to the whaling trade and 'to disuade the use of a trade to the Nave by way through Sweden'. The direct route to Moscow via Narva had already been abandoned in 1581.

Although Stephen Borough had been consulted about Martin Frobisher's plans for exploring a possible north-western passage to Cathay in 1574, his younger brother was reported by Michael Lok to be:

> not so well persuaded of the voyage, that he would enter his money therein; yet in respect of the service of his country, did take paynes to procure a master and many mariners for the ships; and gave good advice in the furniture of the ships; and did consent unto the opinion and mynde of the capitayn in the direction of the ships course in the voyage. (BL, Cotton MS Otho E.viii, fol. 42)

Exchequer records show that William Borough not only sold his own mariner's astrolabe to the venture in 1576 for £3 10*s.*, but that he also sold on a wooden cross-staff with a case for 13*s.* 4*d.* and several ruled-up charts, one of which survives as signed by him in 1576 (Hatfield House, Cecil papers/maps, CPM 69). This was used by Christopher Hall to navigate to Kodlunarn, off Baffin Island, in 1576, 1577, and 1578. In 1578 Borough allowed Lok to charter his new ship, *Judith* (100 tons), for £320 and took out an adventurer's stake of £25. Instructed by the privy council in 1579 to pursue debtors to the venture, Borough as its new treasurer took legal action against his predecessor, Lok, having him imprisoned in Newgate from November 1581 to May 1582.

Meanwhile Borough, who had kept to himself a version of Eden's translation of Taisnier's study of terrestrial magnetism and one of Pellegrine de Maricourt's *De magnete* of 1558, put them into print through John Kingston in 1581 in *A Discourse on the Variation of the Compasse*, reprinted in expanded form in 1585 and 1596. Apart from comments on Mercator's map and projection, Borough's published ideas were largely taken from Spanish teachers or his brother's thoughts. But his preface to the 1585 edition (sig. A3) advised it was 'inadvisable to be tied to Portugale or Spanish marine platts'. His academic and commercial ethics were criticized in cipher by Luke Ward during Edward Fenton's Atlantic voyage in November 1582: 'William Burrows is one who could fill his honeycombs with someone else's honey so far is he accustomed to feed French dogs while they bring in hares' (BL, Cotton MS Titus B.viii, fol. 44). The same year, and acting privately, Borough devised instructions to a potential colonial surveyor of Virginia, Thomas Bavin. In 1592 he was made an assistant of the Levant Company, having given them advice before their new charter was issued.

In 1580 Borough had escaped his difficult duties as treasurer to the Cathay Adventurers with the award of the post of comptroller of the queen's ships, which he shared initially with William Holstock at a salary of £100, plus allowances for two clerks and other expenses. Appointed with Benjamin Gonson as clerk of the queen's ships for life on 24 March 1582, he gained thereby a further annual income of £133 plus expenses. On 15 August 1582 he was asked, as clerk of the ships, to carry out a detailed survey of all naval ordnance, saltpetre, and powder in the hands of the officers of the ordnance. He would later identify the proportions and uses of three main types of ship and compile 'Tables of the prices and lengths of masts' (BL, Harley MS 306, fols. 20–21). He made the case for extensive timber shoring at Deptford on 19 June 1584. His appointment as warden of the Trinity House of Deptford Strond in 1581 was followed by service in 1585–6 as its master. From 6 November 1588 Borough was regularly consulted about naval estimates by the privy council; on 25 October 1597, for instance, he detailed victualling costs associated with taking 540 troops from St Valéry to assault Ostend. On 28 May 1598 the acts of the privy council approved payment to him of arrears of £1546 for 900 troops he had sent to Waterford. Until his resignation from naval office on 6 July 1598 he exerted a strong influence on naval procurement policy.

Borough's career as a naval administrator was not without controversy. He wrote in critical detail about the proposals of Sir John Hawkins and William Pett to refit and build ships for the navy in 1584, and criticized Sir William Wynter in 1587. Yet from 1582 onwards his advice appears gradually to have won the respect of Hawkins and the naval establishment, especially during 1588–9. Consequently his rejection of proposals to convoy ships from London to Bordeaux was not disputed in 1591–2. He also authoritatively resolved disputes with Hanse merchants over the suitability of different types of canvas for ship's sails in 1592, and other issues concerning the English monopoly of the supply of sails in 1596–8. His numerous technical contributions appear in the state papers; other survivals illustrate his compassion, including certificates of disability issued to seamen. His correspondence with Lord Burghley in 1595 and 1596 made the case for new fortifications at Plymouth. In the face of another Armada threat in 1596 he prepared two identical charts to show offshore sandbanks and tidal patterns from Goring to London, and the siltation that adversely affected the port of Rye and exploitation of the Rother valley's naval supplies. One of those charts earned him a commendation from the queen in November 1596.

Borough was unable to confine himself to official paperwork and writing. In June 1583 he was at sea acting as a comptroller of the navy in taking 'outragious sea rovers' and ten pirate ships into custody, and ensuring that all ten masters were hanged at Wapping. In December 1585 he took charge of a squadron sailing from Harwich to Flushing to view the newly garrisoned port and its readiness to support the earl of Leicester's army. In August 1586 he sailed to the Azores with Sir John Hawkins in the *Golden Lion*. In 1587 he sailed with Sir Francis Drake but was indicted for mutiny and cowardice. His response to Lord Burghley shows he was put in irons by Drake well before the crew's mutiny. His defence rested mainly on a chart he drew of the battle before Cadiz on 29 April 1587 showing the dangers of the station assigned to the *Golden Lion*. Duly acquitted, Borough was given the galley *Bonavolia* to patrol the Thames in 1588 lest invaders 'may come in at half tide' as his chart of the estuary shows. On 26 February 1589 he penned a strategic 'Discorse of what course were best should be taken for the resistance of the Spanish navy' (BL, Lansdowne MSS 52/40, 52/42, 52/43). A letter written from Chatham on 28 August shows he was occupied by 'the great business for the dispatch of Sir Martin Frobisher's ships to the sea … in commission for the late Portugayle voyage' (BL, Harley MS 6994/104). It mentions too the 'business' (ibid.) of 'getting a good wife'. This was 'Lady Jane Wentworth, widow' (*b.* *c.*1541), the third wife of Thomas, Lord Wentworth (*d.* 1584). The marriage took place on 8 September 1589 at St Dunstan's, Stepney.

On 31 October 1590 Borough received an anonymous letter threatening his life, which he countered by giving it to Lord Burghley. His continuing concern for his family's security is manifest in his will. He left his wife much more than the value of her own dowry, worth about £74 a year, assigning her rents from the White House at Mile End in Stepney and from another house in Tower Street, Rotherhithe. His will of 26 July 1598 mentions his first wife, Judith Jones, *née* Pike (*d.* *c.*1583), a widow of Stepney, whom he had married on 17 November 1571 and at whose side he was buried at St Dunstan's, Stepney; his son Walter, who would inherit £500; and his daughter, Mary, who could receive up to £2000 on marriage, and £60 a year before that. Borough had died at Stepney by 28 November 1598 when his will was proved. It shows his protestant faith, and that his pastoral concerns ranged from the poor of Stepney, granted £20, and the poor of Northam, also granted £20, to the victims of the *Swallow*'s loss. The will also provided for his brother's widow and her three surviving daughters. The brethren of Trinity House were remembered with £10 towards a dinner.

R. C. D. BALDWIN

Sources R. Hakluyt, *The principall navigations, voiages and discoveries of the English nation*, 1–2 (1589), 280–333, 385–97, 406–7, 425, 437–54, 487 • R. Hakluyt, *The principal navigations, voyages, traffiques and discoveries of the English nation*, 2nd edn, 1 (1598), 232, 363–8, 413–18, 435–7, 455–7 • parish register, St Mary's, Northam, North Devon Record Office, Barnstaple, no. 1 [baptism] • *APC*, *1580–98* • will, PRO, PROB 11/92, sig. 89 • D. W. Waters, *The art of navigation in England in Elizabethan and early Stuart times* (1958) • A. H. W. Robinson, *Marine cartography in Britain: a history of the sea chart to 1855* (1962) • J. L. Chester and G. J. Armytage, eds., *Allegations for marriage licences issued by the bishop of London*, 1, Harleian Society, 25 (1887), 50 • A. H. Johnson, *The history of the Worshipful Company of the Drapers of London*, 5 vols. (1914–22), vol. 2 • J. A. Williamson, *Sir John Hawkins: the time and the man* (1927) • T. S. Willan, *The early history of the Russia Company, 1553–1603* (1956) • T. S. Willan, *The Muscovy merchants of 1555* (1953) • R. A. Skelton and J. Summerson, *A description of maps and architectural drawings in the collection made by William Cecil, first Baron Burghley*, Roxburghe Club (1971), nos. 45, 121, 122 • D. Howse and J. Sanderson, *The sea chart* (1973), 38–9 • T. H. B. Symons, ed., *Meta Incognita: a discourse of discovery, Martin Frobisher's Arctic expeditions, 1576–1578* (1999) • E. G. R. Taylor, 'Instructions to a colonial surveyor in 1582', *Mariner's Mirror*, 37 (1951), 48–62 • E. G. R. Taylor, *The haven finding art: a history of navigation from Odysseus to Captain Cook*, new edn (1971) • M. Oppenheim, *A history of the administration of the Royal Navy* (1896) • *CSP col.*, vol. 2 • G. G. Harris, *The Trinity House of Deptford, 1514–1660* (1969) • PRO, SP 11; SP 12

Archives BL, Add. MSS 12505, fol. 241; 37999; 38823; 41140, fol. 193 • BL, chart of coast, Goring to London, with Ryrap and Goodwin and Thames shoals, Cotton Augustus 1.1., fol. 17 • BL, Cotton MS, Otho E.viii, fols. 43, 67–77 • BL, Cotton MS, Titus B.viii, fol. 44 • BL, plan of Dover harbour alterations, Cotton MS, Augustus, 1.1.7 • BL, Egerton MS 3048 • BL, Harley MSS, 306, fols. 20–21 and 6994/104 • BL, Lansdowne MSS, 10/3, fols. 132–4; 24, fol. 162; 31/76; 43/33; 52/39–42, 99/94; 116, fols. 3–10 • BL, Royal MS 10 D3, fol. 124 • Hatfield House, Hertfordshire, Cecil papers, maps, cat. nos. 45, 69, 121, 122 • LMA, property deed in Stepney in 1590, I/PHI/38 • Magd. Cam., Pepys MSS, 2503, fols. 745–7, and 2876, fol. 423 • NMM, chart of the Baltic, MS G215.1/5 • PRO, exchequer series, E 164/35, fols. 16–17 • PRO, MPF 318 formerly attached to SP 12/208/77 • TCD, MS part of a chart bound within George Legge's atlas, 1209/23

Wealth at death large cash and rental resources: will, PRO, PROB 11/92, fols. 229–30

Borrel, Andrée Raymonde (1919–1944). *See under* Women agents on active service in France (*act.* 1942–1945).

Borrell, Henry Perigal (1795–1851), numismatist, after learning business in London established himself as a trader at Smyrna, where he lived from 1818 until his death. He devoted much of his attention to the discovery of inedited Greek coins, in which he was remarkably successful. The results of his discoveries were given in papers contributed to the *Revue Numismatique*, the *Numismatic Chronicle*, and various German numismatic periodicals. In 1836 he published at Paris a 'Notice sur quelques médailles grecques des rois de Chypre'. His articles entitled 'Coins in Andeda in Pisida' and 'On the coins reading *OKOKLIEŌN*' were published in 1839 and 1841 respectively in the *Numismatic Chronicle*.

Borrell was an associate member of the Numismatic Society of London from 28 November 1839 until his death at the age of fifty-six, at Smyrna on 2 October 1851. His collection of coins, antiquities, and gems was sold by Sotheby and Wilkinson of London in 1851 and his numismatic library was sold at Sothebys on 28 February 1853.

[ANON.], *rev.* JOANNE POTIER

Sources *GM*, 2nd ser., 39 (1853), 324 · 'Proceedings of the Numismatic Society for 24 June, 1852', *Numismatic Chronicle*, 14 (1851–2) [death notice] · Boase, *Mod. Eng. biog.* · R. A. G. Carson and H. Pagan, *A history of the Royal Numismatic Society, 1836–1986* (1986), 79 [honorary members list] · private information (2004) [D. Whitehead]

Borrer, William (1781–1862), botanist, was born at Henfield, Sussex, on 13 June 1781, the eldest of the three sons of William Borrer of Hurstpierpoint, landowner and sometime high sheriff of Sussex, and his wife, Mary, daughter and coheir of Nathaniel Lindfield of Dean House. He received his early education in private schools, at Hurstpierpoint and at that run by John Morphew at Carshalton in Surrey. Although he left school at an early age he continued his studies under tutors and obtained a good knowledge of the classics, French, and theology.

In spite of his own inclination for medicine, Borrer joined in his father's farming business. At first this involved supplying forage to troops stationed around Sussex and for these journeys he travelled on horseback, examining and collecting the plants which he passed. Initially encouraged by some of the military officers, he became acquainted with many of the first botanists of the age, including Joseph Banks, Dawson Turner, and W. J. Hooker. He developed an extensive botanical correspondence in Britain and on the continent.

Borrer travelled widely in the study of plants, in 1810 visiting Scotland with Hooker, who was also his companion on an excursion to Normandy. He made repeated journeys in all parts of Britain, seeking out species reported in unlikely locations and always vigilant for new discoveries. He endeavoured to cultivate every critical British species and all the hardy exotic plants he could obtain, having at one time 6660 species in his garden. By planting species which were only with difficulty distinguished next to one another he made faithful determinations of their distinct qualities.

Borrer's herbarium of British plants, which went on his death to Kew Gardens, was esteemed as one of the best. It was especially rich in the flora of Sussex, which had received little prior attention. His specimens were very reliably named but often lacked date or locality. The comprehensiveness of the herbarium was attributed to Borrer's own application and his willingness to share his knowledge with others, who returned his kindness with specimens.

Borrer's first contribution to the literature was a comprehensive list of and critical notes on Sussex flowering plants, ferns, fungi, lichens, and algae which appeared in Turner and Dillwyn, *Botanist's Guide* (1805), along with some records for Kent, Surrey, and Hampshire. On his own, however, he published little: a few notices in the *Phytologist*; some descriptions in the supplement to *English Botany* (1830), especially of lichens, *Salix*, *Rosa*, and *Rubus*; and, with Dawson Turner, the privately printed

William Borrer (1781–1862), by Maull & Polyblank, *c.*1855

Lichenographia Britannica (1839). His method for the genus *Salix* was adopted by Hooker in *Flora Britannica* (1830), as were his descriptions of *Myosotis*, *Rosa*, and *Rubus*.

Borrer is credited with the identification of twenty-one species of flowering plants, which ranged in location from Cornwall to Caithness, and in addition worked on ferns, lichens, and algae and made several discoveries of rare seaweeds.

Expertise on British plants was Borrer's strongest recommendation: he was considered a reliable authority on the correctness of localities assigned to plants and a good judge of their claims as native productions. His work was characterized by precise description and meticulous detail. The want of a major publication associated with his name has, however, limited the subsequent recognition of his contemporary importance. He was elected a fellow of the Linnean Society in 1805, and of the Royal Society in 1835, and was also a member of the Wernerian Society. Several plants were named after him.

On 28 March 1810, Borrer married Elizabeth, the daughter of Nathaniel Hall, a banker in Brighton. They had five daughters and three sons who survived to adulthood. He served as a justice of the peace for Sussex. While never gregarious, Borrer always welcomed without introduction those who wished to consult his herbarium or garden. He also made many charitable contributions to his community, especially in the development of schools. He helped to establish national schools in Henfield, built a school for girls and one for infants on his own land, and personally undertook the education of three or four boys, subsequently finding them employment. He was active in and generous to the local church.

Borrer's personal fortune made it possible for him to devote his time to those things which interested him. However, in botany, his gentlemanly amateurism was enhanced by application, attention to detail, and precision. He was both zealous and able. He died at his home, Barrow Hill, Henfield, on 10 January 1862 from pleurisy, having been in failing health for a decade. P. E. KELL

Sources *Proceedings of the Linnean Society of London* (1860–62), lxxxv–xc · *GM*, 3rd ser., 12 (1862), 372–4 · *PRS*, 12 (1862–3), xlii · *Journal of Botany, British and Foreign*, 1 (1863), 31–2 · *Phytologist*, 6 (1863), 70–83 · M. A. Lower, *The worthies of Sussex* (1865), 71–3 · A. H. Wolley Dod, *Flora of Sussex* (1937), xl · H. C. P. Smail, 'William Borrer of Henfield', *Watsonia*, 10 (1974), 55–60 · J. C. Loudon, 'Notes on the Brighton and Shoreham gardens', *Floricultural Cabinet & Florist's Magazine*, 14 (Nov 1838), 497–503

Archives Linn. Soc., notes · RBG Kew, corresp. and papers · U. Cam., department of plant sciences, papers | Linn. Soc., corresp. with Sir James E. Smith · NHM, letters to members of the Sowerby family · RBG Kew, corresp. with Sir William Hooker; corresp. with Richard Spruce

Likenesses Maull & Polyblank, photograph, *c*.1855, NPG [*see illus.*] · J. Pannett, drawing (after photograph of portrait, 1847), repro. in Smail, 'William Borrer of Henfield' · portraits, RBG Kew · portraits, Carnegie Mellon University, Pittsburgh, Pennsylvania, Hunt Library

Wealth at death under £70,000: probate, 20 March 1862, *CGPLA Eng. & Wales*

Borrow, George Henry (1803–1881), writer and traveller, was born on 5 July 1803 at East Dereham in Norfolk, the son of Captain Thomas Borrow (1758–1824), adjutant of the West Norfolk militia, and his wife, Ann (1772–1858), daughter of Samuel Parfrement, a farmer. His elder brother was John Thomas Borrow.

The Napoleonic wars ensured that the family put down no roots. The West Norfolks were posted up and down the country, and even after Waterloo saw service in Ireland. Borrow's schooling was sporadic: a year at the high school in Edinburgh in 1813–14 and another at Norwich grammar school in 1814–15 represented his longest continuous periods of education until, in May 1816, the family at last settled in Norwich.

Borrow returned to Norwich grammar school, but in March 1819 he was articled to a firm of solicitors. He did not apply himself to the law, preferring to visit the Gypsies on Mousehold Heath and to study a variety of languages. One of his tutors was William Taylor, Norwich's foremost intellectual and iconoclast, who turned Borrow's thoughts to the literary field. Borrow also showed signs of being fired by Taylor's radicalism, but that did not last. Translations by Borrow—from German, Swedish, Danish, Dutch, and Spanish—started appearing in Sir Richard Phillips's *Monthly Magazine*, and he longed to live by his pen. Two days after his articles expired, and a month after his father's death, he took the coach to London on 1 April 1824. When it became obvious that there would be no other employment than ill-paid hack work for Phillips, the depression from which he had suffered intermittently since childhood returned to plague him. His main task, under Phillips's direction, was to compile

George Henry Borrow (1803–1881), by Henry Wyndham Phillips, 1843 [replica]

Celebrated Trials (6 vols., 1825). He also contributed to Phillips's periodicals and brought out a translation of Klinger's *Faustus* (1825); but a year in Grub Street convinced him that he must escape from London. In *Lavengro*, he would describe writing *The Life and Adventures of Joseph Sell, the Great Traveller* in order to find enough money to do so. None of the attempted identifications of this claimed work has proved valid.

Then came several obscure years, the first few months of which were treated with a liberal seasoning of imagination in *Lavengro* and *The Romany Rye*. Whether there was, in life, someone as important to Borrow as Isopel Berners was to Lavengro is an unsolved puzzle. For the most part Borrow drifted along, alternating between Norwich and London. Much time was spent fruitlessly on translations; only his *Romantic Ballads, Translated from the Danish* appeared in print (1826). Stories of extensive foreign travel must be heavily discounted. Borrow was almost thirty before he found, in 1833, employment with the British and Foreign Bible Society. In maturity, he always expressed allegiance to the Church of England, and a strong antipathy for Roman Catholicism: but in introducing him to the Bible Society, his sponsor said Borrow was 'of no very exactly defined denomination of Christians'. Borrow impressed the society not just by his appearance—he was an imposing 6 foot 3 inches, with prematurely grey hair—but by his linguistic capacities. They sent him to St Petersburg (1833–5) to oversee the printing of a Manchu version of the New Testament, and then to

Portugal and Spain (1835–40) to distribute the scriptures. In Russia and the Peninsula Borrow worked energetically, and sometimes heroically, on the society's behalf. In Spain, civil war made his expeditions risky, while the hostile attitude of the authorities, coupled with his own provocative approach, led twice to his imprisonment. He was still able to pursue his linguistic and translating interests. In St Petersburg he produced *Targum*, a volume of translations from thirty languages, and *The Talisman … with other Pieces*, from Russian and Polish (both 1835). In Madrid the Bible Society financed the printing of St Luke's gospel translated into Spanish Romani by Borrow and Gypsy friends, and also a Basque version, where Borrow's editorial role was minor (both 1838).

By the time his last Spanish tour began, it was clear that Borrow's future with the Bible Society was limited. Increasingly he concerned himself with his own affairs, completing the groundwork for a few books, and thinking up new territory to explore. In mid-1839 he was joined, in the large house he rented in Seville, by a 43-year-old widow and her 21-year-old daughter, Mary and Henrietta Clarke, with whom he had become acquainted shortly before entering the Bible Society's service. Mary Clarke needed to escape from family litigation at home; but all along, she seems quietly to have taken the initiative with Borrow. When he at last complied with the Bible Society's recall, he sailed in the company of the Clarkes. Three weeks later, on 23 April 1840, he married Mary Clarke in London.

Borrow settled on his wife's little estate on the shores of Oulton Broad in Suffolk and began turning his experiences to literary account. After a modest start with *The Zincali* (2 vols., 1841), a book about the Gypsies of Spain and elsewhere, he had a runaway success in 1843 with *The Bible in Spain* (3 vols.), a stirring account of his adventures in the Peninsula which also satisfied the evangelical temper of the 1840s. He then turned to his earlier life, gradually discovering that he had to transform reality into his own apprehension of the truth. He had set himself a standard of unusual incident which was difficult to maintain, and had dropped hints of further adventures which he was ill placed to substantiate. In 1844, dogged by low spirits, he embarked on his last foreign journey, a solitary expedition across Europe to Constantinople, seeking to compose his mind and find new material. Relief was no more than partial and temporary. In the end, he fashioned two books which followed episodically, from birth to early manhood, the fortunes of a complex character (not necessarily always himself as he was or had been), with much satirical comment on society and religion. Only by stopping in mid-narrative was he able to send the part he called *Lavengro* to John Murray, his impatient publisher. When it appeared in 1851, its intermingling of imagination and reality puzzled many readers and irritated others. The sequel, *The Romany Rye* (1857), seemed an even greater mystification.

In 1853 Borrow moved to Great Yarmouth with his wife and stepdaughter, without abandoning their home at Oulton. The Yarmouth years were punctuated by walking tours in which he covered many hundreds of miles in Norfolk, Cornwall, Wales, the Isle of Man, Scotland, and Ireland. From one of them *Wild Wales* emerged (1862)—a classic on Wales and the Welsh, seen through the eyes of a very unusual Englishman. At the same time he completed *Celtic Bards, Chiefs and Kings*, published in 1928, long after his death. He also published a translation of Ellis Wynne's *The Sleeping Bard* in 1860 just before he moved to London, where he did little writing apart from working at translations and the like. After his wife died in 1869, there were few people to turn to for company, and a proposal of marriage to Lucy Brightwell, a Norwich friend from childhood, was declined. He delivered his swansong, *Romano Lavo-Lil*, to Murray and went back to East Anglia—'to die', he said. The book, published in 1874, was poorly received by the new generation of Romani scholars who were following the trail he had blazed. It was the only one of his principal works to make no money during his lifetime; his income from the others amounted to £3366 over forty years.

Borrow died at Oulton on 26 July 1881 (of 'decay of nature' according to his death certificate) and was buried beside his wife in Brompton cemetery. His reputation had long been in decline, but revived towards the close of the nineteenth century. Borrow's bibliography is swelled by articles, reviews, compilations, and, above all, his beloved translations: but his enduring legacy was a handful of original works unlike any others, episodic narratives capturing the imagination with strange and at times superbly presented characters and powerful picaresque sketches. Pervading them all is the opinionated but compelling personality of their narrator. ANGUS FRASER

Sources M. Collie and A. Fraser, *George Borrow: a bibliographical study* (1984) • W. I. Knapp, *Life, writings and correspondence of George Borrow*, 2 vols. (1899) • A. Fraser, 'The unveiling of the veiled period', *Proceedings of the 1987 George Borrow Conference* [Cambridge 1987], ed. G. Fenwick (1988), 1–13 • A. Fraser, 'On the fringes of the George Borrow canon', *George Borrow Bulletin*, 8 (1994) • G. Borrow, *Letters to John Hasfeld, 1835–1839*, ed. A. M. Fraser (1982) • G. Borrow, *Letters to John Hasfeld, 1841–1846*, ed. A. M. Fraser (1984) • A. Fraser, 'George Borrow and Lucy Brightwell', *N&Q*, 220 (1975), 109–11 • parish register (baptism), Norfolk, East Dereham, 17 July 1803 • d. cert.

Archives Ransom HRC • York University, Toronto | BL, Ashley collection • CUL, British and Foreign Bible Society archive • Hispanic Society of America, New York, Knapp collection • Hunt L. • John Murray, London • National Library of Russia, St Petersburg, Tikhanov collection • Norfolk RO • NYPL, Berg collection • PRO • Rutgers University, New Brunswick, papers • Trinity Cam. • U. Leeds, Brotherton L. • University of Kentucky, Lexington

Likenesses J. Borrow, oils, *c*.1824, NPG • life mask, *c*.1824, Castle Museum, Norwich • H. W. Phillips, oils (after his oil painting, 1843), John Murray Publishers, London [*see illus.*] • H. W. Phillips, oils, second version, NPG • photograph, priv. coll.

Wealth at death £519 13*s*. 4*d*.: probate, 31 Oct 1881, *CGPLA Eng. & Wales*

Borsselaer [Bustler], **Pieter** (*fl.* 1664–1687), portrait painter, was most likely of a Dutch burger family of that name long established in Zeeland, the Netherlands. From the fifteenth century onwards members of the family are recorded serving as regents, sheriffs, burgermasters, and taxation clerks in the towns of Middelburg and Goes. Two possible identifications of the artist have been suggested: the Pieter Borsselaer, dissenter, who married Maria Bijsterman in Goes town hall on 24 May 1644; or the Pieter Borsselaer, painter, presumably of a younger generation than the above, who in 1717 recorded his coat of arms, among others, in the privilege book of the Guild of St Luke at Middelburg (until 1940 in the Stedelijke Oudheidkamer of the town hall), of which he was a member from 1716 to 1731.

Borsselaer pursued his early career in England. Nothing is known about his training, or when he arrived in England. Buckeridge, who calls him Bustler and whose information is repeated by Walpole, calls him a history and face painter and refers to a picture of three boors, owned by Mr Elsum of the Temple, a collaborative work by Borsselaer (the figures), Prosper Henry Lankrink (the landscape background), and Abraham Hondius (a 'little Dog to one side'; Buckeridge, 405). Only portraits are known to survive from his English period; these are painted in a distinctive manner closest to that of Gerard Soest but sometimes employing weak perspective. Characteristic of his work is a direct, uncompromising treatment of appearance and character, and the use of particular shades, notably a leaf brown, plum red, and silvery grey. His *Portrait of a Widow* (Rijksmuseum, Amsterdam), signed and dated 1664, is his earliest dated portrait. Bought on the London art market in 1909, it most likely represents Mary Pakington, Lady Yate, related to the staunchly Roman Catholic Throckmorton family of Coughton Court, Warwickshire. A version of the portrait is at Coughton. In 1665 he signed and dated a portrait of the eminent antiquarian and herald Sir William Dugdale (priv. coll.), a powerful and expressive image of the ageing scholar, which has as its pendant a portrait of Lady Dugdale. Possibly dateable to around these years is his portrait (now lost) of the Dutch naval hero Cornelis Evertsen the elder (Evertsen was in England in 1664–5), known through an engraving by Arnold de Jode. Staring suggests an acquaintance between Borsselaer and the Evertsen family, further borne out by a portrait of Evertsen the younger, attributed to Borsselaer, formerly at Middelburg town hall (no longer extant). A significant group of portraits, of members of the Hoby family and other figures, was until recently at Bisham Abbey, Berkshire, but is now partially dispersed. Two of the best, old *Sir Peregrine Hoby* and his wife, *Catherine Dodington*, were sold at Christies on 20 April 1990, while *Catherine of Braganza* and the less good *Charles II*, both inscribed on the reverse 'Peter Burlser, f.', are among those by him remaining at Bisham. It was Borsselaer's practice to make numerous copies of his portraits, especially of well-known sitters, which vary in quality. Several versions of his *Sir Orlando Bridgeman* (created lord keeper in 1667) are known, the earliest probably that formerly at Bisham; others are at Chirk Castle and Weston Park. The attribution to him of the posthumous 'Chesterfield' portrait of Shakespeare (Shakespeare's Birthplace Trust, Stratford upon Avon) is probably correct, as is his authorship of *Samuel Butler* (NPG). One of his latest English portraits is *Admiral Cornelis Van Tromp* (Antony, Cornwall), commissioned by Ambrose Elton in 1675, 'whoe was with him [van Tromp] all the time it was doinge' (these details inscribed on the portrait). Elton's own portrait, by Borsselaer, is at Clevedon Court, Somerset.

So far as Borsselaer's *œuvre* can be reconstructed, his patrons seem for the most part to have been either staunch royalists or Roman Catholics. Borsselaer was probably a Roman Catholic too, and identifiable as the 'Petrus Bustler, Lymnr', of St Peter-le-Poer, Broad Street, in London, indicted for recusancy in 1673, and again in 1678 and 1679, but on the latter two occasions styled 'generosus' of St Gregory's (Bowler, 221, 238). The difficult political and religious climate probably impelled him to leave the country in 1679, or soon after. He is possibly the 'Monsr van Borssele' living in The Hague, at Kleinen Blaesbalch, in 1681, who in October of that year is recorded, with the portrait painter Isaac Paling, paying his membership of the Confrerie Pictura there. His *Five Regents of the Middelburg House of Correction* (Rijksmuseum, Amsterdam; on loan to the Rijksdienst Beeldende Kunst, The Hague) is signed and dated 1683 (the '8' slightly indistinct); and in 1684 and 1687 payments to him are recorded in the Middelburg town archives for two allegorical chimney-pieces for the treasury chamber of Middelburg town hall (des. 1940). Painted on plaster, they celebrated the town's international trade with representations of the Four Continents, Religion, Freedom, and Justice. TABITHA BARBER

Sources A. Staring, 'Weinig bekende portrettisten: Pieter Borsselaer', *Oud Holland*, 51 (1946), 33–42; repr. in *Kunsthistorische Verkenningen* (The Hague, 1948), 37–46 · C. H. Collins Baker, 'Pieter Borsseler: a forgotten seventeenth-century master', *The Connoisseur*, 54 (Sept 1922), 5–15 · [B. Buckeridge], 'An essay towards an English school of painters', in R. de Piles, *The art of painting, and the lives of the painters* (1706), 398–480, esp. 405 · H. Walpole, *Anecdotes of painting in England: with some account of the principal artists*, ed. R. N. Wornum, new edn, 3 vols. (1888), vol. 2, pp. 107–8 · H. Bowler, ed., *London sessions records, 1605–1685*, Catholic RS, 34 (1934), 157, 212, 221, 238 · F. D. Obreen, *Archief voor nederlandsche kunstgeschiednis* (Rotterdam, 1877–90), vol. 2, p. 158; vol. 4, p. 115 · E. Waterhouse, *Painting in Britain, 1530–1790*, 4th edn (1978); repr. (1988), 110, n. 32, 344 · O. Millar, *The age of Charles II* (1960), nos. 232, 470–71, 478 [exhibition catalogue, RA, 1960] · M. Whinney and O. Millar, *English art, 1625–1714* (1957), 184

Borstale, Thomas (*supp. fl.* 1290), supposed Augustinian hermit, is said by Bale to have come from Norfolk and to have studied in England, and taught theology at the University of Paris *c.*1290. Bale adds that Borstale died at the Augustinian convent in Norwich and was buried there; he notes further that Borstale was among the earliest masters in Paris of his order, which would certainly be true if Borstale was indeed a teacher there; the first Augustinian master, Giles of Rome, held his chair from 1285 to 1291. Bale says that he is basing himself on 'the chronicles of the Augustinians', and Bale did have access to some early Augustinian chronicles now lost. Yet Bale's account, followed uncritically by those historians who have noted Borstale's existence, appears to be entirely unsupported by any surviving early evidence, either among the Augustinians' records, or those of the University of Paris—a very strange circumstance if Borstale had the important status of master of theology. Bale attributes to him a commentary on Peter Lombard's *Sentences* (which would have been part of the requirements for becoming a master of theology), and the regular and quodlibetal disputations that would have been part of the teaching of most masters of theology. No copies survive or are recorded.

JOHN MARENBON

Sources Bale, *Cat.*, 1.345 • F. X. Roth, *Sources for a history of the English Austin friars* [1958–61] • F. X. Roth, 'A history of the English Austin friars: sources and literature', *Augustiniana: Tijdschrift voor de Studie van Sint Augustinus en de Augustijnenorde*, 8 (1958), 22–47 • P. Glorieux, *Répertoire des maîtres en théologie de Paris au XIIIe siècle*, 2 (Paris, 1934)

Borthwick family (*per.* c.**1400**–c.**1515**), landowners and administrators, provided some significant servants to the Scottish crown, especially in the second half of the fifteenth century. There are problems in constructing this family's genealogy, as between *c*.1370 and 1544 all the heads of the family bore the Christian name William and before 1500 it is difficult to distinguish between them. The successful petition to the lord Lyon king of arms in the case of John Henry Stuart Borthwick of that ilk to succeed as Lord Borthwick, conducted in 1984–6, altered the previously accepted enumeration of the lords Borthwick by amalgamating the putative first and second lords.

Sir William Borthwick of that ilk (*c*.1385–*c*.1449) was the son of another Sir William Borthwick (*d*. 1429), who, through his particular service to Archibald, fourth earl of Douglas, had brought the family into contact with the royal court. The name of the father's spouse is not recorded. Before the return of King James I from captivity in England in 1424 the younger William was briefly captain of Edinburgh Castle (whose keeper was the earl of Douglas). The accounts of the custumars of Edinburgh show that for some years up to 1420 Borthwick (and others) were abusing their power to seize moneys due to be paid to the crown, and were exporting goods without paying custom. The death of his mentor seems to have resulted in Borthwick's seeking crown patronage instead. He was knighted *c*.1424 and in June 1425 was (with nine others) appointed as ambassador from Scotland to Rome. (The purpose of the embassy may have been to discuss the export of money by Scottish clerics to purchase benefices from the papacy.) While he was in Rome, his father was in England as one of the hostages for the ransom demanded for the king's release. In June 1430 the younger Sir William obtained from James I a licence to build at the mote of Locherworth what became Borthwick Castle, Edinburghshire, which is certainly a building of that period. In 1436–7 Sir David Hay of Yester, whose family had property rights at Locherworth, recorded protests about Borthwick's possession of the mote, but a settlement must have been reached. Sir William, who died about 1449, is stated to have married *c*.1411 Beatrice, possibly daughter of Henry Sinclair, first earl of Orkney. They had at least one son and one daughter.

Their son **William Borthwick**, first Lord Borthwick (*c*.1412–1483), was knighted at the baptism of the infant James II in October 1430. He was created Lord Borthwick in June 1452, a time when James II was anxious to ensure that he had sufficient allies immediately after the stabbing to death of William, eighth earl of Douglas, at whom the king himself had struck the first blow. Borthwick occasionally witnessed crown charters in the next few years and was ambassador during truce negotiations with England. He was regularly present at parliament, however, where he acted as a lord auditor of causes (legal disputes); and he performed in a similar capacity as a lord of the king's council. From mid-1482 he was a frequent witness of crown charters until his death in December 1483. Although he may have married twice, no spouse's name is known. (The peerage petition of 1984–6 was inaccurate in stating that his second wife was Marion Hoppringle.) He had five sons and one daughter, but it is not clear who was the mother of any of the children. His eldest son (who had been knighted by 1468), **William Borthwick**, second Lord Borthwick (*c*.1428–1503), immediately succeeded his father as a witness of crown charters, lord auditor of causes, and lord of council. He was for a time master of the king's household and remained loyal to James III apparently right up to the king's death on the battlefield of Sauchieburn (11 June 1488) during James's conflict with his son and heir. After the accession of James IV, Borthwick was seldom a witness of crown charters, but remained a regular lord auditor and lord of council. By this stage, if not earlier, the family possessed land in Selkirkshire, Peeblesshire, Berwickshire, Aberdeenshire, Edinburgh, and Edinburghshire, where its principal estate lay. The second Lord Borthwick died on 30 April 1503; his spouse's name is not known. The couple seem to have had three sons and perhaps five daughters. The eldest son succeeded as **William Borthwick**, third Lord Borthwick (*c*.1460–1513?). Like his father, he was frequently a lord auditor and lord of council, but was not a witness of crown charters. He was apparently killed at the battle of Flodden, on 9 September 1513. He had married Margaret, daughter of John *Hay, Lord Hay of Yester, about 1491. They had at least one son, William *Borthwick, who succeeded to his father's title. Although the family was not represented constantly at court, from 1450 its heads undertook frequent duties at parliament and council as auditors of causes, and were also often ambassadors.

ALAN R. BORTHWICK

Sources J. M. Thomson and others, eds., *Registrum magni sigilli regum Scotorum / The register of the great seal of Scotland*, 11 vols. (1882–1914), vols. 1–2 • *APS*, esp. 1424–1567 • G. Burnett and others, eds., *The exchequer rolls of Scotland*, 23 vols. (1878–1908) • [T. Thomson] and others, eds., *The acts of the lords of council in civil causes, 1478–1503*, 3 vols. (1839–1993) • [T. Thomson], ed., *The acts of the lords auditors of causes and complaints*, AD *1466–*AD *1494*, RC, 40 (1839) • various collections of manuscript estate and other papers in archive offices and in private hands in Scotland and in England • *CDS*, vol. 4 • *RotS*, vol. 2 • Borthwick of Borthwick muniments, NA Scot., GD 350 • F. McGurk, ed., *Calendar of papal letters to Scotland of Benedict XIII of Avignon, 1394–1419*, Scottish History Society, 4th ser., 13 (1976) • *Scots peerage*, 2.94–109 • G. Crawfurd, *The peerage of Scotland: containing an historical and genealogical account of the nobility of that kingdom* (privately printed, Edinburgh, 1716) • *Minutes of the evidence given before the committee of privileges to whom the petition of Archibald Borthwick, esq. claiming the title and dignity of Lord Borthwick was referred* (1812–14) [repr. (1869)] • NA Scot., C39/1/11 • M. Brown, *The Black Douglases: war*

and lordship in late medieval Scotland, 1300–1455 (1998) • A. Grant, 'Acts of lordship: the records of Archibald, fourth earl of Douglas', *Freedom and authority: Scotland, c.1050–c.1650*, ed. T. Brotherstone and D. Ditchburn (2000)
Archives NA Scot., GD 350

Borthwick, Algernon, **Baron Glenesk** (**1830–1908**), newspaper proprietor, born at Cambridge on 27 December 1830, was the elder son in the family of two sons and a daughter of Peter *Borthwick, who belonged to a Midlothian branch of the ancient Borthwick family of Selkirkshire, and his wife, Margaret (*d.* 1864), daughter of John Colville of Ewart, Northumberland. After education at a school in Paris and at King's College School, London, Borthwick was sent to Paris in September 1850, before he was twenty, as foreign correspondent of the *Morning Post*, of which his father had just become editor. The paper's finances were in poor shape; Borthwick's work was supervised by his father but he soon showed himself to be a resourceful journalist. He reported the *coup d'état* of 1851 and gained access to Napoleon III. He was reported to be in the pay of the French government; even so, he gained the approval of Lord Palmerston, with whose career the *Morning Post* had become closely associated.

On Peter Borthwick's death in December 1852, J. W. Crompton, the owner of the *Morning Post*, appointed Algernon Borthwick, then aged twenty-two, his father's successor as editor. Borthwick continued his father's Palmerstonian editorial line. When Palmerston died, the paper eulogized him as 'the staunchest Conservative in the kingdom' (*Morning Post*, 19 Oct 1865). T. H. S. Escott noted how, under both the Borthwicks, the paper 'mirrored … the prejudices of the Conservative voters who kept a nominally Liberal premier, Lord Palmerston, in office' (Koss, 81). The Turkish ambassador observed that on foreign policy 'The *Post* is Borthwick and Borthwick is Palmerston' (Lucas, 241). Borthwick differed from Palmerston in religion, being influenced by the Tractarians, and to an extent from his father on the economy, for he strongly supported the 1860 free-trade treaty with France. As editor, Borthwick made the *Post* less a journal of fashion and more a paper with news—especially political, military, theatrical, and sporting news. But the paper was even more conservative in its layout than its contemporaries. In 1872 Borthwick appointed Sir William Hardman (*d.* 1890) as the editor in daily charge, and in 1876 he was able to buy the ownership of the paper from W. J. Rideout. In 1881 he reduced the price to 1*d.*, belatedly recognizing the threat posed by the *Daily Telegraph*, then swiftly moving from Liberalism to Conservatism. The *Post* found itself battling with the *Telegraph* for the jingo vote. Borthwick supported fair trade in the 1880s and protection in the 1900s. Side by side with his editorship of the *Post*, in 1864 Borthwick and three friends—Evelyn Ashley, Lord Wharncliffe, and James Stuart Wortley—launched *The Owl*, a society periodical that published fictitious statements by politicians, the names of those about to become engaged, and the like. Borthwick let *The Owl* expire when he decided himself to become engaged.

Algernon Borthwick, Baron Glenesk (1830–1908), by W. & D. Downey, pubd 1891

On 5 April 1870 Borthwick married Alice Beatrice, younger daughter of Thomas Henry *Lister of Armitage Park, Staffordshire, and his wife, Lady Maria Theresa [*see* Lewis, Lady (Maria) Theresa]. Alice's elder sister, Maria Theresa (*d.* 1863), had been the first wife of Sir William Harcourt, with whom Borthwick became a close friend despite their political differences. Alice Borthwick was often ill (though with no clearly diagnosed disease) and spent much of her time abroad, sometimes publishing letters in the *Post* describing her social experiences. When at home she was a lively hostess; the Borthwicks lived in Eaton Place, London, from 1871 to 1884, then at 139 Piccadilly, and from 1886 also at Phyllis Court, Hampstead Heath. They rented the estate of Invercauld and Glen Muick in Scotland, near Balmoral, where they became friendly with Queen Victoria; they also owned the Château St Michel at Cannes.

Alice Borthwick encouraged her husband in his decision to give up daily editing of the *Post*, and to enter politics, preferably as a Liberal (her family was whiggish). In the 1880 general election he stood unsuccessfully for Evesham as a Conservative. Disraeli gave him a knighthood in his resignation honours in April 1880. Borthwick subsequently played a part in popularizing the Primrose League. In 1885 he was elected for South Kensington as a Conservative, and held the seat until becoming a peer in

1895. He associated himself with Lord Randolph Churchill, an alliance that almost guaranteed a career on the back benches. He was not a notable member of the Commons, but in 1888 he carried a measure amending the libel laws to the advantage of newspaper editors. In 1887 he was created a baronet and in 1895, on Lord Salisbury's recommendation, Baron Glenesk, at which time he made over control of the *Morning Post* to his only son, Oliver Andrew. Borthwick was the first newspaper proprietor to be given a peerage. Lady Glenesk died of peritonitis at Cannes in 1898. Oliver Borthwick (*b.* 1873) died on 23 March 1905. Glenesk, aged seventy-five, resumed control of the paper until a month before his death. He arranged that after his death it and the rest of his property would pass to his daughter, Lilias Margaret Frances [*see* Bathurst, Lilias Margaret Frances, Countess Bathurst], who in 1893 had married Seymour Henry Bathurst, seventh Earl Bathurst.

Glenesk thus faced his final years in isolation. In his youth he had been a society figure, with many friends in the theatrical world, and a prominent member of the Garrick Club. Beyond his political career, he had been publicly active as president of the Newspaper Press Fund from 1885, and as a generous supporter of the Newspaper Benevolent Association, the Press Club, the Institute of Journalists, and the Gallery lodge of freemasons. His final years were cheerless. He liked to spend the autumn at Blelack in Aberdeenshire meeting old cronies. In October 1908 he caught a cold there, travelled south, and died of heart failure at 139 Piccadilly, London, on 24 November 1908; he was buried near his wife in St Marylebone cemetery, East Finchley. His peerage became extinct.

H. C. G. MATTHEW

Sources R. Lucas, *Lord Glenesk and the Morning Post* (1910) • S. E. Koss, *The rise and fall of the political press in Britain*, 1 (1981) • W. Hindle, *The Morning Post, 1772–1937: portrait of a newspaper* (1937) • T. H. S. Escott, *Masters of English journalism* (1911)

Archives U. Leeds, Brotherton L., personal and family papers, incl. records of the *Morning Post* | Bodl. Oxf., letters to Lord Beaconsfield • CAC Cam., letters to Lord Randolph Churchill • U. Leeds, Brotherton L., corresp. with Lord Bathurst

Likenesses C. Pellegrini, oils, *c.*1885 • Ape [C. Pellegrini], chromolithograph caricature, NPG; repro. in *VF* (17 June 1871) • W. & D. Downey, woodburytype, NPG; repro. in W. Downey and D. Downey, *The cabinet portrait gallery*, 2 (1891) [*see illus.*] • H. Furniss, pen-and-ink caricature, NPG • B. Stone, photograph, NPG • Walery, photograph, NPG

Wealth at death £400,232 1s. 1d.: probate, 14 Jan 1909, *CGPLA Eng. & Wales*

Borthwick, David (*d.* 1581), lawyer, was the eldest son of the Haddington burgess David Borthwick. A determinant at St Leonard's College, St Andrews, in 1525, he became a burgess of Haddington in July 1531 and within months was one of the bailies of the burgh. He accompanied James V to France in 1536 in the train of the royal secretary, Sir Thomas Erskine, and was rewarded for his services the following year by being appointed captain of Tantallon Castle, where in 1538 he played host to the king. In 1540 he presented a royal letter to the burgh council requiring it to accept a replacement for Archibald Borthwick, prebendar of the burgh's kirk, who was to remain in the king's service. David's career as an advocate grew during the 1530s, while in the following decade he was appointed by the king's advocate, Henry Lauder, as one of his substitutes to act in his absence on the king's behalf. By 1549 Borthwick was one of the nine leading advocates licensed to act before the college of justice. Links to the earl of Arran in the 1540s brought suspicion of protestant sympathies. In 1554 he, along with others including Adam Borthwick, received a remission for treasonably acting against the governor '*super mora de* Glasgow' (Livingstone, 4.2611), presumably with the earl of Lennox when the earl was active against the government in April 1544. However, in 1553 he was appointed to a commission to meet an English delegation in the borders.

Borthwick was retained by Edinburgh town council to act as one of its assessors in 1562 and in the same year he subscribed to raise funds for the building of a new poor hospital within the burgh. During this period he acted as advocate on behalf of the burghs of Aberdeen and Dundee, and also appears to have been advocate for the church. His professional success is reflected in the fact that he was assessed at the highest rate (£100) in Edinburgh council's tax of 1565. In 1573 Borthwick succeeded John Spens as king's advocate and on 20 October became an *ex officio* lord of session. The following year he accompanied the regent, the earl of Morton, to Aberdeen and served on the commission for framing a constitution for the Church of Scotland. Borthwick acquired considerable estates in Haddington and Berwickshire. In 1540 he was given lands in Berwickshire by the commendator and convent of Kelso, and a decade later he and his wife were made jointly infeft in the lands of Lochhill within the constabulary of Haddington. These were augmented in 1553 and 1557 when Borthwick obtained the lands of Fenton in Haddingtonshire in gifts from the crown.

Borthwick died, a wealthy man, on 30 January 1581, leaving a total estate of £11,576 Scots. He married first, before 1550, Marion Blyth (*d.* 24 March 1571) and second Marion Guthrie, who was the executor-nominate of his estate. He had at least two sons from these marriages, David, the elder (*d.* September 1575), and James, and he and Marion Blyth had two daughters, Agnes and Isobel.

JOHN FINLAY

Sources transcript of Haddington burgh court books, NA Scot., CD 1/4B/1 • M. Livingstone, D. Hay Fleming, and others, eds., *Registrum secreti sigilli regum Scotorum / The register of the privy seal of Scotland*, 2–7 (1921–66) • J. M. Thomson and others, eds., *Registrum magni sigilli regum Scotorum / The register of the great seal of Scotland*, 11 vols. (1882–1914), vols. 3–5 • acts of the lords of council and session, NA Scot., CS 6, CS 7 • books of sederunt, NA Scot., CS 1 • register of testaments, NA Scot., CC 8/8/10 • J. Finlay, 'Professional men of law before the lords of council, *c.*1500–*c.*1550', PhD diss., U. Edin., 1997 • G. Brunton and D. Haig, *An historical account of the senators of the college of justice, from its institution in MDXXXII* (1832) • M. H. B. Sanderson, *Cardinal of Scotland: David Beaton, c.1494–1546* (1986) • M. Lynch, *Edinburgh and the Reformation* (1981) • G. R. Hewitt, *Scotland under Morton, 1572–80* (1982)

Wealth at death £11,576 Scots: 16 March 1585, NA Scot., CC 8/8/10, fols. 239*v*–241*v*; CC 8/8/12, fol. 180*r*; CC 8/8/14, fols. 167*r*–169*v*

Borthwick, Jane Laurie (1813–1897), hymn writer and translator, was born on 9 April 1813 in Edinburgh, the first daughter of James Borthwick, insurance manager of the North British Insurance Office, and his wife, Sarah Finlay, both staunch members of the Free Church of Scotland. She collaborated with her sister **Sarah Laurie Findlater** [*née* Borthwick] (1823–1907), who was born on 26 November 1823 in Edinburgh, to produce hymn translations from German.

Jane, the instigator of the translation project and the more prolific of the two sisters, was first introduced to German hymnody in the early 1840s, when she spent several months in Switzerland. On her return she was encouraged by her father to collaborate with Sarah on producing English renderings, some of which were first published in the *Free Church Magazine* in the late 1840s before being collected for inclusion in *Hymns from the Land of Luther* in four series (1854, 1855, 1858, 1862). These pietistic works, for which the Borthwick sisters are best known, confirmed their importance as mediators of German hymnody to Britain in the nineteenth century. Of the sixty-one translations by Jane, those which came into common use included 'Be still, my soul!' and 'Jesus, still lead on'; of Sarah's fifty-three, the best known were 'God calling yet!' and 'O happy home'. The importance Jane attached to her German translations—and indeed the success they attained—are confirmed by her using the pseudonym H.L.L., from the initials of the title, throughout her literary career. In 1875 she published a further book of thirty-three translations under the title *Alpine Lyrics*; these were added to the earlier volume to form a complete edition of *Hymns from the Land of Luther* in 1884.

Among Jane Borthwick's other interests were the education of the poor, and the domestic and foreign missionary work of the Free Church of Scotland. She held large classes in houses of refuge and reformatories in Edinburgh, and donated considerable sums to support large-scale conversion efforts in both Singapore and Labrador. She also used her literary skills to kindle enthusiasm for the Free Church's missionary efforts: she published *Missionary Evenings at Home* (1866) and *Missionary Enterprise in many Lands* (1872), with the acknowledged aim of presenting what she called 'striking and picturesque facts of missionary history' in an effort to recruit young readers to her evangelical cause.

While she developed lasting friendships with individuals in Germany and Switzerland, Jane did little travelling, never married, and lived a quiet, religious life in Edinburgh, largely in the family home at 14 Claremont Crescent. Sarah went to live in Perthshire in 1861, after her marriage on 4 December of that year to Eric John Findlater (1813–1886), a Free Church minister. In her husband's parish of Balquhidder, Sarah inaugurated a coffee house and library, as a diversion from what she considered the excessive drinking habits of the residents. After her husband's death in 1886 Sarah and her daughters Mary, Jane, and Sarah moved to Prestonpans, on the outskirts of Edinburgh. Jane Borthwick, then living at 18 Scotland Street, Edinburgh, was a frequent visitor, and developed a particularly close relationship with her nieces Jane Helen *Findlater [*see under* Findlater, Mary Williamina] and Mary Williamina *Findlater, who later became successful novelists, collaborating on a number of works, including *Crossriggs* (1908) and *Penny Moneypenny* (1911). Mary Findlater also published a tale entitled *A Narrow Way*, for which the character of Miss Cameron was based on Jane Borthwick. The two nieces acknowledged their Aunt Jane's kindness to them, but they grew tired of what they considered her excessive piety, apparent both in daily life and in her journal, which she kept throughout her adult life. They destroyed their aunt's journal after her death.

Jane Borthwick died of cardiac failure at 28 Ann Street, Edinburgh, on 7 September 1897, and was buried on 10 September in Greyfriars churchyard. In 1899 Sarah Findlater, together with her daughters, moved to Torquay; she died there on 25 December 1907. LEON LITVACK

Sources E. Mackenzie, *The Findlater sisters: literature and friendship* (1964) · J. S. Andrews, 'The Borthwick sisters as translators of German hymns', *Expository Times*, 94 (1982–3), 329–33 · J. Julian, ed., *A dictionary of hymnology*, rev. edn (1907); repr. in 2 vols. (1915) · D. Campbell, *Hymns and hymn makers*, 5th edn (1912) · J. Moffatt and M. Patrick, eds., *Handbook to the church hymnary, with supplement*, 2nd edn (1935) · J. S. Andrews, *A study of German hymns in current English hymnals* (1981) · E. Routley, *An English-speaking hymnal guide* (1979) · E. Routley, *A panorama of Christian hymnody* (1979) · old parish register for Edinburgh, NA Scot. [parish of Leith North, 1823; parish of Edinburgh, 1813] · statutory register for 1897, NA Scot. [registration district 685/1, no. 1097] · *The Scotsman* (9 Sept 1897), 8 · Edinburgh register of marriages, NA Scot. [district 685/2, no. 382, 1861]
Wealth at death £2676 14*s*. 9*d*.: inventory, NA Scot., 1897

Borthwick, Sir John (*d.* 1569), soldier and religious activist, is of obscure origins. He was not, as has been claimed, a son of William, third Lord Borthwick, but became son-in-law of the fourth lord [*see* Borthwick, William] when he married the latter's youngest daughter, Margaret, as his first wife. They had at least one son, another John. Unless he was the student of the same name at St Andrews University between 1509 and 1511, which would mean that he was still campaigning in his mid-seventies, the elder John Borthwick is first reliably recorded as a member of the French king's Scottish guard between 1529 and 1538. In 1531 he became an ensign, and was granted Civray, near Poitiers. In 1535 he obtained lands near Wigtown, and also came to the notice of Thomas Cromwell as a supporter of Henry VIII's religious policies. In this he may have been influenced by his kinsman Nicholas Borthwick, who was a student at Wittenberg in 1528. Late in 1538 he received £20 from the English crown as 'a captain of Scotland called Bortyke now passing over to France' (*LP Henry VIII*, 13/2, 535).

By 1539 Borthwick had returned to the court of James V, where in February 1540 he and David Lindsay welcomed the English ambassador Ralph Sadler. However, on 28 May 1540 in St Andrews, now styled knight, he was tried *in absentia* for heresy before Cardinal David Beaton, principally for promotion of 'English heresies', such as the denial of papal authority and the encouragement of the

Scottish king to follow the example of England in despoiling the prelates, who 'do not have the true catholic faith' (Fleming, 1.96–7). Further, he was charged for owning an English New Testament, works by Oecolampadius, Melanchthon, and Erasmus, and the reformist anthology called *Unio dissidentium*. Borthwick was condemned and forfeited, and his likeness burned, but he had fled abroad before he could be tried.

In 1543 Borthwick was commended to Henry VIII as 'singularly dedicate' to the king's service (*LP Henry VIII*, 18/2, no. 522), which by 1545 had taken him to Newcastle, London, and Antwerp, sending information on matters ranging from Edinburgh Castle to the Danish king's religious position; for this he was awarded an English pension of 300 crowns in 1544. Borthwick returned to Dundee after the murder of Beaton in 1546, and was set in free ward in Borthwick Castle that autumn; by April 1547 he had joined the 'Castilians' in St Andrews, and accompanied Henry Balnaves on a secret journey to meet the duke of Somerset in Berwick. Borthwick then entered the service of Edward VI, for whom he went on diplomatic missions to Scandinavia and Germany in order to foster union among protestant rulers, notably in Denmark in 1552.

After Edward's death Borthwick joined the English exiles in Geneva on 21 September 1554, and in 1555 he attempted unsuccessfully to induce the company of pastors to take up his mission of uniting protestant territories. Margaret Borthwick having died, her husband made a second marriage in Geneva, to Jeanne Bonespoir. He was in the company of the young third earl of Arran at the French court by 1558, and returned to England in 1559, when Elizabeth sent him to command 1000 light horsemen in the borders. Borthwick was back in France in 1567–8, evidently in the service of Queen Mary, but when civil war broke out he joined the forces of Regent Moray against the queen, and was slain by members of the Forster family near Bewcastle, Cumberland, on 25 or 26 December 1569.

Well before his death Borthwick had successfully petitioned to be relieved from his sentence for heresy. In 1561 he obtained from the St Andrews kirk session of the reformed church a sentence declaring his opinions reasonable and not heretical, and he was formally rehabilitated by Queen Mary in February 1563. Both Calvin and King Christian III of Denmark had commended his religious zeal, while others described him as 'all given of talking of the Scriptures', and as 'godly, honest, and of great experience' (*CSP for.*, 1559–60, 103n; 1569–71, 156). Well-founded protestant convictions and a sense of mission in his diplomatic efforts remained constant throughout Borthwick's services, performed at court and on the field of battle on behalf of three kingdoms.

Martin Holt Dotterweich

Sources *LP Henry VIII*, 9.21/2 • *CSP for.*, 1559–61; 1569–71 • E. Halle, *Union … of Lancaster and York* (1970), 245v–247r • J. Foxe, *Actes and monuments* (1563), 575–86 • J. Durkan, 'Heresy in Scotland: the second phase', *Records of the Scottish Church History Society*, 24 (1990–92), 342–3, esp. 335–8 • J. Durkan, 'Scottish evangelicals in the patronage of Thomas Cromwell', *Records of the Scottish Church History Society*, 21 (1981–3), 127–56, esp. 132–3 • D. H. Fleming, ed., *Register of the minister, elders and deacons of the Christian congregation of St Andrews*, 1, Scottish History Society, 4 (1889), 89–104 • R. Kingdon, ed., *Registres de la compagnie des pasteurs de Genève au temps de Calvin* (1962), 2.57 • E. Cunitz and E. Reuss, eds., *Corpus reformatorum*, 43 (1876), 278–9 [works of Calvin] • C. Edington, *Court and culture in Renaissance Scotland: Sir David Lindsay of the Mount* (1994) • J. B. Paul, ed., *Compota thesaurariorum regum Scotorum / Accounts of the lord high treasurer of Scotland*, 7–8 (1907–8) • J. M. Thomson and others, eds., *Registrum magni sigilli regum Scotorum / The register of the great seal of Scotland*, 11 vols. (1882–1914), vol. 3, pp. 331, 406 • *Reg. PCS*, 1st ser., 1.43 • J. M. Anderson, ed., *Early records of the University of St Andrews*, Scottish History Society, 3rd ser., 8 (1926), 99, 204 • *Scots peerage*, vol. 2 • M. Livingstone, D. Hay Fleming, and others, eds., *Registrum secreti sigilli regum Scotorum / The register of the privy seal of Scotland*, 5 (1957) • W. Forbes-Leith, *Scots men-at-arms and life guards in France*, 2 vols. (1882) • *The works of John Knox*, ed. D. Laing, 6 vols., Wodrow Society, 12 (1846–64)

Borthwick, Peter (1804–1852), newspaper editor, only son of Thomas Borthwick of Edinburgh, was born at Cornbank, in the parish of Borthwick, Midlothian, on 13 September 1804; he graduated at the University of Edinburgh, and was the private pupil of James Walker, bishop of Edinburgh and Glasgow, and afterwards primus of the Episcopal Church of Scotland. He undertook some tutoring and, despite the objections of her uncle and guardian, married on 8 January 1827 his pupil Margaret (*d.* 1864), daughter of John Colville of Ewart, Northumberland; they had three children. Although he was married, Borthwick matriculated from Jesus College, Cambridge, in 1828, migrating in February 1830 to be a fellow-commoner of Downing College. While at Cambridge, he published *A Brief Statement … Concerning the Second Advent of our Blessed Lord* (1830); at that time he contemplated ordination. He was a good-looking man with an olive complexion and a 'profusion of black hair' (Escott, 187).

In 1832 Borthwick began a series of speeches opposing the abolition of the slave trade, which gained him rapid fame and the thanks of various slave owners and Conservative associations. His views were contested in a lively series of responses by Samuel Bowly and others. Borthwick unsuccessfully stood for Evesham as a Conservative in 1832, but was elected in 1835. He lost the seat on petition in 1838, but was elected for it in 1841. He associated with the Young England group, opposed the move to free trade, and in the general election of 1847 contested—unsuccessfully in both cases—St Ives and Penryn as a Conservative. Borthwick's political career did not reflect his early promise. His speeches 'were apt to provoke not so much cheers as yawns' (Escott, 186). However, he amended the Poor Law Amendment Act through what became known as the 'Borthwick clause', by which married couples over the age of sixty were not required to separate when living in the workhouse.

On 28 April 1847 Borthwick was called to the bar at Gray's Inn. His career at the bar made little headway, and in the late 1840s he failed in his attempt to enter the Foreign Office. In 1849 he resorted to journalism, becoming manager of the *Morning Post*. After a complex series of financial intrigues, he became editor in 1850. Described in 1849 by Lord Malmesbury as 'a paid spy of Palmerston's', Borthwick as editor strongly supported Lord Palmerston, though without estranging Conservative readers (Koss, 80–81) and still supporting protection. Already ill when he became editor, Borthwick's health declined, and he died from pleurisy at his home, 11 Walton Villas, Brompton, London, on 18 December 1852. The editorship of the *Morning Post* soon passed to his son, Algernon *Borthwick, Baron Glenesk. H. C. G. MATTHEW

Sources T. H. S. Escott, *Masters of English journalism* (1911) • Boase, *Mod. Eng. biog.* • Venn, *Alum. Cant.* • *GM*, 2nd ser., 39 (1853), 318–20 • S. E. Koss, *The rise and fall of the political press in Britain*, 1 (1981) • GEC, *Peerage* [Glenesk] • R. J. Lucas, *Lord Glenesk and the Morning Post* (1910) • W. Hindle, *The Morning Post, 1772–1937: portrait of a newspaper* (1937)

Archives BL, corresp. with Sir Robert Peel, Add. MSS 40486–40600, *passim*

Likenesses wood-engraving, repro. in *ILN*, 2 (1843), 8

Borthwick, Sir Thomas (1835–1912), meat importer, was born at Musselburgh, near Edinburgh, on 11 January 1835, the son of Thomas Borthwick of Edinburgh. He worked his way up from apprentice butcher in the family business at nearby Ratho, and at an early age it was clear that his real talent lay in assessing livestock. He was soon an acknowledged expert: it was said that he could walk into a pen holding 500 or more sheep and tell the weight and value of any of them at a glance; he was later to become a judge at the Royal Agricultural Show. He was only twenty-two when he established himself as a livestock agent, initially in Midlothian, but since he also handled Irish cattle landed at Liverpool he was attracted by the prospects there and in 1863 moved to Liverpool. In 1870 he rented a farm near Llanrwst in north Wales, and it was from there that he established a flourishing trade with Liverpool butchers. An indication of his drive is that, occasionally dissatisfied with prices, he slaughtered animals and sold direct to the consumer.

The 1860s and 1870s were years of experimentation in long-distance transport of meat from overseas suppliers. When refrigeration finally made it possible to bring meat across the equator from Australasia and Argentina (the first consignments of frozen meat were arriving by the late 1870s, the first from New Zealand in 1882), Borthwick was quick to recognize the possibilities in international trade in the product. In 1883 he became the selling agent for the New Zealand Loan and Mercantile Agency Co. Ltd. He opened meat depots in Liverpool, Manchester, Glasgow, and Birmingham, and in 1892 transferred the firm's headquarters to London, at the same time securing a stall in Smithfield. This was the real beginning of the large wholesale and distribution business that covered the major livestock products of meat, wool, and tallow. But the main business was meat, and Borthwick was a leading figure in promoting the trade, especially in experimenting with chilling (as opposed to freezing) techniques, which indirectly made him responsible for improving the quality of Australian beef.

Borthwick married Letitia Banks of Liverpool in 1872, and had four sons and three daughters. All the sons went into the business; the eldest son, Thomas Borthwick (*b.* 1875), later Baron Whitburgh, went to Australia and New Zealand in 1904; he purchased meat-processing works and established branch offices at Sydney, Melbourne, Brisbane, and Christchurch. That same year the firm became a limited liability company under the name of Thomas Borthwick & Sons Ltd, registered with a capital of £300,000. More meat works were added later, and the company continued to prosper until the early 1980s, and, together with the Vestey brothers, dominated the Australasian meat trade. At the time of his death in 1912 Borthwick was still chairman of Thomas Borthwick & Sons Ltd and a director of Lancashire Cold Storage Co. Ltd, Thames Cold Storage Co. Ltd, and Thomas Borthwick & Sons (Australasia) Ltd.

Borthwick was a staunch Presbyterian throughout his life, and contributed to church activities both in Midlothian and at Regent Square Presbyterian Church, London. He was in his late sixties before he took an active part in local Midlothian politics. In 1902 he was appointed chairman of the Midlothian Liberal Association, a post he held until his death, and in 1908 he was knighted for his services to the Liberals. He was known for being a plain and blunt man, and while he probably lacked any serious political ambition he was certainly not without friends in high places, being a close friend of Gladstone and later of Lloyd George and Asquith. Weeks before he died he was named as baron in the birthday honours, and so the title of Baron Whitburgh passed to his eldest son. Sir Thomas Borthwick died at his home, Whitburgh Ford, Midlothian, on 31 July 1912. FORREST CAPIE

Sources G. P. Harrison, *Borthwick: a century in the meat trade, 1863–1963* (1963) • *The Times* (2 Aug 1912) • *New Zealand Journal of Agriculture* (1909) • *New Zealand Journal of Agriculture* (1911) • J. T. Critchell and J. Raymond, *A history of the frozen meat trade*, 2nd edn (1912) • A. Chadwick, *The meat trade*, 3 vols. (1934) • F. Capie, 'Borthwick, Sir Thomas', *DBB* • *CGPLA Eng. & Wales* (1912)

Wealth at death £320,569 13*s.* 10*d.*: confirmation, 17 Dec 1912, *CCI*

Borthwick, Sir William, of that ilk (*c.*1385–*c.*1449). *See under* Borthwick family (*per. c.*1400–*c.*1515).

Borthwick, William, first Lord Borthwick (*c.*1412–1483). *See under* Borthwick family (*per. c.*1400–*c.*1515).

Borthwick, William, second Lord Borthwick (*c.*1428–1503). *See under* Borthwick family (*per. c.*1400–*c.*1515).

Borthwick, William, third Lord Borthwick (*c.*1460–1513?). *See under* Borthwick family (*per. c.*1400–*c.*1515).

Borthwick, William, fourth Lord Borthwick (*b.* before 1491, *d.* in or before 1544), nobleman and courtier, was the son of William *Borthwick, third Lord Borthwick (*c.*1460–1513?) [*see under* Borthwick family], and his wife, Margaret Hay, daughter of John *Hay, first Lord Hay of Yester. Borthwick's father died supposedly at Flodden on 9 September 1513, at which time William succeeded to his estates and was soon afterwards appointed to serve as a guardian to the young James V at Stirling. He maintained his guardianship of both the king and his younger brother, the duke of Ross, after the duke of Albany's siege of Stirling Castle on 4 August 1515, sharing these duties with Earl Marischal,

Lord Fleming, and Lord Erskine. Borthwick was continuously listed in the exchequer rolls as the king's guardian until 1 May 1522. In 1524 he severed his links with Albany's regime by taking an oath of loyalty to James, whom he continued to serve at Edinburgh Castle.

Borthwick's personal devotion to the king was rewarded in 1532. When Borthwick became involved in a legal dispute with James Beaton, archbishop of St Andrews, over a lease of Stow church, James wrote personally to Pope Clement VII to prevent further difficulties for his servant, whose house had already been brought 'very low financially' (*Letters of James V*, 250). Borthwick and his wife, whose name is unknown, had five children: Thomas, master of Borthwick (*d.* 1528); John, who became fifth Lord Borthwick; and three daughters, Katherine, Janet, and Margaret, wife of the reformer Sir John Borthwick. William Borthwick died some time before 19 February 1544.

J. R. M. SIZER

Sources *LP Henry VIII*, vol. 1/2 • *Scots peerage*, vol. 2 • GEC, *Peerage*, vol. 2 • *Letters of James V*, ed. R. K. Hannay and D. Hays (1954) • *Report of the Laing manuscripts*, 1, HMC, 72 (1914) • J. B. Paul, ed., *Compota thesaurariorum regum Scotorum / Accounts of the lord high treasurer of Scotland*, 5 (1903) • C. Bingham, *James V, king of Scots, 1512–1542* (1971) • R. Brooke, *Catalogue and succession of the kings, princes, dukes, marquesses, earles, and viscounts of this realme of England, since the Norman conquest, to this present yeere 1622* (1622) • G. Burnett and others, eds., *The exchequer rolls of Scotland*, 15 (1895)

Borthwick, William (1760–1820), army officer, was the eldest son of Lieutenant-General William Borthwick, Royal Artillery, and entered the Royal Military Academy, Woolwich, in 1772. He became a second lieutenant, Royal Artillery, in 1777, lieutenant in 1779, and captain-lieutenant in 1790, serving in Flanders. As brigadier-general he prepared the siege train with which Wellington bombarded Ciudad Rodrigo in January 1812, and was severely wounded during the siege; for this he later received a gold medal. He also prepared the siege train for the final attack on Badajoz; but in April 1812 he was promoted major general, and had to hand over his command to Colonel Framingham, because the number of artillerymen in the Peninsula was insufficient to require a general officer. He died at Margate on 20 July 1820.

H. M. STEPHENS, *rev.* DAVID GATES

Sources F. Duncan, ed., *History of the royal regiment of artillery*, 3rd edn, 2 vols. (1879) • J. T. Jones, *Journals of sieges carried on by the army under the duke of Wellington in Spain*, ed. H. D. Jones, 3rd edn, 3 vols. (1846) • D. Gates, *The Spanish ulcer: a history of the Peninsular War* (1986)
Archives BL, letters to Colonel George Don, Add. MSS 46704–46705

Borton, Sir Arthur (1814–1893), army officer, was born on 20 January 1814 at Blofield, near Norwich, the youngest son of John Drew Borton (1769–1847), rector of Blofield, and of his wife, Louisa, daughter of the Revd Thomas Carthew of Woodbridge, Suffolk. Educated at Eton College, he received a commission as ensign in the 9th (East Norfolk) regiment on 13 July 1832; he became lieutenant-colonel on 10 June 1853, colonel on 28 November 1854, major-general on 1 January 1868, lieutenant-general on 19 October 1875, colonel of the 1st battalion of the West India regiment on 22 May 1876, and general on 4 December 1877, and was transferred to the colonelcy of the Norfolk regiment on 17 October 1889.

Borton joined his regiment in Ireland accompanying it to Mauritius in 1833 and on to India in 1835. He came home in 1838 to study in the senior department of the Royal Military College, and obtained a certificate in November 1839. After his return to India he served with his regiment in Afghanistan under Major-General George Pollock in 1842. He took part in forcing the Khyber Pass on 5 April, when the 9th was broken into detachments which had the honour of leading the columns of attack; he was also engaged in the victory over Muhammad Akbar Khan at the Tezin Pass and the Haft Kotal on 13 September, when, at the head of a party of the 9th, he made a gallant charge. After the force's arrival at Kabul on 15 September he accompanied the column under Major-General John McCaskill into Kohistan, and took part in the assault and capture of the strongly fortified town of Istalif on 29 September. Borton returned to India in October with his regiment, which formed part of the rear-guard and was involved in some fighting in the passes.

Borton served with his regiment in the 5th brigade of the 3rd infantry division in the Sutlej campaign of 1845–6, and was present at Mudki on 18 December 1845, and at Ferozeshahr on 21 and 22 December. In this he succeeded to the command of his regiment when Lieutenant-Colonel A. B. Taylor was killed, and was himself very severely wounded in the right elbow (he never recovered the complete use of his arm). For his services in this campaign he received the brevet of major and a pension for his wound.

The 9th returned home in 1847, and Borton served with the regiment at Winchester until the end of 1848, and during the next six years in Ireland, succeeding to the command on 10 June 1853. He embarked with the regiment for Malta on 18 February 1854, and went on with it to the Crimea on 19 November, where he commanded it at the siege of Sevastopol. He led the regiment in the assault on the Redan by the column under Major-General Eyre on 18 June 1855 and was mentioned in dispatches. He was promoted colonel in the army on 17 July, and made a CB, military division, on 27 July. At the end of the war he received the order of the Mejidiye (third class) and the Légion d'honneur (fifth class). He was also awarded a good service pension.

From the Crimea, Borton took his regiment to Canada in 1856, and brought it home in November of the following year. On 1 March 1865 he was appointed a colonel on the staff to command the troops at Colchester. On 1 April 1866 he was given the command of the infantry brigade at the Curragh, Ireland, with the rank of brigadier-general, until his promotion to major-general on 1 January 1868. On 9 September 1870 Borton was appointed to the command of the Mysore division of the Madras army, which he held for five years. He was promoted to KCB, military division, on 2 June 1877, and on 13 May 1878 was appointed governor and commander-in-chief at Malta. He was made a GCMG on 28

May 1880, and on relinquishing the government of Malta was made GCB, on 24 May 1884.

Borton married, on 9 April 1850, at Drumbanagher, co. Armagh, Caroline Mary Georgina (who survived him), daughter of the Revd John Forbes Close, rector of Mourne, co. Down, and of his first wife, Mary Sophia Brownlow, sister of the first Lord Lurgan. They had two sons: Arthur Close, lieutenant-colonel 13th Somerset (Prince Albert's) light infantry, and Charles Edward, major 9th Norfolk regiment, who served in the Second Anglo-Afghan War. Borton died on 7 September 1893 at his residence, 105 Eaton Place, London, and was buried on 9 September at Hunton, near Maidstone, Kent.

R. H. Vetch, *rev.* James Lunt

Sources *The Times* (8 Sept 1893) · *Admiralty and Horse Guards Gazette* (9 Sept 1893) · *Admiralty and Horse Guards Gazette* (16 Sept 1893) · R. Cannon, ed., *Historical record of the ninth, or the east Norfolk regiment of foot* (1848) · J. A. Norris, *The First Afghan War, 1838–1842* (1967) · H. C. B. Cook, *The Sikh wars: the British army in the Punjab, 1845–1849* (1975) · A. W. Kinglake, *The invasion of the Crimea*, 8 vols. (1863–87) · Boase, *Mod. Eng. biog.*

Archives Bodl. Oxf., corresp. with Lord Kimberley

Likenesses H. Herkomer, oils, priv. coll.; copy in possession of 1st battalion of royal Norfolk regiment, Norfolk, 1901 · group portrait, wood-engraving (after sketch, *Presentation of native Indian officers to the duke of Cambridge in the governor's palace, Malta* by A. Gilmore), NPG; repro. in *ILN* (13 July 1878) · portrait, repro. in *Admiralty and Horse Guards Gazette* (9 Sept 1893) · portrait, repro. in *Admiralty and Horse Guards Gazette* (16 Sept 1893)

Wealth at death £65,971 15*s.* 7*d.* in UK: resworn probate, May 1894, *CGPLA Eng. & Wales* (1893)

Boruwlaski, Joseph [*formerly* Józef Boruslawski], **styled Count Boruwlaski** (**1739–1837**), travelling performer and memoirist, was born in November 1739 near Halicz, Galicia, Poland, the third son of a lower gentry family. The principal source for his life is his own memoirs, published in several editions between 1788 and 1820. When he was nine his father died, leaving a widow with five sons and one daughter. Three sons were very tall, but three children suffered from achondroplasia, an inherited condition in which the cartilage in the bones fails to grow. Boruslawski's eldest brother was 41 inches tall, and his younger sister was even smaller. Józef (known familiarly as Joujou) grew very slowly. At fifteen he had grown to 2 feet 1 inch, at twenty-one he was 2 feet 4 inches, at twenty-five he was 2 feet 11 inches, and at thirty reached his maximum height of 3 feet 3 inches. Boruslawski's mother, left poor, had her achondroplasic children adopted into noble households. Anastasia was 2 feet 4 inches high when she died of smallpox, aged twenty. The eldest brother was at Castellan Inowlowski's wife's court until his death.

Protégé of Madame Humiecka Boruslawski was entrusted first to Madame Jaorlicka, widow of the starostin de Caorliz, one of sixteen regional officers of state, and was well treated and educated. When he was fifteen Madame Jaorlicka married Count de Tarnon, and he was transferred to Madame Humiecka, described as 'Lady sword bearer' (that is, wife of the sword-bearer); she was not a countess as stated in Boruslawski's memoirs. Madame Humiecka travelled Europe with her household, introducing Boruslawski to the most famous European salons. She dressed him as a lieutenant of a great Polish regiment, and her drawing-room contained his diminutive sofa, table, chair, billiard table, and other games. Among the courts they visited were that at Vienna in 1752, where Boruslawski was presented to the empress Maria Theresa and learned dancing from Angelini, the electoral court of Bavaria at Munich, and the court of Stanislaw Leszczýnski, former king of Poland, at Luneville in Lorraine. Here he met Count de Tressan, who described his manners and exceptional intelligence in the *Encyclopédie* in 1766. King Stanislaw introduced Madame Humiecka to his daughter Queen Maria at Versailles, where Boruslawski entertained Louis XV's court. There Count Michal Oginski, grand general of Lithuania, began to teach him music, and arranged further tuition from the leading guitarist Gaviniesa. Music would become a vital source of income.

In 1760 Madame Humiecka took her entourage to The Hague, from where a report on Boruslawski was sent to the *Annual Register* in London, noting his graceful manners, wish to be treated as a nobleman, and his wit, liveliness, memory, and literary and linguistic abilities. When they returned to Warsaw, Madame Humiecka conceded that he was now an adult and he was allowed visits to theatres and parties alone. This independence proved to be limited when Madame Humiecka disapproved of his dissolute companions and threatened to withdraw her protection.

Marriage and independence About 1778 Boruslawski fell in love with Izalina Barboutin (*c.*1763–*c.*1790/91), an attractive dark-haired girl of fifteen, of normal stature; of French descent, she had joined Madame Humiecka as a companion. She mocked him initially; but his persistence and showers of love letters convinced her he was serious. Courtship followed late in 1779, but Madame Humiecka dismissed them both in anger. They married in 1780, under the protection of Prince Kazimierz Poniatowski and his brother, King Stanislaw II. The king granted Boruslawski a carriage and an annual pension of 120 ducats, and may also have allowed him to call himself a count, although there is no evidence for this beyond the memoirs. The couple left for Kraków, where a daughter was born.

Boruslawski had known that the pension would not be enough to support his growing family, and he began the precarious business of earning a living. Madame Humiecka had exhibited him to a select audience as a novelty; as his own man he attempted to be taken seriously as an impoverished gentleman and as a musician, but his diminutive proportion would always be the factor that aroused curiosity. In Vienna in February 1781 a concert was cancelled as the city was still mourning Maria Theresa, but Sir Robert Murray Keith, the British ambassador, suggested that Boruslawski visit England, and provided letters of recommendation. The 1820 edition of the memoirs states that Boruslawski then travelled through the Balkans, Arabia, and Asia as far as Kamchatka and the Bering Strait, but this would have been an impossible journey in the time allowed and is probably an example of the exaggerated traveller's tales he entertained his audiences with in later life. The 1788 memoirs suggest instead that he earned his living seeking hospitality at minor German princely courts.

Arrival in England In late 1781, while visiting Christian Friedrich, margrave of Brandenburg-Ansbach, at Triersdorff, Boruslawski revived the plan to visit England. The margrave agreed to care for his eldest child, and Boruslawski and Izalina left with introductory letters to George III's brothers, William, duke of Gloucester, and Henry, duke of Cumberland, and to William Cavendish, fifth duke of Devonshire, and more importantly to his wife Georgiana, the leading whig political hostess. The Boruslawskis landed at Margate on 21 March 1782 and proceeded to London where Boruslawski was for a period taken up by the Devonshires. The duchess found him accommodation and the duke gave him a suit embroidered with silver and precious stones, and a silver sword. At Devonshire House he met the prince of Wales (afterwards George IV) and the duke of Gloucester, to whom he presented his letter from the margrave of Brandenburg-Ansbach. The Polish ambassador arranged a visit to the royal family on 23 May. There he was treated as a Polish nobleman, and he discussed his travels with George III.

The press reported wrongly that the king gave Boruslawski money. As he needed more than presents, Georgiana arranged a supposedly spontaneous meeting between him and the Irish giant Charles Byrne, known as O'Brien, who was 8 feet 4 inches tall. The publicity failed to have a great effect on Boruslawski's income. Society soon tired of him, and it may have been the need for popular acclaim that led him to simplify his name. Advertisements in the *Public Advertiser* for his concerts on 7 June 1782 and 19 June 1782 at Carlisle House described him as 'Count Boruwlaski'. The concerts were priced at 10*s.* 6*d.*; he later wrote that prices were forced down to 5*s.*, and then to 2*s.* 6*d.* He needed to leave London to earn more, as he now had three daughters, and estimated that he needed £500 annually for travelling, organizing concerts, and hiring rooms for entertaining.

Joined by Izalina's uncle, de Trouville, Boruwlaski and his family left for Bath, but his initial success was eclipsed by a trained pig. He returned to London, where a collection for his benefit failed, the duchess of Devonshire (succumbing to a widespread superstition) refused to admit him lest the sight of him dwarf her expected child, and a concert was unprofitable, partly through the lack of interest of the prince of Wales.

Touring the British Isles In April 1783 Boruwlaski travelled to Ireland, where he was able to renew his success. Thanks to introductions to Frederick Howard, fifth earl of Carlisle, lord lieutenant of Ireland, and his successor, Charles Manners, fourth duke of Rutland, leading Irish families entertained him. Boruwlaski said he spent two years in Ireland, a stay protracted by Izalina's pregnancy, but he was in Cheshire in November 1783 when he became a freemason. Boruwlaski may have realized that it was unlikely that he would enjoy permanent favour from the nobility, and on his return to England, perhaps in early 1785, concentrated his attention on the provinces. He and his family travelled through Liverpool and Manchester to Leeds, and late in 1785 arrived in Birmingham. There Boruwlaski lodged in a house belonging to a man called Hutton where, as usual, he entertained guests for a small admission fee. The Boruwlaskis were invited to Christmas dinner by the Huttons, and Boruwlaski established a lasting friendship with Hutton's daughter, Caroline. She noticed that Boruwlaski had little English but great charm and good manners. Izalina spoke good English, was talkative, laughed easily, and sang French songs, but Caroline thought her character made her an unsuitable wife for Boruwlaski. With them were their pretty middle daughter and the youngest, a baby, the eldest being still at the court of the margrave of Brandenburg-Ansbach. From Birmingham the Boruwlaskis returned to London via Oxford, where Boruwlaski was taken to Blenheim Palace and gave a pair of his shoes to George Spencer, fourth duke of Marlborough, for the duke's collection of curiosities. By 27 March 1786 Boruwlaski was in London, where, as 'Sieur Boruwlaski', he advertised his presence in the *Morning Post*; visitors were invited to call on him at 162 Strand, for the price of 1*s.* An anonymous letter includes a sketch of his guitar performance before the sultan of Turkey, two guards, and three ladies of the harem, indicating that tales of his travels, real or imagined, were an established part of his repertory. His old friend Oginski was now in London, an exile from a Poland torn by political factions and about to be partitioned, and supported a concert on 30 June 1786; the prince of Wales was invited but, although he had lunch with Boruwlaski beforehand, failed to attend. There was a good audience but only Oginski's subsidy averted financial failure. Boruwlaski's long absence from Poland led to his pension being cancelled, as it was rumoured that he had great investments in Britain. Another Polish exile, Princess Lubormirska, arrived in 1787 and generously paid his debts of 50 guineas, when creditors threatened him.

In 1788 *Mémoires du célèbre nain Joseph Boruwlaski* with a parallel English translation by A. J. Des Carrières was published in London. The subscription list of hundreds of names includes the prince of Wales, members of the aristocracy, and several distinguished Poles. It was dedicated to the duchess of Devonshire, perhaps in a bid to renew Boruwlaski's association with the fashionable world, but publication did not improve his finances. A German translation appeared in Leipzig in 1789.

Boruwlaski's advertisements in 1786 had forecast his imminent return to Poland, but he remained in England, probably for financial reasons. His wife, her uncle, and her children disappear from his memoirs at this point; they may have deserted him, perhaps to return to Poland; his regret for neglecting 'a generous man' (*Mémoires*, 1st edn, 245) with Polish connections, in favour of bad advisers, could refer to de Trouville. His narrative, as continued in the 1792 edition, mentions periods at Norwich (where the diarist James Woodforde saw him in 1788) and Edinburgh, the latter visit supported by the family of the earl of Dumfries; the aristocracy was still his preferred milieu. However, the 1820 edition emphasizes his renewed acquaintance in Cambridge at this time with Margaret Metcalfe and her unmarried sisters, whom he had met in London in 1782; they helped to promote successful concerts in Cambridge and on their family estate at Bury St Edmunds. The Metcalfes, presumably of lower gentry or middle-class origin, would be more typical of Boruwlaski's enduring admirers.

From Edinburgh, Boruwlaski travelled south to France, collecting money on the way. He arrived in spring 1789, and performed in Boulogne, in Lille, and in Paris, but attributed his lack of success to the outbreak of revolution that July and two thefts. He returned to England, via Cherbourg and Guernsey, in spring 1790. He then made a final visit to Poland, in 1790 or 1791; his wife died about that time.

On returning to England in 1791 in poverty, Boruwlaski tried the west midlands, where he was unknown, and appeared successfully in Hereford. With a depleted income, he resorted to a paid appearance with a giant. He then returned to Birmingham, where 'guests' paid 1*s*. admission. At the Huttons, Caroline noticed his melancholy and the absence of his wife and family. He was now fifty-three years old with no prospects. Two new editions of the memoirs appeared in Birmingham in 1792, one in French, the other in English, updating the 1788 publication.

According to the 1820 edition of the memoirs Boruwlaski spent much of the succeeding decade in Ireland, where he visited most of the major towns. The account in the memoirs is highly anecdotal and peppered with humorous stories about his Irish servant Noad and observations on the French invasion attempts by Hoche in 1796 and Humbert in 1798. The invasion panic and threat of rebellion 'made such an impression on my strongbox' (*Memoirs*, 4th edn, 327) that he left Ireland, probably in 1798, for the Isle of Man and then England.

The north of England and retirement Boruwlaski then toured the north of England; James Ballantyne published a further edition of the memoirs at Kelso in 1801, probably with the northern English audience in mind. The connections that Boruwlaski made in the north of England at this time were to secure his future. With the help of General Archibald Dickson, he writes, he staged a successful concert at Newcastle, and was introduced by Dickson to Thomas Ebdon, cathedral organist at Durham, who in turn introduced him to 'Mr Smelt', an old friend of George III. The chronological sequence of events in Boruwlaski's memoirs may be confused; a letter in *The Times* in September 1802 states that Boruwlaski stayed with Dickson that May, but if 'Mr Smelt' is Leonard Smelt, the former subpreceptor to the prince of Wales, as seems to be implied, then these events must have taken place before Smelt died on 2 September 1800. To confuse the matter further, the memoirs place Smelt's death after the death of William, duke of Gloucester (in 1805), and an attack of insanity suffered by George III (presumably that same year). It was Smelt who began raising a subscription to provide funds for Boruwlaski's retirement. Boruwlaski, in the meantime, travelled to London, intending to emigrate to America. He was dissuaded from doing so by Margaret Metcalfe and her sisters, who began their own fund for Boruwlaski's retirement; the sums collected in the north and in London were joined so that he was able to buy an annuity. In 1812 he retired to Banks Cottage, South Bailey, Durham, where he lived with the daughters of Thomas Ebdon and paid 2*s*. annual rent to the dean and chapter. The house is illustrated in the 1820 edition of the memoirs.

The annuity, yielding £138 annually, was invested with a local shopkeeper who expected his early demise. Boruwlaski, however, enjoyed excellent health. He enjoyed teasing the shopkeeper, an elderly man many years his junior, asking him how he was, and adding that his own health could not be better. He told his friend the actor Charles Mathews (as related by Mathews's wife, Anne):

> Oh *poor devel*, poor *hold* body. It *macks* me *laffing*, poor *hold hanimal*. Oh, he say prayer for me to die, offen when he *slip*. He *calcoolated dat* dwarf, not live it long *et* I live it forty year to *plag* him … He fifty year *younger den Boruwlaski; minitime* he dead sooner as me … Boruwlaski NEVER die, you may depend. (Mathews, 3.224–5)

The shopkeeper died first, leaving his heirs to continue payments.

Boruwlaski became an honorary member of the Marquis of Granby lodge of freemasons in Durham in 1806, but attended only three times. Another member was the actor Stephen Kemble. The huge Kemble and tiny Boruwlaski became fast friends and were a familiar sight walking on the river banks.

In Durham, Boruwlaski elaborated the earlier text of his memoirs, continuing it to his staying with the Ebdons. The new text was edited by another benefactor, the writer and colliery owner William Burdon, who died before its publication in 1820. This version of the memoirs is the most obviously anecdotal, adding a number of extraordinary travellers' tales to the 1788 text, and reducing the prominence of Izalina, but also placing less emphasis on Boruwlaski's friendships with the higher nobility, instead thanking his lasting, less socially exalted admirers.

Visiting London in July 1821, he wished to call on George IV to present his new book. Although it was the eve of the coronation, Mathews secured an interview. The king greeted him warmly and asked about his wife. Boruwlaski replied: 'Isolina [*sic*] die thirty year. Fine woman! Sweet, beauty body! You have no *idea*, Majesty' (Mathews, 3.219). The king gave him a watch and chain, accepting the book as a souvenir, and interrogated both Boruwlaski and Mathews about Boruwlaski's financial well-being. Mrs Mathews reported that George IV said: 'If I had a dozen sons I could not point out to them a more perfect model of good breeding and elegance than the Count, who really is a most accomplished and charming person!' (ibid., 3.222).

Until the year before his death Boruwlaski visited London annually to stay with the Mathews and other friends. The journalist Peter George Patmore saw him at

Mathews's house in 1823, reporting that at eighty-four 'he played in the house and the garden like a nice puppy or a happy child, gay as a bird' (Mathews, 3.231). He was dignified, however, with strangers.

In the 1830s Boruwlaski became increasingly frail and had to be carried to some of his many social engagements. He continued to correspond with friends such as Caroline Hutton, to whom he wrote in 1833:

Poland was my cradle,
England was my nest,
Durham is my quiet place,
Where my weary bones shall rest.

He died on 5 September 1837 at his home, Banks Cottage, South Bailey, Durham, and was buried near the north tower stair door of Durham Cathedral, at a spot marked by the initials 'J. B.'. Canon Ebdon, Thomas Ebdon's nephew, composed an inscription to which the dean and chapter objected; but it appears on a marble wall slab within the west end of St Mary-the-Less where Canon James Raine, Boruwlaski's friend, was rector.

Boruwlaski was said to have retained the cheerfulness, serenity of temper, and even playfulness, of early youth. He was abstemious, never touched alcohol, had perfect sight, and spent much of his time reading, writing, studying alchemy, and conducting scientific experiments. He was commemorated in Durham by a permanent display of his garments at the town hall, and by the name 'Count's House' given to the folly with a Doric portico erected on a bend of the River Wear, probably designed by Ignatius Bonomi. In death as in life his reputation depended on curiosity towards his physical condition, and both amusement with and respect for his hard-won and carefully maintained dignity. MARGOT JOHNSON

Sources J. Boruwlaski, *Mémoires du célèbre nain Joseph Boruwlaski, gentilhomme polonais, contenant un récit fidelle et curieux de sa naissance, de son éducation, de son mariage & de ses voyages*, trans. A. J. Des Carrières (1788); 2nd edn, trans. A. J. Des Carrières and S. Freeman (1792) [Fr. and Eng.] • J. Boruwlaski, *Memoirs of Count Boruwlaski: containing a sketch of his travels, with an account of his reception at the different courts of Europe*, ed. W. Burdon, 4th edn (1820) • H. Świderska, 'The celebrated Polish dwarf', U. Durham L. [typescript; Eng. trans. of article from *Wiadomósci*, 21 July 1968] • *Annual Register* (1760), 78; (1761), 112 • *N&Q*, 2nd ser., 1 (1856), 154, 240, 358; 2 (1856), 157–8 • *GM*, 2nd ser., 8 (1837), 435 • letters of administration, 27 March 1838, U. Durham L., archives and special collections, Durham probate records • letters to E. George and poem, Czartoryski Library, Kraków, Poland, MS 2798 • U. Durham L., archives and special collections, Boruwlaski collection, SR Cab Ci • R. F. Gould, 'Freemasonry in Cheshire', *Ars Quatuor Coronatorum*, 15 (1902), 41–5, esp. 44 • dean and chapter receivers' books, 1812/13–1850, U. Durham L., archives and special collections • A. Marsden, ed., *A Raine miscellany*, SurtS, 200 (1991), 123–5 • A. Mathews, *Memoirs of Charles Mathews, comedian*, 4 vols. (1838–9), 3.213–32 • T. M. Heron, *Boruwlaski: the little count* (1986) • J. Boruwlaski, *The life and love letters of a dwarf*, ed. H. R. Heatley (1902) • *Public Advertiser* (7 June 1782); (10 June 1782); (19 June 1782) • *Morning Post, and Daily Advertiser* (27 March 1786); (31 March 1786); (5 April 1786); (11 April 1786); (1 May 1786); (10 May 1786) • private information (2004) [L. H. Massey, letter, 16 Oct 1967]

Archives town hall, Durham, collection of memorabilia • U. Durham, collection, SR Cab Ci | Czartoryski Library, Kraków, MS 2798

Likenesses T. Rowlandson, caricature, pubd 1786 • W. Hinks, stipple, 1787, repro. in Boruwlaski, *Mémoires* (1788), frontispiece • R. Hancock, engraving, 1792, repro. in Boruwlaski, *Mémoires* (1792), frontispiece • J. Kay, etching, 1802, NPG • J. Downman, drawing, 1812, BM • E. Landseer, caricature, pen and ink, and wash, 1830–35, NPG • J. Bouet, pen and wash sketch, 1833, U. Durham • T. Bonomi, statue, town hall, Durham • J. Bouet, pen and wash sketch, U. Durham • W. Collins, portrait, BM • J. Downman, engraving (after J. Bouet), U. Durham; repro. in Boruwlaski, *Memoirs* • E. Hastings, oils, town hall, Durham • woodcut, repro. in A. Roberts, *The entertaining medley* (1826)

Wealth at death under £100: administration, 27 March 1838, Durham probate records

Bosa [St Bosa] (*d.* **706**), bishop of York, was trained in the religious life at the monastery of 'Streanæshalch' (Whitby) under Abbess Hild. In 678 or 679 he was intruded into the much reduced see of York, in place of Wilfrid, at the instance of King Ecgfrith and Archbishop Theodore. It was perhaps then that Acca, later one of Wilfrid's leading followers, became a member of his household. When Wilfrid was reinstated, in 686 or 687, Bosa was expelled from York. What became of him then is unknown; with Wilfrid's second expulsion, *c.*691, he was, however, restored, remaining at York until his death. Although commanded by the pope in 704 to attend the council convoked to settle Wilfrid's claims to a diocese covering the whole of Northumbria, it is not certain that he was present at the synod eventually held by the River Nidd in 706; he was probably already a sick man, for he died that year, shortly afterwards.

Bede, who presumably heard about Bosa from Acca, writes of him very warmly, praising his great holiness and humility. The bishop was also remembered with affection at York, where in the time of Alcuin (*d.* 804) he was reputed a 'staunch and upright teacher', who endowed the fabric and caused his clergy to live apart from the common people.

Bosa was commemorated in the late eighth-century metrical calendar of York on 2 October. Later, his feast day was 9 March. ALAN THACKER

Sources Bede, *Hist. eccl.*, 4.12; 5.3, 20 • Alcuin, *The bishops, kings, and saints of York*, ed. and trans. P. Godman, OMT (1982) • A. Wilmart, 'Un témoin Anglo-Saxon du calendrier métrique d'York', *Revue Bénédictine*, 46 (1934), 41–69

Bosan, Bartholomew (*d.* **1400**), merchant, was a native of Lucca in Italy who had established a business in London by the early 1370s. He makes numerous appearances in the city records during the following three decades, mostly as a mainpernor, guarantor, and litigant, and often alongside fellow Italians. Accused at different times of involvement in both usury and forgery, on one occasion he was imprisoned as the result of an action by his fellow Lucchese Francis Vincheguerre. It was with another Lucchese, Thomas Serland, that in 1371 he traded to Bruges, a common centre for commercial activity by Italian merchants living in London at this time. The pattern thus established would appear to have continued, for customs accounts from twenty years later show Bosan frequently receiving consignments from ships captained by north European masters, and the mixture of Italian goods and local European manufactures carried by these ships suggests strongly that they had in their turn come from

Bruges. He imported a wide variety of items, mostly Flemish and Brabant linen thread together with the luxury fabrics for which his native city was well known—rakemas, satins, silk baldachins, Cyprus gold brocades, velvets, taffetas, kerchiefs, and sarsenet—as well as raw silks and small amounts of drugs and spices such as wormseed, rhubarb, and pepper. At his death he owed the wardens of the Mercers' Company £10, perhaps in unpaid quarterage, and was subsequently described as having been a citizen and mercer of London.

Bosan's imports, while finding a natural outlet in sales to London mercers, would have guaranteed him an entrée to aristocratic and clerical households in London. Lucchese fabrics were very popular at Edward III's court, where they were used for royal wedding garments and as gifts to retiring ambassadors, as well as at funerals and obits and for donations to religious houses. Bosan may well have been the Bett Lumbard who supplied eleven lengths of cloth of gold each costing £6 and four lengths of silk worth £2 each that were presented to Waleran de Luxembourg, count of St Pol, and his company when they left England in 1389, having come to swear to the truce between England and France. He sold Cyprus gold baldachins, coloured baldachins, different coloured silk velvets, and satins to the future Henry IV's wardrobe in London during 1391/2; he supplied Henry again in 1397/8, this time with rakemas and silk baldachins. His exports consisted largely of worsted and undyed cloth, tin and tin wares, and old wines. He appears as a debtor to the value of £5 18*s.* in the account book of Gilbert Maghfeld (*d.* 1397), perhaps in connection with a payment owing for customs, as the book contains rough jottings for particulars of customs accounts, and Maghfeld was collector for petty custom and tunnage and poundage in London in 1390.

Bosan was granted letters of denization in 1391 for £50, on condition that he neither belonged to any company of alien merchants nor took advantage of his new nationality by lending his name to cover the passage of alien merchandise through customs. By 1400, when he surrendered letters patent which had granted him the proceeds from property which had belonged to John Export in the parish of St Mary Aldermary, he held the position of king's esquire. In the same year he was named in a grant to Elizabeth, dowager duchess of Norfolk, of the goods and debts due to the king from her late husband, Thomas (I) Mowbray. Although it was said in 1403 that he had fallen sick and made a will at Newark, while accompanying the king on his return from Scotland in 1400, the only surviving record associated with Bosan's death is an enrolment of letters of administration, by which his goods were committed to Peter Burton and William Sowthous in September 1400. However, an action for £200 brought by the mercer Thomas Aleyn in 1403, against Bosan's widow, Joan, and the two administrators, named Joan as his executor along with John Duffeld, John Corne, John Bilte, and John Taillour. Joan had strong English connections. In 1428 the mercer John Shadworth bequeathed property in the parish of St Bartholomew-the-Less to the order of Minoresses outside Aldgate, on condition that they should offer prayers for his own soul and for the souls of Bosan, his wife, Joan, and their daughter Philippa, and in addition the Minoresses were particularly instructed to observe Joan's obit. It is possible that Joan was a blood relative of Shadworth, or perhaps she married him after Bosan's death, bringing their daughter Philippa into Shadworth's household. H. L. Bradley

Sources exchequer of receipt issue rolls, 24 July 1389, PRO, E403/524 · Rymer, *Foedera*, 3rd edn, 3/4.149 · accounts, PRO, duchy of Lancaster, various accounts, 28/1/3, 28/1/6 · husting roll, 7 May 1428, CLRO, 159 (11) · wardens' accounts, 1347, Mercers' Hall, London · wardens' accounts, 1390–1463, Mercers' Hall, London, fol. 17 · CLRO, MC 1/1/27; 1/2/138; 1/2/110 · exchequer, king's remembrancer, curtains accounts, PRO, E122/71/16, 71/13 · exchequer, king's remembrancer, accounts various, PRO, E101/509/19 · 23 Sept 1400, GL, 9171/1/fol. 460 · *CPR*, *1388–92*; *1399–1405* · A. H. Thomas and P. E. Jones, eds., *Calendar of plea and memoranda rolls preserved among the archives of the corporation of the City of London at the Guildhall*, 2–3 (1929–32) · R. R. Sharpe, ed., *Calendar of letter-books preserved in the archives of the corporation of the City of London*, [12 vols.] (1899–1912), vol. H, pp. 27–8, 54, 363

Bosanquet, Sir (Frederick) Albert (1837–1923), judge, was born at Lewes, Sussex, on 8 February 1837, the fourth son of Samuel Richard *Bosanquet (1800–1882) of Forest House, Epping, Essex, and Dingestow Court, Monmouthshire, who belonged to an old Huguenot family. His mother was Emily (1809–1869), eldest daughter of George Courthope, of Whiligh, Sussex. His great-grandfather Samuel Bosanquet (1744–1806) was governor of the Bank of England in 1792; Charles Bosanquet, City merchant and writer, and Sir John Bernard *Bosanquet, judge, were his great-uncles; James Whatman Bosanquet, banker and biblical historian, was his uncle; and Bernard Bosanquet, the philosopher, was his second cousin.

Bosanquet was a scholar of Eton College (1850–56), whence he proceeded to King's College, Cambridge. He obtained a first class in the classical tripos and was senior optime in 1860, becoming a fellow of his college in 1863. In the same year he was called to the bar by the Inner Temple (which he entered in 1860, becoming a bencher in 1889 and treasurer in 1909) and joined the Oxford circuit. On 22 August 1871 he married Albinia Mary (*d.* 1882), daughter of John Curtis-Hayward, of Quedgeley House, Gloucester, with whom he had two sons and two daughters. With J. G. N. Darby he wrote *A Practical Treatise on the Statutes of Limitations in England and Ireland* (1867), which became the standard textbook on the subject. For some years he was junior counsel to the Admiralty. He was appointed recorder of Worcester in 1879 and, on leaving that position, was recorder of Wolverhampton from 1891 to 1900.

In 1882 Bosanquet took silk and acquired a large practice both in London and on circuit, often appearing in local government and rating cases, in which he was regarded as an authority, and to which, an obituarist noted, 'his somewhat dry and funereal style of oratory was well adapted' (*The Times*, 5 Nov 1923). His arguments, which were full and learned, were not always lively: a contemporary directory noted that 'His style of advocacy is far removed from the "showy"; his speeches are epigrammatic in construction and are appreciated more by judges than juries' (Pratt). He was, however, possessed of a certain desiccated wit: to a colleague who chafed him, saying 'Bosey [his nickname], you are the dullest dog at the bar', he reputedly replied: 'Have you considered the case of Gainsford Bruce?' (*The Times*, 5 Nov 1923). As a lawyer his reputation stood high and his elevation to the bench, always regarded as probable, seemed to be foreshadowed by his appointment on two occasions as commissioner of assize. But the times were not propitious for non-politicians, and a judgeship of the High Court was never offered to him. Following the death of his first wife in 1882, on 12 August 1885 he married Philippa Frances (1853/4–1929), daughter of William Bence-Jones, of Lisselan, co. Cork, with whom he had a daughter and a son, Captain William Sydney Bence Bosanquet, who subsequently married a daughter of Grover Cleveland, twice president of the United States of America.

On the promotion in 1900 of Sir Forrest Fulton to the recordership of London, Bosanquet was chosen by Lord Halsbury to succeed him as common serjeant. He at once proved himself to be worthy of higher judicial office. As common serjeant he had both civil and criminal jurisdiction, and was equally at home whether trying prisoners at the central criminal court or cases in the mayor's court: as a judge, he eschewed 'appeals to the gallery, and … irrelevant digressions' (*The Times*, 5 Nov 1923). He retired in 1917 after he had reached his eightieth birthday. In his nominal retirement, he was made an additional judge of the central criminal court and continued to act as chairman of the east Sussex quarter sessions until 1921, an appointment he had held since 1912. He was chairman of the Council of Law Reporting from 1909 to 1917, and a member of the royal commission which in 1888, under the presidency of Lord Herschell, inquired into the old Metropolitan Board of Works. He was interested in religious matters, and was for a time a member of the Canterbury house of laymen. He was knighted in 1907. Bosanquet died at his London address, 12 Grenville Place, on 2 November 1923, and was buried four days later at Quedgeley.

THEOBALD MATHEW, *rev.* H. J. SPENCER

Sources *The Times* (5 Nov 1923) • *Law Journal* (10 Nov 1923) • personal knowledge (1937) • A. T. C. Pratt, ed., *People of the period: being a collection of the biographies of upwards of six thousand living celebrities*, 2 vols. (1897) • Venn, *Alum. Cant.* • m. cert., 12 Aug 1885 • *DWB*

Likenesses Spy [L. Ward], chromolithograph caricature, NPG; repro. in *VF* (21 Nov 1901)

Wealth at death £18,911 16*s.* 7*d.*: probate, 19 Dec 1923, *CGPLA Eng. & Wales*

Bosanquet, Bernard (1848–1923), philosopher and social theorist, was born on 14 June 1848 at Rock Hall, near Alnwick, the youngest of five sons of the Revd Robert William Bosanquet (1800–1880), of Rock, Northumberland, and formerly rector of Bolingbroke, Lincolnshire. Bernard Bosanquet's mother, Caroline (Robert Bosanquet's second wife), was the daughter of Colonel Day Hort Macdowall, of Castle Semple, Renfrewshire. Bosanquet was

Bernard Bosanquet (1848–1923), by Walter Stoneman, 1917

educated at preparatory schools at Sherburn, co. Durham, and Elstree, and then proceeded to Harrow in 1862. He was a classical scholar of Balliol College, Oxford, from 1866 to 1870, and gained first classes in classical moderations and *literae humaniores*. As fellow of University College, Oxford, from 1870, he taught ancient Greek history and philosophy. In 1881 he resigned, having sufficient means to go to London to find more time to write and take up social work.

Intellectual influences The direction of Bosanquet's interests had been foreshadowed at Balliol, where he was strongly influenced by his reading of the Greek philosophers, especially Plato, and the teaching in that field of Richard Lewis Nettleship, by the ideas and social experiments of Arnold Toynbee, and above all by the lectures and tutorials of Thomas Hill Green. Green impressed Bosanquet by his version of idealist philosophy and introduced him to the works of Kant and Hegel. It is possible that Green, who persuaded many of his students to engage in social work, influenced him in that direction too; but Bosanquet also had the example of his half-brother Charles Bertie Pulleine Bosanquet (1834–1905) and his friend Charles Stewart Loch, and like them he soon became prominent in the Charity Organization Society (COS). His role became mainly that of committee man, counsellor, and theorist rather than that of active social worker, for he found direct contact with the poor embarrassing. He also did some university extension lecturing, and later some teaching at the COS's school of sociology and social economics; he also lectured to the London Ethical Society, of which he was a member.

Publications in philosophy and aesthetics Bosanquet made his entrance as a writer on philosophy in 1882–3, when he published two articles in the journal *Mind*, to which he thereafter became a regular contributor. He also joined the Aristotelian Society in 1886, and became not merely a frequent contributor to its *Proceedings*, but also its vice-president in 1888 and its president from 1894 to 1898. His interest in logic had been inspired, as he handsomely acknowledged, by the writings of his contemporary Francis Herbert Bradley. Bradley's *Ethical Studies* had been published in 1876 and his *Principles of Logic* appeared in 1883. Bosanquet declared himself 'blown to the winds' by the quality of the first book; but his response to the second was mixed—he found much to agree with but a deal to disturb him in Bradley's outlook—and he wrote an appreciative but critical study, published in 1885 under the title *Knowledge and Reality*. This was the prelude to his full-scale work *Logic*, which appeared in 1888. Bradley acknowledged the force of some of Bosanquet's criticism. The two philosophers, although not intimate friends or collaborators, established a mutual regard for each other's work. Bosanquet was the more orthodox in his respect for the teachings of the German philosophers Hegel, Lotze, and Sigwart, Bradley more wayward and independent.

Aesthetics occupied Bosanquet's attention next, and there he took the lead. At Oxford he had been attracted by the artistic opinions and the craftsmanship of William Morris. In London, Bosanquet furnished his terrace house at 7 Cheyne Gardens with Morris wallpapers and hangings, De Morgan tiles, and parquet floors. He took an active interest in the Home Arts and Industries Association, founded in 1885 to encourage artistic handiwork in education. Other influences upon him were the writings of John Ruskin and Hegel. He translated the introduction to Hegel's *Philosophy of Fine Art* in 1886, and his own *History of Aesthetic* (1892) covered a period from the Greeks to the nineteenth century, revealing the wide span of his learning and appreciation. It became a standard text in a study rather neglected by British philosophers of his own time.

Politics and the philosophy of public life The depression of the 1880s and early 1890s raised political and social problems, which Bosanquet as a social theorist had to face. He described himself as belonging in the radical wing of the Liberal Party. But the term 'radical' was acquiring a new meaning with the rise of socialism in this period, and the Fabian Society, wishing to discover where he stood, invited him in February 1890 to address them. In his speech he made it clear that he was not an individualist or committed to *laissez-faire* and that he was willing to subscribe to the ideas of 'moral socialism', but he believed 'economic socialists' were on the wrong track. He deplored their disrespect for private property, disparagement of saving, attack on the strict administration of the poor law, and their aim of complete equality and abolition of classes. This marked the beginning of protracted disputes between the COS and Fabians and 'new Liberals' concerning methods of economic reform and remedies for pauperism. The disputes culminated in the great royal commission of inquiry into the poor laws (1905–9), in which Helen Bosanquet and Beatrice Webb played leading roles on opposite sides.

On 13 December 1895 Bernard Bosanquet had married Helen Dendy [*see* Bosanquet, Helen (1860–1925)], a social worker for the COS and a first-class honours graduate in the moral sciences tripos at Cambridge. They combined their talents to improve practical skills in the COS and to justify its policy in terms of the principles of idealist philosophy. A special emphasis on will and character and the communities (especially the family) that fostered them was a key concept both in Bosanquet's social thinking and in his wife's practical COS work. They divided the poor into two categories, which they labelled the 'helpable' and the 'unhelpable' to supersede the COS's earlier terms 'deserving' and 'undeserving', thus avoiding the suggestion that poverty was necessarily a person's own fault. The helpable were those whose character and will to struggle for self-maintenance had not been destroyed. Such persons were fit objects of discriminating charity to set them again on their feet. Undiscriminating charity was an evil to be avoided, for it would weaken the individual will and character and discourage family support. The unhelpable poor should be assigned to the strict state poor law, which might goad their weak wills into strengthening habits. The Bosanquets opposed what they called the 'rough and mechanical' undiscriminating reforms of socialists, such as the provision by the state of free school meals, free medical treatment for the working class, state old age pensions, and child endowment for widows and deserted wives.

In his social philosophy at the theoretical level, Bosanquet was a 'collectivist', and in agreement with Bradley's doctrine of 'my station and its duties', which emphasized the role of the individual as a function of the social organism, and saw his very mind and being as a production of the communities—the family, the neighbourhood, the profession and class, the social groups, the state—to which he belonged. In this view, the basis of the individual's political obligation of loyalty to his state was that its collectivism provided him with the protection and opportunity for developing his talents, not only for the purpose of fulfilling his role in his social station, but also, in the case of gifted individuals, for achieving a perfection in advance of where society at any moment stood, in the arts and the sciences, as well as in social values and personal cultivation.

Bosanquet went on to argue that in the mind of each individual, with varying degrees of consciousness of it, there was a 'real will' as well as an 'actual will'. The actual will sought satisfaction in the individual's immediate desires, including ill-considered and transient impulses; the real will exercised the more critical function of thinking beyond immediate particular ends and means to more permanent and moral satisfactions, including the harmonizing of the individual's wants with those of others. The real will thus became identified with a social way of living—with the 'general will' of the community. Ideally, a state should be in harmony with this general will, for it is then recognized by its members as rightfully exercising legislative and physical compulsion over them; in return, the state should not attempt to go beyond the general will by force. If it did, that would lead ultimately to a repressive 'machine-made utopia', faced with the dangers of disobedience and rebellion. The crucial tests of any social measure of the state were whether it had the approval of the general will, and whether it liberated fresh resources of character, will, and intelligence in the community. Bosanquet's book *The Philosophical Theory of the State* (1889), which embodies these ideas and much besides, still stands as one of the greatest achievements of British idealist philosophy.

Idealism While Bosanquet had been exploring the social implications of idealism, Bradley had plunged deeply into metaphysics. Once again, Bosanquet saluted his priority and welcomed the general argument of his *Appearance and Reality* (1893). Bosanquet's own later books, *The Principle of Individuality and Value* (1912) and *The Value and Destiny of the Individual* (1913), made no great advance on Bradley's brilliant work. Their form of idealism came to be known as absolute idealism because they maintained that logic and the impulsion of human thought to discover ultimate reality implied that an absolute—all-inclusive, completely harmonious—must exist. In the absolute all the contradictions and 'appearances' of everyday life would be transcended in a way that we can only partially (although perhaps increasingly) come to apprehend. Bosanquet took a lively part in professional debates concerning absolute idealism. He was formidable but courteous in disputation with colleagues and opponents, and he had much opposition to contend with, not only from philosophers hostile to idealism, but also from the idealist ranks as well. Absolute idealism treated the Christian deity as merely an 'appearance' of the greater reality of the absolute. This was not welcomed by Christian idealists who sought to identify the absolute with God. Neither did it appeal to personal idealists, who felt that absolutism placed too much emphasis on community values and did not allow enough room for individual personality and initiative; some even claimed that it smacked of 'oriental philosophy'.

The heaviest assault on idealism in general, however, came at the turn of the century from the generation of Cambridge new realists, led by George Edward Moore and Bertrand Russell. During the First World War, idealism suffered a good deal of vilification as a 'Germanic doctrine'; and after the war the development of Cambridge philosophy in the direction of logical positivism and linguistic philosophy captured the attention of the newer generation. Idealism lost its attraction; but in the late twentieth century there were signs of a renewal of interest in it, especially among political philosophers.

Final years After their marriage, the Bosanquets moved out of London, first to Caterham and then, in 1899, to Oxshott in Surrey, where they built a house and rose garden next door to their friends the Lochs. Bosanquet was professor of moral philosophy at the University of St Andrews from 1903 to 1907; but during this appointment they retained the Oxshott cottage, and returned to it in the summer vacations. The only later academic post Bosanquet held was that of Gifford lecturer at Edinburgh in the winters of 1911–12. Oxshott remained the Bosanquets' home until Bernard's health, which had been failing since 1915, made it necessary for them to move back to the London area, to be near relatives in Golders Green; they lived at 13 Heathgate, Golders Green. Bernard Bosanquet died there on 8 February 1923. He had no children. Photographs show him to have been a handsome man of serious and thoughtful appearance, and his grace and courtesy of manner were remarked upon by his many friends.

A. M. McBriar

Sources H. Bosanquet, *Bernard Bosanquet* (1924) · G. L. Lee, *The story of the Bosanquets* (1966) · J. B. Ballie and others, *Contemporary British philosophy: personal statements*, ed. J. H. Muirhead (1924) · J. H. Muirhead, ed., *Bernard Bosanquet and his friends* (1935) · A. M. McBriar, *An Edwardian mixed doubles, the Bosanquets versus the Webbs: a study in British social policy, 1890–1929* (1987) · P. P. Nicholson, *The political philosophy of the British idealists: selected studies* (1990) · P. P. Nicholson, 'A bibliography of the writings of Bernard Bosanquet', *Idealistic Studies*, 8/3 (1978)

Archives U. Newcastle, Robinson L., corresp., MSS, and papers | BL, corresp. with Macmillans, Add. MS 55160 · JRL, letters to Samuel Alexander

Likenesses W. Stoneman, photograph, 1917, NPG [*see illus.*] · H. Glazebrook, portrait, Rock Hall, Northumberland

Wealth at death £8689 17*s*. 0*d*.: resworn probate, 13 March 1923, *CGPLA Eng. & Wales*

Bosanquet, Bernard James Tindal (1877–1936), cricketer, born at home at Bulls Cross, Enfield, Middlesex, on 13 October 1877, was the eldest son in the family of two sons and three daughters of Bernard Tindal Bosanquet (1843–1910) and his wife, Eva Maude Cotton (*d.* 1912), and was grandson of James Whatman *Bosanquet. His father, who was of Huguenot descent, belonged to the banking firm Bosanquet & Co., which was sold to Lloyds Bank in 1884, and then became a partner in Culverwell, Brooks & Co., hide, leather, and fur brokers in the City of London; he was high sheriff of Middlesex (1897–8), honorary lieutenant-colonel in the rifle brigade, and captain of Enfield cricket club. Bernard, the son, attended Sunnymede School, Slough, before going on to Eton College (1891–6), where he scored a century against Harrow at Lord's, and then Oriel College, Oxford (1897–1900), which he left without taking a degree. He had a distinguished sporting career at the university, winning blues for cricket (1898, 1899, and 1900), and half-blues for hammer-throwing (1899, 1900) and billiards (1898, 1900), as well as being an accomplished ice hockey player.

Bosanquet is remembered as the bowler who invented the 'googly', an off-break delivered with a leg-break action from the back of the hand. He had begun, when at Oxford, to pitch a tennis ball on a table so that, with the same action or delivery, he could make it break in one direction, then another. By 1899 he had progressed to a cricket ball. 'I had become a "star turn" for the luncheon interval during our matches at Oxford. The most famous batsman from the opposing side was enticed into a net' (*Wisden*, 1925, 226), Bosanquet bowled two or three leg-breaks to him, and then, with the same action but altering the axis of the spin, deceived him with an off-break. He recorded his first success when, playing for Middlesex at Lord's in 1900, he had the Leicestershire batsman S. Coe stumped on 98, albeit with a delivery which bounced four times before reaching the wicket-keeper. It was at first regarded as something of a joke, and *Wisden* (1901, 129) chose to give him credit instead for his two centuries in the match. The development in this technique, however, marked a revolution in bowling, and transformed Bosanquet from a fairly ordinary medium-pacer into a spinner capable of baffling the most assured batsman with his flight and break.

Between 1898 and 1919 Bosanquet, who had a business career, played 123 matches as an amateur for Middlesex and represented England on six occasions. He took a total of 629 wickets at an average of 23.8 runs per wicket. In his best season, 1904, he captured 132 wickets. He went on six overseas tours but played representative matches only on MCC's 1903–4 tour to Australia, when, in the fourth test at Sydney, his six for 51 in the second innings enabled England to win back the 'Ashes'. His best performance was eight for 107 against Australia at Nottingham in 1905. After 1905, when he was one of the *Wisden* cricketers of the year, his bowling declined, though his batting improved remarkably. Standing 6 feet tall, he was a fine hard-hitting batsman who in 1908 topped the first-class averages with 1018 runs (average 54.05).

As a bowler, Bosanquet remained something of an enigma. A friend once reflected, 'I know old Bose invented the Googly and that sort of thing, but did he ever get any wickets?' (*Wisden*, 1925, 228). His length was notoriously wayward and even his mentor, Sir Pelham Warner, said he bowled more bad balls than any bowler he knew. Yet on his day he was a match-winner, and the long line of googly bowlers who succeeded him (notably the 1907 South African side) was testimony to his achievement. Abdul Qadir of Pakistan was the most notable exponent of the technique in the 1980s, and Shane Warne of Australia in the 1990s.

During the First World War Bosanquet was a temporary lieutenant in the Royal Flying Corps. A convivial and good-natured man, he married, on 5 April 1924, Mary Janet (*b.* 1897/8), daughter of (William) Kennedy *Jones, MP for Hornsey and joint founder of the *Daily Mail*. Their only child, Reginald Tindal Kennedy Bosanquet (1932–1991), became a well-known television newsreader. Following his father's death in 1910 Bosanquet sold the family seat, Claysmore, Enfield, Middlesex, and settled at Wykehurst Farm, Coneyhurst Lane, Ewhurst, Surrey, where he died on 12 October 1936. He was buried three days later in the Lavender Hill cemetery, Enfield. His wife survived him.

GLENYS WILLIAMS

Sources *WWW* • Burke, *Gen. GB* (1937) • P. Bailey, P. Thorn, and P. Wynne-Thomas, *Who's who of cricketers*, rev. edn (1993) • J. Pollard, *The world's greatest leg-spin bowlers* (1994) • D. Frith, *The slow men* (1984) • B. J. T. Bosanquet, 'The googly: the scapegoat of cricket', *Wisden* (1925), 225–8 • B. Green, ed., *The Wisden book of obituaries* (1986) • R. C. Robertson-Glasgow, *Crusoe on cricket* (1966) • C. Martin-Jenkins, *World cricketers: a biographical dictionary* (1996) • *Leading men of London: a collection of biographical sketches* (1895) • J. Eddowes, *The language of cricket* (1997) • m. cert.

Likenesses T. G. Foster, photograph, 1903–4 (*Warner's team series*), Marylebone cricket club • E. Hawkins, photograph, 1904, Marylebone cricket club • G. Whitehead, chromolithograph, 1905 (*The empire's cricketers*), Marylebone cricket club • Spy [L. Ward], chromolithograph caricature, NPG; repro. in *VF* (21 Nov 1901) • Spy [L. Ward], chromolithograph cartoon (*The artful bowler*), Marylebone cricket club; repro. in *VF* (1904) • photograph, repro. in *Wisden* (1905) • photographs, George Beldam collection • postcard, Marylebone cricket club

Wealth at death £2,276 0s. 4*d.*: administration, 30 Nov 1936, *CGPLA Eng. & Wales*

Bosanquet, Charles (1769–1850), merchant and writer, was born at Forest House, Leyton, Essex, on 23 July 1769, the second son of Samuel Bosanquet (1744–1806), a Huguenot merchant, and his wife, Eleanor (*c.*1745–1819), the daughter of Henry Lannoy Hunter of Beechill, Berkshire. When he was seven he was sent to school in Hackney, then from the ages of sixteen to eighteen he was placed in a merchant's house in Lyons. Later, in partnership with J. P. Anderson, he went into the West Indian trade. At the height of the City's fears of attack from France, in 1794, he was gazetted lieutenant of the London and Westminster light horse volunteers. By 1796 he wrote, 'considering myself as well established both in income and respectability, I paid my addresses to Miss Charlotte Holford' (Lee, 81). On 1 June 1796 he married Charlotte Anne (*d.* 1839), the daughter of Peter Holford, a master in chancery; a son and six daughters were born, but five of the daughters died in infancy or youth.

From 1809 Bosanquet was a member of Lloyds (he was also a member of the committee of its patriotic fund) and in 1814 he became trustee to William Balston's paper manufactory. He was sub-governor of the South Sea Company from 1808 to 1838, then governor until 1850. He was appointed a director of the West India Company, which was set up in 1825 to relieve the economic plight of planters in the British Caribbean. He also played an active public role; from 1823 to 1836 he was chairman of the exchequer bill office, and he was governor of the Canadian Land Company and instrumental in bringing vast tracts of land in western Canada into cultivation.

Bosanquet wrote four economic pamphlets, chiefly relating to the sugar and rum trade of the British Caribbean. These included *A letter on the proposition submitted to government for taking the duty on muscovado sugar ad valorem* (1806) and *A Letter to W. Manning, Esq., MP, on the Depreciation of West India Property* (2nd edn, 1807), in which he argued against proposals to tax sugar on the basis of quality and against the discriminatory duties which protected the British Caribbean monopoly of the home market. He advocated the sole use of British West India rum by domestic distilleries and by the navy to boost sales and to exclude foreign competition. His *Thoughts on the value to Great Britain of commerce in general, and the colonial trade in particular* (1807) asserted the importance and profitability of the West India trade, to which William Spence replied in *Radical Cause of the Present Distresses of West India Planters Pointed out* (1807). His *Practical Observations on the Report of the Bullion Committee* (2nd edn, with supplement, 1810) ranks among the most effective statements of the anti-bullionist position and provoked a brilliant rebuttal, which was later upheld as a model essay on political economy, by David Ricardo in *Reply to Mr Bosanquet's Practical Observations on the Report of the Bullion Committee* (1811).

Bosanquet acquired in 1804 a London residence at The Firs, Hampstead, and the former Holford estate at Rock in Northumberland, the gift of his brother-in-law Richard Holford, with its large manor house which had been badly damaged by fire. He set about restoring the house, which served as a summer retreat until his retirement from business, when it became his permanent home. In 1828 he was high sheriff of Northumberland, where he was also justice of the peace and deputy lieutenant. He owned the living of Bolingbroke with Hareby in Lincolnshire, together with stock in the Royal Exchange Assurance Company, and his bequests included £19,000-worth of annuities in the South Sea Company. In old age he underwent treatment for cataract. He died at Rock on 20 June 1850 and was buried in the church there, monuments being placed there and at Hampstead. He was survived by his son, the Revd Robert William Bosanquet, and his daughter Mary Anne, the wife of the Revd Robert Fielde.

ANDREW J. O'SHAUGHNESSY

Sources *GM*, 2nd ser., 34 (1850), 325 • L. C. Meyer, *Genealogy of the family of Bosanquet* (1877) • J. R. McCulloch, *The literature of political economy: a classified catalogue* (1845) • C. Bosanquet, autobiographical sketch, Huguenot Society Library • G. L. Lee, *The story of the Bosanquets* (1966) • will, PRO, PROB 11/2117, sig. 581
Archives UCL, Huguenot Library | JRL, letters to Mary Fletcher
Likenesses portrait, 1824, repro. in Lee, *Story of the Bosanquets*

Bosanquet [*née* Dendy], **Helen** (1860–1925), social theorist and social reformer, was born in Manchester on 10 February 1860. She was the youngest daughter and the fifth child in the family of five sons and four daughters of the Revd John Dendy, who had been a nonconformist minister, and then became a businessman in Manchester, and his wife, Sarah Beard, daughter of a Unitarian minister. Mary *Dendy was an elder sister. Having been educated at home by a German governess, she spent the early part of her adult life keeping house for her brothers. In 1886, at the age of twenty-six, she went to Newnham College, Cambridge, where she and another were the first women to gain first-class honours in the Cambridge moral sciences tripos in 1889. She specialized in political economy. She appears to have had academic ambitions, but no permanent openings were offered in either Cambridge or Oxford. She then moved to London and joined the Charity Organisation Society (COS), a body committed to rationalizing London's vast mass of private charities and to defending orthodox economics. She became organizer and district secretary of the society's Shoreditch branch. She was also active in the London Ethical Society, where she met the philosopher Bernard *Bosanquet (1848–1923), whom she married on 13 December 1895. Thereafter she

Helen Bosanquet (1860–1925), by unknown photographer

took no paid employment for the rest of her life, but pursued an active public career as a theorist and publicist for the COS, as a translator of German philosophy and sociology, and as a collaborator with her husband.

In 1902 Helen Bosanquet had a much publicized exchange of views with Benjamin Seebohm Rowntree in which she questioned both the extent and the causes of primary poverty as set out in Rowntree's survey of York in 1899. At the end of 1905 she was appointed a member of the royal commission on the poor laws, where she defended the role of organized private charity in public welfare, against the bureaucratic socialism of Beatrice Webb. Her health broke down in 1908, but she is nevertheless believed to have drafted many sections of the royal commission's majority report. In 1909 she became editor of the *Charity Organisation Review*, the official mouthpiece of the COS, and in 1914 she published a history of the previous half-century of charitable work in London, *Social Work in London, 1869–1912*. She and her husband lived most of their married life at Oxshott in Surrey, in a rural-cum-suburban community very similar to that described in the writings of their neighbour and contemporary George Sturt (George Bourne). They had no children.

Mrs Bosanquet's reputation was in eclipse for most of the twentieth century, partly because of the disparaging account of her in Beatrice Webb's diaries ('the little woman'), and partly because of her association with a subsequently discredited school of 'social economics'. She was, however, a major figure in the development of British social work; and her theoretical and sociological writings became of more interest in the late twentieth century than they had appeared to be during and shortly after her lifetime (when idealist and *verstehen* modes of thought were being demolished by positivism). She was influential in defining the syllabus of the COS's school of sociology, founded in 1903, which was absorbed into the social science department of the London School of Economics in 1912. It was she who insisted that charitable visiting should be grounded in formal training for objective casework; and it was also she who suggested that social workers needed civic education in history, social structure, and economics, as well as professional skills. That two-tier emphasis on both general and professional learning remained a characteristic of British training for social work.

Helen Bosanquet's major writings were: *Rich and Poor* (1896), *The Standard of Life and other Studies* (1898), *The Strength of the People* (1902), and *The Family* (1906). These books are rather discursive in style, and contain little of the exhaustive empirical detail characteristic of much Edwardian sociological writing. Nevertheless, they all exhibit a coherent underlying social theory. They attempt to fuse an organic, interdependent theory of society with a view of social behaviour that emphasized diversity and idiosyncrasy. The key to social progress lay in the rational will of individuals, and true philanthropy consisted in supporting and strengthening that rational will rather than in the mere mechanical relief of poverty. The way to social understanding lay not in counting heads or in measuring incomes (though accurate collection of such data was a useful secondary tool); it lay rather in cultural interpretation and participant observation. *The Family* challenged the view of many late nineteenth-century sociologists that the family as a social unit would inevitably decline under the pressures of industrial capitalism; and it challenged also the claim of Edwardian anthropologists (echoed by many feminists) that the roots of the family lay in matriarchy. Mrs Bosanquet was herself a feminist and suffragist, though she dissented from most Edwardian feminists in believing that the true expression of women's rights lay not in the public and professional sphere, but in raising the status and functional efficiency of family life. Her views were spelt out in her criticism of the royal commission on divorce (1912), which had recommended the liberalization of the divorce laws. She is often portrayed by historians as upholding an archaic, gentrified, pre-industrial theory of society, and some of her opinions lend support to this view. But in many respects her writing suggests the exact opposite: that she was a proponent of modernity, rationality, and functional efficiency, often at the expense of traditional values and structures. 'The one fundamental cure for poverty is to make the poorer wage-earners more efficient in the widest sense of the term—more efficient as producers, as consumers, and in all the relations of life'.

As a person Mrs Bosanquet appears to have been quiet, ironic, and donnish. Her Newnham nicknames—Tone-Raiser and Aunt Dendy—suggest a certain old-fashioned high-mindedness of manner. Her method of cross-examination on the poor law commission was very low-key and mainly confined to precise verification of points of detail, in marked contrast to the dramatic style and absorption in first principles displayed by Beatrice Webb. In later life she suffered much from ill health and lived largely in retirement with her husband in Oxshott and subsequently in Golders Green. She wrote a short memoir of her husband which was published in 1924. Helen Bosanquet died at her home, 13 Heathgate, Golders Green, on 7 April 1925. JOSE HARRIS, *rev.*

Sources H. McLachlan, *Records of a family, 1800–1933: pioneers in education, social service and liberal religion* (1935) · A. M. McBriar, *An Edwardian mixed doubles, the Bosanquets versus the Webbs: a study in British social policy, 1890–1929* (1987) · *International Journal of Ethics* · *Charity Organisation Review* · *CGPLA Eng. & Wales* (1925)

Archives U. Newcastle, Robinson Library, diaries, corresp., and papers

Likenesses photograph, repro. in McLachlan, *Records of a family* [*see illus.*]

Wealth at death £8750 16*s*. 7*d*.: probate, 22 May 1925, *CGPLA Eng. & Wales*

Bosanquet, James Whatman (1804–1877), banker and biblical historian, was born on 10 January 1804, the second son of Samuel Bosanquet (1768–1843), banker, and his wife, Laetitia Philippa (1774–1855), daughter of James Whatman of Kent. Samuel Richard *Bosanquet was his elder brother. The Bosanquets were a numerous Huguenot family descended through intermarriage from several ancestors who had fled the Cévennes region of France to avoid religious persecutions. Samuel's prosperity derived in part from his bank, founded in 1796 as Bosanquet, Beechroft, and Reeves, of Lombard Street, in the City of London, and although he owned various properties, he was well known as a philanthropist. His own children grew up in the lordly setting of Dingestow Court, Monmouthshire.

James Bosanquet entered Westminster School in 1814 and left in 1817. In 1822 he became a partner in his father's bank, then known as Bosanquet, Pitt, Anderson, and Franks. He subsequently became a governor of the Bank of England and chairman of the income tax commission under Sir Robert Peel, and his earlier publications related to these matters. They included *Metallic, Paper, and Credit Currency* (1842), as well as a *Letter to the Right Hon. G. Cornewall Lewis on the Bank Charter Act of 1844* (1857).

Bosanquet's other interest lay in biblical and Assyrian chronology, reflected in his later writings for the Society of Biblical Archaeology, to which he gave generous financial support, serving as a member of council and treasurer. His third wife and several close relatives were also members of this society. His *Chronology of the Times of Daniel, Ezra, and Nehemiah* appeared in 1848, and was followed by other works, on the fall of Nineveh, the prophecies of Daniel, and the dating of Assurbanipal and Lachish. Bosanquet was described by the president of the society as 'the Maecenas of Assyriology' (*DNB*). He was also a fellow of the Royal Astronomical Society and communicated his findings on solar eclipses in biblical times to the Astronomer Royal.

Bosanquet was married three times, first, on 16 May 1840, to Merelina (1815–1852), daughter of Sir Nicholas Conyngham *Tindal MP, in a major society wedding, the service being conducted by the bishop of London. The couple had five sons and three daughters. His second marriage, on 15 July 1854 to Frances Georgiana Elizabeth (*c.*1817–1862), elder daughter of Lord John Thomas Henry *Somerset [*see under* Somerset, FitzRoy James Henry, first Baron Raglan], was childless. His third marriage, on 25 August 1864, to Emily Dorothy, daughter of James Best of Kent, produced three daughters. They resided at Claysmore, Enfield, Middlesex, where he died of enteric fever and bronchitis on 22 December 1877.

ANITA MCCONNELL

Sources G. L. Lee, *The story of the Bosanquets* (1966) • *The Athenaeum* (19 Jan 1878), 92 • *The Times* (1 Jan 1878), 5a • *The Times* (5 Jan 1878), 9e • *Old Westminsters*, 1.105–6 • *Transactions, Society of Biblical Archaeology*, 6 (1878–9), 592 • *DNB* • J. Clapham, *The Bank of England: a history*, 2 (1944) • d. cert.
Archives UCL, Huguenot Library
Likenesses A. de Salome, portrait, pastel, 1869, priv. coll.
Wealth at death under £30,000: resworn probate, March 1879, *CGPLA Eng. & Wales*

Bosanquet, Sir John Bernard (1773–1847), judge, was born at Forest House, Waltham Forest, on 2 May 1773, the youngest son of Samuel Bosanquet (1744–1806) of Waltham Forest and Dingestow Court, Monmouthshire, governor of the Bank of England in 1792, and his wife, Eleanor (*c.*1745–1819), daughter of Henry Lannoy Hunter of Beechill, Berkshire. He was educated at Eton College and Christ Church, Oxford, where he graduated BA on 9 June 1795 and MA on 20 March 1800. Admitted a student of Lincoln's Inn on 22 January 1794, Bosanquet was called to the bar on 9 May 1800 and joined the home circuit. He also attended the Essex sessions, of which his father was chairman. Before being called to the bar, with Christopher Puller he jointly founded *Reports of Cases Argued and Determined in the Court of Common Pleas and Exchequer Chamber, and in the House of Lords*, which appeared in two series, the first in three volumes from 1796 to 1804, and the second in two volumes from 1804 to 1807.

In 1804 Bosanquet married Mary Anne, the eldest daughter of Richard Lewis of Llantilio Crossenny; they had only one son, who predeceased his father. Family influence ensured early success in Bosanquet's career at the bar and he was appointed standing counsel to the East India Company (1814) and to the Bank of England (1819). On 22 November 1814 he was made a serjeant-at-law, and in thirteen years conducted numerous bank prosecutions, which were widely reported. In 1824 he declined the appointment of chief justice of Bengal, and in 1827 was made king's serjeant. On 16 May 1828 he was appointed to the commission inquiring into the practice of the common-law courts, a committee which he presided over for three years. On the retirement of Sir James Burrough, Bosanquet was made a judge of the court of common pleas on 1 February 1830, and was knighted on the following day. On 4 September 1833 he was sworn a member of the privy council, and from then until 1840 he sat regularly on its judicial committee.

On the resignation of lord chancellor Lyndhurst, Bosanquet, together with Sir Charles Pepys, the master of the rolls, and Sir Lancelot Shadwell, the vice-chancellor, was appointed lord commissioner of the great seal. This commission lasted from 23 April 1835 to 16 January 1836, when Pepys was made lord chancellor.

After eleven years of judicial work Bosanquet was compelled by ill health to retire in 1842. He died at The Firs, Hampstead Heath, on 25 September 1847 and was buried at Llantilio Crossenny, Monmouthshire.

Bosanquet was remembered not simply for his abilities as a judge but also as a man of considerable learning with a taste for biblical scholarship. In an anonymous tract, entitled *Letter of a Layman*, he attempted to demonstrate a connection between the books of Daniel and the Apocalypse.

G. F. R. BARKER, *rev.* HUGH MOONEY

Sources *Annual Register* (1847) • *Law Times* (13 Nov 1847), 122 • *GM*, 2nd ser., 28 (1847), 537–8, 661 • Foss, *Judges*, 9.149–51 • *N&Q*, 6th ser., 10 (1884), 147
Archives NRA, priv. coll., notebooks and corresp.
Likenesses W. J. Ward, mezzotint (after H. W. Pickersgill), BM, NPG • monument, parish church, Dingestow • portrait, Eton

Bosanquet, Mary. *See* Fletcher, Mary (1739–1815).

Bosanquet, Robert Carr (1871–1935), archaeologist, was born on 7 June 1871 in London where his father, Charles Bertie Pulleine Bosanquet (1834–1905), of Rock Hall, near Alnwick, the eldest brother of the philosopher Bernard *Bosanquet, was then acting as honorary secretary to the recently formed Charity Organization Society. His mother, Eliza Isabella (1838–1912), eldest daughter of Ralph Carr (afterwards Carr-Ellison), belonged to a well-known Northumbrian family, the Carrs of Dunston Hill, co. Durham, and Hedgeley, Northumberland. Robert was the elder son in a family of eight children.

After a brilliant career as a king's scholar at Eton College, where he won the Newcastle scholarship, Bosanquet, as a scholar of Trinity College, Cambridge, attracted attention by his light verse, and was awarded a first class in both parts of the classical tripos (1892 and 1894). He was a half-blue for throwing the hammer, and in 1892 had a 12 lb disc made to see if it was possible to match Phayallus' ancient throw of 95 feet.

Bosanquet was first admitted to the British School at Athens in 1892 under the directorship of Ernest Gardner. He was Craven university student in 1894–5 and Craven student (1895–7), travelling in Greece and visiting museums on the continent. In addition to his interest in the archaeology of the Roman frontier, he wrote to his sister Amy from Dresden in November 1895 talking of his great interest in Athenian white-ground pottery; in the same year he was to present a specimen to the Fitzwilliam Museum in Cambridge. J. D. Beazley subsequently attributed several Attic white-ground lekythoi to 'the Bosanquet painter' in recognition of this work. During this period Bosanquet assisted with the British School excavations at Phylakopi on Melos under the new director Cecil Harcourt-Smith; Bosanquet was subsequently involved in the publication of the final report, *Excavations at Phylakopi in Melos* (1904). He also travelled in the Greek islands, taking special interest in the prehistory of the Cyclades. After he recovered from a bout of malaria, his archaeological experience in Greece led him to excavate the Roman fort of Housesteads on Hadrian's Wall in 1898 for the Society of Antiquaries of Newcastle upon Tyne, the results of which he published in 'The Roman camp at Housesteads' (*Archaeologia Aeliana*, 25, 1904).

Bosanquet's excavating expertise led him to be offered the post of assistant director to David George Hogarth of the British School at Athens in 1899, and in 1900 he himself became director. In 1899 he was also elected a fellow of the Society of Antiquaries. One of his first actions as director was to prepare a 'suggested work and teaching scheme' for students of the British School (*Annual of the British School at Athens*, 6, 1900), which was to influence several generations of young scholars. His attention turned to Crete through the creation of the Cretan Exploration Fund (1899). He initially worked at Praesos and Petras, and in 1902 he moved to Palaikastro in eastern Crete, a site which continued to be excavated by the British School at Athens in the early 1960s and late 1980s. One of the students who was to dig with Bosanquet on Crete was John H. Marshall, who went on to be director-general of the archaeological survey of India. On 8 July 1902, between excavations on Crete, Bosanquet married Ellen Sophia (1875–1965), third and youngest daughter of Thomas *Hodgkin, the historian, then living at Barmoor Castle in Northumberland; they subsequently had two sons and four daughters. Ellen had read modern history at Somerville College, Oxford (1896–1900). In 1904 the British School at Athens shifted its focus away from the prehistoric sites of the Greek islands and Crete, to the Greek mainland and in particular Laconia. Excavations were carried out at the sanctuary of Artemis Orthia, work which was to be continued in subsequent seasons by Richard McGillivray Dawkins.

In 1905 the death of his father made it advisable for Bosanquet to live within reach of the Northumbrian estate to which he now succeeded. He therefore resigned the post at Athens, though not before he had acted as British representative with Lord Desborough to the 1906 Olympic Games. In 1906 he was appointed to the newly established chair of classical archaeology in the University of Liverpool. With congenial colleagues and generous financial backing an Institute of Archaeology was soon built up with the help of John Garstang. Although Egypt, Greece, and Crete were the chief fields of research, a beginning was also made on the excavation of Roman sites in Wales, such as Caersŵs, and his appointment enabled him to spend one term in travel or excavation. He served as one of the first commissioners on the newly established Royal Commission on the Ancient and Historical Monuments of Wales and Monmouthshire (1908–1935).

When, therefore, war broke out in 1914, Bosanquet was involved in a variety of interests, domestic and professional, and he had gained a European reputation. He at once put his knowledge of the Near East at the disposal of the War Office, but met with no response, and he was glad to be attached to that part of the Friends' Emergency Committee which was working for the defeated Serbs in Albania and Corfu. In July 1916 he was sent to Salonika as agent of the Serbian Relief Fund and remained there until his health broke down after attacks of malaria and enteric. For this mission and for his work in Greece he received the Serbian order of St Sava and the Greek order of the Redeemer.

In 1920 Bosanquet resigned his chair at Liverpool, partly to make way for younger men returning from the war. Thenceforth he lived at his Northumbrian home, Rock Moor, an adapted farmhouse on the estate, in a 'retirement' which never gave him the leisure which he needed to write the books on Roman trade routes and on the Covenanters in Northumberland for which he had collected material. He retained an interest in Northumbrian archaeology, escorting Queen Mary during a visit to Hadrian's Wall (1924), and serving as president of the Society of Antiquaries of Newcastle upon Tyne. He died, after a short illness, in a nursing home, 9 Windsor Terrace, Jesmond, Newcastle upon Tyne, on 21 April 1935, and was buried on 25 April in Rock churchyard.

E. S. Bosanquet, *rev.* David Gill

Sources E. S. Bosanquet, *Letters and light verse* (1938) · E. S. Bosanquet, *Late harvest: memories, letters and poems* [1970] · *The Times* (23 April 1935) · *The Times* (24 April 1935) · *The Times* (27 April 1935) · *Antiquaries Journal*, 15 (1935), 397–8 · H. Waterhouse, *The British School at Athens: the first hundred years* (1986) · C. Mee and J. Doole, *Aegean antiquities on Merseyside: the collections of Liverpool Museum and Liverpool University* (1993) · personal knowledge (1949) · W. T. Pike, *Liverpool and Birkenhead in the twentieth century: contemporary biographies* (1911) · D. Huxley, ed., *Cretan quests: British explorers, excavators, and historians* (2000) · D. W. J. Gill, 'Collecting for Cambridge: John Hubert Marshall on Crete', *Annual of the British School at Athens*, 95 (2000), 517–26

Archives FM Cam., antiquities (some from excavations) · Rock Hall, Northumberland, family MSS · U. Lpool, antiquities | Bodl. Oxf., corresp. with J. L. Myres · CUL, letters to M. R. James, Add. MS 7481/B226–227 · NL Wales, letters to John Glyn Davies · Sunderland Museum, collection of Greek island embroidery, incl. Rhodian bed tent

Likenesses group portrait (Hadrian's Wall scholars), Housesteads Roman Fort (Hadrian's Wall), Northumberland · photograph, repro. in Waterhouse, *British School at Athens* · photograph, U. Lpool, school of archaeology and Oriental studies

Wealth at death £61,957 1s. 5d.: probate, 24 Aug 1935, *CGPLA Eng. & Wales*

Bosanquet, Samuel Richard (1800–1882), legal and religious writer, was born on 1 April 1800 at Great Russell Street, Bloomsbury, London, the eldest of six sons of Samuel Bosanquet (1768–1843), of the Forest House, Essex, and the family seat of Dingestow Court, Monmouthshire, and his wife, Laetitia Philippa (1774–1855), youngest daughter of James Whatman of Vinters, Kent, and his first wife, Sarah. The Bosanquets were descended from a Huguenot family that came to Britain after the revocation of the edict of Nantes in 1685 and became naturalized by private act of parliament in 1703. They subsequently acquired various banking interests: the author's grandfather, also Samuel Bosanquet (*c.*1747–1806), was a deputy governor of the Levant Company and director of the Bank of England, while generations of the family were employed in the bank of Bosanquet & Co. Samuel Bosanquet was educated at Eton College before matriculating at Christ Church, Oxford, on 17 November 1818. He subsequently gained a second class in classics and a first in mathematics, graduating BA in 1822 and MA in 1829.

Bosanquet entered the Inner Temple as a barrister on 5 May 1826, and was one of the first revising barristers appointed to oversee electoral registration after the passage of the 1832 Reform Act. He began to write leading articles for *The Times* and published a series of legal commentaries, *New Rules of Pleading* (1835), *The Tithe Commutation Act* (1837), and lastly *The Poor Law Amendment Acts* (1839), which insisted that popular hostility to the new poor law was caused by the wilful misapplication of its provisions by the commission's district agents, and argued that the right of interpretation ought properly to belong to JPs, overseers, and boards of guardians. Bosanquet's localist impulses, religious convictions, and pronounced sympathy with the poor briefly aligned him with the high-Anglican paternalism then propounded in the *British Critic* magazine, in Tractarian hands since John Henry Newman's accession to the editorship in 1838. Two of his typically trenchant articles, 'Pauperism and almsgiving' (July 1840) and 'Private alms and poor-law relief' (October 1840), were subsequently revised and published in 1841 as *The Rights of the Poor and Christian Almsgiving Vindicated*, in which Bosanquet employed Mendicity Society reports to demonstrate the hopeless inadequacy of working-class wages and insisted that indigence was overwhelmingly attributable to economic dislocation rather than individual failing. Along with evangelical critics such as Thomas Chalmers and Tractarian commentators such as Thomas Mozley and Frederick Oakeley, Bosanquet insisted that individual charity should vastly supersede public provision, and mourned the effacement of squirearchical by bourgeois values. His 'The age of unbelief', which appeared in the *British Critic* in January 1842, was also published in revised form as part of his *Principia: a Series of Essays on the Principles of Evil Manifesting Themselves in these Last Times in Religion, Philosophy, and Politics* (1843), a virulently anti-liberal polemic which interpreted 'the condition of England' as a portent of the second coming. His *Letter to Lord John Russell on the Safety of the Nation* (1848) was animated by the same hostility to political Liberalism and *laissez-faire* capitalism, and Bosanquet's hallmark reassertion of local paternalist mechanisms in place of the agencies of a centralizing state.

Bosanquet's abhorrence of secular political economy and all things progressive increasingly took him towards theological and philosophical questions. But if his contemporary commentary found a ready audience, Bosanquet's philosophical and biblical studies never enjoyed comparable notice. His first foray into these realms, *A New System of Logic* (1839), added classical humanism to his extensive demonology and endeavoured to displace the 'heathen system' of Aristotelian logic with one of Christian ethics, while a second edition of 1870 appended two lengthy further sections setting out the practical application of his system. Anti-rationalist in spirit and idiosyncratic in method, they were typical of Bosanquet's philosophical *œuvre*. His *'Vestiges of the Natural History of Creation': its Argument Examined or Exposed* (1845) denounced the pre-Darwinian book of that name written by Robert Chambers and published anonymously the previous year, and two lengthy biblical commentaries, *The First Seal: being Short Homilies on the Gospel According to St. Matthew* (1854) and *The Fourth Seal: being Short Homilies on the Gospel According to St. John* (1856), along with *Excelsior* (1865) and *The Bible: its Superiority in Character, Composition, Information, and Authority, to all Uninspired Literature* (1866), evinced an antagonism towards contemporary biblical scholarship which was to preoccupy his subsequent work. Bosanquet began to learn Hebrew in his sixties in order to study the Old Testament, and produced a stream of works asserting the inapplicability of reason to revelation, such as his somewhat vainglorious *Interpretation, being Rules and Principles Assisting to the Reading and Understanding of the Holy Scriptures* (1874), and exemplifying his brand of figurative and typological exegesis, such as *The Successive Visions of the Cherubim Distinguished and Newly Interpreted* (1871), *An Exposition of the First Twenty Chapters of Exodus* (1876), *The Prophecies of Zechariah, Interpreted and Applied* (1877), and *The Interpreter: some Selected Interpretations of Scripture* (1878). Bosanquet's own churchmanship was stoutly Anglican but tolerationist: his *Eirenicon: Toleration, Intolerance, Christianity, Christian Unity, the Church of England and Dissent* (1867) is its clearest expression. His final published work took him towards the interests of his younger brother James Whatman *Bosanquet, the writer on biblical and Assyrian chronology. Entitled *Hindu Chronology and Antediluvian History* (1880), it was an annotated reprint of the first part of the orientalist Alexander Hamilton's *Key to Hindoo Chronology* of 1820, and attempted to synchronize the two subjects by connecting Indian mythology with early biblical characters.

Bosanquet married Emily Courthope (1809–1869), eldest daughter of George Courthope of Whiligh, Sussex, on 4 February 1830. They had nine children, like Bosanquet's siblings all of them boys, and all but one survived him, among them their third son, Admiral George Stanley Bosanquet (1835–1914), veteran of the Crimea, the Taiping uprising, and the Egyptian campaign, and subsequently aide-de-camp to Queen Victoria in 1884, and their fourth son, Sir (Frederick) Albert *Bosanquet (1837–1923), common serjeant of the City of London, 1900–17. At the death of his father in 1843 Samuel Bosanquet succeeded to the family estates at Dingestow Court. For the ensuing thirty-five years he energetically practised the squirearchical paternalism he always preached, serving (like his father before him and his son after) as JP and then chairman of the Monmouthshire quarter session from 1846, and acquiring a high reputation for beneficence to the poor and for the support of myriad local institutions, among them the Monmouth board of guardians, working men's institute, and school and highway boards. He died after a short illness, probably influenza, at Dingestow Court on 27 December 1882 and was buried on 1 January 1883 in the parish churchyard. S. A. SKINNER

Sources Burke, *Gen. GB* (1952), 221–3 • *Monmouthshire Beacon* (30 Dec 1882), 5e • private information (2004) [A. Bosanquet] • *The Times* (20 Jan 1798), 3d • *The Times* (2 April 1800), 3d • *The Times* (7 July 1806), 4a • *The Times* (11 July 1806), 3d • *The Times* (27 Oct 1859), 11a • *The Times* (18 April 1867), 5a • *The Times* (28 Dec 1882), 3f • *The Times* (2 April 1883), 4f • Foster, *Alum. Oxon.* • Boase, *Mod. Eng. biog.*, 1.343 • H. E. C. Stapylton, *The Eton school lists, from 1791 to 1850*, 2nd edn (1864), 73a

Archives priv. coll.

Likenesses G. Richmond, oils, *c.*1850, priv. coll. • J. Edwards, marble, bust, *c.*1855, priv. coll. • A. de Salomé, chalk, 1866, priv. coll. • Fradelle, photograph, *c.*1880, priv. coll.

Wealth at death £49,832 17*s.* 11*d.*: probate, 26 Feb 1883, *CGPLA Eng. & Wales*

Boscawen family (*per. c.*1290–*c.*1850). For members of this family *see* individual entries under Boscawen and related entries; for information on the family *see* Boscawen, Hugh (*bap.* 1578, *d.* 1641).

Boscawen, Sir Arthur Sackville Trevor Griffith- (1865–1946), politician, was born at Trevalyn Hall, Trefalun, Denbighshire, on 18 October 1865, the elder son of Captain Boscawen Trevor Griffith (1835–1904), who assumed the additional name Boscawen in 1875, and his wife, Helen Sophia (*d.* 1930), daughter of Admiral Norwich Duff. His father was a landowner in Denbighshire, where he was high sheriff and chairman of the quarter sessions. Though a son of a thorough-going Conservative family, young Arthur was sent to, and prospered at, Rugby School, which in those years enjoyed a reputation as a forcing house of young radicals. In 1884 he won a classical exhibition at Queen's College, Oxford, where he took a first-class degree in *literae humaniores* in 1888 and a second in history in 1889. He was an enthusiastic member of the Oxford Union Society and was elected first as treasurer and then in 1888 as president.

The young Griffith-Boscawen wished to make a career in politics, and he jettisoned his original plan of reading for the bar when the opportunity arose to be adopted as Conservative candidate for the Tonbridge division of Kent in 1890. He won the seat at the general election of July 1892 and in the same month married Edith Sarah (*d.* 1919), the daughter of a prominent constituent, Samuel Williams of Boons Park, Edenbridge. The marriage was happy, though childless.

Griffith-Boscawen was an ambitious young politician, and, given the Liberals' difficulties caused by Gladstone's commitment to Irish home rule, had every reason to hope that the Unionists—as the alliance of Conservatives and Liberal Unionists under Salisbury and then Balfour called themselves—would enjoy a long period in office. There was plenty for an ambitious and hard-working young MP to do. He gained the notice of the prickly chancellor of the exchequer, Sir Michael Hicks Beach, and was appointed the latter's parliamentary private secretary (1895–1900) and served as parliamentary charity commissioner from 1900 to 1905. He combined this with a special reserve commission in the West Kent militia, which he maintained until 1916.

Griffith-Boscawen became a fervent convert to the tariff reform agitation begun in May 1903 with Joseph Chamberlain's great speech in Birmingham. The campaign split the party and, like his leader and many other party notables, Griffith-Boscawen lost his seat at the general election of 1906. Unsuccessful in a rather quixotic attempt to capture a soundly Liberal seat at the East Denbighshire by-election in July 1906, for the four years that followed while he was out of parliament, Griffith-Boscawen gave his political energies to the tariff reform campaign. He also published a narrative of the parliaments of 1892 to 1906. Always keen travellers—they had already taken a round-the-world voyage in 1896—the Griffith-Boscawens took the opportunity of his enforced idleness to take an extended journey through southern Africa in 1906.

After making what he later called 'the biggest mistake of my life' and declining to remain the candidate of the Tonbridge Unionists, Griffith-Boscawen unsuccessfully contested Dudley in Worcestershire at the general election of January 1910 and watched regretfully as Tonbridge returned to the Unionist fold, where it long remained. To keep his political skills honed, he sought and won election for a three-year term to the London county council. The narrow defeat at Dudley was reversed in December 1910, however, in the second election of the year, and Griffith-Boscawen returned to the House of Commons.

Griffith-Boscawen rejoined his fellow Unionists in opposition to the Parliament Act and Irish home rule and—as a devout Welsh churchman and for many years chairman of the church parliamentary committee—fought disestablishment of the Church in Wales. He and other enthusiastic tariff reformers formed the Unionist Social Reform Committee, dedicated to establishing a programme of social initiatives to rival those of Liberals such as Lloyd George and Winston Churchill. In 1912 (and again in 1913 and 1914) he brought in a private member's bill, grounded in his experience on the London county council, to provide funds to enable local councils to improve working-class housing. The bill, however, died before the combined Liberal–Labour–Irish majority. In 1911, though he had not yet achieved his dream of high office, he was knighted at the recommendation of his party leader.

By 1910 Griffith-Boscawen had risen to the rank of lieutenant-colonel and commanded his special reserve regiment, the West Kents. With the declaration of war in August 1914 he put aside politics and joined the general mobilization. Though he was to be denied a battlefield command because of his age, his repeated requests for foreign service finally resulted in his transfer to a garrison battalion of the Hampshire regiment at St Omer, immediately behind the lines. During his service there he was mentioned in dispatches by the commander-in-chief, Sir Douglas Haig.

In December 1916 Griffith-Boscawen was recalled from France to serve as parliamentary secretary to the Ministry of Pensions in the newly formed coalition government under his old adversary Lloyd George. This fulfilled his long-held ambition for a place on the front bench, and he remained in this post until the end of the war. Following the 1918 election, when he was re-elected for Dudley, he was transferred to the board of agriculture, again as parliamentary secretary. Though essentially unprepared for the work, he developed a deep interest and knowledge of agrarian problems and was delighted when, in February 1921, he at last joined the cabinet as the first minister of agriculture, 'the fulfillment', he later wrote, 'of so many golden dreams' (Griffith-Boscawen, *Memories*, 229). The long-sought reward raised new problems, however. When presenting himself for re-election to his constituents at Dudley in March 1921, the new minister was defeated in the face of a campaign against the government by Lord Beaverbrook's *Daily Express*, which sought to end the embargo on the import of Canadian cattle. He quickly returned to the house through victory in April in a by-election at Taunton.

Griffith-Boscawen's period at the board of agriculture has been described as 'miserable' (Morgan, 325). He took office at a time of growing agricultural depression, through overproduction, the effects of which were compounded by the government's decision, in June 1921, to repeal part of the Agriculture Act (1919), which guaranteed cereal prices to farmers and labourers' wages. As the depression intensified, he found himself having to defend this reversal of agricultural policy, which was highly unpopular among Conservatives with farming interests. In October 1922 he failed to secure cabinet agreement to his proposals to support farmers, but was dissuaded from resignation. By then he was also in opposition to Lloyd George's policy during the Chanak crisis, on which he took a pro-Turkish, non-interventionist line. Soon afterwards he was among the Conservatives who ended the coalition government.

When Bonar Law formed his cabinet, at the end of October 1922, Griffith-Boscawen's reward was promotion to minister of health. Again, though, he suffered electoral defeat, and lost his Taunton seat (where agricultural issues may have been a factor) at the general election in November 1922. Lacking the support of many among the most senior Conservative former ministers, the government badly needed experienced ministers. Yet it proved difficult to find him another seat. More than seventeen constituency committees turned down his candidacy before he was adopted to stand for the normally safe Conservative seat of Mitcham at a by-election in March 1923. As minister of health, though, he was unpopular on account of the government's housing policies, and in addition he faced an independent Conservative candidate, backed by Lord Rothermere and closely associated with Austen Chamberlain. With the Conservative vote split, Labour won the seat, and Griffith-Boscawen's parliamentary career was over; his place at the Ministry of Health was taken by Neville Chamberlain.

After the death of his first wife, Griffith-Boscawen married, on 18 August 1921, Phyllis Maud Dereham, who had served as a secretary at the Ministry of Agriculture. She was the daughter of William Dereham of Rawdon Hall, Holyport. They had a daughter. Shortly after leaving parliament he wrote a volume of memoirs, comprising miscellaneous and generally unrevealing recollections of persons, places, and events, less systematic and comprehensive than his earlier parliamentary narrative. They included sketches of the personalities with whom he served in the coalition cabinet. He attributed his electoral failures to bad luck, and reaffirmed his belief that 'the highest ambition of an Englishman' was 'that of taking part in the public life of the country' (Griffith-Boscawen, *Memories*, 255). Griffith-Boscawen's public activities out of parliament included the chairmanship of the Welsh church commissioners (1923–45), the royal commission on transport (1928–30), and the transport advisory council (1936–45). He died in London on 1 June 1946. His second wife survived him. R. J. Q. Adams

Sources Bodl. Oxf., MSS Griffith-Boscawen · A. S. T. Griffith-Boscawen, *Fourteen years in parliament* (1907) · A. S. T. Griffith-Boscawen, *Memories* (1925) · J. Ramsden, *The age of Balfour and Baldwin, 1902–1940* (1978) · E. H. H. Green, *The crisis of conservatism: the politics, economics and ideology of the Conservative Party, 1880–1914* (1995) · R. J. Q. Adams, *Bonar Law* (1999) · K. O. Morgan, *Consensus and disunity: the Lloyd George coalition government, 1918–1922* (1979) · Burke, *Gen. GB* (1937) · *WWBMP* · *WWW* · *CGPLA Eng. & Wales* (1946)

Archives Bodl. Oxf., corresp. and papers | BL, Arthur James Balfour MSS · Bodl. Oxf., J. S. Sanders MSS · Bodl. Oxf., corresp. with third earl of Selborne · HLRO, corresp. with Andrew Bonar Law · HLRO, letters to David Lloyd George · LPL, corresp. relating to church matters · NL Scot., Arthur Steel-Maitland MSS

Wealth at death £48,926 14*s.* 1*d.*: probate, 15 Oct 1946, *CGPLA Eng. & Wales*

Boscawen, Edward (1711–1761), naval officer and politician, was born on 19 August 1711, the third of five sons of Hugh *Boscawen, first Viscount Falmouth (*c*.1680–1734), politician and courtier, and Charlotte (*d.* 1754), eldest daughter of Charles Godfrey and his wife, Arabella, sister of the duke of Marlborough. He ranks among the most important of the navy's officers in the mid-eighteenth century.

Early career, 1726–1742 Edward Boscawen entered the navy in 1726 and sailed for the West Indies on 9 April in the *Superbe* (60 guns) as part of the squadron under Vice-Admiral Francis Hosier. After service in the *Superbe* lasting nearly three years he served on the *Canterbury*, *Hector*, and *Namur* in home waters and the Mediterranean. After his promotion to lieutenant on 25 May 1732 he was appointed successively to the *Hector* and *Grafton* and then on 12 March 1737 to the command of the *Leopard*. In June 1738 he was appointed to the command of the *Shoreham* (20 guns), and a year later he was ordered to the West Indies where he was stationed at the outbreak of hostilities with Spain. Shortly afterwards the *Shoreham* ran aground near Cape Antonio at the western end of Cuba, and was forced to jettison her guns and stores. As a consequence she was refitting at Jamaica in November 1739 when Admiral Edward Vernon sailed to attack the Spanish at Porto Bello. Boscawen served as a volunteer on the flagship and, after a

Edward Boscawen (1711–1761), by Sir Joshua Reynolds, *c.*1755–6

successful attack, assisted Captain Knowles in the destruction of Porto Bello's fortifications. He spent 1740 cruising with the *Shoreham* off Tortuga and Havana, capturing a small Spanish privateer and in August recapturing two colonial ships. In early 1741 Boscawen took part in Vernon's expedition to Cartagena, commanding seamen and marines in a successful night attack on shore batteries, spiking the guns, and destroying the platforms and carriages. In a letter to the governor of Jamaica, Vernon commented that 'Captain Boscawen, all say made a prudent general in the disposing his men landing in as good order as could be expected for night work in an unknown country' (Ranft, 195–6). He was then put in charge of the destruction of the fortifications at Boca Chica. During the expedition Boscawen was promoted captain and succeeded Lord Aubrey Beauclerk in the command of the *Prince Frederick* (70 guns). Shortly after his return to England in May 1742 he was appointed to the *Dreadnought* (60 guns). On 11 December he married Frances Evelyn Glanville (1719–1805) [*see* Boscawen, Frances Evelyn], great-great-niece of the diarist John Evelyn. They had three sons and two daughters. George, the third son, became third Viscount Falmouth on the death of his uncle.

Captain, 1742–1747 Having been promoted captain in 1742, Boscawen spent the spring of the following year cruising off the Azores with the *Dreadnought* and the *Deptford* to intercept the Spanish trade. Later in 1743 he was attached to the Home Fleet under Sir John Norris. Before any official declaration of war a French fleet commanded by De Roquefeuil cruised in the channel to assist in an invasion on the Thames from Dunkirk. On 24 February 1744 Norris found the French anchored off Dungeness but as the wind was foul he could get no closer to the enemy than 8 miles. Both fleets were dispersed by a gale the following day. On 7 March the *Dreadnought* was ordered to convoy Dutch troops to England. In the following April the *Dreadnought* joined Sir Charles Hardy's squadron escorting victuallers bound for the Mediterranean clear of Brest. On 24 April south-west of Ushant, the French *Medée* (26 guns) was sighted and the *Dreadnought* and *Grampus* were detached in pursuit. After a chase of fifty hours the *Medée* was taken. She was subsequently purchased and fitted out as the *Boscawen*, privateer. May found the *Dreadnought*, in company with the *Prince Frederick*, stationed off Cape Clear to intercept privateers and to warn the homeward trade of the declaration of war with France. On 11 July both ships fell in with a French squadron of thirteen ships 85 leagues south-south-west of the Lizard. The *Dreadnought* kept up a constant fire from her stern chasers as the two ships were pursued throughout the night and into the afternoon of the following day. It was during this skirmish that an incident occurred that would dissuade Boscawen from allowing his officers standing cabins in all his future commands. He remarked that on 'taking down the officer's Cabins to clear ship and bring the stern chasers to bear on the enemy, I found much bottled liquor which being directed to be thrown overboard much of it was drunk by the seamen, that when I engaged soon after were so drunk as not to be able to do their duty, and had the French done theirs, I must have inevitably been taken' (PRO, ADM 1/90, fol. 275).

At the end of the year Boscawen commanded the guardship *Royal Sovereign* at the Nore until appointed to the *Namur* (74 guns) in January 1746. The *Namur* was attached to the western squadron first under Admiral William Martin and then George Anson. The fleet cruised to intercept returning French squadrons and Boscawen was entrusted with the command of an advance squadron. In October 1746 Anson returned to Plymouth leaving Boscawen on station. From letters found in a prize Boscawen anticipated Anson's orders to cruise off Cape Clear and intercept Admiral d'Anville on his return from America. Having been rejoined by Anson, the *Namur* chased and captured d'Anville's hospital ship, the *Mercure*, on 25 November; however, the French, learning that the British fleet lay in wait off Brest, steered for Rochefort and safety.

On 3 May 1747 the first decisive sea battle of the war took place off Cape Finisterre. At about nine in the morning the *Namur* signalled that a fleet was in sight to the south-west. This was Admiral De la Jonquière escorting the India and Canada convoys. Anson signalled a general chase during which the *Namur* was one of the leading ships. According to Boscawen the *Namur* 'came very near three or four of them where we were warmly engaged on both sides for about three-quarters of an hour … we then shot ahead and about half past four engaged the Sérieux (flag) within pistol shot more than half-an-hour when she struck to us' (Richmond, 3.92). Boscawen was close to the top of the captains' list and due for elevation to flag rank and Anson ensured his promotion by writing to the duke of Bedford at the Admiralty: 'Boscawen got a shot in the shoulder, but is almost well; his behaviour in the action pleased me, and I hope your Grace will make him a rear-admiral' (*Correspondence*, 1.214). Such was his professional esteem that Boscawen's name had already been suggested for the overall command of an expedition to India even before the news of the battle off Finisterre reached the Admiralty.

Rear-admiral, 1747–1755 With a squadron of six ships of the line, including the *Namur*, several smaller vessels, fourteen East India Company ships, and an army of 1200 men and 800 marines, Boscawen sailed for the Cape on 4 November 1747. His instructions were not binding but recommended that he proceed from the Cape to take Rodriquez, then Mauritius, proceed to Isle Bourbon and Madagascar, and next sail to the Coromandel coast to take Chandanagar and Mahé. Reaching Mauritius on 23 June, the expedition discovered that with advance warning the French had erected defences along the coast, and after one unsuccessful attempt a council of war agreed that the attack on Mauritius should be abandoned in favour of more important objectives. Accordingly Boscawen proceeded to Fort St David, arriving on 26 July, and after being joined by Admiral Griffith's squadron sailed immediately to attack Pondicherry. The initial attack was repulsed with heavy casualties due to faulty intelligence, provided by the engineers, on the strength of the defences. Cannon were landed from the fleet and the advance defences were eventually taken. The French commander, Dupleix, settled down to a siege knowing that the monsoon would create such difficulties for the British that the siege could not last. Fever soon broke out among the British forces and when the rains began at the end of September Boscawen abandoned the attack and withdrew the army. In any event a peace had been negotiated between Britain and France before the siege of Pondicherry had commenced. Boscawen received news of this in November but was instructed to remain on station until a peace was concluded. While off St David's on 12 April 1749, the *Namur* was lost with all hands in a hurricane. Boscawen and his staff were ashore at the time. He left for England in October and arrived there in April 1750.

In 1749 Boscawen had purchased the estate of Hatchlands near Guildford in Surrey. He had the existing Tudor house demolished and in 1756 began a new house said by Boscawen's wife to have been built at the expense of his country's enemies. This was completed in 1758, and is now a property of the National Trust. Boscawen was appointed a commissioner of the Admiralty on 22 June 1751 and in the same year an elder brother of Trinity House. Boscawen retained his place at the Admiralty despite the political troubles on the formation of the Devonshire ministry in 1756, and again in 1757 when Anson returned to the Admiralty. He had been advanced to the rank of vice-admiral on 6 February 1755 and had developed an unshakeable reputation that was about to see him become one of the foremost naval officers of the time.

The Seven Years' War, 1756–1763 In 1755, as relations between Britain and France rapidly deteriorated, Boscawen was placed in command of a secret expedition to intercept a French squadron bound for Louisbourg in Canada but also carrying troop reinforcements to the French position in Ohio where the war had already broken out. He sailed on 21 April 1755 with his flag on the *Torbay* (74 guns). On passage across the Atlantic the squadron exercised regularly at gun drill and on 3 June encountered thick fogs. On 9 June three large ships were sighted. Boscawen hoisted French colours but when he failed to answer their private signal, the three vessels bore away. They were the *Alcide* (64 guns) and the *Lys*, the latter fitted as a transport, and the *Dauphin Royal*. The *Dunkirk* (Captain Howe) led the chase and coming alongside the rearmost hailed her to shorten sail and speak with the admiral. The French asked if it was peace or war to which Howe replied peace but added that they should prepare for war. Boscawen then made the signal to engage at which point the *Dunkirk* opened her fire, and as the *Torbay* came up to engage the *Alcide* struck her flag. The *Lys* surrendered after a two-hour running fight with the *Defiance* and the third ship escaped. By an unfortunate turn of luck the *Alcide*'s captain, Hocquart, who had also been taken in the *Diamant* at the battle of Cape Finisterre in the last war and in the *Medée* in 1744, now found that he had been captured by Boscawen for the third time.

The news of the engagement was popular with the public but placed the government in an awkward situation. Most of the French armament had arrived safely in Canada and by capturing only an insignificant part of it, Britain was now seen as an aggressor but without the benefit of a successful pre-emptive blow against her enemy. Hardwicke, the lord chancellor, was of the opinion that Boscawen had 'done too much or too little' (Corbett, 1.57–8). He had not been made aware of the political and diplomatic consequences of his instructions though he may have guessed at them. In any event he was not blamed for executing his orders nor is it likely, given the circumstances, that Boscawen would have declined an engagement with the French. He was not to know that the bulk of the French expedition had already reached Louisbourg or that the three ships in sight were not part of a larger fleet still at sea. Retiring to Halifax after the engagement, the squadron was very sickly and suffered the loss of 2000 men before returning to Spithead.

On 6 May 1756, with his flag on *Invincible* (74 guns), Boscawen joined Edward Hawke's fleet off Ushant. As in the previous year his crews were regularly exercised at the guns with live firing at targets. Writing to his wife on 24 June he mischievously commented, 'we are at this minute practising firing, it being calm and many of the fellows hit the mark, *note nobody is firing at them*' (Kemp, 229). It was while off Ushant that Boscawen heard of the debacle of Admiral John Byng and the loss of Minorca. He has been noted as having a share in the responsibility for the trial and execution of Admiral Byng and was therefore a consenting party to his death (*DNB*). Even though he was involved Boscawen was not one of the judges at the court martial and would have gladly avoided any part in the proceedings. His letters, however, make his feelings clear. The conduct of Byng's fleet was a 'scandal' and 'Byng's letters would have written him coward before any jury in the world'. He also expressed the opinion that 'if more regard was had to the characters of men before they are put in the way of high commands, the Service would make a better figure'. Yet he also wrote that if Byng 'was to blame, he was not the only person to be blamed' (Kemp, 228, 231–2, 218).

On 29 July 1756 Boscawen transferred his flag to the *Royal George* (100 guns). The health of the fleet was a preoccupation of many senior officers who appreciated that fresh provisions, adequate rest, and healthy conditions for the men were a prerequisite for efficient operations. However, long cruises in search of enemy squadrons and convoys as well as the close blockade of French naval arsenals required an almost constant presence at sea. Boscawen paid particular care to the health of his officers and men though he was not aware of the precise causes of scurvy. He had Dr Hales's ventilators installed in the *Royal George* and later in the *Namur*. (Hales was his wife's cousin.) These provided a means of circulating fresh air below decks. He was convinced that bad air contributed to the sickness of the men, having had three sailors in the *Torbay* suffocate in the bad air from the well. In August 1756 many of his squadron were sickly, and writing to John Clevland, the secretary of the Admiralty, he gave it as his opinion and that of some of his captains that the sickness among the men was due in part '… to their want of rest when their ships are sent in to clean, being hurried again to sea before they are recovered' (PRO, ADM 1/90, fol. 60). It was also Boscawen's belief that something in the sailors' diet rather than something missing from it was the cause of scurvy; 'I eat very little meat and therefore it is impossible the sea scurvy should ever take hold of me' (Kemp, 245). Many of the measures introduced into the flagship had a positive effect. In September he wrote, 'This ship has now been at sea twelve weeks, which is longer than I ever knew any first-rate ever at sea' (ibid., 248).

On 7 February 1758 Boscawen was made an admiral of the blue and appointed to command the fleet sent to capture Louisbourg as a preliminary to the conquest of Quebec. The expedition sailed on 23 February but due to foul winds and calms took eleven weeks to reach Halifax where the entire fleet at last assembled on 24 May. The French meanwhile had managed to reinforce their position and when Boscawen appeared off Louisbourg on 2 June, the British faced 6000 Frenchmen and five ships of the line anchored to defend the harbour. Landings were made south of Louisbourg at Gabarus Bay. Generals Jeffrey Amherst and James Wolfe laid siege to the town, impeded by the fire of the French warships. On 21 June one of these, the *Célèbre*, caught fire and the flames spread to two of the other ships. By 25 June the town was so battered that only the two remaining warships, the *Bienfaisant* and *Prudent*, were able to maintain a resistance. Boscawen ordered them to be cut out and that night both were boarded, the *Prudent* being set alight and the *Bienfaisant* towed out of the harbour. After the surrender of Louisbourg, Amherst and Wolfe were anxious to press on to Quebec but Boscawen raised objections. Provisions were short, he had 5000 prisoners, and it was late in the season so the descent on Quebec was postponed until the following year. Returning to England with the *Bienfaisant* prize, Boscawen, on 27 October, encountered the homeward bound Quebec squadron, commanded by Du Chaffault, with a captured Indiaman. Boscawen pursued the French, recapturing the Indiaman.

The battle of Lagos, 1759 On 2 February 1759 Boscawen was sworn of the privy council, and in April he sailed with six ships for the Mediterranean with his flag on the *Namur* (90 guns). There he joined Vice-Admiral Broderick and took overall command of the fleet off Toulon. His instructions were to protect trade, secure Gibraltar, and above all prevent the Toulon fleet under de la Clue from passing the strait and joining the French Atlantic squadrons in their attempt to support an invasion of England. He was further instructed to follow the French if they succeeded in breaking out, but how he carried out these orders was left to his discretion. Boscawen was forced to withdraw to Gibraltar to water and refit his ships, arriving there on 4 August. Two frigates were detached to watch for the French. Meanwhile de la Clue had sailed from Toulon on 5 August with twelve ships of the line and hoped to pass Gibraltar undetected by following the north African coast. He was seen by the *Gibraltar* frigate on 16 August and on the following evening the alarm was raised. The British squadron was busy refitting and largely unprepared to sail with many officers and men ashore. There followed a 'stampede' to get on the ships and within three hours, at about 10 p.m., Boscawen with eight ships of the line was in pursuit of the French who were now steering for Cape St Vincent. During the night the French rearguard made for Cadiz, leaving de la Clue with seven ships of the line which were sighted by Boscawen the following morning. At first the French admiral imagined that the British ships were his missing rearguard, but he soon realized his mistake. Off Lagos he was overtaken and at 2.30 p.m. the action opened. At about 4 p.m. Boscawen engaged the French flagship *Ocean*, the *Namur* losing her mizzen mast. With the *Ocean* making off, the *Namur* joined the *Culloden* in the capture of the *Centaur*. Boscawen next shifted his flag from the damaged *Namur* to the *Newark* (80 guns) and continued the chase through the night. At daylight the remaining four French ships were seen making for Lagos Bay. Here the French admiral ran his flagship ashore: she and the *Redoubtable* were then burnt. The *Temeraire* and *Modeste* were captured despite being at anchor in neutral waters. Boscawen then took up station off Cape St Vincent to intercept the remainder of the French; not seeing them, he sailed to join the Channel Fleet as his instructions directed and anchored at Spithead on 1 September. Boscawen's violation of Portugal's neutral waters raised a diplomatic storm but his actions received the full approval of his superiors and the public. For his service he was made a general of marines with an annual salary of £3000. During 1760 Boscawen commanded the fleet in

Quiberon Bay where his ships received fresh meat and vegetables from Ireland. Regular fresh provisions made extended operations at sea possible. In June Boscawen wrote: 'The ships are healthy and I hope to keep them so … As the Monmouth now goes in, not sickly, to clean, she will be in a very short time in a good condition for any service' (PRO, ADM 1/90, fol. 255).

Political career, 1742–1761 Boscawen was a member of parliament, having represented Truro since 1742. The Boscawens were already an important and popular family in local politics, especially as the admiral could provide places and career opportunities for local sons, creating what his wife termed 'a little navy of your own making' (Rodger, '"A little navy"'). In 1753 Boscawen had attempted to break the monopoly of tory families in the county representation by putting up a third tory candidate who subsequently withdrew. In October 1760 Boscawen took the initiative and declared himself a candidate. He was supported by James Buller, one of the sitting members, the other withdrawing from the contest. Boscawen took this action without consultation with his brother, Viscount Falmouth, or any of the political managers, displeasing those who felt that the opinion of the county should have been sought before any change was made. Controversy was avoided by the admiral's death. Boscawen's having taken so much care over the health of his men, it was a cruel twist of fate that he should die of a fever at his home at Hatchlands, on 10 January 1761, depriving Britain of the service of one of its finest naval officers. He was buried that year at the church of St Michael Penkevil, in Cornwall.

Character Boscawen was a determined and confident officer who ensured that those who served him were properly trained and cared for. In his personal life he was devoted to his wife and children. His letters home indicate a happy family life, a sense of humour, and a constant attention not only to the happiness of his family but also to the detail and management of his house and estate. Like every great leader he combined resolution with compassion, single-mindedness with understanding. He had a close working relationship with John Clevland, the secretary of the Admiralty. He applied to Clevland for a sixty-year-old French prisoner-of-war to be exchanged, regarding the man, because of his age, as no great enemy to the nation. He would take the trouble to write to Clevland about the quality of shoes supplied to a marine on one of the ships of his squadron. He would use his own banker to help some of his men to remit their wages to their families, thus saving them expense (PRO, ADM 1/384, 10 April 1759; 1/90, fols. 45, 17; Rodger, *The Wooden World*, 132). He took a constant care over the well-being of his officers and men yet personal feelings and inclinations would not stand in the way of duty. William Pitt remarked to him that 'when I apply to other officers respecting any expedition I may chance to project, they always make difficulties: you find expedients' (Corbett, 2.101). Nicknamed Old Dreadnought by his sailors, he gave his personal following loyal support yet would not suffer fools gladly. His circle of professional friends and followers included John Brett, Francis Geary, and Savage Mostyn with whom he had a fond and effective working relationship. He held an unfavourable opinion of officers like John Byng and Francis Holburne. Holburne had 'contrived to insinuate himself into the good graces of Lord Anson, … I don't like him, nor ever did, having known him from my first entering into the service' (Kemp, 194). Nor would he brook the least action which impaired the efficient running of his squadron. In 1759, when getting under way from St Helens, the fireship *Salamander* failed to weigh anchor. It transpired that the captain was on shore without the admiral's leave. Boscawen not only called for a court martial on the captain but also her lieutenant: 'I think the Lieutenant as much to blame for not making sail, when he saw he must lose company with me by staying behind. I desire that they both be tryed at a court martial for their behaviour' (PRO, ADM 1/384, 20 April 1759). In terms of ability and professionalism, Boscawen prefigured many of the great names that would emerge later in the century. This is well illustrated by the fact that, along with Hawke, he was regularly chosen for the most important commands. He was also the only officer to retain his position at the Admiralty throughout the 1750s, a feat even Anson could not equal. Boscawen was a thoroughly professional naval officer in all respects and his early death was a great loss to his country. CLIVE WILKINSON

Sources *DNB* · admiral's letters, channel fleet, 1756–60, PRO, ADM 1/90 · admiral's letters, Boscawen, 1756–9, PRO, ADM 1/384 · 'Boscawen's letters to his wife, 1755–1756', ed. P. K. Kemp, *The naval miscellany*, ed. C. Lloyd, 4, Navy RS, 92 (1952), 163–256 · H. W. Richmond, *The navy in the war of 1739–48*, 3 vols. (1920) · J. S. Corbett, *England in the Seven Years' War*, new edn, 2 vols. (1992) · W. L. Clowes, *The Royal Navy: a history from the earliest times to the present*, 7 vols. (1897–1903), vol. 3 · L. B. Namier, 'Boscawen, Edward', HoP, *Commons, 1754–90* · N. Rodger, '"A little navy of your own making". Admiral Boscawen and the Cornish connection in the Royal Navy', *Parameters of British naval power, 1650–1850*, ed. M. Duffy (1992), 82–92 · *The Vernon papers*, ed. B. McL. Ranft, Navy RS, 99 (1958) · N. A. M. Rodger, *The wooden world: an anatomy of the Georgian navy* (1986) · R. Furneaux, *The Seven Years War* (1973) · *Correspondence of John, fourth duke of Bedford*, ed. J. Russell, 1 (1842), 214 · H. S. Goodhart-Rendel, *Hatchlands, a property of the National Trust* (1948)

Archives NMM, lieutenant's journal, ADM/L/G93 · PRO, ADM 1/90, 160, 384, 481, 924 | BL, corresp. with duke of Devonshire, Add. MSS 32710–32915, *passim* · CKS, letters to Sir Jeffrey Amherst

Likenesses A. Ramsay, mezzotint, 1747, NMM · J. Reynolds, oils, *c.*1755–1756, NPG [*see illus.*] · J. Macardell, mezzotint, 1757 (after J. Reynolds), BM · A. Ramsay, oils, *c.*1758, Badminton, Gloucestershire · M. Pitcher, graphite sketch, 1912, NMM · J. Faber junior, mezzotint (after A. Ramsay), BM · R. Purcell, mezzotint (after his earlier work), NPG

Boscawen, Edward, first earl of Falmouth (1787–1841), politician, son of George Evelyn Boscawen, third Viscount Falmouth (1758–1808), and Elizabeth Anne (1764–1793), only daughter of John Crewe of Cheshire, was born in London on 10 May 1787. He was educated at Eton College, and became an ensign in the Coldstream Guards. He was MP for Truro in the conservative interest (1807–8), but may not have taken his seat. On succeeding to his father's titles in 1808, he left the army. On 27 August 1810 he married

Anne Frances (1789–1864), elder daughter of Henry Bankes of Kingston Lacy, Dorset. They had one son.

On the coronation of George IV (1821) Falmouth was created an earl, and throughout the reign was constant in his attendance in the House of Lords. He was an ultra-tory, and resisted parliamentary reform and the passage of the Catholic Emancipation Bill, acting as Lord Winchilsea's second in his duel with the duke of Wellington over this issue on 21 March 1829.

Falmouth was the last recorder of Truro, and wrote *A letter on the subject of re-establishing and extending the stannary courts of the dutchy* [*sic*] *of Cornwall* (1836). He died suddenly on 29 December 1841 at Tregothnan House, Truro, which he had rebuilt, and was buried at St Michael Penkevil. His son, George Henry, succeeded him as second earl.

K. D. Reynolds

Sources M. Brock, *The Great Reform Act* (1973), 87, 91 · *The Greville memoirs, 1814–1860*, ed. L. Strachey and R. Fulford, 8 vols. (1938), vol. 1, p. 193 · GEC, *Peerage* · *GM*, 2nd ser., 17 (1842), 208–9 · *The diary and correspondence of Charles Abbot, Lord Colchester*, ed. Charles, Lord Colchester, 3 (1861), 467, 608–10 · HoP, *Commons*

Archives BL, corresp. with second earl of Liverpool, Add. MSS 38248–38249, 38262, 38289, 38323, 38458, 38572–38573 · BL, corresp. with second and third earls of Liverpool, loan 72 · BL, corresp. with Sir Robert Peel, Add. MSS 40386–40426 · Cornwall RO, corresp. with John Hawkins, 5235 · U. Southampton L., letters to first duke of Wellington, 20085

Likenesses J. Opie, oils, *c*.1805, Eton · J. Porter, mezzotint, pubd 1842 (after H. P. Briggs), BM, NPG · G. Hayter, group portrait, oils (*The trial of Queen Caroline, 1820*), NPG

Boscawen [*née* Glanville], **Frances Evelyn** [Fanny] (**1719–1805**), letter writer and literary hostess, was born at St Clere, near Wrotham in Kent, on 23 July 1719, only child of William Evelyn, MP and high sheriff of Kent, and his wife, Frances Glanville (1696/7–1719), the daughter and sole heir of William Glanville of Devon, who died in childbirth, at the age of twenty-two. On their marriage Frances's father had taken her mother's name with her fortune, by special act of parliament. After her death he invested a good deal of his wife's fortune in buying St Clere and other land in Kent. A few years later he married Bridget Raymond, who gave him a second family. Possibly for this reason Frances, known as Fanny, spent much of her childhood with relatives. She was a great-niece, on her mother's side, of the diarist John Evelyn, whose literary skill and love of nature she inherited. Her sprightly and elegant letters, for which she was famous during her lifetime, have remained in private family hands. However, some have been published in collections of bluestocking correspondence, notably in the letters and memoirs of Mrs Delany, Elizabeth Carter, and Elizabeth Montagu. Little is known of her early girlhood and only one letter survives from the period before her marriage. This spirited piece of writing, addressed to her cousin Julia Evelyn, conveys a quiet sense of humour and an easy familiarity with polite literature.

Frances first met her future husband, Edward *Boscawen (1711–1761), third son of Hugh *Boscawen, first Viscount Falmouth, in summer 1738 at the Kent home of his elder sister, Mary (who was married to John Evelyn, great-grandson of the diarist). Edward Boscawen was a rising captain in the navy and had just returned from six years of distinguished service in the West Indies and the Mediterranean. His sister's home was fortuitously close to his naval base at Portsmouth, enabling him to make regular visits to see Fanny. In a letter she wrote to him six years after their marriage, Frances alluded to their meetings of this time, 'when you and I loved one another and told it only by our eyes' (Aspinall-Oglander, *Admiral's Wife*, 11). Their courtship was interrupted in 1739 when Edward set sail for the West Indies. After three years of successful action in the war against Spain he returned to England and was elected member of parliament for the Boscawen family seat of Truro. He was also placed in command of the *Dreadnought* and posted to the Channel Fleet. He and Frances were married on 11 December 1742 and took up residence in a small house in George Street, Hanover Square, London.

Frances's marriage, while extremely happy, was marked by long periods of separation while Edward was engaged in naval service. She kept a journal in her husband's absence, which she loyally sent to him so that he did not feel cut off from the rhythms of family life. On 21 July 1748 she wrote to Edward in India:

> Beauty and I were never acquainted. But may I not hope, dear husband, that you will find charms in my heart, the charms of duty and affection, that will endear me as much to you as if I were in the bloom of youth and beauty. But I must return to my trifles, for talking thus from my heart kills me, and my tears blot my writing! I will go into the garden and take a turn or two. When I have composed myself I will come to you again. (Aspinall-Oglander, *Admiral's Wife*, 96)

In the same year she wrote: 'You know P. P.'s Memoirs are entitled "The importance of a man to himself." Mine might properly enough be called, "The importance of a wife to her husband, and of children to their father"' (ibid.). By this point the Boscawens had three children: Edward Hugh (*b.* 13 Sept 1744); Frances (*b.* 7 March 1746); and Elizabeth (*b.* 28 May 1747), future wife of the duke of Beaufort. On 11 August 1749 William Glanville Boscawen was born.

The Boscawens enjoyed a rare interlude of domestic stability during four years of peacetime between 1750 and 1754. In 1749 they moved to Hatchlands Park in Surrey, where, several years later, they built a new home designed by Robert Adam. When Elizabeth Montagu visited Hatchlands in July 1755 she wrote that 'It resembles the mistress of it, having preserved its native simplicity, though art and care has improved and softened it, and made it elegant' (Aspinall-Oglander, *Admiral's Wife*, 188). Frances took pride in her new home and particular pleasure in overseeing the progress of her garden. In autumn 1754 Frances gave birth to a stillborn daughter and was ill for several months afterwards. On her recovery Edward was called away to fight in America. Frances took charge of the Hatchlands estate, managing the annual sale of wheat in her husband's absence. Her youngest son, George, was born on 6 May 1758, three days before Edward anchored at Halifax in preparation for the capture of Louisburg. When Edward, now an admiral, returned triumphant in 1758 he could spend only a week at Hatchlands before he and Frances moved to London. On 10 January 1761, after a few weeks of high fever, Edward Boscawen died at Hatchlands Park, aged forty-nine, worn out and incapable of recuperating after years of extremely hard conditions at sea. He was buried at the church of St Michael Penkevil, Cornwall; Frances commissioned a tomb from Robert Adam, writing the inscription herself. She praised the way in which 'his concern for the interest, and unwearied attention to the health, of all under his command, softened the necessary exactions of duty and the rigors of discipline by the care of a guardian and the tenderness of a father'. She also referred to material gains he received from war, describing the recently completed Hatchlands Park as built 'at the expense of the enemies of his country' (Aspinall-Oglander, *Admiral's Wife*, 286). He left all his money to Frances, their children thus being dependent on their mother for their inheritance.

Frances was grief-stricken by her husband's death and took some time to recover. However, her long widowhood formed the most sociable period of her life. She returned to her old London house at 14 South Audley Street, where she hosted popular assemblies of bluestocking society; her guests included Elizabeth Montagu, Dr Johnson, James Boswell, Joshua and Frances Reynolds, Elizabeth Carter, and later, Hannah More. Frances was widely known in literary London as a model letter writer and conversationalist, prized for her wit, elegance, and warm heart. Her letters were never formally published, but were treasured by her bluestocking friends. Hannah More first met Frances at Elizabeth Montagu's house in Hill Street in the winter of 1775 and was immediately struck by her vivacity: 'She is at once polite, learned, judicious, and humble, … her letters are not inferior to Mrs Montagu's' (Aspinall-Oglander, *Admiral's Widow*, 72). More later made an interesting comparison between Boscawen and Madame de Sévigné, commenting that both women exhibited an original style that was far preferable to the studied formality and 'affectedness' of Voltaire's letters:

> The same turn of expression, the same ease, which, when imitated, is so stiff, and when natural is so full of grace. The same philanthropy, the same warm feelings, and above all the same excess of maternal tenderness—the same art of dignifying subjects, in themselves of little moment, but which become amiable and interesting by some true, though seemingly random stroke, that shows the hand of a master, but of a master sketching for his amusement, and not finishing for the public.

She praised her model writers for their ability to produce 'a kind of luminous cast, which, like the sunshine of Claude, embellishes the most trifling objects' (More to Boscawen, July 1786; Aspinall-Oglander, *Admiral's Widow*, 73). More also praises Boscawen, alongside Mrs Vesey and Elizabeth Montagu, in her long poem about the bluestocking circle, *Bas bleu, or, Conversation*, first published in 1786, but probably written in the middle of the 1770s, when she first met Montagu and Boscawen. *Bas bleu* emphasizes the importance of intellect over social standing, describing a literary community in which the highest value is placed upon the exchange of thoughts between equals.

Frances acted as a muse and patron to several writers of her day. Edward Young dedicated his poem 'Resignation' (1761) to her, aiming to console her in her new state of widowhood. Hannah More dedicated her impressive poem 'Sensibility' to 'Hon. Mrs Boscawen', making reference to the painful absence of her son William, a young sailor, who was training in Jamaica. Frances heard soon afterwards, in July 1769, that he had drowned on 21 April, while on a routine swimming exercise. As her personal sufferings became widely known, Mrs Boscawen came to symbolize feminine sensitivity, an example of stoic yet delicate endurance. In 1757 Mrs Montagu wrote to her sister, Sarah Scott, describing Frances Boscawen's character:

> She is one of the few whom an unbounded prosperity could not spoil. I think there is not a grain of evil in her composition. She is humble, charitable, pious, of gentle temper, with the firmest principles and with a great deal of discretion, void of any degree of art, warm and constant in her affections, mild towards offenders, but rigorous towards offence. (Montagu, *Queen of the Bluestockings*, 2.118)

While Frances enjoyed town life, she also treasured time spent in the country, first at Glan Villa, a cottage she rented in Enfield between 1772 and 1787, and then at Rosedale in Richmond, Surrey, where she moved in spring 1787. Rosedale was the site of the poet James Thomson's old house, where he lived until he died in 1748. Frances decorated a garden alcove where he had composed *The Seasons* with votive offerings, creating a shrine to her favourite poet of nature.

The last decades of Frances's life were marked by personal sorrows. In 1774 her eldest son, Edward Hugh, died on his way to a health cure in Spa, Germany. She was greatly relieved when her remaining son, George, returned safely from his naval action in America. To her great sorrow her eldest daughter and almost inseparable companion, Frances Leveson-Gower, died in July 1801. Her remaining daughter, Elizabeth, duchess of Beaufort, was widowed in October 1803. In her final years Frances sought solace in the company of her god-daughter, Frances Sayer (daughter of her cousin Julia Evelyn), who collected and saved her letters for posterity. Frances Boscawen died at her home, 14 South Audley Street, London, on 26 February 1805. At her request, she was laid in her husband's tomb in the church of St Michael Penkevil, Cornwall. ELIZABETH EGER

Sources C. Aspinall-Oglander, *Admiral's wife, being the life and letters of the Hon. Mrs. Edward Boscawen from 1719 to 1761* (1940) • C. Aspinall-Oglander, *Admiral's widow, being the life and letters of the Hon. Mrs. Edward Boscawen from 1761 to 1805* (1942) • *The letters of Mrs. Elizabeth Montagu, with some of the letters of her correspondents*, ed. M. Montagu, 3 vols. (1810) • E. Montagu, *Elizabeth Montagu, queen of the bluestockings, 1720–1761*, ed. E. Climenson, 2 vols. (1906) • *Mrs Montagu, 'Queen of the Blues': her letters and friendships from 1762 to 1800*, ed. R. Blunt, 2 vols. (1923) • *The autobiography and correspondence of Mary Granville, Mrs Delany*, ed. Lady Llanover, 2nd ser., 3 vols. (1862) • letters, Hunt. L., Montagu papers • Dr Doran [J. Doran], *A lady of the last century (Mrs Elizabeth Montagu) illustrated in her unpublished letters: collected and arranged, with a biographical sketch and a chapter on blue stockings*

(1873) • S. Harcstark Myers, *The bluestocking circle: women, friendship, and the life of the mind in eighteenth-century England* (1990)
Archives Hunt. L., Montagu collection, letters
Likenesses H. D. Hamilton, crayon (middle age), repro. in Aspinall-Oglander, *Admiral's widow*, 96; priv. coll.

Boscawen, Hugh (*bap.* 1578, *d.* 1641), landowner, was baptized on 28 April 1578 in the parish church of St Michael Penkevil, Cornwall, the only son of Nicholas Boscawen (1540/41–1626), landowner, of Tregothnan near Falmouth, and his wife, Alice (*d.* 1580), daughter of John Trevantin of Trevalster. The Boscawens were a minor gentry family who acquired the Tregothnan estate on the Fal in 1334/5 when John Boscawen of Boscawen Rose married Joan, only daughter and heir of John Tregothnan of Tregothnan. His descendants continued to marry into other Cornish gentry families, adding to their property when possible by soaking up available heiresses. The Boscawens tried not to trouble themselves with matters outside Cornwall: Richard Boscawen paid £5 on 4 July 1505 to avoid going to court to be made a knight of the Bath for 'the creac'on of my Lo. Prince Henrie' (Vivian and Drake, 19), while Hugh Boscawen (*d.* 1559) did likewise on 18 January 1555 in order to get out of attending Philip of Spain's coronation. However, they did resort to the courts of exchequer and Star Chamber from time to time to settle property disputes and benefited from the dissolution of the monasteries. Following the death of his father Hugh on 24 August 1559, Nicholas Boscawen inherited the family estate. He himself died on 1 May 1626 and was buried on 10 May in St Michael Penkevil, leaving Tregothnan and other property to his heir, Hugh Boscawen, who had probably managed his affairs for some years.

Hugh Boscawen was already a substantial figure in local society. He matriculated from Broadgates Hall, Oxford, on 12 October 1594 and entered the Middle Temple on 10 February 1598. He trained as a lawyer at his inn of court, rather than merely rounding out his education as a gentleman there, and became recorder of Truro in 1620, the same year in which he witnessed the heralds' visitation on behalf of his father as chief of the coat armour. On 22 June 1622 he married Margaret (*d.* 1635), daughter of Robert Rolle of Heanton Satchville in Devon and his wife, Joan. The Rolles were a prominent puritan family well known for their austere ways and his brothers-in-law included Henry *Rolle (1589/90–1656) and John *Rolle (1598–1648), who both opposed the collection of tonnage and poundage and government policies in the 1620s and 1630s. Among Hugh and Margaret Boscawen's eleven children were Nicholas (1623–1645/6), who joined the parliamentarian army with a regiment of horse; Joan (*bap.* 1624, *d.* by 1637); Robert (*bap.* and *d.* 1626); Robert (*bap.* and *d.* 1630); Margaret (1631–1655); Alice (*bap.* 1633, *d.* in or after 1637); John (*bap.* 1634, *d.* in or after 1637); and Samuel (*b.* by 1637). Three sons became MPs, Hugh (1625–1701), who supported parliament during the first civil war, Charles (1627–1689), and Edward Boscawen (1628–1685), father of Hugh *Boscawen, first Viscount Falmouth (*c.*1680–1734).

Hugh Boscawen was JP for Powder hundred in 1608 and 1622, a commissioner for the forced loan in 1627, and sheriff of Cornwall between 1634 and 1635. He was not, as commonly believed, knight of the shire in 1626. Boscawen prospered and in 1626 purchased the Tregony estate east of Truro from the Penkivel family. At the time of the 1641 subsidy his income was assessed at over £1000 per annum, placing the Boscawens among the eight leading Cornish gentry families, and he could afford to maintain what was for that county an impressive establishment. He has recently been described as a 'staunch Puritan' (Duffin, 47) and in his last will, which he drew up himself on 23 August 1637 in order to put his 'house in order', he gave sophisticated expression to his protestant beliefs. His body was his 'soules prison' and he instructed that his funeral be 'without any vaine pompous or popish ceremonies' (PRO, PROB 11/188, sig. 10). This apparent anti-Laudianism may explain his ambivalent attitude towards Charles I's policies: on the one hand he collected ship money efficiently and promptly between November 1634 and April 1635, on the other he remained uncommitted to the king after 1638 over the crises in Scotland and Ireland. Boscawen had tried to accommodate both the king and his county, writing in November 1634 to the privy council that 'I have used my best indeavors to advance and hasten the service', while pleading in April 1637 for the poor of the parish of St Mawes near Tregothnan to be remitted from further payment of ship money (Duffin, 159). He did not have to make the choice between king and parliament; his will was proved on 19 February 1641, the day he was interred in the north aisle of St Michael Penkevil.

Boscawen had made careful provision for his family and for his heir's inheritance by conveying his property to several leading Cornish and Devon gentlemen, including his brother-in-law Sir Samuel Rolle and Valentine Rolle, to act as feoffees and executors. These men were also to provide for the continued education of his children and to purchase Nicholas Boscawen's wardship if necessary. Lands were set aside for his younger sons, and his daughters, Margaret and Alice Boscawen, were to receive £1000 each at the age of twenty-one or when they married and a further £1000 each for their marriage portion.

ALAN BRYSON

Sources Burke, *Peerage* • A. Duffin, *Faction and faith: politics and religion of the Cornish gentry before the civil war* (1996) • HoP, *Commons, 1660–90*, 1.685–91 • J. Maclean, *The parochial and family history of the deanery of Trigg Minor in the county of Cornwall*, 3 vols. (1873–9) • *DNB* • will, PRO, PROB 11/188, sig. 10 • J. L. Vivian and H. H. Drake, eds., *The visitation of the county of Cornwall in the year 1620*, Harleian Society, 9 (1874) • J. L. Vivian, ed., *The visitations of Cornwall, comprising the herald's visitations of 1530, 1573, and 1620* (1887) • parish register, St Michael Penkevil, Cornwall • H. A. C. Sturgess, ed., *Register of admissions to the Honourable Society of the Middle Temple, from the fifteenth century to the year 1944*, 1 (1949), 73
Wealth at death income over £1000 per annum in 1641: PRO, E 179/89/324–339

Boscawen, Hugh, first Viscount Falmouth (*c.*1680–1734), politician and courtier, was the eldest surviving son of Edward Boscawen (1628–1685), a wealthy Turkey merchant and MP, and his wife, Jael (*d.* 1730), the daughter of Sir Francis Godolphin. Both parents were of prominent

Cornish landed families, and their connections at the very heart of politics ensured the future path of Boscawen's own career. His mother was the sister of Lord Godolphin and a friend of Sarah, duchess of Marlborough, while his uncle Hugh Boscawen, a county MP for Cornwall, served as a privy councillor under William III. At a young age Boscawen inherited his father's considerable fortune and Cornish estates. In 1698, a year after matriculating at King's College, Cambridge, he was appointed a groom of the bedchamber to the young duke of Gloucester. His marriage took place on 23 April 1700 in Henry VII's chapel, Westminster Abbey, to Charlotte (*d.* 1754), the daughter of Colonel Charles Godfrey, master of the jewel office. The couple had eighteen children, including Edward *Boscawen (1711–1761), admiral. It was a promising match, for Boscawen's mother-in-law, Arabella *Churchill, was the sister of the earl of Marlborough. The death of his uncle Hugh in 1701 brought Boscawen possession of extensive Cornish estates worth £3000 per annum as well as influence in many of Cornwall's twenty-two parliamentary boroughs.

At Queen Anne's accession in 1702 Boscawen was appointed a groom of the bedchamber to Prince George and entered parliament for the family borough of Tregony. Not surprisingly, he was a devoted supporter of the Godolphin–Marlborough ministry (1702–10), and throughout the reign he co-ordinated the whig electoral campaigns in Cornwall, frequently at his own expense. Having been elected for the county in 1705, he was in 1708 appointed warden of the stannaries and high steward of the duchy of Cornwall. His career was curtailed under Oxford's tory ministry (1710–14), when he served once more as a borough MP, first for Truro (1710), then for Penryn (1713), but upon the accession of George I his services in the whig cause were acknowledged in his appointment as comptroller of the household and as a privy councillor. In 1717 he received the lucrative sinecure appointment of joint vice-treasurer of Ireland. Having supported the Sunderland–Stanhope ministry, he was created Viscount Falmouth in 1720, but lost his position at court. Beyond the realms of electoral management his exploits as a politician were invariably blundering, and he was little valued by Sunderland's successor, Walpole. Smouldering annoyance finally goaded him into joining the opposition in the House of Lords in 1733. He died suddenly of an 'apoplexy' on 25 October 1734 at Trefusis, Cornwall, a few months after being dismissed from his remaining offices, and was buried on 6 November at St Michael's, Penkevil. His wife, previously a maid of honour to Queen Anne, died on 22 March 1754 and was buried at Penkevil on 2 April.

A. A. Hanham

Sources E. Cruickshanks, 'Boscawen, Hugh', HoP, *Commons, 1715–54*, 1.475–7 • GEC, *Peerage* • *DNB*

Likenesses M. Dahl, oils, Badminton

Boscawen, William (1752–1811), lawyer and writer, was born on 28 August 1752, the younger son of General George Boscawen and Anne Trevor, and nephew of the admiral Edward Boscawen (1711–1761). He was educated at Eton College, where he was said to have been a great favourite of Dr Barnard. On 10 October 1770 he became a gentleman commoner of Exeter College, Oxford, and on settling in London about 1773 studied law under a Cornish lawyer, Mr Justice Buller, and went on the western circuit.

Boscawen published two or three law treatises, and was appointed a commissioner in bankruptcy. In 1785 he was made a commissioner of the victualling office. He was much attached to literary pursuits, and translated first the *Odes*, *Epodes*, and *Carmen seculare* of Horace (1793), then the *Satires*, *Epistles*, and *Art of Poetry* (1797), the notes for which he was indebted to Dr Foster of Eton College. In 1792 he published a *Treatise on Convictions on Penal Statutes*, and in 1798, 1800, and 1801 some original poems and other works. He was also a contributor to the *Gentleman's Magazine*, and to the *British Critic*. In 1812 T. J. Mathias deprecated Boscawen's translating skills as displaying an 'unresisting imbecility' (Mathias, 260).

With his wife, Charlotte, daughter of the Revd Dr Ibbetson, Boscawen had five daughters. About seven years after his wife's death Boscawen died of asthma on 8 May 1811 at Little Chelsea, and his will was proved there on 2 July of the same year. He was of an affectionate and benevolent disposition, and wrote the annual verses for the Literary Fund until within five years of his death.

W. H. Tregellas, *rev.* Grant P. Cerny

Sources will, PRO, PROB 11/1524, fols. 18–19 • A. Chalmers, ed., *The general biographical dictionary*, new edn, 32 vols. (1812–17) • Foster, *Alum. Oxon.* • *The autobiography and correspondence of Mary Granville, Mrs Delany*, ed. Lady Llanover, 1st ser., 3 vols. (1861) • W. Upcott, *Original letters, manuscripts, and state papers of William Upcott* (1836), 43 • [D. Rivers], *Literary memoirs of living authors of Great Britain*, 1 (1798), 61 • *Poetical Register*, 1 (1801) • W. Beloe, *The sexagenarian, or, The recollections of a literary life*, ed. [T. Rennell], 2 (1817), 223 • J. Taylor, *Records of my life*, 1 (1832), 385, 388; 2 (1832), 397, 401 • T. J. Mathias, *The pursuits of literature: a satirical poem in four dialogues*, 16th edn (1812), 260 • *Literary Panorama*, new ser., 1 (1811) • W. H. Tregellas, *Cornish worthies*, 2 vols. (1884)

Archives Bodl. Oxf., letters to Sir James Burges

Wealth at death see will, PRO, PROB 11/1524, fols. 18–19

Boscombe, Ælfstan of. *See* Ælfstan of Boscombe (*fl.* 1043–1065).

Bose, Satyendranath [Satyendra Nath] (**1894–1974**), physicist, was born on 1 January 1894 in Calcutta, the only son and eldest of the seven children of Surendranath Bose (1867/8–1964), an accountant with the East Indian Railways, and later one of the founders of a small chemical and pharmaceutical company, and his wife, Amodini Devi (*d.* 1939), who had little education but much domestic ability in bringing up a large family. Bose attended the local elementary school in Calcutta until he moved to the Hindu School in 1907. He was much interested in science, in which he was encouraged by the headmaster and mathematics teacher. In 1909 he entered Presidency College, Calcutta, and was awarded science degrees in 1913 (BSc) and 1915 (MSc) with top place in various branches of mathematics. In that year Bose married Ushabala, daughter of

Dr Jogendra Nath Ghosh. They later had two sons and five daughters.

Since Indians were then denied entry to the administrative government service, Bose continued to study physics, in spite of the lack of appropriate textbooks and literature. With much of Europe at war, little was known in India at that time about recent developments of quantum theory in Germany and elsewhere. Moreover, there were no adequate laboratories or equipment for research. In 1914 the University College of Science, for postgraduate studies and research, was established at Calcutta. Some recent European books were obtained, and research was published on new aspects of physics. In 1917 Bose and his lifelong friend Meghnad Saha (1893–1956) became lecturers there, and Bose learned French and German to gain access to recent literature.

Bose developed a special interest in statistical mechanics, and was much stimulated by J. Willard Gibbs's book on *Elementary Principles in Statistical Mechanics* (1902), from which he learned more about phase space and Boltzmann statistics. Arthur Eddington's analysis of the data from the solar eclipse of 1919 verified the deflection of starlight by the sun's gravitational field, confirming one of Einstein's predictions in respect of general relativity, turning Bose's attention to relativity and Einstein's recent papers about it. He translated for circulation in India Einstein's paper of 1905 on the special theory of relativity, and in 1916 that on the general theory of relativity. Although these translations were somewhat defective, they presented the first English texts of Einstein's work.

In 1921 Bose went to the new Dacca University as a reader in physics. He had now studied Planck's theory of heat radiation, and became interested in Planck's radiation formula, the expression which gives the distribution of energy in the radiation from a black body. This had been one of the starting points of the quantum theory. Neither Planck nor Einstein had been satisfied with their attempts to derive this formula by classical methods. The basic assumptions of the quantum theory were not reconcilable with the laws of classical electrodynamics. In this context Bose made his single great contribution. He derived the Planck formula in a logical manner using the principles of Boltzmann statistics. Aware that his derivation was the logical outcome of Einstein's own line of thought, in June 1924 Bose sent his paper to Einstein, who, recognizing its merit, immediately translated it himself. As 'Plancks Gesetz und Lichtquantenhypothese' it was published in August of that year in *Zeitschrift für Physik*, vol. 26. This epoch making paper contained the first correct treatment of the thermodynamics of the photon gas and laid the foundation of quantum statistics. Bose considered his next paper, 'Warmegleichgewicht in Strahlungsfeld bei Anwesenheit von Materie', published later that year in vol. 27 of the *Zeitschrift*, to be his best scientific contribution. It was likewise translated by Einstein, who on this occasion contested Bose's hypothesis about the probability of elementary radiative processes.

Bose longed to meet European scientists, and in 1924 applied to Dacca University for a leave of absence of two years to study abroad. After seeing Einstein's letter to Bose expressing high appreciation of the latter's achievement, the university granted him leave and made adequate financial provision for his family during this period. He first went to Paris, in 1924, where he met Langevin, Madame Curie, and the de Broglies, and among many other things learned something about spectroscopy and crystallography. In October 1925 he went to Berlin and met Einstein, who had made many advances during the previous twelve months, partly arising from Bose's ideas, but who was now mainly interested in a unified field theory. Through Einstein, Bose was delighted to meet many of the distinguished scientists in Berlin at that time. He heard talks by Max Born and others about the new quantum mechanics.

Bose returned to Dacca in 1926 and was appointed a professor of physics in 1927. In the years following 1924 Bose's research interests widened. His forte lay in his profound understanding of basic science, which found expression outside physics, and research workers on other disciplines benefited from discussions with him. In the years 1952–4 he renewed his interest in the theory of relativity. In 1946 he became the Khaira professor of physics at Calcutta University. He retired in 1956, became the vice-chancellor of Viswa-Bharati University, Santiniketan, and in 1958 accepted the honorific appointment of national professor (*Padma Vibhushan*).

Throughout his life Bose tried to improve education, science, and culture in India, and to encourage the use of better technology for the people's welfare. He was proud of his Bengali origins and hoped for Indian independence; he grieved when Bengal was divided in 1947. He was president of the physics section of the Indian Science Congress (1939), general president of the thirty-first session of the Indian Science Congress, Delhi (1944), and president of the National Institute of Science of India (later the National Academy of Sciences) in 1949. In 1958 he was elected a fellow of the Royal Society of London. To those who asked why he had never visited the United States of America, Bose would explain that as he had already visited Russia the American authorities considered him a communist sympathizer (this was in the McCarthy era) and refused him a visa.

It is rare, indeed, for any scientist living in an environment or milieu which could not really teach, or help him, to make an important contribution like that of Bose, and send it to a leading world scientist whom he had never met asking for an assessment of its value. Bose's name is now established by the terms Bose–Einstein statistics, which are used in the interpretation of numerous physical phenomena, and bosons (particles obeying Bose–Einstein statistics).

Plans were in hand at various places in India to celebrate Bose's eightieth anniversary when he died in Calcutta on 4 February 1974. H. W. Thompson, *rev.*

Sources J. Mehra, *Memoirs FRS*, 21 (1975), 117–54 · W. A. Blanpied, 'Bose: co-founder of quantum statistics', *American Journal of Physics*, 40 (1972), 1212–20 · N. N. Ray, 'Professor S. N. Bose: an impression of his personality', *Satyendranath Bose, 70th birthday commemorative volume* (1965) · *Nature*, 249 (1974), 499

Likenesses photograph, repro. in Mehra, *Memoirs FRS*

Bose, Subhas Chandra (1897–1945), Indian political leader, was born on 23 January 1897 in Cuttack, Orissa, the ninth child and sixth son of Janaki Nath Bose (1860–1934), a lawyer and government pleader, and his wife, Prabhabati, *née* Dey (1869–1944). They were high-caste Hindu Bengalis of the Kayastha caste. His eldest brothers, Satish and Sarat, were barristers, and Sarat was an important political leader as well. Another brother, Sunil, was a leading medical doctor in Calcutta.

Bose was educated at the Protestant European School and Ravenshaw Collegiate School, Cuttack, and then at the Presidency College, Calcutta, one of the foremost colleges of India. In 1915 he was expelled from the Presidency College for complicity in the beating of Professor Oaten, a college instructor, whom many students felt had maligned Indians. After a year Bose was admitted to the Scottish Church College, another leading college, and graduated with the highest honours in philosophy in 1919. At the urging of his father he went to England, studied at Cambridge University as a non-collegiate student, and prepared for the Indian Civil Service examination. To the surprise of many he passed the 1920 examination in the fourth position, was appointed, but then resigned to join the Indian national movement headed by M. K. Gandhi nationally and C. R. Das in Bengal. Bose was personally friendly with some British people, but he hated the British presence in India passionately, and his central concern through his adult life was to terminate the raj.

Bose returned to Calcutta, joined the Indian National Congress, and, as a favoured lieutenant of Das, was chosen chief executive officer of the Calcutta Corporation in 1924. He worked for Hindu–Muslim amity and improvement of civic life, but after a few months was gaoled for involvement with acts of violence against the British raj. No formal charges were made and no trial took place, but Bose served about three years in gaol, two of them under unpleasant circumstances in Mandalay, Burma. Released for health reasons in 1927, and with Das now dead, Bose quickly rose to the leadership of the Bengal Provincial Congress. In 1928 he became a general secretary of the Indian National Congress, helped to prepare the Nehru report on Indian self-rule, and became a widely popular leader of the younger leftists in national politics. He had strong support from urban workers, middle-class nationalists in Calcutta and towns through the countryside, women, and students. Bose pressed Gandhi to move more quickly and forcefully for complete independence. He began to call himself a socialist and advocated a socialist programme for the reconstruction of India once independence was gained.

As commander of the Congress Volunteers at the 1928 Congress session, he drilled young Indians to help control the meeting. Some of these Indians later formed an underground revolutionary group, the Bengal Volunteers. Bose's ties to this group, which carried out acts of violence, together with his mass following as a Congress leader, made him a marked man to officials of the raj. His connection to such revolutionaries also made him untrustworthy to Gandhi, a principled non-violent activist. Bose was in and out of gaol from 1930 to 1933 and was even elected mayor of Calcutta in 1930 while imprisoned. He spent a good deal of the period 1933 to 1937 in Europe recovering his health. While in Europe he wrote *The Indian Struggle* (1935), an account of Indian politics from 1920 to 1934, and *An Indian Pilgrim*, a brief, insightful autobiography, eventually published in 1965. Based in Vienna, he also did propaganda work for Indian nationalism and visited many European countries, including Italy and Ireland, where he was warmly welcomed. About 1934 he met an Austrian woman, Emilie Schenkl (1910–1996), who became his secretary. In December 1937, according to Miss Schenkl, they married secretly at Badgastein.

In 1938, with Gandhi's blessing but not complete confidence, Bose became president of the Indian National Congress. He took the initiative in forming the planning committee of the Congress. The next year he decided to run again, against Gandhi's wishes. With the support of the left and strong support in some provinces outside his native Bengal, he defeated Gandhi's candidate, P. Sitaramayya, but then felt compelled to resign his presidency after a controversy about the selection of the working committee, the Congress executive. Bose formed the Forward Bloc, a pressure group within the Congress working for immediate direct action against the raj.

Imprisoned again in 1940, Bose fasted, and was released in December. With the Second World War under way, and now convinced that the British would never leave India peacefully, he determined to flee the country and work with some foreign power hostile to the British. He hoped to recruit and train a military unit which would combine with forces within India to drive the British out by violent means. On 17 January 1941 he slipped out of his Calcutta house, reached the Indian frontier, and walked into Afghanistan. Receiving Italian, German, and Russian help, he travelled as Orlando Mazzotta to Berlin, where he set up the Free India Centre, a propaganda operation, and the Indian Legion, a small fighting force recruited from Indian prisoners taken in north Africa. Unhappy in Europe, Bose was finally allowed by Hitler to leave for south-east Asia in February 1943. He was forced to leave behind in Vienna his wife and his daughter, Anita, born in 1942.

Travelling by German and Japanese submarines, and then by air, Bose reached Tokyo in spring 1943. He courted and impressed Prime Minister Tojo, who supported his efforts to reconstitute the Indian National Army (INA) and to set up the provisional government of Azad Hind, or Free India. Bose's army was constituted mainly from Indian soldiers taken prisoner at Singapore, and was supported by the Free India League, a nationalist organization backed by the Indian community of south-east Asia. Beloved by his followers, Bose was called Netaji, or revered leader. He also recruited a regiment of women headed by Lakshmi Swaminathan, who were trained to fight but never entered combat. Bose worked diligently for communal harmony between Hindus, Muslims, and

Sikhs within his army, and continued to make the broadcasts to India that he had begun in Germany.

In an endeavour to fulfil his slogan of 'chalo Delhi', or 'on to Delhi', Bose induced the Japanese to undertake an invasion of eastern India in 1944. Their forces briefly entered India, but this effort ended in a catastrophic defeat for the Japanese and the INA. Bose fled and was mortally burned in a plane crash in Taiwan on 17 August 1945. He died in a Japanese military hospital nearby, was cremated the following day, and his ashes were delivered by a Japanese officer to Tokyo. There they were turned over to Indian nationalists, who placed them in a Buddhist temple, where they remained, as no subsequent government of India was willing to receive them back into India because of potential controversy about how he died. Many followers of Bose in India and south-east Asia believed that he did not die in the air crash, but escaped, possibly to Soviet territory. For several decades the myth of his imminent return was spread among Indians who hoped that he would emerge to help India combat its many problems by his forceful leadership. He was remembered for his devotion to his country by most Indians, some of whom, like Gandhi, disagreed with his choice of means to reach the goal of independence. Bose was one of those Indian nationalists who believed that violence in a noble cause would not corrupt the end sought.

LEONARD A. GORDON

Sources L. A. Gordon, *Brothers against the raj: a biography of Sarat and Subhas Chandra Bose* (1990) • S. C. Bose, *An Indian pilgrim* (1965) • H. D. Gupta, *Subhas Chandra* (1946) • D. K. Roy, *The Subhash I knew* (1946) • H. Toye, *Subhas Chandra Bose: the springing tiger* (1978) • J. C. Lebra, *Jungle alliance: Japan and the Indian national army* (1971) • S. K. Bose and A. Werth, eds., *A beacon across Asia* (1973) • private information (2004)

Archives Netaji Research Bureau, Calcutta | Nehru Museum, New Delhi, All-India congress committee MSS | FILM BFI NFTVA, 'Enemy of empire', BBC2, 13 Aug 1995 • IWM FVA, documentary footage • IWM FVA, news footage • Netaji Research Bureau, Calcutta | SOUND BL NSA, oral history interview • Netaji Research Bureau, Calcutta

Likenesses B. Bhattacharya, oils; formerly on display at Netaji Bhawan, 38/2 Elgin Road, Calcutta, India • P. Bhattacharya, statue, Calcutta Maidan, Calcutta, India • A. Bose, oils, Netaji Bhawan, 38/2 Elgin Road, Calcutta, India • C. Kar, oils, parliament building, New Delhi, India • S. Pal, bust, Netaji Bhawan, 38/2 Elgin Road, Calcutta, India • S. Pal, engraving, Netaji Bhawan, 38/2 Elgin Road, Calcutta, India • statue, Shyambazar Five-Point Crossing, Calcutta, India • statue, near Red Fort, Delhi, India

Wealth at death share in family house, 38/2 Elgin Road, Bhowanipore, Calcutta, India

Bosgrave, James (*c.*1548–1623), Jesuit, was born at Godmanstone, Dorset, of a staunchly Roman Catholic family. At an early age he was taken to the continent so that he could be brought up in the old faith. After studying humanities at Louvain he found his way to Rome, where he entered the Society of Jesus on 17 November 1564. He made his noviciate and early university studies in Rome, during which time he was a student of Christopher Clavius, the renowned Jesuit astronomer and mathematician.

In 1573 Bosgrave was sent, like many other English Jesuits of his day, to central Europe. Just as the Low Countries and France were the sites of seminaries devoted to training missionaries to evangelize protestant England, so Poland was the site of missionary institutions which trained priests to evangelize the Scandinavian countries and Finland. In November 1573 he was ordained a priest in Krems (Austria). After that he taught Greek and rhetoric at Olomouc in Moravia, Pułtusk in Poland, and Vilna in Lithuania. About this time he seems to have been restless and suffering from bad health. He wrote to the Jesuit general asking for a new assignment. To breathe one's native air was a standard medical cure-all in those days. This might be the reason he set out for England in the summer of 1580, though Bosgrave himself, as far as we know, complained about his health only once in England and that was when he was brought before the privy council.

On his way to England, Bosgrave met John Rogers, an English diplomat on a trade mission to Denmark and Poland. Suspicious of Bosgrave, Rogers intercepted his mail and discovered that he was a Jesuit. This was the summer of the arrival of Persons and Campion in England and anything Jesuit attracted attention. Rogers sent word to England, probably by the same boat on which Bosgrave had taken passage, that he should be arrested on his arrival. This was effected by the mayor of Orford, Suffolk.

Bosgrave was taken to London where he freely admitted that he was a Roman Catholic and a Jesuit. Brought before the privy council he was asked whether he would attend the established church. He agreed to do so and was set free. He was plainly out of touch with the English religious scene. It was a common thing for Catholics in religiously divided countries to visit other churches. But in England for a Catholic to go to another church was almost equal to apostasy. When he was reproached by English Catholics, he repented of his mistake. Afterwards he wrote an eloquent short piece which was appended to William Allen's *A True Report* (1583), entitled *The Satisfaction of M. James Bosgrave*. In it he stated that one of the reasons he attended Church of England services was to recover his ability to speak his native tongue. Bosgrave then refused to 'go to church'. He was once more arrested and came to trial in November 1581 with Edmund Campion and a dozen others for the crime of plotting the assassination of Queen Elizabeth 'in Rome and Rheims'. Bosgrave had some trouble making himself understood when he spoke in his own defence because of his imperfect English. Campion eloquently finished some of the points Bosgrave was trying to make. All the accused were found guilty, but the very day on which Campion, Sherwin, and Briant were executed at Tyburn, Bosgrave and the others convicted with him were sent back to prison.

Bosgrave's case had aroused some interest in Poland, especially in the towns where the English government was trying to negotiate trade agreements. In January 1583 the king of Poland, Stephen Batory, wrote to Queen Elizabeth asking for toleration of Catholics in general and the release of Catholics in prison, particularly his friend James Bosgrave. In January 1585 Bosgrave and twenty-one others imprisoned for religious reasons were released and shipped into exile. Back in Poland, Bosgrave returned to Vilna. But his health was not good and he moved to Braniewo and then to Poznań where he taught Hebrew and mathematics. He died in Kalisz on 27 October 1623.

THOMAS H. CLANCY

Sources T. M. McCoog, ed., *Monumenta Angliae*, 2: *English and Welsh Jesuits, catalogues, 1630–1640* (1992), 240–41 • P. Skwarczynski, 'Elsinore 1580: John Rogers and John Bosgrave', *Recusant History*, 16 (1982–3), 1–16 • H. Foley, ed., *Records of the English province of the Society of Jesus*, 2 (1875), 198–233

Bosham, Herbert of (*d. c.*1194), biographer, was the son of a clerk (later a priest), who may have been one of the ministers of the royal chapel of Bosham in Sussex, at that time an outlier of the diocese of Exeter. Nothing more is known about his parentage and early education; but both must have been good, for he became an excellent Latin scholar and rhetorician, skilled in the arts of letter-writing and diplomacy, and he went on to study theology at Paris under Peter Lombard, a famous teacher who died as bishop of Paris in 1159. Unusually, Herbert acquired a good knowledge of Hebrew.

Early career As a Paris master, he was a member of an élite circle in the English church, and before 1157, having probably been recruited by the royal chancellor, Thomas Becket, another Paris alumnus, he obtained a place in Henry II's itinerant chapel. He certainly made his mark in the chancery, for the king sent from his great council at Northampton in July 1157 'master Heribert and our clerk William' on an embassy to the emperor Frederick I (Leyser, 483) to explain why he could not return the hand of St James, which his mother, the Empress Matilda, had brought to England when widowed in 1125, and which in 1133 her father, Henry I, had transferred to his abbey at Reading. At Würzburg on 28 September the ambassadors presented Henry II's famous letter, witnessed by his chancellor Becket, and possibly drafted by Herbert, so full of 'honeyed words' that it served to promote the theory of imperial domination over other kings. Herbert also made a lasting impression on Henry II, although he was not always remembered with unalloyed approval.

Thomas Becket took Herbert, with four or five other clerks, from the chancery to Canterbury when he was appointed archbishop in 1162. Tall, handsome, high-spirited, and stylish, a smart dresser and by no means austere, Herbert was very much a man to his master's taste, and became his almost inseparable companion. Becket asked him to keep an eye on his deportment as archbishop and report what others thought of it. Herbert was one of the *eruditi*, the scholars, in the archiepiscopal household; and when he came to write the saint's life he listed and gave thumbnail sketches of some of the others, including John of Salisbury, a survivor from Archbishop Theobald's household, with whom, perhaps from the beginning, he did not get on well. Herbert went with Becket to Pope Alexander III's general council at Tours in May 1163, to the royal council at Clarendon in January 1164, when the constitutions, a record of the royal rights in the church, were published, and to Becket's trial at Northampton in October 1164. Another of the archbishop's clerks, William fitz Stephen, remembered, perhaps spitefully, that at the end of the trial, as they fled from the castle, Herbert could not get on his horse and their master had to carry him away on his. He was then sent to Canterbury to collect all the money he could and rendezvous with Becket at the abbey of St Bertin at St Omer.

Exile with Becket Herbert reached the abbey early in November with only a few silver vases and 100 marks in cash, and he had to wait anxiously for Becket's arrival. Soon he was dispatched to trail Henry II's ambassadors to Louis VII of France and Pope Alexander III at Sens, and undo any harm they did, a task he performed very well. He went with Becket to his exile in the Cistercian abbey at Pontigny (November 1164 to November 1166), a situation—'between the rocks and the monks' (Robertson and Sheppard, 3.357)—he heartily disliked, although he soon bought himself a new suit of clothes at Auxerre. He also did his best to cheer up his disconsolate master by arranging seminars for his education. He himself tutored in theology and, at Becket's request, started his edition of Peter Lombard's 'great gloss' on the Psalms and St Paul's epistles. He seems also to have been at the head of Becket's chancery and in charge of the espionage and diplomacy designed to further Becket's cause. John of Salisbury's decision to spend his exile at Rheims made life easier for both. Herbert is the only one of the early memorialists to give a full account of Becket's life in exile, and he was clearly a participant in most of the activities he describes.

Herbert was a man of strong principles and views, although not of simple faith, for his Hebrew studies caused him at times to doubt the truth of the Christian religion. Inevitably he regarded the monastic order as inferior to the clerical, and, until his extreme old age, he particularly despised the Cistercians: at Pontigny he thought that they fed like horses. Like many Paris-educated clerks, including John of Salisbury, he was an ultraist, believing wholeheartedly in the superiority of the church, papal government, and canon law over their secular equivalents. He was a fighter, delighting in martial imagery, and he always dissuaded the archbishop from compromise. They would fight their opponents and enemies to the bitter end. John of Salisbury probably regarded him as their master's evil genius.

Ambassador for the archbishop At Easter 1166, however, Herbert was involved in a peace move. Louis VII, with the archbishop and several of his clerks in attendance, approached Henry at Angers, where Henry was celebrating the festival. Louis could not contrive a meeting between archbishop and king, but Henry did give audience to some of Becket's principal clerks, who were, apparently, prepared to submit if offered honourable terms. After John of Salisbury refused to desert Becket's cause and observe the constitutions of Clarendon, it was Herbert's turn. 'Now we shall see a proud fellow', the king remarked as the clerk went in, dressed very smartly in a tunic and a cloak which hung from his shoulders to his heels in the German fashion, both of green cloth of Auxerre. And Herbert lived up to his reputation. He refused the king's terms, and he discussed at length the evil royal customs that shackled the church, not only in England but also in France and Germany. In his view Henry had made a bad mistake by having them written down at Clarendon. The king took offence when Herbert called Frederick I king, not emperor, of the Germans, and, when the clerk put him right, Henry exclaimed, 'For shame! It's come to a pretty pass when this son of a priest can upset my kingdom and disturb my peace'. 'That's quite untrue', Herbert replied, 'and also that I'm the son of a priest, for I was born before my father became one. Just like you can't be the son of a king if your father wasn't one' (Barlow, *Thomas Becket*, 141). Henry, the son of a count of Anjou, was left speechless by the clerk's audacity. Herbert's only reward for throwing away the chance of recovering his confiscated benefices was the pope's ineffectual recommendation that he be appointed provost of Troyes.

When Henry put pressure on the Cistercian order to expel Becket from Pontigny, it was Herbert who secured from Louis VII what was, for him, a much more attractive refuge at St Columba's Abbey outside Sens, to which the whole party moved in November 1166. But about this time Herbert was almost captured by royalists in Normandy when his courier network was broken. From November 1167 the pope and the French king made a succession of moves to get a reconciliation between Henry and Becket and it is clear, from Herbert's own account, that he used his influence to restrain his master from making the necessary concessions at the conferences of Gisors-Trie (November 1167) and Montmirail (January 1169). But he had probably become a lone voice by November 1169, when most of Becket's clerks, tired of exile, thought that peace could, and should, have been made at St Denis-Montmartre, Paris. And when the reconciliation actually took place at Fréteval, on 22 July 1170, Herbert went forward with the rest of Becket's clerks; and, in contrast to the scene at Angers, they prostrated themselves at Henry's feet and were restored to their possessions, apparently unconditionally. Herbert considered that they had won a great victory, because, at long last, the pope had unsheathed his sword. In August Herbert was sent, exceptionally, with John of Salisbury, on an unsuccessful mission to the king to urge completion of the restoration of the exiles' property, which was one of their conditions for returning to the kingdom; and he was snubbed by Henry. Yet it was he who, standing on the beach at Wissant on 30 November 1170, urged Becket, despite all the dangers that threatened them in England, to press on. The fugitives from Northampton were now soldiers hardened in battle. They should advance, fight, and conquer. Becket accepted his advice.

When the party entered the cathedral church two days later Herbert told his master that it was a day of triumph for the church and Jesus Christ, and entirely thanks to the archbishop. In the three weeks before Christmas Herbert encouraged 'the ram of the Lord's flock, under attack by wolves' (Robertson and Sheppard, 3.483–4) to keep up the fight. But on 26 December Becket prepared him, with another of his clerks, Alexander of Wales, to go to Louis VII, the archbishop of Sens, and other sympathizers in France (another clerk went to the pope) to inform them that the terms of the peace promised at Fréteval had not been implemented in England.

Aftermath of murder Herbert left Canterbury on the 27th at dead of night, and two days later Becket was murdered. For the rest of his life Herbert regretted that he had been deprived of participation in the martyrdom; and there can be no doubt that, if he had been with his lord on the day, events would have taken a different, although not necessarily less bloody, turn. Herbert was apparently at Sens when news arrived of the death, for he wrote a letter for the archbishop to the pope in which he identified the murderers, but refrained from inculpating the king. And he remained almost entirely in France for the rest of his life, being occasionally noticed at Paris as well as Sens. He probably existed by clerking and teaching theology in any welcoming society.

Herbert did not willingly continue his exile. In 1172 he wrote to the papal legates, Albert and Theodwin, and to the pope complaining of the detention of his benefices and the unacceptable terms on which he could return to England. Alexander condoled with him, thanked him for his services to the martyr, and instructed his legates to look after the interests of the victimized clerks. But Herbert seems to have had few, if any, sympathizers in the English church. He did, however, have at least one interview with Henry II, possibly between 1184 and 1186 when he was writing the *Vita*. He questioned the king on how responsible he was for Becket's death; and Henry admitted that, because of his inflammatory words, he had been the unintentional cause. In return Herbert told him that Becket had foreseen in a dream the great rebellions of 1173–4. He had seen the king attacked by a large flock of birds which were tearing him to bits, and, mindful of their old friendship, he had driven them off. But one man, an old courtier now dead, had helped the birds. When Henry asked eagerly who it was, the clerk refused to tell. Henry then told Herbert of the miracle—the defeat and capture of the king of Scots—that Becket had performed for him on 13 July 1174. It was like old friends—or enemies—chatting about old times. In his *Liber melorum* (book of songs), which he appended to his life of Becket, Herbert paid tribute to the king, whose grandeur was impaired only by his unaccountable feud with his archbishop. He dedicated the *Vita* to Archbishop Baldwin of Canterbury, who, when archdeacon of Exeter, had been a regular recipient of news of the exiles from John of Salisbury; he visited Christ Church, Canterbury, in 1187, and, indeed, recovered some of his property.

Possibly even before Henry's death in 1189 Herbert entered the household of William de Longchamp, Richard

I's chancellor, who became bishop of Ely and viceregent. But he could not have stayed there long, for he spent his last days in the Cistercian abbey of Ourscamp, in the diocese of Arras, where he earned his keep by writing a commentary on St Jerome's Hebrew psalter, which he dedicated to the bishop of Arras.

Death and reputation Herbert died, probably at Ourscamp, about 1194, a disappointed and bitter old man. His services to the martyr had not only brought him a largely unpleasant exile, but also earned him no reward after his master's posthumous triumph, to which he thought he had contributed. *Crème de la crème*, a Paris scholar, and a Hebraist, the abrasive edge of his wit and perhaps more than a touch of arrogance could cause offence. Nor have his literary works been greatly esteemed. His letters are over-elaborate; his life of the archbishop, written after most of the other *vitae*, is rambling and verbose; but, since in it he answers, without naming them, some of his predecessors, meditates revealingly on some of the events he records, and gives a unique and intimate account of their life in exile, it is much richer than most of the others. His commentary on the Hebrew psalter and his edition of Peter Lombard's 'great gloss' on the Psalms and St Paul's epistles, which he dedicated to Archbishop William of Sens (*r.* 1169–76), are, however, scholasticism pure and simple, and have had their day. FRANK BARLOW

Sources J. A. Giles, ed., *Herberti de Boseham opera quae extant omnia*, 2 vols. (1845–6) • J. C. Robertson and J. B. Sheppard, eds., *Materials for the history of Thomas Becket, archbishop of Canterbury*, 7 vols., Rolls Series, 67 (1875–85) • B. Smalley, *The Becket conflict and the schools* (1973) • K. J. Leyser, 'Frederick Barbarossa, Henry II and the hand of St James', *EngHR*, 90 (1975), 481–506 • F. Barlow, *Thomas Becket* (1986) • F. Barlow, *Thomas Becket and his clerks* (1987)
Archives Bibliothèque St Vedast, Arras, MS 649 • Bodl. Oxf., Phillipps MS 4622 • Bodl. Oxf., MS Auct. E.inf.6 • CCC Cam., MS 123 • Christ Church Oxf., MS 146 • Trinity Cam., MSS B. 5, 4–7

Boso (*d.* **1178?**), papal official and cardinal, was by the sixteenth century thought to be an Englishman, but was more probably a Tuscan by birth, from Lucca or Pisa, and may have been a canon of Bologna. The only argument in favour of the tradition that he was related to Pope Adrian IV is that he appears in the curia as scriptor and datary of papal letters in 1149, the year when the future pope Adrian was appointed cardinal-bishop of Albano by Eugenius III. There is also the tradition that he accompanied the cardinal-bishop of Albano on his legation to Scandinavia in 1152–4, and it is certainly true that in this period there is no evidence of Boso's presence in Rome. However, Boso's English contacts may not have been made in the course of this journey but rather through Cardinal Guido da Pisa. Six months after the death of Cardinal Guido (1149), who had been papal chancellor, he is found dating papal letters. He was created cardinal-deacon of Santi Cosma e Damiano in 1156. Whether or not he was English has not been finally resolved. He was later said to have been the friend of successive archbishops of Canterbury, Theobald and Thomas Becket. But these acquaintanceships may have been made during Canterbury legations to Rome, rather than in England. Boso was, however, a firm supporter of Becket's cause in the 1160s.

Boso came to prominence in the important office of papal chamberlain, to which he was appointed by Pope Adrian IV, to whom he was certainly close in temperament and purpose. He conducted a vigorous campaign to restore the papal patrimony in the Campagna and Sabina. He received the oaths of fealty from papal vassals and he had troops at his command. Between 1157 and 1159 Boso, as chamberlain, was effectively the head of the papal household and representative of the pope in both the city and the patrimony; this position explains the important part that he played on the death of Pope Adrian in September 1159, when he tried to secure the election of a pope who would continue Adrian's policies. Boso ceased to be chamberlain under Alexander III, but he accompanied Alexander to France during the schism which followed the disputed election of 1159, and, in 1177, to Venice on a mission to make peace with the emperor Frederick Barbarossa. He was promoted cardinal-priest of Santa Pudenziana by Alexander. His importance to curial administration is attested by his revision of the *Liber censuum* but he is also of crucial importance for his revision of and contribution to the *Liber pontificalis*. The biographies of Eugenius III, Anastasius IV, Adrian IV, and Alexander III are first-hand accounts and without Boso, knowledge of the twelfth-century popes would be meagre indeed. His account of Alexander III ends at Easter 1178 and, as he ceased to subscribe as cardinal after July 1178, it may be presumed, in the absence of evidence to the contrary, that he died in that year. JANE E. SAYERS

Sources L. Duchesne and C. Vogel, eds., *Le Liber pontificalis*, 3 vols. (Paris, 1886–1957), vol. 2, pp. 351–446 • P. Fabre and L. Duchesne, eds., *Le Liber censuum de l'église romaine*, 3 vols. (Paris, 1889–1952), vol. 1, pp. 385–400, nos. 98–120 • *The letters of John of Salisbury*, ed. and trans. H. E. Butler and W. J. Millor, rev. C. N. L. Brooke, OMT, 2: *The later letters, 1163–1180* (1979), 774–5 [Lat. orig. with parallel Eng. text] • *Materials for the history of Thomas Becket, archbishop of Canterbury*, 6, ed. J. C. Robertson, Rolls Series, 67 (1882), 57–9 • F. Geisthardt, 'Der Kämerer Boso', *Historische Studien*, 293 (1936) • Z. Zafarana, 'Bosone', in A. M. Ghisalberti, *Dizionario bibliografico degli Italiani* (1971), 13.270–74 • *Patrologia Latina*, 180 (1855), ep. 365, cols. 1400–01 • *Ottonis et Rahewini gesta Friderici I. imperatoris*, ed. O. Waitz and B. von Simson, 3rd edn, MGH Scriptores Rerum Germanicarum, [46] (Hanover, 1912), fol. 320 • J. Garim, 'Boson' (2), *Dictionnaire d'histoire et de géographie ecclésiastiques*, ed. A. Baudrillart and others, 9 (Paris, 1937) • I. S. Robinson, *The papacy, 1073–1198* (1990)
Archives Biblioteca Apostolica Vaticana, Vatican City

Boson family (*per. c.*1675–1730), preservers of the Cornish language, were key figures in the initial revival of Cornish, at a time towards the end of the seventeenth century when it was realized that the language was rapidly dying out. They came from a long-established landowning and merchant family of Newlyn, in Paul parish in west Cornwall, involved in the pilchard fishery.

Nicholas Boson (1624–1708) was born at Newlyn on 25 April 1624, the son of Nicholas Boson (*bap.* 1596, *d.* 1648/9) and Alse Besuerges (*d.* 1669). He was the third of six sons and three daughters, but the first to survive past infancy. At some time before 1653 he married Elizabeth Webber (*d.* 1687), said to be the daughter of John Webber. Nicholas was the author of three important Cornish texts. *Nebbaz gerriau dro tho Carnoack* or 'A few words about Cornish' was written between 1675 and 1708, probably close to the earlier date. *Jowan Chy-an-Horth, py, An try foynt a skyans* or 'John of Chyannor, or, The three points of wisdom' was published in 1707 by Edward Lhuyd, who said it had been written 'some 40 years since', possibly to teach Nicholas's children the language. *The Dutchess of Cornwall's Progress*, written partly in English and existing today only in fragments quoted by other authors, was composed some time between about 1660 and 1670 for the amusement of his children. The first two are the only seventeenth-century Cornish prose compositions which survive.

Nicholas related how his mother forbade their servants and neighbours to talk to him other than in English, so that he did not speak Cornish fluently until it was required in his business dealings with the local fishermen. He was a language informant for both William Scawen and Edward Lhuyd in their efforts to record and preserve the Cornish language. Nicholas was buried on 18 July 1708 at Paul church.

Thomas Boson (*bap.* 1635, *d.* 1719) was baptized on 30 April 1635 at Paul church, the eldest son of Arthur Boson (*bap.* 1603, *d.* 1673)—the second brother of Nicholas (*bap.* 1596)—and Blanch (*d.* 1698) (maiden name unknown). Thomas had three brothers and three sisters. On 2 July 1672 he married Usalla or Ursula Gubbs, daughter of Anthony and Alice Gubbs of Penzance. They had two sons and two daughters. About 1710 Thomas assisted William Gwavas in his research on the Cornish language. He wrote a Cornish inscription for Gwavas's hurling ball and translated Hymn 166, the ten commandments, the Lord's prayer, and the creed into Cornish. He also provided details of the Gwavas family pedigree. Thomas was buried on 5 May 1719 at Paul church.

John Boson (1655–1730) was the second of three sons and one daughter of Nicholas and Elizabeth Boson. He was born on 29 March 1655 according to the Paul parish register. There is no record that he ever married. He was the chief teacher of Cornish to William Gwavas, and thus at one remove from Thomas Tonkin, the Cornish historian. His own works included epitaphs in 1716 for Cornish language scholar John Keigwin in Cornish and for schoolteacher Oliver Pendar in Latin. He wrote the 'Pilchard Curing Rhyme' in Cornish, and Cornish translations of parts of the Bible and the Lord's prayer and creed. He also composed the only surviving lapidary inscription in traditional Cornish, a couplet on the monument in Paul church to Arthur Hutchens (*d.* 1709). John was buried at Paul church on 21 April 1730.

The writings of the Boson family, collected by Padel (1975), are important for the light they throw on vernacular Cornish in the late seventeenth and early eighteenth centuries. Nicholas had learned Cornish as an adult but his son John can be considered a native speaker, as most likely was cousin Thomas. All three were involved in passing on their knowledge of Cornish to future generations through their interactions with scholars of the day. Versions of 'John of Chyannor' are still used to teach the Cornish language to new generations of revivalists.

MATTHEW SPRIGGS

Sources parish register, Paul, Cornwall RO · O. Padel, *The Cornish writings of the Boson family* (1975) · C. Henderson, 'Nicholas Boson and Richard Angwyn', *Old Cornwall*, 2/2 (1931–6), 29–32 · A. Hawke, 'A new Cornish manuscript', *Cornish Studies*, 14 (1986), 5–14 · A. K. H. Jenkin, 'Lhuyd manuscripts in the Bodleian Library, 1: the duchess of Cornwall's progress', *Journal of the Royal Institution of Cornwall*, 21 (1922–5), 401–13 · E. Lhuyd, *Archaeologia Britannica* (1707), 222, 251–3 · R. M. Nance, 'Nicholas Boson's "Nebbaz gerriau dro tho Carnoack"', *Journal of the Royal Institution of Cornwall*, 23 (1929–32), 327–53 · P. A. S. Pool, *The death of Cornish (1600–1800)* (1982), 12–14 · O. Padel, *Exhibition of manuscripts and printed books on the Cornish language* (1975), 1–3 [unpaginated] · W. Scawen, 'Antiquities Cornu-Britannick', [n.d., *c.*1678–1689], Royal Institution of Cornwall · M. Spriggs, 'The Reverend Joseph Sherwood: a Cornish language will-'o'-the wisp?', *Cornish Studies*, new ser., 6 (1998), 54–6 · J. Whetter, *Cornish weather and Cornish people in the 17th century* (1991), 55, 101–2

Archives BL, Add. MS 28554 · Bodl. Oxf., MS Carte 269, fols. 40*r*–45*r* · Cornwall RO, Dd. CN 3460, fol. 3*r* · Cornwall RO, Dd. Enys 2000, pp. 158, 159, 160–62, 165, 169, 173–5 · Diputacion Foral de Bizkaia, Bilbao, Spain, OVR6cmrte collection, T. Tonkin, 'Bilbao MS', MS. BDV m/s Bnv–69 · PRO, MSS E 134 12 Geo I Hil 12, E 134 Geo I East 7 · Royal Institution of Cornwall, Truro, Gatley MS, fols. 9*v*, 15*v* · Royal Institution of Cornwall, Truro, MS Tonkin B, pp. 207c, d–e

Wealth at death estate left to only sister; John Boson: will, proved, 29 April 1730, Cornwall RO

Boson, John (1655–1730). *See under* Boson family (*per.* *c.*1675–1730).

Boson, Nicholas (1624–1708). *See under* Boson family (*per.* *c.*1675–1730).

Boson, Thomas (*bap.* 1635, *d.* 1719). *See under* Boson family (*per.* *c.*1675–1730).

Bossam, John (*fl.* 1550), painter and draughtsman, is of unknown parentage. Bossam had the honour of being noticed by the distinguished limner Nicholas Hilliard, in whose *Treatise Concerning the Arte of Limning* the following account appears:

> If a man be so endued by nature, and live in time of trouble, and under a savage government wherein arts be not esteemed, and himself but of small means, woe be unto him as unto a timely birth! For mine own knowledge it hath made poor men poorer, as among others (many) the most rare English drawer of story works in black and white, John Bossam; one for his skill worthy to have been Serjeant Painter to any king or emperor, whose works in that kind are comparable with the best whatsoever, in cloth, distemper colours, or white and black. Who, being very poor, and belike wanting to buy fair colours, wrought therefore for the most part in white and black; and growing yet poorer by charge of children etc; gave painting clean over; but being a very fair conditioned, zealous and godly person, grew into a love of God's divine service, upon the liberty of the gospel at the coming in of Queen Elizabeth, and became a reading minister: only unfortunate becasse he was English borne, for

euen the strangers would otherwise have set him vpp.
(Hilliard, 67–8)

Of Bossam's work, nothing is known to survive.

[ANON.], *rev.* ANNETTE PEACH

Sources N. Hilliard, *A treatise concerning the arte of limning*, ed. R. K. R. Thornton and T. G. S. Cain (1981), 67–8, 130

Bossewell, John (*fl.* 1572), author, appears to have been a northern man, probably a member of the family of Bosvile from near Doncaster, and possibly the son and heir of Thomas Bosvile of Stainton. He claimed the status of gentleman and seems to have been a notary public. Other details of his life are lacking, including the dates of his birth and death. It is as a heraldist that Bossewell is remembered; his *Workes of Armorie* was published by Totell in 1572. Although this book draws heavily on the writings of his older contemporary Gerard Legh, whom Bossewell terms 'a very fruteful and worthy writer' (Bossewell) in his dedicatory epistle to Lord Burghley, Bossewell's work never achieved the popularity of Legh's *Accedens of Armory*, and it was reprinted only once, in 1597.

Like Legh's book, Bossewell's treatise has been censured as being of little value 'even from an heraldic point of view'. Thomas Moule, writing early in the nineteenth century, considered the book 'strangely connected with the Ancient Mythology, and the Virtues personified' (Moule, 21), and it is true that Bossewell is as interested in the symbolism of the heraldic charges he discusses as he is in blazon. Yet for all its mixture of history, mythology, and mineral and animal lore (mainly in the bestiary tradition), Bossewell's *Workes of Armorie* is an interesting essay in linking heraldry with virtue. He draws on numerous Latin texts, as well as French writers, cites such English authors as Lydgate, Gower, Sir Thomas Eliot, and Richard Grafton, and quotes extensively from Chaucer, including the Wife of Bath on gentility. Arcane and full of remarkable, if implausible, information, Bossewell's work is none the less interesting as an example of the sort of learning that delighted Tudor antiquarians.

J. F. R. DAY

Sources T. Moule, *Bibliotheca heraldica Magnae Britanniae* (privately printed, London, 1822) · *DNB* · J. Bossewell, *Workes of armorie* (1572) · J. Hunter, *South Yorkshire: the history and topography of the deanery of Doncaster*, 2 vols. (1828–31); repr. (1974)

Bossom, Alfred Charles, Baron Bossom (1881–1965), architect and politician, was born at 17 Caledonian Road, Islington, London, on 16 October 1881, the elder son of Alfred Henry Bossom (1854–1919), a stationer, and Amelia Jane (*d.* 1920), daughter of Edmund Henry Hammond of Finsbury. He was educated at St Thomas's Charterhouse Church of England School in Finsbury, and was then articled as an architect, as well as attending the evening school of the Royal Academy. In April 1900 he joined the housing section of the London county council's architects' department as a draughtsman.

Bossom migrated to New York about 1905, in the first instance apparently to assist the English amateur architect and socialite George A. Crawley, who had acquired domestic commissions for Henry Phipps, a partner in US Steel. Doubtless on the strength of this connection and his experience at the London county council, he was put in charge of some industrial housing being built in conditions of urgency by US Steel at Pittsburgh. His involvement in a later crash programme of housing at Bridgeport, Connecticut, for Remington workers making arms for the Russian market at the start of the First World War, enhanced Bossom's expertise in building productivity. But he also worked on the restoration of the historic Fort Ticonderoga, New York, for the Pell family (1908–9).

In 1910 Bossom married Emily (*d.* 1932), daughter of Samuel Gamble Bayne, an oil magnate of Ulster origin and the president of the Seaboard National Bank, set up to deal in oil certificates. This appears to have marked the start of his independent career as an architect of banks and skyscrapers, which he conducted from an elegant office in Manhattan, designing mainly in the 'bankers' Renaissance' style then popular in America. He also took a keen interest in the blend of pre-Columbian and early Spanish–American architecture in Mexico, which he characterized as 'a style so free, so largely suited to our needs that it would seem as if the American point of view had found its expression on this continent centuries ago' (Bossom, *Architectural Pilgrimage*, 6–7). Beside the Seaboard Bank's headquarters in New York, he built: the Liberty Bank, Buffalo, New York; the Virginia Trust Company and First National Bank, Richmond, Virginia; the People's Bank, Harrisburg, Pennsylvania; the Greenwich Trust Company, Greenwich, Connecticut; and the Magnolia Petroleum Building, Dallas, Texas—in its time the tallest structure south of Washington. By the early 1920s Bossom was wealthy, with powerful business and professional connections and a burgeoning taste for politics. Treasurer of the New York Architectural League, he was also honorary secretary of the US Baltic League, chairman of the American Mid-European Association, and founder of the Movement for Co-operation in Government, while his wife was treasurer to the New York Philharmonic Orchestra.

However, Bossom had retained his British citizenship, and in 1926 the couple made their home in England, where their children were already at school. Free of the need to work, Bossom rejoined the London county council, at first as a 'Municipal Reform' member of its housing committee (1927) and then as an alderman (1930–34). In the general election of 1929 he was defeated as a Conservative in Hackney, but in 1931 he triumphed at Maidstone with a majority of over 20,000. He bought an ancient house (Stoneacre, Otham) near Maidstone and for twenty-eight years conscientiously nursed the seat, to which he was regularly re-elected with substantial majorities.

The death of his wife and eldest son, Bruce Bayne (1917–1932), in a flying accident clinched Bossom's commitment to politics and public service. He was totally dedicated to the Conservative Party, and was conspicuously loyal in turn to its successive leaders. From a maiden speech on 'waste in the construction of airfields' he went on to committees involving public expenditure and was resolutely opposed to high taxation. An early mark was made with a trade mission in 1933 to the Baltic states, exploiting his earlier contacts. He acted as a spokesman for architecture and construction in parliament, introducing as a private member in 1938 the second Architects Registration Bill, which secured the 'closed shop' in architecture, and campaigning for the reduction of building costs through American-style efficiency in construction. Long before he had argued that 'commercial buildings have to be commercial … bringing in a revenue commensurate with the amount of investment' (Bossom, *Architectural Pilgrimage*, 9). Bossom fervently admired the American skyscraper, and published *Building to the Skies: the Romance of the Skyscraper* in 1934. But he strenuously opposed the introduction of higher buildings in Europe, and once crossed the Atlantic by liner just to argue the point in a conference.

Bossom was naturally drawn into the wartime investigations into fast construction methods, and in 1943 headed a mission to examine the success of the Tennessee valley authority in assembling prefabricated homes brought to the site in halves, with fittings already complete. This mission had some impact on the British 'prefab' programme. Subsequently he became president of the Modular Society, set up in 1952 to bring dimensional co-ordination to post-war building production. He also took particular interest in the Royal Society of Arts, of which he was chairman. Preferring the variety of delegations, international business and friendship associations, and social and voluntary organizations to the lure of ministerial office, Bossom gloried in giving parties and going on trips to other countries. He amassed dignities and honorary offices with the same enthusiastic acquisitiveness as he collected North American Indian artefacts and police truncheons. A conscientious attender of the Commons when in England, he fell in love with its rituals and procedures, and was moved to publish *Our House* (1948), a brief admiring exposition of its formalities.

In 1934 Bossom was married again, this time to Mrs Elinor Armstrong, daughter of Samuel Gamble Dittenhofer of Minnesota; they divorced in 1947. He received a baronetcy in 1953, and took into his arms a steel building column with three floor girders and the motto *Esto quo es*—'be yourself'—a wry comment, perhaps, on Churchill's witticism: 'Bossom? Funny name—neither one thing nor the other.' In 1959 he finally stood down from the Commons. A life peerage in 1960 took him to the Lords, where he was not conspicuous. He died on 4 September 1965 at his home, 1 St John's House, Smith Square, Westminster, and was buried three days later at Thursley, Surrey, next to his first wife. The baronetcy passed to his second son, Clive (*b.* 1918). A third son, Doric (1922–1959), predeceased him.

IVAN ROOTS

Sources A. C. Bossom, *Some reminiscences* (1953) • A. C. Bossom, *An architectural pilgrimage in Old Mexico* (1923) • D. Sharp, *A. C. Bossom's American architecture, 1903–1926*, 2nd edn (1984) • A. C. Bossom, *Building to the skies: the romance of the skyscraper* (1934) • A. C. Bossom, *Our house* (1948) • *Kent Messenger* (1933–59) • *Kent Messenger* (10 Sept 1965) • *Daily Telegraph* (5 Sept 1965) • *WW* • *WWW* • *Who was who in America* • *Debrett's Peerage* • personal knowledge (2004) • *CGPLA Eng. & Wales* (1965) • b. cert. • m. cert. • d. cert.

Archives priv. coll., family archive | U. Birm. L., corresp. with Lord Avon

Likenesses G. Kelly, portrait, priv. coll.; repro. in Bossom, *Some reminiscences* • miniature (after black and white reproduction of a portrait by G. Kelly), repro. in Bossom, *Some reminiscences* • photographs, repro. in *Kent Messenger*

Wealth at death £92,636: probate, 12 Nov 1965, *CGPLA Eng. & Wales*

Boste, John [St John Boste] (**1544–1594**), Roman Catholic priest and martyr, was born at Wellyng Manor, Dufton, Westmorland, the younger of two sons of Nicholas Boste, of Wellyng Manor, and his wife, Janet Hutton, of Hutton Hall in Penrith. Boste went to Queen's College, Oxford, where he graduated BA on 9 July 1568, was appointed a taberdar on 29 January 1568, and proceeded MA on 18 June 1572. He was elected to a fellowship the same year (31 October 1572). In the winter of 1573–4 he taught at Appleby grammar school, Westmorland. Boste received Church of England orders and subscribed to the royal supremacy. After becoming a Roman Catholic in 1576, presumably at Browne Hall, Suffolk, the house of Sir Thomas Cornwallis, he was expelled from his fellowship for 'ministerium abnegando' ('forsaking his ministry') and contradicting 'sanae et Christianae religioni' ('sound Christian doctrine'; Pollen, 222; Queen's College, register G, fol. 35).

In 1580 Boste left England for the Low Countries. He was a tutor to Gerard Clibborn, with whom he arrived at the English College, then at Rheims, on 4 August 1580. Boste received minor orders in the winter of 1580, and was deaconed (21 February 1581) and priested (4 March 1581) at Châlons-sur-Marne. He was sent back to England soon after (11 April 1581) 'for avoidinge of daunger' (Pollen, 65) associated with the revocation of Englishmen studying abroad. He landed at Hartlepool and commenced his mission to the northern counties and Scotland. He was among the most sought-after priests in the north. Various failed attempts to capture him caused the earl of Huntingdon (lord president of the north) to search Kingston upon Hull for 'John Bost, alias Harckley' (Stanewell, 158).

Boste was eventually betrayed by Francis Ecclesfield, a renegade Catholic, in the house of William Claxton, at Waterhouses near Brancepeth, co. Durham, on 10 September 1593. Sent to Windsor on 2 October 1593, he was examined by Richard Topcliffe on behalf of the privy council a week later. In order to reveal his associates Boste was 'often most cruelly rack'd, insomuch so that he was afterward forced to go crooked upon a staff' (Challoner, 202). His torturer reported that 'since ther Honors knew the world, they never hearde a more resoluyt Traitor' (Pollen, 217). Boste was kept in prison until the summer of 1594 when he was sent back to Durham and tried together with another priest, John Ingram, and a Catholic layman, George Swallowfield. On 24 July 1594 he was accused of leaving and re-entering the country without permission. Later that day he was condemned and hanged, drawn, and quartered in Durham, the others two days later at Gateshead and Darlington.

An incident at Boste's trial speaks of his conviction and courage: Swallowfield, also a former Church of England clergyman, was about to recant his Catholic beliefs, when Boste urged him to stand firm. When Swallowfield asked for forgiveness for his wavering faith Boste gave absolution in open court. Boste was canonized by Pope Paul VI in 1970, and his two companions were beatified by Pope Pius XI in 1929. J. ANDREAS LÖWE

Sources U. Hull, Brynmor Jones L., Knaresborough papers, MSS DDEV/67/1, fols. 500–09 · 'The confession of John Boste', BL, Lansdowne MS, MS 75, no. 22 · J. B. Wainwright, 'John Boste', Jesuit Archives, London · L. M. Stanewell, ed., *City and county of Kingston upon Hull: calendar of the ancient deeds, letters, miscellaneous old documents, &c. in the archives of the corporation* (1951), 158 · Foster, *Alum. Oxon.* · T. F. Knox and others, eds., *The first and second diaries of the English College, Douay* (1878) · R. Challoner, *Memoirs of missionary priests*, ed. J. H. Pollen, rev. edn (1924) · G. Anstruther, *The seminary priests 1: Elizabethan, 1558–1603* [1966], 43f. · J. Morris, ed., *The troubles of our Catholic forefathers related by themselves*, 3 (1877), 185 · *Acts of the apostolic see*, 62 (1970), 745–53 · canonization records, office of the vice-postulation, Jesuit Archives, London · J. H. Pollen, ed., *Unpublished documents relating to the English martyrs*, 1, Catholic RS, 5 (1908) · Queen's College, Oxford, archives, register G, fol. 35

Bostock, Bridget [*called* the Cheshire Doctoress] (*b. c.*1678, *d.* after 1749), faith healer, details of whose parentage are unknown, lived in Coppenhall, Cheshire, throughout her life and was uneducated. 'Aged about 70 years' (*GM*, 18.414), Bostock came to national attention in August 1748 as the result of a report about her in a local newspaper. She had been healing locally for many years with the use of fasting spittle, a little liquor of 'a red complexion', touch, and prayer. In 1748 people of all social ranks began to visit her, and by September she was receiving crowds of 600–700 a day. She was said to cure blind, deaf, and lame people, and those with rheumatism, the king's evil (scrofula), hysteric fits, falling fits, shortness of breath, dropsy, palsy, leprosy, and cancers (though not syphilis). Bostock did not seek such fame or numbers, and by late 1748 she saw only those who had been to her before and those suffering from deafness. She was described as a frequent churchgoer and as a person of great character and faith by her minister, William Harding, whose son claimed that she cured his lameness. John Bennet, a Methodist minister, visited her twice and recorded in his diary his impressions and the reports of others, ultimately declaring himself unable to account for her cures. John Wesley, who heard accounts of her healings, did not doubt them. Sir John Price, a Welsh baronet, wrote asking her to raise his wife from the dead. Bostock refused despite Price's entreaties—peppered with biblical texts concerning resurrection—in his letters to her written between December 1748 and December 1749. Some visitors and commentators sought to explain her cures in natural terms, while others described her as an impostor or cheat who deceived the 'vulgar'. Several also offered accounts of her physical appearance. One described 'an old shrivelled creature seated in an elbow chair in a most dirty attire, and her petticoats not reaching above half-way down her legs', while another spoke less harshly of her dress of 'flannel waistcoat, a green linsey apron, a pair of clogs, and a plain cap, tied with a half-penny lace' (Chaloner, 6, 9–10). There is no record of what happened to Bridget Bostock after 1749, but interest in her continued into the next century, as evidenced by two letters in the *Monthly Magazine* for June and August 1808. JANE SHAW

Sources *GM*, 1st ser., 18 (1748), 413–14, 448, 450, 513 · *GM*, 1st ser., 19 (1749), 343 · *Monthly Magazine*, 25 (June 1808) · *Monthly Magazine*, 26 (Aug 1808) · J. Bennet, MS journal, JRL, Methodist Archives and Research Centre, 20 Sept 1748, 29 March 1749 · H. D. Rack, 'Doctors, demons and early Methodist healing', *The church and healing*, ed. W. J. Sheils, SCH, 19 (1982), 137–52 · W. H. Chaloner, ed., *Bridget Bostock* (1948)

Bostock, Elizabeth Anne [Eliza] (1817–1898), promoter of women's education, was born in Liverpool, the only child of John *Bostock (1772–1846), doctor of medicine, and his wife, Anne Yates (*d.* 1863). Her father, a Unitarian, assumed much of the responsibility for her early education. He taught her Italian, took her to lectures given by Michael Faraday, and nurtured her love of reading. Eliza, as she was known, received some formal education at a day school in Upper Bedford Place in London when she was six years old. The family moved to Paris in 1829 and she was sent to school, where she gained a thorough knowledge of French but, she claimed, learned nothing else. She became caught up in the July revolution of 1830, when a servant had to take her across six barricades to reach the safety of her home.

As a young adult Bostock's time was mainly divided between balls, visits to relatives, travelling to improve her health, and taking care of her mother. Alongside this, her friendship with Elisabeth Jesser Reid led to a growing concern about women's status in society. By the late 1840s she had declared her desire to enable women to 'enjoy the right to work, to labour, to earn independence' (Tuke, 105). She assisted Elisabeth Reid in her plans for a ladies' college in Bedford Square in London, which opened as Bedford College (1849), and later, in 1889, gave public support for women's suffrage. She continued her own education into adulthood, taking the opportunity to attend classes in astronomy, drawing, Italian, and natural history at Bedford College between 1849 and 1863. She also acted as one of the Lady Visitors, who chaperoned younger students and helped to run the college.

In 1860 Elisabeth Reid named Eliza Bostock one of the three Reid trustees, on condition that she remained single. As a trustee she had control over the funds provided by Elisabeth Reid to run Bedford College's boarding-house and to assist women's education. This gave her considerable power in the college, but also enabled her to help other organizations, such as the London School of Medicine for Women. She was determined to improve the standard of girls' and women's education. She worked with Emily Davies in the 1860s to gain agreement for girls to sit the Cambridge local examinations, and for the schools' inquiry commission to investigate girls' schools. She was adamant that Bedford College should prepare students for the University of London examinations: in 1868, in collaboration with Jane Martineau, one of the other Reid trustees, she forced the closure of the school attached to the college, a development which enabled the staff to concentrate on providing higher education for women. She was also a great believer in scholarships for women, arguing that they fostered self-reliance. She provided money for a number of scholarships and prizes at Bedford College. She also donated books and shelves to the library, and made regular gifts of money to help the college expand.

Bostock oversaw the college's move to York Place in 1874, and impressed people with her knowledge of architecture and building. Henrietta Busk noted that by the 1870s her influence was such that she was regarded as 'honorary Principal' of the college (Busk, 9). She was viewed as an awe-inspiring figure, detached and austere, yet friendly and kind when approached for help. Her aloofness can partly be accounted for by her growing deafness, which also limited her contributions to college council and other committees.

By the time Eliza Bostock moved out of London to her Glamorgan home in 1885 all who knew her attested to her devotion to the college, and to what she referred to as 'The Cause' of women's education (Notcutt, obituary, 4). During her retirement, as well as keeping in touch with developments at the college, she indulged her love of gardening and reading. She also encouraged the children in her village to pursue their interests, and on one occasion gave a box of tools to a boy who enjoyed carpentry. An attack of bronchitis led to her death at her home, Cefn Môr, in Penmaen, on 13 April 1898. SOPHIE BADHAM

Sources R. Notcutt, *Bedford College Magazine* (June 1898), 2–4 • E. Lingen, *Bedford College Magazine* (June 1898), 4–5 • E. Davies, *Bedford College Magazine* (June 1898), 5–6 • W. Russell, *Bedford College Magazine* (June 1898), 6 • P. Harding, *Bedford College Magazine* (June 1898), 6–7 • H. Busk, *Bedford College Magazine* (June 1898), 8–10 • E. Sturge, *Bedford College Magazine* (June 1898), 10–11 • E. Garbutt, *Bedford College Magazine* (June 1898), 11–12 • M. J. Tuke, *A history of Bedford College for Women, 1849–1937* (1939) • R. Notcutt, 'Bedford College', *Bedford College Magazine* (March 1887), 1–5 • Bedford College register of students, Royal Holloway College, Egham, Surrey • E. Bostock, letters to Elisabeth Jesser Reid, Royal Holloway College, Egham, Surrey, Elisabeth Jesser Reid MSS • correspondence of the managers of the Residence, Royal Holloway College, Egham, Surrey, Bedford College MSS • d. cert.

Archives Royal Holloway College, Egham, Surrey, Elisabeth Jesser Reid MSS, part of the Bedford College MSS, letters to Elisabeth Jesser Reid

Likenesses photograph, U. Lond.; repro. in Tuke, *History of Bedford College* • photographs, Royal Holloway College, Egham, Surrey

Wealth at death £22,290 2s. 1d.: probate, 8 June 1898, *CGPLA Eng. & Wales*

Bostock, John (1744?–1774), physician, was born in England, but educated at the University of Edinburgh, where he graduated MD in 1769. His inaugural dissertation is his only published work. He dedicated it to William Cullen, under whom he had studied. The dissertation is on gout, and in it Bostock quotes extensively from Thomas Sydenham. He also acknowledges that his work is heavily influenced by Cullen. Bostock became an extra licentiate of the College of Physicians of London in 1770, and began to practise immediately after in Liverpool. He was appointed physician to the Royal Infirmary, and married shortly afterwards Elizabeth (1749–1819), the youngest daughter of John Ashton of Liverpool; the couple had a son, John *Bostock (1772–1846).

Suffering from an incurable disease, Bostock died on 10 March 1774, 'calmly resigning the sweetest blandishments of life, and in his last moments emulating the exit of a Socrates or a Seneca' (Munk, 2.287). Some of his collection of books were preserved in the library of the Royal Medical and Chirurgical Society in London, among them a copy of his dissertation, *Tentamen medicum inaugurale de arthritide* (1769). Three years after her husband's death Elizabeth married the Unitarian minister John Yates (1755–1826). NORMAN MOORE, *rev.* KAYE BAGSHAW

Sources Munk, *Roll*

Bostock, John (1772–1846), physician and medicinal chemist, was born in Liverpool, the son of John *Bostock (1744?–1774), a physician, and Elizabeth (1749–1819), youngest daughter of John Ashton of Liverpool, who later married the Unitarian minister John Yates (1755–1826). He grew up in Liverpool as a member of the town's Unitarian community. In 1792 he attended Joseph Priestley's course of chemical lectures at Hackney College, Middlesex. After returning to Liverpool he studied as an apothecary prior to his move to Edinburgh, in 1794, where he was elected president of the Medical Society. At this time his tutors included Thomas Hope and Joseph Black, joint professors of chemistry, whose lectures were much influenced by H. Lavoisier and J. Dalton. Bostock graduated MD in 1798, having submitted a thesis on bile secretion.

Following graduation Bostock returned to Liverpool, where he became a physician to the General Dispensary. He played key roles in the formation of the botanic gardens, the Fever Hospital, and in 1812 the Liverpool Literary and Philosophical Society. He was also a member of the medical committee of the School for the Blind. Over the next few years Bostock wrote many of the medical and scientific articles for the *Monthly Review* and a large number of original papers for the *Edinburgh Medical and Surgical Journal*, William Nicholson's *Journal of Natural Philosophy, Chemistry and the Arts*, and the *Transactions* of the London Medico-Chirurgical Society. An early interest in physiology led to his *Essay on Respiration* (1804). This in turn led to a commission to write many medical articles for David Brewster's *Encyclopaedia*. Bostock published pamphlets on the new *Edinburgh Pharmacopoeia* (1807), and wrote *Remarks on the Nomenclature of the New London Pharmacopoeia* (1810), which criticized the basis of its terminology in favour of one based on more structured chemical and botanical terms. This had limited effect. One of the last papers he gave in Liverpool was in 1817, to the Liverpool Literary and Philosophical Society, entitled 'The best means of obviating the nuisance arising from the smoke of steam engines', which showed an early awareness of the serious implications of chemical pollution.

Despite having developed an extensive medical and chemical consulting practice in Liverpool, Bostock moved to London in 1817 and gave up the practice of medicine in favour of a full-time career in science. He succeeded his university contemporary and friend Alexander Marcet as chemical lecturer at Guy's Hospital, and for two years he co-edited the *Annals of Physiology*. Later at Guy's he was to work with Richard Bright and Thomas Addison. His works on the chemical composition of body fluids give him a claim to be one of the founders of English chemical pathology. The breadth of his work on normal and pathological urine was unprecedented and he was the first to realize the relationship between the fall of urea in the urine as it 'appeared' in the blood, while the albumin in the blood disappeared as its level in urine increased.

However, it is for a short presentation to the London Medico-Chirurgical Society in 1819 that Bostock is best remembered. His 'Case of a periodical affection of the eyes and chest' (*Medico-Chirurgical Transactions*, 10, 1819, 161–5) is the first recorded description of what became known as catarrhus aestivus or hay fever. Bostock described how he had personally suffered since childhood from a then unknown affliction. Each year at the beginning of June he developed the symptoms of a cold which lasted for about two months and was associated with profuse nasal discharge, repeated paroxysms of sneezing, itching of the eyes, and difficulty in breathing. He described the unique character of the condition. This description is the more remarkable coming from an ex-dispensary physician who would have been very familiar with a wide range of everyday disease, and it provides compelling evidence for the view that hay fever is a post-industrial-revolution disease, with a major environmental component. In the following nine years he collected details of a further twenty-eight cases, and he published these in *Medico-Chirurgical Transactions* in 1828, in an article entitled 'On the catarrhus aestivus or summer catarrh'.

During his early years in London, Bostock published *An Account of the History and Present State of Galvanism* (1818), and between 1824 and 1827 he produced his three-volume *Elementary System of Physiology*, a book which was popular and influential at the time and which had reached a fourth edition by 1844. His interest in chemistry also remained active and in 1829 he published in the *Philosophical Transactions of the Royal Society* 'On the purification of Thames water', in which he discussed the nature of a number of chemical impurities. In addition, in 1828 he had published an incomplete translation of Pliny's *Natural History* and in 1835 he published *A Sketch of the History of Medicine from its Origin to the Commencement of the 19th Century*, which formed part of the introduction to John Forbes's journal, the *Cyclopaedia of Practical Medicine*. Bostock's widening scientific activity and reputation were reflected in his appointments as council member of the Royal Society (elected in 1829, vice-president in 1832), president of the Geological Society (1826), and treasurer of the Medico-Chirurgical Society of London. In addition he served on the council of the Linnean, Zoological, and Horticultural societies and of the Royal Society of Literature.

Bostock married Anne Yates (*d.* 1863), with whom he had a daughter, Elizabeth Anne *Bostock (1817–1898), who became a promoter of women's education. Bostock died of cholera on 6 August 1846 at his home, 22 Upper Bedford Place, London. M. B. EMANUEL

Sources *DNB* • *The Lancet* (15 Aug 1846), 222 • *Abstracts of the Papers Communicated to the Royal Society of London*, 5 (1843–50), 636–8 • J. R. Partington, *A history of chemistry*, 3 (1962), 711–12 • *DSB* • T. J. Pettigrew, *Medical portrait gallery: biographical memoirs of the most celebrated physicians, surgeons … who have contributed to the advancement of medical science*, 4 vols. in 2 [1838–40], vol. 3, pp. 1–20 • M. B. Emanuel, 'Hay-fever, a post-industrial revolution epidemic', *Clinical Allergy*, 18 (1988), 295–304 • R. Finn, 'John Bostock, hay-fever and the mechanism of allergy', *The Lancet* (12 Dec 1992), 1453–5 • d. cert. • T. H. Bickerton and R. M. B. MacKenna, *A medical history of Liverpool from the earliest days to the year 1920*, ed. H. R. Bickerton (1936)

Likenesses W. D. Drummond, lithograph, 1836 (after J. Partridge), BM, Wellcome L. • J. Jenkins, stipple, Wellcome L.

Boston Buriensis. *See* Kirkestede, Henry (*b. c.*1314, *d.* in or after 1378).

Boston, Alison (*fl.* 1424). *See under* Women traders and artisans in London (*act. c.*1200–*c.*1500).

Boston, John (*d.* 1804), radical and merchant in Australia, was born in Birmingham, but nothing further is known of his origins. As a young man he became a disciple of Thomas Paine and a supporter of the London Corresponding Society. At Birmingham he was associated with Joseph Priestley and his radical circle, including the Revd Thomas Fyshe Palmer, and in later life he claimed to have warned Priestley of the approach of the mob that destroyed the latter's house during the church and king riots of 1791. He married, apparently in the early 1780s, but his wife's name and the circumstances of the marriage are unknown.

Following, in September 1793, the sentencing of the 'Scottish martyrs'—Thomas Muir, Palmer, William Skirving, Joseph Gerrald, George Mealmaker, and Maurice Margarot—to transportation to Botany Bay, Boston solicited the government to send him to the colony as a 'settler'. His memorial stated that he was 'brought up a Surgeon and Apothecary but have never since followed that profession'. He added, rather ingenuously, that he had been in business as a distiller—'but was unsuccessfull'—and, having studied those aspects of chemistry useful to trade and industry, had 'therefore a knowledge of Brewing, Distilling, Sugar Making, Vinegar Making, Soap Making, etc … I likewise have a Theoretical and some practical knowledge in Agriculture.' Boston ended his appeal by stating that he would take his wife and three children to New South Wales, where 'my views are not ambitious'.

Boston's radical leanings were well known to the British government, which may have been keen to have him out of the realm. It accepted his offer, and he sailed with Skirving, Margarot, Palmer, and James Ellis (Palmer's servant) on the *Suprize* transport, leaving England on 2 May 1794. With Boston went his wife and two of his three children, aged nine and four. Also on the ship were the Scottish-born gentleman convict John Grant and Sergeant Samuel Reddish of the New South Wales Corps, the illegitimate brother of a future British prime minister, George Canning. The captain of the ship, Patrick Campbell, a veteran of the slave trade, claimed to be an agent of the prime minister, William Pitt.

The voyage of the *Suprize* was marked by conflict. Boston is supposed to have drunk 'Damnation to the King, His Family and all Crowned Heads' (deposition of John Campbell, Archives Office of New South Wales, 5/1156, fol. 18), adding that all monarchs were 'absolute Tyrants' who 'might be extirpated from the face of the Earth' (ibid.). Later he was reported by Grant to have called for a people's war and to have predicted that Europe would soon be engaged in a civil war. Reddish supported Grant, claiming that Boston toasted 'The Rights of Man, The Tree of Liberty', 'The French Revolution', and 'Civil, Religious and universal liberty', and desired that 'a Branch of the Tree of Liberty be transplanted to the Dreary and Desolate Shores of New Holland' (deposition of Samuel Reddish, Archives Office of New South Wales, 5/1156, fol. 33). Campbell claimed, when the *Suprize* landed at Botany Bay on 25 October 1794, that the political exiles had threatened a mutiny, but he had no evidence to support his allegation.

In New South Wales, Boston received government assistance to produce salt and to prepare fish, but his political opinions clearly affronted many of the civil and military officers. Moreover, Boston, Palmer, and Ellis had access to funds in sterling which enabled them to challenge the officers' monopoly of imports, itself based on an accidental monopoly of sterling. By not providing New South Wales with a treasury the British government had made monopoly inevitable. Boston was part of the first significant challenge to this state of affairs.

Boston's failure to disguise his political views and his economic threat to the officer-merchants led to a major confrontation on 29 October 1795, when soldiers under the orders of Quartermaster Thomas Laycock of the New South Wales Corps shot Boston's 'very fine Sow, considerably advanced in pig' (*Historical Records of Australia*, 1st ser., 1.605) in a court owned by Captain Joseph Foveaux. In the ensuing brawl Boston and his spirited wife more than held their own, but the matter did not rest here. Boston sued Quartermaster Laycock, Lieutenant Neil Mackellar, and privates William Eaddy and William Faithfull in the court of civil jurisdiction, demanding damages of £500. On 26 August 1796, in what was a political trial, the bench found for Boston, even arguing that the insult 'rascal' (meaning without testicles) did not justify the actions of the military. Boston was awarded damages of only 20s. each against Laycock and Faithfull, but the rule of law was thus affirmed in convict New South Wales. The verdict was upheld by Governor John Hunter sitting as a court of appeal. The later attempt by the former convict enforcer and debt collector of the New South Wales Corps, Tom Biggars, to assault Boston in the streets of Sydney was futile in these circumstances.

Boston and Palmer shared Paine's belief in the revolutionary and liberating effects of free trade. With Ellis they formed an association, Boston & Co., to acquire ships which they used in the freight trade between Sydney and Norfolk Island and in the coal trade between the principal settlement and Newcastle. The company was also a key player in the burgeoning seal skin trade in the seas around Van Diemen's Land. Finally it was involved in the embryonic manufacturing sector of the colony, particularly in soap making, beer brewing, and distilling.

Boston's mercantile adventures earned him the hostility of Governor Hunter, who in 1797 thought him a 'scoundrel' (Parsons, 171) and now associated him with the officers. However, Hunter was under the influence of the evangelical party in the colony; to him all merchants were involved in monopoly and the destruction of the small settlers. The governor, whom Palmer termed an aristocrat, had also realized that Palmer, Boston, and their business associate, George Bass, were friends of liberty, and so threatened the political order in Great Britain and the colony.

Boston owned a successful farm in the Hawkesbury valley region on which he grew wheat and maize and raised pigs, but lack of capital prevented him from being involved in the much more lucrative business of grazing. However, commerce was his major interest; this was the only real way to make money in New South Wales. Accordingly, in 1800 Boston & Co. purchased a Spanish prize, *El Plumier*, which left the colony in January 1801, probably intending to become involved in the new, developing Pacific sandalwood trade and then to sail illegally to Canton in breach of the East India Company's monopoly.

Boston's wife had died, probably late in 1800. She was apparently buried without religious ceremony, which may suggest the extent of his radical beliefs. With the two children he embarked as supercargo on the *El Plumier*, but the voyage was a disaster. The vessel spent some weeks in New Zealand waters, attempting clandestine deals with New England American sailing captains. She then sailed to Tongataboo and was afterwards damaged on a reef off the Fever Islands. On putting into Guam she was seized as a Spanish war prize and the partners left for Manila on a Spanish vessel. At some point on the voyage both Boston's children died.

Boston arrived back in Sydney in March 1804. He claimed to have made money in a distillery in the Philippines, and he followed up this success by embarking on the American ship *Union* as supercargo. The ship was on its way to Canton with sandalwood and sealskins, with the intention of returning to Sydney with a cargo of manufactured goods. However, on 30 September 1804, at Tongataboo, Boston and six crewmen were killed by the islanders when they ventured ashore for food and water.

Boston was a dedicated, convinced 'friend of liberty' who believed in the liberating effects of commerce. As a merchant his success was limited, but he brought to New South Wales radical ideas which were to be of fundamental importance to future political debate.

GEORGE PARSONS

Sources PRO, CO 201/8; CO 102/12 • Archives Office of New South Wales, 5/1156 (COD 261) • T. G. Parsons, 'Was John Boston's pig a political martyr?', *Journal of the Royal Australian Historical Society*, 71 (1986), 163–76 • M. Flynn, *Settlers and seditionists: the people of the convict ship Suprize, 1794* (Sydney, 1994) • J. Iltis, 'Boston, John', *AusDB*, vol. 1 • B. Kercher, *Debt, seduction and other disasters: the birth of civil law in convict New South Wales* (Sydney, 1996) • *Sydney Gazette* (12 May–

28 Oct 1804) • C. J. Baxter, ed., *Musters and lists: New South Wales and Norfolk Island, 1800–1802* (Sydney, 1988) • *Historical Records of Australia*, 1st ser., 1 (Sydney, 1914)

Boston [*née* Wood], **Lucy Maria** (**1892–1990**), writer, was born on 10 December 1892 at 8 Scarisbrick Street, Southport, Lancashire; she was the fifth of the six children of James Wood (*d.* 1899), engineer and sometime mayor of Southport, and his wife, Mary, *née* Garrett. She was educated at local schools in Southport and Arnside, and latterly at a private Quaker boarding-school in Sussex. In 1914 she entered Somerville College, Oxford, but she left after one year to undertake volunteer nursing during the First World War. After early experience at St Thomas's Hospital in London and Addenbrooke's Hospital, Cambridge, she worked at a military hospital at Houlgate, Normandy. On 21 September 1917 she married a distant cousin, (William) Harold Boston (1891–1969), with whom she had one son, Peter, born in 1918. They lived at Norton Lodge, Norton, Cheshire, near Harold Boston's work as a director of the family tannery. The marriage failed in 1935 and thereafter Lucy spent several years working as an artist in Italy and Austria until the threat of war forced her to return to England. In 1937 she rented a flat in Cambridge, and shortly afterwards she bought the twelfth-century manor at Hemingford Grey, near Huntingdon, a unique and extraordinary house to which she devoted the rest of her life and work.

Lucy Boston found the manor in poor condition, with much of its original structure obscured by later Georgian additions, part of which had been destroyed by fire. Assisted by her son she spent several years in radical and painstaking restoration of the house, completing the work only after the outbreak of war. Over many years she remade the garden, which is distinguished for her topiary and collection of old roses. During the war she held regular concerts of classical music, played on her gramophone in the music room at the manor, to give respite and pleasure to RAF crews serving at nearby bases.

Boston was already in her sixties when her first book, *Yew Hall*, a novel for adults, was published in 1954; as in almost all her later writing the manor is its setting and centrepiece. Later in 1954 her first children's book, *The Children of Green Knowe*, appeared and it proved to be the first of six books in which the manor is characterized as Green Knowe; collectively they form one of the outstanding achievements in modern children's literature. Most of the stories are time fantasies, in which the house's history is evoked and past and present occupants make contact with each other. An exception to this historical preoccupation is *A Stranger at Green Knowe* (1961), widely regarded as her best book, which received the Library Association Carnegie medal for 1961. The tragic story of an escaped gorilla, based on Boston's indignation at the confinement of Guy the gorilla at London Zoo, it is an impassioned plea for freedom and respect for all wild, non-human creatures. The final book in the series, *The Stones of Green Knowe* (1976), written after a gap of twelve years, is notably pessimistic in its verdict on contemporary environmental damage. Having started late in life she continued to write and publish well into her eighties. Her other books include stories for very young children, such as *The Castle of Yew* (1965); two volumes of autobiography, *Memory in a House* (1973) and *Perverse and Foolish* (1979); and a volume of poems, *Time is Undone* (1977).

Lucy Boston was a woman of immense energy and creativity, which she retained into extreme old age. She had very striking dark eyes and large, strong, artisan's hands, which she used not only for vigorous gardening (she was scornful of those who could not use a spade properly) but for a series of delicate and exquisite patchworks, now carefully preserved. Outspoken, independent, and fearless, with fiercely held values and mordant wit, she was also generous and kind, and enjoyed showing complete strangers around the house and garden she loved. She died at the manor, following a stroke, on 25 May 1990; she was buried at the church of St Margaret of Antioch, Hemingford Abbots, on 1 June. PETER HOLLINDALE

Sources L. M. Boston, *Memories* (1992) • D. Boston, ed., *Lucy Boston remembered* (1994) • T. Chevalier, ed., *Twentieth-century children's writers*, 3rd edn (1989) • J. Rose, *Lucy Boston* (1965) • b. cert. • m. cert. • d. cert.

Archives priv. coll., MSS

Likenesses J. Finsey, pencil drawing • N. Youngman, charcoal drawing, priv. coll.

Wealth at death £293,023: probate, 31 Dec 1990, *CGPLA Eng. & Wales*

Boston, Thomas (**1676–1732**), Church of Scotland minister and theologian, was born on 17 March 1676 at Duns, Berwickshire, the youngest of seven children of John Boston (1631–1701), a cooper, and his wife, Alison Trotter (*d.* 1691). Although he laboured in obscure parishes Thomas Boston of Ettrick became a national figure through his involvement in the Marrow controversy and through the evangelical Calvinism of his popular writings. He was a staunch Presbyterian from the time of his conversion. As a small boy he spent time in the local prison with his father, who was incarcerated for failing to conform to the Church of Scotland, then under episcopal governance. During adolescence he accompanied his father to worship services held by Scottish covenanters in nearby fields, later dating his Christian conversion to the open air preaching of Henry Erskine in the summer of 1687. Boston attended the grammar school in Duns between 1685 and 1689. After a brief stint as a notary's assistant there he was sent to Edinburgh University in December 1691 from where he graduated MA in 1694 and to where he returned in the following year to study divinity for four months. His early career was unsettled. He served, in turn, as a schoolmaster in Glencairn, a private tutor in the household of Lieutenant-Colonel James Bruce of Kennet, and as an itinerant preacher in vacant parishes in the presbytery of Stirling. After a series of failed attempts to secure a regular pulpit in the Scottish border country he was finally ordained on 21 September 1699 at Simprin, Berwickshire.

Within the year (on 17 July 1700) Boston married Katharine Brown (1674–1737), whom he had met previously at Barhill, Culross. He was deeply devoted to his wife, especially during the unspecified 'heavy trouble' which began

Thomas Boston (1676–1732), by Robert Scott

in 1720 and frequently confined her to bed. Although the couple had ten children in all, six died in early childhood, and Boston's *Memoirs* (1776) contains touching accounts of his grief over their loss. One of the sons who survived was Thomas *Boston (1713–1767), who succeeded his father as minister at Ettrick (1733) and became a founder of the Relief church in 1761. Thomas Boston the elder was translated to Ettrick, Selkirkshire, on 1 May 1707, the first day of the Union between England and Scotland. In 1717 he was called to the parish of Closeburn, but managed to persuade the presbytery to allow him to remain in Ettrick, where his ministry was finally beginning to make an impression on village life. He was diligent in his pastoral duties, believing that 'ministers by carelessness become the murderers of the souls of their people' (Aberdeen, Boston MS 3245/2.157). Though sometimes discouraged and often in poor health, he never failed to appear for a worship service in more than thirty years of public ministry. In addition to preaching twice on the sabbath and once during the week he visited every household in the parish twice annually for personal conference and catechetical instruction.

It was not Boston's activity as a rural pastor, however, but as a theologian which made him a familiar figure in the Scottish church. He played a significant role in each of the major ecclesiastical controversies of the early eighteenth century. This was the result of conviction rather than design; by his own admission his natural temperament was 'timorous and hard to enter on, but eager in the pursuit once entered' (*Complete Works*, 12.10). Among the laity Boston became popular for opposing the abjuration oaths of 1712 and 1719 which he refused to take, at risk to health and property, because they affirmed the legitimacy of the Church of England in its episcopal form. He was equally unbending in his opposition to the heresies of John Simson, professor of divinity in the University of Glasgow. Simson was first censured in 1717 by the Church of Scotland's general assembly for attributing 'too much to natural reason and the power of corrupt nature' (*Acts of the General Assembly, 1638–1842*, 518). A decade later he was found guilty of Arianism and was eventually suspended from his academic duties. Boston stood alone in the 1729 assembly to issue his dissent. He argued that the sentence was too lenient to express 'the dishonour done by the said Mr. Simson to our glorious Redeemer, the great God and our Saviour' by casting doubt on the deity of Jesus Christ (*Complete Works*, 12.384).

Boston was also at the centre of the most famous ecclesiastical dispute of his day, the Marrow controversy (1717–23). This dispute was prompted by a doctrinal proposition which the Auchterarder presbytery required ministerial candidates to sign: 'It is not sound and orthodox to teach, that we must forsake sin in order to our coming to Christ, and instating us in covenant with God' (*Complete Works*, 12.291). Although the Auchterarder creed was intended to preserve Calvinist orthodoxy by establishing the priority of faith over repentance, it was abolished by the 1717 general assembly. Boston 'believed the proposition to be truth, howbeit not well worded' (*Complete Works*, 12.291). His own convictions about faith and repentance had been shaped by his reading of Edward Fisher's *The Marrow of Modern Divinity* (1645), a work he discovered in the cottage of a parishioner about 1700. The *Marrow* contained a series of dialogues largely quoted from protestant reformers and English puritans. The book was sympathetic to the theology of the Auchterarder creed and showed how orthodox Calvinism could offer assurance of faith without falling into legalism. Boston thus recommended it to James Hog of Carnock, who had it republished in 1718. The *Marrow* aroused opposition from a majority in the church, led by Principal James Hadow of St Mary's College, St Andrews, who considered it antinomian in tendency. The 1720 general assembly condemned the *Marrow* and required ministers to warn their parishioners against it. Boston joined others in drafting a 'representation and petition' protesting the assembly's action. After due process the 1722 general assembly overwhelmingly reaffirmed their prior action and the moderator issued a formal rebuke to the Marrow men. This was the end of the controversy proper, although in 1726 Boston published a carefully annotated edition of the *Marrow* using the pseudonym Philalethes Irenaeus. He later came to believe that the ecclesiastical notoriety he received as a Marrow man prevented him from advancing to a more prominent pulpit. Nevertheless, the controversy helped secure his popularity in the Scottish border country, where the assembly's condemnation had the unintended result of stimulating greater interest in the Marrow theology.

Although Boston's theology sometimes has been viewed as an attempt to moderate the severity of orthodox Calvinism, it is better understood as a recovery of vital

Reformation doctrines, including the 'free offer of the gospel' which became a hallmark of his evangelical preaching. Like the protestant reformers, he taught that assurance of salvation rests on what Christ did rather than on what the Christian does. But this was not to minimize the importance of holy living, which is prompted by the gift of God's grace, not by the fear of God's law. Good works provide, in turn, still further assurance through what Boston termed 'the reflex act' of faith. Boston's popular reputation was further enhanced by his books, the most famous of which was *Human Nature in its Fourfold State* (1720, 1729). The *Fourfold State*, as it was called, became the most frequently reprinted Scottish book of the eighteenth century, going through well over a hundred editions in all. The book consists of a collection of sermons preached early in Boston's ministry and revised throughout his lifetime. It takes its structure from the four conditions of humanity first posited by Augustine: creation, fall, grace, and glory. Boston termed these the states of innocence, nature, grace, and eternity. This simple, practical, and memorable summary of Christian doctrine became a commonplace among Scottish Calvinists. The *Fourfold State's* emphases on the totality of sin, the necessity of being born again, the desirability of being united to Christ, and the reality of the life to come also made it a central text for the rise of evangelicalism in Britain and America. It was a best-seller during the Great Awakening, in part because it came highly recommended by both John Wesley and George Whitefield. The American theologian Jonathan Edwards considered its author 'a truly great divine' (*Works of Jonathan Edwards*, 2.489). Nearly all the rest of Boston's writings were published posthumously and are included in his *Complete Works* (1854). They are distinguished by their simplicity, for Boston had mastered the plain homiletical style so admired by the puritans. His contemporaries lauded his 'peculiar talent for going deep into the mysteries of the gospel, and at the same time for making them plain' (*Complete Works*, 12.451). Most notable among the other writings are *A View of the Covenant of Grace* (1734) and *A View of the Covenant of Works* (1772). Boston's unique contribution to the history of covenant theology was to show that the covenant of redemption (between God the Father and God the Son) and the covenant of grace (between God and his people) are one and the same: God the Father makes a gracious covenant with God the Son, who keeps the covenant as a representative for his people. Although he frequently lamented the inadequacy of his library, Boston was well versed in the literature of international Calvinism. He conducted painstaking independent research into the accent marks of the Hebrew Bible, eventually writing a learned treatise interpreting their significance and defending their divine inspiration (*Tractatus stigmologicus*, Amsterdam, 1738). In addition to numerous individual sermons, many preached on sacramental occasions, Boston wrote a lengthy exposition of the Westminster shorter catechism (*An Illustration of the Doctrines of the Christian Religion*, 3 vols., 1755), as well as shorter treatises on divine providence (*The Crook in the Lot*, 1737) and evangelistic preaching (*A Soliloquy on the Art of Man-Fishing*, 1773). He also produced a spiritual autobiography, primarily for the benefit of his children. These *Memoirs* have become a classic of Calvinist spiritual devotion. They reveal a man earnest in ministry, melancholy in disposition, scholarly in interest, modest in aspiration, sober in judgement, sensitive in conscience, and devout in prayer. It is not surprising that his colleagues greatly admired his 'deep and high sense of divine things' (*Complete Works*, 12.451). Thomas Boston's commitment to his sacred office is perhaps best illustrated by the way he persevered in his pastoral duties during the illness which claimed his life on 20 May 1732. He delivered his final sermons from his deathbed, as the people of Ettrick gathered around the window of the manse to hear their beloved minister preach. He was buried in Ettrick churchyard.

P. G. Ryken

Sources *The complete works of the late Rev. Thomas Boston, Ettrick*, ed. S. M'Millan, 12 vols. (1854) • U. Aberdeen, Boston MS 3245/2 • P. G. Ryken, *Thomas Boston as preacher of the fourfold state* (1999) [incl. bibliography] • W. Addison, *The life and writings of Thomas Boston of Ettrick* (1936) • D. C. Lachman, *The Marrow controversy, 1718–1723: an historical and theological analysis* (1988) • A. T. B. McGowan, *The federal theology of Thomas Boston* (1997) • *Acts of the general assembly of the Church of Scotland, 1638–1842* (1843) • J. E. Smith, ed., *Religious affections* (1959), vol. 2 of *The works of Jonathan Edwards*, ed. P. Miller and others (1957–2001)

Archives Edinburgh Central Reference Library, sermons • NL Scot., sermons, letters, and notes • NL Scot., university notes • Presbyterian Historical Society, Philadelphia • U. Aberdeen, King's College, sermons and notes, some unpublished • U. Edin., New Coll. L., memoirs, sermons, letters, and essays | NA Scot., Simprin kirk session minutes

Likenesses R. Scott, engraving, NPG [*see illus.*] • engraving, repro. in *The complete works*

Boston, Thomas (1713–1767), a founder of the Relief church, was born at Ettrick, Selkirkshire, on 3 April 1713, the youngest son of Thomas *Boston (1676–1732) and Katharine Boston, *née* Brown (1674–1737). After receiving his early education from his father and his brother John, he attended the grammar school in Hawick. In 1728 he entered Edinburgh University, returning home in January 1729 to be educated by his father. In December 1730 he returned to the university to 'attend the school of divinity' (*Memoirs*, 453). He was licensed by the presbytery of Selkirk on 1 August 1732 and ordained to Ettrick on 4 August 1733. On 26 April 1738 he married Elizabeth Anderson (*d.* 1787) of Tushielaw, Tweedsmuir; they had one son, Michael, and four daughters. In 1749 Boston moved to Oxnam in Roxburghshire, where he began his ministry on 10 August.

Soon after the death of their previous minister the elders of the parish of Jedburgh, along with the town council, indicated to their patron, the marquess of Lothian, that they would like Boston to be their next pastor. Oxnam was only 3 miles from Jedburgh, and Boston was a popular preacher. It would appear that a personal dispute had offended the marquess and he presented John Bonar, another member of the popular party within the Church of Scotland. Following various delays the general assembly in May 1756 took the decision that John Bonar should not be called as minister of Jedburgh. The next candidate to be presented and then called was John Douglas, minister of Kenmore. The people of Jedburgh objected to Douglas and Thomas Boston demitted his charge at Oxnam on Sunday 4 December 1757, informing the presbytery of his decision only on the following Wednesday. The fact that he first made his decision known to the kirk session rather than to the presbytery may indicate his own conviction that he was accountable to the local congregation, the community which called him, rather than the presbytery. His appearance at the presbytery on 7 December drew so large a crowd that the Jedburgh church was damaged. A large meeting-house had already been built and Boston was admitted as pastor of the new church on 9 December 1757.

Boston made it clear that his actions were not to be interpreted as being a final break with the Church of Scotland. In a letter to the presbytery of Jedburgh he stated his desire to 'hold ministerial and Christian communion with all who faithfully avouch the Gospel system' and justified his 'partial secession as being a response to the unlawful use of patronage'. When he was inducted to his new independent congregation, he promised to 'hold communion with … his brethren in the Lord, if an opportunity shall be afforded him' and added that he intended to keep himself from 'Sectarianism' (Morren, 2.155–7).

The general assembly of May 1758 prohibited any minister of the Church of Scotland from assisting Boston in any ministerial function. Therefore, when the Jedburgh church decided to celebrate its first communion season in August 1758 Boston turned to Thomas Gillespie, who had been deposed from the ministry in 1752 because of his opposition to the law of patronage. In 1761 Boston joined with Thomas Gillespie to induct Thomas Colier as minister of the Relief congregation in Colinsburgh in Fife and to form the presbytery of Relief and serve as its first moderator. The three men were clear in their conviction that every member of every congregation should have a vote in the election of their own minister. In an age of increasing division among Presbyterian groups within Scotland, the presbytery of Relief sought to maintain fellowship with all Christians within every section of the church. The Relief church became a symbol of the liberality of the grace of God which it preached, and expressed the Enlightenment concepts of toleration and freedom, virtues which would eventually bring about the healing of some of the divisions within Scottish presbyterianism in 1847.

In 1765 a large Relief congregation in Glasgow attempted to call Boston as their minister. Initially he declined the invitation because he was not in good health. A fresh approach was made in which it was suggested that his son, Michael, might be appointed as an assistant minister and successor. The proposal was accepted and Boston went to Glasgow to preach, but the congregation then voted against issuing a call to him. A popular speaker, he was described by David Brogue as being 'the most commanding preacher he had ever heard' (Struthers, 150).

Boston's several published sermons give some indication of the ministry which he exercised as a pastor. One of his most significant publications was the printing of his father's essay on schism (1758), with a preface by Boston, in which he justified the foundation of a separate Presbyterian denomination in Scotland which avoided the censorious attitude of the Original seceders towards the Church of Scotland. Boston died on 13 February 1767 and was buried in the tower at Jedburgh Abbey. He was survived by his wife, who died on 21 June 1787 in the home of her youngest daughter, Margaret, who was married to William Campbell, minister of the Relief congregation in Dysart, Fife. Two more daughters married ministers of the Relief church and his fourth daughter, Christian, moved to South Carolina to marry Dr Tucker Harris in Charleston. Boston's son Michael became minister of the Relief congregation in Falkirk. KENNETH B. E. ROXBURGH

Sources G. Struthers, *The history of the rise, progress, and principles of the Relief church* (1843) • K. B. E. Roxburgh, 'Thomas Gillespie and the origins of the Relief church in eighteenth-century Scotland', PhD diss., U. Edin., 1997 • W. Mackelvie, *Annals and statistics of the United Presbyterian church*, ed. W. Blair and D. Young (1873) • R. Small, *History of the congregations of the United Presbyterian church from 1733 to 1900*, 2 vols. (1904) • *Memoirs of the life, time and writings of … Thomas Boston*, ed. G. H. Morrison, new edn (1899) • *A general account of my life by Thomas Boston*, ed. G. D. Low (1908) • N. M. [N. Morren], *Annals of the general assembly of the Church of Scotland*, 1 (1838) • general assembly records of the Church of Scotland for 1757, NA Scot., CH1/2.101 • minutes of the kirk session of Oxnam, NA Scot., CH2/1232.3 • records of the presbytery of Jedburgh, NA Scot., CH2/198.11 • records of the synod of Lothian and Tweeddale, 1746–80, NA Scot., CH2/252.13 • *Fasti Scot.*, new edn

Archives NA Scot. • U. Edin., New Coll. L., disposition and assignation of the Revd Mr Thomas Boston to Mrs Boston and Mr Michael Boston his eldest son, 21 Jan 1767, Box 2.3.9

Likenesses portrait, repro. in W. W. M. [W. W. Mabon], *Boston church, Jedburgh, 1757–1907: gleanings from old records and the story of Mr. Boston's settlement in Jedburgh* [1907]

Bosville, William (1745–1813), society host and radical, was born on 21 July 1745, the eldest son of Godfrey Bosville of Gunthwaite, Yorkshire, and his wife, Diana, the eldest daughter of Sir William Wentworth, baronet, of West Bretton. Bosville was able to trace his family back to the reign of William I and proved to be the last male descendant of Richard Bosville, who had inherited Gunthwaite during the reign of Henry VI. He was educated at Harrow School, and received a commission in the Coldstream Guards on 24 December 1761. He rose to the rank of lieutenant in January 1769, and served with the regiment during the early stages of the American War of Independence. On retirement from the army in June 1777 he returned to England with a son of Edward, Baron Hawke, via France, Italy, and Morocco.

Back in London, Bosville established a reputation as a generous, if somewhat inflexible, host at his house on Welbeck Street. On each weekday he received no more than twelve guests to dine with him at 5 p.m. precisely. Visitors who missed the appointment by even a couple of minutes were refused entry, a measure Bosville justified with a favoured maxim: 'Some say better late than never; I say better never than late' (*Memoirs*, ed. Sinclair, 2.183).

Among his regular guests, who were expected to sign their name on a slate kept in the hall, were Sir Francis Burdett, the Revd Charles Este, lords Oxford and Hutchinson, and the radical and philologist John Horne Tooke. Tooke repaid Bosville's generosity by including him as one of the circle who visited his Wimbledon house, Chester Lodge, to dine on Sundays during spring and summer.

Politically Bosville was a committed supporter of Tooke, assisting his campaign for the Westminster election in 1796 and acting, unsuccessfully, as an intermediary between Tooke and Charles James Fox. An original member of the Friends of the People (formed in April 1792), Bosville was adjudged soon after his death to have been 'one of the most ultra-liberal spirits of the time' (Sinclair, 2.183). With others from his dining circle, he contributed to Tooke's dwindling finances during the late 1790s as well as donating £1000 to William Cobbett, whom he visited during his imprisonment in Newgate between 1810 and 1812.

Sartorially Bosville proved rather more conservative, indeed eccentric, dressing only in the outmoded powdered wig and frock coat of a mid-eighteenth-century courtier. His clear preference for metropolitan life meant that he made few journeys to his considerable estates in the north of England, notably that of Thorp Hall near Bridlington, which he refused to visit lest he become involved in the responsibilities of landowning. His stories of travelling—to the Isles of Scilly and to Rome during the final days of Clement XIV—were fictions to entertain guests at Welbeck Street. In his will the unmarried Bosville left the majority of his property, including Thorp Hall, to his nephew Godfrey Macdonald, later third Baron Macdonald. He also left 'a large sum of ready money' (*European Magazine*, 64, 1813, 553) and, in addition to landed estates, bequeathed £19,000 to friends including Charles Este.

Though in increasingly poor health, Bosville continued to hold daily dinner parties at Welbeck Street until 16 December 1813, when, with his guests due at 5 p.m., he died earlier in the day. He was buried eight days later in the chancel of St Giles-in-the-Fields, London.

PHILIP CARTER

Sources *Memoirs of the life and works of the late Rt Hon. Sir John Sinclair*, ed. J. Sinclair, 2 vols. (1837) • J. Hunter, *South Yorkshire: the history and topography of the deanery of Doncaster*, 2 vols. (1828–31) • A. Stephens, *Memoirs of J. Horne Tooke*, 2 vols. (1813) • *GM*, 1st ser., 83/2 (1813), 630, 704 • *Annual Register* (1813), 123 • M. C. Yarborough, *John Horne Tooke* (1926) • will, PRO, PROB 11/1551, fols. 25*r*–31*r*

Wealth at death property in Yorkshire and London; 'died [with] a large sum of ready money'; bequeathed legacies of at least £19,000: will, PRO, PROB, 11/1551, fols. 25*r*–31*r*; *European Magazine*, 64 (1813), 553

Boswell, Alexander, **Lord Auchinleck** (1707–1782), judge, was born at Auchinleck, Ayrshire, on 1 March 1707 NS, the eldest of three sons of James Boswell (*c*.1676–1749), laird of Auchinleck and advocate, and Lady Elizabeth Bruce, the youngest daughter of Alexander *Bruce, second earl of Kincardine. Like his father Alexander Boswell studied law at Leiden University, where he passed advocate on 22 July 1727. He was named sheriff of Wigtownshire in 1748 but resigned in 1750, though he was proud that he had been in the first group appointed by royal warrant rather than the holder of a heritable jurisdiction.

On 15 February 1754 Boswell was appointed to the court of session and on 22 July of the following year to the court of justiciary, the highest courts in Scotland for civil and criminal causes respectively. He took his title, as was the custom, from the estate he had inherited in 1749, an extensive barony in Ayrshire which James IV had conferred on Thomas Boswell in 1504. The estate had 600 tenants and yielded an annual income of £1000, to which Lord Auchinleck's judicial appointments added £900 p.a. In 1780 he resigned from the court of justiciary because of ill health but he retained his seat as an ordinary lord, despite diminished faculties, until his death in 1782.

In April 1738 Boswell married his first cousin once removed, Euphemia Erskine (1718–1766), the youngest daughter of Lieutenant-Colonel John Erskine, deputy governor of Stirling Castle, and his third wife, Euphemia Cochrane. Five children were born to the Boswells, of whom three sons survived: James *Boswell (1740–1795), advocate and biographer of Samuel Johnson; John (1743–*c*.1798), briefly lieutenant in the army and periodically deranged from the age of nineteen; and David, later known as Thomas David, or T. D. (1748–1826), merchant in Spain, banker, and finally inspector in the navy pay office. The family lived on the fourth storey of Blair's Land, Parliament Close, Edinburgh, where Boswell himself had grown up. After 1749 they moved during court recesses to Auchinleck, where in 1762 Lord Auchinleck built a beautiful mansion in the Adam style, the third (and surviving) house on his estate.

On 25 November 1769, aged sixty-two and three years a widower, Lord Auchinleck married again, in Edinburgh; his second wife was his cousin, Elizabeth Boswell (*d*. 1799), then aged about forty, the second daughter of John Boswell of Balmuto, Fife. (His outraged son James married his cousin Margaret Montgomerie on the same day.) In January 1782 Lord Auchinleck bought a handsome house in the New Town, Edinburgh, and willed his wife the life-rent, thus further incensing James Boswell. He died in Edinburgh on 30 August 1782, after long suffering from stricture of the urethra, and was entombed on 4 September in the catacombs of the family church at Auchinleck.

Lord Auchinleck was a widely respected judge, upright, learned, hard-working, and skilful at clarifying complicated matters. Stern but reputedly impartial, he spoke broad Scots from the bench and leavened his sobriety with straightfaced irony. He was a staunch whig and a strict Presbyterian, as the world knows from the argument with Samuel Johnson that James Boswell reported, circumspectly, in *Journal of a Tour to the Hebrides*.

Though 'perhaps too anxiously devoted to utility' (James Boswell to William Johnson Temple, 17 April 1764, MS Yale L 1220), Lord Auchinleck was a fine classical scholar and accumulated an impressive library, as attested by the catalogue that Margaret Montgomerie compiled shortly after she had been made mistress of Auchinleck House (the manuscript is at Yale University

Library). A cautious laird in an age of improvement, Lord Auchinleck pioneered an industrial village, chiefly dedicated to weaving (unprofitable to the inhabitants), and divided and enclosed farms, but except for distinctive plantations of trees he was slower than his neighbours in adopting new agricultural methods.

Since the publication of James Boswell's papers in the twentieth century Lord Auchinleck has been identified as the embittered father in a classic struggle: well-meaning and generous on his own terms but authoritarian, cold, and harsh—'If my sons are idiots, can I help it?' (*Laird of Auchinleck*, 467). As he lay dying his heir 'wept; for alas! there was not affection between us' (ibid., 477).

IRMA S. LUSTIG

Sources old parish register, Auchinleck, General Register Office for Scotland, New Register House, Edinburgh • *Scotland and Scotsmen in the eighteenth century: from the MSS of John Ramsay, esq., of Ochtertyre*, ed. A. Allardyce, 1 (1888); repr. with introduction by D. J. Brown (1996) • F. A. Pottle, *James Boswell: the earlier years, 1740–1769* (1966) • *Catalogue of the papers of James Boswell at Yale University*, ed. M. S. Pottle, C. C. Abbott, and F. A. Pottle, 3 vols. (1993) • *Boswell's London journal, 1762–63*, ed. F. A. Pottle (1950), vol. 1 of *The Yale editions of the private papers of James Boswell*, trade edn (1950–89) • *Boswell in Holland, 1763–1764*, ed. F. A. Pottle (1952), vol. 2 of *The Yale editions of the private papers of James Boswell, trade edn* (1950–89) • *Boswell on the grand tour: Germany and Switzerland, 1764*, ed. F. A. Pottle (1953), vol. 4 of *The Yale editions of the private papers of James Boswell*, trade edn (1950–89) • *Boswell on the grand tour: Italy, Corsica, and France, 1765–1766*, ed. F. Brady and F. A. Pottle (1955), vol. 5 of *The Yale editions of the private papers of James Boswell*, trade edn (1950–89) • *Boswell in search of a wife, 1766–1769*, ed. F. Brady and F. A. Pottle (1957), vol. 6 of *The Yale editions of the private papers of James Boswell*, trade edn (1950–89) • *Boswell for the defence, 1769–1774*, ed. W. K. Wimsatt and F. A. Pottle (1959), vol. 7 of *The Yale editions of the private papers of James Boswell*, trade edn (1950–89) • *Boswell's journal of a tour to the Hebrides with Samuel Johnson*, ed. F. A. Pottle and C. H. Bennett (1963), vol. 9 of *The Yale editions of the private papers of James Boswell*, trade edn (1950–89) • *Boswell: the ominous years, 1774–1776*, ed. C. Ryskamp and F. A. Pottle (1963), vol. 8 of *The Yale editions of the private papers of James Boswell*, trade edn (1950–89) • *Boswell in extremes, 1776–1778*, ed. C. M. Weis and F. A. Pottle (1971), vol. 10 of *The Yale editions of the private papers of James Boswell, trade edn* (1950–89) • *Boswell, laird of Auchinleck, 1778–1782*, ed. J. W. Reed and F. A. Pottle (1977), vol. 11 of *The Yale editions of the private papers of James Boswell*, trade edn (1950–89) • *Boswell: the applause of the jury, 1782–1785*, ed. I. S. Lustig and F. A. Pottle (1982), vol. 12 of *The Yale editions of the private papers of James Boswell*, trade edn (1950–89) • *Boswell: the English experiment, 1785–1789*, ed. I. S. Lustig and F. A. Pottle (1986), vol. 13 of *The Yale editions of the private papers of James Boswell*, trade edn (1950–89) • *Boswell: the great biographer, 1789–1795*, ed. M. K. Danziger and F. Brady (1989), vol. 14 of *The Yale editions of the private papers of James Boswell*, trade edn (1950–89) • Boswell, *Life* • A. Stewart, ed., *The minute book of the Faculty of Advocates*, 3: 1751–1783, Stair Society, 46 (1999)

Archives NL Scot., notes on logic lecture • NL Scot., notes on Mackenzie's Institutions • Parliament House, Edinburgh, legal papers and opinions • U. Edin. L., letters; Latin and Greek lecture notes | Yale U., Beinecke L., James Boswell collection and Boswell family MSS

Likenesses A. Ramsay, oils, Tate collection • A. Ramsay?, oils (after A. Ramsay), Yale U. CBA

Wealth at death £1000–£1500 p.a. from estate; £900 p.a. combined as lord of session and of justiciary; could ride horseback 10 miles on Ayrshire estate, which had 600 tenants: Pottle, *James Boswell: the earlier years*; *The correspondence of James Boswell with James Bruce and Andrew Gibb*, ed. N. P. Hankins and J. Strawhorn (1998), 41

Boswell, Sir Alexander, first baronet (1775–1822), poet and politician, was born on 9 October 1775 at Auchinleck, Ayrshire, the first son of James *Boswell (1740–1795), the biographer of Samuel Johnson, and his wife, Margaret (1738?–1789) [*see* Boswell, Margaret Montgomerie], daughter of David Montgomerie of Lainshaw, Ayrshire. When his father moved the family to London in 1786 Alexander briefly attended an academy in Soho Square with his younger brother, James *Boswell (1778–1822); but problems of health and temperament led to his being privately tutored until he went to Eton College in 1789 soon after his mother's death. He entered Edinburgh University in 1792 but did not take a degree. He was nineteen when his father died in May 1795, leaving him a handsome inheritance in land and money. He went to Leipzig to continue his legal studies, but soon gave them up and, after visits to Dresden and Berlin, returned to Britain in 1796. On 23 November 1799 he married, in Edinburgh, Grisel (*d.* 1864), daughter of the late Thomas Cuming, a banker of the city. They had a son, James, born in 1806, and three daughters.

A tall, muscular man, fond of field sports, Boswell practised improving agriculture on his estates and was an active officer of the Ayrshire yeomanry, of which he became lieutenant-colonel in 1816. He had inherited a full measure of his father's literary proclivities. As a young man he composed a number of songs, including 'Jenny's Bawbee' and 'Jenny Dang the Weaver', which were published anonymously in 1803 as *Songs Chiefly in the Scottish Dialect*. He also produced that year the poems *The Spirit of Tintoc* and *Epistle to the Edinburgh Reviewers*. His later poems, which were based on the traditional ballad style, included *Edinburgh, or, The Ancient Royalty* (1810), *Clan-Alpin's View* (1811), and *Sir Albon* (1811). From the Auchinleck archives he published *A Breefe Memoriall of the Lyfe and Death of Dr James Spottiswood, Bishop of Clogher in Ireland* (1811) and a reprint of John Knox's 1561 disputation with Quintin Kennedy, *Ane Oratione* (1812). He contributed to George Thomson's collections of Welsh (1809), Irish (1814), and Scottish (1817) songs. In 1815 he established a private press at Auchinleck, which printed his own poems, *The Tyrant's Fall* (1815), *Skeldon Haughs* (1816), and *The Woo' Creel* (1816). Among the works which he published as editor and printer were *Dialogus pius et festivus inter Deum (ut ferunt) et Evam*, *Dialogus inter Solomon et Marcolphum*, the 1598 edition of *Poems by Richard Barnfield*, and reprints of old poems, which were issued at intervals and subsequently grouped in volumes as *Frondes Caducae*. One of Sir Walter Scott's circle, he became a member of the Roxburghe Club in 1819. He campaigned for a monument to be erected to Robert Burns, whom he venerated, and on 25 January 1820 he laid the foundation-stone of the monument on the banks of the Doon.

In July 1816 Boswell obtained the seat in parliament which had eluded his father by buying one for Plympton Erle, Devon, at a rate of £1000 a session, on the Treby interest. He came in again at the general elections of 1818 and 1820. A thoroughgoing tory who regarded the whigs as dangerous maniacs, he gave general support to Lord Liverpool's administration. In his maiden speech on 10 March

Sir Alexander Boswell, first baronet (1775–1822), by Sir Martin Archer Shee

1817 he stated that Scottish landowners had no wish for parliamentary reform. He opposed reform of the royal burghs on 23 March and 6 May 1819, although on the first occasion he paid lip service to the notion of giving the inhabitants some control over municipal expenditure. In 1819 he introduced a short bill to repeal two old Scottish acts forbidding duelling, which reached the statute book on 3 July (59 Geo. III c. 70). Walter Scott recalled him as a 'proud' and 'very high-spirited man', who 'thought that his father [had] lowered himself by his deferential suit to Johnson' (Croker, 2.32). In 1818 Boswell developed a grudge against ministers, especially Liverpool, for what he perceived as their failure to pay him due attention. In response to the circular requesting attendance for the emergency session of November 1819 he asked the home secretary, Lord Sidmouth, who had evidently been willing to court him, for permission to stay away in order to be ready to deal with any radical disturbances in Ayrshire. However, he was prevailed upon to attend to support the government's coercive legislation. In early 1820 he was conspicuous at the head of his yeomanry in quelling local disaffection, with a mixture of force and reason. Liverpool's well-publicized refusal of his request for a baronetcy in recognition of these services intensified his sense of grievance. Further aggravated by his increasing financial problems, created by rash land purchases and compounded by loss of rental income and heavy expenditure on his parliamentary seat and his yeomanry, Boswell decided to take the Chiltern Hundreds on 7 February 1821, the day after voting in defence of ministers' conduct towards Queen Caroline. Through Sidmouth's influence he obtained the coveted baronetcy on 16 August 1821 as reward for his 'loyalty' in 'supporting his Majesty's ministers in difficult times' (Farington, *Diary*, 16.5713).

Henry Cockburn wrote of Boswell that he was

> able and literary; and when in the humour of being quiet, he was agreeable and kind. But in general he was boisterous and overbearing, and addicted to coarse personal ridicule. With many respectable friends, his natural place was at the head of a jovial board, where everybody laughed at his exhaustless spirits, but each trembled lest he should be the subject of the next story or song. (*Memorials … by Henry Cockburn*, 373)

Boswell's relish for expressing his party rancour through vulgar personal abuse brought about his nemesis. In 1821 two scurrilous Scottish newspapers, *The Beacon* and *The Sentinel*, published a series of pasquinades vilifying the whig James Stuart of Dunearn as a bully and a coward. An unedifying squabble arose between *The Sentinel's* proprietors, Robert Alexander and William Borthwick, who was imprisoned for debt; and early in 1822 Stuart took advantage of this dispute to gain access to office documents which revealed Boswell as the author of the squibs. On his return to Edinburgh from London, where he had been taken by the sudden death of his brother, he was challenged by Stuart. He refused either to deny authorship or to apologize. They met at Auchtertool, near Kirkcaldy, Fife, on 26 March 1822. Boswell deliberately fired wide, but in trying to follow suit Stuart, who had never before handled a gun, sent his shot through Boswell's collar bone. He was removed to Balmuto, Fife, where he died the following day. He was buried at Auchinleck. Stuart was tried for murder on 10 June 1822 and unanimously acquitted. Boswell's financial affairs were found to be in great disarray, with liabilities of over £72,000 set against assets of only £10,000. He was succeeded by his son, on whose death without an heir in 1857 the baronetcy became extinct.

D. R. Fisher

Sources D. Buchanan, *The treasure of Auchinleck: the story of the Boswell papers* (1975) · *The Yale editions of the private papers of James Boswell*, trade edn, ed. F. A. Pottle and others, 14 vols. (1950–89) · *The poetical works of Sir Alexander Boswell*, ed. R. H. Smith (1871) · D. R. Fisher, 'Boswell, Sir Alexander', HoP, *Commons, 1790–1820* · Boswell, *Life* · F. Brady, *James Boswell: the later years, 1769–1795* (1984) · Farington, *Diary*, 5.1633; 16.5713 · *The Croker papers: the correspondence and diaries of … John Wilson Croker*, ed. L. J. Jennings, 2 (1884), 32 · *Memorials of his time, by Henry Cockburn* (1909); repr. with introduction by K. F. C. Miller (1974), 373 · *A true account of the fatal duel, 26 Mar. 1822* (1822) · *A particular account of the trial of J. Stuart* (1822) · *DNB* · *GM*, 3rd ser., 17 (1864), 670

Archives NL Scot., farm journals · NRA, priv. coll., family MSS · Yale U., deeds and estate MSS | BL, letters to G. Thomson, Add. MSS 35263–35265, *passim* · NL Scot., letters to Sir W. Forbes, Acc. 4796 · NL Scot., letters to J. Skene, MS 3854 · U. Edin. L., letters to D. Laing, LA.IV.6 · Yale U., Beinecke L., corresp. with James Boswell and papers, L73-124; C223–303

Likenesses M. A. Shee, oils, priv. coll. [*see illus.*]

Wealth at death bond debts of £40,000; personal debts of £32,000; assets of £10,000: Buchanan, *Treasure of Auchinleck*, 204

Boswell, Claud Irvine, **Lord Balmuto** (**1743–1824**), judge, was born on 23 May 1743 at Kinghorn, Fife, the son of John Boswell of Balmuto, Fife, writer to the signet, and his wife,

Margaret Henderson. Boswell's father died while he was still an infant. He was sent at the age of six to Mr Barclay's school at Dalkeith, finished his education at Edinburgh University, and was admitted a member of the Faculty of Advocates on 2 August 1766. On 25 March 1780 he was appointed sheriff-depute of Fife and Kinross, until the death of James Burnett, Lord Monboddo, whom he succeeded, taking his seat on the bench as an ordinary lord of session, with the title of Lord Balmuto, on 21 June 1799.

Boswell married on 28 April 1783 Anne Irvine, who by the death of her brother and grandfather became the heir of Kingussie; they raised a son and two daughters. The scientific writer Mary Somerville, who as a child used to visit the family, described Boswell as a large coarse man with black hair and beetling eyebrows, a loud voice, and a hot temper. Fond of telling his own jokes, a habit he sometimes indulged in on the bench, he did not enjoy being the butt of other people's wit. Mrs Somerville recalled an occasion when Boswell's son, who had a notion for chemistry, caused a considerable explosion, and she also remarked that Boswell kept his daughters so confined when they were in Edinburgh that one of them, Elizabeth, eloped with her art master, Patrick *Syme (1774–1845).

Boswell never fully recovered from the shock brought about by the death, in his house, of his kinsman Sir Alexander Boswell, following a duel. He died at Balmuto on 22 July 1824. G. F. R. BARKER, *rev.* ANITA MCCONNELL

Sources M. Somerville, *Personal recollections, from early life to old age, of Mary Somerville* (1873), 55–6 • G. Brunton and D. Haig, *An historical account of the senators of the college of justice, from its institution in MDXXXII* (1832), 544 • J. Kay, *A series of original portraits and caricature etchings … with biographical sketches and illustrative anecdotes*, ed. [H. Paton and others], new edn [3rd edn], 1 (1877), 126, 298; 2 (1877), 277–8, 380, 384, 386 • M. F. Conolly, *Biographical dictionary of eminent men of Fife* (1866) • *IGI*
Archives NA Scot., corresp.
Likenesses J. Kay, caricature, etching, 1799, BM, NPG

Boswell, Edward (1760–1842), antiquary, was born at Puddletown, Dorset, on 5 April 1760. He was articled to a solicitor, John Waller of Dorchester, and in 1792 took up practice in Sherborne. In 1793 he was appointed clerk to the lieutenancy of Dorset. In 1794 he joined the Dorset regiment of militia. The following year he began practice in Dorchester.

In 1803 Boswell married Edith, daughter of John Feaver, vicar of St Mary Church, Devon; they had one daughter.

Boswell's major work was *The Civil Division of the County of Dorset* (1795), of which a second, revised edition appeared in 1833. It became the standard account of the civil administration of the county.

Boswell died at Dorchester on 30 October 1842, and was buried in Holy Trinity Church there five days later.

THOMPSON COOPER, *rev.* JONATHAN HARRIS

Sources *GM*, 2nd ser., 19 (1843), 95–6 • [J. Watkins and F. Shoberl], *A biographical dictionary of the living authors of Great Britain and Ireland* (1816)

Boswell, Eve [*real name* Eva Keleti] (1922–1998), popular singer, was born Eva Keleti in Budapest on 11 May 1922, the daughter of a couple who toured the music-halls as a musical act. She was educated in Budapest and later studied the piano at the Lausanne Academy. As a teenager she joined her parents as pianist and singer in an act called the Three Hugos, first appearing under that name in Paris in 1938 when she was sixteen. When the Second World War broke out in 1939 they were on tour in England and, as aliens, had to leave; they moved to South Africa, where they were employed by the Boswell circus. Eva was taught to speak English by Trevor McIntosh, the son of the circus owner, whom she married in 1944. A son, Michael, was born that year. Her husband encouraged her singing talent, became her manager, and suggested she change her name to Eve Boswell—after the circus. She first sang professionally with the Roy Martin band from the Coconut Grove in Johannesburg, and became known through regular broadcasts from there. She was heard and admired by the pianist Adrian Foley, who took some recordings (made by the local disc jockey and producer Alan Dell) to London; they were heard by the band leader Geraldo, who offered her three months' work with his orchestra. The family sailed for England, and she first appeared with Geraldo at the Winter Gardens, Blackpool, on 1 June 1949: she remained with the band for two years.

Boswell made her first recording two months after joining Geraldo and had her first credited record with 'I Can Dream Can't I?' in April 1950, made, as were all her recordings until 1959, for the Parlophone label. She left Geraldo at the beginning of 1952 to embark on a solo career, her first important engagement being with the comedian Derek Roy in a variety tour of his programme *Happy Go Lucky*. Her subsequent radio appearances were in *The Forces Show*, *Workers' Playtime*, and *Henry Hall's Guest Night* and in her own series, *Time to Dream*.

Boswell's first big hit recording was 'Sugar Bush' in August 1952, the final chorus being sung in Afrikaans. She came to be exclusively associated with this song, and was billed as 'the Bush Girl', under which name she appeared in the programme of the royal variety performance in 1953. There was so much demand on her talent that she suffered a collapse through nervous exhaustion in October 1954, but she was back on stage in December in a pantomime with Derek Roy and Tommy Cooper. She continued with many variety appearances in both England and South Africa and in October 1955 had another big recorded hit with 'Pickin' a Chicken', a South African song adapted by Paddy Roberts. She visited the USA in June 1956 and suffered another breakdown in health before launching her first LP, *Sugar and Spice* (1956); she managed to keep up a stream of engagements for radio, television, and stage until 1959. In 1960 she returned for an appearance in her native Hungary, which was followed by a Scottish tour with Jimmy Logan, a pantomime with Tommy Steele in 1961, and a Palladium show with Bruce Forsyth and Morecambe and Wise in 1962. With the onset of the age of the 'beat combo', exemplified by the rise of the Beatles, her appeal declined as the 1960s wore on, and she gradually disappeared from the entertainment world except for the occasional, and usually very successful, revival appearance.

Eve Boswell's first marriage was dissolved in 1965. She again lived in South Africa in the 1970s and ran a school of singing in Durban. She remarried in 1976; her second husband was the South African broadcaster Henry Holloway, who produced her last album, *It's a Breeze* (1979), but they were divorced in 1985. Her third marriage was to an insurance broker, Kenneth Taylor, in 1988, and this ended in 1997. She made her last stage appearance in Britain at the Beck Theatre, Hayes, on 28 July 1998, still in good voice. Eve Boswell died at her home in Durban, South Africa, on 14 August 1998. PETER GAMMOND

Sources *The Independent* (13 Aug 1998) · *The Times* (14 Aug 1998) · *Daily Telegraph* (14 Aug 1998) · *Standard Times* (15 Aug 1998); electronic repr. www.s-t.com/daily/08-98/08-15-98/zzzddobi.htm
Likenesses photographs, Hult. Arch.

Boswell, James (1740–1795), lawyer, diarist, and biographer of Samuel Johnson, was born in Edinburgh on 29 October 1740, probably at the family's house on the fourth storey of Blair's Land, Parliament Close, the eldest son of Alexander *Boswell, Lord Auchinleck (1707–1782), and his first wife, Euphemia, *née* Erskine (*bap.* 1718, *d.* 1766). He was heir to the Auchinleck estate in Ayrshire. His two brothers were Lieutenant John Boswell (1743–*c.*1798), who enlisted in the army but, mentally unstable, spent much of his adult life in supervised confinement; and David Boswell (1748–1826), who later took the name Thomas before David, a merchant and business agent who eventually purchased the estate of Crawley Grange in Buckinghamshire. Boswell prized his distinguished Scottish family connections, especially his mother's descent from the earls of Mar, and cherished his position in the sequence of lairds of Auchinleck descended from Thomas Boswell (*c.*1487–1513), to whom James IV of Scotland awarded the estate in 1504. But the periods of intense depression (usually called 'hypochondria') from which Boswell suffered throughout his life had, as he noted, family precedent; given their generational recurrence modern opinion assigns them a medical basis and deems them hereditary.

In his adult writings about his earliest years, chiefly an 'Ébauche de ma vie' ('Sketch of my life', Yale L 1108; trans. as chap. 1 of Pottle, *Earlier Years*), written in 1764 for Rousseau, and in its drafts and outlines (Yale L 1109–1112), Boswell characterized his boyhood as isolated, lonely, and timid, and described his mother's anxiously loving attentions to him and the simultaneously disturbing effects of her severe Calvinist piety and the Scottish kirk's form of worship. From the age of five to eight he attended James Mundell's academy in Edinburgh's West Bow, where he was unhappy; thereafter a succession of domestic governors tutored him at home. The most influential of them, John Dun (1723/4–1792), taught him from the age of eight to twelve. In later life Boswell deplored the social narrowness of his boyhood governors, holding them in part responsible for feelings of social insecurity and inadequacy, but his confessional 'Ébauche' credited Dun with moderating the effects of his mother's Calvinism, and with delighting him by introducing him to Latin poetry and *The Spectator* essays. Twice in his adolescence Boswell became seriously ill with nervous distresses and was sent

James Boswell (1740–1795), by Sir Joshua Reynolds, 1785

to Moffat spa to recover. He was enrolled in his thirteenth year at the University of Edinburgh, where he attended classes from 1753 to 1759. Here he formed friendships, which remained his closest, with John Johnston of Grange, and William Johnson Temple. With Johnston he shared a warm nostalgia for the Scottish customs, institutions, and buildings whose importance had diminished since the Union of 1707, and an emotional attachment to the Scottish Jacobites. Temple introduced Boswell to the Anglican form of worship, which Boswell continued to prefer to the presbyterianism of his boyhood education. His second bout of nervous distress was at least in part an episode in his continuing adolescent religious crisis, connected with the perplexities into which he was thrown by John Stevenson's course on logic. There he encountered ideas which long disturbed him of divine foreknowledge and the human freedom to choose—the question, as he phrased it, of liberty versus necessity.

During Boswell's second visit to Moffat spa (summer 1757), the sociability—pleasant encounters with new adult acquaintances—helped restore him, and his recovery brought with it a growing rebellion against the strict propriety of his upbringing and his father's expectations that he would follow him into a Scottish legal career. He developed deepened ambitions to be a writer and published author. A restless hunger for literary and social fame and the company of the famous, especially in London, governed much of the conduct of the rest of his life. He began to write and publish verse, and took a delighted interest in the Edinburgh theatre, whose patron, James, Lord Somerville, befriended him and encouraged his writing. Boswell was electrified by the performances of West

Digges, leading man of the Edinburgh company, especially as Macheath in John Gay's *The Beggar's Opera*, which would remain a lifelong favourite play, and Digges's elegant social deportment served as a model for Boswell's own. In autumn 1758, while travelling with his father on the northern circuit, Boswell began to keep a journal. He sent the journal to his friend the actor-manager James Love, whose suggestion it had originally been. In continuing recoil from his boyhood Calvinism, Boswell became attracted at about this time to the idea of converting to Roman Catholicism. He had begun writing theatrical reviews, and in February 1760 published in London pseudonymously ('By a Society of Gentlemen') a pamphlet of fifty pages, *A View of the Edinburgh Theatre During the Summer Season, 1759*, dedicated to Digges. Now ebulliently convivial, he grew fond of clubs and societies, moved in his parents' circles of eminence, and became popular among the literati and leading figures of the Edinburgh Enlightenment. In August 1759 he was admitted a freemason in the Canongate Kilwinning (St John's) lodge, of which his uncle, Dr John Boswell (1710–1780), later president of the Royal College of Physicians of Edinburgh, was depute grand master that year, and he remained an enthusiastic freemason: he was master of his lodge from 1773 to 1775, and in 1776 he was chosen depute grand master of the freemasons in Scotland (when the banker Sir William Forbes was grand master), and re-elected in the following year. Lord Auchinleck, greatly displeased by his son's life, abruptly removed him in 1759 to the University of Glasgow (which city had fewer distractions, and little or no theatre). Though impressed by Adam Smith's lectures in rhetoric and *belles-lettres* and by Smith's social manner, Boswell grew despondent in college life and, on 1 March 1760, fled from the university to London, with a vague plan of becoming a Catholic priest or monk.

In London, Boswell sought out a priest, saw mass celebrated for the first time, and received communion. But eager to experience other delights in London, he explored it, as he later wrote, 'in all its variety of departments, both literary and sportive' (Boswell, *Life*, 1.456) in the company of Samuel Derrick. Lord Auchinleck sought the assistance of Alexander Montgomerie, tenth earl of Eglinton, an Ayrshire neighbour then at his London residence, who diverted Boswell's thoughts from Catholicism and the priesthood by introducing him into the circles of his high-born and rakish friends, including the young duke of York (brother of the future George III). Eglinton's suggestion that he seemed fitted for life as an officer in the guards took a deep hold, as Boswell had long been fascinated by military display, and thought that as a guards officer he could have a permanent base in or near London. He wanted particularly to meet Samuel *Johnson, having read his works with awed delight, and having heard descriptions in Scotland of his imposing social presence and conversation. Derrick promised him an introduction, but failed to bring one about. But Boswell met, among other notables, David Garrick, and the actor turned bookseller Thomas Davies, and visited Laurence Sterne, then the literary toast of London. Giddily exhilarated, Boswell found himself moving among those he termed 'the great, the gay, and the ingenious' ('Memoirs', 234). He consorted for the first time, as habitually in later life, with prostitutes, and as a consequence suffered the first of his many bouts of venereal disease.

Brought back to Edinburgh by Lord Auchinleck, under whose personal instruction he listlessly studied law, Boswell continued his writing and his social escapades and resumed the journal (now private, usually in condensed notes, some in shorthand and some in cipher). He had several clandestine love affairs. He copiously wrote and published poetry, both serious and humorous, and some prose pieces. At about this time he was invited to join the Select Society of Edinburgh, whose members then included Hugh Blair, Sir David Dalrymple, David Hume, Lord Kames, and William Robertson. He had amassed a copious body of juvenilia, most of it, especially the poetry, of little merit, though often biographically revealing. His conduct exasperated his father, and anguished his pious mother. Lord Auchinleck, who was acquiring new lands and having a new mansion house built at Auchinleck, began to talk of disinheriting him and selling the estate, and drew up a document empowering himself to vest the estate after his death in trustees of his choosing. Boswell signed, inaugurating a pattern in which, despite his rebelliousness, he would never fully evade his father's domination, and his father in exchange agreed to provide him with an annual allowance. On 30 July 1762 Boswell passed the private examination in civil law, and earned his father's reluctant consent to return to London to try to pursue a commission (which Lord Auchinleck refused to purchase) in the foot guards through influence. First, he set out from Auchinleck in the autumn for a short tour with Lord and Lady Kames through the border counties of Scotland and England, and he kept a lively and observant 'Journal of My Jaunt, Harvest 1762', his first expansive and fully written journal, for his friends Johnston and William McQuhae.

Boswell left exuberantly for London on 15 November 1762, ostensibly to seek a guards commission, but more actually impelled by his longing for fame and the company of the eminent, and determined to keep a full diary of his sojourn to be sent to Johnston in Edinburgh, and then carefully preserved. He renewed his acquaintance with Eglinton, Garrick, and with the elocution expert Thomas Sheridan, whom he had met in Edinburgh and through whom he hoped now to meet Johnson. As planned, he kept a vivid diary of his activities (supplemented by a series of private daily memoranda, urging himself to a moral programme of discipline and self-improvement) and sent it in weekly packets, with covering letters, to Johnston, reporting his social, literary, and sexual adventures, chief among these last being an affair with a Covent Garden actress, called 'Louisa' in the journal. With his Scots companions, Andrew Erskine and George Dempster MP, he concerted to damn their disliked compatriot David Mallet's tragedy *Elvira* on its opening night, and, though the attempt was unsuccessful, they published *Critical Strictures on the New Tragedy of 'Elvira'* (January 1763).

Boswell persuaded Erskine to join him in a lively and irreverent volume of correspondence, *Letters between the Honourable Andrew Erskine and James Boswell, Esq.* (1763), the first of his publications to bear his name, and one which, in its deliberate violation of norms of public decorum (with the insertion of private and personal material into the domain of publication) is an important early anticipation of Boswell's innovative approach to biography in his later Johnsonian works. Boswell's hopes to meet Johnson through Sheridan came to nothing, as Johnson and Sheridan had become estranged, and the eventual famous first meeting came unexpectedly, when Johnson suddenly entered as Boswell was drinking tea in Davies's back parlour (16 May 1763). Despite Johnson's memorably amusing snub, Boswell began recording in his diaries the distinctive conversational style and opinions that would form a defining part of the *Life of Johnson*, shook off Johnson's initial rudeness, and persisted in his resolve for acquaintance. At later meetings Boswell poured out his soul, described his religious and spiritual perplexities, his restless ambitiousness, and his feelings of being thwarted by his father's will, and listened intently to (and recorded) Johnson's authoritative but sympathetic precepts. Johnson warmed to the charm of Boswell's openly sincere admiration and earnest wish for guidance, and Boswell found a formidable stability and wisdom in one who, unlike his father, remained capaciously tolerant of human waywardness and frailty, despite a tone of moral asperity. Unlike Lord Auchinleck, Johnson valued diary-keeping, and warmly encouraged Boswell in the practice. The diary Boswell kept at this time, unexpectedly recovered among other private papers in the early twentieth century, became an international best-seller on its publication in 1950 as *Boswell's London Journal, 1762–1763*, and has remained the most popular portion of the journal.

The grand tour, and Corsica By mid-1763 Boswell had abandoned his guards scheme and again capitulated to his father, who agreed that if he would study civil law at Utrecht, he might make a European tour before returning to practise at the Scots bar. Once in Utrecht, Boswell suffered an attack of melancholy so severe that he feared for his sanity, and wrote anguished cries for help in letters to his friends. But he recovered, roused and comforted in part by reading several of Johnson's *Rambler* essays, and took a formal course in civil law, studied languages, and conceived a plan of compiling a Scots dictionary (which project he never completed). Late in 1763 he first took notice of Belle de Zuylen (later, as Mme de Charrière, famous as a novelist). The pair met frequently, and afterwards exchanged letters exploring their feelings for one another, and debating gender and marital roles. Boswell, both attracted and disconcerted by her intellect and unconventional moral outlook, considered her a marital prospect, until the correspondence lapsed in 1768. He left Utrecht in June 1764. In the company of George Keith, tenth Earl Marischal, he set off to visit the court of Brunswick, and then see Potsdam. He hoped, vainly, to add Frederick the Great to the list of the many eminences he met, whose characters and conversations he recorded in his journal. At various moments of despondency in Europe, thoughts of Johnson would sometimes restore him, and he urged himself to be 'firm and stable' in imitation of him (Boswell, memorandum, 16 Aug 1764). He wrote from Wittenberg and 'vowed to Mr Johnson an eternal attachment' (30 Sept 1764). After parting company with Lord Marischal, he visited numerous other courts, towns, and cities in the German territories, and, having determined to visit Rousseau and Voltaire, he travelled to Neuchâtel and then to the nearby village of Môtiers. Rousseau—at this time ill and reclusive—was charmed by Boswell's approach, and Boswell visited him, seeking advice on the conduct of his life, four times in December. He wrote and left his 'Ébauche' for Rousseau to read, and recorded in detail in his journals his lively and at times bantering exchanges with the philosopher. From Môtiers he journeyed to Ferney, saw Voltaire later that month, had himself invited to spend two nights under his roof, and conducted a spirited debate with him on the truth of the Christian religion.

His meetings with Rousseau inspired Boswell to make a bold journey to Corsica to meet General Pasquale Paoli, leader of the insurgents seeking the island's independence from the Genoese. In January 1765 Boswell crossed the Alps into Italy, making his way to Naples, where he stayed three weeks with the outlawed John Wilkes, whose wit, gaiety, and knowledge of the classics delighted him in spite of his qualms about Wilkes's political views, disrespect for religion, and libertine conduct. He stayed in Rome until the middle of June, during which time he commissioned a portrait of himself from George Willison. He was much with Andrew Lumisden, and others in the exiled Jacobite circle, and commissioned from Gavin Hamilton a painting, 'Mary Queen of Scots resigning her Crown', a scene chosen from William Robertson's *History of Scotland*. In the company of John Stuart, styled Lord Mountstuart, Bute's eldest son, he travelled to Venice and several other cities. While in Siena (one of his motives in visiting Italy was the hope of amorous intrigues) he won the passionate love of Girolama Piccolomini (1728–1792), wife of the city's capitano di popolo (equivalent to mayor), with whom he had an affair, and from whom he continued to receive affectionate correspondence until 1767. He sailed from Leghorn for Corsica in October. After a difficult inland journey he met and had conversations (22 to 27 October) in Sollacarò with Paoli, who at first suspected he was a spy, but who quickly came to like his improbable young visitor, saw an opportunity for promotion of the Corsican cause in Britain, and consented to a series of interviews. Boswell's trip was both arduous and dangerous. He suffered painfully from ingrowing toenails, the result of trudging long distances in inadequate boots, and he contracted malaria, but the experience none the less exhilarated him. He remarked in 1783: 'I had got upon a rock in Corsica and jumped into the middle of life' (*Boswelliana*, 328).

While in Paris on his way homeward in January 1766, Boswell learned from a newspaper notice of his mother's death. He then gave up a scheme he had formed to travel again to Utrecht to propose formally to Belle de Zuylen, and began preparations to return to Scotland. Rousseau, whom he had hoped to see again in Paris, had already left for England. Thérèse le Vasseur, Rousseau's companion, accepted an offer from Boswell to serve as her escort across the channel, and she and Boswell had a shipboard sexual affair. On arrival in London he delivered her to David Hume, then next day took her to Rousseau at Chiswick. Boswell's ardour for Rousseau and Voltaire cooled quickly. He hurried to London, and to Johnson, who received him affectionately. Boswell lingered in London, saw much of Johnson, whose conversation he now carefully recorded, as well as Oliver Goldsmith and William Johnson Temple, and discussed Corsica in an interview, which he wrote up in detail afterwards, with William Pitt. He left for Edinburgh early in March, travelling almost immediately to the new mansion at Auchinleck with his bereaved father, who began coaching him for the private examination in Scots law, which Boswell passed on 11 July. On 26 July he passed advocate. He continued work, already begun, on his *Account of Corsica*, and set about establishing his legal practice. For much of 1767 he worked as a passionate volunteer in the Douglas interest in the great Douglas cause, and published several pieces in connection with it: *The Douglas Cause* (a short poem) and a companion piece, *The Hamilton Cause*; also *Dorando: a Spanish Tale*; *The Essence of the Douglas Cause*; and *Letters of … Lady Jane Douglas*.

The *Account of Corsica*, marriage, early legal career, Paoli, and Johnson in Scotland His interest in theatre still active, Boswell supported David Ross in his bid to become patentee and manager of Edinburgh's new Theatre Royal, and wrote a prologue for the opening of the theatre on 9 December 1767. His first important work, *An Account of Corsica, the Journal of a Tour to that Island, and Memoirs of Pascal Paoli*, appeared on 18 February 1768. With its reports of the gallant islanders and a Plutarchan depiction of Paoli paralleled with several classical heroes, it was an immediate success. The work was widely read and translated, stimulated great interest in Paoli and the Corsican cause, brought its author wide fame in Britain and Europe, and found an interested readership among the Americans. It attracted the notice of the French government (which had a translation made), and though Boswell's ambition for British intervention was not to be fulfilled, he probably influenced Britain's decision to send secret supplies of arms to the Corsicans. To enjoy his new authorial fame, he set out in March for a three months' jaunt to London, and visited Johnson in Oxford where (though Boswell seems not to have known it, as the matter was long kept secret) he was helping Robert Chambers to prepare his Vinerian lectures. Boswell now wished specifically, among other topics of concern, to consult Johnson on his moral scruples about the profession of law in the Scottish courts (Boswell, journal, 26 March 1768). In London, much acclaimed as the author of the *Account of Corsica*, he received many calls, while confined with another attack of venereal disease (a result of his again consorting with prostitutes), from friends as well as new acquaintances his book had brought him. Amid rumours that France was about to take over Genoese claims to Corsica, Boswell began further newspaper campaigns, and writing and collecting essays by various hands which he brought out as *Essays in Favour of the Brave Corsicans* in December. He published a letter anonymously in the *Public Advertiser* (6 July) urging a voluntary subscription for the Corsican cause. He and his Edinburgh colleague Andrew Crosbie purchased £700 worth of ordnance from the Carron Company for shipment to Corsica. Eventually an estimated £20,000 was raised by subscription and public gift for the Corsicans, before their submission to the French in summer 1769, with Boswell directly or indirectly responsible for all of this aid. In September he attended Garrick's Shakespeare jubilee at Stratford and made a spectacular appearance at a masked ball as an armed Corsican chief. He was known popularly by the designation 'Corsica Boswell' for many years, and he won Paoli's lifelong friendship and gratitude.

By the end of July 1769, after half-hearted pursuits of several eligible young women, and after numerous clandestine affairs (two of which resulted in illegitimate children, one and probably both of whom, to his distress, died in infancy), Boswell was formally engaged to his cousin and close friend and confidante, Margaret Montgomerie (1738?–1789) [*see* Boswell, Margaret Montgomerie] of Lainshaw. The Lainshaw estate had deteriorated and Margaret was virtually penniless. Lord Auchinleck bitterly disapproved of the match and was never reconciled to it, and he distressed Boswell by confirming rumours that he himself intended to remarry. On 22 September, on a last bachelor jaunt south, Boswell was joyously reunited in London with Paoli, now beginning his exile, and set about introducing him to his London acquaintances, among them Sheridan, Garrick, and Johnson. Boswell met Sir Joshua Reynolds, inaugurating another of the most significant of his London friendships, among his closest after Johnson's death (Reynolds would be the *Life*'s dedicatee). The following month he became a co-proprietor of the *London Magazine*, continuing as a partner until late 1784, a year before it ceased publication. On 25 November 1769 Boswell and Margaret Montgomerie were married at Lainshaw, Boswell evidently having chosen the same day on which, in Edinburgh, Lord Auchinleck remarried. Relations between the two families were never anything other than strained. A visit to Auchinleck in 1770 led to an outright rift between Margaret Boswell and her parents-in-law, and she did not visit again (and was probably not invited) during Lord Auchinleck's lifetime. In Edinburgh, Boswell and his wife took up residence in a house in the Cowgate, and moved in May 1770 to a more commodious house in Chessel's Land in the Canongate. They moved once more in May 1771 to a house in James's Court on the north side of the Lawnmarket (it was owned by Hume and had once been his home). In 1773 they moved downstairs to a more spacious house in the same building.

Boswell worked diligently at the law, and in December 1769 was admitted to practise at the bar of the general assembly of the Church of Scotland. But in an anonymous three-part essay, 'On the Profession of a Player' (*London Magazine*, August–October 1770), he expressed again his moral qualms about the profession of law, exploring in particular the theatrical character of a barrister's courtroom conduct. Early the following year Alexander Donaldson brought out an edition of Shakespeare's plays, to which Boswell contributed a fulsome dedication to Garrick. Though he built a creditable practice, he grew restless and unhappy in his Edinburgh life, and developed the habits of heavy convivial drinking and frequent social drunkenness for which he became notorious in his own lifetime, and which linger as an inseparable part of his reputation. They were habits against which, for the rest of his life, he struggled with only intermittent success despite frequent pledges and resolutions. Paoli toured Scotland in September 1771, with Boswell as guide, and Boswell contributed an account to the *London Magazine*. The visit prompted him to resume his journal (a gap from 28 October 1769 to 4 September 1771 being the longest in the surviving journal from its beginning in 1761 until his death).

From March to May 1772, during the court's spring recess, Boswell returned happily to London, where on 14 April he made his maiden speech at the bar of the House of Lords. He had, and carefully recorded afterwards, many lengthy conversations with Johnson, and wrote in his journal for 31 March: 'I have a constant plan to write the life of Mr. Johnson'. The plan, referred to openly here for the first time, had formed earlier, perhaps as early as September 1764, when Boswell wrote to Johnson from the German territories that if Johnson died before him he would endeavour to do honour to his memory. He had written to Wilkes from Venice: 'Could my feeble mind preserve but a faint impression of Johnson, it would be a glory to myself and a benefit to mankind' (Boswell, letter, 13 July 1765, Yale L 1286). He also determined on a plan of visiting London annually during spring court recesses. In Edinburgh he believed himself drudging in provincial obscurity, and longed for the brilliant social company in which he moved in London. He kept up a frequent correspondence and a prolific miscellaneous journalism, acting as Edinburgh correspondent for several London newspapers and magazines. The collapse of the Ayr Bank led to a twenty-five-page pamphlet, *Reflections on the Late Alarming Bankruptcies in Scotland*, a wide-ranging indictment of Scottish manners and culture, written and published in early November. He became sufficiently established in his profession to be made an examiner of the Faculty of Advocates, but his 'constant plan' for Johnson's biography remained active. On 10 September 1772 he wrote to Garrick: 'If I survive Mr Johnson, I shall publish a Life of him, for which I have a store of materials' (*Correspondence*, 4.45).

On 15 March 1773 the Boswells' first surviving child, Veronica (1773–1795), was born. Boswell set out later that month for a six-week jaunt to London, having written beforehand to many of his London acquaintances, including Thomas Percy, Garrick, and Goldsmith. He saw Johnson frequently, and began asking about and recording the details of his early life in Lichfield and his first coming to London. Boswell was now more fully practised in his recording, and large portions of this journal were used almost verbatim in the *Life*. He canvassed assiduously for election to the Club, later briefly known as the Literary Club, and on 30 April he was admitted to membership under Johnson's forceful and enthusiastic sponsorship. Johnson delighted Boswell during this visit by committing himself to a long-proposed scheme to visit Boswell in Scotland later in the year and make a tour of the highlands and Western Isles (the Hebrides). Boswell returned to Edinburgh, reported for the *London Magazine* a series of 'Debates in the General Assembly of the Church of Scotland', and worked as one of Donaldson's counsel in the landmark case on literary property. He prepared his notes on the case for publication, and in early February 1774 brought out *The decision of the court of session upon the question of literary property … published by James Boswell, esq., advocate, one of the counsel in the cause*, in time for Donaldson's successful appeal to the House of Lords against an earlier decision against him of the court of king's bench in London. This case (*Donaldson* v. *Becket*) long remained the basis of British and American copyright law.

Johnson arrived in Edinburgh three days after the rising of the court of session in August 1773, and spent three days at the Boswells' home receiving social visits. For seven weeks of September and October he and Boswell travelled about the highlands and Inner Hebrides, the rugged and at times dangerous travel punctuated by periods of gracious hospitality from the 'great, the learned, and the elegant' (Boswell, *Life*, 2.269). On 22 October they returned to the mainland, then spent an enjoyable six days at Auchinleck, invited by Boswell's father, a visit marred near the end by a violent argument between Johnson and Lord Auchinleck, who, Boswell noted, 'was as sanguine a Whig and Presbyterian, as Dr Johnson was a Tory and Church of England man' (*Journal of a Tour to the Hebrides*, 2 Nov 1773, Boswell, *Life*, 5.376). Boswell resumed legal work almost immediately, while Johnson stayed at the Boswells' home another ten days, receiving social visits. Margaret Boswell acted as hostess at many of them, despite her disapproval of Johnson's 'irregular hours and uncouth habits' and her opinion that 'he had too much influence over her husband' (Boswell, *Life*, 2.269). Lord Auchinleck, talking with a colleague in Edinburgh at the court of session, famously dubbed Johnson 'Ursa Major' (ibid., 5.384). The notes and journals Boswell kept on this trip, revised after Johnson's death with the help of Boswell's friend and editor, Edmond Malone, served as the basis for his innovative travel memoir and the first instalment of his Johnsonian biography, *The Journal of a Tour to the Hebrides* (1785), through which (and Johnson's own *Journey to the Western Isles*) this tour has become one of the most famous of literary journeys, its steps often retraced by later travellers. It had been a remarkable coup to coax the little-travelled Johnson, who passed his sixty-fourth birthday on the trip, to Scotland, against which he had often expressed a prejudice. It affords the most extended and remarkable instance of the many ways in which Boswell as biographer actually broadened his subject's range of experience and acquaintance. Johnson himself read most of Boswell's journal up to the mid-entry for 22 October, and Boswell several times recorded his pleasure and praise and compliments on its accuracy. The tour, as well as Johnson's admiration for the journal, deepened the friendship between the pair, and increased Johnson's respect for and confidence in Boswell as a future biographer.

Heir of Auchinleck Johnson proved a robust but demanding companion, and the tour proved an immense strain on Boswell, leaving him fatigued and depleted. He wrote in June 1774: 'After Mr. Samuel Johnson left me … I was long in a state of languor. My mind had been kept upon its utmost stretch in his company. I had exhausted all my powers to entertain him' (Boswell, journal, 'Review of my life', June 1774, *Defence*, 197). He suffered his first severe depression since his marriage. A dispute with his father festered over the entailing of the estate, and Lord Auchinleck, like Margaret Boswell, ridiculed the association with Johnson, and spoke disparagingly of him. Ideas of transferring to the English bar took a deeper hold. On 20 May the Boswells' second daughter, Euphemia (1774–1837), was born. He did not undertake his usual spring jaunt to London, but remained in Scotland for the whole year, concerned with political activities in Ayrshire. Hopes that he might represent his county as an independent member in parliament remained with him until his last years, despite several ineffectual forays into Ayrshire elections motivated both by a desire to reverse the proportions of his year (to live in London, and visit Scotland) and a sincere disapproval of the way elections were arranged and controlled at this time. The latter half of the year was dominated by his most emotionally wrenching criminal trial, that of a sheepstealer, John Reid, who had in an earlier trial (1766) been his first criminal client. Despite Boswell's strenuous efforts both in court and after the verdict, Reid was hanged, proclaiming his innocence; the case left Boswell profoundly shaken. On his next spring jaunt to London he began to fulfil the requirements for one term's residence at the Inner Temple as a first step towards transfer to the English bar. In summer 1775 he wrote:

> My father's coldness to me, the unsettled state of our family affairs, and the poor opinion which I had of the profession of a lawyer in Scotland, which consumed my life in the mean time, sunk my spirits woefully; and for some of the last weeks of the session I was depressed with black melancholy. … I thought myself disordered in mind. Yet I was able to discharge my duty as a lawyer. (Boswell, journal, 'Review of my life during the summer session', 1775, *Ominous Years*, 158)

On 9 October 1775 Boswell's son Alexander *Boswell (1775–1822) was born. Pleased by the arrival of a male heir, Boswell resumed his journal with greater diligence than at any time since 1763. He followed closely at this time and later the events of the American War of Independence, his feelings—resembling those that produced his youthful attraction to the Corsicans—steadily pro-American. On his spring jaunt of 1776 he accompanied Johnson to Oxford, Stratford upon Avon, Birmingham, Lichfield, and Ashbourne, studying Johnson now in the scenes of his youth. In London, on 22 April, his interest in celebrity (in this case, a glamorous criminal notoriety) having been piqued by press reports of the forgery trials of Margaret Caroline Rudd and her accomplices, Boswell called on her at her lodgings. He wrote a detailed account of his interview, and called on her again several more times. On 15 May occurred the famous dinner at the Dillys', at which he contrived, after much astutely manipulative negotiation, to bring together Johnson and Wilkes, whose libertine morals and politics Johnson found abhorrent—one of the most notable of the many occasions in which Boswell manoeuvred Johnson into complex and even confrontational situations to study his reactions and record his responses. On this occasion, Wilkes's sly tact dissolved Johnson's initial discomposure into pleasant cordiality, and the episode, which Boswell wrote up from brief notes many years later, would become one of the *Life*'s best known.

On 7 July 1776, after his return to Edinburgh, Boswell visited the dying Hume, whose 'infidel' scepticism both fascinated and disturbed him, and recorded their exchanges, enlarging the record from memory on 3 March 1777. Hume died tranquilly on 25 August, and Boswell himself remained long disconcerted by Hume's placidity. Further distresses followed: in the same month Boswell capitulated again to his father's will, and agreed finally to sign the estate entail long sought by Lord Auchinleck (now recurrently ill and in acute pain). On 15 November another son was born, but died in March the following year, and Boswell gave up any idea of a spring jaunt to London. Margaret Boswell had now begun to show symptoms of consumption. In September when Boswell resolved to visit Johnson in Ashbourne, he described himself as 'one going upon a pilgrimage to some sacred place' (Boswell, journal, 10 Sept 1777). After his return to Edinburgh his most important journalism now took the form of his series of monthly reflective essays, eventually seventy in number, for the *London Magazine* in the melancholic persona of 'The Hypochondriack'. The Hypochondriack essays would continue, without a break, from October 1777 to August 1783. Gently meditative in tone, addressed sympathetically to the Hypochondriack's 'atrabilious brethren' (Boswell, *Hypochondriack*, 1.v, February 1778)—his fellow sufferers from inexplicable periods of depression—these essays offer some of Boswell's most considered thoughts on a wide range of moral, social, and political issues, including many of most pressing concern to himself: death, executions (which he attended compulsively throughout his life), war, diary-keeping, marriage, and drinking, among others. In March 1778 Boswell set out for London, where he spoke at the bar of the House of Commons for the first time. Johnson was now at work on his *Prefaces: Biographical and Critical* ('Lives of the Poets'), for which Boswell provided various pieces of research assistance.

On 15 September the Boswells' second surviving son, James *Boswell (1778–1822), was born. In March of the next year Boswell left once more for London. There, his fascination with criminal notoriety again active, he attended the trial and execution of James Hackman (murderer of Martha Ray, mistress of the earl of Sandwich). He met Hackman in prison, and wrote sympathetic letters about him in the London newspapers. His return to Edinburgh was, as usual, dispiriting. Lord Auchinleck was kept away from the court of session by his illness. In July the Boswells were saddened to hear that Lainshaw, Mrs Boswell's family home, had been sold, and Boswell quarrelled later with his former teacher, Adam Smith, over his public eulogy of Hume. He brightened on a jaunt with Colonel James Stuart, Mountstuart's brother, to visit his regiment at Leeds, the journal of which trip Boswell described as a 'log-book of felicity' (Boswell, *Life*, 3.415). He was in London for about two weeks in October and had, as he put it, his only 'second crop' of Johnsoniana in one year (ibid., 3.399–400). In spring 1780 Lord Auchinleck resigned his justiciary gown, and Boswell published anonymously *A letter to Robert Macqueen, Lord Braxfield, on his promotion to be one of the judges of the high court of justiciary*, urging that the circuit criminal courts be conducted 'in the most solemn, exact, and regular way'. The letter testifies to the admiration and regard in which, in spite of their years of bitter contention, he still held his father.

On 15 June 1780 the Boswells' fifth surviving child, Elizabeth (Betsy; 1780–1814), was born. In March 1781 Boswell set off for London to appear as counsel for Hugh Montgomerie (whose election for Ayrshire had been disallowed in favour of Sir Adam Fergusson) before the house committee. The death of Henry Thrale during this visit (on 4 April 1781) aroused Boswell's complex anxieties about Hester Thrale, the rival intimacy which had developed between her and Johnson, and the possibility of a marriage. He composed the scurrilous *Ode by Dr Samuel Johnson to Mrs Thrale upon their Supposed Approaching Nuptials*. He returned to Edinburgh, and to the law, and spent portions of time at Auchinleck with his ailing father. Both his wife and his father were now critically ill, and Boswell was more eager than ever to leave his 'narrow sphere' and secure a remunerative place in London. Lord Auchinleck died on 30 August 1782 at his house in Edinburgh. 'Wept', Boswell wrote in his journal, 'for alas! there was not affection between us' (Boswell, journal, 29–30 Aug 1782, *Laird*, 477). Boswell, though proudly ninth laird of Auchinleck, was ill-trained in estate management, already heavily in debt, and stunned to discover the extent of Lord Auchinleck's settlements on his widow. He was faced for the rest of his life with an impossible financial strain. He and his wife and children came to Auchinleck, which his children had never seen, to take up residence on 18 September. Boswell sought advice from Alexander Fairlie of Fairlie, the agricultural improver, promoter of the successful Fairlie Rotation. Fairlie returned annually until 1789, and again in 1791 and 1794. Despite his love of London, Boswell was fiercely proud of his ancestral estate. He was generally lenient to his tenants, and enlarged and beautified Auchinleck. As one of the late eighteenth-century's 'improving' lowland lairds, he continued his father's campaigns of plantation and development of mining, and introduced new agricultural techniques to supplement the outmoded practices still in operation in the time of his father. But when he made his next spring visit, in 1783, to London—where he was to appear in an appeal before the House of Lords—he consulted his friends with greater earnestness about a transfer to the English bar. Most, including Johnson, advised against it.

Death of Johnson, *The Journal of a Tour to the Hebrides*, and move to London In the autumn of 1783 at Auchinleck, Boswell resumed his laird's duties, became a JP, and was chosen praeses of the quarter sessions at Ayr. Still vainly hoping to attract political notice, he wrote *A Letter to the People of Scotland* in support of the king and Pitt the younger in their opposition to Fox's East India bill, and in Ayrshire the next spring he presented to the county a loyal address to the king, as part of another ill-formed campaign to supplant Sir Adam Fergusson as MP. He set out for London soon afterwards, but hearing of the dissolution of parliament hurried back to Scotland to present himself (in vain) as a candidate. He set out again in April, and while in Lichfield he tried, without success, to flirt with Anna Seward, of whose verse-novel *Louisa* he wrote a fulsome review for the *Public Advertiser* (3 June 1784). This friendship soured later over the *Life of Johnson*, and the pair became embroiled in a lively paper war, since, with mixed feelings about Johnson and on some matters hostile to him, Anna Seward was among those who believed Boswell's estimate of Johnson too generous.

Boswell accompanied Johnson to Oxford, Johnson's first trip since a long confinement through illness, and spent much of the time interviewing William Adams, master of Pembroke, about Johnson's earlier years, and noting his answers. This pleasant Oxford jaunt was to be their last together. Back in London, talk of Johnson's wintering in Italy for his health prompted Boswell to write to Lord Chancellor Thurlow, requesting an increase in Johnson's pension to help with the expense, a gesture that left Johnson deeply moved. Thurlow undertook to press as far as he could, but the application was not granted. On 30 June 1784 Boswell took his last parting from Johnson. He learned in Edinburgh on 17 December 1784 of Johnson's death. Seriously ill himself, he wrote in his journal: 'I was stunned, and in a kind of amaze … My feeling was just one large expanse of stupor. I knew that I should afterwards have sorer sensations' (Boswell, journal, 17 Dec 1784, *Applause*, 271). Letters arrived in quick succession from his publisher Charles Dilly, inviting him to be the editor of Johnson's works, and pressing him to produce his biography. Confronted now with the weight of public pressure and expectation, as well as many years' worth of unsystematic accumulation, and the prospect of many more years of research into the time before he knew Johnson, Boswell resolved that in the spring he would go to London to revise and publish his journal of the Scottish tour, 'a good prelude to my large work, his life' (Boswell, 'Register of letters', 23 Dec 1784). On Fairlie's advice he engaged Bruce Campbell (*c*.1734–1813), his second cousin, a pioneer breeder of the Ayrshire cattle, to see to the needs of his estate farms.

Another political disappointment followed in February 1785. The post of knight marshal of Scotland having become available, Boswell wrote to Henry Dundas to apply for it, and was rejected. He set out for London in late March, and wrote a second *Letter to the People of Scotland*, opposing Ilay Campbell's bill for reducing the number of the lords of session, and venting his considerable anger at Dundas, whose rise to 'prodigious power' in Scotland had both impressed and infuriated him. On 29 April he dined with Malone, the beginning of the critical literary association of the last decade of Boswell's life, one that proved vital to the eventual achievement of both of his Johnsonian masterworks. Malone soon became Boswell's closest London friend and an invaluable prompt and editor. For some months they met several times a week, revising the *Tour* journal. He returned to Scotland and arrived at Auchinleck on 3 October, ending what had been his longest London stay since 1762–3. The *Journal of a Tour to the Hebrides*, seen through the press by Malone (to whom it was dedicated), was published on 1 October 1785, and was the second of Boswell's major publications to be an instant success. The whole impression, of 1500 copies, was sold out by the 17th of that month. Long extracts were published serially in newspapers and magazines, and more space was given in reviews and letters to editors than to any other book (1785–6). Some reviewers were inevitably baffled by its novelty and personal candour, and hostile to its attention to minute quotidian detail, but its success increased Boswell's confidence in his closely personal and anecdotal approach to biography. In letters he and Malone began revising for a second edition, of which Malone supervised the printing while Boswell was in Scotland, and this edition was published on 22 December. A third was published in October 1786, which edition (there were several thereafter) was the last to include revisions by Boswell himself.

Boswell remained at Auchinleck for a month, collecting rents and paying and receiving social visits, then set out in November 1785 for London via Edinburgh. In London he heard again from Margaret Caroline Rudd, and the interest they had shown in each other at their first meetings in 1776 grew into a sexual affair. This affair, with a widely recognized criminal celebrity, shocked even friends such as Reynolds, long accustomed to Boswell's frequent infidelities. When, typically, he confessed it to Margaret Boswell, then gravely ill, it caused her a sharper distress than all his other extramarital affairs and habitual whoring. On 9 February 1786 he completed the requisite number of meals in the Temple commons for admission to the English bar, to which he was called on 13 February, and he joined the northern circuit as junior member. Soon after he had left for the northern circuit, Mrs Piozzi's *Anecdotes of the Late Samuel Johnson* were published. He left the circuit early in order to attend the House of Lords for an appeal in which he was counsel, and he published a reply to Mrs Piozzi in the newspapers, along with 'Piozzian Rhymes', signed 'Old Salusbury Briar'. In May he took a house at 56 Great Queen Street. His journals record further miserable vacillation about transferring to London and conscientious attendance at courts, but (as he had not actually studied to acquire English law) little or no legal business. His entry for 5 June marks the first explicit mention in his journal of work on 'sorting materials' for the *Life of Johnson*, and the entries for 9–11 July show him as beginning to write it. On deciding finally to move to London, he returned to Scotland, having spent less than three of the previous seventeen months with his family, and on 20 September 1786 he left with his wife and their five children, and took up residence in Great Queen Street.

Recorder of Carlisle and death of Margaret Boswell In November, Boswell wrote to the earl of Lonsdale, whose notice he had attracted with complimentary references in his second *Letter to the People of Scotland* (1785) and the *Tour*, seeking the position of recorder of Carlisle. Lonsdale responded by asking if he could go at once to Carlisle as counsel for the mayor at the coming by-election. Boswell accepted, travelled to Carlisle, and saw the election through, but recorded much in his journals of Lonsdale's violently tyrannical manner and the subordination in which he kept his entourage of dependants. In March 1787 there appeared Sir John Hawkins's *Life of Johnson*. This, the most significant and substantial of the several biographies of Johnson before Boswell's, he had been anxiously awaiting, as Hawkins had known Johnson for some forty years and was one of his executors. In May Boswell announced in the *Public Advertiser* that he had delayed his own book in order to see other promised works, and that his own biography would 'correct' the 'erroneous Accounts' of Hawkins and Mrs Piozzi. Mrs Boswell's health worsened seriously in London, and he resolved to take her to Auchinleck with him for a short visit late in August, after which they set off once more for London, where Malone now urged him to put the writing of the *Life* ahead of attendance at courts and other considerations. But he applied again to Lonsdale for the recordership of Carlisle, which, on 20 December, Lonsdale offered, asking him to set out the next day. Boswell complied, but again grew rapidly disheartened with his patron and recorded more in his journals of Lonsdale's brutality and ill temper. On 11 January 1788 he was elected recorder of Carlisle.

Mrs Piozzi's *Letters to and from the Late Samuel Johnson* prompted Boswell to publish his irreverent *Ode by Dr Samuel Johnson to Mrs Thrale*. He had been disappointed by the *Letters*, in which he found 'less able and brilliant writing than I expected', 'proof' of what he saw as Johnson's 'fawning' on Mrs Piozzi, and of Johnson's 'treating me and other friends much more lightly than we had reason to expect'. Even though he found two days later that they 'improved on me', the experience had temporarily 'cooled my warmth of enthusiasm for "my illustrious friend"' (journal, 7 March 1788, *English Experiment*, 194, 196). None the less Boswell resumed work on the *Life*, and by May he could speak of having only his journals of the last two years of Johnson's life to revise. But Mrs Boswell was distressed by the now obviously terminal nature of her illness. In May he yielded to her entreaties, and set out for Auchinleck, where work on the *Life* stalled, and Boswell was often away from home as, having been a declared candidate for the county, he began his canvass. He wrote an address to the real freeholders of Ayrshire dated 30 June, and published it in the *Edinburgh Advertiser* (1–4 July). In October he set out for the Michaelmas quarter sessions at Carlisle, where Lonsdale joined him, and he spoke before the grand jury as recorder. Later that month he left Auchinleck with his sons for London, and was little in Scotland after this date. Work on the *Life* resumed, and by the beginning of 1789 he had nearly finished a first rough draft. In January he took a smaller house at 38 Queen Anne Street West, Cavendish Square, but in April, having received alarming accounts of Mrs Boswell's health, he headed north, with his eldest daughter, Veronica. He again resumed local political activities. On 5 May, as praeses of the general quarter sessions at Ayr, in another attempt to court political notice he proposed and had carried an address to the prince of Wales, expressing 'a grateful sense of his public conduct with regard to the Regency'. Word from Lonsdale came that he wished Boswell to accompany him to London to appear as recorder in an action brought against the Carlisle corporation in the court of king's bench. Boswell hesitated, anguished by, but unwilling and unable fully to confront, his wife's mortal illness, and uncertain about whether to adhere to the association with Lonsdale he had so assiduously sought, and which he thought might yet bring him into parliament. He set out, pausing at Carlisle to meet Lonsdale. He had been in London less than a week, and Lonsdale's case had not yet come on, when letters reached him with the news that Mrs Boswell was sinking. From 4 June he and his sons posted night and day, arriving at Auchinleck to find that his wife had died on the morning of the day he left London.

Guiltily disconsolate, berating himself for his conduct as a husband and for having valued Margaret insufficiently, and inadequate under the burden of sole responsibility for their five children, Boswell set out at the end of the summer once more in pursuit of business on the northern circuit, but, he told Temple, his 'mind was so sore from my late severe loss' that he avoided the 'roaring, bantering society of lawyers'. He continued:

> Every prospect that I turn my mind's eye upon is dreary … The law life in Scotland amidst vulgar familiarity would now quite destroy me. I am not able to acquire the law of England. To be in Parliament unless as an independent member would gall my spirit. To live in the country would either harrass me by forced exertions, or sink me into a gloomy stupor … *The Life of Johnson* still keeps me up. I *must* bring that forth … (23 Aug 1789, *Great Biographer*, 11)

After attending to further business in Carlisle, he set out on 1 October for London with Veronica, James, and Elizabeth, and Alexander joined them at Carlisle. Veronica boarded with a schoolfriend in London, Euphemia went to a boarding-school in Edinburgh, Alexander went to Eton, James continued as a day boy at the Soho Academy in London (and went later to Westminster), and Betsy was sent to a boarding-school in Chelsea. In mid-October in London, Boswell returned to a final burst of work on the *Life*. On 7 December the court of king's bench saw the trial that had been in the offing since Lonsdale called Boswell from the dying Margaret's bedside. Boswell appeared before Lord Kenyon, the lord chief justice, as one of two counsel for the Carlisle corporation. The trial resulted in a victory (though only a temporary one) for Lonsdale.

Boswell worked assiduously at this time, with others of his friends, to erect a monument to Johnson in Westminster Abbey (eventually it was placed in St Paul's Cathedral) and his long association with Paoli, who was returning to Corsica, now neared its end. Paoli had remained, during his London exile of some twenty-one years, an unswerving source of friendship, moral advice, wisdom, and hospitality. Boswell gave a farewell dinner for Paoli on 22 March 1790, and translated Paoli's speech to the Corsican general assembly and published it in the *London Chronicle* for 30 November. He enjoyed a temporary easy sociability with Lonsdale in the aftermath of the trial victory, and felt pleased with his progress on the *Life*. He and Malone had devised an arduous programme of revising later manuscript sections even as the earlier ones were being printed. He launched newspaper campaigns promoting his forthcoming book, and disparaged Mrs Piozzi's. But among other complications Thomas Percy, having grown anxious about the appearance he was to make in Boswell's work, disconcerted him by asking not to be named in it. Boswell altered some material, but rejected the request for anonymity, and Percy long remained profoundly offended by his eventual depiction in the *Life*. Then Boswell found himself summoned (in the middle of a visit from Temple, whom he had not seen since 1783, and his eldest daughter) by Lonsdale to accompany him to his seat at Laleham in Middlesex. Lonsdale, evidently offended when he asked to be excused because of the arrival of his old friend, later spoke abusively, and Boswell 'inwardly resolved to withdraw myself from all connection with him'. But he noted in his journal for 20 May: 'I was now in absolute poverty'. He soon heard enough to know that Lonsdale had no thought of bringing him into parliament or employing him in Westminster Hall. The simmering hostility between them mounted, and the pair came to a violent open quarrel. On the journey north Lonsdale insulted Boswell grossly, Boswell sought pistols from some officers at an inn, and they came almost to a duel before Lonsdale's temper abated and they reached an uneasy calm. Boswell discharged his various legal duties, resigned the recordership (effective 12 July 1790), and his political association with Lonsdale ended.

The *Life of Johnson* In London, Boswell found that Malone had supervised the printing of another forty pages of the *Life*. He was 'put in train again', and resumed his typical patterns of convivial dinners, revising with Malone, and visits to prostitutes. He, Malone, Reynolds, and John Courtenay MP were so often in each other's company that they became known as 'the Gang'. Later in the year he arranged with his brother Thomas David to attend to estate business at Auchinleck as his deputy, on whose recommendation he appointed as overseer Andrew Gibb, a younger brother of Gavin Gibb, to succeed James Bruce, a childhood friend, who had died in August. (Gibb would serve Boswell, his son, and grandson, on the estate for a total of forty-six years.) Still closely and emotionally engaged in estate affairs, Boswell bought, despite his desperate financial state, nearby Knockroon at a cost of £2500. Fairlie lent him £1500 on the security of the land, but how to raise the other thousand remained a persistent anxiety for the winter of 1791. Eventually Dilly and his printer, Henry Baldwin, lent him the money in anticipation of royalties on the *Life*. In November, still vainly hoping for Pitt's interest, he sang his *William Pitt, the Grocer of London* at the lord mayor's feast in the Guildhall, celebrating Pitt's recent success in a favourable trade convention with Spain, and published it in the *Public Advertiser*. In April 1791 he published anonymously a lengthy verse pamphlet, *No Abolition of Slavery, or, The Universal Empire of Love*, containing in part an attack on abolitionism.

In January 1791, as printing of the *Life* proceeded, Boswell moved to 47 Great Portland Street, his home for the rest of his life. On 13 May forty-one London booksellers purchased more than 400 sets (of two large quarto volumes), and on 16 May, the twenty-eighth anniversary of his first meeting with Johnson in Davies's back parlour, the biography was published. Sales exceeded all expectations. Of a total of 1750 sets printed, 800 were sold in the first two weeks, 1200 by the end of August, 1400 by December, and 1600 by August 1792. When he settled accounts with Dilly, the transaction was (he noted) 'very flattering to me as an author' (Boswell, journal, 24 Nov 1792, *Great Biographer*, 201). To promote interest in the *Life*, he wrote a third-person biography of himself in the *European Magazine*, published in two parts in the May and June issues. As tributes to the *Life* poured in from his friends, Boswell continued to attend Westminster Hall, but knew that his transfer to the English bar had been a failure. Convivial dinners, a remarkably extensive and varied range of social acquaintance, frequent heavy drinking, prostitutes, fitful but never plausible schemes of remarriage, and his children's continuing love for him, despite his difficulties as a widower in supervising their lives, punctuated the time which, since the publication of the *Life*, had become essentially idle. In July Reynolds, now in his own last illness, and valuing Boswell's companionship highly, arranged for his election to the honorary post of secretary for foreign correspondence in the Royal Academy, which led later to his joining the Royal Academy Club. On 28 August 1791 he returned to Auchinleck, where he had not been since October 1789, attended desultorily to estate business, and left again in October for London, where he often visited Reynolds, now in rapidly failing health. Reynolds died on 23 February 1792, and Boswell felt his loss severely.

Last years In summer 1792, shortly before a visit with his two elder daughters to Temple and his family in Cornwall, Boswell's characteristic sympathy for impoverished criminals was roused again by the plight of Mary Bryant (or Broad) and the other four survivors of an escape from the penal colony in New South Wales, now confined in Newgate. He appealed on their behalf to Dundas, now home secretary, who set in motion the granting of a royal pardon for Mary Bryant. In October 1793 Boswell arranged for Mary to rejoin her relations in Fowey, and, after seeking to raise money for her through subscriptions, he paid most of a promised annuity of £10 personally. At Auchinleck in spring 1793 he devoted great care and attention to the choice and the appointment of a successor to John Dun, who had died the preceding October, as parish minister. Aware of the kinds of angry broils parish appointments could lead to (they had been pilloried in the poems of his fellow Ayrshireman, Robert Burns), Boswell yielded to his parishioners' choice and presented the Revd John Lindsay to the parish in March. Immediately thereafter he left for London by way of Edinburgh, where he had not been since his move to the English bar in 1786, and this short visit was the last time he saw his native city. In London he worked hurriedly, as publication time drew near, to prepare his second edition of the *Life*. Much new material, including a number of original letters, had come to him, and he added many lengthy new notes, and prefatory matter. The second edition appeared on 17 July, in three octavo volumes, 'corrected and considerably enlarged by additional Letters and interesting Anecdotes …'. The 'Corrections and Additions' were later issued separately to accommodate purchasers of the first edition.

Temple visited London, and on 27 September the friends saw each other for the last time. Boswell continued despondent that he had had never fulfilled his hopes of 'attaining both to consequence and wealth'; 'I tried to soothe myself with the consideration of my fame as a writer' (Boswell, journal, 13 Feb 1794, *Great Biographer*, 287). The entry for 12 April 1794 marks the end of his full journal (only a few later fragmentary notes survive). As secretary for foreign correspondence of the Royal Academy he campaigned in support of William Mitford's candidacy for the professorship of ancient history (having admired his conservative *History of Greece*), in opposition to John Gillies. He returned to Auchinleck in June 1794 with his two elder daughters, who had not been there since their mother's death in 1789, where Alexander (now studying at Edinburgh University) received them. Betsy remained in London at a boarding-school in Soho Square, and James at Westminster. Archibald Montgomerie, eleventh earl of Eglinton, as lord lieutenant of Ayrshire, named Boswell one of his deputies, but Boswell declined the office, having differed with him earlier in Ayrshire political matters, and he yet nurtured hopes of a seat in parliament or a place in government or diplomacy.

In March, Boswell wrote to Dundas, asking to be made minister or commissioner to Corsica, but was rejected, and he wrote to Paoli in Corsica asking that he and his brother T. D. might be remembered, should positions become open in the new administration there. He left Auchinleck for London on 12 January 1795, intending to return in August, and spent his time after his long absence characteristically 'relishing the Metropolis with avidity' (to Le Fleming, 3 March, *Correspondence*, 2nd edn, 2.450) but essentially, as he had been since the first edition of the *Life*, idle, and regretting again that he had never risen to political consequence. The last surviving letter written fully in his hand (13 April 1785), to Malone, concerns Samuel Parr's inscription for Johnson's monument in St Paul's. On 14 April Boswell was taken violently ill at a meeting of the Club, and had to be carried home to Great Portland Street. After about five weeks of severe pain, but without knowing his danger, he died there at 2 a.m. on 19 May 1795, attended during his last illness by Veronica, Euphemia, James, and his brother T. D. A twentieth-century diagnosis names uraemia as the cause of death, 'the result of acute and chronic urinary tract infection, secondary to postgonorrheal urethral stricture' (Ober, 28). His sons set out for Auchinleck to superintend funeral arrangements, and he was interred in the family vault at Auchinleck church on 8 June 1795.

Boswell's legacy In his will made on 28 May 1785 Boswell had named Sir William Forbes executor. He left debts amounting to about £9000. An addition to his will (12 October 1791) nominated his brother T. D. Boswell, along with Forbes, guardian of his children. He left the care of his voluminous private diaries and correspondence and other papers to Forbes, Temple, and Malone, who were to inspect them and decide which if any should be published for the financial benefit of the children other than his heir, Alexander. Temple died the year after his friend, without having inspected the private papers. Forbes and Malone, although they never met, made inspections and corresponded with care and in detail, then left a decision about whether anything in the private writings warranted publication to Boswell's younger son, James. He when he came of age concurred with the executors' general opinion, against publication. In a codicil to his will, Boswell had left particular care of the *Life* to Malone, who discharged his trust with immense dedication, as much a friend to Boswell and the biography as he was in Boswell's lifetime. With occasional help from Forbes he brought out the third edition, 'revised and augmented', in four octavo volumes in May 1799 and the fourth (1804), fifth (1807), and sixth (1811) editions. Boswell's son James contributed notes to the third edition, and read over and corrected the whole of the sixth, which was many times reprinted throughout the nineteenth century. Other major re-edited editions appeared steadily. G. B. Hill's edition of 1887 represented the high point of a long Victorian fascination with Boswell's book, and brought to a vernacular English text for the first time a complex and comprehensive editorial apparatus on a scale then normally reserved for the classics. L. F. Powell's 'revised and enlarged' edition of Hill appeared in six volumes from 1934 to 1964 (the fifth volume containing the *Tour to the Hebrides* and other material, and the sixth volume a comprehensive index). This edition, usually referred to as Hill–Powell, held its position as the standard scholarly version of the work throughout the twentieth century.

Boswell's *Life of Johnson* remains the most famous biography in any language, one of Western literature's most germinal achievements: unprecedented in its time in its depth of research and its extensive use of private correspondence and recorded conversation, it sought to dramatize its subject in his authorial greatness and formidable social presence, and at the same time treat him with a profound sympathy and inhabit his inner life. Boswell both elevated the life of the writer to epic stature, and attended to the minute details of life as lived to provide a steady disclosure of character through their long gradual accretion. To the task of life-writing, Boswell brought his forensic and evidence-sifting habits from his Edinburgh legal training, and the practised journalist's touch for popularizing and rendering accessible a body of complex material. To the conversation scenes (which, based mostly on revisions of his journal entries, remain the best remembered, while making up only about half of the *Life*) he brought the avid eighteenth-century theatregoer's sense of character revelation through dramatically rendered social self-articulation. But though the *Life* has delighted many, putting Johnson's thunderous aphoristic pronouncements into permanent quotable circulation, it remains—like the biographer who produced it—as controversial as it is famous. It has been attacked, in equal measure, for embodying a servile hero-worship and for offering a portrait grotesquely unflattering. While Boswell has been praised for keeping Johnson's name and greatness alive long after a taste for reading him faded, some Johnsonian scholars allege that Boswell's vision of a deeply troubled, frequently combative, and opinionated conversational colossus has unfairly eclipsed in the popular imagination Johnson's own writing, where it is said an intellect far more meditative, capacious, and analytically flexible is to be found. None the less, later scholarship has properly supplemented but never supplanted the *Life*'s basic vision, and has drawn upon Boswell's work as a central source even in those challenges to aspects of its representation.

Boswell's private diaries, letters, and other papers—long suppressed, unsystematically stored, and in some places expurgated by his heirs—came to light in the early twentieth century when his descendants, the Talbots of Malahide, near Dublin, became interested in their literary and commercial value. These papers, and others from later unexpected recoveries from Malahide, then from Fettercairn House, Kincardineshire (home to the descendants of Forbes), and other sources, were eventually assembled after long effort by the American collector Ralph Heyward Isham (1890–1955), who sold his collection (later much augmented) to Yale University in 1949. In that year, under the inaugural general editorship of Frederick A. Pottle (1897–1987), the Yale Boswell Editions were established, and made the publication of selections of the Boswell papers one of the great editorial undertakings of modern times. It brought Boswell a second, posthumous, wave of fame, detached him from the popular myth of a life lived in more or less constant attendance on Johnson, and brought notice to the crowded variety of his own life. It overturned the famously demeaning appraisal of Boswell made by Macaulay in his review of Croker's edition

(1831) of the *Life*, which had done much to fix a distorted image of Boswell in the Victorian popular imagination. A reading edition of Boswell's journal, supplemented as needed by letters and other material, with the popular and bestselling *London Journal, 1762–1763* (1950) appearing as the first in the sequence, ran eventually to fourteen volumes, the last being *Boswell: the Great Biographer, 1789–1795*, edited by Marlies K. Danziger and Frank Brady (1989). The main work of the Boswell editions, the parallel Research Edition series, designed for a specialist scholarly readership, of volumes of correspondence, journals, and a genetic transcription of the manuscript of the *Life of Johnson*, continued into the twenty-first century.

Boswell stood about 5 feet 6 inches tall, and his weight in 1776 was recorded as 11 stone 12 lbs. He had a very dark complexion and a thick crop of very dark hair. His portrait by Willison, in 1765, shows a young Boswell, in Pottle's description, 'odd, eager, egotistical, boyish, sensual—and attractive' (Pottle, *Earlier Years*, 222), and in Brady's, 'a silken Boswell in furred scarlet and green, with graceful hands, a soft alert face, and some determination about him' (Brady, *Later Years*, 293). Reynolds's portrait (1785) shows Boswell aged forty-five in 'blue coat, white stock, and powdered wig, steady and dignified'. Here the 'face has taken on assured and self-conscious importance … [S]ome hint of cheerfulness lingers about the mouth, and the eyes remain always alert' (ibid., 293). George Dance's sketch, of April 1793, shows a 'well-set, double-chinned' Boswell, as does an undated semi-caricature from about the same period by Thomas Lawrence (Yale U., Beinecke L.). Boswell was an ebulliently animated social presence, a fine singer, an energetic anecdotalist, and an entertainingly gifted mimic. In October 1790 Frances Burney, not having seen him for some time, agreed to meet him knowing she would derive 'amusement from his oddity and good humour', and reported that his 'comic serious face and manner' had 'lost nothing of their wonted singularity' (*Journals and Letters*, 1.181–2).

Boswell was and remains a divisive personality, even for modern readers who find the fluent, precise, demotic prose of the journals compelling: an unstable amalgam of vibrant self-advertising vanity and self-tortured insecurity; an able but reluctant Edinburgh lawyer who marred his chances for judicial promotion with over-zealous and occasionally frenetic defences of poor criminal clients, with whom he felt a particular sympathy; a loving but erratic husband; a lenient, beloved, but overburdened father; a kind and improvement-oriented lowland laird who longed for life in London; a sentimental Jacobite who developed an extraordinary veneration for George III; libertinistic, but guilt-stricken at his own recurrent drunkenness and compulsive whoring. The unflinching confessional candour of his journals has found readerships both attracted and disconcerted. 'I have a strange feeling,' he wrote, 'as if I wished nothing to be secret that concerns myself' (journal, 4 Jan 1776). Yet these self-scrutinizing records—like the biography of Johnson—disclose at the same time Boswell's capacious and generous fascination with the mystery of the other, an engagement with men and women striking or distinctive in whatever way. In his travels and social conduct he sought to collect acquaintances and cultivate friendships with the high and the low, the famous, and the notorious, and his collections are drawn—contrary to his Victorian reputation for mere toadying and tuft-hunting—as much from the regions of the humble and the abject as from the eminent and accomplished. Boswell's drive to record himself and others, and his pertinacious pursuit of his two greatest claims on posterity's attention—the journal and his biographical attachment to Johnson—were not explicable to those closest to him: his Edinburgh legal fraternity, his father, or his wife. Others, like Johnson and Malone, understood and encouraged, and Boswell left behind a window on them all, and a record of his times, unrivalled in detail, accuracy, and social range.

GORDON TURNBULL

Sources J. Boswell, journals, memoranda, letters, and other private papers, Yale U., Beinecke L. • *Boswell for the defence, 1769–1774*, ed. W. K. Wimsatt and F. A. Pottle (1959), vol. 7 of *The Yale editions of the private papers of James Boswell*, trade edn (1950–89) • *Boswell: the ominous years, 1774–1776*, ed. C. Ryskamp and F. A. Pottle (1963), vol. 8 of *The Yale editions of the private papers of James Boswell*, trade edn (1950–89) • *Boswell, laird of Auchinleck, 1778–1782*, ed. J. W. Reed and F. A. Pottle (1977), repr. (1993), vol. 11 of *The Yale editions of the private papers of James Boswell*, trade edn (1950–89) • *Boswell: the applause of the jury, 1782–1785*, ed. I. S. Lustig and F. A. Pottle (1981), vol. 12 of *The Yale editions of the private papers of James Boswell*, trade edn (1950–89) • *Boswell: the English experiment, 1785–1789*, ed. I. S. Lustig and F. A. Pottle (1986), vol. 13 of *The Yale editions of the private papers of James Boswell*, trade edn (1950–89) • *Boswell: the great biographer, 1789–1795*, ed. M. K. Danziger and F. Brady (1989), vol. 14 of *The Yale editions of the private papers of James Boswell*, trade edn (1950–89) • *Catalogue of the papers of James Boswell at Yale University*, ed. M. S. Pottle, C. C. Abbott, and F. A. Pottle, 3 vols. (1993) • F. A. Pottle, *James Boswell: the earlier years, 1740–1769* (1966); repr. (1985) • F. A. Pottle, *The literary career of James Boswell* (1929) • [J. Boswell], 'Memoirs of James Boswell, esq.', *European Magazine* (May–June 1791) • [J. Boswell], 'On the profession of a player', *London Magazine* (Aug–Oct 1770) • *The correspondence of James Boswell with David Garrick, Edmund Burke, and Edmond Malone*, ed. G. M. Kahrl and others (1986), vol. 4 of *The Yale editions of the private papers of James Boswell*, research edn (1966–) • Boswell, *Life* • *Boswelliana, the commonplace book of James Boswell*, ed. C. Rogers (1874) • *The Hypochondriack: being the seventy essays by the celebrated biographer James Boswell, appearing in the London Magazine from November 1777 to August 1783*, ed. M. Bailey, 2 vols. (1928) • F. Brady, *James Boswell: the later years, 1769–1795* (1984) • F. Brady, *Boswell's political career* (1965) • *The correspondence of James Boswell with James Bruce and Andrew Gibb, overseers of the Auchinleck estate*, ed. N. P. Hankins and J. Strawhorn (1998), vol. 8 of *The Yale editions of the private papers of James Boswell*, research edn (1966–) • J. Boswell, 'Register of letters', Yale M 255 • *The correspondence and other papers of James Boswell relating to the making of the 'Life of Johnson'*, ed. M. Waingrow, rev. edn (2001) • *The journals and letters of Fanny Burney (Madame D'Arblay)*, ed. J. Hemlow and others, 12 vols. (1972–84), vol. 1 • W. Ober, *'Boswell's clap' and other essays* (1979) • D. Buchanan, *The treasure of Auchinleck: the story of the Boswell papers* (1974) • F. A. Pottle, *Pride and negligence: the history of the Boswell papers* (1982)

Archives NL Scot., legal consultation book • NL Scot., library catalogue • NL Scot., observations on Scottish election laws • priv. coll. • Sheff. Arch., letters to Edmund Burke • Signet Library, Edinburgh • Yale U., Beinecke L., journals, corresp., and papers | BL, letters to William Julius Mickle, RP248(i) [copies] • BL, letters to John Wilkes, Add. MS 30877 • Morgan L., letters to William Temple • NA Scot., letters to Sir Alexander Dick of Prestonfield • NL

Scot., letters to Sir David Dalrymple • NL Scot., letters to Sir William Forbes • NL Scot., letters to Lord Hailes • NRA, priv. coll., letters to the Hon. Andrew Erskine

Likenesses G. Willison, oils, 1765, Scot. NPG • D. Allen, group portrait, etching, 1783, Scot. NPG • J. Reynolds, oils, 1785, NPG [*see illus.*] • T. Rowlandson, etching, 1786 (after S. Collings), V&A • G. Langton, pen and wash drawing, *c.*1790, Gunby Hall, Lincolnshire • T. Lawrence, pencil sketch, *c.*1790–1795, Yale U., Beinecke L., Denham album • T. Lawrence, pencil sketches, *c.*1790–1795, NPG • G. Dance, pencil, crayon, and wash drawing, 1793, NPG • D. G. Thompson, stipple and line engraving, pubd 1851 (after J. E. Doyle), NPG • H. W. Bunbury, chalk drawing (with Dr Johnson), V&A • H. W. Bunbury, pencil drawings (with Dr Johnson), V&A; repro. in J. Boswell, *The journal of a tour to the Hebrides* (1785) • H. Singleton, group portrait, oils (with his family), Scot. NPG • W. S. Watson, group portrait, oils (*The inauguration of Robert Burns as poet laureate of the Lodge Canongate, Kilwinning, 1787*), Scot. NPG

Wealth at death debts approx. £9000: *Correspondence of James Boswell*, ed. Hankins and Strawhorn, 'Introduction', xlii

Boswell, James (1778–1822), barrister and literary scholar, was born on 15 September 1778 at James's Court, Edinburgh. He was the fourth child and second surviving son of James *Boswell (1740–1795) of Auchinleck, advocate, diarist, and biographer of Samuel Johnson, and his wife, Margaret [*see* Boswell, Margaret Montgomerie (1738?–1789)], daughter of David Montgomerie, originally Laing (*d.* 1752), of Lainshaw, Ayrshire, and his wife, Veronica Boswell (sister of Alexander Boswell, Lord Auchinleck). After the family's move to London in 1786, his father, eager for him to have an English education and intending him for the bar, enrolled him in an academy in Soho Square kept by Dr William Barrow, later archdeacon of Nottingham, and sent him to Westminster School in 1790. The elder Boswell's diaries and letters, in which the younger Boswell appears as Jamie, testify to a deep reciprocated affection between father and son, who as a boy consoled his father in his frequent despondencies and frustrations and urged him to take pride in his literary achievements and eminent social circle. He attended his father on his deathbed, and the last letter from the biographer to his closest friend, William Johnson Temple, was dictated to his son.

Raised in his father's circles of friendship, the younger Boswell showed literary aptitudes early, and among his surviving juvenilia are numerous unpublished plays, squibs, poems, and comic operas—including 'The siege of Carthage', in five acts, written when he was ten. His adult correspondence shows continuing cordiality with such figures as the Corsican general Pasquale Paoli, John Courtenay MP, Bennet Langton, his father's publisher Charles Dilly, and in particular Edmond Malone, who became a guardian, mentor, and virtually a second father. Malone wrote of him in 1796, 'He grows every day very like his father, but will not have his vivacity or wit; on the other hand he will be more studious and more steady' (Buchanan, 8). The elder Boswell, in a codicil to his will, had given Malone charge of the *Life of Johnson* (first published 1791), to which Malone, with help from the younger Boswell, added new material and brought out its third (1799), fourth (1804), fifth (1807), and sixth (1811) editions. He went to Brasenose College, Oxford, in 1797, and was admitted to the Inner Temple in January 1799. While still a student at Brasenose, he contributed notes to the third edition and further notes to the sixth, the entire text of which he read and corrected. He was awarded the degrees of BA (1801), and MA (1806), and was made a Vinerian fellow in 1812. He was called to the bar of the Inner Temple in 1805, acted as counsel on the home circuit and Surrey sessions, and was appointed a commissioner of bankrupts, but chose also to pursue his scholarly interests, largely under Malone's direction. His father's executors entrusted to him the decision as to whether the biographer's mass of private papers warranted publication, and when he came of age, he concurred with the executors' general opinion that it did not; the appearance in print of the elder Boswell's journals had to await the twentieth-century rediscoveries at Malahide and Fettercairn.

Boswell joined the Albemarle Street circle of the publisher John Murray, and was elected a member of the Roxburghe Club at its first anniversary dinner in 1813. He wrote a memoir of Malone for the *Gentleman's Magazine* of June 1813, which he reprinted the next year for private circulation. Malone had assigned him work in collecting materials for his vast revised edition of Shakespeare, which at Malone's request Boswell completed and brought out in twenty-one volumes in 1821, nine years after Malone's death. For this edition, commonly referred to as Boswell–Malone or the 'third variorum', Boswell contributed notes, a long preliminary advertisement, and a 'glossarial index', and reprinted his memoir of Malone. The second volume contained Malone's important biography of Shakespeare, assembled by Boswell from materials left in fragmentary form at the time of the editor's death. 'That Malone's life of Shakespeare is available to us in any form we owe to Boswell. He coped heroically with an impossible task' (Schoenbaum, 176).

Boswell died suddenly on 24 February 1822, after a short illness described in a letter by his uncle as an 'inflammatory sore throat', in his rooms at 3 Garden Court, Middle Temple (T. D. Boswell to William Boswell, 25 Feb 1822, Boswell MS C542.7). He had never married. His brother, Sir Alexander *Boswell, travelled to London to settle his affairs, only a short time before his own death from a gunshot wound in a duel, after which in Sir Alexander's pocket book was found his poem to James's memory which concluded, 'He never lost one friend, nor found one foe'.

The Boswell–Malone edition of Shakespeare, reprinting significant earlier prefaces and judiciously selecting material for its annotation from editions as early as Pope's, with substantial new contributions from Malone and a wide network of friends and informants, marked a notable advance in the development of the modern comprehensive variorum edition, and is cited in twentieth-century editions as an authoritative summation of eighteenth-century Shakespearian editing.

Gordon Turnbull

Sources *Boswell, laird of Auchinleck, 1778–1782*, ed. J. W. Reed and F. A. Pottle (1977), repr. (1993), vol. 11 of *The Yale editions of the private papers of James Boswell*, trade edn (1950–89), 16–17 [and passim] •

F. A. Pottle, *Pride and negligence: the history of the Boswell papers* (1982) · Foster, *Alum. Oxon.* · D. Buchanan, *The treasure at Auchinleck: the story of the Boswell papers* (1974), 8–9 · *The correspondence of James Boswell with David Garrick, Edmund Burke, and Edmond Malone*, ed. G. M. Kahrl and others (1986), vol. 4 of *The Yale editions of the private papers of James Boswell*, research edn (1966–), 185 · *Boswell: the applause of the jury, 1782–1785*, ed. I. S. Lustig and F. A. Pottle (1981), vol. 12 of *The Yale editions of the private papers of James Boswell*, trade edn (1950–89) · *Boswell: the English experiment, 1785–1789*, ed. I. S. Lustig and F. A. Pottle (1986), vol. 13 of *The Yale editions of the private papers of James Boswell*, trade edn (1950–89) · *Boswell: the great biographer, 1789–1795*, ed. M. K. Danziger and F. Brady (1989), vol. 14 of *The Yale editions of the private papers of James Boswell*, trade edn (1950–89) · F. Brady, *James Boswell: the later years, 1769–1795* (1984) · records of the Honourable Society of the Inner Temple; law lists, Inner Temple, London · *The plays and poems of William Shakespeare: comprehending a life of the poet, and an enlarged history of the stage*, ed. J. Boswell and others, 21 vols. (1821) · T. D. Boswell to W. Boswell, 25 Feb 1822, Yale U., Beinecke L., Boswell MS C542.7 · S. Schoenbaum, *Shakespeare's lives* (1991)

Archives Bodl. Oxf., letters to Richard Heber · NL Scot., letters to Sir William Forbes · Yale U., Beinecke L., corresp. with James Boswell the elder

Likenesses H. Singleton, group portrait, oils, Scot. NPG

Boswell, James Edward Buchanan (1906–1971), painter and socialist, was born on 9 June 1906 in Westport, New Zealand. His father, Edward Blair Buchanan Boswell (1860–1933), who was born in Stewarton, Scotland, was deputy headmaster of the local high school, an artistic dilettante and amateur watercolourist; his mother, Ida Fair (1876–1956), was born in Charleston, New Zealand, the daughter of a local Irish draper. He was educated in Auckland, New Zealand, at grammar school (1917–24), and then at the Elam School of Art (1924–5). His second-hand enthusiasm for developments in European art apparently convinced his mother that he should study in Britain, and in 1925 he arrived in London with his mother and sisters. From 1925 until 1929 Boswell studied painting at the Royal College of Art, where by his own account his work and views conflicted with the institution's generally anti-modern stance. However, although he was twice dismissed (1926 and 1929) from the college's painting school, his work was accepted by the London Group, with whom he exhibited intermittently from 1927 to 1932 and from 1952 to 1958. When Boswell joined the Communist Party in 1932 he ceased oil painting in favour of illustration. Eight early diminutive lithographs comprising *The Fall of London* (1933; British Museum, London) are archetypes for many later social subjects, real and imaginary. He first rose to prominence as a determinedly socialist artist during the 1930s, when few of his contemporaries equalled his left-wing commitment, and fewer could boast such a hard-hitting body of exhibited and published material in text and image.

In 1933 Boswell, Pearl Binder, James Fitton, and others founded the Artists' International Association (AIA; originally the International Organization of Artists for Revolutionary Proletarian Art), an important, English Marxist artistic pressure group, energetically anti-fascist, and most prominent during the 1930s and 1940s. With William Hogarth as a role model, Fitton taught Boswell how to make satirical prints with social subjects, and these,

James Edward Buchanan Boswell (1906–1971), self-portrait, 1950

with other, mixed-media images, gained him a wider audience when they appeared in the *Left Review* (launched in 1934) and in the *Daily Worker*, for which he used the signature Buchan. As its art editor, Boswell's illustrations for the *Left Review* appeared regularly in the magazine until 1938 as one of 'the three Jameses' (James Holland and James Fitton were the other two) but were not always fully appreciated for their apparently anti-German stance. The point is debatable. Boswell's attractively pugnacious style as an illustrator and cartoonist owes much to the German realist artists George Grosz and Otto Dix and to British artist/illustrators such as Edward Ardizzone; it certainly influenced contemporaries like Fitton and many younger artist/illustrators, including Ronald Searle and Paul Hogarth. However, work for the *Left Review* was unpaid. Boswell married Elizabeth (Betty) Soars, an artist, probably in 1933; they had one daughter, Sarah. To offset penury, in 1936 Boswell became art director of the publicity department of the Asiatic (later Shell) Petroleum Company by day, and continued with his socialist activities after hours. During the period of the Spanish Civil War (1936–9) he exhibited almost continuously with the AIA in anti-war and anti-fascist exhibitions.

After the Second World War was declared, Boswell remained with Shell. In 1941 he was called up, left his home in Parliament Hill, London, and by October was garrisoned in Scotland, a private—and a fully trained radiographer—in the Royal Army Medical Corps. At this time Boswell was in contact with the War Artists' Advisory Committee; they bought some work, took a real interest in his activities, but did not formally commission him. By late spring 1942 he was in Iraq, where he remained for most of 1943. His sketchbooks (Tate collection and Imperial War Museum, London) contain harsh, sometimes re-worked images of army life in the ranks, with annotations, many of them later transformed into fully worked-up watercolours of army life in Scotland and Iraq (Tate collection, Victoria and Albert Museum, and Imperial War Museum): in all, atmosphere, boredom and solitude are magnificently evoked, and eloquently testify to Boswell's real ability and stature as a painter.

Following demobilization and a year as chairman of the AIA, Boswell returned to Shell in 1946. He left them in 1947, allowed his Communist Party membership to lapse (but kept his socialism), became art editor of *Lilliput* magazine (a post he held until 1950), and published *The Artist's Dilemma*, a personal and detailed analysis of the place of art in society. In 1951, after some time with Basil Spence as a Festival of Britain muralist, Boswell joined J. Sainsbury & Co., to edit their house journal. Staying long enough to write the company's centenary history in 1969, Boswell somehow found time to design the entire Labour Party publicity campaign for the general election of 1964. In the post-war period, he also illustrated fourteen books, for authors as diverse as John Pudney, Wolf Mankowitz, and Compton Mackenzie.

In 1950 Boswell resumed painting in traditional and experimental media, and was particularly impressed with New York school painting after its first exhibition at the Tate Gallery (1956). Following a separation from his wife in 1966, Boswell lived with Ruth Abel, who changed her name to Boswell by deed poll in October 1967 and who outlived him. Until his death he exhibited regularly in Britain, at the Royal Academy and elsewhere, and travelled widely in Europe and the UK until 1969. In 1967 he contracted cancer, and fought the disease, ultimately to no avail: his last major work, the mural *The Golden Day* (1971; design Victoria and Albert Museum, London), for BP House in Wellington, New Zealand, was executed between three-weekly chemotherapy treatments. Boswell died in London on 15 April 1971, and was cremated at St Marylebone crematorium on 22 April. Boswell's career is unjustly neglected: in his lifetime he was widely respected for a combination of dynamic personality, intelligence, and artistic integrity. JULIAN FREEMAN

Sources J. Saville, 'Boswell, James Edward Buchanan', *DLB*, vol. 3 • H. Roth, 'James Boswell: a New Zealand artist in London', *Auckland City Art Gallery Quarterly*, 65 (Dec 1977) • *James Boswell, 1906–71: drawings, illustrations and paintings* (1976) [exhibition catalogue, U. Nott. Art Gallery, 22 Nov – 16 Dec 1976] • Tate collection, TGA 8224 • IWM, Second World War artists archive, GP/55/240 • MSS, typescripts, cuttings, reproductive visual records, BM, department of prints and drawings • MSS, typescripts, cuttings, reproductive visual records, V&A, department of prints and drawings • J. Boswell, *The artist's dilemma* (1947) • NL NZ, Turnbull L. • L. Morris and R. Radford, eds., *The story of the AIA, 1933–53* (1983) • R. Garton, ed., *British printmakers, 1855–1955* (1992) • *The modern British artist as printmaker*, Austin/Desmond Fine Art Ltd, 3 (1988)

Archives BM, MSS • NL NZ, Turnbull L., MSS • Tate collection, sketches, corresp., and papers; sketchbooks and loose drawings • V&A, department of prints and drawings, MSS | IWM, Second World War artists archive, MSS, GP/55/240

Likenesses J. E. B. Boswell, self-portrait, drawing, 1950, Tate collection [*see illus.*] • photographs, repro. in Morris and Radford, eds., *Story of the AIA* • photographs, repro. in *James Boswell, 1906–71*

Wealth at death £14,293: probate, 6 Sept 1971, *CGPLA Eng. & Wales*

Boswell [Bozwel], **John** (1698–1757), author and Church of England clergyman, the son of John Boswell or Bozwel, of Puddletown, Dorset, was descended from a Gloucestershire family, and was born at Dorchester on 23 January 1698. After attending the school at Abbey Milton under the Revd George Marsh, he matriculated at Brasenose College, Oxford, in 1715, but migrated to Balliol, where he proceeded BA in 1720. Before taking his bachelor's degree he acted as tutor to Lord Kinnaird. He was ordained deacon at Oxford and priest at Wells, and in 1727 was presented to the vicarage of St Mary Magdalene, Taunton. He was also, from 1736, prebendary of Wells Cathedral. He proceeded MA at King's College, Cambridge, in 1732.

Boswell's published works reveal him as a vehement tory high-churchman. *A Method of Study* (2 vols., 1738–43), written 'to assist the poor Clergyman in his studies, and to encourage the young Gentleman to look into books' (1.iii), commended the influential *Reflections upon Learning* (1699) by the nonjuror Thomas Baker and reflected severely upon Paul de Rapin's whiggish *History of England* (1726). When John Jones, vicar of Alconbury, revived debate about changes to the Church of England liturgy in 1749, Boswell responded immediately. *Remarks upon a treatise, intituled Free and candid disquisitions relating to the Church of England* was a substantial work which appeared in two parts, in 1750 and 1751. In language that frequently recalled the 'church in danger' alarms of the Queen Anne period, Boswell rejected arguments for change, contending that the existing prayer book embodied the excellence of primitive liturgical practice and guarded against the puritan impulses that had produced 'the dreadful Scene of Misery, which we suffer'd in the last Century' (*Remarks*, 1.75). For similar reasons he justified the restrictions on private conscience imposed by the Test Act, defended the practice of demanding subscription to the Thirty-Nine Articles from all clergy, and argued for continuing the frequent public recitation of the Athanasian creed. Like many other high-churchmen of his time, Boswell was devoted to the memory of Charles I. His two-volume study, *The Case of the Royal Martyr Considered with Candour*, published posthumously in 1758, provides a remarkable example of the enduring vigour of old high-tory instincts. This book was provoked by two works. The first, *A Letter to a Clergyman Relating to his Sermon on 30 January*, was written by George Coade, a wool-stapler of Exeter, and published in 1746; the second, Thomas Birch's *Enquiry*, appeared in 1747. Boswell's volumes, which drew heavily from the *Life of James, Duke of Ormonde* (1736) by Thomas Carte, the Jacobite historian, provided detailed refutation of old whig claims that Charles I was a tyrant whose disregard for the welfare of his subjects had been demonstrated supremely during the earl of Glamorgan's negotiations with the Irish Catholics in 1645.

Boswell, who never married, died in June 1757. There is a Latin inscription to his memory in the church of St Mary Magdalene, Taunton, where he was buried.

RICHARD SHARP

Sources Foster, *Alum. Oxon.* • Venn, *Alum. Cant.* • Nichols, *Lit. anecdotes*, 2.507 • *DNB*

Boswell, John James (1835–1908), army officer, was born at Edinburgh on 27 September 1835, the son of Dr John James Boswell of the East India Company's Bengal medical service and his wife, Anna Mary, daughter of Andrew Moffat Wellwood. He was educated at the West Academy, Jedburgh, and at Edinburgh Academy. He entered the Bengal army as ensign on 10 August 1852, became lieutenant on 23 November 1856, and joined the 3rd Punjab infantry on field service in the Miranzai valley in December 1856.

In June 1857, on the outbreak of the Indian mutiny, Boswell went in command of a detachment of the 3rd and 6th Punjab infantry to join the column under John Nicholson at Amritsar. Accompanying the column on its forced march of 44 miles to Gurdaspur, he commanded the native infantry in the actions with Sialkot mutineers on 12 and 16 July at Trimmu Ghat. With his regiment he joined General Sir Sydney John Cotton's field force in 1858 in the expedition to Sitana over the Yusufzai border in the north-west to root out a colony of fanatics and rebel sepoys. Promoted captain on 10 August 1864, he took part in the Hazara campaign of 1868, and was engaged with Colonel Keyes's force against the Bisatis in February 1869. He became major on 10 August 1872 and lieutenant-colonel on 10 August 1878.

Throughout the Afghan war of 1878–80 Boswell commanded the 2nd Sikh infantry, and was at the battle of Ahmed Khel (19 April 1880) and mentioned in dispatches. He was also at the engagement at Ursu near Ghazni (23 April) under Sir Donald Stewart. He accompanied Sir Frederick Roberts on the march to Kandahar and was at the battle of Kandahar, being mentioned in dispatches.

Boswell married in 1860 Esther, daughter of John Elliot, solicitor, of Jedburgh. They had no children. He was made CB on 28 February 1881 and colonel on 10 August 1882. He retired as honorary major-general on 1 May 1885 and was appointed JP for Roxburghshire. He died at his residence, Darnlee, Melrose, Roxburghshire, on 9 October 1908, survived by his wife, and was buried at Greyfriars, Edinburgh.

H. M. VIBART, *rev.* JAMES LUNT

Sources *The Times* (10 Oct 1908) • *Hart's Army List* • H. B. Hanna, *The Second Afghan War*, 3 (1910) • S. Cotton, *Nine years on the north-west frontier of India, from 1854–1863* (1868) • Lord Roberts [F. S. Roberts], *Forty-one years in India*, 2 vols. (1897) • J. G. Elliot, *The frontier, 1839–1947* (1968) • B. Robson, *The road to Kabul: the Second Afghan War, 1878–1881* (1986) • *WWW*

Wealth at death £3908 10s. 8*d*.: confirmation, 10 Dec 1908, *CCI*

Boswell, John Thomas Irvine (1822–1888), botanist, was born John Thomas Irvine Boswell Syme at 4 Queen Street, Edinburgh, on 1 December 1822, the son of Patrick *Syme (1774–1845), a flower painter of repute, and Elizabeth, daughter of Claud Irvine *Boswell, Lord Balmuto, and a second cousin of James *Boswell (1740–1795). Both his parents were keen naturalists and gave him every encouragement to collect plants, insects, and shells. After schooling at Dollar Academy, where his father was drawing-master, he was apprenticed to a firm of Edinburgh-based civil engineers and engaged in surveys for construction projects. The work took him to the Scottish west coast, an ideal environment for botanizing and dredging.

In 1849 Syme spent a holiday with relations in the Orkney Islands, and the following winter he read a paper about his finds there to the Botanical Society of Edinburgh. He made such an impression that he was appointed honorary curator of the society's herbarium and, soon after, he applied for the equivalent but paid post with the Botanical Society of London; he owed this appointment to Hewett Cottrell Watson, who was keen to sustain the society's annual exchanges of herbarium specimens. The post was a half-time one, leaving the holder free to augment the low salary with outside work. Young enough to take the risk, Syme saw this as a springboard to greater things and decided to abandon his engineering profession. He served the London society conscientiously, collecting extensively for its herbarium, but growing teaching commitments, entomological activity, and his marriage in 1856 to Susan Hardwick, the daughter of a London solicitor, all diverted his attention. Unbeknown to him, the society's finances had been neglected, forcing it to be wound up and its property sold.

Watson felt some responsibility for Syme's predicament and proposed employing him as editor of a new journal on British botany which he conceived in 1861. Admitting he would have preferred 'a man of more active and suggestive mind', he saw him as having the advantage of offsetting his own waspishness, being 'very unlikely to give offence' (C. C. Babington letters, Cambridge University); indeed, all his life Syme was as unassuming as he was painstaking and earnest. Watson's plans, however, fell through, not least because Syme received an alternative, more solid offer much to his taste, from the publisher Robert Hardwicke who was planning an ostensible 'third' edition of Smith and Sowerby's classic, *English Botany*, retaining Sowerby's much-admired plates but replacing Smith's scientific text with a wholly new and up-to-date one, and adding sections on popular lore, to be contributed by Mrs [Phebe] Lankester. Syme saw this as a chance to produce the first full-scale, properly 'critical' guide to the British flowering plants and ferns since Sir James Edward Smith's *English Flora* of the 1820s. Encouraged by H. C. Watson and W. W. Newbould, who were to give him much hidden help, Syme took on editorship of the work. He drew up the lengthy species descriptions as far as possible from fresh specimens which he himself had collected. These were submitted to his two mentors for approval and finally copied out in his wife's more legible hand. A notable innovation was the wide adoption of the novel category of subspecies.

In 1868, five years after the first of the eleven volumes appeared (a twelfth, by another hand, was added later), Syme inherited, and moved to, the small ancestral estate of his mother's family at Balmuto in Fife; at this time he took the name Boswell-Syme. Since the London herbaria were now no longer available to him for reference, he volunteered to act as curator of the Botanical Exchange Club, conducting an annual postal exchange of herbarium specimens and publishing a report setting out the names given to these by relevant experts. By taking on this office Boswell-Syme was able to keep himself abreast of the latest state of knowledge; he also did a valuable service to British field botany by preserving this spearhead of the study for seven more years. By the time he stepped down, in 1875, the last volume of *English Botany* had been published, to wide acclaim. However, the appeal of the plates led it to be generally referred to as 'Sowerby', leaving Boswell-Syme to be credited with the work only by the *cognoscenti*. Nevertheless it earned him an honorary LLD from St Andrews in 1875 and honorary fellowship from the Botanical Society of Edinburgh nine years later.

In 1875 Boswell-Syme succeeded to the headship of his branch of the Boswell family and dropped the Syme from his name altogether to become 'Dr Boswell'. However, the role was more impressive in name than in substance: the estate at Balmuto, near Kinghorn, was heavily mortgaged, the mineral rights had been surrendered at the original purchase, the garden was largely overgrown, and the house was dilapidated. Friends reckoned he had barely a living income, and certainly he ceased to travel and made only rare appearances as a magistrate. He was overweight, and from 1886 heart disease and two slight attacks of paralysis confined him to his bedroom; he died on 29 January 1888 and was buried two days later at Kinghorn in the Boswell family vault.

Boswell's collection of British Lepidoptera and beetles (long an active subsidiary interest, on which he also published) was auctioned after his death. His widow sought in vain to interest the British Museum and Kew in buying his many thousands of botanical specimens, but the former eventually received the valuable British herbarium as a gift in 1929 from its purchaser, F. J. Hanbury. A genus of Chilean lilies was named *Symea* in his honour by his friend J. G. Baker, but has had to yield priority to Philippi's *Solaria*. D. E. Allen

Sources *Journal of Botany, British and Foreign*, 26 (1888), 82–4 · W. Bowles Barrett, Botanical reminiscences of T. B. Flower, 1882, Weymouth Central Library, 26–36 · *Transactions of the Botanical Society* [Edinburgh], 17 (1887–91), 516–19 · M. Spence, *Flora Orcadensis* (1914), xliii–xlv · D. E. Allen, *The botanists: a history of the Botanical Society of the British Isles through a hundred and fifty years*, St Paul's Bibliographies (1986), chaps. 5–7 · M. F. Conolly, *Biographical dictionary of eminent men of Fife* (1866)

Archives Manchester Museum · NHM

Likenesses oils, priv. coll.? · photograph, repro. in *ILN* (11 Feb 1888), 142

Wealth at death £6004 6*s*. 1*d*.: confirmation, 10 May 1888, *CCI* · £1258 15*s*. 0*d*.: eik additional estate, 7 June 1888, *CCI*

Boswell, Margaret Montgomerie [Peggie] (**1738?–1789**), wife of James Boswell, was born at Lainshaw, Ayrshire, the fourth of five children of David Montgomerie, formerly Laing (*d*. 1752), of co. Down, and Veronica Boswell (*b*. 1704, *d*. before 1753), daughter of James Boswell, seventh laird of Auchinleck, and Lady Elizabeth Bruce. Both parents died when Margaret was young; her inheritance was an annuity of £1000 with an annual income of £100. On 25 November 1769 she married James *Boswell (1740–1795), author, advocate, and her first cousin (the eldest son of Alexander *Boswell, Lord Auchinleck), at Lainshaw. Samuel Johnson and Pasquale Paoli signed the marriage contract in London and were among the notable visitors to the Boswells' home in James's Court, Edinburgh. Two of their seven children died in infancy; their sons Alexander *Boswell (1775–1822), antiquary and poet, and James *Boswell (1778–1822), editor and author, achieved some prominence.

Margaret Montgomerie Boswell (1738?–1789), by unknown artist

In the noble letter accepting Boswell's proposal of marriage, Margaret had written 'My heart determines my choice … wherever you go I shall willingly accompany you and hope to be happy' (Boswell MS C423). In 1786, though she was ill with consumption, she loyally moved family and furniture to 56 Great Queen Street, London, to satisfy her husband's fruitless ambition to practise at the English bar. By 1788 the gravity of her condition forced her return, with three of the children, to Auchinleck, the Ayrshire estate Boswell had inherited in 1782. She died there on the morning of 4 June 1789; Boswell, despite a frantic journey from London, arrived home that evening. Overcome with grief and guilt, he violated custom by attending the funeral on 11 June 1789. Margaret was entombed in the catacombs of the family church at Auchinleck and was moved, with Boswell and their daughter Veronica, to the vault added to the church after 1864.

Margaret Boswell emerged from obscurity through her

husband's biography of Johnson in the eighteenth century and the publication of his journal and other private papers in the twentieth. Her only known portrait, an oil, anonymous and undated, represents a handsome, full-bodied woman—'a heathen goddess', Boswell wrote in June 1769 (Boswell MS L422)—with a heart-shaped face, strong nose, direct gaze, and crown of dark hair.

In mien and manner a gentlewoman (Johnson said), Margaret Boswell was deferential yet spirited. She was nettled but contrite when Boswell charged her with conversing too freely with men. Capable and informed, though not learned, she catalogued the valuable library at Auchinleck in 1783. Perspicacious and outspoken, even tart, she advised Boswell shrewdly, rebuked him for his compulsive licentiousness, and several times 'divorced' him by forswearing conjugal relations, but yielded to his penitence. His long and frequent absences from home burdened her exceptionally with supervision of the children, their education, and even the estate. An 'abbess' at Auchinleck for the six months in 1785 that Boswell prepared *Journal of a Tour to the Hebrides* in London, she longed for an intimate woman friend, yet professed herself content. The *Life of Johnson* is likewise owed in large part to the endurance of Margaret Montgomerie Boswell.

IRMA S. LUSTIG

Sources *Boswell in search of a wife, 1766–1769*, ed. F. Brady and F. A. Pottle (1957), vol. 6 of *The Yale editions of the private papers of James Boswell*, trade edn (1950–89) · *Boswell for the defence, 1769–1774*, ed. W. K. Wimsatt and F. A. Pottle (1960), vol. 7 of *The Yale editions of the private papers of James Boswell*, trade edn (1950–89) · *Boswell's journal of a tour to the Hebrides with Samuel Johnson*, ed. F. A. Pottle and C. H. Bennett (1963), vol. 9 of *The Yale editions of the private papers of James Boswell*, trade edn (1950–89) · *Boswell: the ominous years, 1774–1776*, ed. C. Ryskamp and F. A. Pottle (1963), vol. 8 of *The Yale editions of the private papers of James Boswell*, trade edn (1950–89) · *Boswell in extremes, 1776–1778*, ed. C. M. Weis and F. A. Pottle (1971), vol. 10 of *The Yale editions of the private papers of James Boswell, trade edn* (1950–89) · *Boswell, laird of Auchinleck, 1778–1782*, ed. J. W. Reed and F. A. Pottle (1977), repr. (1993), vol. 11 of *The Yale editions of the private papers of James Boswell*, trade edn (1950–89) · *Boswell: the applause of the jury, 1782–1785*, ed. I. S. Lustig and F. A. Pottle (1982), vol. 12 of *The Yale editions of the private papers of James Boswell*, trade edn (1950–89) · *Boswell: the English experiment, 1785–1789*, ed. I. S. Lustig and F. A. Pottle (1986), vol. 13 of *The Yale editions of the private papers of James Boswell*, trade edn (1950–89) · *Boswell: the great biographer, 1789–1795*, ed. M. K. Danziger and F. Brady (1989), vol. 14 of *The Yale editions of the private papers of James Boswell*, trade edn (1950–89) · *Catalogue of the papers of James Boswell at Yale University*, ed. M. S. Pottle, C. C. Abbott, and F. A. Pottle, 3 vols. (1993), vols. 1–2 [incl. Margaret Boswell's letters] · F. A. Pottle, *James Boswell: the earlier years, 1740–1769* (1966) · F. Brady, *James Boswell: the later years, 1769–1795* (1984) · Boswell, *Life* · I. S. Lustig, '"My dear enemy": Margaret Montgomerie Boswell in the *Life of Johnson*', *Boswell: citizen of the world, man of letters*, ed. I. S. Lustig (1995) · Yale U., Beinecke L., Boswell papers

Archives Fondazione Sella, San Gerolamo, Biella, Italy, letters · Morgan L., letters · NL Scot., letters · Rosenbach Museum and Library, Philadelphia, letters · Yale U., Beinecke L.

Likenesses oils, unknown collection; copyprint, NPG [*see illus.*]

Wealth at death at marriage, only £100 p.a. from £1000 annuity; husband in debt during her lifetime and at her death: Pottle, *James Boswell: the earlier years*; Brady, *James Boswell: the later years*; Brady and Pottle, *Boswell in search of a wife*

Boswell [*married name* Cattle], **Nellie** [Ellen Clara] (**1858/9–1938**), equestrian performer, was born in Paris, one of the three daughters of James Clements Boswell (1826–1859), an acrobatic circus clown, and his wife, Rebecca (1814–1898), the daughter of the circus proprietor Thomas Taplin Cooke. She was first noted with Hengler's circus at Hull in 1874, and continued to appear with Hengler's circuses for almost twenty years. She was famous for her character delineation, on horseback, of a Newhaven fishwife, then a jolly young waterman, and thirdly a highland laddie, or Rob Roy McGregor, when she changed her costumes with great rapidity and danced a hornpipe and a Scottish reel with as much ease as if she were on terra firma. She also performed a scene entitled 'The Daughter of the Regiment' on horseback. In 1876 she was described as

> a good-looking and unpretentious young lady, appropriately clad in a tunic and trousers of crimson silk … Without further delay she was on the broad, flat saddle … soon she was standing, now on one foot, now on the other, in a series of attitudes which, besides exhibiting her complete mastery of the equestrian difficulties of the situation, were eminently graceful in themselves. (*Liverpool Weekly Albion*, 25 Nov 1876)

On 30 October 1878 Boswell married the widowed circus clown Frederick Isaac Cattle, but she continued to perform until 1892. They had three sons and one daughter. She died at her home, 11 Cyprus Grove, Blackpool, on 21 May 1938 at the age of seventy-nine, her husband having predeceased her.

JOHN M. TURNER

Sources *Liverpool Weekly Albion* (25 Nov 1876) · *World's Fair* (10 Dec 1938) · *Illustrated Sporting and Dramatic News* (12 Dec 1874) · *Huddersfield Examiner* (30 March 1876) · *World's Fair* (21 Feb 1925) · m. cert. · d. cert. · census returns, 1901

Boswell, Percy George Hamnall (**1886–1960**), geologist, was born on 7 August 1886 at Woodbridge in Suffolk, the second son of George James Boswell, master printer, of Ipswich, and his wife, Mary Elizabeth Marshall, of Tasmania. Raised in a strict Victorian household on a diet of English grammar and punctuation, Charles Dickens, and the Bible, Boswell soon acquired a disciplined mind and a flair for lucid writing. While at school in Ipswich, his interest in geology was kindled by fossil collecting in the crag and chalk pits and by poring over displays in the local museum. Rather than join the family's printing business, in 1902 he became a pupil teacher, and in 1905 was appointed a science instructor at the technical school at Ipswich.

While still in his teens Boswell became a founder member of the Ipswich and District Field Club, though his early geological pursuits were carried out mostly alone, and often continued far into the night. They led to his election as a fellow of the Geological Society in 1907. However, by then his excessive zeal had already taken its toll; at the age of eighteen he developed choroiditis in both eyes and was virtually blind for several months, his right eye being so irreparably damaged that he never regained stereoscopic vision.

In 1911 Boswell obtained his London BSc (external) and in 1912 he entered Imperial College to study under W. W. Watts, continuing his researches on the Pliocene–Pleistocene succession in East Anglia, the zoning of the chalk, and the interrelation between the culture stages of palaeolithic Britons and successive phases of the last ice age. These investigations led to the Geological Society's bestowal of the Daniel Pidgeon fund in 1914, the Wollaston fund in 1917, and the award of the degree of DSc by the University of London in 1916. In the years preceding the First World War he also undertook researches into stratigraphic correlation. The dearth of fossils in the Tertiary rocks of the London basin prompted Boswell's prescient concept of using their detrital mineral assemblages for correlation purposes. As a result he acquired an unrivalled knowledge of the mineralogy of a wide range of British rocks, specializing in the qualitative and quantitative aspects of sedimentary petrology which were later to prove so helpful in deciphering the palaeogeography, tectonics, and climatic conditions of past epochs. These pioneer investigations were turned to vital use during the war, when as geological adviser to the Ministry of Munitions he discovered much-needed domestic resources of glass-, foundry-, and furnace-sands. However, he reported himself unable to transform east-coast sands into quicksands to sink German invaders. He was appointed OBE in 1918.

In 1917 Boswell was appointed to the newly founded George Herdman chair of geology at Liverpool, where he quickly organized a department with a high reputation for teaching and research. He undertook researches into the Silurian rocks of north Wales, and oversaw student investigations into the volcanic rocks of Snowdonia and the Lake District, the Carboniferous strata of north Wales, and the Triassic and Pleistocene deposits of the Liverpool district. Always interested in the applications of geology to civil engineering, Boswell advised on the planning and construction of the Mersey road tunnel and on the silting of the Mersey estuary, was consultant to various water undertakings, and geological adviser to the Metropolitan Water Board. With his lucid and incisive mind and ability to present evidence clearly, he was a convincing expert witness.

In 1930 Boswell became professor of geology at Imperial College, undertaking the daunting task of reorganizing and co-ordinating the department. He continued his studies of the Silurian rocks of north Wales, published his classic volume *On the Mineralogy of the Sedimentary Rocks* (1933), and visited east Africa to adjudicate on disputed evidence concerning the age of skeletal hominid remains found by Louis Leakey. However, in 1938 he resigned his professorship. He was suffering from bronchitis and asthma, and mistakenly felt that his scientific reputation had suffered from his misinterpretation of Silurian structures, which had been demonstrated by his Cambridge rival, O. T. Jones. The following year he married Hope, daughter of William Blount Dobell, 'adopted daughter' of Sir Basil Mott, and sister of Clifford Dobell. The couple had no children. After retirement, Boswell continued to work until 1953 on the Denbighshire moors, publishing *The Middle Silurian Rocks in North Wales* in 1949. He also continued to work as a consultant in engineering geology. Gravely incapacitated by 1953, he nevertheless continued to write papers on thixotropy and cognate subjects, and a final book of essays on *Muddy Sediments*, which was published posthumously in 1961.

Boswell had a flair for administration and organization. He was secretary (1932–4) and president (1940–41) of the Geological Society of London, from whom he received the Bigsby medal in 1929. He was president of the Liverpool Geological Society from 1921 to 1923, and of the Prehistoric Society in 1936. He was very active in the British Association, serving as general secretary (1931–5), general treasurer (1935–43), and president of the geology section at the 1932 meeting in York. He was elected FRS in 1931 and was honorary member of numerous scientific societies at home and abroad. His many scientific writings were concerned with East Anglian stratigraphy, the geological relationships of palaeolithic humans, the stratigraphy and tectonics of the Silurian rocks of Denbighshire, the economic and engineering applications of geology, and above all the petrology and physical character of sedimentary rocks.

Despite uncertain health, Boswell loved climbing, especially in the Alps, and was a member of the Alpine Club. He was at his best with students when relaxed, walking and climbing on the Welsh mountains while on field courses. Of medium height and somewhat lean features, he had a ready twinkle, was ever friendly and encouraging to amateur and professional geologists alike, and took immense pride in the accomplishments of his students. His recreations were recorded in *Who's Who* as 'letter-writing and raising professors'. After Boswell's death at Ruthin Castle Clinic in Denbighshire on 22 December 1960, his ashes were scattered on the headland of Great Orme. He was survived by his wife.

David Williams, *rev.* Robert M. Shackleton

Sources G. H. Mitchell, *Memoirs FRS*, 7 (1961), 17–30 · *The Times* (23 Dec 1960) · personal knowledge (1960; 2004) · private information (1960) · *CGPLA Eng. & Wales* (1961) · *WW*

Archives ICL, corresp. and papers · U. Lpool L., autobiography, corresp., and papers | Bodl. Oxf., corresp. with J. L. Myres

Likenesses Lafayette Ltd, photograph, 1935, NPG · W. Stoneman, photographs, 1945, NPG · photograph, repro. in *Memoirs FRS*

Wealth at death £10,832 1s. 0d.: probate, 22 Feb 1961, *CGPLA Eng. & Wales*

Boswell, Robert (1746–1804), Glasite preacher, was a descendant of the Auchinleck family in Ayrshire. He received a classical education and became a writer to the signet in Edinburgh. While still young he became a Glasite, or Sandemanian, and was chosen by the church in Edinburgh to be one of their teaching elders. He published *The Book of Psalms, in Metre; from the Original* in 1784. In his preface he explains his intention of producing as literal a translation as possible, based on Benjamin Kennicott's edition of the Hebrew Bible.

Boswell was on a visit to friends in London when he died in a chapel while preaching a sermon on the text 'All flesh is as grass' on Sunday 1 April 1804; this was probably the Sandemanian chapel, near the Barbican, where Michael Faraday later officiated as elder.

J. H. Thorpe, *rev.* Emma Major

Sources J. Holland, *The psalmists of Britain*, 2 vols. (1843) · *ESTC* · *GM*, 1st ser., 74 (1804), 388

Archives U. Edin. L., corresp. and papers | Yale U., Beinecke L., corresp. with James Boswell

Boswell, Sir William (*d.* 1650), diplomat and patron of learning, was born in Suffolk. He matriculated from Jesus College, Cambridge, in 1600, graduating BA in 1604, becoming a fellow in 1606, and proceeding MA in 1607; he was incorporated at Oxford in 1608. In December 1614 he was granted a pass to travel abroad for three years but he remained absent from England for a total of eight despite remaining a fellow of Jesus until 1629. From at least April 1619 to July 1621 Boswell served as chief secretary to the English ambassador in Paris, Edward Herbert, Lord Herbert of Cherbury; Boswell and the poet George Herbert were dedicatees of Herbert's *De veritate* in December 1622.

Following his return to England Boswell became secretary to the new lord keeper, John Williams, bishop of Lincoln, dealing especially with episcopal revenues. On 11 November 1622 he was appointed clerk to the privy council in extraordinary, specializing in military and naval matters. He also served as MP for Boston, Lincolnshire, in 1624 and 1625, and acted as senior proctor for the University of Cambridge in 1624–5, during which time he liaised with Sir Dudley Carleton in an attempt to persuade the Dutch humanist G. P. Vossius to take up a lectureship in history and political science at Cambridge. As secretary, he accompanied James Hay, earl of Carlisle, on two diplomatic missions: to France in 1624, and to Savoy (via Switzerland, Flanders, the Low Countries, and France) from May 1628 to February 1629. Soon after returning he married his cousin Margaret Boswell or Bosvile, a relation of Sir Ralph Bosvile of Eynsford in Kent, described as already 'well advanced in years' (Davies, 25), although probably aged thirty-four; the marriage appears to have been childless. During 1630 Boswell was absorbed by the appeal of his brother Thomas to be made proctor of Cambridge University. On 21 January 1631 Boswell, Inigo Jones, and Patrick Young were charged with the ordering of the king's ancient coins and medals, while on 12 April 1632, with Peter de Liques, he was created receiver-general of revenues from America. His services were also in demand by the privy council as 'a kind of literary intelligence officer' (Rees, lxxiv), employed in the verification of documents, and in seizing and examining the libraries of Sir Robert Cotton, Captain Henry Bell, Denzil Holles, Sir John Eliot, and John Selden.

Boswell's most important appointment came in July 1632, when he succeeded Sir Dudley Carleton as England's resident agent in the United Provinces at The Hague, arriving in September 1632 and remaining until 1650 (excepting visits to England in 1634 and 1640). On 25 July 1633 he was knighted by Lord Vere at Bokstel, in Brabant. Intimately involved in the household of Elizabeth of Bohemia, he was recalled to England to discuss the case of Elizabeth's servant Francis Nethersole in 1634, and in early 1635 travelled to Germany to invest the elector palatine Charles Louis with the Order of the Garter. Boswell was instrumental in the publication of a tract describing a Jesuit plot to incite Scotland to rebel and overthrow Charles I, which was brought to his attention by Andreas ab Habernfeld; Boswell communicated it to Archbishop Laud, and received royal praise for his actions. He was also active in local religious controversy, supporting Prince Maurice and the Gomarists against Oldenbarneveldt and the Arminian remonstrants, although he also collaborated with Vossius, professor of history at the new remonstrant academy in Amsterdam. After civil war broke out in England Walter Strickland was dispatched by Cromwell to ensure the Netherlands' support for the parliamentary party; Boswell, an ardent royalist, used his influence to secure the country's neutrality; he also attempted to raise funds by pawning the queen's jewels, and to induce Dutch supporters to land an army in England.

A respected diplomat, Boswell was also noted as a patron of learning, bibliophile and manuscript collector, and the hub of an impressive continental network of lettered men. He attributed 'all his proficiency in learning, whatever it be, to the goodness' of John Dee's preface to Euclid, (Worthington, *Diary*, 59–60): and was remembered as 'an excellent philosopher and mathematician' (Worthington, preface), but his interests ranged more widely: from Anglo-Saxon and oriental literatures to the latest scientific experiments. One of the early followers of Galileo in England, Boswell counted among his intellectual contacts William Camden, James Ussher, Henry and John Spelman, John Selden, Thomas Lydiat, Theodore Haak, John Pell, Lodewijck Huygens, Robert Cotton, G. P. Vossius, Fabri de Peiresc, Joseph Mede, Pierre Dupuy, Henry Wotton, Samuel Hartlib, John de Laet, Meric Casaubon, and Simonds D'Ewes; only a tiny proportion of his correspondence survives in two volumes in the British Library (Add. MSS 6394, 6395). Boswell was renowned for his manuscript collection, which contained prized and as yet unpublished works by John Dee, William Gilbert, and Francis Bacon, who had appointed him his literary executor; some of these passed after his death to Isaac Gruter, who published them with the Elsevier press in Amsterdam.

By the time of Charles I's execution Boswell was ill; he died at The Hague in May 1650; much of his library apparently disappeared. His widow, Margaret, died in 1682 at the age of eighty-seven, leaving two Sir William Boswell scholarships to Sevenoaks School boys to attend her late husband's college in Cambridge. In Dr John Worthington's words, Boswell was 'a learned man, a great encourager of learning, zealous for the Church of England, faithful in the execution of his embassy, and highly valued by eminent persons' (Worthington, *Diary*, 59–60).

Alan Stewart

Sources G. Davies, 'Life of Sir William Boswell', in T. Raymond, *Autobiography of Thomas Raymond*, ed. G. Davies (1917) · *DNB* · G. Rees, introduction, in *Collected works of Francis Bacon*, ed. J. Spedding, R. L. Ellis, and D. D. Heath, new edn (1996) · N. Tyacke, 'Arminianism and English culture', *Britain and the Netherlands*, ed. A. C. Duke and C. A. Tamse, 7 (1981) · PRO, SP 14 and 16 · *APC*, *1613–14*, *1621–3*, *1625–31* · BL, Add. MSS 6394, 6395 · BL, Sloane MS 3957 · *The life of Edward, first Lord Herbert of Cherbury written by himself*, ed. J. M. Shuttleworth (1976) · Venn, *Alum. Cant.* · Wood, *Ath. Oxon.: Fasti*, new edn · R. Parr, ed., *The life of the most reverend father in God, James Usher … with a collection of three hundred letters* (1686) · F. Bacon, *Opera* *omnia*, ed. J. Blackbourne (1730) • *The diary and correspondence of Dr John Worthington*, ed. J. Crossley and R. C. Christie, 2 vols. in 3, Chetham Society, 13, 36, 114 (1847–86) • J. Worthington, preface, in *The works of … Joseph Mede*, ed. J. Worthington, 4th edn (1677) • Rymer, *Foedera*, 3rd edn • G. M. Bell, *A handlist of British diplomatic representatives, 1509–1688*, Royal Historical Society Guides and Handbooks, 16 (1990) • M. Feingold, 'Galileo in England: the first phrase', *Novità celesti e crisi del sapere* (1983) • W. A. Shaw, *The knights of England*, 2 vols. (1906), vol. 2, p. 201

Archives BL, letters and papers, Add. MSS 6394–6395 • Magd. Cam., corresp.

Bosworth, Joseph (1787/8–1876), Old English scholar, the third son of Thomas Bosworth of Etwall, Derbyshire, was born at Etwall and was baptized there on 1 June 1788. He was educated at Repton grammar school, and then at the University of Aberdeen, where at an early age he took the degree of MA, and subsequently that of LLD. He later became a member of Trinity College, Cambridge. He was ordained deacon in 1814, and priest in 1815. After serving as curate of Bunny in Nottinghamshire, he was in 1817 presented to the vicarage of Little Horwood, in Buckinghamshire, a preferment that he held for twelve years.

In 1821 Bosworth published two educational works entitled *Latin Construing, or, Lessons from Classical Authors* and *An Introduction to Latin Construing*, the former of which went through six and the latter through five editions. In 1823 appeared his *Elements of Anglo-Saxon Grammar*, which was the earliest work of its kind in the English language. It showed no more scientific knowledge of the structure of the language than did the works of Hickes and Lye, from which it was compiled, but it served to awaken among English speakers an interest in the earliest form of their native tongue. In 1826 Bosworth published *A Compendious Grammar of the Primitive English or Anglo-Saxon Language*, an abridgement of the former work, with some improvements. The author had become acquainted with the epoch-making grammar of Rasmus Christian Rask (1787–1832), and was able to correct several of the most important errors of the original *Elements*, though his grasp of the philological discoveries of the Danish scholar was very imperfect.

During his residence at Little Horwood, Bosworth took great interest in proposals for tackling poverty, and published several pamphlets on this subject. In 1829 he became chaplain in the Netherlands, first at Amsterdam and then in 1832 at Rotterdam. In 1831 the degree of PhD was conferred on him by the University of Leiden. He lived in the Netherlands until 1840, and made occasional visits to England. In 1834 he took the degree of BD at Trinity College, Cambridge, and in 1839 that of DD. While in the Netherlands Bosworth wrote his principal work, the *Anglo-Saxon Dictionary* (1838), to which is prefixed 'An essay on the origin of the English, German, and Scandinavian languages and nations' (reprinted separately in 1848) and a sketch of Old English grammar. The latter, which is condensed from Rask and Grimm, is well arranged and in general accurate; but the dictionary itself shows that the author had only a very superficial acquaintance with the new philology. Nevertheless, despite its unscientific character, and its many errors of detail (partly due to the author's lack of access to English public libraries), the work was a great advance on previous dictionaries in English. Bosworth also published while in the Netherlands *The Origin of the Dutch, with a Sketch of their Language and Literature* (1836); *Scandinavian Literature* (1839); and a translation of the Book of Common Prayer into Dutch, the copyright of which he made over to the Society for Promoting Christian Knowledge. In 1840 Bosworth became vicar of Waith in Lincolnshire, and in 1848 he published, under the title of *A Compendious Dictionary of Anglo-Saxon*, an abridgement of his larger work, omitting the references, but supplying many additional words and corrections (reprinted in 1852, 1855, 1859, and 1882). In 1855 he published an English translation of King Alfred's Old English version of *Orosius*, and also a facsimile of part of its two manuscripts, with a literal English translation and notes. In 1857 he was presented to the rectory of Water Shelford, in Buckinghamshire, and was incorporated a member of Christ Church, Oxford. In 1858 he was appointed Rawlinson professor of Anglo-Saxon at Oxford, and in the following year he issued an edition of the Old English text of Alfred's *Orosius*. His only subsequent publication of importance was an edition in parallel columns of the Gothic and Anglo-Saxon gospels, and the versions of Wycliffe and Tyndale.

Bosworth's works realized for him (according to his own statement quoted in *The Academy* of 10 June 1876) the sum of £18,000. In 1867 he gave to the University of Cambridge £10,000 to establish a professorship of Anglo-Saxon.

After being appointed professor, Bosworth resided either at Oxford or at his rectory of Water Shelford. Until a few days before his death, which occurred when he was eighty-eight, at 20 Beaumont Street, Oxford, on 27 May 1876, he was accustomed to work from nine in the morning until six in the evening, principally on the new edition of his larger dictionary, the publication of which had been undertaken by the Clarendon Press. He also left a mass of annotations on the Anglo-Saxon charters. Bosworth was a fellow of the Royal Society, and a member of many learned societies both at home and abroad. He was three times married, but left no children.

After Bosworth's death the Old English dictionary was committed by the delegates of the Clarendon Press to the editorship of Professor T. N. Toller, of Manchester, and the first and second instalments of the new edition appeared in 1882. Unfortunately Bosworth's material, much of which had already been printed, was very far behind current philological knowledge, and the work was received with general dissatisfaction, especially as the long-standing announcement of its appearance had prevented the preparation of any rival dictionary.

HENRY BRADLEY, *rev.* JOHN D. HAIGH

Sources private information (1885) [Professor Earle] • *The Athenaeum* (3 June 1876), 765–6 • H. Sweet, *The Academy* (3 June 1876), 534 • *The Academy* (10 June 1876) • Crockford (1874) • *IGI* • Foster, *Alum. Oxon.* • *The Times* (29 May 1876), 10d • 'Old English', *The Oxford companion to the English language*, ed. T. McArthur • Boase, *Mod. Eng. biog.* • Allibone, *Dict.* • d. cert.

Archives Bodl. Oxf., corresp. and papers | Hunt. L., letters to Charles O'Conor

Likenesses lithograph, NPG
Wealth at death under £14,000: probate, 4 July 1876, *CGPLA Eng. & Wales*

Bosworth, William (*d.* in or before **1651**), poet, is known only for a volume of verse published posthumously in 1651 by R. C. (and reissued two years later). The volume is entitled *The Chast and Lost Lovers Lively Shadowed in the Persons of Arcadius and Sepha*. The text is prefaced by a dedicatory epistle to John Finch and an epistle to the reader by R. C., and by five verses—by L. B., F. L. (Francis Lovelace), E. G. (Edmund Gayton), S. P., and L. C.—which lament Bosworth's early death.

The chief poem of the volume, 'Arcadius and Sepha', is followed by 'Hinc lachrimae, or, The Author to Aurora', verses 'to the immortall memory of the fairest and most vertuous Lady, the Lady—', and 'to his dear Friend, Mr John Emely, upon his Travells'. In the epistle to the reader R. C. states that Bosworth studied to imitate Ovid, Marlowe (from whose mythological poetry Bosworth takes 'the strength of his fancy, and the shadowing of his wit', Sidney, and Spenser. In his dedication R. C. declares that Bosworth was only nineteen when he wrote the work and that 'had he lived, [he] might have been as well the Wonder as the Delight of the Arts, and been advanced by them amongst the highest in the Temple of Fame'.

An engraving dated 1637, by G. Glover of a young man aged thirty, was identified by Francis Allison in 1811 as a likeness of Bosworth (*GM*, 1st ser., 81/2 1811, 124–5). He wrote that the poet was born in 1607 into an ancient and illustrious family of Boxworth, Cambridgeshire. These facts became standard in accounts of Bosworth's life throughout the nineteenth century but the emphasis in the 1651 volume on the poet's nineteen years and early death makes a birth date of 1607 unlikely.

ELERI LARKUM

Sources J. A. Riddell, 'The life of William Bosworth', *Huntington Library Quarterly*, 49 (1986), 165–74 • *DNB*

Boteler, Edward (*d.* **1670**), Church of England clergyman, was born at Barnwell St Andrews, Northamptonshire, and was probably the son of Noel Boteler, gentleman, and thus brother of William *Boteler. He attended Oundle School in 1627 and matriculated from Magdalene College, Cambridge, in 1635. He graduated BA in 1638 and proceeded MA in 1642. He was ordained deacon in 1641 and priest in 1646. He became a fellow of Magdalene, but on 8 April 1644 he was ejected from his fellowship by the parliamentary visitors. He must have been married by 1655 or 1656, when his son Noel was born. Before 1658 Boteler became rector of Winteringham, Lincolnshire. In that year he preached a funeral sermon for the second earl of Mulgrave, published the following year as *The Worthy of Ephratah*. In 1660 he petitioned the crown, apparently successfully, for presentation to the rectory of Titchmarsh, Northamptonshire, which he claimed he had been given by the patron, the earl of Manchester.

Boteler was a strong, though not an active, royalist. On the return of Charles II he preached a sermon of rejoicing in Lincoln Cathedral, and a similar one at Hull on the occasion of the coronation. He was made one of the king's chaplains. On 29 September 1665 he was installed in the prebend of Southscarle, in Lincoln Cathedral; this he exchanged on 12 October 1668 for the prebend of Leicester St Margaret's, also in Lincoln. He died in 1670.

ALEXANDER GORDON, *rev.* SARAH E. TROMBLEY

Sources Venn, *Alum. Cant.*, 1/1 • J. Walker, *The sufferings of the clergy during the Great Rebellion*, ed. [W. E. Flaherty] (1862) • *Calamy rev.* • *CSP dom.*, 1660–61, 438 • *Fasti Angl.* (Hardy)
Archives Lincs. Arch., historical and heraldic notebook used by him and others

Boteler, Lady Eleanor (*d.* **1468**). *See under* Talbot, John, first earl of Shrewsbury and first earl of Waterford (*c.*1387–1453).

Boteler, Nathaniel. *See* Butler, Nathaniel (*b.* 1577, *d.* in or after 1643).

Boteler, Ralph, first Baron Sudeley (*c.***1394–1473**), soldier and administrator, was the youngest surviving son of Thomas Boteler of Sudeley, Gloucestershire, and Alice (*d.* 1443), daughter of Sir John Beauchamp of Powick, Worcestershire. He was probably born in or about 1394. Thomas Boteler died in 1398, and Ralph became his father's heir only after the deaths without heirs of his elder brothers, John (*d.* 1410) and William (*d.* 1417). Meanwhile, Ralph's long-lived mother in 1406 married Sir John Dalyngrigg of Bodiam, Kent, holding in dower the manors of Sudeley (the Boteler family seat in Gloucestershire), Dassett, and Grift.

Boteler came into his estate and adulthood during Henry V's French wars, and is recorded in 1418 as a knight intending to cross to France. The first stages of his career are obscure, but he soon won recognition for his military and administrative skills. In the English force that landed at Harfleur in May 1420 Boteler captained a company of twenty men-at-arms and sixty archers. He was back in England early in 1421, but returned to France, and in the accounting year of 1421/22 was paid as captain of the royal garrisons of Eu, Monceaux, and Guillemcourt on the frontiers of English conquest. He took part in the military campaigns led by John, duke of Bedford (*d.* 1435), following the death in 1422 of Henry V, and by 1423 was *bailli* of Caux, and was engaged as leader in the siege of Le Crotoy (finally taken in March 1424), becoming captain of that town and of Arques. Also in 1423 Boteler became a councillor to the infant Henry VI, while his mother, Dame Alice, became the king's governess. Alice remained in the king's household throughout his minority. It is uncertain whether Boteler fought in the English victory at Verneuil in 1424, though he was certainly then still serving in France. Boteler may have visited England in 1425 with Bedford, the king's regent in France, and he was certainly in England in 1426, but by early 1427 he was back in France as captain of Le Crotoy. Between late 1428 and early 1429 he was captain of the Bastille in Paris.

Boteler was made a chamber knight of the king (a knight of the body) on 16 February 1430, replacing his recently deceased kinsman Sir Walter Beauchamp, and was part of Henry's bodyguard at his coronation in Notre Dame, Paris, on 16 December 1431. Boteler became chief butler of the royal household on 28 January 1435. By this time he had clearly shifted his ambitions from the French war to the opportunities presented by service in the royal household. He did not, however, entirely lose touch with the war effort. In 1442 he went on a diplomatic mission to the duke of Orléans, as the English government sought for peace with France, and he was engaged in French diplomacy again in 1445, in an effort to extend the truce of Tours (1444) beyond its expiry date of April 1446. He was captain of Calais Castle in 1450–52, and was sent to Calais in 1451 to do what he might for the security of the city.

On 18 July 1433 Boteler became constable and steward of Kenilworth Castle (part of the duchy of Lancaster); the joint appointment became a life tenure on 5 April 1437. He was constable of Kenilworth when Eleanor Cobham was a prisoner there between 1443 and 1446, and took part in the arrest in 1447 of Eleanor's husband, Duke Humphrey of Gloucester. On 27 June 1436 Boteler became constable of Conwy Castle in Wales (which he remained until 1461), and on 14 March in the following year he was named chamberlain of south Wales (an office he held as an absentee for less than two years). He received the usual marks of royal favour, like wardships and offices, was named a justice of the peace, and became a feoffee of duchy of Lancaster estates. As his wealth increased, Boteler rebuilt Sudeley Castle in Gloucestershire, of which little remains, and he built a surviving chapel near the castle where Queen Katherine Parr is buried.

Boteler had been made a Garter knight by April 1440, and on 6 June 1441 he became chamberlain of the king's household (a post he held until 1 April 1447). Three months later, on 10 September 1441, he was created Baron Sudeley by a royal letter patent which was authorized by parliament. He was the first peer to be created by Henry VI. He could have been Lord Sudeley by prescription and inheritance rather than by royal act, for his ancestors were lords of the barony of Sudeley, and John Sudeley had been summoned individually to parliaments in the reigns of Edward I and Edward II, but honouring Boteler as a baron by patent may have been prompted by his mother's still being possessed of the manor of Sudeley, the *caput* of the barony.

On 7 July 1443 Sudeley became treasurer of England, in succession to Ralph, Lord Cromwell, holding that office until December 1446. By this time he had become a close associate of the earl of Suffolk, whom he replaced as steward of the royal household on 3 February 1447. He protested when Suffolk fell from power in 1450, but remained steward until 20 July 1457, even during the first protectorate of the duke of York, Suffolk's bitter rival—no doubt it helped that Sudeley had served with York in France. Sudeley did, however, stand with the king against York at the first battle of St Albans in 1455. After the accession of Edward IV in 1461 Sudeley fell out of national politics, though he attended Edward's first parliament, and remained a JP. He did support the readeption of Henry VI in 1470–71, and his arrest was ordered when Edward recovered the throne, but when he died on 2 May 1473 he was in full possession of his estates. He left no will.

Sudeley married twice. About 1418 he married commercial wealth, in the person of Elizabeth, widow of John Hende (*d.* 1418), late mayor of London. She died in 1462, and in the following year he married Alice (*d.* 1474), daughter of John, Lord Deincourt, and widow of William, Lord Lovel of Titchmarsh, who survived him. Sudeley left no surviving male heir from either marriage, for his son Thomas predeceased him, also without a male heir. Thomas's widow Eleanor was the Lady Eleanor Butler whose alleged precontract of marriage to Edward IV was claimed to have invalidated Edward's marriage to Elizabeth Woodville, and so legitimized the usurpation of Richard III. A. C. Reeves

Sources GEC, *Peerage*, new edn, 12/1.418–22 • J. Ferguson, *English diplomacy, 1422–1461* (1972) • R. A. Griffiths and R. S. Thomas, *The principality of Wales in the later middle ages: the structure and personnel of government*, 1: *South Wales, 1277–1536* (1972) • R. A. Griffiths, *The reign of King Henry VI: the exercise of royal authority, 1422–1461* (1981) • M. C. S. Hanbury-Tracy, 'Medieval Sudeley: the Sudeleys and Botelers of Sudeley Castle', *Family history*, 10 (1977), 9–20 • R. Kretschmer, 'Ralph Butler, Lord Sudeley', BA diss., University of Keele, 1973 • R. A. Newhall, *The English conquest of Normandy, 1416–1424: a study in fifteenth-century warfare* (1924) • H. Nicolas, *The historic peerage of England*, rev. edn (1857) • J. E. Powell and K. Wallis, *The House of Lords in the middle ages* (1968) • R. Somerville, *History of the duchy of Lancaster, 1265–1603* (1953) • G. L. Thompson, *Paris and its people under English rule: the Anglo-Burgundian regime, 1420–1436* (1991) • 13 Edward IV, no.58, PRO, C140

Boteler [Butler], **William** (*fl.* **1645–1670**), parliamentarian army officer and major-general, was the son of Noel (or Neville) Boteler of Barnwell in Northamptonshire; the Anglican clergyman Edward *Boteler was probably his brother. There is little information about his early life but he reputedly attended Oundle School, Northamptonshire. At some point before 1646 he married Elizabeth Brooke of Great Oakley, Northamptonshire.

Boteler rose to the rank of captain of a troop of horse in a local regiment during the first civil war. Over the next few years he was active in, first, local and soon national military affairs: in the summer of 1648 he was a leader of the forces which suppressed a royalist rising in Northamptonshire and the following spring he was active both in maintaining order in the county and in the capture of the Leveller mutineer William Thompson. He acquired a residence in Oundle and land in Derbyshire. Clearly he was on the way up economically.

Boteler's concern for religion was shown by service on the commissions for the propagation of the gospel in Wales (where he became a JP) and by his part in petitions for toleration, which no doubt reinforced contacts with Oliver Cromwell. He had spoken up for religious freedom at the Whitehall debates in January 1649: acutely aware 'that for the most parte truth and light go under the name of errour and heresy', he feared that the state-funded religious teachers proposed in the second *Agreement of the People* would 'raile against us in every pulpitt; and make itt their worke nott to discover truth and preach sound doctrine, butt to raile against honest men' (*Clarke Papers*, 2.173). In 1652, in similar vein, he presented a paper to his fellow-commissioners for the propagation of the gospel in Wales which asked whether it was not God's pleasure that the judgment and condemnation of false teachers and heretics be left to himself [God] alone and whether for civil powers to judge in matters of religion was not against the liberties granted by Christ to his people. An Independent congregation met at his house in Oundle.

Between 1655 and 1657 Boteler was major-general for Northamptonshire, Bedfordshire, and Huntingdonshire. This was a remarkable appointment for one who had so far never commanded a regiment—he was by now major in James Berry's regiment of horse—though he had been engaged in local administration in his home county as JP and judge for the relief of poor prisoners over the preceding years and had recently earned praise for his success in quelling discontent and negotiating civil–military tensions in Bristol in the winter of 1654–5. Boteler was certainly among the most assiduous of the major-generals. He was particularly harsh on Catholics, on Quakers (to George Fox, Boteler was 'a cruel persecutor' and 'a shame to Christianity and religion'), and on vagrants and the disorderly: all of these groups he seems to have lumped together (Durston, 46). Boteler was noted, too, for vigorous, even violent, implementation of the decimation tax upon royalists. He showed little regard for their social sensibilities, gaoling James Compton, third earl of Northampton, when the latter refused to enter into a security bond with no time limitation, and releasing him only when directly ordered to do so by the council of state. According to one royalist account, Boteler had 'carried himself insolently to a royalist of quality, calling him "Sirrah" and telling him he would make him proclayme Charles Steward … a traytor or eate his sworde' (ibid.). He purged Bedford corporation, justifying the legally dubious ends that he had employed by pointing to the consequent strengthening of the position of the godly party in the town; he later managed to restrict the borough franchise and got himself and four allies placed on the aldermanic bench.

Elected for Northamptonshire to the second protectorate parliament (1656–8), Boteler was prominent in the debates over the alleged 'horrid blasphemy' of the Quaker James Nayler, revealing thereby, as in his actions against Friends as major-general, the limitations of his own toleration. His ears tingled and his heart trembled to hear the report of Nayler's entry in Bristol in imitation of Christ's entry into Jerusalem. Such blasphemers by the Mosaic law were to be stoned to death, and for his part he could freely consent to it. When the protector enquired about the grounds for the Commons proceeding to a trial, Boteler was satisfied they had 'a judicatory power' to do so. Not unexpectedly, his defence of the major-generals in the debates over the Decimation Bill was 'hot'. He deplored the house's 'dilatoriness' in voting funds for the war with Spain. Although he was opposed to the offer of the crown to Cromwell in the spring of 1657, with that out of the way he came round in support of the revised draft of the humble petition and advice (June 1657). In the brief second session (January 1658) he argued strongly for transacting with the new 'other House' as a House of Lords, expounding the virtues of government by a single person and a bicameral parliament. In his interventions he displayed a familiarity with the scriptures and a grasp of parliamentary procedure. In the spring of 1658 Boteler was given the command of Oliver Cromwell's own regiment of horse: an appointment which Henry Cromwell put down to his father's belief that 'he may command those more absolutely, who have been most used to obey him' (Thurloe, 7.102).

Boteler did not sit in Richard Cromwell's parliament (1659), where, however, he was assailed for gross abuses as major-general in Northamptonshire. Although he claimed merely to have followed the protector's orders, he was put out of the commission of the peace. When further penalties were proposed Secretary John Thurloe, for political (and perhaps personal) reasons, spoke up for him, pressing—ironically in view of Boteler's attitude in the Nayler trial—that he should be heard before sentence. The abrupt dissolution of the parliament in April rescued him. The restored Rump, however, took away Boteler's regimental command and spurned his nomination as quartermaster-general. Even so, he was given a garrison command at Rockingham.

At the Restoration Boteler's exclusion from the Act of Oblivion was rejected by a small majority. He retired to live quietly at Oatlands Park, Walton-on-Thames, Surrey, maintaining his religious nonconformity, establishing himself in legal practice and, if he was indeed the Mr William Buttler who paid tax on fourteen hearths in 1664, living in some prosperity. He was questioned from time to time about radical plots, and was even for a time held in the Tower of London. In June 1666, after ten months' imprisonment, he pleaded with the secretary of state, the earl of Arlington, for his release: his practice and estate were ruined and he feared that his wife and five children would starve for lack of maintenance (it is uncertain whether this wife was Elizabeth Brooke or another woman). His claim to be moved by conscience and not by political faction seems then to have been accepted. However, he is last visible in the records following his being picked up again at a large conventicle in May 1670, regarded by the authorities as a man 'dangerous, and likely to enflame' (*CSP dom., 1670*, 234). The date and place of his death are unknown.

Boteler's was an unappealing personality. His principles were narrow and his realization of them oppressive: even he conceded to Thurloe in May 1656 that he was almost daily exceeding his legal powers. His career suggests that he was capable of combining a sense of duty with an urge to self-help. But within its strait limits his religion seems to have been genuine enough, and one small incident a few months before Boteler became major-general shows him in an informal moment of curiosity drawn to the utopian vision of Samuel Hartlib. In June 1655 he visited Hartlib to thank him for his recently published *The Reformed*

Common-Wealth of Bees, which presented the hive as the model of a harmonious, ordered commonwealth; Boteler was 'especially taken with the Glass-hives' which Hartlib used to exhibit his argument (Hartlib papers, Sheffield University Library, HP 29/5/35b). IVAN ROOTS, *rev.*

Sources P. H. Hardacre, 'William Boteler: a Cromwellian oligarch', *Huntington Library Quarterly*, 11 (1947–8), 1–11 • Thurloe, *State papers* • *Diary of Thomas Burton*, ed. J. T. Rutt, 4 vols. (1828); repr. (1974) • *CSP dom.*, 1648–70 • *JHC*, 5–8 (1646–67) • C. Durston, *Cromwell's major-generals: godly government during the English revolution* (2001) • C. H. Firth and G. Davies, *The regimental history of Cromwell's army*, 2 vols. (1940) • *The Clarke papers*, ed. C. H. Firth, 4 vols., CS, new ser., 49, 54, 61–2 (1891–1901) • H. I. Longden, *The visitation of the county of Northampton in the year 1681*, Harleian Society, 87 (1935) • J. Wake, ed., *Quarter sessions records of the county of Northampton*, Northamptonshire RS, 1 (1924) • P. Hardacre, 'William Boteler (or Butler)', Greaves & Zaller, *BDBR*, 1.83 • C. A. F. Meekings, ed., *Surrey hearth tax, 1664*, Surrey RS, 17 (1940) • *The fourth paper, presented by Major Butler, to the honourable committee of parliament, for propagating the gospel of Jesus Christ* (1652) • P. R. S. Baker, 'In what way was Samuel Hartlib's interest in bees political?', unpublished paper, 1995 • private information (2004)

Boteler, William Fuller (1777/8–1845), judge, came from an old Kentish family and was the only son of William Boteler FSA of Brook Street, Eastry, Kent, and his first wife, Sarah, daughter of Thomas Fuller, of Statenborough, Kent. His date of birth is given variously as 5 January 1777 and 12 April 1778. He had five half-brothers who rose to high office in the army and navy, and a sixth who was a clergyman. Boteler was educated under Dr Raine at Charterhouse from 1795. He went on to St John's College, Cambridge, where he was senior wrangler and first Smith's prizeman for 1799; the same year he graduated BA and was elected a fellow of Peterhouse, Cambridge. He proceeded MA in 1802. Admitted a student of Lincoln's Inn on 19 November 1801, he was called to the bar on 23 November 1804 and joined the home circuit; he also practised as an equity draftsman and conveyancer. Though his advancement at the equity bar was slow, he eventually became the leading tithe lawyer of the day.

Boteler attended the quarter sessions in Kent and in 1807 he became recorder of Canterbury; he was subsequently appointed recorder of Sandwich, Hythe, New Romney, and Deal, as well as high steward of Fordwich—posts which he held until his death. He was made a king's counsel in Trinity term 1831, and became a bencher of his inn on 27 May 1831 and treasurer in 1843–4. On 29 November 1808 at Betteshanger in Kent, he married Charlotte, daughter of James Leigh Joynes, of Mount Pleasant, near Gravesend; they had three sons (William and Richard, the younger sons, died as infants), and six daughters.

On 16 December 1844 Boteler was appointed senior commissioner of the district court of bankruptcy at Leeds. He died on 23 October 1845 from injuries sustained in a railway accident at Masborough on 20 October 1845.

G. F. R. BARKER, *rev.* BETH F. WOOD

Sources *Law Review*, 3 (1845–6), 245, 327–34 • *Annual Register* (1845), 161–2, 307–8 • *GM*, 2nd ser., 24 (1845), 641–2 • Venn, *Alum. Cant.* • J. L. Smith-Dampier, *Carthusian worthies* (1940) • R. V. Taylor, ed., *The biographia Leodiensis, or, Biographical sketches of the worthies of Leeds* (1865) • W. P. Baildon, ed., *The records of the Honorable Society of Lincoln's Inn* [incl. *Admissions*, 2 vols. (1896), and *Black books*, 6 vols. (1897–2001)] • A. Winnifrith, *Men of Kent and Kentish Men: biographical notices of 680 worthies of Kent* (1913) • d. cert.

Botetourt, John, first Lord Botetourt (*d.* 1324), admiral, emerged from obscurity in the 1280s and became a politically influential baron, an active soldier, and a prominent naval commander. For such a well-connected man Botetourt's origins and parentage are astonishingly obscure. An unsubstantiated reference in the Hailes Abbey chronicle suggests that he was an illegitimate son of Edward I, but it seems more likely that he was connected with Guy Botetourt (*fl.* 1264), an East Anglian landowner. In either case Botetourt's later prominence was unquestionably the result of his long attachment to the royal household rather than of any inherited wealth, and he rose through the ranks to become a knight by Christmas 1284, and a banneret in 1298. Household service brought varied responsibilities, and Sir John's earliest domestic exploits were concentrated in the Welsh marches, including an appointment as keeper of St Briavels Castle, Gloucestershire, in January 1291, and a number of judicial commissions in following years. Botetourt's most important contribution, though, was in the military sphere: his royal connections left him well placed, if not obliged, to participate in a long series of campaigns, including expeditions to Gascony in 1286, 1288, and 1295. Botetourt's estates—so far as they can be identified—may explain this early career focus, for by the turn of the fourteenth century he owned enough property in Gloucestershire and Northamptonshire to qualify for personal military service. In June 1302 he also acquired a stake in the barony of Bedford through his wife, Maud (*c.*1269–1328), who was the daughter of Thomas fitz Otho and Beatrice de Beauchamp and whom he had married by 1292. Long before his death, however, Botetourt's landed interests seem to have shifted almost exclusively to East Anglia, and to Essex in particular, and his career reflected this transition. In March 1294, for example, Sir John was appointed to try alleged maritime crimes against the men of Holland in a period of heightened diplomatic sensitivity. Soon afterwards, in November of the same year, he received his first recorded naval commission as 'subcaptain' of a force sent out from Great Yarmouth; and in March 1297 an existing brief to defend the port's adjacent maritime lands was expanded to include the entire eastern coastline, a sign of Botetourt's growing reputation. Yet any long-term naval responsibilities were interrupted by a period of intense campaigning in Scotland. Botetourt fought alongside his brother Guy at Falkirk in 1298, was present at the siege of Caerlaverock in 1300, and afterwards led, with mixed success, a number of *chevauchées* against the Scots until Edward I's death in July 1307 brought a change of regime, a change of fortunes, and a change of emphasis.

Under Edward II, Botetourt's influence was severely curtailed—his loyalty had evidently been to Edward I rather than the crown, and he was consistently associated with the baronial coalition against the king and his courtiers.

He was a signatory of the so-called 'Boulogne declaration' of January 1308 which was a veiled attack upon Piers Gaveston, Edward II's notorious favourite, whose capture and execution he endorsed in June 1312. Ultimately Botetourt took up arms against the king at Boroughbridge in March 1322, and in the ensuing confusion temporarily fled the country while his eldest son, Thomas, arranged an expensive formal pardon on his behalf. Botetourt also worked as a mediator for the baronial party in the period 1311–13, however, and, ironically, the brief periods of reconciliation between the factions saw his renewed appointment to military and civil office. Personal summonses to parliament from 1305 onwards were combined with an appointment as admiral of the eastern fleet in March 1315, and several judicial commissions in East Anglia. He died on 25 November 1324 leaving property in Norfolk, Suffolk, Essex, and Huntingdonshire. With his wife, Maud, Botetourt had at least two sons, Thomas and John, and possibly a third, William, all of whom appear on contemporary rolls of arms bearing variants of ore a saltire engrailed. Thomas Botetourt predeceased his father in July 1322 and the family estates therefore passed to his son, Sir John's grandson, John (*c.*1317–1339).

RICHARD GORSKI

Sources *Chancery records* • PRO, exchequer accounts various, E101 • PRO, Chancery miscellaneous, C 47 • B. F. Byerly and C. R. Byerly, eds., *Records of the wardrobe and household, 1286–1289* (1986) • M. Prestwich, *War, politics, and finance under Edward I* (1972) • T. Stapleton, ed., *De antiquis legibus liber: cronica majorum et vicecomitum Londoniarum*, CS, 34 (1846) • *Thomae Walsingham, quondam monachi S. Albani, historia Anglicana*, ed. H. T. Riley, 2 vols., pt 1 of *Chronica monasterii S. Albani*, Rolls Series, 28 (1863–4), vol. 1 • M. Prestwich, *Edward I* (1988) • F. Palgrave, ed., *The parliamentary writs and writs of military summons*, 2 vols. in 4 (1827–34) • *CDS*, vol. 2 • *CClR, 1288–96*, 235 • *CPR, 1292–1301*, 106 • *CIPM*, 6, no. 587

Botfield, Beriah (1807–1863), antiquary and industrialist, was born at Earl's Ditton, Shropshire, on 5 March 1807, the eldest son of Beriah Botfield (1768–1813) of Norton Hall, Northamptonshire, and Charlotte, daughter of William Withering MD. Botfield was educated first at Harrow School, where he subsequently established a medal for the encouragement of foreign languages, and then privately. He matriculated at Christ Church, Oxford, in 1824, and graduated BA in 1828. He became MP for Ludlow in 1840 and held his seat until 1847 when he was defeated. In 1857 he was again returned for that borough and held the seat until his death; he was a liberal conservative, and described as one 'who wanted to promote "the greatest happiness of the greatest number"' (*WWBMP*, 41). From 1850 he alone controlled the Shropshire collieries and ironworks that were the basis of the Botfield fortune. The family's foundry at Old Park was once the second largest in England. Botfield married Isabella (*d.* 1911), second daughter of Sir Baldwin Leighton, bt, on 21 October 1858, at Alberbury, Shropshire. There were no children.

Botfield produced a number of volumes that reflected his interests in early printed books and manuscripts. His *Notes on Cathedral Libraries of England* (1849) contained the fruits of much careful examination of what were then little-examined collections. His edition of *Catalogues of the Library of Durham Cathedral* (1840, for the Surtees Society) is also of value. He edited a number of other works: for the Roxburghe Club (of which he was a member), *Manners and Household Expenses of England in the Thirteenth and Fifteenth Centuries* (1841; this edition has also been attributed to T. H. Turner); for the Maitland Club, John Row's *History of the Kirk of Scotland, 1558–1637* (1842); for the Abbotsford Club, Gilbert Hay's translation of *The Buke of Order of Knyghthood* (1847); and, for the Bannatyne Club, *Original Letters on Ecclesiastical Affairs of Scotland* (1851). He also contributed various articles to *Archaeologia*, the *Gentleman's Magazine*, and the *Philobiblon Miscellany*. He set up a private printing press at Norton Hall and printed some of his own writings there in limited editions, including his account of the genealogy of the family of Boteville or Botfield, *Stemmata Botevilliana* (1843) and excerpts from the catalogue of the library of Thomas Hearne, *Bibliotheca Hearneiana* (1848).

Botfield was also a notable book collector, one sufficiently distinguished to be elected a member of the Roxburghe Club. He died at his London home in Grosvenor Square on 7 August 1863, and his collection, primarily of early printed and colour plate books, often in sumptuous bindings, passed on his death to the Thynne family of Bath, with whom he claimed relationship on no very compelling grounds. His widow, Isabella, married Alfred Seymour on 18 August 1866. Most of Botfield's books, which included a number of Caxtons and other incunabula, remained at Longleat, the Thynne family home, although some were sold at sales at Sothebys (11 June 1979) and Christies (30 March 1994). His collection of paintings, mainly Dutch landscapes, also remained at Longleat, largely intact. Botfield produced a catalogue of his picture collection in 1848.

W. P. COURTNEY, *rev.* A. S. G. EDWARDS

Sources 'The papers of the Botfield family, coal and iron masters, Dawley, Shropshire', *Royal Commission on Historical Manuscripts Annual Review, 1992–1993* (1993), 32–3 • B. Trinder, *The industrial revolution in Shropshire*, 2nd edn (1981), 142, 239 • *GM*, 3rd ser., 15 (1863), 645–7 • Burke, *Peerage* (1999) • Burke, *Gen. GB* (1858) • *WWBMP*, vol. 1 • *CGPLA Eng. & Wales* (1863)
Archives JRL, MSS | Bodl. Oxf., letters to Sir Thomas Phillips • U. Edin. L., letters to David Laing
Likenesses T. Phillips, oils, *c.*1828–1830, Longleat House, Wiltshire • L. Macdonald, marble bust, 1846, Harrow School, Middlesex • C. Silvy, carte-de-visite, *c.*1861, NPG • W. Behnes, bust, Longleat House, Wiltshire • W. Behnes, relief figure on marble monument, All Saints Church, Norton, Northamptonshire
Wealth at death under £200,000: probate, 21 Oct 1863, *CGPLA Eng. & Wales*

Botha, Louis (1862–1919), prime minister of the Union of South Africa and army officer, was born on 27 September 1862 at Honigfontein, near Greytown, Natal, the ninth child of Louis Botha (1827–1883), farmer, and his wife, Salomina Adriana Van Rooyen, both of whom had gone on the great trek as children. Until Louis was seven the family lived as British subjects outside Greytown, where he learned Zulu as he was growing up. In 1869 they left northern Natal for the independent Orange Free State, where they settled in the north-east on a large mixed farm near Vrede. His only formal education was two years at a farm

Louis Botha (1862–1919), by Sir James Guthrie, *c*.1919–21

school; he now learned to speak Sesotho as well as Zulu. Having helped his parents to farm he became a farmer himself. From the age of eighteen he took the family's sheep and cattle every winter across the Drakensberg to find pasture on the borders of Zululand.

Early military career In 1884 Botha responded to a call by Lukas Meyer, the landdrost of Utrecht, to serve on a commando (mounted fighting group) to restore Dinuzulu as Zulu king. After a short campaign Dinuzulu was able to defeat his rival Zibhebhu at Entshaneni. In return for their assistance Dinuzulu gave the Boers the land on which the New Republic was established. Botha helped to survey the future town of Vryheid and himself settled on the farm Waterval, east of Vryheid, in 1886. On 13 December of that year he married Annie Frances Bland (1864–1937), eldest daughter of John Cheere Emmett, a descendant of the Irish patriot Robert Emmet. They had three sons and two daughters.

For a time Botha lived a happy married life at Waterval, becoming a prosperous farmer and serving as field-cornet of the district. From 1888 he found himself living in the South African Republic (SAR), for the new republic became part of Paul Kruger's state. In 1895 he was appointed a native commissioner and the following year he won election to the SAR Volksraad (parliament) as representative for Vryheid, gaining more votes than his old friend Meyer. Botha was not, as sometimes alleged, an opponent of Kruger, nor an uncritical supporter of the Uitlander cause, but he did support Piet Joubert in the Volksraad and spoke in favour of concessions on the Uitlander franchise issue. When it was clear that such concessions would not satisfy the British government he spoke out strongly against Britain, and when war was declared in October 1899 he left immediately to muster the Vryheid commando for action.

Since Meyer was ill Botha virtually took over command of the Boer forces at the battle of Talana Hill (Dundee), and he might have delivered a major blow to the British after the battle had his superiors not refused to allow him to pursue the enemy. An imposing man with a warm personality, Botha was revered by those whom he commanded. As Meyer's condition worsened he took over as commandant of the south-eastern Transvaal forces. The aggressive strategy that he favoured would have taken the Boers deep into Natal, but after he routed a British division south of Ladysmith he was again refused permission by his superiors to follow up his victory. Though he was in charge of the commando that took Winston Churchill prisoner he was not himself involved in the capture, although Churchill gained that impression when the two men met after the war. When Commandant-General Joubert became ill Botha was put in command of the Boer forces along the Tugela River and, by anticipating where Sir Redvers Buller, commander of the British forces in Natal, would strike, won one of the greatest Boer victories. With 5000 men he held the small town of Colenso against Buller's 23,000.

Botha followed this with another triumph, on the flat-topped hill of Spioenkop, west of Colenso, where he again outwitted the British and defeated their assault on the summit. After Joubert's death, in March, he was made commandant-general of the Transvaal forces. His meteoric rise to the highest military position in the Boer army in a matter of months, at the age of only thirty-seven, was fully deserved, for he had emerged as probably the greatest of the Boer generals, and on his appointment as commandant-general he was immediately able to infuse new energy into the Boer forces. But by the time he was given the highest command the British had begun to turn the tide of war in their favour.

After trying unsuccessfully to halt the British advance through the Free State, Botha evacuated Pretoria on 5 June and then held up the British attackers long enough to secure for his forces and the Boer government a safe retreat along the line of railway to the east. So, though defeated at Berg-en-Dal on 27 August 1900, in the last set-piece battle of the war, he kept Buller engaged long enough for the republican government to move further east. By then he had realized that the Boers had to adopt guerrilla tactics, and so sent his commandos to their home districts, remaining himself in the south-eastern Transvaal, attacking isolated British units. On several occasions he was extremely fortunate to escape arrest or death.

Peace and union Botha had his first meeting with Lord Kitchener at Middelburg in February 1901 but rejected Kitchener's proposals for ending the war. He continued his guerrilla activities, harassing British forces; on one occasion he invaded Natal and captured a British convoy. But in the face of the British scorched-earth and concentration camp policy he became convinced by early 1902 that the Boers should accept a negotiated peace. When the Boer fighters met at Vereeniging in May of that year, to debate whether to lay down their arms, he urged them to do so. Speaking simply but with great passion he told the assembled men that their land was ruined and that the question before them was whether the Boer nation would die. Those who wanted to fight to the bitter end, he added, did not say what that end would be. 'We must save the nation' was his successful plea.

Milner called the document that closed the war 'terms of surrender' but Botha insisted that it be called a treaty, and he got his way. As soon as he had added his signature to the document in Pretoria he told his burghers in the field that the 'great task of building a South African nation begins tomorrow' (Kruger, 45). Remarkably quick to forget and forgive, he now sought to reconcile British and Boer in a new united nation. Among those whom he influenced in that direction was his fellow general and closest political associate, Jan Smuts.

When he went to England in August 1902 to plead for the Boer orphans and widows Botha had a friendly meeting with Edward VII. An article that Botha published in Britain in that year, 'The Boers and the empire', helped to persuade the House of Commons to grant additional millions of pounds in compensation to the Boers. In England he became a popular figure as the former enemy now reconciled to the idea that South Africa should be part of the British empire. His charming, powerful personality and moderate views greatly impressed a range of British politicians, including the Liberal leader, Sir Henry Campell-Bannerman.

On his return to South Africa Botha bought a farm at Rusthof, near Standerton, south-east of Johannesburg, but most of his time was spent in Pretoria. He refused to sit on the advisory legislative council set up by Sir Alfred Milner in the Transvaal and he protested against the importation of Chinese labour. Meetings that he helped to organize on that issue led to the founding of Het Volk ('the nation') in the Transvaal in May 1904. As leader of this new party he hoped to bring together those Boers who had joined the British cause during the war as well as the 'bitter-enders'. But his aims extended beyond Afrikaner unity to 'conciliation' among all white South Africans and self-government for the ex-republics. He greeted Campbell-Bannerman's decision in 1906 to grant self-rule to the Transvaal as proof of British magnanimity and a triumph for his policy of reconciliation.

In the general election held in 1907, in which Het Volk gained an outright victory, Botha was returned for Standerton. As leader of Het Volk he became prime minister of the Transvaal at the age of forty-four. Taking on the agriculture portfolio himself, he encouraged scientific farming methods and established a land bank. He returned to Britain to attend the Imperial Conference in 1907, where he was able to obtain a further loan and was again showered with praise. But many Afrikaners resented his protestations of loyalty to the empire and were displeased when the Cullinan diamond, the largest to have been discovered, was given to the British monarch to be incorporated into the crown jewels. It was, after all, only half a decade since the war had come to an end.

Botha's main achievement as prime minister of the Transvaal was to take the country into the union of South Africa. He played an important mediating role at the national convention of 1908–9, as head of the Transvaal delegation. He went out of his way to make friends with former enemies, such as Leander Starr Jameson, and was often able to win such people to his cause. The Transvaal delegation was able to secure a centralized union rather than a loose confederation and to insist that in the new united South Africa, though each province would be able to retain its existing franchise provisions, no black person would be able to become a member of the union parliament.

Prime minister of South Africa Botha returned to England in 1909 as a member of the delegation from the national convention that presented the draft legislation for union to the British parliament. And when union arrived in May 1910 it was Botha—and not the veteran Cape politician J. X. Merriman, who did not enjoy the same widespread support—who was asked by the governor-general to become the first prime minister of the new united country, an office that he held until his death.

Botha received a setback in the general election of September 1910. Taking a risk by standing in the Pretoria East constituency, he was to his surprise defeated by Sir Patrick Fitzpatrick. Given a parliamentary seat, he continued as prime minister and in 1911 was able to return to England to attend the Imperial Conference. It was then that he worked out with Viscount Haldane a scheme for a South African defence force that was to prove invaluable when war broke out with Germany in 1914. Though he spoke English in private he nearly always spoke Dutch in public, impressing his audiences in England and South Africa as a man of sincerity, courtesy, and now loyalty to the crown.

One of Botha's chief tasks in the new united South Africa was to fuse the political parties of the ex-colonies into a single new party. In 1911 the South African Party was founded in Bloemfontein with, as the cornerstones of its policies, conciliation at home and continuation of the existing links with Britain. But Botha found himself in an impossible position: the more he leaned towards the English-speaking community the more he offended some Afrikaners. He had tried to keep his strongest critic, J. B. M. Hertzog, out of the first union cabinet but had been unable to do so. Unable to put up with Hertzog's criticisms any longer, he decided to resign as premier in December 1912 in order to form a new government without Hertzog.

One of Botha's first acts as union premier was to release Dinuzulu, the Zulu king, from gaol and settle him on a farm, but Botha was conservative and highly paternalistic in racial matters. He must take responsibility for pushing through parliament in 1913 one of the most notorious pieces of segregationist legislation, the Natives Land Act, which prevented black Africans from acquiring land outside the overpopulated reserves. Though he spoke of allowing black Africans to 'rule themselves under the supervision of the white man' (Meintjes, 200) he did nothing to relieve the harsh conditions in which they lived. Nor had he any time for those white trade unionists who sought to improve conditions for the relatively privileged white miners on the Witwatersrand. In 1913 and again in 1914 he allowed Smuts to take strong action against white workers who went on strike. Critics in England and South Africa denounced the deportation of nine labour leaders without trial or appeal, but Botha was able to win parliamentary support for the action, and an indemnity act was passed.

It was when war broke out in Europe that Botha's greatest trial as premier came. He at once assured Britain that the union would support the war effort and advised that the imperial garrison could be withdrawn from South Africa for use in Europe. When he acceded to the British request that he invade German South-West Africa, however, some of his former Boer generals were so angered that they went into rebellion. To have to take up arms against fellow Afrikaners was, Botha said, 'the saddest experience of all my life' (Meintjes, 251). Though he went out of his way to call out only Afrikaners to deal with the uprising, and showed leniency in dealing with most of the rebels, his suppression of it, and the 'martyrdom' of Jopie Fourie in particular, alienated him from some who had previously supported him.

Early in 1915, having put down the uprising, Botha took personal charge of the invasion of German South-West Africa, and conducted a brilliant campaign there. He decided to advance along the line of rail from Swakopmund, on the coast, leaving Smuts to move up from the south. On 18 May Botha secured the bloodless surrender of Windhoek, the capital, and then continued north to Otavi, where in early July the German governor was finally forced to agree to the surrender of the entire territory. Botha then told his men that 'self-restraint, courtesy and consideration of the feelings of others on the part of the troops whose good fortune it is to be victors are essential' (Williams, 99).

Final years In the campaign before the general election of 1915, which was bitterly fought, Botha was accused of forgetting his Afrikaner roots and the sufferings of his people, and was even labelled a 'Judas, traitor, bloodhound, murderer' (Williams, 100). As a result of the election he no longer enjoyed an outright majority in parliament and had to form an alliance with the pro-British Unionists, which gave his Afrikaner critics more reason to revile him as a traitor. With Smuts out of the country for long periods during the war more work fell on his shoulders, and he began to suffer from periods of depression. He had become overweight; being over-sensitive he was hurt by cartoons that depicted him as clumsy and pot-bellied, and wearing a British military uniform.

By the time that he went, with Smuts, to the Paris peace conference at the end of the war Botha was under continuous medical attention. At the conference he played a moderating role, advising against a triumphal march by the allies to Berlin. He contrasted the magnanimity that Britain had shown to the ex-republics with the punitive measures that the allies wished to impose on the defeated Germany; he reminded his audience that 'he also came from a conquered nation' (Kruger, 25). That he was asked to chair a peace committee concerned with the war in Poland and the Ukraine was a sign of how respected he was as an international statesman. Though bitterly disappointed that permission was not given for South-West Africa to be annexed to the union, as he and Smuts wished, it was secured as a class C mandate under the new League of Nations. Though he added his signature to the peace treaty reluctantly, because he thought it was too harsh, he was proud to sign as leader of a dominion equal to others in the British empire.

Botha returned to South Africa in triumph but the way in which he had been rejected by many of his own people continued to weigh him down. In August 1919, soon after returning to Pretoria, he suffered a heart attack, and he died there, on the 27th, in his fifty-seventh year. He was buried in Rebecca Street cemetery, Pretoria, on 30 August; right-wing Afrikaners boycotted his state funeral. At his graveside Smuts called him 'the sweetest soul of all my days' (Williams, 125) and said that the unity of South Africa had been his life's work. But his vision of a united South Africa within the empire was not shared by those Afrikaners who lacked his capacity to forget the past and see the value of entering into a new relationship with the imperial power. His goal of reconciliation between Boer and Briton was not achieved and, like Smuts, he had no vision of how to bring blacks into the new union. Though he treated individual blacks with respect, as a group they remained non-persons in his eyes.

For a long time Botha's reputation suffered by comparison with that of Smuts. Most Afrikaner writers viewed his career after union as a failure. More recently, however, Afrikaner writers have not questioned his standing as much as that of Smuts, while among British and imperial historians Smuts's reputation has declined as that of Botha has risen. Such historians have come to recognize that he did not live merely in the shadow of Smuts. There is a new admiration for his modest, unassuming personality and his extraordinary willingness to reconcile with his former enemy. A century after the Second South African War—in an era of black majority rule, when reconciliation was again needed after another brutal conflict—statues of Botha still stood, both in the meadow below the union buildings in Pretoria and outside the parliament buildings in Cape Town. CHRISTOPHER SAUNDERS

Sources J. Meintjes, *General Louis Botha: a biography* (1970) • D. W. Krüger, 'Botha, Louis', *DSAB* • A. van Wyk, 'Gen. Louis Botha', *They shaped our century* (Cape Town, 1999) • E. M. Clark, *Louis Botha: a bibliography* (Cape Town, 1956) • B. Williams, *Botha, Smuts and South Africa* (1946) • H. Spender, *General Botha: the career and the man* (1916) • Earl Buxton, *General Botha* (1924) • F. V. Engelenburg, *General Louis Botha* (Pretoria, 1929) • W. K. Hancock, *Smuts: the sanguine years, 1870–1919* (1962) • J. D. Kestell and D. E. van Velden, *The* *peace negotiations between the governments of the South African Republic and … the British government*, trans. D. E. van Velden [Eng. trans. of *De vredesonderhandelingen tusschen …*] • D. W. Kruger, *The age of the generals: a short political history of the Union of South Africa, 1910–1948* (1958) • L. M. Thompon, *The unification of South Africa* (1960) • C. J. Barnard, *General Louis Botha op die Natalse front, 1899–1900* (Cape Town, 1970) • S. B. Spies, 'The outbreak of the First World War and the Botha government', *South African Historical Journal* (Nov 1969) • N. G. Garson, 'Het Volk: the Botha–Smuts party in the Transvaal, 1904–11', *HJ*, 9 (1966)

Archives Bodl. RH, corresp. | BL, corresp. with Lord Gladstone, Add. MSS 46006–46007 • Bodl. Oxf., corresp. with Lord Selborne • Bodl. RH, letters of Sire Matthew Nathan • HLRO, letters to D. L. George • NAM, letters to Earl Roberts • National Archives of South Africa, Pretoria, Transvaal Archives depot, state papers, South African republic • National Archives of South Africa, Pretoria, state papers, union of South Africa • Nuffield Oxf., corresp. with Lord Mottistone | FILM BFI NFTVA, documentary footage • BFI NFTVA, news footage • National Film Archive, South Africa

Likenesses W. Orpen, portrait, 1919, repro. in Engelenburg, *General Louis Botha* • J. Guthrie, oils, *c.*1919–1921, Scot. NPG [*see illus.*] • J. S. Sargent, pencil drawing, *c.*1921, NPG • J. S. Sargent, group portrait, oils, 1922 (General officers of World War I, 1914–18), NPG; study, NPG • J. B. Leighton, oils, 1924, Palace of Westminster, London • J. Guthrie, group portrait, oils, *c.*1924–1930 (Statesmen of World War I, 1914–18), NPG; study, NPG • R. Romanella, statue, Stal Plein, Cape Town • E. Roworth, portrait • RYG, lithograph caricature, NPG; repro. in *VF* (29 May 1907) • C. Steynberg, statue, union buildings, Pretoria • A. Van Wouw, statue, Botha Gardens, Durban • photographs, repro. in Engelenburg, *General Louis Botha*

Wealth at death £67,648: J. Meintjes, *General Louis Botha: a biography* (1970), 123

Bothumley, Jacob (1613–1692), Ranter, was born in 1613 in Leicester, the son of William Bauthumley (1586–1635), a shoemaker, and was baptized on 23 May. He was apprenticed to his father in 1627. Both father and son were members of a semi-separatist group in All Saints parish in the city, and both attracted the attention of the ecclesiastical authorities for repeating sermons in William's house. William had been excommunicated in 1619 and Jacob was excommunicated on 28 June 1634, although he had already refused to kneel at communion in 1627 and 1633. Their identities have been confused: William was probably 'Bottomley the shoemaker' who prayed aloud in the company of the nonconformist ministers Francis Higginson and Jeremiah Burroughs in the later 1620s. Both Bothumleys then were closely involved in the emergence of nonconformity in Leicester, a process which was hastened by the action of the forces attempting to achieve its eradication. The consequence of excommunication for Jacob was economic isolation: he was forced to give up his trade and was given redress for this when he petitioned the Long Parliament in 1640.

Bothumley fought for parliament and rose to be quartermaster in Colonel Cox's regiment. He seems to have had no direct connection with the other publishing Ranters (although Joseph Salmon refers to him), but on 14 March 1650 Bothumley was bored through the tongue with a hot iron for blasphemy, had his sword broken over his head, and was cashiered from the army. He was punished for publishing *The Light and Dark Sides of God* (1650), copies of which were ordered to be burnt, although George Thomason was still able to acquire a copy in November of the same year. By this time Bothumley had probably returned to Leicester, where the tract had already been sent to London as 'very dangerous … a very wide door to atheism and profaneness'.

Bothumley's earlier habit of repeating in private sermons already delivered helps to explain his acquisition of a literacy exceptional for a shoemaker: *The Light and Dark Sides of God* has been regarded as 'a neglected masterpiece of seventeenth-century devotional prose'. It is a work of deep inwardness, where the presence of God in all creatures makes external worship and scriptural authority superfluous: 'God is in all Creatures, Man and Beast, Fish and Fowle, and every green thing, from the highest Cedar to the Ivey on the wall; and that God is the life and being of them all' (Smith, *Collection*, 232). In no place does Bothumley recommend the practical antinomianism of which the other Ranters were accused. The devil and sin exist for him as states of mind in which the true location of the godhead is not recognized, even though such unenlightened awareness still functions as a praise of God. Sinful acts are not Bothumley's concern as such, but it is not difficult to see why *The Light and Dark Sides of God* was regarded as a dangerous work when it appeared to undermine Christian certainties: 'I have made God mutable as my self' (ibid., 233).

When the leading Quaker George Fox met Bothumley at Swannington in January 1655, he referred to him unfavourably as a Ranter, although *The Light and Dark Sides of God* circulated among Quakers. Later on, Bothumley became a minor corporation official at Leicester, in 1658 as serjeant-at-mace, and in 1667 as library keeper. Despite these offices, he was presented for not receiving the holy communion at his parish church, All Saints, Leicester, on 11 September 1667, together with two women. In 1676 he published an abridgement of Foxe's book of martyrs, entitled *A Brief Historical Relation*; it was reissued in 1686. Between 1676 and 1685 Bothumley was keeper of the house of correction, administering relief to the poor in Leicester on behalf of the corporation. He was buried on 30 July 1692. NIGEL SMITH

Sources C. E. Welch, 'Early nonconformity in Leicestershire', *Transactions of Leicestershire Archaeological and Historical Society*, 37 (1961), 29–43 • J. F. McGregor, 'The Ranters: a study in the free spirit in English sectarian religion, 1649–1660', BLitt diss., U. Oxf., 1969 • N. Smith, ed., *A collection of Ranter writings from the seventeenth century* (1983) • J. C. Davis, *Fear, myth and history: the Ranters and the historians* (1986) • N. Smith, *Perfection proclaimed: language and literature in English radical religion, 1640–1660* (1989) • parish register, All Saints, Leics. RO, 1 D 63/1–2 • Leics. RO, D 41/13/76 • private information (2004) [A. Hessayon]

Bothwell. For this title name *see* Hepburn, Patrick, first earl of Bothwell (*c.*1455–1508); Ramsay, John, Lord Bothwell and Lord Balmain (*c.*1464–1513); Hepburn, Patrick, third earl of Bothwell (*c.*1512–1556); Hepburn, James, fourth earl of Bothwell and duke of Orkney (1534/5–1578); Gordon, Jean, countess of Bothwell and Sutherland (*c.*1546–1629); Stewart, Francis, first earl of Bothwell (1562–1612).

Bothwell, Adam (1529?–1593), bishop of Orkney, was the son of Francis Bothwell (*d.* 1535) and his second wife, Katherine Bellenden. He came of an important Edinburgh family with many links to the king's government. His paternal grandfather, William, was a town burgess and dean of guild. His father was provost of Edinburgh in 1523–4, a lord of council and session from 1532, and often a lord of the articles. His uncle Richard Bothwell (*d.* 1549) became provost of St Mary-of-the-Fields, Edinburgh, in 1524, and in the same year was appointed director of the royal chancery. His maternal grandfather, Thomas Bellenden of Auchinoull, was made director of chancery in 1538 and justice-clerk a year later. His mother later married Oliver Sinclair, a favourite of James V and the likely commander of the Scottish army defeated at Solway Moss in 1542. His half-sister Janet, the daughter of his father's first marriage to Janet Richardson, married Sir Archibald Napier of Merchiston, who became general of the mint; the mathematician John Napier was their son.

Nothing is recorded of Adam Bothwell's early life, but he was certainly a university graduate. His father had studied at the University of Orléans and Bothwell may have done the same. It is probably significant that in 1560 he urged his brother-in-law to send the young John Napier 'to the schuyllis: over to France or to Flanderis, for he can leyr na guid at home' (Keller, 115). Nor is it known when he took orders. In 1552 his half-brother William Napier died as parson of Ashkirk, a prebend of Glasgow Cathedral, and shortly afterwards Bothwell succeeded him in this valuable benefice. He also inherited property in the outskirts of Edinburgh at Corstorphine (where he became vicar), Briglands, and Henderstoun, and at Dunsyre, Lanarkshire. In 1555 he went on government business to Orkney, an appointment he could have owed either to his brother-in-law Gilbert Balfour of Westray, the husband of his second sister, Margaret, or to his stepfather, Oliver Sinclair, a near relation of the earls of Caithness. Bothwell's links with the northern isles became much closer four years later, following the death of Robert Reid, bishop of Orkney, on 6 September 1558. After the temporality of the see had been granted to his cousin Sir John Bellenden, Bothwell was himself nominated bishop on 24 July 1559 and provided on 2 August following, the necessary bulls having been secured at Rome and brought home by Balfour. He had most likely been consecrated by 14 October, when he was admitted to the temporality. He was probably then thirty years old.

Bothwell set out for his diocese in February 1560, but was captured by an English ship and held prisoner for several weeks. He arrived in Orkney only in April, to face problems of all kinds: his health was often poor; a large proportion of his revenues had been disposed of in pensions by his predecessor; and his appearance in his diocese was far from welcome to some important members of his flock, notably Henry and Robert Sinclair, who took possession of the episcopal residence at Birsay and, according to Bothwell himself, set upon him as he returned from a visitation, intending 'to haiff alder slaine me, or taiken me' (Donaldson, 27). But Bothwell was not discouraged. From the first he showed himself a committed proponent of the reformed religion and its establishment in his diocese. Later he described how, 'when idolatry and superstitione was suppressed', he curbed 'the same also in his bounds, preached the word, administered the sacraments, planted ministers in Orknay and Shetland, disponed benefices and gave out stipends out of his rents to ministers, exhorters and readers' (Kirk, *Patterns of Reform*, 215).

During 1560 and 1561 Bothwell established the foundations for reform primarily through his cathedral's dignitaries, whom he appointed to the parishes from which their revenues derived. He also imported men sympathetic to the cause of reform. Prominent among them were Gilbert Foulsie, a former monk who had become Bothwell's secretary before being made archdeacon of Orkney; the bishop's cousin Francis Bothwell, who had been a friar and now became treasurer of Kirkwall Cathedral; and William Lauder, a Glasgow notary who succeeded Foulsie as the bishop's secretary. In Shetland Bothwell appointed Archdeacon Jerome Cheyne, who had served Bishop Reid, to act as 'minister in these parts' (Kirk, *Patterns of Reform*, 29), and by 1562 two other priests were acting as readers there. An appeal to the assembly in 1563 shows that elders and deacons had by then been installed in Orkney. The impetus was maintained and the parishes were quickly staffed by reformed clergy, so that by 1567 there were more than thirty ministers or readers in Orkney and Shetland, with almost every parish being served.

Bothwell helped the reformed church to achieve stability in Orkney by quickly making arrangements for paying ministers' stipends. However, while this proved acceptable to the general assembly, his own finances were a continual cause of trouble. At odds with a series of chamberlains, by the time of his death Bothwell claimed to be owed 10,000 merks by the heir of one of them. Nevertheless, he seems to have been resident in his diocese for at least a part of every year in the early 1560s, and between June 1563 and December 1566 he also attended most of the general assemblies. In December 1563 he became a member of the committee set up to revise the Book of Discipline, and he was appointed to committees in 1565 and 1566. In keeping with the approved practice of the reformed church he married; he and his wife, Margaret (*d.* 1608), daughter of John Murray of Touchadam, had six sons and two daughters.

From 1564 Bothwell was increasingly involved in secular affairs, in ways which eventually brought him into conflict with the kirk. On 14 January he was admitted an extraordinary lord of the court of session and on 13 November 1565 an ordinary lord, and he also became a member of the privy council. It was not these promotions as such which first brought trouble upon him, but his marrying Queen Mary to the fourth earl of Bothwell, on 15 May 1567. At first, indeed, the bishop seems to have escaped censure—the order of the reformed kirk had been used, and he was still able to take part in the coronation of James VI on 29 July following, when he anointed the infant king on the head, shoulder blades, and hands.

Earlier that day he had been one of those who received Queen Mary's demission of the crown, and shortly afterwards he took part in the expedition, led by his cousin William Kirkcaldy of Grange, which set off for the northern isles in pursuit of the queen's husband, recently created duke of Orkney. The ship ran upon a rock in Bressay Sound in East Shetland, and the bishop saved his life only by a desperate leap, in full armour, from the wreck into a crowded lifeboat.

Adam Bothwell was not rewarded as he might have expected for his apparent willingness to risk his life in the young king's cause. Instead he seems to have fallen victim to the insecurities of Regent Moray's government, exacerbated by the ambitions of Lord Robert Stewart for control of Orkney (of which he later became earl, in 1581), and perhaps also by the kirk's growing misgivings concerning bishops. In December 1567 several accusations were made against him in the general assembly: he had been lax in visitation; his employment as a lord of session had distracted him from his ecclesiastical ministry; he had associated with Francis Bothwell, allegedly a papist; and he had solemnized the queen's marriage to the earl of Bothwell, contrary to an act of assembly prohibiting the marriage of a divorced adulterer. The bishop admitted that he could not reside continuously in his diocese, 'by reason of the evil air and the weakness of his body' (Kirk, *Patterns of Reform*, 40), but though he made a spirited defence against the other charges he was none the less suspended from all function in the ministry. In July 1568 he was reinstated on condition that he publicly confessed his fault concerning the queen's marriage, but the episode had weakened his position, and, late in September, under heavy pressure from Lord Robert Stewart, Bothwell conveyed to the latter all the lands, rights, and revenues of his see in exchange for the commendatorship of Holyrood Abbey. He remained bishop but was never again appointed by the assembly to oversee his diocese, and he was superseded in his functions by local ministers acting as commissioners.

His bargain with Stewart and his failure thereafter to act as bishop led to further charges being brought against Bothwell in the assembly of March 1570. His exchange of episcopal office for monastic lands was denounced as simoniacal, and he was also criticized for neglecting his diocese, for acting as a lord of session, for failing to preach, and for retaining the title of bishop, especially as he took 'Roman titles as Reverend Father in God which pertaineth to no Ministers of Christ Jesus, nor is given them in Scriptures'. On this last point Bothwell abased himself, admitting that he was just 'a worm of the earth not worthy any reverence' (Kirk, *Second Book of Discipline*, 78). But he defended himself against the other charges, in terms which suggest that he felt he was unjustly used, especially concerning his acting as a lord of session, a position he had accepted:

> with the advice of godly and learned men, compting it not repugnant or contrariouse to any good order as yet established in the Kirke, and alledged that diverse others having benefices, have done the like, and are not condemned for so doing. (Mullan, 31)

The immediate outcome of the assembly's censures is unknown, but thereafter Bothwell had no contact with his diocese besides receiving a few presentations to churches. Nevertheless, he retained his episcopal title and in 1580 was one of the bishops whom the general assembly demanded should submit to its authority.

Instead Bothwell lived in Edinburgh and acted as a government servant, as, indeed, he had long done. A member of the commission which in 1568–9 had brought accusations against Queen Mary in England, in January 1572 he was one of the government's representatives which negotiated the concordat of Leith, regularizing the organization and finances of the kirk. Later that year he represented the king's party in its attempts to make peace with the queen's followers. In 1578 he appears to have supported the earls of Atholl and Argyll against the former regent, Morton. He was a regular attender of privy council meetings from the early 1570s onwards, and was also active as a lord of session. He was present at almost every parliament until his death. When King James returned from Scandinavia in 1590, Bothwell was consulted about the arrangements for Anne of Denmark's coronation, on the basis of his involvement in James's in 1567. He had two residences in Edinburgh, the 'commendator's house' on the north side of Holyrood Palace, and a house in Byres' Close, very near the tolbooth, where the court of session sat.

It is not known where Bothwell kept his library, which its surviving inventory shows to have been impressively large and wide-ranging. He clearly started buying books in his student days, and acquired works by many classical and patristic authors. He added to his collection at least into the 1580s, for instance in the field of theology, when the writings of Beza joined those of earlier Reformation luminaries such as Calvin, Melancthon, and Bullinger. His purchases indicate that he could read Latin, Hebrew, Greek, French, Italian, and Spanish. His judicial employment, as well as his work as a bishop, probably accounts for his owning large numbers of books on canon and civil law, while his continued ill health (in 1582 he excused himself from obeying the kirk's order to take on a congregational ministry on the grounds of sickness) may explain his many books on medicine and surgery. A typical representative of the Scottish Renaissance, if an unusually widely read one, he was interested in political theory, owning books by Buchanan and Bodin, possessed several works of history, and also concerned himself with such subjects as mathematics, geography, philosophy, astronomy, witchcraft, and cookery. Perhaps it was because he lived so close to the royal court that he had a copy of Castiglione's *The Courtier*.

Although financial aspects of his episcopate periodically resurfaced to trouble his peace, as did his deal with Robert Stewart, Bothwell is not known to have visited Orkney again after 1567. He died in Edinburgh on 23 August 1593 and was buried in Holyrood Abbey church. He had resigned as a lord of session a few weeks earlier, on 2 July, when he was succeeded by his eldest son, John, who in 1595 returned to the king 'ane great rubie set in golde' which James had pawned to the bishop for £500 Scots

(*Scots peerage*, 4.432). A courtier and a privy councillor, John Bothwell was created Lord Holyroodhouse on 20 December 1607, and died on 26 November 1609.

DUNCAN SHAW

Sources *Scots peerage*, 4.425–32 · G. Donaldson, 'Adam Bothwell, bishop of Orkney', *Reformed by bishops* (1987), 19–51 · D. Shaw, 'Adam Bothwell, a conserver of the Renaissance in Scotland', *The Renaissance and Reformation in Scotland: essays in honour of Gordon Donaldson*, ed. I. B. Cowan and D. Shaw (1983), 141–69 · *Fasti Scot.*, new edn, 7.352 · D. E. R. Watt, ed., *Fasti ecclesiae Scoticanae medii aevi ad annum 1638*, [2nd edn], Scottish RS, new ser., 1 (1969) · D. G. Mullan, *Episcopacy in Scotland* (1986) · J. Kirk, *The Second Book of Discipline* (1980) · J. Kirk, *Patterns of reform: continuity and change in the Reformation kirk* (1989) · A. R. MacDonald, *The Jacobean kirk, 1567–1625* (1998) · G. R. Hewitt, *Scotland under Morton, 1572–80* (1982) · A. Keller, 'The physical nature of man: science, medicine, mathematics', *Humanism in Renaissance Scotland*, ed. J. MacQueen (1990), 97–122
Archives NL Scot., letters to Sir Archibald Napier · NRA, priv. coll., letters to Sir John Bellenden

Botley, Samuel (1640/41–1677), stenographer, was a son of Robert Botley, citizen of London and cordwainer. The year of his birth has been calculated from the engraved portrait by William Dolle in the first edition of the shorthand manual for which Botley is chiefly remembered, *Maximum in minimo* (first published in late 1674 or more probably early 1675), which gives his age as thirty-three in 1674. Samuel, who was made free of the Cordwainers' Company by patrimony on 12 April 1662, does not appear to have followed his father's profession, and from at least 1668 and probably until 1672 was employed as a messenger in the chamber in the lord chamberlain's department. According to both Botley's *Maximum in minimo* (1675?), sig. K2, and the burial record for their daughter Mary in the register of St Thomas the Apostle, London, on 4 November 1677, his wife's name was Hannah, but nothing else is known of her.

By no later than 1673 Botley was teaching the shorthand system invented by Jeremiah Rich (1630?–1667?), with whom he appears to have had some particular connection, at his house in Thames Street, London, adjacent to Vintners Hall, and subsequently at Colonel Mason's coffee house in Cornhill, London. Botley was among those who subscribed to the publication of later editions of Rich's shorthand edition of the New Testament (1673, 1675) and was supplying both this and Rich's shorthand version of the metrical psalms of Sterngold and Hopkins, *The Whole Book of Psalms in Meter* (1673), from his house in Thames Street. Although in his introduction to *Maximum in minimo* (1675?) Botley addresses scholars in 'London, Bristol and Exeter', it is not known that he himself ever visited the west country, and his treatise may have been designed, at least in part, to foster an early form of distance learning. *Maximum in minimo* was simply a reissue of Jeremiah Rich's *The Penns Dexterity* to which Botley had added his own contribution of 'the whole Terms of the Law in Mr Rich's Character Compleated'; there were at least five subsequent reprints or editions, several of which feature re-engraved versions of William Dolle's original portrait.

On 15 October 1677, according to the register of St James Garlickhythe, Botley died of a gastrointestinal obstruction and was buried in the neighbouring parish of St Thomas the Apostle, Thames Street, London, on 18 October 1677.

FRANCES HENDERSON

Sources W. J. Carlton, *Bibliotheca Pepysiana*, 4: *Shorthand books* (1940), 92–5 · R. C. Alston, *A bibliography of the English language from the invention of printing to the year 1800*, 8: *Treatises on shorthand* (1966), 130–35 · S. Botley, *Maximum in minimo* (1675?) · J. L. Chester, ed., *The parish registers of St Thomas the Apostle, London … from 1558 to 1754*, Harleian Society, register section, 6 (1881), 141 · *CSP dom.*, 1668–9, 105, 278–9; 1671–2, 458 · K. Brown and D. C. Haskell, *The shorthand collection in the New York Public Library* (1935), 191 · [J. Rich], *The whole Book of Psalms in meter according to the art of short-writing* (1674?) · *The book of the New Testament … according to the art of short-writing invented by I. Rich* [1673] · J. Rich, *The penns dexterity* (1675) · E. Arber, ed., *The term catalogues, 1668–1709*, 3 vols. (privately printed, London, 1903–6), vol. 1, pp. 160, 201–2, 249, 305; vol. 3, p. 30 · Wing, *STC*
Likenesses W. Dolle, engraving, repro. in Botley, *Maximum in minimo*, frontispiece · line engraving, NPG; repro. in J. Rich, *The pens dexterity completed, or, Mr Riches short-hand now perfectly taught*, 3rd edn (1674)

Botolph. *See* Botwulf (*fl.* 654–*c.*670).

Botreaux. For this title name *see* Rawdon, Elizabeth, *suo jure* Baroness Botreaux, *suo jure* Baroness Hungerford, *suo jure* Baroness Moleyns, *suo jure* Baroness Hastings, and countess of Moira (1731–1808).

Bott, Thomas (1688–1754), Church of England clergyman, was born at Derby in 1688, the youngest of the six children of a mercer; his grandfather had been a parliamentary major. He was probably the son of Thomas Bott, whose son Thomas was baptized at All Saints', Derby, in June 1688. He was educated for the dissenting ministry, but, after some experience of preaching, he went to London to study medicine, and then took orders in the Church of England, obtaining the rectory of Whinburgh, in Norfolk, through Lord Macclesfield's interest. In 1724 he published a discourse entitled *The Peace and Happiness in this World, the Immediate Design of Christianity*. A defence of this, *The Nature and Design of Christianity Further Considered*, followed in 1727. In 1725 he attacked William Wollaston's peculiar mode of deducing morality from truth, and in 1730 published a sermon on the question entitled *Morality Founded in the Reason of Things*. In 1734 Mr Longe gave him the rectory of Spixworth, which he held, with the neighbouring parish of Croftwick, until his death. On 30 January 1738 he preached a sermon concerning the duty of doing as we would be done by, observing only, by way of application, that if both parties had fulfilled this duty Charles I would not have lost his head. In the same year he attacked Joseph Butler's *Analogy of Religion* (1736). He married Rebecca, daughter of Edmund Britiffe of Hunworth, in 1739. In his chief work, *An Answer to the Rev. Mr Warburton's Divine Legation of Moses* (1743), he censured Warburton for making morality dependent upon the command of a superior being. He also accused Warburton of confusion in his citation of the non-Christian ancients, thereby rendering much of the latter's work unacceptable. In 1747 he was presented to the living of Edgefield, Norfolk. His whole ecclesiastical income was £200 a year. His health broke in 1750, and he died on 19 September 1754 at Norwich. He was a follower of Bishop Benjamin Hoadly, a friend of Samuel Clarke, and a thorough whig. A son, Edmund, was a fellow of Trinity College, Cambridge. B. W. YOUNG

Sources A. Kippis and others, eds., *Biographia Britannica, or, The lives of the most eminent persons who have flourished in Great Britain and Ireland*, 2nd edn, 5 vols. (1778–93) • A. Chalmers, ed., *The general biographical dictionary*, new edn, 32 vols. (1812–17) • *IGI*
Archives BL, letters to Cox Macro, Add. MS 32557

Bott, Thomas (*bap.* 1828?, *d.* **1870**), porcelain painter and designer, was born near Kidderminster, Worcestershire, and was probably the Thomas Bott who was baptized on 25 January 1828 at Bromsgrove, Worcester, the son of Thomas Bott and his wife, Mary. He was brought up to his father's business of making spade handles. He was trained from 1846 at Richardson's glassworks at Wordsley near Stourbridge where he painted glass, examples of which were shown at the Great Exhibition of 1851. On 28 December 1851 he married at St Martin's, Birmingham, Eliza Bourne, with whom he had a son, Thomas John Bott, baptized on 30 November 1854 at St Martin's, Worcester. He worked as a portrait painter in Birmingham and went in 1853 to Worcester, where he became principal artist of the Royal Porcelain works owned by Kerr and Binns. According to the *Worcester Journal*, 'In that year Mr Binns introduced what is known as the Worcester enamel. Mr. Bott made the first trials, and ultimately succeeded in giving the enamel the very important character it has since assumed' (17 Dec 1870). For his work in Worcester enamel Bott obtained distinction at the Paris Exhibition in 1855, and in London in 1862. Enamels by Bott were also shown at the Royal Academy in 1857 and 1860. His enamels are characteristically in the Limoges style, using tinted white enamel designs on dark grounds which are reminiscent of sixteenth-century Limoges enamels. Among his last works were vases in the Limoges style, which formed part of Worcester's 'Norman conquest' exhibit, and which won first prize at Vienna in 1873. A plate featuring a turquoise ground from a dinner service designed by Thomas Reeve for Queen Victoria and painted by Bott can be seen at the Victoria and Albert Museum, London.

Thomas Bott died at his home, 4 Park Hill, in the parish of St Martin, Worcester, on 12 December 1870. His son, Thomas John Bott, continued to work in the Limoges style for the Royal Worcester porcelain works.

ERNEST RADFORD, *rev.* AMANDA GIRLING-BUDD

Sources Redgrave, *Artists* • H. Sandon, *Royal Worcester porcelain* (1973) • G. A. Godden, *Encyclopaedia of British porcelain manufacturers* (1988) • E. Cameron, *Encyclopaedia of pottery and porcelain, the nineteenth and twentieth centuries* (1986) • Boase, *Mod. Eng. biog.* • G. Meissner, ed., *Allgemeines Künstlerlexikon: die bildenden Künstler aller Zeiten und Völker*, [new edn, 34 vols.] (Leipzig and Munich, 1983–) • G. Godden, 'Worcester enamels', *Apollo*, 63 (1956), 122–4 • *Jewitt's ceramic art of Great Britain, 1800–1900*, rev. edn, rev. G. A. Godden (1972) • *CGPLA Eng. & Wales* (1871) • *IGI*
Likenesses portrait, repro. in Godden, 'Worcester enamels', 122
Wealth at death under £600: resworn probate, Jan 1872, *CGPLA Eng. & Wales* (1871)

Bottetourt, John de. *See* Botetourt, John, first Lord Botetourt (*d.* 1324).

Bottlesham [Bottisham], **William** (*d.* **1400**), bishop of Rochester, may have come from the Cambridgeshire village of Bottisham; he was certainly from East Anglia. His origins are otherwise unknown. He became a Dominican friar, and later left bequests (if possible) of £50 and £100 to the houses of that order in Bishop's Lynn, Norfolk, and Cambridge, 'because I owe as much and more' to them (Reg. Arundel, 1, fol. 166*v*): debts of gratitude, not of cash. Cambridge was certainly where he studied, graduating DTh by 17 May 1382, when he was summoned to help Archbishop William Courtenay investigate Wycliffite opinion at the celebrated Earthquake council in London. He had been appointed titular bishop Navatensis by 13 March 1380, when Bishop William Wykeham had appointed him to be his suffragan in the remoter parts of the Winchester diocese, pleading the endless rain, his own ill health, and royal business. In 1383 Bottlesham appears with the grand title of bishop of Bethlehem, but this was purely titular. He was with the Roman pope, Urban VI, albeit only (according to Walsingham) on a mission from England, when the pope was under siege at Nocera by the king of Naples in January 1385. It was probably in appreciation that the pope provided him to the see of Llandaff on 16 October 1385, to which the crown had no objection once personal fealty was given on 21 August 1386. Bottlesham at last had a 'real' bishopric, if a very poor one.

Bottlesham returned to England by the beginning of August 1386, possibly with the papal envoy, Richard Northalis. In the time of the Merciless Parliament, probably in February 1388, certain suspected heretics were summoned before a panel including the bishop. They refused to appear before this 'apostate' and denounced the rest of the panel as inadequate. These are, in effect, the only clues as to Bottlesham's rise to modest eminence; his standing in theology is already known, and whether 'apostate' referred to some particular controversy in his career, or to especial opposition to Wycliffism (a possibility raised by his will), or was just a generic slur on him as a friar, is unknown. It is thin gruel.

On 4 May 1389 the eminent preacher Bishop Thomas Brinton of Rochester died. The monks elected the archbishop's official, John Barnet. Richard II signalled his assent in public, but privately requested the pope's tax collector to secure the see for his own candidate, Richard Wichened. The monks of Christ Church, Canterbury, wanted the see for their own Thomas Chillenden. On 27 August the pope translated Bottlesham; he knew of the current political divisions in England, resented recent attempts to curb his income and patronage, saw the chance to show his muscle over something not too important, and probably did want to reward Bottlesham, his only real appointee on the bench, a little more. The archbishop gave the bishop his temporalities on 15 December, and the king followed suit on 12 February 1390. Both wanted to come to terms with the pope (now Boniface IX) over major difficulties regarding taxation of the clergy and papal patronage, and so probably did not want to make trouble over so relatively small a matter as the see of Rochester.

In any case, Bottlesham was an apposite successor to Brinton in a see too modest to attract the interest of ambitious (and usually heavily pluralist) ecclesiastics. He proved indeed a fully resident and active bishop, although 'aged' by January 1396, a claim supported by his unusual use of a vicar-general and suffragan even while resident, from September 1394. None the less, he preached in the convocation of Canterbury at St Paul's on 7 October 1399, a reportedly nervous assembly, in the immediate circumstances of Richard II's overthrow; perhaps his appearance on such an occasion is a final hint that his career was based on wide respect for his public and personal integrity, not on partisanship.

On 16 February 1400 he made a very sensitive will at his favourite manor of Trottiscliffe, Kent, aware of his parlous financial state, asking for an undemonstrative burial in the church of the Blackfriars in London, requiring that his servants be paid to the end of the quarter, thinking of the poor on his three most familiar properties, having no goods or luxuries at all to direct, recalling very fondly his upbringing in the convents of Lynn and Cambridge, invoking saints Andrew and Dominic, and naming no kin. His chief executor, interestingly, was his fellow Dominican Dr Roger Dymoke, the forceful anti-Wycliffite polemicist.

Bottlesham was dead by 26 February. Archbishop Arundel revoked the will, 'because he was obliged to other diverse creditors in great sums of money and goods' (Reg. Arundel, 1, fol. 167). On 24 May 1402, however, the administrators were able to report that at last they had paid off all the debts and could still hand over a residue of £54 17*s.* 8*d.* This was small comfort to his intended beneficiaries, no doubt, but perhaps they could remember a good, ungreedy master or friend. R. G. DAVIES

Sources R. G. Davies, 'The episcopate in England and Wales, 1375–1443', PhD diss., University of Manchester, 1974, 3.xxxiv–v • Emden, *Cam.*, 76 • Register of Thomas Arundel, LPL, 1, fols. 166*v*–167 [will] • Register of Thomas Arundel, LPL, 1.463 [date of death] • register, Rochester, CKS, DRb ArI/5
Archives CKS, register
Wealth at death £54 17*s.* 8*d.*—after payment of debts: Davies, 'The episcopate in England and Wales'

Bottome [*married name* Forbes-Dennis], **Phyllis** (1882–1963), writer, was born on 31 May 1882 in Rochester, Kent, the third of four children of William MacDonald Bottome (*d.* 1913), an American clergyman, and Margaret Leatham of Yorkshire. She was educated largely at home, except for a brief period from 1890 to 1895 when she attended a Catholic girls' boarding-school in New York, where her family had temporarily relocated. Returning to England in 1896, Bottome studied acting in London, but pneumonia kept her from her stage début. As a young woman Bottome enjoyed reading nineteenth-century women's fiction. In 1899 she wrote her first novel, *Life, the Interpreter*, published in 1902, a story of independent womanhood and an attack on class. Soon afterwards she learned she was afflicted with tuberculosis, and she began a lifelong pattern of travelling in Germany, Austria, and Switzerland for her health while still writing and publishing fiction in Britain and the United States. From 1904 to 1917 Bottome published a series of 'social romances' that were serialized in American magazines. Just before the First World War she was living in London and was part of the literary circle which included Ezra Pound, H. D., and May Sinclair. Her novel *The Dark Tower* (1916; published in England as *Secretly Armed*) was a popular American publication.

In 1917 Bottome married Captain Alban Ernan Forbes-Dennis (*d.* 1972), who was also tubercular (they had met some years previously at St Moritz and had been engaged in 1904 before Bottome broke it off because of her health). While Forbes-Dennis was at the front, Bottome worked as a writer for the Ministry of Information under John Buchan, and as a relief worker for Belgian refugees. Forbes-Dennis's role as a diplomatist after the First World War required that the couple travel widely in Europe where, in Vienna in 1920, Bottome helped the social worker Valerie Adler and her husband the psychiatrist Alfred Adler with relief work.

Between 1917 and 1924 Bottome published seven more novels building on the themes of social ills and women's struggle with identity and success in a patriarchal society. *Old Wine*, released in 1926, brought Bottome critical acclaim for its description of post-war Austria. Bottome was analysed by Alfred Adler in the 1930s before moving to Munich, where she witnessed the Nazi rise to power. She produced a pamphlet in tribute to Stella Benson in 1934, but her next significant publication was *Private Worlds* (1934), a novel about mental illness which was made into a film in 1935 starring Claudette Colbert and Charles Boyer. In 1936 Bottome returned to England and wrote articles warning against the Nazi threat. While these generated little response, her novel *The Mortal Storm* (1937), which explored the same ideas, was an instant best-seller, particularly in America. It was filmed in 1940 with James Stewart and Margaret Sullavan in the leading roles. In 1939 Bottome published a biography of Adler, for which she conducted primary research in Austria, narrowly avoiding Hitler's entry into that country at the start of the Second World War. *Within the Cup* (1943) was also successful for Bottome, who incorporated Adlerian psychological theories, and presented sensitive portrayals of characters in conflict with themselves and society.

In 1947 Bottome published the first of her three autobiographies, *Search for a Soul: Fragment of an Autobiography*. This was followed by *The Challenge* in 1952 and *The Goal* in 1962. These three books provide most of what is known about Bottome. She continued to write and publish novels at a rate of one or two a year between 1940 and 1960.

Bottome died on 22 August 1963 at her home, Little Greenby, 95 South End Road, Hampstead, London. Her friend Daphne Du Maurier edited her collected stories in 1963. In her long career Bottome wrote on a wide range of subjects in several genres, producing popular, feminist novels and, in her non-fiction, raising the public's awareness of political dangers; her recurring theme was personal freedom. Her works were translated into many European languages. BEVERLY E. SCHNELLER

Sources P. Bottome, *Search for a soul* (1947) • P. Bottome, *The challenge* (1952) • P. Bottome, *The goal* (1962) • J. Todd, ed., *Dictionary of British women writers* (1989) • M. Hoder-Salmon, 'Phyllis Bottome', *Late-Victorian and Edwardian British novelists: second series*, ed. G. M. Johnson, DLitB, 197 (1999) • *Living Authors* • *Contemporary Authors*, vol. 179, pp. 96–9 • *New York Times* (23 Aug 1963) • *New York Times* (24 Aug 1963) • P. Lassner, *British women writers of World War II: battlegrounds of their own* (New York, 1998) • P. Lassner, 'A bridge too close: narrative wars to end fascism and imperialism', *Journal of Narrative Theory*, 31/2 (summer 2001), 131–54 • d. cert.

Archives BL, papers • Merton Oxf. • Northwestern University, Illinois, letters • University of Warwick | King's Lond., Liddell Hart C., corresp. with Basil Liddell Hart • U. Reading L., letters to the Bodley Head Ltd

Likenesses portraits, repro. in DLitB, 30, 32

Wealth at death £23,995 5*s.* 2*d.*: probate, 2 Oct 1963, *CGPLA Eng. & Wales*

Bottomley, Arthur George, Baron Bottomley (1907–1995), politician, was born on 7 February 1907 at 7 Sutton Road, Tottenham, Middlesex, the eldest of the five children of George Howard Bottomley, a brass finisher and later an engineer with the firm of Houghton Butcher, and his wife, Alice Louisa, *née* Humphreys, daughter of the postmaster at Mount Pleasant, central London. He attended Gamuel Road council school and Pretoria Avenue Boys' School in Walthamstow. After leaving school at fourteen, he was briefly an office boy in a City textile firm before taking work as a carriage cleaner at the London, Midland, and Scottish railway workshops in Kentish Town. He grew into a tall, plain-featured man with a direct and friendly manner. An active member of the National Union of Railwaymen, he was involved in the general strike and was politicized by it.

For some years Bottomley attended night classes at Toynbee Hall, where he heard, among other university extension lecturers, Norman Angell, George Bernard Shaw, and Sidney Webb. Toynbee Hall also brought him into contact with Clement Attlee, who became his mentor, patron, and, 'in an artless, nice way', his hero (*The Independent*, 7 Nov 1995). With Attlee's encouragement he stood for election to Walthamstow borough council. His election in 1929 initiated what would become a twenty-year tenure of his council seat, including a term as mayor in 1945–6. In 1935, with Attlee as his referee, he was appointed London organizer of the newly formed National Union of Public Employees, a post he would hold until 1945. In 1936 he married Bessie Ellen (*b.* 1906), daughter of Edward Charles Wiles. A teacher and trade unionist, Bessie Bottomley went on to make her own career in the fields of education and health, work for which she was appointed DBE in 1970.

Through the war years Bottomley served with energy and distinction on the home front. Having pioneered civil defence in Walthamstow in the late 1930s, he was chairman of the emergency committee and air raid precautions controller for London during the blitz. This service earned him an OBE in 1941. For the rest of the war he was

Arthur George Bottomley, Baron Bottomley (1907–1995), by Elliott & Fry, 1946

deputy regional commissioner for south-east England. At the 1945 election Bottomley entered parliament as Labour MP for Chatham. In this new role he focused increasingly on overseas policy. Early in 1946 he travelled with a parliamentary delegation to India, a country that had fascinated him since a meeting with Gandhi in 1931; in Delhi he formed lasting friendships with Nehru and Krishna Menon. In May 1946 Attlee brought him into the government as under-secretary for the dominions. He led a government mission to Burma in 1947 and won esteem among the Burmese leaders; long afterwards, in 1981, he was awarded the title of Aung San Tagun, the highest Burmese title available to a foreigner. His next step upwards came in October 1947, when Attlee appointed him secretary for overseas trade, second in command to the Board of Trade's new president, Harold Wilson. A friendly alliance developed between these two, notwithstanding their very different political styles. Wilson was a politician of considerable guile; Bottomley was completely deficient in this quality, invariably believing the best of anyone with whom he had to deal.

Bottomley was sworn of the privy council in 1951, when Labour lost office. During the opposition years he maintained his Commonwealth interests, travelling to Kenya, Ghana, and Cyprus on parliamentary missions. But he also became an enthusiast for Europe, and served in the consultative assembly of the Council of Europe in 1952–4 as well as producing in 1959 a pamphlet, *Why Britain should Join the Common Market*. At the 1959 election he lost his seat. He was forced to return to work for the National Union of Public Employees while searching for another constituency. He found time to write two short anti-communist tracts, *Two Roads to Colonialism* (1960) and *The Use and Abuse of Trade Unions* (1963). A by-election victory in Middlesbrough East in March 1962 revived his career. Eleven months later he strongly supported Wilson against

George Brown for the party leadership. In his capacity as a well-respected trade unionist on the party's right wing, he played an important part in helping to put together Wilson's majority.

Following Labour's return to power in October 1964, Wilson appointed Bottomley secretary of state for Commonwealth relations, with a seat in cabinet. This was Bottomley's political zenith. But now came his misfortune: Rhodesia. His open and straightforward nature did not serve him well in dealing with the devious Ian Smith. Through 1964–5 Bottomley appeared to believe that he was making headway in dissuading Smith from rebellion. Thus Rhodesia's unilateral declaration of independence in November 1965 made him appear naïve. In August 1966 Wilson demoted Bottomley to Overseas Development. He was still in the cabinet but his ministerial career was fading. The end came with Wilson's request for his resignation in August 1967. Bottomley was hurt but, characteristically, not embittered. He involved himself in back-bench assignments, chairing the select committee on race relations and immigration in 1967–70, a committee on Commons services in 1976, and the House of Commons commission in 1980–83. Faithful to Attlee's memory, he chaired the Attlee Foundation from 1978. He served also as treasurer of the Commonwealth Parliamentary Association and as president of the Britain–India Forum and the Britain–Burma Society. Having switched from Middlesbrough East to Teesside (Middlesbrough) in 1974, he carried on as a constituency MP until his retirement from the Commons in 1983. In the following year he was created a life peer, in which capacity he attended the upper house regularly and spoke occasionally, while never seeming altogether at home there. His unrevealing volume of memoirs, *Commonwealth, Comrades and Friends*, came out in 1986 under the aegis of a publisher in India; British publishers had evinced no interest in his 'scandal-free life' (*The Guardian*, 8 Nov 1995).

Bottomley was one of the last of the old-style Labour politicians. A working man with little formal education, he made his way to Westminster through Toynbee Hall, trade unionism, and local government. He was proud of his achievements, but never lost his engaging simplicity of manner. Always a north-east Londoner at heart, he saw out his days in the house at 19 Lichfield Road, Woodford Green, that he and his wife, by whom he was survived (there were no children), had shared since the early 1950s. He died in London on 3 November 1995.

David Goldsworthy

Sources A. Bottomley, *Commonwealth, comrades and friends* (1986) · *The Times* (6 Nov 1995) · *The Independent* (7 Nov 1995) · *The Guardian* (8 Nov 1995) · *WWW* · *Debrett's Peerage* · b. cert.

Archives BL OIOC, memoir on Burma, MSS Eur. E 362 · BLPES, Commonwealth papers · Bodl. RH, corresp. on colonial issues

Likenesses Elliott & Fry, photograph, 1946, NPG [*see illus.*] · group portrait, photograph, 1949 (with N. Hatnell, C. Mortimer, and J. Nixon), Hult. Arch. · H. Todd, double portrait, photograph, 1964 (with Hastings Banda), Hult. Arch. · G. Freston, double portrait, photograph, 1965 (with Harold Wilson), Hult. Arch. · caricature, repro. in *The Guardian* · double portrait, photograph (with Harold Wilson), repro. in *The Independent* · photograph, repro. in *The Times*

Wealth at death £389,541: probate, 24 June 1996, *CGPLA Eng. & Wales*

Bottomley, George (*bap.* **1787?**, *d.* **1868**), surgeon, was, according to *The Lancet*'s obituary, born in Halifax, orphaned at four, and later apprenticed to his maternal grandfather, a retired army surgeon. However, censuses give his place of birth as London, and evidence suggests that he was the son of George and Elizabeth Bottomley who was baptized on 2 October 1787 at St Giles-in-the-Fields, Holborn. Having joined his grandfather John Harris, who had settled at Croydon, Surrey, after serving in North America, Bottomley became a pupil at Guy's Hospital from 22 January 1810 and was elected a member of the Royal College of Surgeons on 4 January 1811. He became Harris's partner and jointly held the post of parish apothecary until Harris's death in 1823, holding it alone thereafter. When the Croydon union was formed in 1836 Bottomley continued as poor-law medical officer both to the parish of Croydon and to its workhouse. He married Harriet Wood (*bap.* 1784, *d.* 1826) on 8 July 1818 and after she died, leaving behind three children, he married Catherine Mary Wood (1793–1866) on 4 September 1828, with whom he had a daughter.

During the 1840s Bottomley achieved some fame as a medical reformer, sharing with Thomas Wakley, editor of *The Lancet*, the conviction that the Royal College of Surgeons was unrepresentative of ordinary provincial surgeons. In 1842 he was elected a vice-president of the short-lived British Medical Association founded by George Webster in 1836. Bottomley was an active member of the Provincial Medical and Surgical Association which took over its name in 1856 and he represented the interests of poor-law medical officers in committees and delegations. His own platform was the Committee of Associated Surgeons, a nebulous organization of which he was chairman. At its peak in the mid-1840s it had several hundred members, declining to double figures by 1850. Though he resented the oligarchic character of the College of Surgeons he vehemently opposed proposals made in 1850 for the formation of a separate college of general practitioners, as degrading to the profession by associating them with midwives and 'retailers of quack medicines'. For his plain-spoken forcefulness in opposition he was called 'the English Brutus'. The revised charter of the Royal College, though it failed to placate its critics, opened the way to his being elected a fellow on 6 July 1852. This belated honour (he had complained to the select committee on medical registration of being passed over for younger men; 'Select committee on medical registration', 15.267) was all the more welcome as his professional career in Croydon was on the wane. Though he held a number of positions, such as surgeon to the Croydon Dispensary, his public career was as a union medical officer. To the select committee on medical poor relief in 1844 he criticized the poor-law guardians for the insanitary state of the workhouse infirmary. An inquiry vindicated the guardians, who claimed that there no longer existed a harmonious relationship between themselves and their medical officer. Nevertheless he was re-elected. The guardians of the more rural parishes continued to criticize his extravagance in providing so much beer, wine, and spirits to the sick poor of the workhouse, for he believed treatment 'should be the same whether Prince or Pauper'.

In 1848 the guardians dismissed Bottomley's associate Julius Berncastle for not attending the fatal pregnancy of Elizabeth Hopkins. But for Bottomley's previous 'unblemished conduct' the guardians would have suspended him for restraining Berncastle from attending her without a medical order. Bottomley resigned in protest since his advice had been consistent with previous policy. The medical press accused the guardians of hypocrisy. *The Lancet* published its reports as a penny pamphlet, no copy of which appears to have survived.

During 1847 Henry Thompson had been Bottomley's assistant. After his medical education Thompson returned to Croydon in 1851 as his partner but finding the practice financially unsatisfactory had the partnership dissolved. In 1854 Bottomley contested the coroner's verdict that the five members of the Atlee (or Atley) family at Coulsdon, south of Croydon, had died of natural causes, his fellow Croydon surgeons Edward Westall and his junior partner Alfred Carpenter having diagnosed typhoid at the post mortem. Suspecting poisoning, Bottomley persuaded the home secretary, Lord Palmerston, to have one of the bodies exhumed. The mother's was examined by the forensic toxicologist Alfred Swaine Taylor, who, despite finding none in the stomach and intestines, detected traces of arsenic in the liver and concluded that she had died of poisoning. Though a textbook case Taylor's examination is now believed to be flawed as arsenic was naturally present in the materials used.

Bottomley's readiness to provoke his fellow surgeons was also demonstrated later in the year when he broke ranks over their boycotting applying for the post of public vaccinator because of poor remuneration. In 1858, when he was seeking re-election to the Croydon board of health at the time of *Chasemore* v. *Richards*, an action brought by the mill owners along the Wandle to prevent the board from drawing on underground water, the local press successfully campaigned against him by accusing him of being an advocate of the mill owners and denigrating the board's achievements.

Bottomley was a competent practical surgeon who contributed some articles to the medical press. He rode to the hounds and played cricket. He died, apparently in debt, aged eighty, on 27 September 1868 at his home, 65 High Street, Croydon; his wife predeceased him by two years. They were buried in Queen's Road cemetery, Croydon, Bottomley on 10 October 1868. BRIAN LANCASTER

Sources *Sussex Agricultural Express* (1848) · *Croydon Chronicle* · minutes of the Croydon local board of health, Croydon Central Library, Croydon Archive Service · 'Select committee on medical poor relief: third report', *Parl. papers* (1844), 9.370–75, no. 531 [minutes of evidence] · W. H. McMenemey, *The life and times of Sir Charles Hastings* (1959) · *London and Provincial Medical Directory* (1855) · *London and Provincial Medical Directory* (1861) · parish register, London, St Giles-in-the-Fields, 2 Oct 1787 [baptism] · registers for Guy's Hospital, 1810, St Thomas's Hospital, London · Z. Cope, *The versatile Victorian: being the life of Sir Henry Thompson, bt, 1820–1904* (1951) · parish register, Middlesex, St Marylebone, 19 Dec 1786 [marriage, George Bottomley] · parish register, Croydon, St John the Baptist [baptism, marriage] · parish register, London, St Martin-in-the-Fields, 5 March 1793 [baptism, Catherine Mary Wood] · parish register, Croydon, 13 Feb 1866 [burial, Catherine Mary Wood] · 'Select committee on medical registration: third report', *Parl. papers* (1847–8), 15.262–6, no. 702 [minutes of evidence]

Wealth at death under £100: administration, 3 April 1871, *CGPLA Eng. & Wales*

Bottomley, Gordon (1874–1948), poet and playwright, was born on 20 February 1874 at Eboracum Street, Keighley, Yorkshire, the only son of Alfred Bottomley, a cashier at a worsted mill and later an accountant, and his wife, Ann Maria Gordon. Educated at Keighley grammar school, he began work as a junior bank clerk. At eighteen the onset of a tubercular condition forced him to give up work and he afterwards spent long periods as an invalid.

Apart from his writing and a little travelling, Bottomley's life was uneventful. He devoted his life to the arts, and even when his name was well known he remained something of a recluse. 'I have no biography', he once said, 'there is nothing that ever happened to me'; but through his work, and a wide correspondence, he led a life 'of singular depth and fullness' (*The Times*). On 24 November 1905 he married Emily (*d.* 1947), the daughter of Matthew Burton, chemist. An artist, she exhibited four works at the Walker Art Gallery, Liverpool, between 1898 and 1901. Their picturesque home, The Sheiling, in Silverdale, Lancashire, welcomed painters and poets, and was celebrated by Edward Thomas in a poem of the same name.

Bottomley's writings, not all published when he died, were profuse: in the period 1902–37 he wrote twenty-three dramatic pieces in verse. He made his début as a poet in 1896 with *The Mickle Drede*, published at Kendal, and was included in the first series of *Georgian Poetry* (1912). The selection was made from his *Chambers of Imagery* (1907, 1912), and the subjects, 'The end of the world' and 'Babel: the gate of the god', attest to his reputation as an elegiac and epic-minded poet. In 1925 Bottomley gathered his representative choice of his work in *Poems of Thirty Years*, which show the influence of Landor and Shelley, though original in certain pictorial, rhythmical, and reflective expressions.

The theatre, however, attracted Bottomley more strongly than poetry; he was one of several poets, from Stephen Phillips to Laurence Binyon, who strove for the revival of a new romantic drama in which poetry should once more dominate. At first he believed that Elizabethan drama, varied by a new age and a new writer, might capture the general audience, but his efforts met only limited success. He later abandoned the Jacobean pattern to concentrate on dramatic poems that combined Celtic legends with the minimalist staging of Japanese Noh drama. Duologues written for John Masefield's Oxford recitations at Boars Hill further convinced him 'that when poetry was perfectly spoken the drama and much of the action would be in the voice' (Bottomley, *Poems and Plays*, 18). In the privately printed *Stage for Poetry* (1948) Bottomley characterized these two phases of personal dramatic development as 'Plays for a theatre outworn' and 'Plays for a theatre unborn'.

Among Bottomley's earlier productions *King Lear's Wife* (1915) and *Gruach* (1921) were nearest to drama. The latter, a prelude to *Macbeth*, won the Femina Vie Heureuse prize (Paris) in 1923. That Bottomley was insufficiently versed in the problems of the theatre was evident, but it was also agreed that he had strength of imagination and eloquence. The best verdict on Bottomley's aspiring poetic plays was that had he been trained as a playwright he might even have been a modern equivalent of John Fletcher. A notable performance of *Gruach* by the Scottish National Theatre Society in March 1923 encouraged Bottomley, whose mother was of Scottish descent, to regard Scotland as a more welcoming home for his experiments in verse drama. Hereafter most of his plays dealt with Scottish themes and he was involved in several movements that aimed to take drama there beyond the limits of established theatre, including the Community Theatre, the Village Drama Society, and the Scottish Association for Speaking Verse. Among his later works were *Singing Sands*, *Ealasaid*, *The White Widow*, and *The Acts of Saint Peter*, the latter the Exeter Cathedral Festival play for 1933.

Bottomley, who had a luxuriant beard and hair well into later life, was liked and admired. He maintained the standards and culture which he knew historically and aesthetically with a generous courtesy. He believed in rural tradition, community, and craftsmanship. His influence on the minority who are sensitive to the power of poetry, and especially of poetry heard communally, was due to his gift of friendship and direct encouragement as well as his writings. Bottomley helped to champion the works of Isaac Rosenberg—they corresponded but never met—and in 1922 he prepared a selection of Rosenberg's poems for publication; he later co-edited, with Denys Harding, the *Collected Works* (1937). He was also friendly with the painter James Guthrie, and together they encouraged the poetry of Edward Thomas, whose letters to Bottomley were published in 1968.

Bottomley's long correspondence with his friend Paul Nash was published in *Poet and Painter* (1955). Nash had designed stage sets and costumes for Bottomley in 1921 and 1922 and his paintings *Gruach* and *Goneril* are in the permanent collection of Carlisle City Art Gallery, with other watercolours and woodcuts inscribed 'to Emily and Gordon Bottomley'. With gifts from their artist friends, including also Guthrie and William Rothenstein, and careful purchases on a restricted budget, the couple built an impressive collection of paintings, drawings, and etchings. It included works by Edward Burne-Jones, Arthur Hughes, William Morris, Samuel Palmer, D. G. Rossetti, and Stanley Spencer. In 1949 the Emily and Gordon Bottomley bequest was given to the Carlisle City Art Gallery, creating the nucleus of the city's art collection.

Gordon Bottomley's reputation was never widespread, and in modern times he has been dismissed as an outdated Georgian belletrist. But he made an important contribution to a vital artistic milieu, and his works were perhaps best understood and most highly valued by his contemporaries. Believing that poetry 'had played itself out of the theatre and into a wilderness', he had the high ambition of seeking to restore it to its rightful setting (Bottomley, *A Stage for Poetry*, 2). He was made a fellow of the Royal Society of Literature in 1926 and was awarded three honorary degrees: LLD (Aberdeen, 1930), DLitt (Durham, 1940), and LittD (Leeds, 1944).

Emily Bottomley, who had nursed her husband and shared in his life to the full, died in 1947, and Gordon Bottomley did not long outlive her. He died at Martinscote, Oare Wilcot, near Marlborough, Wiltshire, on 25 August 1948.

EDMUND BLUNDEN, *rev.* MARK POTTLE

Sources G. Bottomley, *Poems and plays* (1953) · G. Bottomley, *A stage for poetry: my purposes with my plays* (1948) · *Gordon Bottomley and his circle*, University of East Anglia Library (1974) · *The Times* (27 Aug 1948), 7e · *TLS* (9 Dec 1915), 447a; (21 Oct 1920), 681a; (8 Dec 1921), 812b · P. Hartnoll, ed., *The Oxford companion to the theatre*, 4th edn (1983) · M. Banham, ed., *The Cambridge guide to world theatre* (1988) · *Gordon Bottomley, poet and collector: a selection from the collection of Emily and Gordon Bottomley, bequeathed to Carlisle in 1949*, ed. D. R. Perriam [n.d.] [exhibition catalogue, Carlisle City Art Gallery] · *William Rothenstein, a unique collection: Rothstein's purchases for Carlisle 1933-1942* (1970) [exhibition catalogue, Carlisle City Art Gallery] · *Some aspects of British painting, 1890–1945* (1972) [exhibition catalogue, Carlisle City Art Gallery, summer, 1972] · *Emily and Gordon Bottomley bequest: opening exhibition from 16th July to 17th September 1949* (1949) [exhibition catalogue, Carlisle City Art Gallery] · J. Johnson and A. Greutzner, *The dictionary of British artists, 1880–1940* (1976), vol. 5 of *Dictionary of British art* · private information (1959) · d. cert.

Archives BL, corresp. and literary MSS · Hunt. L., letters · Keighley Public Library, corresp. and literary papers · NRA, corresp. and literary papers | Birm. CL, letters to Barry Jackson · BL, corresp. with Sir Sydney Cockerell, Add. MS 52707 · BL, letters to Michael Field, Add. MS 45851 · BL, corresp. with League of Dramatists, Add. MSS 63361 · BL, letters to Charles Ricketts, Add. MSS 58090–58091 · Bodl. Oxf., letters to Evelyn Sharp · Harvard U., Houghton L., letters to Sir William Rothenstein · IWM, letters to Isaac Rosenberg · JRL, letters to John Gray · Keighley Public Library, letters to Hilda Fowlds · LUL, letters to Thomas Sturge Moore, Marie Sturge Moore, Daniel Sturge Moore, and Riette Sturge Moore · NL Ire., letters to Seumas O'Sullivan · NL Scot., letters to Alexander Gray · NL Scot., letters to Sir Herbert Grierson · NL Scot., letters to Neil Gunn · NL Scot., letters to Sir George Henschel · PRO, letters to J. Ramsay MacDonald, PRO 30/69 · Royal Society of Literature, London, letters to the Royal Society of Literature · Somerville College, Oxford, letters to Percy Withers · Tate collection, letters to Paul Nash · TCD, letters to Seumas O'Sullivan · Trinity Cam., letters to J. O. Trevelyan · U. Birm. L., letters to Granville Bantock · U. Birm. L., letters to Allardyce Nicoll, Josephine Nicoll, and John Ramsay · U. Birm. L., letters to Francis Brett Young and Jessica Brett Young · U. Durham, letters to Claude Colleer Abbott · U. Leeds, Brotherton L., letters to Edmund Gosse · U. Reading L., letters to R. L. Mégroz

Likenesses P. Nash, pen and wash drawing, 1912, Carlisle City Art Gallery; repro. in *Poet and painter* (1955) · W. Rothenstein, pencil drawing, 1916, Carlisle City Art Gallery · B. J. Fletcher, charcoal and chalk drawing, 1918, Carlisle City Art Gallery · P. Nash, pencil and crayon drawing, 1922, Carlisle City Art Gallery · W. Rothenstein, chalk drawing, 1922, Carlisle City Art Gallery; repro. in *Twenty-four portraits* (1923) · J. Guthrie, oils, 1923, Carlisle City Art Gallery · C. H. Shannon, chalk drawing, 1924, NPG · T. R. Annan & Sons, photographs, 1930–39, NPG · H. Coster, photographs, 1939, NPG · A. K. Henderson, oils, *c.*1939, Carlisle City Art Gallery

Wealth at death £33,468 2*s.* 5*d.*: probate, 15 Sept 1949, *CGPLA Eng. & Wales* • £1960 2*s.* 6*d.*—save and except settled land: resworn probate, 20 Sept 1949, *CGPLA Eng. & Wales*

Bottomley, Horatio William (**1860–1933**), journalist and swindler, was the only son of William King Bottomley (1827–1863), a tailor's cutter, and his wife, Elizabeth, *née* Holyoake. He was born on 23 March 1860 at 16 St Peter's Street, Bethnal Green, London. Orphaned by the age of four, Bottomley was cared for by his maternal uncle, George Jacob Holyoake, radical agitator and the founder of secularism. In 1869 Bottomley was placed in Sir Josiah Mason's Orphanage, Erdington, Birmingham. To help alleviate his misery and humiliation Bottomley created a world of fantasy from which he never again entirely escaped. When at fourteen he ran away from the orphanage he was shunted between the homes of relatives and various lodging houses in Birmingham and London. Casual jobs preceded five years as a solicitor's clerk. He enrolled at Pitman's College, joined a firm of legal shorthand writers, and became a partner. His introduction to journalism he owed to his uncle and Charles Bradlaugh, serving them as a proof-reader in his spare time. Bottomley bore a striking resemblance to Bradlaugh—not in stature, for he was short and stout, but in features. He countenanced, even encouraged, the rumour that he was the natural child of the great Victorian freethinker.

In May 1880, at twenty, Bottomley impulsively married a dressmaker's counter assistant, Eliza Norton (*c.*1860–1930), daughter of Samuel Norton of Battersea, debt collector. They had one child, a daughter. Poverty spurred Bottomley to a succession of get rich quick schemes. He founded several so-called weekly *Hansards*. They reported the debates of local parliaments, like that at Battersea where Bottomley first discovered his gift for public speaking. He also discovered his unrivalled capacity for separating the credulous from their money. Revenue from advertising was enhanced by the simple expedient of promising special treatment to those who paid him a regular subsidy. By astute buying and selling he quickly acquired a small group of magazines and journals that in 1885 constituted the Catherine Street Publishing Association.

Bottomley's chronic lack of capital prompted him not to caution and parsimony but to ever more expansive and expensive schemes. In 1889 he floated the Hansard Publishing Union. This was popularly referred to on the stock exchange as 'Bottomley's swindle'. Within two years he was obliged to file for bankruptcy and was charged with conspiracy to defraud. It was generally assumed that he would be found guilty but, conducting his own defence brilliantly, he was acquitted. The national press had reported the trial in detail. Bottomley's triumph seemed sufficient to persuade the public that he was a financial genius. Unabashed by the Hansard failure Bottomley founded the Joint Stock Trust and Institute as the vehicle for floating the Western Australian gold mining companies he now promoted. Whatever the consequences for the shareholders, Bottomley invariably did well. The *Financial Times*, of whose board he had been chairman for a few months in 1888, described Bottomley in 1897 as 'a man of millions'. It was a truly amazing success story, the product of reckless audacity, astonishing energy, and extreme good fortune.

Horatio William Bottomley (**1860–1933**), by Bassano, 1918

Despite his prodigious income, the style in which Bottomley chose to live was unsustainable. His simple-minded wife neither understood nor enjoyed the mindless extravagance. She pined for the old days in Battersea, but instead was effectively banished to a villa near Monte Carlo. There, visited occasionally by Bottomley, she lived in ailing if comfortable exile. In Eliza's absence her daughter Florence happily acted as hostess for weekends at The Dicker: the newly purchased, ever expanding, country property near Eastbourne where Bottomley played the squire. His tenants, like his London friends, enjoyed the charade; local society remained quite unimpressed. Bottomley conducted most of his business from his luxury apartment in Pall Mall. Accompanied by his 'stable' of thirsty sycophants—friends, advisers, and general hangers-on—Bottomley became the all too familiar denizen of West End theatres and restaurants, the man about town with an insatiable taste for champagne. Not easily impressed, Frank Harris recorded Bottomley's 'intense greed for all the sensual pleasures' (Harris, 464).

Bottomley bought his first racehorses in 1898. Twice he won the Cesarewitch and numerous lesser races, but never achieved the successes in the Derby or the Grand National which he had grandiloquently forecast when first taking up the sport. For him, racing's real attraction was not the horses but the opportunity it afforded for spectacular gambling. A hopeless judge of equine form, his occasional betting coups never began to compensate for his frequent heavy losses. The bookies loved him because, uncharacteristically, he invariably paid his gambling debts. He enjoyed many mistresses, preferring lively, petite, blonde, working-class girls. He always treated them with courtesy and generosity. The current favourites—he liked to have two if not three in tow at a time—were set up in rented flats and showered with flowers and gifts. None ever seemed to resent it when he chose another as the subject of his fickle, amorous favours. But in 1910 he fell hopelessly and instantly in love with the wife of a fellow ne'er-do-well, Aubrey Lowe. Peggy Primrose (*b*. *c*.1890), a chorus girl with pretensions to being a musical comedy actress, was immediately established as the only permanent member of Bottomley's harem.

Amid this frenetic activity Bottomley nurtured the constant ambition to become an MP. Parliament offered influence and respectability. Also there were obvious advantages for a creative entrepreneur to enter the Commons when parliament increasingly sought to regulate commercial life. The only political conviction he ever convincingly entertained was the determination to gratify his own interests. The opinions he advertised on politics might have amused his constituents by their levity, but were not calculated to impress politicians. 'All parties', he asserted, 'are organised hypocrisies'. Political leaders 'for the most part do nothing or seek only to serve their own ends' (*John Bull*, 12 May 1906). He failed to win a seat in 1887 and again in 1900. But in 1906, as a nominal Liberal, he triumphed in Hackney South, defeating not only the incumbent tory but also another Liberal contender. His dubious financial reputation made him unwelcome at Westminster and his maiden speech was heard in chilling silence. Yet his ebullience and amiable self-deprecation—he referred to himself on one occasion as the chancellor's 'more or less honourable friend'—soon captured his parliamentary audiences. The ingenuity and good sense, particularly of the financial measures he proposed, compelled attention and even grudging admiration. But this parliamentary credit, so skilfully won, he undermined and eventually forfeited by his continued involvement in questionable financial schemes.

Despite the demise of his Hansard Union, Bottomley remained fascinated by journalism. In 1902 he bought a moribund evening newspaper, *The Sun*. Despite the ingenious changes he made, a series of increasingly dubious investigatory stunts, and a highly successful racing tipster, the Scorcher, *The Sun* failed to prosper, and he sold it in 1904. It was two years before Bottomley could persuade Odham's Press to print a new weekly journal that he proposed to edit. He had recruited a small, colourful, and talented editorial team, resurrected his old *Sun* column, 'The world, the flesh and the devil', and from its very first issue, 12 May 1906, *John Bull* was a success—sensational, lively, entertaining, and very profitable. Bottomley, pathologically averse to paying bills, saw no reason why he should pay his printer. Julias Elias (later Viscount Southwood) suggested that Odhams manage the journal. Bottomley agreed, glad to be free of the business details which he always found tiresome. The deal was a brilliant commercial coup for both parties. Bottomley remained editor until 1921. *John Bull*'s masthead asserted that it was written 'without fear or favour, rancour or rant' to uphold the interests of the common man. That claim was as false as Bottomley's repeated assertion 'If you read it in *John Bull*, it is so'. The primary purpose of *John Bull* was to promote Bottomley and his schemes.

In the first general election of 1910, again standing for Hackney South, Bottomley trounced his Unionist opponent. His attachment to the Liberal cause was now so threadbare that he suggested an alliance with a group of ultra tories in order 'to continue to criticise the Liberal party unhampered by Cobdenite shibboleths' (Bottomley to Edward Goulding, 17 June 1910, Wargrave MSS, HLRO). Though nothing came of his proposal he rejected the Liberal whip, claiming he preferred 'to occupy a position of dignified detachment'. He formed the John Bull League as a public assertion of his 'new-found independence'. It was 'opposed to cant and self-righteousness … despised party tactics and party lies', and wanted parliament filled with 'business men of grit', among whose number Bottomley clearly thought he belonged (Hyman, 127). In the general election of December 1910 Bottomley again succeeded, seeing off opponents from both political parties with the help of paid supporters at the hustings. In the High Court, however, he was not so successful. A charge of conspiracy to defraud, brought in November 1908, was dismissed, but he went on to lose a succession of damaging suits arising from his fraudulent schemes. On his return to the Commons members treated him as a pariah. In vain he pleaded with the house that he was the undeserving victim of puritanism, party, and priestcraft, but his reputation for honesty was beyond rescue. In February 1912, facing demands from the Prudential Assurance Company, he admitted that his liabilities exceeded his assets by £200,000. As a bankrupt he could no longer remain an MP, and he applied for the Chiltern Hundreds on 24 May 1912. In public he showed no remorse, telling audiences that parliament was 'played out … quite possibly an illegal assembly', and that the present 'musty, rusty, corrupt system' needed replacement by 'Business government' (*John Bull*, 3 Aug 1912).

With the outbreak of war, in August 1914, Bottomley momentarily promised to mend his ways, but soon succumbed to temptation. War afforded a national stage for his huckstering demagoguery. *John Bull* spewed out venomous chauvinism, demanding that all 'Germ-Huns' in Britain, whether naturalized or no, be exterminated. The old fraudster was inspired to add peddling insurance against Zeppelin raids to his repertoire of familiar swindles—sweeps, lotteries, and rigged prize competitions. But his involvement in the recruiting campaign best demonstrates Bottomley's unrivalled capacity for captious cynicism. From September 1914 he addressed ever larger, more enthusiastic audiences, encouraging men to volunteer and take up arms. He described himself as an 'oratorical courtesan', shamelessly selling himself to the highest bidder. His patriotic appeals were barely disguised music-hall turns. The praise he received served to feed his latent megalomania. His political ambitions had always tended towards fantasy so that when, in December 1916, Lloyd George became prime minister Bottomley declared that he was ready to serve his country in some official capacity or other. He did not seem to realize that he was indelibly associated with dishonesty. Just as the blatant vulgarity of his writing in *John Bull* shamed journalism, so his speeches, with their ignominious appeals for sacrifice, degraded public life. Paid enough (his weekly articles for Northcliffe's *Sunday Pictorial*, launched in 1915, earned him nearly £8000 a year), Bottomley would say or write anything.

Bottomley was eventually betrayed by his growing carelessness, but not before managing his discharge from bankruptcy, partly by launching schemes, publicized in *John Bull*, to invest in war stocks and savings. He once more entered the Commons as the independent member for Hackney South at the general election of 1918. He had the effrontery to congratulate himself upon not being raised to the peerage, an honour that had been given to so many connected with the press. As his investment schemes faltered he moved to France for a time in 1920. An attempted action for criminal libel which he brought in 1921 against a former associate, Reuben Bigland, failed. The case brought damaging revelations that his highly successful Victory Bond Club—through which in 1919 readers of *John Bull* were invited to invest in government Victory Bonds, some £900,000 being raised—was a hopeless swindle. Bottomley complained to readers in the *Sunday Illustrated*, the paper which he had started in 1919, that those, like himself, who sat upon a pinnacle, inevitably became the target of envious mud-slingers. But his business enterprises were being examined by a receiver, and in March 1922 he was charged with fraudulent conversion. Tried before Mr Justice Salter at the Old Bailey, Bottomley was found guilty on twenty-three out of twenty-four counts and sentenced to seven years' penal servitude. His legal appeal was rejected and he was expelled from the Commons.

Prison was a harrowing experience, but his sense of humour never entirely deserted him. A prison visitor seeing Bottomley working on a mail bag inquired, 'Sewing?' 'No, reaping', came the instant reply. He was released from Maidstone gaol in July 1927 after serving five years. The confident belief that he would soon be rehabilitated with his public proved ill-founded. A new journal, *John Blunt*, planned speaking tours, even an act at the Windmill Theatre, all alike failed. He cut a pathetic figure and, a broken old man, he stumbled into obscurity. In 1930 his wife died and his daughter emigrated to South Africa. Of his former friends and acolytes all deserted him except Peggy Primrose, who shared her home with him. He died of a stroke at the Middlesex Hospital, London on 26 May 1933. He was cremated at Golders Green and his ashes were scattered on the Sussex downs in 1937.

Bottomley's obituary notices in the national press emphasized how he had squandered his many gifts. 'He had magnetism, eloquence, enthusiasm, the power to convince … he might have been anything, a captain of industry, a great journalist' (*Daily Mail*, 27 May 1933). All his adult life Bottomley was 'more a series of public attitudes than a person' (Symons, 274). As company promoter, businessman, financier, politician, national recruiting sergeant, bon viveur, sportsman, squire, publisher, journalist, advocate, he claimed to serve the interests of others, but sought only his own gratification. It was his overwhelming egotism that betrayed him and promoted the hubris that condoned ever rasher, more carelessly executed frauds that invited discovery, irredeemable ruin, and disgrace. A. J. A. MORRIS

Sources J. Symons, *Horatio Bottomley: a biography* (1955) · A. Hyman, *The rise and fall of Horatio Bottomley: the biography of a swindler* (1972) · Tenax [E. Bell], *The gentle art of exploiting gullibility* (1923) · R. J. Minney, *Viscount Southwood* (1954) · *WW* · *Daily Mail* (27 May 1933) · *DNB* · G. R. Searle, *Corruption in British politics, 1895–1930* (1987) · J. Camplin, *The rise of the plutocrats* (1978) · T. Jones, *Whitehall diary*, ed. K. Middlemas, 1 (1969) · S. E. Koss, *The rise and fall of the political press in Britain*, 2 (1984) · F. Harris, *My life and loves*, new edn, ed. J. F. Gallagher (1964) · C. Shaw, 'Bottomley, Horatio William', *DBB* · b. cert.

Archives People's History Museum, Manchester, corresp. relating to his Hackney Labour Party candidature | HLRO, Wargrave MSS, letter to Goulding | FILM BFI NFTVA, news footage | SOUND BL NSA, documentary recordings · BL NSA, news recording

Likenesses B. Stone, photograph, 1911, NPG · Bassano, photograph, 1918, NPG [*see illus.*] · E. Kapp, drawing, 1928, Barber Institute of fine Arts, Birmingham · H. W. Bottomley, self-portrait, pencil drawing (aged thirty-three) · photograph (as Sergeant Buzfuz from *Pickwick papers*), repro. in Symons, *Horatio Bottomley* · photographs, repro. in Hyman, *The rise and fall of Horatio Bottomley* · portrait (aged thirty-three; after pencil drawing by H. W. Bottomley), repro. in Symons, *Horatio Bottomley*

Bottomley, Joseph (1786–1858), organist, the son of Enoch and Grace Bottomley, was born in Halifax, where he was baptized on 7 May 1786, and where he played a violin concerto in public at the age of seven. In 1798 he moved to Manchester and studied with Grimshaw, the organist of St John's Church. Three years later he was apprenticed to Lawton, organist of St Peter's, Leeds, and then studied the piano in London with Joseph Woelfl. In 1807 he became organist of Bradford parish church, but lived and taught in Halifax. He was organist of Sheffield parish church from 1820. Bottomley's publications included *Six Exercises for Pianoforte*, twelve waltzes, and *A Dictionary of Music* (1816). He died in 1858. ANNE PIMLOTT BAKER

Sources Grove, *Dict. mus.* · *IGI* · H. W. Shaw, *The succession of organists of the Chapel Royal and the cathedrals of England and Wales from c.1538* (1991)

Bottomley, Sir Norman Howard (1891–1970), air force officer, was born at Bankfield, Soyland, near Halifax, Yorkshire, on 18 September 1891, the son of Thomas Bottomley, a journeyman cotton spinner, from Ripponden, Yorkshire, and his wife, Ellen, *née* Whiteley. He was educated at Halifax secondary school, Borough College in London, and Rennes University in France. On 2 February 1915 he was embodied as a Territorial Force lieutenant in the

3rd battalion, the East Yorkshire regiment, retained at home to provide reinforcements for active service battalions in France. However, he soon crossed the channel to see action and advanced to captain on 9 April 1916. Three days later he was seconded to the Royal Flying Corps (RFC). He frequently flew operationally, and on 22 March 1917 he became a flight commander. The following year he was awarded the AFC, and in 1918–19, as acting major, he carried out staff duties with 1 group at Kenley.

Bottomley secured a permanent commission in the Royal Air Force as a flight lieutenant (captain equivalent) on 1 August 1919. He was posted to the staff of RAF Middle East at Cairo on 23 March 1921, and specifically to operations duties on 7 November 1921. Having advanced to squadron leader on 30 June 1922, he was posted to 4 flying training squadron at Abu Sueir on 19 December 1922. In 1923 he gained second place in the R. M. Groves memorial essay prize competition. He went as a student to the RAF Staff College at Andover on 5 May 1924 and was subsequently appointed to the directorate of operations and intelligence at the Air Ministry on 1 May 1925. In 1927 he married Anne, the daughter of Sir William Biggart Lang, a machine tool manufacturer, and they had a son and daughter.

On 15 October 1928 Bottomley assumed command of 4 (army co-operation) squadron of Bristol Fighters at South Farnborough, and on 1 July 1929 he was promoted wing commander. He entered the Imperial Defence College as a student on 14 January 1930 and, on completing the course, became an instructor at the RAF Staff College on 22 December 1930. Between 1934 and 1938 he was in India, initially at the aircraft park at Lahore, and on 4 October 1934 he took command of 1 (Indian) group at Peshawar as acting group captain (substantive from 1 July 1935). He was mentioned in dispatches for suppressing unrest in Waziristan between January and September 1937, and that year he received the DSO. General Sir Robert Cassels praised Bottomley's 'high example and ready co-operation', with his group playing 'a prominent part in bringing the operations to a successful conclusion' (*The Times*, 15 Aug 1970). He was appointed CIE in the coronation honours list.

Bottomley was made senior air staff officer (SASO) at the headquarters of Bomber Command in Uxbridge on 21 February 1938 and advanced to air commodore on 1 November 1938. At Bomber Command he was reluctant to accept that heavy losses sustained by RAF bombers in the opening months of the war were due to enemy action: 'The failure of the enemy must be ascribed to good formation flying … In our Service it is the equivalent of the old "Thin Red Line" or the "Shoulder to Shoulder" of Cromwell's Ironsides' (Webster and Frankland, 1.194). Bottomley was loyally reflecting RAF doctrine, utterly discredited before the end of 1939, that in daylight bombers flying in tight formation could ward off fighters. He was promoted acting air vice-marshal in March (substantive from 1 July 1940) and was appointed air officer commanding 5 bomber group on 22 November 1940, where he declared himself 'tremendously impressed' by the new Lancaster bomber (Terraine, 491), which did not, however, reach operational squadrons in significant numbers until 1943.

Bottomley moved to deputy chief of the air staff (DCAS) on 13 May 1941, and on 9 July issued a directive about 'dislocating the German transportation system and destroying the morale of the civil population as a whole and of the industrial workers in particular' (Webster and Frankland, 4.136). This foreshadowed the tactic known as area bombing, whereby the centres of urban concentrations were bombed once the inability to strike specific industrial targets had become apparent. In 1941 Bottomley was appointed CB. When the DCAS post lapsed he became assistant chief of the air staff (operations) (5 May 1942), but he was reappointed DCAS when that title was revived (1943).

Bottomley proved himself a careful, thorough administrator and was called upon to chair a number of planning committees, including an *ad hoc* one created by the chiefs of staff to monitor the progress of Barnes Wallis's schemes to breach west German dams and sink the battleship *Tirpitz* with variations of his 'bouncing bomb'. On 16 August 1944 he became a temporary air marshal, made substantive when appointed air officer commanding-in-chief, Bomber Command, on 15 September 1945. In 1943 he was appointed KCB, in 1945 he received the order of merit (USA), and in 1946 a medal from the city of Bordeaux. Bottomley left Bomber Command on 16 January 1947 to become inspector-general of the RAF. Promoted air chief marshal on 23 March 1947, he retired from the RAF in 1948.

For the next eight years Bottomley was director of administration at the BBC, where he established 'a reputation for absolute fairness … a most friendly and humane man' (*The Times*, 15 Aug 1970). When he went to Broadcasting House on 1 January 1948, the BBC was facing decisions about expanding television operations, involving negotiations with six trade unions and the BBC staff association. He knew that the BBC had been granted only a temporary renewal of its charter in 1946 and that the government-sponsored Beveridge committee was currently investigating the future of broadcasting. To ensure that BBC officials, including himself, would be fully prepared, he established an internal working party in March 1948: 'We should start preliminary work at once' to make sure '[we are] fully and accurately informed' (Briggs, 311). By September 1949 this task had been completed, a month before the first BBC representative appeared before the committee. In 1953 Bottomley forecast that, in terms of content and the artists employed, commercial television would be beholden to advertisers. Also its acting director-general for a short period (1956–7), he brought administrative order and clear thinking to the BBC, when it faced severe challenges to its structure and programme content in the immediate post-war years.

Bottomley listed his recreations as golf, fishing, and gardening, and he was a member of the RAF Club. Of his work at the Air Ministry (1941–5) the secretary of state for air, Sir Archibald Sinclair, referred to his being 'cool, alert, wise, indefatigable, indispensable … transparent loyalty and sincerity made him an ideal comrade and diplomat' (Bottomley, 224). Sinclair also drew attention to his ability to focus on main issues: 'His eye was always as true to the ball as the compass needle is to the Pole' (ibid.). In this respect, operational experience during the First World War and inter-war years, including successful command appointments in India, coupled with reflection on theoretical aspects of air power demonstrated by entries to RAF prize competitions early in his career, were invaluable assets. By establishing firm personal friendships he greatly enhanced Anglo-American co-operation during the wartime air offensive against Germany. Bottomley lived at Pipers Wing, Great Kingshill, near High Wycombe, Buckinghamshire, and died from heart disease on 13 August 1970 in St Andrew's Hospital, Northampton.

JOHN SWEETMAN

Sources *Army List* • *Air Force List* • *The Times* (15 Aug 1970) • J. Terraine, *The right of the line: the Royal Air Force in the European war, 1939–1945* (1985) • E. Wyrall, *The East Yorkshire regiment in the Great War* (1928) • *WWW, 1961–70* • A. Briggs, *The history of broadcasting in the United Kingdom*, 4 (1979) • C. Webster and N. Frankland, *The strategic air offensive against Germany, 1939–1945*, 4 vols. (1961) • N. H. Bottomley, 'The strategic bomber offensive against Germany', *Journal of the Royal United Service Institution*, 93 (1948), 224–39 • b. cert. • d. cert.

Archives Royal Air Force Museum, Hendon, papers | Nuffield Oxf., corresp. with Lord Cherwell | FILM IWM FVA, news footage

Likenesses H. Coster, photographs, 1940–44, NPG • T. C. Dugdale, oils, IWM • photograph, IWM

Wealth at death £58,185: probate, 2 April 1971, *CGPLA Eng. & Wales*

Bottomore, Thomas Burton (1920–1992), sociologist, was born on 8 April 1920 at the Collins Trust Maternity Hospital, Waverley Street, Nottingham, the first of the three children of Thomas Joseph Bottomore (1887–1954), milliner, and his wife, Margaret Amy (1894–1977), daughter of James Ernest Bacon, draper, of Nottingham, and his wife, Margaret. Tom, as he was generally known, was educated at Nottingham high school, from 1930 to 1936, and the London School of Economics (LSE), where he graduated in 1943 with an upper second-class BSc (Econ), having worked from 1941 in the Ministry of Economic Warfare. From 1943 to 1947 he did military service, becoming captain and staff captain in the Sherwood Foresters and serving in India and Austria, where he worked in the economics division of the Allied Control Commission. In August 1947, in Vienna, he married Christiane (Christl) von Mosing, a writer and journalist. When he left the army he returned to the LSE, and was awarded his MSc (Econ) in 1950, with a thesis on 'Recent theories of social progress'. In 1951–2 he held a Rockefeller fellowship at the Sorbonne, where he conducted research on the French higher civil service as well as pursuing interests in Marxist theory and workers' co-operatives, and where he got to know many French intellectuals and acquired excellent French and lifelong friends. When he returned to Britain in 1952 he took up an assistant lectureship in sociology at the LSE, and was promoted to lecturer in 1955 and reader in 1959. Meanwhile, having separated from his first wife in 1950 and divorced her early in 1953, on 30 January 1953 he married Mary Kathleen, *née* Greasley (1918–1986), who worked as a translator and for the Citizens' Advice Bureau. They had three children: Katherine Helen (*b.* 1954), Stephen (*b.* 1955), and Eleanor Jane (*b.* 1957).

Bottomore remained at the LSE until 1965, when he left for a professorship at Simon Fraser University in Vancouver, Canada. He returned to Britain in 1967 to become the first professor of sociology at the still new University of Sussex, where he remained (apart from brief periods from 1974 to 1976 at Dalhousie University) until his formal retirement in 1985. In personal appearance he was slim, dark-haired, and of medium height, with a dignified yet quizzical expression, a moustache, a conventional tweed-jacketed style of dress, and a pipe often in his hand. In Sussex he lived at Cherry Tree Cottage, in the village of Ditchling, where he helped dig the swimming pool which he regularly used; he listed his recreations as riding, swimming, gardening, travel, reading, film, and theatre.

The International Sociological Association, founded in 1950, figured largely in Bottomore's life, and he played several important roles in it. In 1953 he became the third executive secretary of the fledgeling association, and held that post until 1959. From 1957 to 1962 he edited its journal *Current Sociology*, which had the important function of providing systematic bibliographical information on major fields of sociological work. From 1970 to 1974 he was vice-president with responsibility for its 'research committees', and from 1974 to 1978 president. (It was for an International Sociological Association commission that he wrote his textbook *Sociology*, published in 1962, designed to provide an introduction suitable for Indian students—though it was widely used outside India.) He was also president of the British Sociological Association from 1969 to 1971; that position was mainly honorific.

As a young man, Bottomore had become interested in socialism as a potential remedy for the poverty he saw in Nottinghamshire mining communities and for the rise of fascism, and briefly became a member of the Communist Party. For the rest of his life he was politically committed to socialism, and strongly interested in Marxism, though he was no orthodox Marxist, and his political activity was mainly on the intellectual front. His time in Paris led to co-editorship with Maximilien Rubel of *Selected Writings on Sociology and Social Philosophy* by Marx (1956), which introduced many sociology students to Marx's thought. He wrote about Marx and Marxists, translated related works, and in 1983 published a *Dictionary of Marxist Thought*. These initially unfashionable interests were in tune with the times in the late 1960s and 1970s, and that did much to enhance his reputation. Other especially influential works, of a high intellectual standard though written for a student audience, were his *Classes in Modern Society* (1955) and *Elites and Society* (1964). Although he drew on empirical work by others, after his time in Paris he was a theorist rather than a researcher. He continued to publish copiously until his death; his later books were largely historical or reference works. His writing was outstandingly clear and readable. He often played a mediating intellectual role, linking Marxism to other social theories and moderating criticisms of either from the other side. His interests and perspectives were always as much international as they were British, and his Marxism was a basis for connections crossing some of the usual boundaries.

Bottomore was widely respected among sociologists both in Britain and abroad. Numerous graduate students of his became prominent theorists themselves. Some of his closest intellectual relationships were reflected in his retirement Festschrift, *Social Theory and Social Criticism* (ed. W. Outhwaite and M. Mulkay, 1987) and in an interview that he gave to *Theory, Culture and Society* (vol. 6/3, 1989). He died at his home, Cherry Tree Cottage, from a sudden aneurysm on 9 December 1992, and was cremated at Woodvale crematorium, Brighton, on 12 December.

JENNIFER PLATT and WILLIAM OUTHWAITE

Sources W. Outhwaite, 'Tom Bottomore's life and work', *Soziologicheskii Zhurnal*, 4 (1994), 96–108 [translated into Russian] • 'Short biography', curriculum vitae, BLPES, T. B. Bottomore MSS, folder 52 • J. Hime, ed., *Debrett's people of Sussex* (1991) • Internationaal Instituut voor Sociale Geschiedenis, Amsterdam, International Sociological Association MSS • *Calendars* [London School of Economics] • personal knowledge (2004) • private information (2004) • *The Times* (18 Dec 1992) • *The Independent* (14 Dec 1992) • b. cert.

Archives BLPES, MSS | Internationaal Instituut voor Sociale Geschiedenis, Amsterdam, International Sociological Association MSS | SOUND BL NSA, performance recordings

Likenesses photograph, repro. in *The Times*

Wealth at death £291,210: probate, 8 April 1993, *CGPLA Eng. & Wales*

Botwulf [St Botwulf, Botolph] (*fl.* **654–*c.*670**), abbot of Iken, began to build his minster of 'Icanho' (now conclusively identified as Iken, Suffolk) in 654 according to the Anglo-Saxon Chronicle. Ceolfrith, the future abbot of Monkwearmouth and Jarrow, is said by his anonymous biographer to have visited East Anglia 'to see the monastic practices of Abbot Botwulf, whom report had proclaimed on all sides to be a man of unparalleled life and learning and full of the grace of the Holy Spirit' (Plummer, 1.389), a visit which would have occurred *c.*670. This suggests that the rule observed at Iken, unfortunately unknown, was a formative one which influenced the practices of other major late seventh-century houses.

Iken Minster, where excavations in 1977 found remains of the early church and monastic settlement, controlled at least one daughter house on the opposite side of England. A charter of 674–90 preserved in the 'Testament of St Mildburg' records the foundation of Much Wenlock Minster, Mercia, on land given by Æthelheah, abbot of Botwulf's monastery of Iken, 'on condition that the said place shall by God's will remain, not on compulsion but willingly, under the tutelage of the church of the venerable Abbot Botwulf' (*AS chart.*, S 1798). A twelfth-century charter records a tradition that Hadstock, Essex, was another minster founded by Botwulf.

These fragments of evidence identify Botwulf as a religious leader of high status in the first years of East Anglian Christianity, almost certainly acting under royal patronage, who extended his monastic federation through cross-kingdom family networks. The much fuller account of his life written by Folcard after *c.*1070, which amplifies the context of royal patronage, states that Botwulf and his brother Adulf were trained in Germany, and gives the year of his death as 680, seems to be largely imaginary. In the tenth and eleventh centuries his relics were divided up and are recorded variously at Peterborough, Thorney, Bury, Ely, and Hadstock, a multiplicity of sites which raises a suspicion that two or more saints called Botwulf may have been conflated in the hagiographical tradition. Botwulf's cult had some success in post-conquest England, especially in East Anglia and London, and sixty-four medieval dedications to him are recorded; there was also a significant cult in Scandinavia. His feast was celebrated on 17 June, that of his translation on 1 December.

JOHN BLAIR

Sources S. E. West, N. Scarfe, and R. Cramp, 'Iken, St Botolph, and the coming of East Anglian Christianity', *Proceedings of the Suffolk Institute of Archaeology and History*, 35 (1981–4), 279–301 • 'Historia abbatum auctore anonymo', *Venerabilis Baedae opera historica*, ed. C. Plummer, 1 (1896), 388–404, esp. 389 • H. P. R. Finberg, *The early charters of the west midlands*, 2nd edn (1972), 197–216 • Folcard, 'Life of St Botolph', *Acta sanctorum ordinis S. Benedicti*, ed. J. Mabillon, 3 (1734), 1–7 • D. Whitelock, 'The pre-Viking age church in East Anglia', *Anglo-Saxon England*, 1 (1972), 1–22, esp. 10–11 • *AS chart.*, S 1798 • J. Toy, 'St Botulph: an English saint in Scandinavia', *The cross goes north: processes of conversion in northern Europe, AD 300–1300*, ed. M. Carver (2003), 565–70 • J. Blair, 'A handlist of Anglo-Saxon saints', *Local saints and local churches in the early medieval west*, ed. A. Thacker and A. Sharpe (2002), 495–565

Bouch, Sir Thomas (**1822–1880**), civil engineer, was born on 22 February 1822 at Thursby, Cumberland, the third son of William Bouch, a captain in the mercantile marine and his wife, Elizabeth Sanderson. At the age of seventeen he was employed for four years on the construction of the Lancaster and Carlisle Railway, for which the engineers were Locke and Errington. He subsequently served four years as resident engineer on the Wear Valley Railway during its construction, and worked on other railways in the north of England.

In 1849 Bouch became engineer and manager of the Edinburgh and Northern Railway (later known as the Edinburgh, Perth, and Dundee Railway). In this capacity he became interested in the problems of railway crossings of the Forth and Tay estuaries, and developed a train ferry or 'floating railway' (partly financed by Sir John Gladstone) for taking goods wagons over the Forth between Granton and Burntisland. The wagons ran on rails directly onto rails on the ferry and were taken off in the same way. This system worked well over a number of years. In 1853 Bouch married Margaret Ada Nelson; they had a son and two daughters.

Shortly after completing the work on the Forth, Bouch left the Edinburgh railway company and set up as a consulting engineer, mainly on the development of railways in the north of England and in Scotland, and for tramways in London, Glasgow, Edinburgh, and Dundee. In total he was the engineer for the construction of about 270 miles of railways, chief of which was the South Durham and Lancashire Union, 50 miles long. His largest railway in Scotland was the Edinburgh to Peebles line, 21 miles in

Sir Thomas Bouch (**1822–1880**), by unknown engraver, pubd 1880 (after John Moffat)

length and for a long time the pattern for cheap construction. His railways demanded many bridges, including the Beelah Viaduct, with sixteen spans of 60 ft each and 196 ft high, and Deepdale, which had eleven spans of 60 ft with a maximum height of 160 ft. These bridges were very economically designed, comprising lattice girders on iron piers composed of groups of braced columns, and carried railway traffic for over a hundred years before being dismantled. Bouch also constructed a remarkable road bridge in 1871 at Newcastle, the Redheugh Viaduct, which consisted of two spans of 260 ft and two of 240 ft. These spans were of lattice girders supported by raking ties and bore a striking resemblance to the cable-stayed bridges of today.

Bouch was thus well equipped to realize the dream of his life, which was to bridge the Forth and the Tay estuaries. His opportunity to bridge the Tay came first, an act being passed in 1870 for the purpose. The scheme proposed by Bouch crossed the river between Wormit and Dundee and was a few yards short of 2 miles long, by far the longest bridge in the world at the time. It consisted of eighty-five spans, of which thirteen, at the deepest part of the channel, formed the navigation spans, longer and higher than the others. They were of lattice girders carried on piers formed of groups of cast-iron columns. The original design had the lattice girders carried on tall brick piers, but owing to misleading information on ground conditions the brick piers had to be replaced by lighter iron construction over most of the bridge length after construction had begun. This change had a significant effect on the strength and stability of the bridge.

The bridge was passed by the Board of Trade and opened in May 1878. Queen Victoria journeyed over during the following year and knighted Bouch on 26 June 1879. He was meantime engaged on his design for a bridge at Queensferry to cross the Forth. Construction of this bridge with two main spans of 1600 ft was begun in 1878, again a gigantic leap forward in bridge design, as the longest railway spans hitherto constructed in Britain were of 460 ft, over the Menai Strait.

However, on 28 December 1879 a violent storm caused the collapse of the navigation spans of the Tay Bridge while a train was crossing, and seventy-five lives were lost. The subsequent inquiry found the cause of the collapse to be inadequate bracing of the ironwork of the tall piers. It seems likely that defects in the casting of the columns also contributed to the collapse. The inquiry did not apportion blame for the disaster, but one of the panel members (a Mr Rothery), in a separate report, placed the blame on Bouch. Work on his Forth Bridge was stopped, and he was relieved of his post as engineer. These events affected Bouch's health, and he died from heart disease the following year, on 30 October 1880, after premature retirement to Moffat. He was buried in Dean cemetery, Edinburgh. He was survived by his wife. It may be said of him that he perhaps designed his bridges with a lower margin of safety than other engineers, but displayed boldness and originality in many of them, and had a distinguished career until the collapse of the Tay Bridge. It could also be said that he pointed the way to the eventual successful bridging of the Forth and Tay at locations which were first chosen by him. J. S. Shipway

Sources *PICE*, 63 (1880–81), 301–08 • *ILN*, 77 (1880), 468 • *The Times* (29 Dec 1879) • *The Times* (30 Dec 1879) • *The Times* (31 Dec 1879) • 'Court of inquiry on … the fall of a portion of the Tay Bridge', *Parl. papers* (1880), vol. 39.1, C. 2616; vol. 39.53, C. 2616-I • d. cert.
Archives NA Scot., corresp.
Likenesses engraving (after photograph by J. Moffat), NPG; repro. in *ILN* [*see illus.*]
Wealth at death £249,859 9*s*. 11*d*.: confirmation, 1 March 1881, *CCI*

Boucher [Bouchier], **George** (*d*. **1643**), royalist conspirator, was probably related—perhaps as a son—to Nathaniel Boucher, a Bristol merchant who was warden (1621) and treasurer (1625) of the Bristol Society of Merchant Venturers, and sheriff of the city in 1624. Little is known of Boucher's family except that he left a wife, who died early in the Restoration, and seven children, of whom the eldest was a son, John; a younger son was named George. Boucher was probably the George Butcher listed as a member of the Merchant Venturers in 1618, who in 1626 was a collector for the company's project to send a ship in search of the north-west passage. He does not appear as a high official of the company. In 1640 or 1641 he was the first of several men sent to Westminster to complain that the actions resulting from the award of the customs farm to the London Vintners' Company had ruined large numbers of Bristol vintners. He was clearly a man of wealth and influence, who allegedly lost £2000 in the plot which cost him his life.

The civic leaders of Bristol were unwilling to take sides in the civil war, but this was at first expressed chiefly in efforts to deflect and delay the admission of parliamentarian forces, who lay closer to the city than their opponents. During the subsequent occupation the behaviour of the parliamentarian commander, Colonel Essex, gave much ground for complaint and, despite his removal and the installation as governor of Nathaniel Fiennes, there was considerable sentiment in Bristol for an approach to the king's forces. The first steps in organizing the attempt were apparently taken before the end of 1642. The chief actors were Richard Yeamans or Yeomans and George Boucher, 'men of good esteem, plentiful estates, known integrity, and true children of the church of England' (Towgood, 21). Boucher's chief role, as he later affirmed, was initially in the political selection and recruitment of the foot-soldiers of the conspiracy in Bristol itself. First he framed an oath which expressed loyalty to the king 'in these words: I do voluntarily protest before Almighty God that I will to the utmost of my power and with my life and fortunes defend and maintain the rights and privileges of my dread sovereign Lord King Charles' (Walker, 6). He himself took this oath on 3 March 1643 and set about administering it to others, providing them also with arms and ammunition. But Boucher's organizational role on the night of 7 March was equally crucial. His house in Christmas Street lay next to St John's Bridge, and backed onto the River Froome. It was selected as one of four rallying points for the plotters, not least because all depended on the first step in their plan, the opening of the Froome gate to admit Prince Rupert and his troops. Boucher's men were to seize the guards stationed at the gate and imprison them in a crypt underneath the adjoining church of St John's. He had also arranged 'to give Prince Rupert a signal when he should make his approaches to the city, by ringing Saint John's and Saint Michael's bells' and had organized locks and chains to bar the movement of any parliamentarian horse, should these appear (Towgood, 15).

The conspiracy, however, was betrayed at the last moment. Alerted to the danger, and expecting the arrival of Rupert under cover of darkness, Captain Thomas Goodier commanded that lanterns be lit by those living close to the Froome gate. His soldiers, proceeding along Christmas Street enforcing the order, found Boucher's residence 'without light' and silent, 'as if there were no person at all in the house', so they set about breaking down the door. Sixty men were crammed inside. Of these, most 'ran out at a water gate on the backside of the house, and went away through the water, it being a low tide, and made an escape' (Walker, 12). The soldiers arrested the twenty-three remaining, and impounded muskets and ammunition.

Four conspirators were singled out as chief organizers. George Boucher was examined at least three times, signing statements on 10 March, 27 April, and 3 May. These amounted to a frank admission of guilt, and the accusers had ample supporting evidence against Boucher and others. Two principals, Edward Dacres and Robert Yeamans's brother William, were pardoned, and parliamentarian officers of the garrison who had been privy to the conspiracy were not prosecuted, but on 8 and 22 May respectively Richard Yeamans and George Boucher were condemned to death by hanging.

In Oxford there was outrage at the death sentences. Patrick Ruthven, earl of Forth, lord general of the king's forces, threatened to execute parliamentarian prisoners taken at Cirencester, but Fiennes responded on 18 May that the four Bristolians had been taken not as soldiers in open warfare but in a conspiracy, and warned of retaliation against royalist prisoners in London if Ruthven did as he had promised. In the circumstances, Fiennes was careful to secure approval at the highest level before carrying out the sentences. On 22 May 1643 the Commons ordered that the earl of Essex, commander-in-chief of the army, should instruct the governor of Bristol to proceed. On 29 May the king himself ordered the mayor and aldermen to prevent the executions by all means. Even had this appeal arrived in time, the civic authorities would have had no means of obeying—and it did not. On the following day Yeamans and Boucher were taken to the scaffold, which had been set up close to Yeamans's house in Wine Street. Fiennes arranged that the city gates be closed and deployed troops to prevent possible disturbances. Yeamans and Boucher had requested that two city divines, Richard Towgood of St Nicholas and Richard Standfast of Christ Church, should preach at the service which would precede their execution. These men were both outspoken supporters of the royalist cause and the request was refused; the three replacements included Walter Cradock, a prominent Independent recently arrived in Bristol.

Yeomans was executed first without incident but Boucher, a devout man even on the testimony of his enemies, was enraged at the choice of preachers. When the time came for his last words, he launched into a bitter speech against 'those beggarly and schismatical rudiments which crafty and malicious men had invented and introduced into the church of God in these last and worst times of the world … Proud (says he) they are, boasters, heady, unstable', continuing in this vein at some length. This appears not to have been well received by one of the ministers, at least, for:

> Rosewell, a levite of their own, and a cract brained separatist, interrupts him in the midst of his devotions, reviles him, and calls him a hypocrite and apostate, that after so strict a conversation, so much time spent in the profession of religion, he should render all suspected for hypocrisie. (Towgood, 25)

George Boucher met his death bravely. The same evening his body was conveyed first to his own house, 'a sad spectacle to his poor widow and seven orphans', and then to be buried at the church of St Werburgh (Towgood, 26–7). His eldest son, John, was banished the kingdom. Charles I granted George's widow a pension of £100 per annum, but she did not receive it until the Restoration, when 'she lived but one year to enjoy it', as her younger son George reported when seeking financial relief from the crown in May 1678. STEPHEN WRIGHT

Sources S. Seyer, *Memoirs historical and topographical of Bristol*, 2 (1823), 341–400 · [R. Towgood?], *The two state martyrs … murther of R. Y. and G. B.* (1643) · N. Fiennes, *An extraordinary deliverance from a cruell plot* (1642) [Thomason tract E92/10] · [C. Walker], *The severall examinations and confessions of the treacherous conspiratours against the citie of Bristoll* [1643] [Thomason tract E104/4] · J. Lynch, *For king and parliament: Bristol and the civil war* (1999) · H. Langrish, *A full declaration of all particulars concerning the march of the forces under Collonel Fiennes to Bristoll, and … the late bloody abominable conspiracy against the city of Bristoll* (1643) [Thomason tract] · P. McGrath, *Bristol and the civil war* (1981) · W. Barrett, *History and antiquities of the city of Bristol* (1789) · J. Latimer, *Society of Merchant Venturers of the city of Bristol*

(1903) · T. K. Rabb, *Enterprise and empire: merchant and gentry investment in the expansion of England, 1575–1630* (1967) · *CSP dom.*, 1674–9, 168 · J. H. Sacks, *The widening gate: Bristol and the Atlantic economy, 1450–1700* (1991) · Clarendon, *Hist. rebellion*, 3.37

Boucher, John (1777–1818), Church of England clergyman, was the son of James Boucher, of Tynemouth. He matriculated at St John's College, Oxford, on 31 October 1795 and graduated BA on 23 May 1799. He was elected fellow of Magdalen College in 1800, took holy orders in 1801, and proceeded MA on 29 April 1802. He was an evangelical and, having been curate in Doddington, from 1803 was vicar of Kirknewton, near Wooler, Northumberland. He married, probably in 1808 or 1809, Salome Letitia, *née* Molesworth; they had six children. He died on 12 November 1818 in Kirknewton and was buried on the 15th in the church there, next to his youngest daughter, Wilhelmina (1816–1817). A posthumous volume of sermons was dedicated to Shute Barrington, bishop of Durham (2nd edn, 1821). JENNETT HUMPHREYS, *rev.* H. C. G. MATTHEW

Sources Foster, *Alum. Oxon.* · J. S. Reynolds, *The evangelicals at Oxford, 1735–1871: a record of an unchronicled movement* (1953) · private information (2004) · parish records, Kirknewton, Northumberland

Boucher, John (1819–1878), Unitarian minister, was born in Moneyreagh, co. Down, the son of David Boucher, a tenant farmer. His educational history is obscure, owing in part to the complex and unfortunately only spottily documented history of the Belfast Academical Institution, from which he was accorded the general certificate from the college department in 1837. He may then have pursued further theological instruction from Henry Montgomery (1788–1865) and John Scott Porter, both of whom had since 1832 lectured to students intended for the non-subscribing ministry and who in 1838 were appointed unpaid professors of divinity to, respectively, the Remonstrant Synod and the presbytery of Antrim, bodies representing the latitudinarian wing of a badly fractured Irish presbyterianism. The Arianism of the latitudinarians—their view, that is, of a limited divinity of Christ as against the full-blooded Trinitarianism of their conservative opponents—easily progressed into belief in the simple humanitarianism of Jesus, and a number of younger remonstrants took up Unitarian pulpits in England.

In 1842 Boucher moved to England and in 1844 he became minister at Union Street, Glasgow, where he healed the serious congregational rift resulting from the extreme theological radicalism of his predecessor, John Taylor (1812–1853), increased attendance, and undertook an only partially successful fund-raising tour in England and Ireland. Boucher's success in Glasgow brought an invitation in September 1846 from the New Gravel Pit Chapel in Hackney, which had been in decline (and some confusion) since the death in 1845 of its pastor of nearly forty years, Robert Aspland. Here, too, Boucher overcame congregational divisions (he had been invited on a split vote of 82–79) and increased both numbers and morale. Rationalistic in outlook at the start, Boucher began to move towards more orthodox positions. A sermon preached in 1852 called into question the central nonconformist principle of private judgement in religious matters. While he retained the votes of a majority of the congregation, he had lost support among the subscribers to the chapel's funds, and his resignation came as a matter of course.

On 9 January 1850 Boucher married Louise (1822/3–1879), daughter of Ebenezer Johnston (*d.* 1850) of Stamford Hill, London; a son and a daughter survived him. His pastorate ended, they moved to Chesterton, Cambridgeshire, and in Easter term 1853 Boucher matriculated at St John's College, Cambridge. He took a first in the moral sciences tripos in 1856 and proceeded BA the next year. His health broke, however, and he had to abandon his intention of taking Anglican orders. He lived on in Chesterton, an invalid, until his death on 12 March 1878.

R. K. WEBB

Sources *The Inquirer* (23 March 1878) · Venn, *Alum. Cant.* · minute book, St Vincent's Street Unitarian Church, Glasgow, 1842, Mitchell L., Glas. · A. R. Ruston, *Unitarianism and early presbyterianism in Hackney* (1980), 27–9 · J. R. Fisher and J. H. Robb, *Royal Belfast Academical Institution: centenary volume, 1810–1910* (1913), 255 · P. Brooke, *Ulster presbyterianism: the historical perspective, 1610–1970* (1987) · *The Inquirer* (1879), 63 · *Christian Reformer, or, Unitarian Magazine and Review*, new ser., 6 (1850), 642 [testimonial on his marriage] · d. cert. · m. cert.

Likenesses photograph (after portrait), DWL

Wealth at death under £4000: administration, 2 May 1878, *CGPLA Eng. & Wales*

Boucher, Jonathan (1738–1804), schoolmaster and Church of England clergyman, was born on 12 March 1738 in Cumberland to James Boucher, schoolmaster and manager of an alehouse, and Anne Barnes, both descendants of Norman aristocracy whose family had fallen on hard times. Although a poor businessman, Boucher's publican father taught him to read at the age of three. His unlettered mother was an efficient household manager who kept Boucher and his siblings just out of poverty and enabled Jonathan to study in the Revd Joseph Blaine's school in Wigdon. In 1756 he secured a teaching post in a school in St Bees run by John and Anne James, who became his mentors and surrogate older siblings.

The Jameses encouraged Boucher to accept a teaching position in Maryland in 1759 as a tutor for the sons of a Virginia merchant, John Younger. In 1761 he returned to London to secure ordination, which he received on 17 January 1762. In July 1762 he became rector of the Hanover parish, Virginia, and in November 1763 accepted a more attractive position in St Mary's parish, Caroline county, Virginia, where he realized his ambition to be a planter as well as a teacher and cleric.

After lengthy manoeuvring Boucher secured appointment to the fashionable parish of St Anne in Maryland in May 1770. In 1771 he married Eleanor (Nelly) Addison (*d.* 1784), the niece of his patron in Maryland, Henry Addison. Addison's patronage made Boucher an intimate of Governor William Eden and chaplain to the Maryland assembly. In 1773 he took the administration's side in a dispute between the governor and anti-proprietary leaders Samuel Chase and William Paca over clerical salaries.

Jonathan Boucher (1738–1804), by Daniel Gardner, *c*.1785

Boucher demolished the anti-proprietary case by demonstrating the historic ecclesiastical supremacy of the Maryland proprietors. 'Uncharitable priest,' Paca and Chase blurted in angry frustration, 'what passion dictated your resentment against us? Was it laudable zeal for the public welfare or was it revenge?' (Calhoon, 223).

It was the central question about Boucher's politics and churchmanship. His transformation from a marginal emigrant in 1759 into an incisive polemicist in 1773 revealed the dependence of the Maryland proprietary regime on maintenance of a cosmopolitan veneer and political operatives willing to expose anti-proprietary republicanism. As tutor to George Washington's hapless stepson Jackie Custis from 1768 to 1773 Boucher took the measure of both the Virginia planter and Chesapeake society. He told Washington that Jackie was 'teeming with all the softer virtues'—'the harmlessness of a dove' without 'the wisdom of the serpent'. 'How will you forgive me', he asked Washington, 'should I suffer him to lose in gentleness, simplicity, and inoffensiveness as much as he gains in address, prudence, and resolution? … a dilemma by no means easily avoided' (Calhoon, 226).

Acting on similar cultural assumptions Boucher laid down his challenge to the American War of Independence. On 20 July 1775, the day set apart by the continental congress for prayer and fasting in support of the American cause, Boucher faced a congregation of 200 armed men in the St Anne's parish church when he attempted to preach on obedience to the magistrate as a religious duty. Armed patriots in the church attempted to force Boucher to leave. Thinking to himself that 'once to flinch was forever to invite danger', Boucher drew his own loaded pistol and, pointing it directly at the head of the leader of the protesters, led a subdued procession out of the church. The next day he returned and without incident preached on Galatians 5: 1 ('Stand fast then in the liberty wherein Christ has made us free'). That passage, Boucher declared, could not, 'without infinite perversion and torture', be 'made to refer to any other kind of liberty' (Calhoon, 230; Bailyn, 315). The very idea of associating Christianity with political radicalism, he suggested, had originated in Judas's politically inspired betrayal of Jesus. The 1797 published text of Boucher's sermon invoked Robert Filmer's doctrine of the divine right of kings to exercise patriarchal authority over their subjects. If Boucher did inject Filmer into the pre-revolutionary controversy, he would have been the only American loyalist to do so. The stronger likelihood is that Boucher added Filmerian patriarchalism to his conservatism during the 1790s in response to the extremism of the French Revolution, and accordingly revised his 1775 sermon just before its publication.

On 14 August 1775 Boucher fled from Maryland, and sailed for England on 22 September. He and Nelly settled in Paddington where he resumed teaching and took into the household John and Anne James's sons, Thomas and John, for whom the Bouchers became surrogate parents, repaying an old emotional debt. He was rector of Paddington from 1776 to 1785, and was appointed the assistant secretary to the Society for the Propagation of the Gospel in 1779. Nelly died in March 1784. In January 1785 he became vicar of Epsom parish in Surrey. Boucher was married twice more—first on 15 February 1787 to Mary Elizabeth Foreman (*d*. 1788), and on 29 October 1789 to Elizabeth Hodgson, who survived him. Among his children was the religious writer Barton *Bouchier (1794–1865). Yearning to become a bishop, Boucher sought unsuccessfully in 1793–4 to effect a merger of the Scottish Episcopal church with Anglican splinter churches in Scotland. During the last years of his life he devoted himself to producing a lexicographical history of the English language. He died on 27 April 1804 in Cumberland and was buried in Epsom churchyard on 4 May. ROBERT M. CALHOON

Sources J. Boucher, *Reminiscences of an American loyalist* (1925) · A. Y. Zimmer, *Jonathan Boucher* (1978) · A. Y. Zimmer and A. H. Young, 'Jonathan Boucher: constitutional conservative', *Journal of American History*, 58 (1972), 897–922 · R. M. Calhoon, *Loyalists in revolutionary America* (1973) · B. Bailyn, *The ideological origins of the American revolution* (1967) · P. Evanson, 'Jonathan Boucher: the mind of an American loyalist', *Maryland Historical Magazine*, 58 (1963), 128–36

Archives College of William and Mary, Williamsburg, Virginia, corresp. · priv. coll., corresp.

Likenesses D. Gardner, pastel drawing, *c*.1785, Yale U. Art Gallery [*see illus.*] · P. Condé, stipple, pubd 1815 (after W. J. Thomson), NPG · L. A. Goblet, bust, Epsom parish church, Surrey

Wealth at death £2200: Zimmer, *Jonathan Boucher*, 345

Boucherett, (Emilia) Jessie (1825–1905), campaigner for women's rights, born in November 1825 at Willingham House, North Willingham, near Market Rasen, Lincolnshire, was the youngest child of Louisa, daughter of Frederick John Pigou and Louisa, *née* Minchin, of Dartford,

(Emilia) Jessie Boucherett (1825–1905), by J. Owen, *c.*1860

Kent, and Ayscoghe Boucherett (1791–1857). Her father, who was high sheriff of Lincolnshire in 1820, was descended from Mathew Boucheret, a French protestant who settled in England in 1644 and became lord of the manor at Willingham. An elder sister, Louisa (1821–1895), a pioneer of the movement for boarding out pauper children, succeeded to the family estates on the death, unmarried, in 1877 of her only surviving brother, Henry Robert, high sheriff of Lincolnshire in 1866. On Louisa's death in 1895 the property (which, according to Bateman, comprised nearly 6000 acres in 1883) passed to Jessie, the last of the family.

Jessie Boucherett was educated at the school run by the Byerley sisters (daughters of Josiah Wedgwood's relative and partner, Thomas Byerley) at Avonbank, Stratford upon Avon, where Elizabeth Gaskell had been a pupil and where the curriculum included the works of women writers of the day. A lover of the country and a 'bold rider to hounds' (*DNB*), she also read widely. Her interest in the condition of women was kindled by Harriet Martineau's seminal article, 'On female industry', in the *Edinburgh Review* (April 1859). A chance purchase of a copy of the *English Woman's Journal* (founded in March 1858), led her to the journal office in central London and a first meeting with Bessie Rayner Parkes and Barbara Leigh Smith Bodichon. It was here that many ideas concerning women's present and future role in society began to germinate, and what came to be referred to as the Langham Place circle became the centre for women's rights activities over the next few years. Supported by her private income and surrounded by like-minded new friends, Boucherett subsequently devoted much of her life to the cause of women's emancipation.

Jessie Boucherett's primary interest was that of employment, and the difficulties encountered by unmarried women of limited means in obtaining suitable and sufficiently remunerative work. Apart from teaching, sewing, and the desultory post of ladies' companion, there were few openings for poorly educated spinsters in mid-Victorian England. With Adelaide Ann Procter and Barbara Bodichon she set up the Society for Promoting the Employment of Women in the winter of 1859, enlisting the support of Lord Shaftesbury, who became the society's first president, and other members of the National Association for the Promotion of Social Science. Based initially at 19 Langham Place and later in Berners Street, they began a law copying office, a school to train women as book-keepers, clerks, and cashiers, and a register of employment. While such measures could clearly help only a few women of the middling classes, the pioneers regarded their innovations as experiments which prepared the ground for future change. Jessie Boucherett never ceased to believe that of all women's grievances, the want of paid employment was the most heartfelt and least difficult to remedy. Lack of training and prejudice against women entering certain trades were obstacles which could and should be removed. She expounded on these views in *Hints for Self-Help: a Book for Young Women* (1863), 'How to provide for superfluous women' in Josephine Butler's edited collection *Woman's Work and Woman's Culture* (1869), and 'The industrial position of women' in *The Woman Question in Europe* (1884), edited by Theodore Stanton. Having been very active in opposing restrictive employment laws, particularly the Factory Act of 1874, in the 1890s she became increasingly concerned with what she regarded as the adverse effect of protective legislation on women industrial workers. While not opposed to factory acts in principle, she feared that legislation directed specifically at women would reduce their wages, restrict employment, and lessen their self-dependence. A staunch Conservative, she founded the Freedom of Labour Defence League with colleagues in 1899 and wrote, with Helen Blackburn, *The Condition of Working Women and the Factory Acts* (1896).

Jessie Boucherett's initial contact with the Langham Place circle had drawn her into the campaigns for women's suffrage and the legal entitlement of married women to their own property and earnings. She joined the Kensington Society, which provided a focus for the discussion of women's rights, and with Barbara Bodichon and Emily Davies drafted the first suffrage petition, which was presented to parliament in 1866 by John Stuart Mill. A leading member of the first Women's Suffrage Committee established in the same year, she remained a staunch supporter of its successors, the London Society for

Women's Suffrage and the National Union of Women's Suffrage Societies, until her death. Her other key contribution to the Victorian women's movement, and perhaps her most lasting memorial, was the founding of the *Englishwoman's Review* (1866–1910). The demise of the *English Woman's Journal* in 1864 had left a great need for a periodical which would address the broad subject of women's emancipation and record the efforts of reformers at home and overseas. Boucherett was its proprietor, a regular contributor, and its first editor until 1870, when she was succeeded first by Caroline Ashurst Biggs, then by Helen Blackburn, and finally by Antoinette Mackenzie; the *Review* is a testament to the Victorian women's movement and its philosophy of liberal individualism.

In later years Jessie Boucherett rekindled her youthful interest in the countryside. She wrote on manorial history, urged a return to the land, and, always alert to the possibilities of encouraging economic self-reliance, advocated poultry and pig farming as occupations for educated women. She died from cancer of the liver on 18 October 1905 at Willingham House, and was buried in North Willingham. She was characterized by her courtesy, a sharp sense of humour, and a wise knowledge of a world which she tried to make more hospitable to the needs and rights of women. LINDA WALKER

Sources H. Blackburn, *Women's suffrage: a record of the women's suffrage movement in the British Isles* (1902) • B. Rayner Parkes, *Essays on woman's work* (1865) • *Englishwoman's Review* (Jan 1904) • *The Times* (21 Oct 1905) • Burke, *Gen. GB* • F. Hays, *Women of the day: a biographical dictionary of notable contemporaries* (1885) • *WWW* • L. Walker, 'The employment question and the women's movement in late Victorian and Edwardian society with particular reference to the *Englishwoman's Review*', MA diss., University of Manchester, 1974 • J. Rendall, '"A moral engine"? Feminism, liberalism and the *English Woman's Journal*', *Equal or different: women's politics, 1800–1914*, ed. J. Rendall (1987), 112–38 • D. Worzala, 'The Langham Place circle: the beginnings of the organized women's movement in England, 1854–1870', PhD diss., University of Wisconsin-Madison, 1982 • J. Bateman, *The great landowners of Great Britain and Ireland*, 4th edn (1883) • d. cert. • *CGPLA Eng. & Wales* (1905) • will

Archives Suffolk RO, Ipswich

Likenesses J. Owen, photograph, *c.*1860, Women's Library, London [*see illus.*]

Wealth at death £38,589 16*s.* 9*d.*: probate, 14 Dec 1905, *CGPLA Eng. & Wales*

Bouchery, Weyman (*bap.* **1684**, *d.* **1712**), Latin poet, was born at Canterbury and baptized on 2 November 1684, at the Walloon or Strangers' Church there, the son of Arnold Bouchery, minister of the church, and his wife, Sara. He was educated at King's School, Canterbury, and Oundle, and was admitted pensioner of Jesus College, Cambridge, aged fourteen, on 3 July 1699. He became scholar in 1700, graduated BA in 1702/3, and MA in 1706; on 23 October 1705 he had migrated as fellow-commoner to Emmanuel College.

Bouchery's sole publication, *Hymnus sacer* (1706), is an accomplished paraphrase, in eighty-eight alcaic stanzas, of the song of Deborah from Judges 5. He dedicates these first-fruits ('primitiae'), to the alma mater and her literary alumni, particularly 'sacrae poeseos amantibus' ('the lovers of sacred poetry'). Biblical paraphrase was a popular neo-Latin genre, in which a young writer could show his skills to good effect; Deborah's dramatic tale was to inspire several other early eighteenth-century versions, most notably by Anthony Alsop and John Burton, against which Bouchery may profitably be compared. In general, Bouchery follows his text closely, though with significant expansion (thirty-one biblical verses produce thirty pages of Latin) so 'they took no gain of money' (v. 19) becomes a whole stanza. Rhetorical flourishes abound; he also makes some material additions (Euphrates and Nile give way to Kishon, p. 21). Jael nails her victim with admirable gusto, though Bouchery's longer version perhaps lacks the full firmness and vigour of Alsop. Nevertheless, Bouchery's *Hymnus sacer* is an elegant production, demonstrating his skill at handling an extended lyric poem: it might (had he continued to write) have led on to greater achievements. Bouchery was ordained deacon in June 1707, and priest in September 1709. He was rector of Little Blakenham, Suffolk, from 1709 until his death at Ipswich on 24 March 1712. His son Gilbert erected a memorial tablet in St George's, Canterbury. D. K. MONEY

Sources Venn, *Alum. Cant.*, 1/1 • D. K. Money, *The English Horace: Anthony Alsop and the tradition of British Latin verse* (1998) • *IGI*

Bouchier [*formerly* Boucher], **Barton** (**1794–1865**), religious writer, born in Epsom, Surrey, was a younger son of the vicar of Epsom, the Revd Jonathan *Boucher (1738–1804), and his third wife, Elizabeth Hodgson, widow of the Revd James of Arthuret. Barton changed his name from Boucher to Bouchier after 1822. He was educated at Balliol College, Oxford, proceeding BA in 1822 and MA in 1827. In 1816 he married Mary, daughter of the Revd Nathaniel Thornbury of Avening, Gloucestershire. Bouchier had read for the bar at Lincoln's Inn in 1813, but was ordained in 1819 by the bishop of Hereford and became curate at Monmouth. A sermon preached by him at Usk in 1822 for the Christian Knowledge Society was published by request. Bouchier held curacies later at Old, Northamptonshire, and (before 1834) at Cheam, Surrey; while resident there he published an edition of Lancelot Andrewes's *Prayers and Offices of Private Devotion* (1834). In 1839 he became rector of Fonthill Bishop, diocese of Salisbury, but remained in Cheam until 1856.

Bouchier was the author of biblical commentaries and devotional works, including *Prophecy and its Fulfilment* (1836) and *Manna in the House* (1852–8). In 1853 he wrote a *Letter* to the prime minister, Lord Aberdeen, against opening the Crystal Palace on Sundays, following up this appeal in 1854 by *The Poor Man's Palace and the Poor Man's Duty*, a pamphlet addressed to the Crystal Palace directors. He also published his *Farewell Sermon* to his Cheam flock, having preached it on 28 September 1856. Bouchier died at the rectory at Fonthill Bishop on 28 December 1865. The editorship of *The Vision*, a humorous illustrated poem on Jonathan Boucher's philological studies, written by Sir Frederick Morton Eden, bt, and published in 1820, has been wrongly attributed to Bouchier.

JENNETT HUMPHREYS, *rev.* MARI G. ELLIS

Sources *GM*, 4th ser., 1 (1866), 431–2 • Foster, *Alum. Oxon.* • Crockford (1865) • *CGPLA Eng. & Wales* (1866)

Wealth at death under £2000: probate, 3 March 1866, *CGPLA Eng. & Wales*

Bouchier, Sir Cecil Arthur (1895–1979), air force officer, was born at La Villetta, Fleet, Hampshire, on 14 October 1895, the son of Arthur Couch Bouchier of Chichester, a hotel proprietor, and his wife, Florence Wootton. Having been educated at Chichester grammar school he joined the Honourable Artillery Company in 1915 as a trooper and served in Palestine. In 1918 he was commissioned in the Royal Flying Corps in Egypt. From March to November 1918, with Squadron Leader Keith Park, he flew Bristol Fighters in 48 squadron RAF on the western front, and in mid-1919 he was a flight commander with Park at both 54 training depot at Fairlop and at London Colney. He then served in the north Russian expeditionary force at Murmansk, where he earned his DFC. This was followed in 1920–21 by service in India and Iraq, which was to stand him in good stead later. For three years he was a resident test pilot at the Royal Aircraft Establishment, Farnborough, and in 1926 he was posted to 41 (F) squadron at Northolt. He married the following year (23 July 1927) Gladys Dorothy Sherwood (*d.* 1964), the daughter of William Alfred Sherwood, a gentleman, with whom he had one son.

In 1929 Bouchier was back in Egypt as a test pilot. He was then selected to study for a year at the RAF Staff College, Andover, from where he was posted to RAF headquarters in India. In 1933 the nucleus of the Indian Air Force, comprising two flights and twelve recent Indian graduates of Cranwell, came into being. As a flight lieutenant Bouchier was the new force's first commanding officer until 1935. For this service he has been called the founder of the Indian Air Force.

Bouchier returned to England in 1936 and commanded 54 (F) squadron at Hornchurch, Essex. During 1938–9 he was at 11 group, shortly to be commanded by his old friend Park (whose dismissal, Bouchier believed, took the heart out of the organization). From December 1939, as a group captain, he was commanding officer of RAF Hornchurch, where he made a name for himself by ordering that the drab, camouflaged station be planted with flowers that bloomed in spring. He also obtained De Wilde ammunition for his aircraft. With nos. 74, 54, and 65 squadrons under his command, Daddy Bouchier's pilots included R. R. Stanford-Tuck, A. G. 'Sailor' Malan, and A. C. Deere. The station was bombed twenty times during the battle of Britain. As a sector controller Bouchier was mentioned in dispatches, as he was in 1941, when he moved to Kenley and 11 group. In 1942 he was once again posted to the Air Ministry, where he strongly argued for posting squadrons not batches of pilots because of morale and *esprit de corps* and in 1943–5 he was with 11 (F) group, where as an air commodore he was heavily involved in planning for Operation Overlord (6 June 1944) and later controlled the fighter umbrella over the beaches.

Early in 1945, at Park's suggestion, Bouchier was appointed commanding officer of 221 group in Burma as acting air vice-marshal while Stanley Vincent was rested. He took over 221 support group for the march to Rangoon at a time when there was no Japanese air opposition. He had first to reposition his squadrons to support the Fourteenth Army in the drive to Rangoon and then to defend Rangoon and the eastern approaches to Burma as far north as Mandalay. Owing to the monsoon season it was difficult to find dry airfields, and the aircraft hopped from one spot to another while 221 took over control from the wings. By 6 May Rangoon was in allied hands and the planning for Operation Zipper, the invasion of Malaya, had begun. Park then called him to south-east Asia command headquarters in Kandy, Ceylon, to prepare plans for the occupation of Japan and the Netherlands East Indies. His subsequent appointment as British senior officer, Japan, although approved by the Air Ministry, was held up by Air Chief Marshal Slessor, who in 1944 had blocked Bouchier's proposed appointment as air officer commanding Aden. Challenged by Park, Slessor replied, 'None of us much care for him here' (Orange, 215), then withdrew his objection.

With the end of the war in the Far East and the establishment of a British Commonwealth air contingent in Japan, Bouchier moved there in command; he remained there until the contingent's disbandment on 15 November 1948. The following year, after commanding 21 group at Swinderby, Lincolnshire, he retired from the RAF. He returned to active service in 1950 on the outbreak of the Korean War, when the British chiefs of staff selected him as their personal representative to the supreme commander of the United Nations forces, General Douglas MacArthur, with whom Bouchier had enjoyed a good working relationship during the allied occupation of Japan. Bouchier arrived in Tokyo on 10 August 1950, and remained as senior British liaison officer to MacArthur and his successors as commanders of the UN forces, Mark Clark and Matthew Ridgway, until his second retirement (28 March 1953), when he was appointed KCB.

Bouchier's honours included OBE (1938), CBE (1941), CB (1945), the order of St Anne of Russia (1919), and commander of the Legion of Merit of the USA (1945). In retirement he became director of the appeal for St Clement Danes, the RAF chapel in the Strand, London. In 1957, on behalf of some contributors, he named a bell Boy, a nickname he had enjoyed in the wartime RAF. It was a well-deserved honour, as he had raised £150,000 in eighteen months. His first wife died in 1964, and four years later, on 14 August 1968, he married Isabella Dorothy Guyner Britton, a composer and writer, of Yokohama, the daughter of Frank Guyner Britton, a mechanical engineer. They then flew to Japan, where they lived until shortly before his death, when he returned to England for medical treatment. He died at Worthing Hospital, Worthing, Sussex, on 15 June 1979, and was cremated privately.

Bouchier loved most sports, but apart from this little is known about his personality. He appears to have been a top second-level officer, not part of the ex-western front clique in the RAF, but able enough to advance in overseas positions. Moreover, he was a fighter pilot in an air force dominated by men with reconnaissance and bomber experience, very much like his friend Keith Park.

ROBIN HIGHAM

Sources *The Times* (20 June 1979) • V. Orange, *Sir Keith Park* (1984) • *WW* (1950); (1960); (1970) • D. Lee, *Eastward: a history of the Royal Air Force in the Far East, 1945–1972* (1984) • S. W. Kirby, *The war against Japan*, 5 (1969) • W. G. Ramsey, *The battle of Britain then and now* (1982) • S. N. Prasad and S. C. Gupta, *History of the Indian air force, 1933–1945* (1961) • J. Rawlings, *Fighter squadrons of the RAF and their aircraft* (1976) • R. A. Hough and D. Richards, *The battle of Britain* (1989) • A. Farrar-Hockley, *The British part in the Korean War*, 1 (1990) • A. Farrar-Hockley, *The British part in the Korean War*, 2 (1995) • Burke, *Peerage* (1959) • m. certs. • d. cert. • J. Douglas-Hamilton, *The air battle for Malta* (1981), 41

Likenesses photograph, repro. in Farrar-Hockley, *The British part*, vol. 1

Wealth at death £42,328: administration with will, 3 Nov 1980, *CGPLA Eng. & Wales*

Bouchier, George. *See* Boucher, George (*d.* 1643).

Bouchier [Bourchier], **Thomas** (**1633–1723**), civil lawyer, was the elder son of James Bouchier (*d.* 1641) of Long Hanborough, near Woodstock, Oxfordshire. He attended Winchester College and then entered Magdalen Hall, Oxford, matriculating as Thomas Boucher on 19 November 1650. He became a fellow of All Souls College, where he received the degrees of BCL in July 1658 and DCL in June 1663. Later that year Bouchier was admitted as an advocate of the court of arches, and on 25 October 1664 he became a member of Doctors' Commons. He did not, however, establish a legal practice in the ecclesiastical or Admiralty courts, nor did he remain an active member of Doctors' Commons. The only judicial post he ever held was that of commissary of the diocese of Canterbury. He married Frances Astell and spent much of his time at Long Hanborough, where he made extensive additions to the estate inherited from his father. He also purchased a farm in Kidlington, where by 1697 he had built up another large estate.

Bouchier spent virtually his entire career at Oxford. He acted as deputy for Sir Giles Sweit, the regius professor of civil law, while Sweit was active in London as dean of the arches, and upon Sweit's death in 1672 Bouchier succeeded him as regius professor. His tenure as regius professor lacked any real distinction. Although he was knowledgeable in the civil law and gave occasional legal opinions as a fellow of All Souls, he made no apparent contribution to legal scholarship. In 1712 Bouchier did the faculty of law serious harm by arranging for his son James (1683–1736), who was also a civil lawyer, to succeed him as regius professor, a strategy that met with considerable opposition within the university. The younger Bouchier, who in Thomas Hearne's opinion was a 'most proud, vain, conceited, impudent and ignorant coxcomb' (*Remarks*, 8.95), knew very little civil law and was considered to be utterly unqualified for the position. When James became assessor of the vice-chancellor's court at Oxford, he was reported to have performed all his duties at his father's direction. Thomas Bouchier was also principal of St Alban Hall from 1678 until 1723. Under his principalship and that of his son, who also succeeded him in that capacity, the hall declined in stature. Twenty members of the hall withdrew after Bouchier accused some of them of the paternity of a child that his son had fathered out of wedlock.

Thomas Bouchier had a reputation for being 'a most vile abominable wretch who would do anything for money' (*Remarks*, 8.74). His son Richard (1691–1725) received the degree of BD from Oxford in 1725, while his son William (*b.* 1694) proceeded DM in 1727. Thomas Bouchier died at Hanborough on 9 May 1723 and was buried on 11 May in Hanborough churchyard, where he had built a small mausoleum in the Gothic style. His son William erected a monument to his parents and other family members in Hanborough church in 1780.

BRIAN P. LEVACK

Sources *VCH Oxfordshire*, vol. 12 • J. R. L. Highfield, 'Stubbins', *Postmaster*, 1 (1956), 12–18 • *The manuscripts of his grace the duke of Portland*, 10 vols., HMC, 29 (1891–1931), vol. 7 • G. D. Squibb, *Doctors' Commons: a history of the College of Advocates and Doctors of Law* (1977) • *The life and times of Anthony Wood*, ed. A. Clark, 3, OHS, 26 (1894) • *Remarks and collections of Thomas Hearne*, ed. C. E. Doble and others, 11 vols., OHS, 2, 7, 13, 34, 42–3, 48, 50, 65, 67, 72 (1885–1921), vols. 4, 8–9 • treasurer's book of Doctors' Commons, PRO, 30/26/8, fol. 200 and *passim* • *Hist. U. Oxf.* 4: *17th-cent. Oxf.*, 558–68 • Foster, *Alum. Oxon., 1500–1714* • C. T. Martin, *Catalogue of the archives in the muniment room of All Souls' College* (1877) • T. F. Kirby, *Winchester scholars: a list of the wardens, fellows, and scholars of … Winchester College* (1888)

Likenesses portrait, possibly Merton Oxf.

Wealth at death estates: *VCH Oxfordshire*

Boucicault, Dion [*real name* Dionysius Lardner Boursiquot] (**1820–1890**), playwright and actor, was born on 27 December 1820 at 28 Middle Gardiner Street, Dublin. He was the fifth and final child of Samuel Boursiquot (1769–1853) and his wife, Anne Maria (1795–1879), the daughter of Arthur Darley and sister of the poet George Darley. Boucicault's natural father was probably the encyclopaedist Dionysius *Lardner, who was lodging with the Boursiquots at the time of Dion's birth and whose relationship with Anne had alienated his own wife. Lardner certainly took charge of the boy's education after 1827, when Samuel's business failed, and evidently encouraged him to adapt his surname to Bourcicault (Boucicault dropped the 'r' in 1845, when he found an authentic French spelling). When Lardner moved to London in 1827, prior to taking up his appointment as professor of natural philosophy and astronomy at the newly established University College, Anne Boursiquot followed him with her four youngest children. Boucicault attended a number of the small, semi-private boarding-schools that flourished during and after the Regency, but his interest was only selectively engaged. Sharing his nominal father's fanciful belief in a noble line of Boursiquots, he was a diligent student of French, and he read plentifully, but his unsystematic approach to learning survived periods at University College School (1834–5), Brentford collegiate school (1836), and a final year, after the ending of Anne's liaison with Lardner, at Dr Geoghegan's academy in Dublin (1837). He was already set on a career in the theatre.

In April 1838, unknown to his family, Boucicault made his acting début at the Theatre Royal, Cheltenham, under

Dion Boucicault (1820–1890), by London Stereoscopic Co., *c.*1865–70

the protective pseudonym of Lee Moreton. His meagre income, augmented until March 1840 by a quarterly allowance from Lardner, did not prevent him from dressing like a dandy, posturing like a star, and spending beyond his means. He was small and agile, with a high forehead that would become domed as his hair thinned to early baldness. Had he been less pushily self-assured, he would have made fewer enemies through his life, but he would have achieved less. Before he was twenty, Lee Moreton had cajoled provincial managers in Brighton, Bristol, and Hull into staging his apprentice work, and it was persistence that led to his first major triumph. Initially thwarted, he eventually persuaded the harassed managers of the Theatre Royal, Covent Garden, Madame Vestris and Charles Mathews, to buy his five-act comedy *London Assurance*. Finely staged, in something approaching an innovatory box-set, it opened to popular acclaim on 4 March 1841. The play is a necessarily bowdlerized imitation of a Restoration comedy, with flirtation replacing seduction, and, though dressed in contemporary clothes, it was, even in 1841, an adroitly crafted period piece. Boucicault now abandoned his pen-name, was elected to the Dramatic Authors' Society, and was welcomed in moderately fashionable society. Immediately, he displayed his lifelong habit of spending more than he had. Sued for debt in September 1841 and February 1842, he escaped only because he was under age when the debts were incurred.

Success had made Boucicault unproductive. Almost a year elapsed between *London Assurance* and the opening, on 7 February 1842, again at Covent Garden, of his next play, *The Irish Heiress*. Such inactivity was rare in a writing life of fifty years and more than 150 dramatic pieces. His long association with the actor–manager Benjamin Webster, which began in April 1842, was a matter of business rather than art, a necessary reining in of poetic aspiration endorsed much later in a comment recorded by the actor J. H. Barnes: 'Ah! when young men get tired of writing clever plays they may write successful ones!' (Barnes, 47). Most of the pieces with which Boucicault fed Webster and himself were avowedly potboilers, though they included the skilfully turned two-act curtain-raiser *Used up* (Haymarket, 6 February 1844), which was a custom-made vehicle for the gentlemanly acting of Charles Mathews as Sir Charles Coldstream, and a competent five-act comedy, *Old Heads and Young Hearts* (Haymarket, 18 November 1844). When Boucicault bemoaned the small remuneration for playwrights, Webster pointed out that it was cheaper for him to pay people to steal plots from the Parisian stage. Needing the money, and drawn by the romance of his own purported French connections, Boucicault sailed for France in December 1844.

There is confusion and some deliberate obfuscation over the events of the next years. It was certainly in Paris that Boucicault met P. T. Barnum, whose eye for publicity, good or bad, he admired and would emulate. He certainly visited theatres, stole plots for shipping back to Webster, and tried to convince himself of his aristocratic descent (he briefly styled himself the Vicomte de Boucicault). It was possibly in Paris that he met the widowed Anne Guiot, whom he married in Lambeth on 9 July 1845. The daughter of Etienne St Pierre, with connections in the lesser nobility, she was older than Boucicault. Since she owned property in France, it was, unsurprisingly, rumoured that he married for her money, and, more far-fetchedly, that he soon pushed her off a glacial peak in the Alps. It is only known that she was dead by the late summer of 1848. Whatever benefits accrued to Boucicault from the marriage were soon squandered. In November 1848 he petitioned for bankruptcy. He had written nothing of note since *Old Heads and Young Hearts*. His career had to be refashioned.

The intervention of Charles Kean, eminent as manager of the Princess's Theatre, was decisive. Kean was conscious of the need to spice his classical repertory with modern work, and Boucicault had an appropriate pedigree. The association began in late 1850 and produced, most significantly, a five-act comedy called *Love in a Maze* (6 March 1851), a clever adaptation of *The Corsican Brothers* (24 February 1852), and a sensational rehandling of *The Vampire* (14 June 1852). The first was approved by Queen Victoria; the second established Kean's credentials in 'gentlemanly melodrama'; the third marked Boucicault's return to acting in the sinister role of the Phantom. The title role in his last play for the Princess's, *The Prima Donna* (18 September 1852), was taken by Agnes Kelly Robertson (1833–1916), who was already his lover and became his wife in New York in September 1853. The relationship caused a rupture between Boucicault and Kean, who had assumed wardship over Agnes, and the young couple resolved to try their luck in America. Boucicault divided the rest of his theatrical life between the New World and the old. Agnes's popularity in America, where she was billed as 'The Pocket Venus', was the foundation of their success there, but Boucicault fashioned the plays that featured her. The first of their six children, baptized Dion, was born on 10 May 1855. Agnes was acting again within a month. Boucicault had made his American début in November 1854, unsuitably as Coldstream in *Used up*. He was at his best only in eccentric character roles, supremely as the roguish Irishman who would be his finest creation both as actor and writer. That was a rich vein he had yet to strike when, after a failed venture into theatre management in New Orleans in 1855–6, he and Agnes became members of the company at Wallack's Theatre, New York.

It was his part in the collaborative composition of *The Poor of New York*, which opened at Wallack's to ecstatic notices on 8 December 1857, that alerted Boucicault, not only to the capital to be made out of vividly staged sensation scenes in melodrama, but also to the marketability of contemporary events. A few months after the relief of Lucknow, *Jessie Brown* opened at Wallack's (22 February 1858), with Boucicault as the evil Nana Sahib and Agnes as Jessie. *Brigham Young* followed on 25 May 1858 and, four days after the execution of John Brown, the famous 'slavery' play *The Octoroon* (6 December 1859). *The Octoroon* marked the end of Boucicault's third American venture into management. After quarrelling with their joint managers over salaries, the Boucicaults stormed out of the Winter Garden, where they had opened in September 1859, to join a rival New York company at Laura Keene's Theatre. It was there, on 29 March 1860, that they opened in *The Colleen Bawn*, with Boucicault outstanding as the lovable wastrel Myles-na-Coppaleen. The play is a model of melodramatic plotting; its splicing of humour and tension captivated audiences. The Boucicaults decided to test it in London, where they opened a run of 230 performances at the Adelphi on 10 September 1860. They remained in England for twelve years.

Boucicault's contract with Webster paved the way for the future prosperity of English playwrights, a cause to which he had been wedded since 1848. The Boucicaults jointly earned £23,000 during their first London year. As always, it was spent. Boucicault bought Hereford House in the Brompton Road, hired whole companies to tour Britain with copycat productions of *The Colleen Bawn*, and, in late 1862, completed the conversion of Astley's Amphitheatre into the New Theatre Royal, Westminster. This ill-starred venture, damaged by the sudden notoriety of his liaison with the actress Emily Jordan, brought Boucicault back to bankruptcy in July 1863. A provincial tour of *The Poor of New York*, adapted and retitled for each city visited, recouped the family finances, and, in July 1864, they settled at 326 Regent Street. *Arrah-na-Pogue*, the second of Boucicault's major Irish melodramas, was warmly received in Dublin in November 1864 and again at the Princess's, where it opened on 22 March 1865. By then, all too characteristically, Boucicault had quarrelled with Webster over money, but his name was a guarantee of audience interest throughout the decade. There were London successes in 1866 (*The Long Strike* and *The Flying Scud*), 1868 (*After Dark*), and 1869 (*Presumptive Evidence*). Rumours of scandal, fanned by Boucicault, attracted audiences to *Formosa* at Drury Lane on 5 August 1869. Was its heroine based on the courtesan Mabel Gray? The secret scandal of the production was Boucicault's affair with its leading lady, Katherine Rogers. She accompanied the Boucicaults on their return to the New York stage in September 1872. The marriage survived only in name. In March 1873 Agnes returned to England, while Boucicault toured his new plays with Katherine. During the prolonged divorce proceedings, concluded in 1889, Agnes named him as the father of Katherine's child.

With one notable exception, Boucicault's later plays are undistinguished. *The Shaughraun*, his masterpiece, began its triumphant history at Wallack's on 14 November 1874. He bought a steam yacht on the American profits, and even persuaded Agnes to play in its London opening at Drury Lane on 4 September 1875. This last attempt at a reconciliation foundered when their eldest son, Dion, was killed in a train crash in January 1876, and there were quarrels over custody of the remaining children. In the event, four of them worked in the theatre, two, Darley George (1859–1929) and Nina (1867–1950), with distinction. Familiarly known as Dot, Darley adopted his father's and dead brother's name on stage [*see* Boucicault, Dion, the younger]. Separated from Agnes, Boucicault continued his American tours, on which his appearance as Conn the shaughraun was almost obligatory. He was still playing the part in 1885–6, when he took a small company to New Zealand and Australia. One of the group was the 21-year-old Louise Thorndyke, whom Boucicault married in Sydney on 9 September 1885. He countered charges of bigamy by denying the legality of his marriage to Agnes, thus burdening his children with the stigma of rumoured illegitimacy. Not until May 1888 did Boucicault discontinue his acting tours with Louise. Out of patience with audiences who found his new work old-fashioned, he accepted an invitation to direct an acting academy at the Madison Square Theatre, New York. But he was determined to write another successful play. During rehearsals for *A Tale of a Coat* in July 1890 he suffered a heart attack. Depressed by the play's failure in New York, he contracted pneumonia, from which, on 18 September 1890, he died. After making and losing several fortunes, the man who had once written of playwriting, 'It's a degrading occupation, but more money has been made out of guano than out of poetry', died poor. He was buried in Woodlawn cemetery, New York, but, on 19 November 1890, Louise had the body moved to the Mount Hope cemetery in Hastings-on-Hudson. When she died in 1956 she was buried under the same stone. PETER THOMSON

Sources R. Fawkes, *Dion Boucicault: a biography* (1979) · S. E. Molin and R. Goodefellowe, *Dion Boucicault, the Shaughraun*, 2 pts. (1979–82) · R. Hogan, *Dion Boucicault* (1969) · *Plays by Dion Boucicault*, ed. P. Thomson (1984) · J. H. Barnes, *Forty years on the stage* (1914)

Archives Harvard TC · Hunt. L., letters; literary MS · NYPL, papers · priv. coll. · Theatre Museum, London, copy of *London assurance* and corresp. · University of South Florida | NL Ire., letters to Ben Webster · University of Kent, Canterbury, Frank Pettingell collection

Likenesses London Stereoscopic Co., carte-de-visite, *c.*1865–1870, NPG [*see illus.*] · J. Rogers, bronze statue, *c.*1875, NG Ire. · J. Rogers, bronze statue, *c.*1875, New York Historical Society, New York · E. H. Corbould, portrait (in *The vampire*), Royal Collection · F. D'Avignon, lithograph, priv. coll. · H. Furniss, pen-and-ink caricature, NPG · Maclure & Macdonald, chromolithograph caricature · Spy [L. Ward], lithograph, NG Ire.; repro. in *VF* (16 Dec 1882) · photographs, priv. coll.

Wealth at death quite poor: consensus

Boucicault, Dion [Darley George], **the younger** (**1859–1929**), actor and theatre manager, the second son of the actor and playwright Dion *Boucicault (1820–1890) and his wife, Agnes Kelly Robertson (1833–1916), was born in New York city on 23 May 1859. He was given the name Darley George, but took that of his elder brother, Dion, who died in 1876. He went to England at an early age and was educated at Esher, at Cuddington, Buckinghamshire, and later in Paris. He served in the army for a short while but soon turned to the stage, and made his début at Booth's Theater, New York, on 11 October 1879, as the Dauphin in *Louis XI*, with his father in the same play. Young Dion first appeared in London at the Gaiety Theatre on 25 November 1880, as Andy Blake in the play of that name. From 1881 to 1882 he performed at the Court Theatre, and the following year he went on tour with Sir Charles Hawtrey, playing, among other characters, the original Harry Marsland in *The Private Secretary* at Cambridge in November 1883. At this time he also adapted two plays, *My Little Girl* (1882) and *Devotion* (1884), both of which were produced at the Court Theatre.

Dion Boucicault the younger (**1859–1929**), by unknown photographer

After reappearing at the St James's Theatre as Archie Hamilton in *A Scrap of Paper* with William Hunter Kendal and Madge Kendal, Boucicault returned to America with his father. He remained there for a year, and appeared at Wallack's Theater, New York, in leading roles in *The Omadhaum* and other plays written by the elder Boucicault. In 1885 father and son sailed for Australia, and at the end of the tour young Dion elected to stay on there. In October 1886 he entered into a partnership with Robert Brough and took up the management of the Bijou Theatre, Melbourne, which he converted into the most important theatre in that city by producing all the principal successes of A. W. Pinero, H. A. Jones, and other leading playwrights of the day. Later they took over the management of the Criterion Theatre, Sydney, until the partnership was terminated in 1896.

Boucicault reappeared in London at the Court Theatre in October 1897 as the Minstrel in *The Children of the King*, and proceeded to become very popular in the role of Sir William Gower in Pinero's *Trelawny of the Wells* (January 1898), as well as in *His Excellency the Governor*, *Wheels within Wheels*, and *A Royal Family*. In 1900 he went to the Criterion, where he was associated with Arthur Bourchier and produced R. C. Carton's *Lady Huntworth's Experiment* and Robert Marshall's *The Noble Lord*. He launched more fully into production, his most important contribution to the world of theatre, when he joined Charles Frohman at the Duke of York's Theatre in 1901.

In that same year Boucicault married the actress Irene *Vanbrugh (1872–1949), whose real name was Irene Barnes. They acted together until his death, and he became her manager in 1915. Boucicault remained with Frohman until the latter's death in 1915, producing plays by Pinero, Carton, Anthony Hope, Sir J. M. Barrie, and others. He was a brilliant stage director and had great success as the original producer in December 1904 of Barrie's *Peter Pan*, which he revived every Christmas until 1918; he was also responsible in June 1913 for the all-star revival of his father's play *London Assurance* at the St James's Theatre, the first of the annual productions given in aid of King George's pension fund for actors and actresses. In December 1913 Boucicault took on the management of the New Theatre in St Martin's Lane, and opened with a revival of *Peter Pan*. He produced a long series of plays there, including *Caroline* by W. Somerset Maugham, *Belinda* by A. A. Milne, and *Mr Pim Passes by* by the same author, in which he had the greatest success of his later years in the part of Carraway Pim (his wife playing Olivia). For a short period he was the manager of the Duke of York's Theatre jointly with A. B. Limpus, and from December 1921 to June 1922 he was the manager of the Globe, but this last venture failed. His last successful production was *Lilac Time* at the Lyric, in December 1922.

In February 1923, accompanied by his wife, Boucicault went to South Africa, where he performed in *His House in Order*, *The Second Mrs Tanqueray* by Pinero, and several plays previously produced by him in England. Next he travelled to Australia and New Zealand, and appeared in Frederick Lonsdale's *Aren't We All?*, Pinero's *The Notorious Mrs Ebbsmith*, and Milne's *The Truth about Bladys*. He returned to London in 1925 but was back again in Australia in 1926 and in South Africa in 1927, then undertook yet another tour of Australia and New Zealand. He arrived in London in May 1929 suffering from a severe illness which he had contracted at the beginning of his return voyage, and died at his home, the Manor House at Hurley, Marlow, Buckinghamshire, on 25 June 1929, survived by his wife. The funeral was held in the church of St Mary the Virgin at Hurley on 28 June 1929.

NILANJANA BANERJI

Sources *Who was who in the theatre, 1912–1976*, 4 vols. (1978) · *The Times* (26 June 1929) · P. Hartnoll, ed., *The Oxford companion to the theatre*, 3rd edn (1967) · *Who was who in America*, 1 (1968) · J. Parker, ed., *Who's who in the theatre* (1912) · Adams, *Drama* · W. Browne and E. de Roy Koch, eds., *Who's who on the stage, 1908* (1908) · *Theatre World Annual*, 1 (1949–50) · *WWW, 1941–50* · D. Hines and H. P. Hanaford, *Who's who in music and drama* (1914) · E. Reid and H. Compton, eds., *The dramatic peerage*, rev. edn [1892] · *Daily Telegraph* (26 June 1929) · *DNB*

Archives Hunt. L., letters; literary MS · NYPL, papers · Theatre Museum, London, corresp. | NL Ire., letters to Ben Webster

Likenesses C. Buchel, lithograph, NPG · Hassall, lithograph (as the Chancellor in *Trelawny of the Wells*), NPG · Sem [G. Goursat], watercolour caricatures, NPG · photograph, Theatre Museum, London [*see illus.*]

Wealth at death £8322 11s.: probate, 16 Aug 1929, *CGPLA Eng. & Wales*

Boudicca [Boadicea] (*d.* AD **60/61**), queen of the Iceni, popularly known as Boadicea since the eighteenth century as a result of misreading manuscripts of the works of the Roman historian Tacitus, was the wife of *Prasutagus [*see under* Roman Britain, British leaders in (*act.* 55 BC–AD 84)], king of the Iceni, a tribe that occupied modern-day Norfolk, eastern Cambridgeshire, and northern Suffolk. Although the Iceni are not documented before the writings of Tacitus, they are probably the same people as the Cenimagni referred to by Julius Caesar in discussing his campaign in 54 BC. Like the Brigantes, the Iceni had also entered into an alliance with the Romans, as Tacitus makes clear; they may have been among the eleven unnamed kingdoms recorded as submitting to Claudius (10 BC–AD 54) in an inscription on a triumphal arch erected in Rome. The Iceni paid tribute, and supplied a quota of troops; but when in AD 47 they were deprived of their weapons, in accordance with Roman law, they rose up in revolt. Tacitus describes how they gathered in what he calls a 'rustic earthwork', possibly Stonea Camp, in the heart of the fens, but were swiftly overwhelmed. Whether Prasutagus was ruler at this time is not known; some assume that he became a client king in AD 43, but it seems more likely that he was installed in this position after the events of AD 47. Evidently, he was untainted by the rebellion, and his wealth was such as to be worthy of note by Tacitus. Some confirmation of the affluence of the region is provided by the discovery of nine hoards of gold and silver torcs, ingots, bracelets, and coins at Snettisham, Norfolk: although dated a century or so earlier, they surely belonged to a ruling clan. Indeed, Boudicca, who is described as coming from a royal house, is said by Cassius Dio (*c.*150–235) to have worn a large golden necklace as invariable attire.

Prasutagus died about AD 60. In his will he made the Roman emperor Nero coheir to his kingdom, together with his two daughters; he hoped in this way to safeguard the future both of his family and of part of his lands, a not uncommon practice in antiquity. In the event, the estates were plundered 'as though the spoils of war' (Tacitus, *Annals*, xiv.31), Boudicca was flogged and her daughters raped. Meanwhile, their neighbours the Trinovantes were suffering from the arrogant behaviour of the Roman colonists now based at Camulodunum (Colchester), who seized what they wanted at will. Furthermore, the procurator of Britain, Decianus Catus, chose that moment to call in grants made by Claudius to pro-Roman Britons, deciding that they should be regarded as loans: thus were sown the seeds for rebellion.

The course of events is described by both Tacitus and, much later, Cassius Dio. Tacitus would have had a first-hand account from his father-in-law, Gnaeus Julius Agricola (later a distinguished governor of Britain, *c.*AD 78–84), for he was on the governor's staff at the time. The governor, Gaius Suetonius Paullinus, was on the island of Mona (Anglesey), suppressing a druidical centre, when the revolt broke out in AD 60 or 61, and thus was powerless immediately to intervene. Camulodunum was first sacked, the final siege, which lasted two days, being of the Temple of Claudius, where the defenders took refuge; it now underlies the Norman castle. Burnt deposits encountered in almost every excavation confirm the ferocity of the assault. The ninth legion and its infantry were then ambushed and the infantry wiped out; and Poenius Postumus, the camp commander of the second legion, based at Isca Dumnoniorum (Exeter), refused to march. Meanwhile Suetonius Paullinus hurried back to London with some of his troops. London was by this time a thriving town, although probably not yet the provincial capital. It was certainly an obvious target for the rebellious Iceni and Trinovantes, and Suetonius realized that, without the support of the second and ninth legions, he could not defend it. He therefore retreated, probably north-westwards along the Watling Street, to join up with the rest of his force. London was then attacked, the buildings fired (as archaeological investigation again shows), and the remaining population butchered. The rebels next moved on to Verulamium (St Albans), which received similar treatment. 'The Britons took no prisoners … [and] wasted no time in getting down to the bloody business of hanging, burning, and crucifying', observes Tacitus (*Annals*, xiv.33). The official figure was that 70,000 were massacred at the three towns, and archaeology offers no dissent from this picture of a huge scale of destruction.

The final denouement probably took place in the midlands, although the exact site is not known. Suetonius had an army of about 10,000, while Cassius Dio estimates the British force at 230,000. The Romans took up a position in a defile, with a plain in front and dense woodland behind. Boudicca's tribesmen entered the plain, drawing up their wagons at the back, together with the women and children, as though in a grandstand. Lured into attack, the Britons were met first with a shower of javelins, and then by a disciplined assault. Hemmed in by the carts, there was a terrible slaughter of the tribespeople: 80,000 according to Tacitus. Boudicca was able to slip away, but died soon afterwards by poison (Tacitus) or illness (*Dio's Roman History*): the former seems the more likely. She was given a costly burial by the Britons. When Poenius Postumus heard the news of the Roman triumph, he too killed himself by falling on his sword, recognizing his indecisiveness in not moving from his base at Isca Dumnoniorum.

Suetonius Paullinus now took his revenge, using reinforcements brought in from the Rhine army. Although not yet satisfactorily attested archaeologically, Tacitus records that the territory of hostile or neutral tribes was laid waste with fire and sword. Fortunately, Julius Alpinus Classicianus, the procurator who replaced Decianus Catus (who had escaped to Gaul), was a provincial, probably from the Trier area of Germany, and thus had some sympathy for the position of the Britons. He made an adverse report on Suetonius and a commission of inquiry was set up: as a result, a pretext was found for the recall of Suetonius. His successor as governor, Petronius Turpilianus, was evidently not a vindictive man, and Classicianus clearly handled the financial side of the aftermath of the revolt with consideration and tact, calming down a still volatile situation.

Boudicca, whose name is best rendered as Victoria, very nearly ended Roman rule in Britain. She emerges in Cassius Dio's description as an awesome but heroic figure, being 'very tall, in appearance most terrifying … [with] a harsh voice, and with a great mass of the tawniest hair [which] fell to her hips' (lxii.2,3). This helps to explain why she became an attractive subject for writers and poets from the sixteenth century onwards, not least as a symbol of national patriotism. She has acquired a firm place in British history, with Thomas Thornycroft's great statue on the Embankment in London, erected in 1902, as a fitting reminder of the leadership and valour of the first Queen Victoria. T. W. POTTER

Sources C. Tacitus, *The histories [and] the annals*, ed. and trans. C. H. Moore and J. Jackson, 4 (1937), bk 14, pp. 29–39 · Tacitus, *Agricola*, ed. and trans. M. Mutton (1914), xvi · *Dio's Roman history*, ed. and trans. E. Cary, 8 (1925), lxii.1–12 · D. R. Dudley and G. Webster, *The rebellion of Boudicca* (1962) · G. Webster, *Boudica* (1978) · D. F. Allen, 'The coins of the Iceni', *Britannia*, 1 (1970), 1–33 · P. Crummy, 'Colchester', *Fortress into city: the consolidation of Roman Britain, first century AD*, ed. G. Webster (1988), 24–47 · R. Merrifield, *London, city of the Romans* (1983), 52–60 · S. S. Frere and M. G. Wilson, *Verulamium excavations*, 2 (1983), 7–8 · I. M. Stead, 'The Snettisham treasure: excavation in 1990', *Antiquity*, 65 (1991), 447–65 · R. P. J. Jackson and T. W. Potter, *Excavations at Stonea, Cambridgeshire, 1980–1985* (1996), 27–44

Likenesses T. Thornycroft, bronze statue, 1902, Embankment, London · A. Sammes, engraving, repro. in *Britannia Antiqua Restaurata* (1676)

Bough, Samuel (1822–1878), landscape and marine painter, was born on 8 January 1822 at Abbey Street, Carlisle, the third of five children of James Bough (1794–1845), shoemaker, and Lucy Walker (1785–1836), a cook. He was baptized at St Mary's Church on 10 February. Bough grew up in a household that lacked material comforts but encouraged a love of literature and the arts, his parents being friends with many local artists. At an early age he began to draw and stage his own theatrical performances for friends, paying off small debts from the proceeds. Although Bough received no formal art education, he assimilated knowledge from an older generation of artists in Carlisle, particularly John Dobson, George Sheffield, and Robert Harrington, and from such visiting artists as Thomas Miles Richardson senior and John Wilson Carmichael. His rambles through Cumberland gave him access to the art collections of the local gentry, which added to his appreciation of the old masters. A few visits to London, including a brief period apprenticed to the engraver Thomas Allom, completed his early schooling in art. Of the many other artists admired by Bough, J. M. W. Turner had the most apparent impact on his subsequent work. For the most part, however, he turned to nature and direct observation for his inspiration. This was to be Bough's approach for the rest of his life.

After an abortive start as a solicitor's clerk, Bough became a professional artist in Carlisle, struggling to make a living there until 1845, when he went to Manchester as an assistant scene painter. There he attended life classes at the Manchester Academy and formed close ties with the artists William Percy and Charles Allen Duval. Despite winning the Heywood silver medal for the best watercolour at the Manchester Exhibition of 1847 Bough had little financial success and took up another scene painting job in Glasgow in 1849. On 30 April of that year he married Isabella Taylor (1824–1900), a young opera singer and harpist. His first major work, *The Baggage Waggons* (1849; Tullie House Museum and Art Gallery, Carlisle), was also painted in 1849. A scene of soldiers approaching his home town with a rainstorm in the distance, it contains most of the elements that marked his work across the rest of his lifetime: humanity set in the context of the elemental forces of nature.

Glasgow failed to offer the breakthrough in art that Bough needed, so he moved on, first to Hamilton and Cadzow Forest in 1851, where his friendship with the landscape painter Alexander Fraser (1827–1899) produced some remarkable pictures of woodland scenes, in both oils and watercolour. Although he was not deemed a great colourist by his contemporaries, Bough's ability to capture the dappled effect of sunlight through trees in works from this period challenges such a judgement.

In 1854 Bough moved to Port Glasgow in order to improve his technique in drawing ships and boats. For a man remembered for his lack of formal art education and with a reputation for being slipshod in his approach, Bough was paradoxically meticulous when he chose to be, as exemplified by his *Gabbarts and Iron Shipyard* of 1855 (NMM), his most important work from this period. Tonally and compositionally a triumph, it depicts the whole spectrum of shipping activity on the Clyde, from the small boy sailing his model boat in the shallows to the construction of an ocean-going ship in the middle distance. From this date marine painting was to be one of Bough's most powerful forms of expression.

To augment his income from painting Bough continued his work as a scene painter and also developed a reputation as a book illustrator, notably of the works of Robert Burns and Sir Walter Scott. He continued both activities throughout his life.

In 1855 Bough moved to Edinburgh. He met with early success at the Royal Scottish Academy exhibitions and was elected an associate in 1856. Thereafter his relationship with the academy was a stormy one and it was not until 1875 that he was elected a full academician, despite being a prolific exhibitor.

Bough's reputation with the art-buying public and the critics continued to rise throughout the 1850s and 1860s and, ultimately, he displaced Horatio McCulloch as the most popular of contemporary Scottish landscape painters. Major works from this period include *The Mail Coach* (1855; Glasgow Museums and Art Gallery), *Cadzow Burn* (1856; Tullie House Museum and Art Gallery, Carlisle), *The*

Weald of Kent (1857; National Gallery of Victoria, Melbourne), *Royal Volunteer Review* (1860; National Gallery of Scotland, Edinburgh), and *Edinburgh Castle from the Canal* (1862).

Bough travelled and painted widely throughout England and Scotland, being mostly identified with his native Cumberland and the Fife coast. He also made occasional forays into Europe, including Norway, the Netherlands, Belgium, France, and Germany. At times, disenchanted by his lack of official recognition in Scotland, he considered resettling in Cumberland or moving to London, but continued to live in Edinburgh for the rest of his life.

Throughout the 1870s Bough's style displayed more impressionistic elements that were later taken further by his younger friend William McTaggart. *St Monance, Fife* (1876; Glasgow Museums and Art Gallery) and *Summer Evening, Cadzow* (1877; priv. coll.) are fine examples of this phase of Bough's work. He continued to produce major works in his more 'commercial' style, including *A Sunny Day in Iona* (1871), *London from Shooters Hill* (1872), *Peel Harbour, Isle of Man* (1875), and *Burns Cottage, Alloway* (1876; Glasgow Museums and Art Gallery).

Renowned for a bohemian lifestyle, Bough made friends at all levels of society. He was widely read, a great storyteller, and an accomplished musician. A kind and generous friend, he could also be sarcastic and boorish towards those he thought pretentious. This latter trait made him significant enemies within the Scottish art establishment.

Bough recommended a palette with a limited range of colours to his students but ignored his own advice when it suited him. He did much of his preliminary sketching outdoors, but returned to the studio to finish the work. His approach was described succinctly by Robert Louis Stevenson:

> Artistic sight is judicious blindness. Sam Bough must have been a jolly blind old boy. … He saw, not the scene, but the watercolour sketch. Where does he learn that? In the studio, I swear. … He learns it in the crystallisation of daydreams; in changing, not in copying, fact. (*Letters of Robert Louis Stevenson*, 2.147)

Always a controversial character, Bough established watercolour as a significant medium in Scottish art. His great facility in both oils and watercolour, and his speed of production, led some to criticize his work for lack of finish. In reality, he overproduced to meet the cost of his way of life. This led to his returning to earlier successful styles and subjects throughout his life and has left posterity with a confusing picture of his development as an artist. The best of his paintings have an energy and freedom of composition and style that mark his capacity for capturing the moment. He was best at portraying nature in its extremes—wonderful skies with fleeting sunsets or storms and raging seas threatening the lives of those who sailed on them. Sentimentality had no part in his art.

In 1877 Bough's health began to fail and he suffered a stroke in January 1878. He appeared to make a good recovery, but fell ill again later that year and died, at Jordan Bank Villa, his home in Morningside, Edinburgh, on 19 November 1878 of cancer of the prostate. He was buried in Dean cemetery, Edinburgh, on 23 November.

Historically, Bough's place in Scottish art is as an artist of transition, marking the change from the traditional themes and style of McCulloch to the impressionistic effects of McTaggart and those who came after.

GIL HITCHON and PAT HITCHON

Sources G. Hitchon and P. Hitchon, *Sam Bough RSA: the rivers in Bohemia* (1998) • S. Gilpin, *Sam Bough RSA* (1905) • Carlisle Reference Library, Sewell collection, E. Pinnington MSS • R. L. Stevenson, 'The late Sam Bough', *Essays literary and critical* (1924), 135–7 • E. Pinnington, 'Sam Bough RSA', *Good Words* (Sept 1897), 597–604 • P. G. Hamerton, 'Etchings from pictures by contemporary artists, no. 17 Sam Bough RSA', *The Portfolio*, 10 (1879), 112–14 • R. Walker, 'Sam Bough', *Magazine of Art*, 19 (1895–6), 425–31 • J. Halsby, *Scottish watercolours, 1740–1940* (1986) • W. D. McKay, *The Scottish school of painting* (1906) • J. L. Caw, *Scottish painting past and present, 1620–1908* (1908) • *The letters of Robert Louis Stevenson*, ed. S. Colvin, new edn, 4 vols. (1911), vol. 2, p. 147 • d. cert. • parish register, Carlisle, St Mary's Church, 10 Feb 1822 [baptism]

Archives NA Scot., trust records

Likenesses W. G. Stevenson, bronze statuette, 1809, Scot. NPG • W. Percy, watercolour drawing, 1846, Tullie House Museum and Art Gallery, Carlisle • J. Mossman, cameo, 1850, Scot. NPG • T. Fairbairn, pencil and wash drawing, 1854, Scot. NPG • J. Philip, oils, 1856, Scot. NPG • D. Macnee, oils, 1878, Art Gallery and Museum, Kelvingrove, Glasgow • R. Anderson, oils, Scot. NPG • S. Bough, self-portrait, oils, Tullie House Museum and Art Gallery, Carlisle • W. Brodie, bronze bust, Dean cemetery, Edinburgh • Nesbitt & Lothian, carte-de-visite, NPG • M. Slee, watercolour (after W. Percy), Scot. NPG

Wealth at death £11,705 18*s*. 6*d*.: confirmation, 4 March 1879, *CCI*

Boughen, Edward (1587–1653), Church of England clergyman and religious controversialist, was born in Buckinghamshire and educated at Westminster School. Elected as a Westminster scholar at Christ Church, Oxford, he matriculated, aged eighteen, on 13 December 1605, graduating BA on 22 June 1609 and proceeding MA on 14 May 1612. In 1619 he became chaplain to the bishop of Oxford, John Howson, who rapidly appointed him rector of Warpsgrave in 1620, and vicar of Bray in 1621 and of Stoke Talmage in 1628.

Boughen was a well-educated conformist and his writings principally offered a staunch defence of the Church of England. He preached on 27 September 1619, at Howson's primary visitation, of the pastoral importance and episcopal function exercised in confirmation. Richard Hooker had long before noted the scandalous neglect into which the practice of confirmation had fallen, repeating criticisms and claims of laxity made to Burghley as early as the 1580s. Although Hooker's contention was championed by George Hakewill in the pamphlet he wrote in 1613 to celebrate the confirmation at Whitehall of Prince Charles, *The Auncient Ecclesiasticall Practise of Confirmation*, it does not seem to have prompted many of the episcopal bench into action any more than had 1604 Canon LX, which required that the bishop confirm triennially at his visitations. Visitation articles tended only to enquire after catechizing, a necessary part of confirmation preparation; those of Howson in 1619, repeated in

1628, on the other hand, expressly enjoined due diligence in preparing candidates for confirmation.

Boughen's agenda at the 1619 visitation was to explain confirmation to the clergy:

> that you … may be the better encouraged, to performe that dutie of seasoning the younger sort of your parishioners with the principles of the Religio, that they may be more fit for that holy *imposition of hands* by the Bishop, and worthily partake the fruits thereof. (Boughen, *A Sermon of Confirmation*, 2)

If this sermon is taken as evidence of an attempt to propagandize the rite—other attempts were made in Scotland in the articles of Aberdeen of 1616 which became the five articles of Perth of 1618—Boughen's success was partial. Little uniformity of practice was achieved until after 1662. In the very next year (1620), in the Oxford schools, Richard Hall roundly answered in the negative the proposition whether confirmation was absolutely necessary as a sacrament instituted by the church.

On 13 April 1633, in succession to Bishop John Bancroft, Boughen was collated to the rectory of Woodchurch, Kent; in 1638 he was appointed to the prebend of Marden in the diocese of Chichester. Removed from Bray in 1640, he was deprived of Woodchurch as a 'delinquent' in February 1641. In 1646 he joined the king in Oxford and on 1 July was made by him DD in the university. Thereafter he lived in Chartham, Kent, where he may have had family links: although nothing is known of his wife, his son Edward, who went to Merton College, Oxford, in 1644, was born there.

Boughen's later writings on the necessity of unity of doctrine and uniformity in discipline are consistent with early opinions. A 1645 treatise 'Observations upon the ordinance of the Lords and Commons', showing the nullity and invalidity of Presbyterian ordinations was, according to Bishop Barlow, part of an intended larger work begun in 1643 that was overtaken by Jeremy Taylor's writings, while he returned to the need for confirmation and value of catechizing in a short exposition of the catechism, *Principles of Religion* (1646). Here he lamented 'that two such useful and excellent means of saving knowledge, as sermons and catechizing be, should the one be advanced to the depressing of the other', noting that 'the inordinate Zeal of people' often demanded two sermons on Sundays at the cost of the catechism. Catechizing 'is a means indispensably necessary to attain the more excellent and only necessary end' (*Principles of Religion*, 1646) of building up the faithful. Shortly before the regicide he discussed the treaty of Newcastle and whether the king could with a safe conscience consent to the abrogation of episcopacy in his *Mr Geere's Case of Conscience Sifted* (1648). His last conformist work was *An Account of the Church Catholick* (1653), a disputation with a New College man, Thomas Read.

Boughen died during the interregnum, on 9 November 1653, and was buried at Southease church, near Lewes. News of his death was not widely known at the time and he was mistakenly entered at the Restoration as vicar of Bray; a successor was appointed later in the year.

Nicholas W. S. Cranfield

Sources Foster, *Alum. Oxon.* • *JHC*, 2 (1640–42) • register books of the proceedings of the committee of the House of Commons … affected ministers who have been plundered, 1645–1647, BL, Add. MSS 15669, fols. 89, 148; 15671, fol. 32 • induction mandates and presentations, 1551–1750, Berks. RO, Archdeaconry MSS • E. Boughen, *A sermon of confirmation* (1620) • J. Howson, *Articles to be enquired of … 1619* (1619) • E. Boughen, 'Observations upon the ordinance of the Lords and Commons', 1645, Bodl. Oxf., MS Linc. C 8.29 [flyleaf] • S. L. Ollard, 'Confirmation in the Anglican communion', *Confirmation, or, The laying on of hands*, 1 (1926), 60–245 • *Sussex Notes and Queries*, 6/2 (1936), 52

Boughton, Sir Charles William Rouse- [*formerly* Charles William Boughton, Charles William Rouse, Sir Charles William Boughton-Rouse], **ninth baronet and first baronet** (**1747–1821**), politician, the son of Shuckburgh Boughton (*d.* 1760) and his wife, Mary, *née* Greville, of Poston Court, Herefordshire, was baptized on 10 December 1747 in the parish of St Nicholas, Worcester.

Boughton was appointed a writer by the East India Company in 1764 to Bengal, and after 1768 used the name Rouse as he had become the heir of his cousin Thomas Rouse. He was appointed supervisor of Nator (Rajshahi district) in 1769, one of the most valuable areas that the East India Company had just acquired in Bengal. The 22-year-old Rouse was expected, according to the new regulations, to report on the tax collections, to give a careful account of the economic conditions of the region, to see that justice was enforced, to extirpate corruption, and to abolish arbitrary fines. In his letters to his superior in Murshidabad, the capital, he acknowledged that he had been criticized for having shown undue concern for the peasants, but he defended himself with the argument that humane treatment was the only way to get the people to accept the rule of foreigners alien in race, religion, and language. He became involved in the debate over the tax system that should be used in Bengal, arguing that the *zamindars* were the actual owners of their lands, not just tax collectors, or tax farmers, to be appointed because they made the highest bid for the office, as many company officials argued. This position aligned him with Philip Francis, a member of the supreme council of Bengal, and against Warren Hastings, the governor-general, in one of the most celebrated disputes over the nature of the company's administration. Francis was impressed by the young Rouse, and, telling him that 'with respect to great fundamental principles, your ideas coincide with mine', used many of Rouse's detailed minutes for his own work (Weitzman, 304). Rouse continued to be helpful to Francis in England in his attacks on Hastings. A competent student of Persian, which he learned in Bengal, he translated part of the great Mughal work on government *A'in-i-Akbari*. He left the company's service in 1778 and returned to England, but remained involved in Indian affairs. According to Edmund Burke, Rouse had an important role in the select committee appointed by parliament in 1781 to investigate the activities of the East India Company and Warren Hastings. Much of the detailed material on land revenue as well as background on Hastings seems to have been supplied in private meetings before and during the meetings of the select committee (*Correspondence*, 4.355–8;

Writings and Speeches, 6.55, 67). In 1791 he published *Dissertation Concerning the Landed Property of Bengal*, in which he showed an unusual knowledge of taxation and land tenures.

Elected MP for Evesham in 1780, Rouse retained the seat until 1790 as a supporter of William Pitt. He was one of the forty-two members in that parliament who belonged to what was known as the 'Indian interest', that is, 'nabobs' who had served in the East India Company. On 3 June 1782 he married Catherine Hall (*d*. 1808), who was the daughter and heir of William Pearce Hall of Downton Hall, Shropshire. They had a son, William, who eventually succeeded to his titles, and two daughters, Louisa and Caroline. His wife's connections, and those of his mother with the Greville family, were factors in his access to William Pitt and other leading politicians. In 1784 he became the secretary of the Board of Control, the body set up by parliament to oversee the affairs of the East India Company, but he was dismissed in 1791, apparently because he had opposed some of the measures of Henry Dundas, the president of the board. In recognition of his services to Pitt's ministry, he was created baronet in July 1791. At this point he added his original family name of Boughton as Boughton-Rouse, but in 1794, when he inherited the family title of ninth baronet, he began using the name Rouse-Boughton.

Rouse-Boughton tried, unsuccessfully, in 1795 to get Pitt to reappoint him as secretary to the Board of Control, pleading that he was in need as his elder brother had left the family estate, valued at £50,000, to his daughter by a maidservant. He was elected as an MP for Bamber in 1796, one of the fifty-seven members of that parliament who belonged to the 'Indian interest'. Rouse spoke occasionally on Indian affairs in parliament, generally defending the East India Company's political activities. He had hoped that Pitt would give him an office that would let him keep his parliamentary seat, but when nothing was forthcoming, he resigned in January 1800 to become an audit commissioner. He died on 26 February 1821 at his home, Downton Hall, Shropshire.

AINSLIE T. EMBREE

Sources biographical index, BL OIOC • minutes of board of control, 1784 • list of the company's covenanted servants, BL OIOC • writers' petitions, BL OIOC • Bengal Letter Room, ed., *Letter copy book of the supervisor of Rajshahi at Nator* (1925) • HoP, *Commons, 1790–1820* • R. Guha, *A rule of property for Bengal: an essay on the idea of permanent settlement* (Paris, 1963) • *The correspondence of Edmund Burke*, 4, ed. J. A. Woods (1963) • *The writings and speeches of Edmund Burke*, ed. P. Langford, 6: *India: the launching of the Hastings impeachment, 1786–1788* (1991) • S. Weitzman, *Warren Hastings and Philip Francis* (1929) • C. H. Philips, *The East India Company, 1784–1834* (1940); repr. with minor corrections (1961) • W. Foster, *The India board, 1784–1858* (1918) • L. S. Sutherland, *The East India Company in eighteenth century politics* (1952) • PRO, Pitt MSS, 30/8/114, fol. 174 • *Debrett's Peerage* • *The Times* (27 Feb 1821)

Archives BL, letters to D. Anderson, Add. MSS 45429–45432 • PRO, Pitt MSS

Boughton, George Henry (1833–1905), painter and illustrator, was born on 4 December 1833 at a village near Norwich, where his father, William Boughton, was a farmer. Taken by his parents to America as an infant, he lived in Albany, New York, where he was educated at the high school. Self-taught as an artist, he sold his first painting, *The Wayfarer*, at the American Art Union exhibition in 1852. Shortly after this he made his first trip to Britain. Back in New York in 1858 he exhibited *Winter Twilight* at the New York Academy of Design. In 1859 he went to Paris, where he spent two years and studied under Edward May, a pupil of Thomas Couture, and later with Édouard Frère, from whom he absorbed elements of the realist tradition and an interest in depicting the activities of the poor. He finally settled in London in 1862. In that year, and again in 1863, he exhibited two pictures at the British Institution. He sent *Through the Fields* and *Hop-Pickers Returning* to the Royal Academy in 1863 thereafter exhibiting annually, a total of eighty-seven pictures, the last one posthumously in the year of his death *Winter in the Marshes* (1905).

George Henry Boughton (1833–1905), by Ralph W. Robinson, 1889

Boughton became an associate of the Royal Academy in 1879, and a full member in 1896. In 1879 he was elected a member of the Institute of Painters in Water Colours. He painted genre, landscapes, portraits, and historical scenes in England, Scotland, France, and from 1881 in Holland. Pretty women, sturdy peasants, and brave and romantic historical scenes, particularly from New England history, including *Hester Prynne* (1881), *Muiden, N. Holland* (1882), *An Exchange of Greetings* (1882), and *Milton Visited by Andrew Marvel* (1885), were popular and financially rewarding subjects in his lifetime. *Puritans Going to Church* (1867) employs a dark palette for the background with the figures distributed across a flat landscape of snow. Many of Boughton's pictures have contemporary, narrative themes which can be sentimental and precious; however, this weakness is often relieved by a strong composition. His *Spring Idyll*, which long remained popular in reproduction, is typical of one aspect of his work: a romantic, idealized, and sentimental female figure. *Weeding the Pavement* (1882), a Dutch scene, was presented to the nation by Sir Henry Tate. *The Road to Camelot* (1898) is in the Walker Art Gallery, Liverpool, and *A Dutch Ferry* (1883) is in the Whitworth Institute in Manchester.

Boughton was also an illustrator, which is apparent in the illustrative, narrative basis of many of the themes of his paintings. Among the books he illustrated were *Rip Van Winkle* (1893), W. Irvine's *Knickerbocker History*, and N. Hawthorne's *The Scarlet Letter*. Boughton wrote well and his *Sketching Rambles in Holland* is a lively account of his travels with the painter Edwin Austin Abbey. They were close friends and part of the community of American expatriate artists in London in the late nineteenth century described by Henry James. Boughton wrote entertainingly, if rather archly, of another friend in *The Studio* (30, 1903–4): 'A few of the various Whistlers I have known'. He had met J. A. M. Whistler, also a friend of Edwin Austin Abbey, in one of the American artist's studios. Boughton also contributed short stories to *Harper's Magazine*. Both his writing and his illustrations for the *Illustrated London News* made a profound impression on Vincent Van Gogh, who wrote at length to his brother Theo about a painting which he called *Pilgrim's Progress*; he appears to be referring to a lost painting of Boughton's entitled *God Speed! Pilgrims Setting out for Canterbury: Time of Chaucer* exhibited at the Royal Academy in 1874. Ruskin, however, was particularly scathing about Boughton's *The Bearers of the Burden*, exhibited at the Royal Academy in 1875, and among other things condemned it in his 'Academy notes' as 'more or less feeble or parsimonious' (Ruskin, 285).

Boughton married Katherine Louise Cullen, daughter of Thomas Cullen MD, on 9 February 1865. He died on 21 January 1905, from heart disease, at his home, West House, Campden Hill, London, which had been designed for him by Norman Shaw; his wife survived him. He was cremated at Golders Green. An exhibition of his remaining works was held at the Leicester Galleries in 1905, and the preface to the catalogue was written by A. L. Baldry. The contents of his studio were sold at Christies on 15 June 1908. New York Public Library holds papers given to it by the artist and a sketchbook. Examples of his work are in the Ashmolean Museum, Oxford, and the Victoria and Albert Museum, London.

MARTIN HARDIE, *rev.* OLIVIA FITZPATRICK

Sources A. L. Baldry, *G. H. Boughton R.A.: his life and work* (1904) [cover title: *Christmas art annual, 1904*] • S. Colvin, 'G. H. Boughton', *The Portfolio*, 2 (1871), 69 • S. Houfe, *The dictionary of 19th century British book illustrators and caricaturists*, rev. edn (1996) • Graves, *RA exhibitors*, vol. 1 • A. Jarman and others, eds., *Royal Academy exhibitors, 1905–1970: a dictionary of artists and their work in the summer exhibitions of the Royal Academy of Arts*, 6 vols. (1973–82) • H. B. Werness, 'Vincent van Gogh and a lost painting by G. H. Boughton', *Gazette des Beaux-Arts*, 6th ser., 106 (1985), 71–5 • X. van Eck, 'Van Gogh and George Henry Boughton', *Burlington Magazine*, 132 (1990), 539–40 • E. Morris, 'Edwin Austin Abbey and his American circle in England', *Apollo*, 104 (1976), 220–21 • G. H. Boughton, 'A few of the various Whistlers I have known', *The Studio*, 30 (1903–4), 208–18 • J. Ruskin, 'Academy notes, 1875', *The works of John Ruskin*, ed. E. T. Cook and A. Wedderburn, 14 (1904), 285 • m. cert. • d. cert.

Archives AM Oxf., MSS • NYPL, MSS • U. Glas., MSS • V&A, MSS | U. Glas. L., corresp. with J. A. M. Whistler

Likenesses G. H. Boughton, self-portrait, oils, 1884, Aberdeen Art Gallery • R. W. Robinson, photograph, 1889, NPG [*see illus.*] • A. L. Baldry, pencil drawing, NPG • J. Pettie, portrait, Metropolitan Museum of Art, New York

Wealth at death £24,916 7*s*. 10*d*.: probate, 7 March 1905, *CGPLA Eng. & Wales*

Boughton, Joan (*c*.1414–1494), Wycliffite heretic, is known only from accounts of her death. The fullest of these, in the great chronicle of London, records that she was a widow and mother, and describes her as 'an old cankyrd heretyke that dotid For age', being at least eighty years old. The chronicle's bitterly hostile account reports that she was a disciple of Wyclif, whom she revered as a saint, and an ardent subscriber to his doctrines. Brought to trial for heresy, she could not be moved from her (unspecified) opinions, in spite of the efforts of 'alle the doctors of london', and was condemned to be burnt at Smithfield. Conducted to the stake on 28 April 1494, 'she spak offtyn of God & ouir lady', but could not be prevailed upon to utter the name of Jesus. She clearly had associates in heresy, since after her death they removed her ashes 'for a precious Relyk' (*Great Chronicle of London*, 252–3). One of them was believed to be her own daughter, Joan, the widow of Sir John Yonge, mayor of London (1466–7). Joan may have followed her mother to the stake, since about 1510 a Kentishwoman declared that Lady Yonge 'died well … a martyr before God' (Brigden, 97), having refused to honour images. But there is no evidence to corroborate this. Sir John appears to have been a man of impeccable orthodoxy, who founded a chantry at Chipping Norton, Oxfordshire. His widow had remarried by 1486; her new husband was Sir Thomas Leukenor. In spite of her great age, there is no evidence that Joan Boughton was a heretic of long standing, and she could have been converted in the 1490s, when there was something of a revival of Lollardy in London [*see* Lollard women (*act. c*.1390–*c*.1520)].

HENRY SUMMERSON

Sources A. H. Thomas and I. D. Thornley, eds., *The great chronicle of London* (1938), 252–3 • C. L. Kingsford, ed., *Chronicles of London* (1905), 200 • R. Fabyan, *The new chronicles of England and France*, ed. H. Ellis, new edn (1811), 685 • *CCIR, 1485–500*, no. 128 • J. C. Wedgwood and A. D. Holt, *History of parliament*, 1: *Biographies of the members of the Commons house, 1439–1509* (1936), 980–81 • S. Brigden, *London and the Reformation* (1989) • J. A. F. Thomson, *The later Lollards, 1414–1520* (1965) • A. Hudson, *The premature reformation: Wycliffite texts and Lollard history* (1988)

Boughton, Rutland (1878–1960), composer, was born in Bicester Road, Aylesbury, Buckinghamshire, on 23 January 1878, the elder son in a family of two boys and one girl of William Rutland Boughton (1841–1905), a grocer at 37 Buckingham Street, and his wife, Grace Martha (1845–1924), the daughter of Francis Bishop, an innkeeper.

Rutland Boughton (1878–1960), by Herbert Lambert, 1921

Although he was educated at the Aylesbury grammar school, he was self-taught in music and began to compose as a child. In 1892 he was apprenticed to a London concert agency, which significantly enlarged his musical horizons so that his compositions now attracted sympathetic interest, and a fund was raised sufficient for a limited period of study (autumn 1898 to spring 1901) under Charles Stanford at the Royal College of Music. On leaving, he endured great poverty before finding work variously in the pit orchestra of the Haymarket Theatre, as music critic on the *Daily Mail*, and as rehearsal pianist to the baritone David Ffrangcon-Davies (who taught him the techniques of voice training). On 16 December 1903 he entered into an ill-judged marriage with Florence Elizabeth Hobley (1885–1973); they had three children, Ruby, Estelle, and Arthur. His financial struggles became known to Granville Bantock, principal of the Birmingham and Midland Institute's School of Music, who offered him a post, which he took up in July 1905.

Success as a singing teacher and choral conductor led to choral compositions, most notably *Midnight*, to words by Edward Carpenter, which, at the Birmingham triennial festival on 5 October 1909, not only established Boughton's reputation as a composer but also advertised his new-found socialist principles. Drawn by the ethos of the Celtic revival, then in full swing, he began to formulate ideas for a cycle of Arthurian music dramas with a large choral content. By chance, this happened to coincide with the work of Reginald Ramsden Buckley, who had just completed *Arthur of Britain*, a cycle of five poetic dramas. The two men met, and by 1908 the composition of *Uther and Igraine*, the first part of the cycle, was well under way. Recognizing the unsuitability of their scheme for the commercial opera house, they now proposed that a temple theatre be built around a commune of like-minded artists who would support themselves by small-scale farming. Their ideals were shared by Christina Anne Stansfield Walshe (1888–1959), a young artist and intellectual equal who had supplanted the rather limited Florence in Boughton's affections, and who, after the completion of a deed of separation in April 1911, became his new partner. Two children were born of their union: Maire and Joy (1913–1964), who won fame as an oboist of great distinction. The children of the first family remained with their father.

The scandal obliged Boughton to resign his post and return to London and musical hack work, from which he was rescued by George Bernard Shaw (with whom he enjoyed a lifelong friendship, fuelled by a mutual delight in provocative correspondence), who proposed his employment as amanuensis to a wealthy musical amateur, Frederick Jackson. Living in a cottage on Jackson's Hindhead estate, Boughton began work on *The Immortal Hour*, a setting of a poetic drama by William Sharp (under the name Fiona Macleod), which had unexpectedly gripped his imagination. In June 1912 he announced a summer school at Hindhead which would culminate in an open-air production of the new music drama. The scheme failed to attract sufficient support, but was revived again, this time successfully, at Bournemouth in 1913 as a preliminary to a festival of music, dance, and mystic drama at Glastonbury in 1914. Although local, and national, support was forthcoming, the proposed theatre and orchestra had to give way to the Glastonbury assembly rooms and a grand piano. Local amateurs provided a sufficient chorus, and Boughton's former pupils and professional friends the soloists. His moral probity having been vouched for by members of the Quaker shoe manufacturing family the Clarks of Street (who also provided vital financial support), the festival began on 5 August and included three performances (26–9 August) of *The Immortal Hour*.

Viability thus having been proved, the festival continued (with a gap from September 1917 to January 1919 during Boughton's service as bandmaster in the Royal Flying Corps) until the end of 1926, each year growing more successful, ambitious, and sophisticated. No fewer than 350 staged performances were eventually mounted (all with Christina Walshe's designs) and more than 100 chamber concerts, thus providing invaluable experience for aspiring young singers and instrumentalists. Operas by Gluck, Purcell, John Blow, Matthew Locke, Edgar Bainton, and Clarence Raybould were heard alongside contemporary British chamber works, and there were lectures and exhibitions. Boughton's own music dramas were premièred in the following sequence: *The Immortal Hour* (August 1914), *Bethlehem* (December 1915), *The Round Table* (August 1916), *The Birth of Arthur* (August 1920), *Alkestis* (August 1922), and *The Queen of Cornwall* (August 1924).

In June 1921 Barry Jackson presented *The Immortal Hour* at his Birmingham Repertory Theatre and, emboldened by its success, transferred the production to the Regent Theatre, London, where, on 13 October 1922, it began an unprecedented run of 216 consecutive performances, followed by a revival of 160 performances in 1923, and further revivals in 1926 and 1932. Boughton was now hailed as the country's leading operatic composer. *Bethlehem* and *Alkestis* also enjoyed London productions, the latter by the

British National Opera Company (Covent Garden, January 1924).

Success gave Boughton the opportunity to air his often controversial opinions, and from now on he began to antagonize his supporters, partly through his membership of the Communist Party (1926–9 and 1945–56, after which complete disillusion set in), but more importantly through his acquisition of a third 'wife', Kathleen Davis (1900–1973), with whom he set up house in April 1923. Events came to a head in December 1926, when, as a gesture of solidarity with the miners' strike, he presented *Bethlehem* at Church House, Westminster, in modern dress, with Christ born in a miner's cottage and Herod as a top-hatted capitalist. The press sensationalized the event to such an extent that Boughton's Glastonbury friends withdrew their support, and on 7 July 1927 the Festival Players went into liquidation.

In November 1927 Boughton took up residence on a smallholding at Kilcot, near Newent, on the Gloucestershire and Herefordshire border. There, with his dependent children (three, Peter, Brian, and Jennifer, were born to Kathleen), he remained for the rest of his life. Two more festivals were attempted (Stroud, 1934, and Bath, 1935). Neither struck root, though each successfully introduced a new music drama: *The Lily Maid* (the third of the Arthurian cycle) and *The Ever Young* respectively. Finding that Boughton's annual income had sunk in 1935 to less than £100, Steuart Wilson petitioned for a civil-list pension. He was supported by, among others, Shaw, Vaughan Williams, Herbert Morrison, and Sir Walford Davies, master of the king's music. The pension was granted in May 1938, supplementing Boughton's uncertain earnings and enabling him to continue his life's work. Between 1943 and 1945 he completed the last two parts of the Arthurian cycle, *Galahad* and *Avalon*. Both were to his own libretto, which by now had departed from Buckley's original concept and taken on an autobiographical slant: the journey from disillusion with the established church to salvation through true communism. He died in his sleep at 30 The Terrace, the house in Barnes, Surrey, of his daughter Joy, on 25 January 1960, and was cremated on 29 January at St Marylebone crematorium. His ashes were later scattered at Kilcot.

Since Boughton was ignored in his later years, and judged mainly by gossip and hearsay, it is only through such modern recordings as *The Immortal Hour* (Hyperion, CDA66101/2; 1984), *Bethlehem* (Hyperion CDA66690; 1993), the second and third symphonies (Carlton Classics, 1565 91892; 1996), and the first and second string quartets and the first oboe quartet (Hyperion CDA66936; 1997) that the range and significance of his achievement has begun to be appreciated. His musical style remained resolutely that of the late nineteenth century, tempered by simple, folk-like melodies. His music dramas depend on a system of leitmotifs, deployed more as a skilful mosaic than as a Wagnerian symphonic argument. Great use is made of the chorus as a commentator on the action.

MICHAEL HURD

Sources M. Hurd, *Rutland Boughton and the Glastonbury festivals* (1993) · R. Boughton, *The self-advertisement of Rutland Boughton* (privately printed, 1909) · R. Boughton, *The Glastonbury festival movement* (1946) · D. Brook, *Composers' gallery: biographical sketches of contemporary composers* (1946) · S. Grew, *Our favorite musicians* (1924) · M. Saremba, *Elgar, Britten & Co.: eine Geschichte der britischen Musik in zwölf Portraits* (Zürich, 1994) · b. cert. · d. cert. · personal knowledge (2004)

Archives BL, letters to Estelle and Stuart Fletcher, Add. MSS 57839–57840 · BL, corresp. with League of Dramatists, Add. MS 63362 · BL, corresp. with G. B. Shaw, Add. MS 50529 · BL, corresp. with Society of Authors, Add. MSS 56671–56673 · BL, corresp. with Marie Stopes, Add. MS 58496 · Bodl. Oxf., corresp. with Gilbert Murray · Durham RO, corresp. with Lady Londonderry · Glos. RO, corresp. with H. W. Sumsion and Alice Sumsion · PRO NIre., letters to Lady Londonderry | SOUND BL NSA, *Bethlehem*, 1946 · BL NSA, 'Scenes from the operas of R. B.', BBC, 1977

Likenesses C. Walshe, pencil drawing, 1911, NPG · H. Lambert, photograph, 1921, NPG [*see illus.*]

Wealth at death £1328 19*s*. 4*d*.: probate, 24 April 1960, *CGPLA Eng. & Wales*

Boulers, Reginald (*d*. 1459), bishop of Coventry and Lichfield, claimed, on the evidence of the heraldic devices on his seals, a connection with the Butler earls of Ormond and Wiltshire, but his family background is otherwise unknown. He was a doctor of theology (probably of Oxford) by 1437, a monk of the Benedictine abbey of St Peter, Gloucester, and may be the monk 'Reynolds of Gloucester' who is recorded as delivering a sermon at Oxford *c*.1432. Royal assent to his election as abbot of Gloucester was granted on 29 October 1437. On 21 November 1440 Henry VI wrote to Pope Eugenius IV (*r*. 1431–47), recommending Boulers for the vacant see of Llandaff, but by 25 December Boulers had declined the offer, presumably in order to stay at the wealthier abbey of Gloucester, and Henry wrote again to the pope, proposing Nicholas Close (*d*. 1452) instead.

During the 1440s Boulers came to be regularly employed as both a diplomatic envoy and a member of the king's council. He was part of the embassy that attended the Reichstag held at Frankfurt am Main to discuss ecclesiastical affairs between March and July 1442, and reported back to the council on 21 August; he was commissioned to go as king's proctor to Rome in August 1444, but then ordered to stay in England; on 12 March 1445, together with Bishop Thomas Beckington of Bath and Wells (*d*. 1465), he informed the papal nuncio of the English clergy's offer of a voluntary grant of 6000 ducats in place of taxation; and on 30 January 1448 he was appointed a member of the plenary embassy to negotiate with the French. He became a regular attender at the council from 1445, and was one of the most frequent witnesses to acts of state.

In parliament in February 1449 Boulers presented, on behalf of Edmund Beaufort, duke of Somerset, the duke's 'credence' which raised the issue of the insecurity of the English position in France in the light of French preparations for a renewal of the war. He was further associated with the government's war effort as one of three commissioners appointed on 18 August 1449 to raise loans on security of certain royal jewels in order to supply Normandy. His close association with the failed Lancastrian policy in France, together perhaps with some underlying anti-clerical feeling and local disputes in Gloucester, left Boulers particularly exposed to attack during the period of popular unrest which beset England in the wake of a series of disastrous reverses in France. In 1449–50 people from Gloucester despoiled the abbey's manor of Wynyards, Gloucestershire, and denounced Boulers for his part in the disasters in France, and in 1450 he was clearly regarded by several groups of critics as a central figure in the reviled government. He was targeted for execution by rebels both in Kent and at Westminster in January 1450; identified as a traitor by discontented royal and magnate retainers in June; satirized in a contemporary ballad for his association with the murdered duke of Suffolk; possibly indicted to commissions of inquiry by supporters of Jack Cade, both in London in July and in Kent in August; and included in a petition submitted in the parliament of 1450–51 which requested that twenty-nine named persons should be debarred for life from coming within 12 miles of the king. At the height of his unpopularity, in September 1450, Boulers, together with John (VI) Sutton, Lord Dudley, fled to Ludlow to seek the protection of Richard, duke of York, whose support may at the time have seemed the best guarantee of survival.

In the event, Boulers not only survived the crises of 1450 but saw his career prosper with no interruption during the next decade. Amid the turmoil he had actually been papally provided to the bishopric of Hereford on 14 August 1450; he received the temporalities on 23 December and was consecrated on 14 February 1451. He was translated to the see of Coventry and Lichfield on 7 February 1453. He was, with others, acquitted of any offence by the Lords in March 1451, and resumed his political role. On 9 January 1452 the duke of York invited Boulers and John Talbot, earl of Shrewsbury (*d.* 1453), his most distinguished neighbours, to Ludlow to hear his declaration of loyalty to Henry VI in advance of the duke's armed demonstration against his rival, the duke of Somerset, at Dartford, Kent. In the wake of this confrontation Boulers was a member of a panel commissioned on 13 March 1452 to arbitrate between the two dukes; nothing came of this. On 23 March 1454 he was included by the Lords in parliament in the carefully chosen delegation to visit Henry VI, then incapacitated by a severe mental collapse, at Windsor. When the delegation reported back two days later, its leader, William Waynflete, bishop of Winchester (*d.* 1486), deferred to Boulers in reporting the outcome, because Boulers had actually undertaken the hopeless task of gaining a response from the king.

Boulers may, like a number of other lords, have been somewhat wary of involving himself too closely with the duke of York's subsequent protectorate administration; he was equivocal about his membership of the council at a meeting held on 3 April 1454 and was chastised for his absence from a meeting of a great council on 1 July 1454, but it is by no means certain that he was definitively an opponent of the duke. Indeed Boulers was one of three mediators sent by Henry VI's council, probably in late April 1455, to meet with York and his Neville allies during the tense period that culminated in the first battle of St Albans (22 May 1455). He continued to attend the royal council even after the Yorkist victory and was appointed to the committee to consider the defence of Calais and Berwick in the parliament of 1455–6.

Thereafter it became harder not to take sides, and Boulers went with the court. He certainly retained the confidence of the king, but much more significantly, that of Queen Margaret. On 28 January 1457 he was appointed to the council of Edward, prince of Wales. On 2 November 1457 he was named as a commissioner to investigate how the king might settle his debts. However, his episcopal register suggests that he may have withdrawn from his more active role in politics from 1456. He is never recorded thereafter as being in London, but indeed the court itself was rarely in the capital. More notably, after 7 June 1457 he is only ever found in his register at his episcopal manor of Beaudesert, Warwickshire. His rather brief will, which states that the bishop was too ill to particularize at greater length, was made at Beaudesert on 23 March 1459, and one of his bequests was of his five books of theology to his old abbey at Gloucester. He died shortly after the will was made, for it was proved on 10 April 1459. He had requested burial in the lady chapel of Lichfield Cathedral. BILL SMITH

Sources A. T. Bannister, ed., *Registrum Reginaldi Boulers, Episcopi Herefordensis*, 2, CYS, 25 (1919) • Registers, Coventry and Lichfield, Lichfield RO, B/A/1/11 • Prerogative Court of Canterbury, Register Stockton, fol. 16 • Emden, *Oxf.* • *RotP* • *Chancery records* • *Memorials of the reign of Henry VI: official correspondence of Thomas Bekynton, secretary to King Henry VI and bishop of Bath and Wells*, ed. G. Williams, 2 vols., Rolls Series, 56 (1872) • N. H. Nicolas, ed., *Proceedings and ordinances of the privy council of England*, 7 vols., RC, 26 (1834–7) • R. A. Griffiths, *The reign of King Henry VI: the exercise of royal authority, 1422–1461* (1981) • M. Harvey, *England, Rome, and the papacy, 1417–1464* (1993)
Archives Lichfield RO, Coventry and Lichfield registers, B/A/1/11

Boulestin, (Xavier) Marcel (1878–1943), restaurateur and writer on cookery, was born at Poitiers, France, where his mother, the daughter of a former lycée teacher, shared the house of his widowed maternal grandmother. Boulestin grew up and attended school in Poitiers, developing strong interests in music and the theatre. He visited his father, who maintained a largely separate existence, only for a month each summer, at the property that he owned at St Aulaye in the valley of the Dronne north-west of Périgueux.

By the time that Boulestin was eighteen both his mother and his grandmother had died. From the latter he had a 1200 franc annuity, which allowed him to follow his aesthetic inclinations with no acute worries about adopting a serious career. Moving to Bordeaux, a city which impressed him with its elegance and sophistication, he settled down for several years, ostensibly to study law at the university there. In fact he became a full-time concert-goer and acquaintance of visiting musicians, contributing a regular 'Bordeaux letter' to the national magazine *Courrier Musical*. Before leaving to perform his military service in 1899, he published his first, unsuccessful book, a dialogue, *Le pacte*, with a foreword by the humorous writer

Willy (Henri Gauthier-Villars, husband of the novelist Colette).

After military service, Boulestin moved to Paris and took a job as secretary to Willy. Ambitious for literary fame, he met many French and English artists and writers, translated Max Beerbohm's *The Happy Hypocrite* (published in the *Mercure de France*, 1905), and enjoyed the smart, Anglophile social life of Paris and Dieppe. With his thickset physique and southern appearance he was frequently caricatured by artist friends, and he was clearly popular for his cheerfully sybaritic approach to life. By 1906, however, he recognized that success had eluded him. In search of a change, he settled that autumn in London, immersing himself in the music-halls and theatres, and the follies and ostentatious luxury of the idle rich. As secretary to a playwright, Cosmo Gordon Lennox, he dabbled in journalism and dramatic translations, and collaborated with a friend, Francis Toye, on a lightweight novel, *The Swing of the Pendulum* (1911).

Switching to a new interest, interior decorating, in 1911, Boulestin equipped his rented flat in Elizabeth Street, Mayfair, with avant-garde materials imported from Paris, Florence, Munich, Vienna, and Berlin, and solicited custom from society friends, who recommended him to others. In August 1914 he was on the point of extending the business by taking a house with the designer Paul Poiret and decorating it entirely in Poiret's own lavish style; instead, he spent the next four years as an interpreter with the British expeditionary force in France. His post-war London shop, Décorations Modernes, proved a failure, as did his *Keepsake* (1921), an anthology bringing together the work of modern artists and writers. For some time Boulestin scraped a living by handicrafts, teaching French, and other means.

Boulestin's first cookery book, *Simple French Cooking for English Homes* (1923), resulted from a casual conversation with a director of Heinemann, followed by a £10 advance. The book was an immediate success, since it suited the new, often servantless, pared-down sophistication of post-war domestic arrangements. Boulestin's explanations of basic French ways with meat, game, poultry, fish, and vegetables, inspired inventions such as sardine butter as an hors d'œuvre, and his revelations of how to cook aubergines or produce a piperade helped to widen the culinary ambitions of British people to whom French cooking had hitherto seemed unattainably exotic.

Although originally a fervent admirer of the solider, more traditional English dishes, Boulestin reconciled this interest with an appreciation of his own earlier gastronomic background. Between 1923 and 1937 he published a dozen recipe books. Some he wrote alone (*The Conduct of the Kitchen*, *A Second Helping*, and *What Shall We Have Today?*); one, in 1930, with Jason Hill (*Herbs, Salads and Seasonings*); and three others (*120 Ways of Cooking Eggs*, *127 Ways of Preparing Savouries and Hors d'œuvres*, and *101 Ways of Cooking Potatoes*) with his close friend and long-term partner, A. H. (Robin) Adair, whom he first met in 1923, and with whom he briefly ran a catering business for dinner parties before opening his first London restaurant in 1925. Editions of his books were still appearing in the 1950s.

The Restaurant Français, on the corner of Panton Street and Leicester Square, flourished for two years despite the absence of a full alcohol licence, and received much fashionable support. In 1927 this gave way to a more ambitious venture, the eponymous Boulestin's (formerly Sherry's) Restaurant in Covent Garden. With its silk velvet curtains designed by Raoul Dufy, and its panelled walls and ceiling by Marie Laurençin and Jean-Emile Laboureur, the restaurant was a striking example of modern Parisian décor, attracting artists and opera-goers alike. The authenticity of the cooking was ensured by Boulestin's choice of chef, Bigorre, who had previously cooked at the famous Restaurant Paillard in Paris.

Once established as an apologist for simple French food and cooking, Boulestin achieved his true role in English life during the inter-war years, and paved the way for successors such as the equally literary Elizabeth David (who quoted with relish his earthy description, in his 1936 autobiographical volume, of the country foods of his childhood summers at St Aulaye). From 1928 he held cookery courses, first on his own, then under the auspices of Fortnum and Mason's store in Piccadilly. In 1937 he gave the first cookery demonstration on British television. He wrote regular columns for the *Daily Telegraph*, *Country Life*, *Harper's Bazaar*, and later the *Evening Standard*. His lightheartedly self-publicizing bent found expression in an autobiography in English, *Myself, my Two Countries* (1936); a gastronomic account of a French tour, *Having Crossed the Channel* (1934); and a volume of reminiscences in French, *A Londres naguère*, translated as *Ease and Endurance* (1948) by Adair.

On the outbreak of war in 1939 Boulestin and Adair were on holiday at Boulestin's house in the Landes. They remained in France, hoping to be able to contribute directly to the war effort. Adair was eventually interned as an enemy alien, and Boulestin moved to Paris in order to be near him. Boulestin was found dead on the morning of 20 September 1943 after a short illness, aged sixty-five.

BRIGID ALLEN

Sources M. Boulestin, *Myself, my two countries* (1936) · D. Hooker, *A salute to M. Boulestin and Jean Emile Laboureur* (1981) · E. David, 'Having crossed the channel', *Wine and Food* (1965); repr. in E. David, *An omelette and a glass of wine* (1985) · E. Firusking and M. Firusking, eds., *The best of Boulestin* (1955)

Likenesses Gromaire and others, caricatures, repro. in Boulestin, *Myself, my two countries*

Boulger [*née* Havers], **Dorothy Henrietta** [*pseud.* Theo Gift] (**1847–1923**), novelist, was born on 30 May 1847 at Thelton Hall, Norfolk, the second daughter of Thomas Havers (*d.* 1870), colonial governor, of Thelton Hall, and his wife, Ellen Ruding, daughter of Rogers *Ruding (1751–1820), the distinguished numismatist. The artist Alice Mary *Havers (later Morgan) (1850–1890) was her sister. Dorothy Havers was educated at home. In 1854 the family moved to the Falkland Islands, where her father had been appointed a colonial manager; from 1861 they lived in

Montevideo, Uruguay. Havers and her brothers and sisters returned to England after their father's death in 1870.

Havers's first magazine contributions date from 1871. She wrote stories for *Once a Week* and *Cassell's Magazine*, both published in London, for the New York periodical *Galaxy*, and for *The Lamp*, a Catholic journal (the Haverses were an old Catholic family). For ten years she worked on a regular basis for *All the Year Round* under the editorship of Charles Dickens jun., and for two years on *Cassell's* under G. Manville Fenn. A prolific and versatile writer of fiction in different genres, Havers wrote under the name Theo Gift, which caused some reviewers to believe that she was a male writer. Her earliest novels are contemporary romances. *True to her Trust, or, 'Womanly Past Question'* (1874) owes something to Charlotte M. Yonge's style, and the influence of her Catholicism is here much more pronounced than in her later works, which are rarely inflected with overt religious references (although *Victims*, 1887, is notably pro-Jewish). Her next novel, and perhaps her best-known, *Pretty Miss Bellew* (1875), is far more lively, recalling Rhoda Broughton's fondness for colloquial asides and spirited dialogue. *Maid Ellice* (1878) is semi-autobiographical, featuring an orphaned girl from Montevideo going to stay in England, and emphasizing the very different upbringing that she had had in Uruguay. On 22 April 1879 Havers married the eminent botanist George Simonds Boulger (1853–1922), professor of botany and zoology at the City of London College, who converted to his wife's religion.

In the years after her marriage Dorothy Boulger published another semi-autobiographical work, *Lil Lorimer* (1885), and *Cape Town Dicky* (1888), illustrated by her sister Alice, written for children and designed to teach a love of animals. In 1889 she published *Not for the Night-Time*, a volume of ghost stories, and in the 1890s two works aimed at the girls' fiction market, *The Little Colonists* (1890) and *An Island Princess* (1893), both set in the Falklands. They give a vivid portrayal of the isolated lifestyle of English settlers there, as well as careful descriptions of landscape and flora: Boulger does not evade topics such as serious alcoholism or over-zealous missionaries, and above all the stories celebrate practical, self-sufficient, confident, and independent-minded young women.

Boulger's work is characterized by a quiet determination to speak up for women, especially for working women, as 'more worthy of respect that those who simply sit and enjoy themselves' (*Dishonoured*, 1890, 2.41). One short story, 'Written to Death' (*A Garden of Girls*, 1880), features a woman who writes art criticism; 'Left Outside' (*Wrecked at the Outset*, 1894), is a gloomy story of a nursery governess betrayed by class and national difference when briefly befriended by an American girl in London, and the other tales in this volume exhibit a sympathetic understanding of the anonymity often experienced by women working in the city.

In 1892 Boulger produced a gift book, *Fairy Tales from the Far East*, and also wrote a number of children's stories with her friend Edith Nesbit, collected in *Dulcie's Lantern and other Stories* (1895). Her last book was the stilted historical romance *The Case of a Man with his Wife* (1901) and she does not seem to have published after 1901. She lived at 12 Lancaster Park, Richmond, Surrey, during the later decades of her life, and died at 26 Cathcart Road, South Kensington, on 22 July 1923, fourteen months after her husband. KATE FLINT

Sources *WWW*, 1916–28 • F. C. Burnand, ed., *The Catholic who's who and yearbook* (1910) • V. F. Boyson, *The Falkland Islands* (1924) • H. H. Stephenson, *Who's who in science* (1913) • *Richmond upon Thames Herald* • J. Sutherland, *The Longman companion to Victorian fiction* (1988) • m. cert. • d. cert.

Boulogne. For this title name *see* Eustace (II), count of Boulogne (*d. c.*1087); Eustace, count of Boulogne (*c.*1129–1153); Mary, countess of Boulogne (*d.* 1182).

Boulsover, Thomas (1705–1788), cutler, was born in Ecclesfield, in the West Riding of Yorkshire, and baptized in the parish church on 18 October 1705, the fifth of the nine children of Samuel Bolsover (1670–1721), farmer and cutler, and Margaret (1673–1716), daughter of George and Alice Brownell. From 1719 he was apprenticed to Joseph Fletcher (*d.* 1746), cutler, in Sheffield. He became a freeman of the Cutlers' Company of Hallamshire, in the county of York, on 26 November 1726 and was assigned the mark 'cross above crescent above finial' with which to stamp his cutlery. In the same year he established a cutlery workshop on Norfolk Street, Sheffield. Also in that year, on 28 October at Sheffield parish church, he married Hannah (1706–1772), youngest of the three children of John Dodworth, of Owlerton, and Sarah Crook, who married in 1695. Thomas and Hannah Boulsover had ten children, of whom only two daughters survived beyond childhood. Mary (1737–1812), their fifth child, married Joseph Mitchell (1728–1788) on 14 February 1760; on the occasion of their wedding Boulsover entered into partnership with Mitchell. Sarah (1739–1810), their sixth child, married William Hutton, a country squire from Kirby West, in the North Riding of Yorkshire, in Sheffield parish church on 30 October 1764.

Tradition relates that in 1743 Boulsover was repairing a knife handle composed of silver and copper, and by heating the adjacent metals fused them together. This 'accidental discovery' resulted in the invention of fused plate (Hatfield and Hatfield, 120). Known as Old Sheffield Plate this was the foundation of Sheffield's fine metalwork and silver industry. Fusing silver to copper creates an alloy that can be worked using silversmithing techniques to produce an article with the external appearance of silver yet at a fraction of the cost of a solid silver article. A brick of copper fused with a sheet of silver is rolled and worked in sheet form.

Boulsover began the manufacture of fused-plate buttons and buckles, costly silver buttons being then in fashion. Fused plate replaced his cutlery manufacture, and by 1747 he had no further cutlery apprentices. However, another cutler, Joseph Hancock (1711–1790), exploited fused plate to make hollow-ware from *c.*1755. Within a decade the manufacture of fused-plate hollow-ware was widespread in Sheffield. However, Boulsover, who had invented fused plate, took no part in developing it for hollow-ware production and did not patent his process.

At the end of the 1750s Boulsover was a man of some means, being both a freeholder and a country gentleman; in 1757 he moved his family from Norfolk Street to Whiteley Wood Hall, a seventeenth-century property on the outskirts of Sheffield, and at the same time moved his workshop to larger premises on Norfolk Street. He was involved in local discussions over a turnpike road from Sheffield to Leeds, and his signature appears as one of twenty-five on a petition of 1759 (also confirming the spelling of his name) for the turnpike from Sheffield to Manchester. He remained committed to improving roads throughout his life.

The 1760s saw a further contribution by Boulsover to the metalwork industry: the development of rolled cast steel for saw making. Rolling cast steel produces a stronger alloy than hammered cast steel. This venture was served by workshops, workers' cottages, an enlarged dam, and an improved water-wheel on the River Porter, below Whitely Wood Hall. Following Boulsover's death Boulsover & Co. continued under the ownership of the Mitchell and Hutton families, and after 1814 was renamed Mitchell & Co.

Thomas Boulsover died at Whiteley Wood Hall on 9 September 1788. He was buried in St Paul's churchyard, Sheffield, with his wife, on 13 September. He was 'typical of the class of men who, by their observation, imagination, industry and ability, laid the foundation of modern Sheffield' (Hatfield and Hatfield, 10). HELEN L. PHILLIPS

Sources J. Hatfield and J. Hatfield, *The oldest Sheffield plater* (1974) • F. Bradbury, History of Old Sheffield Plate (1912)
Archives Company of Cutlers in Hallamshire, papers • Sheffield Central Library, Local History Department, papers • Sheffield Galleries and Museums Trust, biggest public collection of articles of Old Sheffield Plate • University of Sheffield, Ken Hawley Collection Trust, papers

Boult, Sir Adrian Cedric (1889–1983), conductor, was born on 8 April 1889 at 4 Abbots Hayes, Liverpool Road, Chester, the only son and second child of Cedric Randal Boult (1853–1950), an oil merchant, and his wife, Katherine Florence Barman (*d.* 1927). He showed exceptional early musical promise. He entered Westminster School in 1901 and attended London concerts and operas whenever he could. Few schoolboys can have attended as many performances by great artists as Boult heard between 1901 and October 1908, when he went up to Christ Church, Oxford. There music again occupied most of his time (he was also a keen rower, stroking his college boat at Henley), and he was president of the University Musical Club in 1910.

On leaving Oxford, in September 1912 Boult joined the conducting class at Leipzig conservatory. However, the chief attraction was the opportunity to study Arthur Nikisch at work with the Gewandhaus Orchestra. After returning to England in 1913 he became an extra member of Covent Garden music staff and helped in preparations for the first London performance of Wagner's *Parsifal* on 2

Sir Adrian Cedric Boult (1889–1983), by Felix H. Man, 1935

February 1914. Three weeks later, on 27 February, he made his début as a conductor in the public hall, West Kirby, in a programme that included the first performance of Butterworth's *The Banks of Green Willow*. He was unfit for military service when war was declared in August 1914, so he returned to Oxford in October to sit and pass his first doctor of music examination. He then went to London to work for the War Office, but continued his musical activity. In February and March 1918 he organized four concerts in Queen's Hall, at which he conducted the London Symphony Orchestra in contemporary English works. This led to an invitation from Gustav Holst to conduct the first (private) performance of the orchestral suite *The Planets* in September 1918. He conducted the Diaghilev Russian Ballet's 1919 London season, joined the staff of the Royal College of Music, and, in March 1920, conducted Elgar's second symphony, drawing from Elgar the comment: 'I feel that my reputation in the future is safe in your hands' (Kennedy, 73). At the age of thirty-one Boult was now firmly established. In 1924 he was appointed conductor of the City of Birmingham Orchestra, and for the next six years his adventurous programmes attracted widespread attention. He conducted Wagner and Verdi for the British National Opera Company in 1925 and was conductor of the Bach Choir, London, from 1928 to 1931.

In 1930 Boult became the BBC's director of music when Percy Pitt retired. The BBC, with John Reith as director-general, was forming its own symphony orchestra, and Boult conducted the inaugural concert on 22 October 1930, a historic evening in British music-making. This led to his appointment as the orchestra's permanent conductor. He was the ideal choice for a post that in effect made him music educator-in-chief to the nation through broadcasting. He encouraged the engagement of celebrated guest conductors and was willing to conduct works, in programmes chosen by others, which were regarded as important even though they had little appeal for him personally. He was a sound, if not brilliant, trainer in fundamental principles, as was acknowledged by Arturo Toscanini when the latter first conducted the orchestra in 1935 and declared it one of the best he had encountered. As a guest conductor in the 1930s Boult worked with the Vienna Philharmonic, Boston Symphony, and New York Philharmonic orchestras. He conducted the first (concert) performances in England of Berg's *Wozzeck* in 1934 and Busoni's *Doktor Faust* in 1937 and the first London performance of Mahler's ninth symphony, also in 1934. He conducted the first performance of Vaughan Williams's fourth symphony in 1935 (and of his sixth in 1948).

On 1 July 1933 Boult married Ann Mary Grace, the daughter of Captain Francis Alan Richard Bowles RN, of Sittingbourne, Kent. She was previously married to the singer and opera administrator Sir (James) Steuart Wilson, with whom she had four children.

During the Second World War, despite the loss of players to the services (forty out of ninety between 1939 and 1946), Boult kept the standards of the BBC orchestra as high as he could and maintained the enterprising quality of the programmes. In 1942 he handed over the post of director of music to Arthur Bliss. At the end of the war he found a changed attitude to the orchestra in the upper echelons of the BBC and had to fight hard to restore it to its pre-war glory.

Although Reith had told Boult, 'When you get to 60 [the BBC's age for retirement] tell us what extra help you want and we'll draw up a new contract' (private information), Reith had left the BBC in 1938, and Boult's enforced retirement in 1949 was engineered by the head of music, Sir (James) Steuart Wilson, whose divorced first wife Boult had married in 1933. Boult was principal conductor of the London Philharmonic Orchestra from 1950 to 1956. With it he embarked on a busy recording schedule, including the complete cycle of Vaughan Williams's symphonies. In 1953 he conducted the music at the coronation of Queen Elizabeth II (he had served in the same capacity in 1937 for King George VI). In 1959–60, having heard that the City of Birmingham Symphony Orchestra had been unable to find a successor at short notice after its conductor had resigned, he returned to his old haunt with a vintage Boult series of programmes. After 1960 he spent more and more time in the recording studio, making important recordings of Elgar, Vaughan Williams, Holst, Parry, Brahms, and some Wagner. By now he had attained more popularity with the public than he had ever enjoyed. He was especially moved by a return to Covent Garden to conduct the Royal Ballet in Vaughan Williams's *Job*, Mahler's *Das Lied von der Erde*, and Elgar's *Enigma Variations*. His last public appearance was at the London Coliseum on 24 June 1978, when, unannounced, he conducted Elgar's ballet *The Sanguine Fan*. He ended his recording career on 20 December of that year with works by Parry. He died in a West Hampstead nursing home in Christchurch Avenue on 22 February 1983, leaving his body to medical science. He was survived by his wife.

Boult was knighted in 1937 and was made a Companion of Honour in 1969. He was awarded the gold medal of the Royal Philharmonic Society in 1944 and the Harvard Glee Club medal in 1956. He had honorary degrees from five universities: Birmingham (1930), Liverpool (1947), Cambridge (1953), Reading (1976), and Oxford (1979), and was an honorary student of Christ Church. The Royal College of Music conferred the honorary degree of doctor of music of the college on him in 1981.

In the music he admired most, Boult was often a great conductor; in the rest, an extremely conscientious one. His manner was undemonstrative and he liked to use a long baton. If from behind he seemed unexciting and unemotional, the players could see the animation in his face—and he was capable of frightening outbursts of temper at rehearsals. Tall and erect, with something of the military in his appearance (particularly the moustache), he seemed the personification of the English gentleman. But recipients of his cutting wit and occasional sarcasm knew that this was not the whole picture. He was generous to orchestral players and loyal to colleagues, but on certain occasions, when difficulties arose of a quasi-political nature, he took the line of least resistance. How to assess a conductor's lasting influence is difficult if not impossible, but Boult undoubtedly established a tradition of catholic taste at the BBC. His championship of British music was carried on by one of his pupils, Vernon Handley, and he was the inspiration of the career of another pupil, Timothy Reynish, whose work was mainly at the Royal Northern College of Music in Manchester. He wrote two books on conducting, *The Point of the Stick* (1920) and *Thoughts on Conducting* (1963), and his autobiography, *My Own Trumpet*, was published in 1973.

MICHAEL KENNEDY

Sources M. Kennedy, *Adrian Boult* (1987) • A. C. Boult, *My own trumpet* (1973) • N. Kenyon, *The BBC Symphony Orchestra … 1930–1980* (1981) • J. N. Moore, *Music and friends: seven decades of letters to Adrian Boult* (1979) • personal correspondence from Boult to author, priv. coll. [in author's possession] • B. Shore, *The orchestra speaks* (1938) • *CGPLA Eng. & Wales* (1983)

Archives BBC WAC, corresp., diaries, and MSS • BL, corresp. and MSS, Add. MSS 60498–60503 • Royal College of Music, London, collection | BL, letters to Henry Wood, Add. MSS 56419–56430 • Bodl. Oxf., corresp. with Society for Protection of Science and Learning • Bodl. Oxf., corresp. mainly with Lord Woolton • Cumbria AS, Carlisle, letters to Lord Howard of Penrith • Glos. RO, corresp. with H. W. Sumsion and Alice Sumsion | FILM BFI NFTVA, documentary footage • BFI NFTVA, performance footage | SOUND BL NSA, performance recordings

Likenesses K. Ishibashi, oils, 1923, Royal College of Music, London • photographs, 1930–74, Hult. Arch. • E. Kapp, chalk drawing, 1932, Barber Institute of Fine Arts, Birmingham • E. Kapp, lithograph, *c.*1932, NPG • H. Coster, photographs, 1933, NPG • F. Man, photograph, 1935, NPG [*see illus.*] • W. Stoneman, photograph, 1942, NPG • K. Pollak, photographs, 1948, NPG • C. Woodgate, photographs, 1950–59, NPG • W. Stoneman, photograph, 1953,

NPG • W. Bird, photograph, 1963, NPG • J. S. Lewinski, photograph, 1967, NPG • S. Samuels, photographs, 1969, NPG • R. Stone, chalk drawing, 1972, NPG • L. Goehr, photographs, before 1977, NPG • J. Finzi, pencil drawing • W. Narraway, portrait, Royal College of Music, London • W. Redgrave, bronze head, Royal Festival Hall, London • H. Wiener, pencil drawing, Royal College of Music, London

Wealth at death £178,781: probate, 1 June 1983, *CGPLA Eng. & Wales*

Boult, Swinton (1808–1876), insurance company manager, was born on 3 December 1808 in Liverpool, one of several children of Francis Boult, a Unitarian shipowner, and his wife, Anne, *née* Swanwick. While his father was fairly prominent in Liverpool, and a founder of the town's American chamber of commerce in 1801, nothing is known of Boult's early years. In 1831, aged twenty-two, he began in insurance with the local agency of George Booth, who represented two London offices, Albion Life and Protector Fire. In 1833 he married Maria Ann Grundy, eldest child of the Revd John Grundy; they had three sons. In 1834 Boult became Liverpool agent for London Assurance. This was a difficult time for fire insurance agents in Liverpool as London offices sought to maintain high premium rates in the face of consistently poor results, especially on warehouse insurances. Boult believed he saw a market opening for a local office. In 1836 he came together with George Holt, banker, cotton broker, and fellow Unitarian, to found Liverpool Fire and Life Insurance Company, with a paid-up capital of £66,000 and a board selected from local whig nonconformist merchants. Boult became company secretary, a title he held for the next thirty years.

Initially the company's existence remained precarious. Boult was attacked in the press for inviting subscriptions to an enterprise which looked likely to fail. Shareholders became unhappy about slow growth, and the larger London offices were eagerly seeking provincial insurers to swallow up. Sun Fire Office, which targeted Boult's company in 1838, reported that Boult was a 'very young man … [who] has no warm friend or advocate and is thought very inefficient for the situation and has no influence whatever' (J. Toplis to C. Ford, 16 Oct 1838, London, Guildhall Library, MS 15032/7). This opinion, however, soon proved baseless. Boult was determined that Liverpool Fire and Life should survive, and he fought off all attacks, even during the disastrous losses of 1842–3. He launched himself into a campaign to improve Liverpool's water supply and fire-fighting facilities, and eventually succeeded in rallying the other fire offices to the cause. In 1845 the Liverpool Fire Prevention Act was passed, with its provisions based upon an inquiry carried out by Boult into the causes of local fires. In 1846 he organized the Liverpool Fire Salvage Association, which aimed to improve warehouse construction and fire prevention methods. During the 1840s he played a central role in negotiating tariff premium rate agreements among the major fire offices for warehouse and cotton mill risks in Liverpool and Manchester. He also devised a uniform policy form for the tariff offices, which had been another point of competition. His role was further recognized when he was elected chairman of the northern committee of the Fire Tariff Association in 1858, and ten years later he helped to found its successor, the national Fire Offices' Committee.

The early vulnerability of Liverpool Fire and Life was, in part, due to its concentration of risks. As a solution Boult began a series of take-overs which subsumed at least ten offices in Britain and abroad during his career. After the take-over of the London, Edinburgh, and Dublin Insurance Company in 1847, the company's name was changed by act of parliament to Liverpool and London. The culmination of this strategy came in 1864 when the company merged with Globe Insurance (established 1803), in one of the biggest corporate fusions Britain had seen. Boult, who negotiated the merger, was appointed managing director of the renamed Liverpool, London, and Globe (LL&G). At the time some of his compeers thought him a little obsessed with amalgamations, but the strategy had its effect. By 1867 the office was the largest fire insurer in the world, with a premium income of £837,000.

Boult also pursued expansion overseas, particularly following the lines of Liverpool's trading links. From 1848 the first agents were appointed in New York, Newfoundland, and Hamburg, and in 1851 a board of directors was established at New York for the United States. In 1853 Boult made a long journey to Australia, travelling across the USA via San Francisco, where, with a new agency, Liverpool and London opened the first European office on the Pacific coast. New boards were also established by Boult in Melbourne and Sydney. Total premiums more than quadrupled to £222,000 between 1851 and 1856 as Liverpool and London extended its agencies across Europe, Latin America, Africa, India, and the Far East. Increasing use was made by the company of reinsurance, despite Boult's dislike of the business and his opinion that no office should underwrite any one risk or combination of risks, unless it meant to retain it (and had the resources to do so). In 1859 a director resigned in protest at the too rapid expansion, but an inquiry found that, over the long term, foreign underwriting had proved more profitable than home business.

By 1871 the United States generated £423,000 out of a global premium income of £931,000. That year, in which Boult was described by a writer as the 'very Napoleon of fire insurance' (Walford, 354), proved to be disastrous, with losses of over £600,000 in the great Chicago fire, followed by £280,000 paid out in the Boston fire of 1872. All claims were met, and in the long term the company's reputation in the USA was enhanced, but the immediate dividends suffered, and Boult was called to account. Early in 1873 LL&G's board decided not to renew his appointment, ending his career after thirty-seven years. He lobbied the shareholders, but was unable to find a way back, and his attempt to establish a new insurance office failed.

Writing before Boult's departure from LL&G, a journalist referred to 'the cheery voice, the frank manner, the dignified courtesy, the unfailing tact, the power of assimilation and clarification, which carried his board of directors with him' (Walford, 355). Boult was respected by the insurance community on both sides of the Atlantic, and the Americans viewed him as 'an open-hearted and courteous gentleman' (*New York Spectator*, 431), but it seems he was not particularly sociable. Despite his frequent agency tours, it is said he behaved more like a banker than a merchant, sitting in his office to receive callers. He published on a number of topics, including taxation, joint-stock companies, and political economy. He was a firm believer in *laissez-faire*, and criticized, as another example of excessive state interference, the act of 1870 which made the registration of life assurance companies compulsory. He was no orator. In 1867 he gave evidence to the select committee on fire protection, it is said, in 'a sledge-hammer style of delivery, occasionally toned down by a characteristic sarcasm' (Walford, 355).

Boult suffered from acute rheumatic gout, and on 8 July 1876, aged sixty-seven, he collapsed and died in Aigburth Road, Garston, near Liverpool, while hailing the Liverpool omnibus. The county coroner's verdict was death from natural causes. His wife survived him.

ROBIN PEARSON

Sources C. Walford, *The insurance cyclopaedia*, 6 vols. (1871–80) · H. Cockerell, 'Boult, Swinton', *DBB* · J. Dyer Simpson, *1936—our centenary year—Liverpool, London & Globe* (1936) · *Liverpool Mail* (15 July 1876) · *Post Magazine & Insurance Monitor* (15 July 1876) · *New York Spectator*, no. 76, 17/no. 2 (Aug 1876) · 'Correspondence re: Liverpool fire office, 1838–9', James Toplis to C. Ford, 16 Oct. 1838, GL, Sun Insurance Office, MS 15032/7 · *Index of parish registers* · *DNB* · J. C. Rimmer, 'A history of the Liverpool, London and Globe Insurance Company Limited', 1923, Lpool RO, Royal Insurance Plc papers, MS 368 ROY · J. C. Rimmer, results sheets, Liverpool, London, and Globe, 1923, Lpool RO, Royal Insurance Plc papers, MS 368 ROY

Likenesses photogravure, repro. in Dyer Simpson, *1936*, 17

Wealth at death approx. £2000 gross: Cockerell, 'Boult, Swinton'

Boultbee, Thomas Pownall (1818–1884), Church of England clergyman, was born in Hope Street, Liverpool, on 7 August 1818. He was the eldest son of a family of four boys and three girls of the Revd Thomas Boultbee (1793–1883), vicar of Bidford-on-Avon and Salford Priors, Warwickshire, and his wife, Eliza Pownall (1790–1858).

Boultbee was educated privately and then at Uppingham School (1833–7), before proceeding to St John's College, Cambridge, where he was admitted as a sizar in 1837. He graduated BA in 1841 (fifth wrangler), MA in 1844, and LLD in 1871. He was elected to a fellowship of his college in 1841, and was ordained deacon in 1844 and priest in 1845, assisting in the parishes of Wolverton and Bearley in the same area as his father. Between 1846 and 1849 he served a curacy at Oldberrow and Morton Bagot, near Henley in Arden, and tutored private pupils. On 22 December 1846 he married Caroline Frances (1825–1906), daughter of Robert Lawrance (*d.* 1871), rector of Bleadon, Somerset. They had a family of four daughters and three sons (two of whom were ordained).

In 1849 Boultbee became curate to the Revd Francis Close at Cheltenham parish church. They became firm friends and Boultbee was the most able of Close's numerous curates. Between 1853 and 1863 Boultbee was one of the theological tutors (and later housemaster and chaplain) of Cheltenham College. The evangelical outlook of the school was maintained with Close as the chairman of the directors, and by the presence and influence of the theological tutors.

In 1863 Boultbee became the first principal of the London College of Divinity, founded by the Revd Alfred Peache and his sister Kezia, which opened in a former school in Kilburn, London. In 1866 the college was relocated to a former college in Highbury (where it remained until 1940). During Boultbee's principalship 300 men were trained for ordained ministry at home and overseas, and the college buildings were considerably enlarged by the architect Ewan Christian. There were two notable staff appointments, Revd C. H. Waller (who succeeded Boultbee as principal) and Revd H. Gee (who later became master of University College, Durham, and dean of Gloucester).

Islington was the leading evangelical parish in London, and the London College of Divinity became an important centre of learning there, alongside the Church Missionary College (opened in 1825). Boultbee was an evangelical by conviction, and gave strong leadership to the college and within the evangelical party. Committed to the principles of the Reformation, he was judicious, 'soundly and calmly wise', with little 'polemical bitterness' about him (Calthrop, 27–8). His *Commentary on the Thirty-Nine Articles* (1871), based on his theological lectures, was widely approved and used as a textbook in other evangelical theological colleges. He published a number of sermons, gave papers on theological education at church congresses and to lay and clerical associations, and regularly spoke at the Islington clerical meeting.

Boultbee was an examining chaplain to J. C. Ryle, bishop of Liverpool, and in October 1883 was made a prebendary of St Paul's Cathedral by John Jackson, bishop of London. He suffered from gout, and died while convalescing at Bournemouth on 30 January 1884. He was buried at Chesham, Buckinghamshire, where his youngest son was the vicar. Ryle spoke at his memorial service in Christ Church, Highbury, in February 1884.

A. F. MUNDEN

Sources *The Times* (1 Feb 1884) · *The Record* (1 Feb 1884) · *Islington Gazette* (11 Feb 1884) · G. Calthrop, *Quiet strength: a memorial sketch of the life and works of the late Rev T. P. Boultbee LLD* (1884) · P. Boultbee and E. Boultbee, *The history of the Boultbee family* (1994) · G. C. B. Davies, *Men for the ministry* (1963) · A. F. Munden, *The history of St John's College, Nottingham*, 1: *Mr Peache's college at Kilburn* (1995) · notes by F. P. White, St John Cam. · Venn, *Alum. Cant.* · ordination papers for diocese of Ely, CUL

Likenesses Wontner, portrait, 1872, St John's College, Nottingham · portrait, priv. coll.

Wealth at death £4019 8*s.* 5*d.* in UK: probate, 29 April 1884, *CGPLA Eng. & Wales*

Boulter, Hugh (1672–1742), Church of Ireland archbishop of Armagh, was born in London on 4 January 1672, the son of John Boulter of the parish of St Katharine Cree, London. He entered Merchant Taylors' School, London, on 11 September 1685, matriculated at Christ Church, Oxford, in February 1687, but transferred in 1688 to Magdalen College, where he was made fellow in 1696; he graduated BA (1690), MA (1693), and DD (1708). He left Oxford for London

Hugh Boulter (**1672–1742**), after Francis Bindon, *c.*1735–40

in 1700 and was chaplain first to Sir Charles Hedges and then to Archbishop Tennison of Canterbury.

In 1708 Boulter was appointed rector of St Olave's, Tooley Street, Southwark, and in 1715–16 was archdeacon of Surrey. In 1719 he served as chaplain to George I in Hanover; he was also appointed bishop of Bristol and dean of Christ Church, Oxford, being consecrated bishop on 15 November 1719. Three days previously, on 12 November 1719, he had married Elizabeth Savage (*d.* 1754) at the church of St Peter-le-Poer, London; they had no children. In July 1724 Boulter was offered the primacy of the Church of Ireland, which he accepted apparently with great reluctance. Resentment that the archbishop of Dublin, William King, had been passed over for the primacy ensured that a section of Irish opinion was hostile to Boulter from the start. Lord Perceval, whom Boulter met when he went to Richmond to accept the primacy, recorded that Boulter regarded his principal duty in his new post as being to serve the king. Boulter arrived in Dublin on 3 November 1724 in the middle of the 'Wood's Halfpence' dispute, the most serious crisis in Anglo-Irish relations during the first half of the eighteenth century. He immediately warned the ministry of the strength of opposition in Ireland to Wood's patent, and in August 1725 he joined with Lord Lieutenant Carteret and Lord Chancellor West in advising the ministry to withdraw it, a recommendation which was reluctantly followed.

From the start Boulter viewed the Irish political situation in terms of an Irish–English conflict and throughout his primacy argued for a systematic policy of strengthening the 'English interest' through the appointment of English-born bishops, judges, and privy councillors. Although Boulter's appointment did not, as was once thought, represent a radical change in government policy, his arrival was a turning point in the Irish–English conflict which had been afflicting the Church of Ireland since 1716. With Boulter as primate the leadership of the church was removed from Archbishop King, leader of the Irish interest, and Boulter's influence over the crown's ecclesiastical patronage enabled him to strengthen the English interest thereafter. Relations between King and Boulter began uneasily and deteriorated rapidly. Boulter's status among the Irish clergy was damaged by his scheme to augment the church's fund of first-fruits for the purchase of glebes. This well-intentioned plan failed, owing to the opposition of the Ulster and Munster clergy, and Bishop Nicolson of Derry suspected that Archbishop King had suggested the scheme to Boulter in the sure knowledge that it would arouse such opposition. More serious harm to Boulter's reputation quickly followed, as related by Percival:

> The ArchBp. of Dublin and our Primate are now at open enmity, never to be reconciled which among many other things is principally occasioned by the Primate's ordaining and giveing a living to one Power, who was one of the Waltham Blacks, the man came hither recommended by my Lord Townsend and Ld. Fane knowing him, gave the account of his being one of those fellows, and if he had not turned informer and evidence against them, he had bin hanged himself, this story the ArchBp. heard, and spoke of it with great bitterness to the Primate, which you may judge did occasion such resentments as are not to be made up. (BL, Add. MS 21122, fols. 27–8)

Boulter's declared objective was to break up what he called the 'Dublin faction' on the Irish episcopal bench, although this was only finally realized with Archbishop King's death in 1729 (*Letters*, 1.12). Boulter did, however, quickly assert his authority within the church and the House of Lords. While the English-born bishop of Kilmore, Timothy Godwin, wrote that Boulter made 'a very good figure in our House' (Wake MS 14, fol. 297), a less friendly witness, Philip Perceval, reported that the primate was 'looked upon as a dull headed man, who in the house of Lords engrosses all the talk to himself which they say was one reason he was sent over they being tired out with him in England' (BL, Add. MS 47031, fols. 92–4).

Boulter's strongest asset was the firm backing which he received from the British ministry, which normally enabled him to outmanoeuvre his political opponents, one of whom was Lord Carteret, the lord lieutenant. In order to conciliate leading factions in the Irish House of Commons, Carteret often recommended Irishmen for ecclesiastical and judicial positions on the Irish privy council. Boulter regarded such appointments as likely to weaken the English interest and, because he enjoyed better relations with Robert Walpole and the duke of Newcastle than did Carteret, his views normally prevailed. In 1727 Carteret recommended Theophilus Bolton, the Irish-born bishop of Elphin, for the archbishopric of Cashel, despite Boulter's opinion that Bolton was 'as dangerous an Irishman as any on the bench [who] … would set himself, if he had that station, at the head of the Irish interest here' (*Letters*, 1.134, 115–6). This time Boulter blocked Bolton's appointment to Cashel but had to accept it in 1729, in order, as he put it, 'to keep things quiet in this country' (ibid., 1.272). The deaths in the mid-to late-1720s of William King, Timothy Godwin, and William Nicolson—most of the leading actors who had dominated the Irish–English conflict—facilitated the lessening of national tensions within the church. An indication of this changed atmosphere can be seen in Boulter's recommendation, in 1734, of two Irish-born bishops for promotion, describing both as being 'in the English interest' (ibid., 2.80).

Despite his reputation as a staunch defender of the English interest in Ireland, Boulter devoted considerable attention to the problems of the Irish economy. His particular interest was in currency reform, specifically lowering the value of gold relative to silver in Ireland, a scheme which he first proposed in 1726; he finally overcame the opposition of Irish banking interests and various patriot figures, such as Jonathan Swift, in 1738. Over this issue, as with others, Boulter's pro-English reputation was exploited by his opponents to arouse suspicion about his motives. As he complained in 1729, opponents of his scheme were representing it as 'an *English* project, formed in *England*, and carried on by my Lord Chancellor, myself, and other *English* here, with a design to drain this Kingdom of their gold, as they are already drained of their silver' (*Letters*, 1.245). When a riot bill was rejected by the Irish parliament in 1730, one commentator believed that many had opposed it because it was framed by the primate and the lord chancellor, Thomas Wyndham, and that:

> [their] warmth about it was one great means of rejecting it, for some people have a mind to show them, that they shall govern but by the people of Ireland, with whom at present they have little correspondence or confidence, nor endeavour to have any, and yet seem desirous to carry everything as they have a mind. (BL, Add. MS 21123)

In spite of his reputation Boulter does have a claim to some 'patriot' credentials. Following a harvest failure in Ulster in 1728–9, he helped to organize the purchase and transportation of food to prevent famine. He was even prepared to defend the right of Irish protestants to regulate their own affairs without interference from England. In 1735 he asked the duke of Newcastle to oppose a bill in the Westminster parliament 'for securing the title of Protestants'. The primate argued:

> it must be dangerous to give way to passing bills originally in England wholly relating to affairs in Ireland and especially to our private property here, without the least pretence that his Majesty's service or the interest of England are anyways concerned in the affair. (PRO, SP 63/398, fols. 9–10)

Boulter was also actively engaged in a range of philanthropic enterprises. He was vice-president and treasurer of the Incorporated Society in Dublin for Promoting English Protestant Schools in Ireland, a scheme designed to promote protestantism, the English language, and industry among poor Catholic children. Boulter established his own school for forty boys at Santry, co. Dublin. The Charter Schools scheme, however, 'was soon to fall short of the high hopes with which it had been launched' and the schools subsequently achieved notoriety as centres of neglect and abuse (Milne, 34).

Boulter had uneasy relations with successive speakers of the House of Commons with whom he and the lord chancellor served as lords justices. He clashed with William Conolly and Sir Ralph Gore over a range of patronage and policy issues, and in 1733, while supporting Henry Boyle's candidature as speaker, asked that Boyle should not be appointed a lord justice. Like his requests to diminish the Irish presence on the privy council, Boulter's plea went unheeded.

Boulter's correspondence gives the impression of an intelligent, diligent, and determined man. There is no question that he understood his role in Ireland as being the loyal servant of the British government, and this perception was bound to bring him into conflict with anyone who put Irish interests above those of the ministry. As a result his reputation in Ireland has suffered among both contemporaries and later generations; he is generally regarded as the personification of the English interest in Ireland in the early Hanoverian era.

Boulter was a contributor to the *Free Thinker*, a periodical founded in 1718, and published two sermons; a selection of his correspondence (1724–38) was published in 1769–70 under the supervision of his secretary, Ambrose Philips. Boulter died at St James's Palace, London, on 27 September 1742, and was buried in Westminster Abbey. He was survived by his wife, who died on 3 March 1754.

PATRICK MCNALLY

Sources *Letters written by … Hugh Boulter … to several ministers of state*, ed. [A. Philips and G. Faulkner], 2 vols. (1769–70); repr. (1770), vol. 1, pp. 12–13, 114–16, 126–7, 133–4, 243–6, 271–2; vol. 2, p. 80 · J. Stuart, *Historical memoirs of the city of Armagh*, rev. A. Coleman, new edn (1900) · R. Mant, *History of the Church of Ireland*, 2 vols. (1840) · P. McNally, '"Irish and English interests": national conflict within the Church of Ireland episcopate in the reign of George I', *Irish Historical Studies*, 29 (1994–5), 295–314 · Nicolson to Wake, 5 March 1725, BL, Add. MS 6116, fols. 139–40 · Coghill to Southwell, 23 Dec 1725, BL, Add. MS 21122, fols. 27–8 · Coghill to Southwell, 18 April 1730, BL, Add. MS 21123, fols. 1–5 · Lord Perceval to Dering, 7 Aug 1724, BL, Add. MS 47030, fol. 74 · Philip Perceval to Lord Perceval, 1 Feb 1726, BL, Add. MS 47031, fols. 92–4 · Boulter to Newcastle, 18 April 1735, PRO, SP 63/398, fols. 9–10 · Godwin to Wake, 20 Oct 1725, Christ Church Oxf., Wake MS 14, fol. 297 · K. Milne, *The Irish charter schools, 1730–1830* (1997) · *IGI* · *DNB*

Archives Christ Church Oxf. · PRO, state papers (Ireland) · TCD, agent's account book

Likenesses T. Beard, mezzotint, 1728 (after M. Ashton), BM, NPG · after F. Bindon, oils, *c.*1735–1740, NPG; versions, Christ Church Oxf.; Magd. Oxf. [*see illus.*] · F. Bindon, group portrait, oils, 1742, TCD · H. Cheere, monument, 1742, Westminster Abbey · J. Macardell, mezzotint, pubd 1742 (after oil painting by F. Bindon), NG Ire. · J. Brooks, engraving (after F. Bindon), BM, NPG · marble bust, Christ Church Oxf. · portrait, Christ Church Oxf. · two portraits, Magd. Oxf.

Wealth at death approx. £30,000: Stuart, *Historical memoirs*; *GM*

Boulting, John (1913–1985), film producer and director, was born in Bray, Berkshire, on 21 November 1913, the identical twin brother of Roy Boulting and son of Walter Arthur Boulting, financial consultant, of Hove, Sussex, and his wife, Rose Bennett. John and Roy had two brothers—one older than themselves (Peter Cotes, an

John Boulting (1913–1985), by Bert Hardy and Francis Reiss, 1946 [left, with his twin brother, Roy]

actor) and one younger, who died aged eight. Boulting was educated at Reading School, where he was captain of the rugby team, secretary of the dramatic society, and a leading actor. Interested in politics and the local Labour Party, he was a member of the school debating society. John and Roy formed one of the first cinematograph societies in a public school and were film extras in Anthony Asquith's *Tell England* (1931). In 1933 John began work at Ace Films, a small film distribution company owned by a school friend's father in Wardour Street, London, where he discovered his flair for film business.

Early in 1937 Boulting volunteered as a front-line ambulance driver for the International Brigades in Spain. On his return he formed Charter Films with Roy in November 1937. Their first film, *Ripe Earth* (1937), was a documentary, but they soon branched out into features, their first critical success being *Consider your Verdict* (1938). After *Trunk Crime* (1939), a moderately successful thriller, and *Inquest* (1939), John produced *Pastor Hall* (1940), one of the first British anti-Nazi films, and *The Dawn Guard* (1941), a documentary for the Ministry of Information. Early in 1941 he joined the RAF as a flight mechanic but obtained special leave in 1942 to produce *Thunder Rock*. He became a flight lieutenant in the RAF film unit, where he directed his first film, *Journey Together* (1944).

After the war the Boulting brothers worked as independent producers. In 1947 John directed his second film, *Brighton Rock*, the only film of his own work approved by Graham Greene, and produced *Fame is the Spur*, a film about a Labour politician, played by Michael Redgrave. Boulting's preoccupation with social and political issues continued with *The Guinea Pig* (1949), about a lower middle-class schoolboy (played by Richard Attenborough) who attends a public school. The third film John Boulting directed, *Seven Days to Noon* (1950), was the first to deal with the moral implications of the atom bomb, and won an academy award for best original story.

In 1951 Boulting directed *The Magic Box*, which was planned as the film industry's contribution to the Festival of Britain. The film portrayed William Friese-Greene as the inventor of the motion picture camera, a sympathetic, if sentimental, account of his struggle for recognition in the face of financial hardship, rivalry, and conflicts within the film trade. It contained many of the themes which surfaced in subsequent Boulting films: an intense respect for individualism and admiration for those who challenged entrenched interests. Indeed, in his own career as an independent producer, Boulting resented the Rank Organization's stranglehold over film distribution and exhibition. In the following decade he championed the cause of the independent producer and publicly denounced the combines' emphasis on flamboyance and spectacle associated with 'gala' premières.

In the 1950s the Boulting brothers turned to comedy and John became a Liberal. He produced *Brothers in Law* (1957) and *Carlton-Browne of the FO* (1958), and directed *Private's Progress* (1956), *Lucky Jim* (1958), *I'm All Right Jack* (1960), and *Heavens Above!* (1963), films that satirized respectively the legal profession, the civil service, the army, universities, trade unions, and the church. Although *I'm All Right Jack* won British film awards for best screenplay and best British actor (for the performance of Peter Sellers, as a shop steward), the film brought the Boultings into conflict with the film technicians' trade union.

In the 1960s the Boultings did not play a significant part in the 'new wave' British cinema, except perhaps with *The Family Way* (1966). The last film directed by John Boulting was *Rotten to the Core* (1965), but he went on to produce *Twisted Nerve* (1968), *There's a Girl in my Soup* (1970), and *Soft Beds, Hard Battles* (1974). He continued to be interested in film industry politics, particularly the challenge posed by television. He took part in the successful effort to persuade television companies to pay higher fees to film producers for television showings of feature films. He was managing director of British Lion and Shepperton studios (1967–72). British Lion distributed films produced by the independent sector which Boulting championed for many years.

Boulting was married four times. His first wife was Veronica, daughter of John Craig Nelson Davidson, barrister, whom he married in 1938. That marriage ended in divorce and in 1952 he married Jacqueline Helen, daughter of Richard Chilver Robert Rice Allerton, a broker at Lloyds; once again divorced, he married Ann Marion, daughter of Alan Ware, of the Royal Marines, in 1972. Finally, he married Anne Josephine, daughter of Frank Flynn, sales manager, in 1977. He and his first wife had two sons and with his second he had three daughters. He also had another son.

John Boulting's life was dominated by films, his most creative period being the 1940s. He had a close working relationship with his brother throughout his film career.

If John was producing, Roy would invariably be directing, and vice versa. They both liaised closely with scriptwriters and often shared screenwriting credit. John enjoyed cricket, tennis, and horse-riding. His political views clearly influenced his work and while his films were celebrating the individual against authority he was an active local Liberal. He died on 17 June 1985 at his home, 5 The Ridge, Ridgemount Road, Sunningdale, Berkshire.

SARAH STREET

Sources A. Burton, T. O'Sullivan, and P. Wells, eds., *The family way: the Boulting brothers and postwar British film culture* (2000) · *The Times* (19 June 1985) · M. Landy, *British genres: cinema and society, 1930–1960* (1991) · private information (1990) · *CGPLA Eng. & Wales* (1985) · *WWW*

Archives BFI, microfiche jacket of press clippings, film reviews, etc. | JRL, corresp. with Robert Donat | FILM BFI NFTVA, *Cinema*, 3 June 1971

Likenesses B. Hardy and F. Reiss, double portrait, photograph, 1946, Hult. Arch. [*see illus.*] · B. Hardy, photograph, 23 Nov 1946, Hult. Arch.; repro. in *Picture Post* · photographs, 1946–63, Hult. Arch.

Wealth at death £288,594: probate, 20 Aug 1985, *CGPLA Eng. & Wales*

Boulton, Ernest (*b*. 1848?), transvestite, showed from his sixth year an aptitude for playing female characters. He would dress as a parlourmaid, and once waited at table upon his grandmother, who said when he left the room, 'I wonder, having sons, that you have so flippant a girl about you' (*Annual Register*, 223). His parents, who lived near Greenwich or Dulwich, accepted his public cross-dressing. He worked for his uncle, who was a City stockbroker, and as a clerk in the London and County Bank (1866–7). He was thought to be consumptive, suffered from a fistula, and underwent several operations.

Boulton became the inseparable friend of Frederick William Park (whose father was master in the court of common pleas) and the lover of the duke of Newcastle's son, Lord Arthur Pelham Clinton, MP for Newark. From 1867 Boulton and Park, who were known in their set as Stella and Fanny, travelled in the English provinces impersonating female characters at private theatricals. Boulton, who possessed a fine soprano voice, received as many as fourteen bouquets at each performance. Boulton and Park rented a bedroom with sitting room at 13 Wakefield Street, off Regent Square, where they kept an extensive wardrobe of women's clothes and ornaments. They began appearing, dressed as women, at music-halls, theatres, restaurants, shopping arcades, and other resorts near Mayfair. Their conversation, which centred on theatricals, was frivolous and lively. When dressed as women, they painted their faces, chirruped with their lips, and coquetted. Courageous and generous, they were not prostitutes but sometimes asked their admirers for money.

In April 1870 Boulton and Park were arrested in company with a man who believed they were women, although they had repeatedly told him they were men. At his first appearance in the dock Boulton wore a cherry-coloured silk evening dress trimmed with white lace, bracelets on bare arms, a wig, and plaited chignon. They were originally charged with intent to commit a felony,

Ernest Boulton (*b*. 1848?), by Frederick Spalding senior, *c*.1868 [left, with Frederick Park (Stella and Fanny)]

but eight physicians who illegally subjected them to anal examination in Newgate found little evidence of sodomy; instead they were committed for trial in May on milder charges of conspiring to commit felonious crimes and of outraging decency by going about dressed as women. Though their supposed soliciting of men while cross-dressing was central to the prosecution, they prinked themselves to ape the antics of women rather than to seduce men: their intentions seem less sexual than exhibitionistic or even burlesque. The easy-going levity of the throng at their committal proceedings excited the indignation of public moralists. After the Society for the Suppression of Vice requested all evidence to be taken in secrecy, the public were excluded from some police-court hearings. Nevertheless, leaving in a police van, Boulton and Park were saluted in the streets by crowds waving their hats. The police seized a huge mass of correspondence which, though camp, contained not one word of indecency. They failed to cajole the parties to denounce each other or to muster convincing witnesses. Lord Arthur died in June aged twenty-nine (officially of scarlet fever aggravated by anxiety, but perhaps by suicide), yet was vindictively kept on the charge sheet, together with two other young men, Louis Hurt, a clerk in the Post Office, and John Fiske, US consul at Leith.

The trial opened before Lord Chief Justice Cockburn on 9 May 1871, when Boulton was twenty-two, and lasted six days. Prosecuting counsel included Sir Robert Collier (later Lord Monkswell), Sir John Coleridge, Hardinge Giffard (later earl of Halsbury), and Henry James. The case is important for showing that police, physicians, and lawyers were inexperienced in preparing such prosecutions, and that pathological models of homosexuality were not yet established in Britain. Boulton and Park employed as their solicitor George Lewis, who devised an effective defence that the youths were silly but not criminal. It was doubtless at his insistence that Boulton grew a moustache and Park whiskers. When the defendants were acquitted, Boulton fainted.

By Henry Matthews (later Viscount Llandaff) Boulton was described as 'a dainty and pleasing boy who was generally treated as a young girl' (Roughead, 178) and by Simeon Solomon as 'not quite beautiful but supremely pretty, a perfect figure, manner and voice' (Croft-Cooke, 47). Boulton and Park feature in Jack Saul's pornographic *The Sins of the Cities of the Plain* (1881) and are the subject of a Victorian limerick:

There was an old person of Sark
Who buggered a pig in the dark;
The swine in surprise
Murmured: 'God blast your eyes
Do you take me for Boulton or Park?'

RICHARD DAVENPORT-HINES

Sources *The trial of Boulton and Park, with Hurt and Fiske* (1871) • *The Times* (30 April 1870–16 May 1871) • W. Roughead, *Bad companions* (1930), 149–83 • *Annual Register* (1871), 220–24 • H. M. Hyde, *The other love* (1970), 94–8 • R. Croft-Cooke, *Feasting with panthers: a new consideration of some late Victorian writers* (1967) • *The Swinburne letters*, ed. C. Y. Lang, 6 vols. (1959–62), vol. 2, p. 144

Archives PRO, transcript of trial, DPP 4/6

Likenesses F. Spalding senior, double portrait, photograph, *c.*1868, Essex Record Office [*see illus.*]

Boulton, Sir Harold Edwin, second baronet (1859–1935), songwriter and philanthropist, was born at Lower Woolwich Road, Charlton, Kent, on 7 August 1859, the elder son and third of eight children of Samuel Bagster Boulton (1830–1918), of Copped Hall, Totteridge, Hertfordshire, who was created baronet in 1905, and his wife, Sophia Louisa (*d.* 1900), daughter of Thomas Cooper of Newbury, Berkshire. Samuel Boulton was co-founder of Burt, Boulton, and Haywood Ltd, timber merchants and chemical manufacturers; he was also winner in 1884 of the Telford medal for research in the chemical industry, and a founder in 1889 of the London Labour Conciliation and Arbitration Board. Harold Boulton was educated at Harrow School and Balliol College, Oxford, where he was awarded a third in classical moderations in 1879 and a third in *literae humaniores* in 1881. With James Rennell Rodd he founded and edited a magazine of contemporary poetry, and he was runner-up for the Newdigate prize poem in his final year.

Boulton had enjoyed singing at Harrow, where he led the school choir, and after an undergraduate reading party in Scotland he became interested in Scottish folksongs and their preservation, and wrote new words to traditional melodies himself. The most famous of these was *Skye Boat Song* (1884), which tells the story of the escape of Bonnie Prince Charlie (Charles Edward Stuart) after his defeat at Culloden in 1746. He wrote English words for *All through the Night*, the traditional Welsh lullaby, and edited many collections of songs, including *Songs of the North*, in three volumes (1885, 1905, and 1925), gathered from the highlands and lowlands of Scotland; *Songs of the Four Nations* (1892); *National Songs and some Ballads* (1908); and *Prince Charlie in Song* (1933), a collection of Jacobite songs. His lyrics were set to music by well-known composers, including Charles Villiers Stanford, who wrote the music for 'For Ever Mine' (1891), and Granville Bantock, who set 'Song to the Seals'. Edward German wrote the music for many of the songs, including 'Glorious Devon' (1905) and 'The Drummer Boy' (1908). Boulton's published poetry includes *Songs Sung and Unsung* (1894), *The Ballad of Thyra Lee* (1899), and *Lyrics and other Poems* (1902). In 1926 he published *The Huntress Hag of the Blackwater*, a medieval romance in verse, which was followed by *An Unrecorded Miracle of St Columba* (1930) and the verse saga *Olaf and Uaine* (1934), 'a tale of a thousand years ago'. Boulton was an ovate bard of Wales and president of the Scottish Literature and Song Association in 1929, and was made a director of the Royal Academy of Music in 1931. He was also honorary secretary of the Keats–Shelley Memorial Association from 1906 to 1926, and was present at the opening of the memorial in the piazza di Spagna, in Rome.

Boulton became involved in the university settlement movement shortly after leaving Oxford. Toynbee Hall was founded in January 1884 in the East End of London by a group of Balliol men, but Boulton was one of those mainly associated with Keble College and the high-church party, and supported by Octavia Hill, who thought that a settlement should be religious in character: Oxford House opened in the autumn of 1884 in a disused church school in the large slum parish of St Andrew, Bethnal Green, the most densely populated district of east London. There the focus was on setting up clubs for working men—as an alternative to public houses—and for boys. The Oxford House Club, founded in 1885, was the first started in the East End and became a model for other clubs. Among its many other cultural and sporting activities it was famous for its male voice choir. Boulton, with James Granville Adderley, head of Oxford House from 1885 to 1886, founded the Federation of Working Men's Social Clubs, and by the time he was elected president in 1895 there were sixty-five federated clubs. He remained president until 1930. While living at Oxford House he helped to found the People's Palace Horticultural Society, which was an offshoot of the People's Palace which had opened in 1887, and with Charles Bethune he founded the House of Shelter at Bow, where homeless men could find refuge and help in getting employment. In 1932 he was elected chairman of the Mendicity Society. Boulton remained at Oxford House until his marriage, on 26 January 1889, to Adelaide Lucy (*d.* 1926), daughter of Lieutenant-Colonel Duncan Henry Caithness Reay Davidson, of Tulloch Castle, Dingwall, Scotland. They had two sons, the younger of whom was killed in action in 1917, and one daughter.

Boulton had joined the family firm after leaving Oxford and touring Canada, and in 1903 he and his father started the Dominion Tar and Chemical Company in Nova Scotia, setting up tar-distillery companies and creosoting plants. He visited Canada at least once a year until 1918, when he became chairman on the death of his father and inherited the baronetcy. He sold the company in 1929. Before the First World War he was a captain in the Queen's Own Cameron Highlanders, and during the war he served in the City of London yeomanry, the rough riders. He was appointed CBE in 1918. He was president of the Associated Tar Distillers and a member of the Association of British Chemical Manufacturers from its foundation in 1916. First president of the British Association of Wood Preservers in 1930, in that year he published *A Century of Wood Preserving*.

Boulton's interests also extended to medical and nursing organizations: he was a member of the committee of the London Hospital from 1896 to 1921; he helped to organize bush nursing in Australia in 1910; he was vice-president of the Queen's Institute for Nurses, and chairman from 1908 to 1932; from 1909 to 1914 he was honorary commissioner for Canada of the St John Ambulance Association; he was chairman of Queen Mary's Hostel for Nurses from 1918 to 1921; and chairman of the committee for the national memorial to Queen Alexandra from 1926 to 1928.

Following the death of his first wife on 26 April 1926, Boulton remarried on 29 December 1926. His second wife was Margaret Cunningham McKennet (*d.* 1938), widow of Robert Charles Simpson Moodie of Montreal, and daughter of James Lennox Lyons of Montreal. Boulton died at Grosvenor House, Park Lane, London, on 1 June 1935 after a long illness. A requiem mass was held on 4 June at Farm Street Church, London; he was buried at Brookwood cemetery the same day. ANNE PIMLOTT BAKER

Sources *The Times* (3 June 1935) • Burke, *Peerage* • W. Reason, ed., *University and social settlements* (1878) • J. M. Knapp, ed., *The universities and the social problem* (1895) • P. Colson, *Life of the bishop of London* (1935), 24–40 • S. C. Carpenter, *Winnington-Ingram* (1949), 25–61 • J. A. R. Pimlott, *Toynbee Hall: fifty years of social progress, 1884–1934* (1935) • college register, Balliol Oxf. • *WW* • b. cert.

Archives NRA, corresp. | King's AC Cam., letters to Oscar Browning

Wealth at death £23,517 8*s.* 1*d.*: probate, 23 Sept 1935, *CGPLA Eng. & Wales*

Boulton, Matthew (1728–1809), manufacturer and entrepreneur, was born on 14 September 1728 at New Hall Walk, Snow Hill, Birmingham, one of four children, three of whom survived to adulthood, of Matthew Boulton (*d.* 1759), toy manufacturer and merchant, and his wife, Christiana Piers (*d.* 1785) of Chester. He was educated at the academy of the Revd John Hausted in Deritend, Birmingham.

Matthew Boulton (1728–1809), by Carl Fredrik von Breda, 1792 [replica]

Family and friends The 'toy' trade of Birmingham consisted of several distinct branches of the hardware industry. Makers of gold and silver toys produced trinkets, snuff-boxes, inkstands, and a variety of other goods. The tortoiseshell toy makers, as the term implies, worked particularly in that material, while steel toy makers produced corkscrews, buckles, watch-chains, candle-snuffers, and other goods. The largest branch of the toy trade was that of buckle making and chape making (the chape being the part of the buckle by which it was fastened to the strap or ribbon). Buckle making and chape making were independent trades in the eighteenth century.

The elder Matthew Boulton's branch of the Birmingham toy trade was that of steel toys, chiefly buckles for both shoes and knee-breeches. The younger Matthew joined his father on leaving school and is said to have produced an enamelled or inlaid buckle when only seventeen years old, which contributed to the expansion of his father's business. At the age of twenty-one he became a partner in the business and his father entrusted the management to him. About 1756 he married a distant cousin, Mary Robinson (1727–1759/60?), the elder daughter of Luke Robinson, an 'opulent mercer' of Lichfield. Her mother was an heiress and Mary's share of the estate was £14,000. The couple had been married only a few years when Mary died suddenly, probably in 1759 or 1760; there were no surviving children. In 1759 Boulton's father died, leaving the business to his son.

After several years Boulton sought to marry Anne (Nancy) Robinson (1735–1783), Mary's younger sister. This was forbidden by ecclesiastical law but, supported by the view of John Fry in *The Case of Marriage between Near Kindred* (1756), in which it was asserted that 'marriage with a deceased wife's sister is fit and convenient being opposed neither to law nor morals' (p. 80), Boulton pressed his case, and though Anne's brother was opposed to the match it does not appear that the mother-in-law was. The marriage nevertheless took place some time prior to 1767, probably out of Birmingham, the bride also bringing with her £14,000, which was her share of her parents' estate.

Boulton's marriage, and with it the addition to his fortune, was the cause of a number of letters of congratulations from his friends. Later in his life, alluding to his fortune, he remarked that he had had the option of living the life of a gentleman but chose, rather, to become an industrialist.

Matthew and Anne had two children: Anne, who died unmarried in 1829, and Matthew Robinson Boulton (1770–1842). Anne (nicknamed Nancy) developed some crippling ailment from which she never recovered. Matthew Robinson was educated according to the liberal principles espoused by his father and his associates, with much focus on chemistry, mechanics, and geology, as well as the acquisition of French and German. He, in partnership with James Watt jun., directed Soho Foundry and, on his own account, Soho Mint and Soho Manufactory after his father's death.

Ever a sociable individual, Matthew Boulton had a wide circle of friends, especially those of one particular group, whose number swelled eventually to fourteen and became known as the Lunar Society (an allusion to the fact that they met to dine and converse on the night of the full moon). He particularly enjoyed the company of Dr William Small, who had been introduced to Boulton by Benjamin Franklin in 1765. Small became Boulton's personal physician and also a close friend and adviser whose judgement both Boulton and, in due course, James *Watt valued highly. Dr Erasmus Darwin of Lichfield, medical practitioner to a number of families in Warwickshire and Staffordshire, and also an author, was a founder member of the Lunar Society, which met at Boulton's house and, less frequently, at the homes of other members.

Members of the Lunar Society had been interested in the design of steam engines even before Watt joined their number. Boulton had invented a steam engine, the design of which he discussed with Erasmus Darwin and Benjamin Franklin. His toy business was the cause of his interest in metallurgy, an interest shared by William Withering and James Keir. In both Boulton's and Keir's cases intellectual interest produced industrial applications. The potter Josiah *Wedgwood was another member of the society, and the relationship between science and industry is well illustrated in Wedgwood's plan to develop a research establishment in the Staffordshire Potteries. Wedgwood and Boulton collaborated over the production of cameo jewellery set in cut-steel mounts, Boulton, not altogether in jest, suggesting that he might establish a pottery so as to integrate the manufacture of cameo ware more effectively. Interest in chemistry and its practical applications, as, for example, in the manufacture of sulphuric acid, impacted on Boulton's silver plate, Sheffield plate, and minting activities.

Measurement was a concern shared by a number of the members of the Lunar Society; and Boulton's interest in it was crucial to developments in assaying as well as to engine drawing, an essential element in the steam engine business. It is clear, however, that the interplay of science and industry involved both high seriousness *and* merriment; and the latter had highly practical sides as well. Boulton, for example, joined in the late eighteenth-century enthusiasm for balloons and ballooning. When the Derby Philosophical Society sent a message to the Lunar Society by balloon (it was sent off-course by the wind), practical play and scientific experiment were closely engaged; and Boulton made a balloon to entertain his children when in Cornwall. However, as a mark of his involvement with scientific endeavours, he was elected fellow of the Royal Society in 1785. In addition, he was elected a fellow of the Royal Society of Edinburgh in 1783 and was a member of the Society of Civil Engineers from 1792. In 1800 he became a proprietor of the Royal Institution.

Early business Boulton's own career coincided with, and also contributed to, the emergence of Birmingham as a thriving provincial industrial town in the last half of the eighteenth century. Water-wheels were used in rolling and slitting mills, for blade mills (used in the edge tool trades), and in the nearby Black Country forges. Birmingham was noted for the manufacture of a great variety of metal goods. This can be, at least in part, attributed to a long tradition of working in iron and brass. The town had a tradition of liberalism; dissenters settled there and a lively and inventive commercial community emerged. A large number of patents was granted to Birmingham men during the eighteenth century, the majority of them concerned with materials such as metal alloys; with processes such as casting, rolling, and stamping; and with products such as buttons, buckles, and nails. Such was the reputation of the town that it became known as the toyshop of Europe. By mid-century Boulton was the most eminent toy manufacturer, but there were thousands of small masters, each of whose business was conducted in workshops comprising part of, or attached to, their dwelling house. Birmingham industry was characterized by the workshop rather than the factory until well into the nineteenth century.

In 1760 Boulton appeared before the committee of the House of Commons, representing the interests not only of the buckle makers of Birmingham but also those of Warwick and Wolverhampton, the issue being a petition for leave to bring in a bill to prohibit the export of buckle-chapes. A skilful practitioner of 'the Art of Parliamentary Lobbying' (Robinson, 'Parliamentary lobbying', 209), his evidence provided a vivid description of the scale of the buckle trade and the wages of buckle makers and chape makers. The buckle was said to be 'by far the most considerable Article in the Toy Trade' (*JHC*, 901). At this period his business consisted of the manufacture of steel toys and a mercantile business exporting a wider range of midland hardware products.

Soho House and Soho Manufactory Wishing to expand his business, and being constrained at his Snow Hill site, Boulton acquired the lease of a site on Handsworth Heath. The land contained a cottage, the site of which became Boulton's Soho House, while in the valley below, the brook had been dammed and a metal-rolling mill and dwelling house built. In summer 1761 he built dwellings for workmen, workshops, and a warehouse. He demolished the rolling mill and in the following year began to plan the construction of a new factory. The original architect, T. Lightoler, did not provide what was required, and the work was subsequently undertaken by various members of the Wyatt family. The Wyatts of Lichfield and Burton upon Trent were, perhaps, the most famous family of eighteenth-century surveyors and architects. They included in their number John Wyatt, who was the London agent of Boulton and the merchant John Fothergill, the carpenter William Wyatt, and the wooden-screw manufacturer Charles Wyatt, besides the architect and builder members of the family who designed and built Boulton's house, warehouse, and manufactory.

Benjamin Wyatt & Sons were subsequently commissioned to build the Soho Manufactory to the design of William Wyatt. The factory was completed in 1766 and became a showpiece. In the 1790s Boulton engaged the architect James Wyatt to remodel Soho House. James appears to have lost interest in the project, however, and the work was eventually completed by Samuel Wyatt in 1796–8. The house, while designed as a comfortable, yet elegant, family dwelling, contained several novel features. A warm-air convection heating system was installed, while the window frames were made of an alloy invented by fellow 'lunatik' James Keir, and the elevations were slate-hung while appearing to be ashlar. Soho House survives as a museum but the manufactory was demolished in the mid-nineteenth century. Samuel Wyatt was also engaged to design a new Snow Hill warehouse for Boulton.

Soho Manufactory was the focus of Boulton's numerous business enterprises. In 1762 he formed a partnership with John Fothergill, which lasted until 1781. Fothergill had served an apprenticeship in Königsberg and had travelled extensively in continental Europe, probably for Joseph Duncumb of Birmingham as well as for Lewis and Capper. He spoke French and German, his responsibility in his partnership with Boulton being for the mercantile side of the business. He travelled largely in the Baltic for the partnership, though it traded with Italy and France as well. The partners employed a German clerk who acted as a traveller for them in Russia and was probably a contact of Fothergill's from Königsberg. Fothergill was clearly well connected, having friends in the world of banking and finance, but he does not appear to have had sufficient capital for his share of the partnership with Boulton and had to borrow.

Boulton directed his own attention primarily to the organization of production. The range of products was extended to steel jewellery, including Wedgwood's jasperware cameos set in Boulton and Fothergill's cut-steel mountings. Wedgwood also ordered mountings and flutings from Boulton for vases. The threatened pottery at Soho did not materialize and neither did the challenge damage the friendship between the two men. The development of Boulton's and Fothergill's business produced an invitation to Boulton to settle in Sweden, but he declined to meet the Swedish emissary.

The entrepreneurial flair evident in all of Boulton's business activities, and especially his close attention to fashionable design, were most noticeable in the manufacture of buttons. These, along with a wide range of other cut-steel goods, formed an important part of Boulton's output aimed at a mass market. However, like Wedgwood, he specifically targeted royalty and aristocracy in the first instance. 'In future we shall take care to have some thing new in the Button way against every Birth Day of our Sovereign', Boulton wrote, 'and shall present to such of the Nobility as we can make so free with (and such as are most dressy) some setts to garnish their Cloaths with on that Day' (Robinson, 'Eighteenth century commerce and fashion', 47). In his letters he often asked Fothergill to send him sets of new buttons for such special customers as the duke of Marlborough.

Yet unlike John Taylor, whose toy business generated considerable wealth, Boulton and Fothergill made losses over their eighteen years of trading. Fothergill had established many foreign connections, but they did not prove profitable and Boulton's London agent and banker urged that this aspect of the business be closed. As early as 1774 Fothergill had considered the business to be on the edge of bankruptcy. Relations between the partners deteriorated, culminating in charges being made by Fothergill against Boulton, which resulted in the latter's giving his partner notice that the partnership should cease on 31 December 1781; Fothergill died in the following year.

Sheffield plate and ormolu In the early 1760s Boulton acquired the technology for manufacturing Sheffield plate—a sheet of silver fused to one of copper and subsequently rolled. For some years he was the only producer of Sheffield plate outside Sheffield itself, and no other Birmingham manufacturer is known to have been making Sheffield plate until about 1770. While Boulton did not introduce any improvements to the technology, he was one of the first to apply sterling silver thread instead of plated wire thread to articles, thus covering the edges where the most wear occurred and thereby concealing the copper. He manufactured Sheffield plate under the business name of the M. Boulton Plate Company. He supplied a variety of articles, including candlesticks in different patterns, jugs, tureens, and cups, and he was the first to make plated telescope tubes for the London instrument maker Jesse Ramsden. Shortly after the manufacturing of Sheffield plate was established Boulton commenced the manufacture of silver plate (that is, sterling silver ware). The same designs could be used as for Sheffield plate and by the 1780s he was commissioning designs from some of the leading architects of the day. For their part his architect friends, particularly the Wyatts, repaid him for his early commissions by introducing his wares to their landed clientele.

During the late 1760s and early 1770s Boulton commenced the production of another luxury product—ormolu. This was made of a metal—normally brass but sometimes bronze or copper—which was gilded by the process of mercurial gilding and did not require assaying.

Ormolu was used in a wide range of decorative wares, particularly for mounts and vases of various sorts. Production peaked in 1771 and declined soon afterwards. One of the major outlets for Boulton's ormolu, Sheffield plate, and silver plate was Christies, the auction house, in London. Some of his ormolu was purchased by George III and Queen Charlotte, pieces being acquired for Windsor Castle and Buckingham Palace. A sale at Christies in 1772 failed, however, resulting in a number of valuable pieces remaining unsold and having to be reduced in price subsequently.

Another short-lived business was mechanical painting, in which Boulton was partnered by Francis Eginton. Eginton had been employed at Soho as a maker of Japanned ware. However, the business failed to become profitable and Fothergill insisted that it should cease. In June 1780 the agreement with Eginton was terminated. Eginton went on to establish himself as a glass painter and achieved considerable success. Boulton's technique of copying works of art has unfortunately been lost.

Boulton maintained a steady trade in toys to France, from which country he obtained both workmen and tools which enabled him to capture the French trade in ormolu. Besides the quality of his wares he competed on price, consistently undercutting London silversmiths in fashionable markets. Furthermore, because of his reputation as a well-regarded host, distinguished foreigners and members of the British aristocracy visited Soho, and a number of them placed orders. In endeavouring to raise the standards of taste in Britain and to introduce high-quality art wares, Boulton was encouraged by his friend the Hon. Mrs Elizabeth Montague, who remarked on 'our victories over the French in our contention of arts … [and] The achievement of Soho, instead of making widows and orphans, making marriages and Christenings'. She urged: 'Go on then, sir, to triumph over the French in taste and to embellish your Country with useful inventions and elegant productions' (Dickinson, 54). The toy business was continued variously as the M. Boulton Button Company (1782–1809), Boulton and Scale (1782–96), and Boulton and Smith (*c.*1796–1809).

Boulton and Watt partnership As late as September 1778 Boulton was still not convinced 'how far it may be prudent in me to stick to Engines or Buttons for I can consider Buttons as a sheet anchor' (Robinson, 'Eighteenth century commerce and fashion', 39). Yet the business on which Boulton eventually focused most attention was his partnership with James Watt. Watt had visited Soho in 1767 and met Dr Small and Fothergill, though Boulton was absent; he also met Erasmus Darwin in Lichfield. He again visited Soho in 1768 on his journey back to Glasgow from London, where he had been on business associated with the patent which was granted him in 1769 for his improvements to the steam engine. Immediately on returning to Glasgow he informed his patron Dr Roebuck, who had taken over the engine development debts, of Boulton's desire to participate in a steam engine business. John *Roebuck (*bap.* 1718, *d.* 1794), who had studied medicine at Edinburgh and Leiden, was both an industrial chemist and a manufacturer. He developed the manufacture of sulphuric acid, formerly made in glass retorts, to an industrial scale in lead tanks, and established a factory for its production at Prestonpans in Scotland and also, in partnership with Samuel Garbett, in Birmingham. Together, Roebuck and Garbett established the Carron ironworks, Roebuck also leasing coalmines and establishing salt works at Bo'ness. Watt's first experimental engine was built on Roebuck's land. Roebuck was over-extended financially, however, and was therefore more ready to entertain the possibility of involving Boulton in the manufacture and marketing of the Watt engine.

Boulton was offered a licence to manufacture the steam engine in Warwickshire, Staffordshire, and Derbyshire, but he declined, while strongly indicating his desire to be engaged in a joint project with Watt. Roebuck's bankruptcy provided the opportunity for Boulton to take over his share in Watt's engine. In 1774 Watt moved to Birmingham and in 1775 the patent was extended for twenty-five years to 1800 by act of parliament, the Boulton and Watt partnership commencing in that year. Under the terms of the partnership Watt assigned two-thirds of both property and the patent to Boulton, while Boulton undertook to pay the expenses already incurred, to meet the costs of experiments, and to pay for materials and wages. The profits were to be divided in proportion to their shares.

It would be incorrect to stereotype Boulton as the entrepreneur and Watt as the inventor, for Boulton made many suggestions for improvements to the engine and Watt also had a good head for business. But there is no doubt that Boulton's flair for marketing was significant for the early success of the business. He took an order for an engine for Bloomfield colliery in the Black Country. The 50 inch diameter engine was a considerable scale-up from the 18 inch cylinder of Watt's original Kinneil engine. The engine became a showpiece to which prospective customers went and were frequently persuaded of the opportunities afforded by steam power.

In 1769 Boulton had told Watt that he would build a manufactory alongside his Soho Manufactory in which to construct engines for the world. The reality was rather different, as Boulton and Watt was largely a consulting engineering partnership in the early days, and only a small proportion of the engine parts, by value, were made at Soho. The first major market for Boulton and Watt engines was in Cornwall, and, despite the partners' considerable anxieties with the way mines were managed—with the over-production of copper ores and the consequent temporary abandonment of engines—Cornwall proved to be a lucrative market for them. It was Boulton who perceived the potential afforded by the growth of the cotton-spinning industry and urged Watt to develop a rotative engine. Before the expiry of the patent, rotative engines far exceeded the number of reciprocating engines sold per year, though in terms of horsepower they were smaller.

It was during the partners' frequent absences in Cornwall that James Keir (1735–1820), a chemist, glassmaker, and member of the Lunar Society, moved from Stourbridge to Winson Green, giving up direct involvement in glass manufacture in order to be nearer to Soho to assist in the management of Boulton's interests. Both Boulton and Watt had a high opinion of Keir and had hoped to attract him and his capital to their business, but after some long time Keir decided not to commit his own capital to a partnership which would have meant the possibility of servicing Boulton's debts. Yet Keir did not withhold his criticisms on the management of the Boulton and Fothergill business. It seems likely that, with the shelving of the proposed partnership, Keir continued to act as an unpaid manager at Soho to the detriment of his own business interests. But by 1781 Boulton and Keir had settled their business differences and remained affectionate friends.

On the opening of the purpose-built steam engine factory, Soho Foundry, in 1796 Watt effectively retired from active business, though he remained a partner with Boulton and their respective sons. The company became known as Boulton, Watt & Sons from 1795 to 1800 and on Watt's formal retirement in 1800, Boulton, Watt & Co. The sale of steam engines to overseas customers and the attempts to obtain overseas patents were greatly facilitated by Boulton's mercantile connections as well as by his skilful networking.

Soho Mint and assay office While the steam engine business was the most lucrative of Boulton's business adventures, it was the mint that appears to have given him most satisfaction. A mint to supply copper coinage to the government was established at Soho Manufactory. Towards the end of the eighteenth century Boulton undertook the supply of complete mints for overseas customers, the first one being the imperial mint in St Petersburg. Other orders followed and one of his last commissions before his death was the new Royal Mint in London. It was particularly for his mint interests that he sought out expert engravers and die-sinkers from continental Europe to enhance the level of skill at Soho Manufactory. By means of his mint machinery and the flow-production system in which it was deployed he achieved greater accuracy in the finished product.

Boulton's political and negotiating skills are demonstrated in his advice to Watt on the application to parliament for the twenty-five-year extension to the 1769 patent, in the persistence with which those who pirated the steam engine were pursued through the courts in the 1790s, in the creative solution to the export of steam engine parts to France when Britain was at war with that country, in the successful petition for the establishment of an assay office in Birmingham, and in his role in the establishment of the General Chamber of Manufacturers. This organization was intended to be a permanent one, representing the interests of manufacturers nationally. It was short-lived, however, the focus for its endeavours being opposition to the younger William Pitt's proposals for preferential trade between England and Ireland. A modified bill was passed but the Irish parliament had already rejected the English alterations. When Pitt planned a trade agreement with France in 1786, he refused to consult with the General Chamber of Manufacturers as an organization, though he did consult Wedgwood and Boulton, among others, on an individual basis.

Boulton and other manufacturers of silver plate in Birmingham sent their wares to York, Chester, or London for hallmarking prior to being sold. This resulted in delays and sometimes in damage to the goods. Boulton took the lead in the actions which finally resulted in an act of parliament for the establishment of a Birmingham assay office. Birmingham and Sheffield agreed to collaborate rather than compete, with the result that offices were established in both towns. The Birmingham office was opened in 1773 and Boulton was the first manufacturer to use its facilities.

Boulton played a significant role in Birmingham's public life. There was a strong element of self-interest in his promotion of canals, for not only was he an investor but he also depended on canals for transporting engine parts. Moreover, Boulton and Watt pumping engines were purchased by a number of canal companies, particularly those in the midlands. His contributions to the establishment of the general hospital and the dispensary, and his involvement in the Theatre Royal, the new façade of which was designed by his friend Samuel Wyatt, are evidence of his wider social contribution. He became high sheriff of Staffordshire in 1795.

Final years and assessment Towards the end of his life Boulton suffered from stones in the kidneys. He endured considerable pain but even when confined to his room did not cease work. In 1802, seven years before he died, he told a banker, 'My doctors say my only chance of continuing in this World depends on my living quiet in it' (Boulton to Harts, 28 March 1802, Matthew Boulton MS 1788, box H). He died of kidney failure at Soho House, Handsworth, Birmingham, on 17 August 1809. His funeral, 'furnished in the handsomest manner avoiding ostentation' (Dickinson, 192), took place on 24 August, and he was buried in St Mary's Church, Handsworth.

Both Watt and Keir wrote brief memoirs of Boulton. To Watt he was 'not only an ingenious mechanick, well skilled in all the practices of the Birmingham manufacturers, but possessed in a high degree the faculty of rendering any new invention of his own or others useful to the public, by organising & arranging the processes by which it could be carried on' (Dickinson, 203). To this Keir added that Boulton was 'proof of how much scientific knowledge may be acquired without much regular study, by means of a quick & just apprehension, much practical application, and nice mechanical feelings' (ibid., 197).

Of above medium height, Boulton had grey eyes and a slightly receding forehead. He was impulsive, ebullient, and a risk taker. His insights into industrial organization and his ability to realize them were of a high order. Yet he had business failures as well as successes. He did not heed warnings from friends or colleagues when he did not appreciate the message. As Keir said, 'whatever he did or attempted, his success or his failure were all on a large scale' (Dickinson, 196).

Boulton was one of the leading innovating entrepreneurs of the industrial revolution. He found conversation easy, enjoyed entertaining, and was a gracious host. The list of visitors to Soho is a roll-call of British and foreign nobility, many of whom sat at Boulton's table and visited his manufactory. Yet, like Josiah Wedgwood, he produced for the mass market, as well as the aristocratic market, instructing his London agent to promote the goods as widely as possible: 'We think it of far more consequence to supply the people than the nobility only; and though you speak contemptuously of Hawkers, Pedlars and those who supply *Petty* shops, yet we must own that we think they will do more towards supporting a great manufactory, than all the Lords in the Nation' (Dickinson, 39).

Still known today for his support of James Watt and the manufacture of steam engines, Boulton was equally interested in producing fine bronze products for an ever-expanding consumer society. One of the most important and astute of Birmingham manufacturers, his enterprises contributed to an industrial revolution that was 'quintessentially industrial, commercial and urban' (O'Brien, 786). JENNIFER TANN

Sources H. W. Dickinson, *Matthew Boulton* (1937) · J. Watt, *Memorandum concerning Mr Boulton* (1809) · J. Keir, *Memoir of Matthew Boulton … December 3, 1809*, ed. L. Jay (privately printed, Birmingham, 1947) · J. L. Moilliet and B. M. D. Smith, *A mighty chemist: James Keir of the Lunar Society* (privately printed, 1982) · S. Smiles, *Lives of Boulton and Watt* (1865) · A. E. Musson and E. Robinson, *Science and technology in the industrial revolution* (1969) · J. Tann, *Birmingham assay office* (1993) · N. Goodison, *Ormolu: the work of Matthew Boulton* (1974) · M. J. Daunton, *Progress and poverty: an economic and social history of Britain, 1700–1850* (1995) · E. Robinson, 'Matthew Boulton and the art of parliamentary lobbying', *HJ*, 7 (1964), 209–29 · P. K. O'Brien, 'Agriculture and the home market for English industry, 1660–1820', *EngHR*, 100 (1985), 773–99 · *JHC*, 28 (1757–61), 901 · Birm. CL, Matthew Boulton MSS · E. Robinson, 'Eighteenth century commerce and fashion: Matthew Boulton's marketing techniques', *Economic History Review*, 2nd ser., 16 (1963–4), 39–60

Archives Birm. CL, personal and business corresp. and papers, diaries, and notebooks · Birm. CL, letters · RSA, letters to Royal Society of Arts | Birm. CL, letters to James Watt · BL, corresp with first earl of Liverpool; corresp. and papers relating to copper coinage, Add. MSS 38224–38331, 38421–38449, *passim*

Likenesses C. F. von Breda, oils, 1792 (replica), Birmingham Museum and Art Gallery [*see illus.*] · C. F. von Breda, mezzotint, pubd 1796 (after S. W. Reynolds), BM, NPG · W. Beechey, miniature, 1801, NPG · W. Sharp, line print, pubd 1801 (after W. Beechey), BM, NPG · S. Brown, paste medallion, 1807, NPG · L. F. Abbott, oils, Birmingham Museum and Art Gallery · J. Flaxman, marble bust on monument, St Mary's Church, Handsworth, Birmingham · B. Pistrucci, wax medallion, BM · oils, NPG

Boulton, Richard (*bap.* 1674, *d. c.*1724), medical writer, the son of Ralph Boulton, of Chester, and Agnes Brown, was baptized at Ince, Wigan, Lancashire, on 3 December 1674. He matriculated at Brasenose College, Oxford, on 29 November 1697. Boulton was already well versed in medical texts, publishing *A Treatise of the Reason of Muscular Motion* in 1697 and composing another treatise. John Meare, principal of Brasenose, urged Arthur Charlett, master of University College, to lend Boulton help. On 11 February 1698 Charlett wrote to Hans Sloane that Boulton had laboured hard at the books of 'your faculty', desiring to 'become an Early Author', but that because Boulton was only 'a Poor Servitor', he had never had the chance to see patients. Perhaps the letter helped Boulton's second work, *A Treatise Concerning the Heat of the Blood*, to earn the imprimatur of the College of Physicians, London, on 5 March 1698. Dedicated to Meare, the treatise took respectful exception to Thomas Willis's view that heat in the blood was caused by sulphurous particles, advancing instead the mechanical explanation that heat was rarefied matter in swift motion.

By 18 May 1698 Boulton felt able to approach the influential physician Charles Goodall by letter. Goodall replied on 26 May via a third party, asking Boulton to come to London to help with a work of natural history. Near the end of the summer Boulton arrived in London; Goodall asked him to work on books against opponents of the College of Physicians, in return for room and board, and Goodall's influence in advancing Boulton's medical career. Boulton attacked one of the thorns in Goodall's side in *An Examination of Mr John Colbatch* (1698); but he could not resist adding to it an appendix against a pamphlet printed by Charles Leigh, a physician from Manchester, who had attacked the reasoning of Boulton's work on heat in the blood, going on to compare him to the London empiric Gideon Harvey and to Rabelais's Pantagruel. Boulton's appendix replied that Leigh's pamphlet would serve a purpose only in a 'bog-house', although 'most People are afraid of fouling their Fingers with a Piece of Paper the Doctor hath dirty'd already'. Needless to say, Leigh took high exception to such remarks from an Oxford student, and hearing who had backed Boulton, wrote to Goodall. Goodall replied to Leigh in a letter dated 6 December, disowning Boulton, who confronted his patron, only to be kicked out of Goodall's house. To Leigh's *Reply to Mr Richard Bolton* (1698), further cutting at Boulton and printing Goodall's letter, Boulton responded with *A Letter to Dr Charles Goodall* (dated 18 January 1699), which reviewed Goodall's turncoat and underhanded behaviour. Goodall tried to destroy Boulton by publishing *A Two-Penny Answer to R. Boulton's Six-Penny Letter to Dr Charles Goodall* (1699), said to be from William Wilkinson, his footman. It compared Boulton to some famous London quacks and to religious radicals, such as 'W. Pen, G. Whitehead, or one of Muggleton's Successors'. The controversy spread, and when the well-known William Salmon weighed in on Boulton's side, Goodall or one of his defenders replied in turn in the *Post Boy* of 14 February 1699, with an advertisement asking that two quacks be brought to Bedlam (Bethlem Hospital): the first Salmon, the second Boulton, who was described as:

> an odd contriv'd sort of a Country Clown, in a grey Coat, which he cannot change for want of another; … wears his own hair; late of *Brazen Nose* and still of *Brazen Face*; being Impudent, proud, insolent, Atheistical, silly senceless, and a most abominable Lyer, Betrayer of his Trust, and a notorious Contriver and Fomenter of Mischief; with the several signs of a Madman following.

Boulton had obviously fallen into difficulties, and turned to publishing to support himself: he brought out *A System of Rational and Practical Chirurgery* in 1699 and *The*

Works of the Hon. Robert Boyle Epitomised in three volumes, from April 1699 to 1700. According to Wilkinson's *Two-Penny Answer*, the advance offered by the publisher for the Boyle epitome gave Boulton the wherewithal to print his *Letter to Goodall*; Boulton also wrote to Sloane that he undertook the epitome on account of 'misfortunes still attending' him. He later begged Sloane to help him find a way to make a living. He may have turned to medical practice, for between 1714 and 1724 he brought out four more medico-surgical works: a treatise on gout, the king's evil, and venereal disease; a work on external remedies; an essay on plague; and *Some Thoughts Concerning the Unusual Qualities of the Air* (1724). He also published *A Vindication of the Compleat History of Magick* (1722), in which he mentions that he had been out of England for some time. The date of Boulton's death is unknown. HAROLD J. COOK

Sources BL, Sloane MSS • R. Boulton, *An answer to Dr Leigh's remarks* (1698) • R. Boulton, *An examination of Mr John Colbatch, his books* (1698) • R. Boulton, *A letter to Dr Charles Goodall* (1699) • C. Leigh, *Reply to Mr Richard Bolton* (1698) • C. Leigh, *Remarks on Mr Richard Bolton's piece* (1698) • *Post Boy* (14 Feb 1699) • W. Wilkinson, *A two-penny answer to R. Boulton's six-penny letter to Dr Charles Goodall, &c.* (1699) • Foster, *Alum. Oxon.* • H. J. Cook, *Trials of an ordinary doctor: Joannes Groenevelt in 17th-century London* (1994) • IGI

Boulton, Samuel (*fl.* 1656), medical writer, about whom virtually nothing is known, published a work entitled *Medicina magica tamen physica: magical, but natural physick, or, A methodical tractate of diastastical physick*, at London, in 1656. The work was re-issued in 1665. Since he is designated on the title page as 'Samuel Boulton, Salop', it seems reasonable to assume that he was born or at least lived in Shropshire, but it is impossible to say more. In his preface 'To the Reader', dated May 1656 and signed as from London, Boulton says that he was induced to publish the work as a result of a 'short, yet violent fit of sicknesse' (Boulton, sig. A4*r*). Claiming that the work had hitherto been scattered in several places in a small octavo notebook, and on loose sheets, and that some of it was written in 'Characterical figures, only for occultnesse sake', he realized that, had he died, the work would have been either lost or 'never digested into any methodical order' because of the 'confused and occult writing'. He also tells his readers that the work had been written some ten years before, but given what he says about its not being ready for publication until after this life-threatening illness, the date of May 1646 after the dedicatory epistle to the marquess of Dorchester is presumably nothing more than a misprint. This dedication tells readers that Boulton had not acquired Dorchester's 'consent or license', that he knew of Dorchester's interest in 'Aesculapian Mysteries' only from various acquaintances, and that he did not otherwise know him.

In spite of Boulton's detailed description of the state of the work before he finally prepared it for the press, there are good grounds for doubting that he wrote anything but the introductory matter. Chapters 1 to 32 are copied almost entirely verbatim from an anonymous manuscript now in the Sloane collection of the British Library (Sloane MS 1321). This manuscript is as well ordered as Boulton's published version, and none of it is written in secret writing. It seems unsafe to hold it to be the fair and ordered copy of Boulton's confused papers when he first decided to publish, however, since there is no sign of the dedicatory epistle, preface, or introductory chapter, nor of Boulton's extra chapters, 33 and 34.

Boulton 'ingenuously' confesses in his preface that he did not write all of the book, being indebted for what he calls 'some part thereof' (Boulton, sig. A4*v*) to some loose papers of 'an unknown Mr.' which were communicated to him by his close friend, Mr M. B., a 'worthy Gentleman of Kent'. Boulton says that he and his friend believed these loose papers to have been written by 'that late worthy and Reverend chymist Dr. Everard'—presumably John Everard (*c.*1575–*c.*1650), the first English translator of the Hermetic *Poemander*—but he does not say what grounds he has for this belief.

The first twelve chapters of Boulton's book provide a clearly expounded theoretical account of so-called magnetic or diastatic medicine—an occult system of medicine in which medicaments are applied to shed blood, expelled bodily fluids or excrements, or even hair or nail parings, instead of to the sick or injured body itself. It was believed that effluvia or subtle spirits exuding from such bodily excretions were attracted back towards their bodily source and could carry fine particles of the medicaments deep into the body, where they could more efficaciously effect a cure than if the same medicaments were applied directly to the body. Chapters 13 to 32 describe the more practical aspects of this kind of healing. Chapters 33 and 34, which do not appear in the anonymous manuscript, provide lists of herbs and plants which are supposed, by their signatures, to affect certain parts of the body or certain diseases. One or two internal features of these chapters seem to suggest that they too have been copied from another source; certainly there is nothing original in their content. This leaves only the introductory chapter as original to Boulton. Here Boulton defends this kind of medicine as being based upon 'true (yet sublime) natural causes' (Boulton, 2), locating it in the tradition of natural rather than diabolical magic, and insisting that it points the way to useful empirical investigations (ibid., 3). He also insists, with some justification, that this book provides 'the plainest and most methodicallest discourse of this Art, that hitherto is extant' (ibid., 4), having disparaged the earlier discussions of Paracelsus (1493–1541), Tenzelius (Andreas Tentzel; *fl.* 1625), and Dr Floyd, who was almost certainly Robert Fludd (1574–1637), as wrapped up in enigmas and clouds of obscurity. Even though so little is known of Boulton, the reader can conclude from the original part of his book that, like Nathaniel Highmore (1613–1685), for example, Boulton was one of those early modern thinkers who sought to separate what might be pragmatically useful in the natural magic tradition from the more fanciful, semeiological, and superstitious. JOHN HENRY

Sources S. Boulton, *Medicina magica tamen physica: magical, but natural physick, or, A methodical tractate of diastastical physick* (1656); repr.

(1665) • L. Thorndike, *A history of magic and experimental science*, 8 vols. (1923–58), vols. 7–8
Archives BL, Sloane MSS

Bouquet, Henry (1719–1765), army officer and military writer, was born at Rolle in the Pays de Vaud, Switzerland. In 1736 he joined the regiment of Constant in the service of the states general of the United Provinces as a cadet, and in 1738 became an ensign. He distinguished himself while serving with the Sardinian forces in the War of the Austrian Succession, and in 1748 was appointed captain-commandant and lieutenant-colonel of a new regiment of Swiss guards which had been raised by the prince of Orange at The Hague. After liaising with the French in their evacuation of captured Dutch territory, he accompanied Lord Middleton on a tour of France and Italy.

At this time, close-order, linear formations formed the backbone of European armies' tactical systems. But when fighting erupted between France and Britain in America in 1754 their inapplicability to many operations in colonial theatres was quickly revealed. Indeed, the need for light troops capable of countering irregular opponents using sniper rather than volley fire and operating in forested, enclosed, or otherwise broken terrain was highlighted as early as July 1755, when a column of redcoats under General Edward Braddock was destroyed by French skirmishers and Native Americans. Although superior in numbers, Braddock's men, deployed in serried ranks in keeping with the nostrums of European battlefield tactics, proved no match for their dispersed, elusive opponents, who, firing at will and exploiting any available cover, picked off officers and men with virtual impunity.

The British, however, learned from this disaster and soon began supplementing existing small bodies of Canadian auxiliaries and friendly Native Americans with new units which were specifically designed with the realm of *la petite guerre*—the war of outposts, patrols, and skirmishes—in mind. Bouquet, along with another Swiss soldier of fortune, Frederick Haldimand, took command of one such unit, the 60th Royal American regiment. Comprising several battalions, this was specially trained for the 'service of the woods'. After playing a key role in the defence of Virginia and Pennsylvania, in 1763–4 Bouquet was entrusted with two expeditions from Canada. In the first, he was ordered to relieve Fort Pitt. This he duly did, beating off a powerful body of Native Americans near Turtle Creek on 5 August. The 1764 expedition also pitted him against such opponents; striking against the Ohio tribes, he triumphed at Bushy Run and ultimately compelled the Shawanese and Delaware to sue for terms. He was appointed brigadier-general and commandant of all the troops in British America's southern colonies, but he perished at Pensacola, Florida, in an epidemic in the autumn of 1765.

Bouquet's successes against irregular foes contrasted starkly with Braddock's defeat only eight years before. But Bouquet's ruminations on the theory of *la petite guerre* were as significant as his part in its practice. Indeed, persuaded that aptitude had to be moulded by theory, he applied this principle to his innovative training of the 60th regiment. Of all the works produced by the Enlightenment's military thinkers, he had found Count Turpin de Crisse's *Essai sur l'art de la guerre* (1754) particularly engrossing and was recommending it to his colleagues long before it was translated into English in 1761. An account of his own campaign against the Ohio tribes was composed by William Smith and published first in Philadelphia in 1765. A second edition appeared in London the following year, for which Bouquet provided an appendix on the training, tactics, and equipment of light infantry deployed in enclosed terrain against an irregular opponent. Though smaller than John Simcoe's *Operations of the Queen's Rangers* (1844) or Banastre Tarleton's *Southern Campaigns* (1787), his writings rank among the most noteworthy contributions to the illumination of mid-eighteenth-century colonial warfare. DAVID GATES

Sources D. Gates, *The British light infantry arm, c.1790–1815* (1987) • J. A. Houlding, *Fit for service: the training of the British army, 1715–1795* (1981) • W. Smith, *An historical account of the expedition against the Ohio indians in MDCCLXIV* (1766) • D. J. Beattie, 'The adaptation of the British army to wilderness-warfare, 1755–1763', *Adapting to conditions: war and society in the 18th century*, ed. M. Ultee (1986)
Archives BL, corresp. and papers, Add. MSS 21631–21660 • Hunt. L., orderly book • U. Mich., Clements L., orderly books | PRO, corresp. with commander-in-chief in North America, WO34 • U. Mich., Clements L., corresp. with Thomas Gage
Wealth at death see inventory and will, BL, Add. MS 21660

Bouquet, Philip (1670/71–1748), Hebrew scholar, was the son of Thomas Bouquet of La Rochelle, France. He was educated at Westminster School and admitted a pensioner at Trinity College, Cambridge, on 12 June 1689, aged eighteen. Having been elected a scholar in 1690 he graduated BA in 1693 and proceeded MA (1696), BD (1706), and DD (1711). He was elected fellow of his college in 1696 and was ordained priest on 14 March 1703. In 1704 he was temporarily appointed regius professor of Hebrew, in the absence of Henry Sike, the eminent oriental scholar for whom the post was reserved. Sike was elected in August 1705 but, following his death seven years later, Bouquet was elected to fill the chair permanently. He was a tenacious ally of the controversial master of Trinity, Richard Bentley, and refused to sign the petition against him. He was described by the Cambridge antiquary William Cole as 'a meagre, thin man, bent partly double, and for his oddities and way of living was much ridiculed' (BL, Cole MSS).

Bouquet contributed a copy of elegiacs to the university collection of poems on the death of George I and the accession of George II in 1727. He died, senior fellow of Trinity, on 12 February 1748 and was buried in the college chapel on 16 February. According to Cole he left his considerable wealth to French refugees.

JAMES MEW, *rev.* S. J. SKEDD

Sources Venn, *Alum. Cant.* • *Old Westminsters* • *GM*, 1st ser., 18 (1748), 92 • J. H. Monk, *The life of Richard Bentley, DD*, 2nd edn, 1 (1833), 186, 329–30 • BL, Cole MSS

Bourbon, Nicholas (*c.*1503–1549/50), poet and religious reformer, known as Nicholas Bourbon the elder to distinguish him from his namesake and nephew, was the son of

Nicholas Bourbon (*c*.1503–1549/50), by Hans Holbein the younger

Jean Bourbon, an ironmaster from Vandoeuvre in Champagne, and his wife, Marie Galliard (or Gaulier). He studied at the Collège de Troyes, where he met a future patron, Jean de Dinteville. For some time secretary to the bishop of Viviers, Bourbon moved in 1531 to teach and write in Paris. He chose Latin as his vehicle, not the vernacular, which explains why his work has become little known, but his contemporary reputation was endorsed by Erasmus himself. His first book of epigrams, *Nicolai Borbonii Vandoperani nugae* ('Trifles by Nicolas Bourbon of Vandoeuvre'), was published in Paris in 1533. On the reforming wing of French thinking along with his friend Clément Marot, Bourbon savaged the opponents of humanism and reform in his witticisms. He was arrested, brought before the *parlement* of Paris, and imprisoned. His release in March 1534 was on a personal order from François I, conditional on his admitting that his book had gone too far and being warned to be careful. If this humiliation was not enough, the prisoner emerged to find his possessions looted, including his pet nightingale.

As Bourbon's verses make clear, François had responded to an approach from Henry VIII prompted by Anne Boleyn. How she heard about him must be conjectured. He names his contact in England as the king's physician, William Butts, one of the queen's reformist allies, but also hints at Jean de Dinteville, by now several times an envoy to England and a favourite of Anne. Needing to lie low and confident of his reception, Bourbon travelled to England and lodged with Cornelius Hayes, the king's goldsmith, whose wife clearly attracted him. Through Hayes he met many of the foreign experts at Henry VIII's court: Thomas Berthelet, the king's printer, Thomas Soulement, his French secretary, Nicholas Kratzer, the astronomer, and Hans Holbein the younger.

Anne Boleyn recruited Bourbon to teach the children of her circle. These included her nephew Henry Carey, the younger Henry Norris, Henry, the son of John Dudley, and Thomas, the son of Nicholas Harvey, England's ambassador to Charles V. For them Bourbon wrote his second book, the *Paedagogion*, published at Lyons in 1536. He also continued to produce epigrams; nearly fifty of these were written about England, addressed to English people, or composed there. His verses were primarily exercises in form not content, although he did celebrate Cromwell's appointment as vice regent and credit the consecration of Bishop Hugh Latimer to 'the king and Queen Anne who suppress the unworthy and promote the deserving' (*Nugarum libri octo*, 393). What makes the *Nugae* significant, however, is the light it throws on the reformist network at the English court. The queen herself figures in six poems and joins the king in another. There are three verses for Cranmer, two for Cromwell, and one for them together. Latimer is the subject of two poems, as are John Dudley and Henry Knyvet of the privy chamber. Butts gets several mentions in prose as well as verse. So does William Benson (or Boston), abbot of Westminster, whom Bourbon clearly saw as a kingpin of the reformist camp. Bourbon also named Thomas Goodrich, Thomas Thirlby, Francis Bryan, and possibly Henry Norris senior.

Only one of Bourbon's poems, 'De Moribus cui titulus', is hostile to its subject, punning on the name of Sir Thomas More and the two Greek words *moros* ('foolish') and *okumore* ('bubble'). In it Bourbon claims to have met More, most probably when the latter was in William Benson's custody, and he records what may be a genuine pun by Sir Thomas on his stubborn silence: 'I am *Moros* and so safe' (*Nugarum libri octo*, 310).

On his father's death in 1535 Bourbon returned to France to find the religious atmosphere tense following the 'affair of the placards'. He therefore settled away from the *parlement* of Paris, initially at Lyons, where he was tutor to the children of the Gagagne banking family. At Lyons in 1538 he collected his work, including the 1533 *Nugae* and the *Paedagogion*, under the title *Nicolai Borbonii Vandoperani Lingonensis nugarum libri octo ac auctore rescens aucti et recogniti* ('Eight books of trifles by Nicholas Borbonius of Lyons, the Vandoeuvrian, recently enlarged and revised'). Significantly, he did not suppress poems in praise of Queen Anne. He also kept up his association with Holbein, writing verses for the 1539 Lyons publication of the artist's *Historiarum veteris instrumenti iconis*.

Bourbon was then engaged by Marguerite d'Angoulême, queen of Navarre, as tutor to her daughter Jeanne d'Albret, the future mother of Henri IV. In 1539 he wrote for her *Tabellae elementariae pueris ingenuis pernecessariae* and in 1549 an epithalamium on her marriage with Antoine de Bourbon. After Jeanne's marriage Bourbon is said to have retired to a small benefice at Candé, where he was dead by 1550. A chalk likeness by Holbein is extant at Windsor and a woodcut possibly from the (lost) finished painting serves as a colophon to the 1536 *Paedagogion*, with the puff, 'Mantua boasts of Virgil and Greece of Homer, the region of Lyons rejoices in Borbonius'. Dated 1535, it records Bourbon's age as thirty-two. E. W. IVES

Sources *Dictionnaire de biographie française*, 6 (Paris, 1954) • *Nicolai Borbonii Vandoperani nugae* (Paris, 1533) • N. Bourbon, *Paedagogion* (Lyons, 1536) • *Nicolai Borbonii Vandoperani Lingonensis nugarum libri octo* (Lyons, 1538) • E. Lodge, *Biographical and historical memoirs attached to portraits* (1821–34) • E. Saulnier, 'Recherches sur N. Bourbon l'ancien', *Bibl. de l'Humanisme et de la Reform*, 16 (1954), 172–91 • C. Lauvergnat-Gagnière, *Lucien de Samosate et lucienisme en France au xvieme siècle* (Geneva, 1988) • O. Bätschman and P. Griener, *Hans Holbein* (1997) • M. M. Philips, 'The *Paedagogion* of Nicholas Bourbon', *Neo-Latin and the vernacular in 16th-C. France* (1983) • E. W. Ives, 'A Frenchman at the court of Anne Boleyn', *History Today*, 48/8 (1998), 21–6

Likenesses H. Holbein the younger, chalk drawing, Royal Collection [*see illus.*] • woodcut, repro. in Bourbon, *Paedagogion*, title-page

Bourchier, Arthur (1863–1927), actor and theatre manager, was born on 22 June 1863 in Spen, near Newbury, Berkshire, the only son of Charles John Bourchier, a captain in the 8th hussars, and his wife, Fanny, daughter of James Farr, a draper. In 1877 he went to Eton, where he excelled at drama, before going up to Christ Church, Oxford in 1882. After a roving university career, during which he migrated to New Inn Hall in 1884, was attached to Balliol in 1887 (when New Inn Hall was incorporated in that college), and migrated again to Charsley's Hall in 1888, he returned to Christ Church to graduate with a pass degree (BA) in 1888 and an MA in 1889. Once at Oxford he was soon on the committee of the dramatic club, the Philothespians, and appearing as Sir John Vesey in Bulwer Lytton's *Money*. In 1883 the club, of which Bourchier was then president, was formally recognized by the university. He played Shylock in *The Merchant of Venice* later that year and early in 1884 was the prime mover in founding the Oxford University Dramatic Society (OUDS), which succeeded the Philothespians. In early 1885 he played Hotspur in its production of *1 Henry IV*. The New theatre in Oxford was established in February 1886; it opened with an OUDS performance of *Twelfth Night*, Bourchier playing Feste. His subsequent roles at Oxford included Death in *Alcestis* (1887), Falstaff in *The Merry Wives of Windsor* (1888), and Brutus in *Julius Caesar* (1889). He also acted with the Windsor Strollers and the Old Stagers.

After he joined Lillie Langtry's company, Bourchier's first professional appearance was in September 1889 at the Theatre Royal, Wolverhampton, as Jaques in *As You Like It*. He toured in a number of plays before making his London début in the same role at the St James's. He briefly took on the management of this theatre, opening in June 1890 as Jack Daryll in *Your Wife*. For some years following, Bourchier appeared at various London theatres and spent a season (1892–3) with Augustin Daly in New York. In 1894 he married Violet Augusta Mary Barnes (1867–1942), the actress Violet *Vanbrugh, who became his leading lady in many productions. They had one daughter. In 1895 he assumed management of the Royalty, opening in September as Sir Reginald Delamere in *The Chili Widow*. He toured in the USA in 1896–7 before returning to London and one of his best roles, *Dr Johnson*, at the Strand. Wyndham's theatre opened in November 1899 with *David Garrick*, in which Bourchier played Squire Chevy. In early 1900 he became joint manager, with Charles Wyndham, of the Criterion, and in September he became manager of the Garrick where, over the next six years, he oversaw a run of many successful productions, including *The Cricket on the Hearth* (1903), *The Merchant of Venice* (1905), and *Macbeth* (1906), as well as new plays by Arthur Wing Pinero, W. S. Gilbert, Anthony Hope, and Alfred Sutro. In November 1902 he appeared by royal command in *Dr Johnson* before Edward VII at Sandringham, and similarly in November 1905 in *The Merchant of Venice* at Windsor. In 1910 he joined Sir Herbert Beerbohm Tree at His Majesty's, and appeared in numerous Shakespearian roles including Bottom in *A Midsummer Night's Dream*, Brutus in *Julius Caesar* and Sir Toby Belch in *Twelfth Night*. He scored a particular success as the king in *Henry VIII*.

Throughout the rest of his career Bourchier's pace never slowed and there were many highlights. In 1911 he appeared as Stout in a command performance of *Money* at Drury Lane and he was the organizing secretary of a gala performance of *The Critic* at His Majesty's, appearing himself as Puff. Also in 1911 he appeared in the title role in the film *Henry VIII*, and in 1913 he not only appeared on screen as *Macbeth* but also directed the film. In 1913 he played Mark Meddle in an 'all-star' revival of *London Assurance* at the St James's in aid of King George's Actors' pension fund; he also played *Henry VIII* for the same fund at His Majesty's in 1915. In 1914 he played Henry VIII in *Bluff King Hal* at the Garrick. In 1916 he again played Brutus, in an 'all-star' *Julius Caesar* at Drury Lane for the Shakespeare tercentenary. In 1917 he had a particular success as Old Bill the soldier in *The Better 'Ole* at the Oxford music-hall, where it ran for over 800 performances. And in 1920 he was a notable Iago to Matheson Lang's *Othello* at the New. There were further spells of management—of the Garrick (1912–14), of His Majesty's (1916), and of the Strand (1919–23), where, in 1922, he appeared as Long John Silver in *Treasure Island*. He toured with this in 1923, reappearing in it at the Strand in December both that year and the following year.

After his divorce from Violet Vanbrugh in 1917, Bourchier married on 24 December 1918 Violet Marion Kyrle Bellew (*b*. 1887), the actress Kyrle Bellew, daughter of Louis Hance Falck, solicitor, and previously the wife of Allen Martin Reuben Nicholson. They had no children. She too appeared in some of his productions.

Believing himself to be a representative of old theatrical tradition, Bourchier could be overbearing, even dictatorial, in his managerial style, and he was loth to brook criticism, thinking much of his own talents. Yet Bourchier's enthusiasm was as hard to deny as his impatience. While the line he took could often be deemed misguided, as an actor he was never dull, for he had 'an invincible tendency to play for broad effect and to sacrifice delicacy of drawing to richness of colour' (*The Times*, 15 Sept 1927).

Bourchier adapted many plays for production through

the years, and as well as being a patron of theatrical causes he was equally generous towards war charities. Away from the theatre he enjoyed cricket, golf, tennis, cycling, and motoring. Later in life he was interested in politics, and in 1926 he wrote a pamphlet for the Independent Labour Party on *Art and Culture in Relation to Socialism*. At the time of his death he was the prospective Labour Party parliamentary candidate for the city of Gloucester.

In February 1927 Bourchier and his company left England for a tour of South Africa. He fell ill in Johannesburg in September with double pneumonia, and died there in Joubert Park Nursing Home on 14 September 1927. His wife survived him. He was cremated at Johannesburg cemetery on 17 September, and his ashes were interred in the Bourchier family vault at Kensal Green cemetery.

ROBERT SHARP

Sources *DNB* · *WWW* · *Who was who in the theatre, 1912–1976*, 1 (1978) · *The Times* (15 Sept 1927), 14 · *The Labour who's who* (1927) · m. cert. [Kyrle Bellew] · *The Times* (16 Sept 1927), 10

Archives SOUND BL NSA, documentary recordings · BL NSA, performance recordings

Likenesses C. Buchel, watercolour, 1905, Strand Theatre, London · C. Buchel, oils, 1906, Royal Shakespeare Theatre, Stratford upon Avon · C. Buchel, oils, 1910, Strand Theatre, London · G. Kelly, oils, 1923, Garr. Club · F. Lascelles, bronze, 1927, probably priv. coll. · E. J. Macadam, death mask, 1927, Museum of Shakespeare Memorial Theatre · Ellis and Walery, photograph (as Shylock), NPG · H. Herkomer, oils, probably National Gallery, London · Histed, photogravure, NPG · Langfier, photograph, NPG · Spy [L. Ward], caricature, lithograph, NPG; repro. in *VF* (5 March 1896) · oils? (in *The bishop's move*), repro. in *Players of the day* (1902)

Wealth at death £16,277 19s. 10d.: probate, 3 Jan 1928, *CGPLA Eng. & Wales*

Bourchier, Henry, first earl of Essex (*c*.**1408–1483**), magnate, was the son of Sir William *Bourchier, count of Eu (*c*.1374–1420), and of *Anne of Woodstock (*c*.1382–1438), daughter of *Thomas of Woodstock, duke of Gloucester, and widow of two earls of Stafford. Although he was a great-grandson of Robert Bourchier, first Lord Bourchier (*d*. 1349), the first lay chancellor, Henry Bourchier was not in the direct line of succession to the barony of Bourchier, since his grandfather was Lord Robert's younger son. He was half-brother of Humphrey *Stafford, duke of Buckingham, and elder brother of Thomas, Cardinal *Bourchier, William, Lord Fitzwarine, John, Lord Berners, and Eleanor, duchess of Norfolk, all of whom benefited considerably from their mother's royal and aristocratic connections. In 1420 Henry succeeded his father in the French *comté* of Eu, but not yet in the estates in Essex and Suffolk brought to his family by his paternal grandmother, Eleanor Lovaine, for these remained in his mother's possession until her death. He was knighted at Leicester in May 1426, and after obtaining a papal dispensation he married, on 15 October following, at St Peter's Abbey, Gloucester, Isabel (*d*. 1484), the daughter of Richard, earl of Cambridge, and Anne, daughter of Roger Mortimer, earl of March. Isabel was the sister of Richard, duke of York (who gave her an annuity of £100), and the widow of Sir Thomas Grey of Heaton.

Bourchier's service as a military commander began the next year in the duke of Bedford's army in France, and he subsequently also took part in Henry VI's coronation expedition of 1430. Three years later, on the death without children of his kinswoman, Elizabeth, Lady Bourchier, he succeeded to the barony of Bourchier, and was henceforth summoned to parliament either as Lord Bourchier or (as in 1435) as count of Eu. When translating the latter title into English he referred to himself as 'earl', but contemporaries did not accord him precedence above his fellow barons. He may have taken part in the duke of Gloucester's expedition to relieve Calais in 1436, and in 1439 he was one of the diplomatic envoys sent there for peace negotiations. In 1441 he crossed the channel again, this time with a large force in support of his brother-in-law York, who appointed him captain of Neufchâtel and governor-general of the marches of Picardy. Before their departure from England Bourchier also contracted to serve for seven years as captain of the important border fortress of Le Crotoy. The crisis at the exchequer brought about by over-assignment of revenues meant that payment of his salary, set at £1000 p.a., quickly fell into arrears and he was long the crown's creditor, although he eventually recouped some of his losses when he took over as treasurer of England. As reward for his military services he was created Viscount Bourchier during the parliament of 1445–6, and elected knight of the Garter on his third nomination in 1452.

The influence of Buckingham, who always stayed loyal to Henry VI, perhaps counterbalanced Bourchier's links with the increasingly dissatisfied York, whom he served as a councillor. During York's first protectorate in 1454 he assumed a prominent role as a member of the royal council, working in close association with his brother, Thomas, now archbishop of Canterbury, and that summer he was sent to Calais to conduct difficult negotiations with the mutinous garrison. Although it is unclear whether he fought at the battle of St Albans on the Yorkist side, or, intending to do so, arrived the next day in company with his other brother-in-law, Norfolk, he was appointed treasurer just a week later, on 29 May 1455. He and his brother Thomas, the chancellor, both held office until October 1456, when they were 'sodenly discharged' owing to pressure brought to bear on the king by Margaret of Anjou (Davis, 2.165). Certain of Bourchier's sons were retained by their uncle York, but it was not until two of them were attainted with the duke in the parliament of 1459 that Bourchier himself came out in open support of the Yorkist exiles. He fought on their side at Northampton in July 1460, and immediately after their victory he was again appointed treasurer. Even so, he probably did not favour the outright deposition of Henry VI until after the deaths of York and his own son, Edward, at Wakefield in December 1460. He fled the battlefield at St Albans in February 1461 after the Lancastrians won the day, and was among those who set Edward, then earl of March (his wife's nephew), on the throne on 3 March 1461, and advanced with him to Towton.

Edward IV, as he had thus become, confirmed Bourchier in office as treasurer, and on 30 June 1461 created him earl of Essex. His close attendance on the king brought him considerable royal patronage, notably grants of estates forfeited by the earls of Wiltshire and Oxford, in part to compensate him and his wife for an unfulfilled bequest of Isabel's uncle Edmund, earl of March (*d.* 1425), whose heir was now king. Although replaced as treasurer in April 1462, in the next year he carried out important administrative work at Calais and served on an embassy to St Omer for negotiations with France and Burgundy. As steward of the household for at least three years from May 1467 or earlier he stood by Edward throughout the political crises of the late 1460s, and was arrested when Henry VI was restored in the autumn of 1470. After secretly working for Edward's reinstatement and mediating between him and his rebellious brother, Clarence, he raised Essex in his support in April 1471. Having welcomed Edward back to London, he substantially reinforced the royal army, in which, at Barnet, his son and heir apparent, Humphrey, Lord Cromwell, was killed. He then successfully defended the capital against the Kentish rebels led by Thomas Neville, the Bastard of Fauconberg. The influence of Bourchier's family in south-east England was of critical importance for the re-establishment of Edward IV's authority and the stability of the second part of his reign. Edward placed a heavy reliance on his uncle, not only as a councillor and in military matters (as when, in 1473, Bourchier forced the earl of Oxford to re-embark following his landing at St Osyth), but as treasurer and chief steward of the duchy of Lancaster in the south for the full twelve years. Bourchier acted temporarily as keeper of the great seal in 1473 during the chancellor's illness. This was evidently a time of prosperity for him, for he profited from his offices, in particular the treasurership, and from his investments in overseas trade. He dealt extensively in wool and cloth produced on his own estates, as well as in Cornish tin, and imported luxury goods from the Mediterranean. The king confirmed him and his countess in possession of the lordship of Tyndale and Wark, Northumberland, settled on Isabel long before by her uncle Edward, duke of York, and Bourchier's inherited estates gave him at least £1400 a year.

Bourchier died on 4 April 1483, just five days before the king, and was buried at Beeleigh Abbey. His tomb, which later also housed his widow (who survived until 2 October 1484), was subsequently removed to Little Easton church. In furtherance of his dynastic ambitions he had acquired wives for his sons from the ranks of the peerage. Henry (*d.* 1458) was matched with Elizabeth, daughter and heir of Thomas *Scales, seventh Baron Scales, and Humphrey with a niece and coheir of Ralph, Lord Cromwell; while Sir John and Sir Thomas both married rich widows, those of Lord Ferrers of Groby and Humphrey Stafford, earl of Devon. But four of his six sons predeceased him, three of them without surviving children, so he was succeeded by a grandson, also Henry *Bourchier, the child of his son William and Anne Woodville, the queen's sister.

LINDA CLARK

Sources L. S. Woodger, 'Henry Bourgchier, earl of Essex, and his family, 1408–83', DPhil diss., U. Oxf., 1974 • L. Clark, 'The benefits and burdens of office: Henry Bourgchier (1408–83), Viscount Bourgchier and earl of Essex, and the treasurership of the exchequer', *Profit, piety and the professions in later medieval England*, ed. M. A. Hicks (1990), 119–36 • HoP, *Commons, 1386–1421*, 2.315–17 • N. Davis, ed., *Paston letters and papers of the fifteenth century*, 2 vols. (1971–6) • CIPM, C 138/45/34 • CIPM, C 139/59/40 • CIPM, C 141/3/31, 141/7/35 • *Essex Review*, 36 (1927), 28 • chancery masters' exhibits, PRO, C 115/A3/K2/6682, fol. 179v

Archives marquess of Bath's library, Longleat House, Wiltshire, papers

Likenesses H. Addington, brass rubbing, BL, MS Add. 32490 N29 • brass tomb effigy, repro. in F. Chancellor, *Ancient sepulchral monuments of Essex* (1890), pl. 26

Wealth at death approx. £1400 p.a. from estates: estate papers; PRO, C 138/45/34; 139/59/40; 141/3/31; 141/7/35

Bourchier, Henry, second earl of Essex (1472–1540), magnate, was the son of Sir William Bourchier (*d.* 1483) and his wife, Anne (*d.* 1489), daughter of Richard *Woodville (Wydeville), Earl Rivers. His father's death made Henry heir to his grandfather, Henry *Bourchier, first earl of Essex, who died later in 1483. His inherited position was strong in both political and dynastic terms: his grandfather had been a leading Yorkist councillor, his great-uncle Thomas *Bourchier was archbishop of Canterbury, and through his mother he was first cousin to Henry VII's queen Elizabeth. His background fitted him for a central place at the new Tudor court and he was duly prominent in all its great ceremonial occasions, from Henry's coronation in 1485 to Elizabeth's funeral in 1503 and beyond. As he reached maturity in the 1490s he also took a leading part in court jousts and revels. He sat occasionally in the king's council and was named to royal commissions but held no great responsibility in Henry's government. His limited aspirations perhaps helped to preserve him from the political turmoil that engulfed other aristocratic courtiers from 1501, but his service to Henry was not without reward in small grants of land and other favours.

Greater prospects beckoned with the accession of Henry VIII, who made Essex captain of his new guard, the king's spears, in November 1509 and constable of Windsor Castle in July 1511. For the first two years of the new reign Essex jousted and danced with the king as much as anyone, but thereafter he was supplanted by younger favourites. He last jousted at court in June 1517 and began a steady retreat into the life of a country peer. His military career equally never matched those of his forebears. He raised troops and fought loyally in France in 1492 and against the rebels of 1497; he oversaw musters in 1512 and contributed 469 men to Henry's French campaign of 1513, when he led a cavalry charge to rescue captured artillery. Yet in 1521, when his 'hardinesse' brought him to the king's mind as a possible commander for an expeditionary force, it was stressed that he would need 'sad [counsillors] adjoyned to hym', and he was not chosen (*State Papers, Henry VIII*, 1.32).

In the 1520s Essex still appeared at court on occasion, serving as marshal of the English party at the Field of Cloth of Gold in 1520, and attended some sessions of the council. But in the 1530s he generally turned out only for the greatest events. He was licensed to miss every session of the Reformation Parliament and he attended only sparsely in 1536 and 1539. Officially it was ill health and deafness that prevented his attendance, but he could be lively enough at home in Essex, whether on his own business or the king's. His household accounts for 1533/4 show him hunting and travelling between his houses, and in 1539 he reviewed coastal defences in the spring and oversaw the trial of the abbot of Colchester in December. Though his religion was conservative it does not seem to have been passionately so: it was more likely indifference than dissidence that kept him away from the centre of affairs.

At the local level Essex's influence rested on an unusually concentrated body of estates in Essex, Hertfordshire, and Suffolk, sufficient to generate a taxable income just below the mean for the peerage, at £568 11*s.* 2*d.* in 1523 and £850 in 1534. The main inheritance, of which he had livery in September 1493, had been reduced amid the complex politics of 1483–5 to less than half his grandfather's holdings at their peak, but it was subsequently complemented by lands inherited from his uncle Sir Thomas Bourchier in 1491 and from his mother in 1503 on the death of her second husband, the earl of Kent. Essex was not very active on the land market, but he did make some efforts to expand his estates further. His bid for the lands of dissolved Beeleigh Abbey, where his ancestors lay buried, was unsuccessful. More effective, but at the cost of considerable trouble, was his marriage to Mary, one of the two daughters and heirs of the Hertfordshire knight Sir William Say. Their marriage contract of 1497 promised them a share of Say's lands worth £200, but failed to specify which estates should make it up. In 1499 Mary's sister Elizabeth married William, Lord Mountjoy, and it took lawsuits lasting from 1505 to 1515 to settle which of Say's manors would pass to which daughter. Essex could be pleased with the final outcome, which at Say's death in 1529 gave him estates near his own and sufficiently valuable to make up more than a quarter of his income by his death. Mary was alive in 1535, but not at her husband's death in 1540. Essex seems to have been an attentive and effective landlord and though often in debt was never in serious financial difficulties. He maintained a household of about fifty servants and rebuilt his main seat, Stanstead Hall in Halstead, as a moated brick courtyard-house with elaborate turrets and chimneys.

Essex's following among the greater gentry of his region was less impressive than that of his richer and more politically prominent neighbours, the de Vere earls of Oxford. His affinity—a tight network of his tenants and local officers and above them a dozen Essex and Hertfordshire gentlemen of middling rank, frequent occupants of county administrative offices and in several cases highly assiduous justices of the peace—none the less met his rather limited aims. Those aims were perhaps constricted further by his lack of a son. His daughter Anne had married Sir William *Parr in 1527. When Essex fell off a young horse and broke his neck on 13 March 1540, they inherited his estates, but his title was granted to Thomas Cromwell. It was only in 1543, when his sister Katherine married the king, that Sir William followed his father-in-law as earl of Essex. Henry Bourchier was buried at Little Easton, Essex.

S. J. Gunn

Sources S. J. Gunn, 'Henry Bourchier, earl of Essex (1472–1540)', *The Tudor nobility*, ed. G. W. Bernard (1992), 134–79 • GEC, *Peerage* • *State papers published under … Henry VIII*, 11 vols. (1830–52)

Archives Longleat House, Somerset, household accounts, Devereux papers 10

Likenesses drawing, 1539, repro. in 'The last abbot of Colchester', *Essex Review*, 49 (1940), facing p. 1

Bourchier, Henry, fifth earl of Bath (*c.*1587–1654), politician, was born in Ireland, the youngest of five sons of Sir George Bourchier (*d.* 1605) and his wife, Eleanor Howard, daughter of William *Howard, first Lord Howard of Effingham. Sir George, a younger son of John Bourchier, second earl of Bath, ventured to Ireland about 1570 as a captain in the queen's army and made his career there, rising to be master of the ordnance and a member of the Irish privy council. Of his four elder sons two died young in the 1580s, one in the late 1500s, and the fourth, Sir John Bourchier, in 1614: all died childless.

Henry Bourchier was admitted to Trinity College, Dublin, about 1597, graduating BA in 1605 and proceeding MA in 1610; in 1606 he was made a fellow of the college. He was afterwards referred to as 'a learned lord, and a lover of learning', and his widow gave £200 for books for Trinity Library, 'as a Signall Memoriall of the kindness her Lord had for this College' (Fuller, 3.440; GEC, *Peerage*, 2.20). Although he inherited considerable estates in Ireland from his father, by the early 1620s Bourchier appears to have moved to England. He was knighted on 9 November 1621 and in 1623 he was appointed by the privy council to a commission of inquiry charged with investigating the affairs of the Virginia Company. In 1629 he was still in London, where he visited his friend John Selden in the Tower, imprisoned by the king's command. Bourchier inherited the earldom of Bath upon the death of his cousin Edward on 2 March 1637. Although he was the fourth earl's heir male, his cousin left three daughters, and Bath's estate was a slender one—only about £1000 per annum in 1632. His marriage, on 18 December 1638, to Lady Rachel Fane (*bap.* 1613, *d.* 1680), fifth daughter of Francis *Fane, first earl of Westmorland [*see under* Fane, Sir Thomas], in time brought him three daughters but, evidently, very little in the way of fortune.

Bath attempted to tread a moderate course during the crisis of the early 1640s. In April 1640 he opposed a demand that parliament consider supply before grievances, though in August he refused to sign a petition to Charles I to recall parliament. In the Long Parliament, Bath was one of the waverers in the earl of Strafford's trial—he spoke well of Oliver St John's conduct of the prosecution, but he ultimately absented himself at the third reading of the bill of attainder on 7 May 1641. Strafford's fate, however, concerned Bath less than that of the bishops. A friend of episcopacy, he defended the bishops against attack in the Lords, 'publicly professing it one of the greatest honours which ever happily happened to his family, that one thereof … was once dignified with the Archbishopric of Canterbury' (Fuller, 3.440). (He was alluding to Thomas *Bourchier, archbishop from 1454 to 1486.) Although Clarendon dismissed Bath as one with 'no excellent or graceful pronunciation' (Clarendon, *Hist. rebellion*, 1.317), this staunch support for the church probably encouraged the king to name him to the privy council on 8 August. From this point on Bath drifted closer and closer to Charles's cause. In February 1642 he complained that service in the Lords was becoming impossible, thanks to the loss of 'the fundamentall priviledge of parliament, which is free debating and voteing' (Russell, 470–71). Nevertheless, he was present in the house to protest against the passage of the militia ordinance on 15 March. He remained ambivalent, however, as the kingdom slid towards civil war, answering the king's summons to York in May only reluctantly.

Though Bath's family name was an old one, and he was expected to have considerable influence in Devon, where his estate at Tawstock lay, he proved a great disappointment in the summer of 1642, when he travelled there bearing the king's commission of array. Bath was the first name on the Devon commission, issued on 19 July, but his eminence could not have prepared him for his reception in the west. While he publicly pledged 'I have no authority nor will I take the value of sixpence from any man' (*Declaration*), the authorities at Exeter barred the gates, and allowed him entry only after he promised not to publish the commission. About 15 September at South Moulton, only 10 miles from Tawstock, he and his entourage were set upon by an enraged mob, who suspected them of planning to read the commission. He left the village in a hail of stones. On 23 August parliament ordered his arrest, and he was taken to London by a troop of horse on 28 September.

Some royalists were sceptical of Bath's devotion to the cause. He 'never had nor ever meant to do the King the least service, but only out of the morosity of his own nature' had he opposed parliament (Clarendon, *Hist. rebellion*, 2.318). After his release from custody Bath returned to Charles's service, and was appointed keeper of the privy seal on 22 January 1644; later in the year he held a command in the west, where his ineffectual conduct led to conflict with Sir Richard Grenville. Whatever the value of his service, Bath suffered for the king's sake, enduring sequestration. In January 1649 he petitioned the committee for compounding for his release, and was fined £713 on 19 February. He then retired to Tawstock, where he died on 16 August 1654 and was buried the following day, leaving no male heirs, the last of his line.

Bath's widow married again within the year: on 1 May 1655 she wed Lionel Cranfield, third earl of Middlesex (*c*.1625–1674), the son of James I's lord treasurer. The marriage was a failure. Middlesex rapidly sold off 'all her plate, most of the household stuff, and all Lord Bath's library: all goes in rioting and play' (GEC, *Peerage*, 8.691) and in 1661 the countess secured a formal separation on grounds of cruelty and desertion. After she died on 11 November 1680 her body was carried back to Tawstock for burial beside her first husband. VICTOR STATER

Sources GEC, *Peerage* · C. Russell, *The fall of the British monarchies, 1637–1642* (1991) · A. Fletcher, *The outbreak of the English civil war* (1981) · E. A. Andriette, *Devon and Exeter in the civil war* (1971) · Clarendon, *Hist. rebellion* · *A declaration made by the right honourable the earle of Bath* (1642) · T. Fuller, *The church history of Britain*, ed. [J. Nichols], 3 (1837), 440 · M. A. E. Green, ed., *Calendar of the proceedings of the committee for compounding … 1643–1660*, 3, PRO (1891), 885–6 · M. Stoyle, *Loyalty and locality: popular allegiance in Devon during the English civil war* (1994) · W. G. Hoskins, *Devon* (1954) · A. Chambers, *Eleanor, countess of Desmond, c.1545–1638* (1986) · L. Stone, *The crisis of the aristocracy, 1558–1641* (1965), 175

Archives CKS, papers

Likenesses funeral monument, parish church, Tawstock, Devon

Wealth at death income *c*.£1000 p.a. in 1642: Stone, *Crisis of the aristocracy*, 175

Bourchier, James David (1850–1920), journalist, was born at Baggotstown, Bruff, co. Limerick, Ireland, on 18 December 1850, the fourth son of John Bourchier JP, of Baggotstown, and his wife, Sarah, *née* Aher, of La Rive, Castlecomer, co. Kilkenny. Bourchier was a scholar and classics gold medallist at Trinity College, Dublin, and graduated BA there in 1873. He subsequently won a scholarship at King's College, Cambridge, and was placed seventh in the first class of the classical tripos (1876). Shortly afterwards he became a school master at Eton College, near Windsor, where he remained for ten years, despite difficulties caused by his deafness. In 1888 he left Eton for Romania and Bulgaria, where he acted as a special correspondent for *The Times*, becoming the paper's Balkan correspondent in 1892. He had earlier also contributed occasional articles to publications including *The Globe* and *Macmillan's Magazine*.

For fifteen years Bourchier was based in Athens before moving to Sofia. Sociable, with a talent for both languages and music, despite his hearing difficulties, he soon came to know everyone of note in the Balkans and worked behind the scenes of Balkan politics and negotiations for a generation. He also wrote knowledgeably on archaeology and travel. His sympathy with Balkan nationalism, together with his courage and willingness to identify himself with a cause, won for him a unique place in the politics of the Balkan peninsula. He often served as intermediary between the Cretan insurgents and the Greek authorities, and acted unofficially as confidential adviser to Prince George of Greece when, in 1898, the latter became high commissioner of Crete. When Bulgarian peasants in Macedonia rose against Turkish rule in 1903, he alerted the British public to their grievances. In 1911–12 he was entrusted by King George of Greece and the Greek politician Eleutherios Venizelos on one side, and by King Ferdinand of Bulgaria and M. Gueshov on the other, with many of the secret negotiations preceding the Balkan alliance, which he regarded as the only solution to the Balkan question. However, Bourchier's political and professional credibility was severely strained when Bulgaria chose to align itself with Austria-Hungary and Germany in 1915, since his reports had not suggested such a decision. Much as he deplored the part played by Bulgaria in the First World War he did not abandon his empathetic reporting, and *The Times* increasingly sought to distance itself from its long-serving correspondent.

In 1915 Bourchier left Sofia and went to Romania, and in 1917 moved to Odessa and Petrograd to report on the early phases of the Russian Revolution. On returning to England in 1918 he retired from *The Times*, and devoted himself to the forlorn attempt to secure what seemed to him a just and final settlement in the Balkans. Such concern resulted in his being asked, in 1920, to become Bulgaria's consul-general in London. However, before he was able to do so, Bourchier died of heart failure at Sofia on 30 December 1920, and was buried with high honours at Rilo monastery, Bulgaria. He had never married.

E. F. B. Grogan, *rev.* Chandrika Kaul

Sources Lady Grogan, *The life of J. D. Bourchier* (1926) • *WWW* • *The Times* (1 Jan 1921) • [S. Morison and others], *The history of The Times*, 3–4 (1947–52) • private information (1927) • personal knowledge (1927)
Archives News Int. RO, papers
Likenesses N. Michailowz, oils, 1908, Times Newspapers Ltd, London
Wealth at death £9336 4*s*. 7*d*. in England: Irish probate sealed in England, 15 April 1921, *CGPLA Eng. & Wales*

Bourchier, John. *See* Bousser, Sir John (*d.* 1329/30).

John Bourchier, second Baron Berners (*c*.1467–1533), attrib. Ambrosius Benson, *c*.1521–6

Bourchier, John, second Baron Berners (*c*.1467–1533), soldier, diplomat, and translator, was the son of Sir Humphrey Bourchier (*d.* 1471) and Elizabeth (*d.* 1497), daughter and sole heir of Frederick Tilney of Boston, Lincolnshire. His father, a Yorkist, was killed at the battle of Barnet in 1471, and Berners succeeded to the barony at the age of seven when his grandfather died in 1474. The family was a distinguished one: one of his grandfather's brothers was summoned to parliament as Baron Fitzwarine in 1449, another was created earl of Essex in 1461, and a third became archbishop of Canterbury in 1454. His paternal great-grandmother Anne was the daughter of Thomas of Woodstock, sixth son of Edward III.

Early life and employment After the death of Berners's father his mother married Thomas Howard, created second duke of Norfolk in 1514. The first duke, John Howard (*d.* 1485), was Berners's guardian and Berners himself married Katherine (*d.* 1536), John's daughter from his second marriage. (Berners's stepfather, Thomas, was the son of John's first wife, Katherine Moleyns.) Berners had two legitimate children, both daughters. Mary, the elder daughter, married Alexander Unton of Wadley, but was childless and predeceased her father. The younger daughter, Jane, married Sir Edmund Knyvet, sergeant-porter to Henry VIII; heir to Berners's English properties, she lived until 1561. In his will Berners also named three illegitimate sons, Humphrey, James, and George, and he also had a daughter Ursula, who married Sir William Sherington. Berners's portrait, formerly attributed to Holbein, but in fact by an unknown Flemish artist, hangs in the National Portrait Gallery.

Anthony Wood claims that Berners was educated at Balliol College, Oxford, but there is no evidence to substantiate this; Wood probably confused him with his distant relative John Bourchier, son of Lord Fitzwarine. At the time of the marriage of Richard, second son of Edward IV, on 17 January 1478 Berners was knighted. According to Richard Grafton's continuation of Hardyng's chronicle he was involved in the attempt to put Henry Tudor on the throne in 1484 and subsequently fled to Brittany. Probably as a consequence of his connection with Thomas Howard, who was the chief general in England, he contracted in 1492 to 'serve the king in his warres beyond see on hole yeere with two speres' (Rymer, *Foedera*, 12.479), and in 1497 he took part in the suppression of Perkin Warbeck's rebellion. He was first summoned to parliament on 14 October 1495 and was regular in his attendance when in England. He was last summoned on 9 August 1529.

Services overseas In Henry VIII's reign Berners acted as a soldier and diplomat. In 1513 he took part in the French campaign and then seems to have joined his half-brother, Lord Thomas Howard, who had been made lord admiral on 2 May 1513, in Scotland and to have acted as marshal to the army. After peace had been restored with France, Norfolk led the group that escorted Princess Mary to France to marry Louis XII; Howard, now earl of Surrey, was a member of the entourage and Berners was chosen to be Mary's chamberlain. The French, however, demanded the dismissal of all her menservants and Henry Courtenay, earl of Devon, was appointed to wait on her instead. In May 1514 Berners was granted the chancellorship of the exchequer for life in reverson after Sir Thomas Lovell. He received a new grant on 29 May 1516 and finally succeeded to the office after the death of Lovell on 24 May 1524, being admitted on 14 July 1524. In 1518 Berners was sent on a special mission to Spain with John Kite, archbishop of Armagh, as part of a scheme for a general peace in Europe. Throughout the mission the ambassadors were plagued with financial problems, Berners reporting to Wolsey on 26 July that 'we lye here with most charge and expence, horse and man, & in most scarcity of all good things as well meat as drink, that may be thought' (*LP Henry VIII*, 2/2, no. 4342). But although seriously ill with gout for much of the time, he nevertheless sent a spirited report back to Henry VIII on the customs at the Spanish court. Berners was not present at the Field of Cloth of Gold in 1520, as has been generally stated, but remained with the council in London. On 28 November 1520 Henry appointed him deputy of Calais and he occupied that position until 1526 when he was replaced by Sir Robert Wingfield. He then returned to England, but took up the Calais appointment again in 1531, on condition of paying Wingfield 100 marks per annum during his tenure of office. His successor as deputy was Arthur Plantagenet, Viscount Lisle.

Berners became heavily involved in lawsuits over his properties in England, and had to borrow money from the king as early as 1511. His debts continued to grow and in 1532 Henry ordered his agents to watch over Berners's personal effects. After Berners's death at Calais on 16 March 1533 his half-brother Lord Edmund Howard, controller of Calais, was directed to seize all his goods in Calais for the crown. By the terms of his will, dated 3 March 1533 and proved on 4 February 1534, Berners left his great tenement in Calais to Sir Francis Hastings, later second earl of Huntingdon, and one of the executors of his will. He also left Lord Edmund a standing cup of silver. In an attempt to deal with a debt of £500 he requested the king to accept after his wife's death Staffordshire properties settled on her by deed of jointure. He was buried in the parish church in Calais.

Chivalric romances Like his more famous predecessor Sir Thomas Malory, Lord Berners combined an active military life with a strong literary bent—the *post mortem* inventory of his goods listed eighty books in his study—and he was an accomplished translator both of French and Spanish texts. *Arthur of Lytell Brytayne*, probably his earliest work, dates to the second decade of the sixteenth century. It is a translation of *Artus de la Petite Bretagne*, a fourteenth-century prose romance which was first printed in Lyons in 1493; Berners seems to have made use of the second version of 1496. The first surviving edition of Berners's translation was printed by Robert Redborne, perhaps *c.*1560, and there was another edition in 1582 (STC 807, 808). Berners's statement that he gave up the translation after a few pages because of the fantastic nature of the story but picked up again once he realized the text had a moral purpose is probably conventional rather than autobiographical and may be in direct imitation of Caxton, thus showing the literary tradition in which Berners was situating himself. The first edition of the French prose version of *Huon de Bordeaux*, another exemplary chivalric romance of which Berners's *Huon of Burdeux* is a translation, was published by Michel le Noir in 1513. The earliest surviving edition of Berners's translation, now in private ownership and unavailable for inspection, is undated, but the second was printed in 1601 (STC 13998.5, 13999). The undated edition was issued from the press of Julian Notary, perhaps as early as *c.*1515. Although the first edition is described as imperfect at beginning and end, the second has a preface and colophon in which it is stated that the earl of Huntingdon, Lord Hastings, requested the translation and sponsored the printing. It also gives a date of 1570. There are problems determining which earl of Huntingdon is meant, but it is likely that the reference is to Francis Hastings, the second earl. In this case, there must have been a lost edition, in which the preface and colophon first appeared, printed for Hastings between his creation as earl in 1545 and his death in 1561, and perhaps a 1570 edition as well.

Berners's best-known work is his translation of Froissart's chronicles, begun soon after 15 August 1521 when Henry VIII signed the treaty of Bruges, undertaking to declare war on France the following year. According to Berners's preface, the project was undertaken at Henry VIII's express command. The Tudor arms appear on the verso of the title page. The translation, made from one of the early printed editions in four books, was no doubt intended to remind 'noble gentlemen' of their ancient right to France and was meant to spur them on to bravery by enabling them 'to see, behold, and read the high enterprises, famous acts, and glorious deeds done and achieved by their valiant ancestors'. The first volume, completed in 1522, was printed by Richard Pynson on 28 January 1523 (STC 11396). According to the colophon the second volume was finished on 10 March 1525 and was printed on 31 August (STC 11397), that is the day after the treaty to end the war with France was signed at The More. Pynson's device is found at the end of the second volume and he may have shared the costs of publication. Lord Berners's translation of Froissart was republished in the Tudor Translations series in six volumes edited by W. P. Ker (1901–3).

Later translations Berners's first three translations were all of chivalric romances and histories of the type favoured by Caxton, and the prose style tends to be old-fashioned as well. After his return to England in 1526 Berners's choice of material and manner of expression changed—perhaps as a result of exposure to new literary trends—and his last two translations were of more up-to-date works by Spanish authors. Berners himself claimed that he undertook the translations at the request of the children of his sister Margaret, Lady Bryan, both of whom were well connected in court circles. His niece Elizabeth, the wife of one of Henry's former minions, Sir Nicholas Carew, master of the horse, asked him to translate Diego de San Pedro's *Cárcel de amor*. The resulting work, *The Castell of Love*, is a translation from the French version, *La prison damours*, published in 1525, but it includes a preface first found in the French edition of 1526, which thus gives a *terminus a quo* for its production. It also contains a continuation by Nicolas Nuñez, not found in any of the surviving early French editions, and Berners translated directly from the Spanish in this section. He consulted the Spanish original in the earlier parts too. There is no evidence that the *Castell of Love* was published during Berners's lifetime, and the first surviving edition was printed by John Turke *c.*1548, the second by Robert Wyer *c.*1552, and the third by J. King *c.*1555 (STC 21739.5–42). Berners's last work, *The Golden Boke of Marcus Aurelius*, derives from the French translation by René Berthault (1531) of Antonio de Guevara's *Libro aureo de Marco Aurelio*. According to the colophon Berners completed the work on 10 March 1532; it was undertaken at the request of Sir Francis Bryan, who was a close associate of Henry VIII as well as the brother of Lady Carew. Bryan, who himself translated another work by Guevara, was probably responsible for the publication in 1535 by Thomas Berthelet (STC 12436), and the work went through at least ten editions by 1586.

In his *Index Britanniae scriptorum* John Bale attributes two other works to Berners—a comedy, *Ite in vineam* and a *De officiis Calesianorum*—on the authority of unnamed individuals from Calais ('ex testibus Calesiensibus'). There are no records of the former, but the latter may be the 'Ordinances for watch and ward of Calais' (BL, Cotton MS Faustina E. vii, fols. 89–102) printed in *The Chronicle of Calais*, edited by J. G. Nichols (London, 1846), pages 140–62. Bale also claims that Berners translated many books from Italian, but he gives no authority for the statement.

No manuscripts of any of Berners's works survive and no printed books from his library can be identified. When Lady Carew's husband was executed in 1539 his goods were sequestered and Beddington Place fell to Henry VIII. According to a *post mortem* inventory of Henry VIII's possessions, there were twenty books at Beddington. Of these, ten were copies of Froissart—one copy described as 'Frosort', four copies of the 'premier volume of Froscoit', three copies of the 'secund volume de Froscoit/Frosart', and two of the 'third volume'. These were almost certainly books acquired by Lady Carew from her uncle. At Henry's palace at Westminster there were also copies of *La prison damours* and the *Livre doré de Marc Aurele* in the editions used by Berners, but this is no doubt a coincidence.

James P. Carley

Sources GEC, *Peerage*, new edn, 2.153–5 • Bale, *Index* • J. C. Sainty, ed., *Officers of the exchequer: a list* (1983), 38 • G. M. Bell, *A handlist of British diplomatic representatives, 1509–1688*, Royal Historical Society Guides and Handbooks, 16 (1990), 254 • N. F. Blake, 'Lord Berners: a survey', *Medievalia et Humanistica*, new ser., 2 (1971), 119–32 • K. J. Oberempt, 'Lord Berners' "Arthur of Lytell Bryteyne"', *Neuphilologische Mitteilungen*, 77 (1976), 241–52 • G. Kane, 'An accident of history: Lord Berners's translation of Froissart's *Chronicles*', *The Chaucer Review*, 21 (1984), 217–25 • D. J. O'Brien, 'Lord Berners' "Huon of Burdeux": the survival of medieval ideals in the reign of Henry VIII', *Studies in Medievalism*, 4 (1992), 36–44 • *LP Henry VIII*, vols. 1–6 • D. Starkey, ed., *The inventory of King Henry VIII: the transcript* (1998), 349 • P. Neville, 'Richard Pynson, king's printer (1506–1529): printing and propaganda in early Tudor England', PhD diss., U. Lond., 1990, 128–30 • H. Miller, *Henry VIII and the English nobility* (1986) • M. St C. Byrne, ed., *The Lisle letters*, 6 vols. (1981) • J. Bourchier, *The boke of Duke Huon of Burdeux*, ed. S. Lee, 4 pts in 3 vols., EETS, extra ser., 40, 41, 43, 50 (1882–7) • Rymer, *Foedera*, 2nd edn, 12.479

Likenesses oils, *c.*1520–1526 (after unknown Flemish artist), NPG • attrib. A. Benson, portrait, *c.*1521–1526, priv. coll. [*see illus.*]

Bourchier, John (*b.* 1493, *d.* in or after 1577), abbot of Leicester and bishop-designate of Gloucester, was born at Oakington, Cambridgeshire. His parents' names are unknown; in later life numerous variants of his surname appear in official documents. He was educated at Eton College and at King's College and St John's College, Cambridge. In 1534, when an Augustinian canon at St Bartholomew's Priory, Smithfield, Bourchier became abbot of the monastery of St Mary de Pratis, Leicester. His later grovelling letters to Thomas Cromwell show that he obtained the abbacy by promising £100 to Cromwell and the lease of a valuable abbey grange to Cromwell's nephew, though he could not fulfil the latter promise because of the opposition of the canons. After Leicester Abbey was surrendered in 1538 Bourchier received the large annual pension of £200. In a list of proposed new bishoprics (1539) he was named as bishop of Shrewsbury, but this see did not materialize. His activities in the 1540s are not recorded, but in 1554 he was presented to the wealthy rectory of Church Langton, Leicestershire, succeeding the protestant martyr Laurence Saunders.

Letters patent of Philip and Mary, dated 25 October 1558, granted Bourchier custody of the temporalities of the see of Gloucester, describing him as 'bishop nominate'. But Mary died on 17 November following, before Bourchier could be consecrated or even elected, and his nomination to Gloucester was ignored. During the early years of Elizabeth's reign he remained at liberty, though apparently absent from Church Langton. Shortly before August 1570 he was deprived of that benefice, presumably for rejecting the Elizabethan settlement. In 1571 he sold his pension to the statesman Sir Thomas Smith for £900. He left the country, despite his age, some time before January 1577, when a return to the exchequer lists him among 'fugitives over the sea'. According to the Leicestershire historian John Nichols a pardon was issued to him in 1584, but this pardon in fact dated from 1484, and referred to a Leicester priest named John Abbot. The date and place of John Bourchier's death are unknown, but he must have been one of the last surviving former abbots. T. Y. Cocks

Sources T. Y. Cocks, 'The last abbot of Leicester', *Leicestershire Archaeological and Historical Society Transactions*, 58 (1982–3), 6–19 • *LP Henry VIII*, vols. 7, 13 • G. A. J. Hodgett, ed., *The state of the ex-religious and former chantry priests in the diocese of Lincoln, 1547–1574*, Lincoln RS, 53 (1959), 30, 82, 137 • *CPR*, 1476–85, 483; 1557–8, 390; 1569–72, 207 • Lincs. Arch., Lincoln diocesan archives, register 28, fol. 125*v* and fol. 51*v* • J. Strype, *Annals of the Reformation and establishment of religion … during Queen Elizabeth's happy reign*, new edn, 2/2 (1824), 597 • Venn, *Alum. Cant.*, 1/1.187 • Cooper, *Ath. Cantab.*, 1.449 • E. A. Webb, *The records of St Bartholomew's Priory and of the church and parish of St Bartholomew the Great, West Smithfield*, 1 (1921), 238–40 • A. H. Thompson, *The abbey of St Mary of the Meadows, Leicester* (1949), 85–9 • Leics. RO, Archdeaconry papers, 1D 41/13 • W. Sterry, ed., *The Eton College register, 1441–1698* (1943), 43 • J. Nichols, *The history and antiquities of the county of Leicester*, 1/2 (1815), 275

Bourchier, Sir John (*c.*1595–1660), politician and regicide, was the second but eldest surviving son of William Bourchier (1559–*c.*1631) of Beningborough, and his wife, Katherine (*c.*1565–1623), daughter of Sir Thomas Barrington of Hatfield Broad Oak, Essex. He was descended from a family of Norman extraction, a branch of which had settled in Yorkshire during Elizabeth's reign. His father was certified a lunatic in 1598 and upon the death of his grandfather, Sir Ralph Bourchier, that same year, his wardship was granted to his mother and her brother, Sir Francis *Barrington. Bourchier matriculated at Christ's College, Cambridge, in December 1608, and was admitted to Gray's Inn on 6 March 1610. He was knighted on 11 November 1619, and about a year later married Anne (*d.* in or before 1649), daughter of William Rolfe of Hadleigh, Suffolk, with whom he had ten children. By 1625, when he was appointed a JP for all three Yorkshire ridings, his estate was valued at £2200 per annum.

Under the tutelage of his mother and the Barringtons, Bourchier acquired a lifelong commitment to the advancement of godly religion and became closely acquainted with a number of leading puritans, including Sir William Masham, Sir William Strickland, and Henry Darley. His religious convictions may partly explain his refusal to pay the forced loan in 1627, and he gave further offence to the crown in 1633 by pulling down fences in the newly enclosed royal forest of Galtres, near York. His right of access to the forest was not recognized by Strafford or the council of the north, which fined him £1800 and detained him in custody. Deeming him mad like his father, Strafford thought Bourchier had acted 'rather out of animosity towards me … than with the least insolent thought towards his Majesty' (Radcliffe, 1.249). Bourchier looked to Strafford to help mitigate his punishment (apparently travelling to Ireland to attend him), and had his fine reduced to £1000. Although he petitioned parliament against Strafford in February 1641, he apparently disapproved of his case being used as one of the charges at the lord lieutenant's trial.

Bourchier signed almost every Yorkshire petition of 1642 in support of parliament and godly reformation, and against the king's attempts to raise forces in the north. Early in June, while gathering support for a petition at a meeting of the Yorkshire freeholders on Heworth Moor, he had a violent altercation with the royalist peer Thomas, Viscount Savile. Soon after the outbreak of civil war, Bourchier was imprisoned at York by the royalists. Released by June 1643, he took refuge in Hull, where he was involved in the arrest of the Hothams. During 1645–6 he signed almost all the Yorkshire county committee's letters to parliament pleading that the Scottish army be removed from the region. He was returned to parliament for Ripon in the spring of 1647, probably on the interest of Ferdinando, Lord Fairfax, the steward of the borough's manorial courts. He helped to mobilize the Yorkshire parliamentarian forces in 1648, and by late November had emerged as a parliamentary patron of the Independent divine Thomas Brooks. Bourchier retained his seat at Pride's Purge, registering his 'dissent' from the vote that the king's latest answer constituted grounds for further negotiation on 20 December. He attended all four sessions of the king's trial, and signed the death warrant [*see also* Regicides]. A committed Rumper, he was elected to the third and fifth councils of state, figured prominently in the Rump's punishment of delinquents and exploitation of sequestered property, and in July 1651 obtained a grant of £6000 out of Strafford's estate (although there is no evidence that he received any of it). He was active on the Rump's army committees and was a key figure in the committee for plundered ministers and in settling ministers in sequestered livings.

Bourchier apparently supported the Cromwellian religious settlement, being appointed a trier and ejector in 1654. With the restoration of the Rump in May 1659 he returned to Westminster, where he aligned with those anxious to rein in the Quakers. On 18 June 1660 he surrendered himself to parliament, and early in August he died, asserting to the last his support for the regicide: 'I tell you, it was a just act; God and all good men will own it' (E. Ludlow, *Memoirs*, ed. C. H. Firth, 2 vols., 1894, 2.293). He was buried on 8 August at St Mary Magdalen, Milk Street. His son Barrington Bourchier, having aided the Restoration, obtained a grant of his father's estate.

DAVID SCOTT

Sources HoP, *Commons* [draft] • *JHC*, 5 (1646–8) • *JHC*, 6 (1648–51) • *JHC*, 7 (1651–9) • *JHC*, 8 (1660–67) • *CSP dom.*, *1631–60* • J. T. Cliffe, *The Yorkshire gentry from the Reformation to the civil war* (1969) • W. L. F. Nuttall, 'The Yorkshire commissioners appointed for the trial of King Charles the First', *Yorkshire Archaeological Journal*, 43 (1971), 147–57 • *Dugdale's visitation of Yorkshire, with additions*, ed. J. W. Clay, 1 (1899), 305–7 • C. H. Firth and R. S. Rait, eds., *Acts and ordinances of the interregnum, 1642–1660*, 3 vols. (1911) • G. Radcliffe, *The earl of Strafforde's letters and dispatches, with an essay towards his life*, ed. W. Knowler, 1 (1739), 86, 88, 249 • Sheffield Central Libraries, Wentworth Woodhouse muniments, Strafford MSS, 14 (246); 17 (267); 24–5 (36) • PRO, WARD 9/94, fols. 473*v*, 649–50 • PRO, WARD 9/677, fol. 5*v* • Bodl. Oxf., MSS Tanner 59, 60 • Bodl. Oxf., MSS Nalson IV–VI • *Hulls managing of the kingdoms cause* (1644) [Thomason tract E 51(11)] • *The last true newes from Yorke, Nottingham, Coventry, and Warwicke* (1642) [Thomason tract E 116(9)] • *Terrible newes from York* (1642) [Thomason tract E 123(14)] • [W. Prynne], *A full declaration of the true state of the secluded members case* (1660) • PRO, LR 2/266, fol. 1 • PRO, C 142/455/43 • A. W. Hughes Clarke, ed., *The registers of St Mary Magdalen, Milk Street, 1558–1666, and St Michael Bassishaw, London, 1538–1625*, Harleian Society, register section, 72 (1942)

Archives HLRO, main papers 15/2/1642; 6/6/1642 • PRO, C 142/254/69; C 142/455/43; C 181/3; C 181/6; C 231/4; C 231/6; E112; E115; E134; LR 2/266; SP 28; WARD 9

Wealth at death approx. £1200 p.a.: PRO, LR 2/266, fol. 1

Bourchier, Margaret, countess of Bath (1510–1562). *See under* Kitson family (*per. c.*1520–*c.*1660).

Bourchier [Bousser], **Robert, first Lord Bourchier** (*d.* **1349**), administrator, was the son of Sir John *Bousser (*d.* 1329/30), a judge of the common pleas, and his wife, Helen, daughter of Walter of Colchester. The family's estates lay in Essex, where Robert later added substantially to them, especially in and around Halstead. He is first recorded in 1318, and later appears to have been employed by the de Vere earls of Oxford, whose estates were concentrated in Essex, but from the late 1320s he also served the crown. In 1327 he accompanied Sir Bartholomew Burghersh on a diplomatic mission to Charles IV of France. He was returned as a knight of the shire for Essex to the parliaments of 1328–9, 1330 (twice), 1332 (once), and 1339 (both). In 1329 he was a commissioner of the peace in Essex, and during the 1330s he was appointed to a modest number of judicial commissions, nearly all in that county, but there is no evidence that he received a formal legal training, and though in 1334 he was appointed chief justice of the justiciar's bench in Ireland, he never took up office. If anything he pursued a military career. He was ordered to join the invasion of Scotland in the summer of 1335, and though the mistaken belief that he fought at Cadsand in November 1337 is attributable to an error (subsequently often repeated) by his descendant John Bourchier, Lord Berners, in the latter's translation of Froissart, in July 1338 he was in the company of the earl of Northampton, when the earl accompanied Edward III to Flanders. He also established links with Hugh Audley, earl of Gloucester, from whom he was receiving a fee of £100 per annum by 1340.

On 14 December 1340 Bourchier was appointed chancellor of England, the first layman to hold that office. The context of his appointment was Edward III's quarrel with Archbishop John Stratford, over the alleged failure of the English administration to support the king's war effort in Flanders and France. The primate's brother Ralph Stratford, bishop of Chichester, was dismissed as chancellor, and Bourchier was chosen to replace him, presumably as a competent man of affairs who could be relied upon to do the king's bidding. His relative lack of personal means, which led to special arrangements having to be made to finance the chancery clerks in his household, and to the king's providing an annual fee of £100 to replace the one Bourchier had been receiving from Audley, was doubtless a positive advantage in Edward's eyes, since it made the new chancellor more dependent upon royal favour than an ecclesiastical magnate could be trusted to be. Bourchier appears to have fulfilled the king's expectations. In the first parliament of 1341, along with Bishop Orleton of Winchester and Sir John Darcy, he urged the archbishop to submit to the king. And though the parliament extracted the king's assent to articles requiring that officers of state be appointed and sworn in parliament, Bourchier protested against the king's concession, and it was later repealed.

Bourchier resigned as chancellor on 27 October 1341, but continued to serve as a member of the king's council; in 1345 a debt to the crown was specifically remitted for his good services in this respect. He also served the king again as a soldier, in the autumn of 1342 accompanying Edward to Brittany in command of a contingent of men-at-arms. But the 'sires de Boursier' whom Froissart records as fighting in the division of Edward, the Black Prince, at the battle of Crécy in 1346 may well have been Bourchier's son and heir, John, born of his marriage (by 1329) to Margaret, daughter of Sir Thomas Prayers of Sible Hedingham and his wife, Anne, daughter of Hugh of Essex. In the late 1340s Robert Bourchier was once more employed as a diplomat. In 1347 he was among those empowered to negotiate a truce with France, and early in 1348 he was commissioned to accompany the king's daughter Joan to Spain, there to marry the future Pedro I of Castile, but she fell victim to plague at Bordeaux. In November 1348 he received a personal summons to parliament, and is consequently regarded as having become Lord Bourchier. Robert Bourchier died between 12 March and 18 August 1349, probably of the black death, and was buried at Halstead, where he had intended to found a college of eight chaplains. RICHARD K. ROSE

Sources *Chancery records* • *Members of parliament: return to two orders of the honorable the House of Commons*, House of Commons, 1 (1878), 87, 89, 91, 100, 124, 126 • *Adae Murimuth continuatio chronicarum. Robertus de Avesbury de gestis mirabilibus regis Edwardi tertii*, ed. E. M. Thompson, Rolls Series, 93 (1889), 117–18, 323–4 • *The Chronicle of Froissart*, trans. J. Bourchier, 6 vols. (1901–3); repr. (New York, 1967), vol. 1 p. 294 • J. Froissart, *Chroniques*, ed. G. T. Diller (Geneva, 1972), 275, 718 • 'Stephani Birchingtoni historia de vitis archiepiscoporum Cantuarensium', *Anglia sacra*, ed. [H. Wharton], 1 (1691), 1–48, esp. 22–3 • P. Morant, *The history and antiquities of the county of Essex*, 1 (1768), 329–30, 380, 401 • *VCH Essex*, 2.192 • B. Wilkinson, *The chancery under Edward III* (1929) • *CIPM*, 9, no. 239

Bourchier, Thomas (*c.*1411–1486), cardinal and archbishop of Canterbury, was probably the second son of William *Bourchier, count of Eu (*c.*1374–1420), and *Anne of Woodstock, daughter and heir of *Thomas of Woodstock, duke of Gloucester, and granddaughter of Edward III. His mother's second marriage, to Edmund Stafford, fifth earl of Stafford, created links that would be important for the children of her third marriage. Like his brothers (the eldest, Henry *Bourchier, who was created earl of Essex by Edward IV, and William and John, who were to be summoned to parliament respectively as lords Fitzwarine and Berners), Thomas owed much to his mother's royal and aristocratic connections. So, too, did their sister, Eleanor, who married John (VI) Mowbray, third duke of Norfolk (*d.* 1461).

Early promotions At some point after his father's death Thomas Bourchier was sent to Oxford, and despite his youth he rapidly gained preferment in the church. By April 1427 he was master of the hospital of St Mary Magdalene at Paull in Yorkshire; on 1 December following, the council of regency offered him the deanery of St Martin's-le-Grand, London; and prebends in five different cathedrals fell to him within the next six years. He entered holy orders on 24 September 1429, being ordained acolyte and subdeacon in the diocese of London. By his mother's presentation in 1432 he secured a canonry in the royal free chapel of St Mary in Hastings Castle, linked with the prebend of West Thurrock in Essex. When Thomas Polton, bishop of Worcester, died at Basel on 23 August 1433, the candidacy of Bourchier, who by then had graduated MA at Oxford, was promoted by his kinsman Cardinal Beaufort to fill the vacancy, even though he was much younger than the minimum age for consecration as a bishop required under the provisions of the Council of Constance. The process of his elevation to the see lasted over eighteen months and involved lengthy negotiations with the papal court, as Eugenius IV (*r.* 1431–47) had already nominated Thomas Brouns, dean of Salisbury (*d.* 1445), as Polton's successor. Bourchier's election by the prior and chapter on 9 December was prompted by a letter of recommendation from the royal council, and the support of the Commons in parliament, who laid stress on his royal blood and his outstanding abilities. A letter of fulsome praise of his academic record was sent by Oxford University to the pope, to whose ruling Bourchier formally submitted on 27 December. Eventually, on 21 February 1435 Brouns was translated to Rochester and the pope cancelled his previous nomination to Worcester by an antedated bull in favour of Bourchier, whose nomination therefore bears the date 9 March 1434. When Bourchier was consecrated, on 14 March 1435, it was on the strength of a provision in which the pope declared that he had 'hitherto promoted no one of the like age to a cathedral church' (*CEPR letters*, 1427–1447, 213–19). The temporalities of the see were restored to him on 15 April.

In the course of the negotiations, at some point before 20 March 1434, Bourchier had been made chancellor of his university, a position he held for three years. He conducted his business in Nevill's Inn, one of the buildings that occupied the site of what is now Corpus Christi College. On 25 October 1435 the bishopric of Ely fell vacant. The chapter agreed to postulate Bourchier, who sent messengers to Rome to procure bulls for his translation from Worcester, but despite the papal provision in this instance he lacked the support of the king's ministers, who had a number of other preferred candidates for the see, which ultimately went to Louis de Luxembourg, archbishop of Rouen, in 1437. It was not until the latter died in 1443 that Bourchier was nominated by the king and elected by the chapter. Having received a bull for his translation, dated 20 December 1443, he was confirmed and had the temporalities restored to him on 27 February 1444. His conduct as bishop was adversely criticized by the historian of the monastery of Ely, who asserted that Bourchier had never celebrated mass in his own cathedral except on the day of his installation. Although there is ample evidence for his attendance on Henry VI's council at Westminster and elsewhere, Bourchier's registers for Worcester and Ely nevertheless show that he was conscientious about residing in both dioceses. He spent considerably more time at Worcester than he did away from it, at any rate after July 1437, while as bishop of Ely he resided in his diocese at least once a year, usually in the summer. Perhaps it was the fact that he never seems to have stayed at Ely itself that was resented in that house.

Bourchier was increasingly employed as a conciliator in disputes between his peers, a role for which he was apparently qualified not only by profession but also by temperament, for he was evidently regarded with genuine feelings of trust. Sir John Fastolf (*d.* 1459), generally suspicious of the motives of his contemporaries, referred to him as 'one of the lords earthly that I most trust upon' (*Paston Letters*, 2.109). Bourchier intervened to defuse violent local disputes between lords, as part of a process of applying his energies to matters of high political moment. In the critical days of February 1452 he was among the lords most closely occupied in preventing civil war by reaching terms with the duke of York, and on other occasions he engaged in arduous and delicate diplomacy as an arbitrator, reaching complex landed settlements. He was named as a mediator in the quarrels between the dukes of York and Somerset, and between the duke of Exeter and Lord Cromwell.

Chancellor of England Bourchier's stature increased in the winter of 1453–4 after Henry VI was struck by an incapacitating mental illness, and at the beginning of the third session of parliament in February 1454 it was he who, in the king's name, charged the Commons to elect a new speaker. When Cardinal John Kemp, the archbishop of Canterbury and chancellor, died on 22 March, Bourchier joined the deputation of lords in parliament who rode to Windsor the next day to inform the king and seek his guidance, but Henry failed to respond. Accordingly, the Lords appointed York as protector, and on 30 March the council, in compliance with a petition from the Commons, recommended Bourchier's promotion to the see of Canterbury, 'for his great merits, virtues and great blood that he is of' (*Proceedings … of the Privy Council*, 6.168). On 6 April the temporalities of Canterbury were committed to two of his brothers, his half-brother the duke of Buckingham, and other well-wishers. He was translated from Ely on 21 June, and the temporalities were restored to him on 6 August. On 6 September William Paston wrote 'My lord of Canterbury hath received his cross, and I was with him in the king's chamber when he made his homage' (*Paston Letters*, 1.155–6). He was enthroned on 24 January 1455, following the king's recovery. On 7 March he was appointed chancellor, in place of York's ally the earl of Salisbury, and received the seals at Greenwich. Meanwhile, he had helped pave the way for Somerset's release from the Tower of London, yet, remarkably, apparently also retained the confidence of York, despite the failure of his attempts to mediate between them, and his acceptance of office in Henry VI's revived court regime. It was to Bourchier as chancellor and archbishop that York and his allies wrote to declare their peaceable intentions in May 1455, claiming that they were marching south to do the king service and to vindicate their loyalty. Bourchier allegedly sent a special messenger to the king at Kilburn, but this man was not allowed to come into the royal presence, so the opportunity to prevent armed conflict was lost. Following the Yorkist victory at the battle of St Albans on 22 May Bourchier was retained as chancellor, and his brother Henry (York's brother-in-law) was made treasurer a week later. The archbishop made the opening speech to the assembled Lords and Commons on 9 July, and it was he who prorogued the parliament at the end of the month. In October, after news of the murder of Nicholas Radford and the breakdown of order in the west country 'was told to my Lord Chaunceler' (*Paston Letters*, 2.127), the Lords in parliament reluctantly agreed to York's reappointment as protector, and on 17 November Bourchier announced the royal assent. He then survived both York's brief eminence and its peremptory conclusion. In the summer of 1456 he and his brother, the treasurer, attempted to carry on the business of government in London by holding a great council there, but the focus of power was shifting to the midlands, to the queen, Margaret of Anjou, and her supporters. A few months later both brothers were suddenly discharged from office, Thomas Bourchier being dismissed on 11 October. Their half-brother Buckingham, attending a great council at Coventry in October, was reported to have taken their dismissal 'right straungely' (*Paston Letters*, 2.165). Nevertheless, the archbishop continued his endeavours as a peacemaker, and the temporary reconciliation of the factions in the spring of 1458 is largely attributable to his efforts. He needed also to deal with conflict within the church. In the previous year he had cited Reginald Pecock, bishop of Chichester, to appear before him to answer charges of heresy. On receiving an adverse verdict from the commission to which Pecock's works had been committed for examination, he faced him with the alternative of abjuration or burning; when Pecock chose the former and resigned his see, he had him confined at Canterbury. At Bourchier's request the Augustinian friar John Bury wrote his *Gladius Salomonis* as a reply to Pecock's *Repressor*.

Supporter of York Immediately following the flight of the Yorkists, after the confrontation at Ludford on 12 October 1459, Bourchier joined his brothers and Buckingham in taking oaths of allegiance to Henry VI at the Coventry parliament in November. It may have been the attainder of two of his nephews (Thomas and John, the sons of his brother Henry) in the same parliament, and his increasing impotence as the queen's party grew in strength, that made him more partisan. By the summer of 1460 the Yorkist earls were confident of his help. Before crossing the channel from Calais they forwarded to him copies of their manifesto, and he met them at Sandwich and rode with his cross borne before them to London, which admitted them on 2 July. Next day he opened a session of a convocation at St Paul's to which the earls recited their grievances. It was resolved that he and five of his suffragans should accompany the Yorkist army to Northampton to use their diplomatic skills to obtain a peaceful settlement with the king. These efforts failed, and in the ensuing battle, on 10 July, Bourchier's half-brother Buckingham died fighting on the Lancastrian side. Henry VI was escorted into London by the Yorkists, and Bourchier was temporarily given custody of the seals, until the 25th. His brother Henry was again made treasurer, and they and the Nevilles assumed control over the administration. Even so, the archbishop was not yet ready to co-operate in the deposition of the king. York apparently failed to consult him before making his dramatic entry into the parliament chamber to claim the throne on 10 October, and Bourchier immediately showed that he did not condone the duke's repudiation of allegiance. However, two weeks later the Lords including Bourchier agreed to the compromise by which York should succeed after Henry VI's death. Only in February 1461, after York had been killed at Wakefield, and when the triumphant queen's forces were threatening London, did the archbishop concur that York's son Edward, earl of March, should be set on the throne in Henry's place. Initially he had fled with the chancellor, Bishop George Neville (*d*. 1476), to Canterbury, awaiting better news, but they returned to London where, at a meeting of the earl's council on 3 March, they agreed that Edward was now rightful king.

Bourchier's support for Edward IV from the first day of his reign is unquestionable. He was immediately ordained to be a councillor, with a salary of £200 per annum, and on 28 June he set the crown upon Edward's head. Four years later, on 26 May 1465, he also crowned Edward's queen, Elizabeth Woodville. His wholehearted commitment to the new regime extended to financial support, both for the king himself, in the form of loans, and for the king's brothers, whom he assisted 'for a long time at great charges' (*CPR*, *1467–77*, 295–6). Furthermore, he took on the trusteeship of estates belonging to other members of the royal family. It was a sign of his standing that from time to time he was commissioned to prorogue or dissolve parliaments in the king's place. For example, he dissolved parliament during Edward's absence on 2 May 1462, and acted as his locum for part of that of 1463–5. As a reward, and also as a means of obtaining a show of papal support for the Yorkist dynasty, the king petitioned Pope Paul II (*r*. 1464–71) to make Bourchier a cardinal in 1465, and it appears that he was actually named accordingly on 18 September 1467, although several years elapsed before the red hat was sent and his title of cardinal-priest of San Ciriaco in Thermis formally acknowledged in England. In 1469 the pope wrote to the king, promising that it should be dispatched shortly, but the readeption of Henry VI no doubt delayed its transmission further, and it was only sent by the succeeding pope, Sixtus IV (*r*. 1471–84), in 1473. It was reported that Edward IV teased George Neville, now archbishop of York, by sending him the papal letter of 1467 naming Bourchier as a cardinal, when Neville had been blatantly seeking a similar position in Rome, and this may have soured Bourchier's own relations with the Nevilles, who at the start of the readeption had him arrested. Although he was released and summoned to the 1470 parliament, he and his brother Essex secretly worked for Edward's restoration both by mediating with the duke of Clarence, whom they succeeded in winning over to his brother's cause, and by raising armed retinues to bolster Edward's forces. The archbishop sent a timely warning to Edward not to land at Cromer, Norfolk, which was well defended, and following his successful landing further north Bourchier welcomed him to London on 11 April 1471. After the victory at Barnet on the 14th he was among the first to acknowledge Edward's newly born son as prince of Wales, and was one of those appointed to counsel the prince and administer his lands during his minority. In the 1470s Bourchier remained a prominent member of the king's council, and in 1475 when Edward IV set out with his army for France, he was nominated to the executive body left in control of English affairs. In the agreement made between Edward IV and Louis XI at Picquigny, the cardinal was named as one of just four arbitrators (two from each country) to whom the differences between England and France were referred. Rewards for Bourchier's services included valuable wardships, notably those of the heirs of the duke of Buckingham and Lord Latimer.

Last years and death In 1480, feeling the effects of age, Bourchier appointed a suffragan, but three years later, after the unexpected death of Edward IV, he was again called upon to take part in public affairs. On 2 May 1483 the young Edward V, on his way to London, wrote to him requesting him to see to the safety of the Tower and the treasure there, and five days later Bourchier took official custody of the royal jewels and seals, as the executors of Edward IV's will hesitated to act. He saw that the funeral expenses of nearly £1500 were paid. Surprisingly, during the critical two weeks at the end of May and beginning of June he withdrew from London to Knole, but then, on 16 June, as the head of a deputation from the council, he played a crucial part in persuading the king's mother to deliver up her second son, Richard, duke of York, from sanctuary at Westminster to the keeping of his uncle the protector, Richard of Gloucester. To what extent deception was practised on him by the protector remains uncertain. Domenico Mancini, an eyewitness, claimed that Gloucester surrounded the abbey with troops, and that the cardinal, 'suspecting no guile', sought only to prevent violation of the sanctuary (*Usurpation*, 88). There is no reason to suppose that he either encouraged or resisted Gloucester's usurpation, although it may well have caused him unease. He crowned him Richard III on 6 July, although Mancini says he was reluctant to do so, and he did not attend the coronation banquet. His favourite nephew, Sir Thomas Bourchier of Berners, joined the rebellion against the new king in the autumn, and the archbishop thought it prudent to procure a royal pardon for himself on 8 December. Henceforth there is no record of his attendance on Richard's council. He crowned Henry VII on 30 October 1485, and on 18 January 1486 married him to Elizabeth of York.

In 1456 Bourchier had purchased from Lord Saye and Sele the manor of Knole in Sevenoaks, which he adopted as a favourite residence, altered substantially, and bequeathed to the see of Canterbury. Margaret Paston had remarked in 1469 that he was 'an old man' who might 'happe to dye' at any moment (*Paston Letters*, 1.337), but he lived on for seventeen more years. In his will, dated 27 March 1486, he left several valuable images, jewels, and vestments, and a great bowl of gold (this last to be kept as a family heirloom). His bequests of £100 each to the universities for the creation of loan chests to benefit poor scholars, while generous, nevertheless compare poorly with the great foundations at Oxford of his contemporaries Henry Chichele and William Waynflete. He died at Knole three days later, and was buried beneath an imposing monument next to the high altar in Canterbury Cathedral. LINDA CLARK

Sources *Registrum Thomae Bourgchier … 1454–1486*, ed. F. R. H. Du Boulay, CYS, 54 (1957) • *CEPR letters*, vols. 8, 10 • N. Davis, ed., *Paston letters and papers of the fifteenth century*, 2 vols. (1971–6) • N. H. Nicolas, ed., *Proceedings and ordinances of the privy council of England*, 7 vols., RC, 26 (1834–7) • *The usurpation of Richard the third: Dominicus Mancinus ad Angelum Catonem de occupatione regni Anglie per Ricardum tercium libellus*, ed. and trans. C. A. J. Armstrong, 2nd edn (1969) [Lat. orig., 1483, with parallel Eng. trans.] • *RotP*, vols. 5–6 • H. T. Riley, ed., *Registra quorundam abbatum monasterii S. Albani*, 1, Rolls Series, 28/6 (1872) • L. L. Duncan, 'The will of Cardinal Bourgchier, archbishop of Canterbury, 1486', *Archaeologia Cantiana*, 24 (1900), 244–52 • F. R. H. Du Boulay, 'Note on the rebuilding of Knole by Archbishop Bourgchier', *Archaeologia Cantiana*, 63 (1950), 135–9 • [H. Wharton], ed., *Anglia sacra*, 1 (1691), 671–2 • J. Le Neve, *Fasti ecclesiae anglicanae* (1716) • L. S. Woodger, 'Henry Bourgchier, earl of Essex, and his family, 1408–83', DPhil diss., U. Oxf., 1974

Archives BL, Harley MSS

Likenesses monument, Canterbury Cathedral • seal, BL; Birch, *Seals*, 1252

Bourchier, Thomas (*d. c.*1586), Observant Franciscan friar, is of obscure origins. Wadding and Sbaralea suggested that he might be identical with another Franciscan, Thomas Langton, but Parkinson has Langton and Bourchier as two distinct men. Thomas was descended from the Bourchiers who were earls of Bath, but his place of birth is unknown. He was educated at Magdalen College, Oxford, and went to Paris for religious reasons, where he became a Franciscan, if he was not one before then. Wolfgang Eder, the printer of the Ingoldstadt edition (1583) of Bourchier's *Historia*, said on good authority that Bourchier entered the order in 1566, which would suggest that he died in his forties. However, Davenport said that he became a Franciscan at Greenwich in the reign of Queen Mary, and Gillow gives the year 1558.

Bourchier received a doctorate in theology at the Sorbonne, and was highly respected for holiness and learning. He eventually went to Rome, stayed at the Aracoeli friary, and was appointed a penitentiary at the basilica of St John Lateran. He wrote much, said John Pits, who knew him. At the time of his death he was, according to the rather prejudiced Robert Parsons, 'younge, stronge, lustie, and vehement in the faction' against the Jesuits in the setting up of the English College in Rome. In 1585 a 'frier boutser' (*Memoirs*) corresponded with Sir Francis Walsingham, Queen Elizabeth's secretary of state, perhaps officially, about moderation in matters of religion.

Thomas Bourchier's reputation rests principally on his work as an ecclesiastical historian. The first edition of his history was entitled *Historia ecclesiastica de martyrio fratrum ordinis divi Francisci, dictorum de observantia*, and was printed in Paris in 1582. The book covered the period between 1536 and 1582. Well aware of the death of many at home and abroad for religious reasons, Bourchier wrote accounts of five Observant Franciscan martyrs in England; other martyrs in the Netherlands and the Spanish Netherlands; two Irish martyrs, Bishop Patrick *O'Healy and Conn O'Rourke (beatified in 1992); and finally the martyrs of Flanders, including the Scot John Gray. The title and contents were rearranged in the Ingoldstadt edition of 1583. Bourchier's *Historia* was the first published account of the martyrs, and is important for the transmission of the *fama martyrii*. That his work is generally reliable is clear from the detailed account of the two Irish martyrs (*d.* 1579), which he probably got from an Irish source in Paris; Bourchier had, in fact, lived for a while with O'Healy and O'Rourke in the Paris friary, 1578–9. Pages 185–234 read like a long sermon or address on self-defence in the fight against evil and the consequences of being overcome, using examples from the animal world. This is applied to Henry VIII and Elizabeth I, who were learned persons; Bourchier said Elizabeth knew Latin, Greek, French, Italian, Spanish, and German. According to Allison and Rogers the account of the Flemish martyrs is by Florentinus van Oyen of Leiden. There were several further editions of Bourchier's work, which were used by many Franciscan chroniclers and others. He did not edit, as was thought, the Latin translation by Socolovius of *Censura orientalis ecclesiae* by Hieremias II, patriarch of Constantinople. He had hoped to publish the *Liber ad fratres* of the English martyr Thomas Belchiam, written to inspire the friars and others to stand firm in their faith.

Thomas Bourchier died at the basilica of St John Lateran, Rome, about 1586. He was probably buried with the friars of Aracoeli. IGNATIUS FENNESSY

Sources L. Waddingus [L. Wadding], *Scriptores ordinis minorum*, [new edn] (1906) · J. H. Sbaralea, *Supplementum … ad scriptores … S. Francisci*, 3 vols. (Rome, 1908–36) · A. F. Allison and D. M. Rogers, eds., *The contemporary printed literature of the English Counter-Reformation between 1558 and 1640*, 1 (1989) · C. Walmesley, 'The Venerable Thomas Cort', *Archivum Franciscanum Historicum*, 19 (1926), 169–80 · Gillow, *Lit. biog. hist.* · [A. Parkinson], *Collectanea Anglo-minoritica* (1726) · Franciscus à Sancta Clara [C. Davenport], *Manuale missionariorum regularium* (1658) · J. Pits, *Relationum historicarum de rebus Anglicis*, ed. [W. Bishop] (Paris, 1619) · *Dermot O'Hurley, archbishop and companions 1579–1654*, Congregation for the Causes of Saints, 1 (1988) [Prot. N. 114] · Wood, *Ath. Oxon.*, 1st edn · J. H. Pollen, *The English Catholics in the reign of Queen Elizabeth* (1920), 248 · 'The memoirs of Father Robert Persons', ed. J. H. Pollen, *Miscellanea, II*, Catholic RS, 2 (1906), 12–218, esp. 34–5, 206

Bourchier, Sir William, **count of Eu** (*c*.**1374–1420**), magnate and soldier, was the son and heir of Sir William Bourchier (*d.* 1375) and his wife, Eleanor Lovayne (1345–1397).

Background and early career Bourchier's family had risen to prominence during the fourteenth century through an unblemished record of service to the crown, gaining estates concentrated in Suffolk and Essex. Sir Robert *Bourchier, William's grandfather, was the first layman to become chancellor of England, and was duly elevated to the peerage as a reward. Both he and his eldest son, John, the second lord, distinguished themselves in the wars with France, establishing a reputation for military prowess which many of their descendants sought to emulate. Ennoblement brought wealth, and a substantial estate centred upon Halstead in Essex, but since he was only a younger son William's father could expect little in the way of inheritance. He was, however, well placed to make a lucrative marriage, to Eleanor, the second daughter and coheir of Sir John Lovayne (*d.* 1347). She eventually succeeded to all her father's property, which comprised seven manors in Essex and Suffolk, including Little Easton, the family seat. These passed directly to Bourchier's father when she died in 1397, providing him with an income of about £154 a year net and adding greatly to his influence in the region.

The early death of his father, while he was still an infant, drew Bourchier into the orbit of his powerful neighbour, Thomas of Woodstock, duke of Gloucester (*d.* 1397). He may well have spent some of his youth in the ducal household at Pleshey Castle, Essex; and in May 1392, when he was about eighteen, he contracted to accompany the duke to Ireland, where he then held office as king's lieutenant. Gloucester's summary dismissal meant that they never actually set sail, but in 1394 the duke accompanied Richard II on an expedition there, and Bourchier travelled with them. He was knighted shortly afterwards. That he made an extremely favourable impression is evident from Gloucester's decision to engage him for life, in 1396, as a member of his personal retinue at a substantial fee of over £36 a year. His patron's arrest and murder in the following year must have come as a bitter blow to Sir William; although he was too shrewd to show his hand (and even served on a royal commission to levy a fine imposed upon the duke's partisans in Essex and Hertfordshire), he remained in close touch with members of Gloucester's circle. One such was Walter, Lord Fitzwalter, with whom he sailed to Ireland in 1398, possibly remaining there for the rest of Richard II's reign. The value of his services was soon recognized by Henry IV, who arranged in March 1400 for the fee previously granted to him by Gloucester to be assigned directly upon the exchequer at Westminster and thus rendered more secure. Henry, prince of Wales, also thought highly of Sir William, assigning him a similar annuity as a knight of his chamber, in 1401, and entrusting him with the diplomatically sensitive task of negotiating two royal marriages with King Erik of Denmark. He returned to England in the spring of 1403, in time for Henry IV's victory at the battle of Shrewsbury on 21 July that year.

Marriage to Anne of Woodstock Among the many fatalities on the king's side was Edmund Stafford, fifth earl of Stafford, who had been married to Gloucester's daughter, *Anne of Woodstock. As sole heir to the great estates left by the duke and his wife, Eleanor de Bohun, she laid claim to an income worth over £2200 a year net. Although several of the properties in question were currently in other hands, she still ranked as one of the richest women in England and by far the greatest heiress. Then aged about twenty and the mother of one infant son, she offered any prospective husband the promise of great wealth combined with spectacular connections. Such a prize was not, however, within the common reach: Anne's proximity to the throne (she was a granddaughter of Edward III) and the extent of her holdings in eleven English counties, Wales, and Ireland made the question of her remarriage a matter of pressing political as well as financial concern to the crown. Until her cousin Henry V forced her to accept a repartition of the Bohun estates in 1421, she owned swathes of property across the south-east, including Pleshey Castle. In addition, her dower lands (from the third as well as the fifth earl) gave her control of well over half the Stafford inheritance, with a string of castles and lordships along the Welsh border. Fear that the rebels might seize one of these strongholds led Henry IV to entrust Sir William with the task of supervising the defences. He and Anne found themselves together at Huntington Castle in Herefordshire, and it seems to have been then, within a few weeks of Earl Edmund's death, that their clandestine marriage took place. Since they had almost certainly become acquainted at Pleshey in the 1390s, their conduct was less impetuous than it might at first appear. Not even Bourchier, a man of undoubted eloquence and charm, could expect to escape scot-free, but he was clearly prepared to risk the threat of Henry's immediate displeasure. His qualities as a soldier and administrator, as well as his proven loyalty to the beleaguered house of Lancaster, meant that he and his wife were soon excused the 'great sums' that Henry had ordered them to hand over personally in his chamber. Even so, there can be little doubt that, however highly they may have regarded Sir William, neither Henry IV nor his eldest son felt the slightest compunction in obstructing Anne's efforts to recover and retain substantial parts of her inheritance—an inheritance that might, but for Sir William, have been enjoyed by one of their own kinsmen as her new husband. Bourchier's marriage received the unequivocal support of his neighbours in Essex, who had probably learned of it before the elections to the first parliament of 1404. This, his only known return to the House of Commons, reflects the warmth of feeling still felt in the county for the memory of the late duke, as well as the respect that he himself inspired.

Increased wealth and responsibilities During the years immediately after their marriage Bourchier and the countess enjoyed a net annual income of between £1300 and £1700 from her estates, which were administered separately by a staff of experienced bureaucrats. This was considerably less than she might have hoped for, but it represented untold riches for Sir William, who now lived the life of an English nobleman in all but name. Over the year ending September 1409, for example, payments in excess of £894 were made into his own coffers by Anne's officials, she received her customary allowance of £266 for personal expenses, and their joint household cost about £442. Bourchier's private income from this source fluctuated considerably, but never appears to have fallen below £412. His new status brought with it a heavy burden of responsibilities, including the protection of Anne's lordships along the Welsh border, which were still vulnerable to attack. For much of the time he remained in attendance upon Prince Henry, fighting under his banner throughout the summer of 1404, and again, in 1407, when the rebel force supporting Owain Glyn Dŵr at Aberystwyth surrendered after a long siege. As a marcher lord he clearly had a vested personal interest in the suppression of disorder in Wales. He did not, even so, miss the opportunity to extend his own holdings by leasing property in Essex and Norfolk that had been confiscated from a number of alien priories by the government. His membership of the Essex bench, on which he sat for approximately seven years, also bolstered his authority in the region. In this and many other respects, Bourchier profited greatly from his close association with Prince Henry, who mounted the throne in 1413, and (initially at least) looked more favourably upon some of the Countess Anne's claims as a widow and an heiress. He allowed her to recover her father's lordship of Oakham, Rutland, and to collect revenues from the Stafford family estates in Ireland, using these concessions to reward his former companion-in-arms.

Service in France, and death As one of Henry's most trusted advisers Bourchier played a significant part in the diplomatic negotiations that preceded the outbreak of hostilities with France in 1415. He spent several weeks in Paris discussing 'secret matters' with the French king's emissaries (PRO, E404/31/106), being paid £100 in expenses sustained on a mission which, despite its avowed intention of establishing a permanent peace between the two countries, was seen by the English as little more than a cosmetic exercise. Henry V was already mobilizing an army for the invasion of Normandy when Sir William returned home in March. An experienced commander, whose keen intelligence evidently matched his valour in the field, Bourchier now took his place among the leading English captains. He contracted to serve with a large contingent of ninety mounted archers and twenty-nine men-at-arms, and was singled out as one of the beneficiaries of the will that King Henry made in July 1415, just as the army was about to sail. He was promised one of the king's best horses, an appropriate legacy in view of the great bravery he is said to have displayed during the battle of Agincourt in the following October, when 102 men fought directly under him. A number of distinguished prisoners were taken back to England by the victorious army and held in the Tower of London. Since Edward, duke of York, the previous constable, had fallen at Agincourt, Bourchier seemed an ideal replacement. He held the constableship of the Tower from November 1415 until his death, with special responsibility for the safe keeping of the French captives. He was, in addition, granted the less demanding post of master of the royal hounds. As might be expected, given the confidence that he inspired, he was sent as an envoy to receive the visiting emperor, Sigismund, when the latter arrived at Rochester in the spring of 1416. King Henry showed his approval in more concrete ways, too, allowing him to farm some of the estates of his stepson, Humphrey Stafford, future duke of Buckingham (*d.* 1460), and of other royal wards.

Bourchier played an even more important part in Henry V's second expedition to France, which he joined with a personal retinue of 164 men, including 39 mounted lances. This was an army of occupation, whose commanders could expect a share of the conquered territories. After a summer of hard campaigning, in November 1417 Bourchier was given custody of the confiscated estates of the Hermanville family and of a large town house called the Golden Lion in Caen. He spent much of the following year at the sieges of Louviers and Rouen, and in February 1419 assumed the captaincy of Dieppe, which had surrendered to him just a few days before. In order to maintain open lines of supply and communication, it was vital for the English to keep the port firmly under their control, so the appointment was no sinecure.

Bourchier became serjeant of Mantes and Meulan as well, being entrusted with the task of provisioning King Henry's headquarters while he was in the vicinity. It was at this time that Henry decided to take possession of the town and *comté* of Eu (to the north-east of Dieppe), whose lord, Charles d'Artois, then a prisoner in the Tower, had consistently refused to acknowledge his suzerainty. Bourchier was instructed to appoint officials loyal to the English, and then, in June 1419, was himself given the *comté* in tail male. In all, six of Henry V's most valued adjutants were rewarded in this way, as part of a policy designed to strengthen the English presence in Normandy and give leading commanders a personal stake in the success of the enterprise. A few months later Bourchier and his male heirs were likewise confirmed in possession of the Hermanville estates, but he himself did not survive to enjoy them. He died at Troyes on 28 May 1420, his body being sent back to England for burial at Llanthony Priory in Gloucestershire.

The Bourchier legacy As her correspondence with her great friend the prior of Llanthony reveals, the Countess Anne had avidly followed the progress of the English army in France, recording with pride 'the valiant prowess, wisdom and good governance' of her husband (PRO, C115/K2/6682 fol. 129*r*). Her sorrow at his death seems to have been real and lasting: she never remarried and asked, in her will, to be buried beside him. She employed two priests at Little Easton to pray daily for his salvation, and had two masses sung each day at Llanthony for the same purpose. Whatever distress he may have felt at the loss of an old friend, Henry V showed little sentiment in his dealings with Anne, who was forced to accept a repartition of the Bohun estates in 1421, and obliged to struggle on for another decade before all her inheritance was restored to her. This may have intensified her determination to see that her five children with Bourchier did well for themselves, for it was she who promoted their careers and arranged their marriages. They did not disappoint her. Henry *Bourchier, the eldest, succeeded his father as count of Eu and eventually became first earl of Essex; Thomas *Bourchier, archbishop of Canterbury, dominated the political stage for over three decades; and both William and John were elevated to the peerage as, respectively, Lord Fitzwarine and Lord Berners. Their sister, Eleanor, married John (VI) Mowbray, third duke of Norfolk.

CAROLE RAWCLIFFE

Sources HoP, *Commons, 1386–1421*, 2.314–17 • L. S. Woodger, 'Henry Bourgchier, earl of Essex, and his family, 1408–83', DPhil diss., U. Oxf., 1974 • Staffs. RO, Stafford family papers, D.641 • GEC, *Peerage* • *Chancery records* • Longleat House, Wiltshire, Marquess of Bath MSS, Longleat MS 354 [for his own income] • PRO, E404/31/106 • cartulary of Llanthony Priory, PRO, C115/K2/6682

Wealth at death £154 p.a. net from estates; £1500 p.a. net from wife's estates: Longleat House, Wiltshire, Longleat MS 354; HoP, *Commons, 1386–1421*

Bourdillon, Sir Bernard Henry (1883–1948), colonial governor, was born on 3 December 1883 at Emu Bay, Tasmania, the eldest son of the Revd Bernard Keene Bourdillon (1855–1888), cleric, and Laura Elizabeth, daughter of

Sir Bernard Henry Bourdillon (1883–1948), by Walter Stoneman

Richard Townsend of co. Cork. He won scholarships to Tonbridge School in 1897 and to St John's College, Oxford, in 1902. In 1907 he came tenth out of 2706 candidates in the civil service exams, and entered the Indian Civil Service after another year at Oxford. In November 1909, while an assistant magistrate in the United Provinces, he married Violet Grace (1886–1979), daughter of the Revd Henry Godwin Billinghurst of Lynch, Sussex. They had three sons. She took an intense interest in India, as in every country to which her husband was posted, and was a great asset to him. She was referred to in 1935 as 'the perfect Governor's wife' (Pearce, 195). In 1910–11 Bourdillon was seconded to help compile the United Provinces census; in 1913 he became under-secretary to the government of the United Provinces; and in 1915 he was appointed registrar of the high court in Allahabad.

The turning point in Bourdillon's career came in 1918 when he joined the Mesopotamian expeditionary force. He was mentioned in dispatches for bravery during the subsequent Iraq insurrection, and served as land acquisition officer, as political secretary, and as counsellor from 1924 to 1929. Twice he deputized for the high commissioner, Sir Henry Dobbs. In 1926 he used the good relations he had established with King Feisal successfully to negotiate a new Anglo-Iraq treaty. Within a few years, however, he decided that Feisal should be forced to abdicate. Bourdillon also represented Iraq at meetings of the permanent mandates commission.

In 1929 Bourdillon became colonial secretary in Ceylon.

In 1931 the new Donoughmore constitution not only conceded universal suffrage but also saw the appointment of a number of Ceylonese ministers. Bourdillon, who was made KBE in June 1931, was appointed chief secretary, serving as a member of the state council and also as president of the board of ministers. In this position he had to bear the brunt of local criticisms. The poor health of Governor Sir Graeme Thomson added to Bourdillon's difficulties, as did the economic depression, which resulted in unpopular retrenchment and tax rises. The state council vetoed a number of government plans, necessitating the governor's use of reserve powers and leading Bourdillon to call for further reform. He was not popular in Ceylon, and his health suffered from overwork, but he proved himself a capable administrator and debater. It was with relief that in 1932 he obtained his first governorship, that of Uganda.

Inexperienced in Africa, Bourdillon proceeded cautiously. He implemented a levy on official salaries, only sanctioning increased expenditure in 1934 when the economic climate had improved. He also took time to tour all four provinces, getting to know the country and encouraging greater efficiency from the local chiefs. His major reform came in October 1934 with the Bunyoro agreement. The *mukama* wanted an agreement in order to symbolize equality with the other kings in Uganda; but, in return for enhancing the *mukama*'s prestige, Bourdillon insisted that he promise to follow official advice. What seemed to be an old-fashioned measure, preserving chiefly power, was in fact progressive, allowing the British to insist on change. Another reform came in 1933 when he sanctioned the appointment of a second Asian to sit on the legislative council, a measure designed to promote better relations with the Asian settlers. Bourdillon in Uganda was a representative figure in that his eyes were very much on the present rather than the future. Rapid change was thought unwise, especially as there was no consensus about the future of the African colonies. He was made a KCMG in 1934 and left Uganda in August 1935.

The climax of Bourdillon's career was in Nigeria, where he served, from October 1935, for eight years, promotion to the governor-generalship of Sudan in 1940 being vetoed because of the war. His governorship was distinguished by several features: first, helped by his wife, he made Government House in Lagos into a model of interracial harmony, becoming, arguably, the most popular governor in Nigeria's history. His was the human, acceptable face of colonialism. Although a fine actor of majesty—very tall and resplendent on ceremonial occasions in a uniform tailored from tussore silk—he was far from autocratic. In particular he established good relations with the Nigerian Youth Movement and with one of its leading radicals, Dr Nnamdi Azikiwe. Bourdillon saw a chance of guiding nationalism into constructive channels and of avoiding the sterile confrontation of Ceylon. Hence he tried to minimize tribal and regional differences and to lay the foundations for eventual Nigerian nationhood. He also tried to promote economic development: dispatches on this theme helped prepare the way for the 1940 Colonial Development and Welfare Act. He was also an important theorist of indirect rule: his insistence that acceptability to local opinion was the sole criterion for the appointment of a native authority greatly influenced Lord Hailey [*see* Hailey, (William) Malcolm]. In 1938 Bourdillon was appointed GCMG.

During the Second World War Bourdillon showed himself a bold and unorthodox executive. Testing times brought out the best in him. It is doubtful whether, without his help, the French Cameroons or Chad could have rallied successfully to the cause of General de Gaulle, who became godfather to the Bourdillons' first grandchild. Bourdillon also helped set up the west African governors' conference as a means of co-ordinating the war effort. On the domestic front, he pressed for accelerated economic growth, maximizing the colony's aid to Britain, and stimulating local import substitution. He also responded constructively to industrial troubles, instituting in July 1942 a back-dated cost of living allowance which the Colonial Office thought generous. Most important of all, defying his doctor's orders, he toured the northern provinces in February 1943 in order to persuade the emirs to take part in an all-Nigerian legislative council. He levelled a fatal blow at northern separatism, even though ill health meant that he had to leave Nigeria in May 1943, before his plans for the future had fully matured. He and his wife settled at Sandpits, Bepton, Midhurst, Sussex.

In retirement Bourdillon was a member of the Colonial Economic Advisory Council, chairman of the executive committee of the British Empire Leprosy Relief Association, and founding chairman of the Anglo-Iraqi Society. He was also a director of Barclays Bank and a magistrate in Midhurst. He wrote articles, book reviews, and *The Future of the Colonial Empire* (1945), which paid tribute to his wife's 'quite exceptional lack of all sense of class or colour' (Bourdillon, 7). He died of tuberculosis at the Bon Air Nursing Home, St Saviour, Jersey, on 6 February 1948.

ROBERT PEARCE

Sources R. D. Pearce, *Sir Bernard Bourdillon* (1987) • private information (2004) • B. Bourdillon, *The future of the colonial empire* (1945) • *CGPLA Eng. & Wales* (1948) • *DNB*

Archives Bodl. RH, corresp. with Lord Luggard • Bodl. RH, corresp. with R. D. Pearce

Likenesses W. Stoneman, photograph, NPG [*see illus.*]

Wealth at death £10,385 14*s*. 3*d*.: probate, 18 May 1948, *CGPLA Eng. & Wales*

Bourdillon, James Dewar (1811–1883), administrator in India, was the second son of Thomas Bourdillon (*d*. 1854), vicar of Fenstanton and Hilton, Huntingdonshire, and his wife, formerly Miss Dewar. He was educated partly by his father, and partly at a school at Ramsgate; having been nominated to a writership in the East India Company, he went to the East India College, Haileybury, in 1828, and in 1829 to Madras. After serving in various subordinate appointments in the provinces, he was appointed secretary to the board of revenue, and in 1854 secretary to government in the departments of revenue and public works. He was one of three members of a commission appointed to report upon the system of public works in the Madras presidency. The report of the commission, which was written by Bourdillon and published in 1856, emphasized the importance of irrigation and improved communications for the prevention of famines and the development of the country. Bourdillon was also the author of a treatise on the often misunderstood ryotwari system of land revenue, under which land rights were settled and revenues assessed on the ryots (individual cultivators) and which was characteristic of Madras. With Sir Thomas Pycroft he reformed the transaction of public business in the provinces and at the presidency, especially the reporting of the proceedings of local Madras government to the government of India and the secretary of state.

Bourdillon's health failed in 1861, and he was compelled to leave India and to retire from the civil service without achieving as high an appointment as he might have expected. He continued his interest in India, particularly financial questions, occasionally contributing to the *Calcutta Review*. He died suddenly at his home, 10 Calverley Park Gardens, Tunbridge Wells, on 21 May 1883 leaving a widow, Anne, and two sons, one of whom was in the Bengal civil service.

A. J. Arbuthnot, *rev.* Elizabeth Baigent

Sources C. C. Prinsep, *Record of services of the Honourable East India Company's civil servants in the Madras presidency from 1741 to 1858* (1885) · private information (1885) · personal knowledge (1885) · *CGPLA Eng. & Wales* (1884) · Boase, *Mod. Eng. biog.* · Venn, *Alum. Cant.*
Archives BL OIOC, letters to Lord Tweeddale, MS Eur. F 96
Wealth at death £5478 3*s*.: resworn probate, Feb 1884, *CGPLA Eng. & Wales* (1883)

Bourdillon, Thomas Duncan (1924–1956), mountaineer and physicist, was born at 24 Norland Square, North Kensington, London, on 16 March 1924, the elder son of Robert Benedict Bourdillon (1889–1971), scientist, and his wife, Harriet Ada Barnes. He was educated at Gresham's School, Holt, and Balliol College, Oxford (1942–4, 1948–50), where his studies were interrupted by military service. During the Second World War he saw service in Greece and Egypt. In 1950, after leaving Oxford, where he obtained a third-class degree in physics, he was attached to the Ministry of Supply at Westcott, Buckinghamshire, where he worked on the development of rocket engines. On 15 March 1951 he married Jennifer Elizabeth Clapham Thomas (*b.* 1929/30), daughter of Ronald Clapham Thomas, bank official.

In 1951 Bourdillon accompanied Eric Shipton on the Mount Everest reconnaissance expedition which prospected a route through that peak's formidable southern defences, the Khumbu icefall in Nepal. During the trip he also climbed with W. H. Murray to the Nangpa La, a high pass on the Tibetan border, from where a possible route on nearby Cho Oyu was discerned. This was attempted the following year as a warm-up climb for Everest, again with Shipton as leader. Experimenting with oxygen apparatus on this expedition prompted Bourdillon to investigate the practicalities of a 'closed circuit' system. This he developed in conjunction with his father, who worked at the Electro-Medical Research Unit, Stoke Mandeville. Racing

Thomas Duncan Bourdillon (1924–1956), by Alfred Gregory, 1953

against the clock, they produced eight prototype sets for the 1953 Everest expedition, led by John Hunt.

The principle of the closed-circuit system is that the climber receives 100 per cent oxygen from the bottle without air entering the face mask, as it does in the standard 'open-circuit' apparatus. Expired carbon dioxide is 'scrubbed' by passing through soda lime so that a proportion of the breathed oxygen is available for rebreathing, thus extending the life of each bottle of oxygen and reducing the number of bottles required by those using the apparatus. Tests on the mountain were encouraging and, with this closed-circuit system, Bourdillon and Charles Evans on 26 May 1953 made their prodigious climb from the south col to the south summit (28,700 feet) of Everest and back, opening the route for Hillary and Tenzing to go to the summit with open-circuit sets three days later, as the first climbers ever to do so.

Bourdillon—who was described by friends as generous, cheerful, unruffled, dependable, and 'too shy', and by Hunt in *The Ascent of Everest* (1953) as 'huge and hefty, built like a second-row rugby forward'—had climbing in his blood. His father was a founder member of the Oxford University mountaineering club in 1909. Sir Arnold Lunn told the story (in *A Century of Mountaineering*, 1957) that on the premise that 'a scientist must know something about electricity', Bourdillon senior was put in charge of the club's lantern for showing lantern slides; when young Bourdillon joined the club, he too was appointed 'lanternist' to maintain the tradition. An outstanding rock climber and an enthusiast for the new vogue of 'artificial climbing' which so shocked traditionalists, Bourdillon was at the forefront of a post-war renaissance in British alpinism. He took on some of the most difficult alpine routes of the day (north face of Dru, Mer de Glace face of Grépon by Aig du Roc), and he became the first president of the élite Alpine Climbing Group (1954–6), which did so much to raise the profile of British mountaineers on the international stage.

Bourdillon was killed—along with another fine British climber, Richard Viney—in a climbing accident on 29 July

1956 while ascending the east buttress of the Jägihorn in the Bernese Oberland of Switzerland. His widow, their daughter aged nineteen months, and son of ten weeks survived him. AUDREY SALKELD

Sources H. G. Nichol and J. Hunt, *Alpine Journal*, 61 (1956), 357–61 · T. H. B., *Himalayan Journal*, 20 (1957), 137 · *Edinburgh Evening News* (31 July 1956) · J. Hunt, *The ascent of Everest* (1953) · E. Shipton, *Mount Everest reconnaissance expedition 1951* (1952) · A. Lunn, *A century of mountaineering* (1957) · *Report of Medical Research Council* (1952–3) · b. cert. · m. cert. · E. Lemon, ed., *The Balliol College register, 1916–1967*, 4th edn (privately printed, Oxford, 1969)
Archives FILM BFI NFTVA, documentary footage
Likenesses A. Gregory, photograph, 1953, RGS [*see illus.*] · photograph, repro. in Nichol and Hunt, *Alpine Journal*, facing p. 358 · photographs, RGS · photographs, Alpine Club, London
Wealth at death £1388 13*s.* 8*d.*: administration with will, 28 Sept 1956, *CGPLA Eng. & Wales*

Bourdin, Martial (1867/8–1894), anarchist, was born in Tours, France, of working-class parents, and was one of eight siblings. He developed radical sympathies at an early age and when barely in his teens devoted himself to the anarchist cause. During his early years he also learned the trade of tailoring, and by 1884 was probably working as a ladies' tailor in Paris. Anarchist ideas found fertile ground among French artisans of the period, and Bourdin is believed to have joined a group of anarchist tailors, numbering at one time some sixty members, who were known as L'Aiguille ('The Needle'). He apparently adopted the alias of J. Allder for the purposes of his anarchist activities, and in 1884 was sentenced to two months' imprisonment for attempting to organize a meeting in a public thoroughfare.

After release from prison Bourdin went abroad for a time. About 1887 he moved to London to join his brother Henri, who worked there as a master tailor for ladies in a workshop at 18 Great Titchfield Street, Marylebone. From time to time Martial undertook piece-work for his brother. Martial soon made the acquaintance of foreign anarchists who belonged to clubs in the district. He attended meetings at the anarchist-communist Autonomie Club, 'the chief refuge of all Continental Anarchists arriving in London' (Melville, fol. 5), which had premises at 30 (and later 6) Windmill Street, off Tottenham Court Road. In addition to spreading anarchist ideas, one of the club's main purposes was to raise money for penniless anarchists fleeing the continent, and Bourdin energetically organized subscription lists, concerts, excursions, and balls towards this end. For a time he was secretary of the French-speaking section of the club. He also participated in demonstrations in Trafalgar Square.

After a period in London, Bourdin returned to France. Some time later he went back to London, and from there, apparently in possession of ample funds, travelled to America. He spent a year working as a tailor in New York city and the upstate region, and also visited Chicago. From America Bourdin returned to France, and then to London, where he resumed his lodgings at 30 Fitzroy Street, St Pancras, in late 1893.

The events which occurred on Thursday 15 February 1894, ending in Bourdin's death, can be traced in outline, though several crucial elements remain obscure. About noon Bourdin visited his brother's premises to ask for work, but was told there was none available. He took lunch a short distance away, about 2 p.m., at the International Restaurant in Bennett Street, Fitzroy Square, where he was joined by two companions, one of whom was probably his brother-in-law H. B. Samuels (*d.* 1933). Bourdin left the restaurant at 2.50 p.m., and was accompanied, probably by Samuels, as far as Whitehall. At 3.10 p.m. Bourdin boarded a tram, alone, at the Westminster Bridge terminus, and travelled on it to the East Greenwich terminus, where it arrived at 4.19 p.m. He seemed to have missed his stop, for he asked the conductor for directions back to Greenwich Park, and hurried away. A timekeeper at the terminus noticed that he had a bulky item in his pocket. Just after entering Greenwich Park, Bourdin was observed by a park gardener to be carrying a parcel, about the size of a brick, in his left hand. Bourdin began to climb the zig-zag path which led up towards the Royal Observatory. At 4.51 p.m., when he was 46 yards from the observatory, the parcel he was carrying exploded, blowing away part of his left hand and causing severe injury to his abdomen and chest. He managed to retreat a little way down the path. Some schoolboys who were walking through the park heard the explosion and saw a plume of smoke rise through the trees. They ran to the scene and found Bourdin kneeling, covered in blood, his left hand bound with a handkerchief. Bourdin said to them, 'Fetch a cab', and when some park-keepers arrived said, 'Take me home'. A doctor was called, and brandy was administered to Bourdin. He was taken to the nearby Royal Naval Hospital where he was admitted 'in a state of partial collapse' (*Kentish Mercury*, 23 Feb 1894, 3) at 5.15 p.m. After being put to bed he said, 'I'm cold', and could only occasionally be roused. He died twenty-five minutes after admission, at 5.40 p.m.

The questions of where Bourdin obtained his bomb and for what he intended to use it have never been resolved. A recipe for a bomb, copied from a book in the British Museum, was found on his body, and further information about explosives was discovered in his room. It was claimed by David Nicoll in his pamphlet *The Greenwich Mystery* (1897) that Samuels, acting for the police as an *agent provocateur*, supplied Bourdin with the bomb-making chemicals, but Nicoll's account is unreliable. Two months after the explosion an acquaintance of Bourdin, the anarchist Francis Polti, was caught carrying a bomb identical to Bourdin's, and under police interrogation alleged that a friend of his, a mechanic named Giuseppe Farnara, had supplied Bourdin with the fatal bomb.

Newspapers were quick to surmise that the target of Bourdin's bomb was the Royal Observatory at Greenwich, and this view was officially endorsed by Colonel Vivian Majendie, the government's explosives expert, who gave evidence at the coroner's enquiry into Bourdin's death. Majendie's conclusion was repudiated, however, by the anarchists, who pointed out that it was against their principles to attack scientific institutions as these were dedicated to the advancement of humanity. In an obituary in

The Commonweal, Samuels maintained that Bourdin's intention that day had been to test out the bomb in a deserted location, and that he had been on his way to do so when the explosion occurred. The anarchist Max Nettlau suggested another alternative: that Bourdin had aimed to pass the bomb on to a fellow anarchist somewhere by the Thames so that it could be taken over to France. There was also speculation, however, that Bourdin himself intended to deliver the bomb to anarchists in France, and had gone to Greenwich in an attempt to shake off any police spies who might have been following him.

Bourdin's death was widely reported in the newspapers and caused a great sensation. Only three days earlier an anarchist had thrown a bomb in a crowded café in Paris, causing death and injury; and many people feared that the Greenwich explosion heralded the spread of continental anarchist terrorism to British soil. Newspapers queried the wisdom of continuing to give foreign revolutionaries asylum in Britain, and the question was raised in the House of Commons as to whether the government might consider reversing its policy on immigration in the light of the incident.

Bourdin achieved martyrdom in the eyes of certain anarchists, and photographs of him taken after death and memorial cards were circulated in large numbers. The home secretary, Herbert Asquith, fearing that Bourdin's funeral might be turned into an anarchist demonstration, gave orders that the police should prevent any procession from following the hearse and restrain anyone who attempted to make a speech at the graveside. On 23 February, several violent anti-anarchist demonstrations took place, and a noisy, largely hostile crowd of more than 1000 people attended Bourdin's swift interment at St Pancras cemetery, Finchley.

Bourdin was small in stature, at only 5 feet 1 inch, and had fair hair, a fair moustache, and blue eyes. He was described by acquaintances as quiet, reserved, and secretive in nature, tenacious in his devotion to the anarchist cause, but lacking in personal affection. He was not married, though one newspaper article (*Morning Leader*, 24 Feb 1894) makes the dubious suggestion that he was engaged. Several characters in works of fiction have been modelled after him. He appears in the guise of Augustin Myers in Helen and Olive Rossetti's novel (published under the pseudonym Isabel Meredith), *A Girl among the Anarchists* (1903)—a novel which endorses the notion that Bourdin died through the treachery of his brother-in-law Samuels, who was acting for the police. Much modern interest in Bourdin derives from Joseph Conrad's remodelling of him as Stevie in *The Secret Agent* (1907). In creating the character of Stevie, Conrad relied on descriptions, now discredited, of Bourdin as a simpleton who had a childlike admiration for the older man, Samuels. Conrad fashions a sympathetic portrait of Stevie as a just and passionate, if slow-witted, youth, who meets his death while on his way to place a bomb outside the Royal Observatory, Greenwich, at the behest of his brother-in-law, the *agent provocateur* Adolph Verloc. Conrad's novel has helped to sustain Bourdin's reputation as the man who tried to blow up the observatory. Although this is probably an inaccurate charge, Bourdin will remain notorious for the excruciating manner of his death and the impenetrable circumstances that surround it. PAUL GIBBARD

Sources H. Oliver, *The international anarchist movement in late Victorian London* (1983) • H. B. Samuels, *The Commonweal* (10 March 1894) • *Morning Leader* (17 Feb 1894) • *Morning Leader* (19 Feb 1894) • *Morning Leader* (21 Feb 1894) • *Morning Leader* (24 Feb 1894) • *Morning Leader* (26 Feb 1894) • *Morning Leader* (27 Feb 1894) • *The Times* (16–24 Feb 1894) • *The Times* (27 Feb 1894) • *Kentish Mercury* (23 Feb 1894) • *Kentish Mercury* (2 March 1894) • N. Sherry, *Conrad's western world* (1971) [incl. D. Nicoll, *The Greenwich mystery* (1897) in an appx] • H. H. Asquith, instructions for the policing of Bourdin's funeral, 1894, PRO, HO 144/257/A55660, fol. 5 • W. Melville, police report on the Autonomie Club, 1893, PRO, HO 45/9739/A54881, fol. 5 • *ILN* (24 Feb 1894) • *Lloyd's Weekly Newspaper* (18 Feb 1894) • *Daily Graphic* (17 Feb 1894) • *Daily Graphic* (27 Feb 1894) • J. Maitron, *Le mouvement anarchiste en France*, 2 vols. (1975), vol. 1 • J. Quail, *The slow burning fuse: the lost history of the British anarchists* (1978) • I. Meredith [H. Rossetti and O. Rossetti], *A girl among the anarchists* (1903) • J. Conrad, *The secret agent* (1907) • D. Mulry, Popular accounts of the Greenwich bombing and Conrad's *The secret agent*, rmmla.wsu.edu/ereview/54.2/articles/mulry.asp, 1 Aug 2001 • d. cert.

Likenesses drawing, 1894, repro. in *Daily Graphic* (17 Feb 1894) • drawing, 1894, repro. in *Lloyd's Weekly Newspaper* (18 Feb 1894) • drawing, 1894, repro. in *Morning Leader* (17 Feb 1894) • two photographs, 1894 (posthumous)

Wealth at death generally in funds; £12 19*s*. 3½*d*. found on body; various chattels: H. B. Samuels, *The Commonweal* (10 March 1894); *Morning Leader* (27 Feb 1894)

Bourgeois, Sir (Peter) Francis (1756–1811), landscape painter and founder of the Dulwich Picture Gallery, was given to obfuscation and romance where his origins were concerned; but he was born in London, the son of Issac Bourgeois (*b*. 1707/8), who was of Swiss descent, and his wife, Elizabeth Gardin (*d*. *c*.1766), an Englishwoman presumably of Huguenot stock. Issac was a watchmaker in St Martin's Lane, who, Benjamin West told Joseph Farington, left England on the death of his wife, abandoning both the young Francis and his sister. Bourgeois told Farington (who, like West, was a friend) that he was looked after by his future dealing partner Noel Desenfans from the age of ten, his sister being sent to Switzerland. However, Bourgeois's account may not be accurate, given Desenfans's circumstances about 1766, but it does seem certain that Bourgeois was under Desenfans's care from about 1776. He lived thereafter with Desenfans and his wife, Margaret Morris.

Desenfans arranged for Bourgeois to be taught by P. J. de Loutherbourg, whose style of painting he adopted, although hardly justifying his own aim 'to attain Mr. Loutherbourg in execution, Mr. Gainsborough in colour and Mr. [Richard] Wilson in forms and grandeur' (Whitley, 2.142). In 1776, as part of his training, Desenfans sent Bourgeois on a tour of France, the Netherlands, Italy, and Switzerland. The grand design, of forming an important artist out of a minimal talent, culminated in Bourgeois's election first as an associate of the Royal Academy (1787) and then as an academician (1793), following much 'puffing' in the press orchestrated by Desenfans and the lavish entertainment of academicians. The campaign was lent

Sir (Peter) Francis Bourgeois (1756–1811), by Sir William Beechey, *c.*1810

weight by the award in 1791 of a knighthood (or its equivalent) to Bourgeois by Stanisław August, king of Poland, who made him his official painter. The knighthood came about through a visit of Prince Michael Poniatowski, the king of Poland's brother, to London in 1790, when he asked Desenfans to devote himself to creating a major art collection for the king. The title was recognized in the same year by George III, who appointed Bourgeois his landscape painter in 1794. Between 1779 and 1810 Bourgeois exhibited 103 pictures at the Royal Academy (and five at the British Institution). Contemporaries were by no means always impressed with his work, but he was evidently charming in a dandiacal way: the poet and critic Leigh Hunt said of him: 'His oath and buckskin would never allow me to consider him a serious person' (Waterfield, 17).

Bourgeois and Desenfans were very much a dealing partnership, even though Bourgeois was 'officially' a painter first and foremost, and Desenfans liked to pretend that his pictures were merely the collection of a gentleman. They were busy as dealers in the 1780s and, after 1786, when the household moved to 38 and 39 Charlotte Street, Portland Place (now Hallam Street), they might hang as many as 360 important pictures, with no fewer than fourteen Poussins in the dining-room. The Polish collection was the high point of their dealing activities but also very nearly their downfall. In 1795 Poland was partitioned, Stanisław abdicated, and Desenfans and Bourgeois had 180 paintings suddenly 'in stock', after an outlay, so Desenfans claimed, of £9000.

An auction of the Polish paintings held in 1802 was not a success. In any case, Bourgeois was intent upon keeping many of the Polish pictures, as well as others acquired from such sales as that held in 1795 (handled by Desenfans) of pictures from the important collection of Charles-Antoine de Calonne, including Poussin's *Triumph of David* and Rembrandt's *Portrait of a Young Man*. Bourgeois, Desenfans complained, continued to buy pictures 'like a child who wishes for everything in a toy shop' (Waterfield, 22). When, however, Desenfans died in 1807 he left all the pictures to Bourgeois, and the rest of his property to Bourgeois and his widow. It sheds credit on both that they seem to have worked harmoniously from then on to keep the collection intact, aiming to make it freely available to the public.

Although Bourgeois stated late in life that these were the wishes of Desenfans, they were more probably his own. In 1810 he unsuccessfully tried to buy the freehold of the house in Charlotte Street so that the house 'may be gratuitously open to artists as well as to the publick' (Waterfield, 22). By December that year, according to Farington, the British Museum's unpredictable 'aristocracy' had turned him against that institution as a possible destination. In his will he therefore left over 350 pictures to Mrs Desenfans on condition that she left them in turn to Dulwich College. Bourgeois was prompted to make his will after suffering a fall from his horse on 20 December 1810; he died, unmarried, on 8 January 1811.

The Bourgeois bequest included, as something of a poisoned chalice, twenty-one of his own pictures, wildly disparate in subject matter and handling (from *William Tell* to *Tobias and the Angel*, *A Tiger Hunt*, portraits, and landscapes) but uniformly bad in quality. Bourgeois also left an endowment for the collection of £10,000, and £2000 to create a new gallery at Dulwich College after Mrs Desenfans's death. She, however, wanted work to start at once 'to see the wishes and intentions of her dear Friend Sir Francis Bourgeois carried into effect' (Waterfield, 27), and to give the pictures to the college as soon as a gallery was ready. With her additional financial help, a gallery designed by Sir John Soane (as Bourgeois had wished) was swiftly built, incorporating a mausoleum (as had initially been erected in 1807 by Soane for Desenfans's body at the back of the Charlotte Street house). In March 1815 Bourgeois was interred in the mausoleum within the Dulwich Picture Gallery, together with both the Desenfanses. And so in death, as in life, 'they were not divided'.

ROBIN SIMON

Sources G. Waterfield, 'A history of Dulwich Picture Gallery', in I. A. C. Dejardin, D. Shawe-Taylor, and G. Waterfield, *Rembrandt to Gainsborough: masterpieces from Dulwich Picture Gallery* (1999), 11–44 [exhibition catalogue, Dulwich Picture Gallery and New York] · Farington, *Diary* · W. T. Whitley, *Artists and their friends in England, 1700–1799*, 2 vols. (1928); repr. (1968)

Archives Dulwich College, Desenfans archive

Likenesses G. Dance, pencil and chalk drawing, 1793, RA · J. Northcote, oils, exh. RA 1794, Dulwich Picture Gallery, London · P. Sandby, double portrait, watercolour drawing, *c.*1795 (with N. J. Desenfans), Dulwich Picture Gallery, London · S. W. Reynolds, mezzotint, pubd 1796 (after J. Northcote), NPG · G. Dance, drawing, 1798–1800, Dulwich Picture Gallery, London · F. Bourgeois, self-portrait, oils, *c.*1800, Dulwich Picture Gallery, London • W. Ridley, stipple, pubd 1804 (after T. Collopy), BM, NPG • F. Bourgeois?, self-portrait?, mezzotint, *c.*1805, NPG • W. Beechey, oils, *c.*1810, NPG [*see illus.*] • C. Prosperi, marble bust, Dulwich Picture Gallery, London, Mausoleum • H. Singleton, group portrait, oils (*Royal academicians, 1793*), RA

Wealth at death left 371 pictures, £10,000 endowment, and £2000 for building new gallery to Dulwich College: Waterfield, 'A history of Dulwich Picture Gallery'

Bourinot, Sir John George (1836–1902), author and civil servant in Canada, was born on 24 October 1836 at The Esplanade, Sydney, Cape Breton, Nova Scotia, the eldest of the eleven children of John Bourinot (1814–1884), a merchant and member of the house of assembly of Nova Scotia and of the senate of Canada, and (Margaret) Jane Marshall (1810?–1887), the daughter of John George Marshall, a Nova Scotia judge, and his wife, Catherine. Bourinot's father, of French Huguenot descent, was born on the island of Jersey; his mother, born in Nova Scotia, was of English-Irish descent.

Bourinot, an Anglican, was privately educated in Sydney, and in 1854 entered the University of Trinity College, Toronto. In spite of a brilliant academic record, he completed only six of the nine terms required for a BA and left in 1856 without a degree. After a short time working for the Toronto *Leader*, he returned to Sydney in 1858 and entered into articles of clerkship with a lawyer. Soon he decided against the practice of law as a profession and in 1860, in partnership with Joseph Crosskill, he founded the *Halifax Reporter*. During the next seven years the *Reporter*'s editorials were mainly from Bourinot's pen. In addition he reported the debates of Nova Scotia's house of assembly for his newspaper and, in 1861 and again from 1864 to 1867, as official reporter to the house. (There was no official reporting of debates in 1862 or 1863.) In May 1867 he ended his association with the *Reporter* and the house, and soon afterwards returned to Sydney, where he engaged mainly in freelance writing until his appointment in May 1869 as an English clerk in the Canadian senate in Ottawa. To this appointment he added responsibilities as shorthand writer to the senate and committees of the senate (1870) and official reporter of senate debates (1871). In 1873 he transferred to the House of Commons as second clerk assistant. He was promoted first clerk assistant in 1879, and from 1880 until his death he was clerk of the House of Commons.

Bourinot wrote on many subjects, including articles on Canadian history for Canadian newspapers and magazines and prominent British journals, such as *Blackwood's Magazine* and the *London Quarterly*. As a young man he tried his hand at fiction, and wrote a novel, *Marguerite* (published in six instalments in the *New Dominion Monthly* in 1870), and at least five short stories: but the romantic element of his writing was weak, and he was wise in later life to restrict himself to non-fiction. His best and most important work was on parliamentary procedure and constitutional law and history. *Parliamentary Procedure and Practice* (1884) was compared favourably with Erskine May's classic work, and Bourinot came to be known as the Erskine May of Canada. One of his objects was to point out differences between Canadian and British parliamentary practice. His writing on constitutional law and history (*A Manual of the Constitutional History of Canada*, 1888) led to his being consulted on major constitutional issues that would not normally be referred to the clerk of the House of Commons, who is expected to give advice on procedure, but not on law. He became an unofficial adviser on the constitution to successive governors-general, prime ministers, lieutenant-governors, and provincial premiers. In response to requests for information on procedure at meetings of municipal bodies and societies of all kinds, he wrote *A Canadian Manual on the Procedure at Meetings* (complete and abridged versions, 1894); the title *Bourinot's Rules of Order* was adopted sixteen years after his death, and a new edition of the abridged version was published as late as 1995.

Bourinot was a founding member (1882) and for many years honorary secretary of the Royal Society of Canada. He edited the first nineteen volumes of its *Proceedings and Transactions*, to which he contributed many papers. *Our Intellectual Strength and Weakness*, his presidential address to the Royal Society (1893), followed his earlier *The Intellectual Development of the Canadian People* (1881).

Bourinot favoured imperial federation, which he thought grand in its conception although difficult to realize. This befitted one who was a fellow, an honorary corresponding secretary in Canada, and later an honorary fellow, of the Royal Colonial Institute, and an active member of the Imperial Federation League in Canada.

Bourinot married three times: first, on 1 September 1858, Bridget Delia Houck, a widow (1835/6–1861); second, on 3 October 1865, Emily Alden Pilsbury (1842–1887); and third, on 3 July 1889, Isabelle Cameron (1864?–1930). There were two sons from the first marriage, two daughters and one son from the second, and two sons from the third; the son and one of the daughters of the second marriage died in infancy.

Beginning with Queen's University, Kingston, in 1887, many Canadian universities conferred honorary degrees on Bourinot. He was created a CMG in 1890 and a KCMG in 1898. He died at his home, 141 Cooper Street, Ottawa, on 13 October 1902, and was buried on 15 October at Beechwood cemetery. MARGARET A. BANKS

Sources M. A. Banks, *Sir John George Bourinot, Victorian Canadian* (2001) • J. G. Bourinot, 'Bibliography of the members of the Royal Society of Canada', *Proceedings and Transactions of the Royal Society of Canada*, 12 (1894), 1–79 • M. A. Banks, 'Bourinot, Sir John George', *DCB*, vol. 13 • H. F. Gadsby, 'A hard man to follow', *Toronto Star* (3 March 1902) • M. A. Banks, 'New insights on Bourinot's parliamentary publications', *Canadian Parliamentary Review*, 15/1 (1992), 19–25 • P. Benoit, 'The politics and ethics of John George Bourinot', *Canadian Parliamentary Review*, 7/3 (1984), 6–10 • C. Berger, 'Race and liberty: the historical ideas of Sir John George Bourinot', *Canadian Historical Association Annual Report* (1965), 87–104 • M. Macbeth, 'A great Canadian: Sir John George Bourinot', *Dalhousie Review*, 34 (1954–5), 173–80 • *Ottawa Journal* (14 Oct 1902) • *Toronto Star* (14 Oct 1902) • *Sydney Post* (15 Oct 1902) • parish register of St George's Anglican Church, Sydney, Nova Scotia • registrar's records, University of Trinity College, Toronto • marriage register, Trinity Church East, Toronto • private information (1995)

Archives NA Canada • Public Archives of Nova Scotia, Halifax • University College of Cape Breton, Sydney, Nova Scotia, Beaton Institute | National Library of Canada, Ottawa, Arthur Stanley Bourinot MSS

Likenesses Beauchamp, bust, 1949, House of Commons Research Branch Office, Ottawa, Canada • photograph, NA Canada

Wealth at death C$22,000 in Canada: surrogate court records, Carleton county, Ontario (microfilm copy in Public Archives of Ontario, Toronto)

Bourke, Sir Edward Alexander Henry [Harry] **Legge-** (**1914–1973**), politician, was born at Manor Cottage, Clewer Green, Windsor, Berkshire, on 16 May 1914, the only son of Nigel Walter Henry Legge-Bourke, an officer in the Coldstream Guards, of Hayes, co. Meath, and his wife, Lady Victoria Alexandrina Wynn-Carrington, fifth daughter of the marquess of Lincolnshire. His father was killed in action on 30 October 1914, shortly after Harry's birth; his mother married in 1916 Major Edric Weld-Forester. Educated at Eton College, he was for six years a page of honour to George V. After Eton, he went to the Royal Military College, Sandhurst, and in 1934 was commissioned as a second lieutenant in the Royal Horse Guards. He married on 10 June 1938 (Catherine) Jean (*b*. 1917), daughter of Sir Arthur Grant, tenth baronet, of Monymusk: they had two sons and one daughter. During the Second World War he served in the Middle East. He was wounded in action in Greece in 1941. He was aide-de-camp to Sir Miles Lampson, the British ambassador in Cairo 1941–2, and later served in the north Africa campaign. He was promoted major in 1944.

In 1945 Legge-Bourke was released from the army to stand as Conservative candidate in the Isle of Ely constituency, a seat previously held for sixteen years by a Liberal. He won with a majority of over 2000. He established a reputation as a respected, right-wing back-bencher as well as for being a man of impeccable courtesy, candour, and duty. He demonstrated independence in his voting behaviour and his public comments. A Suez rebel, he resigned the Conservative whip on 14 July 1954 in protest at the resumption of Anglo-Egyptian negotiations and two weeks later voted against a motion approving the withdrawal of British forces from the Suez Canal zone. He sat as an independent Conservative until 18 October, when he applied successfully for the whip to be restored to him.

In 1955 Legge-Bourke was one of only two Conservatives to vote against an increase in purchase tax. He felt the country's economic problems could only be solved by having a proper trade policy: the tory party, he told the house, 'should remember its traditional role and get back to protection' (*Hansard 5C*, 545, 27 Oct 1955, 473). In 1962 he said publicly that he thought it was time for the prime minister, Harold Macmillan, to resign and in 1963 he abstained from voting on an opposition motion censuring the home secretary, Henry Brooke, for his handling of the deportation to Nigeria of Chief Enahoro. In 1965 he was, somewhat surprisingly, one of thirty-one Conservatives to vote for the order imposing an oil embargo on Rhodesia, while fifty right-wing Conservatives voted against it (the Conservative line was to abstain). In 1968 he voted against House of Lords reform.

Legge-Bourke was assiduous in his attendance and when not in the chamber he was busy attending committee meetings. In 1953 he was elected to membership of the executive of the 1922 committee, the body comprising Conservative private members. In 1961 he was elected chairman of the Conservative science and technology committee. He was also elected chairman of the Conservative defence committee, though he resigned the post almost immediately following his criticism of the prime minister. His interest in science—he was a well-informed layman—was also reflected in his appointment as a member of the select committee on science and technology and in his election in 1971 as chairman of the all-party parliamentary and scientific committee. His independence may have cost him promotion to ministerial office. He was also hard of hearing, which may have prevented his becoming speaker. Though he served on the chairman's panel, and in 1964–6 was an additional deputy chairman of ways and means (during which time he did not serve on the executive of the 1922 committee), he did not become deputy speaker.

However, Legge-Bourke's independence—and a scepticism about membership of the Common Market—are believed to have contributed to his election in 1970 as chairman of the 1922 committee. He emerged victorious from a field of five candidates. As chairman, he enjoyed an automatic right of access to the party leader, though some members of the 1922 executive took the view that the leader, Edward Heath, was disinclined to listen. In 1972 Legge-Bourke took the unusual step of intervening during the report stage of the Industry Bill, a measure providing for regional development grants, to voice publicly the concern of many Conservative MPs about the bill. Speaking for himself, he described the bill as 'obnoxious for many reasons' and, had some areas not been desperately in need of help, would not have supported it on second reading. 'I believe', he said 'that these thoughts are shared by many of my hon. Friends' (*Hansard 5C*, 841, 28 July 1972, 2402). He was the first chairman of the 1922 committee to provide authorized briefings to the press on meetings of the committee. Legge-Bourke's chairmanship of the 1922 committee was brief. When the house returned after the summer recess in 1972, he announced his retirement following a sudden deterioration in his health. In November Conservative MPs agreed to make a presentation in recognition of his service. He died six months later, on 21 May 1973, at his home, 9 Wilbraham Place, Chelsea, London.

Legge-Bourke's interests were not confined to the House of Commons. He was a landowner and farmer, with 50 acres in the Isle of Ely and 600 acres in Ireland, and had a seat at Hayes, co. Meath. Soon after entering parliament he became a vice-president of the Association of Drainage Authorities. He served from 1950 as chairman of Grant Production Co. Ltd, a firm of photographic equipment and offset printers. He was, from 1966, a vice-president of the Institute of Patentees and Inventors. He was appointed a deputy lieutenant of the county of Cambridgeshire in 1955 and was created KBE in 1960. 'Tall, fair and handsomely moustached' (D. Wood, *The Times*, 17 July 1970), he was a quintessential knight of the shires, a man for whom service was an honour and not a chore. 'He was', in the words of the *Times* obituary,

> one of the last of the English country gentlemen who chose a life of public service from a conviction of duty and obligation, seeking nothing more for himself, certainly not office, but modestly and very effectively, doing his best for his constituents and for the national interest as he saw it. (*The Times*, 22 May 1973)

PHILIP NORTON

Sources *The Times* (22 May 1973) · D. Wood, 'Finding a new chairman for the 1922', *The Times* (13 Nov 1972) · *WWBMP*, vol. 4 · P. Norton, *Conservative dissidents* (1978) · P. Norton, ed., *Dissension in the House of Commons: intra-party dissent in the House of Commons' division lobbies, 1945–1974* (1975) · A. Roth, *The business background of MPs* (1972) · *'Times' guide to the House of Commons* (1950–70) [1950–51, 1955, 1959, 1964, 1970] · 'Legge-Bourke is "1922" chairman', *The Times* (17 July 1970) · 'Diary', *The Times* (16 July 1970) · 'Diary', *The Times* (21 Oct 1970) · 'Diary', *The Times* (12 July 1971) · Burke, *Gen. Ire.* (1958) · Kelly, *Handbk* (1963) · *People of Today* (1992) · b. cert. · d. cert.
Archives U. Leeds, Brotherton L., corresp. and papers | CAC Cam., corresp. with E. L. Spears · U. Leeds, Brotherton L., corresp. with Henry Drummond-Wolff
Likenesses photograph, repro. in *'Times' guide* · photograph, repro. in *The Times* (22 May 1973)
Wealth at death £62,841: probate, 23 July 1973, *CGPLA Eng. & Wales*

Bourke, Sir Richard (1777–1855), army officer and colonial governor, was born on 4 May 1777 in Britain Street, Dublin, the only son of John Bourke of Dromsally, co. Limerick, and his wife, Anne, daughter of Edmund Ryan of Boscable, co. Tipperary. He was educated at Westminster School (1788–93) and at Oriel College, Oxford (BA 1798). He was gazetted ensign by purchase in the Grenadier Guards on 22 November 1798 and while on active service in the Netherlands in 1799 was shot through both jaws. In later life he felt that this wound prevented him from speaking forcefully in public and declined all invitations to stand for parliament. On 22 March 1800 he married Elizabeth Jane, daughter of John Bourke of Carshalton, Surrey. They had seven children: John (who was an invalid), Mary Jane, Anne, Frances, Richard (Dick), and two daughters who died in infancy.

By 27 August 1805 Bourke had attained the rank of major and in 1806 became superintendent of the junior department of the Royal Military College, with the rank of lieutenant-colonel. He was on active service in South America, and as quartermaster-general took part in the storming of Montevideo in 1807. In 1809 he was appointed permanent assistant in the quartermaster-general's department and served in the Peninsular War. He had learned Spanish and was sent by Wellesley to contact Cuesta, the commander-in-chief of the Spanish army. In 1809 Bourke learned that his wife was gravely ill and was granted leave to return to England. On returning to Spain, he was stationed at Corunna as military resident from 1812 to 1814. In addition to his overt duties, he arranged a spy ring to gather information on enemy movements and conditions behind the enemy lines, drawing on a special secret service account to cover expenses. He was promoted colonel on 4 June 1814 and was made a CB.

After the war Bourke retired on half-pay and lived on his estate, Thornfield, Castleconnell, in co. Limerick. He managed his estate, became a magistrate and chairman of the Irish Distress Committee for Limerick. In 1825, finding his income inadequate for the needs of his family, he sought an appointment overseas. The tories were in power and although he was an avowed whig he made a good impression at the Colonial Office and was appointed lieutenant-governor of the Eastern District of Cape Colony. He and his family arrived in Cape Town in February 1826. When the governor, Lord Charles Somerset, returned to England on leave (and later resigned), Bourke assumed office as acting governor of the whole colony.

Bourke's task was not easy. The minority white population, both British and Dutch, were dissatisfied with the government, the laws were uncodified, and many of the officials inefficient and corrupt. The economy was depressed and the colony in debt. Bourke removed local dues and restrictions and by seeking markets in Mauritius and elsewhere increased exports appreciably. Government control of the press was much resented and on Bourke's recommendation its independence was secured by statute in 1829. He was instructed to reorganize the government according to the recommendations of a commission of inquiry appointed by the British government; this difficult task was accomplished by May 1828.

The most controversial part of Bourke's governorship (which was regarded either as 'Bourke's wicked reign' or as most enlightened) was his native policy. He tried to improve the conditions of free persons of colour who were bound by oppressive labour contracts and subject to a pass system which prevented them from moving freely in search of better-paid work. On 17 June 1828, after the courts had been reformed, the council passed ordinance 50 which liberated them from the pass laws and protected them from exploitation; it came to be known as the 'Magna Carta of the Hottentots'.

Bourke and his family left the Cape in September 1828 and returned to Thornfield. When the whigs took office in 1830, he again sought a post and was appointed governor of New South Wales, Australia. He arrived in Sydney in December 1831; to his great sorrow, his wife died at Parramatta in May 1832. He found the colony deeply divided between the 'exclusive' faction made up of free immigrants and their descendants and the 'liberals' who included many emancipists (former convicts). His policies were favoured by the latter and often opposed by the former. One of his controversial measures was the substitution of civil for military juries in criminal cases, which the legislative council, though still wholly nominated, passed only on Bourke's casting vote. Another concerned the criminal law relating to convicts. He found that magistrates were not always impartial and attributed this in part to the complexity of existing regulations. He asked Chief Justice Forbes to draft a single bill consolidating the law and reducing the magistrates' powers. It was passed by the legislature but severely criticized by many landowners and in the press.

Another controversial issue related to religion. Bourke had seen the evil effects of sectarian intolerance in Ireland and believed that there should be no attempt to establish a dominant colonial church. Despite opposition from the Anglican Bishop Broughton, Church Acts were passed by the legislature in 1836 which gave support from public funds to the major denominations in proportion to their numbers.

A further important measure was the Crown Lands Occupation Act of 1836, which provided for the issuing of occupation licences for pastoral purposes on unsurveyed crown land. Much of this had been illegally occupied by squatters to the detriment of the revenue. Under Bourke's legislation commissioners of crown lands were appointed to collect licence fees and also to act as magistrates. Many squatters had crossed the straits from Van Diemen's Land and settled in the Port Phillip district (later Victoria). In 1836 Bourke appointed a resident magistrate for Port Phillip and in 1837 himself visited the area, had a plan of streets drawn up, and the first building sites measured and offered for sale. 'I have had much pleasure in affixing Whig names in the Bush,' he wrote. He travelled widely throughout the colony and he strongly supported the British government's plans for 'assisting' migration by introducing the 'bounty' system, whereby those who arranged to bring out approved migrants were paid a bounty from the crown land revenue. This brought out 50,000 migrants between 1838 and 1842, though while Bourke was governor arriving convicts and free migrants had already raised the population he had to deal with from 51,000 in 1831 to over 97,000 in 1838.

Bourke resigned his office in December 1837. C. D. Riddell, the colonial treasurer, had disobeyed his orders and Bourke dismissed him from the executive council. The secretary of state ruled that he had no power to do so and ordered that Riddell be reinstated. Believing that his personal honour was in jeopardy, Bourke resigned. The popular esteem in which he was held was shown by the great ovation the crowd gave him as he left the colony. A fund was opened, and rapidly filled, to erect his statue, which stands before the Public Library of New South Wales, in Sydney.

Bourke had been made KCB in 1835 and gazetted lieutenant-general and colonel-in-chief of the 64th regiment in 1837. In 1839 he was appointed high sheriff for the county of Limerick; he was offered, but declined, the governorship of Jamaica and the command-in-chief of the forces in India; he was promoted general in 1851. In collaboration with Earl Fitzwilliam, he edited the correspondence of his kinsman Edmund Burke, published in 1844. Bourke died of heart failure at Thornfield, on 13 August 1855, and was buried in the churchyard at Castleconnell.

H. M. STEPHENS, *rev.* HAZEL KING

Sources H. King, *Richard Bourke* (1971) • *AusDB* • G. M. Theal, *History of South Africa since September 1795*, 1, 2 (1908) • Mitchell L., NSW, Bourke MSS, set-403 • NL Ire., Bourke MSS 8473–8478 • Bodl. RH, Bourke MSS [32 vols.] • C. M. H. Clark, *A history of Australia*, 2 (1968) • PRO, Cape of Good Hope series, CO 48/68–133 • PRO, NSW series, CO 201/213–270 • minutes of the Executive Council of NSW, NSW Archives, Sydney, Colonial Secretary's Archives, 1831–1837 • *Votes and proceedings*, New South Wales Legislative Council (1832–7) • [F. Watson], ed., *Historical records of Australia*, 1st ser., 15–19 (1922–3) • G. M. Theal, ed., *Records of the Cape Colony*, 36 vols. (1897–1905)

Archives Bodl. RH, corresp. and papers • Brenthurst Library, Johannesburg, corresp. relating to lieutenant-governorship of the Cape • Mitchell L., NSW, corresp. and papers • NL Ire., corresp. and papers • State Library of Victoria, Melbourne, diary and corresp. | BL, Bathurst MSS • Derbys. RO, letters to Sir R. J. Wilmot-Horton • Mitchell L., NSW, Deas Thomson and Bathurst MSS • priv. coll., letters to Sebb • Royal Artillery Institution, Woolwich, London, letters to Sir John Le Marchant • Royal Military College, Sandhurst, register of officers of the first department

Likenesses E. H. Baily, bronze statue, *c.*1837, Public Library of New South Wales, Sydney, Australia • E. H. Baily, marble bust, Royal Australian Historical Society, Sydney, Australia • lithograph, NL Aus.

Bourke, Richard Southwell, sixth earl of Mayo (1822–1872), viceroy of India, was the eldest son of Robert Bourke (1797–1867), who succeeded his uncle as fifth earl of Mayo in 1849, and his wife, Anne (or Annie) Charlotte Jocelyn (*d.* 1867). Born in Dublin on 21 February 1822, the eldest of ten children, he grew up in an evangelical household at Hayes in co. Meath. Robert *Bourke was a younger brother. He was educated at home, and in 1841 entered Trinity College, Dublin, where, without going into residence, he took an ordinary degree. Bourke was not a highly educated man, but became an accomplished sportsman.

Early career, and marriage In 1845 Bourke visited Russia, and on his return published an acutely observed account of his tour, *St Petersburg and Moscow: a Visit to the Court of the Czar* (2 vols., 1846). In 1847 he was active in famine relief in Ireland, and at the general election was returned as a protectionist for co. Kildare. On 31 October 1848 he married Blanche Julia Wyndham (1826–1918), daughter of George, first Lord Leconfield. They were to have four sons and three daughters; the eldest daughter died an infant in 1851. In 1849 his father succeeded to the earldom of Mayo, and Bourke assumed the courtesy title Lord Naas. In 1852 he was appointed chief secretary for Ireland in Lord Derby's administration, and held the same office in subsequent Conservative administrations until his appointment as viceroy of India by Disraeli in 1868, having succeeded to the Irish earldom in 1867.

Mayo sat in the House of Commons as member for co. Kildare from 1847 to 1852, for Coleraine from 1852 to 1857, and for Cockermouth from 1857 to 1868. As chief secretary, he became the acknowledged manager of the Conservative Party in Ireland, and a significant factor in the relative electoral successes of his party in Ireland at the mid-century. In particular, he was largely responsible for the limited electoral agreement with the Independent Party between 1857 and 1859, which was of great advantage to the Conservatives in Ireland. He opposed the disestablishment of the Church of Ireland, but gradually became less sectarian in his opinions. He was resolute in

Richard Southwell Bourke, sixth earl of Mayo (1822–1872), by John Watkins

his handling of the Fenian crisis of the 1860s, but in 1867 he encountered difficulties in dealing with the Orangeman William Johnstone of Ballykilbeg. Despite initially opposing it, he came to support compensating tenants for improvements made without the consent of their landlords. He has been described as one of those 'efficient, loyal and dedicated politicians of the second rank without whose constant hard work the tedious chores so necessary for success tend to remain undone' (Hoppen, 293).

Governor-general of India In 1868 Disraeli selected him for the governor-generalship of India, which Mayo had long coveted. The Conservative ministry had in fact resigned before the office became vacant, and, despite the fact that Mayo had already sailed for India, Gladstone seriously contemplated cancelling the appointment, believing that a viceroy should not be appointed by a government in its last agony. However, the recall was not issued. Energetic, buoyant, and self-assured, Mayo had no preconceived ideas about India and made his own policies based on the facts as he came to see them.

Sworn in as governor-general at Calcutta on 12 January 1869, the first question which engaged the new viceroy's attention was the relationship with the neighbouring state of Afghanistan. Mayo's predecessor, John Lawrence, advised him to meet the amir, Sher Ali, as the civil war of succession seemed to have ended after six years. Approving of the decision to aid the restoration of settled government in that country, Mayo arranged to meet the amir at Ambala in the Punjab in March 1869. As it had been widely reported that Sher Ali was under the control of Russia and Persia, the effect of such a meeting would be considerable throughout central Asia. Sher Ali, on his part, made no secret of his desire to meet the viceroy. As in March the government of India would be in transit from Delhi to the summer capital, Simla, no impression would be given of deviating from normal arrangements; and by making the venue Ambala and not Peshawar, which was nearer Afghanistan, it was implied that the meeting had been sought by the amir, rather than the viceroy. No approval for the meeting was sought from London, the government merely suggesting that Lawrence's policy of reserve and abstention from central Asian politics be maintained.

In matters of ceremonial Mayo, to the amir's satisfaction, treated him as an equal. The viceroy's main objectives were the creation of a strong and independent government in Afghanistan, total abstinence from interference in its internal affairs, the development and promotion of trade with central Asia, access to information about events in that region, and a frontier that was well policed. A middle path between interference and inaction, a policy of watchful friendly relations, was the safest course. The advance of Russia could be checked mainly by pushing British commerce northwards. The British would assist the amir—without intervening in the domestic affairs of Afghanistan or pushing troops or residents into his country—to form a strong and permanent government in return for increased facilities for trade, and measures to maintain order in those portions of the border over which the amir had any influence. Mayo resisted, on his own responsibility, Sher Ali's demands for British refusal to recognize anybody else as amir, for a fixed and increased subsidy, and for a treaty of mutual assistance. All that he would offer was an assurance of 'cordial countenance and some additional support as it may be advisable', a siege battery, 6000 muskets, and a letter of general support discouraging Sher Ali's foes and viewing with 'severe displeasure' attempts to thwart his 'rightful rule'. Neither side mentioned Russia or central Asia.

Both sides were satisfied with the results of the Ambala conference. The British government was concerned that Mayo might have gone too far in his support for the amir, but the viceroy stood his ground. In 1871 the amir's eldest son, Yakub, imperilled the peace and it was suggested that the government of India should dispatch troops to support Sher Ali. But Mayo preferred to watch and wait, and advised Sher Ali to seek a settlement. Father and son were reconciled, and Mayo had secured peace with dominance.

Mayo also sent his own emissary to St Petersburg, instead of relying on the British ambassador, and secured a statement from the tsar that his government had no intention of extending his empire. A party of Russian troops which had crossed the Oxus was withdrawn, and the Russian government also promised not to meddle in Afghan affairs, and requested the government of India to define the frontiers of Afghanistan. The ruler of Yarkand sent an envoy to Calcutta for support and advice and Mayo decided to send a British mission to Yarkand. Trade with central Asia was promoted and a treaty concluded with the maharaja of Kashmir which provided Britain with transit facilities through his state. A boundary dispute between Afghanistan and Persia, with the possibility of increased influence for Russia, was avoided by persuading Persia to submit the case to arbitration.

Mayo's general policy was to create outworks of the British empire in the border states, and, while assuring them that there was no danger of annexation, to encourage them to seek British support and to ward off interference by any other European power. He hoped thereby to form a cordon of friendly and independent states around the Indian frontier, and claimed that, without firing a shot or moving a soldier, he had made British influence paramount in regions which had been for years the 'hard nut' of Anglo-Indian politics.

Similarly, Mayo's government entertained cordial relations with the princes within the borders of India. Abstaining from needless intervention but not tolerating misgovernment, he sought to convince these princes that the British government sincerely desired to enable them to govern their states in such a manner as to secure the prosperity of the people and to maintain their own just rights. He encouraged the establishment of the Mayo College at Ajmer and the Rajkumar College in Kathiawar for the education of the sons of the chiefs and nobles in the Indian states.

Famine, public works, public finance In India directly under British administration conditions were far from normal during Mayo's tenure of office. Scarcity of food developed in some areas, and, before it deepened into famine, Mayo sanctioned a programme of public works to relieve unemployment, and provided advances for the sinking of wells. To public works generally he devoted much attention and took charge personally of the public works department, as well as of the foreign department. He sought to provide adequate defences for the principal Indian ports and effected large savings in the construction of barracks. Though his aim was to secure an equilibrium in the finances by reducing expenditure and augmenting the revenue, he did not retrench essential public works and expanded the scope of administrative activity. He wished India to be self-sufficient as far as possible and prospected for coal and iron. As private enterprise had failed to locate good iron ore, he wanted the government to show the way and take advantage of the construction of the railways by the state to utilize vast quantities of iron ore. But he was careful not to waste public funds and by 1872 had reduced expenditure by nearly £5 million.

Complementary was the development of sources of revenue. The introduction of an income tax in 1869 led to no great increase of revenue and the financial crisis was severe. By reductions in expenditure on civil and military administration, the increase of salt duties in Madras and Bombay, and raising income tax in the middle of the financial year, Mayo converted the anticipated deficit into a small surplus, and the three following years produced an aggregate surplus of nearly £6 million. He also decided to place a larger proportion of the charges for local requirements onto local resources, which not only reduced central expenditure, but met the political objective of entrusting a large number of Indians with local responsibility and the management of district affairs. Decentralization of finance was resisted by officials both at the centre and in the provinces, but Mayo overruled the opposition.

Mayo also implemented a reform, proposed by John Lawrence, of constructing extensions of the railway system with funds borrowed by the government, rather than entrusting such work to private companies with interest guaranteed by the state. He also adopted the narrow gauge of 3 feet 3 inches for the new state railways. He passed a land improvement act and an act to facilitate by government loans works of public utility in towns.

Growing disaffection in India Mayo cautioned the local governments to effect economy in expenditure and to tax the districts no more than was necessary. Yet he was not sufficiently sensitive to the fact that articulate India was still in an irritable mood. The increase in income tax from 1 to 2.5 per cent and then, in 1870, to 3.225 per cent was severely criticized. The articulate middle-class opposition did not make his task easier. The foreign policy of peace and friendship, commendable in itself, had no healthy effect within the country. Uneasiness, especially among the Muslims, became clear, and Mayo discerned that the task of successfully governing the Indian empire was daily becoming more difficult. A Wahabi conspiracy, seeking to cleanse Islam of idolatry and superstition, had been spreading over the years across northern India. As it was believed that a war against an infidel government could not be carried on by their Muslim subjects, the Wahabis gathered across the frontier. Emissaries toured India, especially Bengal, urging Muslims to join what officials termed a 'crescentade' and contribute funds liberally. Many Wahabi agents were arrested and the Calcutta high court rejected their habeas corpus petitions. This did not seem to deter the conspirators and Wahabi dissent and the discontent caused by novel taxation fed on each other. Mayo, shaken in nerve, decided to reduce the income tax as much as possible; but he was confident that British military strength had so increased that no fresh mutiny need be feared and he blamed a few non-official Europeans for objecting to the income tax. Increase of expenditure and taxation was to him the only real danger. When the income tax was reduced by two-thirds in the budget of 1871, agitation against it ceased.

Disaffection, however, now spread among the Sikhs. The Kukas, in a similar vein to the Wahabis, called on all true believers to abandon temples and mosques, disregard distinctions of caste, and lead lives of abstinence. From such iconoclasm the movement drifted to a zeal for cleansing the Sikh faith and then to a yearning for the revival of Sikh political supremacy. But a policy of firmness tempered with moderation, as in Mayo's foreign policy, seemed to be effective, and in May 1871 he reported to the queen that tranquillity generally prevailed in India. Soon after, in September, he was dismayed when the officiating chief justice of the Calcutta high court was stabbed to death by a Pathan.

Mayo's assassination and its background Though no evidence was discovered to suggest that the murder had been organized, the belief that this was the first political murder in India since 1857 revived an atmosphere of panic. Mayo reassured the public that there was not the least ground for apprehension; all that was required was quiet, though active, watchfulness. In January 1872, when the Kukas attacked Maler Kotla in the Punjab, the provincial authorities had sixty-five men blown away from guns (a form of military execution). Mayo's government condemned these summary executions in the belief that such actions could be justified only by immediate and urgent necessity, which he did not believe existed in this case. Then, on 8 February 1872, Mayo himself was assassinated by a Muslim Afghan convict at Port Blair in the Andaman Islands, where he was on a tour of inspection. His body was returned to Ireland, where he was buried in state at Johnstown church, near Naas, in co. Kildare. His widow was appointed a lady of the bedchamber to Queen Victoria (1872–4), and received a parliamentary annuity of £1000, and a similar pension from the Council of India, together with the sum of £20,000.

Assessment India was to Mayo his destined ground of service and success. He shared the Conservative belief in imperialism, and that racial superiority ensured permanent rule: a self-governing India was not even a distant possibility in a remote future. He did not, therefore, fear the long-term consequences of the promotion of education and the association of Indians with the administration. Believing that such discontent as existed among educated Indians was due to unemployment, he was willing to declare Indians eligible for all posts in the legal and judicial branches of the government, and most posts in the police service. But it was the duty of the British to provide India with efficient administration. 'The days of conquest are past; the age of improvement has begun', he publicly declared. The maintenance of peace, the removal of disaffection, and the promotion of prosperity were the best ways of strengthening the imperial connection. Mayo's objectives were a strong executive, paternal administration with no pretence of promoting self-government, and the maintenance of the rule of law. He worked extremely hard, had an easy command of men, and gave full attention to every problem of administration. He invited even junior provincial officers to be his guests and acquaint him with their work; and he undertook long tours to secure first-hand knowledge of men and matters. He had seen more of India in his three years than most civil servants managed in a lifetime, and knew more about India than any other viceroy until George Curzon at the end of the century. He encouraged popular representations to the central government, instructed the home department to inquire into every allegation of injustice, and reserved the right to communicate directly with any official. It was such energy, drive, and curiosity which led to the occasion of his death. S. GOPAL

Sources W. W. Hunter, *Life of the earl of Mayo* (1875) • J. Strachey, *Minute on the administration of the earl of Mayo as viceroy and governor-general of India* (1872) • J. Strachey and R. Strachey, *Finances and public works of India, 1869–1881* (1882) • *DNB* • S. Gopal, *British policy in India, 1858–1905* (1965) • GEC, *Peerage* • K. T. Hoppen, *Elections, politics, and society in Ireland, 1832–1885* (1984)

Archives CUL, corresp. and papers relating to India • NL Ire., corresp. and papers | BL, letters to Sir Stafford Northcote, Add. MS 50027 • BL, letters to Lord Strathnairn, Add. MS 42608 • BL OIOC, Burne MSS • BL OIOC, letters to Sir Richard Temple, MS Eur. F 86 • Bodl. Oxf., letters to Benjamin Disraeli • Bodl. Oxf., letters to Lord Kimberley • Inveraray Castle, Argyll, letters to the duke of Argyll • Lpool RO, letters to fourteenth earl of Derby • priv. coll., letters to S. H. Walpole • PRO NIre., letters to Lord Abercorn • PRO NIre., letters to Lord Belmore • Som. ARS, letters to Sir William Jolliffe • Suffolk RO, Ipswich, letters to first earl of Cranbrook • W. Sussex RO, letters to the duke of Richmond

Likenesses oils, 1873 (after photograph), BL OIOC • W. H. Thornycroft, bronze statue, *c.*1875, Calcutta, India • J. Brown, stipple (after photograph), BM; repro. in *Baily's Magazine* (1866) • J. Collier, oils (after photograph), Oriental Club, London • H. Gales, group portrait, watercolour (*The Derby cabinet of 1867*), NPG • E. Stodart, stipple and line engraving (after photograph by S. A. Walker), NPG • J. Watkins, carte-de-visite, NPG [*see illus.*] • W & T. Wills, marble statue on monument, Cockermouth, Cumbria • portrait, Victoria Memorial Hall, Calcutta, India • statue, Chowrinqhee, Calcutta, India

Wealth at death under £5000: probate, 23 July 1872, *CGPLA Ire.*

Bourke, Robert, Baron Connemara (1827–1902), administrator in India, born at Hayes, co. Meath, on 11 June 1827, was the third son of Robert Bourke, fifth earl of Mayo (1797–1867), and his wife, Anne (or Annie) Charlotte (*d.* 1867), only child of John Jocelyn, fourth son of the first earl of Roden. Richard Southwell *Bourke, sixth earl of Mayo, viceroy of India, to whom he bore striking physical resemblance, was his elder brother. Educated at Enniskillen Royal School, at Hall Place School, Kent, and at Trinity College, Dublin, he settled in London, being called to the bar at the Inner Temple on 17 November 1852. Besides joining the south Wales circuit and attending the Knutsford sessions for twelve years, he acquired a large practice at the parliamentary bar, and he embodied the decisions of Speaker Shaw-Lefevre, afterwards Viscount Eversley, in a volume entitled *Parliamentary Precedents* (1857).

Returned as Conservative member for King's Lynn at the general election of December 1868, he retained the seat for eighteen years. Known as Bobby Bourke, he was popular in the house and, without shining in debate, held his own in argument. On Disraeli's accession to power in February 1874 Bourke was appointed under-secretary for foreign affairs. As Bourke's successive chiefs, lords Derby and Salisbury, were peers, it fell to him to represent them in the Commons when the Eastern question was at its most acute, and when Gladstone was rousing the country over the Bulgarian atrocities and the Anglo-Afghan War. Although disputation was not altogether agreeable to

Bourke's easy good nature, he performed his tasks at question time and in debate to his chiefs' satisfaction. He was a member of the royal commission on copyright laws appointed in October 1875. On the defeat of the ministry in April 1880 he was sworn of the privy council. He was a severe critic of the foreign policy of the Gladstone government of 1880–85, and in Lord Salisbury's brief 'stopgap' administration (June 1885–February 1886) he again held the foreign under-secretaryship.

When the Conservatives returned to power after the elections of July 1886, Lord Salisbury, the prime minister, nominated him in September to the governorship of Madras in succession to Sir Mountstuart Grant Duff. He assumed the office on 8 December 1886. On 12 May 1887 he was created a baron in recognition of his Foreign Office service, and chose the title of Connemara, in memory of descent from ancestors who once resided there. On 21 June he was made GCIE.

Bourke was the brother of one former governor-general of India (Lord Mayo), and the son-in-law of another (Lord Dalhousie), for he had married, on 21 November 1863, Lady Susan Georgiana Broun Ramsay (*d.* 1898) of Coalstoun, eldest daughter and coheir of James Andrew, first and last marquess of Dalhousie. He thus carried to Madras a reflected prestige. Just before his arrival there had been a local scandal and parliamentary discussions of administrative irregularities in the presidency, where 'blunder had followed blunder' (*Madras Weekly Mail*, 4 Dec 1890). He instituted reforms and restored the administration to equanimity. He made frequent and strenuous tours of the presidency. His versatile private secretary J. D. Rees later published a *Narrative of Tours in India Made by Lord Connemara* (1891). In the midsummer of 1889 he travelled to Ganjam, a famine-stricken district on the extreme north of the presidency, and increased the provision of relief measures. Connemara presided over an active administration. He improved the sanitation of Madras city, and strengthened and reorganized the sanitary department of government. He pressed forward railway communications, particularly the important east-coast line linking Madras with Calcutta. He founded a major public library. A volume of his *Minutes* (1890), mostly written during his tours, and another of his *Speeches* (1891), both edited by J. D. Rees, testify to his administration as 'a bright epoch in the annals of Madras' (*Madras Weekly Mail*, 4 Dec 1890).

But the governorship ended abruptly a year before its normal term under a dark cloud, which closed Connemara's public life. It was announced from India on 8 November 1890 that he had tendered his resignation, to take effect from the following March. Soon afterwards (on 27 November) the divorce court in London heard the petition of his wife for dissolution of marriage on charges of cruelty, adultery with her maidservant, Hannah Moore, and general adultery going back to 1875. Though Bourke's pleadings denied the charge and made a counter-charge of adultery against his wife and Surgeon-Lieutenant-Colonel William Hamilton Briggs, a former member of his staff, he was not represented at the hearing. A decree nisi was pronounced, and was made absolute on 9 June 1891. Lady Connemara and Dr Briggs denied the counter-charge in court; they were subsequently married on 10 October 1894 and she died on 22 January 1898.

Connemara handed over acting charge of the governorship to a civilian colleague on 1 December 1890, and embarked for England on the 7th. He married on 22 October 1894 Gertrude Lawrence Knight, widow of Edward Coleman of Stoke Park, Buckinghamshire, and daughter of J. F. Walsh, a lady of considerable wealth; she died on 23 November 1898. He died at his London residence, 43 Grosvenor Street, after long illness, on 3 September 1902, and was buried at Kensal Green cemetery. There being no children from either marriage, the barony became extinct with his death. A large hotel and the main public library in Madras continue to be named after him.

F. H. BROWN, *rev.* DAVID WASHBROOK

Sources H. W. Lucy, *A diary of the Salisbury parliament, 1886–1892* (1892) · J. D. Rees, *Narrative of tours in India made by Lord Connemara* (1891) · *India List, and India Office List* (1902) · *The Times* (10 Nov 1890) · *The Times* (25 Nov 1890) · *The Times* (28 Nov 1890) · *The Times* (10 June 1891) · *The Times* (4 Sept 1902) · *The Times* (6 Sept 1902) · *Madras Weekly Mail* (13 Nov 1890) · *Madras Weekly Mail* (4 Dec 1890) · Burke, *Peerage* (1902) · Walford, *County families*

Archives BL OIOC, letters to Arthur Godley, MS Eur. F 102 · CUL, corresp. with Lord Mayo · Lpool RO, letters to Lord Derby · NL Scot., letters to Blackwoods · U. Birm., Joseph Chamberlain MSS

Likenesses Spy [L. Ward], caricature, NPG; repro. in *VF* (28 April 1877), pl. 250 · oils, Government House, Madras, India

Wealth at death £38,720 12*s.* 6*d.*: resworn probate, April 1903, *CGPLA Eng. & Wales* (1902)

Bourke, Ulick Joseph (1829–1887), Roman Catholic priest and writer, was born near Castlebar, co. Mayo, in December 1829. He was educated at Errew monastery, Castlebar, where he was said to have been taught Irish by James Hardiman. He then went to St Jarlath's College, Tuam, co. Galway, and to St Patrick's College, Maynooth, where he was ordained in 1858. He returned to St Jarlath's as professor of Irish, classics, and logic, and remained there for twenty years, thirteen of those as president. During this period, Bourke rebuilt the college and acted as private secretary to his cousin John MacHale, archbishop of Tuam. St Jarlath's received as pupils a number of the sons of men who were important figures in Irish nationalism; they included the sons of Jeremiah O'Donovan Rossa, founder-member of the Irish Republican Brotherhood, whose fees were paid by Richard Pigott. Bourke's influence as a tutor of young men preparing to enter a seminary, and his teaching of the Irish language and history, were remembered by future members of the Irish Republican Brotherhood. One of his students was Mark Ryan, Fenian and founder-member of the Gaelic League, who calculated that many of his contemporaries at St Jarlath's subsequently became members of the Fenian movement.

In December 1870 Bourke founded the *Tuam News*, a weekly paper that aimed to provide 'a popular exponent of national and local opinion …'; it claimed to provide special information about the Roman Catholic church and circulated in Tuam and the province of Connaught. The newspaper had a regular column in Irish, for which Bourke had cast a special fount of type. Bourke also founded the *Keltic Journal and Educator* in 1869, but this was short-lived. However, this influenced the publication of *An Gaodhal*, a periodical published in Brooklyn, New York, which printed extracts from the *Tuam News* and articles by Bourke and John MacHale.

Bourke was a founder-member of the Society for the Preservation of Irish. In his *College Irish Grammar* (1856), written while still a student at Maynooth, he said: 'The language of a nation is the exponent of a people's antiquity; the index of their refinement; the mouthpiece of their history.' His *Easy Lessons on Self-Instruction in Irish* (1867), written at the suggestion of A. M. Sullivan, was published in *The Nation* in weekly instalments during the 1860s. This work made Bourke's name known across Ireland and was regarded as a standard treatise on the subject. He was elected a member of the Royal Irish Academy in 1871 for his work on ethnology, which was embodied in his *Aryan Origin of the Gaelic Race and Language* (1879). He was critical of the more fanciful theories of some scholars on the origin of the Irish language, and this book and his *Pre-Christian Ireland* (1887) are serious attempts to dispel some of these myths. He also wrote a life of Archbishop MacHale.

On his retirement from St Jarlath's in the late 1870s, Bourke became parish priest of Claremorris, co. Mayo. Although he was sympathetic to Fenianism, Bourke was not himself a Fenian, but circumstances of time and place, and his influence as a teacher of the Irish language and history, made it inevitable that he was caught up in the politics of the land war. His founding of the *Tuam News* was in part motivated by his drive to give local feelings a voice. He had been influenced by the theories of John Stuart Mill and advocated a peasant proprietary. In 1879, immediately after the meeting in Irishtown, co. Galway, which was the beginning of the Land League, he presided reluctantly at a land meeting in Claremorris, addressed by Michael Davitt. This was the first such meeting to be chaired by a priest and addressed by priests—an important element in the subsequent development of the Land League. Bourke's message was that they should be worthy of the title of free men and should not defy landlords and the government. He wrote a pamphlet addressed to Gladstone on the condition of evicted peasants in co. Mayo (1883).

Bourke died in Castlebar on 22 November 1887 and was buried at Claremorris. At his death he was working on an Irish–English dictionary, which he left incomplete.

MARIE-LOUISE LEGG

Sources P. Diskin, 'Irish scholars and language workers in the west, 1800–1900', *Iarlair* (1961), 90–91 · *Tuam News* (25 Nov 1887) · M. F. Ryan, *Fenian memories*, ed. T. F. O'Sullivan (1945) · T. W. Moody, *Davitt and Irish revolution* (1981) · *Galway Vindicator* (26 Nov 1887) · *Freeman's Journal* [Dublin] (23 Nov 1887)

Wealth at death £82 11*s*. 6*d*.: probate, 22 Feb 1888, *CGPLA Ire.*

Bourn, Samuel (1648–1719), Presbyterian minister, was born at Derby, the son and grandson of clothiers who had 'spent considerable sums … contriving engines' to supply the town with water (*Sermons*, preface), although his parent's names are unknown. These expenses might have hindered Bourn's education had not his uncle Robert Seddon (1629–1696), the ejected vicar of Langley, Derbyshire, taken care to send him to Emmanuel College, Cambridge, in 1671. Unwilling to subscribe to the Thirty-Nine Articles, Bourn left the university without a degree in 1672 and returned to Derby, where he served as a schoolteacher and afterwards as chaplain to Lady Hatton. He was probably ordained as a presbyterian later that decade while living with a Bourn aunt in London. In 1679, through the influence of the London divine Samuel Annesley, he became pastor of the presbyterian congregation at Calne, Wiltshire, at an annual salary of less than £10. Here he remained for the next sixteen years despite receiving more lucrative offers from churches in Bath, Durham, and Lincoln. Between 1690 and 1695 the London Common Fund awarded him yearly grants, ranging from £6 to £8, to encourage his ministry. Shortly after his arrival in Wiltshire he married the daughter of the Revd George Scortwreth (*d.* 1659), of Lincoln. Bourn left Calne in 1696, when the dying Seddon recommended him as his successor at Bolton, Lancashire. Initially unpopular with all save the 'most judicious and serious', Bourn nevertheless resisted calls to return to his former flock at a higher salary. Gradually, 'by his great integrity and inoffensive behaviour', he won over the entire Bolton congregation, which later that year built him a new meeting-house, the Bank Street Chapel, on land given by Seddon (ibid.).

Bourn excelled in the pulpit, according to his son and namesake Samuel *Bourn (1689–1754). If in prayer his 'grimaces … were somewhat peculiar … [and] might perhaps be disagreeable to strangers', he preached as became an orator; in his voice was a 'mixture of softness and vehemence … which tended at once to convince and ravish the souls of the hearers' (*Sermons*, 3.12–13). William Tong (1662–1727), a native of Bolton, who contributed a short memoir to Bourn's posthumous sermons, likewise thought him 'one of the best preachers that ever I heard' (*Sermons*, preface). Considering the meagreness of his stipend, Bourn's charity was as exemplary as his preaching. His success in pleading for the needy earned him a reputation as 'the best beggar in Bolton' (*Sermons*, 3. 25). He not only helped found a school there for twenty poor children, but eventually bore the cost of its maintenance himself. His benefactions culminated in a bequest of £20 to support a weekly lecture in Bolton, as large a legacy as he left to any of his children.

Tragedy struck Bourn's family in 1701 when three of his seven children died, including his eldest son, Joseph, aged twenty-one. His own health had been declining for several years, under the strain of unwearied study and constant preaching, before he died at Bolton on 4 March 1719. His widow had also suffered 'under great decays … of old age', though 'not without some lucid intervals' (*Sermons*, preface). On his deathbed Bourn expressed complete satisfaction with his nonconformist principles. His son Samuel, who had already arrived in Bolton to preach at one funeral, stayed to deliver his father's funeral sermon as well. In 1722 he published this discourse, on 2 Kings 2: 3, along with two sets of the elder Bourn's sermons, 'The transforming vision of Christ' and 'The Believer's Hope … the Reason and Motive of Real Holiness'. He dedicated this volume, his father's only printed work, to a relative, Madam Hacker of Duffield, Derbyshire, wife of Mr Hacker, perhaps the son of the regicide Francis *Hacker. The inclusion of a recommendatory preface by William Tong, a staunch Calvinist, is curious, for he and Bourn's heterodox son, who refused to subscribe to the Westminster assembly's catechism at his ordination, were strange bedfellows indeed. Naturally each offered his own distinctive interpretation of the deceased, making it difficult now to characterize Bourn's theological position. While Tong emphasized his abhorrence of recent departures from traditional Reformed teaching, the younger Bourn minimized his father's attachment to any particular human creeds: men were judged not by the orthodoxy of 'their opinions, but by their hearts and lives' (*Sermons*, 2.50). Both men did agree that, whatever Bourn's doctrinal leanings, tolerance towards those of differing views and an insistence upon 'moral righteousness' constituted the core of his divinity (*Sermons*, 3.8).

ALEXANDER GORDON, *rev.* JIM BENEDICT

Sources *Several sermons preached by the late Revd. Samuel Bourn*, ed. S. Bourn, 3 pts (1722) [preface by W. Tong] • *Calamy rev.*, 429, 431–2 • E. Calamy, *A continuation of the account of the ministers … who were ejected and silenced after the Restoration in 1660*, 2 vols. (1727), vol. 1, p. 232 • J. Toulmin, *Memoirs of the Revd. Samuel Bourn* (1808) • A. Gordon, ed., *Freedom after ejection: a review (1690–1692) of presbyterian and congregational nonconformity in England and Wales* (1917), 123, 218–19 • B. Nightingale, *Lancashire nonconformity*, 6 vols. [1890–93], vol. 3, p. 5 • F. Baker, *The rise and progress of nonconformity in Bolton* (1854) • J. H. Turner, T. Dickenson, and O. Heywood, eds., *The nonconformist register of baptisms, marriages, and deaths* (1881), 83 • J. Hunter, *Familiae minorum gentium*, ed. J. W. Clay, 4 vols., Harleian Society, 37–40 (1894–6), vol. 1, p. 300 • M. Watts, *The dissenters* (1978) • C. G. Bolam and others, *The English presbyterians: from Elizabethan puritanism to modern Unitarianism* (1968)

Likenesses M. Vandergucht, line engraving (after unknown artist), NPG; repro. in Bourn, ed., *Several sermons*

Bourn, Samuel (1689–1754), Presbyterian minister, was born at Calne in Wiltshire, the second son of Samuel *Bourn (1648–1719), dissenting minister, and his wife, Miss Scortwreth. He was taught classics at Bolton and trained for the Presbyterian ministry at the Manchester academy of John Chorlton and James Coningham. He became minister at Crook, near Kendal, in 1711. Probably in the same year he married Hannah Harrison, *née* Taylor (*d.* 1768), of Kendal. They had nine children, three of whom died before adulthood. Of their six surviving sons, two became ministers: Joseph (1713–1765) at Congleton and then Hindley, and Samuel *Bourn (1714–1796) at Norwich. Abraham, who was a surgeon in Market Harborough, Leicester, and Liverpool, wrote several pamphlets in defence of dissent. Benjamin became a London bookseller, publishing some of his father's works, and wrote *A Sure Guide to Hell* (1750). Daniel built an early cotton mill at Leominster, and Miles was a mercer in Dudley.

At first doctrinally orthodox, Bourn's intention not to subscribe to the Westminster assembly catechism at his ordination prompted a number of local ministers to boycott the occasion. When in 1719 the Salters' Hall conference made the trinitarian controversy a burning question among dissenters, Bourn, hitherto 'a professed Athanasian', studied the writings of Samuel Clarke and Daniel Waterland, and accepted Clarke's heterodox scheme. In his ministry at Crook he dedicated a child (probably of Baptist parentage) without baptism, according to a form printed in the memoirs of him by Toulmin. In 1720 he succeeded Henry Winder (*d.* 1752) at Tunley, near Wigan. He declined a call to the neighbouring congregation of Park Lane but accepted one (dated 29 December 1727) to the new chapel at Chorley. On 7 May 1731 he was chosen as one of the Monday lecturers at Bolton, a post which he held along with his Chorley pastorate.

On 19 April 1732 Bourn preached the opening sermon at the New Meeting in Birmingham, which replaced the Lower Meeting, and on 21 and 23 April he was called to be colleague with Thomas Pickard in joint charge of the congregation and a larger one at Coseley. He and his family moved to Coseley and he began his ministry on 25 June. Harassed by the JP John Ward of Sedgley Park, who sought to make him take a parish apprentice, Bourn twice successfully appealed to the quarter sessions. Ward then tried to remove him from Sedgley parish to his last legal settlement on the pretext that he was likely to become chargeable to the parish, to which Bourn wrote a spirited reply, later published by Toulmin. After Pickard's death, Bourn was joined by Samuel Blyth MD. His new colleague was hot-tempered and set about attacking field preachers and Quakers.

Bourn corresponded with Philip Doddridge, with Groome, vicar of Sedgley, and with the Kidderminster dissenters on the subject of subscription. In his catechetical instructions he 'improved upon' the assembly's catechism. Strongly believing that family religion was the first step towards national reformation, Bourn published prayers and catechisms for all age groups. His polemical points in his pamphlets centred on his suspicion of human formulas of doctrine: he accused protestant systematizers of doctrine of behaving like the pope in requiring allegiance to their schemes and urged that confessional subscription should be avoided. He disapproved of the use of technical theological terms not found in the Bible and was equally suspicious of enthusiasm. He argued that an 'Arian' interpretation of the Trinity was appropriate because the orthodox view of the identity of substance of the three persons precluded the idea of equality between them. The Particular Baptist theologian John Gill attacked these views in his defence of Calvinist orthodoxy.

On 18 September 1745 Bourn delivered the charge at the ordination of Job Orton at High Chapel, Shrewsbury, and on 12 September 1750 he 'prayed over' Noah Jones at his ordination at Pensnett meeting-house, Cradley. In 1751 he declined a call to succeed John Buck (*d.* 1750) in his father's congregation at Bolton. He died at Coseley of paralysis on 22 March 1754. He was small, slight, active, and sharp-eyed and somewhat dishevelled in appearance. Although his reputation for heterodoxy went before him, he was seldom polemical in the pulpit and his prayers were notable. With hindsight Joseph Priestley, who ministered at the Birmingham New Meeting from 1780 to 1791, said that his Congregation was 'the most liberal, I believe of any in England; and to this freedom the unwearied labours of Mr Bourn eminently contributed' (Priestley, 1.339).

ALEXANDER GORDON, *rev.* ALAN P. F. SELL

Sources S. Blyth, *The good soldier of Jesus Christ characterized. In a sermon preached at Birmingham, March 31, and at Coseley, April 7. Occasioned by the sudden and much-lamented death of the Reverend Mr. S. Bourn, who died March 22, 1754, in the 66th year of his age* (1754) • J. Toulmin, *Memoirs of the Revd. Samuel Bourn* (1808) • A. P. F. Sell, *Dissenting thought and the life of the churches: studies in an English tradition* (1990), chap. 7 • A. P. F. Sell, *Church planting: a study of Westmorland nonconformity* (1986), 43, 46 • F. Nicholson and E. Axon, *The older nonconformity in Kendal* (1915) • *The theological and miscellaneous works of Joseph Priestley*, ed. J. T. Rutt, 1 (1831–2)

Bourn, Samuel (1714–1796), Presbyterian minister, was born at Crook, near Kendal, the second son of the Presbyterian minister Samuel *Bourn (1689–1754) and his wife, Hannah Harrison, *née* Taylor (*d.* 1768), of Kendal. He was educated at Stand grammar school, Lancashire, and Glasgow University, where he studied under Francis Hutcheson and John Simson. His ministry began in 1742 at Rivington, Lancashire, though he was not ordained until some years after his settlement. In his ordination declaration he specified the duties of the ministry, and elevated the New Testament as the sole authority in matters of doctrine and ethics. While he enjoyed the friendship of Hugh Willoughby, fifteenth Lord Willoughby of Parham, who lived at Shaw Place, Rivington, and was a representative of the last of the Presbyterian noble families, Bourn felt constricted, and was impatient for advancement.

On 12 May 1752 Bourn delivered a sermon on Mark 4: 30 before the Lancashire provincial assembly of ministers at Manchester. In the same year the sermon was published under the title *The Rise, Progress, Corruption and Declension of the Christian Religion*. This led to his being invited to Norwich, where in 1754 he succeeded Peter Finch as the colleague of John Taylor. Bourn was thus present when the Norwich Presbyterians left the building in Little St Mary's (owned by the trustees of the Walloon or French protestants), in which they had been worshipping, for their new Octagon Chapel, which was opened on 12 May 1756. In the following year Taylor left Norwich for the dissenting academy at Warrington, and John Hoyle and Robert Alderson (father of Sir E. H. Alderson) came in succession as Bourn's colleagues. Among those raised under his ministry was Sir James Edward Smith, founder of the Linnean Society.

After losing £1000 speculating on his brother Daniel's cotton mill business, Bourn travelled from place to place in 1758 seeking subscriptions to finance the publication of two volumes of his sermons. He entrusted his manuscript to the rationalist and controversialist Samuel Chandler of the Old Jewry, and in 1759 heard Chandler preach a denunciation of the doctrine of the annihilation of the wicked as utterly inconsistent with Christian teaching. Since Bourn had espoused that doctrine in one of his sermons he took this as a personal attack, and published a letter against Chandler in 1759. John Mason (1706–1763) entered the controversy with his *Christian Morals* (1761), and Bourn appended a rejoinder to his *Discourses on the Parables of our Saviour* (1764).

Bourn was highly respected by those clergy of the Church of England who knew him, and when, about 1775, he became too ill to work and retired on £60 p.a. to Thorpe, Norwich, Dr Mann, bishop of Cork, offered him a sinecure living of £300 p.a. if only he would conform to the established church. Bourn declined—a display of nonconformist integrity which earned the admiration and the practical support of Samuel Parr, later headmaster of Norwich grammar school.

Like his father, Bourn was an Arian in the line of Samuel Clarke. At a time when the preaching of morality was widespread, he was unusually pessimistic in expecting no great improvement in the moral state of humanity. His sermons are forceful, carefully argued, and sometimes solemn. He also published *A series of discourses on the principles and evidences of natural religion and the Christian revelation* (1760), and his last publication comprised *Fifty Sermons on Various Subjects, Critical, Philosophical and Moral* (1777). His projected 'History of the Hebrews' was left unfinished at his death. Bourn married late in life; he and his wife left no children. He died at Norwich on 24 September 1796, and was buried three days later in the graveyard of Octagon Chapel.

ALAN P. F. SELL

Sources J. Toulmin, *Memoirs of the Rev. Samuel Bourn* (1808) • W. Field, *Memoirs of the life, writings and opinions of the Rev. Samuel Parr*, 2 vols. (1828) • J. Taylor and E. Taylor, *History of the Octagon Chapel, Norwich* (1848) • *DNB*

Bourn, Thomas (1771–1832), schoolteacher and educational writer, was born in Hackney, Middlesex, on 19 April 1771, and was educated at a private school in Well Street. He became a teacher at the school of the Revd S. Palmer until 1791 when he became a teacher of writing and geography in the private girls' schools run by William Butler (1748–1822), a Quaker. He married Butler's daughter in 1796 and had a family of eleven children.

Bourn published *A Concise Gazetteer of the most Remarkable Places in the World* (1807; 3rd edn, 1822), a compilation of over 900 pages which sought to make geography more attractive to learners by associating places with historical occurrences, famous persons, and remarkable facts. Drawing upon the educational works of his father-in-law (whose *Arithmetical Questions … for the Use of Young Ladies* he edited in 1829) and the biographical compilations of his friend Stephen Jones, Bourn sought to present useful knowledge in an appealing way, to draw young female readers away from the dangerous frivolities of popular novels. Bourn claimed to use a conversational method of teaching in preference to learning by rote: 'Young people require to be entertained as well as admonished' (*Concise Gazetteer*, viii). He died at his house in Mare Street, Hackney, Middlesex, on 20 August 1832.

THOMPSON COOPER, *rev.* M. C. CURTHOYS

Sources *GM*, 1st ser., 102/2 (1832), 279–80 • J. O. Butler, *A brief memoir of Mr William Butler* (1826)
Likenesses J. Fassell, lithograph, NPG

Bourne, Aleck William (1886–1974), obstetrician and gynaecologist, was born into modest circumstances on 4 June 1886 at Rosebank, Whetstone, Finchley, Middlesex, the only son of the Revd William Charles Bourne, a Wesleyan minister, and his wife, Sarah Wilson Palmer. He was educated at Rydal School, Colwyn Bay (1898–1905), and won an open scholarship to Downing College, Cambridge. Having taken a first-class honours degree in natural sciences in 1908, he won a senior scholarship to St Mary's Hospital, London, qualifying as MRCS LRCP in 1910 and FRCS MB BCh in 1911. From 1910 to 1914 he filled resident and other appointments at St Mary's, Queen Charlotte's, and the Samaritan hospitals. On 3 December 1912 he married Bessie Winifred (*b*. 1886/7), eldest daughter of George Whitfield Hayward, an umbrella manufacturer of Barnet. They had three daughters. From 1914 to 1917 Bourne saw war service as a surgeon in Egypt and France.

Bourne became a leading practitioner of obstetrics and gynaecology and enjoyed a varied and lucrative career as a teaching hospital consultant. In 1934 he was appointed consulting obstetrical surgeon at St Mary's Hospital (whereupon he resigned his appointments at Queen Charlotte's and the Samaritan). He examined for the University of Cambridge; was president of the obstetrical and gynaecological section of the Royal Society of Medicine (1938–9); and was a foundation fellow of the British (later Royal) College of Obstetricians and Gynaecologists (1929), and a member of the Central Health Services Council (1948). He wrote *Recent Advances in Obstetrics and Gynaecology* (1926) and *Synopsis of Midwifery and Gynaecology* (1913), jointly edited with E. Holland *British Obstetric and Gynaecological Practice* (1955), and had several papers published in medical journals. Perhaps his greatest interests were in teaching and in his students, whom he would sometimes invite to join him in his major recreation—sailing.

Bourne is chiefly remembered for his widely publicized trial in 1938 for criminal abortion. A socialist agnostic, he was a member of the Abortion Law Reform Association—a pressure group campaigning for relaxation of the abortion law. He decided to test the law by terminating the pregnancy of a fourteen-year-old rape victim and asking the police to arrest him. They did. He was charged under section 58 of the Offences against the Person Act 1861 and tried at the central criminal court by Mr Justice Macnaghten and a jury. Section 58 prohibited attempts 'unlawfully' to procure a miscarriage and made no explicit exception for therapeutic abortion by medical practitioners. In his summing up, however, the judge directed that the section implied that abortion was not 'unlawfully' performed if carried out to preserve the mother's life and that this included the case where continuation of a pregnancy would leave the woman a 'physical or mental wreck' (Keown, 51). Bourne was acquitted.

This has long been widely perceived as a landmark case, relaxing the law to permit abortion to preserve life or health. There was, however, prior legal authority to this effect, albeit less well known. There were also signs of changing views within the medical profession. In 1936 a British Medical Association committee approved several indications for abortion and at its conference that year the association approved the publication of the committee's report. Furthermore, Bourne, who had been a member of the committee, wrote after his trial that he had never feared conviction and that his reason for inviting prosecution was not to relax the law but merely to obtain a clear ruling that it permitted abortion to preserve physical or mental health. Whether this was his aim remains unclear, for he certainly supported relaxation of the law to permit abortion for victims of rape. He may even, though his pronouncements seem ambivalent, have supported abortion for economic reasons, though he thought that the improved social conditions for which he called would remove the demand for such abortion. In any event, the importance of the case would appear to lie in its clarification, rather than relaxation, of the law. It brought the flexibility of the law dramatically to the attention of both the public and the medical profession and appears to have resulted in an increased willingness of the former to seek, and the latter to perform, abortions. After the case Bourne was, to his dismay, swamped with requests. The case may well have sown the seeds of further relaxation of the law and the controversy it generated may have cost Bourne his chance of high office in the Royal College of Obstetricians and Gynaecologists.

In 1951 Bourne retired from St Mary's. He moved from Burnham-on-Crouch, Essex, to the Red House, Skinners Lane, Ashtead, Surrey, and in 1961 he vacated the flat he had occupied for twenty-three years in Wimpole Street, London. His retirement was active, involving private practice, gardening, reading, travelling, and writing.

Bourne had resigned from the Abortion Law Reform Association in 1945 owing to pressure of work. In the 1960s the association intensified its campaign for substantial relaxation of the law by statute. This Bourne opposed, believing that that the law was not as strict as many believed and required only modest amendment. Indeed, in 1966 he became a founder member of the Society for the Protection of the Unborn Child, though his efforts failed to prevent the major relaxation of the law effected by the Abortion Act 1967.

Bourne died at the Red House, on 27 December 1974. In his autobiography, *A Doctor's Creed* (1962), he summed up his life as having been 'full of the joys of work and the sparkle of so much friendship and fun' (Bourne, 179). He was remembered by his colleagues as a kind and compassionate man of courage and principle; a champion of the cause of women—as his role in securing the admission of women students to St Mary's after the Second World War testified; a superb clinician and an outstanding, inspirational teacher. He will be remembered more widely because of his involvement in abortion law reform, an involvement which contributed to more far-reaching relaxation of the law than he appears either to have expected or desired.

John Keown

Sources A. W. Bourne, *A doctor's creed: the memoirs of a gynaecologist* (1962) • *The Lancet* (11 Jan 1975), 116 • *BMJ* (11 Jan 1975), 99 • J. Keown, *Abortion, doctors and the law* (1988), ch. 3 • M. Simms and K. Hindell, *Abortion law reformed* (1971), 69–72 • *WWW* • b. cert. • m. cert.
Likenesses photograph, repro. in *The Lancet*

Bourne, Francis Alphonsus (1861–1935), Roman Catholic archbishop of Westminster, was born on 23 March 1861 at 10 Larkhall Rise, Clapham, London, the second of two sons of Henry Bourne (1826–1870), a Post Office worker and a convert to Roman Catholicism, and Ellen (1824–1900), daughter of John Byrne, a Dublin merchant. Bourne was baptized at St Mary's, Clapham, on 24 March 1861. The family moved to Greenhithe, near Dartford, in 1868. After the death of her husband on 18 February 1870 Mrs Bourne was influential in the education and religious upbringing of her sons. Both attended St Cuthbert's College, Ushaw, near Durham (Francis from 1869) but after the death of the elder brother, Henry Joseph, on 3 September 1874, Francis went to St Edmund's College, Ware, in 1875 as 'a lay boy in grammar', and began his studies for the priesthood there in 1877.

In 1880 Bourne entered St Thomas's Seminary, Hammersmith, to study theology. He tested his vocation with the Dominicans at Woodchester, Gloucestershire, but he left the Dominicans and went to St Sulpice in Paris to continue his seminary studies. Bourne was ordained subdeacon and deacon there in 1883 by Bishop Francis Richard, coadjutor to the archbishop of Paris. After additional courses at the University of Louvain, the bishop of Southwark, Robert Coffin, ordained him a priest in 1884. Bourne's first assignments were at Blackheath, Sheerness, and Mortlake. His interest in a religious order continued, and in 1887 he visited Don Bosco, the founder of the Salesians, at Turin. Bourne returned to England convinced of his vocation as a secular priest, and in 1887 he was assigned to West Grinstead, where he found work among the young fulfilling. John Butt, who became bishop of Southwark in 1885, wanted a seminary for the diocese and had opened a temporary house of studies at Henfield Place, Sussex, and in 1899 placed Bourne in charge. When the seminary moved to Wonersh, near Guildford, in 1891 Bourne became its first rector. Four years later Leo XIII named Bourne a domestic prelate.

At the age of thirty-five, in 1896, Bourne was consecrated bishop of Epiphania and coadjutor to Bishop Butt with right of succession. In the following year Butt resigned, and Bourne became bishop of Southwark. When Cardinal Herbert Vaughan died in 1903 Rome chose Bishop Bourne, the youngest of the English hierarchy, in spite of Vaughan's preference for Cardinal Rafael Merry del Val. Bourne's enthronement at the new Westminster Cathedral in December 1903 represented the first grand ceremony in the church; Vaughan's funeral had taken place there months earlier. Archbishop Bourne eventually consecrated the cathedral in 1910, and in the following year Pius X made Bourne a cardinal.

As cardinal-archbishop of Westminster, Bourne exercised a prominent role in national affairs. The Balfour Act of 1902 had given some assistance from public funds to the voluntary schools, Anglican and Roman Catholic, but the Liberal government was committed to withdraw aid to voluntary schools, and opponents of Catholic schools campaigned on the slogan 'Rome on the rates'. Bourne angered many Irish, who had placed great hope in the Liberal Party for some measure of home rule, by attacking that government's educational policies. He organized a demonstration at the Albert Hall in 1906 which brought together Catholics of all political parties in defence of their schools. Bourne's leadership helped to defeat three bills hostile to the voluntary schools. Bourne's commitment to Catholic education could be seen in his support for St Edmund's College, Ware, where seminarians and lay students were educated, but some criticized him for neglecting the needs of primary education in the archdiocese.

Anti-Catholic pressures and questions of law forced Prime Minister Herbert Asquith in 1908 to prohibit carrying the blessed sacrament in a procession during the Eucharistic Congress held in London. In dealings with the government Bourne demonstrated his diplomacy, and the procession took place without the blessed sacrament and without incident. Irish politics also brought Bourne national attention. Accused by some of being anti-Irish, the cardinal desired self-government for Ireland, but favoured preserving the essential link with the crown and the empire. The cardinal's role in the 1926 general strike proved more controversial. On 9 May during mass at Westminster Cathedral, Bourne condemned the strike. He believed it lacked moral justification, constituted a direct challenge to lawful authority, and brought hardships to the country.

Bourne represented English Roman Catholics at numerous events abroad. He attended celebrations in France honouring Jeanne d'Arc in 1929 and 1931, the latter as a papal legate, and also attended Eucharistic Congress meetings outside England. In England he supported work among the poor, temperance, Catholic education, Catholic scouting, and the National Catholic Congress, and during the First World War he visited the troops and the fleet. In dealings with Anglicans Bourne initially sympathized with the spirit of the Malines Conversations (1921–6), but he would tolerate no compromise with Catholic doctrine. But by 1926 he had become disillusioned with the meetings.

By 1933 Bourne had begun to cancel engagements because of ill health, and one of his last appearances was in August 1934 when he led a pilgrimage to Norfolk in honour of Our Lady of Walsingham. Cardinal Bourne died peacefully on 1 January 1935 at the archbishop's house, Westminster, London. The archbishop of Cardiff, Francis Mostyn, celebrated the requiem mass on 4 January at Westminster Cathedral. Bourne was buried that day at St Edmund's College, Ware. *The Times* emphasized Bourne's characteristically English firmness and noted that his patience and perseverance helped him to succeed 'where a more superficially brilliant man would probably have failed' (*The Times*, 2 Jan 1935).

Conservative by nature, Bourne performed his ecclesiastical duties with dignity and reserve. Of medium height with a pleasant appearance, he gave the impression of being aloof. Bourne was not a great orator, and his shy nature contrasted with the strong personalities of his three predecessors at Westminster. In addition to pastoral letters and sermons, Bourne published *Ecclesiastical Training* (1926), which dealt with the spiritual formation of seminarians. Both Oxford University and Louvain University gave him honorary doctorates. RENE KOLLAR

Sources E. Oldmeadow, *Francis, Cardinal Bourne*, 2 vols. (1940–44) · *The Times* (1 Jan 1935) · *The Tablet* (5 Jan 1935) · 'A great English cardinal', *The Times* (2 Jan 1935) · R. J. Lahey, 'Cardinal Bourne and the Malines Conversations', *Bishops and writers: aspects of the evolution of modern English Catholicism*, ed. A. Hastings (1977), 81–105 · G. I. T. Machin, 'The liberal government and the Eucharistic procession of 1908', *Journal of Ecclesiastical History*, 34 (1983), 559–83 · R. J. Dingle, *Cardinal Bourne at Westminster* (1934) · F. A. Bourne, *Ecclesiastical training* (1926) · G. Wheeler, 'The archdiocese of Westminster', *The English Catholics, 1850–1950*, ed. G. A. Beck (1950), 151–86 · D. Mathew, *Catholicism in England*, 3rd edn (1955) · A. Hastings, *A history of English Christianity, 1920–1985* (1986) · 'Cardinal Bourne: requiem mass at Westminster', *The Times* (5 Jan 1935) · 'Cardinal Bourne's obsequies', *The Tablet* (12 Jan 1935)

Archives Southwark diocesan archives, London, papers mainly relating to St John's Seminary, Wonersh · Ushaw College, Durham, corresp. and papers · Westm. DA, official papers, corresp. and papers | BL, corresp. with Lord Ripon, Add. MS 43545 · Bodl. Oxf., corresp. with H. Asquith · Bodl. Oxf., corresp. with Sir James Marchant · NL Ire., corresp. with John Redmond · U. St Andr. L., corresp. with Wilfred Ward · University of Sheffield, corresp. with W. A. S. Hewins | FILM BFI NFTVA, news footage | SOUND BL NSA, current affairs recordings

Likenesses two photographs, one 1869?, repro. in Oldmeadow, *Francis, Cardinal Bourne*, vol. 1 · G. C. Beresford, three photographs, 1905–22, NPG · L. Ward, caricature, watercolour, 1910?, NPG · J. Lavery, oils, 1921, Westminster Diocesan Seminary, London, Allen Hall · A. Chevallier Tayler, oils, 1934, archbishop's house, Westminster, London · Bassano, photograph (aged fifty-one), repro. in Oldmeadow, *Francis, Cardinal Bourne*, vol. 2 · Bassano, photograph (late in life), repro. in Dingle, *Cardinal Bourne at Westminster* · Beresford, photograph (aged sixty-three), repro. in Oldmeadow, *Francis, Cardinal Bourne*, vol. 2 · W. & D. Downey, photograph (late in life), repro. in *The Tablet* (5 Jan 1935) · Yevonde, photograph, repro. in *The Tablet* (5 Jan 1935) · photograph (late in life), repro. in G. A. Beck, ed., *The English Catholics, 1850–1950*

Wealth at death £17,308 11s. 9d.: probate, 14 June 1935, *CGPLA Eng. & Wales*

Bourne, Gilbert (*c*.1510–1569), bishop of Bath and Wells, the son of Philip Bourne of Worcestershire, was born *c*.1510 (Foxe reports that Bourne was aged about forty-one in 1551). Having entered Oxford University in 1524, he graduated BA in 1528, became a fellow of All Souls College in 1531, and proceeded MA in 1533. Four years later, in February 1537, he was 'dispensed to take all holy orders outside statutory times and two on [the] same day' (Emden, *Oxf.*, 4.62). He then completed his studies in 1543 when he received the degree of bachelor of theology, also from Oxford.

Between 1541 and 1551 Bourne was given a number of preferments. In 1541 he became rector of Duntisbourne Abbots, Gloucestershire; in 1542, he was made prebendary of the fifth stall of the king's new foundation at Worcester; about 1543 he became chaplain to Edmund Bonner, bishop of London; in 1545 he obtained the prebends of Holborn and Wildland, both at St Paul's, London; in 1547 he was proctor for the clergy of the diocese of London; in 1548 he exchanged the prebend of Wildland for that of Brownswood, also at St Paul's; in 1549 he was made archdeacon of Bedford; in 1550 he became rector of High Ongar, Essex; some time before April 1550 he was vicar of Arlingham, Gloucestershire; and in 1551 he was given the rectory of Minchinhampton, Gloucestershire.

Because he received and maintained so many preferments during such a period of religious turmoil, Bourne must have agreed with or, at the very least, not openly resisted the changes in religion that occurred during that time. As chaplain to Bonner, however, he remained loyal to his superior during Bonner's troubles with the Edwardian government.

On 13 August 1553, less than a month after Mary I's accession, Bourne was almost killed when he preached a sermon at Paul's Cross, denouncing the protestant changes of Edward VI's reign, and singing the praises of Bonner, deprived of the bishopric of London in 1549, but soon to be restored. The crowd that gathered to hear Bourne's sermon became so angry with his remarks that they began to riot, and someone threw a dagger at Bourne that narrowly missed its target.

Probably through the influence of his uncle, Sir John Bourne, who was principal secretary of state during Mary's reign, Bourne was made bishop of Bath and Wells by papal provision, being consecrated on 1 April 1554. The temporalities were restored on 20 April, and he received papal confirmation on 6 July of that same year.

Little can be said of Bourne's secular administration of his diocese, but he did recover the valuable manor of Banwell, lost under Edward VI, albeit at the cost of a reserved rent of £115 per annum. Inevitably religious issues dominated his episcopate, which saw the diocesan clergy deprived of at least 106 benefices—a ratio of one deprivation for every six benefices. The exact cause for many of these deprivations cannot be determined, but in most cases it was probably because the incumbent had married during the Edwardian period when clergy were permitted to do so—something that the Marian religious injunctions of 1554 undid. As for heresy cases, the surviving evidence indicates that Bourne condemned two men, Roger Hues (or Curryer) and Richard Lush, but that only Hues went to the stake. Lush, who was condemned on 5 November 1558, in part for saying that Hues was unjustly executed, must have been spared a fiery end by Mary's death less than a fortnight later.

Outside his diocese Bourne was a member of the commissions that in 1555 examined the martyrs Thomas Tomkins and John Philpot, and (before he became a bishop) he may have been the Dr Bourne who attempted to persuade Walter Mantel to recant. Perhaps for his loyal service to the Marian government, or through the continued influence of his uncle, Bourne was appointed president of the council in the marches of Wales on 29 October 1558, and held this position until February 1559.

After Elizabeth I's accession Bourne refused to take the

oath of supremacy, and was subsequently deprived some time between 18 October 1559 and 11 January 1560—by the middle of November Cecil was proposing Berkeley as his successor. Bourne was then put in the Tower of London on 18 June 1560, and remained there until 1561, when he was turned over to Nicholas Bullingham, bishop of Lincoln. In the following year he was placed in the custody of George Carew, archdeacon of Exeter (who was also the dean of Bristol and of St George's Chapel, Windsor), and probably remained in Carew's keeping until his death at Silverton, Devon, on 10 September 1569. Bourne was buried in Silverton church on the south side of the altar, having bequeathed what possessions he had to his brother Richard. ANGELO J. LOUISA

Sources Emden, *Oxf.*, 4.62 • Wood, *Ath. Oxon.*, new edn, 2.805–7 • Wood, *Ath. Oxon.: Fasti* (1815), 79, 91, 118 • G. Bourne, register, Som. ARS, D/D/B Reg. 14 • H. Maxwell-Lyte, ed., *The registers of Thomas Wolsey, bishop of Bath and Wells, 1518–1523, John Clerke, bishop of Bath and Wells, 1523–1541, William Knyght, bishop of Bath and Wells, 1541–1547, and Gilbert Bourne, bishop of Bath and Wells, 1554–1559*, Somerset RS, 55 (1940), xiii–xvi, 120–57 • *The acts and monuments of John Foxe*, ed. S. R. Cattley, 8 vols. (1837–41), vol. 6, pp. 242, 546–8, 721; vol. 7, pp. 613–15, 656, 658, 671, 674–5, 678–9, 683; vol. 8, pp. 377–8 • BL, Harley MSS, 421/56/111 • *VCH Somerset*, 2.37–9, 65–6 • *Fasti Angl., 1541–1857*, [St Paul's, London], 21, 61 • *Fasti Angl., 1541–1857*, [Bath and Wells], 1 • *Reg. Oxf.*, 1.148 • *CSP dom., 1547–80*, 108, 123 • P. M. Hembry, *The bishops of Bath and Wells, 1540–1640: social and economic problems* (1967), 30, 47, 58, 89–100, 112, 124–9, 134–9, 142 • administration, PRO, PROB 6/1, fol. 150v • A. J. Louisa, 'The Marian bishops: a study of the backgrounds and ecclesiastical activities of the Marian episcopate', PhD diss., University of Minnesota, 1985 • F. Heal, *Of prelates and princes: a study of the economic and social position of the Tudor episcopate* (1980)

Wealth at death all left to brother: administration, PRO, PROB 6/1 (vol. 2), fol. 150v, 1569; Wood, *Ath. Oxon.*

Bourne, Gilbert Charles (1861–1933), zoologist and oarsman, was born at Grafton Manor, Worcestershire, on 5 July 1861, the eldest surviving son of Lieutenant-Colonel Robert Bourne, 54th regiment, of Cowarne Court, near Ledbury, and his wife, Anna Eliza, youngest daughter of Samuel Baker, of Lypiatt Park, Gloucestershire. Diagnosed (possibly incorrectly) as suffering valvular heart disease, he was unable to take part in sports at school in Helidon. He instead took long walks through the Northamptonshire countryside, developing an early interest in natural history. He went to Eton in 1874 and, given a clean bill of health by a physician, became quite a sportsman there. In 1881 he went to New College, Oxford, as an exhibitioner. He spent the summer of his second year in Freiburg-im-Breisgau, studying under August Weismann. He rowed for Oxford in the university boat races of 1882 and 1883, and graduated first class in natural science in 1885. After graduation he visited the atoll of Diego Garcia, in the Indian Ocean. By comparing his observations (and those recently made by HMS *Rambler*) with records from Captain Moresby's 1837 expedition he concluded that the lagoon was silting up and the atoll extending seawards. This lent support to John Murray's hypothesis of atoll formation rather than Charles Darwin's competing theory of subsidence, and Bourne's results were published by the Royal Society in 1888.

In 1887 Bourne married Constance Margaret Graham (*d.* 1954), the eldest daughter of Sir John Frederick Croft, second baronet, of Doddington Place, Kent. The couple had a son, Robert Croft *Bourne, and a daughter. Also in 1887, Bourne was appointed as the first director of the Marine Biological Laboratory at Plymouth. He resigned from the post in 1899 and returned to Oxford, where he became a fellow and tutor at New College. In 1906 he was elected to the Linacre chair of zoology and comparative anatomy with a fellowship at Merton College. He held both positions until 1921, when he succeeded to his father's property in Herefordshire.

Bourne's early researches in Diego Garcia largely determined his later zoological interests. He made studies on the structure, development, and classification of corals and related animals, and many of his findings have passed into the textbooks. Although his later researches were mainly morphological, his interests remained wide. He entered into the preformation–epigenesis controversy and wrote two articles of lasting value in defence of the cell-theory against the attack of Adam Sedgwick.

Bourne's writing was crisp, vigorous, and scholarly, and the illustrations to his morphological papers show considerable artistic ability. His *Introduction to the Study of the Comparative Anatomy of Animals* (1900–02) provided a fresh and readable approach to a subject that is often drily presented. He was also a contributor to the *Treatise on Zoology* (1900–09) by E. R. Lankester. He was considered a stimulating teacher; some of his students had particularly successful careers in zoology. He served as a member of the advisory committee on fisheries of the Development Commission, and in 1931 was appointed chairman. He was elected FRS in 1910.

Apart from his scientific pursuits Bourne devoted much time to boats and oarsmanship. He was an outstanding oarsman and expounder of the theory and practice both of oarsmanship and the design of racing boats. He achieved renown as a rowing coach, and was in no small measure responsible for the success of his college on the river for some fifty years; many university crews also owed much to his coaching in the early days of their training. His *Text Book on Oarsmanship* (1925), a masterpiece of careful detail, was compiled with the help of mechanical experts and mathematicians who worked out innumerable experiments for him. By developing Warre's theories on the lines of racing eights, and from his own observations of the streamlines of fish, he considered that the racing boat should have its greatest beam and draught much farther forward than was usual, so that the waves thrown off by the boat's entry into the water met exactly at the stern. The main features of his design were adopted by several designers of racing eights.

Always a keen soldier, Bourne rose to be second in command of the 4th battalion of the King's Shropshire light infantry (serving in Ireland) during the Second South African War. He represented the University of Oxford on the committee appointed by the War Office in 1906 to consider the provision of an Officers' Training Corps, which proved of the greatest value on the outbreak of war in

1914. In that war he was wounded at Sulva Bay in 1915, and subsequently appointed superintending officer of the young officers' company of the 12th reserve infantry brigade.

From 1920 Bourne was a member of the advisory committee of the Ministry of Agriculture and Fisheries on fishery research, and in 1930 he was appointed chairman. From 1927 he also served as a member of the water pollution research board, and was chairman of its subcommittee set up to develop a programme for a biological and chemical survey on the River Tees. He was still involved in this last project at the time of his death at his home, Tubney House, Tubney, near Abingdon, Berkshire, on 8 March 1933.

JOHN R. BAKER and C. M. PITMAN, *rev.* PETER OSBORNE

Sources *The Times* (10 March 1933) • G. C. Bourne, *Memories of an Eton wet bob of the seventies* (1933) • S. J. H., *Obits. FRS*, 1 (1932–5), 126–30 • *WWW* • private information (1949) • personal knowledge (1949) • *CGPLA Eng. & Wales* (1933)

Archives Marine Biological Association of the United Kingdom, notes on Plymouth fauna • U. Oxf., department of zoology, lecture notes, notes on fauna | UCL, letters to Karl Pearson

Likenesses portrait, repro. in *Obits. FRS*

Wealth at death £79,260 3*s.* 5*d.*: resworn probate, 1 June 1933, *CGPLA Eng. & Wales*

Bourne, Henry (*bap.* **1694**, *d.* **1733**), antiquary, was baptized at Newcastle upon Tyne on 16 December 1694, the son of Thomas Bourne, a tailor. He was bound apprentice to a glazier in 1709, but showed such aptitude for learning that he was allowed to cancel his indentures and was sent to resume his education at the Newcastle grammar school. He was admitted a sizar of Christ's College, Cambridge, in 1717, holding a scholarship of £5 from Newcastle corporation, under the tuition of the Revd Thomas Atherton, a fellow townsman. He graduated BA in 1720 and MA in 1724, and received the appointment of curate of All Hallows Church, Newcastle, where he remained until his death. He married twice; he and his first wife, Margaret (*d.* 1727), had three children, two of whom, Henry and Eleanor, survived infancy. On 30 May 1728 he married Alice Inchbald (*d.* 1773), with whom he had two children who both died young.

In 1725 Bourne published *Antiquitates vulgares, or, The antiquities of the common people, giving an account of their opinions and ceremonies*, which he dedicated to the mayor and corporation in recognition of their encouragement of learning and support for the clergy. This was republished, with additions by John Brand, in 1777 in his *Popular Antiquities*, and forms the groundwork of the later labours of Sir Henry Ellis and W. C. Hazlitt. Consequently, it is often cited as an early example of folklore studies, although Bourne's purpose had been to identify which customs should be retained and encouraged and which abolished or regulated. In 1727 he issued a liturgical manual, *The harmony and agreement of the collects, epistles, and gospels, as they stand in the Book of Common Prayer for the Sundays throughout the year*, in recognition of which he was awarded a lectureship in 1728. He also wrote a history of his native town, which was substantially complete at his death. It was afterwards published by subscription by the printer John White in 1736, in support of Bourne's widow and children, as a folio volume dedicated to Sir Walter Blackett, under the title of *The History of Newcastle-upon-Tyne, or, The Ancient and Present State of that Town*. The history was based on William Grey's *Chorographia, or, A Survey of Newcastle upon Tine* (1649) and followed the tradition of a topographical survey, giving a lively account of Newcastle in the early eighteenth century as well as of its history. Bourne complained in the preface of the difficulties he had met as a humble curate in gathering materials for his work. Christopher Hunter of Durham had plans to publish an edition with considerable additions in 1750, but these never came to fruition. In 1757 a few large paper copies were printed; these are now very rare.

Bourne, who was described by his vicar as 'universally beloved' (Adamson, 'Henry Bourne', 150), died in Newcastle on 16 February 1733 and was buried in All Souls, Newcastle, on 18 February. His widow outlived him for many years and retired to Mrs Davidson's Hospital in Newcastle, where she died in 1773.

C. W. SUTTON, *rev.* R. H. SWEET

Sources R. Welford, *Men of mark 'twixt Tyne and Tweed*, 3 vols. (1895) • E. Mackenzie, *A descriptive and historical account of the town and county of Newcastle upon Tyne*, 2 vols. (1827) • E. H. Adamson, 'Henry Bourne, the historian of Newcastle', *Archaeologia Aeliana*, new ser., 11 (1886), 147–53 • J. Brand, preface, *The history and antiquities of the town and county of the town of Newcastle upon Tyne*, 2 vols. (1789) • E. H. Adamson, *Scholae Novocastriensis alumni* (1846) • *IGI*

Bourne, Henry Richard Fox (**1837–1909**), writer and campaigner for the rights of indigenous peoples, was born at Grecian Regale, Blue Mountains, Jamaica, on 24 December 1837, one of eight children of Stephen Bourne (*c*.1792–1868), a stipendiary magistrate and advocate of the abolition of slavery, and his wife, Elizabeth Quirk. His father, a promoter of the Protestant Society and the Ecclesiastical Knowledge Society, had founded in December 1826 *The Word*, the first nonconformist and exclusively religious journal in England. In 1841 the family moved to British Guiana, but returned to England in 1848. After attending a private school in London, Henry entered London University in 1856 and joined classes at King's College. He also attended the lectures at University College of Henry Morley, who became a lifelong friend.

In 1855 Fox Bourne became a clerk at the War Office, and at the same time undertook a great deal of literary and journalistic work. He contributed to *The Examiner* during Henry Morley's editorship, and to *Household Words* under Charles Dickens. On 1 May 1862 he married Emma Deane, daughter of Henry Bleckly, a Warrington ironmaster. His first independent publication, *A Memoir of Sir Philip Sidney*, appeared in that year, followed by a series of books tracing in a popular style the rise of England's commerce and colonial expansion.

After retiring from the War Office in 1870 during a government economy drive, Fox Bourne used the compensation he had received in lieu of a pension to purchase *The Examiner*, for which John Stuart Mill, Herbert Spencer, and Henry Fawcett wrote from time to time. Distinguished contributors and his own fluent pen did not counterbalance inadequate business skill, however, and three years later he had to dispose of the paper. He stayed in journalism as editor from 1876 until 1887 of the *Weekly Dispatch*, a radical paper aimed at a working-class readership, but his criticisms of the Gladstone government during 1880–85 and of the Home Rule Bill in 1886 brought him into conflict with the paper's owner, Ashton Dilke, and led to his resignation of the editorship. His best-known work, *English Newspapers: Chapters in the History of Journalism* (2 vols.) appeared in that year, and remains a valuable source, particularly for its information about the political complexion of the press in the nineteenth century.

On 4 January 1889 Fox Bourne succeeded F. W. Chesson as secretary of the Aborigines' Protection Society; he also became editor of the society's journal, the *Aborigines' Friend*. As the committee of the society left almost all the initiative and management to its secretary, the position gave considerable scope to a vigorous champion of justice with a flair for advocacy. But Fox Bourne's relations with the Colonial Office were poor and his advocacy met with limited success. His range of interests and literary style were best suited to broad issues, but much of the society's work involved bringing the cases of individuals or small groups of people to the notice of the Colonial Office. Careful reporting was essential, and accurate detail from a distant colony was often hard to come by. Members of the society were disposed to see colonial subjects, and especially non-white ones, as likely victims of oppressive officialdom, and from time to time Fox Bourne took up unworthy cases with excessive zeal and magisterial prolixity. That was of no help when dealing with officials, some of whom had served in the colonies. Self-government had come to the 'white' colonies destined to become dominions and the department had an excuse for declining to intervene in what were seen as internal affairs.

In a number of major causes Fox Bourne's efforts achieved significant results. The campaign against Leopold II's personal fiefdom in the Congo Free State was completed by E. D. Morel's Congo Reform Association, but Fox Bourne's was the pioneering work. He was also a leader of the successful campaign to halt the importation of Chinese labour to the goldfields of Witwatersrand, and his efforts to reveal gross exploitation in Angola and the cocoa plantations of the Portuguese west African islands of San Thomé and Principé met with posthumous success. Setting up the Eastern Sudan famine relief fund in 1890, which involved co-operation between the British government, the Eastern Telegraph Company, and the society, was an effort of a different order and it saved many lives. In such matters Fox Bourne's style was appropriate and effective. Except in the case of the Transvaal, he had the advantage of dealing with a sympathetic Foreign Office, inheritors after the emancipation of slaves in the British empire between 1834 and 1838 of the continuing struggle to suppress slavery and the slave trade.

A stream of well-researched pamphlets on Egyptian maladministration, the liquor trade in Africa, and race relations, among other topics, was part of Fox Bourne's continuing attempt to right perceived wrongs committed by the expanding European nations in the lands of other races. He 'glowed with a constant fire of steady indignation', as one obituarist commented (*The Times*, 6 Feb 1909), and he sometimes clashed with others on his own side stoked with similar fire. Controversy between Fox Bourne and Charles H. Allen, secretary of the Anti-Slavery Society, surfaced in correspondence to *The Times* over the Brussels conference on the slave trade in central Africa (1890), and the treatment of natives of the Rand by the Uitlanders (1901).

Fox Bourne died unexpectedly of bronchitis on 2 February 1909 at the Victoria and Albert Hotel, Torquay, Devon, where he was holidaying. His widow, with two sons and a daughter, survived him. H. C. SWAISLAND

Sources *DNB* · *Aborigines' Friend*, new ser., 8 (1909), 245–55 · *The Times* (10 Jan 1890) · *The Times* (20 Jan 1890) · *The Times* (26 Aug 1901) · *The Times* (28 Aug 1901) · *The Times* (29 Aug 1901) · *The Times* (11 Sept 1901) · *The Times* (12 Sept 1901) · *The Times* (5 Feb 1909) · *The Times* (6 Feb 1909) · *The Times* (8 Feb 1909) · *West African Mail* (23 March 1906) · Colonial office files, PRO · correspondence, Aborigines' Protection Society, Bodl. RH, C 150–3, 165 and ser. G · *CGPLA Eng. & Wales* (1909)

Archives Bodl. RH, corresp. as secretary of the Aborigines' Protection Society | BLPES, corresp. with E. D. Morel · Regent's Park College, Oxford, corresp. with G. W. Macalpine and W. H. Bentley · U. Durham L., letters to third Earl Grey

Likenesses photograph, repro. in *Aborigines' Friend*, 247

Wealth at death £2057 4s. 7d.: probate, 24 June 1909, *CGPLA Eng. & Wales*

Bourne, Hugh (1772–1852), founder of the Primitive Methodist church, son of Joseph Bourne, farmer and wheelwright, and his wife, Ellen Steele, was born at Fordhays Farm, in the parish of Stoke-on-Trent on 3 April 1772, and, after some education at nearby Werrington and Bucknall, worked with his father in his business. The family moved to Bemersley, in the parish of Norton in the Moors, in 1788, and Bourne then took employment under his uncle, William Sharratt, a millwright and engineer at Milton, Staffordshire.

Bourne had been carefully brought up by a pious mother, and his conversion occurred through solitary reading. In June 1799 he joined the Wesleyan Methodists, soon after became a local preacher, and in 1802 built, chiefly at his own expense, a chapel at Harriseahead, Staffordshire. In imitation of the camp meetings which had promoted revivalism in America, Bourne, together with his brother James, William Clowes, and others, held a camp meeting on Mow Cop, near Harriseahead, on Sunday 31 May 1807. The meeting commenced at six in the morning, and prayer, praise, and preaching were continued until eight at night. This successful meeting was the first of many held in that part of the country. The Wesleyan Methodist conference at Liverpool on 27 July 1807 passed a resolution prohibiting such gatherings. The camp meetings, however, continued, and on 27 June 1808 Bourne was expelled from the Wesleyan Methodist Society by the Burslem circuit's quarterly meeting; but he still continued to raise societies, recommending them to join the Wesleyan circuits, and as yet entertained no idea of organizing a separate community. The Wesleyan authorities remained hostile, and a disruption was the consequence.

On 14 March 1810 the first class of the new community was formed at Stanley, near Bemersley. Quarterly tickets were introduced in the following year, and the first general meeting of the society was held at Tunstall on 26 July 1811. The name Primitive Methodist, implying a desire to restore Methodism to its primitive simplicity, was formally adopted on 13 February 1812, but the opponents of the movement often called the members 'ranters'. The first annual conference was held at Hull in May 1820, and a deed poll of the Primitive Methodists was enrolled in the court of chancery on 10 February 1830. Bourne and his brother purchased land and built the first chapel of the new connexion at Tunstall in 1811. After the foundation and settlement of the society Bourne made many evangelizing journeys to Scotland and Ireland. During 1844–6 he travelled in Canada and America, where he obtained large congregations.

Bourne lived to see Primitive Methodism with 1400 Sunday schools, 5300 chapels, and 110,000 enrolled members. He died, unmarried, from a mortification of his foot, at Bemersley on 11 October 1852, aged eighty, and was buried at Englesea Brook, Cheshire. He was, in common with many preachers and members of the Primitive Methodist church, a rigid abstainer. Bourne's preaching skills were limited; he was most notable for the more intimate, 'conversation' and cottage prayer meetings. For the greater part of his life he worked as a carpenter and builder, so as not to become chargeable to the denomination, and it was not until he had reached his seventieth year that he was placed on the superannuation fund. He published widely, including an *Autobiography* (n.d.); an unconventional defence of female preaching in *Remarks on the Ministry of Women* (1808); *A Treatise on Baptism* (1823); a *History of the Primitive Methodists* (1823); and a *Large Hymn Book* (1824). He was also editor of the *Primitive Methodist Magazine* for twenty years. G. C. BOASE, *rev.* W. J. JOHNSON

Sources J. Walford, *Memoirs of the life and labours of the late venerable Hugh Bourne* (1856) • G. Herod, *Biographical sketches of some of those preachers whose labours contributed to the origination and early extension of the Primitive Methodist Connexion* [n.d., c.1855] • J. T. Wilkinson, *Hugh Bourne, 1772–1852* (1952) • J. Simpson, *Recollections and characteristic anecdotes of the late Rev. Hugh Bourne* (1859) • J. S. Werner, *The Primitive Methodist Connexion: its background and early history* (1984) • W. Antliff, *The life of Hugh Bourne* (1892) • H. B. Kendall, *The origin and history of the Primitive Methodist church*, 2 vols. [n.d., c.1906] • H. Bourne, *Autobiography*, typescript copy, JRL, Methodist Archives and Research Centre

Archives JRL, Methodist Archives and Research Centre, autobiography, corresp., journals, and papers

Likenesses portrait, c.1848, repro. in Kendall, *Origin and history of the Primitive Methodist church*, vol. 1, p. 8 • oils, Methodist Publishing House, London • portrait, repro. in Walford, *Memoirs of the life and labours of … Hugh Bourne* • portrait, repro. in J. Petty, *History of the Primitive Methodist Connexion* (1860) • portraits, repro. in *Primitive Methodist Magazine* • portraits, JRL, Methodist Archives and Research Centre

Bourne, Immanuel (1590–1672), Church of England clergyman and religious controversialist, was born on 27 December 1590, the eldest son of Henry Bourne (*d.* 1649), clergyman, and his wife (*née* Bright), of Gray Stones near Sheffield. In 1595 his father became minister of East Haddon, Northamptonshire. Immanuel matriculated from Christ Church, Oxford, on 6 May 1608, graduated BA on 29 January 1612, was ordained deacon at Oxford in February 1613 and priest in March 1614, and proceeded MA on 12 June 1616.

An early indication of Bourne's taste for controversy was his Paul's Cross sermon of 10 June 1617: *The Rainebow*, published that year with a dedication to Robert Spencer of Wormleighton, was a brave, if forlorn, attempt to enlist the support of the arch-encloser of Northamptonshire against depopulating enclosures. Another Paul's Cross sermon, delivered on 22 August 1619 and published as *The Godly Man's Guide* (1620), was addressed to 'merchants and tradesmen'. About 1619 William Piers (the future Laudian bishop of Bath and Wells), another Christ Church man and a former Northamptonshire rector, but by this time rector of St Christopher-le-Stocks, London, appointed Bourne as preacher in his parish. Here he became chaplain to Sir Samuel Tryon and his wife, Elizabeth, in whose household he met his own future wife, Jemima (*c.*1602–1679), daughter of Sir Thomas Beckingham of Tolleshunt Major, Essex; she was Lady Tryon's young cousin and companion. On Tryon's presentation, Bourne was instituted to the living of Ashover, in the Derbyshire Peak District, on 11 July 1621. Further publications followed, *The True Way of a Christian, to the New Jerusalem* appearing in 1622 and *The Anatomie of Conscience*, an assize sermon preached at Derby, in 1623.

In the summer of 1623, by licence dated 7 July, Bourne married Jemima; the couple had at least three sons—Elisha (*b.* *c.*1625), Samuel (*b.* *c.*1628), and Obadiah (*b.* *c.*1634)—and four daughters, Jemima, Mary—who subsequently married the local preacher John Billingsley (1625–1684) and was mother of John Billingsley (1657–1622)—Lidiah, and Dorothy. In 1625 and 1630 Bourne bought extensive property in Ashover, including Eastwood Hall, and he later purchased the advowson of Ashover, thus assuring the future of his sons. Family ties with Derbyshire strengthened further at this period as his younger brothers Nathaniel (*b.* 1601/2) and Elisha (*b.* 1604/5) also gained livings there. Bourne himself sat on the commission of the peace for the county, and was related to another local JP, John Spateman. In 1639 he was prosecuted by high commission for organizing a fast day during time of plague in contravention of a royal proclamation; the case set him back by £300. He also took his own parishioners to court for their lead tithe debts.

Bourne claimed that, at the outset of the civil war, he adopted a neutral position. This did not protect him: indeed, both sides victimized him. When Sir John Gell left Derbyshire to the earl of Newcastle's men, the cavaliers, 'like demons, destroyed all they came neare and left the poore to starve'. Bourne lost, in this way, all his books and 'my Manuscripts, near thirty years studies and pains night and day rent in pieces and taken away' (Bourne, *Light from Christ*, 7). He began to side with parliament. He ceased to pray for the king in public, left marriages to the JPs, and, when 'the kyng's cause became hopeless', accepted an appointment on the committee of sequestration, 'thinking thereby to soften some of the hard measures dealt out to the kyng's friends' (I. Bourne to W. Bourne, 28 Aug 1646, Derby Public Library, Ashover Collection). He was briefly in 1646 rector of Calbourne in the Isle of Wight and became preacher at St Sepulchre, Holborn, in London, because Derbyshire was neither 'safe nor comfortable abiding'. In June 1646, recently returned to Ashover, Bourne found the parliamentary troops were busy taking over his church and hall to prevent their falling into malignants' hands.

Bourne was always a high clericalist by conviction. According to his *A Light from Christ*, a catechism first published in 1645 and reissued, enlarged, in 1646, ministers were 'ordained by Christ, in a special calling above others, to be instruments or outwards of converting men and women unto Christ' (Bourne, *Light from Christ*, 129). Although, as he later explained, his purpose in this work was to help right the 'sad evidences … of deplorable ignorance' (I. Bourne, *A Defence and Justification*, 1659, 5), he felt in 1646 that 'our Church is now in a hopeful way of Reformation' (Bourne, *Light from Christ*, 329) and he supported the introduction of a watered-down form of presbyterianism. By 1656, as a despairing member of the Chesterfield classis debating with James Naylor, he had lost his optimism. That year he became rector of Waltham on the Wolds, Leicestershire, and laid out his position on the ordination controversy in *A Defence of the Scriptures*. In 1659, as his youngest son, Obadiah, a graduate of Corpus Christi College, Oxford, was instituted to the Ashover rectory, he published *A Defence and Justification of Ministers' Maintenance by Tithes*.

Unlike his son-in-law John Billingsley, Bourne retained his living in 1662, but he was still prepared to challenge his social superiors. His *A Golden Chain of Directions to Preserve Love between Husband and Wife* (1669) roundly criticized his patron, the earl of Rutland, for his divorce and remarriage. In 1670 Bourne became rector of Aylestone, Leicestershire. He died at Ashover on 27 December 1672, his eighty-second birthday, and was buried, at his request, in the chancel of Ashover church. He left a substantial library. His will of 1671 made his widow, Jemima, 'with whom I have lived comfortablie fifty yeares', his executor, providing from his private property for her, for his surviving son, Obadiah, still rector of Ashover, and for all future rectors there. His grandson Samuel Bourne (1653–1694), son of his eldest son, Elisha, was designated, and became, Obadiah's successor. ROSEMARY O'DAY

Sources R. O'Day, 'Immanuel Bourne: a defence of the ministerial order', *Journal of Ecclesiastical History*, 27 (1976), 101–14 • R. O'Day, *The English clergy* (1979) • Lichfield Joint Record Office, B/A/1/16 • will and inventory, proved, 10 Feb 1672–1673, Leics. RO • exchequer depositions 1657, Michaelmas, Derby, no. 33, PRO • chancery proceedings, PRO, ser. 2, 396/14; 458/54; WOL 6689 • I. Bourne, *A light from Christ leading unto Christ*, 2nd edn (1646) • I. Bourne, *A defence of the scriptures* (1656) • Derby Public Library, Ashover collection • Bodl. Oxf., ODP c.264, fols. 56v–57v, 61v, 148r–148v • H. I. Longden, *Northamptonshire and Rutland clergy from 1500*, ed. P. I. King and others, 16 vols. in 6, Northamptonshire RS (1938–52), 2.177

Archives Derby Public Library, Ashover collection

Likenesses portrait, Ashover rectory, Derbyshire; copy, Derby Public Library, Ashover collection

Bourne, John (*bap.* 1620, *d.* 1667), naval officer, was baptized on 14 November 1620 at St John-at-Wapping, the younger son of Robert Bourne (*d.* 1625), shipwright, who owned a dockyard at Wapping, and his wife, Mary (*d.* 1630). His elder brother Nehemiah *Bourne emigrated to New England in 1638, and John may have followed him there. During the 1640s he commanded ships on trading voyages to Massachusetts in association with his brother, who had returned home in 1643.

Parliament drew Nehemiah into naval service in 1650, and John accompanied him. He served in the hired ship *Merchant* in the North Sea squadron under his brother in the summer of 1650, and commanded the newly built *Assistance* (thirty-six guns) from the autumn of that year. Bourne served throughout the first Anglo-Dutch War, and fought in the Kentish Knock in December 1652. He was rear-admiral in the squadron of William Penn at the battle off Portland in February 1653; the *Assistance* was boarded by the enemy, and Bourne was wounded in the head with a poleaxe in the course of fierce hand-to-hand fighting. Though still suffering from his wounds, he was persuaded by General Richard Deane, his patron, to return quickly to sea as flag captain to him and George Monck in the *Resolution*. He took part in the major actions off the Gabbard in June and the Texel in July.

During the winter of 1653–4 Bourne served in the channel, and in July 1654 he was named to the *Essex* as commander of a squadron to Newfoundland. The *Essex* lost her mainmast in a storm on the outward voyage and was forced to return, and Bourne thereupon resumed his service in the channel. Early in 1656 he was appointed rear-admiral of the fleet being sent against Spain under generals Robert Blake and Edward Mountagu (later first earl of Sandwich), and took part in the long blockade of Cadiz. When news arrived early in 1657 that a Spanish plate fleet was on its way to the Canaries, Bourne (now vice-admiral) and Richard Stayner, the new rear-admiral, pressed Blake to intercept it. He took part in the ensuing operation at Santa Cruz in April, in which the entire plate fleet was destroyed. He returned to England with Blake later in the year, and was one of the witnesses to the dying admiral's will.

Bourne served as rear-admiral in the *Swiftsure* in 1658 in the channel, and again in 1659 in the *Richard*, commanding the Home Fleet with Mountagu and Lawson away in the sound. Though he was willing to serve under the protectorate, his loyalties were essentially republican, and he welcomed the restoration of the Rump Parliament early in 1659. As Mountagu was a known Cromwellian, the support of Bourne, commanding in the Downs, was of considerable political significance. The *Richard* was paid off in October 1659, however, and was to prove Bourne's last naval command. When the army ousted the Rump in

October 1659 he and a group of other naval officers then ashore wrote to Monck in Scotland, urging him to accept the coup, arguing that divisions would only play into the hands of the cavaliers. The Rump, probably resentful, did not employ him again when it was reinstalled in December, and Mountagu had no wish to recall him. Bourne therefore played no part in the Restoration, returning instead to his earlier career in maritime trade. He became an elder brother of Trinity House in March 1660. He was away at sea for much of the following year, but took the oaths of allegiance and supremacy on 8 June 1661, when he was back in London. There is no record of any further political involvement, and he was often away thereafter, on voyages to the Mediterranean and North America.

As a puritan, Bourne had devoted himself to God's cause, as he saw it. When a storm disabled his ship in 1654 he was dismayed by the thought that God might have judged him unworthy to be an instrument. In 1655 he responded to news of the persecution of the Waldenses by arranging a day of fasting in the Channel Fleet and a collection for the victims.

Bourne died in 1667, probably in July or August and probably in his home parish, St Mary Magdalene, Bermondsey; a successor was elected to his place at Trinity House on 4 September. In a will drawn up two years earlier he bequeathed his estate in Bermondsey to his wife, Mary, and their two sons, Robert and John. BERNARD CAPP

Sources W. R. Chaplin, 'Nehemiah Bourne', *Publications of the Colonial Society of Massachusetts*, 42 (1952–6), 28–155 • B. Capp, *Cromwell's navy: the fleet and the English revolution, 1648–1660* (1989) • *CSP dom.*, 1651–9 • S. R. Gardiner and C. T. Atkinson, eds., *Letters and papers relating to the First Dutch War, 1652–1654*, 6 vols., Navy RS, 13, 17, 30, 37, 41, 66 (1898–1930) • *The Clarke papers*, ed. C. H. Firth, 3, CS, new ser., 61 (1899) • J. R. Powell, 'John Bourne, sometimes vice admiral', *Mariner's Mirror*, 62 (1976), 109–17

Wealth at death land and houses in Bermondsey and in the parish of St Mary Matfelon, Whitechapel: Chaplin, 'Nehemiah Bourne', 149

Bourne, Kenneth (1930–1992), historian, was born at Carshalton, Wick Lane, Wickford, Essex, on 17 March 1930, the son of Clarence Arthur Bourne, a director of a printing and publishing firm, and his wife, Doris English. He attended Southend high school before becoming in 1951 a student at the University College of the South-West (later the University of Exeter). He followed his mentor, Professor William Norton Medlicott, to the London School of Economics (LSE) on the latter's appointment as Stevenson professor of international history in 1953, and obtained his PhD degree from London in 1956. He married on 1 January 1955 Eleanor Anne Wells, a press officer, daughter of Edward Ronald Wells, master grocer. They had one son and one daughter.

Bourne's career was steady rather than dramatic. He was a research fellow at the Institute of Historical Research, London (1955–6), and briefly held a research appointment at the new University of Reading (1956) before returning to the LSE in 1957, initially as an assistant lecturer, working his way upwards until the conferment of a personal professorship at the LSE in 1976, and a fellowship of the British Academy in 1982, marked the crown of his career. He had by then renounced any interest in the Stevenson professorship in favour of a colleague and friend. He retired early in 1992 and later that year died suddenly in his sleep from a heart attack, at Lewisham Hospital, Lewisham, London, on 13 December 1992.

Bourne was the last of a series of major historians of British foreign policy in the nineteenth century, a series which included such men as Harold Temperley, Sir Charles Webster, and R. W. Seton-Watson. He differed from his illustrious predecessors, however, in being without any connections with Oxford or Cambridge, and very much the product of the 1944 Education Act. His master and formative influence was W. N. Medlicott, himself a product of London University. Bourne's place among his predecessors rests on three pillars. Where they had concentrated entirely on British relations with the European great powers, he was the first to bring Britain's relations with the United States into the general picture of Victorian foreign policy. His first book, *Britain and the Balance of Power in North America, 1815–1908* (1967), made him an immediate reputation both in Britain and in the United States. But the merits and new approaches he showed in that book were to figure in his second book, the second pillar to his reputation. He had moved from the traditional diplomatic history practised by his predecessors (drawn mainly from the archives of the Foreign Office and the private papers, such as they were, of major political and diplomatic personalities), to seeing foreign policy and the conduct of relations between one state and its fellows as a composition of the whole structure of government, to be documented from the archives of the palace on the one hand, and the military, naval, financial, secret intelligence, and other such organs of government on the other. Strategic factors figured throughout his narratives, not only when major wars seemed to threaten. He was one of the first to interest himself in the issues of military intelligence and foreign policy. Like his colleagues in the twentieth-century field, he found discontinuities resulting from the failure to resolve the separate approaches of different organs of government, apparent on both sides of the Atlantic as well as among the European great powers, to be no problem. Bourne's second book, *The Foreign Policy of Victorian England* (1970), by comparison, for example, with A. J. P. Taylor's *Struggle for Mastery in Europe, 1815–1914*, clearly reveals that for Bourne 'foreign policy' was made as much in cabinet, Colonial Office, War Office, and Admiralty as by heroic (or muddled) figures in charge of foreign offices. Bourne's work was to be prescribed reading for generations of schoolboys preparing for university entry.

The third pillar on which Bourne's reputation rests is his (alas, unfinished) biography of Lord Palmerston, the first (and only) volume of which, *Palmerston: the Early Years, 1784–1841*, appeared in 1982. It was immediately recognized as the major work it undoubtedly was. Bourne's election to the British Academy followed hot on the heels of its publication. It would not have been possible without the Mountbatten family's decision to grant him access to the Palmerston papers, which they had hitherto denied to historians. But Bourne had also uncovered a series of treasure troves of private papers of Palmerston's many correspondents, containing significant papers not preserved in the Palmerston papers themselves. He had also mastered, and indeed come to own, copies of much of the considerable volume of memoirs, letters, diaries, and so on published by Palmerston's political contemporaries. An indefatigable haunter of antiquarian bookshops throughout the southern counties of Britain, he spent his weekends combing Britain's towns and villages at a time when many of the minor libraries of nineteenth-century dignitaries were being sold by their impecunious and space-starved descendants.

One cannot help thinking that, had Bourne ever met Palmerston face to face, he would have disapproved of him. But his historical view of Palmerston did nothing to denigrate or debunk one of the great heroic figures of early Victorian Britain. Bourne painted Palmerston as an overbearing and often unscrupulous giant, a man who hid his basic integrity and accuracy of judgement behind the manners and feuds of his time. There can be no doubt that, for all the faults which Bourne recognized in his hero, he admired and exalted him.

Bourne's work was such as to awake the admiration of professional historians, especially those who were not absorbed, as were so many of his contemporaries, in the new socio-economic history. But it did not catch the imagination of the general book-reading public, still less the media, who looked for the debunking of the great men of Victorian Britain rather than the confirmation of their existing reputations. He was to spend the latter years of his life in publishing source materials for his period. As well as editing the papers of Francis Horner and the second earl of Minto, he master-minded the massive publication by the University Press of America of 415 volumes of documents selected from the Foreign Office confidential print for the years 1860–1939, as editor-in-chief responsible for the documents deriving from the years before 1914. His biggest disappointment was the inability of information technologists to evolve a workable technique for screening the annual *Foreign Office Lists* in such a way as to make the mechanical compilation of a biographical dictionary of members of the Foreign Office and the diplomatic service from the foundation of the Foreign Office possible. He was to play his part in the celebration at the LSE of the two-hundredth anniversary of the Foreign Office.

When Bourne began his graduate research, British records were accessible only in part for even the end of the nineteenth century. The fifty-year rule was adopted in 1958; by 1967 the closed period had been reduced to thirty years. With the opening not merely of the Foreign Office records but those of cabinet, service ministries, Colonial Office, India Office, Treasury, in fact of all Whitehall, there came a flood of private papers from the twentieth century. Bourne's own contemporaries were the last of British graduate students for whom the death of Queen Victoria was the *ne plus ultra* of archival research. By the time his Palmerston biography appeared, the vast majority of graduate students interested in international history as a field of research were plunged into study of the origins of the Second World War, if not those of the cold war. Only the smallest handful were interested in the fields in which Bourne was the unchallenged master. Thus he left no school of disciples behind him. The disappearance of the deference which he as a young historian had paid his elders, and the intensification of external pressures on all in British universities to justify their practices and record, certainly left their mark on him in his latter years. Indeed he was to spend valuable time and effort on university committees and the like defending the values and culture of independent scholarship against external enemies and internal critics and mischief makers. The possibility that it was the stress which this struggle induced in him which led to his early death cannot be ruled out. To those he respected among his contemporaries (and his judgement like that of Medlicott rested solely on estimates of their professionalism as scholars and historians), he was the best and most loyal of friends and an amusing, witty, if sometimes cynical companion. He was a welcome and frequent visitor at a whole range of American universities and was elected to the American Philosophical Society. D. CAMERON WATT

Sources *WW* (1993) · *The Times* (17 Dec 1992) · personal knowledge (2004) · private information (2004) [family] · b. cert. · m. cert. · d. cert.
Archives BLPES, papers
Wealth at death £369,051: probate, 25 May 1993, *CGPLA Eng. & Wales*

Bourne, Nehemiah (1611–1691), naval officer and official, was born in Wapping, the eldest son of Robert Bourne (*d.* 1625), a prosperous shipwright, and his wife, Mary (*d.* 1630); John *Bourne (*bap.* 1620, *d.* 1667) was his brother. Though his father had hoped he would be educated at Cambridge, Bourne chose to follow in the family business, and married the very young Hannah Earning of Limehouse (*c.*1616–1684) on 18 January 1631. The Bournes belonged to a network of puritan mariners and merchants, and in 1638 they emigrated to Massachusetts in the *Confidence*, owned by William Rainborough. Nehemiah established himself as a merchant and shipowner at Charlestown, Dorchester, and finally Boston, where he became the town's first shipbuilder. He and his wife were admitted to the Boston church in 1641, and two of their five children were born in New England. Bourne returned to England in the winter of 1643–4 to fight for parliament, serving as a major in the regiment raised by Thomas Rainborough, and also leased some of his ships to the state. Resigning his commission early in 1645 he returned to Massachusetts, and in October that year pressed unsuccessfully for its laws against Anabaptists to be dropped. On 19 December 1646 he and his wife sailed again for England, this time intending to remain. Over the next few years Bourne was busy trading to America in his own ships, and was unable to accept an invitation to serve the new Commonwealth's navy in 1649; but when he returned from New England in January 1650 Sir Henry

Vane pressed him again, this time with success, recommending him to the generals-at-sea as a gallant man who would do the state 'both service and honour' (PRO, SP 25/123, 226). Bourne was appointed to the *Speaker*, a newly built second-rate, and commanded the North Sea squadron the following winter, assisting the army in its operations in Scotland. In May 1652, now in the *Andrew*, Bourne was commanding a squadron in the Downs when Tromp appeared with a powerful Dutch fleet; he sent a warning to Blake, and was able to join him in time to play a prominent part in the battle off the Downs on 19 May, which began the First Anglo-Dutch War. Bourne was in action again on 28 September, at the Kentish Knock. His bravery in both actions was admired, but the state had more urgent need of his administrative skills, and on 20 December 1652 he was appointed one of three new navy commissioners, all of them former American settlers, responsible for ships, supplies, and manning. Bourne discharged his duties with immense energy, and in the critical early months of 1653 was busy pressing men in the Thames, securing prize goods, and providing for injured mariners after the battle of Portland. Though he liked to bombard the admiralty with lengthy accounts of his labours and problems, Bourne was undoubtedly an effective administrator and responsible for the development of Harwich as a major naval base, serving in effect as its first resident commissioner. He retained his own shipping interests and, following the closure of the Baltic, contracted to supply masts and other stores from New England.

After the peace with the Dutch in April 1654 Bourne was based at the Navy Office in London, and with two colleagues took on responsibility for naval victualling, with an additional £250 salary. From 1655 he resumed his shipbuilding activities, constructing a new shipyard at Wapping, and also invested in the East India Company. He remained an energetic commissioner throughout the decade, despite mounting problems as the finances of the Commonwealth deteriorated rapidly in its final years. Though Bourne served the protectorate loyally, he suspected that Richard Cromwell's rule would end in a Stuart restoration, and was ecstatic at the restoration of the Rump Parliament in May 1659. 'The Lord Jehovah hath most eminently and signally once more appeared for his own great name', he told a friend in New England (Firth, 3.209). He was dismayed by the king's restoration in May 1660, and his public career ended when new commissioners were appointed on 4 July. He took the oaths enabling him to remain a member of Trinity House, of which he had been an elder brother since 1656, but ceased to be part of its governing body.

By the beginning of 1662 Bourne had resolved to leave England once more, and in May obtained a pass for his family to depart. He crossed to Hamburg and appears to have spent most of the 1660s in Rotterdam, a good base for his mercantile activities. By 1670 he was living in London again, in Abchurch Lane, still engaged in colonial trade. In his last years he was also occasionally involved in Trinity House business, and was consulted by the Navy Board in 1689. His wife, Hannah, had died on 10 June 1684 and was buried at Bunhill Fields on 21 June. Bourne died in the spring of 1691 and was buried beside her. His will, dated 11 February, was proved in May. Bourne was a typical servant of the Commonwealth, a committed radical, energetic, public spirited, yet with a shrewd eye to personal profit.

BERNARD CAPP

Sources W. R. Chaplin, 'Nehemiah Bourne', *Publications of the Colonial Society of Massachusetts*, 42 (1952–6), 28–155 • B. Capp, *Cromwell's navy: the fleet and the English revolution, 1648–1660* (1989) • *CSP dom.*, 1649–62; 1668–70, 1660–85; addenda, 1686–7 • S. R. Gardiner and C. T. Atkinson, eds., *Letters and papers relating to the First Dutch War, 1652–1654*, 6 vols., Navy RS, 13, 17, 30, 37, 41, 66 (1898–1930) • *The Clarke papers*, ed. C. H. Firth, 3, CS, new ser., 61 (1899) • N. B. Shurtleff, ed., *Records of the governor and company of the Massachusetts Bay in New England*, 5 vols. in 6 (1853–4), vol. 3 • admiralty committee MSS, PRO, SP 25/123 • *CSP col.*, vols. 1, 5 • Bodl. Oxf., MS Rawl. A. 468 • *Calendar of the Clarendon state papers preserved in the Bodleian Library*, 5: *1660–1726*, ed. F. J. Routledge (1970) • Bodl. Oxf., MS Carte 73

Archives East Kent Archives Centre, letters, incl. some from Admiral Blake, to the mayor of Sandwich • PRO, state papers, domestic, SP 18

Bourne, Nicholas (*b.* in or before **1584**, *d.* **1660**), bookseller, the son of Henry Bourne, a London cordwainer, was apprenticed on 25 March 1601 to the London printer Cuthbert Burby, who had a shop in Cornhill, near the Royal Exchange. Burby died before Bourne completed his apprenticeship, but bequeathed Bourne the lease of his shop and its stock. Freed by Mrs Burby on 26 March 1608, Bourne spent the rest of his life in those premises. In May 1608 he was granted a loan by the Stationers' Company to assist young members trying to establish themselves in business, and he entered his first title, a religious work, in the Stationers' register on 24 September. Burby's widow signed over part of her husband's copyrights, mostly in religious works, to Bourne the following year, and he was elected to the company's livery in 1616.

Trained as a printer, described as a bookbinder in later life, Bourne is best known as a bookseller. Like Burby, he specialized in theological works, notably the sermons of Arthur Dent and the writings of Daniel Featley. He held the right to sell printed bills of lading and, according to a former apprentice, refused to deal in plays. He also sold the occasional travel narrative as well as accounts of strange occurrences and news of foreign affairs, predisposing him perhaps, like his later business partner Nathaniel Butter, to an interest in publishing newsbooks, the endeavour in which Bourne would achieve his greatest notoriety, if not his greatest success. In 1620 he borrowed further money from the company, probably to finance a new business venture he had embarked on: the publication of news. Initially he collaborated with his fellow apprentice and neighbour Thomas Archer, who dealt primarily in ephemera, then with a small syndicate of news publishers, from which eventually emerged a partnership between Bourne and Butter that dominated news publishing for roughly two decades. It seems that the more flamboyant Butter was the front man for the operation, while the steadier Bourne looked to the business end of the partnership, especially financing. Together they developed the regular weekly newsbooks, known as corantos, reporting about events in the Thirty Years' War. The newsbooks supported the protestant cause in the war and, like the majority of Bourne's publishing collaborations, were consistent with a Calvinist outlook.

If Bourne was not as flamboyant or as cantankerous a figure as Butter, he still had brushes with the regulatory authorities. In March 1630 Bourne and two other booksellers were examined by the high commission for selling dangerous books which all three claimed had been left on their doorstep in the night by unknown persons. A privy council order of October 1632 banned publication of the corantos, and Bourne and Butter were explicitly warned to cease publication. Almost exactly one year later the news partners were chosen as members of the Stationers' Company's governing body. In May 1636 Bourne re-entered in the Stationers' register his lucrative copyright to publish bills of lading printed in French, Italian, and Dutch, as well as indentures for Virginia, St Kitts, and the Somers Islands, and bills of debt for money owed on tobacco. In February 1637 he leased additional warehouse space from the company; in June he was named one of the feoffees for property the company owned in Wood Street, London; and in July he was elected to serve as warden of the company.

The following December Bourne and Butter were granted a royal patent to revive the newsbooks in exchange for £10 a year toward the restoration of St Paul's Cathedral. But the revival was short-lived, and by March 1640 the corantos had folded for good. Bourne and Butter parted ways, and Bourne, focusing on success within the ranks of the company, was re-elected warden in July 1641. A few months later he paid £6 to the company for their attendance at the funeral of his first wife, possibly named Ann, buried on 8 September 1641 at St Michael, Cornhill. In his capacity as warden he seized pirated copies of a work for which he owned the copyright, *The Holy Table, Name and Thing*, but was sued in chancery. He persuaded the company to contribute towards his legal costs, provoking controversy for years. Bourne was elected master of the company in 1643. Throughout the decade he published and republished the popular religious works of Daniel Featley as well as *Le Mercure Anglois*, a news publication for Huguenot exiles in England, and a news serial about the Turks which ran to only four issues. In July 1651 he was again elected master, and during the 1650s he acted as a feoffee for two company properties.

Bourne prospered as a stationer, paying marriage portions of £300 each for three of his daughters, but as his health began to wane in the late 1650s, so did his career as a stationer. He bound his last apprentice in 1657 and made a will on 2 March 1658. He published with his son-in-law, William Hope, who had married his daughter Etheldred before 1641. The parish register of St Michael, Cornhill, records the burial of Nicholas Bourne on 6 April 1660. His will, proved on 17 April 1660, included bequests to a sister, his mother-in-law, an aunt, a number of grandchildren, and a £5 legacy to the company paid by his widow, Jane, in 1661. He left no surviving son to succeed him in his business and so bequeathed a number of copyrights to Etheldred and William Hope. S. A. Baron

Sources L. Rostenberg, 'The debut of English journalism: Nathaniel Butter and Nicholas Bourne, first "masters of the staple"', *Literary, political, scientific, religious and legal publishing, printing and bookselling in England, 1551–1700: twelve studies*, 1 (New York, 1965), 75–96 · *The obituary of Richard Smyth … being a catalogue of all such persons as he knew in their life*, ed. H. Ellis, CS, 44 (1849) · W. Craig Ferguson, *The loan book of the Stationers' Company with a list of transactions, 1592–1692* (1989) · D. F. McKenzie, ed., *Stationers' Company apprentices*, 3 vols. (1961–78), vols. 1–2 · H. R. Plomer and others, *Dictionaries of the printers and booksellers who were at work in England, Scotland and Ireland, 1577–1775* (1910–32); repr. (1977) · W. A. Jackson, ed., *Records of the court of the Stationers' Company, 1602 to 1640* (1957) · Stationers' Company records, Stationers' Hall, London, court bks C and D · PRO, state papers domestic, Charles I, SP16 · W. W. Grey, ed., *A companion to Arber* (1967) · will, PRO, PROB 11/297, sig. 26 · *STC, 1475–1640* · parish register, St Michael Cornhill, 8 Sept 1641, GL [burial: Ann Bourne] · parish register, St Michael Cornhill, 6 April 1660, GL [burial]

Wealth at death legacies to children of approx. £1500; £300 to charities, grandchildren, and friends; copyrights to eldest daughter and her son; debts to be paid: will, PRO, PROB 11/297, sig. 26

Bourne, Reuben (*fl.* 1692), playwright, belonged to the Middle Temple, and left behind him a solitary comedy which has never been acted. The title of this is *The Contented Cuckold, or, The Womans Advocate* (1692). To quote its author, the play 'wants both Language, Wit and Plot' (preface). Its scene is Edmonton, and the principal character, Sir Peter Lovejoy, contends that a cuckold is one of the scarcest of created beings.

Joseph Knight, *rev.* Freya Johnston

Sources Genest, *Eng. stage* · [D. E. Baker], *The companion to the playhouse*, 2 vols. (1764)

Bourne, Robert (1761–1829), physician and chemist, was born at Shrawley, Worcestershire, on 18 August 1761, the second son of Robert Bourne. He was educated at Bromsgrove grammar school and was elected a scholar at Worcester College, Oxford, on 1 July 1777. He took his BA in 1781 and was elected a fellow in 1784 on taking his MA. Following a period of training at St Bartholomew's Hospital in London, he became BM in 1786, and DM in 1787, in which year he was elected honorary physician to the Radcliffe Infirmary at Oxford, a post he held until 1824. According to family tradition he spent a year or longer in the Netherlands to further his knowledge of medicine and natural philosophy.

In September 1790 Bourne became a fellow of the Royal College of Physicians, to whom he delivered the Harveian oration in 1797. In 1794 he succeeded the disgraced Thomas Beddoes as reader in chemistry at Oxford, and he delivered a series of lectures at the Ashmolean Museum that year. His *Introductory Lecture* of 1797 shows that he stressed the need for a knowledge of chemistry among doctors. Like the lectures of Richard Watson at Cambridge, Bourne's lectures were designed to show how a knowledge of chemistry could be useful to students who would later inherit land, become MPs, or take an interest in manufactures and commerce. Understandably, however, given that Bourne's life was given over to medical practice, he made no contribution to the advancement of chemistry. He ceased his chemistry lectures in 1803 on the appointment of John Kidd to the newly endowed chair of chemistry and his own election as the first Aldrichian professor of physic. He resigned this chair in 1824 on election to the Lord Lichfield professorship of clinical medicine.

In 1795 Bourne had married Mary, daughter of James Burr of Spelsbury, Oxfordshire. They had two sons and two daughters. After his first wife's death he married Mary, the widow of the Revd James Griffith, master of University College. Bourne had a large medical practice in Oxford and its county and was active in the modernization of the Radcliffe Infirmary, of which he was a benefactor. He wore his hair in a pigtail long after it had ceased to be fashionable. His only published medical work appeared in 1805. It consisted of twenty-two case histories of pulmonary consumption, in which his treatment had been to use an astringent prepared from the bearberry, *A. uva-ursi*. Although he kept very careful records of all of his patients throughout his career, these histories were destroyed by his son in 1830. Bourne's great-grandson, Gilbert Charles Bourne, rowed at Oxford and was an anatomist there.

Bourne appears to have spent his entire career at Oxford, where he died after prolonged illness on 23 December 1829. An inscription to his memory was erected in Worcester College chapel and is reproduced in Munk's *Roll of the Royal College of Physicians*. W. H. BROCK

Sources Munk, *Roll* • Foster, *Alum. Oxon.* • A. G. Gibson, *The Radcliffe Infirmary* (1926) • R. T. Gunther, *Early science in Oxford*, 1: *Chemistry, mathematics, physics and surveying*, OHS, 77 (1923), 68–9 • R. Bourne, *Cases of pulmonary consumption* (1805) • *Hist. U. Oxf.* 4: *17th-cent. Oxf.*

Archives Magd. Oxf., chemistry course

Bourne, Robert Croft (1888–1938), politician and oarsman, was born at Doddington Place, Kent, on 15 July 1888, the only son of the two children of Gilbert Charles *Bourne (1861–1933), zoologist, and his wife, Constance Margaret Graham (*d.* 1954), eldest daughter of Sir John Frederick Croft, second baronet. His father had been a well-known oarsman and theorist on rowing, and it was for his achievements in this sport that Robert Bourne was also best remembered.

At Eton College Bourne rowed in the eights of 1906 and 1907. He then went to New College, Oxford, where he obtained a second class in modern history in 1911. But it was as the first stroke of a university crew to win the Oxford and Cambridge boat race in four successive years that Bourne achieved his fame. His oarsmanship was described as 'ungainly and not in itself of the highest class' (*The Times*, 9 Aug 1938, 7), and in 1909, at Bourne's first race, the 'critics laughed at Oxford, who were rather rough when they arrived, and none of them liked Bourne's style' (Drinkwater, 104). But they underestimated his strength and leadership of the crew, and Oxford won the race with an enormous spurt towards the finish which completely outclassed their opponents.

The Oxford crew was coached by Bourne's father in this period, and it went on to win the 1910 and 1911 races. Bourne's last university race in 1912 became 'the greatest fiasco in the history of the race' (Drinkwater, 106). In appalling weather conditions both boats sank, partly as a result of both strokes starting their crews off too quickly. The race was replayed, and won by Oxford, two days later. Of the following year's race it was said that by then 'Bourne had gone down, and with him Oxford's period of supremacy' (Burnell, 73). At Henley, Bourne won the Stewards' Cup three times (1912–14) and in 1912 stroked his college crew in the final of the Olympic regatta at Stockholm.

After being called to the bar by Lincoln's Inn (1913), Bourne went in 1915 with his territorial battalion of the Herefordshire regiment to the Mediterranean and lost the use of one hand and had a lung seriously injured at Suvla Bay in August. Further active service being impossible (he had also while at school lost the sight of one eye when playing rounders during the summer holidays) Bourne, now a captain, served on the War Claims Commission (1917) and on the Herefordshire county council (1922). On 7 June 1917 he married Lady Hester Margaret (1895–1985), eldest daughter of Wilfrid Dallas Cairns, fourth Earl Cairns. They had one daughter and two sons, the younger of whom was the barrister Sir (John) Wilfrid *Bourne (1922–1999). Lady Hester was a very active organizer within the Conservative Party, becoming, from 1939 to 1943, president of the National Society of Conservative and Unionist Women Organisers.

In 1923 Bourne contested Oxford City as a Conservative, and, on his opponent being unseated on petition, was returned at the resultant by-election (1924). He retained the seat until his death. In the House of Commons, where he rose to be deputy chairman of ways and means (1931), Bourne's name was canvassed as a possible speaker, for, although on the platform he filled his speeches with too much information for a popular audience, he earned the respect of all parties by his mastery in parliament of the rules of procedure and his fairness. He was sworn of the privy council in 1935. On 7 August 1938, while walking on the moors at Ardgour, Argyll, he suddenly fell dead. He was survived by his wife. The funeral was held five days later at Sandford-on-Thames, Oxfordshire.

L. G. W. LEGG, *rev.* MARC BRODIE

Sources *The Times* (9 Aug 1938) • *The Times* (12 Aug 1938) • personal knowledge (1949) • private information (1949) • Burke, *Peerage* • G. C. Drinkwater, *The boat race* (1939) • R. D. Burnell, *The Oxford and Cambridge boat race, 1829–1953* (1954) • *WWW* • *CGPLA Eng. & Wales* (1938)

Likenesses Ape Junior, caricature, mechanical reproduction, NPG; repro. in *VF* (29 March 1911) • photograph, repro. in *The Times* (9 Aug 1938)

Wealth at death £42,708 13*s.* 3*d.*: probate, 18 Nov 1938, *CGPLA Eng. & Wales*

Bourne, Samuel (1834–1912), photographer, was born at Windy Arbour Farm, Mucklestone, near Market Drayton, Staffordshire, on 30 October 1834, the third son of Thomas Bourne (*b.* 1804), a farmer, and his wife, Harriet *née* Dobson (*b.* 1802). He was educated privately by a clergyman at Fairburn, near Pontefract, Yorkshire, and about 1855 moved

Samuel Bourne (1834–1912), by unknown photographer, *c.*1864

to Nottingham as an assistant at Moore and Robinson's Bank.

Bourne took up photography as an amateur about 1853; by the end of the decade he had acquired a reputation for the outstanding quality of his landscape work. In 1862 he abandoned his banking career and in October set sail for India, for what was initially planned as a two-year residence to exploit the growing photographic market in the subcontinent. He arrived at the hill station of Simla in the Punjab in March 1863 and formed a partnership with William Howard; by the end of the year they had been joined by another photographer, Charles Shepherd. With the departure of Howard in 1865, the business assumed its final form as Bourne and Shepherd. Within a few years it had become the most successful photographic business in the subcontinent.

By a natural division of labour, Shepherd undertook the bulk of the firm's studio work while Bourne took responsibility for topographical and architectural views. From July to October of 1863 Bourne travelled from Simla along the Sutlej valley to Chini and Spiti on the first of three major photographic expeditions. His second journey (March–December 1864) took him to Kashmir, where verdant landscapes inspired some of his finest photographs, while the successfully achieved goal of the third expedition (July–December 1866) was to photograph the source of the Ganges at the base of the Gangotri glacier. The resulting photographs of picturesque and dramatic landscapes—'of scenery which has never been photographed before, and amongst the boldest and most striking on the face of the globe' (*British Journal of Photography*, 11, 1864, 70)—formed the basis of the firm's prosperity. Bourne's own accounts of his adventures, published in a series of articles in the *British Journal of Photography*, established his own reputation both as a sensitive interpreter of the Indian landscape and as a determined traveller willing to undergo hardships and danger to obtain the perfect negative. By the end of the 1860s the Bourne and Shepherd catalogue contained upwards of 2000 views, the overwhelming majority photographed by Bourne. The firm's commercial pre-eminence in India was consolidated by the opening of additional branches in Calcutta (1867) and Bombay (1870), while Bourne's photographic tour of southern India in 1869 further broadened the scope of the studio's coverage.

Bourne visited England in 1867; on 9 May, at the George Street Baptist Church, Nottingham, he married Mary Tolley (1844–1912), the eldest daughter of Abraham Tolley, a silk merchant. His wife accompanied him back to India, where Constance Edith, the first of the couple's five children, was born in 1869. Bourne left India for good in November 1870, but his photographs continued to be marketed for many decades, and Bourne and Shepherd maintained its reputation as the most prestigious photographic studio in the subcontinent up to the Second World War (and, in much attenuated form, still trades in Calcutta under Indian management). This success was not only the product of the technical skills and commercial acumen of its principal photographer but also owed much to Bourne's ability to present a vision of India which coincided with, and reinforced European notions of, a picturesque and exotic East. An impregnable faith in the civilizing power of British rule, allied to strong religious convictions of a Unitarian character, further imbued his work with the pervasive sense of a moral purpose in photography, which 'teaches the mind to see the beauty and power of such scenes as these, and renders it more susceptible of their sweet and elevating impressions' (*British Journal of Photography*, 11, 1864, 69). The qualities of these Indian images place him among the finest nineteenth-century landscape photographers.

Bourne abandoned professional photography on his return to Nottingham (though he continued to practise as an amateur), entering first into partnership with his brother-in-law, James Boraston Tolley, and by 1877 establishing his own successful cotton-doubling business. He died of heart failure at his home, Brightlands, Clumber Road, The Park, Nottingham, on 24 April 1912, and was buried in Nottingham general cemetery on 27 April; his wife survived him by seven months. JOHN FALCONER

Sources G. D. Sampson, 'The success of Samuel Bourne in India', *History of Photography*, 16 (1992), 336–47 · P. F. Heathcote, 'Samuel Bourne of Nottingham', *History of Photography*, 6 (1982), 99–112 · S. Bourne, 'Photography in the east', *British Journal of Photography* (1 July 1863), 268–70; (11 Sept 1863), 345–7 · S. Bourne, 'Ten weeks with the camera in the Himalayas', *British Journal of Photography* (1 Feb 1864), 50–51; (15 Feb 1864), 69–70 · S. Bourne, 'Narrative of a photographic trip to Kashmir (Cashmere) and adjacent districts', *British Journal of Photography* (5 Oct–28 Dec 1866), 474–5, 498–9, 525–5, 559–60, 583–4, 617–19 · S. Bourne, 'Narrative of a photographic trip to Kashmir (Cashmere) and adjacent districts', *British Journal of*

Photography (4 Jan–8 Feb 1867), 4–5, 38–9, 63–4 · S. Bourne, 'A photographic journey through the higher Himalayas', *British Journal of Photography* (26 Nov 1869), 570 · S. Bourne, 'A photographic journey through the higher Himalayas', *British Journal of Photography* (14 Jan–1 April 1870), 15–16, 39–40, 75–6, 98–9, 125–6, 149–50 · typescript obituary, Nottinghamshire County Council Library, Nottingham · *Nottingham Guardian* (25 April 1912) · *The Trader* [Nottingham] (25 June 1910), 2–4

Likenesses photograph, *c.*1864, National Museum of Photography, Film and Television, Bradford, Royal Photographic Society collection [*see illus.*] · G. Hodgson, oils, 1888, Nottingham Society of Artists · photograph, repro. in *The Trader*, 2

Wealth at death £52,016 13*s.* 4*d.*: resworn probate, 14 May 1912, *CGPLA Eng. & Wales*

Bourne, Vincent (*bap.* 1694, *d.* 1747), Latin poet, was the son of Andrew Bourne and his wife, Ann. He was baptized in the church of St Martin-in-the-Fields, Westminster, London, on 22 July 1694. He attended Westminster School, and became queen's scholar in 1710. There he was a pupil of Robert Freind, and became proficient in the art of writing Latin verse; Westminster required its students to compose a number of epigrams in elegiac couplets every week, and it was to this medium that Bourne returned most frequently in later life. A number of his school verses appeared in the popular collection of Westminster compositions entitled *Lusus Westmonasterienses* that appeared in 1730 and went through several later editions.

Bourne was admitted as a pensioner at Trinity College, Cambridge, on 27 May 1714. He became a scholar on 13 May 1715, proceeded BA in 1717, was made a fellow in 1720, and commenced MA in 1721. At Cambridge he distinguished himself as a Latin poet, and was selected to write a set of tripos verses in the spring of 1717. In September of the same year he sent a friendly Latin poem to Joseph Addison to celebrate the latter's recovery from illness (reproduced in Aikin, 2.214). In 1721 Bourne edited a collection of tripos verses entitled *Carmina comitalia Cantabrigiensia*, including, within a section of miscellaneous pieces at the end, five poems from his own pen and two by his friend John Jortin. Of these, Bourne's *Corydon querens*—a translation of Nicholas Rowe's *Colin's Complaint*—was issued separately the same year and again in 1726.

On 14 May 1727 Bourne married Lucia (*b.* 1694?), widow of George Jewell, in St Margaret's, Westminster. (Jewell, who died in 1725 aged thirty-one, had attended Westminster and Trinity at the same time as Bourne, and was an usher at Westminster.) By this point Bourne had probably already become an usher at Westminster School himself, a position he held until his death. He and Lucia had a son, Thomas, and a daughter, Lucia; the family probably divided its time between the house Bourne had built in Westminster and his farm near Bungay, Suffolk.

Though generous and genial, Bourne was ill-suited to teaching: William Cowper, who was one of his pupils at Westminster, recalled that he was slovenly in appearance and idle, and so poor a teacher that 'he seemed determined, as he was the best, so to be the last, Latin poet of the Westminster line' (*Letters and Prose*, 3.234). In 1734 the first collection of Bourne's work, *Poematia*, appeared: it was an instant success. A second edition emerged in 1735, and a third, with additional poems, in 1743; there were three more in the eighteenth century and a further five in the nineteenth (Mitford's, of 1840, is the closest to a scholarly edition). The book was dedicated to the duke of Newcastle, a former schoolmate of Bourne's, who may have been responsible for the poet's appointment as deputy serjeant-at-arms to the House of Commons in November 1734.

Alongside Bourne's translations from English poets (he also wrote versions from David Mallet, Matthew Prior, and John Gay), he produced many occasional pieces, which, though some were probably written as demonstrations for his pupils, are his best work. Bourne wrote without pretension, but with restrained elegance and bold mastery of Latin language and metre. The deceptive simplicity of his verse conceals numerous wry subtleties. A metropolitan, he had a particular genius for providing engaging portraits of contemporary London, and focused sympathetically upon the everyday details of human life. 'Schola rhetorices', for example, recalls the gossiping fishwives of Billingsgate, 'Cantatrices' depicts two ballad singers at Seven Dials, and 'Ad Davidem Cook' is an affectionate reminiscence of the Westminster nightwatchman. All these are rendered with a painterly eye for detail, and Bourne's love of art is visible in his several poems on painters and paintings, foremost among which are his hendecasyllables on Hogarth (*Poems*, 190). The artist, whom Bourne calls 'derisor lepidus' ('elegant mocker') and 'facete censor' ('witty critic'), is an apt recipient of his praise: while the poet lacked some of his addressee's satire, he shared his interests, and was doubtless aware that the same tags could be applied to himself. A certain discontent lies just below the surface of much of his poetry, and sometimes comes to the fore. The epitaph Bourne composed for himself seals this impression: 'in silentium quod amavit descendit' ('he has descended into the silence that he loved'). Moreover, in a letter to his wife written shortly before his death (first printed in the 1772 edition of *Poematia*), he reveals that he refused to enter holy orders from a fear of his own insufficiency, and felt dissatisfaction with his life. Bourne died at Westminster on 2 December 1747, and was buried at Fulham.

Vincent Bourne was one of the most popular English Latin poets of the eighteenth century, but he has not won universal praise. His choice of homely matter and unwillingness to poeticize have led some critics to treat him high-handedly, while others have recognized that he managed to unshackle neo-Latin verse from outright imitation of the classics. The endurance of his fame has largely been due to the translations of his work by Cowper and Charles Lamb, but he merits nevertheless a central place in discussions of Anglo-Latin literature.

Ross Kennedy

Sources L. Aikin, *The life of Joseph Addison*, 2 vols. (1843) · *Old Westminsters* · Venn, *Alum. Cant.*, 1/1 · L. Bradner, *Musae Anglicanae: a history of Anglo-Latin poetry, 1500–1925* (1940); repr. (1966), 266–73 · *The letters and prose writings of William Cowper*, ed. J. King and C. Ryskamp, 5 vols. (1979–86) · D. K. Money, *The English Horace:*

Anthony Alsop and the tradition of British Latin verse (1998), 223–7 • M. Storey, 'The Latin poetry of Vincent Bourne', *The Latin poetry of English poets*, ed. J. Binns (1974), 121–49 • *IGI* • *The poems of Vincent Bourne, with a memoir and notes*, ed. J. Mitford (1840)

Bourne, Sir (John) Wilfrid (1922–1999), barrister and civil servant, was born on 27 January 1922 at Farleigh House, Farleigh Hungerford, Somerset, the second son and youngest child of Robert Croft *Bourne (1888–1938), Conservative MP for Oxford City from 1924 to 1938, and his wife, Lady Hester Margaret, *née* Cairns (1895–1985), the eldest daughter of Wilfrid Dallas Cairns, fourth Earl Cairns. Through his mother he was a great-grandson of Lord Chancellor Cairns, and she herself had a formidable intellect. She was a vice-chairman of the Conservative Party and someone who, as a friend once said, 'could finish the *Times* crossword in the time it took me to open the paper' (private information).

Bourne entered Eton College as a king's scholar in 1934. He had a distinguished academic career, being 'sent up' (commended for good work) to the headmaster on nineteen occasions, and gaining distinction in trials, the school's examinations, ten times. He won trials prizes five times between 1934 and 1938, and a string of other prizes as well. These included the headmaster's French prize, in succeeding years the colleger prize and second prize, a prize for Latin prose and one for Latin verse the year afterwards, and the Duke of Newcastle's Italian prize two years running. In 1939 he was Newcastle medallist and Alfred Lytton scholar, that is, runner-up for the Newcastle scholarship, and the following year he won the scholarship itself. In the same year (1940) he became captain of the school and was also elected to the Eton Society ('Pop'). He left that year with a Davies scholarship, awarded to scholars going to university. He loved the classics, and while only a boy of ten or eleven would trade Greek iambics with his elder brother in the middle of pillow-fights. He went up to New College, Oxford, as the Ella Stephens Greek scholar, and took a first in classical moderations in 1941 before his university career was interrupted by the war. He was commissioned in the rifle brigade and served as signal officer with the 1st battalion from November 1942 to May 1945 in north Africa, Italy, Normandy, and north-west Europe, ending the war as a captain. Demobilized in December 1945, he returned to Oxford, and completed his double first by taking a first in jurisprudence in 1947. He rowed in the New College first eight in 1946 and 1948, and in the coxless four which reached the final of the visitors' cup at Henley in 1947.

Bourne joined the Middle Temple in 1946, and became a pupil in the Hare Court chambers of Melford Stevenson. He was called to the bar in 1948, being awarded the Harmsworth and Eldon law scholarships, and was invited to stay on in Stevenson's chambers. To the surprise and disappointment of Bourne's friends, the bar proved not to suit his temperament. Intellectually he had no difficulty with the work—so much so that his head of chambers said that sending him to do a case in the county court was like using a razor to cut linoleum. But he failed to impress solicitors, perhaps because he was not diplomatic enough. In 1956 he reluctantly took a post in the Lord Chancellor's Office, the headquarters of which were in the House of Lords. He soon became private secretary to the lord chancellor, and rapidly grasped the workings of government. On 2 August 1958 he married Elizabeth Juliet Fox (*b.* 1933), daughter of G. R. Fox of Trewardreva, Constantine, Cornwall; they had two sons. When first married they lived near Bishop's Stortford, Hertfordshire, later moving to Ramsdell, Hampshire, where they lived until Bourne's death.

Despite his disappointment at having been unable to stay at the bar, Bourne derived much pleasure from the more intellectually demanding of the office's legal responsibilities. He served for a long time as secretary to the Law Reform Committee, in which he played an important part. This was his most fulfilling time. He was the mainspring of the committee, and was able to contribute to the development of its proposals, to discuss difficult issues with experts, and to write its reports, notably that reviewing the law of evidence in civil cases, which led to the passing of the Civil Evidence Act (1968). The committee's work was in the heartland of the law, and had a carry-over into political issues, which he found very appealing. He rapidly came to be recognized as the intellectual core of the department, and successive lord chancellors and permanent secretaries, as well as his colleagues, constantly turned to him for advice. His pungent minutes were readily recognizable for their regular inclusion of literary allusions. It was as common to read an aphorism by Sherlock Holmes as it was to find the typescript interrupted by a manuscript quotation from Thucydides. He was principal assistant solicitor from 1970 to 1972, and deputy secretary from 1972 to 1977.

From an early stage it was obvious that Bourne would in due course head the department, and when Sir Denis Dobson retired in 1977 he was appointed to the linked offices of clerk of the crown in Chancery and permanent secretary to the lord chancellor. In the same year he was elected a bencher of the Middle Temple. In the senior ranges of the department he had to concentrate on administration more than law, and when he did so the clash of gears could be heard. He did not like the work, but he recognized its importance and set himself to learn the necessary skills. Because he was very talented, and because he cared much about people, he did so competently and intelligently, but he never pretended to enjoy it. A difficult legal or political issue was what he hungered for. He would complain that he had to consult *Who's Who* all the time, and the law reports almost never. He was a very shy man who found relationships with adults difficult, but he was able to get on extremely well with young people, whom he frequently helped both financially and in other ways.

Bourne was appointed CB in 1975 and promoted KCB in 1979. In 1981 he became a queen's counsel, before retiring the following year. He died of cancer at the Hampshire Clinic, Basingstoke, Hampshire, on 19 October 1999, and was cremated at Basingstoke crematorium on 28 October 1999. He was survived by his wife and their two sons.

Derek Oulton

Sources *The Times* (22 Oct 1999) • *Daily Telegraph* (9 Nov 1999) • *The Independent* (15 Nov 1999) • *WWW* • personal knowledge (2004) • private information (2004) [Lady Bourne]
Likenesses photograph, 1981, repro. in *The Times* • photograph, 1981, repro. in *The Independent* • photograph, repro. in *Daily Telegraph* • photographs, priv. coll.
Wealth at death £267,397: probate, 2 Feb 2000, *CGPLA Eng. & Wales*

Bourne, William (*c.*1535–1582), writer on mathematics, was born at Gravesend, the son of John Bourne (*d.* 1560), who owned property in the town. His exact date of birth is not known. He was appointed a jurat, or town councillor, of Gravesend under the charter of incorporation in 1562 and in 1571–2 served as port-reeve, the equivalent of mayor. In 1573 he made a will, from which it is evident that he had at that time four young sons. He had married Dorothy Beare, a widow with three sons of her own. As well as the four sons mentioned in the will, William and Dorothy Bourne also had a daughter, who was only a child when her mother died in December 1582, also leaving a will.

From both wills it is clear that Bourne and his wife owned considerable property in Gravesend, and lived prosperously. Bourne himself refers to 'the profittes of my houses and Tenements' (Bourne, appx) as sufficient for his wife to bring up the children and give them a good education. He had also inherited from his father a 'tyde', which brought in an income from the service of barges, known as tide barges, plying between the city of London and Gravesend. A residents' list for Gravesend of 1572 records him as serving again as a jurat, and states that he had paid for freedom of the Mercers' Company. A document in his own handwriting (15 March 1571) includes the name of Mr Bourne, port-reeve, as one of fourteen persons fined for selling beer in short measure. One account of his life regards this as conclusive evidence that he was an innkeeper, but it is more likely that the offence was committed by a tenant or employee for whom he was responsible in law.

An active and important citizen of a thriving Thames port, in middle life Bourne set about satisfying a demand for practical textbooks on navigation and gunnery. He was not a university-educated man, unlike other authors dealing with mathematical topics at this time, but he had, from boyhood, everyday contact with seamen, and had practised gunnery as a citizen volunteer with the garrison manning the defensive bulwark at Gravesend. His knowledge of mathematics, of which there is considerable evidence in his writing, must have been acquired through reading and determined study, and was sufficient for him to become a mathematical practitioner, dealing with almanac making, surveying, navigation, and gunnery. According to E. G. R. Taylor, he is 'the earliest unlearned English instructor and writer on mathematical practice known to us' (Taylor, *Mathematical Practitioners*, 176).

Bourne's first book was an *Almanacke and Prognostication for iii Yeres*, printed in 1567, of which a second, updated version appeared in 1571. The almanac customarily contained astrological material, and there was a tradition, particularly on the continent, of including prognostications, often dramatic and alarming. Bourne thought such prophecies 'most vain and foolish', and in his typically practical way included in his almanac a pocket sea-manual, described as 'serten rules of navigation'. One can deduce that the navigational content of the almanac was well received, for probably in 1574 he published *A Regiment for the Sea* (the first edition was not dated but contains a kalendar for 1574). This was his most extensive and important work. A second edition appeared in 1580, and the book went through five further editions after Bourne's death, the last in 1643; it was also translated into Dutch.

The *Regiment* was not, and did not pretend to be, an original work. Bourne's immediate inspiration came from the English translation, published under the title *Arte of Navigation* by Richard Eden in 1561, of Martin Cortes' *Arte de navigar*. Bourne was critical of some aspects of the Spaniard's book, and considered that he could produce a manual of more use to the practical seaman, as indeed proved to be the case. Among much advice to the seaman he describes in detail how to make observations of the sun and stars, using the cross-staff, how to measure the ship's way by log and line, and how to plot coastal features from the ship by taking bearings, using the method of triangulation.

The year 1578 saw the publication of three books by Bourne. One, the *Treasure for Traveilers*, dealt with the practicalities of making measurements, both at sea and on land, including in the latter case methods of surveying. The second, *The Arte of Shooting in Great Ordnance*, drew on his own experience as a gunner. The last, *Inventions, or, Devises*, was the first version in English of a type of book made popular on the continent by authors such as Nicholas Tartaglia and Jacques Besson. In it are described novel devices, such as a geared ship's log, and suggestions for military and naval strategies. For what proved to be his last book, Bourne returned to the almanac form with which he had begun writing, and published in 1580 a ten-year almanac and prognostication. Among Bourne's patrons and dedicatees were: Edward Clinton, earl of Lincoln, lord high admiral; Sir William Winter, master of the queen's ordnance, under whom Bourne had learned his gunnery skills; and Ambrose Dudley, earl of Warwick, general of the ordnance.

Another notable public figure with whom Bourne had dealings was William Cecil, first Baron Burghley. A manuscript pamphlet by Bourne, 'The property or qualytyes of glaces' (written *c.*1572 and addressed to Lord Burghley at Burghley's request), is an assessment of the claims for the discoveries of the effects of perspective glasses made by Leonard Digges, which were published after Digges's death by his son, Thomas, in *Pantometria* (1571). Bourne claims that Burghley made this request because he had, seven years earlier, received from Bourne a paper on buoyancy in water, as affecting the draught of ships. The pamphlet shows that Bourne had some practical knowledge of concave and convex mirrors and their effects, but he disclaims any first-hand experimental information on the crucial aspect of Digges's claim, namely, that a combination of concave mirror and convex lens would produce a telescopic effect. The manuscript was published in the nineteenth and twentieth centuries and used as an argument for the existence of an Elizabethan telescope. However there was neither the conceptual framework nor the technical capability to make such an instrument during this period.

Bourne was a popular author in the very practical sense that he explained technical matters in a comprehensible way for the 'unlettered' man. He owed his success in part to the fact that he lived at the time when the oceans were being opened up to exploration, and the ever-present threat of war with Spain ensured keen interest in all matters military and naval. He died in Gravesend and was buried there on 22 March 1582. G. L'E. TURNER

Sources W. Bourne, *A regiment for the sea*, ed. E. G. R. Taylor (1963) [incl. wills of William and Dorothy Bourne] • E. G. R. Taylor, *Tudor geography, 1485–1583* (1930), 153–61 • D. W. Waters, *The art of navigation in England in Elizabethan and early Stuart times* (1958) • C. Ronan, 'Now it can be told: British scientists beat Galileo by 33 years', *Daily Telegraph* (31 Oct 1991) [presidential address to the British Astronomical Association] • B. S. Capp, *Astrology and the popular press: English almanacs, 1500–1800* (1979) • *DNB* • E. G. R. Taylor, *The mathematical practitioners of Tudor and Stuart England* (1954) • G. L'E. Turner, 'There was no Elizabethan telescope', *Bulletin of the Scientific Instrument Society*, 37 (1993)

Archives BL, Lansdowne MSS, Burghley papers, MS 121 [art. 13] • BL, Sloane MSS, MS 3651

Wealth at death see will and wife's will, Bourne, *Regiment*

Bourne, William Sturges (1769–1845), politician and poor-law reformer, was born on 7 November 1769 as William Sturges, the only son of the Revd John Sturges DD (1736/7–1807), prebendary of Winchester, and his wife, Judith, daughter of Richard Bourne, of Acton Hall, Worcester. Educated first at a private school in Winchester, he entered Winchester College in 1782 and matriculated at Christ Church, Oxford, in Michaelmas term 1786, taking his BA in 1790 and his MA in 1793. In 1831 he was created DCL. He was called to the bar at Lincoln's Inn on 23 November 1793, and practised in king's bench and on the western circuit. At Oxford a lifelong friendship with George Canning was cemented. Canning thought him 'very clever' (*The Letter-Journal of George Canning, 1793–1795*, ed. P. Jupp, 1991, 26), and secured him election as member of parliament for the Treasury borough of Hastings in July 1798. Although Sturges was offered the under-secretaryship at the Home Office in Addington's administration, loyalty to Canning led him to decline. By 1802 he had added George Rose to his circle of political intimates, and was returned with Rose as MP for Christchurch that year.

In 1803 Sturges inherited £2000 p.a. from his uncle Francis Bourne, and happily concurred with the stipulation that he take the name Bourne, whereupon Canning promptly dubbed him 'Scroggs', by which nickname he became generally known in Canningite circles. When Pitt returned to office in 1804 Sturges Bourne became secretary to the Treasury. Relinquishing office in January 1806 following Pitt's death, he returned to public office under Portland as a lord of the Treasury from March 1807 to September 1809, eventually following Canning out of office. On 2 February 1808 he married Anne, daughter of Oldfield Bowles of North Aston, Oxfordshire. Their only child, Ann, was born a year later. After the general election of 1812 Sturges Bourne found himself without a seat, and became increasingly active in county politics in his native Hampshire, serving as chairman of the Hampshire quarter sessions between 1817 and 1822. His return to parliament was again secured by Canning, who insisted that he become a privy councillor (10 August 1814), and an Irish borough open to government nominees, Bandon Bridge, returned Sturges Bourne on 24 March 1815. He held the seat until 1818, when he was again returned for Christchurch. Although loyal to Canning, and firmly committed to Catholic emancipation, he was a comfortable supporter of the Liverpool administration. From September 1814 he served as an unpaid commissioner on the Board of Control, and in June 1818 he was elevated to a salaried commission, an office he held until February 1822.

Between 1817 and 1819 Sturges Bourne was responsible for the most ambitious attempt to reform the poor laws undertaken between 1601 and 1834. As early as November 1801 he had introduced a bill to end the badging of paupers, and in 1807 he successfully opposed Samuel Whitbread's elaborate scheme to reform the poor laws and popular education. In 1817 Sturges Bourne was nominated to a select committee on the poor laws, and in February 1818 assumed its chairmanship. The committee's reports stopped short of recommending abolition of poor relief, the currently orthodox view among political economists, and instead recommended major reform. Although the government was opposed to reform, in 1818 and 1819 Sturges Bourne sponsored a series of bills transforming the administration of poor relief and parish government. Two acts facilitated the appointment of salaried assistant overseers, the establishment of select vestries, and regular minute-keeping in all parish vestries. An act passed in 1819 transformed the local franchise, awarding ratepayers one vote for the first £50 of rateable value and an additional vote for each further £25 of rateable value, up to a maximum of six votes. The Sturges Bourne Acts remained the basis of parish government until the passage of the Parish Councils Act in 1894.

In 1822 Sturges Bourne succeeded to a substantial fortune, and resigned from both the Board of Control and the chairmanship of Hampshire quarter sessions. He remained politically active, serving on the 1824 select committee on artisans and machinery which paved the way for the abolition of the Combination Acts, and sat as MP for Ashburton from 1826 until 1830. Sturges Bourne's lifelong association with Canning reached its climax when Canning appointed him home secretary (he served from April to July 1827). Sturges Bourne's reluctance to accept major office was notorious, and he accepted the seals after prevaricating for a fortnight with Canning's insisting to him on 26 April 1827 that, 'My Administration WHOLLY depends on your helping me for two months as Home Secretary of State' (Aspinall, *Formation of Canning's*

Ministry, 186). Sturges Bourne was as good as his commission, moving to the Office of Woods and Forests when Lansdowne joined the administration. On Canning's death the king sent for Goderich, as his principal political associate, and for Sturges Bourne, Canning's most intimate friend. As Goderich vainly sought to construct a viable administration, the chancellorship of the exchequer was offered twice to Sturges Bourne, who turned it down, much to the dismay of Huskisson, who even accused him of destroying the chances of forming a coherent ministry. Sturges Bourne resigned woods and forests when Wellington assumed the premiership in February 1828. Although he supported Catholic emancipation, and moderate parliamentary reform, he nevertheless opposed the scale and tendency of the Whig Reform Bill, and resigned his seat (Milborne Port, which he had held since 1830) in March 1831. His daughter described his resignation as the product of 'his reluctance to oppose Government in a measure on which their existence, and perhaps our very safety depend, and an equal reluctance to give up the opinions of a lifetime' (Ann Sturges Bourne to Marianne Dyson, 7 March 1831, Hampshire RO, Sturges Bourne–Dyson correspondence, 9M55/F).

Resignation from parliament did not involve retirement from public life. Between 1832 and 1834 Sturges Bourne was an active member of the royal commission on the poor laws, did much to diminish hostility to poor-law reform in London vestries, and finally returned to active involvement in the Hampshire quarter sessions after 1835. He thought Peel's behaviour in office 1834–5 'very judicious'. Although a liberal tory, Sturges Bourne was deeply hostile to whigs and whiggism, even describing Lord Althorp as a republican at heart. In his diary for 18 April 1833, E. J. Littleton recalled that Sturges Bourne 'was a great alarmist. His friend Canning used to invent absurd stories to excite his apprehensions' (Aspinall, *Three Early … Diaries*). Sturges Bourne died at Testwood House, near Southampton, on 1 February 1845 and was buried in Winchester Cathedral. DAVID EASTWOOD

Sources Sturges Bourne–Dyson correspondence, Hants. RO, 9M55/F · *The diary of Henry Hobhouse, 1820–1827*, ed. A. Aspinall (1947) · A. Aspinall, ed., *The formation of Canning's ministry, February to August 1827*, CS, 3rd ser., 59 (1937) · R. Foster, *The politics of county power* (1990) · D. Eastwood, *Governing rural England* (1994) · J. R. Poynter, *Society and pauperism: English ideas on poor relief, 1795–1834* (1969) · A. Aspinall, ed., *Three early nineteenth-century diaries* (1952) [extracts from Le Marchant, E. J. Littleton, Baron Hatherton, and E. Law, earl of Ellenborough] · B. Murphy and R. G. Thorne, 'Sturges (afterwards Sturges Bourne), William', HoP, *Commons* · *The Huskisson papers*, ed. L. Melville [L. S. Benjamin] (1931) · *GM*, 2nd ser., 23 (1845), 433–4, 661

Archives Hants. RO, Sturges Bourne–Dyson MSS | U. Mich., Clements L., corresp. with George Canning

Wealth at death under £60,000: probate, *GM*, 661

Bousfield, Henry Brougham (1832–1902), bishop of Pretoria, was born in London on 27 March 1832, the son of William Cheek Bousfield, barrister, and his wife, Rebecca. He attended Merchant Taylors' School, London, from 1840, and then Gonville and Caius College, Cambridge, where he was an exhibitioner; he graduated BA as junior optime in 1855 and proceeded MA in 1858. He worked for a time for his father, but, believing that he had a vocation to the ministry, he did not pursue a legal career. Ordained deacon in 1855, he was licensed to the curacy of All Saints, Braishfield, Hampshire, and became incumbent of the parish in 1856 following his ordination to the priesthood. On 12 November 1861 he married Charlotte Elizabeth Higginson (*b.* 1840/41), daughter of Jonathan Higginson of Rock Ferry, Liverpool; they had two sons and six daughters. Charlotte died in 1886, and on 8 August 1888 Bousfield married Ellen (*b.* 1840/41), daughter of Thomas Lamb of Andover; he outlived his second wife.

From 1861 to 1870 Bousfield was rector of St Maurice with St Mary Kalendre and St Peter Colebrook, Winchester, and in 1870 he became vicar of Andover with Foxcote. In 1873 he was made rural dean of west Andover. However, from early boyhood Bousfield had been interested in missionary work, especially in British colonies, and during his early career he became secretary of an association supporting missions in the Orange Free State. After the Transvaal was separated in 1877 from the diocese of Bloemfontein, Bousfield refused and then accepted the offer of the new see from the Society for the Propagation of the Gospel. He was consecrated bishop of Pretoria at St Paul's Cathedral in London on 2 February 1878, and he was also made an honorary DD of Cambridge.

Bousfield landed at Durban on 17 September 1878. He trekked to Pretoria, where he found about 3000 inhabitants, of whom 1500 were white, and the church organization only in embryo, the clergy numbering five. Bousfield immediately set about organizing his diocese, travelling between isolated communities and encouraging the establishment of schools and churches. His own record of this work can be found in *Six Years in the Transvaal: Notes on the Founding of the Church there* (1886). He was an eloquent preacher who devoted at least two hours a day to study and reading. However, he was also outspoken and uncompromising in his opinions, with a high notion of episcopal authority. His work was hindered by the Anglo-Zulu War of 1879, and by the First South African War of 1880–81; but under the Boer republic he avoided political entanglement and continued his organization of the diocese. He sought to meet the needs of the white population drawn by the goldfields, and he extended missionary work among the Africans.

Bousfield's last decade was embittered by a serious dispute with J. T. Darragh and other Johannesburg clergy over the administration and finances of St Mary's mission district. The Jameson raid, which Bousfield condemned in a letter to his brother published in *The Times* (30 January 1896), caused him further difficulties within the diocese. However, when war with Great Britain broke out in 1899, the clergy of the diocese numbered thirty-two, and the white church members exceeded 18,000. From October 1899 to April 1901, during the Second South African War, Bousfield was a refugee in Natal, acting for a time as military chaplain at Estcourt and rendering aid to distressed refugees.

Despite failing health Bousfield managed to attend the

episcopal synod of South Africa (3–5 February 1902), but he then died suddenly, at Cape Town, of heart disease on 9 February 1902. He was buried at Rondebosch, and the old cemetery at Pretoria contains a memorial tablet to him.

A. R. BUCKLAND, *rev.* CLARE BROWN

Sources *WWW* · *DSAB* · P. B. Hinchliff, *The Anglican church in South Africa* (1963) · *Record* (14 Feb 1902) · *The Guardian* (12 March 1902) · *The Taylorian* (April 1902) · C. J. Robinson, ed., *A register of the scholars admitted into Merchant Taylors' School, from AD 1562 to 1874*, 2 (1883) · F. S. A. Lowndes, *Bishops of the day: a biographical dictionary of the archbishops and bishops of the Church of England* (1897) · C. F. Pascoe, *Two hundred years of the SPG*, rev. edn, 2 vols. (1901) · m. certs.

Archives University of Witwatersrand Library, Johannesburg, Church of the Province of South Africa Central Record Library, papers | LPL, corresp. with A. C. Tait, mainly relating to the Transvaal mission

Likenesses Standige & Co. Litho, engraving, United Society for the Propagation of the Gospel, Partnership House, 157 Waterloo Road, London

Wealth at death £4005 3*s.* 5*d.*: probate, 21 Aug 1902, *CGPLA Eng. & Wales*

Bousser [Bourchier], **Sir John** (*d.* 1329/30), justice, is first mentioned as deputed by Robert de Vere, earl of Oxford, to represent him in the parliament summoned in 1306. In 1312 he was permitted to postpone the assumption of the rank of knight for three years in consideration of paying a fine of 100*s*. From at least January 1315 he acted as justice of assize in Kent, Surrey, and Sussex, and subsequently in other southern and East Anglian counties. While most of his judicial work remained centred on the south-east of England, the range of his activities increased. From 1316 he participated in Newgate gaol deliveries and he headed many commissions there between 1323 and 1329. He was also entrusted with gaol deliveries at Hertford (1317, 1323–6, 1329) and Colchester Castle (1317–20, 1323–5), and with special commissions at Bury St Edmunds (1319), Dorchester (1321), and Rayleigh (1326). His extensive engagement in commissions of oyer and terminer from 1316 onwards focused on the same region. Bousser was keeper of the peace in Essex in 1317 and 1319/20 and in Nottinghamshire, Derbyshire, and Lincolnshire in 1326. His other tasks included the investigation of abuses committed by purveyors (Kent, Surrey, Sussex, 1317); the alleged corruption of royal officials in the same counties (1318, 1323), in Bedfordshire and Buckinghamshire (1321), and in Nottinghamshire and Derbyshire (1326); allegations against tax collectors in Somerset, Dorset, Wiltshire, Gloucestershire (1320), and Suffolk (1326); and complaints against commissioners of array in Essex, Hertfordshire, Middlesex (1323), and Suffolk, as well as against the keepers of the gaols in London (1326). These and similar tasks did not diminish with his appointment as justice of the common bench on 31 May 1321. Earlier in the same month he was among the thirty-eight judges summoned to attend parliament at Westminster. Already in 1319 he was involved in sensitive business, examining the record and process of a case relating to property in London, where in the following year he was openly accused of partiality by Simon Cofferer, the defendant in another case heard by him. In 1323 he investigated proceedings in the London husting and reviewed a judgment of the London sheriffs' court in the following year.

While Bousser maintained his connections with the de Vere family, he had clearly become a political supporter of the Despensers by 1322, investigating attacks on their possessions in Cambridgeshire and Wales and opening trespass proceedings against Roger Mortimer and others. In addition he appears to have acted as a Despenser agent in their attempts to acquire properties in Gower, Kent, and Worcestershire. In May 1323 he was summoned to attend parliament at York and in October opened an investigation into reports of miracles in Bristol at the place of Henry Montfort's and Henry Wylyngton's execution. In the remaining years of the reign he dealt with confiscated goods of insurgents and was appointed justice of oyer and terminer to investigate complaints made by the Despensers. After Edward II's fall he was summoned to attend a council meeting at Westminster in December 1326. He succeeded in regaining his former position; he took an oath in the London Guildhall to safeguard Queen Isabella and her eldest son in January 1327, acted as justice of oyer and terminer together with Roger Mortimer in Wales in the following month, and was reappointed justice of the common pleas in March.

In 1302 Bousser obtained the manor of Edwardstone in Suffolk for life, and by marriage to Helen, daughter and heir of Walter of Colchester, he acquired the manor of Stanstead. The centre of his properties was in and around Halstead in Essex, where his son Robert *Bourchier held the view of frankpledge after his father's death. Robert became chancellor in 1340 and a younger son, John, was rector of Sible Hedingham. Bousser remained active on the bench until Ascension day 1329 and may have died as early as July of that year; he was certainly dead by October 1330.

JENS RÖHRKASTEN

Sources Foss, *Judges* · N. Fryde, *The tyranny and fall of Edward II, 1321–1326* (1979) · P. Morant, *The history and antiquities of the county of Essex*, 2 (1768), 253 · *Chancery records* · A. H. Thomas and P. E. Jones, eds., *Calendar of plea and memoranda rolls preserved among the archives of the corporation of the City of London at the Guildhall*, 1 (1926), 12–13, 74–5

Boustead, Sir (John Edmund) Hugh (1895–1980), army officer and colonial official, was born on 14 April 1895 on a tea estate above Nawara Eliya, Ceylon, one of the two sons of Lawrence Twentyman Boustead, whose family had a hundred-year connection with Ceylon, and his wife, Ethel Margaret Alers-Hankey. His maternal grandfather served in the Indian Civil Service; and Sir Maurice Hankey, secretary of the war cabinet in the First World War, was his mother's cousin.

After preparatory school at Horton Hall and Cheam School he became a naval cadet at the Royal Naval College, Osborne, in 1908, and later at Dartmouth. In 1913 he joined HMS *Hyacinth* as a midshipman and once had to spend a night 'up the masthead' as punishment for carrying away the admiral's gangway when bringing a sailing launch alongside—a punishment longer than the commander, who had forgotten to call him down earlier, intended. When war came in 1914 he was up the mast of the *Hyacinth* again, in the south Atlantic on look-out for the *Scharnhorst* and *Gneisenau*, and was later involved in actions against the *Konigsberg* and other German ships off east Africa. With the seas cleared of enemy ships, he did not relish a routine security role on the Cape station, but ardently wished to fight in France, particularly as his brother Clive had been killed at Gallipoli serving with the Dublin fusiliers. After leaving his ship he enlisted in the South African Scottish as a private under the name of McLaren, but when the regiment was posted to Bordon camp in Wiltshire, he was traced by his worried parents. Made to face his formidable cousin, Sir Maurice Hankey, he boldly stated that it was out of the question for him to return to the Royal Navy. He was perhaps fortunate to have such a powerful relation, for Sir Maurice arranged for him to continue his service with the South African Scottish, but under his own name—and without stigma.

Boustead fought with his regiment in the brief and successful campaign against the Turks in Libya, marching 180 miles from Mersa Matruh to Sollum with a 94 lb pack, and then went to France in 1916, where his brigade joined the 9th Scottish division between Armentières and Lille in Flanders. Wounded in the fighting near Delville Wood, he was sent home and, having recovered, was commissioned second lieutenant in the field. He was later awarded the MC for bravery in the battle of Arras, during which he was again seriously wounded; but he returned to France in 1918 to serve with the South African brigade. Just before the armistice he volunteered for service in the British mission to assist the White Russians of Denikin's army against the Bolsheviks. Alongside White Cossacks he saw successful action—with the Lewis gunners he had trained—against the Red Cossack cavalry and, while in Russia, received news of a bar to his MC, the Russian order of Vladimir with cross swords (equivalent of the DSO), as well as the welcome news from the Admiralty of the king's pardon for his desertion from the Royal Navy. After the defeat of the White armies, he was withdrawn with the rest of the British force.

Boustead applied for a regular commission in the army, but first had a spell at Worcester College, Oxford, reading Russian and playing a prominent role as a sportsman. Already a well-known lightweight amateur boxer, having been the army champion at this weight, he was called to London at short notice by the president of the Imperial Boxing Association to fight against a French services team. Having knocked his opponent out in the third round, he changed into white tie and tails on the train back to Oxford and attended the Trinity College 'commem' ball with 'some enchanting young Danish girls', dancing the night through and bathing in the Cherwell early next morning. Selected in 1920 for the British team at the Antwerp Olympic games he competed in the modern pentathlon; and was prevented from taking part in the 1924 Paris Olympics only by a motorcycle accident shortly before the event.

Boustead joined the Gordon Highlanders and served with them in 1921 in Constantinople and Anatolia during the war between the Greeks and Turks. In 1924 his battalion was posted to India and, fearing more barrack life there, he applied for a transfer to the Egyptian army. He arrived in Cairo, however, just after it had been decided to create a new British-officered Sudan defence force (SDF), following a mutiny by Egyptian troops in Sudan. He was, therefore, told to remove his kilt and other uniform and proceed to Khartoum in the guise of a civilian official. Thus began a period of twenty-four years' service as soldier and administrator in Sudan.

Boustead joined the camel corps—which was mounted on camels until the late 1930s—and his first station was at Bara in Kordofan province, west of the Nile. Here his temperament and style were ideally suited to the family atmosphere of the companies and the manliness and intense sense of fun of the Sudanese soldier, although he was horrified on one occasion to see a rutting camel seize one of his men by the neck, shake him like a rat and grind his neck to pieces. In 1929 he joined the staff of the British general commanding in Sudan, the 'kaid' of the SDF, and in 1931 was promoted commander of the camel corps with its headquarters at al-ʿUbayd. A great admirer of Douglas Newbold (the governor of Kordofan and later civil secretary of Sudan) for his erudition, wit, and humanity, Boustead always co-operated harmoniously with the civil administration, as for instance in 1933 when the camel corps was called on to stop fighting between the Arab Baggara and the Nilotic Dinka.

A shortish man with—latterly—a face wrinkled like a walnut, Hugh Boustead had a great capacity to inspire and lead, and did extraordinary things as if they were a matter of course. Although not unattracted to women and once engaged, he remained single, preferring a challenging life nearly all spent overseas. When on leave he sought new challenges, as when in 1930 he climbed the Matterhorn, and his mountaineering skills gained him a place on the 1933 Royal Geographic Society's Everest expedition. In the interim his 1932 leave was spent on an extensive survey—led by Ralph Bagnold, founder of the long range desert group—of the Libyan desert, Jebel ʿUwaynat, and the edge of the Tibeste and Ennedi mountains. Responsible for the fauna collection, he collected sixty-seven specimens of migratory birds and joined in the finds of beautiful and wonderfully preserved rock pictures of giraffe, buffalo, gazelle, and antelope.

In 1935 Boustead joined the Sudan political service. Posted to Darfur province, he became resident—with district commissioner's powers—in Zalingei, a district which marched with French Equatorial Africa along the west side of Jebel Marra, a massif rising to 10,000 feet. Boustead's objectives in this area were to stop oppression by local chiefs, and to set up organized local courts, as well as establishing primary schools. He gave priority to the education of boys and, through emphasis on hygiene and cleanliness, made washing and wearing impeccably white clothes fashionable. He also took strong measures for the conservation of the magnificent forest.

Recalled to military service on the outbreak of war in

1939, Boustead raised a new SDF frontier battalion composed of men from all over Sudan. Their role was to open the way, in co-operation with Ethiopian forces, against the Italians for the restoration of Haile Selassie as emperor. Orde Wingate, another former SDF officer, was the kaid's staff officer for the operation, but Boustead did not approve of his tactics. After the capture of Belaya, at over 10,000 feet in the Gojjam, Boustead was given the command of Gideon force consisting of his own frontier battalion and the 2nd Ethiopian battalion. This force achieved further notable successes against the Italians and entered Addis Ababa, where Boustead and his officers were invited to dine with the emperor. 'Boustead Bey' was awarded the DSO and won praise from the historian of the SDF for the way in which he harried the Italians: he had taught the British army new lessons in guerrilla warfare and 'defeated and largely captured or dispersed four Italian brigades with all their equipment. The odds in man-power were ten to one against him; the odds in fire-power far greater' (Orlebar, *Story of the Sudan Defence Force*, 108).

In July 1945 Boustead resumed his previous post in Zalingei, from which he retired in 1949. A chance meeting on leave, however, with Sir Reginald Champion, the governor of Aden, led to his appointment as resident adviser to the Hadhramaut states and British agent to the East Aden Protectorate under the Colonial Office. During his nine years there Boustead came to admire the qualities of the seafaring and mercantile Hadhramis and was enchanted by his new headquarters, the port of Mukalla—a white-walled city with houses fringing the harbour full of dhows. He plunged enthusiastically into his new task in a wild area, where there was still much tribal fighting despite the many truces which his predecessor, Harold Ingrams, had negotiated. Much preoccupied with law and order, he had no fewer than three forces—the Quʿaiti armed constabulary, the Mukalla regular army, and the Bedouin legion—subject to his command. Despite this he was faced with a serious riot in Mukalla, and narrowly escaped a very severe blow to his person. He went on, however, to stamp his unique personality on the area, enjoying the company not only of the Quʿaiti sultan but of qadhis, seyyids, and sultans with their family contacts in Indonesia, Malaysia, and the Far East—and relishing their spicy cooking. He encouraged education, agriculture, and famine prevention, and also successfully ejected a party of Americans from Aramco, the American oil company, who with the backing of the Saudi king, had begun drilling operations 30 miles inside the (disputed) borders of the Aden Protectorate.

In 1958 Boustead became development secretary to the sultan of Muscat and Oman, Sayyed Said bin Taimur, whom he found very half-hearted about plans for health, education, and agriculture. When Boustead suggested establishing a school in every governorate, the sultan refused, saying: 'That is why you lost India, because you educated the people' (private information). This post gave Boustead much less satisfaction than his other posts, and in 1961, shortly after oil had been discovered in Abu Dhabi, he became the political agent of its ruler. However, after a honeymoon period with Sheikh Shakhbut bin Sultan, he suffered, as others had, from the ruler's violent changes of mood and unwillingness to face the responsibility of his new oil wealth.

Boustead nevertheless stayed on in Abu Dhabi as Sheikh Zaid bin Sultan, who succeeded his brother as ruler, persuaded him to look after his large stable of horses in al-ʿAin. He continued to do this until his death in 1980, aged eighty-five. During this time he received many visitors, including young British officers serving in Oman and the United Arab Emirates, who liked to pay a sort of military pilgrimage to an eccentric and lovable figure. Reflecting on his own career, Boustead wrote in his autobiography, *The Wind of Morning* (1971): 'there can be few deeper satisfactions than to have played a part in helping a country forward to a life of peace' (237). In 1966 he was awarded the Lawrence of Arabia medal by the Royal Society for Asian Affairs, 'in recognition of work of outstanding merit in the fields of exploration, research or literature'. Boustead died in Dubai in the United Arab Emirates on 3 April 1980. DONALD HAWLEY

Sources H. Boustead, *The wind of morning* (1971) · J. Orlebar, *Tales of the Sudan defence force* (1981) · J. Orlebar, *The story of the Sudan defence force* (1986) · *WW* · *The Times* (9 April 1980) · *Daily Telegraph* (5 April 1980) · T. Green, *The adventurers: four profiles of contemporary travellers* (1970) · personal knowledge (2004) · private information (2004) · D. Shirreff, *Bare feet and bandoliers: Wingate, Sandford, the patriots and the part they played in the liberation of Ethiopia* (1995)

Archives Bodl. RH, corresp. with Margery Perham · U. Durham L., Sudan archive

Likenesses photographs, repro. in Boustead, *The wind of morning*

Wealth at death £82,324—in England and Wales: probate, 22 July 1980, *CGPLA Eng. & Wales*

Boutel, Mrs. *See* Bowtell, Elizabeth (1648/9–1714/15).

Boutell, Charles (1812–1877), writer on heraldry and antiquities, was born on 1 August 1812 at Pulham St Mary, Norfolk, the son of the Revd Charles Boutell (1771–1855), perpetual curate of Repps-with-Bastwick, Norfolk (1808–48), and his wife, Mary Elizabeth (*née* Day). He entered St John's College, Cambridge, as a sizar in 1829 and graduated BA in 1834. In 1836 he was incorporated at Trinity College, Oxford, took his MA degree, and the same year was ordained as deacon at Ely. He was briefly curate at Hemsby, Norfolk, and then curate at St Leonards, Sandridge, Hertfordshire (1837–46), where he took priest's orders in 1839. In 1847 he returned to Norfolk as rector of Downham Market (1847–50) and vicar of St Mary Magdalen, Wiggenshall (1847–55), before becoming (*c*.1851) curate at Litcham to assist his aged father, who was the incumbent. After moving to London in 1855 he held various positions, including reader at St Luke's, Lower Norwood (1860–67). On 17 April 1838 Boutell married Mary, daughter of the Revd Dr John *Chevallier of Aspall Hall, Suffolk, and his first wife, Caroline. They had four sons, two of whom died young, and two daughters.

Boutell wrote extensively on architecture, brasses, and heraldry. In 1845 he was a founder member and joint secretary of the St Albans Architectural Society; he also acted as the society's treasurer, but was far from reliable. The following year he contributed the text of Britton's *Illustrations of the Early Domestic Architecture of England*. His next work was *Monumental Brasses and Slabs* (1847), 'still an important pioneering work' (Busby, 1996, 10), which was followed two years later by *Monumental Brasses of England*. In 1855, after moving to London, Boutell became a founder member of the London and Middlesex Archaeological Society; on 23 July 1857 he was appointed secretary (against the advice of the Revd Thomas Hugo, a principal trustee). Four months later, on 27 November, at a special meeting, he was dismissed and required to repay the sum of £56 15s. This was not his first or his last financial embarrassment, but his antiquarian zeal appears to have been unimpaired, and *A Manual of British Archaeology* was published in 1858, with illustrations by Orlando Jewitt. *A Manual of Heraldry, Historical and Popular* was an immediate success in 1863 and a second edition was called for in two months, and published as *Heraldry, Historical and Popular*; further editions followed in 1864 and 1867. *Boutell's Heraldry*, as it became known, was his most popular and enduring work, and revised editions were published at intervals up to 1983. In 1891 John Evans praised Boutell 'for popularising heraldry' (Levine, 91). Boutell helped Mary, his elder daughter, to publish *Picture Natural History, Including Zoology, Fossils, and Botany* (1869) while completing *Arms and Armour in Antiquity and in the Middle Ages*, his translation of J. P. Lacombe.

In the *Gentleman's Magazine* (1866) Boutell wrote a series of articles on 'Our early national portraits'; he also contributed to the journals of the British Archaeological Association and the Archaeological Institute, and to *Notes and Queries*. The Robinson Library, University of Newcastle upon Tyne, houses a series of his manuscript notebooks (1865–71), and the British Library has two notebooks on misericords (1872; Add. MSS 32135–32136).

After two years of declining health Boutell died of a ruptured heart on 31 July 1877 at 18 Portsdown Road, London; he was buried on 4 August at Paddington old cemetery, Kilburn. His wife died in 1885. His life was described as 'one of continuous trouble' (*DNB*), but while this may describe his personal life his public persona was different. His financial embarrassments included being 'a prisoner for debt' in 1868 (Busby, 1999, 13); his bankruptcy was announced in *The Times* on 23 December that year, when he was described as 'late of Jermyn Street'. None of this did anything to reduce his considerable popularity as a lecturer or his reputation as an antiquary. He was clearly personable; the obituary in the *Art Journal* states, 'His varied information … always conveyed with great fluency of speech and clearness of description … and his most courteous manners, rendered him at all times a very agreeable companion' (Busby, 1999, 14). COLIN LEE

Sources R. Busby, 'Rev. Charles Boutell', *A history in all men's lives*, ed. B. Moody, St Albans and Hertfordshire Architectural and Archaeological Society (1999), 9–16 • D. Aubrey, 'The society's financial affairs, 1845–1945', *A history in all men's lives*, ed. B. Moody, St Albans and Hertfordshire Architectural and Archaeological Society (1999), 35–46 • R. Busby, *Monumental Brass Society Bulletin*, 71 (Feb 1996), 223–6 • *Transactions of London and Middlesex Archaeological Society*, 1 (1855–9), 209 • private information (2004) [Marie Murphy] • Venn, *Alum. Cant.* • Boase, *Mod. Eng. biog.*, 1.351 • P. Levine, *The amateur and the professional: antiquarians, historians and archaeologists in Victorian England* (1986), 54, 91 • Foster, *Alum. Oxon.* • F. Broomhead, *Orlando Jewitt* (1995), 81, 115 • *IGI* • *The Athenaeum* (11 Aug 1877), 183 • *DNB* • d. cert.

Archives BL, papers relating to misericords, Add. MSS 32135–32136 • priv. coll., scrapbook • U. Newcastle, scrapbooks

Wealth at death bankrupt, so probably negligible

Boutflower, Henry Crewe (1796–1863), Church of England clergyman and headmaster, was the son of John Johnson Boutflower, surgeon, of Salford, and was born there on 25 October 1796. The Boutflowers were an important clerical family in the Manchester area. Henry was educated at Manchester grammar school, and in 1815 entered St John's College, Cambridge. In 1816 he gained the Hulsean theological prize with an essay on the atonement published in 1817. He graduated BA in 1819 and MA in 1822. He was ordained in 1821, when he became curate at Elmdon near Birmingham, having previously acted as assistant master at Manchester grammar school.

In 1823 Boutflower was appointed headmaster of Bury School, Lancashire, and held that position until 1859. On 21 June 1825 he married his cousin, Harriet, daughter of Henry Johnson Boutflower. In 1832 he was presented to the perpetual curacy of St John's Church in Bury. Though during his time Bury School lost prestige—Boutflower being seen as scholarly but ineffective—he was highly respected as an able and conscientious clergyman and a good preacher.

In 1857 Boutflower returned to Elmdon as rector, remaining there until his death, which took place on 4 June 1863, while on a visit to West Felton vicarage, Shropshire. He was buried at Elmdon. He collected materials for a history of Bury, which he left in manuscript, and published a number of sermons, including one on the death of William IV (1837).

W. C. SYDNEY, *rev.* H. C. G. MATTHEW

Sources Venn, *Alum. Cant.* • D. S. Boutflower, *The Boutflower book* (1930) • M. Gray, *History of Bury* (1970)

Wealth at death under £800: probate, 11 Jan 1864, *CGPLA Eng. & Wales*

Boutmy, Emile Gaston (1835–1906), political scientist and commentator on British life and institutions, was born on 13 April 1835 in Paris. He was the son of Laurent-Joseph Boutmy, a journalist and businessman who died in financial ruin in 1848. Educated at the Lycée Louis-le-Grand in Paris, Boutmy became active in liberal journalism in the 1860s, and lectured at the École Centrale d'Architecture in Paris, but he made his name as founder and first director of the independent École Libre des Sciences Politiques (Sciences Po), which opened in Paris in 1872. The school, which set out to counteract the defects of French political culture, became the chief route of entry into the higher civil service, and an immensely important influence on French public life. Its success testified both to the power of its founder's vision, and to his practical genius in translating that vision into reality. He was instrumental in communicating his vision to influential friends and in securing financial backing. Boutmy himself taught constitutional law, and his chief publications ranged over the comparative study of constitutions, political institutions and political cultures: *Études de droit constitutionnel* (1885), *Le développement de la constitution et de la société politique en Angleterre* (1887), *Essai d'une psychologie politique du peuple anglais au XIXe siècle* (1901), *Éléments d'une psychologie politique du peuple américain* (1902). Boutmy, who was almost blind, married the daughter of an eminent protestant pastor, Eugène Bersier, in 1882. He died in Paris on 25 January 1906.

The approach at Sciences Po to the study of the social sciences was empirical and historical rather than abstract and theoretical; it was also comparative, and was orientated towards comparisons with 'Anglo-Saxon' political systems. This was the setting in which Boutmy wrote his own works on English history, constitutional law, and political psychology. A strong Anglophile, he (like his friend H. A. Taine) wrote on England without thinking it necessary to spend much time there. He visited the country only four or five times, and for short periods. His most notable work, the *Psychologie politique du peuple anglais*, was composed at a time when collective psychology was a fashionable intellectual pursuit, and it was as a contribution to that genre that it was enthusiastically reviewed in France, by such authorities as the philosopher Gaston Richard and the Durkheimian sociologist Célestin Bouglé. In England, where Boutmy's constitutional writings had been praised by such authorities as Dicey, his venture into collective psychology was less highly regarded: reviewers in *The Athenaeum* and in *Blackwood's Magazine* were unimpressed, though his work was used by the pioneering social psychologist William McDougall.

Boutmy's emphasis was on the formation of national character through the interaction of the primitive characteristics of the race with its physical and human environment. The English were an active people, not given to abstraction or generalization; an energetic people endowed with foresight and self-control. They were also unsociable: the vigorous associative life of the English, prized by previous French observers such as Taine, was valued by Boutmy too, but he saw it as indicative not of a tendency to sociability, but rather of the individualism and self-reliance of the English. Hence 'the English, though profoundly individual, are nevertheless peculiarly qualified for collective operations; they have a superior power of coalition and ability to work collectively which is unknown among races who are less active and more absurdly vain' (E. G. Boutmy, ed., *The English People: a Study of their Political Psychology*, 1904, 116–7). Like F. Le Play, but unlike Taine, Boutmy emphasized the survival of the patriarchal family in England. He also differed from Taine in playing down the importance of Anglicanism, which he thought merely 'a combination of statesmen' (ibid., 52). It was the dissenters, he thought, who represented 'the heart of the nation' (ibid., 52). H. S. Jones

Sources P. Favre, 'Les sciences d'état entre déterminisme et libéralisme: Emile Boutmy, 1835–1906, et la création de l'École Libre des Sciences Politiques', *Revue Française de Sociologie*, 22 (1981), 429–65 • P. Favre, *Naissances de la science politique en France, 1870–1914* (1989) • G. Vincent, *Sciences Po: histoire d'une réussite* (1987) • P. Rain, *L'École Libre des Sciences Politiques* (1963)

Archives Bibliothèque Nationale, Paris, Ernest Havet MSS • Fondation Nationale des Sciences Politiques, Paris, archives of the École Libre des Sciences Politiques

Bouverie, Edward Pleydell- (1818–1889), politician, the second son of William Pleydell-*Bouverie, third earl of Radnor (1779–1869), and his second wife, Anne Judith (1790–1851), third daughter of Sir Henry St John Mildmay, bt, was born on 26 April 1818. Educated at Harrow School and at Trinity College, Cambridge, he graduated MA in 1838, and became a précis writer to Lord Palmerston at the Foreign Office from January to June 1840. He was called to the bar at the Inner Temple on 27 January 1843, and in the following year he was returned to parliament as Liberal member for Kilmarnock, sitting until his defeat there in 1874. He was a prominent figure in the House of Commons. From July 1850 to March 1852 he was under-secretary of state for the Home department in Lord John Russell's administration, and from April 1853 to March 1855 he was chairman of committees, while Lord Aberdeen was prime minister. In March 1855, when Palmerston became premier, Bouverie was made vice-president of the Board of Trade, and in August was transferred to the presidency of the poor-law board, a position he held until 1858. In 1857 he was appointed one of the committee of the council on education. He was second church estate commissioner from August 1859 to November 1865, and from 1869 he was one of the ecclesiastical commissioners for England. In 1862 he proposed in the Commons the abolition of tests for admission to fellowships in Cambridge.

Though a staunch Liberal, Bouverie belonged to the old whig school, and in his last parliament he often found himself unable to agree with Gladstone's policies. In 1872, when a charge of evasion of the law was made against Gladstone in connection with the appointment of W. W. Harvey to the rectory of Ewelme, Bouverie expressed regret 'that the prime minister should amuse his leisure hours by driving coaches-and-six through Acts of Parliament' (*Hansard* 3, 209.1711).

When the Irish University Bill was introduced, Bouverie finally broke with Gladstone (March 1873). He denounced the measure as miserably bad and scandalously inadequate to its professed object. He voted against the second reading on 10 March, when the government was defeated. During the course of his career Bouverie addressed numerous letters to *The Times* under the signature of 'E. P. B.', and subsequent to this occasion his letters to the newspaper continued his attacks on the measure and its framers. After his retirement from parliament he became in 1877 associated with the corporation of bondholders of the Egyptian and Turkish debt, and was soon made its chairman. Under his guidance the debts of many countries were readjusted; and the corporation's scheme for dealing with the Turkish debt was confirmed by the sultan's irade of January 1882. Bouverie was also director of the Great Western Railway Company and of the Peninsular and Oriental Company.

Bouverie married, on 1 November 1842, Elizabeth Anne, youngest daughter of General Robert Balfour of Balbirnie, Fife, and had two sons and three daughters. He died at his London home, 44 Wilton Crescent, on 16 December 1889.

G. C. Boase, *rev.* H. C. G. Matthew

Sources Boase, *Mod. Eng. biog.* • *The Times* (17 Dec 1889) • J. P. Parry, *Democracy and religion* (1986) • Gladstone, *Diaries*
Archives BL, corresp. with W. E. Gladstone, Add. MSS 44368–44441, *passim* • BL, corresp. with Sir Austen Layard, Add. MSS 39010–39136, *passim* • Bodl. Oxf., letters to Disraeli • Bodl. Oxf., letters to Lord Kimberley • Borth. Inst., letters to Lord Halifax • Castle Howard, North Yorkshire, letters to C. W. G. Howard • NL Scot., corresp. with third earl of Minto • PRO, corresp. with Odo Russell, FO 918 • Wellcome L., corresp. with John Hodgkin
Likenesses lithograph, repro. in *VF* (27 July 1872), 119 • wood-engraving (after photograph by Beard), NPG; repro. in *ILN* (20 July 1850)
Wealth at death £89,730 7*s.* 3*d.*: resworn probate, June 1890, *CGPLA Eng. & Wales*

Bouverie, Sir Henry Frederick (1783–1852), army officer, third son of the Hon. Edward Bouverie (1738–1810)—son of Jacob Bouverie, first Viscount Folkestone (*c.*1694–1761), MP for Salisbury (1761–71) and Northampton (1790–1810)—and his wife, Harriet (*d.* 1831), only daughter of Sir Everard *Fawkener, sometime ambassador to the Porte, was born on 11 July 1783. In 1811 Bouverie's widowed mother married Lord Robert Spencer, son of the third duke of Marlborough, but had no further children. Edward (1767–1858) and John (1779–1855) were Bouverie's brothers; Henrietta (*d.* 1810), Frances, Mary (*d.* 1816), Jane (*d.* 1865), and Diana his sisters. Bouverie went to Eton College in May 1793, and on leaving about 1798 joined the 2nd dragoon guards at Hertford before moving to London as an ensign in the Coldstream Guards on 23 October 1799. He advanced to lieutenant and captain in the Coldstreams (19 November 1800) and served in Ireland, where he was adjutant to a detachment at Bandon. He went with his regiment on Lieutenant-General Sir Ralph Abercromby's expedition to Egypt, landing under heavy fire with its light company at Abu Qir Bay on 8 March 1801. He saw further action on 13 March, and commanded a company during the battle of Alexandria on 21 March. Homeward bound in May, his ship was captured and Bouverie taken prisoner. Swiftly exchanged, before the close of 1801 he was in Scotland as aide-de-camp to Major-General Lord Rosslyn, his sister Henrietta's husband. After the peace of Amiens (March 1802) he travelled to Russia on a military mission, but was recalled to Ireland, once more as aide-de-camp to Rosslyn, when hostilities were resumed (May 1803). In 1806 he accompanied Rosslyn (then lieutenant-general) on a mission to Portugal and was with him the next year during the bombardment of Copenhagen (September 1807).

On 31 December 1808 Bouverie embarked for Portugal with the Coldstreams' 1st battalion, on 27 April 1809 being appointed aide-de-camp and assistant military secretary to Lieutenant-General Sir Arthur Wellesley. He was with Wellesley at the crossing of the Douro (12 May) and battle of Talavera (27–8 July), where he was wounded above the right knee and temporarily deafened after being knocked off his horse. To his mother Bouverie described Talavera as 'the most desperate battle that ever was fought' (Hammersley, 4). On advancing to captain and lieutenant-colonel (28 June 1810), Bouverie went back to the Coldstreams' depot in England, returning to Portugal with regimental reinforcements on 25 December 1811. Shortly after taking part in the successful siege of Badajoz (April–May 1812), Bouverie became assistant adjutant-general to the 4th division, with which he was present at the battles of Salamanca (22 July 1812), Vitoria (21 June 1813), the Nive (10 December 1813, where he was mentioned in dispatches), and Orthez (27 February 1814), as well as the siege and storming of San Sebastian (July–August 1813). After the fighting ended, he was named adjutant-general to a force for the war against the United States, but peace was signed (December 1814) before it sailed.

Bouverie became an extra aide-de-camp to the prince regent and brevet colonel on 4 June 1814. He briefly commanded a Coldstream battalion in Brussels before being superseded by a more senior officer and therefore missing the battle of Waterloo, 'owing to which I am in all probability writing this journal' (Hammersley, 5). Meanwhile, on 2 January 1815, he had been appointed KCB, and for his services in the Peninsula he received the army gold cross and one clasp for Salamanca, Vitoria, San Sebastian, the Nive, and Orthez. Remaining in England, Bouverie obtained a majority in the Coldstreams (18 January 1820), but left the regiment on promotion to major-general (27 May 1825). On 8 July 1826 he married Julia, daughter of Lewis Montolieu and widow of Captain William Wilbraham RN, and they had two children: Henry Montolieu (*b.* 1831?), killed at Inkerman in 1854, and Henrietta (*b.* 1830?). Shortly after his marriage Bouverie commanded the brigade of guards with Lieutenant-General Sir Henry Clinton's expedition to Portugal in support of the young queen being threatened by Spanish-backed opponents. On its arrival in December 1826 the brigade stayed at Cartaxo, then Santarem, before marching to suppress riots in Lisbon. Bouverie left Portugal in April 1828, when the constitutional dispute had been solved. Meanwhile, on 2 February 1827 he had written to congratulate Wellington on his appointment as colonel of the Grenadier Guards, assuring the duke 'that the high character of that distinguished regiment' had been illustrated in the force under his command, however contriving also to inform the duke that his brigade 'is at present very much inconvenienced by the non-arrival of a paymaster' (Hamilton, 92). Three months later, on 8 May, Clinton expressed to Bouverie his 'real satisfaction … [at] the general good conduct and appearance' of the troops which he led (ibid., 93).

From the end of 1828, for almost eight years, Bouverie commanded the northern district in England. Then a widower accompanied by two small children, on 1 October 1836 he was appointed governor and commander-in-chief at Malta, where he was credited with building several new roads, vastly improving the island's water supply, and, less profoundly, personally giving up snuff. Following the death of William IV, Queen Adelaide spent the winter of 1837–8 in Malta as Bouverie's guest and laid the foundation-stone of the first English church located outside the governor's palace. Bouverie received the GCMG on leaving Malta in June 1843. Promoted lieutenant-general (28 June 1838), he became colonel of the 1st West India regiment (13 May 1842), then of the 97th foot (21 November 1843), and was appointed GCB (18 June 1852). In 1846 he was approached to be commander-in-chief in Canada, 'but being grown old and puffy and blind, I wisely declined' (Hammersley, 5). The following year at Woolbeding, near Midhurst, in Sussex, where his clergyman brother John was rector, he declared himself 'blessed with children whom I dearly love … far happier than I deserve to be' (ibid., 5). As he was preparing to attend the duke of Wellington's funeral in London, Bouverie suddenly fell ill at Woolbeding House, bequeathed to his sister Diana (wife of the Hon. George Ponsonby) by their stepfather, and died there on 14 November 1852. JOHN SWEETMAN

Sources *Army List* • H. Hammersley, ed., *Short life of Sir Henry Frederick Bouverie, KCB, GCMG* (1906) • Burke, *Peerage* (1887) • F. W. Hamilton, *The origin and history of the first or grenadier guards*, 3 (1874) • F. W. Walker, *The great deeds of the Coldstream guards* (1916) • D. Mackinnon, *Origin and services of the Coldstream guards*, 2 (1833) • Eton, archives • Fortescue, *Brit. army*, vol. 11 • archives, W. Sussex RO • HoP, *Commons* • GEC, *Peerage* • Boase, *Mod. Eng. biog.*
Archives Lpool RO, letters to Lord Stanley

Bouverie, Katharine Harriot Duncombe Pleydell- (1895–1985), potter, was born on 7 June 1895 at Coleshill House, Berkshire, the youngest of three children of Duncombe Pleydell-Bouverie (1842–1909), second son of Jacob, fourth earl of Radnor, and his wife, Maria Eleanor Hulse. She was brought up in Coleshill House, one of the most striking seventeenth-century stately homes in England; there, surrounded by fine architecture and exquisite blue and white decoration and *famille verte* Chinese porcelain, she acquired her education, together with her elder sister, Mary (known as Molly), and her brother, Edward, who was tragically killed in 1914 in the trenches. The onset of the First World War brought this idyll to an end and Bina, as she was known, joined the British committee of the Red Cross in France. Undecided about a choice of career she studied history at the British Museum with a view to becoming a historian—serious historians were welcomed at Coleshill—or a writer. Two novels were published: *January* (1924) and *The Inn on the Valley* three years later. Although vividly descriptive the novels made little impact and Pleydell-Bouverie did not see herself as a writer, although she produced prize-winning entries for literary competitions in the *Saturday Review* and *Time and Tide*, as well as sensitive poetry.

In 1921 Margaret Fry introduced Pleydell-Bouverie to her brother, the art critic Roger Fry, who set up the Omega Workshops and also made pots, thus alerting her to the qualities of handmade ceramics. Classes in pottery at the Central School of Arts and Crafts followed; there she was much impressed by a skilled thrower named Askew who could produce any shape, but in her view had little sense of form. During a visit to an early show of reduction-fired pots by Bernard Leach at Paterson's Gallery in Bond Street she saw work that she genuinely admired and asked Leach if he would take her as a student. Eventually he agreed and she worked at the Leach Pottery in St Ives from 1924 to 1925, doing what she called general stooging, and became known as Beano. The twelve months were a revelation. Leach prepared his own clay, made his glazes—many from natural local materials such as granite and wood ash—and fired in a large three-chamber kiln, using wood. It was a romantic twelve months in which potting became a way

Katharine Harriot Duncombe Pleydell-Bouverie (1895–1985), by Mayotte Magnus, 1977

of life. Fellow students included Michael Cardew, Ada Mason (known as Peter), and a thirty-ninth generation Japanese potter, Tsurunoske Matsubayashi, known as Matsue, who was rebuilding the three-chamber kiln.

Totally enamoured by reduction-fired wares Pleydell-Bouverie set up a pottery at Coleshill, first with Ada Mason, firing in a two-chamber kiln built in the record time of two weeks by Matsue. Inspired by Leach's idea that whenever possible raw materials should be local Pleydell-Bouverie sought out suitable clays from the estate, using five as part of the clay body. However, it was the clippings from the wide range of trees and bushes that proved the biggest stimulation, for from them Beano obtained pure varieties of wood ash and tested them for use in glazes. Leach spoke glowingly of how various ashes gave widely different results, inspiring Pleydell-Bouverie systematically to research wood-ash glazes. The clippings were carefully burnt and combined with feldspars and clays to produce glazes that ranged from soft blues and greens to pale creams and whites, mostly matt or silky in finish. Endless trials of species such as larch, laurustinus, rose, and honeysuckle were carried out and the results carefully recorded in copious notebooks.

The pots were thrown either on a Japanese wheel operated by a stick or on a treadle wheel. Typically Pleydell-Bouverie made full round vases, bottles, and bowls inspired by the simplicity of Song dynasty stonewares that were intended to show off the richness and depth of the ash glazes. Unlike her partner Norah Braden (known as Lise), who followed Mason and who had also studied with Leach, Pleydell-Bouverie rarely used brush decoration, preferring to create quiet but often spectacular glaze surfaces. Many of her finest pieces were made at this time, the Victoria and Albert Museum acquiring several handsome bowls and bottles in the late 1920s and 1930s. Her work was shown regularly in exhibitions in London galleries, such as Paterson's, Colnaghi's, and Burlington House, and at exhibitions organized by the Red Rose Guild in Manchester.

The Second World War brought production at Coleshill to an end, and after the war the house was sold and Pleydell-Bouverie moved to Kilmington Manor in Wiltshire. Here she set up a pottery in a vast old barn, where she built an oil kiln that proved difficult to fire; in 1960 she installed an electric kiln and continued to experiment with high-fired stonewares and porcelain and ash glazes. Kilmington Manor became a centre for visiting potters and collectors who were royally entertained by Beano and her close friend Robin Spark and their nine cats. The house was filled with classical Chinese ceramics, such as Tang figures, as well as pots made by friends.

In the late 1950s Pleydell-Bouverie became a founder member of the Craftsmen Potters' Association of Great Britain, and served on its council for several years, speaking at meetings, most often on the subject of ash glazes, on which she was an acknowledged expert. Leach had invited her to submit notes for his highly influential *A Potter's Book*, published in 1940. Later she was instrumental in helping to establish the Crafts Study Centre at the Holburne Museum in Bath, to which she presented a large collection of her best pots as well as glaze tests and notebooks. Important London exhibitions included a two-person show with Helen Pincombe at Primavera in 1958, the Craftsmen Potters' Shop in 1965, and the Casson Gallery in 1976. A major retrospective exhibition organized by the Crafts Study Centre in 1980 recognized her achievements. Fine examples of her work are now in York City Art Gallery. Katharine Pleydell-Bouverie died at Kilmington Manor on 9 January 1985.

Ever unassuming and dismissive of claims to be taken seriously as a potter, she was modest in estimation of her skills, while producing some of the strongest and most assured vessels in the merging of oriental form with modernist concepts of simplicity and truth to materials. Her pots, few taller than 30 cm, take on at their best a monumental quality, in which the inner volume is as significant as the outer shape, successfully marrying form, surface, and glaze with a conviction that has rarely been bettered.

EMMANUEL COOPER

Sources B. Roscoe, *Katharine Pleydell-Bouverie: a potter's life, 1895–1985* (1986) • S. Riddick, *Pioneer studio pottery* (1990) • O. Watson, *British studio pottery: the Victoria and Albert Museum collection* (1990) • E. Cooper and E. Lewenstein, 'Katharine Pleydell-Bouverie', *Ceramic Review*, 30 (Nov–Dec 1974), 4–6 • D. Leach, 'Katharine Pleydell-Bouverie', *Ceramic Review*, 92 (March–April 1985), 9 • K. Pleydell-Bouverie, 'At St Ives in the early years', *New Zealand Potter* (1960) [special issue, *Essays in appreciation of Bernard Leach*] • *Katharine Pleydell-Bouverie* (1980) [exhibition catalogue, Holburne Museum of Art, Bath] • *Katharine Pleydell-Bouverie* (1986) [exhibition catalogue, Gainsborough's House, Sudbury]

Archives Surrey Institute of Art and Design, Farnham, Crafts Study Centre collection and archive, notebooks and glaze tests

Likenesses M. Magnus, photograph, 1977, NPG [*see illus.*] • B. Boswell, photograph, repro. in Roscoe, *Katharine Pleydell-Bouverie*, frontispiece • photographs, Crafts Council Archive

Wealth at death £779,753: probate, 12 March 1985, *CGPLA Eng. & Wales*

Bouverie, William Pleydell-, third earl of Radnor (1779–1869), politician, was born on 11 May 1779 at 4 Grafton Street, Marylebone, Middlesex, the eldest son of Jacob Pleydell-Bouverie, second earl of Radnor (1750–1828), and his wife, Anne Duncombe (1759–1829), daughter of Lord Feversham. Viscount Folkestone, as he was styled until his father's death, witnessed the early stages of the French Revolution when sent to Paris as a boy to learn French. He was tutored at home and went for two years to the University of Edinburgh before commencing his studies at Brasenose College, Oxford, in 1795. His education culminated in a grand tour of the northern capitals of Europe from 1797 to 1799. On 2 October 1800 he married Catherine (1776–1804), daughter of Henry Fiennes Pelham-Clinton, earl of Lincoln. She died giving birth to a daughter in 1804. Folkestone's father arranged for his return to the House of Commons for the family borough of Downton in March 1801, followed quickly by translation to the more prestigious Bouverie seat at Salisbury, which he held from 1802 to 1828. The young viscount precociously broke with convention by making his maiden speech within a week of entering the chamber and established himself as a gadfly of government.

Although Folkestone aligned himself with the moderate William Windham during his first years in parliament, he quickly moved on to less conventional associations with Sir Francis Burdett and Samuel Whitbread. A pattern early emerged in his Commons career of impetuous and sometimes spiteful attacks on individuals such as lords Melville, Wellesley, Chatham, and members of the royal family. Folkestone rose to national prominence in 1809 as a principal prosecutor of the duke of York during a scandal involving the latter's mistress, Mary Anne Clarke, and the sale of military commissions, which led to the prince's resignation as commander-in-chief and personal disgrace.

Unfortunately, Folkestone's own subsequent dalliance with Mrs Clarke became public knowledge and undermined his credibility and stature. He recovered some popularity with a spirited attack on the government's repressive legislation in the post-Waterloo years, when he personified his dictum: 'If a nobleman cannot perform his obligation, which is to protect the liberties of all the people, then he has no reason to take part in politics' (Huch, 80). On 24 May 1814 he married his second wife, Anne Judith (1790–1851), daughter of Sir Henry St John-Mildmay, third baronet. They had four daughters and two sons, including the politician Edward Pleydell-*Bouverie.

Folkestone succeeded his father as third earl of Radnor in January 1828, and in the House of Lords he supported parliamentary reform, the new poor law, the abolition of slavery, and repeal of the corn laws. He took the lead in the movement to accord full rights to non-Anglicans at Oxford and Cambridge, bringing in bills to abolish subscription to the Thirty-Nine Articles (1835) and to revise college statutes (1837). He retired from politics in 1848, occupying himself with agricultural experimentation and philanthropy. Radnor died at his seat, Coleshill House, Berkshire, on 9 April 1869, and was buried at Britford, Wiltshire, on 15 April.

Radnor frittered away his influence through intemperance and unwillingness to accept responsibility. He rejected offers of junior office in 1806 and twice declined inclusion in Grey's cabinet, in 1833 and 1834. Though friendly with many whigs, he distrusted all who sought power. His father's repressive influence and a long friendship with William Cobbett distorted Radnor's perceptions of political reality. His hauteur and humourless sanctimony vitiated his considerable talents as a speaker and popular agitator. Canning lampooned Radnor's oratory, delivered 'with all the contortions of a Sybil without her inspiration' (Huch, 105). Radnor's advocacy of universal manhood suffrage, the secret ballot, annual parliaments, and disestablishment of the Church of England made him genuinely radical. His strong evangelical Anglican faith led Radnor to declare the corn laws unchristian. He sought atonement by making 'good use of his riches' (Brent, 125). His uncritical discipleship of the classical economists was, like his radicalism, unusual among the great landed magnates of his era, but Radnor left little in the way of a lasting legacy, except perhaps for *The Economist*, which his generous financial support helped to survive its birth pangs. His mixture of progressive ideas and aristocratic paternalism was more gracefully and effectively espoused by other whig grandees.

ELLIS ARCHER WASSON

Sources R. K. Huch, *The radical Lord Radnor: the public life of Viscount Folkestone, third earl of Radnor, 1779–1869* (1977) • R. G. Thorne, 'Bouverie, William Pleydell', HoP, *Commons* • *The Creevey papers*, ed. H. Maxwell, 2 vols. (1903) • Lord Holland [H. R. V. Fox] and J. Allen, *The Holland House diaries, 1831–1840*, ed. A. D. Kriegel (1977) • E. A. Wasson, *Whig renaissance: Lord Althorp and the whig party, 1782–1845* (1987) • R. Brent, *Liberal Anglican politics: whiggery, religion, and reform, 1830–1841* (1987) • GEC, *Peerage*

Archives Berks. RO, corresp. and papers • NRA, priv. coll., corresp. and papers • Pusey Oxf., corresp. and papers relating to university subscription • Wilts. & Swindon RO, corresp. and papers | BL, Cobbett MSS • BL, Holland House MSS • BL, corresp with Lord Holland, Add. MS 51566 • BL, Spencer MSS • BL, letters to William Windham, Add. MSS 37880–37883 • Devon RO, letters to duke of Somerset relating to estate business • UCL, Creevey MSS • UCL, corresp. with Edwin Chadwick • W. Sussex RO, letters to duke of Richmond

Likenesses M. L. E. Vigée-Lebrun, oils, 1799, Longford Castle, Wiltshire • D. Macdonald, pen-and-ink drawing, 1847, BM • S. Bellin, group portrait, mixed engraving, pubd 1850 (*Anti Corn Law League*; after J. R. Herbert), NPG, BM • oils, c.1860, Longford Castle, Wiltshire

Wealth at death under £160,000: probate, 1869, *CGPLA Eng. & Wales*

Bouyer, Reynold Gideon (1741–1826), Church of England clergyman, was born in London and baptized at the Huguenot church in Threadneedle Street on 6 January 1742, the son of John B. G. Bouyer and his wife, Elizabeth Chevalier. After education at Leiden in the Netherlands he matriculated in 1761 at Trinity College, Cambridge, and was elected as a scholar in 1762. In 1763 he migrated to Jesus College, where he graduated LLB in 1769. Having been ordained deacon in 1764, he served as a curate at Burwell, Cambridgeshire, and later as a chaplain to the duke of Ancaster. From 1771 to 1810 he was rector of Theddlethorpe and Willoughby St Helen, Lincolnshire. He became a prebendary of Sarum in 1785, and a prebendary of Durham in 1791. In 1810 he obtained the vicarage of Eglingham, Northumberland, which he exchanged for that of Northallerton in 1814. In 1812 he was collated to the archdeaconry of Northumberland, which he retained until his death at Durham in January 1826. He was buried in Durham Cathedral.

Bouyer published several sermons, and in 1789 prepared a new edition of *An account … of the society for the promotion of industry in the southern district of Lindsey*. He took an interest in education, instituting the first day school at Northallerton and publishing a short tract, *A Comparative View of the Two New Systems of Education for the Infant Poor* (1811), which reiterated commonplace fears about the influence of dissenting teachers. He established parochial libraries at his own expense in every parish in Northumberland. They contained more than 30,000 volumes, which cost him about £1400, although he was supplied with them by the Society for the Promotion of Christian

Knowledge at 40 per cent discount. These useful libraries were placed under the care of the parochial ministers, and the books were lent free of charge to the parishioners.

THOMPSON COOPER, *rev.* RICHARD SHARP

Sources M. A. Richardson, ed., *The local historian's table book … historical division*, 5 vols. (1841–6), vol. 3, pp. 323–4 • Venn, *Alum. Cant.* • R. G. Bouyer, *A comparative view of the two new systems of education for the infant poor* (1811) • *Fasti Angl.* (Hardy) • *IGI*
Archives Harvard U., Baker Library, notes relating to a bill to amend the poor law

Bovenschen, Sir Frederick Carl (1884–1977), civil servant, was born on 26 March 1884 in Forest Hill, London, he and his older sister being the only children of Carl Bovenschen, silk merchant, of Forest Hill, and his wife, Catherine Hoare. As a scholar of the King's School, Canterbury, his record in work and games was outstanding. He won an open classical scholarship to Corpus Christi College, Oxford, and obtained first classes in both classical honour moderations (1905) and *literae humaniores* (1907).

Bovenschen's initial appointment to the civil service, in March 1908, was as a clerk of the higher division in the War Office, and he remained in that department until his retirement in 1945. In November 1908 he became assistant private secretary to R. B. Haldane, secretary of state for war, whose timely reforms gave the army the strong and elastic structure that stood up to such stern tests in 1914. Four years in Haldane's office gave Bovenschen incomparable opportunities to grasp facts and principles fundamental to military organization. His next three years (1912–15) as private secretary to Sir Charles Harris, whose expertise in the scrutiny of army votes was famous, gave him parallel experience of finance in peace and war. He married on 1 February 1919 Mabel Alice (1891–1975), only daughter of Sir Arthur Herbert Dyke *Acland, thirteenth baronet; they had one daughter. In 1921 he became assistant secretary at the War Office, and in 1931 he was seconded to the government of India to serve on the army retrenchment committee.

Bovenschen had two conspicuous traits: persistent integrity of purpose and painstaking mastery of detail. These dominated his working life for half a century. They were subtly suggested by the strokes of his round, deliberate handwriting and by an occasional quizzical glance above half-moons of gold-rimmed spectacles. These traits together helped to get value for money—sometimes, in the eyes of his military colleagues, with unjustifiable severity—in many aspects of army expenditure for a decade after 1932. He was successively director of army contracts, from 1932; director of finance, from 1936; and finally deputy under-secretary of state for war, from 1936 to 1942. His integrity and conscientiousness combined more conspicuously, and with more unconditional appreciation, during the Second World War when he was charged with building, from inevitably ill-assorted pieces, a strong framework for the administration of occupied enemy territory. This was done through military government and civil affairs staffs set up under Anglo-American co-operation. The completion of this huge, unprecedented task in Europe owed more to Bovenschen than to anyone. From 1942 to 1945, as joint permanent under-secretary of state for war, he chaired the main committees concerned, reconciling conflicting interests of Whitehall departments and within the armed services. It fell to him to force awkward decisions affecting supplies, to enlist American co-operation (he twice visited Washington), and to apply, with the continuity essential in exasperatingly confused conditions, intellectual objectivity and powers of persuasion. It is widely accepted that shortcomings in military government, especially in the control commission for Germany, resulted not from the organization agreed on Bovenschen's committees but primarily from mistakes in staffing.

Retirement from the civil service in 1945 restricted the scope more than the quality of Bovenschen's work. Its benefits to Westminster Hospital and Kent county and Hythe borough councils covered the years until 1960, during which his broadly based if at times over-rigid financial judgement was applied on their governing bodies or main committees. It was also applied in less formal discussions in which, as throughout his public life, he never became heated, endearing himself to a new assortment of colleagues by a characteristic combination of charm and shrewdness.

Bovenschen was a dedicated and good-humoured golfer. On four or five of his favourite Kent courses his small, compact figure would, according to an admirer, 'lead the field like a light infantryman at a good 140 paces to the minute'. He had also enjoyed a slower pace—walking in the queen's coronation procession in his robes as a baron of the Cinque Ports (1953).

Among the pleasures of his eighties were a return to reading classical Greek, and practical interests in education which saw him involved in the managing committees of two schools for young children in Hythe, as well as a long-established role as a governor of the King's School, Canterbury. And there were richer rewards in the happiness of his home life. His wife had studied painting under Walter Sickert and her gentle, artistic temperament complemented her husband's punctilious devotion to duty. He seemed lost when she died in 1975. A solace in the last year of his life was the return of their only child and her husband from South Africa to settle in Hythe, where Bovenschen died on 9 November 1977.

Bovenschen was appointed chevalier of the Légion d'honneur (1920), CB (1927), KBE (1938), and KCB (1943).

V. G. F. BOVENIZER, *rev.* MARK POTTLE

Sources personal knowledge (1986) • private information (1986) • *The Times* (17 Nov 1977) • *WWW* • Burke, *Peerage*
Wealth at death £55,699: probate, 22 Feb 1978, *CGPLA Eng. & Wales*

Bovey, Catharina. *See* Boevey, Catherina (*bap.* 1670, *d.* 1726).

Bovill, Sewal de (*d.* 1257), archbishop of York, is of unknown origins. He attended Oxford University where he was a contemporary of Edmund of Abingdon; he was described by Matthew Paris as the 'disciple in the schools, pupil and fellow scholar' of the future archbishop, whose canonization he was later to support (Paris, 5.691). Edmund, who was greatly attached to Sewal, is said to have foretold his friend's promotion and troubles. By 1244, when he was chancellor of the university, Bovill was a doctor of theology. In 1236 he was made canon and prebendary of York, a position he still held in 1241, and canon and prebendary of Southwell; he also obtained the prebend of Fenton about 1247. Between 1245 and 1248 he was archdeacon of York, after which he became dean of that cathedral, retaining this post until his advancement to the episcopate in 1256. On the death of Archbishop Walter de Gray in 1255 the canons elected him to the vacant see, but the king refused his consent on the ground that Bovill was of illegitimate birth. The chapter appealed to Rome on 1 October, and eventually the pope granted a dispensation removing the defect of birth, and confirmed the election. The king gave his assent on 4 May 1256, and Bovill was consecrated at York on 23 July by Walter de Cantilupe, bishop of Worcester. Shortly after Sewal's consecration, Adam Marsh sent him a long letter of advice urging him to take Bishop Grosseteste as his example. The pope claimed the right to appoint to the now vacant deanery, and in 1257 an Italian, Jordan, was installed by his authority. Bovill resisted the intrusion, and as a consequence was suspended from his office and excommunicated. The dispute was resolved (and the excommunication therefore lifted) by the provision of a pension for Jordan, and Godfrey of Ludham was appointed as dean. In March of that year Bovill was granted a licence to visit the shrine of St Edmund at Pontigny, and on 20 July 1257 he was one of the commissioners appointed to decide the dispute between Alexander of Scotland and his nobles.

Bovill's rule as archbishop was troubled by his quarrel with the pope, whom on his deathbed he summoned to judgement. But his sufferings and resistance to papal intrusion won him great popularity. Matthew Paris describes him as, 'a humble and holy man well skilled in law and other sciences' (Paris, 5.516). However, despite assertions of John Bale (*d.* 1563), his only surviving work is a verse repeated by one of his clerks to Matthew Paris. Sewal de Bovill died on 10 May 1257 and was buried in the south transept of York Minster, where his tomb is marked by a marble slab bearing a cross.

C. L. Kingsford, *rev.* Philippa Hoskin

Sources Paris, *Chron.*, vol. 5 · C. T. Clay, ed., *York Minster fasti*, 2 vols., Yorkshire Archaeological Society, 123–4 (1958–9) · Emden, *Oxf.* · J. S. Brewer and R. Howlett, eds., *Monumenta Franciscana*, 2 vols., Rolls Series, 4 (1858–82) · J. Raine, ed., *The historians of the church of York and its archbishops*, 3 vols., Rolls Series, 71 (1879–94) · *CEPR letters* · *Ann. mon.*

Bovill, Sir William (1814–1873), judge, was born on 26 May 1814 at All Hallows, Barking, Essex, a younger son of Benjamin Bovill, corn merchant, of Durnford Lodge, Wimbledon. He did not go to university, but began his legal career in articles with solicitors in the city of London. He then practised as a special pleader below the bar, but soon joined Middle Temple. He was called to the bar in 1841, joining the home circuit. On 20 August 1844 he married Maria, eldest daughter of John Henry Bolton, of Lee Park, Blackheath; they had many children.

Bovill's familiarity with solicitors helped him at the bar. Another connection, with a firm of manufacturers in the East End of London, gave him some knowledge of engineering, which led to a considerable patent practice, in addition to the commercial cases which were his bread and butter. He became a QC in 1855 and was elected MP for Guildford in 1857, though he was not active in the House of Commons for several years. He did, however, take an interest in legal reform, and was responsible for two acts, the Petition of Right Act and the Partnership Law Amendment Act. In 1865 he pressed for the amalgamation of all the law courts into one building, and in 1866 for a better library at the Patent Office. On 6 July 1866 he was appointed solicitor-general in Lord Derby's last administration; but he held office for only five months. In November 1866 he succeeded Sir William Erle as chief justice of the common pleas, Sir John Karslake replacing him as solicitor-general. He had been elected treasurer of the Middle Temple a few months earlier, but resigned on being raised to the bench. In 1870 he was made honorary DCL of the University of Oxford, and was also elected a fellow of the Royal Society.

Bovill became famous throughout the country as judge in the first Tichborne trial, one of the most celebrated cases of the Victorian period, when he ordered the plaintiff, who claimed to be Roger, the long-lost son of the Tichbornes, to be indicted for perjury. He was much criticized for failing to appear impartial at the trial and was widely believed to have expressed his opinion against the claimant at a lord mayor's dinner before the trial opened. Bovill's admirers claimed that no judge was more learned, forceful, or acute, though even they admitted that he lacked eloquence. He was also praised for his memory and industry, and for scrupulously returning briefs if he did not feel that he could give them due attention. But he was widely believed to leap to conclusions before hearing all of the evidence, and the publicity which was given to his most controversial case continued to tarnish his reputation in public eyes. It was rumoured that he begged people not to mention the case to him, saying 'It weighs upon me' (Woodruff, 393). He fell ill in 1873 and was thought to be recovering when, at noon on 1 November 1873 he died of apoplexy at his home, Coombe House, Kingston upon Thames, Surrey. He had been appointed a member of the judicature commission in the same year, but his work on the midland circuit and then ill health prevented him from taking much part in its activities. His wife survived him.

J. A. Hamilton, *rev.* Mary Heimann

Sources *The Times* (1 Nov 1873) · *Law Journal* (8 Nov 1873), 657 · *Law Journal* (13 June 1874), 365 · *Law Magazine*, new ser., 13 (1862), 362 · *Law Magazine*, 3rd ser., 2 (1873), 28, 79, 368 · *Annual Register* (1873) · *Hansard 3* (1865), 178.194–6, (1866), 910, 930–31, 952, 956–7 · *QR*, 5 (1811), 139, 404, 409 · J. D. Woodruff, *The Tichborne claimant: a Victorian mystery* (1957), 166, 185–7, 190, 211, 242–3, 393 · m. cert. · d. cert. · *CGPLA Eng. & Wales* (1873)

Likenesses C. Silvy, carte-de-visite, *c.*1861, NPG · Ape [C. Pellegrini], caricature, chromolithograph, NPG; repro. in *VF* (8 Jan

1870), pl. 3 • London Stereoscopic Co., carte-de-visite, NPG • wood-engraving, NPG; repro. in *ILN* (15 Dec 1866)
Wealth at death under £60,000: resworn probate, Nov 1874, *CGPLA Eng. & Wales* (1873)

Bowack, John (*fl.* 1705–1737), writing master and topographer, was for many years a writing master at Westminster School. In 1705, when living in Church Lane, Chelsea, he began to publish, in folio numbers, *The Antiquities of Middlesex*, which contained a description of the church monuments in the county with a historical account of each church and parish, and the seats, villages, and names of the most eminent inhabitants. Two parts of this work appeared in 1705–6, comprising the parishes of Chelsea, Kensington, Fulham, Hammersmith, Chiswick, and Acton. A third part was promised, which would have covered Ealing, New Brentford, Isleworth, and Hanwell; but, lacking encouragement, Bowack proceeded no further. His skill in ornamental handwriting is demonstrated in BL, Harleian MS 1809, a thin vellum book containing two neat drawings in Indian ink and various kinds of English text and print hands. This was sent to Lord Oxford in December 1712 with a letter, in which Bowack expressed the hope that his little work might find a place in his lordship's library.

In July 1732 Bowack was appointed clerk to the commissioners of the turnpike roads, and in 1737 assistant secretary to the Westminster Bridge commissioners, with a salary of £100 a year. The date of his death is unknown.

GORDON GOODWIN, *rev.* J. A. MARCHAND

Sources C. R. J. Currie and C. P. Lewis, eds., *English county histories: a guide* (1994), 272 • A. Heal, *The English writing-masters and their copy-books, 1570–1800* (1931), 20 • R. G. [R. Gough], *British topography*, [new edn], 1 (1780), 537–8 • T. Faulkner, *An historical and topographical description of Chelsea, and its environs*, 2 vols. (1829), 1.161 • *GM*, 1st ser., 2 (1732), 877 • *GM*, 1st ser., 7 (1737), 515 • *N&Q*, 164 (1932), 400–02

Bowater, Sir Edward (1787–1861), army officer, was descended from a Coventry family, members of which were established in London and at Woolwich during the eighteenth century. From one of the latter, a wealthy landowner, the government purchased most of the land subsequently occupied by the artillery and others at Woolwich. Sir Edward was the only son of Admiral Edward Bowater of Hampton Court and his wife, Louisa, daughter of Thomas Lane and widow of G. E. Hawkins, sergeant-surgeon to George III. He was born in St James's Palace on 13 July 1787, was educated at Harrow School, and entered the army in 1804 as ensign in the 3rd foot guards, with which he served in the Peninsula from December 1808 to November 1809, in the Peninsula and south of France from December 1811 to the end of the war, and in the Waterloo campaign. He was present at the passage of the Douro, the capture of Oporto, the battles of Talavera, Salamanca, and Vitoria, the sieges of Burgos and San Sebastian, the passage of the Bidassoa, and the battles of Quatre Bras and Waterloo, and was wounded at Talavera and at Waterloo.

In 1837 Bowater left the Scots Fusilier Guards, after thirty-three years' service, on promotion to major-general; he was made a KCH the same year. On 22 May 1839 he married Emilia Mary, daughter of Colonel Michael Barne of Sotterley and Dunwich, Suffolk, sometime MP for Dunwich; they had one daughter, Louisa Mary *Knightley. Soon after the arrival of Prince Albert, Bowater was appointed his equerry; in 1846 became lieutenant-general and groom-in-waiting in ordinary to Queen Victoria, and in 1854 was promoted full general.

In 1861 the queen's youngest son, Prince Leopold, then eight years old, accompanied Bowater and his family to the south of France. Bowater, whose health had been failing, died at Cannes, aged seventy-three, on 14 December 1861, the day of Prince Albert's death.

H. M. CHICHESTER, *rev.* JAMES LUNT

Sources A. W. Woods, 'The pedigree of Sir Edward Bowater', ed. J. J. Howard, *Miscellanea Genealogica et Heraldica*, new ser., 2 (1877), 177–82 • *Hart's Army List* (1862) • *GM*, 3rd ser., 12 (1862), 109 • T. Martin, *The life of … the prince consort*, 5 vols. (1875–80) • Boase, *Mod. Eng. biog.* • *Dod's Peerage* (1858) • *IGI*
Archives W. Sussex RO, letters to duke of Richmond
Likenesses C. Silvy, carte-de-visite, 1860, NPG • W. Salter, group portrait, oils (*Waterloo banquet at Apsley House*), Wellington Museum, Apsley House, London • W. Salter, oils (*Waterloo banquet at Apsley House*), NPG
Wealth at death £2000: probate, 9 May 1862, *CGPLA Eng. & Wales*

Bowater, Sir Eric Vansittart (1895–1962), paper manufacturer and industrialist, was born in London on 16 January 1895, the third child and only son of Sir Frederick William Bowater (1867–1924), paper merchant, of London, and his wife, Alice Emily, daughter of Joseph Sharp, of Bognor Regis, Sussex. He was educated at Charterhouse, leaving there with the ambition of becoming a professional soldier. He was commissioned in the Royal Artillery and served from 1913 to 1917, but suffered wounds at Ypres in 1915 of such severity that he was later invalided out, putting an end to all possibility of following a military career.

During his lengthy and enforced convalescence Bowater gave thought to a new career and eventually joined his father and two uncles, Sir Thomas Vansittart *Bowater, of Hill Crest, first baronet (1862–1938), and Sir Frank Henry Bowater, of Friston, first baronet (1866–1947), in the family business, W. V. Bowater & Sons, in the City of London. At that time the company, which had been founded by his grandfather in 1881, operated purely as paper merchants. Although Bowater had no background technical knowledge of the paper industry he soon realized that the true potential of the family business was not in marketing other firms' products but in manufacturing the goods itself. With this end in view and in the face of some opposition, but with his father's backing, he planned the first Bowater paper mill at Northfleet in Kent. This was opened in 1926; Bowater was now managing director of the company, his father having died two years before.

It was during this stage of his career that Bowater learned to back his own judgement to the limit and, having enlisted the financial support of Lord Rothermere, he bought out his uncles in 1927. Thereafter he took full command of the company as its chairman, a position he continued to hold in the expanding Bowater organization for

Sir Eric Vansittart Bowater (1895–1962), by Wolfgang Suschitzky, 1960

thirty-five years until his death in 1962, when the total assets were close on £200 million.

It was characteristic of Bowater that he would never accept a negative attitude towards plans for future developments and his persistence in questioning every objection proved its worth in the success of his enterprises. It was a mark of the confidence which he inspired in others, as well as his own confidence in the future, that during this early period, in spite of severe financial stringency within the company, he decided to double the capacity of the Northfleet mill, a project completed in 1928. He thus correctly foresaw the need for the supply of newsprint to keep abreast of the accelerating pace of newspaper circulation. In 1929 he opened another newsprint mill at Ellesmere Port in Cheshire. This was designed to supply the press rooms in Manchester which printed northern editions of the London national dailies and the growing markets for provincial newspapers of the north.

In spite of industrial depression, Bowater's confidence in the future ensured for him the support of Lord Beaverbrook as well as Lord Rothermere in the venture at Ellesmere Port, and by the end of 1930 the mill was in production. Only two years later its capacity was doubled and subsequently both Rothermere and Beaverbrook's interests in the mill were acquired by Bowater.

Bowater took further steps towards his eventual goal of making his company one of the largest newsprint manufacturers in the world by acquiring in 1936 the Edward Lloyd paper mills at Sittingbourne and Kemsley in Kent and, setting his sights across the Atlantic, by purchasing in 1938 the newsprint and pulp mills at Corner Brook in Newfoundland. Although Bowaters had had a sales office in New York for many years, this was its first major industrial venture in North America. Soon afterwards the Second World War intervened and further development was temporarily halted.

In 1940, having been invited by Beaverbrook to join him in the Ministry of Aircraft Production, Bowater became its director-general. In 1945 he became controller. It was in recognition of his services in this field that a knighthood was bestowed upon him in 1944. During his five years at the ministry, he continued to control and plan for his firm, and when he eventually returned after the war he began to diversify.

To begin with, Bowater entered the packaging industry. A factory in Croydon, manufacturing corrugated containers, was acquired and extended, as were installations in various parts of the United Kingdom making many types of packaging based mainly on paper but also on plastics and foil. The range of papers made in addition to newsprint was considerably widened and the road transport fleet and other auxiliary services expanded. By the mid-1950s Bowaters was also handling by sea more than 1 million tons of raw materials and finished products. So that the organization might be self-sufficient to the extent of at least one half of its shipping needs, nine new ships were built in British yards.

In 1956 a highly successful partnership was entered into with the Scott Paper Company, one of the largest American manufacturers of domestic tissues. The joint company, called the Bowater-Scott Corporation, with Bowater as its chairman, was set up to manufacture soft tissues in Britain; new mills were built, first at Northfleet and later at Barrow in Furness. A parallel and equally successful development in tissues was embarked upon in Australia. Plans for expansion in North America, which had been interrupted by the war, were also resumed. In 1953, at a time when post-war restrictions and difficulties seemed to make such confidence a thing of the past, Bowater began what was probably his most outstanding enterprise, namely the conception, planning, and construction of a newsprint mill in the state of Tennessee, designed to serve the rapidly growing market in the southern United States. At a cost of $60 million, this was the largest newsprint mill in the United States, and represented the largest investment of British capital in that country since the war. Despite the shortage of dollars, the necessary consents for the equity investment were granted by the Bank of England. The Tennessee mill was extended in 1957 and in 1959, and in 1959 a large new pulp mill was built in South Carolina. Meanwhile Bowater established his company in the Common Market area long in advance of Britain's eventual entry into the EEC.

Bowater was so preoccupied with his business that his inner personality is difficult to assess. His appearance was well known; there could have been few readers of the financial press, and fewer Bowater employees and shareholders, who did not come to know and admire the clean-cut, commanding features. His tall, straight, military bearing and his colouring together combined to present a most distinguished appearance. He gave away little of his true self, however, and while always courteous to all who came into contact with him he remained aloof, though friendly—always a little remote and, to most people, perhaps impenetrable in his reserve; but these mannerisms were the instinctive defences of a fundamentally shy man.

Those who were close to Bowater, however, remembered his sudden smile and unexpected gestures of generosity, things which would break through the reserve. To those who shared his pride in his great organization he was their leader, who by his personal magnetism had welded them together into a family throughout the world, and to whom they owed complete loyalty. This they gave in full measure, holding him always in the highest esteem and affection and, it must be said, some awe. Bowater welcomed change as an ally; he never became comfortable or complacent, nor did he condone cosy half-efficiency, demanding much of those who served him.

Bowater was an officer of the Légion d'honneur and in 1948 was made FRSA. He was twice married. His first marriage, to Blanche Currie, *née* de Ville, in 1915, produced one daughter and ended in divorce. His second marriage, on 23 June 1937, was to Margaret Vivian (*d.* 1995), daughter of Charles Perkins, of Toronto, Canada; they had one daughter and one son. They lived at Dene Place, a 300 acre estate in West Horsley, Surrey, where, although international travel on his business took up much time, he was still able to follow his country pursuits of farming (he maintained a highly prized herd of pedigree Guernsey cattle) and shooting. He died there on 30 August 1962.

ROBERT KNIGHT, *rev.* ANITA MCCONNELL

Sources address by Sir Frank Lee at St Paul's Cathedral, Oct 1962 · personal knowledge (1962) · W. J. Reader, *Bowater, a history* (1981) · m. cert. [Margaret Vivian Perkins] · d. cert.

Likenesses W. Suschitzky, photograph, 1960, NPG [*see illus.*] · A. Zinkeisen, oils (after photograph by D. Glass, 1952), Bowater's United Kingdom Paper Co., London

Wealth at death £495,181 8*s.* 0*d.*: probate, 22 Jan 1963, *CGPLA Eng. & Wales*

Bowater, Sir Thomas Vansittart, first baronet (1862–1938), businessman and politician, was born on 20 October 1862 at Cheetham Hill, Manchester, the eldest child in the family of seven sons and two daughters of William Vansittart Bowater (1838–1907), paper merchant and agent, and his wife, Eliza Jane (*d.* 1912), daughter of Thomas Davey of Islington, London. Educated at Broughton College, Manchester, and at Stourbridge, he left school at a comparatively early age to enter the Manchester textile warehouse of J. and N. Phillips as an apprentice. Soon after the family moved back to London about 1880, he joined the family business. He married, on 8 June 1887, Emily Margaret (1867–1924), daughter of John Spencer of Croydon, with whom he had four sons and two daughters.

In 1889 Thomas Bowater (and two brothers) became partners in W. V. Bowater & Sons. As the buying agents from around 1890 for Alfred and Harold Harmsworth (later respectively viscounts Northcliffe and Rothermere), the company was closely connected with the largest and most successful of all the mass-market publishers and flourished accordingly. By 1900, however, the three brothers rebelled against their father's hard-drinking and tyrannical personality to assume joint control. In 1910 the partnership was turned into a relatively prosperous private company and in January 1914 the brothers decided to enter paper manufacture with the construction of their first paper mill at Northfleet, near Gravesend, Kent, although the intervention of the war ensured that it would not be in operation until 1926.

The company's growth to become by 1938 the world's largest manufacturer of newsprint owed most to the dynamic personality of Bowater's nephew Sir Eric Vansittart *Bowater. Tension between Eric's restless entrepreneurial spirit and his more conservative uncles was resolved with the enforced removal of Thomas Bowater from both the chairmanship and the board (along with his brother Frank) in November 1927. Yet in reality, as the company's historian notes, for some years, the outgoing chairman had 'presided with dignity over the affairs of the firm rather than actively managing them' (Reader, 25).

From at least 1904 Bowater had left his two younger brothers to run the business while he devoted most of his time to public life in the City of London. Having become a freeman in July 1897, he soon became a member of the City board of guardians. After an unsuccessful contest in 1898, he was elected as a common councilman for Vintry ward from 1899 to 1907 serving as chairman of the cattle markets committee in 1903 and the central markets committee in 1905. In 1905 Bowater was also elected as one of the City's two sheriffs and at the end of his term he received a knighthood (June 1906). On 28 August 1907 he was comfortably elected as alderman of Castle Baynard ward, a position he occupied until 1931, when he transferred to the ward of Bridge Without. In 1913 Bowater became lord mayor and soon after (16 July 1914) he was created a baronet. Lord mayor at the outbreak of the First World War (his son Frank held the same office at the outbreak of the Second World War), he was recalled from a motor tour of France only three days before war was declared. He immediately rallied the City, raising a new battalion of the City of London regiment and organizing relief works, particularly for Belgian refugees.

Bowater stood as an independent Conservative in the City of London by-election on 19 May 1922 on a vigorous economy platform. Although the tide had clearly receded since the Anti-Waste League's by-election victories of the previous year, he still polled 6178 votes to the 10,114 for his official Conservative opponent. Standing as a Conservative at another by-election in the City of London in February 1924, he easily defeated his Liberal opponent by 12,962 votes to 5525. He held his seat in this double-member constituency until his death.

Bowater's back-bench parliamentary career was undistinguished: his contribution was confined largely to a few brief questions and interventions either advocating protectionism for the newsprint industry or defending the interests of his constituency. His only significant speech, in March 1931, was a brief but spirited defence of the retention of the business vote for the City of London when all other such qualifications were to be abolished by clause 3 of the unsuccessful Representation of the People (no. 2) Bill. After his first wife's death in 1924, on 12 August 1925 he married Alice Mary (*d.* 1949), widow of Archibald Coysgarne Sim of Harrow Weald Park. Bowater died at his home, 53 Hans Mansions, London, on 28 March 1938.

ROBERT C. SELF

Sources GL, Noble collection [various press cuttings] · *The Times* (29 March 1938) · *Dod's Peerage* · W. J. Reader, *Bowater: a history* (1981) · *The greetings of the ward of Castle Baynard to its alderman, the Rt Hon Sir T. Vansittart Bowater, bt, lord mayor of London, 19 Nov 1913* (1913) [At London Guildhall Library] · A. B. Beaven, ed., *The aldermen of the City of London, temp. Henry III–[1912]*, 2 vols. (1908–13) · m. cert.

Archives GL, Noble collection · GL, diary of mayoralty | FILM BFI NFTVA, news footage

Wealth at death £74,195 4*s.* 1*d.*: probate, 23 May 1938, *CGPLA Eng. & Wales*

Bowden, Sir Frank, first baronet (1848–1921), cycle manufacturer, was born on 30 January 1848 in Bristol, the son of William Bowden (*d.* 1866), a Bristol manufacturer, and his wife, Louise (*d.* 1879), daughter of Henry White of Bath. Bowden's grandfather had also been engaged in manufacturing in the Bristol area. The death of Bowden's father cut short his education and he took up an apprenticeship in a solicitor's office in London. Four years later he secured a post in the office of the principal law officer, Hong Kong, where he rose to a senior position and amassed a personal fortune dealing throughout the Far East in real estate, stocks, and shares.

By 1878 Bowden's health began to break down and he decided to satisfy his interest in travel. He moved to San Francisco and in 1879 met and married Amelia Frances (*d.* 1937), daughter of Colonel Alexander Houston, one of the pioneers of California State. In 1885 he visited Harrogate in England and sought medical advice regarding his ill health. He was advised to take up the pastime of cycling and purchased a second-hand tricycle, on which he rode in the winter and early spring of 1886–7. Impressed by the benefits to his health, and recognizing the potential that cycling had to offer, Bowden visited the makers of his tricycle, Angois, Woodhead, and Ellis of Nottingham, and persuaded the company to accept him as its financial backer.

In January 1889 the Raleigh Cycle Company was incorporated and in 1891, after a disappointing public flotation, Bowden acquired a controlling interest. The 1890s witnessed considerable growth in the cycle industry and the Raleigh Cycle Company Ltd grew significantly through its advertising campaigns, its racing successes, and by building a thriving export business. By 1896 the company had been floated with a capital of £200,000, although Bowden retained a substantial share of this. When the cycle industry witnessed a slump in 1898 Bowden was in a position personally to manage the financial crisis while the firm underwent restructuring. In 1908 another financial crisis arose after substantial debts were incurred by the company, and Bowden was prepared to secure the debts on his personal fortune only if he had complete ownership. Raleigh was to remain a private company until a £2 million public flotation in 1934.

Bowden made a substantial contribution to Raleigh's success. Although seen as an autocrat by some, he was prepared to entrust aspects of the management to those with talents he recognized. He could be single-minded at times, particularly in his severance with Woodhead and Angois who ceased to serve on the board after 1894. There were failed ventures, such as Bowden's promotion of wooden rims for cycles, which demonstrate that he was not infallible, but Bowden did recognize the significance of American manufacturing methods and marketing and his company was among the UK pioneers of sheet steel pressings and liquid brazing in connection with cycle manufacture. Being an active cyclist Bowden was one of the first English manufacturers to recognize the potential benefits which pneumatic tyres and variable gears had to offer. In January 1903 he founded the Three-Speed Gear Syndicate Ltd, which became the Sturmey Archer Gear Company in June 1908.

Bowden became a public figure; at local level he was a JP for Nottingham and at national level he wrote widely on his travels, being elected a fellow of the Royal Geographical Society about 1906. His main publication on cycling was *Cycling for Health and Points for Cyclists* (1913). In 1915 he received a baronetcy for turning the Raleigh works to munitions manufacture. He died of heart failure at his home, Bestwood Lodge, Bestwood Park, Arnold, Nottinghamshire, on 25 April 1921. His only son, Harold, succeeded to the baronetcy and assumed control of the company.

Sir Harold Bowden, second baronet (1880–1960), born in San Francisco on 9 July 1880, was educated at Clifton College, Bristol, then went to Lausanne to study languages before entering Clare College, Cambridge. His studies were prematurely ended in 1899 when his father brought him into the business and in 1905 he was elected to the board as a director. Despite suffering ill health as a boy, as a young man he was a cyclist and keen athlete. In later years he was a supporter of the athletics movement and acted as a fund-raiser for, as well as serving as chairman of, the British Olympic Association in 1931–5. He maintained a high public profile, writing and broadcasting on the activities of the company and promoting cycling in the popular media. Throughout his life he held senior offices in cycle trade associations and employers' associations and at local level served as high sheriff of Nottingham in 1933.

Harold, too, chose to delegate to others, as his father had done. While not a major innovator he did recognize the potential of American methods of scientific management and his visit to Henry Ford's works in America in 1921 clearly had an influence on his policy while managing director. His concern was to retain the reputation for the quality of the product while reducing costs of production. While this led to occasional disputes with the shop-floor workers, he sought harmonious industrial relations and introduced profit-sharing schemes and invested in workers' welfare. In 1938 he retired as managing director of the Raleigh Cycle Company: he retained his chairmanship of the Raleigh Cycle Holdings Company Ltd (which had been founded in 1934), and later served as a director of Lloyds Bank. Among his honours was the appointment as GBE in 1929, and the award of the grand cross of the order of the Phoenix (Greece) awarded in 1932. In 1948 he was elected a fellow of the Royal Society of Arts.

Harold Bowden married four times. His first marriage, to Vera, daughter of Joseph Whitaker JP, on 7 July 1908, was dissolved in 1919. He married Muriel Smythe, divorcée and daughter of William Ker-Douglas, on 18 January 1920. After her death in 1952 he married on 4 November 1952 June Schenker, divorcée and daughter of Christopher T. H. Mackay, who died in the following year. On 11 February 1957 he married Valérie Came-Porter, widow of Albert Renfrew Porter and daughter of Richard Raymont-Came. He had one son, Frank, and one daughter, Ruth, from his first marriage. His home for many years was the Old Farm House, Marsh Court, Stockbridge; he died in the Royal Hampshire County Hospital, Winchester, on 24 August 1960. ANDREW MILLWARD

Sources *Bicycling News and Motor Review* (25 May 1921), 28–9 · *Cycling* (28 April 1921), 313 · *The Times* (25 Aug 1960) · H. Bowden, 'The growth and history of the Raleigh Cycle Co. Ltd' [in possession of the firm] · G. H. Bowden, *The story of the Raleigh cycle* (1975) · A. E. Harrison, 'Growth, entrepreneurship and capital formation in the United Kingdom's cycle and related industries', PhD diss., University of York, 1977 · Raleigh Cycle Co. Ltd, Directors and General Meetings' minutes, 1891–1908 · Raleigh Cycle Co. Ltd Board, General and fortnightly meetings' minutes, 1915–39 · F. Bowden, *Cycling for health and points for cyclists* (1913) · H. Bowden, 'We increased sales 42.8% this year', *System: The Magazine of Business*, 42 (1922), 429–31, 482 · H. Bowden, 'The fork in the road', *Pall Mall Magazine* (May 1929), 67–70 · H. Bowden, 'On cyclists, motorists and others', typescript of BBC radio broadcast, 1930, priv. coll. · *WWW* · Walford, *County families* · d. cert. · d. cert. [Harold Bowden] · A. E. Harrison, 'Bowden, Sir Harold', *DBB* · Burke, *Peerage*

Archives Notts. Arch., The Raleigh Archive

Wealth at death £475,239 1*s*. 7*d*.: probate, 25 Nov 1921 · £932,457 11*s*. 6*d*.—Harold Bowden: probate, 21 Sept 1960

Bowden, Frank Philip (1903–1968), experimental physicist, was born on 2 May 1903, at Hobart, Tasmania, the sixth of the seven children of Frank Prosser Bowden, telegraph and telephone manager for Tasmania, and his wife, Grace Elizabeth Hill. Both his parents were Tasmanian. He was educated at the Hutchins School, Hobart, and, in spite of difficulties with mathematics and having failed at his first attempt, in 1921 he matriculated successfully, entering the University of Tasmania as a science student. He was never good at mathematics and this influenced all his later researches in which he always chose an approach which provided answers without the need for mathematical analysis. In his second year as a student he fell ill and spent six months in the back blocks of New South Wales, but returned completely recovered to continue his university studies with the strong encouragement of A. I. McAuley, later professor of physics. He graduated in 1924. His first researches with McAuley on electrochemistry were

Frank Philip Bowden (1903–1968), by Edward Leigh, 1960

published in 1925 and later that year he became the first recipient of a scholarship provided by the Electrolytic Zinc Company of Australia. In the same year he obtained his MSc degree with first-class honours, and the following year he was awarded an 1851 Exhibition scholarship and left to work under Eric Rideal in Cambridge.

Bowden was admitted as a research student at Gonville and Caius College in 1927 and began research with Rideal on electrode potentials. This, like the earlier work with McAuley, was concerned with the processes occurring at the surface of the electrode during electrolysis and was the precursor of a sustained and broader interest in the general field of surface science. He became a fellow of Caius in 1929. In the 1930s he was involved in a collaborative research project with C. P. Snow on the photochemistry of vitamins and, although the conclusions proved to be faulty, this phase marked the beginning of a lifelong friendship. In his later novels on Cambridge life, Snow drew on Bowden as the prototype of Getliffe, the gifted, wise, and sensitive scientist. In 1931 Bowden married Margot Grace, daughter of Robert Hutchison, architect and engineer, of Hobart, Tasmania. They had three sons and one daughter. His eldest son, Piers Bowden (1937–1974) was a gifted polymer scientist.

Bowden soon moved on to a study of surface phenomena related to friction and lubrication. In this field he pioneered a scientific approach to an applied problem and established for himself and his research group a worldwide reputation in the field. It was during this period that he developed his ideas of the physics of skiing, combining scientific research with pleasurable field experiments. In 1933 he was awarded the Tasmanian DSc degree, and in 1938 the Cambridge ScD.

In 1939 after a lecture tour in America Bowden decided to return via Australia where his wife and first child had meanwhile arrived direct from England. The Second World War broke out and he was asked to establish a research laboratory under the Council for Scientific and Industrial Research (forerunner of the Commonwealth Scientific and Industrial Research Organization) to deal with friction, lubrication, wear, and bearing problems associated with the Australian war effort. The laboratory, later known as the division of tribophysics, also became involved in studies of the initiation and growth of explosions, a field in which Bowden again made original contributions of outstanding importance.

After the war Bowden returned to Cambridge and, with support from the Ministry of Supply (air), set up a research group to continue his work on explosives and friction. The high-speed photographic techniques which he developed for his explosive studies were later applied to the study of impact, erosion, and fracture, and this area of research again proved fruitful and original. It is a reflection of Bowden's catholic interests that he was called upon to organize three Royal Society discussions—on friction, on explosives, and on deformation by impact. Other areas of work included the direct study of surface forces and the mechanical and structural properties of high-temperature solids such as the carbides and borides of transition metals.

It was characteristic of Bowden's attitude to research that he recruited his students from several fields so that, long before it became fashionable, his group was in practice interdisciplinary. He showed a keen interest in applying fundamental science to practical problems, recognizing that applied science could be as intellectually challenging and rewarding as pure science. Although his experiments were basically simple in concept, he recognized the need for sophisticated and specialized equipment, the development of which he did much to foster.

Bowden had been made a director of studies in natural sciences at Cambridge in 1933 and a reader in physical chemistry in 1946. Ten years later, when the physical chemistry department began to move into new accommodation, he changed his affiliations and became a reader in physics (1957). His laboratory became a subdepartment of the Cavendish and in 1966 he was appointed *ad hominem* to a chair in surface physics, an appointment which gave him great pleasure.

Apart from his university commitments Bowden showed a keen interest in co-operating with industry. In 1953 he was appointed adviser to Tube Investments Ltd (TI), and in 1954 established for it a research laboratory at Hinxton with a view to contributing to the general pool of fundamental scientific knowledge and to the commercial needs and benefit of TI. The laboratory proved itself and four of its leading members became fellows of the Royal Society.

In 1958 Bowden was elected a director of the English Electric Company and played an important part in stimulating and co-ordinating its research efforts. He also served on a number of government scientific and technical committees, his most long-term involvement being that as chairman of the executive committee of the National Physical Laboratory (1955–62). He greatly enjoyed his contacts with industry and the broader world of affairs as well as the rewards that these contacts provided, yet he refused several important appointments which would have meant leaving his laboratory in Cambridge. Indeed, his deepest and most sustained interest throughout his life was his laboratory and the challenge and excitement of scientific work.

Bowden served as president of the Cambridge Philosophical Society (1957), as president of the Cambridge Alpine Club (from 1965), and as vice-president of the Faraday Society (1953–6). In later years he was something of an elder statesman, bringing his wisdom and equanimity to bear on complex college problems. He was elected a fellow of the Royal Society in 1948 and awarded its Rumford medal in 1956. He received the Redwood medal of the Institute of Petroleum in 1953, the Elliott Cresson medal of the Franklin Institute in 1955, and the medal of the Société Française de Métallurgie in 1957. In 1954 he delivered the Hawkesley lecture of the Institution of Mechanical Engineers and in 1967 the Kelvin lecture of the Institution of Electrical Engineers. In 1968 he was awarded the Glazebrook medal and prize of the Institute of Physics and the Physical Society and in the same year the Bernard Lewis gold medal of the Combustion Institute of America. He was made CBE in 1956.

Bowden's researches were characterized by simplicity and elegance. His approach was direct and his conclusions clear and uncomplicated. He was recognized as an experimental scientist of great originality and in almost every field which he touched he provided some germinal idea of value and importance. Although his approach was highly individual he was able to establish a research school not once but three times: at Melbourne in tribophysics, at Hinxton for TI, and at the Cavendish. Apart from his gifts as a scientific leader Bowden showed a great personal interest in the well-being of his staff, who recognized that he could be relied upon in times of need. Consequently, all the laboratories in which he was involved were happy institutions.

Bowden was a lightly built man with fine features, a certain measure of reserve, and considerable charm. All his life he showed a capacity for hard work and was possessed of outstanding stamina and reserves of intellectual energy. He had a sensitive and discerning taste in literature and art and an aesthetic sense which was discernible in his science as well as in his broader cultural interests. His hobbies included skiing, mountaineering, and tennis. He died of lung cancer at his home, Finella, West Queens Road, Cambridge, after a protracted illness on 3 September 1968. DAVID TABOR, *rev.*

Sources D. Tabor, *Memoirs FRS*, 15 (1969), 1–38 • T. Bowden, *The way my father tells it* (1989) • 'Profile of Dr F. P. Bowden: penetration, judgement and ideas galore', *New Scientist* (19 May 1960), 1266–7

Likenesses E. Leigh, photograph, 1960, repro. in *Memoirs FRS*, opposite p. 1 [*see illus.*] · photograph, RS
Wealth at death £5126: probate, 23 Jan 1969, *CGPLA Eng. & Wales*

Bowden, Sir Harold, **second baronet** (1880–1960). *See under* Bowden, Sir Frank, first baronet (1848–1921).

Bowden, Herbert William [Bert], **Baron Aylestone** (1905–1994), politician, was born on 20 January 1905 at 16 Taff Embankment, Cardiff, the eldest of eleven children of Herbert Henwood Bowden, baker's assistant, later baker and confectioner, and his wife, Henrietta, *née* Gould. After a council school education, he worked as a shop assistant then commercial clerk, took night classes, and joined the Independent Labour Party. On 4 April 1928 Bert (as he was known) married Louisa Grace (1901/2–1992), daughter of William Brown, dock rigger, of Cardiff. They had one daughter. Following a failed attempt with his own tobacconist's shop, Bowden moved in 1933 with his family to Leicester, where he worked as a radio salesman and in 1938 became a Labour city councillor (having left the Independent Labour Party). During the Second World War he served as a military policeman and then as an administrative officer in the RAF.

Bowden emerged from war service with the rank of flying officer to become the Labour MP for Leicester South, defeating Captain Charles Waterhouse, a tory MP of the old school, by 1100 votes in the general election of 1945. Boundary changes in 1948 made it a safe Labour seat as Leicester South-West during the whole of his Commons service. Bowden's military bearing, ram-rod figure, and neat moustache earned him the sobriquet the Sergeant-Major; his dependability earned him appointment as parliamentary private secretary to the postmaster-general, Wilfred Paling, in 1947, and promotion to junior lord of the Treasury in 1950. When Labour began thirteen years of opposition in 1951 he became deputy chief whip to the veteran William Whitely, in post since 1942. He was made a CBE in 1953. In 1955 Whitely reluctantly made way for Bowden. Bowden immediately showed his mettle as a chief whip by privately convincing an equally reluctant Clement Attlee that it was time to retire and make way for Hugh Gaitskell.

As chief whip, Bowden was known as a 'stickler for standing orders' and a 'real believer in the value of discipline' (*The Independent*, 2 May 1994). He became one of Gaitskell's inner circle, and when Gaitskell died in 1963 it was Bowden who summoned a 'regency council' to deal with the succession. He instructed the opposition whip's office to be studiously neutral in the contest, but privately supported Harold Wilson against George Brown and James Callaghan. Although never as close to Wilson as he was to Gaitskell, Bowden became lord president of the council in the 1964 Labour government. Wilson praised his 'quiet efficiency' as leader of the house, but in August 1966 sought a more inventive approach to parliamentary reform from Richard Crossman. Bowden became, briefly, Commonwealth secretary dealing with the Rhodesian crisis, but much under the shadow of the prime minister; he attended the ill-fated talks with Ian Smith aboard HMS *Tiger*, but resigned shortly after, in August 1967.

Bowden's strength lay in behind-the-scenes handling of affairs, and in 1967 he was glad to leave the Commons with a peerage (as Baron Aylestone) to become the chairman of the Independent Television Authority (later the IBA), where he was a great success. According to the historian of the IBA Bernard Sendall, he had 'a gift for making many friends and few enemies' (Sendall and Potter, 2.90). He served two terms until 1975 as chairman and, in a tribute to his political impartiality in this sensitive role, was made a Companion of Honour. He received the unfavourable publicity of being cited in a divorce case in 1976. Bowden resumed an active political role in 1981 as first leader of the Social Democrat peers in the House of Lords, but made way for Lord Diamond in 1982. He served as a deputy speaker in the House of Lords from 1984 to 1992. His first wife having died in 1992, on 7 May 1993 he married Vera Ivy (Vicki) Clayton, a retired secretary, and daughter of Donald Smith, engineer. He died on 30 April 1994 at Worthing Hospital of heart failure; he was survived by his second wife and the daughter of his first marriage.

GEORGE THOMSON

Sources *WWW*, 1991–5 · *The Times* (2 May 1994) · *The Independent* (2 May 1994) · H. Wilson, *The labour government, 1967–70* (1971) · D. Owen, *Time to declare* (1991) · P. Ziegler, *Wilson* (1993) · R. H. S. Crossman, *The Crossman diaries: selections*, ed. A. Howard (1979) · P. Paterson, *Tired and emotional: life of George Brown* (1993) · B. Sendall and J. Potter, *Independent television in Britain*, 2–3 (1983–9) · private information (2004) · personal knowledge (2004) · b. cert. · m. certs. · d. cert. · *CGPLA Eng. & Wales* (1994)
Archives Independent Television Commission, London | SOUND BL NSA, party political recording · HLRO, television sound archives · Independent Television Commission, London, Independent sound archives
Likenesses photograph, repro. in *The Times* · photograph, repro. in *The Independent*
Wealth at death £146,767: probate, 23 June 1994, *CGPLA Eng. & Wales*

Bowden, John (*d.* 1750), Presbyterian minister, may have been the brother of Samuel *Bowden (*fl.* 1733–1761), physician and poet, of Frome, Somerset, but he also has been identified by Walter Wilson with the Bowden who studied under Henry Grove at Taunton. This is apparently an error, however, for Bowden was settled at Frome before 1700 as assistant to Humphrey Philips, who had been silenced at Sherborne, Dorset, in 1662, whereas Grove did not set up his academy until 1706. Bowden became sole minister on Philips's death in 1707, and the meeting-house in Rook Lane was built for him that year. According to Evans's list he had 1000 hearers in 1717, among whom was Elizabeth Rowe, the dissenting poet, whose funeral sermon he preached in 1737. Bowden himself was a poet: although he does not seem to have published any separate volume of poetry, he contributed two poems to the collection of *Divine Hymns and Poems on Several Occasions* (1704) by Philomela (probably Elizabeth Rowe) and 'several other ingenious persons'. During the last nine years of his ministry Bowden was assisted by Alexander Houston (1741), Samuel Blyth (1742), Samuel Perrott, and Josiah Corrie (1750), who succeeded him.

Bowden published four separate sermons, including *A Sermon Preached at Taunton before an Assembly of Ministers* (1714). With its provocative emphasis on reason, individual judgement, and moral duties, the sermon clearly demonstrates his support for the ideas of the most liberal wing of dissent, which developed into the non-subscribing party after the Salters' Hall controversy. His 'Exhortation' at the ordination of Thomas Morgan was published in 1717, together with the sermon preached on the occasion, 'The conduct of ministers', by Nicholas Billingsley, minister of Ashwick, Somerset. Henry Chandler, minister at Bath and father of Samuel Chandler, added a preface to the work which was published under the title *A Sermon Preached at the Ordination of Mr Thomas Morgan*, and this reached a third edition in 1719. Morgan was Independent minister at Bruton, Somerset, and afterwards at Marlborough, Wiltshire, and an active pamphleteer for the non-subscribers' cause. After being forced from his ministry for heresy, he published the notorious deist work *The Moral Philosopher* (1737). That Morgan, an Independent, went to Frome for Presbyterian ordination has been treated as an indication of the theological divergence of the two bodies, but Bowden's confession of faith appears strongly trinitarian and Calvinistic. It does, however, reveal a fascination with Newtonian science, which suggests his receptivity to the latest intellectual trends.

Bowden's involvement with the future deist Morgan, and with the Arian Billingsley, who sheltered the heterodox Hubert Stogdon and James Foster at his home, provides a clue to his own sympathies. In 1718 he was to participate, again with Billingsley, in the more controversial ordination of Stogdon himself at Shepton Mallet, when it appeared that the Exeter assembly would not approve him. Bowden and Billingsley were greatly blamed by the orthodox ministers in Devon for their involvement in this affair, which prompted a flurry of anxious letters to London lamenting the defection of many younger ministers to Arianism. The controversy culminated in the Salters' Hall debates. Underlying the willingness of Bowden and Billingsley to flout the orthodoxy imposed by the subscription party was a more fundamental commitment to scripture as the only rule of faith, and a consequent antipathy to that 'tyrannical, anti-Christian tenet' which allowed any men to 'domineer and dictate in matters of conscience' (Billingsley, *Sermon … Hubert Stogdon*, 32; J. Bowden, *Sermon Preached at Taunton*, 1714, 24). For them, the partisan divisions engendered by the imposition of human creeds threatened to undermine Christianity itself. Bowden also worked closely with Nicholas Billingsley's nephew and eventual successor at Ashwick, Samuel Billingsley, whose ordination sermon he preached in 1725; this was printed for another Somerset friend, Samuel Chandler, then a bookseller, as well as a minister, in London. Bowden's sermon *The Vanity of All Human Dependence* (1727) was dedicated to the liberal (and heterodox) Benjamin Avery, to whom he was under 'particular obligations'.

Bowden died in Frome on 8 January 1750. A tablet on the front of his meeting-house commemorates him as 'a learned man, an eloquent preacher, and a considerable poet'. Subsequent lines refer to rising 'storms about the good man', which may allude to a Trinitarian secession from his ministry, a charge given weight by Josiah Thompson, who wrote that the meeting at Frome divided as a result of disputes under Bowden's ministry (James, 676; Thompson, fol. 176*r*). Little is known of Bowden's family except that his wife survived him. In January 1750 one Anne Yerbury of Bradford sent his widow a consolatory letter praising Bowden's poetical powers. Bowden was possibly the grandfather of Joseph Bowden, minister at Call Lane, Leeds, for over forty years, from about 1778, who published *Sermons Delivered to the Protestant Dissenters at Leeds* and *Prayers and Discourses for the Use of Families, in Two Parts* (1816). JIM BENEDICT

Sources C. G. Bolam and others, *The English presbyterians: from Elizabethan puritanism to modern Unitarianism* (1968) • T. S. James, *The history of the litigation and legislation respecting Presbyterian chapels and charities in England and Ireland between 1816 and 1849* (1867), 676, 693, 695 • R. Wallace, *Anti-trinitarian biography*, 3 vols. (1850), vol. 3, p. 603 • *N&Q*, 3rd ser., 4 (1863), 431, 504 • 'Memoirs of himself, by Mr John Fox … with biographical sketches of some of his contemporaries; and some unpublished letters [pt 8]', *Monthly Repository*, 16 (1821), 569–75, esp. 573 • T. Belsham, 'A list of students educated at the academy at Daventry [pt 2]', *Monthly Repository*, 17 (1822), 195–8, esp. 196 • N. Billingsley, *A sermon occasioned by the death of the late Revd. Mr. Hubert Stogdon* (1728), 34 • N. Billingsley, *A sermon preached at the ordination of Mr. Thomas Morgan* (1717) • DWL, Wilson MSS • J. Thompson, 'History of protestant dissenting congregations', DWL, MS 38.10 • *DNB*

Bowden, John William (1798–1844), ecclesiastical writer, was born in London on 21 February 1798, the eldest son of John Bowden, a director of the Bank of England, and his wife, Mary Anne. In 1812 he went to Harrow, and in 1817 entered Trinity College, Oxford, at the same time as J. H. Newman. From their first meeting, the day after Newman's arrival, they were inseparable companions throughout their undergraduate career. Together they wrote and published *St Bartholomew's Eve* (1818), a poem in two cantos with a romantic plot of young love thwarted by a scheming priest, and edited *The Undergraduate*, a short-lived periodical that ran to six weekly numbers in 1819. Bowden took mathematical honours in 1820, and proceeded MA in June 1823. In the autumn of 1826 he was appointed a commissioner of stamps and held the office for fourteen years. On 6 June 1828 he married Elizabeth, youngest daughter of Sir John Edward Swinburne, bt, of Capheaton. The poet Algernon Swinburne was her nephew.

From 1833 Bowden was a fervent adherent of the Tractarian movement. To H. J. Rose's *British Magazine* he contributed six of the 178 hymns later published under the title *Lyra apostolica* (1836). His contributions are signed α. He was one of Newman's first collaborators on the Tracts for the Times, to which he himself contributed numbers 5, 29, 30, 56, and 58. Between 1836 and 1841 he published four major articles in the *British Critic*: 'Rise of the papal power', 'On Gothic architecture', 'On British association', and 'On the church in the Mediterranean'.

In the spring of 1839 Bowden felt the first symptoms of

the tuberculosis which five years later proved fatal. In the autumn of 1839 he went abroad with his family and spent the winter in Malta. In the spring of 1840 he published his *Life of Gregory the Seventh*, a work first suggested to him by Hurrell Froude. The last work published during his lifetime, *A Few Remarks on Pews* (1843), was an eloquent protest against a practice he denounced as unchristian and discriminatory.

During the summer of 1843 Bowden's health began to fail rapidly. Newman, then on the brink of his Rubicon, could not bring himself to disturb his friend's peace of mind by discussing his dilemma, but was his constant companion in his last days. Bowden died at his father's house in Grosvenor Place on 15 September 1844 and was buried at Fulham, his childhood home. Though he died in full communion with the Church of England, his widow followed Newman into the Roman Catholic church in July 1846, together with her children. Her two sons later became priests of the London Oratory, and the elder, John Edward, was the biographer of F. W. Faber. One of her two daughters became a nun. She herself lived to attend Newman's funeral. John Bowden's posthumous *Thoughts on the Work of the Six Days of Creation* (1845) was prefaced by a short biographical notice contributed by Newman, who also evoked their friendship in his *Apologia* (1864).

G. MARTIN MURPHY

Sources J. H. N. [J. H. Newman], Preface, in J. W. Bowden, *Thoughts on the work of the six days of creation* (1845), v–viii · *The letters and diaries of John Henry Newman*, ed. C. S. Dessain and others, [31 vols.] (1961–), vols. 1–10 · S. Gilley, *Newman and his age* (1990) · J. H. Newman, *Autobiographical writings*, ed. H. Tristram (1956) · J. H. Newman, *Apologia pro vita sua* (1864) · *Faber, poet and priest: selected letters by Frederick William Faber, 1833–1863*, ed. R. Addington (1974) · Foster, *Alum. Oxon.*

Archives Birmingham Oratory, family papers

Likenesses J. Hoppner, oils, c.1803, Detroit Institute of Arts

Bowden, Samuel (*fl.* **1733–1761**), physician and poet, of Frome, Somerset, the dates of whose birth and death are not known, was the author of two volumes of poetry, *Poetical Essays on Several Occasions* (2 vols., 1733, 1735) and *Poems on Various Subjects. With some Essays in Prose, and a Treatise on Health* (1754). A footnote in the *Gentleman's Magazine*, presumably by John Nichols, the editor of the periodical, states that Bowden

> was a worthy physician and ingenious poet of Frome, a particular friend of Mrs. Rowe (being of the same communion, and living after her death in the same house,) Lord Orrery &. Two volumes of his poems were published by subscription, and several of his pieces have appeared occasionally in our miscellany [the *Gentleman's Magazine*]. (*GM*, 1st ser., 48, 1778, 485)

The word 'was' in the description of Bowden gives a *terminus ad quem* of his life. One piece in Nichols's 'miscellany' appeared in the number for September 1776, a poem titled 'On his Majesty's Intended Marriage to the Princess of Mecklenberg, and her Arrival in England' (*GM*, 1st ser., 46, 1776, 424). The poem, in undistinguished couplets, was from Frome and dated 5 September 1761, making it an occasional poem, as George III was married on 8 September of that year. Bowden's poem begins:

> Britannia's monarch, whom three realms obey,
> And the more spacious kingdoms of the sea,

with its unabashed borrowing, in the opening line, from Pope's *Rape of the Lock*: 'Here Thou, Great *Anna*, whom three Realms obey'. The reference to Mrs Rowe in the 1778 *Gentleman's Magazine* is to the nonconformist poetess Elizabeth Rowe, who was buried in the meeting-house at Frome. James Theobald, earl of Orrery, was one of her correspondents. The Presbyterian minister John *Bowden (*d.* 1750), thought to be Samuel's brother, was in Frome prior to 1700, and it was for him that the meeting-house in Rook Lane was built in 1707. It was he who preached Mrs Rowe's funeral sermon in 1739. In the 1750s a Mrs John Bowden kept lodgings in Bath, where the second of Bowden's works was published, suggesting the possibility of a familial connection.

ARTHUR SHERBO

Sources *DNB* · *The correspondence of Edward Young, 1683–1765*, ed. H. Pettit (1971) · P. J. Wallis and R. V. Wallis, *Eighteenth century medics*, 2nd edn (1988)

Bowden, (Bertram) Vivian, Baron Bowden (1910–1989), scientist and educationist, was born on 18 January 1910 in Chesterfield, Derbyshire, the elder child and only son of Bertram Caleb Bowden, primary school headmaster in Chesterfield, and his wife, Sarah Elizabeth, daughter of John Thomas Moulton, of Throwley Hall, Staffordshire. He was educated at Chesterfield grammar school and became a scholar at Emmanuel College, Cambridge, where he was awarded first-class honours in both parts of the natural sciences tripos (1930 and 1931). He was awarded a PhD at Cambridge for a thesis on the structure of radioactive nuclei.

Bowden then became an Imperial Chemical Industries fellow at the University of Amsterdam (1934–5), sixth-form master at Liverpool collegiate school (1935–7), and chief physics master at Oundle School (1937–40), before moving to the Ministry of Defence Telecommunications Research Establishment, initially at Swanage and then in Malvern (1940–43). Here he investigated the use of radar to detect aircraft and precisely position them. This work began in Malvern, and in May 1943 moved to Washington, where Bowden led a British team working with the Americans at the naval research laboratories. He showed his capacity to earn the trust of people at all levels in an organization, and to cut through delaying bureaucracy to get things done. In 1973 he was given the Pioneer award by the American Institution of Electrical and Electronic Engineers. The citation, which recognized 'work done at least 20 years before but which remains important and in use', applauded Bowden's 'wartime radar identification system that has become an essential aid for modern air traffic control'.

After the war Bowden had a brief period at the Atomic Energy Research Establishment at Harwell (July–December 1946) before becoming a partner with Sir Robert Watson-Watt & Partners (1947–50). He left the partnership when Sir Robert Watson-Watt moved to Canada, and

(**Bertram**) **Vivian Bowden, Baron Bowden** (1910–1989), by Walter Bird, 1965

joined Ferranti (Digital Computers) Ltd to attempt to sell digital computers at a profit. He thought it a most peculiar job until he met a man on the *Queen Mary* who sold lighthouses on commission. In the brief period of this appointment (1950–53) he successfully applied his great energy. He was particularly effective in explaining, with uncanny prescience, the dramatic effect that the digital computer was destined to have. Some of these thoughts he gathered together in his book *Faster than Thought* (1953).

In 1953 Bowden became principal of the Manchester College of Science and Technology. At that time it taught a modest number of students on degree courses of the University of Manchester and a large number of part-time students, who studied for the national certificate and other qualifications. Shortly after Bowden arrived, a period of rapid national expansion in higher education was launched, and he exploited this to the full. He attracted substantial resources, which transformed what he referred to as the surrounding dereliction and slums into an attractive campus with fine buildings. The university numbers expanded by a factor of about ten to the point where the city decided to transfer the non-university work to another college, much to Bowden's regret. The Manchester College then became an independent chartered body, the University of Manchester Institute of Science and Technology (UMIST), and was put on the University Grants Committee's list.

The development of UMIST was Bowden's great achievement. He had drive and energy, and a clear vision of what he wished to achieve. He did things by impulse, offering chairs to outstanding candidates at chance meetings in airport lounges and leaving his efficient and supportive registrar, Joe Burgess, to tidy up the legal processes afterwards. He made UMIST visible to the media by his public statements, in which he generated quotable aphorisms. He employed striking statistics to back his arguments. In these he often used the truth with some economy, but his conclusions were powerful. His national visibility led Harold Wilson to make him a life peer as Baron Bowden of Chesterfield (1963) and to appoint him minister for education and science (1964). Wilson hoped that Bowden would assist the development of the white-hot technological revolution, but it was not to be. Bowden has been described, accurately, as a man possessing candour without guile. This is not a quality that promises success in dealing with permanent civil servants, his relationship with whom Bowden described as 'like fighting a feather bed; you meet no resistance but you cannot get through it'. So he left the ministry in 1965, after having set up the industrial training boards, which was a brave attempt to persuade industry to contribute to the cost of training the skills it needed. He returned to UMIST. Here he continued to twinge consciences. He criticized the government for a fiscal policy that deterred industrial investment in new plant and processes. He counselled against the bifurcation of higher education. He despaired of the inadequate number of engineering and technology graduates entering British industry, and he was forever petitioning the city to act to reduce the 'decaying slums around the UMIST campus'. He retired in 1976.

Bowden was a mixture of the ruthless and the humane. He had a portly figure, which could be recognized at some distance by its rolling gait. As he said, 'I walk as if one leg is always shorter than the next one.' His door was always open. He was continually visible around the campus, and took a keen interest in the problems and successes of all his staff, from the humble to the great. His concern with staff morale led him to pioneer the involvement of students in the decision-making bodies of UMIST. For this he was roundly criticized by the traditionalists, but later UMIST was to avoid the excesses of the student unrest of the 1960s. He was honorary fellow of the Institution of Civil Engineers (FICE) (1975) and had honorary degrees from Rensellaer Polytechnic, USA (1974), Manchester (1976), and Kumasi, Ghana (1977).

Bowden married in 1939 Marjorie Mary (*d.* 1957), daughter of William G. H. Browne, chief government sanitary inspector in British Guiana. They had a son and two daughters. The marriage was dissolved in 1954. In 1955 he married Diana Stewart. They were divorced in 1961 and in 1967 he married Mary Maltby, who died in 1971. She was the daughter of Bernard W. Maltby, of Ilkeston, Derbyshire. In 1974 he married Phyllis, former wife of John Henry Lewis James, and daughter of Stanley Ernest Myson, postman. This marriage was dissolved in 1983. Bowden died on 28 July 1989 in a nursing home in Bowdon, Cheshire. K. M. ENTWISTLE, *rev.*

Sources Citations at the commemoration of the life of Lord Bowden of Chesterfield, *UMIST Times* (13 Oct 1989) • *CGPLA Eng. & Wales* (1989)

Archives ICL, corresp. with Lord Jackson • ICL, corresp. with J. D. McGee • Sci. Mus., corresp. with Stanley Gill

Likenesses W. Bird, photograph, 1965, NPG [*see illus.*] • M. Noakes, oils, *c.*1976, University of Manchester Institute of Science and Technology

Wealth at death £287,828: administration with will, 23 Oct 1989, *CGPLA Eng. & Wales*

Bowdich, Thomas Edward (1791?–1824), writer and traveller in Africa, was born in Bristol, probably on 20 June 1791, though birth dates of 1790, 1792, and 1793 have also been suggested. His father, Thomas Bowdich, was a hat manufacturer and merchant there, and his mother was one of the Vaughans of Painscastle, Radnorshire. He was educated at Bristol grammar school, and (from the age of nine) at Corsham grammar school, Wiltshire, where he soon became head boy. He was keener on classics than mathematics and was noted for his literary style and his skill as a rider. He was originally intended for the bar, and it was much against his wishes that his father put him to the family trade, and for one year, 1813, he was partner in the firm of Bowdich, Son, and Luce. In the same year on 9 January, at the church of St Mary, Newington, Surrey, he married Sarah, daughter of John Eglonton Wallis, of Colchester [*see* Lee, Sarah], and entered himself at Oxford, though he never matriculated. In 1814, with the help of his uncle, a Mr Hope Smith, governor-in-chief of the settlements belonging to the Royal African Company, he secured a writership in the service, and subsequently left England for Cape Coast Castle. His wife followed him soon afterwards, but on her arrival she found he had returned to England for a time. In 1816 the African Company planned a mission to the Asante, and initially contemplated appointing Bowdich to lead it. On reaching Cape Coast Castle the second time, he was judged too young and Frederick James (governor of Fort Accra) was appointed to lead the expedition. In the course of the journey, however, Bowdich superseded his chief (a bold step afterwards sanctioned by the authorities), and, through negotiations which subsequently proved controversial, formed a treaty with the king of the Asante, which promised peace to the British settlements on the Gold Coast in return for commercial and political co-operation. In 1818 he returned to England in poor health, and in the following year published a detailed account of his expedition, *A Mission from Cape Coast Castle to Ashantee*. This work, with its glowing account of Asante society and culture, attracted considerable interest. Bowdich presented a small collection of African objects and specimens to the British Museum.

However, Bowdich's apparent success did not meet with the reward he anticipated. His writings and letters continually speak of unmerited disappointment; the net reward for his great mission amounted to only £200, and it cost him half of this to return home; while a rival, Joseph Dupuis, was appointed consul at Coomassie (Kumasi) with £600 a year. In 1819 he published *The African Committee*, an attack on the corruption and inefficiency of the African Company, and the ensuing controversy resulted in the transfer of the company's forts to the crown. Disappointed by his reception in London, Bowdich left for Paris, where studied mathematics, physical science, and natural history. Soon after, he gained the Cambridge prize of £1000 for a discovery which was dependent on mathematics. In Paris, Humboldt, Cuvier, Denon, Biot, and other eminent savants gave Bowdich a generous reception, and a public *éloge* was pronounced upon him at the Institut de France. Not only were he and his wife introduced to Cuvier and his circle, but for three years Cuvier's extensive library and splendid collections were made available to them as their own. The French government offered him an appointment on generous terms, which Bowdich felt unable to accept, apparently on patriotic grounds. Early in 1820 he wrote an angry response to 'the geographer of the Quarterly Review' (presumably John Barrow) who had published a critical article on his *Mission to Ashantee*. His other writings in Paris included a translation of *Travels in the Interior of Africa to the Sources of the Senegal and Gambia, by G. Mollien* (1820); an account of *British and Foreign Expeditions to Teembo, with Remarks on Civilization* (1821); an *Essay on the Geography of North-Western Africa* (1821) accompanied by a large lithographed map, compiled from his own discoveries; and an *Essay on the Superstitions, Customs, and Arts Common to the Ancient Egyptians, Abyssinians, and Ashantees* (1821), an audacious study which was the first full-length study of west African culture and history. He also published several works on natural history, including *An Introduction to the Ornithology of Cuvier* (1821) and *Elements of Conchology* (1822), both illustrated by numerous lithographs prepared by his wife.

The success of these publications enabled Bowdich and his wife to embark upon a second African expedition, and in August 1822 they sailed from Le Havre to Lisbon. Here, from various manuscripts, Bowdich compiled a complete history of all the Portuguese discoveries in south Africa. They continued to Madeira—where they remained for some months, collecting geological, geographical, and botanical information—and then travelled to the Gambia, where Bowdich began a trigonometrical survey of the river. His enthusiasm for scientific observation was said to have cost him his life there, for while taking astronomical observations at night he caught cold, which was followed by fever, resulting in his death, at the early age of thirty-three, on 10 January 1824. The published account of his last expedition was edited and illustrated by his wife.

Though small in stature, Bowdich was an energetic man. He was an excellent linguist, a graphic writer, and an ardent conversationalist. His reputation as a scholar, enhanced by his association with Cuvier and Humboldt, still survived in the late twentieth century. He left a widow and three children, one of them named after the two companions of his Asante mission.

John Westby-Gibson, *rev.* Felix Driver

Sources T. H. Hale, Introduction, in T. E. Bowdich, *A mission from Cape Coast Castle to Ashantee* (1873) • 'Mr Bowdich, the African traveller', *Literary Gazette* (20 March 1824), 187–8 • *GM*, 1st ser., 94/1 (1824),

279–80 • review, *QR*, 22 (1819–20), 273–302 • P. Curtin, *The image of Africa* (1965) • J. Ajayi and M. Crowder, eds., *History of west Africa*, 2 (1974) • D. Outram, 'Scientific biography and the case of Georges Cuvier', *History of Science*, 14 (1976), 101–37 • S. Bowdich, *Excursions in Madeira and Porto Santo* (1825) • BM, Add. MS 37951 [obituary], fol. 21 • parish register, Newington, Surrey, St Mary [marriage], 9 Jan 1813 • private information (2004) [D. de B. Beaver]

Archives NHM, list of Ashanti plants • U. Birm.

Likenesses engraving, *c*.1819, BM • J. Thomson, stipple (after W. Derby), BM, NPG; repro. in *European Magazine* (1824)

Wealth at death subscription was raised for relief of family after death: *GM*, 94/1

Bowdler [*née* Cotton], **Elizabeth Stuart** (*d*. 1797), religious writer, was the second daughter and coheir of Sir John *Cotton, sixth baronet (*d*. 1752) [*see under* Cotton, Sir Robert Bruce], of Steeple Gidding and Connington, Huntingdonshire, and his wife, Jane, daughter of Sir Robert Burdett, baronet, of Foremark, Derbyshire, and Bramcote, Warwickshire. Elizabeth's father and grandfather, Sir Robert *Cotton (*d*. 1749) [*see under* Cotton, Sir Robert Bruce], were Jacobites who spent periods in exile. On 25 April 1742 she married Thomas Bowdler (*bap*. 1719, *d*. 1785), of the Shropshire Bowdlers, at St Pancras Old Church, Middlesex. They lived mostly in Bath or in Ashley, Somerset, and had five children, four of whom were authors who continued their mother's passion for the Church of England: Jane *Bowdler (1743–1784), John *Bowdler (1746–1823), Henrietta Maria *Bowdler (1750–1830), and Thomas *Bowdler (1754–1825); Frances was their other daughter. Bowdler and her daughters moved on the fringes of literary life at Bath: they knew the blue stockings Lady Miller, of Batheaston vase fame, and Elizabeth Montagu, who admired Jane Bowdler's writings and conduct.

Elizabeth Bowdler was keenly interested in theological matters, and probably studied Hebrew. In 1775 she wrote *Practical Observations on the Revelation of St John*, which was published anonymously in 1787 and posthumously reissued in 1800. The author of the 1800 preface interpreted Bowdler's readings of Revelation as foretelling the apocalyptic events of the French Revolution. According to Bowdler, her *Practical Observations* was published as an educational piece; in it she warns against religious enthusiasm, argues against predestination, and emphasizes the importance of good works and moral responsibility. She may also have written in 1775 a commentary on the Song of Solomon, attributed to her by the New York Public Library catalogue. On her deathbed Bowdler reputedly requested that a special edition of her daughter Jane's *Poems and Essays* be published with an additional essay and a copy given to each of her friends instead of a mourning ring. She died in Bath on 10 May 1797. Her husband had predeceased her, dying in Bath on 2 May 1785.

Bowdler made Henrietta Maria Bowdler her sole executor and residuary legatee, and left various small legacies. She gave each of her surviving children £30 for mourning clothes, Henrietta Bowdler £200, a year's wages to her servants, £20 to the Bath Hospital ('as a testimony of its having been a well conducted charity'; PRO, PROB 11/1292), and £10 to the Magdalen Hospital. She also bequeathed an annuity of £20 to her chaplain Mr Reidford and his wife, and a £10 annuity to a Mrs Margaret Cheyne.

EMMA MAJOR

Sources J. Todd, ed., *A dictionary of British and American women writers, 1660–1800* (1984) • will, PRO, PROB 11/1292, sig. 398 • *ESTC* • J. Bowdler, *Poems and essays* (1798) • Hunt. L., Montagu papers, MO6142, MO6614, MO3620 • *GM*, 1st ser., 55 (1785), 403–4; 67 (1797), 447 • *IGI* [citing parish registers of St Pancras Old Church, 1660–1916] • GEC, *Baronetage* • Burke, *Extinct baronetage*

Wealth at death approx. £500: will, 1797, PRO, PROB 11/1292, sig. 398

Bowdler, Henrietta Maria [Harriet] (1750–1830), writer and literary editor, was born in Conington, Huntingdonshire, the daughter of Thomas Bowdler (*bap*. 1719, *d*. 1785), and his wife, Elizabeth Stuart *Bowdler, *née* Cotton (*d*. 1797). She was one of six children, all of whom were raised in Bath and educated by their literary mother; their father's carefully excised readings of Shakespeare in the evenings also had a considerable influence on the minds of the Bowdler children. Her siblings included Jane *Bowdler (1743–1784), John *Bowdler (1746–1823), and Thomas *Bowdler (1754–1825), the last of whom possessed, until late in the twentieth century, the entire credit (or blame) for the expurgation of Shakespeare that Henrietta Bowdler had in fact originated.

Henrietta Bowdler's first publication was her edition of her sister Jane's *Poems and Essays, by a Lady Lately Deceased* (1786). Jane's health had been ruined by bouts of measles and smallpox, and the volume was originally published for the benefit of the hospital at Bath. It was popular in the region, and had run into seventeen further editions by 1830. It was the *Sermons on the Doctrines and Duties of Christianity* (1801), however, which established Henrietta Bowdler's literary reputation. Beilby Porteus, bishop of London, 'was so struck with their merit', that, believing the volume to have been written by a clergyman, he 'offered through the publisher to confer a benefice on the author' (Gorton). This work passed through nearly fifty editions in almost as many years, and Henrietta Bowdler soon became something of a force in contemporary literary and religious circles: 'half the leaders of high-minded thought in England were in correspondence with her, and many had visited the salon she kept in Bath' (Perrin, 69).

Gilbert Elliot, earl of Minto, describes the young Henrietta Bowdler:

> She is, I believe, a blue-stocking, but what the colour of that part of her dress is must be mere conjecture, as you will easily believe when I tell you that … she said she never looked at [the dancers in operas] but always kept her eyes shut the whole time, and when I asked her why, she said it was so *indelicate* she could not bear to look. (Perrin, 69)

It was this delicacy of mind that led Henrietta Bowdler to produce the work for which her brother assumed the credit, and for which she is known today, *The Family Shakespeare* (1807). Originally published at Bath in four volumes, it contained expurgated versions of twenty Shakespeare plays, from which the editor had 'endeavoured to remove every thing that could give just offence to the religious and virtuous mind' ('Preface', *The Family Shakespeare*, 1807). Henrietta also cut scenes that she deemed trivial or uninteresting, but the excisions primarily consisted of sexual material, or those Roman Catholic references which a good protestant might find distasteful or disturbing. Thomas Bowdler, who later produced a fuller edition of his sister's expurgation in 1818, was in many ways more faithful to the original, restoring the unobjectionable scenes, and confining himself to sexual and religious allusions (although he detected many more of these than his sister had felt necessary to expunge). Henrietta Bowdler's edition of 1807 was published anonymously, but her brother had taken on the mantle of editorship by 1809: an unmarried woman of her stature and beliefs could hardly then acknowledge publicly that she knew enough about sexual impropriety to edit Shakespeare effectively. The later edition of the complete plays that he produced reinforced the notion that he had originated the idea.

Henrietta Bowdler turned to literary projects of other kinds. She edited the *Fragments in Prose and Verse by the Late Elizabeth Smith* (1810), and attached to it a memoir of Smith, an impressive scholar and translator with whom Henrietta Bowdler had shared a long-standing correspondence. The volume was popular in religious circles, and ran into several editions. Henrietta Bowdler has also been credited with the anonymously published *Creation* (1818). She later wrote a novel, *Pen Tamar, or, The History of an Old Maid* (1831), a work that while 'ostensibly defending both virtue and single women, … excuses the hero's prejudice against old maids with one hateful example and harshly penalizes him and the heroine for their filial obedience' (Blain, Clements & Grundy, *Feminist comp.*). Henrietta Bowdler died at Bath on 25 February 1830. She never married.

Henrietta Bowdler's creation of *The Family Shakespeare* brought a more general movement of literary expurgation into play. It is true that her small provincial edition caused little immediate stir on its publication, and her brother's substantive ten-volume revision (retitled *The Family Shakspeare*) also passed largely without comment in 1818. But three years after this second edition appeared, a war of words concerning its merit between *Blackwood's Magazine* and the *Edinburgh Review* caused sales of *The Family Shakspeare* to soar, and the revised work passed into general circulation. The delicacy of mind that had in the late eighteenth century been an object of gentle ridicule from such as the earl of Minto found a more appreciative forum in a growing and varied nineteenth-century reading public, an audience for whom a certain responsibility was felt by the class to which the Bowdlers belonged. As Noel Perrin puts it: 'the gentleman, moved by *noblesse oblige*, kindly sets out to save his inferiors from temptation. *He* can be trusted to read *Hamlet*, but a newly educated grocer will pick up bad ideas' (Perrin, 20). *The Family Shakspeare* ran into many editions and for generations influenced how Shakespeare was edited and read. By 1850 there were seven expurgated editions of Shakespeare on the market, and by 1900 that number had increased to fifty (ibid., xiii). Although the verb that resulted from the Bowdler surname, along with all of its negative connotations, was linked to Thomas Bowdler alone for almost 150 years, it must also be associated with Henrietta Bowdler's literary legacy.

M. CLARE LOUGHLIN-CHOW

Sources *DNB* • N. Perrin, *Dr Bowdler's legacy: a history of expurgated books in England and America*, 3rd edn (1991) • *GM*, 1st ser., 100/1 (1830), p. 567 • *GM*, 1st ser., 100/2 (1830), p. 649 • Blain, Clements & Grundy, *Feminist comp.* • *IGI* • J. Gorton, *A general biographical dictionary*, new edn, 3 vols. (1841) • Allibone, *Dict.* • A. K. Ellwood, *Memoirs of the literary ladies of England*, 2 vols. (1843) • Watt, *Bibl. Brit.*

Archives NL Wales, letters

Likenesses W. Slater, lithograph, pubd 1830 (after J. Slater), BM, NPG

Bowdler, Jane (1743–1784), poet and essayist, was born on 14 February 1743 at Ashley, near Bath, the eldest child of Thomas Bowdler (*bap.* 1719, *d.* 1785) and his wife, Elizabeth Stuart *Bowdler, *née* Cotton (*d.* 1797). She was the sister of John *Bowdler the elder (1746–1823), religious pamphleteer, Thomas *Bowdler (1754–1825), editor of Shakespeare, and Henrietta Maria *Bowdler (1750–1830), religious poet and Shakespearian editor. Throughout her life she suffered from ill health; in 1759 she had a severe attack of smallpox, and from 1771 until her death was a confirmed invalid. She died in the spring of 1784 at her home in Ashley, and was buried in the family vault at the church of St George the Martyr in London.

A selection of the poems and essays that Jane Bowdler had written in her later years was published at Bath for the benefit of the local hospital in 1786 under the title of *Poems and Essays, by a Lady Lately Deceased*, edited by her sister Henrietta Maria. Addressing such subjects as sensibility, politeness, candour, and the pleasures of religion, this volume became extraordinarily popular. Seventeen editions were published at Bath in rapid succession between 1787 and 1830. Other editions appeared at Dublin, in London, and in New York, where the first American edition (from the tenth Bath edition) appeared in 1811. Queen Charlotte is said to have found the poems so comforting that she read them three times. A few of Jane Bowdler's pieces, not previously printed, appear in Thomas Bowdler's *Memoir of the Life of John Bowdler* (1824).

SIDNEY LEE, *rev.* REBECCA MILLS

Sources A. Crawford and others, eds., *The Europa biographical dictionary of British women* (1983), 57 • Blain, Clements & Grundy, *Feminist comp.* • T. Bowdler, *Memoir of the life of John Bowdler* (1824) • will, PRO, PROB 11/1131, sig. 355 • J. R. de J. Jackson, *Romantic poetry by women: a bibliography* (1993) • J. Todd, ed., *A dictionary of British and American women writers, 1660–1800* (1984) • W. Beckett, *A universal biography*, 3 vols. (1835–6) • J. Gorton, *A general biographical dictionary*, 3 vols. (1841)

Likenesses R. M. Meadows, stipple, 1798 (after T. Lawrence), BM, NPG; repro. in J. Bowdler, *Poems and essays* (1798)

Wealth at death under £4000—majority of money and possessions to siblings and their children; generous annuity to servant: will, PRO, PROB 11/1131, fol. 354

Bowdler, John (1746–1823), Church of England layman and religious writer, was born at Bath, Somerset, on 18 March 1746, the eldest son of Thomas Bowdler (*bap.* 1719, *d.* 1785) and Elizabeth Stuart *Bowdler, *née* Cotton (*d.* 1797), religious writer. He was given a strict Anglican religious upbringing by his mother, and at the age of eight was sent to the school kept by Mr Graves at Claverton, near Bath. For unknown reasons he was moved to an academy at Brompton, Middlesex, where he struggled with Greek but learned much about accountancy. In 1762 he was placed under the private tuition of the Revd Nicholas Brett, of Spring Grove, Wye, Kent, only surviving son of the Revd Thomas Brett, the celebrated nonjuring divine. On his death, in 1776, Brett left his pamphlets (many on the nonjuring controversy) and papers to Bowdler.

In November 1765 Bowdler entered the London legal office of Mr Barsham, a special pleader. Between 1770 and 1780 he engaged in the study of law, practising as a chamber conveyancer. During these years his closest friend, or soulmate, was Robert Cobb of Lydd, Kent, with whom he delighted to engage in lengthy discussions of law and theology. He was the victim of frequent bouts of serious ill health during this period. On 28 January 1778 he married Henrietta, eldest daughter of John Hanbury, vice-consul of the English factory at Hamburg, and his wife, the sister of Thomas Lawrence (1711–1783), physician and friend of Dr Johnson. They had ten children, six of whom survived infancy. Bowdler's elder sister Jane *Bowdler died in 1784. On his father's death, in May 1785, Bowdler inherited a small family fortune, which enabled him to retire from the legal profession and move from London to Kent, first, on a seven-year lease, to a house adjacent to Knowle Park, in Sevenoaks. In 1793 he moved from Sevenoaks to Pickhurst Farm, in the parish of Hayes, near Bromley, and finally, about 1806, he moved to Eltham.

Bowdler became part of a distinguished coterie of Anglican high-churchmen that included John Bowles, Charles Daubeny, William Stevens, and, later, Joshua Watson and others. Looking back to the theology of the Laudian and later Caroline divines and nonjurors they emphasized the apostolical authority and descent of the Church of England and the paramountcy of church unity, as well as the divine-right basis and patriarchal rather than contractual origin of the state. Bowdler can be placed in that tradition of high-church Anglican lay spirituality associated with the name of the one-time nonjuror Robert Nelson (1656–1715), of whose devotional writings he was a fervent admirer. Most of his friends were associated with a nucleus of London high-churchmen commonly known as the Hackney Phalanx. Many of them were also members of an influential high-church Anglican dining club known as the Club of Nobody's Friends, founded by the layman William Stevens, the original 'nobody', in 1801. Bowdler was an intimate friend of Stevens and attended him on his deathbed, in 1807.

Bowdler 'admired the principles of the Nonjurors, and held their memory in great veneration' but was 'never disposed to follow them to the extent to which some of them carried those principles' (*Memoir*, 79). None the less he appears not to have doubted the validity of later nonjuring consecrations, and he was in close attendance, in November 1779, on Robert Gordon, the last of the nonjuring bishops, through a fatal illness. He was a firm opponent of the principles of protestant dissent and strongly disapproved of the Anglican evangelical Sir Richard Hill's *An Apology for Brotherly Love* (1799) for its partial justification or extenuation of dissent. Though he declined an offer to review it Bowdler warmly approved Charles Daubeny's uncompromisingly high-church *Guide to the Church* (1798), with its strictures on the sin of schism, against which Hill's *Apology* was a low-church response. He recommended the publishing of an abridgement of the *Guide*, 'in order to procure for it a more general perusal' (ibid., 165). Bowdler planned, but did not complete or publish, his own defence of Daubeny's *Guide* and critique of the Methodists and Hill's *Apology*—a move that was also partly occasioned by the publication of the moderate evangelical William Wilberforce's highly influential *Practical View of the Prevailing System of Professed Christians* (1797). Bowdler also corrected drafts of Daubeny's follow-up 'Letters to Sir Richard Hill', published as *Appendix to the Guide to the Church* (1799), although the author complained that Bowdler had carried the principle of 'removing everything harsh-sounding' 'a little too far' (Daubeny to Boucher, 22 Feb 1799, Boucher MS B/5/6).

Bowdler's high-church principles also found expression from 1806 in his growing interest in, and support for, the once persecuted and downtrodden episcopal church in Scotland, and he became an active member of a committee formed to raise subscriptions for it. His attempts to place the Church of England and the non-established Scottish episcopal church on an apparently equal ecclesiastical footing were privately criticized even by the moderate high-church bishop of Bangor, John Randolph, who complained that Bowdler's view on the subject had 'not a little spice of the nonjuror in it' (Randolph to Thomas Lambard, 15 Feb 1807, Randolph papers, Bodl. Oxf., MS top. Oxon. d.356, vol. 6, 50*v*).

Bowdler was an outspoken and stern moralist and a fierce critic of the social and moral ills of contemporary society. His high-church defence of the spiritual rights of the church co-existed with withering denunciations of economic abuses and moral irregularities and strictures on clerical dancing, card-playing, and sabbath profanation that matched those of his Anglican evangelical contemporaries. In 1796, in published addresses to the archbishop of Canterbury, he proposed that those found guilty of adultery be rendered infamous and incapable of marrying and inheriting land. He also recommended that gaming be punished by imprisonment and new laws introduced to enforce public observance of the Lord's day. Beilby Porteus, bishop of London, responded sympathetically but regretted that several of Bowdler's remedies for moral evils were impracticable and could not be enforced. In 1797 Bowdler again sought to expose what he regarded as the immorality and irreligion of the nation with a strongly worded and lengthy pamphlet, *Reform or Ruin: Take your Choice*. He enunciated the doctrine of apostolic succession but was scathing about what he regarded as abuses in the contemporary church and state. At the root of his panaceas for economic, social, and ecclesiastical reform lay a belief that conduct and principles had first to be reformed.

It is significant that Bowdler's rigid high-church principles did not preclude him being on close terms with prominent Claphamite evangelicals, notably Henry Thornton and his wife, whom he commended for their 'parental' kindness towards his own son John (*Select Pieces*, xx). His own style of churchmanship and spirituality is evident, nevertheless, in the fear that he expressed in his memoir of his son (published in 1816), that readers might suspect that the younger John Bowdler's 'piety bordered on enthusiasm'. He made clear his own position:

> Although no one can be less disposed than myself to become the advocate of enthusiasm, properly so called, for I well know the dangers which attend it, and the dreadful consequences to which it leads; yet, bad as it is, its opposite is surely worse. (ibid., xvii)

The generosity of Bowdler's charitable benefactions was legendary. He was particularly generous in his support for church-building; he was an early advocate of church extension and of the better provision of church accommodation of the poor, and in 1813 responded with enthusiasm to a letter from the banker and Hackney Phalanx ally William Cotton, suggesting the foundation of a church building society. Bowdler helped to form the committee that in 1815 lobbied the bishop of London and then, in 1816, the government, to erect additional churches in the populous parts of England out of public funds. The Church Building Society, formed in July 1817 and formally launched in February 1818, was the fruit of these endeavours. Bowdler was at the forefront of plans to raise £1 million by subscription. He admired Daubeny's appropriation of seatings for the poor at Christ Church, Bath. However, in view of Victorian high-church associations with rich church decoration and furnishings his recommendation of a 'simple, chaste' style of building 'free from all useless or expensive decoration' (*Memoir*, 252) is significant in the light of later perceptions of high-churchmanship.

Bowdler was an early riser and a man of strict devotional habits, being particularly assiduous in the practice of family prayers. He was zealous and could be stern, formidable, and overbearing in his dealings with others, but he also possessed a warm, affectionate personality and made friends easily. As a young man he excelled in boxing, fencing, and horsemanship; he was also an excellent arithmetician and an early advocate of decimalization. His daughter Elizabeth died on 4 December 1810, followed by his son the poet John *Bowdler (1783–1815), on 1 February 1815, at the age of thirty-two. Bowdler developed dropsical symptoms in his last days, and died at Eltham on 29 June 1823, of a 'slight paralysis of the lower abdomen, followed by water effusion'. He was buried at Eltham church, in a vault adjacent to his old friend Bishop George Horne. He was outlived by his younger brother Thomas *Bowdler (1754–1825), famous as the author of the expurgated, or 'bowdlerized', *Family Shakspeare* (1818), and by his younger sister, Henrietta Maria *Bowdler, who originated it.

PETER B. NOCKLES

Sources T. Bowdler, *Memoir of the life of John Bowdler* (1824) · C. Bowdler, *The religion of the heart as exemplified in the life and writings of John Bowdler* (1857) · J. Bowdler, *Select pieces in prose and verse*, ed. J. Bowdler, 2 vols. (1816) · H. Broxap, *The later non-jurors* (1924) · J. Sack, *From Jacobite to conservative* (1993) · Boucher papers, College of William and Mary, Williamsburg, Virginia, Earl Gregg Swem Library · *DNB*

Archives Bodl. Oxf., John Randolph papers, MS Top. Oxon. d.353–356 · Bodl. Oxf., letters to William Wilberforce, Wilberforce MSS c. 52, fols. 68–70; d. 13, 15, 17 · College of William and Mary, Williamsburg, Virginia, Earl Gregg Swem Library, Boucher papers, B/3, B/5 · Harvard University, Houghton Library, letter from R. Cobb

Likenesses M. Gauci, lithograph, BM, NPG

Bowdler, John (1783–1815), religious writer, was born in London on 4 February 1783, one of ten children of John *Bowdler the elder (1746–1823), religious pamphleteer, and his wife, Henrietta Hanbury. Thomas *Bowdler (1782–1856) was his brother.

Bowdler attended Sevenoaks grammar school and Hyde Abbey School before entering Winchester College. Although he wanted to follow his brother to university, or alternatively to be a barrister or join the army, his father had him placed in a London solicitor's office in 1798. Finding the work tedious, he entered Lincoln's Inn and was called to the bar in 1807. Bowdler was a prominent member of the evangelical Clapham Sect, and planned to enter parliament.

However, in 1810 signs of consumption appeared, and Bowdler spent the two following years in the south of Europe with his uncle. (His sister Elizabeth died just weeks after his departure.) He finally settled with an aunt near Portsmouth in 1812. Most of his published work was written while he was ill, in 1812–13, and took the form of contributions to the *Christian Observer*, often under the pseudonym Crito. Bowdler never recovered his health, and died in Portsmouth on 1 February 1815. His father collected and published his *Select Pieces in Prose and Verse* in two volumes in 1816; they were reprinted three times by 1819. His brother Charles later published *The Religion of the Heart as Exemplified in the Life and Writings of John Bowdler* (1857).

SIDNEY LEE, *rev.* JESSICA HININGS

Sources J. Bowdler, *Select pieces in prose and verse*, ed. J. Bowdler, 2 vols. (1816) · C. Bowdler, *The religion of the heart as exemplified in the life and writings of John Bowdler* (1857) · T. Bowdler, *Memoir of the life of John Bowdler*, new edn (1825) · D. M. Lewis, ed., *The Blackwell dictionary of evangelical biography, 1730–1860*, 2 vols. (1995) · will, PRO, PROB 11/1565, fols. 41–2

Likenesses E. Scriven, stipple (after A. W. Devis), BM, NPG; repro. in Bowdler, *Select pieces*

Wealth at death see will, PRO, PROB 11/1565, fols. 41–2

Bowdler, Thomas (1754–1825), writer and literary editor, was born on 11 July 1754 at Ashley, near Bath, the younger son of Thomas Bowdler (*bap.* 1719, *d.* 1785) and his wife, Elizabeth Stuart *Bowdler, *née* Cotton (*d.* 1797). His father, a gentleman of independent fortune, was descended from an ancient family originally settled at Hope Bowdler, Shropshire, and his mother was the second daughter and coheir of Sir John Cotton of Conington, Huntingdonshire, the last baronet in the line of Bruce Cottons. His mother, an accomplished and educated woman, was the first instructor of her six children, who included Jane *Bowdler (1743–1784), John *Bowdler (1746–1823), and Henrietta Maria *Bowdler (1750–1830).

Thomas Bowdler is said to have suffered much from a serious accident when he was nine, which required operations and an extended convalescence. It was about that time, however, in 1765, that he went to Mr Graves's school at Claverton, near Bath, and first met William Anne Villettes, who was to become a military officer and a lifelong friend. In 1770 Bowdler went to study medicine at St Andrews University, and then moved to Edinburgh, where in 1776 he graduated MD and published his thesis *Tentamen medicum inaugurale de febrium intermittentium natura et indole*. He spent the next four years travelling in Europe, where in Lisbon in 1781 he caught a fever from a friend whom he attended during a fatal illness. He returned to England in broken health, with his 'physical aversion to sick people' (Perrin, 69) accentuated. Despite being elected a fellow of the Royal Society and a licentiate of the College of Physicians on 9 April 1781, Bowdler retired from the practice of medicine on the death of his father in 1785.

Thomas Bowdler settled in London, where he lived until 1800. He obtained an introduction to Elizabeth Montagu, 'Queen of the Blues', and became part of a literary and philanthropic circle which included bishops Hinchcliffe and Porteus, Elizabeth Carter, Hester Chapone, and Hannah More. Bowdler devoted himself to charitable work: he acted for many years as chairman of St George's vestry, and was a member of the committee in charge of the Magdalen Hospital. He was also active in the Proclamation Society, formed in 1787 to enforce a royal proclamation against impiety and vice. In 1781 he became a commissioner with Sir Gilbert Elliot and Sir Charles Bunbury to examine the state of the penitentiaries, and he remained an active proponent of prison reform, inspecting gaols throughout the country in 1790. Beginning to feel some disenchantment about the slow progress of his proposed prison reforms Bowdler visited the Low Countries in 1787 and wrote a detailed account of the revolution there in *Letters Written in Holland in the Months of September and October, 1787* (1788). He also travelled in France in 1788.

In 1800 Bowdler left London, partly because of the failure of his prison reform project. The economic advantages of the new scheme of transporting prisoners to Australia meant that parliament lost any interest that Bowdler had been able to generate for reform. He moved to St Boniface, in the Isle of Wight, where he lived for ten years, leasing a country estate. On 13 September 1806, aged fifty-two, he married Elizabeth Frevenen or Trevennen, the widow of a naval officer. The marriage was unhappy, however, and after a few years they lived apart. The relationship was never again mentioned by the Bowdler family, even in the posthumous biography of Bowdler by his nephew, Thomas *Bowdler (1782–1856); as a result, Thomas Bowdler is usually assumed to have been a bachelor. There were no children of the marriage.

In 1814 Bowdler visited Geneva to settle the affairs of his old friend Lieutenant-General Villettes, who had died in Jamaica in 1807, and he also wrote *The Life of Villettes*, published in 1815. In the same year he published *Observations on emigration to France, with an account of health, economy, and the education of children*, which warned Englishmen against France, and English invalids against French watering-places, recommending Malta instead, which he had visited with a nephew in 1810. His *Observations* was eventually appended to later editions of the biography of Villettes.

It was in 1818, however, that Thomas Bowdler produced the work for which he is best-known, *The Family Shakspeare*, an edition of the complete plays best described by its subtitle: *in which nothing is added to the original text; but those words and expressions are omitted which cannot with propriety be read aloud in a family*. This notion of reading aloud was key, as his own father's reading of Shakespeare had had a formative influence on the young Thomas Bowdler. As he later put it:

> In the perfection of reading few men were equal to my father; and such was his good taste, his delicacy, and his prompt discretion, that his family listened with delight … without knowing that those matchless tragedies contained words and expressions improper to be pronounced … It afterwards occurred to me, that what my father did so readily and successfully for his family, my inferior abilities might … be able to accomplish for the benefit of the public. I say, therefore, that if 'The Family Shakspeare' is entitled to any merit, it originates with my father. (preface, *The Family Shakspeare*, 1843, viii)

The edition published by Longman in 1818 was not the first expurgation for which Thomas Bowdler accepted responsibility. His sister Henrietta Maria Bowdler had originated the project at Bath in 1807, with the publication of the first edition of *The Family Shakespeare* (spelt differently in his sister's edition). It had contained only twenty plays, avoiding such perilous works for the editor as *Hamlet*, and throughout had excised sexually explicit passages and religious references which might offend the Anglican reader. Thomas Bowdler had assumed the credit for this edition by 1809, probably in order to protect the reputations of his sister and the family. His own fuller edition of the plays operated on much the same principles as his sister's: in the preface he writes of Shakespeare's language that '[m]any words and expressions occur which are of so indecent a nature as to render it highly desirable that they should be erased' (p. viii). He also complains of the unnecessary and frivolous allusions to scripture, which 'call imperiously for their erasement' (p. ix). But Thomas Bowdler was in some respects more faithful to the original text than his sister had been. While it is true that he detected and excised more religious references than she had felt necessary, he also restored scenes that she had cut because she had found them trivial or uninteresting. As Noel Perrin puts it:

> He substituted very few of his own words for Shakespeare's, and he neither abridged nor (with rare exceptions) added commentary. That is, he treated Shakespeare rather as an unusually scrupulous television producer might now. His sister, who started expurgating Shakespeare ten years before he did, used a similar approach, but also often cut 'an uninteresting or an absurd scene', even though she

> considered it decent. That is, she treated Shakespeare rather as a normal television producer would. (Perrin, xii)

Neither the Bath edition of 1807 nor the London edition of *The Family Shakspeare* (1818) caused much of a stir on publication. In 1821, however, *Blackwood's Magazine* roundly criticized Bowdler's edition, and the *Edinburgh Review* published a defence of his aims and achievement written by Lord Jeffrey, which went so far as to state that all other editions of Shakespeare had been rendered obsolete. The controversy led to increased sales for *The Family Shakspeare*, and it became a best-seller—Lord Jeffrey's review served as a frontispiece to subsequent editions for over sixty years. Bowdler's expurgation ran into many editions, and as late as 1860, when it came out of copyright, demand for it was running high enough for another publisher to bring out a rival edition to Longman's.

During the final years of his life Bowdler wrote *A Short Introduction to a Selection of Chapters from the Old Testament* (1822), intended for a Sunday school society at Swansea, and he also continued his editorial work, attempting to purify Gibbon's *History of the Decline and Fall of the Roman Empire*. This was completed just before 'a cold … falling on his lungs' caused his death at Rhyddings on 24 February 1825 (Bowdler, 326). Bowdler was buried in Oystermouth parish churchyard, near Swansea. His expurgation of Gibbon was published by Longman in the following year, proclaiming itself to be 'for the use of families and young persons, reprinted from the original text with the careful omissions of all passages of an irreligious or immoral tendency'. In his preface Bowdler declared himself confident enough in the worth of his project to assert that Gibbon himself would have approved of it, and he also expressed his hope that his altered work might form the basis for future editions. Bowdler's nephew adds in a note that 'it was the peculiar happiness of the writer' to have so purified Shakespeare and Gibbon that they could no longer 'raise a blush on the cheek of modest innocence nor plant a pang in the heart of the devout Christian' (T. Bowdler, 'Note', *Gibbon's History of the Decline and Fall of the Roman Empire*, ed. T. Bowdler, 1826, xiii).

Bowdler's editing has come in for much criticism for almost two hundred years. The *Dictionary of National Biography* summarized the view which has largely prevailed by commenting that 'Bowdler's prudery makes sad havoc with Shakespeare's text', and by calling attacks on the edition 'deserved'. Most illustrative of this view of his edition is the word 'bowdlerize', derived from the Bowdler surname. The *Oxford English Dictionary* defines this word as 'to expurgate (a book or writing), by omitting or modifying words or passages considered indelicate or offensive', but goes on to offer the secondary, more editorial definition of 'to castrate'. First used in print as early as 1836, and still used to denigrate acts of censorship, the verb encapsulates the commonly held view of Bowdler's editorial philosophy and methods.

It is generally acknowledged that Bowdler's treatment of Shakespeare's text was unacceptable, and its influence can certainly not be denied. His sister's original expurgation and Bowdler's elaboration of her work set a more general movement of literary expurgation into play, and although *The Family Shakspeare* ran into many editions, more importantly it affected how Shakespeare was edited and read for generations. By 1850 there were seven expurgated editions of Shakespeare on the market, and by 1900 that number had increased to fifty (Perrin, xiii). Bowdlerization, however objectionable on intellectual grounds, clearly had a readership. And a defence of Bowdler's effect on the young reading public, if not of his larger philosophy, came from a quarter as unexpected as Algernon Charles Swinburne:

> More nauseous and more foolish cant was never chattered than that which would deride the memory or deprecate the merits of Bowdler. No man ever did better service to Shakespeare than the man who made it possible to put him into the hands of intelligent and imaginative children; it may well be, if we consider how dearly the creator of Mamillius must have loved them, that no man has ever done him such good service. (Swinburne, 'Social verse', *Works*, 15.278)

M. Clare Loughlin-Chow

Sources *DNB* · *IGI* · T. Bowdler, *Memoir of the life of John Bowdler* (1824), pp. 298–331 · N. Perrin, *Dr Bowdler's legacy: a history of expurgated books in England and America*, 3rd edn (1991) · www.findagrave.com · J. Gorton, *A general biographical dictionary*, 3 vols. (1841) · Munk, *Roll*

Archives BL, letters to Sir Robert Keith and Lord Hardwicke, Add. MSS 35524–35539, 35642–35741, *passim* · BL, letters to J. Strange, Egerton MSS 1970, 2001–2002 · Norfolk RO, letters to Silas Neville

Bowdler, Thomas, the younger (1782–1856), Church of England clergyman, the eldest son and heir of John *Bowdler (1746–1823), and his wife, Henrietta, *née* Hanbury, was born on 13 March 1782. John *Bowdler (1783–1815) was a younger brother. He was educated at Hyde Abbey School, Winchester, and at St John's College, Cambridge, where he proceeded BA in 1803 and MA in 1806. On 22 July 1806 he married Phoebe, daughter of Joseph Cotton. They had nine children, four of whom died in infancy. Bowdler was appointed curate of Leyton, Essex, in 1803, and after holding the livings of Ash and Ridley, and Addington, Kent, became incumbent of St Bartholomew's, Sydenham, in 1834. He was a high-churchman of the old school, and opposed both the Romanizing tendencies of the Tractarians, and the evangelicals' attacks upon them. In 1846 he became secretary of the Church Building Society, which his father had been instrumental in founding. On 7 December 1849 he became a prebendary of St Paul's Cathedral. Bowdler was the author of a large number of published sermons, with collected editions in 1820, 1834, and 1846. He wrote a memoir of his father in 1824, and edited with Launcelot Sharpe the Greek version of Bishop Lancelot Andrewes's *Devotions*. He was the editor of the 'Bowdlerized' edition of Edward Gibbon prepared by his uncle, Thomas *Bowdler the elder. Bowdler died on 12 November 1856 at 2 Onslow Square, Brompton, London.

Sidney Lee, *rev.* H. C. G. Matthew

Sources Venn, *Alum. Cant.* · *GM*, 3rd ser., 2 (1857), 241–2

Archives Pusey Oxf., corresp. | BL, letters to W. E. Gladstone, Add. MSS 44361–44369, *passim* · Bodl. Oxf., letters to W. C. Cotton

Bowdoin, James (1726–1790), merchant and revolutionary politician in America, was born on 7 August 1726 in Boston, Massachusetts, the youngest child of James Bowdoin (1676–1747), a prosperous merchant and landowner, and his second wife, Hannah Portage (*d.* 1734). Known in his youth as Jemmy and only posthumously, for the convenience of historians, as James Bowdoin II, he was tall and handsome, but rather plump, with a cleft chin and a long, pointed nose. He prepared for college at South grammar school in Boston under the tutelage of John Lovell, excelled in his studies, especially Latin, and entered Harvard College in 1742. A passionate reader, assiduous student, and keen empirical observer, Bowdoin was mentored at Harvard by John Winthrop, professor of mathematics and natural philosophy. He earned his baccalaureate in 1745 and, with a thesis on the economics of commutative justice, his master's degree in 1748.

One of Bowdoin's two room-mates at Harvard was his future brother-in-law, John Erving jun., for on 15 September 1748 he married Elizabeth Erving (1731–1803), daughter of John Erving sen. and Abigail Phillips. Proceeding from Harvard to his expected place among the élite of colonial Boston, he cultivated strong friendships among businessmen, political leaders, and intellectuals, including Benjamin Franklin, with whom he carried on a lifelong scientific correspondence. He loved to entertain guests frequently and lavishly, and was renowned as a connoisseur of both food and wine. He published much in the natural and social sciences, including *A Paraphrase on Part of the Oeconomy of Human Life* in 1759. He spearheaded the founding of the American Academy of Arts and Sciences (AAAS) in 1780 and served as its first president. In recognition of his leadership in the AAAS, he was elected a fellow of the Royal Society on 31 July 1788.

In 1753 Bowdoin was elected to the general court of Boston and in 1757 to the council of Massachusetts. Being both a political and a personal enemy of Governor Francis Bernard, he was dismissed from the council in 1769. Essentially sober, conservative, and patrician, and therefore the rival of the fiery populist John Hancock, Bowdoin nevertheless grew increasingly offended by the excesses of the royal government of the Massachusetts colony in the 1760s and early 1770s. In sharp contrast to the spirit of most of his publications stands his *Short Narrative of the Horrid Massacre in Boston*, a propaganda pamphlet about the killing of five civilians by British regulars on 5 March 1770.

In the same year Bowdoin was elected to the Massachusetts house of representatives and re-elected to the council in 1772. Subsequent to being dismissed from the council by Governor Thomas Gage in 1774, he was elected chairman of the Boston committee of safety and delegate to the first continental congress, but declined the latter in order to work locally on behalf of the colonists. Even though he was critically ill from spring 1775 until autumn 1778, he contributed what he could to the rebel cause and was elected to a number of high offices during the American War of Independence, including president of the Massachusetts revolutionary council in 1775 and president of the Massachusetts constitutional convention in 1779. After he fled Boston on 14 May 1775, Major-General Sir John Burgoyne occupied his Beacon Hill mansion until that November.

James Bowdoin (1726–1790), by Robert Feke, 1748

In 1784 Bowdoin became president of the Massachusetts Bank, later called the First National Bank of Boston. As governor of Massachusetts for two one-year terms from 1785 to 1787, he was ruthless in crushing Daniel Shays's rebellion. Defeated by Hancock for a third term as governor, he served as a delegate to the Massachusetts convention that ratified the United States constitution on 6 February 1788.

Consumptive and in poor health most of his life, Bowdoin died in Boston on 6 November 1790 from 'putrid fever and dysentery' and was honoured on 10 November with a magnificent state funeral procession to the Granary burial-ground, Tremont Street, Boston. At his death he was probably the wealthiest person in Massachusetts. By his will dated 23 March 1789 he bequeathed £400 to Harvard College, £100 and 1200 books to the AAAS, £100 to the Brattle Square Church, and £50 to its pastor, Peter Thatcher. His widow and two children divided in thirds the remainder of his estate, consisting of cash, securities, silver, *objets d'art*, personal property, and extensive real estate holdings in Boston, western Massachusetts, Connecticut, Vermont, New Hampshire, Maine, Ohio, and offshore islands. Each of the three received over 10,000 acres of land, substantial heirlooms, and at least £7663 and $1183.

On 24 June 1794, with a gift of £1000 and 1000 acres from Bowdoin's son James (1752–1811), the general court of the commonwealth of Massachusetts chartered a college to be founded in Brunswick, Maine, named Bowdoin College after the late governor. ERIC V. D. LUFT

Sources G. E. Kershaw, *James Bowdoin II: patriot and man of the Enlightenment* (1991) · R. L. Volz, *Governor Bowdoin and his family* (1969) · C. C. Calhoun, *A small college in Maine: two hundred years of Bowdoin* (1993) · C. K. Shipton, *New England life in the eighteenth century: representative biographies from Sibley's Harvard graduates* (1963); pbk edn (1995) · D. P. Szatmary, *Shay's rebellion: the making of an agrarian insurrection* (1980) · C. K. Shipton, 'James Bowdoin', *Sibley's Harvard graduates: biographical sketches of those who attended Harvard College*, 11 (1960), 514–50 · G. E. Kershaw, 'Bowdoin, James', *ANB* · W. A. Robinson, 'Bowdoin, James', *DAB* · K. J. Watson, ed., *The legacy of James Bowdoin III* (1994)

Archives Bowdoin College Library, Brunswick, Maine, Bowdoin collection · Harvard U. · Mass. Hist. Soc., cash books and letters

Likenesses J. Smibert, oils, 1736, Bowdoin College Museum of Art, Brunswick, Maine · R. Feke, oils, 1748, Bowdoin College Museum of Art, Brunswick, Maine [*see illus.*]

Wealth at death £25,000; plus 40,000 acres of land: Shipton, 'James Bowdoin', 514–50; will, Suffolk county probate court, Boston, Massachusetts

Bowell, Sir Mackenzie (1824–1917), prime minister of Canada, was born at Rickinghall, Suffolk, on 27 December 1824 (some sources give 1823), the son of John Bowell and Elizabeth Marshall. He emigrated to Canada with his parents in 1833; the family settled in Belleville, Upper Canada, where John Bowell had relatives. Mackenzie Bowell learned his father's trade of cabinet-maker, but went to work at the age of eleven as printer's devil for the Belleville *Intelligencer*, a weekly of which he assumed ownership in the 1850s. By this time he was also a leading member of the Orange order, and from 1870 to 1878 he was grand master of the Orange order in Canada. In December 1847 he married Harriet Louise Moore (*d.* 1884), with whom he had four sons and five daughters.

Bowell's entry into politics came in the 1860s. He was elected in 1867 to the new Canadian House of Commons for Hastings North, a seat he would hold for the next twenty-five years. He was a Conservative, and in 1878, after his party's resounding electoral victory, he was appointed by the prime minister, Sir John A. Macdonald, as minister of customs. Bowell's task was the supervision of the main source of government revenue. It was not easy, and involved an endless procession of things large and little, exacerbated by the fact that 'ignorant impatience of taxation is not confined to the thoughtless or the uneducated', as one of his officials, Charles Belford, put it (Belford to Bowell, 28 Feb 1880, National Archives of Canada, Mackenzie Bowell MSS, 1.212). Bowell's talents were administrative: he was conscientious, hard-working, and scrupulous; but a journeyman he was, and would remain.

After Macdonald's death in 1891 Bowell carried on with some additional responsibilities, but on the accession of Sir John Thompson to the prime ministership in December 1892 he was elevated to the senate, and became government leader there with a new portfolio, minister of trade and commerce. In that capacity he went to Australia in 1893 with Sandford Fleming to discuss trade between the Australasian colonies and Canada, the new Pacific cable, and the new Vancouver–Sydney steamship line. His mission was so successful that, with Thompson's encouragement, it was decided that Canada ought to call an intercolonial conference, to meet in Ottawa in June 1894 to discuss intercolonial trade and imperial preference. The conference had really been Bowell's idea. Six of the seven Australian colonies sent delegates, as did Fiji, Cape Colony, and a still independent Hawaii. The British government did not send a delegate, only an observer; the British were not at all sure they liked such radical colonial initiatives.

That 1894 conference probably represents the furthest reach of Bowell's talents. He was seventy years of age; his younger colleagues called him Grandpa Bowell, and he looked the part, but the appellation also signified intellectual limitations. Sir John Thompson was looking for ways to ease him out of office when Thompson died suddenly in England on 12 December 1894.

Bowell had been senior minister in a cabinet that had been held together by Thompson's strength, suavity, and knowledge. Now it tended to dissolve into its constituent parts. The logical successor to Thompson was Sir Charles Tupper, Canadian high commissioner in London; however, Tupper was disliked by Lady Aberdeen, the strong-minded wife of the governor-general, Lord Aberdeen, and by Thompson's widow. So Lord Aberdeen asked Bowell to become prime minister. Bowell was delighted, especially by his new KCMG, conferred on 1 January 1895. He had never underestimated his own capacities: he believed he could emulate Macdonald and Thompson, but this required a reach of intelligence and finely tuned discrimination that was wholly beyond him. What to Bowell was cleverness was regarded by everyone else as evasion and weakness. Lord Aberdeen found that he liked to have a trapdoor to escape from danger, moral or political, and it was difficult, moreover, to hold him to a point of policy, because he had not sufficiently possessed himself of it in the first place.

In Bowell's defence, it has to be said that, at that time, the Canadian ship of state had a very hard helm. The privy council decision in the Brophy case (29 January 1895) forced the government to redress Roman Catholic grievances in Manitoba. Bowell's Orangeism had faded, and did not block his willingness to do whatever the law dictated. But, to the question of what immediate action was to be taken, the members of Bowell's cabinet returned different answers. If ever a government needed an intelligent, firm, judicious direction, it was now. Parliament had to be dissolved before 26 April 1896. The province of Manitoba deliberately sought to make difficulties. Bowell, in no position to run either his government or the election campaign that was looming, was forced out in April 1896. Sir Charles Tupper was brought over from England to replace him, and though the Liberals, under Wilfrid Laurier, won a working majority at the 1896 general election, the Conservatives under Tupper won a greater share of the popular vote (46 per cent to 45 per cent). Bowell returned amiably enough to the senate, to which he was appointed for life. He was in good health and refused to ease up; he looked twenty years younger than his seventy-two years, and his vanity gloried in the fact. He made many interventions in debate, and retired from the senate only in 1906. In 1913 he was still running the Belleville *Intelligencer*. He died of pneumonia on 10 December 1917 at his home at William and Bridge streets, Belleville. He was buried in Belleville cemetery.

Bowell was not a great law maker; his talent for public life lay in practical administration. He endeavoured to keep the machinery of his customs department functioning smoothly, but in higher offices he must be judged more harshly. His appearance was deceptive, never more than as he grew older: vain, vacillating, and stubborn, he had the pretence and hypocrisy of a weak mind, with only modest talents to redeem him. At the high point of his political career, as prime minister, that was never enough.

P. B. Waite

Sources P. B. Waite, 'Bowell, Sir Mackenzie', *DCB*, vol. 14 • P. B. Waite, *Canada, 1874–1896: arduous destiny* (1971) • *The Canadian journal of Lady Aberdeen, 1893–1898*, ed. J. T. Saywell (1960) • NA Canada, Sir Mackenzie Bowell collection, MG26-E • H. J. Morgan, ed., *The Canadian men and women of the time* (1898) • *The Globe* [Toronto] (11 Dec 1917) • *The Globe* [Toronto] (14 Dec 1917)

Archives Belleville Public Library, Belleville, Ontario, scrapbooks and clippings • NA Canada, MSS | NA Canada, Sir John A. Macdonald MSS • NA Canada, Sir John Thompson MSS

Likenesses photograph, repro. in G. E. Boyce, *Historic Hastings* (1967), 181 • photographs, NA Canada, Photographic Archives

Wealth at death presumed wealthy; owned Belleville *Intelligencer*, perhaps worth C$10,000 in 1917

Arthur Charles Mainwaring Bowen (1922–1980), by unknown photographer

Bowen, Arthur Charles Mainwaring (1922–1980), founder of the British Rheumatic Association, was born on 24 March 1922 at Pentre-bach, Pontyberem, near Carmarthen, the son of Arthur Pendragon Bowen (1887–1942), a timber and builder's merchant, and his wife, Edith Helena Stephenson (1895–1984). He was educated at Gwendraeth infants and junior schools, Pontyberem, and at Gwendraeth Valley secondary school, Dre-fach. Bowen then began a BA in law and history at Aberystwyth. He intended to enter the church and obtained a Welsh church scholarship to go on to Oxford after graduating. However, while still at Aberystwyth, Waring Bowen, as he was known, was diagnosed at the age of nineteen as having ankylosing spondylitis, a painful and progressive rheumatic disease of the spine. During lengthy periods of treatment and rest in hospital he met many young people affected by various forms of arthritis and was determined to try to help them. He was particularly concerned about their chances of gaining qualifications and employment, and extremely conscious of the isolation felt by people in his position, especially those who had been used to an active life.

Bowen eventually obtained an external London BA in 1946 before qualifying in 1950 as a solicitor. Most of his early studies were accomplished lying flat on his back on a plaster bed, as a result of the treatment he was receiving. In spite of his health problems he married Helen Patricia (*b*. 1930), daughter of Egbert John Cope, on 29 August 1953, and they had a son and a daughter. Bowen led a busy life as a solicitor and was a family man who took part in many local activities. He felt passionately that he had, in some small way, to help alleviate the widespread human suffering, both physical and psychological, of arthritis-related diseases, easing the plight of people in a similar situation to himself. It was this which gave him the impetus, at the age of twenty-five, to found the British Rheumatic Association in 1947. In 1959 the name was changed to the British Rheumatism and Arthritis Association and was then changed again, in 1980, at his suggestion to Arthritis Care, the title it still carries. Bowen also founded two other charities. One was the Rehabilitation Loan Society, which helped people who lost their jobs or businesses as a result of contracting arthritis; this society was absorbed into Arthritis Care in the early 1980s. The other charity was the Torbay Arthritis Project, which raised money for a hydrotherapy pool and rheumatology unit; this subsequently became part of the Torbay Hospital. These philanthropic achievements had their roots in his family's history, throughout which there was a strong tradition of public service. His mother's family were devout Methodists. Bowen's uncle gave up his career as a commercial secretary to become a Methodist minister. His grandfather was mayor of Newark in 1933. With this family background it is perhaps not surprising that Bowen devoted his own life to helping others. The greater part of this life was spent encouraging understanding of a disease that at the time was a very neglected branch of medicine, but which he knew only too well. There were virtually no welfare or rehabilitation facilities when he contracted arthritis. This was a situation he was determined to redress.

Bowen was renowned for his depth of feeling and his keen and whimsical sense of humour. His character was such that his extremely fertile imagination encouraged a never-ending stream of ideas and suggestions, but more importantly led to both self-achievement and a sense of spiritual fulfilment. With his determination and idealism as an inspiration, Arthritis Care became the UK's largest voluntary organization working with and for all people with arthritis, from every section of the community. By the 1990s the association which he created was dispensing free advice and information to many of the 8 million men and women, including 1 million under forty-six and 14,500 children, who suffered from the disease.

Waring Bowen died suddenly at the age of fifty-seven at his home, Roundhay, 2 St George's Crescent, Torquay, on 31 January 1980, following a heart attack, and his ashes were buried at Capel Ifan, Pontyberem, on 17 February. Many of the staff who work for Arthritis Care in a paid or voluntary capacity have arthritis and are grateful to Bowen, who proved that the people who best understand living with arthritis are those with arthritis themselves. Practical self-help, talking to other people with the disease, and sharing ideas helped him enormously and this continues, to this day, to be an immensely important part of the ethos of Arthritis Care with its philosophy of user involvement. His widow, Helen, an occupational therapist, was actively involved in the charity both nationally and locally since his death and as one of its vice-presidents.

Bowen's personality, direct approach, ideas, and enthusiasm have continued to flourish. Through his unique compassion for others he left behind an organization with a membership of 62,000 which helped many who have themselves played a major role in developing the charity's work. He left behind a memorial for all those with arthritis. RICHARD GUTCH

Sources *Arthritis care branch manual: notes on arthritis care*, A (1992), 1–12 [Arthritis Care, London] · W. Woodford, 'Arthur Mainwaring—founder of BRAA', *Arthritis News* (April 1980), 2 [Arthritis Care, London] · Memorandum of association of the British Association for Arthritis and Rheumatism. First redraft for initial consideration of the committee of management at its meeting on 19 Jan 1976, Arthritis Care, London · *Some facts about the British Association for Arthritis and Rheumatism (BRAA)* (1979), 1–2 [Arthritis Care, London] · private information (2004) [H. Barbour; M. Ackroyd] · b. cert. · d. certs. [A. P. Bowen and C. H. Bowen, parents] · *CGPLA Eng. & Wales* (1980) · W. Woodford, 'BRAA founder dies, aged 57', *Arthritis News* (April 1980), 1

Likenesses photograph, 1940, priv. coll. · photograph, Arthritis Care [*see illus.*]

Wealth at death £87,680: probate, 25 Sept 1980, *CGPLA Eng. & Wales*

Bowen, Charles Synge Christopher, Baron Bowen (1835–1894), judge, was born on 1 January 1835 at Woolaston, Gloucestershire, the eldest son of the Revd Christopher Bowen (1801/2–1890), clergyman, an Irishman from co. Mayo, and Catherine Emily Steele (1807/8–1902), whose father, Sir Richard Steele, of the 4th dragoon guards, was an Irish baronet, and whose mother was of mixed Austrian and Irish parentage. Edward Ernest *Bowen, schoolmaster, was his younger brother. After attending school in Lille, France, and at Blackheath, Kent, Bowen entered Rugby School at the age of fifteen, already a precocious scholar: he was discovered on his first day reading Euripides' *Alcestis* for 'amusement' (Cunningham, 18). The masters found him 'delightfully clever' (ibid., 17), and the perennial prize-winner was also popular as an outstanding all-round athlete. Well built, outgoing, and adventurous, he was at one point sorely tempted to join the army. In 1853 he won a scholarship at Balliol College, Oxford. His glittering attainments included the Hertford scholarship for Latin, the chancellor's prize for Latin verse, the Ireland scholarship for classics, and the Arnold historical prize. In 1857, while still an undergraduate, he was elected a fellow, subsequently obtaining first-class honours in *literae humaniores*, and graduating with a BA. He was president of the Union in 1858.

Charles Synge Christopher Bowen, Baron Bowen (1835–1894), by J. Thomson

The same year, Bowen began to read for the bar as a student at Lincoln's Inn. The contrast with Oxford he found deeply depressing: so painful was the memory of that time that in after years he would avoid the very vicinity of his former chambers. In 1860 he suffered the first of many breakdowns in health that were to dog his entire career. Very soon after being called to the bar in January 1861, he became engaged to Emily Frances (*d.* 1897), eldest daughter of James Meadows *Rendel, a civil engineer; he joined the western circuit in October and on 7 January 1862 the couple married. Marriage was a bold, perhaps a reckless step for a man without private means who, at twenty-seven, had still to make his way, and who, his constitution already undermined, henceforth enjoyed precarious health, suffering further breakdowns in 1865 and 1868, by which time he had two sons and a daughter. After an unpropitious start on the circuit, he gained the friendship of one of the leaders there, John Duke Coleridge, later lord chief justice, who invited him to join his chambers. With his help, Bowen gradually acquired a reputation for perception and thoroughness. In 1868 he was appointed secretary to the Totnes bribery commission, in 1869 a revising barrister, in 1870 a member of a commission to investigate the operation of the Truck Acts, and later that year he was made recorder of Penzance.

From 1871 to 1874, throughout the protracted hearings of the Tichborne case, Bowen was active as junior counsel for the defendants against the claimant Orton. His senior, John Duke Coleridge, always stressed the immense debt which he owed to Bowen, who, with a diligence and pertinacity which Coleridge classed as 'superhuman' (Cunningham, 133), and aided by a prodigious memory, made himself master of every detail of the case, and who, by painstakingly testing the claimant's minutest allegations, enabled Coleridge successfully to rebut them and to expose Orton as an impostor. Bowen is thought to have devised the preamble much used by Coleridge as a means of avoiding a leading question: 'Would you be surprised to hear that—?' (*DNB*). At Orton's subsequent trial for perjury Bowen was appointed one of four prosecuting counsel. But the cumulative strain proved too much, and he again collapsed. The celebrated Tichborne case later (1998) became the subject of a film.

When Coleridge became attorney-general, he appointed Bowen as junior counsel to the Treasury in 1872. In this capacity Bowen appeared for the crown in many important common-law and commercial cases and rapidly acquired a large commercial clientele. In 1878 his health once more broke down, and he took a tour through Russia to Constantinople. In 1879 he was knighted, and Lord Chancellor Cairns appointed him a judge of the Queen's Bench Division. A year later he again fell seriously ill. In June 1882 he was raised by Lord Chancellor Selborne to the Court of Appeal, where he served for nine years. In Lord Davey's words: 'it is upon his work there that his judicial reputation will rest' (Davey, 215).

According to his entry in the *Biographical Dictionary of the Common Law*, Bowen 'does not rank as one of the greater of the Victorian judges'. This verdict is somewhat harsh. Sir Frederick Pollock considered Willes, Macnaghten, and Bowen 'the greatest English judges I have known' (Pollock, 172); and C. H. S. Fifoot held that a Court of Appeal of which Bowen, Lindley, and Lord Justice Fry were members 'challenges comparison with any before or since' (Fifoot, 20). Liberal and open-minded, Bowen was a reformer, rightly impatient of legal technicalities which impeded justice. His views on the function of law in society were dynamic: 'it changes, it must change, it ought to change' (Bowen, 'Administration of the law', 329); and his judicial activism is exemplified in the case of the armament manufacturer Nordenfelt (1892), where he held that a worldwide covenant in restraint of trade—prima facie void—was enforceable in the public interest. In *The Mogul Steamship Company* v. *McGregor* (1889), he ruled that the elimination of commercial competitors, however robust the means employed, as long as they are not unlawful, is not actionable. *Thomas* v. *Quartermaine* (1887) remains an authority on contributory negligence and the maxim *volenti non fit injuria*.

Bowen was ever the scholarly Oxonian, 'precise, scrupulous, even fastidious, in the spoken and in the written word' (Fifoot, 40). Observers noted his deferential mildness as an advocate, 'that extremely polite and lady-like manner for which he was famed' (Williams, 223) and his 'ineffectiveness' when addressing juries (Lord Justice Mathew, in Coleridge, 2.404). A self-deprecating irony sometimes misfired. In an early case, he prosecuted a burglar who had been apprehended on the roof with the tools of his trade. 'If, gentlemen of the jury', Bowen is supposed to have said:

> you think that the accused was on the roof of the house to enjoy the midnight breeze, and, by pure accident, happened to have about him the necessary tools of a housebreaker, with no dishonest intention of employing them, you will, of course acquit him. (Fifoot, 20)

The jury took him at his word.

Bowen's legal reputation owed more to his intellectual finesse than to his style of advocacy: another contemporary described him as 'a legal archangel who danced with ease on the point of a needle' (Smith, 129). But the ease was deceptive: his forensic triumphs were the hard-earned fruit of strenuous lucubrations, of a self-doubting and almost morbid perfectionism in preparing his cases. 'Cases', he said, 'are won at chambers' (Cunningham, 135); and the fine points which he successfully pleaded were drafted and redrafted beforehand 'with the finest camel-hair pencils' (Smith, 129). Members of his chambers, who included H. H. Asquith, had a very high regard for him. On the bench he demonstrated the same meticulous attention to detail, the same 'mastery of the law, expressed in fastidious prose' (Fifoot, 20), and the same anxious, to some over-anxious, solicitude for justice which characterized what Lord Esher called his 'intense sense of duty' (Davey, 216).

But his heart was not altogether in the law. 'Professional life', he confessed, 'is not worth the sacrifices it entails' (Cunningham, 193). In early years he admitted to hating the law; and for one whom some thought 'perhaps the most brilliant man of his generation' (Biron, 89), ceaseless toil in an essentially uncongenial calling sapped his vitality and was perhaps the underlying cause of his chronic ill health. Even promotion to the bench—which curtailed his hopes, probably illusory, but long nurtured, of a parliamentary career—left him 'a bitterly disappointed man' (Graham, 111). A lifelong friend of Benjamin Jowett, master of Balliol, he might have been happier as a don or man of letters. 'He might have been a poet', Lord Justice Davey reflected, 'as he might have been a good many other things' (Davey, 231). Poetry, classical and English, he relished both as reader and practitioner. He published a verse translation of Virgil's *Eclogues* and the first six books of the *Aeneid* in 1887, and almost his last composition was an exquisite Latin rendering of Landor's valedictory quatrain 'I strove with none'.

To write a legal textbook Bowen dismissed as a task too ephemeral to be worth the effort. In 1868, however, he published a pamphlet advocating Anglo-American arbitration in the *Alabama* dispute; and he wrote several pieces relating to the administration of justice: in 1886 on the effects of the Judicature Acts; in 1887 on law reform across the reign of Victoria. In 1892, having served on a unique committee of judges charged with reviewing the administration of the courts, he compiled and published its far-reaching recommendations; and in 1893, as chairman of a Home Office commission set up following rioting at Featherstone colliery in Yorkshire, he produced a report on the citizen's duty to lend assistance in time of public disturbance. All these writings are compendious, perspicuous, judicious, and authoritative.

Having been snubbed as a young barrister in his first appearance before Lord Justice Cockburn, Bowen never forgot that wounding experience, and he was always gracious and courteous on the bench. Out of court he was remarkably relaxed, companionable, and expansive, 'bright and youthful', as Mr Justice Mathew observed, 'ready to discuss any subject' (Cunningham, 155). He was much sought after for his ready wit, full of whimsy and repartee, often preceded by a misleadingly solemn air. His fellow judges, drafting an address to Queen Victoria, objected to the phrase 'Conscious as we are of our shortcomings'. It was Bowen who demurely suggested: 'Conscious as we are of one another's shortcomings' (Cunningham, 183). Throughout his life Bowen retained his youthful looks and remarkably fine eyes. But his friendly mien and sense of humour concealed a spirit sometimes despondent and sceptical. Behind the kindly smile ran a vein of melancholy, a sense of life's brevity and vanity. Relief and diversion were afforded by the purchase of a country house at Colwood in Sussex, by travel at home and abroad, including a journey across Canada with Lord Coleridge in 1883, which, however, exhaustion obliged him to cut short.

Bowen was an active member of the Council of Legal Education. He was a bencher of Lincoln's Inn in 1879. Oxford granted him a DCL (1883), Balliol elected him its visitor (1885). He was a fellow of the Royal Society (1885) and a trustee of the British Museum. He was elected to a number of clubs, including the Athenaeum (1878), the Literary Society and Grillons (1880), the 'Dilettanti', and 'The Club'. Lord Chancellor Herschell appointed him a lord of appeal in ordinary as Baron Bowen of Colwood in August 1893; but since 1890 illness had again supervened, and after only a few months in the upper house, he died of abdominal cancer on 10 April 1894 at his home at 13 Princes Gardens, Knightsbridge, aged fifty-nine. He was buried in Slaugham churchyard, Sussex, near his country home. A marble tablet was raised to his memory in the vestibule of Lincoln's Inn chapel. A. LENTIN

Sources H. S. Cunningham, *Lord Bowen: a biographical sketch with a selection from his verses* (1897) · H. Davey, 'In memoriam, Lord Bowen', *Law Quarterly Review*, 10 (1894), 211–21 · C. H. S. Fifoot, *Judge and jurist in the reign of Victoria* (1959) · F. Pollock, *For my grandson: remembrances of an ancient Victorian* (1933) · E. Graham, *Fifty years of famous judges* [1930] · A. W. B. Simpson, ed., *Biographical dictionary of the common law* (1984) · C. Bowen, 'The law courts under the Judicature Acts', *Law Quarterly Review*, 2 (1886), 1–11 · C. S. C. Bowen, 'The administration of the law from 1837 to 1887', *The reign of Queen Victoria: a survey of fifty years of progress*, ed. T. H. Ward, 1 (1887), 281–329 · Lord Justice Bowen, *Novel reading: an address* (1891) · *DNB* · E. H. Coleridge, *Life and correspondence of John Duke, Lord Coleridge*, 2 (1904) · C. Biron, *Without prejudice: impressions of life and law* (1936) · M. Williams, *Leaves of a life*, 2 vols. (1890) · K. J. M. Smith, *James Fitzjames Stephen: portrait of a Victorian rationalist* (1988) · *Law reports* · J. Foster, *Men-at-the-bar: a biographical hand-list of the members of the various inns of court*, 2nd edn (1885) · d. cert. · *IGI*

Archives BL, legal opinion and letters to W. E. Gladstone, Add. MSS 44138–44789, *passim* · Devon RO, letters to Sir Thomas Dyke Acland

Likenesses T. Brock, marble bust, exh. RA 1895, Balliol Oxf. · T. Brock, bust, Rugby School · Spy [L. Ward], chromolithograph caricature, NPG; repro. in *VF* (12 March 1892) · J. Thomson, photograph, NPG [*see illus.*] · portrait, Oxford Union

Wealth at death £32,322 19s. 0d.: probate, 18 May 1894, *CGPLA Eng. & Wales*

Bowen, Edmund John (1898–1980), chemist, was born in Worcester on 29 April 1898, the eldest in the family of two sons and two daughters of Edmund Riley Bowen (*b.* 1866), headmaster of St John's Elementary School for Boys, Worcester, and his wife, Lilias, daughter of Thomas Kamester, carpenter, of Clewer, Windsor. He was educated at his father's school and at the Royal Grammar School, Worcester. Bowen won a science scholarship to Balliol College, Oxford, and went into residence in October 1915. In 1916 he volunteered and in April 1917 was posted to France with the Royal Garrison Artillery.

Following demobilization Ted Bowen returned to Oxford in January 1919 and took first-class honours in chemistry in 1920 after only five terms of study. He was one of several highly gifted scientists whose abilities were recognized by their tutor, H. B. Hartley, for whom he and his contemporary C. N. Hinshelwood carried out undergraduate research. Immediately after graduation he was appointed a demonstrator in the Balliol and Trinity laboratories. This was followed by a lectureship (1921) and a fellowship (1922) at University College which he held until his retirement in 1965. In 1924 Bowen married Edith, eldest daughter of Joseph and Margaret Moule, farmers of Hartlebury, Worcestershire. They had a happy marriage, and two children were born, Margaret Lilias (*b.* 1927) and Humphry John (*b.* 1929). From 1938 onwards he was also university lecturer and later Aldrichian praelector. Bowen sat on numerous university committees, but his main contributions to university administration were in connection with the University Museum, the Museum of the History of Science, and the university observatory.

Bowen's scientific work lay almost entirely in the field of photochemistry and the related phenomenon of fluorescence. His pioneer work in the period 1923–35 provided some of the earliest experimental confirmation of the fundamental laws of photochemistry in the theoretical work of Einstein. In 1935 Bowen was elected FRS, and later served on the council (1943–5). During the Second World War he was a member of the Oxford research team working on respirator problems for the Ministry of Supply.

Bowen's early research had been carried out using largely home-made apparatus, often put together using domestic odds and ends. However, from 1945, electrical and optical devices became commercially available, and Bowen used these extensively in his later work on fluorescence. One of the notable results of this work was the demonstration that energy could be transferred from one molecule to another over distances much greater than a molecular diameter. Although no mathematician, he took a keen interest in the developments in quantum theory, which were of basic importance for his experimental work.

Bowen had a remarkable gift for explaining abstruse theories by means of simple diagrams and models. This was put to good use in his book *The Chemical Aspects of Light* (1941) and in discussion with pupils and colleagues. He was widely read in many branches of science outside chemistry, and an avid collector of fossils and antiquities. One ammonite from Dorset, where he had a holiday house, was named *Perisphinctes boweni* after him. He was keenly interested in the history of science, and published several articles on the early history of the Royal Society and of science in Oxford. In 1963 Bowen was awarded the Davy medal of the Royal Society. He also became vice-president of the Chemical Society and of the Faraday Society and was Liversidge lecturer of the Chemical Society in 1966.

Bowen was an inventive scientist, more interested in understanding underlying principles than in accumulation of detail. His enthusiasm and kindness to others were widely acknowledged. He retained his boyish character and youthful appearance until his death at his home, 10 Park Town, Oxford, on 19 November 1980 following a heart attack. R. P. Bell, *rev.*

Sources *The Times* (22 Nov 1980) • R. P. Bell, *Memoirs FRS*, 27 (1981), 83–101 • private information (1986) • personal knowledge (1986)
Archives MHS Oxf., corresp. and papers; research notes and working papers | Bodl. Oxf., corresp. with C. A. Coulson
Likenesses four photographs, RS
Wealth at death £163,362: probate, 24 Feb 1981, *CGPLA Eng. & Wales*

Bowen, Edward Ernest (1836–1901), schoolmaster, was born at Woolaston, near Chepstow, on 30 March 1836, the second of three sons of Christopher Bowen (1801/2–1890) of Hollymount, co. Mayo, an evangelical clergyman who was successively curate of Woolaston and Bath Abbey church, and perpetual curate of St Mary Magdalene's, Southwark. His mother, who died on 1 February 1902 at the age of ninety-four, having survived her three sons and husband, was Catherine Emily, daughter of Sir Richard Steele, third baronet, of Hampstead, co. Dublin. Charles, afterwards Lord *Bowen, was Edward's elder brother. Edward was at school at Lille and at the Revd E. J. Selwyn's school in Blackheath, and after two years at King's College, London, went up to Trinity College, Cambridge, in the autumn of 1854. He was made a scholar of his college, and won the Bell university scholarship in 1855, the Carus Greek testament (undergraduates') prize in 1856, and a prize for an English essay, which was published as *The Force of Habit Considered as an Argument to Prove the Moral Government of Man by God* (1858). In 1856 he was president of the Cambridge Union and in the following year he was elected to the select society of the Apostles. He graduated BA in 1858 as fourth in the first class of the classical tripos, and next year was elected to a fellowship at Trinity. He proceeded MA in 1861. Like his brother Charles, he was a frequent contributor to the *Saturday Review* in its early days.

Bowen was one of the generation of mid-Victorian college fellows who found their vocation as schoolmasters in the revitalized public schools. After one term's work as an assistant master at Marlborough, in January 1859 he became a master at Harrow under C. J. Vaughan. He remained at Harrow for the rest of his life, never marrying, and devoting his energies to the school. As a schoolmaster he was mainly guided by two principles—that the boy must be interested in his lessons and at ease with the teacher. While other teachers were grave and distant, Bowen was always cheerful, vivacious, and familiar, abounding in genial irony and ingenious fancy. Although order and discipline were necessities of his existence, he held that 'boys ought hardly ever to be punished against their will'. 'Punishments, rewards, and marks' he humorously defined as 'the three great drawbacks to education'. Teaching he regarded as an individual gift, and when giving evidence before the secondary education commission of 1894 he opposed any formal training of teachers for secondary schools. He delighted in form-teaching and it was from a sense of duty rather than from choice that in 1863 he accepted a 'small' house which he found 'a nuisance'. In 1881 he became head of The Grove, one of the 'large' houses, where he exercised a strong guidance of the boys.

In order to widen the methods and scope of education, Bowen recommended the creation of the modern side at Harrow. This department was started in 1869, to rank as far as possible on a par with the classical side, with himself as its head. In 1881, at the behest of Henry Montagu Butler, the headmaster, he wrote an exhaustive memorandum on the principles, character, and thoroughly successful results of the new development. Bowen continued the management of the modern side until 1893, when, feeling that under Butler's successor, J. E. C. Welldon, the modern side was silently becoming 'a refuge for the destitute', he resigned his leadership, but continued to teach the two highest forms.

Bowen had strong claims to the headmastership when Welldon was appointed in 1885, but his position as a layman, in a period when governing bodies effectively restricted public-school headships to clergymen, told against him. The author of two articles in the *National Review* (1863), taking a liberal theological position on the

Bishop Colenso controversy and Old Testament criticism, Bowen became increasingly detached from orthodox religion. Opposed to clerical control of education, he was elected as a radical member of Harrow School board in 1877. In 1880 he unsuccessfully stood as a Liberal parliamentary candidate against A. J. Balfour in Hertford, specifically opposing the pro-Turkish policies of the Conservative government. Although he opposed Irish home rule after 1886, he retained democratic sympathies, opposing the Second South African War and militarism generally. He had, however, a deep interest in military tactics and his travels on the continent took him to most of the notable battlefields.

Bowen was one of the earliest and most vigorous promoters of organized games in schools. A formidable pedestrian, walking as an undergraduate from Cambridge to Oxford in twenty-six hours, he was also an accomplished skater and a skilful mountaineer. He rowed in the Trinity College second eight, and played cricket, but his chief influence was as a pioneer of football, which he still played with the boys in the last year of his life. He helped to codify the laws of association football, playing for the Wanderers team in the first FA cup final (1872), but came later to deplore the rise of professionalism in the sport. Though himself a sturdy individualist in matters of political conviction and religious belief, and within the school freely exercised the independence which his position as a housemaster gave him, he expounded the moral virtues of team games as promoting corporate values of 'brotherhood', 'mutual help', and 'social union'. Games almost came to represent for him an ethical substitute for religion: 'There lives more soul in honest play, believe me, than in half the hymn books', he wrote in 1884 (Roach, 131). Like other schoolmasters of the period, such as John Percival and H. H. Almond, he had a spartan loathing of luxury, and saw in games an antidote to materialism. His own literary abilities were turned to writing school songs, set to stirring music by John Farmer, which were intended to increase the sense of corporate union among the boys. His 'Forty Years On', written in 1872, became 'the national anthem of Harrow'. His compositions were collected in *Harrow Songs and other Verses* (1886).

Even sympathetic contemporaries, such as James Bryce, were uneasy about the emphasis which Bowen placed on games, and doubted their results (Bryce, 352). Later writers, taking into account the subsequent excesses of the cult of athleticism in English education, have passed a sterner judgement, declaring that Bowen's 'admiration for Spartan qualities and pluck in games was so intense that his whole sense of values became distorted' (Newsome, 223). In a perhaps fairer assessment Roach emphasizes Bowen's critical intellect and the breadth of his interests, commenting that the promoters of games in subsequent generations were not always men of Bowen's calibre (Roach, 149).

Bowen died suddenly near Moux, in France, on 8 April 1901, while on a bicycle tour in the Côte d'Or with his friend Bryce. He was buried at Harrow, and bequeathed the bulk of his property to Harrow School, having previously added 2 acres to the playing fields at his own expense. [ANON.], *rev.* M. C. CURTHOYS

Sources W. E. Bowen, *Edward Bowen: a memoir* (1902) · J. Bryce, *Studies in contemporary biography* (1903) · E. W. Howson, G. T. Warner, and others, eds., *Harrow School* (1898) · J. Roach, *Secondary education in England, 1870–1902* (1991) · D. Newsome, *Godliness and good learning* (1961) · J. A. Mangan, *Athleticism in the Victorian and Edwardian public school* (1981) · Venn, *Alum. Cant.* · P. M. Young, *A history of British football* (1968) · C. Tyerman, *A history of Harrow School, 1324–1991* (2000)

Archives King's AC Cam., letters to Oscar Browning · Trinity Cam., letters to Henry Sidgwick

Wealth at death £67,899 19*s.* 2*d.*: resworn probate, Jan 1902, *CGPLA Eng. & Wales* (1901)

Bowen, Edward George (1911–1991), radiophysicist, was born on 14 January 1911 in Cockett, Glamorgan, Wales, the youngest of four children of George Bowen (1872–1959), steelworker and later insurance agent, and his wife, Ellen Ann, *née* Owen, who was born in nearby Pembry in 1876. He was educated at Cockett infants' school, Sketty elementary school, and the municipal secondary school, from where he went with a state scholarship to University College, Swansea, graduating with a first-class degree in physics (1930), an MSc (1931), and a fellowship (1932) for PhD studies at King's College, London, with E. V. Appleton. On 27 December 1938 he married Enid Vesta Williams (*b.* 1910/11), daughter of Benjamin Thomas Williams, grocer. She was a science teacher whom he had met at university. They had three sons: Edward, David, and John.

Early in 1935 Bowen was selected by Watson Watt, the 'father' of British radar, to help A. F. Wilkins develop the first air warning equipment at Orfordness, Suffolk; Bowen built the high-power transmitter. A year later the group moved into nearby Bawdsey Manor to plan the vital chain of coastal warning stations. Bowen, however, accepted the challenge of devising radars for aircraft—one type, aircraft to surface vessel radar (ASV), for locating surface vessels, the other, air interception radar (AI), for intercepting night bombers. In September 1937 he unofficially demonstrated his experimental ASV's potential by locating the British fleet, during North Sea exercises, in visibility so poor that Coastal Command aircraft had abandoned their search. His later sets were a major factor in defeating submarines attacking Atlantic convoys. For technical and operational reasons, Bowen's first AI radars were not successful in the RAF in late 1939, but the technical deficiencies were fixed in 1940 with limited modifications and thorough engineering (AI Mk IV). However, Bowen clashed with Superintendent A. P. Rowe, whose deputy, W. B. Lewis, had intervened in the modifications without consulting Bowen. After May 1940 Bowen ceased taking an active part in his group's work, but his AI Mk IV, with the operational problems solved, was decisive in the 1941 night raids.

In August 1940 Bowen became the radar member of Sir Henry Tizard's mission to North America. At the Massachusetts Institute of Technology, Boston, he helped establish the radiation laboratory and its programmes, based on the new British magnetron, the top-secret key to microwave radar. Afterwards he worked to ensure effective liaison with Britain. Late in 1943 he was recruited in Boston by Professor F. W. G. White for Australia's radar centre, the radiophysics laboratory in Sydney. On 1 January 1944 he became White's deputy for research.

Bowen was chief of the radiophysics laboratory from May 1946 to 1971. His first ventures were to edit *A Textbook of Radar* (1947), by the staff, and to develop peacetime radar applications, especially for civil aviation. Later two programmes dominated research. J. L. Pawsey's group studied radio radiation from space. With Pawsey's outstanding scientific ability, supported by Bowen's management skills, it won international recognition in the emerging science of radio astronomy. The second programme, directed by Bowen, explored the physics of rainfall and its stimulation. Systematic cloud seeding over twenty-four years established world leadership. The detailed mechanism underlying Bowen's persistence hypothesis has since been largely explained, but his speculations about the roles of meteor showers and the moon in rainfall periodicities remain controversial.

By the 1950s observational radio astronomers needed much higher resolution. Pawsey's group made progress with interferometric solutions, but Bowen judged correctly that building a giant steerable paraboloid would be quicker. He organized comprehensive London studies of the engineering problems and negotiated substantial American funding. When completed in 1961 at Parkes, New South Wales, the 210 foot telescope was the outstanding instrument of its type, but curtailment of the brilliant interferometry approach split Pawsey's group.

Bowen played a vital role in the Anglo-Australian 153 inch optical telescope (AAT) for Siding Spring Mountain, New South Wales. Between 1968 and 1973 he chaired the majority of the meetings of the interim joint policy committee and its permanent successor, the AAT board, which had overall project responsibility. Design and construction were entrusted to their project office in Canberra. Bowen, who could draw on experience with the new radio telescope technology at Parkes, steered the enterprise through many crises. The result was a telescope in 1974 with an unsurpassed performance for its size. By 1970, however, dissent had surfaced over the facility's eventual management. At a board meeting in 1972 to settle the issue, Bowen voted for the British position. In 1973, when he accepted a three-year appointment as scientific counsellor at the Australian embassy in Washington, DC, the government forced his resignation from the board. After his embassy appointment ended in 1976 he retired to Maryland before returning to Sydney in 1978.

Bowen published sixty-two papers and a second book, *Radar Days* (1987). His honours included the US medal for freedom (1947), appointment as CBE (1962), and fellowship of the Royal Society (1975). Athletic and dynamic, he enjoyed competitive cricket and sailing. He was an ardent Welshman, known to friends as Taffy. In December 1987 he suffered a stroke, and he gradually deteriorated. He died on 12 August 1991, at the Ashley House Nursing Home, Chatswood, Sydney, Australia. His body was cremated at the Northern Suburbs memorial gardens and crematorium, North Ryde, Sydney, four days later.

H. C. Minnett

Sources E. G. Bowen, *Radar days* (1987) • R. H. Brown, *Boffin: a personal story of the early days of radar, radio astronomy and quantum optics* (1991) • P. Robertson, *Beyond southern skies* (1992) • S. C. B. Gascoigne, K. M. Proust, and M. O. Robins, *The creation of the Anglo-Australian observatory* (1990) • E. G. Bowen, 'Biographical notes', 1983?–1985?, Archives of the Australian Academy of Science, Canberra • R. W. Watt, *Three steps to victory* (1957) • R. H. Brown and others, *Historical Records of Australian Science*, 9 (1992–3), 151–66 • E. G. Bowen, ed., *A textbook of radar* (1947) • F. Hoyle, *The Anglo-Australian telescope* (1981) • *WWW*, 1991–5 • m. cert. • personal knowledge (2004) • private information (2004)

Archives Australian Academy of Science, Canberra • CAC Cam., papers on radar development | Australian Academy of Science, Canberra, Sir Frederick White MSS • Australian Academy of Science, Canberra, E. G. Bowen MSS

Likenesses photographs, Commonwealth Scientific and Industrial Research Organization, Sydney

Bowen, Edwin Yorke [York] (1884–1961), pianist and composer, was born on 22 February 1884 in Crouch Hill, London, the youngest of the three sons of Edward Bowen (*d.* 1911), founder of the whisky distillers Bowen and McKechnie, and his wife, Ellen Mary (1854–1906), the daughter of the Revd W. B. Dennis, a Wesleyan minister. He was known as York Bowen from about 1906. He showed musical promise at an early age, and his mother gave him his first piano and harmony lessons. He then attended the North Metropolitan College of Music and, from 1892, the Blackheath Conservatoire of Music, where he studied under Alfred Izard. At the age of eight he performed the solo part in one of Dussek's piano concertos.

When he was fourteen Bowen won the Erard scholarship to the Royal Academy of Music, where he studied composition under Frederick Corder and piano under Tobias Matthay as well as viola and horn, and he was also a proficient organist, enabling him to write idiomatically for a variety of instruments. In 1902 he composed his first symphony and a symphonic poem, *The Lament of Tasso*, which was performed at a Promenade Concert conducted by Henry Wood. Bowen toured Britain, performing his own compositions, including his first piano concerto (December 1903), as well as solos by Chopin, Liszt, Skryabin, and Tchaikovsky. In addition he conducted some of his own orchestral works, which were favourably received. Saint-Saëns praised 'the most remarkable of the young British composers' (Potts), and considered Bowen's potential to be greater than that of his fellow student Arnold Bax, who had made his impact as a prodigious pianist but not yet as a composer. In 1905, having won all the prizes for piano and composition, and having been awarded the Worshipful Company of Musicians medal, Bowen left the academy to teach at the Tobias Matthay Pianoforte School. He was elected a fellow of the academy in 1907 and appointed to the staff there in 1909.

On 23 April 1912 Bowen married (Dorothy) Sylvia Beatrice Dalton (1888–1967), the only daughter of the Revd J. P. Dalton, rector of Creech St Michael, Somerset. Sylvia had acted with the Old Vic Company, but following her marriage to Bowen she studied lieder and later gave recitals with her husband. Their son, Philip, was born on 25 March 1913. During the First World War Bowen joined the Scots Guards and played the horn in the regimental band. He went to France, but returned in 1916 with pneumonia.

Bowen's early musical style was influenced by Liszt, Wagner, Richard Strauss, and the Russian nationalists. He was fascinated by the music of Debussy and Ravel, and temporarily resigned from the Royal Academy following a disagreement on this matter with the principal, Alexander Mackenzie. With his friend Benjamin Dale he frequently attended Wagner operas. He began his compositional career when abstract Romantic music was popular and he continued writing in this lyrical style long after the end of the First World War, when it was considered old-fashioned. The war had signalled a turning point for many European composers, including his contemporaries Bax, Ireland, and Bridge, but Bowen disapproved of all modernist trends, vehemently objecting to music which lacked tonality and melody. His rejection of prevailing fashions won him the admiration of the composer and pianist Kaikhosru Sorabji, who compared him with Rakhmaninov and Medtner, and who hired the Bechstein Hall about 1946 in order to hear Bowen perform his twenty-four preludes and fugues, op. 102.

As one would expect from a pianist-composer, piano music on both a small and large scale dominates Bowen's *œuvre*. His orchestral output includes four symphonies and four piano concertos. Chamber music was frequently performed by his friends, among them Lionel Tertis, Carl Dolmetsch, Leon Goossens, and Aubrey Brain. Bowen composed a number of secular songs for his wife and some piano duets and two-piano pieces, which he performed with Harry Isaacs.

Although he was primarily a performer, Bowen spent much of his life teaching. He wrote pedagogical works for piano students and edited works by Chopin and Mozart. He frequently examined or adjudicated at competitions and festivals and from 1951 he sat on the audition panel for the BBC. In 1959, having reached the age of seventy-five, he retired from the Royal Academy, and in the following year he recorded a selection of his piano pieces for Lyrita. He continued to lead an active life as a composer, recitalist, examiner, and teacher, and he had been preparing for a broadcast when he suffered a fatal coronary thrombosis and died in New End Hospital, Hampstead, on 23 November 1961. He was cremated at Golders Green crematorium.

Monica Watson commemorated Bowen's centenary by writing a biography. While sometimes appearing aloof, he had a sense of humour and was remembered affectionately by friends and pupils. A York Bowen Society was founded by John Lindsay to promote his music and that of other neglected British composers, and Bowen's manuscripts are housed in the Royal Academy of Music.

LISA HARDY

Sources M. Watson, *York Bowen: a centenary tribute* (1984) • K. S. S. Sorabji, *Mi contra fa: the immoralisings of a Machiavellian musician* (1947); repr. with an introduction by D. Garvelmann (1986), 235–9 • L. Hardy, *The British piano sonata, 1870–1945* (2001) • F. Potts, disc notes, *York Bowen: piano music* (Hyperion CDA 66838, 1996) • private information (2004)

Archives BL NSA, performance recordings • Royal Academy of Music, London, collection | SOUND BL NSA, performance recordings

Likenesses photographs, repro. in Watson, *York Bowen*, 55–8

Wealth at death £1283 7*s*. 0*d*.: probate, 1 Feb 1962, *CGPLA Eng. & Wales*

Bowen [*married name* Cameron], **Elizabeth Dorothea Cole** (1899–1973), writer, was born on 7 June 1899 at 15 Herbert Place, Dublin, the only child of Henry Charles Cole Bowen (1862–1930), barrister, of Bowen's Court, Kildorrery, co. Cork, and his wife, Florence Isabella Pomeroy (*c*.1866–1912), daughter of Henry Fitz-George Colley, of Mount Temple, Dublin. The Bowens were Cromwellian settlers of Welsh origin. Elizabeth Bowen's early childhood was happy, with summers spent at Bowen's Court, the house built by Henry Bowen in 1775 (the history of which she told in her family memoir *Bowen's Court*, 1964), and winters in Dublin (recalled in *Seven Winters*, 1942). This idyll ended when her father suffered a mental breakdown in 1905. 'Bitha', as she was nicknamed by the family, and her mother moved to England in 1906, settling in Hythe. Her marked stammer developed at this time. In 1912 her beloved mother died of cancer. Elizabeth Bowen never fully recovered from this trauma, telling a friend that the worst event of her life had occurred when she was thirteen—her fiction abounds in orphaned children. Elizabeth Bowen was largely brought up by her aunts; she attended schools in Hertfordshire and Kent and spent her summers at Bowen's Court. In 1918 her father married Mary Gwynn, sister of Stephen Gwynn.

In 1921 Elizabeth Bowen was briefly engaged to John Anderson, a British officer, and on 4 August 1923 she married Alan Charles Cameron (1893–1952), assistant secretary for education for Northamptonshire. Cameron had fought in the First World War, been badly gassed, and had been awarded the MC. Although the marriage was important to both partners, it was unconsummated. Elizabeth Bowen later told Iris Murdoch that they had decided not to have children because of her desire to write and her husband's horror of the modern world: she came to regret this decision. Alan Cameron is recalled as a Blimpish figure, given to clichés and banal comments. However, he had a passion for education and was an enthusiast for cinema; his report *The Film in National Life* (1932) led to the founding of the British Film Institute. He gave Elizabeth Bowen practical support and was an unqualified admirer of her work—he could recite long passages from her novels, which he knew almost by heart.

Cameron transformed Elizabeth Bowen from a *farouche*, badly dressed young woman into a more worldly, stylish figure. After their move to Waldencote, Old Headington, in 1925, on Cameron's appointment as secretary for education for Oxford, she embraced Oxford life, becoming a close friend of David Cecil, Maurice Bowra, and of Susan

Elizabeth Dorothea Cole Bowen (1899–1973), by unknown photographer

and John Buchan. Her first collection of short stories, *Encounters*, was published in 1923; her first novel, *The Hotel*, was published in 1927. Her first 'Irish' novel, *The Last September*, was published in 1929; *Friends and Relations* and *To the North* followed in 1931 and 1932.

In early 1933 Elizabeth Bowen met Humphry *House (1908–1955), later an eminent Dickens scholar. He had been fellow and chaplain at Wadham, but had resigned after losing his faith. Elizabeth Bowen fell in love with the brilliant, saturnine, much younger House. He was genuinely attached to her, but also admitted to being 'avid for experience' (House to Bowen, undated). Their affair paralleled his established relationship with Madeline Church and continued after his marriage in December 1933—the wedding was arranged while Elizabeth Bowen was in New York, from early November to mid-December 1933. Elizabeth Bowen's animosity towards Madeline House expressed itself in a determination to see Humphry House as 'embracing mediocrity with his eyes open' (Bowen to Berlin, 18 Dec 1933) and as destroyed by claustrophobic domesticity. She expressed outrage to Humphry House on hearing of his wife's pregnancy—he countered by enquiring, 'why, Elizabeth, did you not tell me when we first slept together that you were a virgin?' (House to Bowen, 23 July 1934). Despite these tensions Madeline House and her baby daughter stayed with Elizabeth Bowen at Waldencote in spring 1935. Early in 1936 House went to Calcutta, and this decision caused a serious quarrel with Elizabeth Bowen, although they were to remain friends. A version of this relationship—radically adjusted—is to be found in *The House in Paris* (1935), a novel in which Elizabeth Bowen enshrines her lover's name, and in which her quasi-obsessive theme of orphaned children is intricately tied to a secret affair. In 1935 Alan Cameron was appointed secretary to the Central Council for Schools Broadcasting. Elizabeth Bowen established herself as a notable London literary hostess at 2 Clarence Terrace, the grand house near Regent's Park which they acquired on an eight-year lease. Despite Cameron's director-level salary, they let a bed-sitting-room to help with the rent.

In summer 1936 Elizabeth Bowen arranged a large house party at Bowen's Court, which she had inherited on her father's death in 1930; guests included Isaiah Berlin, Rosamond Lehmann, and Goronwy Rees, journalist, Soviet agent, and fellow of All Souls. It is probable that Elizabeth Bowen saw Rees, a vital young man, as a replacement for Humphry House; however he and Rosamond Lehmann fell in love and began an affair. Elizabeth Bowen's anger at Rees's preference for the exotically beautiful Lehmann erupted in letters to Berlin, in which she accused the couple of defiling Bowen's Court by the 'ruthless incontinence' of their actions (Bowen to Berlin, 23 Sept 1936). Berlin thought her mad with jealousy. The enduring pain caused by this episode provided the central situation for her novel *The Death of the Heart* (1938), in which Rees was, to his consternation, transformed into the egocentric, self-destructive Eddie. Elizabeth Bowen had an intolerance of rejection and this crisis revived her resentment of Humphry House—as she put it 'experience means nothing till it repeats itself' (*The Death of the Heart*, 342). Her uncontrolled behaviour is in contrast to the formal control of the novel—a moving depiction of the crisis of adolescence. She had already confessed to her inability to surrender the 'unchecked power' of the novelist and to realize 'that a close relationship with a person isn't a book' (Bowen to House, 6 June 1934?). As she admitted, 'I am fully intelligent only when I write' (*Why do I Write?*, 20).

Hostility to a married couple with children resurfaced in her affair with Sean O'Faolain (1900–1991), which began in May 1937. Elizabeth Bowen told the American writer May Sarton that the O'Faolain marriage had been a mistake. O'Faolain, a former member of the IRA, brought Elizabeth Bowen to a closer understanding of Irish nationalist politics—she had already dealt with the war of independence in *The Last September*—and put her in touch with contemporary Irish writing. Their affair was effectively ended by the outbreak of war. Elizabeth Bowen also had a brief affair with May Sarton in late May 1937, which she took lightly. She told Sarton that she had had one previous affair with a woman. She distinguished between such relationships between an older woman and younger woman, and lesbianism—of which she disapproved. An important literary friendship with Virginia Woolf was forged in the 1930s; Elizabeth Bowen greatly admired Woolf and valued her rigorous criticism. She stayed regularly with Woolf at Monks House, Sussex, the last time in February 1941.

The Second World War produced Elizabeth Bowen's greatest writing—a great number of short stories emerged, many directly or indirectly concerned with the irruption of the supernatural in wartime London ('The

Demon Lover', 'The Happy Autumn Fields', 'Mysterious Kôr'). She recalled:

> It seems to me that … the overcharged subconsciousnesses of everyone overflowed and merged … Sometimes I hardly knew where I stopped and somebody else began. The violent destruction of solid things … left all of us, equally heady and disembodied. Walls went down. (*The Demon Lover and other Stories*, 217–18)

During the war, Elizabeth Bowen travelled regularly to Ireland and wrote confidential reports for the Ministry of Information; these are brilliant exercises in reportage and analysis, which capture the constriction of neutral Ireland. Despite her own conservative political stance and patriotism—she and her husband acted as ARP wardens during the war—she vigorously defended Irish neutrality:

> It may be felt in England that Eire is making a fetish of her neutrality. But this assertion of her neutrality is Eire's first *free* self-assertion … Eire (and I think rightly) sees her neutrality as positive, not merely negative. She has invested her self-respect in it. (FO 800/310/253)

Elizabeth Bowen's wartime affair with the Canadian diplomat Charles Stewart Almon Ritchie (1906–1995) was the happiest and most equal sexual relationship of her life—it is clear from Ritchie's diaries that he admired and loved her. The affair led to an enduring friendship and he is remembered in her will. Ritchie, who shared Elizabeth Bowen's fascination with the psychology of defeatism, is the unexpected model for Robert, the crypto-Nazi, in *The Heat of the Day* (1949), her supreme achievement as a novelist, and one of the finest novels of civilian life of the Second World War. The love affair between Robert and Stella takes place in a London rendered phantasmagoric by war, a city in which the 'wall between the living and the living became less solid as the wall between the living and the dead thinned' (p. 87). The novel's dreamlike Irish episodes shadow Elizabeth Bowen's war reports and depict a world of fuel shortages, isolation, and obsession with the war.

From 1949 to 1951 Elizabeth Bowen served on the royal commission on capital punishment and successfully pressed the case for verbal provocation. In 1945 Alan Cameron had retired from the BBC—his eyesight was failing and in 1952 they moved permanently to Bowen's Court. Alan Cameron died there that August. He had functioned as a family system for Elizabeth Bowen and she was devastated by his death, using images of amputation to describe her feelings; she later told Iris Murdoch that the most terrible moment of her life had been when she found him dead and told Isaiah Berlin that she had never known what it was like to mourn before and that he had been 'my father and mother … I now have … "no next of kin" … my next of kin is this house' (Bowen to Berlin, 8 Oct 1952).

Elizabeth Bowen continued to entertain at Bowen's Court; guests included Iris Murdoch, a lifelong friend, and, less happily, an infatuated Carson McCullers. Despite heroic efforts, much journalism, lecture tours in the United States, and periods as writer-in-residence at American universities, Elizabeth Bowen was unable to keep up the house, which she sold in 1959 to a farmer, who promptly demolished it. She described this catastrophe as 'a clean end' (*Bowen's Court*, 459), for she had already depicted the more typical fate of a big house—degeneration—in *A World of Love* (1955), her last 'Irish' novel. Elizabeth Bowen returned to England in 1960, living first in Old Headington, and then in 1965 moving to Hythe, where she wrote her last novel, *Eva Trout, or, Changing Scenes* (1968), which reanimates the tensions of her affair with Humphry House. Its genesis was linked to the publication in 1965, of Madeline House's first volume of Dickens's *Letters*, dedicated to Humphry House, who had died in 1955: an episode of *Eva Trout* takes place in Bleak House, Broadstairs, and his letters are quoted at length. In this novel Elizabeth Bowen returns to obsessive themes—displaced, orphaned, and abducted children, the disruption of a marriage by an outsider—in a bizarre, kaleidoscopic work, which gives the reader a 'sense of burning one's finger with the present' (John Bayley to Elizabeth Bowen, undated).

Elizabeth Bowen's output was considerable: ten novels, over eighty short stories, as well as memoirs, travel literature, criticism, and much literary journalism. Her major novels enjoyed critical and commercial success: *The Heat of the Day* sold 45,000 copies on first publication. She was appointed CBE in 1948 and CLitt in 1965. She was a member of the Irish Academy of Letters and received an honorary DLitt from Trinity College, Dublin, in 1949 and Oxford in 1956. Elizabeth Bowen's reputation declined before her death but recently her distinction has been recognized and her standing as a writer is assured. Elizabeth Bowen was tall, large-boned, with red-gold hair and light blue eyes. Attitudes to her varied; some found her kind, generous, and unsnobbish, others thought her arrogant and condescending in a very Anglo-Irish way. In 1972 she developed lung cancer—she was a sixty-a-day smoker—and died on 22 February 1973 in University College Hospital, London. She is buried, as her will directed, in her husband's grave in St Colman's churchyard, Farahy, co. Cork. Virginia Woolf's final pronouncement on Elizabeth Bowen might serve as epitaph for both woman and writer; 'A very honourable horsefaced, upper class hard constricted mind' (*Diary*, 299). DEIRDRE TOOMEY

Sources Elizabeth Bowen's corresp. with Humphry House, priv. coll. • Elizabeth Bowen's corresp. with Isaiah Berlin, Wolfson College, Oxford, Berlin archive • John Bayley to Elizabeth Bowen, undated, Ransom HRC • *The diary of Virginia Woolf*, ed. A. O. Bell and A. McNeillie, 5 (1984) • V. Glendinning, *Elizabeth Bowen: portrait of a writer* (1985) • E. Bowen, *Bowen's Court*, 2nd rev. edn (1964) • E. Bowen, *Seven winters* (1942) • J. Bayley, *Iris: a memoir* (1998) • E. Bowen, letters to William Plomer, U. Durham • E. Bowen, letters to May Sarton, NYPL, Humanities and Social Sciences Library, Berg collection • J. M. Sellery and W. O. Harris, *Elizabeth Bowen: a bibliography* (1981) • C. Ritchie, *The siren years: undiplomatic diaries, 1937–1945* (1974) • 'Royal commission on capital punishment', *Parl. papers* (1952–3), 7.677, Cmd 8932 • private information (2004) [J. Bayley and A. N. Jeffares] • d. cert.

Archives TCD, literary MSS, incl. autobiographical sketches • U. Reading L., corresp. | JRL, corresp. with L. P. Hartley • NYPL, Berg collection, letters to May Sarton • priv. coll., corresp. with Humphry House • Ransom HRC, corresp. with Spencer Curtis Brown • U. Durham L., letters to William Plomer • U. Reading L., corresp. with Longmans • U. Sussex, letters to V. Woolf • Wolfson College, Oxford, corresp. with Isaiah Berlin

Likenesses M. Peake, crayon drawing, 1938 • C. Beaton, photograph, 1943, NPG • A. Durand, oils, 1969, NPG • H. Coster, photograph, NPG • photograph, NPG [*see illus.*] • photographs, priv. coll.
Wealth at death over £30,000: probate, 1975

Bowen, Emanuel (1693/4–1767), engraver and map maker, was the son of Owen Bowen (*d.* 1730), gentleman, of Talley, Carmarthenshire, South Wales, and his wife, Anne (*d.* 1721). On 7 September 1709 he was apprenticed to Charles Price, globe and instrument maker and a member of the Merchant Taylors' Company, and this date suggests that Bowen was born about 1693/4. Price, also from Carmarthenshire, had been apprenticed to John Seller senior.

Bowen married Elizabeth Boreman on 6 February 1714 and their daughter Sarah was born about 1719. During his apprenticeship he engraved maps for George Willdey's *Atlas of the World* (1717). 1720 saw the publication of the *Britannia depicta*, a popular reduced version of John Ogilby's road atlas augmented by fifty-four county maps and historical notes by John Owen. Simultaneously, Bowen was engraving and selling prints and in 1722 one of these, a portrait of the bishop of Rochester, a Jacobite sympathizer, led to his being falsely accused of stirring up 'the minds of the Vulgar to Disaffection against the Government'.

During this period Bowen became a freemason and in 1723 was listed as senior warden of the Newgate Street Lodge in London. Three years later he appeared as master of a newly established lodge meeting at the Naggshead and Starr in Carmarthen and this continuing link to his home locality is significant in that 'A new and accurate map of South Wales … delineated from an actual survey and admeasurement by Eman. Bowen' appeared in 1729. This six-sheet map, superior to previous ones of the region, contains a decorative baroque dedication panel to George, prince of Wales, and topographical views of five towns. Its 500 subscribers were mostly south Wales gentry whose houses are also indicated on the map. The subscribers' list locates two Bowens in his home area and a number of members of the newly formed Carmarthen Lodge. Large-scale maps of Norfolk and Huntingdonshire and 'A new and accurate map of England and Wales' (1734) soon followed. The latter, a large display map with borders containing the coats of arms of 205 MPs who voted against the Excise Bill of 1733, is described by Shirley as a 'tour de force of its kind'. In 1732 and 1735 Bowen took on two apprentices, Thomas Kitchin and Thomas Jefferys, who also became eminent map makers. It was about this time that his son Thomas Bowen [*see below*] was born.

Between 1721 and 1750 Bowen engraved charts for some of the leading hydrographers of his day, including Joseph Avery, Samuel Fearon and John Eyes, Nicholas Dobrée, and Murdoch Mackenzie. His prolific output for British periodicals (1736–63), rivalled only by John Lodge and Thomas Kitchin, includes seventy-six British and foreign maps in the *General Magazine of Arts and Sciences*, the foreign ones illuminating subjects of contemporary interest. In 1763 Bowen produced 'An accurate map of North America describing … the British, Spanish and French dominions as defined in the treaty of Paris 1763'. This four-sheet map, engraved by John Gibson, was reissued a number of times.

Bowen's contribution to eighteenth-century world and British atlases was substantial. Consulting a wide range of contemporary sources, he drew and newly engraved seventy maps for his *Complete System of Geography* (2 vols., 1744–7), most being reissued in his *Complete Atlas* (1752) and *The Maps and Charts to the Modern Part of the Universal History* (published in 1766 under Thomas Kitchin's name). He produced maps for John Harris's *Navigantium atque itinerantium bibliotheca* (1744–8), and all twenty-two new plates in the final edition (1754) of Patrick Gordon's *Geography Anatomized* were also his. Over the period 1749–60, together with Kitchin, who had married his daughter Sarah in 1739, Bowen used the most recent surveys to compile and engrave a set of county maps for his *Large English Atlas* (1760). The commercial success of this important and influential work, the first to cover England and Wales on a large scale, led to the maps being reduced and modified by Bowen and Kitchin for their *Royal English Atlas* (*c.*1763) and then by Emanuel and Thomas Bowen for *Atlas Anglicanus* (1767–8), published after Emanuel Bowen's death by Kitchin. All three works are characterized by detailed texts in the spaces surrounding the maps and by elegant rococo decoration, which became the hallmark of his engraving.

Initially located Next the Stairs in St Katharine's, his address in 1742 was the Progress of the Ship, Clerkenwell. His very active involvement in the affairs of the nearby Barbican Baptist chapel up to a year before his death suggests that he remained in that same area of London. Reporting that he had died in London on 8 May 1767, the *London Magazine* for July 1767 draws attention to 'his reduced circumstances by family extravagances' and reports that he was 'almost blind through age' (July 1767, 372). As a compiler and engraver rather than a publisher of maps, the valuable copperplates he worked would have been owned by others. It is, however, still difficult to understand why he died penniless, since he was industrious and able and had the distinction of being geographer to George II from about 1747 and, according to many sources (particularly Chubb), geographer to Louis XV of France.

Thomas Bowen (1732/3–1790), engraver, was indentured on 7 February 1748 to his father, Emanuel Bowen. This suggests that he was born about 1732/3. In the decade following the end of his apprenticeship he engraved a few maps for the *General Magazine of Arts and Sciences* but, in general, he was overshadowed by his father. Of five maps he engraved in British periodicals, two were by the elder Bowen and two of the three county maps by Thomas Bowen in *The Royal English Atlas* were 'revised, corrected and improved by Eman. Bowen'. After his father's death Thomas informed the subscribers of *Atlas Anglicanus* that, having worked alongside his father in its preparation, he was competent to complete the task. When it appeared in 1768 most of the maps were attributed jointly to them. The same year saw the publication of Philip Morant's *History of Essex*, to which father and son contributed two and four maps respectively. On 25 December of that year Thomas was married to Alice Downes, thought to be from an engraving family, at St John, Clerkenwell.

The next fifteen years, as Bowen became more established as an engraver and compiler of British and foreign maps and charts, were his most productive. Among the British maps he engraved are 'A new and correct map of the countries twenty miles round London' (1770); nine, which include five road maps, in the *Gentleman's Magazine* (1773–9); eight in the *Survey and Maps of the Roads of North Britain or Scotland* (1776) by George Taylor and Andrew Skinner; and 'A map of Great Britain' in Charles Burlington's *Modern Universal British Traveller* (1779). His substantial foreign map output includes three charts relating to James Cook's voyages, jointly engraved with John Gibson for John Hawkesworth's *An Account of the Voyages Undertaken … for Making Discoveries*; a large single-sheet 'Map of the province of South Carolina' and his extension to eleven sheets of the 'Chart of part of the West Indies … by … Joseph Speer', all published in 1773. Numerous maps and further charts by Thomas Bowen are also found in Charles Theodore Middleton's *A New and Complete System of Geography* (1777–9) and Jonathan Carver's *The New Universal Traveller* (1779). Later single works include the three-sheet map of Morea by Peter Bell (1785), and 'A new and complete chart of the world', drawn and engraved by him for *Bankes's New System of Geography* (1790).

Although his output was not as extensive as that of his father, Thomas Bowen's maps and charts, with their simpler post-rococo decoration, made a valuable if modest contribution to the cartography of the last part of the eighteenth century. He spent most of his working life in Clerkenwell, his last recorded address being 9 Charterhouse Lane, and died there in the workhouse in early 1790. It is, again, difficult to understand why he, like his father, should have ended his days in poverty, as the *Gentleman's Magazine* of March 1790 records his death under 'Considerable Persons' and refers to him as 'an eminent engraver of charts … the son of Emanuel B. esq. engraver to his late Majesty' (p. 374). IOLO ROBERTS and MENAI ROBERTS

Sources *British Library map library catalogue* (1998) [CD-ROM] • map catalogue [NL Wales] • L. Worms, 'Thomas Kitchin's "journey of life": hydrographer to George III, mapmaker and engraver', *Map Collector*, 62 (1993), 2–8; 63 (1993), 14–20 [suppl. by private correspondence] • private information (2004) [L. Worms] • DWL • GL • apprenticeship indentures 19/293, Merchant Taylors' Company, archives • Library and Museum Trust of the United Grand Lodge of England, archives • parish records, Carmarthenshire, NL Wales, CLRO CF 1/346 • D. C. Jolly, *Maps in British periodicals*, 2 vols. (1990–91) • *London Magazine*, 36 (1767), 372 • *GM*, 1st ser., 60 (1790), 374 • R. W. Shirley, *Printed maps of the British Isles, 1650–1750* (1988) • R. V. Tooley, *Tooley's dictionary of mapmakers*, ed. J. French, rev. edn, 1 (1999) • *County atlases of the British Isles*, ed. D. Hodson and R. A. Skelton, 3 vols. (1970–97) • H. M. Atherton, *Political prints in the age of Hogarth* (1974) • T. Chubb, *The printed maps in the atlases of Great Britain and Ireland: a bibliography, 1579–1870* (1927) • J. Anderson, *The constitutions of the freemasons* (1723) • *IGI*

Bowen, Emrys George (1900–1983), geographer, was born on 28 December 1900 at 1 Towy View, Carmarthen, the elder child of Thomas Bowen, insurance agent, and Elizabeth Ann Lynch. He was educated at the council school, Pentre-poeth, and from 1912 to 1919 at Queen Elizabeth Grammar School, Carmarthen, before proceeding in 1919 to the University College of Wales, Aberystwyth, where he obtained a first-class honours degree in geography in 1923. The following year he took a teacher's diploma and, after a year's research at Aberystwyth, became the first Cecil Prosser research fellow at the Welsh National School of Medicine at Cardiff, investigating the relationship between 'racial type' and chest disease. From 1928 to 1929 he was an assistant editor with the *Encyclopaedia Britannica* before being appointed in 1929 assistant lecturer in the department of geography and anthropology at Aberystwyth. There he remained for the rest of his academic career, including the war years when he continued to lecture and also taught meteorology to the Royal Air Force initial training wing which was located there. He became Gregynog professor in 1946.

There were three strands to Bowen's academic work. The first was physical characteristics of populations; his master's thesis (1926) was entitled 'South west Wales: a study of physical anthropological characters in correlation with varied distributions'. It was this attempt to relate physical anthropological character to disease, especially to tuberculosis among the population of upland Cardiganshire, which led to his subsequent work at the National School of Medicine. An early paper, 'The incidence of phthisis in relation to race type and social environment in south and west Wales' appeared in the *Journal of the Royal Anthropological Institute* in 1928 (new ser. 31, 363–98). The second was the nature of the social organization, or the way of life, of a people, especially as it was derived from the past, from the process of cultural inheritance. The third was the nature of the physical environment in which the people lived. Essentially Bowen's aim was to integrate all these three strands in the explanation of the variable character of the earth's surface. This is best illustrated in the first book he published, *Wales: a Study in Geography and History* (1941). These themes he had inherited from his mentor, H. J. Fleure, but it was the determination to stress the second, social organization, which had led to the department's being entitled 'geography and anthropology' when it was founded in 1917. Bowen carried forward that emphasis and many of his research students contributed significantly in the field of social anthropology. Against that background, and under Bowen's leadership, the department played a distinctive role in the development of geography in Britain ensuring that both contemporary social structures and the role of historical development were given a significant status in the interpretation of landscape.

If Bowen's early research was in the field of physical anthropology his first published paper (*Geographical Teacher*, 13, 1924–6, 317–26) was 'A study of rural settlement in south-west Wales'. That interest became his specialist concern, more particularly those settlements which had grown about the cells established in the post-Roman period by the so-called Celtic saints. In 1932 he published an article entitled 'Early Christianity in the British Isles: a study in historical geography' (*Geography*,

17, 1932, 267–77), and in 1934 *Aberystwyth Studies* included a paper by him on 'The travels of Saint Samson of Dol' (13, 61–7). His research and writings subsequently broadened to cover the early history of western Britain and its prehistorical antecedents. Its full flowering was represented in his three books, *The Settlements of the Celtic Saints in Wales* (1954), *Saints, Seaways, and Settlements* (1969) and *Britain and the Western Seaways* (1972).

Apart from his specialized field Bowen's interests ranged widely. For many years he was a Sunday school teacher in a Welsh Baptist chapel; in his retirement he lectured on church history in the United Theological College at Aberystwyth. The paper 'Bedyddwyr Cymru tua 1714' in *Trafodion Cymdeithas Hanes Bedyddwyr Cymru* (1957–8, 5–14), ('Welsh Baptists circa 1714' in the *Transactions of the Welsh Baptists Historical Society*, 1957–8, 5–14), and the volume of essays *Geography, Culture, and Habitat* (1975) indicate his versatility, although Wales was always a common denominator. He lived for many years with his sister. After his retirement in 1968 Bowen continued to live at Aberystwyth where he died unmarried after a heart attack on 8 November 1983 at Bronglais General Hospital, Aberystwyth. He was buried at Carmarthen.

Bowen's work was widely recognized. He was president of the Institute of British Geographers in 1958 and president of section E of the British Association in 1962. He was awarded the Murchison grant by the Royal Geographical Society in 1958. In 1949 he was elected a fellow of the Society of Antiquaries and in 1967 he was president of the Cambrian Archaeological Society. He was awarded an honorary LLD by the University of Wales and an honorary DUniv by the Open University. He was an honorary member of the Gorsedd of Bards.

But it was as a teacher and lecturer that Bowen was supreme. His exposition, based on careful structuring, triad upon triad, and the timing of a consummate actor, was masterly. It was in the tradition of Welsh preaching rather than of academic discourse, a feature reinforced by his lively presentation, epitomical short, dark appearance and Bible black clothing. By his devotion to his subject, and his willingness to lecture throughout the country in the smallest and remotest of locations, he did much to establish geography as an academic discipline in Wales.

HAROLD CARTER

Sources H. Carter, 'Emrys G. Bowen, 1900–1983', *Transactions of the Institute of British Geographers*, new ser., 9 (1984), 374–80 [incl. full bibliography] · *Geography, culture, and habitat: selected essays, 1925–1975, of E. G. Bowen*, ed. H. Carter and W. K. D. Davies (1975) · E. G. Bowen, H. Carter, and J. A. Taylor, *Geography at Aberystwyth* (1968) · G. R. J. Jones, 'Emrys George Bowen, 1900–1983', *Welsh History Review / Cylchgrawn Hanes Cymru*, 12 (1984–5), 246–8 · J. E. R. Carson, *Ceredigion* [Cardiganshire Antiquarian Society], 9 (1983), 301 · priv. coll. · *The Times* (12 Nov 1983) · b. cert.

Archives NL Wales, papers | NL Wales, letters to Thomas Iorworth Ellis

Likenesses S. Nisbett, portrait, 1968, NL Wales · D. Tinker, bust, 1984, U. Wales, Aberystwyth, Institute of Geography and Earth Studies

Wealth at death £41,581: administration, 16 Feb 1984, *CGPLA Eng. & Wales*

Bowen, Euros (1904–1988), Church in Wales clergyman and Welsh-language poet, was born on 12 September 1904 at 112 High Street, Treorci, Rhondda, the second of the seven children of the Revd Thomas Bowen (1882–1948), a miner who had become a Congregational minister, and his wife, Ada (1881–1951), daughter of Thomas Griffiths, under-manager of Tyn-y-bedw colliery, and his wife, Sarah. Thomas Bowen, who adopted the poetic name Orchwy, published a volume of lyrics in 1915.

Thomas Bowen's calling meant that the family moved several times. Euros Bowen began his education in primary schools in Treorci and Llanelli. After a year in intermediate school he found work in a furniture shop and then as a clerk in a tin-plate works, going to evening classes at the Llanelli Art School. He resumed his full-time education in 1921, attending Whitland grammar school and New Quay College School.

In 1923 Bowen entered Carmarthen Presbyterian college to prepare for ministry with the Welsh Independents. In September 1924 he moved to the University College of Wales, Aberystwyth, transferring to University College, Swansea, in the following year and graduating with honours in philosophy in 1928. Having returned to Carmarthen to begin a BD degree, he won a scholarship to Mansfield College, Oxford. A serious illness prevented him from sitting his final examinations and he was awarded a BA (*aegrotat*).

In 1933 Bowen joined the Anglican Church in Wales. After training for ordination at St David's College, Lampeter, he was made deacon in St Asaph Cathedral in 1934 and priested the following year. He served his curacy in the parish of Wrexham, where he met Neli Tilston Jones, a secretary with the electricity board. They married in 1936 and had two sons, Gwyn Euros Bowen and Huw Euros Bowen. In 1939 Bowen was appointed rector of Llangywer on the shores of Tegid (Bala) Lake in Merioneth. Responsibility for the parish of Llanuwchllyn was added in 1958. He remained there until his retirement in 1973, when he moved back to Wrexham, where he spent the remainder of his life. In 1946, with the assistance of J. Gwyn Griffiths and Pennar Davies, Bowen began to edit *Y Fflam*, a Welsh-language literary review. It survived until 1952. While snowed into his rectory during the severe weather of 1947 Bowen began to devote himself seriously to writing poetry. In 1948 he won the crown at the Bridgend national eisteddfod, a feat which he repeated at the Caerphilly national eisteddfod two years later. His first collection of poems, *Cerddi*, appeared in 1958. It was the first of twenty volumes of poetry and eight volumes of translations which established him as one of the most prolific Welsh-language writers of the twentieth century.

Bowen deliberately set out to extend the frontiers of Welsh-language poetry. He claimed that he had developed his poetic method before becoming aware of the imagists and symbolists. He described his own poetry as *sacramentaidd* ('sacramental') rather than symbolist, seeing an essential similarity between his office as a poet and as a priest. He was not afraid to experiment with traditional Welsh metres.

Bowen soon became an extremely controversial figure in Welsh-language literary circles. His poems were frequently criticized as being obscure or *tywyll* ('dark'). At the 1963 Llandudno national eisteddfod Bowen's *awdl* was rejected as too difficult to understand. In 1977 the poet and critic Alan Llwyd published a book in which he attempted to 'explain Euros Bowen to others'. Bowen responded with a little volume entitled *Trin cerddi* in which he rejected many of Llwyd's interpretations, souring the relationship between the two writers.

During the last two decades of his life Bowen produced Welsh translations of works by Sophocles, Virgil, and Athanasius. He also produced an influential Welsh anthology of French symbolist poetry. In 1974 he published a bilingual volume containing English versions of some of his own poems. Bowen remains one of the most innovative Welsh literary figures of the twentieth century. He wrote too much, but his work includes several fine poems that have a lasting quality. He died on 2 April 1988 at Ysbyty Maelor, Wrexham, and was buried on 7 April in Wrexham cemetery. PATRICK THOMAS

Sources G. Bowen, 'Llyfryddiaeth Euros Bowen (1904–1988)', *Ysgrifau Beirniadol*, 21 (1996), 228–39 • 'Euros Bowen yn ateb cwestiynau'r golygydd', *Ysgrifau Beirniadol*, 6 (1971), 257–82 • G. Bowen, 'Euros: cip ar ei gefndir teuluol', *Taliesin* (July 1988), 63–70 • G. Bowen, 'Euros', *Taliesin* (March 1990), 55–66 • G. Bowen, *O groth y ddaear* (1993) • G. Thomas, 'Euros Bowen', in D. B. Rees, *Dyrnaid o awduron cyfoes* (1975) • C. Davies and S. Davies, eds., *Euros Bowen: priest-poet/bardd-offeiriad* (1993) • T. H. Davies, *Pwy yw pwy yng Nghymru / Who's who in Wales*, 2 vols. (1981–2) • A. Llwyd, *Barddoniaeth y chwedegau* (1986) • A. Llwyd, *Barddoniaeth Euros Bowen I* (1977) • E. Bowen, *Trin cerddi* (1978) • M. Stephens, ed., *Cydymaith i lenyddiaeth Cymru*, rev. edn (1997)

Archives NL Wales, draft poems, lecture notes, and sermons | NL Wales, letters to W. J. Gruffydd | FILM NL Wales, Aberystwyth, audio-visual department, documentary footage • NL Wales, Aberystwyth, audio-visual department, performance footage | SOUND NL Wales, Aberystwyth, audio-visual department, performance recording

Likenesses photograph, NL Wales, department of pictures and maps, PB906

Bowen, Sir George Ferguson (1821–1899), colonial governor, born in Ireland on 2 November 1821, was the eldest son of Edward Bowen, later rector of Taughboyne, co. Donegal. He was educated at Charterhouse School and as a scholar of Trinity College, Oxford, where he matriculated on 16 June 1840. He was twice president of the Oxford Union. In 1844 he took a first class in classics, was elected a fellow of Brasenose College, and, on 27 May, entered Lincoln's Inn as a student; he never practised law, however. Bowen took his MA in 1847 and became for four years president of the Greek University of Corfu, from where he began a series of travels and publications reflecting his devoted interest in Greece and its surrounds. His *Ithaca in 1850* (1850) was accepted by contemporary Homeric scholars, including W. E. Gladstone, as proving Ithaca to be the island of Odysseus. His reputation was enhanced by *Mount Athos, Thessaly, and Epirus: a Diary of a Journey from Constantinople to Corfu* (1852). Knowledge of the region and its history was put to unusual and effective purpose in *Murray's Handbook for Greece* (1857). Nor were his activities

Sir George Ferguson Bowen (1821–1899), by Bassano, 1897

merely literary: in 1848 he witnessed the capture of Vienna by the imperial troops, and in 1849 journeyed across Hungary, and thence, taking the risk involved in escorting refugees, to Constantinople; he also toured Albania and Montenegro.

In Corfu, Bowen became critical of the constitutional reforms instituted by the then lord high commissioner, Lord Seaton, attacking them in *The Ionian Islands under British Protection* (1850), a considerable work, and in the *Quarterly Review* (1852); following the latter, Seaton contemplated legal action. Approving rather of the controversial policies of Sir Henry Ward in the protectorate, Bowen (back at Brasenose since 1852, supporting university reform and Gladstone's re-election, and contributing leading articles to *The Globe* and other papers) was in 1854 appointed chief secretary to the lord high commissioner, and arrived in Corfu in March. Already fluent in Italian and ancient Greek, he mastered also modern Greek. Ionian agitation for incorporation with the Greek kingdom was then rife. On racial and cultural grounds, Bowen advocated cession of the southern islands to Greece and conversion of Corfu and Paxo into crown colonies; he wrote in this sense the relevant parts of a secret dispatch in 1856 from Sir John Young to Henry Labouchere, a copy of which, stolen from the Colonial Office in October 1858 and published in the *Daily News* in November, became a serious embarrassment to the British government, and to Gladstone, who was then on a mission to report on Ionian grievances. In 1855 Bowen was created CMG, and in 1856

KCMG (raised to GCMG in 1862). Also in 1856 he married the Countess Diamantina Roma, the daughter of the president of the Ionian senate, Count Candiano Roma of Zante, and related to Prince Danilo of Montenegro. This, as well as his views on Corfu, earned him a reputation of being involved to an unseemly extent in Ionian politics.

Bowen thus lost any prospect of realizing his ambition of becoming British minister in Athens; during Gladstone's mission he was even suspected, briefly, of giving information to newspapers. Instead, he was precipitated into a long career in the colonial service, which marks him as perhaps the most notable example of the professional governors who became the rule rather than the exception in the colonial empire in the second half of the nineteenth century. After looking first at Ceylon or Mauritius, and narrowly escaping Dominica, he was sent 'to preside over rising communities of my own countrymen' (Bowen to Gladstone, 21 April 1859, BL, Add. MS 44391), for, on 3 June 1859, thanks to Gladstone and his 'official friends' (ibid.), the secretary of state, Sir Edward Bulwer Lytton, appointed him first governor of Queensland. Bowen landed at Brisbane on 10 December 1859. Though preparing for responsible government, for the first three months he administered Queensland virtually as a crown colony, assisted by an official seconded from New South Wales and an executive council of three. He began also a seven-year association with Robert G. W. Herbert (later permanent under-secretary in the Colonial Office), who had travelled with him from England; the latter became colonial secretary and, on the election of the parliament in April 1860, the first premier of Queensland.

In Queensland, Bowen began to display the qualities which both distinguished and bedevilled his reputation. His attention to public business was constant, his capacity for administration (so far as that was required under responsible government) clear. His public utterances were lucid and usually edifying, if orotund. He dealt comfortably with ministers in ordinary circumstances. Government House hospitality was well maintained; in this he was much helped by the personality and talents of Lady Bowen. In touring over a large territory he was acutely observant as well as sociable, and in both dispatches and private letters he made much of classical and other historical parallels and comparisons: Homer and Horace, as well as seventeenth-century Virginia, provided him with descriptions of the landscape and squatters of Queensland. Public and political affairs engaged a perceptive and enquiring mind reinforced by wide reading in modern as well as ancient works. Bowen had, however, some less edifying qualities. He tended towards the pompous and egotistic, often to a fault. Some colonists regarded him less than respectfully, especially in times of political difficulty. In the Colonial Office he became known as 'an officer who is always obtruding and exaggerating his own merits and claims' (Sir F. Rogers, November 1865, PRO, CO 234/13). Robert Herbert, who maintained a certain friendship with Bowen (and was godfather to his son, William G. H. Bowen, born in Brisbane in 1864) in Queensland and later as head of the Colonial Office, was both amused and irritated by his 'eccentricities' (Knox, *Queensland Years*). Bowen was notable also for his propensity to cultivate and advertise acquaintance with the great and powerful (chiefly, at least until 1874, on the liberal side of politics). For one who was absent from England from 1859 to 1875, such acquaintance could only be made in correspondence. His surviving letters are ample evidence of his ability in this regard. A certain garrulousness and sycophancy aside, they contain much that is insightful and shrewd.

Bowen's success in his first government owed much to Herbert's ability to remain in office for six years. Their accord was especially valuable shortly after Herbert's retirement. In July 1866 a financial crisis struck Queensland as a result of the failure of a London bank. Heavily dependent on borrowed money, the government was unable to meet a range of commitments. The ministry proposed measures to which, Bowen informed them, his instructions forbade him to assent. Ministers resigned, and Bowen called Herbert to form a temporary administration. The crisis was survived by orthodox means, but, though the secretary of state approved, Bowen and Herbert encountered serious popular protests in Brisbane.

Late in 1867 Bowen was promoted to the government of New Zealand, where he assumed office on 9 February 1868. War with the Maori was still in progress. Bowen met chiefs in conference, made official tours through both islands, and received addresses and gave answers in patriarchal style; he perceived a parallel between the social condition of the Maori highlands and that of the Scottish highlands in the first part of the eighteenth century. He pursued a policy of conciliation, endeavouring to promote good feeling between the Maori and the settlers, hoping to mitigate the damage done by government confiscation of Maori land before and during the wars. His relations with the home government were less happy. In 1869 the Gladstone government decreed the removal of all British troops from New Zealand. Bowen strongly objected, in principle and on behalf of his government; in defiance of instructions he delayed the departure of the last regiment. He was rebuked by Lord Granville, the colonial secretary. The changed Colonial Office environment under Lord Kimberley, with Herbert as permanent under-secretary, helps explain why Bowen was nevertheless made, in 1873, governor of Victoria.

The governor's position in Victoria had been difficult ever since the start of the contests—essentially 'property and intelligence' against 'democracy'—between the houses of the legislature in 1865. Sir Charles Darling had been recalled for his partisan behaviour in relation to the 'deadlock', and serious differences had emerged between the colonial and British governments; more recently, Viscount Canterbury had disagreed with premier C. Gavan Duffy over a dissolution of the assembly. Bowen set out to establish harmonious relations between himself, his ministers, and the legislature, as well as with the population generally. In this, as in Queensland, he had the valuable assistance of Lady Bowen. He benefited also from becoming, in 1876, the first occupant of a new Government

House which enabled the governor to entertain the political and social leaders of Victoria in unprecedented style; Bowen could boast that his residence was larger than its equivalents in either Calcutta or Dublin, and its ballroom larger than that in Buckingham Palace. He spent 1875, on his first furlough since 1859, visiting England, where he received the honorary degree of DCL from the University of Oxford on 9 June, and touring the United States and Canada. He met Sir John A. Macdonald and formed views on the differences between Canadian federation and any such development in Australia.

Bowen returned to a troubled colony. In 1877 the ministry attempted to provide 'payment of members' by 'tacking' the item to the general appropriation bill. The council, unable to amend such a bill, rejected it. Faced with serious financial deficiency, the government advised Bowen to sign orders dismissing large numbers of civil servants. Bowen relied on the opinion of Robert Herbert, who privately told him that he could accept the advice of his ministers, whatever it might be, even in financial matters. In Victoria, though a compromise was arranged, he was attacked by opponents of the ministry. Early in 1878, moreover, Lord Carnarvon resigned as secretary of state, and his successor, Sir Michael Hicks Beach, agreed with those who said that Bowen had been too ready to assist his ministers in a dubious policy.

Bowen's term of office in Victoria ended on 31 March 1879. He perceived his transfer to the governorship of Mauritius, rather than to Sydney, to which he had laid serious claim, to be a consequence of Hicks Beach's disapproval. After arriving in Port Louis on 4 April, he found that his administrative talents were in demand in a crown colony whose largest problems arose from the importation and employment of indentured Indian labourers. His and Lady Bowen's social activities continued, in a society which in some ways he found more cultivated than that of Victoria.

On 28 December 1882 Bowen was appointed to Hong Kong. In two years he reconstructed the colonial legislature, concerned himself with public works, and paid visits to China and Japan; the Franco-Chinese war of 1884–5 occurred during his term of office. In 1885 ill health compelled him to return to Europe, and in 1887 he retired from the colonial service. In 1886 he received the honorary degree of LLD from Cambridge University and, on 26 November, was sworn of the privy council; in December 1887 he was appointed head of a royal commission sent to Malta to report on the arrangements connected with its new constitution. Bowen had been elected a member of the Royal Geographical Society in 1844, and served on its council from 1889 to 1892. He was a member of the Royal Colonial Institute, to which, in 1886, he read a paper, 'The federation of the British empire', which was published as a pamphlet and ran to two editions.

Bowen and his wife had a son and four daughters. The first Lady Bowen died on 17 November 1893; on 17 October 1896, at Holy Trinity Church, Sloane Street, Bowen married (Letitia) Florence, the daughter of Thomas *Luby and the widow of Henry White. Bowen died at the Hotel Metropole, Brighton, on 21 February 1899, and was buried at Kensal Green cemetery on 25 February.

BRUCE KNOX

Sources *Thirty years of colonial government: a selection from the papers of Sir G. F. Bowen*, ed. S. E. Lane-Poole, 2 vols. (1889) • B. Knox, 'British policy and the Ionian Islands, 1847–1864: nationalism and imperial administration', *EngHR*, 99 (1984), 503–29 • D. McCaughey, N. Perkins, and A. Trumble, *Victoria's colonial governors, 1839–1900* (1993) • B. A. Knox, ed., *The Queensland years of Robert Herbert* (1977) • H. G. Turner, *A history of the colony of Victoria*, 1 (1904) • BL, Carnarvon MSS, Gladstone MSS • PRO, Carnarvon MSS • Herts. ALS, Lytton papers • Bodl. RH, letters of Sir John Young • PRO, CO 234, 309

Archives NL NZ, Turnbull L., report on Maori rebellion • NRA, priv. coll., press cuttings • Queensland Women's Historical Association, Brisbane, corresp. and papers | Auckland Public Library, letters to Sir George Grey • BL, corresp. with Lord Carnarvon, Add. MS 60802 • BL, corresp. with W. E. Gladstone, Add. MSS 44370–44491, *passim* • BL, letters to Sir John Young, Add. MS 62940 • Bodl. Oxf., letters to Lord Kimberley • Bodl. RH, Labouchere-Young corresp. • Glos. RO, corresp. with Sir Michael Hicks Beach • Herts. ALS, Hertford, corresp. with Lord Lytton • PRO NIre., letters to Lord Belmore

Likenesses photograph, *c*.1864, John Oxley Library, Brisbane, Australia • J. Boterill, hand-coloured photograph, *c*.1875, State Library of Victoria, Melbourne, Australia • Bassano, photograph, 1897, NPG [*see illus.*]

Wealth at death £16,270 1*s*. 8*d*.: probate, 24 March 1899, *CGPLA Eng. & Wales*

Bowen, James [Jemmy] (*fl.* **1695–1701**), singer, has been described as the son of the actor William Bowen, but as William Bowen was probably born in 1666 and they worked for rival theatre companies this seems unlikely. It is possible, but not provable, that he was related to Owen Bowen, a friend of the singer and singing teacher John Freeman, who performed with James Bowen at Drury Lane. He sang Henry Purcell's 'Lucinda is bewitching fair' in Aphra Behn's *Abdelazer* when Drury Lane Theatre, London, reopened after Easter 1695, following the period of mourning for the death of Mary II. He quickly became an important soprano soloist, singing Quivera and the God of Dreams in the dramatic opera *The Indian Queen* by John Dryden and Robert Howard, and songs in several plays. Henry Purcell entrusted him with the affecting and florid 'Whilst I with grief' in Dryden's *The Spanish Fryar*, the risqué dialogue with the girl Letitia Cross 'Clemene pray tell me' in Thomas Southerne's *Oroonoko*, and the eerie recitative 'Thy genius lo' in Nathaniel Lee's *The Massacre of Paris*. Anthony Aston gives an account of the composer's response when other musicians were bothering Jemmy Bowen with advice on ornamentation when rehearsing a Purcell song: '*O let him alone*, said Mr. *Purcell*; *he will grace it more naturally than you, or I, can teach him*' (Aston, 18).

Purcell died in November 1695, and in Jeremiah Clarke's pastoral *Ode on the Death of Mr. Henry Purcell* Bowen sang the key role of the young shepherd who brings news of the composer's death. He remained in the theatre, singing music by Daniel Purcell, Jeremiah Clarke, and Johann Franck, until summer 1696, but a different boy was singing at Drury Lane by summer 1697. In spring 1698 'Young Bowen' sang music by Daniel Purcell in Charles Gildon's *Phaeton*. He was advertised as 'Mr Bowen' for concerts at

York Buildings in May and June 1698 and sang as an alto Bramin in Peter Motteux's *The Island Princess* early in 1699. Song sheets show that he sang in concerts at Richmond and Tunbridge Wells. In 1701 Bowen sang at Hampstead and in plays at Drury Lane, his last recorded appearances being in Richard Steele's *The Funeral*, premièred that December. Roger North ranked him with the most famous singers in London, commenting that 'our gallants and yong ladys' wished to sing exactly like 'Mr. Abell, Fideli, or Jemmy Bowen' (*Roger North's Cursory Notes*, 237). It is not known whether he died soon after December 1701, or left the stage for a different career.

OLIVE BALDWIN and THELMA WILSON

Sources W. Van Lennep and others, eds., *The London stage, 1660–1800*, pt 1: *1660–1700* (1965) • E. L. Avery, ed., *The London stage, 1660–1800*, pt 2: *1700–1729* (1960) • M. Tilmouth, 'A calendar of references to music in newspapers published in London and the provinces (1660–1719)', *Royal Musical Association Research Chronicle*, 1 (1961) • *Roger North's Cursory notes of musicke (c.1698–c.1703)*, ed. M. Chan and J. C. Kassler (Kensington, NSW, 1986) • A. Aston, *A brief supplement to Colley Cibber, esq.: his 'Lives of the late famous actors and actresses'* [n.d., c.1747] • O. Baldwin and T. Wilson, 'Purcell's stage singers: a documentary list', *Performing the music of Henry Purcell* [Oxford 1993], ed. M. Burden (1996), 275–81 • R. Steele, *The funeral* (1702) • G. J. Armytage, ed., *Allegations for marriage licences issued by the vicar-general of the archbishop of Canterbury, July 1679 to June 1687*, Harleian Society, 30 (1890), marriage allegation for John Freeman

Bowen, James (*bap.* **1718**, *d.* **1774**), painter and topographer, was baptized on 29 January 1718 at St Chad's, Shrewsbury, the son of John Bowen and his wife, Anne, *née* Wilding. He collected substantial materials for a history of Shropshire, having taken notes on churches, sketches of monuments, and transcripts of records when he was accompanying John Mytton through the county. One of Bowen's works is a view of the church of Mary in the Battlefield, Shrewsbury (Gough, 2.184), and he produced also some useful maps (ibid., 185). Gough bought all the genealogical and topographical materials which Bowen had amassed, and they form part of the manuscripts which Gough bequeathed to the Bodleian Library, Oxford. James Bowen was the father of the painter and genealogist John *Bowen (1755/6–1832). James Bowen died at Shrewsbury in 1774.

JENNETT HUMPHREYS, *rev.* ASIA HAUT

Sources W. A. Leighton, *A guide, descriptive and historical, through the town of Shrewsbury*, 4th edn (1855) • R. G. [R. Gough], *British topography*, [new edn], 2 (1780), 176–85 • *GM*, 1st ser., 102/2 (1832), 185
Archives BL, Cheshire pedigrees, Add. MS 36663 • Bodl. Oxf., Shropshire collections, notes, and papers • S. Antiquaries, Lond., drawings of monuments, arms, etc. in Shropshire

Bowen, James (**1751–1835**), naval officer, was born at Ilfracombe. He first went to sea in the merchant service, and in 1776 he commanded a ship in the African and West India trade. Shortly afterwards he entered the navy as a master, and he served in that capacity on board the *Artois* with Captain Macbride during 1781–2, being present in the battle of the Dogger Bank on 5 August 1781. He continued with Captain Macbride in different ships until 1789, when he was appointed inspecting agent of transports in the Thames. Following the outbreak of the French Revolutionary War Lord Howe requested Bowen to go with him as master of his flagship, the *Queen Charlotte*, and he had thus the duty of piloting her into the battle of 1 June 1794. It is reported that on Howe's giving the order 'Starboard!' Bowen ventured to say, 'My lord, you'll be foul of the French ship if you don't take care'. 'What is that to you, sir?' replied the admiral, sharply; 'starboard!' 'Starboard!' cried Bowen, muttering by no means inaudibly, 'Damned if I care, if you don't. I'll take you near enough to singe your black whiskers'. He did almost literally fulfil this promise, passing so close under the stern of the French flagship *Montagne* that the French ensign brushed the main and mizen shrouds of the *Queen Charlotte* as she fired her broadside into the French ship's starboard quarter. For his conduct Bowen was made a lieutenant on 23 June 1794. After the action off Lorient on 23 June 1795, in which he was first lieutenant of the *Queen Charlotte*, he was made commander, and on 2 September of the same year he was advanced to the rank of captain. During the two following years he commanded the *Thunderer* in the West Indies. In 1798 he commanded the *Argo* (44 guns) in the Mediterranean, and took part in the capture of Minorca by Commodore John Duckworth; and on 6 February 1799, after a brilliant chase of two Spanish frigates of nearly equal force, he succeeded in capturing one of them, the *Santa Teresa* (42 guns).

For the next three years Bowen was employed in convoy service, in the course of which he was officially thanked by the court of directors of the East India Company, and presented with a piece of plate worth £400 for his 'care and attention' in convoying one of their fleets from England to St Helena. In 1803 he was appointed to command the *Dreadnought* (98 guns), but shortly afterwards, at Lord St Vincent's suggestion, he was nominated a commissioner of the transport board. As first lord of the Admiralty (1802–4) St Vincent relied heavily on Bowen's practical advice. He was sent to Ireland in 1803, on the outbreak of war, to improve the local naval defences. In 1805 he had the charge of laying down moorings for the fleet in Falmouth harbour, and in the following year he served as captain of the fleet to Lord St Vincent off Brest. In January 1809 he superintended the re-embarkation of the army at Corunna, for which he received the thanks of both houses of parliament. He was appointed one of the commissioners of the navy in February 1816, and continued in that office until August 1825, when he was retired with the rank of rear-admiral. He died on 27 April 1835.

Bowen's brother Richard also served in the navy. As captain of the *Terpsichore* in July 1797 he was involved in the attack on Santa Cruz and earned Nelson's commendation as an 'enterprising, able, and gallant officer' (*Dispatches and Letters*, 2.423). Another brother, George, also a captain in the navy, died at Torquay in October 1817. No details remain of Bowen's marriage but his eldest son, James, died captain of the frigate, *Phoenix*, on the East India station, in 1812; and another son, John, also a captain, died in 1828. Both sons had been promoted captain in 1805. According to Sir John Barrow, then second secretary of the

Admiralty, the elder's promotion was the result of his being mistaken for his father. James Bowen's youngest son, St Vincent, was a clergyman. He had also a daughter, Teresa, who died in 1876.

Bowen was an outstanding seaman, as his selection by Howe in 1793 testifies. His resolute conduct during the battle of 1 June 1794 earned him a place on the quarterdeck, and his ability an early rise to captain. He was equally effective in administrative posts, and St Vincent's support is evidence of his all-round ability at the higher level. J. K. LAUGHTON, *rev.* ANDREW LAMBERT

Sources J. Barrow, *The life of Richard, Earl Howe* (1838) · J. M. Collinge, *Navy Board officials, 1660–1832* (1978) · D. Syrett and R. L. DiNardo, *The commissioned sea officers of the Royal Navy, 1660–1815*, rev. edn, Occasional Publications of the Navy RS, 1 (1994) · *Letters of … the earl of St Vincent, whilst the first lord of the admiralty, 1801–1804*, ed. D. B Smith, 1, Navy RS, 55 (1922) · *The dispatches and letters of Vice-Admiral Lord Viscount Nelson*, ed. N. H. Nicolas, 7 vols. (1844–6)
Likenesses I. W. Slater, lithograph (after J. Slater), BM · oils, NMM

Bowen, John (1755/6–1832), painter and genealogist, was born in Shrewsbury, the eldest son of James *Bowen (*bap.* 1718, *d.* 1774), painter and topographer, of that town. He studied the local antiquities under his father, who had compiled notes and sketches towards a history of Shropshire during his travels with John Mytton. Bowen traced out the pedigrees of Shropshire families and became especially skilful in deciphering and copying ancient manuscripts. He almost certainly used his own and his father's materials to compile much of *The History and Antiquities of Shrewsbury* that was published under the name of Thomas Phillips in 1779. He contributed to the *Gentleman's Magazine* drawings and accounts of the seals of the town of Droitwich and of Shrewsbury exchequer. Four of his drawings of views of Shrewsbury were engraved by Vandergucht and his engraving of some Roman inscriptions was published in *Philosophical Transactions* (49.196). He died in Shrewsbury on 19 June 1832, aged seventy-six.
JENNETT HUMPHREYS, *rev.* A. P. WOOLRICH

Sources G. C. Baugh, 'Shropshire', *English county histories: a guide*, ed. C. R. J. Currie and C. P. Lewis (1994), 336–47, esp. 339 · *GM*, 1st ser., 102/2 (1832), 185 · R. G. [R. Gough], *British topography*, [new edn], 2 (1780), 177 · W. A. Leighton, *A guide, descriptive and historical, through the town of Shrewsbury*, 4th edn [1855?]
Archives Bodl. Oxf., collections (made with his father, James) for a history of Shropshire

Bowen, John (1815–1859), bishop of Sierra Leone, son of Thomas Bowen, captain in the 85th regiment, and his third wife, Mary, daughter of the Revd John Evans, chaplain to the garrison at Placentia, Newfoundland, was born at Court, near Fishguard, Pembrokeshire, on 21 November 1815. At twelve years of age he was sent to school at Merlin's Vale, near Haverfordwest, and in 1830 he continued his studies under the Revd David Adams. He emigrated to Canada in April 1835, and had a farm at Dunville, on the shores of Lake Erie. He served in the militia during the rebellion of 1837–8. On Sunday 6 March 1842 he heard a sermon in the Lake Shore church which led him to prepare for the ministry. Disposing of his farm on favourable terms, he returned to England, and in January 1843 entered Trinity College, Dublin, where he graduated BA in 1847, and LLB and LLD ten years later.

Bowen was ordained deacon at Ripon Cathedral on 20 September 1846, and his first appointment was as assistant curate of Knaresborough, Yorkshire, in 1848. An uncle had left him an estate at Haverfordwest, and while at Knaresborough, Bowen asked the Church Missionary Society to allow him to visit its many foreign stations. The society suggested that he go to Jerusalem, confer there with Bishop Gobat, and then visit the missionary stations at Syros, Smyrna, and Cairo; then journey to Mount Lebanon, Nablus, and other places in Syria, and on to Mosul by Constantinople and Trebizond; and finally return by Baghdad and Damascus to Jerusalem. Bowen succeeded, despite many hardships and dangers, and returned to England in December 1851. In 1853 the marquess of Huntly named him rector of Orton-Longueville with Botolph Bridge in Huntingdonshire. With permission from his bishop Bowen again left England, in September 1854, and stayed in the East until July 1856. There he learned Arabic well enough to preach fluently in it.

On 10 August 1857 Bowen was consecrated the third bishop of Sierra Leone by the archbishop of Canterbury and the bishops of Peterborough and Victoria. On 24 November 1857 he married Catharine, daughter of George Butler, the dean of Peterborough. He sailed for his new diocese two days later, on 26 November. Both of his predecessors had died at their posts; Bowen's wife died after giving birth to a stillborn son on 4 August 1858 and Bowen himself died of yellow fever on 28 May 1859, at Freetown. In his short term Bowen served the Yoruba mission, Yorubaland (where Africans had been ordained in 1854), reached the delta of the Niger, and encouraged missionaries to learn the languages of the local people.
G. C. BOASE, *rev.* LYNN MILNE

Sources J. Bowen, *Memorials of John Bowen, compiled by his sister* (1862) · *GM*, 3rd ser., 7 (1859), 187–8 · *Mission Field*, 1 (1856) · *Mission Field*, 2 (1857) · *Mission Field*, 3 (1858) · L. Baillie and P. Sieveking, eds., *British biographical archive* (1984) [microfiche] · E. Stock, *The history of the Church Missionary Society: its environment, its men and its work*, 4 (1916), 497 · Boase, *Mod. Eng. biog.* · *CGPLA Eng. & Wales* (1859)
Archives U. Birm. L., papers relating to Mediterranean mission · U. Birm. L., corresp. and papers relating to Sierra Leone
Wealth at death under £4000: probate, 14 Oct 1859, *CGPLA Eng. & Wales*

Bowen, Marjorie. *See* Long, Margaret Gabrielle Vere (1885–1952).

Bowen, Thomas (1732/3–1790). *See under* Bowen, Emanuel (1693/4–1767).

Bower, Alexander (1774–1837), writer and minister of the Relief church, was born in Edinburgh on 18 March 1774, the son of John Bower, weaver, and Janet Matthew. The elder Bower, according to a relative, John Campbell (1766–1840), was an elder in the Relief church, and Alexander, following attendance at classes at Edinburgh University between 1787 and 1794, trained to be a clergyman. He was licensed to preach by the presbytery of Armagh, before being received as a probationer by the Relief Presbytery of

Edinburgh on 23 May 1799. He married, in Edinburgh on 29 December 1799, Miss Addison Henderson; they had at least two children. He became minister of the Relief congregation of Shiprow church, Aberdeen, on 6 November 1799, but rapidly lost the confidence of a large section of his congregation and in the summer of 1805 attempts were made to have him removed. He resigned on 6 September 1806 and probably moved to Edinburgh shortly thereafter. In the years following 1810 he was employed by both the Advocates' Library and Edinburgh University Library as a cataloguer. In a letter dated 26 November 1813, to an unknown correspondent, Bower declared that 'my life has been devoted to literature' (Edinburgh University, MS La II.501, fol. 336), but in the following year he unsuccessfully attempted to be recognized by the Relief Presbytery of Edinburgh as a probationer. He appears to have sunk further and further into poverty as he got older, and died, probably in Edinburgh, on 23 February 1837.

Bower first appeared in print with *An Address to the Inhabitants of the North of Scotland, upon the Threatened Invasion* (1803), and this was followed by his edition of *An Essay on the Inspiration of the Holy Scriptures* (1806), by an unknown author. His most substantial works are biographies of James Beattie (1804) and Martin Luther (1813) and a *History of the University of Edinburgh* (3 vols., 1817–30). These have long been superseded, apart from some incidental biographical detail in the first- and last-named. He also produced histories of Scotland and Ireland for children (both 1819), as well as *The Edinburgh Student's Guide* (1822) and *A letter to the … lord provost … upon the subject of providing dead bodies for the students of medicine* (1823).

Murray C. T. Simpson

Sources R. Small, *History of the congregations of the United Presbyterian church from 1733 to 1900*, 1 (1904), 10–11, 15 • catalogues of the BL, NL Scot., and U. Edin. L. • *National union catalog*, Library of Congress • matriculation albums, U. Edin. L., special collections division, university archives • A. Bower, letter, 26 Nov 1813, U. Edin. L., MS La II.501, fol. 336 • W. J. Duncan, letter to David Laing, 20 June 1833, U. Edin. L., MS La IV.17, fol. 2816 • W. J. Duncan, letter to David Laing, 28 Sept 1833, U. Edin. L., MS La IV.17, fol. 2817 • parish registers, birth, St Cuthbert's, Edinburgh

Wealth at death died in poverty: letters, 1833, U. Edin. L.

Bower, Archibald (1686x8–1766), religious controversialist and historical writer, was born either on 17 January 1686 or on 17 January 1687 or in September 1688, at or near Dundee. His parents' names are unknown. According to his own account he was descended from an ancient family that had for several hundred years been possessed of an estate in Forfarshire, but as the *Dictionary of National Biography* remarks 'all his statements concerning himself must be received with extreme caution'.

The Society of Jesus In October 1702 Bower was sent to the Scots College at Douai before going on to Rome, where he entered the Society of Jesus on 9 December 1706. After two years of novitiate and of attending lectures in philosophy at the Roman College he was appointed to teach at the Jesuit colleges at Fano (1712–13) and Fermo (1714–16). From 1717 to 1721 he studied theology at the Roman College, during which time he was ordained, in 1719 or 1720. He was then sent to lecture in philosophy at Arezzo in 1721, at Macerata in 1723, and at Perugia in 1725. He was professed at Florence on 2 February 1723.

In 1726 Bower left Perugia for reasons that are less than clear. Those whom he later considered to be his enemies alleged that he had been discovered in a love affair with a nun. He himself described how he escaped from Perugia on account of 'the hellish proceedings' of the inquisition in which, he said, he was a consultor, or judge. In fact the Jesuit records show that he was sent away to England in 1726, perhaps with the hope of enabling him to make a fresh start; if he was truly penitent he could have continued as a Jesuit. He arrived in England in July 1726. The Jesuit records show that as late as 1729 he was in London, nominally as a member of the Jesuit mission to Scotland. To begin with he was in touch with fellow Jesuits but by November 1726 he had abandoned the Jesuits and the Catholic church. Two accounts of his 'flight' from Perugia were published, one by Richard Baron—*A faithful account of Mr Archibald Bower's motives for leaving his office of secretary to the court of inquisition* (1750)—the other by Bower himself, *Mr Bower's Answer to a Scurrilous Pamphlet* (1757).

Conversion? In England Bower made the acquaintance of Dr Edward Aspinwall, a former Jesuit who was at that time prebendary of Westminster and who introduced him to Dr Samuel Clarke; he also met George Berkeley, dean of Londonderry and later bishop of Cloyne. He said that he found a system of religion for himself and was for six years a protestant of no particular denomination. Eventually he conformed to the Church of England. To earn his living he taught the classics and Italian to students, and read the classics with Lord Aylmer, former MP and equerry to George I, to whom he had been introduced by Dr Thomas Goodman, the king's physician. Aylmer in turn introduced Bower to Sir George (later Lord) Lyttelton, who proved to be a steadfast friend when almost everybody else had deserted him. For a year he undertook the education of the son of Mr Thompson of Cooley, in Berkshire, but after a period of ill health he was again employed by Lord Aylmer, this time as tutor to two of his children.

While Bower was living in Aylmer's household he wrote the monthly review *Historia Litteraria, or, An exact and early account of the most valuable books published in the several parts of Europe* which was published from 1730 to 1734. From 1735 to 1744 he was employed by a consortium of London booksellers that was undertaking an ambitious and costly project to publish in monthly instalments a history of the world. One of a group of writers engaged on the history that included George Sale and George Psalmanazar, Bower's contribution to *An Universal History, from the Earliest Account of Time to the Present* was the history of ancient Rome, which came to occupy one third of the seven folio volumes that dealt with ancient history. The final volume of the ancient history appeared in 1744 and the modern history was not completed until 1765; in the interim an octavo edition had appeared and the work had been translated into French, Italian, and German. Bower received £300 for revising the second edition of the *Universal History* but he apparently undertook the task in 'a slovenly and careless manner' (*DNB*). Despite such failings the *Universal History* was a celebrated publishing enterprise that was widely read throughout Europe. Its significance is amply demonstrated by the fact that the writers of the *Encyclopédie* drew on many of its articles in preparing the entries for that publication.

Letters to Jesuits in London from their superior-general in Rome between March 1730 and February 1734 reveal that Bower during these years was nibbling at the idea of returning to the Catholic church and to the Society of Jesus. Then, in 1744, he met the Jesuit Philip Carteret, who in 1745 reconciled him to the church and readmitted him to the society. It was understood that he would go into the country, be provided with books by the Jesuits, and devote himself to writing. A few years before this, wishing to invest his savings (£1100) rather than leave them in the funds and not being able to persuade any of his protestant friends to burden his estate with a life-rent or to find another form of investment, he had transferred his money through Mr Wright, a Catholic banker, to a Mr Hill. Hill was in fact John Hill, the financial agent of the English Jesuits, who gave him for his £1100 (with a further £250) a generous 7 per cent, that is to say £94 10s. a year. This financial negotiation later proved very damaging to his reputation. His opponents believed that he made this arrangement to recommend himself to his superiors and to prove his sincerity. But Bower did not break with his protestant friends, and in 1745 he was engaged in a treaty of marriage that in fact did not take place. He decided to break his vows a second time, and corresponded with Henry Sheldon, provincial superior of the Jesuits in England, asking for the return of his money, which he duly received on 20 June 1747. At St Benet Paul's Wharf, London, on 20 August 1749 Bower married Dorothy Conner, the daughter of a Church of England clergyman and a niece of Bishop William Nicolson. A widow, she brought Bower a fortune of £4000 and a child from her former marriage.

History of the Popes In March 1747 Bower issued proposals for printing by subscription *History of the Popes* 'by Archibald Bower Esq., heretofore public professor of rhetoric, history and philosophy in the universities of Rome, Fermo and Macerata'—a violent attack on papal supremacy 'well qualified to serve the interests of Protestantism' (*GM*, 60/2). He announced that he had begun the work to support the doctrine of papal supremacy but that his researches had led him to change his mind on the subject. In 1748 he presented the first volume to George II, and through the influence of Lyttelton, a commissioner of the Treasury and a friend of the prime minister, Henry Pelham, was appointed keeper of Queen Caroline's library and, in 1754, clerk of the buck-warrants, 'an office of no great emolument' (*European Magazine*, 25.261). The second volume (with a lengthy list of subscribers) and the third appeared in 1750 and 1754, respectively, the fourth in 1759. The final three volumes were rushed through the press in the 1760s, and the recent history of the popes covered in a superficial manner: the period 1600 to 1758 occupied a mere twenty-six pages of the seven volumes. To the fifth volume Bower attached an appendix of 180 pages: 'A summary view of the controversy between the papists and the author … the cruel and unjust persecution which the author of the present history has undergone, in this protestant kingdom, from the Jesuits, encouraged and aided by a protestant clergyman, and the wicked measures, which they have jointly pursued to force him back to the idolatrous church and antichristian order he had left'.

The Sheldon letters The first serious attack on the *History of the Popes* was made in a pamphlet by the Revd Alban Butler published anonymously at Douai under the title *Remarks on the two first volumes of the late lives of the popes, in letters from a gentleman to a friend in the country* (1754), which exposed in 100 pages the author's plagiarism and literary ill faith. This may have had little effect, but about 1750 there had come into the hands of Sir Henry Bedingfield, a Catholic, the letters that Bower had written, signed A—D B—R, to Sheldon during the period of his last coquetting with Catholicism. These letters were written about the time when the prospectus for the *History of the Popes* was issued. While in the prospectus Bower posed as one who had fervent zeal for the protestant faith and was about to publish the results of twenty years of hostile criticism of the papacy, he was writing confidential and respectful letters to Sheldon about the return of his money. Bower maintained that the letters were forgeries designed to destroy his reputation with his protestant friends and produced by the Jesuits in revenge for his attack on the frauds of the priesthood.

One of those who believed the letters were genuine was David Garrick, who had been Bower's friend, and he informed Lyttelton (who took no action) of his belief. Later Garrick threatened to write a farce in which Bower would be introduced as a mock convert and the profligacy of his character exposed. Another who saw the letters was the writer Nathaniel Hooke, who talked of the matter with John Douglas, chaplain to Lord Bath and afterwards bishop of Salisbury, who had already detected the fraud of William Lauder in regard to Milton. Douglas met the historian Dr Thomas Birch, who knew Bower's hand, and he and one Morgan, who had a portfolio of Bower's writings, became convinced, with Douglas, in February 1756 that the letters were genuine.

Sir Henry Bedingfield defied Bower to bring the matter to public trial but Bower replied by asserting that the letters were forgeries and declared that he had had no intercourse with the Jesuits for thirty years; in June he issued a pamphlet entitled *Mr Bower's Affidavit in Answer to the False Accusation Brought Against him by Papists*. The reply by Douglas, published in the same month, was *Six letters from A—d B—r to Father Sheldon, provincial of the Jesuits in England; illustrating with several remarkable facts tending to ascertain the authenticity of the said letters and the true character of the writer.* Douglas found that the letters revealed that in the summer of 1746 and in early 1747, after Bower had been readmitted by the Jesuits, he was writing to Sheldon on matters arising from his return to the society and asking for £500 to pay to a woman for what was later found to be breach of promise. Douglas's tract was a powerful denunciation of Bower and proved the letters were genuine; it showed that want of veracity was not the only defect in Bower's character and that he was as little remarkable for his probity as for his love of truth. He was plainly trading, under false pretences, on the respect of protestants for him and his writings. Douglas also drew attention to the evidence of Mrs Hoyles, a lady converted to Roman Catholicism by Bower years earlier. Her evidence made it clear that Bower was ready to support in secret the church that, for self-interested ends, he was publicly denouncing.

A shattered reputation Bower replied to Douglas with his *Answer to a Scurrilous Pamphlet Intituled 'Six Letters from A—d B—r to Father Sheldon'*, published in two parts, in January and February 1757, respectively, arguing that the Jesuits had asked for his money and that he had agreed because he thought that they were good business people. 'Fancy', said Douglas, 'a deserter from Catholicism, a fugitive from his Order depositing his money with the Jesuit Provincial, that is with the representative of all that he had flouted and injured' (Pollen, 301), whereupon he wrote a second pamphlet, *Bower and Tillemont Compared* (1757), showing how the *History of the Popes*—the first volume especially—was chiefly a translation of a work of the French historian Sébastien Le Nain de Tillemont. Douglas added 'some further Particulars relating to the true character and conduct of the Translator'. In his reply to *Bower and Tillemont Compared* and in two other pamphlets Bower attempted in 1757 to refute the criticism of his character made by Douglas, who in return published *A Full Confutation of All the Facts Advanced in Mr Bower's Three Defences*, which drew from Bower *Mr Bower's Reply to a Scurrilous Tract Intituled A Full Confutation* (1757). Douglas then wrote *A Complete and Final Detection of A—d B—r* (February 1758), to which Bower made no reply.

During his life and after his death there were many who approved of Bower's writings; his views were acceptable to a section of public opinion at that time. In his last years he continued his attacks on his enemies and his attempt to recover his reputation. He published the last volumes of *History of the Popes*, and in 1757 brought out an abridgement of the first four volumes in French. He died on 3 September 1766, probably in London, and was buried in Marylebone churchyard. His widow, to whom he left all his property, wrote from Woodstock Street on 10 October 1766 that during the seventeen years that she had constantly been with him he had always professed himself a protestant. The epitaph on his tomb described him as a man exemplary for every social virtue, justly esteemed by all who knew him for his strict honesty and integrity, a faithful friend, and a sincere Christian.

GEOFFREY HOLT

Sources J. H. Pollen, 'The detection of Archibald Bower', *The Month*, 112 (July–Dec 1908), 290–302 · *DNB* · *Records of the Scots colleges* (1906), 66 · H. Foley, ed., *Records of the English province of the Society of Jesus*, 7 (1882–3), 882 · Roman Archives of the Society of Jesus, Rome, Rom. 175, 97–101, 69; Ital. 68–70 · Epistolae Generalium, 1698–1744, Archives of the British Province of the Society of Jesus, London, 3 (2), 30–71 [photocopies] · J. Douglas, *Six letters from A—d B—r to Father Sheldon, provincial of the Jesuits in England* (1756), 4–24, 41–92 · A. Bower, *Mr. Bower's answer to a scurrilous pamphlet intituled 'Six letters from A—d B—r to Father Sheldon'* (1757), 30–35 · *GM*, 1st ser., 60 (1790), 1187 · *GM*, 1st ser., 61 (1791), 118 · *European Magazine*, 25 (1794), 3, 133, 209, 261 · *European Magazine*, 26 (1795), 32 · H. Bromley, *Catalogue of engraved portraits from Egbert the Great to the present times* (1793), 383 · F. Blom and others, *English Catholic books, 1701–1800: a bibliography* (1996), 45 · A. Bower, *History of the popes*, 2 (1750), iii, xxxv; 5 (1761), appx, 1–186 · G. Abbattista, 'The business of Paternoster Row: towards a publishing history of the *Universal History* (1736–65)', *Publishing History*, 17 (1985), 5–50 · *IGI*

Archives BL, corresp. and papers relating to Jesuits, Add. MS 4234 · Bodl. Oxf., corresp. and papers | Hunt. L., letters to Elizabeth Montagu

Likenesses J. Faber, mezzotint, 1755 (after J. Reynolds), BM · R. Josey, mezzotint (after J. Reynolds), NPG · J. Macardell, mezzotint (after G. Knapton), BM, NPG · engraving, repro. in *European Magazine*, 25, facing p. 3

Bower, Dallas Gordon (1907–1999), film, radio, and television producer and director, was born on 25 July 1907 at 34 Kensington Hall Gardens, London, the only son of Edward Lawrence Oakes Bower, East India merchant, and his first wife, (Gladys) Ethel, daughter of Eugene Dallas Marriott, wine importer. He was a great-great-great-grandson of Sarah Siddons, the actress, and a collateral descendant of George Mifflin Dallas, vice-president of the USA (1845), after whom the city in Texas was named.

What Bower called 'the three conditioning factors' in his life—cinema, Shakespeare, and opera—he owed entirely to family encouragement and sympathetic teachers (Bower, *Playback*, 6). Some of his earliest memories were of Shakespeare readings, Wagner nights, and visits to the cinema with an uncle in 1917 to see D. W. Griffith's epics *Birth of a Nation* (1915) and *Intolerance* (1916). His love of the classical world was fostered at Willingdon School, Putney, by a youthful Antonia White, and at Hurstpierpoint College he was taught by Claude Gurney, later a West End stage director, and by the college organist, John Hawkins, an early champion of Sibelius. Guided by an older boy, he began his first experiments in radio, installing his home-made apparatus in his grandfather's attic.

In the early 1920s Bower joined the Marconi Company as a bench boy, contributing to *Modern Wireless* on radio theory and design (1924), briefly editing *Experimental Wireless* (1926), and writing on radio as a navigational aid. In 1926, at the Radio Society of Great Britain, he heard Campbell Swinton expound his theory of the cathode ray oscillograph, which was to make modern television possible. The lecture made a profound impression on him, and led to meetings with Watson Watt, the inventor of radar. By 1934 Bower was predicting in *Wireless World* that television would eventually take over most of the functions of the traditional film. Meanwhile, on 18 November 1925 he married Violet Florence Collings (1902–1990), elder daughter of William Henry Thomas Collings, estate agent and auctioneer, of Brighton. They had a son and two daughters. The marriage was dissolved in 1945.

In 1927 Bower moved into film production as a sound recordist at Elstree. His technical innovations contributed much to the success of Hitchcock's *Blackmail* (1929) and Hardy's *Under the Greenwood Tree* (1930), the first all-talking

British film. Thereafter he learned film editing from Thorold Dickinson at Cricklewood, and made his début as a director with *Path of Glory* (1934), a satire on war. His radio play *Catastrophe*, his only venture into the genre, was broadcast from Savoy Hill in 1932.

Bower greatly admired the achievements of the silent German cinema, and when Paul Czinner fled to Britain with his production team, Bower became his personal assistant. He was quick to recognize the new role in the sound film that original music by the leading composers of the age could play, and brought in William Walton to write the score for *Escape me Never* (1935), for which Frederick Ashton provided the choreography. Both were again employed in *As You Like It* (1936), Bower's first Shakespeare film, which he latterly directed, with Laurence Olivier playing Orlando. Its magical sets were particularly memorable.

In 1936 Bower published his prophetic *Plan for Cinema*, which called for a new synthesis of the arts within a new form of cinema. He forecast 'the impermanence of the two-dimensional monochromatic cinema and the inevitability of its emergence into colour and giant screen, thence conceivably into an entirely new medium in the form of a circular solid space'—a new kind of three-dimensional theatre which would open up the world of epic and myth to cinema, so that works such as Hardy's *Dynasts* and Wagner's *Ring* cycle, which had hitherto defied production in the naturalistic theatre, could be fully realized for the first time (Bower, *Playback*, 24). Much that he predicted had, by the end of the twentieth century, come about. The book remains challenging, and will hold its place in cinema theory.

When the BBC television service—the first of its kind in the world—went on air from Alexandra Palace in November 1936, Bower became one of its two senior producers, directing the opening programme and the 'demonstration' film, an anthology of the first six months' programmes. Thereafter he triumphed over the cramping restrictions of the pre-war medium to produce a remarkable number of plays, revues, concerts, ballets, and operas, including act II of *Tristan and Isolde*, with miming actors and off-screen singers, the Garrick version of *The Taming of the Shrew*, a modern-dress *Julius Caesar*, and, just before the service closed at the outbreak of war, *The Tempest*, performed for the first time with Sibelius's incidental music. Bower developed the medium with increasing sophistication, and artists such as Margot Fonteyn and Peggy Ashcroft were glad to appear in his productions.

During the Second World War Bower worked alongside John Betjeman and Graham Greene as an executive film producer at the Ministry of Information. His Dunkirk film *Channel Incident* was reputedly one of Churchill's favourites. In 1941–2 he returned temporarily to the BBC as producer of *Alexander Nevsky*, with a script by Louis MacNeice and Prokofiev's music from the Eisenstein film, to celebrate the entry of the Soviet Union into the war. It was followed, after Pearl Harbor, by *Columbus*, to mark the 450th anniversary of the discovery of America, again with a MacNeice script and with a score by Walton, and with Olivier in the title role. These two radio epics were probably the most elaborate live broadcasts ever made from an open studio. After the war Bower again collaborated with MacNeice, on *Pax futura*, a film on the future of aviation, but it never went into production.

Bower's greatest project—the film of Shakespeare's *Henry V* (1944)—started life as a pre-war television script in the aftermath of Munich. In 1944, after the allied invasion of France, he rewrote it as a film scenario which he was to direct, with Olivier in the leading role. In the event, after numerous setbacks, Olivier became director and Bower the producer, but Bower's guiding hand was apparent throughout, in the casting, in the Agincourt battle scenes (filmed in Ireland), and in the choice of Walton for the music. It was an almost faultless film, which transcended its propaganda purpose and presented Shakespeare, perhaps for the first time, in genuine terms of cinematic imagination. Of Bower's uncompleted Shakespeare projects, the loss of *Antony and Cleopatra* is perhaps the most to be regretted. Within a Renaissance setting after Veronese, it was to have included a re-enactment of the battle of Actium.

In 1950 Bower directed an innovative Anglo-French musical version of *Alice in Wonderland*, with puppets; but his 'experimental' film of Berlioz's *Damnation of Faust* failed to go into production. This 'masque for cinema', with designs by Michael Ayrton and choreography by Massine, could have exemplified the new stereoscopic cinema which he had predicted in 1936. But with the decline of the British film industry, his most imaginative projects stood little chance of realization, and he moved into documentaries and commercials. His proposals for Wagner's *Ring* and Berlioz's *The Trojans* (1971) were never taken up. Many of his most inventive ideas survive only as unrealized scenarios, though some, such as his *Hamlet*, became radio productions.

Bower was a genial man, with a great capacity for friendship, but uncompromising where his own high standards were concerned. A master of his craft, he played a unique part in developing the modern media for serious artistic purposes. He will be remembered for his distinctive contribution to the arts in the twentieth century and for his challenging vision of the cinema of the future. He died of heart failure at a nursing home, Denville Hall, 62 Ducks Hill Road, Northwood, Middlesex, on 18 October 1999 and was cremated ten days later at Breakspear crematorium, Ruislip. He was survived by his son Delian and his daughter Tessa; his elder daughter had predeceased him.

ALAN G. HILL

Sources D. G. Bower, *Playback* [forthcoming] · B. McFarlane, ed., *An autobiography of British cinema* (1997), 80–84 · D. Bower, 'Live television drama — 1936', *Journal of the Royal Television Society* (Dec 1986), 338–41 · L. Salter, 'Television opera', *Opera*, 28 (1977) · *Variety* (29 Oct 1986), 125–6 · *From the palace to the grove: Michael Barry* (1992) · J. Stallworthy, *Louis MacNeice* (1995) · *The Independent* (20 Oct 1999) · *The Guardian* (20 Oct 1999) · personal knowledge (2004) · b. cert. · m. cert. · d. cert.

Archives BBC WAC | FILM BFI NFTVA | SOUND BL NSA, BBC sound archives

Likenesses group portrait, photograph, after 1938, BFI; repro. in *The Guardian* · photograph, *c*.1990, repro. in McFarlane, *Autobiography* · photographs, priv. coll.
Wealth at death under £200,000—gross; under £25,000—net: probate, 29 Dec 1999, *CGPLA Eng. & Wales*

Bower [Bowers], **Edward** (*d*. 1666/7), portrait painter, appears to have worked primarily in London, and a number of his portraits after 1637 bear the inscription 'att Temple Barr'. A letter of 1646, plausibly thought to refer to Bower, describes him as 'the workman who was servant' to Sir Anthony Van Dyck (Markham, 428). Bower borrowed something of Van Dyck's style in his backgrounds and accessories but employed them with a less practised hand and demonstrated little understanding of perspective in his portraits of provincial patrons.

The first mention of Bower appears in the minutes of the Painter–Stainers' Company on 27 March 1629, when he was 'informed against' (MS 5667/1, fol. 43, Guildhall Library). Only freemen could have apprentices, so it is interesting to note that on 31 July 1634 Henry Bayly, a blacksmith, complained that Bower was 'not using his Son as an Apprentice ought to be used', but 'fawlying into a great rage', he 'went away discontented because this Court would not agree to his request that was to have him taken away from Bowers and to be bound to Some other of this Companye' (MS 5667/1, fol. 96, Guildhall Library).

Bower's earliest known work, *Unknown Lady*, is dated 1636 (Sothebys, 17 June 1981, lot 59). A noteworthy portrait of this period is of an unknown man (1638), at Dunster Castle, Somerset. The original of Bower's portrait of John Pym (*c*.1640–41) has not been established but is known through versions in private collections and engravings, including one anonymous (1641, NPG) and another by G. Glover (published in 1644, NPG, BM).

On 1 July 1644 Bower was again in trouble with the Painter–Stainers' Company for the non-payment of fines, and on 24 April 1646 he was ordered to be brought before the lord mayor for 'contempt in not obeying the Ordinances and Orders of this Company' (MS 5667/1, fols. 187, 207, Guildhall Library).

In 1646 Bower painted a portrait of the parliamentarian Ferdinando, second Lord Fairfax of Cameron (City of York Art Gallery), probably at Bath in June. A portrait of his son Thomas, later third Lord Fairfax, wearing breastplate and sword, and signed 'Bower at Temple Bar, Fecit 1646', was formerly at Eshton Hall, Yorkshire (Christies, 10 April 1992, lot 4); an equestrian portrait of the general in full armour, engraved by William Marshall after Bower, was published in 1647. Also in 1646 Bower painted the son and daughter of a Devon royalist and his parliamentarian wife: Sir John Drake of Ashe (Tate collection) is depicted in the armour of war; in the companion piece, his sister Lady Elizabeth Drake, later the mother of John Churchill, first duke of Marlborough, holds an olive branch of peace (City of York Art Gallery).

Bower's best-known paintings are of *Charles I at his Trial* (1649). He probably worked up his portraits from drawings taken at Westminster Hall during the trial in January 1649. The three main signed and dated versions are in the Royal Collection, at Belvoir Castle, Leicestershire, and at Antony House, Cornwall (on loan from Sir Richard Carew Pole, bt), with a fourth in a private collection, but numerous variants, copies, and engravings exist because the pattern later became popular with royalists. In the three main versions Bower explores different arrangements of the hands, the silver-headed cane, and the facial expression. The naïve quality of the portraits gives them their emotional power. As Ellis Waterhouse observed, 'If the hand of the painter had been more cunning perhaps something of the unexpected pathos of these portraits would have evaporated' (Waterhouse, *Painting in Britain*, 23).

Despite Bower's earlier conflicts with the Painter–Stainers' Company, he became upper warden in 1656 and master in 1661, and was among those appointed to ride in attendance on Charles II when he arrived in London in 1660. Bower died between 27 December 1666 and 8 January 1667. ARIANNE BURNETTE

Sources 'The booke of orders and constitutions to be made for the good gouerment of the Company of the Painters–Steyners', GL, MSS 5667/1 and 5667/2, pt 1 · E. K. Waterhouse, 'Edward Bower, painter of King Charles I at his trial', *Burlington Magazine*, 91 (1949), 18–19, 21 · C. R. Markham, *A life of the great Lord Fairfax* (1870) · O. Millar, 'Bower [Bowers], Edward', *The dictionary of art*, ed. J. Turner (1996) · *Catalogue of paintings*, City of York Art Gallery, 2: *English school, 1500–1850* (1963) · *Preview, City of York Art Gallery Quarterly*, 14/54 (1961), 519–23 · O. Millar, *The age of Charles I: painting in England, 1620–1649* (1972) [exhibition catalogue, Tate Gallery, London, 15 Nov 1972 – 14 Jan 1973] · O. Millar, *The Tudor, Stuart and early Georgian pictures in the collection of her majesty the queen*, 2 vols. (1963) · E. K. Waterhouse, *The dictionary of British 16th and 17th century painters* (1988) · E. Waterhouse, *Painting in Britain, 1530–1790*, 5th edn (1994) · M. Whinney and O. Millar, *English art, 1625–1714* (1957) · C. H. C. Baker, *Lely and the Stuart portrait painters: a study of English portraiture before and after van Dyck*, 2 vols. (1912) · W. A. D. Englefield, *The history of the Painter–Stainers' Company of London* (1950) · '100 years of the National Trust: 100 treasures chosen by 100 celebrities', *Apollo* (May 1995), 52–3 · D. Piper, *Catalogue of seventeenth-century portraits in the National Portrait Gallery, 1625–1714* (1963) · *Engraved Brit. ports.* · photographs, notes on collections, NPG, Heinz Archive and Library · artist's file, archive material, Courtauld Inst., Witt Library
Archives GL, 'The booke of orders and constitutions to be made for the good gouerment of the Company of the Painters–Steyners', MSS 5667/1, fols. 43, 96, 187, 207; 5667/2, pt 1, fols. 36, 37, 42, 68, 69

Bower, Frederick Orpen (1855–1948), botanist, was born on 4 November 1855 at Ripon, the youngest of the five children of Abraham Bower, wool-stapler and clothier, and his wife, Cornelia Morris, sister of the naturalist Francis Orpen Morris (1810–1893). Bower was educated at Repton School where, by individual study, he became interested in botany and decided that it should be his life's work. In 1874 he went to Trinity College, Cambridge, where he graduated with first-class honours in the natural sciences tripos in 1877. At first he found nothing of the training he expected save for Michael Foster's course in elementary biology. However, in 1876, Sydney Vines (1849–1934) was appointed as a lecturer at Christ's College and introduced instruction in modern botany.

In 1877 Bower went to Würzburg, where he had the

great experience of learning laboratory methods from Julius Sachs. Two years later he went to Strasbourg for a year; he carried out his first original research there, under Heinrich Anton de Bary. After returning to England in 1880 he settled in London for five fruitful years. He became assistant to Daniel Oliver at University College, and in 1882 became a lecturer in botany in the department of T. H. Huxley at South Kensington. However, much of his time was spent in research at the Jodrell Laboratory at Kew.

In 1885, Bower accepted the regius chair of botany in the University of Glasgow. During his forty years in the post he built up a well-equipped department, housed in the first botanical institute built in Great Britain. An all-round botanist, a good organizer, and an inspiring teacher, he was a great mentor to a succession of young botanists. Above all, he was devoted to original work in morphological botany, in which his department had a worldwide reputation.

Bower's research was wide-ranging. He initially dealt with a variety of plants and problems, but from 1890 came to concentrate on the evolutionary morphology of the Pteridophyta. Three major works mark phases of his research into this problem. In *The Origin of a Land Flora: a Theory Based upon the Facts of Alternation* (1908) he suggested a theory about the phylogenetic origin of the land flora. He postulated that the development of the Sporophytic generation had evolved as an adaptation during the colonization of dry land by plants. His book became the accepted exposition of the 'antithetic'—as opposed to the 'homologous'—theory of alternation of generations. There followed during the next twenty years a comprehensive survey of the Filicales, resulting in *The Ferns (Filicales)* in three volumes (1923–8), in which he based the systematic classification of ferns on their phylogenetic relationships, considering recent as well as fossil forms. After his retirement from Glasgow in 1925 Bower's work continued at Ripon. *Primitive Land Plants, also Known as the Archegoniatae* (1935) summed up the position at which he had arrived for all the classes of Bryophyta and Pteridophyta. The changes which had come about in his views were partly due to his own investigations on existing plants, but also to the increase of knowledge of early and primitive fossil plants, unknown at the date of the *Land Flora*.

A digression into physiological morphology which greatly interested Bower in his later years was dealt with in *Size and Form in Plants* (1930), in which he demonstrated that morphological evidence pointed to the necessity in plant tissues to maintain a certain relationship between surface and bulk. His last book, published in 1938, was *Sixty Years of Botany in Britain (1875–1935)*. It was autobiographical and gave an account of the introduction of the 'new botany' in which he had taken part. Although Bower's constructive work had reached its conclusion, the preparation of the fourth edition of *Botany of the Living Plant* (1947; 1st edn, 1919), based on his elementary lectures, carried his botanical activity to the last years of his life.

Bower was elected FRS in 1891 and received a royal medal (1910) and the Darwin medal (1938). He was elected a fellow of the Royal Society of Edinburgh in 1886, was president in 1919–24, and was awarded the Neill prize in 1926. He was president of the British Association meeting at Bristol in 1930 and was three times president of the botany section. He was an honorary member of many foreign societies, and he received the honorary degrees of DSc from Dublin (1919), Sydney (1914), and Leeds (1927), and of LLD from Aberdeen (1919), Glasgow (1925), and Bristol (1930).

Bower was energetic, with a sanguine temperament. Although domesticated and social he never married. He played the cello and was devoted to chamber music, but his scientific work and writing was pursued as his greatest and most continuous pleasure; his clear and vivid style conveyed his personal interest to the reader. He made large additions of new facts, but his tendency was always to get farther by the critical use of his scientific imagination and by pursuing a guiding hypothesis. He was recognized as one of the leading plant-morphologists through a long period of the development of modern botany. Bower died at his home, 2 Princess Terrace, Ripon, on 11 April 1948 in his ninety-third year.

W. H. Lang, *rev.* Thomas Junker

Sources W. H. Lang, *Obits. FRS*, 6 (1948–9), 347–74 · F. O. Bower, *Sixty years of botany in Britain (1875–1935)* (1938) · A. D. Boney, 'Appointment of a "crown" chair of botany: Glasgow, 1885', *The Linnean*, 1/6 (1985), 19–26 · J. Walton, E. J. Salisbury, and L. F. J. Brimble, *Nature*, 161 (1948), 753–5 · S. Williams, 'Frederick Orpen Bower, Sc.D., LL.D., F.R.S.', *Berichte der Deutschen botanischen Gesellschaft*, 68a (1955), 217–20 · A. D. Boney, 'Doing his botany in the intervals of fiddling', *The Linnean*, 9/2 (1993), 29–36 · *CGPLA Eng. & Wales* (1948) · personal knowledge (1959)

Archives RBG Kew, corresp. · U. Glas., department of botany · U. Glas., corresp. and papers; additional corresp., drawings, photographs

Likenesses photogravure, 1889, NPG · W. Orpen, oils, 1927, U. Glas. · W. Stoneman, photograph, 1937, NPG · photograph, repro. in Lang, *Obits. FRS*

Wealth at death £8362 19*s.* 2*d.*: probate, 10 July 1948, *CGPLA Eng. & Wales*

Bower [Bowers], **George** (*d.* **1690**), medallist, was active from 1660 in London. His first recorded medals commemorated the restoration of Charles II, and were followed by several on the royal marriage in 1662 between Charles and Catherine of Braganza. In 1664 he was appointed embosser-in-ordinary, which provided much work in the Royal Mint. During the course of the reign he executed many commissions, often portraits or the commemoration of specific events. Nor was he politically biased: the duchess of Portsmouth (1673), Sir Samuel Moreland, Sir Edmund Godfrey, the acquittal of the earl of Shaftesbury, and the Rye House plot all received his attention.

Bower continued to work under James II, commemorating the royal accession, the battle of Sedgemoor, Monmouth's execution, the duke of Albemarle's exploits in search of treasure ships, and the birth of Prince James. However, in 1688 he produced medals depicting the landing of William of Orange, the destruction of Catholic chapels in London, and the coronation of William and

Mary. Indeed, he was appointed chief engraver at the mint in 1689, his first official post on the mint establishment, and struck the official coronation medal handed out to the participants. He also worked until February 1690 on patterns for the new monarchs' copper coinage. He died on 1 March 1690. Examples of his work are in the British Museum. W. W. Wroth, *rev.* Stuart Handley

Sources H. A. Grueber, *British Museum, department of coins and medals: a guide to the exhibition of English medals*, 2nd edn (1891), 39–68 • C. E. Challis, 'Lord Hastings to the great silver recoinage, 1464–1699', *A new history of the royal mint* (1992), 364 • *Medallic illustrations of the history of Great Britain and Ireland to the death of George II*, British Museum, ed. H. A. Grueber, 3 vols. (1911) • L. Forrer, *Biographical dictionary of medallists*, 8 vols. (1904–30), 1.258–9 • J. Craig, *The mint: a history of the London mint from AD 287 to 1948* (1953), 181 • *N&Q*, 12th ser., 2 (2 Dec 1916)

Bower, Sir John Dykes (1905–1981), organist, was born at Gloucester on 13 August 1905, the third of four sons (there were no daughters) of Ernest Dykes Bower MD, a general practitioner and ophthalmic surgeon, and his wife, Margaret Dora Constance Sheringham. Two of his brothers (Michael and Wilfrid) became well-known doctors, and the other, Stephen Ernest Dykes *Bower, an architect, designed the baldachin at St Paul's Cathedral. All four sons inherited from their parents a powerful interest in music, and as children were daily set to practise the piano during the hour before breakfast. The family worshipped regularly at Gloucester Cathedral.

Dykes Bower was educated at Cheltenham College and at the same time was a pupil of Herbert Brewer, organist of Gloucester Cathedral. From Cheltenham he went in 1922 to Corpus Christi College, Cambridge, and there won the John Stewart of Rannoch university scholarship in music. He was again awarded a Rannoch scholarship, together with his brother Wilfrid, in 1925. At Cambridge he was organ scholar in succession to Boris Ord; his brother Wilfrid succeeded him. Ord and Dykes Bower were lifelong friends, both dedicated to the pursuit of flawless performance of church music and very austere in the demands they made on choirs. Both hated any element of 'show-biz' about the conductor's role.

From Cambridge, Dykes Bower went to be organist at Truro (1926–9), where Bishop Walter Frere as musician and liturgist made his stay congenial. At Truro he succeeded in expelling from his choir a tone-deaf lay clerk who was mayor and a potentate in the city. This difficult achievement commended him to H. A. L. Fisher, warden of New College, Oxford, and Sir Hugh Allen, when New College needed an organist in 1929. In 1933 he was invited to be cathedral organist at Durham, with a university lectureship. His Cambridge college simultaneously elected him a (non-resident) fellow (1934–7). The incomparable acropolis of Durham was congenial to Dykes Bower, but there were also difficulties to contend with (he did not get on well with those who wanted no changes and resented his perfectionism); and in 1936, aged only thirty-one, he was appointed by W. R. Matthews, the dean, to St Paul's Cathedral to succeed Stanley Marchant. Matthews and Dykes Bower became instinctively drawn together in friendship as well as by their common responsibility for cathedral services. They perfectly understood their respective spheres. Moreover, Dykes Bower was a punctilious administrator and letter writer. He enjoyed to the full the great occasions that came to St Paul's, such as the thanksgiving service after the Second World War or Sir Winston Churchill's state funeral in 1965, when the huge congregation singing the 'Battle Hymn of the Republic' was totally controlled by his masterly rhythmic playing.

St Paul's had resources making it possible for Dykes Bower to include music of a complexity that other cathedrals could hardly attempt. Characteristically, unless an anthem were unaccompanied, he would always direct from the organ loft; his intense sense of pulse and rhythm was conveyed with the minimum of external sign. He disliked anything flamboyant or histrionic. In part this reflected the quiet reticence of his personality. But it was more an expression of his deep feeling that the sublimity of church music is diminished or even destroyed if the performance and the performers are perceived to be somehow distinct from the act of worship to which they help to give expression.

During the Second World War the cathedral was under frequent threat from the air. In the destruction of the City of London by firebombs in December 1940 Dykes Bower lost everything, including his exquisite grand piano to which he was devoted; he was at least as fine a performer on the piano as on the organ. In 1940 he joined the Royal Air Force Volunteer Reserve and, with the rank of squadron leader, worked in the Air Ministry with a group which included the viola player Bernard Shore, with whom he used to give occasional wartime recitals when life made such relaxation possible. After the war he combined his continued work at St Paul's with the post of associate director of the Royal School of Church Music (1945–52). He held the professorship of organ at the Royal College of Music (1936–69) and sent out a series of distinguished pupils to many of the major cathedral posts in England. Only Boris Ord at King's College, Cambridge, had a comparable influence on the standard of musicianship in English cathedrals.

In 1967, aged sixty-two, Dykes Bower found his eyesight threatened by cataract, and once, playing some difficult Bach at the end of a service, he suddenly found himself unable to see the printed page. Immediately he decided to retire from the great position he had held so long. He also had such an attachment to W. R. Matthews, with whom he had collaborated for thirty-one years, that he did not want to continue after Matthews's retirement from the deanery. He took a flat near Westminster Abbey, which he attended regularly. Weak sight robbed him of the earlier pleasure of reading Victorian novels and railway timetables, on which he was remarkably expert (he loved to plan imaginary cross-country journeys with *Bradshaw*). But he continued to do much for the Royal College of Organists, of which he was president (1960–62).

Dykes Bower was appointed CVO in 1953 and knighted in 1968. Oxford made him an honorary DMus (1944) and Corpus Christi, Cambridge, made him an honorary fellow

(1980). He was master of the Worshipful Company of Musicians in 1967–8. He did much for the council of *Hymns Ancient and Modern*, of which he was chairman; the hymn writer J. B. Dykes (1823–1876) was his forebear.

Dykes Bower's fastidiousness and relentless quest for flawless performance made him hard to please, and could combine with his quiet reticence to make him silent where a word of encouragement could have been beneficial. A very private man with a horror of the limelight, he asked only to be allowed to offer perfection through music in the worship of the Church of England. He inspired awe but also deep affection in everyone who worked alongside him. He died, unmarried, on 29 May 1981 in a hospital at Orpington, Kent.

HENRY CHADWICK

Sources personal knowledge (2004) · *The Times* (3 June 1981) · *WWW* · *New Grove* · *CGPLA Eng. & Wales* (1981)

Archives FILM BFI NFTVA, news footage | SOUND BL NSA, performance recordings

Wealth at death £132,919: probate, 20 Aug 1981, *CGPLA Eng. & Wales*

Bower, Stephen Ernest Dykes (1903–1994), architect, was born in Gloucester on 18 April 1903, the second of the four sons of Ernest Dykes Bower, general practitioner and ophthalmic surgeon, and his wife, Margaret Dora Constance, the youngest daughter of John William Sheringham, archdeacon of Gloucester. The organist Sir John Dykes *Bower was his brother. His early life was spent in Gloucester, where the cathedral made a strong impression on him. After Cheltenham College, he entered Merton College, Oxford, as an organ scholar in 1921. He graduated with a third-class degree in English in 1924. A meeting with Sir Ninian Comper encouraged him to proceed to study architecture at the Architectural Association. His interest in the Victorian tradition of church architecture was encouraged by a friendship with F. C. Eden (1864–1944), whose refined and scholarly work, with its sensitivity to place, he emulated throughout his life, seeking beauty rather than innovation.

Dykes Bower set up practice in 1931, moving to Quendon Court, near Saffron Walden, Essex, in 1933, where he lived and ran an office for the remainder of his life. His first important new work was the rebuilding after a fire of All Saints' Church, Hockerill, near Bishop's Stortford, in 1936, a Gothic design, but quietly original. After serving with the Ministry of Town and Country Planning in Cambridge during the war, he successfully resumed his practice, with a variety of domestic, institutional, and other work, but always predominantly ecclesiastical. He designed three new churches, built of brick, of which the most impressive was St John's, Newbury (1955–7).

In 1949 Godfrey Allen, the surveyor of St Paul's, commissioned Dykes Bower to design a new high altar for the cathedral. Completed in 1958, this was a bravura performance in design and craftsmanship, recreating Wren's intentions for a baroque baldachin. The American war memorial chapel behind it was included in the design. In 1951 Dykes Bower was appointed surveyor of the fabric of Westminster Abbey and began a programme of cleaning and repair, including gilding and colouring of tombs and Edward Blore's pulpitum. This effected a transformation in the years before his retirement in 1973. He worked with a devoted team of craftsmen and assistants. He encountered opposition over the repair of the roofs and his proposals for a decorative floor in the nave, the latter scheme being abandoned.

Dykes Bower contributed work, large and small, to a great many parish churches, being a notable designer of candlesticks, painted decoration, altar frontals, and vestments. At St Nicholas, Great Yarmouth, he rebuilt most of the extensive church after bomb damage, not only adding sensitive embellishment but rationalizing its liturgical planning. He was not opposed to the post-war trend towards central altars, and gave them dignity and spatial coherence.

Dykes Bower was appointed to complete the cathedral church of St Edmundsbury in Suffolk, formerly the parish church of St James, in 1945. His design for a new choir and crossing was published in 1953, subsequently undergoing revision. The choir and transepts are tall and light, with stencil-painted wooden ceilings, leading naturally out of the fine nave of 1503 by John Wastell. Externally, traditional carved stone details and flint flushwork closely resemble late Gothic work. The crossing lacked its tower during Dykes Bower's lifetime, but his bequest of his estate for the completion of the work enabled it to proceed in the hands of his former assistants Warwick Pethers and Hugh Mathew. His work can also be found in Canterbury, Winchester, Norwich, Ely, Gloucester, Wells, Oxford, Carlisle, Peterborough, and other cathedrals, in Oxford and Cambridge colleges, public schools, the halls of City livery companies, and elsewhere. At Lancing College, Dykes Bower completed R. C. Carpenter's Victorian chapel with the addition of a west front in 1979, containing the largest rose window to be built in England since the middle ages, filled with heraldic glass. His skill in reconstructing Victorian painted decoration was displayed at G. F. Bodley's church of St John, Tue Brook, Liverpool, in 1967.

Several important schemes by Dykes Bower were aborted because they were considered too conservative, and he suffered from a feeling of isolation. He was generous with his professional time for any cause which he considered worthwhile, notably in his restoration and redecoration of St Paul's, Salford, a deprived parish on the edge of Manchester, which became a symbol of regeneration as his work proceeded in the 1970s and 1980s.

Dykes Bower enjoyed writing on architecture, publishing many articles and book reviews. He was interested in all aspects of church architecture, but particularly organ cases. Until his last years he continued to play the organ at Quendon parish church and the piano at home. He was a lay canon of St Edmundsbury Cathedral from 1979 to 1984, and president of the Ecclesiological Society from 1983 until his death. His lectures were impressively cogent and eloquent, delivered without notes, and in conversation he always spoke with a sense of purpose. While viewed by many as a throwback to the nineteenth century, his motoring in a Rolls-Royce and serving dry Martinis before meals were pleasures of his own time. He died at Quendon Court, Essex, on 11 November 1994. He never married. ALAN POWERS

Sources A. Symondson, unpublished monograph • *The Independent* (14 Nov 1994) • *The Times* (14 Nov 1994) • *WWW, 1991–5* • personal knowledge (2004) • private information (2004)
Likenesses G. Butler, photograph, 1987, Art Workers Guild, London
Wealth at death £2,153,070: probate, 20 Jan 1995, *CGPLA Eng. & Wales*

Bower [Bowmaker], **Walter** (1385–1449), abbot of Inchcolm and historian, was born at Haddington. Nothing is known of his parentage, though he may have been related to a John Bowmaker who served as a bailie and custumar at Haddington in the late 1390s. In 1436 he was represented at the Roman court by a John Bowmaker, the rector of a Stirlingshire church; and in 1437 he was a mandatory for a papal provision to an Alexander Bowmaker, an Augustinian canon at St Andrews and teacher of law in the new university there. But no family relationships can be proved.

Since Bower's chronicle contains many references to events over the years in and around Haddington, it may be assumed that he grew up there and afterwards kept in touch. It would be about 1400 that he joined the community of Augustinian canons who served St Andrews Cathedral, for he appears to write about Bishop Walter Trail (*d.* 1401) from personal knowledge. He certainly trained as a novice from 1400 onwards under Prior James Biset, who held office from 1394 to 1416 and was one of the founders of the university at St Andrews. Bower himself describes vividly the celebrations surrounding the arrival in February 1414 of various bulls of privileges for the new university from Benedict XIII, the Avignon pope who was then recognized in Scotland. He was surely an eyewitness. And by 29 November 1417 he had qualified as a bachelor of canon law, when provided on that day by Pope Benedict as abbot of the Augustinian monastery on the island of Inchcolm in the Firth of Forth. He was blessed as abbot by his diocesan, the bishop of Dunkeld, on 17 April 1418. By 22 November 1420 he was claiming to hold the further university degree of bachelor of theology. There is no record of his ever having studied abroad, and so it is presumed that he earned his degrees at St Andrews. At any rate these degrees are a guide to the kind of intellectual training according to scholastic method that is reflected in his writing.

Abbot of Inchcolm Some evidence survives regarding the measures which he took as abbot between 1420 and 1435 to secure his abbey's property. With papal backing for several years he forced the bishop of Dunkeld to compromise in a dispute over the appropriated vicarage of Dalgety nearby in Fife. He took the trouble to obtain a papal protection for the abbey's property on 27 February 1430: as a monastic superior qualified in law, he knew what had to be done to guard the abbey's possessions.

As it turned out Bower was to remain abbot of the modestly endowed abbey on Inchcolm for more than thirty years until his death. He twice became involved in attempts to move to the wealthier house of his order at Holyrood, near Edinburgh. His first attempt was as early as 1420, but his hopes were dashed in 1423 when a candidate supported by the governor of Scotland at the time (Murdoch Stewart, duke of Albany) secured the office. When that abbot quarrelled with one of his canons in 1436–7, Bower was given papal authority to sort things out at Holyrood; yet the main body of canons were successful in having his powers cancelled. Inchcolm remained his base, within sight of Edinburgh.

Involvement in public life As abbot even of that small house Bower ranked as one of the ecclesiastical magnates of Scotland, and after the return of James I from captivity in England in 1424 he was presumably a regular attender at the king's councils and parliaments. He was certainly engaged on duties within the royal administration from time to time. He served several times as a collector of taxes—first for two years from May 1424 to raise funds to pay the king's ransom, and then for other purposes in 1431 and 1433. He tells himself in his book of how unpopular these unfamiliar levies were among all sections of the community. In late 1431 he had to provide custody on Inchcolm for the countess of Ross, the mother of Alexander MacDonald, lord of the Isles, whose power the king was intent on curbing.

In at least one parliament, that which met in January 1435, he was appointed to a committee to hear 'causes and complaints', and in the absence of similar records for other parliaments we may assume that with his legal training he regularly served in this way. But only once do we have information (provided by Bower himself) about his participation in practical politics. This is found in his report of a debate at a council general in October 1433 to discuss a response to a peace embassy from England. Bower was involved in collecting and summing up the views of the majority in favour of rejecting the English advances because of Scotland's prior commitment to France; and he tells with some satisfaction that the abbot of Melrose, who had spoken in favour of peace with England, was soon afterwards forced to recant his opinions when challenged by the inquisitor of heretical deviation. Bower was apparently in favour of an authoritarian alliance of church and state, a stance which he was to develop more theoretically when he came to write his great work. He was clearly a man with considerable administrative and political experience, not a man of the study.

If he had views of this kind about strong government, it is understandable why Bower went to such lengths in his book to lament the murder of King James in 1437. Not much is known about his activities in the first years after the king's death; but by the early 1440s at any rate he can be seen to be involved in the troubled affairs of the minority government of the young James II, attending general councils on 3 April 1441 and 9 February 1442, and serving again as an auditor of causes and complaints in the parliament of July 1445. He had his reward from the government on 8 June 1441, when a crown charter erected the lands of Inchcolm Abbey into a barony to help his community to recover from damage done by pirates.

The *Scotichronicon* It was while Bower was still engaged on such public duties as well as heading his monastic community that, without any known previous experience as a writer, he half unwillingly composed his *Scotichronicon*, the most elaborate work of Latin literature to survive from medieval Scotland. This came about when he was asked by a neighbouring laird, Sir David Stewart of Rosyth, to transcribe the chronicle and annals composed some eighty years earlier by John Fordun, and on the basis of the annals to continue the chronicle from the year 1153 (where Fordun had stopped) to his own day. Between November 1441 and October 1445 Fordun's five books were expanded to sixteen. Bower took the chance to insert in the first five books some passages derived from his own reading, which were carefully distinguished from Fordun's original work; and then he greatly expanded the coverage of the annals with less and less regard for Fordun's text, until by books 15 and 16 he was writing contemporary history of his own down to the king's murder in 1437.

Bower's working fair copy, intended to be kept on Inchcolm, still exists (Cambridge, Corpus Christi College, MS 171), and it shows how he latterly had his scribe make many marginal additions with extra material, all of which after his death came to be incorporated in the main text of all five of the surviving copies which were made in the next sixty years for various other monasteries and individuals. One of the copyists was **Magnus Makculloch** (*fl.* 1477–1484), who was probably born at Tain, Ross-shire, and is recorded as a student at Louvain in 1477. In 1481 and 1483–4 he made full copies of Bower's work for the Augustinian abbey of Scone and Archbishop William Scheves of St Andrews respectively. On the strength of two pages of additional annals relating to the reign of James II (1437–60) which were copied into the latter of these manuscripts, Makculloch has sometimes been given the scarcely deserved status of continuator of Bower's work; but he was a professional scribe rather than a scholar.

As early as 1444 Bower was working also on a shortened version of his main chronicle (now represented by a later copy, NL Scot., MS Advocates 35.1.7), which contains some extra items as well as Bower's own literary improvements. After a period of failing health he died on 24 December 1449. The whole corpus of his two books has been published in Latin and in English translation with commentary.

Outlook and purposes Besides handing on Fordun's work, Bower preserves with convincing reliability a wide range of supplementary information about people and events in Scotland between 1153 and 1437. But his didactic aims (not least with the training of the young James II in mind) led him to expand the scope of the book to include discussion of many other matters. He thought, for example, that his Scottish readers should be better informed about developments on the continent from Roman times onwards, and in general he gave more space to people and events in France than in England. This reflects the experience and intellectual outlook of his putative teachers in St Andrews, who had been students at Paris. He drew on his academic training also for literary allusions and parallels from the works of classical and medieval writers to illumine Scottish history by putting it into proportion in a larger intellectual context. Such features in his book are the product of the culture of fifteenth-century Scotland, and his work (including various later summaries of it) helped to perpetuate this attitude well into the sixteenth century.

Bower shared Fordun's hostility to English aggression and enthusiasm for Scottish liberty, while at the same time he added warning passages of political reflection on how all kinds of people in authority should conduct themselves. His advice was not merely theoretical, but based on personal experience, especially in the light of the factional rivalries in the years following the death of James I which were harming the country as he was writing; and as a practised preacher he knew how to engage the interest of his readers by inserting pithy stories with a moral. His declared intention, indeed, was to entertain, though as a churchman he did not fail to paint the horrors of hell, and particularly those that awaited sinners in high places who disobeyed the laws of the church. He was not just a chronicler preserving all that he could find about the past: he was a sage through whose wide-ranging reflections much can be learned about the customs and attitudes of his time.

D. E. R. Watt

Sources W. Bower, *Scotichronicon*, ed. D. E. R. Watt and others, new edn, 9 vols. (1987–98) • D. E. Easson and A. Macdonald, eds., *Charters of the abbey of Inchcolm*, Scottish History Society, 3rd ser., 32 (1938) • *APS*, 1424–1567 • G. Burnett and others, eds., *The exchequer rolls of Scotland*, 23 vols. (1878–1908), vol. 3 • *CEPR letters*, vols. 7–10 • A. I. Cameron, ed., *The apostolic camera and Scottish benefices, 1418–1488* (1934) • E. R. Lindsay, A. I. Dunlop, and others, eds., *Calendar of Scottish supplications to Rome*, 1–2, Scottish History Society, 3rd ser., 23, 48 (1934–56); 3, Scottish History Society, 4th ser., 7 (1970); 4 (1983) • M. Drexler, 'Attitudes to nationalism in Scottish historical writing from Barbour to Boece', PhD diss., U. Edin., 1979, 278–84 • R. J. Adam, ed., *The calendar of Fearn: text and additions, 1471–1667*, Scottish History Society, 5th ser., 4 (1991), 20–21 • *Johannis de Fordun Chronica gentis Scotorum / John of Fordun's Chronicle of the Scottish nation*, ed. W. F. Skene, trans. F. J. H. Skene, 1 (1871), xvii–xviii • BL, Harley MS 712 • NA Scot., GD 45/26/48 • U. Edin. L., MS 205 • National Library of Medicine, Washington, MS 512
Archives CCC Cam., MS 171 • NL Scot., MS Advocates 35.1.7
Likenesses H. Collins, oils, 1872, Scot. NPG

Bower, Sir (John) William Nott- (1849–1939), police administrator, was born on 20 March 1849 at 17 Micklegate, York, one of the children of John Bower, a barrister and leader of the bar in the ecclesiastical court of the province of York, and his wife, Charlotte, one among the fourteen children of General Sir William Nott GCB (1782–1845), commander of the army which marched from Kandahar to Kabul in 1842, during the First Anglo-Afghan War. In 1858 the family moved to Wales, where his father bought some slate quarries, and in 1862 he was sent to Cheltenham College. From there he entered the Royal Military College, Sandhurst, in 1865, where he won the sword of honour; but after deciding to take up a police career he left the army at the end of 1872, when he managed to get a much sought-after cadetship in the royal Irish constabulary through the Liberal politician W. E. Forster, a friend of his father, who gave him a letter of introduction to Lord Hartington, chief secretary for Ireland. After training at the constabulary depot in Phoenix Park, Dublin, Nott-Bower took charge of a large district in the west of Ireland, and moved to Limerick in 1873, before returning to Dublin in 1876 to command a company at the constabulary depot. Again through influential friends of his father he was appointed chief constable of Leeds in 1878, and during his three years there handled the case of the notorious burglar Charles Peace, tried in Leeds for murder and hanged in 1879.

Nott-Bower was appointed head constable of Liverpool in 1881, and remained there until 1902. On 1 June 1889 he married Florence (*d.* 1920), daughter of Reginald Harrison, a Liverpool surgeon. Two of their five sons were killed in action in the First World War; of the others one, Sir John Nott-Bower (1892–1972), followed his father into the police and served as commissioner of the Metropolitan Police from 1953 to 1958. Liverpool had the largest police force in the country outside London. With high levels of unemployment, over half the working population employed as casual labour in the docks, and large slum areas, the rate of violent crime was rising. In addition there were outbreaks of violence between members of the large Catholic and protestant Irish communities, and shortly before his arrival in Liverpool members of the Fenian Society had attempted to blow up the town hall. He also faced industrial conflict, most notably the great dock strike of 1890, when Nott-Bower, alarmed by the huge processions of dockers, advised the calling in of troops, to be stationed in the docks in order to prevent bloodshed. Not all his problems concerned the working classes: his most famous case was that of Mrs Maybrick, wife of a cotton merchant living in a fashionable suburb, who was sentenced to death in 1889 for poisoning her husband with arsenic, but who was reprieved by the home secretary.

Nott-Bower initiated a number of reforms in the Liverpool police force. With the help of his future father-in-law, Reginald Harrison, he organized the police ambulance system: it was the duty of the police to remove those injured or taken ill in the streets, but when he arrived in Liverpool, this could be done only by stretcher or handcart. In 1884 he persuaded the watch committee to supply horse-drawn ambulances, to be stationed at the hospitals, which would be part of the police force, and also set up a system of telegraph signal boxes to enable the police to summon the ambulances. He instituted the compulsory training of the Liverpool police in first aid, and was created a knight of grace of the order of St John of Jerusalem in recognition of his services to first aid work. In 1886 he formed the Liverpool mounted police to deal with riots and public disorder, and also to control large crowds during public processions, as when Queen Victoria visited Liverpool in 1886. In 1891 he got the watch committee to buy three horse-drawn patrol wagons, on the lines of those introduced in some towns in the United States. He also founded the Liverpool police athletic club, and raised money to build the Liverpool and Bootle police orphanage, which opened in 1895. Although he put pressure on the watch committee to increase the pay of police constables, not enough was done until the implementation of the report of the 1919 Desborough committee. In 1885 his scheme to reorganize the two police divisions into six smaller ones was approved by the home secretary, and after the city boundaries were extended in 1895, increasing the area the police had to patrol from 277 miles of streets to 399 miles, he was able to increase the force from 1294 men to 1460. As his reputation grew, Nott-Bower was asked for advice by police forces as far away as Hong Kong and South Africa, and in 1897 he was asked to give evidence before the royal commission on the liquor licensing laws.

In March 1902 Nott-Bower was elected commissioner of police of the City of London, the second most prestigious position in the police service in the country. A much smaller force than the Metropolitan Police, the City police was responsible mainly for police arrangements at public functions in the Guildhall, including visits by members of the royal family and foreign heads of state. Nott-Bower made the arrangements for the royal progresses through the City during the 1902 and 1911 coronations, when he rode in front of the royal carriage until it passed the City boundary. He was involved in the battle of Sidney Street in January 1911. On that occasion members of the City and Metropolitan Police forces, reinforced by two squads of Scots Guards from the Tower of London, laid siege to a house in Sidney Street, Whitechapel; there two members of a gang of Russian anarchists, who had murdered three policemen during a raid on a jeweller's shop in Houndsditch, were surrounded. In 1911, in response to a circular from the home secretary, Nott-Bower began to recruit members of the City of London police reserve, who could be called on in case of emergency. They were valuable during the First World War, when many of the regular police were away on active service, helping to deal with the Zeppelin raids in 1915 and aeroplane bombing raids on the City later in the war. He was also confronted with the police strikes of 1918 and 1919, called by the National Union of Police and Prison Officers. He was in sympathy with the 1918 strike, acknowledging that the police were underpaid, but he dismissed all those who went on strike in 1919 because he believed that most of their grievances had already been remedied. He retired from the City police in 1925.

Nott-Bower was knighted in 1911 and created KCVO in 1918. He published his autobiography, *Fifty-Two Years a Policeman*, in 1926. He died on 4 February 1939 at his home, the Hotel Stuart, Richmond Hill, Richmond, Surrey, and was buried three days later at Bognor Regis, Sussex.

ANNE PIMLOTT BAKER

Sources J. W. Nott-Bower, *Fifty-two years a policeman* (1926) • W. R. Cockroft, *From cutlasses to computers: the police force in Liverpool, 1836–1989* (1991) • *The Times* (6 Feb 1939) • *WW* • b. cert. • d. cert.
Likenesses photograph, repro. in *The Times* • portrait, repro. in Nott-Bower, *Fifty-two years*, frontispiece

Bowerbank, James Scott (1797–1877), geologist and zoologist, was born on 14 July 1797 in Sun Street, Bishopsgate, London, the fourth of six children of Edward Bowerbank, distiller, and his wife, Fanny. He went to Dr Kelly's school in Finsbury Square, and is said to have developed a love of nature from studying the plants growing alongside the River Lea. He started work in his father's distillery, Bowerbank & Co., at the age of fifteen, and he and his brother Edward became joint heads of the family firm on the death of their father. Bowerbank gained a reputation in the City for being a careful and attentive man of business. He remained associated with the firm until 1847.

In spite of the demands of the family firm, Bowerbank always found time for scientific research. He joined the Spitalfields Mathematical Society in 1818 and soon became one of its most active members, giving lectures on botany in the winters of 1822–4, and on human osteology in 1831. His earliest independent scientific researches were made with a microscope and related to the fine structure of the insect wing. He enjoyed microscopical work throughout his life, and owned many fine instruments. He was one of the founders of the Microscopical Society of London in 1839, and was its president in 1846–7.

Bowerbank lived in Hoxton as a young man and started collecting fossils from the London Clay, particularly the fossil seeds and fruit to be found on the Isle of Sheppey. He joined the Geological Society in 1832, and in 1836, with several geological friends, he founded the London Clay Club, whose members used to meet regularly to display and discuss the fruits of their collecting. In 1840 he published the first, and only, part of a projected monograph on the *Fossil Fruits of the London Clay*, which remained a standard work for many years. This same year Bowerbank moved to Islington where he married Caroline; the couple had no children as far as is known. In 1846 they moved to 3 Highbury Grove, a spacious house with room for Bowerbank's growing geological collections. He was an enthusiastic collector in many branches of geology, and his museum eventually amounted to 100,000 specimens.

Bowerbank was a sociable man, and used to hold 'open house' on Monday evenings, to which young beginners in geology and microscopy were especially welcome. The idea of the aquarium was developed at his house as he experimented with growing algae, other plants, and fish in a large jar. The secretary of the Zoological Society saw what he was doing and adopted the idea, on a much larger scale, for the London Zoo in 1853. The house became celebrated as a scientific centre in London, and is depicted in a lithographed cartoon, 'Highbury Grove in 1846'.

In 1847, after the reading of a paper by Joseph Prestwich at the Geological Society, Bowerbank invited the assembled geologists to meet him in the tea-room. He there proposed the establishment of a society for the publication of undescribed British fossils. This suggestion, which was

James Scott Bowerbank (1797–1877), by Maull & Polyblank, c.1855

supported by William Buckland, Henry De la Beche, William Fitton, and others, was the origin of the Palaeontographical Society. Bowerbank served the society first as honorary secretary and later as president. He was also, in 1844, one of the founders of the Ray Society, and was treasurer from 1845 until 1860, when he did not stand for re-election following criticism of the annual accounts. In 1842 he was elected a fellow of the Royal Society, and he was awarded an honorary degree of LLD by the University of St Andrews in 1857.

A visit to Brighton after a storm in 1841 allowed Bowerbank to collect a large number of fresh sponges, and led to a lifelong interest in the group. He studied the fine structure, and the classification and nomenclature of both living and fossil sponges. He became interested in silicification as a geological process, and developed the idea that most, if not all, flints are composed of sponge material. He published papers on sponges in the *Annals of Natural History*, the *Philosophical Transactions of the Royal Society*, the *Proceedings of the Zoological Society*, and the *Microscopical Society Transactions*. His *Monograph of the British Spongiadae* was published by the Ray Society in four volumes between 1864 and 1882, being edited and completed after his death by the Revd A. M. Norman.

Bowerbank retired from business in 1847. About 1860, concerned for his wife's health, he bought a house in St Leonards, Sussex, and they spent part of each year there. In 1864, apparently after his wife's death, he sold the house in London to move permanently to Sussex. He sold the most important parts of his fossil collection to the British Museum in 1865 and had the remainder auctioned by J. C. Stevens in November of that year, keeping only the sponges. His friends formed a testimonial fund committee which subscribed for a marble bust by Peter Slater, which was presented to the Geological Society in 1865. Bowerbank retained an interest in science throughout the remainder of his life, and continued working on his Ray Society sponge monograph until a few days before his death. He died at his home, 2 East Ascent, St Leonards, Sussex, on 8 March 1877, and was buried in Hollington churchyard. His valuable collection of sponges was acquired by the British Museum in 1877.

JOHN C. THACKRAY

Sources *Monthly Notices of the Royal Astronomical Society*, 38 (1877–8), 144–7 • P. M. Duncan, *Quarterly Journal of the Geological Society*, 34 (1878), 36–7 • C. Tyler, 'Memoir of Dr Bowerbank', in J. S. Bowerbank, *A monograph of the British Spongiadae*, 4, ed. A. M. Norman, Ray Society (1882), xiii–xvii • C. Knight, ed., *The English cyclopaedia: biography*, 6 vols. (1856–8) • *IGI* • census returns, 1851

Archives RGS, secretary's corresp. | CUL, letters to Sir George Stokes • NHM, corresp. with Richard Owen and William Clift • NHM, letters to members of the Sowerby family • Wellcome L., letters to Henry Lee

Likenesses T. H. Maguire, lithograph, 1851, BM • Maull & Polyblank, photograph, *c.*1854, NHM • Maull & Polyblank, photograph, *c.*1855, NPG [*see illus.*] • Maull & Co., photograph, *c.*1860, GS Lond. • P. Slater, marble bust, 1865, GL • E. Edwards, photograph, NPG; repro. in L. Reeve, ed., *Men of eminence* (1864), vol. 2 • engraving, RS • four photographs, RS • group lithograph, RS

Wealth at death under £25,000: probate, 17 April 1877, *CGPLA Eng. & Wales*

Bowerman, Charles William (1851?–1947), trade unionist and politician, was probably born on 22 January 1851 in Honiton, Devon, the son of Charles Bowerman, a tinplater who on finding work in London moved his family to Clerkenwell. After receiving a basic education at Barnsbury national school, Bowerman worked briefly for a watchmaker and jeweller in Clerkenwell before becoming apprenticed to an uncle as a compositor in 1865. In a trade that required a good level of literacy, he improved his education by reading books by the likes of Walter Scott and Charles Dickens.

On completing his apprenticeship in 1872 Bowerman found a place with the *Hour* newspaper before moving after a few months to the compositors' room of the *Daily Telegraph*, where he worked for nineteen years. During this time he became an active trade unionist. He joined the London Society of Compositors (LSC) in 1873; in 1889 he became its news secretary, a post serving the needs of those members who worked on newspapers (as opposed to compositors of books and other printed matter). Although the LSC was a well-established and conservative craft union, it had expanded its membership with the growth of the printing trade in the 1880s. It was in these circumstances that Bowerman became active in seeking to improve conditions of employment in the highly competitive London newspaper market, as well as pressing for the reorganization of the union itself. The general secretary of the LSC, C. J. Drummond, was regarded as out of touch by a self-styled reform group, which included Bowerman, within the union. When this faction gained three seats on the executive committee in 1892 Drummond decided he had lost the confidence of his members; he resigned and was succeeded by Bowerman.

In this full-time, salaried position, Bowerman began to attend the annual congress of the Trades Union Congress. In 1897 he was elected to the TUC's parliamentary committee, and he presided over the congress held in Swansea in 1901. In a presidential address given soon after the setback of the House of Lords judgment in the Taff Vale case, he characteristically advised the delegates to make haste slowly, for he was essentially a conciliator and cautious in negotiating with employers. Although he was a member of the Fabian Society from 1893, his political attitudes were those of the radical Liberal rather than the socialist tradition. However, he was committed to the principle of independent labour politics. In February 1900 he was a delegate at the founding conference of the Labour Representation Committee (LRC). Sponsored by the LSC, he was adopted as LRC candidate for Deptford in 1903. In this role, too, he sought a conciliatory path; as a London county council alderman (from 1901 to 1907) he worked amicably with Liberals as part of the Progressive group. As a result some Liberals favoured him as candidate for Deptford over Herbert Vivian, who was endorsed by the Liberal central office but despite this polled badly in the general election of 1906 when Bowerman took the seat.

Once an MP, Bowerman was designated as the parliamentary secretary of the LSC, which contributed substantially to his expenses. In Deptford, cordial relations between the Labour Association and local Liberals helped to ensure that Bowerman had straight fights, in which he was successful, against the Conservative candidate in the general elections of 1910. In the House of Commons his interventions, when not over constituency issues, usually took the form of questions about working-class interests. His reputation as a good administrator helped him to secure the salaried post of secretary to the TUC in 1911 on the death of W. C. Steadman. Bowerman's involvement in the printing industry meant that he had long advocated the establishment of a daily newspaper to champion the cause of Labour. When the *Daily Herald* was launched, originally as a London printers' strike sheet, along with T. E. Naylor, who had become general secretary of the LSC in 1906, he gave it some support, despite its left-wing views. He switched his allegiance eventually, however, when the official Labour Party paper, the *Daily Citizen*, made its appearance.

In the First World War, in common with most leaders of labour, Bowerman supported the government's war effort, in particular by membership of the joint labour recruiting committee. He was made a privy councillor in 1916. With the end of the war he took part in the discussions which led to the formation of the International Federation of Trade Unions and the International Labour Organization. Neither an innovative nor a visionary official, Bowerman—known as Courteous Charlie, according to Walter Citrine, who later held the TUC secretaryship—operated with an unostentatious paternalism. From 1916 he was assisted in the growing work of the TUC by Fred Bramley, who was regarded by many as a more vigorous organizer. Bramley was expected to succeed him but did so only in 1923, the year after congress had decided that officials had to retire on reaching the age of seventy.

Although Bowerman was by then seventy-two, he continued to represent his Deptford constituency until he was eighty, when he suffered defeat at the general election of 1931. However, he had several more years of activity left ahead of him. In 1935 he was a signatory of the proposals of the Next Five Years Group. He was a member of the council of Ruskin College, thus sustaining an interest that went back to February 1899 when he was present at the founding conference of the college. For several years he was chairman of the board of directors of the Co-operative Printing Society (attending even in the harsh winter of 1946–7, at the age of ninety-six).

Bowerman died at his home, 4 Battledean Road, in the Highbury district of London, on 11 June 1947. He was predeceased by his wife, Louisa Peach, whom he married in 1876 and with whom he had five sons and seven daughters. He was buried on 13 June at Islington cemetery, after a service at Christ Church, Highbury. D. E. MARTIN

Sources P. R. Thompson, *Socialists, liberals and labour: the struggle for London, 1885–1914* (1967) · H. A. Clegg, A. Fox, and A. F. Thompson, *A history of British trade unions since 1889*, 1–2 (1964–85) · B. C. Roberts, *The Trades Union Congress, 1868–1921* (1958) · E. Howe and H. E. Waite, *The London Society of Compositors: a centenary history* (1948) · F. Bealey and H. Pelling, *Labour and politics, 1900–1906: a history of the Labour Representation Committee* (1958) · S. V. Bracher, *The Herald book of labour members* (1923) · *The Times* (12 June 1947) · Lord Citrine [W. M. Citrine], *Men and work: an autobiography* (1964)

Archives Labour History Archive and Study Centre, Manchester, corresp. and papers | U. Warwick Mod. RC, records of the Trades Union Congress | FILM BFI NFTVA, news footage

Likenesses group photograph, 1906 (of the newly formed labour party) · group photograph (general council of the TUC) · group photographs (parliamentary committee of the TUC)

Wealth at death £3668 17*s*. 0*d*.: probate, 18 Oct 1947, *CGPLA Eng. & Wales*

Bowerman, Elsie Edith (1889–1973), suffragette and lawyer, was born on 18 December 1889 at Barnsbury Lodge, Garden Road, Tunbridge Wells, the only child of William Bowerman (*c*.1825–1895) and his wife, Edith Martha Barber (1864–1953). She was educated at Wycombe Abbey School (1901–7), in Paris, and then at Girton College, Cambridge (1908–11), from where she graduated with a second-class degree in medieval and modern languages and a distinction in oral French.

Elsie Bowerman and her mother, now Mrs Chibnall (she had remarried in 1907), both joined the Women's Social and Political Union (WSPU) in 1909. Elsie founded a branch of the WSPU in Girton, inviting such speakers as Lady Constance Lytton to address the undergraduates, despite lack of co-operation from the college authorities. Her mother was active in the WSPU branch at St Leonards, Sussex, and was injured while taking part in a WSPU deputation to the House of Commons in November 1910. Having graduated Elsie Bowerman returned to St Leonards, as a paid organizer for the WSPU. On 15 April 1912, while travelling as first-class passengers to America for a holiday, she and her mother survived the sinking of the *Titanic*.

In September 1916 Elsie Bowerman sailed to Russia as an orderly with the Scottish women's hospital unit, at the request of the Hon. Evelina Haverfield, a fellow suffragette whom she had known for several years. With this unit she travelled via Archangel, Moscow, and Odessa to serve the Serbian and Russian armies in Romania. The women arrived as the allies were defeated, and were soon forced to join the retreat northwards to the Russian frontier. While awaiting her passage home, in March 1917, Elsie witnessed the 'February revolution' in St Petersburg. A diary that she kept, recording her experiences with the hospital unit, is held by the Women's Library, London.

On her return to England Elsie Bowerman joined Emmeline and Christabel Pankhurst's campaign for industrial peace, holding meetings at pitheads and factory gates in Sheffield, Manchester, and south Wales. At the general election of 1918 she was Christabel Pankhurst's agent in Smethwick and, after that defeat, was one of the founders, and took a leading part in the campaigns, of the Women's Guild of Empire (WGE), which denounced trade unions and family allowances and called for an alliance of capital and labour. Elsie Bowerman was honorary secretary of the WGE from 1920 to 1929, and edited the guild's *Bulletin*. She joined the Middle Temple in 1921, read for the bar, and was called—one of the first women barristers—in 1924. She practised on the south-eastern circuit from 1928 until 1946, was involved with the Sussex sessions from 1928 until 1934, and wrote *The Law of Child Protection* (1933). In 1938, with Lady Reading, she founded the Women's Voluntary Service, and from 1938 to 1940 edited its *Monthly Bulletin*. During the Second World War she worked for the Ministry of Information (1940–41) and was liaison officer with the North American Service of the BBC (1941–5). After the war she spent a year in charge of the status-of-women section of the United Nations in New York. She was a governor of Wycombe Abbey School and wrote *Stands there a School* (1965), a history of the school and its founder, Frances Dove.

After a long and active life Elsie Bowerman suffered a stroke, and was declared dead on arrival at the Princess Alice Hospital, Eastbourne, on 18 October 1973. She never married, and left the residue of her estate to the Dove-Bowerman Trust, a fund that she had established to help educationally disadvantaged young people.

ELIZABETH CRAWFORD

Sources Women's Library, London, Elsie Bowerman papers · W. Lord, *A night to remember* (1956) · b. cert. · d. cert. · *CGPLA Eng. & Wales* (1974)

Archives Women's Library, London, papers

Wealth at death £143,007: probate, 29 Jan 1974, *CGPLA Eng. & Wales*

Bowers, George Hull (1794–1872), dean of Manchester, born in Staffordshire, was the son of Francis Bowers. He was sent to the Pembroke grammar school, and from there proceeded to Clare College, Cambridge, in 1819 as a 'ten year man', graduating BD in 1829 and DD in 1849. Ordained in 1819 he was appointed perpetual curate of Elstow, Bedfordshire, and was a tutor in the family of the duke of Bedford, who appointed him to the rectory of St

Paul's, Covent Garden, in 1832. He was select preacher of his university in 1830 and was elected FSA in 1836. He was twice married; his elder son, Francis, was born in 1829.

Bowers was one of the collaborators with the Revd Charles Eaton Plater (1798–1854) in the establishment of a public boarding-school, with modest fees, chiefly for sons of clergymen. He published a scheme for such an institution in 1842; Marlborough College, Wiltshire, opened in the following year. He resigned as honorary secretary of the school in 1844 following evangelical criticisms of its Tractarian tendency. He then became involved with Rossall School, founded at Fleetwood, Lancashire, in 1844 by the Revd St Vincent Beechey (1806–1899) as a safer protestant alternative for clergy sons. Among the early pupils was Bowers's younger son, George Henry Bowers, who entered the church. He also assisted in the foundation of Haileybury College (1862).

In June 1847, following the death of Dean Herbert, Bowers was nominated by Lord John Russell to the deanery of Manchester, an office which he held until 26 September 1871. He was not a frequent preacher in Manchester, but his pulpit discourses were at once simple and scholarly, and his delivery effective. He was a warm advocate of the 'free and open church movement', attacking pew rents in addresses and sermons. He was for this reason instrumental in the erection of St Alban's, Cheetwood, and various addresses which he delivered there were printed. On his resignation of the office of dean of Manchester he retired to Leamington, where he died on 27 December 1872. He bequeathed £300 for the support of the special Sunday evening services at Manchester Cathedral, where a window and a brass were placed by his widow to his memory. One of his daughters, Georgiana Bowers (*b*. 1836), was a noted illustrator of scenes of hunting and country life in *Punch*.

W. E. A. AXON, *rev.* M. C. CURTHOYS

Sources *Manchester Guardian* (30 Dec 1872) • R. Parkinson, *The old church clock*, ed. J. Evans, 5th edn (1880) • Venn, *Alum. Cant.* • Boase, *Mod. Eng. biog.* • A. Boutflower, *Personal reminiscences of Manchester Cathedral, 1854–1912* (1913) • A. G. Bradley and others, *A history of Marlborough College*, 2nd edn (1923) • *CGPLA Eng. & Wales* (1873)
Archives CUL, corresp. and papers
Likenesses C. Mercier, portrait, Rossall School, Fleetwood • photograph, repro. in Boutflower, *Personal reminiscences*, facing p. 49
Wealth at death under £7000: probate, 4 March 1873, *CGPLA Eng. & Wales*

Bowers, Henry Robertson [Birdie] (1883–1912), polar explorer, was born at Greenock on 29 July 1883, the youngest of the three children of Alexander Bowers, a naval captain and independent merchantman, and his wife, Emily, *née* Webb. His father died on the Mergui archipelago, Burma, in 1887, and Bowers and his two sisters were brought up in Sidcup, Kent, by their mother, to whom he always remained devoted. He was educated at Streatham High School for Boys and joined HMS *Worcester* as a cadet on 16 September 1897. He served his indentures in the four-masted iron barque *Loch Torridon*, and on his third voyage around Cape Horn wrote in his diary on 5 December 1902: 'We are in the vicinity of ice ... This nearness to the Antarctic Circle always gives me a longing' (Seaver, 38). His immediate future, though, lay in tropical waters: he was appointed a midshipman in the Royal Naval Reserve in September 1904 and gazetted a sub-lieutenant in the Royal Indian Marine service on 28 February 1905.

Before leaving for India in October, Bowers was introduced by his old commandant at HMS *Worcester*, Captain David Wilson Barker, to Sir Clements Markham, president of the Royal Geographical Society. Talk turned to the recent expedition to the Antarctic of the *Discovery*, under Captain Robert Falcon Scott, which Markham had instigated, and Bowers's enthusiasm for the subject impressed his listeners. It was remembered by them when Scott was recruiting for the *Terra Nova* Antarctic expedition in 1909. In Bombay Bowers joined the Royal Indian Marine service ship *Dufferin* and later the *Sladen* for patrol work on the Irrawaddy, where his father had sailed before him. He took great pride in the service and, as an 'out-and-out Imperialist', viewed with horror 'the effete and jaded existence' of many Anglo-Indians (Seaver, 73). Showing considerable promise, he was given temporary command of the Royal Indian Marine service ship *Bhamo* from June 1907 to February 1908. His future in India seemed assured when, in March 1910, he received a telegraph from Captain Scott inviting him to join the *Terra Nova* as junior officer in charge of stores. He had been specially recommended by Sir Clements Markham and Captain Wilson Barker and was taken on without even an interview. He at once prepared to leave 'the hottest quarter of the globe for the coldest' (ibid., 143).

Bowers, who was unmarried, was 5 feet 4 inches tall with red hair and a beaklike nose, which gave him his expedition name Birdie. Stocky and strong, he had a prodigious appetite for work and a selfless disposition. During the voyage south he showed impressive organizational efficiency, and Scott told him that he was to be included in the shore party: Bowers later wrote that he felt like 'turning a somersault in the cabin' (Seaver, 163). The *Terra Nova* disembarked at Cape Evans in January 1911 and Bowers participated in the depot-laying expedition at the end of the month in preparation for the polar journey. At its conclusion he was charged, with Apsley Cherry-Garrard and Petty Officer Tom Crean, with transporting supplies across the sea ice around Cape Armitage. When the ice began to break up beneath them, on 1 March, Bowers led the others in running the sledges and ponies over the gaps between the floes and towards safety, while killer whales swam in the leads all around. All the sledges, but only one of the ponies, were eventually saved: a severe enough blow to Scott's plans, but nothing like the disaster that initially threatened and which Bowers did much to avert.

A straightforward and at the same time a deeply spiritual character, Bowers was a popular member of the tightly packed expedition hut at Cape Evans. He discovered a special affinity with Edward Wilson, whose strong Christian faith he shared. When Wilson went to collect eggs for his research from the emperor penguin rookery at Cape Crozier, he took Bowers and Cherry-

Garrard with him. The three men left on 27 June and for five weeks pulled their heavy loads in near total darkness and temperatures that fell below −70 °F. They arrived back at Cape Evans on 1 August almost encased in ice and with three eggs (which proved of little scientific value). With this journey Bowers had proved his resilience beyond any doubt, and he was an indispensable element in the polar party that began the march south on 1 November 1911.

Before departure from Cape Evans, Bowers wrote to his mother: 'May God give us what we are striving for, we will do all that man can do, but one realizes more than ever down here how very much man is limited' (Seaver, 227). A man of intense loyalty, he considered 'no sacrifice too great for the main object … I am Captain Scott's man and shall stick by him right through' (ibid.). When on 31 December his team—which included Lieutenant Edward Evans, Tom Crean, and Chief Stoker William Lashly—was ordered to deposit its skis at 87° south, it was assumed that it would be the last returning party. But on 3 January 1912 Scott announced that he was including Bowers in his team of Edward Wilson, Captain Lawrence Oates, and Petty Officer Edgar Evans: it would be five, not four, for the pole. This was an astonishing decision, since all the planning had assumed four-man teams, and Bowers would now be forced to walk while his companions skied. But even with this disability he remained a formidable sledge-hauler. He was also an expert navigator, capable of taking accurate readings in the extreme cold, and it was in this capacity that Scott now most needed him. It was Bowers who spotted, on 16 January, the tell-tale black marker flag left by Amundsen's party weeks earlier. Next day he wrote: 'It is sad that we have been forestalled by the Norwegians, but I am glad that we have done it by good British man-haulage. That is the traditional British sledging method' (Huntford, 513).

The south pole was reached on 18 January 1912, and the return journey became a desperate race to reach each depot before their rations gave out. If Scott's decision to take five to the pole was flawed, it had an unforeseen benefit: when Evans and then Oates succumbed and died, Bowers, the late addition, was there to take the strain. He and Wilson remained strong almost to the last, and their unfailing optimism helped maintain Scott's battered morale. On 18 March they experienced temperatures of −40 °F, and on 20 March a blizzard pinned them in their tent. About 22 March, with Scott incapacitated by frostbite, Bowers and Wilson planned a 22 mile round-trip to 'one-ton depot' for fuel and food. The reason why they did not leave has been the subject of much speculation. Modern research suggests that the blizzard was extremely unlikely to have lasted until 29 March, as Scott's diary states. But even a much shorter blizzard could have detained them beyond the point where they had much strength to move: on Monday 19 March they had only two days' worth of food and barely a day's fuel left. If they were not prevented from moving by the weather or by fatigue, it is possible that they were simply unwilling to abandon Scott, who could not go on, and 'their deaths may have been a matter of choice rather than chance' (Solomon, 327). Bowers and his companions probably died on or about 29 March 1912, the date given by Scott for his last journal entry. On 12 November 1912 the tent was found at 79°50′ south by the relief expedition led by Dr Edward Atkinson. A cairn commemorating also Evans and Oates was built over the bodies.

Bowers made an immense contribution to the *Terra Nova* expedition and especially to its scientific work. At Cape Evans he was assiduous in taking meteorological readings and on the journey south, at considerable cost to himself, he kept a detailed meteorological log. But in spite of his zeal for scientific enquiry he fitted into the mould of the romantic explorer. Before leaving New Zealand in November 1910 he wrote to his mother about his reasons for undertaking the dangerous adventure ahead:

> The chief thing that impels is the indefinable call, that is as unexplainable as it is insistent. Your son is one of the few in this prosaic age who can have the privilege of realizing what must have been a commoner thing when the world was younger. (Seaver, 228)

The Bowers Mountains (71°10′ S, 163°15′ E) and Bowers Piedmont Glacier (77°43′ S, 164°18′ E) in Antarctica are named after him. MARK POTTLE

Sources G. Seaver, *'Birdie' Bowers of the Antarctic* (1938) • R. F. Scott, *The diaries of Captain Robert Scott: a record of the second Antarctic expedition, 1910–1912*, 6 vols. (1968), vol. 2 • R. F. Scott, *Scott's last expedition: the journals* (1951–64) • H. G. R. King, ed., *Edward Wilson: diary of the 'Terra Nova' expedition to the Antarctic, 1910–1912* (1972) • A. Cherry-Garrard, *The worst journey in the world: Antarctic, 1910–1913* (1951) • A. R. Ellis, ed., *Under Scott's command: Lashly's Antarctic diaries* (1969) • T. Gran, *The Norwegian with Scott: Tryggve Gran's Antarctic diary, 1910–1913*, ed. G. Hattersley-Smith (1984) • E. R. G. R. Evans, *South with Scott* (1921); repr. (1962) • H. G. Ponting, *The great white south* (1921) • S. Solomon, *The coldest March: Scott's fatal Antarctic expedition* (2001) • S. Wheeler, *Cherry: a life of Apsley Cherry-Garrard* (2001) • E. Huxley, *Scott of the Antarctic* (1977) • R. Huntford, *Scott and Amundsen* (1993) • G. C. Gregor, *Swansea's Antarctic explorer: Edgar Evans, 1876–1912* (1995) • A. Savours, ed., *Scott's last voyage: through the Antarctic camera of Herbert Ponting* (1974) • *CGPLA Eng. & Wales* (1913)
Archives Scott Polar RI, corresp. and papers, incl. journals
Likenesses photograph, 1911, repro. in Savours, ed., *Scott's last voyage* • photograph, repro. in Seaver, *'Birdie' Bowers*, facing p. 260
Wealth at death £219: probate, 7 July 1913, *CGPLA Eng. & Wales*

Bowery, Leigh (1961–1994), designer and performance artist, was born in Sunshine, a suburb of Melbourne, Australia, on 26 March 1961, the son of Tom Bowery, accountant, and his wife, Evelyn (*d.* 1994). Born into a middle-class family, he was an intelligent and confident boy who excelled at school and achieved grade 8 at piano. Highly creative, he learned to knit and crochet at a young age and went on to study fashion at the Royal Melbourne Institute of Technology. However, he soon tired of the commercialism of his course and the parochialism of his environment and resolved to travel to London, an ambition that he achieved in October 1980. On arriving he focused his energies on joining the capital's alternative nightclub set, who were then wearing the 'new romantic' look, incorporating frills and makeup for women and men. Soon he was designing and selling clothes in Kensington market. In 1984 he moved to what became his main home—a council flat in

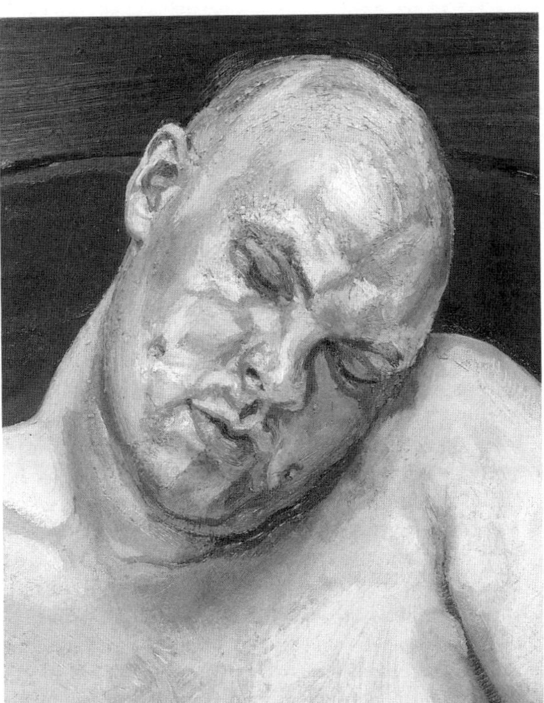

Leigh Bowery (1961–1994), by Lucian Freud, 1991

Farrell House, Ronald Street, in the East End of London. This was initially shared with his close friend Trojan (born Gary Barnes), an artist who collaborated in its bright and elaborate decoration.

Bowery was one of the first fashion designers to promote the 1970s revival, and incorporated into his designs glam-rock elements such as platform shoes, bright colours, fine fabrics, and glitter, which allowed feminine and androgynous looks for men. His costumes were always beautifully made, employing his many crafts and involving long hours of close work. In one of his earliest and best documented designs (which he called 'Pakis from outer space') he began to experiment with full-face makeup in red, green, or blue, which was decorated with jewels and a chain from nose to ear, evocative of Hindu images. The effort that went into both creating and wearing his 'looks' was such that they were not viable commercially, and Bowery was in any case ambivalent towards spreading them widely. His initial model was Trojan, but seeing the attention that his designs created Bowery began to wear them himself. He was a large man, and his clothes achieved additional shock value on his tall, 16 stone frame.

Bowery had by now emerged as a well-known character in London's nightclubs, and in 1985 he consolidated his influence by becoming a partner in a new nightclub, Taboo. He was its public face and centre of attention. Each week he focused on preparing a new outfit for his next appearance. Many were exquisitely tailored, and while emphasizing his bulk they also incorporated traditionally feminine elements. Examples included large polka dots that extended across his yellow-painted face, bustle skirts worn with a First World War German tin helmet, and Lycra costumes with exposed buttocks, worn with high-heeled shoes. All incorporated heavy makeup, generally exaggerating the eyes and lips, and in one memorable look extending over Bowery's entire shaved head, on which coloured paint was dripped from the crown, akin to a broken fluorescent egg. But at Taboo, Bowery was more than just an exhibit; he was also its social centre. His wide networks, wit, charm, and easy sociability attracted a core clientele of designers, artists, and performers, as well as others drawn by the spectacle or who simply wanted to dress up. The club's culture was one of sexual permissiveness, and (like Bowery's looks) of transgressing accepted boundaries of gender and sexuality. As he remarked, 'the name Taboo is a joke really, because there's nothing you can't do there' (Tilley, 61). The culture of permissiveness also extended to drugs, which claimed the lives of Trojan and the club's flamboyant doorman Mark Vautier, both aged twenty, in 1986.

Bowery himself was tremendously strong both physically and mentally—something that he demonstrated by dancing all night in his increasingly constricting outfits, often hoisting others off the floor. After Taboo's closure, in 1986, his looks developed to concentrate increasingly on physical distortion—using corsets and gaffer tape to compress and move his flesh, and sculpted foam to extend it. This was achieved only at the cost of huge physical discomfort. He continued to explore issues of gender and sexuality but his designs became more threatening and disturbing, often incorporating masks or other headwear. Through this work he explored his favourite emotion—embarrassment—and overcame his earlier feelings of physical inadequacy. 'The idea of transforming oneself', he commented, 'gives courage and vigour … Things that used to embarrass me like nudity and gender confusion don't any more' (Tilley, 112).

Bowery had long been an exhibitionist, but in 1988 he was accepted into the art world as a formal exhibit. At the Anthony d'Offay gallery in London he appeared daily, for a week, in a different outfit behind a one-way mirror. Later he began a collaboration with the artist Lucian Freud, for whom he modelled regularly from 1990 until his death. The relationship started in confusion, as Freud assumed that Bowery would pose dressed, and Bowery that Freud wanted him nude. As Bowery stripped fast at his first appointment it was his expectation that prevailed. He found this showing of his private self profoundly liberating, but Freud's paintings depicted a man whom most people who met Bowery would not recognize. Another artistic collaboration, with the photographer Fergus Greer, showed the more familiar Bowery, while cataloguing a large number of his looks and demonstrating their variety, complexity, and artistry.

Bowery's anonymous daytime appearance (generally including a short wig to cover his baldness) enabled him to carry on a sexual life that since his schooldays had centred on casual encounters with men in public toilets and parks. Although entirely open about his sexuality, he found this an efficient way of feeding his considerable sexual appetite, and he entertained friends with many tales of his conquests (although he was also known for his lies and exaggeration). Once diagnosed as HIV-positive, in 1988, he may have been truthful in citing 'unsafe sex with over 1,000 men' as his greatest regret. He had few, if any, conventional relationships, although he married his assistant Nicola Joy Ann Bateman on 13 May 1994. His friend and biographer Sue Tilley later suggested that Trojan was 'the true love of Leigh's life' (Tilley, 77).

Bowery once remarked that 'every time I go out it turns into a performance' (Tilley, 195). Alongside modelling, in his later years he concentrated on formalizing this activity. His first stage appearances were with the dancer and choreographer Michael Clark, for whom he had been designing costumes since 1983. Although large and clumsy, Bowery began dancing with Clark's group in 1987, and sometimes played piano. His independent performances began as repeats of his nightclub appearances but were increasingly designed to shock. He enjoyed incorporating bodily functions, and on one occasion a water enema, which he had administered to himself, went spectacularly wrong on stage. In another celebrated show he 'gave birth' to a naked Nicola Bateman, covered in slime, who had been strapped under his dress throughout a vigorous hour-long performance. Bowery also sang—in his groups the Quality Street Wrappers, Raw Sewage, and Minty—and aspired to release a record of his song 'Useless Man'.

Leigh Bowery's last performance was on 24 November 1994. The authorities shut the show down, somewhat to his relief, as he had been feeling unwell. Four days later he was hospitalized with meningitis—a product of his HIV-positive status, which he had divulged only to Sue Tilley. Still remarkably strong, he fought his illness, but died at the Middlesex Hospital, Westminster, on 31 December 1994. His body was flown to Australia to be buried at Macedon, Victoria, next to that of his mother. As if in final proof of his nonconformism his coffin proved too large for the hole that initially had been dug for it. Certainly not to everybody's taste, Bowery's contribution to design, performance, and art, as well as to the culture of gender and sexuality, was remarkable for his thirty-three years, and after his death has reached a wider audience through a series of exhibitions, publications, and documentaries.

MEG RUSSELL

Sources S. Tilley, *Leigh Bowery: the life and times of an icon* (1997) · H. Als, introduction, *Leigh Bowery*, ed. R. Violette (1998) · F. Greer, *Leigh Bowery looks* (2001) · *Daily Telegraph* (4 Jan 1995) · *The Guardian* (5 Jan 1995) · 'King Dandy', *The Guardian* (1 Aug 1998) · d. cert.

Archives FILM BFI NFTVA, 'The legend of Leigh Bowery' | SOUND BL NSA, performance footage, V2931/01

Likenesses L. Freud, oils, 1990 (*Leigh Bowery (seated)*), priv. coll. · L. Freud, oils, 1991, Tate collection [*see illus.*] · L. Freud, oils, 1992 (*Nude with leg up*), Smithsonian Institution, Washington, DC, Hirshorn Museum and Sculpture Collection · L. Freud, oils, 1993 (*Large head*), priv. coll. · L. Freud, oils, 1995 (*Last portrait of Leigh*), priv. coll. · L. Freud, oils (*And the bridegroom*), Lewis Collection · F. Greer, photographs, repro. in F. Greer, *Leigh Bowery looks*

Bowes [*née* Aske], **Elizabeth** (*bap.* **1505**, *d.* in or before **1572**), protestant exile, was baptized in August 1505 at Aske in Richmondshire, North Riding of Yorkshire, the daughter of Roger Aske (*d.* before 1510), son of William and Felicia Aske, and Margery Wycliffe (*d.* before 1510). By 23 July 1521 she had married Richard Bowes (*c.*1497–1558), youngest son of Sir Ralph Bowes of Streatlam, and had been granted the lands of her grandfather, father, and mother, and of a certain William Curtes, which she inherited with her sister Anne, wife of Ralph Bulmer. Elizabeth and Richard Bowes had five sons and ten daughters; their sons included the soldier Sir George *Bowes (1527–1580) and the ambassador Robert *Bowes (*d.* 1597).

By 1546 Richard Bowes was commander of Norham Castle near Berwick on the Scottish border. Three years later John *Knox, the Scottish reformer, assumed responsibilities at the parish church of Berwick, where Elizabeth Bowes made his acquaintance. Their friendship is documented in twenty-nine letters from Knox to Bowes preserved in a manuscript transcription of 1603 along with the dedicatory letter to Bowes that prefaces Knox's *Commentary on the Sixth Psalm* (U. Edinburgh L., MS La. III. 345; published in *Works of John Knox*, 3.111–56; 3.337–402; 4.217–18). Although Bowes's letters to Knox are not extant, their substance can be reconstructed from his replies. Throughout 1552–3, when the majority were written, Bowes was troubled by doubts regarding her salvation. Her letters contained pointed questions on difficult passages in the Bible, confession of specific temptations and sins, and expressions of anxiety over her status as one of the elect. In response, Knox provided biblical expositions, urged her to regard struggles with sin as a mark of salvation, not damnation, and assured her of the indelible tokens of election. Although Knox assumed the role of mentor, he acknowledged the mutual spiritual benefits of their relationship, noting that Bowes was 'a verie mirrour and glass whairin I beheld my self' (*Works of John Knox*, 3.338). Furthermore, her questions forced him to clarify his own understanding of various doctrines.

By 1553 Knox had contracted to marry Elizabeth Bowes's fifth daughter, Marjorie (*b.* *c.*1534), but the accession of Mary Tudor altered his status from respected court preacher to renegade reformer. As a result Richard Bowes and his brother, Sir Robert Bowes, withdrew their permission for the marriage. Despite opposition from their family, Elizabeth Bowes and her daughter left England for Scotland in 1555; Marjorie and Knox were probably married near the end of that year. In July 1556, however, all three left for the continent, and on 13 September arrived in Geneva, where they remained until the accession of Elizabeth. The rift between Richard and Elizabeth apparently went unhealed: he died in 1558, but neither his wife nor Marjorie is mentioned in his will, and his remaining daughters are strictly forbidden to marry against their brothers' wishes upon pain of forfeiting their inheritance. In 1559 Elizabeth returned to England, while Marjorie joined her husband in Scotland, where they resided until her death in 1560. In 1562 Elizabeth Bowes received permission to travel to Scotland to care for her two grandsons and her son-in-law. When Knox married Margery Stewart in 1564 she returned to England.

The intensity and duration of Bowes's friendship with Knox provoked rumours of an illicit relationship, which Knox refuted in a letter appended to his last work, *An Answer to a Letter of a Jesuit Named Tyrie* (1572). There he notes that their 'great familiaritie and long acquentance … was [based upon] nether fleshe nor bloode, but a troubled conscience' (*Works of John Knox*, 6.513). His further comment that despite the comfort of her friendship 'it was not without some croce: for … my mynde was seldome quyet, for doing somewhat for the comfort of her troubled conscience' (ibid., 6.514), has led some to dismiss Bowes as a spiritual hypochondriac, obsessively attached to her own sins. But her religious anxieties can better be understood within the context of the religious upheavals of the time, and the opposition of her family and community to her fervent protestantism. The assertion by Robert Surtees that Elizabeth Bowes died in Edinburgh in 1568 has been found incapable of substantiation; she certainly died some time before Knox's death in 1572.

SUSAN M. FELCH

Sources *The works of John Knox*, ed. D. Laing, 6 vols., Wodrow Society, 12 (1846–64) • C. M. Newman, 'The Reformation and Elizabeth Bowes: a study of a sixteenth-century northern gentlewoman', *Women in the church on the eve of the dissolution*, ed. W. J. Sheils and D. Wood, SCH, 27 (1990), 325–33 • *LP Henry VIII*, vols. 2/2, 3/2, 21/1 • J. Ridley, *John Knox* (1968) • A. D. Frankforter, 'The chronology of the Knox–Bowes letters', *Manuscripta*, 31 (1987), 28–41 • J. Raine, ed., *Wills and inventories from the registry of the archdeaconry of Richmond*, SurtS, 26 (1853) • J. S. Burn, *Livre des Anglois, à Genève* (1831) • T. McCrie, *The life of John Knox*, 2nd edn, 2 vols. (1813) • W. Hutchinson, *The history and antiquities of the county palatine of Durham*, 3 (1794) • P. Forbes, ed., *A full view of the public transactions in the reign of Queen Elizabeth*, 1 (1740) • C. Sharp, ed., *Memorials of the rebellion of 1569* (1840) • A. D. Frankforter, 'Elizabeth Bowes and John Knox: a woman and Reformation theology', *Church History*, 56 (1987), 333–47 • P. Collinson, '"Not sexual in the ordinary sense": women, men and religious transactions', *Elizabethan essays* (1994), 119–50 • *DNB* • R. Surtees, *The history and antiquities of the county palatine of Durham*, 4 (1840), 118

Archives U. Edin. L., letters from John Knox, MS La. III. 345 • U. Glas. L., letters from John Knox, MS Gen 1219 (Wodrow Folio VII)

Bowes, Sir George (1517–1545), soldier and rebel, was a posthumous son of the landowner Sir Ralph Bowes (*c*.1455–1516) and Elizabeth, daughter of Henry Clifford, Lord Clifford. His wardship was sold to William Eure, Lord Eure, whose daughter Muriel he married. The couple had three daughters: Elizabeth, Anne, and Dorothy. He also had one illegitimate son, Robert. The family owned property in co. Durham and the North Riding, and Bowes was serving in the garrison of Barnard Castle when it was surrendered to the host of the Pilgrimage of Grace in 1536. Like many members of the northern gentry, Bowes himself joined the rebel army. Following the collapse of the rebellion he benefited from the patronage of his influential uncle Sir Robert *Bowes, and was presented to Thomas Cromwell as a young man anxious to devote his youth to the king's service.

Bowes's opportunity came with the war against Scotland in 1542. Surviving the defeat at Haddon Rigg on 24 August 1542, he soon established his reputation as a capable soldier and was entrusted with negotiating with Archibald Douglas, earl of Angus. He also took part in the 1544 expedition to Lothian and was knighted at Leith on 11 May by Edward Seymour, earl of Hertford. Later that year he led a series of brutal forays into Scotland. Jedburgh was sacked, Broom Tower stormed and its occupants massacred, and Dryburgh was burnt to the ground. In November 1544 Bowes seized Coldingham Priory. This was the zenith of his military career and the king agreed to grant him the barony of Coldingham. His ambitions were thwarted, however, when he was taken prisoner outside Dunbar in January 1545. Although he was appointed captain of Norham Castle on his release in March, the barony was withheld, and he does not appear to have played any further prominent role in the war. He died on 26 December 1545 and was buried at Alnwick.

GERVASE PHILLIPS

Sources *LP Henry VIII*, vols. 13, 17–21 • [F. W. Dendy], ed., *Visitations of the north*, 1, SurtS, 122 (1912) • C. Sharp, ed., *Memorials of the rebellion of 1569* (1840); repr. with foreword by R. Wood as *The rising in the north: the 1569 rebellion* (1975) • J. Raine, ed., *Wills and inventories from the registry of the archdeaconry of Richmond*, SurtS, 26 (1853) • 'The late expedition in Scotland, 1544', *Tudor tracts, 1532–1588*, ed. A. F. Pollard (1903), 39–51 • A. G. Dickens, ed., *Clifford letters of the sixteenth century*, SurtS, 172 (1962) • M. Bush, *The Pilgrimage of Grace: a study of the rebel armies of October 1536* (1996) • PRO, C142/75/24

Archives BL, MSS 407, 446–448 • Durham RO, papers relating to the northern uprising • NRA, priv. coll., corresp. • U. Durham L., papers, incl. family papers

Bowes, Sir George (1527–1580), soldier and administrator, was the eldest surviving son of Richard Bowes, esquire (*c*.1497–1558), soldier, and his wife [*see* Bowes, Elizabeth (*bap*. 1505, *d*. in or before 1572)], the coheir of William Aske of Aske in the North Riding of Yorkshire. In 1534 he was contracted to Dorothy (*d*. before 1558), the daughter of Sir William Mallory of Studley, near Ripon in Yorkshire. They had married by 1541 and had seven children, including Sir William Bowes, the heir. George Bowes became head of the Streatlam lordship in co. Durham upon the death of his father in October 1558. He was to prove himself a loyal servant of the crown throughout his career, the high point of which was, undoubtedly, his staunch defence of Barnard Castle, co. Durham, during the northern rising of 1569.

The Bowes family of Streatlam had long participated in the military defence and administration of the Anglo-Scottish border regions and George Bowes was to follow in this tradition. He first gained experience of border conflict during the Scottish wars of the 1540s, with his participation being noted in a raid upon Teviotdale in 1546. Like others of his family he showed particular aptitude in this sphere and he commanded 100 cavalry garrisoned at Douglass in Lothian in 1549. His military capabilities were commended in a dispatch to the privy council that year. During the years of truce, in the early 1550s, Bowes retained his connection with the borders and was named on the commission appointed to oversee the refurbishment of the border fortresses in 1555. Upon the outbreak of war with France in 1557, the government of Mary I took his experience and loyalty into account when considering the state of the once-more vulnerable frontier regions and in January 1558, Bowes was appointed marshal of Berwick. He was knighted there in April 1560.

Border service apart, Bowes's political career remained relatively quiet during the years of the Marian regime. In the summer of 1558 he, now a widower, did seek to advance his prospects through an advantageous marriage on 1 July with Jane Talbot, daughter of Sir John Talbot of Albrighton and Grafton, Worcestershire; they had eight children. She was a kinswoman of the earl of Shrewsbury, lord president of the council of the north. Despite this marriage, his family's close association with protestantism probably inhibited Bowes's political prospects at this time. His uncle, Sir Robert *Bowes (1493?–1555), had been a member of the extreme reformist administration led by John Dudley, duke of Northumberland, during the reign of Edward VI. Moreover, the Streatlam family's close relationship with the charismatic Scottish reformer John Knox (who had married Bowes's sister, Marjorie, probably in 1555), undoubtedly heightened, further, its identification with overt protestantism.

The accession of Elizabeth I, however, brought about an upturn in George Bowes's political fortunes. Indeed, the decision of the new regime to enforce a protestant settlement of religion, as enshrined in the statutes passed in 1559, provided the staunchly protestant Bowes with the opportunity to prove his indispensability in the administration of the north—a region noted for its strong attachment to the 'old religion'. From the early 1560s, his rise to the upper echelons of northern politics was remarkable. In 1561 he was appointed to the council of the north and the ecclesiastical high commission for the province of York. In the following year he was named JP and of the quorum for the bishopric of Durham and the North Riding of Yorkshire and was also appointed sheriff of Yorkshire (1562–3). When, in 1568, Bowes was detailed to attend the 'conduction' of Mary, queen of Scots, from Carlisle to Bolton Castle in the North Riding of Yorkshire, Sir Francis Knollys noted, in a letter to Sir William Cecil, the principal secretary, how Bowes, 'is also a good Protestant, and his brother [Robert] lykewyse, which is a rare matter in this country' (Sharp, 379).

The government's faith in Bowes was well placed, as his loyalty during the rising of the northern earls, which erupted in November 1569, was to demonstrate. Indeed, Bowes's heroic defence of Barnard Castle, of which he held the stewardship, did much to provide a focus for loyal northern sentiment in a region that was out of control for several weeks. Moreover, although he was forced to surrender the castle to the rebels after a siege lasting almost two weeks, Bowes's steadfast loyalty was in contrast to that of some of the other leading members of the Durham political élite who fled the bishopric. At the outset of and during the rising Bowes was subjected to threats regarding his safety and it is clear that the rebels regarded him with great animosity. As a result they laid waste to several of his properties, including Streatlam Castle. The destruction was considerable and Bowes later complained that, in terms of goods, corn, and cattle, he had lost more than £4000. In the wake of the rising he was appointed by Thomas Radcliffe, third earl of Sussex, as his deputy in co. Durham and Richmondshire and provost marshal. As provost marshal Bowes was responsible for the execution of those rebels condemned to die within the localities. The reputation for cruelty he acquired as a result of this was, largely, undeserved; he may in fact have mitigated the severity of the privy council's original orders. Nevertheless, there is little doubt that he carried out his duties with the diligence of a loyal servant of the crown.

Despite his loyalty, Bowes gained scant reward from the crown for his services. Moreover, the losses he incurred during the rising served only to exacerbate the increasing financial difficulties of his later years. Nevertheless, he continued his career in public life up until his death in 1580, retaining his membership of the council of the north and the northern high commission. He was elected to the parliaments of 1571 and 1572, sitting for the boroughs of Knaresborough, in the West Riding of Yorkshire, and Morpeth, Northumberland, respectively, and in 1576 was appointed sheriff of co. Durham. He was added to the commissions of the peace of the East and West Riding of Yorkshire, Cumberland, Northumberland, and Westmorland in 1573. In 1579 he assumed temporary control of Berwick, thereby relieving his brother Robert *Bowes (*d.* 1597), who, as treasurer of the town, undertook day-to-day management of the garrison. However, once more George Bowes's dedication to duty was to cost him dearly, not only in terms of his financial interests but also in terms of his health for he seems to have been dogged by illness for much of his stay in Berwick. Bowes died at Streatlam on 20 August 1580, remaining to the last 'the surest pyllore the Quens Majestie had in these partes' (*CSP dom., addenda, 1580–1625*, 17). He was buried in the family vault of Barnard Castle church.

CHRISTINE M. NEWMAN

Sources C. Sharp, ed., *Memorials of the rebellion of 1569* (1840); repr. with foreword by R. Wood as *The rising in the north: the 1569 rebellion* (1975) · C. M. Newman, 'The Bowes of Streatlam, county Durham: a study of the politics and religion of a sixteenth century northern gentry family', DPhil diss., University of York, 1991 · Bowes letter-books, NRA Scotland [surveyed in National Register of Archives for Scotland, survey 885, and detailed in B. L. H. Horn and F. J. Shaw, 'Bowes bound correspondence and papers', *Archives*, 14, no. 63 (1979), 134–40] · Bowes letter-book, vol. 2, Bowes Museum, Barnard Castle, co. Durham, Bowes MSS · D. Marcombe, 'A rude and heady people: the local community and the rebellion of the northern earls', *The last principality: politics, religion and society in the bishopric of Durham, 1494–1660*, ed. D. Marcombe (1987) · R. Surtees, *The history and antiquities of the county palatine of Durham*, 4 vols. (1816–40), vol. 4 · [F. W. Dendy], ed., *Visitations of the north*, 1, SurtS, 122 (1912) · HoP, *Commons, 1558–1603* · M. E. James, *Family lineage and civil society: a study of society and mentality in the Durham region, 1500–1640* (1974) · *CSP dom., addenda, 1566–79* · A. Fletcher, *Tudor rebellions*, 3rd edn (1983)

Archives BL, family deeds and charters, Add. MSS 66317–66488 · BL, MSS relating to northern rebellion and corresp., Add. MSS 40746–40748 · Bowes Museum, Barnard Castle, corresp. and MSS mainly relating to northern rebellion, Bowes letter-book, vol. 2 · Durham RO, estate and legal family MSS, Strathmore estates S/St/C1; D/St/D03; Hanby Holmes D/HH 5 · Durham RO, papers relating to the northern rebellion · NRA Scotland, priv. coll., corresp. · NRA Scotland, priv. coll., letters, personal and business MSS, MSS relating to the northern rebellion and Scottish affairs, and family MSS · U. Durham L., family and other MSS | N. Yorks. CRO, Clifton Castle archive, Streatlam and Stainton deeds, ZAW/1 (MIC 1764)

Likenesses portrait, 1572, Glamis Castle; repro. in Sharp, ed., *Memorials* [repr. as *The rising in the north* (1975)] · R. Easton, mezzotint, NPG

Wealth at death in 1560 was said to have lands 'better than 600 marks a year'; est. £600 p.a. family patrimony (1569): J. Bain, ed., *Calendar of Scottish papers, 1547–1563* (1899), 375; James, *Family lineage and civil society*, 30

Bowes, George (1701–1760), coal owner and landscape builder, was born on 21 August 1701 at Streatlam Castle, near Barnard Castle, co. Durham, the third son of Sir William Bowes (*bap.* 1657, *d.* 1707), landowner, of Streatlam, and his wife, Elizabeth Blakiston (*d.* 1736), heir of Sir Francis Blakiston of Gibside House, near Rowlands Gill, 3 miles south-west of Newcastle. After the death of Sir Francis Blakiston in 1713, the mineral-rich estate of Gibside became the possession of the Bowes family and thereby transformed its fortunes. William Blakiston Bowes, the first son, who came of age in 1717, was the first of the brothers to enjoy this inheritance. However, he died in 1721, and the second brother, Thomas, died the following year. In 1722, then, at the age of twenty-one, George found himself unexpectedly possessor of both estates. He had been educated first in Newcastle and then at Mr Hill's school in London. As a younger son of a gentry family in need of a profession, he had chosen the army and had become a captain in General Wade's regiment of horse. On inheriting the estates in 1722 he disposed of his commission, and the following year he made an abortive attempt to enter the House of Commons as member for Berwick upon Tweed.

The Streatlam estate was the ancient seat of the Bowes family: their ownership can be traced to the fourteenth century. It was, however, the acquisition of Gibside and its coal that made the family rich. George Bowes was determined to exploit the ownership of coal to its greatest possible extent: he succeeded in becoming member of parliament for co. Durham in 1727 (which he represented until 1760). Membership of the House of Commons brought prestige in the county, but above all it helped to protect the interests of the producers of coal in the north-east of England, in their main market, London. In 1726 he was one of the founder members of the 'Grand Allies'. This, the most important association of coal owners in the eighteenth century, was designed to regulate the production of coal in the north-east. In 1726 George Bowes joined forces with three other large colliery proprietors: the Hon. Sydney Wortley, of Wortley, Yorkshire, with Edward Wortley, his son and heir; Sir Henry Liddell bt, with George Liddell, his guardian, both of Ravensworth Castle; and William Cotesworth. They signed a 99-year agreement to drop suits against each other, to grant each other wayleaves over their land, to refrain from buying or leasing collieries without the consent of the others, and to work all collieries as a joint concern. One of the allies' early joint enterprises was the construction of the Causey Arch, the first railway bridge of a large single span in the world. This crossed the Beckley burn a few miles south-west of Gateshead and carried the wagonway leading the coals of the Grand Allies from Tanfield and Causey to the staithes on the Tyne.

Bowes was by 1731 a convinced advocate of the need for regulation: George Liddell noted in 1731, 'I am of Mr Bowes' opinion that nothing but a Regulation will heale the Coale Trade' (Hughes, 239). By 1739, it had succeeded so well that a pamphleteer, speaking on behalf of the consumers in London, accused the coal owners of 'locking up collieries' (ibid., 247).

All the surviving evidence suggests that Bowes was a dynamic and emphatic personality. The fortune he amassed was worth at least £600,000 at his death, and he used his wealth to transform the grounds at Gibside House. In 1729 extensive plantations began and picturesque buildings of various kinds were erected in the grounds, including in 1736 a bath house in classical style and in 1742 a gothic banqueting house designed by Daniel Garrett—one of the first in this style in the north of England. Among the more striking of the works was the column to British liberty (1750–57) and the mausoleum chapel designed by James Paine. This remained unfinished at Bowes's death and was completed in 1812 by his grandson, the tenth earl of Strathmore. Spencer Cowper, dean of Durham, summed up both the work at Gibside and Bowes's character in a letter in September 1753:

> Last week I was at Glory Bowes' at Gibside, to do it justice, I think it will be one of the finest places in the North when he has finish'd his design. The whole of his works takes in a range of seven miles; which if ever compleated will be worthy his Magnificence and Immensity. (*Letters*, 165)

Bowes was married twice: in October 1724 he married Eleanor Verney (1710–1724), daughter of the Hon. Thomas Verney and heir to George, Lord Willoughby de Broke. She died on 14 December 1724 at the age of fourteen. He married secondly in June 1743 Mary Gilbert (*d.* 1781), heir to her father, Edward Gilbert of St Paul's Walden, Hertfordshire. Bowes's only child and heir, Mary Eleanor *Bowes, was born on 24 February 1749. It was rumoured in 1742 that he was to be offered the Order of the Bath, a prospect he treated with scorn in a letter of 30 December 1742 (Durham RO, D/LO/F743). Bowes died at Gibside in September 1760 and was buried on 26 September in Whickham parish church. In 1812 his body was moved to the mausoleum at Gibside.

JENNIFER GILL

Sources Durham RO, Strathmore papers · Glamis Castle, Strathmore Archives · J. Gill, *Streatlam and Gibside* (1980) · R. Arnold, *The unhappy countess and her grandson, John Bowes* (1957) · M. M. Wills, 'Gibside', PhD diss., U. Newcastle, 1988 · *Letters of Spencer Cowper, dean of Durham, 1746–74*, ed. E. Hughes, SurtS, 165 (1956) · register of baptisms, marriages, and burials in the parish of Barnard Castle, 1688–1719 · register of baptisms and burials in the parish of Whickham, 1696–1773 · E. Hughes, *North country life in the eighteenth century*, 1 (1952) · Durham RO, Londonderry MSS, D/LO/F743

Archives BL, corresp. and family papers, Add. MS 40748 • Durham RO, Strathmore Archives, estate papers • Glamis Castle, Strathmore Archives, papers • NRA, priv. coll., corresp. and papers | Durham RO, letters to George Vane • Gateshead Public Library, Ellison MSS
Likenesses E. Seeman, oils, 1743, Glamis Castle
Wealth at death £600,000: J. Sykes, *Local Records*, 1833; Arnold, *Unhappy countess* • £1,000,000

Bowes, Sir Jerome (*d.* 1616), diplomat and glass maker, was the son of Sir John Bowes, landowner, of Elford, Staffordshire, and his wife, Anne, daughter of Richard Huddleston of Lancashire. For a man of his prominence and considerable notoriety, Bowes is rather an elusive person. He had a sister, Elizabeth, and two brothers, Sir Edward and Ralph Bowes. In 1557 and 1558 a Sir Jerome Bowes was listed together with Ralph Bowes among gentlemen who accompanied Edward Fiennes de Clinton, first earl of Lincoln, on his expedition to France. Since Bowes was knighted at Carlisle by Thomas Radcliffe, third earl of Sussex, on 28 August 1570, this means that either the earlier knighthood was conferred on a different person and namesake or that the note was made after 1570. On 12 August 1562 Bowes married Jane, daughter and coheir of Roger Rookwood of Euston, Suffolk, and widow of Christopher Calthrop of Cockthorpe, Norfolk. She predeceased him. On 14 February 1569 he was granted the wardship of his stepson, James Calthrop, heir of Christopher Calthrop, with an annuity of £2 2*s.* 8*d.* calculated from 11 April 1562.

In the early 1560s Bowes was one of Elizabeth I's household servants and in 1571 acted as surety for a disputant in a property disagreement that was to be settled in combat. The plaintiff belonged to the household of Robert Dudley, earl of Leicester, but Bowes was called to the proceedings after the queen's interference in the dispute. In 1577 he was 'banished Court for a slanderous speech of my Lord Leicester'. The substance of the slander at that time is unknown but, according to Jerome Horsey, Leicester was again furious with Bowes in 1585 when he seems to have been raking up the old rumour concerning the death of the earl's wife, Amy Robsart.

Bowes's diplomatic career began in 1577 when he was among those who accompanied Sir Philip Sidney in his mission to Rudolph II. In the late 1570s and early 1580s he was in France taking part in the marriage negotiations between Elizabeth and François Valois, duke of Alençon. Although his precise role is unknown, he appears to have been resident in Paris for some time and assisted Sir Edward Stafford on his arrival there. In December 1582 Bowes was still in Paris, and the queen instructed Sir Henry Cobham, her resident ambassador in France, to take counsel with him as to how best to proceed in his own mission. Presumably while in France, Bowes had translated into English a book that was published in London in 1579 as *An apology or defence for the Christians in France which are of the evangelicall or reformed religion.*

In June 1583 Bowes was appointed Elizabeth's ambassador to Ivan IV, tsar of Russia. The apocryphal stories about this mission survived until the end of the seventeenth century and references to them can be found in a

Sir Jerome Bowes (*d.* 1616), by unknown artist

number of treatises on Russian history published in London between 1671 and 1699, as well as in Samuel Pepys's diary. In these stories Bowes appears as a valiant subject of the queen who fearlessly defended his sovereign before Ivan the Terrible. His irascibility was admired by the tempestuous Russian tsar who, after many a stormy scene, finally satisfied all the demands presented by the ambassador. Bowes himself had always insisted that the collapse of his mission was brought about by the death of Ivan. This understanding of his mission to Moscow became accepted even at the time although the Muscovy Company, on whose behalf it was undertaken, constantly accused Bowes of mishandling the negotiations. Neither he, nor the company, nor later historians were correct in their interpretation of affairs. Bowes was given the impossible task of procuring the most advantageous trading privileges for the English without giving the tsar anything in return. During the negotiations which lasted from 18 October 1583 until 17 February 1584, Bowes had fourteen audiences with Ivan and his ministers. Termed a plenipotentiary ambassador in the queen's letter, he had no power to conclude anything and was instructed to take away from the tsar even that little which had been given to him during the preceding negotiations with the Russian ambassador in London. He had to bluff his way through the negotiations, which he also sustained by that 'want of temperance' so deplored by the company. On 14 February 1584 he was dismissed by Ivan with these words: 'Since you came to us with nothing, we will send you back with what you brought us.' Bowes was given an official leave on 17 February by the tsar's councillors. Thus his mission was finished a month before Ivan's death on 19 March. Bowes was caught in the turmoil which took place in Moscow after the tsar's death. His relations with Ivan's councillors were extremely strained during the negotiations. Bowes's continuous accusations that they were hampering the talks brought Ivan's wrath on several of them. After the tsar's death, Bowes was placed under house arrest and stood in real fear of his life for some six weeks before he was finally allowed to depart.

In January 1588 Bowes was appointed to command 'some 50 or 60 men … all pikes and cavaliers' during the expedition into Scotland led by Henry Radcliffe, fourth earl of Sussex (*Rutland MSS*, 1.238). The encounter turned out to be more peaceful than had been anticipated. Bowes and his men met with no resistance and the armour was returned to the royal armoury in Newcastle.

Bowes's involvement in commercial enterprise began in 1576 when, as a royal pensioner, he was given a patent for playing cards which he shared with Sir Henry Bedingfield. According to W. H. Price, such patents were given to the household servants in lieu of salaries. Bowes was in perpetual financial trouble and endlessly petitioned for arrears to be paid to him or for a postponement of a debt repayment. In February 1592 he was given a patent for the manufacture of drinking glasses in consideration of his personal services to the crown. The patent was for twelve years, but it was renewed on 5 October 1606. The glass house was situated at Blackfriars, London. The enterprise, unprofitable even at the time of Bowes's entry into it, was further handicapped by an exclusive patent for the use of sea coal in glass making given to Sir Edward Zouch and others. In his commercial enterprise, as in his diplomatic mission to Russia, Bowes gained more notoriety than note. He was continuously involved in disputes with the farmers under his patent and other glass makers. A copy of *Purchas, his Pilgrims* (1626) belonging now to the library of the Academy of Science in St Petersburg contains a piece of doggerel on one of its margins: 'God made men; & men made mony. God made bees; & bees made hony. God made owles, & apes, & asses: God made Sir Jerome Bowes, & S[r] Jerome Bowes made Glasses' (J. S. Lure, *An Unpublished Epigram on an English Ambassador to Russia*, Oxford Slavonic Papers, new ser., 5/7, 1974, 14).

Bowes was an MP for Lancaster in 1601 and for Reading in 1604. He probably owed his election to Sir Robert Cecil, principal secretary, or to Sir John Fortescue, chancellor of the exchequer, and he was reasonably active in parliament. He was appointed to the quorum for Middlesex in 1601 and carried the canopy at the queen's funeral in 1603.

On 20 February 1607 (NS) a murder was committed in Bowes's house near Charing Cross, Westminster. The account of this event, attributed to Bowes, was published in 1607. A female servant of Bowes was killed by the two thieves who came to rob him of his possessions. The thieves were later apprehended in Chester, brought back to London, and eventually executed.

In accordance with Bowes's will, his estate was to be divided between his nephews, nieces, and a god-daughter. His main legatee was 'John Bowes, the sonne of my brother S[r] Edward Bowes knight', and the executors of his will were his nephews, Sir Peter *Manwood and Sir Percivall Hart (PRO, PROB 11/128. sig. 105). Bowes died between 25 and 28 March 1616, when he was buried at Hackney church, Middlesex. A portrait of him was painted in the year of his embassy to Russia: it presents a very tall man of imposing appearance, probably in his mid-thirties.

M. UNKOVSKAYA

Sources J. Bowes, *A true report of the horrible murther, which was committed in the house of Sir Jerome Bowes, knight, on the 22 day of February, anno domini 1606* (1607) • *CPR*, *1560–63*, 16, 21, 212; *1563–6*, 131, 426; *1566–9*, 427; *1572–5*, 500 • *CSP dom.*, *1547–80*, 368–9 • *CSP for.*, *1579–80*, 499, 518, 520; *1583–4*, 44, 374–8, 553 • [S. Collins], *The present state of Russia in a letter to a friend at London* (1671) • HoP, *Commons*, *1558–1603* • W. H. Price, *The English patents of monopoly* (Boston, 1956) • will, PRO, PROB 11/128, sig. 105 • M. V. Unkovskaya, 'Anglo-Russian diplomatic relations, 1580–1696', DPhil diss., U. Oxf., 1992 • T. S. Willan, *The early history of the Russia Company*, *1553–1603* (1956) • W. A. Shaw, *The knights of England*, 2 vols. (1906) • J. L. Chester and G. J. Armytage, eds., *Allegations for marriage licences issued by the bishop of London*, 1, Harleian Society, 25 (1887) • *DNB* • *The manuscripts of his grace the duke of Rutland*, 4 vols., HMC, 24 (1888–1905), vol. 1

Likenesses portrait, 1583 (exh. NPG 1866), priv. coll. • oils, Ranger's House (Greater London Council), Blackheath, London [*see illus.*]

Bowes, John, Baron Bowes of Clonlyon (1691–1767), lord chancellor of Ireland, was born possibly either in Surrey or in Ware, Hertfordshire. He was the second son of Thomas Bowes of Bishopsgate Street, London, a member of the Turners' Company; his mother's surname was North. He entered the Inner Temple in 1712 and was called to the bar in 1718. He went to Ireland in 1725 'in the train of' the new lord chancellor, Richard West, and enjoyed the patronage of Philip Yorke, subsequently Lord Hardwicke, with whom he had studied law (Duhigg, 307). Bowes was called to the Irish bar in Michaelmas 1725 and appointed third serjeant in 1727. At this time he seems to have seen Irish office as a stepping-stone to advancement in England, and complained particularly of the lack of conversation in a society where 'drinking is the business of their leisure hours' (Bowes to Sir Dudley Ryder, 12 July 1727, PRO NIre., T 3228/1/1). He became second serjeant in 1728, solicitor-general in 1730, and in 1731 MP for Taghmon, co. Wexford. When the lord chancellorship fell vacant in 1739 Bowes was one of two candidates recommended by Archbishop Boulter and by Henry Boyle, who cited his parliamentary services. However Sir Robert Walpole and Hardwicke chose Robert Jocelyn, whom Bowes succeeded as attorney-general. He became chief baron of

John Bowes, Baron Bowes of Clonlyon (1691–1767), by John Brooks

the exchequer in 1741 and lord chancellor in 1757. In 1758 he was created Baron Bowes of Clonlyon, co. Meath. He served as a lord justice in 1765 and in 1766.

Bowes was a strong supporter of the English interest in Ireland, hostile to Jonathan Swift and later to Charles Lucas. In the Dublin riot of 3 December 1759 the crowd tried to force on him an oath to oppose the rumoured union of Ireland and Great Britain; he subsequently pressed for the city authorities to be punished for their inaction. When a new dispute arose in 1760–61, about the transmission of finance bills from England, Bowes sharply criticized what he saw as the opportunism of leading politicians, and blamed the money bill dispute of 1753–6 for unsettling the government of the kingdom. In 1757 he opposed proposals to register Roman Catholic clergy on the grounds that this would imply legal recognition. His much quoted judgment, that the law did not suppose any such person to exist as an Irish Roman Catholic, was delivered about 1759 in the case of a Roman Catholic merchant, Laurence Saul, prosecuted for harbouring a woman from relatives who wished to make her conform to the Church of Ireland.

Bowes was regarded as a highly effective speaker, both in court and in the Commons. His performance as prosecutor in the trial for murder of Lord Santry in 1739 was particularly praised. The dedication prefacing a new edition of the Irish statutes in 1762 commended him for making the court of chancery 'a terror to fraud and a protection and comfort to every honest man', while John Scott exempted him from the criticisms he directed at other lord chancellors (Ball, 2.172). By contrast B. T. Duhigg, writing forty years after Bowes's death, in the context of a polemic against the eclipse of Irish lawyers by English placemen, condemned him as the partial tool of political faction. An anonymous poem published in 1730 mocked him as:

> a great beau
> that here makes a show
> and thinks all about him are fools
> (Ball, 2.111)

Bishop Edward Synge of Elphin described him as 'an old fop' (to Alicia Synge, 27 June 1752, in *The Synge Letters*, ed. M.-L. Legg, 1996, 424). He suffered badly from gout; in 1759 he was said to be in 'a miserable state of health, with legs bigger considerably at the ankle than at the calf' (*Autobiography and Correspondence of … Mrs Delany*, 3.554). He died, unmarried, on 22 July 1767 and was buried in Christ Church, Dublin. His brother Rumsey Bowes of Binfield, Berkshire, erected a marble monument to him in the cathedral's crypt.

S. J. CONNOLLY

Sources F. E. Ball, *The judges in Ireland, 1221–1921*, 2 vols. (1926) · J. R. O'Flanagan, *The lives of the lord chancellors and keepers of the great seal of Ireland*, 2 vols. (1870) · GEC, *Peerage*, new edn · B. T. Duhigg, *History of the King's Inns* (1806) · *Report on manuscripts in various collections*, 8 vols., HMC, 55 (1901–14), vol. 4 [M. Eyre Matcham] · R. E. Burns, *Irish parliamentary politics in the eighteenth century*, 2 vols. (1989–90) · J. Gilbert, *A history of the city of Dublin*, 3 vols. (1854) · T. W. Moody and others, eds., *A new history of Ireland*, 9: *Maps, genealogies, lists* (1984) · E. Keane, P. Beryl Phair, and T. U. Sadleir, eds., *King's Inns admission papers, 1607–1867*, IMC (1982) · *The autobiography and correspondence of Mary Granville, Mrs Delany*, ed. Lady Llanover, 1st ser., 3 vols. (1861)

Archives Chatsworth House, Matlock, Derbyshire, letters to fourth duke of Devonshire · Derbys. RO, corresp. with Sir Robert Wilmot · NRA, letters to Chief Baron Willes · PRO NIre., Harrowby MSS, T 3228 · Sandon Hall, Staffordshire, Harrowby Manuscript Trust, letters to Sir Dudley Ryder

Likenesses J. Brooks, mezzotint, 1743?, NG Ire. · mezzotint, *c.*1743 (after J. Brooks), NG Ire. · J. Lodge, engraving, 1779 (after J. van Nost), NPG · J. Brooks, mezzotint, BM, NPG [*see illus.*] · N. Dance, oils, NG Ire. · J. van Nost, relief medallion on monument, Christ Church, Dublin · W. Thomas, line print (after line engraving by R. Pool & J. Cash, 1780), NG Ire.

Wealth at death £200,000: Ball, *Judges in Ireland*, vol. 2, p. 155

Bowes, John (1804–1874), preacher and author, was born on 12 June 1804 in Swineside, Coverham parish, Yorkshire, the son of a farmer. Bowes joined the Wesleyan Methodists in 1817 but, while working for a brewer in Leyburn, he transferred to the Primitive Methodists because of their revivalist successes, becoming a circuit preacher in 1822. He married Susannah Bellwood, a farmer's daughter, on 26 September 1826 and they had several children. One son, Robert Aitken Bowes (1836–1879), became editor of the *Bolton Guardian*. Bowes was assigned to the church's Edinburgh mission, where he became embroiled in a local dispute over the order in belief of faith and reason: he gave priority to the former. Deciding that all religious denominations were sectarian, Bowes helped form the Christian Mission, becoming pastor of its Dundee congregation in 1830. His book *Christian Union* (1835) showed his increasing undenominationalism. After attempting union with various free methodist bodies, he moved to

Liverpool to assist the Revd Robert Aitken, but this association was short-lived. In 1839 he made contact with the (Plymouth) Brethren, and adopted their ecclesiology. Bowes's pamphlet *A Hired Ministry Unscriptural* (1842) showed his extreme anticlericalism, and he became dependent on free-will offerings for his income. Possessing a strong physique and a powerful voice, he was frequently in conflict with the authorities over his street preaching. A tireless itinerant, he devoted the rest of his life to travelling throughout Britain and to pastoring churches in Aberdeen (1841–4), Manchester (1844–52), Cheltenham (1852–9), and Dundee (1859–74).

A vigorous controversialist, Bowes held public debates with, among others, the secularist G. J. Holyoake, the freethinker Charles Bradlaugh, the Swedenborgian Woodville Woodman, and the Church of Christ leader T. H. Milner. He published his debates as well as strictures on movements such as Mormonism and socialism. He espoused pacifism, total abstinence, vegetarianism, and other adjuncts to healthy living. He denied any ecclesiastical affiliations and when challenged to declare his church he claimed, 'No section, I belong to the whole church' (*Truth Promoter*, 1, 1851, 166–7). However, many of Bowes's concerns can be paralleled among individuals such as Joseph Barker and William Trotter in England and Hugh Hart and J. A. Begg in Scotland. A number of the congregations with which he was in contact in the north of England and in Scotland were assimilated into the Open Brethren movement. He was part of the democratization of popular religion which led to a greater desire for ecclesiastical autonomy and, as such, he was an important pioneer of the Brethren among the lower-middle and working classes.

Bowes wrote some 220 tracts during his life (most of them no longer extant). He published two journals, the *Christian Magazine* (1842–51) and the *Truth Promoter* (1849–75). He also translated the New Testament from Greek into English (1870), although it is uncertain how full his knowledge of Greek was, and published an *Autobiography* (1872). He died of bronchitis on 23 September 1874 in Dundee, where he was buried in an unmarked grave.

NEIL DICKSON

Sources J. Bowes, *The autobiography, or, The history of the life of John Bowes* (1872) • newspaper cuttings, Dundee Central Library, Lamb MSS, Box 398 [biographical notices of Dundee men] • G. Herod, *Biographical sketches of some of those preachers whose labours contributed to the origination and early extension of the Primitive Methodist Connexion* [n.d., c.1855], 326–8 • *Old south-east Lancashire*, 1 (1880), 40 • *DNB*

Likenesses T. Annan, photograph, repro. in Bowes, *Autobiography*

Bowes, John (1811–1885), coal industrialist and art collector, was born at 13 South Street, Chelsea, London, on 19 June 1811, the illegitimate son of John Bowes, tenth earl of Strathmore (1769–1820), and Mary (1787–1860), the daughter of George and Ann Milner of Stainton, co. Durham. His grandmother was Mary Eleanor *Bowes, countess of Strathmore. Mary Milner had become Strathmore's mistress about 1809, after his two failed love affairs with members of the Delaval family, and John Bowes was their only child. The earl married Mary on his deathbed with the aim of legitimizing their son by Scots law. Bowes's claim to the title was rejected in 1821, but he succeeded to the estates of Streatlam near Barnard Castle and of Gibside near Newcastle. He was educated at private schools in Ealing and Lincolnshire, and then at Eton College. He went to Trinity College, Cambridge, from 1828, where his tutor was William Hutt (1801–1882); Bowes's mother, Mary, married Hutt in 1831.

Bowes and Hutt entered parliament in 1832. Without party affiliation but supporting reform, the anti-slavery movement, and religious liberty and toleration, Bowes was elected for South Durham. He was re-elected in 1835, 1837, and 1841, but he declined to stand in 1847; he never spoke in the house but was regarded as a good lobbyist.

Bowes, his mother, Hutt, and Nicholas Wood (1795–1865) created the Marley Hill Coal Company in 1839, to exploit the coals on the Gibside estate. Bowes had also inherited his father's stud at Streatlam and he bred four Derby winners. Betting on his own winning horse in the 1843 Derby he won £21,000, which enabled him to meet his 1841 election expenses and put £4000 into the temporarily ailing coal company. In 1844 Charles Mark Palmer (1822–1907) joined the business, and in 1847 the company was renamed John Bowes Esq. & Partners. It soon became one of the greatest companies in British coal history and the source of Bowes's wealth.

Since a continental tour in 1830 Bowes had made several visits to Paris and he decided to settle there in 1847. A keen theatre-goer and an amateur actor from his early days, he bought the Théâtre de Variétés for more than £15,000. There he met Josephine Benoîte Coffin-Chevallier (1825–1874), an actress and painter, whom he married on 23 August 1852. With a town house in the rue de Berlin, Bowes bought a château by the Seine as a country retreat, and stocked it with works of art. It was sold in 1860, and some of the contents were shipped to Streatlam.

Bowes and Josephine had now determined on a museum for their art collections, and in 1869 the Bowes Museum, which was designed in an elaborate French-Renaissance style, was begun at Barnard Castle. Josephine died in February 1874, while the museum was still under construction. Three years later, on 18 August 1877, Bowes married Alphonsine, comtesse de Courten (*b.* c.1837), who was also French. Bowes's second marriage proved to be troubled, as Alphonsine spoke no English and disliked the north of England. She returned to France, leaving Bowes behind, on more than one occasion. He took divorce proceedings against his wife between 1883 and 1885, but a compromise was reached and they remained married, but separate, for the last few months of Bowes's life. Neither marriage produced any children.

Work continued on the museum, at considerable expense, but Bowes's last years were troubled, and he suffered ill health. He died on 9 October 1885 at Streatlam Castle and was buried at Gibside, on 16 October, alongside the remains of his first wife. With his financial affairs in some disarray, his gross personal estate of £147,874 19*s.* 3*d.* was insufficient to meet the very generous bequests of his will. The museum was officially opened in 1892 and remained a major collection of French art at the end of the twentieth century. STAFFORD M. LINSLEY

Sources C. E. Hardy, *John Bowes and the Bowes Museum* (1970); repr. (1989) · C. E. Mountford, *The Bowes railway* (1976) · J. F. Robinson, 'Gibside and its owners', *Monthly Chronicle of North-Country Lore and Legend* (Sept 1889), 390–92 · E. Y. Western, 'The Bowes Museum at Barnard Castle', *Monthly Chronicle of North-Country Lore and Legend* (June 1890), 256–7 · d. cert.

Archives Bowes Museum, co. Durham, archives · Durham RO, corresp. and papers; corresp. and papers relating to Bowes Museum | Durham RO, Strathmore MSS

Likenesses J. Jackson, oils, *c*.1826, Sandringham · J. M. Negelen, crayon drawing, *c*.1832, Bowes Museum, co. Durham · J. E. Feyen, oils, 1863, Bowes Museum, co. Durham

Wealth at death £147,874 19*s*. 3*d*.: probate, 28 Nov 1885, *CGPLA Eng. & Wales*

Bowes, Marmaduke (*d*. 1585), Roman Catholic martyr, is of unknown parentage. He was a substantial Yorkshire yeoman of Angram Grange, near Appleton, in Cleveland. He experienced great personal conflict on religious issues, but refused to declare himself a Catholic, although he sympathized strongly with the Catholic cause. According to the recollections of Grace, wife of Sir Ralph Babthorpe of Babthorpe, Yorkshire, Bowes was married, and 'kept a schoolmaster to teach his children' (Morris, 244). There are several accounts of how Bowes came to be arrested. In one, this tutor, himself a Catholic, was arrested, and subsequently apostatized. The tutor then reported to the queen's council of the north at York that Bowes was known to entertain Catholic priests. Bowes was summoned to answer this complaint, and was ordered to appear at the August assizes of 1585, where he was indicted, condemned, and hanged. In another version, Bowes heard that his friend Hugh Taylor, a Catholic priest who had stayed with him in the past, had been arrested; when Bowes appeared at the York assizes to try to free Taylor, the layman was immediately apprehended, tried, and condemned. His execution took place so quickly that when he was hanged he was still wearing the boots and spurs in which he had ridden to York. What is certain is that Bowes was executed at the same time as Taylor, on 26 November 1585, the first person to be punished under the 1585 statute against harbouring priests. A contemporary report says 'he died very willingly and professed his faith [was openly converted to Catholicism], with great repentance that he had lived in schism' (Morris, 244). He was beatified on 22 November 1987.

SIDNEY LEE, *rev.* SARAH ELIZABETH WALL

Sources R. Challoner, *Memoirs of missionary priests*, ed. J. H. Pollen, rev. edn (1924) · J. Morris, ed., *The troubles of our Catholic forefathers related by themselves*, 2 (1875) · R. Stanton, *A menology of England and Wales* (1887) · J. H. Pollen, ed., *Unpublished documents relating to the English martyrs*, 1, Catholic RS, 5 (1908) · S. Usherwood and E. Usherwood, *We die for the old religion: the story of the 85 martyrs of England and Wales beatified 22 November 1987* (1987)

Bowes, Sir Martin (1496/7–1566), goldsmith and mayor of London, was born in York in the parish of St Cuthbert, Peaseholme. Despite his disclaimer in 1549 that at the time of his going thirty-eight years previously to London at the age of fourteen (HoP, *Commons, 1509–58*, 1.469) he

Sir Martin Bowes (1496/7–1566), by unknown artist, 1562

had been of 'small substance' (Raine, 5.19–20), he came in fact from a family of some prominence, his great-grandfather having been mayor and his grandfather sheriff of York. His father was probably Thomas Bowes, goldsmith, who became free of the city in 1498 and who seems likely to have been related to the man of the same name, who also originated from St Cuthbert's and who went on to pursue an active career at the mint, serving between 1468 and 1476 as attorney to Warden John Wode and then from 1476 until his death on 14 September 1479 as joint warden.

In 1513 Bowes was apprenticed to the prominent London goldsmith Robert Amadas, court supplier and future master of the jewels, under whom he learned the assaying skills that were to be the mainspring of his highly successful career. Made free in 1521 and a liveryman of the Goldsmiths' Company in 1525, he went on to become not just remarkable in his own generation, but perhaps the most remarkable member of the company in the entire Tudor period. Having served as fourth warden in 1532–3, third warden in 1534–5, and second warden in 1535–6 he was elected prime warden on 17 September 1537. Chosen twice more during the years 1540–42, he subsequently occupied the position on no fewer than ten further occasions—1549–51, 1553–7, 1558–62—and by so doing achieved almost uninterrupted control. Even after he had lain down office for the last time, in 1562, Bowes's influence remained undiminished for, time and again, decisions were taken by his successors only after his wishes had first been ascertained.

Closely allied with his Goldsmiths' connection was Bowes's link with the mint, which also began with Amadas—this time through Amadas's being with Ralph Rowlett, deputy to Master Worker William Blount, Lord Mountjoy. Bowes was Amadas's deputy by 1526 and grew so quickly in importance that when, in 1530, Mountjoy called his deputies to account Bowes was accused with them of defrauding him of his rightful profits. Despite their protestations of innocence the deputies were replaced by Hugh Welshe, also a goldsmith, and it was not until his death in 1532, the year in which Amadas also died, that Bowes and Rowlett had the opportunity of returning to the mint. By offering a chain of gold worth £30 to Cromwell to assist their cause and paying dearly for Mountjoy's agreement to surrender his patent, they achieved their end, being appointed joint master workers in April 1533. Surviving an adverse inquiry into mint operations in 1534, Rowlett continued in office until his death in March 1543 and Bowes until the reorganization of the mint in 1544. On 3 June he was appointed under-treasurer of the principal mint in the Tower and remained in control of this, the most important of all the eight mints operating during the debasement of the coinage, until September 1550 when he was pensioned at 200 marks. As a commission of inquiry set up on 3 February 1550 revealed, his stewardship of the mint had left much to be desired. All in all, by virtue of arrears on his accounts, profits arising on bullion provisioning, making coin worse than standard, and profiting from moneys that had not been paid over as promptly as they should have been, Sir Martin was found to be in debt to the tune of £29,762. It is a measure, first, of his massive liquidity that he was able in a matter of months to pay off £22,762 of this and, second, of his standing that he could find sureties for the repayment of the remaining £7000 over the next ten years. In the event, £2000 was remitted by the crown in order to secure more prompt repayment of the rest.

In this year, 1554, Bowes married Elizabeth, daughter of Thomas Harlow and widow of William Billingsley of London. By this and two earlier marriages—(by 1526) to Cecily Eliott and (by 1538) to Anne (*d*. 1553), daughter of John Barrett of Belhus in Aveley, Essex—he had eighteen children, two of whom, Thomas, the eldest son (*d*. 1591), and Martin, the second son (*d*. 1573), served under him at the mint, the first as teller (1545–50), the second as surveyor of the meltings (1547–51). Thomas married Cecily, widow of Thomas Haynes, overseas factor to Sir William Bowyer and merchant adventurer of London, while Martin took as his first wife Frances Scrope, the granddaughter and heir of Robert Amadas. Although both sons were free of the Goldsmiths' Company neither practised the craft, preferring instead to make their way in London as merchants. In his will of 1565 Sir Martin divided his possessions in three, according to the custom of London: one part going to his wife, Elizabeth, one part to William and Charity his orphans (both minors), and one part for the performance of his legacies. Martin inherited Sir Martin's mansion house in Lombard Street and half his household goods in London, the other half going to Dame Elizabeth as part of her portion. After appraisal all Sir Martin's household goods at Woolwich, North Cray, Kent, and Mile End were to pass to William and Charity as part of their legacy. Thomas enjoyed the cancellation of all the debts he owed his father, a blessing indeed, because, as Sir Martin opined, he had cost him 'four times more than ever his part should come to' (PRO, PROB 11/49). By an earlier will of 1562 Sir Martin had defined his legacy to his company as tenements in Lombard Street, Scalding Alley, St Matthew's Alley, and St Botolph without Bishopgate besides a great messuage and twenty-two gardens in the same parish.

During the time when he controlled and benefited from the mint Bowes cut an impressive figure in the city. A commoner in the ward of Langbourn, then alderman from 1536 until his death, he was auditor in 1536, sheriff in 1540–41, the year in which he was knighted, and mayor in 1545–6. In this capacity he participated in the trial of the heretic Anne Askew. In 1547, due partly to the wardens' urging the livery 'by all means to give their whole election' (HoP, *Commons, 1509–58*, 1.470) to him, he was returned as MP for London. According to the limited surviving evidence Bowes was supportive in this, and in the further five parliaments in which he represented London, of the interests of York and, especially, London. Outside parliament the same was true. In 1549 he remembered his northern origins by presenting York with 'a fair sword with a sheath of crimson velvet garnished with pearl and stone set upon silver and gilt' (Raine, 5.20). And it was in the parish of St Cuthbert that, in 1557, he proposed to establish a chantry, possibly an indication of his attachment to the old religion. When, at the accession of Elizabeth, Catholicism was once again eclipsed, his endowment was transferred to poor relief. As far as the metropolis was concerned, Bowes showed similar generosity, presenting in 1558 a jewel of gold embellished with pearls and stones to hang from the mayor's collar. He had similar sympathy for London's poor, endowing five almshouses at Woolwich and playing the key role in the establishment of five hospitals—St Bartholomew's, St Thomas's, Bethlem, Bridewell, and Christ's—of which he became comptroller-general when the scheme was finalized in 1557.

Rich and influential, Bowes was also active in government outside his company and the city. Between 1538 and his death he served on a variety of commissions but made his most continuous contribution as a JP for Kent and Middlesex. Bowes died on 4 August 1566, and was buried in St Mary Woolnoth, Lombard Street. C. E. CHALLIS

Sources HoP, *Commons, 1509–58*, vol. 1 · A. Raine, ed., *York civic records*, 5, Yorkshire Archaeological Society, 110 (1946) · C. E. Challis, ed., *A new history of the royal mint* (1992) · C. E. Challis, 'The debasement of the coinage, 1542–1551', *Economic History Review*, 2nd ser., 20 (1967), 441–65 · C. E. Challis, 'Mint officials and moneyers of the Tudor period', *British Numismatic Journal*, 45 (1975), 51–76 · W. S. Prideaux, *The charities under the management of the Goldsmiths' Company* (1899) · P. Slack, 'Social policy and the constraints of government', *The mid-Tudor polity, c.1540–1560*, ed. J. Loach and R. Tittler

(1980), 94–115 • court minute books, Goldsmiths' Hall, London • PRO, E364/110 • PRO, E101/294/26 no. 1 • PRO, PROB 11/49 • S. Hare and A. Grimwade, 'Our portrait of Sir Martin Bowes', *The Review* [Goldsmiths' Company, London] (May 1980), 19–22 • G. D. Ramsay, ed., *John Isham, mercer and merchant adventurer: two account books of a London merchant in the reign of Elizabeth I*, Northamptonshire RS, 21 (1962) • *The diary of Henry Machyn, citizen and merchant-taylor of London, from AD 1550 to AD 1563*, ed. J. G. Nichols, CS, 42 (1848), 354–5

Likenesses portrait, 1562; Christies, 1 August 1952, lot 26 [*see illus.*] • W. Faithorne, oils, 1679, Goldsmiths' Hall, London • school of Holbein, portrait, priv. coll.

Bowes, Mary Eleanor, countess of Strathmore and Kinghorne (1749–1800), heiress and victim of kidnapping, was born on 24 February 1749, the only child of George *Bowes MP (1701–1760), of Streatlam Castle and Gibside, co. Durham, and his second wife, Mary (*d.* 1781), heir of Edward Gilbert, of St Paul's Walden in Hertfordshire. Her father, a landowner and successful businessman, brought her up at Gibside House, near Rowlands Gill, where she was educated. He had never forgotten his long-dead first wife, Eleanor Verney, whom he had married when she was only fourteen. She had been a prodigy of learning and he was determined that his daughter should emulate her. Fortunately, Mary Eleanor was intelligent. By her own account she could read fluently at the age of four, had a gift for languages, and took a great interest in botany.

Mary Eleanor's father died when she was eleven, leaving her his vast wealth, whereupon her mother promptly took a house in London, first at no. 13 and then at 40 Grosvenor Square. Small and shapely, with dark brown hair, a rather large nose, and a determined chin, Mary Eleanor was soon the centre of attraction for impoverished aristocrats and unscrupulous fortune hunters. Nominally chaperoned by her easy-going aunt, Jane Bowes, she enjoyed a series of flirtations until, at the age of sixteen, she fell in love with 'the beautiful Lord Strathmore', as contemporaries called him (Arnold, 23). **John Lyon**, ninth earl of Strathmore and Kinghorne (1737–1776), landowner, was born on 17 July 1737, the son of Thomas Lyon, eighth earl of Strathmore and Kinghorne (*bap.* 1704, *d.* 1753), and Jean Nicholson (1713–1778). Strathmore was an honest, good-natured, and uncomplicated man, who played no role in public life apart from being one of Scotland's representative peers. It took eighteen months to negotiate the marriage contract, during which time Mary Eleanor realized that he and she had nothing in common. He had no interest in literary or intellectual matters, and she certainly did not want to settle down to a quiet life on his Scottish estates. Too proud to admit her mistake, she married him in St George's, Hanover Square, London, on 26 February 1767, two days after her eighteenth birthday.

By the time Mary Eleanor was twenty-four she had three sons and two daughters, and was finding domestic life unbearably dull. Lord Strathmore had contracted tuberculosis and spent an increasing amount of time away from home, in search of a cure. To amuse herself, Mary Eleanor wrote a poetical play in five acts, entitled *The Siege of Jerusalem*, full of high drama and unrequited love. After the excitement of its publication in 1769, she embarked on a series of affairs. Unscrupulous adventurers were all too ready to divert a bored, wealthy wife, and in 1774 George Grey insinuated himself into her affections, plying her with poems of his own composition. His origins were obscure, but he claimed to have made a fortune in India. They began to meet secretly, and in February 1776 they became lovers. A few weeks later, on 7 March 1776, Lord Strathmore died at sea, *en route* to Lisbon, leaving his wife a farewell letter criticizing her 'extreme rage for literary fame' and her propensity for making ill-natured remarks 'for the sake of sporting a *bon mot*' (Arnold, 41).

Somewhat sobered, Mary Eleanor revived her botanical interests. She purchased Stanley House in Chelsea, built hothouses, and commissioned William Paterson the botanist to collect plants for her in southern Africa. When people enquired about her personal life, she spoke vaguely of marrying Grey, and indeed became engaged to him. However, twice that year when she found that she was expecting his child she had the pregnancies terminated, and in the late autumn she fell in love with Andrew Robinson Stoney (1747–1810), a widowed lieutenant on half pay in the 30th regiment. Undeterred by tales of his ill-treatment of his wealthy first wife, and by the fact that she was once more expecting Grey's child, Mary Eleanor married Stoney on 17 January 1777, in St James's, Piccadilly, London. Mary, her daughter with Grey, was born that summer.

Mary Eleanor and Stoney, now known as Bowes, later had a son, William, but by then her married life was miserable. A few days after their marriage, Bowes discovered that she had signed an antenuptial trust preventing him from having any control over her fortune. Furious, he forced her to revoke the deed and began to abuse her. The servants often saw her bruised and bleeding. In February 1785 she managed to escape, finding refuge in a lodging-house in Holborn under the name of Mrs Jefferies. She raised an action for divorce on the grounds of her husband's ill-treatment and adultery, but on 10 November 1786 he had her abducted. She was carried off to the north of England and held in wretched conditions until she was finally rescued by several local men near Darlington.

Bowes and his accomplices were sentenced to three years in prison and fined £300. Mary Eleanor regained control of her estates, was granted a decree of divorce on 2 March 1789, and spent the rest of her life quietly, in Fludyer Street, London, and then at Purbrook Park, near Cosham, Hampshire. She died at Christchurch, Hampshire, on 28 April 1800, and was buried in her magnificent first wedding dress in the south cross of Westminster Abbey, London, on 10 May. Her story reads like a historical novel, and indeed Thackeray is said to have based Barry Lyndon on Bowes, but the problems caused by her frustrated intelligence and her great wealth were all too real.

ROSALIND K. MARSHALL

Sources R. Arnold, *The unhappy countess and her grandson, John Bowes* (1957) • J. Foot, *Lives of Andrew Robinson Bowes, esq., and the countess of Strathmore, written from thirty-three years' professional attendance, from letters, and other well-authenticated documents* (1810) • *The confessions of the countess of Strathmore: written by herself, carefully copied from the originals lodged in Doctors' Commons* (1793) • *GM*, 1st ser., 56 (1786), 1087 • *GM*, 1st ser., 57 (1787), 635, 933 • *GM*, 1st ser., 59

(1789), 465 · *GM*, 1st ser., 70 (1800), 1285 · *A report of the proceedings in the high court of chancery in the matter of Andrew Robinson Bowes* (1804) · *Scots peerage* · GEC, *Peerage*

Archives Durham RO, papers relating to divorce from Andrew Robinson Stoney · NRA Scotland, priv. coll., legal and literary papers

Likenesses D. Gardner, double portrait, pastels, *c*.1770 (with Lady Maria Jane Bowes-Lyon); Christies, 18 Jan 1972, lot 56; Christies, 14 Nov 1972, lot 67 · J. C. D. Engleheart, miniature, 1800 (after miniature by G. Engleheart); Sothebys, 2 June 1975, lot 119

Bowes, Paul (*d*. 1702), lawyer and antiquary, was born at Great Bromley, Essex, the second son of Sir Thomas Bowes (*d*. 1676), witch persecutor, and Mary (*b*. 1608), third daughter of Paul *Dewes (1567–1631) [*see under* Dewes, Garrat]; his parents had married on 4 December 1626. After being educated at the school at Moulton, Norfolk, he was admitted pensioner of St John's College, Cambridge, on 21 December 1650. He took no degree; indeed, he does not appear to have matriculated. He chose a career in law, and on 12 May 1654 entered the Middle Temple. He was called to the bar on 10 May 1661 and became a bencher on 24 October 1679. By late 1669 he had married Bridget (*d*. 1706), daughter of Thomas Sturges of the Middle Temple. They had three sons, of whom the eldest, Martin, was admitted to St John's College, Cambridge, in April 1686 aged sixteen, and two daughters.

Bowes was an enthusiastic antiquary, and collected enough books to divide them eventually between his first two sons. His interest in the history of parliament led to his judicious and careful edition of the manuscript work of his celebrated uncle, Sir Simonds *D'Ewes. Entitled *The journals of all the parliaments during the reign of Queen Elizabeth, both of the House of Lords and House of Commons*, it was published in 1682, with later editions in 1693 and 1708. Bowes was elected a fellow of the Royal Society on 30 November 1699.

Bowes died in June 1702 and was buried on 3 July at St Dunstan-in-the-West, Fleet Street. His will, dated 5 August 1699, was proved by his widow and sole executor on 16 July 1702. He had made two codicils (dated 17 April and 12 August 1701), the first of which was needed chiefly because of his disappointment with his third son, Francis, who preferred life at sea to the place his father had found for him in chancery. He possessed property in Lincolnshire, Suffolk, Dorset, London, and Essex. Bridget Bowes died in 1706. Their son Martin married Elizabeth, eldest daughter of Edward Thurland of Reigate, Surrey, and afterwards settled at Bury St Edmunds, Suffolk, where he died in 1726, and their second daughter, Anne, became in 1732 the wife of Philip Broke MP, of Nacton, Suffolk.

GORDON GOODWIN, *rev*. DAVID DEAN

Sources *The autobiography and correspondence of Sir Simonds D'Ewes*, ed. J. O. Halliwell, 2 vols. (1845) · P. Morant, *The history and antiquities of the county of Essex*, 2 vols. (1768) · A. Page, *A supplement to the Suffolk traveller*, 2 vols. (1844) · *N&Q*, 3rd ser., 5 (1864), 247, 330 · *N&Q*, 7 (4 June 1853) · *GM*, 1st ser., 3 (1733) · R. F. Scott, *Admissions to the College of St John the Evangelist in the University of Cambridge*, ed. J. E. B. Mayor, 3 vols. in 2 (1893–1903) · H. A. C. Sturgess, ed., *Register of admissions to the Honourable Society of the Middle Temple, from the fifteenth century to the year 1944*, 3 vols. (1949) · will, PRO, PROB 11/465, fols. 164–6

Archives Suffolk RO, Ipswich, journal | BL, Harley MSS

Bowes, Sir Robert (1493?–1555), soldier, lawyer, and rebel, was the second surviving son of Sir Ralph Bowes of Streatlam, co. Durham (*d*. 1512), and Marjorie (*d*. 1524), daughter and coheir of Sir Richard Conyers of South Cowton, North Riding of Yorkshire. He married Alice, a daughter of Sir James Metcalfe of Nappa, in Richmondshire; they had several children, all of whom died young. He became head of the Streatlam family following the death of his nephew Sir George *Bowes (1517–1545). His background and experience in border defence and administrative affairs made Robert Bowes an ideal candidate for royal service in the north, a region where Tudor monarchs struggled to impose their authority. Like other members of his family Bowes had a natural aptitude for border warfare and gained early experience in this sphere during the Anglo-Scottish war of 1522–3. Moreover, he gained wide-ranging expertise and an understanding of the wider political nation as a result of his education at Lincoln's Inn (admitted on 4 May 1511) and his pursuit of a legal career. In 1528 he was noted as a master of the court of requests.

The close connections between royal personnel and the Durham administrative élite provided the channel by which Bowes was first able to enter royal service. He seems to have been a member of the episcopal council of Thomas Wolsey, bishop of Durham from 1523 to 1529, and was appointed escheator for the bishopric in 1529. His appointment to the council in the north in 1525, resurrected under Wolsey's auspices as the duke of Richmond's council, provided Bowes with the initial vehicle for his advancement in royal service. However, his career was undoubtedly furthered as a result of his participation, on the rebel side, in the Pilgrimage of Grace in 1536. In joining the rebellion Bowes was motivated by political considerations: it appears that he, in company with other members of the northern gentry, had become increasingly alienated by the intrusions of central government in the affairs of the region. There is nothing to suggest that he rose in defence of the old religion. Bowes's role in the pilgrimage propelled him into the political limelight and to the notice of the crown, which quickly came to recognize his abilities in the spheres of both law and border defence. Following the breakdown of the rebellion Bowes was quickly reconciled with the Henrician regime, and thereafter began his rise as a faithful servant of the royal administration.

Bowes's legal and administrative expertise ensured his presence on the council in the north after its revitalization in 1537. He retained his seat on that body, serving in his later years as vice-president, until his death in 1555. He was knighted in 1539 and in the same year entered parliament as a knight of the shire for Yorkshire. His growing prominence in the political arena ensured his subsequent return as a member of parliament for Yorkshire in 1542 and for Newcastle upon Tyne in 1545, Westmorland in 1547, and Middlesex in 1553. At the same time his experience of border warfare ensured that he played a prominent role in the Anglo-Scottish hostilities of the 1540s. In 1545 he was appointed warden of the middle marches, and in 1548 his remit was extended to the east marches. In terms of border affairs, he became the acknowledged expert of his generation. His detailed survey of the state of the borders, drawn up in late 1550 or early 1551, is still highly regarded by historians for the insight it gives into the nature of frontier society in the sixteenth century.

By this time Bowes, whose family had become closely associated with the charismatic Scottish reformer John Knox, had become part of the reformist administration of John Dudley, duke of Northumberland. In terms of his legal career this connection enabled Bowes to reach the top of his profession with his appointment as master of the rolls in 1551. In the same year he became a member of the privy council, thus signalling his rise to the highest echelons of political society. Border service, however, remained the recurring theme throughout his career. In the closing years of his life when, following his support for the doomed attempt to settle the crown on the protestant Lady Jane Grey, Bowes was forced to resign his higher offices, the new Marian regime still had need of his expertise in Anglo-Scottish affairs. He died at Berwick on 28 February 1555 while reviewing the defences of the garrison there. CHRISTINE M. NEWMAN

Sources *LP Henry VIII* · J. Bain, ed., *The Hamilton papers: letters and papers illustrating the political relations of England and Scotland in the XVIth century*, 2 vols., Scottish RO, 12 (1890–92) · *APC*, 1542–54 · *CPR*, 1547–53 · PRO, C142/102/46 · admissions book, Lincoln's Inn, London, MS A1A3, vol. 1, fol. 42b · PRO, Durh. 3/76 m.4; 3/77 m.2 · HoP, *Commons*, 1509–58, 1.471–3 · R. R. Reid, *The king's council in the north* (1921), 103–5, 142–55, 181 · W. A. Shaw, *The knights of England*, 2 (1906), 51 · R. Surtees, *The history and antiquities of the county palatine of Durham*, 4 (1840) · J. Hodgson, *A history of Northumberland*, 3 pts in 7 vols. (1820–58), pt 3, vol. 2, 171–248 · J. Ridley, *John Knox* (1968) · I. S. Leadam, ed., *Select cases in the court of requests, AD 1497–1569*, SeldS, 12 (1898), cv · J. G. Nichols, ed., *The chronicle of Queen Jane, and of two years of Queen Mary*, CS, old ser., 48 (1850), 100 · C. M. Newman, 'The Bowes of Streatlam, co. Durham: a study of the politics and religion of a sixteenth-century northern gentry family', DPhil diss., University of York, 1991 · [J. Raine], ed., *Wills and inventories*, 1, SurtS, 2 (1835), 145 · M. H. Dodds and R. Dodds, *The Pilgrimage of Grace, 1536–37, and the Exeter conspiracy, 1538*, 2 vols. (1915) · PRO, E36/44, fol. 133 · *Report of the Deputy Keeper of the Public Records*, 44 (1883), 321, 327, 329, 332

Archives BL, family and estate MSS, add. charters 66317–66488 · Durham RO, MSS | BL, 'Transactions between England and Scotland', state papers, Add. MS 32646

Likenesses G. Vertue, line engraving, 1750 (after group portrait), BM, NPG · etching, NPG · group portrait (*Edward VI granting the charter to Bridewell Hospital in 1553*), Bridewell Hospital, Surrey

Wealth at death £188 2s. 4d.—value of goods: Raine, ed., *Wills and inventories*, 145; *Wills and inventories in the archdeaconry of Richmond*, SurtS (1853), 116–20

Bowes, Robert (*d.* 1597), diplomat, was the fifth but second surviving son of Richard Bowes (*d.* 1558), soldier, of Norham, Northumberland, and his wife, Elizabeth *Bowes (*bap.* 1505, *d.* in or before 1572), protestant exile, daughter and coheir of Roger Aske of Aske, North Riding of Yorkshire, and his wife, Margery. His only surviving brother was Sir George *Bowes (1527–1580), who acted as Elizabeth I's marshal in the suppression of the northern rising of 1569–70. His sister Marjory Bowes (*d.* *c.*1560) married John Knox. The family was experienced in dealing with border warfare, as Richard Bowes had served Henry VIII, leading a force across the Scottish border in August 1542 following the breakdown of Anglo-Scottish negotiations, but was defeated at Haddon Rig. Robert Bowes matriculated at Queens' College, Cambridge, in 1547 but took no degree. He probably attended Lincoln's Inn in 1549. He married first his cousin Anne (*d.* in or before 1566), daughter and coheir of Sir George Bowes of Dalden. They had at least one child, Ralph Bowes (*d.* 1623). In 1566 he married again; his second wife was Eleanor, daughter of Sir Richard Musgrave of Eden Hall, Cumberland. They had no children.

Early Elizabethan career, 1558–1577 Bowes was sheriff of co. Durham in 1564 and again in 1569, in which capacity he assisted his brother in defending Barnard Castle against the northern earls. Following this he was put in command of a mounted force whose purpose was to maintain and enforce order on the western border. He was JP for co. Durham from 1561 and for the North Riding from 1569. In addition to his house at Berwick, Bowes held the manor of Great Broughton, Yorkshire, the extensive improvement of which he later claimed cost him £2300. He was MP for Knaresborough in 1563 and appointed to the succession committee in 1566. He was MP for Carlisle in 1571 and Appleby in 1572, owing his return to the patronage of leading noblemen, and was active in parliament.

Henry capitalized on the disarray of the Scots following the battle of Flodden in 1513 by establishing a system of diplomatic espionage, continued by his daughter Elizabeth. Bowes's position as treasurer of Berwick from 1576 placed him ideally for employment on diplomatic missions, and in the periods when he served as resident English ambassador at the Scottish court he watched over the queen's interests and was briefed to gather and maintain a party of men who supplied information and were in the pay of the English sovereign. He was a member of the queen's council in the north from 1574 and JP for Cumberland, Northumberland, Westmorland, and the East and West ridings from 1577. The purpose of Bowes's actions regarding Scotland was to weaken any inclination by James VI's government to form ties with France and to unite factions of the Scottish nobility favourably disposed towards England. The course of his diplomatic career may be traced through the many letters that survive.

James Douglas, fourth earl of Morton, was established as regent of Scotland in 1572 with the task of administering government for the young king, but his position was challenged in the late 1570s; Bowes recorded the first signs of significant opposition in a letter to Henry Hastings, third earl of Huntingdon, dated 28 June 1577. He noted the formation of a party headed by John Stewart, fourth earl of Atholl, William Grey, fourth Lord Ruthven, and Patrick Lindsay, sixth Lord Lindsay. He suggested that steps were being taken to end the dispute between Atholl and Colin Campbell, sixth earl of Argyll, in the hope of adding Argyll to the coalition aimed at increasing their political influence.

Ambassador in Scotland, 1577–1583 Bowes attempted to broker an accord between the leaders of the two factions and was present at a meeting of Morton, Atholl, and Argyll at Morton's residence at Dalkeith in 1578. In his correspondence Bowes states that the three noblemen agreed to share power amicably, but Morton left for Stirling ahead of the others to take possession of the young king. Such was the tension between the two factions that Argyll and Atholl met Morton, at the head of their respective forces, in the field at Falkirk in August 1578. It was Bowes, in his capacity as English ambassador, who by May 1579 had mediated the truce between the two sides and induced the adversaries to settle their differences without recourse to arms. Nevertheless, it is clear from his correspondence that he seriously doubted whether a formula for peace could be devised. The problem for Bowes was that Elizabeth and her privy council had miscalculated how unpopular Morton's Anglophile regime had become and their mediation, intended to prop the earl up, only worsened their situation and undermined further the Anglo-Scottish amity.

By autumn 1579 a new threat to Morton materialized in the person of Esmé Stewart, seigneur d'Aubigny, who reached Scotland from France in September. Backed by the Guise family, d'Aubigny seems to have been motivated by personal opportunism rather than by a desire to promote Catholicism. He used his French support to appeal to Scottish Catholics and was quick to establish a personal rapport with the thirteen-year-old James, already resentful of Morton's authority. In alliance with James Stewart, captain of the king's guard, d'Aubigny increased his influence at court and drew in Morton's enemies such as Atholl and Argyll. The threat posed to England by a dominant Catholic faction at the Scottish court that could look for support from either France or Spain was not lost on William Cecil, Baron Burghley, lord treasurer, and Sir Francis Walsingham, principal secretary. In April 1580 Bowes, at that time treasurer of the garrison at Berwick, received £500 and instructions to travel to Scotland, where he was to make use of the money to shore up Morton's crumbling regime.

Bowes arrived in Edinburgh on 27 April and his reports to Walsingham indicate that he found Morton's position very fragile, given that d'Aubigny's assiduous attendance at court strengthened his hold on the king. Bowes suggested the provision of financial support for John Erskine, second or eighteenth earl of Mar, and Archibald Douglas, eighth earl of Angus (both more favourably disposed to England), in order to counter this influence. Before departing for Berwick the ambassador sought to secure further support for Elizabeth with the payment of bribes to the captains of Dumbarton and Edinburgh. Upon his return he sent a barrage of messages to Walsingham stressing that immediate action was needed to save the English party in Scotland, but the queen's attention was elsewhere and his proposals seemed too costly, so his pleas were ignored. Verbal assurances of support had lost their appeal to Morton, who sent word to Bowes through Angus that only a pension of 500 marks to him and 2000 marks to the king could save the situation. So far had Morton's faith in Elizabeth evaporated that towards the end of July he was making overtures to d'Aubigny, despite remonstrations from Bowes. When d'Aubigny took Dumbarton, described by Bowes as the gateway of France into Scotland, the English envoy was sent back to Scotland to do what he could, short of using force.

With such restrictions imposed upon him, Bowes's mission was fraught with difficulty. It was complicated further by the fact that Elizabeth was still negotiating with the French, obliging the English envoy to avoid openly antagonizing d'Aubigny. Forbidden to offer more than verbal encouragement and the promise of the queen's approval, Bowes's efforts to discredit the royal favourite were hindered by James's refusal to hear criticism of d'Aubigny unless he was present to defend himself. Bowes nevertheless did what he could to undermine d'Aubigny by spreading rumours that he was planning to abduct James to France. Beyond the court Bowes also made unsuccessful attempts to arrange a meeting of Anglo-Scottish commissioners to discuss border problems, causing him to send a very pessimistic report concerning control of the marches. This stalemate led to his recall from Scotland at the end of October. Clearly frustrated that the duties of his office were so ill-rewarded, he petitioned the queen in 1582 about his expenses and on 14 December wrote to Walsingham asking to be released from service, a request that was denied.

Dissatisfaction with d'Aubigny, created duke of Lennox in August 1581, increased dramatically in the following year, even though Morton had finally fallen and been executed in June 1581. On 7 August, Walsingham wrote to Bowes that he should inform the duke's opponents that Lennox had discovered a plot against him. There followed the Ruthven raid, in which the sixteen-year-old James was tricked into going from Perth to Ruthven Castle, Perthshire, by the earls of Gowrie (Ruthven), Mar, and Lindsay. Bowes was dispatched by Elizabeth to Scotland in order to convey her support and approval. However, the queen was still not prepared to add weight to her words with firm offers of pensions or financial aid, despite his strenuous declaration that all the benefits of the raid would be lost otherwise. He discovered that James was still favourably disposed towards Lennox and that the Ruthven raiders lacked a following. Mar and Thomas Lyon, master of Glamis, he reported, were trustworthy, but the loyalty of the others to the English cause would have to be bought. News that the French ambassador Bertrand de Salignac de la Motte-Fénélon was travelling to Scotland prompted Bowes to work hard for Lennox's departure before the envoy arrived in January 1583. Bowes's fear was that Motte-Fénélon would try to negotiate a French marriage for James and establish a French party to the prejudice of English interests. During his brief sojourn the envoy was able to achieve little, and English concerns over French influence in Scotland were further calmed when Lennox, having alienated the Scottish church's presbyterian leaders, was forced to flee the country in December 1582.

In June 1583 James, with the aid of James Stewart, earl of Arran, Robert Stewart, earl of March, and Patrick Adamson, archbishop of St Andrews, escaped from Ruthven Castle to St Andrews. Bowes conceded that he was taken completely unawares by the king's flight, in no small part because James had repeatedly assured the envoy of his devotion to England and the protestant cause up to the moment of his departure from Ruthven. Having received the information from Bowes on 31 July that the king's affection for Elizabeth was greatly abated, a panicked Walsingham travelled north to Berwick and proceeded with Bowes to Scotland, where they were coolly received and kept waiting until 9 September, when they were granted audience with James at Perth. The king heard their remonstrations, but was in no mood to change course, and Bowes was withdrawn from Scotland shortly after Walsingham's departure.

Final years, 1583–1597 Bowes continued to be involved in Scottish politics and was at Berwick in March 1584 trying to further the plotting of Mar, Angus, and Gowrie against Arran, but he seemed not to know how to influence James, fruitlessly believing that Mary had a strong sway over her son and could be used to help direct his policy. Bowes was MP for Cumberland in 1584, 1586, and 1589, through the patronage of Henry Scrope, ninth Baron Scrope of Bolton. Again, he was an active MP. His diplomatic activity became mundane following James's assumption of personal power, and his long royal service brought him little reward.

On 18 January 1596 Bowes wrote from Edinburgh to his nephew, Sir William Bowes, stating that he was suffering much from ill health and from the broken state of his affairs. He was indebted heavily to the crown and became increasingly inactive. On 15 November 1597 he died at Berwick and was buried there on the following day.

C. A. McGladdery

Sources K. M. Brown, 'The price of friendship: the "well affected" and English economic clientage in Scotland before 1603', *Scotland and England, 1286–1815*, ed. R. A. Mason (1987), 139–62 • *CSP for.*, 1569–89 • G. R. Hewitt, *Scotland under Morton, 1572–80* (1982) • HoP, *Commons, 1558–1603* • R. Lockyer, *James VI and I* (1998) • N. Mears, 'The "personal rule" of Elizabeth I: marriage, succession and Catholic conspiracy, *c*.1578–*c*.1582', PhD diss., U. St Andr., 1999 • C. Read, *Mr Secretary Walsingham and the policy of Queen Elizabeth*, 3 vols. (1925) • C. Sharp, ed., *Memorials of the rebellion of 1569* (1840); repr. with foreword by R. Wood as *The rising in the north: the 1569 rebellion* (1975) • *The correspondence of Robert Bowes, of Aske, esquire, the ambassador of Queen Elizabeth in the court of Scotland*, ed. [J. Stevenson], SurtS, 14 (1842) • Venn, *Alum. Cant.* • *CSP dom.*, 1566–77, 91, 93, 110

Archives Berkeley Castle, Gloucestershire, muniments, letters to G. Carey and H. Carey • BL, letters to Sir G. Bowes, Add. MS 34208 • BL, Cotton MSS, diplomatic corresp. • BL, Harley MSS, diplomatic corresp. • NRA Scotland, priv. coll., letter-books to Sir F. Walsingham and corresp. with Sir G. Bowes • NYPL, letters to Walsingham, Burleigh, Queen Elizabeth

Bowes, Robert (1835–1919), bookseller and publisher, was born at Stewarton, Ayrshire, on 22 August 1835, the third son of Robert Bowes, gardener, of that town, and his wife, Margaret, daughter of Duncan Macmillan (1770–1823). In July 1846 he joined his uncles Daniel *Macmillan and Alexander *Macmillan [*see under* Macmillan family] in their bookselling and publishing business at Cambridge; and a decade later he was to share with members of the university in the founding of the Cambridge Working Men's College.

In 1858 Bowes was placed in charge of the new London branch of Macmillans, in Henrietta Street, Covent Garden. There he remained until 1863, when the whole of the publishing business was transferred to London under the direction of Alexander Macmillan, and Bowes moved back to take charge of the Cambridge bookshop. On 15 April 1868 Bowes married Fanny, youngest daughter of a grocer, Augustine Gutteridge Brimley, alderman and once mayor of Cambridge; they had one son, who was to succeed him as head of the business, and two daughters. Alexander Macmillan died in 1896, and in 1899 Robert Bowes entered into partnership with his own son, George Brimley Bowes; in 1907 the business became Bowes and Bowes, the style it retained until after its sale to the firm of W. H. Smith in 1953.

Among the authors whose acquaintance Bowes made in his youth was Tennyson, and he became well informed on the revisions made in successive editions of the poems. His wife's brother, George Brimley, was librarian of Trinity College in 1845–57, and Bowes's own annotated collection of Tennyson is now in Trinity College Library. He was instrumental in the fate of the manuscript of *Poems by Two Brothers* after it had been sold at auction in 1892 and passed to a New York bookseller. In an early instance of heritage rescue, a body of subscribers recovered it and presented it to Trinity College. In 1893 Macmillan & Co. published a new edition of the volume.

Bowes took a prominent part in Cambridge civil life. He was a town councillor for nine years, an officer in the volunteers, a governor of the Perse School and of the Old Schools, and twice chairman of the free library committee, as well as an officer of the Local Lectures Association. From 1894 to 1910 he served as treasurer of the Cambridge Antiquarian Society, and in 1870 he joined F. D. Maurice, Henry Sidgwick, and others to promote the higher education of women: Newnham College was founded in 1875 partly as a result.

Like the Macmillans, Bowes combined bookselling with publishing, his publications including J. K. Stephen's *Lapsus Calami* (1891) and John Willis Clark's much reprinted *Concise Guide to Cambridge* (1898), as well as his edition of Loggan's *Cantabrigia illustrata* (1905). But his most enduring work was in the field of Cambridge bibliography, in which he was encouraged by Henry Bradshaw and Francis Jenkinson. His investigations into the first Cambridge printer, John Siberch, led to *Biographical Notes on the University Printers in Cambridge* (Cambridge Antiquarian Society *Communications*, 1886), originally a paper read before the Cambridge Antiquarian Society in 1884, a pioneering study based on original sources. This was followed in 1894 by a monumental and still unsuperseded *Catalogue of books printed at or relating to the university, town and country of Cambridge from 1521 to 1893*, in which he combined a bibliographical record of early Cambridge printing (contributed by Francis Jenkinson) with an astonishing array of pertinent books offered for sale, beginning with a copy of Galen's *De temperamentis* printed by Siberch in 1521. In

1906 he collaborated with George John Gray on a monograph, *John Siberch: Biographical Notes, 1886–1905*, and between 1881 and 1896 he published a series of facsimiles of Siberch's works.

In 1918 the university conferred on Bowes an honorary degree of MA. He died at his home, 13 Park Terrace, Cambridge, on 9 February 1919, and his funeral was at St Edward's Church three days later.

David McKitterick

Sources G. J. Gray, 'Memoir', *Cambridge Chronicle* (20 March 1918) · *Cambridge Chronicle* (12 Feb 1919) · C. Morgan, *The house of Macmillan* (1943) · C. L. Graves, *Life and letters of Alexander Macmillan* (1910) · *N&Q*, 8th ser., 3 (3 June 1893) · *N&Q*, 8th ser., 4 (9 Sept 1893) · *DNB* · m. cert.

Archives W. H. Smith archive, Didcot, Bowes and Bowes MSS | BL, Macmillan papers, 54786–56035

Likenesses group portrait, photograph, 1882 (Library Association conference, Cambridge), CUL; repro. in D. McKitterick, *Cambridge University Library: a history: the eighteenth and nineteenth centuries* (1986), fig. 28

Wealth at death £16,582 7s. 2d.: probate, 14 April 1919, *CGPLA Eng. & Wales*

Bowes, Thomas (*fl.* 1579–1589), translator, was educated at Clare College, Cambridge, where he graduated BA in 1579–80 and MA in 1583. Bowes translated the first two volumes of Pierre de la Primaudaye's *Academie Françoise* (1577 and 1583): the first volume, dedicated to Master John Barne, was issued in 1586; the second, printed in 1594 (entered in the Stationers' register in 1589), is dedicated to Sir John Puckering. The contents of the books are accurately summarized by their full titles: *The French academie, wherin is discoursed the institution of maners, and whatsoever els concerneth the good and happie life of all estates and callings, by preceptes of doctrine, and examples of the lives of ancient sages and famous men* and *The second part of the French academie, wherein, as it were by a naturall historie of the bodie and soule of man, the creation, matter, composition, forme, nature, profite and use of all the partes of the frame of man are handled, with the naturall causes of all affections, vertues and vices, and chiefly the nature, powers, workes and immortalitie of the soule*. While the second volume is almost exclusively concerned with the powers and nature of the body and the soul, the first deals with a much wider range of subjects. It contains discussions of the vices and virtues; counsel and counsellors; forms of government; the education of princes and children; death; and various facets of duty, including one's duties to God, to one's community, fellows, and family, as well as the specific duties of princes, magistrates, and soldiers. This moral and philosophical encyclopaedia, written as a dialogue, is a storehouse of exempla, quotations, proverbs, and maxims. Both volumes went through several editions. The *Academie* was pilfered by many subsequent readers and writers, such as Robert Greene and the author of *Boke his Surfeyt*, as cited by Jane Anger (Magnusson, 311–14). Bowes was a devout puritan and condemned literature as dangerous and evil: he denounced plays, mummings, and masks (1.202), and the press is generally rebuked for printing 'lewde and wanton bookes … Termed Stage-playes and Theaters … [and] the Legend of lies, Huon of Burdeaux, King Arthur, with the rest of that rabble' because they are 'the soveraigne place of Satan', responsible for 'the upholding of Atheisme' and possessing 'the force to mainteine Popery in the dayes of ignorance' (vol. 2, 'Epist. to reader'). The date and circumstances of Bowes's death are unknown; it is possible that he was the Thomas Bowes, gentleman, of East Bergholt, Suffolk, whose will was proved in 1598.

Joyce Boro

Sources *The French academie: fully discoursed and finished in foure bookes. 1. Institution of manners and callings of all estates. 2. Concerning the soule and body of man. 3. A notable description of the whole world, &c. 4. Christian philosophie, instruction the true and onely meanes to eternall life. This fourth part never before published in English. All written by the first author, Peter de la Primaudaye, esquire, lord of Barre, chauncellour, and steward of the French kings house*, trans. T. Bowes (1618) · J. Venn, ed., *Grace book Δ* (1910) · Venn, *Alum. Cant.*, 1/1 · A. L. Magnusson, '*Jane Anger her protection, Boke his surfeit*, and the French Académie', *N&Q*, 234 (1989), 311–14 · H. C. Hart, 'Robert Greene's prose works', *N&Q*, 10th ser., 4 (1905), 1–5; 5 (1906), 202–4, 343–4, 424–5, 442–5, 463–5 · J. Parr, 'Robert Greene and his classmates at Cambridge', *Proceedings of the Modern Language Association of America*, 77 (1962), 536–43 · N. Sanders, 'Robert Greene's way with a source', *N&Q*, 212 (1967), 89–91 · G. Aggeler, '"Sparkes of holy things": neostoicism and the English protestant conscience', *Renaissance and Reformation / Renaissance et Reforme*, 14 (1990), 223–40 · J. P. Collier, *The poetical decameron, or, Ten conversations on English poets and poetry, particularly of the reigns of Elizabeth I and James I* (1820), vol. 2 · A. Lake Prescott, 'Pierre de la Primaudaye's *French academy*: growing encyclopaedic', *The Renaissance computer: knowledge technology in the first age of print*, ed. N. Rhodes and J. Sawday (2000), 157–69 · J.-P. Lobies, 'La Primaudaye, Pierre de', *Dictionnaire de biographie française* (1999), vol. 112 · will, PRO, PROB 11/92, sig. 99

Bowes, Sir William (*c.*1389–1465), soldier, was the son of Sir Robert Bowes (*d.* in or before 1410), of Streatlam, co. Durham, and was said to be of full age in 1410. John Leland, writing about 1540, recorded what had by then seemingly become established in family lore: that Bowes served in France for seventeen years under John, duke of Bedford, whose chamberlain he became, and grew so rich that on his return he was able to rebuild his manor house at Streatlam. Further tradition asserts that it was the loss of his wife, Jane, daughter of Ralph, Lord Greystoke, in the first year of his marriage, that prompted him to serve in the wars, and that he was captain of Château Gaillard in Normandy. Evidence in support of these particulars is scant. In 1413 the name of Bowes's wife was recorded as Elizabeth, and there is no known record of his having either been captain of Château Gaillard or associated with Bedford. Following the latter's death in 1435, Bowes's name was not included in the list of the duke's commanders and retainers in France. The issue is further confused by the existence of others of the same or very similar name, including Sir William's own son.

Bowes is not listed in the roll of arms of those present at the battle of Agincourt in 1415. He may have been identical with the William Bowes who mustered in the retinue of the earl of Northumberland, to accompany the latter to France in 1417. And by March 1418 he was certainly in France, acting on behalf of the duke of Clarence at the surrender of the castle of Courtonne, and in September was empowered to receive all brigands and others wishing to perform homage to Henry V in Normandy; he was probably knighted in that year. He joined the spring campaign of 1420 as a captain, departing from Southampton and arriving at Harfleur in May. There is some evidence that Bowes did profit from his part in the wars. Although he was himself a prisoner in France in November 1422, in the following March his prisoner Philippe de Monstreuil was given a safe conduct to travel to France, presumably to arrange for a ransom. And in 1427 a like safe conduct was issued for another prisoner, Thomas Syras, enabling him to go to Scotland, there to raise his ransom due to Bowes.

By the mid-1420s Bowes was back in England, where he played a minor part in the affairs of the north. On 5 April 1424 he and two other commissioners received at Melrose the oath of James I, king of Scots, to observe the conditions of his recent release from English captivity. In 1426 he was licensed to make a pilgrimage to the Holy Land, and may well have completed the journey, as he was certainly abroad in June of that year. In 1434 he was reportedly at odds with the vicar of Gainford, a few miles east of Streatlam; this did not prevent Bishop Langley's appointing him sheriff of Durham in 1436. From this point it becomes impossible to be certain whether all references to William Bowes are to him, or to his son, or to others of the same name. A William Bowes mustered in the retinue of Henry Bourchier, count of Eu, in March 1441, and in 1448 either the same man or a namesake received protection, as he was going to France in the company of Sir Richard Vernon. The Sir William Bowes who fought at Ludford Bridge in 1459, who held Alnwick for Edward IV in 1461, and who received a border commission in 1464, may have been the son of the warrior of forty years earlier. But it was presumably the father whose inquisition post mortem records him as having died before 11 October 1465.

RICHARD K. ROSE

Sources exchequer, king's remembrancer, accounts various, PRO, E 101/51/2; E 101/53/33 · T. D. Hardy, ed., *Rotuli Normanniae*, RC (1835) · *Report of the Deputy Keeper of the Public Records*, 41 (1880) · *Report of the Deputy Keeper of the Public Records*, 48 (1887) · *CEPR letters*, 6.344; 8.134 · *Chancery records* · *The register of Thomas Langley, bishop of Durham, 1406–1437*, ed. R. L. Storey, 6 vols., SurtS, 164, 166, 169–70, 177, 182 (1956–70) · *The itinerary of John Leland in or about the years 1535–1543*, ed. L. Toulmin Smith, 11 pts in 5 vols. (1906–10), pts 2, 9 · R. Surtees, *The history and antiquities of the county palatine of Durham*, 4 (1840), 101–2, 107

Bowet, Henry (*d.* 1423), archbishop of York, was apparently a member of a Cumbrian gentry family who rose to local prominence in the second half of the fourteenth century, making two advantageous marriages (in which Bowet himself had a hand) and producing an MP for Cumberland. His mother was buried at Tupholme in Lincolnshire, but most of his known connections were with the area round Penrith, where kinsmen lived, the family owned land, his father was buried, and many of his servants and officials originated. His educational career suggests that he was born before the mid-1340s. He had probably received a licentiate in laws from Cambridge University by 1368, and his doctorate in canon and civil law from Bologna in 1382. A royal clerk by 1372, and an official of the bishop of Ely in the mid-1370s, by about 1380 he had entered the service of Henry Despenser, the warlike bishop of Norwich, for whom he probably negotiated papal authorization for the Flemish crusade of 1383. As commissary-general to the bishop, he organized the recruitment and finances of the crusade, a role that led to his commitment to the Tower of London when it ended in military fiasco amid charges of corruption. Brought before parliament, Bowet cleared Despenser of the charge of receiving bribes from the French, at the risk of inculpating himself. He was rewarded with his first major preferment, to the deanery of Dublin.

Between 1384 and 1392 Bowet served as royal proctor at the papal court. His courage in remaining with the pope after riots at Lucera in 1385, in which another Englishman was killed, earned him appointment as auditor of causes at the papal court; and his good standing with both the pope and Richard II led to his employment as ambassador between Rome and Westminster on several occasions. In 1387, during Richard II's struggle with the appellants, he acted as his agent in negotiations with pope and emperor which, though ostensibly directed against schismatics, may have been designed to secure aid against the king's domestic enemies. Nothing came of this scheme, but it earned Bowet the enmity of the appellants, who excluded him from the pardon issued at the end of the Merciless Parliament in 1388. He was stripped of his deanery of Dublin and of the archdeaconry of Lincoln granted him by the king in 1386. After Richard II's resumption of the reins of government in 1389 Bowet recovered his preferments and was reappointed proctor at the papal court in 1390. But early in 1392 he left Rome for the last time and returned to England to enter the service of John of Gaunt, duke of Lancaster. In 1393 he was appointed to negotiate with the king of Castile, and in 1394 he sailed with John of Gaunt for Gascony, where he led the negotiations to secure recognition of Gaunt as duke of Aquitaine by the Gascon estates. By July 1396 he had been appointed constable of Bordeaux, and on 19 July 1397 was made chief justice of the superior court of Aquitaine. In the same year he was sent on an embassy to Aragon to negotiate, among other matters, a marriage alliance between Isabella of Aragon and Gaunt's eldest son, Henry Bolingbroke.

In 1398, however, Henry Bolingbroke was banished from England, and Bowet followed him into exile, having first secured for him permission to appoint a proxy to receive his inheritance in the event of the death of his father, Lancaster. When Lancaster died, however, on 3 February 1399, Richard II revoked his grant, and procured Bowet's condemnation in the committee of parliament at Shrewsbury. As the counsellor and abettor of Bolingbroke, Bowet was declared a traitor, and sentenced to execution, a sentence commuted to perpetual banishment in consideration of his clergy. His archdeaconry was again taken away from him. However, after the accession of Bolingbroke as Henry IV in September 1399, Bowet became one of the new king's inner circle of counsellors. He was immediately reappointed constable of Bordeaux. His loyalty was rewarded by restoration to his old preferment at Lincoln, by prebends at London and York, by extensive grants in Aquitaine, and by his appointment in May 1400 as one of the four regents in Aquitaine. His presence there helped to quell a rebellion at Bayonne and to pacify the duchy, shaken by the Lancastrian usurpation; but as soon as quieter circumstances permitted he returned to England, in December 1400, taking care to secure papal absolution for his part in warlike acts, homicides, and mutilations. At the king's insistence he was promoted to the first important bishopric to become vacant, despite opposition from the pope and the Commons, who preferred Richard Clifford (*d.* 1421). Bowet was provided to Bath and Wells, which had been vacant for eighteen months, on 19 August 1401 and consecrated at St Paul's on 20 November.

Bowet initially made an effort to run his diocese from his house near Westminster; but the appointment of a suffragan in June 1402 showed that he was still mainly devoted to cares of state. On 27 February 1402 he became treasurer, though he held that post for only eight months. Between 1402 and 1408, however, he was continually employed by Henry IV in various capacities, and frequently in his company, retained as his personal counsellor. His name appears constantly in the proceedings of the privy council. In 1403 he led an embassy to France and accompanied the king on his Welsh expedition on his return. In 1404 he negotiated with Castile; in 1405 with Scotland. In 1403, 1404, 1406, and 1407, he was a trier of petitions. In 1404 he was one of the king's council nominated in parliament, and in 1406 he swore to observe Henry's settlement of the succession. That same year he accompanied the court to Bishop's Lynn, and was thence dispatched on an important mission to Denmark, to escort Philippa, the king's daughter, to the home of her intended husband, Erik, the heir of the famous Margaret, who had united the three Scandinavian kingdoms. His report of the young king's character and the condition of his country is full of interest. It was his last major diplomatic mission.

Bowet had scarcely returned from his Danish embassy when he was translated by papal provision to York—the archbishopric had been unoccupied for two and a half years since the execution of Richard Scrope on 8 June 1405. His appointment was a victory for the king and his servant and a defeat for the pope, who had pressed the candidature of Robert Hallum (*d.* 1417). Bowet was enthroned on 9 December 1407. With increasing age, and with important duties in the north, Bowet seems henceforth to have had less to do with the court, though, significantly, he was appointed to the council when Henry IV reasserted his control over the government in November 1411, and he was one of Henry IV's executors, and sat on a commission appointed to pay his debts. He was still often in parliament, where in 1413, 1414, 1415, and 1416 he was again trier of petitions; but he was employed on no more embassies, and his name appears less often in the proceedings of the council. In 1409 and 1410 he conducted a thorough primary visitation of his diocese and henceforth resided in the diocese for long periods. His register, though lacking documents of great public interest, is testimony to an orderly and careful administration. Bowet was on good terms with his canons, officials, and suffragans, and had no trouble with convocation after his early years. He built the great hall at Cawood and a new kitchen at Otley, and was a liberal benefactor to his cathedral. He acquired a great reputation for hospitality and sumptuous housekeeping that consumed 80 tuns of claret yearly. The inventory of his property shows him to have been possessed of very considerable wealth, much of which was distributed among his entourage. His rule contributed significantly to the stability of his province after years of turmoil.

In 1410 Bowet showed his zeal against Lollardy by acting as one of Arundel's assistants at the trial of Badby, and in 1421 he wrote a strong letter to the king against another heretic named John Tailor, or Bilton. One of his final public acts was characteristic. In 1417 the Scots profited by Henry V's absence in Normandy to invade England. Bowet, though probably already in his seventies and so infirm that he could only be carried in a litter, 'put himself in great peril' once more for the Lancastrians and accompanied the army with his clergy. His bravery, patriotism, and loyalty largely encouraged the English to victory. He died on 20 October 1423, and was buried at the east end of York Minster, in the fine tomb he had built during his lifetime. T. F. Tout, *rev.* J. J. N. Palmer

Sources PRO · *Chancery records* · *Fasti Angl., 1300–1541*, [Introduction] · [J. Raine], ed., *Testamenta Eboracensia*, 1, SurtS, 4 (1836); [J. Raine], ed., 3, SurtS, 45 (1865) · *RotP* · Rymer, *Foedera* · A. Sorelli, ed., *Il 'liber secretus iuris Caesarei' dell'università di Bologna: 1378–1420*, 1 (1938) · N. H. Nicolas, ed., *Proceedings and ordinances of the privy council of England*, 7 vols., RC, 26 (1834–7) · *The diplomatic correspondence of Richard II*, ed. E. Perroy, CS, 3rd ser., 48 (1933) · T. S. Holmes, ed., *The register of Henry Bowet, bishop of Bath and Wells*, Somerset RS, 13 (1899) · J. J. N. Palmer, 'The career of Henry Bowet, archbishop of York', BLitt diss., U. Oxf., 1964 · Emden, *Oxf.* · Emden, *Cam.*

Archives Borth. Inst., registers

Wealth at death considerable: will and inventory, Raine, ed., *Testamenta Eboracensia*, vol. 1, pp. 398–402, vol. 33, pp. 69–85

Bowhill, Sir Frederick William (1880–1960), air force officer, was born on 1 September 1880 at Morar, Gwalior, India, the son of James Henry Bowhill (1852–1923), then a captain in the 62nd foot, and his wife, Mary Noël Carter. Educated at Blackheath School and in the training ship *Worcester*, he spent sixteen years in the merchant service, which he left with a certificate as extra master square rigged. On leave from P. & O. as a Royal Naval Reserve lieutenant in 1912 he learned to fly, and gained the Royal Aero club aviator's certificate no. 397. In April 1913 he was accepted by the Admiralty as lieutenant RN in the new naval wing of the Royal Flying Corps. After flying training at the Central Flying School and on seaplanes at Eastchurch he was posted as a flying officer to HMS *Hermes*, a light cruiser with a platform over her forecastle, from which he was among the first to fly an aircraft from a ship under way.

With the outbreak of the First World War, Bowhill was placed in command of HMS *Empress*, whose three seaplanes took part in the raid on Cuxhaven on Christmas day 1914. Following a short period at the Admiralty he was promoted squadron commander and commanded the Royal Naval Air Service (RNAS) contingent in Mesopotamia, which dropped some four tons of food for Charles

Sir Frederick William Bowhill (1880–1960), by Bertram Park, 1940

Townshend's besieged force in Kut. Having been posted to command the RNAS squadron on Zanzibar in 1916 and promoted wing commander in June 1917, he commanded the RNAS working with the army in east Africa. Using French Voisin aircraft, he insisted on testing each after assembly on the basis that, if its undercarriage survived a Bowhill landing, it was safe for anyone to fly. In March 1918 he was appointed to the DSO in recognition of services in connection with military operations in east Africa.

With the formation of the Royal Air Force in 1918 Bowhill became a lieutenant-colonel, and after a brief posting in the UK he commanded the 62nd wing in the Mediterranean, where he won a bar to his DSO. He took a squadron to the Caspian Sea to support General Deniken's White Russian forces, was awarded the Russian order of St Vladimir and the Greek order of St Saveur, and on his return was appointed CMG.

Later in 1919 Bowhill received a permanent commission in the RAF as a wing commander and became second in command of the successful operations against Mohammed bin Abdullah Hassan (the so-called Mad Mullah) in Somaliland. Air action against the latter proved both quicker and cheaper than army action and therefore played a significant part in preserving the RAF's independence. This campaign resulted in Bowhill's seventh mention in dispatches. He reported to Coastal Area (forerunner of Coastal Command) in 1920, was promoted group captain in 1921, and was chief staff officer at the headquarters of Coastal Area until his posting to the Middle East area in Cairo in August 1924. There he was chief staff officer before commanding the aircraft depot at Abu Qir. He became chief staff officer in Iraq and air commodore in 1926.

In 1929 Bowhill returned to the Air Ministry as director of organization and staff duties, and in 1931, as air vice-marshal, he became air officer commanding fighting area, air defence of Great Britain. When commanding the 'Redland Fighters' in that year's air defence exercises, he found that London could not be protected successfully and began the RAF's long task of planning more effective air defence systems. On 17 December 1932 he married Dorothy (1896–1966), the daughter of R. H. Arlingham-Davies, of Crickhowell, south Wales, and the widow of wing commander Arthur Bruce Gaskell.

Bowhill was appointed to the very important position of air member for personnel in 1933. As such, he had a seat on the RAF's ruling body, the Air Council, and was in office during the critical early stages of the RAF's massive expansion. During his four years in this post the manpower of the RAF increased from 19,000 to 42,000 and the number of home-based squadrons from thirty-seven to ninety-three. He was appointed CB in 1935 and KCB in 1936, when he became air marshal.

In August 1937 Bowhill became head of Coastal Command, a post he held until 1941. He was promoted air chief marshal in 1939 and appointed GBE in 1941. Coastal Command's primary role was trade protection, reconnaissance, and co-operation with the Royal Navy, for which Bowhill, with his naval experience, was ideally suited. Always short of aircraft, he instituted 'scarecrow patrols' using Tiger Moths over the North Sea to keep U-boats submerged. An early success was when one of his aircraft located the German blockade runner *Altmark* in Josing Fjord, allowing HMS *Cossack* to rescue the British seamen on board. But his main contribution to the eventual winning of the battle of the Atlantic was in planning and developing so many of the means by which it was won in 1943: improved ASV (anti-surface-vessel) radar and depth charges, the Leigh light (an airborne anti-U-boat searchlight), operational research, aircraft camouflage, bases in Iceland and the Azores, and VLR (very long range) aircraft to close the 'Atlantic gap' among them. While he was under orders to move to Canada to set up Ferry Command in May 1941, the German battleship *Bismarck* broke out into the Atlantic, and the Home Fleet lost track of the ship's whereabouts. Bowhill, for purely instinctive sea reasons, suggested that she would first make for Cape Finisterre rather than direct for Brest. He shifted the search by Catalina flying boats south, and as a result *Bismarck* was located and sunk.

Ferry Command was set up as a result of lease-lend when the US government allowed their military pilots to deliver aircraft direct to Montreal, but only to another military organization. Bowhill had the delicate task of taking over from the existing dedicated voluntary group of Canadian businessmen and creating a paramilitary organization. This he did with diplomacy and sheer sincerity, making good friends with all concerned. He and his wife, then a WAAF squadron officer in charge of his cipher office, where she saluted her commanding officer punctiliously, became very popular hosts and highly regarded in Montreal. It was Bowhill himself who proposed the successful but radical solution to the shortage of delivery crews by using the best of the young men trained in Canada and the USA to fly the aircraft over the Atlantic.

In 1943 Bowhill became air officer commanding-in-chief of the new transport command, which included the ferry organization. He and his staff formed the new groups and squadrons needed for the D-day invasion of Europe. He retired in 1945, four years after the normal retirement age.

After the war Bowhill served as chief aeronautical adviser to the Ministry of Civil Aviation until 1957 and was British member on the provisional council of the International Civil Aviation Organization. He was a younger brother of Trinity House and was elected master of the Master Mariners' Company. He received a number of other foreign decorations and was a commander of the American Legion of Merit.

Called 'one of the most colourful personalities of his day', Bowhill possessed 'the capacity to command respect and obedience but without apparent effort he inspired the confidence of his men and won their lasting affection and admiration' (*The Times*). He was spare and compact of figure, with a weather-beaten face and hair which earned him the affectionate nickname Ginge or Ginger. His tremendous beetling eyebrows gave him a rather ferocious appearance, but behind this façade he was kindly and had a keen sense of humour. He died suddenly at Flat 150 Rivermead Court, London, his home by the Thames, on 12 March 1960. ALAN SMITH

Sources *DNB* • Ministry of Defence, RAF records • A. Smith, 'From sail to wing: the career of Air Chief Marshal Sir Frederick Bowhill', 25 (1994), 1–17 • *The Times* (14 March 1960) • *Montreal Star* (14 March 1960) • M. Dean, *The Royal Air Force in two world wars* (1979) • D. Richards and H. Saunders, *Royal Air Force, 1939–1945*, 3 vols. (1953–4) • *A short history of the RAF*, 2nd edn (1936) • C. Bowyer, *RAF operations, 1918–1939* (1988) • J. Golley, *Whittle: the true story* (1987) • J. Terraine, *The right of the line: the Royal Air Force in the European War, 1939–1945* (1985) • C. J. M. Goulter, *A forgotten offensive: Royal Air Force coastal command's anti-shipping campaign, 1940–1945* (1995)
Archives FILM BFI NFTVA, documentary footage • IWM FVA, actuality footage • IWM FVA, documentary footage
Likenesses B. Park, photograph, 1940, NPG [*see illus.*] • Portner, oils, *c*.1941, Royal Air Force Museum, Hendon • Portner, oils, *c*.1941, Honourable Company of Master Mariners, London • O. Birley, portrait • H. Coster, photographs, NPG • T. Gilfillan, oils, Royal Aero Club; on loan to Royal Air Force Museum, Hendon • J. Hughes-Hallett, portrait (after T. Gilfillan); on loan to Royal Air Force Museum, Hendon • R. Jack, portrait • W. Rothenstein, drawing, repro. in W. Rothenstein and others, *Men of the RAF* (1942) • photographs, Royal Air Force Museum, Hendon • photographs, IWM
Wealth at death £7817 8*s*. 8*d*.: probate, 2 May 1960, *CGPLA Eng. & Wales*

Bowie, James (*c*.1789–1869), gardener and botanist, was born in London, son of an Oxford Street seedsman. From 1810 he was employed at the Royal Botanic Gardens, Kew. In 1814 he was chosen by Sir Joseph Banks, with Allan Cunningham, to collect plants for Kew, and set sail for Brazil with the promise that he would enjoy 'the afternoon of life … in ease, comfort, and respectability' (Banks to Bowie, 18 Sept 1815, RBG Kew, 'Kew collectors'). He was ordered two years later to South Africa, where he arrived from Rio de Janeiro in November 1816. He explored the Cape, travelling by 1821 as far east as the Great Fish River. In 1823, however, he was recalled home and dismissed. In part this was due to 'liberal tory' fiscal retrenchment, which in 1822 halved the sum which parliament had annually voted since 1814 for Kew's botanical collectors, but Bowie was also thought to have been dilatory in crown service. He certainly gave false locations for plants, perhaps to ensure that, when his poorly paid and dangerous post finished, his services would remain valuable. He returned permanently to the Cape in 1827, writing that it offered a quality of life 'which did not often fall to the lot of the working classes in Europe' ('Relative merits of the Cape, America and Australia for emigration', *Gardener's Magazine*, 7, 1831, 490–96).

Bowie wrote the earliest guide to the Cape flora printed in South Africa (1829), and his botanical knowledge was famous: he was thought able to identify any plant presented to him, giving its local and Latin names, history, and uses. He advised on gardens, notably Baron Ludwig's botanical collection, and hunted plants with such success that W. H. Harvey considered him to have enriched Europe's gardens with more succulents than any other individual. His feats were honoured in the genera *Bowiea*, named by Harvey, and *Bowiesia*, named by R. K. Greville, but he enjoyed few more tangible rewards, growing old in poverty, an alcoholic dependent on charity. He died at Claremont, outside Cape Town, Cape Colony, on 2 July 1869. RICHARD DRAYTON

Sources *Cape Standard* (6 July 1869) • M. Gunn and L. E. Codd, *Botanical exploration of southern Africa* (1981) • G. F. Smith and A. E. van Wyk, 'Biographical notes on James Bowie and the discovery of *Aloe Bowiea*', *Taxon*, 38 (1989), 557–68 • RBG Kew, 'African letters, 1830–44' • RBG Kew, 'Kew collectors', J. Bowie, A. Cunningham • P. Mac Owan, 'Personalia of botanical collections at the Cape', *Transactions of the South African Philosophical Society*, 4 (1887), xxx–liii • J. Bowie, 'Sketches of the botany of South Africa', *South African Quarterly Journal*, 1 (1829), 27–36 • J. Hutchinson, *A botanist in Southern Africa* (1946) • P. M. Ffolliott, 'Bowie, James', *DSAB* • 'James Bowie', *Gardeners' Chronicle*, new ser., 16 (1881), 568–70 [source on which *DNB* article was based; contains many errors]
Archives Botanical Research Institute, Pretoria, South Africa, Navy Gunn Library • NHM, journal relating to South Africa • RBG Kew, corresp. and papers | Herts. ALS, MSS relating to William Wilshere's garden • Royal Scottish Museum, Edinburgh, William Jardine corresp.

Bowie, James Alexander (1888–1949), economist and educationist, was born at 42 Holburn Road, Aberdeen, on 30 November 1888, the fourth son of William Bowie, a foreman mason, and his wife, Jane Lumsden, who also had four daughters. He attended Central School, Aberdeen, as a pupil teacher and passed first in the king's scholarship for teachers in 1908. He subsequently read philosophy and economic science at Aberdeen University, where he won the Hutton prize for the best student in philosophy, and graduated MA in 1914 with double honours and later DLitt. During the war he rose from gunner to the rank of lieutenant in the Royal Artillery, and saw service in Egypt, Palestine, Greece, and Bulgaria. Two of his elder brothers,

Albert Campbell and John Lumsden Bowie, were killed in France.

In 1919 Bowie joined the staff of the department of industrial administration, Manchester College of Technology, and became its director in 1926. On 26 July 1922 he married Rosa (*b*. 1900/01), daughter of William Henry Tatham of Manchester. In 1931 he was invited by the University of Pennsylvania to deliver a series of lectures there, and later that same year was appointed director of the newly created Dundee School of Economics and Commerce. The school owed its origin to the generous donation of George Bonar, a prominent Dundee industrialist, for the purpose of setting up a school of commerce in Dundee either independent of, or as a faculty of, the University of St Andrews. Bowie was director of the school (apart from when it was closed during the Second World War) until his death.

Bowie was well respected, and was appointed director on the recommendation of Josiah Stamp, who delivered the school's inaugural address, which was also attended by William Beveridge. Three works in particular had established Bowie's reputation prior to his appointment. These were *Sharing Profits with Employees* (1922), *Education for Business Management* (1930), and *Rationalisation* (1930). These works addressed the severe economic problems faced by Britain after the First World War, with respect to both labour relations and the industrial structure. Bowie was much concerned with the antagonism between capital and labour, and called for schemes that would result in co-partnership in industry, where labour had equity stake and shared organizational responsibility. His views were radical and progressive, but he was against violent change, much as he recognized the rights of labour for a greater degree of control—there can be little doubt that the experience of the war and its aftermath played a large part in his attitudes. Additional factors that influenced him were the increasing scale of firms and conglomerates, and the divorce of ownership from control, which implied that the traditional *laissez-faire* doctrine was no longer appropriate as an unquestioned policy guide. Rather, 'rationalization' and 'planning' were advocated, both in production and marketing, and involvement by the state was desirable to encourage change and to protect the community against exploitation.

The new industrial structure that Bowie envisaged would require a well-trained management profession, and it was hoped that the Dundee school would play its part in such professionalization. This goal was clearly enunciated in Stamp's inaugural lecture, and reflected a not uncommon aspiration of the time. Bowie seemed well suited to the task, but the requirement for university status (as expressed by George Bonar and also in broad accordance with Bowie's own views), together with the insurmountable difficulties of incorporation with St Andrews, rapidly led to the school's offering external London University degrees. The connections with the London School of Economics caused recruitment of lecturers to be much influenced by that institution, and the nature of the London syllabus was such that any distinctive course structure was rapidly subordinated. The school became regarded as a mini London School of Economics in Dundee. As a result, Bowie's involvement with the actual teaching in the school became minimal, and instead he threw himself into public relations on behalf of the school and promulgated his views, via newspaper articles, speeches, and the like, on the need for the encouragement of business education and progressive change in industrial organization and labour relations.

Bowie's belief in the importance of economic planning is emphasized in his last major work, *The Future of Scotland* (1939), which specifically addressed problems in regional economics. A Scottish development commission and related state-sponsored institutions, new towns, relocation of industry, rationalization of old industries, and encouragement of new are all trenchantly discussed. Bowie argued for greater Scottish autonomy, but fell short of recommending a separate Scottish parliament in the 'near future' though he did not rule it out for the longer term. These policy goals were reiterated after the war in more popular venues.

Bowie died on 1 September 1949 in Dundee, and was cremated in the city; he was survived by his widow and their daughter and son. With his death support for the school dwindled, and in 1955 it was finally absorbed by Queen's College of St Andrews in Dundee. Though his educational goals did not flourish in Dundee's unfavourable environment, many of them came to fruition in the late twentieth century. On a general level business management courses are now commonplace and the regions are obtaining greater power, and at a specific level road bridges have been built across the Forth and Tay estuaries, as Bowie recommended. J. M. ALEC GEE

Sources University of Dundee Archives, MS 33 · D. Southgate, *University education in Dundee: a centenary history* (1982) · C. Blake and S. G. E. Lythe, eds., *A maverick institution: Dundee School of Economics, 50th anniversary commemorative essays* (1981) · *Aberdeen University Review*, 33 (1949–50), 365–6 · *The Courier* (3 Sept 1949) [Dundee] · *Scottish biographies* (1938) · *WWW* · b. cert. · private information (2004) [A. J. Bowie]

Archives University of Dundee, archives, papers, letters etc., relating to the Dundee School of Economics, MS 33

Likenesses bronze plaque, Dundee University, department of economics

Wealth at death £4109 19*s*. 0*d*.: confirmation, 1 Dec 1949, *CCI*

Bowlby, Sir Anthony Alfred, first baronet (1855–1929), surgeon, was born at Namur, Belgium, on 10 May 1855, the third son of Thomas William *Bowlby (1817–1860), who was then in Belgium acting as correspondent of *The Times*, and his wife, Frances Marion, youngest daughter of Pulteney Mein, formerly surgeon in the 73rd regiment, of Canonbie, Dumfriesshire. Anthony Bowlby was educated at Durham School and entered St Bartholomew's Hospital, London, in October 1876. He qualified MRCS in 1879 and FRCS in 1881. He was a distinguished student, winning the Jacksonian prize (1882) and the Astley Cooper prize (1886) for his work on the diseases and injuries of nerves. His

Sir Anthony Alfred Bowlby, first baronet (1855–1929), by Sir William Llewellyn, 1921

interest in this field led to the publication of a book, *Injuries and Diseases of the Nerves and their Surgical Treatment* (1889).

Bowlby won the Brackenbury scholarship in surgery in 1880, and served at St Bartholomew's as house surgeon to Luther Holden and Thomas Smith in 1881. Here also he filled in succession the offices of curator of the museum (1881–4); surgical registrar (1884–91); assistant surgeon (1891–1903); surgeon (1903–20); and consulting surgeon (1919). In addition he acted as surgeon to the Alexandra Hospital for Diseases of the Hip in Queen Square, Bloomsbury (1885–1918), and as surgeon to the Foundling Hospital. At the Royal College of Surgeons, Bowlby was admitted a member (1879) and a fellow (1881); he was a member of council (1904–20); president, in succession to Sir George Makins (1920–23); and Hunterian trustee (1925). He was Hunterian professor (1887), delivered the Bradshaw lecture (1915), and was Hunterian orator (1919). For many years Bowlby was a member of the BMA. At the annual meeting in 1891 he was secretary of the section of surgery, and in 1895 he was vice-president of the section of pathology and bacteriology. He was a member of the council in the metropolitan counties branch, and in 1922–3 he was a member of the arrangements committee at headquarters.

Although known principally as a surgeon, Bowlby was also a good pathologist. He developed an intimate knowledge of surgical pathology during his early work at St Bartholomew's, both in the museum and in the post-mortem room. In 1882 he published a textbook, *Surgical Pathology and Morbid Anatomy*, which proved immensely popular with students and reached its seventh edition in 1920. It is perhaps a testament to Bowlby's achievements in this area that he was the first surgeon to be appointed to the hospital staff through the museum. At this time it was usual for all surgical staff to have filled the post of demonstrator of anatomy. Bowlby's continued interest in pathology was shown by his successful championing (in the face of strong opposition) of the appointment of a full-time pathologist, at a time when no other London hospital had such a post.

When the Second South African War broke out in 1899 Bowlby went out as senior surgeon in charge of the Portland Hospital, stationed first at Rondebosch and later at Bloemfontein; he was mentioned in dispatches, and was invested with the CMG in 1901. He contributed to a book, *A Civilian War Hospital* (1901), in which he described the nature of the wounds and the surgical work of the war. Largely because of his experiences in South Africa, the development of the military medical services was to remain a paramount concern of his subsequent career.

In 1908 Bowlby accepted a commission as major in the newly formed Territorial Medical Service, and on the outbreak of the First World War in 1914 was called up with the First London General Hospital (Territorial Force). He served for a few days, and then offered his services to the War Office. These were accepted, and he was sent to France on 23 September 1914 as consulting surgeon to the British expeditionary force with the rank of colonel. He was appointed consulting surgeon to the Second Army (in May 1915), and was afterwards general adviser to the director-general, Army Medical Service, and finally advisory consulting surgeon to the whole of the British forces in France, with the temporary rank of major-general.

In these various positions Bowlby did excellent work. He insisted that more surgery should be done at the front and less at the base. He was instrumental in the transformation of the casualty clearing stations into well-equipped hospitals, and in ensuring that these were adequately staffed through the provision of surgical teams from the base hospitals. Immediate surgical treatment was thus provided for cases which were unlikely to have survived the longer journey to the base, and many lives were saved. These developments are examined in the *Official History of the War—Medical Services: Surgery of the War* (2 vols., 1922), which Bowlby edited with Sir W. G. MacPherson and others. Bowlby took a keen interest in the welfare of soldiers, showing particular concern to improve conditions in the trenches, and to minimize the incidence of trench foot. Although a civilian, he possessed a detailed knowledge of military medicine. He was respected for his administrative efficiency and his sound judgement. These qualities proved invaluable in ensuring harmonious relations between the civilian and military branches of the medical profession. He was five times mentioned in dispatches.

Bowlby did not resume active practice at the end of the war, but he did much good work as a member of the executive committee of the British Red Cross Society and as chairman of the Radium Institute. In 1904 he had been appointed surgeon to the household of King Edward VII, and in 1910 he was gazetted surgeon-in-ordinary to King George V. He was knighted in 1911, and created KCMG (1915), KCVO (1916), KCB (1919), and baronet (1923). In total, Bowlby published four books, co-authored two others, and contributed more than one hundred articles to various medical journals.

Bowlby was married, in 1898, to Maria Bridget (1866/7–1957), eldest daughter of Revd the Hon. Hugh Wynne Lloyd Mostyn, rector of Buckworth, Huntingdonshire, and honorary canon of Ely Cathedral. They had three sons and three daughters. Their second son was the distinguished psychoanalyst (Edward) John (Mostyn) *Bowlby (1907–1990). Bowlby died of pneumonia, after a few days' illness, at the Compton Arms Hotel while on a holiday at Stoney Cross, near Lyndhurst, Hampshire, on 7 April 1929; three days later his body was cremated at Brookwood in Surrey. He was succeeded as second baronet by his eldest son, Anthony Hugh Mostyn (1906–1993).

Bowlby was a clear thinker and a dogmatic teacher, a first-rate organizer and a fine administrator. He had a genius for friendship and was extremely popular with students. Educated in the days before the value of Lister's work was recognized in London and without any training in science, he never excelled as a modern operating surgeon, but his large experience and his absolute honesty of purpose made him valuable as a consultant.

D'A. POWER, *rev.* IAN R. WHITEHEAD

Sources W. G. Ball, *St Bartholomew's Hospital Reports*, 63 (1930), 1–17 • D'A. Power and W. R. Le Fanu, *Lives of the fellows of the Royal College of Surgeons of England, 1930–1951* (1953) • *BMJ* (20 April 1929), 747–50 • A. A. Bowlby, diary, RCS Eng. • *The Lancet* (13 April 1929), 796 • *The Times* (9 April 1929) • *The Times* (11 April 1929) • *The Times* (25 May 1929) • Z. Cope, *The Royal College of Surgeons of England: a history* (1959) • R. Cooter, *Surgery and society in peace and war: orthopaedics and the organization of modern medicine* (1993) • personal knowledge (1937) • *WWW, 1981–90* [Bowlby, (Edward) John (Mostyn)] • *CGPLA Eng. & Wales* (1929)

Archives King's Lond., Liddell Hart C., report on steel helmets • RCS Eng., letters and papers • Wellcome L., corresp. and papers incl. diary and photograph album; papers

Likenesses W. Stoneman, photograph, 1919, NPG • W. Llewellyn, oils, 1921, St Bartholomew's Hospital, London [*see illus.*] • M. Ayoub, group portrait, oils (*The council of the Royal College of Surgeons of England, 1926–7*), RCS Eng. • D. V. Jaeger, photograph, Wellcome L. • F. O. Salisbury, group portrait, oils (with George V and Queen Mary visiting the battle areas of France in 1917), Royal Exchange, London

Wealth at death £82,635 18*s.* 1*d.*: resworn probate, 15 May 1929, *CGPLA Eng. & Wales*

Bowlby, (Edward) John Mostyn (1907–1990), psychiatrist, was born on 26 February 1907 at 24 Manchester Square, London, the fourth child and second son in the family of three daughters and three sons of Major-General Sir Anthony Alfred *Bowlby, first baronet (1855–1929), surgeon, and his wife, Maria Bridget, daughter of the Revd Canon the Hon. Hugh Wynne Lloyd Mostyn, rector of Buckworth, Huntingdonshire. Bowlby was educated at the Royal Naval College, Dartmouth. He then read medicine at Trinity College, Cambridge, gaining first-class honours in part one of the natural sciences tripos (1927) and a second class in part two of the moral sciences tripos (psychology, 1932). He went on to qualify in medicine (MB, BChir, 1933) at University College Hospital, London, proceeding to MD (Cambridge, 1939). Upon qualification, he began to specialize in psychiatry by becoming a clinical assistant at the Maudsley Hospital.

(Edward) John Mostyn Bowlby (1907–1990), by Lucinda Douglas-Menzies, 1988

Bowlby was on the staff of the London Child Guidance Clinic from 1936 to 1940, and from 1940 to 1945 he served as a specialist psychiatrist in the Royal Army Medical Corps, attaining the rank of temporary lieutenant-colonel in 1944. From 1946 until his retirement in 1972 he was on the staff of the Tavistock Clinic, where he was director of the department for children and parents (1946–68). From 1962 to 1966 he was president of the International Association of Child Psychiatrists and Allied Professions. He was also consultant in mental health to the World Health Organization (WHO) from 1950 to 1972 and a part-time member of the external scientific staff of the Medical Research Council (1963–72). Bowlby was elected a fellow of the Royal College of Physicians, London (1964), and a foundation fellow of the Royal College of Psychiatrists (1971). He held several visiting chairs abroad.

In 1946 Bowlby published a study of delinquent children entitled *Forty-Four Juvenile Thieves: their Characters and Home-Life*. The work which established his reputation began with an invitation from WHO in 1950 to advise on the mental health of homeless children. This led to the publication of *Maternal Care and Mental Health* (1951). *Attachment*, the first volume of Bowlby's massive trilogy

Attachment and Loss, was published in 1969. Volume 2, *Separation: Anxiety and Anger*, followed in 1973. The trilogy was completed by the publication of *Loss: Sadness and Depression* (1980). Briefer, more popular expositions of Bowlby's views were *The Making and Breaking of Affectional Bonds* (1979) and *A Secure Base* (1988).

Bowlby was the originator of what later became known as 'attachment theory'. Having established that separation from the mother or mother-substitute in early childhood often had dire results, Bowlby set about investigating the way in which human beings establish ties of attachment with one another, and what consequences follow when these ties are severed. His conclusions were invariably backed up by objective research and extensive references. His interest led him to study ethology, and he became acquainted with, and indebted to, Konrad Lorenz, Nikolaas Tinbergen, and Robert Hinde. Bowlby's studies of attachment in other species led him to conclude that the biological roots of attachment originated in the need to protect the young from predators. His interest in biological theory led to his last book, *Charles Darwin* (1990).

Bowlby's studies of attachment had two main consequences. First, his theories prompted a large body of research, ranging from studies of attachment between infants and their mothers to the effects of bereavement and the severance of social ties in adult life. Second, his demonstration that even brief periods of separation of small children from their mothers can have serious emotional consequences led to important changes in hospital practice. It is because of Bowlby's research that it was later taken for granted that parents should be allowed free access to their sick children in hospital (and vice versa). Bowlby reinforced his case that such separations were traumatic by making a series of films with James Robertson, of which *A Two-Year-Old Goes to Hospital* (1952) is the best-known. Bowlby saved hundreds of small children from unnecessary emotional distress. Where most psychoanalysts assume that neurotic symptoms originate from the patient's inner world of fantasy, Bowlby remained firmly convinced that traumatic events in real life were more significant—not only actual separation and loss, but also parental threats of abandonment and other cruelties.

As a psychiatrist, Bowlby was a warm, caring human being who always remained entirely approachable. He was an excellent teacher and lecturer. His contributions to psychiatric knowledge and the care of children mark him as one of the three or four most important psychiatrists of the twentieth century. Underestimated by both biological scientists and psychoanalysts, his recognition was delayed. He was appointed CBE in 1972, and received honorary doctorates from Leicester (1971), Cambridge (1977), and Regensburg (1989). He was elected an honorary fellow of the Royal College of Psychiatrists (1980) and of the Royal Society of Medicine (1987). The British Paediatric Association gave him the Sir James Spence medal (1974) and he was elected a senior fellow of the British Academy in 1989.

Tall and courteous, with the manners of an old-fashioned English gentleman, Bowlby appeared reserved, but was never pompous. In 1938 he married Ursula, daughter of Dr Tom George *Longstaff, mountain explorer and president of the Alpine Club in 1947–9. They had two daughters and two sons. Bowlby died of a stroke while on holiday on the Isle of Skye, on 2 September 1990.

ANTHONY STORR, *rev.*

Sources Wellcome L., Bowlby MSS • personal knowledge (1996) • private information (1996) • *The Times* (14 Sept 1990) • *CGPLA Eng. & Wales* (1991)

Archives CUL, notes and corresp. relating to his work on Darwin • Wellcome L., corresp. and papers

Likenesses L. Douglas-Menzies, photograph, 1988, NPG [*see illus.*] • photograph, repro. in J. Holmes, *John Bowlby and attachment theory* (1993), cover

Wealth at death £88,776: probate, 5 April 1991, *CGPLA Eng. & Wales*

Bowlby, Thomas William (1817–1860), journalist, son of Thomas Bowlby, a captain in the Royal Artillery, and his wife, a daughter of General Balfour, was born at Gibraltar. When very young, Bowlby was taken by his parents to Sunderland, where his father became a timber merchant. Bowlby's education was entrusted to Dr Cowan, a Scottish schoolmaster living in Sunderland. After leaving school he trained as a solicitor under his cousin Russell Bowlby of Sunderland. On completion of his time he went to London and spent some years as a salaried clerk in the office of a large firm in the Temple. In 1846 he began practising in the City as junior partner in the firm of Lawrence, Crowdy, and Bowlby. In his early legal career, Bowlby enjoyed a fair practice, but the law proved uncongenial, and through his many literary acquaintances he felt increasingly drawn to a career in writing. Although remaining a member of the firm until 1854, he went to Berlin as special correspondent of *The Times* in 1848 to report on the continental revolutions. Bowlby married Frances Marion, daughter of Pulteney Mein and sister of his father's second wife, who inherited a considerable fortune on the death of her father. During the railway mania Bowlby got into financial difficulties, which caused him to leave England for a short time, but he made arrangements for the whole of his future earnings to be applied in liquidation of his debts. On returning to England he was associated for some time with Louis Antoine Jullien (1812–1860), the musical director and composer. He next went to Smyrna, where he was employed in connection with the construction of a railway. In 1860 he was engaged to travel to China as the special correspondent of *The Times*. Lord Elgin and Baron Gros were fellow passengers in the steamship *Malabar*, which was lost at Point de Galle on 22 May 1860; his graphic narrative of this shipwreck was considered one of his best pieces of work. His China dispatches were informative and popular with readers of *The Times*. After the capture of Tientsin (Tianjin) on 23 August 1860, Bowlby accompanied Admiral Sir James Hope and four others to Tang-chow to arrange the preliminaries of peace. They were captured and imprisoned by the Tartar general, Senggerinchin. Bowlby died on 22 September 1860 at Tang-chow, from the effects of the treatment he received in prison. His body was afterwards surrendered by the Chinese and buried in the Russian cemetery, outside the Anting (Anding) gate of Peking (Beijing), on 17 October 1860; he left a widow and five young children, among them Sir Anthony Alfred *Bowlby, first baronet.

G. C. BOASE, *rev.* JOSEPH COOHILL

Sources D. Griffiths, ed., *The encyclopedia of the British press, 1422–1992* (1992) • Boase, *Mod. Eng. biog.* • Ward, *Men of the reign* • *ILN* (29 Dec 1860), 615–16 • *Annual Register* (1860), 265–71 • [S. Morison and others], *The history of The Times*, 2 (1939), 292 • D. C. Boulger, *History of China* (1881–4), 3.499–521
Archives News Int. RO, papers

Bowle, John (*d.* **1637**), bishop of Rochester, was born in Lancashire. His father, Richard Bowle (*d.* 1626), auditor to the earl of Bedford, settled at Chesham, Buckinghamshire, where his wife, Marie, died in 1607. John was sent to Westminster School; from there he was elected head of his year to Trinity College, Cambridge, in 1593, matriculating and becoming a scholar in 1594. He graduated BA in 1598 and proceeded MA in 1601, BD in 1608, and DD in 1613, incorporating at Oxford in 1605 and 1615. He became chaplain to Lord Treasurer Salisbury, whose last illness in 1612 he attended and chronicled, and was rector of St Michael-le-Querne, London, from 1 March 1608, vacating by 2 April 1619. On 1 June 1609 he was dispensed to hold additionally the rectory of Upminster, Essex. He acquired the Berkshire rectories of Bradfield and Tilehurst in 1613, and that of Eynsford, Kent, in 1614.

From 1610 Bowle was a regular Lent preacher at court, and in 1615 and 1616 published sermons preached respectively at the funeral of Henry Grey, earl of Kent, and at the request of Sir Richard Blount. His appointment as dean of Salisbury was known by 20 March 1620; he was instituted on 28 July. That September he was a royal chaplain-in-waiting, and the following year published an address to the convocation of Canterbury. Advancement to the see of Rochester was predicted on 16 November 1629; Bowle having meanwhile successfully petitioned to retain Tilehurst, assent was given to his election on 8 January 1630 and he was consecrated on 7 February.

During Bowle's first summer as bishop he was forced by plague to vacate the episcopal seat at Bromley, retreating to Berkshire. In 1631 and 1632 he sat frequently in the court of high commission. Concerned at this time to maintain clerical control of church furnishings, he warned that provision of church seating would 'hatche a lay presbyterye' (Gardiner, 307), although his father had made just such improvements to Chesham church. Bishop Bowle promoted the erection of altar rails but he was a resolute protestant, to whom the pope was 'vicar of hell' (ibid., 227). The papal agent Panzani judged him 'puritanissimo' (Albion, 414). In October 1632 it was rumoured that Bowle would be translated to Lichfield. He preached at Archbishop Abbot's funeral at Croydon on 3 September 1633. He was prompt to commend the 1633 reissue of the Book of Sports, and suspended clergy who would not read it, but told Laud later that year that his visitation of Rochester Cathedral had been impeded by the dean and chapter on a technicality. The remaining years of his episcopate were inactive through illness, described by Laud as 'palsy' (*Works*, 5.324, 345). One Edward Parsons repeatedly abused him as 'a sot' (*CSP dom.*, *1631–3*, 460, 467).

Bowle and his wife, Bridget, sister of Sir George Coppin, had several children including Richard and Mary, and probably also George, Brigitt, and Anne, buried at Chesham within a fortnight in 1614. Bowle promoted his nephew Richard Chase to two of the richest livings in his diocese, later regretting his generosity. He died in London on 9 October 1637 and was buried in St Paul's Cathedral.

C. S. KNIGHTON

Sources *Fasti Angl., 1541–1857*, [Canterbury], 52; [Salisbury], 6 • J. W. Garrett-Pegge, *A transcript of the first volume, 1538–1636, of the parish register of Chesham, in the county of Buckingham* (1904), xi, 294, 304, 324 • *CSP dom.*, *1619–23*, 131; *1629–31*, 97, 130, 183, 368; *1631–3*, 196, 460, 467; *1634–5*, 156 • S. R. Gardiner, *Reports of cases in the courts of star chamber and high commission*, CS, 39 (1886), 184, 225–8, 241, 243, 256, 272, 307, 319–20 • F. Peck, ed., *Desiderata curiosa*, new edn, 2 vols. in 1 (1779), 205–11 • Westminster Abbey Muniments, bk 15, fols. 36–42, 44 • G. Albion, *Charles I and the court of Rome* (1935), 414 • J. Davies, *The Caroline captivity of the church: Charles I and the remoulding of Anglicanism, 1625–1641* (1992), 182, 188, 232 • *The works of the most reverend father in God, William Laud*, 5, ed. J. Bliss (1853), 324, 335, 345, 349 • W. S. Powell, *John Pory, 1572–1636* (1977), microfiche supp., 306 • V. J. Torr, 'Rochester Cathedral in 1634', *Archaeologia Cantiana*, 78 (1963), 39–54 • *Old Westminsters*, vols. 1–2 • Venn, *Alum. Cant.* • J. W. Garrett-Pegge, 'Richard Bowle's book', *Records of Buckinghamshire*, 9 (1904–9), 329–48, 393–414; 10 (1910–16), 1–18 • *DNB*
Archives CKS, episcopal register, DRb Ar/16, fols. 206–20
Wealth at death see will, PRO, PROB 11/175, sig. 132

Bowle, John (**1725–1788**), literary editor, was born on 15 October 1725 at Idmiston, near Salisbury, Wiltshire, the eldest of the four children of John Bowle (*c.*1700–1743), gentleman, and his wife, Sarah (1700–1785), daughter of the Revd Thomas Westley, rector of Brockley, Somerset. A descendant of Dr John Bowle, dean of Salisbury and bishop of Rochester, he was educated at Oriel College, Oxford, where he took his MA in 1750 and, after ordination, became vicar of Idmiston, where his family had long been established. On 7 November 1754 he married Elizabeth, daughter of John Elliott, of Winterbourne Cherburgh, Wiltshire. She died in 1759, leaving two daughters, the elder of whom died in 1769. Bowle was elected FSA in 1776.

Already in his mid-twenties Bowle was acknowledged by the Revd John Douglas, in his *Milton Vindicated from the Charge of Plagiarism* (1751), as the 'Original Detector' of the spurious evidence adduced by William Lauder. His continuing interest in English literature is seen in his publication, in 1764, of the anonymous *Troublesome Raigne of King John*, of 1591, together with various works by John Marston, as also in his contributions to Thomas Warton's *History of English Poetry* and the 1778 Johnson–Steevens edition of Shakespeare. Bowle read Richard Farmer's *Essay on the Learning of Shakespeare*, wrote to Edmund Malone about Edward Capell, praised the 'judicious editor' (Thomas Tyrwhitt) of the 1775 *Canterbury Tales*, and applied to Cervantes Warton's words on Shakespeare in his *Observations on Spenser*: 'If Cervantes is worth reading, he is worth explaining'. This conviction led him to produce the first fully annotated edition of *Don Quixote*.

Bowle received strong encouragement for this undertaking from Thomas Percy to whose *Reliques of Ancient Poetry* Bowle made contributions. Cervantes, according to Percy, was their 'favourite author'. Percy built up a substantial 'Quixotic Library', consisting largely of romances of chivalry, on which he originally proposed to draw for 'an improved Translation [of the *Quixote*] with large Notes and Illustrations: as well containing … Extracts from the old Romances by way of a Key to [Cervantes's] satire' (*Cervantine Correspondence*, 13). This aim (without the translation) became Bowle's own. He thus produced for the *Quixote*, in the same conviction as had animated Lewis Theobald in editing Shakespeare, an edition adorned with a learned apparatus of a kind hitherto generally reserved for classical texts. To this long task of the 1770s Bowle brought wide-ranging literary learning that embraced French and Italian as well as Spanish and English, his own classical education, and an untiring dedication to literary research. His library, at his death, consisted of well over 12,000 works and editions. His edition of *Don Quixote* was published at Salisbury in 1781 at the price of 3 guineas.

Bowle's 300 pages of annotations on Cervantes' text underlie all subsequent work of the kind and have brought him, with time, the highest praise in Spain. In England, in his own time, the reception of his edition brought him disappointment and pain. The auctioneers of his library offered unsold copies at half price and less. Beyond the fact that Bowle's extensive critical apparatus is entirely in Spanish, his scholarly approach to what was seen as an essentially comic masterpiece would have struck many as misconceived. This view was destructively deployed against Bowle by Giuseppe Baretti ('Joseph Baretti')—long resident in London and an associate of Samuel Johnson—in his *Tolondron: Speeches to John Bowle about his Edition of Don Quixote* (1786), where he presented Bowle as a linguistically incompetent pedant. Bowle thus paid a high price for having written disparagingly about Baretti in his *Letter to the Reverend Dr Percy* (1777) announcing his 'new and classical edition' of the *Quixote* to the world. Baretti subsequently made common cause with Captain John Cruickshank RN, whom Bowle had failed to thank in the preliminaries to his edition, even though Cruickshank had, in the mid-1770s, been a warm friend and supportive collaborator. Bowle responded to their criticism of himself and his edition in letters of 1784–5 to the *Gentleman's Magazine* and finally in his *Remarks on the extraordinary conduct of the knight of the ten stars* [Cruickshank] *and his Italian squire* [Baretti], *to the editor of 'Don Quixote': in a letter to the Rev. J. S., D. D.* [probably Joseph Simpson] (1785). It was this that unleashed Baretti's *Tolondron*.

One who had known Bowle since 1760—perhaps the Revd J. Baverstock—commented, in an unsigned note, after the death of 'my old friend' that Bowle's 'great error both as an editor and a Critic, was too fond an acquiescence in his first thoughts and a stubborn unyielding temper that would not allow him to submit to the slightest Retractation'. On the other hand, 'it may be truly asserted that Baretti's Tolondron was the efficient cause of the Death of poor John Bowle' (Bodl. Oxf., MS Eng. misc. d. 244, fol. 108). His final years were further saddened by the death of his young son-in-law, who left Bowle's daughter with two small children. A member of the Essex Club established in 1784 to cheer Dr Johnson in his last days, Bowle himself died on 26 October 1788 at Idmiston, and is buried in the church there. R. W. Truman

Sources R. C. Hoare, *The history of modern Wiltshire*, 5 (1837) • Foster, *Alum. Oxon.* • Bodl. Oxf., MS Eng. misc. d. 244 • *Cervantine correspondence: Thomas Percy and John Bowle*, ed. D. Eisenberg (1987) • correspondence with John Crookshanks [Cruickshank], 14 July 1774–1 Jan 1777, BL, Add. MS 23143 • J. Bowle, *A letter to the Reverend Dr Percy* (1777) • M. de Cervantes, *Historia del famoso cavallero, Don Quixote de la Mancha*, ed. J. Bowle, 6 vols. in 3 (1781) • J. Bowle, *Remarks on the extraordinary conduct of the knight of the ten stars* (1785) • J. Baretti, *Tolondron: speeches to John Bowles about his edition of Don Quixote; together with some account of Spanish literature* (1786) • R. M. Cox, *The Rev. John Bowle: the genesis of Cervantean criticism* (1971) • C. Brooks, 'Thomas Percy, *Don Quixote*, and Don Bowle', *Evidence in literary scholarship*, ed. R. Wellek and A. Ribeiro (1979) • *A catalogue of the library of the Rev. John Bowle* (1790) • Bodl. Oxf., MSS Eng. lett. c. 15, 222 • *Monthly Review*, 68 (1783), 421–4 • *GM*, 1st ser., 54 (1784), 565–6 • *GM*, 1st ser., 55 (1785), 497–8, 608, 760 • *Archaeologia*, 5 (1779), 267–71 • *Archaeologia*, 6 (1782), 76–8 • *Archaeologia*, 7 (1785), 214–21 • *Archaeologia*, 8 (1787), 67–77, 147–51 • J. Douglas, *Milton vindicated from the charge of plagiarism* (1751) • Nichols, *Lit. anecdotes* • Nichols, *Illustrations* • D. Bank and T. Macdonald, eds., *British biographical index*, 2nd edn, 7 vols. (1998) • L. Baillie and P. Sieveking, eds., *British biographical archive* (1984) [microfiche] • D. Bank and A. Esposito, eds., *British biographical archive*, 2nd series (1991) [microfiche]

Archives BL, commonplace book, Add. MS 22667 • University of Cape Town, books, commonplace books, and notes | BL, corresp. with John Crookshanks [Cruikshank], Add. MS 23143 • Bodl. Oxf., corresp. with J. C. Brooke

Likenesses portrait, Oriel College, Oxford • stipple, BM, NPG; repro. in Hoare, *Modern history of south Wiltshire*

Bowler, Henry Alexander (1824–1903), painter and art administrator, was born on 30 November 1824 in Kensington, London, the son of Charles Bowler and his wife, Frances Anne. After attending private schools he studied art at James Matthews Leigh's school of painting in Newman Street, London, and the Government School of Design at Somerset House. In 1851 he was appointed headmaster of the Stourbridge School of Art in Worcestershire, but he was soon transferred to a teaching appointment in the school at Somerset House where he had received his training. On 4 August 1853 he married Ellen Archer Archer, the daughter of Thomas Archer JP, vicar of Whitchurch, Buckinghamshire; they had three sons and one daughter. In 1855 Bowler was appointed an inspector in the Department of Science and Art at South Kensington, and in 1876 he became assistant director for art there. From 1861 to 1899 he was teacher of perspective at the Royal Academy. He also held important posts in organizing the international exhibitions of 1862 and subsequent years.

From 1847 to 1871 Bowler exhibited ten pictures, mostly landscapes, at the Royal Academy, and others at the British Institution and elsewhere. His best-known work is *The Doubt: 'Can these dry bones live?'* (dated 25 August 1854, exh. RA, 1855; Tate collection). This shows a strong Pre-Raphaelite influence in its detailed technique and freshly observed naturalism. The subject, however—a young girl leaning on a gravestone contemplating the bones of a long-dead man—can be related to an older pictorial tradition, inspired by Thomas Gray's *Elegy Written in a Country Churchyard*. There are no known connections between Bowler and members of the Pre-Raphaelite Brotherhood, but he would presumably have been familiar with the works exhibited by them at the Royal Academy in the early 1850s. His response to their work is typical of a large number of painters at this time. Bowler re-exhibited *The Doubt* at the International Exhibition of 1862, but he never found a purchaser for it, and the picture was presented by a member of the family to the Tate Gallery in 1921. It subsequently established a reputation for the artist that he had never achieved in his lifetime, particularly after it was published in Robin Ironside's and John Gere's *Pre-Raphaelite Painters* (1948). Later works are in a different and less intense mode. A watercolour by him, *Luccombe Chine, Isle of Wight*, is in the Victoria and Albert Museum, and the figure of Jean Goujon, among the mosaic decorations of the south court of the museum, was executed from his design. Bowler retired from the Department of Science and Art in 1891. He died at his home, 21 Pembroke Square, Kensington, on 6 August 1903, and was buried at Kensal Green cemetery. WILLIAM VAUGHAN

Sources *DNB* • [L. Parris], ed., *The Pre-Raphaelites* (1984), 130 [exhibition catalogue, Tate Gallery, London, 7 March – 28 May 1984] • R. Ironside and J. Gere, *Pre-Raphaelite painters* (1948), 26–7 • J. Elkan, 'Bowler, Henry', *The dictionary of art*, ed. J. Turner (1996) • B. S. Long and F. W. Stokes, *Catalogue of watercolour paintings by British artists and foreigners working in Great Britain*, rev. edn (1927), 42–3 • Graves, *RA exhibitors* • Graves, *Brit. Inst.* • m. cert. • *CGPLA Eng. & Wales* (1903)

Wealth at death £7856 3s. 3*d*.: probate, 1903, *CGPLA Eng. & Wales*

Bowler, Thomas G. (1826–1893). *See under* Bowler, William (*b*. 1808).

Bowler, Thomas William (1812–1869), landscape painter and printmaker, was born in Tring, Hertfordshire, on 9 December 1812, the son of William Bowler, a labourer, and Sarah Butterfield. He worked for three years in London as a solicitor's clerk, but in 1833, on the recommendation of a local squire, Dr John Lee FRS, who had noticed his talents, he obtained a post as servant and assistant to Thomas Maclear, newly appointed astronomer royal at the Cape of Good Hope. He was employed at the Cape Town observatory from 1834 until July 1835, when he was dismissed. Until 1838 he was tutor to the children of Captain Richard Wolfe, commandant of the prison settlement on Robben Island in Table Bay. He subsequently established himself successfully in Cape Town as a landscape painter and drawing-master; he taught at the South African College (1842–66) and the Diocesan College. He was self-taught as an artist, but in 1854, on a visit to Britain, he studied under James Duffield Harding; in 1857 he published *The Students Hand-Book Intended for those Studying Art, on the System of J. D. Harding*, the first book on the subject to be produced in South Africa.

Influenced by the early works of J. M. W. Turner, Bowler painted sea-, land-, and townscapes, notably a panorama of the Cape Town district (1852); many of his works were purchased by visitors to the Cape. He published *Four Views of Cape Town* (1844); *South African Sketches* (1854), a series of ten lithographs of scenes at the Cape of Good Hope; *The African Sketch Book* (1855); and *The Kafir Wars and British Settlers in South Africa* (1865), a series of twenty views, with descriptive letterpress by W. R. Thomson. He was a committee member of the Cape Town Exhibitions of Fine Arts (1850–59) and won a gold medal at the first exhibition in 1851; he introduced the Art Union of London to the Cape (1851) and became its first secretary in 1853. He received an honourable mention at the British Institution (1857); he also exhibited a drawing of the Royal Observatory, Cape Town, at the Society of British Artists (1857) and two views of Cape scenery at the Royal Academy (1860). Many of his sketches were published as wood-engravings in the *Illustrated London News*.

In 1838 Bowler married Jane Hawthorne, with whom he had four sons and two daughters. His wife died in 1849, and on 26 February 1851 he married Maria Jolly; they had four daughters. He travelled widely in the Cape and Natal, and in 1866 and 1868 visited Mauritius, where he made a number of drawings, but the malaria he caught there weakened his health. He died of bronchitis at the Middlesex Hospital, London, on 24 October 1869. Bowler executed some 800 watercolours, a few oils, and numerous lithographs; there are examples of his work in the Africana Museum, Johannesburg, and the William Fehr collection, Cape Town. DELIA GAZE

Sources F. Bradlow, *Thomas Bowler: his life and work* (1967) • F. Bradlow and E. Bradlow, *Thomas Bowler of the Cape of Good Hope: his life and works with a catalogue of extant paintings* (1955) • G. Ogilvie, *Dictionary of South African painters and sculptors* (1988) • F. R. Bradlow, 'Thomas Bowler of the Cape of Good Hope: artist', *The Connoisseur*, 173 (1970), 162–70 • E. Bradlow and F. Bradlow, 'The English vision in South Africa', *Apollo*, 102 (1975), 262–9

Archives National Archives of South Africa, Cape Town, South Africa, Maclear Mann MSS • National Archives of South Africa, Cape Town, South Africa, MSS • NRA, priv. coll. • Supreme Court Archives, Cape of Good Hope, case no. 67 of 1867 | Bucks. RLSS, corresp. with John Fiott Lee

Likenesses J. A. Vinter, oils, 1854, priv. coll. • photograph, *c*.1863, repro. in Bradlow, *Thomas Bowler*, frontispiece

Bowler, William (*b*. 1808), hatter and feltmaker, was born on 25 January 1808 in Denton, Lancashire, and baptized there on 20 March, one of nine children of William Bowler, hatter, and his wife, Esther, *née* Citlow, who had married in Manchester Cathedral in 1798. The family descended from a long line of hatters in the Manchester area, dating back to 1331, when land was registered in the name of a Thomas Bowler. William Bowler's son **Thomas G. Bowler** (1826–1893) was baptized on 10 December 1826 at Denton, his mother, who gave her name as Nancy Bowler, being present.

Having left strike-troubled Stockport, where the hat industry was in serious crisis, William, who had married Nancy Cook on 23 December 1832, and his son Thomas made their way south to seek work at one of the hatting factories in Southwark, London. William joined John Bowler & Son, and probably took over his cousin's premises at 1 Crescent, Southwark Bridge Road in 1853, trading under the name of William Bowler.

Thomas G. Bowler, having been released from his seven-year indenture with his widowed aunt Dinah Bowler of Denton, joined the business of a French hatter established in London. He became foreman and later took over the company, which prospered under its original name, Victor Jay, and later Jay Hats, managed by consecutive generations of Bowlers. On 3 September 1848 he married Elizabeth Park, daughter of a hatter, at St Mary's Church, Lambeth, London.

The hat which subsequently became known as a bowler was conceived north of the Thames at 6 St James Street, the premises of James Lock & Co., distinguished hatters to royalty and gentry since 1667, and still trading at the same address in the twenty-first century. According to meticulously kept handwritten ledgers, 'stiff round crowned hats' were very much in demand during the late 1840s. A new, more practical hat for young and active gentlemen was required during this period, which prompted the evolution of a round hard hat, which looked smart, was protective on the hunting field, and able to stand up to the smoke and soot of nineteenth-century railway journeys.

James Lock & Co. ledgers record an order placed by the Hon. Edward Coke, son of the first earl of Leicester, dated 25 August 1849, for a shooting hat, giving specific measurements of the brim. Consequent entries of orders by young gentlemen and friends of Edward Coke suggest that he might have started a new trend. The ledger refers to each order as 'a brown Coke hat', leading to the assumption that the first bowler was not black, but made of highly stiffened brown fur felt. To this day, Lock & Co. refer to the hat as a 'Coke hat', named after the first customer who ordered it.

According to the industrial legend recorded by Frank Whitbourn in his history of James Lock & Co., published in 1971, William Bowler was summoned from south London, given Edward Coke's requirements for a new hat, and set about work in his factory at Southwark. After the prototype was delivered to Locks, Edward Coke jumped on it, testing its hardness and durability, and, pleased with the result, ordered the new style of hat for the gamekeepers on his estate. Locks' supplier's book reveals, however, that the Bowler factories never supplied Lock & Co. with felt hats. The established manufacturer was J. Ellwood & Sons of Blackfriars Road, which happened to be very close to the Bowlers in Southwark. The link between the supplier, the manufacturer, and the Bowlers, whose name became synonymous with this style of hat, may lie in the secret recipe for the stiffening of the raw material, the felt hoods, from which the hats were made.

The stiffening of the bowler hat, which is essential to its shape and silhouette, is the result of an arduous manual procedure. Shellac, a dark, treacle-like substance extracted from the secretion of an insect parasite living on trees in south-east Asia, is chipped, heated, and diluted in methylated spirit. The felt hoods are manually rolled in the mixture, with the spirit evaporating, leaving the shellac in the matted felt fibres. The recipe for felt stiffening, which Thomas G. Bowler used at his factory, is alleged to have come from a village in France. It is likely that a French migrant worker, possibly one working for Victor Jay, knew the recipe and that William and Thomas G. Bowler perfected it for the prolific production of bowler hats, thus making their immortal mark on the development of the English gentleman's dress.

In 1890 Thomas G. Bowler headed a household of eleven, residing at 14 Highbury New Park. He served as upper warden of the Worshipful Company of Feltmakers of the City of London and was due to become master when he died of jaundice during a holiday in Guernsey on 5 September 1893, aged sixty-seven. The Bowler dynasty of hat makers continued to thrive at 34 Southwark Bridge Road, and managed a work force of 600 by 1939. Disaster struck in 1940, when the factory was destroyed by two consecutive German air raids during the blitz. The business moved to Great Marlborough Street, London, and manufactured ladies' hats until 1962.

In the twentieth century the bowler hat took on many roles and became a British cultural icon. It became essential for Charlie Chaplin's satirical image, and personified the character John Steed, played by Patrick Mcgee, in the television series *The Avengers* in the 1960s, when it was a symbol not only of probity but also of swinging London. In the 1970s the hat became, on the head of John Cleese, in the television comedy series *Monty Python's Flying Circus*, a lightly satirical symbol of the British upper class. Worn by Alex (Malcolm McDowell) in Stanley Kubrick's film version of Anthony Burgess's novel *A Clockwork Orange* (published 1962, filmed 1971), it became an attribute of gang violence and brutality.

Though the exact nature of the Bowlers' connection remains elusive, with perhaps the formula for stiffening felt forming their part in its creation, the *Oxford English Dictionary* records that, at least from 1861, a low-crowned stiff felt hat had become known as a bowler.

SUSIE HOPKINS

Sources private information (2004) [John Leslie Bowler, great-great-grandson] · papers, London College of Fashion library · papers, Sci. Mus. · papers, LMA · F. M. Robinson, *The man in the bowler hat* (1993) · F. Whitbourn, *Mr Lock of St James* (1971) · *IGI* · *CGPLA Eng. & Wales* (1893) [Thomas Bowler]

Wealth at death £10,530 7*s*. 2*d*.—Thomas G. Bowler: probate, 29 Nov 1893, *CGPLA Eng. & Wales*

Bowles family (*per. c.*1690–*c.*1830), print and mapsellers, came to prominence with **Thomas** [i] **Bowles** (*d.* 1721) who was possibly the son of John Bowles, a joiner of St Lawrence Poultry, whose will was proved in 1652. A Thomas Bowles published a broadside dated 1683 and in that year Harrhman, son of Thomas Bowles and his wife, Anne, was baptized on 1 March at St Gregory by Paul's. The first certain record of the printseller was the publication in 1691 of a print of a triumphal arch, from his house on the corner of Paul's Alley next to the chapter house in St Paul's Churchyard. A plan of the house, which was leased from the bishop of London, is attached to the deeds in the Guildhall Library. It remained the principal family shop for over a century and for most of that time the Bowles were one of two dynasties dominating the flourishing London print trade. Thomas Bowles died on 5 April 1721, 'haveing left off trade and being out of business for some time before his death' (inventory, CLRO, common serjeant's book 6, box 47, fol. 57b). At that time he was described as a citizen and joiner of St Gregory by Paul's; he also owned four tenements in London House Yard and a half-share in two houses in Bloomsbury. Among his most notable publications were views of the new St Paul's Cathedral (1708), and the set of large prints of the duke of Marlborough's victories (1717) after Louis Laguerre, for which Claude Du Bosc was paid the handsome sum of £80 per plate.

This latter undertaking may, in fact, have been the initiative of **Thomas** [ii] **Bowles** (1689/90?–1767), who took over the running of the business from his father about 1714. He was first recorded in 1695 with his sister, Anne, as surviving children of Thomas Bowles. His birth is not recorded in the parish registers of St Gregory which survive up to 1687 but in its report of his death in 1767 the *London Evening-Post* gave his age as eighty-seven. This is inherently unlikely since it would have made Bowles twenty-four years old when apprenticed to his father in 1704 and it is possible that the report erred by exactly ten years. He was made free of the Joiners' Company in 1711 and about that time he married Bethia Stevens.

Although best-known for his ruthless piracy and commercial exploitation of the ideas of artists such as William Hogarth, Thomas [ii] Bowles was also an energetic and enterprising publisher in his own right. In 1720 his *Bubble Cards* and other South Sea Company satires achieved nationwide distribution. During the next decade he undertook an impressive set of sea pieces after Thomas Baston (1726) and an even more ambitious series of historical prints of the life of Charles I (1727) which George Vertue considered 'well deserves being Collected as one of the productions in the Art of Graving here, whereby, alone may be seen the improvements by encouragement this Art has obtaind in London within the space of Twenty Years' (Vertue, *Note books*, 6.191). In 1743 he and his brother John [*see below*] published prints of the paintings that decorated Vauxhall Gardens and from about that date they launched a long series of topographical views depicting the sights of London and the surrounding villages. Thomas [ii] Bowles retired from business in 1763, and on 8 April 1767 'the great printseller' (*GM*, 37, 1767, 192) died at his house in Stoke Newington leaving most of his estate to his daughter Bethia Squire and her two sons, William and Thomas. He was succeeded in the shop (now numbered 69 St Paul's Churchyard) by his nephew Carington [*see below*], as his own son, Thomas, had predeceased him. **Thomas** [iii] **Bowles** (1712?–1762), designer and engraver, is said to have been born in 1712 and was trained as an engraver, producing competent botanical plates for *Pomona, or, The Fruit-Garden Illustrated* (1729) and numerous topographical engravings, some of which were after his own design. His death on 23 December 1762 was recorded four days later in the *Public Advertiser*; his wife, Margaret, survived him.

Most of Thomas [ii] Bowles's ventures were undertaken in partnership with his younger brother **John Bowles** (1701?–1779). He was under twenty-one years old when his father, Thomas [i] Bowles, died in 1721 and is said to have been born in 1701. He was made free of the Joiners' Company by patrimony on 7 May 1723. By his father's will Thomas [ii] Bowles was obliged to pay him £500 at age twenty-one, twenty-three, or twenty-five and another £500 later. He had set up at Mercer's Hall in Cheapside by May 1725 and was still there in 1731, but had moved to the Black Horse, Cornhill, by February 1734. His first notable publication was *Several Prospects of the most Noted Publick Buildings, in and about the City of London* (1724) and maps and topographical views remained a principal speciality of the firm. Beginning with *A Catalogue of Maps, Prints, Books and Books of Maps* (1728), John Bowles issued successive printed catalogues of his stock, facilitating trade with merchants and provincial shopkeepers. By February 1753 he was in partnership with his son—presumably Carington—and the partnership persisted until Carington took over his uncle Thomas's business during 1763. John continued at the Black Horse, subsequently no. 13 Cornhill, until he died in 1779. He married Mary Carington and at his death had four surviving children, John, Carington, Mary, and Margaret. His considerable fortune was divided between his children but John's was to be paid in small allowances to avoid:

> his submitting again to be gulled preyed upon and exhausted by those Monsters in imposture cruelty and wickedness who have already drained him of an handsome ffortune and regardless of the Misery and ruin they bring upon him are ready to assail him entising with diabolic artifice and to bubble him out of any bequest I might bestow. (will, PROB 11/1056/335)

Most of John Bowles's stock of plates and prints passed after his death to Robert Wilkinson.

Carington Bowles (1724–1793), printseller, the son of John Bowles, was born on 1 April 1724. He was apprenticed to his father on 2 March 1741, was made free of the Joiners' Company on 2 March 1752, and soon became his father's partner, trading as John Bowles & Son until he took over his uncle's shop. His father left him only a token legacy 'as I have already advanced him and he is not only in a very flourishing business but possessed of a plentiful ffortune out of Trade' (will, PROB 11/1056/335). Carington's characteristic contribution to the family publishing interest was comic prints, or 'drolls'. He became the principal publisher of the designs of John Collett and later of Robert Dighton and they, with lesser designers, produced hundreds of droll prints which comment with rumbustious humour on the social preoccupations of the time. Carington Bowles died on 30 June 1793 at Kensington Gore, London, and was succeeded in business by his son **Henry Carington Bowles** (1763–*c*.1830). Henry Bowles, born on 31 August 1763, was made free of the Joiners' Company on 7 December 1784 and was in livery by 1792. He traded in partnership as Bowles and Carver until shortly before his death in 1830. TIMOTHY CLAYTON

Sources S. Tyacke, *London map-sellers, 1660–1720* (1978) • T. Clayton, *The English print, 1688–1802* (1997) • A. Griffiths, 'A checklist of catalogues of British print publishers, *c*.1750–1830', *Print Quarterly*, 1 (1984), 4–22 • I. Maxted, ed., *The London book trades, 1710–1777: index of the masters and apprentices recorded in the inland revenue* *registers at the Public Record Office* (privately printed, Exeter, 1983) · *GM*, 1st ser., 63 (1793), 581 · *London Magazine*, 31 (1762), 722 · *GM*, 1st ser., 37 (1767), 192 · Vertue, *Note books*, 6.191 · *London Evening-Post* (9–11 April 1767) · orphans inventories, CLRO, no. 3104 [John Bowles] · will, PRO, PROB 11/928/159 [Thomas [ii] Bowles] · will, PRO, PROB 11/1056/335 [John Bowles] · H. G. Fordham, *Hertfordshire maps* (1907) · D. Hodson, *County atlases of the British Isles published after 1703*, 3 vols. (1984–)

Bowles, Carington (1724–1793). *See under* Bowles family (*per. c.*1690–*c.*1830).

Bowles, Edward (*bap.* 1613, *d.* 1662), clergyman, was baptized on 8 February 1613 at Sutton, Bedfordshire, the son of Oliver Bowles (*d.* in or before 1646), clergyman, author and member of the Westminster assembly. In 1628 Bowles was admitted to St Catharine's College, Cambridge, where he studied under Richard Sibbes and Ralph Brownrigge; he graduated BA in 1633 and proceeded MA in 1636.

Bowles supported parliament in the civil war. At one point chaplain to the second earl of Manchester, from November 1642 to July 1643 he served in the parliamentary army as chaplain to Sir John Meldrum's regiment of foot. In *Plain English*, issued in early January 1643, he criticized parliament for its peace proposals to the king, which had caused divisions and defections and affected morale. Unbreakable guarantees were necessary before peace could be agreed. Religion was in great danger as 'a temporal tyranny is a great step to ecclesiastical; and especially in our Kingdom, where our religion is fenced in with positive law', while peace must provide 'a settlement of the power of the Kingdom, principally of the ships, forts and arms in the hands of them who are known friends of public safety or liberty' but he doubted whether the king would accede to all this, for bad advisers told him 'there can be no new power but what is cut out of his' (pp. 4, 12–13). Bowles urged the founding of an association of counties, based in the south and east, for the maintenance of religion and the army 'by purse and person against the opposite faction'. Although this 'hath been more fully studied by others, than my desire of practice will for the present allow me to do', he thought an association would be 'a good second string in case the Parliament should unhappily miscarry' (pp. 27–8). Bowles also wrote *A letter from a minister … to a brother … from my lord general's quarter before Reading, April 18 1643*, as Essex's artillery pounded the town. His next work, *The Mysterie of Iniquity* (1643), praised puritans and parliament as 'tenacious of just liberty and true religion' (pp. 9–10) and denounced the royalist army as staffed 'from the barren mountains of Wales, Cornwall and the north' (p. 14), that is, 'the dark corners of the land … most void of the knowledge of God … by papists, prelates, courtiers, superstitious clergy-men, dissolute gentry, and a herd of prophane ignorant people' (p. 30).

In the spring of 1644 Bowles wrote newsletters from the Scottish army at Sunderland and gave accounts to parliament of the Scottish army and the battle of Naseby. He was twice voted £100 for his services. He was paid as Sir Thomas Fairfax's chaplain from April to December 1645, writing several news reports of the western campaign of the New Model Army. By 18 January 1646, he had left for York, where he was appointed a minister, and was replaced in the army by William Dell. Bowles published *A Plain and Short Catechism*, of which the first extant edition is dated 1647, in which 'the doctrine of the Trinity can hardly be said to be expressly declared … whilst it is wholly free from the tremendous declarations of the confession of the Westminster assembly' (James, 118).

It was probably in the late 1640s that Bowles married Elizabeth (*bap.* 1619, *d.* 1662), widow of John Robinson of Deighton and daughter of Sir Thomas Hutton of Nether Poppleton; they spent most of the rest of their lives in York. Appointed by the council of state to go to Scotland on 6 February 1649, Bowles did not fulfil the commission. The following year he was one of four ministers at York Cathedral paid a total of £450 out of the proceeds of the dean and chapter lands for the nine months from 25 March 1649. In 1654 Bowles was appointed an assistant to the commissioners for the ministry in the North and West ridings of Yorkshire, and was named for the East Riding on 14 January 1658. The leading presbyterian minister at York, Bowles was a very political divine and may have acted as a link between the city fathers and the government. On 29 December 1657 he wrote to Thurloe from York 'some account of the Christmas spirit that I perceive stirring in this and other places'. One Geldart had preached that it was 'a schismatic who did not observe Christmas day' and 'unless some way is found to purge cities and considerable places of such persons and practices, they will in a short time set all on fire' (Thurloe, 711). In 1660 there was 'a convention of twenty three ministers at Bradford in January under Bowles's leadership' (Woolrych, 506).

Bowles played an important role in helping to facilitate the advance into England of the forces under General George Monck. In late 1659 Monck sent his brother-in-law Thomas Clarges to 'concert definite plans for a rising with Fairfax, Bowles, Colonel Rossiter and other leaders of the Presbyterian gentry' (Woolrych, 487). Convinced by Clarges as to the need for working with the republicans, Bowles took Monck's message to Fairfax at Nun Appleton. It has been remarked that if Fairfax 'leaned on anyone it was on the minister Edward Bowles, whose judgement in counsel and negotiation he trusted far' (ibid.). He instructed Bowles to persuade the royalist Sir Philip Monckton to stay in the background; for Fairfax 'did presently foresee that it was more fit for me to stay with Mr Bowles in York … for some of the Army that joined with him did highly cavil at some old cavaliers' (*Monckton Papers*, 30). In late December, Bowles met Fairfax's cousin Bryan Fairfax in York to hear him rehearse a message from Fairfax to Monck asking him to advance should Major-General John Lambert intervene in Yorkshire. On the day of Fairfax's final advance on the city Bowles, 'who had been menaced by a patrol of horse that if he stirred out of his house he should die', nevertheless went to Philip Monckton's house and requested him 'to send to the citizens to rise which I did' (ibid., 32). The convergence of large numbers upon the minster and two other churches hastened the peaceful surrender of York. With the city occupied by troops loyal to Fairfax, Monck crossed the Scottish border, arriving on 11 January.

During Monck's five-day stay at York, after a dinner with Lord Fairfax, he conferred with Bowles and then told Dr Price that 'Mr Bowles has pressed me very hard to stay and declare for the King, assuring me that I shall have great assistance', but denied he had made any such promise (F. Drake, *Eboracum*, 173). According to one historian:

> It is likely enough that Fairfax urged the almost universal desire for a free parliament, and perhaps he was frank about its inevitable consequence, a return to monarchy. Price's story that Bowles pressed Monck to stay in York and declare at once for the King is not incredible. (Woolrych, 499)

According to Baker, Monck 'very civilly acknowledged Mr Bowles's diligent and industrious acting in his concerns' (R. Baker, *A Chronicle of the Kings of England*, rev. edn, 1670, 594).

Bowles did not much profit from his services to the restored Stuarts. Excluded from the minster, he continued to preach at Allhallows, and lectured at St Peter's. In April 1661 the aldermen and other leading parishioners unsuccessfully petitioned the king for his appointment to the vicarage of Leeds. Richard Baxter thought Bowles 'honest and judicious', and in a letter to Clarendon refusing the bishopric of Hereford, listed him among those who should be considered for the place; Baxter also wrote that Bowles was offered but refused the deanery of York (Keeble and Nuttall, 2.14). Edmund Calamy reported that the eminent clergymen John Tillotson and Edward Stillingfleet unsuccessfully attempted to induce Bowles to conform. The story is told that Bowles's last social call before leaving London was to his old acquaintance, Monck, now the duke of Albemarle: 'My Lord I have buried the good old cause, and am now going to bury myself. I never expect to see your grace more in this world.' And he proceeded to berate Monck for having failed in his duty to help establish a godly commonwealth—'all this you have given up for a feather in your cap'—predicting the early failure of his line and the extinction of his title; the same day, 'the good man went homewards and was met at Doncaster by several of the ministers in that county' (Bradbury, appx, 33–4). Calamy gives Bowles as one of the silenced ministers, but he was buried at Allhallows Pavement in York on 22 August 1662, just before the Act of Uniformity came into force; the funeral sermon was preached by Josiah Hunter. Bowles's wife had been buried on 20 February 1662 at Allhallows Pavement and by his will, signed from the cathedral close on 29 July 1662 and proved at York on 13 October, Bowles left substantial property to his young children Samuel, Thomas, John, Jonathan, and Mary, and to Elizabeth and Anne Robinson, daughters of his late wife by her first marriage. STEPHEN WRIGHT

Sources A. Laurence, *Parliamentary army chaplains, 1642–1651*, Royal Historical Society Studies in History, 59 (1990) • *Calamy rev.* • A. Woolrych, 'Yorkshire and the Restoration', *Yorkshire Archaeological Journal*, 39/155–6 (1958), 483–507 • *The Monckton papers*, ed. E. Peacock, Miscellanies of the Philobiblon Society, 15 (1884) • Venn, *Alum. Cant.* • T. Bradbury, *Eikon basilike, a sermon preach'd the 29th of May, 1715. With an appendix* • will, PC York • E. Calamy, ed., *An abridgement of Mr. Baxter's history of his life and times, with an account of the ministers, &c., who were ejected after the Restauration of King Charles II*, 2nd edn, 2 vols. (1713) • *Calendar of the correspondence of Richard Baxter*, ed. N. H. Keeble and G. F. Nuttall, 2 vols. (1991) • Thurloe, *State papers*, vol. 6 • M. Ashley, *General Monck* (1977) • G. Davies, *The restoration of Charles II, 1658–1660* (1955) • W. A. Shaw, *A history of the English church during the civil wars and under the Commonwealth, 1640–1660*, 2 vols. (1900) • T. James, *The history of the litigation and legislation respecting presbyterian chapels and charities* (1867) • *Diary of Ralph Thoresby*, ed. J. Hunter (1830) • *The proceedings of the army under the command of Sir Thomas Fairfax: from the first of July [1645] to the sixth (1645)* • *Dugdale's visitation of Yorkshire, with additions*, ed. J. W. Clay, 1 (1899), 283

Archives BL, sermons, Add. MS 51054

Wealth at death substantial; Yorkshire and Bedfordshire landed property: will, PC York

Bowles, Edward Augustus [Gussie] **(1865–1954)**, horticulturist and watercolour painter, was born on 14 May 1865 at Myddelton House, Bull's Cross, Enfield, Middlesex, the fourth of five children of Henry Carrington Bowles Bowles (formerly Treacher; 1830–1918), a landowner and governor of the New River Company who had changed his name on inheriting from his maternal uncle, and his wife, Cornelia (1824–1911), daughter of George William Kingdom RN of Sheerness. The versatility of Cornelia's ancestor the Revd Robert Ferryman Cross (1749–1838) in both the planning of gardens and in designing gaol locks became a legend in the Bowles family. A remote Huguenot ancestor was Aimé Garnault (*d.* 1740), merchant-jeweller in Paris, naturalized as British subject in 1700: in 1724 his brother Michael Garnault acquired Myddelton House, which Bowles inherited in 1918. The Garnaults astutely acquired a large block of shares in the New River Company which Bowles's grandparents Edward Treacher (1792–1863) and Ann Bowles inherited in 1799. Bowles lived all his life at Myddelton House.

Although his elder brothers Henry Ferryman (1858–1924), a lawyer, and John Treacher (1860–1887), an army officer, were educated at Harrow School, Bowles was educated at home by a governess and then a tutor, after losing the sight in his right eye at the age of eight. In 1881 the local clergyman taught him Latin and Greek, and in 1884 he entered Jesus College, Cambridge, where he studied theology and Hebrew, intending to become an Anglican clergyman. He graduated BA in 1887. The death, from tuberculosis, of his brother John and his sister Medora (1868–1887) in 1887 put an end to his plan to take orders. Instead his grief-stricken parents encouraged him in outdoor pursuits, such as entomology, ornithology, gardening, and landscape painting. Friendship with the keen gardener and scholar Canon Henry Nicholson Ellacombe (1822–1916), who visited Myddelton House on New River Company business, developed Bowles's interest in horticulture. He often visited Ellacombe at Bicton vicarage in Gloucestershire, where he was able to consult Ellacombe's remarkable library of horticultural and botanical books. In old age Bowles gratefully remembered Ellacombe as 'the foremost both in time and ability of my teachers in garden-craft' (Stearn, 324).

At Myddelton House, Bowles began to amass a similar library for himself, to take over his father's dull garden, to

Edward Augustus Bowles (1865–1954), by unknown photographer

stock it with interesting and beautiful plants, and to construct, in 1893, a rock garden in a meadow remote from the house. The gravel subsoil and low rainfall restricted his range of plants but favoured the cultivation of crocuses, daffodils, and other bulbous plants which specially interested him. In May 1897 he became a life member of the Royal Horticultural Society, and he was made a member of its scientific committee in 1902; from then until within one month of his death he served on various committees including the scientific, library, floral B, narcissus, and tulip committees and the council. In 1916 the society awarded him its highest honour, the Victoria medal of honour.

Bowles was a profoundly religious man, and undertook the tactful relief of distress among the local poor as his father's representative. His father rebuilt the local almshouses and lent him a house for a night school where local boys learned to read and write, or do book-keeping or played games. Bowles also taught in the local Sunday school. From 1913 he became a registered lay reader and churchwarden at Forty Hill church near by. He also became a captain in the Boys' Brigade. Meanwhile Bowles's renown as a horticulturist spread among the best gardeners of the period and the interest of his garden, stocked with uncommon plants, brought many visitors to Myddelton House. Bowles needed no gainful profession. His income came from investments inherited from the Garnaults, from his great-grandfather H. C. Bowles (1763–1830), a publisher and printseller, from the Treachers as navy and tallow chandlers and soapmakers, and from New River revenue.

In December 1912 E. Hooper Pearson, editor of the *Gardener's Chronicle*, suggested to Bowles the writing of three or four books descriptive of his garden season by season. Thus originated Bowles's celebrated trilogy *My Garden in Spring* (1914; repr. 1997), *My Garden in Summer* (1914; repr. 1997), and *My Garden in Autumn and Winter* (1915; repr. 1998); the reprints lack coloured plates but contain revised botanical nomenclature. In these Bowles takes the reader around the garden, commenting on this feature and that, this plant and that, with special attention to early-flowering genera such as Crocus, Galanthus, Narcissus, Tulipa, and Anemone. Reginald Farrer wrote in 1914 that they showed 'how a gentleman can wear his garb of knowledge with a gay air and humour, dignified yet easy, and whimsical and personal' (Stearn, 366). There followed in 1924 *A Handbook of Crocus and Culchicum for Gardeners* (2nd edn, 1952) based on growing, observing, and painting crocuses, his 'first garden love' (Stearn, 367). *A Handbook of Narcissus* followed in 1934. His intended work on Anemone in collaboration with W. T. Stearn was not completed at the time of his death in 1954.

The New River flowing through the Myddelton House estate divided Bowles's garden in two. The southern half had the kitchen garden, a glasshouse, and frames, in which grew crocus seedlings. The northern part, on which stood Myddelton House, was devoted to ornamental and interesting plants and a large ornamental pond originally excavated for gravel. Nearby was the rose garden with the decorative old Enfield Market Cross and the 'lunatic asylum' devoted to plants of abnormal forms. Everywhere in spring were snowdrops and daffodils. Beds of bearded irises lined the path by the New River. All of this was Bowles's creation, marked by a characteristically charming informality. For many years he opened his garden for charitable purposes and delighted in taking parties around and discussing plants in flower.

In 1889 Bowles made his first trip abroad, to Italy, with his brother Henry and sister-in-law Dolly. In 1898 he made a longer Mediterranean journey with Dolly and a friend to Malta, Egypt, Italy, and Greece. On later summer excursions abroad, he went to the Alps in an effort to escape hay fever and in company with Reginald Farrer, the rock garden enthusiast, went to Mount Ceni and the Tyrol. From these journeys he brought back for his garden plants which required dry soil. Plants commemorating E. A. Bowles include the Greek species *Culchicum buculesianum*, the alpine hybrid *Primula* x *bowlesii*, *Vincu* 'Bowles variety' (collected at La Grave, near Grenoble), and many garden plants, among them *Crocus* and *Chrysantus* 'E. A. Bowles', 'Hebe Bowles' hybrid' *Narcissus* 'Bowles white' and *Milium effusum* 'Bowles' golden grass'. Wherever he went, he took his paintbox with him and his exquisite watercolours of flowers and a few of his landscapes are now mostly in private hands.

Bowles visited most of the great gardens in Britain and Ireland before the First World War, when they were in their heyday. A country gentleman following no gainful occupation, he combined high intellectual and artistic gifts with an ever kind and generous disposition. His wide knowledge, unostentatiously shared, his generosity, his integral wisdom, and sense of humour made him many friends, young and old, throughout his life. He died on 7 May 1954 at Myddelton House and was cremated on 11 May. His death thus broke the last links with the great amateur horticulturists of late Victorian times, with H. M. Ellacombe, C. Wolley-Dod, Ellen Willmott, H. J. Elwes, and others. It also ended the Garnault–Bowles association with the property, which had belonged to his family since 1724.

Bowles's garden deteriorated during the two world wars and never completely recovered from them. His much praised rock garden is derelict and the branch of the New River (the haunt of kingfishers and grass snakes), which ran attractively through the garden, has been filled in, its course marked by a lawn. His lasting influence is necessarily through his books and the plant varieties that bear his name. WILLIAM T. STEARN

Sources W. T. Stearn, 'E. A. Bowles (1865–1954): the man and his garden', *Journal of the Royal Horticultural Society*, 80 (1955), 317–26, 366–76 [publications listed] • B. Hewitt, *The crocus king: E. A. Bowles of Myddelton House* (1997) • M. Allan, *E. A. Bowles and his garden at Myddelton House (1865–1954)* [1973] [pubns listed, not always reliably] • b. cert. • d. cert. • Venn, *Alum. Cant.* • Walford, *County families* (1875)
Archives NHM, corresp. and papers • Royal Horticultural Society, London, MSS | Herts. ALS, letters to Lewis Watson
Likenesses photograph, Royal Horticultural Society, Lindley Library [*see illus.*] • photographs, repro. in Allan, *E. A. Bowles and his garden* • photographs, repro. in Hewitt, *Crocus king* • portrait, repro. in *Daffodil Year-Book* (1934)
Wealth at death £89,139 5s. 10d.: probate, 4 Sept 1954, *CGPLA Eng. & Wales*

Bowles, Sir George (1787–1876), army officer and courtier, was born at Heale House, Wiltshire, the second son of William Bowles of Heale House, and Dinah Frankland, daughter of Admiral Sir Thomas *Frankland, bt. William *Bowles was his elder brother. He entered the army as an ensign in the Coldstream Guards in 1804, and served in Germany under Lord Cathcart in 1805–6, at Copenhagen in 1807, in the Peninsula from 1808 to 1814, and in the south of France and Flanders from 1814 to 1818. He was present at the passage of the Douro, the battles of Talavera, Salamanca, and Vitoria, the capture of Madrid, the sieges of Ciudad Rodrigo, Badajos, Burgos, and San Sebastian, the passages of the Nive, Nivelle, and Adour, the investment of Bayonne, the battles of Quatre Bras and Waterloo, and the occupation of Paris. When a brevet major he served as military secretary to the duke of Richmond in Canada in 1818–20, and as deputy adjutant-general in the West Indies from 1820 to 1825. While with his battalion of the Coldstream Guards in Canada, as lieutenant-colonel and brevet colonel, he commanded the troops in the Lower Province during the rebellion of 1838.

Bowles retired on half pay in 1843, and took the post of comptroller of the viceregal household in Dublin under Lord Heytesbury. In 1845 he was appointed master of the queen's household, succeeding Sir Charles Murray, whom Prince Albert had considered incompetent. The household arrangements had recently been reformed, and Bowles took control of the entire domestic establishment. He was promoted major-general in 1846, lieutenant-general in 1854, and general in 1862. He was colonel of the 1st West India regiment from 1 September 1855, and on resigning his appointment in the royal household in 1851 owing to ill health was made KCB and appointed lieutenant of the Tower of London. Prince Albert commented that 'One General Wood, the Lieutenant of the Tower, with £700 a year, has been so good as to die, and Bowles is in rapture at being nominated his successor' (Martin, 2.382–3). He became GCB in 1873. Bowles died, unmarried, at 9 Berkeley Street, Berkeley Square, London, on 21 May 1876. H. M. CHICHESTER, *rev.* K. D. REYNOLDS

Sources W. A. Lindsay, *The royal household* (1898) • T. Martin, *The life of … the prince consort*, [new edn], 5 vols. (1879–80) • Royal Arch. • *Dod's Peerage* (1858) • Boase, *Mod. Eng. biog.* • Burke, *Peerage* • *Men of the time* (1875) • *CGPLA Eng. & Wales* (1876)
Archives University of Toronto, Thomas Fisher Rare Book Library, letters relating to the death of duke of Richmond in Canada
Wealth at death under £90,000: administration with will, 27 Aug 1876, *CGPLA Eng. & Wales*

Bowles, Henry Carington (1763–*c*.1830). *See under* Bowles family (*per. c*.1690–*c*.1830).

Bowles, John (1701?–1779). *See under* Bowles family (*per. c*.1690–*c*.1830).

Bowles, John (1751–1819), barrister and author, was the son of John Bowles, a printseller in Cornhill in the City of London. He is said to have received a bachelor of laws degree from the University of Douai on 25 March 1779 and to have been licensed by the same university on 11 May 1781. While he was reading for the bar he often attended the Robin Hood Debating Society in London with his friend John Taylor, where he was a well-respected speaker. Bowles later also practised as a magistrate in Surrey. He married but his wife's identity remains unknown.

Bowles wrote at least thirty-three pamphlets between 1791 and 1817, most notably and prolifically on the subject of the British wars against revolutionary France. He produced sixteen pamphlets on this conflict, including *The Real Grounds of the Present War with France* (1793), and he also wrote for the *Anti-Jacobin Review*. He was a committee member and leading pamphleteer for the Crown and Anchor Loyal Association, and from 1792 he received government secret service pay for his efforts. He was also made a commissioner of bankrupts, and in 1795 he was appointed a commissioner for the sale of Dutch prize ships. By the mid-1790s, when his writing career was at its height, he had abandoned the legal profession. Despite his various emoluments, his opinions on the war went beyond those of mainstream loyalism, which generally supported the government through thick and thin, and he urged instead a more hardline, Burkean war strategy; that is to say, he was convinced that no peace could be had until revolutionary principles were extinguished in France itself. These views drew him into friendship with men such as John Reeves, John Gifford, William Windham, and William Cobbett. His other writings dealt with such matters as the freedom or restraint of the press, morality, the education of the poor, savings banks, temperance, and the authority of the Church of England.

Bowles's fierce anti-Jacobinism was partly driven by his belief that religious and moral degeneracy were at the root of Britain's political and social troubles. By 1804, when he revised the 1801 edition of his *Reflections on the Moral and Political State of Society at the Close of the Eighteenth Century*, he explicitly declared Britain's moral danger to be greater than that posed by a French invasion. One of the circle of high-churchmen surrounding Joshua Watson and the developing 'Hackney Phalanx', Bowles was briefly, in 1802, a member of the Proclamation Society. Within a year of its foundation (also in 1802) he joined the Society for the Suppression of Vice, and until 1809 he was probably its most active executive member. He led the group within the society which supported the obtaining of evidence against, for example, traders in obscene literature, using somewhat dubious means; this policy led to the alienation of William Wilberforce and other evangelicals from the society's activities.

The controversy over the society's activities was compounded in 1809 by the scandal which surrounded Bowles and the other four Dutch prize commissioners. Allegations of fraud were brought against them in the House of Commons, as part of the anti-corruption drive of the later years of the war which centred around the accusation that the duke of York's mistress had sold army promotions. The commissioners' case was eventually decided against them in the court of exchequer in May 1819. During the ten intervening years Bowles continued to be energetic in public work, such as the foundation, in 1811, of the National Society for the Education of the Poor, but now less conspicuously. He was intensely loyal to his friends although he lost a number of them through his aggressive moralism and his disgrace after 1809. Bowles died on 30 October 1819 at Bath, and a tablet was placed in his memory in the abbey church there. He was survived by his wife. EMMA VINCENT MACLEOD

Sources E. Vincent, '"The real grounds of the present war": John Bowles and the French revolutionary wars, 1792–1802', *History*, new ser., 78 (1993), 393–420 • M. J. D. Roberts, 'The Society for the Suppression of Vice and its early critics, 1802–1812', *HJ*, 26 (1983), 159–76 • E. L. de Montluzin, *The anti-Jacobins, 1798–1800: the early contributors to the 'Anti-Jacobin Review'* (1988), 67–8 • *GM*, 1st ser., 79 (1809), 753 • *GM*, 1st ser., 89/2 (1819), 565–6 • *GM*, 1st ser., 90 (1820), 305 • J. Taylor, *Records of my life*, 2 (1832), 218–20 • E. Churton, ed., *Memoir of Joshua Watson*, 1 (1861) • *Hansard* 1 (1809), 14.291–326 • *JHC*, 64 (1809), 265–6 • E. C. Black, *The Association* (1963) • *The correspondence of Edmund Burke*, 8, ed. R. B. McDowell (1969) • J. Bowles, letters to E. Burke, 19 May 1791, 19 Sept 1792, Sheff. Arch., WWM Bk 1/2387, 2710 • PRO, Home Office MSS, 42/27, fols. 836–836*v*

Bowles, Phineas (1647–1714), naval official, was born on 3 May 1647 at Rochester, Kent, the fourth of five children of Charles Bowles (*d.* 1659) of Chatham, Kent, and his wife, Agnes (*d.* 1661), daughter of Thomas Cole. He was named after Phineas Pett, commissioner of Chatham Dockyard, with whom his family was connected by marriage. Bowles was probably educated locally, perhaps becoming a member of the household of John, first earl of Middleton (1616–1674), governor of Tangier, and accompanying him to Tangier. He possibly married Katherine (*d.* 1716) and had four children: Phineas *Bowles (*d.* 1722), Katherine, Margaret (*d.* 1750), and an unknown daughter mentioned in Margaret's will. When Middleton died in 1674 Bowles was appointed deputy treasurer and collector of revenues for the Tangier corporation. He was accused of dishonesty and inefficiency as he failed to make up his accounts; Bowles alleged in his defence that the shortage in revenue was due to 'the permissive tickets for freedom from Excise' which the mayor freely issued (E. M. G. Routh, *Tangier*, 1903, 153).

The criticisms did not harm Bowles, and in 1674 he was appointed deputy paymaster of the Tangier garrison and the victualler's agent at Tangier. In October 1675 he was appointed storekeeper to the navy at Tangier, a post he possibly owed to 'my patron Mr Pepys' (PRO, ADM 106/316, fol. 321). In November 1677 Bowles wrote to the Navy Board about his salary, which he thought should be £120 a year for himself and £30 a year for a deputy storekeeper, adding 'I have thoughts of coming for England to adjust some accounts' (PRO, ADM 106/321, fol. 542). However, he did not get to England, and, as he wrote to the Navy Board on 18 December 1678, 'this last years receipts have been extraordinary troublesome … as hath forced me to neglect other affairs incumbent on me, which hath not been a little fatal to my reputation', and he asked that a bill of £420 be paid as soon as possible (PRO, ADM 106/331, pt 1, fol. 300). In November 1679 he repeated his plea that the bill for £420 'may no longer lie protested to the ruin of my reputation and the great distress of my family whose subsistence I ordered and depended upon from that payment' (PRO, ADM 106/341, fol. 651). At the beginning of January 1680 he repeated his request to have the bill paid to help his wife: 'charity may incline you to consider the helpless condition of a lone woman with a family and four children' (PRO, ADM 106/341, fol. 653*v*).

Bowles hoped to return to England in the summer of 1680, but he was still at Tangier when, on 13 December 1680, he renewed his pleas to have his bill paid: 'I have been about 5 years in the charge of the stores … but if yet it shall be … my family's misfortune to meet with any obstruction therein, I hope justice or charity will move your honours' (PRO, ADM, 106/347, fols. 316*v*, 321*v*–322). On 18 December, Balthazar St Michel, Samuel Pepys's brother-in-law, arrived at Tangier to take over as storekeeper from Bowles. However, the decision of Arthur Herbert, the commander-in-chief in the Mediterranean, to have stores at Gibraltar and at Tangier meant that St Michel went to Gibraltar in January 1681 and Bowles acted as St Michel's deputy at Tangier, finally returning to England in April 1682.

Following the abandonment of Tangier in 1683 the navy needed a new victualling base for its small Mediterranean Fleet. The Spanish government's initial reluctance to let Gibraltar be used meant that Lisbon was chosen, and on 15 January 1684 Bowles was appointed storekeeper and muster-master there. His letters to the Navy Board show the difficulties he grappled with, partly due to shortage of money and credit; provisions were dearer than had been anticipated and he suggested it would be cheaper to send supplies from England and store them at Lisbon until the fleet needed them, though he also met with further problems with the Portuguese authorities over storing the supplies. Bowles had accepted the Lisbon post:

> in hopes of finding this a cheap place to live in (which I find … quite contrary) and that I might make advantage by way of

trade as a merchant but I find these people so jealous in the matter of their customs. (PRO, ADM 106/369, fol. 402*v*)

In the end, partly because of the problems at Lisbon and partly because the Spanish government had given their approval, the Admiralty decided in 1685 to use Gibraltar as its main victualling base in the region, and Bowles returned to England in 1686.

From 24 September to 24 December 1688 Bowles served as Dartmouth's secretary when he commanded the fleet. Dartmouth also appointed Bowles judge-advocate of the fleet from 11 October 1688 to 14 January 1689, and muster-master despite Pepys's opposition. In January 1689 Bowles travelled from Portsmouth to London 'to attend … the Prince of Orange with the state of the fleet' and to try and secure the prince's support for Dartmouth (PRO, T38/608). Bowles was discharged from Dartmouth's flagship on 14 February 1689. By 1 March he was acting as secretary to Arthur Herbert, the new first lord of the Admiralty, and was appointed secretary to the Admiralty board itself on 9 March 1689, a position he knew was due to Herbert's 'interest and favour' (PRO, ADM 2/377, p. 27; Ehrman, 292).

Bowles's appointment, for which he received a salary of £500 p.a., marked an important change in the functions of the secretary. As Bowles himself recognized, he was the Admiralty board's servant: 'I drudge day and night to give satisfaction to my Patroons, and to discharge the best I can the duty incumbent on me' (PRO, ADM 2/377, p. 28). His relationship with:

external authorities extended only to the communication and never to the initiation of business … It was in what he could not do, rather than in what he did, that he appears as the genesis of that line of permanent salaried administrators. (Ehrman, 293–4)

When Herbert was at sea Bowles kept him informed of the board's meetings, though at the same time he cultivated other members of the board, as well as being on friendly terms with both Sir Cloudesley Shovell and Sir Ralph Delavall. His letters to the captains at times border on unctuousness (Ehrman, 293).

As a political appointment, Bowles was replaced when the new Admiralty commission was issued in January 1690 and returned to Weybridge. He was a signatory on the lease of Loseley House, near Guildford, Surrey, for Herbert (now earl of Torrington). In 1693 he was one of the adventurers who set up the Corporation of Glass-makers, and in the same year he was appointed secretary to the joint admirals of the fleet, Sir Ralph Delavall, Sir Cloudesley Shovell, and Sir Henry Killigrew. Their previous secretary, Abraham Anselme, had been accused of spying for the exiled Stuart court. In 1695 Bowles was appointed assistant victualling commissioner for the English fleet at Cadiz.

In 1702 Bowles was appointed victualling agent to Sir George Rooke's fleet in the Mediterranean. The next year he petitioned the lord high admiral, Prince George, for a pension, stating his previous service, as well as pointing out that arrears were still due to him for his Tangier service and that he had 'served faithfully in several offices concerning the Fleet, without acquiring a competence for self and family'. He was granted a pension of £300 per year 'in consideration of long service', and he was also placed 'on the ordinary establishment of the Navy during pleasure' (*CSP dom.*, *1703–4*, 385, 453). In 1704 he was appointed agent for prizes under Sir Cloudesley Shovell. Bowles was buried on 14 December 1714 in the chancel of the parish church at Weybridge, which was also the place of burial of his wife and children. PETER LE FEVRE

Sources W. H. Bowles, *Records of the Bowles family* (1918) · PRO, admiralty records, navy board letters, ADM 106/321, 331, 341, 347, 369 (Misc. B, 1676–1685) · Phineas Bowles accounts, 1688–9, PRO, T 38/608 · J. Ehrman, *The navy in the war of William III, 1689–1697* (1953), 292–4 · secretary out-letters, PRO, admiralty papers, ADM 2/377, 378 · Admiralty Board Journal, PRO, admiralty papers, ADM 3/1, 2 · parish register, Weybridge, Surrey HC · lease, Loseley House, Surrey HC, Loseley MSS 353/13/1 · *CSP dom.*, *1703–4*, 385, 453 · E. B. Powley, *The naval side of King William's war* (1972) · S. R. Hornstein, *The Restoration navy and English foreign trade, 1674–1688: a study in the peacetime use of sea power* (1991) · PRO, ADM 106/316, fol. 321
Archives PRO, admiralty records, navy board letters

Bowles, Phineas (*d.* **1722**), army officer, was the only son of Phineas *Bowles (1647–1714) of the Chatham branch of the Bowles family. His father was a long-serving official at the Navy Board who briefly held the post of secretary to the navy (1689–90); little is known of his mother, Katherine, or of his three sisters. He was commissioned an ensign in the Queen Dowager's regiment, later the 2nd (Queen's Royal) regiment, on 3 October 1688, in Captain Charles Wingfield's company, and was raised to lieutenant on 21 March 1689. In May 1689 the regiment was sent as part of the expedition to raise the siege of Londonderry under the command of its colonel, Major-General Kirke. Later that year it was charged with the defence of the entrenchments at Dundalk. George Story, in his *A True and Impartial History*, relates that, in December 1689, Bowles, along with two other lieutenants from Kirke's regiment, was court-martialled and shot for killing two ship's masters. However, there must have been some misapprehension, for Bowles was promoted captain-lieutenant on 12 February 1692. By then the regiment was in Flanders, having served through the wars in Ireland until shortly after the second siege of Limerick (1691). In 1693 Bowles's regiment was part of the reserve at Landen, where it suffered slight losses, and in 1695 it was present at the siege of Namur. In March 1696 it was ordered home for duty at the Tower of London following the discovery of a plot against King William, but it returned to Flanders in May before the conclusion of the war by the treaty of Ryswick (1697).

In the general reduction of regimental establishments which followed the peace it is likely that Bowles was himself disbanded—for there is no record of him until 5 February 1705, when he was commissioned colonel of a regiment of foot (the late Colonel Caulfeild's regiment). Originally raised in Ireland in 1703, Bowles's regiment was embarked for Spain in 1705 with the expedition to Catalonia under the command of the earls of Peterborough and Galway; it took part in the siege and capture of Barcelona that September. In October 1706 Bowles was placed in command of a small force at the town of Elche, while the main column retired towards Alicante. On 21 October the French commander, Freville, appeared before the town with a force of 5500 men. Without artillery, Bowles held out for two days, but he was compelled to yield on the 23rd and was taken prisoner. However, his exchange must have been arranged speedily, for he is reported to have been present and in command of his regiment the following April (1707), when he was again forced to surrender at the bloody battle of Almanza.

Narcissus Luttrell reports that Bowles returned to England on parole on 18 September 1707. In December 1708 his regiment was in receipt of a large draft of prisoners to restore it to full strength. Luttrell also relates that, in April 1709, having rebuilt his regiment, Bowles was ordered to Plymouth to join Admiral Baker's squadron, 'supposed to recover our settlements in Newfoundland' (Luttrell, 6.427). This was more than likely a ruse, since Bowles's regiment returned to Spain and distinguished itself at the victory of Saragossa (August 1710).

Bowles was sent home with the captured French colours, and returned via Italy. However, he was left to pay his own expenses and memorialized the Treasury for recompense. In his absence his regiment was one of those British units surprised, surrounded, and eventually captured by superior French forces at Brihuega in December 1710. The regiment was finally disbanded in Ireland after the peace of Utrecht in 1713.

On 12 February 1711 Bowles was raised to the rank of brigadier-general, a non-regimental commission. He remained unemployed until the Jacobite rising in 1715, when he was commissioned in July to raise a corps of cavalry, which became the 12th lancers (later the Prince of Wales's Royal regiment of lancers). Bowles was the regiment's first colonel. Quartered in Berkshire, Bowles's new regiment played little part in the suppression of the rebellion, although in October it escorted some Scottish prisoners to the Tower. Between 1716 and October 1718 it was stationed in the west country, after which it was embarked for Ireland and placed on the Irish establishment.

Bowles married Elizabeth Robinson in 1718. They had one daughter, Elizabeth, who was reported to be living, unmarried, in 1750. In March 1719 Bowles was transferred to the colonelcy of the 8th hussars and on 30 May 1720 was appointed quartermaster-general of Ireland. In May 1722 he was made controller of army accounts. He died intestate on 15 November 1722; administration was granted to his widow in May 1723.

Bowles was described as 'a warm hearted loyalist distinguished for his attachment to the House of Hanover, who had acquired a reputation at the head of a regiment of foot in the Wars of the Spanish Succession' (Cannon, 9–10), but it is as the founder of the 12th lancers that he is chiefly remembered.

Bowles's cousin and namesake, **Phineas Bowles** (*bap.* 1690, *d.* 1749), army officer and politician, was the third son of Phineas Bowles (1664–1718) of Loughbrough House, a partner in the family glass works at Southwark, and his wife, Margaret Dockwra (1665–1740), whose family were London merchants—another branch owned the Putteridge estate in Hertfordshire. Phineas was baptized at St Michael, Crooked Lane, London, on 24 January 1690. In March 1710 he was commissioned a captain in the 27th (Inniskilling) regiment of foot, which between October 1709 and November 1710 was quartered at Alicante before being sent to Minorca for garrison duty. The regiment remained there until 1717, but in 1713 Bowles transferred to the 3rd foot guards (later the Scots Guards), as captain and lieutenant-colonel. In 1715 he was reported to be employed in suppressing the Jacobite rising, and in March 1719 he succeeded his cousin as colonel of the 12th lancers, stationed in Ireland.

Bowles settled in Ireland for the remainder of his life. His marriage in 1724 to Alethea Maria (*d.* 1771), the daughter and heir of Samuel Hill, recently deceased, of Kilmainham, Dublin, brought with it a large Irish estate. Upon Alethea's marriage, portions of the estate were settled absolutely on Bowles and the rest was entailed strictly on the male issue of the marriage, an arrangement which was to cause much family argument and a long-running lawsuit after Bowles's death.

Between 1735 and 1741 Bowles was MP for Bewdly. He had been put in by his elder brother, William, who held a controlling interest. At a time when the Hanoverian succession was being relentlessly buttressed, Bowles's loyalty to the whig administration ensured rapid military promotion. In December 1735 he was raised to brigadier-general, and in 1739 he was promoted major-general and appointed governor of Limerick. In 1740 he was transferred to the colonelcy of the Carabiniers (later the 6th dragoon guards), and in 1745 he was raised to the rank of lieutenant-general and appointed governor of Londonderry and the Culmore forts.

Bowles lived at his town house in Dublin and his county seat, Beaulieu, near Drogheda, where he was falsely reported to have died in 1746. In fact he lived a further three years, and died in his sixtieth year at Bath on 22 October 1749. By his will of 11 September 1749 he left an estate valued at £200,000.

Phineas and Alethea Maria Bowles had two sons, William Phineas and Richard, and a daughter, Anna Maria, who married Lieutenant-Colonel Nathaniel Haywood of the Coldstream Guards. William, the eldest, died unmarried a few years after his father, in 1760, leaving an illegitimate son. The younger son, Richard, then a captain in the Horse Guards, inherited the Irish estates but soon moved to Sayes Court, near Chertsey. For the rest of his life Richard was involved in litigation with his brother's son, a residuary legatee under the father's will, who claimed a portion of the Irish estate and only succeeded in establishing his claim after Richard's death in 1798.

JONATHAN SPAIN

Sources W. H. Bowles, *Records of the Bowles family* (1918) [privately printed] • J. Davis, H. C. Wylly, and R. C. G. Foster, *The history of the second, queen's royal regiment*, 9 vols. (1887–1961) • A. Parnell, *The war of the succession in Spain during the reign of Queen Anne, 1702–1711* (1888); repr. (1905) • N. Luttrell, *A brief historical relation of state affairs* *from September 1678 to April 1714*, 6 vols. (1857) • R. Cannon, ed., *Historical record of the twelfth, or the prince of Wales's royal regiment of lancers* (1842) • C. Dalton, ed., *English army lists and commission registers, 1661–1714*, 6 vols. (1892–1904) • C. Dalton, *George the First's army, 1714–1727*, 2 vols. (1910–12) • R. E. Scouller, *The armies of Queen Anne* (1966) • G. Story, *A true and impartial history of the most material occurrences in the kingdom of Ireland* (1691) • BL, Blenheim MSS, Add. MSS 61132, fol. 39 • BL, Blenheim MSS, Add. MSS 61318, fols. 131–134b • HoP, *Commons, 1715–54* • F. Maurice, *The history of the Scots guards, from the creation of the regiment to the eve of the Great War*, 2 vols. (1934) • *The Royal Inniskilling fusiliers: being the history of the regiment from December 1688 to July 1914*, rev. edn (1934)

Likenesses group portrait (with family), repro. in Bowles, *Records of the Bowles family*, facing p. 74

Wealth at death £200,000—Phineas Bowles: Bowles, *Records*

Bowles, Phineas (*bap.* **1690**, *d.* **1749**). *See under* Bowles, Phineas (*d.* 1722).

Bowles, Thomas (*d.* **1721**). *See under* Bowles family (*per.* *c.*1690–*c.*1830).

Bowles, Thomas (**1689/90?–1767**). *See under* Bowles family (*per.* *c.*1690–*c.*1830).

Bowles, Thomas (**1712?–1762**). *See under* Bowles family (*per.* *c.*1690–*c.*1830).

Bowles, Thomas Gibson (1842–1922), politician and newspaper proprietor, was born on 15 January 1842, the illegitimate son of Thomas Milner-*Gibson (1806–1884) and Susan Bowles, of whom nothing else is known. His father's wife, Susanna, made him welcome with his eight stepbrothers and -sisters. He was educated at Mr Cobley's Preparatory School in Peckham Rye and at a school in northern France. He briefly attended King's College, London, and then, aged nineteen, became an official of the Inland Revenue, and used his post as a sinecure while writing journalism and plays. He left the service in September 1866 for journalism, writing articles and leaders for the *Morning Post* and moving in theatrical society. He later reported the siege of Paris in 1870 for the *Morning Post*, his articles being collected in *The Defence of Paris* (1871); at this time he became friendly with the French artist James Tissot. Financed partly by F. Burnaby, Bowles started in November 1868 a society paper, *Vanity Fair*, which gave coloured cartoons, accompanied by gossip and racy biographical sketches, of public characters (Disraeli by 'Ape' (Carlo Pellegrini) was the first cartoon). Bowles wrote a good deal of the copy and the magazine reflected his pungent wit. He also owned other newspaper interests and in 1884 founded *The Lady*.

In 1875 Bowles married Jessica, daughter of General Evans Gordon, of Kenmure. She died aged thirty-five in 1887, having borne him two sons and two daughters. His journalistic ventures proved profitable—he sold *Vanity Fair* for £20,000 after his wife's death—and Bowles turned his attention to politics. He was active in Salford politics and took a moderately anti-Gladstonian line. At the general election in 1892 he was returned to parliament for King's Lynn as a Conservative, and for three years sat on the opposition side of the House of Commons.

The budget of 1894, introduced by Sir William Harcourt, gave Bowles an opportunity of showing himself an able

Thomas Gibson Bowles (1842–1922), by Théobald Chartran, 1880

and well-informed critic of financial measures. He spoke well on other subjects, and when the Conservatives were returned to office in 1895 seemed a likely candidate for some ministerial post. But he was passed over, and became henceforth a critic rather than a supporter of the government, notably in a speech on the appropriation bill on 6 August 1902 and in his concern for security in Gibraltar (see his pamphlet, 1901), on which he secured a select committee. He was virtually an independent member, and in the tariff-reform controversy of 1903 he declared for free trade, attacking with bitterness both Chamberlain and Arthur Balfour, the leader of his party. The whips refused to recognize him, and put up another Conservative candidate at King's Lynn in 1906. Bowles lost the seat, stood again as a Conservative free-trader for the City of London against Balfour, but received little support, and before the end of the year he had joined the Liberal Party.

Bowles's association with Liberalism was brief. In March 1909 he unsuccessfully contested Central Glasgow as a Liberal, but at the first of the two general elections of 1910, he was returned as a Liberal for his old constituency of King's Lynn. This experience was rendered more curious by the fact that he won the seat as a supporter of Lloyd George's budget, a measure which seemed much at variance with his previous views on taxation. At the second general election in the same year he was turned out again, and this was the end of his political career. In December 1911 he announced his return to the Conservative Party, but he never sat in the Commons again, though he contested South Leicester in 1916. 'Captain Tommy Bowles', as *Punch* called him, usually depicting him with a wooden leg and hook arm, was a popular member of the Commons and added much to the gaiety of its proceedings.

Out of parliament, Bowles pursued his quest for retrenchment in speeches and a series of pamphlets. In 1912 he brought an action against the Bank of England for authorizing the deduction of income tax from dividend warrants on the strength of financial resolutions passed in the committee of ways and means, before the Finance

Act of the year had given legal sanction to new taxation. The object of the practice which he challenged was to prevent forestalling in spirits, tea, and tobacco. Bowles won his case against the bank; Lloyd George, the chancellor of the exchequer, was obliged to get an act passed (colloquially known as the Bowles Act) making legal the provisional collection of taxes. In 1913 friends dissuaded Bowles from bringing an action to test the legality of payment of MPs. In February 1914 Bowles brought out the first number of a journal called the *Candid Quarterly Review*—an anti-corruption journal—but it failed after its second number.

Bowles was an authority on international and maritime law, and published, among other books, *Maritime Warfare* (1878), *The Declaration of Paris of 1856* (1900), and *Sea Law and Sea Power* (1910). He died on 12 January 1922 at Algeciras, and was buried at Gibraltar.

Alfred Cochrane, *rev.* H. C. G. Matthew

Sources L. E. Naylor, *The irrepressible Victorian* (1965) • *The Times* (13 Jan 1922) • *DNB* • R. T. Matthews and P. Mellini, *In 'Vanity Fair'* (1982) • J. B. Osborne, 'The journal "Vanity Fair" and later Victorian politics', *Journal of the Rutgers University Libraries* (Dec 1980)
Archives Duke U., Perkins L., papers | Bodl. Oxf., letters to Herbert Asquith • HLRO, corresp. with Andrew Bonar Law
Likenesses T. Chartran, portrait, 1880, priv. coll. [*see illus.*] • B. Stone, photograph, 1897, NPG • Spy [L. Ward], caricature, chromolithograph, NPG; repro. in *VF* (19 Oct 1905) • Spy [L. Ward], caricature, chromolithograph, NPG; repro. in *VF* (13 July 1889) • photographs, repro. in Naylor, *The irrepressible Victorian* • portrait, repro. in *VF* (1 July 1879)
Wealth at death £59,825 19*s*. 3*d*.: probate, 21 March 1922, *CGPLA Eng. & Wales*

Bowles, William (1705–1780), naturalist, was born in a village near Cork. He was destined for the legal profession but gave it up, and in 1740 went to Paris, where he studied natural history, chemistry, and metallurgy. He subsequently travelled through France, investigating its natural history and mineral and other productions. In 1752 he became acquainted with Don Antonio de Ulloa, afterwards admiral of the Spanish fleet, who persuaded him to enter the Spanish service; Bowles was appointed to superintend the state mines and to form a collection of natural history and establish a chemical laboratory. He first visited the mercury mines of Almaden, which had been seriously damaged by fire but which were successfully brought back into service using his plans. He afterwards travelled through Spain, investigating and collecting specimens of its minerals and natural history, living mainly at Madrid and Bilbao. He married the German Anna Regina Rustein de Clausthal Hartz Hansen, who was pensioned by the king of Spain after her husband's death. Bowles is described as tall and fine-looking, generous, honourable, active, ingenious, and well informed. From at least 1777 he was infirm and confined to his bed. He died at Madrid on 25 August 1780 and was buried in the parish church of San Martin in that city, being an ardent Roman Catholic.

Bowles's principal work was *Introduccion a la historia natural y a la geografia fisica de España* (1775). It is not systematically arranged, but has very considerable value as being the first work of its kind. He was an acute observer and Irish naturalists have found particularly interesting his comparisons of the two countries' flora and fauna (Lusitania and the south-west of Ireland have very similar flora and fauna, a vestige of preglacial connections). Others, too, long found value in his work: the United States Entomological Commission reprinted in 1880 his observations on locusts which had ravaged crops in Spain as in the USA. The second edition of the *Introduccion* (1782) was edited by Don Jose Nicolas de Azara y Perera (1730/31–1804), who helped the author prepare the first edition. It was translated into French by vicomte de Flavigny (1776). An Italian edition, much enlarged by Azara, then Spanish ambassador at Rome, was published in two volumes at Parma in 1784. A microfiche edition was published as late as 1994 and a paper edition in 1982. Bowles was also the author of 'A brief account of the Spanish and German mines' published in the Royal Society's *Philosophical Transactions* (56), and of a letter on the sheep of Spain and other Spanish topics, originally sent to the botanist Peter Collinson and later published in the *Gentleman's Magazine* (1st ser., 34, 1764, 203–6; 206–70). He continued his work on sheep in a volume on merino sheep published in Spanish and English (1811). Sir John Thomas Dillon's *Travels through Spain* (1781) is very largely an adaptation of Bowles's first work. Ruiz and Pavon called a genus of Peruvian plants *Bowlesia* in his honour.

G. T. Bettany, *rev.* Elizabeth Baigent

Sources J. Britten and G. S. Boulger, eds., *A biographical index of British and Irish botanists* (1893) • L. Ruiz and J. Pavon, *Florae Peruvianae et Chilensis prodromus* (1794) • Desmond, *Botanists*, rev. edn • R. L. Praeger, *Some Irish naturalists: a biographical note-book* (1949), 53 • N. Colgan, 'An Irish naturalist in Spain in the eighteenth century', *Irish Naturalist*, 20 (1911), 1–5 • will, PRO, PROB 11/1079, sig. 330

Bowles, Sir William (1780–1869), naval officer and author, was born at his parents' home, Heale House, near Salisbury, Wiltshire. He was the eldest son of William Bowles and his wife, Dinah, third daughter of Admiral Sir Thomas *Frankland. George *Bowles (1787–1876) was his younger brother. He was also related to the earl of Malmesbury. After a good education ashore, to judge from his excellent command of English, French, and Spanish, he joined the navy in September 1796. He was promoted lieutenant on 30 August 1803, and then served for three years on the North American station. He was promoted commander on 22 January 1806, and in 1807 commanded the bomb vessel *Zebra* at the capture of Copenhagen, where he was closely engaged with Danish batteries and gunboats. He reached the rank of captain on 13 October 1807, and in 1810 he was active in coastal and amphibious operations on the north coast of Spain. In July 1812, commanding the frigate *Aquilon* (32 guns), he conveyed the British ambassador to St Petersburg; he then remained in the Baltic theatre for the remainder of the season, capturing vital French transports off Stralsund. His next service was protecting British trade in the River Plate from early 1813 to April 1814.

Bowles returned to the South American station as commodore in May 1816, and remained there until 1820. The station then covered both coasts of the continent. This was a period of great turbulence in the politics of South America, as the region struggled for independence from Spain and then fought over the spoils; Bowles handled his command with skill and judgement. On 9 August 1820 he married the Hon. Frances Temple, the sister of his intimate friend Henry John Temple, second Viscount Palmerston. In 1822 he was briefly appointed to the royal yacht *William and Mary*, a sure sign of favour in the right quarters, before receiving the appointment of comptroller-general of the coastguard in July. The coastguard was then a combination of customs service and naval reserve, paid for by the Treasury. Bowles devoted his efforts to the improvement of naval manning, the subject that would dominate the remainder of his professional life. He became the most active naval writer of pamphlets, in which he generally took a reforming but conservative line. In 1826 he advised the first lord, Lord Melville, to restrict coastguard recruitment to young men with naval experience, and end the practice of linking appointments with party politics. He was ignored, but when the coastguard was called on to serve in 1854 it provided just over 2000 over-age men, some of whom had never been to sea. Bowles also argued that the coastguard should pass under Admiralty control in a crisis. In *Remarks on the Conduct of the Naval Administration of Great Britain* (1830) he advocated the use of steam warships in national defence, the annual commissioning of a squadron of exercise, and a system of naval gunnery. In the last case his advocacy, in combination with the efforts of Sir Howard Douglas, Sir John Pechell, Sir Philip Broke, and George Smith, led to the establishment of HMS *Excellent*. He was appointed an extra aide-de-camp by William IV in 1831. His wife died on 13 November 1838; there were no children. He was elected a fellow of the Royal Geographical Society in 1833, made a CB in April 1839, and became rear-admiral on 23 November 1841, a promotion that ended his command of the coastguard. In *Suggestions* of 1840 he called for the formation of a squadron of six battleships and six frigates, to be ready at twenty-four hours' notice.

Appointed to command the Squadron of Evolution from May 1843 to May 1844, Bowles had an opportunity to test his faith in the radical ship designs of the whig surveyor of the navy, Captain Sir William Symonds. In May 1844 he took office as third naval lord on Lord Haddington's board, where he remained, latterly under Lord Ellenborough, until the fall of Peel's government in June 1846. He tried to alleviate the tory attack on Symonds's system, and to persuade the surveyor to accept criticism, but with little success, as opinions and politics were too entrenched for compromise. He was elected MP for the duke of Northumberland's pocket borough of Launceston in 1844. He retained this until July 1852, when the duke shifted from his Peelite position to join the earl of Derby's ministry, as first lord of the Admiralty. In 1846 Bowles made his political position clear, publishing a defence of Peel. The following year he produced a third edition of his *Remarks* of 1830, this time admitting authorship, and adding a call for a centrally organized system of naval recruitment, with permanent staff at the chief mercantile ports. In 1848 he published *Thoughts on National Defence*, in which he adopted a more alarmist tone and called for the coastal region, up to 10 miles deep, to be prepared to resist invasion. He also worked with his friend Captain Sir Thomas Hastings to develop the concept of a naval militia, which was presented in a memorandum to Sir William Parker's committee on naval manning in 1852. Although this measure, which enrolled men for local service in the event of war, was worthless, it was adopted in 1854. Bowles became a vice-admiral on 3 March 1852.

In 1854 Bowles reprinted most of his earlier works in *Pamphlets on Naval Subjects*; in 1856 he produced *Considerations on the Late Naval War*, and in 1858 *A Recommendation for Abolishing the Rank of Commander in the Royal Navy*. He was an active supporter of efforts to establish a central pension scheme for merchant seamen, masters, and mates, based on a compulsory subscription. In December 1858 he was appointed commander-in-chief at Portsmouth by the tory ministry. He was obliged to resign effective from March 1860 after the Admiralty disapproved of his having published correspondence in the *Morning Post* on 28 December 1859, attempting to vindicate his character from newspaper attacks after a mutiny aboard the *Princess Royal* on 12 November that year. Bowles had stopped shore leave for this ship after a misunderstanding with the captain about the participation of part of the crew in a demonstration ashore. At this time the rapid increase in naval manpower to meet the perceived challenge of imperial France, under a bounty scheme, had brought a large number of poor-quality and unreliable men into the service. Bowles favoured a court martial to assert authority, but Palmerston's Liberal government, unwilling to antagonize the newly raised men, preferred to remove Bowles, a process smoothed by his family connection.

In 1860 Bowles continued his theme with *A Militia our Only Real Naval Reserve*, largely a reprint of the 1856 *Naval War* pamphlet, and defended his views under rigorous cross-examination before the 1861 Commons' select committee on the Board of Admiralty. By then his ideas had hardened into dogma, and he was increasingly out of step with political and naval developments. Having been a liberal conservative, he ended up despairing of the ability of the political system to organize any effective system of naval recruitment and national defence. His later writings were increasingly authoritarian in tone. He became a full admiral on 1 November 1860, a KCB in November 1862, and admiral of the fleet on 15 January 1869. He died at his home at 8 Hill Street, Berkeley Square, London, on 2 July 1869. Bowles was a man of real ability, and his was the leading voice of considered, conservative reform. Like his Canningite brother-in-law, and his Peelite political friends, he was able to adjust tory values to meet new situations. Few officers had as much influence on the navy of the day.

ANDREW LAMBERT

Sources J. S. Bromley, ed., *The manning of the Royal Navy: selected public pamphlets, 1693–1873*, Navy RS, 119 (1974) • *The letters of the third*

Viscount Palmerston to Laurence and Elizabeth Sulivan, 1804–1863, ed. K. Bourne, CS, 4th ser., 23 (1979) • *The Saumarez papers: selections from the Baltic correspondence of Vice-Admiral Sir James Saumarez, 1808–1812*, ed. A. N. Ryan, Navy RS, 110 (1968) • G. S. Graham and R. A. Humphreys, eds., *The navy and South America, 1807–1823*, Navy RS, 104 (1962) • R. Blake, *Disraeli* (1966) • A. D. Lambert, *The last sailing battlefleet: maintaining naval mastery, 1815–1850* (1991) • K. Bourne, *Palmerston: the early years, 1784–1841* (1982) • O'Byrne, *Naval biog. dict.* • D. Syrett and R. L. DiNardo, *The commissioned sea officers of the Royal Navy, 1660–1815*, rev. edn, Occasional Publications of the Navy RS, 1 (1994) • C. J. Bartlett, *Great Britain and sea power, 1815–1853* (1963) • *Dod's Peerage* (1858) • *WWBMP* • *DNB*

Archives Beds. & Luton ARS, corresp. with Earl de Grey

Bowles, William Lisle (1762–1850), Church of England clergyman and poet, was born on 24 September 1762 at Kings Sutton, Northamptonshire, of which his father, William Thomas Bowles (*d.* 1786), was the vicar from 1760 to 1773. In 1776 he was placed at Winchester School, under Joseph Warton, who, discerning his taste for poetry, did his best to foster it; on the death of his old master, Bowles wrote a monody which expressed his regard for his character. On leaving Winchester in 1781 he was elected a scholar of Trinity College, Oxford, of which Joseph Warton's brother, Thomas Warton—professor of poetry at Oxford and eventually poet laureate—was the senior fellow. In 1783 Bowles won the chancellor's Latin verse prize for his poem 'Calpe obsessa, or, The siege of Gibraltar'. After leaving university in 1787 Bowles experienced two thwarted engagements, and turned for consolation to poetry. His first collection, *Fourteen Sonnets Written Chiefly on Picturesque Spots during a Journey*, was published in 1789, and was an immediate success, owing to his ability to harmonize the moods of nature with those of the mind. It attracted the attention of the young Samuel Taylor Coleridge, who paid tribute to Bowles in later years in a sonnet. Having entered holy orders Bowles first officiated as curate of Donhead St Andrew in Wiltshire. In 1792 he was appointed to the rectory of Chicklade in Wiltshire, which he resigned in 1797, on being presented to the rectory of Dumbleton in Gloucestershire. In the same year he was married to Magdalene, daughter of Dr Wake, prebendary of Westminster, whom he survived. In 1804 he became vicar of Bremhill, Wiltshire, where he lived until shortly before his death.

In 1806 Bowles published the work for which he is best known: a ten-volume edition of the work of Alexander Pope with a sketch of his life and strictures on his poetry. His comments on the poet's life were written in a severe, even hostile spirit. Bowles's estimate of Pope as a poet gave rise to a long controversy, in which much bitterness was displayed; Byron, for example, attacked him severely in both verse and prose. While his best work was in the field of poetry, Bowles displayed competence in other areas. He was an antiquary, and in 1828 published a volume entitled *Hermes Britannicus*. He also wrote on ecclesiastical matters, crime, education, and the condition of the poor. His sermons are notable for their dignity and simplicity of style. He was also an active but lenient magistrate. Several honours were bestowed upon Bowles during his lifetime: he was appointed chaplain to the prince regent in 1818, and canon residentiary at Salisbury Cathedral in 1828.

In character Bowles seems to have been ardent and impulsive, but genial and humane. The journal of the poet Tom Moore contains some allusions to him which illustrate his keen susceptibility to impressions, his high-church principles, his love of simple language in the pulpit, together with certain eccentricities, such as his constant refusal to be measured by a tailor. His health had failed some time before his death, which occurred when he was eighty-eight at the close, Salisbury, on 7 April 1850. J. W. MARSTON, *rev.* LEON LITVACK

Sources *The poetical works of William Lisle Bowles, with memoir, critical dissertation, and explanatory notes*, ed. G. Gilfillan (1855) • W. L. Bowles, introduction, *Scenes and shadows of days departed: a narrative accompanied with poems of youth* (1837) • O. Rietmann, *William Lisle Bowles, 1762–1850* (1940) • A. J. A. Waldock, *William Lisle Bowles* (1928)

Archives Harvard U., Houghton L., letters and proofs • Hunt. L., letters • Keswick Museum and Art Gallery, poems and papers • Wilts. & Swindon RO, papers | BL, corresp. with Sir John Allen, Add. MSS 52196–52197, *passim* • Bodl. Oxf., letters to Isaac Disraeli • Bodl. Oxf., letters to James Ingram • Bodl. Oxf., corresp. with Sir Thomas Phillipps • Keswick Museum and Art Gallery, letters to James Bullock • NL Scot., letters to Blackwood & Sons • Northants. RO, letters to Thomas Hutchinson • Rutgers University, New Brunswick, letters to Harriet Wake • Stamford Public Library, Lincolnshire, corresp. with Octavius Gilchrist • Yale U., Sterling Memorial Library, corresp. with James Boswell

Likenesses D. Maclise, lithograph, BM, NPG • D. Maclise, pencil sketch, V&A • J. Thomson, stipple (after Mullar), BM, NPG; repro. in *New Monthly Magazine* (1820)

Bowley, Sir Arthur Lyon (1869–1957), statistician, was born at 12 King's Square, Bristol, on 6 November 1869, the son of the Revd James William Lyon Bowley (1826–1871), vicar of St Philip and St Jacob, and his wife, Maria Johnson. Bowley spent nine years at Christ's Hospital (1879–88), which left a lasting impression on him; in later life he served as a governor of the school for more than ten years. He went to Trinity College, Cambridge, with a major scholarship in mathematics, was bracketed tenth wrangler in 1891, and later obtained both the Cobden and the Adam Smith prizes. He was awarded the ScD by his university in 1913.

On leaving Cambridge, Bowley seemed destined to teach mathematics in schools and he was on the staff, briefly at Brighton College, then at St John's School, Leatherhead, until 1899. His own interests lay in the application of economic analysis to problems of social reform. He published in 1893 his Cobden prize essay, on England's foreign trade in the nineteenth century, then began an extensive series of research projects, mainly with G. H. Wood, on the relationship between movements in wages and prices; he read his first paper to the Royal Statistical Society in 1895. He published many further papers on this subject, all of them put together with great historical and statistical care.

These interests led, in 1895, to a complete and permanent change in Bowley's career. In that year Sidney Webb and others founded the London School of Economics (LSE) and assembled a small staff of part-time experts. Bowley

Sir Arthur Lyon Bowley (1869–1957), by Stella Bowen, 1936

was chosen to take charge of the teaching of statistics, and taught at LSE without interruption for more than forty years. He was never a socialist in Webb's sense but, as a good Liberal, he found the senior common room a congenial and stimulating background to his teaching, research, and public service.

In 1904 Bowley married Julia (1871–1959), daughter of Thomas Hilliam, land agent; they had three daughters, one of whom, Marian Bowley, became professor of political economy at University College, London. Bowley also taught at the University College at Reading from 1900, as lecturer in mathematics (1900–7), in economics (1913–19), and professor in both subjects (1907–13). Meanwhile, at the LSE, he became part-time reader in statistics in 1908 and was given the title of professor in 1915. When the University of London created a full-time chair in statistics in 1919, tenable at the LSE, Bowley became the first occupant. Although he retired from the chair in 1936, he continued many of his activities, both at the LSE and elsewhere, until the early fifties. He acted as director of the Oxford University Institute of Statistics during the war years (1940–44) and received an honorary DLitt in 1943. He was elected FBA in 1922, appointed CBE in 1937, and knighted in 1950.

As a mathematician Bowley was competent but rather old-fashioned. He was one of the founders of the international Econometric Society in 1933 and served later as its president. However, first and foremost he was a practitioner in statistics applied across the whole of the social sciences. He was highly regarded by official statisticians but it was not then the custom for the British government to call upon outside experts for advice, and he exercised his main influence therefore through his teaching and research on the one hand and his extensive international contacts on the other. He was called upon as an expert witness in cases such as the inquiry into dockers' wages (1920).

Two of Bowley's pioneer activities were in the economic field. One comprised a number of studies on the definition and measurement of national income which occupied his attention, on and off, for more than twenty years before the first official estimates were made under Lord Keynes during the Second World War. Without Bowley's careful and precise work the official computations would scarcely have been possible. His other pioneer activity in this field was from 1923 with the London and Cambridge Economic Service, the first venture of this kind in Britain. Bowley was its first editor and he served in this capacity continuously until 1945, remaining a regular contributor until 1953. His editorship was characterized both by the skill with which he pulled together various views in his own succinct assessment of the current economic position for publication in the *Monthly Bulletins* of the service, and by the statistical techniques he used in designing economic series and in devising ways of presenting them. He showed how economic analysis depends on long runs of comparable series, presented in graphical form (for example by the use of ratio scales) and adjusted where necessary for seasonal variation.

The major contribution which Bowley made—and it was one of the utmost importance to statistics—lay in the development of sampling techniques in their application to social studies. He explored, largely for the first time, the appropriate design of sample surveys, the proper formulation of sampling precision, and the ways of interpreting the results in their application. He devised and conducted sample surveys of working-class households in four English towns and, in presenting the results in *Livelihood and Poverty* (with A. R. Burnett-Hurst, 1915), he was far ahead of his time both in explaining the methods used and in formulating the precision of the results. He distinguished four sources of error: incorrect information, loose definitions, bias in selection of samples, and calculable errors of sampling. He may not have been entirely correct in his use of what is now known as cluster sampling, but what he wrote in 1915 remains relevant.

It was natural that Bowley should dominate the committee set up in 1924 by the International Statistical Institute to report on the representative method. At the 1925 session in Rome Bowley's influence was clearly visible in the main recommendation of the committee that:

> the investigation should be so arranged wherever possible as to allow of a mathematical statement of the precision of the results, and that with these results should be given an indication of the extent of the error to which they are liable.

It could also be seen in the technical appendix on the measurement of precisions which accompanied the report. Bowley continued to practise what he preached and he himself regarded as his most important work his contribution to the *New Survey of London Life and Labour* conducted in the period 1930–35.

Bowley was effective, if rather dour, on committees, and held many high offices in the British Association, the Royal Statistical Society, the Royal Economic Society, and the International Statistical Institute. He was shy and retiring, never happier than when talking quietly to his research students or playing Bach with his family. He was respected by all his colleagues and students but intimate with few. One of his close friendships was with the distinguished economist Edwin Cannan, who shared his enthusiasm for cycling. Bowley died at the Otara Nursing Home, Fernhurst, near Haslemere, on 21 January 1957. He was survived by his wife.

R. G. D. ALLEN, *rev.* JOHN BOSNELL

Sources A. H. Bowley, *A memoir of Professor Sir Arthur Bowley* (1972) · R. D. G. Allen and R. F. George, *Journal of the Royal Statistical Society: series A*, 120 (1957), 236–41 · *Nature*, 179 (1957), 398–9 · E. P. Hennock, 'The measurement of urban poverty: from the metropolis to the nation, 1880–1920', *Economic History Review*, 2nd ser., 40 (1987), 208–27 · *The Times* (23 Jan 1957), 12a · *The Times* (12 Feb 1957), 10c · *CGPLA Eng. & Wales* (1957)

Archives BLPES, corresp., lecture notes, and papers · Royal Statistical Society, corresp. and papers | BLPES, letters to Edwin Cannan · King's AC Cam., letters to John Maynard Keynes · U. St Andr. L., letters to Sir D'Arcy Thompson

Likenesses S. Bowen, oils, 1936, London School of Economics [*see illus.*] · photograph, *c*.1939, repro. in Bowley, *Memoir of Professor Sir Arthur Bowley* · photograph, repro. in *The Times* (23 Jan 1957)

Wealth at death £10,549 7*s*. 10*d*.: probate, 13 March 1957, *CGPLA Eng. & Wales*

Bowley, Robert Kanzow (1813–1870), music administrator, was born on 13 May 1813, the son of a bootmaker at Charing Cross. He initially learned his father's trade. At an early age he joined the Benevolent Society of Musical Amateurs, and later became its conductor. He was a member of the committee of the amateur musical festival held at Exeter Hall in 1834, and about the same date was appointed organist of the Independent Orange Street Chapel, Leicester Square. Bowley joined the Sacred Harmonic Society in 1834, and was librarian from 1837 to 1854 and treasurer from 1854 to the year of his death. He published *The Sacred Harmonic Society* (1867).

In 1856 Bowley came up with the idea of celebrating the centenary of Handel's death with a grand musical celebration. A preliminary festival was held in 1857, with a choir of two hundred and an orchestra of 396, and the first large festival took place in 1859. It was a three-day event, held in the Crystal Palace at Sydenham, with *Messiah* performed on the first day and *Israel in Egypt* on the third. From then on Handel festivals were held every three years, conducted from 1859 to 1877 by Michael Costa. In 1858 Bowley was appointed general manager of the Crystal Palace, a post he continued to hold until his death. He committed suicide on 25 August 1870 by jumping into the Thames from a steamboat at Greenwich. He left a widow, Margaret.

W. B. SQUIRE, *rev.* ANNE PIMLOTT BAKER

Sources Grove, *Dict. mus.* · *New Grove* · Brown & Stratton, *Brit. mus.* · Boase, *Mod. Eng. biog.* · *CGPLA Eng. & Wales* (1870)

Wealth at death under £7000: probate, 8 Oct 1870, *CGPLA Eng. & Wales*

Bowlly, Albert Alick [Al] (1899–1941), singer, was born on 7 January 1899 in Delagoa Bay, Portuguese East Africa, the fourth of the ten children of Alick Pauli (1867–1927), a general dealer, and his Lebanese wife, Miriam (Mary) Ayoub-NeeJame (1874–1949). The couple married in Australia; Alick Pauli's surname was written as Bowlly when they left there for Africa and, as he spoke and read only his native Greek, the mistake went unnoticed and the name became permanent when they were naturalized in Pietermaritzburg, Natal, on 21 February 1903. In that year the family moved to Johannesburg, where Al Bowlly was baptized a Roman Catholic (his mother's religion). He later adopted his father's Greek Orthodox faith. He left school at fourteen to work in his uncle's barber's shop, but longed to become an entertainer and soon obtained evening work singing and playing the ukulele and banjo. He took singing lessons from the local pianist and singer Letty Campbell.

Bowlly was naturalized on 12 March 1921 and obtained a passport. In the following year he was offered work by the bandleader Edgar Adler and, in 1923, began a tour of east Africa, India, and Java. He did not return home, accepting instead an engagement as banjoist with the Jimmy Lequime Orchestra in Calcutta, India. When Lequime went to Singapore in 1926, he became the band's singer. He travelled next to Berlin, where he performed with bands such as Arthur Brigg and his Savoy Syncopators, Fred Bird's Salon Symphonic Jazz Band, and George Carhart's New Yorkers Jazz Orchestra. He made his first recordings and enhanced his reputation as a singer in Berlin. From there, he went to London in July 1928, invited by Fred Elizalde to join his band at the Savoy Hotel as vocalist and guitarist. His skill as a guitarist is often overlooked, but can be heard to effect on his and Ella Logan's recording of 'Frankie and Johnnie' (24 November 1930). After Elizalde disbanded he joined the new band put together by Roy Fox at the Monseigneur restaurant, Piccadilly, London, in 1931. During this decade he became immensely popular as a singer and recording artist: over 200 vocal refrains were recorded by him in 1931 alone. In his lifetime he made over 1000 recordings.

Bowlly married a dance hostess, Freda Roberts, on 18 December 1931 at St Martin register office, London, but they broke up three weeks later and finally divorced in January 1934. On what would have been their third wedding anniversary, he got married again, to another dance hostess, Margaret Fairless (known as Marjie). They separated in 1937 but did not divorce; there were no children from either marriage.

In 1932 Bowlly was singing with Lew Stone's band at the Monseigneur, which was really Fox's band under a different leader. With this band he further refined his vocal technique, recorded, broadcast on BBC radio, appeared in variety theatres, and became a crooner to rival the USA's Bing Crosby. He disliked the term 'crooning', and preferred 'modern style singing', the title of a book issued under his name (but probably ghosted) in 1934. The book observes that the modern intimate style of singing depends on the microphone, and that the microphone

Albert Alick Bowlly (1899–1941), by unknown photographer, *c.*1933

gives a new timbre to the voice, amplifying previously unheard harmonics. The techniques of the dance-band style of singing that are described are characteristic of Bowlly: for example, a slight portamento, an added grace-note, a fresh attack, and a dragging behind the tempo followed by a catching up. His technique is heard to advantage in 'The Very Thought of You', recorded with Ray Noble's New Mayfair Orchestra, HMV's house band, in 1934.

Bowlly toured the USA with Noble in 1934, performing at the prestigious Rainbow Room, Fifth Avenue, New York, as well as being given his own NBC radio series. His recording of 'My Melancholy Baby' (New York, 15 March 1935) was the big hit of this period of his life. He returned to the USA in 1937 for a throat operation, which proved successful and allowed him to begin doing freelance work again. In the late thirties he sang with bands led by Maurice Winnick, Lew Stone, and Geraldo, and in 1940 recorded with Ken 'Snakehips' Johnson's West Indian Orchestra.

In the early thirties, when dance-band records announced simply 'with vocal refrain', the singer remaining anonymous, admirers of Bowlly sought out records for his distinctive voice and thus he helped to elevate the status of the popular vocalist. His art ranged from that of the *diseur*, as heard on his recording of 'Is I in Love? I Is' with Arthur Lally and his orchestra (1932), to the jazz improviser, as on his recording of 'Dinah' with Jock McMerdott and his band (1932). He spoke Afrikaans as well as English, and recorded several records in the former language in 1930, under Ray Noble's direction, for the South African market. His dark good looks and silky, sensitive vocal timbre, mellifluous and without breathiness, won him a large following. Surprisingly, perhaps, he smoked heavily, though he drank little. He was warm-hearted, if quick tempered, and physically fit (he took boxing lessons in the mid-1930s).

After the outbreak of the Second World War, session work became scarce and Bowlly teamed up with a fellow guitarist, Jimmy Mesene. His last recordings were made with Mesene two weeks before his death. A bomb exploded near his flat in Dukes Court, Jermyn Street, Piccadilly, London, on the morning of Thursday 17 April 1941, and he was killed by the blast. He was buried on 26 April in a communal grave at Westminster city council cemetery, Hanwell, after a funeral service conducted by the dean of the Greek Orthodox Cathedral in London. The gross value of his estate was £1163 2*s.* 8*d.*, although at the time of his death he had only £3 10*s.* 9*d.* in his bank account, something of an irony given that his signature tune was 'Buddy, Can You Spare a Dime?'. DEREK B. SCOTT

Sources R. Pallett, *Goodnight sweetheart: life and times of Al Bowlly* (1986) [incl. comprehensive discography] · S. Colin and T. Staveacre, *Al Bowlly* (1979) · C. M. Harvey and B. A. L. Rust, *The Al Bowlly discography* (1964) · *Melody Maker* (7 July 1934), 3 · C. Larkin, ed., *The Guinness encyclopedia of popular music*, 4 vols. (1992), 515–16 · P. Gammond, *The Oxford companion to popular music* (1991); repr. with corrections (1993), 74–5 · *Daily Express* (18 April 1941)

Archives FILM BFI NFTVA, performance footage | SOUND BL NSA, performance recordings

Likenesses photograph, *c.*1933, NPG [*see illus.*] · photograph, *c.*1935, Hult. Arch. · photograph, *c.*1936, repro. in P. Cliffe, *Fascinating rhythm* (1990), 243

Wealth at death £1163 2*s.* 8*d.*: administration with will, 1 Oct 1942, *CGPLA Eng. & Wales*

Bowly, Samuel (1802–1884), slavery abolitionist and temperance advocate, the son of Samuel Bowly, a miller at Bibury, Gloucestershire, was born in Cirencester on 23 March 1802. During his youth he attended a Quaker school at Nailsworth and then worked at his father's flour mill. In 1827 he married Jane Shipley, the daughter of John Shipley of Shaftesbury. In 1829 Bowly moved to Gloucester and set up business as a cheese factor. He became chairman of many local banking, gas, railway, and other companies, and for the last twenty years of his life he was looked upon as a leader in commercial circles and affairs. An active participant in the agitation against the corn laws, he also opposed all taxes on essential items. It was one of his endeavours to give the people cheap and universal education, and he was not only one of the founders of the British and ragged schools in Gloucester, but a consistent advocate of a national system. During the early stages of the Crimean War he became involved in the peace movement. Like his father, he belonged to the Society of Friends; throughout the 1850s he spoke at the yearly meetings and in 1863 he was made a minister.

Bowly took an active part in the anti-slavery movement. An effective public speaker, on several occasions he debated with the pro-slavery lecturer Peter Borthwick. He was one of the deputation which went to Downing Street on 14 November 1837 to interview Lord Melbourne concerning the cruelties exercised towards the slaves under the apprenticeship system introduced in 1834, and the following year he took an active part in the formation of the Central Negro Emancipation Committee, which was ultimately instrumental in bringing about full emancipation in 1838.

It was his advocacy of temperance which made Bowly best known. On 30 December 1835 he signed the pledge of total abstinence, and went on to help establish temperance societies and Bands of Hope in the villages around Gloucester. He promoted temperance among the members of his own religious society, and in 1851 he helped found the Friends' Temperance Union. As the leading amateur temperance lecturer in the 1850s and 1860s he specialized in addressing the affluent in drawing-room meetings. Bowly was president of the National Temperance League, a director of the London Temperance Hospital from its foundation, and a director of the United Kingdom Temperance and General Provident Institution, in which roles he was able to draw the attention of scientific men to the damaging physical effects of alcohol. On behalf of the National Temperance League he attended and addressed 107 meetings during the last year of his life, travelling many hundreds of miles. Although he chaired the first public meeting of the United Kingdom Alliance in October 1853, he later moved away from the advocacy of prohibition.

Bowly's first wife, Jane, died in 1868; on 6 August 1873, in Devizes, he married Louisa Cotterell, the widow of Jacob Henry Cotterell of Bath, especially known for his connection with the Rechabite Friendly Society. Bowly published several addresses on anti-slavery and temperance themes, including *Total Abstinence and its Proper Place* (1863). The eightieth anniversary of his birth was celebrated in Gloucester in 1882, and he died there on Sunday, 23 March 1884, his eighty-second birthday. He was buried at Gloucester on 27 March.

G. C. BOASE, *rev.* MARK CLEMENT

Sources F. Sessions, *The life story of Samuel Bowly, a champion of freedom, progress and temperance* (1903) • P. T. Winskill, *The temperance movement and its workers*, 4 vols. (1891–2), vols. 2–3 • B. Harrison, *Drink and the Victorians: the temperance question in England, 1815–1872*, 2nd edn (1994) • L. L. Shiman, *Crusade against drink in Victorian England* (1988) • m. cert. • *CGPLA Eng. & Wales* (1884)

Likenesses B. R. Haydon, group portrait, oils (*The Anti-Slavery Convention, 1840*), NPG

Wealth at death £18,131 14*s*. 4*d*.: probate, 26 May 1884, *CGPLA Eng. & Wales*

Bowman, Alexander [*formerly* Patrick McKeown] (**1854–1924**), trade unionist and politician, was born on 16 March 1854, and baptized as a Roman Catholic, with the name Patrick McKeown. His father, William McKeown, or McKeon (1827–1865), was a Catholic farmer of Derry townland, Dromara, co. Down, and second husband of Elizabeth Bowman (or Boman), *née* Rogers (*b.* 1823), a Presbyterian. His father died in 1865 and his mother moved her family to Belfast, where she had relatives; Catholic Patrick McKeown became Presbyterian Alexander Bowman.

At the age of ten Bowman entered Agnes Street linen mills and became a flax dresser. In the strike year, 1874, his colleagues chose him to present their grievances to their employer; he was dismissed and moved to Ewart's mills. On 30 August 1880 he married Rose Ritchie, whose relative, Robert Ritchie, had organized a short-lived trades council in 1872. In late 1881 Bowman formed a group that canvassed forty organized trades to create the Belfast Trades Council. He became its unpaid secretary and chief organizer. In 1882 he led a successful lobby for the Free Libraries Act to be applied to Belfast. He represented the council at British trade union congresses. However, in the major contemporary industrial dispute, the shipyard lock-outs of 1884–5, Bowman and his council were virtually powerless.

Bowman also became politically active. While Belfast protestant workers were dominated by Orange Conservatism, he was a Liberal radical, upholding Henry George's land nationalization theories and persuading the Belfast Liberal Association to support giving women the parliamentary vote. In October 1885, while still member of the Belfast Liberal Club, Bowman accepted nomination for the new North Belfast seat in the general election of November as a Labour candidate. His platform combined Liberal radicalism's 'unauthorized programme' with women's suffrage and working-class claims for a shorter working day, more factory inspectors, and a more stringent Employers' Liability Act. He upheld the Anglo-Irish parliamentary union, but only 'on the basis of justice'. His campaign was supported by Parnell and by Conservatives in other constituencies; his own Conservative opponents wrecked one of his meetings. He won 1330 votes to the Conservative candidate's 3915.

December saw Gladstone's conversion to home rule revealed. Most Ulster Liberals opposed him, but Bowman feared the Conservative and landlord interest more than he feared nationalism. As trades council secretary he was able to repudiate a unionist workers' delegation, since it was unofficial. However, when he became paid secretary to a protestant home-rule association his colleagues forced his resignation from his trades council post.

In 1889, after three years as home-rule association secretary, Bowman became agent for a vending machine company in Glasgow, where he became president of the Henry George Institute and of the Scottish Land Restoration Federation. By 1891 he had returned to Belfast. In 1894, he was in London. He joined the Social Democratic Federation and stood unsuccessfully for it in elections for Walthamstow urban district council and Essex county council.

At the end of the summer of 1895 he returned to Belfast to become secretary of the city's Municipal Employees' Union, an unpaid post which he had to hold while resuming his old job of flax dressing. In addition, he became lecture secretary to the Belfast branch of the Independent Labour Party (ILP) and, once more, delegate to the trades council. On 25 November 1897 Bowman and five others were elected to the reformed city corporation as the first Belfast Labour Party representatives, winning its largest representation before 1920. Their programme included better health measures, and corporation housing and fair wages for corporation workers and workers in contracting firms. The councillors were able to claim that 'they had adhered to their programme and with very good results', especially for the corporation workers.

In 1898 Bowman was elected to the parliamentary committee of the Irish Trades Union Congress (TUC) and became trades council vice-president. However, he was financially embarrassed: his Duncairn ward party broke its promise to subsidize him and, moreover, his former ILP comrade William Walker opposed trades council payments to him. The 1900 khaki election result showed parliamentary Unionism as strong as ever. The next month Bowman stood down as candidate for re-election to the corporation. In 1901, after presiding at the Irish TUC meeting at Sligo, he accepted the post of superintendent of the Falls Road baths.

From then on Bowman concentrated all his attention on the baths, staying outside politics even after he retired as superintendent on 31 August 1922. He died on 3 November 1924 at 65 Rushfield Avenue, Belfast, survived by his wife, Rose, their daughter Minnie Grimmet (Mrs Thomas Howard), and four of their five sons—William James, Robert Ritchie, Hugh, and Thomas Rodgers. He was buried in the Victoria cemetery, Carrickfergus, co. Antrim. Bowman was no less able than his British Labour contemporaries. However, the Belfast situation proved too much for him, as it would for his successors.

D. R. O'Connor Lysaght

Sources J. W. Boyle, *The Irish labor movement in the nineteenth century* (1988) • *Northern Whig* (31 Oct 1885) • *Northern Whig and Belfast Post* (4 Nov 1924) • *Belfast News-Letter* (27 Nov 1897) • *Belfast News-Letter* (2 Oct 1900) • Belfast Trades Council minutes, 1885–6 • Belfast Trades Council minutes, 1897–1901 • d. cert. • m. cert. • R. J. Griffith, *General valuation of (rateable property in) Ireland*, 204 vols. (1847–64) • *Belfast Directory* (1865–6) • *Justice* (1896) • private information (2004)

Archives Linen Hall Library, Belfast, Belfast Trades Council minutes

Likenesses line drawing, repro. in *Belfast Telegraph* (26 Nov 1897) • photograph, repro. in *Irish T.U.C.: Report of Eighth Congress, 1901*

Wealth at death £182 3s. 5d.: probate, 4 Feb 1925, *CGPLA NIre.*

Bowman, Eddowes (1810–1869), teacher and classical scholar, eldest son of John Eddowes *Bowman the elder (1785–1841), and Elizabeth Eddowes (1788–1859), his cousin, was born at Nantwich on 12 November 1810. He was educated chiefly at Hazelwood, near Birmingham, by Thomas Wright Hill, father of Rowland Hill; the latter was his teacher in mathematics. After leaving school he entered the Eagle foundry, Birmingham, with the intention of becoming an engineer. He became, about 1835, sub-manager of the Varteg ironworks, near Pontypool. Here his educational work among the local population revealed a natural aptitude for teaching. On the closing of the Varteg works in 1840, Bowman undertook further study, graduating MA at Glasgow University. He attended lectures at Berlin, acquiring several modern languages and mastering various branches of physical science. In 1842, while at Glasgow, he engaged in a pamphlet dispute with John Taylor, a Unitarian minister, as to whether the sabbath rested on divine authority.

In 1846 Bowman succeeded F. W. Newman to the classical chair in the Manchester New College, and he held that post until the removal of the college to Gordon Square, London, as a purely theological institution, in 1853. He strongly opposed the move and remained in Manchester where, although he had private means, he continued to be an active teacher. He took a particular interest in the education of girls. As the natural sciences came to be his major interest, he delivered several courses of lectures, at the Manchester Royal Institution and elsewhere, on optics and acoustics. For the study of astronomy he built for himself an excellent observatory; he was elected a fellow of the Royal Astronomical Society in 1864. From 1865, when the Owens scholarship was founded in connection with the Unitarian Home Missionary Board, he was one of the examiners. He was a man of undemonstrative disposition, of wise kindness, and of cultural philanthropy. His chief publication was a learned monograph *On the Roman Governors of Syria at the Time of the Birth of Christ* (1855), reprinted from the *Christian Reformer* (October 1855), a magazine to which he was a frequent contributor. He died, unmarried, at Victoria Park, Manchester, on 10 July 1869.

Alexander Gordon, *rev.* M. C. Curthoys

Sources W. H. Herford, *The Inquirer* (10 July 1869) • *Unitarian Herald* (16 July 1869) • J. Hall, *A history of the town and parish of Nantwich, or Wich-Malbank, in the county palatine of Cheshire* (1883), 505 f. • *Monthly Notices of the Royal Astronomical Society*, 30 (1869–70), 87–8 • *CGPLA Eng. & Wales* (1869)

Wealth at death under £12,000: probate, 2 Sept 1869, *CGPLA Eng. & Wales*

Bowman, Henry (*fl.* 1674–1680), composer and music copyist, is of unknown parentage, but he may have been related to the booksellers Francis and Thomas Bowman, of St Mary the Virgin parish, Oxford. The earliest reference to 'Mr Bowman' is dated 5 February 1674, when his 'new Ayres' were first performed at the Oxford music school (Bodl. Oxf., MSS mus. sch. D.241–244).

Probably during the 1670s Bowman copied a number of manuscripts mainly devoted to the Italian and English vocal music then popular in Oxford. The manuscripts Christ Church Mus. 623–626 contain anthems by Edward Lowe, professor of music at Oxford, while BL, Add. MS 30382 is an early source of two vocal duets by Purcell. Several of Bowman's own vocal compositions, which reflect the influence of the Italian works he transcribed, also appear in the latter manuscript. Some loose autograph papers, now bound in Bodl. Oxf., MSS mus. sch. C.203 and C.204, were performing material for the music school, and other works in the same collection, including the ayres in D.241–244, were copied by Lowe, in some cases in collaboration with Bowman.

In 1677 Bowman's *Songs for One, Two and Three Voices* was published at Oxford, engraved in a style modelled on his distinctive musical handwriting. All copies seem to have been produced with a decorative engraved title-page giving only the composer's name and a short title; some also have a printed title-page, dated 1678, identifying Thomas Bowman as publisher. Copies without this extra page also lack the imprimatur of 12 June 1677 and are assumed to have been issued in that year. A second, corrected, edition was published by Richard Davis in 1679, and a further impression was advertised in 1683. Bowman's songs are notable for the quality of their verses by Abraham Cowley and other poets; the high standard of their engraving, at a time when most London music prints used the Granjon moveable typeface; and their inclusion of some symphony songs possibly earlier than any works in this genre by Blow or Purcell.

The printed title-pages of *Songs* describe Bowman as 'Philo-Musicus', which may indicate that he was not a professional musician. There is no record of his having held an official post in Oxford, but he appears to have had a close relationship with Lowe and to have contributed significantly to Oxford's late seventeenth-century flowering as an independent musical centre with a tendency to cultivate its own musicians and a local if limited tradition of music publication. He is last mentioned in Lowe's comment that Bowman's act song 'My Lesbia, let us live and love' was composed for Saturday 10 July 1680 but not performed (Bodl. Oxf., MS mus. sch. C.120).

ROBERT THOMPSON

Sources P. Holman, 'Bowman, Henry', *New Grove*, 2nd edn, vol. 4, 153–4 • J. P. Wainwright, *Musical patronage in seventeenth-century England: Christopher, first Baron Hatton (1605–1670)* (1997) • C. L. Day and E. B. Murrie, *English song books, 1651–1702* (1940) • M. Crum, 'Early lists of the Oxford music school collection', *Music and Letters*, 48 (1967), 23–34 • P. Holman, 'Original sets of parts for Restoration concerted music at Oxford', *Performing the music of Henry Purcell* [Oxford 1993], ed. M. Burden (1996), 9–19, 265–71 • H. E. Salter, ed., *Surveys and tokens*, OHS, 75 (1923)

Bowman, Henry (1814–1883). *See under* Bowman, John Eddowes, the elder (1785–1841).

Bowman, Sir James, first baronet (1898–1978), trade unionist and industrial administrator, was born at Great Corby, near Carlisle, Cumberland, on 8 March 1898, the fifth of the seven children of Robert James Bowman (1861–1948), blacksmith, and his wife, Mary Murray (1865–1941). On leaving school, Bowman was presented with a watch inscribed 'for being never late and never absent'. At the age of fifteen he started work at Ashington colliery. In the war of 1914–18 he served in the Royal Marines. On returning to Ashington 'big pit', where he was a coal filler, he showed an active interest in trade unionism and became the first full-time official at the pit. On 10 March 1923 he married Jean, daughter of Henry Brooks, a miner, of Ashington, Northumberland.

Bowman's years of active lodge membership gave him a keen understanding of the working miner and fostered his gift for exposition and advocacy. He gained respect for his moderate views combined with a certain toughness. In 1935 he was elected general secretary of the Northumberland Miners' Association. He reached national level within the union in 1936, when he was elected to the executive committee of the Mineworkers' Federation of Great Britain (MFGB). In 1939 he was elected vice-president of the MFGB and he was re-elected, unopposed, until his resignation in 1949. Throughout the 1940s Bowman shared power within the MFGB with William Lawther, president, and Arthur Horner, general secretary. He played a major part in merging the federation, with its deep historical and traditional roots in the district unions, into the National Union of Mineworkers. He successfully urged a more cautious, step-by-step approach to reorganization than was demanded by the Yorkshire miners (Arnot, 422).

In the period immediately after the Second World War Bowman was invited by Sir Stafford Cripps to advise on the reorganization of the German trade unions. In 1946 he was elected to the general council of the TUC and was appointed to serve on its international, economic, education, disputes, and organization committees. In 1947–9 he was a member of the royal commission on the press and in May 1949 became a member of the committee on broadcasting chaired by Lord Beveridge. In January 1950, having resigned his former posts, he was appointed chairman of the Northern Division (Northumberland and Cumberland) of the National Coal Board (NCB) at the instigation of Hugh Gaitskell, then minister of fuel and power. Bowman had no doubts about the move; he believed passionately in nationalization, which he saw as the means to a more efficiently managed industry which would bring increased prosperity and security to those employed within it.

In 1955 Bowman was appointed deputy chairman of the NCB and in 1956, on the death of his predecessor, Sir Hubert Houldsworth, he was appointed chairman. He inherited a revised organization, following the acceptance by the board of the report of a committee chaired by Alexander Fleck, which had recommended a strengthening of functional departments and of the central authority of the board. As chairman he dealt mostly with general matters of policy and left supervision of the board's day-to-day business to the deputy chairman, Joseph Latham. An exception was Bowman's use of his trade union connections to maintain good industrial relations. He supported the introduction of new techniques, such as method study, and did much to secure increased mechanization of production methods. This was undoubtedly his most valuable and enduring legacy to the industry.

In 1957 the board faced a crisis as, with increased use of oil, the market for coal declined rapidly. Over the next three years 124 pits were closed and the number of industrial employees was reduced from 710,000 to 583,000. Although open-cast production was almost halved, undistributed coal stocks rose to 36 million tons. There was much criticism of the NCB during this difficult period. Bowman robustly answered it in a long article in *The Times* (11 December 1958). He pointed out that 'the Board did not aim during the years of scarcity to make the high level of profits which would certainly have been reasonable'. There should be more understanding of the industry's position when the market changed. It was a tribute to Bowman's skill and his understanding of the mining community that, despite the criticism, these policies were effected without opposing industrial action. Meanwhile the pace of mechanization was maintained, with output per man-shift reaching a new record level.

On the expiry of his term of office in 1961 Bowman decided to retire because of ill health. He and his wife returned to Newcastle, which they had always regarded as home. He was succeeded, as chairman of the NCB, by Alfred Robens. In the final annual report of his five years as chairman tribute was paid to him: 'his tenure of office included some of the most difficult years since the industry was nationalised and his resolution and clear vision were an inspiration to everyone in the industry' (NCB annual report, 1960, iv).

Bowman was a powerfully built man of medium height, whose confident physical presence, recalling his early career as a miner, was allied to an ease of manner which enabled him to deal with equal success with trade unionists, mining engineers, civil servants, and politicians. He possessed an outgoing personality which was demonstrated in his strength as a public speaker, whether delivering a prepared set-piece or an impromptu tribute, and in his skill as a raconteur, where he was helped by an accent which retained attractive traces of his Cumbrian origin and Northumbrian upbringing.

Bowman was made a JP in 1935. He was appointed CBE in 1952 and knighted in 1957. In January 1961 he was created a baronet. In October 1958 he was made an honorary DCL of Durham University. Bowman died on 25 September 1978 at his home, Woodlands, Killingworth Drive, West Moor, Newcastle upon Tyne. He had one son, George (*b.* 1923), who succeeded to the baronetcy, and one daughter.

DEREK EZRA

Sources *The Times* (6 Oct 1978) · *The Times* (10 Oct 1978) · *The Times* (12 Oct 1978) · annual reports, 1956–60, national coal board · W. Ashworth and M. Pegg, *The nationalized industry: 1946–1982* (1986), vol. 5 of *The history of the British coal industry* (1984–93) · R. P. Arnot, *The miners: a history of the Miners' Federation of Great Britain*, 3: … *from 1930 onwards* (1961) · J. Bowman, 'Changing demand for coal', *The Times* (11 Dec 1958) · Burke, *Peerage* (1967) · private information (1986) · personal knowledge (2004)

Archives FILM BFI NFTVA, documentary footage

Likenesses D. Low, pencil caricatures, NPG

Wealth at death £20,109: probate, 20 Nov 1978, *CGPLA Eng. & Wales*

Bowman, John (*d.* 1739), singer and actor, was said to have been born at Pillerton, Warwickshire, on 27 December 1664, the son of John Bowman. However, he was stated to be in his eighty-eighth year when he died, implying that he was born in 1651 or 1652. His early stage career indicates a birth date of *c.*1660. He was 'brought into the Duke's Theatre to Sing at Seven Years old' (Betterton, 31). His first known acting roles, Peter Santlow in *The Counterfeit Bridegroom* (1677) (an anonymous adaptation of Thomas Middleton's *No Wit, No Help, Like a Woman's*) and the eighteen-year-old Saunter in Thomas Otway's *Friendship in Fashion* (1678), both included singing. As 'a Youth, and fam'd for his Voice' (Cibber, 317), he sang before Charles II at Nell Gwyn's lodgings. In autumn 1680 Bowman performed Henry Purcell's music as the bass chief priest, Atticus, in Nathaniel Lee's *Theodosius*. He created Priuli, Belvidera's father, in Otway's tragedy *Venice Preserv'd* (1682), a role he played for the last time in October 1738, five months before his death. Bowman acted with the United Company from its formation in 1682 and became a member of the royal private musick in November 1684, singing at court in Purcell's odes for the birthdays of James II (1687) and Mary II (1693). Purcell wrote music for him in Lee's *The Massacre of Paris*, Thomas Southerne's *Sir Anthony Love*, and John Dryden's *Amphitryon* and *Tyrannick Love*. In the Dryden–Purcell opera *King Arthur* (1691) he created the role of the villainous earthy spirit Grimbald. Purcell composed his famous mad song 'Let the dreadful engines' for Bowman to sing as Cardenio in Thomas D'Urfey's *Don Quixote*, part 1 (1694). The 'Gay good Natur'd Boman' (Danchin, *Prologues and Epilogues of the Restoration*, 3.431) developed a line in fop roles, such as Lord Brainless in D'Urfey's *The Marriage-Hater Match'd* (1692) and Lord Froth in William Congreve's *The Double Dealer* (1693), where he sang a song of his own composition, 'Ancient Phillis has young graces'. Later he created Tattle in Congreve's *Love for Love* (1695) and Petulant in *The Way of the World* (1700). On 6 August 1692, at St Marylebone, Bowman married Elizabeth Watson, the adopted daughter of the actor Thomas Betterton, 'a very fine woman and a pleasing actress' (Davies, 3.391), who sang and acted on stage until 1 April 1707. She may have been the Elizabeth Bowman buried at St Martin-in-the-Fields on 21 April 1707. Their son, 'young Bowman', was an actor and stage singer from 1712, but remained a very minor figure. His wife sang at Drury Lane from 1715 until 1728, when she moved with her husband to Norwich. The younger Mrs Bowman was a leading actress in the theatres of East Anglia until 1756; two years later her husband received a share of a London benefit for distressed actors.

After the United Company broke up in 1694, John Bowman became a sharer in Thomas Betterton's Lincoln's Inn Fields Company, where his acting career continued as before and he performed new music by the house composer, John Eccles. He sang in concerts and at Queen Anne's coronation (1702). Tensions developed in Betterton's company, the advent of Italian opera created problems for London actors, and Bowman's career declined. He may have been the Mr Bowman who appeared at the Smock Alley Theatre, Dublin, in 1707–9 and 1714, although the known roles for that actor were very minor. After 1714 he worked steadily as a middle-ranking actor at Drury Lane for the rest of his long career. He specialized in dignified older roles, such as Duncan in *Macbeth* and the Ghost in *Hamlet*, and was particularly praised as the Justice in *Henry IV* and the Judge in Jonson's *Volpone*. 'That Stage Chronicle, Mr. *John Bowman*' (Chetwood, 253) became a source of information and anecdotes for theatre historians. Bowman claimed never to have lost a day's acting because of illness. His last advertised appearance was as Duncan on 1 January 1739, and he died on 23 March 1739. The *London Daily Post* (26 March 1739) called him 'the oldest Player, the oldest Singer, and the oldest Ringer in England … a Man of good Character, a facetious, agreeable Companion, and well respected'.

OLIVE BALDWIN and THELMA WILSON

Sources W. Van Lennep and others, eds., *The London stage, 1660–1800*, pt 1: *1660–1700* (1965) • E. L. Avery, ed., *The London stage, 1660–1800*, pt 2: *1700–1729* (1960) • A. H. Scouten, ed., *The London stage, 1660–1800*, pt 3: *1729–1747* (1961) • A. Ashbee, ed., *Records of English court music*, 1 (1986); 2 (1987); 5 (1991); 8 (1995) • J. Milhous and R. D. Hume, eds., *A register of English theatrical documents, 1660–1737*, 2 vols. (1991) • P. Danchin, ed., *The prologues and epilogues of the Restoration, 1660–1700*, 7 vols. (1981–8), vols. 2–3 • P. Danchin, ed., *The prologues and epilogues of the eighteenth century: a complete edition* (1990–), vol. 1 • C. L. Day and E. B. Murrie, *English song-books, 1651–1702: a bibliography with a first-line index of songs* (1940) • D. Hunter, *Opera and song books published in England, 1703–1726* (1997) • O. Baldwin and T. Wilson, 'Purcell's stage singers: a documentary list', *Performing the music of Henry Purcell* [Oxford 1993], ed. M. Burden (1996), 275–81 [list of printed songs, texts of plays with Purcell's music, MSS] • T. Betterton, [W. Oldys and others], *The history of the English stage* (1741) • C. Cibber, *An apology for the life of Mr. Colley Cibber* (1740) • T. Davies, *Dramatic miscellanies: consisting of critical observations on several plays of Shakespeare*, 3 vols. (1783–4) • W. R. Chetwood, *A general history of the stage, from its origin in Greece to the present time* (1749) • *An account of the life of Mr. Thomas Betterton* (1749) • [J. Hill], *The actor: a treatise on the art of playing* (1750) • [J. Hill], *The actor, or, A treatise on the art of playing* (1755) • [G. Jacob], *The poetical register, or, The lives and characters of the English dramatick poets*, [1] (1719) • J. Downes, *Roscius Anglicanus*, ed. J. Milhous and R. D. Hume, new edn (1987) • W. S. Clark, *The early Irish stage: the beginnings to 1720* (1955) • S. Rosenfeld, *Strolling players and drama in the provinces, 1660–1765* (1939) • parish register, London, St Marylebone, 6 Aug 1692 [marriage] • *London Daily Post and General Advertiser* (26 March 1739) • *GM*, 1st ser., 9 (1739), 161

Bowman, John Eddowes, the elder (1785–1841), naturalist, was born on 30 October 1785 at Nantwich, where his father, Eddowes Bowman (1758–1844), was a tobacconist. A studious child, he was educated at grammar school. His father gave him a taste for botany, and his friend Joseph Hunter (1783–1861), a fondness for genealogy. He initially worked in his father's shop, becoming manager of the manufacturing department, and later traveller. Having been dissuaded by his father from becoming a minister of the Unitarian church, to which his family belonged, in 1813 he joined, as junior partner, a banking business which his father had entered. Its failure in 1816 left him penniless, and he became manager at Welshpool of a branch of the bank of Beck & Co. of Shrewsbury. In 1824 he became managing partner of a bank at Wrexham, and was able to retire from business in 1830.

From 1837 Bowman lived in Manchester, where he pursued his interests in science. He was a fellow of the Linnean and Geological societies, and one of the founders of the Manchester Geological Society. He was chiefly interested in mosses, fungi, and parasitical plants. A minute fossil, which he detected in Derbyshire, is named after him *Endothyra bowmanni*. In the latter part of his life he devoted himself almost entirely to geology.

On 6 July 1809, Bowman married his cousin, Elizabeth (1788–1859), daughter of W. Eddowes of Shrewsbury. The couple had a daughter who died in 1838 and four sons, Eddowes *Bowman (1810–1869), Henry Bowman [*see below*], William *Bowman (1816–1892), and John Eddowes *Bowman the younger (1819–1856). Bowman died on 4 December 1841 in Manchester.

Henry Bowman (1814–1883), the second son of John Eddowes Bowman, was an architect in Manchester. With James Hadfield he was joint author of the *Ecclesiastical Architecture of Great Britain, from the Conquest to the Reformation* (1845), and with his partner, J. S. Crowther, of *The Churches of the Middle Ages* (1857). He died at Brockham Green, near Reigate, on 14 May 1883.

Alexander Gordon, *rev.* Giles Hudson

Sources J. J. Taylor, 'A sketch of the life and character of John Eddowes Bowman', *Memoirs of the Literary and Philosophical Society of Manchester*, 2nd ser., 7 (1846), 45–85 • *Proceedings of the Linnean Society of London*, 1 (1838–48), 135–7 • K. B. Thomas, 'The manuscripts of Sir William Bowman', *Medical History*, 10 (1966), 245–56 • Desmond, *Botanists*, rev. edn

Archives Botanical Garden, Oxford, botanical samples • RBG Kew, letters

Wealth at death £16,880 11*s.* 0*d.*—Henry Bowman: probate, 27 June 1883, *CGPLA Eng. & Wales*

Bowman, John Eddowes, the younger (1819–1856), chemist, was born at Welshpool in north Wales on 7 July 1819, the fourth son of John Eddowes *Bowman the elder (1785–1841), banker and naturalist, and his wife, Elizabeth Eddowes (1788–1859), daughter of William Eddowes of Shrewsbury. An older brother was Sir William *Bowman, ophthalmic surgeon. Bowman was educated at Hazelwood School, Birmingham, and Mr Beard's school, Manchester. A career in the cotton industry was curtailed, in 1839, by persistent lameness. Following initial chemical instruction in Manchester, in 1842 he became a pupil of J. F. Daniell at King's College, London. He then spent a short time at the laboratory of Dumas in Paris, before returning to Manchester to practise as a chemist. He joined the Literary and Philosophical Society and lectured before the Royal Manchester Institution on steam boiler explosions, in 1845.

On 5 January 1844 Bowman married Ellen (1814–1868), daughter of Thomas Paget, surgeon, of Leicester. They had three children: Edith, John Herbert, and George Cyril. In January 1845 Bowman joined the Chemical Society of London and from October of that year he was demonstrator of chemistry in King's College, in succession to W. A. Miller. There he taught practical chemistry to medical and applied science students.

To facilitate this teaching, Bowman wrote *An Introduction to Practical Chemistry, Including Analysis* (1848) and *A Practical Handbook of Medical Chemistry* (1850), updated after his death (until 1885 and 1862 respectively) by C. L. Bloxam. Bowman became professor of practical chemistry at King's College in 1851 and was assisted by his demonstrators, T. F. Hardwich (1851) and Bloxam (1854). His publication of original papers had ceased in 1846, and he was known mainly for his teaching because his frail health precluded active laboratory work. Bowman died, following an attack of influenza, at his home, 5 York Villas, Campden Hill, Kensington, on 10 February 1856 and was buried in Kensal Green cemetery on the 15th.

Robin J. Spring

Sources J. Hall, *A history of the town and parish of Nantwich, or Wich-Malbank, in the county palatine of Cheshire* (1883) • *Quarterly Journal of the Chemical Society*, 9 (1857), 159–60 • private information (2004) •

R. J. Spring, 'The development of chemistry in London in the nineteenth century', PhD diss., U. Lond., 1979 • R. H. Kargon, *Science in Victorian Manchester* (1977) • 'Account of funeral of John Dalton', *Manchester Guardian* (14 Aug 1844), 6 • R. F. Bud, 'The discipline of chemistry: the origins and early years of the Chemical Society of London', PhD diss., University of Pennsylvania, 1980, 393 • Burke, *Peerage* • Kensal Green cemetery records, General Cemetery Company • F. J. C. Hearnshaw, *The centenary history of King's College, London, 1828–1928* (1929) • *DNB* • m. cert. • d. cert.

Archives priv. coll.

Likenesses W. Bowman, pencil sketch, *c.*1833, repro. in *Medical History*, 10 (July 1966), fig. 3

Wealth at death £9163 18*s.* 5*d.*; incl. gift of £8000 to King's College Hospital: PRO, death duty records, IR 2053, f. 162 et seq.

Bowman [*née* Bradford], **Laura** (**1881–1957**), musical entertainer, was born in Quincy, Illinois, USA, on 3 October 1881, the daughter of Charles Bradford (*c.*1850–*c.*1915), bartender, and his wife, Lois Adelaide, *née* Yeates (*c.*1850–1912). After being taken by her aunt for an education in Washington, DC, she rejoined her parents in Cincinnati and, in 1898, married Henry Ward Bowman, railway porter.

Bowman separated from her husband in 1903, moved to London with the very successful negro revue *In Dahomey*, and worked in Britain for several years. Partnering comedian Pete Hampton, who became her husband, she made recordings, including songs from *In Dahomey*, and toured all over the continent, billed as the Darktown Entertainers, working with Will Garland and Fred Douglas. Hampton, born in Kentucky in 1871, made recordings both with Bowman and more often as a banjo soloist and singer, recording more than any contemporary black American. In London in 1906 he recorded with white American Burt Earle, an expert banjo player: such black and white musical co-operation was not possible in the USA for another twenty years.

Bowman and Hampton were active in London in the summer of 1906, recording several discs, then touring the provinces. Much of 1907 was spent in Germany, with some weeks in Italy followed by most of 1908 on tour around Britain. She and Hampton then lived at 14 Marlborough Road, Wimbledon Park, south-west Surrey. They had a successful tour on the Hippodrome circuit, and made an appearance at Buckingham Palace. A tour of France, Belgium, Germany, Russia, and Poland from 1909 to 1910 was followed by a brief return to America and, late in 1910, by yet another tour of British theatres including Southend, Bournemouth, and Southampton. The pair recorded in London in late 1911. By this time Bowman's parents were also living at their London home, and her mother died in London in July 1912. In 1913 Bowman, Hampton, and Bowman's father returned to America, where Bowman's father died about 1915 and Hampton in 1916.

Bowman never reappeared in Britain, but settled in New York. She married Sidney Kirkpatrick (*d.* 1932) and they worked as Hawaiians to avoid negrophobic customers. By 1928 she had moved to California. She appeared on stage and in films into the 1940s, helping to form the Negro Actors Association. Her fame in the USA was as an actress. In 1935 she married LeRoi Antoine, whose unreliable memoir, *Achievement: the Life of Laura Bowman*, appeared in 1961, four years after Bowman's death in Los Angeles, California, on 29 March 1957.

Laura Bowman, whose mixed race is clear in the many photographs with the darker Hampton, presented an elegant show, singing (she was a soprano), playing the banjo, duetting with Hampton (a baritone), and presenting spirituals and American popular songs such as 'My Old Kentucky Home' and 'The Old Folks at Home'. Her experience of British and continental audiences assisted her later fight for black rights in the United States.

JEFFREY GREEN and RAINER E. LOTZ

Sources R. E. Lotz, *Black people: entertainers of African descent in Europe and Germany* (1997) [with audio CD] • J. A. Tanner, 'Laura Bowman', *Black women in America: an historical encyclopedia*, ed. D. C. Hine and others, 2 vols. (1993) • L. Antoine, *Achievement: the life of Laura Bowman* (New York, 1961) • J. Green, '*In Dahomey* in London in 1903', *Black Perspective in Music*, 11/1 (1983), 22–40 • *Variety* (3 April 1957)

Archives SOUND priv. coll., disc and cylinder recordings

Likenesses photographs, repro. in Lotz, *Black people*, pp. 114, 116

Bowman, Walter (**1699–1782**), tutor and antiquary, was the son of Walter Bowman of Logie in Fife. He travelled extensively in Italy, both on his own and with successive pupils. He was tutor to Samuel Rolle on the latter's grand tour of 1724–5, and was enrolled at Padua University each September from 1725 to 1727. From 1730 to 1734 he accompanied Simon Harcourt, later first Earl Harcourt, on a grand tour of France, Italy, and Austria. By April 1743 he had returned to London, and he lived for many years at East Molesey in Surrey. He undertook his final tour abroad in 1764–5, when he travelled as tutor to Francis Seymour-Conway, later second marquess of Hertford. He was rewarded with the place of comptroller of the port of Bristol. A zealous collector and virtuoso, he corresponded with fellow antiquaries and made detailed notes of his travels which survive in manuscript volumes in the Biblioteca Nazionale in Florence and in the National Library of Scotland. In 1735 he was elected a fellow of the Society of Antiquaries and in 1745 of the Royal Society. He contributed several papers, chiefly on classical antiquities, to the former society; three of these were printed in volume one of *Archaeologia*. His only published communication in the *Philosophical Transactions of the Royal Society* (46, 684) was an eccentric letter addressed to Dr Stephen Hales on an earthquake felt at East Molesey on 14 March 1750. He was also a member of the Society of Dilettanti, and a friend of Horace Walpole.

Bowman, who did not marry, spent his last years at Egham in Surrey and died in February 1782. In his will he left singularly minute and meticulous instructions regarding the arrangement and preservation of his fine library at Logie.

GORDON GOODWIN, *rev.* J. A. MARCHAND

Sources J. Evans, *A history of the Society of Antiquaries* (1956) • J. Ingamells, ed., *A dictionary of British and Irish travellers in Italy, 1701–1800* (1997), 113–14 • Nichols, *Illustrations*, 4.795 • J. M. Leighton, *History of the county of Fife*, 3 vols. (1840), 2.50 • Walpole, *Corr.* • will, PRO, PROB 11/1088, sig. 111

Archives Biblioteca Nazionale Centrale, Florence, MS notes on travels in Italy and France • BL, corresp. and papers, Add. MSS 754, 4301, 4055, 6183 • Bodl. Oxf., household and personal account book • NL Scot., album of letters, drawings, and prints • NL Scot., MS notes | priv. coll., letters to Arthur Balfour

Wealth at death numerous small bequests; £250 to the children of his brother and sister: will, 1763, PRO, PROB 11/1088, fols. 127*r*–132*r*

Bowman, Sir William, first baronet (**1816–1892**), ophthalmic surgeon and anatomist, was born at Sweetbriar Hall, Hospital Street, Nantwich, Cheshire, on 20 July 1816, the third of the four sons (there was one daughter) of John Eddowes *Bowman the elder (1785–1841), a banker as well as botanist and fellow of the Linnean Society, and his wife and cousin, Elizabeth (1788–1859), daughter of William Eddowes, a bookseller of Shrewsbury. His brothers were Eddowes *Bowman, Henry *Bowman [*see under* Bowman, John Eddowes, the elder], and John Eddowes *Bowman (1819–1856). At the age of ten he was sent to Hazelwood School, near Birmingham, run by Thomas Wright Hill, father of Sir Rowland Hill. This was a progressive school that had abolished corporal punishment and was regulated by rules drawn up and enforced by the students themselves. At about the age of sixteen Bowman was apprenticed to W. A. Betts of the Birmingham Infirmary, and worked under Joseph Hodgson, later founder of the Birmingham Eye Hospital.

In 1837 Bowman went to London and joined the medical department of King's College, University of London. In the following year he visited seventeen hospitals in the Netherlands, Germany, Austria, and France, travelling with Francis Galton, who had been a fellow pupil under Hodgson. Galton's account of their journey is entertainingly told in his *Memoirs of my Life* (1908). When King's College Hospital was founded in 1839, Bowman was elected to the staff as assistant surgeon, and in the same year he was also appointed junior demonstrator of anatomy and curator of the museum at King's College, working closely with Richard Partridge, the professor of anatomy. On 28 December 1842 Bowman married Harriet Paget (*d.* 1900), fifth daughter of Thomas Paget, a surgeon of Leicester. They had seven children.

In 1846 Bowman was appointed assistant surgeon to the Royal London Ophthalmic Hospital, Moorfields, becoming full surgeon in 1851; he remained there until mandatory retirement at the age of sixty in 1876. Elected joint professor of physiology and general anatomy (with Robert Bentley Todd) at King's College in 1848, he became an honorary fellow in 1855 and a member of the council in 1879. He became full surgeon to King's College Hospital in 1856, and though the claims of private practice (necessitated by his growing family) compelled him to resign this office in 1862, he maintained his interest in the institution until he died. He continued in private practice until the age of seventy and participated in scientific meetings for several years after that.

Bowman was elected a fellow of the Royal Society in 1841, at the unusually early age of twenty-five, and subsequently served on the council and as one of the vice-presidents. He was elected a fellow of the Royal College of

Sir William Bowman, first baronet (1816–1892), by George Frederic Watts, 1865

Surgeons of England in 1844. In 1867 the degree of MD *honoris causa* was granted him by the University of Dublin, and in 1880 the University of Cambridge awarded him the degree of LLD. In 1884 he was made a baronet.

Bowman became the leading ophthalmic surgeon in London after the death of John Dalrymple in 1852. At the Great Exhibition of 1851, held at the Crystal Palace in London, Bowman met Albrecht von Graefe and Frans Cornelius Donders, and their enthusiastic exchange of ideas regarding ophthalmology and their lasting friendship were a great influence on his professional life. Bowman was among the first in England to become expert in the use of the ophthalmoscope. In 1857 he employed and advocated strongly von Graefe's treatment of glaucoma by iridectomy, and he was busy during the years 1864 and 1865 with new methods of treating cases of detached retina and cataract.

In 1880 Bowman was elected the first president of the Ophthalmological Society of the United Kingdom, having played a large role in its founding. During the three years that he held this post, he liberally supported the society through money for its library. A few years later the society established an annual Bowman lecture in his honour; and when in 1965 the society decided to acquire armorial bearings, the arms embodied references to Bowman, including the bowman at the crest. In 1888 the Bowman Testimonial Fund commissioned his portrait to be painted by Walter William Ouless; it was subsequently exhibited in the Royal Academy.

Bowman took a considerable interest in nursing, a concern apparently stimulated by his friendship with Florence Nightingale, whose first nursing post was at the Harley Street Institution for the Care of Sick Gentlewomen, where Bowman was a surgeon. They remained friends, and some of their correspondence has been preserved. In conjunction with Robert Bentley Todd and others, Bowman established the St John's House and Sisterhood, an institution which provided trained nurses for the sick and poor, and a few years later he was able to aid Florence Nightingale by sending out trained nurses to the East during the Crimean War.

Bowman's work divides itself sharply into two periods: one of pure anatomical research, the other concerned with the practice of ophthalmic surgery. His anatomical and physiological investigations were chiefly carried out in the years 1839–42. Many of them were prepared as entries for Robert Bentley Todd's illustrated *Cyclopaedia of Anatomy and Physiology* (5 vols., 1836–59) and read before various meetings of the Royal Society. Muscle tissue was the first structure he minutely examined with his microscope, and this work was followed by a histological study of the kidney, for which he was awarded the Royal Society's medal in 1842. He also collaborated with Todd in producing *The Physiological Anatomy and Physiology of Man* (2 vols., 1843–56). Both works contain numerous illustrations by Bowman himself, who combined accomplished artistic skills with mastery of the microscope. While preparing entries for these two publications, Bowman discovered many new anatomical structures, at least six of which still bear his name, such as the *capsula glomeruli*, still called 'Bowman's capsule'. In 1847 he presented an important paper on the mechanism of accommodation to a meeting in Oxford of the British Association for the Advancement of Science, at which he demonstrated simultaneously with, but independently of, Ernst Willhelm Brueke (1819–1892) the structure and function of the ciliary muscle. After 1850 Bowman's attention turned solely to ophthalmic surgery.

Bowman died of pneumonia at his large country house, Joldwynds, between Dorking and Guildford, Surrey, on 29 March 1892, and was buried on 1 April in the neighbouring churchyard of Holmbury St Mary. To his widow he bequeathed his country estate of Joldwynds, his London residence (since 1850) at 5 Clifford Street, parish of St James, and other properties in London, as well as an estate valued at over £100,000. Bowman had been close friends with the artist George Frederic Watts, and possessed several paintings by Watts, including his own portrait painted in 1865, Watts's portraits of Alfred Lord Tennyson, and Donders, and Watts's self-portrait (the latter now in the Tate collection). Bowman's widow commissioned John Cother Webb to make an engraving of his portrait by W. W. Ouless, copies of which she then distributed to all subscribers to his collected ophthalmological works, which were assembled by friends and published in two volumes in 1892.

Bowman made fundamental contributions to histology and to the knowledge of the structure of the eye, the kidney and striated muscle, and of other structures. These achievements are the more remarkable when it is recalled that he employed relatively simple techniques and that no highly accurate microtome or staining techniques were then available. Bowman profoundly influenced anatomical thinking and teaching by constantly relating minutely described anatomical structures to their physiological functions. Through his skills as an anatomist and microscopist he set a model for future research in physiology and histology.

As an ophthalmic surgeon Bowman maintained a constant interest in new techniques and new technologies, and he modified or developed a number of surgical procedures, including the treatment of lacrimal obstruction, antiglaucoma iridectomy, and the removal of soft cataracts by a suction instrument (which he performed under chloroform anaesthesia). Well known for his manual dexterity, a remarkably light touch, and excellent operative skills, he developed a large private practice in addition to the patients he attended as part of his duties at Moorfields. As a conscientious committee member and organizer, he was noted for his powers of persuasion. A handsome and slender man, who rarely drank, never smoked, and was abstemious in eating, he exemplified certain Victorian virtues through his dignity and reserve, his early rising and constant hard work, and his religious piety (of a dissenting nature). Bowman did not write a book of his own, but through his twenty-three papers and his entries in anatomical encyclopaedias, he became one of the most important English figures of the nineteenth century in the fields of anatomy, histology, and ophthalmic surgery. D'A. POWER, *rev.* EMILIE SAVAGE-SMITH

Sources K. B. Thomas, 'The manuscripts of Sir William Bowman', *Medical History*, 10 (1966), 245–56 • R. R. James, 'Sir William Bowman … 1816–1892', *British Journal of Ophthalmology*, 9 (1925), 481–94 [two plates] • B. Chance, 'Sir William Bowman: anatomist, physiologist, and ophthalmologist', *Annals of Medical History*, 6 (1924), 143–58 • F. W. Law, 'Sir William Bowman', *Survey of Ophthalmology*, 19 (1975), 302–7 • *The collected papers of Sir William Bowman*, ed. J. Burdon-Sanderson and J. W. Hulke (1892) • J. P., *PRS*, 52 (1892–3), i–vii • *Medico-Chirurgical Transactions*, 76 (1893), 10–12 • *Ophthalmic Review*, 11 (1892), 129 • *BMJ* (2 April 1892), 343–5 • *The Lancet* (2 April 1892), 770–81 • J. Hirschberg, *Geschichte der Augenheilkunde*, 4 (1914), 197–224

Archives priv. coll. • RS | BL, corresp. with Florence Nightingale, Add. MSS 45797–45809 *passim* • BL, corresp. with W. E. Gladstone, Add. MSS 44450, 44469, 44161

Likenesses G. F. Watts, oils, 1865, priv. coll. [*see illus.*] • E. Edwards, photograph, 1867, Wellcome L. • Barraud & Jerrard, photograph, 1873, repro. in James, 'Sir William Bowman', following p. 488 • J. C. Webb, mezzotint, exh. 1889 (after painting by W. W. Ouless), Wellcome L. • S. Lawrence, crayon, priv. coll. • Lock & Whitfield, photograph, Wellcome L. • Lock & Whitfield, photograph, woodburytype, NPG; repro. in T. Cooper, *Men of mark: a gallery of contemporary portraits* (1880) • J. H. Lynch, lithograph (after painting by S. Lawrence), RCP Lond. • T. H. Maguire, lithograph, RCP Lond. • Maull & Polyblank, photograph, Wellcome L. • W. W. Ouless, painting, priv. coll. • J. C. Webb, mezzotint (after W. W. Ouless), BM

Wealth at death £107,607 16*s.* 3*d.*: resworn probate, July 1893, *CGPLA Eng. & Wales* (1892)

Bownas, Samuel (1677–1753), Quaker minister and writer, was born on 20 January 1677 at Shap, Westmorland, the second of the two children of Anthony Bownas (*d.* 1677), shoemaker, and his wife, Agnes. Samuel's father died within a month of his birth. Thereafter money was short and he and his brother received only a basic education in reading and writing. At thirteen Bownas was apprenticed to his uncle, a blacksmith, who mistreated him, and later to Samuel Parat, a Quaker of Sedbergh, Yorkshire. Samuel's mother made sure that he was educated as a Quaker, but although he followed the traditional forms of dress, speech, and worship they meant little to him. He went regularly to meeting but confessed that 'the greater part of my time, I slept' (Bownas, *Account*, 5). However, aged about twenty, he was shaken from his lethargy by a visiting travelling minister, Anne Wilson, who rebuked him as 'a traditional *Quaker*' (ibid.), that is, one who came and went from meeting untouched and unchanged.

Bownas was 'convinced' and shortly after felt called to the ministry. For the three remaining years of his apprenticeship he stayed in the Sedbergh area. On completing his seven years Bownas began to travel widely, drawing on the experience and encouragement of many fellow ministers, including James Dickinson and James Wilson. They let him know if he was becoming too pleased with his ministry and urged him to be faithful. On his travels he was careful to remain financially independent and supported himself by harvest-work and other enterprises. About 1701, on a visit to Sherborne in Dorset, Bownas met Joan Slade, his future wife. However, the couple agreed to postpone their marriage as Samuel felt called to travel in the ministry to America, and he set sail for Maryland, by way of Scotland, in 1702.

While in America, Bownas was particularly engaged with challenging the preaching of the renegade Quaker George Keith, who had taken Anglican orders. Keith had Bownas prosecuted for preaching and thrown into gaol on Long Island, where he was held for nearly a year. Samuel learned to make shoes in order to earn a living and received visits from, among others, an 'Indian king' together with 'three of his chief Men' (Bownas, *Account*, 79). After his release in 1703 Samuel travelled in New England in the ministry before returning home at the end of 1706. Early in the following year he and Joan were married and settled in Lymington, Hampshire. In 1708 he visited Ireland, and in 1712 he was imprisoned for tithes in Bristol gaol by the vicar of Lymington. Bownas was soon released after the clergyman tricked Joan into paying the money in question, a mistake which troubled her greatly on her deathbed in October 1719.

On 11 April 1722 Samuel married Elizabeth Nicholls, *née* Priest (*d.* 1746), a widow from Bridport in Dorset, to where he now moved. Samuel used his wife's capital to set up in business and became a prosperous merchant. He also read widely and educated himself, establishing a reputation as a well-known travelling minister. Described as 'of a grave deportment, and of a tall comely and manly aspect' Bownas had a strong, clear voice and preached with 'divine authority and majestic innocence' (Bownas, *Account*, vi).

In 1726 he returned to America, where he met Elizabeth Hanson, from whom he heard the story of her capture, with her children, by Native Americans in 1724. Hanson's narrative was subsequently published as *An Account of the Captivity of E. H. Taken in Substance from her Own Mouth by Samuel Bownas*. Samuel offered his own *Description of the Qualifications Necessary to a Gospel Minister* in 1750; the book, which was well received, reached its fifth edition by 1839.

Towards the end of his life Bownas grew increasingly disillusioned with the Society of Friends. In a letter to an old companion and fellow minister James Wilson he spoke of a church 'very barren of young ministers to what it was in our youth', and with 'but very little convincement to what was then'. To Bownas, the quality of 'convincement' was the main purpose of his ministry, though its importance was often ignored by his audience: '"The man spoke well" say they, and that is all I get for my labours', he wrote to Wilson ('Samuel Bownas to James Wilson'). In spite of his disillusionment Samuel continued to travel extensively for as long as he was physically able. From 1749 he became increasingly infirm, 'his hands shook and his eye-sight failed him much' (Bownas, *Account*, 197), but he continued to attend meetings locally until his death at Bridport on 2 April 1753 aged seventy-six.

Samuel Bownas was characterized by his contemporaries as 'a Man of Peace and Prudence' (Bownas, *Account*, vii) who tried to uphold and pass on the traditions of Quakerism while never giving undue importance to forms for their own sake. His life showed the importance for even those born and brought up as Quakers to come to a living faith for themselves. The autobiographical *Account of the Life, Travels, and Christian experiences … of Samuel Bownas*—'a plain Man's plain and good account of his own Progress in Religion' (ibid., iii)—was published in 1756 with a prefatory note by Joseph Besse.

GIL SKIDMORE

Sources S. Bownas, *An account of the life, travels, and Christian experiences in the work of the ministry of Samuel Bownas* (1756) • S. Bownas, *A description of the qualifications necessary to a gospel minister* (1750) • 'Samuel Bownas to James Wilson', *Journal of the Friends' Historical Society*, 1 (1903–4), 121–3
Archives RS Friends, Lond.

Bownd, Nicholas (*d.* 1613), Church of England clergyman and religious writer, was one of at least three sons of Richard Bound (*d.* in or before 1573), physician to the duke of Norfolk and living in Cambridgeshire, and his wife, Katherine Wood (*d.* 1612). It is not known whether he was educated at Eton College like his elder brother Alexander (1547/8–1622), but like him went to Cambridge, matriculating from Peterhouse in Michaelmas 1568. He graduated BA early in 1572, and that year became a fellow. In August 1573, if not before, he acquired connections among the East Anglian godly when his widowed mother married Richard *Greenham (early 1540s–1594), rector of Dry Drayton, Cambridgeshire. Having proceeded MA in 1575, and received the rectory of Fulbeck, Lincolnshire, in 1576, he followed his brother Alexander into the ministry, being ordained deacon and priest at Ely on 2 June 1580. With John *Dod, who was also ordained at Ely that year and who married Bownd's sister Ann in or after 1585, he formed part of a nucleus of Jacobean clergy trained in Greenham's 'rectory seminary', and he was among the minority of Suffolk ministers who 'resolved not to subscribe' to Archbishop John Whitgift's articles of 1583 targeting nonconformity (R. G. Usher, ed., *The Presbyterian Movement in the Reign of Elizabeth I*, CS, 3rd ser., 8, 1905, xlix). He was instituted on 3 September 1585 to the rectory of Norton, near Bury St Edmunds, Suffolk, a living in his college's gift. At some point he resigned his fellowship, and on 3 October 1592 he married Elizabeth, widow of John More (1542–1592), the late puritan minister of St Andrew's, Norwich; she already had two daughters. He proceeded DD in 1594.

Bownd took on the mantle of More's literary executor and on 24 August 1593 signed the preface of More's *A Table from the Beginning of the World to this Day* (1593), dedicated to Edmund Scambler, bishop of Norwich, and the city corporation. However, Bownd is perhaps best-known for his published works on the Christian sabbath. His early reflections on this subject, dating from about 1586, were presented in a series of sermons, eventually published as *The Doctrine of the Sabbath* (1595) with a dedication to Bownd's patron Robert Devereux, earl of Essex, and a full-page engraving of his arms. Dependent in many parts (as he acknowledged) on Greenham's as yet unpublished sabbatarian treatise, Bownd's work articulated a theological understanding of Sunday observance that had become a growing concern for many godly Elizabethan protestants. He emphasized the morally binding character of the fourth commandment, the divine institution of the sabbath as the Lord's day, the duty to rest and worship on Sunday, and the cessation of non-religious activities (working, festivals, sports, markets) that distracted from devotion and acts of mercy. Because of clerical quarrels in Suffolk and political rivalries surrounding Devereux, *The Doctrine of the Sabbath* was condemned in 1599. Bownd's local clerical protagonist Thomas Rogers tarred his sabbatarian teaching as 'papistry or Brownism' in a sermon delivered on 10 December that year (BL, Add. MS 38492, fol. 104).

In his early career at least, Bownd was an active member of the classis movement and was among those who presided over the celebrated combination lecture at Bury St Edmunds. Following the pastoral example of his stepfather, he occupied himself with preaching and the cure of afflicted consciences. These concerns were reflected in his later publications. The visitation of plague in 1603 gave rise to *A Storehouse of Comfort for the Afflicted*, *The Holy Exercise of Fasting* (dedicated to John Jegon, bishop of Norwich), and *Medicines for the Plague* (dedicated to Humphrey Tyndall, dean of Ely and master of Queens' College, Cambridge), all of which appeared in 1604. By 30 October 1606 Bownd felt sufficiently confident to issue a second edition of his 1595 treatise, now rendered *Sabbathum veteris et novi testamenti, or, The True Doctrine of the Sabbath* (1606), with a dedication to Bishop Jegon, of whose support to a godly preaching ministry in the diocese he expressed his considerable appreciation; it effectively renounced presbyterianism. Perhaps this explains the otherwise puzzling dedication of *A Treatise Ful of Consolation for All that are Afflicted in Minde, or Bodie, or Otherwise* (1608) to Sir Henry Warner (*d.* 1617), who although described by Bownd as a 'professor of the Gospel' (sig. 2), has been seen as hostile to the Bury classis. The co-dedicatee was Warner's wife, Frances, previously widow of Robert Forth (*d.* 1600); her former husband, whose 'zeale to the gospel of Christ' is commended (sig. 3), seems to have belonged to the same circles as Warner. On the same day, 24 June 1608, Bownd signed the address to Sir Robert Gardiner and his wife, Anne, which prefaced his *The Unbelief of St Thomas the Apostle*, but this remained unpublished until 1628.

Bownd's wife, Elizabeth, probably died in 1610. The following year Bownd became minister of her first husband's church, St Andrew the Apostle, Norwich, but was incumbent for only two years before dying in the city. He was buried there on 26 December 1613.

KENNETH L. PARKER

Sources Venn, *Alum. Cant.* • K. Parker, *The English sabbath* (1988) • K. Parker, 'Thomas Rogers and the English sabbath: the case for a reappraisal', *Church History*, 53 (1984), 332–47 • P. Collinson, *The Elizabethan puritan movement* (1967) • P. Collinson, *Godly people: essays on English protestantism and puritanism* (1983) • E. Carlson, ed., *Religion and the English people, 1500–1640* (Kirksville, MO, 1998) • BL, Add. MS 38492, fol. 4 • D. MacCulloch, *Suffolk and the Tudors: politics and religion in an English county, 1500–1600* (1986) • *DNB*

Bowne, Peter (1574–1624?), physician, was a native of Bedfordshire, born on 20 July 1574; at the age of fifteen, on 24 April 1590, he became a scholar of Corpus Christi College, Oxford. He graduated BA in 1593 and MA in 1597, becoming a probationary fellow of his college in the latter year. He never became a full fellow and disappears from the college records at the end of 1597. About 1605 he took up the study of medicine, but there is no evidence of his presence in Oxford until February 1614, when he was admitted as a reader at the Bodleian Library. He proceeded MB and MD on 12 July 1614 and formally incepted on 3 July 1615. Having decided to practise in London, he was admitted a candidate of the College of Physicians on 24 January 1617, and fellow on 21 April 1620. In 1617 he appears in the college annals as informing against an illicit practitioner, and early in 1624 he published *Pseudo-medicorum anatomia*, a Latin poem attacking quacks and impostors, issued as a quarto pamphlet of twelve leaves. This was poorly printed, and a revised and enlarged version in eighteen leaves was soon produced. The principal additional material is a series of dedicatory verses individually addressed to the president and thirty-one fellows of the College of Physicians. Bowne refers several times to his own failing health, and verses addressed to him in a superscription by Matthew Gwinne describe him as 'medicum senem, corpore imbecillum, mente sanum et floridum' ('an aged physician, feeble in body but sound and flourishing in mind'), although Bowne was not yet fifty and Gwinne was some sixteen years older. He had left London before 3

March 1624, when Richard Spicer was admitted a fellow of the College of Physicians in his place, and is presumed to have died soon afterwards. JOHN SYMONS

Sources R. J. Durling, 'Some unrecorded verses in praise of Robert Fludd and William Harvey', *Medical History*, 8 (1964), 279–81 • CCC Oxf. • *Reg. Oxf.*, vol. 2/1–4 • Foster, *Alum. Oxon.* • T. Fowler, *The history of Corpus Christi College*, OHS, 25 (1893) • Munk, *Roll* • *DNB*

Bowness, William (1809–1867), portrait and genre painter, was born at Kendal, Westmorland. He was self-taught, and after some practice in his native town, he went to London about 1829 and met with moderate success as a portrait and figure painter. He exhibited at the Royal Academy from 1836 until 1863, but more often at the British Institution and at the Society (later Royal Society) of British Artists in Suffolk Street. He also wrote a number of poems, in the Westmorland dialect, which were collected under the title *Rustic studies in the Westmoreland dialect, with other scraps from the sketch-book of an artist* (1868). He married the eldest daughter of the marine painter John H. Wilson; they had at least one child. He died a widower on 27 December 1867 at his home at 30 Fitzroy Street, Fitzroy Square, London.

WALTER HEPWORTH, *rev.* EMILY M. WEEKS

Sources Wood, *Vic. painters*, 3rd edn • Redgrave, *Artists* • *Art Journal*, 30 (1868), 34 • Bryan, *Painters* • *Kendal Mercury* (4 Jan 1868) • Allibone, *Dict.* • *CGPLA Eng. & Wales* (1868)

Wealth at death under £200: administration, 10 Feb 1868, *CGPLA Eng. & Wales*

Bowra, Sir (Cecil) Maurice (1898–1971), classical scholar and university administrator, was born in Kiukiang, China, on 8 April 1898, the son of Cecil Arthur Verner Bowra (1869–1947), a senior official in the Chinese customs service, and his wife, Ethel, *née* Lovibond. His childhood was exotic. Chinese servants, carousing Russian soldiers, and the endless prospect of a Japanese invasion made for a colourful upbringing. In later life he admitted that he had been 'spoiled' as a child, but thought 'it was well worth it, and I have nothing but gratitude to those who did it' (Bowra, 5). He had one elder brother, Edward, and two younger sisters, Norah and Francesca, but he was never close to any of his siblings and rather kept them at arm's length. Such a beginning made Bowra a stranger to mainstream English life. He later described himself as a 'nationalist with regard to the past, and to English tradition' only (E. Kantorowicz to C. M. Bowra, 27 April 1949, Bowra MSS). He was not moved by the patriotism of his contemporaries. In 1910 he returned home to take up a scholarship at Cheltenham College, but an English public school was not to his liking. Some masters were kind, but he had few friends, and survived by exploiting his talents to amuse and mimic.

Bowra could not share the euphoria which greeted the outbreak of war in 1914, but dutifully joined the Royal Field Artillery, in which he was commissioned, and served on the western front from August 1917 until the armistice. The grim experiences of these months haunted his imagination ever after, and left him with a detestation of all things military. He long remembered:

Sir (Cecil) Maurice Bowra (1898–1971), by Henry Lamb, 1952

Boys bayonetted in the night
To keep official buttons bright.
(poem, Bowra MSS)

The war also left Bowra with an abiding hatred of all things German, except that country's classical scholarship. In the 1930s he made frequent visits to Austria and Germany, one of which included an interview with Hitler. He never had any doubts about the nature of Nazism, and actively opposed all appeasement policies. As the situation deteriorated, he busily assisted the escape of German friends like Ernst Kantorowicz and Baroness Wangermann. Being as he put it 'very Germanophobe', he could not even enjoy entertaining Konrad Adenauer, deciding not to 'give him a good lunch' and to invite only 'a few old shits' (Bowra to I. Berlin, n.d., Bowra MSS). For the whole of his life, he was sympathetic to the moderate left, a preference confirmed by his friendship with and respect for Hugh Gaitskell.

In 1919 Bowra went up to New College, Oxford. His undergraduate years were in every way successful, except in the tuition offered by the distinguished philosopher H. W. B. Joseph, whose teaching methods 'paralysed' Bowra, and convinced him that he had no future in philosophy (Bowra to Berlin, 20 Nov 1945, Bowra MSS). Joseph insisted that the nuances of every word should be measured, and that precision was more important than imagination. He deeply impressed Bowra, who was left with a feeling that his own writings represented a lesser scholarship, even though they had infinitely more colour and range. Gilbert Murray, not Joseph, became Bowra's patron, and it was largely due to his efforts that Bowra was elected a fellow of Wadham College in 1922, having taken firsts in both classical honour moderations (1920) and *literae humaniores* (1922). Candidly, Bowra expressed pleasure at being able to attend Joseph's funeral.

Bowra was a fellow of Wadham from 1922 to 1938, and warden from 1938 to 1970. The college became the only permanent home he ever knew. It was also a community he transformed, a court he ruled, and a forum in which he established a national reputation. His ideas about the purpose of a university could not have been clearer. He saw an ongoing struggle between those who loved life and those who were interested only in undermining its wonderful possibilities. Jokingly, he declared himself 'anti-prig, anti-élitist, anti-solemn, anti-Balliol'. In a university young people should be invited to break through barriers of class, convention, and national feeling, and to revel in the uninhibited exercise of the mind. He described himself as a member of 'the Immoral Front' (Bowra to Berlin, n.d., Bowra MSS).

In this war between the civilized and the philistine Bowra was at his most combative. Everyone who came within range would be labelled friend or foe. He found it easy to make lists of allies and enemies. Among the first were Isaiah Berlin, John Sparrow, A. J. Ayer, Hugh Trevor-Roper, F. R. Leavis, George (Dadie) Rylands, and Lord Robbins; among the latter C. P. Snow and A. J. P. Taylor. Once a friend had been identified, his career was to be aggressively advanced. Few things pleased Bowra more than the manipulation of elections. The appointment of the right man was reason for celebration. His circle was consciously a band of brothers embattled against the anti-intellectualism so evident on 'Baldwinite faces' (Bowra to Berlin, 20 Jan 1963, Bowra MSS). Loyalty to each other was at a premium. There was no more terrible word in the Bowra vocabulary than 'disloyal'. Those judged guilty of this offence could face crushing anathemas and silences.

In this campaign, Oxford in general and Wadham in particular should become bastions of right thinking. The transformation of Wadham in his time was almost an act of creation. As he put it, 'All Colleges taken in the lump are dim … It does not matter. It is up to oneself to make it enjoyable and reasonably distinguished' (Bowra to Berlin, 11 Nov 1953, Bowra MSS). Talent was to be searched out and encouraged. Grammar-school boys and the beneficiaries of the 1944 Education Act were particularly welcome. Equally, there was to be no provincialism. Bowra's contacts and friendships with members of Ottoline Morrell's circle at Garsington, the Bloomsbury set, and the Sitwell network broadened Oxford's range and enriched it. In England scholarly life lived in Oxford has often been quite separate from the intellectual life lived in London and certain country houses. In Bowra's Wadham the two came together in pleasant and profitable companionship.

Bowra the impresario never overwhelmed Bowra the scholar, however. Parties ended promptly at 10.30, to allow for the possibility of a full day's work on the morrow. His scholarly output was prodigious. Yet it was in one sense personally unsatisfying. He had a clear notion of a hierarchy of classical scholars. At the summit stood Wilamowitz and Fraenkel. Next came Gilbert Murray and J. D. Denniston. Bowra never felt himself the equal of these men. He could never match their meticulous attention to detail in deciphering an inscription or in editing a text, though his own edition (1935) of Pindar's works stands up well. Nor could he, in the last decades of his life, sympathize with new forms of literary criticism coming from France and Germany. In 1936, when he was passed over for the regius professorship of Greek in favour of E. R. Dodds, he was bitterly disappointed but hardly surprised. He was elected a fellow of the British Academy in 1938.

Bowra's classical scholarship was defined by two objectives. First it was 'the task of a Greek scholar … to revive as best he could for the modern world the inner life of the Greeks by a close examination of their literature' (Bowra, 257). He hoped to be an interpreter, making the spirit of Greece intelligible, and he had no doubt about what that spirit was. He told a Cambridge audience just before his death that the essence of Greek thought was 'that man is an individual, who lives among other men in his own right and for his own worth' (speech on Greek Freedom, 21 March 1971, Bowra MSS). The military coup in Greece in 1967 deeply distressed him, and he was happy to allow Wadham to become a base for those trying to restore democracy. His major works included *Ancient Greek Literature* (1933), *Greek Lyric Poetry* (1936), *Periclean Athens* (1971), and *The Greek Experience* (1957).

Bowra's second aim in writing was to shed light on classical literature by comparing it to that of other cultures. His cultural and linguistic range allowed him to do this with effect. He wrote on Valéry and Blok as well as Homer, and he brought new poets like Cavafy and Seferis to the attention of intelligent Englishmen. Works such as *The Heritage of Symbolism* (1943) and *The Romantic Imagination* (1950) broke new ground. Not unreasonably, Edith Sitwell hailed his role as a critic, because he was 'doing a great work in making poetry universal, and abolishing frontiers' (E. Sitwell to Bowra, 17 March 1945, Bowra MSS). Greek literature was never to be assessed as though it stood alone. It was rather to be evaluated as part of an ongoing human experience that transcended particular cultural borders. In making comparisons, what was distinctive about the Greeks would be highlighted, and what they shared with later generations would be underlined. From 1946 to 1951, he held the chair of poetry in Oxford, a position which gave him particular pleasure.

The talents of the scholar were more than matched by those of a formidable administrator. In addition to presiding over the affairs of Wadham, Bowra was vice-chancellor of Oxford University from 1951 to 1954 and president of the British Academy from 1958 to 1962. He claimed that such roles were uncongenial, most of the work being 'dull and difficult, statutes, science, finance, etc.' (Bowra to Berlin, 11 Nov 1953, Bowra MSS). But this was false modesty for the most part. Science and scientists, it is true, presented problems. He never understood the language of scientists and never sympathized with their aims. Relations with Lord Cherwell and Cyril Hinshelwood could be frosty. But, on the other hand, the conducting of campaigns, the marshalling of votes by flattery and bullying, and the securing of favourite projects were all intensely enjoyable.

In coming to a meeting, Bowra was always well prepared and very clear in his own mind about what decisions should be taken. The tempo at which business was taken increased dramatically in university councils. Matters were 'dispatched at high speed and in a loud voice' (Lloyd-Jones, *Bowra*, 123). It was not unusual for other members of committees which he chaired to complain that this breathless approach left them insufficient time to reflect or suggest amendments. But Bowra would assume that such protestations were only further evidence of his methods working. He was not given to doubting. In talking to colleagues he was sure that his instincts were right. In representing Oxford to the University Grants Committee, or to the outside world generally, he was equally sure that Oxford and its values should not be challenged. Such confidence made him formidable in college or university politics. He never feared making enemies or 'making bad blood'. Such things were inevitable in a war against philistinism in all its forms.

Force of argument was matched by force of personality. Short of stature, Bowra yet had bulk. Thickset, bull-necked, and rounding with the years, he was compact and seemingly muscled. His nickname, the Rhino, bore witness to form and character. Yet in one respect it was misleading. No skin was thinner. He was deeply sensitive to criticism and to rejection. He once remarked, 'I create rebuffs before I am rebuffed' (Bowra to Berlin, n.d., Bowra MSS). In particular his homosexuality was always a matter of anxiety. Close friendships with Philip Ritchie, Adrian Bishop, and Ernst Kantorowicz were marred by fears about exposure and blackmail. Although he enjoyed the companionship of many women, among them Iris Murdoch, Elizabeth Bowen, and Penelope Betjeman, he was essentially a member of what he called 'the Homintern' (ibid., 11 Aug [1937]). When his engagement to Audrey Beecham was called off, he reflected that 'it seems that God has decided that I [am] seldom to get what I want and am to be punished for my good actions' (ibid.). Hard work, the loyalty of friends, and wit enunciated in a bittern-booming voice with strange cadences were compensations for emotional disappointment.

In later life Bowra was much honoured. The German government made him a member of the order of merit, and the Sorbonne gave him an honorary doctorate for his writing on French poetry. He once remarked that he collected honorary degrees as a schoolboy collected stamps. He was knighted in 1951 and appointed CH in 1971.

Bowra was not a religious man in any conventional sense, and he detested puritanism in any of its disguises. In the First World War a reluctance to shell Noyon Cathedral was overcome by the recollection that Calvin had been closely associated with the town. Yet he assiduously attended college chapel, and took pleasure in the stateliness of an ordered Anglicanism. It was, in his phrase, 'all marvellous rot'. He died, unmarried, in Wadham College on 4 July 1971, and was buried in St Cross churchyard, Oxford.

In January 1937 Harvard offered Bowra a chair, and he affected to take the matter seriously. His hesitation produced letters from every classicist of note in Oxford begging him not to leave. These appeals not only recognized the value of his scholarship, but also his astonishing capacity to transform the lives of young people. Isaiah Berlin acknowledged, among many others, that his own thinking and behaviour had been moulded by the warden. Young men who arrived in Oxford 'suppressed, un self-expressed, unventilated' (R. Harrod to Bowra, 17 Jan 1937, Bowra MSS) were recast into individuals with something to say. And that, as far as Bowra was concerned, was what a university was for. As a friend remarked, Oxford without Bowra was 'a mutton chop without any chutney' (Mary [?] to Bowra, 16 Dec 1936, Bowra MSS). L. G. MITCHELL

Sources C. M. Bowra, *Memories, 1898–1939* (1966) • Bowra MSS, Wadham College, Oxford • H. Lloyd-Jones, ed., *Maurice Bowra: a celebration* (1974) • H. Lloyd-Jones, *PBA*, 58 (1972) • *DNB* • *The Times* (5 July 1971) • *The Listener* (1 June 1972), 713–15 • A. F. Thompson, ed., 'The Bowra years and after: 1938–1993', *Wadham College*, ed. C. S. L. Davies and J. Garnett (1994) • *Hist. U. Oxf.* 8: *20th cent.*

Archives Bodl. Oxf., corrected copy of *Poetry and politics, 1900–1960* • Wadham College, Oxford, papers | Bodl. Oxf., corresp. with Gilbert Murray • Bodl. Oxf., corresp. with Lord Simon • King's AC Cam., letters to G. H. W. Rylands

Likenesses H. Lamb, oils, 1952, Wadham College, Oxford [*see illus.*] • double portrait, photograph, 1962 (with Charlie Chaplin), Hult. Arch. • M. Black, plaster cast of death mask, 1971, NPG • J. Doubleday, statue, 1977, Wadham College, Oxford • N. Parkinson, photograph, repro. in Thompson, ed., 'The Bowra years and after: 1938–1993', 111 • chalk sketch (after H. Lamb), NPG • photograph, repro. in *PBA*, 58 (1972)

Wealth at death £113,212: probate, 24 Aug 1971, *CGPLA Eng. & Wales*

Bowrey, Thomas (*d.* 1713), merchant and compiler of the first Malay–English dictionary, is of obscure origins. It may be that he was the son of one Thomas Bowrey of Wapping, Middlesex, mariner, and he was certainly kin to some of the Wapping Bowreys associated in this period with the Royal Navy. Almost nothing is known of his education; however, in 1669, presumably while still in his teens, he departed for Fort St George, Madras, India, and he was to spend the next nineteen years sailing about the islands, seas, and coastlines that were known to Europeans as the East Indies. In 1680 Bowrey wrote a memoir of his travels to that date, published in 1905 as *A Geographical Account of Countries Round the Bay of Bengal*. Here he rehearses conventional seventeenth-century English stereotypes about south and south-east Asian religion, expressing much pious horror at Hindu 'idolatry' and alleged popular credulity. However, *A Geographical Account* also supplies careful tables of a variety of local Indian coinage systems, generally with English pound equivalents; discusses boat design along the River Hooghly; contains keen appraisals of trade opportunities and commercial competition in ports in and around the Bay of Bengal and the Malay archipelago; and offers an entertaining account of a ganja or cannabis smoking party organized by a group of sea captains and company officials.

Bowrey was early employed as a pilot on other men's boats, but by the early 1680s he owned at least two ships, a ketch, the *Adventure*, and the *Borneo Merchant*, with which he plied ports about Ceylon and both coasts of India, the Malay peninsula, Sumatra, Java, Bali, Borneo, Celebes, and the Moluccas, carrying spices, cloth, opium, gold, jewels, fine china, and slaves. The perils were many, including conflicts with the East India Company (as an 'interloper' Bowrey had a wary relationship with that powerful body), shipwrecks, regional warfare, and dishonest factors. Bowrey's papers also detail a very narrow escape from Malabar pirates.

During Bowrey's years in the East Indies he learned to speak passable Malay which, as he put it, 'did enable me to Negociate my Affairs, and Converse with those people without the assistance of Prevaricating Interpreters, as they commonly are' (Bowrey, *Dictionary*, preface). Much of this period of his life was spent aboard ship, but accounts survive for a house he maintained in Porto Novo on the Coromandel coast from 1687 to 1688. This sojourn ended abruptly, however: Bowrey assaulted the servant of one of his local suppliers in the course of a business dispute and he was briefly thrown into prison by the local *havildar* (governor). A plea to his old rivals, the East India Company, to intervene on his behalf concludes 'Sir, Your Most humble Servant that would be; but at present weighed down with Irons, Thomas Bowrey' (Bowrey, *Geographical Account*, xxxiii).

Bowrey departed for England in October of 1688. On 17 September 1691 he married his cousin Mary (*d.* 1715), the daughter of Philip Gardiner, a Wapping apothecary, and his wife, Frances. The Bowreys lived for the rest of their lives in Wellclose Square, Wapping (often referred to at the time as Marine Square, because of the number of captains and other sea officers who resided there), within easy walking distance of the Thames docks and shipyards. In 1691 Bowrey was sworn a younger brother of Trinity House. *A Dictionary, English and Malayo* appeared in 1701. Later commentators have found much to criticize in the dictionary's clumsy, error-laden Malay phraseology and eccentric transliterations. None the less this unpretentious merchants' reference book seems to have remained the standard source for a century, and the quaint dialogues at the back convey with some immediacy the atmosphere of seventeenth-century Malayan, Sumatran, and Balinese docks, warehouses, and merchants' compounds.

True to his time Bowrey was an inveterate projector and from the 1690s on he submitted numerous proposals to the East India Company for new trade outlets, plantations in Jamaica, the suppression of piracy, and the like. In 1698 he sailed his yacht, the *Duck*, to the Low Countries and he penned an account of the trip. In 1704 he contracted with the shipwright Richard Wells of Rotherhithe to build a new East India merchant ship, the *Mary Galley*; detailed records, including shipbuilders' accounts, plans, and the like, as well as an account of the ship's later career, have been printed in Bowrey's *Papers*.

In this period Bowrey was part owner or freighter of at least fourteen ships, most of them East India merchant ships. He also invested in London real estate in Wapping and elsewhere, leased an inn in Southwark called the Old King Harry's Head and owned East India and South Sea stock. Bowrey was one of the principal freighters of the *Worcester*, an East India merchant vessel that, at the behest of the Scottish Darien Company, was seized and its crew arrested in Edinburgh in 1704 on a trumped-up charge of piracy. Eventually, despite an avalanche of petitions and affidavits from Bowrey and others, three of her crew (including her captain, Thomas Green) were executed. Neither the owners nor the crew were ever fully compensated. Bowrey wrote his will on 11 March 1713 and he was buried three days later in St Margaret's Church, Lee, Kent. His wife was laid beside him two years later in 1715. The bulk of their estate was made into a trust for the benefit of superannuated seamen and seamen's widows of several Wapping parishes 'with particular regard to such as have been at East India' (PRO, PROB 11/532, fol. 63A).

Although he was not a scholar Bowrey devoted a good part of his life to the public-spirited pursuit and dissemination of practical knowledge, with special reference to the concerns of merchants and seafarers. However, despite his humanitarian care for his countrymen and his commitment to the furtherance of English trade, he clearly experienced difficulty viewing non-Europeans through any wider lens than profit and a reflexive belief in the spiritual and cultural superiority of protestant Christianity. His career thus typifies that inconsistent standard of morality that was to have such an enduring place within British imperialist thought and practice.

MARGARET R. HUNT

Sources T. Bowrey, *A dictionary, English and Malayo, Malayo and English* (1701) • T. Bowrey, *A geographical account of countries round the Bay of Bengal, 1669–1679*, ed. R. C. Temple, Hakluyt Society, 2nd ser., 12 (1905) • *The papers of Thomas Bowrey, 1669–1713; discovered in 1913 by John Humphreys*, ed. R. C. Temple, Hakluyt Society, 2nd ser., 58 (1925) • M. R. Hunt, *The middling sort: commerce, gender and the family in England, 1680–1780* (1996) • R. C. Temple, *New light on the mysterious tragedy of the 'Worcester', 1704–1705: an episode in the long struggle between England and Scotland for union as Great Britain, 1603–1707, with a solution of the mystery* (1930) • Y. Mubayi, 'Status, authority and privilege: the temple as a fulcrum of the balance of power in Orissa (16th–19th centuries)', DPhil diss., Jawaharlal Nehru University, 1999 • correspondence and miscellaneous MSS, GL, MSS 24176–24178 • ledgers and family MSS, GL, MS 3041 • correspondence, travel narratives, accounts, BL OIOC, MSS Eur. A 33; D 1076; D 782; E 192 • *IGI*

Archives BL OIOC, corresp. and papers, MSS Eur. A 33, D 782, E 192 • GL, corresp. and papers • Worcs. RO, travel diary

Bowring [*née* Castle], **Deborah**, **Lady Bowring** (**1816–1902**), local activist, was born on 30 July 1816, one of the fourteen children of Thomas Castle of Clifton and his wife, Mary. Her family were Unitarians, and she was brought up in the Bristol circle which included Lant Carpenter and J. B. Estlin. On 8 November 1860, at the age of forty-four, Deborah Castle became the second wife of the linguist and politician Sir John *Bowring (1792–1872), whose first wife had died in 1858. The couple made their home in Exeter, where they took a prominent part in the life of the city. Lady Bowring was active in local philanthropy, supporting, *inter alia*, the Royal Devon and Exeter Hospital and the Children's Band of Mercy. She was a prominent member of the Unitarian George's Meeting, where she was often to be heard 'hopefully pleading the cause of a large-minded and practical Christianity' (*The Inquirer*, 493). Lady Bowring was a keen advocate of the university extension movement, serving as a member of the Exeter committee, and a promoter of education for the young women of the city. She was a supporter of the Albert Memorial Museum, of which her husband had been among the founders, and to which she left a bust and portrait of Sir John in her will, and a member of the Devonshire Association for the Advancement of Science, Literature and Art.

Lady Bowring was a keen supporter of the women's suffrage movement, becoming in 1871 one of the vice-presidents of the Bristol and West of England Society for Women's Suffrage, a position she retained until her death. She regularly appeared on west country platforms in support of the cause, the last occasion being a meeting at the skating rink, Exeter, in May 1897, when she presided. A committed Liberal, she also spoke at public meetings on other political issues; an 'apt and dignified speaker', she 'blended a good deal of humour with her shrewd and graceful remarks' (*The Inquirer*, 493).

After Sir John's death in 1872, Deborah Bowring edited *A Memorial Volume of Sacred Poetry* (1873), for which she also wrote a fluent memoir of her husband; the memoir was republished in 1895 as a preface to her edition of his *Matins and Vespers*. A woman of 'vigorous grasp of mind and efficient action' (*Englishwoman's Review*, 282), Deborah Bowring died at her home, 7 Baring Crescent, Heavitree, near Exeter, on 28 July 1902, having survived her husband by thirty years. She was buried alongside him on 30 July in the higher cemetery, Exeter. K. D. REYNOLDS

Sources *The Inquirer* (2 Aug 1902) • *Englishwoman's Review*, 33 (1902), 281–2 • private information (2004) • d. cert. • will • *Autobiographical recollections of Sir John Bowring*, ed. L. B. Bowring (1877) • M. Carpenter, *Last days in England of Rajah Rammohun Roy* (1866) • m. cert.
Wealth at death £13,892 13*s*. 11*d*.: probate, 11 Oct 1902, *CGPLA Eng. & Wales*

Bowring, Sir John (1792–1872), politician, diplomatist, and writer, was born on 17 October 1792 at Larkbeare (also known as Great Larkbeare), Holloway Street, Exeter, Devon, the eldest son and second of the nine children of Charles Bowring (1769–1856), a wool merchant, and his wife, Sarah Jane Anne (*d*. 1828), daughter of the Revd Thomas Lane, vicar of St Ives, Cornwall. His mother was an Anglican, but John Bowring, like his father and the rest of the family, was a Unitarian and, as such, subject to restrictions on participation by dissenters in public life until the repeal of the Test Acts in 1828. He was educated first at Mr Bowden's school in Paris Street, Exeter, and then for two years at a Unitarian boarding-school at Moretonhampstead, on Dartmoor. He began work at the age of thirteen, first as a clerk in his father's wool business and then in the counting-house of the local firm of Kennaway & Co. The presence of foreign traders on the Exeter quayside gave him the opportunity of learning and practising languages. He attended the evening study group of Dr Lant Carpenter, minister of George's Meeting-House, the Unitarian chapel in South Street, Exeter. In June 1811 he joined the London branch of Milford & Co., suppliers to the duke of Wellington's forces in the Iberian peninsula. In his early years in London, Bowring lodged near Cheapside, but he soon established links with Hackney, which was then a centre of Unitarianism. He already knew several European languages, and his ability to speak Spanish resulted in 1813 in his first journey abroad, when his firm chose him to go to the area of hostilities near San Sebastian with cargoes of stores for the army. He remained in northern Spain and southern France until late 1814, before returning to London. In 1815 he travelled to Portugal to negotiate settlement of an outstanding claim for supplies to the army. In Unitarian circles in Hackney he had met the family of Samuel Lewin, a corn merchant in the City, and on 16 September 1816 at Hackney he married Lewin's daughter, Maria (1793/4–1858). The couple took up residence in a smart area of Hackney near London Fields, and their first child, Maria, was born at Hackney in 1818. They also had five sons, John, Frederick, Lewin, Edgar, and Charles, born between 1821 and 1828, and three more daughters, Edith, Emily, and Gertrude, born in the 1830s.

Sir John Bowring (1792–1872), by John King, 1826

Early career With Henry Murdoch, in 1817 Bowring established the firm of Bowring & Co. at 23 Bucklersbury,

Cheapside, dealing principally in the shipment of herrings to France and the Iberian peninsula, and the importation of wines. In 1819 he travelled to Spain, France, and the Netherlands, extending his business interests. After a brief period back with his family, he set off again late that year on a tour of northern Europe, passing through Germany to Russia and returning through Scandinavia. Among the celebrities he met in St Petersburg was Friedrich Adelung (1768–1843), who supplied him with German and English prose translations of Russian verse, which he put into English verse for his *Specimens of the Russian Poets* (2 vols., 1820; rev. 2nd edn, 1821). In August 1820 his friend and fellow radical Edward Blaquiere introduced him to Jeremy Bentham, who was delighted to find in Bowring a new disciple. In July 1821 Bowring again set out for the continent on a commercial mission, from which he returned in 1822. Later that year he travelled to Paris, where he developed an association with the Orleanist circle. On arriving at Calais on 5 October on his way home, accompanied by Blaquiere, he was detained and taken to a gaol in Boulogne, accused of complicity in an attempt to secure the release of four sergeants of La Rochelle (who were executed for singing republican songs) and of carrying sealed letters of a treasonable nature. Blaquiere made for England, and following the intervention of Canning, the foreign secretary, Bowring was released, but banned from France. He published his version of the episode in *Details of the Arrest, Imprisonment and Liberation of an Englishman* (1823).

Bowring was secretary of the London Greek Committee, founded in 1823 to assist the Greeks in their rising against the Turks. This brought him into correspondence with Lord Byron, at whose instigation he took steps to negotiate a loan for the Greeks by selling bonds. However, it was mainly Byron's name that attracted investors and his death at Missolonghi in May 1824 resulted in financial difficulties. Bowring was accused of having made a fortune at the expense of both the Greeks and the bondholders, though in reality his finances had suffered. Faced with ruin, he adopted the dubious expedient of putting pressure on the Greek agents in London to relieve him of his bonds at a price higher than their market value. Two years later another disastrous Greek loan, in which Bowring and the Greek Committee played little part, brought the mismanagement of both loans into the public eye, and Bowring and others were alleged to have enriched themselves dishonestly. Bentham, however, refused to listen to Bowring's detractors and in 1824, when the *Westminster Review* was founded, made him the political editor.

Literature and politics Bowring's Russian anthology was followed by similar volumes of verse translations of Dutch (1824), Spanish (1824), Polish (1827), Serbian (1827), Hungarian (1830), and Czech (1832) poetry, sometimes produced with the help of expert collaborators, whose contribution he did not fully acknowledge. He published translations from an even greater variety of languages in the *Westminster Review*, the *Foreign Quarterly Review*, and the *London Magazine*. For a time he worked with George Borrow (1803–1881), whom he had met in 1821, on a volume of Scandinavian translations, but this was never completed. The translations brought him temporary fame, but the public's enthusiasm soon declined. His financial fortunes too were in decline, and by late 1827 Bowring & Co. had collapsed. He was hoping, with Bentham's support, to cure his financial ills by becoming a professor of literature at the newly established London University. His sons John, Frederick, and Lewin were sent to stay with relatives, while he, his wife, their daughter Maria, and the infant Edgar moved to Heidelberg, where he thought associating with German professors would improve his chances. He returned to England in 1828 and took up residence with Bentham at Queen Square, Westminster, while his wife went to live with friends at Hackney. He attributed his failure to get the professorship to Anglican influence at London University. By late 1828 his financial situation was desperate, and a group of friends and fellow Unitarians organized a fund to save him from sequestration. He managed to be nominated a commissioner of public accounts, but the prime minister, the duke of Wellington, prevented his employment. He was, however, permitted, as an unpaid commissioner receiving only expenses, to visit the Netherlands to prepare a review of the Dutch public accounting system. Late in 1828 he moved to 7 North Place, Gray's Inn Lane, Holborn, and the following year to nearby Millmann Street, Holborn. During a visit to the Netherlands in 1829 he received an honorary doctorate from the University of Groningen for services to Dutch literature, and was henceforth often known as the Doctor. He was successful at this time in retaining his position with the *Westminster Review*, when it passed from Bentham's ownership to Colonel Thomas Perronet Thompson, who became a friend of Bowring.

The revolution in France in July 1830 made it again possible for Bowring to visit that country, and following the formation of a whig government that autumn he was engaged as paid secretary to Sir Henry Parnell's commission on the public accounts, which entailed investigating the accounting systems of France and the Netherlands. His fortunes were now improving and he moved with his family into the house at 1 Queen Square, Westminster (next door to Bentham), that was to remain their home for seventeen years. In 1831 Bowring and George Villiers (later Lord Clarendon) were appointed commissioners to investigate commercial relations between Britain and France. In this connection, between 1832 and 1834, Bowring was sent on three long coach journeys through the centre and south of France. His enquiries brought him into conflict with the minister of commerce, Adolphe Thiers. On 6 June 1832 Bowring's mentor Jeremy Bentham died 'in his arms' (L. B. Bowring, 'A brief memoir', 14), leaving him all his manuscripts and a sum of money towards their publication. He now embarked on this formidable task, though, when it eventually came to fruition in *The Collected Works of Jeremy Bentham* (11 vols., 1838–43), much of the work, owing to Bowring's frequent absences abroad or on official duties, had been carried out by others. Anticipating the effect of the Reform Bill, Bentham, in April 1831, had put Bowring's name forward as a parliamentary candidate, and in 1832 Bowring stood for Blackburn but was defeated. In 1835 he stood for the same constituency and was again defeated, but was elected MP for Clyde Boroughs (Kilmarnock). In 1837 he lost his seat, but was sent by Palmerston on an important commercial fact-finding mission to Egypt and Constantinople, which kept him abroad for a full year. On his return, in September 1838, he addressed a meeting in Manchester, at which a proposal was made, leading eventually to the formation of the Anti-Corn Law League. In June 1841 he was elected MP for Bolton as a free-trade candidate and held his seat for over seven years. The issues for which he spoke and voted included the abolition of corn duties, a more humane application of poor relief, the extension of popular education, revision of quarantine regulations, abolition of flogging in the army, the suppression of the opium trade, and the worldwide abolition of slavery. As a supporter of *laissez-faire*, he opposed the regulation of wages. He favoured the introduction of decimal coinage and in April 1847 moved in the House of Commons the introduction of the florin, a coin worth one tenth of a pound, which was first issued in 1849.

Consul at Canton In 1843 Bowring turned once more to commerce and invested his capital in an ironworks in Glamorgan. He also invested in the Llynvi Valley Railway, in the vicinity of his ironworks, and in 1845 became chairman of the directors of the London and Blackwall Railway; but in 1847 his business interests failed and he found himself suddenly in a worse financial position than at any time since 1828. Consequently, when, in October 1848, Palmerston offered him the vacant consulship at Canton (Guangzhou) with a salary of £1800 a year, he accepted, with alacrity, despite his age (he was fifty-six). He arrived at Canton in April 1849, having left his wife and family at Larkbeare. He returned to England on leave in June 1853. During his absence George Borrow had published *Lavengro* (1851), and Bowring thought certain unflattering passages in it applied to him and his family. Relations became strained. While on leave Bowring was appointed plenipotentiary and chief superintendent of trade in the Far East and governor, commander-in-chief, and vice-admiral of Hong Kong. On 16 February 1854 he was knighted and two days later left for China again, accompanied this time by his wife, two of their daughters, and their eldest son, John. At Colombo he was joined by another son, Lewin. In 1855 Bowring visited Siam and successfully negotiated a commercial treaty with King Mongkut, which provoked strong opposition in England from Lord Shaftesbury and Bowring's radical friends owing to the clauses facilitating importation of opium into Siam. Since his arrival in the Far East, Bowring had modified his views on the opium trade, ostensibly because of the difficulty of controlling it, but his son John was a partner in Jardine Mattheson & Co., the largest dealers in opium in the Far East, and this firm acted as Bowring's bankers. He was accused of having sold himself to opium merchants.

Following an incident in October 1856, when a British-registered light vessel, the *Arrow*, was boarded by Chinese soldiers, Bowring authorized the dispatch of a naval force, the bombardment of Canton, and its forcible entry. The Chinese then directed several attacks on the British in the neighbourhood of Canton. In January 1857 an attempt was made to poison the European population of Hong Kong by putting arsenic in their bread. No one died, but about 300–400 people, including Bowring and his family, were made seriously ill. Bowring rejected the implementation of martial law and in the ensuing trial the baker of the poisoned bread and other suspects were acquitted for lack of evidence and allowed to leave the colony. Votes of censure on his conduct and on the government were moved in both houses of parliament, but in the ensuing elections the government was strengthened. Although the prime minister, Lord Palmerston, supported him, he thought Bowring had handled the situation badly and decided that he should be replaced as plenipotentiary while retaining the governorship of Hong Kong. Lady Bowring, suffering from the effects of arsenic poisoning, returned to Britain with her daughter Edith, and died on 27 September 1858 in Taunton, while Bowring remained in Hong Kong, accompanied by two other daughters and his son John. On 3 May 1859 Bowring formally handed over his office and, accompanied by his daughter Maria, left for Britain. As it was passing through the Red Sea, their ship, the *Alma*, struck a submerged coral reef. The passengers were rescued after three days of privation.

Personality and achievement While still in China Bowring had read George Borrow's *The Romany Rye* (1857), which contained a scurrilous attack on him (especially in chapter 11, 'The old radical', of the appendix) and suggested that he had secured his appointment at Canton by exploiting Borrow's work and expertise. This particular slur was without foundation, but there was truth in Borrow's allegation that Bowring was disposed to exaggerate his own reputation as a polyglot and pass off other people's work as his own.

Bowring's personality aroused the antagonism of many besides Borrow. He was often accused of vanity, obsequiousness, and worse. About 5 feet 9 inches tall and of slender build, he had a refined, intellectual face, a long nose, a high forehead, and large grey eyes. He wore spectacles, not only for reading, as may be seen in the portrait painted in 1826 by John King, now in the National Portrait Gallery. Both supporters and detractors noted his volubility, but he was not a success as a speaker in the House of Commons (Bartle, *An Old Radical*, 61). He received many honours from foreign governments and was an honorary member of numerous learned societies. For his Russian anthology he received a diamond ring from Tsar Alexander I, and on 5 June 1856 he was elected a fellow of the Royal Society. Besides his editorial work and many contributions to reviews and magazines on a wide variety of subjects, including political, literary, and philological articles, hymns, poems, and verse translations, he published over thirty books and pamphlets, covering a similar range, and wrote his memoirs, which were published by his son Lewin in 1877. His most successful book, *The Kingdom and People of Siam* (2 vols., 1857), was republished by Oxford University Press in 1969. The volumes of verse translations were also important, for, though not all they pretended to be, they introduced otherwise virtually unknown literatures to the English-speaking world. Bowring's services in diplomacy were valued because of his aptitude for languages, his ability to handle figures, and a 'facility for obtaining access to persons of all stations' (Bartle, *An Old Radical*, 35). His achievement as a radical politician, particularly in the cause of free trade, has tended to be obscured by the controversy over the *Arrow* affair.

On his return to Britain, Bowring was granted a pension and an additional special allowance. He remained active in public life and continued to write and publish. Having failed in 1860 in an attempt to be adopted as the Liberal candidate for Exeter, he accepted in February 1861 a semi-official appointment as commercial agent to the new kingdom of Italy, but with Cavour's death in June 1861 all hope of a commercial agreement with that country came to an end. On 8 November 1860 at Lewin's Mead Unitarian Chapel, Bristol, to the consternation of his children, he married Deborah Castle [*see* Bowring, Deborah, Lady Bowring (1816–1902)], the youngest daughter of Thomas Castle, a prominent Clifton Unitarian. They had no children. As justice of the peace and deputy lord lieutenant for Devon he was active in the cause of prison reform, and in 1865 published *Remunerative prison labour as an instrument for promoting the reformation and diminishing the cost of offenders*. Bowring died of prostate disease on 23 November 1872 at Claremont, Holloway Street, Exeter, the house he had built only a few yards from his birthplace. Late in November following a funeral service at George's Meeting-House, attended by his family and many local worthies, he was buried in Exeter new cemetery. His gravestone bore the opening line of one of his best-known hymns, 'In the cross of Christ I glory'. His second wife, Deborah *Bowring, died on 28 July 1902.

GERALD STONE

Sources G. F. Bartle, *An old radical and his brood* (1994) • J. Youings, ed., *Sir John Bowring 1792–1872: aspects of his life and career* (1993) • *Autobiographical recollections of Sir John Bowring*, ed. L. B. Bowring (1877) • L. B. Bowring, 'A brief memoir of Sir John Bowring', in *Autobiographical recollections of Sir John Bowring*, ed. L. B. Bowring (1877), 1–28 • *A memorial volume of sacred poetry, by the late Sir John Bowring, to which is prefixed a memoir of the author by Lady Bowring* (1873) • Burke, *Gen. GB* (1972) • A. Kowalska, *John Bowring: tłumacz i propagator literatury polskiej w Anglii* (1965) • *The Times* (25 Nov 1872) • G. F. Bartle, 'Sir John Bowring and the "Arrow" War in China', *Bulletin of the John Rylands University Library*, 43 (1960–61) • d. cert. • d. cert. [Maria Bowring]

Archives Duke U., Perkins L., family corresp. • Harvard U., Houghton L., corresp. and papers • Hunt. L., corresp. • JRL, corresp. and papers • U. Cal., Los Angeles, corresp. and papers • U. Cal., Berkeley, corresp. and papers • University of Kentucky, Lexington, Kentucky, corresp. and papers • Wellcome L., corresp. and papers | BL, letters to Lord Auckland, Add. MSS 34459–34460 • BL, letters to Boghos Bey, Add. MS 37461 • BL, letters to Richard Cobden, Add. MSS 43667–43670 • BL, letters to J. C. Hobhouse, Add. MSS 36460–36464 • BL, corresp. with Sir Robert Peel, Add. MSS 40492–40600 *passim* • BL, letters to Francis Place, Add. MSS 37949–37950 • BL OIOC, letters to H. H. Wilson, MS Eur. E 301 • Bodl. Oxf., letters to fourth earl of Clarendon • Bodl. Oxf., corresp. with Lord Kimberley • Bolton Central Library, corresp. with Richard Heywood • Harris Man. Oxf., letters to Carpenter family • NL Scot., letters to John Burton • U. Hull, Brynmor Jones L., corresp. with T. P. Thompson • U. Southampton L., corresp. with Lord Palmerston • University of Amsterdam, letters to W. De Clercq • Woburn Abbey, letters to Lord George William Russell

Likenesses J. King, oils, 1826, NPG [*see illus.*] • W. Brockedon, chalk drawing, 1831, NPG • P. D. D'Angers, bronze medallion, 1832, NPG; repro. in *Autobiographical recollections*, frontispiece • W. Ward, mezzotint, pubd 1832 (after H. W. Pickersgill), BM, NPG • F. Bromley, group portrait, etching, pubd 1835 (after B. R. Haydon, *The reform banquet, 1832*), NPG • J. Doyle, chalk caricature, 1837 (*We, the people of England*), BM • C. Martin, pencil drawing, 1844, BM • J. Stephenson, mixed method engraving, pubd 1844 (after C. A. Duval), BM • S. Bellin, group portrait, mixed media, pubd 1850 (*The Anti-Corn Law League*; after J. R. Herbert, 1847), NPG • pencil drawing, 1854, NPG • E. B. Stephens, bust, *c.*1860, Devon and Exeter Institution, Exeter • photograph, *c.*1865, repro. in Youings, ed., *Sir John Bowring*, 103; priv. coll. • R. Lehmann, drawing, 1867, BM • R. Taylor, wood-engraving, pubd 1871 (after Maull & Fox; after Maull & Polyblank), NPG • Elliott & Fry, carte-de-visite, NPG • B. R. Haydon, group portrait, oils (*The Anti-Slavery Society convention, 1840*), NPG • W. Holl, stipple (after B. E. Duppa), BM, NPG; repro. in J. Saunders, *Political reformers* (1840) • J. H. Lynch, lithograph (after B. R. Green), NPG • carte-de-visite, NPG • engraving (after painting by B. E. Duppa, 1826), repro. in Bartle, *An old radical*, frontispiece

Wealth at death under £16,000: resworn probate, Dec 1873, *CGPLA Eng. & Wales* (1872)

Bowtell [Boutel; *née* Davenport], **Elizabeth** (1648/9–1714/15), actress, was the second daughter of Christopher Davenport and his wife, Frances Ridley. Some time after October 1669 she married Barnaby Bowtell, one of ten children of Barnaby Bowtell of Parham Hall, Suffolk. Mrs Bowtell's husband was commissioned a lieutenant in the Holland regiment of William III on 2 December 1681, a position he retained until 24 January 1705.

The beginnings of Mrs Bowtell's career are hazy. John Downes suggests that she began acting 'some few Years after' the Restoration, and he lists her in three revivals of pre-Commonwealth plays, all most likely produced during the 1663/4 season. Certainly by 1667 Elizabeth Davenport (as she then was) was an active member of the King's Company: in March she played the exuberant ingénue Sabina in Dryden's *Secret Love*. Her career spanned three decades. After 1678 she left the stage for ten years, claiming during that time to have lived 'in a Monastery in France where shee was a Pensioner' (Milhous, 126). She returned to London in spring 1688, performing with the United Company until 1690. In 1692 she surfaced in a Benedictine convent in Paris (Highfill, Burnim & Langhans, *BDA*, 2.261). By the autumn of 1695 Mrs Bowtell was acting with Thomas Betterton's new company at Lincoln's Inn Fields, but she appears to have left the stage permanently after November 1697 to join her husband in the Netherlands. She spent her final years in Middlesex, a prosperous widow who benefited from inheritances on both sides of her family and perhaps from liaisons with lovers.

Mrs Bowtell was a talented actress, popular with audiences and dramatists alike. Dryden wrote several roles for her, aside from Sabina in *Secret Love*: Donna Theodosia in *An Evening's Love* (1668); Benzayda in *The Conquest of Granada* (1670/1671); Melantha in *Marriage a-la-mode* (1671); Laura in

The Assignation (1672); and Cleopatra in *All for Love* (1677). William Wycherley gave her two of his greatest female roles, Margery Pinchwife in *The Country Wife* (1675) and Fidelia in *The Plain Dealer* (1676). Other notable Restoration playwrights, such as Thomas Shadwell, Nathaniel Lee, and Thomas D'Urfey also created roles for Mrs Bowtell, while still others commented upon her skill. In the dedication to his play *The Roman Empress* (1671) William Joyner praised her performance as Aurelia, 'which, though a great, various, and difficult part, was excellently performed' (sig. A2*v*).

Whether deserved or not, Mrs Bowtell had a reputation for promiscuity. One lampoon called her 'chestnut-maned Boutell, whom all the Town fucks' (Wilson, *Court Satires*, 206). Edmund Curll, in his memoir of Thomas Betterton, noted that 'besides what she saved by Playing, the Generosity of some happy Lovers enabled her to quit the Stage before she grew old' (Curll, 21). Her stage roles also capitalized on her sexual appeal. In Thomas Duffett's play, *The Spanish Rogue* (London, 1674), her character is told she should 'know, you'r beauty can Command so large a pow'r ore any heart' (ibid., 16). Curll says 'she was low of Stature, had very agreeable Features, a good Complexion, but a Childish Look. Her Voice was weak, tho' very mellow; she generally acted *the young Innocent Lady* whom all the Heroes are mad in Love with' (ibid., 21). This latter statement best describes the roles of her youth. After 1670 Mrs Bowtell turned to a wider range of parts: cuckolding wives and tragic heroines, especially meek, virtuous women caught up by larger forces, such as Cyara in Lee's *The Tragedy of Nero* (1674). Several times she was coupled with Rebecca Marshall, who played the villainess to Bowtell's innocent. Mrs Bowtell nevertheless continued to play youthful roles, including breeches parts, through her forties. Clara in Joseph Harris's play *The City Bride* (1696) is an unmarried young woman, and Mrs Fantast in Shadwell's *Bury-Fair* (1689) is the 'Daughter to my Lady Fantast by a Former Husband'. She also played parts more suitable to her age: Aurelia in Thomas D'Urfey's *A Fool's Preferment* (1688) is a basset-playing wife who 'rules' her 'half-witted Country-Gentleman' husband.

Mrs Bowtell's life was not without hardship: her sister Frances Davenport, also an actress with the King's Company in its early years (Pepys on 7 April 1668 called her 'a very bad actor'; Pepys, 9.156), died insane in 1696; and Mrs Bowtell was caught up in several legal disputes. Her final years, however, bespeak a fate more clement than that faced by some seventeenth-century actresses. She died between 2 November 1714, when she made her will, in which she was able to leave bequests worth £830 and in which she asked to be buried at Winchester, and 1 September 1715, when it was proved. DEBORAH PAYNE FISK

Sources J. Milhous, 'Elizabeth Bowtell and Elizabeth Davenport: some puzzles solved', *Theatre Notebook*, 39 (1985), 124–34 • Highfill, Burnim & Langhans, *BDA*, vol. 2 • J. Downes, *Roscius Anglicanus*, ed. J. Milhous and R. D. Hume, new edn (1987) • W. Van Lennep and others, eds., *The London stage, 1660–1800*, pt 1: *1660–1700* (1965) • E. Howe, *The first English actresses: women and drama, 1660–1700* (1992) • T. Betterton, [W. Oldys and others], *The history of the English stage* (1741) • will, PRO, PROB 11/548, fols. 9*v*–10*v* • J. H. Wilson, *All the king's ladies: actresses of the Restoration* (1958) • J. H. Wilson, *Court satires of the Restoration* (1976) • Pepys, *Diary*, vol. 9 • P. Danchin, ed., *The prologues and epilogues of the Restoration, 1660–1700*, 7 vols. (1981–8), vols. 1–4 • R. D. Hume, *The development of English drama in the late seventeenth century* (1976)

Wealth at death £830: will, PRO, PROB 11/548, fols. 9*v*–10*v*

Bowtell [Boudle], **John** (1753–1813), bookbinder and philanthropist, the third son of Joseph Boudle (*c*.1722–1757) and his wife, Margery (*c*.1720–1780), was born on 1 August 1753, and baptized John Boudle on 15 September 1753 at Holy Trinity Church in Cambridge, where his parents had been resident at least since 1748. The adoption of the form Bowtell was apparently John's initiative. He may have been apprenticed as a stationer to John ('Maps') Nicholson, and was established as a binder from at least 20 September 1785, the date of the first among many surviving bills for binding for Cambridge University Library, one of which was for an elaborate and skilful piece of repair binding. Most of his work in this line, however, issuing from his shop in Trinity Street in Cambridge, was more workaday, albeit effective, as many of his bindings remain in place today. It has been estimated that between one-third and one-half of Cambridge University Library's manuscripts were repaired and rebound by him, as well as very many printed books, including those from John Moore's library.

Bowtell was also a collector of manuscripts, fossils, and other curiosities. The bulk of his collections were left to the newly founded Downing College, where his books and manuscripts remain. Apart from his notes on the history of the town and university of Cambridge, they contain many items removed from earlier bindings, and a substantial collection of miscellaneous deeds for the town and county of Cambridge and surrounding counties. Among these are a number relating to two tenements in Fairyard Lane, Cambridge, including one by which the property was leased in 1759 by one Mary, widow of John Bowdle of Cambridge, barber, conceivably a relation. Also to be found in his collection are accounts of the Cambridge borough treasurer from 1515 to 1786, with substantial gaps in the eighteenth century. He made many notes for a history of the town of Cambridge and prepared a text in eight volumes, never printed. He was also a keen bell-ringer, and in 1788 rang on the 30-cwt tenor bell of Great St Mary's, Cambridge, 6609 changes 'in the method of *bob maximus* generally termed *twelve-in*' (*GM*).

In October 1786 Bowtell married at St Edward's, Cambridge, Ann Scarr (1742–1807), sister-in-law of his older brother Joseph. They had no surviving children, and after his wife's death on 2 November 1807 a niece, Mary Ann Scarr, kept house for Bowtell, and was rewarded by a legacy of £3000. From his binding, bookselling and transcribing business, and perhaps from the invention of a paper leather-substitute for bindings, for which he claimed in an advertisement of 1798 to have obtained a 'considerable premium', Bowtell amassed considerable wealth. In 1809 he gave to Addenbrooke's Hospital 3 per cent Consols to the value of £100, and by his will he further endowed it with £7000 of the same stock—about half his estate—a bequest which, after its terms had been interpreted by the master in chancery, enabled additional buildings which marked a turning point in the development of the hospital.

Bowtell died in Trinity Street on 1 December 1813 and was buried with his wife in St Michael's Church. His further bequests included, again in 3 per cent Consols: £500-worth, the dividends to be applied by Trinity College to the repair of the church and chancel of St Michael's; £1000-worth, also to be administered by Trinity via the churchwardens for 'repairing and beautifying the church and steeple' of Holy Trinity Church; and £500-worth to the trustees of Hobson's Charity for the apprenticing of poor boys from Cambridge. His portrait was preserved in Addenbrooke's Hospital until its theft in recent years.

John Bowtell is not to be confused with his nephew, also John Bowtell, assistant at Cambridge University Library from *c.*1818, who compiled a catalogue which remained in use until 1861. As both part-author and victim of the chaos into which the library had descended, he was dismissed in 1852, with an annual pension of £100.

ELISABETH LEEDHAM-GREEN

Sources A. B. Gray, *John Bowtell: bookbinder of Cambridge (1753–1813); biographical notes with a further notice of his nephew John Bowtell the younger (1777–1855)* (1907) • D. McKitterick, *Cambridge University Library, a history: the eighteenth and nineteenth centuries* (1986) • A. Rook, M. Carlton, and W. G. Cannon, *The history of Addenbrooke's Hospital, Cambridge* (1991) • Downing College, Cambridge, Bowtell MSS • *Cambridge Chronicle and Journal* (24 Dec 1813) • *GM*, 1st ser., 84/2 (1814), 85 • PRO, PROB 11/1550, sig. 582

Archives CUL, notes, extracts, and collections relating to Cambridge • Downing College, Cambridge, antiquarian collections and papers, incl. MS history of Cambridge

Likenesses photograph (after portrait; stolen), Addenbrooke's Hospital, Cambridge; repro. in Gray, *John Bowtell*

Wealth at death £15,200; plus personal goods and trade materials: will, PRO, PROB 11/1550, fols. 63*r*–64*v*

Bowyer, Sir George, first baronet (1740–1800), naval officer and politician, was baptized on 3 May 1740, at Denham, Buckinghamshire, the third son of Sir William Bowyer, third baronet (1710–1767), of Denham, and Anne (*d.* 1785), daughter of Sir John Stonhouse, baronet, of Radley, Berkshire, MP and comptroller of the household to Queen Anne. On 11 May 1751, as a captain's servant, he joined his first ship, the *Glory* (44 guns), commanded by Richard Howe; in 1752 he moved with Howe to the *Dolphin* (24 guns), in which he stayed until 1755. In her he saw service off west Africa, in the West Indies, and in the Mediterranean. After three years in the *Princess Louisa* (60 guns), the *Lancaster* (66 guns), and the *Royal George* (100 guns), mostly in the Channel Fleet, he was promoted lieutenant on 13 February 1758 and appointed to the *Nottingham* (60 guns), initially in the West Indies and then in the channel. In May 1760 he rejoined Captain Howe in the *Magnamine* (74 guns).

On promotion to commander on 4 May 1761 Bowyer commanded the cutter *Swift*, which was captured off Ushant on 30 June 1762 by a much larger French privateer. Bowyer was acquitted at the subsequent court martial, 'having done everything in his power for escaping the enemy' (PRO, ADM 1/5301). Promoted captain on 28 October 1762, he commanded the *Sheerness* (20 guns) in the Mediterranean until the peace in December 1763. On 11 November 1768 he married Margaret (*née* Price), widow of Sir Jacob Downing, baronet; the couple had no children and Margaret died in 1778.

In 1776, after the outbreak of the American War of Independence, Bowyer commanded the *Burford* (70 guns); he transferred to the *Albion* (74 guns) in 1778, and took part in the battle of Grenada, under Vice-Admiral John Byron, in the West Indies on 6 July 1779, and in Admiral Sir George Rodney's three actions with de Guichen on 17 April, and 15 and 19 May 1780. On 15 May the fleet, 'led by that good and gallant officer Captain Bowyer' (Rodney's dispatch of 31 May, PRO, ADM 1/311/217), engaged fifteen French ships in succession. Inevitably the *Albion*, as the first to engage each ship, suffered severely in men, spars, and hull.

Bowyer returned home at the end of 1781 and on 4 June 1782 married Henrietta (1753–1845), daughter of Admiral Sir Peircy *Brett; they had three sons and two daughters. As a commodore he commanded the *Irresistible* (74 guns), guardship in the Medway, from 1783 for fifteen months. From 1784 to 1790 he was MP for Queenborough, near Sheerness, a seat under Admiralty patronage which his father-in-law had held from 1754 to 1774. In 1785 he was a member of the committee to consider the defences of Portsmouth and Plymouth. On 24 September 1787 he was appointed a colonel of marines. During the Spanish armament in August 1790 he commissioned the *Boyne* (78 guns) and in January 1791 he paid her off. In April 1792 he inherited the Radley estates from his maternal uncle.

Having been promoted rear-admiral on 1 February 1793 Bowyer hoisted his flag in July in the *Prince* (90 guns), commanded by Cuthbert Collingwood, in the Channel Fleet. He and Collingwood transferred to the *Barfleur* (98 guns) in January 1794 and took part in Lord Howe's victory at the battle of 1 June. The *Barfleur* was warmly engaged in the action on 29 May but early on 1 June Bowyer lost a leg, being caught by Collingwood as he fell. He received a pension of £1000 p.a. for his wound, and the gold medal with chain for the victory, and on 16 August 1794 he was created a baronet. Unable to serve again, Bowyer was promoted vice-admiral on 4 July 1794 and admiral on 14 February 1799. He succeeded his brother in the family baronetcy as fifth baronet in April 1799 and died at Radley on 9 December 1800; he was buried at Radley parish church on 16 December. At his house, now Radley College, the union flag is flown annually on 1 June in his memory.

C. H. H. OWEN

Sources PRO, Admiralty MSS • J. Ralfe, *The naval biography of Great Britain*, 1 (1828), 374–6 • J. Charnock, ed., *Biographia navalis*, 6 (1798), 511–14 • J. Brooke, 'Bowyer, George', HoP, *Commons, 1754–90* • Berks. RO, Bowyer MSS • Burke, *Peerage*

Archives Berks. RO, family records

Likenesses J. Reynolds, oils, 1769, council chamber, Abingdon, Oxfordshire • Bartolozzi, Landseer, Ryder and Stow, group portrait, line engraving, pubd 1803 (*Commemoration of the victory of June 1st 1794*), BM, NPG • G. H. Every, mezzotint, pubd 1865 (after J. Reynolds), BM, NPG • attrib. T. Hudson, oils, Abingdon Guildhall, Oxfordshire

Bowyer, Sir George, seventh baronet (1811–1883), jurist and politician, was born on 8 October 1811 at Radley Park, near Abingdon, Berkshire, the eldest son of Sir George Bowyer, sixth baronet (1783–1860), of Denham Court, Buckinghamshire, and his wife, Anne Hammond, daughter of Captain Sir Andrew Snape Douglas RN. He received much of his early education in Italy, before spending a short time as a cadet at the Royal Military Academy at Woolwich. However, Bowyer soon abandoned any idea of a military career and turned instead to the law. He spent a year in Genoa in 1835, studying Roman law, and later compiled a manuscript, *Libro della nobilità di Genova*, with his friend Stacey Grimaldi. On his return to England, he became a member of the Middle Temple on 1 June 1836. He was called to the bar on 7 June 1839, and was awarded an honorary MA at Oxford in the same month. In 1844 he received the degree of DCL. He was also admitted a member of Lincoln's Inn in January 1845.

Although Bowyer practised for some time as a draftsman and conveyancer at the equity bar, this did not suit him for he was more interested in the academic side of law. As a legal writer, he first attracted attention with a book published in 1841, *The English Constitution: a Popular Commentary on the Constitutional Laws of England*. This work sought to place within the reach of educated people the constitutional knowledge to which, in the aftermath of the Reform Act, Bowyer felt it was essential that all voters had access. It sold well, and helped to establish his reputation as a constitutional lawyer. In 1850 he was appointed reader in law at the Middle Temple, and in the following year he published his *Readings Delivered before the Honourable Society of the Middle Temple*. In these lectures, in which he drew widely on Roman and canon law, he sought to show the connection of the various branches of jurisprudence with each other, and to show their place in a general system of moral science. This ambition was echoed in 1854 in his *Commentaries on Universal Public Law*, where he sought to show the universal nature of legal obligation, in the manner of Domat and the civil lawyers. His interest in comparative jurisprudence and Roman law continued, and in 1874 he published his *Introduction to the study and use of the civil law, and to commentaries on the modern civil law*.

In his youth, Bowyer was a follower of the Oxford Movement, and in 1839 he wrote an article on ecclesiastical discipline in Newman's *British Critic*. He converted to Roman Catholicism in August 1850 and immediately became an active spokesman for the Catholic church on legal and constitutional questions. He was soon called on to act as a constitutional adviser to Cardinal Manning, at the time of public agitation against the pope's decision to create the archbishopric of Westminster. In his pamphlet, *The Cardinal Archbishop of Westminster and the New Hierarchy* (1850), Bowyer argued for the legal right of the pope to exercise his spiritual authority by creating a permanent episcopacy in England, saying that the Catholic church was recognized in English law. He remained a regular contributor to the press on religious questions, writing letters frequently to *The Times*, and being a regular contributor to the *Dublin Review*. He was also a consistent defender of Catholic causes in parliament, his attitudes to politics often reflecting his religious rather than strictly party loyalties. For these services he was made a knight commander of the order of Pius IX, as well as a chamberlain to that pontiff; he was also made knight grand cross of the order of St Gregory the Great, and was awarded the grand collar of the Constantinian order of St George of Naples.

Sir George Bowyer, seventh baronet (1811–1883), by William Edward Kilburn

Bowyer was a fervent whig and an enthusiastic supporter of Lord Henry Brougham, as well as being a friend of Henry Fox, fourth Baron Holland. His passion for politics lasted throughout his life. In the late 1830s, he aspired to become Thomas Duffield's successor as MP for Abingdon, the seat which his father had held between 1811 and 1818, and in August 1849 he stood (unsuccessfully) as a Liberal for the parliamentary seat of Reading, in the by-election caused by the elevation to the bench of T. N. Talfourd. He was finally elected to parliament in July 1852, as MP for Dundalk, co. Louth. As an MP, Bowyer was always independent-minded, and he found himself unsuited to the strictures of party discipline. He flirted with Disraeli's Conservatives in the 1860s, and lost his seat in the election of 1868 to a Gladstonian Liberal. Bowyer returned to parliament in 1874 as MP for co. Wexford, having stood in the election as a home-ruler primarily because he realized that this was the only way in which he could continue his political career. He remained thereafter an indisciplined member of an indisciplined group, continuing to sit on the government benches, and remaining a member of the Reform Club, until 23 June 1876, when he was expelled by a two-thirds majority at a general meeting, for frequently voting against the Liberal Party. In March 1880 Bowyer retired from politics.

In 1862 Bowyer was one of the sponsors of a bill in parliament to reform the government of the inns of court and the discipline of the bar, which failed as a result of opposition by the inns. He also played a leading part in the parliamentary agitation of 1873–4, which succeeded in persuading Disraeli's government to retain the appellate jurisdiction of the House of Lords. In addition, he was a member of the royal commission appointed to examine the expediency of digesting the law in 1866, although he did not sign its report.

Bowyer succeeded his father as seventh baronet on 1 July 1860, though the family's landed estate had been leased in 1847 to a nonconformist school (the forerunner of Radley College). He was a magistrate and a deputy lieutenant for Berkshire. He was found dead in his bed at 13 King's Bench Walk on 7 June 1883, having suffered a heart attack. His funeral service was held in his church of St John of Jerusalem, Great Ormond Street, London, and he was buried in the family vault at Abingdon. Bowyer was unmarried, and was succeeded in the baronetcy by his brother William (1812–1893), another barrister of the Middle Temple. MICHAEL LOBBAN

Sources *The Times* (8 June 1883) · *Law Times* (16 June 1883), 137 · *Solicitors' Journal*, 27 (1882–3), 555 · Holdsworth, *Eng. law*, 15.276, 358 · D. Duman, *The English and colonial bars in the nineteenth century* (1983), 56–8 · *The letters and diaries of John Henry Newman*, ed. C. S. Dessain and others, [31 vols.] (1961–), vols. 6, 14 · *Wellesley index* · d. cert. · R. Stevens, 'The final appeal: reform of the House of Lords and privy council, 1867–76', *Law Quarterly Review*, 80 (1964), 343–69
Archives Bodl. Oxf., papers relating to Italy | BL, corresp. with W. E. Gladstone, Add. MSS 44379–44466, *passim* · BL, corresp. with Lord Holland, Add. MS 52021 · Bodl. Oxf., letters to Benjamin Disraeli
Likenesses W. E. Kilburn, photograph, NPG [*see illus.*] · Spy [L. Ward], chromolithograph caricature, NPG; repro. in *VF* (18 June 1879) · portrait, repro. in *ILN*, 36 (1860), 548 · portrait, repro. in *International Studio*, 20 (1903), 182
Wealth at death £9293 4*s*. 6*d*.: probate, 24 Aug 1883, *CGPLA Eng. & Wales*

Bowyer, George Edward Wentworth, **first Baron Denham (1886–1948)**, politician, was born in India at Simla on 16 January 1886, the eldest son of Lieutenant-Colonel Wentworth Grenville Bowyer (1850–1929) of the Royal Engineers and his wife, Eva Mary Lane (*d*. 1954). In 1900 the family returned to north Buckinghamshire, where his father bought the manor and most of the village of Weston Underwood. He was educated at Eton College (1899–1904) and at New College, Oxford, where he graduated with third-class honours in modern history in 1908. He became a barrister of the Inner Temple in 1909, working in criminal practice on the midland circuit. He served as a captain in the Oxford and Buckinghamshire light infantry during the First World War; he was wounded in action on 6 May 1915 and was awarded the Military Cross.

In the 1918 general election Bowyer defeated the sitting Asquithian Liberal and became Conservative MP for the Buckingham division; he represented this rural and now fairly safe seat until his elevation to the peerage in 1937. On 27 February 1919 he married the Hon. Daphne Freeman-Mitford (1895–1996), fourth daughter of Algernon Bertram Freeman-*Mitford, first Baron Redesdale; during the war she had worked on her brother-in-law's estate at Cold Brayfield, not far from Weston Underwood. The Bowyers had a daughter and two sons; the elder son was killed in action with the Royal Air Force in January 1943.

Bowyer made friends easily and was generally liked, and these characteristics shaped his political career. His first step on the ladder was as unpaid parliamentary private secretary to Sir Philip Cunliffe-Lister from 1921 to 1924. He moved into the whips' office as an assistant whip on 15 December 1924 and was a junior lord of the Treasury from 28 December 1927 until the government's defeat in 1929. He enjoyed the work and was a constant attender at the house; during the 1927 session he did not miss a single division. He remained a whip but was not listed in a formal post again until the reshuffle of June 1935: from then until he retired on 6 December 1935 he held the more senior post of comptroller of the household. He was knighted on 10 July 1929 and made a baronet on 21 January 1933.

In the spring of 1930 Bowyer's involvement in the Conservative Party machine took a new direction. The post of deputy chairman of the party had been vacant since July 1929, but on 6 March 1930 the appointments of Bowyer and Lady Iveagh as joint deputy chairmen were announced. The post was one of comparative obscurity, for which the chief qualifications were loyalty and discretion. It is likely that Bowyer was recommended by the chief whip and was an acceptably safe choice. Throughout his career he was firmly in the mainstream of the party, and as well as being a particular friend of Cunliffe-Lister he was also close to Stanley Baldwin and Neville Chamberlain. Bowyer was to remain at central office until December 1935, but from the middle of 1931 the title of deputy seems to have faded away and Bowyer and his colleagues were instead described as vice-chairmen.

The change did not affect his work, which was linked to his role as a whip. His primary responsibility was for parliamentary candidates: interviewing the aspirants, discouraging the undesirables, and seeking to place candidates in suitable seats. From August 1931 onwards matters were complicated by the existence of the National Government. Central office had to balance the sensibilities of the other parties in the coalition against the disgruntlement of those Conservative associations which had to be cajoled into standing aside for the sake of the national picture. It was perhaps a sign of their success that the party managers came under regular fire from both sides. Certainly, they succeeded in keeping the National Government together at the local and electoral level, where it could so easily have unravelled, and in this respect Bowyer deserves a share of the credit for the victories of 1931 and 1935. He knew how to work with the grain of the party, and his tenure laid the foundation for the more formal vetting which began with the establishment in 1935 of the standing advisory committee on candidates. His job was one in which the few who were satisfied went away quietly, while the many who were disappointed made their grievances vocal. Even so, despite seething after one frustrating interview, Cuthbert Headlam noted that Bowyer 'means well and he is always quite civil' (*Parliament and Politics*, 7 May 1931).

Bowyer's connection with Baldwin was underlined by the grant of a peerage in the coronation honours list in 1937, and he took the title of Baron Denham on 24 May. His long involvement in rural life was called upon at the start of the Second World War, when he was parliamentary secretary at the Ministry of Agriculture from 19 September 1939 until Chamberlain's fall in May 1940. For the rest of the war he served in the Home Guard directorate at the War Office, acting as liaison officer with the London division. From 1945 to 1947 he was a Conservative whip in the Lords.

From the early 1920s Bowyer's home was Denham Lodge, Weston Underwood, Olney, until at the end of the Second World War he moved into the Manor House. He was never wealthy and money was always a concern. Bowyer had sandy hair and a moustache; physically he was well proportioned and appeared taller than his 5 feet 10 inches. He enjoyed country pursuits, in particular shooting and coarse fishing; he was an exceptional amateur trainer of gun dogs, keeping his own golden retrievers. Fox-hunting was his favourite sport, but he had to give this up after breaking his pelvis in a fall shortly before the Second World War. In 1935 he became senior steward of the national greyhound racing club. His other pleasures were tennis, cricket, golf, and bridge, and he was mainly a pipe smoker. On one occasion he piloted the liner *Queen Mary* into dry dock, an achievement of which he was proud. A keen Anglican, he was a local churchwarden from his father's death until his own; another facet of his involvement in rural affairs was his service as president of the Urban District Councils Association in 1923–5 and from 1929 until his death.

Bowyer was still politically active when he fell ill with the brain tumour which led to his death at 20 Devonshire Place, Marylebone, on 30 November 1948. His son was to follow in his footsteps, for the second Baron Denham served as Conservative chief whip in the Lords from 1979 to 1991. STUART BALL

Sources private information (2004) [second Baron Denham] • *The Times* (1 Dec 1948) • *Daily Telegraph* (1 Dec 1948) • *Parliament and politics in the age of Baldwin and MacDonald: the Headlam diaries, 1923–1935*, ed. S. Ball (1992) • GEC, *Peerage*
Archives CUL, Baldwin MSS
Wealth at death £12,000: probate, 2 June 1949, *CGPLA Eng. & Wales*

Bowyer, Robert (*c.*1560–1621), parliamentary official and politician, was the younger son of William *Bowyer (*d.* 1569/70) of Wimbledon, Surrey, bailiff of Westminster and keeper of the records in the Tower, and his wife, Agnes, daughter of Sir John Harcourt of Stanton Harcourt, Oxfordshire, and widow of John Knyvet of Ashwellthorpe, Norfolk. His only brother died young; his sister married Richard Highgate. Bowyer's father came from a well-known Sussex family, and left him a lease of Selsey prebend in his will of 15 April 1569.

Bowyer graduated BA at Oxford in March 1579, and went on to Clifford's Inn, and in 1580 to the Middle Temple. He attached himself to the Sussex magnate Thomas Sackville, then Lord Buckhurst and later lord treasurer and first earl of Dorset, who in 1594 recommended him to act as deputy to John Parker in a chancery post as 'of honest sort and behaviour, of such good knowledge and skill for the discharge of such a place, and withall having so good means and ability to live'. He received the appointment, but Parker himself was never sworn into office. Even with Sackville's favour Bowyer failed to secure more than the reversion in 1597 to the clerkship of the parliaments, the successful candidate averring that he was unfit 'by reason of a great imperfection he hath in his speech'. Sackville took him into his own service as secretary, and secured his return to the parliament of 1601 for the Sussex borough of Steyning. He left a distinctive mark of his presence, protesting on 12 December that a member had been 'pulled back' from voting in a close division, and fainting six days later: 'It was said he had a spice of the falling sickness'.

In 1604 Bowyer was appointed with a relative, Henry Elsynge, to his father's post of keeper of the Tower records. On 31 October 1605 he was chosen in a by-election as the member for Evesham, taking the place of a man who had been an exchequer colleague of one of his Bowyer cousins. He was more active as a member of the first Jacobean parliament, often called on in his official capacity to supply precedents, but he is best remembered for his diary of the parliament, which has been described as 'indispensable'. On a more personal level he concerned himself with a land bill for William Essex, who had married a Harcourt, acting as a feoffee for his Berkshire estate. He was sworn clerk of the parliaments on 30 January 1610, relinquishing his seat in the House of Commons. He devoted the rest of his life to bringing order to the parliamentary records after what he called the 'negligence' of his predecessors. Among his achievements was the recovery of the Lords' journal for 1536.

Bowyer died on 14 or 15 March 1621. He had never married, but his will shows that he regarded Elsynge, his successor in the clerkship, more or less as a son. He was particularly grateful to him for the 'extraordinary kindness' he had shown his wife, Bowyer's niece Blanche Highgate, near whom he was buried in St Dunstan-in-the-West.

ALAN DAVIDSON, *rev.*

Sources *Parliamentary diary of Robert Bowyer, 1606–1607*, ed. D. H. Willson (1931) • HoP, *Commons, 1558–1603* • *Catalogue of manuscripts in the library of the Inner Temple* (1972) • Foster, *Alum. Oxon.*

Bowyer, Robert (1758–1834), miniature painter and publisher, was born in Portsmouth, the son of Amos Bowyer, a shipwright, and his wife, Betty Ann. He was baptized there on 18 June 1758. He served first as a clerk to a merchant in Portsmouth and then in London; there are conflicting accounts as to why he changed career. The first ('Bowyer memorials'), recounts that he intended to travel to America as a supercargo at his employer's request but, engaged to Mary Shoveller, he wished to present her with a likeness of himself before setting sail, and, unable to afford the services of a miniature painter, painted his own. Encouraged by a number of commissions, he abandoned his plans to go to America and began to take likenesses from a booth at Coxheath camp. Another version of Bowyer's life cites his need for employment as the motivation for his taking up painting (*N&Q*, 350). Bowyer married Mary in Portsmouth on 14 July 1777; they had one daughter.

At some time, probably in the late 1770s, Bowyer undertook professional training in London with the miniature painter John Smart. He exhibited first at the Free Society of Artists in 1782 (a portrait of a gentleman) and at the Royal Academy in 1783. About this time he moved to 68 Berners Street, London, Smart's former residence. Bowyer enjoyed much success as a miniature painter and his patrons included the duke of Rutland, the marchioness of Salisbury, and Lord Nelson; by April 1790 he described himself as miniature painter to his majesty. However, during the next decade Bowyer's interests became more concerned with print publishing, beginning with a number of his own portraits, including that of Dr Francis Willis, physician to George III, which was exhibited at the Royal Academy in 1789 and published that same year with a dedication to Queen Charlotte.

During the 1790s Bowyer began two major publishing projects: an illustrated edition of the Bible and Hume's *The History of England*. The earliest plates for the *Holy Bible* were published in 1791 and the series included thirty-two engravings by James Fittler after old masters in English private collections and was completed in 1795. The publication of the first part of *The History of England* in 1793 coincided with Bowyer's move from Berners Street to Pall Mall, to what he called the Historic Gallery. There he displayed the paintings commissioned from leading artists such as Benjamin West and P. J. de Loutherbourg for this series. By 1806 Bowyer had published five large folios reaching the year 1688 but the work was never completed owing to the high costs involved, a loss of £30,000 said already to have been incurred.

Bowyer also published a number of engraved series connected with India, probably facilitated by his friendship with Smart, who had gone there in 1785 and to whose children Bowyer acted as guardian. A proposal to publish, in collaboration with the engraver William Sharp and the painter Robert Smirke, the latter's *Lord Cornwallis Receiving as Hostages the Two Sons of Tipoo Sultan* was abandoned; however, Bowyer later published portraits of the three main protagonists by Smart. In 1794 he published *Picturesque Views, with a Descriptive History of the Country of Tipoo Sultan* after drawings by Robert Home and in 1797 *Oriental Scenery: Twenty-Four Views in Hindoostan* after drawings by Thomas Daniell.

The last years of the eighteenth century were difficult for Bowyer personally. The loss of his only daughter at eighteen in summer 1796 caused great personal anguish. In a letter to Warren Hastings he expressed his fear that his loss might be compounded as he was extremely doubtful whether his wife would survive the tragedy. However, in 1799 Bowyer and his wife took into their household a young, orphaned, wax modeller from Bristol named Catherine Andras. She became a member of the family and shared a number of sitters with Bowyer. Bowyer was a member of the Baptist Missionary Society and during the peace of Amiens he, his wife, and Andras travelled to Paris; this visit resulted in the formation of the French Evangelical Society. However, this visit had another important purpose for Bowyer, the collection of prints and engravings of scriptural subjects, which formed the basis of his famous edition of the Bible.

Bowyer's financial difficulties arising from the publication of *The History of England* were compounded by a lawsuit over *Views in Egypt, Palestine and other Parts of the Ottoman Empire* (1803). In 1806 he avoided financial ruin by disposing of the contents of the Historic Gallery by lottery. In that same year he moved to Byfleet in Surrey, although he maintained a house at various addresses in Pall Mall from where he continued to run his publishing business. At Byfleet, Bowyer pursued his evangelism, establishing a Sunday school and giving sermons. He purchased a public house that stood opposite his own residence, pulled it down, and erected a chapel; he also established a day school. Bowyer continued to publish up to his death, including *Works of Raffaelle, Domenichino, Poussin, and Albano*, issued in five volumes in 1819, and his last publication, *A selection of fac-similies of watercolour drawings from the works of the most distinguished artists* in 1825. However, Bowyer was also occupied in the creation of what became known as the Bowyer Bible. The religious prints and engravings he had collected in Paris were augmented by others, purchased by an agent in Paris by special permission during the Napoleonic wars. Bowyer's collection of prints was inserted into a copy of Thomas Macklin's illustrated edition of the Bible, and the resulting work reached forty-five volumes. Bowyer also took up painting again in his later years; George IV, the duke of York, and other members of the royal family sat to him.

However, Bowyer's last years were not free from difficulties. Following the death of his landlord at Byfleet, the duke of York, Bowyer had to purchase his house at a much increased value, which his own improvements had brought about. Further, great expense was incurred when, acting as executor for a friend, he became involved in a lawsuit. His home was mortgaged, only to suffer a fire. He died at Byfleet on 4 June 1834. The publishing business was left to Mary Parkes who, originally a housemaid at Byfleet, had been involved in the business from at least the late 1820s. DEBORAH GRAHAM-VERNON

Sources 'The Bowyer memorials', NPG, Heinz Archive and Library • R. W. Hutton, 'Robert Bowyer and the Historic Gallery: a study of the creation of a magnificent work to promote the arts in

England', PhD diss., University of Chicago, 1992 • *DNB* • B. B., 'The Bowyer Bible', *N&Q*, 5 (1852), 350–51 • *IGI*
Archives V&A, MS biography | BL, letters to W. Hastings, Add. MSS 29174–29180

Bowyer, William (*d.* 1569/70), antiquary, was one of the six sons of Robert Bowyer (*d.* 1552), of Chichester, Sussex, and his wife, Margaret. His father was four times mayor of Chichester, and MP for the borough in 1529 and 1547. His elder brother Robert (*d.* 1567/8) represented Chichester in the parliaments of 1555 and 1559, while Agnes, one of his five sisters, married William Neale, auditor of the exchequer. Bowyer's early life before his entry into the Middle Temple in 1553 is obscure. However, in his will of 15 April 1569 he paid tribute to Alexander Nowell, dean of St Paul's and former master of Westminster School, 'my singular good Master and no lesse approved good frende' for 'my bringing up in the feare and knowledge of god' (fol. 142*v*). By 1560 Bowyer was bailiff of the borough of Westminster, where he came into contact with Sir William Cecil, the high steward. He resided in the parish of Wimbledon, Surrey, alongside Cecil, and at the time of his death was owed £500 by the queen's secretary of state. Bowyer's other residence was in Hand Alley, off London's Fleet Street. He married, at an uncertain date, Agnes, daughter of Sir John Harcourt (*d.* 1566) of Stanton Harcourt, Oxfordshire, and Ellenhall, Staffordshire, and Margaret, daughter of Sir William Barentyne. Agnes was the widow of John Knyvet of Ashwellthorpe, Norfolk. They had two sons, William and Robert, and a daughter, Judith. Bowyer's closest friend was Edward Flowerdew of Norfolk, a lawyer who became a serjeant-at-law and a baron of the exchequer.

Bowyer sat in the parliament of 1563 for Westminster. A year later he was identified as a supporter of the protestant faith and appointed a JP for Surrey. In 1565 he assisted the city of London in the defence of its trading privileges at the Anglo-Netherlandish colloquy of Bruges. By January 1563 Bowyer was occupying the position of keeper of records in the Tower of London, although his patent for that office was not issued until 18 June 1567. His efforts in the latter year to secure custody of the records of parliament and chancery stored in the Rolls Chapel and Rolls House were thwarted by Sir William Cordell, the master of the rolls, but Bowyer still had in his keeping the largest collection of government records, and he was credited by John Strype in the early eighteenth century with being 'the first Digester of them into some Method' (McKisack, 82–3). It was later stated that he devoted eight years and £1000 to his labours, producing digests of the parliament, patent, charter, close, and foreign rolls, from the reigns of King John to Edward IV (now in the College of Arms), as well as a list of escheats, a medieval roll of arms and a heraldic commonplace book. As a collector of manuscripts, Bowyer acquired the Rievaulx Abbey copy of Roger of Howden's *Chronica*, the C manuscript of the Anglo-Saxon Chronicle, William of Malmesbury's *De antiquitate Glastoniensis ecclesiae*, Ranulf Higden's *Polychronicon*, and Laurence Nowell's transcription of the *Vita et mors Edwardi secundi* (part of Geoffrey le Baker's chronicle), among other notable documents of the English medieval past. His second son, Robert *Bowyer (*d.* 1621), who became keeper of the records in the Tower in 1604, inherited many of his father's heraldic and historical manuscripts, some of which are preserved in the library of the Inner Temple. The eldest son, William, acquired the 'bokes escriptes writinges and monuments … as be of my own hande writing … as matters of greater value then all that I leave' (fol. 142*r*). Bowyer died possessed of the leases of his residences, the prebend of Waltham in Chichester Cathedral and parsonage of Selsey, Sussex, and the farm of Little Thetford, Cambridgeshire. Probate of his will was granted on 23 June 1570, his widow being his executor.

J. D. Alsop

Sources HoP, *Commons, 1558–1603*, 1.472–5 • HoP, *Commons, 1509–58*, 1.474–5 • will, PRO, PROB 11/52, fol. 142*r–v* • M. McKisack, *Medieval history in the Tudor age* (1971), 77, 82–3 • L. Campbell and F. Steer, *A catalogue of manuscripts in the College of Arms collections*, 1 (1988), 197–217, 471 • J. C. Davies, ed., *Catalogue of manuscripts in the library of the Honourable Society of the Inner Temple*, 3 vols. (1972), 207, 216–17, 223–4 • L. Fox, ed., *English historical scholarship in the sixteenth and seventeenth centuries* (1956), 16 • *CPR, 1566–9*, 72 • B. R. Masters, ed., *Chamber accounts of the sixteenth century*, London RS, 20 (1984), 125–6 • R. Cooke, *Visitation of London, 1568*, ed. H. Stanford London and S. W. Rawlins, [new edn], 2 vols. in one, Harleian Society, 109–10 (1963), 96
Wealth at death leases of at least two residences; a prebend; a parsonage; a farm; valuable books and MSS

Bowyer, William (1663–1737), printer, was born in July 1663, the son of John Bowyer, grocer of London, and Mary, daughter of William King, vintner of London. He was bound on 1 September 1679 to Miles Flesher (*d.* 1688), printer, and freed on 4 October 1686. His first marriage in 1686 or 1687 to Mary (surname unknown; *d.* 1689) brought two children, Frances and William, said to have died in infancy. On 6 March 1699 Bowyer married Dorothy Allport (1665–1727), widow of Benjamin Allport (bookseller of St Botolph without Bishopsgate, *d.* August 1695), daughter of Thomas *Dawks (1636–1689) [*see under* Dawks, Thomas (*bap.* 1611, *d.* 1670)] and sister to Ichabod Dawks, printers. Their son, also William *Bowyer, was born on 19 December 1699.

In the same year Bowyer set up as master printer at the White Horse in Little Britain, London, the first of his eighteen apprentices being bound on 7 August 1699. Before the end of the year Bowyer moved to Dogwell Court, Whitefriars, London. Called to the livery of the Stationers' Company on 6 May 1700, he advanced no higher in the company hierarchy, perhaps for reasons of conscience.

Fourteen years of progress ended suddenly in the small hours of 30 January 1713: Bowyer's dwelling house and workrooms above were gutted by fire. The loss, including works already printed, totalled £5146. The proceeds of a royal brief with debts forgiven and gifts from friends and members of the trade returned almost half this sum. In October 1713 Bowyer began again in Temple Lane, Whitefriars. Tailpieces depicting a phoenix renewed by fire thereafter ornamented many of the firm's works.

Bowyer brought his son into the firm in 1722, but the father alone continued to be mentioned in imprints and to keep the accounts. The achievements of father and son, best documented of any eighteenth-century London printers, were chronicled in *Literary Anecdotes* by John Nichols, apprentice, partner, and successor to the younger Bowyer, and have been comprehensively studied by Maslen and Lancaster (1991).

Works printed by the father from 1699 to 1737 total more than 2632. Their quantity and diversity are remarkable. The printing of literary works, for instance by Alexander Pope, is only a small part of the story. One class of works stands out, justifying the view that Bowyer aimed to be a scholarly printer in the best continental tradition. To this end he sent his son to university in 1716 to train to be a learned corrector. From the beginning Bowyer printed much in the emergent field of English antiquities, often directly for the authors. Works by the Anglo-Saxonists William and his sister Elizabeth Elstob, Roger Gale, the nonjuror George Hickes (*Linguarum vett. septentrionalium thesauri*, ed. William Wotton, 1708), John Le Neve (*Monumenta Anglicana*, 1716–19), Thomas Rymer (many volumes of the *Foedera* from 1708), David Wilkins (*Leges Anglo-Saxonicae*, 1721), and Moses Williams (proposals issued 1719 for his edition of Humphrey Llwyd, *Britannicae descriptionis commentariolum*, 1731) form a representative few.

Motives for the study of English history included the wish to justify post-Reformation church reform. Bowyer's many nonjuring authors comprised an especially active sub-group of scholars whom Bowyer, a nonjuror himself, served beyond the commercial call of duty. The first work bearing his imprint, the anonymous *Defence of the Vindication of K. Charles the Martyr*, 1699, by Thomas Wagstaffe, nonjuring 'bishop' of Ipswich, reveals the printer's sympathies. Bowyer was nevertheless moderate in his dissent, like his friend Robert Nelson (of whose *Companion for the Festivals and Fasts of the Church of England* he printed sixteen editions between 1704 and 1735). Nonjuring principles governed his choice of private school (under Ambrose Bonwicke) and college (St John's, Cambridge) for his son, and in the 1720s his attendance, with the printer James Bettenham, his step-son-in-law, at meetings to ordain nonjuring priests.

A learned printer required good and exotic types. Bowyer's first Anglo-Saxon types were burnt in the fire. A new fount, used in Elizabeth Elstob's *Anglo-Saxon Grammar* (1715), was later given to Oxford University. In the 1720s Bowyer was an important patron of the typefounder William Caslon. The first recorded use of Caslon's pica roman is in Bowyer's *Anacreontis opera graece*, 1725, while, according to Nichols, Caslon's pica Coptic, used in David Wilkins's *Quinque libri Moysis prophetae in lingua Aegyptia*, typis Gul. Bowyer, 1731, was cut in 1729 under Bowyer's supervision.

There are tantalizing glimpses of Bowyer's journeyman years. Letters written by him in 1696–7, reported by Ord (pp. 340–41) but now presumed lost, imply a serious-minded young man. In one letter, said to display a 'vast mass of erudition', he endeavoured to win back his sister 'Elizabeth Ross', who had 'apostasised to popery, and died a professed nun of St. Clare's, at Dunkirk'. Another, addressed to 'Mr. Bowyer, at Mr. Daniel Sheldon's, in St. Bartholomew's Close' links Bowyer with members of the pre-1688 Anglican establishment. Sheldon (*d.* 1699), whose will Bowyer witnessed on 16 February 1697, was nephew to Gilbert Sheldon, archbishop of Canterbury (*d.* 1677), and brother-in-law to John Dolben, archbishop of York (*d.* 1686).

Bowyer was a highly competent printer, widely respected in the trade and beyond, and able twice in his career to build up a large and successful business. He died in London on 27 December 1737, and was buried at Low Leyton, Essex, where he owned a country retreat. His son raised a monument to his memory in the local church.

KEITH MASLEN

Sources Nichols, *Lit. anecdotes* · *The Bowyer ledgers: the printing accounts of William Bowyer, father and son, reproduced on microfiche with a checklist of Bowyer printing 1699–1777, a commentary, indexes and appendixes*, ed. K. Maslen and J. Lancaster (1991) · D. F. McKenzie, ed., *Stationers' Company apprentices*, [2]: 1641–1700 (1974) · K. I. D. Maslen, *An early London printing house at work: studies in the Bowyer ledgers* (1993) · J. W. Ord, *The history and antiquities of Cleveland* (1846) · M. Treadwell, 'London printers and printing houses in 1705', *Publishing History*, 7 (1980), 5–44 · J. Mosley, 'The early career of William Caslon', *Journal of the Printing History Society*, 3 (1967), 66–81 · K. I. D. Maslen, *The Bowyer ornament stock* (1973) · E. R. Mores, *A dissertation upon English typographical founders and founderies*, ed. H. Carter and C. Ricks, new edn (1961) · K. I. D. Maslen, 'Samuel Negus, his list and "His case"', *The Library*, 6th ser., 4 (1982), 317–20 · private information (2004) [M. Treadwell] · rate books and marriage tax assessments, CLRO

Archives Bodl. Oxf., account books, paper stock ledger, MS Don. b.4 · Grolier Club Library, New York, ledgers A, B, and C, Grolier 19471, 19474, and 19472 [described in *The Bowyer ledgers* (1991)] | Bodl. Oxf., Rawl. MSS · Col. U., Nichols archives [mostly printed in Nichols, *Lit. anecdotes*]

Likenesses J. Basire, line engraving, pubd 1812, BM, NPG; repro. in Nichols, *Lit. anecdotes*, vol. 1, frontispiece · oils, Stationers' Hall, London

Wealth at death estate, incl. business, to son: administration, PRO, PROB 6/114/2

Bowyer, William (1699–1777), printer, was born on 19 December 1699 at Dogwell Court, Whitefriars, London, the only son to survive infancy of William *Bowyer (1663–1737), printer, and his second wife, Dorothy Allport (1665–1727), daughter of Thomas *Dawks (1636–1689) of London, printer [*see under* Dawks, Thomas (*bap.* 1611, *d.* 1670)], and his wife, Anne. Young William attended a private school at Headley, Surrey, kept by Ambrose Bonwicke. Then, most unusually, his father sent him to university. In June 1716 William was admitted to St John's College, Cambridge, as a sizar under Robert Jenkin. There he remained until June 1722, mastering Latin, Greek, and Hebrew. At home, at school, and at university he was much among nonjurors and their sympathizers, which is perhaps why he did not take a degree.

The intention was to place a learned corrector at the heart of the firm, the better to serve the new English scholarship. The success of this plan may be seen in the list of works printed by the Bowyers between 1699 and 1777 given in the Maslen–Lancaster edition of the Bowyer

William Bowyer (1699–1777), by James Basire, pubd 1812

printing ledgers (1991). The two functions of scholar and printer were at best complementary. Often Bowyer acted as a patron of scholarship by encouraging authors to publish on their own account, at times going beyond what was commercially prudent by himself sharing or bearing the financial risk, as when in 1766 he published his friend Samuel Pegge's *Essay on the Coins of Cunobelin*. However, sometimes there were tensions, expressed by Bowyer himself in a letter of 11 January 1767: 'My father, good man, sent me thither [to Cambridge] to qualify me (by a new kind of experiment) for a printer. But it served only in trade to expose me to more affronts, and to give me a keener sensibility of them' (Nichols, *Lit. anecdotes*, 3.13).

In June 1722 young William entered the firm and took over the correcting of proofs; not that he did all himself, for father and son both employed a succession of nonjuring (and hence unbeneficed) clergymen to help with this work. How the complex task of correction was allotted can usually only be guessed. Nichols draws attention to Bowyer's correcting of Selden's *Opera omnia* (1726). Letters between author and printer, some acrimonious, also tell a tale. Unsent letters of 1757 to William Warburton protest vigorously that the bishop unfairly blamed Bowyer for not correcting the author's own mistakes. Nichols notes Bowyer's freedom in correcting the press, citing his letter to Antony Alsop, author of *Odarum libri duo* (1752): 'in the last sheet I made it *obstrepat* against your authority, and will give you leave to advertise me if it is wrong' (Nichols, *Lit. anecdotes*, 2.234–5n).

On 9 October 1728 at St Clement Danes, Strand, London, William married his mother's niece Ann Prudom (*c.*1705–1731), by whom he gained farms in Danby Dale, Yorkshire, and at Navestock, Essex. Their second and only surviving son, Thomas, was born on 5 September 1730. Ann died in childbirth on 17 October 1731.

Meanwhile, Bowyer was venturing in new directions. In 1729, through the friendship of Arthur Onslow, speaker of the House of Commons, he was appointed to print the votes of the House, a profitable employment which remained in the firm until 1940.

The acquisition of copyrights was another line which became increasingly important. At first Bowyer was careful not to be seen to compete with the booksellers, but later his standing in the trade placed him above such question. In any case, for Bowyer owning copy was primarily useful in conferring the right to print. In 1729 Bowyer began to collect copyrights of pieces by Jonathan Swift and his countrymen. George Faulkner, the notable Dublin printer, who had worked not long before as a journeyman for the Bowyers, initiated the lifelong habit of sending Bowyer printed copies of works first published in Dublin, English copyright going to whoever first printed an English edition. Bowyer did as much for Faulkner. Between May 1729 and February 1733 Bowyer thus reprinted a number of pieces of Swiftiana, including, for instance, *A vindication of his excellency the lord C—t, from the charge of favouring none but tories, high-churchmen and Jacobites*. To confirm possession Bowyer secured through the Revd Matthew Pilkington a form of assignment from Swift himself. When Pope protested, meaning to reprint some of these pieces himself, Bowyer insisted on his rights. In later years Bowyer's share of Swift copyrights gave him a valuable stake in the ever expanding editions of Swift's *Works*.

After his father's death on 27 December 1737 Bowyer was on his own. He took charge of the all-important accounts, which William senior had kept almost to the last, and a decline in the standard of bookkeeping soon begins to appear. One more step was necessary. On 4 July 1738 Bowyer was made free of the Stationers' Company by patrimony, and almost immediately called to the livery. Thereafter, being retiring by nature, he refused higher office in the company as he became eligible, and paid the usual fines. On 5 May 1741 he bound the first of seventeen apprentices. Some time in the early 1740s he also took stock of his printing materials and equipment by means of a linked inventory and type specimen, which he occasionally updated. These show his care to renew his text types, for instance by buying regularly from Caslon. Also revealing is his ownership of exotics: Hebrew, Greek (in no fewer than fourteen faces and sizes), Anglo-Saxon, Gothic, and Coptic.

However, output steadily if not alarmingly declined. Complaints by Bowyer about being given only part of a work to print belong to these years. Nevertheless, his learned printing grew in prominence. Bowyer was appointed printer to the Society of Antiquaries in May 1736, and on 7 July was elected to membership. Between 1738 and 1748 he was one of three printers employed by the short-lived Society for the Encouragement of Learning, printing works by Thomas Tanner and others, which brought prestige if not profit.

On 21 August 1747 Bowyer married Elizabeth Bill (*c*.1700–1771), a widow who had long been his housekeeper. She read proofs for him. Less helpfully she favoured William Emonson, son of and apprentice to Bowyer's overseer James Emonson, against her stepson Thomas Bowyer, who had been apprenticed to his father on 5 August 1746. Disappointing his father's hopes, Thomas left home before completing his time, and after other false starts eventually retired to the country under the name Mr Thomas, and died on 17 December 1783.

On 10 October 1754, being 'sick of the World' and hoping to lessen 'the fatigues of Business', Bowyer entered into a partnership with James Emonson (Emonson Partnership MSS). Bowyer soon changed his mind, instancing the bookseller John Knapton's bankruptcy in September 1755 following his partner's death. Emonson cited Bowyer's unfairness in refusing to print the second part of Warburton's *Divine Legation of Moses*, while promising to proof-read it. The causes were deeper. Bowyer found he was not ready to retire or accept a likely change to the character of his press. Emonson moved on to print a newspaper, *Lloyd's Evening Post*. The partnership legally ended on 4 July 1757.

The nonjuring loyalties of Bowyer's father were transformed into a banking service offered by the son to a dozen or so country clergymen, one-time members and fellows of Bowyer's own college of St John's.

Early in 1757 Bowyer took yet another boy for training. John Nichols, not yet thirteen, quickly proved himself to be the helper Bowyer had long desired. Nichols was formally apprenticed on 6 February 1759. On 4 July 1761 Bowyer successfully applied to the earl of Macclesfield, the president of the Royal Society, to follow Samuel Richardson as the society's printer, first completing vol. 52, part 1 of the *Philosophical Transactions*. A later initiative was unsuccessful. During 1765 Bowyer treated with Cambridge University for a lease of its printing privileges. Nichols was freed on 4 March 1766, and made a junior partner on 5 April, with a one-third share in the business. Bowyer cautiously imposed strict conditions. Among Nichols's many duties were keeping most of the accounts and binding the apprentices. Once again, Bowyer was not to be compelled to read proofs.

The year 1767 brought three 'revolutions' in Bowyer's affairs. He complained to his son in a letter of 13 May that Nichols had deceived him by secretly marrying (Nichols MSS). Also, the 'Printing house in White Fryers being propt up & like to fall', he had taken a new one in Red Lion Passage, with access to Fleet Street. There the printing house remained until it too was destroyed by fire, on 8 February 1808. Finally, he had just been appointed printer of the retrospective series of *Journals of the House of Lords*, to be completed in 31 volumes, 1768–77. Nichols was essential to this undertaking, and Bowyer had to overlook his behaviour.

By this time Bowyer's health, long troublesome, was giving way; Elizabeth Bowyer had died on 14 January 1771. On 15 May 1773 Nichols, already effectively in control, was made an equal partner. It was he who superintended the slow passage through the press of *Domesday Book* (1783), using the record type cut to order by Joseph Jackson.

Bowyer's duties as corrector often led him to indulge in the more congenial scholarly tasks of annotating, commenting, emending, epitomizing, indexing, and translating. These works are listed in the index to the *Bowyer Ledgers* (1991), and a selection of such minor pieces was published by Nichols in 1785 as *Miscellaneous tracts, by the late William Bowyer, printer, F.S.A. and several of his learned friends*. Correspondence between Bowyer and these friends, notably Jeremiah Markland and William Clarke (printed in Nichols's *Literary Anecdotes*), was predominantly antiquarian and textual. Roman and English coinage was a favourite topic of inquiry. Bowyer himself was most proud of his *Conjectures on the New Testament, Collected from Various Authors* (1772). This work attracted some later attention.

Bowyer died in London on 18 November 1777, and was buried at Low Leyton, Essex. In his will, having handsomely provided for his errant son, and remembered those who had helped his father after the destructive fire of 30 January 1713, he gave charitable bequests to the Stationers' Company to benefit elderly printers, and also a journeyman compositor aged at least thirty-one 'who shall be able to read and construe Latin, and at least to read Greek fluently with accents' (Nichols, *Lit. anecdotes*, 3.270–89). To John Nichols, his residual legatee, he gave 'all the Books that relate to Cicero, Livy, and the Roman History … my Grammars and Dictionaries, with Swift's and Pope's Works', also his 'Old Bureau … to survey and preserve my Papers in' (ibid.). These materials together with the old printing house books of account formed the nucleus of Nichols's *Literary Anecdotes*.

William Bowyer was surely, as Nichols claimed, 'the most learned [English] Printer of the Eighteenth Century' (Nichols, *Lit. anecdotes*, 1.2). His printing house is also the best documented. His successor's care to preserve the Bowyer business records for posterity allowed the operations of a major London printing house of the hand-press era to be understood in their fullness. Bowyer was a printer not only of works of learning of every sort (including medical and scientific), but of works of imaginative literature from Pope, Swift, and Voltaire to the soon forgotten publications of Grub Street hacks, and parliamentary papers. Interspersed with these were ephemeral pieces of every description. His achievement, like his father's, was to be not only distinctive, but representative of the vigour and service to society of the best of his trade. Bowyer well understood that scholarly printing, however highly valued, was something of a luxury, needing to be subsidized by more commercial work. His devotion to printing the works of the learned stands out as all the more laudable.

KEITH MASLEN

Sources Nichols, *Lit. anecdotes* • *The Bowyer ledgers: the printing accounts of William Bowyer, father and son, reproduced on microfiche with* *a checklist of Bowyer printing 1699–1777, a commentary, indexes and appendixes*, ed. K. Maslen and J. Lancaster (1991) • D. F. McKenzie, ed., *Stationers' Company apprentices*, [3]: 1701–1800 (1978) • K. I. D. Maslen, *An early London printing house at work: studies in the Bowyer ledgers* (1993) • K. I. D. Maslen, *The Bowyer ornament stock* (1973) • private information (2004) [M. Treadwell] • R. F. Scott, *St John's College, Cambridge* (1907) • Emonson Partnership MSS, Bodl. Oxf., MS Eng. misc. c. 141 • Col. U., Nichols MSS

Archives Bodl. Oxf., account books: paper stock ledger, MS Don. b.4 • Col. U., corresp. and papers • Grolier Club Library, New York, ledgers A, B, and C, Grolier 19471, 19472, 19474 | BLPES, Dawes–Bowyer–Nichols notebook, MS Coll. G. 1521 • Bodl. Oxf., Emonson Partnership MSS, MS Eng. misc. c.141 • Bodl. Oxf., Rawlinson papers • CLRO, rate books and marriage tax assessments • Col. U., Nichols MSS

Likenesses J. Basire, engraving, 1782, repro. in Nichols, *Lit. anecdotes*, vol. 2, frontispiece • J. Basire, line engraving, BM, NPG; repro. in *Conjecturae Emendations* (1812) [*see illus.*]

Wealth at death £16,691; farms in Danby Dale (Cleveland and Yorkshire), and Navestock (Essex); plus household goods, plate, old books, coins, and printing business: will, Nichols, *Lit. anecdotes*, vol. 3, pp. 270-89

PICTURE CREDITS

Blackmore, Sir Richard (1654–1729)—© Copyright The British Museum
Blackmore, Richard Doddridge (1825–1900)—© National Portrait Gallery, London
Blackstone, Sir William (1723–1780)—All Souls College, Oxford
Blackton, James Stuart (1875–1941)—Getty Images - Hulton Archive
Blackwell, Sir Basil Henry (1889–1984)—© John Ward
Blackwell, Richard (1918–1980)—© reserved
Blackwood, Algernon Henry (1869–1951)—© National Portrait Gallery, London
Blackwood, Sir (Stevenson) Arthur (1832–1893)—Howarth-Loomes Collection; photograph National Portrait Gallery, London
Blackwood, Lady Caroline Maureen Hamilton-Temple- (1931–1996)—© Lucian Freud; Arts Council Collection, Hayward Gallery, London; photograph National Portrait Gallery, London
Blackwood, Frederick Temple Hamilton-Temple-, first marquess of Dufferin and Ava (1826–1902)—© National Portrait Gallery, London
Blackwood, George Frederick (1838–1880)—© National Portrait Gallery, London
Blackwood, Hariot Georgina Hamilton-Temple-, marchioness of Dufferin and Ava (1843–1936)—© National Portrait Gallery, London
Blackwood, Sir Henry, first baronet (1770–1832)—© National Maritime Museum, London, Greenwich Hospital Collection
Blackwood, William (1776–1834)—Scottish National Portrait Gallery
Blackwood, William (1836–1912)—© reserved; photograph National Portrait Gallery, London
Blades, James (1901–1999)—© Norman Parkinson Ltd., courtesy Fiona Cowan; collection National Portrait Gallery, London
Blagrave, Thomas (*d.* 1688)—Faculty of Music, University of Oxford
Blair, Eric Arthur [George Orwell] (1903–1950)—© Estate of Felix H. Man / National Portrait Gallery, London
Blair, James (1655/6–1743)—Muscarelle Museum of Art, College of William and Mary
Blair, Sir James Hunter, first baronet (1741–1787)—private collection; © reserved in the photograph
Blake, (Dominick) Edward (1833–1912)—© National Portrait Gallery, London
Blake, Katharine Jex- (1860–1951)—The Mistress and Fellows, Girton College, Cambridge
Blake, Dame Louisa Brandreth Aldrich- (1865–1925)—Collection Royal Free Hospital School of Medicine, London; photograph © Courtauld Institute of Art, London
Blake, Sophia Louisa Jex- (1840–1912)—© National Portrait Gallery, London
Blake, William (1757–1827)—© National Portrait Gallery, London
Blakiston, Herbert Edward Douglas (1862–1942)—© National Portrait Gallery, London
Blamey, Sir Thomas Albert (1884–1951)—Australian War Memorial, negative number 054949
Blanch, Stuart Yarworth, Baron Blanch (1918–1994)—© Anne-Katrin Purkiss; collection National Portrait Gallery, London
Blanche, Ada (1863–1953)—© National Portrait Gallery, London
Blanchflower, Robert Dennis [Danny] (1926–1993)—© Mark Gerson; collection National Portrait Gallery, London
Bland, Hubert (1855–1914)—© private collection / National Portrait Gallery, London
Bland, Maria Theresa (1769–1838)—Garrick Club / the art archive
Blane, Sir Gilbert, first baronet (1749–1834)—by permission of the Royal College of Physicians, London
Blaquiere, John, first Baron de Blaquiere (1732–1812)—© National Portrait Gallery, London
Blatchford, Robert Peel Glanville (1851–1943)—© National Portrait Gallery, London
Blech, Harry (1909–1999)—© National Portrait Gallery, London
Blenkiron, William (1807?–1871)—© National Portrait Gallery, London
Bligh, Sir Richard Rodney (1737–1821)—© National Portrait Gallery, London
Bligh, William (1754–1817)—Collection Captain Cook Memorial Museum, Whitby; © reserved in the photograph
Blind, Mathilde (1841–1896)—Christie's Images Ltd. (2004)
Bliss, Sir Arthur Edward Drummond (1891–1975)—© National Portrait Gallery, London
Bliss, Kathleen Mary Amelia (1908–1989)—© News International Newspapers Ltd
Bliss, Philip (1787–1857)—courtesy of the Provost and Fellows of Oriel College, Oxford; photograph © Studio Edmark
Blith, Walter (*bap.* 1605, *d.* 1654)—© Copyright The British Museum
Blixen, Karen Christenze [Isak Dinesen] (1885–1962)—The Royal Library, Copenhagen
Blogg, Henry George (1876–1954)—© reserved; photograph courtesy of the Royal National Lifeboat Institution
Blois, Henry de (*c.*1096–1171)—The British Library
Blom, Eric Walter (1888–1959)—© National Portrait Gallery, London
Blomefield [Jenyns], Leonard (1800–1893)—by permission of the Linnean Society of London
Blomfield, Charles James (1786–1857)—© National Portrait Gallery, London
Blomfield, Sir Reginald Theodore (1856–1942)—RIBA Library Photographs Collection
Blomfield, Sara Louisa (1859–1939)—The Baha'i Publishing Trust
Blood, Sir Bindon (1842–1940)—© National Portrait Gallery, London
Blood, Thomas (1617/18–1680)—The Pepys Library, Magdalene College, Cambridge
Bloomer, Stephen (1874–1938)—W. W. Winter Photographers Ltd / Derby Evening Telegraph
Bloomfield, Robert (1766–1823)—© National Portrait Gallery, London
Blore, Edward (1787–1879)—© National Portrait Gallery, London
Blount, Charles, eighth Baron Mountjoy and earl of Devonshire (1563–1606)—by permission of the Trustees of the Carew Pole Family Trusts; photograph National Portrait Gallery, London
Blount, Sir Henry (1602–1682)—© National Portrait Gallery, London
Blount, Martha (1690–1763)—reproduced by permission of the Mapledurham Trust. Photograph: Photographic Survey, Courtauld Institute of Art, London
Blount, Mountjoy, first earl of Newport (*c.*1597–1666)—Yale Center for British Art, Paul Mellon Collection
Blow, John (1648?–1708)—© National Portrait Gallery, London
Blowitz, Henri Georges Stephan Adolphe Opper de (1825–1903)—© National Portrait Gallery, London
Bloxam, Matthew Holbeche (1805–1888)—reproduced with the kind permission of Warwickshire County Council, Warwickshire Library and Information Service
Blumenfeld, Ralph David (1864–1948)—© National Portrait Gallery, London
Blumlein, Alan Dower (1903–1942)—private collection
Blundell, Sir Michael (1907–1993)—© News International Newspapers Ltd
Blunden, Edmund Charles (1896–1974)—© National Portrait Gallery, London
Blunt, Alfred Walter Frank (1879–1957)—© National Portrait Gallery, London
Blunt, Anne Isabella Noel, *suo jure* Baroness Wentworth (1837–1917)—© Fitzwilliam Museum, University of Cambridge
Blunt, Anthony Frederick (1907–1983)—Snowdon / Camera Press
Blunt, Wilfrid Scawen (1840–1922)—© National Portrait Gallery, London
Blyden, Edward Wilmot (1832–1912)—© reserved
Blythe, Ernest (1889–1975)—Getty Images - Hulton Archive
Blyton, Enid Mary (1897–1968)—© Estate of John Gay; collection National Portrait Gallery, London
Board, Lillian Barbara (1948–1970)—© Empics
Boardman, Peter David (1950–1982)—Alpine Club Photo Library, London
Boase, George Clement (1829–1897)—© National Portrait Gallery, London
Bodichon, Barbara Leigh Smith (1827–1891)—© National Portrait Gallery, London
Bodley, George Frederick (1827–1907)—RIBA Library Photographs Collection
Bodley, John Edward Courtenay (1853–1925)—© National Portrait Gallery, London
Bodley, Sir Thomas (1545–1613)—© Bodleian Library, University of Oxford
Boehm, Sir (Joseph) Edgar, baronet (1834–1890)—© National Portrait Gallery, London
Bogarde, Sir Dirk (1921–1999)—© George Courtney Ward; collection National Portrait Gallery, London
Bohn, Henry George (1796–1884)—© National Portrait Gallery, London
Boileau, Sir John Peter (1794–1869)—photograph by courtesy Sotheby's Picture Library, London
Bolan, Marc (1947–1977)—© Keith Morris; collection National Portrait Gallery, London
Boland, Henry James (1887–1922)—Getty Images - Hulton Archive
Bolt, Robert Oxton (1924–1995)—© Stephen Hyde; collection National Portrait Gallery, London
Bolton, Robert (1572–1631)—© National Portrait Gallery, London
Bolton, Samuel (1605/6–1654)—© National Portrait Gallery, London
Bomberg, David Garshen (1890–1957)—© National Portrait Gallery, London
Bompas, William Carpenter (1834–1906)—© National Portrait Gallery, London
Bonar, Horatius (1808–1889)—© National Portrait Gallery, London
Bond, Sir Edward Augustus (1815–1898)—© National Portrait Gallery, London
Bondfield, Margaret Grace (1873–1953)—© National Portrait Gallery, London
Bone, Henry (1755–1834)—© National Portrait Gallery, London
Bone, Henry Pierce (1779–1855)—Christie's Images Ltd. (2004)
Bone, Sir Muirhead (1876–1953)—© Hunterian Art Gallery, University of Glasgow
Bonington, Richard Parkes (1802–1828)—© Copyright The British Museum
Bonn, Leopold Bernhard (1850–1929)—Royal National Institute for the Deaf
Bonner, Edmund (*d.* 1569)—© National Portrait Gallery, London
Bonomi, Ignatius Richard Frederick Nemesius (1787–1870)—reproduced by kind permission of Durham University Library from Misc. acc. 1985:1/121:219A

Bonomi, Joseph (1739–1808)—© National Portrait Gallery, London

Boole, George (1815–1864)—© National Portrait Gallery, London

Boorde, Andrew (*c*.1490–1549)—© National Portrait Gallery, London

Boot, Jesse, first Baron Trent (1850–1931)—© reserved / The Boots Company plc

Booth, Catherine (1829–1890)—The Salvation Army International Heritage Centre

Booth, Catherine Bramwell- (1883–1987)—Snowdon / Camera Press; collection National Portrait Gallery, London

Booth, Charles (1840–1916)—© National Portrait Gallery, London

Booth, Edwin Thomas (1833–1893)—© National Portrait Gallery, London

Booth, Hester (*c*.1690–1773)—private collection. Photograph: Photographic Survey, Courtauld Institute of Art, London

Booth, Sarah (1789x94–1867)—© National Portrait Gallery, London

Booth, William (1829–1912)—© National Portrait Gallery, London

Boothman, Sir John Nelson (1901–1957)—© National Portrait Gallery, London

Borden, Mary (1886–1968)—© National Portrait Gallery, London

Borden, Sir Robert Laird (1854–1937)—Orpen / National Archives of Canada / C-011238

Borrer, William (1781–1862)—© National Portrait Gallery, London

Borrow, George Henry (1803–1881)—© National Portrait Gallery, London

Borthwick, Algernon, Baron Glenesk (1830–1908)—© National Portrait Gallery, London

Bosanquet, Bernard (1848–1923)—© National Portrait Gallery, London

Bosanquet, Helen (1860–1925)—© National Portrait Gallery, London

Boscawen, Edward (1711–1761)—© National Portrait Gallery, London

Boston, Thomas (1676–1732)—© National Portrait Gallery, London

Boswell, Sir Alexander, first baronet (1775–1822)—private collection; © reserved in the photograph

Boswell, James (1740–1795)—© National Portrait Gallery, London

Boswell, James Edward Buchanan (1906–1971)—courtesy Estate of the Artist & John Gainsborough / Tate Gallery Archive

Boswell, Margaret Montgomerie (1738?–1789)—© reserved

Botha, Louis (1862–1919)—Scottish National Portrait Gallery

Bottomley, Arthur George, Baron Bottomley (1907–1995)—© National Portrait Gallery, London

Bottomley, Horatio William (1860–1933)—© National Portrait Gallery, London

Bouch, Sir Thomas (1822–1880)—© National Portrait Gallery, London

Boucher, Jonathan (1738–1804)—Yale University Art Gallery. Photograph: The Paul Mellon Centre for Studies in British Art

Boucherett, (Emilia) Jessie (1825–1905)—The Women's Library, London Metropolitan University

Boucicault, Dion (1820–1890)—© National Portrait Gallery, London

Boucicault, Dion, the younger (1859–1929)—V&A Images, The Victoria and Albert Museum

Boughton, George Henry (1833–1905)—© National Portrait Gallery, London

Boughton, Rutland (1878–1960)—© Jenny Letton, administered by Composer Prints Ltd.; collection National Portrait Gallery, London

Boult, Sir Adrian Cedric (1889–1983)—© Estate of Felix H. Man / National Portrait Gallery, London

Boulter, Hugh (1672–1742)—© National Portrait Gallery, London

Boulting, John (1913–1985)—Getty Images - Hardy and Francis Reiss Burt

Boulton, Ernest (*b*. 1848?)—reproduced by courtesy of the Spalding Collection, Essex Record Office

Boulton, Matthew (1728–1809)—Birmingham Museums & Art Gallery

Bourbon, Nicholas (*c*.1503–1549/50)—The Royal Collection © 2004 HM Queen Elizabeth II

Bourchier, John, second Baron Berners (*c*.1467–1533)—Galerie Jan der Maere

Bourdillon, Sir Bernard Henry (1883–1948)—© National Portrait Gallery, London

Bourdillon, Thomas Duncan (1924–1956)—The Royal Geographical Society, London

Bourgeois, Sir (Peter) Francis (1756–1811)—© National Portrait Gallery, London

Bourke, Richard Southwell, sixth earl of Mayo (1822–1872)—© National Portrait Gallery, London

Bourne, Samuel (1834–1912)—Royal Photographic Society

Bouverie, Katharine Harriot Duncombe Pleydell- (1895–1985)—© Mayotte Magnus; collection National Portrait Gallery, London

Bowater, Sir Eric Vansittart (1895–1962)—© Wolfgang Suschitzky / National Portrait Gallery, London

Bowden, Frank Philip (1903–1968)—© reserved; photograph National Portrait Gallery, London

Bowden, (Bertram) Vivian, Baron Bowden (1910–1989)—© National Portrait Gallery, London

Bowdoin, James (1726–1790)—Bowdoin College Museum of Art, Brunswick, Maine, Bequest of Mrs Sarah Bowdoin Dearborn

Bowen, Arthur Charles Mainwaring (1922–1980)—© reserved; Arthritis Care

Bowen, Charles Synge Christopher, Baron Bowen (1835–1894)—© National Portrait Gallery, London

Bowen, Elizabeth Dorothea Cole (1899–1973)—© reserved; collection National Portrait Gallery, London

Bowen, Sir George Ferguson (1821–1899)—© National Portrait Gallery, London

Bowerbank, James Scott (1797–1877)—© National Portrait Gallery, London

Bowery, Leigh (1961–1994)—© Lucian Freud / Tate, London, 2004

Bowes, Sir Jerome (*d*. 1616)—© English Heritage Photo Library

Bowes, John, Baron Bowes of Clonlyon (1691–1767)—© National Portrait Gallery, London

Bowes, Sir Martin (1496/7–1566)—unknown collection / Christie's; photograph National Portrait Gallery, London

Bowhill, Sir Frederick William (1880–1960)—© Estate of Bertram Park / Camera Press; collection National Portrait Gallery, London

Bowlby, Sir Anthony Alfred, first baronet (1855–1929)—St Bartholomew's Hospital Archives and Museum. Photograph: Photographic Survey, Courtauld Institute of Art, London

Bowlby, (Edward) John Mostyn (1907–1990)—© Lucinda Douglas-Menzies; collection National Portrait Gallery, London

Bowles, Edward Augustus (1865–1954)—Royal Horticultural Society, Lindley Library

Bowles, Thomas Gibson (1842–1922)—private collection

Bowley, Sir Arthur Lyon (1869–1957)—© reserved; by courtesy of London School of Economics

Bowlly, Albert Alick (1899–1941)—© National Portrait Gallery, London

Bowman, Sir William, first baronet (1816–1892)—private collection; photograph National Portrait Gallery, London

Bowra, Sir (Cecil) Maurice (1898–1971)—Estate of Henry Lamb; Wadham College, Oxford

Bowring, Sir John (1792–1872)—© National Portrait Gallery, London

Bowyer, Sir George, seventh baronet (1811–1883)—© National Portrait Gallery, London

Bowyer, William (1699–1777)—© National Portrait Gallery, London

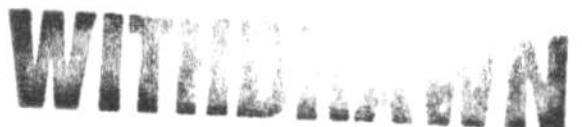